# *Warman's*

# ANTIQUES AND COLLECTIBLES

## PRICE GUIDE

## 35TH EDITION

## EDITED BY ELLEN T. SCHROY

Published by

700 E. State Street • Iola, WI 54990-0001
Telephone: 715/445-2214

**www.krause.com**

Please, call or write us for our free catalog of antiques and collectibles publications.
To place an order or receive our free catalog, call 800-258-0929. For editorial comment and further information,
use our regular business telephone at (715) 445-2214

Library of Congress Catalog Number: 82-643543
ISBN: 0-87341-974-X

Printed in the United States of America

# INTRODUCTION

## Warman's: Serving the trade for more than 50 years

In 1994, *Warman's Antiques and Their Prices* became *Warman's Antiques and Collectibles Price Guide*. The last edition is bigger than ever—physically, that is. Longtime *Warman's* users may find it difficult to imagine that the amount of information in this larger-size book is identical to that found in the earlier smaller-size editions. Yet, it is true. While the page, text, and photograph sizes are larger, the content is the same. You can always expect more, never less, from *Warman's*.

Individuals in the trade refer to this book simply as *Warman's*, a fitting tribute to E. G. Warman and the product he created. *Warman's* has been around for 51 years, 26 years longer than its closest rival. We are proud as peacocks that *Warman's* continues to establish the standards for general antiques and collectibles price guides in 2001, just as it did in 1972 when its first rival appeared on the scene.

*Warman's*, the antiques and collectibles "bible," covers objects made between 1700 and the present. It always has. Because it reflects market trends, *Warman's* has added more and more 20th-century material to each edition. Remember, 1900 was 100 years ago—the distant past to the new generation of 20-something and 30-something collectors. The general "antiques" market consists of antiques (for the purposes of this book, objects made before 1945), collectibles (objects of the post-World War II era that enjoy an established secondary market), and desirables (contemporary objects that are collected, but speculative in price). Although *Warman's* contains information on all three market segments, its greatest emphasis is on antiques and collectibles. In fact, this book is the essential field guide to the antiques and collectibles marketplace, which indicates that Warman's is much more than a list of object descriptions and prices. It is a basic guide to the field as a whole, providing you with the key information you need every time you encounter a new object or collecting category.

## 'Warman's is the key'

*Warman's* provides the keys needed by auctioneers, collectors, dealers, and others to understand and deal with the complexities of the antiques and collectibles market. A price list is only one of many keys needed today. *Warman's* 35th edition contains many additional keys, including: histories, marks, reference books, periodicals, collectors' clubs, museums, reproductions, videotapes, and special auctions. Useful buying and collecting hints also are provided. Used properly, there are few doors these keys will not open.

*Warman's* is designed to be your first key to the exciting world of antiques and collectibles. As you use the keys this book provides to advance further in your specialized collecting areas, *Warman's* hopes you will remember with fondness where you received your start. When you encounter items outside your area of specialty, remember *Warman's* remains your key to unlocking the information you need, just as it has for more than 40 years.

## Organization

**Listings:** Objects are listed alphabetically by category, beginning with ABC Plates and ending with Zsolnay Pottery. If you have trouble identifying the category to which your object belongs, use the extensive index in the back of the book. It will guide you to the proper category. We have made the listings descriptive enough so that specific objects can be identified. We also emphasize items that are actively being sold in the marketplace. Some harder-to-find objects are included to demonstrate market spread—useful information worth considering when you have not traded actively in a category recently.

Each year, as the market changes, we carefully review our categories—adding, dropping, and combining to provide the most comprehensive coverage possible. *Warman's* quick response to developing trends in the marketplace is one of the prime reasons for its continued leadership in the field. Krause Publications also publishes other *Warman's* titles. Each utilizes the *Warman's* format and concentrates on a specific collecting group, e.g., American pottery and porcelain; Americana and collectibles; coins and currency; country, English and continental pottery and porcelain; glass; and jewelry. Several are second or subsequent editions. Their expanded coverage compliments the information found in *Warman's Antiques and Collectibles Price Guide*.

**History:** Collectors and dealers enhance their appreciation of objects by knowing something about their history. We present a capsule history for each category. In many cases, this history contains collecting hints or other useful information.

**References:** Books are listed in most categories to help you learn more about the objects. Included are author, title, publisher, and date of publication or most recent edition. If a book has been published by a small firm or individual, we have indicated (published by author). To assist in finding these sometimes hard-to-locate authors, we have included the address. Many of the books included in the lists are hard to find. The antiques and collectibles field is blessed with a dedicated core of book dealers who stock these specialized publications. You will find them at flea markets and antiques shows and through their advertisements in trade publications.

Books go out of print quickly, yet many books printed more than 25 years ago remain the standard work in a category. Used book dealers often can locate many of these valuable reference sources. Many dealers publish annual or semi-annual catalogs. Ask to be put on their mailing lists.

**Periodicals:** The newsletter or bulletin of a collectors' club usually provides the concentrated focus sought by specialty collectors and dealers. However, there are publications, not associated with collectors' clubs, about which collectors and dealers should be aware. These are listed in their appropriate category introductions. In addition, there are several general interest newspapers and magazines which deserve to be brought to our users' attention. These are:

*Antique & The Arts Weekly*, Bee Publishing Company, 5 Church Hill Road, Newton, CT 06470; http://www.the-bee.com/aweb

*Antique Review*, P.O. Box 538, Worthington, OH 43085

*Antique Trader Weekly*, P.O. Box 1050, Dubuque, IA 52001; http://www.csmonline.com

*AntiqueWeek*, P.O. Box 90, Knightstown, IN 46148; http://www.antiqueweek.com

*Antiques* (The Magazine Antiques), 551 Fifth Avenue, New York, NY 10017

*Antiques & Collecting*, 1006 South Michigan Avenue, Chicago, IL 60605

*Maine Antique Digest*, P.O. Box 358, Waldoboro, ME 04572; http://www.mainantiquedigest.com

*MidAtlantic Monthly Antiques Magazine*, P.O. Box 908, Henderson, NC 27536

*New England Antiques Journal*, 4 Church St., Ware, MA 01082

*New York-Pennsylvania Collector*, Drawer C, Fishers, NY 14453

*Warman's Today's Collector*, 700 E. State St., Iola, WI 54990-0001; (http://www.krause.com)

Space does not permit listing all the national and regional publications in the antiques and collectibles field. The above is a sampling.

**Collectors' Clubs:** Collectors' clubs add vitality to the antiques and collectibles field. Their publications and conventions produce knowledge which often cannot be found elsewhere. Many of these clubs are short-lived; others are so strong that they have regional and local chapters.

**Museums:** The best way to study a specific field is to see as many documented examples as possible. For this reason, we have listed museums where significant collections in that category are on display. Special attention must be directed to the complex of museums which make up the Smithsonian Institution in Washington, D.C.

**Reproductions:** Reproductions are a major concern to all collectors and dealers. Throughout this edition, boxes will alert you to known reproductions and keys to recognizing them. Most reproductions are unmarked; the newness of their appearance is often the best clue to uncovering them. Specific objects known to be reproduced are marked within the listings with an asterisk (*). The information is designed to serve as a reminder of past reproductions and prevent you from buying them, believing them to be period.

We strongly recommend subscribing to *Antique & Collectors Reproduction News*, a monthly newsletter that reports on past and present reproductions, copycats, fantasies, and fakes. Send $32 for twelve issues to: ACRN, Box 12130, Des Moines, IA 50312-9403; (www.repronews.com). This newsletter has been published for several years. Consider buying all available back issues. The information they contain will be of service long into the future.

**Special Auctions:** In the 35th edition, we have chosen to again feature boxes highlighting auction houses. To qualify for placement in one of these boxes, auction houses have to meet several specific requirements. First, they must actively hold auctions solely devoted to that specialty. Second, they must provide a catalog and prices realized. Often the catalogs become an important part of a collection, serving as reference and identification guides. Many of the auction companies featured hold more than one auction annually; some work with a particular collectors' club or society. It is our hope that these boxes will give collectors and those searching for specific objects a better idea of who to contact. *Warman's* is designed to give collectors and dealers a lot of clues to find out what they have, what it is worth, and where to sell it!

These special auction boxes are not intended, however, to diminish the outstanding work done by the generalists, those auctioneers who handle all types of material. The fine auctions like Garth's, Skinner's, and Sloan's, provide us with excellent catalogs all through the year covering many aspects of the antiques and collectibles marketplace. Several categories had too many auction houses to list. For example, most auctioneers sell furniture, clocks, and fine arts. We just couldn't list them all. In addition to these auction-house boxes, we hope you will consult the master list of auction houses included in this edition. We are sure that any one of them will be eager to assist in consigning or selling antiques and collectibles.

**Index:** A great deal of effort has been expended to make our index useful. Always begin by looking for the most specific reference. For example, if you have a piece of china, look first for the maker's name and second for the type. Remember, many objects can be classified in three or more categories. If at first you don't succeed, try, try again.

**Black-and-white photographs:** You may encounter a piece you cannot identify well enough to use the index. Consult the photographs and marks. If you own several editions of *Warman's*, you have available a valuable photographic reference to the antiques and collectibles field. Learn to use it.

## Price notes

In assigning prices, we assume the object is in very good condition. If otherwise, we note this in our description. It would be ideal to suggest that mint, or unused, examples of all objects exist. The reality is that objects from the past were used, whether they be glass, china, dolls, or toys. Because of this, some normal wear must be expected. In fact, if an object such as a piece of furniture does not show wear, its origins may be more suspect than if it does show wear.

Whenever possible, we have tried to provide a broad listing of prices within a category so you have a "feel"" for the market. We emphasize the middle range of prices within a category, while also listing some objects of high and low value to show market spread. We do not use ranges because they tend to confuse, rather than help, the collector and dealer. How do you determine if your object is at the high or low end of the range? There is a high degree of flexibility in pricing in the antiques field. If you want to set ranges, add or subtract 10 percent from our prices.

One of the hardest variants with which to deal is the regional fluctuations of prices. Victorian furniture brings widely differing prices in New York, Chicago, New Orleans, or San Francisco. We have tried to strike a balance. Know your region and subject before investing heavily. If the best buys for cameo glass are in Montreal or Toronto, then be prepared to go there if you want to save money or add choice pieces to your collection. Research and patience are key factors to building a collection of merit. Another factor that affects prices is a sale by a leading dealer or private collector. We temper both dealer and auction house figures.

## Price research

Everyone asks, "Where do you get your prices?"

They come from many sources. First, we rely on auctions. Auction houses and auctioneers do not always command the highest prices. If they did, why do so many dealers buy from them? The key to understanding auction prices is to know when a price is high or low in the range. We think we do this and do it well. The 35th edition represents a concentrated effort to contact more regional auction houses, both large and small. The cooperation has been outstanding and has resulted in an ever-growing pool of auction prices and trends to help us determine the most up-to-date auction prices. Second, we work closely with dealers. We screen our contacts to make certain they have full knowledge of the market. Dealers make their living from selling antiques; they cannot afford to have a price guide which is not in touch with the market.

More than 50 antiques and collectibles magazines, newspapers, and journals come into our office regularly. They are excellent barometers of what is moving and what is not. We don't hesitate to call an advertiser and ask if his listed merchandise sold.

When the editorial staff is doing field work, we identify ourselves. Our conversations with dealers and collectors around the country have enhanced this book. Teams from *Warman's* are in the field at antiques shows, malls, flea markets, and auctions recording prices and taking photographs.

Collectors work closely with us. They are specialists whose devotion to research and accurate information is inspiring. Generally, they are not dealers. Whenever we have asked them for help, they have responded willingly and admirably.

## Board of advisors

Our Board of Advisors is made up of specialists, both dealers and collectors, who feel a commitment to accurate information. You'll find their names listed in the front of the book. Several have authored a major reference work on their subject.

Our esteemed Board of Advisors has increased in number and scope. Participants have all provided detailed information regarding the history and reference section of their particular area of expertise, as well as preparing price listings. Many furnished excellent photographs and even shared with us their thoughts on the state of the market.

We are delighted to include those who are valuable members, officers, and founders of collectors' clubs. They are authors of books and articles, and many frequently lecture to groups about their specialties. Most of our advisors have been involved with antiques and collectibles for more than 20 years. Several are retired, and the antiques and collectibles business is a hobby which encompasses most of their free time. Others are a bit younger and either work full time or part time in the antiques and collectibles profession. We asked them about their favorite publications, and most responded with the names of specialized trade papers. Many told us they are regular readers of *AntiqueWeek* and the *Maine Antique Digest*.

One thing they all have in common is their enthusiasm for the antiques and collectibles marketplace. They are eager to share their knowledge with collectors. Many have developed wonderful friendships through their efforts and are enriched by them. If you wish to buy or sell an object in the field of expertise of any of our advisors, drop them a note, along with an SASE. If time permits, they will respond.

## Buyer's guide, not seller's guide

*Warman's* is designed to be a buyer's guide, suggesting what you would have to pay to purchase an object on the open market from a dealer or collector. It is not a seller's guide to prices. People frequently make this mistake. In doing so, they deceive themselves. If you have an object listed in this book and wish to sell it to a dealer, you should expect to receive approximately 50 percent of the listed value. If the object will not resell quickly, expect to receive even less. Private collectors may pay more, perhaps 70 to 80 percent of our listed price, if your object is something needed for their collection. If you have an extremely rare object or an object of exceptionally high value, these guidelines do not apply.

Examine your piece as objectively as possible. As an antiques and collectibles appraiser, I spend a great deal of time telling people their treasures are not "rare" at all, but items readily available in the marketplace.

In respect to buying and selling, a simple philosophy is that a good purchase occurs when the buyer and seller are happy with the price. Don't look back. Hindsight has little value in the antiques and collectibles field. Given time, things tend to balance out.

## Always improving

*Warman's* is always trying to improve. Space is freely given to long price descriptions, to help you understand that the piece looks like and perhaps what's special about it. With this edition, we've arranged some old formats, using more bold words to help you find what you're looking for. Some categories have been arranged so that if the only thing you know is how high, you can start there. Many times, identifying what you've got is the hardest part. Well, the first place to start is how big— grab that ruler and see what you can find that's a comparable size. You are still going to have to make a determination about what the object is made of, be it china, glass, porcelain, wood, or other materials. Use all your senses to discover what you've got. Ask questions about your object, who made it, and why, how was it used, where, and when. As you find answers to these questions, you'll be helping yourself figure out just what the treasure is all about. Now take that information and you'll be able to look it up and discover the value.

## Eager to hear from readers

At *Warman's* and Krause Publications, we're always eager to hear what you think about Warman's and how we can improve it. Write to either Ellen Schroy, *Warman's* editor, P.O. Box 392, Quakertown, PA 18951-0392 or e-mail at schroy@voicenet.com. The fine staff at Krause Publications can be reached at 700 E. State St., Iola, WI 54990. It's our goal to continue in the *Warman's* tradition and make it the best price guide available.

# STATE of the MARKET

The antiques and collectibles marketplace is in a constant state of change at the moment. To some collectors and dealers, this is a good thing; to others, it represents a challenge. The challenge to collectors is to keep abreast of pricing, reproductions, and other matters that could potentially affect the value of their collections.

Most collectors are very aware of the value of their objects and how much the last great example of their favorite category just sold for. They watch and wait for collections similar to theirs to enter the marketplace so they might glean some new acquisitions. To other collectors, those who collect for the passion of the hobby, sometimes price doesn't matter. It's the thrill of the hunt, the closing of the deal, the addition of that cherished trophy that makes them happy. Dealers have to contend with a slightly different set of perimeters. They need to know what collectors are searching for and what the next "hot" area is going to be—it's that wishing we all had a crystal ball that keeps the antiques and collectible business so fascinating.

The antiques field has changed over the past year due to several influences. One is the Internet. The computer technology now available to collectors and dealers allows them to connect to one another easily. Collectors are no longer restricted to one particular geographic area and can shop from different venues all around the world. Dealers, by the same hand, are now free to offer their items through a virtual shop, through on-line auction, as well as the traditional shows, flea markets, shops, and live auctions. However, because of this, some areas of the antiques marketplace are seeing a decline in their pricing structures. Why? Because so many folks are now dealing on the Internet and more and more examples of antiques and collectibles are becoming easily available. It goes back to that basic supply-and-demand equation. As there are more examples readily available, collectors can be a bit choosier and sometimes able to select from several like objects for their collections. Because of this greater supply, many collectors are focusing on adding objects in as pristine condition as possible, passing up the lesser-quality objects. And, unfortunately, as lesser-quality objects become less desirable, their prices tend to go down.

Many dealers and collectors are now using eBay and other similar on-line auctions to evaluate and price their objects. This is a tricky scenario as the quality, quantity, shipping costs, and other factors must all be analyzed. And, one must remember that just because an item is offered for sale on-line, it does not mean it has been sold. Just like traditional antique shops or shows, many collectors might pass on a particular object for months before it finds a new home. Finding one item on-line that sold for X amount doesn't mean that every similar item is automatically worth as much or more. It's like using price guides, like *Warman's*. It's great to find your exact item listed, but often you've got to find something comparable and make adjustments to the price listed.

Unfortunately, many novice on-line auction participants feel they can afford to wait to get their price, insisting on high reserves. But, when high reserves are dictated, is this really an auction? As the on-line auctions age, perhaps we'll see some more changes coming to the industry.

Many of the *Warman* advisors have taken the time to let me know how their collecting areas are doing right now. James Maxwell tells me that prices of ordinary mechanical banks have taken a down turn. Condition plays a big role in price, as does availability. Because many wonderful rarer examples have turned up in the past few months, the mechanical bank market is suffering. Higher-priced banks, those valued $5,000 and over, are much more stable than the lower end of the scale. Collectors of banks are becoming much more selective. Catalog dealer Ken Schneringer tells me that sales on-line are good, but when I visited with him at the Great Eastern Paper Show in Allentown, PA, he hardly had time to chat as he waited on customers. He feels strongly that dealers need to be at shows, maintain a good customer base, as well as try the on-line markets.

Celluloid advisor Julie Robinson reports her area of collecting is strong, but finds herself spending more time repairing celluloid pieces for other collectors. Julie is delighted about this, as it shows collectors are treasuring their objects and finding it well worth the cost of a repair to bring back the luster or function of a piece.

Arts & Crafts advisor and auctioneer David Rago has merged with Jerry Cohen and John Fontaine to bring even more and higher-quality items to the market. Their first combined auction was very successful. More combined auctions are planned for the next several months, bringing together powerful auctioneers, their wares, and a good clientele. Several of the advisors mentioned to me that finding good quality items is harder than finding buyers. Many spend considerable effort to find quality items for their core customers. Most travel widely and are constantly on the prowl for merchandise.

One aspect of the antiques and collectibles field that is doing well is the growth of interest in collector clubs. Clubs are finding new members and increased interest in education. What a great way to learn about antiques and collectibles while sharing information. Many clubs have excellent newsletters, like the *Early American Pattern Glass Society's New Journal*. It's well written, well illustrated, and keeps educating members.

I had the pleasure of meeting many open salt collectors last summer, at the annual meeting of OSCAR (Open Salt Collectors of the Atlantic Region). They gathered at an annual meeting, enjoyed a well-run business session, and shared through a lively show-and-tell program. After my lecture, we chatted about what makes a good collector club and the benefits to its members. It was the general consensus of the group that the free exchange of ideas, research, and experience leads to the best kind of group. If the meeting I attended was any indication of their sharing nature, OSCAR members will be enjoying each other's company for many years. Not only did they bring treasures to share, they let others carefully handle them; some were looking for more information about their recent acquisitions, others brought something they thought the group would enjoy seeing. Members range in age, type of salts collected, and geographic region. This adds an interesting element of diversity to the group.

I watched quietly as they all greeted one another, eager to hear about their latest adventures. Perhaps it was the mad dash many made to the adjoining room when they opened the door for their sale period that reinforced gathering collectors together is a great way to make friends while adding to one's collection.

Several antique show promoters are also acknowledging the value of encouraging collectors' clubs by allowing them meeting space, etc. This turns out to be a benefit to the club and certainly brings dedicated collectors to the antique dealer booths. Other show promoters are coupling repair services and other extras to encourage attendance. Remembering that most collectors are looking for good prices, as well as interesting items, makes going to added-value antique shows a plus for all.

If the predictions for an economic slow down are right, and folks are looking to make some good investments, now might be the perfect time to invest in some quality antiques and collectibles. A visit to your local antiques shop, mall, flea market, or auction will probably be a great place to start searching for a wonderful addition to your collections.

Making the connection between a dealer and a collector is what the antiques business is all about. Having more and more venues to help make these important connections is what is going to keep this market place alive and vibrant. Collectors, dealers, and auctioneers are learning how to take advantage of the new technology of the new millennium and this trend will only continue. How far it will take us is yet to be seen.

# BOARD of ADVISORS

# AUCTION HOUSES

The following auction houses cooperate with Warman's by providing catalogs of their auctions and price lists. This information is used to prepare *Warman's Antiques and Collectibles Price Guide*, volumes in the Warman's Encyclopedia of Antiques and Collectibles. This support is truly appreciated.

Albrecht & Cooper Auction Services
3884 Saginaw Rd
Vassar, MI 48768
(517) 823-8835

Sanford Alderfer Auction Company
501 Fairgrounds Rd
Hatfield, PA 19440
(215) 393-3000
web site: http://www.alderfercompany.com

American Social History and Social Movements
4025 Saline St.
Pittsburgh, PA 15217
(412) 421-5230

Andre Ammelounx
The Stein Auction Company
P.O. Box 136
Palantine, IL 60078
(847) 991-5927

Antique Bottle Connection
147 Reserve Rd
Libby, MT 59923
(406) 293-8442

Apple Tree Auction Center
1616 W. Church St.
Newark, OH 43055
(614) 344-4282

Arthur Auctioneering
RD 2, P.O. Box 155
Hughesville, PA 17737
(717) 584-3697

Auction Team Köln
Jane Herz
6731 Ashley Court
Sarasota, FL 34241
(941) 925-0385

Auction Team Köln
Postfach 501168 D 5000
Köln 50, W. Germany

Noel Barrett Antiques & Auctions, Ltd.
P.O. Box 1001
Carversville, PA 18913
(610) 297-5109

Robert F. Batchelder
1 W Butler Ave.
Ambler, PA 19002
(610) 643-1430

Bear Pen Antiques
2318 Bear Pen Hollow Road
Lock Haven, PA 17745
(717) 769-6655

Beverly Hills Auctioneers
9454 Wilshire Blvd., Suite 202
Beverly Hills, CA 90212
(310) 278-8115

Bill Bertoia Auctions
1881 Spring Rd
Vineland, NJ 08360
(609) 692-1881

Biders Antiques Inc.
241 S. Union St.
Lawrence, MA 01843
(508) 688-4347

Brown Auction & Real Estate
900 East Kansas
Greensburg, KS 67054
(316) 723-2111

Buffalo Bay Auction Co.
5244 Quam Circle
Rogers MN 55374
(612) 428-8440
web site: www.buffalobayauction.com

Butterfield, Butterfield & Dunning
755 Church Rd
Elgin, IL 60123
(847) 741-3483
web site: http:.//www:butterfields.com

Butterfield, Butterfield & Dunning
7601 Sunset Blvd.
Los Angeles, CA 90046
(213) 850-7500
web site: http:.//www:butterfields.com

Butterfield, Butterfield & Dunning
220 San Bruno Ave.
San Francisco, CA 94103
(415) 861-7500
web site: http:.//www:butterfields.com

C. C. Auction Gallery
416 Court
Clay Center, KS 67432
(913) 632-6021

Cerebro
P.O. Box 327
East Prospect, PA 17317
(717) 252-3685

W. E. Channing & Co., Inc.
53 Old Santa Fe Trail
Santa Fe, NM 87501
(505) 988-1078

Chicago Art Galleries
5039 Oakton St.
Skokie, IL 60077
(847) 677-6080

Childers & Smith
1415 Horseshoe Pike
Glenmoore, PA 19343
(610) 269-1036
e-mail: harold@smithautionco.com

Christie's
502 Park Ave.
New York, NY 10022
(212) 546-1000
web site: http://www.christies.com

Christie's East
219 E. 67th St.
New York, NY 10021
(212) 606-0400
web site: http://www.christies.com

Cincinnati Art Galleries
635 Main St.
Cincinnati, OH 45202
(513) 381-2128

Mike Clum, Inc.
P.O. Box 2
Rushville, OH 43150
(614) 536-9220

Cobb's Doll Auctions
1909 Harrison Road
Johnstown, OH 43031-9539
(740) 964-0444

Cohasco Inc.
Postal 821
Yonkers, NY 10702
(914) 476-8500

Collection Liquidators Auction
Service
341 Lafayette St.
New York, NY 10012
(212) 505-2455
website:
http://www.rtam.com/coliq/bid.html
e-mail: coliq@erols.com

Collectors Auction Services
RR 2, Box 431 Oakwood Rd
Oil City, PA 16301
(814) 677-6070
web site: http://www.caswel.com

Collector's Sales and Service
P.O. Box 4037
Middletown RI02842
(401) 849-5012
web site: http://www.anti-
quechina.com

Coole Park Books and Autographs
P.O. Box 199049
Indianapolis, IN 46219
(317) 351-8495
e-mail: cooleprk@indy.net

Copeke Auction
226 Route 7A
Cokepe, NY 12516
(518) 329-1142

Samuel J. Cottonne
15 Genesee St.
Mt. Morris, NY 14510
(716) 583-3119

C. Wesley Cowan Historic Americana
Terrace Park, OH
(513) 248-8122
e-mail: wescowan@fuse.net

Craftsman Auctions
1485 W. Housatoric
Pittsfield, MA 01202
(413) 442-7003
web site: http://www.artsncrafts.com

Dargate Auction Galleries
5607 Baum Blvd.
Pittsburgh, PA 15206
(412) 362-3558
web site: http://www.dargate.com

Dawson's
128 American Road
Morris Plains, NJ 07950
(973) 984-6900
web site: http://www.idt.net/-
dawson1

DeWolfe & Wood
P.O. Box 425
Alfred, ME 04002
(207) 490-5572

Marlin G. Denlinger
RR3, Box 3775
Morrisville, VT 05661
(802) 888-2775

Dixie Sporting Collectibles
1206 Rama Rd.
Charlotte, NC 28211
(704) 364-2900
web site: http://www.sportauc-
tion.com

Dorothy Dous, Inc.
1261 University Drive
Yardley, PA 19067-2857
(888) 548-6635

William Doyle Galleries, Inc.
175 E. 87th St.
New York, NY 10128
(212) 427-2730
web site: http://www.doylegaller-
ies.com

Dunbar Gallery
76 Haven St.
Milford, MA 01757
(508) 634-8697

Early Auction Co.
123 Main St.
Milford, OH 45150
(513) 831-4833

Fain & Co.
P.O. Box 1330
Grants Pass, OR 97526
(888) 324-6726

Ken Farmer Realty & Auction Co.
105A Harrison St.
Radford, VA 24141
(703) 639-0939
web site: http://kenfarmer.com

Fine Tool Journal
27 Fickett Rd
Pownal, ME 04069
(207) 688-4962
web site: http://www.wow-
pages.com/FTJ/

Steve Finer Rare Books
P.O. Box 758
Greenfield, MA 01302
(413) 773-5811

Fink's Off The Wall Auctions
108 E. 7th St.
Lansdale, PA 19446
(215) 855-9732
web site: www.finksauctions.com

Flomaton Antique Auction
207 Palafox St.
Flomaton, AL 36441
(334) 296-3059

Fontaine's Auction Gallery
1485 W. Housatonic St.
Pittsfield, MA 01201
(413) 488-8922

William A. Fox Auctions Inc.
676 Morris Ave.
Springfield, NJ 07081
(201) 467-2366

Freeman\Fine Arts Co. of Philadelphia, Inc.
1808 Chestnut St.
Philadelphia, PA 19103
(215) 563-9275

Garth's Auction, Inc.
2690 Stratford Rd
P.O. Box 369
Delaware, OH 43015
(740) 362-4771

Greenberg Auctions
7566 Main St.
Skysville, MD 21784
(410) 795-7447

Green Valley Auction Inc.
Route 2, Box 434
Mt. Crawford, VA 22841
(540) 434-4260

Guerney's
136 E. 73rd St.
New York, NY 10021
(212) 794-2280

Hake's Americana & Collectibles
P.O. Box 1444
York, PA 17405
(717) 848-1333

Gene Harris Antique Auction Center, Inc.
203 South 18th Ave.
P.O. Box 476
Marshalltown, IA 50158
(515) 752-0600
web site: www.harrisantiqueauction.com

Norman C. Heckler & Company
Bradford Corner Rd
Woodstock Valley, CT 06282
(203) 974-1634

High Noon
9929 Venice Blvd.
Los Angeles, CA 90034
(310) 202-9010

Randy Inman Auctions, Inc.
P.O. Box 726
Waterville, ME 04903
(207) 872-6900
web site: www.inmanauctions.com

Michael Ivankovich Auction Co.
P.O. Box 1536
Doylestown, PA 18901
(215) 345-6094
web site: http://www.nutting.com

Jackson's Auctioneers & Appraisers
2229 Lincoln St.
Cedar Falls, IA 50613
(319) 277-2256
web site: http://www.jacksonauction.com

James D. Julia Inc.
Rt. 201 Skowhegan Rd
P.O. Box 830
Fairfield, ME 04937
(207) 453-7125
web site: www.juliaauctions.com

J. W. Auction Co.
54 Rochester Hill Rd
Rochester, NH 03867
(603) 332-0192

Lang's Sporting Collectables, Inc.
31 R Turthle Cove
Raymond, ME 04071
(207) 655-4265

La Rue Auction Service
201 S. Miller St.
Sweet Springs, MO 65351
(816) 335-4538

Leonard's Auction Company
1631 State Rd
Duncannon, PA 17020
(717) 957-3324

Howard Lowery
3818 W Magnolia Blvd.
Burbank, CA 91505
(818) 972-9080

Joy Luke
The Gallery
300 E. Grove St.
Bloomington, IL 61701
(309) 828-5533
web site: www.joyluke.com

Mapes Auctioneers & Appraisers
1729 Vestal Pkwy
Vestal, NY 13850
(607) 754-9193

Martin Auctioneers Inc.
P.O. Box 477
Intercourse, PA 17534
(717) 768-8108

McMasters Doll Auctions
P.O. Box 1755
Cambridge, OH 43725
(614) 432-4419

McMurray Antiques & Auctions
P.O. Box 393
Kirkwood, NY 13795
(607) 775-2321

Metropolitan Book Auction
123 W. 18th St., 4th Floor
New York, NY 10011
(212) 929-7099

Gary Metz's Muddy River Trading Company
P.O. Box 1430
Salem, VA 24135
(540) 387-5070

Wm. Frost Mobley
P.O. Box 10
Schoharie, NY 12157
(518) 295-7978

Wm. Morford
RD #2
Cazenovia, NY 13035
(315) 662-7625

Neal Auction Company
4038 Magazine Street
New Orleans, LA 7015
(504) 899-5329
web site: http://www.nealauction.com

New England Auction Gallery
P.O. Box 2273
W Peabody, MA 01960
(508) 535-3140

New Orleans Auction St. Charles Auction Gallery, Inc.
1330 St. Charles Ave.
New Orleans, LA 70130
(504) 586-8733
web site: http://www.neworleansauction.com

New Hampshire Book Auctions
P.O. Box 460
92 Woodbury Rd
Weare, NH 03281
(603) 529-7432

Norton Auctioneers of Michigan Inc.
50 West Pearl at Monroe
Coldwater, MI 49036
(517) 279-9063

Nostalgia Publications, Inc.
21 S. Lake Dr.
Hackensack, NJ 07601
(201) 488-4536
web site: www.nostalgiapubls.com

Old Barn Auction
10040 St. Rt. 224 West
Findlay, OH 45840
(419) 422-8531
web site: http://www.oldbarn.com

Ohio Cola Traders
4411 Bazetta Rd
Cortland, OH 44410
(330) 637-0357

Richard Opfer Auctioneering Inc.
1919 Greenspring Dr.
Timonium, MD 21093
(410) 252-5035
web site: www.opferauction.com

Pacific Book Auction Galleries
133 Kerney St., 4th Floor
San Francisco, CA 94108
(415) 989-2665
web site: http://www.nbn.com/~pbal

Past Tyme Pleasures
PMB #204, 2491 San Ramon Valley
Blvd., #1
San Ramon, CA 94583
(925) 484-6442
Fax: (925) 484-2551
web site: www.pasttyme.com
e-mail: Pasttyme@excite.com

Phillips Ltd.
406 E. 79th St.
New York, NY 10021
(212) 570-4830
web site: http://www.phillips-auc-
tion.com

Postcards International
2321 Whitney Ave., Suite 102
P.O. Box 5398
Hamden, CT 06518
(203) 248-6621
web site: http://www.csmon-
line.com/postcardsint/

Poster Auctions International
601 W. 26th St.
New York, NY 10001
(212) 787-4000
web site: www.posterauction.com

Profitt Auction Company
P.O. Box 796
Columbia, VA 23038
(804) 747-6353

Provenance
P.O. Box 3487
Wallington, NJ 07057
(201) 779-8725

David Rago Auctions, Inc.
333 S. Main St.
Lambertville, NJ 08530
(609) 397-9374
web site: http://www.ragoarts.com

Lloyd Ralston Toys
173 Post Rd
Fairfield, CT 06432
(203) 255-1233

James J. Reeves
P.O. Box 219
Huntingdon, PA 16652-0219
(814) 643-5497
website: www.JamesJReeves.com

Mickey Reichel Auctioneer
1440 Ashley Rd
Boonville MO 65233
(816) 882-5292

Sandy Rosnick Auctions
15 Front St.
Salem, MA 01970
(508) 741-1130

Thomas Schmidt
7099 McKean Rd
Ypsilanti, MI 48197
(313) 485-8606

Seeck Auctions
P.O. Box 377
Mason City, IA 50402
(515) 424-1116
website: www.wil-
lowtree.com/~seeckauctions

L. H. Selman Ltd.
761 Chestnut St.
Santa Cruz, CA 95060
(408) 427-1177
web site: http://www.selman.com

Sentry Auction
113 School St.
Apollo, PA 15613
(412) 478-1989

Skinner Inc.
Bolton Gallery
357 Main St.
Bolton, MA 01740
(978) 779-6241
web site: http://www.skinnerinc.com

Skinner, Inc.
The Heritage on the Garden
63 Park Plaza
Boston, MA 02116
(978) 350-5429
web site: http://www.skinnerinc.com

C. G. Sloan & Company Inc.
4920 Wyaconda Rd
North Bethesda, MD 20852
(301) 468-4911
web site: http://www.cgsloan.com

Smith & Jones, Inc., Auctions
12 Clark Lane
Sudbury MA 01776
(508) 443-5517

Smith House Toy Sales
26 Adlington Rd
Eliot, ME 03903
(207) 439-4614

R. M. Smythe & Co.
26 Broadway
New York, NY 10004-1710
(212) 943-1880
web site: http://www.rm-smythe.com

Sotheby's
1334 York Ave.
New York, NY 10021
(212) 606-7000
web site: http://www.sothebys.com

Southern Folk Pottery Collectors
Society
1828 N. Howard Mill Rd.
Robbins, NC 27325
(910) 464-3961

Stanton's Auctioneers
P.O. Box 146
144 South Main St.
Vermontville, MI 49096
(517) 726-0181

Stout Auctions
11 W. Third St.
Williamsport, IN 47993-1119
(765) 764-6901

Michael Strawser
200 N. Main St., P.O. Box 332
Wolcottville, IN 46795
(219) 854-2859

Swann Galleries Inc.
104 E. 25th St.
New York, NY 10010
(212) 254-4710

Swartz Auction Services
2404 N. Mattis Ave.
Champaign, IL 61826-7166
(217) 357-0197
web site: http://www/SwartzAuc-
tion.com

The House In The Woods
S91 W37851 Antique Lane
Eagle, WI 53119
(414) 594-2334

Theriault's
P.O. Box 151
Annapolis, MD 21401
(301) 224-3655
web site: http://www.theriaults.com

Toy Scouts
137 Casterton Ave.
Akron, OH 44303
(216) 836-0668
e-mail: toyscout@salamander.net

Treadway Gallery, Inc.
2029 Madison Rd
Cincinnati, OH 45208
(513) 321-6742
web site:
http://www.a3c2net.com/treadway-gallery

Unique Antiques & Auction Gallery
449 Highway 72 West
Collierville, TN 38017
(901) 854-1141

Venable Estate Auction
423 West Fayette St.
Pittsfield, IL 62363
(217) 285-2560
e-mail: sandiv@msn.com

Victorian Images
P.O. Box 284
Marlton, NJ 08053
(609) 985-7711
web site: www.tradecards.com/vi

Victorian Lady
P.O. Box 424
Waxhaw, NC 28173
(704) 843-4467

Vintage Cover Story
P.O. Box 975
Burlington, NC 27215
(919) 584-6900

Bruce and Vicki Waasdorp
P.O. Box 434
10931 Main St.
Clarence, NY 14031
(716) 759-2361
web site: www.antiques-stone-ware.com

Web Wilson Antiques
P.O. Box 506
Portsmouth, RI 02871
1-800-508-0022

Winter Associates
21 Cooke St. Box 823
Plainville, CT 06062
(203) 793-0288

Wolf's Auctioneers
1239 W. 6th St.
Cleveland, OH 44113
(614) 362-4711

Woody Auction
Douglass, KS 67039
(316) 746-2694

York Town Auction, Inc.
1625 Haviland Rd
York, PA 17404
(717) 751-0211
e-mail: yorktownauction@cyberia.com

# ABBREVIATIONS

The following are standard abbreviations which we have used throughout this edition of *Warman's*.

4to = 8" x 10"
8vo = 5" x 7"
12mo = 3" x 5"
ABP = American Brilliant Period
ADS = Autograph Document Signed
adv = advertising
ah = applied handle
ALS = Autograph Letter Signed
AQS = Autograph Quotation Signed
C = century
c = circa
Cal. = caliber
circ = circular
cyl. = cylinder
cov = cover
CS = Card Signed
d = diameter or depth
dec = decorated
dj = dust jacket
DQ = Diamond Quilted
DS = Document Signed
ed = edition
emb = embossed
ext. = exterior
eyep. = eyepiece
Folio = 12 x 16"
ftd = footed
ga = gauge
gal = gallon
ground = background
h = height
horiz. = horizontal
hp = hand painted
hs = high standard
HT = hard top
illus = illustrated, illustration
imp = impressed
int. = interior
irid = iridescent
IVT = inverted thumbprint
j = jewels
K = karat
l = length
lb = pound

litho = lithograph
ll = lower left
lr = lower right
ls = low standard
LS = Letter Signed
mfg = manufactured
MIB = mint in box
MOP = mother-of-pearl
n/c = no closure
ND = no date
NE = New England
No. = number
ns = no stopper
r/c = reproduction closure
o/c = original closure
opal = opalescent
orig = original
os = orig stopper
oz = ounce
pat = patent
pcs = pieces
pgs = pages
PUG = printed under the glaze
pr = pair
PS = Photograph Signed
pt = pint
qt = quart
rds = roadster
RM = red mark
rect = rectangular
sgd = signed
S. N. = Serial Number
sngl = single
SP = silver plated
SS = Sterling silver
sq = square
TLS = Typed Letter Signed
unp = unpaged
vert. = vertical
vol = volume
w = width
yg = yellow gold
# = numbered

# ABC PLATES

**History:** The majority of early ABC plates were manufactured in England and imported into the United States. They achieved their greatest popularity from 1780 to 1860. Since a formal education was uncommon in the early 19th century, the ABC plate was a method of educating the poor for a few pennies. ABC plates were made of glass, pewter, porcelain, pottery, or tin. Porcelain plates range in diameter from 4-3/8 to slightly over 9-1/2 inches. The rim usually contains the alphabet and/or numbers; the center features animals, great men, maxims, or nursery rhymes.

**References:** Susan and Al Bagdade, *Warman's English & Continental Pottery & Porcelain, 3rd Edition*, Krause Publications, 1998; Mildred L. and Joseph P. Chalala, *A Collector's Guide to ABC Plates, Mugs and Things*, Pridemark Press, 1980; Irene and Ralph Lindsey, *ABC Plates & Mugs*, Collector Books, 1998; Noel Riley, *Gifts for Good Children*, Richard Dennis Publications, 1991.

**Collectors' Club:** ABC Plate/Mug Collector's Circle, 67 Stevens Ave., Old Bridge, NJ 08857.

## Glass

Beaded Edge, milk white, Westmoreland, 7" d ............................. 50.00
Christmas Eve, Santa on chimney, clear, 6" d ............................ 75.00
Clock face center, Arabic and Roman numerals, alphabet center, frosted and clear, 7" d ................................................................. 75.00
Dog in center, clear, 6-1/2" d ...................................................... 110.00
Duck, amber, 6" d .......................................................................... 45.00
Elephant with howdah, three waving Brownies, Ripley & Co., clear, 6" d ................................................................................................. 135.00
Frosted Stork, flake ...................................................................... 125.00
Girl with bee on cheek, clear, 6-1/2" d ...................................... 125.00
Little Bo Peep, center scene, raised alphabet border, 6" d .......... 50.00
Plain center, clear, white scalloped edge, 6" d .......................... 65.00
Stork, marigold carnival, 7-3/4" d ................................................ 90.00
Young Girl, portrait, clear, 6" d ................................................... 65.00

## Pottery or Porcelain

Brighton Beach, sepia dec of Brighton Beach Bathing Pavilion, 7-1/2" d ....................................................................................... 145.00

Crusoe Finding the Footprints, 7 1/2" d ...................................... 80.00
Fox Hunt, brown transfer, 7" d .................................................... 125.00
Gathering Cotton, 6" d ................................................................. 425.00
Horses for Hire or Sale, brown transfer and polychrome dec, 6-3/4" d ....................................................................................... 145.00
Keep Within Compass, soft paste, enamel, minor damage .......... 85.00
Little Boy Blue ............................................................................... 80.00
Make Hay, soft paste, enamel, minor damage ............................ 55.00
Old Mother Hubbard, brown transfer, polychrome enamel trim, alphabet border, mkd "Tunstall," 7-1/2" d ............................... 200.00
Rooster on Fence, gold rim with alphabet letters, Syracuse China, 8-1/2" d ....................................................................................... 55.00
Take Your Time Miss Lucy, black transfer of money and cat, polychrome enamel, titled, molded hops rim, red trim, ironstone, imp "Meakin," 6" d ............................................................................ 125.00
Wandering Pie, birds, Staffordshire, 1890s ............................... 125.00

## Tin

Girl on swing, lithographed center, printed alphabet border, 3-1/2" d ......................................................................................... 60.00
Mary Had A Little Lamb, light rust, 9" d .................................... 115.00
Two kittens playing with basket of wood, 4-1/2" d ...................... 85.00
Who Killed Cock Robin, 7-3/4" d ................................................ 120.00

**Staffordshire, dog wearing monocle in center, brown transfer, 8-1/2" d, $75.**

# ADVERTISING

**History:** Before the days of mass media, advertisers relied on colorful product labels and advertising giveaways to promote their products. Containers were made to appeal to the buyer through the use of stylish lithographs and bright colors. Many of the illustrations used the product in the advertisement so that even an illiterate buyer could identify a product. Advertisements were put on almost every household object imaginable and were constant reminders to use the product or visit a certain establishment.

**References:** *Advertising & Figural Tape Measures*, L-W Book Sales, 1995; Pamela E. Apkarian-Russell, *Washday Collectibles*, Schiffer Publishing, 2000; Donna S. Baker, *Chocolate Memorabilia*, Schiffer Publishing, 2000; Steve Batson, *Country Store Counter Jars and Tins*, Schiffer Publishing, 1997; Michael Bruner, *Advertising Clocks*, Schiffer Publishing, 1995; ——, *Encyclopedia of Porcelain Enamel Advertising*, 2nd ed., Schiffer Publishing, 1999; ——, *More Porcelain Enamel Advertising*, Schiffer Publishing, 1997; Donald A. Bull, *Beer Advertising*, Schiffer Publishing, 2000; *Collector's Digest Letter Openers: Advertising & Figural*, L-W Book Sales, 1996; Albert and Shelly Coito, *Elsie the Cow and Borden's Collectibles*, Schiffer Publishing, 2000; Doug Collins, *America's Favorite Food: The Story of Campbell Soup Company*, Harry N Abrams, 1994; Irene Davis, *Collecting Paint Advertising and Memorabilia*, Schiffer Publishing, 2000; Fred Dodge, *Antique Tins*, Collector Books, Book I (1995, 1999 value update,) Book II, (1998), Book III (1999); Warren Dotz, *Advertising Character Collectibles*, Collector Books, 1993, 1997 values updated; ——, *What a Character! 20th Century American Advertising Icons*, Chronicle Books, 1996; Robert Forbes and Terrence Mitchell, *American Tobacco Cards: Price Guide and Checklist*, Tuff Stuff Books, 1999; Bill and Pauline Hogan, *Charlton Standard Catalogue of Canadian Country Store Collectables*, Char-

Iton Press, 1996; Bob and Sharon Huxford, *Huxford's Collectible Advertising*, 4th ed., Collector Books, 1999; Don and Elizabeth Johnson, *Warman's Advertising*, Krause Publications, 2000; Ray Klug, *Antique Advertising Encyclopedia*, Vol. 1 (1978, 1993 value update) and Vol. 2 (1985), L-W Promotions; Mary Jane Lamphier, *Zany Characters of the Ad World*, Collector Books, 1995; Rex Miller, *The Investor's Guide to Vintage Character Collectibles*, Krause Publications, 1999; Tom Morrison, *More Root Beer Advertising & Collectibles*, Schiffer Publishing, 1997; Richard A. Penn, *Mom and Pop Stores*, Schiffer Publishing, 1998; Gerald S. Petrone, *Tobacco Advertising*, Schiffer Publishing, 1996; Don and Carol Raycraft, *Wallace-Homestead Price Guide to American Country Antiques*, 16th ed., Krause Publications, 1999; Robert Reed, *Bears and Dolls in Advertising*, Antique Trader Books, 1998; ——, *Paper Advertising Collectibles: Treasures from Almanacs to Window Signs*, Antique Trader Books, 1998; Loretta Metzger Rieger and Lagretta Metzger Bajorek, *Children's Paper Premiums in American Advertising 1890-1990s*, Schiffer Publishing, 2000; Bob Sloan and Steve Guarnaccia, *A Stiff Drink and a Close Shave*, Chronicle Books, 1995; Louis Storino, *Chewing*

## SPECIAL AUCTIONS

Bear Pen Antiques
2318 Bear Pen Hollow Road
Lock Haven, PA 17745
(717) 769-6655

Bill Bertoia Auctions
1881 Spring Rd
Vineland, NJ 08360
(609) 692-1881

Hake's Americana & Collectibles
P.O. Box 1444, Dept. 344
York, PA 17405
(717) 848-1333

James D. Julia, Inc.
P.O. Box 830
Fairfield, ME 04937
(207) 453-7125

Wm. Morford
Rd #2
Cazenovia NY 13035
(315) 662-7625

Richard Opfer Auctioneering
1919 Greenspring Dr.
Timonium, MD 21093
(410) 252-5035

Past Tyme Pleasures
PMB #204, 2491 San Ramon Valley Blvd.
San Ramon, CA 94583
(925) 484-6442

Sandy Rosnick Auctions
15 Front St.
Salem MA 01970
(508) 741-1130

*Tobacco Tin Tags*, Schiffer Publishing, 1995; B. J. Summers, *Value Guide to Advertising Memorabilia*, 2nd ed., Collector Books, 1999; Tom Webster, edited by David D. Kowalski, *Winchester Rarities*, Krause Publications, 2000; Richard White, *Advertising Cutlery*, Schiffer Publishing, 1999; David L. Wilson, *General Store Collectibles*, Collector Books, Vol. 1, 1994, Vol. 2, 1998; Neil Wood, *Smoking Collectibles*, L-W Book Sales, 1994; David and Micki Young, *Campbell's Soup Collectibles from A to Z*, Krause Publications, 1998; David Zimmerman, *The Encyclopedia of Advertising Tins*, Vol. 1 (1994) and Vol. II (1999), Collector Books.

**Periodicals:** (General) *Advertising Collectors Express*, P.O. Box 221, Mayview, MO 64071; *Let's Talk Tin*, 1 S. Beaver Lane, Greenville, SC 29605; *Paper Collectors' Marketplace*, P.O. Box 128, Scandinavia, WI 54917; *Paper & Advertising Collector* (PAC) P.O. Box 500, Mount Joy, PA 17552; *Tin Fax Newsletter*, 205 Brolley Woods Dr., Woodstock, GA 30188; *Tin Type Newsletter*, P.O Box 440101, Aurora, CO 80044; *Trade Card Journal*, 143 Main St., Brattleboro, CT 05301.

**Collectors' Clubs:** (General) Advertising Cup and Mug Collectors of America, P.O. Box 680, Solon, IL 52333; Antique Advertising Association of America, P.O. Box 1121, Morton Grove, IL 60053, www.pastime.org. Ephemera Society of America, P.O. Box 95, Cazenovia, NY 13035, www.ephemerasociety.org. Inner Seal Collectors Club, 4585 Saron Drive, Lexington, KY 40515; National Association of Paper and Advertising Collectibles, P.O. Box 500, Mount Joy, PA 17552; Porcelain Advertising Collectors Club, P.O. Box 381, Marshfield Hills, MA 02051; Tin Container Collectors Association, P.O. Box 440101, Aurora, CO 80044; Trade Card Collector's Assoc., 3706 S. Acoma St., Englewood, CO 80110.

**Museums:** American Advertising Museum, Portland, OR; Creatability Toys Museum of Advertising Icons, Miami, FL; Museum of Beverage Containers & Advertising, Goodlettsville, TN; Museum of Transportation, Brookline, MA; National Museum of American History, Archives Center, Smithsonian Institution, Washington, DC; National Signs of the Times Museum, Cincinnati, OH; U. S. Patent & Trademark Museum, Arlington, VA.

**Additional Listings:** See *Warman's Americana & Collectibles* and *Warman's Advertising* for more examples.

Ashtray, Mail Pouch Tobacco, baby with blue diaper, "Just Found His Mail Pouch," plaster of paris, c1930-40, 5" d, 5" h .................. 120.00
Banner, Chew Old Honesty Plug Tobacco, Always Reliable, linen, St. Bernard, yellow ground, blue letters, water stains at right edge, 50" l, 18" h ............................. 250.00
Bicycle, Hershey's Chocolate Co., Schwinn, 68" l ...................... 375.00
Bill Clip, Heinzelman Bros. Carriage Co., celluloid button bill clip, litho by Ehrman Co., Boston, 2-1/4" l, 2" h ......................... 60.00
Blotter, F. O. Stone Baking Co., Cincinnati, OH, celluloid, dated 1915, by Whitehead & Hoag, Santa and reindeer holiday giveaway, 7-3/4" l, 3" h ............................. 70.00
Bookmark
    Eaton Co., diecut ivory white thin celluloid marker, turning disk wheel picturing aerial view of Toronoto Store and Factories, reverse with full color illus of birthstone f each month, six-year mechanical disk wheel calendar for 1913-1918 ................ 30.00

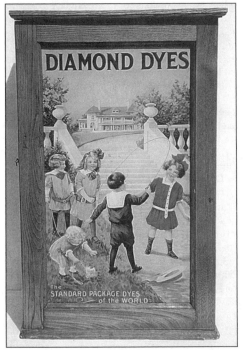

**Cabinet, Diamond Dyes, wooden, counter top, emb tin litho, 15-1/2" w, 9" d, 24-1/2" h, $1,750. Photo courtesy of Past Tyme Pleasures Auction.**

F. F. Pulver Co., diecut thin celluloid marker topped by multicolored image of turkey, lower half black and white Thanksgiving verse by sponsor F. F. Pulver Co., maker of "Pulveroid Novelties That Advertise," blank reverse, early 1900s ...................... 70.00

Standard Mfg. Co., Paris, 1900, celluloid, graphics of lady preparing bath, crossed flags at top, litho by Whitehead & Hoag, 1-1/2" w, 6" h ............................................................... 200.00

Box

Adams Sappota Chewing Gum, 7-1/2" x 8-1/2", two Victorian ladies, graphic labels .......................................... 90.00

Kellogg's Rice Krispies, 5" w, 2-1/2" d, 7" h, 5-3/4 oz, cardboard, little girl in red dress on front "Ladybug, Ladybug," dated 1940 ....................................................... 135.00

Nabisco Barnum's Animals Cookies, c1940, bright colors, 5" l, 1-3/4" d, 2-1/2" h .......................................... 40.00

Roundup Jar Rings, 3" sq, full ........................................... 120.00

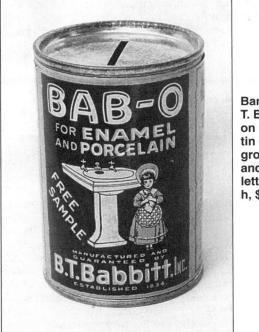

**Bank, Bab-O, B. T. Babbitt, paper on cardboard, tin ends, green ground, white and black lettering, 2" d, 3" h, $35.**

Roylaes Corsets, litho by J. Goosens, Bruxelles, seaside scene with lion, lady, palm trees, 15-3/4" l, 3" d, 3" h ................... 90.00

Calendar

Gus Becht Butchers Supply, famous bull graphics, litho by Gast, St. Louis & NY, 1891, full pad, 10" w, 14" h ...................... 950.00

M. A. Theoford's Black Draught Liver Medicine and McElree's Wine of Cardui Woman's Relief Medicine, 1911, metal edge ....................................................... 40.00

Candy Pail

Lovell & Covel, Queen of Hearts design, 3" x 2-7/8", 3 oz, slot added later to lid .......................................... 110.00

Riley's Rum & Butter Toffee, Halifax, England, 7-1/4" x 7", emb name, silhouettes of children playing with kite, slip lid ....... 50.00

Sharps' Toffee, 10" x 3-1/4", colorful parrot .......................... 55.00

Change Tray, glass

Muriel Cigars, Brunhoff Mgf., Cincinnati, OH, woman in center, unused condition, 7" l, 6" w, 2" h ................................... 100.00

Webster Cigars, by Brunhoff Mfg., Cincinnati, OH, orig label affixed to bottom, unused condition, 7-1/2" l, 6" w ............. 80.00

Cigar Lighter, M. Stachelberg & Co., Havana Cigars, countertop, alcohol burner, 2-1/2" d, 3-1/4" h ................................ 140.00

Clock, Pepsi Cola, Telechron, glass, white ground, red and blue logo, lights up, 1940s, 15" d ............................................. 200.00

Coffee Tin

Arena Coffee, 1 lb size, screw top, litho by General Can, Chicago, same dog image both sides, 4" d, 6" h ............................. 275.00

Astor House Coffee, 4" d, 6-1/4" h, l lb size, screw top ...... 170.00

Baker-ized Coffee, Barrington Hall, 1 lb size, slip lid, graphics of Southern plantation, red ground, dated 1914, 4" d, 5-1/2" h .................................................... 170.00

Beech Nut Coffee, 4 oz sample key wind, by American Can, 3-1/4" d, 2" h .................................................... 50.00

Blanke's Happy Thought Coffee, figural trunk, 9" l, 4-1/2" w, 4-1/2" h .................................................... 70.00

Bueno Coffee, Walker-Smith Co., Brownwood, Texas, l lb size, slip lid, litho by LaCross Can, WI, 4" d, 5-1/4" h .............. 210.00

Canova Coffee, 1 lb, keywind, packed by Canova Foods, Memphis, TN, litho by American Can, 5" d, 3-1/2" h .......... 65.00

Eagle Coffee, litho by Continental Can Co., screw top, same image both sides, minor rust spots bottom edge, 4" d, 6" h .................................................... 90.00

Golden Sheaf Coffee, litho by Passaic Metal Ware, NJ, 1 lb, screw top, 4" d, 6" h .................................................... 120.00

Golden West Coffee, packed by Clossett & Devers, Portland, OR, 2 lb, keywind, dated 1927, same image both sides, 5" d, 7" h .................................................... 150.00

Heart's Delight Coffee, packed by Scoville, Brown & Co., Wellsville, NY, American Can, 1 lb size, 4-1/4" d, 6" h ................ 80.00

Loly Coffee, litho by Passaic Metal Ware, NJ, 1 lb, screw top, 4" d, 6" h .................................................... 250.00

Mokay Coffee, bright litho by American Can Co., 1 lb size, 4" d, 6" h .................................................... 130.00

Monadnock Coffee, by Continental Can, Passaic, NJ, 1 lb size, screw top, same image both sides, 4" d, 6" h .................. 170.00

Perfect Coffee, A. H. Perfect Co., 4" d, 6" h, screw top, 1 lb size, dated 1923 .................................................... 70.00

Progress Dining Room Coffee, litho by Passaic Metalware, NJ, 1 lb size, screw top, same image both sides, 4" d, 6" h ...... 150.00

Red Wolf Coffee, litho by Continental Can, 1 lb size, 5" d, 4" h ..... 210.00

WGY Coffee, litho by Continental Can, Passaic, NJ, 1 lb size, screw top, same images both sides, 4" d, 6" h ................ 120.00

White Label Coffee, litho by American Can Co., MA, 1 lb size, screw top, several scrapes, 4" d, 6" h ................. 50.00

Counter Top Cabinet Diamond Dyes, wooden, emb tin litho, children playing graphics, 15-1/2" w, 9" d, 24-1/2" h .......... 1,750.00

Putnam Dyes, tin litho, bold colors, 19" l, 15" w, 8" d ........ 140.00

Remington Hi Speed .22, wood and glass, hand clock operates front door form back, 16" l, 6" d, 10" h ............... 60.00

**Counter Top Display Box**
  Beemans Pepsin Gum, unused condition,
    4-1/2" l, 3" w, 2" h.............................................45.00
  Havana Sweets Cigar, diecut, 13" w, 9" h...........................40.00
  Marlin High Speed Blades, six full boxes of blades,
    5-1/2" w, 6-1/2" h........................................240.00
**Counter Top Sign**
  Black Cross Teas, emb cardboard, cute girl in pink sunbonnet,
    holding card with adv about teas, 7-1/4" w, 16" h ...........185.00
  Ohio Varnish Co., color samples of floor enamels, 1920-30s, 12"
    w, 18" h .....................................................60.00
  Pabst Blue Ribbon Beer, cardboard, easel back,
    20" w, 26" h .................................................40.00
**Door Push**
  Crystal White Soap, metal, white lettering on dark blue ground,
    3-1/2" w, 8-3/4" h..........................................235.00
  Fleischmann's Yeast, litho by Haeusermann, NY, man made out
    of bread loaves, 3-1/4" w, 9" h .............................90.00
  Dust Pan, Compliments of George Long, Vanderbilt, Mich, emb
    tin, bright colors, 8-3/4" w, 9" h, minor scuff marks ...........50.00
  Jug, Sanford's, 7" d, 10" h, pottery, blue adv,
    orig bail/locking bar ........................................90.00
**Lunch Box, litho tin**
  Blue and Scarlet Plug Cut, Booker Tobacco Co., Richmond, clasp
    missing, some fading .......................................100.00
  Central Union Cut Plug, 7-1/2" l, 5" w, 4" h......................125.00
  Dan Patch Cut Plug, 7" l, 4" w, 4-1/2" h.........................180.00
  Dixie Queen Tobacco, bright graphics,
    7-1/2" l, 4" w, 5-1/2" h.....................................235.00
  Fashion Cut Plug Tobacco, couple strolling.......................360.00
  Great West Tobacco, Canadian, red and black, wear...........60.00
  Winner Cut Plug, same image both sides, minor scrapes,
    8" l, 5" w, 4-1/4" h.........................................385.00
**Match Dispenser, I. W. Harper**, white enamel emb letters "From Old
  Kentucky I. W. Harper," glass, 5" d round base, 5" h .................50.00
**Mirror, pocket, celluloid, oval**
  Bee Hive Overalls Best Maid, 1-3/4" w, 2-3/4" h, made by White-
    head & Hoag, Newark, NJ, c1910, bright image of girl modeling
    blue overalls, mirror broken..................................260.00
  Berry Bros. Varnishes, 2-3/4" l, 1-3/4" h, little boy in overalls,
    straw hat, pulling dog in wagon......................................140.00
  Buckwalter Stove Co., The Enameled Range,
    1-3/4" w, 2-3/4" h...........................................90.00
  Lava Soap, celluloid centered by image of gray soap bar, opened
    container box, yellow ground, early 1900s.........................35.00
  Mascot Tobacco, multicolored portrait of dog, red rim,
    white lettering..............................................85.00
  National Life Insurance, pink and white celluloid centered by rep-

lica of policy certificate, inscriptions for representatives located
    in Kansas City .............................................25.00
  Oliver Typewriter, photo of girl and typewriter, image by Photo
    Jewelry, Chicago, 2" w, 2-3/4" h.............................40.00
  Money Clip, Chesterfield Cigarettes, white enamel on chromed
    metal, sponsored by Liggit & Myers Tobacco Co., each side rep-
    lica of cigarette pack, Robbins Co. maker, c1950.............20.00
**Package, paper label on tin**
  Bomb Buster Popcorn, 2-1/2" d, 5" h...........................60.00
  Lady Adams Oysters, packed expressly for Mebius & Drescher
    Co., Sacramento, CA, paper litho label, opened,
    2-3/4" d, 4-1/4" h..........................................80.00
  Parrot and Monkey Baking Powder, by Sea Gull Specialty Co.,
    Baltimore & New Orleans, unopened, 2-1/2" d, 5" h..........50.00
  Popeye Popcorn, tin by American Can Co., dated 1949 King Fea-
    tures, 3" w, 2" d, 4-3/4" h..................................70.00
**Peanut Butter Pail, tin**
  FI-NA-ST Peanut Butter, 1 lb size, same image both sides,
    3-1/2" d, 3-3/4" h..........................................75.00
  Harvard, Millard Supply Co., Chicago, 10" x 8", 10#, peanut
    dressed as graduating student, "Educate the Taste"........140.00
  Monadnock Peanut Butter, litho by Canco, 1 lb size, same image
    both sides, 3-1/2" d, 3-3/4" h.............................180.00
**Squirrel, Canada Nut Company Limited, Vancouver, BC, snap-top tin**
  3-3/4" x 3", 13 oz .........................................165.00
  4-1/4" x 4", 27 oz .........................................160.00
  4-3/4" x 5-1/4", 48 oz .......................................90.00
  5-1/2" x 5", 57 oz ..........................................95.00
  6-1/2" x 5-1/4", #5, horizontal scratch on front.............120.00
**Pencil Clip**
  Drekorn's Bread, celluloid, silvered tin clip, orange, black, white,
    and yellow wrapped loaf of bread, white ground, c1930....15.00
  Duxbak Sportsman's Clothing, gold luster metal, red, white, and
    blue enamel accents, 1930s .................................25.00
  Shapleigh Hardware Co., 7/8" d, brown and red celluloid, silvered
    clip, Diamond Edge logo in center, 1920s....................18.00
  Worcester Iodized Salt, white lettering outlined in black, orange
    ground, celluloid, silvered clip .............................10.00
  Pennant, Ruhstaller's Gilt Edge Lager, Sacramento, CAL, felt,
    shows bottle, San Francisco maker's tag on reverse,
    8-1/2" w, 29" l ...........................................210.00
**Pinback Button**
  Buster Brown Bread, multicolored .............................25.00
  Cherry Smash, multicolored, portrait of
    George Washington .........................................30.00
  Compliments of Santa Claus & Hales, litho by Whitehead & Hoag,
    dated April 14, 1896, Hales Dept. Store, San Jose, CA, cellu-
    loid, jolly Santa face, 1-1/4" d.............................60.00
  Drink Dukehart's Ale, image of duck, fish, oyster, and crab, cellu-
    loid, 7/8" d ...............................................70.00
  Findlay Carriage Co., sepia celluloid, Model No. 427 buggy, Find-
    lay, OH, early 1900s........................................95.00
  Freeman's Milk, blue bottle, white lettering, 1920s...............15.00
  Golden Sheaf Bread Bungalow, multicolored early ranch-style
    house, 1920s...............................................75.00
  Good Humor Safety Club, blue, white, and orange, 1930s ..18.00
  Majestic, The World in Your Home, blue and white design of elec-
    trical bolt crossing world globe, 1920s .....................20.00
  Maxwell House Coffee, blue and white, "The People's Choice,"
    c1950 .....................................................10.00
  National Spring Bed Co., blue and white logo, inscription "The Rip
    Van Winkle Line," New Britain, CT, store ....................10.00
  Peck-Williamson Furnace, multicolored image of furnace, center
    cut-away, portrait of Sawrie-"The Man Who Made The Under-
    feed Famous in Nashville"..................................75.00
  Puritan Hosiery, multicolored, center image of Puritan lady, red
    trim, white lettering.......................................100.00
  Shoot Peters Shell, celluloid, litho by Whitehead & Hoag,
    7/8" d.....................................................60.00

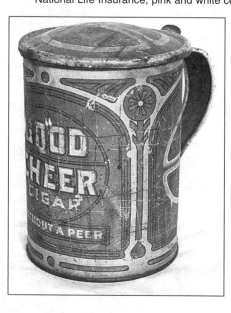

Cigar Tin, Good
Cheer Cigars, mug
form, bottom mkd
"FACT No.
215/25/DIST KAS,"
$70.

Pocket Calendar, Browning, King & Co., 1919, celluloid, graphics of baby in oval "I Want My Clothes and It's Gotta Be A Uniform" with uniformed solider and sailor standing on either side of oval, 2-1/4" w, 3-3/4" h ................................................. 50.00

Pocket Case, The Bachelor Cigar, leather, celluloid inserts on both sides, front with dapper seated gent, other side with risqué four leaf clover, 3" w, 5" h ................................... 130.00

Print, Anheuser Busch

"A Fight for the Overland Mail," by artist Oscar Berninghaus, litho, matted and framed, 16" w, 7-1/2" h ................................ 136.00

"The Father of Waters," by artist Oscar Berninghaus, litho, matted and framed, 16" w, 7-1/2" h ................................ 250.00

Shipping Container, Fairbanks Fairy Soap, wooden, 16" l, 15" w, 8" h, graphic inside paper label ........................................ 325.00

Sign

A. K. Walch's Good Company 3¢ Cigars, tin litho, white letters on red ground, 7-1/2" w, 13-3/4" h ........................................ 185.00

W. L. Brubaker & Bros., 24" x 17", paper, roll-down type, tin strips on top and bottom, portrait of woman on green foliage background, professional restoration to one side, framed ................................. 450.00

Bulldog Seats, 9-3/4" x 6-1/2", oval, emb tin, arrogant looking black and white bulldog standing on toilet seat, "Joints Won't Let Go" ................................. 880.00

Carborundum Scythe Stones, string hung sign, red ground, gold letters, roundel with Indian chief in headdress, 12" l, 3-1/2" h ..... 135.00

Chew Corn Bread Tobacco, 30" x 18", heavy paper, Compton & Sons litho, yellow ground, red and black lettering ........................... 530.00

Duxbak, Servicable Clothes For Life In The Open, tin over cardboard, mallard landing on pond, others flying, 15" w, 18-1/2" h .......... 300.00

Foster Hose Supporters, celluloid, string hung, litho by E. F. Pulver Co., Rochester, NY, lady in green blouse, red skirt, blue garters, 9" w, 17" h ................................................ 500.00

Fritz Bros. Best 5¢ Cigars, 17-1/4" l, reverse foil under glass, framed, some professional repairs ........................................ 250.00

La Flor De Erb 10¢ Cigar, E. S. Erb & Co., Makers, emb tin over cardboard, litho by National Sign, Dayton, OH, 13-1/2" l, 6" h .......... 85.00

Old Reliable Coffee, 9-1/4" x 6-1/2", tin, H. D. Beach Co., Coshocton, Ohio, orig nail holes around edges ........................................ 135.00

Red Coon, Sun Cured Chewing Tobacco, 18" x 12", heavy paper, red and black raccoon, yellow ground, black lettering ...................... 60.00

Smoke A Freelance 5¢ Cigar, cardboard, emb cigar label insert, string handle, 11" l, 9-1/2" h ........................................ 50.00

Squirt, monkeys and bottles, "Why Monkey Drink Squirt," yellow, red, green, white, and black, cardboard diecut, string hanger, double sided, dated 1941, 7-1/2" w, 9-1/2" h ........................................ 70.00

Thirsty? Just Whistle, emb tin, hand holding orange soda bottle, cobalt blue ground, litho by American Art Works, 9-3/4" l, 6-3/4" h .... 650.00

Valley Brew Gold Medal Beer, tin, red ground, white letters, red dot with "Enjoy," 28" l, 10" h ........................................ 50.00

Ziegler's Beer, tin over cardboard, litho by Donaldson Art Sign Co., Covington, KY, 11-1/2" l, 8-1/2" h ........................................ 50.00

Spinner Top

Red Goose Shoes, 2" x 2", diecut cardboard figure attached to wooden base, c1930 ........................................ 30.00

Sun-Proof Paint, celluloid inserted at center by wooden spinner diecut, orange smiling sun on white ground, rimmed in blue, C. A. Loew, Milwaukee, maker, 1930s ........................................ 50.00

Spittoon, Claymore Scotch Whiskey, copper, mkd "J. R. Grant & Son Ltd., London," patina, 3" d, 4" h ........................................ 70.00

Stickpin

B. S. A. Motorcycle, English motorcycle manuf, c1930 ........ 35.00

Holsum Bread, flag, diecut tin celluloid, red, white, and blue banner on brass stickpin, paper backing ................................. 15.00

Store Bin, tin litho

Sweet Barley Tobacco, 8-1/2" w, 10-3/4" h ........................... 195.00

Sweet Cuba Fine Cut, 5¢, 8" w, 8" d, 10" h, minor scrapes 165.00

Sweet Cuba Tobacco, same image both sides, 8-1/2" d, 11-1/2" h ........................................ 170.00

Stud

New Home Sewing Machine, red, white, and black celluloid, metal lapel stud, red lettering "Better Than Silver or Gold" around black and white image of sewing machine, c1896 ........................................ 20.00

Quaker Oats, dark charcoal luster, raised relief image of smiling young boy's head, bow tie, portrait flanked by "Quaker Oats," rim inscription "The Smile That Won't Come Off, Make Somebody Smile Today" ........................................ 12.00

P & F Syrups/Molasses, 3/4", red, white and blue enamel, gold luster ........................................ 10.00

Phantom Bicycles, purple and white celluloid, metal lapel stud, young male figure spreading arms in toga-like garment .... 25.00

Rudge-Whitworth Bicycles, brass, red, white, and blue enamel accents, upraised palm of hand against bicycle spokes, rim inscription "Coventry," Birmingham, England badge maker, late 1890s-early 1900s ........................................ 18.00

Smoke Blackwell's Genuine Durham, celluloid on metal, red drawing of livestock bull, white background, black lettering, c1900 ........................................ 15.00

Sterling Bicycles, litho metal, product name in black and white lettering, dark green ground, "Built Like A Watch" ................. 12.00

World Bicycles, red, white and blue celluloid in metal, world globe under streamer "Ride the World" ........................................ 15.00

Thermometer

David Harum Flour, wooden, dated 1937, 3" w, 12" l .......... 60.00

Drink Double Cola, tin, green ground, 5" w, 17" h ............. 125.00

Fin & Feather Boots & Shoes, emb tin litho, unused, 4-1/2" w, 14" h ........................................ 100.00

Golden Sun Coffee, porcelain, by Beach, Coshocton, OH, dated 1915, 2-3/4" w, 11-1/2" h ........................................ 350.00

Hills Bros. Coffee, porcelain, by Beach, Coshocton, OH, dated 1915, red ground, gent in orange gown, white hat, 8-3/4" w, 21" h ........................................ 825.00

Lash's Kidney Bitters, wooden, black and orange, by American Mfg. Concern, Jamestown, NY, 5-1/4" w, 21" h ................ 475.00

Natures Remedy, porcelain, red, white, and blue, 7" w, 27" h, glass tube broken ........................................ 160.00

Waller Bros. Strawberry Growers, metal, strawberry graphics at top, 6" w, 15" h ........................................ 225.00

Tin

Christmas, sleighing scene, litho by Ginna, NY, graphics on lid and all sides, 6" l, 3-3/4" h ........................................ 275.00

Cigar

Possum Cigar, image of possum on both sides, 5" d, 5" h ........................................ 185.00

War Eagle Cigars, bright luster finish, same image both sides, 5" d, 5" h ........................................ 80.00

Cocoanut, San Blas Cocoanut, mfg by Croft & Allen, Philadelphia, Golden Crown Brand, fading red color, 3" d, 6-1/2" h ........................................ 60.00

Mirror, Ask for Horlicks, gold trim band, brown cow, girl in blue and white, green pasture, trees, blue lettering, 2" d, $70.00

## Gun Powder

Dupont Ballistite Smokeless Powder, litho by American Can, 3-1/4" w, 5" h ..................80.00

Dupont Schuetzen Smokeless Powder, 1 lb size, paper label on tin, some discoloration, 4" d, 5-3/4" h..................65.00

Mathewson's Gun Powder, 3-3/4" w, 6-3/4" h, l lb size.......110.00

Oil, Simoniz Graphite Oil, witch graphics, red, black and yellow, litho by Continental Can, 2" d, 6" h ..................70.00

## Oysters

Christy's Oysters, 1 gal size, graphics of sailor steering with large red wheel, 6-3/4" d, 7" h..................70.00

Mermaid Oysters, packed for Mebius & Drescher, Sacramento, early paper litho, bottom opened, hand soldered, some pcs of label missing, 2-3/4" d, 4" h..................155.00

## Spices

Amocat, packed by West Coast Grocery, Tacoma, WA, litho by American Can, 2 oz size, bright luster finish, same image both sides, 2" w, 3" h..................120.00

Farmers Pride Pure Expertly Ground Rubbed Sage, bright paper label, same image both sides, 2-1/4" w, 3" h..................40.00

Here's Howe's Imperial Pure Spices, Whole Allspice, George J. Howe Co., 2-1/4" w, 4" h..................45.00

## Talcum

A.D.S. Baby Talc, litho by Metal Pkg. Co., Brooklyn, NY, dated 1914, same image both sides, 3" d, 5" h..................80.00

Baby Mine Talc, American Product, Cincinnati, bright blue ground, baby graphics, 2" w, 5" h..................350.00

Colgate Cashmere Bouquet Talc Powder, sample size, 1-1/4" w, 2" h..................45.00

Jap Rose Talc, made by Kirk Chicago, lady graphics, same image on both sides, 2" d, 6" h..................50.00

Richard Hudnut Violet Sec, sample size, same image on both sides, 1-1/4" w, 2" h..................60.00

Sam Toy Talc, litho by Metal Pkg. Co., Brooklyn, NY, 2-1/2" w, 4-1/2" h, top askew..................70.00

Violet Talcum Powder, litho by American Stopper Co., Brooklyn, NY, beautiful lady graphics, 2" d, 6" h..................145.00

Violette Exquisite Talcum Powder, Kirk, Chicago, graphics of pretty girl surrounded by flowers, same image both sides, 2" w, 4-1/2" h..................220.00

Ward's Talcum Powder, Bullock Ward Co., Chicago, baby on front, 2-1/2" d, 4" h..................150.00

Tea, McCormick's Tea, 3-3/4" w, 3-3/4" d, 6" h, litho tin, 1 lb size, dated 1936..................40.00

## Tip Tray

Buffalo Brewing Co., Sacramento, CA, litho by Kaufman & Straus, NY, 4-1/2" d..................250.00

Olympia Beer, It's The Water, minor crazing, 4-1/4" d..................50.00

Resinol Soap and Ointment, beautiful woman graphics, 4-1/4" d..................150.00

## Tobacco Tins, vertical pocket type

Abbey, 10¢, 4" h, full..................370.00

Bagdad, tall version, litho top, 4-1/4" h..................440.00

Bambino, silhouette of the Babe, red ground..................2,930.00

Big Ben..................35.00

Bon Air..................500.00

Briggs, "Complimentary tin, not for sale," full..................165.00

Bulldog, blue, full, 4-1/2" h..................600.00

Cavalier Plug Tobacco, 3" w, 1-1/2" d, 6-1/4" l, bright colors, graphics, labor union sticker attached inside of lid, small ding on bottom center..................80.00

Central Union..................340.00

Checkers, red and black, gold letters, short version..................340.00

Coach & Four..................245.00

Dial, "for pipe and cigarettes"..................140.00

Dill's, concave, girl in red dress..................135.00

Edgeworth Junior..................95.00

Ensign, Washington and Lee, Perfection Cut..................1,210.00

Fairmount, white lid, 10¢..................310.00

Forest & Stream, fisherman, creel top..................125.00

Four Roses, flat top, 4-1/4" h..................545.00

Full Dress, Flip top, overall wear..................200.00

Sears Roebuck & Co...................1,335.00

Gold Bond, 4-1/2" h, 3" w..................235.00

Guide, full..................335.00

Handmade, woman's hand illus..................500.00

Himyar Tobacco, intact with cigarette papers under tax stamp, same image of horse and rider on both sides, 5-1/4" d, 6-1/2" h, 14 oz size..................110.00

Hi-Plane, red ground, white plane and lettering..................60.00

Honeymoon..................600.00

John Middleton Club Mixture..................1,350.00

King Edward..................515.00

Kingsbury, Christian Paper Tob. Co., St. Louis, MO, 4-1/2" h..................755.00

Life..................825.00

London Sherbet Mixture, block letters, green ground..................260.00

Look Out, scratch on front..................1,215.00

Lucky Strike, 4-1/2" h..................100.00

Manhattan Cocktail, rooster and cocktail glass..................1,115.00

Maryland Club, flip top, rust to lid and top left..................250.00

Master Mason..................330.00

Matoaka, some overall wear and rust spots..................1,650.00

Moonshine, dents..................1,180.00

North Star Tobacco, litho by Ginna, NY, lady rising with star, 2-1/4" w, 3-3/4" h..................220.00

Old Colony, silver, 4-3/8" h..................215.00

Peachy..................225.00

Pipe Major, dark variation..................200.00

Plug Crumb Cut..................445.00

Rex..................265.00

Shot, shows rifle and long peace pipe..................275.00

Sun Cured, slight fading to one side..................1,835.00

Stag, tall..................115.00

Three Squares, 2-3/4" x 2", complimentary sample, full..................75.00

Times Square, some rust on lid..................335.00

### Torpedo, Canadian

Destroyer..................1,455.00

Submarine, concave..................7,720.00

Union Leader, five color..................110.00

US Marine, 4-1/4" h, full..................360.00

Wagon Wheel, yellow ground, red and black trim..................1,025.00

Wellington, full..................1,055.00

Yacht Club, red ground, some dents to base, worn....1,100.00

## Trade Sign

Barber, carved and painted wooden razor, black and white, America, 19th C, paint wear, scratches, 43-1/4" l..................920.00

Boot Maker, cast zinc, wrought iron angled bracket holds hanging boot form, painted golden brown, imp "570,"" America, 19th C, paint loss, 22-1/2" h..................1,380.00

### Butcher

Gloeckler's Patent June 25, 1889, cast iron, dimensional, mkd "Pacific Butcher's Supply Co., San Francisco, CAL," orig gold paint, 20" w, 24-1/2" h..................1,100.00

J. W. Goatcher, Butcher, brass, hand chiseled characters, patina, 16" l, 4-1/2" h..................70.00

### Cigar Maker

Cigar, turned wood, red letters "Papa's Best" on brown ground, America, late 19th C, paint losses, 37" l..................420.00

Rectangular, painted wood, black on green ground, "Daniel Spangler Cigar Manufacturer" and "A. M. Wright-Signs, Red Lion, PA" in small lettering at bottom, wear, 30-3/4" l, 14" w..................805.00

Lock Company, Independent Lock Co., Fitchburg, MA, hanging figural cast metal key, 28" l, 1-1/2" w..................335.00

Notary Public, porcelain strip sign, blue ground, red seal, white ground, 15" l, 3" h..................40.00

Watch Maker, pocket watch, cast and sheet zinc, traces of gilt and Roman numerals, 19-1/2" h..................360.00

Tray
  Deer Run Whiskey, Aug. Baetzold's, Buffalo, NY, litho by
    Haeusermann, NY, elk image, 12" d ...............................250.00
  George T. Stagg Co., O.F.C., Bourbon, litho by Haeusermann,
    NY, edge scuffs and minor crazing, 12" d ........................200.00
  Star Brewery, Vancouver, WA, bright luster, 12" d ..............475.00
Whistle, litho tin, double-reed variety
  Buster Brown Shoes, full color image on top, "Tread Straight Fea-
    ture That Helps To Walk Toes Straight Ahead to
    Health"...........................................................................20.00
  Hurd Shoes, inscriptions and logo in red on ivory white
    top ................................................................................15.00
  Poll Parrot Shoes, full color image of parrot on yellow
    ground ...........................................................................15.00
  Red Goose Shoes, full color image of red goose on yellow
    ground, underside mkd "Kirchof Co., Newark, NJ".............25.00

# ADVERTISING TRADE CARDS

**History:** Advertising trade cards are small, thin card-board cards made to advertise the merits of a product. They usually bear the name and address of a merchant. With the invention of lithography, colorful trade cards became a popular way to advertise in the late 19th and early 20th centuries. They were made to appeal especially to children. Young and old alike collected and treasured them in albums and scrapbooks. Very few are dated; the prime years for trade card production were 1880 to 1893; cards made between 1810 and 1850 can be found, but rarely. By 1900, trade cards were rapidly losing their popularity, and by 1910, they had all but vanished.

**References:** Kit Barry, *Advertising Trade Card*, Book 1, published by author, 1981; Dave Cheadle, *Victorian Trade Cards*, Collector Books, 1996, 1998 value update; Robert Forbes and Terrence Mitchell, *American Tobacco Cards: Price Guide and Checklist*, Tuff Stuff Books, 1999; Robert Jay, *Trade Card in Nineteenth-Century America*, University of Missouri Press, 1987; Murray Cards (International) Ltd. (comp.), *Cigarette Card Values*, Murray Cards (International) Ltd., 1994.

**Periodicals:** *Card Times*, 70 Winified Lane, Aughton, Ormskirk, Lancashire L38 5DL England; Trade Card Journal, 109 Main St., Brattleboro, VT 05301.

**Collectors' Clubs:** Trade Card Collector's Association, P.O. Box 284, Marlton, NJ 08053; United States Carto-philic Society, P.O. Box 4020, Saint Augustine, FL 32085.

**Additional Listings:** See *Warman's Americana & Collectibles* for more examples.

Beverages
  Anheuser Busch, 3-1/2" x 6" ................................................24.00
  Arbuckles Coffee, Australia, natives hunting kangaroos, #32 of 50
    pictorial history ..............................................................10.00
  Hires Root Beer, Knapp Litho NY, dated 1891, child in red dress
    pointing towards viewer, 3" w, 5" h...................................40.00
  Hood's Sarsaparilla, adv Catarrah, pre 1900, 3" x 4-3/4" .....12.50
  Union Pacific Tea Company, "We Lead, Let Those Who Can Fol-
    low...We Can't Help It," red on ivory ................................26.00

**Pillsbury XXX Best Flower, two black children floating in tub, flour sack for sale, A. Hoen & Co. Baltimore, $20.**

Clothing
  Chicago Corset Co., pretty darked haired woman,
    3" w, 4-1/2" h................................................................40.00
  Royal Shoe, "We Want the Royal Shoe," downtrodden barefoot
    toddler reading for pair of shoes, c1880, 4-3/4" x 7" ..........50.00
  Warren's Featherbone Dress Stays & Corsets, orange and yellow
    feather, blue ground, Angola, IN, retailer ...........................20.00
  Wilsnap Shoulder Strap Loop, product illus on front............15.00
Food
  Cudahy Packing Co., Rex Brand Hams & Bacon, paper litho
    diecut, pig graphics, 5-1/2" h, 6-1/4" when open..............120.00
  N. K. Fairbanks Lard Refiners, Familiar Quotations, 3" x 4-1/4"
    Paraphrased quote from "Burns, Cotter's Saturday Night," hog
      with spyglass looking from Chicago to Europe, slight crease
      lower right .................................................................15.00
    Paraphrased quote from "Byron, Bards & Scotts, Rev.," hog
      turning on apparatus, pigs rolling along, 3" x 4-1/4" .......8.00
  Fleischmanns, black couple on front, recipes on back, dated
    1877, 2-1/2" w, 4-3/4" h.................................................40.00
  Liebig Extract of Meat, Testu & Massin, printer, 2-3/4" x 4-1/8"
    Children from different nations climbing mountains, two boys
      staking claim on jar, slight corner bruising...................15.00
    Governess serving product to girl and boy .........................18.00
  Magnolia Ham, McFerran, Shallcross & Co., Louisville, KY, 1879
    Alpine mountain climbers packing ham, woman with spyglass
      at apex, Krebs Lithographing Co., Cincinnati ...............10.00
  Trapeze artist dangling ham from teeth, clown on stilts in back-
    ground, Krebs Lithography, Co., Cincinnati,
    2-7/8" x 4-1/2" ...............................................................18.00
  Wilson Packing Co.'s Cooked Meats, Don Quixote, quote below,
    blank back Don and Sancho after Windmill .....................15.00
    Don hugging mule .........................................................15.00
    Don swings his sword.....................................................15.00
    Sancho Panza tossed over a wall ...................................1800
  Woolson Spice Co. Wish You A Merry Christmas, little boy waking
    up as he hears Santa coming down the chimney ..............10.00
Health & Beauty
  Ayers Hair Vigor, mermaid scene .......................................24.00
  Bromo Seltzer, fold-out, 1904 calendar, 5" h .......................75.00
  Dr. Kilmer's Indian Cough Cure, Indian illus .......................35.00
  E. W. Hoyt, Ladies Perfumed Calendar 1893, little girl in blue coat
    and hat, 3-1/2" w, 5-1/2" h..............................................30.00
  Hood's Latest Tooth Powder, Emlet's Drug Store, Hanover, PA,
    smiling man wearing hat .................................................15.00

Miscellaneous

Advance Thresher Co., My Sugar Plum, 1888, Calvert Litho Co.,
Detroit ...................................................................... 18.00
Eastern Woven Wire Mattress, New York City, black white illus of
black man in bed saying, "Go Way White Trash, I want to Get a
rest, For dis am de Swing de Easterns best" ..................... 15.00
Globe Polish, diecut, cat ............................................. 35.00
Great Western Specialty Co., Cincinnati, cherub and heart
motif ........................................................................ 15.00
Kinney Brothers Cigarettes, diecut, straw hat with
streamers ................................................................... 8.00
Lily Corn Starch, three kittens playing ............................. 5.00
National Line Steamship, image of ship, info about rates, steer-
age, etc., 3-1/2" x 6" ................................................. 70.00
Stone & Dunning Tobacco, Rand McNally map of
US illus ..................................................................... 15.00
Virginia Exposition/Walter Wood Machines, showing farm equip-
ment, c1890, 3-1/2" x 6" ............................................ 65.00
Will & Finck, San Francisco, 1884 address, orig 3/4" d round
sticker, 4-3/4" w, 3" h ............................................... 475.00

Sewing Machines

American Sewing Machine Co., Ayer, MA retailer ............... 14.00
Davis Sewing Machine ................................................. 12.00
Domestic Sewing Machine Co., fold-out, black and white .... 25.00
Eldredge Sewing Machine Co., large brown dog image ....... 18.00
Household Sewing Machine Company
Child and cats playing ............................................ 16.00
Children and toys, Bay City, MI, retailer ..................... 18.00
Howe Sewing Machine, Binghamton, NY, retailer .............. 12.00
Leader Sewing Machine, Kalamazoo, MI, retailer .............. 12.00
Royal St. John Sewing Machine Co, Richfield Springs,
NY retailer ................................................................ 18.00
Standard Sewing Maching Co., soldiers from 1776, 1812, 1848 in
uniform ..................................................................... 40.00
Weed Sewing Machine, covered wagon scene .................. 25.00
Wheeler & Wilson, Bellow Falls, VT, retailer .................... 12.00
White Sewing Machine Company
Girl playing baseball, stamped with address of Owosso, MI,
retailer ............................................................... 38.00
The Mail in Holland, New York City retailer .................. 16.00
The Mail in Portugal, Three Rivers, MI, retailer ............. 16.00
Three Flowers, Elkhart, IN, retailer ............................ 12.00

Soap

Babbitts Soap
A Free Bar of Babbitts Soap will Carry the State Every Time,
politican in top hat, black gentleman handing out
soap .................................................................. 24.00
Ahead of Everything, children rowing across lake in Babbitts
Soap boxes ......................................................... 12.00
Fairbank's, pre-1900, 3" x 5" ...................................... 32.00
Higgin's German Laundry Soap, Chas. Higgins, two young
pirates on front .......................................................... 5.00

Stoves

Gold Coin and Gold Metal Stoves and Ranges, litho by Mayer,
Merkel, NY, 3-1/2" w, 6" h .......................................... 30.00
Round Oak Stoves, Ritter & Hubbell, parlor stove with children
playing, 3-1/2" w, 5-1/2" h ......................................... 30.00

Thread

Brooks Sewing Thread, two men ................................... 18.00
Clark's Mile-End Spool Cotton
Oriental lady standing on large spool of thread, fan in one
hand, pointing to dog with other, 4-3/4" x 3" ............... 5.00
Uniformed military officer and castle .......................... 10.00
J & P Coats
Calendar, 1890-91 calendar on back, 2-3/4" x 4" ........... 25.00
Little girl lying in meadow, flowers, large spool of thread,
"White, Black & Colors for Hand & Machine" at top,
2-5/8" x 4" .......................................................... 10.00
Spool Pet #4, Hal the Horse ..................................... 30.00

Two little girls feeding pigeons from apron pocket, large spool
of thread, "White, Black & Colors for Hand & Machine" at
top, more adv on reverse, 2-5/8" x 4" ........................ 10.00
Kerr Thread & Co.
Aesop's Fable, The Wolf & The Crane illus .................... 40.00
Black men carrying spools of Kerr's Thread, country fair
setting ............................................................... 45.00
Merrick Sewing Thread
Diecut, little girl holding two bunnies, 1889 calendar on back,
shaped like spool of thread .................................... 20.00
Little girl ........................................................... 14.00
Man using Merrick's for fishing line .......................... 16.00
The Thread That Binds the Union, color illus of Pres and Mrs.
Cleveland within heart shape design, three cherubs, adv on
reverse for Merrick's Spool Cotton Bobbins for Machine and
Hand Sewing, 4-1/2" x 3" ...................................... 20.00
Starr Embroidery Silk, Brainerd & Armstrong, Lewiston, ME
retailer .................................................................... 16.00
Willimantic
Child in long white dress ......................................... 14.00
Jumbo, 5-1/2" w .................................................. 30.00

# AGATA GLASS

**History:** Agata glass was invented in 1887 by Joseph
Locke of the New England Glass Company, Cambridge,
Massachusetts. Agata glass was produced by coating a
piece of peachblow glass with metallic stain, spattering
the surface with alcohol, and firing. The resulting high-
gloss, mottled finish looked like oil droplets floating on a
watery surface. Shading usually ranged from opaque
pink to dark rose, although pieces in a pastel opaque
green also exist. A few pieces have been found in a
satin finish.

Bowl
5-1/4" d, 3" h, ruffled, deep color, allover bright blue spots. 750.00
8" w, 3-1/2" h, green opaque body, black mottling,
gold border .............................................................. 995.00
8" w, 4" h, green opaque body, gold trim and staining ..... 1,150.00
Celery Vase, 6-1/4" h, sq mouth, glossy peachblow, ground pontil,
some staining remaining ............................................. 750.00
Creamer ........................................................................ 1,200.00
Finger Bowl
5-1/4" d, 2-1/2" h, shiny peachblow, black mottling, lacey gold
tracery, deep crimps ................................................. 685.00
5-1/4" d, 2-5/8" h, crushed raspberry shading to creamy pink, all
over gold mottling, blue accents ................................. 995.00
5-1/4" d, 3" h, ruffled, peachblow opaque body, allover bright blue
staining spots .......................................................... 750.00

**Tumbler, blue ground, black
oil spots, gold trim, $1,150.**

Pitcher, 6-3/8" h, crimped rim ..................................................... 1,750.00
Spooner, 4-1/2" h, 2-1/2" w, sq top, wild rose peachblow ground, small
    areas of wear ............................................................................. 400.00
Toothpick Holder, 2-1/4" h, flared, green opaque, orig blue oil spots,
    green trim .................................................................................... 795.00
Tumbler ........................................................................................... 885.00
Vase
    6" h, lily, crimson peachblow, delicate staining ................... 885.00
    8" h, lily, shiny surface, crimson peachblow ground, large black
        splotches .................................................................... 1,085.00

# AMBERINA GLASS

**1883**

**History:** Joseph Locke developed Amberina glass in 1883 for the New England Glass Works. "Amberina," a trade name, describes a transparent glass which shades from deep ruby to amber. It was made by adding powdered gold to the ingredients for an amber-glass batch. A portion of the glass was reheated later to produce the shading effect. Usually it was the bottom which was reheated to form the deep red; however, reverse examples have been found. Most early Amberina is flint-quality glass, blown or pattern molded. Patterns include Diamond Quilted, Daisy and Button, Venetian Diamond, Diamond and Star, and Thumbprint.

In addition to the New England Glass Works, the Mount Washington Glass Company of New Bedford, Massachusetts, copied the glass in the 1880s and sold it at first under the Amberina trade name and later as "Rose Amber." It is difficult to distinguish pieces from these two New England factories. Boston and Sandwich Glass Works never produced the glass. Amberina glass also was made in the 1890s by several Midwest factories, among which was Hobbs, Brockunier & Co. Trade names included "Ruby Amber Ware" and "Watermelon." The Midwest glass shaded from cranberry to amber, and the color resulted from the application of a thin flashing of cranberry to the reheated portion. This created a sharp demarcation between the two colors. This less-expensive version was the death knell for the New England variety. In 1884, Edward D. Libbey was given the use of the trade name "Amberina" by the New England Glass Works. Production took place during 1900, but ceased shortly thereafter. In the 1920s, Edward Libbey renewed production at his Toledo, Ohio, plant for a short period. The glass was of high quality.

**Marks:** Amberina made by Edward Libbey in the 1920s is marked "Libbey" in script on the pontil.

**References:** Gary Baker et al., *Wheeling Glass 1829-1939*, Oglebay Institute, 1994 (distributed by Antique Publications); Neila and Tom Bredehoft, *Hobbs, Brockunier & Co. Glass*, Collector Books, 1997; Kenneth Wilson, *American Glass 1760-1930*, 2 Vols., Hudson Hill Press and The Toledo Museum of Art, 1994.

**Reproduction Alert:** Reproductions abound.

**Additional Listings:** Mount Washington.

Basket, 8-1/4" h, 6" l, 4" w, sgd "Libbey" ................................. 2,975.00
Boat Centerpiece, 14" l, Daisy and Button,
    Hobbs Brockunier ........................................................................ 950.00
Bon Bon, 7" d, 1-1/2" h, wavy six pointed 1-1/2" w rim, fuchsia shading
    to pale amber, sgd "Libbey" ....................................................... 625.00
Butter Pat, 2-3/4 d, Daisy and Button pattern, sq, notched corners,
    pr ................................................................................................. 250.00
Bowl
    4-1/4" w, 2-3/4" h, Venetian Diamond Pattern, deep color of
        amber to red with fuchsia highlights, bell tone, New England,
        c1880 ................................................................................ 185.00
    4-1/2" w, 2-1/4" h, deep color, Venetian Diamond pattern .. 325.00
    4-1/2" w, 2-1/2" h, twelve wide crimps, Interior Ribbed
        pattern ............................................................................... 375.00
    4-1/2" w, 2-3/4" h, Swirl pattern with blue swirl bands, bell tone
        flint, Mt. Washington ....................................................... 295.00
    5" w by 2-1/2" h, ruffled top with ten ruffles, deep amber shading
        to fuchsia red, New England ............................................ 375.00
    5-1/4" w, 2-1/2" h, 1-1/4" w flaring rim, bulbous bottom, New
        England ............................................................................. 185.00
Celery Vase
    6-3/4" h, 3-3/4" w, sq, IVT, New England, bell tone flint ...... 575.00
    11" h, fancy silver plate holder ............................................ 800.00
Champagne Tumbler, 4" h, 2-1/2" w across top, tapered form, Interior
    Ribbed pattern, very dark amber shading to red ..................... 125.00
Cordial, 4-1/2" h, trumpet shape ............................................... 225.00
Cracker Jar, cov, 8" h, 5-3/4" d, Inverted Thumbprint pattern, barrel
    shape, rare glass cov, applied amber knob finial, attributed to Hobbs,
    c1885 .......................................................................................... 785.00
Cream Pitcher and Sugar, 2-3/4" h, Optic Thumbprint pattern, blood
    red neck and shoulder, honey colored lower half, shape #77, Mt.
    Washington, damage to handle of sugar ................................... 485.00
Decanter
    Optic Diamond Quilted pattern, solid amber faceted stopper, 12"
        h ......................................................................................... 485.00
    Reverse Inverted Thumbprint pattern, ground and polished
        pontil .................................................................................. 125.00
Finger Bowl, 5" d, ruffled rim .................................................... 150.00
Ice Cream Plate, 5-1/2" sq, Daisy and Button pattern, Hobbs
    Brockunier ..................................................................................... 95.00
Jack-in-the-Pulpit Vase, 8" h, 4-1/2" w, ruby red to amber .......... 535.00
Juice Tumbler, 3-1/2" h, tapered cylindrical, applied reeded
    handle .......................................................................................... 150.00
Lamp Shade, deepest fuchsia coloring, shading to deep blue, diamond
    quilted design, 4-1/4" h, 5" d across top, 2" fitter opening ........ 575.00
Lemonade
    3-7/8" h, Interior Ribbed pattern, applied reeded loop handle, Mt.
        Washington ....................................................................... 160.00
    4-7/8" h, 16 optic ribs, upper 2" blushed with color ............. 215.00
Milk Pitcher, 8" h, 5" w, very ruffled top with a wide flange, petticoat
    shape, opalescent lining, clear reeded handle ......................... 650.00
Mug, 3" h by 3-3/4" w, Rose Amber, bulbous, applied loop handle, Mt.
    Washington ................................................................................. 275.00
Pickle Castor Insert, 4-1/4" h, 4" d, Inverted Thumbprint pattern, Mt.
    Washington ................................................................................. 425.00
Pitcher
    5" h, Daisy and Button, Hobbs .............................................. 425.00
    8-1/2" h, tankard, optic elongated diamond quilted design, New
        England ............................................................................. 675.00
    10" h, 4-3/4" d, Optic Diamond Quilted pattern, applied amber
        handle, ground pontil ........................................................ 235.00
Punch Cup
    2-3/4" h, bright magenta rim, Pairpoint, paper Sagamore
        label .................................................................................. 125.00
    3-1/2" w, 2-1/2" h, IVT, applied reeded handle,
        New England ..................................................................... 145.00
Salt Shaker, 4" h, 1-3/4" w, Interior Ribbed pattern, deep color, worn
    two piece silver plated top ......................................................... 285.00
Sauce Dish, Daisy and Button, scalloped, set of 6 ..................... 450.00

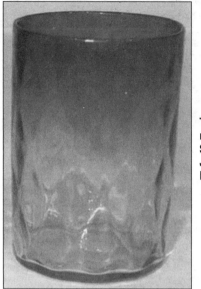

**Tumbler, expanded diamond quilted pattern, $135. Photo courtesy of Joy Luke Fine Art Brokers and Auctioneers.**

Sherbet and Underplate, 5-1/2" h, 8-1/2" d, both pcs sgd "Libbey" ................................................................................. 975.00
Spooner, 4-1/2" h, Inverted Thumbprint pattern, New England Glass Works ........................................................................... 100.00
Sugar Shaker, reverse amberina, inverted thumbprint .............. 200.00
Syrup Pitcher, Hobnail pattern, orig pewter top std "Pat. Jan 29 84," Hobbs, Brockunier & Co, 3 hobs chipped ........................ 300.00
Toothpick Holder
    2-1/4" h, 2-1/2" w, Baby IVT, tri-corner, deep fuchsia color . 350.00
    2-1/2" h, 1-3/4" w, Baby IVT, square top, amberina-fuchsia color ................................................................................. 225.00
    2-1/2" h, 2" w, barrel shape, Baby IVT with 2 rings............. 275.00
Tumbler
    3-5/8" h, cylindrical, faint optic ribs, amber glass rising to red and magenta rim, polished pontil ............................................. 90.00
    3-3/4" h, inverted diamond dec, polished pontil ................. 250.00
Vase
    4" h, flared neck, IVT, enameled white and green floral border ............................................................................... 200.00
    4-7/8" h, scalloped rim, pinched ovoid form, inverted diamond pattern, band of amber rigaree at neck, polished pontil ... 250.00
    6-3/4" h, roll down lip, optic diamond body ........................ 300.00
    9-1/2" h, lily, ribbed trumpet form, tricorn rim, disk base ..... 400.00
    10" h, lily, fuchsia highlights ............................................... 675.00
    10-1/2" h, swagged and ruffled lip, snake form entwined around neck, heavy enameled goldfinches perched on thistle blossoms, attributed to Le Gras, c1890 ....................................... 595.00
    11-1/4" h, shape #3004, sgd "Libbey" ............................. 1,200.00
    15" h, deep ruby red shading to brilliant amber; large lily top, flint.............................................................................. 825.00
Water Set, 8-1/4" h, IVT pitcher, six 3-3/4" h tumblers............. 1,750.00
Whiskey Taster, 2-5/8" h, 2-1/4" w, Baby IVT, barrel shape ........ 245.00
Wine Glass, 4-3/4" h, Mt. Washington ....................................... 300.00

# AMBERINA GLASS, PLATED

**History:** The New England Glass Company, Cambridge, Massachusetts, first made Plated Amberina in 1886; Edward Libbey patented the process for the company in 1889. Plated Amberina was made by taking a gather of chartreuse or cream opalescent glass, dipping it in Amberina, and working the two, often utilizing a mold. The finished product had a deep amber to deep ruby red shading, a fiery opalescent lining, and often vertical ribbing for enhancement. Designs ranged from simple forms to complex pieces with collars, feet, gilding, and etching. A cased Wheeling glass of similar appearance had an opaque white lining but is not opalescent and does not have a ribbed body.

Bowl, 8" w, 3-1/2" h, border of deep dark mahogany, 12 vertical stripes alternating with 12 vertical opalescent fuchsia stripes, off-white casing ................................................................... 7,500.00
Celery Vase.............................................................................. 2,750.00
Cruet, 6-3/4" h, faceted amber stopper................................... 3,200.00
Lamp Shade, 14" d, hanging, swirled, ribbed ......................... 4,750.00
Milk Pitcher, applied amber handle, orig "Aurora" label .......... 7,500.00
Punch Cup, vertical ribs, applied handle................................. 1,500.00
Salt Shaker, vertical ribs, orig top ......................................... 1,200.00
Tumbler, 2-1/2" d, 3-3/4" h, vertical ribbed cylinder, deep fuchsia-red at top shading to golden yellow base, creamy opal lining ......... 1,750.00
Vase, 7-1/4" h, lily shape, raspberry red shading to bright amber, opal white casing ...................................................................... 2,750.00

# AMERICAN HAND-PAINTED CHINA

**History**: The American china painting movement began in 1876 and remained popular over the next 50 years. Thousands of artisans-professionals and amateurs decorated tableware, desk accessories, dresser sets, and many other items with floral, fruits and conventional geometric designs and occasionally with portraits, birds, and landscapes. Some American firms, such as Lenox and Willetts Manufacturing Co. of Trenton, New Jersey, produced Belleek, a special type of porcelain that china painters decorated, but a majority of porcelain was imported from France, Germany, Austria, Czechoslovakia, and Japan.

**References**: Dorothy Kamm, *American Painted Porcelain: Collector's Identification & Value Guide*, Collector Books, 1999; —, *Comprehensive Guide to American Painted Porcelain*, Antique Trader Books, 1999.

**Periodical:** *Dorothy Kamm's Porcelain Collector's Companion Newsletter*, P.O. Box 6460, Port St. Lucie, FL 34985-7460.

**Museums**: Museum of Porcelain Art, International Porcelain Artists & Teachers, Inc., Grapevine, Texas; World Organization of China Painters Foundation Center & Museum, Oklahoma City, Oklahoma.

**Marks:** American-painted porcelains bear foreign factory marks. However, the American style was distinctive, whether naturalistic or conventional (geometric). Some pieces were signed and dated by the artist.

**Notes**: The quality of the artwork, the amount of detail, and technical excellence-not the amount of gilding or the manufacturer of the porcelain itself-are key pricing factors. Unusual subjects and uncommon forms also influence value.

Berry Bowl, 7" d, decorated with cherry clusters, signed "W.Beville," c1900-1915 ....................................................................... 50.00
Bowl, 6" d, 3-15/16" h, pedestal base, decorated with conventional butterfly design, tan luster and burnished gold, burnished gold rim and foot, signed "E. T. Low, Dec. 1909," mkd "O.& E.G., Royal, Austria"............................................................... 60.00

**Berry Bowl, cherry clusters, sgd "W. Beville," c1900-15, 7" d, $50. Photo courtesy of Dorothy Kamm.**

Bread and Butter Plate, 6" d
    Coupe, decorated with violets, burnished gold rim, signed "WANDS," mkd "Favorite, Bavaria," c1910-1916 .............. 20.00
    Round, decorated with border design of pink roses, burnished gold rim and band borders, mkd "Haviland," Limoges, France, c1894-1918 ....................... 15.00

Cake plate, individual, double-handled
    7" d, decorated with central conventional floral bouquet, signed "IFP," mkd "Schuman, Bavaria" .......................... 20.00
    7-1/8" d, decorated with conventional border design, burnished gold rim and handles, signed "LMC," mkd "MADE IN JAPAN," c1925 ...................... 22.00

Celery Dish, 12-1/2" l, 5-3/4" w, decorated with conventional border design, burnished gold rim, signed "L. Amundson," mkd "J. P. L., Limoges, France," 1891-1932 .................. 60.00

Coffee Pot, decorated with conventional design in enamel, outline in raised paste covered with burnished gold finial and base, mkd "CAC, BELLEEK," 1889-1906 ........................... 600.00

Comb and Brush Tray, 10-1/4" l, 7" w, decorated with pink roses, signed "to Isabelle Moore from C. B. Tompson, Christmas, 1889" ..................... 75.00

Cracker and Cheese Dish, 9-3/8" d, decorated with conventional border design of primrose, burnished gold borders and trim, signed "E.S.P., I. M. P.," mkd "T & V, Limoges, France," c1891-1907.. 125.00

Cream Soup Cup, 4-3/8" d, double handled, decorated with conventional border, burnished gold handles and rim, mkd "Bavaria," c1900-1915 ...................... 25.00

Cup and Saucer, decorated with border design of clusters of pink mayflowers, white enamel highlights, burnished gold rims and handle, mkd "O. & E. G. Royal, Austria," 1898-1918 .............................. 20.00

Demitasse Cup and Saucer, decorated with border design of forget-me-nots, burnished gold rims and handle, signed "KEW," mkd "W. G. & Co., Limoges, France," c1901-1920 ....................... 25.00

Dessert Set, three pieces, 7-7/16" d plate, decorated with forget-me-not clusters, cup and saucer, opal luster on cup interior, burnished gold rims and handle, plate mkd with a shield, "Thomas, Bavaria," cup and saucer mkd "JAPAN," c1925-1930 ............ 40.00

Dish, 6-13/16" l, 5" w, decorated with branches of apple blossoms, burnished gold rim, pierced border, signed "F.H.SPEAR," mkd "P.P.A.A., Bavaria," c1920 ..................... 50.00

Humidor, cov, 3-1/4" d, 5-1/4" h, decorated with pipe and swirling smoke on a light green luster ground burnished gold knob, mkd "NIPPON," c1891-1920 ................. 65.00

Milk Pitcher and Plate Set, 5-11/16" h pitcher, 7-3/8" d plate, decorated with conventional design of yellow wild roses on yellow round burnished gold rims and handle trim, signed "M.S.C. '90," pitcher mkd "H & Co., Limoges," plate mkd "CFH/GDM".................. 75.00

Olive or Bonbon Dish, 6" d, ring-handles, decorated with conventional border motif in matt antique green, signed "M.H.Butler," mkd "Thomas Bavaria," c1908-1915 ..................... 35.00

Orange Cups, 3-1/4" d, 2 −3/4" h, ftd, decorated with orange blossoms, white and yellow enamel embellishments, burnished gold rims and interior prongs, signed "CKI," mkd "T & V," c1900-1915, price for pr ......................100.00

Pin Tray and Vase, 5-3/16" l, 3-13/16" w tray, 2-3/8" h vase, decorated in an Arabic-style design in blues, burnished gold rims, signed "FCS," tray mkd "W.G. & Co., Limoges," vase mkd "ADK, France," 1890-1910 ..................... 60.00

Plate
    7-1/2" d coupe, decorated with garden border design, burnished gold rim, signed "Marker," mkd "J. & C., Bavaria," 1902-1920 ..................... 30.00
    9-1/2" d, decorated with raised paste and gilded circle and monogram, surrounded by cluster of pink roses and greenery, burnished bold bands, mkd "Limoges, France," c1891-1914 ..................... 45.00

Powder Box, cov, 3" h, decorated with four panels of monochromatic blue landscapes, green gold borders, feet and knob, mkd "Bavaria," c1900-1920 ..................... 65.00

Rose Bowl, 2-7/8" h, decorated with band of conventional-style violets and bands in burnished gold, mkd "O. & E.G., Royal, Austria," c1898-1918 ..................... 30.00

Salt or Pepper Shaker, 2-7/8"h, decorated with red poppies, burnished gold top and border band, signed "K. Kremep," c1900-1915 ..... 15.00

Sugar Shaker, 4-5/8" h, decorated with conventional floral design in enamels and burnished, gold, burnished gold top, mkd "H.C.Royal, Bavaria," c1905-1920 ..................... 75.00

Talcum Powder Shaker, 4-1/2" h, decorated with pink roses, burnished gold top, mkd "O. & E. G., Royal, Austria," 1898-1918 ............. 85.00

Tea Pot Stand, 6-3/8" d, decorated with border design of forget-me-not-clusters, burnished gold rim, c1900-1920 .......................... 45.00

Tumbler, 3-3/4" h, decorated in conventional Japanesque design, bluebirds on flowering branches, burnished gold rims, signed "MERRY MAN," mkd "Victoria, Austria," c1904-1915, price for pr............. 30.00

Vase, 2-5/8" d, two-handles, decorated with violets, white enamel highlights, burnished gold rim, signed "France," c1880-1900........... 45.00

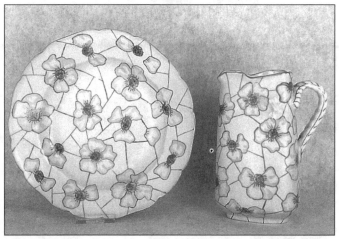

**Milk Pitcher and Plate Set, yellow wild roses, yellow ground, burnished gold rim and handle trim, sgd "M. S. C. '90," 5-11/16" h pitcher mkd "H. & Co. Limoges," 7-3/8" d plate mkd "CFH/GDM," $75. Photo courtesy of Dorothy Kamm.**

# AMERICAN HAND-PAINTED CHINA JEWELRY and BUTTONS

**History:** The American china painting movement began in 1876, about the time the mass production of jewelry also occurred. Porcelain manufacturers and distributors offered a variety of porcelain shapes and setting for brooches, pendants, cuff links, and shirt waist buttons. Thousands of artisans painted flowers, people, landscapes and conventions (geometric) motifs. The category of hand-painted porcelain jewelry comprises a unique category, separate from costume and fine jewelry. While the materials were inexpensive to produce, the painted decoration was a work of fine art.

**References:** Dorothy Kamm, *American Painted Porcelain: Collector's Identification & Value Guide*, Collector Books, 1999; —, *Comprehensive Guide to American Painted Porcelain*, Antique Trader Books, 1999.

**Periodical:** *Dorothy Kamm's Porcelain Collector's Companion Newsletter*, P.O. Box 6460, Port St. Lucie, FL 34985-7460.

**Museums:** Museum of Florida History, Tallahassee, Florida has a collection of hand-painted porcelain jewelry by Olive commons.

**Marks:** American-painted porcelain jewelry bears no factory marks, and is usually unsigned.

**Notes:** The quality of the artwork, the amount of detail, and technical excellence—not the amount of gilding-are the key pricing factors. Uncommon shapes also influence value.

Bar Pin, 2" w, decorated with forget-me-nots, burnished gold rim, brass bezel, 1880-1920 ........................................................ 40.00
Belt Buckle Brooch, 2" w by 2-5/8" oval, decorated with pink roses, burnished gold border, brass bezel, 1900-1917 ...................... 125.00

Pendant, violets, burnished gold border, brass bezel, c1880-1914, 1-5/8" w, 2-1/8" h oval, $60. Photo courtesy of Dorothy Kamm.

Brooch, flapper, burnished gold border, brass bezel, c1924-48, 1-5/8" w, 2-1/8" h oval, $75. Photo courtesy of Dorothy Kamm.

Brooch
    7/8" d, decorated with Colonial man, white enamel on lace, raised paste scrolled border covered with burnished gold brass bezel, c1890-1910 ........................................................ 40.00
    7/8" sq, diamond shape, decorated with waterscape with water lilies, white enamel highlights, burnished with gold border, brass bezel, c1920-1940 .................................................. 35.00
    1" d, decorated with Colonial dame, burnished gold rim, brass bezel, c1890-1910 .................................................. 40.00
    1" d, decorated with white pansy on a matt black background, brass bezel, 1890-1910 .................................................. 30.00
    1" w by 3/4" rectangle, Florida landscape in white on platinum ground, sterling silver bezel, c1920-1940 ........................ 75.00
    1" w by 13/16" oval, decorated with Florida landscape, signed "OC," c1920 .................................................. 45.00
    1-1/8" w by 1-3/8" oval, decorated with forget-me-nots, signed "A. Jibbing," brass bezel, c1900-1920 .................................... 80.00
    1-7/16" w by 1-7/8" oval, decorated with pink roses, burnished gold border, signed "Albrecht," brass bezel........................ 65.00
    1-1/2" w by 2" oval, decorated in a Native American-inspired geometric design, brass bezel, 1915-1935 .............................. 75.00
    1-3/4" d, decorated with daisy, burnished gold border, brass bezel, c1900-1910.................................................. 45.00
    1-7/8" w, crescent shape, decorated with dark pink roses, burnished gold tips, brass bezel, 1900-1920.......................... 45.00
    2" w by 1-5/8" oval, decorated with Art Nouveau-style poppies, burnished gold border, brass bezel, 1856-1915 .................. 75.00
    2" w by 1-1/2" oval, decorated with pink and ruby roses, solid dark blue ground, white enamel highlights, burnished gold border, brass bezel, c1940.................................................. 65.00
    2-1/16" d, decorated with violets, burnished gold rim, brass bezel, 1900-1920 .................................................. 65.00
    2-1/8" w, crescent shape, decorated with forget-me-nots, burnished gold rim, brass bezel .............................................. 40.00
    2-1/2" l, horseshoe shape, decorated with violets, burnished gold tips, brass bezel ............................................................ 100.00
Cuff or Baby Pin, 1" l, decorated with single forget-me-not on burnished gold ground, brass bezel ................................................. 10.00
Cuff Buttons, pr, 3/4" w by 1" ovals, decorated with lavender flowers , border of burnished gold dots and apple green jewels, burnished gold rims, c1890-1920.............................................. 40.00
Cuff Links, pr, 3/4" w by 1" ovals, decorated with forget-me-nots, white enamel highlights, burnished gold borders, gold-plated bezel, c1900-1910 .................................................................... 80.00
Dress Set
    Five pieces: 2" w by 2-5/8" belt buckle brooch, oval brass bezel, pr 1" d shirt waist buttons with shanks, pr 1 " d shirt waist buttons with sew-through backs; decorated with forget-me-nots, black green scalloped borders rimmed in burnished gold, c1900-1917 ... 175.00

Four pieces: 3/4" d shirt waist collar button, three 5/8" d shirt waist buttons, decorated with pink roses, white enamel highlights, burnished gold rims, shank backs ............................60.00
Flapper Pin, 1-5/8" w by 2-1/8" oval, decorated with stylized woman, burnished gold border, brass bezel, 1924-1928 .........................75.00
Hat Pin , 3/4" wide by 1" oval medallion, 6" l shaft, decorated with four-leaf clover on burnished gold ground, brass bezel, 1900-1920 . 75.00
Pendant
   1-5/8" w by 2-1/8" oval, decorated with violets, burnished bold border, brass bezel, c1880-1914.........................................60.00
   1-3/4" w by 1-3/4" oval, decorated with forget-me-nots, white enamel highlights, burnished gold rim, brass bezel, c1900-1920 ...............................................................50.00
Shirt Waist Button, 1" d, decorated with pink and ruby roses, burnished gold stippled border, c1900-1920 ................................20.00

# AMPHORA

**History:** The Amphora Porcelain Works was one of several pottery companies located in the Teplitz-Turn region of Bohemia in the late 19th and early 20th centuries. It is best known for art pottery, especially Art Nouveau and Art Deco pieces.

**Marks:** Several markings were used, including the name and location of the pottery and the Imperial mark, which included a crown. Prior to World War I, Bohemia was part of the Austro-Hungarian Empire, so the word "Austria" may appear as part of the mark. After World War I the word "Czechoslovakia" may be part of the mark.

**Additional Listings:** Teplitz.

Bowl, 12" x 15", reticulated, ftd, applied leaves and chestnuts, 2 double twisted gold handles, sgd.............................645.00
Creamer, 5-1/4" h, gold trim, raised flowers, sgd "Turin, Teplitz, Amphora" ...............................215.00
Ewer, 14-1/2" h, pink, gold, and green floral dec, gold accents, salamander entwined handle, c1900 ...............................575.00

**Pitcher, Art Deco dec, blue, red, yellow, and orange, green mottled ground, mkd "Renee Stellmacher & Kissel," c1900, $225.**

Figure
   16-1/4" h, peasant woman carries basket on back, reaching for another basket at feet, tan clothes, gold highlights, crown mark and "Austria"................................550.00
   18-1/2" h, peasant woman empties apron of greens into basket, tan, gold highlights, crown mark and "Austria".................550.00
Pitcher, 11" h, emb owl sitting on branch ...................165.00
Vase
   7-1/4" h, bulbous inverted rim, pierced leaf dec, tapered neck on swollen body, dec with Art Nouveau style leaves and stems in relief, gilt highlighted turquoise leaves, cream colored ground, imp "Amphora" and red "R. St. K" stamp, early 20th C ....520.00
   10" h, 9-1/2" w, applied blackberry clusters, cream basketweave ground, braided shoulder handles, sgd...........................650.00
   10-3/4" h, inverted rim, hourglass form, four curved handles extending from under rim to base, raised dandelion blossoms and leaves, gray, brown, and green, mottled tan and cream ground, early 20th C......................................250.00
   10-3/4" h, raised rim, oval form, tapering to base, upper portion dec with painted pastoral scene with goat reclining by trees in field in blue tones on cream ground, lower portion with raised repeating scallops, circles, and mottled irid columns, glossy black glaze, imp "Amphora" in lozenge and "32 59".........920.00
   11" h, 5" w, bulbous, two handles, flaring base with four handles, two raised leaves under pink, green, and blue, imp "Crown, Austria, Amphora" ..........................................460.00
   14-1/2" h, bulbous foliate rim with cherry blossoms above tapered body, swollen base, applied high relief leafy branches and cherries, red and purple with gilt highlights, irid green ground, imp mark, early 20th C, minor loss to leaf................................350.00

# ANIMAL COLLECTIBLES

**History:** The representation of animals in fine arts, decorative arts, and on utilitarian products dates back to antiquity. Some religions endowed certain animals with mystical properties. Authors throughout written history used human characteristics when portraying animals. Glass has been a popular material in making animal-related collectibles. Dishes with an animal-theme cover were fashionable in the early 19th century. In the years between World Wars I and II, glass manufacturers such as Fostoria Glass Company and A. H. Heisey & Company created a number of glass animal figures for the novelty and decorative-accessory markets. In the 1950s and early 1960s, a second glass-animal craze swept America led by companies such as Duncan & Miller and New Martinsville-Viking Glass Company. A third craze struck in the early 1980s when companies such as Boyd Crystal Art Glass, Guernsey Glass, Pisello Art Glass, and Summit Art Glass began offering the same animal figure in a wide variety of collectible glass colors, with some colors in limited production. The formation of collectors' clubs and marketing crazes, e.g., flamingo, pig, and penguin, during the 1970s increased the popularity of this collecting field.

**References:** Felicia Browell, *Breyer Animal Collector's Guide*, 2nd ed., Collector Books, 1999; Elaine Butler, *Poodle Collectibles of the '50s & '60s*, L-W Book Sales, 1995; Diana Callow et al., *Charlton Price Guide to Beswick Animals*, The Charlton Press, 1994; Dana Cain, *Film & TV Animal Star Collectibles*, Antique Trader Books, 1998; Jean Dale, *Charlton Standard Catalogue* of *Royal Doulton Animals*, 2nd Edition, The Charlton Press, 1998; ——, *Charlton Standard Catalogue of Royal Doulton Beswick Storybook Figurines*, The Charlton Press, 1994; Candace Sten Davis and Patricia Baugh, *A Treasury of Scottie Dog Collectibles*, Collector Books, Volume I (1998), Volume II (2000); Marbena Jean Fyke, *Collectible Cats*, Book I (1993, 1995 value update), Book II (1996), Collector Books; Lee Garmon and Dick Spencer, *Glass Animals of the Depression Era*, Collector Books, 1993; Everett Grist, *Covered Animal Dishes*, Collector Books, 1988, 1993 value update; Christopher Payne, *Animals in Bronze, Reference and Price Guide*, Antique Collectors' Club, 1999; Patricia Robak, *Dog Antiques and Collectibles*, Schiffer Publishing, 1999.

**Periodicals:** *Boyd Crystal Art Glass Newsletter*, P.O. Box 127, 1203 Morton Ave., Cambridge, OH 43725; *Canine Collector's Companion*, P.O. Box 2948, Portland, OR 97208; *Collieactively Speaking*, 428 Philadelphia Rd, Joppa, MD 21085 *Collie Courier*, 428 Philadelphia Rd, Joppa, MD 21085; *Hobby Horse News*, 5492 Tallapoosa Rd, Tallahassee, FL 32303; *Jumbo Jargon*, 1002 West 25th St., Erie, PA 16502; *MOOsletter*, 240 Wahl Ave., Evans City, PA 16033; *TRR Pony Express*, 71 Aloha Circle, Little Rock, AR 72120.

**Collectors' Clubs:** Boyd Art Glass Collectors Guild, P.O. Box 52, Hatboro, PA 19040; Canine Collectibles Club of America, Suite 314, 736 N. Western Ave., Lake Forest, IL 60045; Cat Collectors, 33161 Wendy Dr., Sterling Heights, MI 48310; Folk Art Society of America, P.O. Box 17041, Richmond, VA 23226; Frog Pond, P.O. Box 193, Beech Grove, IN 46107; National Elephant Collector's Society, 380 Medford St., Somerville, MA 02145; Squirrel Lovers Club, 318 W. Fremont Ave., Elmhurst, IL 60126; Wee Scots, Inc., P.O. Box 1597, Winchester, VA 22604-1597.

**Museums:** American Kennel Club, New York, NY; American Saddle Horse Museum Association, Lexington, KY; Dog Museum, St Louis, MO; Frog Fantasies Museum, Eureka Springs, AR; International Museum of the Horse, Lexington, KY; Stradling Museum of the Horse, Patagonia, AZ.

**Additional Listings:** See specific animal collectible categories in *Warman's Americana & Collectibles*.

## Barnyard

Bottle Opener, rooster, cast iron, orig polychrome paint ............... 95.00
Butter Stamp, 3-3/4" d, wood, goose, half lb size ........................ 165.00
Candy Container, 4-1/2" l, duck, glass, painted ............................ 45.00
Cane, 37" l, carved wood, duck's head handle, chased silver neck band, relief carved leaves on shaft, late 19th C ........................ 800.00
Cookie Cutter, 4-1/2" sq, tin, primitive rooster design,
   spot soldering ................................................................ 65.00
Figure
   Donkey, Metzler ............................................................... 50.00
   Pig, 11-1/4" h, 20-1/4" l, carved wood, glass eyes, leather ears, metal tail, paint dec, 20th C ........................................... 865.00
   Hen on Nest, porcelain Jackfield, black ground, white enamel polka-dots and gilt trim, 5-3/8" h ..................................... 200.00
   Staffordshire, polychrome enameling, imp "P&S XII," 11-1/4" l ...................................................................... 615.00

Poster, Mayo's Plug, linen, 17-3/4" w, 30" h, $700. Photo courtesy of Past Tyme Pleasures Auction.

Unknown maker, polychrome floral enameling, gilt trim,
   7-1/4" h ............................................................................ 275.00
Pie Bird, figural, chicken, glazed ceramic .................................... 50.00
Poster, rooster, chromolithograph, "I Crow for Cleveland and Stevenson," unframed, backed on foam core, some stains and repairs, 44" x 20" ........................................................................................ 200.00
Salt, 2-1/2" l, three pigs around trough ....................................... 60.00

## Birds

Andirons, pr, 8-1/2" w, 17" d, 14-1/4" h, cast iron, owl figures, glass eyes, perched on twigs, raised "407E," America, early 20th C 515.00
Box, 13-1/2" l, walnut, light and dark wood inlay in intricate geometric design with "V. L. Quinn," chip carved eagle, edge damage, age crack, glued repairs ................................................................. 360.00
Cookie Jar, parrot, Metlox ........................................................ 250.00
Figure, 16-3/4" l, 13" h, carved and painted swan, flattened full-bodied figure, painted white with black and yellow features, mounted on carved oblong painted blue and white base, America, 19th C, crackles, small losses on wings ................................................. 14,950.00
Lantern, 14-1/2" h, figural owl, bronze, pierced form, ring at top, dark brown patina, early 20th C ...................................................... 2,750.00
Loving Cup, 7-1/2" x 6", cut glass, three handles, engraved "Corning Poultry Association, 1912," pedestal base, Hawkes ............. 1,000.00
Mantel Carving, A. Elmer Crowell, East Harwich, MA, 1862-1952, orig paint Blue Heron, 6-1/2" l, 7" h, mounted on carved wooden rock, rect "Crowell" stamp, dated 1920 in ink on underside ........... 4,025.00
   Blue Jay, 7-1/2" l, 5-1/2" h, mounted on maple leaves, handwritten signature "A. E. Crowell Cape Cod" ....................... 2,645.00
   Sandpiper, 6" l, 5-1/2" h, mounted on carved clam shell, oval "Crowell" stamp on underside, tiny chip to wing tip ....... 4,600.00
   Wilson's Snipe, 9" l, 6-1/2" n, mounted on carved clam shell, rect "Crowell" stamp, ink signature, paper identification label on underside ..................................................................... 6,325.00
Roof Ornament, 27-3/4" h, full bodied owl standing on hemispherical form, molded zinc, glass eyes, hinged head, painted brown, America, 19th C, split in base, reinforcement, paint loss, dents ........... 2,895.00
Sculpture, 10-1/2" h, sandstone, owl and baby, E. Reed (folk art sculptor known as Popeye) ............................................................. 360.00
Sewer Pipe, 8-1/2" h, owl on log, heavy glaze, 20th C ............... 165.00
Textile, hooked rub, 41" l, 24" h, rooster in center, flanked by tree and flower, yarn hooked in red, various shades of brown, black highlights, oatmeal colored ground, checkered border, America, late 19th/early 20th C, mounted on frame ................................................. 1,495.00

Tumbler, 3-3/4" h, engraved "Happy Days" with chick, 1919 ...... 125.00
Vase, 8-1/2" h, owls, flared colorless glass body, disk foot, enameled snowy night scene of brown owls perched on black branches, reverse painted cobalt blue sky, black enamel base, black enamel signature "De Lucece, France," c1925 ..................................... 230.00

## Cats

Ashtray, cat playing with ball, Bavaria ......................................... 40.00
Bookends, Cheshire cats, brass, c1930 ................................... 140.00
Chimney Flue Cover, 9-1/2" d, picture of golden curled girl holding tabby cat ..................................................................................... 70.00
Doorstop, 7-1/2" h, full bodied sitting cat, old worn repaint ......... 165.00
Music Box, litho tin, Felix the Cat, France ................................. 80.00
Nodder, 3-1/2" h, 6" l, primitive kitten, carved pine, painted black, head bobs and tail moves, late 19th C ..................................... 370.00
Painting, 8-1/2" w, 9" h, oil on board, portrait of gray and white cat in wooden travel crate, wearing red bow, sgd "Gaylord" lower right, American School, late 19th/early 20th C, framed in gilt and black painted shadowbox frame, some surface grime ................. 13,800.00
Sign
    11" x 21", Wrigley's Spearmint Gum, trolley card sign, cardboard, black cat shading to gray image, illus by Shepard .......... 325.00
    14" d, Burke's Ale, counter top reverse painting on glass, cat in center, mounted on tripod base ..................................... 350.00
String Holder, chalkware, kitten's head over ball of yarn, white ..................................................................................... 65.00
Toy, Figaro, litho tin windup ...................................................... 170.00

## Cows

Creamer, 8-1/4" l, gilt dec, Rockingham .................................... 220.00
Drawing, 31" w, 24" h, charcoal on paper, "Feeding the Cow," initialed "E.B.W. 1907," matted and framed, stains ............................. 165.00
Figure, 45" l, papier-mâché, worn black and white paint ........... 190.00
Painting, 10-1/2" w, 7-3/4" h, oil on panel, "Herd with Cattle," sgd "Pingray" lower left, in the manner of Paulus Potter, framed, split to panel, surface grim, prevalent craquelure ..................................... 490.00
Pull Toy, 10" l, cow, wood, hide covering, leather collar with bell, metal wheels ..................................................................................... 120.00
Tin, 3-1/4" d, 5-3/4" h, Buttermilk and Soda Baking Powder, round paper label, woman and cow illus ........................................... 40.00

## Dogs

Bank, 6-1/2" h, seated spaniel, stoneware, applied cobalt blue dec, white Bristol glaze ................................................................... 35.00
Box, cov, 3-1/2" h, silver, rect box, Field Spaniel on cov, engraved and applied detail, Continental, 19th C ....................................... 1,610.00
Broadside, 10-1/2" h, 10-3/4" w, litho, dog dressed in blue jacket, red ascot, glass of whiskey before him, tobacco pouch, printed by Liebler Mass Litho, matted and framed ................................................ 85.00
Calendar, 1937, Du Pont Explosives, two bird dogs, artist sgd "Edm. H. Osthau," 28" h, 15" w, several paint drips on full calendar pad 275.00
Door Stop, Pomeranian, 14" l, painted cast iron, some paint loss ........................................................................... 700.00
Figure, 3-7/8" h, Bulldog, seated on rect platform, pottery, transparent yellow glaze, inscribed around sides "1914, A Happy New Year," "G.A.S.W.," " I should worry," "Phoenix C.W.," large imp Phoenix Pottery mark on base, chips ........................................................ 350.00
Jewelry

**Brooch, Scottie, body covered with coat of blue sapphires in various shapes, sizes, and colors, eye and collar accented with diamond melee, 14kt yg, $2,645. Photo courtesy of Skinner, Inc.**

Brooch, Scottie, 14kt yg, body covered with coat of blue sapphires in various shapes, sizes, an colors, collar and eye accented with diamond melee ..................................... 2,645.00
Cufflinks, 14k yg, textured figural Bulldog faces, diamond set eyes .......................................................................................... 300.00
Letter Opener, 10" l, Dachshund, bronze, two embellished relief heads .......................................................................................... 175.00
Painting
    On The Alert, inscribed "T. Blinks" lower left, oil on canvas, framed, lined, retouched, craquelure, 14" x 18-3/8" ...... 1,955.00
    Sarah Podmore's Dash, titled lower center, unsgd, American School, 19th C, oil on canvas, 21-1/2" h, 29" l, framed, scattered punctures, some repairs, note affixed to stretcher places Sarah and Dash in Boston, c1800 ............................................ 6,900.00
    "Star, an English Setter, 1977," sgd "Will Rannells," watercolor on paper matted and framed, 28-1/2" x 25-1/2" ................... 200.00
Paperweight, 3-1/2" d, colorless dome top, white sulfide of dog, cranberry ground .......................................................................... 275.00
Perfume, 1-1/2" x 1-1/2", figural Scottie, goldtone, plaid blanket, Estee Lauder, orig box .................................................................... 120.00
Sewer Pipe
    10-1/4" h, seated dog with collar, bottom incised "Superior 10-15-70," made by Superior Clay Corp., Tuscarawas County, few firing separators in clay, shallow chip at base ..................... 250.00
    12-1/2" d, seated dog, uneven glaze, imp label "Superior Clay Corp. Uhrichsville, Ohio," incised "Samantha" ................. 350.00
Textile, hooked rug
    39" w, 55" h, large brown dog, black outline, green and tan ground, green leaves, maroon, and black borders, well executed repairs, minor wear ................................................ 385.00
    39-1/2" w, 26" h, portrait of dog in quatrefoil, flanked by cornucopias of flowers, fabric and yarn hooked in shades of brown, cream, red, pink, green, and black, ochre and brown ground, mounted on frame, America, late 19th/early 20th C, minor fading ...................................................................................... 420.00
    44-1/2" w, 35" h, baby in blue dress with shoe button eyes and black dog within pink and red circle, lettered "Baby" within multicolored and ochre rectangle surrounded by border of red, cream, orange, and green floral vine, lettered "Baby Dog" at bottom on black ground, America, 19th C, minor imperfections, one eye missing .............................................................. 2,530.00
Tray, glass, metal rim, illus of two dogs in center .......................... 20.00
Whimsey, 7-7/8" l, 5-3/4", carved wood, dog emerging from shoe, 19th C .......................................................................................... 225.00

## Horses

Bowl, 3" d, 2" h, stallion scene, Rosemeade Pottery .................... 50.00
Calligraphic Drawing, 21-1/2" w, 13-3/4" h, ink on paper, sgd "Goffman" lower left, framed, toning, pale foxing and staining ................. 650.00
Catalog, D. F. Mangels Co. Carousel Works, Coney Island, NY, 28 pgs, 1938 edition ............................................................................ 250.00
Door Knocker, 5-1/2", brass, head ........................................... 140.00
Figure
    9-1/2" l, 7-1/4" h, stallion, medium brown patinated bronze, rect marble base, Gaston Illiers, France, late 19th/early 20th C ........ 815.00

9-3/4" h, Viennese Porcelain, equestrian, "Pirouette Spanische Reitschule, Hofburg Wien" .................................220.00

Jewelry, brooch, platinum, pave-set round brilliant 3.30 ct diamonds, ruby eye, c1935.................................2,300.00

Lunch Box, 7" l, 4-1/2" w, 4-1/4" d, Dan Patch Tobacco, Scotten, Dillin Co., tin litho, brass catch, single handle...................................125.00

Match Safe, 2" l, brass, figural horseshoe with horse and rider in middle, striker......................................200.00

Painting, 7-1/2" w, 9" h, oil on panel, Equestrian Battle Scene, unsigned, identified as manner of Aelbert Cuyp on label from the Museum of the City of New York on reverse, framed, subtle curvature to panel, unobtrusive surface grime, scattered retouch, prevalent craquelure ........................................1,840.00

Print

20" x 26-1/2", "The Famous Roan Horse Capt. McGowan as He Appeared in His 20th Mile," identified in inscription in margin, lithograph on paper with hand coloring, John H. Bufford, lithographer, 1935-71, framed................................850.00

22" x 27-3/4", Brockton Fair Horse Show October 2, 3, 4, 5, 1906, chromolithograph on paperboard, Fred S. Tolman publisher, minor losses ..................................215.00

Pull Toy

11-3/4" h, brown and white leather covered papier-mâché, felt and fabric saddle, glass eyes, carved wooden legs, mounted on green painted board with wheels, German, late 19th C, one felt ear and mane missing, cracks, wear................................375.00

24" l, delivery wagon, carved horse, stenciled wood wagon, German, harness incomplete ..................................275.00

28" l, circus wagon, team of carved horses, polychromed wood, mismatched set ..................................60.00

Watch Fob, horse and horseshoe, gold filled, chain ..................115.00

Windmill Weight, cast iron, bob tail, Dempster Mfg. Co. ............350.00

## Wild Animals

Bell Toy, elephant, cast iron, nickel finish, red wheels, light rust, 7-1/2" l.......................................90.00

Candy Stick Jar, Smokey the Bear ..................................600.00

Chocolate Mold, 6" h, tin, cameo, two parts, hinged.....................70.00

Desk Set, lion, patinated bronze, blotter, standish, and letter holder, dark brown patina, Fredrich Gornick, French, early 20th C...2,250.00

Doorstop, 9" l, lion, cast iron, full bodied, old gold and silver repaint ......................................110.00

Drawing, 10-3/4" x 13-3/4", deer, watercolor on paper, sgd "Victor Schreckengost" lower right, framed ........................400.00

Figure

9" x 5-1/2", reclining lion, stoneware, tooled edge rect base, brown Albany glaze, attributed to NY state, c1850, minor surface wear.......................................385.00

13" l, tiger, patinated bronze, buffed and matte stripes, glass eyes, dark brown patina, Japanese, Meiji period, early 20th C ..................................815.00

Jewelry, brooch, 18k yg, lion, emerald eyes, ruby nose, pave diamond whiskers ..................................485.00

Noah's Ark Set, ninety-one pairs of animals, seventeen singles, three people, animals later replacements, 25-1/4" l ........................2,860.00

Pail, 2-1/2" d, 3-3/4" h, Schepps Cocoanut, monkey in jungle illus ..................................185.00

Pull Toy, 6-3/4" h, tiger, brown and black leather covered papier-mâché, glass eyes, growler mechanism, mounted on wooden base with wheels, Germany, late 19th C, wear, splitting...................395.00

Sewer Pipe, 8-3/8" w, 4-1/8" d, 5-1/4" h, lion, unglazed red clay, rect plinth, reeded edges, incised "4-22-34, W. E. Wadsworth, O" .275.00

Sign, electric, elephant, "Toppie the Elephant" ...........................650.00

Textile, hooked rug, 61" l, 30-1/2" h, recumbent lion among jungle flowers and trees, hooked fabric in shades of brown, green, red, pink, and yellow with red and multicolor diagonal striped border, America, late 19th C, minor imperfections ..................................690.00

# ARCHITECTURAL ELEMENTS

**History:** Architectural elements, many of which are handcrafted, are those items which have been removed or salvaged from buildings, ships, or gardens. Part of their desirability is due to the fact that it would be extremely costly to duplicate the items today. Beginning about 1840, decorative building styles began to feature carved wood and stone, stained glass, and ornate ironwork. At the same time, builders and manufacturers also began to use fancy doorknobs, doorplates, hinges, bells, window locks, shutter pulls, and other decorative hardware as finishing touches to elaborate new homes and commercial buildings.

Hardware was primarily produced from bronze, brass, and iron, and doorknobs also were made from clear, colored, and cut glass. Highly ornate hardware began appearing in the late 1860s and remained popular through the early 1900s. Figural pieces that featured animals, birds, and heroic and mythological images were very popular, as were ornate and very graphic designs that complimented the many architectural styles that emerged in the late 19th century.

Fraternal groups, government and educational institutions, and individual businesses all ordered special hardware for their buildings. Catalogs from the era show hundreds of patterns, often with a dozen different pieces available in each design. The current trends of preservation and recycling of architectural elements has led to the establishment and growth of organized salvage operations that specialize in removal and resale of elements. Special auctions are now held to sell architectural elements from churches, mansions, office buildings, etc. Today's decorators often design an entire room around one architectural element, such as a Victorian marble bar or mural, or use several as key accent pieces.

**References:** Bakewell & Mullins, *Victorian Architectural Sheet-Metal Ornaments*, Dover Publications, 1999; Ronald S. Barlow (comp.), *Victorian Houseware, Hardware and Kitchenware*, Windmill Publishing, 1991; Margarete Baur-Heinhold, *Decorative Ironwork*, Schiffer Publishing, 1996; Louis Blanc, *Decorative French Ironwork Designs*, Dover, 1999; Len Blumin, *Victorian Decorative Art*, available from ADCA (P.O. Box 126, Eola, IL 60519), n.d.; Michael Breza and Craig R. Olson (eds.), *Identification and Dating of Round Oak Heating Stoves*, Southwestern Michigan College Museum (58900 Cherry Grove Rd, Dowagiac, MI 49047), 1995; Henri Clouzet, *Art Deco Decorative Ironwork*, Dover Publications, 1997; A. Dureanne, *Ornamental Ironwork*, Dover Publications, 1998; Maude Eastwood wrote several books about doorknobs which are available from P.O. Box 126, Eola, IL 60519; David A. Hanks, *The Decorative Designs of Frank Lloyd Wright*, Dover Publications, 1999; Barbara Israel, *Antique Garden Ornaments: Two Centuries of*

*American Taste*, Harry N. Abrams, 1999; Joan Kahr, *Edgar Brandt: Master of Art Deco Ironwork*, Harry N. Abrams, 1999; Alistair Morris, *Antiques from the Garden*, Antique Collectors' Club, 1999; Ernest Rettelbusch, *Handbook of Historic Ornament from Ancient Times to Biedermeier*, Dover Publications, 1996; Edward Shaw, *Modern Architect* (reprint), Dover Publications, 1996; *Turn of the Century Doors, Windows and Decorative Millwork*, Dover Publications, 1995 reprint; Stanley Shuler, *Architectural Details from Old New England Homes*, Schiffer Publishing, 1997; Web Wilson, *Great Glass in American Architecture*, E. P. Dutton, New York, 1986; — *Antique Hardware Price Guide*, Krause Publications, 1999; Myra Yellin and Eric B. Outwater, *Garden Ornaments and Antiques*, Schiffer Publishing, 2000.

**Periodical:** *American Bungalow*, P.O. Box 756, Sierra Madre, CA 91204.

**Collectors' Club:** Antique Doorknob Collectors of America, Inc., P.O. Box 126, Eola, IL 60519.

**Museum:** American Sanitary Plumbing Museum, Worcester, MA.

**Additional Listings:** Doorknobs & Builders' Hardware, Stained Glass.

Architectural Element, 89" l, 16" h, rect form, multi-shaped wooden pieces nailed and arranged to depict five radiating flower blossoms, attributed to H. H. Richardson, America, late 19th C .............. 600.00
Basket, 19" w, 9" d, 19" h, wirework, polychromed, scrolling, lattice, and interlacing patterns, French Provincial, fourth quarter 19th C ................................................................. 525.00
Bird Bath
    19" d, 45" h, cast stone, form of Atlas supporting stylized flower formed basin on his back, socle base ........................... 1,760.00
    20-1/2" d, 33" h, cast stone, lotus shape base, circular leaf molded standard, octagonal base .................................... 460.00
Birdcage
    20" w, 15-1/2" d, 23-1/2" h, Victorian, brass, rect wirework form centered by handle, fitted with pull-out tray, fourth quarter 19th C................................................................. 300.00
    26" w, 18" d, 42" h, Victorian-style, polychromed, form inspired by Italianate-villa, corners and peak mounted with vermilion finials, 26" w, 18" d, 42" h ..................................................... 495.00
Bracket, 20" w, 30" d, carved wood, bird plucking at stamen of flower, boldly carved scrolls, traces of tinting, Portuguese, late 18th/early 19th C, worming, price for pr..................................... 1,725.00
Column
    18-1/4" h, sienna marble, Corinthian column topped by cast metal figure of a Roman, socle inscribed "Colonna Foca," stepped base, rouge marble mount, Italian "Grand Tour," late 19th C ...... 1,150.00
    112" h, carved wood, Corinthian capitals above fluted shafts, foliate carving at both ends, raised on carves stone pilasters on a socle base, c1840, price for pr ..................................... 2,450.00
    Curtain Tiebacks, 10", green and white candy swirl, silver ends, price for set of five............................................... 75.00

Door
    76-1/4" h, 23-3/4" w, grain painted, two fielded panels painted mustard brown, dark brown exotic wood graining, New England, early 19th C.................................................. 490.00
    77-3/4" h, 28" w, upper half of leaded glass with stylized red rose on long stem with green leaves, textured colorless glass ground segmented by stylized Art Nouveau leading, oak frame with Gothic-style int. arch, lower half framed by six vertical boards joined by exposed butterfly joints, orig medium brown finish, Arts & Crafts-style, c1905, some wear and loss to edges 635.00
Eagle, 12" x 11-1/2", cast lead, holding shield, mounted on threaded rod, America, some corrosion ................................. 400.00
Fan, 19-3/4" h, 35-5/8" w, painted pine, America, 19th C, minor wear ........................................................... 650.00
Fernery, 32" w, 13" d, 37" h, tôle peinte, molded rect planter inset in arched wirework frame, raised on elaborate cabriole-shaped legs ending in scrolled toes, painted pale yellow with blue accents, French Provincial, fourth quarter 19th C ............................. 775.00
Fountain
    23-1/2" d, 45" h, cast iron, putto struggling with large fish, lattice edged basin with reeded body, floral pedestal ending with three applied swans, concave triangular base ........................ 750.00
    26" d, 46-3/4" h, cast iron, attributed to J. W. Fiske, NY, 19th C, basin with cast leaf exterior, cranes and cat o'nine tails base, molded circular platform, old white paint, weathered .... 2,875.00
Fountain Figure
    17" l, 9" h, bronze, alert frog ............................... 360.00
    23-1/2" d, 48-1/2" h, patinated bronze, putto kneeling with one leg on acanthus-like form, holding hand on grapevine, other supporting shell form basin atop his head, circular base molded with clusters of grapes spilling out of barrel ................. 1,320.00
    32" w, 42" h, patinated bronze, kneeling boy playing with frog, naturalistically molded base, applied lotus leaves ........ 1,210.00
    35" h, bronze, naked boy holding goose, socle surrounded by four goslings with open beaks as fonts, greenish gold patina, 20th C 6,325.00
Frieze, 39" l, 32" h, central laurel wreath, mottoed band centered by rocaille shell mounted with two heraldic cartouches, wreath topped by fruit-filled urn and flanked by two cherubs, scrolled arched base with sea serpent insets on corners, Rococo-style, late 19th/early 20th C.......................................................... 1,610.00
Garden Armillary Sphere, Victorian, third quarter 19th C, 38" w, 64" h, later patinated bronze sphere raised on heavily molded cast iron base, fruit, floral and paw designs, plinth base .................... 3,520.00

**Font, carved Carrara marble, Italian, late 19th C, high relief carving of frolicking infant bacchantes, grape bunches, masks, circular painted wood socle, repairs, 42" d, 29" h, $21,850. Photo courtesy of Skinner, Inc.**

**Garden Bench**
49" l, 14" d, 27" h, cast iron, polychromed, out-scrolling slatted back, conforming seat, rope-twist arms, molded klismos base, price for pr .................................................................. 750.00
49" l, 41-1/2" d, 29" h, cast iron, slatted construction, naturalistically formed arms, interlocking snake and grapevine legs, leaf shaped feet, price for pr ................................................ 1,650.00
61-1/2" l, 20" d, 32" h, cast iron, out-scrolling slatted back, conforming seat, scrolled arms, interlocking acanthus legs, plinth feet, price for pr .................................................................. 275.00
63" l, 22" d, marble, rect seat, backrest carved with Neoclassical scene, satyr and corbel carved supports, Continental 10,925.00

**Garden Chair**, cast iron, painted and gilded, backrest with drapery and masks above two warriors, openwork frieze, cabriole legs, two painted black, four painted red, gilt highlights, price for assembled set of six ........................................................................... 4,350.00

**Garden Gate**, 42-1/2" w, 70-1/2" h, cast iron, domed form, centered scrolling design, price for 4 pc set ................................ 3,500.00

**Garden Seat**, 32-1/2" h, painted arrow-back, curving crest above arrow-back spindles, shaped arm supports, plank seat, sq splayed legs with stretchers, orig green paint, 19th C, repairs ........... 1,725.00

**Garden Suite**, cast iron, two 38" h arm chairs, 49" l, 14-1/2" d, 38" h bench, each with arched back, centered armorial within a rosette, surrounded by interlacing branches, topped by trefoils, slatted seat, down-swept scrolling arms and legs, Victorian, price for 3 pc set ......................................................................................... 1,760.00

**Garden Urn**, cast iron
16" d, 29" h, egg and dart molded lip above neck dec with spray of flowers and wheat over fluted body, circular molded standard, applied scrolling handles, price for pair ........................... 750.00
16" d, 31" h, campana form, egg and dart molded lip, partially reeded body on circular pedestal, pyramidal molded base, price for pr ................................................................................... 425.00
16-1/2" d, 25-1/2" h, campana form, egg and dart molded lip, basketweave molded body, conforming circular base standard, socle, price for pr ........................................................... 825.00
21-1/2" d, 24" h, campana form, egg and dart molded lip, body dec with scrolling arabesques, circular reeded standard, socle base, applied lion head centered handles, price for pr .... 500.00
25" d, 45" h, campana form, everted molded lip, body dec with pr of winged mythical creatures, each centering mosaic with high relief, fluted circular standard, socle base, applied scrolling snake intertwined handles, price for pr ......................... 1,200.00
25" w, 12" d, 12-1/2" h, rect, rococo manner, serpentine lip above garland and floral motifs dec body, splayed scroll feet, price for pr ......................................................................... 350.00
31-1/2" h, three piece construction, scrolled borders with flowers beneath, swallows on wells, scrolled cast detail around base, old worn white repaint, one with welded repair, price for pr ......................................................................... 550.00

**Garden Urn**, cast stone, 18" d, 27" h, everted lip above a partially reeded bulbous body, circular standard, socle base, Italian..... 650.00

**Garden Urn**, terra cotta, 28" d, 52" h, campana form, crested molded lip above body with two Bacchic masks among grapevines, lower fluted part with two rams heads, raised on reeded circular standard, socle base, price for pr ......................................................... 1,100.00

**Gate**, 29" w, 41" h, cast iron, vine cresting manner "Edward R. Dolan" above willow tree with doves in branches, flanking lambs and flowers below on grassy mound, old black, green, and white paint, America, c1860 ........................................................................... 1,380.00

**Mantel**
55" w, 12" d, 41-1/4" h, carved Sienna marble, Louis XVI taste, pilasters carved with anthemion and bellflowers ........... 1,000.00
60" w, 12" d, 47-1/2" h, carved white marble, Napoleon III neoclassical style ........................................................... 4,500.00

**Mantel Tile**, 8-1/2" w, 8-1/8" d, 4-1/8" h, molded pottery, four shaped tiles, two end sides are glazed, mottled yellow and taupe matted glaze, Arts and Crafts style, America, early 20th C, edge chips .................................................................. 175.00

**Obelisk**, 22-1/2" h, ecru marble, Continental, price for pr ........ 1,210.00

**Over Door Panel**, 51" l, 13" h, carved pine, overhanging cornice with foliage and egg and dart carving, central floral swag, flanked on either side by acanthus panels, Adam taste, second quarter 19th C .............................................................................. 2,100.00

**Panel**, 13" h, 68-1/2" w, carved cherry, rect frame with carved interwoven panel centering two quarter fans bordered by spindles and balls, America, late 19th C .............................................................. 700.00

**Pedestal**
37" h, Baroque style, iron, inset circular white marble top joined to two lower graduated inset shelves, cabriole supports, lion's head and intricate molding, scrolled toes, price for pr ...... 400.00
50" h, 14" w, Louis XVI-style, gilt bronze mounted marble, sq top, Corinthian capital, standard applied with foliate cast mounts, stepped base, late 19th C ............................................ 3,750.00

**Roof Ornament**, 50" h, tin and sheet iron, molded five point star about sphere above crescent with round cutouts, resting on larger sphere, mounted on hollow tapering shaft, attributed to Crescent Manuf Co., Rutland, VT, late 19th C, corrosion, four bullet holes .............. 980.00

**Roof Tile**, 15-3/4" l, redware, tulip design, Zoar, OH, few edge chips, price for pr ......................................................................... 200.00

**Rosette**, 11" d, terra cotta, English, 19th C .................................. 40.00

**Shelf Brackets**, pr
6-3/4" w, 4-3/4" d, 10-1/4" h, neoclassical style, carved giltwood, Italian ......................................................................... 475.00
9" w, 4-1/8" d, 9-3/4" h, lyre-form supports, carved beechwood, lyres strung with brass wire, Italian ................................... 100.00

**Valance Rod**, gilt bronze, Neo-Renaissance style, male head at each terminal, Austro-German, c1890 ............................................. 350.00

**Wall Bracket**
11-1/2" l, 8-3/4" d, 16" h, carved giltwood, oval shelf with beaded trim, carved eagle perched on rockery, America, 19th C, minor bead and gilt losses .................................................... 2,185.00
24" w, 22-1/2" d, 36" l, giltwood, tapered top centered by rocaille shell, above carved cherub's head flanked by wings and surrounded by carved clouds, C-scrolls, fruit, and flowers, shaped ground, Baroque, 18th C .............................................. 2,300.00

**Wall Planter**, 16" w, 37" l, patinated bronze, semi-circular scroll molded front, surmounted by lyre form backplate, price for pr ............. 300.00

**Window**, 63" w, 19-1/2" h, wood, two section framework in old white paint, geometric design inside old red paint, wear ................... 650.00

# ART DECO

**History:** The Art Deco period was named after an exhibition, "l'Exposition Internationale des Arts Déecorative et Industriels Modernes," held in Paris in 1927. Its beginnings succeed those of the Art Nouveau period, but the two overlap in time, as well as in style. Art Deco designs are angular with simple lines. This was the period of skyscrapers, movie idols, and the Cubist works of Picasso and Legras. Art Deco motifs were used for every conceivable object being produced in the 1920s and 1930s (ceramics, furniture, glass, and metals) not only in Europe but in America as well.

**References:** Victor Arwas, *Glass: Art Nouveau to Art Deco*, Rizzoli, 1977; Bryan Catley, *Art Deco and Other Figures*, Antique Collectors' Club, 1999; Alastair Duncan, *American Art Deco*, Thames and Hudston, 1999; Alfred W. Edward, *Art Deco Sculpture and Metalware*, Schiffer Publishing, 1996; Mary Gaston, *Collector's Guide to Art Deco*, 2nd ed., Collector Books, 1997, 2000 value update; Ken Hutchinson and Greg Johnson, *Affordable Art Deco*, Collector Books, 1999; Colin Mawston, *British Art Deco Ceramics*, Schiffer Publishing, 2000; Betty Ward and Nancy Schiffer, *Weller, Roseville, and Related Zanesville Art Pottery and Tiles*, Schiffer Publishing, 2000; Joan Kahr, *Edgar Brandt: Master of Art Deco Ironwork*, Harry N. Abrams, 1999; Jim Linz, *Art Deco Chrome*, Schiffer Publishing, 1999; Henrie Martinie, *Art Deco Ornamental Ironwork*, Dover Publications, 1996; Theodore Menten, *Art Deco Style*, Dover Publications, n.d.; Paula Ockner and Leslie Piña, *Art Deco Aluminum: Kensington*, Schiffer Publishing, 1997; Leslie Piña and Paula Ockner, *Depression Era Art Deco Glass*, Schiffer Publishing, 1999; Tina Skinner, *Art Deco Era Textile Designs*, Schiffer Publishing, 1998; Wolf Uecker, *Art Nouveau and Art Deco Lamps and Candlesticks*, Abbeville Press, 1986; Howard and Pat Watson, *Collecting Art Deco Ceramics*, Kevin Francis, 1993.

**Periodical:** *Echoes Report*, P.O. Box 2321, Mashpee, MA 02649.

**Collectors' Clubs:** Canadian Art Deco Society, #302-884 Bute St., Vancouver, British Columbia V6E 1YA Canada; Carlton Ware International, P.O. Box 161, Sevenoaks, Kent TN15 6GA England; Chase Collectors Society, 2149 W. Jibsail Loop, Mesa, AZ 85202; International Coalition of Art Deco Societies, One Murdock Terrace, Brighton, MA 02135; Miami Design Preservation League, P.O. Box Bin L, Miami Beach, FL 33119; Twentieth Century Society, 70 Cowcross St., London EC1M 6DR England.

**Museums:** Art Institute of Chicago, Chicago, IL; Copper-Hewitt Museum, National Museum of Design, Smithsonian Institution, New York, NY; Corning Museum of Glass, Corning, NY; Jones Museum of Glass and Ceramics, Sebago, ME; Virginia Museum of Fine Arts, Richmond, VA.

**Additional Listings:** Furniture; Jewelry. Also check glass, pottery, and metal categories.

Bust, 8-1/4" h, porcelain, female, blond coiled hair, wearing ethnic sash dec with scrolling floral pattern, stamped "Roman, made in Italy," mid-20th C, price for pr .......... 290.00
Car Mascot, 14-1/4" h, pale topaz glass, stylized draped woman with outstretched arm, threaded disk base, attributed to Etling, France, c1927, later cylindrical black stand with light, stress cracks.. 1,150.00
Chair, club, mahogany and leather, French, first quarter 20th C 29-1/2" h, padded rect back joined to cushioned seat, padded arms, tapering sq feet ................. 550.00
30" h, shaped back, large padded arms, cushioned seat, tapering sq feet, tan leather with black piping, price for pr.......... 2,450.00
Chair, side, chromed metal rod frame, triangular linear back over triangular upholstered seat and rod legs, 32" h, price for pr .......... 100.00
Clock, desk
5-5/8" h, 7-1/2" l, General Electric, rect black glass clock face with chrome numerals, etched leaf and scallop dec on chrome rect at center, imp marks on back, second quarter 20th C, wear to chrome .......... 175.00
8-3/4" h, Sessions, round alabaster form surrounding clock face attached to gilt metal band over elongated oval alabaster base, raised gilt and black painted numerals, second quarter 20th C, hand-set screw missing.......... 150.00
Clock Garniture, marble, 12-1/2" h diamond-shaped clock, matted silvered metal face, sgd "Uteau and Bordeaux," set into marble frame

on rect marble standard flanked by two gilt seated metal female figures, all raised on rect platform of striated white and black marble, two 7-3/4" h marble garnitures with geometric dec, France, c1935, chips, separations, cracks, price for 3 pcs .......... 490.00
Cocktail Shaker, 15-3/4" h, tapered black amethyst body, silver overlay scenes of stylized deer in landscape, red Bakelite knob on silver spout, imp "Sterling," attributed to Rockwell Co., c1925, minor wear .......... 175.00
Demitasse Cup and Saucer, 2-1/2" h cup, 4-5/8" d, floral dec rim, yellow, pink, blue, green, and black, cream colored ground, maker's stamp on base, Honiton Pottery, Devon, England .......... 90.00
Dresser, miniature, 30" w, 10" d, 27-1/2" h, mahogany, serpentine backsplash surmounted by circular beveled mirror plate, two shelves, flanked on either side by two graduated satinwood inlaid drawers, tapering stepped plinth base.......... 200.00
Figure
5-1/2" h, carved rearing horse within upright horseshoe, polished black granite, scratches, minor chips .......... 190.00
11" h, bronze, dancer, patinated, ivory dec, brass inlaid malachite box base, French, c1920-25 .......... 275.00
16" h, dancing woman, gilt bronze body, modeled in dimpled body suit, carved ivory hands and face, stained details on face, attributed to Demetre Chiparus, French.......... 6,325.00
Fruit Bowl, 11" d, 2-1/2" h, Lotus Fan dec, silver plate, Rogers, c1923-25 .......... 90.00
Garniture Figure
Crystal, stylized goldfish, c1930, price for pair .......... 90.00
Porcelain, 12-1/2" h, ancient Greek inspired "Red Figure," mkd "Limoges," c1920-25, price for pair .......... 880.00
Jar, cov, 8-1/8" h, flared cylindrical body, stepped faceted foot, faceted finial cover, transparent blue layered in violet, acid etched and deeply engraved with Art Deco geometric dec, sand textured ground, illegible signature, France, c1925, minor rim nicks .......... 350.00
Lamp, 16-1/2" h, metal-framed ochre paper shade, two-socket fixture with slender metal standard above ceramic base designed as a sphere within a cub, cream and gray crackle glaze, imp "Editions Etling" within a triangle, "Marcel Guillard," and "J. Martin" on base, c1927, minor chips .......... 690.00
Magazine Rack, 4-1/2" w, 11-7/8" l, 12" h, bronze, upright circular sides with openwork design of greyhound in stride, scrolling leaf border, c1930 .......... 375.00
Mirror, 44-1/2" w, 56" h, wooden crest with stylized doves among flower and leaves, elongated hexagonal frame, fleur-de-lis at sides, one with antique gold finish, other silvered, wear to finish and mirrors, price for pr .......... 1,725.00
Salad Servers, fork and spoon, 11-3/4" l, Swedish, c1930-35 ...... 50.00
Sideboard, 86-1/4" w, 19-1/2" d, 37-1/2" h, Louis XVI taste, brass mounted mahogany, French, c1925-30 .......... 1,200.00
Smoking Stand, 27-1/2" h, Statue of Liberty, bronze patinated metal stand, eagle finial on tray, removable cov matched canister, two ash trays, small lighted amber dome, tray dec with raised images of Presidents Washington and Lincoln, American landmarks, tray supported by Statue of Liberty figure, round stepped base, minor wear to patina .......... 230.00
Table
13-3/4" w, 23-3/4" l, 20-1/2" h, rect black lacquered wooden top over three curved flat chromed metal bands with two connecting bands at lower center, four circular band feet, some corrosion... 115.00
39-1/2" w, 44-1/2" l, 29-3/4" h, mahogany veneer rect top, symmetrical design, contrasting dark edge, curved stepped supports over medial shelf, ebonized feet, wear.......... 850.00
Tea Cart, 29" w, 17" d, 27" h, chrome, glass, and Lucite construction, 1930s .......... 450.00
Tea Service, silver plate, Wm. Hutton & Sons and J. Dixon & Sons, Sheffield, England, c1930, cylindrical bodies, stepped and canted feet, 6-1/4" h coffeepot with taupe colored composition finial and handle, teapot with black composition finial and handle, creamer and open sugar, imp marker's marks, assembled set, wear.......... 290.00

**Vase, cast metal, flaring buttressed sides, brass patina, unmarked, 14-1/2" h, 8-1/2" w, $110. Photo courtesy of David Rago Auctions.**

Toast Holder, 6-1/2" l, 2-1/2" w, 2-1/4" h, Carlton Ware, ceramic, black and orange edged wedges, yellow glazed ground, loop handles .......................................................................... 150.00

Vase, glass

6-1/4" h, flattened rim, elongated stem over ovoid vessel, transparent green deeply acid etched with braid motif, inscribed "Daum (cross) Nancy France" at base, rough rim ............ 650.00

8-1/2" h, cone-form, heavy walled and textured black amethyst, sq foot, inscribed "Daum (cross) Nancy France," c1935 .................................................................... 1,495.00

9-3/4" h, flared rim, double bulbed frosted colorless body, raised stylized roses, stained pale pink and orange, molded "Muller Freres" signature on base, minor nicks ............................ 300.00

10" h, flared rim, swollen cylindrical body, translucent opal, engraved and etched with two stylized nude women supporting polished disk, etched initials "A.N.B." at bottom of dec and "Gray-...(illegible)" around pontil on base, minor staining 260.00

11-3/4" h, raised and gently tapered neck on ovoid body, pronounced ribs, textured panels of mottled amber and colorless glass, acid signature "Daum (cross) Nancy France," c1930 ...................................................................... 920.00

13-1/4" h, flared rim on molded body of opalescent glass, domed foot, dec as overlapping palm leaves, frosted and polished, base with acid stamp "Ovington, New York, France, H. Dieupa...," c1925, (attributed to Henri Dieupart,) c1925, rim chips... 460.00

Vase, pottery, 8-3/4" h, flared raised rim, tapered neck, oval body, incised lines around rim, shoulder and body, glossy dark turquoise blue glaze ........................................................................ 200.00

Vide-Pochie, 4" d, green onyx, gilt spelter Borzoi, c1920-30 ........ 70.00

Wall Sconces, pr, 18" w, 9-3/4" w, mixed metal, elongated shield shape, emb overlapping circles at top, etched linear dec on white metal, beveled mirrors, brass brackets, double candleholders and studs, minor corrosion ............................................ 520.00

Wristwatch, lady's, Swiss, 18kt white gold, tonneau shape, ivory-tone dial with black Arabic numerals, diamond bezel, 14kt white gold, snake charm strap .......................................................... 350.00

# ART NOUVEAU

**History:** Art Nouveau is the French term for the "new art," which had its beginning in the early 1890s and continued for the next 40 years. The flowing and sensuous female forms used in this period were popular in Europe and America. Among the most recognized artists of this period were Gallé, Lalique, and Tiffany. The Art Nouveau style can be identified by flowing, sensuous lines, florals, insects, and the feminine form. These designs were incorporated into almost everything produced during the period, from art glass to furniture, silver, and personal objects. Later wares demonstrate some of the characteristics of the evolving Art Deco style.

**References:** Victor Arwas, *Glass: Art Nouveau to Art Deco*, Rizzoli, 1977; Graham Dry, *Art Nouveau Domestic Metalwork*, Antique Collectors' Club, 1999; Alastair Duncan, *The Paris Salons 1895-1914, Vol. IV, Ceramics and Glass*, Antique Collectors' Club, 1998; Albert Christian Revi, *American Art Nouveau Glass*, reprint, Schiffer Publishing, 1981; Wolf Uecker, *Art Nouveau and Art Deco Lamps and Candlesticks*, Abbeville Press, 1986; Kenneth Wilson, *American Glass 1760-1930*, 2 vols., Hudson Hill Press and The Toledo Museum of Art, 1994.

**Museum:** Virginia Museum of Fine Arts, Richmond, VA.

**Additional Listings:** Furniture; Jewelry. Also check glass, pottery, and metal categories.

Ashtray, 3-3/8" w, 5-1/4" l, 7/8" h, rect, molded colorless glass, reverse relief of Leda and Swan, c1925, ground spot at base, nicks to bottom edge ...................................................................... 175.00

Box, cov, 4" h, domed sq cover on broad shouldered four paneled box of rust brown shaded to colorless cased glass, acid etched dec with textured surface, gilt highlights, script gilt mark "H 57" on base, Continental, early 20th C .................................................. 350.00

Candlesticks, pr, l" h, tricorn, raised stylized floral and leaf motifs, bronze patina ............................................................ 150.00

Center Bowl, 18" d, 15-1/4" h, alabaster bowl with everted rim, figural bronze base of three crouching nude male figures, green marble base, restorations .................................................. 2,415.00

Desk Set

Cast Bronze, emb with stylized thistle motif, inkstand, pen tray, stamp moistener, letter opening, 15-1/4" h candlestick, stamped "J. Preston/Chicago" ...................................... 1,800.00

Copper, enameled and overlaid, each with silver dragon set with green cabochon and green enamel detail, four blotter ends, letter holder, letter opening, stamp box, inkwell, stamp sponge holder, paper clip, pen tray, perpetual calendar, medium patina, stamped mark "Art Crafts Shop," patent date "July 21, -06" ...................................................... 1,700.00

Dinner Gong, 12" w, 10-1/2" d, 10" h, mahogany, five graduated bronze bells, exotic wood floral marquetry on each side, bells restrung ................................................................ 450.00

Dish, 10-1/4" h, faience, foliate shaped bowl, int. painted in naturalistic colors with wild flowers in front of shore landscape, gilded rim, base with red stamp "E. (cross) G depose, Emile Galle a Nancy," restored .............................................................. 320.00

Ewer, 9-1/2" h, pottery, silver overlay, slender form, sinuous loop handle neck wrapped by reclining young woman, shaped base extending from handle ........................................................ 415.00

Figure

17" h, Fame, gilt-spelter, standing on Langeudoc marble base, figure after E. Villianis, French ...................................... 275.00

**Wall Plaque, ceramic, polychrome dec, center woman's portrait surrounded by irises, mkd "Made in Austria/Ernst Wahliss/Turn Wien," chips, minor glaze flakes, 13" d, $395. Photo courtesy of David Rago Auctions.**

22-1/4" h, poised female dancer, onyx, paintated metal, celluloid hands and face, lighted circular green onyx base surrounded by gold patinated elephants, electrified, early 20th C ........... 650.00

Group, 17" w, 7" d, 15" h, patinated bronze, floral mounted bowl attended by cherubs, rocaille base on rectilinear plinth ........... 415.00

Inkstand

3-1/2" w, 10-1/4" l, 2-5/8" h, two sq glass ink bottles with hinged caps set in conforming pewter stand with raised vine and leaf dec, imp marks "English Pewter, 2, 0715" and "Made in England"........................ 375.00

3-7/8" h, brass, two tiered letter holder, hinged lid on inkwell, etched floral dec, base imp "D.R.G.M. 237670 Ges Gesch".................. 120.00

Jar, 13-1/2" h, brass lined, patinated, ovoid body dec with flowers, foot resting on frogs, domical cover with knopped finial.................. 375.00

Lamp

Desk, 13-7/8" h, bronze, helmet-shaped textured shade, raised heavy vine border, flattened bar and double rod shaft on flared base, front band of raised petal dec.................. 865.00

Figural, 40" h, polychromed, three lights with frosted shades issuing from foliate standard, pair of classical maidens and child below on sq base, hoof feet .................. 300.00

Table, 22-1/4" h, early 20th C, bronze flower blossom finial, frosted bent panel domed glass shade, metal overlay frame with Art Nouveau floral and scroll motif, two-socket vasiform standard with stylized heron handles on flared round base, dark brown patina.................. 1,150.00

Lavabol, 14" w, 13-1/2" d, 19" h, brass, corner fitting, emb figural dogs at splash back corners, curvilinear dec, spigot center, round basin with stylized woven strap border, dents .................. 230.00

Medal, silver gilt, depicting winged figure slaying bat, stamped "PW 1903," verse emb "1907 Longchamps fleuri," stamped "Wolfers Freres" for Phillip Wolfers.................. 690.00

Mirror, 13" w, 18-1/2" l, patinated bronze, girl on swing motif, Continental .................. 220.00

Pitcher, 7-1/4" h, earthenware, tapered hexagonal form, angular handles, stylized roseheads and floral drops, green, pink, and gold glazes, French, made by Frie, Onnaing, early 20th C, price for pr .................. 150.00

Parlor Suite, America, early 20th C, mahogany and birch, 52" l, 29", 39-1/4" l loveseat, 30" w, 37" d, 39" h rocking chair, 30-1/2" w, 30" d, 40-1/2" h arm chair, each with closed arms, lion carved masks terminating in paw feet, reupholstered .................. 1,870.00

Screen, 73" l, 63-1/4" h, pyrographic dec, three part oak frame, hinged, pierced, red, green and gilt painted dec of birds and cascading foliage, reverse covered in fabric, paint wear, heavy wear to fabric .................. 420.00

Server, English, fourth quarter 19th C, 36" w, 18" d, 52" h, back piece surmounted by shaped foliate carved crest, green tiles with foliate pattern, lower section with white marble top over frieze raised on turned legs, casters .................. 275.00

Vase

4" h, 7-3/4" d, porcelain, round bulbous from, five sq feet, raised bellflower dec and leafy gilt swags, speckled buff colored ground, gilt highlights, Austria.................. 435.00

6" h, 6-1/2" d, silver plate, stylized relief waterlily dec, English, c1900-15 .................. 175.00

7-1/8" h, glass, quarter form, ruffled rim, ribbed stem, bulbed base, green glass cased to opaque pink int., slight irid sheen, rough pontil, attributed to Union Glass Co., Somerville, MA ....... 115.00

8" h, etched glass, flared rim, four panel body of colorless glass, etched stylized flower blossoms and stems, price for pr..300.00

9-1/4" h, pottery, molded and shaped vessel flanked by two draped figures, matte black glaze, irid green glazed ground, central panels with red flowers and gilded highlights, base imp "Made in Austria," shape numbers, rubbed marks .................. 635.00

# ART POTTERY (GENERAL)

**History:** America's interest in art pottery can be traced to the Centennial Exposition in Philadelphia, Pennsylvania, in 1877, where Europe's finest producers of decorative art displayed an impressive selection of their wares. Our young artists rose to the challenge immediately, and by 1900, native artisans were winning gold medals for decorative ceramics here and abroad. The Art Pottery "Movement" in America lasted from about 1880 until the first World War. During this time, more than 200 companies, in most states, produced decorative ceramics ranging from borderline production ware to intricately decorated, labor intensive artware establishing America as a decorative art powerhouse. Below is a listing of the work by various factories and studios, with pricing, from a number of these companies. The location of these outlets are included to give the reader a sense of how nationally-based the industry was.

**References:** Susan and Al Bagdade, *Warman's Americana Pottery and Porcelain*, 2nd ed., Krause Publications, 2000; Carol and Jim Carlton, *Colorado Pottery*, Collector Books, 1994; Paul Evans, *Art Pottery of the United States*, 2nd ed., Feingold & Lewis Publishing, 1987; Lucile Henzke, *Art Pottery of America*, revised ed., Schiffer Publishing, 1996; Norman Karlson, *American Art Tile, 1876-1941*, Rizzoli Publications, 1998; Ralph and Terry Kovel, *Kovels' American Art Pottery*, Crown Publishers, 1993; Richard and Hilary Myers, *William Morris Tiles*, Richard Dennis (distributed by Antique Collectors' Club), 1996; David Rago, *American Art Pottery*, Knickerbocker Press, 1997; Jim Riebel, *Sanfords Guide to Nicodemus*, Adelmore Press, 1998; Dick Sigafoose, *American Art Pottery*, Collector Books, 2001.

**Periodicals:** *Style 1900*, 17 S. Main St., Lambertville, NJ 08530.

**Collectors' Clubs:** American Art Pottery Association, P.O. Box 834, Westport, MA 02790-0697, http://www.amartpot.org; Pottery Lovers Reunion, 4969 Hudson Dr., Stow, OH 44224.

**Museums:** Cincinnati Art Museum, Cincinnati, OH; Everson Museum of Art of Syracuse and Onondaga County, Syracuse, NY; Los Angeles County Museum of Art, Los Angeles, CA; Metropolitan Museum of Art, New York, NY; Newcomb College Art Gallery, New Orleans, LA; Zanesville Art Center, Zanesville, OH.

**Additional Listings:** See Clewell; Clifton; Cowan; Dedham; Fulper; Grueby; Jugtown; Marblehead; Moorcroft; Newcomb; North Dakota School of Mines; Ohr; Paul Revere; Peters and Reed; Rookwood; Roseville; Van Briggle; Weller; Zanesville.

**Notes:** Condition, design, size, execution, and glaze quality are the key considerations when buying art pottery. This category includes only companies not found elsewhere in this book.

**Advisor:** David Rago.

**Arequipa**

Bowl, 9" d, 4-1/4" h, light blue glossy glaze, molded flower and leaf dec, rolled rim, mkd .......................... 55.00

Vase, 8" x 5", eight sided, tapering rim, emb leaves, matted red-brown glaze, imp mark, small base bruise, minor glaze flakes inside rim ...................... 950.00

**Bybee, Seldon**, vase, 5-7/8" h, three handles, strong crystalline glaze over brown glaze, mkd with outline of Kentucky enclosing name, early 1930s ...................... 85.00

**California Faience**

Bowl, 4-1/2" d, medium blue, glossy glaze ......................... 125.00

Flower Frog, sailboat shape ................................. 65.00

Vase, 5" h, 2-3/4" d, bottle shape, flared rim, feathered blue matte finish, incised mark .......................... 515.00

**Cincinnati Faience**, umbrella stand, 20" h, applied sea life, blue glaze, gold accents, sgd, c1890 ......................... 995.00

**Denver Denaura**, vessel, 2-3/4" h, 5-3/4" d, closed-in rim, emb with violets and leaves, matte green glaze, stamped mark "Denver Denaura/174" ...................... 1,900.00

**Jervis**, 4" h, 3" d, vessel, incised stylized trees and mountains, greens, blues, and ivory, incised mark, two minor glaze nicks at base, stilt pill 2,600.00

**Durant Kilns**, center bowl, turquoise crackled glaze, incised and dated 1917, very shallow bruise to side ...................... 450.00

**Merrimac**, 7-3/4" h, 4-1/2" d, closed-in rim, tooled and applied swirling leaves, feathered matte glaze, carved "EB," several nicks to edges of leaves ...................... 3,750.00

**Overbeck**

Chalice, 6" h, 5-1/4" d, incised yellow and gunmetal camels and mountains, raspberry ground, incised "OBK/E/F," tight rim crack 1,500.00

Musicians, seven 4-1/2" h figures, whimsical yellow, green, pink, and white glazes, incised "OBK," few small chips ......... 2,100.00

Tea Set, teapot, creamer, sugar, trivet, four cups and saucers, all dec with panel of stylized lily of the valley in cuerda seca, celadon matte ground, mkd "OBK/E/H," minor nick to rim of creamer, small stilt pull chips on cups ......................... 2,200.00

Tumbler, 3-3/4" h, 3" d, emb green crickets, beige ground, stamped "OBK/E/F," price for set of four ........................ 1,300.00

**Pewabic**

Bowl, 6-3/4" d, 3-3/4" h, hemispherical, gunmetal and turquoise dripping lustered glaze, circular stamp mark .................. 1,800.00

Jardiniere, 9" d, 8" h, lustered cobalt blue glaze, stamped "Pewabic/Detroit" .................................. 2,200.00

Vase

5" h, 5" d, spherical, ribbed body, orange matte glaze, circular stamp mark, restoration to small base chip ................ 400.00

7-3/4" h, 5-1/2" d, bulbous, lustered blue and turquoise mottled glaze, stamped "Pewabic/Detroit" .................... 1,200.00

9-3/4" h, 6-1/2" d, baluster, brilliant pulled cobalt blue and turquoise lustered glaze, stamped "Pewabic/Detroit" .. 5,000.00

10-1/2" h, 5" d, tapering, frothy, dripping celadon and gold lustered glaze, stamped "Pewabic/Detroit," drilled hole in bottom ....................... 2,100.00

11" h, 8-1/2" d, emb with numbs around shoulder, rare dripping matte mustard glaze on caramel ground, stamped "Pewabic" with leaves ........................... 10,000.00

**Pisgah Forest**

Cream Pitcher, 4-1/2" h, 5-1/4" d, white cameo relief of pioneering scene, blue marbled ground, dec by Walter Stephen, raised potter's mark, mkd "1951/Stephen" ...................... 195.00

Mug, 3-3/8" h, cameo dec of finely detailed clog dancers, dec by Walter Stephen, raised logo on base ............................. 120.00

Vase, 12-1/4" h, 8" d, stove-pipe neck, bulbous base, shaded ivory glaze, blue and pearl crystals, raised potter's mark and "Stephan/1946," firing lines around base of neck ............ 700.00

**Robertson, Fred, Los Angeles**, vase, 7-1/2" h, 4-3/4" d, classical shape, celadon glaze, tightly packed crystals, mark obscured by glaze ...................... 3,250.00

**Shearwater**

Bowl, 5-1/2" d, 1-1/2" h, underglaze painted stylized bird, black and white, beige ground, ext. with band of waves, stamped "Shearwater" ................................. 1,000.00

Vase

5-1/4" h, 6" d, bulbous, pierced shoulder, emb primrose, sheer blue and pink semi-matte glaze, stamped "Shearwater," incised "MA," burst bubble on rim ........................... 2,100.00

7-1/2" h, 5" d, double gourd shape, mottled turquoise, celadon, and gunmetal glaze, stamped "Shearwater" ....... 850.00

9" h, 4-1/2" d, cylindrical, incised with stylized carp, sheer blue and purple semi-matte glaze, incised "MA," 3" crack, bruise, and tight line to rim, few tight firing lines to base ........ 850.00

10-3/4" h, 6-1/2" d, classical shape, stylized fish and sea plants in sgraffito, brushed cobalt blue ground, incised "MA&PA" ................................. 8,000.00

Vessel, 12" h, 7-1/2" d, emb stylized Art Deco zodiac icons, ivory on gunmetal ground, stamped "Shearwater" ................. 4,500.00

**Teco**

Box, cov, 3-1/2" l, 2-1/2" w, 2-1/4" h, squatty, smooth matte green glaze with charcoaling, stamped "Teco," bruise to base .. 700.00

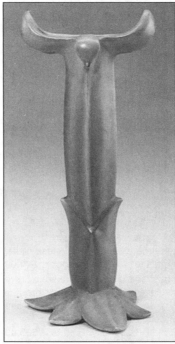

**Teco, bud vase, organic form, heavily charcoaled matte green glaze, imp "Teco/153/4," three tiny chips to base, 12-1/2" h, 5-1/2" d, $2,415. Photo courtesy of David Rago Auctions.**

**Wheatley, jardinière, molded with 2 rows of leaves, matte dark green glaze, incised "WP," restoration to 2 handles and section of rim, $1,100. Photo courtesy of David Rago Auctions.**

Chamberstick, 10-3/4" h, 5" d, bulbous, emb stylized flowers and leaves, smooth matte green glaze, paper label ............... 800.00

Pitcher, 8-1/2" h, 5" d, sinewy handle, mottled matte green and charcoal glaze, stamped "Teco" ..................................... 750.00

Tiffany

Vase, 10" h, 4-1/2" d, cylindrical, bisque, emb with wisteria, incised "LCT," 2" hairline on rim .................................. 4,500.00

Vessel, 5" h, 7-1/2" d, closed-in, vines, berries, and leaves, Old Ivory glaze, incised "LCT," acid etched "Favrile Pottery/P22Y Tiffany," three chips ..................................................... 4,000.00

Walley, W. J.

Vase

7-1/4" w, 3-1/4" d, tapering, mottled brown and gold matte glaze, stamped "WJW," few small grinding chips at base .......................................................................... 1,200.00

7-1/2" h, 5-1/2" d, bulbous, fine frothy semi-matte green glaze, stamped "WJW," minor glaze flake to rim ................ 1,300.00

Wheatley

Lamp Base

11-1/2" h, 10-1/2" d, gourd shape, four buttressed handles, leathery matte green glaze, orig oil font, incised "WP/672," several burst bubbles............................................... 2,500.00

16-1/4" h, 10" d, broad circular form, emb tall stems, leaves, and buds, fine leathery matte green glaze, unmarked............................................................................... 1,400.00

Vase

6-3/4" h, 3" d, ribbed leaves, mottled matte green glaze, mark partially obscured by glaze, several clay pimples....... 850.00

12-1/2" h, 6" d, emb arrowhead leaves, medium matte green glaze, mark obscured by glaze, several clay pimples, burst bubbles ........................................................................ 1,600.00

14-1/4" h, 8" d, lobed rim, four webbed handles, leathery matte green glaze, incised "WP," several burst bubbles, few glaze chips, grinding chips to base.......................... 2,800.00

26-1/2" h, 10-1/2" d, faceted, emb tall leaves, stylized buds, leathery matte green glaze, incised "WP," two glaze chips on ribs ................................................................................ 3,500.00

Vessel

7-1/4" h, 7-1/4" d, ribbed neck, emb rows of leaves, frothy light green and amber glaze, mkd "WP," several burst glaze bubbles ........................................................................ 800.00

7-1/4" h, 9" d, flat rim, four buttresses, flowing dead-matte green glaze, marked "61".......................................... 1,600.00

13" h, 9" d, gourd shape, emb with broad leaves, leathery green matte glaze, after G. P. Kendrick, mkd "WP," two small chips ................................................................................ 3,500.00

Wall Pocket, 8" l, 9-1/4" w, hemispheric, emb with broad leaves alternating with buds, curdled medium matte green glaze, unmarked ........................................................................ 600.00

# ARTS and CRAFTS MOVEMENT

**History:** The Arts and Crafts Movement in American decorative arts took place between 1895 and 1920. Leading proponents of the movement were Elbert Hubbard and his Roycrofters, the brothers Stickley, Frank Lloyd Wright, Charles and Henry Greene, George Niedecken, and Lucia and Arthur Mathews. The movement was marked by individualistic design (although the movement was national in scope) and re-emphasis on handcraftsmanship and appearance. A reform of industrial Society was part of the long-range goal. Most pieces of furniture favored a rectilinear approach and were made of oak. The Arts and Crafts Movement embraced all aspects of the decorative arts, including metalwork, ceramics, embroidery, woodblock printing, and the crafting of jewelry.

**References:** Steven Adams, *Arts & Crafts Movement*, Chartwell Books, 1987; *Arts and Crafts Furniture: The Complete Brooks Catalog of 1912*, Dover Publications, 1996; Annette Carruthers and Mary Greensted, eds., *Simplicity of Splendour Arts and Crafts Living, Lund Humphries*, distributed by Antique Collectors' Club, 1999; David Cathers, *Furniture of the American Arts and Crafts Movement: Revised Edition*, Turn of the Century Editions, 1996; —, *Stickley Style: Arts and Crafts Homes in the Craftsman Tradition*, Simon & Schuster, 1999; Michael E. Clark and Jill Thomas-Clark (eds.), *J. M. Young Arts and Crafts Furniture*, Dover Publications, 1994; Douglas Congdon-Martin, *Arts & Crafts Designs for the Home*, Schiffer Publishing, 2000; Paul Evans, *Art Pottery of the United States*, 2nd ed., Feingold & Lewis Publishing, 1987; *Furniture of the Arts & Crafts Period With Prices*, L-W Book Sales, 1992, 1995 value update; *Charlotte Gere and Geoffrey Munn, Pre-Raphaelite to Arts & Crafts Jewelry*, Antique Collectors' Club, 1999; Bruce Johnson, *Pegged Joint*, Knock on Wood Publications, 1995; Elyse Zorn Karlin, *Jewelry and Metalwork in the Arts and Crafts Tradition*, Schiffer Publishing, 1993; *Limbert Arts and Crafts Furniture: The Complete 1903 Catalog*, Dover Publications, n.d.; Thomas K. Maher, *The Jarvie Shop: The Candlesticks and Metalwork of Robert R. Jarvie*, Turn of the Century Editions, 1997; James Massey and Shirley Maxwell, *Arts & Crafts*, Abbeville Press, 1995; —, *Arts & Crafts Design in America: A State-By-State Guide*, Chronicle Books, 1998; Kevin McConnell, *More Roycroft Art Metal*, Schiffer Publishing, 1995; Richard and Hilary Myers, *William Morris Tiles*, Richard Dennis (distributed by Antique Collectors' Club), 1996; David Rago, *American Art Pottery*, Knickerbocker Press, 1997; Roycrofters, *Roycroft Furniture Catalog*, 1906, Dover Publications, 1994; Paul Royka, *Mission Furniture from the American Arts & Crafts Movement*, Schiffer Publishing, 1997; Joanna Wissinger, *Arts and Crafts: Metalwork and Silver and Pottery and Ceramics*, Chronicle Books, 1994.

**Periodicals:** American Bungalow, P.O. Box 756, Sierra Madre, CA 91204; Style 1900, 333 N. Main St., Lambertville, NJ 08530. American Bungalow focuses on the contemporary owner of Period homes and the refurbishing of same. Style 1900 has a more historically oriented approach to the turn of the century artisans.

**Collectors' Clubs:** Foundation for the Study of the Arts & Crafts Movement, Roycroft Campus, 31 S. Grove St., East Aurora, NY 14052; Roycrofters-At-Large Association, P.O. Box 417, East Aurora, NY 14052; William Morris Society of Canada, 1942 Delaney Dr., Mississaugua, Ontario, L5J 3L1, Canada. Students of the Arts and Crafts Movement are encouraged to participate in the two major conferences now available. The Grove Park Inn Conference is held annually in Ashville, NC, in February, by Bruce Johnson.

**Museums:** Cooper Hewitt Museum, Manhattan, NY; Elbert Hubbard Library-Museum, East Aurora, NY; Los Angeles County Museum of Art, Los Angeles, CA; Metropolitan Museum of Art, Manhattan, NY; Museum of Modern Art, New York, NY; Richmond Museum of Art, Richmond, VA.

**Advisor:** David Rago.

**Additional Listings:** Roycroft; Stickleys; art pottery categories.

Bookcase, 55" w, 12" d, 55-3/4" h, Lifetime, three doors with glass panels, orig hardware, int. shelves, orig medium brown finish, Lifetime decal, "Grand Rapids Furniture Co." paper tag .................... 2,500.00
Box, cov
    7-3/4" d, 3-3/4" h, round, pyrography dec, landscape of trees and mountains, browns and golds, orig green silk lining, small rim chip, unmarked, attributed to Arthur Grinnell ................... 550.00
    9-1/2" d, 6-1/2" h, round, hammered copper, floriform rim, ivory and silver pineapple shaped finial, medium orig patina, stamped "CAUMAN" .................................................................. 550.00
Bowl
    5" d, 1-3/4" h, hammered silver, stamped "Sterling, Hand Beaten at the Kalo Shops, Park Ridge, Illinois," 4 troy oz ............ 395.00
    6-1/2" d, 2-3/4" h, hammered copper, rolled, closed-in rim, orig patina, windmill stamp with "D'Arcy Gaw/Dirk Van Erp" 1,000.00
Cabinet, 19" w, 15" d, 67" h, mirrored, single door painted with monk pouring wine, pewter strap hinges, paper "Shop-Of-The-Crafters" label on back, skinned finish .................................................. 1,300.00

---

# SPECIAL AUCTIONS

Craftsman Auctions
1485 West Housatonic
Pittsfield, MA 01201
(413) 448-8922

David Rago Auctions, Inc.
333 North Main St.
Lambertville, NJ 08530
(609) 397-9374

Treadway Gallery, Inc.
2029 Madison Rd
Cincinnati, OH 45208
(513) 321-6742

---

Candlesticks, pr
    14-1/2" h, 7" d, brass, flat bobeches, flaring stems, wide circular base, orig inserts, attributed to Jessie Preston ............... 650.00
    14-3/4" h, 5-3/4" d, copper, enameled blue and red flowers, green stems, stamped "ART CRAFTS SHOP/8001," minor nicking to enamel .......................................................................... 750.00
    15" h, hammered silver, tulip shape, stamped "Sterling, Hand Wrought at the Kao Shops, G152H," 42 troy oz ............ 3,600.00
Carpet, 35-1/2" w, 12' 13-1/2" l, silk, William Morris, Wilton style, c1890, acanthus leaves, stylized blossoms, gold, teal blue, and salmon pink ........................................................................... 6,000.00
Chair, arm
    27" w, 22-1/2" d, 37" h, three vertical back slats, drop-in spring seat recovered in rust leather, orig dark finish, branded Limbert mark, minor wear to arms ................................................ 550.00
    35-1/2" w, 22-1/4" d, 36-3/4" h, carved floral motif on crest rail, posts and leg fronts, narrow vertical slats on back and sides, flaring lobed armrests, black vinyl-covered drop-in seat pad, orig dark finish, unmarked ............................................. 2,000.00
China Cabinet, 45-1/2" w, 17-1/4" d, 61-3/4" h, Rome Furniture Co, GA, two doors, orig glass in doors and in sides, three shelves, paneled back, paper label ........................................................... 1,200.00
Cigarette Box, cov, 3-1/2" sq, 2" h, hammered pewter, enameled top with polychrome seascape with sailboat, cedar lined, sgd "Made in England/Tudric/Pewter/01021/Made by Liberty and Co." ......... 775.00
Clock, 4" x 2-3/4" x 1-3/4", sterling silver, mother-of-pearl inlay, turquoise cabochons, enameled face, Archibold Knox, sgd "L & Co./Anchor/Lion/G/5217" ..................................................... 7,750.00
Coat Rack, 24" d, 67" h, brass, four-sided post, flaring base, four double hooks, old patina ............................................................. 200.00
Desk Set, sterling on bronze, overlaid with pine bough motif, dark patina, pen tray, perpetual calendar/letter holder, blotter roller, inkwell, orig dark patina, stamp mark "Heintz", foil label .............. 275.00
Dining Chair, Limbert, one arm and four side chairs, narrow crest rail, three vertical slats, branded mark, reupholstered seat cushions, refinished, price for set of five ............................................... 2,100.00
Dining Table, Limbert, 48" d, 29-1/2" h, flaring cut-out base, two leaves, refinished top, orig finish on base, branded mark ..... 2,600.00
Game Table, 44" d, 30-1/2" h, circular, sq posts, broad apron with four drawers, orig dark finish, unsigned, attributed to McHugh .... 3,250.00

**Lamp, table, Limbert, Windmill, copper and brass, octagonal shade with caramel and green opalescent glass behind repeating diecut scene of windmills and children, octagonal lighthouse-shaped base with reticulated window panels lined with green slag glass, orig patina, 25" h, 27" d, $8,500. Photo courtesy of David Rago Auctions.**

**Wall Cabinet, oak, turned corner finials, scalloped base, single door inset with Grueby blue, ivory, and tan tile dec in cuenca with masted ship, 28" h, 14-1/4" w, 11" d, $2,990. Photo courtesy of David Rago Auctions.**

Garden Stool, 14-3/4" sq, 15-1/2" h, terra cotta, designed by Archibald Knox, cube form, Celtic knot motif, loose tufted seat cushion, imp "Liberty & Co.," couple of firing breaks and chips, price for pr .........4,500.00
Humidor
    6-3/4" h, 6" sq, copper, pagoda shape, acid etched panels of floating swans, stamped "CC" for Carence Crafters ........ 750.00
    8-1/4" h, 5-1/2" d, hammered copper, riveted to circular oak base, arrowhead leaves fastened with sterling bands, orig patina, Shreve, one missing base rivet, dents to rim and lid..... 1,300.00
    9-1/2" h, 5-1/2" d, silver on bronze, figure of golfer, overlaid with silver shields, slight wear to orig verdigris finish, Silvercrest stamp ............................ 800.00
Lamp, floor, 65" h, 14" d, wrought iron, hammered copper lantern fixture, cylindrical mica shade, unmarked ................................... 250.00
Lamp, table, Dirk Van Erp, hammered copper
    13" h, 8" d, conical shade with three mica panels, bulbous base, single fixture, open box mark, some wear to orig patina ........................ 9,500.00
    18" h, 18" d, conical shade with four mica panels, vented cap, trumpet shaped base, two fixtures, med orig patina, open box mark, restoration to small hole in orig mica................ 55,000.00
Library Table
    48" l, 27-3/4" w, 29" h, single blind lift-top drawer, arched sides and back, through-tenon lower shelf, branded Limbert mark, refinished................ 1,400.00
    48" l, 30" w, 29" h, turtle top, cutout sides, long corbels and lower shelf, unmarked, new finish to top, orig finish on base .3,250.00
Hall Bench, 47" l, 18" d, 38" h, Lifetime, tapering posts, paneled back and sides, dark orig finish ................ 4,500.00
Hall Chair, 31-1/2" w, 16" d, 77" h, lift seat, beveled glass mirror, new medium dark finish, one replaced hook .................. 900.00
Magazine Stand, 20" w, 15" d, 42" h, flaring cut-out sides, four shelves, new medium brown finish, branded Limbert mark................. 1,100.00
Mirror, 35" w, 77-1/4" h, cheval, walnut, beveled glass, stretcher, shoe feet, unmarked .................... 1,500.00
Plant Stand, 17" d, 32" h, Charles Rohlfs, c1901, hammered copper jardinière set with rivets on top rim, four carved legs, reticulated medallion shaped lower shelf, orig finish, carved mark "CR/1901".......................... 20,000.00
Print, woodblock, by Arthur Wesley Dow, archival mat
    3" d, circular, four quadrants depicting stylized landscapes, orange ink on beige, used as cover image for Dark and Light, Dow Assoc publication, c1903-05 ................... 300.00
    4-3/4" w, 2-3/4" h, woodblock, Ipswich Bridge, c1895-1905 ................ 1,100.00

Rocker
    22-1/4" w, 30" d, 34" h, rounded posts, two narrow back slats flanking broad one carved with stylized teasel, replaced rush seat, orig finish, unmarked, some stains to rush............. 750.00
    29-1/2" w, 35" d, 34" h, cube, flaring back posts, five vertical back slats, loose seat and back cushions, orig medium finish, reupholstered in burgundy leather........................................ 1,100.00
Screen, three 19-3/4" w x 68-1/4" panels, oak, pyrography etched poppy frieze, painted red and green, skinned oak dark finish, unmarked ................................................................. 1,200.00
Settle, 72" l, 32" d, 32-1/2" h, Lifetime, broad paneled back, arms mortised through legs with sq tenons, slatted sides, new leather cov seat, two loose cushions, skinned finish, paper label .......... 3,250.00
Settee, Limbert
    46-1/4" l, 24" d, 37-1/2" h, drop-arm, eight vertical back slats under straight rail, curved arms, drop-in spring seat, recovered in rust leather, orig finish, branded Limbert mark, minor wear to arm ........................................ 2,400.00
    49-1/4" l, 25" d, 38-3/4" h, twin-back, vertical slats, cutout panels, cutout front posts, new leather cov drop-in seat, unmarked, cleaned orig finish ......................................... 5,000.00
Sideboard
    60" l, 21" d, 46" h, Limbert, plate rail, small drawer, drop-front cabinet, two doors over linen drawer, arched apron, orig condition and finish, branded mark, two ring stains on top.......... 2,600.00
    72" l, 25" w, 57-1/2" h, unmarked, arched and mirrored backsplash over four drawers, two doors, linen drawer, dark overcoat to orig finish, casters ...................................... 3,500.00
Smoking Set, hammered copper, 12" d tray, match holder, cigarette holder, humidor with scrolled brass feet, stamped "Benedict Studios" marks, some cleaning to reddish patina, price for set.............. 550.00
Vase
    8" h, 3-1/2" d, sterling on bronze, corset shape, flowering branch, dark orig patina, stamp mark "Heintz" ............................ 450.00
    10" h, 3" d, sterling on bronze, cylindrical, overlaid with bird on branch, pewter finish, stamp mark "Heintz,"" small base dent ................................................................. 300.00
Vice Cabinet, 20" w, 12-1/2" d, 32" h, backsplash, single drawer, carved door with green slag glass panel, new medium brown finish, replaced drawer bottom and glass ........................... 800.00
Wardrobe, 53" w, 20" d, 80" h, mahogany, carved poppy motif panels, single mirrored door, lower drawer, orig finish, English......... 2,600.00

# AUSTRIAN WARE

**History:** More than 100 potteries were located in the Austro-Hungarian Empire in the late 19th and early 20th centuries. Although Carlsbad was the center of the industry, the factories spread as far as the modern-day Czech Republic. Many of the factories were either owned or supported by Americans; hence, their wares were produced mainly for export to the United States.

**Marks:** Many wares do not have a factory mark but only the word "Austrian" in response to the 1891 law specifying that the country of origin had to be marked on imported products.

**Additional Listings:** Amphora; Carlsbad; Royal Dux; Royal Vienna.

Bowl, 10-1/2" d, glazed pottery, gnarled branch section, grape bunch at one end, incised mark, c1900 ............................................. 325.00
Celery Tray, 12" l, scalloped border, pink roses, green leaves, gold trim 75.00
Demitasse Cup and Saucer, scenic panels, price for pr .............. 80.00
Ewer
    5-5/8" h, 2-7/8" d, dark green, maroon, tan, and cream, gold trim, Alhambra pattern............................................................. 90.00

**Dinner Service, Augarten pattern, pink roses, green accents, price for 40 pc set, $150. Photo courtesy of Joy Luke Fine Art Brokers and Auctioneers.**

11-3/4" h, 6" d, rococo gold scroll, hp pink and yellow wild roses, gold outlines, 4 ftd .............................................. 125.00

Figure
   3-3/4" h, bronze, huntsman, cold painted, c1920 ............... 320.00
   4" h, bronze, monkey holding shell, cold painted, ............... 230.00
   4" l, bronze, recumbent puppy, cold painted in brown tones, c1920 ....................................................................... 290.00
   4-1/4" h, bronze, courting couple, cold painted ................... 750.00
   5" h, cold painted bronze, bird and chicks, painted in natural colors, Bergman stamp ................................................ 325.00
   6" h, bronze, Harem Girl with leopard, Oriental carpet form base, A. Chotka, c1920 .............................................. 815.00
   8" l, cold painted bronze, black bird, white chest, wing bands, late 19th C, dent to beak ................................................. 375.00
   8" h, porcelain, five children in various poses, mounted on circular base, printed beehive mark, late 19th C, restoration ....... 175.00
   14" h, bronze, farmer, dark brown and green patina, sgd "Andor Ruff" ....................................................................... 460.00

Lamp, 15-1/2" h, 9" d metal shade dec with three red glass inserts, three foliate stem arms, reticulated bronzed Secessionist-inspired base ................................................................................. 750.00

Pin Tray, 5" l, portrait of Josephine, blue border ....................... 30.00

Pitcher, light green ground shaded to brown, purple grapes with white and green leaves, brown handle, gold rim, mkd "Vienna, Austria" ............................................................................ 200.00

Portrait Vase, 34-1/2" h, cov, oval cartouche, polychrome enameled female portrait, burgundy luster ground, raised gilt scrolled foliate design, sgd " Rosley," beehive mark, early 20th C, rim repair, lines to handles .............................................................................. 2,875.00

Rose Water Sprinkler, 12-1/2" h, floriform rim pulled to a point on elongated and curved neck, bulbous body of green glaze, irid blue textured surface, applied disk foot, inclusions, early 20th C ......... 290.00

Salt, 3" h, figural, donkey, 2 dish shaped baskets on back, c1915 ............................................................................... 265.00

Stamp Box, cov, 4-1/4" x 3-1/8", ftd, two compartments, hp, roses, gold trim ................................................................................... 50.00

Tankard, 14" h, hp Dutch scene, mkd "Made in Austria, 159 Haag" ..................................................................... 400.00

Tray, 7" h, 2 bronze dancers, round green and white marble base, imp mark, c1925, abrasions ....................................................... 175.00

Urn on Stand, 25" h, painted and parcel gilt, dancing classical maidens and putti on one side, maidens lounging by statuary on other side, gold stippled ground, base with geometric and scroll reserves, heron roundels, two rect handles, domed lid with pineapple finial, Vienna, late 19th C ............................................................. 2,415.00

Vase
   4-1/4" h, organic pod-shaped form pottery body, three angled branch supports, gold, green, blue, and purple irid glaze, stamped "Hellosine Ware (crown), Austria" in black, early 20th C, rim chip ....................................................................... 320.00

   4-1/4" h, raised rim, pinched oviform, semi-opaque pink glass, pulled purple swirls and silver spots, irid luster, spurious acid stamp in polished pontil, rim possibly ground, attributed to Loetz, c1900 .................................................................. 1,840.00
   10" h, divided rim forms 2 spouts, large dolphin handles, gold scales, raised gold florals, cream ground ........................ 125.00
   10-1/2" h, 4-1/2" w, pedestal, reticulated handles, peacock on balcony scene, aqua, roses, green, brown, mkd "Carlsbad, Austria"" ....................................................................... 265.00

# AUTOGRAPHS

**History:** Autographs appear on a wide variety of formats—letters, documents, photographs, books, cards, etc. Most collectors focus on a particular person, country, or category, e.g., signers of the Declaration of Independence.

**References:** Mark Allen Baker, *All-Sport Autographs*, Krause Publications, 1995; ——, *Advanced Autograph Collecting*, Krause Publications, 2000; ——, *Collector's Guide to Celebrity Autographs*, 2nd ed., Krause Publications, 2000; *Standard Guide to Collecting Autographs*, Krause Publications, 1999; Kevin Keating and Michael Kolleth, *The Negro Leagues Autograph Guide*, Tuff Stuff Books, 1999; Kevin Martin, *Signatures of the Stars*, Antique Trader Books, 1998; Tom Mortenson, *Standard Catalog of Sports Autographs*, Krause Publications, 2000; Kenneth W. Rendell, *Forging History: The Detection of Fake Letters & Documents*, University of Oklahoma Press, 1994; ——, *History Comes to Life*, University of Oklahoma Press, 1996; George Sanders, Helen Sanders and Ralph Roberts, *Sanders Price Guide to Sports Autographs*, 2nd ed., Alexander Books, 1997; ——, *Sanders Price Guide to Autographs*, 5th ed., Alexander Books, 2000.

**Periodicals:** *Autograph Collector*, 510-A S Corona Mall, Corona, CA 91720-1420, http://www.autographcollector.com/acm.htm; *Autograph Review*, 305 Carlton Rd, Syracuse, NY 13207; *Autograph Times*, 1125 W. Baseline Rd., #2-153-M, Mesa, AZ 85210-9501, http://celebrityconnection.com/at.htm; *Autographs & Memorabilia*, P.O. Box 224, Coffeyville, KS 67337; *The Collector*, P.O. Box 255, Hunter, NY 12442; *Celebrity Access*, 20 Sunnyside Ave., Suite A241, Mill Valley, CA 94941-1928; *V.I.P. Autogramm-Magazine*, 3000 W. Olympic Blvd., Blvd. 3, Suite 2415, Santa Monica, CA 90404, http://www.vip-entertainment.com.

**Collectors' Clubs:** International Autograph Collectors Club & Dealers Alliance, 4575 Sheriden St., Suite 111, Hollywood, FL 33021-3575, http://www.iacc-da.com; Manuscript Society, 350 N Niagara Street, Burbank, CA 95105-3648, http://www.manuscript.org; Universal Autograph Collectors Club, P.O. Box 6181, Washington, DC 20044; Washington Historical Autograph & Certificate Organization, P.O. Box 2428, Springfield, VA 22152-2428, http://www.whaco.com.

**Additional Listings:** See *Warman's Americana & Collectibles* for more examples.

**Notes:** The condition and content of letters and documents bear significantly on value. Collectors should know their source, since forgeries abound and copy machines compound the problem. Further, some signatures of recent presidents and movie stars were done by machine rather than by the persons themselves. A good dealer or advanced collector can help spot the differences.

**Abbreviations:** The following are used to describe autograph materials and their sizes.

## Materials:

| | |
|---|---|
| ADS | Autograph Document Signed |
| ALS | Autograph Letter Signed |
| AQS | Autograph Quotation Signed |
| CS | Card Signed |
| DS | Document Signed |
| FDC | First Day Cover |
| LS | Letter Signed |
| PS | Photograph Signed |
| TLS | Typed Letter Signed |

## Sizes (approximate):

| | |
|---|---|
| Folio | 12 x 16 inches |
| 4to | 8 x 10 inches |
| 8vo | 7 x 7 inches |
| 12mo | 3 x 5 inches |

Colonial America

Adams, Samuel, ALS, as Congressman to Henry Bromfield, telling military news, sgd "Saml. Adams," Philadelphia, Sept. 2, 1777, 1 pg, folio, addressed and docketed on verso ............... 9,200.00

Austin, Stephen Fl, DS, Texian Loan Certificate, issued to Robert Triplett in the amount of $32, first installment of $320 loan to the Government of Texas, 8% interest, partially printed, New Orleans, Jan. 11, 1836, cross-cut cancellation, triangular piece missing at top of cancellation, also sgd by other Commissioners, B. T. Archer and W. H. Wharton.................................................................. 1,100.00

Burr, Aaron, ALS, to his Aunt Mary Clarke, sending requested funds and expressing mortification that she would be hesitant to ask for anything in his power, sgd "A. Burr," 1 pg, 8vo, integral address leaf .............................................................................. 1,150.00

Dalton, Trestram, ALS, to Elbridge Gerry, Chairman of the Committee of Supply, about supplying Indians in Maine and keeping their friendship, pleading for additional supplies, especially gunpowder, Newburyport, Oct 21, 1775, 4 pgs, 4to, on 2 sheets, minor repairs ................................................................................ 1,265.00

Dayton, Jonathan, ALS, to Jacob Burnet, concerning land holdings in Cincinnati, 1 pg, folded, 8vo sheet, integral blank and holograph address, remnants of seal ............................................. 920.00

Hamilton, Alexander, ALS, as Secretary of Treasury, to clerk Daniel Brent, regarding his disappointment over Brent's decision to leave the Treasury, wishing him well, Dec 26, 1793, Philadelphia, 1 pg, folded 4to sheet, integral address leaf, reattached, bit toned, visible folds................................................................................. 2,760.00

Hancock, John, ALS, to Mr. Williams, thanking him for letter, sending

gift of pound of green tea, Oct 22, 1772, Boston, 1 pg, single 4to sheet, inlaid and entirely mounted to cardboard, hole from opening repaired, appears to have been washed and pressed ......... 5,520.00

Harrison, Benjamin, DS, as Governor of VA, land grant for Joseph Con, July 4, 1783, Richmond, 1 pg, folio, separations at folds repaired, framed .................................................................. 375.00

Morris, Robert, partially printed DS, promissory note to William Bell for 100 pounds, signed by Bell on verso, 4-1/2" x 9-1/2", Feb. 16, 1787, Philadelphia..................................................................... 460.00

Washington, George, LS, to Captain Brewster, discussing prisoners and his inability to release more troops, sgd "Go. Washington," Headquarters, New Windsor, Feb. 23, 1781, 1 pg, folio, silked, uniformly browned, chips in right edge ............................................... 10,350.00

Foreign

Bonaparte, Napoleon, DS, 1 pg, 17" x 23-1/2", sgd as Emperor of France, 29 Oct. 1809, concerning Senator Giassano being awarded title of Count of the Empire of France, sgd as "Napol," 4-1/2" d wax seal showing Napoleon on his throne, Giassano's coat of arms hand painted in upper left of document, framed........................................................................... 2,530.00

Charles I, King of England, 1625-1649, DS, license for foreigners to fish in English waters, countersigned by Sir Balthazar Gerbier, 1 pg folio, mid-1630s............................................................ 2,250.00

Louis XVI, King of France, 1774-1792, DS, tax of officers of justice for the district of Auch, district of Armagnac, offices of Senechal and President, account of sums payable, 6 pgs folio, Jan 31, 1789, some chipping and soil to edges, text and signatures unaffected ......................................................... 1,250.00

Rosenberg, Alfred, Nazi, sgd and inscribed book, copy of his Schriften und Reden, Munich, 1943, 624 pgs, 8vo, bound in gold-stamped blue cloth, German inscription on fly-leaf regarding thanks for work in office to Party member G. Ebert, some wear on covers............................................................... 875.00

General

Barton, Clara, ALS, personal letter to Miss Kensel, regarding busy schedule of travel and activities, ..."Don't work too hard—There is a Hereafter...," 1 pg, small 8vo, Glen Echo, MD, May 7, 1908 ................................................................................. 450.00

Chagall, Marc, PS, mount below image of artist and his wife viewing exhibit in Israel, 7" x 9", David Harris photographer's stamp on verso .......................................................................... 175.00

Dalton, Emmett, American outlaw, sgd and inscribed 8vo pg from his personal copy of his book, When the Daltons Rode, in blank area above heading for Chapter V ............................... 1,100.00

Einstein, Albert, TLS, sgd "A. Einstein" to Menorah Assoc, in German, declining invitation, Nov 22, 1933, Princeton, 1 pg, single 4to sheet, Institute for the Advanced Study stationery, folds, mounted to page from oblong 8vo autograph album, identification in ink on verso ................................................... 1,610.00

Fulton, Robert, LS, recommendation for Mr. Smith, for service in North River Steamboat, Oct 24, 1809, New York, half page, 4to sheet, silked, writing on verso visible on recto affecting paraph of signature, hinged to mat........................................... 1,725.00

Hay, John Milton, TLS, as Secretary of State, to Robert S. Chilton, accepting his resignation as Commercial Agent of US at Goderich, Ontario, praising him for years of service, Sept 21, 1901, Washington, 1 pg, folded, small folio sheet, integral blank, mourning stationery........................................................ 230.00

Lindbergh, Charles A., book We, 8vo, 1/2 vellum, worn, backstrip defection, one of 1,000 numbered copies signed by Lindbergh, New York, 1927 ................................................................. 43500

Schwab, Charles, TLS, to Maurence T. Fleisher of Philadelphia regarding permission to order photograph of a painting lent by Schwab to the Metropolitan Museum of Art, 1 pg 4to, personal letterhead, NY, Feb 25, 1937 ........................................... 450.00

Rockefeller, John D., TLS, to Charles H. Brown, Jr., of Yonkers, NY, with orig envelope, thanking him for gift of a putter, 1 pg, 8vo, letterhead of Pocantico Hills, NY, Jan 12, 1912 .... 1,400.00

# 44    AUTOGRAPHS

## Literature

Cummings, E. E., ANS, thanking for good wishes, Oct 4, 1944, New York, 3-1/4" x 5-1/2", postcard, holograph address on verso ......................................................................... 110.00

Hemingway, Ernest, ALS, sgd "Ernie" at age 17, to father about canoe trip, 3-1/4" x 5-1/2" postcard, written in pencil, April 5, 1917, Channahon ................................................ 2,990.00

Holmes, Oliver Wendell, AQS, "And if I should live to be/The last leaf upon the tree/In the Spring,/Let them smile as I do now/At the old forsaken bough/Where I cling," July 3, 1885, Beverly Farms, 1 pg, 3" x 4-1/2" sheet, corner mounted to larger sheet ........................................................................ 230.00

Lawrence, T. E., ALS, sgd "T. E. Shaw" to Benhem, regarding sending him a copy of Seven Pillars of Wisdom, Oct 12, 1932, Plymouth, half page, single small 4to, usual folds ........ 5,290.00

Mitchell, Margaret, TLS, "Margaret Mitchell Marsh" to Doctor Mayos, thanking him for photographs of Rock Island Arsenal Confederate cemetery and the list of Georgians buried there, Dec 18, 1937, Atlanta, 1-1/4 pgs, folded small 8vo sheet, integral blank .......................................................... 1,380.00

Shaw, George Bernard, English playwright, ALS, to Gilbert Murray, 2 pgs, oblong 8vo, Old House, Harmer Green, Welwyn, June 21, 1905 .................................................... 875.00

Stowe, Harriet Beecher, AQS, Biblical quote, 1 pg, 8vo, Andover Jan 24, 1864 ......................................................... 475.00

Twain, Mark, (Samuel L. Clemens,) ALS, 2 separate pgs, 4to, Hartford, April 11, 1883 ................................... 2,750.00

Whitman, Walt, American poet, book sgd, on title page of conclusion of printed poem, and on flyleaf Dr. Benjamin from the author, May 26, 1883, author's edition of Leaves of Grass, accompanied by orig photo of Dr. Benjamin, taken in 1925, cloth folding case .................................................... 4,000.00

Whittier, John Greenleaf, American poet, AQS, last stanza from poem "Child Songs," 1 pg, 8vo, Amesbury, June 5, 1874 385.00

## Military

Grant, U. S., ALS, to Captain Edward Brown turning down invitation for Declaration Day parade, New York City, 12 April, 1882, 1 pg, small 8vo, matted with engraving of Grant with his horse and sgd card from Chicago, 1879 ...................... 1,150.00

Jackson, Andrew, DS, 1 pg, 19-1/4" x 15", military appointment of Alfred Morton as 2nd Lieutenant in 9th US Infantry, sgd as Pres of US ......................................................... 200.00

MacArthur, Douglas, TLS, to Dorothy Kukla, thanking her for birthday wishes, Feb 6, 1956, 1 pg, single 4to sheet, folds....................................................................... 220.00

Santa Anna, Antonio Lopez De, Mexican General, DS, military commission for Don Julio Castaneda, sgd as dictator, in Spanish, partially printed, 1 pg folio, Palace of the National Government, June 5, 1854 ........................................ 1,400.00

Toombs, Robert A, Confederate general, Secretary of State, ALS, to Navy Secretary John P. Kennedy, asking if there is a vacancy as a surgeon's make for Dr. Whitlock of Washington, 1 pg, 4to, Washington, O t 3, 1852..................................... 285.00

## Music

Berlin, Irving, TLS, to writer Mark Sullivan, regarding prospects of making movie based on Our Times, 1 pg, single 4to sheet, personal stationery, Feb 18, 1936, New York ................ 260.00

Bernstein, Leonard, PS, "For Ray Fisher," bust post, casually holding cigarette, 11" x 14"................................. 865.00

Blake, Eubie, sheet music "I'm Just Wild About Harry," inscribed and sgd on cover, small folio, 6 pgs, including wrappers . 315.00

Glazunov, Alexandre, musical quotation signed, 4 bars, headed "Moderato," sgd and dated "le 30 Nov 1909 St. Petersbourg," 3" x 4-1/2" card, mounted, framed with portrait, 10" x 8" overall........................................................... 635.00

Horowitz, Vladimir, PS, sgd and dated "To Ray Fisher," image taken during performance, 11" x 14", inscription and dated on lower black border, also sgd by photographer Fisher, Nov 1988.................................................................. 375.00

Kern, Jerome, DS, contract with publisher T. B. Harms Co., for song Day Dreaming, partially printed, 4 pgs, 4 to, New York Sept 10, 1941, sgd on 4th pg................................... 375.00

Liszt, Franz, ALS, to Steinway and Company, in Germany, praising performance of Steinway piano at Festspiel auf Wartburg, Sept 1873, Weimar, 1-1/2 pgs, single 8vo sheet, folds, minor soiling, staple holes................................................ 1,035.00

Ravel, Maurice, French composer, musical quotation sgd, inscribed to Mlle. Thérèse Moss, 4 bars of music, mkd "Simplicidato," 1 pg, 4to, Nov 21, 1927................................. 3,500.00

Sousa, John Philip, American composer and bandmaster, ALS, to "Dear Little Lady," Mrs. Ralph Willis, 1 pg 8vo, Feb 19, 1925, with orig envelope .................................................. 250.00

Smith, Samuel Francis, AQS, sgd "S. F. Smith," 4 stanzas of hymn America, 2 pgs, 2 single 8vo sheets, ruled paper, with full length portrait silver print, March 29, 1887, Boston....... 1,265.00

## Presidents

Adams, John Quincy, ALS, to Mary Talbot, sending her quote from Psalm 104, single 8vo, emb stationery, Sept 10, 1841, Washington ......................................................... 1,150.00

Buchanan, James, ALS, to David Mann, Esq., asking to be paid "liberal compensation for work in case of Commonwealth vs Aurand," Lancaster, Aug 26, 1829, 1 pg, oblong 8vo....... 690.00

Bush, George, LS, as VP, to Jim Hier, providing letter for collection, 1 pg, 8vo, vice-presidential stationery, framed with photo sgd by George and Barbara Bush................................. 330.00

Carter, James, PS, sgd and inscribed, color, 8" x 10", standing in library, American flag to right............................... 250.00

Cleveland, Grover, TLS, to H. H. Hart, thanking him for badges, August 13, 1892, Gray Gables, 1 pg, single 4to, folds..... 175.00

Fillmore, Millard, on partial manuscript document, Senate Resolution, countersigned by Edward Everett as Secretary of State, 7" x 10-3/4", Washington, 1853, some staining and soiling, vertical folds................................................................ 230.00

Harding, Warren G., portrait engraving, inscribed and sgd, to Ted Booth, May, 1922, Washington, 11-3/4" x 8-1/2", trimmed, repaired tears at edges ..................................... 260.00

Jefferson, Thomas, ALS, to William Brent, offering him a job as his private secretary, Jan 20, 1804, Washington, half page, folded 4to, integral blank, address leaf inlaid, some staining, minor separations........................................... 8,625.00

Kennedy, John F., book, Profiles in Courage, inscribed and signed to Barbara Halpern, on front free endpaper, 8vo, publisher's cloth, worn at edges, dust jacking missing, New York, 1948 ................................................................ 2,990.00

Lincoln, Abraham, note signed "A. Lincoln" to Secretary of State Seward appointing Allen Francis, Nov 16, 1861, Washington, 2" x 3-1/8" notecard, browned........................................ 3,680.00

McKinley, William, PS, bust portrait, 8-1/4" x 6", on 11" x 8-1/2" mount ................................................................ 575.00

Polk, James, partially printed vellum document sgd, commission appointing Theodore Talbot as Second Lieutenant in the First Regiment of Artillery, countersigned by W. L. Marcy as Secretary of War, Feb 12, 1848, Washing, 1 pg, folio, folds...... 920.00

Roosevelt, Franklin D., TLS, to Dorothy McAllister, thanking her for presentation, Feb 5, 1941, Washington, 1 pg, folded 8vo sheet, integral blank, White House stationery, orig envelope............................................................. 520.00

Washington, George, ALS, to Daniel Carroll, informing him of travel plans to Philadelphia, April 24, 1795, Mount Vernon, half page, 4to folded sheet with holograph address leaf, mounted to larger sheet of paper................................... 10,925.00

## Show Business

Allen, Woody, signed book, Side Effects, 8vo, cloth, dust jacket, first edition, New York, c1980......................... 230.00

Bogart, Humphrey, DS, adv release for Arnold, Schwinn & Co. giving them the right to use his name in connection with adv for Schwinn bicycles, Jan 31, 1947, Burbank, 1 pg, single 4to sheet, staple holes at top ..................................... 815.00

Gone with the Wind, Margaret Mitchell book signed by 14 members of cast and crew, Victor Fleming, Harry Davenport, Eric A. Stacey, Hattie McDaniel, Clark Gable, Alicia Rhett, Olivia de Havilland, Ward Bond, Leslie Howard, Sidney Howard, Vivien Leigh, Arthur Arling, David O. Selznick, and Leona Roberts, all signatures excepts Roberts on front free endpaper, Roberts signature on front pastedown as it was her copy, 8vo, publisher's cloth, dust jacket, minor repairs, minor toning, later edition, New York 1937 .................................................................... 10,925.00

Hepburn, Katharine, two ALS, each to Proctor Jones, one thanking him for lovely visit, other thanking him for sending her a present, each 1 page, single 8vo sheet, personal stationery, April 20, 1981 and April 22, 1981 ..................................... 320.00

Powell, Eleanor, PS, 8 x 10", black and white, inscribed "Harriet, a sweet girl I'm happy I know-you couldn't be anything else with the wonderful mother you have, Good Luck," sgd in ink, 1939 ................................................................................. 41.00

Sinatra, Frank, TLS, agreement granting Arnold, Schwinn & Co. right to use his image for adv and publicity of Schwinn bicycles, September 1945, half page, single 4to sheet, folds ......... 350.00

Sports

Carnera, Primo, PS, inscribed "To Lillian and Eddie from Primo Carnera," 10" x 8", full length portrait of boxer in fighting stance.................................................................... 260.00

Dimaggio, Joe, album, complied and edited by Richard Whittingham, New York, illus with repro photographs, programs, newspaper and magazine clippings, 2 volumes in publisher's slip case, 4to, Yankee logo, one of 700 numbered sets, sgd by Dimaggio, 1989 ................................................. 635.00

Statesmen

Adams, Charles Francis, ALS, to Senator Wm. S. Seward, complimenting him on recent Senate speech, 2 pgs, single small 8vo sheet, April 5, 1858, Boston, folds............................. 145.00

Benton, Thomas Hart, ALS, as Senator to Mrs. Talbot, forwarding letter from his daughter, Senate Chamber, Dec 14, 1843, 1 pgs, 4to, integral address leaf, vertical fold through signature. 200.00

Bryan, William Jennings, ALS, to Mark Sullivan, inviting him to FL to discuss League question, Jan 28, (no year), Miami, 2 pgs, single 4to sheet, personal stationery, paper clip stain...... 145.00

Carneige, Andrew, ALS, to "Editor Tribune," recounting instance when Mr. Gladstone refused a peerage, Dec 16, 1909, Washington, 2 pgs, single 4to sheet ........................................ 415.00

Clay, Henry, ALS, as Secretary of State, to D. Brant, thanking him for public service, March 3, 1829, Washington, 1 pg, folded 4to sheet, integral address leaf, minor separations at folds... 460.00

Crockett, David, ALS, to publishers E. L. Cary and A. Hart, informing them of his travel plans back to Washington, telling them of the status of Jacksonianism in Tennessee, October 9, 1834, Weakley County, TN, 1 pg, single folio sheet, separations at folds, expertly repaired vertical fold.......................... 21,850.00

# AUTOMOBILES

**History:** Automobiles are generally classified into two categories, vehicles manufactured before World War II, and those manufactured after the conflict. The Antique Automobile Club of America, the world's oldest and largest automobile historical society considers motor vehicles manufactured before 1930 officially "antique." The Contemporary Historical Vehicle Society, however, accepts cars and trucks that are twenty-five years old. There are scores of clubs dedicated to specific marques, like the Willys/Kaiser/AMC Jeep Club, and the Edsel Owners Club. Some states, such as Pennsylvania, have devised a dual registration system for older cars—antique and classic. Models from the 1960s and 1970s, especially convertibles and limited production vehicles (under 10,000 produced), fall into their "classic" designation if they are not used as daily transportation.

Many states have also allowed collectible vehicles to sport "year of issue" license plates, thus allowing the owner of a 1964 1/2 Mustang to legally use a 1964 license plate from his or her home state. Many older cars, especially original and unrestored models, are worth well more than $20,000. Restoration costs have skyrocketed, making it advisable to purchase a complete, running and original vehicle or one that has been completely restored rather than a car or truck needing thousands of dollars invested for mechanical, body and paint work. Prices of high-powered 1964 to 1972 "muscle cars" will continue to escalate, while the value of pre-war cars will remain steady for all but unique custom-built roadsters and limousines. The prices of old pickup trucks will remain steady as vintage trucks remain popular with consumers for their style and usefulness. Look for vintage sports cars, especially European marques like the Porsche and Ferrari, and even Datsun's "Z" cars to become more popular with collectors.

Auctions, more than any other source, determine the value of antique and classic automobiles. Values have remained steady for some years, but the combination of increased demand and fewer available vehicles is sure to drive prices up.

**References:** Robert C. Ackerson, *Standard Catalog of 4x4s, 1945-2000*, Krause Publications, 2000; Dennis A. Adler, *Corvettes*, Krause Publications, 1996; John Chevedden & Ron Kowalke, *Standard Catalog of Oldsmobile, 1897-1997*, Krause Publications, 1997; James M. Flammang, *Standard Catalog of American Cars, 1976-1999*, 3rd ed., Krause Publications, 1999; ——, *Standard Catalog of Imported Cars, 1946-1990*, 2nd ed., Krause Publications, 2000; ——, *Volkswagen Beetles, Buses and Beyond*, Krause Publications, 1996; Patrick R. Foster, *American Motors, The Last Independent*, Krause Publications, 1993; *The Metropolitan Story*, Krause Publications, 1996; Gordon Gardner and Alistair Morris, *Automobilia, 20th Century International Reference with Price Guide*, 3rd ed., Antique Collectors' Club, 1999; Robert Genat, *The American Car Dealership*, MBI Publishing, 1999; John Gunnell, *American Work Trucks*, Krause Publications, 1994; ——, *Marques of America*, Krause Publications, 1994; —— (ed.), *100 Years of American Cars*, Krause Publications, 1993; ——, *Standard Catalog of American Light Duty Trucks, 1896-1986*, 2nd ed., Krause Publications, 1993; ——, *Standard Catalog of Chevrolet Trucks, Pickups & Other Light Duty Trucks, 1918-1995*, Krause Publications, 1995; Beverly Kimes and Henry Austin Clark Jr., *Standard Catalog of American Cars, 1805-1942*, 3rd ed., Krause Publications, 1996; Ron Kowalke, *Old Car Wrecks*, Krause Publications, 1997; ——, *Standard Guide to American Cars, 1946-1975*, 3rd ed., Krause Publications, 1997; ——, *Standard Guide to Amercian Muscle Cars, 1949-1995*,

2nd ed., Krause Publications, 1996; ——, *2001 Standard Guide to Cars & Prices, Prices for Collector Vehicles, 1901-1993*, 13th ed., Krause Publications, 2000; James T. Lemzke, *Standard Catalog of American Light-Duty Trucks, 1896-2000*, 3rd ed., Krause Publications, 2000; ——, *Standard Catalog of Cadillac, 1903-2000*, 2nd ed., Krause Publications, 2000; Jim Lenzke and Ken Buttolph, *Standard Guide to Cars & Prices*, 12th ed., Krause Publications, 1999; Albert Mroz, *The Illustrated Encyclopedia of American Trucks & Commercial Vehicles*, Krause Publications, 1996; Robert Murfin (ed.), *Miller's Collectors Cars Price Guide*, Reed International Books (distributed by Antique Collectors' Club), 1996; Gerald Perschbacher, *Wheels in Motion*, Krause Publications, 1996; Edwin J. Sanow, *Chevrolet Police Cars*, Krause Publications, 1997; Ed Lindley Peterson, *First to the Flames*, Krause Publications, 1999; Donald F. Wood and Wayne Sorensen, *Big City Fire Trucks, 1951-1997*, Krause Publications, Volume I, 1996, Volume II, 1997; Peter Winnewisser, *The Legendary Model A Ford*, Krause Publications, 1999. Krause Publications' Standard Catalog series includes special marque volumes, including *Standard Catalog of Cadillac, 1903-1990*; *Standard Catalog of Chrysler, 1925-1990*; *Standard Catalog of Pontiac, 1926-1995*; *Standard Catalog of Ford, 1903-1990*; *Standard Catalog of Chevrolet, 1912-1990*; *Standard Catalog of American Motors, 1902-1987*; *Standard Catalog of Oldsmobile, 1897-1997*; *Standard Catalog of Buick, 1903-1990*.

**Periodicals:** *Automobile Quarterly*, 15040 Kutztown Rd, P.O. Box 348, Kutztown, PA 19530; *Cars & Parts*, P.O. Box 482, Sydney, OH 45365; *Classic Car Source*, http://www.classicar.com; *Hemmings Motor News*, P.O. Box 256, Bennington, VT 05201; *Old Cars Price Guide*, 700 E. State St., Iola, WI 54990; *Old Cars Weekly, News & Marketplace*, 700 E. State St., Iola, WI 54990.

**Collectors' Clubs:** AACA Library and Research Center, 501 Governor Road, P.O. Box 417, Hershey PA 17033; Antique Automobile Club of America, 501 West Governor Road, P.O. Box 417, Hershey, PA 17033; http://www.aaca.org; Contemporary Historical Vehicle Association, P.O. Box 98, Tecumseh, KS 66542; Horseless Carriage Club of America, 128 S. Cypress St., Orange CA 92866; http://www.horseless.com; Milestone Car Society, P.O. Box 24612, Indianapolis,IN 46224; Veteran Motor Car Club of America, P.O. Box 360788, Strongsville OH 44136.

**Websites:** Antique Auto Trader: http://www.traderonline.com; Classic Car Source: http://www.classicar.com; Krause Publications: http://www.krause.com.

**Advisors:** Jim and Nancy Schaut.

**Notes:** The prices indicated are for cars in running condition, with either a high proportion of original parts or somewhere between 60 and 80 percent restoration. Prices can vary by as much as 50 percent in either direction for lesser vehicles.

**AMC**
- 1960 Rambler Station Wagon .......................... 5,500.00
- 1968 AMX Fastback coupe .......................... 8,500.00

Amphicar, 1962 conv ........................... 19,500.00

**Auburn**
- 1929 Auburn boattail speedster ............... 58,000.00
- 1935, Model 6-653, 4d sedan, 6cyl ............ 23,000.00

Bricklin, 1975, Model SV-1, gullwing coupe ......... 12,500.00

**Buick**
- 1911 Model 38 Roadster, conv, 4cyl ........... 26,500.00
- 1941 Roadmaster, 4dr sedan, 8cyl ............. 17,500.00
- 1986 Regal, Grand National ..................... 10,500.00

**Cadillac**
- 1931 Model 370, Cabriolet, V-12 ............. 147,000.00
- 1957 Eldorado Barritz Conv, V8 ............... 28,000.00

Checker, 1963, Aerobus ......................... 6,500.00

**Chevrolet**
- 1932 Model AE, 2dr sedan, 6cyl ............... 12,000.00
- 1953 Bel Air Conv ............................. 25,000.00
- 1955 Cameo Pickup Truck ...................... 19,500.00
- 1964 Chevelle Super Sport, coupe ............. 15,000.00
- 1969 Camaro Convertible ...................... 18,000.00
- 1967 Corvette Stingray Coupe ................. 32,000.00

**Chrysler**
- 1932 Imperial Sedan, 6cyl .................... 18,000.00
- 1956 New Yorker, Hemi engine, 2dr hardtop .... 15,000.00
- 1970 300, 2dr. "Hurst" edition ............... 9,500.00

Cord, 1931 4dr. convertible sedan, celebrity owned ......... 225,000.00

Crosley, 1950 "Hot Shot" Roadster ............. 8,900.00

**Dodge**
- 1915, 2dr roadster ........................... 14,500.00
- 1932 2dr RS conv ............................. 25,000.00
- 1948 Power Wagon ............................. 9,500.00
- 1957 "Sweptline" Pickup, 101 made ............ 14,000.00
- 1970 Challenger T/A .......................... 25,000.00

Essex, 1929 Challenger Series, 4dr Town Sedan ......... 9,500.00

Edsel, 1958 Ranger 2dr HT ..................... 12,000.00

Ferrari Testarosa coupe, 1985 ................. 52,000.00

**Ford**
- 1924 Model T coupe ........................... 8,500.00
- 1931 Model A rds ............................. 18,500.00
- 1934 5W coupe ................................ 22,000.00
- 1956 F-100 pickup ............................ 7,500.00
- 1959 Thunderbird 2dr HT ...................... 19,500.00
- 1970 Mustang Boss 302 ........................ 30,000.00

Henry J, 1953, Allstate ....................... 8,500.00

**Hudson**
- 1937 Terraplane pickup, 1 of 5 known ......... 49,000.00
- 1951 Hudson Hornet ........................... 18,000.00

Hummer, 1985, government sale, served in Desert Storm .... 21,500.00

International Scout, 4x4, 1966 ................. 6,500.00

Jaguar, 1964 XKE, roadster .................... 52,000.00

Jeep, 1966 Wagoneer, 4dr, 4x4 ................. 8,500.00

Julian, 1922 Model 60 coupe, 6cyl ............. 9,500.00

**Kaiser**
- 1953 Manhattan, 4dr sedan .................... 12,000.00
- 1954 Kaiser Darrin 2dr, 1 of 435 ............. 50,000.00

Lambert, 1909, roadster, 6cyl ................. 12,500.00

Lamborghini, 1975, P200 ....................... 90,000.00

**La Salle**
- 1928 2dr business coupe ...................... 32,000.00

**Lincoln**
- 1935 Dietrich conv. Coupe, V-12 .............. 38,000.00
- 1957 Continental Mark II, 2dr HT ............. 32,000.00
- 1973 Lincoln Cont. Mark IV, 10,000 miles .... 6,000.00

Mercedes-Benz, 1964 300Se Coupe ............... 25,000.00

**Mercury**
- 1940 convertible, 8 cyl ...................... 25,000.00
- 1966 Comet Cyclone GT ........................ 12,000.00
- 1969 Cougar XR-7 HT .......................... 7,500.00

Nash
  Ambassador, 1954, 2dr HT ............................................. 4,500.00
  Metropolitan, 1956, conv .................................................. 8,500.00
  Oakland, 1930 sedan ......................................................... 7,500.00
Oldsmobile
  1901 Curved dash, 1cyl ................................................... 34,000.00
  1934 Business coupe ........................................................ 11,000.00
  1967 Toronado .................................................................... 9,500.00
  1970 Vista Cruiser Station Wagon ............................. 6,500.00
Packard
  1930 Model 745 Deluxe Eight, limo ............................ 72,000.00
  1946 Clipper, sedan .......................................................... 12,000.00
Plymouth
  1942 Model P14S, 2dr. sedan, 6cyl .............................. 6,500.00
  1959 Sport Fury convertible ......................................... 24,000.00
  1970 Barracuda, 1 of 1,554 .......................................... 11,000.00
Pontiac
  1934 2dr sedan ................................................................. 9,500.00
  1955 Star Chief custom Safari .................................... 19,500.00
  1966 2+2 convertible ...................................................... 13,500.00
  1970 GTO 2dr HT .............................................................. 15,000.00
Porsche, 1961, 356B, Rds ................................................ 35,000.00
Rolls Royce, 1951 Siilver Wraith .................................... 49,000.00
Studebaker
  1932 Rockne, 2 passenger coupe ............................... 12,500.00
  1963 Avanti coupe ........................................................... 17,000.00
  1962 Lark .......................................................................... 4,500.00
  1962 Gran Turismo Hawk .............................................. 12,750.00
Toyota, 1967 2000GT .......................................................... 75,000.00
Triumph, 1956 TR-3, rds ..................................................... 11,000.00
Volkswagen
  1949 sedan ...................................................................... 10,500.00
  1974 Super Beetle ............................................................ 6,500.00
Willys-Knight, 1928 Model 70, roadster ........................ 22,000.00
Willys, 1954, Eagle .............................................................. 8,500.00

# AUTOMOBILIA

**History:** Automobilia is a wide-ranging category that covers just about anything related to automobiles and trucks from fine art costing thousands of dollars to new diecast toys costing less than one dollar. Car parts are not usually considered automobilia, although there are a few exceptions, like beautiful glass radiator ornaments by Renee Lalique or an upholstered sofa made from the tail fins of a 1959 Cadillac.

Advertising from dealers and manufacturers comprise a major part of most automobilia collections. Signs, salesman's jewelry and desk ornaments, and metal or plastic promotional model cars are hot sellers. As more manufacturers turn to the internet for advertising, look for the color advertising brochure to become rarer, and more collectible. Automobilia is not restricted to antique automobiles and it is not necessary to actually own an antique car to enjoy automobile, bus, truck and motorcycle advertising. Modern automobilists often collect advertising brochures or diecast models depicting their daily driver, be it Jeep Grand Cherokee or Toyota truck.

The most popular automobilia reflects the most popular collector cars. Right now, muscle cars from the late 1960s are hot and the market for Mustang, Pontiac GTO, Oldsmobile 4-4-2 and Chevrolet Chevelle memorabilia remains strong. Up and coming are the foreign sports cars, like the Datsun/Nissan "Z" cars and even the dependable Honda Civic, which enjoys almost cult status with the younger generation. Vintage VW Beetle memorabilia and toys have become less sought after, as collectors seek models and advertising from the "new" Volkswagen.

Racing memorabilia is always popular with collectors. Look for NASCAR diecast to cool off as the market gets supersaturated with it, while we enjoy a sports car renaissance and an exciting market for vintage road racing programs, pennants and pins. Most material changes hands at automobile swap meets, specialty auctions like Krause and internet auction venues held throughout the year. eBay Motors continues to be an interesting specialty arena, while Mobilia magazine has ceased print publication in favor of their website.

**References:** Mark Anderton, *Encyclopedia of Petroliana, Identificatin and Price Guide*, Krause Publications, 1999; Mark Anderton and Sherry Mullen, *Gas Station Collectibles*, Wallace-Homestead/Krause, 1994; Mark Allen Baker, *Auto Racing Memorabilia and Price Guide*, Krause, 1996; Leila Dunbar, *Motorcycle Collectibles*, Schiffer Publishing, 1996; John A. Gunnel, *Car Memorabilia Price Guide*, Krause, 1995; James K. Fox, *License Plates of the United States: A Pictorial History 1903 to the Present*, Interstate Directory Publishing Co., 1996; Don and Elizabeth Johnson, *Warman's Advertising*, Krause Publications, 2000; Ron Kowake and Ken Buttolph, *Car Memorabilia Price Guide*, 2nd ed., Krause Publications, 1997; Jim and Nancy Schaut, *American Automobilia*, Wallace-Homestead, 1994.

**Periodicals:** Hemmings Motor News, P.O. Box 256, Bennington, VT 05201; Check the Oil, 30 W. Olentangy St., Powell, OH 43065-9764; Old Cars Weekly, Krause, 700 E. State, Iola WI 54990; Toy Cars & Vehicles, Krause, 700 E. State, Iola WI 54990.

**Collectors' Clubs:** Automobile License Plates Collectors Association, 226 Ridgeway Drive, Bridgeport, WV 26330; National Indy 500 Collectors Club, 10505 N. Delaware, Indianapolis IN 46280; International Petroliana Collectors Association, P.O. Box 937, Powell, OH 43065-9764.

**Advisors:** Jim and Nancy Schaut.

Ashtray, figural
  Pot bellied stove, orange and black ceramic, decal says "'49
    Nash, hotter than a depot stove" ........................................ 75.00
  Tire, green depression glass insert, 1936 Texas exposition 125.00
Badge, attendant's hat
  Sinclair Grease, celluloid, 3" diameter ............................... 350.00
  Texaco, 1930s era, with Scottie dogs ................................. 750.00
Badge, driver's hat, Trailways Bus Lines, enamel ..................... 225.00
Bank, shaggy dog, "Ford" on collar, marked "Florence Ceramics" 65.00
Blotter, Sunoco advertising, Disney's Goofy character, near mint 60.00
Box, Mobil oil "Gargoyle" logo, designed to hold lubrication
  charts ............................................................................................ 45.00
Calendar, 1966 Texaco station, "girlie" type, unsigned ............... 15.00
Can, motor oil
  D-A Speed Sport, racing oil, yellow tin with black and white
    checkered flags, near mint full quart ................................... 50.00
  Duplex, 8oz. Tin, Outboard Motor Oil, Quaker State,
    near mint ...................................................................................... 60.00

**Hood Ornament, Lalique, Cyrysis, clear and frosted glass, sepia patina, stenciled "R. Lalique," Art Deco-style ebonized wood base, $4,975. Photo courtesy of David Rago Auctions.**

Ronson, Wayne Oil Company, Philadelphia, racing streamlined car, airplane and car, full quart ........................................ 900.00

Clock
    Atlas Tires and Batteries, wall clock, 1950s ........................ 175.00
    Pontiac Service, glass front, dark blue painted rim ............ 300.00
    Studebaker, 15" tall, gold metal rim, red/blue emblem, electric ..... 400.00

Compression Tester, Hasting's Piston Ring advertising on dial, original metal storage box ........................................................ 45.00

Credit Card, Husky, 1961, fair to good condition .......................... 25.00

Decanter, figural race car, Lionstone, Al Unser's Johnny Lightning Special, 1970 and 1972 Indianapolis 500 Winner ........................... 75.00

Display
    Champion Spark Plugs, 12" h, 19" w, 5 1/2" d, tin, yellow with black lettering ................................................................ 200.00
    Exide battery, 40" high, tin and metal, black with orange lettering ........................................................................... 150.00

Display Cabinet
    Gates fan belts, hangers inside for various sizes, painted tin front, 15" long, 30" wide, 24" h ........................................ 75.00
    Auto Lite Spark Plug, 18 1/2" h, 13" w, painted metal cabinet, glass front ................................................................ 125.00
    Schrader tire gauge cabinet, figural tire gauge, opens to reveal parts ........................................................................ 350.00

Emblem, Wolverine, model made only a few years by Reo .......... 50.00

Gas Pump Globe
    Mobilgas Special, red pegasus logo ................................... 275.00
    Shell, figural white Shell ..................................................... 450.00
    Thorobred, horse head ................................................... 2,800.00

Gas Pump Salt & Pepper set, plastic, decals crazed, Phillips . 66 45.00

Grill Badge, Sports Car Club of America, black and red wire wheel logo, cloisonné, early 1960s era ............................................ 50.00

Hood Ornament, 1955 Chevrolet, mint, unused .......................... 275.00

Key Fob
    1960 Oldsmobile, color print in clear Lucite .......................... 10.00
    Esso Tiger logo, 1960s, engraved serial number for lost key return ....................................................................... 10.00

Knife, Cadillac Crest, 1958 Certified Mechanic, orig box ............. 80.00

Light, red bubble light for roof, 6 volts, early 1950s emergency vehicle ...................................................................... 225.00

Lighter, Zippo, 1953 Buick Suggestion Winner, Buick Crest engraved, mint and unused in orig box ...................................................... 125.00

Map
    1938 Standard Oil Map of Idaho ........................................ 25.00
    1967 Texaco, map of Texas ................................................. 5.00

Map Rack, gas station display, Conoco, "branding iron" logo ....... 95.00

Motometer, Boyce, unpitted chrome, working condition ............. 135.00

Nodder, Chrysler advertising, "Little Profit" .............................. 60.00

Paperweight
    1938 Pontiac, cast pot metal car on base, probably by Banthrico ...................................................................... 95.00
    Laughing Bear cast metal on base, advertising Bear Wheel Alignment, 4" h ................................................................ 200.00

Pencil, mechanical, "floating" 1953 Cadillac in clear top, dealer advertising on side ........................................................................ 45.00

Pin, "Chevrolet Corvette Owner," 10K, makers' mark on reverse 300.00

Plate, Ford Rotunda logo, 10" d dinner plate ........................... 125.00

Playing cards, AMC Pacer Wagon, still sealed, dealer giveaway . 25.00

Service Pin
    Buick, 25 years, screwback,10K gold, 1930s logo .............. 50.00
    Lincoln-Mercury Registered Mechanic, 10K gold filled ......... 25.00
    Shell oil 15 year tiebar, 10K gold, dated 1944 ..................... 75.00

Sign
    Oilzum, 10" by 15 1/2", double sided, few chips ................ 450.00
    Reo Sales & Service, 18" by 24" .................................... 1,000.00
    Triple X Trucking, Phoenix, Arizona, porcelain over steel... 250.00

Thermometer
    Buick Motor Cars, 27" tall, porcelain, blue, c1918 ............. 300.00
    Texaco, Plastic Pole Thermometer, 6" h ............................ 75.00

Tin
    American Motors, 1 quart all season coolant, no rust .......... 20.00
    Cadillac, Blue Coral Wax, no rust, light scratches .............. 25.00

Mopar, tin, polishing cloth, red/yellow/blue tin, 1950s Chrysler Corp. logo, excellent condition ........................................................ 35.00

Tie Bar, replica of 1950s Ford truck grill ................................... 60.00

Tire Patch Repair Kit, Belnord/Cornell Tires, (Pep Boys), tin, with contents ....................................................................... 25.00

Tissue Dispenser, chrome, Buick logo affixed, mounts under dash and swivels out for access, mint with orig box ................................... 40.00

Vase, bud vase, Fostoria glass, with hard-to-find mounting bracket, unusual pattern ...................................................................... 150.00

Watch Fob
    "Good Roads," celluloid logo affixed to metal fob ............... 75.00
    Thomas Flyer, cloisonné, reverse unmarked ...................... 250.00

Weathervane, 27" by 32", Mobil service station, double sided, porcelain, flying red horse ........................................................... 1,500.00

**Watch Fob, Golden Shell Oil, dark bronze luster finish brass, porcelain enamel center, 1-3/8" d, $165. Photo courtesy of Hake's Americana & Collectibles.**

# BACCARAT GLASS

**History:** The Sainte-Anne glassworks at Baccarat in Voges, France, was founded in 1764 and produced utilitarian soda glass. In 1816, Aime-Gabriel d'Artiques purchased the glassworks, and a Royal Warrant was issued in 1817 for the opening of Verrerie de Vonâoche éa Baccarat. The firm concentrated on lead-crystal glass products. In 1824, a limited company was created. From 1823-1857, Baccarat and Saint-Louis glassworks had a commercial agreement and used the same outlets. No merger occurred. Baccarat began the production of paperweights in 1846. In the late 19th century, the firm achieved an international reputation for cut-glass table services, chandeliers, display vases, centerpieces, and sculptures. Products eventually included all forms of glassware. The firm still is active today.

**Reference:** Jean-Louis Curtis, *Baccarat,* Harry N. Abrams, 1992; Paul Jokelson and Dena Tarshis, *Baccarat Paperweights and Related Glass,* Paperweight Press, 1999.

**Additional Listings:** Paperweights.

Ashtray, 4-1/2" d, Pinwheel, sgd ................................. 85.00
Atomizer, 5" h, 3-1/2" l, oval, etched crystal body, metal chrome top, sgd ......................................................... 90.00
Biscuit Jar, cov, 6" h, crystal, etched ground, cranberry flowers, leaves, and vines, marked inside lid ................................. 600.00
Bookends, pr, 12" h, crystal, serpentine tube on molded rocky form base, etched "Baccarat, France" ............................. 150.00
Bowl, 5-1/2" d, cameo, colorless etched leaf ground, carved chartreuse floral dec ................................................... 100.00
Brandy Snifter, crystal, gilded foliate cartouche, monogrammed "N," set of 12 ........................................................ 275.00
Calling Card Holder, 5-1/2" h, opaline, fan shape, pedestal base, relief butterflies, trees, and flowers, sgd ......................... 195.00
Candlesticks, pr, 9" h, swirled ..................................... 225.00

**Atomizer, amberina, 6" h, $70.**

Celery Tray, 9-1/2" l, 3-1/2" w, Rose Tiente ................................. 45.00
Champagne Bucket, 9-1/4" h, tapering cylinder, rect stop fluted molded sides, stamped "Baccarat, France" ......................................... 400.00
Cologne Bottle, 5-1/2" h, Rose Tiente, Diamond Point Swirl, orig stopper ...................................................................... 125.00
Creamer, 4-1/2" h, lacy, colorless, minor chips ........................... 90.00
Decanter, 8-1/2" h, crystal, cut, orig stopper, mkd "Baccarat France" ............................................................ 110.00
Desk Obelisk, 10" h, cut crystal, sgd with acid "decanter" stamp 250.00
Dish, 8-3/4" l, oval, lacy, colorless, minor chips ........................ 80.00
Dresser Jar, cov, 2-1/2" h, 4-1/2" w, cranberry cut to green base, finely textured bark-like ground, finely cut tiny flowers and leaves, irregular border bands, gold checkerboard type pattern, mkd in pontil, monogrammed lid marked "Sterling" .............................................. 2,350.00
Fairy Lamp, 3-7/8" h, shaded white to clear ............................. 275.00
Finger Bowl and Underplate, 4" d, blue cut to clear, flute and punties motif ...................................................................... 200.00
Goblet, Perfection pattern ............................................... 40.00
Jar, cov
    6" h, 3-3/4" d, sapphire blue, Swirl, mkd ........................... 95.00
    7" d, cameo cut, gilt metal mounts, imp "Baccarat" ........... 350.00
Jewelry Box, cov, 4" d, 2-3/4" h, hinged lid, Button and Bow pattern, sapphire blue, brass fittings ............................................. 145.00
Mustard Jar, cov, 3" d, 5" h, Rose Tiente, Swirl ......................... 85.00
Perfume Bottle, black, Art Deco style, D'Orsay ......................... 225.00
Ring Tree, 4" h, blue cut to clear, diamond and fan motif .......... 225.00
Rose Bowl, 3" d, cranberry, lace enamel dec .......................... 155.00
Sugar Bowl, cov, 7-1/4" h, lacy, colorless, rim chips ................... 95.00
Sweetmeat Jar, cov, cranberry colored strawberries, blossoms, and leaves, cut back to clear ground of ferns, silver plated cover and handle, sgd ................................................................. 350.00
Toasting Goblet, 7" h, #340103, pr ....................................... 150.00
Tumbler, 3-1/2" h, Rose Tiente ............................................. 5.00
Tumble-Up, carafe and tumbler, Rose Tiente, Swirl pattern ....... 350.00
Vase
    9-1/4" h, ovoid, crystal, large thumbprint design, acid stamped mark ................................................................... 200.00
    10-1/4" h, inverted bell form, five etched urns with tall scrolling branches, printed factory mark, 20th C ........................... 800.00
Wine Goblet, set of eight 8" h red wine goblets, and eight 7" h white wine goblets, all signed with acid "decanter" stamp ................. 825.00

# BANKS, MECHANICAL

**History:** Banks which display some form of action while accepting a coin are considered mechanical banks. Mechanical banks date back to ancient Greece and Rome, but the majority of collectors are interested in those made between 1867 and 1928 in Germany, England, and the United States. Initial research suggested that approximately 250 to 300 different or variant designs of banks were made in the early period. Today that number has been revised to 2,000–3,000 types and varieties. The field remains ripe for discovery and research. More than 80% of all cast-iron mechanical banks produced between 1869 and 1928 were made by J. E. Stevens Co., Cromwell, Connecticut. Tin banks are usually of German origin.

**References:** Collectors Encyclopedia of Toys and Banks, L-W Book Sales, 1986, 1993 value update; Al Davidson, Penny Lane, A History of Antique Mechanical Toy Banks, Long's Americana, 1987; Don Duer, A Penny Saved: Still and Mechanical Banks, Schiffer Publishing, 1993; Bill Norman, The Bank Book: The Encyclopedia of Mechanical Bank Collecting, Collectors' Showcase, 1984.

**Collectors' Club:** Mechanical Bank Collectors of America, P.O. Box 128, Allegan, MI 49010.

Reproduction Alert: Reproductions, fakes, and forgeries exist for many banks. Forgeries of some mechanical banks were made as early as 1937, so age alone is not a guarantee of authenticity. In the following price listing, two asterisks indicate banks for which serious forgeries exist, and one asterisk indicates banks for which casual reproductions have been made.

**Notes:** While rarity is a factor in value, appeal of design, action, quality of manufacture, country of origin, and history of collector interest also are important. Radical price fluctuations may occur when there is an imbalance in these factors. Rare banks may sell for a few hundred dollars while one of more common design with greater appeal will sell in the thousands. The mechanical bank market is being greatly affected by the on-line auctions found on the Internet. This past year has seen more examples of banks being offered for sale than has been seen in decades. Many of these previously unavailable examples are being eagerly purchased by collectors. However, because of large numbers of more common banks also coming into the market, this past year represents a drop in the price of many banks, especially those in the under $3,500 range. The values in the list below accurately represent the selling prices of mechanical banks in the specialized collectors' market. As some banks are hard to find, and the market is quite volatile both up and down in price structure, consultation of a competent specialist in mechanical banks, with up to the moment information, is advised prior to selling any mechanical bank. The prices listed are for original old mechanical banks with no repairs, in sound operating condition, and with at least 90% of the original paint intact.

**Advisor:** James S. Maxwell, Jr.

**Note:** Prices quoted are for 100% original examples, no repairs, no repaint, and which have at least 90% bright original paint. An * indicates casual reproductions; † denotes examples where casual reproductions and serious fakes exist.

| | |
|---|---:|
| †Acrobat | 900.00 |
| †Afghanistan | 465.00 |
| African Bank, black bust, back emb "African Bank" | 450.00 |
| American Bank, sewing machine | 510.00 |
| *Artillery | 1,100.00 |
| Atlas, iron, steel, wood, paper | 450.00 |
| Automatic Chocolate Vending, tin | 450.00 |
| Automatic Coin Savings, predicts future, tin | 150.00 |
| Automatic Fortune Bank, tin | 3,700.00 |
| Automatic Savings Bank, tin, soldier | 270.00 |
| Automatic Savings Bank, tin, sailor | 120.00 |
| Automatic Surprise Money Box, wood | 6,500.00 |
| †Baby Elephant X-O'clock, lead and wood | 1,100.00 |
| *Bad Accident | 1,920.00 |
| Bambula, black bust, back emb "Bambula" | 4,700.00 |
| Bank Teller, man behind 3-sided fancy grillwork | 5,500.00 |
| Bank of Education and Economy, must have orig paper reel | 1,600.00 |
| Barking Dog, wood | 300.00 |

| | |
|---|---:|
| Bear, tin | 270.00 |
| †Bear and Tree Stump | 3,500.00 |
| †Bear, slot in chest | 240.00 |
| †Bill E. Grin | 300.00 |
| †Billy Goat Bank | 210.00 |
| Bird In Cage, tin | 150.00 |
| †Bird on Roof | 750.00 |
| †Bismark Bank | 20,350.00 |
| Bonzo, tin | 210.00 |
| Book-Keepers Magic Bank, tin | 24,200.00 |
| Bow-ery Bank, iron, paper, wood | 1,500.00 |
| Bowing Man in Cupola | 1,920.00 |
| †Bowling Alley | 5,500.00 |
| †Boy Robbing Birds Nest | 1,050.00 |
| *Boy Scout Camp | 1,500.00 |
| †Boy and bull dog | 8,500.00 |
| †Boy on trapeze | 6,000.00 |
| †Boys stealing watermelons | 850.00 |
| Bread Winners | 1,620.00 |
| British Clown, tin | 13,200.00 |
| †Bucking Mule | 4,500.00 |
| *Bull Dog, place coin on nose | 3,700.00 |
| †Bull and Bear | 75,000.00 |
| Bull Dog Savings, clockwork | 660.00 |
| †Bull Dog, standing | 1,500.00 |
| Bureau, wood, Serrill patent | 5,500.00 |
| Bureau, Lewando's, wood | 22,000.00 |
| Bureau, wood, John R. Jennings Patent | 7,500.00 |
| Burnett Postman, tin man with tray | 3,500.00 |
| †Butting Buffalo | 510.00 |
| †Butting Goat | 1,620.00 |
| †Butting Ram | 225.00 |
| *Cabin, black man flips | 720.00 |
| Caller Vending, tin | 3,500.00 |
| †Calamity | 4,500.00 |
| †Called Out | 1.680.00 |
| Calumet, tin and cardboard, with Calumet kid | 120.00 |
| Calumet, tin and cardboard, with sailor | 15,000.00 |
| Calumet, tin and Cardboard, with soldier | 18,500.00 |
| †Camera | 660.00 |
| *Cat and Mouse | 720.00 |
| †Cat and Mouse, giant cat standing on top | 40,000.00 |
| Chandlers | 1,200.00 |
| Chandlers with clock | 210.00 |
| *Chief Big Moon | 1,080.00 |
| Child's Bank, wood | 510.00 |
| Chinaman in Boat, lead | 3,500.00 |
| Chinaman with queue, tin | 240.00 |
| Chocolate Menier, tin | 1,050.00 |
| †Chrysler Pig | 480.00 |
| Cigarette Vending, tin | 420.00 |
| Cigarette Vending, lead | 1,200.00 |
| Circus, clown on cart in circular ring | 1,200.00 |
| †Circus, ticket collector | 210.00 |
| Clever Dick, tin | 120.00 |
| Clown Bust, iron | 1,500.00 |
| Clown, Chein, tin | 45.00 |
| †Clown on Bar, tin and iron | 1,350.00 |
| *Clown on Globe | 5,500.00 |
| Clown and Dog, tin | 150.00 |
| Clown with arched top, tin | 150.00 |
| Clown with black face, tin | 1,200.00 |
| Clown with white face, tin | 125.00 |
| Clown with white face, round, tin | 3,700.00 |
| Cockatoo Pelican, tin | 120.00 |
| Coin Registering, many variants | 25-1,000.00 |
| Columbian Magic Savings, iron | 120.00 |
| Columbian magic Savings, wood and paper | 15,500.00 |
| Confectionery | 1,320.00 |

| | |
|---|---|
| Coolie Bust, lead | 240.00 |
| Cowboy with tray, tin | 210.00 |
| †Creedmoor | 675.00 |
| Crescent Cash Register | 4,120.00 |
| Cross Legged Minstrel, tin | 210.00 |
| Crowing Rooster, circular base, tin | 6,500.00 |
| Cupid at Piano, pot metal, musical | 450.00 |
| †Cupola | 650.00 |
| Dapper Dan, tin | 1,500.00 |
| *Darktown Battery | 3,500.00 |
| Darky Bust, tin, tiny size | 120.00 |
| †Darky Fisherman, lead | 8,500.00 |
| †Darky Watermelon, man kicks football at watermelon | 7,500.00 |
| †Dentist | 3,700.00 |
| Dinah, iron | 300.00 |
| Dinah, aluminum | 150.00 |
| Ding Dong Bell, tin, windup | 3,500.00 |
| Dog on turntable | 571.00 |
| †Dog with tray | 392.00 |
| Domed vending, tin | 4,000.00 |
| Driver's Service Vending, tin | 1,680.00 |
| Droste Chocolate | 900.00 |
| *Eagle and Eaglettes | 70.00 |
| Electric Safe, steel | 1,320.00 |
| *Elephant and Three Clowns | 1,110.00 |
| *Elephant, locked howdah | 270.00 |
| Elephant, made in Canada | 11,500.00 |
| Elephant, man pops out, wood, cloth, iron | 330.00 |
| †Elephant, no stars | 3,700.00 |
| *Elephant, pull tail | 60.00 |
| Elephant, three stars | 720.00 |
| *Elephant, trunk swings, large | 210.00 |
| *Elephant, trunk swings, small | 150.00 |
| Elephant, trunk swings, raised coin slot | 900.00 |
| †Elephant with tusks, on wheels | 300.00 |
| Empire Cinema, tin | 465.00 |
| English Bulldog, tin | 270.00 |
| Feed the Goose, pot metal | 480.00 |
| 5 cents Adding | 150.00 |
| Flip the Frog, tin | 270.00 |
| Football, English football | 1,080.00 |
| Fortune Savings, tin, horse race | 750.00 |
| Fortune Teller, Savings, safe | 1,320.00 |
| †Fowler | 1,320.00 |
| †Freedman's Bank, wood, lead, brass, tin, paper, etc. | 75,000.00 |
| Frog on arched track, tin | 720.00 |
| Frog on rock | 840.00 |
| *Frog on round base | 570.00 |
| †Frogs, two frogs | 720.00 |
| Fun Producing Savings, tin | 1,920.00 |
| *Gem, dog with building | 1,700.00 |
| German Sportsman, lead and iron | 900.00 |
| German Vending, tin | 1,200.00 |
| †Germania Exchange, iron, lead, tin | 1,200.00 |
| †Giant in Tower | 720.00 |
| †Giant, standing by rock | 1,320.00 |
| Girl Feeding Geese, tin, paper, lead | 24,000.00 |
| †Girl Skipping Rope | 16,500.00 |
| †Girl in Victorian chair | 1,200.00 |
| Give Me A Penny, wood | 8,000.00 |
| Grenadier | 1,125.00 |
| Guessing, man's figure, lead, steel, iron | 8,800.00 |
| Guessing, woman's figure, iron | 1,320.00 |
| Guessing, woman's figure, lead | 900.00 |
| Gwenda Money Box, tin | 3,500.00 |
| Hall's Excelsior, iron, wood | 450.00 |
| Hall's Liliput, no tray | 240.00 |
| Hall's Liliput, with tray | 150.00 |
| †Harlequin | 7,500.00 |
| Harold Lloyd, tin | 270.00 |
| Hartwig and Vogel, vending, tin | 900.00 |
| Hen and Chick | 990.00 |
| Highwayman, tin | 380.00 |
| Hillman Coin Target | 900.00 |
| *Hindu, bust | 450.00 |
| †Hold the Fort, 2 varieties, each | 650.00 |
| Home, tin building | 570.00 |
| *Home, iron | 240.00 |
| Hoop-La | 5,500.00 |
| *Horse Race, 2 varieties, each | 1,200.00 |
| †Humpty Dumpty, bust of clown with name on back, iron | 1,680.00 |
| Humpty Dumpty, aluminum, English | 210.00 |
| Huntley and Palmers, tin, vending | 1,080.00 |
| *I Always Did 'spise a Mule, black man on bench | 630.00 |
| *I Always Did 'spise a Mule, black man on mule | 930.00 |
| Ideal Bureau, tin | 3,700.00 |
| *Indian and Bear | 750.00 |
| †Indian Chief, black man bust with Indian feathered headdress, aluminum | 450.00 |
| Indiana Paddlewheel Boat | 650.00 |
| †Initiating Bank, first degree | 600.00 |
| Initiating Bank, second degree | 720.00 |
| Japanese Ball Tosser, tin, wood, paper | 900.00 |
| Joe Socko Novelty Bank, tin | 270.00 |
| John Bull's Money Box | 1,200.00 |
| John R. Jennings Trick Drawer Money Box, wood | 16,500.00 |
| Jolly Joe Clown, tin | 1,920.00 |
| *Jolly Nigger, American | 390.00 |
| *Jolly Nigger, English | 210.00 |
| Jolly Nigger, lettering in Greek | 225.00 |
| Jolly Nigger, lettering in Arabic | 1,080.00 |
| *Jolly Nigger, raises hat, lead | 900.00 |
| *Jolly Nigger, raises hat, iron | 1,320.00 |
| *Jolly Nigger, stationary ears | 150.00 |
| *Jolly Nigger, stationary eyes | 270.00 |
| Jolly Nigger, with fez, aluminum | 450.00 |
| Jolly Sambo Bank | 1,680.00 |
| *Jonah and The Whale Bank, large rectangular base | 1,200.00 |
| †Jonah and The Whale Bank, stands on 2 ornate legs with rectangular coin box at center | 8,500.00 |
| †Jumbo, elephant on wheels | 300.00 |
| Kick Inn Bank, wood | 1,500.00 |
| Kiltie | 390.00 |
| Lawrence Steinberg's Bureau Bank, wood | 13,000.00 |
| †Leap Frog | 1,320.00 |
| Lehmann Berlin Tower, tin | 210.00 |
| Lehmann, London Tower, tin | 240.00 |
| †Light of Asia | 270.00 |
| †Lighthouse Bank | 300.00 |
| Lion, tin | 345.00 |
| Lion Hunter | 990.00 |
| †Lion and Two Monkeys | 1,110.00 |
| *Little High Hat | 900.00 |
| Little Jocko, tin | 390.00 |
| *Little Joe Bank | 570.00 |
| Little Moe Bank | 210.00 |
| Lucky wheel Money Box, tin | 4,120.00 |
| *Magic Bank, iron house | 400.00 |
| Magic Bank, tin | 200.00 |
| Magic, safe, tin | 270.00 |
| †Magician | 1,080.00 |
| †Mama Katzenjammer | 1,590.00 |
| †Mammy and Child | 1,200.00 |
| *Mason | 1,680.00 |
| Memorial Money Box | 240.00 |
| *Merry-Go-Round, mechanical, coin activates | 1,680.00 |
| †Merry-Go-Round, semi-mechanical, spin by hand | 510.00 |
| Mickey Mouse, tin | 1,450.00 |

Mikado Bank ...................................................... 7,500.00
†Milking Cow ..................................................... 3,600.00
Minstrel, tin ...................................................... 2,8800.00
Model Railroad Drink Dispenser, tin ................... 15,500.00
Model Savings Bank, tin, cash register ................. 4,120.00
*Monkey and Coconut ........................................... 960.00
Monkey and Parrot, tin .......................................... 850.00
†Monkey Bank ....................................................... 850.00
Monkey, chimpanzee in ornate circular bldg, iron ..... 650.00
Monkey Face, tin with arched top ......................... 1,920.00
Monkey, pot metal, nods head ............................... 450.00
†Monkey, slot in stomach ...................................... 225.00
Monkey, tin, tips hat ............................................. 270.00
Monkey with Tray, tin ............................................ 570.00
Mosque ................................................................ 270.00
Motor Bank, coin activates trolley ....................... 1,200.00
Mule Entering Barn .............................................. 1,125.00
Music Bank, tin .................................................... 225.00
Musical Church, wood ........................................... 345.00
Musical Savings Bank, Regina ............................. 1,680.00
Musical Savings, tin .............................................. 195.00
Musical Savings, velvet covered easel ................... 270.00
Musical Savings, velvet covered frame ................... 300.00
Musical Savings, wood house ................................ 570.00
National Bank ....................................................... 570.00
National, Your Savings, cash register ................... 1,680.00
Nestle's Automatic Chocolate, cardboard, vending ..... 1,680.00
*New Bank, lever at center .................................... 240.00
*New Bank, lever at left ........................................ 180.00
†New Creedmoor Bank ......................................... 200.00
Nodding Clown, pewter and brass ......................... 450.00
Nodding Dog, painted tin ...................................... 225.00
†North Pole Bank ................................................ 1,125.00
*Novelty Bank ....................................................... 870.00
Octagonal Fort Bank ............................................ 960.00
Old Mother Hubbard, tin ....................................... 450.00
*Organ Bank, boy and girl ..................................... 570.00
*Organ Bank, cat and dog ..................................... 450.00
*Organ Bank, medium, only monkey figure ............. 270.00
*Organ Bank, tiny, only monkey figure ................... 210.00
Organ Grinder and Dancing Bear .......................... 410.00
Owl, slot in book .................................................. 165.00
Owl, slot in head .................................................. 195.00
*Owl, turns head ................................................... 240.00
*Paddy and the Pig ............................................. 1,110.00
Panorama Bank ................................................... 1,050.00
Pascal Chocolate Cigarettes, vending, tin ............ 1,080.00
Patronize the Blind Man ....................................... 720.00
Pay Phone Bank, iron .......................................... 1,680.00
Pay Phone Bank, tin ............................................. 510.00
†Peg-Leg Beggar ................................................. 410.00
*Pelican, Arab head pops out ................................ 345.00
*Pelican, Mammy head pops out ............................ 315.00
*Pelican, man thumbs nose ................................... 300.00
*Pelican, rabbit pops out ....................................... 270.00

†Perfection Registering, girl and dog at blackboard ..... 1,110.00
Piano, musical ...................................................... 450.00
*Picture Gallery .................................................. 1,650.00
Pig in High Chair .................................................. 270.00
Pinball Vending, tin ............................................. 1,320.00
Pistol Bank, iron ................................................... 345.00
Pistol Bank, iron, Uncle Sam figure pops out ....... 1,320.00
Pistol Bank, litho, tin .......................................... 3,700.00
Pistol Bank, sheet steel ...................................... 1,120.00
Policeman, tin ...................................................... 300.00
Popeye Knockout, tin .......................................... 1,650.00
Post Office Savings, steel .................................... 1,200.00
†Preacher in the Pulpit ....................................... 9,500.00
†Presto, iron building ........................................... 570.00
Presto, mouse on roof, wood and paper ................ 570.00
*Presto, penny changes optically to quarter ........... 675.00
*Professor Pug Frog 4 .......................................... 120.00
Pump and Bucket ............................................... 4,700.00
*Punch and Judy, iron ......................................... 1,570.00
Punch and Judy, iron front, tin back ...................... 450.00
Punch and Judy, litho tin, circa 1910 .................... 275.00
Punch and Judy, litho tin, circa 1930 .................... 165.00
†Queen Victoria, bust, brass ............................... 1,680.00
†Queen Victoria, bust, iron .................................. 4,120.00
Rabbit in Cabbage ............................................... 210.00
†Rabbit Standing, large ........................................ 410.00
†Rabbit Standing, small ........................................ 225.00
Reclining Chinaman with cards ............................ 1,500.00
Record Money Box, tin scales .............................. 6,700.00
†Red Riding Hood, iron ....................................... 1,900.00
Red Riding Hood, tin, vending .............................. 900.00
†Rival Bank ........................................................ 1,950.00
Robot Bank, aluminum .......................................... 390.00
Robot Bank, iron .................................................. 620.00
Roller-Skating Bank ............................................ 1,710.00
Rooster .............................................................. 1,200.00
Royal Trick Elephant, tin ..................................... 5,500.00
Safe Deposit Bank, tin, elephant .......................... 990.00
Safety Locomotive, semi ..................................... 1,110.00
Sailor Face, tin, pointed top ................................ 1,920.00
Sailor Money Box, wood ....................................... 270.00
Saluting Sailor, tin ............................................... 510.00
Sam Segal's Aim to Save, brass and wood ............. 780.00
Sam Segal's Aim to Save, iron ............................ 1,080.00
*Santa Claus ..................................................... 1,000.00
Savo, circular, tin ................................................. 390.00
Savo, rectangular, tin ........................................... 345.00
†Schley Bottling Up Cevera .................................. 585.00
Schokolade Automat, tin, vending ....................... 1,200.00
School Teacher, tin and wood, American ................ 920.00
School Teacher, tin, German ................................. 410.00
Scotchman, tin ................................................... 1,125.00
Seek Him Frisk ................................................... 1,920.00
Sentry Bank, tin ................................................... 375.00
Sentry Bugler, tin ................................................ 165.00
†Shoot That Hat Bank ......................................... 1,620.00
†Shoot the Chute Bank ........................................ 1,380.00
Signal Cabin, tin ................................................. 1,275.00
†Smith X-ray Bank ............................................... 765.00
Snake and Frog in Pond, tin .............................. 12,500.00
*Snap-It Bank ...................................................... 840.00
Snow White, tin and lead ..................................... 525.00
*Speaking Dog .................................................. 1,125.00
Spring Jawed Alligator, pot metal ......................... 150.00
Spring Jawed Bonzo, pot metal ............................ 150.00
Spring Jawed Bulldog, pot metal .......................... 135.00
Spring Jawed Cat, pot metal ................................ 168.00
Spring Jawed Chinaman, pot metal ....................... 850.00
Spring Jawed Donkey, pot metal .......................... 135.00
Spring Jawed Felix the Cat, pot metal ................. 3,700.00

**Paddy and the Pig,
J & E Stevens Co.,
$1,110.**

| | |
|---|---|
| Spring Jawed Mickey Mouse, pot metal | 13,500.00 |
| Spring Jawed Monkey, pot metal | 135.00 |
| Spring Jawed Parrot, pot metal | 150.00 |
| Spring Jawed Penguin, pot metal | 165.00 |
| Springing Cat | 4,120.00 |
| †Squirrel and Tree Stump | 410.00 |
| Starkies Aeroplane, aluminum, cardboard | 13,000.00 |
| Starkies Aeroplane, aluminum, steel | 17,000.00 |
| Stollwerk Bros., vending, tin | 650.00 |
| Stollwerk Bros., 2 penny, vending, tin | 840.00 |
| Stollwerk Bros., Progressive Sampler, tin | 330.00 |
| Stollwerk Bros., Victoria, spar-automat, tin | 570.00 |
| Stollwerk Bros., large vending, tin | 960.00 |
| *Stump Speaker Bank | 1,680.00 |
| Sweet Thrift, tin, vending | 345.00 |
| Symphonium Musical Savings, wood | 1,440.00 |
| †Tabby | 225.00 |
| *Tammany Bank | 225.00 |
| Tank and Cannon, aluminum | 1,200.00 |
| Tank and Cannon, iron | 1,680.00 |
| †Target Bank | 252.00 |
| †Target In Vestibule | 570.00 |
| *Teddy and The Bear | 990.00 |
| Ten Cent Adding Bank | 2,800.00 |
| Thrifty Animal Bank, tin | 510.00 |
| Thrift Scotchman, wood, paper | 4,500.00 |
| Thrifty Tom's Jigger, tin | 1,500.00 |
| Tid-Bits Money Box, tin | 210.00 |
| Tiger, tin | 270.00 |
| Time Is Money | 750.00 |
| Time Lock Savings | 345.00 |
| Time Registering Bank | 450.00 |
| *Toad on Stump | 450.00 |
| Toilet Bank, tin | 390.00 |
| Tommy Bank | 570.00 |
| Treasure Chest Music Bank | 150.00 |
| *Trick Dog, 6 part base | 1,380.00 |
| *Trick Dog, solid base | 510.00 |
| *Trick Pony Bank | 720.00 |
| Trick Savings, wood, end drawer | 650.00 |
| Trick Savings, wood, side drawer | 650.00 |
| Tropical Chocolate Vending, tin | 1,800.00 |
| Try your Weight, tin, semi | 570.00 |
| Try Your Weight, tin, mechanical | 1,560.00 |
| †Turtle Bank | 1,920.00 |

| | |
|---|---|
| Twentieth Century Savings Bank | 300.00 |
| Two Ducks Bank, lead | 9,000.00 |
| U.S. Bank, Building | 510.00 |
| †U.S. and Spain | 720.00 |
| †Uncle Remus Bank | 765.00 |
| †Uncle Sam Bank, standing figure with satchel | 1,125.00 |
| †Uncle Sam, bust | 240.00 |
| †Uncle Tom, no lapels, with star | 255.00 |
| †Uncle Tom, lapels, with star | 240.00 |
| †Uncle Tom, no star | 210.00 |
| United States Bank, safe | 330.00 |
| Viennese soldier | 650.00 |
| Volunteer bank | 570.00 |
| Watch Bank, blank face, tin | 120.00 |
| Watch Bank, dime disappears, tin | 165.00 |
| Watch Bank, stamped face, tin | 90.00 |
| Watchdog Safe | 390.00 |
| Weeden's Plantation, tin, wood | 510.00 |
| Weight Lifter, tin | 390.00 |
| Whale Bank, pot metal | 510.00 |
| *William Tell, iron | 1,315.00 |
| William Tell, crossbow, Australian, sheet steel, aluminum | 1,920.00 |
| Wimbledon Bank | 900.00 |
| Winner Savings Bank, tin | 660.00 |
| Wireless Bank, tin, wood, iron | 525.00 |
| Woodpecker Bank, tin | 525.00 |
| World's Banker, tin | 450.00 |
| *World's Fair Bank | 720.00 |
| Zentral Sparkasse, steel | 850.00 |
| Zig Zag Bank, iron, tin, papier-mâché | 4,120.00 |
| *Zoo | 900.00 |

# BANKS, STILL

**History:** Banks with no mechanical action are known as still banks. The first still banks were made of wood or pottery or from gourds. Redware and stoneware banks, made by America's early potters, are prized possessions of today's collectors. Still banks reached a golden age with the arrival of the cast-iron bank. Leading manufacturing companies include Arcade Mfg. Co., J. Chein & Co., Hubley, J. & E. Stevens, and A. C. Williams. The banks often were ornately painted to enhance their appeal. During the cast-iron era, banks and other businesses used the still bank as a form of advertising.

The tin lithograph bank, again frequently a tool for advertising, reach its zenith during the years 1930 to 1955. The tin bank was an important premium, whether a Pabst Blue Ribbon beer can bank or a Gerber's Orange Juice bank. Most tin advertising banks resembled the packaging of the product.

Almost every substance has been used to make a still bank—die-cast white metal, aluminum, brass, plastic, glass, etc. Many of the early glass candy containers also converted to a bank after the candy was eaten. Thousands of varieties of still banks were made, and hundreds of new varieties appear on the market each year.

**References:** *Collector's Encyclopedia of Toys and Banks,* L-W Book Sales, 1986, 1993 value update; Don Duer, *Penny Banks Around the World,* Schiffer Publishing, 1997; Earnest Ida and Jane Pitman, *Dictionary of Still Banks,* Long's Americana, 1980; Beverly and Jim Mangus, *Collector's Guide to Banks,* Collector Books,

**Trick Dog, solid base, $510.**

**Bank, salt glaze, globe shape, relief, blue accents "World'ls Fair My Expenses to Chicago, pat Applied for," central relief design of train and track with blue accents, attributed to Whites, Utica, NY, factory, 4-1/2" h, $3,750. Photo courtesy of Vicki & Bruce Waasdrop.**

1998; Andy and Susan Moore, *Penny Bank Book, Collecting Still Banks,* 3rd ed., Schiffer Publishing, 2000; Tom and Loretta Stoddard, *Ceramic Coin Banks,* Collector Books, 1997.

**Periodicals:** Glass Bank Collector, P.O. Box 155, Poland, NY 13431; Heuser's Quarterly Collectible Diecast Newsletter, P.O. Box 300, West Winfield, NY 13491.

**Collectors' Club:** Still Bank Collectors Club of America, 4175 Millersville Rd, Indianapolis, IN 46205.

**Museum:** Margaret Woodbury Strong Museum, Rochester, NY.

## Cast Iron

Advertising
 Building, Economy Accumulates Wealth, Branch of 3rd Piqua Building and Loan, worn nickel finish, old silver overpaint, dome rotates to reveal slot in each corner, 7-1/4" h .................. 150.00
 Satchel, Peoples Savings Bank and Trust Co., Covington, Ky, two-tone bronze finish, 6" l ................................. 150.00
 Aunt Jemima, wear to orig polychrome paint, M168, 5-3/4" h ................................................................ 200.00
 Bank, double door, old gold and silver, M1125, 5-1/2" h ..... 250.00
Battle Ship
 Maine, dark brown japanning, gold trim, some wear, M1440, 4-1/2" l ................................................................ 385.00
 Oregon, very worn brown japanning, gold trim, M1450, 5" l 425.00
Bear Stealing Pig, very worn old gold paint, some rust, M683, 5-5/8" h ................................................................ 220.00
Billy Goat, with tails, old worn polychrome, 4-3/4" h .................. 330.00
Blackpool Tower, dark brown japanning, M984, 7-1/2" h ........... 220.00
Boston Bull Terrier, wear to orig white and brown paint, M421 or M425, 5-1/2" h ................................................................ 175.00
Boy Scout, wear to polychrome paint, M47, 5-7/8" h ................. 165.00
Buster Brown and Tige, worn old gold and polychrome paint, M241, 5-1/8" h ................................................................ 165.00
Camel, old gold repaint with red, M767, 7-1/4" h ...................... 360.00
Campbell Kids, old worn green repaint, M163, 3-1/2" h ............. 150.00
Captain Kidd, worn polychrome paint, light rust, M38, 5-5/8" h .... 80.00
Castle, old red repaint, gold trim, M954, 3-1/8" h ...................... 1,100.00
Circus Elephant, orig pain, minor wear, replaced screw, M462, 3-7/8" h ................................................................ 200.00
City Bank, old gold repaint, replaced screw, M1097, 5-1/2" h ....... 90.00
City Bank, worn gold paint, M111, crack in back, 4" h ................ 150.00
Columbia Bank, worn old silver paint, light rust, trap missing, M1070, 5-7/8" h ................................................................ 275.00
County Bank, old brown repaint, M1110, 4-1/4" h ...................... 150.00
Crown Bank, old brown japanning with gold trim, M1226, 3-1/2" h ................................................................ 360.00
Dormer, old polychrome paint, steeple missing, top edge incomplete, M953, 3-3/4" h ................................................................ 3,960.00

Do You Know Me? old polychrome paint with good color and minor wear, M75, 6-1/8" h ................................................ 330.00
Elephant, stiff legged, old silver, red, and gold paint, M469, 4-3/8" h ................................................................ 315.00
Fidelity Trust Vault, old white paint with orange wash, two finials missing, edge and foot damage, M901, 6-5/8" h ......................... 110.00
Finial Bank, worn old two-tone bronze finish, M1158, 6" h ......... 800.00
Flat Iron Bank, old gold repaint, orig combination trap, two cracks in base, glued chip, 5-7/8" h ........................................ 140.00
Flat Iron Bank, worn silver and gold paint, M1161, 5-1/2" h ........ 250.00
Globe, Enterprise Mfg. Co., wear to orig red and black paint, 5-5/8" h, M781 ................................................................ 420.00
Globe on Arc, minor wear to old red and gold paint, M789, 5-1/2" h ................................................................ 385.00
Golliwog variant, old polychrome paint, probably second period, M86, 6-1/8" h ................................................................ 140.00
Graf Zeppelin, worn rusted silver paint, on wheels, M1431, 8" l 200.00
High Rise, worn gold and silver, crack in base plate, M1216, 7" h ................................................................ 1,320.00
High Rise, worn old black and gold, M1219, 5" h ....................... 385.00
Home Savings Bank
 M1201, worn nickel finish, wear, light rust, orig coin retainers, 10-1/2" h ................................................................ 1,240.00
 M1236, worn red and green paint, 3-1/2" h ....................... 220.00
 M1237, worn brown japanning, gold trim, light rust, 6" h .... 175.00
Independence Hall, wear to old bronze repaint, M1244, 9" h ..... 420.00
Independence Hall Tower, old gold repaint, M1202, 9-1/2" h ..... 250.00
Indiana Silo, old gold paint, M1247, 3-6/8" h ........................... 2,650.00
Indian with Tomahawk, minor wear to polychrome paint, M228, 6" h ................................................................ 360.00
Kido Bank, traces of paint, M36, 5-1/4" h ................................. 140.00
Lion, quilted, old gold, red, and black paint, some wear, M758, 3-3/4" h ................................................................ 440.00
Main Street Trolley, old worn red and green paint, no people, M1469, 6-3/4" l ................................................................ 250.00
Mary and Lamp, traces of paint, M164, 4-3/8" h ....................... 115.00
Merry Go Round, very worn nickel finish, M1617, 4-3/4" h ......... 220.00
Mosque, dome, combination lock, green repaint, M1176, 5-1/4" h ................................................................ 90.00
Mulligan, worn polychrome paint, faded, M177, 5-3/4" h .............. 85.00
Mulligan variant, Murphy the Shoeman on back, wear to orig polychrome paint, M178, 5-3/4" h ........................................ 1,485.00
Mutt and Jeff, old gold paint, M157, 5-1/8" h ............................ 110.00
New England Church, nickel finish, M986, 7-1/2" h .................... 220.00
Owl, worn polychrome paint, light rust, M597, 4-1/4" h .............. 110.00
Pig, "I Made Chicago Famous," old black, red, silver, and gold paint, wear, M629, 4" l ................................................ 175.00
Possum, traces of silver paint, light rust, M561, 4-1/2" l ............. 300.00
Radio Bank, old red and gold, nickel finish, labeled "Kenton Toys, Kenton, Ohio," M829, 4-1/2" l ................................. 315.00
Radio, GE, orig red and gold paint, Arcade decal, minor wear, M822, 4" h ................................................................ 250.00
Recording Bank, nickel finish, M1062, 6-5/8" h .......................... 90.00
Rhino, old unpainted surface, some old paint chips, M721, 5" l 200.00
Roof Bank, old brown japanning with gold trim, break in base plate, M1122, 5-1/2" h ................................................ 220.00
Rose Window, traces of black paint, M1170, 2-1/4" h ................. 200.00
Safe
 Jewel Safe, worn and rusted nickel finish, M896, 7-38" h .. 115.00
 Star Safe, old black and green paint, M876, 2-1/2" h .......... 90.00
 The Bank of Industry, shiny nickel finish, labeled "Kenton Branch," 5-1/2" h ................................................ 225.00
Savings Chest, register type, worn nickel finish, rust, one side panel loose, M948, 6-1/4" l ................................................ 165.00
Sea Lion, gold repaint, M732, 3-1/2" h ..................................... 165.00
Skyscraper, six panels, worn old gold and silver, trap missing, M1241, 6-1/2" h 140.00 Stove, worn nickel finish, some rust, black finished tin on sides and back, labeled "Klotz Mfg Co. U. S. Patent," 4-1/2" h ................................................................ 175.00

Stove Pipe, worn old black, nickel finish insert, 3" h ................... 150.00
Tally-Ho, brown japanning, gold trim, minor war, M535,
   4-3/8" h ................................................................................ 1,715.00
Taxi, Yellow Cab Co., Arcade, orig paint, very minor wear,
   7-3/4" l ................................................................................. 2,310.00
Teddy Bear, old gold paint, slight rust, M698, 3-7/8" l ................. 275.00
Town Hall, red and silver repaint, screw replaced, M998,
   4-3/4" h ................................................................................. 275.00
Turkey, old bronze japanning, red and gold trim, some wear, M585,
   4-3/8" h ................................................................................. 425.00
Washington Monument, worn old gold, replaced screw, M1048 . 165.00
Woolworth Tower, old gold paint, M1242, 5-3/4" h ...................... 200.00
Woolworth Tower, old silver repaint, M1041, 8" h ........................ 90.00

## Ceramic/Pottery

Advertising, figural acorn, "Acorn Stoves will save half your fuel
   money," green glaze, 3" h ...................................................... 70.00
Cat's Head, white clay, green glaze, 3" h ................................... 115.00
Cylindrical, emb hen and chicks, redware, 12" h ........................ 500.00
Dog's Head, molded fur and retriever-type features, green glaze on
   dark brown clay, 3-1/2" h ...................................................... 265.00
Dutch Girl, worn polychrome, 4-3/4" h, chips ............................... 60.00
Elf's Head, white clay, brown glaze, 3-5/8" h .............................. 60.00
Jug, wide ovoid body, tapering from button finial, Albany brown slip
   glaze, 6-3/8" h ...................................................................... 200.00
Lion, Hubert, Lefton ..................................................................... 45.00
Pear, naturalistic yellow-green glaze, pink blush, 3-7/8" h .......... 120.00
Pig
   4-3/8" l, two tone marbleized blue and brown glaze, small edge
      chips ................................................................................... 65.00
   6-1/4" l, red, brown, and cream marbleized glaze, small edge
      chips ................................................................................... 50.00
   6-1/2" l, brown, olive, and cream marbleized glaze .............. 95.00
Uncle Sam, blue and white, 4-1/2" h ............................................ 20.00

## Chalk

Dove, 11" h, worn green, red, and yellow ochre paint ................. 250.00
Pig, 7-1/8" l, old white repaint, pink ears .................................... 90.00

## Glass

Bank of Independance Hall, clear, tin base, 7-1/4" h, chips .......... 65.00
Clock, mantle type, painted, tin closure, 3-3/4" h .......................... 40.00
Devil, worn red paint, 4-1/2" h ..................................................... 165.00
Dog, sitting on drum, 4-1/8" h ....................................................... 85.00
Donkey, polychrome dec, 7" h ..................................................... 140.00
Duck, round, polychrome dec, 4" h ............................................. 190.00
Elephant, gold and red, replaced tin wheels, 4" h, minor wear ... 190.00
Log Cabin, milk glass, paper insert, worn gold, 3-7/8" h .............. 40.00
Pig, painted gold, 4-1/4" l ............................................................. 30.00
Radio, clear, emb details ............................................................... 35.00
Skookum, clear, mkd "S. Sears, 1916," 3-1/2" h ........................... 35.00

## Papier-mâché

Advertising, James Taffy, tin top, 7" h ........................................... 20.00
Charlie McCarthy, "Feed Me...," worn polychrome ....................... 45.00
Kewpie, worn polychrome, trap missing, 5" h ............................... 40.00
Scottie, pink and white, 5-3/4" h ................................................... 35.00

## Tin

Advertising, Red Circle Coffee, yellow, black letters, red circle,
   3-7/8" h ................................................................................... 35.00
Andy Gump, 4-3/8" h, 3" w, 7/8" d, litho images of Gump cartoon char-
   acters on front and back .......................................................... 140.00
Barrel, Happy Days, J. Chein & Co. .............................................. 45.00
Mailbox, emb "Save for Savings Bonds," red, white, and blue,
   9" h ......................................................................................... 60.00

## Wood

Fidelity Trust, black and gold, decoupage scenes on sides and top,
   drawer, 8-1/2" h ...................................................................... 120.00

First National Bank, worn decoupage, 5-3/4" h ............................ 90.00
Fort, oak, pull-out coin slot, 6-1/8" h, worn ................................... 25.00
Tramp Art, secret access to coins, 4" w, 4" d, 6" h ...................... 335.00

# BARBER BOTTLES

**History:** Barber bottles, colorful glass bottles found on shelves and counters in barber shops, held the liquids barbers used daily. A specific liquid was kept in a specific bottle, which the barber knew by color, design, or lettering. The bulk liquids were kept in utilitarian containers under the counter or in a storage room. Barber bottles are found in many types of glass—art glass with various decorations, pattern glass, and commercially prepared and labeled bottles.

**References:** Barbershop Collectibles, L-W Book Sales, 1996; Keith E. Estep, Shaving Mug & Barber Bottle Book, Schiffer Publishing, 1995; Richard Holiner, Collecting Barber Bottles, Collector Books, 1986; Ralph & Terry Kovel, Kovels' Bottles Price List, 11th ed., Three Rivers Press, 1999.

**Museums:** Atwater Kent History Museum, Philadelphia, PA; Barber Museum, Canal Winchester, OH; Lightner Museum, Saint Augustine, FL.

**Note:** Prices are for bottles without original stoppers unless otherwise noted.

Amethyst, enameled flowers ......................................................... 135.00
Art Glass, cylindrical, bulbous body, long bulbous neck, amethyst and
   light yellow amber mottled design, all over pink irid, ground mouth,
   smooth base, 7-1/4" h ............................................................ 325.00
Blue, horizontal brown band design, applied white enamel floral pat-
   tern, sheared lip, exposed pontil, 8" h .................................... 115.00
Canary, Hobnail pattern, three pouring rings, round lip, smooth base,
   7-1/4" h .................................................................................... 85.00
Clambroth, emb "Water" in red letters across front, porcelain stopper,
   8" h .......................................................................................... 50.00
Cobalt Blue, bell shape, raised white and orange enameled flowers,
   sheared lip, exposed pontil, 8-1/2" h ...................................... 125.00
Colorless, ribbed, dec band around center, gold trim, raised enamel
   dot pattern, pontil, 6-1/2" h ....................................................... 75.00
Crackle, cranberry, swirl .............................................................. 220.00

**Hobnail Opalescent, blue, 7-3/4" h, $150.**

Cranberry, rings of hobnails on neck, 6-3/4" h ............................ 175.00
Cut Glass, hobstar base, pewter top, 5" h ................................ 90.00
Electric Blue, cylindrical corset waisted form, long neck, opalescent wandering vine dec, tooled mouth, smooth base, 7-1/2" h ...... 210.00
Emerald Green, cylindrical modified corset waisted form, long neck, lighter green enamel and floral gilt dec, tooled mouth, pontil scar, 7-1/2" h ......................................................... 275.00
Milk Glass, Bay Rum, hand painted pink and white flowers, green leaves, pastel ground, rolled lip, pontil, 9" h ............................ 150.00
Opalescent
    Hobbs Hobnail, cranberry .................................. 225.00
    Seaweed, cranberry, teepee shape ................................... 495.00
Satin, Hobnail, dark green ........................................... 250.00
Spatter, cranberry ground, opalescent white mottling, sq, long neck, tooled mouth, smooth base, 8-1/2" h ........................................ 160.00
Tiffany, Favrile, irid gold, purple highlights, unsigned, 7-1/2" h, 4-1/4" d ........................................................ 395.00

# BAROMETERS

**History:** A barometer is an instrument which measures atmospheric pressure, which, in turn, aids weather forecasting. Low pressure indicates the coming of rain, snow, or storm; high pressure signifies fair weather. Most barometers use an evacuated and graduated glass tube which contains a column of mercury. These are classified by the shape of the case. An aneroid barometer has no liquid and works by a needle connected to the top of a metal box in which a partial vacuum is maintained. The movement of the top moves the needle.

**Reference:** Nicholas Goodison, English Barometers, 1680-1860, Antique Collectors' Club, 1999.

2-3/4" d, pocket, brass, pocket watch shaped case, mkd "Made in England," worn orig cardboard case with paper label "Henry J. Green, Brooklyn, NY, 1899" ............................. 275.00
5-1/2" h, Aneroid, Holosteric, brass, ring hanging mount, mkd "France, USLH Establishment" from New London Lighthouse ............... 295.00
6" h, desk, Gustave Keller, gilt bronze, barometer, thermometer, and clock, c1900 ........................................ 1,200.00
15-3/8" l, 5" w, 2-1/4" d, cistern, Currier & Simpson, pat'd Jan 31, 1860, glass front mahogany case, silver wash barometer and thermometer scales, old instruction sheet ........................................ 920.00
19" h, 17" w, 5-1/2" d, carved and ebonized walnut, rectangular with rounded corners, barometer with enamel plaques indicating weather conditions, matching clock with applied brass numbers, French, c1880, price for pr ........................................ 550.00
35-1/4" h, A. S. and J. A., West Rochester, NY, c1840, walnut, rippled molded cornice above glazed panel, framing engraved silvered dial showing temperature and barometric pressure, ripple molded box mirrored base, maker's label on back ........................................ 635.00
35-3/4" h, 3-1/2" w, 1-5/8" d, stick, Charles Wilder, Peterborough, NH, mahogany, patent date June 5, 1860, cockbeaded case with applied rosette and oval aperture with printed label ........................ 1,725.00
37" h, stick, William IV, rosewood, waited case, ivory scale with brass border, sgd "S. A. Callie, Newcastle," c1835 ......................... 1,750.00
37-1/2" h, 4-3/8" w, stick, Charles Wilder, Petterborough, NH, wood case, silver wash and black wax scales, case needs repair .... 635.00
38" h, banjo, James Kirby, St. Neotes, early 19th C, walnut, swan's neck cresting above thermometer and barometer, engraved silvered dials, shaped case ........................................ 425.00
38" h, wheel, S. Crocker, Kingston, mahogany, thermometer and hydrometer ........................................ 500.00
38-3/8" h, 8-1/2" d, banjo, broken pediment, temperature gauge flanked by paterae and "Sheraton shell" inlay, barometer with siphon tube mechanism, face sgd "Pozzi & Co.," further inlaid paterae, Regency, English, early 19th C ........................................ 1,610.00

39" h, wheel, late George III, Holbn, London, inlaid mahogany, inlaid shell dec ........................................ 850.00
40" h, W. Fraiser, Cleveland, Ohio, c1860, walnut, shaped and molded edge, white printed dial with thermometer to the left, continuing to vase and ring split baluster ending in applied turned boss at base ........................................ 575.00
40-1/2" h, stick, oak case, "Pinkam and Smith," molded case with white painted rect dial above throat thermometer, beveled glass, base with raised panel, molded bracket, England, 19th C .................... 1,200.00
42-1/2" h, wheel, late Georgian, F. Amadio & Son, London, satinwood, rosewood crossbanding, shrinkage ........................................ 2,070.00
44" h, split baluster, George III, D. Luvate, Preston, faded mahogany, hygrometer, thermometer, convex mirror, barometer, and level, late 18th C ........................................ 750.00
44-1/8" h, wheel, scroll pediment over hygrometer, thermometer and central siphon-run barometer, above level sgd "Ja. Basmett, Liverpool," first half 19th C ........................................ 1,380.00
50-1/2" h, banjo, V. Zanetti, Manchester, mahogany, 12" d silvered scale, mercury thermometer, hygrometer, spirit level, inscribed name ........................................ 2,600.00

# BASKETS

**History:** Baskets were invented when man first required containers to gather, store, and transport goods. Today's collectors, influenced by the country look, focus on baskets made of splint, rye straw, or willow. Emphasis is placed on handmade examples. Nails or staples, wide splints which are thin and evenly cut, or a wire bail handle denote factory construction which can date back to the mid-19th century. Decorated painted or woven baskets rarely are handmade, unless they are American Indian in origin. Baskets are collected by (a) type—berry, egg, or field, (b) region—Nantucket or Shaker, and (c) composition—splint, rye, or willow.

**Reference:** Don and Carol Raycraft, Collector's Guide to Country Baskets, Collector Books, 1985, 1994 value update.

**Museums:** Heard Museum, Phoenix, AZ; Old Salem, Inc., Winston-Salem, NC.

**Note:** Limit purchases to baskets in very good condition; damaged ones are a poor investment even at a low price.

Bread, 15" d, rye straw, PA, early 20th C, coil work, open handles ........................................ 120.00
Buttocks, woven splint, bent wood handle
    10-1/2" d, 7-1/2" h, America, late 19th C, minor wear ........ 290.00
    12-3/4" w, 12-1/2" h, half-buttocks style, twenty-eight ribs, minor breaks ........................................ 250.00
    13" x 15" x 9" h, twenty-six ribs, splint breaks .................... 110.00
Cheese
    17-3/4" d, 6-1/2" h, splint, round, six shaped wooden fixed handles, America, 19th C ........................................ 850.00
    21-1/4" d, 8-1/2" h, woven splint, round, pentagonal base, America, 19th C, minor breaks ........................................ 300.00
Cotton Picking, 18" d, woven splint, worn blue paint, leather shoulder strap ........................................ 400.00

## Reproduction Alert:

Modern reproductions abound, made by diverse groups ranging from craft revivalists to foreign manufacturers.

**Nantucket, with lid, $650.**

Covered, 9" l, 13-1/4" w, 7-3/4" h, rectangular, woven splint, paint dec on three sides, alternating black and natural horizontal splints, four-petal blossoms and berry sprigs alternating with vertical splints, cover dec with black dots, New England, 19th C, losses to splint cover and basket top edge, wear ................................................ 650.00
Feather, 34-1/2" h, woven splint, painted green, round baluster form, traces of white paint, America, 19th C, minor losses ............ 1,725.00
Field
    22" h, oak splint, oval, plaited weaving pattern, carved hickory handle ............................................................................................. 250.00
    25" d, 14" h, splint, carved notched handles, rounded body, sq base, America, late 19th C ............................................................. 350.00
Gathering
    11" l, 10" d, 7" h, plus bentwood handle, woven splint, finely woven .................................................................................................... 240.00
    14" d, splint, painted red and green dec, imperfection ........ 750.00
Indian
    16-1/4" d, 15-1/4" h, Apache, c1900, burden, twined weave, worn dyed design, wear and missing stitches, native leather repair .................................................................................................... 250.00
    17-1/2" l, 14-1/8" w, 9-3/4" h, woven splint, rect, carved handles, green and blue polychrome dec banding, 19th C, minor breaks ................................................................................................ 550.00
Key, 3-1/4" h, 10" l, 5" w, leather, tapering oval form, decorative tooling and stitching, imp mark "J. H. Laymeyer, Petersburg, VA" on bottom, 19th C, hand reinforced with glue ........................................... 1,400.00
Miniature, 4" l, 3-3/4" h, melon, sgd and dated in ink on handle "Louise 1908," very minor cracks and breaks ....................................... 265.00
Nantucket
    9" d, 8-1/4" h, woven cane and splint construction, round wooden bottom, wrapped rim, swivel bentwood handle, old printed paper label "Mrs. L. M. Foskett, Gardner, Mass. Given by Harriet Sawyer," good patina, minor break on rim .............................. 715.00
    9-1/2" l, 6-1/2" d, 5-3/4" h, oval, covered, bottom inscribed "W&J Sayle 1980," cherry plaque and base, ivory seagull sgd "C. F. Sayle" .................................................................................................... 575.00
    10-1/4" d, 9" h, round, turned wooden base, swing handle, early 20th C .................................................................................................. 2,070.00
Paint Decorated
    11-1/2" w, 12-1/4" d, 4-1/2" h, woven splint, orig darn green paint, sq design, tightly woven narrow splints, 19th C, few minor breaks and paint wear ....................................................................... 365.00
    13-1/2" d, 6" h, round woven splint, square base, floral painted splint bands in blue and red on yellow on rim and base, blue painted accent bands, 19th C, minor breaks ...................... 350.00
    13-3/4" d, 7-3/4" h, round woven splint, carved loop handles, sq base, yellow and brown painted dec bands, minor wear . 175.00
Picnic, 10-1/4" l, 16" h, twenty-two ribs, woven natural and colored splint, bentwood handle, double hinged cov ............................ 225.00
Rectangular, 12-3/4" w, 11-1/4" d, 6-1/4" h, tightly woven wide splint base, loosely woven narrow splints on top, breaks .................. 110.00
Stamped Decoration, cov, 5" d, 4" h, woven splint, blue and red geo-

metric potato stamp dec, sq base, round top, few breaks on lid ................................................................................................................ 935.00
Storage, 18" h, rye straw, swollen oval form, woven coils, attributed to PA, losses ........................................................................................ 320.00
Weaver's, 10-1/2" d, 18" h, woven splint, orange and blue watercolor designs, divided in., rounded corners ...................................... 250.00

# BATTERSEA ENAMELS

**History:** Battersea enamel is a generic term for English enamel-on-copper objects of the 18th century. In 1753, Stephen Theodore Janssen established a factory to produce "Trinkets and Curiosities Enamelled on Copper" at York House, Battersea, London. Here the new invention of transfer printing developed to a high degree of excellence, and the resulting trifles delighted fashionable Georgian society. Recent research has shown that enamels actually were being produced in London and the Midlands several years before York House was established. However, most enamel trinkets still are referred to as "Battersea Enamels," even though they were probably made in other workshops in London, Birmingham, Bilston, Wednesbury, or Liverpool. All manner of charming items were made, including snuff and patch boxes bearing mottos and memory gems. (By adding a mirror inside the lid, a snuff box became a patch box). Many figural whimsies, called "toys," were created to amuse a gay and fashionable world. Many other elaborate articles, e.g., candlesticks, salts, tea caddies, and bonbonnières, were made for the tables of the newly rich middle classes.

**Reference:** Susan Benjamin, English Enamel Boxes, Merrimack Publishers Circle, 1978.

Bonbonnier
    Otter's head, natural colors, floral slip on lid, c1770, Bilston ................................................................................................ 2,650.00
    Spaniel, King Charles, oval, black and white, yellow ground, pastoral scene lid, c1770, Bilston ...................................... 3,200.00
Box, 2" x 1-1/2" d, yellow, bird on nest, inside top fitted with mirror, minor cracking ................................................................................. 300.00
Candlestick, 10-1/2" h, white ground, landscape vignettes within pink ground, gilt scroll borders, c1770, Bilston ........................... 4,200.00
Cloak Hooks, 2" l, oval, rose festooned anchors, white ground, c1775, South Staffordshire ............................................................................ 650.00

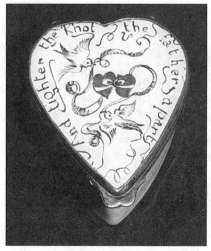

**Box, heart shaped, yellow base, white ground, black and red lettering "And tighten the knot the farther apart," doves and heart motif, $550.**

Patch Box
  "x 1-1/2" x 1", rect, light blue, concave sides, lid with grisaille dec of fishing scene, motto "No Toil is Pain When Love's the Gain," int. fitted with mirror, enamel damage and repair............500.00
  1-1/2" l, oval, "Always the Same," love birds on white lid, pink base, c1780, Bilston......................750.00
  2-1/4" l, oval, red checked gingham, green raised ivy, c1770, Bilston......................700.00
Scent Bottle Holder, 1/2" x 1-1/4" x 2-1/4", allover pink floral with trellis, leafy green, c1775, Bilston......................400.00
Snuff Box, 2-1/2" l, white, lovers in pastoral setting, ruin background, c1780, Bilston......................825.00

# BAVARIAN CHINA

**History:** Bavaria, Germany, was an important porcelain production center, similar to the Staffordshire district in England. The phrase "Bavarian China" refers to the products of companies operating in Bavaria, among which were Hutschenreuther, Thomas, and Zeh, Scherzer & Co. (Z. S. & Co.). Very little of the production from this area was imported into the United States prior to 1870.

Bowl, 10" d, 2 1/4" h, deeply scalloped and scrolled rim, brushed gold trim, large pink roses and buds, green leaves, castle mark and "RC Monbijou"......................35.00
Bread Plate, Isabelle pattern, set of seven......................35.00
Celery Tray, hp, multicolored parrots, white ground......................40.00
Chocolate Set, roses and floral bouquets, gold trim, cov chocolate pot, six cups and saucers, price for 13 pc set......................225.00
Coffee Set, 9 1/4" h cov coffeepot, creamer, cov sugar, scrolled and melon ribbed blank, multicolored floral dec, gold rim and trim, crown mark with "Bavaria, Creidlitz, Germany," price for 5 pc set......125.00
Compote, 8 1/4" d, openwork edge, fruit dec......................35.00
Demitasse Set, porcelain, white ground, polychrome birds transfer dec, gilt trim, teapot, creamer, sugar, five cups, six saucers, Schwarzenhammer, 20th C, price for 16 pc set......................45.00
Dinner Service, partial, Spring Flowers pattern, c1920-25, mkd "Thomas, Bavaria," service for six plus oval meat platter, two handled bowl, vegetable tureen, gravy boat with integral stand, price for 28 pc set......................100.00
Dish, 7 3/4" x 11 1/4", fluted and scalloped rim, two sections, center scrolled handle, medallions of Venus, Mars, Neptune, blue ground, gold tracery and trim, crown mark with "Royal Bavarian, Germany"......................75.00
Dresser Set, hand mirror and brush, hp portrait of lady, long flowing hair entwined with gold streamers and flowers, ornate handles, mkd "R.C. Bavaria," price for 2 pc set......................165.00

**Stein, cream ground, red currants and flowers, $60. Photo courtesy of Joy Luke Fine Art Brokers and Auctioneers.**

Dresser Tray, 11" l, white, scene of two women on balcony, rose border......................60.00
Fish Set, fish in underwater setting, different scene of each of ten plates and serving platter, mkd "Mignon, Bavaria," price for 11 pc set......................1,800.00
Marmalade Jar, cov, matching underplate, two handles, hp pink roses, cream ground, black and gold trim......................115.00
Oyster Plate, 9" w, crescent shape, shaded blue ground, five shell shaped depressions, one round shell......................115.00
Plaque, 12" d, hp, deer, gold border......................85.00
Plate
  7 3/4" d, Arbutus pattern, pink and green draped flowers border, gold trim......................12.00
  8 1/2" d, cat and roses......................35.00
  10 3/4" d, white center, wide gold encrusted rim band, delicate floral design, mkd "Bavaria," price for 12 pc set......................430.00
  11" d, encrusted gold surface with fairies, minor wear and scratches, sgd "Bavaria, Germany"......................50.00
  Portrait Plate, 10 1/2" d, Edwardian woman, crown mark and "Bayreuth"......................100.00
  Stein, red currants and flowers dec......................65.00
  Table Set, hp roses and gold trim, artist sgd, mkd "J & C," creamer, cov sugar, salt and pepper shakers, toothpick holder, price for 5 pc set......................150.00
  Toothpick Holder, pink flowers, green leaves, shaded ground, gold rim, mkd "Versailles/R C Bavaria"......................45.00
Vase
  9-1/4" h, 8" d, oval, two applied ring handles, four applied feet, poppies and daisies dec, sgd "Osborne," mkd "H & C Bavaria"......................400.00
  11-1/2" h, gold luster, floral dec, sgd "Sisters of Notre Dame"......................95.00

# BELLEEK

**History:** Belleek, a thin, ivory-colored, almost-iridescent porcelain, was first made in 1857 in county Fermanagh, Ireland. Production continued until World War I, was discontinued for a period of time, and then resumed. The Shamrock pattern is most familiar, but many patterns were made, including Limpet, Tridacna, and Grasses. There is an Irish saying: If a newly married couple receives a gift of Belleek, their marriage will be blessed with lasting happiness. Several American firms made a Belleek-type porcelain. The first was Ott and Brewer Co. of Trenton, New Jersey, in 1884, followed by Willets. Other firms producing this ware included The Ceramic Art Co. (1889), American Art China Works (1892), Columbian Art Co. (1893), and Lenox, Inc. (1904).

**Marks:** The European Belleek company used specific marks during given time periods, which makes it relatively easy to date a piece of Irish Belleek. Variations in mark color are important, as well as the symbols and words.

First mark......................Black Harp, Hound, and Castle 1863-1890
Second mark..Black Harp, Hound, and Castle and the words "Co. Fermanagh, Ireland" 1891-......................1826
Third mark......................Black "Deanta in Eirinn" added 1926-1946
Fourth mark.......Green same as third mark except for color 1946-1955
Fifth mark......................Green "R" inside a circle added 1955-1965
Sixth mark..............Green "Co. Fermanagh" omitted 1965-March 1980
Seventh mark......................Gold "Deanta in Eirinn" omitted ......................April 1980-December 1992
Eighth mark......Blue Blue version of the second mark with "R" inside a circle added January ......................1993-present

**References:** Susan and Al Bagdade, *Warman's English & Continental Pottery & Porcelain,* 3rd Edition, Krause Publications, 1998; Richard K. Degenhardt, *Belleek,* 2nd ed., Wallace-Homestead, 1993.

**Collectors' Club:** The Belleek Collectors' Society, 144 W. Britannia St., Taunton, MA 02780.

**Museum:** Museum of Ceramics at East Liverpool, East Liverpool, OH.

**Additional Listings:** Lenox.

## American

Bowl, 9-1/4" w, 4-1/2" h, ovoid, painted sprays of violets, ruffled gilded rim, two short gilded handles, mkd "Willets Manufacturing Co." ......... 200.00

Chalice, 12" h, hp, monk smoking cigar, Willets .......................... 690.00

Charger, 10-1/2" d, hp, gold and bronze enamel floral center, scalloped rim, Willets.................................................................... 190.00

Creamer, 4" h, pale pink ground, gold paste flowers, lavender palette mark, Ceramic Art Co................................................... 90.00

Cup and Saucer
    Bouquet pattern, Coxon ...................................................... 140.00
    Gold paste floral dec, wishbone handle, Ott & Brewer ....... 150.00

Demitasse Set, cov coffeepot, creamer, cov sugar, four ftd cups and saucers, hp, Harvard University tiger and crest, white ground, gold trim, c1899 .................................................................... 1,200.00

Egg Stand, ftd flat plate pierced with six holes, figural dolphin center handle, applied gold floral dec, sponged gold dec, Ott & Brewer ............................................................................ 125.00

Goblet, 6" h, Princeton University, Willets.................................... 75.00

Hatpin Holder, gold scrolling, green enameled dots on top and base, gold trim .............................................................................. 245.00

Lemonade Pitcher, 7" h, 8" d, scalloped top, gold trim, gold scroll handle, yellow, orange, green, and white water lilies dec, Willets..275.00

Mug, 6" h, dragon handle, Willets ................................................. 275.00

Mustache Cup, gold leaves, butterflies ...................................... 100.00

Stein, 7-1/4" h, hp, monk drinking from bottle, other bottles tucked in his apron, green palette mark ............................................. 165.00

Tray, 5" l, lotus leaf shape, hp currents and violets, sgd Willets, pr..............................................................................................160.00

Vase
    6" h, narrow neck tapers to bulbous body, lemon, tan, and light green Art Nouveau florals and swirling ribbons, artist sgd, palette mark .......................................................................... 375.00
    10-1/2" h, Roses of Morning, c1918-25 .............................. 200.00

**Willets, tea set, teapot, creamer, and cov sugar, white ground, gilded finials and handles, monogrammed "HGG," $160. Photo courtesy of Joy Luke Fine Art Brokers and Auctioneers.**

## Irish

Basket, Forget Me Not, #524, 2nd black mark........................... 200.00

Belleek Pot, #538, 2nd black mark .............................................. 300.00

Biscuit Jar, 8" h, Diamond Pattern, Victoria Tea Ware, 1st black mark ................................................................................... 1,200.00

Bust, 10" h, Sorrow, 2nd black mark.........................................2,850.00

Butter, cov, cottage, figural, 6th mark......................................... 160.00

Candelabrum, 14" l, 9" h, putti musicians about urn, scrolled base, painted and gilded, white ground, black mark ...................... 600.00

Compote, 9-3/4" d, 4-3/4" h, openwork edge, Green pattern, aqua trim, 2nd black mark .................................................................. 675.00

Cornucopia, 7" h, figural cherub holding cornucopia base, 1st black mark ................................................................................... 1,800.00

Creamer
    3" h, Irish pattern, ftd, yellow irid int. and handle, 3rd black mark ................................................................................. 65.00
    3" h, Lotus pattern, pink handle and trim, 2nd black mark.... 70.00
    3-1/2" h, Lily pattern, green handle and trim, 2nd black mark ................................................................................. 70.00
    4" h, Shamrock, green mark ............................................... 195.00

Creamer and Sugar
    Ivy pattern, 3rd black mark ................................................ 125.00
    Ribbon pattern, 1st green mark ............................................ 80.00
    Shamrock pattern, 3rd black mark ..................................... 150.00

Cup and Saucer
    Grass pattern, 1st black mark ............................................ 265.00
    Harp Shamrock pattern, 3rd black mark ........................... 120.00
    Shell pattern cob luster, 3rd black mark ............................. 85.00
    Dish, coral and shell, 6th mark ............................................ 35.00

Heart Basket
    4" x 4-1/2", #464, 3rd black mark...................................... 250.00
    5" x 5", #464, 3rd black mark............................................ 350.00
    Mustache Cup, Tridacna pattern, first black mark ............. 125.00

Plate
    8" d, Shell pattern, cob luster, 3rd black mark ..................... 85.00
    10-1/2" d, Basketweave pattern, 1st green mark................. 40.00

Spill Vase, Flower, #509, black mark ......................................... 150.00

Sugar, cov, Shamrock Basketweave pattern, 2nd black mark .... 140.00

Teapot, cov
    Limpet pattern, 3rd black mark .......................................... 285.00
    Neptune pattern, green trim, 2nd black mark .................... 325.00
    Trinket Tray, 4" d, scalloped edge, two chimney sweepers dec, c1910 .................................................................................. 45.00

Vase
    5-1/4" h, bud, Shamrock, green mark................................. 150.00
    7" h, 3-1/2" d, Vintage, 6th mark ........................................ 75.00
    8" h, owl, 6th mark ............................................................. 65.00
    10" h, Calla Lilies, baluster form, black mark...................... 250.00

# BELLS

**History:** Bells have been used for centuries for many different purposes. They have been traced as far back as 2697 B.C., though at that time they did not have any true tone. One of the oldest bells is the "crotal," a tiny sphere with small holes, a ball, and a stone or metal interior. This type now appears as sleigh bells. True bell making began when bronze, a mixture of tin and copper, was invented. Bells are now made out of many types of materials—almost as many materials as there are uses for them. Bells of the late 19th century show a high degree of workmanship and artistic style. Glass bells from this period are examples of the glassblower's talent and the glass manufacturer's product.

Ships Bell, bronze, emb "W. Taylor, Oxford, 1847," 11" d base, $700.

**Collectors' Clubs:** American Bell Association, Alter Rd, Box 386, Natrona Heights, PA 15065; American Bell Association International, Inc., 7210 Bellbrook Dr., San Antonio, TX 78227.

**Museum:** Bell Haven, Tarentum, PA.

Altar, 2-1/2" h, brass, emb angels and Latin script........................90.00
Cigar Counter, brass, cast iron base, marked "Russel & Erwin Mfg Co, New Britain, CT, USA, Pat'd Aug 1, 96, Rd No. 269895".........275.00
Church
    20" d, steeple, molded signature "Made by Meneely Bell Co. at Troy, N.Y., 1911," orig mounting bracket, wooden base...325.00
    27" h, triple, graduated stand, domed cross finial.................95.00
Commemorative, 6" h, metal, R.A.F. Victory, 1939-45, R. A. F. Benevolent Fund, emb head of Stalin, Churchill, and Franklin Roosevelt .......................................................120.00
Cut Glass, American Brilliant Period
    4-1/2" h, hollow handle and stem, cut and engraved flowers, sgd "Seneca".......................................................................150.00
    5" h, Corinthian pattern, faceted handle, Strass .................125.00
    5" h, notched and plain prisms, band of alternating diamond shaped stars, crosshatching and fans..............................125.00
    5-1/2" h, Ivy pattern, Sinclaire.............................................300.00
    5-1/2" h, Jewel, cut handle, orig clapper, Clark..................400.00
    5-1/2" h, strawberry diamond and fan, handle cut, Dorflinger........................................................................350.00
    6" h, hollow handle, cut and engraved floral, notched base and top, cork attached clapper ..............................................100.00
    6" h, Premier pattern, Bergen ...........................................400.00
    7" h, Colonial pattern, Dorflinger.......................................600.00
Desk
    Side tap, bronze, white marble base, c1875........................45.00
    Twister type, double chime, c1850 .....................................75.00
Elephant, 4" h, bronze, Khmer, 14th C.......................................175.00
Fire, 11 1/2" l, hand, metal, iron spring loaded clapper, turned wood handle ...................................................................................225.00
Hand
    Brass, figural
        Napoleon, raised Battle of Waterloo scene .....................75.00
        Victorian Lady, plumed hat .............................................70.00
    Bronze, figural, windmill, turning blades, emb stonework.....90.00
    French Faience type, figural, lady......................................125.00
    Glass, 5" h, Bohemian, pink ext. overlay, cream int., amber glass handle, rigaree, and clapper, applied pink and cream flower, green glass leaves ........................................................195.00
Pot Metal, police helmet shape, Queen Elizabeth II coronation ...38.00
Pottery, 5 1/4" h, Southern Belle, Ceramic Arts Studio.................75.00

Silver, 4 5/8" h, sterling, cupid blowing horn, figural handle, frosted finish, foliate strapwork border, Gorham Mfg Co, c1870 ..........725.00
Liberty Bell, 19-1/2" h, brass, black metal holding bracket .........400.00
School
    Desk type.............................................................................25.00
    Hand held, brass, No. 7, wood handle..................................45.00
Sleigh
    28 brass graduated bells from 1 1/8 to 3 3/4" d, 105" l leather strap .................................................................................300.00
    34 bells, leather strap ..........................................................75.00
    42 bells, straight throats, leather strap.................................70.00
Souvenir, 5 3/4" h, glass, 1893 World's Far, clear, circular logo surrounded by acid etched florals and banners, int. shoulder emb "1893 WORLD'S COLUMBIAN XPOSITION (sic)," frosted finish twisted handle with star at top, metal clapper, attributed to Libbey Glass ...............................................................................285.00
Temple Bell, 50" h, bronze, support molded with pair of dragons, shoulder with lotus petals, apron with eight tri grams, China, 18th C or earlier .............................................................................7,475.00
Trolley Car, brass.....................................................................150.00

# BENNINGTON and BENNINGTON-TYPE POTTERY

**History:** In 1845, Christopher Webber Fenton joined Julius Norton, his brother-in-law, in the manufacturing of stoneware pottery in Bennington, Vermont. Fenton sought to expand the company's products and glazes; Norton wanted to concentrate solely on stoneware. In 1847, Fenton broke away and established his own factory. Fenton introduced to America the famous Rockingham glaze, developed in England and named after the Marquis of Rockingham. In 1849, he patented a flint enamel glaze, "Fenton's Enamel," which added flecks, spots, or streaks of color (usually blues, greens, yellows, and oranges) to the brown Rockingham glaze. Forms included candlesticks, coachman bottles, cow creamers, poodles, sugar bowls, and toby pitchers.

J NORTON
BENNINGTON
VT.

Fenton produced the little-known scroddled ware, commonly called lava or agate ware. Scroddled ware is composed of differently colored clays which are mixed with cream-colored clay, molded, turned on a potter's wheel, coated with feldspar and flint, and fired. It was not produced in quantity as there was little demand for it. Fenton also introduced Parian ware to America. Parian was developed in England in 1842 and known as "Statuary ware." Parian is a translucent porcelain which has no glaze and resembles marble. Bennington made the blue and white variety in the form of vases, cologne bottles, and trinkets.

The hound-handled pitcher is probably the best-known Bennington piece. Hound-handled pitchers were made by about 30 different potteries in more than 55 variations. Rockingham glaze was used by more than 150 potteries in 11 states, mainly in the Midwest, between 1830 and 1900.

**Marks:** Five different marks were used, with many variations. Only about 20 percent of the pieces carried any mark; some forms were almost always marked, others never. Marks include:

- 1849 mark (4 variations) for flint enamel and Rockingham
- E. Fenton's Works, 1845-1847, on Parian and occasionally on scroddled ware
- U. S. Pottery Co., ribbon mark, 1852-1858, on Parian and blue and white porcelain
- U. S. Pottery Co., lozenge mark, 1852-1858, on Parian
- U. S. Pottery, oval mark, 1853-1858, mainly on scroddled ware.

**References:** Richard Carter Barret, How to Identify Bennington Pottery, Stephen Greene Press, 1964; William C. Ketchum, Jr., American Pottery and Porcelain, Avon Books, 1994.

**Museums:** Bennington Museum, Bennington, VT; East Liverpool Museum of Ceramics, East Liverpool, OH.

**Additional Listings:** Stoneware.Bennington Pottery

Book Flask, flint enamel, minor edge wear
    5-5/8" h, Departed Spirits.....................500.00
    5-3/4" h, Life of Kossuth, "J" mark, 1849-58 , Barret,
        plate 411.....................490.00
    6" h, Battle of Bennington, one corner chipped .................400.00
Bottle, 10" h, coachman, running brown glaze with hint of yellow, imp 1848 mark, "Lyman Fenton & Co. 1849, Bennington, Vt," chips and spider in base.....................385.00
Bowl, 11 7/8" d, flint enamel, imp 1849 mark.....................145.00
Bust, 5" h, parian, girl with bird on shoulder.....................75.00
Candlestick
    6 5/8" h, flint enamel glaze, Barret Plate 198.....................465.00
    6 7/8" h, flint enamel glaze, Barret Plate 198.....................715.00
    7 3/4" h, Rockingham glaze, Barret Plate 197.....................360.00
    8" h, Rockingham glaze with black flecks, Barret Plate 198.....................470.00
    8 3/8" h, mottled olive glaze, Barret Plate 196, lip has old professional repair.....................360.00
Coffeepot, 12 3/4" h, flint enamel, paneled sides, helmet shaped cov, pale cream underglaze, flowing tan, deep blue, and orange glaze, Barret Plate 136, professional restoration to tip of spout and edges.....1,980.00

**Bank, Uncle Sam, minor mold imperfection at hat rim in back, 4" h, $250. Photo courtesy of Vicki & Bruce Waasdrop.**

**Preserve Jar, 3 gallon, large compote of flowers dec, J. & E. Norton, c1855, minor glaze flaking at left lug handle, 13" d, $880. Photo courtesy of Vicki & Bruce Waasdrop.**

Crock
    7-1/4" h, stoneware, two handles, cobalt blue dec of house flanked by fencing, tree, label "J. & E. Norton, Bennington," 1850-61, minor chips, hairlines.....................2,760.00
    10-1/4" h, stoneware, two handles, two gallon, label "J. & E. Norton, Bennington," cobalt blue foliate devices, chips, cracks, staining, drilled base.....................200.00
Curtain Tiebacks, 4 1/2" h, 4 1/2" d, flint enamel, pale cream underglaze, flowing medium brown to dark brown, semi-flowing green, Barret, plate 200, price for pr.....................440.00
Cuspidor, 9" d, paneled, Rockingham glaze, imp "1849" mark... 110.00
Ewer, 7" h, parian, raised grapevine dec.....................195.00
Name Plate
    7 3/8" l, Rockingham glaze, one white letter "F," scrolling type shape, Barret Plate 203.....................250.00
    8 1/4" l, Rockingham glaze, rect shape, Barret Plate 203, chip on one end.....................250.00
Pie Plate, 8 1/4" d, imp 1849 mark.....................175.00
Pitcher
    8-1/8" h, flint enamel, Alternate Rib pattern, 1849 mark, Barret, plate 24.....................375.00
    10" h, flint enamel, lobed alternate rib form, 1849 mark on base, hairline, base chip, glaze wear.....................325.00
    12-1/2" h, flint enamel, tapering panel design, 1849 mark.. 425.00
Relish Dish, 10" l, Rockingham glaze.....................350.00
Teapot, cov, flint enamel glaze, Alternate Rib pattern, pierced pouring spout, period cov.....................420.00
Toby Bottle, 10-1/2" h, Rockingham glaze, 1847, imp mark on base, Barret, plate 419.....................460.00
Toothbrush Holder, cov, flint enamel, Alternate Rib pattern.....................500.00
Vase, 10" h, tulip shape, black olive flint enamel, Barret Plate 213, pinpoint flakes.....................910.00
Wash Bowl and Pitcher, 4-1/2" h, 13-1/2" d bowl, 12-1/2" h pitcher, flint enamel, Alternate Rib pattern, scrolled handle, emb scrolls on bowl, pale cream underglaze with yellow and brown bowl, additional blue on pitcher, imp "United States Pottery Company\Bennington, VT" on bowl, Barret Plate 169, minor glaze rubs on bowl.................4,200.00

## Bennington-Type

Candlesticks, pr, 9-1/4" h, Rockingham glaze, circular kiln separations.....................725.00
Frame, 8" x 7", oval, Rockingham glaze.....................325.00
Marbles, assorted sizes
    Blue glazed, 86 pcs.....................220.00
    Brown glazed, 88 pcs.....................200.00
Mixing Bowl, 9-1/2" d, 4-1/2" h, Rockingham glaze, small chip on foot rim.....................110.00
Pitcher, 9 1/4" h, hound handle, emb hunt scenes, base hairlines, wear and chip on table ring.....................330.00
Plate, 9 sq, emb design, Rockingham glaze.....................290.00
Soap Dish, round, Rockingham glaze.....................85.00
Spittoon, 11" d, 5" h, relief seashell border, Rockingham glaze, c1853-55.....................175.00

**Loetz, green glass body, unmarked lid and handle, 7-1/4" d, 5" h, $345. Photo courtesy of David Rago Auctions.**

# BISCUIT JARS

**History:** The biscuit or cracker jar was the forerunner of the cookie jar. Biscuit jars were made of various materials by leading glassworks and potteries of the late 19th and early 20th centuries.

4" h, jasper, three-color dip, green ground with yellow latticework alternating with white scrolled bands below zigzag border, silver plated rim, cover, and handle, imp Wedgewood mark, c1882, slight surface flake ................................................................................. 435.00

5-1/8" h, jasper, three-color dip, applied white classical relief on central green ground, wide lilac borders, silver plated rim, cover, and handle, imp Wedgwood mark, late 19th C, handle damaged ............... 425.00

5-1/4" h, 5-1/2" d, jasper, royal blue and white, cylindrical, white classical relief, silver plated rim, cover, and handle, imp Wedgwood mark, c1870-75, silver plate worn through to brass base .................. 330.00

5-1/2" h, 5" d, jasper, blue and white, cylindrical, white relief of riders and horses, silver plated rim, cover, and handle, Brownhills Pottery, Staffordshire, c1875-90, plating form to brass base metal....... 220.00

5-1/2" h, 5-1/2" d, jasper, royal blue and white, cylindrical, white relief of classical figures and children in landscape, silver plate rim, cover, and handle, Edwardian, c1900-10, silver plate worn through to brass base .................................................................................. 300.00

6" h, egg crate mold, white ground, blue floral dec, unmarked Wavecrest ............................................................................. 150.00

6-1/4" h, clear glass body, enameled floral dec, brass lid and bail ..................................................................................... 100.00

6-1/2" h, white ground, pink floral dec, gilt lid and bail handle, paper Wavecrest label ..................................................................... 450.00

6-3/4" h, 4" d, opalescent glass, watermelon striping, dark green ground, vertical white stripes opalescent stripes, SP lid and handle ................................................................................... 375.00

7" h, sq, floral design, Royal Bonn, SP top and handle ............. 145.00

7-1/2" h, Britannia Ware, cylindrical, white on blue, classical figure and tree dec, swing handle, ball feet, Wedgwood, late 19th or early 20th C ................................................................................... 225.00

7-1/2" h, 6" d, Opal Ware, Mount Washington, peach shading to pale yellow ground, purple and yellow pansies dec, base sgd "M.W.," and numbered #3926, lid mkd "M.W.4404" ................................ 650.00

8" h, cut glass, hobstar, strawberry diamond, and fan motif ....... 650.00

9-1/2" h, Carlton Ware, multicolored floral dec, cobalt blue trim, SP handle, Staffordshire ........................................................... 125.00

9-1/2" h, 5-1/2" d, shaded yellow to opal, morning glories dec, pewter lid and bail, sgd Wavecrest ................................................. 230.00

# BISQUE

**History:** Bisque or biscuit china is the name given to wares that have been fired once and have not been glazed. Bisque figurines and busts, which were popular during the Victorian era, were used on fireplace mantels, dining room buffets, and end tables. Manufacturing was centered in the United States and Europe. By the mid-20th century, Japan was the principal source of bisque items, especially character-related items.

**References:** Susan and Al Bagdade, *Warman's English & Continental Pottery & Porcelain,* 3rd Edition, Krause Publications, 1998; Elyse Karlin, *Children Figurines of Bisque and Chinawares,* Schiffer Publishing, 1990; Sharon Weintraub, *Naughties, Nudies and Bathing Beauties,* Hobby House Press, 1993.

Bathing Beauty
  4-1/2" l, unjointed body in lying position, hands coming up to face, left leg bent at knee, delicate painted pale blue eyes, single stroke brows, closed mouth, orig mohair hair with ribbon trimmed hat, painted calf-high stockings, molded and painted dark gray high heels, mkd "1740 2/0 B" on bottom of right leg ........................................................................... 400.00
  5" l, 3-3/4" h, unjointed bisque body in sitting position, playing banjo, finely painted pale blue eyes, single stroke brows, open-closed mouth, orig wig and turban, lavender high heel shoes molded on feet, black stamp mark "Bavaria," bottom incised "2739 B" .................................................................. 625.00
  Bottle, 4" h, figural, sailor boy, cork stopper, paper label, "Verbena" ....................................................................... 65.00
Bust
  11" h, 6 1/2" d, young man, blond hair, blue eyes, gray hat, colored flowers, tan vest with pink and blue, allover dainty pink florals on shirt, blue base, imp "M. B." ............................... 325.00
  16" h, young boy, after Houdon, cobalt blue base, French . 175.00
Cake Figures, bride and groom, traditional clothing, c1947, mounted on white base, floral garland overhead ................................. 150.00
Candleholder, 8" h, double, figural, girl leaning against bridge in woods, Germany, late 19th C .............................................. 50.00
Cigar Holder, 4 1/4" h, tree stump, bird chasing insect, Germany, 19th C ......................................................................................... 45.00
Doll
  4 3/4" h, Betty Boop-style, blond bobbed molded hair, large painted blue eyes to one side, one piece body and head, arms need re-stringing, Japan ...................................................... 45.00
  6-1/2" h, moveable arms, original clothes, mkd "Nippon," damage to clothes ..................................................................... 95.00
  Dresser Tray, green, white high relief cupids, floral border... 80.00
Figure
  3" h, Nun, white habit, gold rosary painted waist and trailing down left front, holding book open, singing, mkd "La Bomboniera Sicilia Catania Corso Sicilia 3," blue and gold foil label ..... 30.00
  3-1/2" h, bird, gray, crown on head ...................................... 15.00
  7-1/2" h, elegantly dressed couple, French, late 19th C, price for pr ..................................................................................... 230.00
  12-1/4" h, 3-3/4" d, French style blond couple, girl carrying tambourine, boy with horn, fancy pink hats and baskets, raised gold dot dec, German, price for pair ......................................... 325.00
  13" h, The Engagement, price for pair ................................. 400.00
  18" h, 18th C French maiden, green anchor mark, stamped "Exposition 1878 Medaille Do'or, Paris" ......................... 145.00
  18-1/2" h, Medieval courting couple, stamped "M.F. #122". 290.00
  27" h female, 27-3/8" h male, gardeners in 18th C dress, female with watering can, male with basket and spade, yellow and gilt dec, late 19th/early 20th C, price for pr ........................ 2,650.00
Half Doll, 5" h, 3" d, gray hair, band in hair, both hands and arms away from body, nude bust, marked "5275 Germany" ...................... 150.00
Lamp Base, 9-3/4" h, figural, candlestick type, shepherdess and shepherd, pr .......................................................................... 40.00
Match Holder, 8" h, figural, hunter with pipe, dog with bird in mouth, marked "Made in Germany," c1900 ....................................... 105.00

**Match Holder, seated baby and chamber pot with "Scratch my back," 4-3/4" h, $60.**

Nodder, 4-3/4" h, poodle and bulldog, oval base ......................... 165.00
Pen Wipe Doll, 2-1/2" h, blond hair, articulated arms, gray wool felt dress, red silk sash ...................................................................... 65.00
Piano Baby, 7-1/4" h, boy and girl, Heubach ................................ 75.00
Planter, figural, fox with boots, jacket, pipe and musket, Germany ............................................................................................. 110.00
Plaque
    11" h, 14" w, shepherdess with sheep on one, shepherd with pipe on other, pr .................................................................................... 450.00
    19" h, 16" w, multicolored foliate still life, molded in high relief, set of four plaques mounted in giltwood shadowbox frame, early 20th C ............................................................................................. 1,265.00
Sugar Shaker, egg shape, shaded ecru ground, Easter lily dec, Austria mark ................................................................................................... 40.00
Toothbrush Holder, Three Little Pigs, Walt Disney Productions, mkd "Made in Japan," c1930 ......................................................... 125.00
Toothpick Holder, 4 1/2" h, figural, dwarf, blue pants, green hat...30.00
Vase, 6 1/4" h, 3 1/2" d, figural, Indian Chief head, feather headdress, braids, blue crown and "NP" mark, c1900 ............................... 155.00

# BITTERS BOTTLES

**History:** Bitters, a "remedy" made from natural herbs and other mixtures with an alcohol base, often was viewed as the universal cure-all. The names given to various bitter mixtures were imaginative, though the bitters seldom cured what their makers claimed. The manufacturers of bitters needed a way to sell and advertise their products. They designed bottles in many shapes, sizes, and colors to attract the buyer. Many forms of advertising, including trade cards, billboards, signs, almanacs, and novelties, proclaimed the virtues of a specific bitter. During the Civil War a tax was levied on alcoholic beverages. Since bitters were identified as medicines, they were exempt from this tax. The alcoholic content was never mentioned. In 1907, when the Pure Foods Regulations went into effect, "an honest statement of content on every label" put most of the manufacturers out of business.

**References:** Ralph and Terry Kovel, *Kovels' Bottles Price List,* 11th ed., Three Rivers Press, 1999; John Odell, *Digger Odell's Official Antique Bottle and Glass Collector Magazine Price Guide Series,* Vol. 2, published by author (1910 Shawhan Rd, Morrow, OH 45152), 1995; Carlyn Ring, For Bitters Only, published by author 203 Kensington Rd, Hampton Falls, NH 03844), 1980; J. H. Thompson, *Bitters Bottles,* Century House, 1947; Richard Watson, *Bitters Bottles,* Thomas Nelson and Sons, 1965; Jeff Wichmann, *Antique Western Bitter Bottles,* Pacific Glass Books, 1999; —, *The Best of the West Antique Western Bitters Bottles,* Pacific Glass Books, 1999.

**Periodicals:** Antique Bottle and Glass Collector, P.O. Box 187, East Greenville, PA 18041; Bitters Report, P.O. Box 1253, Bunnell, FL 32110.

Alpine Herb Bitters, amber, sq, smooth base, tooled lip, 9-5/8" h ................................................................................. 175.00
Baker's Orange Grove Bitters, yellowish-amber, smooth base, applied mouth, 90-1/2" h ............................................................... 185.00
Bell's Cocktail Bitters, Jas. M. Bell & Co., New York, amber, applied ring, smooth base, 10-1/2" h .................................................. 450.00
Browns Celebrated Indian Herb Bitters/Patented Feb. 11, 1868, figural, emb, golden amber, ground lip, smooth base, 12-1/4" h.......... 350.00
Bourbon Whiskey Bitters, barrel shape, cherry puce, applied sq collar, smooth base, 9-3/4" h ................................................... 500.00
Caldwell's Herb Bitters/The Great Tonic, triangular, beveled and lattice work panels, yellowish-amber, applied tapered lip, iron pontil . 395.00
Clarke's Vegetable Sherry Wine Bitters, aqua, smooth base, applied mouth, 14" h ............................................................................ 575.00
Dr. Loew's Celebrated Stomach Bitters & Nerve Tonic, green, smooth base, tooled lip, 9-1/4" h .................................................. 150.00
Drake's Plantation Bitters, puce, Arabaseque design, tapered lip, smooth base, , 9-3/4" h .................................................... 295.00
Godfrey's Celebrated Cordial Bitters, NY, aqua, pontil, applied mouth, 10" h ................................................................................. 1,225.00
Greeley's Bourbon Bitters, barrel shape, smokey gray-brown, sq collared lip, smooth base, 9-1/4" h .......................................... 225.00
Hibernia Bitters, amber, sq, smooth base, tooled lip, 9-1/4" h .... 125.00
Hops & Malt Bitters, golden amber, tapered collar lip, smooth base, 9-1/8" h .............................................................................. 250.00
J. C.& Co, molded pineapple form, deep golden amber, blown molded, 19th C, 8-1/2" h ..................................................................... 460.00
Kelly's Old Cabin Bitters, cabin shape, amber, sloping collar lip, smooth base, 9" h ................................................................... 725.00
Keystone Bitters, barrel shape, golden amber, applied tapered collar, sq lip, smooth base, 9-3/4" h ............................................ 175.00
McKeever's Army Bitters, amber, sloping collared lip, smooth base, 10-5/8" h ........................................................................... 1,700.00
Mist of the Morning Sole Agents Barnett & Lumley, golden amber, sloping collar lip, smooth base, 9-3/4" h .................................... 300.00
National Bitters, corn cob shape, puce amber, applied ring lip, smooth base, 12-5/8" h ................................................................... 350.00
Red Jacket Bitters, Monheimer & Co, sq, amber, tooled lip, smooth base, 9-1/2" h .......................................................................... 100.00
Simon's Centennial Bitters, George Washington bust shape, aqua, applied mouth, smooth base, 9-1/8" h ................................. 650.00
Suffolk Bitters, Philbrook & Tucker, Boston, pig shape, amber, applied mouth, smooth base, 10-1/8" l ............................................ 600.00
Sunny Castle Stomach Bitters, Jos. Dudenhoefer, Milwaukee, sq, amber, tooled lip, smooth base, 9" h ...................................... 125.00

**Pottery, emb "Grenade Sauvient Malakoff Seine," 3-3/4" h, $30.**

Tippecanoe, Warner & Co, amber, applied mushroom lip, 9" h .... 95.00
Warner's Safe Bitters, amber, applied mouth, smooth base,
    8-1/2" h ................................................................................ 275.00
Zingan Bitters, amber, applied mouth, smooth base, 11-7/8" h .. 165.00

# BLACK MEMORABILIA

**History:** The term "Black memorabilia" refers to a broad range of collectibles that often overlap other collecting fields, e.g., toys and postcards. It also encompasses African artifacts, items created by slaves or related to the slavery era, modern Black cultural contributions to literature, art, etc., and material associated with the Civil Rights Movement and the Black experience throughout history. The earliest known examples of Black memorabilia include primitive African designs and tribal artifacts. Black Americana dates back to the arrival of African natives upon American shores.

The advent of the 1900s saw an incredible amount and variety of material depicting Blacks, most often in a derogatory and dehumanizing manner that clearly reflected the stereotypical attitude held toward the Black race during this period. The popularity of Black portrayals in this unflattering fashion flourished as the century wore on. As the growth of the Civil Rights Movement escalated and aroused public awareness to the Black plight, attitudes changed. Public outrage and pressure during the early 1950s eventually put a halt to these offensive stereotypes.

Black representations are still being produced in many forms, but no longer in the demoralizing designs of the past. These modern objects, while not as historically significant as earlier examples, will become the Black memorabilia of tomorrow.

**References:** Douglas Congdon-Martin, *Images in Black: 150 Years of Black Collectibles,* 2nd ed., Schiffer, 1999; Dee Hockenberry, *Enchanting Friends: Collectible Poohs, Raggedies, Golliwoggs & Roosevelt Bears,* Schiffer Publishing, 1995; Kyle Husfloen (ed.), *Black Americana Price Guide,* Antique Trader Books, 1997; Kevin Keating and Michael Kolleth, *The Negro Leagues Autograph Guide,* Tuff Stuff Books, 1999; Jan Lindenberger, *Black Memorabilia for the Kitchen: A Handbook and Price Guide,* 2nd ed., Schiffer, 1999; —, *More Black Memorabilia,* 2nd ed., Schiffer Publishing, 1999; J. L. Mashburn, *Black Postcard Price Guide*, 2nd ed., Colonial House, 1999; Dawn Reno, *Encyclopedia of Black Collectibles,* Wallace-Homestead/Krause, 1996; J. P. Thompson, *Collecting Black Memorabilia,* L-W Book Sales, 1996; Jean Williams Turner, *Collectible Aunt Jemima,* Schiffer Publishing, 1994.

## Reproduction Alert:

Reproductions are becoming an increasing problem, from advertising signs (Bull Durham tobacco) to mechanical banks (Jolly Nigger). If the object looks new to you, chances are that it is new.

**Periodical:** Blackin, 559 22nd Ave., Rock Island, IL 61201; Doll-E-Gram, P.O. Box 1212, Bellevue, WA 98009-1212; International Golliwogg Collectors Club, P.O. Box 612, Woodstock, NY 12498, http://www.teddy-bears.com/golliwog; Lookin Back at Black, 6087 Glen Harbor Dr., San Jose CA 95123.

**Collectors' Club:** Black Memorabilia Collector's Association, 2482 Devoe Ter, Bronx, NY 10468.

**Museums:** Great Plains Black Museum, Omaha, NE 68110; Museum of African American History, Detroit, MI.

Ashtray, boy with alligator, fishing pole ......................................... 50.00
Autograph
    Carver, George Washington, letter signed, 4 pages 4to, Tuskegee Institute letterhead, orig envelope addressed by Carver, Aug 4, 1931, to Ralph Douberly of Columbus, GA, young poet friend ......................................................................... 585.00
    Ellington, Duke, Edward Kennedy, first-day cover honoring Edward MacDowell, American composer, postmarked May 13, 1940 ............................................................................ 250.00
    Bill Hook, 7-1/2" h, 3" w, Deluth Flour adv, cardboard, flour sacks, black baker holding loaf, minor wear, some damage to hanging hole ............................................................................. 325.00
Book
    Blacks in the Marine Corps .................................................. 25.00
    Through Missouri on a Mule, Thomas Jackson, 1904 .......... 65.00
    Uncle Tom's Cabin, Harriet Beecher Stowe .......................... 20.00
Cabinet, 20" h, 12-1/8" w, 8-1/8" d, Mammys' Favorite Extract, wood and glass display case, orig wood shelves, orig label with black woman on box of "Mammys' Favorite Extract" ...................... 2,600.00
Carnival Mask, 14" h, figural, carved and painted wood, black man with hair wig, America, 19th C, minor losses, scattered paint loss .. 750.00
Coffee Tin, 6" h, 4-7/8" w, 3" d, Mity Good Coffee, cardboard litho, tin top and bottom, H & K brand, I lb, black waiter serving coffee. 240.00
Coin Operated Jazz Band, "The Five Pence Band," men playing piano, drum, horn, and bass, 5¢, 66" h, 44" w, 22" deep, minor chip to one band member ................................................................... 2,000.00
Cookie Jar
    Chef, National Silver ............................................................ 250.00

**Advertising Tray, Cottolene Shortening, made by N. K. Fairbank Co., 4-1/4" d, $75.**

Mammy, blue, Mosaic Tile .................................................. 425.00
Mammy, yellow, Mosaic Tile.............................................. 375.00
Mammy, National Silver ..................................................... 200.00
Dart Board, 14" h, 10-1/2" w, tin over cardboard, stereotype black boy as bull's eye................................................................... 225.00
Dexterity Puzzle, silvered tin rim holding glass over multicolored emb metal playing surface, German made, early 1900s
Black Man, caricature of man in gray top hat, white collar, red bow tie, blue shirt, green ground, slot to form teeth ............................. 65.00
Two Little Nigger Boys, youngsters in frolic play while seated in sudsy bath tub, caricature features .................................................... 300.00
Doll
    Beloved Melindy, Georgene, 18" h ..................................... 800.00
    Uncle Mose, cloth, uncut ..................................................... 225.00
Figure
    11" h, 3-1/2" d, bisque, African princess, blue tunic, red and gold belt, pink scarf draped over shoulders, multicolored striped turban with upright feathers, cornucopia of flowers in one hand, bird perched on other, white circular base with gold scrolls and trim, French, c1860 .............................................................. 525.00
    19" h, carved and painted wood, African colonial soldier, separately carved red-dyed fez with tassel, carved cylindrical head resting on flat body form with intricately carved uniform detail, applied carved wooden cartridge box and bayonet, aluminum buttons, shorts carved with side satchel, two tubular legs mounted in separately carved and attached bare feet, c1900 .............................................................................. 500.00
    64-3/4" h, painted and carved, standing Blackamoors, polychrome turbans, jackets, pantaloons, holding spears, mounted on maroon painted, octagonal wooden pedestals, giltwood trim, Venetian, 19th C, losses, price for pr .......................... 23,000.00
Hose Caddy, 35-1/2" h figural, boy wearing coveralls, striped shirt, straw hat, one arm extended to hold hose, orig polychrome paint, orig hose fittings, early 20th C, unused condition.......................................................................... 175.00
Humidor, cov, 7-1/2" h, Black Arab, purple striped turban .......... 225.00
Inkwell, Johnny Griffin ............................................................. 350.00
Lunch Box, tin, Dixie Kid, worn top ........................................... 450.00
Manuscript Document Signed, Bill of Sale
    1821, 1 pg, 8" x 10", Washington, DC, Sept 12, for four slaves, "...A Negro woman named Milley with her three children, Charity, Henry, and Annette...," sold by Brooke Williams to Margaret Dashiell for $400 ......................................................... 250.00
    1843, 2 pgs, small folio, Washington, DC, Nov 28, combined bill of sale and manumission for "...negro slave Catharine Murry, aged now about twenty one years...," sold by James Dodds to John Smith for term of five years after which she is to be "...entirely free from bondage or slavery..." ..................... 300.00
Match Holder, black Nubian ...................................................... 250.00
Match Safe
    Figural, 5" h, ceramic baby doll.......................................... 100.00
    Wall, De Handy Man, little boy holding pouch for matches, "Don't scratch your matches on de wall, scratch 'em on my overalls".......................................................................... 250.00
Original Art, framed
    16-1/2" h, 18" w, shows product from start as raw cotton ending up as finished box of Johnson Bandages, Mammy says "Yas-Suh Johnson Bandages are only 25¢".............................. 400.00
    22" h, 14" w, stereotype black boy in colorful clothing holding emb bottle of Rochette orange soda, heavily soiled ............... 400.00
    35" h, 9-1/2" w, four pc set, pin and ink sketches by Edwin Kemble, raccoon angry at black boy in coon skin cap, final scene raccoon wearing black boys' clothes, cartoon appeared in Feb 1913 Cosmopolitan Magazine............................. 300.00
Pancake Flour Sack, Aunt Jemima ............................................ 225.00
Paper Holder, Johnny Griffin .................................................... 100.00
Perfume Bottle, 2-1/2" h, Golliwog, orig box ............................. 450.00
Pillow Cover, framed
    21-1/2" sq, humorous wedding scene, elegantly dressed couple, friends and family tossing old shoes ................................. 225.00

**Pinback Button, "Score Against Hitler, Lift Ban on Negro Player," red baseball stitching, blue letters, white ground, 1-1/4" d, $500. Photo courtesy of Hake's Americana & Collectibles.**

    22" h, black scene of three city boys playing craps with shoe shine money............................................................................ 250.00
Pipe Rack, Johnny Griffin .......................................................... 350.00
Plate, 9" d, Famous and Dandy, white ground, multicolored center, 1930s .................................................................................... 115.00
Post Card
    Aunt Shug, "Who makes the pralines at Afton Village, Famous Ante Bellum House, St. Francisville, Louisiana," cook with pralines, black and white........................................................ 30.00
    Cranberry Scooper, Ocean Spray Cranberry Sauce and Cranberry Cocktail adv, smiling youth in field with scoop, Curt Teich, linen.................................................................................. 95.00
    Happy New Year, black caricature, published in England..... 35.00
    Hedspath, American Champion on his bicycle, L'Albatros, tires Le Persan, French, black rider.................................................. 60.00
    Negro Baptism, near Norfolk, VA, crowds of blacks gathered in boats and on shore, used, 1924, Norfolk ........................... 30.00
    Poor family, real photo of large family posed in front of shack home, "Greetings from the Sand Hills of North Carolina," photo by E. D. Putnam & Son, Atrim, NH.................................... 45.00
Poster, paper, framed
    22-1/2" h, 19-1/2" w, titled "5 cent limit," black poker game, humorous dialogue between Uncle Remus and Bruer Gumson, advertising Red Crow Cigars, artist sgd "Van," some restoration ....................................................................... 1,100.00
    23-1/2" h, 29-1/2" w, Lime Kiln Club Cigars, comical scene of black town meeting, © 1882, some overall scratching..... 750.00
    65-1/2" h, 46-1/2" w, paper, Bougie Oleo Huile Auto'D, black face with huge red lips, artist sgd "Raoul Vion"........................ 600.00
    79" h, 40-1/2" w, black banjo player, big red lips, oversized polka dot bow-tie, forty people in band and orchestra, multiple folds and overall creasing ....................................................... 400.00
    88" h, 39-1/2" w, three sheet, paper, Uncle Tom's Cabin, unusual black face with enlarged facial features, "Jes Yo come along an 'laff at Uncle Tom's Cabin," artist sgd "Robt Kemp" ...... 1,000.00
Print, 15-1/2" h, 19-1/2" w, log cabin scene of black family, father plays banjo, son struts, © 1898, framed, some staining in background .......................................................................... 150.00
Quilt, pieced cotton gauze, Sawtooth/Target pattern, red, blue, green, and white spiral design, trimmed in white border with white and red stripes, hand pieced, machine finished ................................. 1,600.00
Salt and Pepper Shakers, pr, Luzianne Mammy, F. F. Mold Works, Dayton, OH, 2-1/2" d, 5-1/2" h ............................................... 210.00
Sign
    5" h, 28" l, emb tin, Gold Dust Twins holding package of washing powder, titled "Let The Gold Dust Twins Do Your Work," Chas W. Shonk Co. litho................................................................ 550.00
    11-1/2" h, 7" w, diecut cardboard, scene of elderly black rural doctor helping constipated black child with his satchel of Ayers remedies, framed ................................................................. 175.00
    13-1/2" h, 19-1/2" w, curled corner tin sign, titled "The temptation of St. Anthony," black father uncorking bottle of Paul Jones Whiskey while Aunt Jemima looking mother holds watermelon, Meek Co. litho, some minor fading to sky and roof of house ...... 1,000.00
    14" h, 7-1/2" w, diecut cardboard, easel back, one of Gold Dust Twins, creased, some damage ....................................... 225.00

16" h, 6-1/2" w, two sided diecut cardboard, black man holding sign "Shut the Door," wearing hat advertising German Syrup and August Flower with cures Coughs, Consumption, Dyspepsia & Liver Ailments, framed ............................175.00

21-3/4" h, 31-1/2"n w, paper, Great Atlantic & Pacific Tea Co., titled "Ten Minutes for Refreshments," very busy coffee house scene, customers frantically finishing refreshments before they board train, black waiters serving coffee from great copper urns, framed .............................1,250.00

23-3/4" d, Green River Whiskey, tin litho charger, trademark black man and mule on front .......................700.00

39" h, 22" w, three piece diecut cardboard, Sealy All Cotton Beds, little black boy and girl carrying cotton representing twin beds, while father carries large basket of cotton representing Sealy full size cotton mattress, children are 39" h x 22" w, father 73" h, 29" w, some wear.........................1,000.00

47" l, 11-3/4" w, wood, folk type hand painted store sign, Olewine's General Store, Hazleton, PA, black man in chair smoking pipe ....................1,000.00

48" h, 12" w, set of five roadside signs, designed to be placed a mile apart, each different, one mile sign with Will Rogers type minstrel in black face, two mile marker with alligator bait scene, three mile marker with little boy being rammed by goat, four mile sign with little boy showing bagged possum, five mile marker with Aunt Jemima type woman, each read "Short's Cash and Carry, Use Your Sense And Save Your Dollars, Sutherland, Iowa," produced by Ithaca Sign Works ....................1,700.00

51" h, three-dimensional plaster, life size black boy wearing straw hat, straddling wooden crate while holding sign reading "Giletts Lye Eats Dirt," wooden crate lettered "Mammy Beverage"........................3,500.00

Slave Tax Badge, Charleston, SC, early 19th C
1-5/8" x 1-5/8", stamped "Charleston 12 Porter 1852," wear, cleaned, dents.........................1,725.00
2" x 2", stamped "Charleston 1812 No. 500 Servant," stamped on reverse "Lafar" in rectangle, wear, traces of glue on reverse...... 2,900.00
2" x 2", stamped "Charleston 1831 No. 218 Servant," wear, some surface cleaning, traces of glue on reverse, tag number may be a restrike ..........................1,725.00

Statue, 12" h, three-dimensional, chalk, black boys watching cock fight through split rail fence, ©1898, some paint chips.....500.00

String Holder
Chef, chalkware, flowers.........................350.00
Mammy, ceramic, flowers .........................275.00
Mammy, chalkware, flowers.........................350.00
Mammy, scissors in apron .........................350.00

Tin
2-1/2" w, 2-1/2" l, 3/4" h, Old Hickory Brand Typewriter Ribbon, southern plantation scene, black man resting under tree, other blacks picking cotton in field............550.00
2-3/4" h, 2" d, Fairbanks, Gold Dust Scouring Cleanser, mkd "Free Sample," dated 1931 ............................100.00
6-1/2" h, 5-1/2" d, 6-1/2" h, Niggerhair Smoking Tobacco, by Leiderdort Co., Milwaukee, same image both sides .............210.00
9-1/2" h, 8-1/2" d, Pickaninny Brand Peanuts, orig litho lid, F. M. Hoyt & Co., 10 lb size............................200.00

Tip Tray, 4-1/4" d, Cottolene, black woman and child picking cotton, titled "Best for Shortening, Best for Frying," some overall crazing.........................75.00

Tobacco Card, set of six
Sweet Lavender Tobacco, 9-1/4" x 10" cardboard card, comical story told scene by scene, titled "A Sure Thing on a Possum," hunting to last scene titled "Fo' De Lawd It's A Skunk," set of six cards matted and framed as 35" h x 25-1/2" ....................950.00

Toy, hand painted tin
Seated black figure holding musical drum in hand, feet attached to spoke wheels and pulley for drum, tube on back used as handle to pull toy, 8" l ....................660.00

Seated black figure in rocking chair, cloth suit, clockwork mechanism activates rocking motion, 6-1/2" h, 7" w................1,210.00

Tray, 12" d, Green River Whiskey, titled "She was bred in old Kentucky," black man holding nag with oversized jug of Green River Whiskey hanging from saddle, "The Whiskey without a headache," Chas. W. Shonk & Co. litho.......................200.00

# BLOWN THREE MOLD

**History:** The Jamestown colony in Virginia introduced glassmaking into America. The artisans used a "free-blown" method. Blowing molten glass into molds was not introduced into America until the early 1800s. Blown three-mold glass used a predesigned mold that consisted of two, three, or more hinged parts. The glassmaker placed a quantity of molten glass on the tip of a rod or tube, inserted it into the mold, blew air into the tube, waited until the glass cooled, and removed the finished product. The three-part mold is the most common and lends its name to this entire category. The impressed decorations on blown-mold glass usually are reversed, i.e., what is raised or convex on the outside will be concave on the inside. This is useful in identifying the blown form. By 1850, American-made glassware was relatively common. Increased demand led to large factories and the creation of a technology which eliminated the smaller companies.

**Reference:** George S. and Helen McKearin, *American Glass*, reprint, Crown Publishers, 1941, 1948.

**Collectors' Club:** Early American Pattern Glass Society, P.O. Box 266, Colesburg, IA 52035; National Early American Glass Club, P.O. Box 8489, Silver Spring, MD 20907.

**Museum:** Sandwich Glass Museum, Sandwich, MA.

Bird Cage Fountain, 5-1/4" h, colorless, ground mouth, pontil scar, McKearin GI-12 ....................50.00

Bowl, colorless
5" d, rounded sides, outward folded rim, rayed base, pontil scar ....................200.00
6" d, 1-3/4" h, outward folded rim, straight slanting sides, sixteen diamond base, pontil....................140.00
6-3/8" d, 5-3/4" h, folded rim, sixteen diamond base, ftd, pontil, tilts to one side, McKearin GII-18 ..................4,800.00

Carafe, 9-1/4" h, dark yellow amber, rayed base, deep pontil scar ....................2,400.00

Creamer, 3" h, colorless, applied handle, rigaree on end of handle ground, some residue under rigaree, McKearin GII-18............200.00

Cruet, 5-3/8" h, colorless, plain base, formed pouring lip, pontil, McKearin GII-28 ....................150.00

Cup Plate, 3-7/8" d, folded rim, rayed base, pontil scar, three McKearin labels, ex-collection George McKearin and TMR Culbertson, McKearin GII-1 ....................600.00

Decanter
6-3/4" h, colorless, orig stopper, minor stains, McKearin GI-15 ....................225.00
9-3/4" h, colorless, sunburst and diamond pattern, orig stopper ....................300.00
13-3/4" h, colorless, paneled neck, band of geometric motifs above hobnail body, quilted stopper..................350.00

Dish, colorless
5" d, outward rolled rim, pontil scar, McKearin GIII-21........130.00
6-3/8" d, folded rim, rayed base, iron ponti!.........................90.00

Flip Glass, colorless, 6" h, McKearin GII-18 ......................125.00

**Hat**
    2-1/8" h, colorless, fifteen diamond base, pontil, folded rim 275.00
    2-1/4" h, colorless, swirled rayed base, pontil, folded rim ... 125.00
**Inkwell**
    1-7/8" h, 2-3/4" d, amber, drum shape, faint ringed base, pontil
      scar .................. 125.00
    2" h, 2-5/8" d, olive green, McKearin GII-18 ............ 125.00
**Lamp**
    4" h, 3" d, peg, colorless, heavy applied solid pegs, period tin matching double burners, short factory ground neck, McKearin GII-18, pr .................. 1,450.00
    6-1/2" h, colorless, double paw pressed base, orig brass collar, mkd "BTM font/Mt Vernon Works," McKearin GI-30 ......... 800.00
**Mustard**, 5" h, colorless, clear sheared ball finial, flanged, folded lip, pontil, orig matching cov .................. 125.00
**Pan**, 1-1/2" h, 5" d, colorless, McKearin GI-6 ............ 185.00
**Pitcher, colorless**
    8-1/2" h, tool mark at lower part of applied handle ......... 250.00
    10-3/4" h, McKearin GV-17 .................. 420.00
**Plate**, 5-3/8" d, colorless, folded rim, plain base, pontil ...... 150.00
**Salt**, 2-3/8" h, colorless, pinpoint lip flakes, McKearin GII-21 ..... 165.00
**Salt Shaker, colorless**
    4-5/8" h, pontil base, orig metal cap .................. 75.00
    5" h, sheared lip, orig metal cap and pontil ............ 75.00
**Sugar**, 2-1/" h, 5" d, brilliant sapphire blue, rolled flanged lip, solid applied base with pontil attributed to Boston & Sandwich, c1820, McKearin GI-29 .................. 3,250.00
**Toddy Plate**, 4-1/4" d, colorless, folded rim, rayed base, pontil .. 265.00
**Toilet Water Bottle**, 6-3/4" h, violet, flared lip, smooth base, period tam-o-shanter stopper .................. 650.00
**Tumbler, colorless**
    3-1/4" h, McKearin GII-18 .................. 200.00
    5-1/2" h, McKearin GII-18 .................. 210.00
    5-5/8" h, McKearin GII-18 .................. 300.00
    5-3/4" h, McKearin GII-18 .................. 275.00
**Whiskey Taster**, colorless, 1-5/8" h, ringed base, pontil ......... 200.00

# BOEHM PORCELAINS

**History:** Edward Marshall Boehm was born on Aug. 21, 1913. Boehm's childhood was spent at the McConogh School, a rural Baltimore County, Maryland, school. He studied animal husbandry at the University of Maryland, serving as manager of Longacre Farms on the Eastern Shore of Maryland upon graduation. After serving in the air force during World War II, Boehm moved to Great Neck, Long Island, and worked as an assistant veterinarian. In 1949, Boehm opened a pottery studio in Trenton, New Jersey. His initial hard-paste porcelain sculptures consisted of Herefords, Percherons, and dogs. The first five to six years were a struggle, with several partnerships beginning and ending during the period. In the early 1950s, Boehm's art porcelain sculptures began appearing in major department stores. When Eisenhower presented a Boehm sculpture to Queen Elizabeth and Prince Philip during their visit to the United States in 1957, Boehm's career accelerated. Boehm contributed the ideas for the images and the techniques used to produce the sculptures. Thousands of prototype sculptures were made, with more than 400 put into production. The actual work was done by skilled artisans. Boehm died on Jan. 29, 1969. In the early 1970s, a second production site, called Boehm Studios, was opened in Malvern, England. The tradition begun by Boehm continues today. Many collectors specialize in Boehm porcelain birds or flowers. Like all of Boehm's sculptures, pieces in these series are highly detailed, signed, and numbered.

**Reference:** Reese Palley, *Porcelain Art of Edward Marshall Boehm,* Harrison House, 1988.

**Collectors' Club:** Boehm Porcelain Society, P.O. Box 5051, Trenton, NJ 08638.

**Birds**
    Baby Blue Jay, No. 436, 4-1/2 h .................. 170.00
    Baby Crested Flycatcher, #458, 5" h .................. 150.00
    Baby Robin, No. 437D, 3-1/2" h .................. 175.00
    Carolina Wren, mushrooms, Malvern Studio, England ....... 625.00
    Catbird, two hyacinths base .................. 1,320.00
    Chick, No. 412, yellow glaze, 3-1/2" h .................. 200.00
    Jenny wren, No. 201, Malvern Studio, England, 4" x 6" ..... 350.00
    Junco, No. 400-12, pyracantha base, 10-1/2" x 11-1/2" ..... 875.00
    Little Owl, No. 1002, Malvern Studio, England, 6" x 9" ....... 600.00
    Orchard Oriole, No. 400-11, tulip, 14" h .................. 570.00
    Ptarmagin Birds, #463, 18" h, price for pr .................. 950.00
    Ruffled Grouse, No. 456, 12" h .................. 1,350.00
    The Great Egret, #40221, limited edition #798/1029 ....... 2,200.00
    Warblers .................. 1,320.00
    White Throated Sparrow, #430, 9-1/2" h .................. 250.00
**Other**
    Daisies, #3002 .................. 800.00
    Magnolia Grandiflora, #300-12 .................. 1,600.00
    Orchid, pink .................. 460.00
    Panda Cub, No. 400-47, reclining on bamboo, 6-1/2" x 8" . 425.00
    Polo Player, a 1964 replica of a piece commissioned in 1957 by President Eisenhower for Queen Elizabeth .................. 1,210.00
    Rose on log, 6" l, yellow flower, English .................. 175.00

# BOHEMIAN GLASS

**History:** The once-independent country of Bohemia, now a part of the Czech Republic, produced a variety of fine glassware: etched, cut, overlay, and colored. Their glassware, which first appeared in America in the early 1820s, continues to be exported to the U.S. today. Bohemia is known for its "flashed" glass that was produced in the familiar ruby color, as well as in amber, green, blue, and black. Common patterns include Deer and Castle, Deer and Pine Tree, and Vintage. Most of the Bohemian glass encountered in today's market is from 1875 to 1900. Bohemian-type glass also was made in England, Switzerland, and Germany.

**References:** Dr. James D. Henderson, *Bohemian Decorated Porcelain,* Schiffer Publishing, 1999; Sylvia Petrova and Jean-Luc Olivie (eds.), *Bohemian Glass,* Abrams, 1990; Robert and Deborah Truitt, *Collectible Bohemian Glass, 1880-1940,* R & D Glass, 1995; —, *Collectible Bohemian Glass*, Volume II, 1915-1945, R & D Glass, 1998; —, *Mary Gregory Glassware,* 1880-1990, R & D Glass, 1992, 1998 value update.

Reproduction Alert.
**Beaker**
    4 1/2" h, blue and white overlay, arched panels with gilt ivy and stylized foliage on oval white overlay, flaring base, mid 19th C. 225.00
    5 1/4"h, white on amethyst overlay, quatrefoil and circular cut windows, painted trailing roses .................. 250.00

Bottle, 16" h
    Bulbous, slim neck, painted floral and gilt design, long, slender
        stopper ........................................................................... 115.00
    Cylindrical, gilt dec green body and stopper ...................... 90.00
Biscuit Jar, 6-1/2" d, 9 h, Brilliant Period style cut glass, cylindrical,
    Buzz and Hobstar dec, cover with one magnum
    buzz....................................................................................... 175.00
Cake Stand, 9-1/2" h, 14-1/2" d, white overlay, painted springs of foli-
    age, gilding, late 19th C, wear.................................................. 800.00
Candelabra Lusters, 21-3/8" h, green flashed and cut glass, three-light,
    molded clear glass sconces on clear glass candle arms, green
    flashed bobeches, hung with faceted prisms, cut and flashed slender
    baluster form stem with spreading foot, late 19th/early 20th C, price
    for pr .............................................................................. 1,840.00
Canister, cov, 9" h, ruby overlay, landscape scene, cut with
    foliage.................................................................................... 150.00
Center Bowl, 9" d, 11 1/2" h, ribbed and ruffled green irid glass bowl,
    elaborate metal base with three cherubs playing flutes ........... 520.00
Cream Pitcher and Sugar, panoramic rustic scene of peasants, vil-
    lages, castles, well-dressed couple, nobleman with walking stick,
    wandering troubadour, three hollow bun feet on cream pitcher, sugar
    bowl with pedestal and three hollow bun feet, Schwarzlot, Lobmeyer
    signature, price for pr ............................................................ 1,250.00
Cruet, amber cut to clear, carved floral arrangement intaglio, three oval
    panels with ruby flashing, carved floral swags, five cut to clear neck
    panels with gold scrollwork, sixteen dec cut panels on amber cut to
    clear stopper, gold edges, base sgd "4," stopper base sgd "4,"750.00
Decanter
    15 1/2" h, ruby cut to clear, geese dec, cut stopper............ 140.00
    15 3/4" h, ruby cut to clear, floral dec, orig stopper............. 120.00
Finger Bowl, 4-1/4" d, 3" h, heliotrope stained, vintage engraving,
    c1895-1910, price for set of six .................................................. 250.00
Garniture Vase, 29-1/2" h, white to cobalt overlay, gilt detailing,
    mounted as table lamps, ivory painted and parcel gilt trimmed wood
    base, price for pr ....................................................................... 550.00
Goblet
    5-1/4" h, cup shaped bowl, low spreading foot, white overlay cut
        to purple-edged clear glass, central hand painted roundel with
        courting couples, painted floral sprays, late 19th C,
        price for pr.......................................................................300.00
    6-3/8" h, enameled, ruby flashed ground, paneled octagonal
        body, floral and scrolled foliate design, gilt wear, pr.........690.00
Jar, cov, 5-1/4" d, frosted colorless base and top, cased to off-white,
    layered on enameled orange and black, etched leaves and bellflow-
    ers, cameo mark at side........................................................... 575.00
Mantel Lusters, 14" h, blown, cut, enameled, and parcel-gilt, ruby
    ground, dressed with alternating back-cut spears and ball-end
    prisms, c1885-95, price for pr ................................................. 225.00
Mug, 5-1/2" h, cobalt blue overlay, gilt dec, baluster shaped cut panels,
    early 20th C.............................................................................. 415.00
Oil and Vinegar, 7-3/4" h, 7-1/2" w, fish-form, clear molded glass, bright
    green tail stoppers, imported by Paul Straub, c1930 ............... 225.00
Refreshment Set, tapered cylindrical 9-5/8" h pitcher, eleven 4-1/2" h
    tumblers, applied ear shaped draw handle, amber flashed grounds,
    etched with scrolled cartouches, deer, castles, late 19th C, price for
    twelve pc set .......................................................................... 575.00
Rose Bowl, 6-1/2" d, 6-1/2" h, garnet cased overlay, Brilliant period
    rose cutting, c1900-10................................................................. 45.00
Salt, open, 2-3/4" h, 1-7/8" d, raised rim on squat form, colorless glass
    dec internally with concentric rings and arcs of millefiori canes, base
    facet-cut and centered by starburst, 19th C ........................... 550.00
Service Plate, 10-3/4" d, porcelain, burgundy ground border, gilt scrolls
    and foliage, 20th C, set of 15 ................................................... 865.00
Sherry, 4-3/8" h, cup-shaped bowl flashed with color, then star and
    cross cut, short stem with single faceted knop, star-cut flat foot, two
    green, two purple, two pink, two cranberry, two yellow, and one dark
    pink, fitted satin-lined case................................................... 1,380.00
Tumbler, 4 1/4" h, clear, leaded glass, pontil scar, enameled German
    inscription, florals, heart, two hands shaking, dated 1727 ....... 550.00

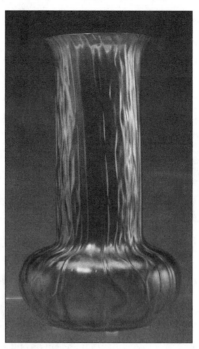

**Vase, Neptune, rubena verde, polished rim, 10-1/2" h, $230. Photo courtesy of David Rago Auctions.**

Vase
    3-7/8" h, mold blown form, flared rim, bulbous yellow-green glass
        body, light blue, white, tan, red, and black enamel dec of drag-
        onflies and frogs by pond, early 20th C, rim nicks ........... 115.00
    4-5/8" h, baluster, trefoil rim, white overlay cut to apple green, gilt
        details, price for pr............................................................ 400.00
    5" h, malachite glass, molded to form nude women under grape
        arbor, Schlevogt Ingrid series, mid 20th C ....................... 175.00
    5-1/2" h, satin, mother-of-pearl, brown shading to white, swirl
        body, airtraps on ribs, flared top, very pale green lining, attrib-
        uted to Harrah ............................................................. 1,250.00
    10" h, white overlay cut to cranberry, squat baluster form, slightly
        everted lip, spreading foot, gold enamel detailing, late 19th C,
        price for pr.................................................................... 645.00
    16" h, cranberry, medallion of princess, heavy gold enameling,
        crown shield in oval mark................................................. 700.00
Wine Glass
    8" h, flared bowl, colorless glass overlaid in deep red facet-cut to
        clear with diamond-form gilt and green highlights on paneled
        sides, facet-cut stem and disk foot................................... 120.00
    8" h, flared bowl, colorless glass overlaid in amethyst facet-cut to
        clear, dec with gilt trailing scrolls and dots, facet-cut stem and
        disk foot........................................................................ 120.00

# BOOKS, REFERENCE

**History:** The 1920s saw the first real concentration of books about antiques and collecting. Some of those early titles, such as Wallace Nutting's Furniture Treasury, are considered classics today. Well past the first half of the 20th century, the focus of those books was objects and their histories.

The first general-line price guide, Antiques and Their Current Prices, was a breakthrough idea when published by Edwin G. Warman in 1949. Not until the 1960s did authors of single-category books covering topics such as glassware begin including values along with informational content.

Largely ignored by collectors and dealers even just a few years ago, out-of-print antiques reference books are now recognized for the wealth of information they contain. Buyers are saving shelf space for early reference books, seeing them as perfect go-withs for their collections. As an example, many Depression glass collectors are no longer content with searching for their favorite patterns, wanting to add early glassware reference books that trace the history of and changes in the hobby. Two condition grades are used whenever a book has a dustjacket. The first grade is the book, the second is the dustjacket.

**References:** Allen Ahearn, *Book Collecting: A Comprehensive Guide,* G. P. Putnam's Sons, 1995; Allen and Patricia Ahearn, *Collected Books: The Guide to Values,* F. P. Putnam's Sons, 1997; *American Book Prices Current,* Bancroft Parkman, published annually; Geoffrey Ashall Glaister, *Encyclopedia of the Book,* 2nd ed., available from Spoon River Press, 1996; John R. Gretton, *Baedeker's Guidebooks: A Checklist of English-Language Editions 1861-1939,* available from Spoon River Press, 1994; Sharon and Bob Huxford, *Huxford's Old Book Value Guide,* 11th ed., Collector Books, 1999; Ian C. Ellis, *Book Finds,* Berkley Publishing, 1996; Norma Levarie, *Art & History of Books*, available from Spoon River Press, 1995; Catherine Porter, *Collecting Books,* available from Spoon River Press, 1995; Caroline Seebohm, Estelle Ellis, and Christopher Simon Sykes, *At Home with Books: How Book Lovers Live with and Care for Their Libraries,* available from Spoon River Press, 1996; Henry Toledano, *The Modern Library Price Guide 1917-1995,* available from Spoon River Press, 1995; John Wade, *Tomart's Price Guide to 20th Century Books,* Tomart Publications, 1994; Nancy Wright, *Books: Identification and Price Guide*, Avon Books, 1993; Edward N. Zempel and Linda A. Verkler (eds.), *Book Prices: Used and Rare 1996*, Spoon River Press, 1996; ——, *First Editions: A Guide to Identification*, 3rd ed., Spoon River Press, (2319C W Rohmann, Peoria, IL 61604) 1995.

**Periodicals:** *AB Bookman's Weekly,* P.O. Box AB, Clifton, NJ 07015; *Biblio Magazine,* 845 Wilamette St., P.O. Box 10603, Eugene, OR 97401; *Book Source Monthly,* 2007 Syosett Dr., P.O. Box 567, Cazenovia, NY 13035; *Firsts, The Book Collector's Magazine,* P.O. Box 65166, Tucson, AZ 85728, http://www.firsts.com; *Rare Book Bulletin,* P.O. Box 201, Peoria, IL 61650.

**Collectors' Club:** Antiquarian Booksellers Association of America, 20 West 44th St., 4th Floor, New York, NY 10036.

**Web Sites:** www.abebooks.com, www.bibliofind.com

**Advisor:** Don Johnson

**Note:** The Internet has greatly simplified the once-tedious search for many out-of-print titles. Tens of thousands of antiques reference books can be found at a number of multi-dealer Web sites, and want lists can be created for titles not immediately available.

## Ceramics

Barrett, Richard Carter, Bennington Pottery and Porcelain: A Guide to Identification, Crown Publishers, 1958, 1st ed, hardcover, dj, VG+/VG .................................... 50.00

Clement, Arthur & Bishop, Edith, The Pottery and Porcelain of New Jersey, 1688-1900, Newark Museum, 1947, 1st ed, softcover, 100 pgs, G/G ..................................... 125.00

Collard, Elizabeth, Nineteenth-Century Pottery and Porcelain in Canada, McGill University Press, 1967, 1st ed, hardcover, dj, 441 pgs, VG-/G+ ..................................... 35.00

Hayden, Arthur, Royal Copenhagen Porcelain: Its History and Development from the Eighteenth Century to the Present Day, T. Fisher Unwin, 1911, 1st ed, hardcover, 452 pgs .......... 375.00

Klamkin, Marian, White House China, Charles Scribner's Sons, 1972, 1st ed, hardcover, dj, 184 pgs, G/G ..................... 60.00

Liverani, Giusepgse, Five Centuries of Italian Majolica, McGraw-Hill, 1960, hardcover, missing dj, 258 pgs ..................... 195.00

Osgood,Cornelius, The Jug and Related Stoneware of Bennington, Charles E. Tuttle Co., 1971, 1st ed. ......................... 65.00

Pitkin, Alfred H., Early American Folk Pottery, Including the History of the Bennington Pottery, privately printed, 1918, limited to 260 copies, 152pgs plus 26 plates, G/G ...................... 425.00

De Ricci, Seymour, Catalog of Early Italian Majolica, Mortimer L. Schiff Collection, 1927, limited to 250 copies .................. 650.00

Webster, Donald, Decorated Stoneware and Pottery of North America, Charles Tuttle Co., 1972, hardcover, dj, slip case, 232 pgs, G .................................................. 125.00

Williams, G.C., The Book of Famille Rose, Methuen & Co., 1927, 1st ed, limited to 750 copies, hardcover, dj, 231 pgs plus 62 plates, G/G .............................................. 350.00

## Furniture

Cescinsky, Herbert, English Furniture from Gothic to Sheraton, Grand Rapids, 1929, 1st ed, hardcover, 438 pgs .............. 85.00

Cescinsky, Herbert & Hunter, George Leland, English and American Furniture, Garden City Publishing Co., 1929, 1st ed, hardcover, dj, 311 pgs, VG/VG- ........................... 45.00

Downs, Joseph, American Furniture: Queen Anne and Chipgsendale Periods in the Henry Francis Du Pont Winterthur Museum, Bonanza Books, copyright 1952, later reprint, hardcover, dj, VG/F ................................................. 48.00

Hackenbroch, Yvonne, English Furniture With Some Furniture of Other Countries in the Irwin Untermeyer Collection, Harvard University Press, 1958, hardcover, dj, 519 pgs ............... 475.00

Hinckley, F. Lewis, A Directory of Antique Furniture: The Authentic Classification of European & American Designs, for Professionals and Connoisseurs, Bonanza Books, 1953, 1st ed, hardcover, dj, NF/VG .......................................... 75.00

Jobe, Brock, Portsmouth Furniture: Masterworks from the New Hampshire Seacoast, University Press of New England, 1993, 1st ed, hardcover, dj, 454 pgs, G/G ............................. 300.00

Lyon, Irving W., The Colonial Furniture of New England: A Study of the Domestic Furniture in Use in the Seventeenth and Eighteenth Centuries, Houghton Mifflin and Co., 1924, 3rd ed, limited to 515 copies, hardcover, 285 pgs plus 113 plates ...200.00

Nutting, Wallace, Furniture Treasury (Mostly of American Origin), Old America Co., 1928, 1st ed, 2 Vol. .............................225.00

Nutting, Wallace, Furniture Treasury, Macmillan, 1948, hardcover, 2 vol, VG .........................................................................50.00

Otto, Celia Jackson, American Furniture of the Nineteenth Century, Castle Books, 1965, 1st ed, hardcover, dj, 229 pgs, G/G .................................................................................150.00

Shea, John, The American Shakers and Their Furniture, Van Nostrand & Reinhold, 1971, 4th printing, hardcover, dj, 208 pgs, VG .........................................................................95.00

Schiffer, Herbert F. and Peter B., Miniature Antique Furniture, Livingston, 1972, 1st ed, hardcover, dj, VG/G....................34.00

## Glassware

Archer, Douglas and Margaret, The Collector's Encyclopedia of Glass Candlesticks, Collector Books, 1983, hardcover, 176 pgs, · G .......................................................................................125.00

Felt, Tom & O'Grady, Bob, Heisey Candlesticks, Candelabra, and Lamps, Heisey Collectors of America, 1984, 1st ed, hardcover, dj, 436 pgs, VG/VG ...............................................127.50

Florence, Gene, Collector's Encyclopedia of Depression Glass, Collector Books, 1972, 1st ed, softcover, spiral-bound, 142 pgs, G+ ...................................................................................35.00

Garmon, Lee & Spencer, Dick, Glass Animals of the Depression Era, Collector Books, 1993, 1st printing, hardcover, 237 pgs, G .........................................................................................48.00

Klamkin, Marian, The Collector's Book of Bottles, Dodd, Mead & Co., 1971, 1st ed, hardcover, dj, 248 pgs, G/G..................30.00

Klamkin, Marian, Collector's Guide to Depression Glass, Hawthorn Books, 1973, 1st ed, hardcover, dj, 225 pgs, G+/G ..65.00

Wiener, Herbert & Lipkowitz, Freda, Rarities in American Cut Glass, Collectors House of Books, 1975, hardcover, dj, 294 pgs, G/G..................................................................................100.00

## Jewelry

Bradford, Ernle, Four Centuries of European Jewellery, Philosophical Library, 1953, 1st ed, hardcover, dj, 226 pgs, G/G .........................................................................................60.00

Gere, Charlotte, American and European Jewelry 1830-1914, Crown, 1975, hardcover, missing dj, VG............................62.50

Schofield, Anne & Kevin Fahy, Australian Jewellery, 19th and Early 20th Century, Antique Collectors' Club, 1991, hardcover, dj, 286 pgs, G/G .............................................................110.00

## Lighting

Grove, John R., Antique Brass Candlesticks 1450-1750, privately printed, 1967, 140 pgs, G/G............................................250.00

Willis, Geoffrey, Candlesticks, Clarkson Potter, 1974, 1st ed, VG/VG.................................................................................35.00

## Metalware

Culme, John, The Directory of Gold and Silversmiths: Jewelers & Allied Traders 1838 -1914, Antique Collectors' Club, 1987, 1st ed, 2 Vol, hardcover, dj, slipcase, G/G ............................300.00

Ebert, Katherine, Collecting American Pewter, Scribner, 1973, hardcover, dj, 160 pgs, G ...................................................45.00

Ensko, Stephen G.C., American Silversmiths and Their Marks, privately printed, 1927, 1st ed, limited to 310 copies, hardcover, 219 pgs, VG ...........................................................................300.00

Kerfoot, J. R., American Pewter, Crown, 1942, 2nd printing, hardcover, dj, 236 pgs, VG+/VG- .........................................25.00

Laughlin, Ledlie I., Pewter in America, Its Makers and Their Marks, Boston, 1940, 2 Vol, VG/G ...................................150.00

Laughlin, Ledlie Irwin, Pewter in America, Its Makers and Their Marks, Three Vol. in One, American Legacy, 1981, hardcover, dj, 276 pgs, VG/G ...........................................................100.00

*Pottery*, copyright 1929, containing illus of Roseville Pottery, no author or publisher given, $165. Photo courtesy of David Rago Auctions.

Powers, Beatrice F. & Floyd, Olive, Early American Decorated Tinware, Hastings House, 1957, hardcover, dj, 267 pgs.... 45.00

Schiffer, Herbert, Peter and Nancy, Antique Iron: Survey of American and English Forms, Fifteenth Through Nineteenth Centuries, Schiffer Publishing, 1979, hardcover, dj, 348 pgs, VG/G ......................................................................................60.00

Thomas, John Carl, American and British Pewter, Universe Books, 1972, 1st ed, softcover, G ......................................42.00

## Miscellaneous

Armstrong, Nancy, A Collector's History of Fans, Clarkson Potter, 1974, 1st ed, hardcover, dj, 208 pgs, G/G .......................85.00

Bolle, Bert, Barometers, Antique Collectors' Club, 1984, hardcover, dj, reprint, VG/VG ...................................................27.50

Crandell, Bernard W., Mason Decoys, Hillscrest Publications, 1974, 1st ed, hardcover, dj, 166 pgs, G/F ......................50.00

Flayderman, E. Norman, Scrimshaw and Scrimshanders: Whales and Whalemen, N. Flayderman & Co., 1972, 2nd printing, hardcover, dj, VG/G ............................................................300.00

Frost, T.W., The Price Guide to Old Sheffield Plate, Antique Collectors' Club, 1971, 1st ed, hardcover, dj, 396 pgs, NF/NF 50.00

Haertig, Evelyn, Antique Combs and Purses, Gallery Graphics Press, 1983, hardcover, dj, 304 pgs, VG+/VG+ .................70.00

Harris, Ian, The Price Guide to Victorian Silver, Antique Collectors Club, 1971, loose 1973 updated price guide, hardcover, dj, 276 pgs, VG/VG ..................................................................40.00

Haweis, H.R., Old Violins, no date, hardcover.....................45.00

Hinckley, F. Lewis, Queen Anne & Georgian Looking Glasses, Old English and Early American, Washington Mews, 1987, hardcover, dj, 254 pgs, EXC .............................................37.50

Jokelson, Paul, Antique French Paperweights and Related Objects, Colyer-Roux Printing Co., no date, limited to 2,000 copies, hardcover, 253 pgs ............................................150.00

Kauffman, Henry J., Early American Gunsmiths 1650-1850, Stackpole Co., 1952, 1st ed, hardcover, missing dj, 94 pgs, G .........................................................................................40.00

Meyer, John D., A Handbook of Old Mechanical Penny Banks, Aurora Art Publishers, 1952, 2nd ed, hardcover, dj, 119 pgs, G/G.........................................................................................75.00

Miller, Andrew Hayes, Survey of American Clocks: Calendar Clocks, Antiquitat Pub., 1976, 3rd, F/VG- ..........................75.00

Morton, Robert, Southern Antiques & Folk Art, Oxmoor House, 1976, hardcover, dj, VG/NF..................................................20.00

Powell, Robert Blake, Antique Shaving Mugs of the United States, self-published, ltd 1st ed, 1972, hardcover, dj, signed, VG/G- ...................................................................................200.00

**Lyre shape, cast iron, 10-1/4" l, $65.**

Rapaport, Benjamin, A Complete Guide to Collecting Antique Pipes, Schiffer Publishing, 1979, hardcover, dj, NF/VG ... 250.00
Tallis, David, Music Boxes, Stein & Day, 1971, 1st printing, hardcover, dj, VG .................................................................................... 60.00
Tarassuk, L., Antique European and American Firearms at the Hermitage Museum, Iskusstvo Publishing House, 1972, 1st ed, hardcover, dj, 224 pgs .......................................................... 60.00
Thomas, Denis, Price Guide to English Watercolours 1750-1900, Antique Collectors' Club, 1971, hardcover, dj, 340 pgs, with 1975 update booklet, VG/VG ............................................. 45.00

# BOOTJACKS

**History:** Bootjacks are metal or wooden devices that facilitate the removal of boots. Bootjacks are used by placing the heel of the boot in the U-shaped opening, putting the other foot on the back of the bootjack, and pulling the boot off the front foot.

Advertising, Mussleman's Plug Tobacco, cast iron ..................... 125.00
Bronze, 9 1/2" l, Naughty Nellie .................................................. 175.00
Cast Iron
    9 1/4" l, beetle, worn black paint .......................................... 40.00
    10 1/2" l, cricket, labeled "Boot Jack, the Tri State Foundry Co, Cincinnati, Ohio," worn black paint ..................................... 40.00
    13" l, open heart and circle, scalloped sides ....................... 220.00
    19" l, two pheasants, brushes .............................................. 225.00
Wood
    11" l, folding ......................................................................... 40.00
    17" l, pine, primitive, hole for hanging .................................. 40.00
    22" l, walnut, hearts and diamonds openwork ..................... 50.00

# BOTTLES, GENERAL

**History:** Cosmetic bottles held special creams, oils, and cosmetics designed to enhance the beauty of the user. Some also claimed, especially on their colorful labels, to cure or provide relief from common ailments. A number of household items, e.g., cleaning fluids and polishes, required glass storage containers. Many are collected for their fine lithographed labels. Mineral water bottles contained water from a natural spring. Spring water was favored by health-conscious people between the 1850s and 1900s. Nursing bottles, used to feed the young and sickly, were a great help to the housewife because of their graduated measure markings, replaceable nipples, and the ease with which they could be cleaned, sterilized, and reused.

**References:** Hugh Cleveland, *Bottle Pricing Guide*, 3rd ed., Collector Books, 1999 value update; Kyle Husfloen, *Antique Trader's American Pressed Glass & Bottles Price Guide*, 2nd ed., Krause Publications, 2000; Ralph & Terry Kovel, *Kovels' Bottles Price List*, 11th ed., Three Rivers Press, 1999; Peck and Audie Markota, *Western Blob Top Soda and Mineral Bottles,* 2nd ed., published by authors, 1994; John Odell, *Digger Odell's Official Antique Bottle and Glass Collector Magazine Price Guide Series,* Vols. 1 through 8, published by author (1910 Shawhan Rd, Morrow, OH 45152), 1995; Diane Ostrander, *Guide to American Nursing Bottles,* 1984, revised ed. by American Collectors of Infant Feeders, 1992; Michael Polak, *Bottles*, 2nd ed., Avon Books, 1997; Dick Roller (comp.), *Indiana Glass Factories Notes,* Acorn Press, 1994; Jeff Wichmann, *Antique Western Bitter Bottles*, Pacific Glass Books, 1999; —, *The Best of the West Antique Western Bitters Bottles*, Pacific Glass Books, 1999.

**Periodicals:** *Antique Bottle and Glass Collector*, P.O. Box 187, East Greenville, PA 18041; *Canadian Bottle and Stoneware Collector,* 179D Woodridge Crescent, Nepean, Ontario K2B 7T2 Canada.

**Collectors' Clubs:** American Collectors of Infant Feeders, 5161 W. 59th St., Indianapolis, IN 46254; Antique Bottle Club of Northern Illinois, P.O. Box 571, Lake Geneva, WI 53147; Baltimore Antique Bottle Club, P.O. Box 36031, Townson, MD 21296-6061; Empire State Bottle Collectors Association, 22 Paris Rd., New Hartford, NY 13413; Federation of Historical Bottle Collectors, Inc.; 88 Sweetbriar Branch, Longwood, FL 32750; First Chicago Bottle Club, P.O. Box A3382, Chicago, IL 60690; Forks of the Delaware Bottle Collectors Association, P.O. Box 693, Easton, PA 18042; Historical Bottle Diggers of Virginia, 1176 S. Dogwood Dr., Harrisonburg, VA 22801; Las Vegas Antique Bottle & Collectibles Club, 3901 E Stewart #16, Las Vegas, NV 89110-3152; Midwest Antique Fruit Jar & Bottle Club, P.O. Box 38, Flat Rock, IN 47234; New England Antique Bottle Club, 120 Commonwealth Rd, Lynn, MA 01904; North Jersey Antique Bottle Collectors Association, 117 Lincoln Place, Waldwick, NJ 07463-2114; Pennsylvania Bottle Collector's Association, 251 Eastland Ave., York, PA 17402-1105; San Bernardino County Historical Bottle and Collectible Club, P.O. Box 6759, San Bernardino, CA 92412; Southeastern Antique Bottle Club, 143 Scatterfoot Dr., Peachtree City, GA 30269-1853.

**Museums:** Hawaii Bottle Museum, Honolulu, HI; National Bottle Museum, Ballston Spa, NY, http://www.crisny.org/not-for-profit/nbm; Old Bottle Museum, Salem, NJ.

**Additional Listings:** Barber Bottles; Bitter Bottles; Figural Bottles; Ink Bottles; Medicine Bottles; Poison Bottles; Sarsaparilla Bottles; Snuff Bottles. Also see the bottle categories in Warman's Americana & Collectibles for more examples.

## Baby and Nursing

Acme, clear, lay-down, emb ................................................. 65.00
Baby's Delight ...................................................................... 45.00
Binky's Nip Cap .................................................................. 210.00
Bunny, Hazel Atlas ............................................................. 15.50
Cala Nurser, oval, clear, emb, ring on neck, 7-1/8" h ............. 8.00
Cat, Anchor Hocking ........................................................... 25.00
Cats and Kittens, enamel dec with oz measurements ......... 21.50
Comfy, bottle with orig nipple ........................................... 15.00
Dominion Glass Co, Canada, 8 oz, narrow mouth, orig filled with Vanilla Extract from Pure Standard Products, orig label, nursery rhyme, "I had a little hobby horse," imp image of little boy riding rocking horse, 1940s ........................................... 15.00
Empire Nursing Bottle, bent neck, 6-1/2" h ......................... 50.00
Evenflo, 4 oz, black plastic ring, flat cap, rubber nipple orig cardboard sleeve, paper adv flyer, date 1956 on sleeve ........... 12.00
Fire King, sapphire blue 8 oz ............................................. 60.00
Griptight, banana shape, hole at both ends, colorless, emb name ................................................................................. 25.00
Hailwoods Graduated Feeding Bottle, aqua, applied top, flattened bladder shape, 2" neck, markings up to 8 oz on back, front emb with name, 7" h ................................................................ 75.00
Happy Baby .......................................................................... 10.00
Hygeia, adv on panels ........................................................ 15.00
Hygienic Feeder, emb, open on both ends ......................... 30.00
Manx Feeding Bottle, bulbous, clear, tooled sq collar, emb "Patent July 4, 1876," 3" h ............................................... 200.00
Marguerite Feeding Bottle, inside screw, daisy on top ......... 35.00
Mother's Comfort, clear, turtle type .................................. 25.00
Nonpareil Nurser, aqua, 5-1/2" h ....................................... 20.00
Nursery Rhyme, enameled Jack and Jill ............................. 15.00
Ovale Nurser, Non-Rolling, Whitall Tatum & Co, 6 oz, applied lip, narrow mouth .................................................................... 10.00
Pottstown, PA, dairy giveaway, set of five bottles, each enameled with nursery rhyme, one with bank top, other with plastic closure, nipple, yellow and blue congratulations box, never used ................................................................................... 25.00
Steri-Seal Nipple Cover, colorless, emb on cover ............... 25.00

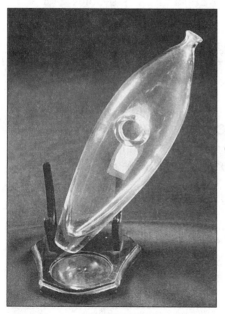

**Nursing, blown, early, 8-3/4" l, $270.**

Pyrex
4 oz, narrow mouth, orig cardboard sleeve ................... 12.00
8 oz, air vent feature, six-sided, narrow top, pink and blue graphics, orig box ......................................................... 20.00
Sure Feed Ltd Carfidd, flat turtle shape, long neck, colorless, emb on top ............................................................................. 40.00
Sweet Babee Nurser, colorless, emb "Easy Clean, Pat'd May 3, 1910" .............................................................................. 15.00
Teddy's Pet, Peaceful Nights, colorless, emb, turtle shape, 4 oz ................................................................................. 70.00
The Hygienic Feeder, banana shape, hole at both ends, colorless, emb name .............................................................. 25.00
Tuffy Kap, nipple cov, colorless, emb "Tuffy KAP U.S.A." around cap, "B" in circle on flat top ............................................ 10.00

## Beverage

Drink Howel's Original Orange-Julep, 12" h, cylindrical, colorless, white, gold, red, and yellow orange label under glass, sheared mouth, metal cap, smooth base, America, 1880-90 ......... 125.00
Frontier Lemon Extract, hunting scene on paper label, 5-1/2" h .......................................................................... 35.00
Gin, olive amber, flared rim, taper body, America, early 19th C, 13-1/2" h ........................................................................ 320.00
Grapette, 1946 .................................................................... 10.00
J. M. Roseberry & Co, Alexandria, VA, eagle wreath and shield, soda water, attributed to Baltimore Glass Works, Baltimore, MD, 1845-60, squat cylindrical form, yellowish green, applied sloping collared mouth, iron pontil mark, half pint, overall ext. wear, 3/8" flat chip ............................................................................ 800.00
Port Wine, brown glass, backbar type, emb, oval reverse painted label, 12" h ....................................................................... 155.00
Port Wine, green glass, backbar type, colorful applied reverse painted label, cork stopper, metal top chained to bottle, 13" h, minor chipping on edges of label ..................................... 125.00
Steinke & Kornahrens/Soda Water/Return This Bottle/Charleston SC, America, 1845-60, octagonal, cobalt blue, applied sloping collared mouth, iron pontil mark, oversize half pint, 7-3/4" h, professionally cleaned to orig luster, some remaining scratches ........................................................................ 650.00

## Cosmetic

Boswell & Warner's Colorific, rect, cobalt blue, indented panels, tooled sq lip, c1880, 5-1/2" h ........................................... 85.00
Edwards Harlene Astol Hair Colour Restorer, three sunken panels, cobalt blue, 7" h .................................................... 55.00
Ferd. Muhlens Inc., New York No. 4711 Bath Salts, orig label ................................................................................. 20.00
Harrisons Hair Colour Restorer, Amber, Reading, sunken panel, emb on front, 6" h ........................................................... 18.00
Hind's Honey and Almond Cream, 5-1/2" h ........................ 7.50
Hyacinthia Toilet hair Dressing, rect, aqua, crude applied lip, open pontil, 6" h ....................................................................... 25.00
Lavender Salts, cylinder, recessed reverse painted label, raised bottom with same pattern as ribbed stop, ground stopper, 6-3/4" h ........................................................................... 100.00
Mrs. S. A. Allens World's Hair Restorer, amber, rect, three sunken panels, emb name and "London" on base, 7 h ................. 30.00
Oriental Lotion The Persian Secret Beautifier, blue, emb, paper label, lady admiring her image in mirror, back emb "Elysian Mfg'g Co. Chemists & Perfumers," unopened, 7" h ........... 95.00
Prichard & Constance, London & New York, Tonic Bath Crystals, orig label ......................................................................... 20.00
The Mexican Hair Renewer, rounded shoulder, rect emb on edges, cobalt blue, 7" h .................................................. 35.00

## Household

Ammonia, Parson's, aqua, 1882 ........................................ 20.00
Blueing, Jennings, aqua, blob top, 7" h ............................... 8.00
Cleaning, Lysol, amber, Lysol Boots All British around shoulder, jug, 6-1/2" h ................................................................... 20.00

DeLaval Oil, orig box, 1-1/2" w, 3-1/2" h .............................. 190.00
Furniture Polish
Alma Polish, aqua, name emb on shoulder, mkd "M & Go" on
   base, 5" h ..................................................................... 8.00
Gordon's Chafola Furniture Polish, emb, open pontil ......... 150.00
Osborn's Liquid Polish, cylindrical, yellow olive, inward rolled
   mouth, tubular pontil scar, American, 1840-60, 3-5/8" h .. 475.00
Oil, Standard Oil Co, colorless, orig label, 6" h ...................... 7.50

## Mineral or Spring Water

Artesian Water, round, golden chocolate amber, twelve panled
   base, iron pontil, 1850-60, pint ......................................... 450.00
B. R. Lippincott & Co, Stockton Superior, Mineral Water, Union
   Glass Works, 1852-58, cobalt blue, applied top, iron pontil,
   7-3/8" h ............................................................................. 450.00
Buffalo Mineral Water Springs Natures, Materia Medica Trade
   Mark, yellow, lady sitting on stool, 10-1/2" h ................... 125.00
Chase & Co Mineral Water, San Francisco, CA, green, applied
   top, iron pontil, 7-3/8" h ..................................................... 60.00
Clarke & Co, New York, America, 1840-60, cylindrical, olive
   amber, applied sloping collared mouth with ring pontil scar,
   quart .................................................................................. 170.00
D. A. Knowlton, Saratoga, NY, America, 1960-80, high shoul-
   dered cylinder, olive green, applied sloping collared mouth with
   ring, smooth base, quart ..................................................... 100.00
G. W. Weston & Co., Saratoga, NY, America, 1840-60, cylindrical,
   yellow olive, applied sloping collared mouth with ring, pontil
   scar, pint, 1" vertical body crack on reverse ..................... 375.00
Lancaster Glass Works, round, sapphire blue, applied blob top,
   iron pontil, 1850-60, 7" h ................................................... 120.00
Lynch & Clarke, New York, America, 1840-60, cylindrical, yellow-
   ish olive, applied sloping collared mouth with ring, pontil scar,
   pint .................................................................................... 275.00
Lynde & Putnam, Mineral Waters, San Francisco Cala, Union
   Glass Works, Philada, teal blue, applied top, iron pontil,
   7-1/2" h ............................................................................. 100.00
M. T. Crawford/Springfield-Superior Mineral Water, Union Glass
   Works, Philadelphia, PA, 1845-60, squat cylindrical form, mug
   base, cobalt blue, heavy applied collared mouth, iron pontil
   mark, half pint, some int. stain, 1/2" bruise on top of
   mouth ................................................................................. 160.00
Oak Orchard Acid Springs, H. W. Bostwick, Broadway, NY,
   golden olive green, whittled three part mold, bottom emb "Glass
   from F. Hitchins Factory Lockport, NY," applied sloping lip with
   small flakes, 9" h ............................................................... 200.00
Round Lake Mineral Water, red amber, 9-1/4" h ................ 750.00
Rutherford's Premium Mineral Water, ground pontil, dark olive,
   7-1/2" h ............................................................................... 60.00
San Francisco Glass Works, tapered neck, blob top, sea green,
   6-7/8" h ............................................................................... 15.00
Saratoga Highrock Spring (fancy rock) Saratoga, NY, America,
   1860-80, cylindrical, bright medium green, applied sloping collared mouth with ring, smooth base, pint, 1/2" shallow chip on
   mouth ................................................................................. 850.00
Saratoga Seltzer Water, cylindrical, teal blue-green, applied ring
   lip, c1890, 7-1/2" h .............................................................. 85.00
Veronica Mineral Water, amber, sq ...................................... 10.00

## Utility

3-5/8" h, freeblown, flattened chestnut form, short neck, bright
   green, sheared mouth, pontil scar, American, 1800-30 ... 300.00
7-7/8" h, freeblown, rect, chamfered corners, dark olive amber,
   applied sloping collared mouth with ring, pontil scar, America,
   1800-30, ext. wear ............................................................. 275.00
9-1/4" h, freeblown, globular, golden amber, heavy applied mouth,
   pontil scar, attributed to Midwest America, 1800-30, some int.
   stain .................................................................................. 230.00

# BRASS

**History:** Brass is a durable, malleable, and ductile metal alloy consisting mainly of copper and zinc. The height of its popularity for utilitarian and decorative art items occurred in the 18th and 19th centuries.

**References:** Mary Frank Gaston, *Antique Brass & Copper*, Collector Books, 1992, 1998 value update; Rupert Gentle and Rachael Feild, *Domestic Metalwork 1640-1820*, Revised, Antique Collectors' Club, 1994; Henry J. Kaufmann, *Early American Copper, Tin & Brass*, Astragal Press, 1995.

**Additional Listings:** Bells; Candlesticks; Fireplace Equipment; Scientific Instruments.

Andirons, pr, 12-5/8" h, ball top, matching ball log stops, early .. 470.00
Appliques, pr, Belle Epoque
   11" l, Louis V taste, c1900-10, frosted rose glass shade in form of
     a blossom ........................................................................ 250.00
   40" h, Louis XVI taste, c1900-15, each of five lights fitted with
     frosted glass floriform shade, gilted, electrified ............... 950.00
Bed Warmer
   40" l, floral engraved lid, turned wooden handle with old
     finish ............................................................................... 420.00
   42" l, engraved lid, turned wooden handle, age crack in
     handle ............................................................................. 275.00
   43" l, brass and copper, engraved lid, turned wooden handle, old
     repairs ............................................................................ 220.00
   43-3/4" l, foliage engraved lid, turned wood handle, minor
     imperfections .................................................................. 200.00
Bird Cage, sq, ornate, brass and copper, 19th C ...................... 300.00
Bookends, pr, 7 3/4" h, George Washington, red, white, and gold paint,
   1932 ..................................................................................... 75.00
Box
   3-3/8" d, hexagonal, gilded, inset ivory with miniature painting of
     man and woman, sgd .......................................................... 110.00
   11" l, repousse dec, rampant lions, Victorian-style ............. 100.00
Candelabrum, 14" d, 25-1/2" h, Belle Epoque, Louis XVI style, c1900-
   1910, six lights, dressed with faceted bead festoons, cut glass
   bobeches, cut, faceted spears, white marble base, electrified. 175.00
Candlestick
   Set, graduated set, baluster shaft, pr 14-1/2" h Ace of Diamonds,
     pr 12-1/4" h King of Diamonds, pr 11 3/4" Queen of Diamonds,
     pr 11-3/4" h, Diamond Prince, pr 10 3/4" h, Diamond Princess,
     English ......................................................................... 1,350.00
   Single, 9" h, Queen Anne, Continental, first half 18th C, very
     minor dents ..................................................................... 290.00
Candy Thermometer, 12" l ...................................................... 80.00
Carriage Lamp
   9 1/2" h, marked "Neverout Insulated Kerosene Safety, Rose Mfg.
     Co, Philadelphia, USA," price for pr .............................. 250.00
   23 1/2" h, ball finials, two etched glass side panels, ball ends,
     price for pr ...................................................................... 160.00
Chandelier, 40" d, 48" h, Italian Renaissance-style, patinated, eight-
   light, circular corona, above tier of projecting cherubs, scrolled arms
   issuing putti with hands raised supporting urn-form candle
   nozzles .............................................................................. 1,870.00
Clock Jack, 15" h, mkd "No. 7 Warranted," John Linwood, heart
   shaped key ........................................................................... 300.00

## Reproduction Alert:

Many modern reproductions are being made of earlier brass forms, especially such items as buckets, fireplace equipment, and kettles.

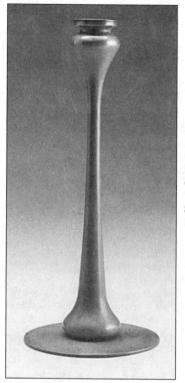

**Candlestick, Jarvie, Kappa, bulbous bobeche and base, orig patina, incised "Jarvie/K/4," 14" h, 6" d, $10,350. Photo courtesy of David Rago Auctions.**

Coal Hod, 24" h, urn form, lion's heads and pendant handles, acanthus-topped beaded legs, scrolled toes, pineapple finial, Regency-style, late 19th C ................................................................. 320.00

Fireplace Fender, 42" l, three-bar design above pierced skirt, molded base ......................................................................................... 275.00

Fireplace Set, 16-1/2" h belted ball top andirons, matching tongs, and shovel, America, late 19th C, repairs to dogs ......................... 425.00

Heater, 8 1/4" d, 7 1/2" h, octagonal, pierced, four turned feet, bail handle, four lines inscribed on top in Dutch ................................. 300.00

Icon, Russian, cast. 7" x 15 l/2" open, folding, Church Feasts, each leaf divided into quadrants with different feast, back panel displaying cross and outer walls of Jersualem ......................................... 440.00

Jardiniere, 14" w, 7-1/2" d, 8-3/4" h, oval, two handles, emb, rococo taste, conforming removable galvanized metal liner, Belle Epoque, c1890 ............................................................................................... 325.00

Kettle Stand, 15-3/8" w, 4-3/4" h, wrought iron framework, button feet, tall legs, brass top plate pierced at center, turned curly maple handle, repair at handle ................................................................................ 110.00

Lamp
    10 1/2" h, gimbal, saucer base .......................................... 140.00
    20" h, cranberry flash receptacle and shade, trefoil shaped stem and base, faceted prisms, marked "J & I Cox, New York," c1880, electrified .................................................................................. 550.00
    25" h, Baroque Revival, oil, molded high relief figures and foliage, scrolled base, converted, price for pr .......................... 1,610.00
    28" support tube, hanging, gas light, two burners, etched crystal shades, black and copper stripes .................................... 165.00
    Noodle Maker Roller, 8-1/2" w, marked "F Crafts, Rochester, NY" .............................................................................................. 60.00

Pail, 9-1/2" h, 6" h, spun, iron bale handle, marked "Haydens Patent" .............................................................................................. 75.00

Sauce Pan, 5-3/4" to 8-1/2", wrought iron handles, price for assembled set of 5 ............................................................................................. 330.00

Signal Cannon, barrel with crowned shield and two applied dolphins, wood and metal bound caisson, applied flowerheads and exposed nailheads, French, 19th C ................................................................ 1,955.00

Skimmer, 18-1/4" l, star flower shape holes, wrought iron handle 60.00

Steelyard, 18-1/4" l, mkd "Wm. B Preston, Boston" ....................... 95.00

Stencil, 13" d, revolving, used for marking barrels or feed sacks, "Patented Aug 11, 1866, May 30, 1871" ................................................ 200.00

Sundial Compass, sunburst on lid, 1940s.................................. 275.00

Taper Jack, with wick, English, early 19th C .............................. 380.00

Tea Kettle, 8" h, gooseneck spout, turned wooden handle.......... 60.00

Telescope, five sections, orig lens cap.................................... 165.00

Tool, leg calipers ...................................................................... 60.00

Trivet
    7-1/4" x 12-1/4" x 5-1/2" h, reticulated, lion and unicorn, English........................................................................................195.00
    10-5/8" l, punch engraved date 1826, replaced feet............ 60.00

Wall Sconces, pr, 13-1/2" h, 8" w, hand wrought, double light, hammered on front "A.N.N.O. 1698" and "A.N.N.O. 1693" ............. 475.00

Wick Trimmer, 9-1/2" l, orig tray..................................................... 90.00

# BREAD PLATES

**History:** Beginning in the mid-1880s, special trays or platters were made for serving bread and rolls. Designated "bread plates" by collectors, these small trays or platters can be found in porcelain, glass (especially pattern glass), and metals. Bread plates often were part of a china or glass set. However, many glass companies made special plates which honored national heroes, commemorated historical or special events, offered a moral maxim, or supported a religious attitude. The subject matter appears either horizontally or vertically. Most of these plates are oval and ten inches in length.

**Reference:** Anna Maude Stuart, *Bread Plates and Platters*, published by author, 1965.

**Additional Listings:** Pattern Glass.

Cut Glass
    13-1/2" d, Propeller pattern, Marshall Field & Co. ............. 350.00
    14" l, Bengal pattern, sgd "Sinclaire" ................................... 900.00

Historical Glass
    Beecher ............................................................................... 65.00
    Garfield Memorial ............................................................... 45.00
    Liberty and Freedom............................................................ 65.00
    Three Presidents, frosted ................................................... 75.00
    US Grant............................................................................... 50.00

Majolica
    Etruscan, emb fern leaves and wheat sheaves.................. 265.00
    Pond Lily pattern.................................................................. 200.00

Pattern Glass
    Basketweave, amber ............................................................ 40.00
    Beaded Loop ........................................................................ 30.00
    Crying Baby, frog on plate, 13" d ........................................ 99.00

**Sterling Silver, reticulated border, center monogram, hallmark for H. Muhr's Sons, 14-1/2" l, $235. Photo courtesy of Sanford Alderfer Auction Co.**

| | |
|---|---|
| Deer and Pine Tree | 45.00 |
| Finecut and Panel, amber | 48.00 |
| Garden of Eden, 9-1/4" x 12-1/2" | 40.00 |
| Minerva | 60.00 |
| Rock of Ages, clear, milk glass center | 125.00 |
| Royal Lady, vaseline | 130.00 |
| Scroll with Flowers | 30.00 |
| Three Graces | 50.00 |
| Wheat | 30.00 |

Silver, sterling, 12" l, 6-1/2" w, reticulated and ribbed, navette form, Gorham, c105-10 .................................................................. 50.00

# BRIDE'S BASKETS

**History:** A ruffled-edge glass bowl in a metal holder was a popular wedding gift between 1880 and 1910, hence the name "bride's basket." These bowls can be found in most glass types of the period. The metal holder was generally silver plated with a bail handle, thus enhancing the basket image. Over the years, bowls and bases became separated and married pieces resulted. If the base has been lost, the bowl should be sold separately.

**Reference:** John Mebane, *Collecting Bride's Baskets and Other Glass Fancies*, Wallace-Homestead, 1976.

**Reproduction Alert:** The glass bowls and silver plated holders have been reproduced.

7-1/2" w, 8-3/4" h, crystal pot-shaped body, handle in loop with deep pink and white latticino stripes, three matching feet................. 850.00

7-3/4" d, opalescent and colorless shading to lavender, applied flowers, looped thorn handle .......................................... 140.00

8" d, cased, red to white, small elegant SP frame ...................... 250.00

8" d, 10-1/2" h, Loetz-type glass, irid blue, and purple, recessed indentations, ruffled, ground pontil, ftd metal stand ......................... 345.00

8" d, 10-1/2" h, sq crimped edge bowl, white cased to rose-red, cameo cut winged griffins, floral bouquets and swags, fitted SP metal frame with leaf and berry embellished handle, Mt. Washington Glass Co bowl, frame mkd "Pairpoint" ...................................... 825.00

8-1/2" d, spiral white and turquoise dec, ruffled, colorless thorn handle ........................................................................ 125.00

8-1/2" d, 14-1/2" h, heavenly blue satin glass shading to pale white, diamond quilted design, pie crust crimped edge, orig fancy silver plated holder, Mt. Washington .................................. 400.00

9" d, overshot, green shaded to pale pink, thorn handle............. 135.00

9" d, Peachblow, shiny finish bowl, applied amber rim, SP Wilcox holder .............................................................................. 215.00

9" d, 12" h, Mt. Washington, Rose Amber, Coin Spot pattern, deep color, fancy silver plated Pairpoint stand .................................. 875.00

9-1/4" d, blue opalescent, crimped rim, reticulated SP holder mkd "Wallingford, Biggins & Rodgers Co" ...................................... 225.00

9-1/2" d, MOP satin, Diamond Quilted pattern, deep blue shading to pale blue int., blue shading to white ext., applied frosted crimped edge, Mt. Washington ............................................... 600.00

9-1/2" d, pigeon blood, enamel floral dec, SP holder................. 225.00

9-3/4" d, 11" h, off-white ext., shaded rose int., crystal ruffled edge, Rogers & Bros. SP basket with two small hands, chains, fruit design on holder ............................................................ 300.00

10" d, 2-1/2" h, deep rose shading to pink satin bowl, ruffled, enameled floral dec. ...................................................... 225.00

10-1/2" h, colorless frosted bowl, overlaid in pink crystal, etched acorn and oak leaf dec, gilt metal frame with basket handles, Victorian ............................................................ 250.00

10-1/2" d, 10-3/4" h, MOP satin, Diamond Quilted pattern, deep pink shading to pale pink to off-white, Mt. Washington rectangular form bowl, applied frosted edge, orig fancy silver plated Victorian "Manhattan Silver Company," holder has been resilvered.................... 400.00

10-1/2" d, 12-1/2" h, oval satin bow, blue int., white ext., pleated rim, applied frosted ribbon edge, ornate ftd Forbes frame ............. 250.00

11" d, cased, pink ext., peachblow int., gold stylized flowers, ornate SP holder with aquatic marine life motif, mkd "Pairpoint Mfg. Co." 825.00

11" d, 10-1/2" h, white and vaseline bowl, all over floral enamel dec, fancy silver plated frame, sgd "Meriden," minor handle restoration ............................................................... 300.00

11-1/2" h, sapphire blue bowl, applied ruffled rim, gold tracery and courting scene dec, ornate ftd Meriden stand .......................... 325.00

11-1/2" d, 12" h, dark red satin glass shaded to cream, ruffled and crimped rim, SP stand ............................................... 275.00

11-1/2" d, 13-1/2" h, ruffled white shading to pink to raspberry bowl, cased in white, plum dec, gold ranches, hanging ferns, gold dotted florals, ornate double handled silver frame, figural flowers on handle and base .......................................................... 400.00

13" l, 12-1/2" h, oval satin bowl, shaded raspberry ext., brilliant turquoise int., tightly ruffed pleated and fold-in edge, rect shape, white and gold enameled floral leaf and berry dec on ornate ftd rope handled silver plated orig frame ..................................... 650.00

# BRISTOL GLASS

**History:** Bristol glass is a designation given to a semi-opaque glass, usually decorated with enamel and cased with another color. Initially, the term referred only to glass made in Bristol, England, in the 17th and 18th centuries. By the Victorian era, firms on the Continent and in America were copying the glass and its forms.

Vases, window and curtain motif, flared scalloped edge, gold highlights, 11-1/8", price for pr, $90.

**Pink interior, purple ruffled rim, silver plated pedestal holder, $90.**

Biscuit Jar, cov
    5" d, 7-1/2" h, apple green body, enameled green and yellow flowers and plants, SP rim, cov, handle, and base, figural strawberry finial.................................................................................195.00
    5-1/4" d, 6-1/2" h, satin finish, opaque beige ground, pink roses, gold leaves, gray foliage, SP top, rim, and handle...........195.00
Bowl, colorless, cinched, ruffled, crimped, hp.......................65.00
Box, cov
    1-5/8" l, 1" h, turquoise body, gold dec.............................110.00
    5-3/4" l, 3-5/8" h, egg shape, white body, pink, cream, blue, and yellow flowers.....................................................................225.00
Compote, fluted, white body, hand painted cat scene, metal base...............................................................................................95.00
Condiment Set, cov mustard pot, pepper shaker with orig lid, open salt, milk white, pink and blue flowers and green leaves dec, 4-1/4" x 5-3/4" SP holder.............................................................................175.00
Creamer and Sugar, cov, white body, multicolored floral dec.......65.00
Cruet, 6-3/4" h, enameled floral dec.......................................50.00
Decanter
    8-3/8" h, gray, encrusted floral engraving, butterflies, gilt trim, vase-like stopper.................................................................60.00
    9-1/4" h, 3-1/2" d, apple green body, reeded gold trimmed green handles, matching stopper.................................................120.00
Egg Cup, white body, gold bands.............................................25.00
Ewer, 4-1/2" h, 2-3/4" d, turquoise, enameled pink flowers, white and green leaves, yellow scrolls, gold trim, applied turquoise handles, pr......................................................................................190.00
Garniture Set, 19-1/2" h cov jar, 14-1/2" vases, pink, dec with courtship scenes, black and gold highlights, green vines, small chip to vase rim...............................................................................................300.00
Goblet, 10-3/4" h, pedestal base, opaque blue ground, polychrome enamel floral dec, gilt trim.....................................................95.00
Lamp
    13-1/4" h, blue body, enameled white egret, multicolored flowers and foliage, brass oil fittings, black base...........................300.00
    31" h, black ground, white enameled scene of woman on tree branch................................................................................180.00
Mantle Vase, 11" h, painted transfer scene of boy with poodle, large hand painted florals, 19th C, pr.............................................150.00
Miniature Lamp, 10" h, 4-3/4" d, white shaded to soft blue, dainty enameled orange flowers, green leaves, sq ruffled shade, base with matching flowers, brown flying bird, applied opalescent shell feet, orig burner and chimney...........................................................885.00
Patch Box, 1" h, 1-1/4" d, hinged, soft pink ground, enameled brown and white bird............................................................................100.00
Perfume Bottle, 3-7/8" h, hourglass shape, opaque blue, silver mounted cap..............................................................................175.00
Pitcher, 8-1/4" h, light green body, enameled bird and flowers, applied clear handle.............................................................................95.00
Plate, 14-1/2" d, white body, hand painted, lavender and ochre French lilacs, green leaves..........................................................................80.00
Ring Box, cov, 1-3/4" h, 1-3/4" d, turquoise body, gold flowers and leaves.............................................................................................50.00
Rolling Pin, Sailor's Valentine, 15-3/4" l, façade with worn polychromed and gilt poem and scene of frigates, knob terminals fitted with brass hanging chain, c1825-40..................................................................200.00
Salt, 2-3/4" d, light gray body, enameled herons and foliage, SP rim and handle....................................................................................48.00
Sugar Shaker, yellow satin glass body, flying birds scene............75.00
Sweetmeat Jar, 4-1/2" d, 5-1/2" h, floral garlands and butterflies dec, SP top and bail handle..............................................................125.00
Tumbler, 6-3/4" h, 2-3/4" d, turquoise body, gold and white rope garlands, gold foot...................................................................................72.00
Vase
    4" h, caramel acid finish, hand painted scenic and floral dec, remnants of French retailer's label............................................50.00
    8" h, 2-3/4" w, Fireglow, beige ground, white flowers, green and gold leaves, worn gold accents, matched pr...................100.00
    8-1/2" h, light pink shading to dark pink, hp enameled design...................................................................................65.00
    8-1/2" h, white body, enameled floral and leaf dec, ruffled top, ram's head handles..................................................................75.00
    9" h, white body, portrait of young boy and girl, facing pr...165.00
    9-3/8" h, white body, hand painted, flowers, gold trim, raised enameling, pr...........................................................................150.00
    10" h, blue body, cut-out base, enameled floral dec, pr......120.00

# BRITISH ROYALTY COMMEMORATIVES

**History:** British commemorative china, souvenirs to commemorate coronations and other royal events, dates from the 1600s, with the early pieces being rather crude in design and form. With the development of transfer printing, c1780, the images on the wares more closely resembled the monarchs. Few commemorative pieces predating Queen Victoria's reign are found today at popular prices. Items associated with Queen Elizabeth II and her children, e.g., the wedding of HRH Prince Andrew and Miss Sarah Ferguson and the subsequent birth of their daughter HRH Princess Beatrice, are very common. Some British Royalty commemoratives are easily recognized by their portraits of past or present monarchs. Some may be in silhouette profile. Royal symbols include crowns, dragons, royal coats of arms, national flowers, swords, scepters, dates, messages, and monograms.

**References:** Susan and Al Bagdade, *Warman's English & Continental Pottery & Porcelain,* 3rd Edition, Krause Publications, 1998; Douglas H. Flynn and Alan H. Bolton, *British Royalty Commemoratives,* Schiffer Publishing, 1994; Lincoln Hallinan, *British Commemoratives,* Antique Collectors' Club, 1999; Eric Knowles, *Miller's Royal Memorabilia,* Reed Consumer Books, 1994.

**Collectors' Club:** Commemorative Collector's Society, The Gardens, Gainsborough Rd, Winthrope, New Newark, Nottingham NG24 2NR England.

**Periodical:** *The Commemorative Collector Newsletter,* Douglas H. Flynn, P.O. Box 294, Lititz, PA 17543-0294.

**Additional Listings:** See Warman's Americana & Collectibles for more examples.

Autograph
    Christmas Card, Elizabeth II, 1954, photo showing Queen, Prince Philip flanking 6 year old Prince Charles and 4 year old Princess Anne, sgd in lower blank margin by Queen, "Elizabeth R" and Prince "Phillip," 1 page, oblong 8vo, emb royal crown on cover............................................................................................250.00
    Document Signed, Charles II, Dec 20, 1680, London, instructing Sir Robert Howard to pay sum, 1 page 4to, soiled...........690.00
    Manuscript Document, Charles II, countersigned by Samuel Pepys, Sept 29, 1674, London, reassigning naval cook, 1 page, small folio, matted with reproductions of early Charles II and Pepys portraits.....................................................................980.00
    Note Signed, Edward VIII, sgd "Edward" in pencil, both sides of 3-1/2" x 4 1/2" printed Marlborough House card, dated London July 3, 1904, note regarding forgotten prayer book........850.00
    Typed Letter Signed, Duke of Windsor, sgd "Edward," Sept 1940, to John Royal, Vice President of NBC............................220.00
Beaker, 3 1/2" h
    Elizabeth II, 1953 Coronation, Poole....................................35.00

George V/Mary, 1911 Coronation, Bishop and Stonier .........75.00

Bell, metal, police helmet shape, Queen Elizabeth II....................38.00

Bottle, Coca-Cola, Royal Wedding, 7/29/81, illus of Diana ...........60.00

Bowl

Edward VIII, 1937 Coronation, Grindly, 6 1/4" d ...................45.00

Elizabeth II, crown shaped, marked "Queen Elizabeth II, 2 June 1953" to commemorate coronation, 8" d, 4" h....................50.00

Victoria, In Memoriam, 1901, pressed glass, 9-1/2" d ........120.00

Box, Elizabeth II, 1977 Jubilee, raised flowers, Crown Staffordshire, 1-7/8" d ............................................................................................20.00

Bust, Victoria, parian, circular plinth base, inscribed "To Commemorate the 60th Year of Her Reign 1837-1897" ......................................750.00

Cake Plate, Victoria, 1907 Jubilee, sepia portraits, residences, Man of War, 10-3/4" d....................................................................................140.00

Coronation Chair, 4-5/8" h, sterling silver, gold overlay, Stone of Scone under seat, chair supported by four lions, commemorative plaque, fitted case, Birmingham, 1953, 11 troy oz ....................................750.00

Cup and Saucer, Edward VII/Alexandria, 1888 Silver Wedding Anniversary, coat of arms, oversized.................................................175.00

Folio, Edward VIII Collection, 9" x 11" cover, 8-1/2" x 10-3/4" commemorative tribute folder, orig envelope, following 1936 abdication..30.00

Glass, George IV Coronation, 3-3/4" h, red finish design, one with portrait and inscription "H. M. King George IV Coronation May 12, 1937," second with different portrait view, royalty symbols, inscription "May 1937 Coronation," pr ................................................................................60.00

Invitation, Honorable Mayor La Guardia, New York City's welcome of King George VI and Queen Elizabeth, June 1939, 8" h .............45.00

Jug, George VI\Elizabeth 1937 Coronation, musical, sepia portraits, Princess Elizabeth\Margaret on reverse, Shelley....................275.00

Lithophane, crown, and cypher, 2-3/4" h

Alexandra, 1902, cup ................................................................200.00

George V, 1911, mug .................................................................175.00

Mary, 1911, cup...........................................................................275.00

Loving Cup, Elizabeth II, 1972 Silver Wedding Anniversary, Paragon, 3" h ......................................................................................................150.00

Match Book Cover, celebrates "Their Most Gracious Majesties Canada Tour," May/June 1939...........................................................................18.00

Match Safe

1-5/8" h, brass, relief of King Edward VII on front, "Long Live the King" on back, c1902 ........................................................................85.00

2-1/8" h, Vulcanite, encased picture of King Edward VI......160.00

Mug

Charles, 1969 Investiture as Prince of Wales, gold dragon, feathers, black ground, Portmerion Pottery, 4" h..........................45.00

Charles & Diana wedding, 1981, emb "Made in England"....65.00

Duke and Duchess of Windsor, In Memoriam, black and white portraits, Dorincourt, 3-3/8" h ..............................................60.00

Edward VIII, Coronation........................................................................50.00

Victoria, 1887 Jubilee, color beaded crown and ribbon, William Whiteley, 3-1/4" h ................................................................95.00

Paperweight, Victoria\Albert, black and white portraits, color, glitter, 2-7/8" d ................................................................................45.00

Photograph, formal wedding photograph by Soper, Duke and Duchess of Windsor, sgd "Edward Duke of Windsor" and "Wallis Duchess of Windsor," dated in Duke's hand, June 3, 1937, 11-1/2" x 9-1/2", mounted, photographer's signature on mount, period standing frame ...................................................................................................3,910.00

Pinback Button

Edward VII and Alexandria, multicolored portraits, gold trim, c1902 ....................................................................................................60.00

Edward VIII

1920, Prince of Wales, black and white military portrait, blue rim, white letters ....................................................................................35.00

1937, Coronation, multicolored portrait, white trim ..............30.00

Elizabeth II, Coronation, 7/8" d, black and white, bright luster rim, inscribed "Coronation of Elizabeth II, 1953" ........................15.00

George V, blue portrait, military uniform, light blue rim inscribed "Unley-April 21, 1917," Gallipoli Day ..................................20.00

George VI, Elizabeth I, red, white, and blue portrait, 1939 Canadian visit ................................................................................................20.00

Queen Victoria, Diamond Jubilee, 1897, two sided cello disk, color images of her as young queen in 1837 and reigning in 1897, reverse inset black and white commemorative text, made by Whitehead & Hoag .......................................................................75.00

Prince Philip and Princess Elizabeth, black and white photo, early 1950s ....................................................................................................20.00

Pin Tray, George VI, 1937 Coronation, sepia portrait, Royal Crown Derby, 3" sq ...................................................................................40.00

Pitcher, William\Adelaide Coronation, white china, portraits and decorative floral accents, in lavender and violet tones, "King William IV & Queen Adelaide, Crowned Sept 6, 1831," tribute inscriptions, chips to pitcher spout, some wear, 8" h.................................................90.00

Plate

Edward VII\Alexandra, 1902 Coronation, color portraits, scalloped edge, 9-1/2" d.....................................................................................60.00

Elizabeth II, 1953 Coronation, back mkd "Confederation Series Canada, Clarice Cliff, Royal Staffordshire, Burslem, England, Approved by the Council of Industrial Design," 10-3/4" d 125.00

Elizabeth II, 60th Birthday, large color portrait, Coalport.......75.00

George\Mary, white china, full color royalty symbols, sepiatone oval portraits, "Crowned June 22, 1911," inscribed "Long May They Reign," artwork of St. George slaying dragon, 6" d...65.00

Princess Margaret, birth, parakeets, flowers, Paragon, 6" d.75.00

Victoria, 150th Anniversary of Coronation, gold portrait, 10-1/2" d..........................................................................................140.00

Portrait Plaque, Duke and Duchess of York, oval, three color jasper, solid light blue ground, applied black laurel molded frame, white portrait posts, Wedgwood, imp marks, and oval "O," attributed to Bert Bentley, 20th C, 5-1/2" h, 4-1/2" w, price for pr ......................635.00

Ribbon, Queen Victoria Reign Anniversary, 2" x 6-1/2", blue silk, inked in black, profile portrait, inscription "H.R.H. Queen Victoria 1837/1887 Jubilee Anniversary June 21"...................................90.00

Shaving Mug, Edward VIII, 1937 Coronation, sepia portrait .........75.00

Stickpin, Queen Victoria, Jubilee 1887, diecut thin brass holding sepia paper inset photo ........................................................................60.00

Teapot

Edward VII\Alexandra, 1902 Coronation, color portraits, 4-3/4" h .......................................................................................................75.00

George V\Mary, 1911 Coronation, color portraits with Prince of Wales, bone china.............................................................................250.00

**Plate, commemorating King George VI and Queen Elizabeth's US visit, blue and white, mkd "John Maddock & Sons, Ltd., England," Royal Ivory, $45.**

Tea Set
Elizabeth II, 1953 Coronation, teapot, creamer, and sugar, relief portraits, Jasperware, white on royal blue, Wedgwood. price for set ........................................................................................ 350.00
George VI and Queen Elizabeth, 5" h teapot, creamer, sugar, dark blue jasper dip, applied white relief, imp Wedgwood marks, c1937 ......................................................................... 250.00
Tin, color portrait
Edward VII\Alexandra, 1902 Coronation, Ridgway Ltd. Tea .... 120.00
Elizabeth II, 1953 Coronation, red ground, British flags, portrait, "Long May She Reign," info about Her Majesty on lid int., 2-1/2" x 3-1/2" ................................................................................ 20.00
Tumbler, H. M. Queen Elizabeth II, porcelain, white, full color portrait, Coronation June 2, 1953 ............................................................ 60.00

# BRONZE

**History:** Bronze is an alloy of copper, tin, and traces of other metals. It has been used since Biblical times not only for art objects, but also for utilitarian wares. After a slump in the Middle Ages, the use of bronze was revived in the 17th century and continued to be popular until the early 20th century.

**References:** Harold Berman, *Bronzes: Sculptors & Founders 1800-1930,* Vols. 1–4 and Index, distributed by Schiffer Publishing, 1996; James Mackay, *The Dictionary of Sculptors in Bronze,* Antique Collectors' Club, 1999; Christopher Payne, *Animals in Bronze, Reference and Price Guide,* Antique Collectors' Club, 1999; Stuart Pivar, *The Bayre Bronzes, A Catalogue Raisonné,* Antique Collectors' Club, 1999.

**Notes:** Do not confuse a "bronzed" object with a true bronze. A bronzed item usually is made of white metal and then coated with a reddish-brown material to give it a bronze appearance. A magnet will stick to it but not to anything made of true bronze. A signed bronze commands a higher market price than an unsigned one. There also are "signed" reproductions on the market. It is very important to know the history of the mold and the background of the foundry.

Bookends, pr, 6-3/4" h, kneeling youth, partially clothed, mkd "J. Konti, 1911" ...................................................................................... 450.00
Box, cov, 3-5/8" w, 6-1/4" l, 1-1/2" h, rect, hinged, etched central six-sided oval reserve flanked by scroll devices and geometric outline, mottled texture on recessed areas, wood-lined int., imp marks for manuf Silver Crest, 20th C ............................................................ 45.00
Bust, child, blackish patination, black marble base, French, early 20th C .............................................................................................. 490.00
Candlesticks, pr, 8" h, Belle Epoque, Louis XVI taste, c1890-95 .. 70.00
Cast Register, 21" h, labeled "Lincoln Hotel," National Cash Register .. 650.00
Center Bowl, 23-1/4" l, 13-3/4" h, gondola form, young gondolier with paddle, floral swags, stylized wave pedestal with seahorse, oval base with bird's foot, shell, and grotesque mask feet, amber glass liner, Continental, late 19th/early 20th C ............................... 1,050.00
Chandelier, 20-3/8" l, six-light, central black patinated standard with husk wrap, gilt bronze scrolled candle arms topped by goat's head, scroll ending in perched bird joined by fruit and flower swags suspended in their beaks, Louis XV-style, late 19th/early 20th C .................................................................................. 4,600.00
Cup, two handles
5-1/2" h, modeled in high relief, classical figures and masks, Continental, 19th C ............................................................................ 375.00

**Figural Group, by French artist Julies Moigniez (1835-94), 11" x 16", $3,000. Photo courtesy of Jackson's Auctioneers & Appraisers.**

10-3/4" w, 8" h, relief band of boisterous putti fighting butterflies, high loop handles topped by lion's heads and lizards below, slender fluted trumpet foot, flattened beaded knop, sgd "F. Barbedienne," French, late 19th C .................................... 290.00
Dresser Tray, 14" l, twin handles, scrolling Baroque border, polychrome champleve enamel dec, French ................................. 500.00
Figure
8-1/4" h, Leda and Swan, classically draped figure, circular pedestal, Continental, 19th C .................................................. 460.00
10" h, conquistador, light brown patina, Emile Guillemin, French .. 815.00
11-1/8" h, female snake charmer, seminude, stylized headpiece, outstretched arms supporting entwined snake, chocolate brown patina, incised signature "Arthur Bock, Hamburg," imp founders mark for Brandstettner, Muncheon, c1920-30 ............... 1,725.00
12" h, blacksmith, sgd "P. Ludwig Kowalczewski," brown patination, circular marble socle, early 20th C .......................... 690.00
12" h, classical nude, dolphin and cherub, patinated, Italian, late 19th C ...................................................................................... 490.00
12" h, Napoleon, standing figure, arms crossed, sq stepped base, Continental, third quarter 19th C ..................................... 990.00
12-1/4" h, Vingtans, light brown patination, red marble base, Raoul Lanche, French, c1900 ............................................... 815.00
17" h, boy with geese, chocolate brown patina, C. Philipp, Continental, late 19th C ..................................................... 1,100.00
17" h, classical-style male athlete, nude figure bending to put on sandals, seal applied to base for "Reduction Mechanique" by A. Collas, late 19th C ..................................................... 1,955.00
18" h, Revoluntary Hero Danto, patinated, French, c1875-90 .................................................................................. 800.00
20-1/2" h, seated imp, young figure with wings and horns, leafy ground, sated on part of quadripartite column, paterae and flowers, light brown patina, by Eugene Nicolas Celement, Conne D'Astaniere ..................................................................... 4,900.00
22" h, young woman, Neoclassical costume, French, late 19th/early 20th C ......................................................... 1,100.00
23" h, Dancing Faun with Cymbals, standing nude figure leaning against tree stump, incised signature, late 19th/early 20th C .................................................................................. 1,100.00
25" h, nude bather, classical undress, M. Amadio, Naples, late 19th C ................................................................................. 1,380.00
27" h, classical archer, nude figure with quiver of arrows, standing beside tree stump with entwined snake, Reduction Mechanique seal for A. Colias, late 19th/early 20th C ..................... 1,610.00

28" h, reveling Bacchus, figure poised in dance, grape leaf drapery and circlet, upraised hand holding cup, sq base, incised signature "M. Pritzsche," greenish patina, 20th C.............. 1,495.00

29" h, young goatherder, nude figure carrying kid around shoulders, staff in one hand, sq base, late 19th C................. 2,300.00

30-3/4" h, Le Coup Double, hunter holding up bird and hunting dog presenting rabbit, naturalistic base with incised signature and title on front, E. Delabrierre, late 19th/early 20th C 6,325.00

31-1/2" h, Winner of the Cockfight, young nude man with fighting fowl, incised signature "Jean-Alexandre Joseph Falguiere" and "Thiebault Freres, Paris" foundry seal.......................... 3,750.00

34" h, Dionysus Playing Flute, seated figure accompanied by young satyr sneaking up from behind, dark greenish-brown patina, after Antonine Coyzevox, incised F. Barbedienne foundry mark, signature on base, "Reduction Mechanique" seal, late 19th C................................................................ 4,600.00

Inkwell, 5" l, gilt bronze, figural, barrel of fish, anchor, and ropes, rocky base, green marble stand, French, late 19th C ........................ 350.00

Lamp Base

20-1/4" h, figure of Bacchus holding serpent in upraised hand, supporting flat leaf inverted trumpet sconce, round base with band of grapes and grape leaves, electrified ................... 815.00

23" h, six-sided faceted finial above three-socket fixture, faceted standard tapering to round base, brown patina, woven fabric Handel, Meriden, CT, tag on base, two replaced pull chains, some corrosion, early 20th C ........................................... 575.00

Letter Opener, 11-3/4" l, bust of woman in relief .......................... 85.00

Medallion, 8-1/2" d, portrait of Marat, inscribed "L'aimi Du Peuple…," patinated, French, 19th C................................................ 425.00

Photograph Frame, 8-1/2" l, 4" h, oblong, Belle Epoque, Louis XVI-style, c1900-1910, gilt ......................................................... 250.00

Plaque, 13-3/8" w, 16-1/2" h, Bacchus supported by satyrs, figures in high relief, grape vine arch, 20th C ........................................ 520.00

Smoking Stand, 8" h, central figural finial, two match urns, inscribed base, foliate feet, French, early 20th C ................................... 450.00

Standish, 15" l, 9" h, patinated bronze, bird perched on naturalistic base, two inkwells, sgd "A. Marionnet," c1900 ......................... 520.00

Wall Sconce

18-1/2" l, two-light, patinated, blue and white oval jasperware plaque with classical woman set in flat leaf surround, topped by acanthus, paterae, and husk drops, two scrolling candle arms with flat leaf nozzles, floral lappets above vasiform tapering base, electrified, Classical Revival, 20th C ...................... 450.00

25-1/2" l, two-light, central black patinated standard with husk wrap, topped by foliate finial, gilt bronze scrolled candle arms topped by goat's head, ending in two perched birds, joined by fruit and flower swag, centered by woman's head, Louis XV-style, late 19th/early 20th C, price for pr ...................... 4,900.00

# BUFFALO POTTERY

**History:** Buffalo Pottery Co., Buffalo, New York, was chartered in 1901. The first kiln was fired in October 1903. Larkin Soap Company established Buffalo Pottery to produce premiums for its extensive mail-order business. Wares also were sold to the public by better department and jewelry stores. Elbert Hubbard and Frank Lloyd Wright, who designed the Larkin Administration Building in Buffalo in 1904, were two prominent names associated with the Larkin Company.

Early Buffalo Pottery production consisted mainly of semi-vitreous china dinner sets. Buffalo was the first pottery in the United States to produce successfully the Blue Willow pattern. Buffalo also made a line of hand-decorated, multicolored willow ware, called Gaudy Willow. Other early items include a series of game, fowl, and fish sets, pitchers, jugs, and a line of commemorative, historical, and advertising plates and mugs. From 1908 to 1909 and again from 1921 to 1923, Buffalo Pottery produced the line for which it is most famous—Deldare Ware. The earliest of this olive green, semi-vitreous china displays hand-decorated scenes from English artist Cecil Aldin's Fallowfield Hunt. Hunt scenes were done only from 1908 to 1909. English village scenes also were characteristic of the ware and were used during both periods. Most pieces are artist signed.

In 1911, Buffalo Pottery produced Emerald Deldare, which used scenes from Goldsmith's The Three Tours of Dr. Syntax and an Art Nouveau-type border. Completely decorated Art Nouveau pieces also were made. Abino, which was introduced in 1912, had a Deldare body and displayed scenes of sailboats, windmills, or the sea. Rust was the main color used, and all pieces were signed by the artist and numbered. In 1915 the manufacturing process was modernized, giving the company the ability to produce vitrified china. Consequently, hotel and institutional ware became the main production items, with hand-decorated ware de-emphasized. The Buffalo firm became a leader in producing and designing the most-famous railroad, hotel, and restaurant patterns. These wares, especially railroad items, are eagerly sought by collectors. In the early 1920s, fine china was made for home use. Bluebird is one of the patterns from this era. In 1950, Buffalo made their first Christmas plate. These were given away to customers and employees primarily from 1950 to 1960. However, it is known that Hample Equipment Co. ordered some as late as 1962. The Christmas plates are very scarce in today's resale market.

The Buffalo China Company made "Buffalo Pottery" and "Buffalo China"—the difference being that one is semi-vitreous ware and the other vitrified. In 1956 the company was reorganized, and Buffalo China became the corporate name. Today Buffalo China is owned by Oneida Silver Company. The Larkin family no longer is involved.

**Marks:** Blue Willow pattern is marked "First Old Willow Ware Mfg. in America."

**Reference:** Seymour and Violet Altman, *Book of Buffalo Pottery*, reprinted by Schiffer Publishing, 1987.

## Blue Willow

Butter Pat.......................................................................... 14.00
Cup and Saucer.................................................................. 35.00
Plate, 9" d ......................................................................... 20.00
Platter, 13" x 11", dated 1909.............................................. 100.00
Vegetable Bowl ................................................................. 50.00

## Commercial

Bowl, 6" d, made for Roycroft Inn, East Aurora, NY ............ 75.00
Calendar Plate, 8" d, 1911, red open touring car................. 45.00

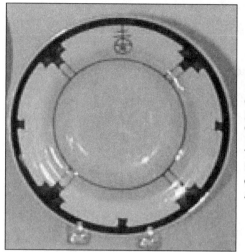

Bowl, green and maroon orb and cross Roycroft pattern, designed by Dard Hunter, 7-1/4" d, $195. Photo courtesy of David Rago Auctions.

Compote, 9-1/4" d, 3-3/4" d, semi-vitreous stamp, for Roycroft..... 1,000.00
Cup and Saucer, George Washington ............................... 275.00
Plate
  Automobile Club of Buffalo......................................... 25.00
  Hotel Astor, Art Nouveau ......................................... 25.00
  Tea Set, teapot, creamer, sugar, waste saucer, for Roycroft, 1925 stamp mark ............................................. 1,500.00

## Deldare

Ashtray/matchbox ....................................................... 675.00
Bowl, 8" d, Ye Village Tavern, 1908 ................................. 300.00
Calling Card Tray
  Fallowfield Hunt, 1908.......................................... 250.00
  Ye Lion Inn, sgd by artist M Gerhardt .......................... 300.00
  Candlestick, shield shape...................................... 700.00
  Chop Plate, 14" d ............................................. 600.00
  Cup and Saucer, Fallowfield Hunt, 1908 ....................... 350.00
  Fruit Bowl .................................................... 500.00
  Hair Receiver................................................. 425.00
  Humidor ...................................................... 800.00
Mug
  3-1/2" h .......................................................... 300.00
  4-1/2" h .......................................................... 350.00
  Ye Lion Inn........................................................ 310.00
  Pin Tray, 6-1/2" x 3-3/4", Ye Olden Days, artist's signature, mkd "Deldare Ware underglaze, Made at Ye Buffalo Pottery 1909".................................................... 355.00
Pitcher
  6" h, The Vicar of Wakefield, hand painted by Lanna, 1908 550.00 9" h, The Vicar of Wakefield, hand painted by Ball, 1908.................................................... 850.00
Plate
  6-1/2" d .......................................................... 180.00
  8-1/4" d, Town Crier............................................. 175.00
  9" d, The Start, hand painted by L. Newman, 1909....... 250.00
  10" d, Village Gossips, 1909 .................................. 125.00
  13-3/4" d, An Evening at Ye Lion Inn........................ 625.00
  Tankard........................................................... 950.00
  Teapot, cov, large ............................................. 350.00
  Tea Tile .......................................................... 300.00
  Tea Tray.......................................................... 550.00
  Vase, 7" h ....................................................... 400.00

## Emerald Deldare

Charger, 12 1/2" d, Dr Syntax Sketching the Lake, polychrome dec of man on horseback, emerald border, green ink stamp mark .......................................................... 850.00
Cup and Saucer, Dr Syntax at Liverpool...................... 500.00
Fern Dish, 8" d, butterflies and flowers ..................... 850.00

Plate, 8 1/4" d, Art Nouveau dec....................................... 400.00
Vase, 8" h, kingfisher, dragonflies, iris, and waterlilies .... 1,200.00

## Historical and Commemorative

Mug, 3 1/2" h, Beechland Farms ............................... 100.00
Pitcher
  5 1/8" h, Geranium pattern, strong blues, transfer type logo ........................................................275.00
  6 1/2" h, Landing of Roger Williams, scenes include view of Betsy Williams' cottage, logo and dated 1906 and 1907 on base .......................................................... 400.00
  6 3/4" h, The Whirl of the Town - Fox Hunt, unique logo, obscured date, c1906 .................................... 500.00
Plate
  7 1/2" d, Niagara Falls .......................................... 65.00
  10" d, Capitol Building, Washington, DC, canton green, eagle and banner mark, c1905 ................................... 55.00
  10 1/4" d, Independence Hall, Philadelphia, PA, blue-green transfer, back mark with eagle perched on American flag, banner "Buffalo Pottery, Warranted" ...................... 55.00

## Miscellaneous

Butter Pat, Gaudy Willow............................................. 35.00
Child's Feeding Dish, Mary Had A Little Lamb .................... 65.00
Dinner Service, Maple Leaf, price for 100 pc set................ 400.00
Dresser Tray, 10 1/2" x 13 3/4", Abino Ware, rect, band of sheep on village street, blue highlights, 1913 ..................... 1,750.00
Grill Plate, 10" d, hand decaled flowers and orange trim, 1920s.............................................................15.00
Hair Receiver, Abino Ware, sailing ship, blue highlights, 1913, sgd "WE Simpson" ........................................... 650.00
Plate
  9" d, Restaurant Ware, pink floral border, unused.......... 18.00
9 1/4" d
  American Herring Gull ......................................... 65.00
  Ducky Goose ................................................... 65.00
  Wild Ducks .................................................... 65.00
  10 1/2" d, Gaudy Willow ....................................... 150.00
Platter, Restaurant Ware
  9-1/2" l, 7-1/4" l, white, black stripe, scalloped edge ....... 15.00
  13-1/2" l, green trim, green flowers and leaves, back stamp "Buffalo China #N3, Made in USA".......................... 15.00

# BURMESE GLASS

**History:** Burmese glass is a translucent art glass originated by Frederick Shirley and manufactured by the Mt. Washington Glass Co., New Bedford, Massachusetts, from 1885 to c1891. Burmese glass colors shade from a soft lemon to a salmon pink. Uranium was used to attain the yellow color, and gold was added to the batch so that on reheating, one end turned pink. Upon reheating again, the edges would revert to the yellow coloring. The blending of the colors was so gradual that it is difficult to determine where one color ends and the other begins. Although some of the glass has a glossy surface, most pieces were acid finished. The majority of the items were free blown, but some were blown molded in a ribbed, hobnail, or diamond-quilted design. American-made Burmese is quite thin and, therefore, is fragile, and brittle. English Burmese was made by Thos. Webb & Sons. Out of deference to Queen Victoria, they called their wares "Queen's Burmese Ware."

**Reference:** Kyle Husfloen, *Antique Trader's American & European Decorative and Art Glass Price Guide,* 2nd ed., Krause Publications, 2000.

**Collectors Club:** Mount Washington Art Glass Society, P.O. Box 24094, Fort Worth, TX 76124-1094.

**Advisors:** Clarence and Betty Maier.

Bon Bon Dish
    5-1/4" l, 1-1/2" h, satin finish, rect, bulged out optic ribbed sides, turned-in edges Mt. Washington ......................................285.00
    6-1/2" l, 4-3/4" w, 2-3/8" h, shiny finish, three applied lemon yellow prunts, applied handle, heart shaped rim, Mt. Washington ................................................835.00
Creamer, 2-5/8" h, enameled vintage dec, ruffled rim.................295.00
Cruet, 7" h, shiny finish, thirty ribs with light pink, blush intensifies on neck and stopper, mushroom stopper, applied handle, Mt. Washington ............................................................1,250.00
Epergne, 14" h, 8" center floriform vase, satin finish, pastel yellow stripes, unique pink blush borders, undecorated, shallow bowl-shaped base with muted Burmese color, cone-shaped center rising to support brass fittings that hold three petite Burmese bud vases, Webb ..............................................................1,950.00
Fairy Lamp
    3-3/4" h, Burmese shade, clear glass base, mkd "S. Clarke's Pyramid Fairy," Webb .......................................335.00
    5-1/2" h, 7-1/2" d base, dome shade, frilly pleated skirt, clear glass candle cup sgd "Clarke's Criklite Trade Mark" .....1,350.00
Finger Bowl, 2-3/4" d, shiny finish, refired crimped rim, Mt. Washington .........................................................435.00
Jack-In-The-Pulpit, 12-1/2" h, elongated prunus blossom dec, gold detail stripes, row of white dots on wafer base, Mt. Washington .........................................................1,750.00
Mustard Pot, 4-1/2" h, shiny finish, barrel shape, vertical ribs, bail, metal collar, hinged lid, Mt. Washington...............................425.00
Pitcher, 6-3/4" h, 8-1/2" w, satin finish, unadorned, Mt. Washington .........................................................950.00
Salt Shaker, 4-1/4" h, lemon-yellow lower half, intense color on upper half, two part metal top, Mt. Washington .......................265.00
Toothpick Holder, 2-1/2" h, shiny finish, Optic Diamond Quilt pattern, Mt. Washington .........................................................535.00
Tumbler, 3-3/4" h, shiny finish, pastel salmon shading to creamy yellow, Mt. Washington ............................................285.00

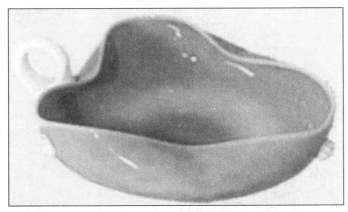

**Bon Bon, three applied lemon yellow prunts, applied handle, re-fired heart-shaped rim, Mt. Washington, 6-1/2" l, 4-3/4" w, 2-3/8" h, $835. Photo courtesy of Clarence & Betty Maier.**

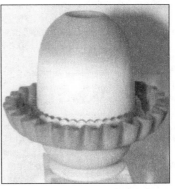

**Fairy Lamp, base sgd "Thomas Webb & Sons Queens Burmeseware," 5-3/4" d, 5-1/2" h, $1,285. Photo courtesy of Clarence & Betty Maier.**

Vase
    4" h, shiny finish, ruffled top, Webb ...................................485.00
    4-1/2" h, shiny finish, scalloped rim, unadorned, Shape 52-1/2 C, Mount Washington .......................................................585.00
    6" h, floriform shape, hp fern leaf dec, fitted into gold sgd "Dunham Mfg Co. Triple Plate" holder with Egyptian motif, Mt. Washington .......................................................545.00
    6-1/2" h, shiny finish, scalloped rim, unadorned, Shape 52-1/2 S, Mt. Washington .......................................................565.00
    10" h, tall tapered cylindrical, stick neck, two blossoms, one blue and white, other brown, black, and white, tiny raised pink-gold enamel dots, Mt. Washington ....................................1,785.00
    11" h, 6" d, white daisies, lemon-yellow ground, No. 146, Mt. Washington .......................................................1,850.00
    12" h, lily, satin finish, yellow border as blush to lily, Mt. Washington .......................................................665.00

# BUSTS

**History:** The portrait bust has its origins in pagan and Christian traditions. Greek and Roman heroes dominate the earliest examples. Later, images of Christian saints were used. Busts of the "ordinary man" first appeared during the Renaissance. During the 18th and 19th centuries, nobility, poets, and other notable persons were the most frequent subjects, especially on those busts designed for use in a home library. Because of the large number of these library busts, excellent examples can be found at reasonable prices, depending on artist, subject, and material.

**Additional Listings:** Ivory; Parian Ware; Soapstone; Wedgwood.

4-1/2" h, Caesar, youthful pose, patinated bronze, turned wooden base, French ...........................................................375.00
5-1/2" h
    Galileo, bronze, three quarter view, medium brown patination, onyx socle, Continental, 19th C ..................................550.00
    Woman, wearing whimple, white marble bust, shaped gray marble base, early 20th C ....................................................375.00
6" h, woman, carved mahogany, America, 19th C, contemporary stand, minor losses ...........................................................750.00
6-3/4" h, Magellan, bronze, black patination, green marble socle base, Continental, 19th C ........................................................230.00
8" h, Blackamoor, painted terra cotta, glass bead jewelry, Continental, 19th C.......................................................................690.00
8-1/2" h, Reverend John Wesley, creamware, gray hair, pink tinted flesh, black and white clerical robes, black self socle base, inscribed "The Revd John Wesley M. Died Mar 2, 1891, Aged 88, Enoch Wood Sculp. Burslem," Staffordshire, c1791, chips to base..............400.00
8-3/4" h, January (young woman), reddish-brown patinated bronze, red marble socle, Georges Van der Straeton, French..............690.00

9-1/2" h, Joseph de Carayon La Tour, bronze, sgd "h. Chapu" (Henri Michel Antoine Chapu,) inscribed "E. Coni & Co. fondeur," ..... 275.00

9-3/4" h, 7" l, young woman, green marble base, sgd "E. Battiglia," Italian, some chips ................................................................. 350.00

11" h, 11" d, pheasant woman, white alabaster, Italian .............. 400.00

11-1/4" h, Charles Dickens, parian, raised circular base, attributed to Robinson & Leadbeater, late 19th C ...................................... 290.00

11-3/4" h, Alexandra, parian, pedestal base, imp "Crystal Palace Art Union, F M Miller Sculpt, Pub'd Feb 11, 1863, Copeland" ....... 225.00

12" h, 7-1/4" l, Busto di Donna Vecchia," bronze, reddish and greenish brown patina, sgd "Gemito" (Vincenzo Gemito), inscribed "V-VIII'" and indecipherable foundry seal ........................................ 325.00

12-1/2" h, Au Vieil Ami M. B. Monvel, medium brown patina, red marble socle, Paul Paulin, French, early 20th C .......................... 550.00

14" h, girl with large ruffled hat, looking down on bird perched on shoulder, lace dressed, carved flowers, alabaster, mounted on small alabaster circular pedestal atop wood platform, 1" chip to hat ...... 350.00

14-3/8" h, Scott, Carrara, mounted on waisted circular socle, imp title, mark, and E. W. Wyon F., Wedgwood, England, c1855 ........... 750.00

17" h, woman, porcelain, pastel tones, flower and feather hair ornament, ruffled off-shoulder corseted bodice, English, late 19th/early 20th C ....................................................................... 750.00

17-3/4" h, maiden, bronze, parcel gilt, gilt and dark brown patina, socle base, inscribed "G" .............................................. 1,950.00

19" h, young girl with dove, textured shawl on shell background, carved Italian marble, sgd "P. Romanelli, Firenze" on base .. 5,175.00

20-1/2" h, Neoclassical beauty, composition, terra-cotta finish, tapered socle, 20th C ................................................... 320.00

21" h, 14" d, Napoleon, marble, incised "A. Cipriani," Italian, 19th C, losses ...................................................................... 490.00

21-1/4" h, Caesar Augustus, marble, Continental, c1900 ........ 1,950.00

22" h, 16" d, Sara Bernhardt, marble, platform base, incised "Pineschi G" ..................................................................... 1,265.00

23-1/4" h, Benjamin Franklin, bronze, after Jean-Antoine Houdon, French, 19th C, green patina ...................................... 750.00

24" h

    Caesar Augustus, carrara marble and gilded bronze, seal "Pinedo Bronzes Paris" ...................................................... 6,325.00

    Maiden, terra cotta, sgd "A Carrier-Belleuse," French, c1850 ................................................................. 6,000.00

25" h, Venice, three-quarters length, sq base, marble ............ 1,150.00

25-1/2" h

    Greek Slave, after Hiram Powers, c1850-70, nude, bead and leaf tip molded edge on circular sole, carved carrara marble, Italian .............................................................. 8,050.00

    Venus, clamshell and pearl headdress, shell covered bust, carved carrara marble, Italian ............................................ 5,750.00

26" h

    Young lady, pierced and carved lace hat with flowers, 5" h turned pedestal, alabaster .................................................. 1,550.00

    Young maiden, intricate coiffure, sq base, alabaster, Continental ............................................................... 1,955.00

29" h, marble, lady, 18th C costume, 42-1/4" h mottled marble column ....................................................................... 1,600.00

31-1/2" h, Lincoln, bronze, George Edwin Bissell, copyright 1904, cast by Gorham Foundries, Inc. ........................................... 4,840.00

32" h, Hera, cast stone, circular plinth base, early 20th C .......... 700.00

75" h, Roman emperor, cast stone, raised on two part fluted column, early 20th C, price for pr .............................................. 5,280.00

# BUTTER PRINTS

**History:** There are two types of butter prints: butter molds and butter stamps. Butter molds are generally of three-piece construction—the design, the screw-in handle, and the case. Molds both shape and stamp the butter at the same time. Butter stamps are generally of one-piece construction but can be of two-piece construction if the handle is from a separate piece of wood. Stamps decorate the top of butter after it is molded. The earliest prints are one piece and were hand carved, often heavily and deeply. Later prints were factory made with the design forced into the wood by a metal die. Some of the most common designs are sheaves of wheat, leaves, flowers, and pineapples. Animal designs and Germanic tulips are difficult to find. Prints with designs on both sides are rare, as are those in unusual shapes, such as half-rounded or lollipop.

**Reference:** Paul E. Kindig, *Butter Prints and Molds,* Schiffer Publishing, 1986.

**Reproduction Alert:** Reproductions of butter prints were made as early as the 1940s.

## Mold

    Cherries, carved wood, oblong, almond shaped indented mold carved with stylized cluster of cherries, leafy twig, serrated border, two part, dark finish, 10-1/2" l ................................ 90.00

    Cornflower, hand carved maple, round, c1830, 4-3/4" x 9" 125.00

    Cow pattern, hinged wood frame .................................... 360.00

    Four Leaf Clover, carved wood ..................................... 95.00

    Grapes pattern, porcelain, individual size ...................... 85.00

    Heart, anchor, and cross, carved wood, dished form, fluted sides, old brown patina, 4-5/8" d, 2" h .............................. 90.00

    Klappmodel, Maltese cross, five sections, woman drawing water from pump house with pine tree, flowers, tree in bloom, radiating tulips in center pc, 6 1/2" d ................................. 420.00

    Morvavian Star, carved wood, 5-1/4" h, 4-1/2" d ................ 90.00

    Rectangular, eight individual carved designs, including strawberries, vintage, acorns, etc., varnish finish, 5-1/2" x 11" ...... 140.00

    Swan, carved wood, cased, old finish, 5" d ..................... 190.00

## Print

    Acorn with two leaves, deeply carved maple, round, knob handle, c1820, 3-1/4" d .................................................. 250.00

    Berries and leaves, round, cross-hatched design above cluster of long pointed serrated leaves, three round berries, serrated rim, one piece turned handle, old patina, 4-1/2" d ................. 80.00

**Woman, flowers in hair, bronze, black marble base, 13-1/2" h, $200. Photo courtesy of Joy Luke Fine Art Brokers and Auctioneers.**

**Print, carved deer, $175.**

Bird and flowers, rect, chip carved border, old patina and dark stains, inserted turned handle, 1-3/4" x 2-1/2" x 4-3/4" .... 250.00

Cow, tree, poplar, round, one piece turned handle, dark patina, 4 1/2" d .................................................................. 195.00

Double

Carved intaglio star and leaves with chip carved fluted border, floral pattern on reverse, lathe turned from single piece of wood, c1840, 5" d, small age crack ........................... 220.00

Chip carved, falling leaves pattern, small leaf print on handle ..................................................................... 75.00

Eagle and rose, pedestal form, highly chip carved, whittle marks ....................................................................... 600.00

Palm held, deep gouge and chip carved rosette designs, concentric border ................................................... 220.00

Pestle shape, chip carved radiating leaf patterns, notched border ..................................................................... 200.00

Eagle, scrubbed poplar, round, one piece turned handle, 4 1/4" d, minor age cracks ......................................... 385.00

Elliptical, lightly carved two way design, primitive form ... 55.00

Floral over leaf, lollipop handle, deeply carved from one pc of wood, PA, c1830, age crack in handle ....................... 210.00

Flower on one side, pinwheel on other, scrubbed poplar, lollipop, handle marked "Grandma's Butter Printer," 7 3/4" l ................................................................ 360.00

Fox, running, carved, scrubbed finish, one piece turned handle, 3-1/2" d .......................................................... 675.00

Geometric starflower scrubbed poplar, lollipop, 9" l ...... 250.00

Intaglio floral design, round, fluted border, c1840, 4-1/2" d ................................................................... 80.00

Leaf, round, carved wood, sprig of three large serrated leaves in center, thin chip-carved border, turned handle, 3-3/4" d ................................................................... 75.00

Maple Hill Dairy, relief carved ........................................ 65.00

Pennsylvania Crown Tulip, chip carved ......................... 85.00

Pineapple, semi-circular, pine, 3 3/8 x 7", worn patina, replaced turned inserted handle ................................ 110.00

Rosette, chip and gouge carved, chip carved fluted border, round, c1850, 3 1/2" d .................................................. 55.00

Rosette, six pointed design alternating crosshatch and striated designs, chip and gouge carved, round, c1850, 3 1/2" d ........................................................................ 95.00

Starflower, concave circle, carved wood, old patina, 3-3/4" d ................................................................... 80.00

Striated Tulip, deeply gouge carved, border of chip and gouge carved radiating triangles, round, PA, 1830, 4" d........ 270.00

Swan, carved wood, round, carved border, 4-1/8" d ..... 365.00

The Union, hearts and stars, butternut, scrubbed finish, 3-1/8" x 5", added tin hanger ...................................... 360.00

Tulip, stylized, pine, old patina, 3" h, 4-7/8", added tin hanger .................................................................... 250.00

# CALENDAR PLATES

**History:** Calendar plates were first made in England in the late 1880s. They became popular in the United States after 1900, the peak years being 1909 to 1915. The majority of the advertising plates were made of porcelain or pottery and the design included a calendar, the name of a store or business, and either a scene, portrait, animal, or flowers. Some also were made of glass or tin.

**Periodical:** *The Calendar*, 710 N Lake Shore Dr., Barrington, IL 60010.

**Additional Listings:** See *Warman's Americana & Collectibles* for more examples.

1907, 9-1/4" d, Santa Claus center, River Falls, Wisconsin, advertising ...................................................................... 85.00
1908, 8" d, holly sprays, Russell Clothing House adv .................. 20.00
1908, 9-1/4" d, four cat faces, "Merry Christmas, B. L. Schermerhorn, Lowville, New York" ........................................ 65.00
1909, 8 1/2" d, flower girl, souvenir Abrams, WI ......................... 40.00
1909, 9" d, John Kemper Harness Maker, Butler, PA, Mediterranean woman in center, marked "Vorrey" ....................... 30.00
1909, 9 1/2" d, Gibson girl type portrait, calendar months, fruit, and floral border, WI adv .................................................. 35.00
1910, 6 7/8" d, compliments of Geo H Farguhasson, Cooperstown, NY, marked "Semi Porcelain" .............................. 35.00
1910, 7" d, violets with ribbon banner, emb gold scalloped edge, JL McCue adv .................................................................. 30.00
1910, 7-1/4" d, United States Bank, bank note in center payable to Bearer, Three Hundred and Sixty Five Bright, Happy, Prosperous Days, green border, gold trim, green Carrolton Pottery Co. mark with crown and eagle ................................................................. 50.00
1910, 10" d, woman in garden center, calendar months border ...30.00
1911, 6-1/2" d, Compliments of H. B. Schanley, Jewelers, Quakertown, PA, early red roadster with four figures, months strong across road as banner ................................................................. 95.00
1911, 8 1/2" d, gray fence with three rabbits and two birds, JW Morey adv ................................................................................. 30.00
1912, 7-1/2" d, owl on open book, calendars on pages, August, Illinois, advertising ..................................................................... 45.00
1912, 8-1/4" d, Indian husking corn .......................................... 40.00
1912, 8-1/2" d, flowers and cherubs center ............................... 35.00
1912, 8 1/2" d, hot air balloon ................................................... 75.00
1913, 8" d, calendar months center, rose garland and holly border ................................................................................... 30.00
1913, 8-1/4" d, sweet peas, pink and lavender ground ................ 50.00
1914, 9 1/4" d, Washington's Tomb, Milford, DE, artist sgd "A Smith" ............................................................................... 40.00
1914, 9-1/2" d, sandpiper center, sgd "R. K. Beck" .................... 50.00
1916, 8 1/4" d, American flag, eagle with shield ........................ 35.00

1919, 8 1/4" d, American flag, John J Rutgers Co, Holland, MI adv ...................................................................................... 40.00
1919, 8" d, Walnut Grove, MN ................................................... 50.00
1928, 8-1/2" d, deer looking at road sign "To Old Orchard Beach, Maine" ................................................................................. 60.00

# CALLING CARD CASES and RECEIVERS

**History:** Calling cards, usually carried in specially designed cases, played an important social role in the United States, from the Civil War until the end of World War I. When making formal visits, callers left their card in a receiver (card dish) in the front hall. Strict rules of etiquette developed. For example, the lady in a family was expected to make calls of congratulations and condolence and visits to the ill. The cards themselves were small, embossed or engraved with the caller's name and often decorated with a floral design. Many handmade examples, especially in Spencerian script, can be found. The cards themselves are considered collectible and range in price from a few cents to several dollars.

**Note:** Don't confuse a calling card case with a match safe.

## Calling Card Case
Gold
    Elaborately chased and engraved, fan design within floral motifs, textured background, monogrammed curved lid, European hallmarks, 50.1 dwt ......................................................... 1,100.00
    Tiffany & Co., 18K yellow gold, rect design, textured black leather and yellow gold frame, sgd "Tiffany & Co." ................... 320.00
Ivory, 4-1/4" x 3" .................................................................... 50.00
Mother-of-pearl, tortoiseshell and pique work, English, c1855-70, 2-5/8" w, 5-3/4" h ................................................................... 70.00
Silver, English, Victorian, maker's mark, Birmingham,
    Rect, bright-cut engraved foliate surface dec, hinged flip-top lid, central lever device to push cards out of case, on chain with ring, monogram, 1898, 3-1/4" l, 2 troy oz .................................. 300.00
    Rect, hinged flip-top lid, chain, monogram, 3-7/8" l, c1900, 2 troy oz ............................................................................... 150.00

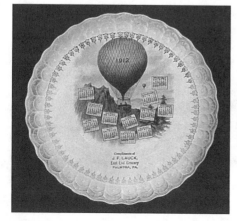

**1912, Compliments of J. F. Lauck, Palmyra, PA, hot air balloon, mkd "Sterling China," $75.**

**Case, sterling silver, Christ Church, Phila on one side, other side with Fairmount Waterworks, 2-3/8" x 3-3/8", $275.**

Rect, maker R. T., Birmingham, 1869, elaborately engraved, 4" l, 2 troy oz ...................................................200.00

Slim rect shape, hinged lid, engine-turned surface dec, engraved foliate frame border, central medallion with monogram, illegible maker's mark, 1872, 3-7/8" l, 2 troy oz ...........................250.00

Tortoiseshell

Inset silver shield, engraved crest, mother-of-pearl inlay, 4-1/8" x 3-1/8".................................................................200.00

Regency, 4" x 3"..................................................................165.00

## Calling Card Receiver

Arab and woven basket, 9-3/4" h, bronze, 19th C .............420.00

Butler, 33-1/4" h, cast iron, African-American, holding tray 225.00

Cut Glass, 6" l, rolled edge, strawberry diamond and fan motif, sold with "Mr. & Mrs. Samuel Hawkes" calling card .........500.00

Flower shape, 6-1/2" d, green five-petaled blossom in center of amber plate, overall gold irid, base inscribed "L. C. T. N9511" for Tiffany Studios.................................................................575.00

Frog shape, 7-1/2" l, hammered surface, Tiffany & Co., 1875-91, 5 troy oz ...................................................................1,100.00

Shell shape, 18kt yellow gold wash over sterling silver, sgd "Tiffany & Co."...............................................................260.00

Shell shape, engraved mermaid, ftd, SP, Rogers ...............100.00

Sterling Silver

5-1/8" h, sterling, easel back, projecting rect card holder, molded scroll border, top pointed arch, America, 20th C, 2 troy oz ......... 100.00

9" l, Colonial style, America, c1905-15, 5.9 troy oz ..............50.00

# CAMBRIDGE GLASS

**History:** Cambridge Glass Company, Cambridge, Ohio, was incorporated in 1901. Initially, the company made clear tableware, later expanding into colored, etched, and engraved glass. More than 40 different hues were produced in blown and pressed glass. The plant closed in 1954. Some of the molds were later sold to the Imperial Glass Company, Bellaire, Ohio.

**Marks:** Five different marks were employed during the production years, but not every piece was marked.

**References:** Tom and Neila Bredehoft, *Fifty Years of Collectible Glass, 1920-1970*, Volume 1, Volume II, Antique Trader Books, 2000; Gene Florence, *Elegant Glassware of the Depression Era*, 8th ed., Collector Books, 1998; ——, *Glass Candlesticks of the Depression Era*, Collector Books, 1999; National Cambridge Collectors, Inc., *Cambridge Glass Co., Cambridge, Ohio* (reprint of 1930 catalog and supplements through 1934), Collector Books, 1976, 1998 value update; ——, *Cambridge Glass Co., Cambridge, Ohio, 1949 through 1953* (catalog reprint), Collector Books, 1976, 1996 value update; ——, *Colors in Cambridge Glass*, Collector Books, 1984, 1999 value update; ——, *Nearcut* (reprint of 1910 catalog), 1997; Naomi L. Over, *Ruby Glass of the 20th Century*, Antique Publications, 1990, 1993-94 value update; Miami Valley (Ohio) Study Group, *Etchings by Cambridge*, Volume 1, Brookville Publishing, 1997; Bill and Phyllis Smith, *Cambridge Glass 1927-1929* (1986) and *Identification Guide to Cambridge Glass 1927-1929* (updated prices 1996), published by authors (4003 Old Columbus Rd., Springfield, OH 45502).

**Periodical***: The Daze*, P.O. Box 57, Otisville, MI 48463.

**Collectors' Club***: National Cambridge Collectors, Inc., P.O. Box 416, Cambridge, OH 43725.

**Museums:** Cambridge Glass Museum, Cambridge, OH; Museum of the National Cambridge Collectors, Inc., Cambridge, OH.

Ashtray

Caprice, Blue Alpine ...........................................................30.00

Portia, sq..............................................................................45.00

Basket, Rose Point, #3500/55, 2 handles on turned up sides, 6" sq, 3-1/4" h, pie crust edge ..............................................................100.00

Bon Bon

Apple Blossom, #3400/1180, blue, 5-1/4" d......................60.00

Caprice, 2 handles, 6"..........................................................15.00

Rose Point, #205 ...............................................................200.00

Bouillon, Decagon, light blue ..................................................20.00

Bowl

Azurite, 8" d, cupped, gold trim............................................75.00

Caprice, blue, 11" d, 4 ftd, crimped ...................................115.00

Gloria, #3400/185, 10" d, 2 handled, silver encrusted ebony, some wear and tarnishing..............................................125.00

Rose Point, 9-1/2" d, 12-1/2" l, ruffled, oval, 4 ftd, two handles...............................................................................425.00

Tally Ho, red, 12-1/8", flat rim............................................75.00

Wildflower, 9-5/8" d, flared rim ............................................85.00

Windsor Blue, 10" d, seashell, 3-toed................................250.00

Brandy, Nudes

Amber .................................................................................185.00

Amethyst..............................................................................195.00

Forest Green .......................................................................185.00

Bridge Hound, emerald green..................................................65.00

Bud Vase, Rose Point, 6" h......................................................95.00

Butter, cov, #3400/52

Apple Blossom, pink ...........................................................500.00

Wildflower ...........................................................................200.00

Cake Plate

Rose Point, #3500/110, ftd, 13" d .....................................145.00

Wildflower, 13" d .................................................................145.00

Candlesticks, pr

Apple Blossom, #3400/646, pink .......................................110.00

Caprice, 3-lite, #1338, 6" h ..................................................75.00

Decagon, Carmen red, keyhole ...........................................75.00

Martha, 2-lite, 8-1/2" w, 5-1/2" h .........................................65.00

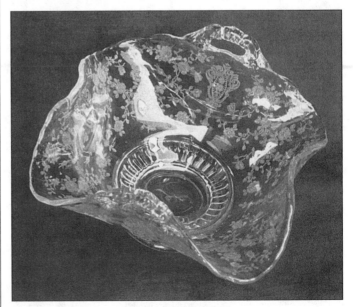

Bowl, Rose Point, handle, 5-1/2" d, $32.

Rose Point, 2-lite, keyhole, etched bobeches and prisms .. 550.00
Twist, Jade, opaque blue-green, 8-1/2" h ............................. 95.00
Wildflower, #646, 1-lite ......................................................... 75.00
Candy Box, cov
    Cascade, yellow ................................................................... 60.00
    Washington, No. 77 Wedgwood etch, 2 lb size, round ....... 110.00
Candy Dish, cov
    Blossom Time, Martha blank, 3 ftd, 6" h, 6-1/4" d .............. 165.00
    Cleo, #103, 3-part ............................................................. 115.00
    Portia, Carmen, gold encrusted, four small feet .............. 2,230.00
    Rose Point, Crown Tuscan, gold edge, 3-part ................... 165.00
    Wildflower, 3-part .............................................................. 150.00
Celery/Relish
    Apple Blossom, #3500/152, 4-part ..................................... 65.00
    Diane, 5-part .................................................................... 60.00
    Rose Point, 3-part, 9" l ...................................................... 70.00
    Tally Ho, forest green, 12" l ............................................... 35.00
    Wildflower, #397 ................................................................ 60.00
Centerpiece Bowl, Apple Blossom, 12-1/2" d, #3400/2, draped
    edge ..................................................................................... 65.00
Champagne
    Decagon, light blue ............................................................ 25.00
    Wildflower, #3121 35.00
Cheese and Cracker Set, Wildflower ........................................ 110.00
Cheese Comport, Wildflower ...................................................... 50.00
Cheese Dish, cov, Cordeilia, #980, 5" d .................................... 85.00
Cigarette Box, cov
    Nudes, Carmen ................................................................. 600.00
    Rose Point, 3-1/2" w, 1-1/2" l ......................................... 500.00
Cigarette Holder
    Caprice, blue, 2-1/4" h ..................................................... 75.00
    Diane, gold encrusted, ashtray foot ................................. 300.00
Claret
    Nudes, Carmen ................................................................. 175.00
    Tally Ho, red, 4-1/2 oz ....................................................... 45.00
    Wildflower, #3121, 4-1/2 oz ............................................... 42.00
Cocktail
    Caprice, blue, #3 ............................................................... 65.00
    Chantilly, #3775 ................................................................ 25.00
    Diane, #3122 ..................................................................... 28.00
    Gloria, #3122, pink .......................................................... 165.00
    Hunt's Scene, #3077 ......................................................... 60.00
    Nudes, La Rosa Pink ........................................................ 170.00
    Regency/Stradivari ............................................................ 15.00
    Rose Point, #3121 ............................................................. 32.50
    Tally Ho, forest green, 3 oz ............................................... 18.00
Cocktail Shaker, Rose Point, 32 oz .......................................... 325.00
Compote
    Apple Blossom, yellow, 7" h .............................................. 85.00
    Azurite, 8-1/4", ftd, silver trim .......................................... 95.00
    Daffodil, 6-1/2" d, low, ftd, handles ................................... 40.00
    Farber, Grape pattern, 5-1/2" h, brass holder, green glass
        insert ................................................................................ 40.00
    Krome Statuesque, amber glass insert .............................. 55.00
    Nudes, Carmen, cupped .................................................. 300.00
    Rose Point, 5-1/2" ............................................................ 125.00
Console Set, Apple Blossom, 10-1/2" d #674 bowl, pair 3-1/2" h #628
    candlesticks ......................................................................... 80.00
Cordial
    Chantilly, 1 oz. .................................................................. 80.00
    Portia ............................................................................... 125.00
    Rose Point ......................................................................... 75.00
    Tally Ho, red, thick ............................................................ 65.00
    Wildflower, #3121, 1 oz ..................................................... 60.00
Cornucopia, Sea Shell #47, Crown Tuscan ............................. 195.00
Cracker Plate, Apple Blossom, #3400/6, yellow ....................... 50.00
Creamer, individual size
    Chantilly ............................................................................. 22.50
    Gadroon, amber ................................................................ 17.50

Creamer, table size
    Cleo, amber, ftd ................................................................ 20.00
    Decagon, pink, lightning bolt handle ................................. 15.00
Cruet
    Caprice, Blue Alpine ........................................................ 175.00
    Nautilus, amethyst ............................................................ 60.00
Cup and Saucer
    Portia ................................................................................. 45.00
    Rose Point ......................................................................... 55.00
Decanter
    Portia, #3400/113 ............................................................ 300.00
    Rose Chintz, amber ......................................................... 400.00
    Rose Point, ftd, #3121 ..................................................... 450.00
    No. 1380, etched "Scotch," etched thistles, 26 oz ............... 95.00
Decanter Set, Caprice, LaRosa pink, 35 oz decanter with orig stopper,
    four 2 oz tumblers ............................................................ 800.00
Finger Bowl, Heatherbloom, #3111, optic ................................. 60.00
Flower Frog
    Blue Jay, crystal, 5-1/2" h ................................................ 135.00
    Draped Lady, 8-1/2" h, pink .............................................. 250.00
    Heron, crystal, 9" h .......................................................... 135.00
    Two Kid, pink ................................................................... 325.00
Flower Holder, Crown Tuscan .................................................. 175.00
Goblet, water
    Chantilly, #3775 ................................................................ 25.00
    Elaine ................................................................................. 60.00
    Nudes, Carmen ................................................................. 275.00
    Portia ................................................................................. 35.00
    Rose Point, #3121 ............................................................. 32.50
    Tally Ho, red, 10 oz, thick .................................................. 35.00
Honey Dish, cov, Rubina, 8" h ................................................. 175.00
Ice Bucket
    Cleo, light blue ................................................................. 225.00
    Diane, No. 3400/851, orig handle and tongs ..................... 225.00
    Oaken Bucket, pink, hammered metal handle, "C" in triangle
        mark ................................................................................. 60.00
    Rose Point, metal handle, #3400/851 ............................... 235.00
    Wildflower, #3400/851 ...................................................... 225.00
Iced Tea Tumbler
    Chantilly, #3625 ................................................................ 30.00
    Gloria, #3122, pink .......................................................... 165.00
    Roselie, blue ..................................................................... 65.00
    Wildflower, #3121, 12 oz ................................................... 32.50
Ivy Ball
    Gold Krystol, ftd, 4-1/2" w, 5-3/4" h .................................. 35.00
    Nudes, Carmen ................................................................. 500.00
    Rose Point ......................................................................... 585.00
Lemon Plate, Caprice, blue, 6" d, handle .................................. 40.00
Jelly, Caprice, blue, 7" d, crimped ............................................ 65.00
Jug
    Elaine, 80 oz .................................................................... 400.00
    Farber, amethyst, 5" h ....................................................... 75.00
    Nautilus, crystal, silver overlay fruits ............................... 210.00
    Rose Point, ball, 80 oz ..................................................... 325.00
Juice Tumbler
    Elaine, ftd ......................................................................... 35.00
    Rose Point, #3121, ftd ...................................................... 35.00
Marmalade, cov
    Diane ................................................................................ 185.00
    Portia, ftd .......................................................................... 75.00
    Rose Point, #147, 1 oz, sterling lid, glass spoon .............. 150.00
    Wildflower ......................................................................... 175.00
Martini Pitcher, Portia, orig plunger, 60 oz ............................ 1,500.00
Mayonnaise
    Diane, SS base .................................................................. 85.00
    Portia, Tally Ho blank, divided .......................................... 40.00
    Wildflower, pink, liner ...................................................... 165.00
Muddler, rooster, 5-1/2" l .......................................................... 27.50
Mug, Martha Washington, Carmen red, 12 oz, clear applied
    handle ................................................................................ 45.00

Mustard, cov, Two Town, amber ..............................50.00
Nappy, Rose Point, 6" d ...........................................85.00
Oyster Cocktail, Portia ............................................40.00
Parfait
    Hunt's Scene ...................................................85.00
    Portia ................................................................95.00
Pickle Dish
    Rose Point, 9" l ...............................................65.00
    Wildflower, 9-1/2" l ..........................................48.00
Plate
    Cleo, blue, 8-1/4" d .........................................30.00
    Diane, 8-1/2" d, #3400/62 ...............................22.00
    Imperial Hunt Scene, pink, 8" d ......................45.00
    Portia, 6" d ......................................................15.00
    Tally Ho, red, 8" d ...........................................20.00
Platter, Apple Blossom, #3400/1186, 12-1/2" l ...175.00
Punch Bowl Set, Tally Ho, red, ftd bowl, 8 mugs ........800.00
Punch Mug, Tally Ho, red .........................................35.00
Relish
    Blossom Time, Martha blank, 3 part, 8-1/2" l, four tab
       handles ..........................................................75.00
    Candlelight, 3-part, 12" l ..................................55.00
    Elaine, 3-part ...................................................85.00
    Rose Point, 3-part, center handle, 7-1/2" d.........165.00
    Wildflower, cloverleaf shape, 3 part, 3 handles, #3400/91 ...55.00
Rose Bowl
    Caprice, 6" h ...................................................80.00
    Gold Krystol, 6" d, 5-1/2" h.............................50.00
    Salad Bowl, Caprice, #80, pink, cupped, 13" d..................500.00
Salad Dressing
    Caprice, blue, twin, handle ..............................500.00
    Decagon, #1263, amber ....................................110.00
    Tally Ho, crystal, #1402/95, 5-3/4" d bowl, 8" d plate............45.00
Salt and Pepper Shakers, pr, Decagon, cobalt blue .................125.00
Sandwich Plate, Everglades, #57, 3 toes, 15" d .................55.00
Seafood Cocktail, icer with liner, Rose Point, #968 ...................125.00
Server, center handle
    Aero Optic, moonlight blue, 11-1/2" d .............68.00
    Apple Blossom, pink .........................................60.00
    Azurite, gold trim .............................................85.00
    Decagon, mulberry, keyhole handle .................75.00
    Decagon, Regal blue ........................................75.00
Sherbet
    Apple Blossom, amber, #3130, 6 oz .................18.00
    Diane, low ........................................................24.00
    Forest Green, No. 3035, low.............................15.00
    Rose Point, #3121, tall .....................................22.00
    Wildflower, #3121, 6 oz, tall ............................20.00
Sherry
    Diane, 2 oz .......................................................75.00
    Trumpet, amethyst, 2-1/2 oz .............................30.00
Sugar Bowl, cov
    Caprice, moonlight blue, 3" ..............................25.00
    Decagon, light blue ..........................................20.00
Sugar Pail, Cleo, bail handle, green ......................350.00
Sugar Shaker, Decagon, pink ................................165.00
Syrup, cov, Decagon, pink .....................................125.00
Swan
    Type I, ebony, 3" h ..........................................110.00
    Type II, crystal, 8-1/2" h ...................................95.00
    Type II, pink, 3" ...............................................45.00
    Type IIIB, Mandarin gold, 3" .............................75.00
Sweet Pea Vase, Wildflower, green, 3-3/4" h..........300.00
Tankard Pitcher, Portia.............................................500.00
Torte Plate
    Chantilly, Martha blank.....................................85.00
    Rose Point, 12-1/2" d, 3 ftd, 3900 line ...............125.00
    Tray for creamer and sugar, Decagon, black........45.00

Tumbler, water
    Apple Blossom, yellow, 12 oz, ftd ....................40.00
    Heatherbloom, #3111, optic, 12 oz, ftd .............55.00
    Marjorie, #7606, 10 oz .....................................35.00
    Nautilus, amethyst, 4-3/4" h, 12 oz ..................25.00
    Rosalie, #119, amber .......................................45.00
    Rose Point, #3121, 12 oz, ftd ...........................35.00
    Tally Ho, Carmen red, 12 oz .............................60.00
Vase
    Caprice, blue, 3-1/2" h .....................................200.00
    Castle, 11-3/4" h, 5-1/2" w, black, silver castle scene in oval
       medallion, silver border at top and on short pedestal ... 1,675.00
    Cleo, #1023, pink, 9-1/2" h ..............................450.00
    Portia, Crown Tuscan, gold inlay, 6" h, 6" d....................185.00
    Rose Point, Crown Tuscan, gold edge, 10" h ..................250.00
    Two Tone, forest green, 12" h ...........................75.00
Wine
    Chantilly, #3775 ...............................................32.50
    Decagon, amethyst ...........................................30.00
    Nude, amber .....................................................325.00
    Portia ................................................................50.00

# CAMEO GLASS

**History:** Cameo glass is a form of cased glass. A shell of glass was prepared; then one or more layers of glass of a different color(s) was faced to the first. A design was then cut through the outer layer(s) leaving the inner layer(s) exposed. This type of art glass originated in Alexandria, Egypt between 100 and 200 A.D. The oldest and most famous example of cameo glass is the Barberini or Portland vase which was found near Rome in 1582. It contained the ashes of Emperor Alexander Serverus, who was assassinated in 235 A.D. Emile Gallé is probably one of the best-known cameo glass artists. He established a factory at Nancy, France, in 1884. Although much of the glass bears his signature, he was primarily the designer. Assistants did the actual work on many pieces, even signing Gallé's name. Other makers of French cameo glass include D'Argental, Daum Nancy, LeGras, and Delatte. English cameo pieces do not have as many layers of glass (colors) and cuttings as do French pieces. The outer layer is usually white, and cuttings are very fine and delicate. Most pieces are not signed. The best-known makers are Thomas Webb & Sons and Stevens and Williams.

**Marks:** A star before the name Gallé on a piece by that company indicates that it was made after Gallé's death in 1904.

**References:** Victor Arwas, *Glass Art Nouveau to Art Deco*, Rizzoli International Publications, 1977; Alastair Duncan and George DeBartha, *Glass by Gallé*, Harry N. Abrams, 1984; Ray and Lee Grover, *English Cameo Glass*, Crown Publishers, 1980; Kyle Husfloen, *Antique Trader's American & European Decorative and Art Glass Price Guide*, 2nd ed., Krause Publications, 2000; Albert C. Revi, *Nineteenth Century Glass*, reprint, Schiffer Publishing, 1981; John A. Shuman III, *Collector's Encyclopedia of American Art Glass*, Collector Books, 1988, 1999 value update.

## American

Durand, vase, 6" h, cut floral rose color ext., white int., sgd "V. Durand" .......................................................385.00

Gillander American Glass Co,
Lamp Shade, 4-1/2" h, 3-7/8" fitter ring, crimped rim, flared cased body, Pink, three birds among blossoms, minor rim chips................................250.00
Vase, 4" h, overlaid in white, cameo etched morning glory blossoms, buds, and leafy vines, shaded blue cased to white oval body ......................................825.00

Honesdale, vase
8" h, 4" d, bright yellow over crystal, stylized blossom design, sgd in gold on base.....................975.00
8" h, 7" d base, Art Nouveau motif, oily irid to some portions, some loss to gold edges .........................750.00
9-3/4" h, 5" d, brilliant deep amber over crystal, five bright yellow chrysanthemums, carved leaves, two leaf borders, gold trim ........................................2,250.00

Mount Washington
Bowl, 9" w, 4" h, bulbous, deep pink over creamy white, scrolls, flowers, and woman design ............................950.00
Parlor Lamp, 21" h, 10" w shade, parlor, brilliant yellow over white, woman and baskets of flowers on base, matching floral design on side, fancy brass base and font, original chimney ...................................8,500.00

## English

Carder, Frederick, attributed to, vase, 8" h, baluster, olive green body, thickly layered in white, deeply carved blossoms on convoluted leafy stems .....................4,350.00

Richardson, vase, 8" h, clear golden amber, lily blossoms nestled among shiny golden foliage, honeycomb design body, sgd "Richardson's Rich Cameo" in pontil mark ...................1,350.00

Stevens and Williams
Bowl, 6-1/4" d, 4" h, ftd, cased yellow ground, carved seaweed, applied glass prunt .............................250.00
Decanter, 15-1/2" h, citron yellow and colorless ground, sapphire blue overlay, wheel cut and engraved cactus rose blossoms on spiked leaf-forms, matching teardrop stopper .............................................1,265.00

Vase
4-1/4" h, 3-1/4" w, pale blue ground, dainty carved leaves, single large butterfly, band of white beaded cutting at throat, base fully sgd "Stevens & Williams Art Glass, Stourbridge".....................................1,250.00
4-1/2" h, broad bright blue oval, overlaid in opaque white glass, cameo etched and cut clusters of cherries on leafy boughs, circular mark on base "Stevens & Williams Art Glass Stourbridge"......................................1,265.00
5-1/2" h, buttercup yellow body, dolce-relievo dec of soft pink cherry blossoms, gnarled and twisted branch, pink borders .............................................1,450.00

Unknown Maker
Lamp Shade, 5" h, 8-1/2" d, 4" d fitter, gaslight, powder blue ground, four detailed sprays of white Maidenhair Fern alternating with four sprays of Forest Fern, white border at lower edge and collar .......................................1,245.00
Plaque, 5-1/2" l, 3-1/2" w, citron yellow ground, white carved carnation and leaf ...............................1,275.00
Vase, 5" h, frosted red body, white cameo blossoms and leafy stems, reverse with two butterflies..............................750.00

Webb, Thomas & Sons
Bowl, 6" d, 1-3/4" h, powder blue ground, white old fashioned roses, foliage, and butterfly, white border, incised "L/6107" in pontil ........................................985.00
Cologne Bottle, 6-1/4" h, citron body, white over red dec of criss-crossed pussy willow twigs, push-on silver cap ...............................................1,250.00
Ewer, 5-3/4" h, Grecian shape, custard colored body, formal dec, amber handle, imp "Thomas Webb & Sons," neck broken off, ground smooth ...........................385.00

Perfume Bottle
2-1/2" h, sphere, opalescent translucent body, white overlay, cameo etched with repeating blossom and vine tracery, mounted with mkd "sterling" silver rim and hinged wreath dec cap, orig glass stopper.....................1,035.00
3-1/8" h, sphere, ruby red, cameo cut shell and seaweed motif, fitted with hallmarked silver rim, hinged dome cov...........................................2,100.00
4" l, teardrop, green oval, white snowdrop blossoms and buds dec, hallmarked silver rim, hinged cover with glass int...........................................1,400.00
5" h, cased oval, red ground, white cameo overlay, etched blossom motif, three applied thorny camphor glass feet, hallmarked silver rim fitted with silver clad glass stopper, silver over-cover................................1,850.00
Plaque, 7-3/4" h, 4-3/4" w, attributed to George Woodall, yellow amber overlaid in white, cameo etched lilac blossoms, bordered and scalloped at edge, mounted to foil lined metal frame for hanging......................4,900.00

Rose Bowl
2-1/4" h, 2-1/2" d, etched blackberry dec in white, dark plum ground................................920.00
6" h, translucent ruby red, white overlay carved and etched with brambles and thorny rosa rugosa bushes, butterfly and caterpillar at reverse, base stamped for retailer "Theodore B. Starr, New York".....................2,875.00

Scent
2" h, sphere, frosted colorless cased to opal, overlaid with white over red, cameo etched trumpet blossoms and leafy vine, hallmarked silver threaded rim and screw cap 1,380.00
2-1/4" l, sphere, red body, detailed white floral spray, screw rim, chased cap with elaborate foliate design, cross threaded...........................................1,100.00
3" h, cylinder, deep amber ground, white carved flowers and leaves, borders above and below, hallmarked hinged rim and silver cap (dented) ...........................1,495.00

Vase
3" h, 3-1/4" d, squat bulbous, raisin brown ground, white blossoming leafy vines, borders above and below, Webb medallion on base ................................690.00
3-1/2" h, oval red body, white fuchsia blossoms, linear borders .............................................1,265.00
4" h, design attributed to George Woodall, oval body, deep cobalt blue, overlaid in pastel cornflower blue, cameo carved six Japanesque floral medallions, latticework foliate and geometric ground, polished top rim .........................6,900.00
5" h, small flared rim on ovoid body, chartreuse ground, white overlay, engraved with double bands at top and bottom, fuchsia blossoms and leaves, butterfly on reverse, minor chips to cameo band at rim, minor abrasion..............575.00
5-1/4" h, flared Northwood blue oval body, deeply overlaid in white, cameo etched and carved with sculptural blossoming plants obverse and reverse with insects in flight at sides ...............................................3,650.00
5-3/4" h, bulbous lily, chartreuse yellow cased body, overlaid in white over deep red, cameo etched orchid lilies, butterfly at reverse, linear borders.......................2,500.00
7" h, small flared rim on ovoid body, chartreuse ground, red and white overlay, cameo etched fuchsia blossoms and leaves, butterfly on reverse, double bands at top and bottom rim, rim possibly ground, minor nicks .....................1,100.00
7-1/2" h, complex oval body, transparent ice blue overlaid at top quarter in stippled ruby red with white layer below, etched and carved as pond lilies and leaf pods, clear blue water background, base borders center "Webb" medallion, possible restoration to center base......................20,700.00
7-3/4" h, Peking tricolor, bright olive green overlaid on ivory, lined in raspberry pink, etched and carved blossoms and foliate devices in Asian manner, elaborate borders interspersed, framed mark on base "Thos. Webb & Sons"..............6,900.00

**La Verre Francais, table lamp, acid etched and carved, brown bell flowers and leaves, yellow and orange ground, sgd in script on base, 12" d shade, 20" h, $2,530. Photo courtesy of Joy Luke Fine Art Brokers and Auctioneers.**

8" h, flared trumpet form, bright blue overlaid in white, oak leaves dec, elaborate lower border........................... 1,725.00

8-1/2" h, flared cone, bright yellow-green cased to opal, over-laid in white over deep blue, cameo etched and carved blackberry branches, bumblebee below .................. 3,450.00

9" h, 6-1/2" w, deep amber ground, carved white oriental pop-pies, leaves, stems, and buds, reverse with carving of morn-ing glories, leaves, vines, and buds......................... 3,950.00

10" h, flared baluster, yellow-green body overlaid in white over ruby red, cameo etched and carved chrysanthemums and bumblebee and butterfly at reverse, linear borders, small surface scratch at center ........................................ 1,200.00

## French

Chouvenin, vase, 9-1/8" h, tapered mouth on cylindrical gray ves-sel, etched and enameled trees by mountainous lake, brown, rust-orange enamel on stained orange to yellow ground, enamel signature, c1900.............................................. 650.00

D'Argental

Box, cov, 3-1/2" d, 3-1/4" h, cylindrical, amber layered in bur-gundy-red, cameo etched Art Deco style blossoms in over-lapping designs, flower mkd "D'Argental" .................. 600.00

Vase

8" h, oval body, fiery golden amber, overlaid in bright and burgundy-red, cameo etched expansive riverside scene with mountains, tall trees in foreground, sgd "D'Argental" in motif............................................... 1,150.00

12" h, bottle form, fiery golden amber, overlaid in red-amber and maroon, etched landscape and riverside scenes, framed in scrolling arches, etched "D'Argental (cross)"................................................ 950.00

Daum Nancy Cabinet or Miniature Vase

3/4" h, 1-3/4" w, oval, fall scene, sgd........................ 800.00
1-1/2" h, 1-3/4" w, oval, summer scene, sgd ............. 1,100.00
1-3/4" h, summer scene, sgd........................................ 900.00
1-3/4" h, trees and lake scene, fall colors, sgd............ 750.00
1-3/4" h, winte scene, sgd ........................................... 850.00
2-1/2" h, corset shape, sunset scene, sgd ................ 1,000.00
2-3/4" h, bud type, rain scene, sgd........................... 2,000.00

Lamp

14" h, matching base and shade, purple-aubergine at top shaded to mottled green at lower edge, overlaid in white and green, cameo etched as broad leafy trees, crowns on shade, trunks o base, period bronze lamp fittings, inscribed "Daum Nancy (cross)" under base and on shade rim.......... 5,175.00

19" h, matching base and ball shade, green and black glass layered over turquoise blue, cameo etched riverside scene with tall trees and grass on foreground shore, island views beyond, sgd "Daum Nancy (cross)" on both, black metal fit-tings with sockets above and below ...................... 12,650.00

Miniature Pitcher, 2-3/4" h, frosted pink ground, carved black leaves, gold flowers, applied handle, sgd ................... 900.00

Salt Dish, 2" h, 3" l, angular oval, ftd, one fiery golden amber, other emerald green cased to clear, etched gilded maiden hair fern motif, four applied glass ball feet, each inscribed in gold "Daum (cross) Nancy," price for pr.................. 1,400.00

Vase

4-3/4" h, flared, cushioned triangular base, green, acid etched alternating bands of raised and relief stylized blossoms on textured ground, black and gold enamel highlights, base with etched signature "Daum (cross) Nancy," minor wear to enamel................................................. 320.00

6" h, Rain scene, sgd ................................................ 6,200.00

8-1/2" h, detailed flowers, shades of brown, yellow frosted and modeled ground, cameo sgd ................................... 1,600.00

14" h, flared mottled gold and red-amber oval body, acid-etched forest scene, enhanced by vitrified autumn colors on falling leaves, sgd "Daum Nancy (cross)" in middle. 4,600.00

DeVez

Vase, 3-3/4" h, frosted colorless oval, overlaid in pink, cameo etched five-petaled blossoms, cameo sgd "deVez" at side, top edge smoothed................................................... 300.00

Galle

Atomizer, 7" h, deeply cut blue trees, blue mountain range, green lake, frosted and yellow sky, cameo sgd .......... 800.00

Bowl, 5-3/4" d, 1-1/2" d, colorless and yellow overlaid in aub-ergine, cameo etched in organic leaf forms, sgd "Galle" at rim................................................... 350.00

Lamp, 14" h, cameo shade and base, 9" d shade carved with blue eagles, frosted and blue ground, base with deep blue evergreens, light blue mountains, green lake, both cameo sgd, shade cracked............................................ 1,200.00

Perfume Bottle

5-1/4" h, oval body, frosted yellow overlaid in green-brown, etched spring flowers, sgd "Galle" at side, fitted with gilt metal atomizer top, some parts missing ..................... 520.00

5-3/8" h, conical, cased yellow overlaid in brown, cameo etched leafy stems and blossoms, sgd "Galle" at reverse, top sheared................................................... 550.00

6-3/4" h, oval body, frosted golden amber, amethyst disk foot, overlaid in lavender and brown, cameo etched blossoms above spiked leaves, sgd "Galle" on reverse.............. 500.00

Vase

2-1/2" h, raised rim, broad ovoid body, gray layered in ame-thyst, etched violets, cameo signature........................ 460.00

5-1/8" h, raised rim, flattened circular body, , two applied loop handles, gray and pale yellow layered in burnt orange, etched and engraved primroses, cameo signature with star, polished pontil ................................................ 1,495.00

5-1/4" h, frosted ovoid, bright fiery golden-amber glass layered in ruby and maroon-red, cameo etched upright butterfly cyclamen blossoms and buds above dense leaves, cameo sgd "Galle" on reverse ............................................. 2,200.00

6-1/2" h, elongated neck, flattened oval body, pale gray and pink layered in periwinkle and green, etched hydrangea blossoms on branch, cameo signature with star........ 373.00

7-1/4" h, flattened oval, frosted aqua-blue layered in blue and aubergine, cameo etched riverside scene, tall trees in fore-ground, cameo sgd "Galle" on reverse .................... 1,610.00

7-3/4" h, stick, elongated neck on squat body, melon pink and gray, layered in white and shades of green, cameo-etched trailing leafy branches, cameo signature with star, old distrib-utor label on base, c1904, rim has been ground ........ 690.00

8-1/8" h, double spout on elongated neck, shouldered vessel, amber and gray layered in amber, etched chrysanthemums, highly polished surface, vertical Galle in cameo on side, c1920 ................................................ 1,200.00

9" h, narrow mouth, vessel swelling to base, blush and gray layered in chartreuse and brown, etched landscape scene, trees by water, inscribed Galle on lower side, large polished pontil .................................................................... 1,725.00

Legras Vase

8-1/8" h, elongated ovoid body, olive green etched with trailing leaves and tassels seed pods, textured ground, enameled brown and gold dec, enameled cameo signature at side, ground base............................................................ 865.00

8-1/4" h, inward rim on ovoid body, heavy walled olive green ground, acid-etched fruit laden branches on textured ground, gilt and enameled ochre and gray highlights, sgd in enameled cameo, c1920, wear to enamel.................. 460.00

Muller Fres

Vase, 9" h, flared elongated oval, cased white overlaid in orange, green, and black, cameo etched lakeside scene with tall trees on shore, islands beyond, cameo sgd "Muller," some restoration .......................................... 900.00

Schneider LeVerre, vase

11-1/2" h, mottled orange on yellow oval, three stylized etched horseshoe crabs alternating with repeating design elements, candy cane signature at lower edge ........................ 1,200.00

19-1/2" h, tall tapered pale orange oval, layered in aubergine-brown, etched pendant seed clusters and spiked leaves, embedded candy cane signature................................ 950.00

St. Louis

Box, cov, 3" d, 2" h, frosted snowflake background, cranberry cut floral scene.............................................................. 325.00

Cologne Bottle, 7-1/2" l, frosted snowflake background, cranberry cut floral scene .................................................. 250.00

# CAMERAS

**History:** Photography became a viable enterprise in the 1840s, but few early cameras have survived. Cameras made before the 1880s are seldom available on the market, and when found, their prices are prohibitive for most collectors. George Eastman's introduction of the Kodak camera in 1888, the first commercially marketed roll film camera, put photography in the hands of the public. Most collectors start with a general interest that becomes more defined. After collecting a broad range of Kodak cameras, a collector may decide to specialize in Retina models. Camera collectors tend to prefer unusual and scarce cameras to the most common models, which were mass-produced by the millions. Because a surplus exists for many common cameras, such as most Kodak box and folding models, collectors are wise to acquire only examples in excellent condition. Shutters should function properly. Minimal wear is generally acceptable. Avoid cameras that have missing parts, damaged bellows, and major cosmetic problems.

**References:** Brian Coe and Paul Gates, *The Snapshot Photograph*, Ash and Grant Ltd., 1977; John F. Maloney, *Vintage Cameras and Images*, Books Americana, 1981; James and Joan McKeown, *McKeown's Price Guide to Antique & Classic Cameras, 1997-1998*, Centennial Photo Service, 1996; Beaumont Newhall, *The History of Photography*, The Museum of Modern Art, 1982.

**Periodicals:** *Camera Shopper*, P.O. Box 1086, New Cannan, CT 06840; *Classic Camera*, P.O. Box 1270, New York, NY 10157-2078; *Shutterbug*, 5211 S. Washington Ave., Titusville, FL 32780.

**Collectors' Clubs:** American Photographic Historical Society, Inc., 1150 Avenue of the Americas, New York, NY 10036; American Society of Camera Collectors, 4918 Alcove Ave., North Hollywood, CA 91607; International Kodak Historical Society, P.O. Box 21, Flourtown, PA 19301; Leica Historical Society of America, 7611 Dornoch Lane, Dallas, TX 75248; National Stereoscopic Association, P.O. Box 14801, Columbus, OH 43214; Nikon Historical Society, P.O. Box 3213, Munster, IN 46321; Photographic Historical Society, P.O. Box 39563, Rochester, NY 14604; The Movie Machine Society, 50 Old Country Rd, Hudson, MA 01749; Zeiss Historical Society, 300 Waxwing Drive, Cranbury, NJ 08512.

**Museums:** Cameras & Images International, Boston, MA; Fleetwood Museum, North Plainfield, NJ; George Eastman Museum, Rochester, NY; International Cinema Museum, Chicago, IL; Smithsonian Institution, Washington, DC.

**Additional Listings:** See *Warman's Americana & Collectibles* for more examples.

**Advisor:** Tom Hoepf.

Agfa, Munich, Germany, Agfamatic 1008, c1976, simple 110 cartridge camera ................................................................................ 10.00

Ansco, Binghamton, N.Y.

Memo, c1927, half-frame 35mm camera, wooden vertical box body, black leather, knob on back advances film .............. 75.00

Vest-Pocket No. 2, c1917, strut-type folding camera, 120 roll film, f7.5 Modico Anastigmat or f6.3 Ansco Anastigmat lens, Bionic shutter, hinged lens cover .................................................. 30.00

Berning, Dusseldorf, Germany Robot II, c1939, 35mm miniature camera, 1x1 inch exposures, spring motor automatic film advance, various Zeiss Tessar lenses ......................................................... 150.00

Braun, Nuremberg, Germany, Paxette Reflex, c1959, single lens reflex camera with interchangeable lens in front of leaf shutter........... 50.00

Contessa-Nettel, Stuttgart, Germany, Taxo, c1921, 9x12 cm folding plate camera, f6.8/135mm Trinastigmat lens, Derval shutter..... 50.00

Detrola Corp., Detroit, Mich., Detrola G, basic 1940s miniature camera, Ilex or Detrola Anastigmat f4.5 lens ................................... 34.00

Eastman Kodak, Rochester, N.Y.

Film Premo No. 1, c1917, drop-in film pack folding bed camera, leather-covered wooden body, meniscus achromatic lens ..... 35.00

Kodak Bantam f8, c1940, f8/40mm Kodalinear lens, Bakelite camera body (watch for chipped corners) with telescoping front lens............................................................................................. 20.00

**Ansco, Memo, c1927, $75. Photo courtesy of Tom Hoepf.**

**Yashica Electro, 35 GSN, c1972, $40. Photo courtesy of Tom Hoepf.**

Kodak Instamatic 500, 1963-66, Germany, f2.8/38mm Schneider-Kreuznach lens, Compur shutter........................................35.00

Graflex Inc., Century 35, c1961, 35mm camera made by Kowa in Japan, f3.5/45mm Prominar, Seikosha-MX 1/500 shutter..........25.00

Houghton, London, Ensign Double-8, 1930s compact strut-type folding camera, 3 x 4 cm exposures on 127 film, f4.5 Ensar lens..........60.00

Konishiroku Kogaku, Japan, Konica II, c1951-58, 35mm camera, f2.8/50mm Hexanon lens, Konirapid-S 1/500 shutter ................75.00

G.A. Krauss, Stuttgart, Germany, Rollette, 1920s vest-pocket folding roll-film camera, f6.8/9cm Rollanar Anastigmat lens, hinged wire frame finder....................................................40.00

Leitz, Wetzlar, Germany, Leica IIIb, c1938, 35mm, with f2/50mm Summar, lens coupled range finder.................................500.00

Minox, Wetzlar, Germany, Minox B, c1958-71, subminiature, built-in meter, chrome body ..................................................120.00

M.I.O.M., France, Photax, c1938-50s, streamlined black Bakelite body, molded lens cap bears name of camera ....................................25.00

Welta Kamera-Werke, Freital, Germany, Weltaflex, c1955, twin lens reflex camera, 6 x 6 cm exposures on 120 film, f.3.5/75mm lens...............................................................80.00

White, Milwaukee, Wis., Stereo Realist, 1950s 35mm stereo camera, f3.5 lenses, hinged lens cover.................................................125.00

Yashica, Japan, Electro 35 GSN, 1970s, rangefinder camera, automatic exposure, f1.7/45mm Yashinon lens...............................40.00

Zeiss Ikon, Germany, Bob 510/2, c1935 folding camera, f7.7/10.5cm Nettar lens...............................................................40.00

# CANDLESTICKS

**History:** The domestic use of candlesticks is traced to the 14th century. The earliest was a picket type, named for the sharp point used to hold the candle. The socket type was established by the mid-1660s. From 1700 to the present, candlestick design mirrored furniture design. By the late 17th century, a baluster stem was introduced, replacing the earlier Doric or clustered column stem. After 1730, candlesticks reflected rococo ornateness. Neoclassic styles followed in the 1760s. Each new era produced a new style of candlesticks; however, some styles became universal and remained in production for centuries. Therefore, when attempting to date a candlestick, it is important to try to determine the techniques used to manufacture the piece.

**References:** Margaret and Douglas Archer, *Collector's Encyclopedia of Glass Candlesticks*, Collector Books,

1983; Veronika Baur, *Metal Candlesticks*, Schiffer Publishing, 1996; Gene Florence, *Glass Candlesticks of the Depression Era*, Collector Books, 1999; Ronald F. Michaels, *Old Domestic Base-Metal Candlesticks*, Antique Collectors' Club, 1999; Sherry Riggs and Paul Pendergrass, *20th Century Glass Candle Holders: Roaring 20s, Depression Era, and Modern Collectible Candle Holders*, Schiffer Publishing, 1999; Kenneth Wilson, *American Glass 1760-1930*, 2 vols., Hudson Hills Press and The Toledo Museum of Art, 1994.

Art Glass, 8-7/8" h, jade green rim wrap on flared cup, custard yellow tapered stem and disk foot, ground pontil, c1925 ...................200.00

Brass

6" h, beehive, push-ups, mkd "England," Victorian, pr........175.00

6-1/4" h, Queen Anne, sq base, scalloped corners, well turned columns, engraved initials "J.H.D.," dated "1772," light pitting, pr ........................................................770.00

6-7/8" h, Queen Anne style, scalloped bases, turned columns, push-ups missing, 19th C, pr .........................................220.00

9-5/8" h, tapered baluster, fluted shaft, domed paneled sq base with dentil borders, 19th C, small base loss, wear, pr......420.00

9-3/4" h, French, octagonal, well shaped baluster stems, conforming sockets, int. of foot has white metal plating, early, pr.....440.00

10-1/2" h, Modern Gothic style, set with paste cabochons in opal, moonstone, ruby, sapphire, turquoise, and topaz, Edwardian, c1900-1910, pr..........................................................625.00

10-3/4" h, machine turned classical and floral dec, 19th C, one slightly crooked ...............................................420.00

11" h, Diamond Knop, Edwardian, c1900-1910, pr.............100.00

12-3/8" h, Dutch, domed base, baluster stem, mid-drip pan .......................................................................3,520.00

26-1/2" h, long turned shaft supported by tall multi-tiered dome, shaped drip pan, tall turned and long socketed candle holder, 17th C..........................................................1,450.00

Bronze

10-1/4" h, cylindrical rope twist standard, acanthus cast flaring nozzle, acanthus, anthemion, and flowerhead cast stepped circular base, late 18th C ......................................1,800.00

10-5/8" h, figural, satyr holding candle sconce aloft, round base with three hairy paw feet, late 19th/early 20th C, price for pr ..........................................................1,725.00

12-1/2" h, figural, youthful Aurora, Belle Epoque, c1890-95, pr 220.00

13" h, neoclassical taste, patinated, Louis Philippe, c1840-50, pr..........................................................1,550.00

**Roseville Pottery, Pine Cone pattern, triple, green, imp mark "1106-5-1/2," pr, $325. Photo courtesy of David Rago Auctions.**

17-1/2" h, blown glass inserts, orig patina, one orig bobeche imp "Tiffany Studios, New York" ............................... 2,600.00
Copper, hammered, 8" h, Princess style, Karl Kipp, minor cleaning to patina ................................................................................ 500.00
Cut Glass
    9" h, controlled center, notched and beaded mitres, 16-point hobstar base ................................................................... 175.00
    10" h, air controlled center, faceted knob, notched and beaded mitres, 24 point hobstar base ......................................... 200.00
    10" h, Honeycombed Flute pattern, six petal shaped base 425.00
    10" h, notched panels, flashed hobstar base ..................... 200.00
    10-1/4" h, hollow center, flute neck with ball cut in strawberry diamond ................................................................................ 125.00
Iron, 6-5/8" h, hogscraper, pushup and hanging lip, mkd "Shaw" 275.00
Majolica, 9" h, 3-3/4" w, Choisy-le-roi, Orientalist taste, shafts and candle sockets molded as Moroccan water sellers and vases, c1880, pr ..................................................................................... 275.00
Marble
    9" h, carved ecru marble, form of ancient Ionic columns, price for set of four .................................................................... 175.00
12" h, carved beige marble, form of ancient Ionic columns, price for set of four .................................................................... 200.00
    12" h, carved ecru marble, form of ancient Ionic columns, price for pr ..................................................................................... 200.00
Pewter, 9-3/4" h, unmarked, married pr ..................................... 255.00
Pottery, 6-1/2" h, handled form, green matte glaze, imp Teco mark, cov with wax, glued crack to bottom edge ..................................... 110.00
Silver
    3-1/2" d, traveling type, circular dished form, detachable candle socket, loop handle, monogram, Black, Starr & Frost, NY, late 19th C ................................................................................ 400.00
    4-1/2" d, traveling type, circular form, shaped edges, bright-cut dec, Hebrew text, unmarked, late 19th/early 20th C ..... 1,100.00
    9-1/4" h, repousse, spiral column form, domed bell shaped foot, heavily foliate dec, mkd "A.B.," Continental, late 18th/early 19th C .............................................................................. 2,650.00
Silver Plate
    11" h, Reed and Barton, Louis XV taste, c1855-70, price for pr ............................................................................... 275.00
    14" h, overall cast foliate and winged griffin's heads, paw feet, mkd "WMF,"" German, late 19th C, minor damage to one 350.00
Tin, 11-1/2" h, double wedding ring, hogscraper type base ........ 625.00
Wrought Iron, 19-5/8" h, primitive, spring loaded splint holder, tripod base ........................................................................................ 470.00

# CANDY CONTAINERS

**History:** In 1876, Croft, Wilbur and Co. filled small glass Liberty Bells with candy and sold them at the Centennial Exposition in Philadelphia. From that date until the 1960s, glass candy containers remained popular. They reflect historical changes, particularly in transportation. Jeannette, Pennsylvania, a center for the packaging of candy in containers, was home for J. C. Crosetti, J. H. Millstein, T. H. Stough, and Victory Glass. Other early manufacturers included: George Borgfeldt, New York, New York; Cambridge Glass, Cambridge, Ohio; Eagle Glass, Wheeling, West Virginia; L. E. Smith, Mt. Pleasant, Pennsylvania; and West Brothers, Grapeville, Pennsylvania.

**References:** *Candy Containers*, L-W Book Sales, 1996; Douglas M. Dezso, J. Lion Poirier & Rose D. Poirier, *Collector's Guide to Candy Containers*, Collector Books, 1998, 2001 value update; George Eikelberner and Serge Agadjanian, *Complete American Glass Candy*

*Containers Handbook*, revised and published by Adele L. Bowden, 1986; Jennie Long, *Album of Candy Containers*, published by author, Vol. I (1978), Vol. II (1983).

**Collectors' Club:** Candy Container Collectors of America, P.O. Box 352, Chelmsford, MA 01824-0352.

**Museums:** Cambridge Glass Museum, Cambridge, OH; L. E. Smith Glass, Mt. Pleasant, PA.

**Additional Listings:** See *Warman's Americana & Collectibles* for more examples.

**Notes:** Candy containers with original paint, candy, and closures command a high premium, but beware of reproduced parts and repainting. The closure is a critical part of each container; if it is missing, the value of the container drops considerably. Small figural perfumes and other miniatures often are sold as candy containers.

o/c = orig closure, n/c = no closure, r/c = reproduction closure

E&A refers to George Eikelberner and Serge Agadjanian, *Complete American Glass Candy Containers Handbook*.

Long refers to Jennie Long, *Album of Candy Containers*.

Airplane
    Musical Toy, o/c, E&A 3, Long 331 ..................................... 66.00
    P-38 Lightning, orig candy, o/c, E&A 12, Long 326 ........... 310.00
    Spirit of Goodwill, o/c, 50% orig paint, orig propeller, E&A 8b ................................................................................ 125.00
    Spirit of St. Louis, clear, all orig tin, E&A 9, Long 321 ........ 425.00
Amos and Andy, 70% orig paint, o/c, E&A 21, Long 77 ............. 580.00
Automobile
    Coupe with Long Hood, U.S.A., green glass, roughness on roof, r/c, E&A 51b, Long 359 ...................................................... 80.00
    Electric Coupe, pat Feb 18, 1913, chip on roof corner, n/c, E&A 49, Long 354 ...................................................................... 45.00
    Hearse #2, r/c, E&A 40, Long 361 ................................... 100.00
    Limousine, rear trunk and tire, 95% orig blue paint, tiny nick on truck, o/c, E&A 38, Long 367 ......................................... 200.00
    Streamlined, orig paint, o/c, E&A 34, Long 372 ................... 42.00
    V.G. Co. Sedan, 70% orig yellow paint, small chips on running board, replaced wheels and closure, E&A 57b, Long 370 . 72.00
    West Bros. Co. Limousine, orig wheels, chip under closure, o/c, E&A 43, Long 350 .............................................................. 95.00
    Barney Google and Ball, repainted, o/c, E&A 72, Long 79 . 200.00
Battleship, 3 stacks, orig tin base ................................................. 40.00
Bell, Liberty Bell with Hanger, E&A 85, Long 229 ...................... 110.00
Big Show Candy Box, four giraffes .............................................. 16.50
Black Cat
    2-1/2" h, composition, US zone, set of 3 ............................. 60.00
    5" h, composition ............................................................... 25.00
    6" x 9", emb, scrap pictures ............................................... 45.00
Boat, Submarine F6, E&A 101, Long 337 ................................... 440.00
Buddy Bank, o/c, Long 449 ........................................................ 245.00
Bus, Jitney, orig wheels, small chip under front grill, o/c, E&A 114b, Long 340 ............................................................................. 290.00

Candlestick, with handles, "Souvenir of South Fork, PA," o/c, E&A 119b, Long 203.................................................245.00
Cannon, two wheel mount #1, all orig, o/c, E&A 123, Long 137.210.00
Carpet Sweeper, "Baby Sweeper," all orig, o/c, E&A 132, Long 242 ..... 385.00
Charlie Chaplin, Borgfeldt, 80% orig paint, o/c, E&A 137, Long 83 .......................................................................175.00
Chicken on Sagging Basket, traces of paint, tiny corner chip under closure, o/c, E&A 148a, Long 8 ......................................50.00
Clock
   Mantel, orig dial, mkd on reverse "Contents 3 oz. Av.," o/c, E&A 104a, Long 116 ........................................235.00
   Octagon, 80% orig paint, orig dial, tiny crack front corner, o/c, E&A 163, Long 117 ..............................275.00
   "Souvenir of Platte, S. D.," milk white, o/c, E&A 162, Long 114 ........................................................235.00
Dirigible, Los Angeles, 95% orig paint, o/c, E&A 176a, Long 322 ..........................................................................195.00
Duck on Plain Top Basket, 80% orig paint, o/c, E&A 197, Long 30 ...........................................................................110.00
Easter, composition
   6-1/2" h, boy, round body shape ...............................40.00
   6-1/2" h, duck, egg body shape ................................45.00
   6-1/2" h, chick, egg body shape ...............................45.00
   6-1/2" h, girl, round body shape ...............................40.00
Elephant with Howdah, camphor glass, chipped foot, n/c, Long 32 ...........................................................................35.00
Fire Engine
   Fire Dept. No. 99, o/c, E&A 214, Long 384 ...............50.00
   Ladder Truck, chip on left running board, orig wheels, o/c, E&A 216, Long 384 ......................................165.00
Football, 19" h, figure, painted composition and cloth, dressed, German ...................................................................5,700.00
Gas Pump, Gas 23c today, 70% orig paint, replaced hose, o/c, E&A 240a, Long 316 ...............................................320.00
Girl, with two geese, n/c, E&A 241.................................22.00
Halloween, candy box, 5" x 7" .......................................10.00
Hen on Nest, 6"................................................................50.00
Horn, trumpet, two bears, worn, age cracks, o/c, E&A 313, Long 280 ........................................................................100.00
House, "All Glass," 95% paint, o/c, E&A 324b, Long 75 .............205.00
Independence Hall, minor edge nick, o/c, E&A 342, Long 74.....275.00
Jack O Lantern, 95% orig paint, blue glass, orig bail and rim, E&A 349a, Long 159 .......................................................330.00
Kewpie by Barrel, 90% orig paint, o/c, E&A 359, Long 91 ..........110.00
Kiddie Kar, 75% orig paint, small chip under closure, o/c, E&A 360, Long 253 ........................................................125.00
Lamp
   Inside Ribbed Base, "Souvenir Boston, Mass," o/c, E&A 367, Long 208 ............................................125.00
   Kerosene, o/c, E&A 371, Long 212 ......................55.00
Lantern, "Beveled Panel Square," o/c, E&A 396, Long 175..........72.00
Locomotive
   American Flyer Type #23, blue glass, r/c, E&A 480, Long 417 ......................................................110.00
   "Jeant. Glass C. #888," orig wheels, small chip on wheel flange, o/c, E&A 485a, Long 395 ..................165.00
   "Mapother's 1892," o/c, E&A 494a, Long 404..............80.00
Mail Box, 80% gray paint, o/c, E&A 521, Long 254 ....................190.00
Midget Washer, E&A 526 ...............................................50.00
Milk Bottle Carrier, four bottles, Long 451 .....................25.00
Mule Pulling Two Wheeled Barrel, with driver, o/c, E&A 539a, Long 38 ............................................................................70.00
Opera Glass, Swirl Ribs, o/c, E&A 559, Long 260 ......................125.00
Phonograph
   Inkwell Type, orig horn, orig record faded, o/c, E&A 575a, Long 287 ....................................................290.00
   With Glass Horn, 80% orig paint, o/c, E&A 576, Long 286.300.00
Piano, upright, 95% orig paint, o/c, E&A 577, Long 289............275.00

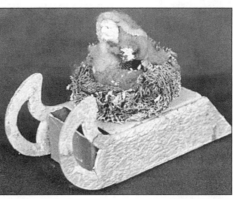

St. Nicholas, on sled, papier-mâché, fur, paper, 3-5/8" l, $45.

Pipe, glass, blue ..............................................................160.00
Powder Horn with Hanger, E&A 588h............................18.00
Pumpkin Man, papier-mâché, 5-1/2" h, wire neck .......25.00
Puss & Boots, Long, 468 ................................................140.00
Rabbit
Glass, crouching, 80% orig paint, o/c, E&A 615, Long 41 ..........155.00
Glass, feet together, sq nose, o/c, E&A 614 ................85.00
Glass, in egg shell, 80% orig paint, o/c, E&A 608b, Long 48......125.00
Glass, laid back ears, 95% orig paint, o/c, E&A 616a, Long 40..100.00
Glass, legs apart, 95% orig paint, o/c, E&A 611b, Long 50 ........110.00
Glass, Peter Rabbit, all orig, o/c, E&A 618a, Long 55 .................30.00
Papier-mâché...................................................................600.00
Racer
   "6," #4 on grill, o/c, E&A 641b, Long 430.....................90.00
   "12," 90% orig paint, o/c, E&A 642, Long 432...............350.00
Radio, "Tune In," 90% orig paint, o/c, E&A 643a, Long 290 ........100.00
Rocking Horse, small chip under front, o/c, E&A 651, Long 58 ..155.00
Safe, clear, o/c, E&A 661b, Long 268.............90.00Santa Claus, glass
   By square chimney, 80% orig paint, o/c, E&A 672a, Long 99 ........................................................430.00
   Double cuff, 95% orig paint, o/c, E&A 671, Long 101........355.00
   Leaving chimney, 60% orig paint, o/c, E&A 673a, Long 102 ......................................................100.00
   Paneled Coat, o/c, E&A 670, Long 98 ....................175.00
   Plastic head, all orig, o/c, E&A 674, Long 103.....................35.00
Skookum by tree stump, 75% orig paint, o/c, E&A 681, Long 106 ........................................................................220.00
Snowman, composition or papier-mâché 4-1/2" h, round body .... 15.00
   5" h, round body, glass eyes, marked "Germany"................40.00
   5-1/2" h, top hat, glass eyes .....................................30.00
   6-1/4" h, glass eyes ...................................................24.00
   6-1/2" h, umbrella.......................................................40.00
   7-1/4" h, top hat, tree, carrot nose .........................30.00
   9" h, stick, musical hat ...............................................40.00
Spark Plug, 60% orig paint, rough under closure, r/c, E&A 699 . 115.00
Stop and Go, all orig tin, o/c, E&A 706, Long 317 .....................360.00
Suitcase, milk glass, bear decal, orig handle, o/c, E&A 707, Long 216 ........................................................................220.00
Swan Boat, rabbit and chick, 95% orig paint, r/c, E&A 713, Long 60 ..........................................................................825.00
Tank, World War I, o/c, E&A 721, Long 434................................160.00
Telephone
   Millstein's ToT, all orig, o/c, E&A 744, Long 306 ..........50.00
   Tall V.G. Co., all orig, o/c, E&A 746, Long 299 ..................160.00
Toonerville Depot Line, traces of paint, large chip on rear, o/c, E&A 767, Long 111................................................................90.00
Top, "Spinning Top," all orig, winder, o/c, E&A 775, Long 271 ....100.00
Trunk, round top, milk glass, 90% orig paint, o/c, E&A 789a, Long 219 ........................................................................125.00
Turkey, papier-mâché
   3" h, Tom...................................................................24.00
   4-1/4" h, Hen............................................................28.00
   4-1/2" h, Tom............................................................40.00
   5-1/2" h, Hen............................................................40.00
   5-1/2" h, Tom............................................................50.00

Village

    Bank, insert, E&A 804, Long, 76b..................................190.00

    Church, insert, replaced clip, replaced cross, E&A 809,
      Long 76c .....................................................100.00

    City Garage, insert, E&A 811, Long 76g............................100.00

    Confectionery, insert, E&A 812, Long 76q.........................100.00

    Drug Store, insert, E&A 810, Long 76d .............................110.00

    Engine No. 23, insert, E&A 815, Long 76e .........................140.00

Wagon, "U. S. Express," all tin replaced, E&A 821b, Long 440 ..110.00

Well, "Ye Old Oaken Bucket," 50% paint, replaced handle, o/c, E&A
  831a, Long 137 .....................................................27.50

Windmill

    Dutch Wind Mill, orig blades, n/c, E&A 243, Long 448 .........50.00

    Five Windows, ruby flashed, replaced blades, o/c, E&A 844a,
      Long 446 ......................................................220.00

    Teddy Wind Mill, replaced tin super structure, tiny corner bottom
      chip, o/c, E&A 860, Long 276......................................90.00

    World Globe, orig stand, o/c, E&A 860, Long 276 ..............330.00

# CANES

**History:** Canes and walking sticks were important accessories in a gentleman's wardrobe in the 18th and 19th centuries. They often served both a decorative and utilitarian function. Glass canes and walking sticks were glassmakers' whimsies, ornamental rather than practical. The year 2000 is going to always be remembered for that amazing political campaign. Before that occurred, auctioneer C. Wesley Cowan sold a wonderful collection of political canes and walking sticks, all belonging to one Ohio collector who had been collecting canes for over twenty-five years. Many of these unique canes feature a bust portrait of the candidate or a motif readily identified with a particular campaign.

**References:** Linda L. Beeman, *Cane Collector's Directory*, published by author, 1993; Joyce E. Blake, *Glasshouse Whimsies*, published by author, 1984; Catherine Dike, *Cane Curiosa*, Cane Curiosa Press (250 Dielman Rd, Ladue, MO 63124), 1983; ——, *Canes in the United States*, Cane Curiosa Press (250 Dielman Rd, Ladue, MO 63124), 1994; ——, *La Cane Object díAr,*; Cane Curiosa Press (250 Dielman Rd, Ladue, MO 63124), 1988; Ulrich Klever, *Walkingsticks*, Schiffer Publishing, 1996; George H. Meyer, *American Folk Art Canes*, Sandringham Press, 1992.

**Periodical:** *Cane Collector's Chronicle*, 99 Ludlum Crescent, Lower Hutt Welling, New Zealand.

**Collectors' Club:** International Cane Collectors, 24 Magnolia Ave., Manchester-by-the-Sea, MA 01944; The Cane Collector's Chronicle, 99 Ludlum Crescent, Lower Hutt, Weelington, New Zealand.

**Museums:** Essex Institute, Salem, MA; Remington Gun Museum, Ilion, NY; Valley Forge Historical Society, Valley Forge, PA.

**Notes:** Carved wood and ivory canes are frequently considered folk art and collectors pay higher prices for them.

## Cane

    34" l, ebony shaft, gold dog's head handle, patterned neck,
      c1901 ..........................................................900.00

    34-1/4" l, maple, pistol handle, shaft with high relief carving of
      cow, chicken, home, two dogs' heads, two plants, mother with
      child..............................................................260.00

35" l

    Pine, carved and painted, handle carved in form of recumbent
      striped cat tugging at a plaque, relief carved American eagle,
      crossed cannon, flag and stars and "GAR," with two hearts,
      tapering shaft relief carved with another striped cat figure, late
      19th C............................................................2,000.00

    Rounded ivory knob above tapering whalebone shaft,
      19th C...........................................................200.00

    Wood, handle carved with stylized bearded man head, tasseled
      cord carved on shaft, attributed to Bally Carver, southeastern
      PA, 19th C, split at top..........................................750.00

36" l

    Bamboo, sterling silver knob set with small clock, enameled face,
      mkd "Brevete," silver mkd "Sterling"..............................250.00

    Glass, colorless cased over 1" w opalescent ribbon, red stripe
      down one edge, blue stripe down other, shepherd's crook
      handle, fancy knurl .............................................275.00

    37" l, carved wood, figural, knob in form of antelope's head, glass
      eyes, polychrome highlights, 19th C, minor cracks..........250.00

    44" l, ivory handle over arching horn shaft, ivory top, minor
      cracks, 19th C ..................................................200.00

    52" l, glass, pale green, ribbed tapered twist last 18", twist in
      handle ..........................................................295.00

## Political Canes and Walking Sticks

    James Blaine, bronze-colored metal portrait bust, label "Chicago,"
      referring to 1884 Republican National Convention ..........550.00

    William J. Bryant, cast metal bust, 1908 campaign ............750.00

    James Buchanan, sterling head engraved "Presented to James
      Maxfield by the Goshen Democratic Club, 1856 Buchanan &
      Breckridge"................................................1,000.00

    Jimmy Carter, cast metal peanut, name and date
      inscription......................................................325.00

    Grover Cleveland and Allen Thurman, pewter-colored metal double sided bust portraits, molded inscription "Cleveland" on one
      side, "Thurman" on other side .....................................2,200.00

    Dwight Eisenhower, painted porcelain-like cane ...............325.00

    Gerald Ford, aluminum curved handle, inscribed "Gerald F. Ford
      for President"...................................................150.00

    James Garfield, bronze-plated metal bust .........................800.00

    Benjamin Harrison, metal top hat, inscribed "1776, Wm. H. Harrison, 1841, Ben I. Harrison 1833-92" ..............................950.00

    Benjamin Harrison and running mate Levi Morton,
      portraits ......................................................2,300.00

    William Henry Harrison, gold plated knob engraved with Harrison's log cabin and barrel of cider, some dents ...............850.00

    Andrew Jackson, carved horn bust ...................................290.00

    Lyndon B. Johnson, "Walk Away with LBJ," used by Texas delegates to Democratic Convention ..................................400.00

    John F. Kennedy, copper-plated metal bust.......................900.00

    Abraham Lincoln, hard rubber handle, finely molded bust of
      Lincoln.......................................................1,300.00

    William McKinley and Garret Hobart, 1896, muslin flag with portraits and inscriptions ...............................................2,700.00

    William McKinley and T. R. Roosevelt, folk art, carved portraits
      and inscription "Four Years More of Peace and Prosperity if
      McKinley Triumphs," eight pointed start carrying Roosevelt's
      name .......................................................2,100.00

    Alton B. Parker, inset celluloid image, inscribed
      "For President" ................................................800.00

    Franklin D. Roosevelt, pencil cane, red and black lettering, "Pencil to be used to Balance 4 Years of Hoover, Prosperity, Elect
      Roosevelt & Gardner and Let's Have a New Deal".........750.00

    Theodore Roosevelt, plaque inscribed in blue "You Can't Monkey
      with Teddy," 1904 campaign.......................................700.00

    William Howard Taft, emb sterling portrait disk.................475.00

Woodrow Wilson, Britannia metal golf club head, inscribed "Wilson for President" on one side, "Notion 1917" on other side............................................................................. 150.00

## Walking Stick

30-3/4" l, carved wood, eagle head knob, swelled tapering shaft, relief dec of two swimmers, lion, dog, and ballerina, inscribed "George Hynes Waterbury Conn. Cut from Camp Bradley Aug 17th, 1894".................................................. 500.00

32-1/2" l, carved hardwood, two snakes grabbing both ends of small quadruped, roothead handle with some burl, very worn black and yellow paint ...................................... 480.00

32-1/2" l, curly maple, octagonal, good old finish .............. 125.00

33" l, tin, cast white metal knob with McKinley bust, 1896.. 200.00

33-1/4" l, sapling, dog head handle, two tone relief carved figure, leaf, alligator, and giraffe ................................... 110.00

34-1/4" l, carved softwood, snake with fist handle, branded inscription "A. M. Gregg, Dec. 3, 1891, Waulpgy Pike, Ohio," old brown crusty finish, some edge damage......................... 175.00

35" l, gold plated knob with cased scrolling design, inscribed "J. H. Hynes Waterbury Ct," tapering ebonized wood shaft, minor cracks, late 19th C .................................................. 400.00

35" l, mahogany, open grip handle, relief carved arms and hands, old alligatored varnish, dovetail joining handle and shaft with damage, old repair ......................................... 85.00

35-1/4" l, carved roothead, two snakes, old black and brown paint, brass top.......................................................... 110.00

36" l, bamboo, natural bark on handle ................................ 30.00

36" l, carved softwood, snake with fist handle, carved name "J. F. Williams," old varnish ...................................... 165.00

36" l, hardwood, cast white metal man's head handle, carved bamboo-like shaft.......................................................... 165.00

36-1/2" h, wood, painted black, gold accents, horse's hoof terminal to handle, late 19th/early 20th C, minor paint loss ..... 250.00

37" l, Indian head, lizard, bird, snake, and dated "1926," two tone brown and red finish............................................. 550.00

37-1/2" h, primitive, tattoo type, pony, gazelle, fish, crane, lizard, and snake, knob handle ...................................... 325.00

# CANTON CHINA

**History:** Canton china is a type of Oriental porcelain made in the Canton region of China from the late 18th century to the present. It was produced largely for export. Canton china has a hand-decorated light- to dark-blue underglaze on white ground. Design motifs include houses, mountains, trees, boats, and bridges. A design similar to willow pattern is the most common. Borders on early Canton feature a rain and cloud motif (a thick band of diagonal lines with a scalloped bottom). Later pieces usually have a straight-line border. Early, c1790-1840, plates are very heavy and often have an unfinished bottom, while serving pieces have an overall "orange-peel" bottom. Early covered pieces, such as tureens, vegetable dishes, and sugars, have strawberry finials and twisted handles. Later ones have round finials and a straight, single handle.

---

## Reproduction Alert:

Several museum gift shops and private manufacturers are issuing reproductions of Canton china.

---

Cup and Saucer, loop handle, $70.

**Marks:** The markings, "Made in China" and "China" indicate wares which date after 1891.

Bowl
9-1/4" d, 4-3/4" h, cut-corner, minor area of restoration, hairline............................................................... 435.00
10-1/4" d, 4-5/8" h, cut-corner, minor rim chips, price for pr .................................................................... 1,955.00
10-1/2" d, shallow, deeply scalloped rim, rim chip .............. 110.00
10-1/2" d, 3" h, scallop edge................................................. 375.00
10-3/4" d, scalloped, low, very minor rim chip.................... 920.00
12" d, 2" h, round .................................................................. 425.00
13-3/4" x 10-3/4" x 2-1/4" h, cut corner, rect ...................... 250.00

Box, dome top, sq, cloud and rain border, first half 19th C, pr. 6,270.00
Butter Dish, domed lid, pierced insert, mismatched, repaired .... 440.00
Cann, 5-1/8" h .......................................................................... 175.00
Cider Jug, 11-1/2" h, cracks, staple repair to lid, 19th C .......... 1,500.00
Creamer, 4-1/4" h, helmet shape, 7-1/4" x 5-1/4" leaf shaped underdish ............................................................................ 500.00
Dinner Plate, 10" d, set of 14, very minor chips, hairlines ....... 1,150.00

Dish
7-3/8" l, leaf shape, small chips ...................................... 95.00
10-1/2" l, almond shape, small chips .............................. 110.00

Fruit Basket with Undertray, 10" d, 3-3/4" h basket, 10-1/4" d undertray, oval, reticulated, China, 19th C, minor edge chips.................. 850.00
Ginger Jar, 7" h, 7" d, hardwood turned and carved cover ......... 150.00
Pitcher, 4-1/4" h ...................................................................... 220.00
Planter, 13" w, 10" h, hexagonal, ftd trays, 20th C, pr................. 300.00

Plate
7" d, set of nine, minor rim chips........................................ 200.00
8-1/2" d, set of six, minor rim chips.................................... 175.00
9-1/2" d, rim chips, short hairlines...................................... 50.00

Platter
11-1/4" l, rect........................................................................ 315.00
12-1/2" x 15-1/2", octagonal, deep blue and white ............ 450.00
12-3/4" l, octagonal, pearlware .......................................... 375.00
13-3/4" l, deep, very minor chips ........................................ 375.00
15-7/8" l, very minor rim chips, rim roughness.................... 260.00
16-7/8" l, 13-3/4" w, octagonal, 19th C ............................. 750.00
17-1/8" l, 13-3/4" w, eight-sided oval, deep center filled with strainer, 19th C, minor glaze irregularities, color variations....................................................................... 980.00
17-1/2" l................................................................................. 550.00
17-3/4" l, 15" w, cut corner................................................. 475.00
18-1/2" l, well and tree ......................................................... 750.00

Sauce Tureen, cov, undertray
6-3/4" h, 3-3/4" h, mismatched ......................................... 600.00
7" l, 8" d undertray, cut corner rect, conforming lid with finial, boars head handles............................................ 500.00
7-1/8" l, very minor chips ................................................... 500.00

Shrimp Dish, 10-1/2" d, , minor chips ...................................... 450.00
Soup Tureen, 10" l, 6" h.......................................................... 875.00

Sugar Bowl, cov
5" h, intertwined strap handles........................................ 150.00
5-7/8" h, ear handles, mismatched lid................................ 275.00

Syllabub, set of eight................................................900.00
Tea Caddy, cov, 6" h, pr .........................................275.00
Teacup, cov, 3-3/4" h, intertwined strap handles, similar finial on
   lid.........................................................................100.00
Teacup and Saucer, minor chips and hairlines, set of ten...........250.00
Teapot, cov
   6-1/4" h ........................................................500.00
   6-1/2" h, barrel-form, foo dog handle, mismatched lid, chips........
      690.00
   6-1/2" h, twined handle, mismatched lid ...........420.00
Tray
   8-3/4" x 9", chip on table ring..........................220.00
   10" l, oval ......................................................165.00
Tureen, cov, 13" l, 8-1/2" h, rect bowl with rounded corners, flared
   base, lid dec with leaf shaped knob, boar's head handles, minor
   small firing cracks............................................1,955.00
Umbrella Holder, 24-1/2" h, 8-1/2" d, side dec with deer, trees, and
   landscape ......................................................600.00
Vegetable, cov
   9" l, mismatched lid........................................200.00
   9" l, pine cone finial.......................................275.00
   9-1/2" l, pine cone finial..................................200.00
   10" l, pine cone finial, orange peel glaze ..........330.00
   10-1/4" l, mismatched lid.................................400.00
   13-1/2" l, 8-3/4" d, 9" h, blue and white, cut corner form, boars
     head handles, raised base, large finial on lid ..................850.00
Warming Dish, cov, 11-1/2" d, 5-1/4" h, round, minor chips........650.00

# CAPO -DI-MONTE

**History:** In 1743, King Charles of Naples established a soft-paste porcelain factory near Naples. The firm made figurines and dinnerware. In 1760, many of the workmen and most of the molds were moved to Buen Retiro, near Madrid, Spain. A new factory, which also made hard-paste porcelains, opened in Naples in 1771. In 1834, the Doccia factory in Florence purchased the molds and continued production with them in Italy. Capo-di-Monte was copied heavily by other factories in Hungary, Germany, France, and Italy.

**Museums:** Metropolitan Museum of Art, New York, NY; Museo of Capodimonte, Naples, Italy; Woodmere Art Museum, Philadelphia, PA.

Bowl, 14" d, relief molded leopard scene, c1860 ........................190.00
Box, cov
   6" x 4" x 3-1/2", c1940, minor flakes ..................145.00
   8" l, hinged, molded classical Roman bacchanalian scene 500.00
Cachepot, 11" d, 11-1/2" d, polychromed Bacchic Revelers in relief
   around body, c1920...........................................200.00
Chocolate Cup and Saucer, relief molded figures, cupid finial cov,
   c1870 ............................................................165.00
Coffeepot, cov, 6" h relief molded nude figures and trees near lake,
   pear finial, c1890.. 225.00 Compote, 13" d, shell shape, relief molded
   cherubs and classical figures, scroll base ...............125.00
Demitasse Cup and Saucer, maiden, dog, tree, and mountain scene,
   pastels, branch handle ......................................90.00
Figure, 11" h, dancing woman, 18th C dress .............200.00
Jewelry Box, 3-1/4" h, Roman and biblical motif on lid ...............165.00

---

## Reproduction Alert:

Many of the pieces in today's market are of recent vintage. Do not be fooled by the crown over the "N" mark; it also was copied.

Plate, molded figures in border, hp flowers, gilding, crown N mark, $100. Photo courtesy of Joy Luke Fine Art Brokers and Auctioneers.

Pitcher, 8" h, relief molded satyrs and cherubs, polychrome enameling,
   gilt trim.........................................................90.00
Plate, multicolored, raised classical figure border, crown
   N mark...........................................................200.00
Snuff Box, 3" l, oval, polychrome, molded relief of bottle and Neoclassical scenes, 19th C...........................................435.00
Tankard, cov, 13" h, relief molded classical scenes, elephant head
   handle, relief molded cherubs on rim cov, cupid finial, blue underglaze crown N mark .........................................500.00
Tea Set, teapot, creamer, cup and saucer, relief carved classical
   scenes, gold overglaze crown N mark ....................425.00
Tile, paneled, relief molded nude maidens and Roman bath
   scene.............................................................190.00
Tureen, cov, undertray, 13" l, ovoid body, relief molded with cavorting
   figures, int. dec with floral springs, cover surmounted by drunken
   cherub finial, matching undertray, losses ...............750.00
Urn, 12" h, relief molded classical scenes, blue overglaze crown N
   mark, pr .........................................................850.00
Urn, cov, 15" h, baluster shape, domed cov, relief molded sides with
   cupids and grapevines, relief molded florals on cover, molded Bacchus heads at base of handles, pr ........................600.00

# CARLSBAD CHINA

**History:** Because of changing European boundaries during the last 100 years, German-speaking Carlsbad has found itself located first in the Austro-Hungarian Empire, then in Germany, and currently in the Czech Republic. Carlsbad was one of the leading pottery manufacturing centers in Bohemia. Wares from the numerous Carlsbad potteries are lumped together under the term "Carlsbad China." Most pieces on the market are post-1891, although several potteries date to the early 19th century.

Vegetable Tureen, cov, blue bachelor buttons and light brown floral motif, white ground, molded pattern, shaped handles, 8-1/2" l, 6-1/2" w, $45.

Biscuit Jar, cov, 5-1/2" d, 6-3/8" h, multicolored florals, gold trim, mkd "Victoria-Carlsbad" ................................................ 70.00
Bowl, 12" w, sq, pale peach shading to pale blue, center transfer of five classical maidens, gold foliage, mkd "Victoria-Carlsbad" .......... 75.00
Cake Plate, 12" d, violets, pierced gold handles, mkd "Victoria, Carlsbad, Austria" .......................................... 45.00
Chocolate Pot, 10" h, multicolored daisies, gold trim, white ground ......................................................... 110.00
Dessert Set, 9-1/2" d master bowl, twelve 5-1/2" d bowls, scalloped and fluted, four winter scenes, apple blossom boughs, cream ground ...................................................... 200.00
Ewer, 10" h, divided rim forms two spouts, large dolphin handles with gold scales, raised gold florals on cream, mkd "Victoria, Carlsbad" .................................................. 125.00
Miniature Lamp, 8-1/2" h, porcelain base, Bristol glass shade, orange, blue, and lavender flowers, scrolling gold trim, nutmeg burner, mkd "Victoria, Carlsbad, Austria" ..................... 450.00
Mug, 4" h, decal portrait of monk, violin, mkd "Victoria-Carlsbad" 80.00
Pitcher, 11" h, cobalt blue bands, gold trim, pink ground ............ 100.00
Portrait Plate, cherubs, rich dark green and cream background, ruffled edges, sgd "Kaufman" ........................................ 145.00
Relish, pierced handles, multicolored flowers, pink border, cream ground .......................................................... 40.00
Teapot, cov, relief scrolls, hp flowers, mkd "Carlsbad, Austria 1892" .................................................... 70.00
Vase, 13-3/8" h, 6-1/2" d, hp flowers and holly, colorful shaded ground, raised enameling, gold tracery, pr ............................. 320.00

# CARNIVAL GLASS

**History:** Carnival glass, an American invention, is colored pressed glass with a fired-on iridescent finish. It was first manufactured about 1905 and was immensely popular both in America and abroad. More than 1,000 different patterns have been identified. Production of old carnival glass patterns ended in 1930. Most of the popular patterns of carnival glass were produced by five companies—Dugan, Fenton, Imperial, Millersburg, and Northwood.

**Marks:** Northwood patterns frequently are found with the "N" trademark. Dugan used a diamond trademark on several patterns.

**References:** Gary E. Baker et al., *Wheeling Glass*, Oglebay Institute, 1994 (distributed by Antique Publications); Elaine and Fred Blair, *Carnival Hunter's Companion: A Guide to Pattern Recognition*, published by authors (P.O. Box 116335, Carrolton, TX 75011), 1995; Carl O. Burns, *Collector's Guide to Northwood Carnival Glass*, L-W Book Sales, 1994; ——, *Dugan and Diamond Carnival Glass, 1909-1931*; Collector Books, 1998; ——, *Imperial Carnival Glass*, Collector Books, 1996, 1999 value update; Dave Doty, *A Field Guide to Carnival Glass*, Antique Trader Publications, 1998; Bill Edwards and Mike Carwile, *Standard Encyclopedia of Carnival Glass*, 7th ed., Collector Books, 2000; ——, *Standard Encyclopedia of Carnival Glass Price Guide*, 12th ed., Collector Books, 2000; Marion T. Hartung, *First Book of Carnival Glass to Tenth Book of Carnival Glass* (series of 10 books), published by author, 1968 to 1982; published by authors (36 N. Mernitz, Freeport, IL 61032), 1996; Diane C. Rosington, *Carnival Glass Club Commemoratives, 1964-1999*, published by author (P.O. Box

348, North Greece, NY 14515-0348), 2000; Glen and Steven Thistlewood, *Carnival Glass, The Magic & The Mystery*, Schiffer Publishing, 1998; Margaret and Ken Whitmyer, *Fenton Art Glass: 1907-1939*, Collector Books, 1996, 1999 value update.

**Periodical:** *Network*, PageWorks, P.O. Box 2385, Mt. Pleasant, SC 29465.

**Collectors' Clubs:** American Carnival Glass Association, 9621 Springwater Ln, Miamisburg, OH 45342; Canadian Carnival Glass Association, 107 Montcalm Dr., Kitchner, Ontario N2B 2R4 Canada; Collectible Carnival Glass Association, 3103 Brentwood Circle, Grand Island, NE 68801; Heart of America Carnival Glass Association, 4305 W. 78th St., Prairie Village, KS 66208; International Carnival Glass Association, P.O. Box 306, Mentone, IN 46539; Lincoln-Land Carnival Glass Club, N951, Hwy 27, Conrath, WI 54731; National Duncan Glass Society, P.O. Box 965, Washington, PA 15301; New England Carnival Glass Club, 27 Wells Rd, Broad Brooks, CT 06016; Tampa Bay Carnival Glass Club, 101st Ave. N., Pinellas Park, FL 34666; WWW.CGA at http://www.woodsland.com.

**Museums:** National Duncan Glass Society, Washington, PA; Fenton Art Glass Co, Williamstown, WV.

**Notes:** Color is the most important factor in pricing carnival glass. The color of a piece is determined by holding it to the light and looking through it.

Acorn Burrs, Northwood
    Punch Set, 8 pcs, green ................................. 3,500.00
    Punch Cup, marigold, set of 5 ......................... 145.00
African Shield, English maker, vase, wire flower arranger, marigold ....................................................... 145.00
Amaryllis, Dugan, compote, stemmed, flared, miniature, purple 150.00
Apple Blossom Twigs, Dugan, bowl, low, ruffled, peach opal ..... 150.00
April Showers, Fenton, swung vase, tight crimped edge, 11" h, amethyst opal ...................................... 1,300.00
Arched Flute, unknown maker, toothpick, ice green ............ 300.00

Beaded Cable, rose bowl, marigold, $50.

Asters, unknown maker, plate, 5" d, marigold............................125.00
Banded Diamonds, Australian maker, tumbler, marigold............175.00
Band of Roses, unknown maker
    Cordial Set, decanter, six cordials, undertray, marigold......575.00
    Tumbler, marigold.......................................................185.00
Barley & Hops, unknown maker
    Beer Pitcher, marigold, painted..................................160.00
    Tumbler, marigold, painted .........................................50.00
Beaded Bull's Eye, Imperial, vase, flared, 6" h, 6-1/2" d,
    dark marigold ..........................................................95.00
Beaded Cable, Northwood, rose bowl, ftd, aqua opal.................400.00
Beaded Spears, unknown maker
    Pitcher, marigold .......................................................425.00
    Tumbler, marigold .....................................................145.00
    Tumbler, teal ..............................................................30.00
Beaded Swirl, English maker, miniature lamp, marigold.............115.00
Big Basketweave, Dugan, vase, 10-3/4" h, white .......................165.00
Birds and Cherries, Fenton
    Chop Plate, flat, 10-1/2" d, amethyst ...........................16,000.00
    Ice Cream Bowl, flat, 9-3/4" d, blue .............................2,000.00
Blackberry, Fenton, hat, open edge, 2 rows, red .......................375.00
Blackberry Wreath, Millersburg, sauce, deep, 5" d, dark marigold, dark
    radium finish ..............................................................35.00
Blossomtime, Northwood, compote, marigold ...........................375.00
Boggy Bayou, Fenton, vase, 5" h, lime green opal.....................950.00
Bull's Eye & Loops, Millersburg, vase, amethyst ......................350.00
Bushel Basket, Northwood, round, handle
    Aqua Opal...............................................................600.00
    Marigold, pastel ........................................................95.00
    Sapphire Blue with Aqua Opal.....................................650.00
Butterfly, Fenton, ornament, miniature, marigold......................1,000.00
Butterfly & Berry, Fenton
    Creamer, blue ............................................................75.00
    Hatpin Holder, ftd, blue ............................................2,500.00
    Swung Vase, 8-1/2" h, green .....................................425.00
Butterfly and Tulip, Dugan, whimsey, flared bowl, 4 ftd, peach
    opal .......................................................................9,000.00
Buzz Saw, Cambridge, cruet, small, green ...............................350.00
Cane Panels, unknown maker, tumble-up, marigold ..................175.00
Captive Rose, Fenton
    Plate, flat, 9-1/4" d, blue..............................................900.00
    Plate, flat, 9-1/4" d, marigold......................................700.00
    Plate, flat, 9-1/2" d, amethyst......................................900.00
    Plate, flat, 9-1/2" d, green ..........................................4,500.00
Christmas Compote, Dugan, purple...........................................4,500.00
Classic Arts, Czechoslovakian maker, powder box, marigold.....280.00
Coin Spot, Dugan, compote, celeste blue..................................550.00
Colonial Flute, Imperial, toothpick, two handles, marigold,
    old mark .....................................................................235.00
Colonial Lady, Imperial
    Vase, marigold ..........................................................700.00
    Vase, purple ...............................................................850.00
Color Burst, unknown maker, perfume, marigold.......................105.00

Concord Grape, Fenton, plate, flat, 9-1/4" d, amethyst ...........2,750.00
Constellation, Dugan, compote, stemmed, ruffled, white...........100.00
Corinth, Dugan, jack in the pulpit vase, blue opalescent ..........300.00
Corn, Imperial
    Bottle, helios ............................................................165.00
    Bottle, smoke ...........................................................350.00
    Vase, green..............................................................600.00
    Vase, ice green .........................................................375.00
    Vase, white, lavender tint ..........................................300.00
Cosmos and Cane, US Glass
    Lady's Spittoon, 3-1/2" d, 1-3/4" h, honey amber ...........4,750.00
    Rose Bowl, volcano shape, honey amber ......................475.00
    Tumbler, white............................................................335.00
Country Kitchen, Millersburg, spooner, marigold ......................175.00
Curved Star, unknown maker, child's dish, marigold ................175.00
Cut Cosmos, Millersburg, tumbler, marigold ............................135.00
Daisy Cup, unknown maker, bell, marigold................................215.00
Daisy Squares, unknown maker, goblet, crimped, flared out edge,
    green ......................................................................200.00
Dandelion, Northwood
    Mug, handle, aqua opal ............................................1,300.00
    Tumbler, ice blue.......................................................175.00
Diamond Fountain, Higbee, cruet, marigold ..............................325.00
Diamond Point, Northwood, vase, amethyst................................90.00
Dimples and Brilliants, maker unknown, hatpin, purple .............115.00
Double Loop, Northwood, chalice, aqua opal ............................180.00
Double Scroll, Imperial, candlesticks, pr, red with amberina
    base ......................................................................500.00
Dragon and Lotus, Fenton
    Bowl, 3 in 1, amethyst................................................125.00
    Bowl, 3 in 1, peach opal.............................................275.00
    Ice Cream Bowl, amber opalescent.............................2,800.00
    Ice Cream Bowl, red ..................................................4,500.00
    Plate, marigold...........................................................900.00
Dragon and Strawberry, Fenton
    Bowl, ruffled, 9-1/2" d, blue........................................250.00
    Ice Cream Bowl, 8-3/4" d, marigold.............................250.00
Drapery, Northwood
    Swung Vase, 7" h, dark marigold.................................375.00
    Swung Vase, 8-1/2" h, white........................................195.00
Elephant, unknown maker, paperweight, miniature, marigold ....700.00
Embroidered Mums, Northwood, bowl, sapphire blue .............1,200.00
Fan, Dugan
    Bowl, flared, ftd, peach opal .......................................55.00
    Gravy Boat, ftd, peach opal .......................................160.00
Farmyard, Dugan, bowl, 3-in-1 edge, 10-3/4" d, purple...........5,300.00

## Feathered Serpent, bowl, 5" d, marigold 30.00

Feather Stitch, Fenton, bowl, ruffled, 9-1/4" d, dark marigold.......95.00

Dandelion, Northwood, tumbler, purple, $65.

**Fisherman, mug, marigold, $245.**

Field Thistle, US Glass plate, 6" d, scalloped edge, marigold .... 275.00
Fine Rib, Fenton
    Swung Vase, 8-3/4" h, red, streaked effect......................... 325.00
    Swung Vase, 9-3/4" h, dark amber .................................... 125.00
    Swung Vase, 10" h, aqua opal............................................ 375.00
    Swung Vase, 10-1/2" h, aqua ............................................ 100.00
    Swung Vase, 12" h, light amber ........................................... 45.00
Fishscale and Beads, Dugan, plate, 7-1/2" d, amethyst ............. 500.00
Five Hearts, Dugan, compote, marigold ..................................... 275.00
Fleur De Lis, Millersburg, bowl, ruffled, vaseline ..................... 6,500.00
Floral and Grape, Fenton
    Tumbler, blue ..................................................................... 35.00
    Water Pitcher, blue............................................................ 400.00
Floral Spray, unknown maker
    Pitcher, clear, very good iridescence ................................. 375.00
    Tumbler, clear, very good iridescence ................................. 30.00
Flowers & Frames, Dugan, bowl, ftd, purple............................. 450.00
Formal, Dugan, hatpin holder, marigold..................................... 700.00

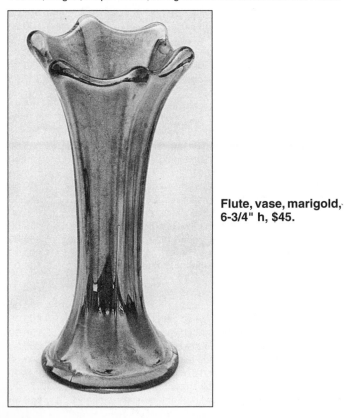

**Flute, vase, marigold, 6-3/4" h, $45.**

Fruits and Flowers, Northwood
  Bon Bon, stemmed, handled
    Aqua opal ......................................................................... 700.00
    Electric blue...................................................................... 350.00
    Green ............................................................................... 295.00
    Ice blue............................................................................ 575.00
    Lavender .......................................................................... 500.00
    Marigold, dark .................................................................. 165.00
    Purple .............................................................................. 145.00
    White ............................................................................... 150.00
  Bowl, ruffled, basketweave ext., 7-1/4" d, aqua ............ 400.00
  Garden Mums, Northwood, plate, 6" d, amethyst...........300.00
  Garden Path Variant, Dugan, chop plate, 11-1/4" d, purple,
    soda gold ext. .............................................................. 6,750.00
  Garland, Fenton, rose bowl, blue ................................. 165.00
Good Luck, Northwood
  Bowl, ribbed ext., pie crust edge, aqua opal................... 8,750.00
  Bowl, ribbed ext., ruffled, aqua opal .......................... 5,000.00
Grape, Imperial, water set, 6 pcs, purple .................................. 425.00
Grape & Cable, Northwood
  Bon Bon, basketweave ext., handle, stippled, dark
    amethyst ......................................................................160.00
  Bowl, 9" d, basketweave ext., marigold ................................ 85.00
  Bowl, ribbed ext., ruffled, 8-3/4" d, white .......................... 500.00
  Bowl, stippled, ribbed ext., pie crust edge, 8-1/2" d........ 3,750.00
  Hatpin Holder, ice blue, small chip on foot..................... 1,100.00
  Miniature Lamp, purple .................................................... 200.00
  Plate, purple...................................................................... 200.00
  Powder Jar, purple............................................................ 200.00
  Punch Cup, handle, aqua opal .......................................... 700.00
  Sweetmeat Compote, cov, dark marigold.......................... 1,800.00
  Tobacco Jar, cov, stippled, blue ...................................... 1,100.00
Grape & Gothic Arches, Northwood
  Tumbler. Blue...................................................................... 45.00
  Tumbler, purple .................................................................. 25.00
  Water Pitcher, blue............................................................ 275.00
Grapevine Lattice, bowl, 5" d, white.......................................... 55.00
Greek Key, Northwood, plate, ribbed ext., dark marigold ........ 4,500.00
Hanging Cherries, Millersburg, ice cream bowl, amethyst........... 300.00
Hattie, Imperial, rose bowl, marigold......................................... 650.00
Heart and Vine, Fenton, plate, flat, 9-1/4" d
  Amethyst, satiny irid........................................................ 500.00
  Blue, reddish irid .............................................................. 800.00
Hearts and Flowers, Northwood
  Bowl, ruffled, ribbed ext., aqua opal ............................. 13,000.00
  Bowl, ruffled, ribbed ext., ice blue, pink highlights ............. 350.00
  Compote, stemmed, ruffled, aqua ................................. 1,050.00
  Compote, stemmed, ruffled, ice blue, frosty,
    pink highlights .............................................................. 1,000.00
  Compote, stemmed, ruffled, marigold, dark....................... 350.00
  Plate, ribbed ext., marigold, dark ................................. 2,000.00
  Plate, ribbed ext., purple, multicolored irid...................... 2,500.00
Hobnail, Millersburg, rose bowl, amethyst 425.00
Hobnail Swirl, Millersburg
  Cuspidor, green ............................................................. 1,700.00
  Cuspidor, purple ............................................................... 600.00
Hobstar & Fruit, Westmoreland
  Card Tray, marigold over milk glass................................... 775.00
  Sauce, 5" d, aqua opal...................................................... 225.00
Hobstar & Shield, unknown maker, tumbler, marigold ............... 265.00
Holly, Fenton
  Bowl, ruffled, 8-3/4" d, dark amber .................................. 200.00
  Bowl, ruffled, 9" d, peach opal ....................................... 1,100.00
  Bowl, 3-in-1 edge, 9-1/4" d, powder blue........................... 225.00
  Plate, flat, 9-3/4" d, amethyst........................................ 1,250.00
  Plate, flared, 9-1/2" d, blue ............................................ 375.00
  Plate, flared, 9-1/2" d, green ........................................... 700.00
Holly Whirl, Millersburg, bowl, ruffled, 9-1/2" d, green, radium and gold
  highlights ........................................................................ 200.00
Homestead, Imperial, chop plate, green ................................. 1,350.00

Horsehead Medallion, Fenton, plate, 7-1/2" d, crystal ............... 175.00
Inverted Fan and Feather, Dugan, fruit bowl, ftd, marigold .......... 85.00
Inverted Feather, Cambridge, cordial, marigold ........................ 500.00
Interior Panels, Imperial, vase, flared, 8-3/4" h, 8-3/4" d, wheel etched
 floral design, marigold, sgd with iron cross mark .................... 450.00
Iris, compote, blue .................................................................... 85.00
Jockey Club, Northwood, bowl, 6" d, amethyst ....................... 1,500.00
Kittens, Fenton
 Banana Boat, 2 sided, amethyst .................................... 525.00
 Bowl, 4-1/4" d, ruffled, crystal ..................................... 225.00
Lattice and Grape, Fenton, water set, tankard pitcher, 7 pcs,
 white ......................................................................... 950.00
Lattice and Poinsettia, Northwood
 Bowl, ruffled, ribbed ext., ftd, aqua opal ..................... 6,500.00
 Bowl, ruffled, ribbed ext., ftd, ice blue ...................... 3,000.00
Leaf and Beads, Northwood, nut bowl, flared, ftd, aqua opal .. 2,250.00
Leaf Chain, Fenton
 Bowl, ruffled, 7-1/2" d, red ........................................ 900.00
 Ice Cream Bowl, 8-1/4" l, reverse amberina ................... 2,250.00
 Plate, flat, 7-1/2" d, white .......................................... 625.00
 Plate, flat, 9-1/4" d, electric blue ............................... 3,100.00
Lined Lattice, Dugan
 Swung Vase, 4-3/4" h, 51/4" d, flared, dark peach opal ...... 425.00
 Swung Vase, 9" h, light amethyst/horehound .................... 275.00
 Swung Vase, 9-1/2" h, purple ...................................... 300.00
 Swung Vase, 10-1/2" h, white, frosty, sun-colored lavender tint ....
  165.00
Little Stars, Millersburg, bowl, 3 in 1 edge, dark marigold .......... 375.00
Loganberry, Imperial
 Vase, amber .............................................................. 400.00
 Vase, green ............................................................... 575.00
Lotus and Grape, Fenton, plate, flat, 9-1/2" d, green ............... 3,250.00
Lotus and Poinsettia, Fenton, sauce, ruffled, ftd, ice green
 opal ........................................................................ 1,350.00
Luster Rose, Northwood, open sugar, green ............................. 30.00
Maple Leaf, tumbler, purple ..................................................... 45.00
Mikado, Fenton
 Compote, stemmed, ruffled, electric blue ....................... 1,000.00
 Compote, stemmed, ruffled, marigold .............................. 200.00
Millersburg Courthouse, Millersburg, bowl, low, ruffled, 7-3/4" d, ame-
 thyst, radium finish ................................................... 1,050.00
Millersburg Diamond, Millersburg
 Tumbler, dark marigold ................................................. 55.00
 Water Pitcher, marigold ............................................... 235.00
Morning Glory, Imperial, vase, 3-3/4" h, purple ........................ 215.00
Nesting Swan, Millersburg, bowl, ruffled, 9-1/2" d, pastel
 marigold ..................................................................... 90.00
Nippon, Northwood
 Bowl, ribbed ext., 8-1/2" d, white, frosty ....................... 155.00
 Bowl, ribbed ext., pie crust edge, 9" d, purple ................ 300.00
Open Edge, unknown maker, basket, red, two sides up ............. 350.00
Octagon, water pitcher ........................................................... 95.00
Omnibus, U. S. Glass, tumbler, blue ......................................... 275.00
Open Edge, basket, Blackberry interior, marigold, 5-1/2" x 7" ...... 45.00
Open Rose, Imperial, sauce, ruffled, 5-3/4" d, blue ................. 1,100.00
Orange Tree, Fenton
 Ice Cream Bowl, 8", marigold and moonstone ................. 1,000.00
 Loving Cup, handle, amethyst ....................................... 700.00
 Loving Cup, handle, blue ............................................. 550.00
 Loving Cup, handle, green ............................................ 650.00
 Mug, flared, handle, brick red, silvery irid ...................... 175.00
 Plate, flat, 9-1/2" d, electric blue ................................ 1,500.00
 Plate, flat, 9-1/2" d, marigold, dark .............................. 800.00
 Powder Jar, cov, marigold with vaseline highlights ............ 125.00
Orange Tree Orchard, Fenton, tumbler, white ........................... 55.00
Oriental Poppy, Northwood, tumbler, ice blue .......................... 175.00
Panther, Fenton
 Berry Bowl, individual, ftd, 5" d, amethyst ...................... 275.00
 Berry Bowl, individual, ftd, ruffled, 5-3/4" d, aqua ........... 350.00
 Berry Bowl, individual, ftd, ruffled, 5-3/4" d, red ............. 2,200.00

**Peacock, Millersburg, master ice cream bowl, amethyst, $3,000. Photo courtesy of Seeck Auctions.**

 Berry Bowl, master, ftd, ruffled, 8" d, blue .......................... 425.00
 Berry Bowl, master, ftd, ruffled, 8" d, marigold ................... 175.00
Pansy, Imperial
 Bowl, ruffled, 9" d, smoke ........................................... 300.00
 Plate, low, ruffled, 9-1/4" d, light amethyst ..................... 235.00
Parlor Panels, Imperial. vase, 3-3/4" h, 5-3/4" d, ruffled, squatty,
 smoke, slight peeling to one edge .................................. 340.00
Peacock, Millersburg, sauce, ruffled, 6-1/4" d
 Amethyst .................................................................. 175.00
 Marigold, dark ........................................................... 550.00
Peacock at the Fountain, Northwood
 Compote, stemmed, white, frosty .................................. 315.00
 Punch Bowl, base, marigold ........................................ 500.00
 Punch Cup, aqua opal ................................................. 900.00
 Punch Set, 4 pcs, purple ............................................ 1,700.00
 Punch Set, 8 pcs, marigold, dark .................................. 850.00
 Punch Set, 8 pcs, Renninger Blue ................................. 1,500.00
 Tumbler, marigold 45.00
 Water Pitcher, purple, electric blue highlights .................. 400.00
 Water Pitcher, white ................................................... 900.00
Peacock at the Urn, Fenton
 Compote, stemmed, ruffled, amethyst ............................ 325.00
 Plate, flat, 9-1/2" d, dark marigold ............................... 350.00
Peacock at the Urn, Northwood
 Ice Cream Bowl, individual size, aqua opal ..................... 4,000.00
 Ice Cream Bowl, individual size, electric blue .................. 250.00
 Ice Cream Bowl, individual size, green ........................... 650.00
 Ice Cream Bowl, individual size, purple .......................... 155.00
 Ice Cream Bowl, large, electric blue .............................. 7,250.00
 Ice Cream Bowl, large, ice blue, dark ............................ 1,000.00
 Ice Cream Bowl, large, marigold, dark ........................... 600.00
 Peacocks, Northwood
 Bowl, ruffled, stippled, ribbed ext., pie crust edge,
  aqua opal ............................................................. 3,700.00
 Bowl, ruffled, stippled, ribbed ext., pie crust edge, blue ...... 800.00
 Bowl, ruffled, stippled, ribbed ext., aqua opal ................. 3,250.00
 Bowl, ruffled, stippled, ribbed ext., Renninger Blue .......... 1,050.00
 Plate, ribbed ext., electric blue ................................... 1,600.00
 Plate, ribbed ext., lavender ......................................... 950.00
Perfection, Millersburg, tumbler, amethyst ............................... 275.00
Persian Garden, Dugan, bowl, 10" d, ten ruffles, amethyst ........ 650.00

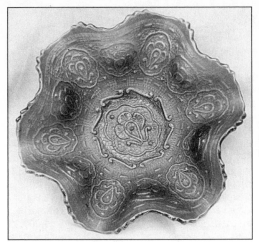

**Persian Medallion, Fenton, bowl, blue, 7" d, $80.**

Persian Medallion, Fenton
    Compote, large, green ........................................... 400.00
    Compote, small, white .......................................... 215.00
    Fruit Bowl, Grape & Cable ext., marigold............................ 200.00
    Plate, 6" d, black amethyst ........................................ 275.00
Pine Cone, Fenton, plate, flat, 7-1/2" d, root beer amber ........... 400.00
Poppy, Northwood, relish tray, ribbed ext., ruffled, aqua opal.. 3,250.00
Poppy Show, Imperial
    Vase, marigold, pastel............................................. 900.00
    Vase, purple ...................................................... 400.00
    Vase smoke ...................................................... 2,250.00
Poppy Show, Northwood
    Bowl, ruffled, electric blue ..................................... 1,850.00
    Bowl, ruffled, green .............................................. 2,000.00
    Bowl, ice green .................................................. 1,100.00
    Bowl, marigold, dark .............................................. 850.00
Pulled Loop, Dugan
    Swung Vase, 8-1/4" h, purple ...................................... 475.00
    Swung Vase, 11" h, celeste blue.................................... 375.00
Raspberry, Northwood, water pitcher, marigold ...................... 175.00
Rays and Ribbons, Millersburg, ice cream bowl, 8-1/2",
    amethyst........................................................... 250.00
Regal Cane, unknown maker, clock, marigold.......................... 800.00
Ripple, Imperial, vase, 11" h, purple ............................... 120.00
Rising Sun, US Glass
    Juice Tumbler, marigold............................................. 75.00
    Tumbler, blue .................................................... 300.00
    Tumbler, marigold ................................................ 135.00
Rococo, Imperial, vase
    Vase, dark marigold ............................................... 155.00
    Vase, smoke ...................................................... 175.00
Rosalind, Millersburg, bowl, 10" d, amethyst ........................ 220.00
Rosalind Variant, compote, green.................................... 600.00
Rose Show, Northwood
    Bowl, ruffled, aqua opal ......................................... 2,600.00
    Bowl, ruffled, electric blue ...................................... 850.00
    Bowl, ruffled, green ............................................. 1,150.00
    Bowl, ruffled, ice blue .......................................... 1,000.00
    Bowl, ruffled, lime ice green .................................... 1,050.00
    Bowl, ruffled, purple ............................................. 750.00
    Plate, electric blue, flake on one rose petal .................... 2,850.00
    Plate, emerald green, small chip ................................. 3,750.00
Rustic, Fenton, 15-1/2" h, 4" d base, swung vase, white............. 165.00
Sailboats, Fenton, plate, 6" d, blue ................................ 900.00
Sand and Shell, Imperial, bowl, ruffled, deep, 7-1/2" d, purple ... 250.00
Scroll Embossed, Imperial
    Compote, small, purple ............................................ 315.00
    Plate, amber ..................................................... 350.00
    Plate, purple .................................................... 425.00
Singing Birds, Northwood
    Berry Bowl, green ................................................. 55.00

    Berry Bowl, purple ................................................ 35.00
    Water set, 7 pcs, green............................................ 800.00
Six Petals, Dugan
    Bowl, 3 in 1 edge, purple ......................................... 135.00
    Bowl, 7" d, peach opalescent....................................... 70.00
Skaters, unknown maker, bowl, dark marigold ........................ 225.00
Stag and Holly, Fenton, bowl, ftd, ruffled, 10-3/4" d, blue .......... 350.00
Starfish, Dugan, compote, stemmed, ruffled, dark pastel opal ... 150.00
Star of David, Imperial, bowl, ruffled, 8-3/4" d, purple.............. 160.00
Strawberry, Northwood
    Bowl, ruffled, basketweave ext., marigold, opal tips ........ 1,950.00
    Plate, basketweave ext., marigold, opal tips...................... 700.00
Sunflower, Millersburg, pin tray, amethyst ................................ 400.00
Swirl Hobnail, Millersburg, rose bowl, purple, radium, roughness on
    hobs .............................................................. 200.00
Ten Mums, Fenton, bowl, tight candy ribbon edge, 8-1/2" d,
    amethyst.......................................................... 300.00
The States, US Glass, butter dish, marigold.......................... 375.00
Thin Rib, Fenton, vase, 7-1/2" h, blue .............................. 155.00
Three Fruits, Northwood, plate, purple .............................. 175.00
Tree Trunk, Northwood
    Funeral Vase, 17" h, 5-3/4" d base, green ...................... 4,000.00
    Swung Vase, 9-3/4" h, aqua ........................................ 950.00
    Swung Vase, 11-1/2" h, green ...................................... 375.00
    Swung Vase, 12" h, 4-1/2" d base, purple ......................... 300.00
    Swung Vase, 12-3/4" h, 4-1/2" d base, green ...................... 325.00
Trout & Fly, Millersburg, bowl, 8-1/2" d, scalloped, marigold ...... 500.00
Tulip & Cane, Imperial, cordial, marigold ........................... 200.00
Vintage, Fenton, Millersburg, Northwood
    Bowl, 6-3/4" d, ruffled, cherry red ............................. 2,200.00
    Epergne, large, green ............................................. 300.00
    Epergne, small, amethyst, some roughness on base......... 155.00
Vintage Grape, Fenton, bowl, 3-in-1 edge, 8-3/4" d, red ........ 1,400.00
Weeping Cherry, Dugan, bowl, crimped edge, marigold.............. 95.00
Western Thistle, unknown maker
    Tumbler, blue .................................................... 215.00
    Vase, marigold ................................................... 500.00
Wild Rose, Westmoreland, syrup jug, handle, dark marigold ..... 600.00
Wide Panel, Millersburg, compote, stemmed, ruffled, 8-3/4" h, dark
    marigold .......................................................... 575.00
Wishbone, Northwood, plate, ftd, marigold.......................... 800.00
X-Ray, US Glass, cruet, marigold, enameled flowers ................ 225.00
Zig-Zag, Millersburg
    Bowl, tri-corner, green............................................ 800.00
    Bowl, tri-corner, crimped edge, amethyst, radium ............. 350.00
    Ice Cream Bowl, amethyst, radium.................................. 600.00

# CAROUSEL FIGURES

**History:** By the late 17th century, carousels were found in most capital cities of Europe. In 1867, Gustav Dentzel carved America's first carousel. Other leading American firms include Charles I. D. Looff, Allan Herschell, Charles Parker, and William F. Mangels.

**References:** Charlotte Dinger, *Art of the Carousel*, Carousel Art, 1983; Tobin Fraley, *The Carousel Animal*, Tobin Fraley Studios, 1983; Frederick Fried, *Pictorial History of the Carrousel*, Vestal Press, 1964; William Manns, Peggy Shank, and Marianne Stevens, *Painted Ponies*, Zon International Publishing, 1986.

**Periodicals:** *Carousel Collecting & Crafting*, 3755 Avocado Blvd., Suite 164, La Mesa, CA 91941; *Carousel News & Trader*, Suite 206, 87 Park Ave. West, Mansfield, OH 44902; *Carousel Shopper*, Zon International Publishing, P.O. Box 6459, Santa Fe, NM 87502.

**Collectors' Clubs:** American Carousel Society, 3845 Telegraph Rd, Elkton, MD 21921; National Amusement Park Historical Association, P.O. Box 83, Mount Prospect, IL 60056; National Carousel Association, P.O. Box 4333, Evansville, IN 47724.

**Museums:** Herschell Carrousel Factory Museum, North Tonawanda, NY; International Museum of Carousel Art, Portland, OR; Merry-Go-Round Museum, Sandusky, OH; New England Carousel Museum, Inc., Bristol, CT.

**Notes:** Since carousel figures were repainted annually, original paint is not a critical factor to collectors. "Park paint" indicates layers of accumulated paint; "stripped" means paint has been removed to show carving; "restored" involves stripping and repainting in the original colors.

Bull, Heyn, Germany, c1904, old red park paint, brass horns..2,000.00
Camel, Charles Dare, c1890, restored by Tina Veder .............5,750.00
Cat, Dentzel, fish in mouth, c1915, professionally restored...26,000.00
Chariot Seat, Looff, 1884, complete, early park paint.............4,000.00
Deer
    Dentzel, leaping, early paint, real antlers......................10,500.00
    E. J. Morris, stander converted to jumper by C. W. Parker in 1925,
        early paint.................................................................12,00.00
    PTC, standing, antlers ....................................................26,400.00
Frog, Herschell-Spillman, North Tonawanda, NY, c1914, leaping, green painted body, yellow waistcoat, orange shorts, 42" l.20,000.00
Giraffe, E. Joy Morris, Philadelphia, old park paint ...............15,000.00
Horse
    Anderson, English, named "Nina" on neck ......................2,000.00
    Carmel, Charles, stander, later heavily jeweled by
        Borelli.........................................................................25,000.00
    Dentzel, Gustave
    Listener, ears cocked, dapple gray, c1905, restored by Layton
        Studios, New Castle, PA ..........................................13,500.00
    Prancer, restored by Layton Studios, New Castle, PA...12,000.00
    Prancer, second row, restored by Layton Studios, New Castle,
        PA...............................................................................12,000.00
    Second row jumper, old paint ...........................................8,000.00
Herschell, Allan, second row jumper, c1920, Navajo symbols in glass jewels on blanket, restored ....................................................2,600.00

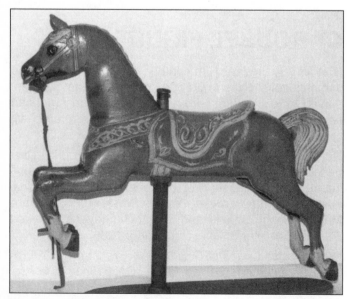

**Horse, carved and painted wood, repaint, 51" l, $1,300. Photo courtesy of Richard Opfer Auctioneering, Inc.**

Illions & Sons, M. D., jumper, flame mane, restored......30,000.00
Looff, Charles I. D.
    Inside row prancer, good condition............................4,250.00
    Outside row stander, restored, starburst mirrors and tassels...
        8,500.00
    Outside row stander, three legs replaced.................11,500.00
    Second row prancer, c1900.....................................4,000.00
    Parker, C. W., Abiliene, KA, c1905, carved mane, saddle,
        American flag, glass eyes, old polychrome repaint, 56" h,
        added bass and brass post, replaced tail and stirrups, old
        sheet metal repairs over seams and breaks in legs 1,760.00
Spillman
    Jumper, restored ........................................................3,500.00
    Stander, animal pelt.....................................................4,600.00
    Stein & Goldstein, jumper............................................2,850.00
    Unidentified Maker, second row stander, stripped, restored
        woodwork..................................................................9,000.00
Lion, PTC, standing, 51" h.................................................49,500.00
Ostrich, Savages of King's Lynn, England, c1875, running, carved leathers and saddle, hinged neck, 56" h, 58" l, refinished ....3,500.00
Running Board (cornice), 10' l, 2' h, orig paint, portrait of Sir Harcourt, elaborate dec, English.............................................................1,600.00
Tiger, Gustav Dentzel, Daniel Muller, c1895, walking, raised head, carved saddle, restored........................................................24,000.00
Wolf, PTC, leaping.............................................................24,400.00

# CASTLEFORD

**History:** Castleford is a soft-paste porcelain made in Yorkshire, England, in the 1800s for the American trade. The wares have a warm, white ground, scalloped rims (resembling castle tops), and are trimmed in deep blue. Occasionally pieces are decorated further with a coat of arms, eagles, or Lady Liberty.

Bowl, 5" d, scalloped, white ground, blue bands .........................200.00
Creamer, 3-1/2" h, three brown oval medallions, one with white applied eagle and shield, second with Lady Liberty, third with cherubs and eagle on cloud.................................................................................315.00
Sugar, cov, round, mythological scenes, vertical panels, twisted rope band near top, scalloped edge with oval medallions, blue enamel lines, double lid, floral knob....................................................240.00
Tea set, 6-1/2" h teapot, molded white salt glaze, blue enameled trim, 3 pcs, all with some damage.......................................................235.00

# CASTOR SETS

**History:** A castor set consists of matched condiment bottles held within a frame or holder. The bottles are for condiments such as salt, pepper, oil, vinegar, and mustard. The most commonly found castor sets consist of three, four, or five glass bottles in a silver-plated frame.

**Castleford Teapot, blue stripe, hairline at handle, 9" l, 5-1/4" h, $225.**

Although castor sets were made as early as the 1700s, most of the sets encountered today date from 1870 to 1915, the period when they enjoyed their greatest popularity.

2 Bottle, silver mounted cut glass bottles, engraved crest on hinged bottles, pierced and forked handles, open frame with applied shell-work cartouche, engraved crest, four scroll supports, rococo shell terminals, George II period, Samuel Wood, London, 1750, 10-1/4" h ..................................................... 2,500.00
3 Bottle, Bristol glass, enameled flowers, SP holder .................. 150.00
3 Bottle, green glass shaded to clear bottles, cut panels, ornate SP frame, 3-1/2" x 4" x 5" h ............................................. 190.00
3 Bottle, Mt. Washington glass, opaque white bottles, hp floral dec on salt and pepper, hummingbird dec on mustard, pastels, round hammered SP frame, mkd "Pairpoint 724" ...................................... 200.00
3 Bottle, opalescent glass, apple blossom mold, one cranberry, white, and blue, silver plated lids, 15" h, needs minor soldering ..... 2,000.00
4 Bottle, blown three mold glass, cruet with solid ball stopper, mustard with ribbed cov, two shakers with orig metal caps, sq tin frame painted red, McKearin GI-7 ...................................... 450.00
4 Bottle, cobalt blue glass bottles, SP tops, fitted in oval galleried SP frame, four columns supporting pierced cupola, Germany, c1795, 14-1/2" h .......................................................... 4,200.00
4 Bottle, Fenton, opaque turquoise glass bottles, matching holder ............................................................. 120.00
4 Bottle, opalescent glass bottles, horizontal ribbing, vertical enameled band with multicolored flowers, ornate SP ftd and handled frame, mkd "Simpson, Hall, Miller & Co." ............................ 275.00
4 Bottle, Daisy and Button pattern, blue patterned glass bottles, matching blue glass holder with metal center handle ...................... 180.00
5 Bottle, cut glass bottles with unmarked lids, silver, Robert Hennell, London, 1777, three ball and claw feet, frame pierced with scrolling foliage between bands of engraved guilloche, beaded rim, mahogany base, beaded stem, 8-3/4" h .................................... 985.00
5 Bottle, Daisy and Button pattern, clear patterned glass bottles, ornate SP frame with bell at top, resilvered ............................ 500.00
5 Bottle, Heavy Paneled Finecut pattern, SP holder .................. 200.00
5 Bottle, ivory, mahogany case, SP tops ..................... 200.00

**6-bottle, cut and etched bottles, silver plated holder, 14" h, $145.**

5 Bottle, vaseline glass, fern engraving, orig tops and stoppers, handled frame sgd "Meriden" ...................................... 290.00
5 Bottle, willow ware china, blue dec, white ground, matching ceramic holder .......................................................... 180.00
6 Bottle, amberina glass, metal holder, mkd "Aurora 487" ....... 2,400.00
6 Bottle, cut glass, SP oval Sheffield holder, baluster stem, loop handle, 9-3/4" h ................................................... 395.00
7 Bottle, cut glass, SS collars and caps, George II silver galleried canoe-shaped tray, scroll feet, mkd "Peter, Ann & William Bateman, London," 1801, 8-1/2" h ....................................... 1,400.00

# CATALOGS

**History:** The first American mail-order catalog was issued by Benjamin Franklin in 1744. This popular advertising tool helped to spread inventions, innovations, fashions, and necessities of life to rural America. Catalogs were profusely illustrated and are studied today to date an object, identify its manufacturer, study its distribution, and determine its historical importance.

**References:** Ron Barlow and Ray Reynolds, *Insider's Guide to Old Books, Magazines, Newspapers, Trade Catalogs*, Windmill Publishing (2147 Windmill View Rd, Cajon, CA 92020), 1995; Lawrence B. Romaine, *Guide to American Trade Catalogs 1744-1900*, Dover Publications, n.d.

**Museums:** Grand Rapids Public Museum, Grand Rapids, MI; National Museum of Health and Medicine, Walter Reed Medical Center, Washington, DC.

**Additional Listings:** See *Warman's Americana & Collectibles* for more examples.

**Advisor:** Kenneth Schneringer.

Abercrombie & Fitch Co., Play Hours-Vacation at Home, New York, NY, c1938, 40 pgs, 6-3/4" x 9-1/2", croquet, lawn hi-li, archery, lawn games, golf & tennis accessories, water sports, music, bicycles, summer outdoors furniture, garden and lawn groupings, play houses, playground equipment, picnic kits ............................... 18.00
Aluminum Goods Mfg. Co., Manitowoc, WI, c1956, 20 pgs, 2-3/8" x 3", "Mirro" Aluminum Kitchen Products, percolators & whistlers, dish pan, strainer pan, bun warmer, molds, mixing bowls, boilers, tea kettles, cookie sheets, muffin pans, colanders, juice catcher, pressure cooker, etc., fifty items shown .................................... 12.00
American Printing Co., Fabrics We Are Printing & How We Do It, Fall River, MA, c1929, 28 pgs, 8-1/2" x 10-3/4", hard cover, 12 colored sheets, dyeing and printing of fabrics, picture and information about the plant, various mills, cuts of indigo, blue and white, Calcutta light blue, dyed reds, dyed clarets, etc. .............................. 60.00
American Steel & Wire Co., New York, NY, c1913, 22 pgs, 6" x 7", colorful wraps, fence posts with cuts of the fence and posts, fence post construction, driving line post, fastening fence to posts, anchoring line posts, stapling fence, gates, plus all parts and fences ........ 20.00
Atlas Boat Supply Co. Inc., Marine Equipment Catalog, New York, NY, c1948, 172 pgs, 7-3/4" x 10-3/4", mooring buoys, anchors, ropes, bolts, sockets, spinnaker pole fittings, winches, blocks, combination lights, stern and pole lights, marine lights, pumps, oar locks, compasses, flags, waterproof clothing, etc. ...................................... 26.00
Atwater Kent Mfg. Co., Cat. Of Atwater Kent Tuned Radio Frequency Receivers, Philadelphia, PA, c1928, 28 pgs, 6" x 9", featuring Model 29 compact with cuts of design, manufacturing, home settings, factory, other models, radio speakers .................................... 50.00
Baker-Vawter Co., Baker-Vawter Steel Filing Sections Catalogue, Holyoke, MA, c1920, 68 pgs, 8" x 10", drawers, followers, compressors, combination drawers, filing conveniences, combinations of drawers, shelves & sections, etc., lots of illustrations in light green color .......................................................... 38.00

Bastian- Blessing Co., Superior Soda Fountain Equipment, Cat. S-155, Chicago, IL, 1948, 32 pages, 8-1/2" x 10-3/4", cuts of soda fountain, fountain luncheonette assemblies, creamer units, work boards, sandwich units, steam tables, service units, counters etc. .......... 88.00

Belmont Stamping & Enamel, Catalog G, New Philadelphia, OH, c1924, 96 pgs, 6" x 9", high grade enameled ware, dinner pails, roasters, tea pots, kettles, rice boilers, convex sauce pots, pie and dish pans, sauce and stew pans, colanders, soup strainers, dippers, etc. .................................................. 180.00

Berks Building Block Co., National Cinder Concrete Products Assoc, Reading, PA, 1925, 207 pgs, 8-1/2" x 11", hard cover, Straub Cinder Building Blocks, cuts of buildings using blocks, residences, small houses, bungalows, garages, schools, churches, institutions, hotels, etc. .................................................. 36.00

Bethlehem Steel Co., Catalog W-1, Bethlehem, PA, c1928, 62 pgs, 3-1/2"x 6", wire nails and other wire products, galvanized nails, standard bright wire nails, box or siding, fence, dowel pin, foundry, shingle, slating, roofing, plaster board, barrel, berry box, clinch nails, barbed wire, etc. .................................................. 24.00

Bindley Hardware Co., Fall & Winter House Furnishings, Pittsburgh, PA, c1893, 79 pgs, 9-1/4" x 12-1/4", cuts of 4 lanterns, 12 coal vases, 2 coal hods, fire place equipment, kettle, wringers, coffee mills, pots and pans, slaw cutters, glass, vases, hanging lamps, cutlery....75.00

Braybar Co., Graybar Interphones & Accessories, Chicago, IL, c1930, 44 pgs, 8-1/2" x 10", interphone systems, desk and hand set interphones, wall interphones, master station interphones, outlying station interphones, master annunciator phones, two station private lines, code ringing .................................................. 55.00

Brunswick-Balke-Collender, Chicago, IL, 1914, 48 pgs, 3-5/8" x 6-3/8", rules to playing the various games of billiards and pocket billiards, also illustrating Brunswick Billiard tables for home use, cuts of right and wrong ways to cue a ball, 1 colored picture of accessories, 8 cuts of the various pool tables .................................................. 215.00

Buckley Of Binghamton, Binghamton, NY, c1929, 79 pgs, 6-1/4" x 9", early American antiques of chairs, tables, stands, chests of drawers, sideboards, desks, mirrors, beds, clocks, Currier & Ives prints, glassware, bottles, quilts, items of pewter, brass, hooked rugs, china , iron, lamps, etc. .................................................. 55.00

Cleveland Foundry Co., The Puritan Wickless Blue Flame Oil Cooking Stoves Cleveland, OH, c1900, 19 pgs, 5-1/2" x 8", several styles, 2 burner with 1 step burner for an oven, 3 burner with enclosed oven, Japanned top ornamented, etc., good cuts of the units, repair list of parts and prices.................................................. 50.00

Corliss, Coon & Co., New York, NY, c1909, 36 pgs, 7-1/4" x 8-1/4", line of collars and cuffs for gentleman-Country-Club, Touring, Gotham, Varisty, Boss, Fairfax, Sitka, Jerome, Glerngarry, Dartmouth, Norfolk., Fenwickascot, Georgia, Kent, Bronx, Golden Gate, Puritan, Alaska., over 200 illus .................................................. 36.00

Division Street Fair, Chicago, IL, c1907, 19 pgs, 4-1/4" x 7-1/2", watches, jewelry, men's scarf pins, cuff buttons, brooch pins, vest chains, fobs, ladies' silver plate purses, bracelets, Valier chain festoon rings, perfume atomizers, mantel clocks, baby place settings, etc. .................................................. 22.00

Donley Brothers Co., Book of Successful Fireplaces & How to Build Them, Cleveland, OH, c1940, 64 pgs, 8-1/4" x 11", cuts of side, end or corner units, period treatments, Colonial fireplaces, rugged type hearth and flue construction, ash pit, smoke chamber, etc. ....... 24.00

Lawrence Ellerbrock, Inc., Baltimore, MD, c1923, 76 pgs, 9" x 11-1/4", complete kitchen and serving equipment for hotels, etc., large steel ranges, Vulcan broilers, steam tables, serving tables, urns, ovens, dish washers, etc. .................................................. 60.00

Floyd Wells & Co., Cat. #10, Stoves, Heaters, Ranges, Royersford, PA, c1910, 218 pgs, 6" x 9", oven, coal or wood stoves, Irving ranges, rock Irving, rose Irving, vent and tall oak heaters, grand social open face heaters, wood cook stoves, box woods, furnaces.................42.00

Frigidaire Corporation, Dayton, OH, c1930, 487 pgs, 6" x 9", hard cover, 2 screw add-to wraps, installation and service manual on advanced refrigeration with information and illustrations, refrigeration, compressor units, cooling coils, walk-in coolers, cases, counters, ice cream cabinets, storage & makers, etc.................24.00

Funk Wig Co., Chicago, IL, 1919, Cat. #15, 32 pgs, shows some use, 6" x 9", $18. Photo courtesy of Kenneth E. Schneringer.

Funk Wig Co., Cat. No 15, Chicago, IL, 1929, 32 pgs, 6" x 9", wigs beards, mustaches, and theatrical cosmetics, court, colonial, Shakespeare and character wigs, clowns, comedy and devil's skulls, minstrel wigs, professional make-up box, etc. .......................... 18.00

General Electric Co., Bulletin 4891, Schenectady, NY, c1911, 5499 pgs, 8" x 10-1/2", electric railway equipment, cuts of railway power stations, portable substations, eight locomotives, forty different elevated and ground railway, rapid transits..................................... 80.00

Girl Scouts, Inc., New York, NY, c1936, 7-1/2" x10", official uniforms, make-up sets, material for uniforms, sportswear, camping & hiking equipment, flags, archery, Brownie equipment, gift items, arts & crafts material, first aid equipment ........................................... 40.00

Grand Union Tea Co., Premium Catalog Given For Purchase Of Grand Union Goods, Brooklyn, NY, c1912, 30 pgs, 6" x 9", light tears on wraps, linens, stoves, furniture, glassware, clocks, sewing machines, silverware, lamps, kitchen, washer, china, lighting..................... 32.00

Herter's, Inc., Cat. No. 57, Fall, Winter & Spring, Waseca, MN, c1956, 190 pgs, 8-1/2" x 10-3/4", cuts of gunstocks and fittings, decoys, game calls, outdoor clothing, trailers and boat carriers, lots of boats, gifts and novelty items, camping supplies, checkering tools, choke devices, gun supplies, etc. ...................................................... 35.00

Kimball Tire Case Co., The Kimball Steel Armor for Pneumatic Tires, Council Bluffs, IA, c1913, 18 pgs, 3-1/2" x 6", cuts of the products ......................................................................... 16.00

Kittanning Church Seating, Kittanning, PA, c1909, 32 pgs, 6" x 9", church seating, pulpit furniture, church pews, pulpits, pulpit chairs, communion tables, altars, altar railings, shrines arcs, reading desks, book rack, collection plates, etc. ............................................... 42.00

Lane Brothers, Manufacturers Of Hardware Specialties, Poughkeepsie, NY, c1900, 42 pgs, 6" x 8-3/4", timber & door hangers, parlor & fire door hangers, store rolling ladders, tackle blocks, carriage jacks, swift mills for grinding spice, corn, drugs, coffee mills, root cutter, etc. .................................................................... 55.00

Larkin Co., Spring & Summer Products & Premium Merchandise, Buffalo, NY, c1913, 160 pgs, 8-1/4" x 10-1/4", foods, toiletry, pharmacy products, hardware, cutlery, clothing, table linens, towels, rugs, furniture, musical, stoves, pottery, cut glass, lamps, leather, goods, outdoor furniture, etc. .................................................................... 45.00

Chas. E. Marshall, Lockport, NY, 1894, 32 pgs, 8" x 11-1/2", new & useful inventions, Dresden metal novelties, chenille monkey, rooster horn, automatic jumping jacks, Nuremberg magic box, wigs, wizard's pack of toys, sewing items, brushed brushes, books, emblems, tricks, games, etc. .................................................................... 44.00

Mills Sales Co., More For Your Money, Boston, MA, c1940, 120 pgs, 8" x 10-1/4", discount drugs, sundries, pharmaceuticals, dental needs, razor blades, balloons, balls, toys, Christmas items, fishing needs, clocks, radios, watches, sporting goods, cameras, movie equipment, etc. ..................................................................................... 20.00

Murphy Door Bed Co., New York, NY, c1927, 48 pgs, 8" x 9-1/2", illustrations of how Murphy In-A-Door Beds are used in various buildings, floor plans, plus seven models in color ...................................... 45.00

National Car Spring Co., Catalogue Of Railway Springs, New York, NY, c1878, 23 pgs, 4-1/4" x 6", cuts of rubber center spiral, equalizer or bolster, nest spiral spring, dinsmore nest spiral, volute buffer, group spiral bearing springs, paragon buffer, elliptic spring, etc. ......... 15.00

Emil J. Paidar Co., Cat. No. 32, Chicago, IL, 1930, 20 pgs, 10" x 12", barber and beauty parlor equipment, mirror cases, hydraulic barber chairs, electric barber poles that revolve, enameled wall and floor lavatories.................................................................................. 175.00

Pan-American Navigation, Navigation Service Catalog, Aeronautical Supplies & Navigation Equipment, N. Hollywood, CA, 8-1/2" x 11", watches, Dalton computers, navigation computers, slide rules, aircraft sextants, aerial cameras, sun glasses, texts, publications, flight records, log books, etc. ................................................................. 44.00

Perfection Mfg. Co., St. Louis, MO, c1930, 52 pgs, 3-5/8" x 7", "Rock-a-Bye" baby items, folding carriages, high chair attachment, folding strollers, nursery seats, metal porch gates, auto seats, beds, hammocks, swings, stands, bath tubs, tables, dressing tables, doll bathinette, doll carriages, etc. ...................................................... 48.00

Pittsburgh Plate Glass Co., Vetter Mfg. Co., Stevens Point, WI, Pittsburgh, PA, c1942, 8-1/2" x 11", nature's colors in lasting beauty, building morale through the proper use of color, cuts of rooms inside the home showing the various combinations of color ................ 12.00

Roderick, Payne, Inc., Bird Houses & Outdoor Decorations From The "Bird House Man," Springfield, OH, c1928, 16 pgs, 7" x 10", pottery for gardens, birth bath, sun dial, glazing gloss, oil jars, pots, saucers, door stops, foot scrapers, plus birdhouse tree feeders, novelty window feeder, martin house, etc. ...................................................... 25.00

Scranton Stove Works, Scranton, PA, c1901, 28 pgs, 7-1/4"x 10-1/4," Dockash stoves with fine cuts of various cabinet ranges with nickel trimmings, cabinet Garnet ranges, Dockash piano base ranges, Glen Hudson, Grand Dockash, Gem Hudsons, etc. for coal or wood. 55.00

J. Elliot Shaw & Co., Philadelphia, PA, c1903, 80 pgs, 4-3/4" x 7-1/2", electrical novelties, dynamos, motors, electrical apparatus, gas engines-electrical railways, cars, bridges, tracks, toy steam engines, dynamos, water power plants, electric motors, railway stations, etc. ......................................................................................... 85.00

Shaw Supply Co., Inc, Tacoma, WA, c1929, 458 pgs, 6" x 9", hard cover, standard surgical instruments w/cuts of centrifuge instruments, forceps, operating scissors, directors, probes, some drills, curettes, bone instruments, needles, gowns, eye specula, mastoid instruments, etc........................................................................... 135.00

Slingerland Drum Co., Catalog 67, Niles, IL, 1965, 64 pgs, 8-1/2" x 11", drums in color, duet and jazz outfits, jam session, complete outfits, cocktail drums, be bop, snare and bass drums, Latin American drums, parade drums, pedal Timpani, concert outfits, etc. plus sticks, etc. ........................................................................................ 58.00

Standard Chair Co., Union City, PA, c1912, 47 pgs, 3-1/4"x 10-3/4", straight back and saddle seat rockers, rockers with and with-out arms, padded back rockers, plain rockers, straight back chairs, chairs for the desk and offices, armed chairs, stools, etc. sold by dozen to dealers ...................................................................... 40.00

Stilwell-Bierce & Smith, Dayton, OH, c1897, 94 pgs, 6" x 9", special machinery for heating and purifying feed waster for steam boilers, cuts of lime-extracting heater and filter combined, round heaters, heater and filter combined, combined feed water heater, purifier, etc. ......................................................................................... 33.00

Times Square Theatrical & Studio Supply Corp, Cat. No. 22, New York, NY, c1979, 66 pgs, 8-1/2" x11", spots lens and patterns, follow spots, strip lights, light control devices, electronic dimmer boards, electrified tracks, facet foils, flexible lighting, etc. ...................................... 22.00

Webber Lumber & Supply Co, Building Materials Catalog #89, Fitchburg. MA, c1920, 146 pgs, 9" x 12", doors, side lights, glazed windows, blinds, art sash, side lights for front doors, builders hardware, office desks, chairs, wicker furniture, furniture, row boats, campers supplies, etc. ................................................................................ 46.00

West Haven Mfg., Co., New Haven, CT, c1930, 8 pgs, 3-3/8" x 6-1/4", 6-1/4" x 13-1/2" sheet folded as issued, black ink on green paper, universal hack saws, hack saw frames, utility band saws with prices and descriptions, plus four cuts of the hack saw frame, utility hack, band saws, and power blade ...................................................... 12.00

# CELADON

**History:** The term "celadon," meaning a pale grayish green color, is derived from the theatrical character Celadon, who wore costumes of varying shades of grayish green, in Honore d'Urfe's 17th-century pastoral romance, *L'Astree*. French Jesuits living in China used the name to refer to a specific type of Chinese porcelain. Celadon divides into two types. Northern celadon, made during the Sung Dynasty up to the 1120s, has a gray to brownish body, relief decoration, and monochromatic olive green glaze. Southern (Lung-ch'uan) celadon, made during the Sung Dynasty and much later, is paint-decorated with floral and other scenic designs and is found in forms which would appeal to the European and American export market. Many of the southern pieces date from 1825 to 1885. A blue square with Chinese or pseudo-Chinese characters appears on pieces after 1850. Later pieces also have a larger and sparser decorative patterning.

Reproduction Alert.

Bottle, Korean, 12th C, Koryo Dynasty ....................................... 500.00
Bowl
    6-1/2" d, 3" h, Ching Par ware, blue-green glaze, carved combed lotus scroll dec, Southern Sung Period, 1127-1279 ......... 230.00
    7-3/4" d, foliate form, shallow draft, pale green-blue, Ying Ching, Sung period, 960-1270.................................................... 175.00
Buddha, 16" h, figure of maitreya seated on lotus throne, Korea, early 20th C................................................................................ 460.00
Cup, 6" d, tan colored glass, Korean Koryo, 13th C ................... 150.00
Dish, 10-1/2 d, incised peony blossom, crackled deep green glaze, everted rim, Ming Dynasty ...................................................... 300.00
Ewer, 3-5/8" h, ovoid form, ribbed, plain shoulder, loop handle, upright spout, blue-green glaze, burnt orange foot rim, Southern Sung Dynasty ................................................................................. 950.00
Garden Seat, 19" h, floral dec, barrel form, China, late 19th C .. 550.00
Jar, 5" h, globular form, pale green glaze, Yongzheng mark, 1723-35 .. 5,000.00
Urn, cov, 6" h, low relief carved Indian lotus motif, exotic bloom carved handles, surmounted by lotus form knot cover, Moghul style 2,950.00
Vase
    8" h, mallet shape, carved dragon roundels, underglaze blue double-circle mark, 19th C, pr............................................... 320.00
    13" h, inlaid floral dec, Korean, mounted as lamp ............. 350.00
Water Dropper, bird shape, Korean, Koryo Dynasty, 12th/13th C.............................................................................. 785.00

# CELLULOID ITEMS

**History:** In 1869, an Albany, NY printer named John W. Hyatt developed and patented the world's first commercially successful semi-synthetic thermoplastic. The moldable material was made from a combination of camphor—the crystalline resin from the heart of a particular evergreen tree, and collodion—a type of nitrated cellulose substance (also called Pyroxylin), which was extremely flammable. Hyatt and his brother Isaiah called their invention Celluloid, a name which they made up, by combining the words cellulose and colloid. By 1873 the Hyatts' were successfully producing raw pyroxylin plastic material at the Celluloid Manufacturing Company of Newark, NJ. In the early days of its commercial development, Celluloid was produced exclusively in two colors; flesh tone - for the manufacture of denture base material and off white - which was primarily used for utilitarian applications like harness trimmings and knife handles. However during the late 1870s advances in plastics technology brought about a shift in the ways that Celluloid could be used. Beautiful imitations of amber, ivory, tortoise shell, jet and coral were being produced and used in the fabrication of jewelry, fashion accessories and hair ornaments. Because the faux luxury materials were so realistic and affordable, Celluloid quickly advanced to the forefront of consumerism by the working and middle classes.

Throughout the 1880s and 1890s, competition in the infant plastics industry was rampant and a number of newly organized fabricating companies were aggressively molding their brands of pyroxylin plastic into a variety of consumer products. However, since there was such limited knowledge about the nature of the material, many companies failed due to inferior products or devastating fires. By the early 20th century, there were four major American manufacturers firmly established as producers of quality pyroxylin plastics. In addition to the Celluloid Company of Newark, NJ, there was the Arlington Manufacturing Company of Arlington, NJ, which produced Pyralin; Fiberloid Corporation of Indian Orchard, MA, makers of Fiberloid; and the Viscoloid Company of Leominster, MA. Even though these companies branded their plastic products with their registered trade names, today the word "celluloid" is used in a general sense for all forms of this early plastic.

Celluloid-type plastic became increasingly popular as an alternative for costly and elusive natural substances. Within the fashion industry alone, it gained acceptance as a beautiful and affordable substitute for increasingly dwindling supplies of ivory and tortoise shell. However, it should be noted that celluloid's most successful application during the late 19th century was realized in the clothing industry; sheet stock in imitation of fine grade linen was fashioned into stylish waterproof cuffs and collars. In sheet form, Celluloid found other successful applications as well. Printed political and advertising premiums, pinback buttons, pocket mirrors and keepsakes items from the period between 1890-1920 were turned out by the thousands. In addition, transparent sheet celluloid was ornately decorated by embossing, reverse painting and lamination, then used in the production of decorative boxes, booklets and albums. The toy industry also capitalized on the used of thin celluloid sheet for the production of blow molded dolls, animal toys and figural novelties.

The development of the motion picture industry helped celluloid fulfill a unique identity all its own; it was used for reels of camera film, as well as in sheet form by animation artists who drew cartoons. Known as animation cels, these are still readily available to the collector for a costly sum, but because of the depredation of old celluloid, many early movies and cels have been lost forever. By 1930 and the advent of the modern plastics age, the use of celluloid began to decline dramatically. The introduction of cellulose acetate plastic replaced the flammable pyroxylin plastic in jewelry and toys and the development of non-flammable safety film eventually put an end to its use in the movies. By 1950, the major manufacturers of celluloid in the United States had ceased production; however, many foreign companies continued manufacture. Today Japan, France, Italy and Korea continue to manufacture cellulose nitrate plastics in small amounts for specialty items such as musical instrument inlay, ping pong balls and designer fountain pens. Beware of celluloid items that show signs of deterioration: oily residue, cracking, discoloration, and crystallization. Take care when cleaning celluloid items—it is best to use mild soap and water, avoiding alcohol or acetone-based cleansers. Keep celluloid from excessive heat or flame and avoid direct sunlight.

**References:** Shirley Dunn, *Celluloid Collectibles*, Collector Books, 1999, 2001 value update, Keith Lauer and Julie Robinson, *Celluloid, A Collector's Reference and Value Guide*, Collector Books, 1999, 2001 value update; Karima Parry, *Bakelite Bangles, Price & Identification Guide*, Krause Publications, 1999; Joan Van Patten and Elmer and Peggy Williams, *Celluloid Treasures of the Victorian Era*, Collector Books, 1999.

**Collectors' Club:** American Plastics History Association, 534 Stublyn Rd., Granville, OH 43023-9554.

**Museum:** National Plastics Center & Museum, Leominster, MA 01453.

**Marks:** Viscoloid Co. manufactured a large variety of small hollow animals that ranged in size from 2 to 8 inches. Most of these toys are embossed with one of three trademarks: "Made in USA," an intertwined "VCO," or an eagle with a shield.

**Advisor:** Julie P. Robinson.

## Advertising & Souvenir Keepsake Items

Bookmark, 4-1/2" l, diecut ivory grained celluloid, poinsettia motif in red, yellow & green, Psalm 22, David C. Cook Publishing Co. .. 25.00
Clothing Brush, 3" d, circular brush, shows black and white photograph of Gettysburg Memorial, Gettysburg, PA .................................... 35.00
Combination ruler, ink blotter, 8-3/4" x 1-1/2" wood grained celluloid, tan and light brown tones, features 1917 calendar for "Jennison Co. Engineers & Contractors," mfg. By Brown & Bigelow, St. Paul .. 30.00
Compact
    1-1/4" x 2" metal powder compact with celluloid top, featuring scenic view of Cypress Gardens ........................................ 15.00
    1-3/4" octagonal metal compact with inset pearlized celluloid lid in light amber tone, pink & blue floral motif; reverse has shield shaped medallion of Harrisburg, PA .................................. 12.00

**Counter, Compliments of Kennedy Furniture Co., Chicago, merchandise list on back, 3" l, $20.**

Fan, 4" h, mottled turquoise and cream celluloid Brise, light blue ribbon, shows the Washington Monument and words "Washington D.C." in gold tone paint ............................................. 15.00

Ink Blotter, 2-1/2" x 6" rect, booklet of blotters with decorative celluloid cover, shepherds overseeing sheep; A Merry Christmas; Keller Mfg. Co. of Allentown, PA, Christmas 1921, printed by Whitehead and Hoag Co ............................................................ 25.00

Letter Opener, 6-3/4" l, round bookmark medallion features Indian profile while the pointed letter knife mkd "SOUVENIR OF QUEBEC" .....18.00

Match Safe
   2-1/2" x 1-1/2" ivory grained, blue and black graphics "New England Made Cigars, Carry This Blue Union Label On The Box & Before Purchasing A Cigar Be Sure & See that This Blue Label is on The Box" ........................................... 65.00
   2-1/2" x 1-1/2", celluloid photo dec in green tones feature scenic views of Atlantic City, NJ ..................................... 15.00

Note Pad, 4-1/4" x 2-1/2" leather bound celluloid cover, children with bird and advertisement "Presented By Germania Savings Bank, Pittsburgh, PA," reverse has 1906 Calendar .............................. 25.00

Pocket Mirror
   Oval shaped, pink rose motif; "Use Mennen's Flesh Tint Talcum Powder" ............................................................... 50.00
   Round, 1-1/2" d, Bedford Peanut Butter, colorful graphics on cream ground features a jar of peanut butter ..................... 75.00

Pyro Print, 7-7/8" x 4-5/16" black ink over ivory grained celluloid sheet, featuring image of boy and girl at waters edge, "Smoke Mellow Mixture" printed by the Pyro Photo Company, NY, imp patent date Aug. 11, 1891 ............................................. 110.00

Shoe Horn, 5-1/2" l, two-tone amber and cream pearlescent, "HR Holden & Co. Inc - Shoe Store Supplies, 184 Summer St. Boston," c1925 ................................................................... 15.00

Tape Measure
   1-1/4" d with pull out tape; colorful picture of pretty girl with flowers, advertisement for "The First National Bank of Boswell, The Same Old Bank in its New Home" printed by P.N. Co. (Parisian Novelty Co. of Chicago) and Patent 7-10-17 emb in the side ................................................................. 65.00
   1-1/2" d, cream, black lettering, "JR Kramer Inc. Butter, NY.," mfg. by JB Carroll Co. of Chicago .................................... 15.00
   2-5/8" h, red celluloid bear on round pink tape measure base, Souvenir of Old Orchard Beach, Maine .............................. 65.00

Template, 3-7/16" x 1-13/16", typewriter correction template, "Remtico Typewriter Supplies" Remington Typewriter Co., printed by Whitehead & Hoag of Newark, NJ........................................... 20.00

## Decorative Items and Fancy Goods

Autograph Album, 4" x 5-1/2", printed celluloid with ocean scene, sea gulls, predominately green and blue colors.............................. 45.00

Candle Holders, pr, 6-1/2" h, with round weighted base, trademark Tuskoid in triangular outline ......................................... 65.00

Clock
   3-1/2" w x 4-1/2" h, ivory grained rect mantle clock .............. 30.00
   6-1/2" x 5-1/2", classical design with columns, pink pearlescence celluloid, round clock face, working order, c1930.............. 45.00

Collar Box, triangular shape, 10" on w end and 5" on back, 6-1/2" h, completely covered in brown imitation wood grained celluloid with bright yellow rose motif on the top ........................................... 55.00

Dresser Box
   3-1/2" deep, 8" x 6-1/4" embossed white celluloid with floral motif, fitted with imitation ivory brush, mirror, salve box, file and nail cleaner, mkd "Celluloid, 62" on the mirror, deep maroon satin lining, c1890 ............................................ 150.00
   4-1/2" w , 4-1/2" h, , grained ivory celluloid fashioned in the shape of a grand Piano, lift top with celluloid prop, blue velvet lining, no trademark ........................................ 70.00

Dresser Set
   Arch Amerith, Beverly Pattern, Ivory with amber edging, scalloped beveled edge, mirror, comb, rect clothing brush, imitation ivory tray with amber trimming, matching powder jar and hair receiver, perfume bottle with celluloid holder, ivory pin cushion base with scalloped amber trim, mkd Arch Amerith, Beverly .................................................. 125.00
   Black with green pearlescent surface, dresser tray with oval glass center, comb, brush, mirror, glass powder jar with matching celluloid lid, c1930 .......................................... 35.00
   Fiberloid, Fairfax pattern, variegated brown and gold, Fairfax pattern, includes 11 pieces, powder box, hair receiver, mirror, brush, comb, file, 2 button hooks, scissors and clothing brush .................................................. 85.00
   Pyralin, DuBarry pattern, vanity set in ivory, brush and comb, button hook, clothing brush, dresser tray, hair receiver, hand mirror, manicure implements, buffer and slave box, powder box, vase and frame ............................................... 145.00

Frame
   2-3/4" x 4-1/4" filigree lace edge with oval opening, easel back ................................................................ 20.00
   5-1/2" x 4" peach celluloid, semi-oval with footed scalloped bottom, oval metal decoration in black and gold floral design, oval 3" x 5" opening 15 ...................................... 20.00
   6" x 8" oval in ivory celluloid, celluloid easel back .............. 18.00

Glove Box, 13" x 4", blue satin lining, reverse painted Arts & Crafts type geometric design in cream, brown and coral..................... 65.00

Handkerchief Box, 3-1/2" h, 6" x 6" square, pale green embossed celluloid with reverse painted center motif in cream of a classical woman petting a little dog, Wedgwood type design............................ 75.00

Hat Pin Holder
   Circular weighted base from cream celluloid with cranberry colored velvet cushion, 5" h, center post with round circular disc on top features various openings to hold hat pins.................. 85.00
   Conical shaped holder fashioned from cream colored celluloid, weighted rect base, very plain........................................ 15.00

Manicure Set, rolled up leather pouch with fitted manicure tools, salve jars and scissors, deep purple velvet lining, mkd "French Ivory" 35.00

Music Box, 14" x 9" x 6" h, green floral embossed celluloid with center motif of a beautiful woman in a flowing gown.......................... 175.00

Photograph Album
   8" x 11", picture of a pretty child holding kitten, yellow and turquoise ............................................... 125.00
   18" x 6", printed picture of standing lady in red draped flowing dress ............................................... 250.00

Vase
   7" h, yellow, bulbous bottom, narrow opening with fluted top, painted pink and blue floral motif on bottom, no trademark20.00
   12" h, conical shape with round weighted base, imitation tortoise shell............................................... 30.00

## Fashion Accessories

Bar Pin
   2-1/2" l ivory grained rect, hp floral pink and green motif ........ 10.00
   3" black, flared ends, applied pink, blue and yellow celluloid flowers, c-clasp.................................................. 12.00

Belt, 22" l, 3-4" x 1-1/2" rect mottled green celluloid slabs, applied silver tone filigree decorations, slabs linked together by chain.................................................................35.00

Brooch

1-1/4" oval, imitation coral, molded flowers, filigree edging, mkd "Made In Japan," blue ink on back.......................20.00

1-1/2" x 1-1/8" oval brooch in amber pearlessence with black silhouette of a swan, c1926.......................................25.00

Bracelet, 3" d

Link, 4 oblong two tone cream and ivory links, attached with round creme links of smaller size, unusual........................30.00

Molded imitation coral, imitation ivory or imitation jade celluloid bangle with all over floral designs, Made in Japan, blue ink stamp inside.................................................15.00

Cuff Links

Kum-a-Part, separable links, square brown celluloid face with circular center opening for metal disc, orig paper display......25.00

Toggle back, realistic molded celluloid owls, glass eyes, c1896.... 95.00

Dress Clips, pr, molded lily in semi-translucent cream celluloid mkd "Japan".............................................................25.00

Eyeglasses, Harold Lloyd type with black frames.........................20.00

Hair Comb

Imitation ivory back comb with regal filigree design topped with celluloid balls, English, c1890.................................70.00

Imitation tortoise shell back comb with decorative metal work with scarab beetles among flowers and leaves, rhinestone trim, wide row of multiple teeth, c1900............................85.00

Pale amber celluloid with embedded red rhinestones in a whimsical floral motif, c1926.........................................40.00

Side combs, pr of 4-1/2" imitation amber side ornaments shaped like long hair pins, painted with delicate floral motif...........25.00

Hat Pin

4" l imitation ivory elephant head with tusks and black glass eyes 95.00

12" l, imitation tortoise, hollow tusk shape...........................18.00

12" l, Question mark shape, pearlized gray and cream swirled, hollow.................................................................45.00

Hat Ornament

3-1/2" h, Art Deco ornament with pearlized red and pearlized cream half circles, rhinestone trimming.........................32.00

4" translucent pale amber feather with black center, studded with rhinestones........................................................10.00

4-1/2" calla lily, amber celluloid with applied gold paint, studded with yellow rhinestones..........................................30.00

Necklace

1" imitation ivory elephant pendant on celluloid linked chain 35.00

2" elegant Art Nouveau filigree pendant, cream celluloid with oval cameo, profile of a beautiful woman, suspended from 20" cream celluloid beaded necklace, fine detailing............................95.00

Purse

4-1/2" h, x 3" w, oval cream molded basket weave design, dyed olive green, celluloid chain........................................120.00

6" long linked chain bag with satin lining, lid is solid celluloid, 4" x 3" oval shaped with painted flowers, 4" w at top and goes to a point at the bottom...........................................135.00

## Holiday Items

Christmas

Nodder, Santa, 4-1/2" h, Made in Japan..............................95.00

Ornament, roly-poly type house with opening in back for a small bulb, shows Santa approaching door, red and white, intertwined VCO/USA trademark............................................85.00

Santa, 4-1/2" figure, holding lantern in one hand and waving the other, Made In Japan.............................................40.00

Easter

Car, 3" peach with mottled green movable wheels, driven by bunny, VCO/USA.............................................65.00

Rabbit, 3-1/2" Roly Poly, cream with aqua trim, VCO/USA... 75.00

**Miniature Painting, seated girl with large hat, ribbons, black stained wood frame, 6-3/4" x 6", $225. Photo courtesy of Joy Luke Fine Art Brokers and Auctioneers.**

Woven Basket with lid, 1-3/4" tall, 1-1/2" diameter, bright red, string handle, bright blue Easter bunny with egg in hand painted on lid........................................................35.00

Independence Day, 5-1/4" Uncle Sam figural in white celluloid with painted red white and blue patriotic clothing.........................80.00

Halloween

2-3/4" witch driving a pumpkin vehicle, VCO.....................150.00

3" owl, roly poly, VCO trademark.................................85.00

4" h, horn, favor, orange celluloid with black stencil witch, VCO.................................................................45.00

St. Patrick's Day, toy, Paddy riding the Pig, 4-3/4" tall figure of a pig with movable legs, little boy with dunce cap riding on the back, Japan.................................................................185.00

Thanksgiving, 2-1/2" realistic turkey in gray with molded detailing highlighted with red and black, on roly-poly base.........................55.00

## Novelties

Bookmark, child's, 4-1/2" l x 1/2" w, thick cream colored celluloid, folded over to clasp onto paper, top formed into a cute bunny head with painted pink and blue features.........................22.00

Compact, 1-1/2" d, dark blue celluloid base with lid with reverse painted dancing girl, decorated with glitter, "Made in France"....65.00

Comb, 2-1/2" folding, comb, tear drop shaped, cream celluloid with black embossed floral trim and rhinestones........................25.00

Comb with Case, 3-1/4" x 1" pearlized red and gray rhinestone studded case, 3" cream colored comb.................................15.00

Letter Opener

5" curved sword with butterfly motif on handle, hand painted garish colors over thin ivory celluloid......................10.00

7-1/4" l, cream, bull dog figural top, VCO trademark...........30.00

8" l, saber shape, embossed fern motif, heavy thick ivory grained celluloid, mfg. by Celluloid Novelty Co., c1898.................90.00

Pocket Mirror, round, 2-1/8" d, black dwg, cream ground, 1920s style woman holding hand mirror, scene reverses to naughty scene when turned upside down.................................................25.00

Tape Measure, figural

Billiken, cream colored, applied brown highlights, sitting on circular tape measure base, mkd "Japan" on tape measure...125.00

Dice, 1-1/8" sq, cream colored, black dots.......................120.00

Fruit, 1-1/4" pear with lady bug tape measure pull.............175.00

Girl, basket of flowers and little dog near skirt, cream, blue, and maroon, Japan.............................................110.00

Pig with piglet, cream colored, mkd "Made in Occupied Japan".............................................................60.00

Toys

Alligator, 5-3/4" tan with red and black detailing, facing left, VCO/USA trademark............................................32.00

Bear

5" w, ream bear with pink & gray highlights, VCO/USA... 15.00

5" w, cream bear with pink & gray highlights, VCO/USA . 15.00
5-1/4" l, white polar bear, made in USA............................5.00
Bison, 3-1/4" long dark Brown, eagle and shield
   trademark ...............................................................18.00
Boar, 3-1/4" brown, Paul Haneaus of Germany/PH
   trademark ...............................................................65.00
Camel, 3-1/2" tan with brown highlights, Diamond S2 trade-
   mark, mkd "Made In Japan".......................................15.00

Cat
   3" peach with black highlights, floral trademark, mkd
     "JAPAN"..............................................................25.00
   5-1/4" cream cat with pink & black highlights, molded collar
     and bell, Made In USA trademark, rare ........................50.00
   Chicken, 3" standing hen in grass, cream with gray, yellow
     feet, VCO/USA trademark ......................................15.00
   Circus animals, elephant, gorilla, giraffe, tiger, lion, and hippo,
     garish bright colors, mkd "Made In Occupied Japan" ... 45.00
   Cow, 7-1/2" gray cow with purple highlights, eagle and shield
     trademark...............................................................35.00

Dog
   3" sitting German Shepherd, cream, plaster filled, MC, mkd
     "Made In Japan".....................................................40.00
   3-1/4" collie, yellow and tan, excellent realistic detail, Noris
     trademark...............................................................55.00
   3-1/4" St. Bernard, tan with black highlights, VCO/Circle 15.00
   4-1/2" Scotty, all black with VCO/USA............................20.00
   4-3/4" bull dog, cream with black highlights, VCO/USA .. 25.00
   5-3/4" hound dog with long tail, gray, VCO/Circle mark... 25.00
   5-3/4" Scotty, purple & gray with red rhinestone eyes, Royal
     Japan ...................................................................20.00
   Donkey, 2-1/4" cream with pink and black highlights, Made in
     USA ......................................................................15.00
   Duck, 3-1/2" yellow with green highlights, VCO/USA &
     Circle....................................................................12.00
   Elephant, 3-1/2" cream elephant with painted red floral blan-
     ket, Made In USA....................................................12.00
   Fish, 6-3/4" white and red fish, smooth shiny surface, molded
     fin, VCO/USA.........................................................15.00
   Frog, 1-1/4" yellow frog with stripe on back, VCO/USA .. 10.00
   Giraffe, yellow with brown spots, excellent molding by Petti-
     colin of France, eagle head trademark .........................75.00
   Goat, 3-1/2" white with gray, Billy Goat with beard & horns,
     VCO/USA...............................................................22.00
   Hippopotamus, 3-1/2" peach with open mouth, Made in Tokyo
     Japan, TS .............................................................15.00

Horse
   4" yellow horse with orange highlights, painted reigns and
     saddle, rattles, Made in USA ....................................20.00
   7" cream with purple & pink highlights, Made in USA ..... 25.00
   Lion, 3" orange with black highlights, Made in USA ........ 12.00
   Pig, 4-1/2" or 1-1/8" pink pig with painted eyes, Made in
     USA ......................................................................22.00
   Ram, 2-1/2" cream with gray highlights, Made in USA...... 9.00
   Rhinoceros, 2-1/2" gray and peach rhino, Made in USA. 15.00
   Seal, 4-1/2" gray balancing red ball, VCO/USA ..............55.00
   Squirrel, 2-7/8" brown celluloid, holding a nut, Made in
     USA ......................................................................30.00
   Stork, 6-3/4" standing stork, white with pink legs, flower mark
     & Japan.................................................................18.00
   Swan, 4" cream swan with gray, pink and orange highlights,
     VCO/USA...............................................................18.00
   Tiger, 4" tan with black stripes, 2 stickmen trademark &
     Japan ...................................................................15.00
   Turkey, 2-1/2" cream with dark blue, wire spring legs,
     PH ........................................................................35.00

Turtle
   1-3/8" two tone, brown top, yellow bottom......................12.00
   3" cream with brown highlights, VCO/USA with Circle .... 12.50

**Prince on Pig, joined legs, 4-1/2" l, 4" h, $25.**

## Dolls, Toys & Rattles

Doll
   4-3/4" realistic child doll with movable arms and legs, short blond
     molded hair, Shell trademark on back................................55.00
   6" side glancing Kewpie carnival doll with top hat, cane and feath-
     ers, crossed circle, Japan .................................................18.00
   9-1/2" girl and boy dressed in ethnic costumes, Turtle in Diamond
     trademark, Rheinische Gummiund Celluloid Fabrik Co, of Ger-
     many, pr . 125.0010" Carnival Kewpie with feathers, top hat and
     cane, Royal Japan, fleur-de-lis trademark ........................30.00
   12" realistic baby doll, Made in USA by Viscoloid Co ..........95.00
Figural Toy
   4" double figural showing two little girls with umbrella in pink and
     green bathing suit, floral trademark, mkd "Made in Japan" 55.00
   4-1/2" flesh tone Aviator with purple highlights, gray and black
     detailing, Made in Japan ..................................................35.00
   6-1/4" Beefeater with British Flag, standing on bright green base,
     House in Circle with Japan.................................................35.00
Rattle
   Egg shape on solid handle with ring, cream, pink, and blue floral
     motif ...............................................................................12.00
   Stork, 6" long, Made in Japan, rabbit trademark..................35.00
   Roly Poly
     1-1/2" Commodore Vanderbilt Navy Blue Officers Suit, PH
       trademark................................................................115.00
     2-1/2" aqua and cream ball with balancing elephant, trunk
       raised, no trademark....................................................35.00
     3-1/2" clown, pink & white base with balancing clown, feather
       on hat, Germany .........................................................55.00
     Toy Boat, 3-3/4" Gun Boat, purple with cream and pink flag,
       bow trademark, Made In Japan ....................................20.00
     Toy Dish, 3-3/4", cake on round platter, brightly colored, inter-
       twined VCO.................................................................95.00
     Whistle, 2", bird, red ......................................................12.00

## Utilitarian Items

Cutlery, solid imitation ivory grained handle utensils, 8 forks and 8
   knives in original box, Standard Mfg. Co....................................30.00
Crumb Tray Set, two dust pan shaped trays in ivory colored celluloid,
   one large and one small, scalloped and curved rim, no
   trademark .............................................................................12.00

**Cow, black and white, Japan, 5-1/2" l, 3" h, $35.**

Napkin Ring, 1-1/2" wide, lacy embossed ivory celluloid .............. 10.00
Soap Container, two piece cream box, rectangular with round corners, overall emb fleur-de-lis motif ...................................................... 12.00
Powder Box with Puff, 3-1/4" h, 2-3/4" h, hand painted forget-me-not motif, marked "Celluloid" with an easel trademark ..................... 35.00
Straight Razor, molded cream celluloid, handle formed to represent an ear of corn, Germany ............................................................ 20.00
Toothbrush, imitation ivory with hog hair bristles, no trademark ..... 4.00
Toothbrush Case, rectangular, 1" x 7" peach mottled celluloid, hinged opening on top with ventilating holes ........................................... 9.00

# CHALKWARE

**History:** William Hutchinson, an Englishman, invented chalkware in 1848. It was a substance used by sculptors to imitate marble and also was used to harden plaster of paris, creating confusion between the two products. Chalkware pieces, which often copied many of the popular Staffordshire items made between 1820 and 1870, was cheap, gaily decorated, and sold by vendors. The Pennsylvania German folk art pieces are from this period. Carnivals, circuses, fairs, and amusement parks gave away chalkware prizes during the late 19th and the 20th centuries. These pieces often were poorly made and gaudy.

**Additional Listings:** See Carnival Chalkware in *Warman's Americana & Collectibles.*

**Notes:** Don't confuse the chalkware carnival giveaways with the earlier pieces.

Bank, 10-1/2" h, seated cat, black and red ribbon collar and pipe, PA, 19th C .............................................................................. 225.00
Bust, 11-1/2" h, woman, pedestal base, titled "Micaela," numbered on back .................................................................................... 145.00
Figure
    5-3/4" h, deer, reclining, polychrome dec, red, ochre, brown, and black, America, 19th C, repair, paint wear, price for pr .... 490.00
    6-1/4" h, doves, molded, polychrome green, red, black, and ochre dec, America, 19th C, paint wear, chips, price for pr ........ 950.00

**Bust, woman, black, mkd "Micaela," 11-1/4" h, $165.**

8" h, rooster, molded, polychrome green, red, black, and ochre dec, America, 19th C, paint wear, chips .......................... 850.00
40" h, Abraham Lincoln, standing, painted ......................... 400.00
Mantel Ornament
    5-5/8" h, dog, full figured, oval base .................................. 225.00
    5-5/8" h, pr of lovebirds, plinth base .................................. 250.00
    7-1/4" h, dog, facing left, stepped rect base ...................... 275.00
    16" h, fruit in footed urn, red, yellow, green, and tan paint, America, 19th C, repair ...................................................... 2,185.00
Match Holder, 6" h, figural, man with long nose and beard, Northwestern Insurance Co., c1890 ...................................................... 115.00
Plaque, 9" h, horse head, orig polychrome paint ....................... 115.00
Urn, 9" h, shades of brown and green, Arts and Crafts style floral motif at neck, two handles formed by kneeling male figures ........... 175.00
Watch Hutch, 14" h, figural, compote of fruit, polychrome dec, 19th C .............................................................................. 350.00

# CHARACTER and PERSONALITY ITEMS

**History:** In many cases, toys and other products using the images of fictional comic, movie, and radio characters occur simultaneously with the origin of the character. The first Dick Tracy toy was manufactured within less than a year after the strip first appeared. The golden age of character material is the TV era of the mid-1950s through the late 1960s. Some radio premium collectors might argue this point. Today, television and movie producers often have their product licensing arranged well in advance of the initial release. Do not overlook the characters created by advertising agencies, e.g., Tony the Tiger. They represent a major collecting subcategory.

**References:** Bill Blackbeard (ed.), *R. F. Outcault's The Yellow Kid*, Kitchen Sink Press, 1995; Bill Bruegman, *Cartoon Friends of the Baby Boom Era*, Cap'n Penny Productions, 1993; ——, *Superhero Collectibles*, Toy Scouts, 1996; *Cartoon & Character Toys of the 50s, 60s, & 70s*, L-W Book Sales, 1995; Albert and Shelly Coito, *Elsie the Cow and Borden's Collectibles*, Schiffer Publishing, 2000; James D. Davis, *Collectible Novelty Phones*, Schiffer, 1998; Warren Dotz, *Advertising Character Collectibles*, Collector Books, 1993; ——, *What a Character! 20th Century American Advertising Icons*, Chronicle Books, 1996; Ted Hake, *Hake's Guide to Cowboy Character Collectibles*, Wallace-Homestead, 1994; ——, *Hake's Price Guide to Character Toys*, 3rd ed., Collector Books, 2000; Jim Harmon, *Radio & TV Premiums*, Krause Publications, 1997; Clark Kidder, *Marilyn Monroe: Cover to Cover*, Krause Publications, 1999; Jack Koch, *Howdy Doody*, Collector Books, 1996; Mary Jane Lamphier, *Zany Characters of the Ad World*, Collector Books, 1995; Cynthia Boris Liljeblad, *TV Toys and the Shows That Inspired Them*, Krause Publications, 1996; Jan Lindenberger with Cher Porges, *Peanuts Gang Collectibles; An Unauthorized Handbook and Price Guide*, Schiffer, 1998; David Longest, *Character Toys and Collectibles* (1984, 1992 value update), 2nd Series (1987, 1990 value update), Collector Books; Rex Miller, *The Investor's Guide To Vintage Collectibles*, Krause Publications, 1999; Andrea Podley with Derrick Bang, *Pea-*

nuts Collectibles, Identification and Value Guide, Collector Books, 1999; Jon R. Warren, Collecting Hollywood: The Movie Poster Price Guide, 3rd ed., American Collectors Exchange, 1994; David and Micki Young, Campbell's Soup Collectibles from A to Z, Krause Publications, 1998.

**Periodicals:** Autograph Times, 2303 N. 44th St., #225, Phoenix, AZ 85008; Baby Boomer, P.O. Box 1050, Dubuque, IA 52004; Big Reel, P.O. Box 1050, Dubuque, IA 52004; Button Pusher, P.O. Box 4, Coopersburg, PA 18036; Celebrity Collector, P.O. Box 1115, Boston, MA 02117; Classic Images, P.O. Box 809, Muscatine, IA 52761; Collecting Hollywood, American Collectors Exchange, 2401 Broad St., Chattanooga, TN 37408; Cowboy Collector Newsletter, P.O. Box 7486, Long Beach, CA 90807; Frostbite Falls Far-Flung Flier, P.O. Box 39, Macedonia, OH 44056; Hollywood & Vine, Box 717, Madison, NC 27025; Hollywood Collectibles, 4099 McEwen Dr., Suite 350, Dallas, TX 75224; Movie Advertising Collector, P.O. Box 28587, Philadelphia, PA 19149; Movie Collector's World, 17230 13 Mile Rd., Roseville, MI 48066; Television History Magazine, 700 E Macoupin St, Staunton, IL 62088; TV Collector Magazine, P. O. Box 1088, Easton, MA 02334.

**Collectors' Clubs:** All About Marilyn, P.O. Box 291176, Hollywood, CA 90029; Beatles Fan Club, 397 Edgewood Ave., New Haven, CT 06511; Betty Boop Fan Club, P.O. Box 42, Moorhead, MN 56561; C.A.L./N-X-211 Collectors Society, 2820 Echo Way, Sacramento, CA 95821; Camel Joe & Friends, 2205 Hess Dr., Cresthill, IL 60435; Charlie Tuna Collectors Club, 7812 NW Hampton Rd, Kansas City, MO 64152; Dagwood-Blondie Fan Club, 541 El Paso, Jacksonville, TX 75766; Dick Tracy Fan Club, P.O. Box 632, Manitou Springs, CO 80829; Dionne Quint Collectors, P.O. Box 2527, Woburn, MA 01888; Howdy Doody Memorabilia Collectors Club, 8 Hunt Ct, Flemington, NJ 08822; Official Popeye Fan Club, 1001 State St., Chester, IL 62233; R. F. Outcault Society, 103 Doubloon Dr., Slidell, LA 70461; Three Stooges Fan Club, P.O. Box 747, Gwynedd Valley, PA 19437.

**Additional Listings:** See Warman's Americana & Collectibles for expanded listings in Cartoon Characters, Cowboy Collectibles, Movie Personalities and Memorabilia, Shirley Temple, Space Adventurers, and TV Personalities and Memorabilia.

Buster Brown, pinback button, multicolored, back paper label "Look for Buster's Picture on the Sole of Every Shoe Manufactured by Buster Brown Shoe Co., St. Louis," $200. Photo courtesy of Hake's Americana & Collectibles.

## Character

**Boop, Betty**

Animation Art, 8 1/2" x 11", Betty in top hat, ink on paper, Max Fleischer Studios, c1930, unframed................................. 950.00

Perfume Bottle, 3 1/2" h, glass, figural, painted facial features, dark red plastic cap, c1930 ................................................. 50.00

Pin, 1" h, enamel on silvered brass, Betty playing violin, 1930s................................................................................200.00

Pinback Button, 7/8" d, "Betty Boop A Paramount Star Created By Fleischer Studios," black and white, 1930s, backpaper from Phila. Badge Co. ........................................................... 100.00

String Holder, wooden, wall mounted, souvenir type decal ..50.00

**Bounce, Billie**, W. W. Denslow character, pinback button, 1 1/4" d

"Billie Bounce in the Sunday Sentinel," multicolored, Billy with white bear holding blue umbrella, man holding lunch pail, orig backpaper ........................................................................ 300.00

"Compliments of Billie Bounce," red ground, blue uniform, 1904 T C McClure copyright......................................................... 250.00

**Brown, Buster**

Child's Book, My Resolutions, R. F. Outcault, black and white illus, Frederick A Stokes Co., 1906, 6" x 5"...................... 35.00

Christmas Tree Light Bulb Cover, 5" h, celluloid, Buster Brown hiding Tige...................................................................... 125.00

Doll, 25" h Buster Brown, 16-1/2" h Tige, composition head and hands, stuffed Tige with composition head ................... 1,150.00

Mechanical Display, 50" h, 53-1/2" w, three-dimensional, Buster Brown and Tige swimming at "Old Swimming Hole" with Tom Sawyer, Huckleberry Finn, and Becky Thatcher, some fading ...................................................................... 1,550.00

Sign

14" h, 14-1/2" l, Buster Brown Shoes, Buster Brown and Tige in center.................................................................. 60.00

19-3/4" h, 27-3/4" l, Buster Brown Bread, emb tin, shows Buster Brown and Tige and sheaf of wheat, some paint splatters, trimmed at top ............................................. 350.00

89" h, 42" w, wood, "Hand-Up Matches, First In Safety," Buster Brown standing on stool, arm up stretched unable to reach "Hand-up noiseless licenses matches," National Match, Joliet, Ill, large lettering "Spohn & Thaner Sole Agents," green ground, ivy and red stripe border, two board construction ............................................................. 1,100.00

Statue, 29" h, composition, Buster wearing sailor's hat, red jacket, red checked shorts, Tige sitting beside him, base reads "Buster Brown" with picture of Buster Brown and Tige playing tug-of-war, Buster redressed ......................... 225.00

**Brownies, Palmer Cox**

Stud, 1-3/8" h, white porcelain oval, hp dancing Brownie, wearing tam, brown, c1890................................................ 70.00

Tray, 10-1/2" w, 13-1/4" h, Benham's Ice Cream, H. D. Beach Co. Coshocoton, OH, litho tin .............................................. 175.00

**Campbell Kids**

Doll, squeeze, Chef, painted hollow rubber, early 1950s.... 170.00

Feeding Dish, Buffalo Pottery ............................................ 50.00

Spoon, 6" l, SP, boy on handle, c1920................................. 15.00

## Elsie, Borden's

Apron, cloth............................................................85.00
Book, Funbook Cut Out Toys and Games, 7" x 10", 1940s, mint, unused ........................................................70.00
Buttons, 3" x 4-1/4" store card, full color Elsie image as cut-out after buttons removed, 3/4" d diecut white plastic Elsie in daisy ring border, copyright 1949 ............................25.00
Christmas Card, 4-3/4" x 6-1/2", glossy stiff paper, color pop-up center of Elsie and family, printed greeting, Borden copyright, 1940s .......................................................40.00
Clapper, tin............................................................160.00
Coffee Mug .............................................................125.00
Flashlight, tractor trailer .........................................150.00
Ice Cream Container, 1940s, pink, illus of Elsie and slogan "If It's Borden's, It's Got To Be Good," 4" h .....................10.00
Lamp Base, 4" x 4" x 7", glazed ceramic, 3" h metal bulb socket, Elsie reading book to baby Beauregard in diaper ...........185.00
Push Puppet, 2-1/2" x 2-1/2" x 5-1/2" h, jointed wood, Mesgo Products Co., late 1940s, brown and pink figure, white muzzle, green base, played-with condition....................................80.00

## Felix the Cat

Clicker, 1 1/2" h, black Felix, dark reddish brown ground, angry expression, 1930s ...................................................50.00
Mug, 2-1/2" h, porcelain, four different leaping poses, Rudolstadt ...........................................................45.00
Pinback Button
    1" d, black and white, portrait center, "Member Katz Kitten Klub," 1930s..................................................125.00
    1 1/8" d, litho, red and black center reads "31 Comics In Color Sunday Detroit Times, Felix, Skippy, Papa Katzenjammer, Jiggs, Barney Google, the Toonerville Trolley Skipper, and two female characters peeking around of center, yellow ground. 1930s......................................................40.00
Tie Bar, black enamel figure, with arms behind back, on silvered brass bar, mkd "Felix the Cat, Made in England," 1920s ...85.00
Toy, painted wood, joined, orig label, 4" h.......................120.00
Valentine, mechanical, German, framed........................65.00

## Google, Barney, pinback button

1" d, "Detroit Times Barney Google," black, white, red, and flesh-tone, serial number on front, plus backpaper describing prizes.................................................................50.00
1 1/8" d, "Sunday Herald and Examiner 30 Comics," litho, dark blue on white, bright orange ground, 1930s.....................20.00

## Gump, Andy

Bank, 4 3/8" h, cast iron, worn polychrome, newspaper missing .................................................................600.00
Pinback Button, 7/8" d, "Andy Gump For Congress," black and white, "The Gumps in the Courier," c1928 ........................40.00
Sheet Music, 9 1/4" x 12 1/4", full color images on front cov, 1923 copyright......................................................35.00

## Hooligan, Happy, pinback button, 1 1/4" d, "Is Everybody Happy?" full Happy figure, cream ground, light red type, c1910 ...................20.00

## Howdy Doody

Bank, 4" x 7", china, red and blue striped shirt, blue neckerchief, rubber trap, 1950s................................................450.00
Mask, 8" x 9", molded rubber, orig red, white, and blue tag with characters, Bob Smith copyright, c1948-51 ........................85.00
Plaque, Howdy, Clarabelle, Mr. Bluster, multicolored .........100.00
Prize, Doodle Booklet, 1954 ......................................10.00
Shake-Up Mug, directions .........................................75.00
Watch, silvered metal case, plastic crystal over Howdy dial, diecut eyes slowly move clockwise, plaid fabric band, Bob Smith copyright, 1948-51 ..............................................195.00

## Jiggs and Maggie

Ashtray, 38" h, carved and painted flat wood silhouette, metal tray, c1930................................................................150.00
Pin, 1-1/4" h, enamel dec, blue and white Jiggs with cigar, Maggie in purple dress, yellow waist sash..................................100.00

Pinback Button
    7/8" d, litho, full color portrait of Jiggs, yellow background....... 18.00
    7/8" d, litho, shows Maggie and Jiggs, 1950s .................15.00
    1" d, Detroit Times Contest, black, white, and red, lucky number...............................................................25.00
Puzzles, set of 4, 1932 ............................................45.00

## Katzenjammer Kids, pinback button, 1 1/8" d, "Sunday Herald and Examiner 30 Comics," dark blue on white, bright orange ground, Papa Katzenjammer smoking cigar, 1930s...............................25.00

## Krazy Kat

Pin, 1 1/4" h, brass, black enamel, white enamel bow, yellow rhinestone eyes, c1920......................................80.00
Pinback Button
    1" d, black on white, Ignatz, 1970s...............................15.00
    1-1/4" d, black, white, and red, New York Evening Journal, serial number..................................................40.00
    1 3/8" d, dark green, black image and printing, Los Angeles Evening Herald & Express, serial number .................25.00

## Lil Abner

Charm, 1" h, figural plastic, white Shmoo, late 1940s ..........45.00
Comic Strip Orig Artwork, Al Capp, daily strip, 4-9-43, Moonbeam McSwine...........................................................450.00
Keychain Puzzle, 2" h, white Shmoo, green and dark red, late 1940s ...................................................................60.00
Pin, Shmoo, 1-1/2" h, figural brass, late 1940s..................30.00
Pinback Button
    13/16", Li'l Abner, Saturday Daily News, black litho, cream ground, newspaper name in red .................................20.00
    15/16" d, dark blue and white, Abner running with arms in fighting position, "Get In The Scrap! McKeesport," facsimile of All Capp ............................................................65.00
    1-5/8" d, Knoxville Shmoo Booster - Be a Shmoo, black and white, c1940....................................................100.00
Tab, litho tin, 2 1/4" h, Sealtest Ice Cream Shmoo Club, black and white Shmoo, orange ground, c1949 .............................25.00

## Little Orphan Annie

Clicker, Secret Guard......................................................70.00
Coin Collection Folder, complete with coins, orig mailer ......75.00
Dog Whistle, 3-1/4" l, brass tube extends to 5-1/4", flat diecut image of Sandy, 1940 Ovaltine premium .........................80.00
Magic Transfers, complete ..........................................60.00
Manual, orig mailer, 1941 ........................................125.00
Mug, 3" h, plastic, Ovaltine premium ..............................30.00
Nodder, 4" h, bisque, Germany.....................................90.00
Pinback Button, Voters ..............................................525.00
Ring, magnifying .....................................................800.00
Shadowettes, contest, orig mailer, fold-out, instructions, unfinished.............................................................185.00
Watch, brass, compass and sundial combination, Egyptian hieroglyphics on back, Ovaltine, 1938 ....................................70.00

## MAD

Model Kit, Alfred E Neuman, plastic pieces, orig instruction sheet, uncut sign sheet, orig box, 1965 E C Publications copyright....................................................................225.00
Pinback Button
    1 1/2" d, full color, Easter rabbit holding basket ready to descend down chimney on snow covered roof, subscription premium, copyright 1987 ........................................20.00
    2-1/2" d, Alfred E. Neuman For President, full color portrait, bright red and blue background.....................................70.00

## Mr. Peanut, Planters

Coloring Book, 8 x 11", Planters Nut & Chocolate Co publication, c1920, 32 pages, only one page colored .........................50.00
Top, 2 1/2" h wooden spinner, red, yellow and blue decal on large end with Mr. Peanut, c1930s...........................................80.00
Tray, 5-3/4" d, 4-1/2" h, brass finish, base mkd "Planters Peanuts/1906-1956," Mr. Peanut inscription on hatband ........40.00

## Morris, Philip, Johnny, table card, diecut stiff paper, 3-1/2" h, 3-1/2" w, c1960 ...................................................................20.00

**Mullins, Moon**, pinback button
  13/16" d, Kellogg's Pep, white background .......................... 15.00
  1-3/8" d, dark green, black image and printing, Los Angeles
    Evening Herald & Express, serial number ...................... 25.00

**Mutt & Jeff**
  Blotter, 4" x 9", black, white, and red, "The Musical Comedy Sen-
    sation of the Age," unused ....................................... 30.00
  Movie Poster, 28" x 41", "A Tropical Eggspedition," 1920s. 425.00
  Pinback Button, 1-1/4" d
    Join The Evening Telegraph Mutt & Jeff Club, black on cream,
      c1920 ........................................................ 75.00
    Meet Us At Forest Park, striking blue and white illus, bright
      yellow background, Parisian Novelty, early 1930s........ 90.00

**Peanuts Gang**
  Commemorative Medal, 1-1/2" d, Snoopy Moon Landing, silver,
    Snoopy in space suit and helmet, inscribed "All Systems Are
    Go!," reverse with Snoopy in space helmet seating on top of
    doghouse and slogan "First Landing On The Moon/Commemo-
    rative 1969," facsimile Schulz signature, 1969 copyright on back
    30.00
  Pin, 1-5/8" h, Charlie Brown, heavy brass, enameled orange shirt,
    black shoes ...................................................... 75.00
  Pinback Button
    1-3/4" d, "Happy Birthday America, 1776-1976," red, white,
      blue, and yellow, Woodstock and Snoopy with birthday cake,
      Simon Simple Originals, various UFS copyrights on
      curl ......................................................... 20.00
    2-1/4" d, "U of M Homecoming," white, maroon, and bright yel-
      low, Charlie Brown in Indian headdress in a pot over camp-
      fire as Snoopy and other Peanuts characters look on, curl
      reads "Peanuts © United Features Syndicate, Inc. Appear
      Daily in Minneapolis Star and Sunday Tribune"............ 40.00

**Pillsbury Doughboy**
  Bank, 7" h, 2-1/2" d base, figural, ceramic, c1985 ............... 20.00
  Cookie Jar, 5" x 5-1/5" x 10-1/2", heavy ceramic, 1970s ...... 70.00

**Popeye**
  Bank, dime register, 1929 ....................................... 90.00
  Big Little Book, Popeye, Saalfield, 1934, Elzie Cristler
    Segar............................................................ 35.00
  Cereal Bowl, 1935 ............................................... 60.00
  Egg Cup, china, figural ......................................... 120.00
  Fountain Pen, 1930 .............................................. 25.00
  Pin, enamel, 1-1/4" h, fleshtone body, silvery white outfit, blue
    accented hat, 1930s ............................................ 100.00
  Pinback Button
    1-3/8" d, dark green, black image and printing, Los Angeles
      Evening Herald & Express, serial number .................. 25.00
    1-1/4 d", "I Yam Strong For King Comics," blue and white Pop-
      eye, c1936 .................................................. 70.00
    1-1/4" d, "Popeye for President," multicolored, 1980 KFS
      copyright .................................................... 10.00
    1-5/8" d, "Onward Popeye," white figure, blue outline, light
      blue ground, c1960 ......................................... 15.00

**Reddy Kilowatt**
  Counter Display Figure, 12" h, jigsawed wood, finished on both
    sides, wooden base, one foot mkd "Pat. 94261," c1935 ..200.00
  Cookbook, Reddy Killowatt's Holiday Favorites, folio, 8-1/2" x 11",
    Christmas season recipes ...................................... 20.00
  Keychain Flashlight, 3" l, red and white plastic .................... 35.00
  Mechanical Pencil, 5" l, hard plastic and chrome, pocket clip,
    c1950 .......................................................... 20.00
  Plate, 9" d, Syracuse China, 1940s ............................ 125.00
  Playing cards, complete deck, 2-1/4" w, 7/8" d, 3-3/4" h, slightly
    use ............................................................. 42.00
  Switch Plate, 7" x 9-1/2" blister card holding 4-1/2" x 5" plastic
    cover for single toggle wall switch ............................ 50.00
  Skippy, pinback button, 1" d, Detroit Times contest button, black,
    white, and red.................................................. 20.00

**Smokey Bear**
  Key Ring and Fob, 3 1/4" h, bright brass luster, darker brass fob,
    c1970 .......................................................... 15.00
  Pinback Button
    1" d, red and yellow litho, "Keep California Green and
      Golden/Smokey's Reading Club," c1960 .................... 25.00
    2-1/8" d, Smokey's Timbertennial, bright red and white, 1964
      International Falls, MN, event, pr of small bears stand by
      Smokey's legs and slogan ................................... 85.00
  Ring, plastic, raised brown image, yellow plastic, c1970 ...... 15.00
  Tab, litho tin, 2-1/4" d, "I'm Helping Smokey Prevent Forest Fires,"
    brown lettering, bright yellow ground, unbent, 1980s ......... .00
  Token, 1-1/4" d, aluminum, illus of Smokey saying "Please! Only
    You Can Prevent Forest Fires," reverse with pledge to protect
    fires, US Dept. of Agriculture-Forest Service and Your State
    Forester ....................................................... 10.00

**Tarzan**
  Advertising Poster, 5" x 18", "Delicious Ice Cream in Tarzan
    Cups," full color illus, 1930s ................................ 115.00
  Better Little Book, The Son of Tarzan, Whitman, Edgar Rice Bur-
    roughs, 1939 copyright....................................... 60.00

**Tracy, Dick**
  Big Little Book, *The Super Detective*, Whitman Better Little
    Book, 1939, Chester Gould artist and author, 432 pages,
    hardcover...................................................... 30.00
  Camera, orig box ............................................... 175.00
  Children's Book, Dick Tracy Meets the Night Crawler, orig dust
    jacket.......................................................... 25.00
  Comic Strip Orig Artwork
    Fletcher, Rick, Sunday page, 12-9-79 ........................ 200.00
    Gould, Chester, daily strip, 8-1-47........................... 600.00
  Pinback Button, Dick Tracy Secret Service Patrol,
    1940s .......................................................... 35.00
  Toy, tin, ramp walker, Nurse Nora figure pushing Bonnie Braid in
    carriage, orig box ............................................ 175.00

**Uneeda Kid**, Nabisco
  Doll, 16" h, composition, orig yellow slicker and hat, holding pack-
    age, orig box ............................................... 2,000.00
  Store Scoop, china, decal on inside and ext...................... 250.00

**Yellow Kid**
  Doll, 8" h, composition head, wooden jointed body, all orig, yellow
    cloth outfit, some damage to left hand ...................... 425.00
  Gum Tin, 7/8" w, 3" l, 3/8" h, Pulver's Kola Pepsin 5¢ Gum, litho
    tin, Yellow Kid Gum machines on back, substantial wear on
    base .......................................................... 525.00
  Pin Cushion, 4" h, 3" w, 1-1/5" d, figural, pot metal, carrying red
    pin cushion at side .......................................... 350.00
  Sheet Music, 11-1/2" h, 8-1/4" w, Hogan's Alley Songster, ©1897
    Press Publishing Co.......................................... 925.00

# Personality
## Allen, Jimmie
  Album, Skelly Oil Club, complete........................... 40.00
  Member Certificate, 8" x 11", parchment paper, green border, red
    seal, "Full Fledged Pilot Member,"" Richfield Oil issue,
    c1934 ......................................................... 50.00
  Whistle, secret signal ......................................... 20.00

## Autry, Gene
  Badge, 1-1/4", "Gene Autry Official Club Badge," black and white,
    bright orange top rim, c1940 ............................... 50.00
  Child's Book, *Gene Autry and Thief River Outlaws*, Whitman Pub-
    lishing Co., 1944, 5-1/2" x 7", 249 pgs ..................... 35.00
  Pinback Button, 1-1/4" d
    "Gene Autry," black and white image, dark red shirt accents,
      face, kerchief, and hat band, bright yellow ground ....... 15.00
    "Gene Autry/Durst Bros Dairy," Gene holding six gun in black
      over yellow printing, black and yellow rim................. 125.00
  Watch, orig band.............................................. 140.00

Hopalong Cassidy, wallet, leather, metal fringe, multicolored cover, made by Top Secret, $35.

## Bergan, Edgar and Charlie McCarthy
Bank, 7 1/2" h, white metal, polychrome dec ......................... 85.00
Pinback Button
   3/4" d, black and white "Charlie McCarthy," late 1930s ... 60.00
   1" d, black and white, "An Effanbee Play-Product," late 1930s ..................................................................... 150.00
   Radio Show Ticket, 1 1/2 x 3 1/2", tan and black, from "Edgar Bergan With Charlie McCarthy," March, 1951 show, Columbia Broadcasting System, Coca-Cola sponsor ... 25.00
   Sheet Music, Love Walked In, 1938 Goldwyn Follies musical ................................................................. 85.00

## Cassidy, Hopalong
Button, 1/2" d, silvered brass, black lettered name ............... 15.00
Charm, 1" h, silvered plastic, inset glossy real photo, c1960 15.00
Compass Ring, black metal hat missing .............................. 40.00
Employee Button, 4" d, "Hoppy's Favorite Bond Bread," black and white photo, red and black ground, used by delivery men and/or store clerks ........................................................ 50.00
Pinback Button, 2-1/4" d, "Hopalong Cassidy's Saving Rodeo (Bar 20) Foreman," black and gold, pale cream rim ......... 200.00
Tab, 2" h, litho tin, "Burry's Hopalong Cassidy Cookies," multicolored, Sheriff, unbent ...................................... 45.00
Tie Slide, 2-1/2" w, Long-Horn Steer, white metal, bright silver luster, inset red rhinestone eyes ................................. 40.00

## Chaplin, Charlie
Figure, 2-1/2" d, lead ............................................. 95.00
Pencil Box, tin, sgd "H. Clive" ................................... 75.00
Pinback Button, 7/8" d, "Charlie Chaplin in Modern Times," blue, bright yellow round, string holding celluloid charm of Charlie with cane, red outfit, black derby, 1936 ..................... 50.00
Premium, figure, 13" h, "Dancing Charlie Illusion," jointed, orig package and instructions ....................................... 145.00

## Crabbe, Buster
Pinback Button
   1-1/4" d, black and white photo, bright orange ground, c1950 ............................................................. 35.00
   1-5/8" d, litho, black and white photo, red ground, white rim "Member Buster Crabbe Western Club," c1950 .......... 80.00
   Program, Aqua Parade, 1948 ................................... 20.00

## Dionne Quintuplets
Bowl, five girls illus ............................................ 170.00
Broadside, 14-3/4" h, 32" l, five girls promoting Quaker Oats, multicolored ........................................................ 100.00
Cake Plate, serving knife ........................................ 300.00
Candy Box, Baby Ruth ............................................. 190.00
Magazine Adv, 31-1/2" x 14 1/2" h, color, 1935, girls and house adv .............................................................. 125.00
Mug, one girl illus ............................................... 75.00

**Durante, Jimmy**, puppet, hand, Umbraigo, sidekick, composition face, mustache and hat, 1945 .......................................... 120.00

**Fields, W C**, pinback button, 2-1/4" d, black and white, litho, "W. C.," slogan "Be Safe-We Care," Upjohn, 1970s .................... 12.00

**Gish, Lillian**, pinback button, 13/16" d, black and white photo, Egyptian Oasis Cigarettes, c1920 ................................... 20.00

## Laurel & Hardy
Figure, Knickerbocker, bend-em's, rubber faces, clothed soft bodies, price for set ................................................. 75.00
Mask, 9" h, paper, printed caricature face, marked "Laurel & Hardy's Laughing 20's," c1966, price for pr ...................... 40.00
Planter, 7-1/2" h, porcelain, standing together, planter in back, 1940s ............................................................. 145.00

## Lone Ranger
Badge, "The Lone Ranger - A Republic Picture," 1-1/4" horseshoe-shaped, brass, luster worn, Lone Ranger riding Silver ........................................................... 35.00
Charm, 1" d, dark red plastic frame, inset full color cardboard photo of Tonto, 1950s ........................................... 12.00
Comic Strip Orig Artwork, Charles Flanders, four consecutive daily strips, 1-20 to 1-23-63 .................................. 100.00
Deputy Kit, orig mailer, 1980 ................................... 12.00
Frontier Town, four sections, unpunched, blue backs, orig mailers ........................................................ 850.00
Game Token, 1" d, aluminum disk, portraits of Lone Ranger and Tonto, c1950 ................................................... 15.00
Good Luck Token, 1 1/2" h, aluminum casing, 1948 penny, good luck symbols, "Keep Me And Never Go Broke," reverse reads "Pioneer/Belts/Braces/Wallets/Superman-Lone Ranger For Boys" ......................................................... 100.00
Ring, Six Gun ................................................... 75.00
Silver Bullet, 1-1/4" l, removable end cap holds compass, 1940s, scattered tarnish ............................................. 25.00

**Marx Brothers**, program, 8 1/2 x 11", Curtain Time Variety Show, 16 pgs, 1945, black, white, and maroon cov 70.00

## Mix, Tom
Belt Buckle, 1-1/2" x 1-3/4", solid brass, facsimile signature stamped vertically on left side, 1930s .......................... 200.00
Big Little Book, Tom Mix in the Range War, Buck Wilson, Hal Arbo, Whitman, 1937 ........................................... 65.00
Bracelet, leather ............................................... 45.00
Branding Iron .................................................. 45.00
Fountain Pen ................................................... 75.00
Magnetic Compass Gun with Whistle, orig mailer ............... 160.00
Pinback Button
   7/8" d, dark brown and light tan litho, Tom surrounded by lasso as border, issued by Canvas Products Co, 1935 .......... 75.00
   1-3/4" d, Tim Mix Circus, black and white photo, black ground, 1930s ...................................................... 120.00
Ring, cat's eye, orig mailer, directions ...................... 275.00

## Monroe, Marilyn
Bridge Set, two decks of cards .................................. 32.00
Calendar, 1954, unused ......................................... 20.00
Candy Dish ...................................................... 8.00
Snow Dome ...................................................... 15.00
Statue, 4" h, porcelain, pink dress ............................ 15.00
Our Gang, box, "Our Gang Junior Stationery," dimensional diecut of six Our Gang stars, dated 1937, Hal Roach Studios, 5" w, 1" d, 6" h .......................................................... 45.00

## Pervis, Melvin
Premium Photo .................................................. 65.00
Ring, scarab .................................................. 600.00

## Presley, Elvis
Christmas Ornament ............................................. 12.00
Coloring Book ................................................... 5.00
Locket, 5/8" h, heart shape, name in black, c1956 ............. 40.00
Miniature TV Film Viewer, 1" l black plastic television set, loop on one edge to serve as key fob, front with white plastic screen, reverse with viewing hole, six black and white photos to be viewed, also shows Pat Boone, Ava Gardner, Deborah Kerr, Sandra Dee, and Connie Francis, late 1950s, mkd "H0 597 Made in Hong Kong" .......................................... 85.00
Newspaper, death headline ...................................... 12.00
Pinback Button, 7/8" d
   Any Way You Love Me, 1956, black and white photo, gold rim ........................................................... 20.00
   Love Me Tender, red, white, and blue litho ................ 15.00

**Rogers, Roy**
  Bowl ......................................................................85.00
  Charm, 1" h, blue plastic frame, black and white glossy paper photo, seated sideways, face turned front ........................35.00
  Paint Set, Post, orig box ........................................80.00
  Pinback Button, 13/16" d, Post's Grape-Nut Flakes, Canadian, 1953 copyright Buttermilk................................................65.00
    Dale Evans ..........................................................65.00
    Roy Rogers, yellow ground.....................................70.00
  Poster, Ranch Set ................................................125.00
  Ring, sterling, image of Roy on rearing Trigger, crossed branding irons on each side .........................................................200.00

**Sky King**
  Dectecto Microscope, orig box, complete ....................350.00
  Magni-Glo Writing Ring ...........................................45.00
  Mystery Picture Ring, 1948 Peter Pan premium, adjustable brass base, propeller and wing design, top with glow-in-dark white plastic square with dark gray plastic circular inset on top, image visible .....................................................................900.00
  Photo, 4" x 5" ........................................................12.00
  Radar Ring.............................................................80.00
  Stamping King, 1-1/4" x 1-3/4" white tin box with red designs, rubber stamp with name and address, felt ink pad on lid, 1953 .....................................................................80.00

**Temple, Shirley**
  Children's Book, Birthday Book, 6th birthday, unused ..........65.00
  Paper Dolls, ten outfit, cut, orig box......................35.00
  Pin, 7/8" disk, real black and white photo, thin silvered rim, silvered metal English-style safety pin.................................100.00
  Pinback Button
    15/16", Kline's Shirley Temple Beret Club, blue on white, 1930s ...................................................................200.00
    1 1/4" d, browntone photo, light pink rim, Ideal Dolls, 1930s....75.00

**Wayne, John**
  Charm, 7/8" h, white plastic frame holds inset black and white photo, wearing cowboy outfit, early 1950s .........................15.00
  Dixie Cup Lid, 2-3/4" d, bluetone photo ...................5.00
  Pinback Button
    1-1/4" d, black and white portraits of Wayne and Ronald Reagan, c1968 .....................................................30.00
    2-1/4" d, black and white photo, red, white, and blue flag ground.....................................................................15.00

**Wynn, Ed**, figure, 10" h, cardboard, bright paper label, Fire Chief outfit, movable arms, legs, and leg, c1930 ..................................65.00

# CHELSEA

**History:** Chelsea is a fine English porcelain which was designed to compete with Meissen. The factory began operating in the Chelsea area of London, England, in the 1740s. Chelsea products are divided into four periods: Early (1740s), 1750s, 1760s, and Derby (1770-1783). In 1924, a large number of the molds and models of figurines were found at the Spode-Copeland Works, and many items were brought back into circulation.

**References:** John C. Austin, *Chelsea Porcelain at Williamsburg*, Colonial Williamsburg Foundation, 1977; Susan and Al Bagdade, *Warman's English & Continental Pottery & Porcelain*, 3rd Edition, Krause Publications, 1998; John Bedford, *Chelsea & Derby China*, Walker & Co., 1967.

**Museums:** Colonial Williamsburg Foundation, Williamsburg, VA; Fine Arts Museums, San Francisco, CA; Fitzwilliam Museum, Cambridge, England; Gardiner Museum of Ceramic Arts, Toronto, Canada; Henry E. Huntington Library & Art Gallery, San Marino, CA; Museum of Fine Arts, Boston, MA; Seattle Art Museum, Seattle, WA; Victoria & Albert Museum, London, England; Wadsworth Atheneum, Hartford, CT; Walters Art Gallery, Baltimore, MD.

**Marks:** Different marks were used during the different Chelsea periods:

Early incised triangle and raised anchor

1750s red raised anchor

1760s gold anchor

Basket, 12-1/8" l oval, deep reticulated sides, upright end loop handles, rose, blue, iron-red, yellow, green, gray, and brown floral bouquet, scattered sprigs and two insects, ext. molded with open wickerwork, brown edge scalloped rim, puce-bound stem end handles, yellow and brown mottled branches, iron-red blossoms, green leaves, c1775, slight glaze chips, handle chipped ...................700.00
Dessert Plate, 8-1/2" d, c1755, red anchor mark....................3,450.00
Dish
    8-1/8" d, puce, iron-red, and yellow painted tulip and flowers bouquet, scattered flowers, brown edged shaped rim, c1755, red anchor mark .................................................................255.00
    9-7/8" l, leaf shape, two overlapping cos lettuce leaves, puce veins, edged in bright green, c1755, red anchor mark.. 1,500.00
Figure
    6" h, drummer, light green jacket, puce pantaloons, black drumsticks in hands, drum at side, flower encrusted circular base, imp "R" mark, restored .....................................................925.00
    7-1/16" h, young sportsman, black hat, turquoise jacket, gold, black, and iron-red waistcoat, pale yellow pants, tan topped black boots, holding bird in right hand, another between feet, brown riffle to left, recumbent brown spotted white hound to right, tree stump with iron-red berries and green leaves, scroll molded mound base trimmed in turquoise and gold, c1765, gold anchor mark, chips.........................................................1,250.00
Flower Holder, 9-1/2" h, figural, seated fisherman, green hat, light mauve coat, iron-red breeches, open pierced basket between knees, 1758 .............................................................................520.00
Pipe Tamper, 3-5/8" h, modeled bust, brown hair, ruffle, tapered pedestal, orange, yellow, and blue lines, blue flower on base, c1780 ...........................................................................2,250.00
Plate
    8-1/2" d, silver shape, painted exotic birds, green and brown foliage, three molded rose-pink and gilt shells on border, painted leaf on reverse, gold anchor mark, repaired .................1,850.00
    9-5/16" d, scalloped border, rose, iron-red, yellow, blue, purple, brown, green and gray, small floral sprigs, brown edged rim, c1755, red anchor mark .....................................................650.00
Tea Bowl and Saucer, octagonal, multicolored painted bouquets and insects, scattered floral sprays, c1760 ...................................310.00

# CHILDREN'S BOOKS

**History:** Because there is a bit of the child in all of us, collectors always have been attracted to children's books. In the 19th century, books were popular gifts for children, with many of the children's classics written and published during this time. These books were treasured and often kept throughout a lifetime. Developments in printing made it possible to include more attractive black and white illustrations and color plates. The work of artists and illustrators has added value beyond the text itself.

**References:** E. Lee Baumgarten, *Price Guide for Children's & Illustrated Books for the Years 1880-1960 Sorted by Artist and Sorted by Author*, published by author, 1996; David & Virginia Brown, *Whitman Juvenile Books*, Collector Books, 1997, 1999 value update; Richard E. Dickerson, *Brownie Bibliography*, 2nd ed., Golden Pippin Press, 1995; Glenn Erardi, *Collecting Edgar Rice Burroughs*, Schiffer Publishing, 2000; Virginia Haviland, *Children's Literature, a Guide to Reference Sources (1966)*, first supplement (1972), second supplement (1977), third supplement (1982), Library of Congress; John Henty, *The Collectable World of Mabel Lucie Attwell*, Richard Dennis Publications, distributed by Antique Collectors' Club, 1999; Alan Horne, *Dictionary of 20th Century British Book Illustrators*, available from Spoon River Press, 1994; Simon Houfe, *Dictionary of 19th Century British Book Illustrators*, revised ed., available from Spoon River Press, 1996; E. Christian Mattson and Thomas B. Davis, *A Collector's Guide to Hardcover Boys' Series Books*, published by authors, 1996; Diane McClure Jones and Rosemary Jones, *Collector's Guide to Children's Books, 1850 to 1950*, Vol. I and II, Collector Books, 2001 value update; —, *Collector's Guide to Children's Books, 1950-1975*, Vol. III, Collector Books, 2000; Jack Matthews, *Toys Go to War*, Pictorial Histories Publishing, 1994; Edward S. Postal, *Price Guide & Bibliography to Children's & Illustrated Books*, M & P Press (available from Spoon River Press, 2319C W. Rohmann, Peoria, IL 61604), 1995; *Price Guide to Big Little Books & Better Little, Jumbo Tiny Tales, A Fast Action Story*, etc., L-W Book Sales, 1995; Steve Santi, *Collecting Little Golden Books*, 4th ed., Krause Publications, 2000; Albert Tillman, *Pop-Up! Pop-Up*, Whalesworth Farm Publishing, 1997.

**Periodicals:** *Book Source Monthly*, 2007 Syosset Dr., P.O. Box 567, Cazenovia, NY 13035; *Firsts: The Book Collector's Magazine*, P.O. Box 65166, Tucson, AZ 85728, http://www.firsts.com; *Martha's KidLit Newsletter*, P.O. Box 1488, Ames, IA 50010, http://www.kidlitonline.com; *Mystery & Adventure Series Review*, P.O. Box 3488, Tucson, AZ 85722; *The Authorized Edition Newsletter*, RR1, Box 73, Machias, ME 04654; *Yellowback Library*, P.O. Box 36172, Des Moines, IA 50315.

**Collectors' Clubs:** Horatio Alger Society, 4907 Allison Dr., Lansing, MI 48910; Movable Book Society, P.O. Box 11645, New Brunswick, NJ 08906; Society of Phantom Friends, P.O. Box 1437 North Highlands, CA 95660.

**Libraries:** American Antiquarian Society, Worcester, MA; Free Library of Philadelphia, Philadelphia, PA; Library of Congress, Washington, DC; Lucile Clark Memorial Children's Library, Central Michigan University, Mount Pleasant, MI; Pierpont Morgan Library, New York, NY; Toronto Public Library, Toronto, Ontario, Canada.

**Additional Listings:** See *Warman's Americana & Collectibles* for more examples and an extensive listing of collectors' clubs.

**Abbreviations:**

| | |
|---|---|
| dj | dust jacket |
| n.d. | no date |
| pgs | pages |
| teg | top edges gilt |
| unp | unpaged |
| wraps | paper covers |

*Adventures of Paddy Beaver, The*, Thornton Burgess, Toronto, McClelland & Stewart, 1943, 1st ed, drawings, dj ............................ 20.00
*Alice's Adventures in Wonderland*, 42 illus by Tenniel, McMillan, 1914, blue cover, gold Alice, gold edges on pages ............................ 25.00
*Alice in Wonderland with Cut Out Pictures*, cover by Julia Green, 1917 148.00
*Alphabet Book*, Whitman, 1935, linen finish, soft cov, 10" x 13" ... 10.00
*Anthology of Children's Literature*, Edna Johnson and Carrie E. Scott, Boston Houghton Mifflin, 1935, first edition ............................ 25.00
*American Boys Book of Birds & Brownies of the Woods*, Woodcraft Series, Lippincott, 1931, 242 pgs, dj ............................ 18.00
*Andrew Henry's Meadow*, Doris Bun, Weekly Reader Book Club, 1965 .................................................................... 200.00
*Billy Bunny and The Friendly Elephant*, David Cory, Hugh Spencer, Cupples & Leon, Co., 1920 ............................ 35.00
*Black Beauty*, Edgar Lee version, illus by H. L. Miller, Saalfield, 1905 ...................................................... 20.00
*Blondie Who's Boss*, Chick Young, Whitman Publishing, 1952 .... 25.00
*Bobbsey Twins on the Deep Blue Sea*, Laura Lee Hope, Grosset & Dunlap, 1918, first edition ............................ 25.00
*Boys and Girls of Book Lane*, Nora Smith, 1923, 11 stories, Jessie Wilcox Smith plates ....................................... 300.00
*Camel with the Wrinkled Knees*, Johnny Gruelle, Volland ............ 75.00
*Chaga*, William Lipkind, Nicholas Mordvinoff illustrator, Harcourt, Brace and Co., 1955, first edition ............................ 6.00
*Charlotte's Web*, E. B. White, Harper, 1952, 1st edition, Garth Williams illus, child's name on flyleaf ............................ 110.00
*Chatterbox for 1928*, J. Erksine Clarke, Boston, 1928 ................. 40.00
*Children's Classics Illustrated*, 5-book series ............................ 60.00
*Child's Garden of Verses*, A, Robert Louis Stevenson, illus by Jesse Wilcox Smith ................................................ 35.00
*Comical Doings*, Ernest Nister, dressed animals, Lewis Wain illus ........................................................ 175.00
*Daddy Long Legs*, J Webster, Thrushwood Books, 1940 ............. 10.00
*Danny Decoy*, John Held, A. S. Barnes, 1942, author sgd .......... 20.00
*Doings of Little Bear*, Frances Margaret Fox, color and black and white illus by Warner Carr, Rand McNally & Co., 1932 ...................... 10.00
*Dr. Rabbit & Grumpy Bear*, Thomas Clark Hinkle, illus by M. Winter, Rand McNally, 1934 ............................................. 15.00

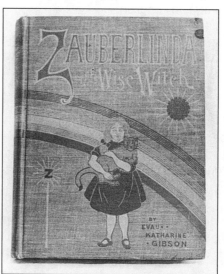

***Zauberlinda the Wise Witch*, Eva Katharine Gibson, Chicago, 1901, $48.**

*Edith and the Bear Lend A Hand*, Dare Wright, dust jacket.......... 45.00

*Flower Children*, Elizabeth Gordon, M. T. Ross illus, 1910, Volland, 78th ed ............................................................................. 70.00

*Friendly Fairies*, Johnny Gruelle, 1919, Volland, 27th ed ............. 60.00

*Girl in the Woods, The*, Grace L Hill, Lipcott, 1st ed, 1942 .......... 10.00

*Golden Arrow*, Bill and Bernard Martin, Tell-Well Press, 1950, 1st ed, sgd by Bill Martin ........................................................... 25.00

*Grimm's Fairy Tales*, Anderson, matched set in slip box, 1945, bright blue pictorial covers, 373 and 343 pgs, lavish color ................... 45.00

*Honey Bunch Her First Tour of Toy Town*, Helen L. Thorndyke, 1951, 180 pgs ............................................................................... 8.00

*Hunting for the Hidden Gold*, Hardy Boys, F. W. Dixon, 1928, gray cover ..................................................................................... 10.00

*Jolly Jump-Ups*, The, R. L. Stevenson, McLoughlin, 1941, pop-up, loose hinge ............................................................................ 25.00

*Kantner's Illustrated Book of Objects*, 1895, 2,000 engravings, explanations in English and German .................................................. 95.00

*Kids Cooking - A Very Slightly Messy Manual*, Klutz Press, 1987, 78 pgs, spiral bound ................................................................... 10.00

*King Arthur and His Knights*, Chicago, 1924, colored plates ........ 15.00

*Lands of Pleasure*, First Reader, Teacher's Edition, McMillian, 1965 ................................................................................... 20.00

*Little Brown Bear*, The, Johnny Gruelle, P. F. Volland Co., 1920, 34th edition ................................................................................ 35.00

*Little Brown Koko Has Fun*, 2nd edition, 1945, dust jacket.......... 95.00

*Little Engine That Could*, The, Lois Lenski, retold Watty Pipe, 1930 ..................................................................................... 25.00

*Little Garden People*, Marion Bryson, illus by Ann Pearsal Sharp, Akron, Saalfield, 1938, 8" x 10" ............................................ 45.00

*Lone Ranger at the Haunted Gulch*, Fran Striker ......................... 20.00

*Lost Princess, The, A Fairy Tale*, Maple Lucie Attwell, Fred Warne pub, six tip-in color pictures, 1st edition ..................................... 45.00

*Lost Wagon Train*, The, Zane Grey, 1936, binding loose................ 5.00

*Mistress Mary The Secret Garden*, Frances H. Burnette, Ottenheimer, retold by Andrea Leach, pop-ups ............................................. 8.00

*Modern Explorers*, Thomas Frost, McLoughlin Bros., Arctic explorers on cov .................................................................................. 55.00

*Mrs. Piggle Wiggle*, Betty MacDonald, black and white Hillary Knight illus, J. B. Lippincott Co., 1957, dj ....................................... 20.00

*Nancy Drew Cookbook Clues to Good Cooking*, Keene, NY, 1974, 159 pgs ............................................................................... 15.00

*Peter Puzzlemaker*, John Martin Puzzle Book, George Carlson compiler, Platt & Munk Co., 1929........................................... 20.00

*Popeye and the Pirates*, animated, Julian Wehs, 1943 .............. 125.00

*Puppy Stories*, Evien Beaudry, illus by Diana Thorne, Akron, Saalfield, Pub, 1934, pictorial cov ......................................................... 20.00

*Puss N Boots*, animated by Julian Wehr, Duenwald Printing Corp., NY, 1944, dj ................................................................................. 65.00

*Raggedy Ann Stories*, Johnny Gruelle, Volland ........................... 75.00

*Return of Tarzan*, The, Edgar Burroughs, 1967, Western Pub ..... 10.00

*School Days*, handkerchief book with orig handkerchief, 1930s... 50.00

*Seven Ages of Childhood*, Jessie Wilcox Smith, 1st ed.............. 175.00

*Strawberry Girl*, Lois Lenski, author and illus, Lippincott, 1945, 8" x 6-1/2", Sunbonnet girl on cover.................................... 25.00

*Sunbonnet Babies Book*, The, E O Grover, 1902, orig jacket....... 55.00

*Sunny Bunny*, Nina Wilcox Patnum, Johnny Gruelle illus, P. F. Volland Co., 1918, 5th edition ...................................................... 50.00

*Tale of Mr. Tod*, The, Beatrice Potter, 1939, dust jacket ............. 50.00

*Tale of Peter Rabbit*, The, Beatrice Potter, Fern Bisel Peat illus, Harter, 1931, soft cover, 9" x 13" ...................................................... 45.00

*Tarzan and the Jewels of Opar*, Edgar Burroughs, 1918 ............. 10.00

*Tasha Tudor's Bedtime Book*, Tasha Tudor, 1977 ........................ 45.00

*Tawny Scrawny Lion*, Little Golden Book, Western Publishing Co. & Applause, 1991, includes clear vinyl tote bag, book, hangtag, and stuffed 8" h, 4-1/2" w, Tawny Scrawny Lion, blue plastic Applause tag in ear .................................................................................... 40.00

*Teddy Bears in Hot Water*, The, 1907 ........................................ 75.00

*Ten Seconds to Play*, Chip Hilton, Clair Bee, black and white illus, 1960s .................................................................................... 10.00

*Three Bears*, The, linen, 1933 ................................................. 552.00

*Through the Looking Glass*, Tenniel illus, McMillan, 1914 ........... 25.00

*Thundering Herd*, The, Zane Grey, Harper's, 1925, 1st ed.......... 24.00

*Tip and Mitten*, Paul McKee, 1950s........................................ 300.00

*Tom Swift & His Sky Racer*, Victor Appleton, 1911, 207 pgs, ads in back...................................................................................... 10.00

*Treasure Island*, Robert Louis Stevenson, Rand McNally Co., 1916, cover worn............................................................................. 35.00

*Twins in the West*, The, D. Whitehall, Barse & Hopkins, 1920, 1st ed, bright cov ............................................................................. 10.00

*Uncle Wiggly & Jackie & Pettie Bow Wow*, Howard Garis, Louis Wisa color illus A. L. Burt Co........................................................ 18.00

*Uncle Wiggly Goes Camping*, Howard Garis, Lang Campbell, Whitman Publishing Co., 1931 ............................................................. 35.00

*Winnie The Pooh*, Dutton, Shepard illus, 1945 ......................... 15.00

*Wizard of Oz* Series, illus by John R. Neill

*Dorothy and the Wizard of Oz*, L. Frank Baum, Chicago, 1908.. 125.00

*Kabumpo in Oz*, Ruth Plumly Thompson, Reilly & Lee, Chicago, 1922.................................................................................... 200.00

*Ozma of Oz*, L. Frank Baum, Chicago, 1907 ........................... 180.00

*Rinkitink In Oz*, L. Frank Baum, Chicago, 1916 ......................... 70.00

*The Cowardly Lion of Oz*, Ruth Plumly Thompson, Chicago, 1923.................................................................................... 65.00

*The Emerald City of Oz*, L. Frank Baum, Chicago, 1910............. 75.00

*The Magic of Oz*, L. Frank Baum, Chicago, 1919...................... 95.00

*The Road to Oz*, L. Frank Baum, Chicago, 1909...................... 115.00

*The Scarecrow of Oz*, L. Frank Baum, Chicago, 1915 .............. 70.00

*The Tin Woodsman of Oz*, L. Frank Baum, Chicago, 1918 .......... 90.00

*The Wishing Horse of Oz*, Ruth Plumly Thompson, Chicago, 1935 .................................................................................. 200.00

*Tic-Tok of Oz*, L. Frank Baum, Chicago, 1914............................ 95.00

# CHILDREN'S FEEDING DISHES

**History:** Unlike toy dishes meant for play, children's feeding dishes are the items actually used in the feeding of a child. Their colorful designs of animals, nursery rhymes, and children's activities are meant to appeal to the child and make mealtimes fun. Many plates have a unit to hold hot water, thus keeping the food warm. Although glass and porcelain examples from the late 19th and early 20th centuries are most popular, collectors are beginning to seek some of the plastic examples from the 1920s to 1940s, especially those with Disney designs on them.

**References:** Maureen Batkin, *Gifts for Good Children, Part II*, 1890-1990, Antique Collectors' Club, 1996; Doris Lechler, *Children's Glass Dishes, China and Furniture*, Vol. I (1983), Vol. II (1986, 1993 value update), Collector Books; Noel Riley, *Gifts for Good Children: The History of Children's China, Part I, 1790-1890*, Richard Dennis Publications, 1991; Margaret and Kenn Whitmyer, *Collector's Encyclopedia of Children's Dishes: An Illustrated Value Guide*, Collector Books, 1993.

Bowl, 6-5/8" d, Yellowstone Zoo pattern, imp and printed Wedgwood marks, designed by Daisy Makeig-Jones, c1916..................... 175.00

Cereal Bowl, seven nursery rhyme scenes and captions ............ 60.00

Cereal Set, cereal bowl, mug, and 6" d plate, Nursery Rhyme, Jack and Jill, marked "Royal Bayreuth"........................................ 145.00

Cup Plate, 3-1/2" d, children at play, rust-brown transfer, imp "Woods".................................................................................. 75.00

Dish, 6-1/2" d, 1-1/2" h, Peter Rabbit and Farmer, Beatrix Potter, Wedgwood ............................................................................. 40.00

**Plate, multicolor transfer of Buster Brown playing with Tige, 5-1/4" d, $50.**

Feeding Dish
    Animals, divided, Walker China ............................................. 20.00
    Birds perched on branch, dressed in clothes, children's toys on border, red "Made in Czechoslovakia" mark, 5-1/2" d ........ 65.00
    Campbell Kids, 7-1/2" d, 1-1/2" deep, some wear to Kids decal.... 65.00
    Duck in Hat, Blue Ridge Pottery ........................................... 55.00
    Girl feeding teddy, 8" d .......................................................... 65.00
    Jigsaw, Blue Ridge Pottery .................................................... 90.00
Peter Rabbit and Mr. McGregor, multicolored, Wedgwood, 6-3/8" d ..... 45.00
    Scottie and girl, 7" d .............................................................. 65.00
Jug, 3-3/8" h, Golliwog pattern, imp and printed Wedgwood marks, designed by Daisy Makeig-Jones, c1916 ................................ 195.00
Mug
    1-3/4" h, motto, "Idleness Brings Disgrace," transfer dec, pink luster highlights ..................................................................... 150.00
    2-1/4" h, For My Dear Girl, black transfer, pink luster trim .. 225.00
    2-3/8" h, Ann, black transfer, geometric rim, applied leaf tip handle, pearlware ...................................................................... 20.00
    2-1/2" h, Franklin's Maxim, "keep thy shop and thy shop will keep thee," black transfer dec, handpainted red highlights, imp applied handle, England, 19th C, repairs to handle and rim, hairline.......................................................................................... 200.00
    2-1/2" h, 4" d, black transfer of sign language ...................... 35.00
    3" h, Hazel Atlas, red animal characters, white ground, 1930-40 .. 25.00
    3-1/2" h, Little Bo Peep, milk glass ....................................... 65.00
Place Setting, Bunny pattern, 7" d plate, two 9-5/8" bowls, tea cup and saucer, green enamel band below rabbit border, imp and printed Wedgwood marks, designed by Daisy Makeig-Jones, c1938 .. 325.00
Plate
    5-1/2" d, Punch and Judy, red transfer, Allerton, early 20th C ....... 85.00
    6" d, sleeping girls and angels, polychrome transfer ............ 70.00
    6-1/8" d, My Pretty Bird, girl with bird on wrist, black transfer, emb floral border ....................................................................... 125.00
    6 1/2" d, Dr Franklin Maxim, "It Is Hard For An Empty Bag to Stand Free," pawn shop scene, black line border .............. 95.00
    6-1/2" d, Hey Diddle Diddle, blue ........................................... 30.00
    8" d, Little Tommy Tucker, Royal Doulton ............................. 65.00

# CHILDREN'S NURSERY ITEMS

**History:** The nursery is a place where children live in a miniature world. Things come in two sizes. Child scale designates items actually used for the care, housing, and feeding of the child. Toy or doll scale denotes items used by the child in play and for creating a fantasy environment which copies that of an adult or his own. Cheap labor and building costs during the Victorian era encouraged the popularity of the nursery. Most collectors focus on items from the years 1880 to 1930.

**References:** Marguerite Fawdry, *International Survey of Rocking Horse Manufacture*, New Cavendish Books, 1992; Marcia Hersey, *Collecting Baby Rattles and Teethers: Identification and Value Guide*, Krause Publications, 1998; Sally Kevill-Davies, *Yesterday's Children, The Antiques and History of Childcare*, Antique Collectors' Club, 1999; Elizabeth Kurella, *The Complete Guide to Vintage Textiles*, Krause Publications, 1999; Doris Lechler, *Children's Glass Dishes, China and Furniture*, Vol. I (1983), Vol. II (1986, 1993 value update), Collector Books; Patricia Mullins, *Rocking Horse: A History of Moving Toy Horses*, New Cavendish Books, 1992; Lorraine May Punchard, *Playtime Kitchen Items and Table Accessories*, published by author, 1993; Herbert F. Schiffer and Peter B. Schiffer, *Miniature Antique Furniture: Doll House and Children's Furniture from the United States & Europe*, Schiffer Publishing, 1995; Tony Stevenson and Eva Marsden, *Rocking Horses: The Collector's Guide to Selecting, Restoring, and Enjoying New and Vintage Rocking Horses*, Courage Books, 1993.

**Museum:** The Victorian Perambulator Museum of Jefferson, Jefferson, OH.

**Additional Listings:** Children's Books; Children's Feeding Dishes; Children's Toy Dishes; Dolls; Games; Miniatures; Toys.

Bowl and Spoon, sterling silver, Wm. B. Kerr & Co., early 20th C, acid-etched design of children riding different animals from seven countries, minor dents, Gorham monogrammed spoon, 5 troy oz ... 200.00
Cart, 39" w, 16-1/2" d, 23-1/2" h, old green repaint, decal eagle and shield dec, corner decals, spoked wheels with rubber tires, moveable handle, some paint wear ............................................ 175.00
Chair, George III style, library, late 19th or early 20th C, mahogany, serpentine back, scrolled arms, plain legs, rust velvet upholstered seat, 33" h ............................................................................ 550.00

**Print, framed bookplate, little girl picking flowers, mkd "Bessie Collins Pease," c1905, 8" x 10", $75. Photo courtesy of Michael Ivankovich Antiques & Auction Co., Inc.**

Christening Outfit, gown, slip, and cap, white cotton, c1920 ........ 85.00

Cup, Bowl, and Plate, sterling silver, International Silver Co., early 20th C, acid-etched animals, fitted case, 7 troy oz .......................... 400.00

Desk and Chair, America, first quarter 20th C, oak and chestnut, knee-hole desk with slanting lift top, mounted by leatherette writing surface, each pedestal with bank of three drawers, adjustable chair with rotating seat and spindle back, 32" w, 18-1/2" d, 35-1/2" h desk, 29-1/4" h chair ................................................................ 650.00

Doll Baby Carriage, 34" l, 26" h, wood and metal, orig yellow and orange paint, white and red striping, very worn folding old leatherized sun screen, wooden spoke wheels with metal rims ................. 330.00

Doll Cradle
    18-3/4" l, 10-3/4" w, 13-5/8" h, poplar, old red finish, gold striping, scalloped head and foot boards with shaped and scrolled side boards, simple incised leaf detail inside, birch rockers with red repaint, glued crack in head board, edge wear ................ 110.00
    19" l, poplar, hickory, old reddish brown finish, dovetailed with cut-out rockers, bent wood hood has age cracks, traces of orig cloth lining ................................................................ 110.00

Flatware Set, sterling silver, fork, knife, and spoon
    Bright-cut shell and flower dec, monogram, Bingham, Walk & Mayhew, c1883, fitted case, 4 troy oz ....................... 135.00
    Engraved leaf dec, rope carved MOP handles, Victorian, George Unite maker, Birmingham, 1881, inscription, fitted case .. 175.00
    Leaf and fern engraved design, HW LD makers, Sheffield, England, 1911, fitted case, 2 troy oz ................................. 90.00
    Low relief scroll dec, monogram, fitted case, Gorham, c1871, 2 troy oz ................................................................ 115.00

Gliding Horse, 33" l, 31-1/2" h, painted dapple gray, leather and leatherette, harness and saddle, leather ears, steel and celluloid eyes, horsehair tail, dark red base with white striping, early 20th C, some paint lose, wear to mane ......................................... 750.00

High Chair, 21-1/2" h, Windsor, New England, 1820-30, arrow-back, shaped and incised seat, foot rest, turned played legs, early red paint, 21-1/2" h seat, 36" h ...................................... 2,875.00

Morris Chair, Arts and Crafts, America, early 20th C, oak, adjustable back, flat arms over two side slats, simulated leather upholstered seat and back, 16-3/4" l, 19-1/4" d, 27" h, adjusting rod missing, wear .................................................................. 320.00

Perambulator, 55" l, 24" w, 41" h, convertible leatherette top, faille tufted and upholstered seat, wooden spoke wheels with iron rims, yellow paint on body with dark blue and orange striping, cream wheels with similar color accents, America, 1860 ................... 460.00

Portrait
    7-3/4" h, 6" w, watercolor and pencil on paper, portrait of Joan Elizabeth Cook, aged 5, four months, 1835, full length profile, wearing white dress, holding bouquet of flowers, calligraphic identification info beneath portrait, by Joseph H. Davis, descended thru family ............................................. 46,000.00
    25" h, 20" w, oil and graphic on canvas, portrait of Francis E. West as a Child, holding toy lamp, period frame, craquelure, descended thru family ............................................. 68,500.00

Rattle
    3-3/4" l, Palmer Cox Brownie head with bells, sterling and mother-of-pearl, late 19th C ................................................. 150.00
    5-1/2" l, Santa, celluloid, colorful ................................ 75.00

Rocker, 18" w, 20" d, 25" h, ladder back, open arms, new brown leather seat cover, orig finish, paper Gustav Stickley label, red decal .............................................................. 500.00

Rocking Horse
    32" l, 24" h, carved and polychromed wood, genuine horsehair, crimson leather seat, America, 19th C ......................... 225.00
    34" l, wood, worn orig red paint, black and white trim, some edge damage ................................................................ 110.00
    34-1/2" l, platform type, mohair, wood, and leather horse, painted wood stand ............................................................ 400.00
    40" l, cloth covered horse, wheels attached to rockers ....... 325.00
    46" l, 23" h, worn orig paint, red runners, white stretchers, white horse, black rings, damage, partial saddle remaining, ears, bridle, and tail missing .......................................... 660.00

**Rocker, wicker, child size, $100. Photo courtesy of Joy Luke Fine Art Brokers and Auctioneers.**

    73" l, 39-1/2" h, J. A. Yost, 1860-90, fully carved red-brown horse, leather saddle rocks on black painted platform, American flag, red pin striping and stars, stenciled "J. A. Yost Manufacturer's of Children's Carriages, 214 Dock Street, Philadelphia," imperfections ................................................................ 1,725.00

Sailboat Model, 49" h, wood and wire, old paint, some damage 385.00

Settee, Windsor, New England, early 19th C, arrow back, sq crest about shaped spindles, incised blank seat and raked legs joined by rect stretcher with pointed ends, orig red paint with yellow striping to simulate inlay on crest, painted yellow and black leafage and highlights, all orig, 25-3/4" l, 9" d, 21-3/4" h ............................... 12,650.00

Sled, 36-1/2" l, extra top enclosure, painted wood, restoration .. 275.00

Wagon
    22" l, 8" h, painted wood, "The Flyer," rect red body, mustard wheels, black lettering on sides, paint wear, repairs ........ 175.00
    34" l, wood and steel, wood spoke wheels, old worn red repaint, hand brake ............................................................ 330.00
    39" l, Sherwood Springs, coaster, brake, cast iron and wood ........ 375.00

Wheelbarrow, 42" l, removable sides with designs, painted wood and metal ................................................................ 350.00

# CHILDREN'S TOY DISHES

**History:** Dishes made for children often served a dual purpose—playthings and a means of learning social graces. Dish sets came in two sizes. The first was for actual use by the child when entertaining friends. The second, a smaller size than the first, was for use with dolls. Children's dish sets often were made as a sideline to a major manufacturing line, either as a complement to the family service or as a way to use up the last of the day's batch of materials. The artwork of famous illustrators, such as Palmer Cox, Kate Greenaway, and Rose O'Neill, can be found on porcelain children's sets.

**References:** Doris Lechler, *Children's Glass Dishes, China and Furniture*, Vol. I (1983), Vol. II (1986, 1993 value update), Collector Books; Lorraine May Punchard, *Playtime Kitchen Items and Table Accessories*, published by author, 1993; ——, *Playtime Pottery & Porce-*

lain from Europe and Asia, Schiffer Publishing, 1996; ——, *Playtime Pottery and Porcelain from the United Kingdom and the United States*, Schiffer Publishing, 1996; Margaret and Kenn Whitmyer, *Collector's Encyclopedia of Children's Dishes*, Collector Books, 1993.

**Collectors' Club:** Toy Dish Collectors, P.O. Box 159, Bethlehem, CT 06751.

## Akro Agate

Tea Set, Interior Panel, green cups and saucers, green creamer, pink sugar, pink teapot, white lid, small size .............. 290.00
Water Set, Stippled Band, green, pitcher, six tumblers ....... 110.00

## China

Creamer and Sugar, cov, Willow Ware, blue and white ........ 30.00
Cup and Saucer, green luster, saucer with scene of girl and Golliwog.............................................................................. 48.00
Set, Toy Ware, Brownie pattern, polychrome dec transfer, 2-3/4" h beaker, 5" h bud vase, 3-1/4" h jug, 3-3/8" h jug, 4-1/2" l cov pin box, 3" h oval cov soup tureen, 3-3/4" h cov teapot, imp Wedgwood marks, designed by Daisy Makeig-Jones, c1913 1,725.00
Teapot, 5-1/8" h, dome top, Pearlware, blue transfer dec, small flake on flange lid ............................................................... 385.00
Tea Set, 7 pcs, transfer scene of Santa Claus in balloon, dropping gifts to children, pink trim, 5-5/8" h teapot, six cups and saucers, some damage, replaced teapot lid .................................. 200.00
Vase, cut glass, 5-3/4" h, trumpet shape, cut allover in hobstars, fans, sawtooth cut rim, American Brilliant Period............. 110.00

## Milk Glass

Basket, cov, emb "Peepers".................................................. 185.00
Candleholders, pr, Swirl pattern, opaque green ................... 65.00

## Pattern Glass

Butter Dish, cov, Pennsylvania, dark green, gold trim ................ 110.00
Cake Stand, Thistle, 6 1/2" d, 3 1/2" h .......................................... 75.00
Creamer
    Amazon ....................................................................... 20.00
    Liberty Bell ................................................................. 90.00
Cup, Dahlia, apple green ....................................................... 85.00
Cup and Saucer, Wee Branches................................................. 90.00
Dish, Sandwich, lacy, oval, minor damage ............................ 60.00
Mug, Wee Branches .............................................................. 30.00
Pitcher, Hobb's Hobnail, cranberry ..................................... 275.00
Punch Set, Thumbelina, 7-pc set............................................. 50.00
Spooner, Sultan, chocolate glass............................................ 375.00
Sugar, cov, Rooster, dog finial ............................................ 250.00
Table Set
    Colonial, No. 2630, Cambridge, creamer, sugar, spooner, crystal................................................................... 65.00

**Pattern Glass, Oval Star table set, $175.**

Doyle's 500, cov butter, creamer, spooner, sugar, amber... 325.00
Stippled Vine and Beads, cov butter, creamer, spooner, sugar .................................................................... 350.00
Tin
    Mug, 2-1/2" h, Little Bo Peep................................................. 20.00
    Tea Set, dogs and cats, red, blue, and white, marked "Germany," price for 9-pc set ............................................................. 95.00

# CHINESE CERAMICS

**History:** The Chinese pottery tradition has existed for thousands of years. By the 16th century, Chinese ceramic wares were being exported to India, Persia, and Egypt. During the Ming dynasty (1368-1643), earthenwares became more highly developed. The Ch'ien Lung period (1736-1795) of the Ch'ing dynasty marked the golden age of interchange with the West. Trade between China and the West began in the 16th century when the Portuguese established Macao. The Dutch entered the trade early in the 17th century. With the establishment of the English East India Company, all of Europe sought Chinese-made pottery and porcelain. Styles, shapes, and colors were developed to suit Western tastes, a tradition which continued until the late 19th century. Fine Oriental ceramics continued to be made into the 20th century, and modern artists enjoy equal fame with older counterparts.

**References:** Carl L. Crossman, *The Decorative Arts of the China Trade*, Antique Collectors' Club, 1999; Gloria and Robert Mascarelli, *Warman's Oriental Antiques*, Wallace-Homestead, 1992; Nancy N. Schiffer, *Imari, Satsuma, and Other Japanese Export Ceramics*, Schiffer Publishing, 1997.

**Periodical:** *Orientalia Journal*, P.O. Box 94, Flushing, NY 11363-0094.

**Collectors' Club:** China Student's Club, 59 Standish Rd, Wellesley, MA 02181.

**Museums:** Art Institute of Chicago, Chicago, IL; Asian Art Museum of San Francisco, San Francisco, CA; George Walter Vincent Smith Art Museum, Springfield, MA; Morikami Museum & Japanese Gardens, Delray Beach, FL; Pacific Asia Museum, Pasadena, CA.

**Additional Listings:** Canton; Fitzhugh; Imari; Kutani; Nanking; Rose Medallion; Satsuma.

## China

Bowl, large, silvery blue underglaze blue design of kylin in int., rim design of cranes and clouds, ext. of bowl with Buddhist lion, elephant, horse, and ram supporting Shou characters, ground strewn with clouds, unidentifiable shop mark on base, Ming period, probably Wan Li, 1573-1619, rim chips............... 900.00
Brush Pot, 7" d, 6-1/2" h, deep sapphire blue, diaper patterns surrounding two reserves of deer and cranes in mountain scene, other reserve with fisherman at work, K'ang His period ...................................................................... 10,350.00
Charger, 15" d, brilliant sapphire blue pattern of birds and flowers reserved with diaper borders, ext. with sprigs of flowers, base with shop mark, K'ang Hsi period, 1662-1722 ................... 1,725
Figure, 11-1/2" h, Blanc de Chine, seated goddess Kuan Yin, 19th C...................................................................... 1,380.00

Jardiniere, 15" d, 15-1/2" h, enamel dec of scholars in mountain rustic retreat, sixty-character inscription and single seal on reverse, 19th C 350.00

Lamp, Sang de Bouef vase, relief carved dragons, China, 19th C, mounted as lamp, some damage ............................................320.00

Teapot, 12-1/2" h, blue and white, stationary loop handle, Celestial Dragons dec, sgd in calligraphy on base, Hsien-Feng, c1850-60....... 275.00

Vase

7" h, Flambé, pomegrante form, lavender magenta glaze, 19th C.................................................................550.00

9" h, reversed pattern of white flowers on blue ground, transitional period, 1600-50 .............................................750.00

11-1/2" h, Ming-style, heaped blue dec, Hu Chun form, Kuang Hsu period and mark, 1874-1908.................................1,840.00

13-1/4" h, fen tsai, hexagonal, chartreuse ground, upper register with stylized banana leaves, flower register with ju-i and banana leaves, central register of archaic dragon kuei in coral red, pale celadon int., finely drawn six-character seal mark on base, Ch'ien Lung period and mark, 1736-95..........................5,175.00

14" h, Meiping, dragon and wave motif, underglaze red dec, Ch'ien Lung six character mark......................................1,150.00

15" h, 7-3/4" h, blue and white, baluster, multiple blue Tzou symbols on floral ground, Kuang-Hsu, c1880-85....................250.00

15-1/2" h, 8-1/2" d, blue and white, baluster, multiple blue Tzou symbols, Kuang-Hsu, c1880-85 .........................220.00

16" h, globular body, tall flaring mouth, bowstring marks around body, pale blue glaze, Ch'ien Lung mark, 1735-96 .........490.00

16" h, 7-1/2" d, blue and white, baluster, multiple blue Tzou symbols on floral ground, Kuang-Hsu, c1880-85....................275.00

## Chinese Export

Basin, 16-1/2" d, 5" h, sacred bird and butterfly pattern, orange, gilt highlights, 19th C, chip, hairline .........................1,380.00

Bough Pot, 8" h, applied shapes of squirrels among grapes and Famille Rose painted panels, made for the European market, pr....... 13,800.00

Bowl

8-7/8" d, 4-7/8" h, armorial, multicolored flower sprig center, draped shield with initials "RI" and unicorn over lion shield on side, diaper and spearhead border, blue, green, and purple, gilt highlights, 19th C, wear............................375.00

11-5/8" d, butterfly and chrysanthemum, pink, blue, green, red, and brown floral vine border, gilt highlights, third quarter 19th C.................................................................230.00

Brush Pot, 4" h, ivory ground, pierced relief carving of people and pavilions in garden, cash/coin design ground, 19th C......200.00

Creamer, 3-1/4" h, hog spout, brown eagle, red, white, and blue shield, flower sprigs, gilt highlights, early 19th C.................................575.00

Cup and Saucer

1-1/2" h, armorial, Arms of Bishop impaling Campbell," 18th C, rim chips, glaze wear .........................................525.00

3" h cup, 5-1/2" d saucer, Tobacco Leaf, blue leaves, pink and green floral sprigs, gilt highlights, early 19th C, glaze flakes, rim nicks ...................................................................175.00

Garden Seat, barrel form

12-3/4" h, all over light green foliage with pink buds, celadon ground, speckled blue cashes and gilt bosses, late 19th C, minor glaze and gilt wear, hairline...................................575.00

18-1/2" h, two large panels with figures alternating with cashes, floral ground, pastel aqua, pink, blue, yellow, and green glazes, late 19th C, price for pr.................................................1,380.00

Gravy Boat, 3-1/4" h, oval scalloped rim, hog nose spout, center flower basket dec, pink and iron-red floral swag and spearhead dec around rim, gilt highlights, 18th C, rim chips, repair to spout................290.00

Mug, 5-1/2" h, 19th C, rim repair...........................................260.00

Plate

8-7/8" d, center painted with potted flowers, incense burner and bat, potted plants, flowers, and spearhead rim border, pink,

blue, yellow, green, orange, and brown, gilt highlights, 19th C, glaze wear, chip, price set of six ......................................635.00

9" h, center painted with basket of flowers, red, blue, yellow, and green, cell pattern rim dec, repeating panels of flowers, gilt highlights, 18th C, glaze wear...........................................230.00

9-3/4" d, scalloped rim, painted center floral spray, iron-red, purple, yellow, pink and green, looped pink, green, and blue floral swag border, gilt edge, 18th C, glaze wear, chips, hairlines, price for set of six...........................................................490.00

12-1/4" d, metal banded, grisaille dec, flesh tone enamels of Achilles bath, 18th C, surface wear...........................................2,185.00

12-1/4" d, round, center dec with cornucopia and flower sprigs, floral and purple wavy line border dec, gilt highlights, late 17th/early 18th C, minor chips and hairlines ....................230.00

13-3/4" d, round, painted bird, dog perched on rock, peony, and bamboo, blue peony border, gilt highlights, 19th C, minor gilt wear, firing imperfections ......................................575.00

Platter, 12-7/8" l, 9-5/8" w, eight-sided oblong, lion, anchor and crown crest, surrounded by flower sprigs, insects, and fruit, green border bands with gilt leaf dec, 19th C .......................................850.00

Punch Bowl, 15-1/4" d, 6-1/2" h, armorial, Arms of Jongkers, four monograms in reserves, gilt and red spearhead interior rim border, late 18th C, repairs...............................................2,875.00

Punch Bowl and Underplate, 11" d, 4" h bowl, 9-7/8" d underplate, multicolored center flower bouquet, foliage, and squash border, 19th C, glaze wear, hairline, base chips ....................................375.00

Tea Service, partial, armorial, gilt star spangled cobalt blue and iron-rd borders, some pieces with mantle-draped shield with birds perched on top and initials "I. R.," smaller pieces with gilt star spangled cobalt blue oval with initials "AEC" within, two teapots, five large teacups, eight saucers, twelve smaller plates, six bowls, creamer, cov sugar, two small saucers, small tea cup, early 19th C, damage and repairs . 1,610.00

Urn, 15" h, scenic sepia dec around shoulder, oval reserve depicting manor, surrounded by multicolored butterflies, flowers, and birds, simulated marble stepped square base, griffin shaped gilt handles, 19th C, covers missing, losses, wear, price for pr.................8,625.00

Wash Basin, 16" d, 5" h, butterfly, bird, and foliate border, center diapered field, reserves of precious objects, restoration, gilt and enamel wear ......................................................................250.00

Water Dropper, 9-1/2" h, iron-red and cobalt blue Imari palette foliate designs...................................................................115.00

## Japanese

Bowl, 11-1/2" d, Arita Ware, blue and white, foliage edge, ribbed body, floral dec, late 19th C ...........................................220.00

Charger, 15-1/2" d, blue and white, large flower-filled basket, Meiji, c1890 .....................................................................275.00

Figural Group, 10" l, 10" w, 10" h, frolicking shishi, underglaze blue accents, bisque eyes, Hirado, 19th C, one minor chip........12,650.00

Plate, 8-1/4" d, Kakiemon, lobed form, straw rope edge, relief dec of three friends, pine, bamboo, and prunus, center with pair of pheasants and flowers, red, yellow, blue, turquoise, and black enamel, gilt accents, three spur marks on base, late 17th/early 19th C, small chip and hairline...............................................................520.00

Vase

6-3/4" h, monogram sang de boeuf glaze, sgd "Kozan sei" within sq in underglaze blue for Makuzu Kozan, c1900 .............575.00

7-1/2" h, celadon glaze with band of peach bloom across body and mouth, sgd in underglaze blue "Tai Nihon Kozan Sei" within a sq for Makuzu Kozan, c1900......................................575.00

## Korea

Jar, 6" h, stoneware, faceted sides covered with thick green-brown glaze, sandy foot, 19th C .................................................300.00

Water Dropper, 3" l, fish form, lapis lazuli glaze, Choson dynasty, 18th/19th C...............................................................815.00

# CHINTZ CHINA

**History:** Chintz china has been produced since the 17th century. The brightly colored exotic patterns produced on fabric imported from India to England during this century was then recreated on ceramics. Early chintz patterns were hand painted and featured large flowers, fantastical birds and widely spaced patterns. The advent of transfer printing resulted in the development of chintz dishes which could be produced cheaply enough to sell to the masses. By the 1830s a number of Staffordshire potteries were producing chintzware for everyday use. These early patterns have not yet attracted the interest of most chintz collectors.

Collectors typically want the patterns dating from roughly 1920 until the 1950s. In 1920, A.G. Richardson "Crown Ducal" produced a range of all-over-transfer chintz patterns, which were very popular in North America, particularly the East Coast. Patterns such as Florida, Festival, and Blue Chintz were originally introduced as tea sets and then expanded to full-dinner services. Florida is the most popular of the Crown Ducal patterns in North America, but Peony has become increasingly popular in the past year or two. What most collectors consider the first modern chintz was designed by Leonard Grimwade in 1928 and named Marguerite. This pattern was very successful for many years but has never been highly regarded by collectors. Every year at the British Industries Fair factories vied with each other to introduce new patterns which would catch the buyers' eye. From the late 1920s until the mid-1950s, Royal Winton produced more than 80 chintz patterns. In some cases, the background color was varied and the name changed: Hazel, Spring and Welbeck is the same pattern in different colorways. After the second world war, Royal Winton created more than fifteen new patterns, many of which were more modern looking with large flowers and rich dark burgundy, blue or black backgrounds—patterns such as May Festival, Spring Glory and Peony. These patterns have not been very popular with collectors, although other 1950s patterns such as Florence and Stratford have become almost as popular as Julia and Welbecki in the past year.

The 1930s were hard times in the potteries and factories struggled to survive. They copied any successful patterns from any other factories. James Kent Ltd. produced chintzes such as DuBarry, Apple Blossom and Rosalynde. These patterns were sold widely in North America and complete dinner sets still occasionally turn up. The most popular pattern for collectors is the white Hydrangea, although Apple Blossom seems to be more and more sought after. Elijah Cotton "Lord Nelson" was another factory which produced large amounts of chintz. Cotton had always been known for the hundreds of utilitarian jugs it produced and it continued to be great producers of institutional ware. The workers at Elijah Cotton were never as skilled as the Grimwades' workers and usually the handles and the spouts of teapots and cof-feepots were left undecorated. The shapes are chunky and the pottery thicker than the other factories. Collectors, however, love the Nelson Ware jugs and stacking teapots especially in Black Beauty and Green Tulip. Although a number of factories produced bone china after World War II, only Shelley Pottery seems to be highly desired by today's collector.

By the late 1950s, young brides didn't want the dishes of their mothers and grandmothers but preferred the clean lines of modern Scandinavian furniture and dishes. Chintz gradually died out by the early 1960s and it was not until the 1990s that collectors began to search for the dishes their mothers had scorned.

**References:** Eileen Busby, *Royal Winton Porcelain*, The Glass Press Inc.1998; Susan Scott, *Charlton Standard Catalogue of Chintz*, Charlton Press, 3rd Edition; 1999; Heller/Feljoy, *Chintz by Design*, Chintz International, 1997; Muriel Miller, *Collecting Royal Winton Chintz*, Francis Joseph Publications, 1996, Jo Anne Welch, *Chintz Ceramics*, 2nd Edition, Schiffer Publishing 1998.

**Collectors' Clubs:** Royal Winton International Collectors' Club, Dancer's End, Northall, Bedfordshire, England LU6 2EU; Royal Winton Collectors' Club, 2 Kareela Road, Baulkham Hills, Australia 2153

**Reproduction Alert:** In the last couple of years with the rising prices of chintz, both Royal Winton and James Kent have started to reproduce some of their more popular patterns. Royal Winton is reproducing Welbeck, Florence, Summertime and Julia, while James Kent has so far reproduced Du Barry and Hydrangea. The Old Chintz Company has bought the Lord Nelson backstamp and there are plans to reproduce some of the Elijah Cotton patterns as well. The new Royal Winton backstamp has a black circle around the original deco backtamp; the new James Kent backstamp includes 100-year anniversary. Contact the factories for current production lists to avoid confusing old and new chintz.

**Advisor:** Susan Scott.

## Elijah Cotton "Lord Nelson"

Cake Plate, tab handles, Black Beauty pattern............................250.00
Cup and Saucer
    Rosetime pattern .................................................150.00
    Royal Brocade pattern.........................................75.00
Plate, 8-1/2" sq, Pansy pattern ....................................175.00
Stacking Teapot, totally patterned, Heather pattern................1,695.00
Teapot, cov, six cup, Briar Rose pattern ......................850.00
Grimwades Royal Winton
    Breakfast Set, Royalty pattern ...........................1,800.00
    Butter Dish, rect, Ascot shape, Summertime pattern..........295.00
    Cake Stand, 3 tier, metal handle, Summertime pattern......425.00
    Coffeepot, Perth shape, Fireglow white pattern...............1,150.00
    Cream and Sugar, Balmoral pattern ..................................225.00
    Cream and Sugar ,on tray, May Festival pattern ...............195.00
Cup and Saucer, Bedale pattern................................................95.00
Hot Water Pot, Countess shape, Welbeck pattern....................995.00
Jug, Albans shape 4-1/2", Cotswold pattern..........................475.00
Plate, 10" sq, Sweet Pea pattern ...........................................225.00
Salt and Pepper, on tray, Chelsea pattern .................................345.00
Stacking Teapot, Balmoral pattern...........................................1,850.00

Teapot, cov
    Four cup, Albans shape, Eleanor pattern ...................... 1,100.00
    One cup, Countess shape, Majestic pattern ...................... 795.00
Toast Rack, five bar, Julia pattern .............................................. 750.00
Vase, Gem shape, Hazel pattern ............................................... 395.00
Wall Pocket, Nita shape, Evesham pattern ............................... 950.00

## James Kent Ltd.

Breakfast Set, Apple Blossom pattern .................................. 1,200.00
Cream and Sugar, Rosalynde pattern ........................................ 195.00
Egg Cup Set, four egg cups on tray, Marigold pattern ............... 395.00
Mint Sauce, liner, Du Barry pattern ........................................... 375.00
Nut Dish, 3" sq, Florita pattern ................................................... 95.00
Plate, 7" round, Rosalynde pattern ............................................ 135.00
Toast rack, five bar, large, Du Barry pattern .............................. 550.00

## Midwinter Ltd.

Biscuit Barrel, chrome lid, Brama pattern .................................. 350.00
Chop Plate, 11" d, Lorna Doone pattern .................................... 225.00

## A.G. Richardson "Crown Ducal"

Bowl, 9-1/2" octagonal, Florida pattern ...................................... 495.00
Breakfast Set, Peony pattern ................................................... 3,000.00
Cup and Saucer, Pansy pattern ................................................. 195.00
Plate, 8" d, Ivory Chintz pattern .................................................. 95.00
Teapot, cov, four cup, Priscilla pattern ...................................... 495.00

## Shelley Potteries Ltd.

Bonbon Dish, tab handles, 4-3/4", Maytime pattern ..................... 65.00
Cup and Saucer, Primrose pattern ............................................. 115.00
Plate, 6" d, Rock Garden pattern ................................................. 95.00
Teapot, cov, three cup, Melody pattern ...................................... 875.00

# CHRISTMAS ITEMS

**History:** The celebration of Christmas dates back to Roman times. Several customs associated with modern Christmas celebrations are traced back to early pagan rituals. Father Christmas, believed to have evolved in Europe in the 7th century, was a combination of the pagan god Thor, who judged and punished the good and bad, and St. Nicholas, the generous Bishop of Myra. Kris Kringle originated in Germany and was brought to America by the Germans and Swiss who settled in Pennsylvania in the late 18th century. In 1822, Clement C. Moore wrote "A Visit From St. Nicholas" and developed the character of Santa Claus into the one we know today. Thomas Nast did a series of drawings for Harper's Weekly from 1863 until 1886 and further solidified the character and appearance of Santa Claus.

**References:** Robert Brenner, *Christmas Past*, 3rd ed., Schiffer Publishing, 1996; ——, *Christmas through the Decades*, Schiffer Publishing, 1993; Barbara Fahs Charles and J. R. Taylor, *Dream of Santa*, Gramercy Books, 1992; Beth Dees, *Santa's Guide to Contemporary Christmas Collectibles*, Krause Publications, 1997; Jill Gallina, *Christmas Pins Past and Present*, Collector Books, 1996; George Johnson, *Christmas Ornaments, Lights & Decorations* Vol. I, (1987, 1998 value update), Vol. II (1996, 1997 value update), Vol. III (1996, 1997 value update), Collector Books; Constance King, *Christmas Customs, Antiques, Decorations & Traditions*, Antique Collectors' Club, 1999; Chris Kirk, *Joy of Christ-*

Pinback Button, Victor & Co. Toys, Santa holding wreath, dated 1925, starry sky background, $200. Photo courtesy of Hake's Americana & Collectibles.

*mas Collecting*, L-W Book Sales, 1994; James S. Morrison, *Vintage View of Christmas Past*, Shuman Heritage Press, 1995; Mary Morrison, *Snow Babies, Santas and Elves: Collecting Christmas Bisque Figures*, Schiffer Publishing, 1993; Margaret Schiffer, *Christmas Ornaments: A Festive Study*, Schiffer Publisher, 1984, 1995 value update; Clara Johnson Scroggins, *Silver Christmas Ornaments*, Krause Publications, 1997; Lissa Bryan-Smith and Richard Smith, *Holiday Collectibles, Vintage Flea Market Treasures Price Guide*, Krause Publications, 1998; Margaret and Kenn Whitmyer, *Christmas Collectibles*, 2nd ed., 1994, 1996 value update, Collector Books.

**Collectors' Club:** Golden Glow of Christmas Past, 6401 Winsdale St., Golden Valley, MN 55427.

**Reproduction Alert:** Almost all holiday decorations including Christmas are now being skillfully reproduced. Only by knowing the source of a possible purchase, trusting the dealer, and careful observation can you be sure you are obtaining an antique.

**Additional Listings:** See *Warman's Americana & Collectibles* for more examples.

**Advisors:** Lissa Bryan-Smith and Richard M. Smith.

## Advertising

Bank, molded rubber, Santa Clause holding a coin, toys in pack, mkd "Christmas Club A. Corp, N.Y. 1972" ........................................... 6.00
Booklet, "When All The World Is Kin," 5" x 4", collection of Christmas stories, Christmas giveaway, Fowler, Dick, and Walker, The Boston Store, Wilkes-Barre, PA .......................................................... 7.00
Calendar, 3" h, 7" l, celluloid, Christmas scene with holly border and 1929 calendar, giveaway from the Penny Specialty Shop, Selinsgrove, PA ............................................................................ 15.00
Candy Tin, 9" l, rect, red and green holly on white ground, mkd "Satin Finish, hard candies, div. of Luden's Inc., Reading, PA" ........... 18.00
Catalog, Boston Store, Milwaukee, WI, 1945, 48 pgs, 8-1/2" x 11", "For An American Christmas" ........................................................ 20.00
Cracker Tin, 2-1/2" h, 11" l, 8" w, Christmas scene on hinged lid, red and gold trim on sides, mkd "NBC" on base ............................. 25.00
Matches, 4" x 2", "Season's Greetings," winter scene on cover, intact matches create Christmas scene, Boehmer's Garage, Milton, MA ............................................................................................. 15.00
Trade Card, child holding snowballs, "The White is King of all Sewing Machines, 80,000 now in use," reverse reads "J. Saltzer, Pianos, Organs, and Sewing Machines, Bloomsburg, Pa." .................... 10.00

## Candy Box, cardboard

4-1/2" l, 3" h, Christmas Greetings, three carolers, USA ............... 4.00
6" x 5", pocketbook style, tuck-in flap, Merry Christmas, Santa in store window with children outside, mkd "USA" ............................... 15.00
8" h, four sided cornucopia, Merry Christmas, Santa, sleigh, and reindeer over village rooftops, string bail, USA ........................... 35.00

## Children's Book

*The Night Before Christmas*, Clement C. Moore, Corrine Malvern illustrator, A Golden Book, Golden Press, 1975 ................................ 8.00
*Rudolph The Red-Nosed Reindeer*, Robert I. May, Maxton Publishers, Inc., 1939 ................................................ 12.00
*The Littlest Snowman*, Charles Tazewell, Grosset Dunlap, NY, 1958 ................................................ 18.00

Feather Tree
    24" h, painted wood base .................................. 240.00
    48" h, green goose feather wrapped branches with metal candleholders, painted white with green trim round wooden base, mkd "Germany" .................................. 400.00

## Figure

Father Christmas
    7" h, composition, pink face, red cloth coat, painted blue pants, black boots, mounted on mica-covered cardboard base, mkd "Japan" .................................. 90.00
    8" h, papier-mâché, hollow molded, plaster covered, white coat, black boots, sprinkled with mica .................................. 300.00
Friar choir, on wooden accordion base, 7 friars, two trees and church, mkd, Japan, 1930s .................................. 15.00
Nativity, 7" h, composition, shepherd holding lamb, mkd "Germany" .................................. 12.00
Reindeer
    1" h, pot metal, mkd "Germany" .................................. 18.00
    4" h, celluloid, white .................................. 7.00
Santa Claus
    3" h, bisque, long red coat, mkd "Japan" .................................. 25.00
    3" h, cotton batting, red, attached to cardboard house, mkd "Japan" .................................. 48.00
    3" l, celluloid, molded, one-piece Santa, sleigh, and reindeer .................................. 35.00
    5" h, hard plastic, Santa on green plastic skis, USA .................................. 120.00
    10" h, pressed cardboard, red hat and jacket, black boots ... 90.00
    12" h, painted face, Japan .................................. 70.00
    14" h, pressed cardboard, head, store display .................................. 95.00
Sheep, 3" h, composition body, carved wooden legs, covered with cloth or wool, glass eyes .................................. 40.00

## Greeting Card

"Christmas Greetings," booklet style, emb diecut cov, color litho pictures on int. pgs, The Art Lithographic Publishing Co. ............... 18.00
"Loving Greetings," flat card, two girls pictured hanging garland, c1910, mkd "Germany" .................................. 8.00
"Merry Christmas," series of 6 envelopes, decreasing in size, small card in last envelope, American Greeting Publishers, Cleveland, USA, 1933 .................................. 12.00
"Sincere Good Wishes," purple pansy with green leaves, greeting inside, Raphael Tuck & Sons, 1892 .................................. 7.00

## House, cardboard

2" x 2", mica covered, wire loop on top, mkd "Czechoslovakia" ..... 7.00
4" x 5", house and fence, sponge trees, mkd "USA" .................................. 10.00
**Lantern**, 8" h, four sided, peaked top, wire bail, metal candleholder in base, black cardboard, colored tissue paper scenes, 1940s ..... 25.00

## Ornament

Angel
    4" h, wax over composition, human hair wig, spun glass wings, cloth dress, Germany .................................. 55.00
    8" h, chromolithograph, tinsel and lametta trim, pr ............... 15.00
Ball, 2" d, silvered glass, any color .................................. 3.00
Beads, 72" l, glass, half inch multicolored beads, paper label mkd "Japan" .................................. 8.00
Bulldog, 3" h, Dresden, three-dimensional, mkd "Germany" ....... 250.00
Camel, 4" h, cotton batting, Germany .................................. 160.00
Cross, 4" h, beaded, 2-sided, silvered, wire hanger, paper label mkd "Czechoslovakia" .................................. 18.00

Print, A Christmas Kid, mkd "Bessie Collins Pease," c1905, gold frame, 8" x 10", $75. Photo courtesy of Michael Ivankovich Antiques & Auction Co., Inc.

Drummer Boy, 3" h, wax, hollow, metal ring hanger, USA ............. 5.00
Father Christmas on Donkey, 10" h, chromolithograph, blue robe, tinsel trim .................................. 25.00
Mandolin, 5" h, unsilvered glass, wrapped in lametta and tinsel .. 45.00
Parakeet, 5" h, multicolored glass, spun glass tail, mounted on metal clip .................................. 23.00
Pear, 3" h, cotton batting, mica highlights, paper leaf, wire hanger, Japan .................................. 12.00
Santa Claus in Chimney, 4" h, glass, Germany .................................. 75.00
"SparklingTinsel Icicles," original red and white box, 20 twisted metal wire icicles, National Tinsel Manufacturing Co., Manitowoc, Wis .................................. 15.00
Swan, 5" x 6", Dresden, flat, gold with silver, green, and red highlights .................................. 150.00
Tree Top, 11" h, 3 spheres stacked with small clear glass balls, silvered, lametta and tinsel trim, attached to blown glass hooks ... 90.00
Wax figural ornaments, original box, one dozen, includes three of each: toy soldier, Santa, Angel, Deer, all 3 - 3-1/4"h, painted, Tavern Candle Co., USA .................................. 40.00

## Postcard, Germany

"Happy Christmas Wishes," Santa steering ship .................................. 10.00
"May Your Christmas Be Merry and Gay," photo card, sepia tones, Father Christmas peeking between 2 large wooden doors, wearing fur cap .................................. 18.00

## Putz

Brush Tree, 6" h, green, mica-covered branches, wooden base .... 8.00
Christmas Tree Fence
    Cast iron, silver, ornate gold trim, fifteen 10" l segments with posts, Germany .................................. 600.00
    Wood, folding red and green sections, 48" l, USA .................................. 35.00
Choir Boy, 3" h, hard plastic, red and white .................................. 4.00
Penny Wooden, two children on seesaw, hand carved wood, multicolored, Nurenberg or Erzgebrige .................................. 32.00

## Sheet Music

"Have You Seen Our Santa?," words and music by Will A. Harding, Fillmore Music House, Cincinnati, Ohio, 1910, light green cover with dark green printing and sketch of early Father Christmas holding a Christmas Tree and carrying a pack of toys ... 25.00
"Santa Claus is Coming To Town," words by Haven Gillespie and music by J. Fred Coots, Leo Feist Co., New York, 1934, green, white and red cover with Santa over rooftops .................................. 20.00
"Ye Christmas Piano Book - Christmas Carols," by Mary Bacon Mason, Oliver Ditson Company, New York, 1931, beautiful illustrated cover, children caroling .................................. 15.00

## Toy

Jack-in-the-Box, 9-1/2" h, "Santa Pops," hard plastic, red felt hat, orig box, Tigrette Industries, 1956 .................................. 30.00

Merry-Go-Round, wind-up, celluloid, green and red base, 4 white reindeer heads, Santa sitting under umbrella, Santa spins around, stars hanging from umbrella bounce of bobbing deer heads, orig box, Japan .................................................................................. 65.00
Santa, 10" h, battery-operated, metal, covered with red and white plush suit and hat, soft plastic face, holding metal wand with white star light, wand moves up and down and lights up while Santa turns head .............................................................................. 110.00
Wagon, painted wood, added Santa and package, plaque reads "St. Claus-Dealer in Good Things," 25" l ........................................ 775.00

# CIGAR CUTTERS

**History:** Counter and pocket cigar cutters were used at the end of the 19th and the beginning of the 20th centuries. They were a popular form of advertising. Pocket-type cigar cutters often were a fine piece of jewelry that attached to a watch chain.

**Reference:** Jerry Terranova and Douglas Congdon-Martin, *Antique Cigar Cutters and Lighters*, Schiffer Publishing, 1996; —, *Great Cigar Stuff for Collectors*, Schiffer Publishing, 1997.

1-5/8" l, 1" w, gold filled, blimp shape, 15" l watch fob chain ...... 110.00
1-3/4" l, pelican, sterling silver, pocket type ............................... 200.00
2" h, sterling silver, naughty girl .................................................. 530.00
2" x 2-1/2", gold colored metal, steel blade, pocket type, c1900 .. 95.00
3" h, front emb "Smoke Country Gentleman 5 cent. American Thoroughbred 10 cents, Bennett, Sloan & Co., N.Y.," manuf by Brunhoff Mfg. Co. ...................................................................................... 150.00
3-1/4" h, nickel plated cast iron
    Front emb "R. G. Sullivan's 7-20-4-10 cent cigar," manuf by Brunhoff Mfg. Co., Pat'd May 19, 1891, orig condition, light surface rust and wear ...................................................................... 210.00
    Top emb "Smoke Dona Marina Mexican Cigars - Highest Grade Imported," clockwork mechanism, manuf by Erie Specialty Co., Pat'd 1889, professionally restored ................................. 325.00
3-1/2" h, cast iron
    Emb fancy filigree on front and base, front lever operates cutter, spring missing .......................................................................... 200.00
    Nickel plated, top emb "Automatic Cigar Tip Cutter, Pat'd in U.S. and European Countries," clockwork mechanism, mounted on wood base .................................................................................. 415.00
    Nickel plated, top emb "Hermann cent cigar, Stoddard, Gilbert & Co.," image of elf, clockwork mechanism, missing base plate, restored ...................................................................................... 450.00
    Top emb "We Sell the J. U. Divilbiss Co.'s Celebrated Fine Cigars, Try Them," clockwork mechanism, c1889 .......... 450.00
3-3/4" h
    Cast iron, base, reverse painting on glass adv "Mi Favorita Cigars," cameo of lady, clockwork mechanism, Brunhoff Mfg. Co., some loss to reverse painting ................................... 400.00
    Nickel plated cast iron, adv "Flor De Melba The Cigar Superior," highly dec patter on base, some paint loss to revere glass on sign, worn nickel plating ..................................................... 500.00
4-3/4" h, marquee emb "Waitt & Bond's Blackstone, Leads the World," professionally restored with copper tiger striping ..................... 300.00
5" h, reverse painting on glass sign on front reads "B-Y's and buy Y-B's," cutter operates mechanically when customer pulls down lever in front, Brunhoff Mfg. Co. ............................................................. 450.00
5-1/4" l, scissors type, chicken on handle, mkd "Germany" .......... 30.00
5-1/2" h, cast iron machine emb "Havana High Grade Cigars," paper picture showing open box of cigars, one wooden match dispensed with cigar cut with lever action ............................................... 850.00
6" h, front emb with shield adv "Kenteria Hanna Cigars Kent's Extra 5 cents, Mac's Best, I. S. Kent - McCathy Co., Jacksonville, IL," cast iron top and front, Pat'd Aug 7, 1906, missing base plate ........ 500.00

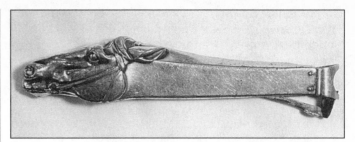

**Horse, figural head, silver plated, 5-3/4" l, $120.**

7" h, cast iron body, emb with embellishments on all four sides of body, shield with stars and stripes on top, Yankee, Pat'd July 13, 1909, also dispensed one lit match at a time, top of shield copper flashed .................................................................................... 700.00
7-1/2" h
    Metal marquee, figural cast iron cigar center, engraved "The New York Specials, Havana Cigars, Bondy & Lederer, N.Y. Makers," Brunhoff Mfg. Co. ................................................................. 750.00
    Table top, detailed frame with painting of cows, farm house, stream, and wild life, frame titled "H. A. Schneck Allentown Cigars of Quality Maker," minor rusting ......................... 1,300.00
8" h, cast iron
    Figural marquee emb "Above the Average" atop the world, perimeter and cigar copper plated, rest painted, Brunhoff Mfg. Co. ...................................................................................... 1,200.00
    Figural, portly man singing from hymnal, man mouth is cutter, operated by moving left arm, cast iron base, pot metal figure, orig paint, wear ............................................................... 600.00
8-1/2" h, 7" w, donkey, cast iron, cigar cutter and trade stimulator, overall wear to paint, 1890s ................................................... 1,250.00
8-3/4" h, nickel plated cast iron, shape of customer's cigar determined whether left round hole or right oval hole was used, two bulbous handles mechanically operate cutter, marquee emb "Declarencia Havana Cigars" with trademark, ornate base also ashtray, Brunhoff Mfg. Co. ...................................................................................... 900.00
9" h, figural cast iron, marquee emb "Havana Cigars of Excellent Quality" around paper picture of H. W. Longfellow, emb base also ashtray, Brunhoff Mfg. Co. ................................................................. 750.00
10" h, figural, giraffe shape, brass, holder for matches and butting tray on base, raise giraffe's neck up to cut cigar, wear on neck ...... 225.00
11" h, figural, parrot shape, brass wings, raise head up to cut cigar ...................................................................................... 350.00
19-1/2" h, combination cigar cutter and cigar lighter, mail box shape with lamp post and fence post, lever on side of cast iron chest opens cigar cutter, cast lighter, finials atop fence posts become wicks, could be lit from lantern at top of lamp post ...................................... 375.00

# CIGAR STORE FIGURES

**History:** Cigar store figures were familiar sights in front of cigar stores and tobacco shops starting about 1840. Figural themes included Sir Walter Raleigh, sailors, Punch figures, and ladies, with Indians being the most popular. Most figures were carved in wood, although some also were made in metal and papier-mâché for a short time. Most carvings were life size or slightly smaller and were brightly painted. A coating of tar acted as a preservative against the weather. Of the few surviving figures, only a small number have their original bases. Most replacements were necessary because of years of wear and usage by dogs. Use of figures declined when local ordinances were passed requiring shopkeepers to move the figures inside at night. This soon became too much trouble, and other forms of advertising developed.

**References:** Edwin O. Christensen, *Early American Wood Carvings*, Dover Publications, out of print; A.W. Pendergast and W. Porter Ware, *Cigar Store Figures*, The Lightner Publishing Corp., out of print.

Counter-top, painted black, except feathers, possible repaint . 5,500.00
Indian, standing
    65" h, full costume, holding hands out, sq base with four iron wheels, repainted .......... 2,600.00
    69" h, full headdress with 11 feathers, painted red, green, and cream, base reads "Cigars 5 Cents" ............... 450.00
    70" h, polychrome paint over gesso over carved wood, full figured Indian with "Illinois" stamped on back, one cigar broken .......... 2,240.00
    77-1/2" h, brightly painted, full dress.............. 29,900.00
Princess, carved and painted, muted polychrome dec .......... 29,900.00
Punch Figure, carved and painted pine, inscribed "Cigars" on front and "Tobacco" on sides, America, 1850-75.............. 107,000.00
Squaw, 57-1/2" h, carved and painted, holding tobacco leaf in left hand .......... 15,000.00

# CINNABAR

**History:** Cinnabar, a ware made of numerous layers of a heavy mercuric sulfide, often is referred to as vermilion because of the red hue of most pieces. It was carved into boxes, buttons, snuff bottles, and vases. The best examples were made in China.

Bowl, cov; 13" d, shallow............. 715.00
Box, cov
    3" d, 1" d, Oriental carving on lid.......... 75.00
    9-3/4" sq, carved cinnabar lacquer, Chinese, 18th C, pr 20,700.00
Brooch, 2" x 3/4", carved Chinese symbol and floral motif, silver over copper fittings, sgd "China," c1910 .......... 145.00
Cabinet, 10-1/2" w, 22" d, 5" h, upper case of staggered shelves, two short drawers, pair of cupboard doors, gilt landscapes, 20th C 475.00
Cup, 4-1/2" d, dragon handles, c1900 .......... 225.00
Dish, 10-3/4" d, deeply carved, leafy melon vines, black lacquer base .......... 900.00
Dress Clip, 2" l, 1-3/4" w, carved floral motif, brass metal clip, mkd "China" .......... 65.00
Incense Burner, pagoda type, Taoist mask design, c1900....... 1,300.00
Jar, 4" h, flowering plants, carved floral scrolls, diaper ground, domed cov, gilt metal rim and finial, price for pr .......... 150.00
Money Clip, 2-1/4" x 1-1/2", carved cinnabar plaque, brass fittings, mkd "Made in China" .......... 125.00
Necklace, 26" l, knotted between each bed, clasp mkd "Sterling".......... 125.00
Netsuke, carved high relief with dragons and auspicious emblems on diapered ground, Manjo, 19th C.......... 375.00
Plate, 12 3/4" d, double dragon design .......... 375.00
Snuff Bottle
    Baluster shape, 2" h, carved Oriental figures and pagodas, celluloid spoon .......... 325.00
    Cylindrical, carved figures in landscape, chrysanthemum borders and top, metal mounted base with gold four-character Ch'ien Lung mark on black ground.......... 250.00
Stand, 14-1/2" l, 30" h, sq top, lacquered mountain scenes, brass pan, Chinese, c1900 .......... 240.00
Tray, 15" l, bird and flower scene, reddish brown .......... 625.00
Vase, 10 1/2" h, ovoid, long cylindrical neck, carved lotus flowers and leaves, high foot rim with scrolling floral band, price for pr....... 295.00

# CLEWELL POTTERY

**History:** Charles Walter Clewell was first a metal worker and secondarily a potter. In the early 1900s, he opened a small shop in Canton, Ohio, to produce metal overlay pottery. Metal on pottery was not a new idea, but Clewell was perhaps the first to completely mask the ceramic body with copper, brass or "silvered" or "bronzed" metals. One result was a product whose patina added to the character of the piece over time. Since Clewell operated on a small scale with little outside assistance, only a limited quantity of his artwork exists. He retired at the age of 79 in 1955, choosing not to reveal his technique to anyone else.

**Marks:** Most of the wares are marked with a simple incised "Clewell" along with a code number. Because Clewell used pottery blanks from other firms, the names "Owens" or "Weller" are sometimes found.

**References:** Paul Evans, *Art Pottery of the United States*, 2nd ed., Feingold & Lewis Publishing Corp., 1987; Ralph and Terry Kovel, *Kovels' American Art Pottery*, Crown Publishers, 1993.

**Museum:** John Besser Museum, Alpena, MI.

Ashtray, 3-1/4" d, copper, circular imp mark "Clewell, Canton, OH," 1922 .......... 200.00
Bowl, 4-1/2" d, riveted overlay finish, sgd, circular imp seal "Clewell Coppers" .......... 215.00
Jardiniere, copper-clad pottery
    6-1/2" d, 5-1/4" h, verdigris and bronze patina, incised "Clewell 418-2-9".......... 950.00
    12" d, 9" h, uneven patina, incised mark .......... 450.00
Urn, 9" h, 4-1/2" d, copper-clad, bronze and verdigris patina, incised "C. W. Clewell/520-220," few patina chips on base.......... 1,000.00
Vase, copper-clad pottery
    5" h, 4-1/4" d, spherical, fine verdigris and bronze patina, incised "Clewell 300-25" .......... 1,100.00
    6" h, 3" d, ovoid, fine verdigris patina, incised "Clewell 331-6".......... 475.00
    7-1/2" h, 3-1/2" d, classic shape, fine verdigris and bronze patina, incised "Clewell 351-24".......... 1,900.00
    7-3/4" h, flared rim tapering to bulbous foot, inscribed "Clewell 293-29".......... 575.00
    8-1/2" h, 7" d, classic shape, fine brown to verdigris patina, incised "Lcewell/463-26" .......... 1,800.00
    8-3/4" h, 7" d, classic shape, fine verdigris patina, incised "Clewell 323-6".......... 1,100.00
    10" h, 3-1/2" d, faceted, verdigris and bronze patina, incised "Clewell 439-2-6".......... 2,400.00
    10" h, 5" d, flat shoulder, fine verdigris patina, unmarked 1,000.00

**Vessel, shouldered, bronzed and verdigris patina, incised "Clewell/323-2-6," 8-3/4" h, 6-1/4" d, $575. Photo courtesy of David Rago Auctions.**

10-1/4" h, 4-1/2" d, squatty base, fine verdigris patina, incised "Clewell 5-2-6" ............ 1,700.00
11" h, bulbous shoulder, orig orange, green and blue patina, incised "Clewell 272-2-6" ............ 1,300.00
11-1/2" h, orig patina, incised mark ............ 375.00
11-1/2" h, orig patina, orange, green, and blue drip effect, sgd "Clewell 302-2-6" ............ 1,300.00
12" h, exceptional orig patina ............ 4,750.00
19" h, orig patina, orange, green, and blue, sgd "Clewell 430-2-6" ............ 6,000.00

# CLARICE CLIFF

**History:** Clarice Cliff, born on January 20, 1899, in Tunstall, Staffordshire, England, was one of the major pottery designers of the 20th century. At the age of thirteen, she left school and went to Lingard, Webster & Company, where she learned freehand painting. In 1916, Cliff was employed at A. J. Wilkinson's Royal Staffordshire Pottery, Burslem. She supplemented her in-house training by attending a local school of art in the evening. In 1927, her employer sent her to study sculpture for a few months at the Royal College of Art in London. Upon returning, she was placed in charge of a small team of female painters at the Newport Pottery, taken over by Wilkinson in 1920. Cliff designed a series of decorative motifs which were marketed as "Bizarre Ware" at the 1928 British Industries Fair.

Throughout the 1930s, Cliff added new shapes and designs to the line. Her inspiration came from art magazines, books on gardening, and plants and flowers. Cliff and her Bizarre Girls gave painting demonstrations in the stores of leading English retailers. The popularity of the line increased. World War II halted production. When the war ended, the hand painting of china was not resumed. In 1964, Midwinter bought the Wilkinson and Newport firms. The original names for some patterns have not survived. It is safe to rely on the handwritten or transfer-printed name on the base. The Newport pattern books in the Wilkinson's archives at the Hanley Library also are helpful. Since 1999 marks the centenary of Clarice Cliff's birth, there are several major exhibitions of her work planned. Christie's South Kensington, in London, is having three Clarice Cliff auctions this year. They now include a section on the Wedgwood Reproductions from 1992 and later.

**Marks:** In the summer of 1985, Midwinters produced a series of limited-edition reproductions to honor Clarice Cliff. They are clearly marked "1985" and contain a special amalgamated backstamp.

**References:** Susan and Al Bagdade, *Warman's English & Continental Pottery & Porcelain*, 3rd Edition, Krause Publications, 1998; Helen C. Cunningham, *Clarice Cliff and Her Contemporaies: Susie Cooper, Keith Murray, Charlotte Rhead, and the Carlton Ware Designers*, Schiffer Publishing, 1999; Richard Green and Des Jones, *Rich Designs of Clarice Cliff*, published by authors, 1995 (available from Carole A. Berk, Ltd, 8020 Norfolk Ave, Bethesda, MD 20814); Leonard R. Griffin,

*Clarice Cliff: The Art of Bizarre*, Pavilion Books, 1999; —, *The Fantastic Flowers of Clarice Cliff*, Pavilion Books, 1998; Leonard R. Griffin and Susan Pear Meisel, *Clarice Cliff*, Harry N. Abrams, 1994; Howard and Pat Watson, *Clarice Cliff Price Guide*, Francis-Joseph Books, 1995.

**Collectors' Club:** Clarice Cliff Collector's Club, Fantasque House, Tennis Drive, The Park, Nottingham, NG7 1AE, England.

**Advisor:** Susan Scott.

**Notes:** Bizarre and Fantasque are not patterns. Rather, they indicate the time frame of production—Bizarre being used from 1928-1937 and Fantasque from 1929-1934.

Cup and Saucer
Bizarre, conical shape, Orange Autumn, printed factory marks ............ 425.00
Fantasque Bizarre, Pastel Melon, printed factory marks .... 550.00
Honey Pot
3-3/4" h, Bizarre, Orange Roof Cottage, printed factory marks ............ 1,565.00
4" h, Beehive, Crocus, printed factory marks ............ 585.00
Lotus Jug
11-1/2" h, Fantasque Bizarre, twin handles, Autumn between orange bands ............ 3,125.00
12" h, Bizarre, single-handle, Viscaria, printed factory marks ............ 1,475.00
Plate, Fantasque Bizarre
7" d, Red Gardenia inside orange and yellow bands, printed factory marks ............ 625.00
9" d, House & Bridge inside orange, yellow, and black bands, printed factory marks ............ 1,465.00
10" d, Windbells inside green, yellow, and orange bands, printed factory marks ............ 1,270.00
Preserve, 4-1/4" h, Bon Jour shape, Rhodanthe, printed factory marks ............ 395.00
Sugar Shifter
5" h, Bizarre, Bon Jour shape, Blue Firs, printed factory marks ............ 3,125.00
5" h, Bizarre, Lynton shape, Newlyn, printed factory marks 785.00
5" h, Bon Jour Shape, Coral First, printed factory marks. 1,750.00
5-1/2" h, Bizarre, Conical, Mountain, printed factory marks ............ 3,715.00
Vase
2" h, miniature, ovoid, Sliced Fruit, between yellow and orange bands, printed factory marks ............ 585.00
6" h, Original Bizarre, shape 186, band of triangles in red, blue, and yellow between red and blue bands, printed factory marks ............ 780.00
8" h, Bizarre, shape 358, Appliqué Avignon between orange and black bands, printed and painted marks ............ 3,500.00
8" h, Fantasque Bizarre, shape 360, Floreat between yellow and orange bands, printed factory marks ............ 1,175.00
Zodiac Sign, 6-3/4" d, star shape, modeled in low relief, "Pisces" ............ 875.00
Wedgwood Reproductions

Bowl, 7" d, conical, Tennis, orig box with certificate 89/250 875.00
Figure, Age of Jazz, double dancer, orig box with certificate 26/150 ................................................................. 700.00
Sugar Shifter, conical, May Avenue, orig box with certificate 444/500 ............................................................. 400.00
Vase, 12" h, Meiping, Solitude, orig box with certificate 142/250 ................................................................. 875.00

# CLIFTON POTTERY

**History:** The Clifton Art Pottery, Newark, New Jersey, was established by William A. Long, once associated with Lonhuda Pottery, and Fred Tschirner, a chemist. Production consisted of two major lines: Crystal Patina, which resembled true porcelain with a subdued crystal-like glaze, and Indian Ware or Western Influence, an adaptation of the American Indians' unglazed and decorated pottery with a high-glazed black interior. Other lines included Robin's-Egg Blue and Tirrube. Robin's-Egg Blue is a variation of the crystal patina line but in blue-green instead of straw-colored hues and with a less-prominent crushed-crystal effect in the glaze. Tirrube, which is often artist signed, features brightly colored, slip-decorated flowers on a terra-cotta ground.

**Marks:** Marks are incised or impressed. Early pieces may be dated and impressed with a shape number. Indian wares are identified by tribes.

**References:** Paul Evans, *Art Pottery of the United States*, 2nd ed., Feingold & Lewis Publishing Corp., 1987; Ralph and Terry Kovel, *Kovels' American Art Pottery*, Crown Publishers, 1993.

Biscuit Jar, cov, 7" h, 4-1/4" d, gray-brown ground, enameled running ostrich and stork, florals, bail handle ....................................... 300.00

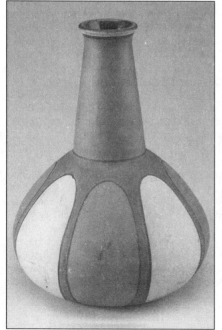

**Vase, Indian Ware, bulbous, rounded panel design, tan, brown, and terra cotta, mkd "Clifton/231,"" and "Middle Mississippi Valley," several glaze nicks around rim, 12-1/4" h, 8-1/2" h, $325. Photo courtesy of David Rago Auctions.**

Cruet, 5-3/4" h, hp swallows, blue ground, orig stopper ............... 45.00
Decanter, 11-1/2" h, rose shading to deep rose, purple flowers, gilt butterfly on neck, applied handle, marbleized rose and white stopper ................................................................. 150.00
Jardiniere, 8-1/2" h, 11" d, Four Mile Ruin, Arizona, incised and painted motif, buff and black on brown ground, imp mark and incised inscription, hairline to rim ................................................. 400.00
Sweetmeat Jar, 4" h, hp ducks and cranes, robin's egg blue ground, cow finial ............................................................. 375.00
Teapot, 6" h, brown and black geometric design ........................ 200.00
Vase, 8-1/2" h, 5" d, bottle shape, Crystal Patina, incised "Clifton" and dates 1906 and 1907, pr ............................................. 450.00

# CLOCKS

**History:** The sundial was the first man-made device for measuring time. Its basic disadvantage is well expressed by the saying: "Do like the sundial, count only the sunny days." Needing greater dependability, man developed the water clock, oil clock, and the sand clock, respectively. All these clocks worked on the same principle—time was measured by the amount of material passing from one container to another. The wheel clock was the next major step. These clocks can be traced back to the 13th century. Many improvements on the basic wheel clock were made and continue to be made. In 1934, the quartz crystal movement was introduced.

The first carriage clock was made about 1800 by Abraham Louis Breguet as he tried to develop a clock that would keep accurate time for Napoleon's officers. One special feature of a carriage clock was a device that allowed it to withstand the bumpy ride of a stagecoach. These small clocks usually are easy to carry with their own handle built into a rectangular case. The recently invented atomic clock, which measures time by radiation frequency, only varies one second in a thousand years.

**References:** Robert W. D. Ball, *American Shelf and Wall Clocks*, Schiffer Publishing, 1992; F. J. Britten, *Old Clocks and Watches & Their Makers*, Antique Collectors' Club, 1999; Cesinsky & Webster, *English Domestic Clocks*, Antique Collectors' Club, 1999; J. E. Connell, *The Charlton Standard Catalogue of Canadian Clocks*, 2nd ed., Charlton Press, 1999; Brian Loomes, *Brass Dial Clocks*, Antique Collectors' Club, 1999; —, *Painted Dial Clocks*, Antique Collector's Club, 1994; Tran Duy Ly, *Seth Thomas Clocks & Movements*, Arlington Book Co., 1996; Derek Roberts, *Skeleton Clocks*, Antique Collectors' Club, 1999; Tom Robinson, *The Longcase Clock*, Antique Collectors' Club, 1999; Ronald Rose, *English Dial Clocks*, Antique Collectors' Club, 1999; Robert and Harriet Swedberg, *Price Guide to Antique Clocks*, Krause Publications, 1998; John Ware Willard, *Simon Willard and His Clocks*, Dover Publications, n.d.

**Periodicals:** Clocks, 4314 W. 238th St., Torrance, CA 90505.

**Collectors' Club:** National Association of Watch and Clock Collectors, Inc., 514 Poplar St., Columbia, PA 17512.

**Museums:** American Clock & Watch Museum, Bristol, CT; Greensboro Clock Museum, Greensboro, NC; National Association of Watch and Clock Collectors Museum, Columbia, PA; National Museum of American History, Washington, DC; Old Clock Museum, Pharr, TX; The Time Museum, Rockford, IL; Willard House & Clock Museum, Grafton, MA.

**Notes:** Identifying the proper model name for a clock is critical in establishing price. Condition of the works also is a critical factor. Examine the works to see how many original parts remain. If repairs are needed, try to include this in your estimate of purchase price. Few clocks are purchased purely for decorative value.

## Advertising

Calumet Baking Powder, Time to Buy Best By Test, Regulator, Sessions, oak case, 38-1/2" h .......................................... 400.00
Chew Friendship Cut Plug, face of man with moving mouth, chewing Friendship Tobacco, patent March 2, 1886, 4" h ...................... 900.00
Ever-Ready Safety Razors, tin litho, man shaving in center of face, some scattered rust and scuffs, 17-3/4" h, 12-1/2" .............. 1,550.00
Ford, octagonal, center trademark, neon, 18" d ........................ 650.00
John Deere Quality Farm Equipment, round, electric, mkd "Pam Clock Co., Inc., Brooklyn, NY, USA" ...................................... 350.00
Old Mr. Boston, figural painted metal bottle case, eight day movement, c1910, 22" h, 10" w ................................................ 325.00
Pepsi, "Say Pepsi Please" at top center, Pepsi-Cola in black across bottle cap at bottom center, yellow ground, black numbers, white border, 1950s ............................................................. 1,265.00
Wolf's Head Motor Oil, rect, shows oil can and round clock, outlined in pink neon, 19" h, 30" l ...................................... 1,500.00

## Clocks

Alarm
  Attleboro, 36-hour, nickel-plated case, owl dec, 9" h ............ 75.00
  Bradley, brass, double bells, Germany ................................. 40.00
  Champion, 30-hour, American movement, metal frame, ornamental feet, 9" h ............................................................. 75.00
  New Haven, c1900, 30-hour, SP case, perfume bottle shape, beveled glass mirror, removable cut glass scent bottle, beaded handle ................................................................. 185.00
  Philadelphia Light and Electric, image of Reddy Kilowatt, Westclox, 5" d .............................................................. 350.00
  Thomas, Seth 1919, one day time and alarm movement, second bit, metal case, 10-1/4" h ..................................................... 50.00
Automation, George III, 3rd quarter 18th C, bracket, gilt bronze mounted mahogany, quarter striking, made by Thomas Gardner, triple fusee, striking nest of eight bells, elaborately engraved backplate, dial with dials for strike/silent and chime/not chime and date aperture, arch with automation of blacksmith's shop, domed case fitted with figural and foliate mounts, ogee bracket feet, 20" h, 14-1/2" w, 9" d ........................................... 18,700.00
Blinking Eye, figural, owl, unknown maker, c1920, nickel plated white metal front, green eyes, 30 hour level movement, hardwood case, paper dial, nickel plated bezel, beveled glass, 6-1/2" h .......... 375.00
Boat, Seth Thomas, Thomaston, CT, 1880, nickel plated brass case, painted dial, seconds indicator, 8-day double wind movement with lever escapement, 6-1/4" d .......................................... 100.00
Bracket
  French, late 19th C, pressed brass, two-train chiming and weighted movement, pull repeater, set in black painted tin case, enameled dial sgd "E. Leclerc, a Vire," brass surround pressed with scrolls and flowerheads, wagon, wheat sheaves, and barrel to top, similar pressed brass oversized pendulum, later walnut wall mount, 13-1/8" w, 54-1/4" l ...................................... 300.00

George III, signed
  John Ferry, London, c1770, ebonized and brass mounted, chiming and quarter striking, inverted bell top, pierced spandrels and dial in each for jig/minuet, engraved backplate and nest of eight bells, 20" h, 13-1/2" w .................... 5,465.00
  Steph. Rimbault, London, gilt metal mounts, ebonized, etched backplate, date aperture, phases of moon, strike/silent and pendulum adjustment, nest of four bells, 19" h, restorations ............................................................ 4,890.00
Regency, Bennett & Co., Norwich, c1810, brass inlaid and gilt bronze mounted mahogany, dial and backplate sgd, oak leaf spandrels, case inlaid with scrolls, gadrooned bun feet, 17" h, chips .................................................................. 4,325.00
Regency, London, c1800, mahogany, painted dial, double fusee movement, hour strike with repeat lever, painted face and openwork brass panels, 14" h, minor losses .................... 1,380.00
Tiffany & Co., bronze, stepped rect shaped top, four acorn finials, cast foliate frieze, four capitals with reeded columns, shaped and foliate cast base, beveled glass door and panels, circular face dial with Roman numerals, mkd "Famiel Marti Medaille...Paris 1900, Tiffany & Co." 13" h ................... 600.00
Calendar, parlor, Ithaca Clock Co., Ithaca, NY, c1875, walnut case with fine carved dec, black and silver hour dial, glass silver calendar dial, cut glass pendulum bob, maker's label, 10-1/4" w, 5-1/4" d, 20-1/2" h 1,800.00
Carriage
  Belle Epoque, gilt bronze mounted black lacquer, Louis XVI taste, c1890, alarm mechanism, black and white enameled dial, 4" w, 3" d, 5" h ................................................................. 175.00
  J. E. Caldwell & Co., late 19th C, mahogany case, gilt brass mounts and face, works by Furtwangler, Germany, 13-1/2" h .............................................................. 300.00
French, c1900
  Brass, movement sgd "Geo. Burchall," enamel face, Roman numberals, brass case with handle on top, 4-3/8" h ............. 230.00
  Glass and brass, fluted columnar corners, openwork face, borders dec with blind fretwork, alarm ................................. 450.00
  Glass, brass, gilt bronze, milled face, enameled dials, neoclassical dec, alarm, 6-1/2" h ...................................... 920.00
  Glass, brass, leather case, quarter-chiming two-train movement, plain enamel dial with Roman numerals, satin lined leather case with glass inset panel on front, 7" h ................................. 490.00
  Gubelin, 20th C, lapis lazuli case, gilt-metal mounts, 5-1/2" h ................................................................ 425.00
  Garniture, French, early 20th C, cut and etched glass, ormolu, and jasperware, rect clock with glass columns on each corner, frosted glass panels on sides and back, jasperware mounts on

**French, brass case, beveled glass inserts, painted enamel face, mkd "J. E. Caldwell & Co.," damage to one panel, 4-1/2" h, $385. Photo courtesy of Sanford Alderfer Auction Co.**

top and bottom, round face with beaded surround and jasperware mounted pendulum, case topped by glass sphere with scrolled ormolu mounts, two vasiform glass garnitures, 18-1/2" h clock, 10" h garnitures.................................................5,750.00

Gaslight, American, 1900, cast brass bezel and feet, 30 hour lever movement, milk glass shade, 5-3/4" d ....................................175.00

Gravity

American, c1925, brass case, powered by weight of clock movement descending along two posts, lifting movement back winds the clock for another 24 hours, marked "Patented 8/2/21," 10-1/4" h..........................................................................................200.00

French, c1940, retailed by Shreve, Crump & Low, Boston, powered by the fall of the movement along brass rails, reminding accomplished by lifting the movement back to the top of rails, mahogany case, turned columns and brass finials, 30-hour movement, porcelain dial, polished stone drum case, 17" h.................................................................................................800.00

Lantern, John Cotsworth, London, 1670, brass dial with engraved chapter ring, alarm mechanism engraved with maker's name "John Cotsworth Londini," brass weight driven movement housed in iron and brass four column case, cross arched bell supports terminating in urn finials, clock set in oak wall shelf, restorations, 13" w, 6" d, 15" h..........................................................................................5,175.00

Mantel

Biedermeier, late, second half 19th C, temple, marquetry inlaid, two-train quarter-strike movement, pull repeat mechanism, enameled dial, top of case with band of ebonized reeding over fruitwood scroll and fruit inlay, dial between four ebonized columns, fruitwood stringing, brass end caps, base with further ebonized reeded and fruitwood inlay, 10-1/8" l, 6" d, 17" h...................................................................................................650.00

Continental, late 19th/early 20th C

Figural, gilt-metal, two-train chiming movement, young male scholar reclining on rocky base set with engine-turned dial, Roman numerals, beaded surround, two-tiered rect base with band of flat leaves and shells, scrolled supports, glass dome, 14-1/4" h ...................................................1,860.00

Neoclassical-style, ebonized gilt metal, round hood topped by patinated bust of neoclassical youth, rect base with mirrored angled niche to front, central gilt metal rose vine, stepped base, 10-3/4" w, 5-1/8" d, 21" h ...................................900.00

Edwardian, c1900-1910, brass mounted ebonized oak, windmill form, façade with period glazed lithograph panel of worldly monk, 8" w, 3-1/2" d, 16-1/2" h ........................125.00

Egyptian Revival, America, retailed by A. Stowell and Co., Boston, late 19th C, single-train chiming movement sgd "Boston Clock Co.," enamel face, Arabic numerals in roundels, sgd by retailer, tapered rect case topped by gilt-metal sphinx on striated marble slab, side of case similarly mounted with smaller sphinxes, front of case mounted with plaque of winged Egyptian mask, 15-1/2" l, 6-1/4" d, 14" h .....................................................................................2,550.00

Empire, Continental, 19th C, mahogany and inlay, two-train movement with pull repeater, face with animated gilt metal dec of cupid sharpening an arrow on foot pedal lathe, enameled Arabic numeral bezel, tapered rect case with demilune hood, set to front with gilt metal flowers, band of stylized reeded inlay, later ogee bracket base, fitted with later independent music box, 9-3/4" l, 5-1/2" d, 14-1/2" h ......1,380.00

Empire-Style, late 19th C

Ebonized and ormolu mounted temple, two-train chiming movement mkd "FC," pediment mounted with ormolu fruit swags, round engine-turned face in cast floral frame flanked by columns with ormolu mounts top and bottom, plinth base with ormolu mount of swan above fruit, flanked by fairies and scrolls, flattened bun feet, 9-3/8" h .............................500.00

Marble, three-train quarter striking movement with hour gong and seven bells, rectilinear black marble body, dial with gilt metal bezel, front of case with multicolored slab of marble, 10-1/4" w, 6-3/4" d, 18-1/8" h .....................................375.00

Empire-Style, early 20th C, mahogany veneered temple, two-train chiming movement, enamel dial with Roman numerals, top with ormolu scroll mount, supported on four columns with ormolu caps, further ornament on base, four flattened ball feet, 20" h ..........................................................................815.00

Figural, bronze figure of Mercury lacing his sandals, clock set into naturalistic rocky base, two-train chiming movement, engine turned dial with Roman numerals, marble rect base with bronze flat leaf band, bronze acanthus feet, late 19th C, 19-5/8" h ............................................................................1,380.00

French

Brass, onyx, and glass, columnar stiles, bracket feet, retailed by Tiffany & Co., c1900, 11" h.....................................460.00

Bronze and champleve, face enameled with floral swags, beveled glass sides, early 20th C, 11" h...............................1,380.00

Figural, ormolu and marble, two-train chiming movement incised "L. K. Brevete S.G.D.G.," Medialle d' Argent seal, enamel face painted with delicate floral swags set into rect glass and ormolu mounted case, set to one side with figure of cupid with portrait medallion of a beauty, white marble and ormolu stepped base, late 19th C, 17" h .................2,645.00

Figural, sienna marble and gilt bronze, mounted with standing bronze figure of maiden playing lute beside marble arch set with mechanism, enameled dial with Arabic numerals, body set with lyre, topped by finial shaped like sheet music, rect marble base, beaded bronze feet, late 19th C, 5-5/8" l, 8-1/8" h ...................................................................................900.00

Gilt bronze and champleve, putti finial shaped case modeled with foliage, blue and yellow foliate enamel ground, late 19th C, 5-1/2" h..................................................................................1,495.00

. Onyx and cloisonné, two-train chiming movement with Medialle d' Argent seal, enamel face pained with delicate floral swags in cloisonné dial, ovoid case with stepped green onyx top, over four curved glass panels with cloisonné accent stripes, green onyx base with flattened cloisonné ball feet, late 19th/early 20th C, 12" h ....................................2,200.00

Gubelin, Switzerland, 20th C, marble and enamel, rect, two front doors with enamel plaques of medieval falconer and lady, clock face enameled with three further figures and Latin motto, int. of doors enameled with figures, face sgd "Richay," green marble sides and base, eight-day movement, 5-1/8" w, 1-1/2" d, 5-1/8" h.............................2,875.00

Louis XVI Style, third quarter 19th C, lyre form, gilt bronze, mounted porcelain, illegible signature, foliate cast mounts .........................................................................................4,325.00

Napoleon III, c1870-75, polished black slat and inset Brescia marble, enameled circular dial, marble basal plaque missing on right, 14-1/4" w, 7" d, 9" h ......................................660.00

Napoleon III, late 19th C, marble and slate, pair of 10-1/2" h coupes, 17" h clock marked "C. DeFouche," open escapement and time and strike movement, circular face, beveled glass revealing pendulum ..........................................990.00

New Haven Clock Co., French Empire style, cast iron and cast metal, bronze finish, brass works, porcelain dial mkd "New Haven Clock Co.," wear, damage, chips to beveled glass, 15-1/2" h, 20" l ............................................................500.00

Regency, English, first half 19th C, mahogany veneered and inlaid, two-train chiming movement, rounded hood with tapered pediment topped by brass ball finial, inlaid to front with fruitwood and ebony stringing, rect plinth base with engaged reeded brass columns on front, four brass ogee bracket feet, 28" h............................................................5,475.00

Royal Bonn-Style, Germany, late 19th/early 20th C, porcelain, enamel and gilt dec, dark blue ground, scrolled floral relief, molded front hoof feet, 15-1/2" h .............................1,035.00

Miniature

French, late 19th C, three section screen form, enamel plaques with figures in 18th C costume, rococo style bronze frames, 6-3/4" h .......................................................1,725.00

Silver and Agate, Cartier, white porcelain dial with decorative gold bands, black enameled Roman numerals, silver base numbered "1200," orig fitted box with dedication, sgd .......... 3,220.00

Viennese, onion dome shape, enameled panels, ormolu frames, late 19th C, 5-1/2" h .......... 1,725.00

Night Light, Standard Novelty Co, NY, nickel plated case, 30 hour lever Ansonia movement, revolving milk glass dome, 6" h .......... 225.00

Paperweight, E. N. Welch, Bristol, CT, 1860, Briggs Rotary Patent, rotary escapement mounted on turned wood base, cast feet, orig glass dome, nickel plated pendulum ball, 8" h .......... 300.00

Plateau, Continental, late 19th/early 20th C, marble and bronze mounted, corners mounted with bronze flower-form finials, gilt metal scroll mounts to three sides, front set with two-train chiming movement with Roman numerals, round glass face, 11-3/4" w, 11-3/4" d, 6-1/8" h .......... 920.00

Pillar and Scroll, shelf, Eli Terry

Mahogany and curly maple refinished case with mahogany veneer, wooden works, painted wooden face and weights, pendulum, and key, paper label "Eli Terry, Plymouth Hollow, Connecticut," orig reverse glass painting very worn and flaking, replaced brass finials, repairs to case, 31-1/4" h .......... 2,000.00

Mahogany, Federal, c1822, miniature, swan's neck cresting above glazed door with eglomise tablet showing classical building, white painted gilt dec wooden dial, thirty-hour wooden weight driven movement, case with freestanding turned columns, cutout feet, old refinish, 22-1/2" h, 13-1/2" w, 4" d .......... 7,475.00

Regulator, jeweler's, standing, carved mahogany case, large door fitted with dome top beveled edge glass pane, large enameled brass ring supporting large brass pendulum, 66" h, 27-1/2" w, 10" d .......... 2,000.00

Shelf

Ansonia, Victorian, walnut case, old finish, brass works mkd "The King Clock by Ansonia," orig glass with gold enameling, missing 3 medallions, loose finial, 23-1/2" h .......... 250.00

Atkins and Downs

Eight day triple, reverse painted glass with buildings, pendulum window and split columns, middle section with mirror and full columns, top section with dec dial, split columns, top crest with spread eagle, most of orig label remains, 38" h, 17" w, 6" d .......... 450.00

**Seth Thomas, brass case, beveled glass panels, mfg for Shreve, Crump & Low, Boston, $110. Photo courtesy of Joy Luke Fine Art Brokers and Auctioneers.**

**E. N. Welch, walnut case, teardrop shaped finials, 8 day movement, wear to gilt trim on door, $300.**

Reverse painted portrait of Henry Clay, stenciled top crest, half columns, orig paper label, 32" h, 16-1/4" w, 4-1/2" d .......... 800.00

Botsford's Improved Patent Timepiece, Coe & Co. 52 Dey St, New York, papier-mâché, scrolled front, gilt, polychrome embellishments, mother of pearl floral designs, circular enamel dial inscribed "Saml. S. Spencer," lever spring-driven movement, mounted on dec oval base, brass ball feet, glass dome, 11" h .......... 1,265.00

Classical, Norris North, Torrington, CT, c1825, mahogany, flat cornice above glazed door, eglomise tablet of young woman flanked by engaged black paint stenciled columns, polychrome and gilt white painted dial, thirty-hour wooden weight driven movement, 23-3/4" h, 13-1/2" w, 5-1/4" d .......... 4,900.00

Empire, mahogany veneer, ebonized and stencil gilded pilasters and crest, wooden works with weights, key, and pendulum, very worn paper label "William Orion & Co.," door with mirror in base, replaced reverse painted glass in middle section, finials missing, some veneer damage and repair 350.00

Federal, New England, early 19th C, mahogany and mahogany veneer, shaped fretwork joining three plinths and brass urn finials, flat cornice, glazed veneer door, white painted wood dial with red painted drapery, lower projecting base with crossbanded frame and flame mahogany panel pierced for viewing pendulum, slightly flaring French feet, 39" h, 13-3/4" w, 5-1/2" d, imperfections, replaced old movement .......... 1,500.00

Eli Terry, Plymouth, CT, c1817-18, mahogany, flat cornice above glazed door enclosing painted and gilt wooden dial, thirty-hour wooden weight-driven movement with outside escapement, flanking freestanding columns, flat molded base, engraved label "Patent invented, made and sold by Eli Terry, Plymouth, Conn," old finish, imperfections, 16" w, 20-3/4" h .......... 4,255.00

Treat and Bishop for George Mitchell, Bristol, CT, c1830, miniature, scrolled crest and square plinths above glazed door with engraved columns, eglomise tablet enclosing white painted and gilt dial, thirty-hour wooden weight-driven movement, refinished, imperfections, 11-1/4" w, 21" h .......... 2,530.00

Willard, Aaron, Boston, c1825, Federal

Mahogany and mahogany veneer, mahogany case with pierced fretwork centering fluted plinth and brass ball finial, flat half-round molded cornice, glazed door with half-round molding framing eglomise tablet with shield spandrels, inscribed "Aaron Willard Jr. Boston," iron concave white and gilt dial, brass eight-day weight driven striking movement, lower mahogany hinged door, rounded base, ball feet, refinished and restored, 36-1/4" h, 13" w, 6" d ............... 2,990.00

Mahogany, molded plinth above glazed door, eglomise tablet of lyre spandrels and foliate designs, oval inscribed "Aaron Willard Boston," wooden framed white painted concave iron dial, eight-day weight-drive brass movement, lower section with mirror, framed by rounded moldings, ball feet, refinished, imperfections, 31" h............................... 7,500.00

Ship, Chelsea, 1920, 8 day time brass movement, second bit, 5-1/4" d ........................................................ 200.00

Skeleton, metal figure of man and dog on wood base, glass dome missing, 19" h .................................................. 900.00

Tall

American, John Field, Cumberland, RI, 1760-80, carved cherry, molded hood with carved rosettes and piral carved finials mounted on fluted plinths, glazed door with arched top opening to engraved brass dial with silvered engraved arch inscribed "Soon Man's Hour Is Up and We Are Gone" over Father Time figure moving against painted landscape, silvered chapter ring with numerals for date, hour, and seconds, silvered plat engraved "John Field Cumberland No. 2," eight-day brass weight-driven movement, flanked by fluted free-standing columns above thumb-molded shell carved free-standing columns, thumb-molded shell carved blocked waist door, blocked and shell carved base, ogee bracket feet, old surface, imperfections, 95" h.................. 61,900.00

Chippendale

New Hampshire, Issac Blasdel, Chester, curly maple, hood with flat molded cornice above tombstone arch and glazed door flanked by full standing columns, brass dial with pewter boss in arch engraved "Issac Blasdel, Chester," with cast pewter spandrels framing engraved chapter ring and calendar aperture, pull-up posted frame single-weight movement, waist with thumb molded tombstone door with glazed opening, molded stepped base, refinished, minor imperfections, 85" h .................................................... 23,000.00

Pennsylvania, walnut, dark orig finish, engraved signature on back of works "Wilson" (attributed to William Wilson, Newtown, PA), dovetailed bonnet with free standing turned columns, arched door and molded cornice with goose neck pediment with brass rosettes and turned flame finial, overhanging door with scalloped top corners, cove molding between sections, ogee feet with inset panel in base, brass works with second hand and calendar movement, painted iron face with pheasant crest and rose spandrels, weights and pendant, minor restoration, replaced brass rosettes, 97" h ...................................................... 7,150.00

Continental, mid 19th C, craved oak, face sgd "Mezaize, orfeure, Horloger a Bacquevelle," two train movement, enameled face with Roman numerals, hood elaborately carved with crest of urn with cascading fruit and flowers, face flanked by further fruits and flowers, plain case with glass door with husk carving on all four sides, short plinth base, 21" w, 92-1/2" h.............................................. 1,495.00

English

Figured mahogany veneer with inlay, scalloped crest, rope carved columns with brass Corinthian capitals, cove molding between sections, bracket feet, brass works, painted metal face with phases of moon dial, ship, and calendar movement, weights and pendulum, second hand missing, replaced eagle finials, center finial missing, replaced feet, 82-3/4" h ............................................................ 3,250.00

George III, mahogany, J. McKibain, Lisburn, c1800, arched bonnet, brass dial with lunar aperture and subsidiary dial, waisted case, plinth base......................................... 1,610.00

George III, mahogany, inscribed "Martin Crosby," c1775, engraved face with brass chapter ring, date aperture, subsidiary seconds dial and cherub spandrels, rolling moon in arch, hood with broken pediment, gilt-glass frieze and freestanding columns, shaped trunk door flanked by reeded quarter columns, outset molded base with paneled front, canted corners, and ogee bracket feet, 95" h.......... 6,250.00

Gothic Revival, mahogany, old finish, brass works, phase of moon dial, cast and engraved detail, labeled "Elliott, London," tubular Westminster and Whittington chimes, weights, key, and pendulum (with mercury removed), 97" h.. 7,700.00

Renaissance Revival, late 19th C, carved oak, face sgd "Whitehurst Derby," phases of moon and date to crest, allegorical figures of the seasons on four corners, two-train chiming movement, hood with swan's neck cresting topped with three brass ball finials, door with chip carving, flanked by applied dec of grotesque mask above scrolls, case carved to two front edges with crowned male herms in pediments, door carved with crowned bearded male figure holding sword, grotesque mask below, plinth base carved to front edges with lion herms, foliate scroll carving on front and base, 18-1/2" w, 9-5/8" d, 92-1/2" h ........................ 2,650.00

Straus Farringdon, dial dec with fox hunting scene at top, dec floral corners, brass works, oak case with mahogany veneer dec banding, dec diamond shaped inlaid bird on branch in door, split column front with matching split columns on hood, scroll top, ogee bracket base, glass cracked in door, minor chips to veneer, 86" h ............................................... 2,200.00

Federal

Massachusetts, Boston or Roxbury, William Cummens, mahogany inlaid, hood with pierced fretwork joining three inlaid plinths and brass finials above the arched cornice molding, inlaid tombstone glazed door with brass beaded liner framing the white painted iron dial with polychrome and gilt floral dec, second hand, calendar aperture inscribed "Warranted by Wm. Cummens," flanked by reeded brass stop fluted columns, waist with inlaid molded rect door, string inlaid base, ogee bracket feet, finials appear to be orig, old refinish, minor imperfections, 96-1/2" h ................. 34,500.00

New York or New Jersey, c1800, inlaid mahogany, scrolled pediment with brass rosettes above a frieze with central inlaid keystone and edge inlays, polychrome painted iron dial with second hand and calendar aperture, eight-day brass movement, hood flanked by free standing inlaid column, shaped waist door flanked by inlaid engaged quarter columns above base with cyma curved skirt, delicate bracket feet, case ornamented with neoclassical stringing and banding, patterned and pictorial inlays, inlaid carved circles and rectangles, old refinish, veneer losses, glass cracked, provenance includes 178? Letter stating name of original purchaser, Long Island, NY, 93" h.............................. 13,800.00

New York or New Jersey, c1800-10, inlaid mahogany, hood with scrolling crest and cast brass rosettes center plinth of contrasting stringing on keystone, frieze with inlaid fluting at corners above free-standing fluted columns which flank glazed door enclosing floral painted arched dial with calendar aperture and second hand, eight-day brass weight driven movement, waist with three bands of inlaid fluting at top, fluted quarter columns at corners, door with elliptical inlay within rect on bottom, base with cove molding at top, circular inlay on front, replaced bracket feet, old refinish, 92" h............................................................... 7,475.00

New York or New Jersey, c1815-20, mahogany and mahogany veneer, hood with molded swan's neck cresting above glazed tombstone door flanked by reeded columns, painted iron dial with polychrome and gilt designs of urn in the arch, shield spandrels with seconds hand, calendar aperture, eight-day brass weight-driven movement, waist with shaped door flanked by reeded quarter columns on base, cutout feet, old finish, minor imperfections .......................... 6,900.00

Ohio, cherry, figured mahogany veneer cross banding, bonnet with free standing columns, arched pediment with goose necks and turned finials, chamfered corners, cove molding between sections, scrolled apron, cut-out feet, mellow finish, brass works stamped "J. E. Stretcher," (John Stretcher, Cincinnati, OH, 1826-29), second hand and calendar movement, painted metal face with polychrome flowers in crest, shells in spandrels, touch-up on face, pendulum, weights, key, 94" h ....................................... 6,200.00

French Provincial, third quarter 19th C, polychromed, kettle form, enameled dial above faux-bois case, scrolling floral accents, bracket feet, dial signed "Lethiec/à/Bain-de-Pretagne," 19-1/2" w, 8" d, 92" h............................ 1,320.00

Ohio, Watson, decorated, pine, orig reddish brown vinegar grained paint, face with orig painted dec, gilded spandrels, crest with red swag in arch, sgd "L. Watson, Cincinnati" (Lumen Watson, Cincinnati, OH, c1820-35), bonnet with free standing reeded columns, molded and curved cornice with fretwork, three brass finials, reeded quarter columns with brass trim, molded waist, scalloped apron, cut out feet, few areas of touch-up, one finial replaced, orig pain inside door shows bright unaged color, 91" h........................... 27,500.00

Renaissance Revival-style, late 19th C, carved oak, three-train movement chiming on Westminster or Whittington bells, dial with Arabic numerals, subsidiary dials for seconds, chimes, chime/strike, phases of the moon, arch top hood with gadroon carving, door flanked by two musicians, case carved on front with further gadrooning and lions' heads, front door with applied carved strapwork flanked by putto heads, plinth base with carved inset of revelers flanked by lion's head herms, 92" h ....................................... 14,950.00

Waterbury Clock Co., late 19th C, labeled on back "Hall Clock no. 62," two-train movement, Arabic numerals, subsidiary seconds dial and gilt mounts, rounded hood with C-scrolls on top, flanked by urn form finials, tapered case with further C-scroll and bead detailing around glass-fronted door, tapered plinth, veneer inlaid beaded roundel, 90-1/2" h ................................................................. 3,450.00

**Adv, Baird Clock Co., Chicago, IL, Seth Thomas 15 day movement, blue, cream dial, c1890, working order, 19-3/4" d, 30-1/2" h, $1,590.**

Wall Banjo

Federal, Massachusetts, c1820, mahogany and gilt gesso, circular molded brass bezel, convex glass, white painted iron dial, brass weight driven-movement above throat and pendulum box, eglomise tablets inscribed "Patent" and shows classical building, framed by spiral gilt gesso moldings, flanked by pierced brass brackets, 30" h ................. 1,850.00

Federal, Boston, c1815, mahogany case, gilt finial, molded brass bezel, white painted iron dial, eight-day brass weight driven movement with T-bridge escapement above throat and pendulum mirror tablets, framed by mahogany cross-banding flanked by brass side pieces, old finish, 34" h ......................................................... 8,625.00

E. Howard & Co., Boston, #5, rosewood grained, circular molded bezel enclosing white painted metal dial inscribed "Howard & Co., Boston," eight-day weight-driven movement above half round moldings framing throat and pendulum box eglomise black and maroon tablets, very minor imperfections, 28-1/2" h........................................................ 2,450.00

A. Willard, Jr., mahogany case, brass trim and façade, old gold repaint, brass works, painted steel faced mkd "A. Willard Jr., Boston," reverse painted glass panels are old replacements, bottom panel with ship flying American flag, eagle finial, orig weight and pendulum, 33" h .......... 1,100.00

Cartel, George III, fourth quarter 19th C, carved giltwood, twin fusee striking movement, sgd silvered dial with subsidiary dials and date, Roman and Arabic numerals, case topped with eagle with outstretched wings above C-scroll surround, 28" w, 41-1/2" h...................................................... 12,650.00

European, 24" h, ebonized convoluted oval frame with inner facade with nacre inlay around brass ring, repainted metal face, brass works, pendulum and key, repairs............ 225.00

French, Ferdinand Berthoud, white enamel dial with black second and hour numbers, sgd "Fd. Berthoud A PARIS," round brass housing with applied ormolu cornucopias of flowers on sides, intertwined with bow at bottom, works sgd "L. Moinet A PARIS," key and pendulum present, weights missing, 13" h, 11" ................................................... 1,500.00

French Normandy, embossed brass facade and pendulum, brass works in sheet steel case, enameled face with "Andre Spéth à la Charité" and flowers, hairlines and yellowed repair to face, weights and key, replacement wrought iron shelf, 56" l.................................................................... 950.00

Swiss, Regulator, late 19th C, walnut, three-train weighted chiming movement, enameled dial sgd "Jos. Stand, Zwittan," shell carved pediment flanked by finals over stepped cornice, tapered base flanked by further finials, carved shell, 52" h ....................................................................... 1,265.00

# CLOISONNÉ

**History:** Cloisonné is the art of enameling on metal. The design is drawn on the metal body, then wires, which follow the design, are glued or soldered on. The cells thus created are packed with enamel and fired; this step is repeated several times until the level of enamel is higher than the wires. A buffing and polishing process brings the level of enamels flush to the surface of the wires. This art form has been practiced in various countries since 1300 B.C. and in the Orient since the early 15th century. Most cloisonné found today is from the late Victorian era, 1870-1900, and was made in China or Japan.

**Reference:** Lawrence A. Cohen and Dorothy C. Ferster, *Japanese Cloisonné*, Charles E. Tuttle Co., 1990.

**Collectors' Club:** Cloisonne Collectors Club, P.O. Box 96, Rockport, MA 01966.

**Pot, cov, 2 arms, 3 applied feet, wooden stand, dragons motif, 33" h, $2,000. Photo courtesy of Joy Luke Fine Art Brokers and Auctioneers.**

**Periodical:** *Orientalia Journal*, P.O. Box 94, Flushing, NY 11363-0094, http://members.aol.com/Orientalia/index.html

**Museum:** George Walter Vincent Smith Art Museum, Springfield, MA.

Box, cov, silver wire, chrysanthemums, pale mustard ground, Meiji period ................................................................ 300.00
Candelabra, moon flask shape, ormolu mounts, sgd "F. Barbedienne, France," c1870, pr .............................................. 8,250.00
Censer, cov
    Archaism dec, ornate finial, 18th C ............................... 34,100.00
    Chinese, Qianlong period, 13" d .................................... 48,875.00
    Namikawa Sosuke style, tripod, wireless ........................ 6,100.00
Charger, 18" d, five clawed dragons, turquoise ground, formalized lotus scrolls on ext., 19th C, price for pr ................................ 1,100.00
Figure, 10" h, parrot, green and yellow, perched position, carved wood, 4" d x 1-1/2" h base, 19th C, pr .................................................. 500.00
Hot Water Pot, 11-1/2" h, formalized lotus plants, turquoise ground, repousse gilt-metal mounts with Buddhistic emblems, China, late 19th C ................................................................................. 400.00
Incense Burner
    4" h, tsuiki-jippo technique on silver, form of stylized hydrangea flowers, blue body, three green leaves, hydrangea flower at top, Japan, late 19th/early 20th C, minor loss ...................... 2,100.00
    7" h, covered, floral dec globular form, foo lion mask handles, tripod base, Chinese, 19th C ............................................... 125.00
Tray, 10-3/4" sq, rounded corners, design of bird on rose bush, shaded gray ground, sgd with two characters and seal, reverse with flower, late 19th C ......................................................................... 3,335.00
Vase
    7-1/2" h, silver wire work of seasonal flowers, one on celadon ground, other midnight blue, late 19th/early 20th C, price for pr ...................................................................................... 690.00
    9-1/2" h, hexagonal, silver wire, iris design, midnight blue ground, Japanese.............................................................................. 690.00
    10" h, tall, thin shaped, six panels to tapered center, flaring lip and base, black ground, decorative panels of birds, dragons, and flower bands ........................................................................... 200.00

10-7/8" w, 7-1/2" w, flared neck, jade green ground, silver mounts at top and bottom, stylized leaf and Greek key design top border, stylized leaf designs around center, Greek Key design at base, apple green counter enamel, silver wire, Art Deco Style, c1920, Ando Jubei mark on base in silver wire ............. 4,500.00
11-1/2" h, silver wire work of flowers and insects, teal blue ground, ornate brocade borders, Japan, Meiji period, c1880, price for pr ............................................................................. 1,610.00
12" h, silver wire work, lobed form, long trumpet neck, finely detailed brocade pattern, stylized phoenix and dragon panels, goldstone border, Japan, Meiji period, c1890 ................. 690.00
13-1/2" h, one side with perched bird, other with foliage, Japanese, early 20th C ...................................................... 1,265.00
23" h, hexagonal, hundred antiques dec, turquoise ground, Chinese, c1900, price for pr .............................................. 1,700.00

# CLOTHING and ACCESSORIES, DESIGNER and COUTURE

**History:** For many of us, watching the award shows is a good place to study current fashions and accessories. But what happens to those beautiful garments after the event is over? Some are consigned to auction, others donated to charities and museums, while still others are used as patterns for knock-off designs for the masses. For this edition, there is a concentration on designer and couture clothing. Vintage clothing and fashion is becoming a hot segment of the antiques and collectible market. Some buyers are looking for vintage clothing with interesting designs, fabrics, and colors to collect and enjoy. Other buyers are looking for clothes they can wear and enjoy. Perhaps they sometimes pause to think about what kind of exciting life this particular dress or accessory might have all ready had. Some collectors concentrate on clothing they feel exemplifies a certain period of history, style, or a particular designer.

Clothing, by it's very nature, is often short lived as natural materials age and fade. Add the stress of wearing an article for many seasons, laundering techniques that might have been too harsh, giving clothing a shorter life than many other kinds of antiques. Look for clothing with interesting designs, in good repair, sturdy fabrics, and always remember to check the label for a designer's name or retailer's name. Skinner, Inc. and many other auction houses regularly auctions these couture and designer clothing allowing collectors the chance to bid on glitter and glamour, and perhaps owning some special dress at a fraction of the original price. Cared for properly, these designer and couture clothing will appreciate in value.

**References:** LaRue Johnson Bruton, *Ladies' Vintage Accessories*, Collector Books, 2000; Blanche Cirker (ed.), *1920s Fashions From B. Altman & Company*, Dover, 1999; Paula Jean Darnell, *Victorian to Vamp, Women's Clothing 1900-1929*, Fabric Fancies, 2000; Roseann Ettinger, *Handbags*, 3rd ed., Schiffer Publishing, 1999; Roselyn Gerson, *Vintage & Contemporary Purse Accessories*, Collector Books, 1997; —, *Vintage& Vogue Ladies*

*Compacts*, 2nd ed., Collector Books, 2000; —, *Vintage Vanity Bags and Purses*, Collector Books, 1994, 1997 value update; *Michael Jay Goldberg, The Ties That Blind*, Schiffer Publishing, 1997; Carol Belanger Grafton, *Fashions of the Thirties*, Dover Publications, 1993; —, *Shoes, Hats and Fashion Accessories*, Dover Publications, 1998; —, *Victorian Fashion: A Pictorial Archive*, Dover Publications, 1999; Helenka Gulshan, *Vintage Luggage*, Phillip Wilson Publishers, 1998; Kristina Harris, *Authentic Victorian Dressmaking Techniques*, Dover Publications, 1999; —, *Collector's Guide to Vintage Fashions*, Collector Books, 1999; —, *Victorian & Edwardian Fashions for Women*, Schiffer Publishing, 1995; —, *Vintage Fashions for Women*, Schiffer Publishing, 1996; Richard Holiner, *Antique Purses*, Collector Books, 1999 value upate; Erhard Klepper, *Costume Through The Ages*, Dover Publications, 1999; Elizabeth Kurella, *The Complete Guide to Vintage Textiles*, Krause Publications, 1999; Susan Langley, *Vintage Hats & Bonnets, 1770-1970*, Collector Books, 1997, 1999 value update; Ellie Laubner, *Fashions of the Roaring '20s*, Schiffer Publishing, 1996; —, *Fashions of the Turbulent 1930s*, Schiffer Publishing, 2000; Jan Lindenberger, *Clothing & Accessories from the '40s, '50s, & '60s*, Schiffer Publishing, 1996; Sally C. Luscomb, *The Collector's Encyclopedia of Buttons*, Schiffer Publishing, 1997; Rosanna Mihalick, *Collecting Handkerchiefs*, Schiffer Publishing, 2000; Laura M. Mueller, *Collector's Encyclopedia of Compacts, Carryalls & Face Powder Boxes*, Collector Books, Vol. I (1999 values), Vol. II (1997 values); Herbert Norris, *Ancient European Costume and Fashion, Dover Publications*, 1999; Mary Brooks Picken, *A Dictionary of Costume and Fashion: Historic and Modern*, Dover, 1999; Leslie Piña, Lorita Winfield, and Constance Korosec, *Beads in Fashion, 1900-2000*, Schiffer Publishing, 1999; Maureen Reilly, *Hot Shoes, 100 Years*, Schiffer Publishing, 1998; Desire Smith, *Fashion Footwear, 1800-1970*, Schiffer Publishing, 2000; —, *Hats*, Schiffer Publishing, 1996; —, *Vintage Styles: 1920-1960*, Schiffer Publishing, 1997; Pamela Smith, *Vintage Fashion & Fabrics*, Alliance Publishers, 1995; Jeffrey B. Snyder, *Stetson Hats & The John B. Stetson Company 1865-1970*, Schiffer Publishing, 1997; Diane Snyder-Haug, *Antique & Vintage Clothing*, Collector Books, 1996; Geoffrey Warren, *Fashion & Accessories, 1840-1980*, Schiffer Publishing, 1997; Lorita Winfield, Leslie Pina, and Constance Korosec, *Beads on Bags, 1880s to 2000*, Schiffer Publishing, 2000; Debra Wisniewski, *Antique and Collectible Buttons*, Collector Books, 1997.

**Periodicals:** *Glass Slipper*, 653 S. Orange Ave., Sarasota, FL 34236; *Lady's Gallery*, P.O. Box 1761, Independence, MO 64055; *Lill's Vintage Clothing Newsletter*, 19 Jamestown Dr., Cincinnati, OH 45241; *Vintage Clothing Newsletter*, P.O. Box 88892, Seattle, WA 98138; *Vintage Connection*, 904 N. 65th St., Springfield, OR 97478; Vintage Gazette, 194 Amity St., Amherst, MA 01002.

**Collectors' Clubs:** Textile Group of Los Angeles, Inc., 894 S. Bronson Ave., Los Angeles CA 9005-3605; The Costume Society of America, P.O. Box 73, Earleville, MD 21919, http://www.costumesocietyamerica.com; Vintage Fashion and Costume Jewelry Club, P.O. Box 265, Glen Oaks, NY 11004.

**Museums:** Bata Shoe Museum, Toronto, Canada; Fashion Institute of Technology, New York, NY; Los Angeles County Museum (Costume and Textile Dept.), Los Angeles, CA; Metropolitan Museum of Art, New York, NY; Museum of Costume, Bath, England; Philadelphia Museum of Art, Philadelphia, PA; Smithsonian Institution (Inaugural Gown Collection), Washington, DC; Wadsworth Athenaeum, Hartford, CT; Whiting and Davis Handbag Museum, Attleboro Falls, MA.

Caftan
> Arden, Elizabeth, floor length, pale pink sari fabric woven with metallic gold, burgundy, and green floral pattern, long full sleeves, V-neck, center front buttons, labeled "Elizabeth Arden, the Salon" at neckline, size 8, 1970s .............................. 140.00
>
> Trigère, Pauline, three-quarter length, brown silk chiffon and metallic gold, A-line, embroidered with stripes of diamond-patterned metallic gold thread, round neckline, fitted shoulders, very long cape sleeves fall to hem, labeled "Pauline Trigère" and "Ted Saunders, the Ritz Carlton Hotel, Boston," size 8, 1964 .............................................................................. 360.00

Coat
> Courrèges, three-quarter length, green and white wool and acrylic blend, fitted silhouette, center front button closure, long sleeves, pointed collar, welted seam detail, two front stand pockets, white plastic Courrèges logo on center front, ivory acetate lining, labeled "Courrèges, Paris, Made in France, 88142" at neckline and "Made in France for I. Magnin & Co." at side seam, size 6, 1970s .......................................................................... 920.00
>
> Dior, Christian, three-quarter length, gray wool, cocoon silhouette, wide pointed collar, large center front buttons, side slash pockets, removable brown nutria lining, labeled "Boutique Christian Dior, Paris" and numbered, size 6-8, 1950s..................... 575.00
>
> Gucci, below-the-knee length, fitted red suede, center front closure with horseshoe insignia buttons, long fitted sleeves, pointed collar, four front flap pockets, labeled "Gucci, Made in Italy" at side seam, size 6, 1975....................................... 435.00

**Cocktail Dress, Christian Dior, periwinkle blue silk taffeta, large bow at center front bodice, orig label, $690. Photo courtesy of Skinner, Inc.**

Magnin, I., below-the-knee length, black cashmere, cocoon silhouette, wide pointed collar, oversized center front buttons, black satin lining, labeled "I. Magnin" at back neckline, size 6-8, 1950s ............................................................................. 350.00

Revillon, knee length, white mink, full silhouette and white fox trim at collar, cuffs, shoulders, and hem, white silk lining, labeled "Revillon, London-Paris-New York" at neckline, size medium to large, 1980s .................................................................... 550.00

**Cocktail Dress**

Carneige, Hatti, below-the-knee length, midnight blue raw silk, printed with black floral pattern, fitted bodice with round neckline, cap sleeves, natural waist leading to full skirt, four wide inverted pleats at back, wide rolled hem, labeled "Hattie Carnegie" at bodice side seam, size 6, 1950s ........................ 115.00

Chanel, sheer striped silk, floor length, shades of pink and purple, sleeveless bloused bodice with high ruffled collar, elasticized waistband, flowing two-layer skirt, lilac satin bow at back neck and waist, fuchsia silk skirt lining, labeled "Chanel, Creations-Paris" and "Neiman Marcus" at neckline, size 8, 1970s...375.00

Chapman, Ceil, below-the-knee length, black crepe, allover sequins in vermicelli pattern, fitted camisole bodice, natural waist, flared skirt, labeled "Ceil Chapman" at bodice, size 6, mid 1950s .......................................................................... 1,035.00

Dior, Christian, tea length

Periwinkle blue silk taffeta, round neckline, short sleeves, full skirt, large bow at center front bodice with fringed ends hanging below waist, chiffon lining, labeled "Christian Dior-New York" and "Bergdorf Goodman on the Plaza" at skirt seam, size 8-10, mid-1950s.......................... 690.00

Strapless, bodice of black chantilly lace over ivory satin, sweetheart neckline, black silk taffeta cummerbund wraps around to tie at front waist, accordion-pleated taffeta skirt, boned int. bodice, labeled "Christian Dior-New York Original" at waist, size 2-4, 1950s, light soil on skirt and int. ...... 225.00

Galanos, knee length, black and lime green tufted velvet in oversized paisley pattern, long dolman sleeves, V-neck, black beads and rect rhinestones adorn neckline and waist area, form faux necklace, black chiffon lining, labeled "Galanos" at waist, size 6, 1980s ..................................... 165.00

Greer, Howard, three-quarter length, ivory cotton dress, allover bugle beads and rhinestones in wave like pattern, fitted silhouette with sweetheart neckline, short sleeves, side slash pockets, narrow skirt, flesh colored ivory lining at bust, labeled "Howard Greer, Hollywood" at back waistline, slight bead loss, size 4, 1950s ............................................ 690.00

Heim, Jacques, silver silk satin, hand embroidered with foliate design in pale blue silk, silver bugle beads, crystal seed beads, pink sequins, fitted camisole bodice with dropped waistline, attached belt with self-tie at center front, crinolined below-the-knee length skirt, labeled "Heim Actualité, Cannes, Paris, Biarritz" and "20930" written in ink on back of label, size 6-8, 1950s................................................. 350.00

Mackie, Bob, mini-dress, gold beaded, upper bodice with high band collar, padded shoulders, bugle bead fringe yoke, flesh-colored mid-section with rhinestones in diamond pattern, adorned with goldtone coins, bugle bead fringe also adorns zig-zag hem, flesh colored silk and net lining, labeled "Bob Mackie" at back bodice, size 6, 1970s ............ 1,840.00

Pertegaz, Manuel, black paper taffeta and chantilly lace, wrapped taffeta sleeveless bodice, very full skirt with alternating layers of chantilly lace and ballooned taffeta, together with lace shawl, taffeta cummerbund, int. boned bodice, size 4, 1951 .................................................................. 460.00

Pucci, Emilio, floor length, silk jersey, black skirt, printed bodice in black, white, and shades of gray and pink, fitted bodice with low round neckline, short sleeves, empire waist, biascut full skirt, labeled "Emilio Pucci, Florence-Italy" at neckline, size 6, 1970s .................................................. 520.00

Rosenstein, Nettie

Below-the-knee length, black silk, blousy bodice, bracelet sleeves, black taffeta band collar, fitted natural waist with black taffeta sash that hangs below hemline, straight skirt, labeled "Nettie Rosenstein" at neckline, size 8-10, late 1940s .......................................................................... 130.00

Cocktail length, black silk, sleeveless sheath, high-waisted cap sleeved bodice of black guipure lace over flesh-colored net, fitted skirt with silk flower at front waist and pleated, flying panel at back waist, lined in china silk, labeled "Nettie Rosenstein" in skirt seam, "The French Shops, Filene's-Boston" at center back, size 6, c1958.............................. 290.00

**Cocktail Ensemble**

Balenciaga, black brocaded silk, below-the-knee length straight skirt, boxy sleeveless top, boxy jacket with wide three-quarter length sleeves and wide shawl collar, one center front button, hand-sewn, size 8, 1950s ............................................... 575.00

Mori, Hanae, pantsuit, over-tunic, and wrap, silk and chiffon printed with flowers, trees, butterflies, and birds in orange, blue, white, green, yellow, and pink, pantsuit with sleeveless silk bodice, chiffon palazzo pants, loose-fitting sheer orange over-tunic with round neckline and bishop sleeves, self-tie rope belt, 34" wide sheer wrap, labeled "Hanae Mon," size 8-10, 1970s230.00

Pucci, Emilio, printed silk jersey dress, bolero jacket with black, brown, pink, and orange vine and leaf pattern, beige ground, fitted dress with V-neck, spaghetti straps, floor length skirt, fitted double breasted bolero jacket with notched lapel and very full, very long bishop sleeves, labeled "Emilio Pucci, Florence-Italy" and "Exclusively for Saks Fifth Avenue" at neckline, size 8, 1970s ....................................................................... 825.00

**Cocktail Suit**

Blass, Bill, sequined jacket and pants, long-sleeved jacket with three broad stripes of yellow, red, and black with large gold beaded central medallion at center front, black sequined pants with black satin waistband, fully lined, both items labeled "Bill Blass," size 8, early 1980s ................................................. 635.00

Saint Laurent, Yves, burgundy velvet, Edwardian-inspired skirt and jacket, fitted jacket with high collar, taffeta neck ruffle, center front button closure, full peplum three-quarter length skirt, burgundy silk lining, labeled "Saint Laurent Rive Gauche" at neckline, size 6, c1980................................................... 290.00

Scherrer, Jean-Louis, metallic gold crochet jacket and skirt, fitted mid-though length unlined jacked, fitted shoulders, open front, long sleeves, A-line mid-calf length skirt lined with textured lamé, labeled "JLS Paris, Scherrer Boutique B10878" at neck and waist, size 4-6, mid 1970s......................................... 435.00

Valentino, jacket and skirt with allover sequined leopard and floral pattern in black, white, shades of gold, red, yellow, and purple, V-neck short sleeve jacket with center front closure, purple satin lining, knee length straight skirt with elastic waistband, labeled "Valentino Boutique" at neckline and waistband, size 10, early 1980s .......................................................................... 575.00

**Day Dress**

Beene, Geoffrey, below-the-knee length, forest green wool tweed, dress with high square neckline, raglan sleeves, fitted waist, circular skirt, fully lined in red tartan plaid silk, knit bolero jacket with high sq neckline, center front buttons, ruffled hem, labeled "Geoffrey Beene, New York" at neckline, size 8-10, 1970s .......................................................................... 290.00

Dior, Christian

Knee length, shirtwaist, black and brown gingham taffeta, black satin stripes, V-neck blousy bodice with lapel collar, elbow length sleeves, full skirt with inverted pleating at waist, labeled "Boutique Christian Dior, Paris" with "1526407" stamped on front, size 6, 1950s.................................. 575.00

Below-the-knee length, gray wool, round neckline, sloped shoulders, elbow length sleeves, fitted at natural waist, balloon skirt with fitted hemline, center front bow, black taffeta lining, size 8, 1950s .................................................... 325.00

Norell, Norman, three-quarter length, oatmeal colored wool knit, turtleneck, long fitted sleeves, brown leather belt at natural waist, "Norman Norell" stamped on belt, labeled "The French Shops, Filene's-Boston" at neckline, size small, 1960s ........................ 260.00

Pucci, Emilio, below-the-knee length, printed silk jersey, black, white, and shades of green, purple, and blue, fitted silhouette, round neckline, long sleeves, straight skirt, matching self-tie rope belt with beaded tassels, labeled "Emilio Pucci, Florence Italy" and "Made Exclusively for Saks Fifth Avenue" at neckline, matching sunglasses, size 6, 1970s ........ 825.00

## Evening Dress

Allard, Isabelle, floor length, black taffeta, sweetheart neckline, gathered taffeta bodice fitted to knees, skirt flares out to floor, three large center front bows and detachable puffed sleeves, black silk lining, labeled "Isabelle Allard Paris," 1980s 230.00

De la Renta, Oscar, floor length, white bodice with diagonal rows of white beads and rhinestones covering one shoulder, black silk organza skirt gathered to left side with large front bow, ruffled slit and hem, labeled "Oscar de la Renta" at neckline, size 4, 1980s ...................... 635.00

Gordon, Billy, floor length, black chiffon and crepe, halter top embroidered with celadon green sequins and rhinestones in floral pattern, fitted at natural waist with sheer two-tiered skirt, black chiffon and taffeta underskirt, labeled "California Billy Gordon Original" and "Bullocks Wilshire" at underskirt side seam, size 4-6, 1954, worn by Mrs. Van Johnson to Academy Awards ...................... 490.00

Halston, floor length, black wrap dress, accordion pleated silk, V-necked bodice with full bishop sleeves, flowing skirt, ruffled hemline, labeled "Halston" and "Sarah Fredericks" at waist, size 8, early 1980s .................... 375.00

Mackie, Bob, floor length, brown, gold, white, and silver beading, brown net beaded with bugle beads and rhinestones, high-necked bodice adorned with trompe l'oeil necklace and twisted bead rope that forms yoke above bust and across shoulders to back, long sheer beaded sleeves, center front slit from hem to knee, size 6, late 1970s, provenance includes photo of orig owner Yolanda, Boston, one of the first retailers to carry Mackie's designs ............... 750.00

Milgrim, Sally, floor length, black satin, net overdress, sleeveless satin dress with V-neck and plunging V-back, bias-cut skirt, net overdress with gathered ruffles trimming neckline and sleeves, eight rows of horizontal ruffles extending from hips to hem, overdress is slit from hem to waist at center front, labeled "Milgrim" with "Mrs. Griffith 3/2/37, No. 965" written in pen on label, size 6, 1937 ...................... 490.00

Saint Laurent, Yves, knee length, black silk crepe, V-neck bodice wraps to left and falls to form asymmetric draped front, long bishop sleeves, matching belt with long sash, labeled "Yves Saint Laurent, Rive Gauche" at neckline, size 8, c1980 .. 350.00

### Unknown Maker

Floor length, black silk crepe and organza, fitted sheet black bodice with black ostrich feathers at shoulders, ostrich feather trimmed net peplum over straight crepe skirt with center front slit, black rayon underdress, labeled "Jenkins, New York" at side seam, size 4, 1953, worn by Mrs. Van Johnson to Beverly Hills party ...................... 920.00

Floor length, blue-green and metallic gold, sari fabric, one-shouldered asymmetric bodice, straight skirt with flying panel extending from back right waist, green chiffon and taffeta lining, hand-sewn, matching wrap, size 6, early 1960s ...................... 215.00

Floor length, sequined and bugle beaded, sleeveless, fitted silhouette, round neckline, seed bead fringe zig-zags across dress from top to bottom, slit from hem to knee, black silk lining, size 10, early 1960s .................... 245.00

Mid-calf at front, floor length at back, sheer net with allover gold sequins in Art Deco inspired pattern, fitted silhouette with

sleeveless bodice, wide V-neck and cape collar at back, size 6, late 1920s, evidence of previous repair, alterations ........ 330.00

Three quarter length, peach silk crepe, sleeveless, bodice with rounded neckline, allover rhinetone and simulated pearl beading in circular pattern, dropped waistline, petal hemline with large beaded circle adornment, size 6, 1920s ..... 200.00

Evening Ensemble, Pierre Balmain, coral brocade silk, two piece, ankle length cheongsam tunic with long sleeves, bold coiled metallic gold cuffs, side slits from hem to waist, matching slim pants, labeled "Balmain Paris" at neckline, attached tape with number, size 6, 1960s .................. 460.00

## Evening Gown, floor length

Arden, Elizabeth, pale aqua and metallic gold, fitted bodice with short sleeves, wide shawl collar, trimmed with black passementerie, attached self covered belt at natural waist, full bias-cut skirt with two side pockets, labeled "Elizabeth Arden, New York-Paris" at neckline, size 8-10, late 1940s ......................... 175.00

Balenciaga, silver floral brocade and lamé, sleeveless fitted bodice with jewel neckline, low round back, bow at center front waist, full skirt, matching boxy jacket with three-quarter length sleeves, center front self-covered buttons, jacket labeled "Balenciaga, 10 Avenue Georges V, Paris" and "84483" written on pencil on tape attached to back of label, size 8, late 1950s, light soil spot on front skirt................... 750.00

Balmain, Pierre, black silk velvet, fitted silhouette, sweetheart neckline with spagetti straps, silk velvet extends to knees, adorned with large circular velvet flowers, flaring black tulle skirt extends from knees to floor, labeled "Boutique Balmain Paris" at waistline, size 6, 1950s ...................... 550.00

Bergdorf Goodman, Grecian-style white crepe, vertical silver bugle bead stripes, sleeveless wrap bodice with V-neck and back, heavily beaded faux belt at waist, according pleated skirt, white crepe lining, labeled "Made to Order, Bergdorf Goodman on the Plaza, Mrs. M. Bruce, date 12-3-67, No. 17593" at skirt seam, size 6, 1967 ......................... 450.00

Dior, Christian, black velvet, strapless, fitted bodice, 2-1/2" grosgrain band extending horizontally around bust, grosgrain band at dropped waistline with bow to left side, full skirt with three rows of grosgrain extending from hem to knee, labeled "Christian Dior-New York" at skirt side seam, "G. Fox, The Speciality Shop" at neckline, size 6, late 1950s .......................... 1,150.00

Heim, Jacques, mint green silk, sleeveless, fitted bodice with jewel neckline, plunging back, trimmed with band of small white appliqué flowers, rhinestones, crystal seed beads, pendant crystals, wide attached sash at waist, full skirt trimmed with two symmetric bands of embroidery, wide bow at center back, skirt with seven layers of crinoline, labeled "Jaques Heim, Paris" and "93530" written on ink on tape attached to back of label, matching floor length cape, size 8, lot includes oversized invitation/program to which dress was worn, soiree hosted by General de Gaulle at the Theatre Louis XV to honor President John F. Kennedy, June, 1 1961 ...................... 575.00

Jeran Design, strapless, allover bugle beading, white ground, large multicolored beaded butterfly on bodice, green beads in grass and butterfly pattern extends from hem to waist, side slit from hem to knee, white silk lining, labeled "Jeran Design" at center back, size 6, 1980s ............................. 1,265.00

### Mackie, Bob

Black, sequin, and bugle beads, purple fuchsia, red, gold, blue, and aqua stripes, fitted sheath with sweetheart neckline, spaghetti straps, front left slit, black silk lining, labeled "Yolanda Designer's Shop" at back bodice, size 6, late 1970s ...................... 920.00

Ivory silk charmeuse and beaded net, flesh-colored net over-bodice adorned with gold and white bugle beads and faux pearls in Egyptian-inspired design, round neckline and long sleeves, ivory underdress forms skirt, attached beaded and tasseled belt, ivory silk and chiffon linings, labeled "Bob Mackie" at bodice, size 8-10, 1980s ........................... 225.00

Taj Mahal, strapless silk chiffon, beaded bodice of ivory net with white and gold bugle beads and pearls in Taj Majal design on center front, full skirt of ivory silk chiffon with white underskirt, bodice lined in flesh-colored silk, labeled "Yolanda Designer's Collection" at back bodice, size 6-8, 1970s .................................................................................. 575.00

Macrin, Rosalie, beaded ivory silk satin, fitted camisole bodice and natural waist, skirt with wide inverted pleats at waist to create fullness, bodice and skirt embroidered with abstract circular pattern in silver bugle beads and irid sequins, ivory satin stole, hand and machine sewn, labeled "Rosaline Macrin, New York" at skirt seam, size 4, early 1950s . 200.00

McFadden, Mary, white, silver, and gold, long-sleeved floral lace bodice with round neckline, bodice embroidered with pearls, white sequins, seed beads, sequins, silver diamantes, and bugle beads, small gold braid, gold bugle beads and white silk embroidery thread, white finely pleated skirt with fishtail train, labeled "Mary McFadden" at neckline, size 6, late 1970s, garment was model from first Mary McFadden wedding gown line ....................................................................................... 575.00

Molyneux, orange silk with metallic gold trapunto quilting in abstract pattern, camisole bodice, empire waist, back slit, matching 15" wide floor length wrap, orange silk lining, hand finished interior, labeled "Molyneux, Paris" at center back, size 6, 1960s ........................................................................ 375.00

Unknown Maker
Silver bugle beads, fitted sleeveless sheath with round neckline, side slit, lined in ivory satin and china silk, hand-finished interior, size 8, 1960s ............................................................ 290.00

## Evening Jacket

De la Renta, Oscar, knee length, black silk organza, nine rows of large ruffles, round neckline, elbow length ruffled sleeves, very full silhouette, black chiffon lining, labeled "Oscar de la Renta" and "Saks Fifth Avenue" at neckline, size small to medium, early 1960s ....................................................................................... 435.00

Kamali, Norma, Ono, faux zebra, wrap-type jacket, belt, labeled "Norma Kamali" at neckline, size 8, early 1980s ............... 115.00

Saint Laurent, Yves, pink marabou feathers, long sleeves, center front opening, pink ostrich feather trim at neckline, hem, and wrists, pink acetate lining, labeled "Saint Laurent Rive Gauche" at neckline, size small to medium, 1980s ......................... 980.00

## Evening Top and Matching Bag, Loris Azzaro, 1970s

Gold crocheted top, attached goldtone chain fringe imitating chain mail, fitted bodice with bateau neck, chain elbow length sleeves, looped chain hem, matching 9" x 5-1/2" evening purse ... 690.00

Silver crocheted top, attached silver chain fringe, fitted silhouette with low V-neck, center front snap closure covered by 20" fringe, long chain sleeves, chain fringe from below bust to hips, matching 9" x 15" evening purse .................................... 815.00

## Hat

Ben, Bes, close fitting velvet and net headpiece adorned with papier-mâché yellow bananas and green leaves, gold leaf embellishment, labeled "Bes Ben, Made in Chicago" ...... 550.00

Jones, black satin, mini-pillbox, ornamental white puff at top, purple satin lining, labeled "Stephen Jones, Handmade in England" ....................................................................................... 75.00

Schooler, small disk with black taffeta bow, black net, stand-up irid feathers ....................................................................... 50.00

## Purse

Bon Ton, 9-1/2" x 7-1/2" x 3", brown crocodile box bag, goldtone hardware, short crocodile handle, brown satin lining with "Bon Ton & Co," 1930s ............................................................. 320.00

Chanel, 7-1/2" x 4-1/2" x 1-1/2", black quilted shoulder envelope bag, long black leather and goldtone chain shoulder strap, double "C" logo on front, burgundy leather lining stamped "Chanel, Made in France," closure also stamped "Chanel Paris," 1980s .. 260.00

Gucci, 9-1/2" x 7" x 3", black satin, petal-inspired design, three compartments, rhinestone clasp, rhinestone vines handle attach-

ments, black silk lining with three interior pockets, stamped "Gucci" on lining, 1940s ................................................... 375.00

Hermès
10" x 7" x 2", rect taupe alligator shoulder bag, front flap, circular goldtone clasp, shoulder strap, taupe leather lining, "Hermès, Paris, Made in France" stamped on lining, 1970s ...................................................................................... 1,150.00

12-1/2" x 9-1/2" x 5", chestnut brown alligator Kelly bag with lock and key, detachable shoulder strap, brown leather lining, "Hermès, Paris, Made in France" stamped in gold under flap, "Hermès,-Paris" stamped on hardware, 1970s 9,200.00

13" x 9" x 5", black pebble grain leather Kelly bag, black leather int. with three inner pockets, "Hermès, Paris, Made in France" stamped in gold under flap, "Hermès,-Paris" stamped on hardware, 1980s ................................... 1,840.00

Langolis & Jargeais, 8" x 6" x 1", red, gold, and silver cut-steel beads in foliate pattern, goldtone frame with rhinestone clasp, short beaded handle, labeled "Langlois & Jargeais, 4 Rue Vaucanson, Paris" on interior, red satin lining, 1933 ........................................................................................ 460.00

Leiber, Judith
9" x 3-1/2" x 4", lozenge shape, hard-sided black leather, top closure, short round handle, black satin lining, "Judith Leiber" printed in gold on lining, 1980s ........................ 635.00

13" x 8" x 2", white clutch, alternating overlapping bands of lizard and leather, amethyst and stone encrusted strip at top closure, white grosgrain lining, matching change purse, gold-plated comb and mirror, detachable thin shoulder strap, "Judith Leiber" stamped goldtone plate on interior, 1970s .......... 250.00

Rosenstein, Nettie, 8-1/4" x 4" x 4-1/2", champagne pink velvet barrel bag embroidered with metallic goldtone yarns, rhinestones, gold seed beads in allover vine pattern, short top handle, champagne silk lining, one interior pocket, lining stamped "Nettie Rosenstein," 1950s ......................... 175.00

Unknown Maker, 7" l, 5" w, beaded, jeweled and reticulated gilt-brass frame, paste cabochon pearls, Belle Epoque, c1910-15, one jewel missing, rose silk lining disintegrated ................................................................... 75.00

Veneta, Bottega, 5-1/4" x 5" x 3", small sq red leather bag, front flap, long thin shoulder strap, black leather lining, plate on int. stamped "Bottega Veneta, Made in Italy," 1974 ................. 85.00

Versace, Gianni, 14" x 13-1/2" x 4", rect, black mesh with embroidered flowers, leather to handle and bottom, labeled "Gianni Versace Couture" on interior, 1990s............................... 185.00

Vuitton, Louis, 12" x 11-1/2" x 6", black epi leather, sack-shaped shoulder bag, plain leather band encircling top, plain wide lether strap, suede interior, stamped "LV" on outside band, hardware stamped "Louis Vuitton," 1990s ..................................... 260.00

## Skirt

Carnegie, Hattie, "Pineapple," midnight blue silk taffeta, below-the-knee length, panels of knife pleats turned at right angles to one another to form pineapple effect, fitted waist, full skirt, two front pockets, lined in black net, labeled "Hattie Carnegie" at side seam, size 4-6, 1950s ............................................. 260.00

De la Renta, Oscar, fuchsia, forest green, white, black, and orange sequined plaid, knee length, fuchsia silk satin waistband, multicolored bugle bead fringe at hem, black silk satin lining, black velvet belt with self covered buckle, labeled "Oscar de la Renta" at back waistline, size 8, 1980s ....................... 320.00

Valentino, below-the-knee length, black and white suede, stripes of suede woven to form plaid pattern, fitted waist and hips, slightly A-line at hem, black silk lining, labeled "Mario Valentino, Made in Italy" and "Neiman Marcus" at side seam, size 6-8, 1973 ....................................................................................... 165.00

## Suit, lady's

Chanel, navy wool knit skirt and jacket, white braid trim, boxy jacket with center front opening, two patch pockets, goldtone shamrock buttons at wrist pockets, braid trim at neckline, opening, pockets, and cuffs, straight above-the-knee length skirt, navy silk lining, labeled "Chanel Boutique" and "Neiman Marcus" at neckline, size 6, 1980s .........................................175.00

Givenchy, brown, hunter green, camel, and beige checked wool, fitted hip length jacket with center front button closure, pointed collar and two front patch pockets, below-the-knee length skirt with wide inverted pleat at center front, green lining, labeled "Givenchy Nouvelle Boutique" at back neckline, size 6, 1970s ..............................................................................100.00

Suit, man's

Cardin, Pierre, navy and white checked wool, single-breasted jacket, notched lapel, flap pockets, blue lining, narrow pants with two front and two back slit pockets, labeled "Pierre Cardin, Paris, New York" at neckline, 1970s.................................100.00

Versace, Gianni, pale gray linen, single breasted jacket, three slit pockets, cuffed wide leg pants, labeled "Gianni Versace" and "Made in Italy," 1980s ...................................................125.00

Tuxedo, Ralph Lauren, black velvet suit, jacket with wide label, narrow waist, pants with narrow ribbon tuxedo stripe at sides, two side pockets, two back pockets, one slip pocket, other with triangular flap, labeled "Polo Ralph Lauren" inside jacket, early 1970s .............................................................................150.00

Waistcoat, gentleman's, English, 18th C, embroidered on front with feather and boat motif, floral and dotted border, buttons embroidered with floral sprigs ...........................................550.00

# COALPORT

**History:** In the mid-1750s, Ambrose Gallimore established a pottery at Caughley in the Severn Gorge, Shropshire, England. Several other potteries, including Jackfield, developed in the area. About 1795, John Rose and Edward Blakeway built a pottery at Coalport, a new town founded along the right-of-way of the Shropshire Canal. Other potteries located adjacent to the canal were those of Walter Bradley and Anstice, Horton, and Rose. In 1799, Rose and Blakeway bought the Royal Salopian China Manufactory at Caughley. In 1814, this operation was moved to Coalport. A bankruptcy in 1803 led to refinancing and a new name—John Rose and Company. In 1814, Anstice, Horton, and Rose was acquired. The South Wales potteries at Swansea and Nantgarw were added. The expanded firm made fine-quality, highly decorated ware. The plant enjoyed a renaissance from 1888 to 1900. World War I, decline in trade, and shift of the pottery industry away from the Severn Gorge brought hard times to Coalport. In 1926, the firm, now owned by Cauldon Potteries, moved from Coalport to Shelton. Later owners included Crescent Potteries, Brain & Co., Ltd., and finally, in 1967, Wedgwood.

**References:** Susan and Al Bagdade, *Warman's English & Continental Pottery & Porcelain*, 3rd Edition, Krause Publications, 1998; Michael Messenger, *Coalport 1795-1926*, Antique Collectors' Club, 1995; Tom Power, *The Charlton Standard Catalogue of Coalport Figures*, 2nd Edition, Charlton Press, 1999; —, *The Charlton Standard Catalogue of Coalport Figures*, Millennium Edition, Charlton Press, 1999; Alf Willis, *The Charlton Standard Catalogue of Coalport Collectables*, Charlton Press, 2000.

**Collectors' Club:** Coalport Collector Society, P.O. Box 99, Sudbury, CO10 6SN England.

**Museums:** Cincinnati Museum of Art, Cincinnati, OH; Coalport China works Museum, Ironbridge Gorge Museum Trust, Shropshire, England; Victoria & Albert Museum, London, England.

Cake Set, Revelry, 9" cake plate, four serving plates, mkd "Coalport, Made in England, Est. 1750, Revelry".......................................95.00

Compote, 11" x 8-3/4" d, 1-3/4" h, ftd, apple green pierced border with raised relief leaf handles, hp floral dec in center, dated 1830 .. 325.00

Cottage

3-1/4" h, 8" l, Farmhouse, issued 1980, retired 1983 .........200.00

4" h, Pagoda House, issued 1976, retired 1984 .................200.00

4-1/2" h, Parasol House, removable lid ..............................275.00

5" h, Bridge House, issued 1976, retired 1981 ..................210.00

5" h, Castle ......................................................................225.00

5" h, Old Curiosity Shop, issued 1977, retired 1990 ..........200.00

5-1/4" h, Toll House, issued 1974, retired 1981 .................200.00

5-1/2" h, Dove Cote, issued 1972, retired 1981 .................200.00

5-1/2" h, Dower House, issued 1980, retired 1983............200.00

8-1/2" h, 6-1/2" l, 5" w, American Church..........................250.00

Decanter, 12" h, limited edition, base mkd "Coalport, Made in England"...................................................................................68.00

Figure, limited edition

8-1/4" h, Miss 1925, Vogue Series, orange dress, matching shoes, carrying large white feather, designed by John Bromley, 1981 ...................................................................................200.00

8-1/2" h, Miss 1928 with borzoi, Vogue Series, yellow dress, jacket trimmed in black, designed by John Bromley, 1981 ...................................................................................225.00

9" h, L. A. Gala, hp, lemon and lilac, numbered "502" of 1,000, David Shilling, 1986 ........................................................300.00

12" h, Pippa with borzoi, Roaring Twenties Series, bisque, burgundy coat, fur collar and cuffs ........................................175.00

Gravy Boat with Underplate

Marilyn .............................................................................220.00

Rosalinda..........................................................................220.00

Lamp Base, 10" h, Paddington Bear, standing against lamp post, clutching jar of marmalade .......................................................320.00

Place Setting

Cairo, blue and white ........................................................245.00

Hazelton, white .................................................................315.00

Rosalinda..........................................................................245.00

Plate, pierced, apple green ground, floral center, hand gilded, orange painted #2 over 62.56 and three dots mark, c1830..................250.00

Platter

Hazelton, white, large .......................................................465.00

Ming Rose, medium, scalloped...........................................235.00

Rosalinda, medium ............................................................275.00

Rosalinda, large.................................................................360.00

Soup Tureen, cov, Queen Elizabeth, turquoise and ivory...........400.00

**Platter, Urn and Florals, orange and blue, white ground, c1800, 14-1/2" w, 19-1/2" l, $375.**

Teapot, cov, Rosalinda..............................................290.00
Trophy Vase, cov, 12-1/4" h, bone china, manufactured for the bicentenary of St. Leger, 1776-1976, gilt trimmed and enamel dec, portrait of rider on horseback, titled on reverse "Memnon 1825 after J. F. Herring, Snr.," numbered 65 in limited edition of 200, printed mark, c1976 ......................................175.00
Vase, 9" h, Indian Tree Temple, ram's head handles..................200.00
Vegetable Dish, cov, Rosalinda .....................................435.00
Vegetable Dish, open
    Hazelton, white, round ........................................260.00
    Marilyn, round ................................................200.00
    Ming Rose, oval ..............................................235.00
    Rosalinda, round .............................................200.00

# COCA-COLA ITEMS

**History:** The originator of Coca-Cola was John Pemberton, a pharmacist from Atlanta, Georgia. In 1886, Dr. Pemberton introduced a patent medicine to relieve headaches, stomach disorders, and other minor maladies. Unfortunately, his failing health and meager finances forced him to sell his interest. In 1888, Asa G. Candler became the sole owner of Coca-Cola. Candler improved the formula, increased the advertising budget, and widened the distribution. A "patient" was accidentally given a dose of the syrup mixed with carbonated water instead of still water. The result was a tastier, more refreshing drink. As sales increased in the 1890s, Candler recognized that the product was more suitable for the soft-drink market and began advertising it as such. From these beginnings, a myriad of advertising items have been issued to invite all to "Drink Coca-Cola."

**References:** Gael de Courtivron, *Collectible Coca-Cola Toy Trucks*, Collector Books, 1995; Steve Ebner, *Vintage Coca-Cola Machines*, Vol. II, published by author (available from FunTronics, Inc., P.O. Box 448, Middletown, MD 21769; Bob and Debra Henrich, *Coca-Cola Commemorative Bottles*, 2nd ed., Collector Books, 2000; Deborah Goldstein Hill, *Price Guide to Vintage Coca-Cola® Collectibles: 1896-1965*, Krause Publications, 1999; Allan Petretti, *Classic Coca-Cola Calendars*, Antique Trader Books, 1999; ——, *Classis Coca-Cola Collectibles Cardboard & Paper Signs*, Krause Publications, 2000; —, *Petretti's Coca-Cola Collectibles Price Guide*, 10th ed., Antique Trader Books, 1997;—, *Petretti's Soda Pop Collectibles Price Guide*, 2nd ed., Antique Trader Books, 1998; Allan Petretti and Chris Beyer, *Classic Coca-Cola Serving Trays*, Antique Trader Books, 1999; B. J. Summers, *B. J. Summers' Guide to Coca-Cola*, 3rd ed., Collector Books, 2000; Jeff Walters, *Complete Guide to Collectible Picnic Coolers & Ice Chests*, Memory Lane Publishing, 1994; Helen and Al Wilson, *Wilson's Coca-Cola Price Guide*, 3rd ed., Schiffer Publishing, 2000.

**Collectors' Club:** Cavanagh's Coca-Cola Christmas Collector's Society, 1000 Holcomb Woods Parkway, Suite 440B, Roswell, GA 30076; Coca-Cola Collectors Club, 400 Monemar Ave., Baltimore, MD 21228-5213; Coca-Cola Collectors Club International, P.O. Box 49166, Atlanta, GA 30359-1166; The Coca-Cola Club, P.O. Box 158715, Nashville, TN 32715.

**Museums:** Coca-Cola Memorabilia Museum of Elizabethtown, Inc., Elizabethtown, KY; World of Coca-Cola Pavilion, Atlanta, GA.

**Additional Listings:** See *Warman's Americana & Collectibles* for more examples.

**Notes:** Dates of interest: "Coke" was first used in advertising in 1941. The distinctively shaped bottle was registered as a trademark on April 12, 1960.

Blotter, 1955, children at party scene..............................5.00
Bottle, 9-1/2" h, 2-1/4" d, 1986 Penn State Championship, unopened, 10 oz, Coke trademark on neck, blue and white Penn State logo, reverse with tribute to coach Joe Paterno..............................20.00
Bottle Carrier, sic holder, cardboard, 1930s.........................40.00
Bottle Opener, eagle head, 1912-20.................................100.00
Broadside, 24" h, 18-1/2" w, Baseball Greats series, Stan Musial, action shot and brief write-up........................................50.00
Button, 3/4" d, uniform type, c1910.................................45.00
Calendar Top, 8-1/8" h, 6-1/8" w, 1903, image of Victorian woman holding early Coke fountain glass, glossy cardboard.....................825.00
Chalkboard, tin, 1958.............................................95.00
Clock, electric, wall, "Drink Coca-Cola," 18" d litho metal, plastic cover, Telechron, General Electric, early 1950s........................250.00
Coke Dispenser, child's, plastic, 10" h, one glass...................45.00
Cooler, 32" h, 20" d, 38" w, lead lined wood, c1934 ...............1,750.00
Crossing Guard Sign, tin, double sided, diecut of policeman on one side, logo and bottle on other, two bases, c1950.................1,870.00
Cuff Links, pr, 1/2" d silvered brass with red and white paper insert under celluloid, two paper adv on threaded center spindle, red ground, orig card, c1921 ........................................50.00
Display Case, watches, 1950.......................................145.00
Door Push, plastic, bottle shape, c1950 ...........................145.00
Game, Game of Health, 8-1/2" x 17-1/4" folded cardboard game board, 1934 Canadian copyright, youthful health activities from rising to bedtime, full color bottled Coke and Canadian maple leaf symbol 125.00
Glass, bell shape, 1929-40.........................................5.00
Glass, 4" h, 2-1/2" d, etched, fountain type, set of four..............160.00
Magazine, Pause for Living, 1960s.................................4.00
Mechanical Pencil, 5-1/2" l, silvered metal and celluloid, red barrel inscribed in silver "Drink Coca-Cola in Bottles," imprint for local bottler, pencil clip bright silver luster miniature replica of Coke bottle ..............................................................50.00
Menu Board, tin, 1939.............................................75.00
Needle Case, 2" w, 3" h, 1925, girl with glass on one side, bottle and tumbler on other side ...........................................30.00
Pencil Clip, cello disk mounted on bright silver luster tin clip, red ground, 1940-50 Drink Coca-Cola, yellow lettering...................22.00
Drink Coca-Cola In Bottles, white lettering ........................20.00
Pencil Sharpener, metal, bottle shape, orig full box with twelve unused sharpeners, c1920 ............................................350.00
Pinback Button, Hi Fi Club, yellow and green lettering, brown Coke bottle, red 45 rpm record, 1950s ................................25.00
Pocket Knife, two stainless blades, marked "Remington," c1930 100.00
Pocket Mirror, 2-1/2" h, 1-3/4" w, celluloid, Duster Girl, mfg. by Cruver Mfg. Co., 1911 ..............................................6,750.00
Pocket Watch, "Time for Cold Bottle of Coca-Cola," 1920s........750.00
Premium, tie, 15" l red cord bolo tie, emb brass 1" slide clasp, frontal portrait of Kit Carson by Coca-Cola bottle, two small brass balls on ends, sponsorship premium for TV series "The Adventures of Kit Carson," c1951................................................85.00
Salesman's Sample, cooler, Glasscock, 1929, four miniature cases of bottles, 13-1/4" h ............................................19,550.00
Script, Coke Time TV Broadcast, 8-1/2" x 11" mimeographed paper 16 page typewritten script, Wed, July 22, 1953, starring Eddie Fisher, host Don Ameche, DeMarco Sisters as special guests ............35.00
Shooting gallery, 50" h, Coca-Cola on side panels, marquee, backfield, and gun barrel ...............................................1,100.00

**Tray, Elaine, c1916, $125.**

## Sign

11" h, 9" w, wood, metal trim, two glasses of Coca-Cola, Kay Displays, Inc., c1930, part of three pc display set ................ 450.00

11-3/4" h, 28" l, porcelain, "Drink Coca Cola Fountain Service," bright yellow, red, green, and white .................................. 950.00

27-3/4" h, 19-1/2" l, tin, "Take Home a Carton," six-pack carrier with metal handle, c1951 ................................................ 750.00

34" h, 62" w, cardboard, "Hospitality," young man with red bow-tie sitting on sofa with two attractive young ladies, orig gold-colored wood molded frame .......................................................... 800.00

48" h, round porcelain, minor scratch ............................... 950.00

50" h, 30" w, cardboard, lady wearing ice skates, sitting on log, enjoying bottle of Coca Cola, 1941, some warping and staining ............................................................................... 250.00

57" h, 36" w, cardboard, lady in full length gown holding glass of Coca Cola waiting for her partner, artist sgd, 1936, orig frame ................................................................................ 375.00

62" h, 30-1/2" d, standing, round porcelain sign, orig base emb "Drink Coca Cola," considerable porcelain loss and wear 225.00

Table Knife, 9" l, stainless steel blade, tan solid early plastic handle, inscribed "Drink Coca-Cola," 1930s-40s .................................. 30.00

Tip Tray, 6" l, 4-1/4" w, titled "Relieves Fatigue," lady enjoying beverage in flared glass, Chas. W. Shonk Co. litho, some age spotting ..................................................................................... 250.00

Toy, plane, 24" l, painted pressed steel ..................................... 250.00

## Tray

1914, 15-1/4" h, 12-1/4" w, Betty, wearing bonnet, Passaic Metal Ware Co. litho, color loss, chips, poor condition .............. 200.00

1931, Norman Rockwell design, boy in straw hat sitting on ground with puppy ............................................................................ 665.00

1934, 10-1/2" h, 13-1/4" w, Maureen O'Sullivan and John Weissmuller both enjoying bottles of Coca Cola, American Art Works Inc. litho, some rubbing and chipping .................. 725.00

1935, Madge Evans ............................................................. 415.00

1937, 13-1/4" h, 10-/2" w, rect, lady in full length gown holding glass, Canadian version, titled in French "Baviez Cocae Cola" .................................................................................... 125.00

Umbrella, 1920s ..................................................................... 750.00

Vending Machine, 36" h, 24" w, V-23, "Coca-Cola 10 Cents, Drink Coca-Cola In Bottles," revolving white top, orig working condition ................................................................................ 1,895.00

Vienna Art Plate, 10" tin litho, issued by Western Coca-Cola Bottling Co., orig ornate gold leaf frame, 16" sq ornate shadow box frame, 1905 ...................................................................................... 925.00

Window Display, Bathing Beauty, water skiing, trifold, 1922 .... 6,000.00

# COFFEE MILLS

**History:** Coffee mills or grinders are utilitarian objects designed to grind fresh coffee beans. Before the advent of stay-fresh packaging, coffee mills were a necessity. The first home-size coffee grinders were introduced about 1890. The large commercial grinders designed for use in stores, restaurants, and hotels often bear an earlier patent date.

**Reference:** Edward C. Kvetko and Douglas Congdon-Martin, *Coffee Antiques*, Schiffer Publishing, 2000; Joseph Edward MacMillan, *MacMillan Index of Antique Coffee Mills*, Cherokee Publishing (657 Old Mountain Rd., Marietta, GA 30064), 1995; Michael L. White and Derek S. White, *Early American Coffee Mills*, published by authors (P.O. Box 483, Fraser, CO 80442).

**Collectors' Club:** Association of Coffee Mill Enthusiasts, 5941 Wilkerson Rd, Rex, GA 30273.

## Commercial

Elgin, #40, double-wheel, missing finial and handle ........... 550.00

### Enterprise

#3, double wheel, orig red paint and stenciling, 1875 ... 990.00

#5, double wheel, worn orig paint .................................. 600.00

Landers, Frary & Clark, No. 10, double wheel, cast iron, orig condition ................................................................... 950.00

Simmons Koffee Krusher, double wheel, orig dark blue paint, gilt stenciling, mkd "KK 13" on front of drawer ......... 1,350.00

Star Mill, 28" h, cast iron, red and gold repaint over pitted iron, damaged brass hopper, replaced coffee container, crank and gear case with welded repair, mkd "Star Mill, Philadelphia" ............................................................... 500.00

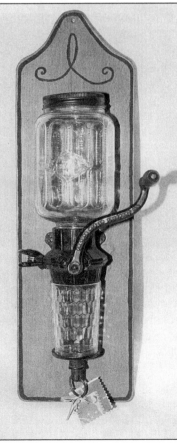

**Wall Mounted, Freidac Mfg. Co., glass canisters, cast iron mechanism, replaced wood plaque with pinstriping, $350.**

Domestic

    Arcade No. 25, wall type, cast iron, clear glass base, metal lid..... 70.00

    Imperial No. 705, long cast iron crank handle, domed cast-iron top, molded scrolls above dovetailed case, small drawers, remnants of label above drawer, 6" h, 11" h..............60.00

    Parker No. 50, wall type, tin and iron, orig mounting board..90.00

    Pine, fingered joints, one drawer, iron pull, iron top cup and handle, wooden knob, c1880, 5-3/4" sq, 6" h..........90.00

    Poplar, round pewter cup on top, iron turn handle, wooden knob grip, dovetailed sq wooden base, single drawer, old soft finish, 9-1/4" h..........140.00

    Walnut, Louis XIV, 18th C, mkd "Martin Laisnez," small old repair..........4,850.00

# COIN-OPERATED ITEMS

**History:** Coin-operated items include amusement games, pinball machines, jukeboxes, slot machines, vending machines, cash registers, and other items operated by coins. The first jukebox was developed about 1934 and played 78-RPM records. Jukeboxes were important to teenagers before the advent of portable radios and television. The first pinball machine was introduced in 1931 by Gottlieb. Pinball machines continued to be popular until the advent of solid-state games in 1977 and advanced electronic video games after that. The first three-reel slot machine, the Liberty Bell, was invented in 1905 by Charles Fey in San Francisco. In 1910, Mills Novelty Company copyrighted the classic fruit symbols. Improvements and advancements have led to the sophisticated machines of today. Vending machines for candy, gum, and peanuts were popular from 1910 until 1940 and can be found in a wide range of sizes and shapes.

**References:** Michael Adams, Jurgen Lukas, and Thomas Maschke, *Jukeboxes*, Schiffer Publishing, 1995; Michael F. Baute, *Always Jukin' Official Guide to Collectible Jukeboxes*, published by author (221 Yesler Way, Seattle, WA 98104), 1996; Richard M. Bueschel, *Collector's Guide to Vintage Coin Machines*, Schiffer Publishing, 1995; ——, *Guide to Vintage Trade Stimulators & Counter Games*, Schiffer Publishing, 1997; —, *Lemons, Cherries and Bell-Fruit-Gum*, Royal Bell Books, 1995; —, *Pinball 1*, Hoflin Publishing, 1988; ——, *Slots 1*, Hoflin Publishing, 1989; Richard Bueschel and Steve Gronowski, *Arcade 1*, Hoflin Publishing, 1993; Herbert Eiden and Jurgen Lukas, *Pinball Machines*, Schiffer Publishing, 1992, values updated 1997; Bill Enes, *Silent Salesmen Too, The Encyclopedia of Collectible Vending Machines*, published by author (8520 Lewis Dr., Lenexa, KS 66227), 1995; Eric Hatchell and Dick Bueschel, *Coin-Ops on Location*, published by authors, 1993; Bill Kurtz, *Arcade Treasures*, Schiffer Publishing, 1994; Joseph E. Meyer, *Protection: The Sealed Book*, 10th ed., Mead Publishing Co., 1999.

**Periodicals:** *Always Jukin'*, 221 Yesler Way, Seattle, WA 98104; *Antique Amusements Slot Machines & Jukebox Gazette*, 909 26th St. NW, Washington, DC 20037; *Around the Vending Wheel*, 5417 Castana Ave., Lakewood, CA 90712; *Coin Drop International*, 5815 W. 52nd Ave., Denver, CO 80212; *Coin Machine Trader*, 569 Kansas SE, P.O. Box 602, Huron, SD 57350; *Coin-Op Classics*, 17844 Toiyabe St., Fountain Valley, CA 92708; *Coin Slot*, 4401 Zephyr St., Wheat Ridge, Co 80033; *Gameroom Magazine*, 1014 Mt. Tabor Rd, New Albany, IN 47150; *Jukebox Collector*, 2545 SE 60th St., Des Moines, IA 50317; *Loose Change*, 1515 S. Commerce St., Las Vegas, NV 89102; *Pin Game Journal*, 31937 Olde Franklin Dr., Farmington, MI, 48334; *Scopitone Newsletter*, 810 Courtland Dr., Ballwin, MO 63021.

**Collectors' Club:** Bubble-Gum Charm Collectors, 24 Seafoam St., Staten Island, NY 10306

**Museum:** Liberty Belle Saloon and Slot Machine Collection, Reno, NV.

**Additional Listings:** See *Warman's Americana & Collectibles* for separate categories for Jukeboxes, Pinball Machines, Slot Machines, and Vending Machines.

**Advisor:** Bob Levy.

**Notes:** Because of the heavy usage these coin-operated items received, many are restored or, at the very least, have been repainted by either the operator or manufacturer. Using reproduced mechanisms to restore pieces is acceptable in many cases, especially when the restored piece will then perform as originally intended.

## Arcade

Fortune Teller, Grandma, Genco, c1940..........1,800.00
Grip Strength Test, Gottlieb, c1940..........200.00
Merchandiser Digger, exhibit, c1930..........2,200.00
Rifle, Williams, c1968..........300.00
Shuffle Alley, United, c1953..........300.00
Gum Machine

    Atlas

        Bantam, c1947, tray type, 11"..........100.00

        Deluxe, c146, bulk vendor, 16'..........100.00

        Master, c1954, penny/nickel, 16"..........40.00

        Midget, c1950, 14-sided, 11'..........125.00

        Columbus, Model "A," c1915, round globe, 15-1/2"..........200.00

        Intl Mutoscope, Old Mill, c1930, floor model..........2,000.00

        Manikin Vendor, Baker Boy, c1927, automated, 16"..2,500.00

        Mansfield, Automatic Clerk, beveled glass, flips package of gum, c1902, 16"..........600.00

        Norris Mfg., Master Special, c1923, 4-sided porcelain, 16"..........225.00

## Jukebox

AMI, Model D-40, c1951..........1,300.00
Rockola, Model 1455, c1957..........3,000.00
Seeburg

    Model 147, c1947..........2,500.00

    Model HF-100R, c1954..........3,500.00
Wurlitzer

    Model 1100, c1948..........6,000.00

    Model 1800, c1955..........3,500.00

## Slot Machine

Caille

    Dough Boy, c1935, three reel, inferior, 5¢..........700.00

    Upright Centaur, 1907, single wheel, magnificent, 5¢...14,000.00
Jennings

    Dutch Boy, c1930, three reel, nice wood cabinet, 25¢.....1,200.00

    Silver Moon Chief, c1840, three reel, jackpot, club machine, 10¢..........1,100.00

**Vending Machine, Rosebud Matches, by Northwestern, 13-1/2" h, 5-1/2" w, $525. Photo courtesy of Past Tyme Pleasures Auction.**

Mills
| | |
|---|---:|
| Black Cherry, c1946, three reel, first after World War II, 5¢ | 1,000.00 |
| Poinsettia, c1929, three reel, fancy design, 5¢ | 1,200.00 |
| War Eagle, c1931, three reel, 10¢ | 1,500.00 |

Pace
| | |
|---|---:|
| Bantam, c1928, three reel, three-quarter size, 1¢ | 1,000.00 |
| Comet Vendor, c1933, three reel, vends mints, 5¢ | 1,400.00 |

Watling
| | |
|---|---:|
| Bird of Paradise, c1937, three reel, very desirable, 10¢ | 3,500.00 |
| Blue Seal, c1928, three reel, jackpot, plain, 5¢ | 800.00 |
| Treasury, c1936, three reel, twin jackpot, beautiful gold coins, 5¢ | 3,500.00 |

## Vending Machine

| | |
|---|---:|
| Cigaret Special, Rowe Mfg., c1935, 36" | 700.00 |
| Fresh Gum, 6-column tabs, c1940, 18-1/2' | 75.00 |
| Hershey's Bar, Shipman Mfg., c1937, 16" | 125.00 |
| Model D Match Vendor, Specialty Mfg., c1920, 14-1/2" | 250.00 |
| National Postage, Northwestern, c1940, 13" | 75.00 |
| Novelty Card, exhibit, c1930, 12" | 150.00 |
| Pocket Combs, Advance Machine, c1950, 10" | 50.00 |
| Pulver Short Case, c1930, 21" | 600.00 |
| Reed's Aspirin, Kayem Prod., c1940, 13-1/2" | 175.00 |

# COMIC BOOKS

**History:** Shortly after comics first appeared in newspapers of the 1890s, they were reprinted in book format and often used as promotional giveaways by manufacturers, movie theaters, and candy and stationery stores. The first modern-format comic was issued in 1933. The magic date in comic collecting is June 1938 when DC issued Action Comics No. 1, marking the first appearance of Superman. Thus began the golden age of comics, which lasted until the mid-1950s and witnessed the birth of the major comic book publishers, titles, and characters. In 1954, Fredric Wertham authored *Seduction of the Innocent*, a book which pointed a guilt-laden finger at the comic industry for corrupting youth, causing juvenile delinquency, and undermining American values. Many publishers were forced out of business, while others established a "comics code" to assure parents that their comics were compliant with morality and decency standards upheld by the code authority. The silver age of comics, mid-1950s through the end of the 1960s, witnessed the revival of many of the characters from the golden age in new comic formats. The era began with Showcase No. 4 in October 1956, which marked the origin and first appearance of the Silver-Age Flash. While comics survived into the 1970s, it was a low point for the genre; but in the early 1980s a revival occurred. In 1983, comic book publishers, other than Marvel and DC, issued more titles than had existed in total during the previous 40 years. The mid- and late 1980s were a boom time, a trend which appears to be continuing into the 1990s.

**References:** *Comic Buyer's Guide Annual*, Krause Publications, issued annually; Alex G. Malloy, *Comics Values Annual 1999*, 6th ed., Antique Trader Books, 1998; Robert M. Overstreet, *Overstreet Comic Book Price Guide*, 29th ed., Avon Books, 1999; —, *The Overstreet Comic Grading Guide*, published by author, 1999; Don and Maggie Thompson (eds.), *Comic Book Superstars*, Krause Publications, 1993; —— (eds.), *Marvel Comics Checklist & Price Guide*, Krause Publications, 1993; Maggie Thompson and Brent Frankenhoff, *2001 Comic Book Checklist & Price Guide*, 7th ed., Krause Publications, 2000; Maggie Thompson and John Jackson Miller, *Comic Buyer's Guide 1997 Annual*, 6th ed., Krause Publications, 1996; Stuart W. Wells, III, *Science Fiction Collectibles: Identification & Price Guide*, Krause Publications, 1999.

**Periodicals:** *Archie Fan Magazine*, 185 Ashland St., Holliston, MA 01746; *Comic Book Market Place*, P.O. Box 180900, Coronado, CO 92178; *Comics Buyer's Guide*, 700 E. State St., Iola, WI 54990, http://www.krause.com; *Comics Interview*, 234 Fifth Ave., New York, NY 10001; *Comics Journal*, 7563 Lake City Way, Seattle, WA 98115, http://www.tcj.com; *Comics Source*, P.O. Box 2512, Chattanooga, TN 37409; *Duckburg Times*, 3010 Wilshire Blvd #362, Los Angeles, CA 90010; *Overstreet Comic Book Marketplace*, 1996 Greenspring Dr., Suite 405, Timonium, MD 21093-4117; *Overstreet's Advanced Collector*, 1996 Greenspring Dr., Suite 405, Timonium, MD 21093-4117; *Western Comics Journal*, 1703 N. Aster Place, Broken Arrow, OK 74012; *Wizard: The Guide To Comics*, 151 Wells Ave., Congers, NY 10920.

**Collectors' Clubs:** *American Comics Exchange*, 351-T Baldwin Rd, Hempstead, NY 11550; *Fawcett Collectors of America*, P.O. Box 24751, Minneapolis, MN 55424-0751, http://shazam.imginc.com/fca.

## Reproduction Alert:

Publishers frequently reprint popular stories, even complete books, so the buyer must pay strict attention to the title, not just the portion printed in oversized letters on the front cover. If there is any doubt, look inside at the fine print on the bottom of the inside cover or first page. The correct title will be printed there in capital letters. Also pay attention to the dimensions of the comic book. Reprints often differ in size from the original.

**Museums:** International Museum of Cartoon Art, 300 SE 5th Ave., #5150, Boca Raton, FL 33432; Museum of Cartoon Art, Rye, NY.

**Note:** The comics listed below are in near-mint condition, meaning they have a flat, clean, shiny cover that has no wear other than tiny corner creases; no subscription creases, writing, yellowing at margins, or tape repairs; staples are straight and rust free; pages are supple and like new; generally just-off-the-shelf quality.

*Action Comics*, D. C.
| | |
|---|---|
| # 23, April 1940 | 1,975.00 |
| #55 | 290.00 |
| #100 | 1,200.00 |
| #122 | 240.00 |
| #228 | 95.00 |
| #252 | 400.00 |
| #254 | 160.00 |

*Adventure*, D. C.
| | |
|---|---|
| #102 | 375.00 |
| #222 | 100.00 |
| #258 | 40.00 |
| #273 | 40.00 |
| #369 | 5.00 |

*All-American Men of War*, D. C., #23 ... 45.00
*All Star*, #105 ... 20.00

*Amazing Spider-Man*, Marvel
| | |
|---|---|
| #6 | 180.00 |
| #12 | 100.00 |
| # 28 | 650.00 |
| #37 | 18.00 |

*Aquaman*, D. C.

**Walt Disney's Comics & Stories, Dell, #131, $4.50.**

| | |
|---|---|
| #6 | 35.00 |
| #21 | 70.00 |
| #50 | 12.00 |

*Archie's Pal, Jughead*, #4 ... 400.00
*Atom and Hawkman*, D. C., #40 ... 25.00

*Avengers*, Marvel
| | |
|---|---|
| #17 | 145.00 |
| #23 | 400.00 |
| #129 | 64.00 |

*Banana Splits*, Gold Key, #1 ... 45.00

*Batman*, D. C.
| | |
|---|---|
| #71 | 75.00 |
| #109 | 105.00 |
| #131 | 50.00 |
| #213 | 30.00 |

*Blackhawk*, D. C., 1st D.C. issue, #108 ... 120.00
*Bonanza*, Gold Key, #35 ... 44.00
*Brave and the Bold*, D. C., #7 ... 40.00

*Captain America Comics*, Marvel
| | |
|---|---|
| # 6, Sept 1941 | 1,275.00 |
| #100 | 105.00 |
| #108 | 30.00 |

*Conan*, Marvel
| | |
|---|---|
| #1 | 105.00 |
| #8 | 15.00 |

*Daredevil*, #4 ... 65.00
*Dark Mansion of Forbidden Love*, D. C., #1 ... 32.00

*Dark Shadows*, Gold Key
| | |
|---|---|
| #2 | 85.00 |
| #5 | 60.00 |
| #12 | 40.00 |

*Detective Comics*, D. C.
| | |
|---|---|
| # 54, Aug 1941 | 450.00 |
| # 87, June 1944 | 625.00 |

*Fantastic Four*, Marvel
| | |
|---|---|
| # 5, July 1962 | 875.00 |
| # 10, Dec 1962 | 875.00 |
| # 12, March 1963 | 850.00 |
| #57 | 55.00 |
| #99 | 25.00 |

*Flash Comics*, D. C.
| | |
|---|---|
| # 12, Dec 1940 | 700.00 |
| # 15, March 1941 | 700.00 |
| # 26, Feb 1942 | 975.00 |

*G. I. Combat*
| | |
|---|---|
| #22 | 30.00 |
| #25 | 30.00 |
| #246 | 5.00 |
| #267 | 4.00 |

*G. I. Joe*
| | |
|---|---|
| #5 | 11.00 |
| #6 | 12.00 |
| #69 | 3.00 |

*Green Hornet*, Gold Key
| | |
|---|---|
| #1 | 135.00 |
| #3 | 110.00 |

*Green Lantern*, D. C.
| | |
|---|---|
| #1 | 2,500.00 |
| #22 | 165.00 |
| #80 | 35.00 |

*Hot Wheels*, D. C., #1 ... 65.00
*House of Mystery*, D. C., #1 ... 400.00
*House of Secrets*, D. C., #2 ... 100.00

*Incredible Hulk*, Marvel
| | |
|---|---|
| # 3, Sept. 1962 | 375.00 |
| # 4, Nov. 1962 | 450.00 |
| #107 | 40.00 |

*Iron Man*, Marvel
| | |
|---|---|
| #2 | 80.00 |
| #3 | 55.00 |

*Justice League of America*, D. C. #31 ........................................30.00
*Laurel & Hardy*, D. C., #1 ...............................................45.00
*Legion of Super Heroes*, #3 .............................................12.00
*Mars Patrol*, Gold Key, #9 ..............................................20.00
*Marvel Super Heroes*, Marvel, #1 ....................................60.00
*Marvel Mystery Comics*, # 5, March 1940 ..................1,200.00
*Munsters*, Gold Key, #15 ................................................30.00
*Mystery in Space*, D. C., #4 ..........................................200.00
*My Greatest Adventure*, D. C., #23 ...............................55.00
*Night Nurse Marvel*, #1 ...................................................55.00
*Our Army At War*, D. C., #185 ........................................10.00
*Rawhide*, Gold Key, #1160 ...........................................100.00
*Rifleman*, Gold Key, #2 ...................................................30.00
*Rocky and his Friends*, Gold Key, #1 .............................65.00
*Scooby Do*, Gold Key, #8 ...............................................28.00
*Silver Surfer*, Marvel, #2 ...............................................110.00
*Star Spangled War Stories*, D. C., #141 ........................25.00
*Star Trek*, Gold Key
    #4 .....................................................................................70.00
    #5 ...................................................................................105.00
    #38 ....................................................................................21.00
*Strange Adventures*, D. C., #8 .......................................75.00
*Strange Tales*, Marvel
    #69 22.00
    #78 200.00
*Tales of Suspense*, Marvel, #24 .....................................36.00
*Tales to Astonish*, Marvel, #10 .....................................140.00
*Teen Titans*, D. C., #20 ...................................................36.00
*Thor*, Marvel, #142 .........................................................30.00
*Witching Hour*, D. C., #3 .................................................28.00
*World's Finest*, D. C.
    #20 ..................................................................................265.00
    #99 ..................................................................................120.00
    #119 ................................................................................100.00
*Wyatt Earp*, Gold Key, #7 ...............................................20.00
*X-Men*, Marvel
    #2 ...................................................................................630.00
    #8 ...................................................................................800.00
    #10 ..............................................................................1,600.00
    #12 ...................................................................................75.00
*Young Romance*, D. C., #197 ........................................120.00
Zip
    #39 ..................................................................................225.00
    #43 ..................................................................................150.00

# COMPACTS

**History:** In the first quarter of the 20th century, attitudes regarding cosmetics changed drastically. The use of make-up during the day was no longer looked upon with disdain. As women became "liberated," and as more and more of them entered the business world, the use of cosmetics became a routine and necessary part of a woman's grooming. Portable containers for cosmetics became a necessity. Compacts were made in myriad shapes, styles, combinations and motifs, all reflecting the mood of the times. Every conceivable natural or man-made material was used in the manufacture of compacts. Commemorative, premium, souvenir, patriotic, figural, Art Deco, and enamel compacts are a few examples of the types of compacts that were made in the United States and abroad. Compacts combined with other forms, such as cigarette cases, music boxes, watches, hatpins, canes, and lighters, also were very popular. Compacts were made and used until the late 1950s when women opted for the "au naturel" look. The term "vintage" is used to describe the compacts from the first half of the 20th century as distinguished from contemporary examples.

**References:** Juliette Edwards, *Compacts*, published by author, 1994; Roselyn Gerson, *Ladies Compacts*, Wallace-Homestead, 1996; ——, *Vintage and Contemporary Purse Accessories, Solid Perfumes, Lipsticks, & Mirrors*, Collector Books, 1997; ——, *Vintage Ladies Compacts*, Collector Books, 1996; ——, *Vintage Vanity Bags and Purses: An Identification and Value Guide*, 1994, 1997 value update, Collector Books; Frances Johnson, *Compacts, Powder and Paint*, Schiffer Publishing, 1996; Laura M. Mueller, *Collector's Encyclopedia of Compacts, Carryalls & Face Powder Boxes* (1994, 1999 value update), Vol. II (1997), Collector Books.

**Collectors' Club:** Compact Collectors Club, P.O. Box 40, Lynbrook, NY 11563.

**Additional Listings:** See *Warman's Americana & Collectibles* for more examples.

**Advisor:** Roselyn Gerson.

Arden, Elizabeth, 3" d, 1/4" h
    Black satin, beaded red, white, and green flowers on cover, 1950s ........................................................................65.00
    Pin satin, beaded butterflies on cover, powder puff printed "Ardena Invisible Veil, Elizabeth Arden," 1950s ................75.00
    Red satin, white straw hat embroidered onto cover embellished with red, white, yellow, and green beads, 1950s................65.00
Cartier, 3" x 2-3/8", two side clasps, orig mirror and powder screen, mkd "Cartier 14K" .....................................5,250.00
Continental, 4-1/4" l, 3-1/4" w, gold washed and enameled, center enameled scene of courting couple by river landscape, engraved surround, reserves of aqua enamel embellished with stylized ribbons, underside engraved with leafy scrolls and flowerheads, mirror int., 800 fine, early 20th C ........................320.00
Coty, #405, envelope box .................................................85.00
Daniel, black leather, portrait of lady encased in plastic dome, Paris.... 95.00
Dejer-Kiss
    German Silver, 2" x 2", sunburst ribbing, mythical winged image and floral dec, patent 1925................................125.00
    Hammered case, center lid monogram cartouche, orig loose powder and puff, orig box and brochure ................................150.00
Dorothy Gray 5th Ave., 2-3/4", goldtone, used .............35.00
Doyle & Co., 2-1/4" x 3" oval, lilac painted enamel, two engraved fan designs and bouquet on sides, loose powder, mirror, rouge, orig pads, c1920..........................................................210.00
Elgin American
    Bell shape, 3-1/4" x 2-1/2", goldtone, white matte enameled case, relief bar and Greek Key lid design, crème rouge liner, framed mirror, sgd puff ..........................................145.00
    Heart shape, goldtone, deeply chased with lateral lid banding, rococo border, powder door and pressed powder disk compartment, case sgd, orig puff, orig protective pouch, 1948 ....125.00
    Octagonal, 2-1/2", goldtone, pave faux pearls and gemstone ornamentation, cased mirror, puff, orig flannel case sgd "Elgin America," case sgd "American Beauty, Made in USA".....125.00
    Rainbow, goldtone, enameled rainbow, letters "B F C L R" and pair of shaking hands, wear to ext. ...................................50.00
Evans
    Art Deco, 2" x 3/8", white metal, vanity, engine turned case, enameled circle, floral design, chased border in sunray design on back, short single medium bar ring on chain, loose powder style compact, pressed rouge, case framed mirror.........155.00

Carryall, 5-1/2" x 3-1/8" x 7/8", silvertone, applied silvertone vines and clear rhinestone flowers, int. with goldtone pattern, hinged two-sided mirror, loose powder make-up compact, sq lipstick, snake wrist chain, int. shows signs of use ...................... 210.00

Flapjack, Rex Fifth Avenue, goldtone, Brocado emb rococo lid with initial cartouche in aqua enamel, orig puff with logo, sifter screen, c1956 .................................................................................. 135.00

Flowerton, 2-1/2" d, golden mesh ......................................... 95.00

Goldtone top studded with gemstones, mkd puff ....................... 110.00

Fiato, goldtone, jeweled horse and carriage mounted on lid, blue velvet protective case, sleeve for jeweled lipstick ........................... 90.00

Foster & Bailey, vanity case, blue cloisonné suspended from enameled perfume container, powder and rouge compartments, lipstick attached at base, tassel and black enameled finger carrying ring ..................................................................................... 950.00

French, 1-3/4" x 5/8", gilded metal, filigree lid with prong-set blue and red cabachons, domed shaped painted enamel disk center, mkd "Made in France," orig puff, wear to mirror ............................... 225.00

Kigu of London
Enamel and Marcasite, 2-7/8" x 3/8", goldtone, black enamel, marcasite bowknot bijou, caes and puff sgd, mkd "Made in England, patented," c1950, unused .................................. 275.00
Goldtone, floral decal, orig cloth case .................................. 85.00

Lampi, light blue enamel, five colorful three dimensional scenes from *Alice in Wonderland* enclosed in plastic domes on lid .............. 185.00

Madame Pomadour, 4" d, round, gold plated, basket design on top, sgd powder puff, mkd "Gold Plated" .................................... 125.00

Marian Bilac New York Paris, compact and lipstick, applied green stones, lipstick set with prong set rhinestones, orig puff and sifter, orig pink carry pouch ...................................................... 85.00

Rex Fifth Avenue, 3-3/4" sq
Goldtone top with palm trees and enameling, brass base, orig powder puff, some wear to brass ................................... 65.00
Goldtone, engine turned feather and mirror motif, orig logo puff, case glued beveled mirror ............................................... 155.00

Souvenir
2-1/8" x 1-7/8", Boston State House, lithographed celluloid, int. with metal mirror separating rouge from powder, two orig puffs .............................................................................. 45.00
2-1/8" sq, Statue of Liberty, silvered metal ........................... 65.00
2-1/4" sq, Carlsbad Caverns, showing caverns and Indian, unused ............................................................................ 40.00

Stratton, 3-1/2" d, goldtone, round, mkd "Made in England" ......... 95.00

Tiffany & Co.
14K yellow gold, mirrored compartment, engraved case, engine turned design, sgd "Tiffany & Co.," minor dents ............... 325.00
Sterling silver and 14K yellow gold, Art Deco, reeded silver sunburst, ruby and gold accents, brushed gold int. .............. 350.00

Unknown Maker
2-1/2" sq, green enamel, center scalloped champleve enamel with pink rose, swivel int. lid, c1930 ................................. 185.00
2-7/8" x 2-7/8" x 1/2", transparent pink Lucite, round sterling silver medallion with lovebird, orig puff ..................................... 275.00
3" d, dark blue enamel, edged l gold, hp flowers on inside, screen, remnants of powder ......................................... 175.00
3" x 1", combination compact, mirror, comb, lipstick holder, money clip, coin purse, and cigarette case, rhinestone covered, goldtone, 1940-50s .......................................................... 150.00
3-1/4" d, goldtone, enameled pink and green floral lid .......... 75.00
4" x 3", carryall, basketweave, lipstick holder on side of case, one side for cigarettes, other with comb and compact, snake link chain, cloth case ............................................................. 165.00
4-1/4" l, combination compact and cigarette case, goldtone, two Scotties, black enamel back, orig box ............................... 200.00
5-1/4" x 3-1/8" x 1", carryall, goldtone, brushed finish, rhinestones and pearl crown bijou on lid, broad mesh wrist strap, loose powder, puff, comb, pop-up lipstick tube, case glued mirror, gray flannel coin case and case protector, unused .................. 265.00

Victorian, 3-1/2" x 2-1/2", sterling silver, compact and coin purse, interior with two coin holders, mirror on one side, money clip on other, mirror opens to reveal power compartment ............................. 150.00

Volupte
3" sq, goldtone, slight wear on ext., cloth case ................... 85.00
4" l, sterling, raised flowers and balls, reverse side monogrammed ..................................................................... 125.00
5-1/4" l, 3" w, envelope shape, rhinestoned ribbon as seal, orig box and cloth case ......................................................... 95.00
Whiting and Davis, 3-1/2" l, 2-3/4" w, gold mesh case with compact ............................................................................. 80.00
Whiting & Davis Co., vanity bag, purple, black, and silver mesh, purple enameled vanity case on outside corner of frame, lined int., powder sifter, metal mirror, and rouge compartment on lid, carrying chain .................................................................... 500.00

# CONSOLIDATED GLASS COMPANY

**History:** The Consolidated Lamp and Glass Company was formed as a result of the 1893 merger of the Wallace and McAfee Company, glass and lamp jobbers of Pittsburgh, and the Fostoria Shade & Lamp Company of Fostoria, Ohio. When the Fostoria, Ohio, plant burned down in 1895, Corapolis, Pennsylvania, donated a seven-acre tract of land near the center of town for a new factory. In 1911, the company was the largest lamp, globe, and shade works in the United States, employing more than 400 workers. In 1925, Reuben Haley, owner of an independent design firm, convinced John Lewis, president of Consolidated, to enter the giftware field utilizing a series of designs inspired by the 1925 Paris Exposition (l'Exposition Internationale des Arts Décorative et Industriels Modernes) and the work of René Lalique. Initially, the glass was marketed by Howard Selden through his showroom at 225 Fifth Avenue in New York City. The first two lines were Catalonian and Martele. Additional patterns were added in the late 1920s: Florentine (January 1927), Chintz (January 1927), Ruba Rombic (January 1928), and Line 700 (January 1929). On April 2, 1932, Consolidated closed it doors. Kenneth Harley moved about 40 molds to Phoenix. In March 1936, Consolidated reopened under new management, and the "Harley" molds were returned. During this period, the famous Dancing Nymph line, based on an eight-inch salad plate in the 1926 Martele series, was introduced. In August 1962, Consolidated was sold to Dietz Brothers. A major fire damaged the plant during a 1963 labor dispute and in 1964 the company permanently closed its doors.

**References:** Tom and Neila Bredehoft, *Fifty Years of Collectible Glass, 1920-1970*, Volume 1, Volume II, Antique Trader Books, 2000; Ann Gilbert McDonald, *Evolution of the Night Lamp*, Wallace-Homestead, 1979; Jack D. Wilson, *Phoenix & Consolidated Art Glass, 1926-1980*, Antique Publications, 1989.

**Collectors' Club:** Phoenix and Consolidated Glass Collectors, 41 River View Dr., Essex Junction, VT 05452, http://www.collectoronline.com/club-PCGCC-wp.html.

**Bowl, Ruba Rombic, jungle green, light rim chips, 8-1/2" d, $750. Photo courtesy of David Rago Auctions.**

Ashtray, Santa Maria, green wash ............................. 195.00
Berry Bowl, master, Criss-Cross, cranberry opalescent, 8" d ..... 175.00
Bon Bon, Ruba Rhombic, 6" d, smoky topaz ............................. 145.00
Bowl
    5-1/2" d, Coronation, Martelé, flared, blue ............................. 75.00
    8" d, Dancing Nymph, dark blue wash ............................. 365.00
Box, cov, 7" l, 5" w, Martelé line, Fruit and Leaf pattern, scalloped
    edge ............................. 85.00
Butter Dish, cov, Cosmos, pink band ............................. 200.00
Candlesticks, pr
    Hummingbird, Martelé line, oval body, jade green, 6-3/4" h 245.00
    Ruba Rhombic, smoky topaz ............................. 215.00
Cocktail, Dancing Nymph, French Crystal ............................. 90.00
Cologne Bottle, orig stopper, 4-1/2" h, Cosmos ............................. 120.00
Cookie Jar, 6-1/2" h, Regent Line, #3758, Florette, rose pink over white
    opal casing ............................. 370.00
Cruet, orig stopper, Florette, pink satin ............................. 225.00
Cup and Saucer, Dancing Nymph, ruby flashed ............................. 265.00
Goblet, Dancing Nymph, French Crystal ............................. 90.00
Humidor, Florette, pink satin ............................. 225.00
Jar, cov, Con-Cora, #3758-9, pine cone dec, irid ............................. 165.00
Jug, Spanish Knobs, 5-1/2" h, handle, pink ............................. 125.00
Lamp
    Cockatoo, 13" h, figural, orange and blue, black beak, brown
      stump, black base ............................. 450.00
    Elk, 13" h, chocolate brown, blue clock mounted between horns,
      black bass base, shallow annealing mark ............................. 1,000.00
    Flower Basket, 8" h, bouquet of roses and poppies, yellows,
      pinks, green leaves, brown basketweave, black glass
      base ............................. 300.00
Mayonnaise Comport, Martelé Iris, green wash ............................. 55.00
Miniature Lamp, Cosmos, 7" h, fish net ground ............................. 350.00
Night Light, Santa Maria, block base ............................. 450.00
Old Fashioned Tumbler, 3-7/8" h, Catalonian, yellow ............................. 20.00
Pitcher, water, Florette, pink satin ............................. 200.00
Plate
    7" d, Catalonian, green ............................. 25.00
    8-1/4" d, Bird of Paradise, amber wash ............................. 40.00
    8-1/4" d, Dancing Nymph, French Crystal ............................. 85.00
    8-1/2" d, Five Fruits, green ............................. 40.00
    10-1/4" d, Catalonian, yellow ............................. 40.00
    12" d, Five Fruits, white ............................. 65.00
    12" d, Martelé, Orchid, pink, birds and flowers ............................. 115.00
Platter, Dancing Nymph, Palace, dark blue wash ............................. 1,000.00
Puff Box, cov
    Hummingbirds, milk glass ............................. 75.00
    Lovebirds, blue ............................. 95.00
Salt and Pepper Shakers, pr
    Cone, pink ............................. 75.00
    Cosmos ............................. 185.00
    Guttate, green ............................. 85.00
Sauce Dish, Criss-Cross, cranberry opalescent ............................. 55.00
Sherbet, ftd
    Catalonian, green ............................. 20.00
    Dancing Nymph, French Crystal ............................. 80.00
Snack Set, Martelé Fruits, pink ............................. 45.00
Spooner, Criss-Cross, cranberry opalescent ............................. 75.00

Sugar Bowl, cov
    Catalonian, green ............................. 30.00
    Guttate, cased pink ............................. 120.00
Sugar Shaker, orig top
    Cone, green ............................. 95.00
    Guttate, cased pink, pewter top ............................. 200.00
Sundae, Martelé Russet Yellow Fruits ............................. 35.00
Syrup
    Cone, squatty, pink ............................. 295.00
    Cosmos, SP top ............................. 275.00
Toilet Bottle, Ruba Rhombic, cased jade green ............................. 650.00
Toothpick Holder
    Florette, cased pink ............................. 75.00
    Guttate, cranberry ............................. 185.00
Tumbler
    Catalonian, ftd, green, 5-1/4" h ............................. 30.00
    Cosmos ............................. 85.00
    Dancing Nymph, frosted pink, 6" h ............................. 175.00
    Guttate, pink satin ............................. 60.00
    Katydid, clambroth ............................. 165.00
    Martelé Russet Yellow Fruits, ftd, 5-3/4" h ............................. 5.00
    Ruba Rhombic, jade, 5-1/2" h ............................. 325.00
Umbrella Vase, Blackberry ............................. 550.00
Vase
    Catalonian, #1183, three tiers, honey, 6" h ............................. 175.00
    Con-Cora, milk glass, hp flowers, 12" h, 8-1/2" d ............................. 115.00
    Dancing Nymph, crimped, ruby stain, reverse French Crystal
      highlights, 5" h ............................. 135.00
    Florentine, collared, flat, green, 12" h ............................. 275.00
    Freesia, white ceramic wash, fan ............................. 225.00
    Hummingbird, #2588, turquoise on satin custard, 5-1/2" h ... 90.00
    Katydid, blue wash, fan shaped top, 8-1/2" h ............................. 300.00
    Lovebirds, custard yellow ground, pale green birds, coral colored
      flowers, 11-1/4" h, 10" w ............................. 600.00
    Poppy, green cased ............................. 550.00
    Purple leaf and berry design, opalescent, 9-3/4" h ............................. 225.00
    Regent Line, #3758, cased blue stretch over white opal, pinched,
      6" h ............................. 185.00
    Ruba Rhombic, French Silver, 9-1/2" h ............................. 4,000.00

# CONTINENTAL CHINA and PORCELAIN (GENERAL)

**History:** By 1700, porcelain factories existed in large numbers throughout Europe. In the mid-18th century, the German factories at Meissen and Nymphenburg were dominant. As the century ended, French potteries assumed the leadership role. The 1740s to the 1840s were the golden age of Continental china and porcelains. Americans living in the last half of the 19th century eagerly sought the masterpieces of the European porcelain factories. In the early 20th century, this style of china and porcelain was considered "blue chip" by antiques collectors.

**References:** Susan and Al Bagdade, *Warman's English & Continental Pottery & Porcelain*, 3rd Edition, Krause Publications, 1998; Rachael Feild, *Macdonald Guide to Buying Antique Pottery & Porcelain*, Wallace-Homestead, 1987; Geoffrey Godden, *Godden's Guide to European Porcelain*, Random House, 1993.

**Additional Listings:** French—Haviland, Limoges, Old Paris, Sarreguemines, and Sevres; German—Austrian Ware, Bavarian China, Carlsbad China, Dresden/Meissen, Rosenthal, Royal Bayreuth, Royal Bonn, Royal Rudolstadt, Royal Vienna, Schlegelmilch, and Villeroy and Boch; Italian—Capo-di-Monte.

French Faience, plate, blue, red, and green florals, mkd "Revon," 9-3/4" d, $185.

## Bohemian

Unknown maker
>Garniture Vase, 7-1/2" w, 4" d, 12-1/4" h, Rose Du Barry, two handles, floral and galants reverse, price for pair .................. 500.00
>Vase, 23" h, cylindrical form, two handles, vieux rose ground, obverse with well painted reserves of parrots among exotic foliage, reserves with sprays of asters, c1875-80.............. 1,540.00

## Faïence

>Soup Tureen, c1820-30, blue, white, and yellow, full relief apple finial, age cracks in bowl of tureen, 8-1/2" d, 9-1/2" h ...... 440.00
>Tureen On Stand, 18th C Rowen style, c1900-1915, blue and white, 19-1/2" l, 12" w.................................................. 880.00
>Vase, 12-1/2" h, 8" w, 7" d, first quarter 19th C, ovoid, blue ground dec with allegorical figures, serpentine handles above grotesque masks, circular foot, price for pr ........................ 3,100.00

## French

Chantilly
>Dish, 9 3/4" l, quatrefoil, Kakiemon palette, chrysanthemum, chocolate rim, c1740....................................................200.00
>Plate, 9 1/2" d, blue and white, carnations, basketwork border, blue hunting horn mark, c1845, price for 12 pc set.....750.00

## Galle Faience

>Compote, 9" d, scalloping rim, waisted cylindrical base, dark blue and yellow, blossom sprays, central unicorn and centaur, sgd "E Galle Nancy," price for pr .................................................990.00
>Figure, 13-1/4" h, seated brown tabby cat, green glass eyes, sgd "Galle Nancy," minor restoration ......................................500.00

## German

>Ansbach, coffeepot, 8" h, pear shape, dome cov with fruit finial, scrolling handle, short spout, molded female mask and feathers, loose bouquets and scattered flowers dec, c1765, blue coat of arms and "A" mark, restored finial................................ 1,200.00
>Altwasser, serving bowl, 13-1/2" w, 13-1/2" d, 5" h, sq, compartmented, floral dec, white ground, gilt detailing, c1875-85..75.00
>Berlin, plaque, 8-1/2" l, oval, peasant boy with recorder, imp marks, early 20th C ......................................................980.00
>Blanc-de-Chine, cachepot, 6-3/4" d, 5-7/8" h, Romeo and Juliet at wellhead, c1885-90 ........................................................ 110.00
>Furtstenburg, charger, 15-1/4" d, blue floral dec, 18th.... C 800.00

## Herend

>Dinnerware Service, green band and floral spray dec, 11 soup plates, 12 dinner plates, 9 salad plates, 5 bread plates, sauce boat with two handles, low fruit bowl, oval 14" platter ... 1,100.00
>Fruit Bowl, 10-1/2" l oval, open work, hp center, pink, gold, and blue dec....................................................................250.00
>Hoechst, figure, 5-1/2" w, 5-1/2" h, two children dancing, painted factory marks, mid-19th C ................................................ 375.00

## Longwy

>Box, cov, 7-1/2" d, circular, polychrome parrot on lid..........225.00
>Plaque, 8" x 6-1/2" oval, crane in marsh, cobalt blue field....90.00

## Lunéville

>Asparagus Server, majolica, c1885-95, 12-1/2" w, 11" d, 7-1/2" h, scroll form, matching oblong tray, molded as 23 parallel stalks of white asparagus, twig feet, platter with relief floral and asparagus ornament, platter sgd "Lunéville," imp underglaze mark ................................................................... 660.00
>Dinner service, partial, Faïence, Moustiers-style, c1920-30, 22 dinner plate, two elliptical relief dishes, two circular cov tureens, cov soup tureen, circular platter, price for 29 pc set...... 1,100.00

## Nymphenburg

>Cup and Saucer, 3-3/4" d, bell shaped bowl, Maximillian Joseph Platz, burnished gilt int. and scroll handle, c1835 .........1,900.00
>Figure, 3-1/4" h, sparrow, realistic color enamels ...............125.00
>Tea Set, black border, magenta rim, magenta floral sprays, spherical teapot, creamer, 12 teacups and saucers, cake plates, circular tray, damage to teapot.............................................550.00

## Paris

>Centerpiece Bowl, 21" w, 11-1/2" d, 12-1/2" h, oval, Sevres style, Louis Philippe blue ground, large floral reserves, gilt brass mounts in Louis XVI taste, c1865-70 ..........................2,900.00
>Centerpiece Corbeille, 16" w, 11" d, 11" h, reticulated, ftd, rococo taste...................................................................425.00
>Coffeepot, 10" h, Anneu d'Or, anthropomorphic spout, c1820-25 ........................................................... 175.00
>Encrier, 7-3/4" w, 3" d, 4-1/2" h, nautilus form, scalloped shell gilded within, fitted with ink bowl and sand caster, pink, coral, and brown, rect plinth, second quarter 19th C, restored rim chip................................................................. 200.00
>Garniture Basket, 14" w, 9-1/2" d, 9-3/4" h, oval, ftd, Rose du Barry ground, each façade with well painted reserve of fruits, Rococo taste, c1850-65, one tip broken off .....................360.00
>Garniture Vase, 16-1/2" h, two handles modeled as full figured Bacchic cherubs, facades with large reserves of summer flowers, gilt detailing of the Vintage elements, c1850-65, price for pr ...............................................................2,860.00

## Potschappel

>Basket, 16-1/4" w, 11-3/4" d, 5" h, reticulated, two handles, ftd, floral appliqués, Carl Thieme, c1910............................... 100.00
>Centerpiece Corbielle, 10-1/2" w, 9" d, 15" h, in the Meissen style, reticulated, ftd, floral appliqués, 1890-1900 .....................325.00
>Garniture Vase, cov, 12-1/2" d, 30" h, in the Meissen style, each façade with large figural reserve, two handles modeled as seated semi-nude female figures holding floral sprays, flower bedecked cover with two putti displaying armorial shield, Carl Thieme, c1888-1901 ...................................................... 1,980.00

## Samson

>Figure, 9-3/8" h, 9-5/8" h, children as Winter and Spring, second as Summer and Autumn, late 19th C, price for pr............750.00
>Jar, 14" h, Famille Rose, Phoenix, floral, and dragon dec, mounted as lamp..............................................................500.00
>Salts, cov, figural, 7-1/2" h, male and female figures supporting oval two handled baskets on their laps, enamel dec, late 19th C, pr ......................................................................... 350.00
>St. Cloud, cup and saucer, 2 3/4" d, white, plum tree branches, mid-18th C, price for pr ................................................ 1,700.00
>Unknown Maker, centerpiece, 12" l, oval porcelain dish, Commedia del Arte figures in landscape on gilt and sky blue ground, four scrolling legs terminating in oval base, ormolu mounts ......................................................................... 1,200.00

## Sitzendorf

Banquet Lamp, 28" h, courting scene .................................. 600.00
Cachepot, 16" w, 14" d, 12" h, trapezoidal, applied flowers bedeck shell supported by three putti, high relief, c1890-95, one foot of putti repaired .............................................................. 775.00
Candelabrum, five-light, scrolled arms and putti form standard, courting couple, base with plethora of foliage, late 19th C, restorations, chips ............................................................... 460.00
Compote, 10" h, maiden with bird and cage in bocage surrounded with lamp, late 19th C, minor chips ................................. 300.00
Potpourri Urn, 11" h, cupid handles, high relief modeling with flowering vines, late 19th C, minor chips ............................... 200.00

## Thieme, Carl, Saxonian Porcelain Factory

Candlesticks, pr, 6-1/2" h, enamel dec scrolled panels of cherubs between gilt lattice and enameled floral designs ............. 150.00
Teapot, cov, 6" h, globular form, applied flowers and leaves, figural landscape, floral panels, mark for Carl Thieme Saxonian Porcelain Factory, chips ................................................... 400.00
Schiere-Alsback, centerpiece corbeille, 17" w, 10" d, 9-1/2" h, reticulated, ftd, Moss Rose dec, full relief rose blossoms and foliage on ext., polychromed Moss Rose spray in center of int., c1885-1890 ........................................................................ 200.00

## Thuringia Factory

Compote, 4-1/4" h, figural, pierced dish with floral and fruit dec, supported by three cherubs, Thuringia mark, late 19th C .............. 175.00

## Unknown Maker

Fruit Bowl, ftd, 15" h, openwork basket, cupid standard, foliate molded base, chips, repairs .......................................... 350.00
Woflsohn, Helene, urn, cov, 13" h, magenta ground, painted reserves of battle scenes on both sides, attributed, Dresden, late 19th C, pr ........................................................... 1,725.00
Volkstedt, figure, 13-3/4" h, 27" l, white glazed, eight figures clad in 18th C dress, surrounding piano, rococo framed oval base, underglazed printed mark, restorations, hairline .......... 1,495.00
Italian
  Deruta, jar, 7-1/4" h, majolica, scrollwork, grotesques and leaf forms, inscribed "Ghoma di Lava" ............................... 500.00
Doccia
  Cup and Saucer, flaring cylindrical cup, C-scroll handle, purple highlights, c1755, price for pr ..................................... 145.00
  Dish, 9-5/8" w, shell shape, central bouquet of purple flowers surrounded by floral sprays, continuous twisting branches of leaves and nuts border, five point purple star mark, c1780 ................................................................ 165.00
  Istoriato, charger, 16" d, majolica, underglaze blue, yellow, and red luster enamels dec, central scene of Roman legions rallying around their standards, wide scrolling grotesque border ................................................................. 200.00
  Savona, compote, 14" d, blue and white dec, floral border, pierced, blue lighthouse mark ................................... 1,200.00

# COOKIE JARS

**History:** Cookie jars, colorful and often whimsical, are now an established collecting category. Do not be misled by the high prices realized at the 1988 Andy Warhol auction. Many of the same cookie jars that sold for over $1,000 each can be found in the field for less than $100. Cookie jars often were redesigned to reflect newer tastes. Hence, the same jar may be found in several different variations.

**Marks:** Many cookie jar shapes were manufactured by more than one company and, as a result, can be found with different marks. This often happened because of mergers or separations, e.g., Brush-McCoy which became Nelson McCoy. Molds also were traded and sold among companies.

**References:** Fred and Joyce Roerig, *Collector's Encyclopedia of Cookie Jars*, Book I (1991, 1997 value update), Book II (1994, 1999 value update), Book III (1998), Collector Books; Mike Schneider, *The Complete Cookie Jar Book*, 2nd ed., Schiffer, 1999; Mark and Ellen Supnick, *Wonderful World of Cookie Jars*, L-W Book Sales, 1995, 1998 value update; Ermagene Westfall, *Illustrated Value Guide to Cookie Jars*, Book I (1983, 1997 value update), Book II (1993, 1997 value update), Collector Books.

**Periodical:** *Cookie Jarrin'*, RR 2, Box 504, Walterboro, SC 29488-9278.

**Collectors' Club:** American Cookie Jar Association, 1600 Navajo Rd, Norman, OK 73026, http://cookiejar-club.com.

**Museum:** The Cookie Jar Museum, Lemont, IL.

## Abingdon

Choo Choo ........................................................... 225.00
Humpty Dumpty .................................................. 295.00
Jack in Box ......................................................... 450.00
Jack O'Lantern .................................................... 350.00
Old Lady, #471 ................................................... 235.00

## American Bisque

Baby Elephant ..................................................... 175.00
Casper the Friendly Ghost .................................... 450.00
Cow Jumping Over The Moon, flasher ................... 975.00
Donkey pulling cart ............................................... 75.00
Humpty Dumpty .................................................. 455.00
Lamb ..................................................................... 75.00
Mohawk Indian ................................................ 2,200.00
Paddle Boat ........................................................ 275.00
Seal, igloo .......................................................... 350.00

## Appleman, Glenn

Rolls Royce ......................................................... 850.00

## Brayton Laguna

Matilda ............................................................... 900.00
Plaid Dog ........................................................... 360.00

## Brechner, Dan

Mickey Mouse School Bus ................................... 750.00
Mickey's 60th Anniversary, giant cake, 1988 ...... 425.00

## Brush

Covered Wagon .................................................. 500.00
Davy Crockett ..................................................... 225.00
Dog, basket ........................................................ 350.00
Hillbilly Frog ................................................... 4,200.00
Little Red Riding Hood ........................................ 795.00

## California Originals

Koala on Stump .................................................. 275.00
Pinocchio ............................................................ 950.00
Tigger ................................................................ 200.00

## Cavanaugh, Henry

Good Humor Truck .............................................. 225.00

## Disney

Bambi on Tree Stump, small chip ..................... 1,000.00
Donald Duck, on pumpkin ................................... 400.00
Dumbo with Timothy ............................................ 175.00
Mickey in car ...................................................... 450.00

## Doranne of California

Brown Shoe ........................................... 40.00
Cow Jumped Over the Moon, green ................... 200.00
Dragon ................................................. 275.00

## Enesco

Betsy Ross ............................................ 75.00
Sugar Town General Store .......................... 65.00

## Fitz and Floyd

Busy Bunnies Tree................................... 150.00
English Garden Wheelbarrow ....................... 165.00
Hydrangea Bears .................................... 170.00
Rolls Royce .......................................... 175.00
Santa, in airplane .................................. 200.00
Sock Hoppers ....................................... 300.00

## Goode, George

Tazmanian Devil in Whirlwind ..................... 200.00

## Hull

Apple ................................................. 150.00

## Lefton

Bluebird.............................................. 165.00
Miss Priss ........................................... 85.00
Old Lady ............................................. 110.00
Pixie Baby ........................................... 125.00
Scottish Mist ........................................ 200.00
Young Lady .......................................... 95.00

## McCoy

Cat on Coal Bucket................................. 200.00
Christmas Tree ...................................... 725.00
Clyde Dog ........................................... 200.00
Football Boy......................................... 295.00
Liberty Bell .......................................... 36.00

## Metlox

Frosty the Penguin.................................. 100.00
Koala Bear .......................................... 100.00
Little Red Riding Hood .......................... 1,275.00
Pinocchio Head ..................................... 235.00
Pretty Anne ......................................... 205.00
Rabbit on Cabbage ................................. 110.00
Scottie Dog, black .................................. 75.00
Squirrel on Pine Cone .............................. 75.00
Walrus................................................ 235.00
Watermelon .......................................... 365.00

## Mosaic Tile

Mammy, yellow ..................................... 500.00

## Napco

Bo Peep ............................................. 175.00
Cinderella............................................ 175.00
Little Red Riding Hood ............................. 175.00

## Regal

Chef .................................................. 475.00
Diaper-Pin Pig....................................... 450.00
Fifi Poodle .......................................... 525.00
Goldilocks ........................................... 225.00
Hobby Horse ........................................ 275.00
Three Bears ......................................... 325.00

## Shawnee

Smiley Pig, shamrock dec .......................... 400.00
Winnie, green hat, #61.............................. 475.00

## Sigma

Circus Lady .......................................... 200.00

## Star Jars

Wizard of Oz, complete set, Dorothy and Toto, Cowardly Lion, Scarecrow, Tin Man, Wicked Witch, Glenda, Winged Monkey, Munchkin Mayor, Wizard of Oz, Professor Marvel, Emerald City, Ruby Slippers............................... 1,900.00

## Starnes

Barn Happy Face.................................... 300.00
Bear Blocks.......................................... 150.00

## Twin Winton

Ark ................................................... 150.00
Bambi................................................ 180.00
Dutch Girl ........................................... 115.00
Gunfighter Rabbit................................... 250.00
Jack In Box .......................................... 500.00
Santa, black ......................................... 625.00
Smokey the Bear .................................... 90.00

## Warner Bros.

Roadrunner and Acme TNT......................... 400.00
Superman ........................................... 110.00

## Webster

School House ........................................ 70.00

# COPELAND and SPODE

**History:** In 1749, Josiah Spode was apprenticed to Thomas Whieldon and in 1754 worked for William Banks in Stoke-on-Trent. In the early 1760s, Spode started his own pottery, making cream-colored earthenware and blue-printed whiteware. In 1770, he returned to Banks' factory as master, purchasing it in 1776. Spode pioneered the use of steam-powered pottery-making machinery and mastered the art of transfer printing from copper plates. Spode opened a London shop in 1778 and sent William Copeland there about 1784. A number of larger London locations followed. At the turn of the century, Spode introduced bone china. In 1805, Josiah Spode II and William Copeland entered into a partnership for the London business. A series of partnerships between Josiah Spode II, Josiah Spode III, and William Taylor Copeland resulted. In 1833, Copeland acquired Spode's London operations and seven years later the Stoke plants. William Taylor Copeland managed the business until his death in 1868. The firm remained in the hands of Copeland heirs. In 1923 the plant was electrified; other modernization followed. In 1976, Spode merged with Worcester Royal Porcelain to become Royal Worcester Spode, Ltd.

**References:** Susan and Al Bagdade, *Warman's English & Continental Pottery & Porcelain*, 3rd Edition, Krause Publications, 1998; Robert Copeland, *Spode & Copeland Marks*, Cassell Academic, 1993; —, *Spode's Willow Pattern & Other Designs After The Chinese*, Blanford

Press, 1990; D. Drakard & P. Holdway, *Spode Printed Wares*, Longmans, 1983; L. Whiter, *Spode: A History of the Family, Factory, and Wares, 1733-1833*, Random Century, 1989; Sydney B. Williams, *Antique Blue & White Spode*, David & Charles, 1988.

**Museums:** Cincinnati Art Museum, Cincinnati, OH; City of Stoke-On-Trent Museum, Hanley, England; Jones Museum of Glass & Ceramics, Sebago, ME; Spode Museum, Stoke-on-Trent, UK; Victoria & Albert Museum, London, England.

Bowl
    8-1/2" d, Imari type, blue, green, and orange, scalloped edge, pedestal base, c1850 .................................... 85.00
    9-3/4" sq, cut corner, Imari-style dec, c1825, Spode mark, minor gilding and over glaze enamel wear ................... 650.00
Bust, 8-1/4" h, Sir Walter Scott, parian, mounted to raised circular base, imp Copeland mark, c1875 .................... 230.00
Centerpiece, 12" h, majolica, shell molded bowl surmounted by putto supporting small shell molded bowl on head, molded coral base, imp mark, c1875, rim chip repair ................ 990.00
Charger, 13-1/2" d, Imari style, red and blue enamels, gilt trim, floral border with scroll pattern and Chinese motif, imp "Spode New Stone China," c1810 .................................... 550.00
Creamer and Sugar, 3-1/4" h, Blue Willow, marked "Copeland's China England" .................................... 200.00
Demitasse Cup and Saucer, 4-1/2" d, gilt trim enamel floral design, pink ground, c1900, set of six .................. 700.00
Dinner Service, elegant gold and multicolored floral design, large, c1805-15 .................................... 5,500.00
Figure
    12" h, Lady of the Lake, nude figure, loosely draped cloth, seated on back, molded fish and reeds below, parian, imp marks "Marshall Fect SC, Copeland," mid-19th C ............. 400.00
    19-1/8" h, Young Shrimper, holding shell, dragging net, parian, c1880, imp Copeland marks, chips ............. 550.00
Flower Pot, 5" h, ftd base, gilted sea serpent head handles and trim, hp floral panels, striped bodies, painted Spode mark, gilt rim wear, price for pr .................................... 2,185.00
Luncheon Service, pattern 1721, Kakiemon style, enameled and gilt dec, twenty-one 8-1/2" d plates, four shrimp dishes, four 9-1/2" oval vegetable dishes, 10-1/4" d oval vegetable dish, three 9" d round vegetable dishes, two 7" cov oval sauce tureens with underplates, 14" l oval compote, Spode, early 19th C, price for 40 pc set 2,875.00
Oyster Plate, hp, insects and flowers .................... 50.00
Pitcher, jasper, blue, 19th C .................... 150.00

Plate
    8" d, scalloped edge, underglaze blue and orange floral pattern, gilt enamel accents and rim, price for set of 6 ................. 175.00
    8" d, scalloped edge, underglaze orange floral pattern, gilt enamel accents and rim, price for set of 6 ................. 150.00
    8-3/8" d, Aesthetic Movement, third quarter 19th C, octagonal, transfer and enamel Japonesque dec of birds, flowers, and fans, gold enamel details and rim, price for set of 10 ....... 300.00
    10-1/2" d, Louis XVI taste, Rose Pendant dec, retailed by Daniell, London, c1900-1910, price for set of 12 ................. 350.00
Platter, 21" l 15-1/2" w, Imari-style, well and tree, c1840, mkd "Copeland & Garrett" .................................... 450.00
Punch Bowl, 12-1/2" d, multicolored, Chinese garden scene, gold trim, c1810 .................................... 750.00
Salt and Pepper Shakers, pr, Red Tower pattern ..................... 20.00
Service Plate, 10-1/4" d, wide blue ground rim bounded by emb gilt bands, 20th C, set of twelve .................... 690.00
Tea and Dessert Service, semi-porcelain, Black Bird pattern, red on white, teapot, cov sugar, creamer, cov warm milk jug, eight dessert plates, seven cups and saucers, sq serving plate, minor damage, price for 31 pc set .................... 75.00
Tureen, cov, Imari palette, ironstone, c1833, Copeland and Garrett mark .................................... 690.00
Wall Brackets, parian, from Mississippi antebellum mansion, mkd "Copeland," pr .................................... 3,750.00

# COPPER

**History:** Copper objects, such as kettles, teakettles, warming pans, and measures, played an important part in the 19th-century household. Outdoors, the apple-butter kettle and still were the two principal copper items. Copper culinary objects were lined with a thin protective coating of tin to prevent poisoning. They were relined as needed.

**References:** Mary Frank Gaston, *Antique Brass & Copper*, Collector Books, 1992, 1998 value update; Henry J. Kauffman, *Early American Copper, Tin, and Brass: Handcrafted Metalware from Colonial Times*, Astragal Press, 1995.

**Reproduction Alert:** Many modern reproductions exist.

**Additional Listings:** Arts and Crafts Movement; Roycroft.

**Notes:** Collectors place great emphasis on signed pieces, especially those by American craftsmen. Since copper objects were made abroad as well, it is hard to identify unsigned examples.

Bed Warmer, 45" l, engraved floral and bird, turned wood handle ......... 375.00
Bookends, pr, 5-1/2" h, hammered, Dirk van Erp, imp mark, cleaned patina .................................... 300.00
Bowl
    8-1/2" d, 3-1/2" h, hand hammered, curving rim, light patina, imp Kalo Shops mark .................... 195.00
    15-1/2" d, 4" h, symbol shape, rolled edge, light patina, imp Marie Zimmerman mark, No. 95 .................... 1,495.00
Box, 7" l, 2-1/2" h, hammered, cedar lined, Dirk van Erp, imp mark, lightly cleaned patina .................... 550.00
Bud Vase, 8" h, 3-3/4" d, cylindrical, hammered woodgrain pattern, three buttresses, applied nickel-plated faceted squares, orig patina, stamped "M" .................................... 500.00
Candleholder, four holders, sgd "W L Fletcher" .................... 40.00
Chafing Dish, 11" h, dish supported by three realistically modeled rabbits, wooden base, marked "Black, Starr & Forest" ................. 450.00

**Plate, Marathon pattern, white center, cream border with blue floral dec, gold trim, 10-1/4" d, $25.**

**Measure, one gallon, handle, $90.**

Coal Hod, 17" h, brass handles, 19th C .................................... 165.00
Coffeepot, 11" h, wrought, tapering, lift lid with small turned copper fin- ial, curved spout, side apple wood handle, attached to stylized cop- per heart mounting .................................................................... 350.00
Coffee Urn, 14-1/2" h, brass fittings, label inside lid "Parkinson's Manu- factory, London" .................................................................... 225.00
Dipper, 80" l, orig pole with wrought iron fittings ......................... 650.00
Fish Cooker, 10" w, 7" h, punched tin insert, hinged top, handles 40.00
Hotwater Bottle, 17-1/2" l, oval, pewter fittings, screw cap with ring, old patina ...................................................................................... 140.00
Jardiniere, 14" h, 18-1/2" d, hammered, Secessionist style, four riveted strap handles, new dark patina, unmarked .......................... 1,400.00
Kettle, 18" d, 16-1/2" h, wrought iron rim, bale handle, old patina ...................................................................................... 165.00
Lamp, 9" h, 5-3/4" w, compressed sq, circular foot rim, beaded mid molding, patinated, applied silver seaweed, fish, seashells, and crab dec, orig wick holder now fitted for electricity, marked "Gorham," 1884 ..................................................................................... 3,850.00
Measure
    5" d, 3-7/8" h, cylindrical, brass rim, labeled "Fairbanks & Co, US Standard New York" ........................................................ 300.00
    6-1/4" h, haystack, Continental, 19th C ............................... 75.00
Mirror, 27-1/2" l, 18" h, repoussé copper mounted tooled russet leather covering, period beveled mirror, English, c1890-1895 ............. 495.00
Pitcher, 9-1/4" h, tankard shape, marked "D Bentley & Sons, N 3rd St., Phila" ....................................................................................... 75.00
Preserving Pot, 28" d, loop wrought iron handle, 19th C ............ 450.00
Sauce Pan, 8" d, dovetailed, wrought copper handle ................... 75.00
Tea Kettle
    5" h, dovetailed, polished, swivel handle, replaced lid ........ 200.00
    6" h, dovetailed, polished, swivel handle, dents, pinpoint holes in bottom .............................................................................. 200.00
    6-1/2" h, dovetailed, stamped "D. M. D." ............................. 160.00
    7-1/4" h, dovetailed, goose neck spout .............................. 165.00
    8" d, circular, brass knob finial, flat serving handle, marked "P Apple, Philadelphia," 18th/19th C .................................... 575.00
    8-1/2" d, circular, brass knob finial, flat serving handle, marked "C Tryon" .............................................................................. 550.00
Trade Sign
    8" d, Pawn Broker, three orig copper balls, old patina, new bracket .............................................................................. 250.00
    16" w, 14" h, coppersmith's, candle with candleholder shape, Arts and Crafts era, American ................................................ 275.00
Vase, 9" h, 9" w, hammered, bulbous form, rolled rim, Arts & Crafts style, attributed to San Francisco School, orig patina .............. 800.00
Vessel, 11" d, 7-1/2" h, hammered copper, warty design, rich red patina, applied handle, Arts & Crafts style, attributed to San Fran- cisco School ............................................................................. 750.00

# CORALENE

**History:** Coralene refers to glass or china objects which have the design painted on the surface of the piece along with tiny colorless glass beads which were applied with a fixative. The piece was placed in a muffle to fix the enamel and set the beads. Several American and English companies made glass coralene in the 1880s. Seaweed or coral were the most common design. Other motifs were Wheat Sheaf and Fleur-de-Lis. Most of the base glass was satin finished. China and pottery cor- alene, made from the late 1890s until after World War II, is referred to as Japanese coralene. The beading is opaque and inserted into the soft clay. Hence, it is only one-half to three-quarters visible.

## China

Box, cov, 1-1/2" x 2" x 3", copper matte ground, pink, lavender, and green thistle, mkd "Kinran Pat. 16132 Japan" .......................... 140.00
Sugar Shaker, white ground, orange coralene seaweed dec, orig top .. 180.00
Vase, 8" h, bulbous, scalloped and fluted rim, shaded lavender to light blue ground, multicolored snapdragons ................................. 250.00

## Glass

Bowl, 5-1/2" d, peachblow, ruffled, yellow coralene seaweed dec ......... 190.00
Miniature Lamp, rect satin base, Rainbow mother-of-pearl, applied pink and yellow coralene flowers, green leaves, applied clear scal- loped shell rigaree forms feet, orig fittings, shade and globe later replacements ........................................................................... 300.00
Pickle Castor, 7" h, rubena inverted thumbprint insert, coralene butter- flies, floral wreath, bird finial cov, cucumbers and leaves on vine, ring handle, low silverplated frame, marked "Derby Silver Co. #147" ...................................................................................... 825.00
Pitcher
    5-1/4" h, cased white ground, bright pink lining, gold seaweed coralene, applied amber reeded handle ............................ 225.00
    6-1/4" h, shaded yellow ground, white lining, coralene seaweed dec .................................................................................. 350.00
    6-1/2" h, pink and white satin stripes, yellow branch coralene, rose int., bulbous shape, tricorner mouth, amber applied handle, polished pontil .................................................................. 500.00
Sweetmeat, blue ground, flowers and leaves, SP holder ........... 400.00
Toothpick Holder, 2-1/2" h, glossy peachblow, sq raised rim, bulbous body, opaque lining, yellow seaweed coralene dec ................. 275.00
Vase
    4-1/2" h, Snowflake pattern, golden amber blending to pastel pink, cased in ivory ......................................................... 425.00
    4-1/2" h, 3-3/8" d, Diamond Quilted pattern, shaded pink, yellow beaded coralene starts in centers of diamonds, white enameled beading around top edge ................................................ 500.00
    5" h, yellow satin ground, blue coralene overlay, sgd "Webb," some beading missing ...................................................... 150.00
    5-3/8" h, golden yellow snowflake MOP satin ground, white lining, yellow wheat coralene dec ............................................... 520.00
    5-1/2" h, 4-5/8" d, fan shaped top, opaque pink satin ground blends to frosted base, all over dec of yellow three leaf sprays with coralene beads ...................................................... 235.00

# Reproduction Alert:

Reproductions are on the market, some using an old glass base. The beaded decoration on new coralene has been glued and can be scraped off.

**Vase, orange to yellow cased baluster body, allover seaweed coralene dec, 5" h, $425. Photo courtesy of Joy Luke Fine Art Brokers and Auctioneers.**

6" h, white cased to yellow, yellow coralene beading, ruffled rim ................................................................................. 250.00

7" h, ruffled pink top shading to white mother of pearl, coralene flowers and butterfly ............................................. 90.00

7-1/2" h, blue ground, bulbous, yellow coralene seaweed dec ...... 265.00

7-1/2" h, peachblow satin, deep rose shading to pale pink, yellow coralene seaweed dec, gold trim top, white casing, polished pontil, c1870, mkd "PATENT" ........................................... 850.00

7-3/4" h, 4-3/4" d, pink and green striped satin ground, off-white lining, heavy yellow beaded coralene .............................. 475.00

8" h, crimped wave mouth, yellow seaweed pattern, shaded pink ground .......................................................................... 200.00

8" h, 5" d, alternating pink, white, and green striped satin ground, shades to white base, yellow coralene beading ................ 520.00

8-1/2" h, green shaded ground, green beading, gold tracery .......................................................................... 350.00

Water Set, 9" h satin glass MOP pitcher, DQ, glossy finish, yellow coralene seaweed dec, bulbous, three-spout top, applied reeded shell handle, three matching 4" h tumblers, two small blisters on pitcher, Mt. Washington ...................................................................... 750.00

# CORKSCREWS

**History:** The corkscrew is composed of three parts: handle, shaft, and worm or screw. The earliest known reference to "a Steele Worme used for drawing corks out of bottles" is 1681. Samuel Henshall, an Englishman, was granted the first patent in 1795. Elaborate mechanisms were invented and patented from the early 1800s onward, especially in England. However, three basic types emerged: T handle (the most basic, simple form), lever, and mechanism. Variations on these three types run into the hundreds. Miniature corkscrews, employed for drawing corks from perfume and medicine bottles between 1750 and 1920, are among those most eagerly sought by collectors. Corkscrew styles tend to reflect the preferences of specific nationalities. The English favored the helix worm and often coppertoned their steel products. By the mid-18th century, English and Irish silversmiths were making handles noted for their clean lines and practicality. Most English silver handles were hallmarked. The Germans preferred the center worm and nickel plate. The Italians used chrome plate or massive solid brass. In the early 1800s, the Dutch and French developed elaborately artistic silver handles. Americans did not begin to manu-

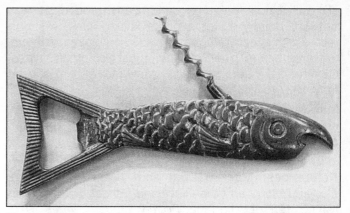

**Brass, fish, combination bottle opener and corkscrew, 5-1/2" l, $65.**

facture quality corkscrews until the late 19th century. They favored the center worm and specialized in silver-mounted tusks and carved staghorn for handles.

**References:** Donald A. Bull, *Bull's Pocket Guide to Corkscrews*, Schiffer Publishing, 1999; Fred O'Leary, *Corkscrews*, Schiffer Publishing, 1996.

**Collectors' Clubs:** Canadian Corkscrew Collectors Club, 670 Meadow Wood Rd, Mississaugua, Ontario, L5J 2S6 Canada; Just For Openers, 3712 Sunningdale Way, Durham, NC 27707.

Bone Handle
    Mechanism type, English rack and pinion corkscrew, polished, brush and hanging ring, four plain post open barrel, narrow rack, long wire helix, side handle, sgd "Verinder" ............. 410.00
    T-handle, Henshall, incised button, helical worm, c1820 .... 125.00
Brass Case, mechanism type, secondary wood swivel jointed handle, brush, applied Royal supporters, marked "Thomson Patent New Plus Ultra" ........................................................................ 300.00
Brass, rack and pinion type, double, steel shaft, center worm, cap lifter in handle, Italian, 1920 ............................................. 40.00
Bronzed Steel, lever, Heeley A1, double lever patent, helical worm ......................................................................... 65.00
Cast Iron, clamp on mechanism type, lacy openwork, emb "Phoenix," patented 1887 ............................................................ 200.00
Celluloid, novelty type, figural mermaid, bends at waist, marked "Geschutz" .................................................................. 275.00
Chrome, lever, zig-zag design, French, 10-1/2" l extended .......... 65.00
Ebony Handle, mechanism type, steel frame, foliate scrolling raised arm, steel ciphered worm, marked "Champion, Made in USA" 110.00
Ivory Handle, miniature, crescent shape, chromed turned steel shaft wire helix, c1790-1820 ..................................................... 75.00
Palmette Handle, miniature, carved handle with MOP, helical worm ......................................................................... 30.00
Silver, novelty type, gaucho and horse, oblong platform handle, Archimedian screw ......................................................... 775.00
Staghorn Handle, T-handle, ornate SS cap .............................. 100.00
Wood Handle, duck bill cap, simple Archimedean screw, German ........................................................................ 85.00

# COWAN POTTERY

**History:** R. Guy Cowan founded the Cowan Pottery in 1913 in Cleveland, Ohio. The establishment remained in almost continuous operation until 1931, when finan-

cial difficulties forced closure. Early production was redware pottery. Later a porcelainlike finish was perfected with special emphasis placed on glazes, with lustreware being one of the most common types. Commercial wares marked "Lakeware" were produced from 1927 to 1931.

**Marks:** Early marks include an incised "Cowan Pottery" on the redware (1913-1917), an impressed "Cowan," and an impressed "Lakewood." The imprinted stylized semicircle, with or without the initials "R. G.," came later.

**References:** Mark Bassett and Victorian Naumann, *Cowan Pottery and the Cleveland School*, Schiffer Publishing, 1997; Leslie Piña, *Pottery, Modern Wares 1920-1960*, Schiffer Publishing, 1994; Tim and Jamie Saloff, *Collector's Encyclopedia of Cowan Pottery: Identification and Values*, Collector Books, 1994.

**Museums:** Cowan Pottery Museum, Rocky River Public Library, Rocky River, OH; Everson Museum of Art, Syracuse, NY.

Bookends, pr, Push and Pull Elephants.................................. 1,400.00
Bowl
    8" d, irid blue luster glaze, minor roughness on base .......... 50.00
    12" d, irid blue luster glaze, ink mark .................................. 70.00
Candlesticks, pr, 5-1/2" h, 10-1/2" l, swirling molded floral design, ivory with yellow tint, imp mark .......................... 170.00
Cigarette Holder, ashtray, figural duck, yellow ........................... 85.00
Console Set, Art Deco styled bowl with radial lines, Nubian design, April Green glaze, matching pr of candlholders ...................... 400.00
Decanter, Standing Queen from Alice in Wonderland, Oriental Red, by artist Waylande DeSantis Gregory ..................... 675.00
Figure
    Bird on Wave, by Alexander Blazys, 12" h, melon green, broken and repaired .................................................................. 775.00
    Horse, 9" l, by Ralph Howard Cowan, Egyptian blue glaze.................................................................................. 1,500.00
    Nautch Dancer, by Waylande Gregory ,17-3/4" h .......... 10,450.00
    Russian Accordion Player (#34), artist Alexander Blazys 1,000.00
    Russian Balalaika Player (#44), by Alexander Blazys ..... 1,800.00

**Flower Frog, ivory glaze, 1920s, mkd "Lakewood, Ohio," 7" h, $165.**

Flower Frog
    6-1/2" h, Pavlova flower figure (#698), designed by R. Guy Cowan and Walter Sinz.................................... 270.00
    7-3/4" h, figural, two dancing girls with clasped hands, oval base, stylized wave motifs, glossy cream colored glaze, imp "R. G. Cowan" on base, c1925 .................... 520.00
Lamp, 19" h, molded squirrel and birds, brown and ivory, imp mark, orig fittings, later fabric shade .................... 350.00
Lamp Base
    16-1/2" h, Art Deco birds, wing-like handles, Guava glaze. 800.00
    19" h, molded leaves, gray and ivory semi-gloss glaze, orig fittings.......................................... 100.00
Sculpture, 14" h, 7" d, Colonial Head, by Waylande Gregory, peach crackled glaze, circular mark.................... 3,250.00
Vase
    5" h, shouldered form, pink and maroon high glaze, imp mark ..................................................70.00
    6-1/4" h, 5-1/4" d, spherical, stylized fish, seaweed and bubbles, light green sgraffito, emerald green ground, circular mark and "Cowan," small int. rim repair .......................... 950.00
    7" h, molded design, nude woman, long flowing hair, red hi-glaze, imp mark, minor line to lip .................... 1,000.00
    11-1/4" h, 8" w, pillow shape, phoenix base, flaring rim, crackled green glaze, circular mark, small manufacturing bruise to base of one, price for pr .......................... 1,200.00

# CRANBERRY GLASS

**History:** Cranberry glass is transparent and named for its color, achieved by adding powdered gold to a molten batch of amber glass and reheating at a low temperature to develop the cranberry or ruby color. The glass color first appeared in the last half of the 17th century but was not made in American glass factories until the last half of the 19th century. Cranberry glass was blown, mold blown, or pressed. Examples often are decorated with gold or enamel. Less-expensive cranberry glass, made by substituting copper for gold, can be identified by its bluish purple tint.

**Reference:** William Heacock and William Gamble, *Encyclopedia of Victorian Colored Pattern Glass: Book 9*, Cranberry Opalescent from A to Z, Antique Publications, 1987.

**Reproduction Alert:** Reproductions abound. These pieces are heavier, off-color, and lack the quality of older examples.

**Additional Listings:** See specific categories, such as Bride's Baskets; Cruets; Jack-in-the-Pulpit Vases; etc.

Basket
    5" d, 7" h, deep color, ruffled edge, petticoat shape, crystal loop handle, Victorian, c1880.................... 250.00
    7" h. 5" w, petticoat shape, ruffled edge, colorless loop handle, Victorian .......................... 250.00
    7-1/2" h, 6-3/4" w, boat-shaped basket, dark cranberry, all over gold dec, white florals, wide gold band, brass ftd vase with flower form handle.......................... 200.00
    8" h, 5" w, deep color, ruffled edge, applied colorless handle, Victorian .......................... 90.00
    8-1/2" h, 5" w, rose bowl form, Diamond Quilted pattern, ruffled edge, applied wishbone feet, V-shaped loop handle........ 150.00
    9" h, 5" w, deep cranberry int., amber casing on ext., white and gold aventurine flecks, applied amber feet, amber U-shaped handle .......................... 90.00

**Cruet, enameled white blossoms and berries, gold branches, orig hollow cranberry stopper, 7-1/2" h, $350. Photo courtesy of Clarence & Betty Maier.**

9" h, 5" w, very deep cranberry int., slight ribbed int., applied colorless wishbone rigaree around top, twelve applied feet, applied colorless twisted loop handle, Victorian, flake on one foot ............................................................................................... 100.00

Biscuit Barrel, frosted, bear finial top ......................................... 450.00

Bottle, 9-3/4" h, 3-1/2" d, dainty white enameled flowers around middle, white enameled dots dec, colorless teardrop stopper ....... 175.00

Box, cov, 6" d, hinged, Mary Gregory type dec of two birds on wall ................................................................................................ 325.00

Bride's Bowl, 9" sq, 3-1/2" h, finely executed enameled apple blossom dec, fancy ornate SP orig holder mkd "Middletown Silver Co.," Mt. Washington ..................................................................................... 950.00

Candlesticks, pr
8-1/2" h, prisms ...................................................................... 225.00
10-5/8" h, heavily encrusted gold and polychrome dec ...... 190.00

Celery Vase, 10" h, Thumbprint pattern, enameled flowers and birds, ornate handles, ftd mount, orig silverplated Jas. Tufts Co. frame ........................................................................................... 550.00

Claret Jug, 10-3/4" h, 4-5/8" h, French emb pewter hinged top, foot, and handle ................................................................................ 320.00

Cologne Bottle, 8-5/8" h, 2-3/8" d, gold scrolls, small gold flowers, matching sq cranberry bubble stopper ..................................... 185.00

Creamer, 5" h, 2-3/4" d, Optic pattern, fluted top, applied colorless handle .......................................................................................... 95.00

Cruet, orig stopper
6-1/2" h, 2-3/4" d, applied colorless wafer foot, applied colorless twisted rope handle with flower prunt at base, colorless ribbed bubble stopper ................................................................. 135.00
7-1/2" h, enameled white and blue blossoms, white berries, gold branch, orig hollow cranberry stopper with cranberry core ............................................................................................ 350.00
10-1/2" h, 3-7/8" d, acid cut herringbone double band around middle, applied colorless foot, applied colorless handle, colorless cut faceted stopper ........................................................... 190.00

Decanter
10" h, cut to colorless, flattened colorless oval, obverse medallion engraved "Mollies Pony 1869" centering scene with horse, cut star on reverse, conforming teardrop stopper, some internal bubbles ................................................................................. 990.00
10-1/2" h, 3-1/4" d, cut to colorless, matching mushroom bubble stopper ................................................................................. 250.00
11-1/2" h, 3-7/8" d, bulbous base, pinched-in sides, lacy gold enamel dec, dark red flowers, gold enameled centers, applied colorless handle, colorless cut faceted stopper ............... 250.00

Epergne, 19" h, 11" d, 5 pc, large ruffled bowl, tall center lily, three jack-in-the-pulpit vases ............................................................... 1,150.00

Finger Bowl and Underplate, 5-1/2" d, 6-1/2" d underplate, swirl pattern ........................................................................................ 65.00

Jack In The Pulpit Vase, 9" h, 5" w, deep cranberry, white opal edge, applied crystal base, Hobbs ..................................................... 325.00

Lamp, oil
Hobnail cranberry glass font, opaque white shade ............... 75.00
Opaque white cut to cranberry font, replaced metal base .. 275.00

Lantern, masthead type, cranberry glass lens, heavy Reverse Coin Dot design, orig brass maker's label mkd "Shubert & Cottingham Philadelphia," removable fuel container patented by Hugh Sangster in 1851, 1854, and 1867 ....................................................... 4,600.00

Mantel Luster, Victorian, electrified ............................................. 190.00

Mug, 4" h, 2-3/4" d, Baby Inverted Thumbprint pattern, applied colorless handle and pedestal foot ...................................................... 65.00

Music Box, 12-1/4" h, 5-1/4" d decanter, emb ribs with etched leaves and stars, orig colorless cut bubble stopper, not working ........ 310.00

Night Light, 6-1/4" h, 3-1/4" d, cranberry shade with white sanded scallops, grapes, and leaves, openwork brass top rim, gold-washed ormolu ftd frame ...................................................................... 275.00

Perfume Bottle, 2-1/4" d, round, filigree, gilt collar ..................... 695.00

Pickle Castor, 12-1/2" h, 7" jar with floral enameling, silver plate frame, lid, and tongs ........................................................................ 1,000.00

Pickle Jar, 3-1/2" h, apple blossom mold, pewter emb floral lid, Northwood .......................................................................................... 175.00

Pitcher
7-1/2" h, Coin Spot, shading to white base, rippled top, applied reeded colorless glass handle ............................................ 250.00
8-3/4" h, 6-3/4" d, hand blown, bell flower engraving, applied crystal loop handle, c1880 ...................................................... 375.00

Rose Bowl
3-3/4" h, 3-3/4" d, worn gold rim, six-crimp top .................... 90.00
4" h, optic ribs, scalloped turned in rim, colorless ruffled applied pedestal base ...................................................................... 125.00

Salt, open, 2-1/2" d, 1-1/2" h, six clear glass applied feet, silver rim with hallmarks ................................................................................. 200.00

Sugar Shaker
Argus Swirl .......................................................................... 150.00
Inverted Thumbprint ............................................................... 75.00
Optic pattern, bulbous base ................................................. 130.00

Tumbler, 3-3/4" h, hand blown, bell flower engraving, c1880 ..... 125.00

Vase
5-1/2" h, cranberry cut to clear to white, heavy raised gold dec, accent stripes around cutouts and borders ..................... 385.00
8" h, vertical bands below diamond points, deep cut to colorless ............................................................................... 315.00

Wine Decanter, 12" h, opaque white cased over cranberry, enameled flowers and gilt scrollwork dec, pr .......................................... 500.00

# CROWN MILANO

**History:** Crown Milano is an American art glass produced by the Mt. Washington Glass Works, New Bedford, Massachusetts. The original patent was issued in 1886 to Frederick Shirley and Albert Steffin. Normally, it is an opaque-white satin glass finished with light-beige or ivory-colored ground embellished with fancy florals, decorations, and elaborate and thick raised gold.

**Collectors Club:** Mount Washington Art Glass Society, P.O. Box 24094, Fort Worth, TX 76124.-1094

**Marks:** Marked pieces have a purple enamel entwined "CM" with a crown on the base. Sometimes paper labels were used. Since both Mount Washington and Pairpoint supplied mountings, the silver-plated mounts often have "MW" impressed or a Pairpoint mark.

**Advisors:** Clarence and Betty Maier.

Creamer and Sugar, 3-3/4" h creamer, 4-1/2" h cov sugar, pink cabbage roses, blue cornflowers, other colorful blossoms strewn over creamy surface, tan border, edged with raised gold scrollwork, ribbed handle on creamer, two tiny shell handles on sugar, logo mark ....................................................................................... 2,750.00

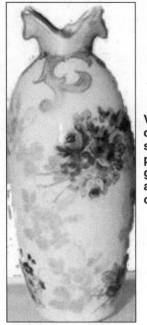

Vase, 9" h, Colonial Ware, sprays of colorful enamel blossoms, shadow foliate branches of single petaled roses and buds, neck with gold embellishments, sgd logo and "0615," $945. Photo courtesy of Clarence & Betty Maier.

Demitasse Cup and Saucer, 2" h, 5" d, golden vine with single petaled blossoms, buds, and tiny leaves, each with raised gold, coral and black rings of dots, sepia-colored rococo scrolls, satin-white ext., both mkd with logo .................................................... 1,750.00

Lamp, banquet, 23" h, 9" d, Colonial Ware, shiny ground, base and globe-shaped shade dec with sprays of golden roes an blossoms, touches of gold accent molded-in dec of florals, swags, and geometric designs, opaque white chimney, brass burner sgd "Made in United States of America" .......................................... 2,950.00

Muffineer, melon ribbed, butter yellow tint, swags of dainty powder blue and cream daisies, metal collar, lid emb with butterfly, dragonfly, and blossoms ............................................................. 535.00

Vase

    6" h, 5-3/4" d, butter yellow neck, mouth with four fold-down sides, twenty-four swirling molded-in ribs, cream colored body, blue and white forget-me-nots in heavily applied enamel, leaves and foliage ........................................................... 1,350.00

    6" h, 5-3/4" d, cream colored body, twenty-four swirling molded-in ribs, white peony blossoms, each petal outlined in raised gold, pearlescent scene, randomly placed medallions of light blue squiggly lines ................................................. 1,450.00

    8" h, huge mauve, creamy white, and peach-yellow peony blossoms, soft lemon ground, green and sepia foliage, gold dec around neck ............................................................... 765.00

    9" h, Colonial Ware, sprays of colorful enamel blossoms, shadow foliate branches of single petaled roses and buds, neck with gold embellishments, sgd logo and "0615" ..................... 945.00

    10-12" h, petticoat shape, white body, pastel pansies, freeform gold accents ................................................. 750.00

# CRUETS

**History:** Cruets are small glass bottles used on the table and holding condiments such as oil, vinegar, and wine. The pinnacle of cruet use occurred during the Victorian era when a myriad of glass manufacturers made cruets in a wide assortment of patterns, colors, and sizes. All cruets had stoppers; most had handles.

**References:** Elaine Ezell and George Newhouse, *Cruets, Cruets, Cruets*, Vol. I, Antique Publications, 1991; William

Opaque White, New England Glass Works, 6" h, $850. Photo courtesy of Clarence & Betty Maier.

Heacock, *Encyclopedia of Victorian Colored Pattern Glass: Book 6, Oil Cruets from A to Z*, Antique Publications, 1981.

**Additional Listings:** Pattern Glass and specific glass categories such as Amberina, Cranberry, and Satin.

5" h, satin, Diamond Quilted, MOP, pink, thorn handle and stopper ...... 595.00

5-1/2" h, cut glass, Chrysanthemum pattern, Hawkes ............... 150.00

5-1/2" h, opalescent glass, white Swirl pattern, applied sapphire blue handle, sapphire blue stopper .................................................. 285.00

6" h, Cone pattern, pink ............................................................... 70.00

6" h, white opaque, applied white handle, orig white stopper, attributed to New England Glass Works ...................................................... 850.00

6-1/2" h, threaded glass, vaseline............................................... 100.00

6-3/4" h, 4" d base, peachblow, petticoat form, three lip top, acid finish, New England ......................................................................... 1,950.00

7" h

    Custard Glass, Chrysanthemum pattern ............................ 250.00

    Cut glass, Vintage pattern, three pour spout, sgd "Tuthill".. 200.00

7-1/4" h, lavender, blown, ftd spherical body, slender cylindrical neck, gold flowers and bows, applied colorless handle and foot, colorless facet cut stopper ....................................................................... 225.00

7-1/2" h

    Art Glass, blue, fancy metal handle and band .................... 120.00

    Art Glass, lavender, white floral dec ................................. 100.00

    Opalescent, cranberry, Hobnail pattern ............................ 175.00

    Vaseline, Hobnail pattern .................................................. 400.00

8" h

    Amber, blown, ftd ovoid body, short neck, tricorn rim, blue daisies and gold leaves, applied handle, amber ball stopper....... 125.00

    Amazon pattern, amber, orig bar-in-hand stopper, Bryce Bros, c1880-95 .......................................................................... 500.00

8-1/4" h, Amazon pattern, clear, orig bar-in-hand stopper, Bryce Bros, c1880-95 ................................................................................ 125.00

9" h, cut glass, Alhambra pattern, orig stopper, Meriden ........... 550.00

10" h, cut glass, Greek key engraved border, pedestal ................ 50.00

# CUP PLATES

**History:** Many early cups were handleless and came with deep saucers. The hot liquid was poured into the saucer and sipped from it. This necessitated another plate for the cup, hence the "cup plate." The first cup plates made of pottery were of the Staffordshire variety. From the mid-1830s to 1840s, glass cup plates were favored. The Boston and Sandwich Glass Company was one of the main manufacturers of the lacy glass type.

**References:** Ruth Webb Lee and James H. Rose, *American Glass Cup Plates*, published by author, 1948, Charles E. Tuttle Co. reprint, 1985; Kenneth Wilson, *American Glass 1760-1930*, 2 vols., Hudson Hills Press and The Toledo Museum of Art, 1994.

**LR-82, Acorn and Leaves, opaque blue, fiery opalescence, $75.**

**Notes:** It is extremely difficult to find glass cup plates in outstanding (mint) condition. Collectors expect some signs of use, such as slight rim roughness, minor chipping (best if under the rim), and, in rarer patterns, portions of scallops missing. The numbers used are from the Lee-Rose book in which all plates are illustrated. Prices are based on plates in average condition.

## Glass

LR 13, deep blue, A-type mold, plain rim, New England .............. 65.00
LR 15 ............................................................................ 95.00
LR 28, colorless, 17 even scallops, New England or Sandwich origin .. 35.00
LR 36, opal opaque, 17 even scallops ...................................... 475.00
LR 42 ............................................................................ 100.00
LR 46, lavender, 15 even scallops ........................................... 125.00
LR 70, plain rope, Midwest origin ........................................... 125.00
LR 82, acorn and leaves, silver opaque blue, fiery opalescent... 575.00
LR 95, opal opaque, 10 sided, rope top and bottom.................. 175.00
LR 109, George Washington, 6" d, small chips ......................... 150.00
LR 135, 24 bull's eyes, Midwest origin..................................... 75.00
LR 163, light green, 34 scallops, Midwest origin......................... 65.00
LR 179, lavender, 10 scallops, rope top and bottom, Philadelphia
    origin ....................................................................... 135.00
LR 197-E....................................................................... 65.00
LR 200, 96 sawtooth scallops, Midwest orig................................ 40.00
LR 216-C....................................................................... 35.00
LR 257 ......................................................................... 35.00
LR 271 ......................................................................... 30.00
LR 272, 43 scallops ......................................................... 65.00
LR 323, opalescent .......................................................... 75.00
LR 332-B....................................................................... 30.00
LR 343-B....................................................................... 45.00
LR 399 ......................................................................... 119.00
LR 412, 10 sided, Sandwich origin ......................................... 100.00
LR 439-C....................................................................... 40.00
LR 440-B....................................................................... 35.00
LR 455, 48 even scallops, Sandwich origin ............................... 275.00
LR 456 ......................................................................... 40.00
LR 458-A....................................................................... 15.00
LR 465-F....................................................................... 15.00
LR 477 ......................................................................... 15.00
LR 479 ......................................................................... 25.00
LR 500 ......................................................................... 65.00
LR 522, amber, flint.......................................................... 375.00
LR 526 ......................................................................... 35.00
LR 547 ......................................................................... 20.00
LR 561-A, octagonal, clear, gray striations, Washington, tilted head,
    Midwest origin ........................................................... 4,000.00
LR 565-A....................................................................... 30.00
LR 575 ......................................................................... 65.00

## Glass, Historical

LR 576, medium blue, Sandwich origin ..................................... 95.00
LR 580, colorless, Victoria & Albert, 5-1/8" d, lacy..................... 100.00
LR 605-A, octagonal, ship................................................... 95.00
LR 619 ......................................................................... 185.00
LR 653, eagle, laurel wreath ............................................... 165.00
LR 658, emerald green, Boston & Sandwich origin, two tiny scallops
    missing ..................................................................... 4,250.00
LR 670 ......................................................................... 65.00
LR 676, 60 even scallops, Curling's Ft Pitt Glass Works............. 75.00
LR 677-A....................................................................... 40.00
LR 836, Geo. Peabody, Heart & Crown, 4-3/4" d......................... 85.00
LR 888 ......................................................................... 30.00

## Porcelain or Pottery

Davenport, pink luster, imp mark, 3-7/8" d ................................ 35.00
Mulberry, floral dec.......................................................... 25.00

## Pearlware, free-brushed

Eagle dec .................................................................... 660.00
Green scalloped edge, polychrome flowers, 4-1/2" d ............. 1,485.00
Octagonal, brown band, 4" d ............................................ 1,130.00

## Ridgway

Blind Boy pattern, scene of boy and mother seated on bench, floral
    border, medium blue transfer, c1830, 4-1/4" d .......................... 85.00
India Temple pattern, blue, emb white border, 3-7/8" d ............... 50.00
**Spatter Ware**, 5-1/8" d, blue morning glory center................. 3,245.00

## Staffordshire

American Eagle with Shield pattern, paneled sides, medium blue and
    white, 3-3/4" d ........................................................... 385.00
Asian landscape scene, imp "Opaque Granite China, W. R. & Co.,"
    light blue and white, 4" d, light stain.................................. 20.00
Basket of Flowers, imp "Adams," dark blue transfer, 4" d........... 155.00
Ben Franklin, boy with kite, blue and white, 3-1/2" d ................. 110.00
Bosphorous pattern, marked "T Mayer," c1840, light blue and white,
    4" d .......................................................................... 45.00
Boy with hoop, blue and white, 3-1/2" d.................................. 90.00
Center fruit cluster with bird, flowers, and scroll border, c1830, dark
    blue transfer, 4-1/4" d .................................................. 125.00
Cottage in woods scene, spearhead and trefoil border, marked
    "Clews," 3-5/8" d........................................................ 125.00
Landing of Lafayette, blue transfer ....................................... 275.00
William Penn's Treaty, Thomas Goodwin, 1830-40, brown and white,
    3-3/4" d...................................................................... 100.00
Woodlands Near Philadelphia, Joseph Stubbs and Stubbs & Kent,
    1790-1831, blue and white, 3-3/4" d ................................... 265.00

# CUSTARD GLASS

**History:** Custard glass was developed in England in the early 1880s. Harry Northwood made the first American custard glass at his Indiana, Pennsylvania, factory in 1898. From 1898 until 1915, many manufacturers produced custard glass patterns, e.g., Dugan Glass, Fenton, A. H. Heisey Glass Co., Jefferson Glass, Northwood, Tarentum Glass, and U.S. Glass. Cambridge and McKee continued the production of custard glass into the Depression. The ivory or creamy yellow custard color is achieved by adding uranium salts to the molten hot glass. The chemical content makes the glass glow when held under a black light. The more uranium, the more luminous the color. Northwood's custard glass has the smallest amount of uranium, creating an ivory color; Heisey used more, creating a deep yellow color. Custard glass was made in

## Reproduction Alert:

L. G. Wright Glass Co. has reproduced pieces in the Argonaut Shell and Grape and Cable patterns. It also introduced new patterns, such as Floral and Grape and Vintage Band. Mosser reproduced toothpicks in Argonaut Shell, Chrysanthemum Sprig, and Inverted Fan & Feather.

patterned tableware pieces. It also was made as souvenir items and novelty pieces. Souvenir pieces are include a place name or hand-painted decorations, e.g., flowers. Patterns of custard glass often were highlighted in gold, enameled colors, and stains.

**References:** Gary E. Baker et al., *Wheeling Glass 1829-1939*, Oglebay Institute, 1994, distributed by Antique Publications; William Heacock, *Encyclopedia of Victorian Colored Pattern Glass, Book IV: Custard Glass from A to Z*, Peacock Publications, 1980; William Heacock, James Measell and Berry Wiggins, *Harry Northwood: The Early Years 1881-1900*, Antique Publications, 1990.

**Additional Listings:** Pattern Glass.

Banana Boat
  Grape and Gothic Arches, Northwood, 6" h, 12" l............200.00
  Grape and Thumbprint, Northwood..................375.00
Berry Bowl, master
  Argonaut Shell, Northwood, 10-1/2" l..............150.00
  Beaded Circle, Northwood........................185.00
  Cherry and Scale, Fenton.......................120.00
  Intaglio, ftd.................................125.00
  Ring Band, Heisey............................125.00
  Victoria, Tarentum............................175.00
Bowl
  Delaware, US Glass............................65.00
  Wild Bouquet, 5" l, 2-3/4" h, slight loss to gold edge.........235.00
Butter Dish, cov
  Argonaut Shell, Northwood.....................250.00
  Beaded Circle, Northwood......................275.00
  Cherry and Scale, Fenton......................240.00
  Chrysanthemum Sprig, Northwood, blue...........750.00
  Fan, Dugan..................................225.00
  Geneva, Northwood, red and green dec...........165.00
  Intaglio, gold and green enamel dec, 6-1/5" h, 7-3/4" d......250.00
  Inverted Fan and Feather, Northwood............250.00
  Jefferson Optic, Jefferson.....................200.00
  Maple Leaf, Northwood.........................200.00
  Wild Bouquet, Northwood.......................275.00
  Winged Scroll, Heisey, dec.....................185.00
Celery
  Ivorina Verde, Heisey.........................250.00
  Victoria, Tarentum, gold trim..................190.00
Cigarette Box, Ivorina Verde, Heisey................250.00
Cologne Bottle, orig stopper
  Ivorina Verde, Heisey.........................250.00
  Northwood Grape, Northwood, nutmeg stain.......425.00
Compote, Intaglio, Northwood, 9" d.................385.00
Condiment Set
  Chrysanthemum Sprig, Northwood, 4 pcs.........2,000.00
  Ring Band, Heisey, 5 pcs.......................800.00
Cracker Jar, cov, Grape and Cable, Northwood, two handles....700.00
Creamer
  Argonaut Shell, Northwood.....................150.00
  Beaded Circle, Northwood, 4-1/2" h, slight gold loss.........350.00
  Cherry and Scale, Fenton......................145.00
  Delaware, US Glass, rose dec...................85.00

  Diamond with Peg, Jefferson....................90.00
  Fan, Dugan..................................100.00
  Fluted Scrolls, Heisey........................85.00
  Intaglio, gold and green enamel dec, 5-1/4" h, slight loss of gold at rim......225.00
  Inverted Fan and Feather, Northwood............150.00
  Jackson, Northwood...........................100.00
  Jefferson Optic, Jefferson.....................95.00
  Louis XV, Northwood...........................85.00
  Maple Leaf, Northwood.........................125.00
  Northwood Grape, Northwood, nutmeg stain.......115.00
  Ribbed Drape, Jefferson.......................120.00
  Ring and Beads, Heisey........................50.00
  Vermont, US Glass Co..........................100.00
  Victoria, Tarentum............................125.00
  Wild Bouquet, Northwood.......................145.00
  Winged Scroll, Heisey, dec....................110.00
Cruet
  Argonaut Shell, Northwood, gold trim...........885.00
  Beaded Circle, Northwood, 6-1/2" h, slight gold loss......1,250.00
  Georgia Gem, Tarentum, green, orig stopper.....300.00
  Louis XV, Northwood, clear faceted stopper.....185.00
  Maple Leaf, Northwood.........................950.00
  Ribbed Drape, Jefferson.......................400.00
  Ring Band, Heisey............................400.00
  Wild Bouquet, Northwood.......................525.00
Custard Cup
  Empress, Riverside, green, gold trim...........45.00
  Winged Scroll, Heisey.........................65.00
Goblet
  Beaded Swag, Heisey..........................75.00
  Grape and Cable, Northwood....................70.00
  Humidor, Winged Scroll, Heisey................225.00
Jelly Compote
  Argonaut Shell, Northwood.....................110.00
  Beaded Circle, Northwood......................365.00
  Chrysanthemum Sprig, Northwood................200.00
  Geneva, Northwood............................100.00
  Intaglio, Northwood, gold trim.................150.00
  Maple Leaf, Northwood.........................375.00
  Ribbed Drape, Jefferson.......................190.00
  Ring Band, Heisey............................200.00
Lamp, Heart with Thumbprint, Tarentum, kerosene.....400.00
Mug
  Diamond with Peg, Jefferson....................60.00
  Punty Band, Heisey...........................70.00
  Ring Band, Heisey............................60.00
Nappy, Winged Scroll, Heisey......................65.00
Pickle Dish
  Beaded Swag, Heisey..........................265.00
  Vermont, US Glass............................60.00
Pin Dish, Delaware, US Glass, dec..................80.00
Pitcher
  Cherry and Scale, Fenton......................350.00
  Chrysanthemum Sprig, Northwood................375.00
  Intaglio, gold and green enamel dec, 8-1/2" h..425.00
  Inverted Fan and Feather, Northwood............400.00
  Maple Leaf, Northwood.........................385.00
  Ring Band, Heisey, floral dec..................450.00
  Vermont, US Glass............................250.00
  Winged Scroll, Heisey, dec....................290.00
Plate
  Grape & Cable, Northwood, nutmeg stain.........60.00
  Prayer Rug, Imperial, 7-1/2" d.................45.00
  Three Fruits, Northwood, 7-1/2" d..............35.00
Punch Bowl, matching base, Grape and Cable, Northwood....900.00
Punch Cup
  Grape and Cable, Northwood....................50.00
  Inverted Fan and Feather, Northwood............200.00
  Ring Band, Heisey............................60.00

Salt and Pepper Shakers, pr
- Argonaut Shell, Northwood ...................................... 350.00
- Beaded Circle, Northwood ...................................... 275.00
- Carnelian, Northwood ........................................... 450.00
- Fluted Scrolls with Flower Band, Northwood ...... 150.00
- Geneva, Northwood .............................................. 185.00
- Georgia Gem, Tarentum, orig top ....................... 100.00
- Heart, Northwood ................................................. 175.00
- Intaglio, gold and green enamel dec, 3-1/4" h .... 175.00
- Louis XV, Northwood ............................................ 350.00
- Maple Leaf, Northwood ........................................ 475.00
- Trailing Vine, Couderspot Glass ......................... 165.00

Sauce/Berry Bowl, individual size
- Argonaut Shell, Northwood, dec ............................ 90.00
- Beaded Circle, Northwood ..................................... 65.00
- Chrysanthemum Sprig, Northwood ........................ 85.00
- Delaware, US Glass, rose stain ............................. 65.00
- Fan, Dugan ........................................................... 70.00
- Geneva, Northwood, oval ...................................... 45.00
- Georgia Gem, Tarentum ........................................ 40.00
- Intaglio, gold and green enamel dec, 2-3/4" h, wear to gold at
  rim ...................................................................... 100.00
- Inverted Fan and Feather, Northwood ................... 55.00
- Louis XV, Northwood, gold trim ............................. 45.00
- Maple Leaf, Northwood .......................................... 80.00
- Peacock and Urn, Northwood ................................ 45.00
- Ribbed Drape, Jefferson ....................................... 45.00
- Victoria, Tarentum ................................................. 50.00

Spooner
- Beaded Circle, Northwood, 4-1/4" h, slight gold loss .......... 350.00
- Chrysanthemum Sprig, Northwood ....................... 125.00
- Everglades, Northwood ........................................ 145.00
- Fan, Dugan ........................................................... 85.00
- Intaglio, gold and green enamel dec, 4-3/4" h, some loss to gold
  trim ..................................................................... 225.00
- Louis XV, Northwood ............................................. 75.00
- Ribbed Drape, Jefferson ....................................... 65.00
- Trailing Vine, Couderspot Glass, blue ................... 70.00
- Victoria, Tarentum ................................................. 65.00
- Wild Bouquet, Northwood ...................................... 70.00
- Winged Scroll, Heisey ......................................... 100.00

Sugar, cov
- Argonaut Shell, Northwood ................................. 150.00
- Beaded Circle, Northwood, 6-3/4" h, slight gold loss .......... 485.00
- Cherry and Scale, Fenton ................................... 145.00
- Chrysanthemum Sprig, Northwood, blue, gold dec .......... 395.00
- Delaware, US Glass, rose dec .............................. 85.00

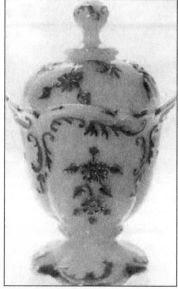

**Sugar Bowl, cov, Intaglio, slight loss to gold and green dec, 7-1/2" h, $225. Photo courtesy of Clarence & Betty Maier.**

- Diamond with Peg, Jefferson ............................... 110.00
- Everglades, Northwood ........................................ 125.00
- Fan, Dugan ......................................................... 100.00
- Fluted Scrolls, Heisey .......................................... 85.00
- Intaglio, gold and green enamel dec, 7-1/2" h, some loss to gold
  trim at rim .......................................................... 225.00
- Jackson, Northwood ............................................ 100.00
- Northwood Grape, Northwood, nutmeg stain ...... 115.00
- Ribbed Drape, Jefferson ..................................... 120.00
- Ring and Beads, Heisey ........................................ 50.00
- Vermont, US Glass Co. ........................................ 100.00
- Winged Scroll, Heisey ......................................... 175.00

Syrup, orig top
- Geneva, Northwood ............................................. 250.00
- Ring Band, Heisey ............................................... 315.00

Table Set, cov butter, creamer, cov sugar, spooner
- Carnelian ........................................................... 850.00
- Geneva, Northwood ............................................. 550.00
- Georgia Gem, Tarentum, gold trim ...................... 300.00
- Louis XV, Northwood, gold trim ............................ 500.00
- Ring Band, Heisey ............................................... 550.00

Toothpick Holder
- Argonaut Shell, Northwood, dec .......................... 465.00
- Chrysanthemum Sprig, Northwood, blue, gold trim .......... 315.00
- Diamond with Peg, Jefferson ................................ 85.00
- Ivorina Verde, Heisey ............................................ 85.00
- Maple Leaf, Northwood ........................................ 475.00
- Ribbed Drape, Jefferson ..................................... 150.00
- Vermont, US Glass, green dec ............................ 145.00

Tumbler
- Argonaut Shell, Northwood .................................... 90.00
- Chrysanthemum Sprig, blue, gold trim, 3-3/4" h .......... 185.00
- Delaware, US Glass, green dec ............................. 65.00
- Fan, Dugan ........................................................... 60.00
- Fluted Scrolls, Heisey .......................................... 45.00
- Grape and Cable, Northwood, nutmeg stain ......... 50.00
- Grape and Gothic Arches, Northwood, , 6" h ....... 65.00
- Prayer Rug, Imperial ............................................. 80.00
- Punty Band, Heisey, souvenir ............................... 40.00
- Ribbed Drape, Jefferson, floral dec .................... 100.00
- Winged Scroll, Heisey ........................................... 70.00

Vase
- Grape Arbor, Northwood, nutmeg stain .................. 85.00
- Prayer Rug, Imperial ............................................. 65.00
- Victorian, baluster, crown-style top, gold dec, intertwining foliage
  around center, 15" h, 4-1/2" h, matched pr ......... 2,500.00

Whiskey, Diamond with Peg, Jefferson souvenir .......... 45.00

Wine
- Beaded Swag, Heisey ............................................ 70.00
- Diamond with Peg, Jefferson ................................ 50.00
- Punty Band, Heisey ............................................... 50.00
- Tiny Thumbprint .................................................... 50.00

# CUT GLASS, AMERICAN

**History:** Glass is cut by grinding decorations into the glass by means of abrasive-carrying metal or stone wheels. A very ancient craft, it was revived in 1600 by Bohemians and spread through Europe to Great Britain and America. American cut glass came of age at the Centennial

Exposition in 1876 and the World Columbian Exposition in 1893. The American public recognized American cut glass to be exceptional in quality and workmanship. America's most significant output of this high-quality glass occurred from 1880 to 1917, a period now known as the Brilliant Period.

**Marks:** Around 1890, some companies began adding an acid-etched "signature" to their glass. This signature may be the actual company name, its logo, or a chosen symbol. Today, signed pieces command a premium over unsigned pieces since the signature clearly establishes the origin. However, signatures should be carefully verified for authenticity, since objects with forged signatures have been in existence for some time. One way to check is to run a finger tip or fingernail lightly over the signature area. As a general rule, a genuine signature cannot be felt; a forged signature has a raised surface. Many companies never used the acid-etched signature on their glass and may or may not have affixed paper labels to the items originally. Dorflinger Glass and the Meriden Glass Co. made cut glass of the highest quality, yet never used an acid-etched signature. Furthermore, cut glass made before the 1890s was not signed. Many of these wood-polished items, cut on blown blanks, were of excellent quality and often won awards at exhibitions.

**References:** Bill and Louis Boggess, *Identifying American Brilliant Cut Glass*, 3rd ed., Schiffer Publishing, 1996; ——, *Reflections on American Brilliant Cut Glass*, Schiffer Publishing, 1995; Jo Evers, *Evers' Standard Cut Glass Value Guide*, Collector Books, 1975, 2000 value update; Kyle Husfloen, *Antique Trader's American & European Decorative and Art Glass Price Guide*, 2nd ed., Krause Publications, 2000; Bob Page and Dale Fredericksen, *A Collection of American Crystal*, Page-Fredericksen Publishing, 1995; ——, *Seneca Glass Company 1891-1983*, Page-Fredericksen Publishing, 1995; J. Michael Pearson, *Encyclopedia of `American Cut & Engraved Glass*, Vols. I to III, published by author, 1975; Albert C. Revi, *American Cut & Engraved Glass*, Schiffer Publishing, 1965; Jane Shadel Spillman, *American Cut Glass, T. G. Hawkes and His Competitors*, Antique Collectors' Club, 1999; Martha Louise Swan, *American Cut and Engraved Glass*, Krause Publications, 1998. Kenneth Wilson, *American Glass 1760-1930*, 2 vols., Hudson Hills Press and The Toledo Museum of Art, 1994.

**Collectors' Club:** American Cut Glass Association, P.O. Box 482, Ramona, CA 92065.

**Museums:** Corning Museum of Glass, Corning, NY; High Museum of Art, Atlanta, GA; Huntington Galleries, Huntington, WV; Lightner Museum, St. Augustine, FL; Toledo Museum of Art, Toledo, OH.

Ashtray, 4" x 3", billiard table shape, engraved Kingfisher, sgd "Hawkes" ...............................................................100.00
Basket
    4", egg shaped, two large pinwheels, hobstar, crosshatch and fan motif, twist handle ....................................................150.00
    7" x 7", two large Florentine stars, hobstar, crosshatch, rope twist handle, attributed to Meriden ......................................350.00

Bell
    4-1/2" h, Monarch pattern, J. Hoare............................225.00
    4-1/2" h, starred top, beaded flutes on handle, large feathered band with vesicas of hobstars and crosshatching............225.00
    4-1/2" h, three large hobstars with pillar of crosshatching, fan in between, notched handle .................................................150.00
    4-3/4" h, Delft pattern, J. Hoare .................................175.00
    5-1/2" h, strawberry diamond bands, crosshatching in fan, handle cut to pattern ..............................................................325.00
    7" h, Colonial pattern, Dorflinger................................600.00
    8" h, hobstars, fans, crosshatching, cut handle, cut by Thomas Hazelbauer for Hawkes............................................850.00
Berry Bowl, 8" d, Expanding Star.................................250.00
Bonbon Dish
    7-1/2" l, 6" w, loop handle, Hobstar and Gothic Arch dec, c1900 ........................................................................75.00
    9" l, Arcadia pattern, scoop shape, by Sterling.................175.00
Bowl
    3-1/2" x 13", rolled top, silver diamond in thistle shape, notched miters on base, thistle and flower top border ...................700.00
    7" x 4" x 3", oval, Rosaceae pattern, sgd "Tuthill".............800.00
    8" d, Napoleon pattern, sgd "Hawkes" .........................550.00
    8" x 11", pedestal, large hobstars, bands of cane and stars, 32-point hobstar base, triple notched handles, very heavy blank............................................................3,250.00
    8-3/4" d, low, cranberry cut to clear, Venetian pattern .....2,100.00
    9" d, demonstration type, cutting process shown through four divided sections, sgd "J. Hoare"................................2,500.00
    9" d, divided, Garland pattern, hobstars, feathered fan, and crosshatching, sterling rim, Gorham ..............................250.00
    9" d, low, large feathered hobstars, hobstar, cane, and fan motif ........................................................................500.00
    9" w, sq, #98 pattern, sgd "Sinclaire" ..........................850.00
    9-1/2" d, Bermuda pattern, blown out and crimped, Bergen............................................................................325.00
    9-1/2" d, 2" h, low, engraved fish swimming in swirling water, sgd "Sinclaire, Fish #1" ................................................400.00
    10" d, 4" h, rolled rim, Harvard pattern, Mt. Wasington.......350.00
Bud Vase, 3" h, green cut to clear, split miters and punties, floral engraving, silver rim, pattern "Stone Engraving #2" by Dorflinger............................................................900.00
Bunsen Burner, 5", Harold pattern, brass fittings and cover, Hawkes ......................................................................450.00
Butter Pat
    2-1/2" d, flat stars and crosshatching, price for set of four.. 150.00
    2-1/2" d, ray center, split vesica and star border, sgd "Unger Bros," price for pr ...........................................................200.00
Cake Stand
    8" d, 3-1/2" h, Vintage pattern, scalloped rim, sgd "Tuthill" ......................................................................800.00
    9-1/2" x 7-1/2", Alhambra pattern, tear drop stem, pattern cut base, Meriden ...........................................................1,100.00
Candelabra
    15" h, Prism pattern, five sterling holders, Meriden .........1,250.00
    16" h, Clarke cricket lights, hollow stems with diamond cuts, brass fittings, sgd with Clarkes patent, price for pr .................1,000.00
Candlestick
    7-1/2" h, Flutes, Hawkes.......................................175.00
    9" h, Paul Revere pattern, sgd "Hawkes".....................300.00
    10" h, honeycomb, large 24 point hobstar base .................400.00
    10-1/4" h, hollow center, flute neck with ball cut in strawberry diamond ......................................................................125.00
    10-1/2" h, Victoria pattern, sgd "Eggington".....................600.00
    10-3/4" h, Colonial pattern, Bergen.............................200.00
    10-3/4" h, rolled top, Vintage pattern, Tuthill.................275.00
Candy Dish, cov, 9" d, Marlboro pattern, Dorlinger.................650.00
Canoe
    3-1/2" l, Harvard .................................................80.00
    10" l, ends in shape of "Woodbark & String" boat ends, crosscut diamond, Hawkes.....................................................1,200.00

Caviar Dish, cov
    6" x 8-1/2", stars, hobstars, crosshatching, blind miters .. 1,150.00
    8" h, hobstar, strawberry diamond, and fan ........................ 650.00
Celery Boat, 11-1/2" w, 4-1/2" d, 2" h, elliptical, Hobstar and Fan dec,
    c1895-1905 ........................................................................ 175.00
Celery Dish
    12" x 8", side compartments for dip, fancy feathered heart
        pattern .......................................................................... 1,000.00
    13", folded, etched floral with hobstar, vesica, and fan....... 175.00
Celery Vase, 10" h, notched prisms with band of hobstars, faceted
    knob, skirt base, attributed to J. Hoare .................................. 675.00
Center Bowl, 9-1/2" d, 4-1/2" h, Kohinoor & St. Louis motif, sgd
    "Hawkes".................................................................................. 250.00
Chalice, 14", hobstar and fan motif, one fan left out for monogram, tear
    drop stem ................................................................................ 650.00
Chamberstick
    2" x 4", star of crosshatching and hobstars with notched border,
        notched handle, sgd "Hawkes"........................................ 800.00
    2-1/2" x 4-1/2", base cut in notched prisms, four ball feet, swirled
        cut handle, sterling silver holder..................................... 750.00
Champagne, 5-1/4" h, hollow stem, hobstar, crosshatch, star and fan
    motif ........................................................................................ 125.00
Champagne Jug, 12-3/4" h, large 36 point hobstars, cane, prism,
    strawberry diamond, star, and fan motif, pattern cut handle . 1,300.00
Cheese Dish, 7" x 6", dome cover, matching underplate, all over cop-
    per wheel engraving of farmhouse, trees, cows, lambs, and
    deer ...................................................................................... 3,700.00
Cheese and Cracker
    9" d, Aberdeen pattern, Jewel............................................... 850.00
    10" d, center spire, Dorlinger's #18..................................... 260.00
Cigar Holder, 3-1/2" l, notched miters and stem in swirl miter .... 350.00
Claret Decanter
    9-1/2" h, whiskey jug form, shoulder step-cut, loop handle lapi-
        dary cut, Lancet Hobstar dec, discoloration on int. base, c1890-
        95 ...................................................................................... 165.00
    10" h, Buzz and Hobstars dec, cut spherical stopper, notch-cut
        handle, c1905-15 ............................................................. 110.00
Cocktail Glass, 4-1/4" h, Greek Key, three engraved flowers and
    leaves, Pairpoint....................................................................... 70.00
Cologne Bottle
    4" d, 6" h, sterling silver cap with fitted secondary glass stopper,
        c1895-1900 ...................................................................... 490.00
    8-3/4" l, lay-down, diamond of hobnail with clusters of punties .....
        110.00
Comport
    7-1/2" d, 8" h, hobstar, cane, strawberry diamond motif, scalloped
        rim, 32 point hobstar scalloped foot base ........................ 400.00
    8" x 5", Kenwood pattern, sgd "Maple City" ........................ 200.00
Condiment Bowl, 8" d, Interlaced Hobstars dec, c1895............. 100.00
Cookie Tray, 7" x 8-1/2", hobstar, Harvard, and silver diamond, side-
    bands of hobstar and crosshatching, fully cut .......................... 275.00
Cordial
    3-3/4" h, feathered star with curved miters, hobstar and fan, apple
        core stem with double teardrop, star base ....................... 375.00
    6" h, Uncatena, Pairpoint, straight stem, price for pr .......... 175.00
    6-1/2" h, engraved floral and ribbon, elongated punties ....... 40.00
Creamer, 4" h, Propeller pattern, distributed by Marshall Fields... 75.00
Creamer and Sugar
    Pedestal, Dorcas pattern ....................................................... 450.00
    Pedestal, 6", strawberry diamond and fan, sterling base, sgd
        "Hawkes".......................................................................... 175.00
    Tri-corner, Monarch pattern, J. Hoare................................... 325.00
Cruet, 6" h, hobstars, crosshatching and double miter cuts, triple pour
    spout ........................................................................................ 150.00
Cup and Saucer, star pattern, triple notched handle, Dorlinger .. 300.00
Decanter
    13-3/4" h, Buzz dec, period cut glass snake stopper,
        c1905-15 .......................................................................... 75.00

**Grain Cart, Harvard pattern, 11-1/2" l, 4" d, 4" h, $2,000.
Photo courtesy of Woody Auction.**

    15" h, Mercedes pattern, lapidary cut ring, pattern stopper,
        Clarke................................................................................. 950.00
Dish, 10" d, three-sections, engraved strawberries, currents, and
    gooseberries, Gorham sterling silver handle connected to center, sgd
    "Sinclaire" ............................................................................ 1,550.00
Epergne
    14", four lilies, copper wheel engraved floral and fern,
        John Illig.......................................................................... 900.00
    14-1/2" x 11", engraving #8, heavy blank, pedestal bowl, two
        piece, sgd "Sinclaire"....................................................... 650.00
Figure, dog, 2-1/2" l, frosted, fashioned after Faberge Dog, cut by Dor-
    flinger, 1920............................................................................. 125.00
Finger Bowl, 4-1/2" d, engraving #4 pattern, sgd "Sinclaire" ...... 250.00
Flask, 11" l, lay-down, strawberry diamond, clear sides, sterling top,
    attributed to Dorflinger............................................................. 200.00
Flower Center
    4-1/2", Bengal pattern, sgd "Sinclaire" ................................. 700.00
    5-1/2", Kings pattern, wafer base, sgd "Hawkes"................ 900.00
    6-1/2" x 8", Queens pattern, sgd "Hawkes" .................... 1,100.00
    10" d, 6-1/2" h, Grecian pattern, sgd "Hawkes" .............. 4,900.00
    12" d, 8" h, large hobstars, strawberry diamond, crosscut bar
        motif, sgd "J. Hoare"......................................................... 800.00
Fruit Bowl, 8" d, 3-1/2" h, Interlaced Hobstars dec, c1895 ......... 110.00
Ginger Jar, cov, 5" h, Russian pattern....................................... 325.00
Grain Cart, 11-1/2" x 4" x 4", Harvard pattern, very rare.......... 2,000.00
Gravy Boat
    6" l, blowout panels, scalloped standard, stepcut neck and
        spout ................................................................................. 550.00
    8" l, matching underplate, hobstar and fan, stepcut lip....... 450.00
Honey Jar, cov, 6" h, Boston pattern, sterling silver rim and lid, Mt.
    Washington ............................................................................. 400.00
Horseradish Jar, cov
    4-1/2" h, Brunswick pattern, triple notched handle, sterling finial,
        Higgins & Seiter............................................................... 525.00
    5" h, Boston pattern, Gorham sterling silver lid, Mt.
        Washington ...................................................................... 225.00
Ice Bucket
    6" x 7-1/2", Crescent pattern, two handles, Higgins and
        Seiter................................................................................. 375.00
    6-1/2" d, 5-1/2" h, Hobstar and Fan dec, c1895-1910 ........ 150.00
Ice Cream Bowl, 10" d, 4" h, Interlaced Hobstars dec,
    c1895-1900 ............................................................................. 200.00
Ice Cream Set, 15" x 9" Cluster pattern tray, six 7" d matching plates,
    Eggington .............................................................................. 3,100.00
Ice Cream Tray, 10" x 10-1/4", Carolyn pattern, sgd "J. Hoare" and "F.
    W. Hoffman" ......................................................................... 2,750.00
Jelly Compote
    4-1/2" d, 9" h, hobstar, band of flat star, attributed to Clark 350.00
    8" d, hobstar, vesica, strawberry diamond and cane, tear drop
        stem .................................................................................. 250.00
Lamp, table, 21-1/2" h, 12" d mushroom shade, hobstar pinwheel
    motif ...................................................................................... 2,000.00
Letter Opener, 11-1/2" l, engraved hollow handle with seaweed motif,
    ivory blade, sterling silver fitting .............................................. 600.00

Liquor Decanter, 14-1/2" h, Creswick pattern, long narrow neck, triple notched handle, pattern cut stopper, sgd "Eggington" ............ 900.00

Loving Cup, 5" h, bow time of crosshatch and fan, star base, three handles ................................................................................. 175.00

Mayonnaise Set, Tiger Lily pattern, sgd "Sinclaire" .................... 475.00

Miniature

    Banana Bowl, 4" d, hobstar, miter, nailhead diamonds, attributed to Hawkes ................................................................... 200.00

    Dish, 2-1/2" d, double handles, cut hobstars, zippered miters, and fans ............................................................................ 100.00

    Flower Center, 2-1/2" x 3", hobstar, bow tie of crosshatching and fans ............................................................................ 200.00

    Loving Cup, 3" h, Pattern #20, sterling silver rim, Dorflinger .................................................................... 300.00

    Paperweight, 1-1/2" x 2", miniature, cut in double miter, Harvard ...................................................................... 300.00

    Pitcher, 2-1/2" h, large fans, alternating diamonds of strawberry diamond and crosshatching, star base, triple notched handle ..................................................................... 225.00

    Punch Bowl, 3" w, 3" h, two piece bowl and stand, strawberry diamond .................................................................... 600.00

    Vase, 5" h, Brunswick pattern, sgd "Hawkes" .................... 500.00

Mint Set, Star of David center, sterling rims, sterling handle on master, master dish and four individuals, price for five pc set .............. 250.00

Mustard Pot, sterling top, 3" d, 5" h, ftd, bands of punties, notched oblong flutes ............................................................................ 200.00

Napkin Ring, 1-1/2" x 2", cut in band of diamond shaped stars with crosshatching ..................................................................... 80.00

Nut Dish, 7" d, swirl effect, hobstar, beading, crosshatch and fan motif 110.00

Paperweight

    2-1/2" w, 4" h, book shape, Russian pattern ...................... 400.00

    3" d, eight sided, zipper cut, ray base, Gorham sterling silver top ............................................................................ 175.00

    3" d, hobstar shape, cut hobstar and prisms, sterling silver top ............................................................................ 250.00

Parfait, 7" h, two hobstars alternating with two large fans around top, bottom notched with fans and hobnails ................................. 110.00

Picture Frame, 5" x 6-1/2", strawberry diamond border, sgd "Hawkes" ............................................................................. 275.00

Pitcher

    7-1/2" h, tusk shape, Russian pattern, button strap handle, J. Hoare ........................................................................ 800.00

    11" h, pedestal, rock crystal, engraved iris, carnation, tulip, daisy, and lily panels, pattern cut handle, sgd "Hawkes Gravic" ..................................................................... 1,600.00

    12-1/2" h, Wild Rose pattern, pedestal, sgd "Tuthill" ........ 5,200.00

Place Card Holder, 2-1/2" x 2", faceted ball on faceted base, attributed to Dorflinger ......................................................................... 150.00

Plate, 7" d

    Aberdeen pattern, Jewel Cut glass ............................... 1,100.00

    Acme pattern, J. Hoare .................................................. 800.00

    Albion pattern, sgd "Hawkes" ....................................... 800.00

    Alexandria pattern, sgd "Hawkes" ............................... 1,150.00

    Bands of cane and fans in center, hobstars and crosshatching border, attributed to J. Hoare ....................................... 200.00

    Bands of hobstars with notched miters, alternating with flat stars and feathered fans, large center hobstar with hobnail and fan ............................................................................ 400.00

    Carolyn pattern, sgd "J. Hoare" ..................................... 800.00

    Genoa pattern, sgd "Clark" ............................................ 300.00

    Glenda pattern, sgd "Libbey" ......................................... 500.00

    Hindu pattern, J. Hoare .................................................. 400.00

    Hobstar, intersecting miters, crosshatching ...................... 125.00

    Hobstars surrounded by tusks, hobdiamonds, crossbands of hobstars ......................................................................... 550.00

    Mars pattern, Pitkins and Brooks .................................... 550.00

    Paul Revere pattern, sgd "Hawkes" ............................... 275.00

    Russian pattern ............................................................. 125.00

Russian pattern, hobstar center ........................................... 275.00

Salem, heart shaped, Pairpoint ........................................... 125.00

Zella pattern, Irving ........................................................... 175.00

Powder Jar, cov

    3" d, 3" h, emb florals on sterling silver lid, c1890-1900 ..... 100.00

    4" x 5", Wild Rose pattern, engraved roses on lid, hobnail band on bowl, on standard, sgd "Tuthill" ................................... 700.00

    5-1/2" d, Venetian, Hawkes ......................................... 350.00

Punch Bowl

    12" d, 10" h, interlaced hobstars dec, stand base, c1895-1900 ................................................................. 385.00

    14" d, two piece, large stars with fields of cane and crosshatching ............................................................. 2,300.00

Punch Cup, 4-1/2", Monarch pattern, pedestal, sterling silver base mkd "Shreve & Co., San Francisco," J. Hoare, price for four pc set 525.00

Ramekin, underplate, 3" x 1-3/4", Hobnail pattern, Dorflinger .... 125.00

Relish, 8" l, 3" w, double handles, hobstars, fans, and crosshatching ..................................................................... 120.00

Ring Tree, 4" x 3", green cut to clear, hobstar and strawberry diamond motif ............................................................................. 900.00

Rum Jug, 7-1/2" h, strawberry diamond pattern, faceted stopper ................................................................................... 275.00

Salad Set, 9" salad bowl, 11" d matching underplate, fan, crosshatching, stars and miter cuts, large 24 point hobstar center .......... 700.00

Salt, master, 3" d, pedestal, scalloped base, serrated rim, crosshatch diamond motif ......................................................................... 75.00

Salt Shaker, 3-1/4" h, Alhambra pattern, sterling top mkd "Meridan" ................................................................................. 175.00

Sherry, 4-1/2" h

    Russian pattern, Dorflinger .......................................... 80.00

    Russian pattern with star buttons .................................. 45.00

Spooner, 4-1/2" h, Crescent pattern, two handles, Higgins & Seiter ................................................................................. 250.00

Sweet Pea Vase, 5-1/2" x 8-1/2", hobstar, cane, crosshatching and fan motif ................................................................................. 200.00

Swizzle Stick, 6" l, pinwheel and diamond cut body ................... 200.00

Syrup, 4" x 3-1/2", hobstar, miter and cane cutting, sterling flip top lid .. 300.00

Tankard

    11" h, vertical rows of hobstars and stars, crosscut diamond and fan motif ................................................................... 240.00

    13" h, bowling pin shape, alternating vertical bands of hobnail and engraved wild florals, attributed to Tuthill ...................... 3,000.00

Tazza, 6-1/2" d, 8" h, Pattern #100, Elmira ............................... 375.00

Teapot, 7" h, Old Irish pattern, long elegant spout, Hawkes ....... 900.00

Toilette Ewer, 10-1/2" h, panel-cut, attributed to Boston and Sandwich Glass Co. or New England Glass Co., c1845-55 ...................... 90.00

Tonic Bottle, 6-1/2" h, Victoria pattern, sterling top, sgd "Hawkes" ............................................................................. 500.00

Toothpick Holder

    3" h, on standard, notched top, feather intersecting miters with crosshatching, sgd "Hawkes" ....................................... 200.00

    3" h, Queens pattern, sgd "Hawkes" ............................. 800.00

Tooth Powder Bottle, 4" h, flat, stars, hobnail, and notched prisms, sterling dispenser and lid ....................................................... 750.00

Tray, 12" d, engraved cherries, plus, strawberries, and gooseberries, sgd "Hawkes Gravic" ......................................................... 2,700.00

Tumble-Up, 6-1/2" h, alternating panels of cut large diamond and engraved grapes, attributed to Pairpoint ................................. 450.00

Vase

    10" h, chalice shape, hobstar, vesica, hobnail, crosshatch, prism, and fan motif, faceted cut knob, hobstar base ................. 750.00

    10" h, corset shape, hobstar, crosshatching, prism and punty motifs .................................................................... 275.00

    10" h, fan shape, hobstar base with panels of flutes on side ......... 300.00

    10" h, 8" d, bulbous, Roosevelt pattern, Quaker City ......... 700.00

    12" h, corset shape, vertical rows of punties, prism and crosshatching, attributed to Clark ......................................... 250.00

    12" h, pedestal, Stratford pattern, Herbeck ...................... 600.00

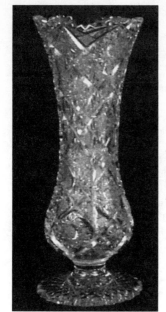

**Vase, Stratford pattern, Herbeck, pedestal, 12" h, $600. Photo courtesy of Woody Auction.**

12" h, pedestal, tulip, hobstar and geometric cane motif . 1,150.00
16" h, 5-1/2" d, trumpet form, circular foot with sunburst, Vertical Graduated Hobstars dec, c1895-1900 ............................ 110.00
19" h, corset shape, alternating vertical Russian and Buzz and Snowflake panels ......................................................... 220.00
22-1/2" h, 11" d, baluster shape, alternating Buzz and Harvard Spear dec.......................................................... 220.00
Vase/Candleholders Combination, 10" h, floral cut, sgd "Sinclaire," price for pr ....................................................... 500.00
Water Bottle, 7" h, Bengal pattern, sgd "Sinclaire"...................... 325.00
Water Set, Bengal pattern, pitcher with six tumblers, sgd "Sinclaire" ...................................................... 2,400.00
Whiskey Bottle
    12" h, pinwheel, crosshatching, stars, and fan motif, St. Louis Diamond neck and stopper..................................... 400.00
    13-1/2" h, Aberdeen pattern, Jewel Cut Glass Co. ............. 850.00
Whiskey Jug, 8" h, Laurette pattern, pinwheel, crosshatch and hobstar buttons, corncob stopper, strap handle, Lucerne .................... 400.00
Wine
    4-1/2" h, Vintage, sgd "Egginton" ....................................... 250.00
    4-3/4" h, Hobdiamond pattern, vaseline, Dorlinger ............. 325.00
    4-3/4" h, Hoblace pattern, yellow cut to clear, Dorlinger ..... 500.00
Wine Hock
    7-1/2" d, vesica, crosshatch, cane and fan, tear drop stem .. 70.00
    8-1/2" h, rock crystal, lotus flowers with clear fingers, diamond cut round base of bowl, sgd "Brierly" ..................................... 200.00

# CUT VELVET

**History:** Several glass manufacturers made cut velvet during the late Victorian era, c1870-1900. An outer layer of pastel color was applied over a white casing. The piece then was molded or cut in a high-relief ribbed or diamond shape, exposing portions of the casing. The finish had a satin velvety feel, hence the name "cut velvet."

Basket, 11-1/2" h, 9" w, brilliant yellow ext., Diamond Quilted pattern, bright pink shaded int., tightly crimped and ruffled edge, applied crystal loop handle ....................................................... 300.00
Biscuit Jar, cov, pink, SP mountings and lid................................ 275.00
Celery Vase, 6-1/2" h, deep blue over white, Diamond Quilted design, box pleated top........................................................ 725.00

Creamer, 5-1/4" h, raised ribbed pattern, butterscotch body, white lining .......................................................... 200.00
Finger Bowl, 4-1/2" d, Diamond Quilted pattern, blue................ 185.00
Rose Bowl, 3-1/4" d, 3-3/4" h, egg shape, raised Diamond Quilted pattern, rose body, white lining, six crimp top............................... 195.00
Vase
    4-1/4" h, 3" d, bulbous, deep pink shading to pale pink, DQ pattern, ruffled top, Mt. Washington ...................................225.00
    6-1/2" d, stick type, raised Diamond Quilted pattern, rose body, white lining ......................................................... 250.00
    7-1/2" h, 3-1/2" w, bulbous shape, ruffled top, Herringbone pattern, Alice Blue, white lining, c1880 ............................... 450.00
    9" h, cylindrical, raised Diamond Quilted pattern, blue body, ruffled rim ........................................................... 250.00
    9" h, deeply ruffled top, deep orange body, DQ pattern...... 675.00
    9" h, slight flare to end of elongated neck, robin's egg blue, diamond quilt body, daisy blossom like design at base ........ 385.00
    9" h, 6" tall cylinder over short bulbous base, deeply ruffled 9" w top, deep orange Diamond Quilted pattern ...................... 675.00
    10" h, ruffled and crimped top, purple cased to opal white body, Diamond Quilted pattern, Victorian ................................. 575.00
    11-1/2" h, 6" w, glossy satin, Herringbone pattern, deep blue shading to pale blue, bright opaque white lining, applied crystal edge .......................................................... 250.00
    13-1/2" h, 6" w, double gourd, long pumpkin stem neck, pale gold Diamond Quilted body..................................................... 650.00

# CZECHOSLOVAKIAN ITEMS

**History:** Objects marked "Made in Czechoslovakia" were produced after 1918 when the country claimed its independence from the Austro-Hungarian Empire. The people became more cosmopolitan and liberated and expanded the scope of their lives. Their porcelains, pottery, and glassware reflect many influences.

**Marks:** A specific manufacturer's mark may include a date which precedes 1918, but this only indicates the factory existed during the years of the Bohemian or Austro-Hungarian Empire.

**References:** Dale and Diane Barta and Helen M. Rose, *Czechoslovakian Glass & Collectibles* (1992, 1995 values), Book II (1997) Collector Books; *Bohemian Glass*, n.d., distributed by Antique Publications; Ruth A. Forsythe, *Made in Czechoslovakia*, Antique Publications, 1995 value update; Jacquelyne Y. Jones-North, et. al., *Czechoslovakian Perfume Bottles and Boudoir Accessories*, Revised Ed., Antique Publications, 1999.

**Periodical:** *New Glass Review*, Bardounova 2140 149 00 Praha 4, Prague, Czech Republic.

**Collectors' Club:** Czechoslovakian Collectors Guild International, P.O. Box 901395, Kansas City, MO 64190.

**Museum:** Friends of the Glass Museum of Novy Bor, Kensington, MD.

Bowl, woman figure, emb yellow iris, flower frog cover .............. 200.00
Candy Dish, multicolored spatter, black feet................................ 45.00
Compote, 7-1/2" d, 5-3/4" h, art glass, bright orange cased to colorless glass, pulled black stripes, wafer, and rim rap, attributed to Michael Powolny....................................................... 415.00
Console Set, porcelain, Art Deco style, turquoise raised drapery with knotted corners, 10" x 6" x 2-1/2" bowl, pr candlesticks............. 85.00
Creamer, gold luster ex., black handles and trim, marked "Czechoslovakia"........................................................... 15.00

**Console Set, bowl and pr matching candlesticks, white threading, all mkd with acid stamp mark, 7-1/2" d, 7" h bowl, $115. Photo courtesy of David Rago Auctions.**

Figure, 3-1/2" h, girl with basket.....................................25.00
Gravy Boat, 10-1/8" l, 5-1/4" h, silver, attached trays, Colonial Revival style, triple ribbed rim detail, hallmarked, 800 fine, 41 troy oz, price for pr..............................635.00
Jack-In-The-Pulpit Vase
    10-7/8" h, pulled and folded irid cobalt rim on tapered body of opal glass, irid pearl mottled surface, cobalt blue trailing threads, c1920 .........................................650.00
    12-1/4" h, pulled and folded chartreuse rim, tapered body, dome foot, opal glass with opal gold mottled surface, chartreuse trailing threads, c1920..........................700.00
    Jardiniere, 4-1/2" h, cameo, white cased to colorless, maroon and pink layers, acid etched grape vines and clusters, partial oval mark on base "Czecho Slovakia" ...................260.00

Lamp
    Basket, 10-1/2" h, colorful faceted fruit and flower form beads form lampshade, basket frame, electrical base imp "Made in Czechoslovakia"................................525.00
    Desk, two figural Scottie dogs, multicolored spatter geometric glass globe..............................265.00
    Hanging, 17" l, swirled orange, purple, and yellow............350.00
Luncheon Set, flowing irid, magenta, orange, brown, and lavender on MOP, teapot and lid, creamer, sugar, cov butter, handled cake plate, twelve 7-1/2" d plates, 5-3/4" bowl, eight cups and saucers, sgd .....................................280.00
Lemonade Set, 10" h pitcher, two matching tumblers, sapphire blue, green, and aubergine ground, sapphire blue threaded shoulder, blue ribbed handles, sgd, c1930 ...................250.00
Perfume, 6-1/4" h, diagonally faceted red bottle, curvilinear etched colorless glass stopper, c1925, minor staining........................420.00
Pin Tray, 3-3/8" l, yellow-green glass, intaglio of nude woman, frosted int., cut edges...............................100.00
Pitcher, 8-1/2" h, goat's head......................................375.00
Plate, sq, green border, floral dec................................37.50
Scent Bottle, amber, 1" h, paneled cut glass, sterling silver hinged emb lid................................195.00
Vase
    7-1/8" h, narrow mouth on ovoid body, cased orange glass with black linear overlay, black tripod base, flat ribbed feet, c1930 .....................................175.00
    7-1/4" h, raised rim, flattened spherical form, red cased to colorless ground, internally dec with lavender windings, c1930, minor scratches to surface.......................190.00
    9-1/2" h, heavy walled flared cylindrical colorless glass body, heavily etched with cameo of rampant lion with shield, portrait of man, banner, and flowering branch, dated 1918-1938, frosted and polished to enhance design, rim flake......................450.00
Wine Glass, amethyst panels and gilding, price for set of six.... 150.00

# DAVENPORT

**History:** John Davenport opened a pottery in Longport, Staffordshire, England, in 1793. His high-quality light-weight

wares are cream colored with a beautiful velvety texture.

The firm's output included soft-paste (Old Blue) products, luster-trimmed pieces, and pink luster wares with black transfer. Pieces of Gaudy Dutch and Spatterware also have been found with the Davenport mark. Later Davenport became a leading maker of ironstone and early flow blue. His famous Cyprus pattern in mulberry became very popular. His heirs continued the business until the factory closed in 1886.

**Reference:** T. A. Lockett and Geoffrey A. Godden, *China, Earthenware & Glass, 1794-1884,* Random Century, 1990.

**Museums:** British Museum, London, England; Cincinnati Art Museum, Cincinnati, OH; Hanley Museum, Stoke-on-Trent, England; Liverpool Museum, Liverpool, England; Victoria & Albert Museum, London, England.

Biscuit Jar, 6-1/2" h, Imari style dec, SP cover and bail, c1870.. 150.00
Bowl, 5" d, Cyprus, mkd "Cyprus Davenport" ............................... 55.00
Compote, 10-1/4" d, romantic landscape scene, gilt border, apple green ground, two handles ....................................................... 120.00
Cup and Saucer
    Clifford pattern ..................................................................... 115.00
    Hawthorn pattern, blue transfers, handleless ....................... 95.00
Dessert Service, 20-pc set, multicolored floral sprays, scroll surrounds, gilt stylized foliage on green border, puce printed mark, c1850 ............................................................................................. 1,250.00
Dish, 9-1/2" l, molded cobalt and gilt handle, Oriental style gilt dec outlined in blue, yellow, green, and red exotic birds, orange-red chrysanthemums, pink and magenta flowerheads on scrolling branches, blue "Davenport Stone China" anchor mark, c1820.......................... 295.00
Ewer, 9" h, multicolored floral dec, c1830 .................................. 200.00
Gravy Boat, blue and white flowers .............................................. 90.00
Jug, 5-7/8" h, "The Litchfield Jug," black outlined white Greek warriors, orange ground, white handle, title on bottom, c1850 ............... 395.00
Plate
    8" d, white ground, green panels, orange Gaudy Welsh flowers, gold trim, mkd "Davenport, Longport Staffordshire," incised "England".............................................................................. 90.00
    8-3/4" d, earthenware, medium blue transfer, English landscape, ruined abbey, imp "Davenport"........................................... 60.00

**Cup and Saucer, Clifford pattern, $115.**

9" d, Blue Willow pattern, imp mark, c1820 ........................ 175.00
9-1/2" d, flow blue, sgd "Davenport Wood & Sons" in ribbon, "Royal Semi-Porcelain, England," crown, two small chips .............. 95.00
10" d, Muleteer pattern, man riding mule, C-scroll and flower border, blue transfer ............................................................. 100.00
10-1/2" d, Indian Festoon pattern, red, green, and yellow bower and flowers in center, green floral transfer border............ 125.00
Platter, 18-3/4" l, rect, cut corners, blue transfer, large house with Chinese junk in front in center, willow trees on shore, floral border............. 675.00
Sauce Tureen, cov, underplate, 8-1/4" l, Japan pattern, iron-red, cobalt, and gilt, gilt curved horizontal handles, pr ................. 1,450.00
Soup Tureen, 15" l, 9-1/2" h, Java pattern, flowers, bird, and fruit, blue and white.............................................................................. 395.00
Tray, 11" w, 9" l, cloverleaf design, c1850.................................. 150.00
Vegetable Bowl, cov, hot water liner, 9-3/4" l, 7" w, Chinoiserie Bridgeless, c1810 ................................................................................. 690.00

# DECOYS

**History:** During the past several years, carved wooden decoys, used to lure ducks and geese to the hunter, have become widely recognized as an indigenous American folk art form. Many decoys are from the years 1880 to 1930 when commercial gunners commonly hunted using rigs of several hundred decoys. Many fine carvers also worked through the 1930s and 1940s. Fish decoys were also carved by individuals and commercial decoy makers.

Because decoys were both hand made and machine made, and many examples exist, firm pricing is difficult to establish. The skill of the carver, rarity, type of bird, and age all effect the value.

**References:** Joel Barber, *Wild Fowl Decoys*, Dover Publications, n.d.; Russell J. Goldberger and Alan G. Haid, *Mason Decoys—A Complete Pictorial Guide,* Decoy Magazine, 1993; Loy S. Harrell Jr., *Decoys: North America's One Hundred Greatest,* Krause Publications, 2000; Carl F. Luckey, *Collecting Antique Bird Decoys and Duck Calls: An Identification & Value Guide*, 2nd ed., Books Americana, 1992; Donald J. Peterson, *Folk Art Fish Decoys*, Schiffer Publishing, 1996.

**Periodicals:** *Decoy Magazine*, P.O. Box 787, Lewes, DE, 19558; *North America Decoys*, P.O. Box 246, Spanish Fork, UT 84660; *Sporting Collector's Monthly*, RW Publishing, P.O. Box 305, Camden, DE 19934; *Wildfowl Art*, Ward Foundation, 909 South Schumaker Dr., Salisbury, MD 21801; *Wildfowl Carving & Collecting*, 500 Vaughn St., Harrisburg, PA 17110.

**Collectors' Clubs:** Midwest Collectors Association, 1100 Bayview Dr., Fox River Grove, IL 60021; Minnesota Decoy Collectors Association, P.O. Box 130084, St. Paul, MN 55113; Ohio Decoy Collectors & Carvers Association, P.O. Box 499, Richfield, OH 44286.

**Museums:** Chesapeake Bay Maritime Museum; Saint Michaels, MD; Havre de Grace Decoy Museum, Havre de Grace, MD; Museum at Stony Brook, Stony Brook, NY; Noyes Museum of Art, Oceanville, NJ; Peabody Museum of Salem, Salem, MA; Refuge Waterfowl Museum, Chincoteague, VA; Shelburne Museum, Inc., Shelburne, VT; Ward Museum of Wildfowl Art, Salisbury, MD.

# Special Auction

Gary Guyette & Frank Schmidt Inc.
P.O. Box 522
West Farmington, ME 04992
(207) 778-6256

Reproduction Alert.

**Notes:** A decoy's value is based on several factors: (1) fame of the carver, (2) quality of the carving, (3) species of wild fowl—the most desirable are herons, swans, mergansers, and shorebirds—and (4) condition of the original paint.

The inexperienced collector should be aware of several facts. The age of a decoy, per se, is usually of no importance in determining value. However, age does have some influence when it comes to a rare or important example. Since very few decoys were ever signed, it is quite difficult to attribute most decoys to known carvers. Anyone who has not examined a known carver's work will be hard pressed to determine if the paint on one of his decoys is indeed original. Repainting severely decreases a decoy's value. In addition, there are many fakes and reproductions on the market and even experienced collectors are occasionally fooled. Decoys represent a subject where dealing with a reputable dealer or auction house is important, especially those who offer a guarantee as to authenticity.

Decoys listed below are of average wear unless otherwise noted.

Black-Bellied Plover
    Cobb, Nathan, Cobb Island, VA, c1895 ..................... 18,700.00
    Dilley, some damage ........................................................... 990.00
    Holmes, Lothrop, Kingston, MA ..................................... 11,550.00
Black Duck, 17-1/2" l, 6-1/2" h, A. Elmer Crowell, East Harwich, MA, oval "Crowell" brand on underside, orig paint, minor paint loss, repairs ............................................................................... 1,380.00
Blue-Breasted Plover, unknown maker, Long Island, carved wings, split tail, old paint .................................................................. 400.00
Bluebill
    Drake, old label attributes it to Jim Foote, Pte Moulle, MI, wood and cork, old worn working repaint, glass eyes, 14" l ...... 165.00
    Drake, G. W. Stevens Factory, Weedsport, NY, orig paint, replacement eyes, branded "G W Stevens" ................. 1,500.00
    Hen, Hayes Decoy Factory, orig paint, age split ................. 175.00
Blue Goose, Ben Schmidt, early ........................................... 11,550.00
Brant
    Cobb, Nathan, VA, hollow carved, slightly turned head, cocked down, "V" detail, c1860 ................................................. 5,750.00
    Parker, Lloyd, hollow carved, old repaint ........................... 900.00
    Shourds, Harry V., Tuckertown, NJ, hollow, branded .......... 385.00
Waterfield, Amos, swimming position, hollow body, old repaint, added inscription "1930, Ridgeway, N.J. Amos Waterfield 3/21/80, " 19" l ................................................................................... 385.00
Bufflehead
    Drake, J. L. Saltonstall ....................................................... 100.00
    Drake, unsigned, contemporary, carved, orig paint, glass eyes, good details, 9-1/2" l ....................................................... 110.00
    Hen, Eric Nelson, relief carved, orig paint, glass eyes, sgd "Eric V. Nelson," incised "EVN '81," 9-1/2" l ................................. 360.00
    Hen, Harry V. Shourds, Tuckertown, NJ, c1890, hollow carved ............................................................................... 18,700.00

Canada Goose
    Crowell, A. Elmer, East Harwich, MA, rect "Crowell" stamp on underside, orig paint, 23-1/2" l, 11" h, age split to underside ............................................................................ 3,450.00
    Reeves, Phineas, Point, Ontario, c1870, hollow carved 10,120.00
    Schmidt, Marvin, Peru, IL, early 1900s, 19" l, 13" h, neck reattached ................................................................................ 100.00
    Unknown carver, black and white paint over waxed canvas covered hollow body, carved neck and head, glass eyes, 15-1/2" l ............................................................................ 300.00
    Unknown carver, preening, old gray, black, and white paint, 20-1/2" w, 8" h, ................................................................. 250.00
    Watson, Dave "Umbrella," Chincoteague, VA, hollow carved, c1920 ........................................................................... 11,000.00
    Wheeler, Shang, Stratford, CT, c1935 ........................... 18,700.00
    Wheeler, Shang, Stratford, CT, hollow-carved, sleeping, c1910 ........................................................................... 27,500.00
Canvasback
    Fennimore, Harry, Bordentown, NJ ................................ 4,675.00
    Schoenheider, Charles, Peoria, IL, hollow carved .......... 9,200.00
Cape Cod Shore Bird, 10" l, 5" h, underneath sgd "J. Mulak L. Cayman Chatham, 84," head reattached, some paint loss ................... 100.00
Common Yellow Throat, 4" x 6", round wood pedestal .............. 275.00
Curlew
    Boyd, George, Seabrook, NH .......................................... 4,840.00
    Bowman, William, Long Island, NY, 1870-90, hunched up in cold weather ....................................................................... 90,500.00
    Bowman, William, Long Island, NY, 1870-90, standing ...... 57,500.00
    Crowell, A. Elmer, East Harwich, MA ............................. 6,380.00
    Gelston, Thomas, Quogue, Long Island, New York, long billed, head repair, replaced bill, 1890 .................................. 11,550.00
    Unknown maker, MA, c1890, running, sickle-billed, 21-1/2" l ..................................................................... 335,500.00
    Unknown maker, Brigatine, NJ, c1800, long-billed ........ 18,000.00
    Unknown maker, VA, c1880 .......................................... 20,900.00
    Verity, Obediah, Seaford, NY, c1870, oversized ........... 30,800.00
    Wheeler, Shang, unique .................................................. 7,150.00
Dowticher, William Bowman, Long Island, NY, 1870-90 ........ 13,475.00
Eider Drake, wide-bodied, oversized ...................................... 4,070.00
Eider Hen, Gus Wilson, South Portland, mussel in bill ........... 5,500.00
Goldeneye, Maurice Eaton, Deer Island, ME
    Drake ............................................................................... 2,530.00
    Hen .................................................................................. 2,090.00
Golden Plover, A. Elmer Crowell, East Harwich, MA .............. 7,260.00
Gull, Bill Cranmer, hollow carved, orig paint, weathered ........... 450.00
Hutchins Goose, preening, unknown maker ........................... 9,900.00
Ice Fishing
    9" l, cream colored body, dark lateral line, fine gold sand glued to the back above the line, gold tin tail and fins, pressed painted eyes, and multi-loop line tie, Leroy Howell ....................... 365.00
    9" l, tan, black markings on back, red gill and mouth lines, metal fins, a wooden tail, and large tack eyes, wear on belly and fins, gently curved Cadillac style by Leonard Zelinski ............... 50.00

**Canvasback, unknown maker, some wear to orig paint, $50.**

12" l, cedar, red nailed bead eyes, heavy copper fins, wood tail, burned or carved gill lines, possibly stripped and repainted ... 25.00
Labrador Duck, Northeast, 19th C, ........................................ 5,500.00
Loons, miniature, George Boyd, Seabrook, NH, made for display at 1939 New York World's Fair
- Drake ................................................................. 2,970.00
- Hen ................................................................... 1,210.00

Mallard
- Drake, Mason's standard grade, old worn repaint, tack eyes, some damage, 15-1/2" l ............................................... 250.00
- Drake, Charles Perdew, Henry, IL River area, hollow carved, painted by his wife Edna ................................................ 3,575.00
- Pair, Nathan Rowley Horner, West Creek, NJ, hollow carved ..................................................................... 71,500.00

Merganser
- Drake, George Huey ...................................................... 4,180.00
- Hen, Mason Factory Premier-grade ................................ 7,150.00

Swimmer, carved, orig paint, glass eyes, sgd "Richard C. Watson, Fair Haven, Mich," 23" l, contemporary, small edge chips .............. 385.00
Oldsquaw, canvas covered, Clinton Keith, Kingston, MA ........... 770.00
Pied Bill Grebe, Jim Polite, carved minnow in mouth, sgd and dated 1974 ...................................................................... 375.00

Pintail
- Drake, John Blair, Philadelphia, c1895, hollow carved .. 19,800.00
- Hen, Charles Perdew, Henry, IL, c1930 .......................... 6,600.00
- Standing, Schoenheider, Charles, Peoria, IL, hollow carved ................................................................ 85,000.00
- Swimming, Graves, Bert, Peoria, IL, hollow carved ......... 3,520.00

Red-breasted Merganser
- Crowell, A. Elmer, East Harwich, MA, drake, oval "Crowell" brand on underside, orig paint, 19-1/2" l, 5-1/2" h, horizontal age split through eye right side, minor paint loss ......................... 8,625.00
- Gelston, Thomas, Long Island, NY .................................. 8,250.00
- Shourds, Harry V., Tuckerton, NJ, hollow carved, c1890 ................................................................... 13,200.00
- Smith, Ben, Martha's Vineyard, MA, c1900, hollow carved, restored to orig paint ................................................. 3,300.00
- Unknown, horseshoe weights, Maine, pr ........................ 2,970.00
- Wilson, Gus, South Portland, ME .................................. 55,000.00

Rig Plover, Morton ........................................................... 7,700.00
Ruddy Turnstone, William Bowman, Lawrence, NY .............. 57,750.00
Shovelier Hen, Bob Schaber .............................................. 300.00
Snowy Egret, branded "H. Conklin" on bottom ...................... 500.00
Surf Scoter, with mussell, Gus Wilson, Portland, ME ........... 28,600.00
Swan, 25" l, 18-1/2" h, horseshoe weight, over painted, some paint flaking ..................................................................... 825.00

Teal
- Drake, Mason Factory, Premier-grade, blue wings ........... 4,400.00
- Drake, Mason Factory, Premier-grade, green wings ..... 19,800.00
- Hen, Mason Factory, Premier-grade, green wings ........ 10,725.00

Tern, life size, A. Elmer Crowell, East Harwich, MA ................. 5,280.00

Wigeon
- Crowell, A. Elmer, East Harwich, MA ........................... 33,000.00
- Lincoln, Joe, Accord, MA, restored bill top ................... 12,650.00

Woodcock, A. Elmer Crowell, East Harwich, MA ................... 13,200.00

Wood Duck
- Crowell, A. Elmer, East Harwich, MA, three-quarter size, flying ................................................................... 11,500.00
- Lincoln, Joe, Accord, MA ......................................... 165,000.00
- Mason Factory, Detroit-grade, tack eyes, price for pr ...... 6,050.00

Yellowlegs, feeding, Fred Nichols, Lynn, MA ...................... 25,850.00

# DEDHAM POTTERY

**History:** Alexander W. Robertson established a pottery in Chelsea, Massachusetts, about 1866. After his brother, Hugh Cornwall Robertson, joined him in 1868 the firm was called A. W. & H. C. Robertson. Their father, James Robertson, joined his sons in 1872, and the name Chelsea Keramic Art Works Robertson and Sons was used.

Their initial products were simple flower and bean pots, but the firm quickly expanded its output to include a wide variety of artistic pottery. It produced a very fine redware body used in classical forms, some with black backgrounds imitating ancient Greek and Apulian works. The firm experimented with underglaze slip decoration on vases. The Chelsea Keramic Art Works Pottery also produced high-glazed vases, pitchers, and plaques with a buff clay body with either sculpted or molded applied decoration.

James Robertson died in 1880 and Alexander moved to California in 1884 leaving Hugh C. Robertson alone in Chelsea where his tireless experiments eventually yielded a stunning imitation of the prized Chinese Ming—era blood-red glaze. Hugh's vases with that glaze were marked with an impressed "CKAW." Creating these red-glazed vases was very expensive, and even though they received great critical acclaim, the company declared bankruptcy in 1889.

Recapitalized by a circle of Boston art patrons in 1891, Hugh started the Chelsea Pottery U.S., which produced gray crackle-glazed dinnerware with cobalt blue decorations, the rabbit pattern being the most popular.

The business moved to new facilities in Dedham, Massachusetts, and began production in 1896 under the name Dedham Pottery. Hugh's son and grandson operated the business until it closed in 1943, by which time between 50 and 80 patterns had been produced, some very briefly.

**Marks:** The following marks help determine the approximate age of items:
"Chelsea Keramic Art Works Robertson and Sons," impressed, 1874-1880
"CKAW," impressed, 1875-1889
"CPUS," impressed in a cloverleaf, 1891-1895
Foreshortened rabbit only, impressed, 1894-1896
Conventional rabbit with "Dedham Pottery" in square blue stamped mark along with one impressed foreshortened rabbit, 1896-1928
Blue rabbit stamped mark with "registered" beneath, along with two impressed foreshortened rabbit marks, 1929-1943

**References:** Lloyd E. Hawes, *Dedham Pottery and the Earlier Robertson's Chelsea Potteries*, Dedham Historical Society, 1968; Paul Evans, *Art Pottery of the United States*, Feingold & Lewis, 1974; Ralph and Terry Kovel, *Kovels' American Art Pottery*, Crown Publishers, 1993.

**Collectors' Club:** Dedham Pottery Collectors Society, 248 Highland St., Dedham, MA 02026.

## Reproduction Alert:

Two companies make Dedham-like reproductions primarily utilizing the rabbit pattern, but always mark their work very differently from the original.

**Bowl, Rabbit, blue ink stamp mark, 8" d, 3" h, $630. Photo courtesy of David Rago Auctions.**

**Museum:** Dedham Historical Society, Dedham, MA.

**Advisor:** James D. Kaufman.

Bowl
    6" d bowl, style #4, Butterfly pattern, reg ............................. 325 00
    7" d bowl, style #3, Rabbit pattern, reg .............................. 275.00
    8" d bowl, style #2, Rabbit pattern, reg .............................. 450.00
Candlesticks, pr
    Elephant pattern, reg blue stamp........................................ 750.00
    Rabbit pattern, reg. blue stamp .......................................... 325.00
    Rabbit pattern with ring handles .......................................... 525.00
Creamer and Sugar, type #1, Turkey pattern, 3.25" h, blue
    stamp ................................................................................. 650.00
Demitasse cup and saucer, Rabbit pattern, blue stamp ............. 300.00
Knife Rest, rabbit form, blue reg stamp ..................................... 575.00
Mug or Stein, 6"
    Elephant pattern, blue stamp............................................. 875.00
    Rabbit pattern, blue stamp 650.00
Olive Dish, 8-1/4" h, Rabbit pattern, blue reg stamp.................. 450.00
Paperweight, rabbit form, blue reg stamp ................................... 495.00
Pitcher
    5" h, Rabbit pattern, blue stamp ........................................ 325.00
    5-1/2" h, Oak Block style, blue reg stamp.......................... 975.00
    7" h, Chicks pattern, blue stamp ........................................ 950.00
    9" h, Rabbit pattern, blue stamp ........................................ 700.00
Place Card Holder, rabbit form, blue stamp ............................... 575.00
Plate
    6" d, Azalea, blue stamp, "O"Maude Davenp. ..................... 280.00
    6" d, Clover, blue reg stamp............................................... 685.00
    6" d, Dolphin pattern, blue reg stamp, chip......................... 375.00
    6" d, Elephant pattern, blue stamp...................................... 575.00
    6" d, Rabbit pattern, blue stamp ......................................... 175.00
    6" d, Rabbit pattern, blue stamp, Maude's "O".................... 205.00
    6" d, Water Lily pattern, blue stamp .................................... 145.00
    7-1-2" d, Rabbit pattern, blue stamp ................................... 190.00
    8" d, Azalea, reg stamp...................................................... 230.00
    8-1/2" d, Central lobster design, blue stamp....................... 575.00
    8-1/2" d, Central crab design, blue stamp........................... 550.00
    8-1/2" d, Central crab design, blue stamp, "O" ................... 875.00
    8-1/2" d, Duck pattern, blue stamp, "O" Maude D.............. 375.00
    8-1/2" d, Duck pattern, blue stamp .................................... 300.00
    8-1/2" d, Elephant pattern, blue reg stamp ........................ 750.00
    8-1/2" d, English Mushroom, blue reg stamp...................... 850.00
    8-1/2" d, French mushroom, blue stamp.......................... 1,100.00
    8-1/2" d, Magnolia pattern, blue stamp............................... 165.00
    8-1/2" d, Rabbit pattern, blue stamp................................... 200.00
    8-1/2" d, Rabbit pattern, blue stamp, with Maude Davenport's "O"
      rebus ............................................................................. 235.00
    8-1/2" d, Snow Tree pattern, blue stamp "O" ..................... 255.00

    8-1/2" d, "Upside down dolphin," C.P.U.S.mark ................. 900.00
    10" d, Clover, blue stamp.................................................... 825.00
    10" d, Dolphin pattern, blue reg stamp ............................... 875.00
    10" d, Pine Apple, C.P.U.S. cloverleaf mark ...................... 700.00
    10" d, Swan pattern, blue reg stamp................................... 475.00
    10" d, Swan pattern, blue reg stamp, with small rim nicks.. 250.00
    10" d, Turkey, blue stamp, "O"Maude Davenp.................... 525.00
    10" d, Turtle pattern, reg blue stamp ............................... 1,225.00
Platter, 16" x 10" Rabbit pattern, blue reg stamp.................... 1,025.00
Tea Cup and Saucer
    Azalea pattern, reg stamp.................................................. 180.00
    Butterfly pattern, blue stamp............................................... 345.00
    Duck pattern, reg stamp ..................................................... 260.00
    Iris pattern, reg stamp........................................................ 195.00
    Rabbit pattern, reg stamp................................................... 225.00
    Turtle pattern, reg stamp.................................................... 680.00
    Water Lily pattern, reg stamp.............................................. 190.00
Tea Pot, 8-1/4" h, Rabbit pattern, blue stamp ........................... 875.00

# DELFTWARE

**History:** Delftware is pottery with a soft, red-clay body and tin-enamel glaze. The white, dense, opaque color came from adding tin ash to lead glaze. The first examples had blue designs on a white ground. Polychrome examples followed.

The name originally applied to pottery made in the region around Delft, Holland, beginning in the 16th century and ending in the late 18th century. The tin used came from the Cornish mines in England. By the 17th and 18th centuries, English potters in London, Bristol, and Liverpool were copying the glaze and designs. Some designs unique to English potters also developed.

In Germany and France the ware is known as Faience, and in Italy as Majolica.

Bowl
    11-5/8" d, shallow, polychrome flowers and squirrel, English, edge
      chips.............................................................................. 935.00
    13" d, 6" h, polychrome floral dec with butterfly, wear, rim hairline,
      and small chips ........................................................... 1,705.00
Bust, 11-3/4" h, Napoleon, ceramic, artist sgd "S.B.," dated
    1809 ................................................................................. 500.00
Charger
    12-1/8" d, blue and white floral dec, wear and rim
      restoration ..................................................................... 385.00
    13-1/2" d, Adam and Eve, polychrome, English ............. 7,475.00
    13-1/2" d, blue and white, central scene of house and tall tree, styl-
      ized birds, Liverpool, 18th C, small glaze edge chips .......... 350.00
    13-3/4" d, polychrome floral dec, Holland, late 18th/early
      19th C ........................................................................... 550.00
    15-1/2" d, blue and white, Rembrandt portrait, mkd "Delft," imp
      "Joost Thooft & Labduchere" .......................................... 200.00
Dish, 10-5/8" d, blue and white floral dec, Dutch, 18th C .......... 150.00
Flask, 7" h, flattened round base, narrow short neck, round foot, blue,
    white, and black floral dec, windmill landscape scene of man and harp,
    loops for rope, sgd "AK," Holland, minor edge chips ................. 300.00
Garniture Set, three 17-1/2" h baluster covered vases, two 12" h, trumpet-
    form open vases, blue and white, bird finials, Dutch, c1800 ...... 2,300.00
Ginger Jar, blue and white, birds, flowers, and human figures, 18th C,
    set of three .......................................................................... 3,960.00

Inkstand, 9-3/4" l, cov central pot, raised pen stand, blue and white landscape, floral, and insect dec, Dutch, late 18th C, glaze wear, rim chips..................................................................................460.00
Jar, 8-1/4" h, chicken-shape, polychrome, pink and green dec, sgd, chips..................................................................................400.00
Plate
   8-3/4" d, flowers and bird, polychrome dec, English, small chips.............................................................................385.00
   8-7/8" d, polychrome, profiles of regal couple, mkd "FSW-PVOR," chips and glued rim repair.............................770.00
   9-1/2" d, blue tin glaze, landscape and border dec, 18th C, price for pr.......................................................................350.00
   10-1/2" d, blue tin glaze, garden dec, 18th C......................260.00
Posset Pot, cov, 10" h, polychrome floral and floral dec, Dutch, c1770, glaze loss to spout rim, restorations.....................................1,495.00
Pot, cov, 4" h, two handles, blue and white dec bird and floral designs, English, mid-18th C, rim chip to cov, glaze loss.......................550.00
Soup Plate, 8-3/4" d, blue and white floral dec, Dutch, 18th C...150.00
Tile, 5-3/4" x 12-1/4", painted blue and white, cows on coast, framed, late 19th/early 20th C.................................................................280.00
Tobacco Jar, 10" h, blue and white dec, pipe smoking Indian seated by large cov jar, titled "St Domingo," Dutch sailing ships in distance, brass cov, Dutch, late 18th/early 19th C, glaze wear to rim, old repair to body.........................................................575.00
Trivet, 8-1/2" l, triangular form, black outlined blue and white leaves dec, circular frieze of figures in landscape, Dutch, early 19th C, slight glaze loss to rim.........................................................100.00
Vase
   3-1/8" h, shaped flaring rim, ribbed baluster form body, figural and foliage devices, 18th C, minor chips, hairline.................350.00
   8-1/4" h, blue and white floral dec, oval scene of youth in landscape with windmills, chips, hairline, repair.....................275.00
   8-1/2" h, tin glazed blue and white earthenware, bishop praying in landscape dec, dated 1742, repairs, Continental.............40.00
   20" h, 9-1/2" d, double gourd form, Faience, Orientalist style blue and white dec, price for pr.........................................3,750.00

# DEPRESSION GLASS

**History:** Depression glass was made from 1920 to 1940. It was an inexpensive machine-made glass and was produced by several companies in various patterns and colors. The number of forms made in different patterns also varied.

Depression glass was sold through variety stores, given away as premiums, or packaged with certain products. Movie houses gave it away from 1935 until well into the 1940s.

Like pattern glass, knowing the proper name of a pattern is the key to collecting. Collectors should be prepared to do research.

**References:** Tom and Neila Bredehoft, *Fifty Years of Collectible Glass, 1920-1970*, Volume 1, Volume II, Antique Trader Books, 2000; Shirley Dunbar, *Heisey Glass, The Early Years, 1896-1924*, Krause Publications, 2000; Gene Florence, *Anchor Hocking's Fire-King & More*, 2nd ed., Collector Books, 2000; ——, *Collectible Glassware from the 40's, 50's, 60's*, 5th ed., Collector Books, 2000; ——, *Collector's Encyclopedia of Depression Glass*, 14th ed., Collector Books, 2000; ——, *Elegant Glassware of the Depression Era*, 9th ed., Collector Books, 2001; ——, *Florence's Glassware Pattern Identification Guide*, Collector Books, Vol. I, 1998,

Vol. II, 1999; ——, *Glass Candlesticks of the Depression Era*, Collector Books, 2000; ——, *Pocket Guide to Depression Glass & More, 1920–1960s*, 12th ed., Collector Books, 2000; ——, *Stemware Identification Featuring Cordials with Values, 1920s–1960s*, Collector Books, 1997; ——, *Very Rare Glassware of the Depression Era*, 1st Series (1988, 1991 value update), 2nd Series (1991), 3rd Series (1993, 1995 value update), 4th Series (1996, 1997 value update), 5th Series (1996, 1999 value update), Collector Books; Philip Hopper, *Forest Green Glass*, Schiffer Publishing, 2000; Ralph and Terry Kovel, *Kovels' Depression Glass & American Dinnerware Price List*, 5th ed., Crown, 1995; Carl F. Luckey and Mary Burris, *Identification & Value Guide to Depression Era Glassware*, 3rd ed., Books Americana, 1994; Jim and Barbara Mauzy, *Mauzy's Comprehensive Handbook of Depression Glass Prices*, 2nd ed., Schiffer, 2000; James Measell and Berry Wiggins, *Great American Glass of the Roaring 20s & Depression Era*, Book 2, Antique Publications, 2000; Leslie Piña and Paula Ockner, *Depression Era Art Deco Glass*, Schiffer Pubilshing, 1999; Sherry Riggs and Paul Pendergrass, *20th Century Glass Candle Holders: Roaring 20s, Depression Era, and Modern Collectible Candle Holders*, Schifer Publishing, 1999; Ellen T. Schroy, *Warman's Depression Glass*, 2nd ed., Krause Publications, 2000; Kent G. Washburn, *Price Survey*, 4th ed., published by author, 1994; Hazel Marie Weatherman, *Colored Glassware of the Depression Era*, Book 2, published by author 1974, available in reprint; ——, *1984 Supplement & Price Trends for Colored Glassware of the Depression Era*, Book 1, published by author, 1984.

**Periodical:** *The Daze*, P.O. Box 57, Otisville, MI 48463.

**Collectors' Clubs:** Canadian Depression Glass Club, 1026 Forestwood Drive, Mississauga, Ontario L5C 1G8, Canada; National Depression Glass Association, Inc., P.O. Box 8264, Wichita, KS 67209; 20-30-40 Society, Inc., P.O. Box 856, LaGrange, IL 60525, plus many local and regional clubs.

**Additional Listings:** See *Warman's Americana & Collectibles* for more examples.

## Reproduction Alert:

The number of Depression Glass patterns that have been reproduced continues to grow. Reproductions exist in many patterns, forms, and colors. Beware of colors and forms that were not made in the original production of the pattern. Carefully examine every piece that seems questionable and look for loss of details, poor impressions, and slight differences in sizes.

## Adam

Manufactured by Jeannette Glass Company, Jeannette, Pennsylvania, from 1932 to 1934. Made in crystal, Delphite blue, green, pink, some topaz and yellow.

**Reproductions:** † Butter Dish in pink and green.

| Item | Green | Pink |
|---|---|---|
| Ashtray, 4-1/2" d | 25.00 | 32.00 |
| Berry Bowl, small | 20.00 | 18.50 |
| Bowl, 9" d, cov | 85.00 | 75.00 |
| Bowl, 9" d, open | 45.00 | 30.00 |
| Bowl, 10" l, oval | 40.00 | 40.00 |
| Butter Dish, cov † | 325.00 | 145.00 |
| Cake Plate, 10" d, ftd | 32.00 | 30.00 |
| Candlesticks, pr, 4" h | 125.00 | 100.00 |
| Candy Jar, cov, 2-1/2" h | 100.00 | 95.00 |
| Casserole, cov | 90.00 | 75.00 |
| Cereal Bowl, 5-3/4" d | 46.00 | 46.00 |
| Coaster, 3-1/4" d | 22.00 | 32.00 |
| Creamer | 22.00 | 20.00 |
| Cup | 24.00 | 26.00 |
| Dessert Bowl, 4-3/4" d | 18.50 | 16.50 |
| Iced Tea Tumbler, 5-1/2" h | 60.00 | 65.00 |
| Lamp | 285.00 | 265.00 |
| Pitcher, 32 oz, round base | - | 125.00 |
| Pitcher, 32 oz, 8" h | 48.00 | 45.00 |
| Plate, 6" d, sherbet | 12.00 | 12.50 |
| Plate, 7-3/4" d, salad, sq | 18.00 | 19.50 |
| Plate, 9" d, dinner, sq | 32.00 | 38.50 |
| Plate, 9" d, grill | 20.00 | 20.00 |
| Platter, 11-3/4" l, rect | 38.00 | 35.00 |
| Relish Dish, 8" l, divided | 27.00 | 20.00 |

| Item | Green | Pink |
|---|---|---|
| Salt and Pepper Shakers, pr, 4" h | 130.00 | 95.00 |
| Saucer, 6" sq | 12.00 | 10.00 |
| Sherbet, 3" | 40.00 | 35.00 |
| Sugar, cov | 48.00 | 42.00 |
| Tumbler, 4-1/2" h | 30.00 | 35.00 |
| Vase, 7-1/2" h | 60.00 | 250.00 |
| Vegetable Bowl, 7-3/4" d | 30.00 | 30.00 |

Delphite 4" h candlesticks are valued at $250 a pair. A yellow cup and saucer is valued at $200, and a 7-3/4" d yellow plate is valued at $115. Production in topaz and yellow was very limited. Crystal prices would be approximately 50% of the prices listed above for green.

## Avocado,

*No. 601*

Manufactured by Indiana Glass Company, Dunkirk, Indiana, from 1923 to 1933. Made in crystal, green, pink, and white.

**Reproductions:** † Creamer, 8" pickle, 64-oz pitcher, plates, sherbet, sugar, and tumblers. Reproductions can be found in amethyst, blue, dark green, frosted green, frosted pink, pink, red, and yellow, representing several colors not made originally.

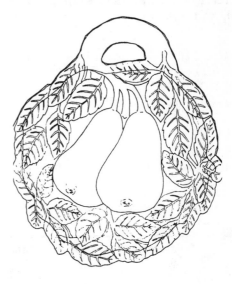

| Item | Crystal | Green | Pink |
|---|---|---|---|
| Bowl, 5-1/4" d, 2 handles | 12.00 | 38.00 | 27.50 |
| Bowl, 8" d, 2 handles, oval | 17.50 | 30.00 | 25.00 |
| Bowl, 8-1/2" d | 20.00 | 60.00 | 50.00 |
| Bowl, 9-1/2" d, 3-1/4" deep | 35.00 | 155.00 | 125.00 |
| Cake Plate, 10-1/4" d, 2 handles | 17.50 | 60.00 | 40.00 |
| Creamer, ftd † | 17.50 | 40.00 | 35.00 |
| Cup, ftd | - | 36.00 | 30.00 |
| Pickle Bowl, 8" d, 2 handles, oval † | 17.50 | 30.00 | 25.00 |
| Pitcher, 64 oz † | 365.00 | 1,100.00 | 800.00 |
| Plate, 6-3/8" d, sherbet † | 6.00 | 22.00 | 15.00 |
| Plate, 8-1/4" d, luncheon † | 7.50 | 25.00 | 20.00 |
| Preserve Bowl, 7" l, handle | 10.00 | 32.00 | 28.00 |
| Relish, 6" d, ftd | 10.00 | 32.00 | 28.00 |

| Item | Crystal | Green | Pink |
|---|---|---|---|
| Salad Bowl, 7-1/2" d | 9.00 | 55.00 | 37.50 |
| Saucer | 6.00 | 24.00 | 15.00 |
| Sherbet, ftd † | - | 75.00 | 55.00 |
| Sugar, ftd † | 17.50 | 40.00 | 35.00 |
| Tumbler † | 25.00 | 250.00 | 150.00 |

## Beaded Block

Manufactured by Imperial Glass Company, Bellaire, Ohio, from 1927 to the 1930s. Made in amber, crystal, green, ice blue, iridescent, milk white (1950s), opalescent, pink, red, and vaseline. Some pieces are still being made in pink and are embossed with the "IG" trademark. Values comparable for Ice Blue, Opal, and Vaseline.

| Item | Amber | Crystal | Green | Ice Blue | Irid. | Pink |
|---|---|---|---|---|---|---|
| Bowl, 4-1/2" d, lily | 8.00 | 6.00 | 10.00 | 18.00 | 15.00 | 15.00 |
| Bowl, 4-1/2" d, 2 handles | 10.00 | 8.00 | 10.00 | 18.00 | 16.00 | 10.00 |
| Bowl, 5-1/2" sq | 8.50 | 6.00 | 8.50 | 9.00 | 7.50 | 8.50 |
| Bowl, 5 -/2 d, 1 handle | 8.50 | 6.00 | 8.50 | 9.00 | 7.50 | 18.00 |
| Bowl, 6" deep | 12.00 | 10.00 | 12.00 | 12.50 | 10.00 | 15.00 |
| Bowl, 6-1/4" d | 9.00 | 7.00 | 9.00 | 9.50 | 9.00 | 8.00 |
| Bowl, 6-1/2" d, 2 handles | 9.00 | 7.00 | 9.00 | 9.50 | 9.00 | 8.00 |
| Bowl, 6-3/4" d | 12.00 | 10.00 | 12.00 | 11.00 | 12.00 | 11.00 |
| Bowl, 7-1/4" d, flared | 12.00 | 10.00 | 12.00 | 11.00 | 12.00 | 11.00 |
| Bowl, 7-1/2" d, fluted | 22.00 | 20.00 | 22.00 | 21.00 | 18.00 | 21.00 |
| Bowl, 7-1/2" plain | 20.00 | 18.00 | 20.00 | 18.50 | 18.50 | 18.00 |
| Candy Dish, cov, pear shaped | | - | - | 275.00 | - | - |
| Celery, 8-1/4" d | 15.00 | 12.00 | 15.00 | 16.00 | 15.00 | 14.00 |
| Creamer, ftd | 20.00 | 16.00 | 20.00 | 18.50 | 18.50 | 25.00 |
| Jelly, 4-1/2" h, stemmed | 10.00 | 8.00 | 10.00 | 10.00 | 9.00 | 9.00 |

Jelly, 4-1/2" h,

| Item | Amber | Crystal | Green | Ice Blue | Irid. | Pink |
|---|---|---|---|---|---|---|
| stemmed, flared lid | 12.00 | 10.00 | 12.00 | 11.00 | 12.00 | 12.50 |
| Pitcher, 1 pt, 5-1/4" h | 85.00 | 95.00 | 100.00 | 95.00 | 90.00 | 175.00 |
| Plate, 7-3/4" sq | 7.50 | 5.00 | 7.50 | 7.50 | 7.00 | 6.00 |
| Plate, 8-3/4" | 20.00 | 16.00 | 20.00 | 20.00 | 17.50 | 16.00 |
| Sugar, ftd | 20.00 | 16.00 | 20.00 | 20.00 | 17.50 | 25.00 |
| Syrup | - | - | - | - | - | - |
| Vase, 6" h, ftd | 15.00 | 12.00 | 18.00 | 25.00 | 15.00 | 14.00 |

## Chinex Classic

Manufactured by MacBeth-Evans Division of Corning Glass Works, from the late 1930s to early 1940s. Made in Chinex (ivory) and Chinex with Classic Bouquet or Classic Castle dec.

| Item | Chinex | Chinex Classic Bouquet decal | Chinex, |
|---|---|---|---|
| Bowl, 11" d | 20.00 | 36.00 | 48.00 |
| Butter Dish, cov | 55.00 | 80.00 | 135.00 |
| Cake Plate, 11-1/2" d | 10.00 | 15.00 | 25.00 |
| Cereal Bowl, 5-  " d | 6.00 | 8.50 | 15.00 |
| Creamer | 8.50 | 12.00 | 20.00 |
| Cup | 6.00 | 9.50 | 17.50 |
| Plate, 6-1/4" d, sherbet | 3.50 | 4.50 | 8.00 |
| Plate, 9-3/4" d, dinner | 4.00 | 8.00 | 16.00 |
| Sandwich Plate, 11-1/2" d | 8.00 | 15.00 | 25.00 |
| Saucer | 2.00 | 4.00 | 7.00 |
| Sherbet, low, ftd | 7.50 | 12.00 | 29.00 |
| Soup Bowl, 7-3/4" d | 14.00 | 25.00 | 40.00 |
| Sugar, open | 9.50 | 12.50 | 20.00 |
| Vegetable Bowl, 7" d | 15.00 | 25.00 | 35.00 |
| Vegetable Bowl, 9" d | 15.00 | 25.00 | 35.00 |

## Coronation

*Banded Fine Rib, Saxon*
Manufactured by Hocking GlassCompany, Lancaster, Ohio, from 1936 to 1940. Made in crystal, green, pink, and Royal Ruby.

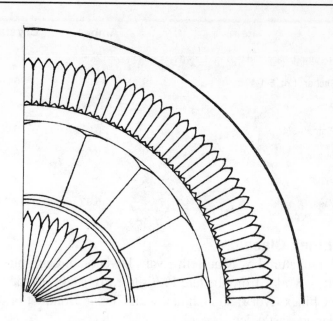

| Item | Crystal | Green | Pink | Royal Ruby |
|---|---|---|---|---|
| Berry Bowl, 4-1/4" d | - | 34.00 | 8.50 | 8.00 |
| Berry Bowl, 8" d, handle | - | - | 18.00 | 20.00 |
| Berry Bowl, 8" d | - | 150.00 | - | - |
| Cup | 5.00 | - | 6.00 | 7.50 |
| Nappy Bowl, 6-1/2" d | 15.00 | - | 7.50 | 15.00 |
| Pitcher, 68 oz, 7-3/4" h | - | - | 500.00 | - |
| Plate, 6" d, sherbet | 2.00 | - | 4.50 | - |
| Plate, 8-1/2" d, luncheon | 5.00 | 42.00 | 12.00 | 8.50 |
| Saucer | 2.00 | - | 4.00 | - |
| Sherbet | - | 70.00 | 7.00 | - |
| Tumbler, 10 oz, 5" h, ftd | - | 165.00 | 35.00 | - |

## Diana

Manufactured by Federal Glass Company, Columbus, Ohio, 1937-1941. Made in amber, crystal, and pink.

**Reproductions:** † A 13-1/8" d scalloped pink bowl has been made which was not original to the pattern.

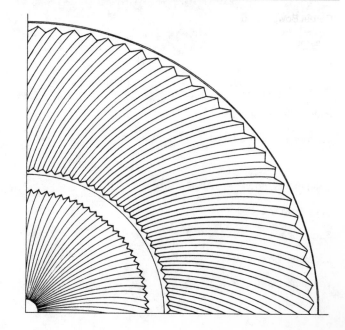

| Item | Amber | Crystal | Pink |
|---|---|---|---|
| Ashtray, 3-1/2" d | - | 4.00 | 5.00 |
| Bowl, 12" d, scalloped edge | 20.00 | 10.00 | 32.00 |
| Candy Jar, cov, round | 40.00 | 18.50 | 48.00 |
| Cereal Bowl, 5" d | 15.00 | 6.50 | 13.00 |
| Coaster, 3-1/2" d | 12.00 | 4.00 | 7.00 |
| Console/Fruit Bowl, 11"d | 10.00 | 20.00 | 44.00 |
| Cream Soup Bowl, 5-1/2" d | 18.00 | 14.00 | 24.00 |
| Creamer, oval | 9.00 | 4.00 | 12.50 |
| Cup | 7.00 | 4.00 | 19.00 |
| Demitasse Cup and Saucer, 2 oz, 4-1/2" d saucer | - | 15.00 | 50.00 |
| Junior Set, 6 cups and saucers, rack | - | 125.00 | 300.00 |
| Plate, 6" d, bread & butter | 3.50 | 3.00 | 5.50 |
| Plate, 9-1/2" d, dinner | 9.00 | 7.00 | 18.50 |
| Platter, 12" l, oval | 15.00 | 12.00 | 28.00 |
| Salad Bowl, 9"d | 18.00 | 15.00 | 20.00 |
| Salt and Pepper Shakers, pr | 100.00 | 30.00 | 75.00 |
| Sandwich Plate, 11-3/4" d | 10.00 | 8.00 | 28.00 |
| Sandwich Plate, 11-3/4" d, advertising in center | - | 15.00 | - |
| Saucer | 2.25 | 2.00 | 6.00 |
| Sherbet | 10.00 | 7.00 | 12.00 |
| Sugar, open, oval | 10.00 | 10.00 | 16.00 |
| Tumbler, 9 oz, 4-1/8" h | 27.50 | 18.00 | 45.00 |

## Doric

Manufactured by Jeannette Glass Company, Jeannette, Pennsylvania, from 1935 to 1938. Made in Delphite, green, pink, and yellow (rare).

| Item | Delphite | Green | Pink |
|---|---|---|---|
| Berry Bowl, 4-1/2" d | 45.00 | 12.00 | 12.00 |
| Berry Bowl, 8-1/4" d | 135.00 | 25.00 | 17.00 |
| Bowl, 9" d, two handles | - | 45.00 | 45.00 |
| Butter Dish, cov | - | 90.00 | 75.00 |
| Cake Plate, 10" d, 3 legs | - | 30.00 | 30.00 |
| Candy Dish, cov, 8" d | - | 42.50 | 45.00 |
| Candy Dish, three part | 10.00 | 9.50 | 12.50 |
| Cereal Bowl, 5-1/2" d | - | 65.00 | 90.00 |
| Coaster, 3" d | - | 28.00 | 20.00 |
| Cream Soup, 5" d, 2 handles | - | 385.00 | - |
| Creamer, 4" h | - | 17.00 | 14.00 |
| Cup | - | 10.00 | 10.00 |
| Pitcher, 36 oz, 6" h, flat | 1,200.00 | 50.00 | 45.00 |
| Pitcher, 48 oz, 7-1/2" h, ftd. | - | 1,000.00 | 750.00 |
| Plate, 6" d, sherbet | - | 7.50 | 7.50 |
| Plate, 7" d, salad | - | 20.00 | 18.00 |
| Plate, 9" d, dinner | - | 24.00 | 12.00 |
| Plate, 9" d, grill | - | 20.00 | 25.00 |
| Platter, 12" l, oval | - | 32.00 | 35.00 |
| Relish Tray, 4 x 4" | - | 12.00 | 14.00 |
| Relish Tray, 4 x 8" | - | 10.00 | 11.00 |
| Salt and Pepper Shakers, pr | - | 40.00 | 45.00 |
| Saucer | - | 7.00 | 7.00 |
| Sherbet, footed | 10.00 | 17.50 | 15.00 |
| Sugar, cov | - | 35.00 | 32.00 |
| Tray, 8" x 8", serving | - | 30.00 | 42.50 |
| Tray, 10" l, handle | - | 25.00 | 16.00 |
| Tumbler, 9 oz, 4-1/2" h, flat | - | 100.00 | 75.00 |
| Tumbler, 10 oz, 4" h, ftd. | - | 90.00 | 65.00 |
| Tumbler, 12 oz, 5" h, ftd. | - | 125.00 | 85.00 |
| Vegetable Bowl, 9" l, oval | - | 35.00 | 30.00 |

## English Hobnail *Line #555*

Manufactured by Westmoreland Glass Company, Grapeville, Pennsylvania, from the 1920s to 1983. Made in amber, cobalt blue, crystal, crystal with various color treatments, green, ice blue, pink, red, and turquoise blue.

**Reproductions:** † A creamer and sugar with a hexagonal foot have been reproduced as well as a nut bowl, and pickle dish.

| Items | Amber | Crystal | Green | Ice Blue | Pink |
|---|---|---|---|---|---|
| Ashtray, 3" d | 20.00 | 20.00 | 22.00 | - | 22.00 |
| Ashtray, 4-1/2" d | 9.00 | 9.00 | 15.00 | 24.00 | 15.00 |
| Ashtray, 4-1/2" sq | 9.50 | 9.50 | 15.00 | - | 15.00 |
| Basket, 5" d, handle | 20.00 | 20.00 | - | - | - |
| Basket, 6" d, handle, tall | 40.00 | 40.00 | - | - | 43.00 |
| Bonbon, 6-1/2" h, handle | 15.00 | 17.50 | 30.00 | 40.00 | 30.00 |
| Bowl, 7" d, 6 part | 17.50 | 17.50 | - | - | - |
| Bowl, 7" d, oblong spoon | 17.50 | 17.50 | - | - | - |
| Bowl, 8" d, ftd | 30.00 | 30.00 | 48.00 | - | 48.00 |
| Bowl, 8" d, hexagonal foot, 2 handles | 38.00 | 38.00 | 75.00 | 115.00 | 75.00 |
| Bowl, 8", 6 pt | 24.00 | 24.00 | - | - | - |
| Bowl, 9-1/2" d, round, crimped | 30.00 | 30.00 | - | - | - |
| Bowl, 10" d, flared | 35.00 | 35.00 | 40.00 | - | 40.00 |
| Bowl, 10" l, oval, crimped | 40.00 | 40.00 | - | - | - |
| Bowl, 11" d, bell | 35.00 | 35.00 | - | - | - |
| Bowl, 11" d, rolled edge | 35.00 | 35.00 | 40.00 | 85.00 | 40.00 |
| Bowl, 12" d, flared | 32.00 | 32.00 | 40.00 | - | 95.00 |
| Bowl,12" l, oval crimped | 32.00 | 32.00 | - | - | - |
| Candelabra, 2 lite | 20.00 | 20.00 | - | - | - |
| Candlesticks, pr, 3-1/2" h, round base | 24.00 | 32.00 | 36.00 | - | 60.00 |
| Candlesticks, pr, | | | | | |

| Items | Amber | Crystal | Green | Ice Blue | Pink |
|---|---|---|---|---|---|
| 5-1/2" h, sq base | 30.00 | 32.00 | - | - | - |
| Candlesticks, pr, | | | | | |
| 9" h, round base | 50.00 | 40.00 | 72.00 | - | 125.00 |
| Candy Dish, 3 foot | 35.00 | 38.00 | 50.00 | - | 50.00 |
| Candy Dish, cov, | | | | | |
| 1/2 lb, cone shape | 35.00 | 40.00 | 55.00 | - | 90.00 |
| Celery, 12" l, oval | 24.00 | 45.00 | 36.00 | - | 36.00 |
| Celery, 9" d | 18.00 | 20.00 | 32.00 | - | 32.00 |
| Champagne, | | | | | |
| two ball, round foot | 8.00 | 7.00 | 20.00 | - | 20.00 |
| Chandelier, 17" shade, | | | | | |
| 200 prisms | 425.00 | 400.00 | - | - | - |
| Cheese, cov, 6" d | 40.00 | 42.00 | - | - | - |
| Cheese, cov, 8-3/4" d | 50.00 | 48.00 | - | - | - |
| Cigarette Box, cov, | | | | | |
| 4-1/2 x 2-1/2" | 24.50 | 24.50 | 30.00 | - | 55.00 |
| Cigarette Jar, cov, round | 16.00 | 18.00 | 25.00 | - | 65.00 |
| Claret, 5 oz, round | 15.00 | 17.50 | - | - | - |
| Coaster, 3" | 5.00 | 5.00 | - | - | - |
| Cocktail, 3 oz, round | 8.50 | 12.00 | - | - | 37.50 |
| Cocktail, 3-1/2 oz, | | | | | |
| round, ball | 15.00 | 17.50 | - | - | - |
| Compote, 5" d, | | | | | |
| round, round foot | 22.00 | 20.00 | 25.00 | - | 25.00 |
| Compote, 5" d, | | | | | |
| round, sq foot | 24.00 | 24.00 | - | - | - |
| Compote, 5-1/2" d, bell | 12.00 | 15.00 | - | - | - |
| Compote, 5-1/2" d, | | | | | |
| bell, sq foot | 20.00 | 20.00 | - | - | - |
| Console Bowl, | | | | | |
| 12" d, flange | 30.00 | 30.00 | 40.00 | - | 40.00 |
| Cordial, 1 oz, round, ball | 16.50 | 16.50 | - | - | - |
| Cordial, 1 oz, round, foot | 16.50 | 16.50 | - | - | - |
| Cream Soup Bowl, 4-5/8" d | 15.00 | 15.00 | - | - | - |
| Cream Soup Liner, | | | | | |
| round, 6-1/2" d | 5.00 | 5.00 | - | - | - |
| Creamer, hexagonal foot † | 20.00 | 20.00 | 25.00 | - | 48.00 |

| Items | Amber | Crystal | Green | Ice Blue | Pink |
|---|---|---|---|---|---|
| Creamer, low, flat | 10.00 | 10.00 | - | - | - |
| Creamer, sq foot | 24.00 | 24.00 | 45.00 | - | 45.00 |
| Cruet, 12 oz | - | 25.00 | - | - | - |
| Cup | 6.50 | 6.50 | 18.00 | - | 25.00 |
| Decanter, 20 oz | 55.00 | 55.00 | - | - | - |
| Demitasse Cup | 17.50 | 17.50 | 55.00 | - | 55.00 |
| Dish, 6" d, crimped | 15.00 | 15.00 | - | - | - |
| Egg Cup | 15.00 | 15.00 | - | - | - |
| Finger Bowl, 4-1/2" d | 7.50 | 7.50 | 15.00 | 35.00 | 15.00 |
| Finger Bowl, 4-1/2" sq, foot | 9.50 | 9.50 | 18.00 | 40.00 | 18.00 |
| Finger Bowl Liner, 6" sq | 6.50 | 6.50 | 20.00 | - | 20.00 |
| Finger Bowl Liner, 6-1/2" d, round | 12.00 | 12.00 | 10.00 | - | 10.00 |
| Ginger Ale Tumbler, 5 oz, flat | 10.00 | 10.00 | 18.00 | - | 20.00 |
| Ginger Ale Tumbler, 5 oz, round foot | 10.00 | 10.00 | - | - | - |
| Ginger Ale Tumbler, 5 oz, sq foot | 8.00 | 8.00 | 32.00 | - | 35.00 |
| Goblet, 8 oz, 6-1/4" h, round, water | 11.00 | 11.00 | - | 50.00 | 35.00 |
| Goblet, 8 oz, sq foot, water | 9.00 | 9.00 | - | - | 50.00 |
| Grapefruit Bowl, 6-1/2" d | 12.00 | 12.00 | 22.00 | - | 24.00 |
| Hat, high | 18.00 | 18.00 | - | - | - |
| Hat, low | 15.00 | 15.00 | - | - | - |
| Honey Compote, 6" d, round foot | 18.00 | 18.00 | 35.00 | - | 35.00 |
| Honey Compote, 6" d, sq foot | 18.00 | 18.00 | - | - | - |
| Ice Tub, 4" h | 18.00 | 18.00 | 50.00 | - | 85.00 |
| Ice Tub, 5-1/2" h | 36.00 | 36.00 | 65.00 | - | 100.00 |
| Iced Tea Tumbler, 10 oz | 14.00 | 14.00 | 30.00 | - | 30.00 |
| Iced Tea Tumbler, 11 oz, round, ball | 12.00 | 12.00 | - | - | - |
| Iced Tea Tumbler, 11 oz, sq foot | 13.50 | 13.50 | - | - | - |
| Iced Tea Tumbler, | | | | | |

| Items | Amber | Crystal | Green | Ice Blue | Pink |
|---|---|---|---|---|---|
| 12-1/2 oz, round foot | 14.00 | 14.00 | - | - | - |
| Iced Tea Tumbler, 12 oz, flat | 14.00 | 14.00 | 32.00 | - | 32.00 |
| Icer, sq base, patterned insert | 45.00 | 45.00 | - | - | - |
| Ivy Bowl, 6-1/2" d, sq foot, crimp top | 35.00 | 35.00 | - | - | - |
| Juice Tumbler, 7 oz, round foot | 27.50 | 27.50 | - | - | - |
| Juice Tumbler, 7 oz, sq foot | 6.50 | 6.50 | - | - | - |
| Lamp Shade, 17" d | 175.00 | 165.00 | - | - | - |
| Lamp, 6-1/2" h, electric | 45.00 | 45.00 | 50.00 | - | 50.00 |
| Lamp, 9-1/2" d, electric | 45.00 | 45.00 | 115.00 | - | 115.00 |
| Lamp, candlestick | 32.00 | 32.00 | - | - | - |
| Marmalade, cov | 40.00 | 40.00 | 45.00 | - | 70.00 |
| Mayonnaise, 6" | 12.00 | 12.00 | 22.00 | - | 22.00 |
| Mustard, cov, sq, foot | 18.00 | 18.00 | - | - | - |
| Nappy, 4-1/2" d, round | 8.00 | 8.00 | 15.00 | 30.00 | 15.00 |
| Nappy, 4-1/2" w, sq | 8.50 | 8.50 | - | - | - |
| Nappy, 5" d, round | 10.00 | 10.00 | 15.00 | 35.00 | 15.00 |
| Nappy, 5-1/2" d, bell | 12.00 | 12.00 | - | - | - |
| Nappy, 6" d, round | 10.00 | 10.00 | 17.50 | - | 17.50 |
| Nappy, 6" d, sq | 10.00 | 10.00 | 17.50 | - | 17.50 |
| Nappy, 6-1/2" d, round | 12.50 | 12.50 | 20.00 | - | 20.00 |
| Nappy, 6-1/2" d, sq | 14.00 | 14.00 | - | - | - |
| Nappy, 7" d, round | 14.00 | 14.00 | 24.00 | - | 24.00 |
| Nappy, 7-1/2" d, bell | 15.00 | 15.00 | - | - | - |
| Nappy, 8" d, cupped | 22.00 | 22.00 | 30.00 | - | 30.00 |
| Nappy, 8" d, round | 22.00 | 22.00 | 35.00 | - | 35.00 |
| Nappy, 9" d, bell | 25.00 | 25.00 | - | - | - |
| Nut, individual, ftd † | 6.00 | 6.00 | 14.50 | - | 14.50 |
| Oil Bottle, 2 oz, handle | 25.00 | 25.00 | - | - | - |
| Oil Bottle, 6 oz, handle | 27.50 | 27.50 | - | - | - |
| Old Fashioned Tumbler, 5 oz | 15.00 | 15.00 | - | - | - |
| Oyster Cocktail, 5 oz, sq foot | 12.00 | 12.00 | 17.50 | - | 17.50 |
| Parfait, round foot | 17.50 | 17.50 | - | - | - |
| Pickle, 8" d † | 15.00 | 15.00 | - | - | - |
| Pitcher, 23 oz, rounded | 48.00 | 48.00 | 150.00 | - | 165.00 |
| Pitcher, 32 oz, straight side | 50.00 | 50.00 | 175.00 | - | 175.00 |

| Items | Amber | Crystal | Green | Ice Blue | Pink |
|---|---|---|---|---|---|
| Pitcher, 38 oz, rounded | 65.00 | 65.00 | 215.00 | - | 215.00 |
| Pitcher, 60 oz, rounded | 70.00 | 70.00 | 295.00 | - | 295.00 |
| Pitcher, 64 oz, straight side | 7500 | 75.00 | 310.00 | - | 310.00 |
| Plate, 5-1/2" d, round | 7.00 | 7.00 | 10.00 | - | 10.00 |
| Plate, 6" w, sq | 5.00 | 5.00 | - | - | - |
| Plate, 6-1/2" d, round | 6.25 | 6.25 | 10.00 | - | 10.00 |
| Plate, 6-1/2" d, round, depressed center | 6.00 | 6.00 | - | - | - |
| Plate, 8" d, round | 9.00 | 9.00 | 14.00 | - | 14.00 |
| Plate, 8" d, round, ftd | 13.00 | 13.00 | - | - | - |
| Plate, 8-1/2" d, plain edge | 9.00 | 9.00 | - | - | - |
| Plate, 8-1/2" d, round | 7.00 | 9.00 | 17.50 | - | 28.00 |
| Plate, 8-3/4" w, sq | 9.25 | 9.25 | - | - | - |
| Plate, 10" d, round | 15.00 | 15.00 | 45.00 | - | 65.00 |
| Plate, 10" w, sq | 15.00 | 15.00 | - | - | - |
| Plate, 10-1/2" d, round, grill | 18.00 | 18.00 | - | - | - |
| Plate, 12" w, sq | 20.00 | 20.00 | - | - | - |
| Plate, 15" w, sq | 28.00 | 28.00 | - | - | - |
| Preserve, 8" d | 15.00 | 15.00 | - | - | - |
| Puff Box, cov, 6" d, round | 20.00 | 20.00 | 47.50 | - | 80.00 |
| Punch Bowl and Stand | 215.00 | 215.00 | - | - | - |
| Punch Cup | 7.00 | 7.00 | - | - | - |
| Relish, 8" d, 3 part | 18.00 | 18.00 | - | - | - |
| Rose Bowl, 4" d | 17.50 | 17.50 | 48.00 | - | 50.00 |
| Rose Bowl, 6" d | 20.00 | 20.00 | - | - | - |
| Salt and Pepper Shakers, pr, round foot | 27.50 | 27.50 | 150.00 | - | 165.00 |
| Salt and Pepper Shakers, pr, sq, foot | 15.00 | 15.00 | - | - | - |
| Saucer, Demitasse, round | 10.00 | 10.00 | 15.00 | - | 17.50 |
| Saucer, Demitasse, sq | 10.00 | 10.00 | - | - | - |
| Saucer, round | 2.00 | 2.00 | 6.00 | - | 6.00 |
| Saucer, sq | 2.00 | 2.00 | - | - | - |
| Sherbet, high, round foot | 7.00 | 7.00 | 18.00 | - | 37.50 |
| Sherbet, high, sq foot | 8.00 | 8.00 | 18.00 | - | - |
| Sherbet, high, two ball, round foot | 10.00 | 10.00 | - | - | - |

| Items | Amber | Crystal | Green | Ice Blue | Pink |
|---|---|---|---|---|---|
| Sherbet, low, | | | | | |
| one ball, round foot | 12.00 | 10.00 | - | - | 15.00 |
| Sherbet, low, round foot | 12.50 | 7.00 | - | - | - |
| Sherbet, low, sq foot | 6.50 | 6.00 | 15.00 | - | 17.50 |
| Straw Jar, 10" h | 65.00 | 60.00 | - | - | - |
| Sundae | 9.00 | 9.00 | - | - | - |
| Sugar, hexagonal, ftd † | 9.00 | 9.00 | 25.00 | - | 48.00 |
| Sugar, low, flat | 8.00 | 8.00 | - | - | - |
| Sugar, sq foot | 9.00 | 9.00 | 48.00 | - | 55.00 |
| Sweetmeat, | | | | | |
| 5-1/2" d, ball stem | 30.00 | 30.00 | - | - | - |
| Sweetmeat, 8" d, ball stem | 40.00 | 40.00 | 60.00 | - | 65.00 |
| Tidbit, 2 tier | 27.50 | 27.50 | 65.00 | 85.00 | 80.00 |
| Toilet Bottle, 5 oz | 25.00 | 25.00 | 40.00 | 65.00 | 40.00 |
| Torte Plate, 14" d, round | 35.00 | 30.00 | 48.00 | - | 48.00 |
| Torte Plate, 20-1/2" round | 55.00 | 50.00 | - | - | - |
| Tumbler, 8 oz, water | 10.00 | 10.00 | 24.00 | - | 24.00 |
| Tumbler, 9 oz, | | | | | |
| round, ball, water | 10.00 | 10.00 | - | - | - |
| Tumbler, 9 oz, | | | | | |
| round, ftd water | 10.00 | 10.00 | - | - | - |
| Tumbler, 9 oz, | | | | | |
| sq foot, water | 10.00 | 10.00 | - | - | - |
| Urn, cov, 11" h | 35.00 | 35.00 | 350.00 | - | 350.00 |
| Vase, 6-1/2" h, sq foot | 24.00 | 24.00 | - | - | - |
| Vase, 7-1/2" h, flip | 27.50 | 27.50 | 70.00 | - | 70.00 |
| Vase, 7-1/2" h, | | | | | |
| flip jar with cov | 55.00 | 55.00 | 85.00 | - | 85.00 |
| Vase, 8" h, sq foot | 35.00 | 35.00 | - | - | - |
| Vase, 8-1/2" h, flared top | 40.00 | 40.00 | 120.00 | - | 235.00 |
| Whiskey, 1-1/2 oz | 10.00 | 10.00 | - | - | - |
| Whiskey, 3 oz | 12.00 | 12.00 | - | - | - |
| Wine, 2 oz, round foot | 13.00 | 13.00 | - | - | - |
| Wine, 2 oz, sq ft | 15.00 | 15.00 | 35.00 | - | 65.00 |
| Wine, 2-1/2 oz, ball, foot | 10.00 | 10.00 | - | - | - |

Values for cobalt blue, red, or turquoise blue pieces would be approximately 25% higher than ice blue values. Currently a turquoise basket is valued at $150. A red basket $100. Crystal pieces with a color accent would be slightly higher than crystal values.

## Floral *Poinsettia*

Manufactured by Jeannette Glass Company, Jeannette, Pennsylvania, from 1931-1935. Made in amber, crystal, Delphite, green, Jadite, pink, red, and yellow.

**Reproductions:** † Reproduction salt and pepper shakers have been made in cobalt blue, dark green, green, pink, and red.

| Item | Delphite | Green | Jadite | Pink |
|---|---|---|---|---|
| Berry Bowl, 4" d | 40.00 | 25.00 | - | 25.00 |
| Butter Dish, cov | - | 95.00 | - | 90.00 |
| Candlesticks, pr, 4" h | - | 90.00 | - | 95.00 |
| Candy Jar, cov | 80.00 | 45.00 | - | 45.00 |
| Canister Set | - | - | 60.00 | - |
| Casserole, cov | - | 45.00 | - | 28.00 |
| Coaster, 3-1/4" d | - | 15.00 | - | - |
| Comport, 9" | - | 875.00 | - | 795.00 |
| Cream Soup, 5-1/2" d | - | 735.00 | - | 735.00 |
| Creamer, flat | - | 24.00 | - | 24.00 |
| Cup | - | 15.00 | - | 15.00 |
| Dresser Set | - | 1,350.00 | - | - |
| Dresser Tray, 9-1/4" l, oval | - | 200.00 | - | - |
| Flower Frog | - | 695.00 | - | - |
| Ice Tub, 3-1/2" h, oval | - | 850.00 | - | 825.00 |
| Juice Tumbler, ftd | - | 24.00 | - | 27.50 |
| Juice Tumbler, 5 oz, 4" h, flat | - | 35.00 | - | 35.00 |
| Lamp | - | 275.00 | - | 260.00 |
| Lemonade Pitcher, 48 oz, 10-1/4" h | - | 265.00 | - | 350.00 |
| Lemonade Tumbler, | | | | |
| 9 oz, 5-1/4" h, ftd | - | 60.00 | - | 55.00 |
| Pitcher, 23 or 24 oz, 5-1/2" h | - | 50.00 | - | - |
| Pitcher, 32 oz, ftd, cone, 8" h | - | 36.00 | - | 42.00 |

| Item | Delphite | Green | Jadite | Pink |
|---|---|---|---|---|
| Plate, 6" d, sherbet | - | 8.50 | - | 8.50 |
| Plate, 8" d, salad | - | 15.00 | - | 17.00 |
| Plate, 9" d, dinner | 145.00 | 30.00 | - | 27.50 |
| Plate, 9" d, grill | - | 185.00 | - | - |
| Plate, 10-3/4" l, oval | - | 20.00 | - | 17.50 |
| Platter, 11" l | 150.00 | 25.00 | - | 25.00 |
| Refrigerator Dish, cov, 5" sq | - | - | 15.00 | - |
| Relish, 2 part oval | 165.00 | 24.00 | - | 18.50 |
| Rose Bowl, 3 legs | - | 500.00 | - | - |
| Salad Bowl, 7-1/2" d | - | 40.00 | - | 40.00 |
| Salad Bowl, 7-1/2" d, ruffled | 65.00 | 125.00 | - | 120.00 |
| Salt and Pepper Shakers, pr, 4" h, ftd † | - | 45.00 | - | 45.00 |
| Salt and Pepper Shakers, pr, 6" flat | - | - | - | 60.00 |
| Saucer | - | 12.50 | - | 12.50 |
| Sherbet | 90.00 | 20.00 | - | 20.00 |
| Sugar, cov | - | 26.00 | - | 30.00 |
| Sugar, open | 75.00 | - | - | - |
| Tray, 6" sq, closed handles | - | 195.00 | - | - |
| Tumbler, 3 oz, 3-1/2" h, ftd | - | 18.00 | - | 25.00 |
| Tumbler, 7 oz, 4-1/2", ftd | 175.00 | 25.00 | - | 25.00 |
| Tumbler, 5-1/4" h, ftd | - | 60.00 | - | 55.00 |
| Vase, flared, 3 legs | - | 485.00 | - | - |
| Vase, 6-7/8" h | - | 475.00 | - | - |
| Vegetable Bowl, 8" d, cov | - | 50.00 | - | 40.00 |
| Vegetable Bowl, 8" d, open | 80.00 | - | - | 30.00 |
| Vegetable Bowl, 9" l, oval | - | 35.00 | - | 35.00 |

Production in amber, crystal, red, and yellow was very limited. A crystal 6-7/8" h vase would be valued at $295.

# Harp

Manufactured by Jeannette Glass Company, Jeannette, Pennsylvania, from 1954 to 1957. Made in crystal, crystal with gold trim, limited pieces made in ice blue, iridescent white, pink, and shell pink.

| Item | Crystal | Ice Blue | Shell Pink |
|---|---|---|---|
| Ashtray | 6.00 | - | - |
| Cake Stand, 9" d | 35.00 | 45.00 | 45.00 |
| Coaster | 6.00 | - | - |
| Cup | 28.00 | - | - |
| Parfait | 20.00 | - | - |
| Plate, 7" d | 20.00 | 25.00 | - |
| Saucer | 12.00 | - | - |
| Snack Set, cup, saucer, 7" plate | 48.00 | - | - |
| Tray, 2 handles, rectangular | 35.00 | 35.00 | 65.00 |
| Vase, 7-1/2" h | 35.00 | - | - |

# Iris *Iris and Herringbone*

Manufactured by Jeannette Glass Company, Jeannette, PA, from 1928 to 1932, 1950s, 1970s. Made in crystal, iridescent, some green and pink. Recent color combinations of yellow and red and blue and green and white have been made.

**Reproductions:** † Some collectors and dealers feel strongly that the newer re-issues of this pattern are actually reproductions. Forms that have the potential to fool buyers are the 4-1/2" berry bowl, covered candy jar, 10" d dinner plate, 6-1/2" h ftd tumbler, and vase. Careful examination of the object, plus careful consideration of the color should help determine age.

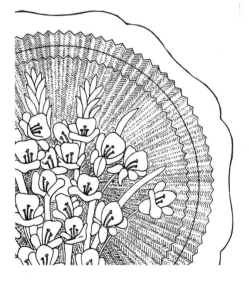

| Item | Crystal | Green | Iridescent | Pink |
|---|---|---|---|---|
| Berry Bowl, 4-1/2" d, beaded edge † | 50.00 | | 20.00 | - |
| Berry Bowl, 8" d, beaded edge | 110.00 | - | 30.00 | - |

| Item | Crystal | Green | Iridescent | Pink |
|---|---|---|---|---|
| Bowl, 5-1/2" d, scalloped | 10.00 | - | 23.00 | - |
| Bowl, 9-1/2" d, scalloped | 17.50 | - | 14.00 | - |
| Bread Plate, 11-3/4" d | 20.00 | - | 38.00 | - |
| Butter Dish, cov | 50.00 | - | 55.00 | - |
| Candlesticks, pr | 48.50 | - | 48.00 | - |
| Candy Jar, cov † | 150.00 | - | - | - |
| Cereal Bowl, 5" d | 150.00 | - | - | - |
| Coaster | 105.00 | - | - | - |
| Cocktail, 4 oz, 4-1/4" h | 29.50 | - | - | - |
| Creamer, ftd | 15.00 | 150.00 | 17.50 | 150.00 |
| Cup | 20.00 | - | 17.50 | - |
| Demitasse Cup and Saucer | 210.00 | - | 350.00 | - |
| Fruit Bowl, 11" d, straight edge | 15.00 | - | - | - |
| Fruit Bowl, 11-1/2" d, ruffled | 15.00 | - | 18.00 | - |
| Fruit Set | 110.00 | - | - | - |
| Goblet, 4 oz, 5-3/4" h | 30.00 | - | 135.00 | - |
| Goblet, 8 oz, 5-3/4" h | 27.50 | - | 175.00 | - |
| Iced Tea Tumbler, 6-1/2" h, ftd | 42.00 | - | - | - |
| Lamp Shade, 11-1/2" | 90.00 | - | - | - |
| Nut Set | 90.00 | - | - | - |
| Pitcher, 9-1/2" h, ftd | 50.00 | - | 50.00 | - |
| Plate, 5-1/2" d, sherbet | 16.00 | - | 15.00 | - |
| Plate, 7" d | 95.00 | - | - | - |
| Plate, 8" d, luncheon | 125.00 | - | 115.00 | - |
| Plate, 9" d, dinner † | 65.00 | - | 48.00 | - |
| Salad Bowl, 9-1/2" d, ruffled | 20.00 | 150.00 | 20.00 | 135.00 |
| Sandwich Plate, 11-3/4" d | 20.00 | - | 38.00 | - |
| Sauce, 5" d, ruffled | 12.50 | - | 24.00 | - |
| Saucer | 15.00 | - | 11.00 | - |
| Sherbet, 2-1/2" h, ftd | 30.00 | - | 15.50 | - |
| Sherbet, 4" h, ftd | 22.00 | - | 15.50 | - |
| Soup Bowl, 7-1/2" d | 165.00 | - | 80.00 | - |
| Sugar, cov | 32.00 | 150.00 | 23.00 | 150.00 |
| Tumbler, 4" h, flat | 125.00 | - | 18.00 | - |
| Tumbler, 6" h, ftd | 30.00 | - | 25.00 | - |
| Tumbler, 6-1/2" h, ftd † | 40.00 | - | - | - |
| Tumbler, flat, water | 135.00 | - | - | - |

| Item | Crystal | Green | Iridescent | Pink |
|---|---|---|---|---|
| Vase, 9" h † | 38.00 | - | 35.00 | 225.00 |
| Wine, 4" h | 20.00 | - | 33.50 | - |
| Wine, 4-1/4" h, 3 oz | 24.00 | - | - | - |
| Wine, 5-1/2" h | 27.50 | - | - | - |

## Laurel

Manufactured by McKee Glass Company, Pittsburgh, Pennsylvania, 1930s. Made in French Ivory, Jade Green, Poudre Blue, and White Opal.

| Item | French Ivory | Jade Green | Poudre Blue | White Opal |
|---|---|---|---|---|
| Berry Bowl, 4-3/4" d | 9.00 | 12.50 | 16.00 | 14.00 |
| Berry Bowl, 9" d | 28.50 | 32.00 | 55.00 | 30.00 |
| Bowl, 6" d, three legs | 15.00 | 18.00 | - | 15.00 |
| Bowl, 10-1/2" d, three legs | 37.50 | 50.00 | 68.00 | 45.00 |
| Bowl, 11" d | 40.00 | 50.00 | 85.00 | 37.50 |
| Candlesticks, pr, 4" h | 50.00 | 60.00 | - | 45.00 |
| Cereal Bowl, 6" d | 12.00 | 20.00 | 28.00 | 20.00 |
| Cheese Dish, cov | 60.00 | 80.00 | - | 75.00 |
| Creamer, short | 12.00 | 20.00 | - | 18.00 |
| Creamer, tall | 15.00 | 24.00 | 40.00 | 24.00 |
| Cup | 9.50 | 12.50 | 20.00 | 12.00 |
| Plate, 6" d, sherbet | 6.00 | 12.00 | 10.00 | 8.00 |
| Plate, 7-1/2" d, salad | 10.00 | 15.00 | 17.50 | 12.00 |
| Plate, 9-1/8" d, dinner | 15.00 | 20.00 | 30.00 | 18.50 |
| Plate, 9-1/8" d, grill, round | 15.00 | 20.00 | - | 18.50 |
| Plate, 9-1/8" d, grill, scalloped | 15.00 | 20.00 | - | 18.50 |
| Platter, 10-3/4" l, oval | 32.00 | 35.00 | 45.00 | 30.00 |
| Salt and Pepper Shakers, pr | 48.00 | 75.00 | - | 65.00 |

| Item | French Ivory | Jade Green | Poudre Blue | White Opal |
|---|---|---|---|---|
| Saucer | 3.25 | 3.75 | 7.50 | 3.50 |
| Sherbet | 12.50 | 18.00 | - | 18.00 |
| Sherbet/champagne, 5" | 50.00 | 62.00 | - | 60.00 |
| Soup Bowl, 7-7/8" d | 35.00 | 40.00 | - | 40.00 |
| Sugar, short | 12.00 | 20.00 | - | 18.00 |
| Sugar, tall | 15.00 | 24.00 | 40.00 | 24.00 |
| Tumbler, 9 oz, 4-1/2" h, flat | 40.00 | 60.00 | - | 60.00 |
| Tumbler, 12 oz, 5" h, flat | 60.00 | - | - | - |
| Vegetable Bowl, 9-3/4" l, oval | 18.50 | 20.00 | 45.00 | 20.00 |

| Children's Item | Plain | Green or Decorated | Scotty Dog Green | Scotty Dog Ivory |
|---|---|---|---|---|
| Creamer | 25.00 | 50.00 | 155.00 | 100.00 |
| Cup | 20.00 | 36.00 | 85.00 | 50.00 |
| Plate | 10.00 | 17.50 | 55.00 | 35.00 |
| Saucer | 8.00 | 10.00 | 55.00 | 25.00 |
| Sugar | 25.00 | 50.00 | 155.00 | 100.00 |

## Miss America *Diamond Pattern*

Manufactured by Hocking Glass Company, Lancaster, Ohio, from 1935 to 1938. Made in crystal, green, ice blue, jade-ite, pink, and royal ruby.

**Reproductions:** † Reproductions include the butter dish, (including a new importer,) creamer, 8" pitcher, salt and pepper shakers, sugar, and tumbler. Reproductions are found in amberina, blue, cobalt blue, crystal, green, pink, red.

| Item | Crystal | Green | Ice Blue | Pink | Royal Ruby |
|---|---|---|---|---|---|
| Berry Bowl, 4-1/2" d | - | 15.00 | - | - | - |
| Bowl, 8" d, curved at top | 48.00 | - | - | 95.00 | - |
| Bowl, 8" d, straight sides | - | - | - | 85.00 | - |
| Bowl, 11" d, shallow | - | - | - | - | 800.00 |
| Butter Dish, cov † | 200.00 | - | - | 550.00 | - |
| Cake Plate, 12" d, ftd | 27.50 | - | - | 45.00 | - |
| Candy Jar, cov, 11-1/2" | 65.00 | - | - | 175.00 | - |

| Item | Crystal | Green | Ice Blue | Pink | Royal Ruby |
|---|---|---|---|---|---|
| Celery Dish, 10-1/2" l, oval | 19.50 | - | 160.00 | 38.50 | - |
| Cereal Bowl, 6-1/4" d | 12 | 18.00 | - | 25.00 | - |
| Coaster, 5-3/4" d | 19.50 | - | - | 35.00 | - |
| Comport, 5" d | 20.00 | - | - | 35.00 | - |
| Creamer, ftd † | 12.50 | - | - | 24.00 | 215.00 |
| Cup | 12.50 | 12.00 | 14.00 | 28.00 | 235.00 |
| Fruit Bowl, 8-3/4" d | 39.50 | - | - | 60.00 | 450.00 |
| Goblet, 10 oz, 5-1/2" h | 22.50 | - | - | 60.00 | 250.00 |
| Iced Tea Tumbler, 14 oz, 5-3/4" h | 25.00 | - | - | 85.00 | - |
| Juice Goblet, 5 oz, 4-3/4" h | 27.50 | - | - | 95.00 | 250.00 |
| Juice Tumbler, 5 oz, 4" h | 20.00 | - | 150.00 | 60.00 | 200.00 |
| Pitcher, 65 oz, 8" h † | 45.00 | - | - | 175.00 | - |
| Pitcher, 65 oz, 8-1/2" h, ice lip | 75.00 | - | - | 135.00 | 50.00 |
| Plate, 5-3/4" d, sherbet | 7.50 | 9.00 | 55.00 | 12.50 | - |
| Plate, 6-3/4" d | - | 12.00 | - | - | - |
| Plate, 8-1/2" d, salad | 9.00 | 14.00 | - | 32.00 | 150.00 |
| Plate, 10-1/4" d, dinner | 16.50 | - | 150.00 | 45.00 | - |
| Plate, 10-1/4" d, grill | 15.00 | - | - | 37.50 | - |
| Platter, 12-1/4" l, oval | 18.00 | - | - | 45.00 | - |
| Relish, 8-3/4" l, 4 part | 30.00 | - | - | 35.00 | - |
| Relish, 11-3/4" d, divided | 35.00 | - | - | 40.00 | - |
| Salt and Pepper Shakers, pr † | 35.00 | 300.00 | - | 65.00 | - |
| Saucer | 4.00 | - | - | 7.00 | 60.00 |
| Sherbet | 10.00 | - | 60.00 | 20.00 | 135.00 |
| Sugar | 12.00 | - | - | 24.00 | 175.00 |
| Tumbler, 10 oz, 4-1/2" h, flat † | 20.00 | 45.00 | - | 40.00 | - |
| Tumbler, 14 oz, 5-3/4" h | 28.00 | - | - | - | - |
| Vegetable Bowl, 10" l, oval | 18.00 | - | - | 47.50 | - |
| Whiskey | 24.00 | - | - | - | - |
| Wine, 3 oz, 3-3/4" h | 25.00 | - | - | 85.00 | 250.00 |

## Old English *Threading*

Manufactured by Indiana Glass Company, Dunkirk, Indiana, late 1920s. Made in amber, crystal, green, and pink.

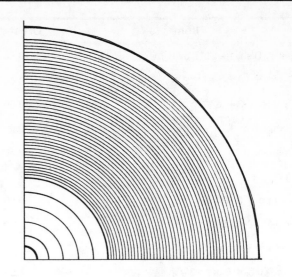

| Item | Amber | Crystal | Green | Pink |
|---|---|---|---|---|
| Bowl, 4" d, flat | 20.00 | 18.00 | 22.00 | 20.00 |
| Bowl, 9-1/2" d, flat | 35.00 | 25.00 | 35.00 | 35.00 |
| Candlesticks, pr, 4" h | 35.00 | 25.00 | 35.00 | 35.00 |
| Candy Dish, cov, flat | 50.00 | 40.00 | 50.00 | 50.00 |
| Candy Jar, cov | 55.00 | 45.00 | 55.00 | 55.00 |
| Cheese Compote, 3-1/2" h | 17.50 | 12.00 | 17.50 | 17.50 |
| Cheese Plate, indent | 20.00 | 10.00 | 20.00 | 20.00 |
| Compote, 3-1/2" h, 6-3/8" w, 2 handles | 24.00 | 12.00 | 24.00 | 24.00 |
| Compote, 3-1/2" h, 7" w | 24.00 | 12.00 | 24.00 | 24.00 |
| Creamer | 18.00 | 10.00 | 18.00 | 18.00 |
| Egg Cup | - | 10.00 | - | - |
| Fruit Bowl, 9" d, ftd | 30.00 | 20.00 | 30.00 | 30.00 |
| Fruit Stand, 11" h, ftd | 40.00 | 18.00 | 40.00 | 40.00 |
| Goblet, 8 oz, 5-3/4" h | 30.00 | 15.00 | 30.00 | 30.00 |
| Pitcher | 70.00 | 35.00 | 70.00 | 70.00 |
| Pitcher, cov | 125.00 | 55.00 | 125.00 | 125.00 |
| Sandwich Server, center handle | 60.00 | - | 60.00 | 60.00 |
| Sherbet | 20.00 | 10.00 | 20.00 | 20.00 |
| Sugar, cov | 38.00 | 14.00 | 38.00 | 38.00 |
| Tumbler, 4-1/2" h, ftd | 24.00 | 12.00 | 28.00 | 24.00 |
| Tumbler, 5-1/2" h, ftd | 35.00 | 17.50 | 35.00 | 35.00 |
| Vase, 5-3/8" h, 7" w, fan-shape | 48.00 | 24.00 | 48.00 | 48.00 |
| Vase, 8" h, 4-1/2" w, ftd | 45.00 | 20.00 | 45.00 | 45.00 |
| Vase, 8-1/4" h, 4-1/4" w, ftd | 45.00 | 20.00 | 45.00 | 45.00 |
| Vase, 12" h, ftd | 60.00 | 32.00 | 60.00 | 60.00 |

## Pioneer

Manufactured by Federal Glass Co., Columbus, Ohio, starting in the 1940s. Originally made in pink, crystal was added later. The crystal 11" fluted bowl and 12" dinner plate were made until 1973.

| Item | Crystal | Pink |
|------|---------|------|
| Bowl, 7" d, low, fruits center | 8.00 | 10.00 |
| Bowl, 7-3/4" d, ruffled, fruits center | 10.00 | 12.00 |
| Bowl, 10-1/2" d, fruits center | 12.00 | 14.00 |
| Bowl, 10-1/2" d, plain center | 10.00 | 12.00 |
| Bowl, 11" d, ruffled, fruits center | 15.00 | 18.00 |
| Bowl, 11" d, ruffled, plain center | 12.00 | 15.00 |
| Nappy, 5-3/8" d, fruits center | 8.00 | 10.00 |
| Nappy, 5-3/8" d, plain center | 6.00 | 8.00 |
| Plate, 8" d, luncheon, fruits center | 6.00 | 8.00 |
| Plate, 8" d, luncheon, plain center | 6.00 | 8.00 |
| Plate, 12" d, fruits center | 10.00 | 12.00 |
| Plate, 12" d, plain center | 10.00 | 12.00 |

## Roulette *Many Windows*

Manufactured by Hocking Glass Company, Lancaster, Ohio, from 1935 to 1939. Made in crystal, green, and pink.

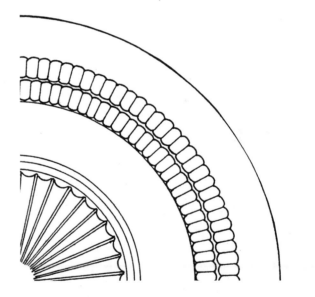

| Item | Crystal | Green | Pink |
|------|---------|-------|------|
| Cup | 35.00 | 8.00 | 8.50 |
| Fruit Bowl, 9" d | 12.00 | 18.00 | 18.00 |
| Iced Tea Tumbler, 12 oz, 5-1/8" h | 24.00 | 40.00 | 35.00 |
| Juice Tumbler, 5 oz, 3-1/4" h | 10.00 | 20.00 | 24.00 |
| Old Fashioned Tumbler, 7-1/2 oz, 3-1/4" h | 24.00 | 40.00 | 40.00 |
| Pitcher, 65 oz, 8" h | 30.00 | 35.00 | 45.00 |
| Plate, 6" d, sherbet | 3.50 | 4.50 | 5.00 |
| Plate, 8-1/2" d, luncheon | 7.00 | 8.00 | 6.00 |

| Item | Crystal | Green | Pink |
|------|---------|-------|------|
| Sandwich Plate, 12" d | 15.00 | 18.50 | 20.00 |
| Saucer | 2.50 | 4.00 | 3.00 |
| Sherbet | 8.00 | 10.00 | 12.00 |
| Tumbler, 9 oz, 4-1/8" h | 15.00 | 20.00 | 22.00 |
| Tumbler, 10 oz, 5-1/2" h, ftd | 18.00 | 30.00 | 35.00 |
| Whiskey, 1-1/2 oz, 2-1/2" h | 10.00 | 18.00 | 18.00 |

## Sharon *Cabbage Rose*

Manufactured by Federal Glass Company, Columbus, Ohio, from 1935 to 1939. Made in amber, crystal, green, and pink.

**Reproductions:** † Reproductions include the butter dish, cov candy dish, creamer, cov sugar, salt and pepper shakers. Reproduction colors include dark amber, blue, green, and pink.

| Item | Amber | Crystal | Green | Pink |
|------|-------|---------|-------|------|
| Berry Bowl, 5" d | 8.50 | 5.00 | 18.50 | 15.00 |
| Berry Bowl, 8-1/2" d | 10.00 | 12.00 | 40.00 | 35.00 |
| Butter Dish, cov † | 48.00 | 20.00 | 85.00 | 65.00 |
| Cake Plate, 11-1/2" d, ftd | 30.00 | 10.00 | 65.00 | 50.00 |
| Candy Dish, cov † | 45.00 | 15.00 | 100.00 | 65.00 |
| Cereal, 6" d | 24.00 | 12.00 | 32.00 | 30.00 |
| Champagne, 5" d bowl | - | - | - | 12.00 |
| Cheese Dish, cov † | 225.00 | 1,500.00 | - | 950.00 |
| Cream Soup, 5" d | 28.00 | 15.00 | 60.00 | 50.00 |
| Creamer, ftd † | 15.00 | 14.00 | 22.00 | 24.00 |
| Cup | 9.00 | 6.00 | 18.00 | 15.00 |
| Fruit Bowl, 10-1/2" d | 24.00 | 18.00 | 40.00 | 55.00 |
| Iced Tea Tumbler, ftd | 125.00 | 15.00 | - | 65.00 |
| Jam Dish, 7-1/2" d | 40.00 | - | 48.00 | 215.00 |
| Pitcher, 80 oz, ice lip | 145.00 | - | 150.00 | 165.00 |
| Pitcher, 80 oz, without ice lip | 140.00 | - | 150.00 | 150.00 |
| Plate, 6" d, bread and butter | 16.00 | 5.00 | 9.00 | 16.50 |
| Plate, 7-1/2" d, salad | 16.50 | 6.50 | 8.00 | 30.00 |

| Item | Amber | Crystal | Green | Pink |
|------|-------|---------|-------|------|
| Plate, 9-1/2" d, dinner | 17.00 | 9.50 | 27.50 | 24.50 |
| Platter, 12-1/2" l, oval | 24.00 | - | 35.00 | 40.00 |
| Salt and Pepper Shakers, pr † | 40.00 | - | 80.00 | 65.00 |
| Saucer | 6.50 | 4.00 | 36.00 | 15.00 |
| Sherbet, ftd | 14.00 | 8.00 | 35.00 | 19.50 |
| Soup, flat, 7-3/4" d, 1 7/8" deep | 60.00 | - | - | 65.00 |
| Sugar, cov † | 35.00 | 12.00 | 55.00 | 60.00 |
| Tumbler, 9 oz, 4-1/8" h, thick | 30.00 | - | 65.00 | 45.00 |
| Tumbler, 9 oz, 4-1/8" h, thin | 38.00 | - | 65.00 | 42.00 |
| Tumbler, 12 oz, 5-1/4" h, thick | 55.00 | - | 95.00 | 50.00 |
| Tumbler, 12 oz, 5-1/4" h, thin | 55.00 | - | 95.00 | 52.50 |
| Tumbler, 15 oz, 6-1/2" h, thick | 125.00 | 18.00 | - | 63.00 |
| Vegetable Bowl, 9-1/2" l, oval | 25.00 | - | 35.00 | 42.50 |

## Twisted Optic

Manufactured by Imperial Glass Company, Bellaire, Ohio, from 1927 to 1930. Made in amber, blue, canary, green, and pink.

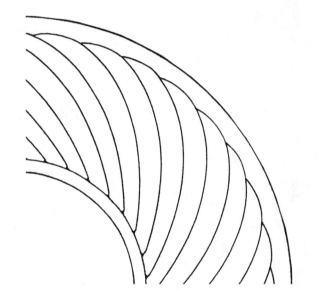

| Item | Amber | Blue | Canary | Green | Pink |
|------|-------|------|--------|-------|------|
| Basket, 10" h | 42.00 | 75.00 | 75.00 | 45.00 | 45.00 |
| Bowl, 7" d, ruffled | - | - | - | 8.00 | - |
| Bowl, 9" d | 18.50 | 28.50 | 28.50 | 18.50 | 18.50 |
| Bowl, 11-1/2" d, 4-1/4" h | 24.00 | 48.00 | 48.00 | 24.00 | 24.00 |
| Candlesticks, pr, 3" h | 22.00 | 40.00 | 40.00 | 22.00 | 22.00 |
| Candlesticks, pr, 8" h | 30.00 | 50.00 | 50.00 | 30.00 | 30.00 |
| Candy Jar, cov, flat | 25.00 | 50.00 | 50.00 | 25.00 | 25.00 |
| Candy Jar, cov, flat, flange edge | 35.00 | 60.00 | 60.00 | 33.00 | 33.00 |
| Candy Jar, cov, ftd, flange edge | 35.00 | 60.00 | 60.00 | 33.00 | 33.00 |
| Candy Jar, cov, ftd, short | 40.00 | 70.00 | 70.00 | 40.00 | 40.00 |

| Item | Amber | Blue | Canary | Green | Pink |
|---|---|---|---|---|---|
| Candy Jar, cov, ftd, tall | 40.00 | 65.00 | 65.00 | 40.00 | 40.00 |
| Cereal Bowl, 5"d | 6.50 | 10.00 | 10.00 | 6.50 | 6.50 |
| Cologne Bottle, stopper | 45.00 | 65.00 | 65.00 | 45.00 | 45.00 |
| Console Bowl, 10-1/2" d | 25.00 | 35.00 | 35.00 | 25.00 | 25.00 |
| Cream Soup, 4-3/4" d | 12.00 | 18.00 | 18.00 | 12.00 | 12.00 |
| Creamer | 8.00 | 14.00 | 14.00 | 8.00 | 8.00 |
| Cup | 7.50 | 10.00 | 12.50 | 5.00 | 6.00 |
| Mayonnaise | 20.00 | 35.00 | 35.00 | 20.00 | 20.00 |
| Pitcher, 64 oz. | 32.00 | - | - | 30.00 | 32.00 |
| Plate, 6" d, sherbet | 2.50 | 4.50 | 5.00 | 2.50 | 2.00 |
| Plate, 7" d, salad | 3.50 | 6.50 | 7.00 | 3.50 | 3.50 |
| Plate, 7-1/2 x 9" l, oval | 6.00 | 10.00 | 10.00 | 6.00 | 6.00 |
| Plate, 8" d, luncheon | 6.00 | 9.00 | 10.00 | 6.00 | 5.00 |
| Powder Jar, cov | 38.00 | 65.00 | 65.00 | 38.00 | 38.00 |
| Preserve Jar | 30.00 | - | - | 30.00 | 30.00 |
| Salad Bowl, 7"d | 12.00 | 15.00 | 15.00 | 12.00 | 12.00 |
| Sandwich Plate, 10" d | 10.00 | 17.50 | 17.50 | 10.00 | 10.00 |
| Sandwich Server, center handle | 22.00 | 35.00 | 35.00 | 22.00 | 22.00 |
| Sandwich Server, two-handles, flat | 15.00 | 20.00 | 20.00 | 15.00 | 15.00 |
| Saucer | 2.50 | 4.50 | 4.50 | 2.50 | 2.50 |
| Sherbet | 7.50 | 12.00 | 12.50 | 7.00 | 7.50 |
| Sugar | 8.00 | 14.00 | 14.00 | 8.00 | 8.00 |
| Tumbler, 4-1/2" h, 9 oz | 6.50 | - | - | 6.50 | 7.00 |
| Tumbler,.5-1/4" h, 12 oz | 9.50 | - | - | 9.50 | 10.00 |
| Vase, 7-1/4" h, 2 handles, rolled edge | 20.00 | 50.00 | - | - | - |
| Vase, 8" h, 2 handles, fan | 32.00 | 65.00 | 65.00 | 30.00 | 30.00 |
| Vase, 8" h, 2 handles, straight edge | 30.00 | 65.00 | 65.00 | 30.00 | 35.00 |

**Vernon** *No. 616*

Manufactured by Indiana Glass Company, Dunkirk, Indiana, from 1930 to 1932. Made in crystal, green, and yellow.

| Item | Crystal | Green | Yellow |
| --- | --- | --- | --- |
| Creamer, ftd | 12.00 | 25.00 | 25.00 |
| Cup | 10.00 | 15.00 | 18.00 |
| Plate, 8" d, luncheon | 7.00 | 10.00 | 12.00 |
| Sandwich Plate, 11-1/2" d | 14.00 | 25.00 | 25.00 |
| Saucer | 4.00 | 6.00 | 6.00 |
| Sugar, ftd | 12.00 | 25.00 | 25.00 |
| Tumbler, 5" h, ftd | 15.00 | 35.00 | 35.00 |

# DISNEYANA

**History:** Walt Disney and the creations of the famous Disney Studios hold a place of fondness and enchantment in the hearts of people throughout the world. The 1928 release of "Steamboat Willie," featuring Mickey Mouse, heralded an entertainment empire.

Walt and his brother, Roy, were shrewd businessmen. From the beginning they licensed the reproduction of Disney characters on products ranging from wristwatches to clothing.

In 1984, Donald Duck celebrated his 50th birthday, and collectors took a renewed interest in material related to him.

**References:** Ted Hake, *Hake's Guide to Character Toys*, Gemstone Publishing (1966 Greenspring, Ste. 405, Timonium, MD 21093), 1998; Robert Heide and John Gilman, *Disneyana*, Hyperion, 1994; Maxine A. Pinsky, *Marx Toys: Robots, Space, Comic, Disney & TV Characters*, Schiffer Publishing, 1996; Rex Miller, *The Investor's Guide to Vintage Character Collectibles*, Krause Publications, 1999; Carol J. Smith, *Identification & Price Guide to Winnie the Pooh Collectibles*, Hobby House Press, 1994; Tom Tumbusch, *Tomart's Illustrated Disneyana Catalog and Price Guide*, vols. 1, 2, 3, and 4, Tomart Publications, 1985; ——, *Tomart's Illustrated Disneyana Catalog and Price Guide, Condensed Edition*, Wallace-Homestead, 1989.

**Periodicals:** *Mouse Rap Monthly*, P.O. Box 1064, Ojai, CA 93024; *Tomart's Disneyana Digest*, 3300 Encrete Ln, Dayton, OH 45439; *Tomart's Disneyana Update*, 3300 Encrete Ln, Dayton, OH 45439.

**Collectors' Clubs:** Imagination Guild, P.O. Box 907, Boulder Creek, CA 95006; Mouse Club East, P.O. Box 3195, Wakefield, MA 01880; National Fantasy Fan Club for Disneyana Collectors and Enthusiasts, P.O. Box 19212, Irvine, CA 92713.

**Archives/Museum:** Walt Disney Archives, Burbank, CA 91521.

**Additional Listings:** See *Warman's Americana & Collectibles* for more examples.

**Advisor:** Theodore L. Hake.

## Bambi

Figure
    1-1/4" x 3-1/4" x 4-5/8", Bambi, painted and glazed, foil Shaw label, 1940s...................................................................... 100.00
    2" x 4" x 3-1/4", Bambi and Thumper, Goebel, full bee mark, 1950s .......................................................................... 190.00
Push Puppet, 2-3/4" h, 1940s, yellow base, gold foil sticker, Kohner Brothers #3990 copyright Walt Disney Productions, c1960, label slightly faded ........................................................... 24.00
Salt and Pepper Shakers, pr, 2-1/2" h, Flower, Goebel ............... 110.00
Tiny Golden Book, 2-1/8" x 31/8", full color, 20 pgs, *Bambi,* Simon & Schuster, copyright 1950, art by Campbell Grant ...................... 10.00

## Davy Crockett

Children's book, *Davy Crockett Big Golden Book,* Simon & Schuster, 1955 copyright, 8-1/2" x 11", color hardcover, 48 pgs, color illus on every page ................................................................... 40.00

## Disneyland

Brochure Map, 3-1/2" x 9", Welcome to Disneyland, copyright 1958, detailed illus overhead map of park on one side, other side with information on attractions.................................................. 35.00
Contest Entry Bank, 6" x 6", two sided paper sheet, "Trip To Disneyland Contest Entry Blank," sponsored by Plastic Division of Monsanto Chemical Co., 1956........................................... 15.00
Guide Book
    8-1/4" x 11-1/2", *Disneyland Guide,* 28 pgs, copyright 1957, color photos, cover photo of Sleeping Beauty's castle ............... 90.00
    10-1/2" x 10-1/2", *Walt Disney's Disneyland,* glossy full color softcover, 32 pages of photos and illus of park attractions, copyright 1965, one page fold-out for new Haunted Mansion .......... 45.00
Miniature Cup and Saucer and Plate, 2-3/4" d x 1-3/4" h cup, image of Tinker Bell on inside, Sleeping Beauty's castle on outside, matching 4-1/2" d plate with color art of Disneyland castle, "Disneyland Copyright Walt Disney Productions" stamp, c1950 ............................ 65.00
Pennant, 8-1/2" x 26-1/2", orange felt, large name in white and design of Tinker Bell and castle in red, white, and blue, pair of purple streamers, first year .................................................. 28.00
Postcard Folder, 4" x 6", color, unfolds to 54" l, 26 different photo scenes, plus introduction from Walt Disney, c1960..................... 35.00
Salt and Pepper Shakers, pr, 2-1/2" h, glazed china, figural bells, white, gold accents, colorful image of Disneyland castle, other with flying Tinker Bell, "Disneyland" stamped in gold on front, Japan sticker on underside, c1950, plastic stopper ............................. 30.00
Shopping Pass, 2-1/4" x 4", card, Disneyland Employee Family Christmas, design in green and red on white, reindeer illus on front, text on back indicates 15% discount ............................................. 20.00
**Disney Studios,** stock certificate, 8" x 12-1/4", Walt Disney Productions Common Stock, unissued, purple, black and white logo, bank

**Book, *Dumbo,* copyright 1941, Walt Disney Productions, 8 pgs, 10-1/8" h, $30.**

note imprint, smiling image of Walt at top in simulated TV screen, Mickey on his shoulder, Fantasyland castle background, masthead showing various Disney characters smiling at Walt and Mickey, "Void" stamped on blue ink three times at bottom where offer's facsimile signatures are printed, including "Michael Esner," two punch holes at bottom as issued, c1980 ........................................... 30.00

## Donald Duck

Bank, 4-1/2" x 6" x 1", *Donald Duck Ideal Bank Book,* deep yellow hard plastic, black, white, red, and orage designs, book shape, coin slot on top, copyright 1964.................................................. 35.00
Big Little Book, *Donald Duck in Volcano Valley,* Whitman #1457, copyright 1949 ............................................................ 24.00
Birthday Card, 3-1/2" x 4-1/2", color art, Hallmark, copyright 1943 ............................................................... 30.00
Drinking Glass, 4-1/2" h, blue/green image of Donald and bird, flowers, and grass around bottom rim, Chocolate Milk is Good, late 1940s ............................................................... 60.00
Easter Card, 4-3/4" x 7-1/2", white paper, bright blue, yellow, orange, and brown, White and Wyckoff copyright 1938, Donald playing flute, "Donald Duck Toots A Tune at Easter Time, Don't You Love It". 40.00
Figure, 3-1/4" h, bisque, Donald with hands on hips, head titled upward smiling, 1930s ....................................................... 75.00
Fork and Spoon, 5-3/4" l, figural, Donald wearing sailor suit, left hand raised, Bonny, Japan, copyright Walt Disney Productions, c1980 ............................................................... 19.00
Ink Blotter, 3-3/4" x 6", Sunoco Oil, color illus of Donald driving car out of garage and into snow, 1942, printed "Buy War Bonds" logo on bottom, station imprint.................................................. 60.00
Pencil, 7-1/2" l, unused, red and blue design on white, text "Harvest Donald Duck Bread/Ungles Baking Company," illus of bread loaf with Donald images on wrapper ............................................ 35.00
Salt and Pepper Shakers, pr, glazed ceramic, 3-1/4" h smiling and waving Donald, dark green shirt, brown cap, pink tie, orange beak and feet, pink flower in right hand, 3" h Daisy dressed like mother hen, green sweater, purple scarf, red apron, pink hat with "Souvenir of Endicott, N.Y." decal on front brim, unlicensed, made in Japan, late 1940s ............................................................... 55.00
Sheet Music, 9" x 12", *Der Fuehrer's Face,* four pages of words and music by Oliver Wallace, from film *Donald Duck in Nutzi Land,* copyright 1942, Donald hitting Hitler in eye with tomato while reverse has victory garden symbol design with Disney characters ............... 60.00
Straws, 4-1/2" x 12-1/4", Donald Duck Sunshine Straws, unused, orange stiff paper, color image of Donald on one side, holding straw to beak with bottom of straw going into cellophane-covered diecut window, reverse with colorful images of Donald, Mickey, Pluto, and Mickey with Donald, Herz Mfg. Crop, New York City, 1950s .................... 18.00

## Fantasia

Original Art, 10" x 12" sheet of animation paper, concept drawing, 6" x 7-3/4" outlined area at center with 4-1/2" x 7-3/4" lead and orange pencil drawing of baby Pegasus sitting on large tree branch, minor pinpoint holes, scattered traces of soiling ............................... 325.00
Souvenir Album, 9-1/2" x 12-1/2",*Walt Disney Presents Fantasia,* softcover, orig 1940 movie release, Western Printing Co., color plates, black and white photos of Disney and other contributors to film............... 45.00

## Mickey Mouse

Bank, Mickey Mouse Bank Book, 4-1/2" x 6" x 1", hard plastic bank, Ideal, copyright 1964.................................................. 35.00
Big Little Book, *Mickey Mouse in the World of Tomorrow,* Whitman #1444, copyright 1948................................................. 48.00
Bobbing Head, 6" h, painted composition figure, 1960s, "Made in Japan" foil sticker ....................................................... 75.00
Candy Box, 5-3/4" x 9" x 2-3/4", Mickey Mouse Sugar Babies, cardboard, countertop box, originally contained 24 five-cent packages of candy, tan and red lid, design of Mickey holding birthday cake with test "Free Mickey Mouse Surprise Birthday Party Comic Strip And Card Game Offer On Each Bag," same design on four sides ............... 35.00
Cereal Box, 11" x 12", Post Toasties Mickey Mouse Cut-Outs, back panel, attached right, left, and bottom flaps, copyright 1934...... 48.00

Figure

1-3/4" h, bisque, smiling full figure, hand on right hip, light green shorts, brown shoes, 70% orig paint .................................... 25.00

3-1/2" h, Mickey dressed as hunter, holding book, sitting on log, log with silver oil sticker reading "Walt Disney Character W.D.P. FFM Copyright," incised "78," and Goebel full bee mark, 1950s ................ 225.00

5" h, glazed ceramic, smiling full figure, yellow shirt, red bow tie, blue pants, green shoes, dark green base, stickers missing .................................. 38.00

Fork and Spoon, 5-1/2" l spoon with 2" full figure of smiling Mickey wearing T-shirt and shorts, 5-1/2" l fork with 2" smiling seated image of Pluto, Bonny, Japan, copyright Walt Disney Productions, c1980 .......................... 18.00

Ice Cream Lid, 2-3/4" d, Mickey Mouse Southern Dairies Ice Cream, stiff paper, black and orange design of Mickey holding ice cream cup which features his image, 1930s, blank reverse ........................ 35.00

Ink Blotter, 3-1/2" x 6", Sunoco Oil, color illus of Mickey as artillery man giving victory symbol, standing behind artillery gun with Sunoco oil bottle as it's body, bottom printed label "Keep 'Em Flying! Buy Defense Bonds," 1942 .................. 75.00

Planter, 3-1/2" x 6" x 6", Mickey as Santa, holding sack, standing next to sleigh, unmarked, Leeds China Co., late 1940s .................... 65.00

Premium Folder, 5-3/4" x 8", "The Happy Homemakers Weekly," April 17-22, 1938 issue, four pages, color front and back covers, black and white inside .................. 70.00

Sheet Music, *Fun and Fancy Free,* 9" x 12", copyright 1947 Santly-Joy Inc., song "To Good To Be True," black, white, and red illus of Mickey and Donald in front, photo scene of Donald and Goofy on back along with Charlie McCarthy and Mortimer Snerd .................. 15.00

Spoon, 5-1/2" l, 1-1/2" h smiling full figure relief image of Mickey on handle, c1934, offered by Post Toasties as cereal premium .............. 28.00

Toothbrush Holder, 2-1/4" x 2-1/4" x 5-1/8", bisque, movable right arm, 1930s .................. 200.00

Toy, 2-3/8" x 6-1/2" x 3-1/2" h, Sun Rubber fire truck, bright red soft rubber, hard rubber white wheels, Mickey wearing fireman's helmet, smiling as driver while Donald stands on rear of truck holding his hat, most of paint on Mickey's head worn off, no paint on Donald, rest 80% complete, early 1950s .................. 55.00

Watch, 4" x 4-1/2" x 5-3/4" h, boxed, U.S. Time, c1958, white box with illus on rd on all sides of Mickey, Minnie and nephews, lifts off to reveal yellow cardboard box bottom/display, 5" h colorful hard plastic figure and watch with 1" d silvered metal case, dial features Mickey image and his hands point at numerals, orig red leather straps, running, orig warranty card .................. 325.00

Watch Figure, 5-1/4" h, three-dimensional, originated with 1958 boxed US Time watch .................. 20.00

## Mickey Mouse Club

Brush-Up Kit, 7-1/2" x 8" x 2", black, white, and red box with display window, unused set, Dupong, 1950s ...................... 45.00

Certificate, 8-1/2" x 11", tan parchment-like paper, black text, black and white image of Mickey in center, red accents, simulated full color seal with him at lower left, smiling black art images of Mouseketeers around margins, copyright Walt Disney productions, c1970s .................. 28.00

Letterhead, 8-1/2" x 11", "Walt Disney's Mickey Mouse Club," unused white paper sheet, light red design of Mickey as band leader, c1950 .................. 12.00

Magazine, *Walt Disney's Mickey Mouse Club Magazine*, 8-1/4" x 11-1/2", 42 pages, Western Printing

Vol. 2, #1, Dec, 1956, Christmas theme cover ...................... 60.00

Vol. 3, #3, 1958, Zorro cover ...................... 30.00

Pencil Case, 4-3/4" x 10" x 2" deep, stiff cardboard, red paper cov, snap closure, full color paper label on lid with clubhouse, Mickey, Pluto, Donald, and nephews, copyright Walt Disney Productions, mid-1950s .................. 40.00

Poster, 19-3/4" x 44", full color, "Walt Disney's Mickey Mouse Club," Welch's, full-color Mickey holding club sign as cartoon Indians and fox holding Welch's products, ride around on roller coaster, copyright Walt Disney Productions ABC-TV, mid-1950s, rolled ................ 95.00

## Minnie Mouse

Animation Cel, 10" x 12-1/2" acetate sheet, 3-1/4" x 6-3/4" cel image of Minnie in pink and cranberry outfit, "24" of numbered sequence, 1970s .................. 125.00

Figure, 3-3/4" h, wood and wire, Fun-E-Flex, 70% of orig decal on chest, orig tail, professionally replaced ears, light paint wear .... 75.00

Plate, 5" d, glazed white ceramic, red trim, Minnie as falling down Jill, mkd "J. & G. Meakin, England," 1930s ...................... 50.00

## Pinocchio

Bank, 7-3/4" h, hard vinyl, smiling image of Pinocchio in black chair, looking up, yellow shirt, hat, and shoes, blue shorts, red tie, copyright Walt Disney Prod. Play Pay Plastics Inc., c1970, no coin trap .............. 28.00

Doll, Jiminy Cricket, 3" x 5" x 9-3/4", composition, Knickerbocker, moveable head and arms, fabric jacket, hat missing, 1940 ..... 175.00

Figure

3" h, bisque, blue, red, and yellow outfit, brown shoes, c1940.. 40.00

41/2" h, composition wood, Jiminy Cricket, blue coat and hat, red tie and hat band holding red umbrella, name incised on base, copyright Walt Disney Prod. Multi Products, Chicago, c1940 ........ 95.00

5" h, composition wood, smiling full Pinocchio figure, nicely painted brown wood design, red shorts, blue tie, yellow hat, red feather, name on base, copyright Walt Disney Prod., Multi Products Chicago, c1940 .................. 95.00

Sheet Music, 9" x 12", *When You Wish Upon A Star,* 6 pages of words and music, copyright 1940 Irving Berlin Inc., front cover with black, white, and orange image of smiling Pinocchio and Jiminy Cricket .................. 24.00

Shovel, 3-1/2" x 5" tin litho shovel blade, 13" long wood rod handle, c1939, illus of Pinocchio as donkey boy crying and holding tail as Jiminy shouts at him, Spanish .................. 135.00

Song Folio, 9" x 12", *Pinocchio Song Hit Folio,* 16 pgs of words and music, copyright 1950, Australian issue by Allan & Co. Pty. Ltd., front cover with black, white, and red illus .................. 28.00

Spoon, 5-3/8" l, relief of Pinocchio with name and donkey with his name on handle, Duchess Silver Plate, c1939, lightly tarnished around edges of bowl .................. 28.00

## Pluto

Figure

3-1/4" h, bisque, smiling seated Pluto looking at green crab, yellow base, Disney Gift-Ware stamped on base, gold foil UCGC Taiwan sticker, c1970 .................. 35.00

3-3/4" x 6" x 3", painted and glazed, by Brayton Laguna, c1940, fleshtone, black and red accents, blue outline on eyes ........ 100.00

Hand Puppet, 10-1/2" h, molded vinyl head and fabric body, orange, black, white, and red accents, Gund, 1960s .................. 20.00

Soaky, 8-1/2" h, one-piece, empty, deep orange, black and red accents, 1960s .................. 15.00

Toy, push bottom, 2-1/2" x 3" x 2-1/2" h, hard plastic, Pluto's doghouse, white, orange, roof, Kohner Brothers, 1970s .................. 22.00

## Snow White

Bread Label Picture, 11" x 11-1/2" full color, Snow White cottage with background of forest setting, wood grain design margins, white silhouettes for application of cut-out bread characters, red, white, and blue design on reverse with directions from sponsor Skylark Bread, Safeway Stores, 1950s .................. 85.00

Glass, 4-3/4" h, Walt Disney All Star Parade, wrap-around design of Snow White and the Seven Dwarfs, dark blue, title at top in light blue .................. 45.00

Paper Dolls, 10" x 12-3/4", *Snow White and the Seven Dwarfs Paperdolls' Book*, Whitman, copyright 1972, full color covers, two stiff paper pages with punch-outs, price sticker on front cover ...................... 38.00

Valentine, 3" x 5-3/4", mechanical, diecut, stiff paper, smiling image of Snow White sweeping, tab on one side which lifts up to smiling squirrel from under broom holding valentine heart, caption "You Are The Fairest in The Land, If You'll Be My Mine-Twil Be Just Grand," copyright 1938 W.D. Ent., ink inscription on back .................. 35.00

## Three Little Pigs

Glass, 4-7/8" h, 2nd Little Pig, blue accent, smiling and dancing Fiddler Pig next to his name, copyright WD, c1936 ...............................35.00

Spoon, 4-1/4" l, 2-1/2" l handle, image of three pigs, titled on reverse "Wm. Rogers & Son" imprint, bit tarnished, c1933.....................35.00

Tiny Golden Book, 2-1/8" x 31/8", full color, 20 pgs, *Three Little Pigs, Bambi, Bongo,* Simon & Schuster, copyright 1950, art by Campbell Grant ....................................................................................10.00

Toothbrush Holder, 4" l x 4" h, 1-1/4" deep, bisque, Practical Pig with bricks in center between Fiddler and Fifer Pigs, 95% complete paint, Made in Japan, copyright Walt Disney incised on reverse.........95.00

## Zorro

Action Figure, 6" x 9", blister card, 3-3/4" poseable figure, accessories
    Captain Ramon, Gabriel #32714, copyright 1981.................30.00
    Sergeant Gonzalez, Gabriel #32716, copyright 1981...........30.00
    Zorro, Gabriel #32710, copyright 1981 ...............................75.00
Children's Book, *Zorro,* Whitman, copyright 1958, 5-1/2" x 7-3/4", hardcover, full-color wraparound cover.............................15.00

# DOLLHOUSES

**History:** Dollhouses date from the 18th century to modern times. Early dollhouses often were handmade, sometimes with only one room. The most common type was made for a young girl to fill with replicas of furniture scaled especially to fit into a dollhouse. Specially sized dolls also were made for dollhouses. All types of accessories in all types of styles were available, and dollhouses could portray any historical period.

**References:** Evelyn Ackerman, *Genius of Moritz Gottschalk,* Gold House Publishing, 1994; Mary Brett, *Tomart's Price Guide to Tin Litho Doll Houses and Plastic Doll House Furnishings,* Tomart Publications, 1997; Nora Earnshaw, *Collecting Dolls' Houses and Miniatures,* Pincushion Press, 1993; Charles F. Donovan Jr., *Renwal-World's Finest Toys, Dollhouse Furniture,* L-W Book Sales, 1999; Flora Bill Jacobs, *Dolls' Houses in America: Historic Preservation in Miniature,* Charles Scribner's Sons, 1974; Margaret Towner, *Dollhouse Furniture,* Courage Books, 1993; Dian Zillner, *American Dollhouses and Furniture from the 20th Century,* Schiffer Publishing, 1995.

**Periodicals:** *Doll Castle News,* P.O. Box 247, Washington, NJ 07882; *International Dolls' House News,* P.O. Box 79, Southampton S09 7EZ England; *Miniature Collector,* 30595 Eight Mill, Livonia, MI 48152; *Miniatures Showcase,* P.O. Box 1612, Waukesha, WI 53187; *Nutshell News,* 21027 Crossroads Circle, P.O. Box 1612, Waukesha, WI 53187.

**Collectors' Clubs:** Dollhouse & Miniature Collectors, 9451 Lee Hwy #515, Fairfax, VA 22302; National Association of Miniature Enthusiasts, P.O. Box 69, Carmel, IN 46032; National Organization of Miniaturists and Dollers, 1300 Schroder, Normal, IL 61761.

**Museums:** Art Institute of Chicago, Chicago, IL; Margaret Woodbury Strong Museum, Rochester, NY; Museums at Stony Brook, Stony Brook, NY; Toy and Miniature Museum of Kansas City, Kansas City, MO; Washington Dolls' House and Toy Museum, Washington, DC.

R. Bliss, litho on board, hinged, 2 int. rooms, 11-1/2" w, 16-1/4" h, $750.

## Buildings

Butcher Shop, 17-1/2" l, Metzgerei...Leipold, painted, papered wood, orig composition meat, German ................................................550.00

Gazebo, 14-1/2" h, with colorful flower boxes, painted wood .. 1,000.00

Stable, 16" w, Bliss, paper lithograph, wood, some replaced parts ......................................................................................175.00

## Doll Houses

Bliss, 10" x 13" x 13", Wild Rose Cottage, litho paper on wood, potted geraniums and Little Red Riding Hood at the door on front facade ................................................................................1,600.00

Christian Hacker, Nuremberg, Germany, 34" h, painted, front stucco facade, five rooms, 2-1/2 story, steeple roof, two chimneys, bay window, papered int., FAO Schwartz label .................................750.00

McLoughlin Bros., 18-1/2" h, 12-5/8" w, 1-1/2" d, Dolly's Playhouse, litho paper on board, folding two room house, folded printed paper furniture, orig worn box .........................................................375.00

Schoenhut, 28" h, 23" w, 23" d, eight rooms, attic, gray blocks, c1917 ...............................................................................1,400.00

Stirn & Lynn, 15" h, wood "Combination Dollhouse," patent 1911, litho paper illus on cover, stenciled wood building sections, crayon dec ......................................................................................175.00

Unknown Maker, Victorian
    23" h, 26"l, 22-3/4" d, cottage, yellow with red trim, green shingled roof, two rooms down, one room up, early 20th C, miscellaneous furniture and accessories ......................................500.00
    36" h, 25" w, mansard roof, belvedere, mustard yellow, brown trim, gray roofs, red accents, two rooms down, two rooms up, attic, staircases, cast iron fence, cast iron lions on wooden plinths, wooden outhouse, 49" sq lawn, late 19th C, some restoration needed .............................................................2,875.00

## Room Settings

General Store, 22" l, Konsum, painted, papered wood, some added newer accessories, German .....................................................500.00

General Store Countertop, 12-1/2" w, three working accessories, paper roll, scale, register plus paper pad and pencil, tin litho and wood, German.........................................................................160.00

Kitchen Set, Marklin, #16041, mint in orig box ..........................350.00

# DOLLS

**History:** Dolls have been children's play toys for centuries. Dolls also have served other functions. From the 14th through 18th centuries, doll making was centered in Europe, mainly in Germany and France. The French dolls produced in this era were representations of adults and were dressed in the latest couturier designs. They were not children's toys.

During the mid-19th century, child and baby dolls, made in wax, cloth, bisque, and porcelain, were introduced. Facial features were hand painted; wigs were made of mohair and human hair; and the dolls were dressed in the current fashions for babies or children.

Doll making in the United States began to flourish in the 1900s with companies such as Effanbee, Madame Alexander, and Ideal.

**Marks:** Marks of the various manufacturers are found on the back of the head or neck or on the doll's back. These marks are very important in identifying a doll and its date of manufacture.

**References:** J. Michael Augustyniak, *Thirty Years of Mattel Fashion Dolls, 1967 Through 1997: Identification and Value Guide,* Collector Books, 1998; Kim Avery, *The World of Raggedy Ann Collectibles,* Collector Books, 1997, 2000 value update; Mary Caruso, *Care of Favorite Dolls, Antique Bisque Conservation,* Hobby House Press, 1999; Jurgin and Marianne Cieslik, *German Doll Studies,* Gold Horse Publishing, 1999; Carol Corson, *Schoenhut Dolls,* Hobby House Press, 1993; Linda Crowsey, *Madame Alexander Collector's Dolls Price Guide #25,* Collector Books, 2000; —; *Madame Alexander Store Exclusives & Limited Editions,* Collector Books, 2000; Maryanne Dolan, *The World of Dolls, A Collector's Identification and Value Guide,* Krause Publications, 1998; Jan Foulke, *Doll Classics,* Hobby House Press, 1997; —, *Insider's Guide to China Doll Collecting,* Hobby House Press, 1995; —, *Insider's Guide to Doll Buying and Selling,* Hobby House Press, 1995; —, *Insider's Guide to Germany "Dolly" Collecting,* Hobby House Press, 1995; —, *14th Blue Book Dolls and Values,* Hobby House Press, 2000; Sandra Ann Garrison, *The Raggedy Ann and Andy Family Album,* 2nd ed., Schiffer Publishing, 1999; Dawn Herlocher, *Antique Trader's Doll Makers & Marks,* Antique Trader Books, 1999; —, *200 Years of Dolls,* Antique Trader Books, 1996; R. Lane Herron, *Warman's Dolls,* Krause Publications, 1998; Judity Izen, *Collector's Guide to Ideal Dolls,* 2nd ed., Collector Books, 1998; Judith Izen and Carol Stover, *Collector's Guide to Vogue Dolls,* Collector Books, 1998, 2000 value update; Polly Judd, *African and Asian Costumed Dolls,* Hobby House Press, 1995: —, *Cloth Dolls,* Hobby House Press, 1990; Polly and Pam Judd, *Composition Dolls, Vol. I* (1991), *Vol. II* (1994), Hobby House Press; —, *European Costume Dolls,* Hobby House Press, 1994; —, *Glamour Dolls of the 1950s & 1960s,* revised ed., Hobby House Press, 1993; —, *Hard Plastic Dolls,* 3rd ed. (1993), Book II (1994), Hobby House Press; Michele Karl, *Composition & Wood Dolls and Toys: A Collector's Reference Guide,* Antique Trader Books, 1998; Constance King, *Collecting Dolls Reference and Price Guide,* Antique Collectors' Club, 1999; Kathy and Don Lewis, *Talking Toys of the 20th Century,* Collector Books, 1999; A. Glenn Mandeville, *Glenn Mandeville's Madame Alexander Dolls, 3rd Collector's Price Guide,* Hobby House Press, 2000; —, *Ginny,* 3rd ed., Hobby House Press, 1998; Marcie Melilo, *The Ultimate Barbie Doll Book,* Krause Publications, 1997; Ursula R. Mertz, *Collector's Encyclopedia of American Composition Dolls, 1900 to 1950,* Collector Books, 1999; Patsy Moyer, *Doll Values, Antique to Modern,* 4th ed., Collector Books, 2000; —, *Modern Collectible Dolls,* Collector Books, 1997, *Vol II.* (1997, 1998 value update), *Vol. III* (1999), *Vol. IV* (2000); Myra Yellin Outwater, *Advertising Dolls,* Schiffer Publishing, 1997.

Lydia and Joachim F. Richter, *Bru Dolls,* Hobby House Press, 1989; Cindy Cabulis, *Collector's Guide to Dolls of the 1960s and 1970s,* Collector Books, 2000; Jane Sarasohn-Kahn, *Contemporary Barbie,* Antique Trader Books, 1997; Patricia N. Schoonmaker, *Patsy Doll Family Encyclopedia, Vol. II,* Hobby House Press, 1998; Patricia R. Smith, *Antique Collector's Dolls,* vol. I (1975, 1991 value update), vol. II (1976, 1991 Value update), Collector Books; —, *Collector's Encyclopedia of Madame Alexander Dolls, 1965-1990,* Collector Books, 1999; —, *Effanbee Dolls,* Collector Books, 1998 values update; —, *Madame Alexander Dolls 1965–1990,* 1991, 1997 values update, Collector Books; —, *Modern Collector's Dolls,* Series I through VIII (1973–1996 value updates), Collector Books; —, *Patricia Smith's Doll Values Antique to Modern,* Eleventh Series, Collector Books, 1995; —, *Shirley Temple Dolls and Collectibles,* vol. I (1977, 1992 value update), vol. II (1979, 1992 value update), Collector Books; Evelyn Robson Stahlendorf, *Charlton Standard Catalogue of Canadian Dolls,* 3rd ed., Charlton Press, 1997; Marci Van Ausdall, *Betsy McCall,* Hobby House Press, 2000.

**Periodicals:** *Antique & Collectables,* P.O. Box 12589, El Cajon, CA 92002, http://www.collect.com/antiquesandcollectables; *Antique & Collectible Dolls,* 218 W. Woodin Blvd., Dallas, TX 75224; *Antique Doll Collector,* 6 Woodside Ave., Suite 300, Northport, NY 11768, http://www.antiqueDollCollector.com; *Cloth Doll Magazine,* P.O. Box 2167 Lake Oswego, OR 97035-0051, http://www.theclothdoll/com; *Costume Quarterly for Doll Collectors,* 118-01 Sutter Ave., Jamaica, NY 11420; *Doll Castle News,* P.O. Box 247, Washington, NJ 07882-0247, http://www.dollcastlenews.com; *Doll Collector's Price Guide,* 306 East Parr Rd, Berne, IN 46711; *Doll-E-Gram,* P.O. Box 1212, Bellevue, WA 98009-1212; *Doll Life,* 243 Newton-Sparta Rd, Newton, NJ 07860; *Doll Magazine,* Avalon Court, Star Rd, Partridge Green, West Sussex RH13 BRY +44(0) 1403 711511, http://www.doll-magazine.com; *Doll Reader,* 741 Miller Drive, SE, Harrisburg, PA 20175, http://www.cowles.com/maglist.html;

*Doll Times*, 218 W Woodin Blvd., Dallas, TX 75224; *Doll World*, 306 East Parr Rd, Berne, IN 46711; *Dollmasters*, P.O. Box 151, Annapolis, MD 21404; *Dolls—The Collector's Magazine*, 170 Fifth Ave., 12th Floor, New York, NY 10010; *Patsy & Friends,* P.O. Box 311, Deming, NM 88031, http://www.zianet.com/patsyandfirends; *Rags,* P.O. Box 823, Atlanta, GA 30301.

**Collectors' Clubs:** Annalee Doll Society, P.O. Box 708, Meredith, NH 03253, http://www.annalee.com; Doll Collector International, P.O. Box 2761, Oshkosh, WI 54903; Doll Costumers Guild, 7112 W. Grovers Ave., Glendale, AZ 85308; Doll Doctor's Association, 6204 Ocean Front Ave., Virginia Beach, VA 23451; Ginny Doll Club, P.O. Box 338, Oakdale, CA 95361; International Golliwogg Collectors Club, P.O. Box 612, Woodstock, NY 12498, http://www.teddybears.com/golliwog; Ideal Toy Co. Collector's Club, P.O. Box 623, Lexington, MA 02173; Madame Alexander Doll Fan Club, P.O. Box 330, Mundeline, IL 60060; United Federation of Doll Clubs, 10920 N Ambassador Drive, Suite 130, Kansas City, MO 64153, http://www.ufdc.org.

**Museums:** Aunt Len's Doll House, Inc., New York, NY; Children's Museum, Detroit, MI; Doll Castle Doll Museum, Washington, NJ; Doll Museum, Newport, RI; Toy and Miniature Museum of Kansas City, Kansas City, MO; Gay Nineties Button & Doll Museum, Eureka Springs, AR; Margaret Woodbury Strong Museum, Rochester, NY; Mary Merritt Doll Museum, Douglassville, PA; Mary Miller Doll Museum, Brunswick, GA; Prairie Museum of Art & History, Colby, KS; Washington Dolls' House & Toy Museum, Washington, DC; Yesteryears Museum, Sandwich, MA.

**Additional Listings:** See *Warman's Americana & Collectibles* for more examples.

**Alt, Beck & Gottschalck,** 16-1/2" h, 912, solid dome bisque shoulder head, orig mohair wig, large oval brown eyes, multi-stroke brows, painted upper and lower lashes, open-closed mouth with white space and accent lines between lips, cloth body with leather arms, individually stitched fingers, red lower legs with leather boots, peach two-piece outfit, matching bonnet, antique underclothing, mkd "912" No. "4" on bottom of rear shoulder plate, "2" on body, aged body with spots on torso, light wear on leather arms, upper torso and arms recovered .......................................................................... 725.00

**American Character,** 8" h, Betsy McCall, hard plastic head, orig wig, blue sleep eyes with molded lashes, single stroke brows, painted

lower lashes, closed mouth, hard pastic child body with jointed knees, orig nylon teddy, socks, and shoes, mkd "Betsy McCall" on box, mint in lightly aged box, unplayed with On the Ice and Sunday Best outfits ..................................................................... 1,050.00

**Georgene Averill,** 16" h, Bonnie Babe, solid dome bisque flange head, lightly molded and painted hair, brown sleep eyes, softly blushed brows, painted upper and lower lashes, open mouth with molded tongue, cloth body with composition arms and legs, orig blue romper, tagged lace-trimmed bib, matching bonnet, orig long cotton socks, black shoes, mkd "Copr. By Georgene Averill, 7055 13652, Germany" on back of head "Bonnie Babe, Copyrighted, Georgene Averill, Made by K and K Toy Co." on tag on bib, small rub on left cheek, teeth missing, tongue cracked, cloth body aged ......................................... 400.00

**Bahr & Proschild,** 12-1/2" h, 224 Belton, bisque socket head, flat area and three holes on top, set blue threaded eyes, feathered brows, painted upper and lower lashes, closed mouth, accented lips, accent line and white space between lips, pierced ears, orig mohair wig, jointed wood and composition body with straight wrists, old pale blue print dress, eyelet trim, underclothing, socks, and shoes, marked "224, 5" on back of head, slight damage to body finish, neck socket loose.................................................................................. 1,500.00

**Beecher,** 20" h, Baby, stockinette head, looped yarn hair, painted and needle sculptured features, applied ears, stockinette body jointed at shoulders, hips, and knees, antique white baby dress, antique underclothing, knit wool knee high socks, crocheted bonnet, unmarked, light wear to cheeks, looped hair worn................................. 2,000.00

**C. M. Bergmann**

16" h, Character, bisque head, brown glass sleep eyes, open mouth, bent limb composition body, imp "Spezial," needs restringing ......................................................................... 375.00

24" h, bisque socket head, set blue eyes, real and painted lashes, feathered brows, open mouth, four upper teeth, synthetic wig, jointed wood and composition body, antique blue and white dress, underclothing, new socks, and shoes, marked "C. M. Bergmann, Simon & Halbig, S & H, 3" on back of head, tiny flake on lower right lid, broken eyes set with plaster showing, unmatched legs, foot repaired ......................................... 250.00

30" h, bisque socket head, brown sleep eyes, real lashes, molded and feathered brows, painted lower lashes, open mouth, accepted lips, four upper teeth, pierced ears, human hair wig, jointed wood and composition body, antique low-waisted dress, antique underclothing, stockings, high button shoes, marked "C. M. Bergmann, Simon & Halbig, 13 1/2" on back of head, light rub on cheek, finish worn on front of torso ...................... 400.00

**Bisque,** unknown makers

6" h, character, bisque socket head, orig blond mohair wig, blue sleep eyes, single stroke brows, painted upper and lower lashes, open-closed mouth with hint of teeth, all bisque body jointed at shoulders and hips, bare feet, possibly orig white organdy dress and underwear combination, mkd "141,4" on back of head, right thumb missing, flakes to other fingers ............................... 450.00

7" h, bisque socket head, orig mohair wig, set dark pupilless eyes, feathered brows, painted upper and lower lashes, closed mouth with accent line between lips, five-piece all bisque body joined at shoulders and hips, molded and painted socks and one-strap shoes, illegible mark ....................................... 825.00

**Borgfelt,** 24" h, bisque head, orig blond mohair wig, blue glass sleep eyes, open mouth, fully jointed composition body, imp "GB" mark, some paint wear................................................................... 230.00

**Casimir Bru**

17" h, pressed bisque head, brown paperweight eyes, outlined open/closed mouth, cork pate, pierced ears, wood jointed body, key wound mechanical music box, marked "Bte S.G.D.G."............................................................. 6,600.00

23" h, bisque swivel head, shoulder plate, brown paperweight eyes, highlighted lids, outlined open/closed mouth, cork pate, pierced ears, kid body, bisque lower arms, repainted wood lower legs, circle dot mark "Bru Jne 19"...................... 1,320.00

## Bye-Lo

5" h, bisque swivel head, tiny brown sleep eyes, softly blushed brows, painted upper and lower lashes, closed mouth, all bisque body, jointed at shoulders and hips, orig crocheted diaper with belly band, white baby dress, crocheted sweater, marked "12" on front of neck, "6-12, Copr. by Grace S. Putnam, Germany" on back, "20-32" on top of right leg .......................................... 275.00

18" h, bisque flange head, blue sleep eyes, softly blushed brows, painted upper and lower lashes, closed mouth, lightly molded and painted hair, cloth body with frog legs, celluloid hands, antique white lace trimmed christening dress, underclothing, baby booties, embroidered bib, bonnet, marked "Copr. by Grace S. Putnam, Made in Germany" on back of head, turtle mark on celluloid hands, very fine flake at upper left eye rim, light rub to cheek............................................................................ 525.00

## Chase Type

18-1/2" h, oil painted stockinette head, stiff neck, painted brown eyes, single stroke brows, painted hair, applied ears, cloth body with sateen covering, oil painted stockinette lower arms and legs, jointed at shoulders, hips and knees, pink tint on stitched fingers and toes, plain white baby dress, underclothing, old blue cotton socks, light wear, slight flaking, left ankle repaired, unmarked........................................... 550.00

## China Head

21" h, china shoulder head, light pink tint, painted brown eyes with red accent line, single stroke brows, closed smiling mouth with white space between lips, molded and painted black hair with center part, cloth body, leather arms, individually stitched fingers, orig red print dress, black velvet ribbon trim, underclothing, socks, old hand made leather shoes, unmarked, well repaired hairline on left side of shoulder, dark spot of kiln debris on left shoulder, fragile dress .............................................. 350.00

24" h, boy, china shoulder plate, painted blue eyes, red accent line, single stroke brows, closed mouth, molded and painted curly hair, cloth body, leather lower arms, redressed in black and white checked two piece suit, underclothing, black socks, marked "880 11" on back of shoulder plate...................... 275.00

## Door of Hope

11" h, Bride, carved wooden head, painted black hair with carved braided bun with carved and painted flowers, painted dark eyes, single stroke brows, closed mouth, cloth body with carved wooden hands, orig red embroidered bride's outfit with beaded head piece, long tassels on sides, orig underclothing, embroidered slippers, mkd "Made in China" on wrist tag ...................................... 1,350.00

11" h, Groom, carved wooden head, painted black hair with side part, painted dark eyes, single stroke brows, closed mouth, cloth body with carved wooden hands, orig deep purple robe with embroidered square on front, matching hat, orig underclothing, black cloth high boots, mkd "Made in China" on wrist tag ............................................................................... 1,100.00

Door of Hope, Bride, 11" h, $1,350 and Groom, 11" h, $1,100. Photo courtesy of McMasters Doll Auctions.

11" h, Widow, carved wooden head, painted black hair with carved bun, painted eyes, single stroke brows, closed mouth, cloth body with carved wooden hands, orig clothing made of coarse fabric tied with reed belt, linen underclothing, hood partially covering face, and shoes, wooden stick with strips of fabric in right hand, mkd "Made in China" on paper tag ................................. 1,400.00

11-1/2" h, Mourner, carved wooden head, painted black hair with side part, painted eyes, single stroke brows, closed mouth, cloth body with carved wooden hands, orig clothing made of coarse fabric tied with reed belt, linen underclothing, hat and shoes, wooden stick with strips of fabric in right hand, mkd "Made in China" on paper tag, "Kimport Dolls, Independence, MO, This Doll Was Made In China" on tag on back of clothing ................................. 1,425.00

## Effanbee

7" h, Baby Tinyette Quintuplets, composition heads, molded and painted hair, painted brown eyes, single stroke brows, painted upper lashes, close mouths, composition bent limb baby bodies, orig long white organdy baby dresses, birdseye diapers, organdy lace-trimmed bonnets, mkd "Effanbee" on back of head, "Effanbee, Baby Tinyette" on backs, "Effanbee Durable Dolls, Made in USA" on dress tags, "F.A.O. Schwarz, 745 Fifth Avenue, New York, Quintuplets" on label on case, unplayed with condition in orig case, orig clothing, orig glass bottles, orig pink and white blanket trimmed with pink ribbon rosettes ...................... 1,200.00

11" h, Patsy Jr., composition head, molded and painted head, painted brown eyes to side, single stroke brows, painted upper lashes, closed mouth, five-piece composition child body, dressed in orig red print dress with white bodice edge in red ruffle, matching underwear, orig socks and red side snap shoes, mkd "Effanbee, Patsy Jr. Doll" on back, light crazing on head, touch-up on left toes ......................................................... 300.00

15" h, Patricia as Anne Shirley, composition head, orig human hair wig in braids, brown sleep eyes with real lashes, single stroke brows, painted lower lashes, closed mouth, five-piece composition child body, dressed in orig tagged blue dress with bolero jacket look, matching underwear and hat, orig socks and tie shoes, mkd "Effanbee, Patricia" on back, "Effanbee Durable Dolls, Made in USA" on dress tag, light crazing to face, general light crazing on body, finish flaking on right arm ............................................ 450.00

20" h, Charlie McCarthy, composition should head, molded and painted hair, painted brown eyes, multi-stroke brows, painted upper and lower lashes, wire monocle attached to right eye, bottom jaw attached to string in back of head to operate, cloth body, composition white hands for gloves, feet with molded black shoes, orig bacl tuxedo, white skirt, and vest, black tie and black silk top hat, mkd "Edgar Bergen's Charlie McCarthy, an Effanbee Product" on back of shoulder plate, few fine craze lines from edges of mouth, hole from monocle, mouth elastic stretched so mouth stays open ....................................... 300.00

22" h, Patsy Lou, composition head, molded hair under mohair wig, brown, sleep eyes, real lashes, feathered brows, painted upper and lower lashes, closed mouth, five-piece composition child body, tagged white organdy dress, underwear, and hat with blue polka dots, rayon socks, black snap shoes, mkd "Effanbee, Patsy Lou" on back and bracelet, "Effanbee Durable Dolls, Made in USA" on dress tag, light crazing to face, eyes cloudy............................................................................. 675.00

26" h, Patsy Ruth, composition head, composition shoulder plate, mohair wig, green sleep eyes, real lashes, feathered brows, painted upper and lower lashes, closed mouth, cloth mama doll body, composition arms and lower legs, redressed in blue organdy copy of orig dress, replaced underclothing, new socks and shoes, mkd "Effanbee Patsy Ruth" on back of head, "Effanbee Lovums, ©, Pat. 1283558" on shoulder plate, "Effanbee Durable Dolls" on metal heart bracelet, light crazing to face, shoulder plate and legs.................................................... 900.00

**French Fashion,** 16" h, bisque socket head, bisque shoulder plate, set cobalt blue eyes, multi-stroke brows, painted upper and lower lashes, closed mouth, accented lips, pierced ears, orig mohair wig, kid body with gussets at hips, individually stitched fingers, dark brown velvet suit with long train and bustle, lace trim, flowers on blue hat, hand made shoes, marked "B 3 S" on bottom of rear shoulder plate, minor repairs ................................................................ 1,600.00

**Frozen Charlie**, 15-1/2" h, pink tint china head with stiff neck, molded and painted blond hair, painted blue eyes, heavy black shading on lids, two tone brows, closed mouth with accent line between lips, unjointed china body with arms held out, hands closed in fists, finger and toe nails outlined, knit one piece underwear, unmarked, nose rub, minor rubs on cheeks and forehead .................................. 525.00

**Francois Gaulthier,** 26" h, bisque swivel shoulder head, Ethel, cork pate, orig mohair wig, stationary blue paperweight eyes, open/closed mouth, pierced ears, cloth shoulder and legs, kid upper arms, fragments of celluloid hands, mkd "F 9 G," right shoulder mkd "FG," c1870, imperfection to neck, front of shoulder plate damaged ............ 4,320.00

**Georgene,** 13" h, Nancy and Sluggo, cloth swivel head, molded mask faces, painted black eyes, single stroke brows, closed smiling mouth, cloth bodies stitch-jointed at shoulders and hips, gold flannel feet for shoes, Sluggo has applied ears, dressed in orig blue pants, yellow knit shirt, black flannel jacket, orange flannel hat, Nancy has early floss hair, orig dress with orange skirt, black bodice, white collar and sleeves, mkd "A Georgene Doll, Sluggo, Georgene Novelties, Inc., New York, NY, Made in USA" on Sluggo's wrist tag, price for pr .......................... 825.00

**Greiner,** 28" h, papier-mâché shoulder head, painted blue eyes, single strike brows, painted upper lashes, closed mouth, molded and painted hair with twelve vertical curls, cloth body, leather lower arms, orig black and gold plaid dress, underclothing replaced socks and shoes, white apron, marked "Greiner's Improved Patent Heads, Pat. March 30, '58" on label on back shoulder plate, very light touch-up on face, light crazing on face, left ankle mended, water stains on orig body, lower kind arms discolored, orig silk dress deteriorating badly in places ................................................................................ 450.00

**Heinrich Handwerck**

17-1/2" h, 109, bisque socket head, orig human hair wig, blue sleep eyes, molded and feathered brows, painted upper and lower lashes, open mouth, accented lips, four upper teeth, pierced ears, jointed wood and composition body, white dress with black dots, red trim, antique underclothing, new socks, old shoes, mkd "109 7-1/2", Germany, Handwerck" on back of head, several wig pulls, light rubs on nose and cheeks, normal wear at joints, hands repainted ........................................ 420.00

19" h, 109, bisque socket head, orig blond mohair wig, brown sleep eyes, feathered brows, painted upper and lower lashes, open mouth with distinct modeling, accented lips, four upper teeth, pierced ears, jointed wood and composition body, antique white embroidered dress, antique underclothing new replaced socks and shoes, feather trimmed bonnet, mkd "109 10-1/2x, Germany, Handwerck, 2-1/4" on back of head ................................... 450.00

**Huret, lady, 17" h, wooden body, $7,000; man, 17" h, gutta percha body, $17,500. Photo courtesy of McMasters Doll Auctions.**

24" h, bisque socket head, synthetic wig, blue sleep eyes, molded and feathered brows, painted upper and lower lashes, open mouth with four upper teeth, pierced ears, jointed wood and composition toddler body, pink print dress with lace panel, underclothing, new cotton socks, old leather tie shoes, mkd "Germany, Heinrich Handwerck, Simon & Halbig, 3-1/2" on back of head, 1/2" hairline from neck socket, hip joints repaired, lower arms and hands repainted ............................................... 350.00

**Max Handwerck,** 17" h, 421, bisque socket head, orig mohair wig, blue sleep eyes, feathered brows, painted upper and lower lashes, open mouth with well accented lips, four upper teeth, pierced ears, jointed wood and composition body, antique white dress with lacy ruffle around neck, underclothing, socks and shoes, red straw hat, mkd "421, 7, Germany, Handwerck, 1" on back of head, "Handwerck" stamped in red on right hip, teeth replaced, lower legs do not match color on rest of body .............................................................. 300.00

**Hertel, Schwab & Co.,** 11" h, 151 Baby, solid dome bisque socket head, lightly molded and brush stroked hair, blue sleep eyes, feathered brows, painted upper and lower lashes, open mouth with two upper teeth, bent-limb composition baby body, blue-green lace trimmed romper, rayon socks, new replaced shoes, mkd "151, 2" on back of head, rub on lower right cheek, body finish worn ....................... 400.00

**Ernst Heubach,** 17" h, 300 Baby, bisque socket head, orig mohair wig, blue sleep eyes with real lashes, feathered brows, painted upper and lower lashes, open mouth with accented lips, four upper teeth, composition bent-limb baby body, fragile antique white baby dress, lace trim, matching bonnet, mkd "Heubach, 300-3, Germany" on back of head, tiny wig pulls, normal wear at body joints, right middle fingers reglued ................................................................................ 250.00

**Gebruder Heubach**

7" h, Character, solid dome bisque socket head, molded and painted hair, blue intaglio eyes, single stroke brows, open-closed mouth with two upper teeth and tongue, crude five-piece body, black and white print pants and shirt, mkd "Heubach" in square, "5/0 Germany" on back of head, light rub on right cheek, body repainted .................................................................. 350.00

9-1/2" h, 7602 Baby, solid dome bisque socket head, lightly molded and painted hair, blue intaglio eyes, single stroke brows, closed pouty mouth, composition bent limb baby body, white shirt, blue shorts, red and white embroidered suspenders, new socks and shoes, mkd "I (sunburst) 76 DEP 02, Germany" on back of head, toes repaired, clothing stitched on ..................................... 325.00

**Huret**

17" h, man, china shoulder head, orig skin wig, painted blue eyes with lightly molded eyelids, multi-stroke brows, painted upper and lower lashes, closed mouth with accented lips, gutta percha body jointed at shoulders, elbows, hips, and knees, dressed in possibly orig shirt-type chemise, vest, and straw hat, very well made brown suit, replaced socks, old shoes, mkd "Brevet D'Inv: S.G.D.G., Maison Huret, Boulevard Montmartre, 22, Paris, Exposition Universelle de 1855, Napoleon III Empereur" stamped on kid attaching head to body ............................................. 17,500.00

17" h, woman, china shoulder head, antique mohair wig, painted blue eyes with lightly molded eyelids, multi-stroke brows, painted upper and lower lashes, closed mouth with accented lips, wooden body jointed at shoulders, elbows, hips, and knees, swivel joints in upper arms and upper legs, dressed in antique black and white two-piece outfit, antique underclothing, socks, and boots, black straw hat, illegible stamp on kid attaching to body, pieces broken off left knee and right elbow, toes of both feet broke off at ends, flakes off body finish ........................... 7,000.00

**Ideal,** 14" h, Betsy McCall, vinyl head, orig brunette saran wig, brown sleep eyes, real lashes, feathered brows, closed smiling mouth, five-piece hard plastic child body, dressed in orig red cotton dress trimmed with white, orig underclothes, socks, and shoes, orig labeled box, wrist tag, curlers, McCall's pattern for apron, mkd "McCall Corp" on back of head, "Ideal Doll, P-90" on back, "Ideal's Official Betsy McCall Doll, Copyright 1951, McCall Corporation" on wrist tag, unplayed with in orig labeled box .............................................. 725.00

## Jumeau

16-1/2" h, Tete Jumeau, bisque socket head, blond mohair wig, bulbous blue paperweight eyes, feathered brows, painted upper and lower lashes, closed mouth with accented lips, pierced ears, jointed wood and composition body, straight wrists, separate balls at shoulders, elbows, hips, and knees, antique blue dress with ribbon trim, antique underclothing, black lace stockings, antique leather shoes, mkd "Depose, Tete Jumeau, Bte. S.G.D.G., 7," red and black artist marks on back of head, "Jumeau, Medaille d'Or, Paris" on lower back, tiny wig pull, touch-up and repaint on torso and lower legs, normal wear on fingers .......................... 3,700.00

19" h, bisque socket head, human hair wig, bulbous blue paperweight eyes, heavy feathered brows, painted upper and lower lashes, closed mouth with white space between accented lips, pierced ears, jointed composition body with straight wrists, working mama/papa pull string crier, antique embroidered white dress, underclothing, socks and shoes, bonnet with floral trim, mkd "Depose, E. 8 J.," incised "H" in red on back of head, "Jumeau Medallie d'Or, Paris" stamped in blue on lower back, two small firing lines in left ear, body well refinished ........................... 4,900.00

## Kämmer & Reinhardt, K * R

9-1/2" h, 126 Toddler, bisque socket head, mohair wig, set blue sleep eyes, real lashes, feathered brows, painted upper and lower lashes, open mouth with two upper teeth, chubby five-piece composition toddler body with starfish hands, antique blue dress, matching underwear, replaced socks, center snap leatherette shoes, mkd "K * R, Simon & Halbig, 126, Germany, 23" on back of head, left fingers repaired ............................... 675.00

19" h, 100 Baby, solid dome bisque socket head, painted blue eyes, molded lids, single stroke brows, open-closed mouth, bent-limb composition baby body, dressed in antique long embroidered baby dress, mkd "K * R, 100, 50" on back of head .................................................... 550.00

## Kestner

16" h, 160, bisque socket head, human hair wig, brown sleep eyes, feathered brows, painted upper and lower lashes, open mouth with lightly accented lips, four upper teeth, jointed wood and composition body, dressed in antique red low-waisted dress, antique underclothing, replaced socks and shoes, red straw hat with flower trim, mkd "Made in Germany, C, 160, 7, Dep" on back of head, "Germany, 1" stamped in red on right lower back, eyes loose in sockets, touch-up on all joints of body, hands and feet repainted ................................... 750.00

16" h, 164, bisque socket head, synthetic wig, blue sleep eyes, feathered brows, painted upper and lower lashes, open mouth with lightly accented lips, two upper teeth, jointed wood and composition body, redressed in red plaid dress, antique underclothing, replaced socks and shoes, red hat with black trim, mkd "C Made in Germany, 7, 164" on back of head, "Germany, 1" stamped in red on right lower back, two teeth missing, light general wear to body, middle finger of right hand missing ....................... 475.00

16" h, 12-1/2" circ., Kestner Century Baby, solid dome bisque flange head, lightly molded and painted hair, blue sleep eyes, softly blushed brows, painted upper and lower lashes, open-closed mouth with two upper teeth, molded tongue, cloth body with non-working crier, composition hands, disk-jointed hips, orig pink organdy dress, matching bonnet, diaper, booties, mkd "Century Doll Co., Kestner, Germany" on back of head, very light rub on right cheek, overall soil on body, light crazing on hands, neck edge of cloth body is worn with wire showing, three extra handmade dresses, sweater, matching bonnet, bib, two blankets .......................... 500.00

19" h, 128, bisque socket head, auburn mohair wig, set brown eyes, feathered brows, painted upper and lower lashes, closed mouth with accent line between lips, jointed composition body with separate balls at shoulders, elbows, hips, and knees, straight wrists, antique white dress with lace trim, antique underclothing, old replaced socks and shoes, mkd "H, made in Germany 12, 128" on back of head .............................. 2,100.00

25" h, Baby, solid dome bisque socket head, lightly molded and brush stroke hair, set brown eyes, feathered brows, painted upper and lower lashes, open mouth with two upper teeth, molded tongue, composition bent-limb baby body, dressed in antique pink baby romper, mkd "Made in Germany, 19" on back of head, "Made in Germany" stamped on rear torso below neck, normal wear, some aging to finish .................................. 400.00

30" h, 164, bisque socket heat, synthetic wig, brown sleep eyes with real lashes, heavy feathered brows, painted upper and lower lashes, open mouth, four upper teeth, jointed wood and composition body, dressed in antique white dress, lace and tucks trim, antique underclothing, socks, old baby shoes, mkd "M made in Germany 16, 164" on back of head, hands repainted, minor repair at hip joints................................... 900.00

**Kley & Hahn**, 12" h, 525 Baby, solid dome bisque socket head, lightly molded and brush-stroked hair, blue intaglio eyes with molded lids, feathered brows, open-closed mouth, composition bent-limb baby body, pink knit outfit, matching bonnet, mkd "K & H" in banner, "525, 4" on back of head, "Germany" stamped on back of left shoulder, body shows light overall wear, repair at top of right leg at hip........................... 300.00

**Kathe Kruse**, 20" h, boy, oil painted cloth swivel head, orig wig, painted blue eyes, single stroke brows, closed mouth, five-piece cloth body, orig red and white shorts and shirt, tie, underwear, socks, and shoes, faintly mkd "Kathe Kruse 40740" on left foot, other black marks on both feet, orig paper tag ............................................ 950.00

**Gebruder Kuhnlenz**, 12", 41, bisque socket head, mohair wig, set brown eyes, heavy feathered brows, painted upper and lower lashes, open mouth with two molded upper teeth, pierced ears, jointed wood and composition body, factory chemise, underclothing, new socks and shoes, mkd "41-22" on back of head, light rub on nose, body lightly touched up ...................................................... 420.00

**Leather**, unknown maker, 21" h, pressed leather socket head, orig human hair wig, painted blue eyes with real lashes inserted into slits, feathered brows, shapely closed mouth, painted leather body jointed at shoulders and hips, long individually stitched fingers, applied separate thumbs, individually stitched toes, possibly orig pale blue silk two-piece dress outfit and bonnet, antique underclothing, socks, and shoes, unmarked, aged body with wrinkles and natural creases, wig sparse in back .................................................... 2,000.00

**Lenci**, 20" h, Modestina, pressed felt swivel head, orig curly mohair wig, large painted eyes to side, molded and lightly feathered brows, painted upper lashes, accented nostrils, open-closed two tone mouth, five-piece body with cloth torso, upper torso felt covered, felt arms and legs, orig felt dress with colorful plaid skirt, felt trimmed organdy sleeves and bloomers with ruffles, gold felt flower-trimmed bonnet, illegible marks on feet .............................. 1,000.00

## Madame Alexander

9" h, Cissette, hard plastic head, orig wig in orig set, blue sleep eyes with molded lashes, single strike brows, painted lower lashes, closed mouth, hard plastic body joined at shoulders, hips, and knees, molded high heel feet, orig lace teddy, nylon stockings, silver high heels with elastic straps, mkd "Mme Alexander" on back, "Cissette, © Madame Alexander, New York, USA" on dress tag, unplayed with orig condition, orig box, extra pink taffeta dress and straw hat outfit in orig box.............................. 1,000.00

14" h, Emelie Dionne Toddler, composition head, molded and painted brown hair, brown sleep eyes with real lashes, feathered brows, painted lower lashes, closed mouth, composition five-piece toddler body, orig lavender romper, tapped lavender snowsuit with pants, coat, and bonnet, replaced shoes, mkd "Alexander" on back, "Genuine Dionne Quintuplet Dolls. All Rights Reserved Madame Alexander, NY" on tags ...................... 425.00

21" h, Judy, composition h4ad, orig elaborate mohair wig with flower dec, amber sleep eyes with real lashes, mauve eye shadow, multi-stroke brows, painted lashes at corners, closed mouth, composition five-piece body, elaborate peach taffeta dress with pinch-pleated insets at bottom of skirt, pink half slip, matching panties, pink silk shoes, flower bouquet, mkd "Alexander" on back, "Madame Alexander, All Rights Reserved:" on foil wrist tag, "Madame Alexander, New York USA" on tag on slip, top layer of composition cracked and lifted on back of head under wig, piece of finish missing on outside of left foot, one of portrait series, inspired by Judy Garland in "Meet Me In St. Louis" movie, unplayed-with condition ........................... 2,500.00

**Armand Marseille, A. M.**

9" h, 323 Googly, bisque socket head, orig blond mohair wig in orig curls, large blue sleep eyes to side, single stroke brows, painted upper and lower lashes, closed smiling mouth, five-piece composition chubby body, possibly orig white dress, antique underclothing, old socks, new leather shoes, pink ribbon trimmed cape, matching hat with ribbons, mkd "Germany, 323, A. 6/0 M." on back of head ..................................... 1,000.00

20" h, A. M. 370, Florodora, bisque shoulder head, orig human hair wig in orig set, brown sleep eyes, real lashes, feathered brows, painted upper and lower lashes, open mouth with four upper teeth, kid body with bisque lower arms, rivet joints at hips, gussets at knees, fragile orig pink silk dress, orig underclothing, pink mesh socks, pink cloth shoes, mkd "370, A.M. –I-, DEP, Armand Marseille, Made in Germany" on back of shoulder plate, "Real Hair, Florodora, Germany" on label on front of body, unplayed with condition, orig box ..................................... 425.00

33" h, child, bisque socket head, orig mohair wig, blue sleep eyes, feathered brows, painted upper and lower lashes, open mouth, jointed wood and composition body, pink nylon dotted Swiss dress with attached slip, pants, orig socks, pink cloth shoes, mkd "A 15 M" on back of head, touch-up to body, wrists, hands, and lower arm ...................... 550.00

**Mascotte,** 23" h, fine quality bisque head, bulging blue paperweight glass stationary eyes, pierced ears, closed mouth, long brown curls, real French hair wig, French composition jointed body, straight wrists, marked "M," blue satin dress with lace, matching blue hat with ostrich plume ...................... 2,900.00

**Morimura,** 19-1/2" h, bisque shoulder head, orig strawberry blond wig, blue glass sleep eyes, open mouth, oil cloth body and legs, bisque hands, imp mark, several pcs of clothing, early 1920s .............. 200.00

**Parian,** unknown maker, 19" h, lightly tinted bisque shoulder head, molded and painted café au lait hair with black bow and jeweled tiara, blue glass eyes, feathered brows, painted upper and lower lashes, closed with, pierced in-ears, kind body with bisque lower arms, cloth lower legs, gussets at hips and knees, white white lace trimmed blouse, antique light bleu skirt, underclothing, old socks, white leather tie shoes, unmarked ....................... 1,425.00

**Poupee Pea, orig clothing, 17" h, $3,000. Photo courtesy of McMasters Doll Auctions.**

**Poupee Peau,** 17" h, bisque socket head, bisque shoulder plate, orig mohair wig, set light blue eyes, multi-stroke brows, painted upper and lower lashes, closed mouth with accented lips, pierced ears, kid fashion style body with gussets at elbows, hips, and knees, individually stitched fingers, olive green and gold striped silk two-piece outfit, antique underclothing, high button boots, faint mark "3" on back of head ..................................... 3,000.00

**Revalo**

16-1/2" h, 22 Toddler, bisque socket head, mohair wig, blue sleep eyes with real lashes, feathered brows, painted lower lashes, open-closed mouth with two upper teeth, jointed wood and composition toddler body with straight legs and diagonal hip joints, antique fabric clothing, replaces socks and shoes, mkd "Germany, Revalo, 22-7" on back of head, body repainted, light cracking to finish of legs and torso ................................... 350.00

24-1/2" h, bisque socket head, replaced human hair wig, blue sleep eyes, real lashes, feathered brows, painted lower lashes, open mouth with four upper teeth, jointed wood and composition body, redressed in maroon flowered dress, new underclothing, socks, and shoes, by Ohlhaver, mkd "8, Revalo, 3 Germany" on back of head, light kiln dusk under chin, touch-up on arms, hands, torso, hip joints and left knee, normal wear at joints .................... 625.00

**Bruno Schimdt**

12" h, 2097 Toddler, bisque socket head, blond mohair wig, set brown eyes, feathered brows, painted upper and lower lashes, open mouth with two upper teeth and molded tongue, jointed wood and composition body, two-piece light blue corduroy suit, white shirt with lace trimmed collar, cotton socks, black leatherette tie shoes, mkd "O, BSW (in heart), 2091-0" on back of head, "Germany, 2/0" stamped in red on right hip, replaced eyes, body shows light wear, left knee ball replaced, right lower arm and right foot repainted ............................. 350.00

19-1/2" h, 2072 Toddler, bisque socket head, orig mohair wig, brown sleep eyes, feathered brows, painted upper and lower lashes, closed mouth with accented lips, dark area between lips, fully jointed wood and composition toddler body with diagonal hip joints, old knit outfit with knit top, sweater, pants, cap, socks, replacement shoes, mkd "B & P, 0" on top of back of head, "BSW" in heart, "2072, 5" on back of head, faint hairline from crown to top of left ear shows with black light, finger repairs, discolored old repaint on hands, wear on toes, wear and finish chips at hip joints ............................. 750.00

**Franz Schmidt,** 19" h, Character, bisque head, orig light brown mohair wig, blue glass sleep eyes, open mouth, pierced nostrils, bent limb composition body, imp "F S & Co. 1271/50" ............................. 490.00

**Schoenau Hoffmesiter,** 19" h, 170 toddler, painted bisque socket head, blue sleep eyes, real lashes, feathered brows, open mouth, two upper teeth, replaced synthetic wig, five piece composition toddler body, black corduroy jumper, new socks, and shoes, marked "S PB [in star] H, 170 3 1/2" on back of head, light wear, crazed replaced arms, torso finish cracked and damaged, legs repainted ............................. 215.00

**Schoenut,** 14" h, Toddler Walker, wooden socket head, orig very blond mohair wig, painted blue eyes, single stroke brows, closed mouth, wooden toddler body jointed at shoulders and hips, possibly orig navy two-piece dress and jacket, lace trimmed cotton underclothing, old replaced socks and shoes, mkd "Schoenhut, © 1913" on round label on head, "Schoenhut Doll, Pat. Jan 17th, 1911, USA" on oval label on back, "Patent Applied For" stamped in purple on back .............. 575.00

**Simon & Halbig**

7" h, 890, bisque socket head, mohair wig, dark brown sleep eyes, single stroke brows, painted upper and lower lashes, open mouth with four upper teeth, all bisque body jointed at shoulders and hips, black over the knee stockings, brown one strap shoes, pale blue silk dress made from parts of her orig dress, orig underclothing trimmed with lace and tucks, orig bonnet, mkd "890, 3" on back of head ................. 525.00

9" h, 1078, bisque socket head, replaced wig, set blue eyes, feathered brows, painted upper and lower lashes, open mouth with four upper teeth, five-piece composition body with molded and painted socks and one-strap shoes, pink and white dress, white organdy pinafore, knit underclothing, mkd "1078 Simon & Halbig, S & H, 0, Germany" on back of head, touch-up to body, arms, and legs................................................. 300.00

16" h, 1039, bisque socket heat on bisque shoulder plate, orig mohair wig, set dark brown eyes, feathered brows, painted upper and lower lashes, open mouth with four upper teeth, pierced ears, cloth body, bisque lower arms, stitch-jointed at hips and knees, orig ethnic-type outfit, orig underclothing, black shoes and socks, mkd "SH 1039, 4 DEP" on back of head, some aging to cloth body................................. 600.00

23" h, 570, bisque socket head, orig blond mohair wig, brown sleep eyes, feathered brows, painted upper and lower lashes, open mouth with four upper teeth, wood and composition body, antique maroon two-piece outfit, lace trimmed blouse, hat, antique underclothing, socks, and shoes, mkd "570, Germany, Halbig, S & H" on back of head, several wig pulls, hands repainted.......................................... 500.00

27" h, 1079, bisque socket head, replaced wig, dark brown sleep eyes, feathered brows, painted upper and lower lashes, open mouth with four upper teeth, pierced ears, jointed wood and composition body, redressed in new sailor outfit, white top, red trim, navy blue pleated skirt, antique underclothing, replaced shoes, mkd "S & H 1079, DEP, Germany, 13-1/2" on back of head, wear to finish of lower arms and hands, repair around neck socket, minor repairs at hip joints .......... 700.00

34" h, 1079, bisque socket head, orig human hair wig, brown sleep eyes, feathered brows, painted upper and lower lashes, open mouth with four upper teeth, pierced ears, jointed wood and composition body, ecru antique silk child dress, antique underclothing, old cotton socks, old leather child's shoes, mkd "1079, S & H, DEP, 16, B, Germany" on back of head, light kiln dust on cheeks, minor wig pulls on back, body shows normal wear .......................................... 1,300.00

### Societe Francaise de Bebes et Jouets, S. F. B. J.

13" h, 236 Toddler, bisque socket head, human hair wig, blue sleep eyes with real lashes, feathered brows, painted lower lashes, open-closed mouth with two upper teeth, jointed wood and composition toddler body, diagonal hip joint, redressed, mkd "S. F. B. J. 236, Paris, -4-" on back of head, partial S. F. B. J. label on back .................... 400.00

21" h, Character, boy, fine quality bisque head, open/closed mouth, two upper molded teeth, blue glass open/close eyes, dark blond orig hair, orig chunky French toddler composition jointed body, jointed wrists, white shirt, black and white striped shorts, red and white striped cap, new shoes, marked "S.F.B.J. 247 Paris".................................. 2,750.00

22" h, 301, bisque socket head, replaced wig, set blue eyes, molded and feathered brows, painted lower lashes, open mouth with accented lips, four upper teeth, jointed wood and composition French body, white organdy lace trimmed dress, mkd "S. F. B. J., 301, Paris, -9-" on back of head, "Fabrication Francaise, Paris, S.F.B.J." on paper label on back, three small flakes at neck socket, right hand touch-up ...................... 375.00

### Sonneberg Taufling

18" h, papier-mâché head, composition shoulder plate, lightly painted wisps of hair on sides of head, set dark pupilless eyes, light single stroke brows, closed mouth, wooden arms and legs, composition hands, feet, and hip section, dressed in antique white gown, crochet bonnet, unmarked, touch-up on nose, left check, repaint on front of composition lower torso, other minor paint touch-ups.......................... 600.00

### Jules Nicholas Steiner

16-1/2" h, Le Parisien, bisque socket head, human hair wig, brown paperweight eyes, feathered brows, painted upper and lower lashes, accented nostrils, closed mouth, pierced ears, jointed light weight composition body, antique clothing and bonnet, mkd "Le Parisien, Bte S.G.D.G. A 9" stamped in black on back of head, incised "A-9," "Le Petite Parisien, Bebe Steiner, Medaille d'Or, Paris 1889" stamped on left hip, small wig pull, orig body finish, one finger reglued, wear at both knee joints ............3,400.00

24" h, bisque socket head, blue paperweight eyes, pierced ears, closed mouth, brown wig, composition jointed body, marked "Steiner/Paris/Fre A.17" ..................................... 4,675.00

**Unis France**, 13-1/2" h, bisque socket head, blue sleep eyes, real lashes, feathered brows, open mouth, four upper teeth, jointed composition body with jointed wrists, orig labeled regional costume, underclothing, socks, and shoes, orig paper label on skirt, paper wrist tag "fabrication Jumeau Paris, Made in France," marked "Unis France, 71 301 149" on back of head, "Made in France" circular stamp, facial coloring pale......................................... 475.00

### Vogue

7-1/2" h, Ginny, hard plastic head, mohair wig, painted blue eyes to side, single stroke brows, painted upper lashes, closed mouth, five-piece hard plastic body, dressed in orig tagged outfits with red plaid shirts, red overalls with plaid trim, red cotton socks, green leatherette center snap shoes, replaced red felt caps, mkd "Vogue" on back of head, "Vogue Doll" on backs, "Vogue Dolls Inc., Medford, Mass" on "ink spot" label on clothing, price for pr .................................... 450.00

7-1/2" h, Toodles Draf-Tee, composition head, orig mohair wig, painted blue eyes to side, single stroke brows, painted upper lashes, closed mouth, five-piece composition toddler body, orig brown military uniform, brown leather belt with small gun, matching cap, socks, brown side snap shoes, mkd "Vogue" on head, "Doll Co." on back, round gold "Vogue" tag on right front uniform, unplayed-with condition ...................................... 350.00

**Walker, Izannah**, 17" h, painted brown hair and eyes, closed mouth, dark brown orig clothes, kid boots, 1860s, paint wear and fiber loss, arms repaired .......................................... 2,415.00

**Walkure**, 19-1/2" h, bisque socket head, replaced wig, blue sleep eyes, molded and feathered brows, painted upper and lower lashes, open mouth with accented lips, four upper teeth, pierced ears, jointed wood and composition body, blue and white dress, trimmed with lace and bow, underclothing, new black socks, black leatherette tie shoes, mkd "I, 8, Walkure, Germany" on back of head, light rubs on nose and left cheek, old water damage on finish of left lower leg and foot, hands different color from body.............................. 350.00

**Wax**, 5-1/4" h, wax shoulder head, molded and painted hair, tiny glass eyes, single stroke brows, closed mouth, cloth body with wax lower arms and lower legs, molded and painted black shoes, dressed in orig green and white dress, white bodice and sleeves, orig underclothing, ribbon trimmed bonnet, unmarked, unplayed with condition, fingers missing from left hand ................................ 775.00

**Wax Over Composition**, 26" h, shoulder head, orig mohair wig, set blue eyes, single stroke brows, closed mouth, cloth body with kid lower arms, individually stitched fingers, jointed at shoulders, hips, and knees, possibly orig white blouse trimmed with eyelet and tucks, blue plaid silk jumper, antique underclothes, socks, red leather shoes, lace and flower trimmed bonnet, unmarked, flake of wax off chin, circular crack and discoloration on right cheek, rub on nose, wig sparse in back, normal aging to body ..................................... 750.00

# DOORKNOBS and OTHER BUILDER'S HARDWARE

**History:** Man's home has always been his castle, whether grand and ornate, or simple and homey. The use of decorative doorknobs, back plates, door bells, knockers, and mail slots helped decorate and distinguish one's door. Creating a grand entrance was as important to our ancestors as it is today.

Before the advent of the mechanical bell or electrical buzzer and chime, a door knocker was considered an essential door ornament to announce the arrival of visitors. Metal was used to cast or forge the various forms; many cast-iron examples were painted. Collectors like to find door knockers with English registry marks.

Collectors of doorknobs and other types of builders hardware are growing as we learn to treasure the decorative elements of our past. Often old house lovers seek out these elements to refurbish their homes, adding to the demand.

**References:** Ronald S. Barlow (comp.), *Victorian Houseware, Hardware and Kitchenware*, Windmill Publishing, 1991; Margarete Baur-Heinhold, *Decorative Ironwork*, Schiffer Publishing, 1996; Len Blumin, *Victorian Decorative Art*, available from ADCA (P.O. Box 126, Eola, IL 60519), n.d.; Maude Eastwood wrote several books about doorknobs which are available from P.O. Box 126, Eola, IL 60519; Constance M Greiff, *Early Victorian*, Abbeville Press, 1995; Philip G. Knobloch, *A Treasure of Fine Construction Design*, Astragal Press, 1995; Henrie Martinie, *Art Deco Ornamental Ironwork*, Dover Publications, 1996; James Massey and Shirley Maxwell, *Arts & Crafts*, Abbeville Press, 1995; Ted Menten (comp.), *Art Nouveau Decorative Ironwork*, Dover Publications, n.d.; *Ornamental French Hardware Designs*, Dover Publications, 1995; Ernest Rettelbusch, *Handbook of Historic Ornament from Ancient Times to Biedermeier*, Dover Publications, 1996; Alan Robertson, *Architectural Antiques*, Chronicle Books, 1987; Edward Shaw, *Modern Architect* (reprint), Dover Publications, 1996; *Turn of the Century Doors, Windows and Decorative Millwork*, Dover Publications, 1995 reprint; Web Wilson, *Antique Hardware Price Guide,* Krause Publications, 1999,—, *Great Glass in American Architecture,* E. P. Dutton, New York, 1986.

**Periodical:** *American Bungalow*, P.O. Box 756, Sierra Madre, CA 91204.

**Collectors' Club:** Antique Doorknob Collectors of America, Inc., P.O. Box 126, Eola, IL 60519.

**Additional Listings:** Architectural Elements, Stained Glass.

**Advisor:** Web Wilson.

Doorbell
 Cast Iron, Aesthetic design ................................................... 65.00
 Nickel plated, lever action, fancy, dated 1870 ..................... 160.00
Doorbell Pull and Backplate, nickel-plated, Neo-Grec style ........ 140.00
Doorbell Pull, glass and cast iron, 1860s .................................... 20.00
Doorbell Push Button Plate, La Grande pattern by Reading ........ 75.00
Doorknob
 Geisha Girl, Russell & Erwin, c1774 ............................... 1,600.00
 Gothic design, c1900, entry size ........................................ 50.00
 Hexagonal, fancy, c1875, entry size .................................. 170.00
 Millefiori, knurled brass shank, c1850, small .................... 475.00
 New York City Public School, oval ...................................... 35.00
 Nickel-plated, Art Deco circle design ................................ 165.00
 Walnut, fancy pressed design............................................. 40.00

Wedgwood, blue and white medallion, cast with classical ladies, entry size ................................................... 375.00
Doorknob and Plate
 Hummingbird, figural backplate, entry size, R & E ............. 500.00
 Knights of Pythias ................................................................ 65.00
 Statler Hotel, New York City, cast iron ............................... 375.00
Doorknob and Rosette, gutta percha, fancy design, dated 1860 ................................................................................... 40.00
Door Knocker
 10-3/4" h, 5-1/2" w, 7" d, patinated bronze, modeled as putti suspended from draped boss, Renaissance-style, Continental, third quarter 18th C ............................................................... 715.00
 11" h, 7" w, brass, ringed lion mask, Beaux Arts-style, c1890-1910 .......................................................................... 315.00
Doorplate, large, single keyhole, Bamboo pattern by Branford .. 160.00
Door Pull
 Bronze, store type, dated July 22, 1879, pr ....................... 220.00
 Cast Iron, Egyptian Pharaoh face, 20th C .......................... 100.00
 Hinges, pr, bronze, Aesthetic design, 4" ............................ 110.00
 Keyhole Doorplate, single, Windsor pattern ........................ 35.00
 Keyhole Escutcheon, large, swing cover, Ekado pattern ...... 95.00
Knob
 Clear acrylic, pink roses inside, set of three ...................... 45.00
 Oval, painted, French ......................................................... 65.00
Mail Slot, bronze, orig spring ...................................................... 75.00
Passage Knob
 Aesthetic design ................................................................. 90.00
 Argillo Glass, red and black swirl pattern............................ 55.00
 Masonic Crest...................................................................... 55.00
 Newark Public Schools ........................................................ 60.00
 Odd Fellows logo ............................................................... 140.00
 Pressed Glass, amber ......................................................... 55.00
Passage Knob and Backplate
 Broken Leaf pattern ........................................................... 170.00
 Bronze, triangle backplate, R & E, c1870 .......................... 550.00
 Gothic ................................................................................. 180.00
 Rice pattern, Yale ............................................................... 45.00
Rim Lock, entry size, keeper and key, early 19th C ................... 325.00
Sash Lifts, cast iron, fancy, set of eight...................................... 70.00
Shutter Latches, bronze, Veroccio pattern, four sets ................. 55.00
Thumb Latch, entry, Arts & Crafts style, bronze ....................... 200.00

**Door Knocker, parrot on branch, oval base, painted, cast iron, 4-1/2" h, $45.**

# DOORSTOPS

**History:** Doorstops became popular in the late 19th century. They are either flat or three dimensional and were made out of a variety of different materials, such as cast iron, bronze, or wood. Hubley, a leading toy manufacturer, made many examples.

All prices listed are for excellent original paint unless otherwise noted. Original paint and condition greatly influence the price of a doorstop. To get top money, the piece must be close to mint original paint. Chipping of paint, paint loss, and wear reduce the value. Repainting severely reduces value and eliminates a good deal of the piece's market value, thereby reducing it's value. A broken piece has little value to none.

**References:** Jeanne Bertoia, *Doorstops*, Collector Books, 1985, 1996 value update; Douglas Congdon-Martin, *Figurative Cast Iron*, Schiffer Publishing, 1994.

**Advisor:** Craig Dinner.

**Notes:** Pieces described below contain at least 80% or more of the original paint and are in very good condition. Repainting drastically reduces price and desirability. Poor original paint is preferred over repaint.

All listings are cast-iron and flat-back castings unless otherwise noted.

Doorstops marked with an asterisk are currently being reproduced.

Basket, 11" h, rose, ivory wicker basket, natural flowers, handle with bow, sgd "Hubley 121" ............................................................ 145.00
Bear, 15" h, holding and looking at honey pot, brown fur, black highlights ..................................................................................... 1,500.00
Bellhop
    7-1/2" h, carrying satchel, facing sideways, orange-red uniform and cap ..................................................................... 400.00
    8-7/8" h, blue uniform, with orange markings, brown base, hands at side ......................................................................... 300.00
Bobby Blake, 9-1/2" h, boy holding teddy bear, blue shirt, pink socks, black pants, blond hair, Hubley .......................................... 350.00
Bowl, 7" x 7", green-blue, natural colored fruit, sgd "Hubley 456" ................................................................................... 135.00
Boy, 10-5/8" h, wearing diapers, directing traffic, police hat, red scarf, brown dog at side ............................................................. 665.00
Caddie, 8" h, carrying brown and tan bag, white, brown, knickers, red jacket* ............................................................................. 625.00
Cat
    8" h, black, red ribbon and bow around neck, on pillow* .... 135.00
    10-3/4" h, licking paw, white cat with black markings, mkd "Sculpture Metal Studios" ................................................. 425.00
    Cat Scratch Fever, 8-3/4" h, girl in blue dress, blond hair, black cat at side, scratches on arm, mkd "CJO 1271" .............. 800.00

---

**Child, reaching, naked, short brown curly hair, flesh color, 17" h, $1,250. Photo courtesy of Craig Dinner.**

Child, 17" h, reaching, naked, short brown curly hair, flesh color ............................................................................. 1,250.00
Clipper Ship, 5-1/4" h, full sails, American flag on top mast, wave base, 2 rubber stoppers, sgd "CJO" .................................... 65.00
Clown, 10" h, full figure, 2 sided, red suit, white collar, blue hat, black shoes ................................................................... 875.00
Cosmos Flower Basket, 17-3/4" h, blue and pink flowers, white vase, black base, Hubley ............................................... 1,125.00
Cottage, 8-5/8" l, 5-3/4" h, Cape type, blue roof, flowers, fenced garden, bath, sgd "Eastern Specialty Mfg Co. 14" ............. 150.00
Dancer, 8-7/8" h, Art Deco couple doing Charleston, pink dress, black tux, red and black base, "FISH" on front, sgd "Hubley 270" .. 1,275.00
Dog
    7" h, three puppies in basket, natural colors, sgd "Copyright 1932 M. Rosenstein, Lancaster, PA, USA" .............................. 350.00
    8" x 7-1/2", Beagle pup, full figure, cream with darker markings ....................................................................... 685.00
    9" h, Boston Bull, full figure, facing left, black, tan markings ....................................................................... 175.00
    10-1/2" x 3-1/2", St. Bernard, lying down, full figure, cream with brown markings, Hubley ............................................ 775.00
    14" x 9", Sealyham, full figure, Hubley, cream & tan dog, red collar ........................................................................... 650.00
Dolly, 9-1/2" h, pink bow in blond hair, holding doll in blue dress, white apron, yellow dress, Hubley ................................... 365.00
Doorman in Livery, 12" h, twin men, worn orig paint, mkd "Fish," Hubley ................................................................. 1,760.00
Drum Major, 12-5/8" h, full figure, ivory pants, red hat with feather, yellow baton in right hand, left hand on waist, sq base ............... 250.00
Duck, 7-1/2" h, white, green bush and grass ........................... 335.00
Dutch Boy, 11" h, full figure, hands in pockets, blue suit and hat, red belt and collar, brown shoes, blond hair .......................... 425.00
Elephant, 14" h, palm trees, early 20th C, very minor paint wear .... 210.00
Fisherman, 6-1/4" h, standing at wheel, hand over eyes, rain gear ................................................................................. 185.00
Frog, 3" h, full figure, sitting, yellow and green ...................... 50.00
Giraffe, 20-1/4" h, tan, brown spots, squared off lines to casting .. 2,400.00
Girl, 8-3/4" h, dark blue outfit and beanie, high white collar, black shoes, red hair, incised "663" .............................................. 475.00
Golfer, 10" h, overhand swing, hat and ball on ground, Hubley* ...... 475.00
Halloween Girl, 13-3/4" h, 9-3/4" l, white hat, flowing cape, holding orange jack-o-lantern with red cutout eyes, nose, and mouth* ........... 2,000.00

## Reproduction Alert:

Reproductions are proliferating as prices on genuine doorstops continue to rise. A reproduced piece generally is slightly smaller than the original unless an original mold is used. The overall casting of reproductions is not as smooth as on the originals. Reproductions also lack the detail apparent in originals, including the appearance of the painted areas. Any bright orange rusting is strongly indicative of a new piece. Beware. If it looks too good to be true, it usually is.

Indian Chief, 9-3/4" h, orange and tan headdress, yellow pants, and blue stripes, red patches at ankles, green grass, sgd "A. A. Richardson," copyright 1928............................................................................295.00

Lighthouse, 14" h, green rocks, black path, white lighthouse, red window and door trim ..........................................................................385.00

Mammy

    8-1/2" h, full figure, Hubley, red dress, white apron, polka-dot bandanna on head ............................................................................225.00

    10" h, white scarf and apron, dark blue dress, red kerchief on head* ..........................................................................................425.00

Monkey

    8-1/2" h, 4 5/8" w wrap around tail, full figure, brown and tan ..............................................................................................295.00

    14-3/8" h, hand reaching up, brown, tan, and white ..........650.00

Old Mill, 6-1/4" h, brown log mill, tan roof, white patch, green shrubs .......................................................................................350.00

Owl, 9-1/2" h, sits on books, sgd "Eastern Spec Co" ...............285.00

Pan, 7" h, with flute, sitting on mushroom, green outfit, red hat and sleeves, green grass base ...........................................................165.00

Parrot, 13-3/4" h, in ring, two sided, heavy gold base, sgd "B & H" .....................................................................................265.00

Peasant Woman, 8-3/4" h, blue dress, black hair, fruit basket on head ..........................................................................................250.00

Penguin, 10" h, full figure, facing sideways, black, white chest, top hat and bow tie, yellow feet and beak, unsgd Hubley ...................435.00

Policeman, 9-1/2" h, leaning on red fire hydrant, blue uniform and titled hat, comic character face, tan base, "Safety First" on front .....725.00

Prancing Horse, 11" h, scrolled and molded base, "Greenlees Glasgow" imp on base, cast iron ......................................................175.00

Quail, 7-1/4" h, two brown, tan, and yellow birds, green, white, and yellow grass, "Fred Everett" on front, sgd "Hubley 459"* ..............335.00

Rabbit, 8-1/8" h, eating carrot, red sweater brown pants............300.00

Rooster, 13" h, red comb, black and brown tail .........................360.00

Squirrel, 9" h, sitting on stump eating nut, brown and tan ..........275.00

Storybook

    4-1/2" h, Humpty Dumpty, full figure, sgd "661" ..................375.00

    7-3/4" h, Little Miss Muffett, sitting on mushroom, blue dress, blond hair ........................................................................175.00

    9-1/2" h, Little Red Riding Hood, basket at side, red cape, tan dress with blue pattern, blond hair, sgd "Hubley" .............395.00

    12-1/2" h, Huckleberry Finn, floppy hat, pail, stick, Littco Products label.....................................................................................475.00

    Sunbonnet Girl, 9" h, pink dress .........................................265.00

Whistler, 20-1/4" h, boy, hands in tan knickers, yellow striped baggy shirt, sgd "B & H" .................................................................2,750.00

Windmill, 6-3/4" h, ivory, red roof, house at side, green base* ... 115.00

Woman, 11" h, flowers and shawl*...............................................245.00

Zinnias, 11-5/8" h, multicolored flowers, blue and black vase, sgd "B & H" .....................................................................................185.00

# DRESDEN/MEISSEN

**History:** Augustus II, Elector of Saxony and King of Poland, founded the Royal Saxon Porcelain Manufactory in the Albrechtsburg, Meissen, in 1710. Johann Frederick Boettger, an alchemist, and Tschirnhaus, a nobleman, experimented with kaolin from the Dresden area to produce porcelain. By 1720, the factory produced a whiter hard-paste porcelain than that from the Far East. The factory experienced its golden age from the 1730s to the 1750s under the leadership of

Samuel Stolzel, kiln master, and Johann Gregor Herold, enameler.

The Meissen factory was destroyed and looted by forces of Frederick the Great during the Seven Years' War (1756-1763). It was reopened, but never achieved its former greatness.

In the 19th century, the factory reissued some of its earlier forms. These later wares are called "Dresden" to differentiate them from the earlier examples. Further, there were several other porcelain factories in the Dresden region and their products also are grouped under the "Dresden" designation.

**Marks:** Many marks were used by the Meissen factory. The first was a pseudo-Oriental mark in a square. The famous crossed swords mark was adopted in 1724. A small dot between the hilts was used from 1763 to 1774, and a star between the hilts from 1774 to 1814. Two modern marks are swords with a hammer and sickle and swords with a crown.

**References:** Susan and Al Bagdade, *Warman's English & Continental Pottery & Porcelain*, 3rd Edition, Krause Publications, 1998; Robert E. Röntgen, *The Book of Meissen*, revised ed., Schiffer Publishing, 1996.

**Museums:** Art Institute of Chicago, Chicago, IL; Cincinnati Art Museum, Cincinnati, OH; Dresden Museum of Art & History, Dresden, Germany; Gardiner Museum of Ceramic Art, Toronto, Canada; Meissen Porcelain Museum, Meissen, Germany; Metropolitan Museum of Art, New York, NY; National Museum of American History, Smithsonian Institution, Washington, DC, Robertson Center for the Arts and Sciences, Binghamton, NY; Schlossmuseum, Berlin, Germany; Stadtmuseum, Cologne, Germany; Wadsoworth Atheneum, Hartford, Ct; Woodmere Art Museum, Philadelphia, PA; Zwinger Museum, Dresden, Germany.

**Cup and Saucer, cobalt blue, gilded tracery, hp portrait of Marie Antoinette, $300. Photo courtesy of Joy Luke Fine Art Brokers and Auctioneers.**

## Dresden

After-Dinner Coffeepot, 12-3/4" h, floral Cannele pattern, Helena Wolfson, c1900-15 ............................................................... 100.00

Centerpiece, 15" h, Art Deco-style female, gilt hair and shoes, peach bathing suit, lilac wrap, standing on octagonal base, round center bowl with molded floral gilt rim, ivory and gilt ground ............ 1,200.00

Charger, 18" d, soldiers receiving provisions, flower garland border, black enamel pseudo AR cipher, 19th C ................................. 650.00

Compote, 18" h, three detailed figurines playing around tall stem, multicolored flowers, white ground, round pedestal base, c1870 1,500.00

Figure, 6-1/4" h, male flute player, floral pantaloons, mauve coat, seated dog, 19th C ................................................................... 200.00

Fruit Dish, circular, low front, scalloped, open wide sides, floral panels, floral center, price for pr ........................................................... 300.00

Miniature, 2-5/8" w, 3-3/8" h, painted porcelain, young woman in profile, gilt copper frame with Art Nouveau style enamel scrolling flowers, early 20th C ...................................................................... 350.00

Mirror, 13-3/4" h, scrolled foliate porcelain encrusted frame, female figure and cherubs, late 19th/early 20th C ................................. 435.00

Plaque, 2-1/2" x 3-1/4" and 3-1/2" x 4-1/2" d, oval, female portrait, mounted in giltwood frame, c1900, pr ...................................... 375.00

Punch Bowl, cover, stand, 11-3/4" d, 15-1/4" d stand, sliced lemon finial, enamel dec, titled figures depicting the "Punch Society," c1750 ................................................................................. 27,600.00

Relish Dish, 7-1/2" l, 4-part, handled, hp flowers ...................... 125.00

Shrimp Server, circular, floral dec, openwork border .................. 125.00

Urn, cov, 17-1/4" h, baluster, scroll handles, reticulated neck and cov, floral and landscape cartouches, white ground, floral spray dec............ 750.00

Vase, cov, 20-1/2" h, 9" w, white ground, two Victorian multicolored romantic scenes, multicolored floral dec on each side of detailed white and gold handles, neck and base with gilt and white pebble border, gold border with magenta and orange roses, green leaves, detailed elongated oval gilt design at base, gilt short pedestal with floral dec, Dresden mark on bottom with crown on top, number 11018, c1883 ................................................................ 1,600.00

Wall Sconce, 33" h, shaped mirror plate and frame, elaborately modeled with putti and foliate, three-light standard, 20th C, cracks, minor losses .................................................................................. 635.00

## Meissen

Candelabra, pr, 22-3/4" h, seven-light, underglaze blue dec, applied flowers and figures of children playing musical instruments, crossed swords marks ....................................................................... 2,990.00

Clock, mantel, 18" h, figural, rococo-style body, classical female figures and putti, retailed by Tiffany & Co., New York, crossed swords mark, late 19th C ................................................................... 6,100.00

Coffee Service, coffeepot, creamer, sugar, cup and saucer, 17-3/4" l rect tray, Baroque-style, broad blue borders, new gold dec, late 19th C ................................................................................... 750.00

Compote, 20-3/4" h, three tiers, blue floral dec, figure of female flower seller mounted to top of three graduated dishes, late 19th/early 20th C .......................................................................... 1,380.00

Cream Jug, cov, 5-1/2" h, scenes of miners at work, 19th C ...... 650.00

Cup and Saucer, 5-1/4" d, scenes of miners at work, 19th C ..... 700.00

Demitasse Set, 8" h cov baluster-form pot, creamer, cov sugar, four cups and saucers, polychrome and underglaze blue floral dec, gilt enamel dec, price for eleven pc set .......................................... 575.00

Desk Set, 7-1/2" x 11-1/4" shaped rect tray, 9" l oval pen tray, 3" h sander, 3-1/4" h cov ink pot, underglaze blue bird and floral ground, overglazed iron red enamel and gilding, late 19th C ................ 650.00

Figure

5-1/2" h, female in 18th C costume showing her dog to image in mirror, 19th C .......................................................... 1,495.00

5-1/2" h, seated male and female figures playing flute and lyre, incised "W56," crossed swords mark, late 19th C, losses ..2,300.00

7-1/8" h, cupid with burning heart, marbleized and gilt edged socle base, late 19th/early 20th C ................................... 1,265.00

7-1/2" h, Autumn, supporting sheaf of wheat, crossed swords mark, late 19th C ................................................................ 520.00

8-1/8" h, cupid with broken heart, marbleized and gilt edged socle base, late 19th/early 20th C .......................................... 1,385.00

8-3/4" h, hunter, polychrome dec, incised "1285," crossed swords mark, 19th C ..................................................................... 460.00

11-1/2" h, modeled as five figures in various gardening acts, freeform circular base, crossed swords mark, late 19th C ............... 1,840.00

12" h, allegorical female subjects set on oval base, one holding ribbon at wings of cupid, other feeding doves, crossed swords mark, 19th C ................................................................. 5,175.00

16-1/4" h, allegorical female figure holding scepter, inscribed "no. 369," crossed swords mark, 19th C ............................ 1,7225.00

16-1/2" h, allegorical female figure holding script, inscribed "no. 369," crossed swords mark, late 19th/early 20th C ........ 1,610.00

16-1/2" h, allegorical female figure playing musical instrument, inscribed "no. 369," crossed swords mark, late 19th/early 20th C .................................................................................. 1,850.00

Plate

8-5/8" d, raised gilt foliate dec, set of six ........................... 550.00

9" d, monochrome white, molded foliate and cattail dec, gilt rim ..................................................................................... 75.00

9-3/4" h, Apple Picker, group, enamel dec, gilt trim, model 2229, losses .................................................................................. 865.00

Salt, figural

5" h, modeled as male and female figures seated between two basket form bowls, crossed swords mark, early 20th C, losses, price for pr ............................................................................ 690.00

5" h, 5-1/2" l, modeled as seated child between two baskets, foliate sprays, late 19th C, price for pr .............................. 2,100.00

Serving Tray, 10" x 13-3/8" oval, molded laurel leaves and grape border, gilt framed central cartouche, enamel dec figural landscape scene, late 18th C/early 19th ................................................ 1,840.00

Soup Plate, 9-5/8" d, scrolled gilt vine borders, enameled landscape and floral dec, early 19th C, pr ................................................ 230.00

Standish, 14" w, 9-1/2" d, 10" h, figural sander and inkwell, center Chinoiserie figural group with small well, scrolled base, late 19th C, minor restorations .................................................................. 4,025.00

Tea Service, partial

Cobalt blue ground, cartouche of colorful flowers, gold dec, cov teapot, creamer, cov sugar, tray, eleven cups, twelve saucers, twelve 7" d plates ......................................................... 1,100.00

Enamel floral dec, 4-1/4" h teapot, two tea bowls and saucers, 4" h cream jug, 6-3/4" d waste bowl, 19th C ........................ 690.00

Miners dec, scrolled gilt trim, central enamel dec of miners at work, 3-1/2" cov teapot, 5" h cov tea canister, six cups and saucers, 18th C ................................................................ 13,800.00

Tray, 16-1/4" w handle to handle, sq, molded edge with rocaille shells, blue floral dec, polychrome floral dec in center, gilt enamel dec, late 19th C ................................................................................ 1,100.00

Vase, 15" h, baluster form, cobalt blue glaze, parcel-gilt, snake handle, 20th C ................................................................................... 635.00

# DUNCAN and MILLER

**History:** George Duncan, Harry B. and James B., his sons, and Augustus Heisey, his son-in-law, formed George Duncan & Sons in Pittsburgh, Pennsylvania, in 1865. The factory was located just two blocks from the Monongahela River, providing easy and inexpensive access by barge for materials needed to produce glass. The men, from Pittsburgh's south side, were descendants of generations of skilled glassmakers.

The plant burned to the ground in 1892. James E. Duncan Sr., selected a site for a new factory in Washington, Pennsylvania, where operations began on February 9, 1893. The plant prospered, producing fine glassware and table services for many years.

John E. Miller, one of the stockholders, was responsible for designing many fine patterns, the most famous being Three Face. The firm incorporated and used the name The Duncan and Miller Glass Company until the plant closed in 1955. The company's slogan was "The Loveliest Glassware in America." The U.S. Glass Co. purchased the molds, equipment, and machinery in 1956.

**References:** Tom and Neila Bredehoft, *Fifty Years of Collectible Glass, 1920-1970, Volume 1, Volume II*, Antique Trader Books, 2000; Gene Florence, *Elegant Glassware of the Depression Era*, 9th ed., Collector Books, 2001; Naomi L. Over, *Ruby Glass of the 20th Century*, Antique Publications, 1990, 1993-94 value update, *Book II,* 1999.

**Collectors' Club:** National Duncan Glass Society, P.O. Box 965, Washington, PA 15301.

**Additional Listings:** Pattern Glass.

Animal, donkey .................................................. 225.00
Ashtray, clear
    Canterbury ................................................. 18.50
    Duck, ruby.................................................. 120.00
    Fish, blue opalescent.................................. 45.00
    Tulip ........................................................... 30.00
Basket, Canterbury, 8-1/2" h, blue opalescent............................. 95.00
Bowl
    Canterbury, 5" d, crimped, blue opalescent........................ 25.00
    Caribbean, 5" d, blue ................................. 20.00
    Sandwich, 5" d............................................ 10.00
Butter, cov, Tear Drop, clear, silverplated lid.................................. 30.00
Cake Plate, King Arthur, clear, 9-1/2" d, skirted........................... 55.00
Candlesticks, pr, Canterbury, clear, etched.............................. 30.00
Candy Box, cov, Canterbury, etched Charmaine Rose, 8" d, 3-part, handles .................................... 125.00
Canoe, Daisy and Button, blue ...................... 145.00
Celery and Relish Tray, First Love, #30, 12" l.................. 90.00
Cheese Compote, Tear Drop, clear .............. 20.00
Cheese Stand, Canterbury, chartreuse, 5-1/2" w, 3-1/2" h .......... 35.00
Cigarette Jar, Nautical, crystal, frosted, sterling lid...................... 95.00
Cocktail
    Canterbury, clear, 4-1/4" h, 3-1/2" oz........... 10.00
    Spiral Flutes, green, ftd, 3-3/8" h................. 8.00
Cologne, stopper, Hobnail Opalescent Blue, 9 oz .................... 120.00
Comport
    First Love, 5-1/2"......................................... 50.00
    Terrace, amber, 7"...................................... 45.00
Cordial, Indian Tree, 1 oz............................... 65.00
Cornucopia Vase, Three Feathers, #117, pink opalescent, 8" h, ftd.............................. 140.00
Creamer and Sugar
    First Love, stacking.................................... 95.00
    Plaza Punties, amber.................................. 45.00
Cruet, Caribbean.............................................. 70.00
Cup and Saucer
    Caribbean, blue .......................................... 70.00
    Sandwich ..................................................... 13.00
    Terrace......................................................... 20.00
Decanter, Laguna, #154/49, 32 oz, Biscayne Green ................. 130.00
Deviled Egg Plate, Sandwich, clear.............. 50.00
Flower Basket, Teardrop, loop handle, 12" h.................... 175.00
Flower Bowl, Murano, 9-1/2" d........................ 65.00
Fruit Bowl, Sandwich, flared, 12" d................ 70.00
Gardenia Bowl, Canterbury, clear.................. 35.00

Goblet
    Croesus ...................................................... 35.00
    Eternally Yours............................................ 25.00
    Hobnail Opalescent Blue, 9 oz .................. 40.00
    Sandwich, 9 oz ........................................... 18.00
Hat, Hobnail Opalescent Blue, 6" h............... 200.00
Hors D'oeuvre Plate, American Way, 9-1/2" d........ 35.00
Iced Tea Tumbler, clear
    Canterbury, 7" h ......................................... 15.00
    Croesus ...................................................... 35.00
    Indian Tree, ftd, 6" h .................................. 22.00
Ivy Bowl, Hobnail, black, pedestal ................ 48.00
Jelly Compote, Caribbean, clear.................... 30.00
Juice Tumbler, Eternally Yours....................... 18.00
Lemon Tray, Puritan, green, clear handle...... 25.00
Mayonnaise, 3 pc set
    Canterbury, chartreuse.............................. 75.00
    Language of Flowers, crystal...................... 37.50
Nappy
    Canterbury, 5" d, chartreuse ...................... 15.00
    Indian Tree, clear, triangular, handle........... 20.00
    Murano, clear, ruffled, 6" d......................... 20.00
Nut Bowl, Sandwich, 3-1/2" d......................... 10.00
Olive Dish, Tear Drop, clear, divided, 6" l...... 15.00
Pickle/Olive, Indian tree, 8-1/2" l.................... 40.00
Plate
    Canterbury, 8" d, lily of the valley cutting..... 15.00
    Caribbean, dinner, blue............................... 125.00
    Sandwich, 16" d........................................... 90.00
Puff Box, cov, Hobnail Opalescent Blue, 4".... 100.00
Relish
    Sanibel, 2-part, 8-1/2" d, blue opalescent... 45.00
    Sandwich, 3-part, 10-1/2" d, rect............... 42.00
Salad Plate, Sanibel, 8-1/2" d, blue opalescent........ 35.00
Salt and Pepper Shakers, pr
    Caribbean, blue, salt cloudy ...................... 70.00
    Sandwich, 2-1/2" h, metal lids.................... 18.00
Serving Plate, Sandwich, clear, 13" d............ 40.00
Sherbet
    Sandwich ..................................................... 10.00
    Tear Drop, clear, tall................................... 10.00
Sugar, clear
    Canterbury................................................... 10.00
    First Love .................................................... 15.00
    Language of Flowers................................... 18.00
Swan
    7", Pall Mall, chartreuse............................. 65.00
    7", Pall Mall, ruby....................................... 55.00
    7-1/2", Sylvan, blue opalescent ................. 145.00
    11" w wingspan, blue opalescent............... 235.00
    11" w wingspan, crystal.............................. 90.00
    12", Sylvan, pink opalescent...................... 295.00
Torte Plate, Sandwich, 12" d.......................... 50.00
Tumbler, Sandwich, 9 oz, ftd.......................... 15.00
Vase
    Canterbury, chartreuse, 8-1/2" h, flower arranger............... 95.00
    Caribbean, blue, flared, 7-1/2" h................ 60.00
    Sandwich, 10" h, ftd, #41........................... 90.00
Wine, Indian Tree, 3 oz.................................... 35.00

# DURAND

**History:** Victor Durand (1870-1931), born in Baccarat, France, apprenticed at the Baccarat glassworks where several generations of his family had worked. In 1884, Victor came to America to join his father at Whitall-Tatum & Co. in New Jersey. In 1897, father and son leased the Vineland Glass Manufacturing Company in Vineland,

New Jersey. Products included inexpensive bottles, jars, and glass for scientific and medical purposes. By 1920, four separate companies existed.

When Quezal Art Glass and Decorating Company failed, Victor Durand recruited Martin Bach Jr., Emil J. Larsen, William Wiedebine, and other Quezal men and opened an art-glass shop at Vineland in December 1924. Quezal-style iridescent pieces were made. New innovations included cameo and intaglio designs, geometric Art Deco shapes, Venetian Lace, and Oriental-style pieces. In 1928, crackled glass, called Moorish Crackle and Egyptian Crackle, was made.

Durand died in 1931. The Vineland Flint Glass Works was merged with Kimble Glass Company a year later, and the art glass line was discontinued.

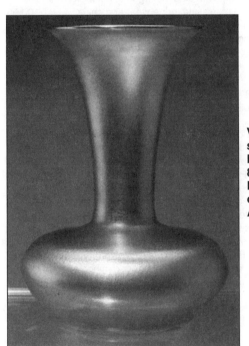

**Vase, gold irid, sgd "V Durand/1990-8," 8" h, $520. Photo courtesy of David Rago Auctions.**

**Reference:** Edward J. Meschi, *Durand: The Man and His Glass,* Glass Press, 1998.

**Marks:** Many Durand glass pieces are not marked. Some have a sticker with the words "Durand Art Glass," others have the name "Durand" scratched on the pontil or "Durand" inside a large V. Etched numbers may be part of the marking.

Bowl, 8" d, 6-1/2" h, orange cased to opal, overall irid green leaf and vine dec, sgd in V ............... 1,500.00
Candlesticks, pr, 9-1/2" h, baluster, amber, pulled blue feather tips, flanged rim with etched wheat and leaves ............... 300.00
Chandelier, baluster-form central blue glass shaft, conforming irid threading mounted on six-light ceiling lamp, adjustable drop ..... 350.00
Compote, 8" d, white feather dec, blue ground, pale green stem and foot ............... 750.00
Lamp, 14" h, shade with gold and green hearts and vines, irid opal ground, applied heavy gold threading, yellow int., bronze tree-form standard ............... 2,250.00
Lamp Shade, 6-3/4" h, craquelle, blue and white, gold threading ... 725.00
Torchieres, pr 70-3/4" h, trumpet form transparent green shades with heart shaped leaf and vine motifs over opaque white glass, single socket brass fixture with scroll and leaf flanking seated satyrs on six-sided shaft, paneled domed cast iron base, rim flake, patina wear to shaft ............... 1,495.00
Vase
　6" h, flared, tapered body, white heart and vine dec, blue ground, sgd ............... 1,200.00
　6-7/8" h, flared neck on squat oval body, cobalt blue with overall strong blue irid, polished pontil, Meschi shape number 1730, c1925, slight wear to iridescence ............... 700.00
　8" h, baluster, pulled feather, blue and white ............... 1,200.00
　8-1/2" h, baluster, threaded and feathered, sgd "Durand 2028" ............... 1,800.00
　8-1/2" h, 5-1/2" d, red, white, and gold craquelle ............ 2,500.00
　9-1/4" h, baluster, pulled feather ............... 1,750.00
　10" h, King Tut, broad shouldered cased oval body, strong green pulled and coiled dec, lustrous irid gold surface, gold int. over opal, base inscribed "Durand 1964-10" ............... 2,450.00
　15-1/2" h, Genie, bulbous cobalt ribbed body, elongated slender neck, lustrous blue-silver irid, mirror bright near base .. 2,415.00
　18-3/4" h, Fireglow, burnt orange flowers, brown leaves, beige ground, price for pr............... 700.0

# EARLY AMERICAN GLASS

**History:** The term "Early American glass" covers glass made in America from the colonial period through the mid-19th century. As such, it includes the early pressed glass and lacy glass made between 1827 and 1840.

Major glass-producing centers prior to 1850 were Massachusetts (New England Glass Company and the Boston and Sandwich Glass Company), South Jersey, Pennsylvania (Stiegel's Manheim factory and many Pittsburgh-area firms), and Ohio (several different companies in Kent, Mantua, and Zanesville).

Early American glass was popular with collectors from 1920 to 1950. It has now regained some of its earlier prominence. Leading auction sources for early American glass include Garth's, Heckler & Company, James D. Julia, and Skinner, Inc.

**References:** William E. Covill, *Ink Bottles and Inkwells*, William S. Sullwold Publishing, out of print; George and Helen McKearin, American Glass, Crown, 1975; ——, *Two Hundred Years of American Blown Glass*, Doubleday and Company, 1950; Helen McKearin and Kenneth Wilson, *American Bottles and Flasks*, Crown, 1978; Dick Roller (comp.), *Indiana Glass Factories Notes*, Acorn Press, 1994; Jane S. Spillman, *American and European Pressed Glass*, Corning Museum of Glass, 1981; Kenneth Wilson, *American Glass 1760-1930*, 2 vols., Hudson Hills Press and The Toledo Museum of Art, 1994; ——, *New England Glass and Glassmaking*, Crowell, 1972.

**Periodicals:** *Antique Bottle & Glass Collector*, P.O. Box 187, East Greenville, PA 18041; *Glass Collector's Digest*, Antique Publications, P.O. Box 553, Marietta, OH 45750.

**Collectors' Clubs:** Early American Glass Traders, RD 5, Box 638, Milford, DE 19963; Early American Pattern Glass Society, P.O. Box 266, Colesburg, IA 52035; Glass Research Society of New Jersey, Wheaton Village, Glasstown Rd, Millville, NJ 08332; National Early American Glass Club, P.O. Box 8489, Silver Spring, MD 20907.

**Museums:** Bennington Museum, Bennington, VT; Chrysler Museum, Norfolk, VA; Corning Museum of Glass, Corning, NY; Glass Museum, Dunkirk, IN; Glass Museum Foundation, Redlands, CA; New Bedford Glass Museum, New Bedford, MA; Sandwich Glass Museum, Sandwich, MA; Toledo Museum of Art, Toledo, OH; Wheaton Historical Village Association Museum of Glass, Millville, NJ.

**Additional Listings:** Blown Three Mold; Cup Plates; Flasks; Sandwich Glass; Stiegel-Type Glass.

## Blown

Bottle
   8-1/4" h, globular, amber, twenty-four swirled ribs, Zanesville, OH, wear and bruise at bubble on side .................................... 275.00
   9-1/2" h, globular, aqua, twenty-four swirled ribs, Zanesville, OH, residue, large ext. broken blister and stone ..................... 325.00
Bowl
   5-5/8" d, 3-3/4" h, colorless, applied sapphire blue rim, late ..................................................................................... 125.00
   8-1/4" d, 2-7/8" h, light green, folded rim, ftd, Eastern ........ 550.00

Candlestick
   7" h, opaque medium blue, hexagonal, wafer, minor edge damage and damage to base of socket ................................... 185.00
   7-3/8" h, canary, petal detail, mated pair, some damage on both ..................................................................................... 120.00
   7-1/2" d, canary, hexagonal, flaring base, wafer, broken blister inside socket ....................................................................... 150.00
   7-5/8" h, canary, hexagonal, wafer, small chips .................. 150.00
   8-1/8" h, colorless, blown hollow socket, baluster stem, pressed base, firing checks in base, pr ......................................... 400.00
   9-1/4" h, canary, opalescent socket, hexagonal socket and stem, round base, pewter insert missing, Pittsburgh, chips and crack in socket ............................................................................. 135.00
   9-1/8" h, colorless, hollow socket with two knob stem, stepped pressed base, pewter insert, chips on base .................... 150.00
   9-3/8" h, grass-green, hexagonal, Pittsburgh, chips, check in socket ................................................................................... 75.00
   9-1/2" h, opaque medium blue, hexagonal, Pittsburgh, sanded finish, pewter socket missing, edge wear and chips ............ 100.00
   9-5/8" h, opaque medium blue, hexagonal, Pittsburgh, pewter socket missing, small edge chips .................................... 250.00
Canister, 9-1/2" h, colorless, two applied sapphire rings, matching ring on lid, colorless finial ...................................................... 995.00
Compote
   4-5/8" h, 5-5/8" d, blue bowl cased in clambroth-colored glass, deep cobalt blue base, applied foot, baluster stem, worn int. .............................................................................. 550.00
   6-7/8" h, 8" d, colorless with slight amber tint, cut ovals, strawberry diamonds and fans on bowl, applied foot with star, Pittsburgh, wear, pinpoints and scratches .............................. 200.00
   7" d, 6-1/2" h, Pittsburgh, colorless, blown, pillar molded, applied tooled lip, eight ribs, baluster stem, applied foot .............. 360.00
   7-1/4" h, 9-1/2" d, colorless, flared bowl with folded rim, engraved vining floral design on bowl, knob step, applied foot, wear, New England Glass Co. ......................................................... 250.00
   11-1/4" d, green .............................................................. 550.00
Decanter, 8-1/4" h, Pittsburgh, cut panels, strawberry diamonds, and fans, three applied rings, mismatched stopper, minor wear and stain ................................................................................. 100.00
Gemel Bottle, 10" h, Pittsburgh, double gemel, opaque white, cranberry looping, applied rigaree and foot, McKearin PL 229 #5 ................................................................................. 500.00
Lamp
   3-1/2" h, sparking, colorless, blown, bulbous font, wafer stem, applied foot, tin drop burner ............................................ 250.00
   3-3/4" h, sparking, colorless, blown bulbous font, detailed pressed base, tin drop burner, base chips .................................. 315.00
   4-1/4" h, sparking, colorless, blown, bulbous font, wafer stem, applied foot, tin drop burner ............................................ 250.00
   7-7/8" h, opaque white, onion font, baluster stem, applied foot, reset brass collar ............................................................ 110.00
   8-1/2" h, colorless, blown conical font, pressed sq and water fall base, pewter collar marked "A. C. Hobbs," small chips on base .................................................................................. 220.00
   8-3/4" h, opaque white, ribbed onion font, double stem with knob, applied foot, brass collar ............................................... 250.00
Mug, 5-3/8" h, opalescent, enamel dec floral sprays, reserve of gentleman smoking, very minor enamel wear ................................. 550.00
Pan, 5-3/4" d, aqua, folded rim ................................................... 115.00
Pitcher
   5-3/4" h, colorless, squatty, cut swags and fans in bowl, applied foot and handle, cut rayed foot, grinding at base of handle and on spout, attributed to Pittsburgh ..................................... 185.00
   7" h, South Jersey, deep amber, four drawn fingers on bowl, applied handle, threaded neck, flared lip, applied and tooled foot, base of handle chipped, wear, stain ........................ 110.00
Sugar Bowl, cov, 9-1/2" h, flint, fiery opalescent, Colonial pattern, minor roughness and shallow foot flake, glued finial, attributed to Pittsburgh area .......................................................... 330.00

## Vase

7-1/2" h, Pittsburgh, blue opalescent molded and cased bowl, applied double ear handles and foot in opaque white ...... 715.00

8-1/2" h, Pittsburgh, flint, colorless, blown, flared bowl with cut panels and sheaves, knop stem, wide applied foot, wear and scratches .......................................................................... 350.00

## Lacy

Bowl

6" d, rope rim, eight spoke center, minor chips ................... 250.00

7-3/8" d, 1-5/8" h, Nectarine, chips ..................................... 100.00

9-3/4" d, Thistle and Beehive, octagonal, shallow, edge chips .................................................................................... 50.00

Candlesticks, pr, 6" h, reeded and ribbed socket attached with wafer, reeded stem, sq stepped base, chips, checks in socket .......... 450.00

Compote, cov, 9-1/2" h, 8-1/4" d, Sawtooth, flint, chips ............. 150.00

Compote, open, 8" h, 8-1/2" d, Diamond Point, flint, wear and small flakes ............................................................................... 145.00

Miniature Lamp, 4" h, lacy cup plate base, blown spherical font, knob stem, chips on base ............................................................. 385.00

Plate

5-3/8" d, side wheeler, Pittsburgh, round ........................... 220.00

7" d, eagle, chips ............................................................. 160.00

Relish, 7-1/2" l, Peacock Eye, Midwestern, chips ......................... 65.00

Tea Plate, 6-1/2" d, octagonal, side wheeler, Pittsburgh ............. 800.00

Toddy Plate, 7-1/8" d, Peacock Eye, chips, set of six ................. 200.00

## Pillar Mold

Bowl, 4-3/8" h, emerald green, cut design at top of each rib, applied foot, ground pontil, attributed to Pittsburgh ........................... 1,100.00

Cologne Bottle, 5-5/8" h, cobalt blue, eight ribs, two applied rings, flared lip, mushroom stopper, stopper base chipped ............... 400.00

Decanter

9-3/4" h, cobalt blue, applied handle and collar, pewter jigger cap .............................................................................. 7,920.00

10-1/2" h, apple green, eight ribs swirled to the right, double ringed lip, polished pontil, pewter stopper, 1840-50, price for pr, one with minor stain ......................................................... 700.00

Pitcher, 5-5/8" h, colorless, applied handle, Pittsburgh, bottom ground flat, minor wear .................................................................... 275.00

# ENGLISH CHINA and PORCELAIN (GENERAL)

**History:** By the 19th century, more than 1,000 china and porcelain manufacturers were scattered throughout England, with the majority of the factories located in the Staffordshire district.

By the 19th century English china and porcelain had achieved a worldwide reputation for excellence. American stores imported large quantities for their customers. The special-production English pieces of the 18th and early 19th centuries held a position of great importance among early American antiques collectors.

**References:** Susan and Al Bagdade, *Warman's English & Continental Pottery & Porcelain*, 3rd Edition, Krause Publications, 1998; John A. Bartlett, *British Ceramic Art: 1870-1940*, Schiffer Publishing, 1993; Peter Bradshaw, *English Eighteenth Century Porcelain Figures, 1745-1795*, Antiques Collectors' Club, 1980; John and Margaret Cushion, *Collector's History of British Porcelain*, Antique Collectors' Club, 1992; Rachael Feild, *Macdonald Guide to Buying Antique Pottery & Porcelain*, Wallace-Homestead, 1987; Geoffrey A. Godden, *God-*

**Lowestoft, saucer, Chinese style blue dec, 4-3/4" d, $75.**

*den's Guide to Mason's China and the Ironstone Wares*, Antique Collectors' Club, out of print; ——, *Godden's Guide to English Porcelain*, Wallace-Homestead, 1992; Pat Halfpenny, *English Earthenware Figures 1740-1840*, Antique Collectors' Club, 1992; R. K. Henrywood, *Relief Molded Jugs, 1820-1900*, Antique Collectors' Club; Llewellyn Jewitt, *Ceramic Art of Great Britain*, Sterling Publishing, 1985 (reprint of 1883 classic); Griselda Lewis, *Collector's History of English Pottery*, 5th ed., Antique Collectors' Club, 1999

**Additional Listings:** Castleford; Chelsea; Coalport; Copeland and Spode; Liverpool; Royal Crown Derby; Royal Doulton; Royal Worcester; Staffordshire, Historical; Staffordshire, Romantic; Wedgwood; Whieldon.

## Ashworth

Plate, 9-1/4" d, wide cobalt blue border with enamel and gilt dec Japanese floral design, c1885, price for set of 12 .......................... 300.00

## Bow

Coffee Cup and Saucer, Golfer and Caddy pattern, blue, c1758 475.00

Dish, 10-5/8" l, rect, cur corners, oval reserve f Chinese water scene, border with four fan reserves of Oriental landscapes, four round reserves of flowers, powder blue, c1765 .................................. 690.00

Figure, 3-1/2" h, goldfinch, iron-red patches on black head, puce back, black tail, black and yellow wings, seated on flowered branch, 1760, repairs, pr ......................................................................... 1,950.00

Salt, 7-5/8" w, white, molded scallop shell, shell covered coral base, c1755, chips and cracks ........................................................ 920.00

**Newport Pottery Co., Ltd., Burslem, wash bowl and pitcher, band transfer with Japanese motif, Kutani bird, cherries, floral Geisha in oval medallion on black ground, lavender ground, $265.**

## Bristol

Charger, 12" d, man standing with boy, balcony overhead, oval panels of leaves border, criss-cross and dots between, blue and white, c1720-60, pr ............................................................................ 2,100.00
Dish, 9" d, Cracked Ice pattern, blue and manganese............. 1,350.00
Mug, 7-1/8" h, polychrome stylized peacock, large stylized flower-heads and insects, scroll design on rim, dot handle, mid 18th C, repairs ...................................................................................... 400.00
Plate, 9" d, light blue ground, blue center scene of Oriental village, fisherman on dock and boat, bianco soopra bianco border band of white flowerheads, fruit, and leaves, hairline and chips .................... 200.00

## Caughley

Dessert Plate, 8" d, four floral sprigs painted in center cavetto, floral garlands dec, blue edged scalloped rim, blue "S" mark ........... 185.00
Mug, 4-3/4" h, blue printed dec, late 18th century, crescent mark, rim restoration ............................................................................. 175.00
Pitcher, 7-1/2" h, leaf molded body, blue printed bouquets of garden flowers, mask spout, scroll handle with thumbrest, c1785 ....... 460.00

## Derby

Cream Jug, 2-3/8" h, painted Chinoiserie scene, pagoda flanked by rockwork and pines, int. with boulder and grasses, brown lined rim, c1760 .................................................................................... 2,465.00
Dish, 9-7/8" x 7-1/4", diamond shape, green scattered floral bouquets and sprigs, gilt lined and dentil rim, gilt anchor and "D" mark, Chelsea-Derby, c1775 ...................................................... 425.00
Figure, 6-1/8" h, standing shepherd, flower in hand, pink hat, light yellow coat, striped waistcoat, iron-red breeches, gilt accents, leaning on flower encrusted stump, hound at side, mound base, c1765, chips and repairs ................................................................................. 300.00
Plate, 8-7/8" d multicolored center, exotic birds in landscape, stiff gilt leaves border, pale blue ground, gilt stylized flower heads on rim bands, c1820, iron-red crown mark, crossed batons and "D" mark, gilder's mark attributed to John Moscrop ................................. 360.00
Potpourri, cov, 8-3/4" h, deep pink enamel and gilt dec pot supported by three goat's mask columns, hood feet, coiled snake, red baton mark, early 19th C, rim cov nicks, snake restored, one horn repaired, gilt wear .................................................................................. 650.00

## Flight, Barr, & Barr

Coffee Cann and Saucer, painted yellow and black, moonlight classical ruins scene, gilt scroll panel, dark blue ground, incised mark, c1807, pr .................................................................................... 4,450.00
Crocus Pot, 9" w, 4" h, D-form, molded pilasters and panels, arcaded base, pale salmon ground, gilt stylized anthemion and foliage, painted still-life panel of shells and coral, conforming top pierced panel, early 19th C ........................................................... 8,000.00
Plate, 8" d, Exotic Birds by G. Davis, c1807-13, wear to gilding. 350.00

## Ralph Wood

Bust, 9-1/4" h, Handel, brown wig, green lined puce drapery, blue coat, waisted socle, imp mark, c1790, repainted ............................... 990.00
Figure, 5-1/4" h, Admiral Rodney, uniform with open coat, green enamel with manganese dots, emblems of war at feet, molded tree stump with name, sheathed sword, c1780, restored................ 950.00
Spill Vase, 10-3/8" h, seated shepherd and shepherdess with sheep, gnarled tree with three openings, rocky mound base, late 18th C, restored ............................................................................... 1,000.00

## Worcester

Coffeepot, 7-1/2" h, 6-1/2" handle to spout, Rock & Strata Island pattern, Dr. Wall, c1770, very minor chips and wear to floral finial 950.00
Creamer, 3-1/2" h, pear shape, blue Oriental dec, 18th C .......... 250.00
Dish, 3-3/4" h, sheep shape, blue and white, Two Peony Rock Bird pattern, scrolls, underglaze blue workman's mark, c1755 ............ 575.00
Plate, 6-1/4" d, Pine Cone pattern, underglaze blue, scalloped rim, crescent marks, 18th C, shallow foot rim chips, price for pr..... 320.00

# ENGLISH SOFT PASTE

**History:** Between 1820 and 1860 a large number of potteries in England's Staffordshire district produced decorative wares with a soft earthenware (creamware) base and a plain white or yellow glazed ground.

Design or "stick" spatterware was created by a cut sponge (stamp), hand painting, or transfers. Blue was the predominant color. The earliest patterns were carefully arranged geometrics which generally covered the entire piece. Later pieces had a decorative border with a central motif, usually a tulip. In the 1850s Elsmore and Foster developed the Holly Leaf pattern.

King's Rose features a large, cabbage-type rose in red, pale red, or pink. The pink rose often is called "Queen's Rose." Secondary colors are pastels—yellow, pink, and, occasionally, green. The borders vary: a solid band, vined, lined, or sectional. The King's Rose exists in an oyster motif.

Strawberry China ware comes in three types: strawberries and strawberry leaves (often called strawberry luster), green featherlike leaves with pink flowers (often called cut-strawberry, primrose, or old strawberry), and relief decoration. The first two types are characterized by rust-red moldings. Most pieces have a cream ground. Davenport was only one of the many potteries which made this ware.

Yellow-glazed earthenware (canary luster) has a canary yellow ground, a transfer design which is usually in black, and occasional luster decoration. The earliest pieces date from the 1780s and have a fine creamware base. A few hand-painted pieces are known. Not every piece has luster decoration.

Because the base material is soft paste, the ware is subject to cracking and chipping. Enamel colors and other types of decoration do not hold well. It is not unusual to see a piece with the decoration worn off.

**Marks:** Marked pieces are uncommon.

**Additional Listings:** Gaudy Dutch; Salopian Ware; Staffordshire Items.

## Adams Rose

Bowl, 9" d, early, rare size, mint condition ................................. 500.00
Creamer, 5 3/4" h, early ............................................................ 325.00
Cup and Saucer, handleless
    Early................................................................................. 215.00
    Late, rose dec on saucer, blue spatter................................ 115.00
Pitcher, 7" h.............................................................................. 550.00
Plate
    6-7/8" d, two purple luster bands on border.......................... 65.00
    7 1/2" d, single rose, rust and green florals, raised basketweave border, two purple luster bands on border ...................... 125.00
    8 1/2" d, red, blue, green, and black flowers, imp "Adams," wear, minor pinpoints, stains, price for pr ................................. 250.00
    9" d, red, green, and black design ........................................ 75.00
    10 1/2" d, red, green, and black design .............................. 150.00
Platter, 17 5/8" d, early, emb scalloped rim................................ 450.00
Soup Plate, 10 1/4" d ................................................................ 175.00
Sugar Bowl, cov, early ............................................................. 345.00
Teapot, cov, late ...................................................................... 265.00
Vegetable Dish, cov, 12 5/8" d, early ........................................ 500.00

## Creamware

Pitcher, 8" h, polychrome dec, floral swags, sheath of wheat, various farm implements, dated 1793, hairlines, glaze wear, minor base chip................................................................. 1,725.00

Plaque, 5-7/8" h, 5-1/2" l, oval, transfer dec, "Fayette The Nation's Guest," portrait reserve of Lafayette, hairlines, second quarter 19th C.....300.00Plate, 10" d, Last Rites scene, dec for Dutch Market 250.00

Stirrup Cub, 4-7/8" h, figural cow, late 18th C, restored, hairlines.......................................................................345.00

## Design Spatterware

Bowl, 9-1/2" d, serrated rim, blue, white, and black trim.............300.00
Cup and Saucer, floral, blue, green, ochre, and red ...................150.00
Mug, 6" h, rosettes, blue, green bands ......................................100.00
Plate, 9-3/4" d, red concentric center circles, narrow red line border, stars circled in blue ...............................................................145.00

## King's Rose

Creamer, helmet shape, brick red rose.......................................260.00
Cup and Saucer, solid border ....................................................190.00
Plate, 7-1/2" d, vine border ......................................................150.00
Platter, 11" l, pierced edge, hairline crack .................................825.00
Soup Plate, 9" d ......................................................................190.00
Sugar, cov, pink rose................................................................200.00

## Pearlware

Bowl, 14-3/4" d, transfer dec, polychrome dec, various foliate devices, 19th C, hairline, very minor base chip .....................................250.00
Cup and Saucer, handleless
    Bird dec...........................................................................1,240.00
    Floral pattern, yellow and green ..........................................550.00
    Gaudy blue, green, yellow and yellow-ochre floral dec, imp "Wood & Sons," stains and wear .................................................275.00
Cup Plate, free-brushed, eagle dec ...........................................660.00
Pitcher
    Black transfer "Country Lad and Lass" with "Sailor's Farewell" and vase, polychrome enamel and pink luster, wear .......550.00
    Chinoiserie, 6" h, 6-3/4" w handle to lip, vibrant polychrome dec ................................................................................575.00
    Three color, 8-1/4" h ..........................................................990.00
    Plate
        7-1/2" d, blue feather-edge, Peafowl dec .....................600.00
        7-1/2" d, green shell edge, hexagonal, Peafowl dec ..1,210.00
        7-1/2" d, green shell scalloped-edge, pineapple and urn decoration................................................................1,100.00
        7-1/2" d, green shell edge, five color floral dec .........1,705.00
        8-1/4" d, scalloped edge, five color floral, brown band, running vine border...............................................................935.00
        10" d, blue shell edge, bold floral design...................2,860.00
Toddy Plate, 4-1/2" d, chicken transfer .......................................550.00
Wash Bowl and Pitcher, blue, yellow, and tan flowers .............1,595.00

## Strawberry China

Bowl, 6-1/4" d, pink luster, red and green enamel, wide strawberry border, c1820 ......................................................................200.00
Creamer, 6-1/4" h.....................................................................225.00
Cup and Saucer, handleless.......................................................150.00
Plate, 8-1/4" d, Cut Strawberry .................................................225.00
Sugar, cov, raised strawberries, strawberry finial......................225.00

## Yellow Glaze

Child's Mug
    Come Up Donkey, transfer dec, 2" h, second quarter 19th C, minor rim chips, hairlines .............................................375.00
    Polychrome and luster dec .................................................825.00
Child's Teapot, 3-1/2" h, floral dec, spout repaired, hairline crack.....................................................................................635.00
Cup and Saucer, handleless, brown transfer, couple at tea........300.00
Jug, 5-1/4" h, black transfer print, silver-luster dec, inscribed "Accept this trifle from a friend whose love for thee shall never end," and "George Lawton, 1809" under spout ......................................700.00
Cup and Saucer, handleless
    Luster print of mother and children .....................................360.00
    Transfer print of fishing scene............................................495.00
Mug, 2-1/2" h, yellow ground, pink luster dec .............................330.00
Pitcher, bulbous, floral dec........................................................600.00
Plate
    6-1/2" d, floral pattern, yellow border ................................247.50
    7-1/2" d, floral dec, scalloped edge...................................440.00
    8-1/4" d, deep, emb fruit and floral border ......................2,750.00
    8-1/4" d, floral pattern .....................................................415.00
Tea Bowl, 4-3/8" d, repair on base .............................................412.50
Teapot
    6" h, 8" w handle to spout, black transfer, lady with urn in medallion, florals, Staffordshire, minor chips to spout foot rim ..800.00
    7" h, 8-1/2" w handle to spout, black transfer scenic view, Staffordshire...............................................................1,000.00

**Strawberry, plate, pink luster band and vine, 8" d, $70.**

# FAIRINGS, MATCH-STRIKERS, and TRINKET BOXES

**History:** Fairings are small, charming china objects which were purchased or given away as prizes at English fairs in the 19th century. Although fairings are generally identified with England, they actually were manufactured in Germany by Conte and Boehme of Possneck.

Fairings depict an amusing scene, either of courtship and marriage, politics, war, children, or animals behaving as children. More than 400 varieties have been identified. Most fairings include a caption. Early examples, 1860-1870, were of better quality than later ones. After 1890, the colors became more garish, and gilding was introduced.

The manufacturers of fairings also made match safes and trinket boxes. Some of these were also captioned. The figures on the lids were identical to those on fairings. The market for the match safes and trinket boxes was the same as that for the fairings.

**Reference:** Janice and Richard Vogel, *Victorian Trinket Boxes*, published by authors (4720 S.E. Ft. King St., Ocala, FL 34470), 1996.

## Figure

Goat, 3" h, 2-3/4" w, 1-1/4" d, white, brown, and green details...125.00
God Save The Queen, children singing around piano ................365.00
Peep Through A Telescope, sailor and child..............................195.00
Present From Llangollen, bootie shape, Elfin Ware, Dresden, 2-1/2" l, 2" h ............................................................................................95.00

## Trinket Box

Angel and Sleeping child, 3" h, 3" w, 2-1/2" d, hp front and back, c1860, unmarked, attributed to Conte & Boehme ....................375.00
Child and Goose, 4-3/4" h, 3" w, 2" d, child confronting goose, incised "Conte & Boehme" inside lid, c1870, minor loss to mirror........290.00
Child, seated in chair, feeding bird and squirrel, hp front and back, 2-3/4" h, 2-3/4" w, 2" d, c1870, slight chipping to flowers at edges, loss of gold on base.........................................................................265.00
Commode, 2" h, 1-5/8" d, with pitcher, bowl, and tumbler, worn dec .75.00

**Three O'Clock in the Morning,** woman in bed, husband sitting on edge of bed holding baby, 3-5/8"l, 3" h, $245.

Dog, red and white dog reclining on purple pillow, horn and ball, c1870-80, 2-1/2" h, 2-1/2" w, 1-1/2" d .....................................225.00
Monkey in Hat, 3-1/8" h, 2-3/4" w, 2" d, monkey opening hat box, hp monkey, hat bands, and flower centers, incised "Conte & Boehme" inside lid, c1870, some chipping, loss of color.........................265.00
Red Riding Hood, 3" h, 2" l, fading to colors, part of animal next to Red Riding Hood broken and missing ..............................................60.00
Swan, 2" h, 2-1/2" d, worn dec.......................................................75.00
Train Engine, 3" h, 2-3/4" w, 2" d, unmarked, c1870, professional repair, chipping to flowers at edge, loss of gold on base .........190.00
Two Children, 3-3/8" h, 3" w, 1-3/8" d, sleeping girl, holding doll, being awakened by boy blowing a horn, unmarked, attributed to Conte & Boehme, professional repair to horn and boy .........................365.00

# FAIRY LAMPS

**History:** Fairy lamps, which originated in England in the 1840s, are candle-burning night lamps. They were used in nurseries, hallways, and dim corners of the home.

Two leading candle manufacturers, the Price Candle Company and the Samuel Clarke Company, promoted fairy lamps as a means to sell candles. Both contracted with glass, porcelain, and metal manufacturers to produce the needed shades and cups. For example, Clarke used Worcester Royal Porcelain Company, Stuart & Sons, and Red House Glass Works in England, plus firms in France and Germany.

Fittings were produced in a wide variety of styles. Shades ranged from pressed to cut glass, from Burmese to Nailsea. Cups are found in glass, porcelain, brass, nickel, and silver plate.

American firms selling fairy lamps included Diamond Candle Company of Brooklyn, Blue Cross Safety Candle Co., and Hobbs-Brockunier of Wheeling, West Virginia.

Two-piece (cup and shade) and three-piece (cup with matching shade and saucer) fairy lamps can be found. Married pieces are common.

**Marks:** Clarke's trademark was a small fairy with a wand surrounded by the words "Clarke Fairy Pyramid, Trade Mark."

**References:** Bob and Pat Ruf Pullin, *Fairy Lamps*, Schiffer Publishing, 1996; John F. Solverson (comp.), *Those Fascinating Little Lamps: Miniature Lamps Value Guide*, Antique Publications, 1988.

**Periodical:** *Light Revival*, 35 West Elm Ave., Quincy, MA 02170.

**Collectors' Club:** Night Light Club, 38619 Wakefield Ct., Northville, MI 48167.

**Reproduction Alert:** Reproductions abound.

3-1/2" h, figural monkey, natural coloring, amber eyes ...............375.00
4-1/2" h, figural owl's head, frosted green, red enameled eyes, sgd Clarke clear candle holder ......................................................315.00
4-7/8" h, cranberry, Florentine dec, white enamel floral and geometric design, matching base ...........................................................500.00
5" h, Nailsea, blue ground, white loopings, sgd Clarke clear candle holder .....................................................................................385.00
5" h, satin glass, Diamond Quilted shade, sgd Clarke clear candle holder .....................................................................................150.00
5" h, 5-1/2" d, Nailsea, sweeping white loopings, ruby-red ground, dome shade, bowl-shaped base, clear candle cup holder sgd "S.

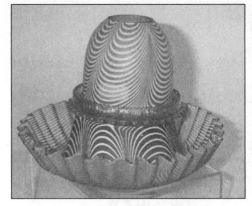

Nailsea, light blue ground, white loopings, clear mkd Clarke base, 5" h, $395. Photo courtesy of Joy Luke Fine Art Brokers and Auctioneers.

Vase, Mandarian figures in reserves, c1820, 10-1/2" h, $600.

Clarke Patent Trade Mark Fairy" .............................................. 985.00
5" h, 6-1/2" h, Verre Moire, profuse white loopings over citron, dome shade, bowl-shaped base with turned up sides with 36 piecrust crimped pleats around rim, clear glass candle cup holder sgd "Clarke's Criklite Trade Mark" .................................................... 985.00
5-1/4" h, peachblow, sgd Clarke clear candle holder .................. 265.00
5-1/2" h, 5-3/4" d, Burmese, Webb, slight blush of color, crimped base sgd "Thomas Webb & Sons Queens Burmese-Ware" ........... 1,285.00
7" h x 7" d, cut glass, cranberry cut to clear, Russian, cane, and prism motif, Clarke inserts .................................................... 1,350.00
5-3/4" h, 8-1/2" d, ruby red Criklite, profuse white loopings, dome shaped shade, bowl shaped base with eight turned-up/turned down scallops, clear glass candle cup sgd "S. Clarke Patent Trade Mark Fairy" ....................................................................... 1,135.00

# FAMILLE ROSE

**History:** Famille Rose is Chinese export enameled porcelain on which the pink color predominates. It was made primarily in the 18th and 19th centuries. Other porcelains in the same group are Famille Jaune (yellow), Famille Noire (black), and Famille Verte (green).

Decorations include courtyard and home scenes, birds, and insects. Secondary colors are yellow, green, blue, aubergine, and black.

Rose Canton, Rose Mandarin, and Rose Medallion are mid- to late 19th-century Chinese export wares which are similar to Famille Rose.

**Famille Noir,** vase, 19" h, sq form, birds and flower landscapes, China, 19th C460.00

## Famille Rose

Basin, 17" d, multicolored scene of pheasants perched on pierced rockwork, peonies and chrysanthemums, cavetto border with suspended pomegranates alternating with ruyi heads, stylized hibiscus blossoms with gilt highlights, four iron-red peony sprigs on underside ....................................................................... 10,750.00
Bowl
7-1/4" h, Boys' Festival, Qianlong seal mark, 20th C .......... 235.00
10" w, 5" h, sq, pink, purple, iron red, and green sprig dec, gilt highlights, Chinese Export, early 19th C, glaze wear, price for pr .......................................................................... 920.00
Figure, 8-1/2" h, rooster, early 20th C, price for pr .............. 215.00
Jar, cov, 22" h, reserves from *Story of the Stone,* leaf-shaped reserves on green ground with flowers, China, 18th C, price for pr ..... 4,320.00
Jardiniere, 20-1/2" d, foo lion mask handles, China, late 19th/early 20th C, price for pr ......................................................... 3,740.00
Plate
9-1/8" d, octagonal, round, floral center, gilt spearhead border, Chinese Export, late 18th C, rim chips, glaze wear, hairline ....... 160.00
9-1/8" d, round, floral center, gilt spearhead border, Chinese Export, late 18th C, rim chips, glaze wear ....................... 190.00
Tankard, 6" h, cylindrical, rose, iron-red, turquoise, green, and blue, trailing branch of flowering peonies, iron-red scalloped band, ribbed base, brown rim with gilt blossoms and leaves, S-scroll handle, iron-red heart shaped terminal, c1745 ........................................... 750.00
Tureen, cov, 15" w, octagonal, armorial, hare's head handles, pomegranate finial, painted iron-red, turquoise, pale green, yellow, and blue opaque enamels, cartouche-shaped coat of arms below rampant lion crest, c1750 .................................................. 11,500.00
Vase
12" h, finely enameled dec of children playing, Ch'ia Ching mark, but probably Republican period, c1910, price for pr ........ 460.00
24" h, bottle form, dec with magpies, flowering trees, ling chih, China, 19th C ................................................... 2,185.00

## Famille Verte
Vase
14" h, rocks, birds, and flowering trees, China, 19th C, price for pr .......................................................................... 450.00
17" h, 9" d, baluster, each façade with large floral, avian scene, separated by multiple floral reserves on ice-blue vermicule ground, Kuang-Hsu, c1880-90 ........................................ 770.00
17-3/4" h, baluster, warriors in garden scenes, China, late 19th C .......................................................................... 450.00
19-1/4" h, sq form, seasonal flowers and birds, artemesia leaf mark on base in underglaze blue, K'ang Hsi period, 1662-1722 ............................................................. 5,750.00

# FENTON GLASS

**History:** The Fenton Art Glass Company began as a cutting shop in Martins Ferry, Ohio, in 1905. In 1906 Frank L. Fenton started to build a plant in Williamstown, West Virginia, and produced the first piece of glass there in 1907. Early production included carnival, chocolate, custard, and pressed glass, plus mold-blown opalescent glass. In the 1920s stretch glass, Fenton dolphins, jade green, ruby, and art glass were added.

In the 1930s, boudoir lamps, Dancing Ladies, and slag glass in various colors were produced. The 1940s saw crests of different colors being added to each piece by hand. Hobnail, opalescent, and two-color overlay pieces were popular items. Handles were added to different shapes, making the baskets they created as popular then as they are today.

Through the years Fenton has beautified their glass by decorating it with hand painting, acid etching, and copper-wheel cutting

**Marks:** Several different paper labels have been used. In 1970, an oval raised trademark also was adopted.

**References:** Tom and Neila Bredehoft, *Fifty Years of Collectible Glass, 1920-1970, Volumes I and II,* Antique Trader Books, 2000; Robert E. Eaton, Jr., (comp.), *Fenton Glass: The First Twenty-Five Years Comprehensive Price Guide 1998,* Glass Press, 1998; —, *Fenton Glass: The Second Twenty-Five Years Comprehensive Price Guide 1998,* Glass Press, 1998; *Fenton Glass: The Third Twenty-Five Years Comprehensive Price Guide, 1998,* Glass Press, 1998; William Heacock, *Fenton Glass: The First Twenty-Five Years* (1978), *The Second Twenty-Five Years* (1980), *The Third Twenty-Five Years* (1989), available from Antique Publications; Alan Linn, *Fenton Story of Glass Making,* Antique Publications, 1996; James Measell (ed.), *Fenton Glass: The 1980s Decade,* Antique Publications, 1996; Naomi L. Over, *Ruby Glass of the 20th Century,* Antique Publications, 1990, 1993-94 value update, —, *Book II,* Antique Publications, 1999; Ferill J. Rice (ed.), *Caught in the Butterfly Net,* Fenton Art Glass Collectors of America, Inc., 1991; John Walk, *The Big Book of Fenton Glass, 1940-1970, Revised 2nd Edition,* Schiffer, 1999; Margaret and Kenn Whitmyer, *Fenton Art Glass 1907-1939,* Collector Books, 1996, 1999 value update; —, *Fenton Art Glass, 1939-1980,* Collector Books, 1996, 2000 value update; —, *Fenton Art Glass Patterns 1939-1980,* Collector Books, 1999.

**Periodical:** *Butterfly Net,* 302 Pheasant Run, Kaukauna, WI 54130.

**Collectors' Clubs:** Fenton Art Glass Collectors Of America, Inc., P.O. Box 384, Williamstown, WV 26187; National Fenton Glass Society, P.O. Box 4008, Marietta, OH 45750; Pacific Northwest Fenton Association, 8225 Kilchis River Rd, Tillamook, OR 97141.

**Videotape:** *Making Fenton Glass, 1992,* Fenton Art Glass Co. Museum, 1992.

**Museum:** Fenton Art Glass Co., Williamstown, WV.

**Advisor:** Ferill J. Rice.

**Additional Listings:** Carnival Glass.

Ashtray
   #3648 OR Ball, Colonial Orange ...........................................15.00
   #3877 French Opalescent Hobnail octagon ashtray, medium
     size.................................................................................... 45.00
   #3877 Jonquil Yellow Hobnail octagon ashtray, medium
     size.................................................................................... 75.00
   #3773 MI Pipe ash tray, milk glass hobnail........................ 115.00
   #5175 Crystal Velvet Pelican, Ca: 1978 .............................. 45.00
   Blue Opalescent Hobnail, nesting ashtray set (3)................50.00
Basket
   #1616 Pink Ming, wicker handle .......................................... 95.00
   #7257 Burmese, 10 " hand painted roses........................... 125.00

**Bell, Rosaline, orig paper label, c1970, 7" h, $35.**

   #7446 6-1/2" milk, mauve roses inside, dtd. 7-25-88, hand
     painted, Louise Piper .........................................................175.00
   7" Chocolate Roses on Cameo Satin, hand painted, Louise
     Piper................................................................................65.00
Bell
   #7565 BD Blue Dogwood on Cameo Satin...........................75.00
   #7667 EE, "Majestic Flight" on White Satin ........................95.00
   #7667 TL, "Smoke & Cinders" on white satin .....................85.00
   #8267 BC Bluebirds on custard, medallion...........................30.00
   #9065 Cameo Opal Sable Arches .......................................30.00
   #9168 Bride & Groom Bell, White Satin................................30.00
Bottle
   "Gems" Blue Opalescent made for DeVilbiss & made into oil
     lamp .....................................................................................75.00
   1934 Wine, Flower Stopper, c1935.....................................125.00
Bowl
   #249, 7-1/2" Snow Fern, cupped, ftd ..................................195.00
   #950 Centerpiece Bowl, Mongolian Green ..........................165.00
   #5626 TUI, 8-1/2" w, Turquoise Block & Star.......................32.00
   #7424 Rose, Violets on Burmese, small (LeVay)...............125.00
   #8223 LS Rose, Lime Sherbet, Leaf & Orange Tree ...........38.00
   #8226 BA Planter or Hexagon .............................................95.00
Candy Jar or Box
   #3886 MB Hobnail w/lid ......................................................35.00
   #9088 Lime Sherbet Wild Strawberry Candy Box ...............95.00
Candlesticks
   #1523 Cornucopia, Ivory Crest, pr......................................150.00

#3570 SC Spanish Lace, Milk Glass ................................... 45.00
#318 Cameo Opalescent, pr ........................................... 50.00
Three hole Butterfly Candleholder, Ruby iridized, FAGCA
1989 ................................................................ 125.00
Comport
#1533 6" Crimp, Dolphin, Jade .......................................35.00
#7252 DB, Scenic Burmese 7", signed "Louise Piper" ....... 165.00
#8476 Jefferson, Independence Blue ...............................95.00
Blue Opalescent, 11", ftd ...........................................60.00
Holly, red, 6" ruffled, Carnival .................................... 750.00
Creamer, Aqua Crest, crimped top ..................................... 60.00
Fairy Light
#2092 Blue Burmese, 1 pc. (for FAGCA) ........................... 175.00
#2092 Green Swirled Feather, 1 pc ................................. 390.00
#5108 BA Owl .......................................................65.00
#7501 PD Burmese, Pink Dogwood, 3 pc ......................... 225.00
#9401 FT Nativity Florentine Blue ...................................45.00
Figurine
#5151 Bear Cub, Blue Burmese, shiny .............................60.00
#5160 Fawn, Ruby ...................................................30.00
#5197 PY happiness Bird, Pink Blossom .............................45.00
#5418 Mouse, Blue Burmese, iridized ...............................50.00
Marigold Carnival Butterfly Ornament........................... 1,000.00
Twilight Blue iridized Happy Cat (FACGA) ..........................65.00
Flower Pot, with underplate, Jade
#1554, small .........................................................55.00
#1555, large ..........................................................65.00
Hat
#1923 Cranberry Snowcrest .........................................65.00
Holly, 2 sided, red, Carnival ........................................ 950.00
Hobnail
#3746 Milk Glass, Egg Cup .........................................125.00
#3837 RW Milk Glass 7" h, Basket with Roses &
Forget-Me-Nots ................................................60.00
#3904, Milk Glass, of four napkin rings, orig box ............... 200.00
Jug or Pitcher
#8964 Turquoise Hanging Heart, c1976 ........................... 350.00
Blue Overlay Melon Ribbed 5-1/4" h, squatty jug ................55.00
Lamp
#9101 24" Gone-With-The-Wind, Poppy, Lavender Satin .. 450.00
#9101 24" Gone-With-The-Wind, Poppy, Lime Sherbet ..... 250.00
Oil, Custard Satin, Poppy ........................................... 200.00
Lavabo, #3867 Wild Rose, 3 pcs ..................................... 495.00
Macaroon Jar, #1681, Big Cookies, 7" h, c1933
Jade Green .........................................................95.00
Lilac ................................................................ 250.00
Mongolian Green ................................................... 185.00
Periwinkle Blue .................................................... 250.00
Perfume Bottle, Cranberry satin, Swirled Feather .................. 250.00
Plate
Peacock/UM, Blue Carnival ........................................ 500.00
10" d, 1938, Lincoln Inn pattern, Marietta, OH, Crystal ...... 150.00
Powder Box, Cranberry satin, Swirled Feather.................... 340.00
Praying Boy & Girl
#5100 LN Lavender Satin ...........................................60.00
#5100 VE Crystal Velvet ............................................35.00
Salt and Pepper Shakers, pr
#2206 Polka Dot, Cranberry Opalescent, 1955 ....................99.00
#4408 Thumbprint, Colonial Blue ..................................30.00
Sherbet, #1620 Amber Plymouth......................................16.00
Sugar, #9100 Jacqueline, Honey Amber ..............................30.00
Tobacco Jar, cov, #9188 Grape & Cable
Colonial Orange ....................................................95.00
Rosalene............................................................ 135.00
Vase
#183 7" h, Wild Rose Satin etched ................................ 150.00
#183 8" Crystal, San Toy ...........................................55.00
#184 12" Jade, c1931 ...............................................55.00
#3758 PO Plum Opalescent Hobnail 12" medium swung... 115.00

#9155 BA 8" Blue Satin ............................................... 55.00
Bittersweet, 8" h, off-hand, center hole, sample from Robert Barber era, c1976 ...................................................... 725.00
Peachblow Barcelona ................................................. 135.00

# FIESTA

**History:** The Homer Laughlin China Company introduced Fiesta dinnerware in January 1936 at the Pottery and Glass Show in Pittsburgh, Pennsylvania. Frederick Rhead designed the pattern; Arthur Kraft and Bill Bensford molded it. Dr. A. V. Bleininger and H. W. Thiemecke developed the glazes.

The original five colors were red, dark blue, light green (with a trace of blue), brilliant yellow, and ivory. A vigorous marketing campaign took place between 1939 and 1943. In mid-1937, turquoise was added. Red was removed in 1943 because some of the chemicals used to produce it were essential to the war effort; it did not reappear until 1959. In 1951, light green, dark blue, and ivory were retired and forest green, rose, chartreuse, and gray were added to the line. Other color changes took place in the late 1950s, including the addition of a medium green.

Fiesta ware was redesigned in 1969 and discontinued about 1972. In 1986, Fiesta was reintroduced by Homer Laughlin China Company. The new china body shrinks more than the old semi-vitreous and ironstone pieces, thus making the new pieces slightly smaller than the earlier pieces. The modern colors are also different in tone or hue, e.g., the cobalt blue is darker than the old blue. Other modern colors are black, white, apricot, and rose.

**References:** Susan and Al Bagdade, *Warman's American Pottery and Porcelain*, 2nd ed., Krause Publications, 2000; Mark Gonzalez, *Collecting Fiesta, Lu-Ray & Other Colorware,* L-W Books Sales, 2000; Homer Laughlin China Collectors Association, *Fiesta, Harlequin, Kitchen Kraft Tablewares,* Schiffer Publishing, 2000; Sharon and Bob Huxford, *Collector's Encyclopedia of Fiesta*, 8th ed., Collector Books, 1998; Ronald E. Kay and Kathleen M. Taylor, *Finding Fiesta: A Comprehensive Price Guide,* Fiesta Club of America, Inc., 1998 (P.O. Box 15383, Loves Park, IL 61132-5383; Richard Racheter, *Post 86 Fiesta Identification and Value Guide,* Collector Books, 2000; Jeffrey B. Snyder, *Fiesta, Homer Laughlin China Company's Colorful Dinnerware,* 3rd ed., Schiffer Publishing, 2000.

**Collectors' Clubs:** Fiesta Club of America, P.O. Box 15383, Loves Park, IL 61132-5383; Fiesta Collectors Club, 19238 Dorchester Circle, Strongsville, OH 44136; Fiesta Collector's Quarterly, P.O. Box 471, Valley City, OH 44280.

Reproduction Alert.

**Additional Listings:** See *Warman's Americana & Collectibles* for more examples.

After Dinner Coffeepot, cov, stick handle
    Cobalt Blue ............................................................550.00
    Light Green, 8" h..................................................375.00
After Dinner Cup and Saucer
    Charcoal ..............................................................550.00
    Chartreuse ...........................................................625.00
    Cobalt blue ............................................................95.00
    Gray ......................................................................550.00
    Green .....................................................................85.00
    Ivory ......................................................................25.00
    Yellow, 2-1/2" h cup, 5" d saucer .........................80.00
Ashtray, Ivory, 5" d ......................................................75.00
Bowl
    5-1/2" d, green, small chip ...................................75.00
    8-1/4" d, Green, wear to glaze ...........................125.00
Bud Vase, yellow, 6-1/2" h, 3" d ................................60.00
Cake Plate, green .................................................1,950.00
Candlesticks, pr
    Bulb
        Ivory..............................................................125.00
        Turquoise......................................................110.00
    Tripod
        Cobalt blue ...................................................950.00
        Turquoise......................................................890.00
        Yellow ...........................................................550.00
Carafe
    Turquoise ............................................................380.00
    Yellow...................................................................275.00
Casserole, cov
    Red .......................................................................275.00
    Turquoise .............................................................135.00
Casserole, French
    Yellow...................................................................275.00
Chop Plate, 13" d
    Gray .......................................................................95.00
    Ivory ......................................................................45.00
Coffeepot, cov, Turquoise Blue, 10-1/2" h...............275.00
Comport, 12" d, Ivory, mkd........................................225.00
Creamer, ring handle, 3" h, 6" w
    Green ...................................................................115.00
    Rose ......................................................................40.00
Creamer, stick handle
    Ivory ......................................................................75.00
    Red .........................................................................75.00
    Turquoise .............................................................115.00
    Yellow.....................................................................45.00
Cream Soup
    Gray .......................................................................60.00
    Ivory ......................................................................60.00
    Rose ......................................................................95.00
Cup
    Cobalt blue............................................................35.00
    Dark green ............................................................45.00
    Light green ............................................................25.00
    Medium green .......................................................70.00
    Turquoise ..............................................................25.00
    Yellow....................................................................25.00
Dessert Bowl, 6" d
    Chartreuse .............................................................55.00
    Red .........................................................................45.00
    Rose ......................................................................45.00
    Yellow....................................................................40.00
Egg Cup
    Green .....................................................................50.00
    Red .........................................................................70.00
Fruit Bowl, 4-3/4" d
    Cobalt blue............................................................25.00
    Medium green .....................................................550.00
Fruit Bowl, Turquoise, 11-1/4" w, 7-1/2" h, some flakes and
   hairlines ..................................................................220.00

Gravy Boat, 8" l
    Ivory ......................................................................20.00
    Turquoise ..............................................................45.00
Gravy Pitcher, Gray, 32 oz.........................................125.00
Juice Pitcher, Celadon green, 6" h..............................385.00
Juice Tumbler, 4" h
    Ivory ......................................................................60.00
    Rose ......................................................................65.00
    Yellow....................................................................40.00
Marmalade, cov, Cobalt Blue, 3" h, some chips to lid ...............285.00
Mixing Bowl
    #1, cobalt blue ...................................................375.00
    #2, cobalt blue ...................................................195.00
    #2, red, 6" d, 4" h, mkd "Fiesta Made in USA 2"..................90.00
    #2, yellow ............................................................140.00
    #4, green .............................................................195.00
    #5, ivory ..............................................................275.00
    #7, ivory ..............................................................580.00
Mug
    Dark green ............................................................90.00
    Gray, 3" h, 1950s .................................................80.00
    Medium Green .....................................................110.00
    Rose .....................................................................125.00
    Yellow, 3" h ...........................................................85.00
Nappy, 5-1/2" d, turquoise...........................................25.00
Onion Soup, cov
    Green ...................................................................895.00
    Ivory ....................................................................950.00
Pitcher, disk
    Sapphire Blue, 7-1/2" h .....................................150.00
    Turquoise, 7" h ...................................................145.00
    Yellow, 7-1/2" h ..................................................150.00
Pitcher, ice lip
    Green ...................................................................135.00
    Turquoise .............................................................195.00
Plate, deep
    Gray .......................................................................42.00
    Rose ......................................................................42.00
Plate, 6" d
    Dark green ............................................................13.00
    Ivory ........................................................................7.00
    Light green ..............................................................9.00
    Turquoise ................................................................8.00
    Yellow......................................................................5.00
Plate, 7" d
    Chartreuse .............................................................14.00
    Ivory ......................................................................10.00
    Light green ..............................................................8.50
    Medium green .......................................................40.00
    Rose ......................................................................15.00
    Turquoise ................................................................8.50
Plate, 9" d
    Cobalt blue............................................................17.00

Onion Soup, cov, turquoise, $11,000. New record set by auctioneer Michael G. Strawser.

| | |
|---|---|
| Red | 18.00 |
| Yellow | 10.00 |

Plate, 10" d, dinner

| | |
|---|---|
| Gray | 42.00 |
| Light green | 28.00 |
| Medium green | 125.00 |
| Red | 35.00 |
| Turquoise | 30.00 |

Plate, 15" d, cobalt blue ........ 62.00

Platter, oval

| | |
|---|---|
| Gray | 35.00 |
| Ivory | 25.00 |
| Red | 45.00 |
| Yellow | 22.00 |

Relish Tray, yellow base, red, cobalt, and two green trays, cobalt blue center dish, 11" d, some roughness to base ........ 300.00

Salt and Pepper Shakers, pr, round, rose, 2-1/2" h, 2-1/2" d ........ 50.00

Saucer

| | |
|---|---|
| Light green | 5.00 |
| Turquoise | 5.00 |

Soup Plate

| | |
|---|---|
| Ivory | 36.00 |
| Turquoise | 29.00 |

Sugar Bowl, cov

| | |
|---|---|
| Chartreuse | 65.00 |
| Gray | 75.00 |
| Rose | 75.00 |

Syrup

| | |
|---|---|
| Green | 450.00 |
| Ivory | 600.00 |
| Red | 795.00 |

Sweets Compote, yellow ........ 65.00

Tea Cup, flat bottom, cobalt blue ........ 100.00

Teapot, cov

| | |
|---|---|
| Cobalt blue, large | 335.00 |
| Green, chips on lid, flakes on spout | 175.00 |
| Rose, medium, 7" h | 225.00 |

Tumbler, 5" h

| | |
|---|---|
| Cobalt blue | 75.00 |
| Green | 85.00 |

Utility Tray, red ........ 55.00

Vase

| | |
|---|---|
| 8" h, green | 595.00 |
| 10" h, cobalt blue | 850.00 |
| 12" h, yellow | 950.00 |

# FIGURAL BOTTLES

**History:** Porcelain figural bottles, which have an average height of three to eight and were made either in a glazed or bisque finish, achieved popularity in the late 1800s and remained popular into the 1930s. The majority of figural bottles were made in Germany, with Austria and Japan accounting for the balance.

Empty figural bottles were shipped to the United States and filled upon arrival. They were then given away to customers by brothels, dance halls, hotels, liquor stores, and taverns. Some were lettered with the names and addresses of the establishment, others had paper labels. Many were used for holidays, e.g., Christmas and New Year.

Figural bottles also were made in glass and other materials. The glass bottles held perfumes, food, or beverages.

**References:** Ralph & Terry Kovel, *Kovels' Bottles Price List, 11th ed.,* Three Rivers Press, 1999; Kenneth Wilson,

*American Glass 1760-1930*, 2 vols., Hudson Hills Press and The Toledo Museum of Art, 1994.

**Periodical:** *Antique Bottle and Glass Collector*, P.O. Box 187, East Greenville, PA 18041.

**Collectors' Clubs:** Federation of Historical Bottle Clubs, 88 Sweetbriar Branch, Longwood, FL 32750; New England Antique Bottle Club, 120 Commonwealth Rd, Lynn, MA 01904.

**Museums:** National Bottle Museum, Ballston Spa, NY; National Bottle Museum, Barnsley, S Yorkshire, England; Old Bottle Museum, Salem, NJ.

Barrel Form, 4-7/8" h, yellow olive green, fancy rigaree trailing around body, two sleigh runner feet serve as base, each emb with repeating sunburst motif, tooled mouth, pontil scar, Europe, 18th C ........ 450.00

Bear, 10-5/8" h, dense yellow amber, sheared mouth, applied face, Russia, 1860-80, flat chip on back ........ 400.00

Big Stick, Teddy Roosevelt's, 7-1/2" h, golden amber, sheared mouth, smooth base, flat flake at mouth ........ 170.00

Boy crying against brick wall, "I'm So Discouraged" ........ 100.00

Fish, 11-1/2" h, "Doctor Fisch's Bitters," golden amber, applied small round collared mouth, smooth base, America, 1860-80, some ext. highpoint wear, burst bubble on base ........ 160.00

Garfield, James, President, 8" h, colorless glass bust set in turned wood base, ground mouth, smooth base, America, 1880-1900. 80.00

Huntsman with snooty dog, comical expression, Goebel crown mark, 10" h ........ 275.00

Indian Maiden, 12-1/4" h, "Brown's Celebrated Indian Herb Bitters," yellow amber, inward rolled mouth, smooth base, America, 1860-80 ........ 600.00

Man, Toasting Your Health, flask shape, bisque front, tree bark back, 4-1/2" x 4" ........ 40.00

One of the Boys, man in tux, tall stool, Schafer & Vater ........ 165.00

Pig, pottery, Kirkpatrick Brothers, Anna, Illinois; incised "From the World's Fair/ With a little good Old Rye in [arrow] 1893/Cut Rates/To All Points East," 7-1/4" l ........ 1,760.00

Pig, Suffolk Bitters, America, 1860-90, shaded yellow amber, applied double collared mouth, smooth base, 10-1/8" l, minor ext. high point wear ........ 750.00

Pineapple, 8-3/4" h, "W & Co./N.Y.," America, 1845-60, brilliant yellow green with strong olive tone, applied double collard mouth, iron pontil mark, 8" meandering crack through body ........ 425.00

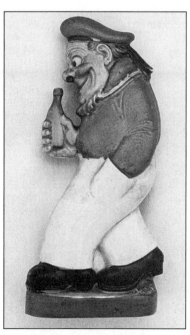

**Sailor, high gloss front, white pants, blue blouse, and hat, mkd "Made in Germany," 6-1/2" h, $50.**

Shoe, dark amethyst, ground mouth, smooth base .................... 125.00
Washington, George, 10" h, "Simon's Centennial Bitters," aquamarine,
applied double collared mouth, smooth base, America,
1860-80 ................................................................................. 650.00

# FINDLAY ONYX GLASS

**History:** Findlay onyx glass, produced by Dalzell, Gilmore & Leighton Company, Findlay, Ohio, was patented for the firm in 1889 by George W. Leighton. Due to high production costs resulting from a complex manufacturing process, the glass was made only for a short time.

Layers of glass were plated to a bulb of opalescent glass through repeated dippings into a glass pot. Each layer was cooled and reheated to develop opalescent qualities. A pattern mold then was used to produce raised decorations of flowers and leaves. A second mold gave the glass bulb its full shape and form.

A platinum luster paint, producing pieces identified as silver or platinum onyx, was applied to the raised decorations. The color was fixed in a muffle kiln. Other colors such as cinnamon, cranberry, cream, raspberry, and rose were achieved by using an outer glass plating which reacted strongly to reheating. For example, a purple or orchid color came from the addition of manganese and cobalt to the glass mixture.

**References:** Neila and Tom Bredenhoft, *Findlay Toothpick Holders*, Cherry Hill Publications, 1995; James Measell and Don E. Smith, *Findlay Glass: The Glass Tableware Manufacturers, 1886-1902*, Antique Publications, 1986.

**Collectors' Club:** Collectors of Findlay Glass, P.O. Box 256, Findlay, OH 45839.

Bowl
    7" d, 2-3/4" h, silver onyx ..................................................... 320.00
    7-1/2" d, cream onyx ............................................................. 390.00
    7-1/2" d, raspberry onyx ....................................................... 425.00
Butter Dish, cov, 5-1/2" d, silver onyx ......................................... 850.00
Celery, cream onyx, gold florals ................................................... 400.00
Cream Pitcher
    4-1/2" h, platinum blossoms, cream onyx ........................... 550.00
    4-3/4" h, cinnamon onyx ................................................... 5,675.00
Jar, cov, 6" h, silver blossoms, cream onyx ............................... 995.00
Mustard, cov, 3" h, hinged metal cov, orig spoon mkd "sterling"
    Cream onyx .......................................................................... 400.00
    Raspberry onyx .................................................................... 600.00
Pitcher, 8" h, cream onyx, amber florals and handle, minor bubbles in
inner liner ................................................................................. 700.00
Salt and Pepper Shakers, pr, 3" h, platinum onyx ...................... 550.00
Spooner, 4-1/4" h, platinum blossoms, raspberry ground ........ 3,495.00
Sugar Bowl, cov, 5-1/2" h
    Cream onyx .......................................................................... 475.00
    Raspberry onyx .................................................................... 650.00
Sugar Shaker, 6" h, silver onyx ................................................... 400.00
Toothpick Holder, 2-1/2" h, cinnamon onyx ................................ 425.00
Tumbler, raspberry onyx, Floradine pattern ................................ 785.00

# FINE ARTS

**History:** Perhaps it was first the cave man who decided to brighten his surroundings with paintings. No one is sure at what point, but some one cleverly made his paintings on canvas or other mediums that could be moved from abode to abode. Today we find paintings and all types of fine arts at almost every auction, antique show, flea market, and antique shop.

In any calendar year, tens, if not hundreds of thousands of paintings are sold. Prices range from a few dollars to millions. Since each painting is essentially a unique creation, it is difficult to compare prices.

Since an essential purpose of *Warman's Antiques and Collectibles Price Guide* is to assist its users in finding information about a category, this Fine Arts introduction has been written primarily to identify the reference books that you will need to find out more about a painting in your possession. The listings of American Paintings that follow are to give a general idea of paintings sold at auction recently.

**Artist dictionaries:** *1999 ADEC International Art Price Annual,* ADEC, 1999; E. H. H. Archibald, *The Dictionary of Sea Painters of Europe and America,* Antique Collectors' Club, 1999; Russell Ash, *Impressionists' Seasons,* Pavilion, 1999; Emmanuel Benezit, *Dictionnaire Critique et Documentaire des Peintres, Sculpteurs, Dessinateurs et Graveurs*, 10 volumes, Grund, 1999; John Castagno, *Old Masters: Signatures and Monograms,* Scarecrow Press, 1996; Ian Chilvers, *Concise Oxford Dictionary of Arts & Artists,* 2nd ed., Oxford University Press, 1996; Peter Hastings Falk, *Dictionary of Signatures & Monograms of American Artists,* Sound View Press, 1998; Mantle Fielding, *Dictionary of American Painters, Sculptors and Engravers,* Apollo Books, 1983; Franklin & James, *1988-1998 Decade Review of American Artists at Auction,* Franklin & James, 1999; Christine E. Jackson, *Dictionary of Bird Artists of the World,* Antique Collectors' Club, 1999; David Joel, *Charles Brooking and the 18th Century British Marine Painters,* Antique Collectors' Club, 1999; J. Johnson and A. Greutzner, *Dictionary of British Artists, 1880-1940: An Antique Collector's Club Research Project Listing 41,000 Artists,* Antique Collector's Club, 1976; Blake McKendry, *A to Z of Canadian Artists & Art Terms,* published by author, 1997.

**Introductory information:** Alan Bamberger, *Buy Art Smart,* Wallace-Homestead Book Company, 1990; ——, *How to Buy Fine Art You Can Afford*, Wallace-Homestead, 1994.

**Price guide references, basic:** *Art at Auction in America,* 1998 ed., Krexpress, 1998; William T. Currier (comp.), *Currier's Price Guide to American Artists 1645–1945 at Auction,* 6th ed., Currier Publications, 1994; —— (comp.), *Currier's Price Guide to European Artists 1545–1945 at Auction,* 4th ed., Currier Publications, 1994.

**Price guide references, advanced:** R. J. Davenport, *1999-2000 Davenport's Art Reference & Price Guide,* Davenport Publishing, 1998; Peter Hastings Falk (ed.), *Art Price Index International '98,* Sound View Press, 1998; Richard Hislop (ed.), *Annual Art Sales Index,* 28th ed., Art Sales Index Ltd., 1996; Enrique Mayer, *International Auction Record,* Paris, Editions Enrique Mayer, since 1967; Judith and Martin Miller (comps. & eds.), *Miller's Picture*

*Price Guide*, Millers Publications, 1994; Susan Theran (ed.), *Leonard's Price Index of Art Auctions*, Auction Index, since 1980.

**Museum directories:** *American Art Directory*, R. R. Bowker, 1995; American Association of Museums, *Official Museum Directory: United States and Canada*, R. R. Bowker, updated periodically.

**Collectors' Club:** American Art Collectors, 610 N Delaware Ave., Roswell, NM 88201.

Albright, Henry J., *The Mystic Pool,* oil on board, wisteria blossoms overhanging pond at sunset, Impressionist style, carved period frame, sgd on front, reverse with ink name, title, and "Glenmount, NY," 20" x 16" ................................................... 1,800.00

Baker, Ernest, (19th C), *New York Harbor,* sgd and dated "Ernest Baker '79," titled in inscription on stretcher, oil on canvas, 29" x 48", framed, lined, retouched ........................ 1,495.00

Baker, George A., (1821-1880)
  *Portrait of a Young Lady in a White and Blue Gown and Holding a Rose,* sgd and dated "G. A. Baker 1809" center right, faint canvas stencil on reverse, inscribed on stretcher, oil on canvas, 27-1/4" x 22", ornately carved period (repainted) frame, repaired puncture lower right, craquelure.................................. 1,380.00
  *The Lavender Ribbon/A Portrait,* sgd and dated "G. A. Baker 1869" center left, canvas stencil on reverse, oil on canvas, 27" x 22", ornate carved period frame.................................. 1,265.00

Batcheller, Frederick S., (1837-1889)
  *Greetings from Across the Field,* genre scene with children, sgd "Batcheller" lower right, oil on canvas, 16" x 24", framed ...1,495.00
  *Landscape with Grazing Cattle,* sgd "Batcheller" lower left, oil on canvas, 16" x 24", framed ................................................ 3,335.00
  *Still Life with Grapes,* sgd "Batcheller" lower left, oil on canvas, 12" x 18", framed, strip lined, scattered retouch, craquelure .......3,335.00

Baum, Walter E.
  *Autumn Landscape,* sgd "W. E. Baum" lower right, oil on panel, 4" x 6", framed .................................................................. 3,850.00
  *Pennsylvania Dutch Village,* "W. E. Baum" lower left, oil on canvas, winter scene, 25" x 30", framed........................... 22,200.00
  *Pennsylvania Scene,* sgd "W. E. Baum" lower right, oil on canvas, winter scene, 30" x 36", framed ................................. 38,500.00
  *River Landscape in Autumn,* sgd "Baum" lower right, oil on canvas, 1940 gift dedication on stretcher bat, 16" x 20", framed.....4,400.00
  *Springtime Landscape,* sgd "W. E. Baum" lower left, oil on board, 10" x 8".................................................................. 2,860.00
  *Tylersport 1944,* sgd "W. E. Baum/1944" lower left, oil on canvas, winter scene, 20" x 30", framed ..................................... 13,750.00

Blackburn, Morris, (1902-1979), *Abstract Harbor,* sgd and dated '47 lower left, gouache on paper, 19" x 25"................................. 1,680.00

Brackett, Walter M., (1852-1910), *Trout, Rod and Reel on a Riverbank,* sgd and dated "W.M. Brackett 1894" lower left, oil on canvas, 20" x 32", framed................................................................. 18,400.00

Bradford, William, (1823-1892), *Midnight Sun in Norway,* sgd and dated "Wm Bradford '79" lower right, identified on label on reverse, oil on canvas, 18-1/4" x 30", period frame........................... 21,850.00

Brown, George Loring, (1814-1889), *Old Maccaroni* [sic] *Mill in the Gorge at Amalphi* [sic], sgd "Geo. L. Brown" lower left, titled, sgd, identified, dated "...Gulf of Salerno, Italy by Geo. L. Brown 1877" on reverse, oil on canvas, 22" x 36, scattered retouch, prevalent craquelure to sky .................................................................. 2,875.00

Campbell, Hugh, (20th C), *After A Shower,* sgd and dated "H. Campbell 44" lower right, titled, sgd, dated, and inscribed "...Summer 1944 Below Seaside Park by Hugh H. Campbell of Mt. Holly NJ" in pencil on reverse, oil on canvas, 27" x 40", retouched, scattered craquelure..........4,600.00

Clime, Winfield Scott, (1881-1958), *Yellow Barn,* sgd "Winfield Scott Clime" lower left, sgd, titled, and inscribed "...Old Lyme Connecticut Bright 1947" on reverse, oil on canvas board, 20" x 23-3/4", framed, varnish inconsistencies ........................................................ 2,185.00

Coppedge, Fern I., (1883-1951)
  *Gloucester Harbor Scene,* sgd "Fern I. Coppedge" lower left, oil on canvas, dusk scene, 25" x 20", framed .................. 20,350.00
  *Twin Churches Overlooking Delaware River,* sgd "Fern I. Coppedge" lower left, oil on canvas, 16" x 16", framed, minor paint loss ..................................................................... 19,800.00

Cornover, Paul, (1864-1923), *December-Gloucester,* sgd "PAUL CORNOVER" lower left, identified on labels including one from R. H. Love Galleries, Chicago, on reverse, oil and graphite on canvas, 22-1/4" x 27", framed.................................................................. 9,775.00

Culverhouse, Johann Mongels, (1820-1891), *Family at Supper,* oil on canvas, 16" x 13-1/2" ............................................................ 2,465.00

Dickinson, Howard Clinton, *Summer Lakeside,* oil on canvas board, sgd, framed, 23" x 33-1/2"........................................................... 375.00

Dufner, Edward, (1872-1957), *Fishing Boat at Low Tide,* sgd and dated "E DUFNER-1906" lower left, oil on canvas, 25" x 32", framed, lined, scattered retouch, fine craquelure.................................... 8,050.00

English, Frank F., (1854-1922), *Farm in Autumn,* sgd lower right, watercolor, 14" x 26-3/4", framed ..................................... 2,920.00

Enneking, John Joseph, (1841-1916)
  *Autumn Twilight,* sgd and dated "Enneking 01" lower right, oil on canvas, 12-1/2" x 16-1/4", framed, lined, minor retouch3,450.00
  *Spring Pastures,* sgd and dated "Enneking 89" lower right, oil on canvas, 22" x 30", framed, scattered craquelure ........ 29,900.00

Gerry, Samuel Lancaster, (1813-1891)
  *Apple Blossoms,* sgd "S. L. Gerry" lower right, oil on board, 12-1/4" x 18-1/4", framed ........................................................ 1,380.00
  *Bar Harbor-Mt. Desert-Maine,* sgd "S. L. Gerry" lower right, titled and identified in inscription on stretcher, oil on canvas, 17" x 25", lined, scattered retouch ..................................... 6,900.00
  *Fisherman and Footbridge,* sgd "S. L. Gerry" lower right, oil on canvas, 11-1/2" x 17-3/8", framed, lined onto metal.... 1,495.00
  *Lakeside in Autumn/A White Mountain View,* sgd "S. L. Gerry" lower right, indistinctly inscribed on stretcher, oil on canvas, 20" x 35-3/4", framed, surface grim, scattered retouch, craquelure .......14,950.00

Gifford, Charles Henry, (1839-1904), *Sailboats off the Coast,* sgd and dated "C. H. Gifford 88" lower left, watercolor on paper, 8-1/2" x 12-5/8", framed, toning unobtrusive staining............................. 1,150.00

Greaves, Harry E., (1854-1919)
  *Coastal Surf by Midnight,* monogram signature and date "HEGreaves 1899" lower left, oil on canvas, 24-3/4" x 50-1/4", framed, prevalent craquelure with minute losses.......... 1,150.00
  *The Tempest from David Copperfield,* monogram signature and date "HEGreaves 1894" lower left, fragmentary label on reverse, oil on canvas, 25-1/4" x 51", framed ............... 4,890.00

Griggs, Samuel W., (1827-1898), *Haying Time,* sgd and dated "S. W. Griggs 1865" lower right, oil on canvas, 9" x 15", framed, scattered loses, scattered retouch, surface grime ................................ 1,955.00

Gruppe, Emile Albert, (1896-1978), sgd "Emile A. Gruppe" lower right, oil on canvas
  *Fall Birches,* 29-1/2" h, 24-1/2" w, dec wood frame with linen and gold liner.................................................................... 5,000.00
  *On Fish,* identified in inscription on stretcher, 20" x 24", framed.................................................................... 13,800.00
  *Sponge Boats,* 19-1/2" h, 23-1/2" w, dec wood frame with linen liner .................................................................... 6,000.00

Halsall, William Formby, (1841-1919)
  *Sailing Vessels in the Harbor,* sgd "W. F. Halsall" lower right, oil on canvas, 12" x 18", framed, lined, retouched, scattered craquelure ..................................................................... 9,200.00
  *The Coming Tide,* sgd "W. F. Halsall" lower left, identified on exhibition label on reverse, oil on canvas, 11-1/4" x 37-1/4", period frame, puncture and minor losses.................................. 8,050.00

Harrison, Lowell Birge, (1854-1929), *Early Morning Low Tide,* sgd "Birge Harrison" lower left, pastel on paper, 23-1/2" x 31-1/2", framed, tear upper right, foxing .................................... 6,325.00

Hart, James McDougal, (1828-1901), *Twilight,* sgd and dated "James M. Hart 1863" lower center, identified on label on reverse, oil on canvas, 28" x 20", period frame, lined, scattered retouch, craquelure .......... 7,475.00

Hart, William M., (1823-1894), *Cattle by a Pool,* sgd and dated "WM HART 1873" in ink lower right, oil on canvas, 18" x 13-7/8", unframed, scattered retouch, craquelure ............................. 6,325.00

Hassam, Frederick Childe, (1858-1935), *Rain and Mist Gloucester Harbor,* sgd "Chide Hassam" lower left, identified on fragmentary label affixed to reverse, watercolor on paper, 14" x 20", framed, toning and staining, retouched .................................................. 40,250.00

Hilliard, William Henry, (1836-1905), *Bear Paw Creek, Adirondackis,* sgd and dated 1868 lower left, oil on canvas, 29" x 36-1/2" .. 4,600.00

Hills, Laura Coombs, (1859-1952), *Newburyport Marshes at Dusk,* inscribed "L. C. Hills" on stretcher, oil on canvas, 14" x 20", framed, strip lined, scattered retouch ................................................ 3,450.00

Key, John Ross, (1837-1920)
> *Marshes with Heron, Twilight,* sgd "John R. Key" lower left, oil on canvas, 10" x 16", period frame, lined, retouched center left, scattered retouch, fine craquelure ................................. 5,465.00
> *Watching the Boats, Newport,* sgd and dated "John R. Key 77" lower left, oil on canvas, 12" x 20", framed, lined, retouched, craquelure ...................................................................... 12,650.00

Knight, Louis Aston, (1873-1948), *Nassandres Morning,* sgd and inscribed "Aston Knight Launzy" lower right, identified on label, inscription on reverse, oil on board, 18" x 21-3/4", framed, subtle toning, surface grime .................................................................. 2,990.00

Lazer, Charles "Shorty," (1856-1945), *River Landscape with Boats,* sgd lower left, oil on canvas, 17" x 24", framed ........................... 1,065.00

Leavitt, Edward Chalmers, (1842-1904), *Still Life with Roses and Goblet,* sgd and dated "E. C. Leavitt 89" lower left, oil on canvas, 20" x 12", framed, scattered craquelure ........................................ 2,300.00

Lewis, Edmund Darch, (1835-1910)
> *Mt. Washington and Conway Village,* sgd and dated "Edmund D. Lewis 1873" lower right, identified in inscription and on label from Vose Galleries, Boston, on reverse, oil on canvas mounted onto Masonite, 24" x 36", framed .................................. 5,465.00
> *The Squall,* sgd, dated, titled, "Edmund D. Lewis 1910" lower right, watercolor with gouache and graphite on paper, 19-1/4" x 29", framed .................................................................... 1,035.00

Martin, William A. K., (1817-1867), *Portrait of Lieutenant James B. McCauley,* sgd and dated 1854, oil on canvas, oval, 30" x 25" .. 1,235.00

McCord, George Herbert, (1848-1909), *A December Evening,* sgd and dated '76 lower left, label on reverse "The Albany Gallery, Stuyvesant Plaza, Albany, New York," 14" x 12", framed .......................... 2,355.00

Meeker, Joseph Rusling, (1827-1889), *Bayou Scene,* oil on canvas, sgd lower left, 18" x 28" ............................................................. 5,880.00

Moffett, Ross E., (1888-1971), *Being Neighborly,* sgd "Moffett" lower right, landscape study on reverse, oil on board, 12" x 16-1/4", framed ........................................................................................ 3,335.00

Moran, Peter, (1841-1914), *Walking the River/A Southern Landscape,* sgd and dated "...Moran 1881" lower left, oil on canvas, 21" x 17", framed, strip lined, scattered retouch, craquelure ................. 9,775.00

Murphy, John Francis, (1853-1921)
> *Arkville Landscape,* sgd and dated "J. Francis Murphy - 1901" lower right, identified on labels including one from William Macbeth, NY, on reverse, oil on canvas, 16" x 22", period frame, under glass ............................................................................. 10,350.00
> *Fading Sunset,* sgd and dated "J. Francis Murphy '95" lower left, identified on label from Babcock Galleries, NY, on reverse, oil on canvas, 12" x 16", period frame .......................................... 7,475.00
> *House on the Knoll, Late Afternoon,* sgd and dated "J. Francis Murphy '89" lower right, oil on canvas, 12" x 19", framed ........ 4,320.00

Nicholson, George W., (1832-1912)
> *Fishing in the Tidal Pools,* sgd "G.W. Nicholson" lower left, oil on canvas, 18" x 32", period frame, scattered craquelure . 3,750.00
> *Morning in the Market Place,* sgd "G.W. Nicholson" lower left, oil on canvas, 27-1/8" x 21-3/4", framed, lined, retouched, craquelure .................................................................... 2,300.00

Noyes, George Loftus, (1864-1951)
> *European Market Scene,* sgd "G. L. Noyes" lower right, oil on canvas, 29-1/2" x 39-1/2", thin gold frame ...................... 3,200.00
> *Gloucester Harbor,* sgd "G. L. Noyes" lower right, oil on canvas

mounted on Masonite, 25" x 24", Copley Gallery frame, scattered retouch ............................................................................. 28,750.00

Page, William J., *Half Dome, Yosemite,* oil on board, initialed lower right, pencil and identified on label on reverse, framed, 3-1/4" x 3-1/4" . 350.00

Peale, Charles Wilson (1741-1827), *Portrait of Joseph Sansom,* oil on canvas laid down on Masonite, reverse inscribed, "Joseph Sansom, my great-uncle on my mother's side, a man of culture in his day and an early antiquarian," 20-1/2" x 16-3/4" .............................. 34,720.00

Riecke, George, (1848-1924), *The Little Flock,* sgd "Geo. Riecke" lower left, oil on canvas, 16" x 24", framed, varnish inconsistencies ... 3,335.00

Rockwell, Norman, (1894-1978), *Organ Grinder,* sgd "Norman Rockwell" lower right, oil on canvasboard, 22-1/2" x 22-1/2", framed, c1920, minor scattered retouch, craquelure ...................... 145,500.00

Rouland, Orlando, (1871-1945), *Stream in Winter,* sgd "Orlando Rouland" lower left, identified on label from Milch Galleries, NY, on reverse, oil on canvas, 14" x 17", period frame, surface grim ........................... 1,150.00

Smith, Alice Ravenal Huger, (1876-1945), *Flying Egrets,* sgd "Alice R. Huger Smith" lower right, watercolor on paper, 20-5/8" x 15-7/8", framed, subtle toning ........................................................... 25,300.00

Smith, Frank Vining, (1879-1967)
> *Shortening Sail,* sgd "Frank Vining Smith" in ink lower right, label from Findlay Galleries, Chicago, on reverse, identified on presentation plaque, oil on canvasboard, 16" x 19-3/4", framed, surface grim .................................................................... 1,265.00
> *South Shore Road,* sgd "FRANK VINING SMITH" lower left, sgd, dated, and identified "1910..." on stretcher, oil on canvas, 24" x 28", framed, minor damage near tacking edges, prevalent craquelure .................................................................... 2,415.00

Smith, Russell William Thompson, (1812-1898)
> *Ben Ley from the Orchy,* initialed lower right, oil on canvas, 12" x 18" ........................................................................ 815.00
> *Llyn Cwellyn, Wales,* initialed lower right, titled and sgd verso, 12" x 17" ........................................................................ 815.00

Stover, Allen James, (born 1887), *The Quiet River,* sgd "A. Stover" lower left, identified in presentation plaque, oil on canvas, 10-3/4" x 14", framed, scattered retouch .................................................. 5,100.00

Stull, Henry, (1851-1913)
> *Braw Lad and Jockey,* sgd and dated "Henry Stull 1902" lower left, identified on label on reverse, oil on canvas, 23-1/2" x 28", framed, lined, scattered old retouch, craquelure ........... 8,050.00
> *Favor, by Pat Malloy-Favorite,* sgd and dated "Henry Stull 1894" lower left, identified in information affixed to reverse, oil on canvas, 25" x 30", framed, scattered old retouch, craquelure ......... 8,625.00

Thompson, Albert, (born 1853), *Cows in a Landscape,* sgd "Albert Thompson" lower left, oil on canvas, 13-3/4" x 19-3/4", framed . 1,100.00

**Wilder Darling (1856-1933), oil on canvas, 24" x 19", $8,400. Photo courtesy of Jackson's Auctioneers & Appraisers.**

Tyler, James Gale (1855-1931), *Moonlit Dory on the Shore,* sgd "James G. Tyler" lower left, oil on canvas, 11" x 17", Newcombe-Macklin frame ................................................................. 2,530.00
Van Deusen, C. C., (19th C), *Lovers on a Swing,* sgd lower right, oil on canvas, 16" x 10" ....................................................... 1,960.00
Van Loan, Dorothy, (born 1904), *Circus Scene,* oil on canvas, 36" x 42" .................................................................... 3,360.00
Wall, William C., (1810-1886), *Landscape Scene*, sgd "W. C. Wall" lower left, oil on canvas, 15" x 25", framed, scattered repairs, retouch, craquelure .......................................... 12,650.00
Webber, Wesley, (1839-1914), *The Lighthouse on the Point,* sgd "Wesley Webber" lower left, oil on canvas, 26" x 36", framed, surface grime, craquelure ............................................. 2,070.00
Wilder, Arthur B., (1857-1943), *Summer,* sgd and dated 1933 lower right, oil on canvas, 24" x 30" ....................................... 1,065.00
Williams, Frederick Dickenson, (1928-1915)
   *Charles River,* sgd and dated "F. D. Williams 1865" lower right, titled and identified on presentation plaque, oil on canvas, 11" x 15", split to panel upper right, scattered retouch, scattered craquelure and alligatoring ........................................ 3,450.00
   *Shepherdess and Flock on the Road to Pasture,* sgd and dated "F. D. Williams 1877" lower left, Paris canvas stenciled on reverse, oil on canvas, 18-1/4" x 15", framed ............... 1,495.00

# FIREARM ACCESSORIES

**History:** Muzzle-loading weapons of the 18th and early 19th centuries varied in caliber and required the owner to carry a variety of equipment, including a powder horn or flask, patches, flints or percussion caps, bullets, and bullet molds. In addition, military personnel were responsible for bayonets, slings, and miscellaneous cleaning equipment and spare parts.

During the French and Indian War, soldiers began to personalize their powder horns with intricate engraving, in addition to the usual name or initial used for identification. Sometimes professional hornsmiths were employed to customize these objects, which have been elevated to a form of folk art by some collectors.

In the mid-19th century, cartridge weapons replaced their black-powder ancestors. Collectors seek anything associated with early ammunition—from the cartridges themselves to advertising material. Handling old ammunition can be extremely dangerous because of decomposition of compounds. Seek advice from an experienced collector before becoming involved in this area.

**References:** Ralf Coykendall, Jr., *Coykendall's Complete Guide to Sporting Collectibles,* Wallace-Homestead, 1996; Jim Dresslar, *Folk Art of Early America—The Engraved Powder Horn*, Dresslar Publishing (P.O. Box 635, Bargersville, IN 46106), 1996; John Ogle, *Colt Memorabilia Price Guide,* Krause Publications, 1998; Nick Stroebel, *Old Gunsights, A Collector's Guide, 1850-1965,* Krause Publications, 1999.

**Periodical:** *Military Trader,* P.O. Box 1050, Dubuque, IA 52004.

**Museums:** Fort Ticonderoga Museum, Ticonderoga, NY; Huntington Museum of Art, Huntington, WV.

**Reproduction Alert:** There are a large number of reproduction and fake powder horns. Be very cautious!

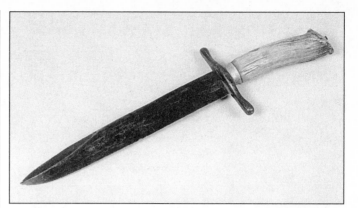

**Bowie Knife, stag grip, blade mkd "Kingman & Hassam Boston," some chips, few nicks, $4,670. Photo courtesy of Jackson's Auctioneers & Appraisers.**

**Notes:** Military-related firearm accessories generally are worth more than their civilian counterparts.

**Additional Listings:** Militaria.

Advertising Display, 11" w, 21" h, counter stand-up, diecut cardboard, Western Super X Shells, cut-away of shell ............... 585.00
Award Fob, 1-3/4" d, 2-sided, celluloid, 1899 shooting tournament
   DuPont Powder ..................................................... 600.00
   Hazard Powder ..................................................... 575.00
Belt, 36" l, 2" w, thirty nickel metal clips for holding shot shells, canvas shoulder straps, nickel plated buckle with Savage Arms logo cast into it, nickel plated hook .................................. 350.00
Book
   *Custom Guns,* Richard Simmons, illus, 1949 ................ 30.00
   *Western Ammunition Handbook,* 1938, 72 pgs ............. 35.00
Bullet Mold, 9", brass, casting six round buttons with central raised letter "I" for infantry, one 25 mm, one 18 mm, and four 14.5 mm d, American, 18th C ..................................................... 750.00
Calendar
   26-3/4" h, 13-3/4" w, Harrington & Richardson Arms Co., 1908, hunter taking bead on caribou, oilcloth, orig metal rim top and bottom, calendar pad missing ........................... 800.00
   27" h, 13-3/4" w, Peters Cartridges, 1910, titled "The First Lesson STEADY," mother pointer teaching pups, © 1908, artist sgd "A. Muss Arnolt," oilcloth, framed ............................. 1,100.00
   29-1/2" h, 14-1/2" w, Winchester, 1915, eagle attacking mountain goats, Forbes Litho Mfg. Co., artist sgd "Lynn Bogue Hunt," paper, framed, calendar pad missing ..................... 1,500.00
Cartridge Board, 30 1/4 x 32 1/4", US Cartridge Co, plaster casting of early board, displaying line of self contained ammunition, bullets, and primers, rifle, handgun, and shot shell ammunition, laminated oak frame, refinished c1960, provenance includes display at 1892 Chicago Expo and 1904 St. Louis World's Fair ................. 1,800.00
Cartridge Box
   3-7/8" x 2" x 1", Hall & Hubbard, cal. 22, green and black label "100 No. 1/2 2-100/PISTOL CARTRIDGES," molted cream and black paper, empty, half green side label missing ........... 350.00
   4" x 2-1/8" x 1-1/4", Union Metallic Cartridge Co., cream and black label "FIFTY .32 CALIBRE/No. 2/PISTOL CARTRIDGES," engraving of Smith & Wesson 1st Model 3rd Issue, checkered covering, orange and black side labels, unopened .......... 250.00
Catalog, Colt's Patent Fire Arms, Hartford, CT, 1920s, 40 pgs, 3-1/4" x 5-1/4" ................................................................. 50.00
Display Cabinet, 56" l, 7 1/4" d, 33 1/2" h, oak, glass front lift door, three drawers across bottom, rests for two Thompson carbines, back lined with red cloth, USMC logo in center, key locks at each end ......... 500.00
Holster, Colt Single Action Holster, tooled dec along borders on both sides, brown leather ................................................. 125.00

Powder Flask
    7-3/4" h, copper, pear shape, emb on both sides with group of hounds fighting with bear in woods, script initials below, brass top ........................................................................ 100.00
    8-1/4" h, brass, body emb "Rifle Horn" within a curved panel surrounded with a toothed design, orig lacquer finish, orig faded green carrying cord .......................................................... 170.00
Powder Horn
    9" l, engraved ship, hearts, house, trees, two inscriptions "Jeremiah Donohue, Age 21, M. 11, 1871," and "Patrick Donohue born 1866," another date of 1885, crack in end, may be cut down, very worn old plug ................................................ 150.00
    10-1/2" l, engraved map of fort and roads leading to it, stag hunt scene, plug engraved "JR," very minor loss to plug ...... 2,760.00
    11-1/4" l, engraved stags, foliate, and geometric devices, name "Samuel Evens," late 18th/early 19th C, minor cracks ..... 650.00
Powder Keg, 9-1/4" h, 6-1/4" d, wood, black painted number 56, 3-1/4" h black and white "Oriental Powder Mills" label, 2" "Eastern Sporting FFG Gun Powder," other end with 5" "Oriental Powder Mills Boston FF Western Sporting Powder G" purple and gold label, orig wooden screw plug with slight chips ........................................................ 500.00
Sign, framed paper
    24-1/4" h, 13-3/4" w, Marlin Firearms, two determined hunters in canoe in hot pursuit of pray, © 1907, artist sgd Philip B. Goodwin ........................................................................ 1,800.00
    24-1/4" h, 15" w, Marlin Rifles and Shotguns, hunting scene with hunter, two shot ducks, © 1908 ...................................... 1,600.00
    26-1/2" h, 16" w, Ithaca Guns, wild turkey in winter scene, © 1908, artist sgd Louis Agassiz Fuertes ......................... 1,800.00
    29" h, 15-1/4" w, Winchester, hunter standing tall with his Winchester as ferocious wolves attack, © 1906 .................. 3,300.00
    29" h, 18-3/4" w, Remington Shotgun, oil cloth, flock of ducks landing among decoys at dawn, both Remington Repeating Shotgun and Remington Auto Loading Shotgun pictured, © 1908 .......................................................................... 2,250.00
    29-1/4" h, 15" w, UMC Shot Shells, flying covey of quails, © 1908, textured paper ............................................................ 1,100.00
Target Ball, 2-3/4" d, molded amber glass, overall net pattern, bottom with raised sunburst pattern, middle 1/2" band emb "Bogardus Glass Ball Ptd April 10' 1877," chips at neck ...................................... 200.00

# FIREARMS

**History:** The 15th-century Matchlock Arquebus was the forerunner of the modern firearm. The Germans refined the wheelock firing mechanism during the 16th and 17th centuries. English settlers arrived in America with the smooth-bore musket; German settlers had rifled arms. Both used the new flintlock firing mechanism.

A major advance was achieved when Whitney introduced interchangeable parts into the manufacturing of rifles. Continued refinements in firearms continued in the 19th century. The percussion ignition system was developed by the 1840s. Minie, a French military officer, produced a viable projectile. By the end of the 19th century cartridge weapons dominated the field.

**References:** Robert W. D. Ball, *Mauser Military Rifles of the World*, Krause Publications, 1996; ——, *Remington Firearms*, Krause Publications; ——, *Springfield Armory Shoulder Weapons, 1795–1968*, Antique Trader Books, 1997; Ralf Coykendall Jr., *Coykendall's Complete Guide to Sporting Collectibles*, Wallace-Homestead, 1996; Norman Flayderman, *Flayderman's Guide to Antique American Firearms And Their Values*, 7th ed., Krause Publications, 1998; *Gun Trader's Guide*, 15th ed., Stoeger Publishing, 1992; Herbert G. Houze, *Colt Rifles and Muskets from 1847-1870*, Krause Publications, 1996; ——, *History of Winchester Repeating Arms Company*, Krause Publications, 1994; David D. Kowalski, *Standard Catalog of Winchester*, Krause Publications, 2000; Harold A. Murtz, *Guns Illustrated 2000*, 32nd ed., Krause Publications, 1999; ----, *Handguns 2000*, 12th ed., Krause Publications, 1999; John Ogle, *Colt Memorabilia Price Guide*, Krause Publications, 1998; Russell and Steve Quertermous, *Modern Guns Identification & Values*, 13th ed., Collector Books, 2000; Ken Ramage, ed., *Gun Digest 2001*, 55th ed., Krause Publications, 2000; ——, *Guns Illustrated 2001*, 33rd ed., Krause Publications, 2000; ——, *Handguns 2001*, 13th ed., Krause Publications, 2000; Ned Schwing, *Browning Superposed*, Krause Publications, 1996; Ned Schwing, *Standard Catalog of Firearms*, 9th ed., Krause Publications, 1999; Jim Supica and Richard Nahas, *Standard Catalog of Smith & Wesson*, Krause Publications, 1996; John Taffin, *Action Shooting: Cowboy Style*, Krause Publications, 1999; ——, *Big Bore Sixguns*, Krause Publications, 1997; ——, *Modern Custom Guns*, Krause Publications, 1997; Tom Turpin, *Custom Firearms Engraving*, Krause Publications, 1999; John Walter, *Rifles of the World*, Krause Publications, 1998; Ken Warner (ed.), *Gun Digest 2000*, 54th ed., Krause Publications, 1999; Tom Webster, edited by David D. Kowalski, *Winchester Rarities*, Krause Publications, 2000.

**Periodicals:** *Gun List*, 700 E. State St., Iola, WI 54990; *Gun Report*, P.O. Box 38, Aledo, IL 61231; *Historic Weapons & Relics*, 2650 Palmyra Rd, Palmyra, TN 37142; *Man at Arms*, P.O. Box 460, Lincoln, RI 02865; *Military Trader*, P.O. Box 1050, Dubuque, IA 52004; *Sporting Gun*, P.O. Box 301369, Escondido, CA 92030; *Wildcat Collectors Journal*, 15158 NE 6 Ave., Miami, FL 33162.

**Collectors' Clubs:** American Society of Military History, Los Angeles Patriotic Hall, 1816 S. Figuerora, Los Angeles, CA 90015; Winchester Arms Collectors Association Inc., P.O. Box 6754, Great Falls, MT 59406.

**Museums:** Battlefield Military Museum, Gettysburg, PA; Museum of Weapons & Early American History, Saint Augustine, FL 32084; National Firearms Museum, Washington, DC; Remington Gun Museum, Ilion, NY; Springfield Armory National Historic Site, Springfield, MA; Winchester Mystery House, Historic Firearms Museum, San Jose, CA.

**Notes:** Two factors control the pricing of firearms—condition and rarity. Variations in these factors can cause a wide range in the value of antique firearms. For instance, a Colt 1849 pocket-model revolver with a 5-inch barrel can be priced from $100 to $700 depending on whether or not all the component parts are original, whether some are missing, how much of the original finish (bluing) remains on the barrel and frame, how much silver plating remains on the brass trigger guard and back strap, and the condition and finish of the walnut grips.

Be careful to note a weapon's negative qualities. A Colt Peterson belt revolver in fair condition will command a much higher price than the Colt pocket model in very fine condition. Know the production run of a firearm before buying it.

## Derringer
Colt
No. 1, Cal. 41, standard engraved frame, nickel barrel, plain steel frame, 80% nickel on barrel, bare steel frame, 30% case color on hammer ..... 800.00
No. 2, Cal. 41, checkered wood drips, standard engraved frame ..... 500.00
No. 3, Cal. 41, Thieur, last type, nickel plated frame and barrel, walnut grips ..... 375.00
Henry, medium size, Cal. 47, 4" barrel, overall 8-1/4", mkd "Deringer Philadela" on lock and barrel, German silver mounted with ramrods, all mounts engraved, shield shaped thumb pieces inscribed "WBJ," pair ..... 1,750.00
Marston, William, .32 Cal., three barrel, 4" barrels, bold signature and brass frame, rosewood grips, spots of pitting, 7" l overall ..... 550.00
Mossberg Brownie, Cal. 22, 4 shot, 2-1/2" tip down barrel, serrated wood grip panels, missing ejector pin, fair bores, cracked left grip ..... 95.00
Philadelphia
Early, Cal. 45, 3" barrel stamped "Deringer/Philadel'a," two gold bands at breech and single "P" proof, 6-3/4" overall, scroll engraved lock sgd "Deringer/Philadel'a," well grained walnut stock, engraved silver barrel key plates, side plate, small inlay below nipple bolster, trigger guard and shield shaped wrist escutcheon, lightly engraved German silver butt cup with plain iron cover, ramrod and horn forend cap missing, modern replacement nipple ..... 800.00
Vest Pocket, Cal. 42 Perc, 2-1/2" octagon round barrel with markings on lock and breech, single "P" proof, normal German silver fittings, lightly engraved with checkered butt and grip ..... 950.00
Sharp's Four Barrel, Model 2, Cal. 30, rimfire, medium size, nickel plated brass frame, 2 pc checkered ivory grips, no orig finish, pin does not revolve ..... 350.00

## Musket
Confederate, Richmond Armory, Cal. 58, 40" round barrel, three bands, walnut stock, lockplate mkd "CS/Richmond, VA," dated 1863, 1855 type rear sight, iron mounted with brass butt plate ..... 2,000.00
Flagg, B., 1842 Pattern, percussion, Cal. 69, usual 1842 pattern, 42" barrel, usual proofs, lock plate markings with eagle obliterated over "US" with maker's name and address over "1849" behind hammer, three barrel bands, trumpet ramer, rocket bayonet mkd "GL" on flat without scabbard ..... 700.00
Springfield Cadet, Cal. 57 Perc., 1851 dated lock and tang, made for Virginia Military Institute, slim 40" barrel, three bands, iron mounted on walnut stock, bottom bayonet lug, trumpet ramrod, middle band and 2 pc trigger guard fitted with sling swivels, lock and small eagle over "US" ahead of hammer, "Springfield 1851" behind hammer, tan also dated 1851, breech mkd with small "VP" proof and eagle head, left flat with crisp tiny cartouche, orig cadet socket 14-1/4" l bayonet ..... 4,150.00
US Model 1855 Harpers Ferry, Cal. 58, 40" round barrel, three barrel bands, iron mounted, brass nose cap, walnut stock, lockplate dated "1857," long range rear sight, no patch box, dark brown uncleaned patina on all metal parts, medium to heavy pitting hear breech . 2,000.00
Winchester Low Wall Winder, Cal. 22 short, regular musket configuration, 28" barrel, ramp front sight, no barrel sight, receiver with Lyman side mount sight, full length wood forestock, military style butt stock, marked "US" and flaming bomb on top tang, 93-94% barrel blue turning plum, scattered surface rust, thinning near muzzle, some heavier pitting at muzzle, stock with pinned wrist, normal handling and use marks, strong bore ..... 330.00

## Pepperbox
Allen & Thurber, Worcester
Dragoon, Cal. 36, 6" barrel group, ribbed, long curved grip, trigger guard made without second finger spur, engraved frame, engraved nipple shield, 1845 date on hammer, no finish, overall dark gray/black with scattered light pitting and discolorations, one nipple missing, trigger guard needs resecuring, orig grips ..... 300.00
6-shot, Cal. 31, 4-3/4" barrel group, Norwich style engraved frame, engraved nipple shield, silver spangled grips, cased in orig mahogany Allen case, cylindrical plunger flask mkd "J. Camm" on top, orig accessories ..... 1,050.00
Robbins & Lawrence, Cal. 31, 5-shot, mkd Leonard's patent 1848, ring trigger, concealed hammer, 2-pc rosewood grips, engraved frame and barrels, traces of factory finish, light pitting in small areas ..... 550.00
Spies, A. W., Cal. 31, 3-3/4" barrel, engraved frame, narrow ribs on barrel, 1837 patent barrel, mkd "Allen" ring trigger, shieldless, light gray to black engraved frame, engraving on left side, 75% on right side, hammer markings clear, no finish on barrels, light speckling and dings, grips and spangles intact, right grip with 17 notches cut in it, no finish on grips, mechanically fine ..... 350.00
Stocking & Co., Worcester, Cal. 31, 4" barrel group with ribs, engraved frame, second finger spur on trigger guard, rounded spangled walnut rips, worn overall, no finish remaining, light to medium pitting on nipple shield, mottled medium gray barrels, bright steel frame, clear hammer and barrel markings ..... 450.00

## Percussion Rifle
Half stock, curly maple, refinished, gold curl, brass butt plate, nickel silver inlays, and patchbox, restoration with replacements, 50-1/2" l ..... 400.00
Half stock, walnut stock, beaver tail cheek piece, engraved German silver cap box with squirrel and eagle, 30" octagonal barrel with silver bands, hook breech with bright finish, 48" l ..... 1,550.00
Half stock, walnut stock, 36" barrel, brass hardware, Golcher lock, stock has been varnished, minor age cracks, 53-1/2" l ..... 350.00

## Pistol, flintlock
Danish, Revolutionary War Period, Calvary, 10-3/4" barrel, Danish proof at breech, brass blade sight, relief carved walnut stock, heavy cast brass furniture, ramrod assembly with swivel and iron swivel mounted to butt cap, large convex banana shaped flintlock ..... 1,550.00
European, walnut stock, brass hardware, horn nose cap, 8-1/4" octagonal to round barrel, dark surface with pitting, lock bolts stripped, 13-1/2" l ..... 330.00
US Model 1819, contract by Simeon North, dated 1821, Cal. 54, 10" round barrel with swivel ramrod, iron furniture, walnut stock, markings clear, cleaned, minor pitting, orig flintlock ..... 1,200.00
US Model 1836, contract by Robert Johnson, dated 1838 on lock plate, Cal. 54, 8-1/2" round barrel, iron mounted, walnut stock, dark gray uncleaned patina, minor pitting, double stamped on lock plate, visible inspector's cartouche on stock, orig flintlock ..... 1,050.00
US Model 1837, contract by Asa Waters, dated 1837, Cal. 54, 8-1/2" round barrel, iron furniture, walnut stuck, light peppery pitting near breech, clear inspector's cartouches ..... 1,500.00

## Pistol, percussion
Allen & Thurber Grafton Tubehammer, Cal. 38, 2-5/8" round/octagon barrel, engraved frame, sharp drop grip with spangles, mkd "cast sleeve/warrented" on one barrel flat, "pocket rifle" on next flat, "Allen &

Thurber" on next flat, "Grafton, Mass," on next flat, and "P. M.E.A. 183" on another, mkd "Allens Patent" on side plate, no finish, cleaned bright overall, light pitting and metal deterioration lightly scattered.......1,400.00

Allen & Wheelock

Double Barrel, 2-shot, Cal. 34, 3-1/8" barrel, two hammer single trigger system, 40% faded blue on barrels, traces of blue on frame, right grip replaced ...................300.00

Single Shot, medium frame, orig Allen combination mold/wrench, Cal. 36, 3" round/octagon barrel mkd "Allen & Wheelock" on top flat, standard engraved frame, walnut grips, one handle is octagonal barrel wrench, no finish, steel gray metal with mottled brown, 75% varnish grips.................200.00

Stocking & Co., Worcester, MA, single shot, Cal. 34, 4-1/8" round/octagon barrel, engraved frame, single action hammer with spur, walnut grips, excellent barrel and hammer markings, gray barrel with some light dark pitting at muzzle, cleaned gray frame, overall speckled pitting, orig grips, 40% varnish...................200.00

## Pistol, semi-auto

Astra Cub, Cal. 22 short, tiny pocket model, full coverage factory arabesque engraving pattern, silver plated, artificial pearl grips, spare mag and orig owner's manual ...................150.00

High Standard Model, HD Military, Cal. 22 LR, blued finish, 6-3/4" barrel, adjustable sights, full checkered walnut grips, Lt. Col., insignia stuck on left grip ...................225.00

## Revolver

Allen & Wheelock

Belt Model, lip fire, converted to rimfire, Cal. 32, 5-7/8" barrel, no blue remaining except on striker level which is 50%, rest gray steel, with metal surfaces fairly good, 80% varnish on grips, mechanically fine...................400.00

.25 lip fire, Cal., 25, 3" barrel, no markings, blue finish overall, nicely figured walnut grips, 80% orig bright blue barrel, 25% on cylinder, balance flaked brown, 15-20% on frame, balance flaked, grips with 80% varnish, mechanically fine ...........300.00

.32 side hammer, Cal. 32, 4" barrel, brass frame, traces of silver, replaced cylinder pin, bare stele barrel, weak cylinder scene, no finished on cylinder, 85% orig varnish on grips, mechanically fine ...................300.00

Colt

Army Special, Cal. 38, regular configuration, 6" barrel, blued finish, black Colt composition grips, orig hinged lid maroon box and instruction sheet ...................300.00

Detective Special, Cal. 28 Spel., nickel finish, 2" bbl with reproduction stag grips, Tyler grip adapter ...................200.00

Model 1851 Navy, Cal. 36, six shot, 7-1/2" barrel, brass back strap and trigger guard, "US" marked on left side of frame, cleaned with areas of light pitting, 20% seam remains on cylinder, worn grips...................1,250.00

Model 1851 Navy, Cal. 36, Perc., 4-screw, scarce shoulder stock model, extended screws each side of receiver, iron trigger guard, back strap with small swivel installed just to front of trigger guard, 1 pc wood grips...................1,200.00

Model 1860 Army, Cal. 44, Perc, 8" round barrel, three screw frame, brass trigger guard, 1 pc walnut grips, no orig finish, dark gray patina overall, 50% cylinder scene, mechanically sound ...1,600.00

**Colt Model 1851 Navy Revolver, 2nd Model, 36 cal., $7,975. Photo courtesy of Jackson's Auctioneers & Appraisers.**

Police Positive Flattop Target, Cal. 22, small frame, 6" barrel, adjustable front and rear sights, checkered medallion wood grips, checkered trigger and back strap, 94-96% strong blue, thin and turning at muzzle, grip frame and sharp edges, moderate wear to sound grips, bright bore...................350.00

Ethan Allen & Co.

Lip Fire, Cal. 32, 5" barrel, full silver plate finish, 75% silver finish, 90% clear markings, 40% varnish on grips, inoperable cylinder stop ...................475.00

Side Hammer, Cal. 32, last variety, 3-7/8" octagon barrel mkd on top flat, no cylinder engraving, iron frame, walnut grips, traces of blue in protected areas, balance turned mottled gray/brown, orig grips, 75% varnish, hammer with 50% case colors, mechanically fine ...................200.00

Moore, Belt Model, Cal. 32, RF, blued finish, engraved brass silver plated frame, trigger guard with back strap, 1 pc varnished walnut grips complete with ejector rod, traces of finish on barrel, 40-50% thinning blue on cylinder, 75-80% silver plate on brass, most varnish finish on wood, excellent bore...................600.00

Rogers & Spencer

Army, Cal. 44, 7-1/2" barrel, military inspected, excellent grips with triangular repair to toe of right grip, excellent cartouche, 25% bright blue, balance thin blue/gray to brown, mechanically excellent, apparently unfired ...................1,200.00

Percussion, Cal. 44, all matching serial numbers, 7-1/2" octagonal barrel, 2 pc walnut grips, sharp US Inspector's marks, 40% bright factory blue remains...................1,200.00

US Military, Cal. 44, Perc, 7-1/2" barrel, military inspected, dings and small areas of pitting, 50% blue overall, no finish on cylinder, grips not original, mechanically fine ...................800.00

Ruger Bearcat, single action, Cal. 22, standard configuration, blued finish, brass coated trigger guard, 2 pc varnished wood grips, orig box and papers ...................300.00

Smith & Wesson

M28-2 Highway Patrolman DA, Cal.357 Mag., blued finish, 4" barrel, adjustable sights and checkered medallion walnut grips, strong orig finish...................175.00

No 1-1/2 Spur Trigger, Cal. 32, nickel finished, 3" ribbed barrel, half moon sight, black composition logo grips, orig green cloth cov hinged lid box ...................400.00

Star Number 38, Prescott Pistol Co., Hatfield, MA, Cal. 38, 2-7/8" octagon barrel, marked only with star and "No. 38" on top strap, wood grips color of walnut but with tight dark grain, nickel finish, case colored hammer, orig black label picture box, 60% nickel on barrel, 85% on brass frame, 40% cylinder, 70% case colors on hammer, excellent grips, 95% varnish, one ding, mechanically fine ...................625.00

## Rifle

Ballard Single Shot, Sporting, Cal. 22, 22-1/2" octagonal barrel, iron frame, ring style lever, walnut stocks with iron butt plate, 90% factory blue barrel, orig varnish on stock, excellent bore...................1,700.00

Jenks Mule Ear Navy, Cal. 54 Perc., 30" round barrel, three brass bands, bayonet lug at bottom of muzzle, lock with Ames and Jenks marks, mkd on breech with usual marks, dated 1844, full length wood stock...................2,500.00

Kimber Model 82 Bolt Action, Cal. 22 LR, early model, 22" tapered round barrel, straight grain checkered 1 pc stock, 13-5/8" over a flat checkered steel butt plate, grooved receiver and 5-shot mag. ...................475.00

Marine Corps 1903 Sniper, Cal. 30-06, Regulation 1903, scope blocks mounted to barrel and rear sight, barrel markings "SA/5-21," mounted with Lyman 48 receiver sight with bright bolt and rails, straight grip stock cartouche "WJS," with "T" in cutoff recess, Unertl 8X scope mkd "USMC-Sniper," military mounts, white paint on target knobs, clean smooth wood, 97-98% gray/black parkerizing thin over front barrel area, muzzle recrowned during period of use, brilliant bore, excellent optics ...................2,600.00

Remington

Flintlock, barreled full stock, Bedford County, KY, type, Cal. 50, 39" octagon barrel mkd on top flat "Remington," stepped lock plate with teardrop at back, lightly engraved with name "Spencer/Stafford/Warranted," recent reconversion using nice period hammer and older parts, full length curly maple stock secured with three oval head wedges, brass furniture including three ramrod guides, nose cap, trigger guard, butt plate, pierced plain patchbox, release on toe tiny beavertail push, full iron sideplate secured with three wood screws, two lockplate screws ...........................1,500.00

Military, Rolling Block, Cal. 58 center fire, 39" round barrel with M1864 type rear sight, three iron bands on walnut stock, unmarked except for Remington name and patent data on tang, manuf utilizing altered Civil War musket stock, bayonet standard cal. 58 triangular socket, mkd "US," light to medium overall pitting, heavy patches on frame and butt plate, missing ramrod, stock heavily worn, worm damage on end ......................450.00

Model 1867 Navy Cadet, rolling block, 32-1/2" round barrel, .50/45 center fire cadet cal., right side of frame mkd "P/F.C.W.," left side frame mkd with anchor stamp, Remington patent info on tang, butt plate stamped "U.S." with rack No. 158, right side of butt stock stamped "B/103," single leaf Springfield musket type rear site, knurled slotted ramrod, two barrel bands with retaining springs on black walnut stock, lightly cleaned, light gray patina, clean sharp bore, hammer and block blued............................................2,100.00

Model 1903A3 Military, Cal. 30-06, regular 03A3 configuration, barrel marking "RA/9-43" and various cartouches, old military sling, pristine condition, new, unfired, very minor handling and storage, some roughness, couple of bruises to handguard and forend top ........................................................................400.00

Model 1917 Military, Cal. 30-06, barrel mkd "R/9-18," regular 1917 configuration, bright blued metal, British proofed Remington bayonet with green leather scabbard and leather sling.................400.00

Springfield

Air Force M-1 Garand Match, Cal. 30-06, National Match configuration, "NM" marked sights, op-roc, barrel and gas cylinder, glass bedded stock, barrel dated "4-63," Air Force paperwork.......950.00

M-1 Garand, Cal. 30-06, usual configuration, barrel dated "6-43," early battled sight, small wheeled "EM c F" cartouche, "114" at left toe, 90-99% dark green parkerizing, thin gas tube, dark oiled wood, bright shiny bore ........................................................750.00

M-1 Gas Trap Garand, Cal. 30-06, early configuration, all numbered parts including wood, replacement gas trap, barrel, cylinder, sight, plug, ferrule, follower rod and springs, early stock without butt trap and checkered steel butt plate inspected "SPG," 96-98% orig gray/green parkerizing, restored finish to wood, pins through wrist ................................................1,750.00

Winchester Model 677, single shot, Cal. 22, normal Model 67 with smooth stock, never fitted with signs, mounted with target scope blocks on barrel, British proofed with British military broad arrow marking, nickeled bolt, no serial no., 98-99% orig barrel blue, solid wood showing light handling and use marks, filled knot bottom of forearm, bright shiny bore ........................................................775.00

## Shotgun

Browning, pre-war GR-1, Over-Under, Cal. 20 ga., long tang, round knob model with 26-1/2" barrels, imp cyl/mod, narrow vent rib, checkered round forearm and round knob grip, 14" over a Pachmayr pad, single trigger and ejectors ........................................................600.00

Daly, Charles, Over-Under, Cal. 28 ga., early Browning infringement model, 26" barrels, choked Skeet/Skeet, checkered rounded forearm and round knob painted grip stock 15" over black composition butt plate, single selective trigger and ejectors, 97-99% orig blue on barrels, sound clean wood with 2 bruises to forearm checkering, few light handling and use marks ........................................................650.00

Winchester Model 1887, lever action, Cal. 10 ga., regular configuration, 32" steel barrel, wood forestock panels, semi-pistol grip stock, refinished wood, replaced tang screw, butt plate missing ........325.00

# FIREHOUSE COLLECTIBLES

**History:** The volunteer fire company has played a vital role in the protection and social growth of many towns and rural areas. Paid professional firemen usually are found only in large metropolitan areas. Each fire company prided itself on equipment and uniforms. Conventions and parades gave the fire companies a chance to show off their equipment. These events produced a wealth of firehouse-related memorabilia.

**References:** Andrew G. Gurka, *Hot Stuff! Firefighting Collectibles*, L-W Book Sales, 1994; Ed Lindley Peterson, *First to the Flames: The History of Fire Chief Vehicles*, Krause Publications, 1999; James Piatti, *Firehouse Memorabilia: Identification and Price Guide*, Avon Books, 1994; Donald F. Wood and Wayne Sorensen, *American Volunteer Fire Trucks*, Krause Publications, 199_; — *Big City Fire Trucks, 1900-1950*, Krause Publications, 1996 (Volume I), 1997 (Volume II).

**Periodical:** *Fire Apparatus Journal*, P.O. Box 141295, Staten Island, NY 10314, http://fireapparatusjournal.com; *Vintage Vehicle & Fire Engine Magazine*, Rt. 3, Box 425, Jasper, FL 32052, http://www.vintagevehicle.com/MASTOF97.htm.

**Collectors' Clubs:** Antique Fire Apparatus Club of America, 5420 S. Kedvale Ave., Chicago, IL 60632; Fire Collectors Club, P.O. Box 992, Milwaukee, WI 53201; Fire Mark Circle of the Americas, 2859 Marlin Dr., Chamblee, GA 30341; Gibson Road Antique Fire Association, 1545 Gibson Road, Crum Lynne, PA 19022, http://www.firefighting.com/grafa; Great Lakes International Antique Fire Apparatus Association, P.O. Box 2519, Detroit, MI 48231; International Fire Buff Association, Inc., 7509 Chesapeake Ave., Baltimore, MD 21219; International Fire Photographers Association, P.O. Box 8337, Rolling Meadows, IL 60008; Society for the Preservation & Appreciation of Motor Fire Apparatus in America, 5420 S. Kedvale Ave., Chicago, IL 60632, http://www.spaamfaa.org.

**Museums:** American Museum of Fire Fighting, Hudson, NY, http://www.firemumsumnetwork.org; Fire Museum of Maryland, Lutherville, MD; Hall of Flame, Phoenix AZ, http://www.halloflame.org; Insurance Company of North America (INA) Museum, Philadelphia, PA; New England Fire & History Museum, Brewster, MA; New York City Fire Museum, New York, NY, http://nyfd.com/museum.htlm; Oklahoma State Fireman's Association Museum, Oklahoma City, OK, http://tulsaweb.com/FIREMUS.HTM; San Francisco Fire Dept. Memorial Museum, San Francisco, CA; Smokey's Fire Museum, Chamblee, GA; Toledo Firefighters Museum, Toledo, OH, http://www.toledolink.com/~matgerke/~thm.

**Additional Listings:** See *Warman's Americana & Collectibles* for more examples.

Advertising Pinback Button, 7/8" d, The Vajen-Bader Patent, Firemans Smoke Protector, celluloid, litho by Whitehead & Hoag, July 21, 1896 date ....................................................................................285.00

Alarm Box

Gamewell Excelsior, cast iron, code wheel and number plate telegraph door, orig weathered paint .....................................300.00

Utica Fire Alarm and Telegraph, telegraph door ................500.00

**Alarm Gong**

Star Electric, Binghamton, NY, fancy case with star on top, 12" ..................................................................... 1,800.00

US Fire and Police Telegraph, maple "Moses Crane" case, fig leaf finial, 8" ........................................................... 1,250.00

**Badge**

Eureka Fire Co., bronze luster, metal link, "Compliments of Eureka Fire House Co., N.Y.," pendent rimmed in coiled hose design, center eagle, "Eureka/Paragon/Red Cross," early 1900s ............. 40.00

Union Hose Co., bright silver luster brass, also inscribed "Annville, PA," fire symbols of primitive pumper, hook and ladder, c1930s ............................................................... 25.00

**Bell**, American La France, 700 series type base, eagle finial, orig, 12" ................................................................. 550.00

**Belt, leather**

32" l, brass trim "Old Town," one side painted white, buckle stamped "Dirigo No. 1," some paint flaking ...................... 150.00

48" l, brown leather, applied brass "2nd Assistant," large "2" by buckle, wear ...................................................... 100.00

**Catalog**, Daly & Bryan, Boston, MA, 1886, 26 pgs, 4-1/2" x 6-1/4", "Illustrated Catalog & Price List of Firemen's Equipment," 19 illustrations ...................................................... 135.00

**Child's Book**, *Five Little Firemen*, Little Golden Book, 1949, 6-3/4" x 8" .................................................................. 5.00

**Extinguisher**, foam type, 2-1/2 gal

Ahrens Fox ................................................................... 215.00

Mack, nickel and glass .................................................. 175.00

**Fire Bucket**, 12-3/4" h, leather, painted "Benj. Pitman 1830" on scrolling banner design, painted in black and yellow, green ground, break and losses to handle, paint loss ............................... 460.00

**Fire Wagon Lantern**, 23-1/4" h, nickel plated, mkd "DeVoursney Bros. makers 389 Broome St. New York," acid etched and engraved blue, red, and clear glass panels showing fire fighting equipment, geometric and foliate device, and "Prospect 4," removable oil font.............. 1,725.00

**First Day Cover**, commemorating 300th anniversary of volunteer fireman, 3 cent stamp, dated Dover, Delaware, Oct 4, 1948 .......... 15.00

**Hat**, 13" x 11-3/4" x 6", leather, top hat style, black paint, gold writing on front "Good Will 1802," back with "G.W.," top with "T.M.S.," number "15734" on brim, piece missing from brim .................... 2,750.00

**Helmet**, 14" l, leather, brass eagle, painted leather shield with "10, LFD," very work, old added brass gimbal lamp on top ............. 350.00

**Horn**

17" h, brass, painted red int., inscribed "From Mrs. PH Bowman to GP Mason" ....................................................... 500.00

17" h, brass, plain ....................................................... 450.00

18" h, silverplated, inscribed "Presented to EB Ackerman of Lafayette Co. No. 1" ............................................... 700.00

23" h, silverplated, repousse flowers, unsigned................... 700.00

**Hose Box**, 38-1/4" l, 10" d, 10-1/4" h, wooden, from early fire hose wagon, long rect wooden box, hinged lid, chamfered front panel with painted scene of chip in water near rocky shore, to and sides painted red with yellow dec trim, wear to paint, loose locking mechanism, 19th C .......................................................... 230.00

**Hose Nozzle**, 19-1/2" l, "Chief" model, two man type, Elkhart Brass Mfg. Co., professionally restored ................................. 150.00

**Lapel Stud**, York Fire Co., blue and white celluloid, bull head image, "Vigilient S & C F. E. Co. No. 1," metal lapel stud, late 1890s/early 1900s ........................................................ 25.00

**Pin**

Western PA Firemen's Assoc. 18th Annual Convention, Monongahela Delegate, August 1911, made by Whitehead and Hoag............................................................... 85.00

Western PA Firemen's Assoc. 20th Annual Convention, Punxatawney Delegate, August 1913, made by Whitehead and Hoag............................................................... 85.00

**Pinback Button**, 1-1/4" d, "Firemen's Celebration" with illus of fireman, "1958 Celebration" on red ribbon ................................ 18.00

**Poster**, 22" x 27", Fire! Fire! Fire!, "Chicago Lost But J. Dearman of Knoxville, Penna. Continues to Roll Up, Bundle Up, and Box Up As Many Goods As Ever!" red and black, some replacement to border, Oct 15th, 1871 ...................................................... 225.00

**Print**, lithograph with hand-coloring, "The American Fireman, Rushing to the Conflict," Currier and Ives, Louis Maurer lithographer, 1858, identified in inscriptions in matrix, 22-1/2" x 17-1/4" sheet size, framed .......................................................... 700.00

**Ribbon**, convention, brass scroll, 1922, San Francisco Fire Chiefs, hanging blue glove fire lantern ..................................... 195.00

**Shot Glass**, 2-3/4" h, silver plated, fire bucket shape, Gorham Co., white badge with ladder, and fire hydrant, blue lettering "Little Giant Engine Company 1871, Chicago Fire Department" ................ 150.00

**Siren**, hand crank, sterling silver, orig mounting bracket ........... 450.00

**Stereocard**, The Summer St Fire, Boston, Mass, Nov 9 & 10, 1872, shows rubble of burned out buildings, people ..................... 25.00

**Tie Tac**, 1/2" d, enamel dec "Member, County Fireman's Ass'n," keystone shaped back, mkd "10K" ..................................... 30.00

**Toy, cast iron**

Fire Patrol Wagon, 16" l, red and yellow wagon, driver missing leg, seat missing, horse, poor paint, some rust............... 275.00

Fire Patrol Wagon, 17" x 7", three horses, bell on chassis, orig fireman and driver, blue paint, red trim, some paint loss to figures .......................................................... 750.00

Fire Pumper, 11-1/2" l, 4-1/2" h, two horses, yellow metal spoked wheels, overall paint loss ....................................... 75.00

Fire Truck, 6-1/2" l, driver, worn red paint, replaced wheels, Kenton .......................................................... 100.00

Fire Wagon, 15" l, red paint, yellow wheels, orig figures and horses, two ladders, Dent ...................................... 150.00

Ladder Wagon, 21" l, red and yellow painted wagon, ladders missing, non-matching nickel plated figure at rear, painted three horse team .................................................... 100.00

Ladder Wagon, 30" l, horse-drawn, red and white painted wagon, one complete and one broken ladder, two repainted figures, horse painted black and white, Hubley ........................ 100.00

**Toy, plastic**, rampwalker, Marx, fireman holding hose, yellow jacket, red and yellow hat ...................................................... 110.00

**Toy, tin**, ladder truck, tin, four tin firemen, hard rubber wheels, Gunthermann, 14" x 5" .......................................................... 200.00

**Watch Fob**, double sided cello, York County Convention, Red Lion, Pennsylvania, Sept. 4, 1916, red lettered inscription, black and white firehouse, red, white, and blue US flat at top, back with tinted color image of woman in showgirl outfit, dark brown background ...... 35.00

# FIREPLACE EQUIPMENT

**History:** In the colonial home, the fireplace was the gathering point for heat, meals, and social interaction. It maintained its dominant position until the introduction of central heating in the mid-19th century.

Because of the continued popularity of the fireplace, accessories still are manufactured, usually in an early-American motif.

**References:** John Campbell, *Fire & Light in the Home Pre 1820*, Antique Collectors' Club, 1999; Rupert Gentle and Rachael Field, *Domestic Metalwork 1640–1820*, Revised, Antique Collectors' Club, 1994; George C. Neumann, *Early*

**Pinback Button, from June 17, 1908, Napoleon, OH event, multicolored portrait of fireman, $30. Photo courtesy of Hake's Americana & Collectibles.**

*American Antique Country Furnishings*, L-W Book Sales, 1984, 1993 reprint.

**Reproduction Alert:** Modern blacksmiths are reproducing many old iron implements.

**Additional Listings:** Brass; Ironware.

Andirons, pr

16-3/4" h, 10" l, 17" d, sun face, finials depicting radiating sun rays centering by face, ribbed and curvilinear standard with additional rays, raised "B & H 9510" marks, Bradley and Hubbard, Meriden, CT, early 20th C ........................................ 600.00

17-5/8" h, cast iron, figural, classical male herms, plinth stands, torch detail, dolphin base, late 19th C ............................ 850.00

18" h, brass, double lemon tops, early polished ................. 425.00

19-3/4" h, 10-1/2" w, 21-1/4" d, brass, engraved belted ball top, sq plinths engraved with flowers and bow knotted wreath surrounding "B" monogram, stylized flower on two flanking sides, arched spurred legs on ball feet, attributed to R. Wittingham, NY, early 19th C, surface scratches, grime .................................. 4,315.00

23" h, brass, bulbous turned finish, Georgian-style ........... 400.00

23" h, brass and wrought iron, late Baroque-style, c1900-10 ..220.00

23-1/2" h, brass and wrought iron, knife blade, penny feet, urn finials, brass trim at base of stem ........................................ 250.00

31" h, 28" d, wrought iron, obelisk-form, decorative studded strapwork and scrolls, Arts & Crafts-style, early 20th C, one ball finial missing .................................................................. 600.00

56" h, 19" w, 38" d, wrought iron, stylized floral baskets at top and front, accented with leaves and protruding serpents heads, standards wrapped with stylized serpents, Arts and Crafts, attributed to Samuel Yellin, c1920.................................... 865.00

Bellows

Decorated, 15" l, very worn orig rose wood graining, floral dec, old worn leather, brass nozzle........................................... 85.00

Decorated, 16-1/2" l, orig yellow paint, green and black striping, stenciled and free hand floral dec in red, green, gold, and black, brass nozzle, professionally re-leathered, minor wear ..... 325.00

Edwardian, 27" l, brass and horse brass mounted yewwood, c1900-1910 ...................................................................... 165.00

Victorian, brass, nailhead mounted yewwood and wrought iron, c1890-1900 ...................................................................... 140.00

Billiard Ball Holder and Firescreen, 26" w, 48-1/4" h, rosewood veneered, fitted with two open shelves on one side, framed needlepoint and beaded panel of courting couple, trestle base, labeled William Morron, New York, Victorian, late 19th C ........................... 980.00

Bird Spit and Broiler, 11" w, 11-3/4" d, 10-3/4" h, wrought iron, adjustable rack, six prongs, pull handle, penny feet .......................... 200.00

Chenet, 40" l, Louis XVI-style, gilt and patinated bronze, mounted with two bacchanalian putti, fender and base molded with foliate, late 19th C.................................................................... 3,150.00

Chimney Cover, 12" h, oval, marked "Compliments of C. D. Denny Co., Kaufmann & Strauss Co., N. Y. 1058," metal cover with picture of two little girls having tea party in lush spring garden, large bunny seated at table, eight smaller bunnies on ground, doll lying under table. gold border.................................................................. 210.00

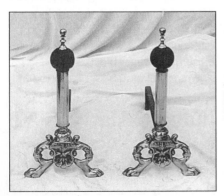

**Andirons, pr, brass plated, black metal ball and finial, 20-1/2" h, $145.**

Clock Jack, 19" h, brass, cast iron rotating wheel for roasting small game, replaced key, working.................................... 715.00

Coal Box, 12" w, 12" d, 13" h, copper, emb laurel wreath dec.... 150.00

Coal Bucket, 15" d, 20" h, mahogany, brass liner, open slat sides, tripod base, Regency, early 19th C, price for pr........................ 2,645.00

Coal Grate, 32" w, 17" d, 38 1/2" h, bell metal, rect basket, cast iron back plate, dancing maidens ornament, pierced front skirt, surmounted by urns, straight tapered legs, spade feet, George III, late 18th C.................................................................. 315.00

Crane, 41" h, 39" w, wrought iron, attached kettle tilter, scrolled detail, pitted and rust damage ...................................................... 615.00

Fender

42" l, 9" d, 8" h, cut brass and sheet iron, paw footed, English, c1875-90 ...................................................................... 110.00

42" l, 10-1/2" h, cut brass, paw footed, D-configuration, English, c1875-90 ...................................................................... 200.00

49" l, 11-1/2" d, 7" h, cut brass, Leaf dec, English, c1890-95 ...................................................................... 220.00

49-1/2" l, 15" d, 10" h, brass and white, brass top rail, scroll dec on vertical wirework, America or England, late 18th/early 19th C.................................................................. 2,875.00

Fire Back, 21 3/4" w, 27" h, cast iron, curved crest with cherubs and garlands, heat damage, crack in base .................................. 125.00

Fire Board, 22 3/4 x 36 1/4", painted, geometric blue, yellow, green, sienna, black, and white pattern, American, 19th C............. 2,000.00

Fire Screen, 24" w, 18" d, 38-3/4" h, Classical, Boston, 1815, carved rosewood veneer and grained giltwood, black floral needlework panel set in frame with simulated brass inlay, flanked by faux rosewood columns, brass capitals and bases above gilded acanthus leaves, curving legs ending in brass paw feet on casters, surface imperfections.................................................... 32,220.00

Fireplace Set, gilt bronze, pr andirons, matching set of tools, ornate winged sphinx heads, Egyptian Revival................................ 2,760.00

Fireplace Tool Set

25" l, shovel and tongs, matching brass handles................ 220.00

29-1/4" h, five mismatched tools, steel and brass, stone base, two tongs, shovel, poker, and stand ...................................... 110.00

31" l, pair of tongs, matching shovel, brass and iron, paneled steeple top, attributed to New York, early 19th C............. 575.00

Hearth Broom, 28" l, orig red paint, black, yellow, and gold striping, stenciled and free hand dec in bronze powder and black, horse hair bristles, wear and flaking........................................... 250.00

Kettle Shelf, 12" h, wrought iron, twisted iron cross member, ring top, smaller inner ring, penny feet................................... 200.00

Pole Screen

Edwardian, 56" h, painted satinwood, tripod base, needlework panel with circular satin stitch of fruit still life, base painted with pendant fruit, finial missing, c1895.................................. 690.00

Regency, 14-1/4" w, 8-1/4 d, 57-1/2" h, early 19th C, Chinoiserie lacquered, oriental dec adjustable panel housed on rod raised on turned ebonized and gilt dec stem, stepped down plinth base on flared legs, price for pr .......................................... 1,540.00

Victorian, second quarter 19th C, 25-1/2" w, 23" d, 74" h, rococo taste, walnut, scalloped adjustable frame fitted with vintage needlework panel, carved and fluted tripodal base, cabriole legs,............................................................... 420.00

Victorian, second quarter 19th C, 54" h, mahogany, oval frame with figured mahogany veneer, watercolor on silk scene of birds and flowers, urn finial, turned column and pole, tripod base with snake feet, stains on silk, repairs to base of column..... 1,760.00

Steelyard, 37" l, brass inlay, brass weight .......................... 330.00

Surround, white marble, carved

Baroque Style, rect mantel over stepped leaf carved arched opening, flanked on either side by male and female leaf-carved terminals, central putti supporting cartouche ............... 6,325.00

Rococo Style, serpentine mantel, central carved cartouche issuing carved foliage and C-scrolls continuing to side supports, slip with urn, floral and rope carving................................... 3,163.00

Tinder Lighter, 7" l, flint lock, wooden pistol grip, engraved and cast detail................................................................ 500.00

Trammel, wrought iron, sawtooth, simple tooling, "B.S. 1781," adjusts from 36" ....................................................................................... 165.00

# FISCHER CHINA

**History:** In 1893, Moritz Fischer founded his factory in Herend, Hungary, a center of porcelain production since the 1790s.

FISCHER J. BUDAPEST.

Confusion exists about Fischer china because of its resemblance to Meissen, Sevres, and Oriental export wares. It often was bought and sold as the product of these firms.

Fischer's Herend is hard-paste ware with luminosity and exquisite decoration. Pieces are designated by pattern names, the best known being Chantilly Fruit, Rothschild Bird, Chinese Bouquet, Victoria Butterfly, and Parsley.

Fischer also made figural birds and animal groups, Magyar figures (individually and in groups), and Herend eagles poised for flight.

**Museum:** Victoria & Albert Museum, London, England.

**Marks:** Forged marks of other potteries are found on Herend pieces. The initials "MF," often joined together, is the mark of Moritz Fischer's pottery.

Bowl, 10" d, 5-1/2" h, reticulated, leaf shape, sgd "J. Fischer, Budapest" .......................................................................... 750.00
Ewer
    12-1/2" h, 6-1/4" d, reticulated, white ground, gilt dec, long handle, sgd "J. Fischer, Budapest," price for pr ...................... 750.00
    13-1/2" h, 6-1/2" d, long handle and spout, white ground, applied flowers, sgd "J. Fischer, Budapest" .................................. 350.00
Garniture Set, 12" d center bowl, pr 18" h vases, ornate rococo form, pierced work, polychrome and gilt dec, early 20th C, price for 3 pc set ........................................................................................... 1,610.00
Jug, 10-3/4" h, Oriental style multicolored florals, butterflies, and fans, gold outlines .......................................................................... 200.00
Planter, 19" w, painted green and brown flowerheads, cream ground, green and brown reticulated raised diamonds around base, blue "J. Fischer, Budapest" mark ....................................................... 1,650.00
Plaque, 11-1/2" h, 8-1/4"" l, seated lady, wearing 18th C costume, low cut bodice, rose in one hand, table with open book and glove by side,

**Vase, cornucopia body, pierced rim, painted floral motif, four feet with fish scales, stamped and imp mark, orig paper label, 13-3/4" h, $295.**

two figures in distance in formal garden setting, script title "Mondespan C Netscher, Dresden Museum," imp "CF" for Christian Fischer, c1860-80, framed .................................... 8,500.00
Plate, 9-1/2" d, reticulated, gold, rose, and turquoise medallions, marked "Budapest, Hungary" price for pr ................................. 350.00
Puzzle Jug, 13" h, brown transfer of three gentlemen, polychrome and gilt accents, marked "Fischer, Budapest" ................................. 175.00
Vase, 13" h, moon flask shape, two loop handles, Iznik design, red flowerheads and green vines, cream ground, gold brocade ground on sides, base, and handles, mkd "Fischer, J., Budapest," c1882 ............................................................................... 850.00

# FITZHUGH

**History:** Fitzhugh, one of the most-recognized Chinese Export porcelain patterns, was named for the Fitzhugh family for whom the first dinner service was made. The peak years of production were 1780 to 1850.

Fitzhugh features an oval center medallion or monogram surrounded by four groups of flowers or emblems. The border is similar to that on Nanking china. Occasional border variations are found. Butterfly and honeycomb are among the rarest.

**Notes:** Color is a key factor in pricing. Blue is the most common color; rarer colors are ranked in the following ascending order: orange, green, sepia, mulberry, yellow, black, and gold. Combinations of colors are scarce.

Cider Jug, cov, 11 1/2" h, underglaze blue, 19th C .................. 2,500.00
Hot Water Dish, 10 5/8" d, underglaze blue, center pine cone and beast medallion, four clusters of flowers and precious objects in trellis diaper border, spearhead and dumbbell border, blue spouts, c1840 ................................................................................... 450.00
Plate, 9" d, green, 19th C, chips, gilt wear, price for nine pc set ...................................................................................... 1,150.00
Platter, 18" l, oval, 19th C, rim chip ........................................ 865.00
Punch Bowl, 11" d, white underglaze blue, Fitzhugh border, famille rose floral sprays and shield shaped cartouche, monogram, scalloped rim, restoration ..................................................... 500.00
Salt, 4" l, oval, underglaze blue, center pine cone and beast medallion, four clusters of flowers and precious objects spearhead and dumbbell border, ruffled rim, Mared pattern border, feathered edge, fluted sides, c1820, price for pr ...................................... 1,450.00
Serving Dish, ogee-shaped, crest of the Manigault family of Charleston, SC ....................................................................... 7,765.00
Tureen, 14" l, underglaze blue dec, braided handles, restored pineapple knop finial ..................................................................... 1,400.00
Vegetable Dish, 9-1/2" w, 8-1/4" h, 2" h, blue and white ............ 110.00

# FLASKS

**History:** A flask, which usually has a narrow neck, is a container for liquids. Early American glass companies frequently formed them in molds which left a relief design on the front and/or back. Historical flasks with a portrait, building, scene, or name are the most desirable.

A chestnut is hand-blown, small, and has a flattened bul-

## Reproduction Alert:

Spode Porcelain Company, England, and Vista Alegre, Portugal, currently are producing copies of the Fitzhugh pattern. Oriental copies also are available.

bous body. The pitkin has a blown globular body with a spiral rib overlay on vertical ribs. Teardrop flasks are generally fiddle-shaped and have a scroll or geometric design.

**References:** Gary Baker et al., *Wheeling Glass 1829-1939*, Oglebay Institute, 1994, distributed by Antique Publications; Ralph and Terry Kovel, *Kovels' Bottles Price List*, 11th ed., Three River Press, 1999; George L. and Helen McKearin, *American Glass*, Crown Publishers, 1941 and 1948; John Odell, *Digger Odell's Official Antique Bottle and Glass Collector Magazine Price Guide Series*, Vol. 3, published by author (1910 Shawhan Rd, Morrow, OH 45152), 1995; Michael Polak, Bottles, Avon Books, 1994; Kenneth Wilson, *American Glass 1760-1930*, 2 vols., Hudson Hills Press and The Toledo Museum of Art, 1994.

**Periodical:** *Antique Bottle & Glass Collector*, P.O. Box 187, East Greenville, PA 18041.

**Collectors' Clubs:** Federation of Historical Bottle Clubs, 88 Sweetbriar Branch, Longwood, FL 32750; The National Early American Glass Club, P.O. Box 8489, Silver Spring, MD 20907.

**Notes:** Dimensions can differ for the same flask because of variations in the molding process. Color is important in determining value—aqua and amber are the most common colors; scarcer colors demand more money. Bottles with "sickness," an opalescent scaling which eliminates clarity, are worth much less.

**Silver, leather covering, engraved bass and "4th of July Derby 1915, Heddon's of Dowagiac," $1,045. Photo courtesy of Lang's Sporting Collectables, Inc.**

## Ceramic

Bennington-type, book shape, glazed, chips
    5" h, Comin thro the Rye.....................................175.00
    5-3/4" h, History of Holland................................175.00
    7" h, *History of Burbon County,* blue glaze ...........225.00

## Chestnut

5-1/8" h, citron, half pint, fifteen vertical ribs, attributed to OH
    maker ..................................................................675.00
6" h, cobalt blue, eighteen swirled ribs ........................715.00
10" h, Germany, 1650-1700, freeblown, olive yellow, sheared mouth,
    applied decorated string rim, smooth base .............325.00

## Historical

Baltimore Monument-Sloop, Baltimore Glass Works, Baltimore, MD, 1840-60, light yellow with olive tone, sheared mouth, pontil scar, half pint, some ext. high point wear and scratches ......................2,100.00
Clasped Hands-Cannon, Pittsburgh district, Pittsburgh, PA 1860-80
    Aquamarine, applied collared mouth with ring, smooth base, pint, McKearin GXII-41, some minor int. haze ..........................70.00
    Golden yellow, applied collared mouth with ring, smooth base, pint, McKearin GXII-41, some minor ex. Scratches below cannon, 1/8" chip on top of mouth .........................................300.00
Eagle, pint, blown
    Deep olive green, double eagle and "Pittsburgh, PA" in oval, broken blister on lip, some other surface chips, small star at stone..125.00
    Green, McKearin GII-64, minor rim chip ...........................750.00
    Eagle-Cornucopia, attributed to Keene Marlboro Street Glassworks, Keene, NH, 1830-50
    Bright aquamarine with bluish bone, sheared mouth, pontil scar, pint, McKearin GII-74 ......................................................140.00
    Emerald green, sheared mouth, pontil scar, pint, McKearin GII-74, pinhead sized flake on top of mouth, two 3/8" potstone cracks.............................................................................210.00
    Pale aquamarine, sheared mouth, pontil scar, pint, McKearin GII-72, some minor int. stain near base ................................130.00
    Yellowish olive amber, sheared mouth, pontil scar, pint, McKearin GII-72 .....................................................................150.00
Eagle-Westford Glass Co., Westford Glass Co, Westford, CT, 1860-73, bright medium reddish amber, malformed applied double collared mouth, smooth base, half pint, McKearin GII-65 ......................120.00
Horse and Cart-Eagle, Coventry Glass Works, Coventry, CT, 1830-48, bright light yellow amber with olive tone, sheared mouth, pontil scar, pint, McKearin GV-9 ...............................................170.00
Lowell/Railroad-Eagle, Coventry Glass Works, Coventry, CT, 1830-48, yellow amber with olive tone, sheared mouth, pontil scar, half pint, McKearin GV-10, some minor ext. highlight wear, lettered emb weak .....................................................................170.00
Masonic-Eagle, Keene Marlboro Street Glassworks, Keene, NH, 1815-30, deep bluish aquamarine, shared mouth, pontil scar, pint, McKearin GIV-27 ............................................................275.00
Masonic-Eagle, New England, possibly CT glasshouse, 1815-30, brilliant aquamarine, inward rolled mouth, pontil scar, pint, McKearin GIV-16 ............................................................3,000.00
Masonic-Eagle, White Glass Works, Zanesville, OH, 1820-30
    Light blue green, sheared mouth, pontil scar, pint, McKearin GIV-32 .................................................................325.00
    Light yellow amber, sheared mouth, pontil scar, pint, McKearin GIV-32, shallow bubble burst on left column of Masonic emblem ..............................................................500.00
Masonic-NEG Eagle, attributed to New England Glass Bottle Co, Cambridge, MA, 1820-30, deep greenish aquamarine, sheared mouth, ground pontil, half pint, McKearin GIV-26 ...........................1,200.00
Seeing Eye Masonic, attributed to Stoddard glasshouse, Stoddard, NH, 1846-60, olive amber, sheared mouth, pontil scar, pint, McKearin GIV-43, moderate ext. highpoint wear....................................150.00
Success to the Railroad, olive amber, pint, GV-3, minor wear,
    7" h.....................................................................150.00

## Pictorial

Baltimore/Glass Works and anchor-Resurgam Eagle, Baltimore Glass Works, Baltimore, MD, 1860-70, variegated yellow amber, applied collared mouth, smooth base, pint, McKearin GXIII-54, two 1/4" shallow flakes at side of base ...................................................... 475.00

Cornucopia-Large Medallion, Midwest America, 1820-40, very pale blue green, sheared mouth, pontil scar, half pint, McKearin GIII-1 ................................................................................ 3,000.00

Cornucopia-Urn, attributed to New England, 1830-50, yellow olive, sheared mouth, pontil scar, half pint, McKearin GIII-2, small chip .................................................................................. 130.00

Isabella/Glass Works and anchor-Factory, Isabella Glass Works, Brooklyn, NJ, 1850-60, aquamarine, sheared mouth, pontil scar, qt, McKearin GXIII-55, 3/4" open bubble burst to right of factory .. 210.00

Sailor-Banjo Player, Maryland Glass Works, Baltimore, MD, 1840-60, aquamarine, inward rolled mouth, pontil scar, half pint, McKearin GXIII-8 ................................................................ 180.00

Sheaf of Wheat-Star, attributed to Bulltown Glass Works, Bulltown, NJ, 1858-60, bright medium green, applied double collared mouth, pontil scar, pint, McKearin GIII-39 .......................................... 750.00

Sheaf of Wheat-Westford Glass Co, Westford Glass Works, Westford, CT, 1860-73

    Golden amber, reddish tone, applied double collared mouth, smooth base, pint, McKearin GXIII-35 .............................. 120.00

    Reddish amber, applied double collared mouth, smooth base, pint, McKearin GXIII-35 .................................................. 140.00

    Yellow olive, applied double collared mouth, smooth base, pint, McKearin GXIII-36 ............................................................. 120.00

    Yellow olive, applied double collared mouth, smooth base, pint, McKearin GXIII-37 ............................................................. 120.00

Summer-Winter, attributed to Baltimore Glass works, Baltimore, MD, 1860-70, citron with olive tone, applied double collared mouth, smooth base, pint, McKearin GX-15 ........................................ 900.00

Urn and Cornucopia, olive green, pint, GIII-4, wear, minor residue, 6-3/4" h ...................................................................... 220.00

## Pitkin Type

Midwest, 1800-30, 5-1/4" h, light green, sixteen ribs broken swirl, Midwestern, worn ext. ............................................... 450.00

New England, 1783-1830, sheared mouth, pontil scar

    5" h, 36 ribs swirled to the right, yellow olive ..................... 400.00

    5-1/4" h, 36 swirled ribs, olive green, half post neck........... 255.00

    6-3/4" h, olive green, 36 ribs, broken swirl......................... 220.00

## Pocket

6-3/4" l, colorless, fiery opalescent ribs................................. 225.00

7-5/8" l, opaque white, blue spatter...................................... 195.00

## Portrait

Lafayette, Thomas Stebbins, Coventry, CT, 19th C, olive amber, pint, reverse with DeWitt Clinton, McKearin GI-80, 8-1/2" h ............ 575.00

Lafayette-Masonic, Coventry Glass Works, Coventry, CT, 1824-45, yellowish-olive, sheared mouth, pontil scar, half pint, McKearin Gi-84, some minor exterior highpoint wear ...................................... 1,700.00

Rough and Ready Taylor-Eagle, Midwest, 1830-40, aquamarine, sheared mouth, pontil scar, pint, McKearin GI-77 ................ 1,200.00

Washington-Albany Glass Works/NY, Albany Glass Works, Albany, NY, 1847-50, greenish-aquamarine, sheared mouth, pontil scar, half pint, McKearin GI-30 .......................................................... 2,200.00

Washington-Eagle, Kensington Glass Works, Philadelphia, PA, 1820-38, bright aquamarine, sheared mouth, pontil scar, pint, McKearin GI-14 ............................................................................. 375.00

Washington-Jackson, Coventry, CT, Glass Works, olive amber, half pint, reverse with portrait of Jackson, McKearin GI-34, 5-1/2" h........... 250.00

Washington-Taylor, Dyottville Glass Works, Philadelphia, PA 1840-60

    Bright bluish-green, applied double collared mouth, pontil scar, quart, McKearin GI-42 .................................................. 400.00

    Brilliant olive yellow, sheared mouth, pontil scar, pint, McKearin GI-38 .................................................................... 900.00

## Scroll

America, 1845-60

    Brilliant golden amber, applied collared mouth, iron pontil mark, pint, McKearin GIX-10.................................................... 425.00

    Medium lime green, sheared mouth, iron pontil mark, McKearin GIX-11, 1/4" flat flake on top of mouth .......................... 325.00

Miniature, America, 1845-60, cobalt blue, inward rolled mouth, pontil scar, 2-5/8" h, approx. 1 oz, McKearin GIX-40, extremely rare, deep color .......................................................................... 5,000.00

## Sunburst

Baltimore Glass Works, Baltimore, MD, 1820-30, attributed to, sheared and tooled mouth, pontil scar

    Colorless, light gray hue, pint, McKearin GVIII-26, some light overall int. haze ................................................................. 375.00

    Olive green, half pint, McKearin GVIII-27 ....................... 3,000.00

Coventry Glass Works, Coventry, CT, 1814-30

    Brilliant light olive yellow, sheared mouth, pontil scar, pint, McKearin GVIII-3.................................................................. 450.00

    Variegated brilliant yellowish amber with olive tone, sheared mouth, pontil scar, half pint, McKearin GVIII-18.............. 850.00

Keene Marlboro Street Glassworks, Keene, NY, 1815-30

    Brilliant yellow amber with olive tone, sheared mouth, pontil scar, half pint, McKearin GVIII-8, 3/4" faint fissure in one of rays......... 200.00

New England, 1820-30, attributed to, blue green, inward rolled mouth, pontil scar, half pint, McKearin GVIII-29 ................................ 190.00

# FLOW BLUE

**History:** Flow blue, or flown blue, is the name applied to china of cobalt and white china whose color, when fired in a kiln, produced a flowing or blurred effect. The blue varies from dark royal cobalt to a navy or steel blue. The flow may be very slight to a heavy blur where the pattern cannot be easily recognized. The blue color does not permeate through the body of the china. The amount of flow on the back of a piece is determined by the position of the piece in the sagger during firing.

Flow blue was first produced around 1830 in the Staffordshire area of England and credit is generally given to Josiah Wedgwood. He worked in the Staffordshire area of England. Many other potters followed, including Alcock, Davenport, Grindley, Johnson Brothers, Meakin, and New Wharf. Early flow blue, 1830s to 1870s, was usually of the ironstone. Variety. The later patterns, 1880s to 1900s, and modern patterns, after 1910, usually were made of the more delicate semi-porcelain. Approximately 90% of the flow blue was made in England, with the remainder made in Germany, Holland, France, Belgium, Wales and Scotland. A few patterns were also made in the United States by Mercer, Warwick, and the Wheeling Pottery companies.

**References:** Susan and Al Bagdade, *Warman's English & Continental Pottery & Porcelain*, 3rd Edition, Krause Publications, 1998; Mary F. Gaston, *Collector's Encyclopedia of Flow Blue China*, Collector Books, 1983, 1993 value update; —, *Collector's Encyclopedia of Flow Blue China*, 2nd Series, Collector Books, 1994; Ellen R. Hill, *Mulberry Ironstone: Flow Blue's Best Kept Little Secret*, published by author, 1993; Norma Jean Hoener, *Flow Blue China, Additional Patterns and New Information*, Flow Blue International Collectors' Club, Inc. (P.O. Box 1526, Dickensen, TX 77539), 1996; Jeffrey Snyder, *Fascinating Flow Blue*,

Schiffer Publishing, 1997; —, *Flow Blue, A Collector's Guide to Pattern, History, and Values,* Schiffer, 1992; —, *Historic Flow Blue*, Schiffer Publishing, 1994; Petra Williams, *Flow Blue China: An Aid to Identification*, revised ed. (1981), *Flow Blue China II* (1981), *Flow Blue China and Mulberry Ware: Similarity and Value Guide*, revised ed. (1993), Fountain House East (P.O. Box 99298, Jeffersontown, KY 40269).

**Collectors' Club:** Flow Blue International Collectors' Club, Inc., P.O. Box 168572, Irving, TX 75016.

**Museum:** The Margaret Woodbury Strong Museum, Rochester, New York.

**Advisor:** Ellen G. King.

**Acme**, Hancock, teapot with lid ................................. 275.00
**Albany,** Johnson Bros., gravy boat with undertray ..................... 150.00
**Amoy**, Davenport
    Cup and Saucer, handleless ............................... 285.00
    Cup Plate ................................................ 165.00
    Pitcher, 7-1/2" h ....................................... 850.00
    Toddy Plate, 5" d ....................................... 275.00
    Vegetable Tureen, cov ................................... 495.00
**Andorra,** Johnson Bros., large centerpiece bowl ..................... 250.00
**Arabesque,** Mayer
    Creamer .................................................. 325.00
    Plate, 10-1/2" d ........................................ 135.00
**Argyle,** Grindley
    Creamer, 4-1/2" h ....................................... 175.00
    Gravy Boat .............................................. 225.00
    Vegetable Bowl, 9-1/2" l, oval, open .................... 255.00
**Argyle,** Myott, teapot with lid ............................... 475.00
**Athens,** Meigh, tazza, pedestal .............................. 320.00
**Babes In The Wood,** Doulton, vase, 7" h ..................... 650.00
**Balmoral,** Burgess & Campbell, relish tray ................. 165.00
**Beaufort,** Grindley
    Egg Cup ................................................. 100.00
    Gravy Boat with undertray ............................... 195.00
**Beauties of China,** Mellor-Venables, butter dish, covered ........ 325.00
**Bentick,** Cauldon
    Centerpiece Bowl ........................................ 450.00
    Soup Tureen, lid, footed ................................ 700.00
**Brushstroke, Spinach,** maker unknown, plate, 9" d ......... 85.00
**Cabul,** Challinor, wash bowl and pitcher .................. 950.00
**Canton,** Edwards
    Chamber Pot, cov ........................................ 450.00
    Sauce Tureen, lid, ladle ................................ 475.00
**Carlton,** Alton, individual vegetable dish ................. 50.00
**Carro,** Grimwades, wash bowl set, pitcher, bowl, lidded soap dish, chamber pot .............................................. 850.00
**Cashmere,** Morley
    Plate, 8-1/4" d ......................................... 125.00
    Platter, 15" l .......................................... 600.00
    Platter, 17" l, scalloped ............................. 1,050.00
    Platter, 17-1/2" l ...................................... 750.00
    Soup Tureen, cov ...................................... 3,200.00
    Sugar Bowl, cov ......................................... 425.00
    Vegetable Bowl, open, 9-3/4" d .......................... 575.00

**Chatsworth,** Grindley, shaving mug ......................... 250.00
**Chinese,** Dimmock
    Pitcher, 7-1/2" h, bulbous .............................. 350.00
    Plate, 8-1/2" d ......................................... 200.00
**Chinese Bells,** Cochran, sugar bowl, cov .................. 500.00
**Chinese Sports,** Furnivals, child's teapot with lid ...... 325.00
**Chusan,** Morley
    Punch Cup, footed ....................................... 150.00
    Shaving Mug ............................................. 325.00
**Clare,** Royal Albion, creamer ............................. 150.00
**Clarence,** Grindley, fruit bowl, ftd ...................... 225.00
**Cow,** Doulton, plate, 11" d ............................... 200.00
**Dainty,** Maddock
    Gravy Boat with undertray ............................... 200.00
    Tea Cu and Saucer ....................................... 110.00
**Daisy,** Burgess & Leigh
    Butter Pat .............................................. 40.00
    Tea Cup and Saucer ...................................... 80.00
**Del Monte,** Johnson Bros., relish tray, 8-1/2" l ......... 165.00
**Delph,** Globe Pottery
    Bowl, 10-1/2" d, open, round ............................ 175.00
    Sauce Ladle, 8" ......................................... 165.00
**Dog Rose,** Ridgway, punch bowl, edge restoration ......... 350.00
**Duchess,** Wood, wash bowl and pitcher ................... 1,100.00
**Eastern Flowers,** Mellor-Venables, platter, 15-1/2" l .... 250.00
**Eclipse**, Johnson Bros.
    Bone Dish ............................................... 65.00
    Butter Pat .............................................. 55.00
    Cereal Bowl ............................................. 75.00
    Coffee Cup and Saucer ................................... 110.00
    Tea Cup and Saucer ...................................... 95.00
**Excelsior,** Fell
    Bowl, 10-1/2" d, open ................................... 135.00
    Pitcher, 7-1/2" h ....................................... 375.00
    Plate, 10-1/4" d ........................................ 120.00
**Fairy Villas,** Adams
    Butter Pat .............................................. 50.00
    Bowl, 10-1/2" d, open, round ............................ 225.00
    Teapot with lid ......................................... 800.00
**Florida,** Grindley
    Bowl, 10" d, open ....................................... 245.00
    Platter, 12" l .......................................... 275.00
**Florida,** Johnson Bros., creamer .......................... 320.00
**Formosa,** Ridgway
    Plate 9-1/2" d .......................................... 150.00
    Platter, 19-1/2" l ...................................... 850.00

**Chinese Bells, covered sugar bowl, $500. Photo courtesy of Ellen G. King.**

**Fairy Villas, bowl, 10-1/2" d, $225. Photo courtesy of Ellen G. King.**

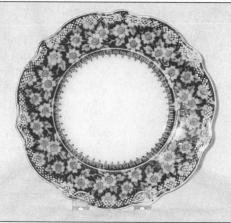

**Grace, plate, 9" d, $85. Photo courtesy of Ellen G. King.**

**Gainesborough,** Ridgway, platter, 14-1/2" l .. 325.00 **Galleon,** Doulton, ale pitcher, 6-1/4" h ............................................................. 350.00
**Geneva,** Doulton, relish tray, 8" l ...................................... 225.00
**Gironde,** Grindley
    Pitcher, 4-1/4" h ...................................................... 275.00
    Plate, 10" d ............................................................. 95.00
    Vegetable Bowl, individual ..................................... 45.00
**Grace,** Grindley, plate, 9" d ............................................. 85.00
**Haddon,** Grindley
    Butter Pat ............................................................... 65.00
    Cup Plate ................................................................ 125.00
    Plate, 10-3/4" d ...................................................... 225.00
    Soup Plate, 10-5/8" d ............................................. 250.00
**Holland,** Johnson Bros.
    Milk Pitcher, 6-1/2" h .............................................. 425.00
    Platter, 12" l ........................................................... 250.00
    Sauce Boat ............................................................. 200.00
**Hudson,** unknown maker, butter pat ................................. 48.00
**Idris,** Grindley
    Bowl, 9" l, oval, open ............................................ 175.00
    Tea Cup and Saucer .............................................. 85.00
**India,** Villeroy & Boch, teapot with lid ........................... 750.00
**Indian,** Pratt
    Soap Dish, lid and drainer ..................................... 500.00
    Teapot with lid ....................................................... 625.00
**Indian Stone,** Furnivals, soup tureen, cov ................... 1,650.00
**Japan,** Fell, plate, 10-1/4" d ........................................... 115.00
**Japan,** Minton, soup plate, 10" d .................................... 110.00
**Japan Flowers,** Meigh, syrup pitcher, 10-1/2" h ............ 575.00
**Jenny Lind,** Newport Pottery, wood and silver encased sauce dish .................................................................................. 300.00
**Kaolin,** Podmore, Walker, platter, 15-1/2" l ................... 250.00
**Kirkee,** Meir, plate, 10-1/2" d ......................................... 150.00
**Kremlin,** Alcock, cake plate, 10-1/2" d, self handles ...... 225.00
**Kyber,** Adams
    Cup and Saucer, handleless .................................. 225.00
    Plate, 9" d .............................................................. 120.00
**LaBelle,** Wheeling
    Bowl, 11-3/4" d, ruffled rim .................................... 600.00
    Celery Tray ............................................................. 250.00
    Charger Plate, 12" d ............................................... 275.00
    Cracker Jar, cov ..................................................... 650.00
    Dresser Tray .......................................................... 295.00
    Gravy Boat ............................................................. 320.00
    Ice Cream Tray, 13-1/2" l ....................................... 285.00
    Pitcher, 7" h, bulbous ............................................ 275.00
    Sugar Bowl, with lid ................................................ 450.00
    Syrup Pitcher ......................................................... 300.00
**Lahore,** Phillips, tea cup ............................................... 100.00
**Lintin,** Godwin, pancake dish, covered .......................... 325.00
**Lois,** New Wharf, plate, 9-3/4" d .................................... 80.00

**Lorne,** Grindley
    Creamer, 3-14" h ................................................... 200.00
    Tea Cup and Saucer .............................................. 85.00
**Madras,** Doulton, tea set, cov teapot, creamer, cov sugar ......... 675.00
**Manilla,** Podmore & Walker
    Gravy Boat .............................................................. 275.00
    Sugar Bowl, with lid ................................................ 425.00
**Marble,** Spode, pitcher, 8-3/4" h .................................... 250.00
**Marble,** unknown maker, tea cup and saucer ................. 100.00
**Marechal,** Grindley, platter, 12" l ................................... 225.00
**Marie,** Grindley, pitcher, 6" h ......................................... 150.00
**Morning Glory,** Ridgway, pitcher, 7" h ........................... 495.00
**Nankin,** Doulton
    Relish, 9-1/4" l, shell shape
    Teapot, cov ............................................................ 550.00
**Non Pareil,** Burgess & Leigh
    Egg Cup ................................................................. 195.00
    Platter, 18" l ........................................................... 500.00
    Soup Tureen with lid .............................................. 650.00
    Tea Cup and Saucer .............................................. 125.00
**Normandy,** Johnson Bros.
    Child's Plate, 4-1/4" d ............................................ 150.00
    Plate, 10" d ............................................................ 125.00
**Nymphia,** Wedgwood, compote, stemmed ...................... 450.00
**Okent,** Globe Pottery, wall picture, 10" .......................... 250.00
**Olympia,** Grindley
    Berry Bowl, 4-3/4" d, individual .............................. 45.00
    Butter Pat ............................................................... 40.00
    Creamer, 3-5/8" h ................................................... 165.00
    Tea Cup and Saucer .............................................. 85.00
**Oregon,** Mayer
    Berry Bowl, 5" d, individual .................................... 135.00
    Creamer, 5-1/4" h ................................................... 450.00

**Pelew, teapot, cov, $1,200. Photo courtesy of Ellen G. King.**

| | |
|---|---|
| Plate, 8-1/2" d | 100.00 |
| Teapot with lid, bulbous | 550.00 |
| Vegetable Tureen, cov | 475.00 |

**Oriental**, Ridgway, soup tureen with lid and undertray ............. 495.00
**Pansy**, Haynes, milk pitcher, 5" h ................................. 375.00
**Pekin**, Regout, tea cup and saucer ................................. 120.00
**Pelew**, Challinor

| | |
|---|---|
| Cup and Saucer, handleless | 210.00 |
| Plate, 10" d | 150.00 |
| Sugar Bowl with lid | 450.00 |
| Teapot with lid | 1,200.00 |

**Persian Moss**, Utzschneider

| | |
|---|---|
| Berry Bowl, 5" d, individual | 40.00 |
| Butter Pat | 55.00 |
| Plate, 6-1/4" d | 35.00 |

**Persian Spray**, Doulton

| | |
|---|---|
| Fruit Compote, stemmed | 250.00 |
| Plate, 9-7/8" d | 75.00 |

**Rhone**, Furnivals, platter, 20" l, well and tree ............................ 450.00
**Richmond**, Meakin

| | |
|---|---|
| Tea Cup and Saucer | 95.00 |
| Waste Bowl | 145.00 |

**Roseville**, Maddock, soup tureen with lid ................................. 575.00
**Royal Blue**, Burgess & Campbell, butter dish with lid ............... 250.00
**Royston**, Johnson Bros.

| | |
|---|---|
| Plate, 10" d | 75.00 |
| Tea Cup and Saucer | 85.00 |

**Saskia**, Ridgway, lady's spittoon ......................................... 250.00
**Scinde**, Alcock

| | |
|---|---|
| Compote, footed | 2,100.00 |
| Mug, 3-1/2" h | 500.00 |
| Plate, 10-1/2" d | 195.00 |
| Platter, 16-1/4" l | 550.00 |
| Platter, 18" l | 750.00 |
| Soup Plate, 10-1/2" d | 210.00 |

**Seville**, Wood, plate, 9-3/4" d ............................................. 95.00
**Shanghae**, Furnivals, plate, 9" d ......................................... 85.00
**Shell**, Challinor

| | |
|---|---|
| Milk Pitcher, 8" h | 1,500.00 |
| Platter, 18" l | 795.00 |
| Teapot with lid | 775.00 |

**Sloe Blossom**, Ridgway, syrup pitcher, pewter lid .................... 450.00
**Surrey**, Keeling, wash bowl, oval ......................................... 475.00
**Syria**, Grindley, pitcher, 7-1/2" h ........................................ 350.00
**Talli,** Godwin, platter, 21-1/4" l ........................................... 475.00
**Temple**, Podmore & Walker

| | |
|---|---|
| Bowl, 12" d | 375.00 |
| Vegetable Bowl, 9-1/2" d, open | 275.00 |

**Tonquin**, Adams, chamber pot, covered ................................. 650.00
**Tonquin**, Heath

| | |
|---|---|
| Pitcher, 6-1/2" h | 350.00 |
| Sugar Bowl with lid | 325.00 |

**Touraine**, Alcock

| | |
|---|---|
| Berry Bowl, oval individual | 175.00 |
| Butter Dish with lid | 350.00 |
| Creamer | 195.00 |

**Weir, sauce tureen, 4 pcs, $495. Photo courtesy of Ellen G. King.**

| | |
|---|---|
| **Turkey**, Cauldon, platter, 19-3/4" l | 625.00 |
| **Turkey**, Ridgway, plate, 10" d | 135.00 |
| **Tyrolean**, Ridgway, charger, 12-1/4" d, round | 275.00 |

**Vermont**, Burgess & Leigh

| | |
|---|---|
| Berry Bowl, 5" d, individual | 45.00 |
| Plate, 7-3/4" d | 65.00 |
| Plate, 10" d | 110.00 |

**Verona**, Wood, plate, 10-3/4" d ........................................... 75.00
**Waldorf**, New Wharf

| | |
|---|---|
| Bowl, 9" d, round | 125.00 |
| Platter, 10-3/4" l | 160.00 |
| Platter, 11" l | 175.00 |

**Warwick**, Johnson Bros., gravy boat with undertray ................. 225.00
**Watteau**, Doulton

| | |
|---|---|
| Compote, stemmed | 500.00 |
| Loving Cup, three handles | 475.00 |
| Pitcher, 6-1/2" h | 250.00 |
| Teapot with lid | 420.00 |

**Weir**, Ford & Sons, sauce tureen, four pcs ............................ 495.00
**Whampoa**, Mellor-Venables, wash basin ................................ 450.00
**Wild Rose**, Warwick, syrup pitcher ....................................... 275.00
**Yedo**, Ashworth, plate, 10-3/8" d ......................................... 95.00
**Yedo**, Wilkinson, berry drainer with tray, footed ...................... 450.00
**Zuyder,** Meakin, waste jar (to wash set) ................................. 375.00

# FOLK ART

**History:** Exactly what constitutes folk art is a question still being vigorously debated among collectors, dealers, museum curators, and scholars. Some want to confine folk art to non-academic, handmade objects. Others are willing to include manufactured material. As in many areas of the antiques and collectibles marketplace, collectors have the final word in what they wish to include in their collections.

**References:** Edwin O. Christensen, *Early American Wood Carvings*, Dover Publications, n.d.; Country Living Magazine, *Living with Folk Art*, Hearst Books, 1994; Catherine Dike, *Canes in the United States*, Cane Curiosa Press, 1995; Jim Dresslar, *Folk Art of Early America—The Engraved Powder Horn*, Dresslar Publishing (P.O. Box 635, Bargersville, IN 46106), 1996; Wendy Lavitt, *Animals in American Folk Art*, Knopf, 1990; Jack L. Lindsey, *Worldly Goods, The Arts of Early Pennsylvania, 1680-1758,* Pennsylvania Museum of Art, distributed by Antique Collectors' Club, 1999; Jean Lipman, *American Folk Art in Wood,*

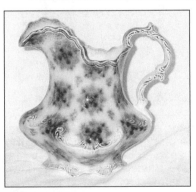

**Syria, pitcher, 7-1/2" h, $350. Photo courtesy of Ellen G. King.**

*Metal, and Stone*, Dover Publications, n.d. George H. Meyer, *American Folk Art Canes*, Sandringham Press, Museum of American Folk Art, and University of Washington Press, 1992; Donald J. Petersen, *Folk Art Fish Decoys*, Schiffer Publishing, 1996; Beatrix Rumford and Carolyn Weekly, *Treasures in American Folk Art from the Abby Aldrich Rockefeller Folk Art Center*, Little Brown, 1989.

**Periodical:** *Folk Art Illustrated*, P.O. Box 906, Marietta, OH 45750.

**Museums:** Abby Aldrich Rockefeller Folk Art Center, Williamsburg, VA; Daughters of the American Revolution Museum, Washington, DC; Landis Valley Farm Museum, Lancaster, PA; Mercer Museum, Doylestown, PA; Museum of American Folk Art, New York, NY; Museum of Early Southern Decorative Arts, Winston-Salem, NC; Museum of International Folk Art, Sante Fe, NM.

Box, cov, 6" h, wood, oval, orig red and black floral dec, cut-out double bird head crest and lift lid, minor edge damage .................... 1,430.00
Carving, Popeye Reed, OH
    6-1/2" h, woman, sgd "E. Reed," marked in pencil "Indian Flat Head, 1982," sandstone.................... 275.00
    6-3/4" h, owl, double, sgd "E. Reed," limestone................. 385.00
    7-3/4" h, bearded man, sgd "E. Reed," sandstone ............. 385.00
Doll, America, late 19th C
    22" h, black cotton, embroidered features, plaid cotton dress .............. 175.00
    22" h, cotton, pen and inked features, brown calico dress, blue and white striped bonnet.................... 850.00
Family Memorial, 24-3/4" w, 17-1/2" h, Hammond-Bradley Family, MA, 1822-29, unsigned, "Painted by Harriet M. Hammond about 1830, Miss Lois B. Batchelder, Teacher" inscribed in pencil on reverse, watercolor on paper, three classical memorials, each inscribed on plinth, "sacred to the memory of Mrs. E. W. Bradley Obt. Oct 23, 1825 aged 16 years, 10 months," "Edward W. Hammond Obt. Oct 10, 1822, aged 1 year 10 months, 20 days," "Andrew L. Hammond Obt. Dec 27, 1829 aged 1 year 3 months 22 days," fourth memorial is partially obscured by shrubbery, all beneath trees in landscape, river, bridge, church and buildings in background, framed, minor foxing, staining, and cockling, small tear lower center.....................2,990.00
Family Record
    15-3/4" w, 13" h, ink and watercolor on paper, Decost Family, floral dec, grain painted frame, creases, toning ................2,300.00
    16-1/2" w, 13-1/2" h, watercolor on paper, Dover, NH, 1823-90, Stevens/Smith family, sgd V. R. "Dover NH Sept 1823 Presented by John B. Stevens," on reverse "A Distaff Side of my Family..., Sept 18 1823 J B. Stevens," vining plant, heart and circles with family info, creases, tears, staining, toning .........................1,610.00
Game Board, America, 19th C, painted wood
    Checkerboard, rectangular shaped checkerboard at center, painted dark red and taupe, frame losses, paint wear, 17-1/2" w, 31-1/2" l.................... 175.00

Checkerboard, rectangular form, rounded ends and chamfered edges, scribed checks painted black on red ground, minor paint wear, 13-1/2" w, 25-1/2" l .................................................. 750.00
Checkerboard, sq, dark red swirl and sponge dec, grain painted mustard ground, black checks, linear scroll dec, molded border, 16-1/2" sq.................................................................... 1,955.00
Folding, hinged at center, checkerboard pattern on red ground, interior with backgammon and star motifs, shades of red, green, orange, yellow, and black on white ground, paint wear, 14-1/2" x 17-1/4", folds to 14-1/2" x 8-3/4" ...................................... 350.00
Parcheesi, dark green border on one side, checkerboard on dark red ground on reverse, paint wear, some rough edges. 5,290.00
Parcheesi, shades of dark red, mustard, and black, painted on one side, backgammon game in red, green, and yellow on reverse, minor wear, some edge roughness, 18-3/4" w, 18" h.........2,070.00
Parcheesi, shades of red, blue, yellow, gray, brown, and gilt, off-white ground, black frame, minor paint wear, 18-5/8" l, 18-1/4" ....................................................................... 17,250.00
Memorial Stickpin, 5/8" w, 1" h lozenge-shaped grisaille watercolor on ivory, mourning figures at classical monument and urn, inscribed above "Be What Your Mother Was and Claim the Skies," 2-1/2" l gold plated mount, initialed "A.I.H." on reverse................................. 260.00
Schnerenschnitte paper cutting
    4-3/4" h, 2-3/4" w, tree with four birds, cut from lined school paper, green backing, old carved 7-1/2" h, 5-7/8" h frame, collector notes on back "Pa. Dutch Cutout, Lancaster County"...... 475.00
    16-5/8" h, 21" w, paper cut-out, birth record, lattice work border with leaves and tulips on top, bottom with "Jannens Stratingh, Ge Boren Den 4 October 1812," two other names with leaf dividers, margin stains, early mahogany veneer 21" h, 25-3/4" w frame ...................................................................... 1,320.00
Theorem, on paper
    5-3/4" h, 7" w, bird, nest with eggs, foliage, and cherries, shades of green, brown, red, and blue, sgd in pencil "L. Lewis," reds somewhat faded, old 7-7/8" h, 9-3/8" w frame ................ 360.00

**Memorial Picture, watercolor and pencil on paper, tom inscribed "Sacred to the Memory of Sally McFarland who died August 1807 aged 32 years...," sgd on eglomise mat "Ann Bradley," old gilt gesso frame, 10-3/4" w, 11-3/4" w, $1,380. Photo courtesy of Skinner, Inc.**

**Theorem, still life of fruit and nuts, blue and white export bowl, painted by Morgan Stoddard, (1768-1865), 11-1/2" x 15-1/2", $910. Photo courtesy of Sanford Alderfer Auction Co.**

12-1/2" h, 10" w, bouquet of mixed pink, yellow, and blue flowers with green foliage in brown vase, oval format, framed, unsigned, minor toning, staining .......................................................... 490.00

15-1/4" h, 19-1/4" w, still life of flowers in blue bowl, unsigned, New England, early 19th C, framed, toning, creases, abrasions ..................................................................... 4,315.00

Theorem, on velvet

7" h, 9-1/2" w, fruit still life, shades of green, yellow, and dark blue, New England, early 19th C, framed, foxing, fabric abrasions .......................................................................... 920.00

12-7/8" h, 14-3/8" w, magnolia and lilies with foliage, well executed in blue, burgundy, and green, frame has black repaint with gilt liner and eglomise border with crazing, stains ........... 525.00

16" h, 20-1/4" w, basket of fruit and foliage, green, blue, yellow, and brown, scrap of paper with pen and ink inscription, "Taken from frame by Carlton P. Crittenden at Fredonbourg 1862," unframed ....................................................................... 3,630.00

17-3/4" h, 15" w, basket of fruit on fringed mat, shades of dark blue, green, and mustard, New England, early 19th C, framed, minor staining, toning ............................................................ 7,475.00

18-1/2" h, 22-1/2" w, still life, over turned Canton fruit bowl on marble table, red, blue, green, yellow, and yellow, some wear and minor age stains, old frame ...................................... 2,860.00

21" h, 24-1/2" w, still life in decorated bowls, and basket, unsigned, framed ......................................................... 12,650.00

Toy, America, late 19th C

19" h, Jumping Jack, carved wood, polychrome dec .......... 115.00

41-1/2" w, 16" d, 38-1/2" h, jig dancers, carved wood and wrought iron, articulate figures with period clothing, remnants of hair wigs, imperfections ........................................................... 825.00

# FOOD BOTTLES

**History:** Food bottles were made in many sizes, shapes, and colors. Manufacturers tried to make an attractive bottle that would ship well and allow the purchaser to see the product, thus giving assurance that the product was as good and as well-made as home preserves.

**References:** Ralph & Terry Kovel, *Kovels' Bottle Price List*, 11th ed., Three Rivers Press, 1999; John Odell, *Digger Odell's Official Antique Bottle and Glass Collector Magazine Price Guide Series*, Vol. 6, published by author (1910 Shawhan Rd, Morrow, OH 45152), 1995.

**Periodical:** *Antique Bottle and Glass Collector*, P.O. Box 187, East Greenville, PA 18041.

**Collectors' Club:** Federation of Historical Bottle Collectors, Inc., 88 Sweetbriar Branch, Longwood, Fl 32750.

Banana Flavoring, Herberlings, paper label, 8" h ........................ 10.00

Candy, Prices Patent Candie Company, England, 1840-60, rect wedge form, cobalt blue, applied sloping collared mouth with ring, pontil scar, 7" h ................................................................... 350.00

Catsup

Curtis Brothers, colorless, blue label .................................... 12.00

Quickshank, paper label ....................................................... 5.00

Extract

Baker's Flavoring Extracts, 4-3/4" h, aqua, sq ring lip .......... 15.00

L. C. Extract, label, orig box ................................................ 180.00

Honey, Land of Lakes, honeycomb, metal cap ............................. 8.00

Horseradish, Heinz Nobel & Co., emb, two anchors, horse head on lid, 1873, 5" h .......................................................................... 275.00

Lemonade, G. Foster Clark & Co, Eiffel Tower, 2-3/4" h .............. 10.00

Lemon Extract, Louis & Company ............................................... 10.00

Lime Juice, 13" h, tapered cylinder, blob top, overall emb lime foliage, emb "L. Rose & Co" .............................................................. 35.00

Malted Milk, Horlick's Malted Milk, Racine, half pint ................... 20.00

Olive, Chef, 5" h ....................................................................... 5.00

Pepper Sauce, 8" h, S & P Pat. Appl. For, teal blue, smooth base, tooled lip ............................................................................. 50.00

Pickle, cathedral, America, 1845-80, sq, beveled corners,

10-5/8" h, 4 fancy cathedral arch designs, medium green, tooled rolled mouth, smooth base .......................................... 650.00

11-1/2" h, 3 fancy cathedral designs, greenish-aqua, tooled rolled mouth, smooth base .......................................... 150.00

11-3/4" h, 4 different fancy cathedral arch designs, protruding irregular panels, aquamarine, tooled sq mouth, iron pontil mark ... 170.00

Valentine's Vanilla, rect, recessed reverse painted label, Pat'd Apr 2, 1889, ground stopper with flat top, 10" h, light crazing and staining to label ................................................................................... 100.00

Vinegar, jug shape, Whitehouse, 10" h ....................................... 20.00

# FOOD MOLDS

**History:** Food molds were used both commercially and in the home. Generally, pewter ice cream molds and candy molds were used commercially; pottery and copper molds were used in homes. Today, both types are collected largely for decorative purposes.

The majority of pewter ice cream molds are individual serving molds. One quart of ice cream would make eight to ten pieces. Scarcer, but still available, are banquet molds which used two to four pints of ice cream. European-made pewter molds are available.

**Marks:** Pewter ice cream molds were made primarily by two American companies: Eppelsheimer & Co. (molds marked "E & Co., N.Y.") and Schall & Co. (marked "S & Co."). Both companies used a numbering system for their molds. The Krauss Co. bought out Schall & Co., removed the "S & Co." from some, but not all, of the molds, and added more designs (pieces marked "K" or "Krauss"). "CC" is a French mold mark.

Manufacturers of chocolate molds are more difficult to determine. Unlike the pewter ice cream molds, makers' marks were not always used or were covered by frames.

Eppelsheimer & Co. of New York marked many of their molds, either with their name or with a design resembling a child's toy top and the words "Trade Mark" and "NY." Many chocolate molds were imported from Germany and Holland and were marked with the country of origin and, in some cases, the mold-maker's name.

**Reference:** Judene Divone, *Chocolate Moulds*, Oakton Hills Publications, 1987.

**Museum:** Wilbur's American Candy Museum, Lititz, PA.

**Additional Listings:** Butter Prints.

Cake
    Rabbit, cast iron, Griswold ...................................... 225.00
    Ring, 6" d, adv "Mother's Oats," aluminum ........................... 10.00
    Swirl, copper, domed half round shape, bold design,
      6-5/8" d ............................................................. 90.00
    Turk's Turban, redware, reddish glaze, brown flecks, white slip
      and dark brown dec at top, 10-1/4" d, minor chips ........... 125.00
Chocolate
    Alligators, Anton Reiche, 1885, price for four pc set .......... 125.00
    Bulldog, tin, 5" h ................................................... 90.00
    Camel, tin, two-part, 6" h .......................................... 80.00
    Cat, bird and rabbit, three cavities, relief carved wood, 3-3/8" x
      11-3/4", frame type ............................................. 125.00
    Clown, 10-1/2" h, 4-1/2" w .......................................... 65.00
    Dog with hat, tin, 6-1/2" h ........................................ 120.00
    Duck, clamp and hinge, Germany ..................................... 70.00
    Egg with star, 1-1/2" h, mkd "Made in USA" .......................... 20.00
    Hen on nest, tin, removable handled base, orig long clipped top,
      sgd "K & M," 7" h, 7" w ......................................... 300.00
    Lamb, two rows of three seated lambs ............................... 65.00
    Rabbit and chicken, six rows, 11" x 17", tray type .............. 100.00
    Rooster, 12" x 10", single cavity, tray type ...................... 75.00
    Snowman, wearing hat, two pc type .................................. 50.00
Cookie, 8" h, 11-7/8" w, carved mahogany board, well detailed relief carving, large eagle with banner and "E. Plurbis Unum," Washington, Lady Liberty, harvest goddess, cornucopia, and stars .......... 4,625.00
Ice Cream, pewter
    Black boy killing turkey, L & Co, 4" h .............................. 95.00
    Boy swinging golf club, 1900s ..................................... 145.00
    Child, 5" h ......................................................... 45.00
    Cucumber, E & Co, #228, 4-1/2" w, 2" h .............................. 42.00
    Drum, 2-1/2" h ...................................................... 40.00
    Eagle with shield, 5" h ........................................... 200.00
    Halloween Witch, 511/2" h ......................................... 175.00
    Horse, 3" h ......................................................... 65.00
    Girl, golfer, 1900s ............................................... 150.00
    Orange, 2-1/2" d
      D & Co, #120 .................................................... 32.00
      E & Co, #807 .................................................... 35.00
    Pear, E & Co, 4" w, 2-1/2" h ....................................... 35.00

    Pears, three joined pears, L & Co, 3 5/8" l ........................ 45.00
    Plum, D & Co, #121, 2-1/2" d ....................................... 32.00
    Wedding Bells, 3" h ................................................ 45.00
Lollipop, tin
    4-1/4" x 4-1/4", pumpkin .......................................... 16.50
    4-1/2" x 3-7/8", rabbit ........................................... 20.00
Pastry, two-sided, horse on one side, two chickens on other, cast iron, late 19th/early 20th C, 6-1/2" ....................................... 300.00
Pudding
    Basket of flowers, china, 7" x 7" x 3", Germany .................... 45.00
    Ear of Corn, copper, rect, rounded corners, deep ruffled sides,
      design stamped in top, tin-washed, 4" x 6" .................... 165.00
    Fish, copper, 7-1/2" d, 4" h, round ................................ 45.00
    Fruits, apple, grapes, and cherries, copper and tin ............. 135.00
    Grapes, pottery, oval, 3-3/4" l, 2-1/2" w, 1-1/2" h ................ 35.00
    Lion, ironstone .................................................... 95.00
    Melon, tin, two mark, marked "Kraemer" ............................. 48.00
    Pear, tin, oval, deep ruffled sides, design stamped in top, framed
      by raised rim band, 3-1/2" x 5-1/2" ............................ 90.00
    Pomegranate, tin, oval sides, inset top with stamped design of
      large and small fruit, scrolling leaves, 7-1/4" l ............. 80.00
Rice Cake, carved wood, self handle, old worn finish, 10-1/4" l ... 30.00

# FOSTORIA GLASS

**History:** Fostoria Glass Co. began operations at Fostoria, Ohio, in 1887, and moved to Moundsville, West Virginia, its present location, in 1891. By 1925, Fostoria had five furnaces and a variety of special shops. In 1924, a line of colored tableware was introduced. Fostoria was purchased by Lancaster Colony in 1983 and continues to operate under the Fostoria name.

**References:** Frances Bones, *Fostoria Glassware; 1887-1982*, Collector Books, 1999; Tom and Neila Bredehoft, *Fifty Years of Collectible Glass, 1920-1970*, Volume 1, Volume II, Antique Trader Books, 2000; Gene Florence, *Elegant Glassware of the Depression Era*, 9th ed., Collector Books, 2001; —, *Glass Candlesticks of the Depression Era*, Collector Books, 1999; Ann Kerr, *Fostoria: An Identification and Value Guide of Pressed, Blown, & Hand Molded Shapes* (1994, 1997 values), *Etched, Carved & Cut Designs* (1996, 1997 values) Collector Books; Milbra Long and Emily Seate, *Fostoria Stemware*, Collector Books, 1995, 1998 value update, ——, *Fostoria Tableware, 1924-1943*, Collector Books, 1999; ——, *Fostoria Tableware 1944-1986*, Collector Books, 1999, —, *Fostoria, Useful and Ornamental: The Crystal for America*, Collector Books, 2000; L-W Book Sales, *Fostoria: Fine Crystal & Colored Glassware, Cut, Etched, and Plain*, L-W Book Sales, 2000; Gary Schneider, Melanie Hildreth, Therese Ujfalusi and Irene Gardner, *Navarre by Fostoria*, Past Reflections, 1998; Sidney P. Seligson, *Fostoria American, A Complete Guide*, printed by author, 1999.

**Periodical:** *The Daze*, P.O. Box 57, Otisville, MI 48463.

**Collectors' Clubs:** Fostoria Glass Collectors, Inc., P.O. Box 1625, Orange, CA 92856; Fostoria Glass Society of America, P.O. Box 826, Moundsville, WV 26041.

**Museums:** Fostoria Glass Museum, Moundsville, WV; Huntington Galleries, Huntington, WV.

Cake Mold, lamb, #866, $75.

After Dinner Cup and Saucer
     Beverly, green ................................................30.00
     June, blue ....................................................160.00
     Versailles, yellow .........................................48.00
Almond Dish, Colony, ftd............................................15.00
Ashtray
     Fairfax, yellow, 4" d .....................................12.00
     Manor, yellow, sq .........................................40.00
     Terrace, red, 3-1/2" sq .................................35.00
Baker
     June, oval ....................................................180.00
     Trojan, yellow .............................................100.00
Basket, Heirloom Opalescent, blue.........................35.00
Berry Bowl, Heather ..................................................17.50
Bon Bon
     Baroque, blue, 3 toes..................................40.00
     Lafayette, burgundy, 5" d, handle .............40.00
     Meadow Rose, 7" d, 3 legs .......................35.00
     Teardrop, 6" h, 4 handles ..........................18.00
Bouillon, liner
     Beverly, green ..............................................22.00
     June ..............................................................40.00
Bowl
     America, 8" d, 5-1/8" h, ftd........................250.00
     Baroque, blue, 11" d, rolled edge..............95.00
     Chintz, 10-1/2" d, 4 toes ...........................70.00
     Coin, 9" l, oval, olive ..................................33.50
     Heirloom, 15" d, pink opalescent ..............85.00
     Navarre, 12" d, flared .................................62.50
Brandy Inhaler, Navarre ..........................................115.00
Bud Vase, Coin, olive.................................................27.50
Butter Dish, cov
     America, round ...........................................125.00
     Colony, 1/4 lb ..............................................60.00
Cake Plate
     Chintz, 2 handles, 10" d..............................40.00
     Coin, crystal ...............................................135.00
Cake Stand
     American, 10", square .................................125.00
     Bouquet, ftd ................................................135.00
Candlesticks, pr
     American, #282, 3" h, round, ftd ................40.00
     Baroque, blue, 4" d .....................................35.00
     Camelia, duo................................................130.00
     Chintz, #2496, duo......................................75.00
     Coin, blue, small .........................................55.00
     June, blue, 3 ftd .........................................110.00
     June, yellow, 3" h .......................................75.00
     Lido, 5-1/2" h..............................................90.00
     Meadow Rose, #2496, double ....................70.00
     Morning Glory cutting, 2 lite .......................70.00
     Versailles, pink, mushroom shape ..............135.00
Candy Dish, cov
     American, 3 part ..........................................90.00
     Coin, amber, 6" d, round.............................60.00
     Corsage, 3 part ..........................................150.00
     Lido, crystal, 3 part ....................................85.00
Celery
     Baroque, blue ..............................................85.00
     June, blue .....................................................130.00
Centerpiece Bowl
     American, 11" d ...........................................175.00
     Seascape, blue, ftd .....................................140.00
Cereal Bowl
     Beverly, green ..............................................30.00
     Vernon, orchid.............................................55.00
     Versailles .....................................................70.00
Champagne
     Beacon.........................................................15.00
     Chintz, saucer.............................................22.00

Deauville, saucer, etched Indian Tree............20.00
     Florentine, yellow .........................................18.00
     June, blue .....................................................50.00
     Meadow Rose, saucer ..................................22.00
     Navarre, saucer............................................24.00
     Rambler, hollow stem ..................................30.00
     Romance, saucer..........................................20.00
     Westchester, saucer, amethyst.....................22.50
Cheese and Cracker
     Chintz..........................................................145.00
     Navarre ........................................................150.00
     Vernon, orchid.............................................90.00
Cheese Stand, Teardrop, 3-1/4" h ............................25.00
Chop Plate, June, pink, 13" d....................................230.00
Cigarette Urn, Coin, olive...........................................22.50
Claret
     Navarre, 4-1/2 oz ........................................45.00
     Wilma, pink ..................................................40.00
Cocktail
     American Lady .............................................12.00
     Buttercup .....................................................18.00
     Chintz..........................................................24.00
     Colony.........................................................27.00
     Fairfax, #5299, yellow ................................18.00
     Hermitage, yellow, cone .............................10.00
     Meadow Rose, #6016, 3-1/2 oz, 5-1/4" h ...25.00
     Navarre ........................................................30.00
     Romance ......................................................23.50
     Versailles, yellow, 3-1/2 oz .........................25.00
Compote, cov, Colony, low........................................45.00
Compote, open
     Baroque, blue, 5-1/2" d, 6-1/2" h ...............140.00
     Beverly, amber, 8" d, ftd.............................85.00
     Navarre, #2396, 4-3/4" ..............................80.00
     Romance, 8" d, Sonata...............................130.00
     Trojan, yellow, 4-1/2" d ..............................40.00
Console Bowl, June, blue, scroll...............................200.00
Cordial, Corsage.........................................................50.00
Creamer
     Fairfax, blue ................................................25.00
     Meadow Rose, 3-3/4" h ..............................18.00
     Navarre ........................................................20.00
     Romance ......................................................20.00
     Terrace, ruby ...............................................65.00
     Willowmere ..................................................18.00
Creamer and Sugar on Tray, individual size
     Fairfax, amber.............................................55.00
     Mayfair, green .............................................65.00
     Teardrop, crystal .........................................35.00
Cream Soup, June, blue ............................................100.00
Cup and Saucer
     Baroque, blue ..............................................40.00

**Console Set, Heather etching, 11-1/2" d bowl, pr 4-5/8" h candlesticks, $90.**

Century ............................................. 18.00
Fairfax, blue ..................................... 13.00
Heather ........................................... 22.50
Lafayette, wisteria ........................... 28.00
Meadow Rose ................................. 22.50
Navarre ............................................ 24.00
Romance ......................................... 27.00
Terrace, red ..................................... 75.00
Versailles, yellow ............................ 22.00

Decanter
American, Rye ................................ 180.00
Heirloom, orig stopper, topaz ........ 130.00
Hermitage, azure ........................... 260.00

Dessert Bowl, two handles
Century ............................................ 45.00
Lido ................................................. 65.00

Epergne, Heirloom Opalescent, large, green .......... 175.00
Figurine, Chinese Lotus, silver mist ................... 200.00

Finger Bowl, liner
Beverly, green ................................. 25.00
June, yellow ..................................... 60.00

Floating Garden, American, 10" d ........... 60.00

Fruit Bowl
Buttercup, 13" d ............................... 75.00
Colony, 10" d .................................... 35.00

Goblet, water
American Lady, amethyst ................. 35.00
Arcady .............................................. 28.00
Baroque, blue ................................... 30.00
Capri, cinnamon ............................... 20.00
Chintz, 7-5/8" h ................................ 30.00
Colonial Dame, green ...................... 19.00
Colony, 9 oz ..................................... 20.00
Deauville, etched Indian Tree .......... 25.00
Florentine, yellow ............................ 25.00
Jamestown, blue ............................... 20.00
June, blue ......................................... 80.00
Meadow Rose, #6016, 10 oz, 7-5/8" h ... 30.00
Navarre ............................................. 30.00
Neo Classic, amethyst ..................... 35.00
Patio, Starlyte cutting ...................... 45.00
Shirley .............................................. 27.50
Wilma, pink ...................................... 30.00

Grapefruit, liner, June, crystal ................ 125.00

Gravy, liner
June, pink ....................................... 500.00
Versailles, green ............................. 260.00

Ice Bucket
Arcady ............................................ 125.00
Baroque, blue ................................. 190.00
June, yellow ................................... 140.00
Navarre, Baroque style .................. 160.00
Versailles, blue .............................. 210.00

Iced Tea Tumbler, ftd
Baroque, blue, 6" h .......................... 90.00
Chintz, 13 oz ................................... 30.00
Colonial Dame, green ...................... 22.00
Colony .............................................. 24.50
Holly ................................................. 18.00
Jamestown, amber ........................... 12.00
June, pink ......................................... 70.00
June, yellow ..................................... 45.00
Laurel, gray ...................................... 26.00
Meadow Rose, #6016, 13 oz, 5-7/8" h ... 35.00
Navarre, pink .................................... 55.00
Neo Classic, amethyst ..................... 25.00
Trojan, yellow, 12 oz ....................... 36.00

Jelly, cov
Baroque, blue ................................. 200.00
Garland ........................................... 100.00

Jewelry Box, America, 5-1/2" x 2-5/8" .......... 500.00

Jug, ftd
Arcady ............................................ 490.00
Beverly, amber ............................... 400.00
Hermitage, yellow .......................... 130.00

Juice Tumbler
Chintz, 5 oz, ftd .............................. 30.00
Fairfax, #2375, 5 oz, ftd, yellow .... 11.00
Jamestown, amber ........................... 14.00
Plymouth .......................................... 12.00

Mayonnaise, 3 piece, (bowl, liner, spoon)
Buttercup .......................................... 90.00
Chintz ............................................. 100.00
Lido ................................................ 230.00
Meadow Rose ................................... 90.00
Morning Glory cutting ...................... 75.00

Mint Tray
Baroque, blue, tab handle ................ 28.00
Seascape, blue, 7" l ......................... 45.00

Muffin Tray, Colony, 2 handles ................ 28.00

Nappy
Baroque, blue, 5" w, handle, ftd ...... 55.00
Glacier, 5-1/4" d .............................. 15.00
Lido, tricorn ..................................... 30.00

Nut Cup
Baroque, blue, 3 toes ....................... 40.00
Chintz, 3 toes ................................... 50.00
Fairfax, yellow ................................. 25.00

Nut Dish, Teardrop, 6" d, 2-part, handles .......... 18.00

Oil Bottle, stopper
Baroque, yellow ............................. 225.00
June, crystal, ftd ............................ 400.00
Mayfair, topaz .................................. 98.00

Old Fashioned Tumbler, Baroque, blue ........... 95.00

Oyster Cocktail
Colony .............................................. 12.50
Meadow Rose ................................... 25.00
Rambler ............................................ 20.00

Pansy Bowl, Seascape, 4" d, blue ............. 25.00

Parfait
June .................................................. 70.00
Vernon, orchid .................................. 55.00
Versailles, pink ................................. 90.00

Pickle Dish
Baroque, blue ................................... 55.00
Romance ........................................... 40.00

Pin Box, cov, Jenny Lind, 5" d, milk glass .......... 70.00

Pitcher
Century, pint ..................................... 70.00
Colony, 48 oz, ftd, ice lip .............. 215.00
Heather ........................................... 500.00
Vernon, orchid ................................ 500.00
Versailles, green, #5000 ................ 760.00

Plate
Baroque, blue, 8" d .......................... 20.00
Baroque, 8" d, crystal ...................... 10.00
Beacon, 7-1/2" d ................................ 9.00
Chintz, 7-1/2" d ................................ 14.00
Fairfax, 6" d, topaz, used ................... 2.00
June, 8-1/4" d, pink .......................... 22.00
Kashmir, grill, blue .......................... 58.00
Lafayette, 8-3/8" d, wisteria ............ 25.00
Mayfair, 6" d, rose ........................... 10.00
Meadow Rose, 7-1/2" d ..................... 14.00
Navarre, 7-1/4" d .............................. 16.50
Teardrop, 8" d ..................................... 8.00

Platter
America, 12" l ................................... 60.00
June, 12" l ........................................ 75.00

Pomade Box, cov, American ..................................... 200.00
Punch Bowl Set, Coin, crystal, punch bowl, base, twelve cups .. 625.00
Relish
    Baroque, blue, 2 part, 6-1/2" l ................................ 55.00
    Buttercup, 3 part .............................................. 60.00
    Chintz, 2 part ................................................ 30.00
    June, 2 part, pink ........................................... 70.00
    Meadow Rose, 3 part ........................................ 45.00
    Navarre, 3 part .............................................. 48.00
    Rambler, 5 part, gold trim ................................... 70.00
    Terrace, 2 part, ruby, 6" l .................................. 45.00
    Versailles, yellow, #2375, 2 part ........................... 35.00
Salad Bowl, Morning Glory cutting, 12" d ...................... 55.00
Salad Dressing Bottle
    Buttercup, #2063 ........................................... 460.00
    June, crystal ................................................ 290.00
    Navarre ..................................................... 490.00
Salad Plate, Romance, crescent shape ........................ 100.00
Salt and Pepper Shakers, pr
    American, glass tops ......................................... 50.00
    Baroque, blue, individual size .............................. 340.00
    Baroque, crystal ............................................. 45.00
    June, yellow ................................................ 185.00
    Navarre, glass tops, #2375, ftd ............................ 160.00
    Versailles, pink ............................................. 190.00
Sauce Boat
    Chintz, #2496, oval .......................................... 75.00
    June, yellow ................................................ 115.00
Sauce Boat, liner
    Baroque, blue .............................................. 150.00
    Lafayette, red .............................................. 125.00
Sauce Dish
    Baroque, blue .............................................. 135.00
    Lafayette, #2440, pink ...................................... 65.00
    Navarre, #2496 ............................................. 125.00
    Shirley, 6-1/2" x 5-1/4" ...................................... 95.00
Server, center handle
    Brocade, Oakwood, blue .................................... 200.00
    Buttercup .................................................... 50.00
    Chintz ....................................................... 80.00
    June, pink, 11" d ............................................ 75.00
    Morning Glory cutting ........................................ 50.00
    Vernon, orchid ............................................... 90.00
    Willowmere, #2560 ........................................... 48.00
Sherbet
    Baroque, yellow, 3-3/4" h, 5 oz ............................. 17.00
    Chintz ....................................................... 20.00
    Colonial Dame, green ........................................ 18.00
    Colony ........................................................ 9.00
    Fairfax, #2375, yellow, 4-1/4" ............................... 10.00
    Jamestown, amber ........................................... 10.00
    June, yellow ................................................. 26.00
    Laurel, gray ................................................. 15.00
    Meadow Rose, low ........................................... 20.00
    Plymouth .................................................... 14.00
Sherry, Neo Classic, amethyst ................................. 40.00
Snack Tray, Colony, 10-1/2" d .................................. 45.00
Sugar Bowl, cov
    Fairfax ...................................................... 25.00
    June, pink ................................................... 38.00
    Meadow Rose, 3-3/4" h ...................................... 18.00
    Navarre ...................................................... 22.00
    Romance ..................................................... 20.00
    Willowmere ................................................... 18.00
Sugar Cuber, America, orig tongs ............................. 325.00
Sugar Pail, Trojan, yellow ..................................... 240.00
Sweet Meat
    Beacon ...................................................... 25.00
    June, pink ................................................... 60.00
    Versailles, yellow ........................................... 15.00

Tidbit
    Baroque, blue, 3 toe ........................................ 45.00
    Chintz, 3 ftd, 8-1/4" d ....................................... 24.00
Torte Plate
    American, 13-1/2" l, oval .................................... 70.00
    Heather, 14" d .............................................. 37.50
    Lido, 13" d .................................................. 70.00
Tumbler, water
    American Lady, 10 oz ........................................ 12.00
    Baroque, blue, 12 oz, ftd ................................... 40.00
    Beacon, 9 oz, ftd ........................................... 12.00
    Chintz, 10 oz, ftd ........................................... 22.00
    Colony, 12 oz, ftd ........................................... 35.00
    Jamestown, amber, 9 oz ...................................... 7.00
    Jamestown, amber, 12 oz ..................................... 7.00
    June, pink ................................................... 48.00
    Lido, crystal, 12 oz, ftd ..................................... 22.00
    Meadow Rose, 13 oz, ftd ..................................... 35.00
    Navarre, 13 oz, ftd ......................................... 32.50
    Romance, 12 oz, ftd ......................................... 25.00
    Willowmere, #6024, 12 oz, ftd .............................. 28.00
Vase
    American, 9-1/2" h, flared, swung ........................... 400.00
    Arcady, #2470, 10" h, ftd ................................... 260.00
    Baroque, yellow, 7" h ........................................ 95.00
    Brocade, #4105, pink, palm leaf, 8" h ...................... 220.00
    Morning Glory cutting, #2577, 14" h ........................ 400.00
Vegetable Bowl, Century, oval ................................. 45.00
Wedding Bowl, cov, America, milk glass ....................... 90.00
Whipped Cream Bowl
    Fairfax, yellow .............................................. 15.00
    Versailles, yellow ........................................... 15.00
Whipped Cream Pail
    June, pink .................................................. 300.00
    Versailles, blue ............................................ 240.00
Whiskey
    June, yellow, ftd ............................................ 90.00
    Manor, ftd .................................................. 25.00
Wine
    Colony ...................................................... 28.00
    Jamestown, amber ........................................... 15.00
    Laurel, gray ................................................ 25.00
    Meadow Rose ................................................ 37.50
    Navarre ..................................................... 40.00
    Romance ..................................................... 40.00

# FRAKTUR

**History:** Fraktur, the calligraphy associated with the Pennsylvania Germans, is named for the elaborate first letter found in many of the hand-drawn examples. Throughout its history, printed, partially printed/partially hand-drawn, and fully hand-drawn works existed side by side. Frakturs often were made by schoolteachers or ministers living in rural areas of Pennsylvania, Maryland, and Virginia. Many artists are unknown.

Fraktur exists in several forms—geburts and taufschein (birth and baptismal certificates), vorschrift (writing examples, often with alphabet), haus sagen (house blessings), bookplates and bookmarks, rewards of merit, illuminated religious texts, valentines, and drawings. Although collected for decoration, the key element in fraktur is the text.

**References:** Corinne and Russell Earnest, *Fraktur: Folk Art and Family,* Schiffer Publishing, 2000; Donald A. Shelley, *Fraktur-Writings or Illuminated Manuscripts of the*

# SPECIAL AUCTION

Sanford Alderfer Auction Company
501 Fairgrounds Rd
Hatfield, PA 19440
(610) 368-5477

*Pennsylvania Germans*, Pennsylvania German Society, 1961; Frederick S. Weiser and Howell J. Heaney (comps.), *Pennsylvania German Fraktur of the Free Library of Philadelphia*, 2 vols., Pennsylvania German Society, 1976.

**Museum:** The Free Library of Philadelphia, Philadelphia, PA.

**Notes:** Fraktur prices rise and fall along with the American folk-art market. The key marketplaces are Pennsylvania and the Middle Atlantic states.

**Birth Certificate**, Geburts and Taufschein

6" h, 8" w, pen and ink and watercolor on laid paper, red frame topped with stylized tulips and other flowers, red, brown, blue, and black, text in red and black, 1904 birth in Berks County, Manheim Township, by Martin Brechall, stains and some paper damage, 10" h, 12" w modern painted frame...................750.00

8-1/4" h, 13" w, printed and hand dec, records 1840 birth of Adam Schafer, Centre County, sgd "Daniel Diefenbach," red, yellow, green, and blue, stains, edges of paper worn, geometric inlaid 14-3/4" h, 18-1/2" w frame ...............660.00

12-1/2" h, 15-1/4" w, hand colored print, 1838 Lebanon County birth, printed in Lancaster by Jacob Silver, wood block printed flowers and leaves, shade shaped reserve and eagle in black, red, yellow, blue, and green, stains and wear, 15-1/2" h, 18-1/2" w frame .........................500.00

12-1/2" h, 15-1/2" w, ink and watercolor on paper, inscribed for Johannes Zeller, 1797, red, gold, and brown birds and flowers, framed, laid down, tears, creases, staining, toning.........525.00

12-1/2" h, 15-1/2" w, lithograph, ink, and watercolor on paper, for Catharina Nonnenmacher, April 27, 1795, Berks County, PA, large central heart flanked by two smaller hearts, surrounded by handpainted flowers and vines, framed, staining, toning, creases.......................635.00

13" h, 15-1/2" w, pen and ink and watercolor on laid paper, printed format with heart recording 1813 birth in North Hampton County, labeled "F. Krebs," parrots, tulips, stars, orange, brown, green, and yellow, some damage and glue stains from old rebacking on paper, 15-3/4" h, 18-1/2" w frame...........1,100.00

13-1/2" h, 9-1/4" w, printed, dec by Martin Brechall, printed text, verse, and eagle, hand done dec in pen and ink on paid paper, red, blue, and yellowish-gray watercolor, records 1812 Berks County birth, stains, damage, and some color bleeding, 15-3/4" h, 11-5/8" w frame ........................385.00

14-3/4" h, 18-1/2" w,..... printed and hand colored, printed by D. P. Lange, Hanover, 1833, angels, birds, strong red, blue, yellow, and green, paper damage, unfilled in birth and baptismal info, framed, .....................1,100.00

16" h, 13" w, printed and hand colored, 1820 Berks County, PA, birth, printed by Rotter, Reading, angels with cherub and birds, yellow, blue, orange, red, and purple, stains, margin tears, unframed .................................200.00

19" h, 16-1/4" w, printed and hand colored, 1849 "Schulhl" County (PA) birth, printed by "J. T. Werner, Pottsville, Pa," red and green, stains and some damage at fold lines, old reeded frame......325.00

19-1/2" h, 17-1/2" w, printed and hand colored, printed by "Ruth, Rube, and Young, Allentown," records 1831 Schuykill County birth, angels, birds, red, green, yellow, and blue, some wear and fading, framed ...................................1,760.00

**Bookplate, watercolor, Jenette Trumbauer, PA German inscription and calligraphy, dated 1841, red, blue, green, yellow, and black, in orig book, 7" h, 4" w, minor edge loss, $315. Photo courtesy of Sanford Alderfer Auction Co.**

**Bookplate**

6-1/2" x 4", attributed to Andreas Kolb (1749-1811) of Berks, Bucks, Chester, Lehigh, Montgomery, and Northampton counties, dated 1797, translates as "This New Testament belongs to Elizabeth Schei-mer...25th day March...1797..." ..........5,980.00

6-1/2" x 4", signed by George Gerhart (1791-1846) of Lehigh or Washington County, dated February 12, 1837, illustrated in Pastor Frederick Weiser's *The Gift Is Small, the Love Is Great*........................27,600.00

17" x 21", double, fraktur artist Christian Strenge of Lancaster County, PA, for Christian Steman................18,000.00

**Copybook**, Vorschriften

Christian Frederick Helener, 6-1/2" x 8-1/8" ...................1,495.00

Wilhelm Munch, 5" x 8-1/8"...............................6,900.00

**Drawing**, pen and ink and watercolor on laid paper, 3-1/8" h, 2-5/8" w, bird on scrolled leafy branch with flying butterfly, green and black "18" in corner, black, green, and faded yellow border stripes, some wear, later 5-3/4" h, 4-1/2" w frame........................425.00

**Drawing**, pen and ink and watercolor on wove paper

3-1/4" h, 3-7/8" w, red and yellow heart and stars, black inscription, edges trimmed, backed on paper dated 1801, modern 6-1/8" h, 7" w frame..........................350.00

6" h, 7-3/4" w, brown, yellow, and blue heart, interior heart, flowers, and foliage, and "Maria Hoffert" in yellow, white, green, and brown, minor stains, very small amount of flaking, short edge tear, old 8-1/4" h, 10-1/4" w frame...............2,200.00

6-1/4" h, 7-3/4" h, primitive scene of two story half timber house with fence, dog and trees with vintage, shades of green, red, blue, black, and yellow, stains, wear, edge damage, old fold lines, old decorated red and yellow 8-1/4" h, 10-3/8" w frame ..........................2,530.00

6-1/2" h, 9-1/2" w, yellow eagle with branch, two stars, "For a Good Boy" in red, stains and tears, old curly maple 10-1/4" h, 12-1/4" w frame..............................350.00

12-1/2" x 15-1/2", sgd "Carl Munch, Heidelberg Township, Dauphin Co., 1799," decorated with a basket of flowers and a vase of tulips flanking an interior scene of a woman spinning, and featured a Windsor and a ladder-back chair and a six-plate stove, paper has darkened over the years..............................22,000.00

**Family Record**, 15-1/4" h, 11-1/4" w, pen, ink, and watercolor on paper, gilt highlights, Mayberry Family, Windham, Maine area, framed, some scattered staining, minor tears, old repairs....................500.00

**House Blessing**, Haus Segen, 16" h, 12" w, printed and hand colored, printed in Reading by John Ritter, cherubs, birds, fruit, and grain, yellow, orange, blue, and green, stains, 18-1/4" h, 14-1/4" w frame.........250.00

**Marriage Certificate**, watercolor, Col. Edward Anderson of Windham, Maine, born 1753 and married in 1774, water-stained..........2,750.00

**Portrait,** pen, ink, and watercolor, wove paper, full length portrait of woman in yellow dress, holding purse and bouquet of flowers, inscribed "Miss Susannah Kern her Picture AD 1831," red, yellow, pink, green, and black, Centre County, PA, artist, 10-5/8"h, 7-1/2" w, orig walnut frame, 11-3/4" h, 9-5/8" w .................................. 21,010.00

**Print,** 9" h, 7" w, wood block, hand colored, two birds on branch, black, red, and green, old 12-1/4" h, 8-1/2" w frame with beaded edge, old crusty black paint ....................................................................... 660.00

**Religious Text,** pen, ink, and watercolor on paper
14" x 12" religious text fraktur by Heinrich Engelhard, dated 1830, text in Pennsylvania German ......................................... 2,420.00
17" h, 13-3/4" w, text in English, excerpt from Exodus, Chapter 20, architectural frame work with columns, picket fence, gable roof and steeples with plumes of flowers, red, green, yellow, and black, paper has darkened and very fragile, 1889 presentation inscription on old gilt frame backing ............................... 2,860.00

**Tauf Zedel,** 9" h, 7" w, hand colored print, dated 1850, red, green, yellow, and blue floral design, minor stains, and damage at fold lines, old 10-3/8" h, 8-3/8" w frame ...................................................... 500.00

**Writing Book** (Schreibbuch), Catherine Rohr, New Britain Township, PA, 1784-1824, and her husband, John Frick of Hatfield Township, Montgomery County, legal-size softcover manuscript, for years 1784-1788, 1798-1800, and 1823-24, 45 pages written mostly in German script with several full pages of fraktur ................................... 4,400.00

# FRANKART

**History:** Arthur Von Frankenberg, artist and sculptor, founded Frankart, Inc., in New York City in the mid-1920s. Frankart, Inc., mass produced practical "art objects" in the Art Deco style into the 1930s. Pieces include aquariums, ashtrays, bookends, flower vases, and lamps. Although Von Frankenberg used live female models as his subjects, his figures are characterized by their form and style rather than specific features. Nudes are the most collectible; caricatures of animals and human figures were also produced, no doubt, to increase sales.

Pieces were cast in white metal in one of the following finishes: cream—a pale iridescent white; bronzoid—oxidized copper, silver, or gold; french—medium brown with green in the crevices; gunmetal—iridescent gray; jap—very dark brown, almost black, with green in the crevices; pearl green—pale iridescent green; and verde—dull light green. Cream and bronzoid were used primarily in the 1930s.

**Ashtray, kneeling nude, arms extended to hold ash opaque green glass tray, Roman Green finish, 9-1/4" h, $260.**

**Marks:** With few exceptions, pieces were marked "Frankart, Inc.," with a patent number or "pat. appl. for."

**Note:** All pieces listed have totally original parts and are in very good condition unless otherwise indicated.

Bookends, pr
6" h, owls, Art Deco style, c1920 ...................................... 225.00
6-1/4" h, 7-1/4" l, 3-3/8" w, gazelles ................................. 225.00
6-1/2" h, Cocker Spaniels, c1934 .................................... 165.00
7" h, horse heads, 1920s .................................................. 100.00
Centerpiece Bowl, 15" d dish, 8-1/2" h nude flower frog............ 275.00
Incense Burner, 5" h, female head on burner base, leaning back to blow smoke through mouth .................................................... 195.00
Lamp
9" h, two kneeling nudes, embracing 8" d crackle glass globe ............................................................................... 495.00
23" h, two female figures wearing pajamas and wide brimmed hats, strolling across base, silk shade............................. 400.00
Match Holder, 8" h, burrow, pack on back ................................. 165.00
Smoker's Set, 7" h, nude, seated and leaning back, geometric base, arms resting on removable glass cigarette box, 3" d removable glass ashtray at feet ........................................................................... 300.00
Wall Plaque, 6"h, seated nude, floral framework ........................ 275.00

# FRATERNAL ORGANIZATIONS

**History:** Benevolent and secret societies played an important part in America from the late 18th to the mid-20th centuries. Initially, the societies were organized to aid members and their families in times of distress. They evolved from this purpose into important social clubs by the late 19th century.

In the 1950s, with the arrival of the civil rights movement, an attack occurred on the secretiveness and often discriminatory practices of these societies. Membership in fraternal organizations, with the exception of the Masonic group, dropped significantly. Many local chapters closed and sold their lodge halls. This resulted in the appearance of many fraternal items in the antiques market.

**Museums:** Iowa Masonic Library & Museum, Cedar Rapids, IA, http://www.gl-ia.org/museums.htlml; Knights of Columbus Headquarters Museum, New Haven, CT, http://www.kofc-supreme-council.org; Masonic Grand Lodge Library & Museum of Texas, Waco, TX, http://www.gltexas.org; Museum of Our National Heritage, Lexington, MA, http://www.mnh.org; Odd Fellows Historical Society, Caldwell, ID.

**Additional Listings:** See *Warman's Americana & Collectibles* for more examples.

**Benevolent & Protective Order of the Elks** (BPOE)
Badge, metal
1913, Rochester ....................................................... 30.00
1940, Houston .......................................................... 25.00
Bowl, 1910, Detroit, Fenton, amethyst carnival glass ................ 650.00
Calling Card Case, 1-1/2" x 2", sterling silver, inscribed and dated 1913 ....................................................................... 100.00
Cap, Keokuk, IA, purple and white............................................ 5.00
Mug, purple, elk's head and clock, silver handle and trim ........... 40.00
Pinback Button
1-1/4" d, East Orange, NJ, Lodge 630, 1-1/2" l ribbon reads "Visiting Brother" ....................................................... 28.00

1-1/2" d, Dedication, New Home, Dunellen Lodge, No. 1488, October 27, 1927, ribbon torn ............................................ 38.00

Pipe Holder, ceramic, white, gold trim, "Elks Lodge, South Bend, Ind." ............................................................................... 22.00

Pitcher, 12" h, china, purple shaded elk's head and clock emblems, white ground, marked "National Art China, Trenton, NJ" ......... 115.00

Program, souvenir, 1940 .............................................................. 10.00

Shaving Mug, gold on white, elk emblem ..................................... 50.00

## Fraternal Order of Eagles

Match Safe, 2-3/4" h, plated metal, metal inserts, encased wording, "Compliments of H. Fetter, Toledo, Ohio," very worn ................. 15.00

Pinback Button, 2" d, celluloid, attached 4" l red, white, and blue ribbon, "Guest, Plainfield Aerie F.O.E., Instituted Oct 11, 1904" .... 28.00

Stein Set, tankard, six matching steins .................................... 1,250.00

## Independent Order of Odd Fellows, IOOF

Badge, 1-3/8" d, emb image of 1834 Independent Order of Odd Fellows logo with two goddesses ..................................................... 30.00

Brooch, 5" l, coppered brass, Odd Fellows symbols hang from pin at top ............................................................................................. 185.00

Certificate, 16" h, 19" w, Grand Lodge of Ontario ......................... 50.00

Collar, scarlet, sateen lining, 2" long silver fringe and trim, six silver stars .............................................................................................. 75.00

Degree Chart, 31-1/2" h, 25-1/2" w, framed, stains ................... 100.00

Match Safe, 2-3/4" h, plated metal, metal inserts ....................... 130.00

Plaque, 7" h, 5" w, painted cast iron, horseshoe shape with emblems ......................................................................................... 65.00

Quiver with Arrows, 5-1/2" h, silver plated pendant with scroll, quill pens, and heart in hand ............................................................. 85.00

Receipt, 2-1/2" x 4", 1955 ............................................................. 15.00

Secretary, 31-1/4" w, 24-1/2" d, 81-1/2" h, two pc, oak, molded cornice with Odd Fellows insignia on crest, top door with single pane of glass, two drawers, slant top writing surface, one drawer base, fluted and turned legs, old worn finish ............................................. 700.00

Shaving Mug, symbols, wear to name in gold letters .................... 80.00

Staff of Life, 62-1/2" l, serpent, worn polychrome ........................ 90.00

## Knights of Pythias

Goblet, green, 1900 ...................................................................... 50.00

Match Safe, 2-3/4" h, plated metal, inserts with Knights of Pythias emblems and Friendship, Charity and Benevolence wording, some wear ............................................................................................... 90.00

Medal with bar pin, "Conn Lodge 37," name on back ................... 38.00

Rug, hooked, 36" l, 24" w, oval with knight and crossed arms, red/brown border, late 19th or early 20th C, needs rebinding .. 250.00

Tankard and Mug Set, 11-1/2" h tankard, six 5" h mugs, multicolored decal transfers, mkd "Roseville," minor flaws ........................... 350.00

## Masonic

Apron, 13-1/2" l, 15" w, silver bullion embroidery and fringe, scrolling foliate, crossed swords, crossed keys, skull and crossbones, open book with crossed quills, Masonic compass and sq, all-seeing eyes, velvet ground, painted highlights, 19th C, some loss and fading ............. 100.00

Bookmark, 1-1/4" x 4", white silk, finely detailed stitched inscriptions and Indian head art, 1907 Ladies Night event, purple and red lettering ...................................................................................... 20.00

Chest, 30-1/2" l, 13-1/2" w, 14" h, wood, nailed construction, Masonic emblem no top, int. till, metal escutcheon, faint name on int., c1900, warp to till cover, slight damage to edge molding, wear ........... 225.00

Cufflinks, pr, blue and white enamel inlay, brassy gold links ......... 50.00

Flag, 33" w, Grotto of the Mystic Order of the Veiled Prophets of the Enchanted Realm, Masonic emblem on both sides ................... 35.00

Hat

Jester, white, goldtone jester, red stone in navel, green stone eyes, purple sash around crown ...................................... 40.00

Scottish Rite 32 Degree, black, gold trim, double eagle and 32 in red triangle, orig owner's name in top ............................... 45.00

Scottish Rite 50 Year, light blue, gold and green trim, "50" inside wreath on front ............................................................... 50.00

**Masonic, silk apron, designed by T. Kensett, Cheshire, CT, 1812, applied border, creased, minor fabric loss, 13" x 16-1/4", $75.**

Light Bulb, 3-3/4" l, 2-1/4" d, mkd "Aerolux, NY," dated 1903, working order, glows warm orange-gold color ..................... 70.00

Loving Cup, St. Paul, MN, 1907, Pittsburgh PA ........................... 65.00

Match Safe, 2-3/4" h, plated metal, metal inserts with Masonic emblem on both sides .................................................................... 90.00

Panel, 50" sq, painted on canvas, yellow rayed sun face on yellow ground surrounded by three intersecting triangles of white, dark green, and black, upper most points with black letters "E.A.J.J.Y.A.O.A.H.," surrounded by green serpent swallowing its tail, red ground, black border, abrasions, staining, fading ............. 920.00

Photograph, 10-1/2" x 8-1/2", President McKinley in full Masonic outfit, sgd "Courtney, Canton, Ohio," matted and framed ................. 110.00

Pin, Grand Lodge of VA, 25 Years, silver pin, dark blue circling Masonic emblem, mkd "Balfour," orig box .................................. 70.00

Ring, Eastern Star, 14K white gold, emerald cut synthetic ruby with inset Eastern Star emblem ....................................................... 125.00

Tie Clip, sterling Masonic emblem suspended from chain ............. 32.00

Tumbler, "Landmark Lodge No. 127, Baltimore, 1866-1916," milk glass ............................................................................................. 45.00

## Shriner

Fez, Khiva, gold-tone sabre tassel clip, some wear to leather liner .............................................................................................. 70.00

Goblet, ruby stained, St. Paul, 1908 ............................................. 60.00

Mug, 5-1/4" h, 4-1/4" d, Islam logo, sword and crescent on fez, hand painted ...................................................................................... 70.00

Planter, 4" h, fez, Klay Kraft, Nebraska, red, gold insignia, black tassel, two rim chips ............................................................................... 30.00

Shot Glass, cranberry, gold sheaf of wheat pattern, Shrine symbol, marked "Syria Temple Pittsburgh 1908, Brown, Motheral, Moore, Robinson" .................................................................................. 175.00

Statue, 5" h, painted white metal, felt on bottom, some damage to paint ............................................................................................. 50.00

Wine Glass, sgd "Buffalo 1899," clear, gold dec ......................... 115.00

# FRUIT JARS

**History:** Fruit jars are canning jars used to preserve food. Thomas W. Dyott, one of Philadelphia's earliest and most innovative glassmakers, was promoting his glass canning jars in 1829. John Landis Mason patented his screw-type canning jar on November 30, 1858. This date refers to the patent date, not the age of the jar. There are thousands of different jars and a variety of colors, types of closures, sizes, and embossings.

**References:** Douglas M. Leybourne Jr., *Red Book No. 8*, published by author (P.O. Box 5417, N. Muskegon, MI 49445), 1997; Jerry McCann, *Fruit Jar Annual*, published by author (5003 W. Berwyn Ave., Chicago, IL 60630), 1995; Dick Roller (comp.), *Indiana Glass Factories Notes*, Acorn Press, 1994; Bill Schroeder, *1000 Fruit Jars: Priced and Illustrated*, 5th ed., Collector Books, 1987, 1996 value update.

**Periodical:** *Fruit Jar Newsletter*, 364 Gregory Ave., West Orange, NJ 07052.

**Collectors' Clubs:** Ball Collectors Club, 22203 Doncaster, Riverview, MI 48192; Federation of Historical Bottle Collectors, Inc., 88 Sweetbriar Branch, Longwood, FL 32750; Midwest Antique Fruit Jar & Bottle Club, P.O. Box 38, Flat Rock, IN 47234.

**Additional Listings:** See *Warman's Americana & Collectibles* for more examples.

Mason's, Patent Nov. 30th 1858, emb iron cross, name, and patent date, 1-1/2 qt, clear, $10.

All Right, aquamarine, qt, cylindrical, ground mouth, metal cap, wire clamp, smooth base, wispy amber streaks in neck, 1868-1880, old closure, crudely made jar .......................................................225.00

American Fruit Jar, light green, qt, handmade, glass lid, wire bail..............................................................................................100.00

Anchor Hocking, clear, qt, machine made, glass lid, wire bail, anchor emb on side H superimposed on anchor .....................................5.00

Atlas Mason's Patent, apple green, quart......................................75.00

Ball, Mason, blue, half gallon, zinc lid, rubber jar ring...................15.00

Belle, Pat. Dec 14th, 1968, aquamarine, qt, three raised feet, ground lip, lid, metal neck band, wire bail ......................................775.00

Blue Ribbon, clear, qt, glass lid, wire clip......................................8.00

Cadiz, aqua, ground lip.................................................................450.00

Clark's Peerless, blue, quart, wire bail..........................................35.00

Cohansey, clear, half gallon, wire glass closure ...........................40.00

Conserve, clear, qt, handmade, glass lid, wire bail.........................9.00

Dexter, aqua, ground lip, glass insert and screw band, patd Aug 8th, 1865 ...........................................................................................35.00

Doolittle, aqua, qt, handmade, glass lid, emb "Doolittle The Self Sealer" ........................................................................................65.00

Eagle, aquamarine, qt, applied mouth, lid, cast iron yoke ..........125.00

Economy, amber, pt, metal lid, spring clip......................................5.00

Electric, blue, pint, name in circle on front, "t" in circle on bottom, wire bail.............................................................................................30.00

F & S, blue, pint, wire bail, logo in circle .....................................30.00

Gayner Glass Works, Salem, NJ, clear, pint, name emb on front.20.00

Hazel Atlas, light green tint, half gallon, zinc lid with rubber jar ring ............................................................................................18.00

H. W. Pettit, blue, quart, mkd "H. W. Pettit," steel clamp closure ..35.00

Imperial, clear, 3 quarts, front mkd "The Imperial" in emb letters, glass closure, several small rim chips ..............................................125.00

Improved Gem, L G Co, aqua, ground lip, glass insert, screw band............................................................................................400.00

Kerr, self sealing trademark, patented Mason, sky blue, pt, smooth lip, 2 pc lid.......................................................................................95.00

Lafayette, aqua, script..................................................................2.50

Mason
    Aqua, ground lip, X patent Nov 30th 1858...........................15.00
    Green, qt, hand made, zinc lid, emb "S Mason's Patent 1858".........................................................................................5.00

Millville Atmospheric Fruit Jar, NJ, aqua, cast iron lid fastener, aqua lid marked "Whitall's Patent," chip on lid, 9" h................................50.00

Ohio Quality Mason, clear, 2 qt, handmade, zinc lid.....................15.00

Perfecto Fruit Juices, Crane & Godley Co., light blue, half gallon, wire bail............................................................................................125.00

Porcelain, white ext., lined in blue, quart, patent date No. 26, 67 and Feb 4 on bottom, large #154 in middle.......................................65.00

Potter & Bodine/Air Tight/Fruit Jar, aquamarine, cylindrical, barrel form, tooled mouth, pontil scar, 1840-60, two flat mouth chips, some int,. minor stain, 9" h .......................................................................500.00

Protector, aquamarine, qt, cylindrical, ground mouth, smooth base, 1867-90, no closure .................................................................45.00

Safety Valve, clear, half gallon, patent May 2, 1895, with "H_C" in triangle, steel clamp closure.............................................................28.00

Sure, aqua, qt, handmade, glass lid, spring wire clip..................225.00

The Clyde, clear, half gallon, name in circle, wire bail .................48.00

The Gem, Rutherford Co., clear, quart, large "B" on bottom, glass closure ...........................................................................................45.00

The Ideal, light blue, quart, name emb on front ...........................35.00

The Liquid Carbonic Co., clear, half gallon, 11-1/2" h, wire bail, name emb on bottom ..........................................................................35.00

Tillyer, aquamarine, qt, ground lip, lid, wire clamp ......................60.00

Trade Mark Lightning, light yellow amber, qt, cylindrical, ground mouth, smooth base, yellow glass lid, wire bail, 1882-1900 .................65.00

Wan-eta, brown, quart, front "J. Wan-eta, Cocoa, Boston," with "14" on bottom ........................................................................................50.00

Western Pride, aquamarine, qt, cylindrical, applied collared mouth, smooth base, 1875-90, no closure ..........................................120.00

Woodbury Improved WGW, aquamarine, qt, cylindrical, ground mouth, smooth base, 1880-90 .............................................................40.00

Yeoman's Fruit Bottle, aqua, wax cork closure ............................50.00

# FRY GLASS

**History:** The H. C. Fry Glass Co. of Rochester, Pennsylvania, began operating in 1901 and continued in business until 1933. It first products were brilliant-period cut glass. It later produced Depression glass tablewares. In 1922, it patented heat-resisting ovenware in an opalescent color. This "Pearl Oven Glass," which was produced in a variety of pieces for oven and table, included casseroles, meat trays, and pie and cake pans.

Fry's beautiful art line, Foval, was produced only in 1926 and 1927. It is pearly opalescent, with jade green or delft blue trim. It is always evenly opalescent, never striped like Fenton's opalescent line.

**Marks:** Most pieces of the oven glass are marked "Fry" with model numbers and sizes. Foval examples are rarely signed, except for occasional silver-overlay pieces marked "Rockwell."

**Reference:** Fry Glass Society, *Collector's Encyclopedia of Fry Glass*, Collector Books, 1989, 1998 value update.

**Collectors' Club:** H. C. Fry Glass Society, P.O. Box 41, Beaver, PA 15009.

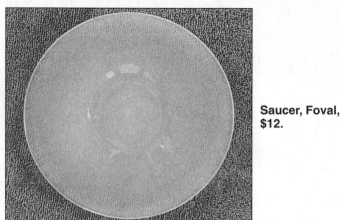

Saucer, Foval, $12.

Basket, 5", cut glass, bucket shape, Trojan pattern, triple notched handle, sgd .................................................................... 225.00
Bowl, 9" square, low, cut glass, Chicago pattern ........................ 550.00
Candlesticks, pr, 10-3/8" h, Foval, gently flared opalescent cup, translucent blue bobeche, opalescent standard with spiral blue threading, blue connector on opalescent disc foot, one with faint Fry shield acid stamp ........................................................................ 350.00
Casserole, Pearl Oven Ware, etched gold dec lid, metal holder, 1938 ................................................................................... 75.00
Celery Dish, 11-1/2" l, cut glass, Chicago pattern, sgd .............. 550.00
Compote, 6-3/4" d, Foval, alabaster white bowl and foot, jade green stem ....................................................................................... 120.00
Creamer, 3-1/2" h, Foval, opal, blue "C" handle, c1927 ............... 95.00
Creamer and Sugar, 3-1/4" h, sugar, 3" h, sterling silver overlay dec and rim, pearly white to almost clear smoky white ground, jade-green handles ............................................................................... 850.00
Cup and Saucer, Foval, pearl white, Delft blue handles ............... 75.00
Goblet
    Rose etch, #7816, 10 oz ...................................................... 24.00
    Royal Blue, 6-1/4" h ............................................................ 35.00
Grill Plate, 10-1/2" d, mkd "Pearl Oven Ware" .......................... 35.00
Iced Tea Set, Japanese Maid, deeply etched, ftd pitcher, six handled, ftd tumblers ...................................................................... 525.00
Ivy Ball, Emerald Green, crystal swirl connector ....................... 60.00
Lemonade Pitcher, 6" h, Pearl Ware, Delft blue handle ............. 165.00
Pie Plate, Pearl Oven Ware ...................................................... 35.00
Pitcher, 9-1/4" h, Diamond Optic pattern, chrome green, ground pontil ................................................................................... 85.00
Plate
    7-1/2" d, jade, sterling silver floral overlay ........................ 185.00
    9-1/2" d, Foval, pearl white, Delft blue rim .......................... 75.00
Soda Tumbler, Wild Rose etch, 5" h, 12 oz, handle, 16 point cut star base ..................................................................................... 30.00
Sugar, 3" h, Foval, opal, blue "C" handle, c1927 ...................... 115.00
Teapot, Foval, pearl white, cobalt blue spout, handle and knob . 250.00

---

## Reproduction Alert:

In the 1970s, reproductions of Foval were made in abundance in Murano, Italy. These pieces, including items such as candlesticks and toothpicks, have teal blue transparent trim.

---

Toothpick Holder, Foval, pearl white, Delft blue handle ............... 85.00
Tumbler, Wild Rose etch, #51, 3-1/2" h, 8 oz, cut fluted base ...... 24.00
Vase, 9-3/4" h, Foval, opal, applied disk foot, c1927 ................. 100.00
Wine Glass, 5-1/4" h, cut glass, Wild Rose etch, cut fluted stem . 28.00

# FULPER POTTERY

**History:** The Fulper Pottery Company of Flemington, New Jersey, made stoneware pottery and utilitarian ware beginning in the early 1800s. It switched to the production of art pottery in 1909 and continued until about 1935.

Its earliest artware was called the Vasekraft line (1910-1915), featuring intense glazine and rectilinear, Germanic forms. Its middle period (1915-1925) included some of the earlier shapes, but it also incorporated Oriental forms. Its glazing at this time was less consistent but more diverse. The company's last period (1925-1935) was characterized by water-down Art Deco forms with relatively week glazing.

Pieces were almost always molded, though careful hand-glazing distinguished this pottery as one of the premier semi-commercial producers. Pieces from all periods are almost always marked.

**Marks:** A rectangular mark, FULPER, in a rectangle is known as the "ink mark" and dates from 1910-1915. The second mark, as shown, dates from 1915-1925, it was incised or in black ink. The final mark, FULPER, die-stamped, dates from about 1925 to 1935.

**References:** Susan and Al Bagdade, *Warman's American Pottery and Porcelain*, 2nd ed., Krause Publications, 2000; Ralph and Terry Kovel, *Kovels' American Art Pottery*, Crown Publishers, 1993; David Rago, *American Art Pottery,* Knickerbocker Press, 1977; —, *Fulper Pottery,* Arts & Crafts Quarterly Press, n.d.

**Collectors' Clubs:** American Art Pottery Association, P.O. Box 834, Westport, MA 02790-0697, http://www.amart-pot.org; Stangl/Fulper Collectors Club, P.O. Box 538, Flemington, NJ 08822.

**Advisor:** David Rago.

**Left: Vaz-Bowl with flower holder, 3 ftd, Blue Wisteria and Mirrored Green, rect ink mark, Pan-Pacific and orig Fulper labels, 7-1/4" d, 5" h, $520; center (back), vessel, emb collared rim, frothy Flemington Green flambé glaze, rect ink mark, 6-1/2" d, 4-1/2" h, $400; right: vessel, gourd-shape, lobed ext., green and Chinese Blue flambé glaze, ink racetrack mark, 5" d, 4" h, $625. Photo courtesy of David Rago Auctions.**

Bookends, pr, 9" h, 7-1/2" w, eagles, Cucumber matte Crystalline glaze, rect ink stamp mark, restoration to beak and neck of one ............. 950.00
Bowl
    8" d, 5" h, flower holder, blue-green crystalline glaze, rect ink mark ................................................................................. 100.00
    10" d, 4" h, low, collar neck, Flemington Green flambé glaze, mustard matte base, rect ink mark ................................... 900.00
    Bud Vase, 9" h, 2-1/2" d, baluster shape, Butterscotch flambé glaze, ink racetrack mark ................................................ 275.00
Floor Vase, 17" h, 8" d, Chinese Blue and brown mirror flambé glaze, rect ink mark, drilled hole in bottom ....................................... 1,500.00
Incense Burner, 4" d, 5" d, pierced lid, four buttresses, four feet, matte green Crystalline glaze, unmarked, bruise to lid int., restored chip ............................................................................................ 950.00
Lamp, table, mushroom cap shape shade, baluster shaped base
    24" h, 15-1/2" d, Chinese Blue and Butterscotch flambé glaze, shade inset with blue leaded glass, rect ink mark, two small cracks in shade ........................................................... 11,000.00
    24" h, 17" d, Café-au-Lait glaze, shade inset with leaded green and yellow slag glass, rect ink mark, circular stamp mark, patent mark, three small base chips, hairline to shade rim ...... 8,500.00
Pipe Holder, 6-1/2" l, 3-1/4" h, figural, fox on logs, glossy Mahogany glaze, unmarked, repair to ears and log ................................. 800.00
Urn
    9-1/2" h, 8" d, two angular handles, corseted shoulder, frothy blue to Famille Rose flambé glaze, ink racetrack mark ........ 1,400.00
    12" h, 7-1/2" d, two handles, fine Mirrored Green, Mahogany, and Ivory Flambe glaze, rect ink mark ................................. 1,200.00
    13" h, 12" d, Roman style, Mirror Black crystalline glaze, incised racetrack mark, restoration to four handles, two short tight lines at rim, short scratches ....................................... 700.00
    15" h, 9" d, scrolled handles, Mirror Black to Copperdust Crystalline glaze, paper label and "MR" in red, glaze drip to one handle ........................................................................ 1,400.00
Vase
    6-1/4" h, 3-1/4" d, bulbous, Rose Famille glaze, squat rect ink mark/121/McConnel ..................................................... 1,300.00
    9-1/2" h, 5" d, corseted, Fool's Cap, Flemington Green flambé glaze, rect ink mark ........................................................ 600.00
    9-3/4" h, 6-1/2" d, classical shape, Leopard's Skin crystalline glaze, ink racetrack mark ...................................... 600.00

    11-1/4" h, 5" d, Vasekraft, two long buttressed handles, cobalt blue crystalline glaze, ink racetrack mark, restoration to one handle ................................................................................ 325.00
    12" h, 4-1/2" d, baluster shape, Butterscotch flambé glaze, ink racetrack mark ........................................................... 550.00
Vessel, 10" h, 10" d, bulbous, Chinese Blue flambé glaze, raised racetrack mark, minor scratches near rim .................................. 1,700.00
Wall Pocket, 10-1/2" l, 4-3/4" w, Pipes of Pan, Cucumber matte glaze, rect ink mark .................................................................. 400.00

# FURNITURE

**History:** Two major currents dominate the American furniture marketplace—furniture made in Great Britain and furniture made in the United States. American buyers continue to show a strong prejudice for objects manufactured in the United States. They will pay a premium for such pieces and accept them above technically superior and more aesthetically appealing English examples.

Until the last half of the 19th century, formal American styles were dictated by English examples and design books. Regional furniture, such as the Hudson River Valley (Dutch) and the Pennsylvania German styles, did develop. A less-formal furniture, often designated as "country" or vernacular style, developed throughout the 19th and early 20th centuries. These country pieces deviated from the accepted formal styles and have a charm that many collectors find irresistible.

America did contribute a number of unique decorative elements to English styles. The American Federal period is a reaction to the English Hepplewhite period. American designers created furniture which influenced, rather than reacted to, world taste in the Gothic Revival style and Arts and Crafts, Art Deco, and Modern International movements.

## Furniture styles and approximate dates:

| Style | Dates |
|---|---|
| William and Mary | 1690-1730 |
| Queen Anne | 1720-1760 |
| Chippendale | 1755-1790 |
| Federal (Hepplewhite) | 1790-1815 |
| Sheraton | 1790-1810 |
| Empire (Classical) | 1805-1830 |
| Victorian | |
|     French Restauration | 1830-1850 |
|     Gothic Revival | 1840-1860 |
|     Rococo Revival | 1845-1870 |
|     Elizabethan | 1850-1915 |
|     Louis XIV | 1850-1914 |
|     Naturalistic | 1850-1914 |
|     Renaissance Revival | 1850-1880 |
|     Néo-Greek | 1855-1885 |
|     Eastlake | 1870-1890 |
| Art Furniture | 1880-1914 |
| Arts and Crafts | 1895-1915 |
| Art Nouveau | 1896-1914 |
| Art Deco | 1920-1945 |
| International Movement | 1940-Present |

**References:** *Antique Wicker from the Heywood-Wakefield Catalog*, Schiffer Publishing, 1994; Edward Deming Andrews and Faith Andrews, *Masterpieces of Shaker Furniture*, Dover Publications, 1999; John Andrews, *British Antique Furniture Price Guide and Reasons for Values*, Antique Collectors' Club, 1999; —, *Victorian and Edwardian Furniture Price Guide and Reasons for Values*, Antique Collectors' Club, 1999; Luke Beckerdite (ed.), *American Furniture 1998*, Chipstone Foundation, University Press of New England, 1998; Joseph T. Butler, *Field Guide to American Furniture*, Facts on File Publications, 1985; David Cathers, *Furniture of the American Arts and Crafts Movement: Revised Edition*, Turn of the Century Editions, 1996; —, *Stickley Style: Arts and Crafts Homes in the Craftsman Tradition*, Simon & Schuster, 1999; Victor Chimnery, *Oak Furniture, The British Tradition*, Antique Collectors' Club, 1999; Frances Collard, *Regency Furniture*, Antique Collectors' Club, 1999; Douglas Congdon-Martin, *Arts & Crafts Designs for the Home*, Schiffer Publishing, 2000; Bernard D. Cotton, *The English Regional Chair*, Antique Collectors' Club, 1999; Anna Tobin D'Ambrosio, (ed.,) *Masterpieces of American Furniture from the Munson-Williams-Proctor Institute*, Syracuse University Press, 1999; Eileen and Richard Dubrow, *American Furniture of the 19th Century: 1840-1880*, Schiffer Publishing, 2000; —, *Styles of American Furniture, 1860-1960*, Schiffer Publishing, 1997; Nancy Goyne Evans, *American Windsor Chairs*, Hudson Hills Press, 1996; —, *American Windsor Furniture: Specialized Forms*, Hudson House Press, 1997; *Fine Furniture Reproductions*, Schiffer Publishing, 1996; Helaine Fendleman and Jonathan Taylor, *Tramp Art: A Folk Art Phenomenon*, Stewart, Tabori & Chang, 1999; Oscar P. Fitzgerald, *Four Centuries of American Furniture*, Wallace-Homestead, (Krause Publications,) 1995; Tim Forrest, *Bulfinch Anatomy of Antique Furniture*, Bulfinch Press, 1996; Don Fredgant, *American Manufactured Furniture*, revised and updated ed., Schiffer Publishing, 1996; Phillipe Garner, *Twentieth-Century Furniture*, Van Nostrand Reinhold, 1980; Cara Greenberg, *Op To Pop: Furniture of the 1960s*, Bulfinch Press, 1999; David Hawkins, *Close Encounters with American Furniture: A Restorer's Story*, Sage Crest Press, 1999; Barbara Israel, *Antique Garden Ornament: Two Centuries of American Taste*, Harry N. Abrams, 1999; Bruce Johnson, *The Pegged Joint*, Knock on Wood Publications, 1995; Edward Joy, *Pictorial Dictionary of British 19th Century Furniture Design*, Antique Collectors' Club, 1999; John Kassay, *The Book of American Windsor Furniture: Styles and Technologies*, University of Massachusetts Press, 1998;

Myrna Kaye, F*ake, Fraud, or Genuine*, New York Graphic Society Book, 1987; —, *There's a Bed in the Piano: The Inside Story of the American Home,* Bullfinch Press, 1998; William C. Ketchum Jr., *American Cabinetmakers*, Crown, 1995; Ralph Kylloe, *History of the Old Hickory Chair Company and the Indiana Hickory Furniture Movement*, published by author, 1995; —, Rustic Traditions, Gibbs-Smith, 1993; David P. Lindquist and Caroline C. Warren, *Colonial Revival Furniture with Prices*, Wallace-Homestead, 1993; —, *English & Continental Furniture with Prices*, Wallace-Homestead, 1994; —, *Victorian Furniture with Prices*, Wallace-Homestead, 1995, distributed by Krause Publications; Jack L. Lindsey, *Worldly Goods, The Arts of Early Pennsylvania, 1680-1758,* Pennsylvania Museum of Art, distributed by Antique Collectors' Club, 1999; Paul McCobb, *Fifties Furniture,* Schiffer Publishing, 2000; Robert F. McGiffin, *Furniture Care and Conservation*, revised 3rd ed., American Association for State and Local History Press, 1992; *Herman Miller 1939 Catalog, Gilbert Rohde Modern Design,* Schiffer Publishing, 1998; John Morley, *The History of Furniture: Twenty-Five Centuries of Style and Design in the Western Tradition,* Bulfinch Press, 1999; Marie Purnell Musser, *Country Chairs of Central Pennsylvania*, published by author, 1990; Milo M. Naeve, *Identifying American Furniture*, W. W. Norton, 1998; John Obbard, *Early American Furniture, A Practical Guide for Collectors,* Collector Books, 1999; Peter Philip, Gillian Walkling, and John Bly, *Field Guide to Antique Furniture*, Houghton Mifflin, 1992; Leslie Piña, *Dunbar: Fine Furniture of the 1950s,* Schiffer Publishing, 2000; —, *Fifties Furniture*, Schiffer Publishing, 1996; Rudolf Pressler and Robin Staub, *Biedermeier Furniture*, Schiffer Publishing, 1996; Don and Carol Raycraft, *Wallace-Homestead Price Guide To American Country Antiques, 16th Edition,* Krause Publications, 1999; Steve and Linda Rouland, *Knoll Furniture, 1938-1960,* Schiffer Publishing, 1999; Steve and Roger W. Rouland, *Heywood-Wakefield Modern Furniture*, 1995, 2001 value update, Collector Books; Paul Royka, *Mission Furniture ,from the American Arts & Crafts Movement,* Schiffer Publishing, 1997.

Albert Sack, *New Fine Points of Furniture*, Crown, 1993; Nancy N. Schiffer, *The Best of Golden Oak Furniture,* Schiffer Publishing, 2000; Ellen T. Schroy, *Warman's American Furniture,* Krause Publications, 2000; Harvey Schwartz, *Rattan Furniture,* Schiffer Publishing, 1999; Klaus-Jurgen Sembach, *Modern Furniture Designs, 1950-1980s,* Schiffer Publishing, 1997; Nancy A. Smith, *Old Furniture,* 2nd ed., Dover Publications, 1990; Robert W. and Harriett Swedberg, *Collector's Encyclopedia of American Furniture*, Vol. 1 (1990, 1998 value update), Vol. 2 (1992, 1999 value update), Vol. 3 (1998, 2000 value update), Collector Books; —, *Encyclopedia of American Oak Furniture,* Krause Publications, 2000; —, *Furniture of the Depression Era*, Collector Books, 1987, 1999 value update; —, Thonet Co., *Thonet Bentwood and Other Furniture* (1904 catalog reprint), Dover Publications, 1980; Treadway Gallery, Inc., *The 1950's/Modern Price Guide: Furniture, Volumes 1 and 2,* Treadway Gallery, Inc., 1999;

## Reproduction Alert:

Beware of the large number of reproductions. During the 25 years following the American Centennial of 1876, there was a great revival in copying furniture styles and manufacturing techniques of earlier eras. These centennial pieces now are more than 100 years old. They confuse many dealers, as well as collectors.

Clifford A. Wallach and Michael Cornish, *Tramp Art, One Notch At A Time,* Wallach-Irons Publishing, (277 W. 10th St., New York, NY 10014) 1998; Elizabeth White, ed., *Pictorial Dictionary of British 18th Century Furniture Design,* Antique Collectors' Club, 1999; S. Whittington & C. Claxton Stevens, *18th Century Furniture,* Antique Collectors' Club, 1999; Eli Wilner, *Antique American Frames: Identification and Price Guide,* Avon Books, 1999; Ghenete Zelleke, Eva B. Ottillinger, and Nina Stritzler, *Against the Grain*, The Art Institute of Chicago, 1993.

There are hundreds of specialized books on individual furniture forms and styles. Two of note are: Monroe H. Fabian, *Pennsylvania-German Decorated Chest*, Universe Books, 1978, and Charles Santore, *Windsor Style In America*, Revised, Vols. I and II, Dover Publications, n.d.

**Additional Listings:** Arts and Craft Movement; Art Deco; Art Nouveau; Children's Nursery Items; Orientalia; Shaker Items; Stickley.

**Notes:** Furniture is one of the types of antiques for which regional preferences are a factor in pricing. Victorian furniture is popular in New Orleans and unpopular in New England. Oak is in demand in the Northwest, not as much so in the Middle Atlantic states.

Prices vary considerably on furniture. Shop around. Furniture is plentiful unless you are after a truly rare example. Examine all pieces thoroughly—avoid buying on impulse. Turn items upside down; take them apart. Price is heavily influenced by the amount of repairs and restoration. Make certain you know if any such work has been done to a piece before buying it.

The prices listed below are "average" prices. They are only a guide. High and low prices are given to show market range.

# Beds

**Arts and Crafts**, America, early 20th C, oak, straight headboard and footboard crest rail over nine vertical spindles, wide plank side rails, wear, age cracks, 81" l, 38-3/4" w, 48-3/4" h .............................. 260.00

**Baroque**, Italian, simulated marble high scrolling headboard dec in patiglia with vacant cartouches and foliage, carved scrolling feet, painted, green and blue marbleized dec, losses to paint and gilt, pr, 45-3/4" w, 84" h ................................................. 3,750.00

**Biedermeier,** figured mahogany veneer, octagonal posts, turned feet and finials, paneled head and footboards, orig rails, some veneer damage, 38" w, 72" l, 45" h, pr ................................................. 750.00

**Chippendale**, tall post, curly maple, turned posts, scrolled headboard with poplar panel, orig side rails, old mellow refinishing, minor repairs to posts, 60" w, 72" l, 80" h.................................. 3,000.00

**Classical**
   America, first quarter 19th C, cherry, tall post, twist-reeded posts joined by single headboard and footboards, rails missing, 52" w, 81" h.............................................................. 470.00
   New England, c1820, low post, carved mahogany, pineapple carved finials on leaf spiral and ring-carved posts ending in vase and ring-turned legs, brass cuffs and casters, joined by scrolled and shaped headboard, old refinish, imperfections, 72" l, 49-1/4" w, 60" h ............................................................. 2,875.00

**Classical Revival**, America, fourth quarter 19th C, tall post, pineapple and acanthus carved posts, paneled headboard with foliate and acorn-mounted roll, 77" l, 55" w, 88" h .................................. 2,860.00

**Colonial**. West Indies, second quarter 19th C, tall post, mahogany, tester frame supported by boldly proportioned reeded and twist posts, headboard surmounted by waterfall crest centered by contrasting light wood panel, 77" l, 54" w, 92-3/4" h, alternations and restorations .............................................................. 4,200.00

**Empire**, American
   Single, fitted as daybed or sofa, mahogany and mahogany figured veneer, turned and acanthus carved posts, upholstered cushion, 31-1/2" x 80" x 43-3/4" h.................................... 825.00
   Tall Post, curly maple posts, poplar scrolled headboard with old soft finish, turned detail, acorn finials, rails and headboard replaced, 57-1/4" w, 72-1/2" l rails, 89" h ..................... 1,650.00

**Empire Style**, cannonball, mahogany, bold detail, replaced headboard with carved eagle, originally rope bed, side rails changed, other repairs, replaced rails, 78" l, 54" w, 59" h.............................. 1,200.00

**Federal**
   Massachusetts or New Hampshire, tall post, maple and birch, vase and ring-turned, reeded, and swelled foot posts joined to tapering pencil head posts, shaped pine headboard with arched tester frame, old red stain, later urn finials, imperfections, 71" l, 51-1/2" w, 69-1/2" h......................................... 1,725.00
   New England, 19th C, tall post, maple and birch, tapering pencil headposts flanking arched headboard, joined by rails to reeded vase, cup, and ring-turned footposts on casters, surmounted by arched tester, old refinish, 75" l, 53-1/2" w, 78-1/4" h with tester ...................................................................... 1,380.00
   Southern States, early 19th C, tall post, carved mahogany, sq tapering birch posts flank arched pine headboard, reeded tapering footposts have tobacco leaf carving, reeded legs ending in turned feet, rails, flat tester, restoration, 79-1/2" l, 56-1/4" w, 83-1/2" h.......................................................... 4,025.00

**George III,** four poster, carved walnut, brass mounted, circular tapered head posts, shaped mahogany headboard, reeded and acanthus-carved footposts, ring-turned feet, casters, 9-1/2" h ........... 10,000.00

**Queen Anne**, Pennsylvania, early 19th C, low poster, turned and painted pine, head and footposts with flattened ball finials, shaped head and footboards, tapered feet, orig rope rails, orig green paint, 48-1/2" w, 74-3/4" h ............................................. 3,600.00

**Rope,** poplar and pine, old red paint, suppressed ball finials, turned legs, high turned feet, orig rails, 71" l, 47-1/2" w, 37" h headboard........ 400.00

**Sheraton**
   Canopy
      Carved mahogany, headboard posts simple turned with ring and block turnings, simple headboard, heavily carved footboard posts with spiral turnings and acanthus leaf bell, sq tester with curtains, 58" w, 73-1/2" l, 88" without finials.................. 3,200.00
      Painted, headboard with D-type cut outs on side, footboard with reeded and turned posts, canopy frame, painted red, 52" w, 76" l, 68" h........................................................ 750.00

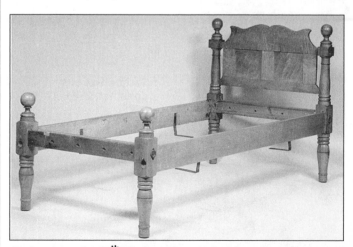

**Federal, early 19th C, maple, paneled headboard, turned posts with cannonball finials, 40" w, 84" d, 42" h, $1,320.**

Tall post, refinished maple an birch, pine headboard, turned posts with reeded detail on foot posts, rope end rails, replaced side rails, curved canopy frame covered in white cotton with floral embroidery, matching bed clothes included, 55" w, 78" l, 66-3/4" h ................................................. 1,550.00

**Victorian**

Elizabethan Revival, America, tall post, bobbin turned posts joined to head and footboard with spool turned galleries, 46" w, 89" h ................................................................................ 395.00

Renaissance Revival, America, third quarter 19th C, walnut and burl walnut, high back, headboard with broken arch pediment centered by cartouche, flanked by finials, conforming foot-boards each with burled panels, applied carving, 76-1/2" l, 52-1/4" w, 83" h, price for pr ................................................. 1,800.00

Renaissance Revival, America, third quarter 19th C, walnut and burl walnut, suite, half tester bed, 81" l, 68" w, 118" h, double door armoire, 58" w, 25" d, 116" h, deep well dresser, 51" w, 18-1/2" d, 91" h, each with anthemion and scroll carved crests ................... 8,250.00

Rococo Revival, America, third quarter 19th C, half tester, walnut, canopy with bracketed supports jointed to tapering octagonal posts, supporting headboard with shell carved crest, 82" l, 64" w, 100-3/4" h ................................................................. 1,800.00

Rococo Revival-Style, America, mid-20th C, mahogany, high back, headboard with shell carved crest over pair of panels, footboard with wrap-around ends, made to accommodate modern queen sized mattress, 86" l, 67" w, 92-1/2" h .......... 1,870.00

## Benches

**Arts & Crafts,** oak, rect top with raised edge, pierced and arched apron supported by side slabs, scrolled cut-outs at base, refinished top, orig finish to base, 42" w, 14" d, 18" h ............................ 1,600.00

**Classical,** window

Boston, 1835-45, carved mahogany veneer, upholstered seat, veneered rail, leaf-carved cyma curved ends, joined by ring-turned medial stretcher, 48" w, 16-1/4" d, 17-1/2" h ...... 2,185.00

New York, 1815-25, mahogany veneer, curving upholstered seat flanked by scrolled ends, scrolled base, old refinish, some veneer cracking and loss, 20th C olive green velvet upholstery, 39-1/2" w, 14" d, 23-5/8" h ................................................ 3,500.00

New York, c1820, mahogany and mahogany veneer, upholstered slip seat, veneered rect frame, beaded curule legs joined by vase and ring-turned stretcher, old finish, 24-1/4" w, 15" d, 19" h .............................................................................. 1,035.00

**Saddle Maker's, chestnut, 25" l, 41" h, $225.**

**Classical Revival,** mahogany, carved paw feet and lion's heads, maroon velvet cushion, old finish, 16-1/2" l, 29-1/4" w, 23" h... 600.00

**Courting** (tête à tête), country, maple, some figure and traces of old paint, shaped back rest, curved and molded arms, woven cane seat with flaked finish, turned and tapered feet with ring turned posts, some damage, refinished, glued crack in one foot, 43" w, 23" d, 31-5/8" h ......................................................................... 1,210.00

**Long,** Baroque, Continental, late 17th/early 18th C, pained, shaped trapezoidal case, painted with scrolls and shells, hinged lift top, 91" l, 16" d, 21" h .............................................................. 2,070.00

**Neoclassical-Style,** Italian, 19th C, giltwood, worn leather top, 44-1/2" w, 20" d, 21" h .................................................................. 2,530.00

**Settle**

Arts and Crafts, Paine Furniture Co., Boston, early 20th C, oak, drop arm, curved crest rail above six wide vertical slats, three vertical side slats, medium brown finish, metal tag, marring, small losses, 74" l, 32" d, 28" h ................................ 2,415.00

Jacobean, England, late 17th C, oak, rect paneled backrest, scrolled arms, rope seat, plank legs joined by stretchers, 75" l, 41-1/2" h ...................................................................... 6,325.00

**Wagon Seat,** New England, mid 19th C, painted, square crest above tapering spindles, seat rail, early splint seat, turned legs joined by stretchers, orig red paint, imperfections, 17" h seat, 34-1/4" h 460.00

**Wicker,** painted white, hooped crest rail flanked by rows of dec curlicues, spiral wrapped posts and six spindles, pressed-in oval seat, dec curlicue apron, wrapped cabriole legs, X-form stretcher, 35" w, 31" h ............................................................................ 500.00

**Window**

Classical, America, c1840, mahogany, upholstered back, serpentine crest rail, seat with serpentine seat rail edged in beaded molding, scroll feet, 46" w, 31" h ...................................... 350.00

Classical, America, mid 19th C, mahogany, tufted back with scrolling top rail, ogee-molded apron, bracket feet, 44" w, 22" d, 31" h .................................................................................. 425.00

George III, English, mid-18th C, mahogany, rect seat, scrolling arms, later velvet cov, straight legs, blind fret craved, H-form stretcher, pr, 38" l ........................................................... 4,750.00

Louis XVI-Style, carved cherry, overstuffed seat, channeled rails, flanked by molded, overscroll arms carved with be-ribboned foliate sprays, turned, tapered, and leaf-capped legs ........... 200.00

Queen Anne-Style, incorporating 18th C elements, mahogany, scrolled arms, cabriole legs, paw feet, 33" w, 18" d, 26" h ................................................................................. 800.00

Regency-Style, mahogany, slightly out-scrolled arms, X-form splat, centered by brass medallion with urn, padded seat, molded skirt, saber legs, headed by giltwood patera, 44-3/4" w, 17" d, 31" h ...................................................................... 450.00

**Windsor,** America, 19th C, oak, crest rail joined to plank seat by spindle gallery, 98" l, 18" d, 33" h .................................................. 650.00

## Bentwood

In 1856, Michael Thonet of Vienna perfected the process of bending wood using steam. Shortly afterward, Bentwood furniture became popular. Other manufacturers of Bentwood furniture were Jacob and Joseph Kohn; Philip Strobel and Son; Sheboygan Chair Co.; and Tidoute Chair Co. Bentwood furniture is still being produced today by the Thonet firm and others.

Box

6-3/4" h, oval, Shaker, Harvard type, finger construction, steel tacks, presentation inscription on inside of lid, old varnish finish, lid has some damage ....................................................... 175.00

8" d, 7" h, round, worn orig paint resembles wallpaper, yellow and black foliage scrolls on blue ground, some edge damage to lid .............................................................................. 750.00

10" d, pine and beech, lapped seams with steel tacks, lid with primitive carved inscription "Jew Denmnia S J C," old dark finish, edge damage ............................................................ 250.00

12" d, round, old dark finish, swivel handle, minor lid edge damage ............................................................................... 200.00

**Rocking Lounge Chair, cane paneled back and seat, Thonet, 40" x 26" x 38, $125. Photo courtesy of David Rago Auctions.**

14-3/4" l, oblong, pine, laced seams, old blue paint, edge damage ........................................................................ 250.00

17-1/4" l, band, pine, orig blue paint, unusual decoupage paper scene of black man, woman, and child, foreign inscription, wear and loose bottom board ................................... 550.00

Chair

> Austrian, Vienna Secession-style, c1910, side, back splat with three circular perforations, three slender spindles, painted black, set of eight ............................................. 5,500.00
>
> Thonet, arm, c1935, lacquered, pine frame, upholstered back and seat, 43" h ....................................................... 600.00

Cradle, 41" l, 39" h, ivory fittings ................................. 440.00

Hall Tree, Thonet, c1910, bentwood frame, contrasting striped wood inlay, coat hooks with central beveled mirror above one door, metal drip pan, orig label, 57" w, 13" d, 76" h ................................. 2,750.00

Rocker, Thonet, arched twined top rail, cut-velvet fabric fitted back, armrests, and seat, elaborate scrolling frame, curved runners, 53" l .................................................................. 750.00

Stool, Thonet, attributed to Marcel Kammerer, Austria, 1901, beech, sq seat, four legs, U-shaped braces forming spandrels, shaped bronze sabot feet, 14-1/4" sq, 18-1/2" h ............................ 1,500.00

Table, Josef Hoffman, c1905, circular top, wooden spheres dec below rim, 21-1/4" h ........................................................ 500.00

# Blanket Chests

**Chippendale**, country, pine, molded rect and hinged top, storage well, front with two simulated drawer fronts over two drawers, molded surrounds, outset molded base with bracket feet, 37-1/2" w, 20" d, 41" h .................................................................. 750.00

**Decorated**

> Massachusetts, 1825-35, rect hinged to lifts above well, two drawers, cyma-curved skirt, high French feet, top, sides, and skirt with red and black paint simulating rosewood, façade is putty and sponge painted in shades of gold, green, and red, orig brass and surface, very minor imperfections, 42-3/4" w, 18-5/8" d, 37" h ..................................................... 63,000.00
>
> Massachusetts, early 19th C, six board, pine, rect hinged top, conforming base, straight front, cut-out ends, orig brown and mustard paint dec, 42-1/2" w, 18-1/2" d, 25-1/2" h ........ 5,175.00

New England, late 18th C, six board, walnut, hinged top with molded edge overhangs nailed box, orig red ground with black stems with white blossoms on top and three sides, orig painted surface, imperfections, 24-1/2" w, 12-3/4" d, 11-1/2" h ................... 1,035.00

New England, early 19th C, hinged top opens to interior with till over single short drawer, case with one long drawer with wooden pulls on cutout feet, orig all over yellow putty design, imperfections, 38-3/4" w, 18" d, 30-3/4" h .................... 2,300.00

New England, 19th C, six-board, top lifts, cavity with lidded till, base with arched feet, orig yellow ground point with orig burnt sienna fanciful graining and inlay simulation, paint wear, loss to top, restored molding, 38" l, 17" d, 22-1/4" h .............. 10,350.00

New York, attributed to Schoharie County, early 19th C, poplar, molded lift-top, dovetailed case with four recessed panels, four short drawers with wooden pulls, cutout feet joined by shaped skirt, hardwood heart shaped escutcheon, initials "EPH," old blue-green, white, and yellow paint, imperfections, 41-3/4" w, 18" d, 23-1/4" h ............................................... 1,725.00

Pennsylvania, poplar, faded red graining over bright yellow, red showing on top edge of case, hidden by lip, molded edge lid, dovetailed case, turned feet, till with lid, sgd on back "Eli mma Beecher 1848," 37-1/4" l, 19-1/2" d, 26" h ...................... 990.00

**Dower**

> Berks County, PA, 1780s, walnut, hinged top with molded edge, dovetailed case with cavity and till, heavy molded base with two drawers, spurred shaped bracket feet, old refinish, replaced pulls, imperfections, 50-3/4" w, 23-1/4" h, 31" h ..................... 1,3800.00
>
> Lebanon County, PA, late 18th C, attributed to Christian Selzer (1789-1831), painted and decorated, white pine top with molded edge, strap hinges, heavy molded base and bracket feet, front of dovetailed pine case has three arched floral painted panels with white ground outlined in red, each contains a blue vase with red, blue, and yellow flowers, brown leaves, paint appears orig, height loss, other imperfections, 51-1/2" w, 22-1/4" d, 23" h ............................................................. 6,325.00

**Grain Painted**, northern New England, c1830, pine, molded top lifts above cavity over two drawers, shaped bracket feet, side shaping, orig putty red, green, and yellow with umber tones paint, brasses not orig, very minor surface imperfections, 38" l, 17-3/8" w, 36-1/2" h ... 16,100.00

**Jacobean**, oak, paneled construction with relief carving, drawer and feet replaced, repairs to lid and molding, old dark finish, 44-1/2" w, 19-1/2" d, 31-3/4" h ............................................... 825.00

**Italian Renaissance-Style**, walnut, antique elements, 60-1/2" w, 20" d, 21-3/4" h ............................................................ 4,000.00

**Mule**, America, pine, thumb-molded top, two overlapping dovetailed drawers, bracket feet, old dark finishing, int. lined with 1875 Boston newspaper, pierced repairs to feet and drawer fronts, 40" w, 18" d, 34-3/4" h ................................................................ 700.00

**Painted**

> Massachusetts, western, 18th C, pine, hinged top with molded edge, lidded molded till, single base drawer, molded bracket feet, old green paint over red, old replaced glass pulls, paint wear on top, 45" w, 17" d, 31-5/8" h .............................. 2,650.00
>
> Milford, Connecticut, early 18th C, yellow pine, six board construction, vestiges of painted dec, replaced ball feet, imperfections, 42-1/2" w, 20" d, 26-1/2" h ...................................... 950.00
>
> New England, c1780, six-board, molded hinged top, dovetail constructed base, bracket feet, orig red paint, minor imperfections, 43-3/4" w, 19" d, 26" h .......................................... 700.00
>
> New England, late 18th C, molded lift top, two thumb-molded drawers on bracket base, old blue paint, brasses and hinges replaced, 36" w, 19" d, 44" h ....................................... 1,955.00
>
> New England, late 18th C, pine, hinged molded lid, dovetailed box, applied carved ropetwist beading, applied molded base, orig blue paint, 43-1/2" w, 18" d, 17" h .......................... 2,645.00
>
> New York, attributed to Schohaire County, early 19th C, six-board, poplar, hinged molded top, dovetailed constructed box, white painted panel with blue stenciled floral border with center initials "J.T.K.," cutout bracket feet, old paint, restorations, 36" w, 18-3/4" d, 21-3/4" h ....................................................... 2,990.00

Pennsylvania, c1780, pine, green and blue paint, one board top with breadboard ends, applied lower molding, dovetailed case, strap hinges, till with molded lid, ogee feet, 45" w, 19" d, 25-1/4" h ....................................................................1,500.00

Pennsylvania, poplar, old brownish-red finish, dovetailed case, hinged lid, three dovetailed drawers, dovetailed bracket feet, applied moldings, till with lid, tattered printed Haus Segen fraktur on int. of lid, bear trap lock, 50-1/4" w, 23" d, 30" h ............2,100.00

**Pilgrim Century,** attributed to Peter Blin, Wethersfield, CT, 1675-1710, carved, painted, and ebonized oak, rect hinged lid, storage well with till, front carved with two rect inset panels of stylized tulips and leaves, center octagonal panel carved with sunflowers, ebonized splint balusters, mid molding, two long drawers with egg appliqués, stiles continue to form feet, replaced lid, reduced feet, traces of orig red and black pigment, 47-1/2" w, 20-3/4" d, 34-1/4" h ....... 12,000.00

**Scratch Decoration,** Marshfield or South Scituate, late 17th C, scratch decorated, pine, molded lift top opening on pintail hinges, front façade dec with geometric patterns and initials "A.S.," sides continuing to cutwork feet, refinished, repairs, 38-3/4" w, 16" d, 21" h ........... 8,100.00

**Sheraton,** country, pine and poplar, orig red paint, molded edge top, paneled front and ends, sq corner posts, mortised and pinned frame, scalloped apron, turned feet, 44" w, 19-1/2" d, 25-1/2" h ......... 900.00

**Rococo Revival, c1870, ebonized oak, upper section with carved cornice above egg and dart molding, frieze with applied floral and leaf molding, 2 large beveled glass doors flanked by craved columns, curved glass sides, lower section with wreath carved edge, central double door cupboard carved with musical instruments, curved sides with applied basket of fruit and flowers carving, surrounded by branches and ribbon wreath, 95" w, 21-1/2" d, 110-1/2" h, $6,600.**

**William and Mary,** New Haven Colony, CT, 1680-1740, pine and oak joined and paneled, overhanging thumbmolded hinged white pine top, three paneled façade with applied moldings over drawer flanked by shadow molded stiles, recessed panel sides, drawer stippled "1707 H I," interior open till, old dark stained surface, minor imperfections, 40" w, 19-1/4" d, 31-1/2" h ........................................... 9,775.00

# Bookcases

**Anglo-Indian,** fourth quarter 19th C, bamboo and sea grass
Rectangular top, inset sea grass panel, three like-inset open shelves, splayed bamboo legs, 37" w, 11-3/4" d, 42-1/2" h ..500.00
Rectangular top, three open shelves, bamboo legs, 29-1/2" w, 13" d, 39" h ..........................................................................................500.00

**Arts & Crafts**
Paine Furniture Co., three sliding doors, arched leaded glass panel at top with organic design over single pane of glass, eight adjustable shelves, missing backsplash, orig dark finish, sgd with metal tag, 60" w, 14" d, 59" h ................................. 2,200.00
Stickley Brothers, oak, three door form, arched gallery top, leaded stained glass at top above two vertical panes on each door, orig copper hardware, orig finish, unsigned, 59" w, 12" d, 60" h ..............................................................................4,750.00
Stickley, L. & J. G., #645, oak, double door with twelve panes of glass in each, orig copper hardware, keyed tenon construction at sides, orig finish, sgd "The Work of...," 53" w, 12" d, 55" h ...............................................................................7,000.00
Viking, oak, four stacking units, single drawer base, orig copper hardware, orig finish, paper label, 34"w, 13"d, 60"h ......... 650.00

**Biedermeier-Style,** c1900
Birchwood, ogee rect cornice above frieze ornamented by brass rosettes, four doors with elliptical brass grillwork, int. lined in moiré, filled with glass shelves, projecting lower case with four raised diamond paneled doors dec with ebonized outlines, molded plinth base, 82" l, 19-1/2" d, 96" h ................... 6,500.00
Fruitwood, black and white flecked rect marble top, conforming frieze, pair of doors fitted with ebonized geometric glazing bars, sq tapered legs, 48" w, 16" d, 38-1/4" h ........................ 2,000.00
Inlaid cherry, outset molded cornice with ebonized bead, front with two recessed glazed doors, four shelves, outset molded base raised on black feet, burr poplar panels, ebonized stringing, 53-1/2" w, 21" d, 72" h.................................................. 700.00
Mahogany, outset molded top, front with two glazed doors, three shelves, sq section stile feet, 35-3/4" w, 15" d, 52" h ....... 375.00

**Chippendale,** Maryland or Pennsylvania, 1765-65, mahogany, three sections, upper: dentiled triangular pediment, plinth with contemporary bust of William Shakespeare, plain veneered frieze; center: bookcase with double glazed cupboard doors, astragal mullions, Chinoiserie pattern, molded base; lower: chest with short thumb-molded central drawer flanked by two similar box drawers, two graduated long box drawers, two graduated long drawers, flanked by fluted quarter columns, ogee bracket feet, 44-3/4" d, 25-1/4" d, 106-1/4" h ........................... 18,500.00

**Classical-Style,** Late, America, c1840, upper section with glazed doors over pair of cupboard doors, made from armoire, 63" w, 26" d, 82" h ...................................................................................... 300.00

**Empire,** America, third quarter 19th C, walnut and mahogany, ogee molded cornice over pair of glazed doors, each with Gothic arch, set on base with fold-over writing surface over three long drawers, 45-1/2" w, 23-1/2" d, 82" h............................................................. 900.00

**Federal,** Philadelphia, 1790-1810, mahogany veneered, four part construction: long rect top with detachable molded cornice; two bookcase sections each with pairs of glazed cupboard doors, twelve rect panes below top row of arched panes, adjustable shelves int.; lower: center butler's fall-front desk drawer, kneehole area flanked by bands of three cockbeaded short drawers, large paneled cupboard doors, molded base, 119" w, 17-1/2" d, 105-3/4" h ........................ 27,500.00

**George II,** mid 18th C, walnut and parcel-gilt, rect molded cornice over pair of glazed mullioned doors, base with pair of short drawers over two long drawers, flattened bun feet, restorations, 43" w, 19" d, 86" h ....................................................................................6,900.00

**George III**, late 18th C, mahogany, carved and reticulated crest over pair of glazed mullioned doors, base with deep fitted drawers over pair of paneled cabinet doors, bracket base, 49-1/4" w, 20-1/4" d, 97-1/2" h ................................................12,075.00

**Georgian-Style**, breakfront, mahogany, shaped and pierced pediment above four astragal-glazed doors, lower section fitted with central bank of four long graduated drawers, flanked on either side by paneled cupboard door, plinth base, 87-1/2" w, 20" d, 95" h ....... 4,180.00

**Louis XVI-Style**, 19th C, inlaid mahogany, parquetry top, low three-quarter gallery and center oval panel inlaid with fleur-de-lis, open shelf raised on sq-section tapered legs, conforming sabots, 24" w, 8-1/4" d, 27-1/4" h, pr ...............................................900.00

**Neoclassical**, Baltic, first quarter 19th C, kingwood and tulipwood parquetry, rect galleried top with canted cornice above drawer over pair of glazed doors, sq tapered legs ending in flattened balls, ivory pulls and escutcheons, minor losses, 33-1/4" w, 16-1/4" d, 57-1/2" h ...............................................2,300.00

**Queen Anne**, early 18th C, walnut, molded cornice above mirrored door and slide, lower section with slant front desk above three long drawers, bun feet, altered, 31" w, 22" d, 84" h .......................6,325.00

**Queen Anne Revival**, late 19th C, mahogany, upper section fitted with doors and candle-slides, lower section fitted with slant-lid bureau with two short drawers over two long drawers, turned feet, 36-1/2" w, 22" w, 86" h ...........................................5,175.00

**Regency**

England, c1830, mahogany, variegated white and lavender marble top, two open shelves, molded plinth base, 44" w, 11" d, 34-1/2" h ...................................................550.00

England, early 19th C, mahogany and satinwood, raised platform cornice crest with applied detailing above band of mahogany veneer, two glazed doors with diamond astragals, lower section with two cabinet doors, ebony line inlay on low plinth base, alternations, 42-5/8" w, 19-5/8" d, 92-1/2" h ...............10,925.00

**Regency-Style**, closed, mahogany, rect molded cornice above plain frieze, glazed doors fitted with classical grillwork, cabinet base with conforming designed doors, rect plinth base, 69-1/2" l, 14-3/8" d, 78" h .............................................3,200.00

**Regency-Style**, open

Carved mahogany, four ogee-edged open shelves supported by turned posts joined by X-form stretchers, centering stylized stars, 41-1/2" w, 18" d, 85" h ...........................................600.00

Mahogany, molded cornice, case fitted with four shelves, flanked on either side by ebonized engaged columns, headed by gilt brass Corinthian capitals, reeded toupie feet, 41" w, 18-1/2" d, 76" h ...............................................825.00

Rosewood, pierced and shaped back, four graduated open shelves, fall-front cupboard below, bun feet, first quarter 19th C, 40-1/2" w, 12" d, 55-1/2" h ...........................................2,800.00

**Victorian**, late, America, early 20th C, quarter-sawn oak, stacking, each section with fold-out glazed door, scrolled top and base, 34" w, 14" d, 57-1/2" h ...........................................715.00

## Boxes

**Band,** Hannah Davis, New Hampshire, c1830, oval, Napoleon patter paper, shades of green and white, gilt touches, orig yellow ground, paper label, also booklet about Hannah Davis reprint from Boston Evening Transcript, Sat. Nov 14, 1925, imperfections, 19" d, 16-1/2" h ...............................................425.00

**Bible**, chestnut, some curl in lid, molded edges, front panel with punched design, initials and date "L. T. 1705," int. with cov till and single drawer, wrought-iron lock, old dark patina, hasp missing, some edge damage, pulls added to drawer, 27" l .............................650.00

**Book**, walnut, dovetailed, old varnish on cover and marbleized paper, minor age cracks, edge damage, 12-1/2" l .............................350.00

**Bride**, 18-1/2" l, pine, orig blue paint, polychrome flowers and fruit, lid with bowl of flowers, wear, some edge damage, glued split on lid ........880.00

**Candle**

12" l, 4-1/2" w, 4-1/4" h, dovetailed, rect, sliding lid, cherry lid, pine box ...............................................300.00

14" l, 20" h, hanging, pine, two compartments, old red repaint, minor wear ...............................................625.00

22" l, 10" d, 6-3/8" h, pine, slide top, painted red, America, early 19th C ...............................................425.00

**Cheese**, 6-1/2" h, 12-1/8" d, pine, circular, incised "E. Temple" on lid, painted blue, America, 19th C, cracks, paint wear, minor losses ..175.00

**Collar**, 13" l, 5" h, wallpaper covering, oval, mkd "E. Stone no. 116 1/2 William Street, New York"...............................................575.00

**Decorated**

Pine, orig dark red paint, red, black, yellow, and green stylized floral dec, two painted panels on front and two on lid with hears on corners, stenciled back with freehand inscription "J. K. Hoadle, So. Woodstock, Jan. 1816," dovetailed case, molded edge lid, staple hinges, oval brass bale handles, int. baffle removed, some alligatoring and flaking of paint on lid, 20-1/2" w, 10-5/8" d, 10-1/2" h ...............................................2,750.00

Poplar, worn orig red paint, black striping, Roman numerals and decals of children, made to look like stack of books, floral wallpaper-lined int., secret compartment in base, keyhole hidden by sliding book, some edge damage, 9-3/4" l .......................325.00

Walnut and poplar, vinegar grained, worn orig brown graining, wrought iron lock, incomplete hasp, 31" l .......................295.00

**Desk**, English, c1850-1865, brass inlaid rosewood, drop down front folds out to reveal velvet writing surface, compartmented lift-out tray lined in marbleized Florentine paper, int. fitted with pen compartment and period glass ink bottle in orig compartment, 11-3/4" l, 6-1/2" h ...............................................325.00

**Document**

Decorated, hinged lid, rect box, repeating rows of squiggle patterns, linear border, brown on tan ground, iron latch, America, 19th C, 26" l, 13-1/2" l, 13-3/4" w...............................................815.00

Decorated, poplar, orig floral dec, green ground, yellow and black striping, dovetailed, molded lid and base, int. with till, lock and key, wear and some fading, 16" w, 8-1/4" d, 6-3/4" h .......690.00

Rosewood veneer, ebonized edges, brass escutcheons, lid medallion, some edge damage, 8" l ...............................................315.00

**Dome Top**, America, 19th C

Grain painted, rect box, initials "A. H." outlined in red and mustard oval, ovolo corner, linear outlines, minor paint and edge wear, 10-1/2" l, 6-5/8" w, 5-1/4" h ...........................................1,150.00

Painted, hinged lid, wrought iron handles and lock, green sponged dec, 24" l, 12-3/4" d, 10" h, America, early 19th C .............2,530.00

Vinegar Graining, poplar, orig brown graining dec, dovetailed, wrought iron lock, hasp missing, wear, 23" w, 12" d, 11-5/8" h ...............................................150.00

**Dough**, pine and poplar, rect removable top, tapering well, splayed ring-turned legs, ball feet, Pennsylvania, 19th C, 38" w, 19-3/4" w, 29-1/2" h ...............................................500.00

**Hatbox,** wallpaper covered

10-3/4" h, 16-3/4" l, birds among foliage, architectural view, imperfections...............................................500.00

11" h, 17-3/4" l, scene of stagecoach among hunters, imperfections ...............................................150.00

12-1/4" h, 17-3/4" l, 12-1/2" d, Clayton's Ascent, showing hot air balloons in flight, labeled on underside of lid "From J. M. Hulbert's paste board band box manufactory no. 25 Court Street, Boston," imperfections ...............................................980.00

**Knife**

5-1/4" h, 13-1/8" l, ivory inlaid rosewood, attributed to New England, 19th C, very minor cracks, minor inlay loss ... 1,850.00

8-3/4" h, 15-3/4" l, walnut, dovetailed, high sides, scalloped divider with heart cut out handle ...............................................880.00

16" h, 9-3/4" w, 14-1/2" d, Federal, flamed grained mahogany, serpentine and block front, reeded front columns, fitted int., orig keys, pr ...............................................2,500.00

**Letter Box**, Georgian, c1800, banded mahogany, knife box shape, int. knife grille removed to form letter box, 8-1/2" w, 8-1/2" d, 14-1/2" h...............................................500.00

**Officer's Valet**, Napoleon III, c1855-70, inlaid mahogany, int. elaborately fitted with shaving mirror, pair of bone-mounted strap razors, pair of scissors, corkscrew, pair of boot pulls, bone folding nail file, pair of silver-topped cut glass pomade jars sgd "M. Foy," cut glass cologne bottle, lower element fitted with silver-topped glass ink bottle, silver-topped glass powder jar, silver-topped cut glass dentifrice bottle, mahogany hairbrush, ivory brush, ivory toothbrush, period steel keep, 11" w, 6-1/2" d, 3" h ............................................. 1,430.00

**Painted**, America, 19th C, sliding lid, rect box, painted in argyle pattern, shades of red, black, brown, and yellow, wear, 12" l, 6" w, 6-3/4" h ........................................................................ 1,610.00

**Pantry**, circular, nailed construction, swing handle
    7-1/2" d, 3-1/2" h, green, two finger construction, orig paint.....250.00
    10-7/8" d, 7" h, orig red painted surface, 19th C, chip to top and bottom, paint wear............................................................550.00
    12" d, 6-3/4" h, orig green painted surface, 19th C, minor surface abrasion .................................................................550.00

**Pipe**, hanging
    America, early 19th C, carved and painted pine, pierced heart-shaped backboard, lower drawer with brass pull, old red paint, losses, wear, 5-1/4" l, 5" d, 15-3/4" h ............................ 3,105.00
    New England, early 19th C, painted pine, pierced and scrolled back, sides, and front, single drawer, red paint, shield, wreath, monogrammed "B" in green, red, blue and yellow, red and yellow linear outlines, losses, 15" h .................................. 2,875.00

**Salt**, 11-1/2" w, 7-1/4" d, 9" h, oak, dovetailed, lift lid, crest, divided int., old finish ...................................................................... 120.00

**Sewing**, 9-1/2" l, 6-3/4" w, 7-3/4" h, bird's eye maple and inlaid walnut, tiered, one drawer, America, mid-19th C, very minor losses to finials..........................................................................375.00

**Spice**, 9-3/8" d, circular, maple, eight spice containers with stenciled names, America, late 19th C ..............................................450.00

**Spill**, 10-1/8" h, 3" w, 2-3/4" d, hanging, walnut and poplar, New England, late 18th/early 19th C, old refinish, front molding replaced .............................................................................550.00

**Storage**, 15-1/2" x 28" x 15", dome top, dark brown paint, interior lined with newspaper "Brother Jonathon, New York, June 19, 1852, A Double Sheet Fourth of July Pictorial Paper," cover lining with scenes of Battle of Lexington, box with portraits of thirteen presidents of United States, partial segments of facsimile of the Declaration of Independence, some staining and wear ................................................230.00

**Tantalus**, Belle Epoque, c1900-10, case formed as stack of four antique books, fitted with liqueurs decanter and eight liqueurs glasses of different colors, 10" w, 8" d, 7" h ............................660.00

**Wall**, America, early 19th C, painted pine, slanted hinged lid on upper compartment, open lower compartment, painted dark red, minor split, wear, 6-3/4" w, 13-3/4" l..............................................490.00

**Whimsical**, figural bedsteps, mahogany, lidded well on each of two treads, turned legs, late Georgian, 19th C, 5" l, 4-3/4" h ..........425.00

**Work**, 12" w, 10-1/2" d, 7-1/4" h, European, marquetry inlaid mahogany veneer, pine secondary wood, slant top lid with pincushion covered in old burgundy velvet, paper lined int., till with lid, engraved strap hinges, old finish, repairs ..............................................275.00

# Cabinets

**Bar**, Art Deco, walnut, sarcophagus form, two doors, sq top with drop-front cabinet on left, mirrored bar, small drawer on right between two open bays, 48" w, 21" d, 54-1/2" d .........................................600.00

## China
    Art Moderne, mahogany, double doors, floral-carved relief panels, int. shelves, two drawers below, 45" w, 17" d, 62" h .....2,000.00
    Arts & Crafts, Limbert, #428, trapezoidal form, two doors, each with four windows at top over one large window, orig copper pulls, sides with two windows over one, refinished, branded, 40" w, 19" d, 63" h ....................................................................4,250.00
    Biedermeier-style, mahogany, double arched pediment with ebonized scroll ends, case fitted with two astragal-glazed doors, flanked on either size by ebonized columns, headed by gilt-brass Corinthian capitals above two short drawers, ogee-molded bracket feet, 55" w, 15-1/2" d, 82-1/2" h...........1,350.00
    Edwardian-Style, curved glass sides, single flat glazed door, illuminated int., mirrored back, 42""w, 16""d, 64""h, pr ......1,675.00

**Late Regency, mahogany, rect top, pr of frieze drawers, pr cupboard doors with arched panels, plinth base, 38" w, 15-1/2" d, 37" h, $2,100.**

    International Movement, Gilbert Rhode, manufactured by Herman Miller, glass-sided china cabinet top over two doors with burled fronts, brushed steel pulls, refinished, glass doors and shelves missing, 36" w, 17" d, 58" h...............................................800.00
    Victorian, late, America, c1900, oak, convex glass ends, flanking an upper central door surmounted by log-roll crest, larger glazed cupboard door below, carved paw feet, 49" w, 114-1/2" d, 70" h .........................................................................1,100.00

**Chinoiserie**, two drawers, double doors, two adjustable int. shelves, walnut veneer with inlay and black lacquer, gilded detail, attached base with turned legs, 20th C, 43" w, 15-1/2" d, 63" h ............625.00

**Corner, hanging**, George III, 18th C, black japanned, bow front, fitted with two doors opening to shelves, allover Chinese scenes, losses, 24" w, 35-3/4" h ............................................................1,265.00

**Curio**, Louis XV, French, mahogany and mahogany veneer, well detailed ormolu with cherubs, marble top, beveled glass panel in door and plain glass in sides, lighted int., lined with very work silk moiré, 20th C, 28" w, 14" d, 65" h ......................................3,410.00

**Demilune**, Neoclassical, Baltic, late 19th C, gilt bronze mounted tulipwood and marquetry, plain top, inlaid frieze with drawers, two drawers flanked by cabinet doors, circular tapering legs ending in brass caps, 37" w, 15-1/2" d, 34-1/2" h ...........................................1,150.00

## Display
    Biedermeier-style, poplar and burr-poplar, single door, outset molded cornice, three-pane glazed door flanked by similar stiles and sides, three mirror-backed shelves supporting shaped half shelves, block feet, 41" w, 16" d, 68" h ...........................800.00
    Continental, mid-19th C, mahogany and marquetry, corner type, arched molded cornice, glazed door, shelved int., shaped plinth base, minor damage, one lacking glass, veneer loss, 33-1/2" w, 23" d, 75-1/4" h, price for pr .........................................3,750.00
    Italian, Milan, c1880, ivory, tortoiseshell, and lapis lazuli mounted ebony, arched cresting with ivory balustrade above pair of glazed doors, base fitted with two drawers, bun feet, allover openwork ivory inlay, tortoiseshell and lapis lazuli plaques, losses, 48-1/2" w, 20" d, 91-1/2" h ....................................3,500.00
    Neoclassical-style, London, late 19th/early 20th C, oak and parcel-gilt, presentation plaque inscribed "Presented by Mr. and Mrs. Sidney H. Cotton (The Knoll 1874-1876)," ivory plaque for F. Sage & Co. (1905), 37" w, 31" d, 78" h ....................4,900.00

Rococo, South Germany, 18th C, walnut, scrolling heavily molded open pediment, center gilt-bronze cartouche plate, two arched doors of fielded panels, mahogany figures of court ladies, basal-molded and conforming stand, shaped apron, cabriole legs, 46" w, 19-1/2" d, 71-1/2" h ............................................... 4,750.00

**Filing**, American, c1910, golden oak, plain vertical stack, five drawers, orig brass nameplates and pulls ............................................... 650.00

**Ledger**, American, 19th C, walnut and mixed hardwoods, poplar secondary wood, dovetailed case, single paneled door, int. with divided compartments, later salmon paint, pr, 15-1/2" w, 12" d, 24" h.............. 600.00

**Liquor**, Chippendale-style, 20th C, steel mounted walnut, shelved superstructure, pair of doors on sq legs, 19" w, 11" d, 45" h ................... 550.00

**Music**, walnut, two dovetailed drawers, two paneled doors, molded and punched designs, four adjustable shelves, old varnish finish, orig castors, 22" w, 16-1/4" d, 37-1/2" h ............................................ 450.00

**Side**

Biedermeier, late 19th C

Fruitwood parquetry, rect top, canted corners, pr of cabinet doors enclosing shelves, bracket feet, 55-1/4" w, 24-3/4" d, 40-1/2" h ............................................... 1,725.00

Inlaid walnut, single door, outset molded cornice, door with arched, sunken panel, flanked by bowed stiles continuing to molded stile feet, three int. shelves, 39-1/2" w, 19" d, 65-1/4" h ............................................... 1,500.00

Empire-Style, late 19th/early 20th C, gilt bronze mounted mahogany, rect marble top, conforming case fitted with cabinet door, pull-out shelves, plinth base, 20-3/4" w, 16-1/4" d, 52-1/4" h ...... 750.00

Louis XIV-Style, third quarter 19th C, boullework, bronze mounted, ebonized, brass and tortoiseshell marquetry, satyr and foliate bronze mounts, 32" w, 18" d, 44" h .............. 1,265.00

Louis XV-Style, late 19th C, marble top, demilune, Vernis Martin, foliage cast bronze mounts, painted with cherub scene, cabriole legs, 30-1/2" w, 16" d, 45" h ............................................... 1,495.00

Louis XVI-Style, 20th C, gilt bronze mounted, beige marble top, frieze drawer, two drawers mounted with cherub plaques, circular turned feet, 21" w, 14-1/2" d, 34" h ............................................... 2,070.00

Napoleon III, 1850-70, fruitwood marquetry and gilt bronze mounts, serpentine crest, conforming case, shelved int., drawer, two doors, figural, foliage and mask cast mounts ............................................... 4,025.00

Napoleon III, third quarter 18th C, gilt bronze mounted part ebonized amboynawood, Sevres-style porcelain mounts, central section with mirrored int. flanked by two cabinets above inlaid surface, frieze fitted with writing compartment raised on fluted supports joined by shelf stretchers, shaped feet, two porcelain knobs missing, restorations, 48-1/2" l, 22-1/2" d, 65-1/2" h ........ 3,750.00

Victorian

English, c1870, Wedgwood mounts, inlaid ebony, reverse breakfront top above pair of glazed doors and central door, bun feet, inlaid allover with palmettes and scrolled vines, 70-1/2" w, 17" d, 43" h ............................................... 1,750.00

Renaissance Revival, c1860-70, carved walnut, marble top, canted case elaborately carved with figural stiles, foliate and putti, base drawer, scrolled feet, 34-1/2" w, 17" d, 32" h ............................................... 4,320.00

**Vitrine**

Edwardian, c1900, mahogany and boxwood inlay, rect, Gothic-style mullioned glazed doors, sq tapering legs, spade feet, 41-1/2" w, 14-1/4" d, 63-1/4" h ............................................... 1,200.00

George III-Style, late 19th/early early 20th C, mahogany, rect lift top, chamfered legs, joined by shelf stretcher and fretwork, 21-1/4" l, 15-1/2" d, 31-3/4" h ............................................... 850.00

Georgian-Style, mahogany, molded cornice, case fitted with two astragal-glazed doors, ogee molded bracket feet, 47-1/2" w, 17" d, 84-1/2" h ............................................... 2,100.00

Louis XV-Style, late 19th/early 20th C, giltwood, boxed glass on each side, cabriole legs, 19" w, 17" d, 38" h ................... 800.00

Louis XVI-Style, c1850, giltwood, outset molded rect top, frieze with beribboned floral garlands, front with glazed door with inset corners, flanked by fluted stiles, opening to two shelves, glazed sides, paneled skirt with swags, turned, tapered, and fluted legs with paterae, 27-1/4" w, 16" d, 61-1/2" h ...................... 1,200.00

## Candle Shields

**Chippendale**, Philadelphia, c1770, attributed to Thomas Afleck, carving attributed to Bernard and Jugiez, carved mahogany, turned cylindrical pole, adjustable screen with intricately carved frame, tapering fluted shaft, acanthus carved baluster, swirl gadroon, carved ball, acanthus carved tripod cabriole legs overlaid with trailing husk and vines, carved hairy paw feet, 60" h ...................... 68,000.00

**George II**, English, mid 18th C, carved mahogany, turned standard surmounted by urn shaped finial, spirally fluted multi-knopped shaft, acanthus carved tripod base, claw and ball feet, adjustable rect screen with beaded edge, orange, red, blue, and green needlepoint panel of floral bouquet, reverse inset with painted leather panel of Chinese figures in parquetry floored pavilion in garden, finials added, some damage to fabric, 59-1/2" h ........................................ 3,750.00

**Regency-Style**, giltwood, rect panel with molded border, scrolling frame, shells, and ornaments at corners with volutes, 33" w, 48" h ............................................... 1,500.00

**Victorian**, English, c1840, fluted stem surmounted by an urn finial, circular plinth base on three scrolled feet, adjustable shield shaped frame carved with scrolling leaves and enclosing floral needlework screen, 24" w, 77" h ............................................... 1,400.00

## Candlestands

**Chippendale**

Bristol County, MA, early 19th C, imp "A. Shove," (Abraham Shove), cherry, sq top, scratch beaded edge, swelled ring-turned pedestal, cabriole leg base ending in pad feet, old refinish, replaced leg, 15-1/4" w, 14-7/8" d, 27" h ................ 1,495.00

Norwich, CT, attributed to, late 18th C, painted black, circular molded top with scalloped lower edge, vase and ring-turned post, tripod cabriole leg base ending in pad feet, imperfections, 13-3/4" d, 27-1/2" h ...................................... 9,775.00

**Classical**

New England, c1820, bird's eye and tiger maple, tilt-top, top with canted corners, vase, ring-turned and urn form pedestal, tripod scrolling legs, old refinish, minor imperfections, 20-3/4" w, 17-1/2" d, 28-1/2" h ........................................ 1,100.00

New England, c1825, tiger maple, rectangular top with canted corners, vase and ring-turned post and tripod base, scrolled legs, old finish, 16-3/4" w, 21-3/4" d, 28-1/2" h.............. 1,380.00

New England, c1825, tiger maple, shaped top, vase and ring-turned support, tripod base of scrolled legs, ball feet, old refinish, imperfections, 19" w, 16-1/4" w, 28-1/2" h ................ 920.00

**Federal**

Massachusetts, c1800, mahogany, octagonal tilt-top, vase and ring-turned post, tripod spider leg base, spade feet, refinished, 21-1/4" w, 15-3/4" d, 29-1/2" h ................................... 1,500.00

Massachusetts, c1810, red painted birch, octagonal tilt top, vase and ring-turned post and tripod base, three shaped scratch beaded legs tapering to space feet, 16" w, 23" d, 30" h 4,025.00

New England, c1790, maple, octagonal top, vase and ring-turned post, tripod cabriole leg base, pad feet, old finish, imperfections, 15" w, 15-1/8" d, 27" h .................................. 1,610.00

New England, early 19th C, painted, octagonal shaped top, outlined in black, painted checkerboard and four gilt scrolled flourishes dec, pedestal, cabriole legs with similar Victorian dec, 18" w, 17-3/4" d, 29" h ...................................... 12,650.00

New Hampshire, c1810-20, maple, carved tilt top, swelled reeded post, chip-carved detail, old red varnish, minor imperfections, 20" x 15-5/8" top, 29-1/2" h ...................................... 1,000.00

**Hepplewhite**, American, cherry, one-board octagonal top, turned column with chip carving, tripod base, spider legs, old refinishing, minor damage, old repair, 17-1/4" x 18-1/8" top, 27" h ...................... 500.00

**Queen Anne**, Norwich, CT, area, late 18th C, cherry, circular molded top with scalloped carved lower edge, vase and ring-turned post ending in tripod cabriole leg base, fad feet, refinished, 15-1/2" d, 28-1/2" h ........................................................6,900.00

# Chairs

### Arm

Anglo-Indian, fourth quarter 19th C, bamboo and sea grass, arm, back with central sea grass panel joined by open bamboo arms, matching seat, bamboo legs joined by stretchers, 40" h.......350.00

Edwardian, England, c1895, painted and caned satinwood, oval backrest inset with portrait roundel, foliate painted frame, losses, price for arm chair and matching side chair ......2,185.00

French Provincial

Second quarter 19th C, fruitwood, back with nicely pierced and carved splat, joined to rush seat by scrolling arms on turned supports, turned circular legs, joined by like stretchers, 36-3/4" h .................................................550.00

Third quarter 19th C, fruitwood, scalloped crest above Gothic-arch patterned slatted back, joined by scrolled arms to rush seat, saber legs, 37" h .................................................500.00

Third quarter 19th C, fruitwood, trapezoidal-inset rail above like rails, joined to rush seat by scrolled arms, tapering cabriole legs, joined by box stretcher, 38" h, price for pr ....700.00

Georgian, early, mid 18th C, walnut, yoke back, vasiform splat, open shepherd's crook arms, slip seat, cabriole legs joined by stretchers, pad feet, 36-3/4" h, price for pr....................1,495.00

Georgian-Style, first quarter 19th C, mahogany, top rail inlaid with stringing over a row of reeded vertical spindles, whole supported by tapered reeded Hepplewhite legs, 33" h ..........400.00

Regency, first quarter 19th C, mahogany, curving tablet crest over carved foliate scroll ends, leaf-carved horizontal back support, reeded scrolling arms and saber legs, seat upholstered in later floral needlepoint, 34" h...................................................450.00

Regency-Style, c1920, ebonized and parcel gilt, caned oval in open back, open downswept arms, caned trapezoidal seats, reverse saber legs, labeled "Parker & Sons, Ltd., 20 Newman Street W, made in England," surface wear, 33-1/3" h, price for pr ....................................................................1,380.00

Victorian

Empire Revival, America, first quarter 20th C, mahogany, closed arms with scroll ends, supported by Queen Anne legs, pad feet, 27" w, 25" d, 35" h .................................90.00

Rococo Revival, third quarter 19th C, walnut, corseted back, scroll carved crest, open arms, cabriole legs, reupholstered, 46" h .................................................................250.00

Rococo Revival, third quarter 19th C, walnut, medallion back, finger-roll carving, open arms, cabriole legs, later tufted pale blue upholstery, 40" h and 43" h, price for pair ...........400.00

Rococo Revival, third quarter 19th C, walnut, medallion back surmounted by carved grapes and leaf, open arms, cabriole legs, reupholstered, 45" h.............................................250.00

William and Mary, New England, mid-18th C, maple and ash, banister back, arched crest over four molded banisters joining vase and ring-turned stiles surmounted by ball finials, shaped arms with scrolled terminals, trapezoidal rush seat, cylinder and ring-turned legs joined by swelled vase and ring-turned double stretchers, old finish, 18" h seat, 47-1/2" h....................8,100.00

Windsor

Combed Fan Back, child's, labeled "Wallace Nutting, Saugus, Mass," serpentine crest with scrolled ends above spindles, shaped plank seat, splayed legs joined by stretchers, dark stain, surface imperfections, 10-1/2" h seat, 27" h........1,380.00

Sack Back, bowed crest over seven spindles joining shaped arms on vase and ring-turned supports, incised seat resting on vase and ring-turned legs joined by H-form swelled stretchers, refinished, imperfections, 18" h seat, 36-1/4" h.............1,265.00

### Bergère

Empire-Style, mahogany, curved padded backs joined to like seat by giltwood swan-shaped arms, tapering saber legs, 31-1/2" h, price for pr .........................................................1,200.00

Louis XV to Louis XVI-Style Transitional, fourth quarter 19th C, fruitwood, padded back surmounted by foliate carved crest, joined by shaped sides, padded arms, cushioned seat, floral-carved skirt, cabriole legs, 40" h ......................................750.00

Louis XV-Style

c1850, fruitwood, serpentine molded crest, conforming padded back, cushioned seat, padded arms, cabriole legs, scroll feet, 34" h, price for pr .............................................1,320.00

Late 19th C, mahogany, floral carved crest, scrolled upholstered arms, floral carved seat, cabriole legs with floral carved knees, scrolled feet, ecru upholstery, 38-3/8" h, price for pr ....................................................................2,415.00

**Campechy**, lower Mississippi Valley, first quarter 19th C, mahogany, tablet form top rail, black leather-covered back and seat outlined in brass nail heads, reverse curve armrests raised on out-curved supports, curule legs joined by stretchers, 28-1/2" w, 24" d, 37-1/2" h.................4,100.00

### Corner

Queen Anne, Boston, c1740-90, walnut, shaped crest above out-scrolled arms, vase and ring-turned supports flanking two vasiform splats, slip seat on shaped seat frame, frontal cabriole leg ending in pad feet, remaining legs are turned and end in diminutive pad feet, joined by block and vase turned stretchers, old surface, imperfections...................................................6,900.00

Victorian, Renaissance Revival, c1880, carved walnut, elaborately carved seraphs, dolphins, and foliage, circular legs, 31-1/2" h..........................................................................700.00

### Dining

Arts & Crafts, English, early 20th C, two arm chairs, four side chairs, sq top back posts, shaped crest rail with heart and scroll cut-out over three back slats, shaped arms, upholstered seats, tapered legs, medium brown, 23" w, 20" d, 42-1/4" h, price for set of six....................................................................3,565.00

Chippendale-Style, c1920, one arm chair, seven side chairs, carved mahogany, pierced shaped ladder-back, burgundy faux-leather seat with brass nail upholstery, sq legs joined by stretchers, 37" h, price for set of eight ....................................1,870.00

Chippendale-Style, early 20th C, two arm chairs, four side chairs, mahogany, shaped crest over pierced splat with tassel carving, slip seat, cabriole legs headed by acanthus carving, claw and ball feet, 39-1/2" h side chairs, 37" h arm chairs, price for set of six....................................................................................600.00

Chippendale-Style, early 20th C, two arm chairs, six side chairs, mahogany, serpentine crest, pierced and carved spat, cushioned seat, cabriole legs headed by acanthus carving, claw and ball feet, 39-1/2" h, price for set of eight .........................800.00

Jacobean-Style, late 19th C, two arm chairs, four side chairs, mahogany, shaped scrolling crest flanked by turned finials above caned back flanked by turned uprights, padded seat, block and turned legs joined by stretchers, ending in ball feet, arm chairs 50" h, side chairs, 45" h, price for set of six .........................1,200.00

Neoclassical, Italian, c1810, two arm chairs, six side chairs, parcel-gilt fruitwood, each backrest with carved figureheads above faux bamboo and rope twist lattice, carved bird head handholds, slip seat, saber legs headed by figureheads, stiles and legs with incised calligraphy, 36" h, price for set of eight ...........48,300.00

Queen Anne Style, late 19th C, two arm chairs, six side chairs, yoke back, vasiform splat with green Chinoiserie dec, cabriole legs joined by turned stretchers, pad feet, striped silk upholstery, 37-1/4" h, price for set of eight............................9,200.00

Regency, c1810, two arm chairs, ten side chairs, mahogany, paneled cresting, shaped slat carved with diamond, over-upholstered seat, circular turned legs, price for set of fourteen...........16,100.00

Regency-Style, two arm chairs, six side chairs, mahogany, rope-twist crest above scrolling brass inlaid splat, slip-in seat, saber legs, price for set of eight................................................1,100.00

Restauration-Style, American, c1900, gondola form, mahogany, floral carved crest, shaped splat, bowed seat, saber legs, 34" h, price for set of six ............................................. 600.00

Rococo, Continental, late 18th/early 19th C, one arm chair, nine side chairs, carved walnut, crest carved with rocaille shell over vasiform splat, shaped slip seat with central carved shell, rear block legs, cabriole front legs with shell on flat leaf carved knees, claw and ball feet, legs joined by H-stretcher, 40-1/8" h, price for assembled set of ten ........................................ 4,025.00

Victorian, after the tenets of Charles Cocke Eastlake, cherry, each with carved crest rail over fan-carved splat, turned legs joined by paired stretchers, 35" h, price for set of eight ......................... 750.00

Victorian, Empire Revival, first quarter 20th C, oak, carved Northwind mask in top rail, price for set of five ......................... 500.00

Windsor, MA, c1815-25, arrow back, one arm, six side chairs, inscribed in chalk "A. Wills" (for A. Williams) on underside, old paper affixed to underside of one "This chair came from Abethas Wiliams old homestead on Chappel St., Raynham, Massachusetts," curving crests above arrow back spindles, balloon shaped incised seats, shaped medial stretchers and ring-turned legs and stretchers, old dark red ground paint with indistinct yellow and green stencil dec on crests and stiles, old surface, some surface imperfections, 17-3/4" h, price for set of seven .................. 2,645.00

### Fauteil

Louis XV, third quarter 18th C, foliate carved frame, later 17th C Flemish verdure tapestry upholstery, painted green, similarly upholstered Louis XV-style footstool, upholstery later restoration, price for pr, 36" h ................................................... 2,185.00

Louis XV-Style, early 20th C, polychromed, shaped padded back surmounted by floral carved crest, joined by padded arms to like seat, cabriole legs headed by floral carving, scroll toes, upholstered in floral pattern needlepoint, 33" h, price for pr ......................... 650.00

Restauration, first quarter 19th C

Fruitwood, padded back and seat, joined by scrolled arms, bowed seat frame on scroll legs headed by lappets, 35" h, price for pr............................................................. 1,800.00

Fruitwood, slightly domed crest above padded back, joined by scrolled arms to padded seat, saber legs, 33" h, price for pr................................................................ 1,100.00

Mahogany, padded back joined to like seat by lotus carved arms fronted by ormolu patera, sq legs, 35-1/2" h...... 850.00

Oak, padded back surmounted by slightly curved crest, joined to padded seat by down-swept arms, bellflower carved uprights, saber legs, 34" h, price for pr .................... 1,350.00

**Folding,** Victorian, Renaissance Revival, America, third quarter 19th C, walnut and burl walnut, carved crest, arms terminating in dog's heads, labeled "Holmes Patent Folding Chair, 1871," 40" h, price for pr .............................................................................. 900.00

### High, Child's

Sheraton, America, country, 19th C, back with concave tablet crest rail, scroll arms, cane seat, 34-3/4" h ...................... 200.00

Victorian, America, c1900, walnut, arched crest rail and splat, scroll arms, cane seat, 34" h............................................. 150.00

Windsor

Braced Back, continuous armchairs, stamped "EB Tracy," Lisbon, CT, late 18th C, bowed crests with beaded edges above tapering spindles, tail pieces, shaped seats, and splayed bulbous turned legs joined by swelled stretchers, imperfections, 17-1/4" h seat, 37" h, price for pr .................. 4,025.00

Painted, semi-circular crest rail supported by turned spindles, cane seat, America, country, c1900, 34" h ................. 150.00

Poplar, semi-circular semi-circular crest rail supported by turned spindles, plank seat, America, country, c1900, 31-1/2" h ......................................................................... 100.00

Sack Back, painted, bowed crest over seven spindles joining shaped arms with vase and ring turned supports, shaped and incised seat on splayed vase and ring turned legs joined by swelled H-form stretchers, old worn black over green paint, New England, c1790, imperfections, 17-1/2" h seat,

39" h ....................................................................... 14,950.00

**Library**

George III, c1770, mahogany, upholstered backrest, scrolled arms, over-upholstered seat, sq molded legs joined by stretchers, 38" h ................................................................. 1,610.00

George III, third quarter 18th C, Chinese Chippendale, mahogany, upholstered back and seat, scrolled arms and squat legs, stretchers carved with blind fretwork............................. 1,495.00

Victorian, Renaissance Revival, c1875, carved walnut, sloped backrest and hound's head carved handholds, fluted circular legs, casters, 40-1/2" h ................................................. 5,175.00

William IV, second-quarter 19th C, mahogany, domed back-scrolled back, scrolling arms, reeded toupie feet headed by carved patera, ending in brass caps and casters, upholstered in burgundy leather, 37" h ................................................. 3,750.00

**Parlor,** Victorian, Elizabethan Revival, America, third-quarter 19th C, cabochon centered crest among oak leaves, backs mounted with c1870 needlepoint executed by Sarah Fenner Mallet, granddaughter of first governor of Rhode Island, initials "L.,G. F.," for family surnames of Lee, George, and Fenner, price for set of four ........ 825.00

**Side**

Biedermeier, first quarter 19th C, fruitwood, spoon back, needle-work upholstered seat, circular tapering legs, 34-1/2" h .. 250.00

Biedermeier-Style, late 19th C, fruitwood and part ebonized, shaped back with ebonized wreath, upholstered seat, slightly flared sq tapering legs, 32-1/2" l, price for set of four ... 3,335.00

Chippendale

Massachusetts, c1780, grain painted, serpentine crest rail with shaped ears, pierced vasiform spat with heart shaped cutout joining raked and chamfered stiles over trapezoidal rush seat, square front legs, relief rear legs joined by square stretchers, all over red brown mahogany grain paint ......................... 1,150.00

Philadelphia, 1755-70, carved walnut, serpentine crest with beaded edges, raked ears, central carved shell above reverse curved pedestal splat with C-scrolls, trapezoidal seat frame with central carved shell over front cabriole legs, ball and claw feet, rear rounded legs with chamfered edges, old refinish, 18" h seat, 42-1/2" h............................. 6,900.00

**Rococo Revival, rosewood, elaborate carved back panel, demi-arms, spool turned legs, needlepoint back panel with figure of seated lady, bird, and flowers, 48" h, $240. Photo courtesy of Joy Luke Fine Art Brokers and Auctioneers.**

Classical

America, second quarter 19th C, maple and bird's eye maple, top rail over vasiform splat, carved seat, saber legs, 33" h, price for pr.................................................................300.00

Boston, c1825-35, carved mahogany and mahogany veneer, concave veneered crests with leaf-carved terminals above carved curving splats flanked by molded stiles continuing to molded front seat rail, curving front legs, old refinish, 17-1/2" h seat, 35-1/4" h, price for set of four......................2,300.00

Classical, late, New York, c1835-45, mahogany veneer, curving crests with classical carving above serpentine stiles and splats which terminate in C-scrolls above veneered serpentine front seat rails, Grecian-style curving front legs, old refinish, 20th C, red and gold textile with classical covers seats, minor imperfections, 33-1/4" h, price for set of six...............................3,000.00

Colonial Revival, c1900, Chippendale-style incorporating influence of Art Nouveau design, back with serpentine crest rail, foliate carved splat, upholstered seat, cabriole legs, 38" h ...............................................................990.00

Country, PA, c1840, painted and decorated, shaped crests above pierced vasiform bootjack shaped splats, plank seats with rolled front rails and ring-turned legs and stretchers, old light brown ground paint with polychrome floral designs highlighted with soft yellow bordered by black, highlighted with gold striping, minor surface imperfections, 17-1/4" h seat, 33-5/8" h, price for set of six ...................................3,335.00

Directorie, first quarter 19th C, mahogany, crest with diamond curving centering carved patera to padded seat, ring-turned circular legs headed by floral carving, toupie feet, 34" h, price for set of eight.......................................................4,200.00

French Provincial, c1880-90

Fruitwood, scalloped crest centered by carved fruit basket, two like-shaped rails, rush seat, cabriole legs joined by stretchers, 37" h, price for set of four...........................550.00

Fruitwood, scalloped crest centered by shell and foliate carving, two like shaped rails, rush seat, cabriole legs joined by shaped front stretcher, 34-1/2" h, price for set of six1,100.00

Oak, scalloped crest centered by carved shell over two shaped rails, rush seat, cabriole legs joined by turned H-form stretcher, scrolled toes, 38" h, price for set of six950.00

George III-Style, late 19th/early 20th C, in the Chinese taste, stylized pagoda crest, pierced shaped back splat with slip seat, tapered rear supports ending in pad feet, cabriole front legs with claw and ball feet, 38-1/8" h, price for pr.........................920.00

Georgian, late, carved mahogany, foliate and tassel carved openwork splat, slip-seat, sq legs, price for pr ......................1,150.00

Neo-Baroque, c1860, laminated rosewood, stylized Baroque back, upholstered seat, slender cabriole legs, losses, 35" h.......900.00

Neoclassical, Italian, c1790-1800, painted green and parcel-gilt, dipped crest rail, open anthemion splat above serpentine slip seat, tapered fluted legs, restorations, price for set of six, 36-1/2" h..........................................................8,625.00

Queen Anne, MA, c1740-60, maple, yoked crest rail over vasiform splat and molded shoe flanked by raked and chamfered stiles, over-upholstered balloon seat on frontal cabriole legs ending in pad feet, joined to rear shaped and raked legs by block, vase, and ring-turned stretchers, old refinish, minor restoration .........................................................4,315.00

Venetian, early 20th C, polychrome and parcel gilt, ladder back, triangular seat, incised scrolling design, tapered saber legs, price for set of six, 39-1/2" h...........................................800.00

Victorian, America, Renaissance Revival, attributed to John Jeliff, c1865-70, carved walnut, high back, architectural carved cresting centered by maidenhead, serpentine seat and circular turned legs on casters, red silk upholstery, price for pr, 38-1/2" h 990.00

Victorian, Continental, Renaissance Revival, c1880, carved walnut, whimsical, profusely carved with cherubs, nude maidens, foliage, and other devices, shaped trestle legs, 47" h......850.00

Victorian, English, c1860, Wedgwood mounted, painted black, open splat, circular splayed legs, inset with neoclassical jasperware medallion, 34" h.....................................................435.00

Victorian, English, third quarter 19th C, walnut, foliate crest over carved banister back, barley-twist stiles and legs, 19-1/2" w, 20" d, 44-1/4" h.........................................................190.00

Victorian, Renaissance Revival, America, c1870, walnut, foliate and lappet carved cresting, incised dec, circular turned legs, 38-3/4" h, price for pr........................................................400.00

Victorian, Rococo Revival, America, third quarter 19th C

Balloon back, rosewood, crest, cabochon-mounted cartouche, carved serpentine seat rail, cabriole legs, 39" h, price for pair.................................................................200.00

Gondola form, mahogany, carved crest rail over scrolling splat, bowed seat rail, saber legs, 34" h, price for pr..350.00

Whimsical, Continental, late 19th C, carved walnut, figural lyre back surmounted by carved cherubs, seraphim, and foliage, upholstered section on back, upholstered seat, carved cabriole legs with peg feet, shaped apron, price for pr....2,100.00

Windsor

Birdcage, MA, c1810, concave crest rail above seven spindles, shaped seats, splayed legs joined by stretchers, painted old putty green with red pin striping, 16-1/2" h, 35" h, price for pr..............................................................3,565.00

Bow Back, New England, 1790-1810, arched crests above tapering spindles, shaped incised seats, splayed bamboo turned legs joined by similar stretchers, orig cream colored paint with dark green striping, imperfections, minor paint wear, heights vary from 35-3/4" h to 37-5/8" h, price for assembled set of six ...............................................4,025.00

**Slipper**

Aesthetic Movement, c1870-80, in the manner of Louis Comfort Tiffany, oak, brass knobs, leather back and seat, molded legs joined by stretchers, distressed, 31" h ............................850.00

Victorian

Renaissance Revival, America, c1870, mahogany, tufted upholstery, circular turned legs, casters .....................375.00

Rococo Revival, America, mid 19th C, attributed to J and J. W. Meeks, NY, rosewood, pierced carved back with gadrooned crest, fruit and scroll carving, carved legs, 43" h .....1,100.00

**Tub**, Edwardian, first quarter 19th C, mahogany and leather, deep button back joined to seat by slightly out-scrolled arms, cabriole legs, pad feet, 35" h.................................................................1,100.00

**Wing**

Georgian-Mid, English, mid-18th C, mahogany, shaped wings, scrolled arms, shell carved cabriole legs, 46" h...............980.00

Louis XV, provincial-style, early 20th C, walnut, leather upholstered back, seat, and arms, cabriole legs, 45-1/2" h arm chair and matching rect upholstered ottoman, price for two pcs....................................................................1,150.00

**George II, second quarter 18th C, walnut frame, blue upholstery, shaped side wings, padded C-scroll arms, cabriole legs, front feet replaced, $750.**

Queen Anne, early 18th C, ebonized, shaped wings, cabriole legs, pad feet, 49" h ......................................................3,000.00

# Chests of Drawers

**Art Deco,** Quigley, France, c1925, parchment covered, rect top, three tapering drawers, pyramid mirrored stiles, bracket feet, back branded, 44-1/2" x 35".............................................2,750.00

**Chippendale**

America, bow front, cherry, two board top with molded edge, four dovetailed drawers with beaded trim, reeded quarter columns, well shaped replaced ogee feet, old mellow finish, replaced brasses, top molding reset, 42" w, 23-1/4" d, 36-1/2" h......................3,575.00

Boston, c1760-80, oxbow, mahogany, overhanging molded top with shaped front, square corners, cockbeaded case, four reverse serpentine drawers with blocked ends, conforming bracket feet, orig brass hardware, old refinish, back stenciled "H. A. Hancock," minor restoration, 32-1/2" w, 22" d, 31" h .................................. 58,600.00

Boston, c1760-80, serpentine, mahogany, overhanging molded top with serpentine front and serpentine sides, conforming cockbeaded case, four graduated drawers, molded base, carved ball and claw feet, replaced brasses, old refinish, 36" w, 20" d, 32-1/4" h ...........................................34,500.00

Massachusetts, c1760-80, serpentine, mahogany, shaped molded top, cockbeaded case of four graduated long drawers, molded base, carved claw and ball feet, old replaced brasses, old refinish, bottom of top drawer inscribed in chalk "Basle Williams," minor restorations, 37-1/2" w, 18-3/4" d, 33-3/4" h.......................... 16,100.00

**Chippendale to Hepplewhite,** transitional, America, mahogany, pine and poplar secondary woods, case with reeded quarter columns, four dovetailed drawers with string inlay and corner fans (possibly a later addition), full dust shelves, molded base, ogee feet, old worn refinishing, replaced brasses and locks, some replaced facing on feet, 39-1/2" w, 20-3/4" d, 34-1/2" h ................................. 2,750.00

**Classical**

America, second quarter 19th C, mahogany, two parts, upper section with paneled splash over pair of shallow drawers, base with convex top drawer over bank of three drawers flanked by columns, bun feet, 43-1/4" w, 18-1/2" d, 50" h.......................600.00

Massachusetts, c1825-35, Faux Bois, splashboard with scrolled and spurred ends, four drawers flanked by spiral carved columns over bulbous ring-turned feet ending in balls, top with red stain, drawers with early graining simulating mahogany, some orig pulls, imperfections, 43" w, 20-1/2" d, 43-1/2" h........600.00

**Classical, Late,** America, fourth quarter 19th C, mahogany and poplar, projecting convex upper drawer over bank of three drawers, flanked by scrolling pilasters, 42-3/4" w, 22-1/4" d, 45-1/4" h ............ 1,000.00

**Empire,** America, mid-19th C, mahogany, two parts, mirror frame with arched pediment, resting on lift-top compartment, base with molded top drawer over bank of graduated drawers, 42" w, 20-1/2" d, 84" h...250.00

**Federal**

Hubbardton, Vermont, attributed to Asahel Jones (1766-1822), c1810-20, cherry and bird's eye maple veneer, cherry top with veneered edge overhangs case, four cockbeaded drawers of bird's eye veneer with mahogany cross-banded veneer surrounds, cyma-curved veneered skirt, replaced brasses, old refinish, 40" w, 18-1/2" d, 36-1/4" h ............................. 4,500.00

Massachusetts, early 19th C, birch and mahogany veneer, birch top with ovolo corners, case with mahogany veneer drawers flanked by spiral-turned legs, flanking central drop pendant, orig brasses, orig façade surface, old refinish to top, 42" w, 19-1/2" d, 37-3/4" h .......................................................... 1,840.00

New Hampshire, c1810, cherry and mahogany veneer, top with inlaid edge above scratch-beaded drawers, cyma-curved veneered skirt, central panel bordered by cross-banded maple veneer, replaced brasses, old refinish, imperfections, 42" w, 21-1/2" d, 37-1/2" h ........................................................2,300.00

North Shore, MA, early 19th C, wavy birch and grained cherry, curving splash board with scrolled terminals above top with ovolo front corners over turned colonettes which end in tapering

turned front feet, flank thumb-molded graduated wave birch drawers, old refinish, replaced brasses, imperfections, 39-1/2" w, 17-1/2" d, 49" h.................................................... 1,380.00

Portsmouth, NH, attributed to, c1805-15, mahogany and tiger maple, bowed top with double string inlay edge above case of four cockbeaded drawers, each with maple veneer panels outlined with stringing and mahogany cross banding, string inlaid base on shaped cutout feet, old finish, possibly orig brasses, imperfections, 39-3/4" w, 21-1/2" d, 34" h, .................. 18,400.00

Vermont, c1820, carved cherry and bird's eye maple veneer, rect overhanging top with reeded edge, case of four cockbeaded graduated drawers with flanking reeded panels, vase and ring-turned feet, replaced brass pulls, old refinish, 39-1/2" w, 19" d, 39-1/2" h................................................................. 2,415.00

**George II,** first half 18th C, walnut and inlay, molded top above two short and three graduated long drawers, turned feet, restoration, 40" w, 21-1/2" d, 38" h........................................................2,990.00

**George III,** c1800, mahogany and inlay,
Bow front, cross-banded top, four graduated drawers, French feet, veneer loss, restoration, damage, 37" w, 21" d, 35-1/2" h .... 1,850.00
Serpentine top, pair of short drawers over three graduated drawers, shaped bracket feet, 43" w, 21-3/4" d, 37-1/2" h...................4,140.00

**George III, Late,** early 19th C, mahogany, bowfront, plain top, pair of drawers over three graduated drawers, French feet............. 1,380.00

**Georgian,** first quarter 19th C

Mahogany, bow front, case fitted with two short drawers over three graduated drawers, ogee-molded bracket feet, 37" w, 20" d, 39-1/2" h ...................................................... 1,200.00

Mahogany, bow front, frieze with inlaid burled panels, two short drawers, three long graduated drawers below, splayed bracket feet, 44" w, 18" d, 44-1/2" h............................................ 1,550.00

Mahogany, c1810 and later, rect top, case fitted with two short drawers over three long graduated drawers, ogee-molded bracket feet, 43" w, 21" d, 41-1/2" h............................... 1,570.00

Mahogany, figured, bow front, case fitted with two short drawers over three graduated drawers, slightly splayed bracket feet, 42" w, 21" d, 44-1/2" h............................................... 1,540.00

Mahogany, rect top, case fitted with three concealed frieze drawers over two short drawers and three long graduated drawers, all flanked by engaged cluster of columns, ogee-molded bracket feet, 47-1/2" w, 22" d, 49" h........................................... 1,450.00

**Georgian-Style,** first quarter 19th C and later, yewwood, top quarter veneered, inlaid ebonized stringing above case fitted with two banks of five drawers, all banded, raised on bun feet, 45" w, 20-1/2" d, 38-1/2" h ..................................................................... 1,430.00

**George III-Style,** late 19th C, serpentine, mahogany, molded serpentine top, four graduated cockbeaded drawers flanked by carved supports, ogee bracket feet, 45" w, 21" d, 39-1/2" h...................4,900.00

**Gothic Revival, Cottage Style,** MA, late 19th C, pine, pediment and molded scalloped cornice over rect mirror flanked by frame with candle plateaus, shelf under mirror, four drawers, brown and orange comb-graining, black and gold accent striping on olive green, rose and gold floral motif on top, painted round reserve with landscape scene on front, castors, orig brass and paint, 38" w, 18-3/4" d, 76" h .........................................................................950.00

**Hepplewhite,** country, maple and birch with some curl, dovetailed case, five dovetailed overlapping drawers with orig brasses, scalloped apron, bracket feet, period replacement key escutcheons, old mellow finish, small well-done old repairs, 39-1/4" w, 19-1/4" d, 42-3/4" h ................................................................. 6,600.00

**Louis XV-Style,** bureau-plat, kingwood, parquetry, and gilt-metal mounts, rect top, leatherette-lined writing surface, cast acanthus edge, frieze with central drawer flanked by shaped drawers, keeled cabriole legs, molding, chutes, and sabots, 33" w, 70" l, 30-1/2" h................................................................2,100.00

**Queen Anne**

New England, mid 18th C, old dark brown stain, overhanging top, case of four graduated drawers, high arched feet, turned wooden pulls, imperfections, 36" w, 16-1/4" d, 40-1/2" h ................2,990.00

**Hepplewhite, America, 18th C, inlaid maple and curly maple, swell front, 40" l, 47" h, $3,200.**

New England, late 18th C, maple, cornice above split drawers over four full length graduated drawers, shaped molded base, refinished, replaced brasses, imperfections, 41" w, 19" d, 46" h ............................................................................ 2,070.00

**Regency,** first quarter 19th C and later, mahogany, bow front, molded edge top, case fitted with two short drawers over three long graduated drawers, bracket feet, 43" w, 22-1/2" d, 41-1/2" h ......... 1,760.00

**Sheraton**

America

Bowfront, mahogany and mahogany veneer, pine secondary wood, four drawers with applied edge beading, molded stiles with reeding, turned feet, old finish, orig oval brasses, wear and minor edge damage, filed age cracks in top, one foot with age crack, 41-3/8" w, 23-1/2" d, 38-1/2" h ........ 1,100.00

Cookie Corner, mahogany, shaped backsplash, three quartered reeded corner columns, shaped apron, turned feet, orig hardware, 42-1/2" w at front, 39-3/4" h ............... 1,50.00

Ohio, c1820-30, walnut, white pine secondary wood, four graduated drawers, scratch bead and inlaid diamond escutcheons, double lined inlay on stiles and on top board, 41-1/2" w, 20" d, 46-1/4" h ....................................... 1,650.00

**Victorian**

American, c1870, mahogany, rounded top with molded edge, case fitted with two short drawers over three long graduated drawers, finely figured veneers and carved ribbon formed pulls, bun feet, 48-1/2" w, 22" d, 47" h ........................................ 990.00

American, c1900, mahogany, large oval mirror with floral carved crest supported by well-carved conforming brackets, bow front base with three smaller drawers over pair of full width drawers, 54" w, 26" d, 74-1/2" h ...................................................... 360.00

American, fourth quarter 19th C, pine, molded edge, case fitted with two short drawers over three long drawers, turned bulbous feet, 39-1/2" w, 38-1/2" h ................................................... 660.00

American, third quarter 19th C, pine, molded edge, case fitted with two short drawers over two long drawers, bulbous toupie feet, 32" w, 17" d, 32" h ...................................................... 425.00

Eastlake, America, fourth quarter 19th C, walnut, marble top over bank of four drawers, each centered by figured panel, mirrored back, 40" w, 19-1/4" d, 33-1/2" h ...................................... 525.00

**William IV**

Second quarter 19th C, mahogany, bow front, case fitted with two short drawers over three graduated long drawers, bulbous reeded and ring-turned legs, toupie feet, 42" w, 21" d, 47-1/2" h ...1,485.00

Second quarter 19th C, mahogany, string-inlaid top, case fitted with two short drawers over three long drawers, turned bulbous toupie feet, 39" w, 17-1/2" d, 47" h ................................. 1,100.00

Second quarter 19th C, rosewood, rounded edge top, conforming case fitted with two short drawers over three graduated long drawers, plinth base, 45-1/2" w, 19" d, 45-3/4" h ............. 360.00

Third quarter 19th C, mahogany, bow front, curv3ed top, conforming case fitted with two short drawers over three graduated long drawers, flanked on either side by reeded pilasters, serpentine carved skirt, bulbous toupie feet, 47-1/2" w, 19" d, 45-1/2" h ........... 950.00

**William and Mary**

American, oak, molded edge top, five dovetailed drawers, facade with applied moldings, bracket feet, old worn finish, orig engraved brasses, repairs, feet replaced, 36" w, 35-3/4" h ............... 1,350.00

Southern Massachusetts or Rhode Island, tiger maple, graduated drawer construction, two over four drawers, applied moldings to top and bottom, turned turnip feet, old grunge finish, 3 escutcheon plates present, rest of hardware missing, some repair, 36-1/4" w, 18-1/4" d, 48" h.................................................. 2,950.00

## Chests of Drawers, Other

**Bachelor,** late George III, English, early 19th C, mahogany, rect top with molded edge, slide, four graduated cockbeaded drawers, bracket feet, veneer damage, restoration to feet, 37" l, 33-1/2" h.................... 2,750.00

**Campaign,** mahogany, pine secondary wood, brass trim, dovetailed case, int. with lift-out tray, one dovetailed drawer, some shrinkage to lid, 30-3/4" w, 18-1/4" d, 19" h .................................................. 385.00

**Cartonniere,** Louis XVI-Style, late 19th C, mahogany and burgundy gilt tooled leather, sloped lift top above drawer, five leather compartments, plinth base, 23" w, 14-1/4" d, 46-1/2" h .................... 4,600.00

**Cedar,** America, early 20th C, top fitted with pair of raised panels, dovetailed construction, brass plaque inscribed "B. T. Montgomery & Co. New Orleans," 54" w, 32" d, 32-1/2" h ............................... 350.00

**Cellarette,** Regency, Irish, first quarter 19th C, mahogany, sarcophagus form, ebony and brass strung rect hinged top, divided int. with twelve blown-glass decanters, twin lidded tôle storage box, six rect compartments with mahogany covers, banded front and sides set between reeded corners, ebonized feet raised on stepped plinth, faux marble base of later date, provenance: Mallett's, London, 36" w, 21" d, 28" h.......................................................... 10,000.00

**Chest on Chest**

Chippendale

Connecticut, Peter Newcomb, Lebanon, 1768, cherry, carved rosettes, scrolled, molded cornice, three small drawers, central one with carved sunburst, above four graduated drawers flanked by fluted engaged quarter columns with lamb's tongues above and below, lower case of drawers, fluted column flanking, molded base with pierced central drop, large shaped ogee bracket feet ending in platforms, side shaping with scrolled spurs, early surface, replaced brass pulls, imperfections, 37-1/2" w, 17-1/2" d, 91" h.............. 37,950.00

Connecticut, 18th C, cherry, scrolled molded top flanks central plinth above three small drawers, central one with carved pinwheel over three long drawers flanked by fluted engaged quarter columns, mid-molding and four additional thumb molded drawers, shaped bracket feet, old refinish, replaced brasses, imperfections, 34" w, 18-1/2" d, 84" h ..... 13,800.00

George III, late 18th/early 19th C, mahogany and inlay, plain cornice over boxwood and ebony banding, upper structure with two short drawers over three long drawers, diamond shaped ivory escutcheons, canted corners with feather banding, lower structure with three graduated long drawers with ivory escutcheons, further checker banding and shaped bracket base, 44" w, 20-3/4" d, 78-3/8" h................. 3,500.00

Georgian, walnut and Elmwood, molded cornice above pair of short drawers and three long drawers, base with pair of short drawers over two long drawers, bracket feet, 41-1/2" w, 22" d, 67" h ......................................................... 8,625.00

**Chest on Frame**

Queen Anne, New England, last half 18th C, maple, pine, and cherry, rect molded slightly overhanging top, case with five thumb-molded graduated drawers, frame with skirt and drop pendant, cabriole legs, pad feet on platforms, replaced brasses, refinished, restoration, 36" w, 19" d, 52-1/2" h ....................................1,380.00

Queen Anne style, English, walnut and burl veneer, mahogany secondary wood, case with four dovetailed drawers, brass teardrop pulls, cabriole legs, duck feet, 20th C, 19-1/4" x 33-1/2" base, 38-1/2" h .......................................825.00

Southeastern New England, early 18th C, painted maple, cherry, oak, and pine, top with flat molded cornice, double arch molded case, two short drawers, frame with valanced skirt, four ring turned legs, disc feet, old engraved brasses, old Spanish brown paint, imperfections, 35" w, 19" d, 54-1/2" h ....................................3,500.00

**Chest on Stand,** William and Mary, walnut, rect molded cornice over secret drawer above three short drawers, three long drawers, base raised on baluster-turned supports joined by shaped stretcher, ball feet, 40" w, 21-1/2" d, 67" h ....................................1,840.00

**Commode**

Biedermeier-Style, fourth quarter 19th C, bedside, mahogany, variegated gray marble top, case fitted with frieze drawer over cupboard door, bulbous feet, ebonized accents, 14-1/2" w, 14" d, 30" h, price for pr ....................................750.00

Charles X, second quarter 19th C, bedside

Mahogany, variegated gray marble top with canted corners, conforming case fitted with single frieze drawer over cupboard, paneled block feet, 15" w, 13-1/2" d, 30-1/4" h 500.00

Mahogany, variegated gray marble top, case fitted with cushion frieze drawer over three long graduated drawers, concealed plinth drawer, molded block feet, 48-1/2" w, 21-1/4" d, 37-1/2" h ....................................4,000.00

Directorie-Style, mahogany, rect projecting top, conforming frieze drawer, centered by ormolu-mount, two graduated drawers, flanked on either side by engaged columns, headed by carved capitals, splayed saber feet, 48" w, 22" d, 34" h ..............900.00

French Provincial, fourth quarter 19th C, bedside, stained fruitwood, bow front top with three-quarter scalloped gallery above open compartment, each with heart cutouts, cabriole legs, 15-3/4" w, 11-1/4" d, 27-1/2" h, price for pr ...........................770.00

Louis Philippe

Composed of antique elements, walnut, variegated charcoal marble top, canted corners, conforming case fitted with frieze drawer over three long paneled doors, molded block feet, 48" w, 20-1/2" d, 37-1/2" h ...............................1,500.00

Second quarter 19th C, rosewood, inset gray marble top with canted corners, conforming case fitted with secretary frieze drawer, leather inset writing surface with a variety of drawers, three long drawers, concealed plinth drawer below, molded feet, 50-1/2" w, 21-1/2" d, 36-1/2" h ............2,400.00

Louis XV-Style, 20th C, kingwood, marquetry inlaid, tulipwood, serpentine marble top, case on angular legs, foliate cast mounts, 27-1/2" w, 16" d, 31" h................................1,265.00

Louis XV/XVI-Style, 20th C, tulipwood, ormolu mounts, breche d'alep marble top, three long drawers, angular cabriole legs, 50" w, 22" d, 38" h...................................2,415.00

Louis XVI-Style, bedside

Mahogany, late 19th C, banded and quarter-veneered top, case fitted with three drawers, all with matchbook veneers, tapering sq legs ending in brass caps, 14-1/4" w, 11-1/2" d, 28-1/2" h ....................................400.00

Walnut, composed of antique parts, variegated green marble top, case fitted with three long drawers, bun feet, 24-1/2" d, 17-1/4" d, 36" h ....................................1,200.00

Restauration-Style, mahogany, rect top, case fitted with two tambour doors, flanked on either side by ebonized and parcel gilt engaged columns, slightly splayed tapering legs, 47-1/2" w, 18-1/2" d, 35" h ....................................500.00

**Credenza,** attributed to Horner, New York, ebonized, marquetry inlaid, shaped inset marble top, ormolu bronze figural mounts, two drawers over two doors with concave sides, side panels inlay with flowers on green ground, front door panels inlay with baskets of flowers with bow tie ribbon, int. fitted with shelves, 67-1/2" w, 19-1/2' d, 41" h......8,000.00

**Highboy**

Queen Anne

American, maple, curly facade, molded cornice, top dovetailed case with seven overhanging dovetailed drawers, four overlapping dovetailed drawers in base, scrolled apron, cabriole legs with trifid feet, orig brasses, refinished, pine secondary wood, base reworked, several brasses incomplete, one escutcheon missing, 35" w, 20-7/8" d, 70-1/4" h......7,500.00

American, walnut with figured veneer, herringbone cross banding on drawers, applied moldings, top: molded cornice, dovetailed case, five dovetailed drawers, scrolled apron with turned drops and three dovetailed drawers, cabriole legs, duck feet, old refinishing, replaced brasses, cornice and molding between sections replaced, facade veneer has damage and restoration, apron drops replaced, other repairs, 35-1/2" w, 22" x 39-3/4" cornice, 21-1/2" d, 38-1/2" w base, 64-1/4" h ....................................3,300.00

Massachusetts, c1740-80, walnut and maple, upper section with flat cornice above two short and three long thumb molded drawers, lower case of one long and three short thumb molded drawers, cabriole legs, pad feet on platforms, orig brasses, old mellow surface, minor imperfections, 38" w, 20" d, 70-3/4" h ....................................17,250.00

New England, 19th C, maple, cornice molding on upper case, five graduated thumb-molded drawers, lower case with similar drawers, shaped skirt, cabriole legs, high pad feet, replaced brasses, old refinish, minor restoration, 38" w, 17" d, 70-7/8" h ....................................12,650.00

North Shore, MA, 18th C, walnut and maple, cove molding, five graduated thumb-molded drawers, lower case with small drawers centered by fan-carved drawer, shaped skirt, cabriole legs, pad feet, some old brasses, old refinish, restoration, 37" w, 19-3/4" d, 72" h ....................................8,100.00

Salem, MA, c1760-75, carved walnut, cornice molding above three small drawers, central one with fan-carving, four thumb-molded graduated drawers, lower case with one long drawer above three small drawers, central one fan-carved, scrolled skirt, cabriole legs ending in arris pad feet, old brasses, refinished, two replaced moldings, 37" w, 19-3/4" d, 72-1/4" h ....................................16,100.00

Victorian, late, America, c1900, oak, two parts, mirror with log roll crest and beveled plate, serpentine base with two over four drawers, 34-1/2" w, 21-1/2" d, 60" h................................450.00

William and Mary, southeastern New England, early 18th C, painted pine, top section with flat molded cornice, single arch molded case with two short drawers and three long graduated drawers, base with three short drawers, four turned legs joined by flat shaped stretchers, turned feet, brasses may be orig, painted dark brown, restoration, 33" w, 18" d, 55" h ...16,100.00

**Linen Press,** Federal, New York, c1820, mahogany inlaid, top section with arched molding above inlaid frieze flanked by ball finials, two cupboard doors with applied molding opening to mahogany, cedar, and pine linen drawers, lower case with two cockbeaded short drawers, three graduated long drawers, flaring French feet joined by valanced skirt, old finish, 48" w, 22" d, 87-3/4" h .......................9,775.00

**Liquor,** England, late 18th C, oak, two handles, iron mounts, compartmented int. with thirteen etched foliate dec bottles, ten pressed brass and cork stoppers, 17-5/8" w, 12-3/8" d, 11-3/4" h ...................460.00

**Low Boy,** Queen Anne, burl walnut, molded edge top, matched veneer rectangles, bordered in two borders with matching veneers, front has two sq drawers flanking central drawer with burl walnut veneer, center with shaped apron, four cabriole legs, pad feet, old brasses, 29-1/2" w, 18-3/4" d, 28" h ....................................3,000.00

**Lowboy, Chippendale, Delaware Valley, c1760, walnut, rect molded top, one wide and three small thumb molded drawers, recessed reeded side columns, shaped apron, cabriole legs with shell carved knees, claw and ball feet, 33-1/2" w, 20-3/4" d, 28-1/2" h, $22,000.**

**Spice,** Pennsylvania, 1780-1800, walnut, dovetailed, cove-molded cornice, raised panel hinged door, opens to int. of eleven small drawers, brass pulls, molded base, old surface, 15-1/2" w, 11" d, 18-1/4" h .................................................. 14,950.00

**Tall Chest of Drawers**
Chippendale
    Connecticut, attributed to, 18th C, cherry and maple, flat molded cornice, case of central fan carved short drawer flanked by two sets of small drawers, six graduated long drawers, tall bracket feet, possibly orig oval brass pulls, old finish, minor restoration, casters added, 37" w, 18" d, 62-3/4" h .......................................... 46,000.00
    New England, 18th C, tiger maple, cornice flares above case of seven graduated drawers, orig brasses, old refinish, new base, 36" w, 19" d, 59-1/4" h .................................. 8,625.00
    New Hampshire or Massachusetts, cherry and pine, flat molded cornice above case of five thumb molded graduated corners, bracket feet, center drop pendant, old refinish, minor imperfections, drawers never had hardware, 36" w, 18-1/2" d, 48-1/4" h .................................. 4,600.00
    Queen Anne, southeastern New England, c1750, tiger maple, molded cornice, case of four small, two half-size, and four graduated thumb molded long drawers, bracket feet, replaced Queen Anne style brasses, old refinish, minor imperfection, 34-3/4" w, 18" d, 49-1/2" h ................ 21,850.00
**Wardrobe,** Classical, mid Atlantic states, 1840, mahogany veneer, two recessed panel doors, similar sides, int. with veneered drawers, base with platform feet, small int. drawers added, 65" w, 26" d, 79-1/2" h ................................................................ 3,200.00

# Cradles
Chippendale-Style, birch, canted sides, scalloped headboard, turned posts and rails, refinished, 37-1/2" l ......................................... 400.00
Country
    Attributed to Connecticut River Valley, MA, early 19th C, paint decorated, shaped sides joining arched head and foot boards, scrolled rollers, orig green painted exterior mustard and brown vinegar, putty grained interior, 40-1/2" l, 15" d, 22" h .... 1,750.00
    New England, 18th C, painted pine, arched hood continuing to shaped and carved dovetailed sides, rockers, old light green paint, old repairs, 40" l ............................................... 300.00
    New England, early 19th C, crib, stenciled and yellow painted, scrolled head and footboards joined by side rails, vasiform spindles on ring-turned tapering legs and feet, orig yellow and black

paint, stenciled floral and fruit designs on head and footboards, imperfections, 52" l, 25-1/2" w, 33" h ................................. 450.00
    Pennsylvania, late 18th C, dovetailed, refinished curly maple, cut-out hearts, age cracks and shrinkage, 41" ..................... l550.00
    Pennsylvania, 19th C, walnut, scrolled back and sides, shaped rockers, old refinish, repaired crest, 39" l, 18-1/4" d, 21" h .......... 250.00
Eastlake, 1875, walnut, paneled headboard, footboard, and sides, scrolling crest above short turned spindles, platform support, orig finish, dated................................................ 495.00
Federal, America, early 19th C, rocking, walnut, hooded canopy, single board sides joined with finely crafted dovetails, 42-1/2" w, 23" d, 26-1/2" h ................................................................ 200.00
Italian, third quarter 19th C, crib, carved polychrome, tapering form, shaped and paneled sides, each end fitted with carrying handles, cabriole feet, painted cream, gilt accents, 38" w, 24-1/2" d, 27" h ......... 700.00
Victorian, America, third quarter 19th C, mechanical, walnut, banister gallery supported by trestle base, patent ironwork rocking mechanism missing, as-found condition, 43" w, 20-1/2" d, 35" h ........ 250.00
Windsor, New England, c1800-20, bamboo turned spindles, worn finish................................................ 850.00

# Cupboards
## Armoire
    Classical, America, second quarter 19th C, mahogany, arched pediment centered by carved palmette, pair of paneled doors, segmented int., bracket feet, 52" w, 22" d, 92" h .......... 1,950.00
    Empire to Rococo Revival, transitional, America, mid-19th C, walnut, double ogee molded cornice, pair of doors, each with glazed panel terminating in Moorish arch, ogee-bracket feet, now fitted as a bookcase, 57" w, 22-1/2" d, 86" h ........ 1,210.00
    Empire to Rococo Revival, transitional, America, mid-19th C, walnut, ogee molded cornice, pair of doors, each with Gothic arched panel, ogee bracket feet, 58" w, 23" d, 89" h .... 1,900.00
French Provincial
    First quarter 19th C, fruitwood, molded, domed cornice above two long doors, each inset with molded panels, raised on molded block feet, maker's stamp "I. Martiny," 51" w, 26-1/2" d, 95" h .................................................. 6,000.00
    Made of old pieces, fruitwood, single door, molded cornice above case fitted with double serpentine paneled door, trefoil carving, sq bracket feet, 32" w, 14-1/2" d, 82" h.... 955.00
    Louis Philippe, second quarter 19th C, fruitwood and Elmwood, ogee-molded cornice above pair of paneled doors, plinth outlined in scrolls, concave block feet, 52" w, 23-1/2" d, 92-1/2" h .. 2,250.00
    Louis XV, Provincial, 18th/19th C, fruitwood, arched molded cornice, pair of carved drawers, short cabriole legs, scrolled toes, worming, restorations, 56" w, 24-1/2" d, 95" h ............. 1,725.00
    Louis XV/XVI, Provincial, late 18th C, cherry and Elmwood, later rect molded cornice over pair of paneled doors, shaped skirt, short cabriole legs, restorations, worming, 55" w, 24-1/2" d, 80" h ................................................ 1,150.00
    Napoleon III, third quarter 19th C, rosewood, single door, floral carved crest over stepped cornice, mirror plate surmounted by foliage carving, drawer fitted with sliding bird's eye maple dust cover, slipper drawer below, 41" w, 19" d, 98" h ........... 2,900.00
Victorian
    Eastlake, America, fourth quarter 19th C, walnut and burled walnut, stepped cornice with burled panel and line incising, single door retaining period mirror plate, projecting base fitted with drawer, 46" w, 25-1/2" d, 89" h .................. 1,350.00
    Late, America, c1900, oak, crest with log roll surmounted by foliate carving, pair of doors with arched beveled mirror plates, not in verdigris paint, 50" w, 17-1/4" d, 91" h.......................... 675.00
**Bonnetière,** French Provincial, c1860, fruitwood, ogee molded cornice above two paneled cupboard doors, separated by single drawer, bracket feet, 31" w, 23" d, 74-1/2" h ...................... 1,500.00
**Chiffonnier,** Regency, first quarter 19th C, mahogany, rect top surmounted by shelf on scrolled supports, single drawer over pair of grillwork doors, French bracket feet, 36-1/2" w, 15-1/4" d, 45" h .....1,100.00

**Corner, New England, early 19th C, pine, flat molded cornice, case with glazed door, projecting lower case of two cupboard doors with cockbeaded panels on base, applied molding, old refinish, replaced hardware, imperfections, 57" w, 29-1/2" d, 88-3/4" h, $1,725. Photo courtesy of Skinner, Inc.**

## Corner

Architectural, American, curly maple, arched cornice with molded details, carved rosettes, turned finials, arched upper paneled cupboard doors over paneled cupboard base doors, ogee feet, old refinishing, finials, upper sections of goosenecks, and feet replaced, 44-1/2" h, 99-1/2" h ...................................... 10,450.00

Chippendale, Pennsylvania, early 19th C, carved cherry, scrolled molded pediment flanking fluted keystone with flame finial, arched door flanked by reeded columns, three serpentine-shaped painted shelves, recessed panel doors also flanked by reeded columns, single shelf base int., cyma curved skirt, old refinish, hardware changes, minor patching, 41-1/2" w, 17-3/4" d, 95" h..........9,200.00

Hepplewhite

One piece, refinished cherry with inlay banding around base, waist and top, inlaid fan in apron, line inlay with invected corners on doors, cove molded cornice, paneled doors with molded edge stiles and rails, cut-out feet and scrolled apron, replaced feet, repairs, 42-1/4" w, 82-1/2" h.............. 3,300.00

Two piece, cherry, old dark finish, figured wood veneer on door panels, drawers, and cornice, molded cornice, top with double doors, each with eight panes of old glass, arched top lights, three drawer fronts with chamfered edges, center drawer dovetailed, two flanking faux drawers, paneled base doors, orig brass "H" hinges, other hardware replaced, bracket feet are old replacements, top int. covered in old worn yellow-green brocade, minor repairs to cornice, 54" w, 86" h................................3,850.00

Middle Atlantic States, cherry, flaring cornice above glazed door, three-shelved interior, lower case with two recessed panel doors which open to single interior shelf, molded base, replaced hardware, refinished, height loss, other repairs, 44" w, 28-1/4" d, 85-3/4" h.....................4,315.00

New England, late 18th/early 19th C, red washed pine, cornice molding above four serpentine shelves which flank middle one with straight front edge, molded base with frontal cyma curving, orig red wash, restoration and losses, 32-1/2" w, 20-1/4" d, 65" h .......................................... 2,990.00

## Hanging

America, decorated, pine and chestnut, orig red paint, floral dec, mortised and pegged door with four inset panels with tulips, side panels with vines and flowers, one board back with age crack, two int. shelves, old replaced brass pull, minor wear, 19-1/4" w, 9" d, 29" h..................................................................3,575.00

English, corner, mahogany, open curved shelves, shaped top edge, old finish, center of three base drawers missing, 22-3/4" w, 39" h ............................................................................... 770.00

## Linen Press

Federal, New York, c1840, labeled "Thomas Burling," mahogany veneer, flaring cornice above veneered frieze, recessed panel doors opening to interior with three adjustable shelves, lower case with butler's desk above two full width drawers, recessed panel doors, molded bracket base, old refinish, replaced pulls, lower case of different origin, 49" w, 23-1/2" d, 88-1/2" h ................................................................1,840.00

Georgian, c1810, in the style of Thomas Sheraton, mahogany, molded cornice above two paneled doors, sliding shelves, lower section fitted with two short drawers over two long graduated drawers, inlaid ebonized stringing, splayed bracket feet, 48" w, 23 d, 75" h ....................................................2,200.00

Georgian, first quarter 19th C, mahogany, molded cornice, two paneled doors, lower case fitted with three long drawers, ogee-molded bracket feet, 49" w, 23" d, 93-1/2" h ................. 2,650.00

**Kas,** Long Island, NY, c1730-80, cherry, pine, and polar, architectural cornice molding, two raised panel thumb-molded doors flanked by reeded pilasters, applied moldings, single drawer, painted detachable disc and stretcher feet, replaced hardware, refinished, restored, 65-1/2" w, 26-1/4" d, 77-1/4" h ............................................. 4,500.00

**Kitchen** (Hoosier), American, early 20th C, oak, scalloped cornice over three cupboard doors, two glazed over two larger paneled doors, outset lower section with aluminum-lined work surface, over cupboard door flanked by three graduated drawers, 39-1/2" w, 28" d, 71-3/4" h ................................................................ 650.00

**Pewter,** two part, top: cornice molding, two six glass pane doors, two shelves, open pie shelf; base: two drawers over raised panel doors, one shelf int., short turned feet, 56" w, 20" d, 87" h .............. 2,250.00

**Slant Back,** New England, late 18th C, pine

Flat molded cornice above beaded canted front flanking shelves, projecting base with single raised panel door, old refinish, doors missing from top, imperfections, 37-1/2" w, 18" d, 73" h.................................................................2,300.00

Flat overhanging cornice, cockbeaded front, three shelves, paneled door with wrought iron "H" and "L" hinges, old refinish, replaced door, 29-1/2" w, 12-3/4" d, 39" h..................... 1,650.00

**Spice,** northern Europe, last half 18th C, wall-type, painted, flat molded cornice, hinged cupboard door, molded recessed panel opening, compartmentalized int., molded base, old dark green paint bordered by red, int. drawers missing, imperfections, 16" w, 8" d, 17" h .................................................................................1,500.00

## Step-Back

New England, early 19th C, painted pine, cornice above two doors, opens to three-shelved interior, open compartment, stepped-out surface above two doors opening to three-shelved base interior, interiors painted red, exterior painted light blue, surface losses and repairs ............................................ 2,990.00

New England, early 19th C, painted, two raised panel doors, four shelf int., stepped out lower case with similar raised panel doors with two-shelf int., old blue paint, imperfections, 36-1/2" w, 17 d, 80-1/2" h ................................................................................. 7,475.00

## Wall

Country, refinished pine and poplar, top: molded cornice, double doors with "H" hinges, nine panes of glass, high pie shelf, base: three dovetailed drawers, paneled doors (probably from earlier piece), 64-1/2" w, 18" d, 85" h ....................................... 2,550.00

New England, early 19th C, red painted pine, one-pat, double raised panel upper door, three-shelved painted int., similar base door with one shelf int., shaped skirt, orig red paint, int. repaint, hardware changes, minor height and cornice loss, 43-1/2" w, 19-1/4" d, 81" h ............................................................. 1,200.00

New England, southeastern, 18th C, pine, molded cornice, two sliding doors, int. with three shelves, gadrooned molding, four paneled hinged door, flanked by paneled pilasters on molded capitals and bases, old refinish, remnants of blue-green paint, minor imperfections, 37-1/2" w, 19-1/2" d, 78" h .......... 9,775.00

Ohio, early 19th C, cherry inlaid, flat molded cornice, door with flush cockbeaded panel inlaid with two symmetrically arranged leafy branches, rect escutcheon, int. with three shelves, flanked by ring-turned columns, flat molded base, 19-1/2" w, 7-1/2" d, 27-1/4" h ............................................................................ 1,495.00

Pennsylvania, 19th C, pine, two sections, upper: cavetto cornice, two six-pane doors over arched open shelf; lower: outset with three drawers over two sunken-panel doors, shield int., short turned feet, 51" w, 19" d, 81" h .......................................... 2,500.00

**Wardrobe,** William IV, second quarter 19th C, mahogany, molded cornice above two long molded doors, each inset with highly figured domed panel, bun feet, 52-1/2" w, 20" d, 85" h ..................... 1,210.00

## Day Beds

**Art Deco,** Jules Leleu, c1925, walnut, two high scrolling ends, rectangular plinth, tapered everted feet ending with scrolls, upholstered cushion and rolled pillows ................................................... 4,500.00

**Charles X,** England, c1830, burl walnut, carved to one side with scrolling and shell motifs, arched headboard and footboard joined by scrolled veneered panel, molded feet, 72" l, 50-1/2" d, 42-1/2" h ........................................................................... 1,250.00

### Classical

New England, sleigh, carved mahogany, veneered crests, scrolled sides with crossbanded veneer on edges and in middle, shaped carved feet on casters, very minor surface imperfections, 59-1/2" w, 102" l, 34-3/4" h footboard, 41-1/2" h headboard ......................................................................... 4,025.00

New York, c1820, rosewood, painted and molded crest rail with stenciled acanthus decoration, dolphin carved gilded and verde antico arms, torus molded seat rail, dark green worsted wool upholstery with brass tack decoration, carved cornucopia gilded verde antico brackets, carved hairy paw feet with casters ..................... 6,950.00

New York, c1830, sleigh, carved mahogany veneer, scrolled head and footboards with foliate carving, gadrooned sides and rails, leaf carved shaped legs with brass caps on casters, 59" w, 103-1/2" l, 40" h footboard, 41" h headboard ..................... 31,050.00

Pennsylvania, Philadelphia, c1825, mahogany, low incurvate crest rail, rounded flowing shell carved arm rests, acanthus and beaded legs, ball feet with casters, 72" l, 20" d, 28" h ..................... 4,975.00

**Duncan Phyfe-Style,** recamier, ormolu-mount, rush seat, scrolled ends, horizontal splat, large scrolled back, 58" l, 18-1/2" d, 32-1/2" h ..1,450.00

**French Provincial,** Louis XV style, third quarter 19th C, fruitwood, shaped and padded back removable for conversion from settee to daybed, outscrolled arms above cushioned seat, cabriole legs headed by floral carving, scrolled toes, 81-1/2" w, 35" d, 36" h ................................... 4,850.00

**French Restauration,** America, c1840, mahogany, down scrolled serpentine crest rail, plain seat rail, champagne colored silk upholstery, scalloped bracket feet with casters, 79" l, 27" w, 27" h ......... 1,675.00

**Louis Philippe,** second quarter 19th C, fruitwood, headboard and footboard both with rounded crests fronted by flower-patterned ormolu patera above engaged pilaster, turret-form feet, 77" l, 42" w, 44" h ....825.00

**Louis XVI-Style,** white painted, arching head and footboards with ribbon carving, pine cone finials, upholstered in off-white fabric, fluted legs, ball feet, pair of matching bolsters, 82-1/2" l, 36-1/2" w, 45" h ...........2,400.00

### Victorian

Bauer, Gustav, c1870, récamier, red velvet and silk tassel upholstery, double cushion backrest, scrolled arm, over-upholstered frame, circular turned legs, losses, 66" l ....................... 1,150.00

English, late 19th C, récamier, mahogany, one corner mounted with button-tufted chair back extending to low top rail, cabriole legs, 68" w, 31" d, 32" h ................................................ 450.00

**William and Mary,** maple, adjustable headboard with urn splat, scalloped crest with fixed chains, turned and canted posts, boldly turned stretcher base with eight legs, mellow old refinishing, old replaced rush bottom, headboard is well executed replacement, top of posts ended out, 68" w, 22" d, 38-1/2" h............................................. 2,200.00

**Windsor,** New England, early 19th C, painted and decorated, triple-section back, hinged fold-out bed, bamboo turned arms and tapered spindles, orig yellow ground paint with orig brown leaf and berry stencil dec and striping, replaced seat with 20th C textile cover, minor surface imperfections, 84" l, 26" d, 36-1/2" h .............................. 4,025.00

## Desks

**Architect's,** English, Provincial, 19th C, pine, rect molded top above two long drawers, circular tapering ring-turned legs, 53-1/2" w, 35" d, 38" h ................................................................................ 800.00

### Arts & Crafts

McHugh, oak, partners, four drawers on each side, Mackmurdo feet, X-design applied to sides, orig dark finish, one knob replaced, 56" w, 37" d, 29" h ......................................... 1,300.00

Stickley Brothers, #6515, oak, slant front, copper strap hinges, over single drawer, orig oval copper hardware, four tapered posts on shoefoot base, cleaned orig finish, unsigned, 30" w, 15" d, 47" h.................................................................. 1,900.00

### Chippendale

Boston, c1760-80, reverse serpentine, slant front, interior of one short drawer flanked by two long drawers over five short drawers and ten valanced compartments, cockbeaded case with arced top drawer over three graduated drawers, ogee bracket feet, old replaced brasses, old refinish, repairs to lid, 41-1/2" w, 22" d, 43-1/2" h .......................................................... 6,900.00

Connecticut, late 18th C, mahogany, block front, slant front lid, fitted tiered int. with nine dovetailed drawers, pigeonholes, two pull-out letter drawers with fluted columns, flame carved finials and door with blocking and fan carving, dovetailed case, four dovetailed drawers, conforming apron, bracket feet, replaced brasses, old refinishing, feet replaced, repairs to case, 41-3/4" w, 21-1/2" d, 42-3/4" h................................................. 3,850.00

Delaware River Valley, c1770, walnut, slant front, int. of central prospect door with recessed thumb-molded tombstone panel opening to valanced two-drawer int. flanked by document drawers with engaged columns and four valanced compartments and four short drawers, case with four thumb-molded graduated drawers, flanked by reeded quarter columns, ogee bracket feet on platforms, orig Chippendale brass pulls and escutcheons, old finish, minor imperfections, provenance: made for Captain John Lambert, Revolutionary War captain for whom Lambertville, NJ, was named ............................................. 25,300.00

Massachusetts, c1760-80, maple, slant front, two-stepped int., four balanced compartments, fourteen drawers, case with four thumb-molded graduated drawers, bracket feet, old refinish, minor imperfections, 35" w, 19-3/4" d, 41-1/2" h ........... 4,200.00

Massachusetts, 18th C, carved mahogany, reverse serpentine, slant lid, two-stepped int. of valanced compartments and small drawers, case with four graduated scratch beaded serpentine drawers, conforming molded base with central drop, frontal ball and claw feet, shaped bracket rear feed, old refinish, repairs, 42" w, 22" d, 44-1/2" h.................................................... 5,175.00

New England, c1760-80, maple, slant front, int. with tan-carved concave drawer, conforming drawer below flanked by shaped valanced compartments above shaped drawers, two projecting compartments, case with four thumb-molded graduated drawers, bracket feet, replaced pulls, old finish, imperfections, 35-3/4" w, 17" d, 40-3/4" h................................................. 5,175.00

New England, c1780, maple, slant front, int. of eight valanced compartments, two document drawers, five drawers, case with four thumb-molded graduated drawers, bracket feet, replaced brasses, refinished, 35" w, 18-1/8" d, 41-1/2" h ........... 3,800.00

New England, 18th C, maple, slant front, walnut stepped int. with valanced compartments above small drawers, some with end blocking, central convex end blocked drawers with flanking document drawers with turned columns, case with four thumb-molded graduated drawers, bracket base, replaced brasses, old refinish, repairs, 35-1/4" w, 19-1/2" d, 40" h.................. 3,450.00

Northern New England, mid to late 18th C, slant front, birch, slant lid opens to two stepped interior with open valanced compartments above small drawers, central opening all above drawers with cockbeaded surrounds, molded base with shaped bracket feet, refinished, replaced brasses, imperfections, interior drawer inscribed "Nathan Emery," 39" w, 18" d, 43" h .............. 3,200.00

Rhode Island, 18th C, cherry and maple, slant front, two-tiered int. of small compartments and drawers, thumb-molded case ad four graduated drawers, shaped bracket feet, casters, replaced brasses, old refinish, repairs, 36-3/4" w, 18-1/4" d, 40-1/2" h ................................................................2,675.00

Rhode Island, late 18th C, cherry, slant front, stepped int. of small drawers, central one with shaping, case of beaded graduated drawers, ogee bracket feet, orig brasses, old refinish, restoration, 39" w, 20" d, 43" h ................................................3,800.00

**Chippendale,** country, slant front

Birch, pine secondary wood, four dovetailed drawers with beaded edges, fitted int. with seven int. drawers and pigeonholes, molded base, replaced bracket feet, old refinishing, period replaced brasses, few repairs, 43-1/2" w, 19" d, 42" h ......................1,350.00

Maple with some curl, pine secondary wood, dovetailed case, four dovetailed overlapping drawers with replaced brasses, fitted int. with six dovetailed drawers in stepped arrangement, eight pigeon holes, molded base, scalloped bracket feet and center drop, old mellow refinishing, repairs and replacements to bracket feet, veneer replaced on ext. of drawers, 39" w, 18-1/2" d, 42-1/4" h ..........................3,575.00

**Eastlake,** lady's, walnut, two part, top section sits on pegs, top: mirror with two columns supported shelves, fancy carving, pressed dec; base section: double hinged writing surface with dec floral carving, writing surface with two panels of green felt, lifts to reveal compartment desk int. with two drawers, one side fitted with two long drawers, gallery shelf in base, dec applied pieces, shoe foot base, metal asters, 31-1/2" w, 19" d, 57" h ................................. 1,150.00

**Edwardian,** c1900, kneehole, mahogany, rect crossbanded top with central oval medallion, front canted corners, long frieze drawer, two banks of three drawers, center cupboard door, foliate marquetry dec, 37-1/2" w, 31" h ......................................................... 600.00

**Empire,** butler's, cherry and curly maple, poplar secondary wood, scrolled crest with turned rosettes, pull-out desk drawer with arched pigeon holes and three dovetailed drawers, three dovetailed drawers with applied edge beading, turned and carved pilasters, paneled ends, paw feet, old finish, some edge damage, 44-1/2" w, 23" d, 57-3/4" h ............................................................................1,925.00

**Federal**

Massachusetts, c1810, lady's, mahogany and mahogany veneer, flat molded cornice above upper section of two beaded and veneered doors enclosing three shaped document drawers

**Eastlake, walnut, center mirror plate surmounted by gallery, side shelf brackets with decorative banding, turned columns, slant front with emb dec on lid, brass escutcheon, galleried lower shelf, $3,000. Photo courtesy of Jackson's Auctioneers & Appraisers.**

flanked by two short drawers above three valanced compartments, lower projection section with fold-out writing surface, case of three cockbeaded veneered drawers, ring-turned legs joined by shaped skirt, old glass pulls, old refinish, imperfections, 39-1/2" w, 53" h ................................................3,220.00

Massachusetts, c1820, tiger maple and mahogany inlaid, top section with cross-banded cornice board over two tambour doors, int. of nine valanced compartments over fifteen drawers with mahogany cockbeaded surrounds, center prospect door, pen and ink on paper "Commandments 10" within arched glass panel set in mahogany panel framed by tombstone stringing, lower section: fold-out writing surface, two cockbeaded long drawers, straight skirt joining block ring-turned tapering legs, old refinish, replaced pulls, minor restoration, 39-1/4" w, 18-1/2" d, 54" h ......................................17,250.00

New England, early 19th C, mahogany and mahogany veneer inlaid, top section shaped gallery above flat molded cornice, two glazed doors enclosing compartments and drawer, flanking door and small drawer; projecting base with fold-out writing surface, two cockbeaded short drawers, two graduated long drawers, four sq tapering legs, inlaid cross-banding, old refinish, some restoration, inscribed "22 Geo. L. Deblois Sept 12th 1810," 37-1/8" w, 20" d, 51-1/2" ...................................3,000.00

New York State, early 19th C, mahogany veneer inlaid, slant lid and three graduated drawers outlined in stringing with ovolo corners, int. of veneer and outline stringing on drawers, valanced compartments, prospect door opening to inner compartments and drawers, flanking document drawers, orig brasses, old surface, veneer cracking loss and patching, other surface imperfections, 41-1/2" w, 21-1/2" d, 44" h ....................2,550.00

Pennsylvania, early 19th C, walnut inlaid, slant front, lid and cockbeaded drawers outlined in stringing, base with band of contrasting veneers, int. of small drawers above valanced compartments, scrolled dividers flanking prospect door which opens to two small drawers, three drawers, old refinish, repairs, 40" w, 20" d, 44-1/2" h...................................................3,550.00

Pennsylvania or New York, c1790, mahogany inlaid, slant front, string inlaid lid opens to multi-compartmented int., center prospect door, case of four graduated drawers, inlaid stringing flanked by inlaid lambrequin corners, inlaid flaring French feet, old replaced brasses, refinished, repairs, 41-1/2" w, 20-1/4" d, 42-3/4" h...................................................................2,770.00

**George III,** c1800, cross-banded satinwood, tambour toll top, interior fitted with small drawers, pigeonholes, and sliding ratcheted leather topped writing surface, over two short drawers on sq tapered legs, casters, 36-3/4" l, 24" d, 38-1/2" h.........................................8,625.00

**George III, late,** English, burl elmwood, slant front with rect crossbanding, fitted int. of pigeonholes and drawers, three graduated crossbanded drawers, serpentine apron, bracket feet, restorations, 30-1/2" w, 38" h ...................................................................... 1,800.00

**George III-Style,** early 20th C

Partner's, mahogany, rect molded top inset with gilt tooled burgundy leather, sides fitted with drawers, cabriole legs ending in claw and ball feet, 61-1/2" w, 36" d, 31" h.....................3,220.00

Pedestal, mahogany, rect top fitted with leather surface, three drawers, each pedestal fitted with drawers, 60" w, 41" d, 30" h.................................................................................3,150.00

**Gothic Revival,** English, late 19th/early 20th C, oak, upper section fitted with two doors, lower section with writing slide and door, carved tracery throughout, 37-1/2" w, 19" d, 53" h.............................. 400.00

**Hepplewhite,** country, slant front, cherry, poplar secondary wood, dovetailed case, four dovetailed drawers with banded inlay, fitted interior with ten dovetailed drawers and door with curly maple veneer, banded inlay across base, scalloped apron, bracket feet, old dark finish, replaced brasses, replacements and wear, 41" w, 19-3/4" d, 46-1/4" h ..................................................................... 1,650.00

**Louis XV-Style,** early 20th C, polychromed, serpentine top above like frieze fitted with three drawers, cabriole legs headed by acanthus and floral carving, pad feet, blue floral and scrolling designs on ochre ground, 49-1/2" w, 27" d, 31" h.............................................1,200.00

**Louis XVI-Style,** late 19th C, mahogany, brass mounts, molded rect top, leather-lined writing surface, outset corners, frieze drawer over kneehole, flanked by three graduated drawers on each side, opposing faux drawers, toupee feet, 59-1/4" w, 25" d, 30-1/4" h ....... 900.00

**Neoclassical,** northern Italian, first quarter 19th C, fruitwood and ebony inlaid, rect top above retreating ebony-striped cylinder lid simulating tambour, opening to desk int. fitted with three drawers, pull-out writing surface, frieze containing single drawer centered by diamond, sq tapered ebony-outlined legs, 36-1/2" w, 20-1/2" d, 42" h .......... 2,400.00

**Queen Anne**

Northern Maine, 19th C, maple, slant front, int. with valanced compartments above small drawers, end drawers separated by scrolled dividers, case of three thumb-molded drawers, molded bracket base with central drop pendant, old darkened surface, 35-1/2" w, 17-1/2" d, 40-1/4" h ...................... 5,175.00

Vermont, c1750, tiger maple and cherry, slant front, int. with central fan-carved drawer, two valanced compartments flanked by molded document drawers, four valanced compartments, three drawers, case with four thumb-molded graduated drawers, bracket feet, replaced brasses, old refinish, imperfections, and repairs, 36" w, 18" d, 41-1/2" h...................... 3,220.00

**Regency-Style,** lady's, inlaid mahogany, oval parcel gilt leather inset serpentine top fitted with various cubby holes and drawers, conforming case fitted with satinwood banded central bow front drawer, flanked on either side by like banded shorter drawer, tapering sq legs, headed by patera inlay, toupie feet, 32" w, 19" d, 39" h...................... 495.00

**Renaissance Revival,** English, partner's, carved oak, rect top with rounded corners, molded edge, front and back each carved with three frieze drawers, one pedestal with three drawers, other with paneled door opening int. with drawers and shelves, canted corners with figural pilasters, conforming molded plinth base, compressed bun feet, profusely carved with fruiting swags, grotesque masks, and heraldic devices, 72" w, 39-1/2" d, 30" h ...................... 5,500.00

**Sheraton,** Maine, birch, slant front, three drawers, dec inlaid skirt, tapering ridge feet, int. with five drawers and five cubbyholes, turned legs, refinished, 37-1/2" w, 19" d, 45" h...................... 1,200.00

**Stand-Up,** New England, early 19th C, red stained pine, lid with lipped edge lifts to interior with four open compartments, stand on turned tapering legs joined by square H-stretchers, surface imperfections, 30" w, 17-3/4" d, 44" h ...................... 1,380.00

**Victorian,** English, second half 19th C, davenport, carved walnut, three-quarter galleried rect top, tooled green leather slant writing surface, int. drawers, bank of four drawers, turned and carved supports, plinth base, distressed leather, veneer chips, 23" w, 34" h ...................... 1,400.00

**Victorian,** late, America, c1880, oak, pedestal, gilt tooled leather writing surface, frieze and pedestal fitted with drawers, casters, 41" w, 24" d, 29" h...................... 800.00

**William and Mary,** attributed to CT, early 18th C, tulipwood and oak, fall-front lid with raised panel, int. of four compartments, three drawers, well with sliding closure, double arched molded front, base with long drawer, four turned legs, joined by valanced skirt, shaped flat cross stretchers, turned feet, replaced brasses, old refinish, minor imperfections, 24-3/4" w, 15" d, 42-1/2" h ...................... 17,250.00

## Hall Trees and Hat Racks

Bench

Arts and Crafts, America, early 20th C, oak, curvilinear crest rail on paneled back, lift top seat with storage below, arched front and back apron, medium brown finish, 38-1/2" w, 17-3/4" d, 36-1/2" h, minor abrasions and losses, newer finish ............ 425.00

Colonial Revival, Baroque-Style, American, 1910, cherry, shell carved crest over cartouche and griffin carved panel back, lift seat, high arms, mask carved base, paw feet, 39-1/2" w, 21-1/2" d, 51" h ...................... 700.00

Classical, Late, transitional, America, c1850, mahogany, serpentine top rail centered by carved crest, serpentine seat rail edge with beaded molding, bracket feet, 48" w, 24" d, 38" h .... 475.00

Victorian, Rococo Revival, America, mid-19th C, mahogany, top rail centered by foliage carved crest, serpentine apron raised on cabriole legs, 41" w, 21" d, 30" h...................... 525.00

Coat/Umbrella Stand, mahogany and bentwood, splayed legs, Edwardian, early 20th C...................... 350.00

Hall Rack, Art Nouveau, France, early 20th C, mahogany, flaring mahogany panel, five brass curved coat hooks centered by mirror, umbrella stand below, 47" w, 85" h ...................... 1,200.00

Hall Tree, 80" h, Colebrookdale, England, late 19th C, wrought iron, rustic backrest and scrolled hooks, modeled with foliate dec .. 700.00

Hat Rack, Windsor, American, pine, bamboo turned, six knob like hooks, orig yellow varnish, black striping, 33-3/4" w ............... 200.00

Seat, Queen Anne-style, second quarter 20th C, birch, lift-top, scroll ends joined by turned handles, liner and marquetry stringing, 20-1/2" w, 13-1/2" d, 25" h ...................... 100.00

Stand, Victorian-style, carved mahogany, broken crest above central mirror and shelf, flanked by coat pegs, lower section with frieze drawer flanked by spindled umbrella compartments, bun feet, 43" w, 15" d, 87" h...................... 500.00

Tree

Arts & Crafts, attributed to Charles Rohls, early 20th C, oak, tall sq shaft, two tiers of four wooden hooks, each near the top, half buttresses running up from the cross base on all four sides, sq wafer feet, 64" h ...................... 1,100.00

Victorian, late, America, c1900, quarter-sawn oak, back with carved crest over arched beveled mirror plate flanked by garment hooks, base with arms on scroll brackets, lift-top seat, 47-3/4" w, 18" d, 84-1/2" h...................... 2,100.00

## Magazine Racks

**Anglo-Indian,** bamboo and lacquered, 4th quarter 19th C, two slotted compartments over lower shelf, splayed bamboo legs, inset with foliage dec lacquer panels, 16" w, 12" d, 29" h...................... 460.00

**Arts & Crafts,** attributed to L. & J. G. Stickley, New York, c1916, model no. 40, arched side stretchers above three side slats, four open shelves with arched lower side rails, unfilled holes on slats, rough, 21" l, 12" d, 41-1/2" h ...................... 575.00

**Edwardian,** c1900, brass and mahogany, rect form, three diagonal shelves, lower shelf, chamfered supports, brass cup casters, 17-1/2" w, 11" d, 39-1/2" h ...................... 575.00

**Empire-Style,** mahogany, four compartments separated by open slats, fronted by brass medallions, case fitted with one drawer, turned legs, brass casters, 18-1/2" w, 15" d, 24-1/2" h...................... 300.00

**Federal,** attributed to Boston, c1815-25, mahogany, curving tops of three sections divided by flat column-like supports, flanked by ring-turned tapering corners, cockbeaded drawer, ring-turned legs ending

**Arts & Crafts, J. & L. G. Stickley, 3 slats on each side, 4 shelves, skinned finish, "The Work of ..." decal, 21" w, 12" d, 42" h, $2,070. Photo courtesy of David Rago Auctions.**

in casters, wooden pull appears orig, old refinish, minor imperfections, 18-1/8" w, 12-1/2" d, 20-1/8" h ..................................... 4,600.00
**George III,** early 19th C, mahogany, three compartments, two graduated drawers, turned legs, castors, 20" l, 16" d, 22-1/4" h .... 1,000.00
**Regency,** first quarter 19th C, rosewood, typical form, four vertical dividers, reeded and ring turned feet, casters, 22" w, 16" d, 19-3/4" h................................................................... 4,025.00
**Rococo-Style,** carved mahogany, four elaborate pierce-carved partitions on base, single drawer, bulbous turned feet, 22-1/2" w, 16-3/4" d, 26-3/4" h .......................................... 300.00

## Mirrors

**Art Deco,** French, c1930, giltwood, frame closed at bottom and sides, carved chevrons, stylized sundials and Chinese scrolls, hung by gilt thread rope, tapered rect beveled mirror plate, 27" w, 37" h. 1,500.00
**Arts & Crafts**
  Boston Society of Arts and Crafts, 1910, carved wood, rect, carved and gilded frame, ink mark, initials, orig paper label, 11-1/4" w, 18-1/2" h ............................................................ 700.00
  Limbert, oak, frame with geometric inlaid design over rect cane panel shoefoot base, recoated orig frame, orig glass, 20" w, 8" d, 22" h .............................................................. 600.00
**Cheval,** German, ebonized, swivel rect mirror, rounded ends, low sq mount, artist sgd, 70" h .......................................... 425.00
**Chippendale,** scroll
  Mahogany, England, late 18th C, gilt stenciled star on crest over molded liner, orig finish, 12-1/4" w, 19-3/4" h ................... 600.00
  Mahogany, old finish, molded frame, old replaced ears, some edge damage, replaced mirror, Philadelphia paper label in very poor condition, 16-1/2" w, 30" h ...................................... 420.00
  Mahogany, orig finish, molded frame with gilded liner, composition eagle in crest with old gilding, orig mirror glass with minor wear to silvering, 19-3/4" w, 40-1/2" h........................... 3,575.00
  Mahogany veneer and giltwood, England, 18th C, scrolled and pierced crest with central gilded Hoho bird above molded and parcel-gilt mirror surround over scrolled pendant, old surface, minor repairs, 31-3/4" h................................................. 1,100.00
  Walnut, England, last half 18th C, scrolled crest, pierced foliate and scroll device, gilt molded liner, remnants of orig label on back, imperfections, 21-1/2" w, 41-1/2" h ...................... 1,725.00
**Classical**
  Dressing, America, first quarter 19th C, mahogany, rectilinear mirror plate in molded frame, supported by finial capped columns resting on base with pedestal ends, each with narrow over deep drawer, pedestals joined by wide central joined by a wide cen-

**Chippendale, England, 19th C, walnut and parcel gilt, scrolled frame, center gilt foliate device, molded gilt incised liner, 43" h, 21-1/2" w, $3,115. Photo courtesy of Skinner, Inc.**

tral drawer over scalloped apron, all drawers edged in contrasting light wood cock beading, case raised on molded ogee bracket feet, 21-1/2" w, 8" d, 25" h ................................... 500.00
  Girandole, America or England, 1810-20, gilt gesso, crest with eagle flanked by acanthus leaves, convex glass, ebonized molded liner with affixed candle branches, foliate and floral pendant, imperfections, 23" w, 35" h.................................. 5,175.00
  Over Mantel, New York, c1830, giltwood, molded cornice over split baluster frame, anthemion and floral squares at each corner enclosing three part mirror, applied leaf molded composition liner, old gilding, mirror glass appears to be replaced, minor imperfections, 62" l, 26" h ................................ 1,150.00
**Classical-Style,** America, c1900, over mantel, giltwood, tripartite form, turned foliate pilasters, old mirror plates, 65" w, 26-1/2" h ....... 850.00
**Courting,** Northern Europe, late 18th C, molded rect frame, shaped crest enclosing reverse painted glass panels, etched mirror glass, imperfections, 11-1/4" w, 18-1/2" h ...................................... 3,750.00
**Empire**
  Architectural, two part glass replaced, orig gilding, touch up repair, 20-1/2" w, 40-1/2" h.............................................. 250.00
  Convex, c1820, giltwood, eagle finial, carved, gessoed, and gilded frame, foliage, acorns, and oak laves, replaced mirror, repairs, 32" h.............................................................. 2,400.00
**Federal**
  Architectural, old gold repaint, 26" w, 38-3/4" h .................. 360.00
  Girandole, America or England, 1810-20, gilt gesso carved, eagle with outstretched wings on rocky plinth, flanking foliate devices, circular frame with acanthus leaves, ebonized reeded liner with flanking candle sconces, foliate and floral drop pendant, regilding, 24" w, 43" h ...................................................... 5,475.00
  Dressing, engraved label "I. Richman's Looking Glass Store No. 59 Maiden Lane near...Street, New York...," mahogany and mahogany veneer, shield form mirror glass, conforming veneered surround with string inlaid edge flanked by scrolled and incised supports, ringed bosses at terminals, stepped and shaped trestle feet joined by incised shaped stretcher, old refinish, imperfections, 14" w, 8-3/4"d, 21-1/4" h.................. 1,265.00
  Overmantel, Boston, MA, c1820, gilt gesso, rect frame, central frieze of shell and grape vines in relief, mirror plate flanked by floral panes and mirrors, framed by spiral moldings, corner blocks with lions' heads, regilded, replaced mirrors, 56" w, 28" h......... 4,615.00
  Shaving mahogany veneer on pine, oval beveled mirror with scrolled posts, four dovetailed drawers, edge and veneer damage, one foot missing, 24-3/4" w, 9-1/4" d, 29-1/4" h ....... 300.00
  Wall
    Gilt and eglomise, Boston or North Shore, MA, early 19th C, molded cornice with gilt spherules overhangs reverse painted tablet with light blue paint, white rect reserve with gilt urn and gilt flowerettes, imperfections and regilding, 22-1/2" w, 38" h.............................................. 2,100.00
    Giltwood, labeled "Parker and Clover Looking Glass and Picture Frame Makers 180 Fulton St. New York," molded cornice with applied spherules above eglomise table of girl in pasture landscape holding dove, mirror flanked by spiral carved pilasters, 13-3/4" w, 29-1/8" h ...................... 2,875.00
**George II-Style,** English, 19th C, carved gesso and giltwood, C-scroll and shell carved arched crest, serpentine and rect mirror plate, scrolled foliate corner pendants, C-scroll, shell, and acanthus carved shaped apron, 29" w, 65-1/2" h ............................................. 1,800.00
**George III-Style,** late 19th C, retailed by Edwards and Roberts, giltwood and composition, over mantel, five spherule mounted cresting and frieze modeled with neoclassical procession scene, three-part beveled mirror, flanked by engaged columns, 58-1/2" w, 35-1/2" h..................... 2,645.00
**Louis XV Revival**
  Mantel, late 19th C, giltwood, foliate and floral carved crest over horizontal oval mirror plate with gadrooned perimeter, 68" w, 8" d, 44" h................................................................. 800.00
  Pier, third quarter 19th C, giltwood, arched plate surmounted by open scroll and floral carving, with later marble-top console base, alternations and restorations, 34" w, 14" d, 96" h ...................... 500.00

**Napoleon III**, third quarter 19th C, 25-1/2" w, 3-1/2" d, 32-1/2" h, cushion, giltwood, rect beveled glass mirror plate within guilloche-molded frame, rect mirrored surrounds bordered by medallions .......... 900.00

**Neoclassical-Style**, fourth quarter 19th C

Continental, giltwood, flower and fruit filled urn flanked by scrolled cornucopia, rect frame with paterae to corners, flat leaf and scroll surround, 22-1/2" w, 54-1/2" h ............................ 1,380.00

Italian, giltwood, rect beveled glass mirror plate within conforming frame dec by classical mounts, 24" w, 28" h .................... 200.00

Swedish, pier, gilt composition, bow surmount above rect frieze centered by beaded octagon, rect mirror plate within ribbon molded frame, 31" w, 60-1/2" h ......................................... 200.00

**Queen Anne**, country, pine, orig black floral dec on red ground, molded frame, scalloped crest, orig backboard, written provenance taped to back listing owners from 1825 thru 1941, minor age crack and worn silvering, 11-1/2" w, 21-1/2" h ................. 3,190.00

**Regency**

20-1/2" w, 30" h, carved giltwood and plaster, oblong, pediment ornamented with relief festoons, c1810 ............................ 625.00

25" d, 40" h, convex, giltwood, circular plate surmounted by winged eagle and acanthus carving, framed by ebonized reeded frame, applied ebonized balls, second quarter 19th C ................ 2,640.00

**Regency-Style**, over mantel

54-1/2" w, 4" d, 35-1/4" h, giltwood and ebonized, cove molded cornice ornamented with spheres, bas-relief frieze with chariot procession, three beveled glass mirror plates flanked by engaged Corinthian columns on outset platforms ......... 1,450.00

55" w, 36" l, giltwood, projecting cornice above frieze ornament, demi-spherules and rosettes, rect mirror plate flanked by engaged columns ............................................. 200.00

**Shaving**, English, bow front, mahogany veneer, pine secondary woods, three finely dovetailed drawers with brass pulls, middle drawer with replaced diamond shaped inlay, turned bail finials, replaced feet, refinished, 19-1/8" w, 11-1/4" h ......................... 175.00

**Rococo Revival**, America, third quarter 19th C, pier, giltwood, arched mirror plate surmounted by gadrooned cornice, foliate carved cartouche, 38" w, 5" d, 95" h ............................................. 1,210.00

**Victorian**

25" w, 47" h, carved oak, spindled frieze surmounted by domed acanthus carved pediment, plate flanked on either side by turned columns, third quarter 19th C .............................. 250.00

25-1/2" w, 52" h, walnut and parcel giltwood, arched mirror plate within conforming finger molded frame, third quarter 19th C ............................................................ 250.00

38" w, 3-1/2" d, 75" h, pier, giltwood, arched mirror plate within molded frame, scrolled shell cresting flanked by cherub heads, third quarter 19th C ......................................... 525.00

**Victorian-Style**

40-1/2" w, 3" d, 60" h, gilt composition, oval mirror plate, conforming frame surmounted by symmetrical cartouche, terminating in scrolled cabochon .............................................. 615.00

49" w, 3-1/2" d, 61-1/2" h, gilt composition, rect beveled glass within elaborate frame, floral scrolled corners joined by diapered panels .............................................................. 900.00

# Rockers

### Arts and Crafts

Paine Furniture Co., Boston, early 20th C, oak, four curved horizontal back slats, shaped plank armrests with through tenons over four vertical side slats, spring cushion seat, medium brown finish, metal Paine Furniture tag, wear, scratches, 27-1/2" l, 33" d, 36" h ......................................................... 750.00

Stickley, Charles, five slats under each arm, thru-tenon construction, recovered cushions, minor wear to orig finish, remnant of decal, 34" w, 37" d, 41" h ........................................... 1,400.00

Stickley, L. & J. G., #831, Morris-type, adjustable back, open under arms, orig finish, sgd "The Work of…," back bar replaced, 30" w, 35" d, 38" h ........................................... 1,500.00

**Boston**, American, 19th C, maple, spindle back ...................... 200.00

**International Movement**, Charles Eames, manufactured by Herman Miller, salmon fiberglass zenith shell, rope edge, black wire struts, birch runners, c1950, 25" w, 27" d, 27" h ............................ 1,400.00

**Ladderback**, vase turned front posts, four arched panels on back, turned finials on real posts, notched arms, shaped rockers, replaced splint seat, old repairs to one arm, refinished, 46" h ............... 850.00

### Victorian

Empire Revival, early 20th C, mahogany and oak, wing back, generous proportions, 25-1/2" w, 37" w, 43" h, price for pr .... 700.00

Renaissance Revival, George Huntzinger, NY, 1876, walnut, ring turned armrests and stretchers, cloth wrapped wire seat and back, dated, 21" w, 33" h ..................................................... 400.00

### Windsor

New England, c1830, combed arrow-back, paint dec, comb-back above rect crest and four arrow-form spindles flanked by raked stiles on scrolled arms and bamboo supports, shaped seat with splayed legs on rockers, joined by stretchers, orig yellow and green foliage designs, mottled brown and black background, imperfections, 15-1/2" h seat, 38" h ................................. 650.00

New England, early 19th C, bow back, bowed crest rail above eight spindles, shaped pommel seat, bamboo turned legs joined by swelled H-form stretchers on rockers, old brown paint, rockers added mid 19th C, minor imperfections, 16-3/4" h seat, 32" h .................................................................. 700.00

New England, early 19th C, comb back, curving rect crest above tapering spindles, incised seat, splayed bamboo turned legs on rockers, off-white paint highlighted with gilt, surface imperfections, 13" h seat, 40-5/8" h ................................................. 300.00

# Secretaries

### Biedermeier-Style

Inlaid walnut, molded rect top, four drawers, top drawer with fall front, fitted int. with ebonized writing-surface, molded block feet, 50-1/4" w, 23-3/4" d, 35-1/2" h ..................................... 1,000.00

Walnut and parquetry, cavetto-molded cornice, front with frieze drawer, fall front opening to fitted int. with box-fronted cupboard and similar drawers, base of two door cupboard, flanked by convex stiles, molded plinth base, 42-1/2" w, 21-1/4" d, 67" h ............................................................. 2,300.00

**Centennial**, inlay mahogany, two part: top with four drawers over six cubbyholes center, line inlay door opening to reveal two cubbyholes

**Baroque, South German, two sections, top: broken pediment, pr parquetry paneled doors, lower: hinged slant front writing surface, fitted int., 2 frieze drawers over 3 graduated long drawers, all with geometric parquetry panel, bun feet, 44" w, 24" d, 83" h, $12,000.**

and large drawer, sliding tambour doors flanked by inlay panels with simulated columns; lower: fold-over line inlay lid, two drawers with line inlay, diamond inlay on legs, some lifting to veneer, replaced cloth writing surface, 37-1/4" w, 19-3/4" d, 46" h ..................... 800.00

**Chippendale**

Massachusetts, c1770-90, carved mahogany, scrolled and molded pediment above tympanum with projecting shell and arched raised panel doors flanked by fluted pilasters, candle-slides, raised panel slant lid with blocked facade, molded conforming base, bracket feet, int. of upper bookcase divided into nine open compartments above four small drawers, int. of lower case with two fan-carved blocked drawers, similar prospect door, small blocked and plain drawers, scrolled compartment dividers, replaced brasses, old finish, restored, 39" w, 22" d, 93-1/2" h ............................. 19,550.00

New England, c1780, cherry, two pc, top section: flat cove molded cornice, two cupboard doors, molded recessed panels, projecting base with slant lid opening to int. of central prospect door flanked by three valanced compartments and drawers; lower section: case of four thumb-molded graduated drawers, bracket feet, replaced brasses, refinished, restored, 39-1/4" w, 20-1/8" d, 86" h ............................. 4,500.00

**Classical**, Baltimore, c1825-35, carved and glazed mahogany veneer, cylinder fall, cornice flares above veneered frieze and doors with arched glass panels, interior with two shelves, lower case with butler's desk with six small drawers over nine valanced compartments, felt-lined writing surface over two small stepped out cockbeaded drawers, two similar long drawers flanked by columns topped by carved foliage, ending in large turned ball feet on casters, early surface, orig brasses, imperfections, 46" w, 24" d, 78-1/4" h ..... 2,100.00

**Colonial Revival,** Colonial Desk Co., Rockford, IL, c1930, mahogany, broken arch pediment, center finial, two glazed mullioned doors, fluted columns, center prospect with acanthus carving flanked by columns, four graduated drawers, brass eagle, carved claw and ball feet, 41" w, 21" d, 87" h ............................. 1,000.00

**Eastlake,** American, burl walnut and mahogany, shaped cornice, pair of glazed cabinet doors, cylinder front, writing surface, two doors in base, shaped apron, 27" w, 22" d, 66" h ............................. 1,500.00

**Empire-Style,** late 19th C, gilt bronze mounted mahogany, rect top, fall front with fitted int., over pr of recessed cupboard doors, flanked by columns, paw feet, 44-1/4" w, 23-1/2" d, 49-1/4" h ........... 1,955.00

**Federal,** Boston or North Shore, MA, early 19th, mahogany inlaid, top section: central panel of bird's eye maple with cross-banded mahogany veneer border and stringing joined to the plinths by a curving gallery above flat molded cornice, glazed beaded doors with Gothic arches and bird's eye maple panels and mahogany cross-banding and stringing enclosing shelves, compartments, and drawers; lower: projecting section with fold-out surface inlaid with oval bird's eye maple panel set in mitered rect with cross-banded border and cockbeaded case, two drawers veneered with bird's eye maple panels bordered by mahogany cross-banding and stringing, flanked by inlaid panels continuing to sq double tapered legs, lower edge of case and leg cuffs with lunette inlaid banding, old finish, replaced brasses, imperfections, 41" w, 21-3/4" d, 74-1/2" h ............................. 9,775.00

**George III**

England, c1800, butler's, mahogany and inlay, rect top, deep drawer fitted as writing compartment over three graduated drawers, French feet, restoration 44-1/4" w, 20-3/4" d, 41-1/2" h ............................. 2,775.00

England, early 19th C, japanned, swan neck pediment, rosette carved terminals, two glazed cupboard doors, fitted int. of compartments and small drawers, fall front writing surface with cubbyholes and drawers, four graduated drawers, shaped apron, bracket feet, gilt and polychrome warrior and figural landscape scenes, birds, and flowering trees, green ground, over painting and minor reconstruction, 40-1/4" w, 21-1/2" d, 96-1/2" h ............................. 5,000.00

**George III-Style,** mahogany and inlay, swan's neck cresting and central fretwork urn finial, two glazed doors, lower section with slant lid with inlaid central shell and corner fans, two short and two long drawers, ogee bracket feet, 30-3/8" w, 50" d, 82-1/2" h ............... 3,800.00

**Georgian-Style**, second quarter 19th C, mahogany, molded cornice above two paneled doors, lower section fitted with three long graduated drawers, upper with fall-front opening to inset-leather writing surface and drawers, splayed bracket feet, 32" w, 13-3/4" d, 71-1/2" h ............................. 1,800.00

**Hepplewhite**, two pc, walnut and figured walnut veneer with inlay, pine and poplar secondary wood, top: removable cornice with high goose-necks, keystone and turned finials, double doors with adjustable shelves, stringing inlay with invected corners and inlay on cornice, base: slant front lid, fitted int., with pigeon holes and ten dovetailed drawers, center door, four dovetailed drawers with applied edge beading, bracket feet, old finish, period replaced brasses, pieced repairs, some edge damage, replaced finials, 39-5/8" w, 11" h x 42-1/4" cornice, 21" d x 40-1/2" w base, 90" h ......................... 20,900.00

**International Movement,** Gilbert Rhode, manufactured by Herman Miller, upper bookcase with drop front desk over four doors, carved wooden pulls in burl and paldio veneers, refinished, c1940, 66" w, 15" d, 72" h ............................. 2,600.00

**Renaissance Revival,** American, c1865, walnut, two sections, upper: bookcase section, S-curved pediment with center applied grapes and foliage carving, two arched and molded glazed doors, shelved int., three small drawers with applied grapes and foliage carved pulls; lower: fold-out writing surface, two short drawers over two long drawers with oval molding and applied grapes and foliage carved pulls, matching ornamentation on skirt, 48" w, 21" d, 95" h ........... 5,000.00

**Sheraton**, late, American, c1925, walnut and oak, projecting molded cornice, pair of glazed doors, fold-out writing surface, long drawer, turned tapering legs, 35" w, 1-1/2" d, 75" h ............................. 900.00

**Victorian**, two pc, walnut, top: crown molding cornice, two glazed doors with burl and walnut buttons; base: burl cylinder roll with two drawer walnut int., pigeon holes, slide-out writing surface, base: three long drawers with burl dec, tear drop pulls, refinished, 40" w, 23" d, 86" h ............................. 1,850.00

## Settees

### Arts & Crafts

Limbert, #939, oak, eleven back slats, corbels under arm, recovered orig drop-in cushion, branded, refinished, 75" w, 27" d, 40" h ............................. 800.00

Stickley, L. & J. G., oak, drop-arm form, twelve vertical slats to back and drop-in orig spring cushion, recovered in brown leather, refinished, unsigned, 65" w, 25" d, 36" h .......... 1,800.00

**Baroque Revival,** Flemish, scroll, mahogany, old cane in back medallion, cane seat has been upholstered, old dark finish, 66" w, 50" h ............................. 750.00

**Biedermeier,** curved rect back, sides pierced with stylized flower-form ebonized splat, upholstered back and seat, sq section tapered legs ............................. 2,500.00

**Biedermeier-Style,** first quarter 20th C, mahogany, padded seat surmounted by scrolling inlaid crest, padded seat, flanked on each side by rounded cupboard door above larger rounded cupboard, doors inlaid with classical designs, plinth bases, 91" w, 50-1/2" d, 52-1/2" h ............................. 3,750.00

**Arts & Crafts, Gustav Stickley, cube, horizontal slats, top one mortised through front legs, fitted with 3 loose cushions, box mark, thin overcoat to finish, 78" l, 33" d, 27" h, $7,475. Photo courtesy of David Rago Auctions.**

**Child's**, New England, 1830-40, painted and decorated, orig red and brown grained surface highlighted with gold striping which outlines rect crest, horizontal splat above seat, rolled front rail, gold striping on turned tapering legs, minor surface imperfections, 25" l, 11" d, 21-1/2" h .................................................................. 1,610.00

**Classical**, American, c1850, mahogany, serpentine front, carved crest, transitional rococo design elements, 82" l ...................... 600.00

**Country**, New York, 1815-25, painted and stenciled decorated, triple chair back crest continues to scrolled arms, seat rail with similar paint dec, reeded seat, scrolled drop pendants over turned tapering legs, similar stretchers, ground painted to simulate rosewood, gold stenciled dec of compotes of fruit and foliate, old surface, losses, reeded repairs, 70-3/4" l, 17-1/4" h seat, 35-1/2" h ............................... 920.00

**Empire-Style**, late 19th/early 20th C

Mahogany and parcel-gilt, two seat canapé, curved and padded back, reeded frame continuing into arms with swan-form supports, overstuffed seat, sabre legs ................................... 400.00

Mahogany, two seat, curved backs, each armrest ending on ram's head, hoof-foot feet ...................................................... 2,100.00

**French Restauration,** New York City, c1840, rosewood, arched upholstered back, scrolled arms outlined in satinwood terminating in volutes, rect seat frame with similar inlay, bracket feet, 80" l, 27" d, 33-1/2" h .......................................................... 1,200.00

**Louis XVI-Style**, third quarter 19th C

Gilt bronze mounted ebonized maple, Leon Marcotte, New York City, c1860, 55-1/2" l, 25" d, 41-1/2" h .......................... 2,185.00

Giltwood, two-seat canapé, upholstered with Fortuny fabric, flaking, 55" l, 36" h .......................................................... 1,610.00

**Regency**, c1810, caned, painted, ebonized, triple chair back, painted with reserves of putti and foliage, circular splayed legs, 45-1/2" l ...................................................................... 2,530.00

**Victorian**

Gothic Revival, American, c1850, carved walnut, shaped crest rail surmounted by center carved finial, stiles with arched recessed panel and similarly carved finials, upholstered back and seat, open arms with padded armrests and scrolled handholds, carved seat rail, ring turned legs, ball feet, 67-1/2" w, 23-1/2" d, 49-3/4" h .................................................. 800.00

Renaissance Revival, America, attributed to Johh Jeliff, c1856-70, carved walnut and parcel-gilt, low back, raised and tufted ends, carved foliage, pendants, and masks on arms, turned circular legs, casters, 81" l .............................................. 2,100.00

Rococo Revival, rosewood, laminated curved backs, Stanton Hall pattern, attributed to J. & J. Meeks, rose crest in scrolled foliage and vintage, tufted gold velvet brocade reupholstery, age cracks and some edge damage, 65-1/2" l ................................. 5,500.00

**Windsor**

New England, c1810, ash, pine, and maple, bamboo turnings, straight crest rail with bowed ends, twenty-five spindles, slightly scrolled arms, shaped seat, eight legs joined by stretchers, old refinish, restored, 85-1/8" l, 20-1/2" d, 35-1/8" h ............. 5,175.00

New England, c1810, maple and pine, bamboo turnings, straight crest rail with bowed ends, three shaped panels, parallel rail, twenty-one spindles and four stiles, flanking arms, shaped seat, eight splayed legs joined by stretchers, old refinish, imperfections, 78" l, 20-1/2" d, 33" h .......................................... 3,220.00

# Sideboards

**Arts & Crafts**, English, early 20th C, oak, rect top over arched, mirrored back, flanked by two shelves and two pedestal supports with applied copper repousse floral dec hardware, two half-drawers above double-door cabinet, copper and brass hardware, medium brown finish, minor wear, 60" l, 23-1/2" d, 66" h .................. 2,450.00

**Centennial**, Chippendale-Style, America, late 19th C, mahogany, block front with shell carving, four drawers, front cabinet doors, gadrooned apron, cabriole legs, claw and ball feet, 68" w, 24" d, 40" h .............................................................. 950.00

**Classical**

America, second quarter 19th C, figured walnut and mahogany, crotch-veneered splash flanked by pilasters, base with pair of

doors over three cupboard doors, bun feet, 60" w, 22-1/4" d, 56" h ................................................................ 1,320.00

Boston or New York, c1830, mahogany and mahogany veneer, gallery with beaded edge joining to end plinths with brass inlay and rosewood panels, white rect marble top, two recessed panel doors, shelved int., flanked by brass mounted columns continuing to acanthus carved feet, stenciled dec dies and frieze, orig finish, restoration, 42" w, 18-1/2" d, 47" h .......................................... 4,320.00

New York, c1815-25, carved mahogany veneer, rect gallery with simulated end columns above top which overhangs veneered case, three small drawers over three recessed panel doors, each opening to single shaped shelf, flanked by columns with frontal carved leafage over paw feet, ring-turned and tapered real feet, early surface, veneer damage and other imperfections, 60-3/4" l, 23-3/4" d, 54-3/4" h .............................. 2,185.00

**Empire, late,** mahogany, three drawers over four drawers, mahogany veneer front on center drawer, two pull-out working surfaces above two smaller drawers, four mahogany turned front posts, four front hairy paw feet, two turned rear feet, glass pulls, 73" w, 24" d, 42" h .............. 750.00

**Federal**

Baltimore, MD, or Norfolk, VA, c1800, mahogany veneer, serpentine top with ovolo corners, conforming case with central drawer over two single shelved cupboards flanked by bottle drawers and end cupboards, edge of top outlined in stringing, as are cupboards and drawers, top of legs with satinwood inlaid panels, lower sections with four oval drops descending in size separated by inlaid circles and surrounded by stringing in outline to inlaid cuffs, replaced brasses, old refinish, imperfections, 80" w, 26-5/8" d, 39" h .......................................... 23,000.00

Boston, 1810-20, mahogany, maple, and rosewood veneer, two-tiered case, demilune superstructure, maple inlaid panels surrounded by cross-banded rosewood veneer above cockbeaded end drawers, small central drawer flanked by end cupboards, six ring turned tapering legs, case with concentric turnings, reeding, cockbeading, and scenic landscape jointed on underside of arched opening, old surface, replaced pulls, replaced leg, veneer loss, later landscape painting, 74-1/2" l, 24-1/2" d, 44-3/4" h ............................................................ 9,200.00

Maryland, c1810, butler's, mahogany veneer, top with ovolo corners overhanging case with oval central reserve outlined in ebonized inlay embellishing hinged centered desk of twelve small veneered drawers and one larger drawer with felt-lined writing surface flanked by single drawers, above two cupboard doors opening to interior, square tapering legs with cuff banding, outlined ebonized bandings on doors, drawers, skirt, and cuffs, replaced brass, old surface, imperfections, 64-1/2" l, 28" d, 43-1/2" h ................................................. 13,800.00

Middle Atlantic States, c1790, attributed to, mahogany and cherry inlaid, overhanging top with canted corners and serpentine front, central cockbeaded door inlaid with cherry panel with quarter fan inlays and mahogany mitered border, cockbeaded wine drawer with three-drawer facade at one end, three cockbeaded graduated drawers on other, ends with cherry veneered panels, four sq inlaid tapering legs ending in molded spade feet, lower edge of case with molding, old finish, minor imperfections, 48-1/2" w, 21-5/8" d, 37" h .......................................... 19,950.00

New Bedford, MA, Reuben Swift, c1815-20, mahogany and mahogany veneer, rect top, boxed center section, three cockbeaded drawers and cabinets, four sq tapering legs ending in brass caps with casters, orig drawer pulls and surface, veneer cracks and losses, other repairs needed, 69-1/2" l, 28" d, 43-3/4" h .......................................................... 1,850.00

New England, c1790, mahogany and mahogany veneer, overhanging top with shaped front, conforming case, central pullout surface, bowed cockbeaded drawers, two cupboard doors flanked by concave drawers and cupboard doors, six sq tapering legs, replaced brasses, old refinish, imperfections, 64" w, 20-1/8" d, 37-1/2" h .................................................... 5,500.00

Providence area, RI, 1790-1825, mahogany inlaid, rect top, cross-banded veneer outlining overhanging edge, case of cockbeaded

**Hepplewhite, America, c1800, inlaid mahogany, serpentine, 75-1/2" l, 40" h, $4,650.**

drawers flanking similar central cupboard, two working drawers on left, single deep drawer on right, all outlined with stringing, ovolo corners flanked by two front legs also delicately outlined in stringing, terminating in cuff inlays, replaced brasses, old refinish, minor imperfections, 50" l, 21-1/2" d, 39" h ................................. 20,700.00

**French Provincial**, third quarter 19th C
Fruitwood, banded and hinged top opening to narrow storage space, two paneled cupboard doors, bracket feet, 53" w, 24-1/2" d, 40" h................................................................................... 1,850.00
Walnut, variegated cream marble top with canted corners, conforming case fitted with two inlaid and floral carved frieze drawers, two paneled doors, frieze centered by shell carving, tapering acanthus carved feet, 41-1/2" w, 18-1/2" d, 31-1/2" h........................1,100.00

**George III**, late 18th C, mahogany and inlay, cross-banded breakfront top above drawer and cabinet doors, sq tapering legs ending in spade feet, restoration, 59" w, 20-1/2" d, 37-1/2" h...............3,350.00

**Georgian-Style**, c1890, mahogany, bow front, bowed top above central cutlery drawer, flanked on either side by two drawers to one side and deep drawer, faced as two drawers, 62" w, 27" d, 36" h .............2,750.00

**Gothic**, Kimbel & Cabus, New York, c1875, design no. 377, walnut, galleried top over two cupboard doors over open self over slant front over central drawer over open well flanked by two cupboard doors, galleried base shelf, bracket feet, 39-1/4" w, 17-3/4" d, 73" h...................9,775.00

**Henri II-Style**, carved walnut, upper section with three-carved doors divided by fluted, free-standing columns, surmounted by foliate crest, raised on baluster turned columns, lower section with two molded frieze drawers over carved doors, similar columns, molded base on compressed bun feet, 58-3/4" w, 21-3/4" d, 98" h .................1,900.00

**Hepplewhite**, mahogany and mahogany veneer with inlay, bowed center section with conforming doors and dovetailed drawer, two flat side doors, sq tapered legs, banding and stringing with bell flowers on legs, corner fans on doors and drawers, reworked, repairs, replaced brasses, 58-1/4" w, 18-1/2" d, 37-3/4" h .................2,200.00

**Regency**, England, early 19th C, inlaid mahogany, rect top, drawers and doors on sq tapered legs ending in spade feet, 66" w, 20-1/2" d, 37" h .......................................................................... 1,150.00

**Sheraton-Style**, c1890, inlaid mahogany, serpentine top, conforming case fitted with central satinwood string-inlaid drawer, flanked on either side by deep inlaid drawers, tapering sq legs, toupie feet, 59" w, 25" d, 36" h .........................................................................3,300.00

**Victorian**, late, America, c1900, quarter-sawn oak
Façade with band of molded drawers over cupboard doors, full-width drawer below, flanked by foliate carved scrolling pilasters, carved paw feet, 72" w, 25" d, 40" h..............................1,210.00
Top with pair of frieze drawers raised on foliate carved columns joined by low shelf, whole supported by carved paw feet, 48" w, 21-1/2" d, 37-1/2" h ......................................................... 650.00

## Sofas

**Aesthetic Movement**, America, late 19th C, walnut, tripartite back, ends with taller chair backs, joined by foliate carved crest rail cen-

tered by masque, later lime and fuchsia velvet upholstery, 74" w, 27" d, 38" h.............................................................................450.00

**Art Nouveau,** Carlo Bugatti, 1900, ebonzied wood, rect back, mechanical seat, slightly scrolling rect arms, parchment upholstery, painted swallows and leafy branches, hammered brass trim, four block form feet, 68-3/8" l ........................................................ 1,900.00

**Classical**
Mid Atlantic States, 1805-20, carved mahogany and bird's eye maple veneer, Grecian style, scrolled and reeded arm and foot, punctuated with brass rosettes, continuing to similar reeded seat rail with inlaid dies, reeded saber legs flanked by brass flowerettes, brass paw feet on castors, old surface, 75" l, 14-1/2" h seat, 35" h .................................................................. 3,680.00
New England, 1820-40, carved mahogany veneer, cylindrical crest ends, leaf carved volutes, upholstered seat and rolled veneer seat rail, leaf carved supports, carved paw feet, 92" w, 16-1/2" h seat, 34-3/4" h ............................................... 1,650.00

**Edwardian-Style**, Chesterfield
Brown leather, deep button back cushioned seat, conforming arms, mahogany bun feet, 68" l, 31-1/2" d, 27" h.......... 1,100.00
Maroon leather, deep button back, cushioned seat, out-scrolling arms, mahogany bun feet, 69-1/2" l, 26-1/2" d, 24" h ... 1,320.00

**Empire,** mahogany and figured mahogany veneer frame, well detailed carving with sea serpent front legs, turned back legs, lyre arms with relief carved flowers and cornucopia, rope turned crest rail, refinished, reupholstered in floral tapestry on ivory ground, bolster pillows, 107" l ...................................................................... 3,850.00

**Federal**
Boston or North Shore, MA, c1815-50, mahogany and mahogany veneer, reeded crest rail above molded arms continuing to reeded arm supports, veneered seat rail and reeded tapering legs ending in brass casers, square rear raking legs, old refinish, imperfections, some height loss, 76" l, 13" h seat, 34-1/8" h ..................... 7,475.00
Massachusetts, c1800, mahogany veneer, square back, crest above reeded arms and arm supports, maple inlaid rectangular die above reeded tapering legs ending in swelled and turned feet, square rear legs, old surface, imperfections, 76" l, 33-1/2" h.........2,530.00

**George III,** England, c1780, mahogany, camel back, serpentine crest and foliate carved out-scrolled arms, upholstered seat, sq molded legs joined by stretchers, 82" l, 36" h ..................................... 3,450.00

**George III-Style,** English, carved oak, double arched upholstered high backrest, scrolled arms, loose cushion seat, acanthus carved legs, claw and ball feet, 58" l ........................................................ 1,200.00

**Louis XV-Style,** 19th C, walnut, shaped, foliate carved crest rail, padded back, out-scrolled arms, foliate carved scrolled armrests, conforming molded seat rail, cabriole legs, pad feet, 85" l............. 800.00

**Neoclassical-Style,** Grecian, mahogany, reeded crest rail joined to scroll ends, gilt-winged paw feet, 72" w, 28" d, 36" h ............. 1,200.00

**Regency,** English, c1800, ebonized, serpentine back, scrolled arms, sq tapered legs, casters, losses, 77" l ................................... 3,200.00

**Victorian**
Renaissance Revival, America, suite, attributed to Pottier and Stymus, New York, c1865-75, walnut, parcel-gilt, and patinated metal mounts, pair of settees, arm chair, four side chairs, all carved with elongated leaf tips and acorn finials, classical portrait medallions, incised gilt dec, 64" l, 39" h settee, price for suite.............................................................................. 6,900.00
Rococo Revival, America, third quarter 19th C
Rosewood, tripartite back, each section with button-tufted damask surmounted by floral carved crest, serpentine seat rail with cabochon and shell carved cartouche, cabriole legs, 60" l, 25" d, 39" h ......................................................... 950.00
Walnut, medallion tripartite back, serpentine apron, four cabriole legs, 69" w, 26" d, 40" h, reupholstered, as found condition.............................................................................. 525.00

## Stands

**Basin**
Classical, attributed to North Shore, MA, c1825, mahogany and veneer, cyma-curved splash board, bow front top with openings

for chamber set, veneered skirt flanked by small drawers over medial shelf with drawer below, spiral carved legs ending in turned feet, refinished, replaced hardware, minor imperfections, 20-1/2" w, 14-1/2" d, 51-1/4" h ....................................... 1,150.00

Federal, Charleston, SC, 1790-1800, corner type, mahogany inlaid, top with openings for chamber set, veneered inlaid skirts, lower one with single working drawer flanked by faux drawers, sq tapered legs outlined on sides with stringing, old refinish, repairs, height loss, 21-1/2" w, 15" d, 29-1/8" h ........... 2,990.00

**Bedside,** Edwardian-Style, mahogany, top with bowed front over conforming case, pullout slide over four graduated drawers, turned circular legs, 14" w, 12-1/2" d, 30-1/2" h ........................................ 70.00

**Bird Cage,** wicker, painted white, tightly woven quarter moon shaped cage holder, wrapped pole standard, tightly woven conical base, 74" h ................................................................................... 225.00

**Cellaret,** George III, English, mid-19th C, mahogany, lozenge form, brass bands, twin loop carry handles, racked chamfered tapering legs, 24" w, 17-1/2" d, 27-1/2" h .......................................... 7,500.00

**Dressing,** grain painted, labeled "J. G. Briggs, Charlestown, New Hampshire," 1830-33, shaped splashboard above two small drawers, long drawer, four ring-turned tapered legs, orig black and gold graining to simulate rosewood, minor imperfections, 36-3/8" w, 16" d, 39" h ................................................................... 920.00

**Dumbwaiter,** Queen Anne style, walnut, three circular shelves, splayed legs, pad feet, 21" d, 39" h ......................................... 300.00

**Easel**

Aesthetic Movement, attributed to Cincinnati furniture maker, cherry, intricate carved sunflowers and oak leaves, orig finish, 23" w, 36" d, 75" h ....................................................... 2,500.00

Louis XVI-style, mahogany and parcel-gilt, picture support hung with berried laurel swags, trestle-end frame carved with acanthus, imbrication, and dolphins, 25" w, 23-1/2" d, 82" h ... 950.00

**Étagère**

Aesthetic Movement, c1870, fruitwood and ivory inlaid, shelved and mirrored superstructure, cabinet door, open shelves, circular feet, 27-1/2" w, 17" d, 82" h ....................................... 2,300.00

Anglo-Indian, fourth quarter 19th C

Bamboo and lacquer, pagoda form top, asymmetrical arrangement of seven shelves of various sizes, splayed bamboo feet, 23" w, 13-1/2" d, 63-1/2" h ................................ 995.00

Corner, bamboo and sea grass, three shelves joined by bamboo supports, splayed legs, 22" w, 10" d, 58-3/4" h ...... 450.00

Edwardian, fourth quarter 19th C, inlaid mahogany, fitted with small upper shelf over three lower shelves, all inlaid with stringing and urn design, joined by turned supports, raised on turned toupie feet, 22" w, 14" d, 50" h .......................................... 360.00

Louis XVI taste, hanging, carved giltwood, five shelves, back plate mirrored, bowknot finial, 38" w, 43-1/2" h ............... 325.00

Napoleon III, c1870, boullework and ebony, three-tiers, serpentine shelves, angular supports, 16" w, 14" d, 33" h .......... 650.00

Victorian, Rococo Revival, America, third quarter 19th C, console base, walnut

Upper section with central mirror plate flanked by graduated shelves supported by scrolled brackets, serpentine base with frieze drawer, cabriole legs, 40" w, 20" d, 70-1/2" h ......... 500.00

Upper section with pair of shelves, carved scroll brackets, top-shelf surmounted by pierced floral and foliate carved crest, serpentine base with frieze drawer supported by cabriole legs, 45" w, 17" d, 68-1/2" h .......................................... 3,300.00

Victorian, late, America, c1900, cherry, four tier, top shelf with fretwork gallery, each shelf with reeded edge, turned columns, fitted with lower drawer, 19" w, 14" d, 36-1/2" h .................. 425.00

**Fern,** Victorian, late 19th C, brass, onyx type, scrolling cartouche centered frieze, cabriole legs, joined by pierced shelf stretcher centering finial, scroll feet, 10-1/2" w, 10-1/2" d, 35-1/2" h ...................... 200.00

**Folio,** Victorian, c1840, rosewood, ratchet leaves, trestle base, casters, 30" w, 38-1/2" h ............................................................. 3,115.00

**Guèrdon,** Empire-style, fourth quarter 19th C

Mahogany and brass mounts, circular marble top supported by three scrolling legs, joined by pair of marble stretchers with brass galleries, 13-1/2" d, 34-1/2" h ................................. 900.00

Verde Antico, parcel giltwood, circular brass bound top centered by rouge variegated marble, griffin supports raised on triangular plinth, turned feet dec with leaves, 25-1/2" d, 29-1/4" h ............... 2,875.00

**Luggage,** William IV, second quarter 19th C, oak, turned bulbous legs, 24" w, 18" d, 17-1/2" h ................................................................. 50.00

**Music,** Napoleon III, second half 19th C, ebonized and parcel-gilt, lyre fronted upper section with folio rack divided by spindle galleries, open shelf, lower section with open shelf, turned, tapered, and fluted supports, incised dec of floral arabesques, gilt-metal mounts, 21-3/4' w, 11-1/4" d, 54-1/2" h ............................................................. 600.00

**Night,** Classical

New England, c1830, tiger maple, overhanging sq top, conforming base with single drawer, ring-turned and swelled legs, ball feet, old refinish, imperfections, 20" w, 19" d, 29" h ...... 2,070.00

Philadelphia area, c1825, carved mahogany and mahogany veneer, rect top with gadrooned edge, single convex drawer flanked by leaf carved panels, vase and ring-turned carved posts continuing to turned ball feet, joined by shaped medial shelf, minor imperfections, refinished, 25" w, 17" d, 29" h 990.00

**Plant**

Arts & Crafts, Limbert, ebon-oak line, overhanging top, four caned panels on each side, recent finish, branded signature, 14" w, 14" d, 34" h ................................................................... 2,100.00

Victorian, wirework, painted, late 19th C, demilune, three-tier, each tier with ornately curled rim, four slender legs heading by scrolled wire design, joined by single stretchers, X-bracing at back, casters, 45" l, 40" h ................................................ 750.00

**Portfolio,** William IV, English, c1830, carved rosewood, folding mechanism ................................................................................ 3,500.00

**Shaving,** Victorian, Empire Revival, America, third quarter 19th C, mahogany, circular mirror on wishbone support, extending and adjustable port, top fitted with shallow frieze drawer, 19" w, 13-1/4" d, 50" h ................................................................................ 150.00

**Side,** Federal, MA, early 19th C, mahogany and bird's eye veneer, sq top with ovolo corners overhanging single veneered drawer, ring-turned tapered legs ending in ball feet, old refinish on top, orig dark stained surface on base, old brass pull, minor imperfections, 15-1/4" w, 15" d, 27-3/4" h ................................................................ 2,760.00

Music Stand, Victorian, musical devices carved on single door, shelved int., hairy paw front feet, late 19th C, 39" h, $2,688. Photo courtesy of Jackson's Auctioneers & Appraisers.

**Teapot**, William IV, second quarter 19th C, rosewood, rect molded hinged top, int. fitted with compartments and spaces for tea mixing bowls, baluster support on circular base, paw feet on casters, 14" l, 12-1/2" w, 29" h ............................................ 850.00

**Tier**, Sheraton, English, three tiers, rosewood, single dovetailed drawer, turned finials, posts, and legs, old finish, 15" x 19" x 42" h .......................................... 1,450.00

**Tilt-Top**, Chippendale
Boston or coastal Essex County, MA, 1775-1800, mahogany, serpentine folding top above block, incised "I. Young," turned tapering pedestal above cabriole legs ending in arris pad feet, old surface, imperfections, 21-3/4" w, 2" d, 29-1/2" h ......... 2,185.00
New England, late 18th C, cherry, tilt-top dish top with molded edge, pedestal, cabriole tripod base, arris pad feet, old refinish, imperfections, 25-3/4" d, 28-1/2" h ............................. 3,450.00

**Vitrine**, transitional Louis XV/XVI style, kingwood, hinged, glazed, rect top, quilted int. with glazed sides, keeled cabriole legs, gilt-brass beading, chutes and sabots, 29-1/2" w, 20" d, 32" h ................ 375.00

**Wash**
Classical, Maryland, mahogany and mahogany veneer, sides with scrolled terminals, marble top, single drawer, mahogany veneer platform flanked by tapering columns which end in ball feet, refinished, imperfections, 29-5/8" w, 21-1/4" d, 33-1/2" h .......... 1,495.00
Federal, New England, early 19th C, stained, flaring scrolled splashboard, solid board top, straight skirt flanked by turned supports over single drawer, ring-turned tapering legs, orig pull, lightly cleaned old surface, minor imperfections, 20-1/2" w, 13-3/4" d, 35" h ............................................ 460.00
Hepplewhite, American, polar and pine, painted yellow ground, black blocking and linear dec, shaped gallery, cutouts for bowls and accessories, sq tapering legs, base shelf, emb brass pulls, nailed drawer, 18-1/2" w, 15-1/2" d, 37-1/4" h .................. 650.00
Victorian, Eastlake, America, late 19th C, walnut, rectilinear white marble top over pair of drawers, line-incised pedestal, legs joined by lower shelf with openwork gallery, 20" w, 14-1/2" d, 42" h ............................................ 425.00

**Work**
Hepplewhite, New England, c1810, cherry inlaid, sq top, outline stringing and quarter fan inlays on ovolo corners, line inlaid drawer and skirt, line inlaid sq tapering legs, crossbanded cuffs, brass drawer pull, refinished, 19" w, 19" dc, 27" h ........ 2,650.00
Victorian, Renaissance Revival, American, c1860, lift top opening to real satinwood interior fitted with compartments, narrow drawer above semi-circular bag drawer, pair of stylized lyre form ends jointed by arched stretcher surmounted by turned finial ........ 875.00

# Steps

Bedside
Classical, American, second quarter 19th C, mahogany, three-tier form, each step with inset green leatherette panel, turned legs, 24-1/2" w, 27-1/4" d, 19" h .......................................... 450.00
Regency, first quarter 19th C, mahogany and inlay, three steps, two with hinged lids, gilt-tooled green morocco inset on step, ebony geometric banding, four ring turned feet, 26-1/2" h ............ 1,725.00
Regency-Style, mahogany, three steps, all leather-inset panels, upper one opening to commode storage compartment, turned toupie feet, 15-1/2" w, 28-1/2" d, 27" h ............................. 275.00

Library
George III, English, late 18th C, mahogany, rect molded hinged top, eight steps, 49-1/2" w, 53-1/2" h ............................. 2,500.00
Regency, English, early 19th C, mahogany, three steps, inset green leather treads, scrolling banister, sq balusters, feet with brass casters, 46" w, 27" w, 56" h ............................. 2,400.00
Regency-Style, mahogany, five rungs, each fronted by brass tread, 62" h .......................................... 330.00

# Stools

**Cricket**, Arts & Crafts, Limbert, #205-1/2", rect top covered with new leather, splayed sides, inverted heart cut-out, single stretcher with thru-tenon, replaced keys, orig finish, branded, 20" w, 15" d, 18" h ...... 950.00

**Foot**
Arts & Crafts, oak
Barber Brothers, oak, nicely replaced leather seat, some color added to orig finish, paper label, 13" w, 13" d, 11" h ........ 110.00
Limbert, cricket, #205-1/2, rect orig leather top and tacks, splayed sides with inverted heart cut-out having single stretcher with thru-tenon construction, orig finish, branded and numbered, 20" w, 15" d, 19" h ........................ 2,000.00
Orig leather and tacks, slightly arched rails, orig finish, 12" sq, 8" h .......................................... 90.00
Worn orig drop-in leather cushion with four vertical slats to side, orig finish, 16" w, 14" d, 14" h ............................. 260.00
Classical, Boston, 1825-29, carved mahogany, over-upholstered, curule base with leaf carving, C-scrolls, central concentric circles plus ring-turned medial stretcher, old surface, imperfections, 22-1/2" w, 15-1/2" d, 15" h ............................. 1,265.00
Louis XV Revival, French, early 20th C, triangular form, tufted cut-velvet upholstery, shell-carved apron, cabriole legs, 22-1/2" w, 21" d, 14" h, price for pr ............................. 525.00
Louis XVI-style, fourth quarter 19th C, giltwood, padded top, carved frieze, center patera carving, turned legs, toupie feet, 13" w, 10-1/2" d, 7" h .......................................... 650.00
Queen Anne, 18th C, walnut, rect frieze, four cabriole legs each with shell carving on knees, pad feet, slip seat, 22-1/2" w, 17" d, 17" h .......................................... 1,950.00
Rococo taste, Italian, rococo taste, fourth quarter 19th C, carved, polychromed, and parcel gilt, ecru corduroy upholstery, 17-1/2" w, 22-1/2" d, 17" h .......................................... 1,100.00
Sheraton, curly and bird's eye maple, old finish, cane top, minor damage to top, 7-3/4" w, 13" l, 6-1/2" h ............................. 440.00
Victorian, walnut, floral needlework top with brown ground, 14" x 17 3/4" x 14" h .......................................... 220.00
Hepplewhite, mahogany with old finish, sq tapered and reeded legs, upholstered top recovered in gold brocade, 17" w, 17" l, 19-1/2" h .......................................... 935.00

**Joint**
Early, oak, old finish, wear and age cracks, 11" w, 16-1/2" l, 17-3/4" h .......................................... 990.00
Jacobean, 17th/18th C, oak
17" w, 7-1/2" d, 19" h .......................................... 490.00
17-1/2" w, 10-1/2" d, 22" h .......................................... 635.00

**Piano**
Louis XVI-Style, late 19th C, carved beech, circular, adjustable, close-nailed over stuffed top, petal-carved frieze, leaf-capped turned, tapered, and fluted legs, wavy cross-stretcher .... 850.00
Renaissance Revival, American, 1870, walnut, sq upholstered seat, acanthus carved baluster supports, four outswept legs, hoof feet .......................................... 350.00

**Seat-type**
Country, folk art, attributed to Fredericksburg, PA, late 19th/early 20th C, painted and dec, octagonal seat, chamfered edge, trimmed with border band of carved hearts, tall splayed and chamfered legs also trimmed with carved hearts and joined by slender rungs, overall polychrome ............................. 1,850.00
George III, late 19th C, mahogany, gold floral satin upholstered rest seat, sq tapering supports, molded H-form stretchers, pr, 19-1/2" l, 17" h .......................................... 1,650.00
Neoclassical-Style, cast iron, curule form, dished seats, later cream paint, 15" w, 14" d, 16-1/2" h, price for pr ............. 400.00
Regency, first quarter 19th C, mahogany, turned circular legs ending in brass caps on casters, missing upholstered seat, 17-1/2" w, 14" d, 17" h .......................................... 315.00
Windsor, American, 19th C, oblong plant seat raised on three tall, turned and slightly swelled legs joined by T-stretcher, traces of old green paint, 15" w, 24-1/2" h ............................. 200.00

# Tables

**Architect's**, George III, English, late 19th C, mahogany, hinged tooled leather work surface above opposing hinged work surface, turned pedestal on three splayed legs, pad feet, some reconstruction, 29" w, 19-1/4" d, 29-1/2" h ............................................. 2,300.00

**Banquet,** Federal, New England, c1800, two part, mahogany and mahogany veneer, two parts with D-shaped tops, conforming straight skirts, cross-banded lower edge continues around sq tapering legs, both with hinged rect drop leaves, old refinish, imperfections, 43" w, 84" d, 29" h.................................................. 2,645.00

**Breakfast**

Classical, American, c1840, mahogany, top with pair of drop leaves, molded frieze supported by vasiform pedestal, scroll legs, 40" w, 24" d, extends to 76" l, 29" h ......................... 550.00

George III-Style, second half 19th C, mahogany and inlay, circular tilt top, cross-banded in satinwood, turned support raised on four splayed legs ending in brass paw feet on casters, 49" d, 28-1/2" h ................................................................ 1,150.00

Georgian-Style, Victorian, c1880, mahogany, circular top, molded edge, turned vasiform standard, four splayed legs, headed by scroll carving, ending in brass paws on casters, 52" d, 30" h ............................................................ 1,450.00

Victorian, early, mid 19th C, mahogany, circular top raised on paneled baluster support, circular base ending in paw feet, restoration, 48" d, 29-1/2" h...................................................... 1,150.00

**Bureau,** Queen Anne, Boston, 1735-40, walnut inlaid, molded edge top outlined in stringing, single drawer, two banks of small drawers flanking raised panel door which opens to single shelf, pulls forward, molded base with bracket feet, all drawers thumb molded and outlined in stringing, repairs, 33-3/4" w, 30-1/2" h .................. 25,300.00

**Card**

Chippendale, New Hampshire, c1790, birch, overhanging rect folding top, straight skirt with single drawer, four molded straight legs, old finish, minor imperfections, 35" w, 16-1/2" d, 27-1/8" h ............................................................ 4,025.00

Classical, Philadelphia, PA, c1830, carved mahogany veneer, rect tops with rounded front corners above concave skirts with anthemion carved corners, ring-turned and waterleaf carved pedestals, shaped veneered platforms above leaf-carved paw feet, old refinish, casters missing, imperfections, 36" w, 17-3/4" d, 28-1/4" h, price for pr................................................... 6,325.00

Federal

Boston, c1790, mahogany inlaid, sq top with elliptical front, serpentine ends, inlaid edge above skirt with central inlaid oval in inlaid rectangle, double tapered legs, topped by inlaid oval dies outlined in stringing and ending in cuff inlays, old refinish, imperfections, 36-1/8" l, 16-7/8" d, 29-1/2" h.................. 4,025.00

Boston, c1805-15, mahogany and flame birch veneer, serpentine top with ovolo corners, half serpentine sides, inlaid edge on conforming base, skirt with three flame birch panels outlined in stringing and with cross banded mahogany surrounds, flanked by ring turned colonettes, sides similarly veneered and inlaid, four ring-turned and reeded tapering legs, imperfections, 36-1/4" w, 17" d, 20" h ........... 17,250.00

Boston or North Shore, MA, c1800, mahogany inlaid, folding top with half-round ends, sq corners, serpentine front, string inlaid edge above conforming base with sq central panel bordered by stringing and cross-banding, lower edge cross-banded, four sq double tapering legs with inlaid panels in the dies, stringing continuing to banded cuffs, refinished, minor imperfections ........................................... 2,990.00

Newburyport, MA, early 19th C, mahogany inlaid, rect hinged top with ovolo corners, skirt with oval reserved outlined in stringing and rectangular inlaid dies, similarly outlined above sq tapering legs with stringing, old refinish, imperfections, 35-3/4" w, 17-1/2" d, 29-1/4" h ................................. 5,750.00

New Hampshire, c1800, birch and cherry inlaid, folding top with elliptical front, half-serpentine ends and square corners, conforming skirt centering wavy birch panel bordered by stringing and mahogany cross-banding, four square double-tapered legs with inlaid dies and stringing continuing to banded cuffs, refinished, minor imperfections, 35" w, 16" d, 31" h ............................................................ 2,990.00

Northern Massachusetts or Portsmouth, NH, c1815-20, carved mahogany and mahogany veneer, folding top with cross-banded edge half serpentine ends, serpentine front, beaded conforming skirt, engaged leaf carved vase and ring-turned reeded and swelled frontal legs, rear legs with plain paneled dies, refinished, 35-1/4" w, 14-3/4" d, 29-3/4" h ............................................................ 1,955.00

North Shore, MA, c1800, mahogany inlaid, elliptical front top with ovolo corners, veneered skirt with central figured maple panel outlined with cross-banded mahogany veneer and tiger maple banding, similar outlining on skirt and tops of ring-turned tapered legs, rear legs topped by fluting, old refinish, very minor imperfections, 36" w, 17-1/4" d, 9" h ........................... 9,200.00

North Shore, MA, c1800, mahogany inlaid, mahogany top above undercut lower top, skirt with inlaid edge, each leg with inlaid fan patera above descending veined leafage ending in a dot with outline stringing ending at cuff inlays, old refinish, imperfections, 36" w, 17-3/4" d, 29" h ........ 4,025.00

Salem, MA, c1800, labeled "Thoms Needham Charter Street Salem, Mass," mahogany inlaid, rect top with ovolo corners and edge inlay, veneered skirt with central oval reserve in a rect mitred panel above a cockbeaded skirt with oval inlays centering by conch shells over the two front sq tapered legs, cuff inlays, old refinish, repair, 36" w, 17" d, 29-3/4" h ......... 6,325.00

Salem, MA, mahogany and flame birch veneer, top with serpentine front and ends, ovolo corners, skirt with central rectangular flame birch veneer panel above inlaid lower edge flanked by ring-turned and reeded legs, minor imperfections, 37-5/8" w, 18-3/4" d, 30-1/2" h .............................. 4,600.00

Southern States, c1800, cherry and tiger maple veneer, demilune top, tiger maple veneer skirt with cockbeaded edge over sq tapering legs, old refinish, imperfections, 32-1/2" w, 15-3/4" d, 30-1/2" h ............................................. 2,750.00

Napoleon III-Style, French gilt-brass mounted mahogany and marquetry, swivel top, int. fitted with compartments for counters and gaming pieces, playing surface in gilt-tooled turquoise leather, 27-1/2" w, 18-1/4" d, 30-3/4" h ........................... 800.00

William IV-Style, fourth quarter 19th C, mahogany, fold-over top, heavily molded scrolling frieze, turned bulbous standard, four splayed cabriole legs, scrolling feet, 36-1/2" w, 18-1/2" d, 29-1/2" h.......................................................... 400.00

**Center**

Biedermeier-Style, mahogany, banded oval top, plain frieze, columnar legs, ebonized plinths, shelf stretcher, 35-1/2" w, 29-1/2" d, 29-1/2" h .................................................. 700.00

Charles X, second quarter 19th C, mahogany, circular variegated brown marble top with raised edge, bulbous paneled standard, three scrolling supports, carved paw feet, 39-1/2" d, 27" h ................................................................ 3,600.00

Classical, America, second quarter 19th C, mahogany, shaped top over conforming molded apron, tripodal pedestal, scrolling legs, reduced in height, 36" d, 21-1/2" h ......................... 350.00

Edwardian, c1895, marquetry inlaid satinwood, top inlaid with pendant bellflowers, circular reeded legs, 26-3/4" d, 28" h ................................................................ 2,415.00

George III-style, Irish, late 19th C, mahogany, 36" d, 21-1/2" d, 31-1/2" h ................................................................ 2,875.00

International Movement, Wienerwerkstatte, c1930, mahogany and brass, circular top with crossbanded edge, conforming frieze, sq-section support flanked by four further cylindrical supports, raised on truncated pyramidal base, 25-1/4" d, 30-1/2" h ................ 550.00

Louis XV-Style, 19th C, mahogany inlaid, ormolu mounted walnut, shaped rect top, one short drawer, opposite faux drawer, cabriole legs, cast sabots, 35" w, 22" d, 28" h ......... 600.00

Regency, second quarter 19th C, mahogany, circular top, paneled standard, tripartite base, carved scrolled feet, 48" d, 29" h .................................................................... 1,750.00

Victorian

Egyptian Revival, c1865, probably New York, walnut and gilt incised, shaped oval top inset with brocatelle marble, frieze with masks and palmettes, stylized urn form support with Egyptian heads, carved hairy paw feet on casters, minor losses, shrinkage, 45" w, 30" d, 29-3/4" h.............. 10,925.00

Renaissance Revival, third quarter 19th C, walnut, marquetry, part-ebonized, parcel gilt, shaped top over frieze mounted with porcelain roundels, tapering fluted legs joined by shaped stretcher with finial, turned feet with casters, shrinkage to top, 42-1/2" w, 27" d, 30-1/4" h ..................... 4,025.00

Rococo Revival, America, mid 19th C and later, rosewood and faux-rosewood, tortoise-form top, conforming carved apron, pedestal joined to scrolling dolphin-carved legs, 39" w, 27-1/2" d, 30" h ................................................................... 900.00

William IV, second quarter 19th C, mahogany, highly figured circular top, paneled bulbous standard on scalloped molding, circular base raised on paw feet ending in casters, 51" d, 32" h ...............................................................................1,650.00

**Chair,** New England, 18th C, painted pine, round top attached by dowels above chair with shaped arms and plank seal, shoe feet, early red paint, minor losses, top reshaped, 54-1/4" w, 48-3/4" d, 27-1/2" h.................................................................6,900.00

**Console**

Georgian, first quarter 19th C, mahogany, demilune top with molded edge, sq tapering legs, 45-1/2" w, 21-1/2" d, 33-1/2" h, price for pr ....................................................................3,100.00

Georgian-Style, early 20th C, variegated green marble top over wave-carved frieze, standard in form of winged eagle on rocky perch, socle base, 32" w, 14-1/2" d, 33" h, price for pr.......4,650.00

Louis XV-Style, giltwood, shaped top raised above floral garland-carved frieze, tapering sq legs, pad feet, 29" w, 12-1/2" w, 30-1/4" h ...................................................................... 400.00

Louis XVI, c1785-90, giltwood, D-shaped fossilized yellow marble top, fluted and beaded frieze, leaf carved circular fluted and tapered legs, 48" d, 21" d, 33-1/2" h .............................9,775.00

Neoclassical-Style, Paine Furniture, Boston, early 20th C, demilune, reeded top above plain frieze with drawer, sq tapering legs ending in spade feet, polychrome dec, 36" w, 16" d, 30-1/4" h, price for pr ....................................................................3,750.00

**Dining**

Biedermeier, 19th C, birch and part ebonized, oval top, circular support, shaped base raised on stylized cabriole legs, restoration, 44-3/4" l, 33-1/2" d, 31" h .......................................2,875.00

Chippendale, MA, c1760-80, mahogany, drop leaf, overhanging rect top, valanced skirt, cabriole legs, claw and ball feet, old refinish, leaves reshaped, 46-1/2" w, 27-3/4" h.............1,610.00

Georgian-Style, mahogany and polychrome, rect banded top with rounded corners, gilt-molded edge, ivory polychromed frieze, cabriole legs headed by gilt acanthus carving, toupie feet, five leaves, 66-1/2" w, 49-1/2" d, 30" h ...................................800.00

Louis XV-Style, c1920, burled walnut, carved, rounded rect top with molded edge, cabriole legs, French toes, 71-1/2" w, 36-1/2" d, 31" h....................................................................500.00

Louis XVI-Style, brass mounted mahogany, drop leaves, circular tapering legs ending on brass caps on casters, three 17-1/2" leaves, 29" h ...............................................................7,475.00

Regency-Style, mahogany

Banded rounded rect top, two triangular pedestals, scrolling and acanthus carving, palmetto carved bun feet, two 19-1/4" leaves, 125-1/2" l extended, 48" d, 29-1/2" h...........2,450.00

Rectangular central section, two D-shaped ends, three turned urn-form standards, reeded downswept legs with brass paw caps on casters, two 18" leaves, 96-1/4" l without leaves, 47-1/4" w, 29-1/4" h......................................................5,465.00

Victorian, late, America, c1900, quarter-sawn oak, circular top, split pedestal, central column quartered by foliate carved scroll brackets with lion masks, carved paw feet, four leaves, 56" d, 29" h ...............................................................................1,540.00

**Display,** Louis XV-style, early 20th C, marquetry, brocade lined top above scalloped skirt, inlaid with satinwood acanthus and patera designs, tapering cabriole legs, headed by ormolu mounts, joined by X-stretcher centered with round shelf, 38" w, 29-1/2" h.........2,450.00

**Dressing**

Classical, New England, c1820, faux, scrolled backboard and chamfered top, conforming base with single long drawer, ring-turned tapered legs, all over red fanciful graining, old bras, 29-1/4" w, 14" d, 32-1/2" h.................................................................575.00

Federal, Newburyport, MA, c1820-30, painted and decorated, backsplash above two small indented drawers and one long drawer, flanked by boldly turned and dec front legs ending in small ball feet, old yellow ground paint with olive green and gold highlights, orig striping and fruit and foliage stenciled dec, orig brass, minor surface imperfections, 35-3/4" w, 17-1/2" d, 40-1/2" h ...............................................................................4,600.00

Neoclassical

Continental, first quarter 19th C, mahogany, oval beveled mirror plate within brass frame, surmounted by floral crest, joined by brass scrolling foliage uprights fitted with candleholders, rect top, frieze fitted with central long drawer, flanked by shorter drawers on each side, centered by bone plaque, circular legs, acanthus-molded brass toupie feet, joined by H-stretcher, 44-1/2" w, 15" d, 55" h .......... 1,100.00

Danish, first quarter 19th C, mahogany, rect top divided into three sections, opening to reveal fitted compartments, frame once containing dressing mirror, case with five drawers, sq tapered legs, 31" w, 18-1/2" d, 34-1/4" h ................. 1,650.00

Queen Anne

Massachusetts, 1730-50, carved walnut, top with molded edge and notched front corners, case of thumb molded drawers, one long drawer over three short drawers, central one fan carved, skirt with flat headed arches, cabriole legs ending in pad feet, replaced brasses, old surface, minor repairs and losses, 34-1/2" w, 19-1/2" d, 28-1/2" h.....................................................................28,750.00

Coastal Massachusetts, New Hampshire, or Maine, 1750-80, carved cherry, overhanging thumb molded top, case with cockbeaded drawers, central fan carved drawers, cyma curved skirt, four cabriole legs with spurs and arris knees, high pad feet, orig brasses, old refinish, imperfections, 33" w, 20" d, 30" h......................................................29,900.00

Victorian, Rococo Revival, America, mid-19th C, rosewood and walnut, upper section with shell and scroll carved mirror supported by foliate carved brackets, black and gold Egyptian marble inset in gadrooned edge, serpentine drawer, cabriole legs, 40" w, 26" d, 62" h ............................3,100.00

**Drop-Leaf, Arts & Crafts, L. & J. G. Stickley, c1910, sq top, cut-out plank legs, shoe feet, orig finish, "The Work of ..."" decal, 24" sq open, 24" h, $5,360. Photo courtesy of David Rago Auctions.**

## Drop Leaf

Country, New England, 1820s, tiger maple, rounded hinged leaves flank straight skirts above swelled ring-turned legs ending in turned feet, old refinish, minor imperfections, 38-1/4" w, 40-3/4" d, 30" h ........................ 1,150.00

Federal

America, mahogany, rect hinged leaves flank straight cock-beaded skirts, reeded tapering legs, turned feet on casters, refinished, minor repairs, 62-1/5" l, 46-3/4" w, 29-1/4" h ........................ 1,495.00

New England, c1820, tiger maple, rect overhanging drop leaf top with rounded corners, straight skirt, baluster and ring-turned legs on tapering feet, old refinish, imperfections, 44" l, 20" w, 29-1/2" h ........................ 1,150.00

Napoleon III, c1870, fruitwood marquetry and gilt-metal mounts, floral marquetry, frieze drawer, circular fluted legs, 24" w, 17-1/4" d, 29-1/2" h ........................ 990.00

Neoclassical-style, Dutch, 19th C, fruitwood marquetry inlaid, D-shaped leaves, frieze drawer, sq tapered legs, inlaid with foliage and birds, 38" w, 46" d open, 28-1/2" h ........................ 2,415.00

Queen Anne, America, c1774 and later, mahogany, each leaf with pair of cut shells on corners, tapering legs, pad feet, restorations, alternations, provenance includes documentation of descending in family of James Fenner, first governor of Rhode Island, 33" w, 14-1/4" d, 38-1/2" l extended, 28" h .......... 990.00

## Game

Classical, America, mid 19th C, mahogany, fold-over top, molded apron, supported by lyre-form pedestal on scroll legs, 35" w, 17-1/4" d, 34-1/2" l extended, 30" h ........................ 450.00

Classical, America, second quarter 19th C, mahogany, D-shaped fold-over top, conforming molded frieze, columnar pedestal joined by platform with beaded molding, carved paw feet, 36" w, 18" d, 32" h, price for pair ........................ 1,980.00

French Provincial, fourth quarter 19th C, fruitwood, rounded rect top with central inset chess board, flanked by inlaid diamonds, baize-lined gaming surface, scalloped apron, cabriole legs, 31-3/4" w, 15-3/4" d, 30" h ........................ 1,210.00

Louis XV Revival, 19th C, rosewood, hinged top, felt lined interior swiveling to reveal well, foliate carved base, 34" w, 18" d, 30" h ........................ 700.00

Victorian, America, fourth quarter 19th C

Renaissance Revival, walnut, serpentine fold-over top, conforming frieze, turned legs, int. bearing stenciled label "From McCracken & Brewster Wholesale Retail Furniture Dealers, Royal St. New Orleans," 34-1/2" w, 18" d, 29-1/2" h... 800.00

Rococo Revival, George Hunzinger, New York, walnut, circular removing top with inlaid gaming surface and baize verso, shaped supports joined by stretcher ending in paw feet, brass tag, 36" d, 29" h ........................ 1,000.00

William IV, English, c1830, rosewood, rect top, leather cov playing surface, apron with bead edge panel extending to pair of leaf carved brackets, turned columns, concave plinth base, scroll feet ........................ 975.00

**Harvest,** New England, late 18th/early 19th C, painted pine, scrubbed top with natural color pine, with hinged leaves, painted olive green base with ring-turned tapering legs, early surface, imperfections, 102-3/4" l, 18-1/4" w, extends to 39-3/4" w, 20-1/2" h ........................ 11,500.00

## Library

Arts and Crafts, Charles F. Limbert Co., Grand Rapids and Holland, MI, early 20th C, similar to model no. 1131, oak, rect top, arched skirt, single drawer that opens to lift top writing desk with inkwell and pen tray, medial shelf below, medium brown finish, branded mark, stains, wear, scratches, 48" l, 28" w, 29" h ........................ 1,955.00

George III, c1800, mahogany and inlay, circular drum top, alternating working and faux drawers, inset gilt tooled green leather top, 42" d, 31" h ........................ 8,625.00

Modernism Era, Frank Lloyd Wright, designed for Sherman Booth residence, Glencoe, IL, c1915, walnut, rect top over central drawer, lower shelf, flanked on one side by cabinet fitted with two shelves, two door and cabinet and shelf, whole cantilevered over square legs, 108" l, 38" w, 28" h ........................ 85,000.00

Victorian, Eastlake-style, America, late 19th C, carved oak, rect top, curved edges, scalloped skirt, curved legs with carved scrolls, medial shelf with open box at center, wear, 54" l, 25-3/4" w, 30-1/2" h ........................ 230.00

**Nesting,** Chippendale-style, first quarter 20th C, mahogany, each with rect top, acanthus carved edge, serpentine frieze, cabriole legs headed by acanthus carving, pad feet, 21" w, 15-3/4" d, 21-1/2" h, price for group of three ........................ 250.00

## Occasional

Belle Epoque, fourth quarter 19th C, marble-top mahogany, kidney-shaped top, inset brèche d'Aleps marble top, partial pierced brass gallery above single frieze drawer, joined on like-shaped lower shelf by sq supports, turned toupie feet, 16-1/4" w, 13" d, 29-1/2" h ........................ 250.00

French Provincial, third quarter 19th C, fruitwood, ovoid top with gallery and recessed front, single frieze drawer, galleried lower shelf, shaped supports, trestle base, 27-1/2" w, 16" d, 30" h ......... 550.00

Victorian, fourth quarter 19th C, black lacquer and naturalistic wood, rect top centered by oriental birds and floral branches, supports dec with diagonal braces and diamond shaped shelf, 21" w, 28-1/2" l, 27-1/2" h ........................ 1,100.00

## Parlor

Renaissance Provincial, America, third quarter 19th C, walnut, ovoid white marble top, molded apron, quadruped base centered by bowl finial flanked by turned supports, 34-1/2" w, 25-1/2" d, 30" h ........................ 900.00

Victorian, Rococo Revival, America, third quarter 19th C, walnut, tortoise shaped top, conforming frieze, cabriole legs joined by lower shelf centered by final, 34" w, 25" d, 31" h ........................ 975.00

## Pembroke

Federal, New York, early 19th C, mahogany veneer, hinged shaped leaves flank single drawer at each end, one working, one faux, reeded tapering legs ending in tapering feet on balls, old refinish, replaced brass, very minor imperfections, 22-1/2" w, 36" d, 28-1/2" h ........................ 1,380.00

George III, c1790, string inlaid satinwood, oval inlaid top, cross banded border, sq tapered legs, spade feet, 43-1/2" w, 29" d, 28-5/8" h ........................ 2,185.00

George III, c1800, boxwood string inlaid mahogany, shaped drop leaves, frieze drawer, sq tapered legs inlaid with pendant flowers, 33" d, 28" h ........................ 1,785.00

Fourth quarter 18th C, mahogany, rect top with drop leaves, frieze fitted with single drawer, sq tapered legs with brass cup casters, 21-1/2" w, 43-1/2" l extended, 28-1/2" h ........................ 1,000.00

**Pier,** George III, late 19th C, giltwood and mahogany, rect inlaid tops, giltwood bases, sq tapering legs, adapted, price for pr ......... 7,475.00

**Reading,** Regency, second quarter 19th C, mahogany, rounded rect extending top, sq shaft on rounded X-form base, toupie feet on brass caps and casters, 29-1/2" w, 46-1/2" h ........................ 2,650.00

**Side, Victorian, shaped white marble top with beveled ledge, ornate skirt, carved legs, wooden casters, 21" x 29" top, 29" h, $700. Photo courtesy of Joy Luke Fine Art Brokers and Auctioneers.**

## Side

Chippendale, Irish, third-quarter 18th C, walnut, veneered, banded, and inlaid top above beaded and rosette-carved frieze, cabriole legs, headed by lion mask carving, paw feet, 32-1/2" w, 23-1/2" d, 29" h ................................................. 3,300.00

Georgian, mid-18th C, English, oak, circular dished tilt top, turned standard, tripod cabriole legs, 21" d, 28" h .................... 1,955.00

Empire, first-quarter 19th C, figured walnut, variegated charcoal marble top with curved corners, frieze drawer, scrolling ormolu-mounted supports, shelf stretcher, plinth base, 28" w, 15-1/2" d, 32-1/2" h............................................................... 1,100.00

French Provincial, late-19th C, fruitwood, serpentine parquetry top, scalloped frieze, shell and floral carving, cabriole legs, acanthus carving, scroll feet, 33-1/2" w, 21-1/2" d, 28-1/2" h .......................................................................... 525.00

French Provincial-Style, cherry, long rect top, molded edge frieze, tapering cabriole legs, 60" w, 18-3/4" d, 30" h.................. 500.00

Georgian-Style, mahogany, slightly bowed top, frieze fitted with two drawers, tapering sq legs, 37" w, 19" d, 35" h .......... 360.00

Queen Anne-Style, mahogany, dished top, scalloped frieze, cabriole legs, each end with pull-out candle stand, 20" w, 30" d, 26" h..............................................................200.00

## Silver

George III, c1765, carved mahogany, galleried tray top, low relief carved everted lip, repeating border of C-scrolls and foliage, swirling scroll bordered apron, molded sq cabriole supports with trailing acanthus carving at knees, Spanish feet, alternations to top, repairs, 31-3/4" l 28-3/4" h ..................................... 2,000.00

George III-style, c1900, mahogany, tripod, dished top carved with shells and leaves, bulbous acanthus and fluted stem, leaf-clad legs, claw and ball feet, 36" d, 27-1/2" h ..................... 3,200.00

## Sofa

Hepplewhite, Salem, MA, 1790-1810, mahogany, satinwood inlaid, rect top flanked by D-shaped drop leaves, skirt fitted with two cockbeaded inlaid working and two faux drawers, drawers flanked by diamond inlaid dies, stringing on lower skirt edge, two upright rect columns each continuing to two line inlaid tapering down curving legs, brass animal paw casters, ring-turned transverse stretcher, repairs to legs and uprights, 53-3/4" w extended, 27-1/4" d, 28-1/2" h ................................. 82,500.00

Neoclassical, Continental, second quarter 19th C, brass and ivory inlaid rosewood, 52-1/2" w extended, 28-1/4" d, 29-1/2" h...............................................................3,335.00

## Tavern

New England, mid 18th C, Baroque, maple and pine, rect overhanging breadboard top, straight molded skirt, block, vase, and ring-turned legs joined by box stretchers, vase and ring-turned feet, old red washed surface, repairs, 52" l, 30" d, 37" h.................1,850.00

New England, 18th C, maple and pine, stretcher base, top with breadboard ends overhangs single drawer, four block and baluster turned legs joined by sq stretchers, old color, repairs to two feet, 31-1/2" w, 22-3/4" d, 26-7/8" h........................2,070.00

## Tea

Federal, New England, c1790, cherry, octagonal tilt-top, vase and ring turned post, tripod shaped tapering legs, old finish, 22" w, 14-3/4" d, 28" h ............................................................. 4,025.00

George II-Style, mahogany, two tiers, graduated dished tops, columnar tripodal pedestal, 20-1/2" d, 31" h .................... 750.00

Queen Anne, Rhode Island, c1750, maple, painted, rectangular top overhangs shaped skirt, cylindrical tapering legs ending in diminutive pad feet on discs, brown stain, pencil inscription on bottom relating to previous owners, imperfections, 25" x 33" top, 28" h ...........................................................4,485.00

## Tray

Edwardian, c1900, satinwood and inlay, two oval tiers, removable wood and glass tray, slightly splayed sq tapering legs joined by stretcher, 36" w, 20-1/4" d, 32" h .................................. 1,150.00

George III, late-18th/early-19th C, mahogany, butler's type, later base with molded legs joined by stretchers, imperfections to finish, 17" w, 27-1/4" l, 22" h .............................................. 275.00

## Vitrine

Edwardian, early 20th C, mahogany, glazed octagonal top hinged, opens to display area, sides also glazed, turned standard, four scrolling supports, spade feet, 38" d, 28" h ...................... 440.00

Neoclassical-Style, Dutch, late 19th C, walnut and floral marquetry, kidney shape, inset glass top and sides, sq tapering legs, spade feet, 33" w, 19-1/4" d, 30" h................................. 1,725.00

Queen Anne-Style, early 20th C, mahogany, glazed serpentine top over conforming frieze, cabriole legs, pad feet, 25" w, 17-1/4" d, 28-1/2" h ............................................................... 250.00

## Wine, French Provincial

Fruitwood, c1840, tilting circular top, two end supports, splayed plinth base, 44" d, 28" h ................................................. 1,350.00

Oak, c1860, tilting circular top, rust leather surface, two end supports on trestle bases, 35-1/2" d, 28" h ............................. 350.00

## Writing, French Provincial

Fourth quarter 19th C, pine, rect top, frieze fitted with central drawer, tapering sq legs, 50-1/2" w, 29" d, 28-1/2" h ....... 700.00

Third quarter 19th C, fruitwood, partially galleried top, frieze drawer, tapering sq legs, 31-1/2" w, 16" d, 27-1/2" h ....... 400.00

Third quarter 19th C, fruitwood, rect top, frieze fitted with central drawer, tapering sq legs, 26" w, 16-1/2" d, 28" h.............. 450.00

## Work

Anglo-Indian, 4th quarter 19th C, bamboo and lacquer, hinged top opens to sea grass-lined int., two lower small shelves, raised on splayed bamboo legs, lacquer panels with foliage dec, 20-1/2" w, 15-1/2" w, 29-1/2" h ............................................................ 500.00

Biedermeier-Style, cherry wood and burr popular, rect top, molded frieze with drawer, inverted, pierced, and lyre-form supports joined by pole stretcher, 22-1/2" l, 15-3/4" w, 25-1/4" h.................... 650.00

Classical

    American, late 19th C, mahogany and cherry, top with pair of drop leaves over pair of drawers, spiral-turned Sheraton legs, 21" w, 21" d, 27-1/2" h........................................ 250.00

    American, second quarter 19th C, mahogany, pair of drawers raised on spiral reeded legs, 22" w, 18" d, 29" h ........ 940.00

    Boston, c1830, mahogany veneer, top with hinged leaves which flank veneered drawers, top drawer with fittings, tapering pedestal with four concave sides above conformingly shaped platform with three turned discs, turned tapering feet on casters, old refinish, orig pulls, imperfections, 18-1/8" w, 19" d, 29-3/4" h ........................................... 1,380.00

    New England, c1820-30, mahogany and mahogany veneer, cross-banded rect top over veneered case, two drawers, four turned drops, ring-turned and acanthus leaf carved pedestal ending in four claw feet, casters, old refinish, replaced brasses, minor imperfections, 24" w, 18" d, 29" h.... 1,265.00

    New England, c1820-30, tiger maple, rect drop leaf top, two drawers with convex fronts, sq tapering pedestal, stepped sq platform, four turned and belted feet, old finish, 16-1/2" w, 17" d, 30-1/2" h ...................................................... 1,500.00

    Pennsylvania, c1825, bird's eye maple, tiger maple, and cherry, rect top, two drawers, straight skirt joining four vase and ring-turned tapering legs, old refinish, imperfections, 21-1/2" w, 19" d, 29" h ............................................... 1,610.00

Classical, Classical Revival, America, early 20th C, mahogany, gadrooned top with pair of drop leaves, frieze with bank of three drawers, acanthus carved pedestal, paw feet, 17" w, 16" d, 31" h................................................................475.00

Classical-Style, American, second quarter 20th C, mahogany, drop leaf top, gadrooned edges over bank of three drawers, foliage carved pedestal supported by cabriole legs, claw and ball feet, 18" w, 16-1/2" d, 46" l extended, 30-1/2" h.............. 385.00

Empire, America, second quarter 19th C, mahogany, pair of drop leaves flanked by pair of molded drawers, tapering pedestal on bun feet, 17-1/4" w, 17" d, 29-1/4" h ................................ 250.00

Federal

    New England, c1800, mahogany and mahogany veneer, rect top, two drawers, straight skirt joining four sq tapering legs, replaced brass pulls, old finish, 18-3/4" w, 15-1/8" d, 29-1/2" h ....................................................................980.00

New York, c1815-20, mahogany astragal-end carved and mahogany veneer, rect top flanked by hinged tops above conforming case of two cockbeaded drawers flanked by reeded pilasters and acorn-turned drop pendants and compartments, vase and ring turned pedestal, four acanthus leaf carved and molded shaped legs, cast brass hairy paw feet, replaced brasses, imperfections, some sun-bleaching, 25-1/4" w, 14" d, 30-1/4" h ............................................. 2,300.00

Louis Philippe-Style, Provincial, Elmwood, partially constructed from antique elements, oval top, long drawer, sq tapered legs, 52-1/2" l, 38-1/2" w, 29-1/2" h........................................ 1,450.00

Queen Anne

Black walnut and pine, painted, PA, c1760-1800, removable blank three-board pine top, supported by cleats and four dowels, two thumb-molded drawers, straight skirt with breaded edge above straight cabriole legs ending in pad feet, orig apple green paint, old replaced wooden pulls, surface imperfections, cracked foot, 48-1/2" w, 32" d, 27" h........................2,500.00

Maple and pine, New England, late 18th C, scrubbed top, straight skirt with beaded edge, turned tapering legs ending in turned button feet, old surface, remnants of red on base, 28" w, 28-1/2" l, 27" h................................................2,530.00

Painted Pine, New England, 18th C, overhanging oval scrubbed top, straight molded skirt, splayed ring-turned legs ending in turned feet, orig red paint on base, 35" w, 26-3/8" l, 26-1/4" h ...................................................14,950.00

Pine and maple, two board pine bread board top with good old patina, mortised and pinned apron, turned tapered legs, button feet, maple base with traces of old paint, reddish brown finish, one corner of top has damage, 31-3/4" w, 64-1/2" l, 27-3/4" h ...................................................... 550.00

Walnut, removable three board top, two dovetailed overlapping drawers, mortised and pinned apron with edge beading, turned legs, weathered duck feet, old refinishing, period replaced brasses, pieced repairs to top, age cracks, 32" w, 49-1/2" l, 28" h .......................................................... 2,750.00

Sheraton, mahogany and mahogany veneer, three dovetailed drawers, turned legs with ring turned detail, orig gilded lion head brasses, old finish, top drawer is fitted with tilt-up writing surface, age cracks in sides, some veneer damage to writing tablet, 16" w, 18" l, 27-3/4" h ................................................ 1,430.00

Victorian, Rococo Revival, America, third quarter 19th C, mahogany, lift top opens to reveal fitted int. mounted with mirror, frieze drawer with wooden bag drawer below, molded trestle base with shaped stretcher, 20-1/2" w, 15" d, 29" h ......................... 900.00

William and Mary-Style, walnut, ebonized trim, two board top, one dovetailed drawer, turned stretchers and legs, repairs and old replacements, 22-3/4" w, 34" d, 27-1/4" h............................. 935

# GAME PLATES

**History:** Game plates, popular between 1870 and 1915, are specially decorated plates used to serve fish and game. Sets originally included a platter, serving plates, and a sauce or gravy boat. Many sets have been divided. Today, individual plates are often used as wall hangings.

## Birds

Plaque, 14-1/2" d, multicolored flying ducks over marsh, printed under glaze, gold trim, #1044-9030, Mettlach ................................. 350.00
Plate
　8-3/4" d, hp, brown quail standing in green and tan landscape, white ground, inner border of yellow flowers and green leaves, raised outer border with gilt leaves, shaped rim, sgd "C. T." and eagle mark ........................ 55.00
　9-1/2" d, sgd "Max," Limoges Coronet ................................. 65.00
　9-3/4" d, blue grouse, brown grouse, shielded green field, shaded brown border, brown lined rim, Bavaria............................. 25.00
　10" d, duck, white, gray, and black body, emerald green head, standing in marsh, gadrooned gilt border within traditional border, Royal Copenhagen .......................... 990.00
　10-1/2" d, Asiatic Pheasants, R Hall ................................. 3.00
　12-1/4"" d, birds in flight, hp, gold scalloped edge, marked "Limoges" ................................. 200.00
Platter
　13-3/4" x 9-1/2", oval, duck, p, natural setting, gold handles, artist sgd, Limoges blank .......................... 225.00
　18" l, pheasants, multicolored center scene, marked "R K Beck" .......................... 500.00
　Set, 16-1/2" l platter, nine 9" d plates, various game birds, each mkd "Limoges, Corunet, France," early 20th C, price for set ................................. 425.00

## Deer

Plate, 13-3/4"" h, stag in woods, hp, raised enamel dec............. 200.00
Platter, 15-1/4" x 12-1/8", antlered deer fighting, muticolored transfer, cobalt blue border, gold stencil trim, gold striped rim ................. 50.00
Set, platter, twelve plates, deer, bear, and game birds, yellow ground, scalloped border, marked "Haviland China," artist sgd "MC Haywood" ................................. 3,000.00

## Fish

Plaque, 14" d, multicolored hanging fish and lobster, printed under glaze, gold trim, Mettlach ......................... 375.00
Plate
　9" d, bass, artist sgd "Morley," marked "Lenox" ................... 75.00
　10-1/2" d, trout, cobalt blue border, marked "M Z Austria"....85.00
Platter, 16-1/2" l, bass, water lilies, emb, artist sgd "Max," marked "Limoges" ................................. 175.00

**Fish Platter, majolica, oval, yellow ground, molded salmon, leaves, imp "Wedgwood," c1880, light staining, 25-1/4" l, $5,465. Photo courtesy of Skinner, Inc.**

Set
　21" platter, nine 8-1/2" d plates, sauceboat with undertray, hp reserves of leaping trout, seaweed border, heavy gold accents, Limoges................................................ 990.00
　23-1/2" platter, twelve plates, different species on each plate, yellow border, gold trim, marked "Limoges, France"............. 500.00

## Miscellaneous

Plaque, 11-5/8" d, brown moose in woods, dark blue shaded border, gold overlay, pierced for hanging ............................................. 45.00
Plate
　9" d, elk, natural colors, scalloped edge ............................. 45.00
　10" d, wild boar, multicolored, Limoges ............................. 160.00
Platter, 18" l, weasel carrying red squirrel in mouth, winter scene, sky blue ground, paneled and beaded border, dentil rim, gilt and ground highlights, numbered, Royal Copenhagen ............................ 1,200.00

# GAMES

**History:** Board games have been commercially produced in this country since at least 1822, and card games since the 1780s. However, it was not until the 1840s that large numbers of games were produced that survive to this day. The W. & S. B. Ives Company produced many board and card games in the 1840s and 1950s. Milton Bradley and McLoughlin Brothers became major producers of games starting in the 1860s, followed by Parker Brothers in the 1880s. Other major producers of games in this period were Bliss, Chaffee and Selchow, Selchow and Righter, and Singer.

Today most games from the 19th century are rare and highly collectible, primarily because of their spectacular lithography. McLoughlin and Bliss command a premium because of the rarity. The quality of materials, and the extraordinary art that was created to grace the covers and boards of their games.

In the 20th century, Milton Bradley, Selchow and Righter and Parker Brothers became the primary manufacturers of boxed games. They have all now been absorbed by toy giant Hasbro Corporation. Other noteworthy producers were All-Fair, Pressman, and Transogram, all of which are no longer in business. Today the hottest part of the game collecting market is in rare character games from the 1960s. Parker Brothers and All-Fair games from the 1920s to 1940s also have some excellent lithography and are highly collectible.

**References:** *Board Games of the 50's, 60's & 70's with Prices*, L-W Books, 1994; Lee Dennis, *Warman's Antique American* Games, 1840-1940, Wallace-Homestead, Krause Publications, 1991; *Dexterity Games and Other Hand-Held Puzzles*, L-W Book Sales, 1995; Alex G. Malloy, *American Games Comprehensive Collector's Guide,* Antique Trader Books, 2000; Jack Matthews, *Toys Go to War*, Pictorial Histories Publishing, 1994; Rex Miller, *The Investor's Guide to Vintage Character Collectibles,* Krause Publications, 1999; Rick Polizzi, *Baby Boomer Games*, Collector Books, 1995; Rick Polizzi and Fred Schaefer, *Spin Again*, Chronicle Books, 1991; Desi Scarpone, *More Board Games,* Schiffer Publishing, 2000; Bruce Whitehill, *Games: American Boxed Games and Their Makers,* Wallace-Homestead, Krause Publications, 1992.

**Periodicals:** *The Games Annual,* 5575 Arapahoe Rd, Suite D, Boulder, CO 80303; *Toy Shop,* 700 E. State St., Iola, WI 54990.

**Collectors' Clubs:** American Game Collectors Association, P.O. Box 44, Dresher, PA, 19025; Gamers Alliance, P.O. Box 197, East Meadow, NY 11554.

**Museums:** Checkers Hall of Fame, Petal, MS; Essex Institute, Salem, MA; Margaret Woodbury Strong Museum, Rochester, NY; University of Waterloo Museum & Archive of Games, Waterloo, Ontario, Canada; Washington Dolls' House and Toy Museum, Washington, D.C.

**Additional Listings:** See *Warman's Americana & Collectibles*.

**Notes:** While people collect games for many reasons, it is strong graphic images that bring the highest prices. Games which are collected because they are fun to play or for nostalgic reasons are still collectible but will not bring high prices. Also, game collectors are not interested in common and "public domain" games such as checkers, tiddley winks, Authors, Anagrams, Jackstraws, Rook, Pit, Flinch, and Peter Coodles. The game market today is characterized by fairly stable prices for ordinary items, increasing discrimination for grades of condition, and continually rising prices for rare material in excellent condition. Whether you are a dealer or a collector, be careful to buy games in good condition. Avoid games with taped or split corners or other box damage. Games made after about 1950 are difficult to sell unless they are complete and in excellent condition. As games get older, there is a forgiveness factor for condition and completeness that increases with age.

These listings are for games that are complete and in excellent condition. Be sure that the game you're looking to price is the same as the one described in the listing. The 19th century makers routinely published the same title on several different versions of the game, varying in size and graphics. Dimensions listed below are rounded to the nearest half inch.

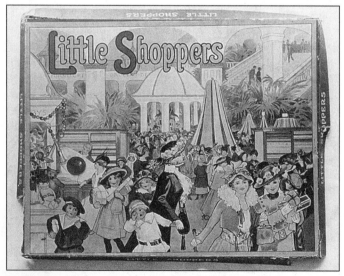

**Little Shoppers, Gibson Game Co., c1910, $35.**

After Dinner, Frederick H. Beach, 1933, 8" x 11" .........................70.00

American Boys, McLoughlin Bros., early 1900s, boxed board game, 11" x 20", some damage to orig box.......................200.00

Auto Race Game, Milton Bradley, c1925, boxed board game, 16-7/8" x 8-3/4", 8 pcs ...............................................125.00

Bagatelle, early push-type, 1-5/8" x 9-15/16" x 19-1/4"", wooden, multicolored litho pasted to face marking points, wooden stick with wooden block to push ball, one wood and one clay ball, instructions pasted on back.......................................135.00

Bicycle Race, McLoughlin Bros., c1890, boxed board game......925.00

Big Trail Game, boxed board game, 13-1/2" x 17" x 1-1/2", 1930 Movietone picture with John Wayne and Tyrone Power Sr., 14" x 26" multicolored board, wagon train illus, instruction booklet, wooden pawns, metal figures, full color illus box, several pawns and four figures missing .......................................75.00

Bradley's Toy Town Post Office, Milton Bradley, c1910, educational, 8-3/4" x 11", 10 pcs........................................110.00

Buster Brown and Tige, Bliss, target game...............................575.00

Champion Game of Baseball, Proctor Amusement, c1900, boxed board game, 9" x 12", instructions inside cov, unused score card, litho heavy paper gameboard with baseball diamond, attached spinner, bleachers, and stands, paper markers in orig envelopes..140.00

Charlie Chan, Whitman, 1939, boxed card game, 5" x 6" x 1", 35 playing cards, instruction card, black, white, and red crime fighting scenes, multicolored box............................................75.00

Cinderella, Milton Bradley, c1900, card game, 6-3/4" x 5-1/2", 33 cards ............................................20.00

Comic Conversations, Parker Bros., card game, 5" x 6-1/2" ........45.00

Dixie Pollyanna, Parker Brothers, 1952, 8" x 18"........................100.00

Down the Pike with Mrs. Wiggs at the St. Louis Exposition, Milton Bradley, c1904, card game, 7-1/2" x 5-1/2", instructions on front of reading booklet, small cards..............................................20.00

Excursion to Coney Island, Milton Bradley, c1885, card game, printed cards, reading booklet .................................................35.00

Flap Jacks, Alderman-Fairchild, 1931, skill game, 15-1/2" x 12-1/2", 30 pcs..............................................35.00

Game of Balloon, R Bliss Manuf, 1889, skill game, 31" x 10-1/2", 17 pcs, wooden stand and hoop, all wood dovetailed and hinged box......275.00

Game of Bang, McLoughlin Bros., 1912, boxed board game, 15" x 8", orig spinner, game board on box bottom, playing pcs...............85.00

Game of Boy Scouts, McLoughlin Bros. ....................................290.00

Game of Louisa, McLoughlin Bros., 1888, platform type board, repairs to orig box ...............................................625.00

Game of Old Mother Hubbard, Milton Bradley, c1890, boxed board game, 15" x 16", 8 pcs .................................................95.00

Game of Parlor Baseball, McLoughlin Bros, 1897, boxed board game, 17" x 19", vivid litho cov of early baseball players, board with playing field, two litho spinners, 18 wooden playing markers............1,600.00

Game of Poor Jenny, Alderman-Fairchild, c1927, boxed board game, 11-1/2" x 11-1/2", 9 pcs .............................................50.00

Game of Zulu, McLoughlin Bros, target game, 12" x 20", 8 parts110.00

Gypsy Fortune Telling Game, Milton Bradley, 1930, fold out board, fortune telling cards .................................................150.00

Honey Bee Game, Milton Bradley, c1913, boxed board game, 12-3/4" sq, 26 pcs............................................60.00

Jack and the Bean Stalk, Parker Bros., 1901, box bottom is playing board, two playing pieces, teetotum, cover edge wear, 15" l, 9-1/2" w, 5/8" h ............................................115.00

Japnese Games of Mon, Blind Pilgrim, and Cash, McLoughlin Bros, 1890, book type.............................................275.00

Klondyke Nugget Game, c1890, boxed board game, 4" x 8" x 1", full color illus of mine, miner holding "Boss Nugget," multicolored game board, mine covers, gold nuggets .............................................85.00

Lee at Havana Game, c1898, boxed board game, 5" x 7" x 1", Spanish-American War, set of 52 cards, instruction sheet, full color paper label on lid ............................................75.00

Magnetic Fish Pond, Parker Bros., c1930, boxed board game ....75.00

Mansion of Happiness, Henry P. Ives, 1864, hand colored board, 15" x 18", slight damage to box.......................................250.00

Motor Cycle Game, Milton Bradley, c1905, boxed board game, 9" sq, 5 pcs .......... 40.00
One Two Button Your Shoe! Master Toy Co., 11" x 12" .......... 150.00
Oriental Color Game, McLoughlin Bros, 1875, 7-1/2" x 4-1/2", wooden box, 54 multicolored litho cards, litho double arrowed block spinner, instruction booklet .......... 85.00
Peter Coddles Trip to New York, 6" x 8-1/2" .......... 50.00
Pike's Peak or Bust, Parker Brothers, 1895, 7" x 7" .......... 150.00
Psychology of the Hand, Baker & Bennett Co, card game, 8-3/4" x 12-1/4" x 1-1/2", copyright by Getrude Ann Lindsay, five cards of hands, instruction booklet .......... 35.00
Raggedy Ann's Magic Pebble Game, Johnny Gruelle Co, Milton Bradley, 1941, 15-1/2" x 8-11/16" x 1-3/4", 18 pcs .......... 65.00
Round the World with Nellie Bly, c1895, Statue of Liberty on board .......... 125.00
Strange Game of Forbidding Fruit, Parker Bros, c1900, boxed card game, 4" x 5-1/2", forty cards, full color paper label on lid of three men steeling apples, charging farm yard dog .......... 75.00
Tally-Ho, Snow, Woodman & Co, c1880, 11-1/4" x 11-1/4", thirty-six white wooden pegs, thirty-six black wooden pegs, lift out board, instruction sheet, multicolored litho board with red star center .......... 60.00
The Two Friends, French, 19th C, litho paper on wood, flat picture blocks, view of people in national costumes, 9-5/8" w, 7-1/2" d, 1-1/8" h .......... 288.00
The Wonderful Game of Oz, Parker Brothers, 1931, 10" x 19", some damage to box .......... 275.00
Tiddle Tennis, Schonlat, 1930s, tiddly wink type, 6" x 12-1/2", 8 playing pcs .......... 45.00
Tug of War, Chafee/Selchow, 1898, boxed board game, 10-1/2" x 19-1/2", repairs to orig box .......... 425.00
When My Ship Comes In, George S. Parker, & Co, c1888, 5-1/2" x 4", boxed card game, 84 cards, instruction sheet .......... 30.00

# GAUDY DUTCH

**History:** Gaudy Dutch is an opaque, soft-paste ware made between 1790 and 1825 in England's Staffordshire district.

The wares first were hand decorated in an underglaze blue and fired; then additional decorations were added over the glaze. The over-glaze decoration is extensively worn on many of the antique pieces. Gaudy Dutch found a ready market in the Pennsylvania German community because it was inexpensive and extremely colorful. It had little appeal in England.

**Museums:** Henry Ford Museum, Dearborn, MI; Philadelphia Museum of Art, Philadelphia, PA; Reading Art Museum, Reading, PA.

**Marks:** Marks of various potters, including the impressed marks of Riley and Wood, have been found on some pieces, although most are unmarked.

**References:** Susan and Al Bagdade, *Warman's English & Continental Pottery & Porcelain*, 3rd Edition, Krause Publications, 1998; Eleanor and Edward Fox, *Gaudy Dutch*, published by author, 1970, out of print; John A. Shuman, III, *Collector's Encyclopedia of Gaudy Dutch & Welsh*, Collector Books, 1990, 1998 value update.

**Collectors' Club:** Gaudy Collector's Society, P.O. Box 274, Gates Mills, OH 44040.

**Advisor:** John D. Querry.

Butterfly
Bowl, 11" d .......... 3,900.00
Coffeepot, 11" h .......... 9,500.00
Cup and Saucer, handleless, minor enamel flakes, chips on table ring .......... 950.00
Plate, 7-1/4" d .......... 645.00
Soup Plate, 8-1/2" d, wear and scratches .......... 1,275.00
Sugar Bowl, cov .......... 900.00
Teapot, 5" h, squat baluster form .......... 2,400.00
Carnation
Bowl, 6-1/4" d .......... 925.00
Creamer, 4-3/4" h .......... 700.00
Pitcher, 6" h .......... 675.00
Plate, 8" d .......... 950.00
Plate, 9-3/4" d .......... 1,265.00
Teabowl and Saucer .......... 575.00
Teapot, cov .......... 2,200.00
Toddy Plate .......... 975.00
Waste Bowl .......... 675.00
Dahlia
Bowl, 6-1/4" d .......... 1,800.00
Plate, 8" d .......... 2,800.00
Teabowl and Saucer .......... 8,000.00
Double Rose
Bowl, 6-1/4" d .......... 545.00
Creamer .......... 650.00
Gravy Boat .......... 950.00
Plate, 8-1/4" d .......... 675.00
Plate, 10" d .......... 935.00
Sugar Bowl, cov .......... 750.00
Teabowl and Saucer .......... 675.00
Teapot, cov .......... 1,900.00
Toddy Plate, 4-1/2" d .......... 675.00
Waste Bowl, 6-1/2" d, 3" h .......... 850.00
Dove
Creamer .......... 675.00
Plate, 8-1/8" d, very worn, scratches, stains .......... 245.00
Plate, 8-1/2" d .......... 770.00
Teabowl and Saucer .......... 500.00
Waste Bowl .......... 650.00
Flower Basket, plate, 6-1/2" d .......... 375.00
Grape
Bowl, 6-1/2" d, lustered rim .......... 475.00
Plate, 6-1/4" d .......... 580.00
Sugar Bowl, cov .......... 675.00
Teabowl and Saucer .......... 475.00
Toddy Plate, 5" d .......... 475.00
Leaf, bowl, 11-1/2" d, shallow .......... 4,800.00
No Name
Plate, 8-3/4" d .......... 17,000.00
Teapot, cov .......... 16,000.00
Oyster
Bowl, 5-1/2" d .......... 675.00
Coffeepot, cov, 12" h .......... 10,000.00
Plate, 9-1/2" d .......... 575.00
Plate, 10" d .......... 1,550.00
Soup Plate, 8-1/2" d .......... 550.00
Teabowl and Saucer .......... 1,275.00
Toddy Plate, 5-1/2" d .......... 475.00
Single Rose
Bowl, 6" d .......... 650.00

Coffeepot, cov ................................................. 8,500.00
Cup and Saucer, handleless, price for pr ........................... 850.00
Plate, 8-1/4" d ................................................. 650.00
Plate, 10" d ................................................. 975.00
Quill Holder, cov ................................................. 2,500.00
Sugar Bowl, cov ................................................. 700.00
Teapot, cov ................................................. 1,200.00
Toddy Plate, 5-1/4" d ................................................. 250.00
Waste Bowl, 5-1/2" d, wear, hairlines, stains, flake on table ring, glaze rim flakes ................................................. 365.00

Sunflower
Bowl, 6-1/2" d ................................................. 900.00
Coffeepot, cov, 9-1/2" h ................................................. 6,500.00
Creamer ................................................. 850.00
Cup and Saucer, handleless, wear, chips ................................................. 575.00
Plate, 9-3/4" d ................................................. 825.00

Urn
Creamer ................................................. 475.00
Cup and Saucer, handleless ................................................. 550.00
Plate, 8-1/4" d ................................................. 910.00
Plate, 9-7/8" d, very worn, scratches, stains, rim, chips ..... 225.00
Sugar Bowl, cov, 6-1/2" h, round, tip and base restored ..... 295.00
Teapot ................................................. 895.00

War Bonnet
Bowl, cov ................................................. 225.00
Coffeepot, cov ................................................. 9,500.00
Cup and Saucer, handleless ................................................. 575.00
Plate, 8-1/8" d, pinpoint rim flake, minor wear ................... 880.00
Teapot, cov ................................................. 4,400.00
Toddy Plate, 4-1/2" d ................................................. 975.00

Zinna, soup plate, 10" d, impressed "Riley" ................................................. 4,675.00

# GAUDY IRONSTONE

**History:** Gaudy Ironstone was made in England around 1850. Ironstone is an opaque, heavy-bodied earthenware which contains large proportions of flint and slag. Gaudy Ironstone is decorated in patterns and colors similar to those of Gaudy Welsh.

**Museums:** Henry Ford Museum, Dearborn, MI; Philadelphia Museum of Art, Philadelphia, PA; Reading Art Museum, Reading, PA.

**Marks:** Most pieces are impressed "Ironstone" and bear a registry mark.

Coffeepot, cov, 10" h, Strawberry pattern ................................................. 650.00
Compote, 8-1/4" d, 4" h, molded ironstone, floral designs, Gaudy floral dec, underglaze blue, red, green, and luster, minor wear and scratches ................................................. 360.00
Creamer and Sugar, 6-3/4" h, fruit finial, Blackberry pattern, underglaze blue, yellow, and orange enamel and luster, wear, small flakes, int. chip on sugar ................................................. 990.00
Cup and Saucer
Blackberry pattern, handleless, underglaze blue, yellow, and orange enamel and luster, imp label or registry mark with "E. Walley," price for set of ten ................................................. 1,375.00
Morning Glory pattern, underglaze blue, polychrome enamels ................................................. 170.00
Seeing Eye pattern ................................................. 180.00
Jug, 7-1/2" h, yellow, red, white, and blue tulips on sides, light blue pebble ground, luster trim, rim outlined ................................................. 350.00
Pitcher
8-1/2" h, Strawberry pattern. paneled ................................................. 1,045.00
11-3/4" h, Blackberry pattern, black, yellow, and orange enamel and luster, molded handle with branch and leaf design, unmarked, short hairline in foot, black areas have some iridescent ........ 425.00

Plate
6-1/4" d, Morning Glories and Strawberries pattern, underglaze blue, polychrome enamel and luster trim ................................................. 80.00
7-7/8" d, Urn pattern ................................................. 70.00
9-1/2" d, Blackberry pattern, underglaze blue, yellow, and orange enamel and luster, some wear, set of seven ................. 1,320.00
Platter, 13-3/8" l, Gaudy blue and white floral dec, scalloped border, molded fish scale and feather design, minor wear ............... 1,540.00
Soup Plate, 9-7/8" d, Blackberry pattern, underglaze blue, yellow, and orange enamel and luster, one imp "Elsmore & Forster, Tunstall," price for set of three ................................................. 650.00
Sugar Bowl, cov, 8-1/2" h, Strawberry pattern ........................... 425.00
Toddy Plate, 4-3/4" d, Urn pattern, underglaze blue, polychrome enamel and luster ................................................. 210.00
Vegetable, open, 8-3/4" d, Blackberry pattern, underglaze blue, yellow, and orange enamel and luster ................................................. 350.00

# GAUDY WELSH

**History:** Gaudy Welsh is a translucent porcelain that was originally made in the Swansea area of England from 1830 to 1845. Although the designs resemble Gaudy Dutch, the body texture and weight differ. One of the characteristics is the gold luster on top of the glaze.

In 1890, Allerton made a similar ware from heavier opaque porcelain.

**Museums:** Royal Institution of South Wales, Swansea Mills; St. Fagen's Welsh Folk Museum, Cardiff, Wales; Welsh National Museum, Cardiff, Wales.

**Marks:** Allerton pieces usually bear an export mark.

**References:** Susan and Al Bagdade, *Warman's English & Continental Pottery & Porcelain*, 3rd Edition, Krause Publications, 1998; John A. Shuman, III, *Collector's Encyclopedia of Gaudy Dutch and Welsh*, Collector Books, 1990, 1991 value update, out-of-print; Howard Y. Williams, *Gaudy Welsh China*, Wallace-Homestead, out-of-print.

**Collectors' Club:** Gaudy Collector's Society, P.O. Box 274, Gates Mills, OH 44040.

Columbine
Bowl, 10" d, 5-1/2" h, ftd, underglaze blue and polychrome enamel floral dec ................................................. 400.00
Plate, 5-1/2" d ................................................. 65.00
Tea Set, c1810, 17 pc set ................................................. 625.00
Daisy and Chain
Creamer ................................................. 175.00
Cup and Saucer ................................................. 95.00
Sugar, cov ................................................. 195.00
Teapot, cov ................................................. 225.00
Flower Basket
Bowl, 10-1/2" d ................................................. 190.00
Mug, 4" h ................................................. 90.00
Plate ................................................. 65.00
Sugar, cov, luster trim ................................................. 195.00
Grape
Bowl, 5-1/4" d ................................................. 50.00
Cup and Saucer ................................................. 75.00
Mug, 2-1/2" h ................................................. 65.00
Plate, 5-1/4" d ................................................. 65.00
Oyster
Bowl, 6" d ................................................. 80.00
Creamer, 3" h ................................................. 100.00
Cup and Saucer ................................................. 75.00
Jug, 5-3/4" h, c1820 ................................................. 85.00
Soup Plate, 10" d, flange rim ................................................. 85.00

Strawberry
  Creamer ........................................................... 90.00
  Cup and Saucer ............................................... 75.00
  Mug, 4-1/8" h ................................................. 125.00
  Plate, 8-1/4" d ............................................... 150.00
Tulip
  Bowl, 6-1/4" d .................................................. 50.00
  Cake Plate, 10" d, molded handles ................... 120.00
  Creamer, 5-1/4" h ............................................ 90.00
  Sugar, cov, 6-3/4" h ....................................... 110.00
  Teapot, 7-1/4" h ............................................. 175.00
Wagon Wheel
  Cup and Saucer ............................................... 75.00
  Mug, 2-1/2" h ................................................... 95.00
  Pitcher, 8-1/2" h ............................................. 195.00
  Plate, 8-3/4" d ................................................. 85.00
  Platter ............................................................. 125.00

# GIRANDOLES and MANTEL LUSTRES

**History:** A girandole is a very elaborate branched candleholder, often featuring cut glass prisms surrounding the mountings. A mantel lustre is a glass vase with attached cut glass prisms.

Girandoles and mantel lustres usually are found in pairs. It is not uncommon for girandoles to be part of a large garniture set. Girandoles and mantel lustres achieved their greatest popularity in the last half of the 19th century both in the United States and Europe.

## Girandoles

13" h, pink opaque, enameled dec, large prisms, price for pr ..... 475.00
16-3/4" h, three cast floral branches with candle sockets, cut glass prisms, man and woman on stem, white marble base, brass, good patina ................................................................. 165.00
17-3/4" h, 16-1/2" w, silver plated figures of Indians and frontiersmen with three candle sockets, white marble base, back sgd "Cornelius, Pat. Dec 1848," some prisms missing ...................................... 200.00
18-1/4" h, 15-1/4" h, gilt metal figural centerpiece depicting capture of Major Andre, flanked by eagle, flag, shield, and arms, embellished with grapevines and crystal prisms, stepped marble bases, some prisms missing, chips on marble edges, America, mid-19th C, price for three pc set .......................................................... 690.00

**Frosted pink, enameled floral dec, orig prisms, 10-1/2" h, $170. Photo courtesy of Joy Luke Fine Art Brokers and Auctioneers.**

## Mantel Garnitures

10-1/4" h, urn form, two short scroll handles, incised on side side with Japonesque florals in silver and gold coloration, trumpet foot further dec with Japonesque patterning and insects, sq section marble base, inset to front with mixed metal-style patinated plaque depicting drummer and dancer, Aesthetic Movement, third quarter 19th C, price for pr ..... 690.00
14" h, 12" h, three cov baluster jars and two vases, Hundred Antiques dec, in famille rosé enamels, China, 19th C, price for five pc set .................................................... 2,185.00
20-5/8" h, bronze and crystal, three-light candelabra, stylized lyre form garniture hung with cut and pressed glass prisms, above three scrolled candlearms, trefoil base, price for pr ......................... 980.00

## Mantel Lusters

12" h, ruby glass, overlay and enameled plaques, fluted, heavy gilt, cut glass prisms, France, 19th C, price for pr ........................... 2,645.00
13" h, overlay glass, white cut to green, enamel flowers, gilt accents, cut glass prisms, Bohemian, mounted as lamp, 19th C, .......... 290.00

# GOLDSCHEIDER

**History:** Friedrich Goldscheider founded a porcelain and faience factory in Vienna, Austria, in 1885. Upon his death, his widow carried on operations. In 1920, Walter and Marcell, Friedrich's sons, gained control. During the Art Deco period, the firm commissioned several artists to create figural statues, among which were Pierrettes and sleek wolfhounds. During the 1930s, the company's products were mostly traditional.

In the early 1940s, the Goldscheiders fled to the United States and re-established operations in Trenton, New Jersey. The Goldscheider Everlast Corporation was listed in Trenton City directories between 1943 and 1950. Goldscheider Ceramics, located at 1441 Heath Ave., Trenton, New Jersey, was listed in the *1952 Crockery and Glass Journal Directory* but was not listed in 1954.

**Reference:** Susan and Al Bagdade, *Warman's English & Continental Pottery & Porcelain*, 3rd Edition, Krause Publications, 1998.

Bust, 8-1/4" h, Indian Prince, turban, teal shirt ........................... 110.00
Charger, 18-1/2" d, earthenware, riverscape scenes with cottages, one sgd "A. Keller," other sgd "A. Wagner," pr ............................. 1,200.00
Figure
  4" h, hummingbird, teal, purple, light green, black beak, green leaves, mkd "Goldscheider Everlast Corp., USA Fine China, #1124" ..................................................................... 165.00
  7" h, Oriental couple, lady with green komona with rose colored flowers, gentleman in green costume, price for pr ........... 120.00
  15" h, 11" w, 8-1/5" d, dancing minstrel twins .................. 7,500.00
  14" x 11-1/2" x 8", girl stooping down to pick up large basket, Austro-Hungary seal, initialed "HIG," stamped number, crack in base ......................................................................... 1,350.00
  14" x 11" x 10", seated Gypsy dancer, resting feet on pillow, sgd "Kostral," incised number, 1923, small chip .................. 1,850.00
  16" x 10-1/2" x 7", lady with borzoi, mkd, few chips ......... 3,500.00
  18" x 14" x 6-1/2", Europa, black glaze mark with faint traces of logo, also sgd "Schmidt & Kestner," incised number ..... 4,500.00
  18" x 13" x 7", Laurenzl, blue floral harem outfit, logo and stamped "Goldscheider Wein," incised number, dated 1923 ............ 4,000.00
  19" h, 16" w, 6-1/2" d, girl with arms extended, holding out cape, blue dress and cape, sgd "Lorenzl," stamp mark .......... 4,750.00
  21" x 17" x 11", three dancing young ladies, paper label, sgd "Podany," initialed "D. L.," incised number ................... 4,500.00

Dancer, Dakon, artist sgd, mkd "7195/374/2," 14-1/2" h, $1,450.

Lamp Base, 18" x 10" x 7", two figures dressed as Pierot, white costumes, trying to light cigarettes, pre WWI mark, artist initials, incised number ...................................................................... 3,500.00

Plaque, 13-1/2" w, 25-1/8" h, earthenware, rect, molded, maiden in profile, garland of blossoms and berries in hair, large blossom and cluster on left, earth tones, designer sgd "Lamassi," Goldschneider mark, c1900 ........................................................................ 1,200.00

Vase, 8-7/8" h, thistle form, stylized leaf and heart motifs, blue and white glazes, black ground with orange banding ..................... 500.00

Wall Mask, 7-1/4" h, woman's face, dark brown hair, red lips, light beige face ................................................................................ 295.00

# GONDER POTTERY

**History:** Lawton Gonder established Gonder Ceramic Arts, Inc., at Zanesville, Ohio, in 1941. He had gained experience while working for other factories in the area. Gonder experimented with glazes, including Chinese crackle, gold crackle, and flambé. Lamp bases were manufactured under the name "Eglee" at a second plant location.

The company ceased operation in 1957.

**Marks:** Pieces are clearly marked with the word "Gonder" in various forms.

**References:** Susan and Al Bagdade, *Warman's American Pottery and Porcelain*, 2nd ed., Krause Publications, 2000; Ron Hoppes, *Collector's Guide and History of Gonder Pottery*, L-W Book Sales, 1992.

**Collectors' Club:** Gonder Collectors Club, 917 Hurl Drive, Pittsburgh, PA 15236.

Basket, pale aqua body, peach floral dec ..................................... 24.00
Bowl, 8" d, gray, pink int., mkd "H-29" ......................................... 32.00
Bulb Bowl, 8-1/4" d, 3" h, melon ribbed, pale blue ext., pink int., imp "H-29 USA" ................................................................................ 45.00
Candlesticks, pr, 5" h, cornucopia shape, light gray, pink highlights, mkd "Gonder USA 552" ............................................................. 32.00
Console Bowl, 15-1/2" l, 4-3/4" w, 7" h, Art Deco, mkd "557" ..... 165.00

Mark from base of vase.

Cornucopia, 9" h, shaded green, brown, and pink, mkd "Gonder USA H14" ....................................................................................... 60.00
Ewer, 8" h, shaped angular handle, pink, gray, and purple glaze, mkd "H-73" .................................................................................... 75.00
Figure, 12-1/2" h, 7" w, Chinese woman, hands on hips, silver label, mkd "765" on bottom .............................................................. 45.00
Pitcher, twist body, crimson, mkd "Gonder" ................................ 65.00
Planter, dolphin-type dec on sides, mkd "Gonder 556" ................ 65.00
Sculpture, 11" h, 12" w, 8-1/2" d, Chinese man bust, celadon green glaze, mkd "541" .................................................................... 500.00
Swan, 5-1/2" h, 5" l, 4" w, mother-of-pearl luster, light blue highlights, coral pink int., mkd "Gonder USA E-44" ................................. 35.00
Urn, handles, gray, pink int., paper label on side, incised "H-49" .. 48.00
Valse
    6" h, flared baluster, yellow, mkd "Gonder E-68" ................. 25.00
    6" h, inverted baluster, mustard yellow and green-brown, mauve int., mkd "E-64, Gonder, USA" ........................................ 20.00
    7" h, light gray shading to pink, darker pink int., mkd "Gonder E-5" ................................................................................. 30.00
    8" h, shoulder handles, stylized rim, mottled peach and aqua blue, solid peach int., incised "Gonder USA," c1941-55 .... 45.00
    9" h, lavender, mkd "H-67" ................................................. 30.00
    12" h, 10" w, feather, pale blue, pink int., mkd ..................... 95.00

# GOOFUS GLASS

**History:** Goofus glass, also known as Mexican ware, hooligan glass, and pickle glass, is a pressed glass with relief designs that were painted either on the back or front. The designs are usually in red and green with a metallic gold ground. It was popular from 1890 to 1920 and was used as a premium at carnivals.

It was produced by several companies: Crescent Glass Company, Wellsburg, West Virginia; Imperial Glass Corporation, Bellaire, Ohio; LaBelle Glass Works, Bridgeport, Ohio; and Northwood Glass Co., Indiana, Pennsylvania, Wheeling, West Virginia, and Bridgeport, Ohio.

Goofus glass lost its popularity when people found that the paint tarnished or scaled off after repeated washings and wear. No record of its manufacture has been found after 1920.

**Marks:** Goofus glass made by Northwood includes one of the following marks: "N," "N" in one circle, "N" in two circles, or one or two circles without the "N."

**Periodical:** *Goofus Glass Gazette*, 9 Lindenwood Ct, Sterling, VA 20165.

Ashtray, red rose dec, emb adv ..................................................... 15.00
Basket, 5" h, strawberry dec ......................................................... 50.00
Bon Bon, 4" d, Strawberry pattern, gold, red, and green dec ....... 40.00
Bowl
    6-1/2" d, Grape and Lattice pattern, red grapes, gold ground,
       ruffled rim ........................................................................... 45.00
    7" d, Iris pattern, gold and red dec ........................................ 35.00
    7" d, thistle and scrolling leaves, red dec, gold ground, ruffled
       rim ....................................................................................... 35.00
    8" d, 3-3/4" h, scalloped edge, gold leaves, cranberry flashed
       flowers ................................................................................ 75.00
    9" d, 3" h, Narcissus, Indiana Glass, c1915-30, some paint
       loss ..................................................................................... 35.00
    10-1/2" d, 2-1/2" h, Cherries, gold leaves, red cherries ........ 35.00
Bread Plate, 7" w, 11" l, Last Supper pattern, red and gold, grapes and
    foliage border ........................................................................... 65.00
Candy Dish, 8-1/2" d, figure eight design, serrated rim, dome foot .... 60.00
Coaster, 3" d, red floral dec, gold ground ..................................... 12.00
Compote
    4" d, Grape and Cable pattern ............................................... 35.00
    6" d, Strawberry pattern, red and green strawberries and foliage,
       ruffled ................................................................................. 40.00
    6-1/2" d, Poppy pattern, red flowers, gold foliage, green ground,
       sgd "Northwood" ................................................................. 40.00
    9-1/2" d, red and green floral and foliage dec, green ground, crimped
       and fluted rim, pedestal foot, sgd "Northwood" ...................... 40.00
Decanter, orig stopper, La Belle Rose ........................................... 50.00
Dresser Tray, 6" l, Cabbage Rose pattern, red roses dec, gold foliage,
    clear ground ............................................................................. 35.00
Jar, cov, butterflies, red and gold ................................................. 35.00
Jewel Box, 4" d, 2" h, basketweave, rose dec .............................. 50.00
Mug, Cabbage Rose pattern, gold ground ..................................... 35.00
Nappy, 6-1/2" d, Cherries pattern, red cherries, gold foliage, clear
    ground ...................................................................................... 35.00
Perfume Bottle, 3-1/2" h, pink tulips dec ....................................... 20.00
Pickle Jar, aqua, molded, gold, blue, and red painted floral design .... 50.00
Pin Dish, 6-1/2" l, oval, red and black florals ................................ 20.00
Plate
    6"d, Rose and Lattice pattern, relief molded ......................... 20.00
    6" d, Sunflower pattern, red dec center, relief molded .......... 20.00
    7-3/4" d, Carnations pattern, red carnations, gold ground .... 20.00
    10-1/2" d, grapes dec, gold ground, irid pink edge .............. 35.00
    11" d, Cherries, some paint worn off ..................................... 35.00
    11" d, Dahlia pattern, red and gold ....................................... 40.00
Platter, 18" l, red rose dec, gold ground ....................................... 65.00
Powder Jar, cov
    3" d, puffy, rose dec, red and gold ........................................ 40.00
    4-1/2" d, Cabbage Rose pattern, white cabbage rose, relief
       molded ................................................................................ 35.00
Salt and Pepper Shakers, pr, Grape and Leaf pattern .................. 45.00
Syrup, relief molded, red roses dec, lattice work ground, orig top 85.00
Toothpick Holder, red rose and foliage dec, gold ground ............. 40.00
Tray, 8-1/4" d, 11" d, red chrysanthemum dec, gold ground ........ 45.00
Tumbler, 6" h, red rose dec, gold ground ...................................... 35.00
Vase
    6" h, Cabbage Rose pattern, red dec, gold ground .............. 45.00
    6-1/2" h, Grape and Rose pattern, red and gold dec, crackle glass
       ground ................................................................................. 35.00
    9" h, Poppies pattern, blue and red dec, gold ground ........... 45.00
    10-1/2" h, Peacock pattern ................................................... 75.00

# GOUDA POTTERY

**History:** Gouda and the surrounding areas of Holland have been principal Dutch pottery centers for centuries. Originally, the potteries produced a simple utilitarian tin-glazed Delft-type earthenware and the famous clay smoker's pipes.

MADE IN

Zuid Holland

Gouda potteries turned to art pottery. Influenced by the Art Nouveau and Art Deco movements, artists expressed themselves with free-form and stylized designs in bold colors.

**References:** Susan and Al Bagdade, *Warman's English & Continental Pottery & Porcelain*, 3rd Edition, Krause Publications, 1998; Phyllis T. Ritvo, *The World of Gouda Pottery,* Font & Center Press, 1998.

**Periodical:** *Dutch Potter*, 47 London Terrace, New Rochelle, NY 10804.

Biscuit Jar, cov, 8" h, multicolored ................................................ 135.00
Bowl
    5-1/2" d, 3-1/2" h, Damascus mark ...................................... 60.00
    11-1/2" l, 4-1/2" w, 4-1/4" h, stylized floral black, yellow, orange
       and teal design ................................................................... 265.00
    Candlestick
    3" h, 6-1/2" d, circular, handle, matte green, yellow, blue, and
       cream dec, marked "0139 DAM II Holland," c1885 .......... 100.00
    3-3/4" h, green, rust, cobalt blue, ochre, marked "Candis 1137"
       and house mark ................................................................... 55.00
Clock Garniture, 20-1/2" h clock, 16-3/4" h pr candlesticks, circular clock mouth with painted ceramic face supported by four ceramic arms on baluster shaped body and flared base, candlesticks of similar form, all dec with Art Nouveau style flowers, glossy glaze pink, purple, blue, green, and tan, sgd "Zuid Holland" and imp house and "R" on base, repairs to candlesticks ..................................... 2,875.00
Charger, 12" d, multicolored flowers, rope border, black trim ..... 150.00
Compote, 7-5/8", black ground, geometric design, multicolored scroll int. ............................................................................................. 175.00
Ewer, 7-3/4" h, flared rim, extended neck over oval body, bands of stylized leaves and wavy dotted lines, yellow, blue, green, orange, and gray, blue painted marks ............................................................. 130.00
Incense Burner, 8" h, Roba, flowers and geometric designs, green ground ....................................................................................... 110.00
Jug, 10" h, multicolored dec, black matte ground, orig stopper .. 195.00
Match Holder, striker on bottom, mkd "Regina Holland" ............... 45.00
Pitcher
    6-1/4" h, 3-1/4" w, Peggy .................................................... 100.00
    9-3/8" h, 9-1/8" w, Rosalie .................................................. 200.00
    13-1/2" h, 9" w, Sammy, floral dec ..................................... 325.00
Plate, 10-1/2" d, matte multicolored dec ..................................... 100.00
Tobacco Jar, cov, 5" h, Verona pattern ......................................... 100.00
Tumbler, 4-3/8" h, 3-5/8" d, multicolored flowers, green leaves, black ground, satin finish, marked "Neri" and house mark ................. 65.00

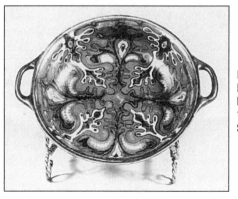

**Bowl, two small handles, red, blue, green, gold, 10-1/4" d, 2" h, $140.**

Vase

    5-1/2" h, 5" w, bright florals ....................................75.00
    7-3/4" h, raised rim, oval body tapering to base, central band with
        upside down stylized tulip blossoms in blue, green, and cream,
        green ground, painted marks include "Holland 091/1 R"..175.00
    8-1/2" h, raised rim, bulbed neck over oval body, stylized leaves
        and diamond motif, blue painted marks ...........................100.00

# GRANITEWARE

**History:** Graniteware is the name commonly given to enamel-coated iron or steel kitchenware.

The first graniteware was made in Germany in the 1830s. Graniteware was not produced in the United States until the 1860s. At the start of World War I, when European companies turned to manufacturing war weapons, American producers took over the market.

Gray and white were the most common graniteware colors, although each company made its own special color in shades of blue, green, brown, violet, cream, or red.

Older graniteware is heavier than the new. Pieces with cast-iron handles date between 1870 to 1890; wood handles between 1900 to 1910. Other dating clues are seams, wooden knobs, and tin lids.

**References:** Helen Greguire, *Collector's Encyclopedia of Granite Ware: Colors Shapes and Values*, Book 1 (1990, 1994 value update), Book 2 (1993, 2000 value update), Collector Books; David T. Pikul and Ellen M. Plante, *Collectible Enameled Ware: American & European,* Schiffer Publishing, 1998.

**Collectors' Club:** National Graniteware Society, P.O. Box 10013, Cedar Rapids, IA 52410.

**Reproduction Alert:** Graniteware still is manufactured in many of the traditional forms and colors.

**Additional Listings:** See *Warman's Americana & Collectibles* for more examples.

Bacon Platter, blue and white swirl .............................. 115.00
Baking Pan, 11-1/2" l, gray mottled, wire handle ..........................25.00
Basin, 9-1/2" d, blue and white swirl ..............................75.00
Berry Bucket, cov, brown and white swirl, tin lid, bail handle......120.00
Bowl, 9" d, marble blue and white, some rust on edges, used condition ................................................................55.00
Bread Dough Riser, cov, gray mottled .........................100.00
Bread Pan, robin's egg blue, 9" l.............................35.00
Bucket, 8-1/2" d, 10" h, white, red rim trim, orig red wooden handle, small Mendit repair on base ..........................45.00
Butter Churn, blue and white swirl, orig lid................950.00
Cake Carrier, white with blue trim, orig clasp and hinge, several enamel chips, used condition .....................................50.00
Cake Pan, 10" x 14", blue and white swirl, molded handles .......150.00
Candleholder, cobalt blue and white, medium spatter .................90.00
Canning Kettle, cov, 11-1/2" h, 14-1/2" w, gray, orig jar rack, some rusting to lid.................................................145.00
Coffee Boiler
    9" d, 10-3/4" h, brown, white swirl, 1940s, used condition....45.00
    11" d, 14-1/2" h, gray speckled body, tin lid, bail handle, small chips, slight rust on lid.......................................165.00
Coffeepot
    10" h, green, chip on spout ..................................75.00
    13" x 12-1/2", teal green and white, wood knob on lid, some wear on edge and lid........................................500.00
Colander, ftd, blue and white mottled...........................80.00
Cream Can, 6-1/4" h, black and white mottled body, lid painted black .............................................................225.00

**Lunch Pail, cov, oval, pressed tin bail, 8" l, 6-3/4" h, $120.**

Creamer, multicolored dec.......................................325.00
Dipper, gray mottled...............................................25.00
Double Boiler, cov, yellow and black...........................200.00
Dutch Oven, 7" h, yellow and black, used condition ...................60.00
Egg Poacher, 4-1/4" d, 3" h, red ext., blue and white insert........110.00
Fold Mold, 12-1/4" l, 8-3/4" w, mkd "Graniteware Cream City Ware, Milwaukee, G & P & F"..............................................50.00
Frying Pan, brown and white swirl ..............................80.00
Funnel, gray spatter ...............................................18.00
Grater, cream and green, flat .................................100.00
Ladle, 12" l, gray mottled .........................................20.00
Lunch Bucket, 5-1/2" h, English
    Brown and white, tray insert missing .................................85.00
    Green, white, and yellow, light wear around lid, tray insert missing ......................................................70.00
Measure, pitcher shape, gray, darker gray speckles, applied spout and handle, small pinpoint hole in bottom......................115.00
Milk Pan, 11" d, gray mottled ....................................40.00
Milk Pitcher, large blue and white swirls ....................190.00
Muffin Pan, 8 cup, brown and white swirl.....................140.00
Mug, blue and white swirl.........................................90.00
Pan, 13-1/2" l, 11" w, red and white marble ...........................500.00
Pie Pan, 9-3/4" d, blue and white..................................35.00
Pitcher, 14-1/2" h, 7-1/2" d, dark blue mottle, slight rust around mouth.............................................................200.00
Plate
    8" d, blue-gray speckled ........................................15.00
    10" d, gray mottled..............................................20.00
Roaster, cov, tan, green trim, large ...........................180.00
Salt Box, cream and red .........................................125.00
Spittoon, red and white swirl....................................160.00
Sugar Bowl, tin cover, gray mottled, mkd "L & G Mfg. Co." ........325.00
Teapot, 9-1/2" h, green crystallite, some chips on base, lid detached .............................................................525.00
Tea Strainer, blue, star perforations...........................70.00
Wash Board, dark blue insert, mkd "Enamel King" .......................65.00

# GREENAWAY, KATE

**History:** Kate Greenaway, or "K.G." as she initialed her famous drawings, was born in 1846 in London. Her father was a prominent wood engraver. Kate's natural talent for drawing soon was evident, and she began art classes at the age of 12. In 1868, she had her first public exhibition.

Her talents were used primarily in illustrating. The cards she decorated for Marcus Ward are largely unsigned. China and pottery companies soon had her

Toothpick Holder, seated girl, brown hat, gray dress, yellow-green floral holder, imp "#10257," 5-1/8" h, $85.

drawings of children appearing on many of their wares. By the 1880s, she was one of the foremost children's book illustrators in England.

**Reference:** Ina Taylor, *Art of Kate Greenaway: A Nostalgic Portrait of Childhood*, Pelican Publishing, 1991.

**Collectors' Club:** Kate Greenaway Society, P.O. Box 8, Norwood, PA 19074.

**Reproduction Alert:** Some Greenaway buttons have been reproduced in Europe and sold in the United States.

Bowl, 8-1/2" h, 3-1/4" h, mottled opaque white glass on clear ground, painted and enameled three young children standing in garden, enamel spray of pink daisies on reverse, cut edge, brass-plated stand ................. 300.00
Box, cov, three girls sitting atop log ........................... 200.00
Calling Card Holder, 6-1/4" w, 6" h, little girl holding puppy standing next to pedestal stem, silver plate, mkd "Rogers" ................... 300.00
Children's Book
    *All Alone House*, Ruth Campbell, 1923 ............................. 60.00
    *That Pink and Blue Affair*, Ruth Campbell, 1923 ................. 60.00
Children's Feeding Dish, nursery rhyme dec with children and dog, Haviland ................................................................. 100.00
Children's Play Dishes, tea set, children and dachshund pulling tablecloth, price for 7 pc set .......................................... 150.00
Cup and Saucer, 4" cup, 7-1/2" d saucer, Victorian girl in garden scene, standing by fence, holding nosegay, feathers, bows, and streamers on bonnet, mkd "Germany" .................................. 175.00
Figure, 9-1/2" h, children jumping rope, price for pr ................... 600.00
Match Holder, girl helping little girl over log, place for matches and striker .................................................................. 100.00
Nodder, bisque, elderly couple, wearing eyeglasses, cloak, bonnet, and high hat .............................................................. 135.00
Plate, 9" d, children playing, oversized fruit, birds, and flowers .. 100.00
Print, Don't Push, c1900, matted and framed ............................. 25.00
Salt and Pepper Shakers, pr, 2-3/4" h, little girls in white dresses, mkd "Germany" ........................................................... 115.00
Sugar Shaker, boy in long coat, white ground ............................. 95.00
Thimble Holder, girl holding sterling silver thimble ..................... 125.00
Tile, Pipe Thee High, scene with small boy and horn, Wedgwood 85.00
Vase, 4" h, figural girl, holder with orig frosted dec bud vase, sq ornate ftd base, marked "Tufts" ............................................. 150.00

# GREENTOWN GLASS

**History:** The Indiana Tumbler and Goblet Co., Greentown, Indiana, produced its first clear, pressed glass table and bar wares in late 1894. Initial success led to a doubling of the plant size in 1895 and other subsequent expansions, one in 1897 to allow for the manufacture of colored glass. In 1899 the firm joined the combine known as the National Glass Company.

In 1900, just before arriving in Greentown, Jacob Rosenthal developed an opaque brown glass, called "chocolate," which ranged in color from a dark, rich chocolate to a lighter coffee-with-cream hue. Production of chocolate glass saved the financially pressed Indiana Tumbler and Goblet Works. The Cactus and Leaf Bracket patterns were made almost exclusively in chocolate glass. Other popular chocolate patterns include Austrian, Dewey, Shuttle, and Teardrop and Tassel. In 1902, National Glass Company bought Rosenthal's chocolate glass formula so other plants in the combine could use the color.

In 1902, Rosenthal developed the Golden Agate and Rose Agate colors. All work ceased on June 13, 1903, when a fire of suspicious origin destroyed the Indiana Tumbler and Goblet Company Works.

After the fire, other companies, e.g., McKee and Brothers, produced chocolate glass in the same pattern designs used by Greentown. Later reproductions also have been made, with Cactus among the most-heavily copied patterns.

**Reference:** James Measell, *Greentown Glass*, Grand Rapids Public Museum, 1979, 1992-93 value update, distributed by Antique Publications.

**Collectors' Clubs:** Collectors of Findlay Glass, P.O. Box 256, Findlay, OH 45839; National Greentown Glass Association, P.O. Box 107, Greentown, IN 46936.

**Videotape:** *Centennial Exhibit of Greentown Glass* and *Reproductions of Greentown Glass*, National Greentown Glass Association, P.O. Box 107, Greentown, IN 46936.

**Museums:** Grand Rapids Public Museum, Ruth Herrick Greentown Glass Collection, Grand Rapids, MI; Greentown Glass Museum, Greentown, IN.

**Additional Listings:** Holly Amber; Pattern Glass.

**Reproduction Alert.**

Animal Covered dish
    Bird with Berry, blue ............................................. 475.00
    Cat, hamper base, amber ......................................... 465.00
    Hen on Nest, chocolate ........................................... 725.00
    Robin, nest base, opaque white ................................. 225.00
Berry Set, Leaf Bracket, chocolate, 7 pcs .......................... 275.00
Bowl
    Cactus, 6-1/4" d, chocolate ..................................... 120.00
    Geneva, 10-1/4" d, chocolate ................................... 465.00
Butter, cov
    Cactus, chocolate ................................................ 300.00
    Daisy, opaque white .............................................. 100.00

**Butter Dish, Cactus pattern, chocolate, 7-1/2" d, 5-1/4" h, $300.**

| | |
|---|---:|
| Herringbone Buttress, green | 250.00 |
| Leaf Bracket, chocolate | 250.00 |
| Oval Lattice, colorless | 75.00 |
| Shuttle, chocolate | 1,100.00 |
| Compote, Geneva, 4-1/2" d, 3-1/2" h, chocolate | 150.00 |

Cordial
| | |
|---|---:|
| Austrian, canary | 125.00 |
| Overall Lattice, colorless | 45.00 |
| Shuttle, colorless | 45.00 |

Creamer
| | |
|---|---:|
| Austrian, colorless | 40.00 |
| Cactus, chocolate | 125.00 |
| Cord Drapery, colorless | 65.00 |
| Cupid, Nile green | 400.00 |
| Indian Head, opaque white | 450.00 |
| Indoor Drinking Scene, chocolate, 5-1/2" h | 500.00 |
| Shuttle, colorless, tankard style | 65.00 |

Cruet, orig stopper
| | |
|---|---:|
| Cactus, chocolate | 325.00 |
| Chrysanthemum Leaf, chocolate | 1,275.00 |
| Dewey, vaseline | 300.00 |
| Geneva, chocolate | 1,000.00 |
| Dish, Dolphin, chocolate, sawtooth | 200.00 |
| Dresser Tray, Wild Rose and Bowknot, chocolate | 350.00 |

Goblet
| | |
|---|---:|
| Beehive, colorless | 65.00 |
| Diamond Prisms, colorless | 70.00 |

Jelly Compote
| | |
|---|---:|
| Cactus, chocolate | 200.00 |
| Pleat Band, chocolate | 130.00 |
| Lemonade Tumbler, Cactus, chocolate | 100.00 |

Mug
| | |
|---|---:|
| Elf, green | 115.00 |
| Herringbone Buttress, chocolate | 80.00 |
| Serenade, colorless | 75.00 |
| Troubadour, 6-1/2" h, opaque white, cov | 70.00 |
| Nappy, Leaf Bracket, chocolate, triangular | 85.00 |

Pitcher, water
| | |
|---|---:|
| Cord Drapery, colorless | 95.00 |
| Fleur De Lis, colorless | 265.00 |
| Racing Deer and Doe, colorless | 200.00 |
| Ruffled Eye, chocolate | 550.00 |
| Squirrel, colorless | 200.00 |
| Teardrop and Tassel, cobalt blue | 200.00 |
| Punch Cup, Shuttle, colorless | 18.00 |
| Relish, Cord Drapery, amber | 110.00 |
| Rose Bowl, Austrian, colorless | 45.00 |
| Salt, wheelbarrow shape, Nile green | 350.00 |

Sauce
| | |
|---|---:|
| Cactus, chocolate, ftd | 65.00 |
| Leaf Bracket, chocolate | 50.00 |
| Water Lily and Cattails, chocolate | 100.00 |
| Wild Rose and Bowknot, chocolate | 95.00 |

Spooner
| | |
|---|---:|
| Austrian, colorless | 65.00 |
| Cactus, chocolate | 80.00 |
| Cupid, colorless | 145.00 |
| Wild Rose and Bowknot, chocolate | 150.00 |
| Stein, Serenade, colorless | 50.00 |
| Sugar, cov, Cupid, opaque white | 115.00 |
| Syrup, Cord Drapery, chocolate | 350.00 |

Tumbler
| | |
|---|---:|
| Cord Drapery, chocolate | 250.00 |
| Geneva, chocolate | 115.00 |
| Icicle, chocolate | 150.00 |
| Teardrop and Tassel, blue | 65.00 |
| Wildflower, amber | 48.00 |
| Wine, Shuttle, colorless | 25.00 |

# GRUEBY POTTERY

**History:** William Grueby was active in the ceramic industry for several years before he developed his own method of producing matte-glazed pottery and founded the Grueby Faience Company in Boston, Massachusetts, in 1897.

The art pottery was hand thrown in natural shapes, hand molded, and hand tooled. A variety of colored glazes, singly or in combinations, were produced, but green was the most popular. In 1908, the firm was divided into the Grueby Pottery Company and the Grueby Faience and Tile Co. The Grueby Faience and Tile Company made art tile until 1917, although its pottery production was phased out about 1910.

Minor damage is acceptable to most collectors of Grueby Pottery.

**References:** Paul Evans, *Art Pottery of the United States*, 2nd ed., Feingold & Lewis Publishing, 1987; Ralph and Terry Kovel, *Kovels' American Art Pottery*, Crown Publishers, 1993; Susan Montgomery, *The Ceramics of William H. Grueby,* Arts and Crafts Quarterly Press, 1993; David Rago, *American Art Pottery,* Knickerbocker Press, 1997.

**Advisor:** David Rago.

Fountain and Architectural Tiles, tiles with medieval motifs designed by Addison B. Le Boutiller, 6" sq low relief and glazed designs
| | |
|---|---:|
| 45" x 31", 23" l, 17" d, 7-7/8" h petal form fountain with matte yellow glaze, 11 Monk with Book, 9 Monk with Cello, 22 4" sq with matte brown glaze, some imp "G34" on side, c1915, chips | 6,900.00 |
| 55" x 48" total, 23" l, 17" d, 7-7/8" h petal form fountain with matte yellow glaze, 15 Cupid with Cymbals, 24 Cupid with Cornucopia, 3 Eros, 5 Mermaids, red clay with matte yellow glaze, some tiles imp "Grueby Boston," c1915, chips | 13,800.00 |

Scarab Paperweight
| | |
|---|---:|
| 3" l, 2" w, matte ochre glaze, Grueby Faience stamp and paper label | 650.00 |
| 3-3/4" l, 2-3/4" w, matte green-brown glaze, Grueby Faience stamp, small glaze flake on front | 650.00 |
| 4" l, 2-3/4" w, matte blue-gray glaze, Grueby Faience stamp | 500.00 |
| 4" l, 2-3/4" w, matte green glaze, imp pottery mark, partial paper label | 635.00 |
| 4" l, 2-3/4" w, matte mustard glaze, Grueby Faience stamp and paper label, glaze flake to bottom | 600.00 |

**Vessel, squatty, tooled broad leaves, leathery matte green glaze, by Wilhelmina Post, circular pottery mark, incised "155," few minute flecks to edges of leaves, 5-3/4" h, 6-1/2" d, $10,350. Photo courtesy of David Rago Auctions.**

Tile

4" w, sq, dec in cuenca, stag underneath tree, browns, green, and blue, unmarked, new Arts & Crafts style frame ................ 950.00

6" w, sq, dec in cuenca, cherub with cornucopia in matte oatmeal glaze, gray-blue ground, illegible imp number on side, design by Addison Le Boutiller, glaze bursts, minor edge chips ....... 290.00

6" w, sq, dec in cuenca, rabbit in cabbage patch, green and blue, initialed by artist, new Arts & Crafts style frame ............ 3,000.00

6" w, sq terra cotta tiles, dec in cuenca, Celtic woven quatraform pattern in matte light blue, dark blue ground, imp "697" on side, minor edge chips, price for pr ........................................... 690.00

6" w, sq terra cotta tiles, dec in cuenca, knight in matte gray-blue, creamy yellow ground, imp "655" on side ........................ 550.00

6" h, 4-1/2" w, rect, dec in cuenca, chamberstick and yellow candle and "Grueby Tile," initialed by artist, new Arts & Crafts frame ....................................................................... 4,000.00

8" w, sq terra cotta tiles, dec in cuenca, three-masted ship on water, matte glazes in brown, mustard, cream, and green, light blue ground, imp "82" on side ......................................... 690.00

8-1/4" w, sq terra cotta, dec in cuenca, kneeling angel, matte oatmeal glaze, gray-blue ground, imp "33" on side, design by Addison Le Boutiller, crack ....................................................... 460.00

Vase

6-1/4" h, 5" d, bulbous, collared and ribbed rim, speckled blue-gray matte glaze, Grueby Pottery stamp, touch-up to rim nick ..... 800.00

7" h, 3" d, thick matte oatmeal glaze, Grueby Faience stamp ............................................................................... 850.00

7-1/4" h, 4-1/2" d, bulbous, tooled broad leaves, matte green glaze, Ellen Farmington, Grueby Faience stamp, mkd "ERF," minor nick to one leaf edge .......................................... 2,600.00

7-1/4" h, 4-3/4" d, bulbous, applied leaves alternating with buds, leathery matte green glaze, stamped circular Faience mark/LEM, several minor flecks to leaves .................... 2,500.00

8" h, flared rim tapering to bulbous base, repeating raised bud on long flower stem and leaves, matte green glaze, imp "Grueby Faience Co., Boston, USA" and "22," glaze hairlines near base ................................................................. 3,165.00

Vessel, 7-1/4" h, 7-3/4" d, bulbous, tooled and applied leaves, leathery matte green glaze, "Grueby Pottery stamp/WP/6/8," restoration to rim, touch-ups to leaf edges ......................................... 2,50

# HAIR ORNAMENTS

**History:** Hair ornaments, among the first accessories developed by primitive man, were used to remove tangles and keep hair out of one's face. Remnants of early combs have been found in many archaeological excavations.

As fashion styles evolved through the centuries, hair ornaments kept pace with changes in design and usage. Hair combs and other hair ornaments are made in a wide variety of materials, e.g., precious metals, ivory, tortoiseshell, plastics, and wood.

Combs were first made in America during the Revolution when imports from England were restricted. Early American combs were made of horn and treasured as toiletry articles.

**References:** Mary Bachman, *Collector's Guide to Hair Combs, Identification and Values,* Collector Books, 1998; Evelyn Haetig, *Antique Combs and Purses*, Gallery Graphics Press, 1983.

**Collectors' Club:** Antique Comb Collectors Club International, 8712 Pleasant View Road, Bangor, PA 18013; Antique Fancy Comb Collectors Club, 3291 N. River Rd, Libertyville, IL 60048; National Antique Comb Collectors Club, 3748 Sunray Dr., Holiday, FL 34691.

**Museums:** Leominster Historical Society, Field School Museum, Leominster, MA; Miller's Museum of Antique Combs, Homer, AK.

Back Comb
　Bakelite, coral and gold-wash filigree, c1890 ..................... 290.00
　Imitation goldstone, green stone, Victorian style, c1900 ..... 150.00
Barrette, Edwardian, 119 rose-cut diamonds, silver topped gold mount, French hallmark and assay marks ........................................ 1,150.00
Clip, rhinestone dec, c1930, pr ...................................................... 40.00
Comb
　Tortoiseshell, wide plain top .................................................... 30.00
　Tortoiseshell, set four graduated combs with 14kt yellow gold beaded dec ............................................................................ 40.00
Hairpin
　Silver, butterfly shape, celadon green jade wings, 7" l, Sung Dynasty ................................................................................... 200.00
　Staghorn, hand with insect on wrist, 19th C ......................... 80.00
　Tortoiseshell, openwork naturalistic carving ......................... 45.00
Headband, 14K yellow gold, double band, engraved scroll and leaf dec, Edwardian, matching gold hairpins .................................. 275.00
Ornament, Art Nouveau, tortoiseshell, c1910 .............................. 90.00

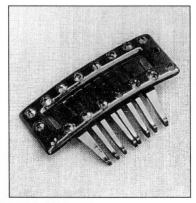

**Comb, red plastic, 18 red rhinestones, 1-1/4" l, $12.**

# HALL CHINA COMPANY

**History:** Robert Hall founded the Hall China Company in 1903 in East Liverpool, Ohio. He died in 1904 and was succeeded by his son, Robert Taggart Hall. After years of experimentation, Robert T. Hall developed a leadless glaze in 1911, opening the way for production of glazed household products.

The Hall China Company made many types of kitchenware, refrigerator sets, and dinnerware in a wide variety of patterns. Some patterns were made exclusively for a particular retailer, such as Heather Rose for Sears.

One of the most popular patterns was Autumn Leaf, a premium designed by Arden Richards in 1933 for the exclusive use of the Jewel Tea Company. Still a Jewel Tea property, Autumn Leaf has not been listed in catalogs since 1978 but is produced on a replacement basis with the date stamped on the back.

**References:** Susan and Al Bagdade, *Warman's American Pottery and Porcelain*, 2nd ed., Krause Publications, 2000; Harvey Duke, *Hall China: Price Guide Update Two*, ELO Books, 1995; ——, *Official Price Guide to Pottery and Porcelain*, 8th ed., House of Collectibles, 1995; C. L. Miller, *Jewel Tea Grocery Products with Values*, Schiffer Publishing, 1996; ——, *Jewel Tea: Sales and Housewares Collectibles*, Schiffer Publishing, 1995; Jim and Lynn Salko, *Halls Autumn Leaf China and Jewel Tea Collectible*, published by authors (143 Topeg Dr., Severna Park, MD 21146); Margaret and Kenn Whitmyer, *Collector's Encyclopedia of Hall China*, 2nd ed., Collector Books, 1994, 1997 values update.

**Periodicals:** *The Daze*, P.O. Box 57, Otisville, MI 48463; *Hall China Encore*, 317 N. Pleasant St., Oberlin, OH 44074.

**Collectors' Clubs:** Hall Collector's Club, P.O. Box 360488, Cleveland, OH 44136, http://www.chinaspecialties.com/hallnews.html; National Autumn Leaf Collectors Club, P.O. Box 162961, Fort Worth, TX 76161-0961.

**Additional Listings:** See *Warman's Americana & Collectibles* for more examples.

## Patterns Autumn Leaf

Berry Bowl, small ........................................................................ 6.50
Bowl, 6" d .................................................................................. 22.00
Bowl, 7-1/2" d ............................................................................ 27.00
Coffeepot, cov ........................................................................... 50.00
Cream Soup ............................................................................... 15.00
Custard Cup ............................................................................... 10.00
Gravy Boat and Liner ................................................................ 65.00
Jug, worn gold ........................................................................... 48.00
Plate, 8" d .................................................................................. 15.00
Plate, 10" d, ruffled .................................................................... 20.00
Platter, 9" l ................................................................................. 20.00
Saucer ......................................................................................... 3.00
Sugar, cov .................................................................................. 32.00
Teapot, long spout ..................................................................... 45.00
Tray, glass and wood ............................................................... 135.00
Vegetable, oval .......................................................................... 25.00

## Blue Blossom

Bean Pot, New England type ............................225.00
Casserole ...........................................................95.00
Cookie Jar, five band .....................................240.00
Jug, loop handle..............................................195.00
Pepper Shaker, handle ....................................30.00
Syrup, cov, five band .....................................165.00

## Blue Bouquet

Creamer and Sugar ........................................40.00
Teapot, Aladdin ...............................................135.00

## Chinese Red

Batter Bowl.......................................................125.00
Bean Pot, New England type ..........................85.00
Custard .............................................................12.00
Donut Jar ..........................................................70.00
Jug, loop handle...............................................100.00
Teapot, Streamline ..........................................125.00

## Crocus

Cup and Saucer ...............................................25.00
Leftover, cov, set of 3 .....................................300.00
Plate, 9" d, dinner ............................................25.00
Pretzel Jar ........................................................195.00
Teapot
       Boston...................................................225.00
       Medallion ..............................................65.00
       New York...............................................275.00

## Game Birds

Coffee Pot, electric perk..................................95.00
Cookie Jar, cov ................................................250.00

## Mount Vernon

Berry Bowl, 5" d ................................................7.00
Cup and Saucer ...............................................11.00
Platter, 13" l, oval ............................................20.00
Plate, 6" d .........................................................4.00
Plate, 7" d .........................................................7.00
Plate, 10" d .......................................................12.00
Soup Plate, flat, 7-3/4" d .................................14.00

## Orange Poppy

Baker, fluted .....................................................25.00
Bean Pot, New England type ..........................110.00
Casserole, cov, oval.........................................40.00
Cup and Saucer ...............................................10.00
Jug, Radiance ..................................................45.00
Plate, 9" h .........................................................12.00
Pretzel Jar, cov ................................................110.00
Spoon.................................................................145.00
Teapot
       Boston...................................................210.00
       Melody ..................................................400.00
       Streamline.............................................35.00

## Red Poppy

Milk Jug, Daniel................................................60.00
Recipe Box........................................................52.00
Teapot, New York .............................................90.00

## Rose Parade

Casserole..........................................................50.00
Jug, pert ............................................................40.00
Salt and Pepper Shakers, pr, pert....................45.00

## Royal Rose

Ball Jug .............................................................95.00
Mixing Bowl, large............................................30.00

## Wildflower

Berry Bowl ........................................................11.00
Bowl, oval .........................................................45.00
Creamer and Sugar, cov ..................................50.00
Cup and Saucer ...............................................18.00
Custard Cup......................................................38.00
Plate, 7" d .........................................................18.00
Plate, 9" d20.00
Platter, 11" l......................................................32.00
Platter, 13" l......................................................38.00
Salt and Pepper Shakers, handles, pr .............45.00
Soup Bowl .........................................................25.00
Tid-Bit Server, 3 tiers .......................................55.00
Vegetable Dish, 9-1/4" .....................................38.00

## Miscellaneous

Casserole, cov, Fantasy....................................45.00
Coffee Pot
       Duse Drip-O-Later ................................50.00
       Golden Glow, #2 ...................................200.00
       Waverly Minuet .....................................65.00
Tankard, Silhouette ..........................................75.00
Tom and Jerry Set, bowl, 12 cups, ladle, ivory, gold trim,
  orig box ..........................................................235.00
Water Server
       Hercules, cobalt blue ...........................125.00
       Montgomery Ward .................................40.00
       Phoenix .................................................65.00

## Teapots

Addison, globe, dripless, gold trim, 6 cup .......95.00
Airflow, 6 cup
       Cobalt blue, gold...................................95.00
       Warm Yellow, gold ................................95.00
Aladdin, 6 cup
       Blue, oval lid .........................................50.00
       Blue Bouquet ........................................135.00
       Cobalt Blue, gold trim ...........................95.00
Albany, mahogany, gold trim, 6 cup .................95.00
Biggin Stock, brown, 2 cup ..............................110.00
Birdcage, maroon, gold, 6 cup ........................335.00
Boston, white, gold lettering, 2 cup .................35.00
Connie, celadon green, 6 cup ..........................50.00
Coverlet, white, gold cover, 6 cup ....................40.00
Donut, Chinese red, 6 cup ...............................425.00
French
       Maroon, gold trim, 6 cup ......................45.00
       Seaspray, gold trim, 2 cup ...................40.00
Hollywood, maroon, gold dec............................65.00
Illinois, maroon, gold spirals............................240.00
Indiana, warm yellow, gold trim, 6 cup ............350.00
Manhattan, warm yellow, 6 cup........................85.00
McCormick, mahogany, gold trim .....................85.00
Nautilus, turquoise, gold trim ...........................225.00
Ohio, brown, gold trim.......................................200.00
Parade, Chinese Red, flake ..............................160.00

**Teapot, blue, gold trim, hooks cover, $40.**

Rhythm, yellow, gold trim, 6 cup ............................................... 125.00
Royal Rose, French ...................................................................... 100.00
Streamline, Chinese Red .............................................................. 110.00
Sundial
    Canary, gold trim ................................................................. 75.00
    Yellow, gold trim .................................................................. 95.00
T-Ball, black, gold label, 6 cup ..................................................... 195.00
Tip Top, yellow, 6 cup, stand missing............................................ 95.00
Windshield, maroon, gold rose dec................................................ 45.00

# HAMPSHIRE POTTERY

**History:** In 1871, James S. Taft founded the Hampshire Pottery Company in Keene, New Hampshire. Production began with redwares and stonewares, followed by majolica in 1879. A semi-porcelain, with the recognizable matte glazes plus the Royal Worcester glaze, was introduced in 1883.

Until World War I, the factory made an extensive line of utilitarian and art wares including souvenir items. After the war the firm resumed operations but made only hotel dinnerware and tiles. The company was dissolved in 1923.

**References:** Susan and Al Bagdade, *Warman's American Pottery and Porcelain*, 2nd ed., Krause Publications, 2000; Ralph and Terry Kovel, *Kovels' American Art Pottery*, Crown Publishers, 1993.

Bowl, 10" d, 3" h, emb water lily pads and buds, leathery matte brown-green glaze, emb mark ............................................................ 400.00
Dresser Tray, 8" x 6-1/2", cream, pink florals, gold trim, "Mt. Mansfield" in gold script, sgd "Hampshire Pottery, Keene, NH".................. 110.00
Lamp Base
    10-1/4" h, 5-1/2" d, thick leathery matte green glaze, imp mark, restoration to kiln pull ....................................................... 160.00
    16" h, 7" d, twining lilypads, smooth olive green glaze, verdigris patina to fittings, stamped "Hampshire Pottery/0018" ...... 900.00
Pitcher, emb band of leaves at rim, smooth matte green glaze, slight glaze wear ................................................................................ 150.00
Plate, 6-1/2" d, Royal Worcester-style, oyster white, light green rim, gold edge, imprinted with Hampshire majolica mark, age discoloration ............................................................................................ 50.00
Urn, 15" h, 9" d, reticulated handles, emb Greek key bands, matte green glaze, stamped "Hampshire Pottery/88," light abrasion to bulbous base............................................................................. 1,700.00

**Vessel, squatty, green frosty glaze, incised "Hampshire Pottery," 3-1/2" h, 3-1/4" d, $295. Photo courtesy of David Rago Auctions.**

Vase
    4-7/8" h, cylindrical, swollen base, shaded matte green and mauve glaze, imp "Hampshire Pottery 155" and "M" with an O cipher, by Cadmon Robertson......................................... 350.00
    6-7/8" h, raised rolled rim, oval form tapered to base, imp columns around body, mottled matte mauve glass over light green, incised "Hampshire Pottery 157" and "M" with an O cipher, by Cadmon Robertson .......................................................... 750.00
Vessel
    6" d, 4" h, ovoid, mottled green and brown matte glaze, imp "Hampshire Pottery/1812," typical short firing lines in base from manufacture ................................................................... 300.00
    4" d, 4-3/4" h, bulbous, incised geometric band, smooth matte green glaze, imp "Hampshire Pottery/152" ..................... 380.00

# HATPINS and HATPIN HOLDERS

**History:** When oversized hats were in vogue, around 1850, hatpins became popular. Designers used a variety of materials to decorate the pin ends, including china, crystal, enamel, gem stones, precious metals, and shells. Decorative subjects ranged from commemorative designs to insects.

Hatpin holders, generally placed on a dresser, are porcelain containers which were designed specifically to hold these pins. The holders were produced by major manufacturers, among which were Meissen, Nippon, R. S. Germany, R. S. Prussia, and Wedgwood.

**Reference:** Lillian Baker, *Hatpins & Hatpin Holders: An Illustrated Value Guide*, Collector Books, 1983, 2000 value update.

**Collectors' Clubs:** American Hatpin Society, 20 Montecillo Drive, Rolling Hills Estates, CA 90274; International Club for Collectors of Hatpins and Hatpin Holders, 1013 Medhurst Rd, Columbus, OH 43220.

**Museum:** Los Angeles Art Museum, Costume Dept., Los Angeles, CA.

## Hatpin

Bead, 6" l, black filigree around oblong red glass bead............... 20.00
Brass
    1-1/8" d, Egyptian coin motif, 8" l pin ................................. 135.00
    1-1/4" d, round, profile of classical woman, 9" l pin, orig finish ............................................................................ 100.00

**China, Rosenthal, poppies dec, white ground, gold band and top dec, 4-3/8" h, $95.**

1-1/4" x 1", Indian face, wearing headdress, 9" l pin, orig
finish ...................................................................... 150.00
1-3/4" x 1/2", woman with long hair, sunflowers on each side of
her face, 9" l pin, orig finish .............................. 125.00
2" l, 1-3/4" oval, woman's face, flowing hair, 9" l pin, orig
finish ...................................................................... 125.00
2-1/4" d, four panels with citrine-colored accents, oxidized brass
finish ...................................................................... 315.00
Cloisonné, foil back, mkd in Japanese script ................. 90.00
Crystal, 10" l ...................................................................... 25.00
Gold, 6-3/4" l, 14kt yg, scrolling leaves and flowers .... 175.00
Ivory, elephant, hand carved .......................................... 95.00
Jet Glass, 3-1/4" d, cut and faceted, wire frame, japanned
shank ..................................................................... 200.00
Mosaic, brass button sleeve type metallic mounting, gold wire trim, 8"
brass pin, stamped "GS," c1875 ............................ 80.00
Pearl, 2.5mm natural pearl, balloon shape setting with applied Etrus-
can type granulation work, natural pearl finial, hatpin shaft
damaged ................................................................. 55.00
Porcelain, 1-1/2" d round painted disc, Art Deco Eye of Horis motif,
bezel mount, brass button type sleeve, c1920 .......... 70.00
Rhinestones, large domed round head ............................ 145.00
Turquoise, 6" l, pewter mounting and pin ....................... 25.00

## Holder

Austria, hp violets dec, mkd "Royal Austria" ................. 90.00
Bavarian, floral dec ........................................................ 75.00
Bisque, 4" h, old woman wearing purple beret ............... 95.00
Carnival Glass
Orange Tree pattern, marigold, 6-3/4" h ............. 450.00
Sun's Up, lavender ............................................... 275.00
Nippon, 4-3/4" h, white ground, small red roses, "M" in wreath
mark ........................................................................ 65.00
R. S. Germany, 4-1/2" h, hp roses, shaded green to white ground, mkd
"R. S. Germany" ................................................... 320.00
Silver, etched and engraved, holes for sixteen hatpins, 5-1/2" h,
unmarked, c1880 ................................................. 135.00
Torquay Pottery, hp rooster dec, "Keep Me on the Dressing Table," ftd,
5" h ....................................................................... 120.00

# HAVILAND CHINA

**History:** In 1842, American
china importer David Haviland moved to Limoges,
France, where he began
manufacturing and decorat-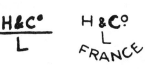
ing china specifically for the U.S. market. Haviland is synony-
mous with fine, white, translucent porcelain, although early
hand-painted patterns were generally larger and darker colored on heavier whiteware blanks than were later ones.

David revolutionized French china factories by both
manufacturing the whiteware blank and decorating it at
the same site. In addition, Haviland and Company pioneered the use of decals in decorating china.

David's sons, Charles Edward and Theodore, split the
company in 1892. In 1936, Theodore opened an American division, which still operates today. In 1941, Theodore bought out Charles Edward's heirs and
recombined both companies under the original name of
H. and Co. The Haviland family sold the firm in 1981.

Charles Field Haviland, cousin of Charles Edward
and Theodore, worked for and then, after his marriage in

1857, ran the Casseaux Works until 1882. Items continued to carry his name as decorator until 1941.

Thousands of Haviland patterns were made, but were
not consistently named until after 1926. The similarities
in many of the patterns makes identification difficult.
Numbers assigned by Arlene Schleiger and illustrated in
her books have become the identification standard.

**References:** Susan and Al Bagdade, *Warman's American Pottery and Porcelain*, 2nd ed., Krause Publications, 2000; Mary Frank Gaston, *Haviland Collectibles & Art Objects*, Collector Books, 1984; Charles E. & Carol M. Ulrey, *Matching Services for Haviland China*, published by author, (P.O. Box 15815, San Diego, CA 92175); Arlene Schleiger, *Two Hundred Patterns of Haviland China*, Books I-V, published by author, 1950-1977; Nora Travis, *Haviland China*, Schiffer Publishing, 1997, 1998 value update; —, *Evolution of Haviland China Design,* Schiffer Pubilshing, 2000.

**Collectors' Club:** Haviland Collectors International Foundation, P.O. Box 802462, Santa Clarita, CA 91380.

Bouillon Cup and Saucer, small green flowers and leaves ........... 30.00
Bowl, 5-1/2" d, Greek Key dec, black and yellow ....................... 15.00
Bread and Butter Plate, Davenport pattern ................................. 12.00
Cake Plate, open handles, Schleiger #705 .................................. 45.00
Coffee Service, coffeepot, creamer, and sugar, Wedding Anniversary
pattern, marked "H & Co" ..................................................... 140.00
Compote, 9" d, 2-3/4" h, blue and pink flowers, gold scalloped
edge ....................................................................................... 65.00
Cup, Autumn Leaves pattern ....................................................... 23.00
Dresser Set, hair receiver, cov powder jar, fitted tray with handle,
yellow florals, gilt borders ...................................................... 150.00
Gravy Boat, cov, attached underplate, oval, green and gold geometric
dec .......................................................................................... 50.00
Oyster Plate, 7-1/2" d, white and gold, mkd "Charles Field Haviland,
Limoges," c1900-1905, price for set of six ............................. 360.00
Plate
Autumn Leaf pattern, 6" d ................................................ 15.00
Baltimore Rose pattern, 8-1/2" d, pink, Ranson blank, marked
"Haviland & Co" ........................................................... 25.00
Blank 211, blue flowers, set of 5 ...................................... 55.00
Silver Anniversary pattern, 8-1/2" d ................................. 25.00
Platter, 11-3/4" l, Arbor pattern ................................................. 60.00
Ramekin and Saucer, No. 24 pattern, Ranson blank .................. 35.00
Relish, white, scattered pink flowers, scalloped edge ................. 30.00
Seafood Plate, 8" l, sq, canted corners, painted ocean creatures,
printed floral border, late 19th C, price for set of eleven .......... 275.00
Tureen, cov, two handles, border of flowers, large irises ............. 500.00
Vegetable Dish, cov, 9-1/2" w, octagonal, Persia pattern ........... 200.00

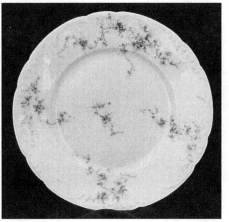

**Plate, pink floral dec, 8" d, $20.**

# HEISEY GLASS

1900–58

**History:** The A. H. Heisey Glass Co. began producing glasswares in April 1896, in Newark, Ohio. Heisey, the firm's founder, was not a newcomer to the field, having been associated with the craft since his youth.

Many blown and molded patterns were produced in crystal, colored, milk (opalescent), and Ivorina Verde (custard) glass. Decorative techniques of cutting, etching, and silver deposit were employed. Glass figurines were introduced in 1933 and continued in production until 1957 when the factory closed. All Heisey glass is notable for its clarity.

**Marks:** Not all pieces have the familiar H-within-a-diamond mark.

**References:** Neila Bredehoft, *Collector's Encyclopedia of Heisey Glass, 1925-1938*, Collector Books, 1986, 1999 value update; —; *Fifty Years of Collectible Glass, 1920-1970, Volume 1, Volume II,* Antique Trader Books, 2000; Lyle Conder, *Collector's Guide to Heisey's Glassware for Your Table*, L-W Books, 1984, 1993-94 value update; Shirley Dunbar, *Heisey Glass, The Early Years, 1896-1924,* Krause Publications, 2000; Gene Florence, *Elegant Glassware of the Depression Era*, 9th, Collector Books, 2001; —, *Glass Candlesticks of the Depression Era,* Collector Books, 1999; Frank L. Hahn and Paul Kikeli, *Collector's Guide to Heisey and Heisey by Imperial Glass Animals,* Golden Era Publications, 1991, 1998 value update.

**Collectors' Clubs:** Bay State Heisey Collectors Club, 354 Washington St., East Walpole, MA 02032; Heisey Collectors of America, 169 W Church St., Newark, OH, 43055; National Capital Heisey Collectors, P.O. Box 23, Clinton, MD 20735.

**Videotape:** Heisey Glass Collectors of America, Inc., *Legacy of American Craftsmanship: The National Heisey Glass Museum*, Heisey Collectors of America, Inc., 1994.

**Museum:** National Heisey Glass Museum, Newark, OH.

Almond Dish, #1469 Ridgleigh....................................20.00
Ashtray
    #1401, Empress.............................................45.00
    #1435, individual, Orchid etch ..............................35.00
Bar Glass, #2052, 1-1/2 oz, Tally Ho etch....................25.00

## Reproduction Alert:

Some Heisey molds were sold to Imperial Glass of Bellaire, Ohio, and certain items were reissued. These pieces may be mistaken for the original Heisey. Some of the reproductions were produced in colors which were never made by Heisey and have become collectible in their own right. Examples include: the Colt family in Crystal, Caramel Slag, Ultra Blue, and Horizon Blue; the mallard with wings up in Caramel Slag; Whirlpool (Provincial) in crystal and colors; and Waverly, a 7-inch, oval, footed compote in Caramel Slag.

Bowl
    Lariat, 10-1/2" d .........................................45.00
    Titania, #1519, 11" d, 3 seahorse feet ...............115.00
Candle Block
    Crystolite, rosette, pr.....................................25.00
    Lariat....................................................18.00
Candlesticks, pr
    Plantation, duo ..........................................150.00
    Queen Anne, 3" h, 3 ftd ..................................45.00
Candy Dish, cov
    #1503 Crystolite, shell ...................................65.00
    #1506 Whirlpool, ftd......................................70.00
    #3947, ladle, cut, blue dec, "H" mark...................225.00
Celery
    #407 Coarse Rib, marigold flashed, metal holder..............25.00
    #1401 Empress, 10" ......................................25.00
Centerpiece Vase, #1405 Ipswich, ftd, candle holder missing......70.00
Champagne
    #3390 Carcassone, 6 oz, cobalt bowl, saucer ............80.00
    #4069 Ridgeleigh, 5 oz, Mariemont cutting .............85.00
    #4083 Stanhope, 4-1/2 oz, zircon bowl and foot, saucer......50.00
    #5025 Tyrolean, 6 oz, Orchid etch, saucer .............35.00
    #5057 Suez, 6 oz, Sultana stem.........................45.00
    #5072 Rose, 6 oz, Rose etch, saucer ...................30.00
Cheese Dish, Octagon, #1229, hawthorne ....................35.00
Claret, #3390 Carcassone, 4 oz, cobalt bowl ...............85.00
Coaster, Plantation............................................60.00
Cocktail
    #5025 Tyrolean, 4 oz, Orchid etch......................35.00
    #5038 Rooster .........................................65.00
    #5072 Rose, 4 oz, Rose etch ..........................25.00
Compote, cov, Pleat and Panel, flamingo, gold trim ..........95.00
Cordial, 1 oz
    #5010 Symphone, Minuet etch ........................115.00
    #5022 Graceful, Orchid etch ..........................125.00
    #5072 Rose, Rose etch ...............................105.00
Creamer, #1425 Victorian, silver deposit .....................20.00
Creamer and Sugar, #1469 Ridgleigh, individual size, oval handled tray ....................................................65.00
Cruet, faceted stopper
    #305 Punty & Diamond Point, 6 oz, slightly cloudy ..............50.00
    #1201 Fandango, 6 oz.................................50.00
Cup, Empress, Sahara.......................................30.00
Cup and Saucer #1509 Queen Ann, Orchid etch .............60.00
Dessert, #1637A Town and Country, 5 oz, flared, dawn ...........25.00
French Dressing Bowl, underplate, ladle, #412 Tudor, Moongleam green ....................................................75.00
Gardenia Bowl, orchid etch.................................250.00
Goblet
    #1425 Victorian .......................................20.00
    #4069 Ridgeleigh, 8 oz, cutting, monogram .........25.00
    #5025 Tyrolean, 10 oz, tall, Orchid etch ..............65.00
    #5072 Rose, 9 oz, Rose etch .........................40.00
Hors D'oeurve, #1401 Empress, 10" d, 7 part ...............35.00
Iced Tea Tumbler, Puritan, ftd...............................30.00
Ice Tub, #393 Narrow Flute, pat'd...........................30.00
Jello Dish, #1495 Fern, 12" d, zircon .......................50.00
Mayonnaise, cov, #1509 Queen Ann, Rosalie etch .............25.00
Mayonnaise, open, #1401 Empress, Sahara, dolphin feet..........60.00
Mint Dish, Octagon, #1229, hawthorne......................45.00
Nappy
    #380, Scalloped Octagon, ground bottom, mkd ..........75.00
    #1225 Sawtooth Band, 4" d, scalloped .................20.00
Nut Cup
    #1229 Octagon, moongleam, diamond optic ............25.00
    #1401 Empress.........................................12.00
Party Plate, #1519 Waverly, unknown floral etch, 13" d .............20.00
Pickle and Olive, #1401 Empress, 13" l, 2 part

**Powder Box, Crystolite, clear, 5" d, $60.**

Plate
| | |
|---|---|
| Twist, green, 7" d | 10.00 |
| #1183 Revere, Westpoint etch, 8" d | 25.00 |
| #1228 Swirl, Moongleam green, 10" d | 45.00 |
| #1229 Octagon, Moongleam, 8" d | 20.00 |
| #1236 Eagle, Moongleam green, 8" d | 25.00 |
| #1401 Empress, Alexandrite, 7" d | 150.00 |
| #1401 Empress, Sahara, 6" sq | 15.00 |
| #1401 Empress, Sahara, 6" round | 20.00 |
| #1509 Orchid Etch, 10-1/2" d | 175.00 |
| Punch Bowl, Colonial | 135.00 |

Punch Cup
| | |
|---|---|
| Empress | 35.00 |
| Greek Key | 20.00 |

Relish
| | |
|---|---|
| #1401 Empress, 16" l, 4 part | 65.00 |
| #1540 Lariat, 8-1/2" d, round, 4 part | 35.00 |
| Salt, master, #1503 Crystolite, swan | 35.00 |
| Sandwich Platter, #1401 Empress, two handles | 45.00 |
| Server, center, #1401 Empress, cut | 55.00 |

Sherbet
| | |
|---|---|
| #349 Colonial, 4 oz, ftd | 20.00 |
| #349 Colonial, 4-1/2 oz, flared | 35.00 |
| #1425 Victorian | 12.00 |
| #4085 Kohinoor, 5-1/2 oz, zircon | 175.00 |
| #5025 Tyrolean, 6 oz, low, ftd, Orchid etch | 25.00 |
| #5072 Rose, 6 oz, Rose etch | 20.00 |

Soda Tumbler
| | |
|---|---|
| #2041 Oakwood, fisherman etch | 55.00 |
| #3381 Creole, Sahara, 8 oz, ftd | 95.00 |
| Swan, #1503 Crystolite, 6-1/2" h | 45.00 |
| Torte Plate, Rose Etch, #1519, 14" d | 95.00 |
| Tray, #1503 Crystolite, 12" l, oval | 45.00 |

Tumbler
| | |
|---|---|
| Old Sandwich, Sahara, 12 oz, ftd | 45.00 |
| Plantation, 12 oz, ftd, pressed | 80.00 |
| Twist, green, ftd, 9oz | 50.00 |
| 300-1/2 Flamingo, 8 oz | 50.00 |
| #1506 Whirlpool, 9 oz, limelight | 40.00 |
| #2351 Tally Ho etch, 14 oz | 50.00 |

Vase
| | |
|---|---|
| #1503 Crystolite | 45.00 |
| #4045 Wide Optic, cobalt blue, ball, 7" h | 180.00 |

Wine
| | |
|---|---|
| #1425 Victorian | 25.00 |
| #5025 Tyrolean, 3 oz, Orchid etch | 55.00 |

# HOLLY AMBER

**History:** Holly Amber, originally called Golden Agate, was produced by the Indiana Tumbler and Goblet Works of the National Glass Co., Greentown, Indiana. Jacob Rosenthal created the color in 1902. Holly Amber is a gold-colored glass with a marbleized onyx color on raised parts.

Holly (No. 450), a pattern created by Frank Jackson, was designed specifically for the Golden Agate color. Between January 1903 and June of that year, when the factory was destroyed by fire, more than 35 different forms were made in this pattern.

**Reference:** James Measell, *Greentown Glass, The Indiana Tumbler & Goblet Co.*, Grand Rapids Public Museum, 1979, 1992-93 value update, distributed by Antique Publications.

**Collectors' Club:** National Greentown Glass Association, 19596 Glendale Ave, South Bend, IN 46637.

**Museums:** Grand Rapids Public Museum, Ruth Herrick Greentown Glass Collection, Grand Rapids, MI; Greentown Glass Museum, Greentown, IN.

**Additional Listings:** Greentown Glass.

| | |
|---|---|
| Bowl, 7-1/2" l, oval | 375.00 |
| Butter, cov | 1,200.00 |
| Cake Stand | 2,400.00 |
| Compote, cov, 8-1/2" h, 12" d | 2,500.00 |
| Creamer, 4-1/2" h | 650.00 |
| Cruet, orig stopper | 1,850.00 |
| Honey, cov | 850.00 |
| Mug, 4-1/2" h, ring handle | 550.00 |
| Nappy | 385.00 |
| Parfait | 600.00 |
| Salt & Pepper Shakers, pr | 500.00 |
| Sauce | 250.00 |
| Spooner | 475.00 |
| Syrup, 5-3/4" h, SP hinged lid | 2,000.00 |
| Toothpick, 2-1/4" h | 585.00 |
| Tumbler | 400.00 |

# HORN

**History:** For centuries, horns from animals have been used for various items, e.g., drinking cups, spoons, powder horns, and small dishes. Some pieces of horn have designs scratched in them. Around 1880 furniture made from the horns of Texas longhorn steers was popular in Texas and the southwestern United States.

**Tumbler, Honey Amber, 3-7/8" h, $400.**

**Tablespoon, tapered handle, $20.**

**Additional Listings:** Firearm Accessories.

Arm Chair, 36-1/2" h, arched back, orig upholstered back and seat, fringe, and braid trim, curved legs ending in casters, upholstery distressed, Victorian, c1870 ...................................................... 1,035.00
Beaker
    5-1/8" h, harvest scene dec, sgd "Ion Stead," 19th C, minor losses and cracks to rim............................................. 250.00
    7-1/2" h, silver mounted rims, and crest, Victorian, pr ........ 600.00
Box, cov, 2-3/4" d, brass hinges.................................................. 35.00
Corkscrew, 7" l, staghorn, sterling silver end cap stamped with lily, American, late 19th C .......................................................... 475.00
Figure, 8-1/2" h, courtesan, standing, carrying branch and basket, Chinese, 18th/19th C.......................................................... 345.00
Flask, 8-1/2" h, dark patina, silver mounds, 19th C ................... 250.00
Foot Stool, hide covering, horns form legs ............................... 165.00
Libation Cup. 4" h, carved rhinoceros horn, lotus blossom carving, carved hardwood stand, Chinese, minor damage.................... 920.00
Parlor Chair, 39-1/2" h, rect back splat, shaped seat, scrolling horns as crest rail, side supports, apron, and legs, Victorian, third quarter 19th C.......................................................................................... 920.00
Snuff Box, 2-1/4" x 1-1/2", carved bust, textured ground, gold hinge, inlaid dec, Continental, 19th C, losses, cracks .......................... 200.00
Tumbler, 5" h, engraved hunt scene ........................................... 70.00
Vinaigrette, curled horn surmounted by pierced screen, silver cap with repousse acorns and oak leaves, faceted foil-backed quartz, trace link chain and ring, minor crack in horn................................ 290.00

# HULL POTTERY

**History:** In 1905, Addis E. Hull purchased the Acme Pottery Company, Crooksville, Ohio. In 1917, the A. E. Hull Pottery Company began making art pottery, novelties, stoneware, and kitchenware, later including the famous Little Red Riding Hood line. Most items had a matte finish with shades of pink and blue or brown predominating.

After a disastrous flood and fire in 1950, J. Brandon Hull reopened the factory in 1952 as the Hull Pottery Company. New, more-modern-style pieces, mostly with glossy finish, were produced. The company added dinnerware patterns, and glossy finished pottery. The company closed its doors in 1986.

**Marks:** Hull pottery molds and patterns are easily identified. Pre-1950 vases are marked "Hull USA" or "Hull Art USA" on the bottom. Many also retain their paper labels.

Post-1950 pieces are marked "Hull" in large script or "HULL" in block letters.

Each pattern has a distinctive letter or number, e.g., Wildflower has a "W" and a number; Waterlily, "L" and number; Poppy, numbers in the 600s; Orchid, in the 300s. Early stoneware pieces are marked with an "H."

**References:** Joan Hull, *Hull, The Heavenly Pottery,* 7th ed., published by author (1376 Nevada, Huron, SD 57350), 2000; —, *Hull, The Heavenly Pottery Shirt Pocket Price List,* 4th ed., published by author, 1999; Brenda Roberts, *The Ultimate Encyclopedia of Hull Pottery,* Collector Books, 1995, 1999 value update; Mark and Ellen Supnick, *Collecting Hull Pottery's Little Red Riding Hood, Revised Edition,* L-W Books, 1998.

**Periodical:** *Hull Pottery Association,* 11023 Tunnel Hill NE, New Lexington, OH 43764.

**Additional Listings:** See *Warman's Americana & Collectibles* for more examples.

**Advisor:** Joan Hull.

## Pre-1950
### Matte Bowknot
| | |
|---|---|
| B-4 6-1/2" h vase | 250.00 |
| B-7 cornucopia | 325.00 |
| B-11 10-1/2" h vase | 500.00 |
| B-12, 10-1/2" h basket | 750.00 |
| B-16 console bowl | 325.00 |
| B-17 candleholders, pr | 225.00 |

### Calla Lily
| | |
|---|---|
| 500-32 bowl | 200.00 |
| 520-33, 8" h vase | 150.00 |

### Dogwood (Wild Rose)
| | |
|---|---|
| 501, 8-1/2" h basket | 300.00 |
| 508 10-1/2" window box | 195.00 |
| 513, 6-1/2" h vase | 125.00 |

### Little Red Riding Hood
| | |
|---|---|
| Creamer and Sugar, side pour | 400.00 |
| Dresser or Cracker Jar | 800.00 |
| Lamp | 2,500.00 |
| Matchbox for wooden matches | 900.00 |
| Salt and Pepper Shakers, pr, small | 120.00 |
| Teapot, cov | 395.00 |
| Wall Pocket Planter | 620.00 |

### Magnolia
| | |
|---|---|
| 3 8-1/2" h vase | 125.00 |
| 9 10-1/2" h vase | 200.00 |
| 14 4-3/4" h pitcher | 75.00 |
| 20 15" floor vase | 500.00 |

**Cornucopia, green tones, pink int., high glaze, mkd "Hull 64 USA," $24.**

## Open Rose/Camellia

106 13-1/2" h pitcher ................................. 650.00
114 8-1/2" h jardiniere .............................. 375.00
119 8-1/2" h vase ...................................... 175.00
127 4-3/4" h vase ........................................ 75.00

## Orchid

301 4-3/4" h vase ....................................... 95.00
302 6" h vase ............................................ 175.00
303 8" h vase ............................................ 195.00
304 10-1/2" h vase .................................... 350.00
310 9-1/2" jardiniere ................................. 450.00

## Poppy

601 9" h basket ......................................... 800.00
607 10-1/2" h vase .................................... 450.00
610 13" pitcher ......................................... 900.00
613 6-1/2" h vase ...................................... 200.00

## Rosella

R-2 5" h vase ............................................. 35.00
R-6 6-1/2" h vase ....................................... 45.00
R-15 8-1/2" h vase ..................................... 75.00

## Tulip

101-33 9" h vase ....................................... 245.00
103-33 6" h vase ....................................... 250.00
107-33 6" h vase ....................................... 125.00
109-33-8" pitcher ...................................... 235.00

## Waterlily

L-14, 10-1/2" basket .................................. 350.00
L-16, 12-1/2" vase .................................... 395.00

## Wild Flower, No. Series

53 8-1/2" h vase ....................................... 295.00
61 6-1/2" h vase ....................................... 175.00
66 10-1/4" h basket ................................ 2,000.00
71 12" h vase ........................................... 450.00

## Woodland

W9 8-3/4" h basket ................................... 245.00
W11 5-1/2" flower pot and saucer ............... 175.00
W13 7-1/2" l wall pocket, shell ................... 195.00
W14 10-1/2" window box ............................ 200.00

## Post 1950
## Blossom Flite

T4 8-1/2" h basket .................................... 125.00
T13 12-1/2" h pitcher ................................ 150.00

## Butterfly

B9 9" h vase .............................................. 55.00
B13 8" h basket ........................................ 150.00
B15 13-1/2" h pitcher ................................ 200.00

## Continental

C29 12" h vase ........................................... 95.00
C55 12-1/2" basket ................................... 150.00
C62 8-1/4" candy dish ................................. 45.00

## Ebb Tide

E-1 7" h bud vase ....................................... 75.00
E-8 ashtray with mermaid ......................... 225.00
E-10 13" h pitcher ..................................... 275.00

## Parchment and Pine

S-3 6" h basket .......................................... 95.00
S-11 and S-12 tea set .............................. 250.00
S-15 8" h coffeepot .................................. 175.00

## Serenade

S1 6" h vase .............................................. 55.00
S-15 11-1/2" d fruit bowl, ftd .................... 125.00
S11 10-1/2" h vase .................................. 100.00
S17 teapot, creamer and sugar ................ 275.00

## Sunglow

53 grease jar ............................................. 60.00
82 wall pocket, whisk broom ....................... 75.00
85 8-3/4" h vase, bird ................................ 60.00

## Tokay/Tuscany

3 8" h pitcher ............................................ 95.00
8 10" h vase ............................................ 150.00
10 11" l cornucopia .................................... 65.00
12 12" h vase .......................................... 125.00

## Tropicana

T53 8-1/2" h vase .................................... 550.00
T55, 12-3/4" h basket .............................. 750.00

## Woodland (glossy)

W1 5-1/2" h vase ....................................... 45.00
W15 8-1/2" h vase, double .......................... 75.00
W19 14" d console bowl ............................ 100.00

# HUMMEL ITEMS

**History:** Hummel items are the original creations of Berta Hummel, who was born in 1909 in Massing, Bavaria, Germany. At age 18, she was  enrolled in the Academy of Fine Arts in Munich to further her mastery of drawing and the palette. Berta entered the Convent of Siessen and became Sister Maria Innocentia in 1934. In this Franciscan cloister, she continued drawing and painting images of her childhood friends.

In 1935, W. Goebel Co. in Rodental, Germany, began producing Sister Maria Innocentia's sketches as three-dimensional bisque figurines. The Schmid Brothers of Randolph, Massachusetts, introduced the figurines to America and became Goebel's U.S. distributor.

In 1967, Goebel began distributing Hummel items in the U.S. A controversy developed between the two companies, the Hummel family, and the convent. Law suits and counter-suits ensued. The German courts finally effected a compromise: the convent held legal rights to all works produced by Sister Maria Innocentia from 1934 until her death in 1946 and licensed Goebel to reproduce these works; Schmid was to deal directly with the Hummel family for permission to reproduce any pre-convent art.

**Marks:** All authentic Hummel pieces bear both the signature "M. I. Hummel" and a Goebel trademark. Various trademarks were used to identify the year of production:

| | |
|---|---|
| Crown Mark (trademark 1) | 1935-1949 |
| Full Bee (trademark 2) | 1950-1959 |
| Stylized Bee (trademark 3) | 1957-1972 |

| | |
|---|---|
| Three Line Mark (trademark 4) | 1964-1972 |
| Last Bee Mark (trademark 5) | 1972-1979 |
| Missing Bee Mark (trademark 6) | 1979-1990 |
| Current Mark or | |
| New Crown Mark (trademark 7) | 1991 to the present. |

**References:** Ken Armke, *Hummel: An Illustrated History and Price Guide*, Wallace-Homestead, 1995; Carl F. Luckey, *Luckey's Hummel Figurines and Plates: A Collector's Identification and Value Guide*, 11th ed., Krause Publications, 1997; Robert L. Miller, *No. 1 Price Guide to M. I. Hummel: Figurines, Plates, More...*, 6th ed., —, *Hummels 1978-1998: 20 Years of "Miller on Hummel" Columns*, Collector News, 1998; Portfolio Press, 1995.

**Collectors' Clubs:** Hummel Collector's Club, Inc., 1261 University Dr., Yardley, PA 19067; M. I. Hummel Club, Goebel Plaza, Rte 31, P.O. Box 11, Pennington, NJ 08534.

**Museum:** Hummel Museum, New Braunfels, TX.

**Additional Listings:** See *Warman's Americana & Collectibles* for more examples.

Ashtray
    Boy with bird, #166, trademark 3 ...........................................95.00
    Joyful, #33, trademark 2, 6" x 3-1/2" ...................................165.00
Bell, 1980, third issue, 6-1/4" h, MIB..............................................70.00
Bookends, pr, Farm Boy and Goose Girl, #60/A and B, trademark 1, 4-3/4" h ...................................................................................775.00
Candleholder, Silent Night, #54, trademark 2, 3-1/2" x 4-3/4" ....265.00
Candy Box, cov, Happy Pastime, #111/69, trademark 4, 5-1/4" h.........125.00
Figure
    Apple Tree Boy, #142/I, trademark 2, 6" h .........................400.00
    Apple Tree Girl, #141/I, trademark 3, 6" h .........................290.00

Auf Wiedersehn, #153/0, trademark 3 ...............................175.00
Be Patient, #197/0, trademark 2, 1948 ...............................390.00
Bookworm, trademark 3...................................................490.00
Brother, #95, trademark 3...............................................150.00
Chicken Licken, trademark 4 ...........................................240.00
Chimney Sweep, trademark 2 ...........................................300.00
Coquettes, #179, trademark 2 ...........................................280.00
Duet, #130, trademark 2 ..................................................275.00
Heavenly Protection, #88, trademark 3 ................................90.00
Hello, #124/0, trademark 3 ...............................................175.00
Home from Market, #198/2/0, trademark 4 ...........................100.00
Joyful, #53, trademark 2 ..................................................215.00
Just Resting, #112/3/0, trademark 4 ...................................100.00
Light the Way, trademark 4 ...............................................115.00
Little Sweeper, #171/0, artist sgd, trademark 6, 4-1/2" h....195.00
Not for You, #317, trademark 3..........................................375.00
She Loves Me, #174, trademark 2.......................................250.00
Shepherd, #214F, trademark 7 ...........................................110.00
Sign of Spring, #203, trademark 6 ......................................550.00
Stormy Weather, #71/I, trademark 2, 6" h.............................700.00
Trumpet Boy, #97, trademark 5, 4-5/8" h.............................195.00
Village Boy, #51/1, trademark 5 .........................................300.00
Wayside Harmony, #111/1, trademark 3 ..............................195.00
Font
    Angel Shrine, #147, trademark 3, 3" x 5"..........................40.00
    Holy Family, #246, trademark 3, 3-1/8" x 4-1/2" ..................65.00
Lamp
    Culprits, #44, trademark 1, c1930, orig wiring, 9-1/4" h......475.00
    Happy Days, #235, trademark 2 ......................................400.00
Nativity
    Madonna with Child, white, #151 ....................................250.00
    Set, #214/A-O, trade mark 3, color, 14 pcs.......................850.00
Plate, first edition, 1971, angel...........................................550.00
Wall Plaque
    Flitting Butterfly, #139, trademark 1, 2-1/2" x 2-1/2" ..........275.00
    Swaying Lullaby, #165, trademark 1, 4-1/2" x 5-1/4" ..........700.00

# IMARI

**History:** Imari derives its name from a Japanese port city. Although Imari ware was manufactured in the 17th century, the pieces most commonly encountered are those made between 1770 and 1900.

Early Imari was decorated simply, quite unlike the later heavily decorated brocade pattern commonly associated with Imari. Most of the decorative patterns are an underglaze blue and overglaze "seal wax" red complimented by turquoise and yellow.

The Chinese copied Imari ware. The Japanese examples can be identified by grayer clay, thicker glaze, runny and darker blue, and deep red opaque hues.

The pattern and colors of Imari inspired many English and European potteries, such as Derby and Meissen, to adopt a similar style of decoration for their wares.

**Reference:** Nancy N. Schiffer, *Imari, Satsuma, and Other Japanese Export Ceramics,* Schiffer Publishing, 1997.

**Reproduction Alert:** Reproductions abound, and many manufacturers continue to produce pieces in the traditional style.

Bowl
    8-1/2" d, floral brocades around central landscape, late 19th C .................................................. 150.00
    10-1/2" d, hexagonal, pronounced lip, floral motifs, brocade patterns, fuku mark, early 19th C .................... 490.00
Charger
    16" d, central panel of three friends, brocade border with phoenixes and foliage, 19th C ................................ 350.00
    16" d, hexagonal, central landscape with borders dec with cranes and foo dogs, late 19th C .................................. 435.00
    18" d, scene from *47 Ronin* story, late 19th C ..................... 460.00
    18-3/8" h, scroll frame panels with figural, landscape, and floral designs, Japan, 19th C ........................................ 490.00
    21-3/4" d, floral and dragon reserves surrounding central foliate pattern medallion, Japanese, Meiji, c1890 .................... 1,100.00
Dish
    12-1/4" l, sq form with cut corners, floral basket design, center foliate borders, Japan, 19th C, price for pr ...................... 850.00
    14-1/2" l, oval, floral and foliate design, Japan, 19th C ....... 260.00

Garniture, 10-1/4" h, 12-1/5" h, two vases, three covered jars, flowering branch and butterfly dec, iron-red and blue, traces of gilt, Japan, 19th, chips, hairline, restoration, price for five piece set ........ 2,990.00
Jar, cov
    12" h, tall domed lid, floral pattern dec, 19th C ................... 435.00
    12-1/2" h, hexagonal form, domed lid surrounded by shishi, floral dec, late 19th C, repair to cov ........................................... 290.00
    11-1/2" h, ribbed form, lid surmounted by shishi, dec with various floral patterns, late 19th C, price for pr ........................... 500.00
Plate
    7-1/2" d, blue and white dec, grapes and foliage, late 17th/early 19th C ........................................................ 150.00
    8-1/2" d, *rouge-de-fer* and black palette, floral border encircling phoenix tondo in black on white ground, Japanese, Meiji, c1880-90 ........................................................ 70.00
    11-1/4" d, piecrust edge, floral elements on underglaze blue ground, central panel of flowering branch, Japan, 12th C 300.00
    12" h, central phoenix medallion surrounded by border of prunus flowers, brick-red ground, late 19th C .............................. 175.00
Saki Bottle, 10" h, tokkuri, sq form, design of ships and Europeans, orig wooden box, late 19th C ................................................ 1,380.00
Vase
    9-3/4" h, bottle form, floral roundels, late 19th C ................. 175.00
    12" h, swirled ribbed form with scalloped mouth, peacocks and brocade pattern, 19th C ...................................................... 290.00
    22" h, 7" d, ovoid, floral panels dec, 4th quarter 19th C, mounted as lamp, pierced brass foot, electrified ........................... 470.00
    23-3/4" h, bottle form, fluted body, foliate designs, Japanese, 19th C ......................................................................... 815.00
Vase, cov
    14" h, hexagonal, foo lion finials, Japan, 19th C, price for pr ...................................................................... 1,380.00
    14-1/2" h, Temple Jar form, ribbed, multiple floral reserves, Japanese, Meiji, c1880-1885, price for pr .............................. 1,100.00

# IMPERIAL GLASS

**History:** Imperial Glass Co., Bellaire, Ohio, was organized in 1901. Its primary product was pattern (pressed) glass. Soon other lines were added, including carnival glass, Nuart, Nucut, and Near Cut. In 1916, the company introduced Free-Hand, a lustered art glass line, and Imperial Jewels, an iridescent stretch glass that carried the Imperial cross trademark. In the 1930s, the company was reorganized into the Imperial Glass Corporation, and the firm is still producing a great variety of wares.

Imperial recently acquired the molds and equipment of several other glass companies—Central, Cambridge, and Heisey. Many of the retired molds of these companies are once again in use.

**Marks:** The Imperial reissues are marked to distinguish them from the originals.

**References:** Margaret and Douglas Archer, *Imperial Glass,* Collector Books, 1978, 1998 value update; Tom and Neila Bredehoft, *Fifty Years of Collectible Glass, 1920-1970, Volume 1, Volume II,* Antique Trader Books, 2000; Carl O. Burns, *Imperial Carnival Glass,* Collector Books, 1999; Gene Florence, *Elegant Glassware of the Depression Era,* 8th ed., Collector Books, 1998; Myrna and Bob Garrison, *Imperial's Boudoir,*

**Platter, iron-red, cobalt blue, green, and gold, c1875, 12-3/8" l, $125.**

*Etcetera,* 1996; National Imperial Glass Collectors Society, *Imperial Glass Encyclopedia: Volume I, A-Cane,* Antique Publications, 1995; ——, *Vol. II: Cape Code- L,* Antique Publications, 1998; ——, *Imperial Glass 1966 Catalog,* reprint, 1991 price guide, Antique Publications; Virginia R. Scott, *Collector's Guide to Imperial Candlewick,* published by author (275 Milledge Terrace, Athens, GA 30606); Mary M. Wetzel-Tomlka, *Candlewick: The Jewel of Imperial* Books I and II, published by author (P.O. Box 594, Notre Dame, IN 46556-0594); ——, *Candlewick The Jewel of Imperial, Personal Inventory & Record Book,* published by author, 1998; ——, *Candlewick The Jewel of Imperial, Price Guide 99 and More,* published by author, 1998.

**Collectors' Clubs:** National Candlewick Collector's Club, 275 Milledge Terrace, Athens, GA 30606, plus many regional clubs; National Imperial Glass Collectors Society, P.O. Box 534, Bellaire, OH 43906.

**Periodicals:** *Glasszette,* National Imperial Glass Collector's Soc., P.O. Box 534, Bellaire, OH 43528; *Spyglass Newsletter,* Michiana Association of Candlewick Collectors, 17370 Battles Rd, South Bend, IN 46614; *The Candlewick Collector Newsletter,* National Candlewick Collector's Club, 6534 South Avenue, Holland, OH 43528; *TRIGC Quarterly Newsletter,* Texas Regional Imperial Glass Collectors, 2113 F. M. 367 East, Iowa Park, TX 76367.

**Videotapes:** "National Imperial Glass Collectors Society, Candlewick: at Home, In Any Home," Vol. I: "Imperial Beauty," Vol. II: "Virginia and Mary," RoCliff Communications, 1993; ——, "Glass of Yesteryears: The Renaissance of Slag Glass," RoCliff Communications, 1994.

**Additional Listings:** See Carnival Glass; Pattern Glass; and *Warman's Americana & Collectibles* for more examples of Candlewick Pattern.

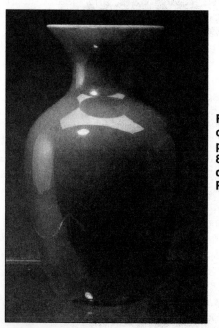

**Free Hand, vase, orange ext. and int., polished white pontil, 8" h, $300. Photo courtesy of David Rago Auctions.**

## Art Glass

Bowl, 11" d, low, inward rim, opal white glass flashed overall with brilliant orange stretched irid, c1920, minor wear to irid ............... 200.00
Candlesticks, pr, 9-1/4" h, Free Hand Ware, orange mirror luster.... 275.00
Compote, 7-1/2" d, Jewel Ware, irid teal blue ............................. 75.00
Creamer, Jewel Ware, amethyst, pearl, and green luster ............. 80.00
Rose Bowl, 6" d, Free Hand Ware, irid orange, white floral cutting.... 85.00
Vanity Jar, 7-5/8" h, Spun, pink, reeded ........................................ 95.00
Vase
    4-3/4" h, 8" d, opaque white body, irid golden-orange ext., impressionistic blue dec of eight heart-shaped blossoms, blue vines, blue rim, brilliant irid golden-orange int., gold paper label .......... 1,000.00
    6" h, Free Hand Ware, bulbous yellow, orange int. rim ....... 200.00
    6-1/2" h, Mosaic, deep cobalt blue body, shaded and swirled with opal, irid orange lining ..................................................... 550.00
    6-5/8" h, 4-1/8" d, Free Hand Ware, ovoid tapering body, short neck, flattened flaring rim, oyster white irid body, green hearts and vines dec, deep bronze int. ...................................... 350.00
    8" h, Jewel Ware, flared rim, irid silver, mulberry ground.... 180.00
    8-1/8" h, flared mouth over slender waisted body, flared base of cobalt blue and opal swirled glass, golden orange luster int., polished pontil, c1924 ............................................. 425.00
    8-1/2" h, 4-1/2" w, deep blue Heart and Vine dec, applied cobalt blue glass rim, apricot colored throat ........................... 1,495.00
    11-1/4" h, Free Hand Ware, tall slender ovoid body, tapering slightly to flared rim, glossy cobalt blue ext., white hearts and random vine dec, orig irid int. ......................................... 600.00
    11-1/2" h, Free Hand Ware, orange ground, deep blue Drag Loops over white, iridescent surface ............................... 875.00

## Pressed

Animal, owl, milk glass ............................................................ 50.00
Basket, miniature, basketweave, marigold carnival ................... 275.00
Bowl
    7-1/2" d, Beaded Block, green ........................................ 45.00
    9" d, Roses pattern, milk glass ...................................... 25.00
Bowl, cov, purple slag, #680 ...................................................... 65.00
Bud Vase, Candlewick, fan, floral cutting, 8-1/2" h ...................... 90.00
Candy Jar, cov, 1 lb, Cape Cod ................................................ 100.00
Cigarette Holder, Candlewick, eagle .......................................... 95.00
Coaster/Ashtray, Cape Cod ........................................................ 5.00
Cocktail, Cape Cod .................................................................. 12.00
Cologne Bottle, Hobnail, blue milk glass, ruffled stopper, pr......... 75.00
Compote, Hobnail, 5", crimped, green ........................................ 15.00
Creamer and Sugar
    Beaded Block, deep blue .............................................. 95.00
    Cape Cod, crystal ......................................................... 25.00
    Diamond Quilted, green ................................................. 25.00
Cruet, stopper, Cape Cod, verde green ...................................... 35.00
Goblet
    Cape Cod .................................................................... 12.50
    Tradition ...................................................................... 35.00
Ivy Ball, Hobnail, 6-1/2" h, green opalescent .............................. 45.00
Mayonnaise, Laced Edge, blue opalescent ................................. 75.00
Parfait, Cape Cod .................................................................... 12.00
Pitcher, Windmill, red slag........................................................ 60.00
Plate, Katy, blue opalescent, 8" d .............................................. 65.00
Salt and Pepper Shakers, pr, Cape Cod, fern green ................... 75.00
Sherbet, Mt. Vernon, ruby ........................................................ 30.00
Toothpick, Ivory, orig label........................................................ 24.00
Vase, Beaded Block, deep blue opal ......................................... 95.00

# INDIAN ARTIFACTS, AMERICAN

**History:** During the historic period, there were approximately 350 Indian tribes grouped into the following regions: Eskimo, Northeast and Woodland, Northwest Coast, Plains, and West and Southwest.

American Indian artifacts are quite popular. Currently, the market is stable following a rapid increase in prices during the 1970s.

**References:** C. J. Brafford and Laine Thom (comps.), *Dancing Colors: Paths of Native American Women,* Chronicle Books, 1992; Harold S. Colton, *Hopi Kachina Dolls,* revised ed., University of New Mexico Press, 1959, 1990 reprint; Lois Sherr Dubin, *North American Indian Jewelry and Adornment,* Harry N. Abrams, Inc., 1999; Gary L. Fogelman, *Identification and Price Guide for Indian Artifacts of the Northeast,* Fogelman Publishing, 1994; Lar Hothem, *Arrowheads & Projectile Points,* Collector Books, 1983, 1999 value update; ——, *Collecting Indian Knives, Identification and values, Second Edition,* Krause Publications, 2000; ——, *Collector's Guide to Indian Pipes,* Collector Books, 1999; ——, *Indian Artifacts of the Midwest,* Book I (1992, 1996 value update), Book II (1995, 1999 value update), Book III (1997, 1999 value update), Book IV (2000), Collector Books; ——, *Indian Axes & Related Stone Artifacts,* Collector Books, 1996; *North American Indian Artifacts,* 6th ed., Krause Publications, 1998; Preston E. Miller and Carolyn Corey, *The Four Winds Guide To Indian Trade Goods and Replicas,* Schiffer, 1998; Karen and Ralph Norris, *Northwest Carving Traditions,* Schiffer Publishing, 1999; Robert M. Overstreet, *Overstreet Indian Arrowheads Identification and Price Guide,* 6th edition, Avon Books, 1999; Lillian Peaster, *Pueblo Pottery Families,* Schiffer Publishing, 1997; Dawn E. Reno, *Native American Collectibles,* Avon Books, 1994; Nancy N. Schiffer, *Indian Dolls,* Schiffer Publishing, 1997; Peter N. Schiffer, *Indian Jewelry on the Market,* Schiffer Publishing, 1996; Lawrence N. Tully & Steven N. Tully, *Field Guide to Flint Arrowheads & Knives of North American Indians,* Collector Books, 1997, 2000 value update; Sarah Peabody Turnbaugh and William A. Turnbaugh, *Indian Baskets,* Schiffer Publishing, 1997; Barton Wright, *Hallmarks of the Southwest,* Schiffer Publishing, 2000.

**Periodicals:** *American Indian Art Magazine,* 7314 E. Osborn Dr., Scottsdale, AZ 85251; *American Indian Bas-*

**Blanket, Navajo, c1920, pictorial, corn stalk with birds, feather, bows and arrows, finely woven, gray, ivory, brown, black, and green, 33" w, 36" l, $825. Photo courtesy of Jackson's Auctioneers & Appraisers.**

*ketry Magazine,* P.O. Box 66124, Portland, OR 97266; *Indian-Artifact Magazine,* RD #1 Box 240, Turbotville, PA 17772; *Indian Trader,* P.O. Box 1421, Gallup, NM 87305; *Whispering Wind Magazine,* 8009 Wales St., New Orleans, LA 70126.

**Collectors' Club:** Genuine Indian Relic Society, Int., 8117 Preston Road, Dallas, TX 75225-6324; Indian Arts & Crafts Association, Suite B, 122 Laveta NE, Suite B, Albuquerque, NM 87108.

**Museums:** Amerind Foundation, Inc., Dragoon, AZ; The Heard Museum, Phoenix, AZ; Colorado River Indian Tribes Museum, Parker, AZ; Favell Museum of Western Art & Indian Artifacts, Klamath Falls, OR; Field Museum of Natural History, Chicago, IL; Grand Rapids Public Museum, Grand Rapids, MI; Indian Center Museum, Wichita, KS; Institute of American Indian Arts Museum, Sante Fe, NM; Maryhill Museum of Art, Goldendale, WA; Museum of Classical Antiquities & Primitive Arts, Medford, NJ; Museum of the American Indian, Heye Foundation, New York, NY; US Dept. of the Interior Museum, Washington, DC; Wheelwright Museum of the American Indian, Sante Fe, NM.

**Note:** American Indian artifacts listed below are prehistoric or historic objects made on the North American continent.

Bag
    11-3/4" l, Plateau, beaded asymmetrical flora pattern, mauve ground, backed with yarn adorned corn husk bag fragment, c1910 ............................................................................. 175.00
    18" l, Nez Perce, Plateau, cornhusk, dyed husk, repeated diamonds and stepped geometric motifs, blue, orange, pink, and yellow, slight fading .......................................................... 980.00
    22" l, 16" w, Nez Perce, Plateau, cornhusk, dyed husk and yarn geometric motifs, one side in purple and green repeating parallelogram motif, ................................................................ 1,610.00
Bandoleer, 40" l, Ojibwa, Great Lakes, c1880, beaded cloth, backed in cotton and wool trade cloth, shoulder strap with beaded bilateral geometric and flora design, heart and rhombodial devices, pumpkin, greasy yellow, navy, and bottle green beads, white field, bag sides bound with olive worsted tape with pumpkin, white, and yellow-amber beadwork, central panel of bilateral design of beads similar to strap, loom beaded tabs of repeated heart and rhomboidal devices, red and olive wool yard tassels, c1880 ............................................. 3,780.00
Basket, cov, 4" d, 3" h, Wakeshan, Northern region, twined, cov, finely woven with branching design around body and top of lid ........ 275.00
Basket, open
    3-1/4" h, 14" d, Pima, shallow, geometric pattern dec ........ 225.00
    3-1/2" h, 7-1/8" d, Alaskan Eskimo, lidded, diamond design in light and dark fiber, missing stitches, rim splits ................ 200.00

4-3/4" d, 4" h, Tinglit, Yakutat, deep berry type, rect and diamond eye designs, beargrass and bracken fern root, spruce body, old tag reads "grass utility basket, Yucatat Alaska," some wear to rim ........................................................................................ 380.00

7-1/2" h, 5" h, Tinglit "eye-hole," spruce root dec with orange dyed beargrass, fern false embroidery in firewood design ....... 615.00

8" h, 10" w, Pima, stepped geometric pattern dec, damage to bottom .......................................................................................... 100.00

8" h, 10-1/2" w, Pima/Papago, sides dec with geometric pattern ................................................................................. 100.00

11" h, Apache, Southwest, burden-style, twined, two rows of tin cone danglers, inverted cone at base, early 20th C ......... 350.00

13-1/4" d, 26" h, Taconic, oblong cylindrical form, two wooden fixed handles, hinged cov, 19th C, cover detached, minor breaks .................................................................................... 250.00

Bird Effigy Jar, 5" h, pottery, Casa Grandes, Southwest, cream, red, and brown slip painted geometric devices, 12th/13th C, loss and cracks ..................................................................................... 300.00

Blanket Strip, 58" l, 3-1/2" w, Lakota, beaded buffalo hide, repeated cross-roundel device separated by barred designs, white heart red, apple green, dark blue, and faceted metallic beds, white field, c1880, minor bead loss .................................................................. 2,100.00

Bracelet

1/2" w, Navajo, silver and turquoise, sq stone, stamped design, applied silver beading, c1920.......................................... 400.00

3/4" w, Navajo, silver and turquoise, round and elliptical turquoise stones, stamped and twisted silver, c1930...................... 575.00

3-1/2" h, Navajo, silver, 2 pcs of turquoise, berry and leaf silver work, soldered repair on back ................................... 140.00

Bottle, basketry, 10-1/2" h, Nootka, Northwest, twined, finely woven, decorative bands, sea birds, and boats, early 20th C ...........320.00

Bowl, basketry

6-1/2" d, 4" h, Northern CA, Kanuk, half twined overlay, stepped design of beargrasses and maidenhair fern, red dyed woodwards fern ground, three faint white smudges on one side.............615.00

11" d, Washoe, Southwest, finely coiled, unusually patterned geometric devices, c1800 ................................................. 1,955.00

14" d, Pima, Southwest, coiled, abstract rosette pattern with geometric devices ............................................................ 980.00

15" l, Apache, Southwest, oval, shallow, positive/negative stepped devices, four sets of paired dogs, c1920......... 1,150.00

17-3/4" d, Yokuts, CA, finely woven, two rows of hourglass devices, pair of small bear paw like motifs, c1800 ........ 1,265.00

Bowl, pottery

3" h, Santa Clara Pueblo, Southwest, sgd "Joy Cain" in slip, deeply carved geometric motifs ......................................... 15.00

3-3/4" h, Hopi, Southwest, sgd "Adelle Nampeyo," highly stylized bear paw motif, some abrasion at lip ............................... 345.00

**Basket, Winnebago, Northern WI, c1850, ash splint with red stained dec, remnants of 1843 newspaper lining, 18" x 12" x 11", $165. Photo courtesy of Jackson's Auctioneers & Appraisers.**

4-3/4" d, Zuni, Southwest, red, cream, and brown slip designs, geometric neck band with deer, heart lines, and floral motif, c1920, minor surface wear............................................... 350.00

5" d, Southwest, black and red geometric devices, cream ground, applied snake at rim, mid-20th C ................................... 115.00

5" h, Acoma Pueblo, Southwest, body painted in geometric and foliate motif, labeled in pencil "Acoma $1.00" at shoulder, indented base, chipped, surface discoloration, pitting ... 230.000

5-1/4" d, Hopi, Southwest, sgd "Nellie Nampeyo" at base, creamy orange ground, brown slip flora design .......................... 150.00

Canteen, pottery, 4-1/2" d, Hopi, Southwest, red and black painted Kachina head design, creamy orange ground ........................ 690.00

Cradle Board

27" l, 9" w, carved wood head with painted eyes, wrapped in green cloth, deerskin wrapping with white bead dec........ 200.00

33" l, Paiute, Great Basin, wicker frame and damaged sun shade, covered in buckskin hide, applied and loomed beadwork, beaded cotton cloth pillow fastened to wicker structure, double rows of fringed danglers with shells and large multicolored beads, back with elongated fringe, top front with loomed strips and two applied beaded celestial motifs, c1900............... 460.00

44" l, Central Plains, beaded buffalo hide calico lined cradle, edge roll beaded in bottle green and devices to white field, form beaded in stepped geometric devices, crossed, forked linear devices, hourglasses and arrows, pumpkin, light and dark blue, white heart red, greasy yellow, white ground, stained yellow hide ties, side trim of barley corn beads and skeleton key suspensions, profusely tacked wood slats, c1880............59,700.00

Cradle Cover, 13-1/2" l, Plains, beaded and quilled, native tanned hide, roll beaded edge, white, apple green, and greasy yellow beads, continuous-lopped lined faded red and cream quillwork on sides, yellow quilled "elk dreamer" motif top, c1880, damage, loss, tears to hide and quillwork, some old repairs............................................... 690.00

Cribbage Board, 20" l, Eskimo, carved ivory, incised and carved animal motifs, seals, whales, caribou, fox, fish, an sea birds, repaired and unrepaired cracks............................................................... 460.00

Dance Kilt, 30" h, 41" w, Santa Domingo Pueblo, painted single cloth panel, pair of classic facing Avanyo (plumed serpents) in black, tin cone rattles, red band at bottom, aged patina, fold lines, soiling, few missing cones ....................................................................... 440.00

Doll

Arapaho, Southern Plains, beaded hide, cloth form, white fringed leggings and dress, white, wine, red, powder blue, and green dec, braided horsehair coiffure, beaded facial features, c1890, 12" h............................................................................... 1,265.00

Eskimo, inked facial features, muslin body, sealskin parka, mitten, one mukluk. 15" l................................................................. 250.00

Iroquois, cornhusk, male and female, well clothed in stroud cloth and cotton, edge beaded satin trim,13" h, late 19th C, pr 635.00

Katsina, Hopi, mudhead clown or Koyemsi, three gourds on head, body paint, and kilt, old tag says "Mudhead...," 9" h, age crack, one foot broken ........................................................................ 370.00

Mohave, painted clay, late 19th C................................................. 920.00

Skookum, man wrapped in blanket, moccasins on feet, crying papoose in cradle board, 12" l, damage to faces .......... 1,485.00

Ute, Plains, beaded hide, cloth form, hide leggings, clothes, and head, yellow paint on leggings and yoke, multicolored beadwork, beaded and modeled facial features, plaited horse hair, late 19th C.................................................................................. 865.00

Yuma, maternity, painted clay, cloth, beads, and horsehair, 19th C.....................................................................................2,875.00

Yuma, polychrome figure, face, and torso painted in linear tattoo motif, skirt, sash, hair, and band of organic matter, damage, one leg partially missing, 5-1/2" h ........................................ 1,035.00

Dough Bowl

11-1/2" d, Acoma Pueblo, Southwest, black and orange stepped geometric devices, cream ground, int. with band of elliptical devices, deeply patinated, c1920, repaired cracks at lip .................... 575.00

19-1/2" d, Santo Domingo Pueblo, Southwest, band of dec geometric devices, drill hole at base, paint loss, major surface abrasion.................................................................................... 865.00

Drum

16" d, 3-1/2" d, hand held, painted rawhide head, reinforced wood frame, flat side painted yellow, green dot center, sgd in several different places, two old sinew repairs, green painted edges, rawhide lacing and hand hold .......................................... 450.00

25" d, Southwest, attributed to Tarahumara, hide covered, painted brick red cross, multi-pointed star, c1940 ......................... 490.00

Hat

3-1/2" h, 7" d, basketry, Northern California, attributed to Hupa, decorative bands, main one triangles with bracken fern root, minor wear ............................................................................. 310.00

6" h, 15" d, basketry, Northwest, Nootka or Tingit, cone shaped outside, inner round attached insert to hold to head, yellow, blue, red, green, and black paint dec, one side is face, other eyes and patterns, rough rim edge ............................... 2,600.00

7-1/2" h, Eastern Woodlands Iroquois, four black velvet triangular panels, white, yellow, red, blue, green, and opalescent floral beading, some bead loss, wear, damage to silk lining ..... 660.00

Jar, basketry

5" h, Tulare, CA, finely woven, polychrome, double rattlesnake bands, some minor loss ................................................. 1,265.00

9-1/2" d, Tubatulatal, CA, finely coiled, repeated cross devices in four rows at neck and shoulder, followed by two rows of rhomboidal devices with male and female figures, 19th C .... 3,110.00

Jar, pottery

3" h, Southwest, sgd "Fannie Nampeyo," cream, orange, and brown highly stylized geometric bear paw motif ............... 320.00

3-1/2" h, San Ildefonso Pueblo, Southwest, sgd "Maria" and "Santana" at base, highly polished gunmetal finish, decorative band of repeated geometric devices at neck, minor abrasion to finish ................................................................. 375.00

4-3/8" h, 5" d, Acoma Pueblo, Southwest, white polished slip with umber and red heartline deer, base sgd "Lucy M. Lewis, Acoma Pueblo, Southwest, N.M.," small scratches and flakes .... 275.00

5-1/2" h, Acoma Pueblo, Southwest, sgd "Lucy M. Lewis," brown and creamy slip, linear and geometric design, minor surface wear ......................................................................... 920.00

6-1/4" h, Santa Clara Pueblo, Southwest, sgd "Tina Garcia" at base, Blackware, highly polished surface ...................... 230.00

6-1/2" h, Santa Domingo Pueblo, Southwest, black and cream repeated geometric devices ........................................... 300.00

12-1/4" h, San Ildefonso Pueblo, Southwest, sgd "Marie," highly polished gunmetal finish, repeated geometrics motifs below lip, anther decorative band below neck with Avanyu water serpent and rain cloud motifs, abrasions and small chips to mouth ............. 1,610.00

Kachina, 10" h, Southwest, Hopi, felt kilt and tunic clad priest figure, articulated arms, 20th C ...................................................... 320.00

Kayak, 27" l, Eskimo, hide covered, wood frame, two person, 19th C ..................................................................................... 635.00

Leggings, pr, 33" l, Plains Apache, natural hide, fringed outside edges, bottoms finished with short fringe and scalloped edges, c1880 .... 865.00

Mask

11-1/2" h, 7-1/2" w, Northwest Coast, painted and carved wood, white highlights around crescent-shaped eyes, red nose and lips, black ground .............................................................. 2,000.00

8-1/2" h, 14-1/2" l, 8" w, Northwest Coast, wolf, articulated form, wolfs teeth and bone teeth, abalone eyes, copper eyebrows, painted red, blue, and black, movable jaw, early 20th C ....2,400.00

Moccasins, pr

7" l, Plains, attributed to Arapaho, youth, white beaded bands with medium blue fields, checkered terraced dark blue, lavender, and pink bands ............................................................... 330.00

10" l, Cheyenne, full spot stitch beading, concentric medallions on fronts surmounted by cross, red, dark blue, and green beads on white ground, some beads missing ................................ 615.00

10-1/2" l, Northern Plains, Cheyenne, blue, dark blue, green, soft gold, dark red, and white beads, tongue and cuffs stained with yellow ochre, one tongue forked, damage to one cuff, minor bead loss ....................................................................... 1,485.00

10-1/2" l, Plains, attributed to Eastern Sioux, white roses with blue, yellow, and green stems, overall dark red ground with some orange beading on tongue, scalloped yellow beads at edge of cuff and tongue, repaired hole in one, minor bead loss .............. 440.00

Necklace

12-1/2" l, Pueblo, four-strand disk carved clamshells, polished shell, turquoise, and other stone nuggets, strung on organic cording, c1880 ................................................................. 320.00

16" l, Navajo, squash blossom, silver, 18 pcs of turquoise, support chain broken, minor dents to blossoms ........................... 385.00

Olla

7-1/2" h, Zia Pueblo, Southwest, flared form, black and white, repeated geometric forms with hatching, indented base, c1920 ................................................................................. 1,610.00

7-3/4" d, Acoma Pueblo, Southwest, geometric stepped and elliptical devices, hatching in black and light orange, white ground, base indented, c1920, small puncture ............................ 750.00

8-1/2" h, 11" d, Acoma Pueblo, Southwest, black and white geometric pattern of feathers and arrowheads ..................... 450.00

9" h, Zia Pueblo, Southwest, upper body painted in cream, black, and red, alternating road runner and avian form, floral motifs, banded arched devices, indented base, c1920, minor slip loss ..................................................................... 1,495.00

11" h, 13" w, Acoma Pueblo, Southwest, three red, black, and white parrots, three large flowers and geometric patterns, pieced together from several parts, one 2-1/2" sq missing dec ........ 400.00

Olla, cov, 10-1/2" h, Tesuque Pueblo, Southwest, black stylized cloud and rain motif, geometric motifs, white ground, lid with conforming dec, labeled "3780" inside, indented bottom, c1900, some burn marks ..................................................................................... 11,500.00

Ornament, 10" l, Plains, c1885, rect, white bead ground with cranberry white heart reds, green and blue centered with cut brass beaded stepped rectangles, blue bead looped border with quill wrapped parfleche at bottom, quilled rawhide, cone and dentalium dangles, remnant horsehair inside ..................................................... 385.00

Paddle, 42" l, Northwest Coast, carved cedar, one side carved with eagle motif, other with stylized bear, 19th C .......................... 175.00

Pipe Bag, 21" l, western Sioux, Lakota, native tanned hide, roll beaded top with descending three row beaded edgework, lower panel with geometric devices topped with coup feather, teepee, and cross devices, faceted metallic, dark blue, white heart red, apple green, and cobalt blue beads, white ground, lowest panel of aniline-dyed quillwork with fringe, c1880 ................................................ 2,415.00

Pitcher

6" h, Southwest, Roosevelt, black slip geometric motifs, white ground, repair to handle, chip at lip ................................. 230.00

8-1/2" h, Cochiti Pueblo, Southwest, black flora and foliate design, cream ground, handle, light fire spots ................ 145.00

Plate, 5-3/4" d, San Ildefonso Pueblo, Southwest, sgd in slip "Marie-Popovi," polished gunmetal finish, abstract feather design, 20th C ..1,380.00

Rug

2'9" x 4'8", Navaho, bands of hourglass shades surrounding central diamonds in stripe segments, carded reds, oranges, and russet with gray and black, natural color background ...... 415.00

2'10" x 4'11", South America, Peruvian, pictorial, woven, three llamas, zig-zag border, natural hand carded colors, damage, folded and stitched ends ................................................. 200.00

3' x 4'4", Navaho, simple stripe and corner fringe, central net area with small orange and yellow diagonal figured stripes, gray strip and red ends, turn of century transitional style, loss at one end, repair, some damage ..................................................... 525.00

3'6" x 5'9", Ganado Navaho, double bar cross in center, red, white, and black three banded border, carded gray/tan, c1905, minor color bleeding, damage, stitch repair, restitched over all selvages ................................................................................... 355.00

Saddle Blanket, 2'11" x 47", Navaho, carded tan central field, small nahokas figures in corners and border, red band, orange, natural, and dark brown stepped fret design, c1910, minor color bleeding and stains ................................................................................... 495.00

Seed Jar, pottery

4" h, San Ildefonso Pueblo, Southwest, sgd "Blue Corn," repeated black and tan feather motif, light umber ground .............. 490.00

5-1/2" h, Hopi, Southwest, sgd "Dextra" with ear of corn at base, sq opening, intricate geometric design on shoulder and body ...920.00

6-1/4" h, Hopi, Southwest, sgd "Clinton Polacca Nampeyo," red and brown slip, creamy ground, stylized bear paw motif, 20th C ........................................................230.00

Serape, 3'5" x 5'7", Navaho or Rio Grande Pueblo (Hopi and Zuni), heavyweight stripe, red, natural, and dark carded wool, 19th C, damage, edge loss, stabilization repairs ........................ 275.00

Shirt, 18" l, youth's, Plains Apache, buckskin with Southern Plains long fringe and ochre paint, poncho cut neck hemmed on both sides with sparsely spaced white beads, center front with thirteen inches of narrow fringe, body and sleeves painted dark ochre, shoulder seams surrounded by fine long fringe, edged in white, navy, and translucent wine red beads, each sleeve with red-ochre stripe with traces of dark horizontal stripes of varying width, outside sleeve edge trimmed with long fringe running about three-quarters of the length, cuff trimmed with single lane of lazy stitch white, wine red, black, and pony trader blue beadwork, c1880 ......................... 6,900.00

Shirt and Leggings, 21" l each, child's, Southern Plains, native tanned hide, trace yellow ochre, shirt fringed at yoke, shoulder, sleeves, and bottom, front and back yoke trimmed with narrow bands of white, translucent dark blue and pumpkin beads, front with cross device, cuffs with similar double band of beadwork, thicker hide leggings with outseam joined by leather straps, edged in double banded single row beadwork of white, light blue, and dark blue, fringe at outseams and cuff, c1900 ......................... 2,645.00

Shirt and Pants, man's, Northeast, buckskin, laced front pull-over shirt, machine sewn, scalloped edge yoke and fringe across back and back of sleeves, fancy stitched wide cuffs with red cotton edging, same red cloth lining down front, around collar and top of yoke, sleeves lined with natural cotton cloth; pants with wide waist band, four pockets of white cotton cloth, seven button fly, early trade buttons, watch pocket, outside seam with fine fringe, cuffs with eleven silvery buttons in gusset, all lined with red wool, some wear, and repairs, bullet hole .............................1,550.00

Slippers, 10" l, Eskimo, seal skin, hand pink felt trim, tag "Louis H. Werner Co.," early 20th C ........................................ 175.00

Spoon, 16-1/2" l, Northwest Coast, carved horn, pierced and incised goat horn totem handle attached to sheep horn ladle with nail 375.00

Storyteller Bear, 9" h, Cochiti Pueblo, Southwest, sgd "Seferina Ortiz," black, cream, and orange, seated, open mouth, four listening cubs ...............................................................825.00

Textile, 2'2" x 4'2", Navaho, finely woven regional with stylized Storm Pattern design elements, red, black, and natural, carded gray ground ...............................................................690.00

Totem Pole, 25-1/2" h, Northwest Coast, tongue and groove, sliding parts, some labeled on back, shaman, frog, raven, and eagle motifs ...............................................................460.00

Tray

10" d, Hopi, Second Mesa, basketry, fine coil, four lobed flower or butterfly design in soft aniline colors ............................... 110.00

12-3/4" d, Pima, Southwest, basketry, maze motif, coiled rim and Navajo silver and turquoise button ................................... 690.00

Vessel, pottery

4-1/2" h, Hopi, Southwest, sgd "S" with feather (Sylvia Naha Humphrey), globular, painted with stylized turtles and intricate geometric devices ............................................................. 865.00

6-1/2" h, Zuni, Southwest, olla-form, stepped geometric devices, flora and deer motifs, red and brown slip, white ground, corrugated band at lip, three sets of applied coupling frogs, late 19th C....................................................................3,105.00

7-3/4" h, Cochiti Pueblo, Southwest, horned owl form, small outlet under each wing, red and brown abstract feather motif on cream ground ............................................................. 1,095.00

8" h, Cochiti Pueblo, Southwest, clay form, surprised feline, black slip, creamy ground, hairline crack at neck ...................... 865.00

Vest

17" l, Lakota, Central Plain's, man's, fully beaded, native tanned buckskin, abstract teepee and geometric designs, white heart, red, greasy yellow, dark blue, medium blue, and faceted metallic beads, white ground, fringed bottom, late 19th C ..... 1,840.00

18" l, Northern Plains, beaded buckskin and cloth, asymmetrical floral motif, multicolored beads, pearl button closure, lined in brown cotton, printed tan cotton cloth backing, c1920 ..... 750.00

Vest and Belt, Woodlands, flora beaded and fringed buckskin vest, cotton lining, 40" l commercial leather belt with orange, blue, and white beads in geometric design, c1920 ......................................... 400.00

Wall Pocket, 23-3/4" l, Tlingit, Northwest Coast, edge beaded seal skin, two stroud cloth panels, bilateral beading of avian and flora forms ................................................................... 550.00

# INK BOTTLES

**History:** Ink was sold in glass or pottery bottles in the early 1700s in England. Retailers mixed their own formula and bottled it. The commercial production of ink did not begin in England until the late 18th century and in America until the early 19th century.

Initially, ink was supplied in often poorly manufactured pint or quart bottles from which smaller bottles could be filled. By the mid-19th century, when writing implements had been improved, emphasis was placed on making an "untippable" bottle. Shapes ranging from umbrellas to turtles were tried. Since ink bottles were usually displayed, shaped or molded bottles were popular.

The advent of the fountain pen relegated the ink bottle to the back drawer. Bottles lost their decorative design and became merely functional items.

**References:** Ralph & Terry Kovel, *Kovels' Bottles Price List*, 11th ed., Three Rivers Press, 1999; John Odell, *Digger Odell's Official Antique Bottle and Glass Collector Magazine Price Guide Series*, Vol. 4, published by author (1910 Shawhan Rd, Morrow, OH 45152), 1995.

**Periodical:** *Antique Bottle and Glass Collector*, P.O. Box 187, East Greenville, PA 18041.

**Additional Listings:** See *Warman's Americana & Collectibles* for more examples.

Bell

2-1/2" h, aqua ................................................................... 10.00

3-1/2" h, "M" emb on body, colorless ................................... 35.00

Boat

Cobalt blue, shear top......................................................... 28.00

Moss green, sear top, two pen rests, 2-1/2" h ...................... 30.00

**Waterman, emb "Pat'd 01759866," dug bottle with some sickness, $5.**

Cylindrical
    2" h, cobalt blue, ringed neck.................................28.00
    4-1/4" h, Waterman's, colorless, paper label with bottle of ink, wooden bullet shaped case, orig paper label....................10.00
    5-1/2" h, ice blue, 2 rings at bottom, 2 at top, 1-1/2" neck with pour lip ..................................................30.00
    6" h, Hyde London, cobalt blue, emb, 1-1/2" neck with pour lip.................................................60.00
Figural, America, 1860-90
    2" h, house, domed offset neck for, emb architectural features of front door and 4 windows, colorless, sheared mouth, smooth base, Carter's Ink, some remaining int. ink residue, C #614..........650.00
    2" h, locomotive, aquamarine, ground mouth, smooth base, C #715....................................800.00
    2-5/8" h, house, 1-1/2 story cottage form, full label on reverse "Bank of Writing Fluid, Manuf by the Senate Ink Co Philadelphia," aquamarine, tooled sq collared mouth, smooth base, small area of label slightly faded, C # 682 .......................300.00
    3-1/8" h, rect log cabin, colorless, ground mouth, smooth base, 1/8" bruise on int. of mouth, possibly done at manufacture..........375.00
Hexagonal, 9-7/8" h, America, 1900-20, "Carter," cathedral panels, colorless with pale yellow cast, machined mouth, smooth base, similar to C #820...............................700.00
Inverted Concial
    2-3/8" h, Stoddard, NH, 1846-60, deep yellow-olive, sheared mouth, pontil scar, pinhead flake on mouth edge, C #15..................170.00
    2-1/2" h, America, 1840-60, "Woods/Black Ink/Portland," aquamarine, inward rolled mouth, pontil scar, C #12, unearthed with some remaining stain .......................170.00
Master
    6" h, cobalt blue, round, pour spout, emb "Hyde London" ....85.00
    8-1/2" h, aqua, 2" neck, crude applied pour lip, some bubbles.................................................40.00
    10-1/2" h, eighteen sides, cobalt blue.................................95.00
Octagonal
    Aqua, cut away base to lay on side ........................20.00
    Harrison's Columbian Ink, light green ....................60.00
    Light forest green with slight amber swirls, burst top, 3-1/2" h.18.00
Square, Temple London, emb top, one pen rest, aqua................24.00
Teakettle, sapphire blue, long curved spout, orig metal cap, 2" h, C #1257 ..................................................500.00
Tent, light cornflower blue, ribbing from bottom of neck to base, single pen rest ..................................................85.00
Triangular, Derby's All British, emb, aqua, sheared lip .................30.00
Umbrella, America, 1840-60
    2-1/4" h, New England, 1840-60, octagonal, golden amber, sheared mouth, C #145....................160.00
    2-3/8" h, octagonal, sapphire blue, inward rolled mouth, pontil, scar, C #141 .......................700.00
    2-5/8" h, octagonal, lime green, labeled "Williams/Black/Empire/Ink/New York," tooled mouth, smooth base, label 95% intact, C #173 ..............................175.00
    2-5/8" h, octagonal, sapphire blue, inward rolled mouth, pontil, scar, C #129 ..............................950.00

# INKWELLS

**History:** Most of the commonly found inkwells were produced in the United States or Europe between the early 1800s and the 1930s. The most popular materials were glass and pottery because these substances resisted the corrosive effects of ink.

Inkwells were a sign of the office or wealth of an individual. The common man tended to dip his ink directly from the bottle. The years between 1870 and 1920 represent the golden age of inkwells when elaborate designs were produced.

**References:** Veldon Badders, *Collector's Guide to Inkwells: Identification and Values*, Book I (1995, 1998 value update), Book II, 1998, Collector Books; William E. Covill Jr., *Inkbottles and Inkwells*, William S. Sullwold Publishing, out of print; Jean and Franklin Hunting, *The Collector's World of Inkwells,* Schiffer Publishing, 2000.

**Collectors' Clubs:** St. Louis Inkwell Collectors Society, P.O. Box 29396, St. Louis, MO 63126; The Society of Inkwell Collectors, 5136 Thomas Ave. So, Minneapolis, MN 55410, http://www.soic.com.

**Additional Listings:** See *Warman's Americana & Collectibles* for more examples.

Art Glass
    3" h, flattened sphere of colorless glass with spiral air trap pattern, polished pontil, sterling silver hinged monogrammed cap, silver mkd "Sterling 2246" ................................375.00
    6-1/4" h, irid gold glass lid, hinged bronze inkwell, mounted on blown amber glass body with gold irid, set within conforming bronze base with six arrow shaped arms, six bulbed feet, glass reservoir, attributed to Tiffany, early 20th C, base plate missing, stress crack to glass lid and glass base.......................3,450.00
Basalt, 2-1/2" d, black, circular form, banded anthemion border in iron red and white Encaustic dec, imp Wedgwood mark, late 18th C, slight rim nicks ..................................................825.00
Brass, 4-1/2" sq inkwell, 9" l, 5" w tray, Clarence Crafters, butterfly design, brass patina, green highlights, imp mark....................110.00
Bronze
    4-3/4" x 4-1/2", elephant with chicken top, Chinese, sgd, c1850 ..................................................400.00
    10-1/4" h, figural, bust of satyr with hinged bask lid, flat leaf standard, tripartite base with scroll legs ending in hoof feet, late 19th/early 20th C ....................290.00
Cast Iron, 5" h, seated rotund man, eating turkey, polychrome dec, late 19th C..................................................350.00
Copper, 5" h, tooled and riveted, Forest Craft Guild, orig patina, imp mark..................................................400.00
Cut Glass, 4-1/2" h, floral engraved, monogrammed lid, sgd "Hawkes".................................................550.00
Gilt Metal, 7-5/8" w, 12" h, Egyptian Revival, ebonized wood base supported by gilt metal scrolled legs with scroll and foliage edge, topped by balusters, connected by ropetwist gallery, mounted to center with sphinx, flanked by squat obelisks enclosing ceramic inkwells, late 19th C, losses ....................420.00
Pewter, honeypot with underplate, blown-out bees, Kayserzinn. 400.00
Pottery, 1-7/8" h, 5" l, 6" w, double, orig lids, blue ground, white clouds dec, emb emblem, American Encaustic Tile Co......................125.00
Sheffield Silver, 11" w, 9" d, 5 h, Regency, mahogany, one drawer box, set of four silver ball feet, top section in silver over copper, two pen trays, silver topped inkwell, silver topped sander, central ring holder, inlay to drawer, small silver drawer knob ................................600.00
Silver, round hinged lid, front hinged compartment with gold wash int. for stamps, Birmingham, England, 20th C ..............................260.00
Staffordshire, 4-5/8" h, salmon and gray enameled, gilt trim, stag and doe dec, pr ..................................................275.00
Stag's Head, 10" l, 5" h, gilt metal, rect, trefoil feet, border of leaves, mounted to center with stag's head pen rest, flanked by two pressed glass inkwells, Bradley and Hubbard, late 19th C ...................350.00

# IRONS

**History:** Ironing devices have been used for many centuries, with the earliest references dating from 1100. Irons from the medieval, Renaissance, and early industrial eras can be found in Europe, but are rare. Fine engraved brass irons and hand-wrought irons predominated prior to 1850. After 1850, the iron underwent a series of rapid evolutionary changes.

Between 1850 and 1910, irons were heated in four ways: 1) a hot metal slug was inserted into the body, 2) a burning solid, e.g., coal or charcoal, was placed in the body, 3) a liquid or gas, e.g., alcohol, gasoline, or natural gas, was fed from an external tank and burned in the body, or 4) conduction heat, usually drawing heat from a stove top.

Electric irons are just beginning to find favor among iron collectors.

**References:** Dave Irons, *Even More Irons by Irons,* published by author, (223 Covered Bridge Rd, Northampton, PA 18067), 2000; ——, *Irons by Irons,* published by author 1994; ——, *More Irons by Irons,* published by author, 1997; ——, *Pressing Iron Patents,* published by author, 1994; Carol and Jimmy Walker, *Year 2000 Pressing Iron Price Guide,* Iron Talk, 1999.

**Periodical:** *Iron Talk,* P.O. Box 68, Waelder, TX 78959.

**Collectors' Clubs:** Club of the Friends of Ancient Smoothing Irons, P.O. Box 215, Carlsbad, CA 92008; Midwest Sad Iron Collectors Club, 24 Nob Hill Dr., St. Louis, MO 63138.

**Website:** www.ironsantiques.com

**Museums:** Henry Ford Museum, Dearborn, MI; Shelburne Museum, Shelburne, VT; Sturbridge Village, Sturbridge, MA.

**Additional Listings:** See *Warman's Americana & Collectibles* for more examples.

**Advisors:** David and Sue Irons.

## Charcoal, box

Bronze, India, massive 10-1/2" vertical size, vent holes ............. 130.00
Dragon, German, full bodied head of dragon as chimney, c1890 ....600.00
Everready, 1917, flat top ................................................... 120.00
Tall chimney, Vulcan face damper ...................................... 100.00

## Children's

Chattanooga, cast, 3-1/2" .................................................. 190.00
English, box slug, 4" ......................................................... 300.00
French, cast, boar or rooster emb on top surface ...................... 200.00
Goffering, Kenrick, brass (2-3/8"), with slug holder .................... 250.00

**Charcoal, wood handle, #3, $55.**

Mexican, engraved with flowers ................................................. 275.00
Spanish, tall chimney, charcoal, Mondragon, 3-5/8" .................. 500.00
Swan, cast, 2-1/2" to 3-1/4"
    No original paint ...................................................... 125.00
    Original paint, pin striped feathers .............................. 450.00
Toy Enterprise, mini handle, Centennial give-away, 7/8" ........... 500.00
Victor, #10, wood grip, 3" .......................................................... 200.00

## Flat Iron

Dover, No. 912, 4-1/8" .................................................................. 45.00
Enterprise, Star Iron, flat back with holes in handle .................... 110.00
Indicator, temperature indicator on top ...................................... 500.00
Mexican, wrought, bell in handle ................................................. 150.00
Ober
    #6, cast, 1912, 6" ................................................................ 45.00
    Two piece, size 3, 1895 ...................................................... 60.00
Sensible, No. 4, 5-1/4" ................................................................ 130.00
Simmons Special, 2 piece cold handle ........................................ 95.00
Two Piece, knob release under handle .......................................... 60.00
Weida's 1870, flip back handle, 4-1/2" ....................................... 400.00

## Fluter

Combination Type
    Flip over, revolving, alcohol heated ................................... 800.00
    Hewitt, clamp on fluter plate ............................................. 450.00
Machine Type
    Companion, clamp-on, gold paint ...................................... 600.00
    Crown, Am. Machine Co., Phila., orig paint and pin striping....300.00
    Dudley, 1816, orig paint and details ................................... 600.00
    English box type, small flutes ............................................ 500.00
    The Original Knox, orig paint .............................................. 400.00

## Goffering

Double barrel, Queen Anne tripod base, all brass ...................... 650.00
Single barrel, cast with paw feet .............................................. 400.00
Single barrel, decorative openwork base ................................... 450.00

## Hat

Egg on rod, wood handle ............................................................ 70.00
Electric, stretcher with crank ................................................... 150.00
McCoys, curved bottom ............................................................. 160.00
Shackle, moveable edge with groove ........................................ 150.00

## Liquid Fuel, gasoline

Am. Gas Machine Co. 1912, side tank ....................................... 250.00
Coleman, blue, model 4A, common ............................................. 80.00
Coleman, red, model 4, Canadian, excellent condition .............. 500.00
Imperial ...................................................................................... 100.00
Iwantu Gas Iron, 1910 ................................................................. 90.00

## Miscellaneous

Acme Tie Press, wood, with clamps ............................................. 60.00
Entrekin's Swing Back Burnisher, 1873, looks like a machine fluter with no flutes ................................................................................ 500.00
Mangle Machine, looks likes large wringer ................................ 500.00
Ober, cast sleeve, #1, 4-1/2" ..................................................... 300.00
Seam Iron, narrow body, all cast ................................................ 140.00
Tailor's, A. Griffith & Co. Balt., iron, give-away, 3-1/2" .............. 300.00

## Natural Gas

English, G. L. C. Kenrick, gray agate .......................................... 250.00
English, Metro, blue body, 1930 ................................................. 200.00
European, gas jet, ox tongue ....................................................... 80.00

## Polisher

Enterprise, Star Polisher, 1872, rounded edges, 5-1/2" .............. 110.00
French, dimpled bottom, Repose ................................................. 250.00
Geneva, diamond grid bottom, round nose ................................. 170.00
Gleason, round back type, heat shield ......................................... 130.00
Sweeney Iron, 1896, 5-3/4" ....................................................... 175.00

## Rocker Type
Geneva, most common, 1866.................................................80.00
The Best, two piece .................................................75.00
The Star, two piece .................................................150.00

## Roller Type
Am. Machine Co., wood handle.................................120.00
Clarks, 1879, cast carved handle..............................200.00

## Slug, box
Austrian, brass
    Box, turned post, swing gate .............................350.00
    Ox tongue slug, 3-1/2".....................................300.00
Belgium, round back ................................................400.00
Danish, all brass, decorative posts ............................250.00
Deans, L. F., top lifts off, can be used with fluter plate.........200.00
German, wrought, 1800 ............................................300.00
Italian, hand made, "L" posts ...................................400.00
Kendrick, top hinged at side......................................250.00
Scottish, round back, "S" posts .................................800.00

# IRONWARE

**History:** Iron, a metallic element that occurs abundantly in combined forms, has been known for centuries. Items made from iron range from the utilitarian to the decorative. Early hand-forged ironwares are of considerable interest to Americana collectors.

**References:** *Collectors Guide to Wagner Ware and Other Companies*, L-W Book Sales, 1994; Douglas Congdon-Martin, *Figurative Cast Iron*, Schiffer Publishing, 1994; *Griswold Cast Iron*, L-W Book Sales, 1997; Jon B. Haussler, *Griswold Muffin Pans,* Schiffer Publishing, 1997; Joan Kahr, *Edgar Brandt: Master of Art Deco Ironwork,* Harry N. Abrams, 1999; Kathryn McNerney, *Antique Iron Identification and Values*, Collector Books, 1984, 2001 value update; George C. Neumann, *Early American Antique Country Furnishings*, L-W Book Sales, 1984, 1993 reprint; David G. Smith and Chuck Wafford, *The Book of Griswold & Wagner,* 2nd ed., Schiffer Publishing, 2000.

**Periodicals:** *Cast Iron Cookware News*, 28 Angela Ave., San Anselmo, CA 94960; *Kettles 'n Cookware*, Drawer B, Perrysburg, NY 14129.

**Collectors' Club:** Griswold & Cast Iron Cookware Association, P.O. Drawer B, Perrysburg, NY 14129-0301.

**Additional Listings:** Banks; Boot Jacks; Doorstops; Fireplace Equipment; Food Molds; Irons; Kitchen Collectibles; Lamps; Tools.

Andirons, pr, wrought iron
    15" h, goose neck, triple-split holder, England or America, 18th C.................................................720.00
    17-1/2" w, 33" d, 29-3/4" h, wrought, Arts and Crafts, squared caps on sq standard, shaped handles and crossbar, shaped tripod feet.................................................230.00
Bed Warmer, 42-1/2" l, wrought iron, tooled brass lid is old mismatched replacement .................................................60.00
Bill Clip, 2" x 2-3/4", cast, figural Indian Chief, headdress and earrings, facing left, old brass color, hole for hanging................................90.00
Bird House, 13" h, 12" x 10" base, cast iron, two story sq house, bow windows and doorway, large back open door, red paint with gold trim, cupola on top, Victorian, one corner of roof gone .................1,750.00

Bookends, pr, 6" h, cast, Indian with full headdress, painted dec, late 19th C.................................................125.00
Bottle Opener, cast
    3-1/4" l, steel worker, worn polychrome dec .................140.00
    5-1/8" l, lion, gold dec .................................................75.00
    5-1/2" l, parrot on perch, polychrome dec.................65.00
    5-3/4" h, man with top hat, orig polychrome dec................150.00
Broiler, 12" d, 27" l, wrought iron, twisted detail, wavy lines, circular revolving top.................................................165.00
Candleholder, 21-1/2" h, 12" w, wrought iron, double adjustable, table top, center shaft with turned stopping knob, tripod base, penny feet, candleholder adjusts on metal springs, horizontal bar holds two candleholders with drip pans, two decorative hooks on side of metal supports .................................................2,750.00
Candlestand, 36" h, primitive, wrought iron, pricket, tripod base, pitted with rust.................................................420.00
Candlesticks, pr, 54-1/2" h, tripod base, adjustable sockets with push-ups, wrought iron.................................................1,430.00
Coffin Stand, 24-1/4" h, 49-3/4" w, 13" d, wrought iron, America, 19th C.................................................150.00
Doorstops, pr, 8" w, 12-1/2" h, Punch and Judy, Punch with dog, Judy with doll, cast, English, c1825-40.................................................275.00
Dough Scraper, 4-1/4" w, hand wrought, snake head, bent handle .................................................150.00
Garniture Vase, 5-1/2" d, 13-1/2" h, cast, campana form, tall sq base, relief on sides with neoclassical trophies, Restauration, c1825-30........700.00
Holder, 2-1/4" h, wrought iron, snake-form, clasping ball joint caliper form clamp, coiled body forms base, America, 19th C..........2,530.00
Kettle Shelf, 11-1/4" x 17", cast, reticulated top, straight narrow lets.................................................75.00
Mailbox, cast, Griswold No. 106 .................................................90.00
Paper Clip, cast, wall-type, figural, collie ...................................160.00
Parlor Stove, 24" w, 26" w, 23" d, 27-1/2" h base, cast iron, labeled "Campbell, Elisson and Co., Cincinnati, Ohio," bow front, four sliding doors, scrolled pilasters, cast with three scrolled feet, shell insert in base, emb "The Violet #4" on top and "1856".........500.00
Pie Crimper, 9-1/2" l, wrought iron wheel and handle, curly maple handle .................................................120.00
Pipe Tongs, wrought iron
    15-3/4" l, pierced tobacco tamp, 18th C.........1,000.00
    16-1/2" l, England or America, 18th C, very minor losses ..635.00
Plant Stand, 14" w, 12" d, 55" h, wrought, sq top above Corinthian-formed capitals, scrolling floral shaft, scroll-end plinth base, French Victorian, fourth quarter 19th C, price for pr.........2,400.00

**Kettle, three small feet, orig handle, $65.**

Plate Warmer, 13" w, 10" d, 28-1/2" h, cast and wrought-iron, four paw feet, America, c1830-40 ............................................. 660.00

Roaster

12" l, wrought iron, pierced pan, hinged lid, wooden handle....360.00

27-1/2" h, wrought iron, standing, ball finial above double and single pronged meat holders, sliding circular frame, tripod base, penny feet, England, late 18th C .................................... 500.00

Rush Light, 11-1/2" h, candle socket counter weight, twisted detail, turned wooden base with age cracks, wrought iron ................ 385.00

Sconce

10-1/2" w, 11" l, wrought iron and polished iron, Yellin manner, c1915-20, electrified, price for set of four ...................... 1,760.00

19" l, wrought iron, single light, ivy leaf motif, Italian, c1925-30, not electrified, price for pr.................................... 200.00

Shooting Gallery Figure, 4-1/2" h, cast, rooster, black finish 35.00

Spatula, 11" l, wrought iron, some wear.................................... 115.00

Spur, 6" l, wrought iron, lady's leg, brass trim, stamped initials in two places "V. O. W.," very worn old tooled leather ......................... 75.00

Stand, 53-3/4" w, 22-1/2" h, wrought iron, English or America, late 18th/early 19th C ................................................... 490.00

Trivet, 14-1/2" h, wrought, scrolled and pierced heart dec.......... 160.00

Trough, 26" l, 11" w, 4-7/8" h, cast iron, painted blue, corrosion, 19th C .............................................................. 300.00

Umbrella Stand, 42" d, 28-1/4" h, cast iron, figural, sailor with stylized loop of rigging, standing on crow's nest surrounded by anchor, paddle, and ship's stores, ovoid flat leaf base, removable drip pan, imp mark for Corneau Freres, Charleville, France, late 19th C ....... 990.00

Urn, 32" h, cast, classical-style, painted black, two handles, figures on sides, waisted socle on sq plinth base, early 20th C............. 2,070.00

Wall Sconce, wrought iron, America, late 18th/early 19th C, corrosion

19-1/2" l, cutout pinwheel design ..................................... 425.00

26" h, trammel bracket..................................................... 450.00

Windmill Weight, cast, horse, Dempster, repainted .................... 300.00

# IVORY

**History:** Ivory, a yellowish white organic material, comes from the teeth or tusks of animals and lends itself to carving. Many cultures have used it for centuries to make artistic and utilitarian items.

A cross section of elephant ivory will have a reticulated crisscross pattern. Hippopotamus teeth, walrus tusks, whale teeth, narwhal tusks, and boar tusks also are forms of ivory. Vegetable ivory, bone, stag horn, and plastic are ivory substitutes which often confuse collectors. For information on how to identify real ivory, see Bernard Rosett's "Is It Genuine Ivory" in Sandra Andacht's *Oriental Antiques & Art: An Identification and Value Guide* (Wallace-Homestead, 1987).

**References:** Edgard O. Espinoza and Mary-Jacque Mann, *Identification for Ivory and Ivory Substitutes*, 2nd ed., World Wildlife Fund, 1992; Gloria and Robert Mascarelli, *Oriental Antiques*, Wallace-Homestead, out of print.

**Periodical:** *Netsuke & Ivory Carving Newsletter*, 3203 Adams Way, Ambler, PA 19002.

**Collectors' Club:** International Ivory Society, 11109 Nicholas Dr., Wheaton, MD 20902.

**Note:** Dealers and collectors should be familiar with The Endangered Species Act of 1973, amended in 1978, which limits the importation and sale of antique ivory and tortoiseshell items.

Box, 4" d, carved, lid surmounted by rampant dragon in clouds motif, body of box with lozenge pattern, China, 19th C ...................... 490.00

Bust

7-1/2" h, General Sherman, Continental............................... 525.00

10-1/2" h, carved head and headdress, some seams and cracks poorly glued................................................................ 370.00

Carving

4-1/2" x 4-1/2", general on horseback with his attendants, carved wooden stand, China, late 19th C..................................... 260.00

6-3/4" h, Sciobo, female divinity, polychrome and gilt dec, sgd on base within circular cartouche, Japan, Taisho period, c1915........... 425.00

7" l, Ebisu with large fish, mother-of-pearl inlay, stained details, Japan .......................................................................... 520.00

8" h, group of women in garden vignette, carved fitted stand, China, late 19th C....................................................... 460.00

8" h, toba on mule, stained details, sgd, Japan ................. 815.00

8-1/4" h, goddess Kuan yin with her attendant, carved fitted rosewood stand, China, late 19th C....................................... 260.00

9" h, two farmers struggling with cart of vegetables, sgd "Goto," Japan ...................................................................... 500.00

12" l, branch of apples, fruit and foliage, polychromed natural colors, Taisho period, c1920............................................. 575.00

19-1/2" h, woman holding branches of flowers, fitted silver inlaid stand, China, orig box ................................................. 2,645.00

Chess Piece, drum shape, engraved with single character, China, 19th C or earlier ......................................................................... 220.00

Chess Set, 6-1/2" h, figures of immortals and warriors, China, 19th C .............................................................................. 1,150.00

Coffer, 4-1/2" w, 4" h, Victorian, mid 19th C, simulated straps and ivory studs, orig key ....................................................................... 375.00

Cup, 5-1/2" h, relief carved dec of retriever, Continental ........... 500.00

Cylinder, 7" h, pierce carved scenes, pagodas, trees, animals, people, Oriental carved........................................................................... 440.00

Diptych, 3-1/4" w, 5-3/8" h, carved ivory panels set in hinged wooden frame, one panel depicting Madonna and Child with heavenly Host, other with Christ on the cross, both in gothic arches, Continental, late 19th/early 20th C ................................................................ 1,265.00

Figure

6-1/2" h, musical band, each piece differing instrument, all standing on treenware barrel, Continental, late 19th C, price for 8 pc set ............................................................................... 2,875.00

6-3/4" h, old man, robed figure holding peach, gilt and polychrome accents, sgd on cinnabar cartouche on base, Taisho period ......................................................................... 460.00

7" h, mandolin players, 18th C dress, turned wood base, French, late 19th C, price for pr ........................................... 3,780.00

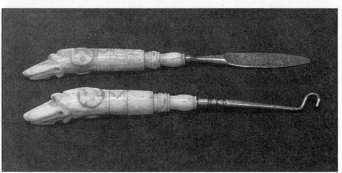

**Top: Manicure implement, bottom, button hook, both with carved dog's head handle, each $35.**

7-1/2" l, bull, finely modeled, textured fur, sgd "Kanko," Taisho period, lines ..................................................... 920.00

8" l, physician's figure, woman, Oriental carved, wooden base .............................................................................. 525.00

8-3/4" h, St. Sebastian, figured tied to tree trunk, arrow wounds, Continental, late 18th/early 19th C ................................. 1,150.00

9" h, Meirin holding fan and flower, Chinese ....................... 250.00

9" h, woman with flowers, bright colored polychrome, Oriental carved, attached wooden base ........................................ 220.00

10-1/4" l, woman with flower, colored beads set on costume, Oriental carved, wooden bench, glued head rest and floor .. 275.00

11-1/4" h, woman with fan and cage on chains, polychrome detail, Oriental carved, attached wooden base ........................... 330.00

14-1/2" h, Mu Lan, woman warrior, sword in hand, bow over her shoulder, dressed in armor, tinted with ink, 19th C, fitted rosewood stand, mounted as lamp, ivory finial ....................... 750.00

18-1/4" l, two elephants and two big cats, Indian carved, glued to wooden base ................................................................. 425.00

30" l, dragon, fully articulated, Japanese, Meiji period, minor losses ......................................................................... 2,185.00

Hemming Clamp, carved ivory figure of whale atop clamp, ivory disk thumbpiece, America, 19th C, age cracks ................................. 815.00

Jar, cov, 10-1/2" h, Archaic-style, darkly stained and inlaid with turquoise, coral, and carnelian cabochons, silver inlaid rosewood stands, China, lines .............................................................. 425.00

Letter Set, Aesthetic Movement, third quarter 19th C, carved, letter opener, seal, and pen, all with carved ivory handles with foliate spray, perched bird and naturalistically painted ladybug, fitted velvet lined morocco case ......................................................................... 350.00

Memorandum Tablet, 22" l, engraved with Kuan yin on one side and three Buddha, Simhavana Manjushri, Samantrabadra, and Manjushri Boddhisattva, probably Ming period, 1368-1644 ...................... 690.00

Miniature, vase and stand, 2-3/4" h, pomegranate shape, relief carving of gardens, pavilions, and mountains, sgd, base carved with flowers, Japanese ............................................................................... 460.00

Necessaire, 4" l, paint dec, fitted, tools, French, 1870 ............... 230.00

Necklace, 30-1/2" l, six carved ivory balls with Chinese motifs spaced by fancy silver ink chain, shrinkage cracks to ivory ................. 550.00

Okimono
Bishamonten and Hoitei, sgd "Gyokusan," 19th C .......... 1,850.00
Man and boy dancing, sgd, 19th C ..................................... 980.00

Panel, 13" l, 5" h, high relief carving of deities in palace garden, China 1,380.00

Pilgrim's Orb, 2-1/4" d, ext. carved with geometric motifs, hinged front cover opening to triptych depicting the Nativity, Continental, 19th C ............................................................................. 300.00

Plaque, 20" l, 10-3/4" h, painted, scene of conquering army receiving keys to a keep, sgd lower right "Meriller," ivory veneered frame with etched scroll dec, Continental, late 19th C ........................... 2,875.00

Sewing Clamp, carved screw top depicting man's head wearing Civil War period cap, clamp carved as set of teeth, incised heart motif, carved ivory thumbscrew, America, 19th C, age cracks .......... 690.00

Standish, 7-1/4" l, ivory and tortoiseshell Boullework, Continental, late 19th C, minor losses ............................................................ 690.00

Snuff Bottle, 3" h, flattened round shape, tall neck, foot rim, carved on both sides with masks, brocade carving on sides and neck, polychrome dec, two-character seal from signature to base, Japanese .................. 375.00

Tankard, 9-3/8" h, silver fittings, detailed relief carving, scenes of Dionysian revelry, mermaid handle, cherub finial, age cracks in ivory, silver base loose, old repair to hinge .................................... 5,300.00

Vase
9-1/2" h, carved, people in garden scenes, lion mask handles with jump rings, lids carved with foo dogs, 19th C, pr .......... 2,300.00
10-1/2" h, carved and pierced, ornate scenes of figures in garden vignettes, China, c1860, boxed, price for pr ................. 2,300.00
20" h, Buddhist and Taoist figures in landscape setting, iron mask handles with jump rings, lid surmounted by figure of an immortal with demon, small child and peacock, Chinese, mid 19th C, inlaid stand, mounted without drilling to lamp base ....... 6,150.00

Vase, cov, 14" h, high relief carving, two reserves of figures in palace setting, lid with two warriors locked in combat, archaic-style dragon handles, four-character Ch'ien Lung mark on base, China ............. 1,100.00

Wrist Rest
8" l, carved as bamboo section, int. with various naturalistically colored insects, China, price for pr .............................. 1,725.00
10-1/4" l, carved Buddhist divinities on one side, reverse with boat being towed, Ch'ien Lung period, 1735-96 ..................... 5,465.

# JADE

**History:** Jade is the generic name for two distinct minerals: nephrite and jadeite. Nephrite, an amphibole mineral from Central Asia that was used in pre-18th-century pieces, has a waxy surface and hues that range from white to an almost-black green. Jadeite, a pyroxene mineral found in Burma and used from 1700 to the present, has a glassy appearance and comes in various shades of white, green, yellow-brown, and violet.

Jade cannot be carved because of its hardness. Shapes are achieved by sawing and grinding with wet abrasives such as quartz, crushed garnets, and carborundum.

Prior to 1800, few items were signed or dated. Stylistic considerations are used to date pieces. The Ch'ien Lung period (1736-1795) is considered the golden age of jade.

**Periodical:** *Bulletin of the Friends of Jade*, 5004 Ensign St., San Diego, CA 92117.

**Museum:** Avery Brundage Collection, de Young Museum, San Francisco, CA.

Beads, double strand of jadeite beads graduating from 4.60 to 9.90 mm, 14kt yg, jade, and diamond clasp entered by marquise-shaped cabochon jade measuring 17.70 x 7.50 mm, stamped "Birks," 21-1/2" l ................................................................. 2,100.00
Belt Buckle
    Horse form, gray color stone, blue, black, and tan inclusions, reverse with two bosses for suspension, 3/4" x 2-3/4" .. 3,565.00
    Three-part type, celadon colored stone, tan veins, relief carved lotus and two foo dog heads, 19th C ................................ 230.00
Bottle, Nephrite, even celadon colored, rounded four-side oblong form, flat sq foot, finely carved bamboo and lotuses ...................... 2,300.00
Boulder, carved, 8" x 6", mountain landscape, three figures, nephrite stone with celadon color, brown, black, and gray markings ........ 1,495.00
Bracelet
    Bangle, jadeite, hinged, 14kt yg chased dragon design, hallmark ................................................................. 575.00
    Lavender and tomato red, even tone stone, bright red markings, fitted embroidered box, 3-1/2" d, pr .............................. 7,200.00
    Uniform pale green stone, brilliant apple green inclusions . 920.00
Brush Washer, 3-1/8" h, peach on gnarled branch form, slender leaves encompassing sides, gray with dark brown, calcified to opaque buff base, Ming Dynasty ................................................................. 2,400.00

**Centerpiece, pink and green florals, 12-1/2" h, 21-1/2" d, $325.**

Buddha, 1-3/4" h, apple green stone, Pu Tai seated with rosary around his neck, 19th C .............................................................. 115.00
Chrysanthemum Bowl, carved in form of flower, Mughal-style, 19th C
    4" d, highly translucent celadon color stone, white inclusions ........................................................................ 290.00
    4-3/4" d, 1-1/4" h, gray stone, white clouds and mossy inclusions, raised flower shaped foot, Mughal-style, 19th C ............. 460.00
Clasp, 3" l, dragon, carved lotus button, 19th C ......................... 90.00
Ewer, cov, 9-3/4" h, mottled gray stone, baluster body, six vertical lobes, barbed rim encircled with key fret border, faceted spout and handle carved with clouds and surmounted by chliong, handle with tab, sage figure sleep amidst rocks and pine on conforming cov, Ming Dynasty ................................................................. 3,500.00
Figure
    Ebisu with large fish, mother-of-pearl inlay, stained details, Japan, 7" h ................................................................. 520.00
    Horse, green stone, brilliant apple green marking, darker inclusions, Chinese, 19th C, 2-1/2" l ........................................ 230.00
    Kylin, yellow jade with cinnabar, giving red and orange hue, carved openwork motif of birds and exotic animals, Chinese ........ 7,770.00
    Pair of crabs on lotus pod, tied with silk ribbon, pure white stone, slight greenish blue tone, 3" l ........................................ 325.00
Pendant
    2-1/2" l, 2" w, gray stone, bright amber brown skin, carved bats and peaches, 19th C ........................................ 260.00
    3-1/2" l, green spinach stone, form of lock composed of chih lung dragons and phoenix around a central medallion, four character seal, script inscription on reverse, mounted in enameled gilt silver box, 19th C ................................................................. 1,035.00
Pendant and Necklace, 2" l bright olive green pendant, carved with bird and pair of cucumbers, necklace of cord stung with six 1/2" d jade beads, two 1-1/2" l ornately carved peach pits ....................... 230.00
Ring, jadeite, collet-set marquise-shape within 14kg yg chased mount, applied bead and wiretwist dec, Chinese hallmarks, size 3-1/2 .... 225.00
Snuff Bottle, natural form pebble, off-white with yellow and brown skin, carved dragon, stem-shaped green Peking glass top .............. 300.00
Tray, 5" x 4", highly translucent stone, rect, carved allover with chrysanthemum petals radiating from central medallion, Mughai-style, 19th C ................................................................. 2,185.00
Water Coupe, 6" l, highly translucent very white stone, carved in form of basin with branches, leaves, and Buddha's hand, citrons, finely carved hung mu base with ling chih and foliage, China, 18th/19th C ...... 2,990.00
Wine Ewer, 6" x 3-1/2", burnt opaque green-gray stone with black veining, animal-form handle and spout, body and lid in flowering lotus form ................................................................. 230.00

# JASPERWARE

**History:** Jasperware is a hard, unglazed porcelain with a colored ground varying from the most common blues and greens to lavender, yellow, red, or black. The white designs, often classical in nature, are applied in relief. Jasperware was first produced at Wedgwood's Etruria Works in 1775. Josiah Wedgwood described it as "a fine terra-cotta of great beauty and delicacy proper for cameos."

In addition to Wedgwood, many other English potters produced jasperware. Two of the leaders were Adams and Copeland and Spode. Several Continental potters, e.g., Heubach, also produced the ware.

**References:** Susan and Al Bagdade, *Warman's English & Continental Pottery & Porcelain*, 3rd Edition, Krause Publications, 1998; R. K. Henrywood, *Relief-Moulded Jugs, 1820-1900*, Antique Collectors' Club.

**Museums:** British Museum, London, England; Memorial Hall Museum, Philadelphia, PA; Museum of Fine Arts, Boston, MA; Victoria & Albert Museum, London, England.

**Reproduction Alert:** Jasperware still is made today, especially by Wedgwood.

**Note:** This category includes jasperware pieces which were made by companies other than Wedgwood. Wedgwood jasperware is found in the Wedgwood listing.

Biscuit Jar, 5-1/2" d, light green jasper dipped body, applied yellow trellis, white floral dec, SP rim, handle, and cov, imp mark ........... 900.00
Bookends, pr, 6" h, white figural colonial man with cane, woman with basket, blue ground, Germany ................................................. 140.00
Bowl, 7" d, white classical figures, dark blue ground .................. 225.00
Box, cov, 5" l, oval, white relief carved cherub and nymph, blue ground, mkd "Schafer & Vater, Germany" ........................................ 70.00
Buckle, 3-3/8" d, solid blue, oval medallion with applied white classical relief, unmarked, c1800 ............................................................ 375.00
Candelabra, 19-1/2" h, dark blue dip, drums applied with white classical and foliate relief, mounted to later gilt-metal five-light stands, unmarked, late 18th C, chips and hairlines, price for pr ........... 460.00
Chandelier, 22" h, light blue dip, dish with applied white classical relief, gilt metal mounted with jasper knop centering supports, no visible mark, late 19th C ..................................................................... 635.00
Cheese dish, cov, 11" d, 11-1/4" h, high domed blue cov, white relief figures of classical ladies in panels, rolled base rim with white relief flower and leaf band, acorn finial, Dudson Bros., England ...... 575.00
Hair Receiver, 3-3/8" d, 3-1/2" h, white relief classical ladies and flowers, cupids on lid, blue ground, mkd "Germany" ......................... 75.00
Jardiniere, 7-1/2" h, light blue ground, white relief scene of Columbus landing, mkd "Copeland" ................................................... 225.00
Jug, 4-7/8" h, 4-3/8" d, blue ground, white relief hunting scene, man on horse with dogs and stag, white relief band, Copeland, 19th C . 90.00
Medallion, 2-1/2" x 3", oval, yellow dip, applied white classical subjects, spurious imp mark, England, 19th C, price for pr ........... 215.00
Pin Dish, green ground, white relief figures of Indian Chief holding bow and arrow, sgd "Heubach" ......................................................... 70.00
Pitcher
　6-7/8" h, 4-1/8" d, cylindrical, dark green ground, white relief classical ladies in panels, gray-green rim band with white relief band, Dudson Bros., England, 19th C ............................... 125.00
　7-7/8" h, 5" d, cylindrical, dark blue ground, band of small white relief classical figures around base, band of white relief floral Swags around rim, angled white handle, Copeland, 19th C ............. 150.00
Plaque, pierced for hanging
　Angel holding baby, cupid beside her, sage green ground, white relief figures and floral border, Germany, late 19th C ......... 90.00
　Chief Painted Horse, Indian in full headdress, owl border, white relief figures, green ground ............................................... 125.00
　Cupid kissing bust of lady, sage green ground, white relief figures and floral border, Germany, 6" d ..................................... 120.00

**Cheese Dish, tan ground, white classical figures, mkd "Adams," c1820, $365.**

Fisherman in rowboat being embraced by young lady, blue ground, white relief figure and floral border, Germany, 7-7/8" ............ 150.00
Potpourri Vase, cov, 11-3/8" h, dark blue dip, applied white relief with portraits above fruiting grapevine festoons terminating in ribbons, unmarked, attributed to Adams & Bromley, England, c1875 ......... 350.00
Sugar Shaker, hunt scene, dome top, cobalt blue ground, mkd "Adams" ............................................................................... 100.00
Tray, 6" x 5", oval, green ground, Indian on horseback aiming arrow at running buffalo, sgd "Heubach" ............................................... 135.00
Urn, 8" h, dark blue ground, white classical hunting scene, mkd "Adams, Tunstall, England" ....................................................... 210.00
Vase
　3-7/8" h, three-color, Diceware, engine turned dark blue ground, green quatrefoils, white foliate borders, unmarked, attributed to Wedgwood, England, early 19th C, covers missing, chip to socle rim, price for pr ...................................................... 2,645.00
　9-1/8" h, light blue dip, footed owl with white arabesque floral relief, mounted on drum base with dancing hours figures, imp "Adams," late 19th C, covers missing, price for pr ............ 635.00

# JEWEL BOXES

**History:** The evolution of jewelry was paralleled by the development of boxes in which to store it. Jewel-box design followed the fashion trends dictated by furniture styles. Many jewel boxes are lined.

Art Glass, 5" d, hinged, enameled pink morning glory dec ......... 175.00
Brass Mounted Leather, cushion form, fitted with foliate mask and mounts, red leather, lidded well and drawer, lined with silk, paw feet, orig key, Charles X, c1820-30 ............................................. 1,150.00
Ebony and Pietra Dura, 13-1/8" l, shaped octagon, inset with foliate and insect panels, red velvet int., Italian, cracks to case and one panel ........................................................................... 1,725.00
Enamel and Ebony, 8" h, enamel plaques with figures in 19th C garb, brass columns, lion's feet and capitals, Viennese, late 19th C ...1,495.00
Enamel and Silver, egg shaped, enamel dec of figures in landscapes, int. with landscape and putti, gilt silver mount, Viennese, 19th C ..... 1,265.00
Etched Metal and Glass, 9" l, 6-1/4" w, 3-1/8" h, rect, hinged lid, Pine Needle pattern overlay with beaded rim, green slag glass panels, int. fitted with green velvet lining, two lift-out trays, initials "M.F.T." engraved on lid, unsigned, attributed to Tiffany Studios, New York, early 20th C, one cracked panel, corrosion .......................... 1,610.00
French Enamel, 3" d, hinged, round, pink ground, floral dec, black and gold border, tiny enameled jewels, mounted on ornate French gilt holder ............................................................................... 300.00
Ivory, 8-1/2" x 8-1/2" x 3-1/2", rect, two doors including two drawers, two drawers below, stone appliqué and gilding, Oriental, losses to gilding ................................................................................ 775.00
Mount Washington, 5" d, hinged, green textured glass, colored floral dec ................................................................................... 375.00
Porcelain
　3-1/2" l, bombe, cobalt blue ground with landscapes, classical scenes with gilt accents, int. with flowers, brass mounts, Sevres-type .................................................................. 600.00
　6-1/2" l, shaped ovoid, burgundy ground, gilt scrollwork, lid printed and painted with mythological scene of Cupid and couple, sgd "Rita," int. of lid and box printed with floral sprays, maker's mark "BFS," French, 20th C ............................... 300.00
　9-1/2" w, 6-1/2" d, 4" h, Belle Epoque, Old Paris style, turquoise ground, edges mounted with gilt-brass in rococo taste.... 250.00
Silver Plate, Belle Epoque, rococo taste, c1890-1915, oval, worn to copper base at several points, 7-1/2" w, 6" d, 3" h ................... 165.00
Silver, sterling
　3-1/2" l, oval, repousse crown and laurel wreath with monogram, engraved sides, lid set with colored glass jewels and two miniature portraits on ivory, mkd "930" and partial European hallmarks ............................................................................ 385.00

Wave Crest, blue mottled background, pink florals, 12 sided, sgd "Kelva," 6" $1,050. Photo courtesy of Woody Auction.

7" l, rect, repousse floral design, maroon velvet lining, Jacob & Jenkins, early 20th C, 18 troy oz ................................... 1,100.00
9-1/2" w, 7" d, 7" h, Victorian, "R. C." maker, London, various relief reserves of knights and trophies emb on ext., int. lined in dark blue velvet ............................................................. 1,250.00
Silver Wirework, 10-3/8" l, 6" d, 4-1/2" h, rect, hinged lid, open wirework top and sides with fleur-de-lis and scroll dec, overlaid on blue moiré, ball feet, inside fitted with two compartmentalized lift-out trays ............ 900.00
Wavecrest, 4-1/2" w, Bella Ware, Helmschmeid Manufacturing Co, Meriden, CT, pale lavender ground, violet bunches within scroll, orig brass hardware, sgd on base ................................................... 250.00
Wood, 6" sq, 15-1/2" h, burl veneer, inlaid fans, watch hutch with lift top jewelry compartment, revolving center section with door and watch holder window, four black painted columns surround revolving box, sq base, round black feet, urn finish ..................................... 1,000.00

# JEWELRY

**History:** Jewelry has been a part of every culture. It is a way of displaying wealth, power, or love of beauty. In the current antiques marketplace, it is easiest to find jewelry dating after 1830.

Jewelry items were treasured and handed down as heirlooms from generation to generation. In the United States, antique jewelry is any jewelry at least 100 years old, a definition linked to U.S. Customs law. Pieces that do not meet the antique criteria but are at least 25 years old are called "period" or "heirloom/estate" jewelry.

The names of historical periods are commonly used when describing jewelry. The following list indicates the approximate dates for each era.

| | |
|---|---|
| Georgian | 1714-1830 |
| Victorian | 1837-1901 |
| Edwardian | 1890-1920 |
| Arts and Crafts | 1890-1920 |
| Art Nouveau | 1895-1910 |
| Art Deco | 1920-1935 |
| Retro Modern | 1935-1945 |
| Post-War Modern | 1945-1965 |

**References:** Lillian Baker, *Art Nouveau & Art Deco Jewelry*, Collector Books, 1981, 1997 value update; ——, *Fifty Years of Collectible Fashion Jewelry, 1925-1975*, Collector Books, 1997 values; ——, *100 Years of Collectible Jewelry, 1850-1950*, Collector Books, 1978, 1999 value update; Joanne D. Ball, *Costume Jewelers: The Golden Age of Design*, Schiffer Publishing, 2000; Joel A. Batech, *Kremlin Gold: 1000 Years of Russian Gems & Jewels*, Harry N. Abrams, 2000; Howard L. Bell Jr., *Cuff Jewelry*, published by author (P.O. Box 11695, Raytown, MO 64138), 1994; C. Jeanenne Bell, *Answers to Questions about Old Jewelry*, 5th ed., Krause Publications, 1999; ——, *Collector's Encyclopedia of Hairwork Jewelry: Identification and Values*, Collector Books, 1998; David Bennett and Daniela Mascetti, *Understanding Jewellery*, Antique Collectors' Club, 1999; France Borel, *Splendor of Ethnic Jewelry*, Harry N. Abrams, 1994; Marcia Brown, *Unsigned Beauties of Costume Jewelry*, Collector Books, 2000; Shirley Bury, *Jewellery 1789-1910*, Vols. I and II, Antique Collectors' Club, 1991; Deanna Farneti Cera, *Costume Jewellery*, Antique Collectors' Club, 1999; — *The Jewels of Miriam Haskell*, Antique Collectors' Club, 1999; Monica Lynn Clements and Patricia Rosser Clements, *Cameos: A Pocket Guide*, Schiffer Publishing, 1999; Franco Cologni and Eric Nussbaum, *Platinum By Cartier, Triumphs of the Jewelers' Art*, Harry N. Abrams, 1996; Genevieve Cummins and Neryvalle Taunton, *Chatelaines*, Antique Collector's Club, 1994.

Lydia Darbyshire and Janet Swarbrick (eds). *Jewelry, The Decorative Arts Library*, Chartwell Books, 1996; Ginny Redington Dawes and Corinne Davidov, *Victorian Jewelry*, Abbeville Press, 1991; Daniel J. Dennis, Jr., *Gems: A Lifely Guide for the Casual Collector*, Harry N. Abrams, 1999; Ulysses Grant Dietz, Janet Zapata et. al., *The Glitter & the Gold, Fashioning America's Jewelry*, The Newark Museum, 1997; Janet Drucker, *Georg Jensen, A Tradition of Splendid Silver*, Schiffer Publishing, 1997; Lois Sherr Dubin, *North American Indian Jewelry and Adornment*, Harry N. Abrams, Inc., 1999; Alastair Duncan, *Paris Salons 1895-1914*, Jewelry, 2 vols., Antique Collectors' Club, 1994; Martin Eidelberg, (ed.), *Messengers of Modernism, American Studio Jewelry 1940-1960*, Flammarion, 1996; Lodovica Rizzoli Eleuteri, *Twentieth–Century Jewelry*, Electa, Abbeville, 1994; Martha Gandy Fales, *Jewelry in America 1600-1900*, Antique Collectors' Club, 1999; Fritz Falk, *Lalique and His Circle*, Arnoldsche, distributed by Antique Collectors' Club, 1999; Charlotte Gere and Geoffrey Munn, *Pre-Raphaelite to Arts & Crafts Jewelry*, Antique Collectors' Club, 1999; Stephen Giles, *Jewelry, Miller's Antiques Checklist*, Reed International Books Ltd., 1997; Geza von Habsburg, *Fabergé in America*, Thomas and Hudson, 1996; S. Sylvia Henzel, *Collectible Costume Jewelry, Third Edition*, Krause Publications, 1997; Helmet Kahlert, Richard Mühe, Gisbert L. Brunner, *Wristwatches: History Of A Century's Development*, Schiffer Publishing, 1999; George Frederick Kunz and Charles Hugh Stevenson, *Book of the Pearl*, Dover Publications, 1973; David Lancaster, *Art Nouveau Jewelry, Christie's Collectibles*, Bulfinch Press, Little Brown and Co., 1996.

Daniel Mascetti and Amanda Triossi, *Bulgari*, Abbeville Press, 1996; Daniel Mascetti and Amanda Triossi, *The Necklace, From Antiquity to the Present,* Harry N. Abrams, Inc., 1997; Antionette Matlins, *The Pearl Book,* GemStone Press, 1996; Patrick Mauries, *Jewelry by Chanel*, Bulfinch Press, 1993; Anna M. Miller, *Cameos Old and New*, Van Nostrand Reinhold, 1991; ——, *Illustrated Guide to Jewelry Appraising: Antique Period & Modern*, Chapman & Hall, 1990; Penny C. Morrill, *Silver Masters of Mexico,* Schiffer Publishing, 1996; Penny Chittim Morrill and Carol A. Beck, *Mexican Silver: 20th Century Handwrought Jewelry and Metalwork*, Schiffer Publishing, 1994; Gabriel Mourey et al., *Art Nouveau Jewellery & Fans*, Dover Publications, n.d.; Karima Parry, *Bakelite Bangles, Price & Identification Guide,* Krause Publications, 1999; Clare Phillips, *Jewelry, From Antiquity to the Present,* Thames and Hudson, 1996; Michael Poynder, *Jewelry, Reference & Price Guide,* Antique Collectors' Club, 1999; —, *Price Guide to Jewellery 3000 B.C.–1950 A.D.*, Antique Collectors' Club, 1990 reprint; Penny Proddow and Marion Fasel, *Diamonds, A Century of Spectacular Jewels,* Harry N. Abrams, 1996; Penny Proddow, Debra Healy, and Marion Fasel, *Hollywood Jewels*, Harry L. Abrams, 1992; Dorothy T. Rainwater, *American Jewelry Manufacturers*, Schiffer Publishing, 1988; Christie Romero, *Warman's Jewelry*, 2nd ed., Krause Publications, 1998; Fred Rezazadeh, *Collectible Silver Jewelry,* Collector Books, 2000; ——, *Costume Jewelry,* Collector Books, 2000; Judy Rudoe, *Cartier 1900-1939,* Harry N. Abrams, 1997; Nancy N. Schiffer, *Silver Jewelry Designs*, Schiffer Publishing, 1996; —, *The Best of Costume Jewelry,* 3rd ed., Schiffer Publishing, 1999; Sheryl Gross Shatz, *What's It Made Of? A Jewelry Materials Identification Guide*, 3rd ed., published by author (10931 Hunting Horn Dr., Santa Ana, CA 92705), 1991; Cherri Simonds, *Collectible Costume Jewelry,* Collector Books, 2000; Doris J. Snell, *Antique Jewelry with Prices, Second Edition,* Krause Publications, 1997; Ralph Turner, *Jewelry in Europe and America, New Times, New Thinking,* Thames and Hudson, 1995; Fred Ward, *Opals,* Gem Book Publishers, 1997; Janet Zapata, *Jewelry and Enamels of Louis Comfort Tiffany*, Harry N. Abrams, 1993.

**Periodicals:** *Auction Market Resource for Gems & Jewelry*, P.O. Box 7683, Rego Park, NY 11374; *Gems & Gemology*, Gemological Institute of America, 5355 Armada Drive, Carlsbad, CA 92008; *The Estate Jeweler,* Estate Jewelers Association of America, 209 Post St., Suite 718, San Francisco, CA 94108; *Professional Jeweler,* Bond Communications, 1500 Walnut St., Suite 1200, Philadelphia, PA 19102.

**Collectors' Clubs:** American Hatpin Society, 2101 Via Aguila, San Celemnte, CA 92672; American Society of Jewelry Historians, Box 103, 133A North Avenue, New Rochelle, NY 10804; Leaping Frog Antique Jewelry and Collectable Club, 4841 Martin Luther Blvd., Sacramento, CA 95820; National Antique Comb Collectors Club, 3748 Sunray Rd., Holiday, Fl 34691; National Cuff Link Society, P.O. Box 346, Prospect Heights, IL 60070; Society of Antique & Estate Jewelry, Ltd., 570 7th Ave., Suite 1900, New York, NY 10018.

**Videotapes:** C. Jeanne Bell, "Antique and Collectible Jewelry Video Series," Vol. I: "Victorian Jewelry, Circa 1837-1901," Vol. II: "Edwardian, Art Nouveau & Art Deco Jewelry, Circa 1887-1930's," Antique Images; Leigh Leshner and Christie Romero, "Hidden Treasures," Venture Entertainment (P.O. Box 55113, Sherman Oaks, CA 91413).

**Notes:** The value of a piece of old jewelry is derived from several criteria, including craftsmanship, scarcity, and the current value of precious metals and gemstones. Note that antique and period pieces should be set with stones that were cut in the manner in use at the time the piece was made. Antique jewelry is not comparable to contemporary pieces set with modern-cut stones and should not be appraised with the same standards. Nor should old-mine, old-European, or rose-cut stones be replaced with modern brilliant cuts.

The pieces listed here are antique or period and represent fine jewelry (i.e., made from gemstones and/or precious metals). The list contains no new reproduction pieces. Inexpensive and mass-produced costume jewelry is covered in *Warman's Americana & Collectibles.*

## SPECIAL AUCTIONS

Beverly Hills Auctioneers
9454 Wilshire Blvd., Suite 202
Beverly Hills, CA 90212
(310) 278-8115

Butterfield & Butterfield
220 San Bruno Ave.
San Francisco, CA 94103
(415) 861-7500

Christie's
502 Park Ave.
New York, NY 10022
(212) 546-1000

Dunning's Auction Service
755 Church Rd
Elgin, IL 60123
(847) 741-3483

Phillips Fine Art Auctions
406 E. 79th St.
New York, NY 10021
(212) 570-4830

Skinner, Inc.
The Heritage on the Garden
63 Park Plaza
Boston, MA 02116
(617) 350-5400

Sotheby's
1334 York Ave.
New York, NY 10021
(212) 606-7000

**Victorian, bangle, 14kt rolled gold, engraved throughout, black enamel tracery, $490. Photo courtesy of Skinner, Inc.**

## Bar pin

Victorian, pearl and citrine, center marquise-shaped citrine with oval citrine terminals outlined by freshwater pearls, 14kt yellow gold mount, two pearls missing.......................................................320.00

## Bracelet, bangle

Art Deco, channel-set alternating pattern of French-cut onyx and old European and single-cut diamonds, platinum topped 18kt yg mount, out of round, solder evident, 7" d ..........................................2,300.00

Edwardian, 14kt yg and enamel
    Curb links, suspending heart-shaped charm, surmounted by light pink and blue enamel florets, enamel chipped.................300.00
    Ropetwist design, surmounted by light pink and blue enamel florets, enamel chipped.......................................................375.00

Victorian, gold and enamel, engraved throughout with black enamel tracery, 14kt rolled gold, 16.3 dwt............................................490.00

## Bracelet, chain

Art Nouveau, gold, scroll motifs within oval-shaped open links, French assay marks, 8,7 dwt., 7-3/4" l .............................................635.00

Edwardian, gold, fancy link design, French assay mark, 7" l......690.00

## Bracelet, cuff

Retro Modern, Spratling, Mexico, c1940, silver band of repeating linear dec, gold toned pyramid forms, imp "WS" print circle and oval mark, wear, loss, 9-1/2" l.................................................................320.00

## Bracelet, line, Art Deco

Diamond and synthetic sapphires, alternating pattern of twenty bead-set diamonds, twenty calibre-cut synthetic sapphires, platinum mount, 2.00 cts, c1930.......................................................2,300.00

Platinum and diamond, flexible form, centered by three collet-set marquise-cut diamonds, 63 old European-cut, transitional, and single-cut diamonds (approx 3.23 cts), four calibre-cut rubies and emeralds, one wire bracket needs repairs, cracks to 2 emeralds, 6-1/2" l..........3,450.00

Platinum and diamond, twenty-eight squares set with single-cut diamonds, black enamel diagonal pattern, French hallmarks, numbered 50504, 7" l, some enamel missing ......................................24,150.00

Platinum and diamond, forty-three brilliant-cut slightly graduated diamonds set in engraved box links, 4.67 cts, 6-3/8" l ...............7,475.00

## Bracelet, links

Art Nouveau, seven bezel-set moonstones set in diamond-shaped cartouche alternating with seven freshwater pearls, 14kt yg, 7-3/4" l...1,380.00

Post-War Modern, Taxco, Mexico, mid-20th C, sq shaped links with staggered mottled brown inlay, imp "Taxco" and "Sterling," scratches..................................................................................220.00

Retro Modern
    14kt yg, alternating pattern of rose and yellow gold flat rect links surmounted by three cabochon sapphires and two circular-cut diamonds, 0.80 approx total weight, 13.1 dwt, 6-1/4" l.....980.00
    14kt yg, textured gold links, 51.0 dwt, 7-1/2" l ....................920.00

Victorian
    Enamel and 14 kt yg, trace-links dec with cobalt blue enamel, 9 kt engraved padlock charm, 7-1/2" l....................................635.00

Hand, flexible gold and white enamel links, foliate repousse spacers completed by hand clasping basket of blue enameled flowers, surmounted by pink stones, French assay mark, chips and repair to enamel ........................................................................2,300.00

Yellow gold, etched link band, floral engraved clasp, 6-1/2" l, 1-3/4" oval with miniature portrait on ivory, young child in ringlets, paper label on reverse with attribution to J. Carlin, dated 1869, late 19th C .......................................................................................900.00

## Brooch

Art Deco

    Center bezel-set opal doublet within 14kt yg engraved openwork foliate mount....................................................................550.00

    Center oval bezel-set 14.50 x 17.10 x 4.30 mm opal, further set with demantoid garnet and ruby florets, platinum and diamond openwork mount with millegrain dec, repair to back .....4,600.00

    Emerald and diamond, centered by 0.65 old European-cut diamond, 162 single-cut 3.50 cts diamonds, 84 square and calibre-cut 2.50 cts emeralds, platinum mount ........................6,650.00

    Platinum and diamond, center French-cut 2.00 ct diamond, lacy platinum and diamond mount, sgd "Tiffany & Co.," minor lead solder ....................................................................23,000.00

    Platinum and diamond, centered by three 2.69 ct old European-cut diamonds, set with 104 diamonds in platinum millegrain mounts, 18kt white gold pin stem...................................4,890.00

    Platinum and diamond, six collet-set 2.96 ct old European-cut diamonds, openwork and pierced geometric further set with 146 full and single-cut diamonds, platinum mount with millegrain dec, 18kt white gold curved pin stem, repair to mount..4,025.00

    Platinum, diamond, and jade, five jadeite jade leaves, red, blue, and yellow enamel flowers, fancy shape diamond leaves, sgd "Kohn," minor black enamel loss....................................7,015.00

Art Nouveau

    Diamond, set throughout with single-cut diamonds, suspending flexibly set pearl, trillion-shaped red stone accent, platinum-topped 18kt yg mold with millegrain dec .........................980.00

    Plique-a-jour, sq openwork naturalistic design, centered by three graduated fluted emerald beads within 18kt yg, gold, green plique-a-jour frame with diamond accents, sgd "Marcus & Co.," minor enamel loss ......................................................18,400.00

    Scallop shape, pink irid champlevé enamel portrait, rose-cut diamond accent, French assay mark, 18kt yg ...................1,610.00

    Woman smelling poppy, polychrome enamel, diamond accent, 14kt yg, hallmark for Krementz & Co. ..............................575.00

Edwardian

    Open work scroll design, 2.50 cts old European-cut diamonds, white gold chain ..........................................................4,715.00

    Stylized bow, set with 56 rose-cut diamonds in pierced and millegrain mount framed by 52 pearls, platinum topped 18kt yg, two diamonds missing....................................................1,610.00

    Post-War Modern, 18kt yg, foxtail tassel fringe suspended from asymmetrical openwork abstract mount with curved pave diamond segments and nine brilliant-cut diamond accents, hallmarked, 1.43 cts, 18.5 dwt. .........................................1,725.00

**Victorian, cameo, Three Graces, engraved frame, retractable bail, 10kt yg, minor hairline cracks, $320. Photo courtesy of Skinner, Inc.**

Retro Modern

Bouquet of flowers, 18kt yg, opening to reveal prong-set ruby clusters, stems tied with wiretwist, 22.8 dwt.....................815.00

Sprating, Mexico, c1940, stylized pre-Columbian motif, imp "WS" print circle and oval mark, 1-1/2" l, 1-3/8" w .....................230.00

Stylized floral spray set with ten moonstones, twenty prong-set sapphires, thirty-one bead-set diamonds, platinum-topped 14kt yg mount, sgd "Trabert & Hoeffer Mouboussin, Reflection no. 4383" ..............................................................................5,175.00

Stylized yellow and rose gold bow, centered by three bead-set diamonds mounted in platinum, circular and calibre-cut bi-color sapphire terminals, verso inscribed "E. H. from Tau Beta 1944" ............................................................1,725.00

Victorian

Amethyst and gold, crescent-shape, 14kt yg bead and wiretwist dec, suspending round faceted amethyst within bead and wiretwist frame ................................................................520.00

Garnet and diamond, openwork foliate mount centered by 9.00 ct garnet, set throughout with old mine and roe-cut diamonds, suspending three pear-shaped light yellow sapphire drops, 24.00 cts, silver topped gold mounts, accompanied by GIA certificate ........................................................3,565.00

Scottish Agate, scabbard design, set with foil backed citrines and various agates, faceted citrine terminal, 10kt yg chased mount ...........................................................................575.00

## Buckle

Art Nouveau, silver, pierced abstract design, cabochon green stone accents, hallmark for T. Fahrner, sgd "K. Poe" ......................3,750.00

## Cameo

Bracelet, eight oval coral, shell, mother-of-pearl and onyx cameos, 14kt yg wiretwist mounts spaced by textured roundels ............920.00

Brooch, Victorian

Hardstone, round, bust portrait of left-facing classical female, 18kt gold setting, French hallmark ...........................................635.00

Shell, flower-filled urn with bow and arrow, floral motif, 14kt yg and seed pearl frame, verso inscribed, one seed pearl missing .......................................................................320.00

Earpendants, pr, shell, circular tops designed with applied wiretwist and gold balls suspending carved portrait of Mercury, 14kt yg, signature partially obliterated, later fittings ........................................750.00

Earpendants, pr, tortoiseshell and cameo, oval tops suspending openwork scrolled tortoiseshell frame centered by oval shell cameo.............320.00

Pendant/Brooch, Victorian, shell cameo, oval

Three graces, engraved frame, retractable bail, 10kt yg, minor hairline cracks ..............................................................320.00

Woman's profile, long wavy hair, carved pearl necklace, draped costume, 14kt yg octagon-shaped filigree frame .............320.00

Ring, shell, classical woman's profile, 18kt yg ropetwist oval mount .........................................................................375.00

## Chain

Art Nouveau, 14kt yg, scrolls and beads as modified floret links, 20.5 dwt, hallmark, 30-1/2" l ......................................................1,265.00

Victorian, fancy trace and curb reeded links, barrel clasp with applied wiretwist design, 14kt yg, 17-1/8" l, 17.2 dwt ...........................450.00

## Circle Pin

Art Deco, ruby and diamond, band of channel-set rubies and single-cut diamonds surmounted by diamond floret, platinum and millegrain mount ............................................................................2,760.00

## Clip

Art Deco, ruby and diamond, eight oval cabochon rubies, set throughout with bead-set circular-cut diamonds, twelve baguette diamond accents, 2.85 cts, platinum mount.......................................6,325.00

Art Nouveau, gold and plique-a-jour, rect cartouche, chased and etched, bloomed gold work designed as curving vines, flower heads, and leaves, gray-mauve plique-a-jour enamel, French hallmark and assay marks ............................................................2,875.00

## Cufflinks, pr

Art Deco

Hammered design, oval form, English hallmarks for 1926, stamped "F. C.," 9.8 dwt...................................................420.00

Platinum, diamond, and enamel, four French-cut diamonds in center, framed by calibre-cut onyx and single-cut diamonds, set in geometric design, millegrain accents ......................7,765.00

Art Nouveau, oval rose gold bar cuff links, repousse swirl design, 14kt ..............................................................................350.00

Bacchus, 18kt yg, chased and engraved design, collet-set old mine-cut diamond accents, 7.6 dwt ....................................................1,725.00

Pistol, revolving barrel, 14kt yg, stamped "Jost," 9.4 dwt...........750.00

## Demi Parure

Brooch and pr earpendants, Victorian

Agate cameo, profile of classical female with lyre, oval frame highlighted with black enamel and seed pearls, 14kt yg ..............2,185.00

Micromosaic, oval onyx brooch with spaniel, 18kt yg ropetwist frame, earpendants depicting birds, cracks to onyx, solder repairs . 1,035.00

Paste and enamel, collet-set colorless pastes surrounded by black and white enamel ornamentation earpendants, pin ensuite, 14kt yg ...635.00

## Earpendants, pr

Edwardian, flexible and open work filigree design suspending three fringes, mounted with numerous round-cut diamonds, 1.40 cts, c1910 ..............................................................................1,955.00

Etruscian Revival

Balls, dec with granulation and wiretwist accents, 14kt yg, later findings.................................................................550.00

Day/night, top with sq bezel-set bloodstone with applied bead dec suspending detachable capped drop, 18kt yg mount.......490.00

Victorian

Agate and 14kt yg, round pictorial agate top surmounted by foliate design suspending triangular-shaped agate flanked by gold drops ...................................................................700.00

Day/night, bead-set turquoise tops suspending turquoise florets centered by pearl, 14kt yg, glue evident .........................635.00

Enamel, shaped champlevé enamel cartouche with polychrome floral motif outlined in white enamel, gold ball terminal, 14kt yg, enamel loss ............................................................280.00

Gold and diamond, floret shape, each set with seven old mine-cut diamonds, 18kt yg mount.......................................1,265.00

Pliqué, oval tops suspending three graduated oval rings ...............................................................................1,725.00

## Earrings, pr

Arts & Crafts, pearl, each centered by bezel-set cultured 7.20 mm pearl, scroll and foliate motif frame, 14kt yg, attributed to Edward Oakes.......................................................................2,070.00

Edwardian, diamond hoops, bead-set old mine-cut diamonds set both inside and outside the hoop, platinum topped 14kt yg ..........2,990.00

## Festoon Necklace

Art Nouveau, citrine and freshwater pearl festoon, set with three pear-shaped citrines, four freshwater pearls joined by trace-link chain, 14k yg, 15" l ......................................................................575.00

Edwardian, platinum, bow and swag motif, set with pearls and one mine-cut diamonds within filigree and millegrain mount, detachable 14kt white gold fine trace-link chain, one fringe and one pearl missing, needs minor repair ......................................................20,700.00

Victorian, 14kt yg and agate, snake chain suspending three oval shaped banded agate disks centered by star-set seed pearls and amphora-shaped drops, invisible barrel clasp, 16" l, orig fitted box, includes three additional agate disks with star-set pearl findings, chips to agate................................................................1,495.00

## Lavaliere, Edwardian

Amethyst, centered by oval faceted amethyst suspended within 15kt yg foliate and seed pearl frame, suspending pear-shaped citrine, fine trace-link chain with citrine highlight, 10-3/4" l ........................490.00

**Edwardian, platinum and diamond festoon, bow and swag motif, set with pearls and old mine-cut diamonds, filigree and millegrain mount, detachable 14kt white gold fine trace link-chain, $20,700. Photo courtesy of Skinner, Inc.**

Diamond, openwork foliate mount, collet and bead-set diamonds ranging from 0.03 to 0.50 carats, silver-topped yellow gold mount with bead accents, suspended from silver box-link chain with diamond accents, 11-1/2" l, break to mount .........................................2,760.00

**Memorial Locket/Pendant,** Victorian, pavé-set turquoise pendant with Gothic-revival pearl initial, pavé-set turquoise terminals with rose diamond accents suspended from bail with simulated diamonds, gilt-metal mount, verso with beveled glass compartment, 14kt yg trace link chain with twelve gilt-metal bezel-set light blue opaque glass beads, 30" l, solder evident, chips to glass ..............................920.00

## Necklace

Etruscan-Revival

14kt yg, groups of elliptical and round beads, allover applied wiretwist dec spaced by amethyst roundels and gold beads, hallmark for Carter, Gough & Co., 17-38" l ....................1,265.00

18kt yg, beads with applied wiretwist dec spaced by smaller plain gold beads, invisible clasp, 18.5 dwt, 16-1/2" l..............1,725.00

Victorian, coral, triple strand of coral beads suspending detachable carved brooch with foliate, bird, and fruit motifs, orig box, some leaves missing, chips to coral, pin stem missing......................435.00

## Pearls

Post-War Modern

33 round gray cultured South Sea pearls, graduating from 12.0 to 14.4 mm, greenish overtone, 18kt white gold ball clasp with diamond accents, 18-1/2" l................................................11,500.00

36 South Sea black pearls ranging from 9.60 to 13.50 mm, ruby, diamond, silver, and gold round clasp..........................2,900.00

38 cultured pearls ranging from 9 to 9.5 mm, 18kt white gold and diamond ball clasp .......................................................1,380.00

105 pearls, approx 7.80 mm, platinum barrel-shaped clasp set with 38 single-cut diamonds, 36-1/2" l...............................980.00

## Pendant

Art Deco

Light blue enamel baton links spaced by sq periwinkle blue enamel links, suspending geometric plaque with red stone highlights, textured gilt-metal mount, 10" l ...........................1,495.00

Platinum and diamond solitaire, 12.10 x 7.35 mm old European-cut diamond, suspended from chain spaced by 84 collet-set old European-cut diamonds, each weighing 0.04 cts, diamond bail, orig fitted Drecier & Cie box, 18" l .............................156,500.00

Platinum, onyx, and diamond, centered by 0.25 ct old European-cut diamond, onyx circular frame, 3 collet-set old European-cut and 36 rose-cut diamonds, pierced and millegrain mount, suspended from trace link chain, 16" l ...............................2,300.00

Sapphire and diamond, flexible bail suspending lozenge-shaped plaque set throughout with old European-cut and single-cut diamonds, calibre-cut sapphire accents, millegrain and platinum ............................................................3,565.00

Art Nouveau

Griffin, rose-cut diamond wings, yg body, tail wrapped around open rose-gold circle set with cabochon rubies, French assay marks, three stones and wing missing .............................920.00

Octagon form, portrait of woman with flowers in hair, wearing draped fringe shawl, row-cut diamond necklace, holding tambourine, chased 18kt yg, 2.2 dwt ......................................350.00

Edwardian

Diamond and ruby, collet-set old mine-cut and rose-cut diamonds within pierced and openwork frame, center highlighted with calibre-cut rubies suspending diamond and pearl drop, platinum-topped gold, French import assay marks ........................1,725.00

Grape cluster with seed pearls, diamond leaf accents, suspended from platinum trace-link chain, platinum-topped gold mount, 9" l ..............................................................690.00

Imperial topaz and diamond, center oval-shaped mixed-cut 15.10 x 11.80 x 7.40 mm topaz, surrounded by 87 old mine cut diamonds, yellow diamond briolette weighing approx 2.55 cts, platinum topped 14kt yg, minor abrasion, lead solder, one diamond missing ...............................................................17,250.00

Platinum and diamond, open diamond heart, diamond set arrow, 0.85 cts, c1910 .................................................................2,530.00

Renaissance Revival, Holbeinsque, centered by foil-back carbuncle garnet surrounded by bezel-set chyrsolites alternating with cobalt blue champlevé enamel motifs, completed by diamond-shaped cartouche drop, 18kt yg.................................................................1,840.00

Retro Modern, Spratling, Mexico, c1940, amethyst frog set I sterling silver frame, fine link chain, imp "WS" print circle and oval mark, wear and abrasions to amethyst, 19" l................................................260.00

## Pendant/Brooch

Art Nouveau, enamel, designed as orchid, light pink, lavender, and green enamel petals, 14kt yg, maker's mark for Whiteside and Blank.......................................................................................520.00

Edwardian

Enamel and seed pearl, four-leaf clover, leaves outlined with seed pearls, retractable bail, 14kt yg, hallmark for Krementz & Co. ........................................................................1,265.00

Laurel garland with bow and swag motif centered by flexibly set 0.20 old European-cut diamond, freshwater pearl terminal, suspended from trace link chain with swag links, European hallmarks, 18kt gold........................................................4,025.00

Victorian, diamond and enamel, portrait of Jane Seymour, framed with seventy-two rose-cut diamonds, bow and swag crest, reverse inscribed "E. G. Wade, Oct 1888," stamped "T. B. Starr," mounted in silver and 14kt yg .................................................................2,415.00

**Pendant/Brooch Locket,** Victorian, oval lapis framed by pearls within 18kt yg mount, applied foliate design, verso with hinged compartment ........................................................................690.00

## Pin

Art Deco, figural articulated girl, painted enamel features, gold body, seated on 15kt yg safety pin, fine safety chain, c1915, minor enamel loss ..................................................................................980.00

Edwardian, swallow, body and wings composed of pave-set diamonds, ruby eyes, gold beak, platinum topped 18kt yg....................2,185.00

Retro, bow, 14kt pink and green gold, stamped "H.S.B.," 11.40 dwt...........................................................................375.00

Victorian, horseshoe nail, centered by old 0.50 cts mine-cut diamond, surrounded by rose-cut diamonds, silver-topped gold mount.............865.00

## Ring

Art Deco

Diamond and amethyst, centered by 2.50 ct colleg-set oval diamond, framed by calibre-cut amethysts, pierced platinum mount with diamond accents, sgd "M & Co." for Marcus & Co. .................1,265.00

Pearl and emerald, centered by 10.0 mm cultured pearl, flanked by table-cut emeralds, diamond shoulders, pierced and millegrain platinum mount, one emerald cracked ..............3,450.00

Platinum and ruby, centered by 10.80 x 9.70 x 4.00 mm cabochon ruby, flanked by trapezoid and circular-cut diamonds, numbered 2842, scratches to ruby ............................................. 2,875.00
Sapphire and diamond, center oval 13.40 x 11.00 x 7.05 mm sapphire, framed with six circular-cut diamonds in scalloped design, platinum topped 18kt yg mount with pierced gallery and diamond shoulders, European hallmarks ........................... 6,325.00
Sapphire and diamond, centered 10.20 x 7.60 x 6.90 mm sugarloaf sapphire, surrounded by 76 old mine-cut diamonds, 16 French-cut sapphires, platinum mounts ...................... 10,100.00

Art Nouveau
Diamond, centered by 0.35 ct old European-cut diamond, foliate and scroll motif shoulders, 18kt yg mount ..................... 1,495.00
Emerald and diamond, center sugarloaf cabochon emerald surrounded by fifteen old mine-cut diamonds, chased shoulders, 18kt yg ............................................................... 2,645.00
Snake, 14kt rose gold, two entwined snakes, blue stone eyes .......................................................................... 460.00

Arts & Crafts
Citrine, center faceted oval citrine, pierced mount, chased and engraved in grapevine design, 18kt yg, sgd "Kohn" ...........2,185.00
Moonstone and garnet, bevel-set carved moonstone, faceted garnet, seed pearl accents ............................................375.00
Pearl, bezel-set blister pearl surrounded by four old mine-cut diamonds, eight demantoid garnets, floral motif shoulders, 14kt yg mount, demantoids abraided ........................ 1,725.00

Edwardian, amethyst, prong-set oval 13.40 x 9.80 x 7.60 mm amethyst, surmounted by rose-cut diamond initials in Gothic-revival style, engraved decorative shoulders, 10kt yg ................................. 290.00
Retro Modern, center cabochon 12.50 x 9.10 x 4.90 ruby, framed by scroll of twenty-two circular and pave-set diamonds, platinum mount ......................................................................1,035.00
Victorian, snake, 18kt yg, triple coil design, head set with five graduated old European-cut diamonds, hallmark for Birmingham, date letter for 1863, no. 285 ...................................................... 490.00

## Stickpin, Art Nouveau
Double-sided cabochon sapphire, chased floral and scroll motif, 14kt yg mount, blemish to back of sapphire .................................... 460.00
Enamel, sweet pea blossom shape, lavender and white enamel, old European-cut diamond accent, 14kt yg .................................. 920.00

## Suite
Etruscan Revival, knot-shaped brooch centered by old mine-cut diamond, applied wiretwist and bead dec, cabochon emeralds and seed pearls, matching earrings, 14kt yg, sgd "FROV" ...................... 700.00
Post War Modern, Kitzbunel, Leni Kuborn-Grothe, 28-1/2" necklace, 1-1/4" l drop earrings, center cluster of multicolored pastel glass beds on gilt, braided metallic thread necklace with applied sequins and glass beads, braided thread laces tie to fit, matching clip earrings, sgd ................................................................................ 115.00
Victorian
Brooch and pr earpendants, 10kt gold, shield-shaped brooch suspending three marquise-shaped onyx drops, seed pearl accents, matching earpendants with later fittings ..............................435.00
Brooch and pr earpendants, clusters of cabochon coral beads suspending three coral drops, 18kt yg mount with applied gold bead dec, matching earpendants, fitted box .................. 1,495.00
Locket and earpendants, 18kt yg, locket with enamel portrait of angel, wings outlined in onyx and rose-cut diamonds, platinum-topped bail set with two rose-cut diamonds, matching earpendants (originally cuff buttons) ........................................... 1,840.00

Tiara, Victorian, tortoiseshell band surmounted by swags of rose-cut diamonds and pearls, mounted in silver ................................ 2,300.00

## Watch Chain and Slide
Victorian
Engraved opal slide, 10kt gold chain, hand-form clasp ...... 150.00
Suspended 14kt yg slide with black enamel and seed pearl accents, 10kt yg fancy trace-link chain, mark for "Hamilton & Hamilton Jr.," 32" l, 34.8 dwt ............................................... 815.00

## Watch Fob
Center rectangular faceted 22.70 x 19.10 x 10.03 mm citrine, foliate chased and engraved 18kt yg mount with similar ring, suspended in grosgrain ribbon, 35.1 dwt........................................865.00
Seal
Rectangular bezel-set carnelian intaglio surmounted by 14kt yg chased and engraved serpent ring...................................320.00
Rectangular bloodstone intaglio surmounted by 14kt yg chased and engraved ring ............................................280.00
Rectangular bloodstone intaglio lion surmounted by 14kt yg foliate chased and engraved ring.........................................345.00

# JUDAICA

**History:** Throughout history, Jews have expressed themselves artistically in both the religious and secular spheres. Most Jewish art objects were created as part of the concept of Hiddur Mitzva, i.e., adornment of implements used in performing rituals both in the synagogue and home.

For almost 2,000 years, since the destruction of the Jerusalem Temple in 70 A.D., Jews have lived in many lands. The widely differing environments gave traditional Jewish life and art a multifaceted character. Unlike Greek, Byzantine, or Roman art which have definite territorial and historical boundaries, Jewish art is found throughout Europe, the Middle East, North Africa, and other areas.

Ceremonial objects incorporated not only liturgical appurtenances, but also ethnographic artifacts such as amulets and ritual costumes. The style of each ceremonial object responded to the artistic and cultural milieu in which it was created. Although diverse stylistically, ceremonial objects, whether for Sabbath, holidays, or the life cycle, still possess a unity of purpose.

**References:** Anton Felton, *Jewish Carpets,* Antique Collectors' Club, 1999; Penny Forstner and Lael Bower, *Collecting Religious Artifacts (Christian and Judaic),* Books Americana, 1996; Eric and Myra Outwater, *Judaica,* Schiffer Publishing, 1999.

**Collectors' Club:** Judaica Collectors Society, P.O. Box 854, Van Nuys, CA 91408.

**Museums:** B'nai B'rith Klutznick Museum, Washington, DC; H.U.C., Skirball Museum, Los Angeles, CA; Jewish Museum, New York, NY; Yeshiva University Museum, New York, NY; Judah L. Magnes Museum, Berkeley, CA; Judaic Museum, Rockville, MD; Spertus Museum of Judaica, Chicago, IL; Morton B. Weiss Museum of Judaica, Chicago, IL; National Museum of American Jewish History, Philadelphia, PA; Plotkin Judaica Museum of Greater Phoenix, Phoenix, AZ.

**Notes:** Judaica has been crafted in all media, though silver is the most collectible.

Amulet
3-1/4" h, silver, oval shape, applied cast dec to edges, glass inset on front and verso, Italian-style ........................................ 400.00
3-1/4" h, silvered metal, oval shape, crenelated surround, reverse painted tablet depicting binding of Isaac, verso with amulet against evil eye, Italian-style ........................................... 635.00

5-3/4" h, enamel dec and parcel-gilt porcelain, rect, painted star, gilt-metal mounts, painted mark on reverse, attributed to Limoges, France, 20th C ............................................ 800.00

**Belt Buckle, Yom Kippur**

5" d, silver-gilt and jewel mounted, domed circular form, various inset stones, unmarked, Polish, 18th/19th C .................... 875.00

8" l, silver, silver filigree, and gem mounted, double paisley form, repousse silver panels depicting binding of Isaac and Jonah and the whale, unmarked, Italian ................................. 6,900.00

Candlesticks, pr, 7-1/2" h, silver and silver filigree, tapering form, dished bobeche, domed circular foot, stylized dec, applied mark, Bezalel, early 20th C, dents ................................................. 1,850.00

**Charity Container**

7" h, domed cylindrical form, slop on top, door to side, dec with Jewish subjects, Hebrew text, Damascene, 20th C ......... 800.00

7-1/2" h, brass, cylindrical form, hasp and loop handle, Polish, late 19th/early 20th C ....................................................... 400.00

10-3/4" h, paint dec pine, rect box, hinged lid, slot on top, back with swan's neck cresting, painted with deer holding an oval inscribed "Torah Fund," flanked by columns, plain base, painted yellow and dark green, attributed to Philadelphia, PA, area, late 19th/early 20th C ..................................................... 4,600.00

Charity Collection Dish, 5-1/2" d, silver, circular bowl, applied handle, foliate engraved thumb-piece, engraved Hebrew inscription on rim, fitted with small candle socket, Continental, late 18th C ....... 3,795.00

Children's Game, "The New and Fashionable Game of the Jew," London, J. Wallis, M. Dunnet and J. Wallis Junr, 27 May 1807, uncut broad-sheet game board, hand colored engravings, minor old repairs, matted and framed ........................................................................ 2,760.00

**Esther Scroll, silver cased, vellum scroll, unmarked**

8" h, Salonic, heavy floral repousse, floral-form finial, turned winder, hand lettered ink, 18th/19th C .......................... 1,495.00

15-1/4" h, North African, repousse floral dec, crown finial, handwritten ink, vellum scroll, unmarked, late 19th/early 20th C ........ 875.00

Etrog Container, 7-1/2" l, carved walnut, fruit fork, hinged top, realistically carved leafy base, America, late 19th C .......................... 920.00

**Hanukah Lamp**

5" h, bronze, arched and scrolled backplate above row of eight oil fonts, Italian Renaissance, late 16th/early 17th C, replaced servant lamp ............................................................. 1,725.00

8-3/4" h, brass, cartouche-shaped backplate stamped with lions, crowns, and foliage, central etched menorah design, rect base with eight candleholders, cast feet, Polish, 19th C, lacking servant light ................................................. 1,265.00

9-3/4" h, silver, paneled baluster stem, eight thin arms holding candle sockets, removable snuffer with star of David finial, servant light, domed paneled foot, obscured maker's mark, Birmingham, England, 1929, bent ......................................... 325.00

10-1/2" h, silver, paneled tapering stem, eight thin arms holding candle sockets, servant light to side, Star of David finial, sq domed foot, maker "A. S.," Birmingham, England, 1963 .................. 575.00

11-3/4" h, brass, arched backplate pierced with exotic beasts, tree branches, central heart device, over row of eight oil fonts, rect drip-pan, servant light above right, Dutch, 18th C .. 2,070.00

**Kiddush Cup**

4-1/4" h, silver, finely chased floral motifs, engraved Hebrew text, illegible maker's mark, Continental, 19th C ..................... 920.00

5" d, 2-1/2" d, repousse silver, int. gilded, one reserve with Hebraic script, Continental, c1855-70 ............................. 265.00

5-1/2" h, silver-gilt, paneled form, cast foliate dec, Hebrew text, molded octagonal foot, German-style, 20th C .............. 9,200.00

Laver, 4-3/4" h, copper, applied loop handle, engraved Hebrew text, Continental, 18th/19th C ...................................................... 175.00

Magazine, *Der Hammer Worker's Monthly,* New York, 1926, cov illus designed by Gropper, Lozowick, Yiddish text, orig pictorial wrappers, no. 1 to 10 bound into contemporary cloth volume, folio .......... 290.00

**Manuscript**

*Bible, Pentateuch,* Hebrew, 1740-42, "[The Pentateuch] with the order of the Haftarot that belong to each of the books. According to the rites of Germanic Jews with vocalization and accents," written on vellum, drawings, Simha ben Yona Segal, Scribe, Mannheim, five volumes, orig leather binding, marbleized end papers, fitted leather case ........................................ 145,500.00

*Seder Tefillah M'Kol Hashanah,* (The Order of Prayers for the whole year), according to rites of German, Polish, Lithuania, and Russian Jews, Hebrew and Yiddish, Raphael de Gedalia Halevi Luria, Scribe, Vilna, 1827, enameled and jeweled binding, later name plate for Helene Ratner, fitted leather slip-case ........................................................................... 5,630.00

Map, 21-1/2" x 25-1/4", Holy Land, etching, later hand coloring, Generalle Kaart van het Beloofde Land, Jan Berend Elwe, Amsterdam, 1792 ......................................................................................... 650.00

Marriage Bowl, 5-1/4" d, silver, silver-gilt, and niello, inscribed with text relating to seven benedictions of marriage, Buchara, Persia, dated 1683, modern fitted box ......................................................... 12,650.00

Marriage Contract (Ketubah), 13" x 18-1/4", illuminated parchment, Livorno, dated 1817, rect, flowers, foliage, and text, framed ... 865.00

Mennorah, 13" l, 6-1/2" w, porcelain, figural family members dancing in line, holding hands, hand printed bright clothing ........................ 85.00

**Mezuzah**

3-3/4" h, cast bronze, architectural form, lion, inscribed in Hebrew "Shadai" and "Yerushaliem," Bezalel, early 20th C .......... 700.00

4" h, Ottoman silver and stone inset, rect form, hand and "Shadai," rounded scroll case set with gemstones, overall engraved geometric and foliate dec, bosses to sides, indistinctly marked, 19th/20th C ..................................................................... 575.00

9-1/2" h, German silver, cylindrical, peaked top and bottom, adjustable bracket, Anton Gutwein, maker, Augsburg, c1800 ..................................................................................... 2,415.00

Oil Can, one gallon, Planters Edible Oil Co., Suffolk, VA, shows fried foods along sides, Star of David, Hebrew writing on front and back, red ground, yellow and black lettering, unopened, large dent in back ............................................................................................. 400.00

**Preserve Jar, stoneware, 1 quart, "Remmey 1882" with cobalt blue Star of David, c1882, professional restoration to hairlines, 6-3/4" h, $1,870. Photo courtesy of Vicki & Bruce Waasdrop.**

Painting
13-3/4" h, 10-1/8" w, oil on panel, "The Marriage Broker," sgd and inscribed "PR. B. Schatz, Jerusalem" (Boris Schatz, 1866-1932), lower left, monogram and inscribed "Jerusalem" in Hebrew lower right, titled on label on reverse, repousse brass frame, under glass ....................................... 25,300.00

24" h, 20" w, oil on canvas, "Portrait of a Rabbi," sgd "Bromberg," lower right, framed ........................................... 350.00

Picture Frame, 9" h, silver, clasps depicting Moses and Aaron, small with hallmarks, int. 5" x 7" ........................................ 345.00

Plaque
7-1/4" h, 5" w, bronze, titled "In The Old City," mounted on patinated bronze frame, M. Murro, early 20th C .................... 350.00

8-1/2" h, 6-1/2" w, hammered brass, titled "At The Kotel," mounted on silvered metal and ebonized wood frame, mkd "Bezalel," M. Murro, early 20th C ..................................... 230.00

9-3/4" h, scene titled "Blessing of the Rabbi," arched frame, stylized dec, title, easel back, reverse with paper label for Bezalel, numbered A15, Boris Schatz, c1906............................ 3,450.00

Prayer Book, Austria, 1857, written in Hebrew and English, celluloid cover dec, 4-3/4" h, 3-1/2" w, 1-1/4" thick, gilded edges, ornate clasp........................................................... 350.00

Purim Noisemaker (Gregger), 7" h, wood, maple handle, later applied silver dec depicting Haman and Purim scenes, late 19th C ..... 500.00

Rose Water Container, 11-1/4" h, silver, flattened inverted heart-shaped form, domed pierced top, oval domed foot, chased with foliage, unmarked, Persian, late 19th/early 20th C ....................... 375.00

Rug, wool, double candelabra device, Bezalel, early 20th C
50-1/2" x 28-1/2", mosque, green, blue, beige, and rust, overall wear ..................................................... 520.00

55-1/4" x 21", panorama of Jerusalem, blue, rust, and beige, overall wear, borders re-woven .............................. 460.00

Seal, 5" h, silver, for Bassevi von Trefeld, created 1622, formed as rampant lion holding shield, crest three stars and two lion/leopards, Austrian, Baroque-style ........................................... 575.00

Shabat Bottle Opener, bronze, key-form, incised blessing for wine, early 20th C............................................... 920.00

Shabat Knife, 5-1/2" l, metal and mother-of-pearl, inscribed in Hebrew, Czechoslovakian ........................................... 290.00

Shabat Table Cover, 23-1/2" w, 20-1/2" h, Balkan, gilt-metal thread embroidered silk, purple ground, sequined dec, early 20th C, minor discoloration ................................................ 230.00

Shabat Tray, 15-3/4" l, Sheffield silver, oval, repousse dec of braided challah loafs, vintage border, Hebrew text, base mkd "England," 20th C........................................................ 345.00

Sheet Music, *The Titanic Disaster,* New York, Hebrew Publishing Co., copyright 1912, blue and white cover art work by J. Keller ...... 260.00

Shofar, 13-1/4" l, ram's head, geometric carving at edge, scalloped end section, Continental, 19th/20th C ......................... 200.00

Snuff Box
2-1/4" h, silver-gilt mounted polychrome dec porcelain, rect, painted with Biblical scenes, French, 19th C, restoration to lid........................................................ 2,185.00

2-3/4" h, silver-gilt, later worked lid with binding of Isaac, George III, London, c1778, adapted ........................... 575.00

3" d, silver-mounted enamel, circular, painted with Biblical scenes, base with moth, German, 18th/19th C, some restoration to lid.................................................... 1,380.00

3" d, silver-mounted enamel, circular, painted with Biblical scenes, base with floral de, German, 18th/19th C ........ 1,725.00

Spice Container, silver
2-1/4" h, grand piano form, hinged lid, ivorine keys, hallmarked, 20th C.................................................... 345.00

3-1/2" l, round openwork container, tapering stem, filigree cover, Russian, 19th C............................................ 980.00

4" l, horn form, heavily dec with birds, foliage, and scrollwork, lid engraved with crest of Sir Moses Montefiore, carnelian mount, chain, London, 1871, maker "T.J.".......................... 1,955.00

4-1/4" h, two compartments, rooster finials, dolphin-form legs, Birmingham, England, 1808, maker "M.L." ...................... 750.00

6" h, fruit-form, curved stem, applied leaves, apple set on leaf-form base, Polish, 19th C.............................. 1,035.00

Spice Tower, spire with pendant
7-1/4" h, silver, 800 fine, hexagonal compartment, floral repousse panels, hinged door, tapering stem, hexagonal domed foot, German, late 19th/early 20th C ......................... 635.00

7-1/4" h, silver and silver filigree, central filigree compartment, emb dec, tapering stem, domed circular foot, attributed to Berlin, early 19th C ........................................ 520.00

9" h, silver and silver filigree, sq filigree compartment, hinged door, flags, and bells, baluster stem, domed circular foot, London, 1902, maker "H.A." .................................. 690.00

10-1/4" h, silver and silver filigree, sq compartment with hinged door and flags, tapering stem, circular domed foot, Continental, late 19th/early 20th C ..................................... 600.00

Tefflin Case, 1-1/4" h, miniature, silver, engraved dec, late 19th C, pr..................................................... 1,265.00

Torah Binder, 112" l, painted linen, dated 15th day of Elul, 1870, inscribe to Yehuah ben Eli Gold, printed in bright colors, Hebrew inscriptions and birds, some staining ...................... 750.00

Torah Crown, 19-1/4" h, silver and silver filigree, heavily pierced and cast, foliate dec, surmounted by bird perched on ball, pendant bells, J. Perlman, maker, Warsaw, c1900, some bells replaced..... 2,300.00

Torah Pointer, silver
9" l, tapering form, heavily cast with rococo style dec, tapering knopped finial, lower section terminating in cuffed hand, hallmarked, Dutch, 19th C ..................................... 375.00

11" h, oval stem cast with leaf-tip and molded dec, finial formed as rampant lion holding shield, lower section terminating in cuffed hand, unmarked, Bohemian, late 19th/early 20th C.............. 800.00

12" l, tapering cylindrical stem, baluster shaped chased with foliage, ovoid knop finial, lower section terminating with hand, loop, and chain, hallmarked, Polish-style, 20th C .................... 350.00

12-1/2" l, silver, hand shaped, Polish/Russian hallmarks, 1865, Hebrew inscription............................................ 825.00

Torah Shield, 14" h, silver, 950 fine, cartouche form, crown above two winged griffins, lions, and tablets to center, supported by scroll-work, suspension chain, Johann Aiehrer maker, Austro-Hungary, c1880, repairs .................................................... 750.00

Vase, Bezalel, bronze, early 20th C
6" h, tapered hexagonal form, stylized designs and Hebrew text on sides, mkd on base ........................................ 350.00

11-3/4" h, flattened moon-flask form, circular stylized dec, flaring rim, loop handles, domed foot, applied mark ............... 1,495.00

# JUGTOWN POTTERY

**History:** In 1920, Jacques and Julianna Busbee left their cosmopolitan environs and returned to North Carolina to revive the state's dying pottery-making craft. Jugtown Pottery, a colorful and somewhat off-beat operation, was located in Moore County, miles away from any large city and accessible only "if mud permits."

Ben Owens, a talented young potter, turned the wares. Jacques Busbee did most of the designing and glazing. Julianna handled promotion.

Utilitarian and decorative items were produced. Although many colorful glazes were used, orange predominated. A Chinese blue glaze that ranged from light blue to deep turquoise was a prized glaze reserved for the very finest pieces.

**Vase, bulbous, flaring rim, emb medallions, Chinese blue glaze, circular pottery mark, 7-1/2" h, 3-3/4" d, $745. Photo courtesy of David Rago Auctions.**

Jacques Busbee died in 1947. Julianna, with the help of Owens, ran the pottery until 1958 when it was closed. After long legal battles, the pottery was reopened in 1960. It now is owned by Country Roads, Inc., a non-profit organization. The pottery still is operating and using the old mark.

Bowl
    5" d, 2-1/2" h, orange .......................................... 85.00
    7" d, 4-1/2" w, Chinese Blue glaze, turned under rimq255.00
    8-3/4" d, 2-7/8" h, frogskin glaze, white flowers dec .......... 335.00
Cabinet Vase
    3" h, Chinese Blue glaze, stamped "Jugtown Ware" .......... 375.00
    3-3/4" h, Chinese Blue glaze, stamped "Jugtown Ware" .... 325.00
    4" h, Chinese Blue hi-glaze, imp mark ............................... 150.00
Candlesticks, pr
    4 1/2" h, tapered stems, broad cups supporting candleholders, mottled blue and black high glaze, imp mark ................... 110.00
    13-1/2" h, Mirror Black glaze, imp mark ............................ 600.00
Urn, 7" h, 5-1/4" d, bulbous, predominately red Chinese Blue glaze, stamped "Jugtown Ware" ...................................... 3,500.00
Vessel
    4-1/2" h, Chinese Blue glaze .............................................. 350.00
    5-1/2" h, 4" d, pear shaped, red Chinese Blue glaze, stamped "Jugtown Ware" .......................................... 1,400.00
    5-1/2" h, 4-1/4" d, bulbous, thick, dripping purple and green glossy glaze, stamped "Jugtown Ware" ....................... 1,500.00
    5-1/2" h, 6-1/2" d, flaring, incised band on top, red and turquoise Chinese Blue glaze, stamped "Jugtown Ware" ............. 2,500.00
    5-3/4" h, 6-1/2" d, bulbous, Chinese Blue glaze dripping over brown clay bisque body, stamped "Jugtown Ware" ....... 1,300.00
    6-1/4" h, 7" d, bulbous, tapered shoulder, Chinese Blue glaze, stamped "Jugtown Ware" ................................................. 700.00
    7-1/2" h, 4" d, two applied medallions, predominately red Chinese Blue glaze, stamped "Jugtown Ware," restoration to two rim chips ...................................................... 2,400.00
    8" h, two small handles at neck, Mirror Black glaze, orange int. ............................................................ 1,400.00
    8-3/4" h, 8" d, two handles, Chinese Blue glaze, stamped "Jugtown Ware" ................................................. 2,200.00
    9-1/2" h, 7" d, classic shape, light Chinese Blue glaze, stamped "Jugtown Ware" .......................................... 1,200.00
    11" h, 7-3/4" d, Chinese Blue glaze, stamped "Jugtown Ware" ...................................................... 3,500.00

# KPM

**History:** The "KPM" mark has been used separately and in conjunction with other symbols by many German porcelain manufacturers, among which are the Königliche Porzellan Manufactur in Meissen, 1720s; Königliche Porzellan Manufactur in Berlin, 1832-1847; and Krister Porzellan Manufactur in Waldenburg, mid-19th century.

Collectors now use the term KPM to refer to the high-quality porcelain produced in the Berlin area in the 18th and 19th centuries.

Cassolettes, cov, urn on pedestal shape, yellow ground, gilt foliate dec, mask handles, late 19th C, price for pr ................................... 1,150.00

Cup and Saucer, topographical, Bavarian mountainscape with castle on cup, paw feet, 19th C ...................... 750.00

Dessert Plate, 7-3/4" d, porcelain and biscuit, one with medallion featuring "The Birth of Venus," other with "The Dolphin Boy," c1925-30, price for pr ..................... 150.00

Dinner Service, burgundy borders and gilt scrolls, twelve 9-3/4" dinner plates, twelve 9-1/4" d soup plates, cov tureen, cov vegetable, sauce boat, 25" fish platter, two 9-1/4" open bowls, five platters, ftd salt, late 19th C .............. 4,025.00

Flagon, 13-1/4" h, incised brown glazed body, blue glazed jewelling, late 19th C ................ 250.00

Lamp Base, 28" h, painted porcelain, procession of frolicking putti, molded masks, late 19th C ........... 1,035.00

Plaque, painted porcelain
  6" w, 9" h Der Gratulant, giltwood frame within frame, c1900 .................... 2,990.00
  6" w, 9" h, Expectations, raised gilt highlights, after H. Coomans, c1900 ..................... 3,450.00
  6" w, 9" h, portrait of young monk holding turnips and beer stein, framed ..................... 900.00

**Plaque, hand painted religious scene, ornate gold fran $9,240. Photo courtesy of Jackson's Auctioneers & Appraise**

10" w, 15-1/2" h, Greek maiden with water jug, sgd "Fr. Till," c1900, giltwood frame ................................ 6,900.00

Scent Bottle, molded scrolls, multicolored painted bouquets of flowers, gilt trim, gilt metal C-scroll stopper, mkd, mid 19th C .............. 220.00

Stein, 6-1/4" h, molded body with raised bands of flowers flanking central scrolled foliate band, blue glaze, pewter lid, incised marks, 19th C ...................... 250.00

# KAUFFMANN, ANGELICA

**History:** Marie Angelique Catherine Kauffmann was a Swiss artist who lived from 1741 until 1807. Many artists who hand-decorated porcelain during the 19th century copied her paintings. The majority of the paintings are neoclassical in style.

**References:** Susan and Al Bagdade, *Warman's English & Continental Pottery & Porcelain*, 3rd Edition, Krause Publications, 1998; Wendy Wassying Roworth (ed.), *Angelica Kauffmann*, Reaktion Books, 1993, distributed by University of Washington Press.

Biscuit Jar, cov, 7" h, 5" d, scenic panel of three ladies and gentleman, pastels, alternating gold and maroon panels, gold grim, SP rim, cov, and handle ...................... 165.00

Bowl, 9-1/2" d, two maidens and child ..................... 65.00

Condensed Milk Can Holder, cov, matching underplate, classical maiden, green ground, gold tracery .................. 115.00

Demitasse Cup and Saucer, scenic panels with figures ............... 45.00

Dresser Set, green ground, multicolored portraits on each of 3 cov pots, matching tray .................. 150.00

Marmalade jar, cov, Three Graces scene .................. 90.00

Plate, 8-5/8" d, scalloped edge, gilt and magenta border with gilt foliage and 3 cartouches of multicolored floral sprays, cream ground with gilt leaves, center painting of chariot with cupid, 3 maidens, artist sgd "Angelica Kaufmann" on front, mkd "Imperial Crown China Austria" with crown and wreath mark with "Austria" underneath on back .......... 550.00

Portrait Plate, 8-1/2" d, emerald green, gold, and cream, fancy edges, ladies in orange and purple gowns, cherub, sgd, mkd "Carlsbad, Austria" ...................... 100.00

Tobacco Jar, cov, portrait front, muted dark green, orange and yellow trim, SP rim and lid, pipe finial ..................... 325.00

Vase, 8-3/8" h, medallion of classical maidens, gold filigree and trim, sgd, mkd "Austria" .................. 125.00

# KEW BLAS

**History:** Amory and Francis Houghton established the Union Glass Company, Somerville, Massachusetts, in 1851. The company went bankrupt in 1860, but was reorganized. Between 1870 and 1885, the Union Glass Company made pressed glass and blanks for cut glass.

Art-glass production began in 1893 under the direction of William S. Blake and Julian de Cordova. Two styles were introduced: a Venetian style, which consisted of graceful shapes in colored glass, often flecked with gold; and an iridescent glass, called Kew Blas, made in plain and decorated forms. The pieces are similar in design and form to Quezel products but lack the subtlety of Tiffany items.

The company ceased production in 1924.

**Museum:** Sandwich Glass Museum, Sandwich, MA.

Bowl, 5-1/2" d, irid gold ground, shaped rim, shallow round bowl, sgd "Kew Blas" on base ........................................................ 250.00

Compote, 7" h, irid gold ground, pink highlights, ribbed bowl, twisted stem ........................................................ 550.00

Console Set, 10" d compote, 6-3/4" h pr candlesticks, Alexandrite, heat reactive red shaded to blue, chocolate shading, central air trap bubble stem ........................................................ 1,265.00

Cuspidor, 5-3/4" d, 2-1/2" h, amber ground, irid gold dec, squatty, flattened flared rim, sgd "Kew Blas" ........................................ 285.00

Decanter, 14-1/2" h, gold, ribbed and painted stopper, purple-pink highlights, sgd on base ........................................................ 1,450.00

Finger Bowl and Underplate, 5" d, 7" d plate, twelve ribbed body, scalloped edge, gold irid, inscribed and numbered ....................... 425.00

Goblet, 4-3/4" h, irid gold ground, curved stem ........................... 250.00

Pitcher, 5" h, King Tut, white ground, green and gold irid dec, irid blue lining, blue handle, sgd ........................................................ 2,000.00

Rose Bowl, 3-1/2" h, 4-1/4" w, butterscotch ground, irid green and gold chain dec, 16 rows of green dots ............................................. 950.00

Tumbler, 3-1/2" h, 3" d, brilliant irid gold exterior, purple irid interior, sgd ........................................................ 275.00

Vase

4-1/4" h, 5-1/4" d, deep emerald green, honeycomb pattern, highly irid purple int., sgd ................................................. 800.00

4-1/4" h, 5-1/4" d, flared amber ribbed trumpet form, pulled emerald green int. dec, base engraved "Kew-Blas" ................. 815.00

7" h, cased ambergris oval body, gold irid feathers on opal body, folded irid rim, base inscribed "Kew-Blas" ........................... 980.00

8-1/4" h, elongated goblet form, gold irid luster, splotched and spotted technique, base inscribed "Kew Blas" ................. 450.00

10" h, tooled spiked top rim, flared amber cylinder, green pulled feather dec, irid luster, base inscribed "Kew Blas" ........... 550.00

# KITCHEN COLLECTIBLES

**History:** The kitchen was the focal point in a family's environment until the 1960s. Many early kitchen utensils were handmade and prized by their owners. Next came a period of utilitarian products made of tin and other metals. When the housewife no longer wished to work in a sterile environment, enamel and plastic products added color, and their unique design served both aesthetic and functional purposes.

The advent of home electricity changed the type and style of kitchen products. Fads affected many items. High technology already has made inroads into the kitchen, and another revolution seems at hand.

**References:** E. Townsend Artman, *Toasters: 1909-1960*, Schiffer Publishing, 1996; Ronald S. Barlow, *Victorian Houseware*, Windmill Publishing, 1992; Ellen Bercovici, Bobbie Zucker Bryson and Deborah Gillham, *Collectibles for the Kitchen, Bath and Beyond,* Antique Trader Books, 1998; *Collector's Digest Price Guide to Griswold Mfg. Co. 1918 Catalog Reprint*, Edward C. Kvetko and Douglas Congdon-Martin, *Coffee Antiques,* Schiffer Publishing, 2000; L-W Book Sales, 1996; *Collectors Guide to Wagner Ware and Other Companies*, L-W Book Sales, 1994; Linda Fields, *Four & Twenty Blackbirds: A Pictorial Identification and Value Guide for Pie Birds,* published by author, 1998, (158 Bagsby Hill Lane, Dover, TN 37058); Gene Florence, *Kitchen Glassware of the Depression Years*, 5th ed., Collector Books, 1999; Linda Campbell Franklin, *300 Years of Housekeeping Collectibles*, Books Americana, 1992; ——, *300 Hundred Years of Kitchen Collectibles*, 4th ed., Krause Publications, 1997; Ambrogio Fumagalli, *Coffee Makers*, Chronicle Books, 1995; Michael J. Goldberg, *Collectible Plastic Kitchenware and Dinnerware*, Schiffer Publishing, 1995; ——, *Groovy Kitchen Designs for Collectors*, Schiffer Publishing, 1996; Helen Greguire, *Collector's Guide to Toasters & Accessories*, Collector Books, 1997; Susan E. Grindberg, *Collector's Guide to Porcelier China*, Collector Books, 1996; Jon B. Haussler, *Griswold Muffin Pans,* Schiffer Publishing, 1997; *Griswold Cast Iron*, L-W Book Sales, 1997; Frances Johnson, *Kitchen Antiques*, Schiffer Publishing, 1996; Jan Lindenberger, *Black Memorabilia for the Kitchen,* 2nd ed., Schiffer Publishing, 1999; ——, *The 50s & 60s Kitchen*, Schiffer Publishing, 1994; ——, *Fun Kitchen Collectibles*, Schiffer Publishing, 1996; Barbara Mauzy, *Bakelite in the Kitchen,* Schiffer Publishing, 1998; ——, *The Complete Book of Kitchen Collecting,* Schiffer Publishing, 1997; Gary Miller and K. M. Mitchell, *Price Guide to Collectible Kitchen Appliances*, Wallace-Homestead, 1991; Jim Moffett, *American Corn Huskers*, Off Beat Books (1345 Poplar Ave., Sunnyvale, CA 94087), 1994; David T. Pikul and Ellen M. Plante, *Enameled Kitchenware American & European,* Schiffer Publishing, 2000; Don and Carol Raycraft, *Wallace-Homestead Price Guide to American Country Antiques,* 16th ed., Krause Publications, 1999; James Rollband, *American Nutcrackers*, Off Beat Books (1345 Poplar Ave., Sunnyvale, CA 94087), 1996; David G. Smith and Charles Wafford, *Book of Griswold & Wagner*, Schiffer Publishing, 1996; Diane Stoneback, *Kitchen Collectibles*, Wallace-Homestead, 1994; Don Thornton, *Apple Parers,* Off Beat Books, (1345 Poplar Ave., Sunnyvale, CA 94087) 1997; ——, *Beat This: The Eggbeater Chronicles*, Off Beat Books, 1994; ; ——, *The Eggbeater Chronicles,* 2nd edition, Thorton House, 1999; *Toasters and Small Kitchen Appliances*, L-W Book Sales, 1995; April M. Tvorak, *Fire-King Fever '96*, published by author, 1995.

**Periodicals:** *Cast Iron Cookware News*, 28 Angela Ave., San Anselmo, CA 94960; *Kettles 'n' Cookware*, P.O. Box B, Perrysburg, NY 14129; *Kitchen Antiques & Collectible News*, 4645 Laurel Ridge Dr., Harrisburg, PA 17110; *Piebirds Unlimited*, 14 Harmony School Rd, Flemington, NJ 08822.

**Collectors' Clubs:** Cook Book Collectors Club of America, P.O. Box 56, St. James, MO 65559-0056; Cookie Cutter Collectors Club, 1167 Teal Rd, SW, Dellroy, OH 44620; Eggcup Collectors' Corner, 67 Steven Ave., Old Bridge, NJ 08857; Glass Knife Collectors' Club, 4448 Ironwood Ave., Seal Beach, CA 90740; Griswold & Cast Iron Cookware Association, 3007 Plum St., Erie, PA 16508; International Society for Apple Parer Enthusiasts, 17 E. High, Mount Vernon, OH 43050; Jelly Jammers, 6086 W. Boggstown Rd, Bottstown, IN 46110; Kollectors of Old Kitchen Stuff, 501 Market St., Mifflinburg, PA 17844; National Cookie Cutters Collectors Club, 2763 310th St., Cannon Falls, MN 55009; National

Reamer Collectors Association, 47 Midline Court, Gaithersburg, MD 20878; Pie Bird Collectors Club, 158 Bagsby Hill Lane, Dover, TN 37058.

**Museums:** Corning Glass Museum, Corning, NY; Kern County Museum, Bakersfield, CA; Landis Valley Farm Museum, Lancaster, PA.

**Additional Listings:** Baskets; Brass; Butter Prints; Copper; Fruit Jars; Food Molds; Graniteware; Ironware; Tinware; Woodenware. See *Warman's Americana & Collectibles* for more examples including electrical appliances. See *Warman's Flea Market Treasures* also.

Apple Peeler, cast iron, Hudson Co, Leominster, MA, patent 1882 ...75.00
Bread Stick Pan, cast iron, Griswold #23 ......................................75.00
Broiler, 6-1/2" d, wrought iron, wavy cross bars ..........................75.00
Butter Churn, 8-3/4" d, 26" h, wood, blue painted, America, late 18th/early 19th C, wear to paint ......................................375.00
Butter Paddle, 10" l, maple, curved handle, some curl, old worn patina, age crack in bowl ..................................................55.00
Cake Board, 13" x 17", carved walnut, three lozenge-shaped molds of dog, soldier on horseback, and flower filled base, imp mark "J. Conger, New York," 19th C ..................................................825.00
Cookie Board, 3-7/8" x 7", pewter, fifteen segments, well detailed animals, flowers, and buildings, walnut back ................................220.00
Cream and Egg Whip, Whippit, Durometal Products Co, 14" l .....25.00
Dutch Oven, cov, cast iron, Griswold #8, large trademark ..........100.00
Egg Beater
    Dover, 13" l, 4 hole wheel standard, pat. Dec 27-98 .............65.00
    Instant Whip, 11-1/2" l, aluminum, Pat April 20, 1920 ...........25.00
    Taplin Improved Dover Pattern, 10-1/2" l, Pat Feb 9, 1904 ..45.00
Fish Broiler, 18" l, wrought iron, America, late 18th/early 19th C 175.00
Flour Scoop, 14" l, maple, Shaker type, carved, shaped handle, finger grip ................................................................170.00
Food Grinder, cast iron, Griswold #4 ............................................25.00
Grater, 9-5/8" l, tin, pine box with sliding lid and drawer, old brown varnish, wire nail construction ..........................................95.00
Griddle, 11-1/2" d, 21-1/8" w, 4" h, cast iron, round cast griddle plate, handle with hole for hanging, three legs, America, 18th C .......350.00
Herb Grinder, 15" l, 6-3/4" h, cast iron, iron disk blade with wooden handles, elongated oval slant-sided trough, America, 19th C ..920.00
Ice Chest Refrigerator, 34" w, 20-1/2" d, 30-1/4" h, poplar, old worn refinishing, metal lined int. with double wooden lid, turned feet with castors, paper label "Eddy Refrigerator, Boston…" ..................250.00
Kettle, cast iron, 5 qt, Wagnerware and Griswold trademarks ......80.00
Kraut Cutter, 13" x 41", ash, cherry dovetailed hopper, refinished 80.00
Muffin Pan, cast iron, Griswold #10 ..............................................40.00
Nutmeg Grater, 5-1/4" l, tin, wood handle ....................................65.00
Pie Bird

**Lemon Squeezer, Arcade No. 9, cast iron, porcelain slotted insert, $90. Photo courtesy of Joy Luke Fine Art Brokers and Auctioneers.**

**Colander, yellow ware, applied cream colored Bristol glaze, relief arch panel design, full length hairline extending from rim, 12" d, 5-1/4" h, $180. Photo courtesy of Vicki & Bruce Waasdrop.**

    Blackbird ............................................................................55.00
    Duck, yellow ........................................................................65.00
Pie Crimper, 7" l, wood handle, brass crimper ..............................75.00
Pot Scraper, 3" h, 3-1/2" l, King Midas Flour adv, diecut, black ground, Sunbonnet girl in white, orange lettering and trim ..................300.00
Rice Jar, cov, 5-1/2" h, blue and white stripes, T. G. Green, England, c1930 ................................................................250.00
Rolling Pin, 15" l, glass, blown, amethyst, worn painted floral dec 135.00
Salesman's Book, 6" h, 4" w, Cream of Wheat, black simulated leather case, celluloid oval on front of Cream of Wheat Chef, selling pointers and product info inside ..........................................135.00
Salt Box, 4-1/4" h, blue and white stripes, T. G. Green, England, c1930 ................................................................345.00
Skewer Holder, six flat skewers, wrought iron, 12-3/4" l, imp "RE" mark, 18th C ................................................................550.00
Skillet, cast iron
    Griswold #0, heat ring, large trademark ...............................65.00
    Griswold #9, hinge, small trademark ....................................35.00
    Victor, #8 ............................................................................50.00
    Wagnerware, #0, Randall Wagnerware paper label .............15.00
    Wapak, #8, heat ring ...........................................................100.00
Sugar Nippers, wrought steel and brass, turned wooden handle, molded edge base, 11" l ..........................................175.00
Trivet, 7-3/4" l, heart shape, wrought iron, penny feet, some damage ................................................................325.00
Wafer Iron, 28" l, 5-1/2" w, eagle motif, late 18th/early 19th C....550.00

# KUTANI

**History:** Kutani originated in the mid-1600s in the Kaga province of Japan. Kutani comes in a variety of color patterns, one of the most popular being Ao Kutani, a green glaze with colors such as green, yellow, and purple enclosed in a black outline. Export wares made since the 1870s are enameled in a wide variety of colors and styles.

Berry Set, master bowl, six serving bowls, multicolored enamel floral dec, red border, price for 7 pc set ..........................................175.00
Bowl
    4-3/4" sq, polychrome, gold flowers, unglazed foot, sgd gold seal form ................................................................320.00
    11-1/2" d, tethered hawk and brocade pattern, ext. with cranes, 19th C ................................................................200.00
Candleholders, pr, 11-1/2" h, late 19th C ....................................100.00

**Plate, cream and beige ground, multicolored dec of poppies, gold, black, and red border, mkd, 8-1/4" d, $85.**

Charger, 14" d, figural landscape, multicolored, gold border ...... 225.00

Chocolate Pot, 8-1/2" h, red, orange, and gold, reserve panels of peonies and birds, people in gardens ............................................. 165.00

Ewer, 8-1/4" h, duck on floral base, keyfret band, green, yellow, aubergine, and blue enamel .......................................................... 195.00

Ginger Jar, cov, 5" h, blue, green, and carmine enamel dec, foo dog finial ............................................................................................. 150.00

Jar, cov, lid damaged, late 19th C .................................................. 50.00

Low Bowl, 13-1/2" d, yellow, blue, green, and aubergine enamels, central reserve of scholar and attendant in pavilion, wide lappet border .. 650.00

Sake Cup, 1-7/8" h, floriform rim, short ring foot, enamel and gold dec, painted rim band, gold scrolling flower and trellis dec .............. 125.00

Umbrella Stand, 28" h, multicolored butterflies, flowers, foliage, and medallions ................................................................................... 500.00

Vase, 26" h, medallions of birds and flowers, gold brocade dec orange ground, Aka-Kutani, late 19th C, mounted as lamp ................ 300.00

# LACE and LINENS

**History:** Lace, lacy linens, embroidery, and hand-decorated textiles are different from any other antique. They are valued both as a handmade substance and as the thing the substance is made into. Thread is manipulated into stitches, stitches are assembled into lace, lace is made into handkerchiefs, edgings, tablecloths, bedspreads. Things eventually go out of style or are damaged or worn, and just as the diamonds and rubies are taken from old jewelry and placed into new settings, fine stitchery of embroidery and lace is saved and reused. Lace from a handkerchief is used to decorate a blouse, fragments of a bridal veil are made into a scarf; shreds of old lace are remounted onto fine net and used again as a veil.

At each stage in the cycle, different people become interested. Some see fragments as bits and pieces of a collage, and seek raw materials for accent pieces. Others use Victorian whites and turn-of-the-century embroidered linens to complement a life style. Collectors value and admire the stitches themselves, and when those stitches are remarkable enough, they will pay hundreds of dollars for fragments a few inches square.

Until the 1940s, lace collecting was a highly respected avocation of the wealthy. The prosperity of the New World was a magnet for insolvent European royalty, who carried suitcases of old Hapsburg, Bourbon, Stuart, and Romanov laces to suites at New York's Waldorf hotel for dealers to select from. Even Napoleon's bed hangings of handmade Alencon lace, designed for Josephine and finished for Marie Louise, found their way here. In 1932, Fortune magazine profiled socially prominent collectors and lace dealers. For the entire first half of this century, New York City's Needle and Bobbin Club provided a forum for showing off acquisitions.

Until 1940, upscale department stores offered antique lace and lacy linens. Dealers specializing in antique lace and lacy linens had prominent upscale shops, and offered repair, restoration, remodeling, and cleaning services along with the antique linens. In addition to collecting major pieces—intact jabots from the French Ancient Regime, Napoleonic-era Alencon, huge mid-Victorian lace shawls, Georgian bed hangings appliquéd with 17th-century needle lace—collectors assembled study collections of postcard-size samples of each known style of antique lace.

When styles changed round the 1940s and 1950s and the market for antique lace and linens crashed, some of the best collections did go to museums; others just went into hiding. With renewed interest in a gracious, romantic lifestyle, turn-of-the-century lacy cloths from the linen closets of the barons of the industrial revolution are coming out of hiding. Collectors and wise dealers know that many of the small study-pieces of irreplaceable stitchery—fragments collectors will pay ten to hundreds of dollars for—still emerge in rummage and estate sales.

Very large banquet-sized lace tablecloths, especially those with napkins, continue to be especially popular. Appenzell, a white-on-white embroidered lacework of 19th C Switzerland, has become one of the hottest collector's items. Strong interest continues in patterned silk ribbons, all cotton lace yardage, and other lacy materials for heirloom sewing and fashion.

The market for antique lace definitely is changing. Interest is still rising for elaborate lace for home decorating and entertaining, and interest in fine quality lace collars is increasing. Large lace shawls and veils, especially for bridal wear, continue to be in demand. Internet auctions and chat groups make it possible for a dealer in Wyoming to link up with a collector in Louisiana, and find a home for an interesting piece. Those interested in fine quality lace are realizing they need to start buying at market prices instead of waiting for that lucky find that they alone recognize. Current market prices, although rising, still are usually far below what the pieces would have cost when new, or during the early twentieth century heyday of lace collecting.

As prices rise, buyers more often want an accurate identification: what is it, where was it made, how old is it? What makes it worth the price? Word spreads quickly over the Internet when it is obvious a dealer has mislabeled something, especially labeling something as handmade that is obviously machine. Lace has long been a sideline for most dealers, and they did not bother to learn to identify it. As long as they could turn it over quickly for a small markup, they were satisfied. That is changing. More sophisticated buyers won't put up with that without comment.

The basic techniques are bobbin lace, needle lace, crochet, tatting, knitting, knotting, and needleweaving. Identifying how a piece was made is the easy part, and there is no excuse for a dealer not being able to separate crochet from bobbin lace. Anyone can identify the technique after just a weekend workshop, or by comparing a piece to pictures in a good textbook. The technique, plus the quality of the design, and the condition, provides nearly all the information anyone needs to decide what a piece is worth.

After identifying the technique, many like to apply a name to the style (Duchesse bobbin lace, Point de Gaze needle lace, Irish crochet). This serves as a useful shorthand in talking about lace, but adds nothing to the value of the piece. This is often the confusing part. Unlike most antiques, there is no uniformity in labeling styles of lace. Names changed at different points in time, different names were used for similar products made in different countries, and foreign names often were translated differently. Any dealer should be expected to be able to explain why they chose to use any specific style name.

The Internet offers a unique access to a wide variety of kinds of lace and lacy linens. The small pictures available on the Internet, however, rarely show enough detail to know just what you are buying. Insist on a return policy for any lace purchased sight unseen on the Internet. Even well intentioned dealers may miss details that significantly affect the value of lace. Handmade meshes cannot be positively identified without high powered magnification. Repairs often go unnoticed and unreported. Color and texture make a great deal of difference in determining whether a piece of lace is attractive or not.

Whether purchasing fine quality collector's study samples, or boxes and bags of recyclable fragments for sewing, it is worth taking a close look at all the details. It is not uncommon for good quality study samples that a collector will pay $10 to $100 for in the "rag bags."

Those who learn to recognize the artistry and value of old stitchery will not only enhance their lives with beauty, they may find a windfall.

**References:** Pat Earnshaw, *Identification of Lace*, Lubrecht and Cramer, 1989; Frances Johnson, *Collecting Antique Linens, Lace, and Needlework*, Wallace-Homestead, 1991; —, *Collecting More Household Linens,* Schiffer Publishing, 1997; Elizabeth Kurella, *Guide To Lace and Linens,* Antique Trader Books, 1998; —, *Secrets of Real Lace*, The Lace Merchant, 1994; —, *Pocket Guide to Valuable Old Lace and Lacy Linens*, The Lace Merchant, 1996; —, *The Complete Guide To Vintage Textiles,* Krause Publications, 1999; Marsha L. Manchester, *Vintage White Linens A to Z,* Schiffer Publishing, 1997; Emily Reigate, *An Illustrated Guide to Lace,* Antique Collectors' Club; Elizabeth Scofield and Peggy Zalamea, *Twentieth Century Linens and Lace*, Schiffer Publishing, 1997.

**Collectors' Club:** International Old Lacers, P.O. Box 554, Flanders, NJ 07836, http://members.aol/com/iolinc/ioli.html.

**Museums:** Chicago Art Institute, Chicago, IL; Cooper Hewitt (Smithsonian), New York, NY; Metropolitan Museum of Art, New York, NY; Museum of Early Southern Decorative Arts (MESDA), Winston-Salem, NC; Museum of Fine Arts, Boston, MA; Rockwood Museum, Wilmington, DE; Shelburne, Museum, Shelburne, VT; Smithsonian Institution, Washington, DC.

**Advisor**: Elizabeth M. Kurella.

---

## SPECIAL AUCTIONS

Christies South Kensington
85 Old Brompton Road
London, England SW7 3LD
011-44-171-581-7611

William Doyle Galleries
175 E. 87th St.
New York, NY 10128
(212) 427-2730

Phillips
Blenstock House
Blenheim Street
101 New Bond St.
London, England W1Y OAS
011-44-171-629-6602

---

## Collars

Honiton English bobbin lace, traditional design of roses, thistles, and shamrocks, inch-long robin-like bird hidden in each lapel, 38" l, 9" deep at center back, mid-19th C ............................................... 385.00
Irish Crochet, round cape-like collar, exceptional design of heavy flowers with lots of raised work, imitates 17th C Gros Point needle lace, 12" deep .................................................................... 325.00
Maltese bobbin lace, round style, honey color silk, geometric design with Maltese crosses, background grid of fat wheatears, c1900, 7" deep .................................................................. 285.00
Needle lace, large stylized flowers with raised outlines, c1900 ..375.00
Tape lace, heavy millinery-style cotton tape in scrolling design, simple looping and needlewoven stitches, deep beige, early 20th C .. 175.00
Vieux Flandre Berthe, combination of bobbin lace motifs with needle lace background, deep beige, early 20th C, 5" x 56" ............... 185.00

## Collector's Lace

Alencon needle lace lappets (headdress streamers) with stylized floral design, c1730, 28" l, pr............................................................ 725.00
Brussels bobbin lace flounce fragment in exceptional design of full-blown roses with shaded petals, unusual bobbin lace fillings, 16" deep, 28" l ................................................................................ 485.00
Dutch bonnet, late nineteenth century, decorated with about a yard of four-inch deep handmade Beveren bobbin lace ........................ 54.00
Gros Point de Venise, design of stylized flowers with heavy raised outlines decorated with picots, background repaired, 2" x 18"...... 125.00
Point de France needle lace border fragment, with a Berainesque design of small, symmetrical flower vases and stylized flowers, background of hexagonal bars covered with buttonhole stitches and decorated with picots, 3.8" x 25"...................................................... 125.00
Point de France needle lace engegeant (sleeve ruffle) with a hunting scene design including fox and hounds in exotic floral and foliage background, c1720................................................................. 1,100.00
Point de Gaze needle lace, flounce fragment with design of traditional rose and scroll, 6" x 14" ............................................................ 45.00
Point de Gaze needle lace. tablier (dress front) with design of flower bouquets and scrolls with two heraldic shields each with tree, castles, and fleur-de-lis, 42" l ......................................................... 3,700.00

## Doilies

Bobbin lace, design of butterflies typical of 20th C Chinese, 8" d round.............................................................................................5.00
Bobbin lace, meandering scrollwork design, probably early 20th C, Chinese, 8" d round....................................................................... 5.00
Crochet, unusual dragon-like design, probably eastern European, early 20th C, 8" d round. ....................................................... 35.00
Needle lace, well-designed rose motif with shaded petals, fine thread, 20th C, 9" d round .................................................................. 25.00

## Handkerchiefs

French embroidery, drawnwork, and needle lace inserts, large satin stitch leaves design, 10" sq, fair condition ................................. 75.00
Irish Youghal needle edge, 4" w lace in stylized foliate design, background of bars with picots, 14" sq ........................................... 425.00
Linen, 12" sq
    Edged with 1/4" of tatted rings with picots ............................ 8.00
    Edged with 2" of scallops of crochet chain stitch and double crochet..............................................................................5.00
Point de Gaze needle lace edged with 4" of design of cattails and flower sprays, c1870 ................................................................ 375.00

## Tablecloths

Combination of bobbin lace and needle lace, scrolling design including dragon-like figures, early 20th C, 68" x 108".......................... 1,250.00
Crochet, round design of scallop chain stitch, 38" d, some small repairs ...................................................................................28.00
Normandy work, a patchwork of machine, crochet, torchon bobbin lace, needle lace, filet in good symmetrical design, ecru, 48" x 68" .................................................................................750.00

## Veils and Shawls

Brussels bobbin lace flowers and bouquets appliquéd on machine net, c1870, 96" x 28" ...................................................................... 1,800.00

Brussels needle and bobbin lace flowers arranged in bouquets at the corners and in sprays at the border, applied to machine net, sprigs and spots scattered across the net, 51" x 78" ...................... 1,530.00

Brussels needlelace flowers appliquéd in scalloped border on machine net, scattered sprigs, 74" x 69 " ............................................... 625.00

English Honiton bobbin lace appliqué on machine net, spray of flowers at each corner, scattered springs and scalloped border, late 19th C, 71" x 69" ............................................................................... 238.00

English Honiton bobbin lace appliqué on machine net, stylized posies at each corner and roses along the border, late 19th C, 75" x 73" ....660.00

Shawl, machine-made black lace, imitating Chantilly, opulent design of flower bouquets and garlands of flowers and foliage, triangular, 105" l x 54" w ..................................................................................145.00

Veil, rect, large, bouquet of flowers at each corner, formal posies at border, sprigs and spots scattered across net in fine tambour embroidery, 92" x 74" ...........................................................325.00

# LALIQUE

**History:** René Lal-
ique (1860-1945)
first gained promi-
nence as a jewelry
designer. Around
1900, he began experimenting with molded-glass
brooches and pendants, often embellishing them with
semiprecious stones. By 1905, he was devoting himself
exclusively to the manufacture of glass articles.

In 1908, Lalique began designing packaging for the
French cosmetic houses. He also produced many
objects, especially vases, bowls, and figurines, in the Art
Nouveau and Art Deco styles. The full scope of Lalique's
genius was seen at the 1925 Paris l'Exposition Internationale des Arts Décorative et Industriels Modernes.

**Marks:** The mark "R. LALIQUE FRANCE" in block letters
is found on pressed articles, tableware, vases, paperweights, and automobile mascots. The script signature,
with or without "France," is found on hand-blown objects.
Occasionally, a design number is included. The word
"France" in any form indicates a piece made after 1926.

The post-1945 mark is generally "Lalique France"
without the "R," but there are exceptions.

**References:** Fritz Falk, *Lalique and His Circle,* Arnoldsche, distributed by Antique Collectors' Club, 1999; Kyle
Husfloen, *Antique Trader's American & European Decorative and Art Glass Price Guide,* 2nd ed., Krause Publications, 2000.

**Collectors' Club:** Lalique Collectors Society, 400 Veterans Blvd., Carlstadt, NJ 07072; Lalique Society of America, 400 Veterans Blvd., Carlstadt, NJ 07072.

## Reproduction Alert:

The Lalique signature has often been forged, the most common fake includes an "R" with the post-1945 mark.

Animal

Fox, 2-3/4" h, frosted, circular, engraved script sgd "R. Lalique France".......................................................................... 550.00

Frog, 5" x 4" x 2-3/4", crystal, script mark "Lalique, France," paper "Made in France" label ...................................................... 375.00

Rabbit, 2-1/4" h, stylized, seated, smoky topaz, facet design, cir-cular base, inscribed "R. Lalique," c1925, price for pair, one damaged and repaired..................................................... 1,035.00

Rooster, 9" h, numbered, sgd "R. Lalique, France," orig paper label.............................................................................. 2,000.00

Ashtray, 3-1/2" h, Soucis, opal figure of vase with flowers at center, base stamped "R. Lalique France"........................................ 460.00

Atomizer, cylindrical, 3-3/4" h, relief molded frieze of six nude maidens, holding floral garland, waisted gilt metal mount, Le Provencal fra-grance, molded "R Lalique, Made in France" ........................ 265.00

Auto Mascot, 8-1/4" h, rooster, molded, polished and frosted, ruffled tail feathers, low disk base, etched block mark, numbered on base ..750.00

Bookends, pr

6-1/4" h, florals, birds, sgd .............................................. 500.00

7-1/8" h, three molded putti bearing garlands, frosted, stenciled "Lalique France" .............................................................. 600.00

Bowl

8-1/2" d, Volubilis, colorless, molded underneath with three opal-escent morning glory blossoms, centers form feet, sgd "R. Lal-ique" in mold, inscribed "France," model created 1921, Macilhac 383, nicks to rim .............................................................. 635.00

9-7/8" d, 2-3/8" h, Daisy, untulating rim, molded colorless body, alternating raised flower heads and recessed leaves, frosted and polished, inscribed "Lalique France" on base, paper label, late 20th C, rim flake....................................................... 150.00

Box, cov, 3-1/2" d, Emiliane, frosted, molded flowerheads, engraved "R. Lalique France"............................................................. 250.00

Carafe, 7-1/4" h, clear, indented and molded large blossoms, brown patine in recesses, inscribed "R. Lalique" ............................ 450.00

Champagne Glass, 4-1/2" h, Strasbourg, frosted androgynous nude couple on stem, Art Deco pattern exhibited at Paris Exhibition, 1925, Rene Lalique, set of 6 ........................................................ 920.00

Chandelier, 13-1/2" d domed shade, Charmes, frosted all over leaf pat-tern, rect components with similar pattern, orig metal fixtures, molded "R. Lalique".................................................................... 4,000.00

Charger

12" d, Peacock Feather ..................................................... 550.00

14-1/2" d, Martigues, opalescent, deeply molded swimming fish, molded mark "R. Lalique"............................................... 2,700.00

Cigarette Lighter, 5" h, highly emb frosted lion's heads, pedestal, sgd in script.............................................................................. 90.00

Clock, 8-1/2" l, 6" h, demilune, circular mate finished silvered metal face, stylized dahlia encircled by polished Arabic numerals, arching frosted glass case, relief molded pairs of finches among flowering vines, inscribed in block letters "R. Lalique France," dial inscribed "ATO" and impressed "Made in France," c1930 ................... 2,750.00

Cordial Set, Wingen, 8" h bulbous bottle, conforming stopper, two 3" h wine glasses, each with fine vertical striping, molded "R. Lalique" .............................................................................575.00

Candleholder, 3-1/2" h, frosted and colorless, molded flower, block mark ................................................................................ 160.00

Coupe, 3-1/2" h, 9-1/2" d, Coquilles, molded overlapping scallop shell design, strong opal blue color at base, inscribed in block letters "R. Lalique France" ................................................................ 500.00

Dresser Box, cov, 4" d, Emiliane, LeLys, floral dec, colorless pressed molded glass, retains some sepia patine ................................ 250.00

Jardiniere, 18-1/4" l, 5-1/8" h, Saint Hubert, frosted elliptical bowl, ends spreading to form reticulated ear shaped handle, molded relief of leaping antelope among clear leafy branches, wheel cut block letters "R. Lalique/France," incised script "No. 3461," c1932........... 3,500.00

Light Bowl, 13-1/2" d, partial luster, press molded design, four exotic birds among stylized berries and foliage, sepia patina in recesses, pierced at four panels and base for hanging, panel inscribed "Lalique France"............................................................................ 500.00

**Perfume Bottle, Perles, opalescent, sepia patina, molded "R. Lalique," 5-1/2" h, $1,380. Photo courtesy of David Rago Auctions.**

Paperweight, Tete D'Aigle, eagle head, clear and frosted, sgd in mold at side "R. Lalique" .............................................. 1,200.00

Perfume Atomizer, 5-1/8" h, gilt metal press button cap, cylindrical press molded bottle of frosted colorless glass, frieze of nude woman with flower garlands, molded signature "R. Lalique Made in France" on base, model created 1925, burst bubble at top, wear to gilt .................... 460.00

Perfume Bottle

    3-1/4" d, 2" h, flattened circular molded colorless body, dec with asymmetrical flock of butterflies, stopper with circular dec, molded signature "R. Lalique" ......................................... 750.00

    8-1/8" h, circular form, molded as dahlia blossom, highlighted with black enamel stamens, base acid stamped "Lalique France," stuck stopper ................................................................ 690.00

Pin Tray, 6" l, Medicis, press-molded oval, opalescent, two pairs of nude women among garlands of flowers, sgd "R. Lalique" in mold and inscribed "France No. 280," model created 1924, Marcilhac 280, nicks ............................................................................... 400.00

Place Card Holder, 1-5/8" h, demilune form, clear and frosted, molded baskets of flowers and fruit, engraved "R. Lalique," set of 8 ......... 850.00

Plaque, 4" h, 3-1/2" w, frosted and clear, floral design, mkd "Lalique," orig velvet lined box .............................................. 100.00

Plate

    7-7/8" d, crescent-form, colorless, frosted thistle dec, pr.... 125.00

**Statuette, Suzanne, opalescent, orig bronze illuminated stand, molded "R. Lalique," $25,400. Photo courtesy of David Rago Auctions.**

    12-1/2" d, molded swirling fish, opalescent, raised signature, few scratches.....400.00Table Ornament, 8" h, Luxembourg, catalog no. 11619/11620, selectively frosted colorless crystal, molded three full-length cherubs in half circle, semi-circular platform foot, inscribed "Lalique France," price of pr..................... 900.00

Tray, 10-1/2" d, blue opalescence, all over shell pattern, sgd "R. Lalique" ............................................................................... 300.00

Vase

    6" h, flared rim, colorless body molded with wide band of berries on the vine, frosted to enhance dec, acid signature on base "Lalique France," mid-20th C ........................................... 415.00

    6-3/4" h, oval colorless body, dec with trailing garlands of multi-petaled flowers, acid stamp "Lalique France," mid-20th C ......... 635.00

    7-3/4" h, Cariatides, rim on ovoid colorless body, eight female torso columns on leafy ground, frosted, alternating with arched panels of polished glass, base imp "R. Lalique," inscribed France, model created 1920, Marcilhac 924........................................... 4,600.00

    9-1/2" h, Bornco, flared rim, press-molded form, lower portion decorated with black enameled birds among exotic foliage, frosted and polished to enhance design, model created 1930, Marcilhac 1056, minor nicks to rim, minor bubble burst.................. 2,645.00

    10-1/2" h, Enfants, press molded, colorless vase supported by two putti with grapes, disk foot, acid stamp "R. Lalique," model crated 1931, Marcilhac 1070, wear, nicks .................... 1,035.00

# LAMP SHADES

**History:** Lamp shades were made to diffuse the harsh light produced by early gas lighting fixtures. These early shades were made by popular Art Nouveau manufacturers including Durand, Quezal, Steuben, and Tiffany. Many shades are not marked.

Acid Etched, 8" d, hummingbirds and leaves, clear and frosted, c1870, price for pr ............................................................................... 195.00

Burmese, 8 3/4' d, birds, butterflies, and floral dec, gas style fitter ring.................................................................................... 275.00

Cut Glass

    7-1/4" d, 6" h, ball form, engraved and etched leaves and diamonds, America, second quarter 19th C ......................... 175.00

    9-3/4" d, 4" h, chandelier type, tulip form, floral etched glass, price for set of four....................................................................... 125.00

Durand, 3 1/2" d, irid gold, candle lamp type ............................. 150.00

Fostoria, 5"h, gold, green leaves and vines, white luster ground 150.00

Hobbs Bruckunier, 4 1/2" h, 7" d, Coinspot pattern, opalescent and amber optic, c1880.................................................................. 75.00

Iridescent, 3-1/4" d fitter ring, 5-3/4" h, Steuben, catalog 907, tenribbed bell form, amber ground, strong gold irid, traces of silver fleur-de-lis mark, minor dark inclusions............................................. 300.00

Leaded

    14" d, 5-3/4" h, Tiffany Studios, hemispherical, mottled green segments with band of mottled amber and green acorns, rim tag stamped "Tiffany Studios New York" ............................. 7,500.00

    15-5/8" d, 6-1/2" h, Tiffany Studios, domed, radiating mottled green tiles, band of mottled amber-green fleur-de-lis motifs, rim imp "Tiffany Studios New York, 1437-5," out of round, cracked segments...................................................................... 6,100.00

**Cameo Glass, gaslight, powder blue ground, 4 white sprays of Maidenhair fern alternating with 4 white sprays of Forest fern, English, 8-1/2" d, 4" d fitter ring, 5" h, $1,245. Photo courtesy of Clarence & Betty Maier.**

Lustre Art, 4-7/8" h, 2-1/4" d, bud form, opal glass, scalloped rim, five pulled gold feathers on ext., irid gold flashed int., minor chips to top rim .................................................................................. 115.00
Muller Fres, art glass, blue and orange, sgd, price for pr ........... 350.00
Opalescent Glass, 2-1/4" d, 5" h, scalloped rim, colorless glass with spiral optic ribbing shading to opalescent white, minor rim nicks ..............60.00
Quezal, sgd
    Art glass, threading............................................................225.00
    Butterscotch......................................................................130.00
    Gold irid, price for pr .........................................................500.00
    Opaque white, hearts and threaded dec, sgd, price for set of three .................................................................................900.00
    White, feathered dec...........................................................250.00
Tiffany
    3" h, 5-1/4" d lower opening, Candlelamp, Pine Needle pattern, conical, reticulated etched metal, imp "Tiffany Studios," price for pr .......................................................................................280.00
    5" h, 3" d top opening, opal glass, optic-ribbed, pink damascene striping, rim mkd "L. C. T.," both cracked, price for pr ......300.00
    6-3/4" h, 16" d, leaded, Pomegranate pattern, band of yellow fruit, segmented two-tone green ground, imp "Tiffany Studios/New York/1-57-109"..............................................................8,750.00

# LAMPS and LIGHTING

**History:** Lighting devices have evolved from simple stone-age oil lamps to the popular electrified models of today. Aimé Argand patented the first oil lamp in 1784. Around 1850, kerosene became a popular lamp-burning fluid, replacing whale oil and other fluids. In 1879, Thomas A. Edison invented the electric light, causing fluid lamps to lose favor and creating a new field for lamp manufacturers. Companies like Tiffany and Handel became skillful at manufacturing electric lamps, and their decorators produced beautiful bases and shades.

**References:** James Edward Black (ed.), *Electric Lighting of the 20s-30s* (1988, 1993 value update), *Volume 2 with Price Guide* (1990, 1993 value update), L-W Book Sales; John Campbell, *Fire & Light in the Home Pre 1820,* Antique Collectors' Club, 1999; J. W. Courter, *Aladdin Collectors Manual & Price Guide #19,* published by author (3935 Kelley Rd, Kevil, KY 42053), 2000; —, *Aladdin, The Magic Name In Lamps, Revised Edition,* published by author, 1997; *Electric Lighting of the 20s-30s, Vol. 1* (1994, 1998 value update), *Vol 2, (1994),* L-W Book Sales, Carole Goldman Hibel, John Hibel, John Fontaine, *The Handel Lamps Book,* Fontaine Publishers, 1999; Marjorie Hulsebus, *Miniature Victorian Lamps,* Schiffer Publishing, 1996; Donald B. Johnson and Leslie Pina, *1930s Lighting: Deco & Traditional by Chase,* Schiffer Publishing, 2000; Jan Lindenberger, *Lamps of the 50s & 60s,* Schiffer Publishing, 1997; L-W Book Sales, *Better Electric Lamps of the 20s & 30s,* L-W Book Sales, 1997; Calvin Shepherd, *50s T. V. Lamps,* Schiffer Publishing, 1998; Richard Miller and John Solverson, *Student Lamps of the Victorian Era,* Antique Publications, 1992, 1992-93 value guide; Bill and Linda Montgomery, *Animated Motion Lamps 1920s to Present,* L-W Book Sales, 1991; Denys Peter Myers, *Gaslighting in America,* Dover Publications, 1990; Henry A. Pohs, *Miner's Flame Light Book,* Hiram Press, 1995; Sam and Anna Samuelian, *Collector's Guide to Motion Lamps,* Collector Books, 1998; Tom Santiso, *TV Lamps,* Collector Books, 1999; Jo Ann and Francis Thomas, *Early Twentieth Century Lighting Fixtures,* Collector Books, 1999; Jo Ann Thomas, *Early Twentieth Century Lighting Fixtures: Selections from the R. Williamson Lamp Catalog,* Collector Books, 1999; —, *Lighting Figures of the Depression Era,* Collector Books, 2000; Catherine M. V. Thuro, *Oil Lamps,* Wallace-Homestead, 1976, 1998 value update; —, *Oil Lamps II,* Collector Books, 1983, 2000 value update; John J. Wolfe, *Brandy, Balloons & Lamps: Ami Argand, 1750-1803,* South Illinois Univ Press, 1999.

**Periodical:** *Light Revival,* 35 West Elm Ave., Quincy, MA 02170.

**Collectors' Clubs:** Aladdin Knights of the Mystic Light, 3935 Kelley Rd, Kevil, KY 42053; Coleman Collector Network, 1822 E. Fernwood, Wichita, KS 67216; Historical Lighting Society of Canada, P.O. Box 561, Postal Station R, Toronto, Ontario M4G 4EI, Canada; Incandescent Lamp Collectors Association, Museum of Lighting, 717 Washington Place, Baltimore, MD 21201; International Coleman Collectors Club, 2710 Nebraska St., Amarillo, TX 79106; International Colmean Collector's Network, 3404 West 450 North Rochester, IN 46975-8370; Night Light, 38619 Wakefiled Ct, Northville, MI 48167; Rushlight Club, Inc., Suite 196, 1657 The Fairway, Jenkintown, PA 19046.

**Museums:** Kerosene Lamp Museum, Winchester Center, CT; Pairpoint Lamp Museum, River Edge, NJ.

## Astral

11" h, socket, marble base, two tone gilding, mkd "Cornelius & Co., Philda," drilled and fitted as electric table lamp, pr...................200.00
13" h, molded opalescent stem, brass font labeled "Patented by J. G. Webb, NY, Oct 14, 1851," marble base, font altered and collar replaced ............................................................200.00
13-1/2" h, molded cranberry stem, brass font labeled "Patented by J. G. Webb, NY, Oct 14, 1851," marble and brass base, font altered and collar added, rings for prism and globe, top of glass insert chipped........225.00
16" h, gilded stem with resist floral dec, stepped marble base, font labeled "Cornelius & Baker, Philadelphia," mismatched parts, drilled and fitted as electric table lamp....................................................60.00
17" h, brass fluted columnar stem, Corinthian capital, ornate scroll base, marble base, font mkd "Cornelius & Co., Philad," labeled "Patent April 1st 1843," drilled and fitted as table lamp............165.00
21" h, Classical, ormolu and etched glass, mid-19th C...............690.00
25-1/2" h, ormolu and etched glass, elaborate, electrified.......1,150.00
26" h, gilt brass, wheel-cut and acid finished foliate and swag dec shade, Corinthian column standard on C-scroll and foliate dec sq base, Cornelius & Co., Philadelphia, dated April 1, 1843 .....1,035.00
27-1/4" h, banquet, frosted cut to clear shade, late font, brass and marble base ............................................................400.00

## Boudoir

Classique, 14" h, 8" d, reverse painted shade with landscape along river bank, sgd and numbered bronzed metal base, orig patina............900.00
Moe Bridges, 18" h, 8" d reverse painted shade, landscape dec, bronzed metal base, orig patina, mkd ...................................900.00
Muller Fres, France, c1925, 12" h, mushroom form cased glass shade, int. mottled blue and purple on orange ground, three-arm patinated metal arms, elongated bulbed cased glass base, int. streaked blue and orange on yellow ground, both with acid signature, nick to shade rim, shade signature rubbed ...................................................490.00
Pairpoint, 13-1/2" h, 8-1/2" d reverse painted shade, Art Deco orange flowers with green centers, ivory ground, green leaves, black stems, nickel plated bronzed metal base, imp mark, shade sgd .........950.00
Unknown Maker
   15-1/4" h, 8" d domed reverse painted frosted shade, pink, green, and yellow rose blossoms, buds, foliage, single socket trumpet-form painted metal base with raised shell motif, brown highlights on cream colored ground, minor wear, minor rim chips ...350.00

**Handel, gold ground, red flowers with yellow centers, sgd "Handel/7808," 8" h, 5" d, $1,380. Photo courtesy of David Rago Auctions.**

15-1/4" h, 8-1/4" d eight-sided conical shade, striated green slag glass panels, bronze floral motif overlay, four arm spider over sq shaft, stepped base, shade slightly bent ..........................230.00

## Ceiling

Pittsburgh Glass Co, 10" d amber glass globe with etched crackle surface, painted blue parrot motif repeated on obverse, 16" d round flush-mount bronzed metal ceiling fixture, four figural whorl heads applied to edge surface .........................................1,150.00

## Chandelier

Arts and Crafts, America, early 20th C, 20" h, hammered bronze, two tiered domed ceiling mount terminating in three waisted shades of opal glass, amber and gold colored serpentine dec, shades sgd "Quezal" .............................................................2,415.00
Cut Glass, 23" h, late 19th/early 20th C, five –light, standard suspending tier of cut drops from top, five serpentine scrolled candle arms, ribbed bobeche and suspending drapes, bell-shaped nozzle, further cut drops, electrified ...................................................475.00
Dutch Rococo-style, 50" d, 28" h, brass, 24 light, bulbous standard joined by two tiers of scrolled branches ..................................250.00
Empire-Style, c1900, 37" h, gilt and verde antico patinated brass, 9 lights, circular corona above tazzae supporting trio of standing maidens holding stylized cornucopias, bowl joined by scrolled branches issuing urn-shaped nozzles, pineapple pendant...................1,200.00
Italian, late 18th/early 19th C, 39-1/2" h, 46" d, giltwood and iron, old surface, fitted with electrified sockets and external wiring, formerly used in First Church of Deerfield, Deerfield, MA................19,550.00
Neoclassical-style, 20th C, 26" l, gilt bronze, seven-light, topped by husk swags above three slender scrolls ending in flat leaves, suspending tapered body with single central light, frosted glass flame-form globe, three ram's heads joined by drapery swags between six candlearms ending in reeded nozzles, six small paper shades, electrified ..............................................................650.00

## Desk

Emerlite, 50" h, 4-1/2" x 9" x 5" green cased glass shade, tag on inside of shade bracket....................................................275.00
Faries Manufacturing Co., Decatur, IL, mid-20th C, 12" h, 20" l, streamline design, copper plated metal, elongated rect shade raised on long rect standard over round stepped base, wear to metal finish ..260.00
Tiffany Studios, 15" h, 7" d gold Favrile glass shade, bright gold and rose irid, three-arm bronze base, orig patina, shade mkd "L. C. T. Favrile," base mkd "Tiffany Studios, N.Y., #322" ..................5,000.00
Unknown maker
   Brass, 17-1/2" h, slender curved arm suspending light aqua shade with white opalescent striations, irid oil spot dec, baluster shaped brass standard, stepped circular base, shade with chips on top rim, imperfections...................................................115.00
   Metal, 10-1/2" h, helmet shaped shade with two geometric pierced bands of silvered metal over bronze patina, centered by ceramic cameo of female nude in white on blue ground, shade supported by swivel harp above flared base with similar metal overlay, wear to patina, dents ..........................................435.00

## Early American

Betty Lamp
   4" h, wrought iron, brass plated top crest with engraved initials "P.R.R."...................................................................200.00
   5-3/4" h, iron, hinged brass lid, plus hanger ......................115.00
   12" h, wrought iron, old pitted finish, wood base with old worn black patina, iron hanger...............................................220.00
Grease, hanging, 28-1/4" h, wrought iron, sq pan, one corner partitioned, twisted post, ratchet trammel.......................................315.00
Loom Light, 23" h, wrought iron, adjustable betty lamp and candle socket on rod with ring top finial, round base with punched brass washer trim, three feet, wire link wick pick ..........................1,100.00
Rush Light Holder, 7-1/4" h, wrought iron, three feet, twisted detail ...................................................................385.00

Time Lamp, 12-3/4" h, pewter, clear blown font, orig wick support, burner cover missing................................................250.00

Whale Oil, 8-1/2" h, cast brass, oval font, candlestick base, double copper burners, price for pr....................................1,955.00

## Floor

Arts & Crafts style, 63" h, 20" d domed shade, central woven design, ribbed base, wicker, natural finish, relined............1,100.00

Empire Style, 73-1/2" h, carved wood, griffin base, old ebonized finish, gold trim, black and gold velvet brocade fringed shade, wear and damage to shade....................................450.00

Gurschner, Gustave, 40-1/4" h, bronze, amorous couple in embrace, bowl-lie globe shade with colored glass circles in copper foil, bronze top rim, sgd.........................................1,870.00

Handel

   55-1/2" h bronze frame, unsigned 10" d Steuben brown aurene with platinum border shade, base mkd "Handel," worn gilding....................................................3,300.00

   57" h, 10" d brown chipped ice shade, bronzed metal harp, recent patina, shade and base sgd...................2,300.00

   58" h bronze frame, old patina, 10" d, Steuben green shade, platinum irid rim, band of green and white, minor chips on top edge of unmarked shade.............................3,150.00

   58" h bronze frame, old patina, 10" d gold irid Tiffany-style shade cased white, minor chips to metal ring on shade..........3,795.00

## Fluid

9-1/8" h, purple cut to clear font, brass collar and fluted stem, marble base....................................................375.00

10" h, white cut to cranberry font and stem insert, brass fittings and collar, black ceramic base.................................565.00

10-1/4" h, white cut to cranberry overlay font, brass connector and collar, opaque white base, minor chips to base............350.00

11-5/8" h, opaque blue font, clambroth base, lightly sanded, Acanthus, chips and bruise on edge of font, replaced brass collar.........395.00

12-1/4" h, clear pressed font with cut panels and engraved floral band, brass collar and stem, stepped marble base with brass trim...125.00

13-1/4" h, blue cut to white to clear font, brass connector and collar, fluted column on opaque white base.....................935.00

15" h, cobalt blue cut to clear font, brass plated figural stem and font fittings, black stone base, Victorian.........................500.00

20-3/4" h, banquet, emerald green cut to clear font, brass collar, ornate gilded brass stem, marble base..............................400.00

## Hall

Belle Epoque, Louis XVI taste, c1905-15, gilt brass, frosted and cut faceted bead, treillage-patterned basket element, further dressed at base with cut faceted spears, 10-3/4" d, 22" h..........900.00

Duffner & Kimberly, 12" h, leaded glass, closed teardrop form, stylized floral repeating motif, deep red-amber scrolls, single socket mount, large cap...........................................825.00

Unknown Maker, 12" h, polished and lacquered brass frame, red swirled cylindrical insert, no burner, orig chain and pulleys......350.00

## Hanging

Daum Nancy, France, c1925, 32-1/2" l, hammered finish on round bronze ceiling cap, shaft of etched sq rods and tendril rods, three-part frame embellished with grape leaves and clusters, supporting elongated helmet-shaped mottled orange and yellow glass shade, tassel finial, etched "Daum (cross) Nancy" on side, repair to bronze mount...................................................1,725.00

Handel, Meriden, CT, early 20th C, 28" drop, 6" drop shade, bronze patinated metal circular stepped ceiling plaque with gadrooned rim, chain and similar dec shade mount, spherical textured amber shade dec with green and blue parrot, leafy grapevines, tassel finial, shade sgd "Handel 7006 RA" on rim, minor rim nicks......2,550.00

Steuben, attributed to, chain metal ceiling mount supporting sphere of opal glass cased to amber, strong gold irid, cast metal tassel, unmarked, c1925, wear....................................2,500.00

**Unknown Maker, Gone With The Wind style, rainbow colored molded acanthus leaves, brass oil font and base, $550. Photo courtesy of Joy Luke Fine Art Brokers and Auctioneers.**

**Parlor**, 21-1/2" h, 10-1/2" d, America, c1900-1910, kerosene, frosted, Colonial style, shade edge with faceted spears, brass mounted, electrified.......................................................175.00

## Piano

Handel, Meriden, CT, early 20th C

   7-1/2" h, 6-1/8" w sq shade of four mottled green and amber panels, striated yellow border, patinated metal overlay frame with geometric motif, single-socket lamp with reeded curved arm attached to round weighted base, imp "Handel"" on base, metal tag on shade, cracks.....................................1,380.00

   12-1/2" h, 10" w, bronze, swiveling cylindrical slag glass shade in brick and harp motif, orig patina, ribbon label, short tight line in shade..................................................750.00

Steuben, Corning, NY, early 20th C, 8-1/4" h, 3-1/2" h shade variant catalog 2545, bell-shaped mount with calcite and gold Aurene ribbed shade, silvered metal curved arm on stepped dome base, silver Steuben fleur-de-lis stamp on shade, wear to silver finish on base....................375.00

## Table

Benedict, 32" h, 20" d, copper and mica conical shade, hammered copper tapered and banded base, orig patina and mica........................3,250.00

Bigelow Kennard, 23" h, 18" d leaded glass shade, sunflower blossom configuration, green lappet motif above petal-form border, deep gold amber "granite" glass, bronze spider and socket, green matte glaze Grueby pottery base............................................9,200.00

Bradley & Hubbard

   23" h, 20" d, domed yellow slag glass shade, bronzed metal base with Celtic knot motif, stamped mark............................2,700.00

   26" h, 18" d, ribbed glass flaring shade, reverse painted with stylized flowers and leaves, patinated bronze base emb with oak leaves, stamped mark....................................2,300.00

Moe Bridges, 21" h, 15" d reverse painted shade, tree and lake scene, sgd.......................................................2,000.00

Duffner & Kimberly, 22-1/2" h, 19-1/2" d leaded glass mosaic shade, gold leading, multicolored domed shade, six repeating red-orange shell forms space by green scrolls and sky blue glass segments, yellow-amber shield reserves, Duffner gilt bronze four-socket base, bowed tripartite shaft, elaborate paw feet............................13,800.00

E M & Co., 26" h, 17-1/2" d eight-sided shade of caramel glass with patinated metal overlay in urn motif, bud finial, two-socket standard, reeded and foliate dec on flared round base, base mkd "E M Co.," some panels replaced ........................................................865.00

Erp, Dirk van

    20" h, 17" d, hammered copper and mica four panel shade, supported by four socket trumpet base, recent mica and patina..............................................................................4,500.00

    22" h, 19" d hammered copper and mice four panel shade, four light base, imp marks, recent patina, replaced mica ................8,500.00

French, Bouillotte, green tolé-peinte shade, three-light, adjustable, Restauration-style, electrified, 16-1/4" d, 28" h ........................935.00

Grueby and Tiffany, 22" h, 18" d, domed green and yellow leaded glass Lemon Leaf pattern shade, orig bronze Tiffany insert, shade mkd "Tiffany Studios, NY, No. 468," ovoid Grueby vase base with tooled and applied buds and leaves, covered in leathery matte green glaze, circular pottery mark and "RE" ............................................19,000.00

Handel, Meriden, CT, early 20<sup>th</sup> C

    18-1/2" h d leaded glass shade, ring accented by geometric border of blue-green glass, parasol shaped shade with radiating panels of light green glass, drop apron with border of diamond shaped segments of blue green and opalescent white, light green ground, bronze metal flared, rich red brown patina floriform base with shaped feet, base mkd "Handel,"..............................1,725.00

    18-3/4" h, reverse painted domed shade, cabin on rocky shore at sunset, shades of brown, yellow, and purple, partial paper label, two socket fixture, pod shaped patinated base, four molded feet, raised floral motifs, woven Handel label on base ...............2,875.00

    26" h, 16" d, Arts & Crafts style reverse painted glass shade, stylized red, green, and yellow flowers and leaves, three sockets, bronze base emb with leaves, base stamped "Handel," shade unmarked, grinding chips on rim ...........................................3,250.00

    27" h, 19-1/2" d shade of eight bent amber slag glass panels, Art Nouveau linear metal overlay, green painted highlights, three socket fixture on baluster form patinated metal base, molded serpentine dec over four sq bracket feet, raised and imp "Handel" marks on shade rim and base, replaced handle, possible retouching to paint dec..........................................................4,325.00

    30" h, broad conical shade with lapped arch motif, striated green amber and white slag glass segments, five socket standard with slender shaft swelling to round slightly domed base, dark brown patina, raised Handel mark on base, c1907, patination wear, two panels with cracks ....................................................9,200.00

Heintz, 15" h, 14" d, sterling on bronze, mushroom cap shade overlaid with leaves on verdigris patinated ground, stamped mark..........1,100.00

Jefferson

    21-1/2" d, 16" d domed glass shade, pebbled surface, hp on int. with riverside scene, including fence and red-roofed buildings, lower edge numbered "2365," mounted on cat metal two-socket ribbed base inscribed "Jefferson" at lower edge ..............1,650.00

    21-1/2" d, 16" d domed glass shade, pebbled surface, reverse painted with three repeating border elements of purple iris blossoms, buds, and stylized leaf forms, deep orange-amber ground, two-socket ribbed cast metal baluster base, shade rim and base imp "Jefferson" ............................................920.00

    22" h, 18" d conical reverse painted shade, yellow, green, and brown landscape, scene of trees surrounding body of water, bulbous green textured glass base, worn orig patina, shade sgd, minor chips to base under fittings.........................1,800.00

    22-3/4" h, 18" d conical shade, reverse painted, int. painted with lilac and woodland scene in naturalistic tones, two socket fixture on tapered five sided standard, dark green patinated metal on flaring petal form base, shade indistinctly sgd "Jefferson Co. WJS," minor shade imperfections .................................2,645.00

    23" h, 18" d reverse painted shade, multicolored landscape, bronzed metal base, orig patina....................................2,200.00

Modern, late 20<sup>th</sup> C, 31-1/2" h, 18" d flared oval shade with light tan pierced suede covering, telescoping two-socket chromed metal fixture, rounded Lucite base .....................................................1,035.00

Pairpoint, New Bedford, MA, early 20<sup>th</sup> C, reverse painted shade

    20-1/4" h, 15" d Exeter reverse painted flared shade, two urn and griffin mounts space by floral reserves, two-socket balus-

ter form base, imp "Pairpoint" and numbered, two small rim chips ....................................................................................1,200.00

    22" h, 18" d shade, Garden of Allah, Carlisle shape, base #D3058 .............................................................................3,900.00

    22-1/4" h, 16-1/2" d conical frosted shade with textured surface, birch trees and boats on water in mountainous landscape, hp in naturalistic tones, three-socket patinated metal baluster shaped base, shade unsigned, base imp "Pairpoint, D3063," minor rim chips at top.......................................................................2,530.00

Pittsburgh, 18-1/2" h, 14" d conical shade, reverse painted with winter scene of evergreens, snowy landscape, orange-purple sky, obverse accented with snow-capped dark trees, single-socket cast metal foliate base ....................................................................1,100.00

Tiffany

    18-1/4" h, 12" d Damascene green and gold shade, cased in white, mkd "favrile," bronze base with verdigris finish, mkd "Tiffany Studios New York," crack in top edge of shade ...................2,860.00

Unknown American Maker

    Leaded, 26-1/4" h, 18-1/2" d dome shade, radiating bands of rect mottled amber, green, and brown glass segments, upper border of stylized green leaves, lower border of pinecones and leaves, three sockets, reeded bronze standard over round base, dark brown patina, wear to base patina, restoration to shade .............2,990.00

    Reverse painted, 24" h, 18" d dome shade, scene of farm by lake in mountainous landscape, two-socket baluster patinated metal standard with two handles, raised floral dec, flared round base.......................................................................2,420.00

Wilkinson & Suess, 24" h, 19-1/2" d parasol shaped leaded glass shade, radiating panels of caramel and light green glass segments, dropped with square opalescent and red triangular shaped jewels, three-socket ribbed standard with scroll and foliate dec, ftd Suess base, some cracked segments ................................................2,100.00

## Torchères

Classical-style, patinated metal, molded with satyr masks, ribbed standard and foliate molded three-sided base..............................1,035.00

Continental

    56-1/2" h, wrought iron, single nozzle formed by four curled flat leaves, sonce supported by four scrolls, twisted standard with applied scrollwork to center, tripartite base, price for pr .....1,725.00

    67-3/4" h, wrought iron, three-light, central pricket flanked by two further lower-set prickets conjoined by scrollwork, standard incised with line dec, three ogee legs with carved toes, traces of gold patination, 19<sup>th</sup> C, price for pr...............................1,725.00

    73" h, wrought iron, three-light, central pricket as tulip form nozzle, dragon's heads above bell mounted on bracket, pull chain on one side, grotesque mask on other, bell flanked by two further pricket nozzles, standard mounted with scrollwork, quadripartite base formed by four scroll legs ending in further dragon's heads and legs, standard with incised linework, worn gold colored finish.......................................................................750.00

Victorian, wrought iron and brass, Gothic taste, each with three scrolled branches centered by central branch, columnar standard raised on splayed strapwork legs, fourth quarter 19<sup>th</sup> C, 80" h, price for pr.......................................................................................660.00

# LANTERNS

**History:** A lantern is an enclosed, portable light source, hand carried or attached to a bracket or pole to illuminate an area. Many lanterns have a protected flame and can be used both indoors and outdoors. Light-producing materials used in early lanterns included candles, kerosene, whale oil, and coal oil, and, later, gasoline, natural gas, and batteries.

**References:** *Collectible Lanterns*, L-W Book Sales, 1997; Anthony Hobson, *Lanterns That Lit Our World*,

**Hammered copper, faceted overhanging top, trellis grid over hammered yellow glass, orig chain, hanging wall bracket, and faceted ceiling plate, stamped "Als ik Kan," Gustav Stickley, 10" h, 6" sq, price for pr, $5,750. Photo courtesy of David Rago Auctions.**

Hiram Press, reprinted 1996; Neil S. Wood, *Collectible Dietz Lanterns*, L-W Book Sales, 1996.

**Collectors' Club:** Coleman Collectors Network, 1822 E. Fernwood, Wichita, KS 67216.

Barn, 11 1/2" h, wood, pine, worn red finish, hinged door, wire bail handle, age cracks, top board cracked ................................. 440.00
Bicycle, 7 3/4" h, Majestic model, nickel plated, clear lens, faceted red and green side lights, c1900 ......................... 175.00
Buggy, 13-1/2" h, brass, fixed handles, orig index burners, Manhattan Lamp Works, price for pr ..................................... 290.00
Campaign, 30" l, brass, weighted base on font, gimbal holder, turned ash handle, small split in font .................................. 55.00
Candle, 10" h, tin, candle, pierced and tooled pyramid top, traces of brown japanning, ring handle ..................................... 110.00
Dashboard, 15" h, spring clips, reflector, orig red paint, sgd brass label, Kemp Mfg. Co, c1900 ............................................. 165.00
Fireman's
    19" h, all brass, red globe, emb "Dietz King Fire Dept," missing reservoir cap ...................................................... 460.00
    19" h, mkd "Dietz King Fire Dept" ...................................... 290.00
Hall, 9-1/2" d, 12" l, patinated brass-mounted blown glass, inverted bell form in Biedermeier style, fitted with suspension chains and smoke shades, one with acid stamp "R. Ditmar/Vienna, Austria," price for pr ............................................................. 330.00
Halloween, 6-1/2" d, 36" l pole, ribbed tin, jack-o-lanterns with cut-out face, worn orig orangish-yellow paint, black detail, candle socket burners, one on wooden pole with orig swivel open design to access candle, other soldered together, socket inserts from bottom, price for pr ......................................................................... 1,760.00
Hanging, 21-1/2" h, tin and glass, sq form, wire guard, tall vent stack with handle, orig tin font with chimney ..................... 290.00
Miner, 6" h, brass and glass, mkd "E. Thomas & Williams, Ltd., Made in Wales" ...................................................................... 95.00
Onion
    11" h, punched tin design and burner ................................. 345.00
    15-1/2" h, punched tin, pierced star and diamonds ........... 290.00
    20" h, pierced tin top, candle holder .................................. 345.00
Paul Revere Type, 13" h, punched tin, dented, ring handle ........ 140.00
Pocket, 5 3/4" h, folding, black and gold lithograph f man seated on train, ruby glass panel, c1870 ................................................. 200.00
Post, 26" h, tin, orig glass globe, orig brass burner, marked "Dietz Tubular Globe #3," old worn green paint, light rust ................. 220.00
Railroad, 11 1/8" h, NL Piper Railway Supply Co. Ltd., bull's eye front lens, orig red and green side glass, corrugated reflector lined door, Simplex burner ....................................................................... 200.00

Rayo, No. 60 CB ..................................................................... 90.00
Skater's, 7" h, brass, bail, kerosene burner, clear globe ............. 145.00
Tin
    12 1/2" h, clear blown globe, pierced air vents in diamond design, five and six point stars, removable front, whale oil burner, mismatched parts, wire guard missing, ring handle .............. 215.00
    14-3/4" h, pierced tin and blown colorless glass, star and diamond design on tin, base separates for removable font, 19th C ........................................................................... 1,955.00
Wall, Prairie School
    8" l, 5" sq, zinc and slag glass, alternating bands of cream and yellow glass, orig dark patina on metal, price for pr ......... 400.00
    9 1/2" h, 6" sq, four sided brass and leaded glass, yellow, opalescent and frosted glass, orig gas fittings, price for pr ......... 650.00

# LEEDS CHINA

**History:** The Leeds Pottery in Yorkshire, England, began production about 1758. Among its products was creamware that was competitive with that of Wedgwood. The original factory closed in 1820, but various subsequent owners continued until 1880. They made exceptional cream-colored wares, either plain, salt glazed, or painted with colored enamels, and glazed and unglazed redware.

**Marks:** Early wares are unmarked. Later pieces are marked "Leeds Pottery," sometimes followed by "Hartley-Green and Co." or the letters "LP."

**Reproduction Alert:** Reproductions have the same marks as the antique pieces.

Bough Pot, 9" l, D-shaped, silver resist luster fruiting vine dec within arched panels, pierced cov, c1815 ......................... 750.00
Charger, 15-1/2" d, five color urn, floral spray, blue feathered edge 450.00
Chestnut Bowl, cov, reticulated band, twisted rope handles, c1790 ........................................................................ 775.00
Creamer, 3-3/8" h, brown, yellow dec ....................................... 145.00
Cup and Saucer, five color, floral and cross hatched dec .......... 125.00
Fruit Basket and Stand, 10" l, creamware, oval, pierced body, molded angel figures, foliate, late 18th/early 19th C, edge nicks ........ 1,380.00
Jug, 4-1/2" h, baluster, transfer print, underglaze blue, iron-red, yellow, green, and brown enameled scene of hunter and two hounds, silver resist border, blue floral garland, c1815 ................................. 295.00
Pitcher, 8-1/2" h, pearlware, ovoid body, painted spout and strap handle, blue hp three-leaf sprig, surrounded by small stylized flowers and leaf sprigs, early 19th C ..................................................... 900.00
Plate
    7" d, spatterware, peafowl and green dec, green border, early 19th C ........................................................................... 1,650.00

**Platter, blue border, scalloped edges, raised border design of beaded bands and leaves, 17-1/2" l, 14-3/8" w, $90.**

8" d, earthenware, molded shell edge, green glazed rim, center dec of stylized American eagle crest, early 19th C .......... 650.00

9 5/8" d, cream, blue edge, some damage and variation to sizes, price for five pc set ......................... 150.00

Potpourri, cov, 4-5/8" h, basket form, pierced cover, silver resist leaf and berry dec ................... 275.00

Sauce Tureen, cov, underplate, basketweave, green edges, floral finial, early 19th C, one handle repaired ........................ 450.00

Snuff Box, cov, 2 3/4" d, waisted cylinder, iron-red, puce, yellow, and green painted floral sprays, floral wreath, inscribed "When This You See, Remember Me, W. G. 1779," and "A Pinch of This Deserv's A Kiss" ................... 595.00

Tea Caddy, cov, 5-1/4" h, pearlware, deep rect body, short block feet, low domed cov with center loop handle, hp, bouquet of stylized green, dark, brown and yellow ochre flowers, thin band edge trim, chips, minor edge wear ......................... 1,200.00

Teapot, cov, 5-1/2" d, creamware, fluted body, green glaze striping, pierced trellis rim, late 18th C, restored spout and trellis, rim chip to cover ......................... 435.00

# LEFTON CHINA

**History:** China, porcelain, and ceramic with that now familiar "Lefton" mark has been around since the early 1940s and is highly sought by collectors in the secondary marketplace today. The company was founded by George Zoltan Lefton, a Hungarian immigrant who arrived in the United States in 1939. In the 1930s, he was a sportswear designer and manufacturer, but his hobby of collecting fine china and porcelain led him to a new business venture.

After the bombing of Pearl Harbor in 1941, Mr. Lefton aided a Japanese-American friend by helping him to protect his property from anti-Japanese groups. As a result, Lefton came in contact with and began marketing pieces from a Japanese factory owned by Kowa Toki KK. At this time, he embarked on a new career and began shaping a business that sprang from his passion for collecting fine china and porcelains. Though his funds were very limited, his vision was to develop a source from which to obtain fine porcelains by reviving the postwar Japanese ceramic industry, which dated back to antiquity. As a trailblazer, George Zoltan Lefton soon earned the reputation of "The China King."

Figurines and animals, plus many of the whimsical pieces such as the Bluebirds, Dainty Miss, Miss Priss, Angels, Cabbage Cutie, Elf Head, Mr. Toodles, and the Dutch Girl, are popular with collectors. All types of dinnerware and tea-related items are eagerly acquired by collectors. As is true with any antique or collectibles, prices vary, depending on location, condition, and availability.

**Marks:** Until 1980, wares from the Japanese factory include a "KW."

**Reference:** Loretta DeLozier, *Collector's Encyclopedia of Lefton China*, Vol. 1 (1995), Vol. 2 (1997), Vol. 3 (1999), Collector Books; *1998 Lefton Price Guide.*

**Collectors' Club:** National Society of Lefton Collectors, 1101 Polk St., Bedford, IA 50833.

**Advisor:** Loretta DeLozier.

Animal
  4" h, camel, Bethlehem Collection, #05381 ......................... 35.00
  5" h, spaniel, #80521 ......................... 50.00
  7" h, cat, luster, stones, #871 ......................... 35.00
Baby Set, bowl and mug, Bluebirds, #435 ......................... 80.00
Bank, 7-3/4", kangaroo with baby, #2778 ......................... 25.00
Beer Mug, 5" h, Paul Bunyan, #609 ......................... 28.00
Bird
  5-1/2" h, bobwhite, #300 ......................... 40.00
  6-3/4" h, bird of paradise. #140 ......................... 85.00
  7" h, seagull. #02715 ......................... 60.00
  7-1/2" h, owl and waxwing. #8018 ......................... 250.00
  12" h, pheasant, closed wings, #210 ......................... 200.00
Box, cov, 5" d, round, Flower Garden, #2152 ......................... 80.00
Butter Dish, Mr. Toodles, #3294 ......................... 95.00
Candleholders, pr, Vineyard line, #3035 ......................... 30.00
Candy Box, 9", Santa in rocker, #7923 ......................... 65.00
Canister Set, 4 pieces
  Americana, #946 ......................... 215.00
  Blue Plum, #4981 ......................... 125.00
Cheese Dish, cov, Honey Bee, #1285 ......................... 55.00
Cigarette Set, 4 pieces, Violets with stones, #4557 ......................... 65.00
Coffee Pot, cov
  Gingham, #3265 ......................... 80.00
  Green Heritage, #3065 ......................... 165.00
  Magnolia, #2518 ......................... 175.00
  Rose Garden, 8-1/2" h, #6570 ......................... 110.00
Cookie Jar, 10-1/4" h, Honey Bear, #7439 ......................... 85.00
Creamer and Sugar
  Bossie the Cow, #6512 ......................... 35.00
  Dutch Girl, #2698 ......................... 85.00
  Festival, #2615 ......................... 65.00
  Heavenly Rose, #2689 ......................... 65.00
  Magnolia, #2520 ......................... 65.00
Cup and Saucer
  Americana, #963 ......................... 38.00
  Magnolia, #2523 ......................... 35.00
Dish
  6" l, leaf, sponge gold and raised pink roses, #961 ......................... 60.00
  7" l, butter, Sweet Violets, #2854 ......................... 28.00
Eggcup, Bluebirds, #286 ......................... 60.00
Egg Tray, 12-1/2" d, Country Squire, #1601 ......................... 35.00

**Figure, Victorian woman with umbrella, early 1950s, 7-1/2" h, $140.**

# LENOX CHINA

**History:** In 1889, Jonathan Cox and Walter Scott Lenox established The Ceramic Art Co. at Trenton, New Jersey. By 1906, Lenox formed his own company, Lenox, Inc.
Using potters lured from Belleek, Lenox began making an American version of the famous Irish ware. The firm is still in business.

**Marks:** Older Lenox china has one of two marks: a green wreath or a palette. The palette mark appears on blanks supplied to amateurs who hand painted china as a hobby. The Lenox company currently uses a gold stamped mark.

**References:** Susan and Al Bagdade, *Warman's American Pottery and Porcelain*, 2nd ed., Krause Publications, 2000.

**Additional Listings:** Belleek.

**Figure, Revolutionary War soldiers, four of set of six, mid-1960s to early 1970s, 7" h, each $60.**

Figure
    8" h, Don Quixote and Sancho Panza, #4721 .................... 120.00
    10-1/2" h, Colonial man and woman, pr, #2256 ................. 350.00
    11" h, Napoleon on horse, #4908 ....................................... 285.00
Jam Jar
    Fruit, teapot-shape, #6973 .................................................... 35.00
    Grapes, 5", #4852 .................................................................... 30.00
    Miss Priss, #1515 .................................................................. 105.00
Mug, Winter Holly, #6066 ............................................................... 12.00
Nappy, 8" sq, Roses, #2874 ............................................................ 35.00
Pin Box, 2-1/4" d, pink, rhinestones, #90254 ............................... 35.00
Planter
    5", bucket, Mardi Gras, #50442 ......................................... 45.00
    9", cherub holding urn, antique ivory, #193 ..................... 48.00
Plate
    7-1/2" d, Fruit, latticed, #711 ............................................... 35.00
    8" d, Elegant Rose, #2854 .................................................... 28.00
    8" d, Moss Rose, #3169 ......................................................... 20.00
    10-1/2" d, Americana, #963 .................................................. 40.00
Religious, 5", Sacred Heart of Jesus, #479 ................................ 32.00
Salt and Pepper Shakers, pr
    Chicks with hats, #4926 ....................................................... 12.00
    Fruit, jug-shape, #4418 ......................................................... 12.00
Sleigh, 8" l, Green Holly, #1346 ................................................... 50.00
Snack Set
    Elegant Rose, #2124 ............................................................. 35.00
    Magnolia, #2599 ..................................................................... 25.00
    Rose Heirloom, #1376 ........................................................... 32.00
    To A Wild Rose, #2580 ......................................................... 25.00
    White with violets. #20054 .................................................... 28.00
Swan, 3-1/2" h, pink, lily of the valley, #194 .............................. 18.00
Teapot, cov
    Fleur De Lis, #1799 ................................................................ 70.00
    Miss Priss, #1516 ................................................................. 155.00
    Poinsettia, #4388 .................................................................. 175.00
    Violets, Dresden-shape, #2439 .......................................... 215.00
Tray, 2 tier
    Green Heritage, #1153 .......................................................... 85.00
    Green Holly, #1364 ............................................................... 70.00
Vase
    4" h, Italian Romance, beige, #781 .................................... 18.00
    5" h, lyre, white china, #955 ................................................ 85.00
    6-1/4" h, fan, milk china, #840 ............................................ 85.00
    6-1/2" h, tree trunk with child, #840, pr ........................... 180.00
Wall Plaque, 8"
    Fruit, #094 .............................................................................. 20.00
    Fruit, latticed edges, #6350 ................................................ 25.00

Bon Bon, Shell
    Brushed gold rim, blue mark ............................................... 100.00
    Small sawtooth edge, green mark ....................................... 45.00
Bouillon Cup and Saucer, Detroit Yacht Club, palette mark ........ 565.00
Bowl, 2 handles, etched told trim, pre 1930 ............................... 45.00
Box, cov, 3-3/4" x 4-3/4", spray of flowers, green wreath mark .... 50.00
Cake Set, Mimosa pattern, 10-1/2" d low pedestal plate, six 7-1/2" d plates, green wreath mark, 7 pc set ......................................... 225.00
Compote, 2" h, 5" d, brown rim, white ground, hp black insignia, pre-1930 ............................................................................................ 40.00
Creamer and Sugar, 3-1/2" w creamer, 4-1/2" w open sugar, silver overlay dec, palette mark, c1910-20 ...................................... 115.00
Cup and Saucer, Kingsley pattern, X445 ...................................... 30.00
Decanter Set, ivory, gold trim, green wreath mark, price for decanter and five shot glasses .............................................................. 125.00
Demitasse Cup and Saucer, 2" h, 2" d cup, 4-1/2" d saucer, silver overlay dec, crosshatching and fleur-de-lis ................................... 145.00
Figure, 7-1/4" h, 7" w, Wind Dancers, swallows, gold eyes ........ 100.00
Mug, cobalt blue, sterling silver overlay bands .......................... 75.00
Salt, open, palette mark ................................................................. 15.00
Salt Shaker and Pepper Mill, Lido, 8" h ..................................... 150.00
Swan
    4-1/2" h, green mark ............................................................. 55.00
    5" h, green mark .................................................................... 40.00
    9" h, green mark .................................................................. 100.00
Teapot, 4-1/4" h, individual, salmon color, metal lid and handle, made for Waldorf Astoria, 1931 ....................................................... 125.00
Toby, William Penn, 7-1/2" h, yellow, green mark ..................... 300.00
Vase
    7" l, basket form, round loop center handle, silver bands down center and around rims, c1930 ........................................ 120.00
    9-3/4" h, cylindrical, rounded shoulder, short rolled neck, cobalt blue ground, silver overlay, small pierced scrolls ............. 650.00

## Dinnerware, sample prices
Bread and Butter Plate
    Country Garden ...................................................................... 30.00
    Lenox Rose ............................................................................. 12.00
    Kingsley, X445 ........................................................................ 15.00
    Olympia 303 ............................................................................ 15.00
Coffeepot, cov
    Biltmore ................................................................................. 225.00
    Gramercy ............................................................................... 260.00

## Creamer

| | |
|---|---|
| Blue Royale | 140.00 |
| Brookdale | 130.00 |
| Castle Garden | 125.00 |
| Gramercy | 100.00 |

Cream Soup, Weatherly, D517 .............................. 200.00

## Cup and Saucer

| | |
|---|---|
| Autumn | 100.00 |
| Beacon | 60.00 |
| Jefferson | 55.00 |
| Sachet | 82.00 |
| Tuxedo | 50.00 |

## Dinner Plate

| | |
|---|---|
| Blue Ridge | 55.00 |
| Buchanan | 48.00 |
| Empress | 42.00 |
| Lenox Rose | 25.00 |
| Kingsley, X445 | 30.00 |
| Meadow Song | 20.00 |
| Snow Flower | 55.00 |

## Fruit or Dessert Bowl

| | |
|---|---|
| Cretan | 55.00 |
| Starlight | 42.00 |

## Gravy Boat with underplate

| | |
|---|---|
| Essex | 255.00 |
| Golden Wreath | 190.00 |
| Ming | 200.00 |

Pitcher, Cottage pattern ...................................... 75.00
Place Setting, 5 pcs, Autumn ............................ 100.00

## Platter

| | |
|---|---|
| Aristocrat, medium | 260.00 |
| Barclay, medium | 350.00 |
| Bellaire, large | 310.00 |
| Boheme, medium | 210.00 |
| Brookdale, large | 400.00 |
| Castle Garden, medium | 315.00 |
| Country Holly, medium | 140.00 |
| Flirtation, large | 300.00 |
| Golden Wreath, large | 230.00 |
| Laurent | 175.00 |
| Lenox Rose, 13" l | 75.00 |
| Kingsley, X445, 16" l | 100.00 |
| Ming, medium | |
| Weatherly, D517, large | 515.00 |

## Salad Plate

| | |
|---|---|
| Cinderella | 35.00 |
| Fresh Meadow | 34.00 |
| Lenox Rose | 18.00 |
| Kingsley, X445 | 20.00 |
| Tuscany | 50.00 |

## Sugar Bowl, cov

| | |
|---|---|
| Blue Royale | 175.00 |
| Brookdale | 180.00 |
| Castle Garden | 170.00 |
| Courtland | 100.00 |
| Eclipse | 100.00 |
| Weatherly, D517 | 235.00 |

Vegetable, cov, Aristocrat ................................ 700.00
Vegetable, open, oval .........................................

| | |
|---|---|
| Boheme | 190.00 |
| Brookdale | 215.00 |
| Cretan | 155.00 |
| Gramercy | 190.00 |

# LIBBEY GLASS

**History:** Edward Libbey established the Libbey Glass Company in Toledo, Ohio, in 1888 after the New England Glass Works of W. L. Libbey and Son closed in

East Cambridge, Massachusetts. The new Libbey company produced quality cut glass which today is considered to belong to the brilliant period.

1896–1906

In 1930, Libbey's interest in art-glass production was renewed, and A. Douglas Nash was employed as a designer in 1931.

The factory continues production today as Libbey Glass Co.

**References:** Tom and Neila Bredehoft, *Fifty Years of Collectible Glass, 1920-1970, Volume 1, Volume II,* Antique Trader Books, 2000; Bob Page and Dale Frederickson, *Collection of American Crystal*, Page-Frederickson Publishing, 1995; Kenneth Wilson, *American Glass 1760-1930*, 2 vols., Hudson Hills Press and The Toledo Museum of Art, 1994.

**Additional Listings:** Amberina Glass; Cut Glass.

## Art Glass

Bowl, 11" d, 3-3/4" h, Cleuthra, pink and crystal, numerous large pink bubbles, sgd ............................... 395.00
Celery Vase, 6-1/2" h, 5" w, Maize pattern, amber kernels, blue leaves ....................................... 385.00
Compote
    8" d, 4" h, Amberina, 1-3/4" wide crimson rim, honey amber bowl, applied standard, wafer base, sgd ................... 985.00
    10-1/2" d, 4" h, colorless, pink Nailsea type loops look like flower petals, sgd ..................................... 595.00
Vase
    8" h, amberina, flared rim with twelve scallops, twelve optic ribs, knob and wafer base, factory drilled hole at base, sgd slightly off center of pontil ................................ 575.00
    12" h, amberina, slender, Shape #3003, deep fuchsia at top shades to honey-amber, half original Libbey paper label remains and encircles signature on pontil ............. 985.00

## Cut Glass

Berry Bowl, 5" d, Regis pattern, sgd ................... 50.00
Bowl
    8" d, Colonna pattern, crimped edge ........... 350.00
    8" d, Comet pattern, sgd ........................... 550.00
    9" d, Gloria pattern ................................. 325.00
    9" d, 4" h, Snowflake pattern, sgd ............... 950.00
Candlestick
    6" h, Flute pattern, sgd ........................... 100.00
    8" h, cut in flutes with multiple woven air controlled swirl stems, sgd ................................................. 175.00
    8" h, #0493 pattern, twisted stem, sgd ......... 110.00
    10" h, Empress pattern, sgd, price for p ..... 2,200.00
Chamberstick, 5" h, Pannel pattern, hollow core, star base, sgd .... 550.00
Cordial, 5" h, hobstar, strawberry diamond and hob diamond, sgd... 150.00

**Amberina, comport, shape #3023, applied standard, wafer base, sgd, 8" d, 4" h, $985. Photo courtesy of Clarence & Betty Mair.**

**Decanter**
    9-1/2" h, hobstar, prism, and strawberry diamond cutting, sgd ................................................................425.00
    11-1/2" h, Colonna pattern, sterling wheat stopper, sgd .....375.00
**Flower Center**
    6" x 8", Kingston pattern, unusual shape ...........................400.00
    10-1/2" d, 6-1/2" h, Venetia pattern....................................600.00
    12" d, 7-1/2" h, Gloria pattern, sgd.................................1,600.00
**Grapefruit Stemware**, 7" x 5", hobstar and notched mitres, stars, and fans ........................................................................225.00
**Jug**, 11" h, Harvard pattern, pattern cut handle, heavy cut deep blank ...............................................................................2,300.00
**Perfume Bottle**, 7-1/2" h, cobalt blue cut to clear, engraved floral motif, two handles, sgd ................................................................450.00
**Plate**
    6" d, Sultana pattern, shows four stages of cutting, large engraved "Libbey" in center, sgd "Libbey".....................2,300.00
    7" d, Azora pattern ............................................................375.00
    7" d, Diana pattern, sgd ..................................................2,750.00
    7" d, Delphos pattern .......................................................2,300.00
    8" d, Ellsmere pattern, sgd .................................................675.00
    10" d, Isabella pattern.......................................................2,000.00
**Punch Ladle**, 13" l, hobstar, strawberry diamond and fan motif, Gorham sterling silver shell shaped dipper .............................1,10.00
**Salad Bowl**, 9" d, 4" h, Savona pattern, hobstar, star center, engraved fruit and wreath, sgd..........................................................1,900.00
**Toupee Stand**, 3" x 6", hobstar, cane, and vesica motif, sgd ...1,300.00
**Tray**
    9" d, Aztec pattern, sgd....................................................7,000.00
    11-1/2" d, Regis pattern, sgd ...........................................1,300.00
    12" d, large hobstars, strawberry diamond, star, and crosshatch motif, very thick blank...........................................900.00
**Tumbler**, 4", Herringbone pattern, sgd ..................................700.00
**Tumble-Up**, 5-3/4" h, medicine jar insert, engraved corn pattern, sgd "Libbey" on all four pcs ........................................1,600.00
**Vase**
    7" h, Empress pattern, trumpet shape, sgd .......................300.00
    9" h, 7" w, flared, Comet pattern, sgd ...............................375.00
    9" h, 9" w, rippled top, multiple scenes of engraved houses, church, boats, and forest, sgd "Libbey"......................2,000.00
    10" h, Harvard pattern, trumpet shape..............................125.00
    Water Carafe on Stand, 9" h, Ellsmere pattern, sgd...........700.00
    Water Set, pitcher and six tumblers, engraved cherries, sgd .......................................................................5,500.00
**Whipped Cream Bowl**, 8-1/2" d, 3-1/2" h, shooting stars cutting, engraved ivy border, presentation piece to bookkeeper who left to serve in World War I......................................................250.00
**Wine**, 4-1/2" h, cranberry cut to clear, Venetia pattern................550.00

# LIMITED EDITION COLLECTOR PLATES

**History:** Bing and Grondahl made the first collector plate in 1895. Royal Copenhagen issued its first Christmas plate in 1908.

In the late 1960s and early 1970s, several potteries, glass factories, mints, and artists began issuing plates commemorating people, animals, and events. Christmas plates were supplemented by Mother's Day plates and Easter plates. Speculation swept the field, fostered in part by flamboyant ads in newspapers and flashy direct-mail promotions.

**References:** Jay Brown, *The Complete Guide To Limited Edition Art Prints*, Krause Publications, 1999; *Collectors' Information Bureau Collectibles Market Guide & Price Index*, 18th ed., Krause Publications, 2000; Beth Dees, *Santa's Price Guide To Contemporary Christmas Collectibles*, Krause Publications, 1997; Carl Luckey, *Luckey's Hummel Figurines & Plates*, 11th Edition, Krause Publications, 1997; Mary Sieber (ed.), *2001 Price Guide to Limited Edition Collectibles*, 6th ed., Krause Publications, 2000.

**Periodicals:** Collector Editions, 170 Fifth Ave., 12th Floor, New York, NY 10010; Collectors Mart Magazine, 700 E. State St., Iola, WI 54990; Collectors News, 506 Second St., P.O. Box 156, Grundy Center, IA 50638; Insight on Collectibles, 103 Lakeshore Rd, Ste. 202, St. Catharines, Ontario L2N 2T6 Canada; International Collectible Showcase, One Westminster Place, Lake Forest, IL 60045; Plate World, 9200 N. Maryland Ave., Niles, IL 60648; Toybox Magazine, 8393 East Holly Rd, Holly MI 48442.

**Collectors' Clubs:** Franklin Mint Collectors Society, US Route 1, Franklin Center, PA 19091; Hummel Collector's Club, Inc., P.O. Box 257, Yardley, PA 19067; International Plate Collectors Guild, P.O. Box 487, Artesia, CA 90702; M. I. Hummel Club, Goebel Plaza, Rte. 31, P.O. Box 11, Pennington, NJ 08534.

**Museum:** Bradford Museum of Collector's Plates, Niles, IL.

**Additional Listings:** See *Warman's Americana & Collectibles* for more examples of collector plates plus many other limited edition collectibles.

**Notes:** The first plate issued in a series (FE) is often favored by collectors. Condition is a critical factor, and price is increased if the original box is available.

Limited edition collector plates, more than any other object in this guide, should be collected for design and pleasure and only secondarily as an investment.

## Bing and Grondahl (Denmark)

**Christmas Plates**, various artists, 7" d
    1895 Behind the Frozen Window......................................3,450.00
    1896 New Moon over Snow Covered Trees ...................1,975.00
    1897 Christmas Meal of the Sparrows...............................725.00
    1898 Christmas Roses and Christmas Star........................700.00
    1899 The Crows Enjoying Christmas .................................900.00
    1900 Church Bells Chiming in Christmas ...........................800.00
    1901 The Three Wise Men from the East...........................450.00

**Bing & Grondahl, 1930, Yule Tree in Town Hall Square of Copenhagen, $85.**

1902 Interior of a Gothic Church.......................285.00
1903 Happy Expectation of Children ..................150.00
1904 View of Copenhagen from Frederiksberg Hill ...........125.00
1905 Anxiety of the Coming Christmas Night ...................130.00
1906 Sleighing to Church on Christmas Eve .......................95.00
1907 The Little Match Girl.......................................125.00
1908 St Petri Church of Copenhagen...............................85.00
1909 Happiness over the Yule Tree................................100.00
1910 The old Organist ...........................................90.00
1911 First It Was Sung by Angels to Shepherds in the Fields ...80.00
1912 Going to Church on Christmas Eve .........................80.00
1913 Bringing Home the Yule Tree...............................85.00
1914 Royal Castle of Amalienborg, Copenhagen.................75.00
1915 Chained Dog Getting Double Meal on Christmas Eve....120.00
1916 Christmas Prayer of the Sparrows .........................85.00
1917 Arrival of the Christmas Boat ...............................75.00
1918 Fishing Boat Returning Home for Christmas ..............85.00
1919 Outside the Lighted Window ...............................80.00
1920 Hare in the Snow .........................................70.00
1921 Pigeons in the Castle Court ................................55.00
1922 Star of Bethlehem ........................................60.00
1923 Royal Hunting Castle, The Hermitage ......................55.00
1924 Lighthouse in Danish Waters .............................65.00
1925 The Child's Christmas.....................................70.00
1926 Churchgoers on Christmas Day............................65.00
1927 Skating Couple ..........................................110.00
1928 Eskimo Looking at Village Church in Greenland..........60.00
1929 Fox Outside Farm on Christmas Eve......................75.00
1930 Yule Tree in Town Hall Square of Copenhagen ...........85.00
1932 Lifeboat at Work..........................................95.00
1934 Church Bell in Tower .....................................70.00
1936 Royal Guard Outside Amalienborg Castle in
   Copenhagen.............................................75.00
1938 Lighting the Canles ......................................115.00
1940 Delivering Christmas Letters .............................175.00
1942 Danish Farm on Christmas Night...........................150.00
1944 Sorgenfri Castle .........................................125.00
1946 Commemoration Cross in Honor of Danish Sailors Who
   Lost Their Lives in World War II .........................90.00
1948 Watchman, Sculpture of Town Hall, Copenhagen .......80.00
1950 Kronborg Castle at Elsinore...............................145.00
1952 Old Copenhagen Canals at Wintertime with Thorvaldsen
   Museum in Background ..................................90.00
1954 Birthplace of Hans Christian Andersen, with
   Snowman...............................................110.00
1956 Christmas in Copenhagen ...............................150.00
1958 Santa Claus .............................................110.00
1960 Danish Village Church ...................................175.00
1962 Winter Night ............................................85.00
1964 The Fir Tree and Hare ...................................60.00
1966 Home for Christmas ......................................55.00
1968 Christmas in Church .....................................50.00
1970 Pheasants in the Snow at Christmas.......................25.00

**Mother's Day Plates**, Henry Thelander, artist, 6" d
1969 Dog and Puppies ........................................400.00
1971 Cat and Kitten ...........................................20.00
1973 Duck and Ducklings ......................................20.00
1975 Doe and Fawns...........................................20.00
1977 Squirrel and Young .......................................25.00
1979 Fox and Cubs ............................................30.00
1981 Hare and Young..........................................40.00
1983 Raccoon and Young.......................................45.00
1985 Bear and Cubs ..........................................40.00
1987 Sheep with Lamps .......................................40.00
1989 Cow with Calf............................................45.00
1990 Hen with Chicks .........................................65.00

## Reed & Barton (United States)
**Audubon Series, various artists**
1970 Pine Siskin, FE .........................................165.00

1971 Red-Shouldered Hawk............................75.00
1972 Stilt Sandpiper ...................................70.00
1974 Boreal Chickadee ................................60.00
1975 Yellow-Breasted Chat ............................60.00
1977 Purple Finch......................................65.00

**Christmas Series**, Damascene silver, 11" d through 1978, 8" d 1979
to present
1970 A Partridge in a Pear Tree, FE...................200.00
1971 We Three Kings of Orient Are...................65.00
1973 Adoration of the Kings ..........................75.00
1975 Adoration of the Kings ..........................65.00
1977 Decorating the Church..........................60.00
1979 Merry Old Santa Claus .........................65.00
1981 The Shopkeeper at Christmas ..................75.00

## Rosenthal (Germany)
**Christmas Plates**, various artists, 8 1/2" d
1910 Winter Peace .................................550.00
1911 The Three Wise Men ..........................325.00
1912 Shooting Stars ...............................250.00
1913 Christmas Lights .............................235.00
1915 Walking to Church............................180.00
1917 Angel of Peace ...............................200.00
1919 St Christopher with the Christ Child...........225.00
1920 The Manger in Bethlehem ....................300.00
1922 Advent Branch ...............................210.00
1924 Deer in the Woods ...........................200.00
1926 Christmas in the Mountains ..................175.00
1928 Chalet Christmas .............................185.00
1930 Group of Deer under the Pines................190.00
1932 Christ Child ..................................200.00
1934 Christmas Peace .............................210.00
1936 Nuremberg Angel.............................185.00
1940 Marien Church in Danzig .....................250.00
1942 Marianburg Castle ...........................300.00
1944 Wood Scape .................................275.00
1946 Christmas in an Alpine Valley ................250.00
1948 Message to the Shepherds....................875.00
1950 Christmas in the Forest.......................190.00
1952 Christmas in the Alps ........................195.00
1954 Christmas Eve ...............................190.00
1956 Christmas in the Alps ........................190.00
1958 Christmas Eve ...............................185.00
1960 Christmas in Small Village ...................210.00
1962 Christmas Eve ...............................185.00
1964 Christmas Market in Nuremberg..............220.00
1966 Christmas in Ulm ............................250.00
1968 Christmas in Bremen .........................200.00
1970 Christmas in Cologne ........................175.00

## Royal Copenhagen (Denmark)
**Christmas Plates**, various artists, 6" d 1908, 1909, 1910; 7" 1911 to
present
1908 Madonna and Child............................1,750.00
1909 Danish Landscape .............................150.00
1910 The Magi .....................................120.00
1911 Danish Landscape .............................135.00
1912 Elderly Couple by Christmas Tree .............120.00
1913 Spire of Frederik's Church, Copenhagen.........125.00
1914 Sparrows in Tree at Church of the Holy Spirit,
   Copenhagen ................................100.00
1915 Danish Landscape .............................150.00
1916 Shepherd in the Field on Christmas Night .......85.00
1917 Tower of Our Savior's Church, Copenhagen .......90.00
1918 Sheep and Shepherds .........................80.00
1919 In the Park ...................................80.00
1920 Mary with the Child Jesus .....................75.00
1921 Aabenraa Marketplace ........................75.00
1922 Three Singing Angels ..........................70.00
1923 Danish Landscape.............................70.00

1924 Christmas Star Over the Sea and Sailing Ship .......... 100.00
1925 Street Scene from Christianshavn, Copenhagen ........ 85.00
1926 View of Christmas Canal, Copenhagen ..................... 75.00
1927 Ship's Boy at the Tiller on Christmas Night ............... 140.00
1928 Vicar's Family on Way to Church ............................. 75.00
1929 Grundtvig Church, Copenhagen .............................. 100.00
1930 Fishing Boats on the Way to the Harbor ................... 80.00
1931 Mother and Child ................................................... 90.00
1932 Frederiksberg Gardens with Statue of Frederik VI ...... 90.00
1933 The Great Belt Ferry .............................................. 110.00
1934 The Hermitage Castle ............................................ 115.00
1935 Fishing Boat off Kronborg Castle ............................. 145.00
1936 Roskilde Cathedral ................................................ 130.00
1937 Christmas Scene in Main Street, Copenhagen .......... 135.00
1938 Round Church in Osterlars on Bornholm ................... 200.00
1939 Expeditionary Ship in Pack-Ice of Greenland ........... 180.00
1940 The Good Shepherd ................................................ 300.00
1942 Bell Tower of Old Church in Jutland .......................... 290.00
1944 Typical Danish Winter Scene ................................... 150.00
1946 Zealand Village Church ........................................... 175.00
1948 Nodebo Church at Christmastime ............................ 160.00
1950 Boeslund Church, Zealand ...................................... 175.00
1952 Christmas in the Forest .......................................... 125.00
1954 Amalienborg Palace, Copenhagen ........................... 160.00
1956 Rosenborg Castle, Copenhagen .............................. 170.00
1958 Sunshine over Greenland ........................................ 145.00
1960 The Stag ............................................................... 150.00
1962 The Little Mermaid at Wintertime ............................. 220.00
1964 Fetching the Christmas Tree .................................... 80.00
1966 Blackbird at Christmastime ...................................... 60.00
1968 The Last Umiak ...................................................... 45.00
1970 Christmas Rose and Cat ......................................... 115.00

**Mother's Day Plates**, various artists, 6 1/4" d
1971 American Mother .................................................... 125.00
1973 Danish Mother ....................................................... 60.00
1975 Bird in Nest ........................................................... 50.00
1977 The Twins .............................................................. 50.00
1979 A Loving Mother ..................................................... 30.00
1981 Reunion ................................................................ 40.00

# Wedgwood (Great Britain)

**Christmas Series**, jasper stoneware, 8" d
1969 Windsor Castle, FE ................................................. 225.00
1970 Christmas in Trafalgar Square ................................. 30.00
1971 Piccadilly Circus, London ........................................ 45.00
1972 St Paul's Cathedral ................................................ 40.00
1973 The Tower of London .............................................. 45.00
1974 The Houses of Parliament ....................................... 40.00
1975 Tower Bridge ......................................................... 50.00
1976 Hampton Court ...................................................... 45.00
1977 Westminster Abbey ................................................ 55.00
1978 The Horse Guards .................................................. 55.00
1979 Buckingham Palace ................................................ 60.00
1980 St. James Palace ................................................... 70.00
1982 Lambeth Palace ..................................................... 80.00
1981 Marble Arch ........................................................... 75.00
1983 All Souls, Langham Palace ...................................... 80.00
1984 Constitution Hill ..................................................... 80.00
1985 The Tate gallery ..................................................... 80.00
1986 The Albert Memorial ............................................... 80.00
1987 Guidhall ................................................................ 80.00
1988 The Observatory/Greenwich ..................................... 90.00
1989 Winchester Cathedral ............................................. 85.00

**Mothers Series**, jasper stoneware, 6 1/2" d
1971 Sportive Love, FE ................................................... 25.00
1972 The Sewing Lesson ................................................ 20.00
1973 The Baptism of Achilles ........................................... 30.00
1974 Domestic Employment ............................................ 30.00
1975 Mother and Child .................................................... 35.00
1976 The Spinner ........................................................... 35.00

1977 Leisure Time .......................................................... 30.00
1978 Swan and Cygnets .................................................. 35.00
1979 Deer and Fawn ....................................................... 35.00
1980 Birds ..................................................................... 48.00
1981 Mare and Foal ........................................................ 50.00
1982 Cherubs with Swing ................................................ 55.00
1983 Cupid and Butterfly ................................................. 50.00
1984 Musical Cupids ....................................................... 55.00
1985 Cupid and Doves .................................................... 50.00
1986 Cupids Fishing ....................................................... 50.00

# LIMOGES

**History:** Limoges porcelain has been produced in Limoges, France, for over a century by numerous factories in addition to the famed Haviland.

**Marks:** One of the most frequently encountered marks is "T. & V. Limoges," which is on the wares made by Tressman and Vought. Other identifiable Limoges marks are "A. L." (A. Lanternier), "J. P. L." (J. Pouyat, Limoges), "M. R." (M. Reddon), "Elite," and "Coronet."

**References:** Susan and Al Bagdade, *Warman's English & Continental Pottery & Porcelain*, 3rd Edition, Krause Publications, 1998; Mary Frank Gaston, *Collector's Encyclopedia of Limoges Porcelain*, 3rd ed., Collector Books, 2000; Raymonde Limoges, *American Limoges,* Collector Books, 1998; Faye Strumpf, *Limoges Boxes,* Krause Publications, 2000; Keith and Thomas Waterbrook-Clyde, *The Decorative Art of Limoges Porcelain and Boxes,* Schiffer Publishing, 1999.

**Additional Listings:** Haviland China.

Box, cov, 2" d, hinged, mythological scene on lid, multicolored .. 225.00
Cabinet Vase, 7-1/2" d, 4-1/2" d, les Roses dec, elaborate Pickard gilding, fully signed by Jean Pouyat, hp and retailed for W. A. Pickard China Company, c1900-1910 ................................................ 250.00
Champagne Pitcher, 5" d, 15" h, dragon handle, gold ground, overall chased floral pattern, Jean Pouyot, c1895-1900 ..................... 425.00
Charger, 16" d, still life fruit, gold rococo rim, sgd "Duval" .......... 350.00
Chocolate Service, cov chocolate pot, eight chocolate cups and saucers, floral dec, rich gilding, Louis XVI taste, Jean Pouyat, c1895-1900, each pc signed, price for 17 pc set ............................... 425.00
Cracker Jar, cov, ivory ground, flowers, green and gold trim, TV mark ....................................................................................... 250.00
Cup and Saucer
    Dark browns, leaf dec ............................................... 90.00
    Poppies dec ........................................................... 40.00
Garniture Vase, 7-1/2" d, 6-1/2" h, near spherical form, roses dec, rich gilding, Jean Pouyat, c1890-95 ............................................... 100.00
Oyster Plate, indentations for oysters outlined in gold, small pink flowers dec, mkd "GDA France" ................................................... 150.00
Plate
    8-1/4" d, hp, blackberries, gold border and dec, sgd, c1900 ......................................................................... 125.00
    8-1/4" d, hp, cherries, gold border and dec, sgd, c1900 ..... 125.00
    9-1/2" d, hp, Cupid's Sail with Cupid, playing lyre, leading lovers across water, Flora's Triumph with woman crowned by putto and attendants; Harvest with scene of women lying in wheat field; Spell with scene of putto eating berries; all with scrolling gilt borders, sgd "Soustre," retailed by Tiffany I Co., New York, set of 4 ......................................................................... 400.00
    10" d, scenic, hp, boats, day scene, Flambeau China ........ 165.00
Portrait Plaque, 4" x 3", enameled elegant woman in 19th C dress, sgd "Sandrina," shagreen case ................................................... 435.00
Pot De Creme, set of eight, matching lids and tray, polychrome transfer of birds and flowers, gilt trim, mkd "Limoges France" ............. 325.00

Vase, two handles, pink roses, gilding, base sgd "Emily Chase," 11" h, $200. Photo courtesy of Joy Luke Fine Art Brokers and Auctioneers.

Powder Box, cov
    Courting couple on lid, dark pink bowl, small Elite mark.....200.00
    Hand painted, sgd by two artists, early 1900s ....................110.00
Salt and Pepper Shakers, pr, poppy dec .......................................35.00
Table Box, 5-1/4" w, 3-1/2" d, 2" h, brass mounted, rouge-de-fleur flowers, parcel gilt trellising, Belle Epoque, c1900-15 ....................100.00
Vase
    7-1/2" d, gently flared form, dome foot, glaze dec with Art Deco raised thistles in black and gray, matte pink ground, glossy white int., glossy black foot, black stamp mark "Tharaud Limoges France" on base, second quarter 20th C ......................90.00
    12" h, 9" w, bulbous body, small neck opening with brass rim, floral arrangement on front and back, raised white daisies with yellow centers, shaded coral poppies with mauve centers, mauve and blue shaded poppies with dark purple centers, pink shaded with white poppies with yellow and black centers, yellow daisies with orange centers, light and dark shaded foliage, flowers on silver-foil backed mottled background of mauve, emerald green, light and deep turquoise, and pink, copper base, sgd in gold "Faure, Limoges, France," c1930..................................7,800.00

# LITHOPHANES

**History:** Lithophanes are highly translucent porcelain panels with impressed designs. The designs result from differences in the thickness of the plaque; thin parts transmit an abundance of light while thicker parts represent shadows.

    Lithophanes were first made by the Royal Berlin Porcelain Works in 1828. Other factories in Germany, France, and England later produced them. The majority of lithophanes on the market today were made between 1850 and 1900.

**Collectors' Club:** Lithophane Collectors Club, 2030 Robinwood Ave., P.O. Box 4557, Toledo, OH 43620.

**Museum:** Blair Museum of Lithophanes and Carved Waxes, Toledo, OH.

Candle Shield, 9" h, bronze collar, rococo frame, two country boys, goat and castle in background .................................................265.00
Cup and Saucer, nude lady, moriage and dragon dec..................60.00
Fairy Lamp, lady leaning from tower window, two panels, rural romantic scene ...................................................................1,400.00
Lamp, 23-1/2" h, double student type, four scenes, brass base, mkd "Germany" ........................................................................1,950.00
Lamp Shade, bone china
    3-3/4" h, four paneled sides, intaglio classical relief and acanthus leaf border, printed mark, Wedgwood, England, late 19th C ........175.00

Lamp, brass, four panels with woodland scenes, electrified, $125.

    3-7/8" h, hexagonal, intaglio angel figures on each side, printed mark, Wedgwood, England, c1900, one with rim repair, price for pr ..............................................................................175.00
    4" l, octagonal, white classical cherub intaglio enamel and gilt dec, printed marks, Wedgwood, England, late 19th C, set of 3 ....375.00
    12" d, hanging type, light blue ground, intaglio fruiting grapevine festoons terminating at Bacchus masks, acanthus leaves and bellflowers radiating from center, bronze frame, printed mark, Wedgwood, England, c1900 ......................................1,100.00
    13" d, white glazed body with intaglio Dancing Hours figures surrounding central acanthus leaf and bellflower design, printed mark, Wedgwood, England, 20th C, glaze staining ..........350.00
Panel
    4-1/2" x 5", PR Sickle, cupid and girl fishing......................220.00
    6-1/2" x 8", PPM, elderly lady teaching girl to knit, lead mounted edge ........................................................................195.00
    8" x 16", KK, General Zachary Taylor, holding telescope in left arm, men fighting battle in background, wreath, eagle, and two flags, leaded frame, ruby flashed ....................................750.00
Stein, half liter, dancing couple ...................................................115.00
Tea Set, cov teapot, creamer, cov sugar, six cups and saucers, romantic scenes ...............................................................175.00
Tea Warmer, 6" x 6", four panels, scenic, pierced top, metal frame, molded ftd base, Germany......................................................195.00

# LIVERPOOL CHINA

**History:** Liverpool is the name given to products made at several potteries in Liverpool, England, between 1750 and 1840. Seth and James Pennington and Richard Chaffers were among the early potters who made tin-enameled earthenware.

    By the 1780s, tin-glazed earthenware gave way to cream-colored wares decorated with cobalt blue, enameled colors, and blue or black transfers.

    The Liverpool glaze is characterized by bubbles and frequent clouding under the foot rims. By 1800, about 80 potteries were working in the town producing not only creamware, but soft paste, soapstone, and bone porcelain.

**References:** Susan and Al Bagdade, *Warman's English & Continental Pottery & Porcelain*, 3rd Edition, Krause Publications, 1998; Robert McCauley, *Liverpool Transfer Designs on Anglo-American Pottery*, Southworth-Anthoensen Press; Bernard M. Watney, *Liverpool Porcelain of the Eighteenth Century,* Antique Collectors' Club, Ltd., 1997.

**Museums:** City of Liverpool Museum, Liverpool, England; Henry Ford Museum, Dearborn, MI; Potsdam Public Museum, Potsdam, NY.

Bowl, 10-1/2" d, int. painted with two men standing next to ale cask, border of blue alternating panels of trellis and half flowerheads, ext. painted blue vignettes of Chinese houses and rockery, c1754 ................9,200.00

Charger, 13-3/4" d, black, iron-red, yellow, green and blue Fazackerly floral pattern, scattered flowers on rim ...................................... 825.00

Commemorative Bowl, 10-1/4" d, Delft, inscribed, "A Ship at Launch/Jonathan Greenleaf/1752," dec of ship with three Union Jacks flying, ten figures on deck, five at dock, ext. painted with farmhouse and figure walking toward a barn, one of three bowls made to commemorate launching of ship built in Newburyport by Greenleaf and his partner Thomas Cottle, Edinburgh merchant, painting attributed to decorator William Jackson, sold with silhouette portraits of Greenleaf and his wife, Mary Presbury ............................. 112,500.00

Cream Jug, 3-1/4" h, spiral fluted base, rocaille scrolls, iron-red, blue, turquoise, green-yellow, and black painted Chinese man beside tree, another holding stick, scalloped rim, C-scroll handle, c1776 ... 460.00

Cup and Saucer, handleless, Washington and Lafayette portraits on cup, bust of Washington and "Washington, His Country's Father" on saucer, black transfers, hairlines ............................................... 330.00

Jug, transfer dec, early 19th C

    5-1/2" h, black and white transfer dec, obverse with portrait of naval hero Commodore Stephen Decator (sic), reverse with military hero Major General Jacob Brown, repairs, early 19th C ............2,100.00

    8" h, reserve of masons congregating "Vertias Prevalerus," various Masonic and regalia motifs, "Holiness to the Lord, it is found," cracks, staining, minor glaze wear........................ 450.00

    8-1/4" h, reserve of Ship *Caroline*, Shipwrights Arms, spread eagle with shield, "James Leech," polychrome highlights, minor spout chips, cracks, staple repair...................................... 350.00

    9-3/4" h, reserve of portrait of Washington surrounded by Justice, Liberty, and Victory, encircled by fifteen stars, names of fifteen states, reserve of Peace, Plenty, and Independence, "Phillip & Jane Gilkey" under spout, base chip, minor staining, rim roughness............................................................1,725.00

    9-3/4" h, Proscribed Patriots of America, three-masted hip flying American flag, spread eagle with American shield, polychrome highlights, restoration, minor abrasions to transfers ........1,725.00

## Reproduction Alert:

Pitcher, transfer dec, ship on one side, Masonic emblems on other, captioned "United States" above Jefferson quotation, "Peace, Commerce, and honest Friendship, with all Nations-Entangling Alliances with none-Jefferson/Anno Domini 1804," small chip on spout, hairline cracks, 11" h, 7" d, $4,025. Photo courtesy of Skinner, Inc.

    10-1/8" h, reserve of three-masted ship under sail, flying American flag, Masonic elements, "United for the Benefit of Mankind," spread eagle with shield, polychrome highlights, shadows of gilt highlights, chips to spout, minor cracks, staining, transfer wear ......... 1,150.00

    10-1/2" h, "Washington in Glory America in Tears," reverse with transfer of Masonic elements, below spout monogram and eagle, "SOS" within Masonic reserve, staining, old repair to handle, minor hairlines ....................................................... 1,380.00

    11-3/8" h, three Masonic reserves "United for the Benefit of Mankind," reserve of woman with three children "to judge with candor…," various Masonic elements, "EW" under spout, polychrome and gilt highlights ................................................................. 1,380.00

Pitcher, transfer dec

    5-1/2" h, reserve of naval battle, "Lepervier and Peacock," restoration to spout, cracks, minor rim chips, surface abrasions ..... 700.00

    10-5/8" h, frame of ribbon bearing names of fifteen states, sgd at base "F. Morris Shelton," reverse dec with American three-masted ship under sail, spread eagle, polychrome highlights, cracks, minor chips, and staining..................................... 875.00

Plate, creamware

    7-3/4" d, Nelson's Monument in Liverpool harbor, black transfer, black lined rim ................................................................. 165.00

    10" d, Hope, woman seated under tree, sailing ship in background, bird border, black transfer, polychrome enamel accents, c1800 ................................................................................... 195.00

Puzzle Jug, 7-1/2" h, neck pierced with outlined hearts and ellipses, body inscribed with rhyme, blue Chinese landscape, c1760..............2,185.00

# LOETZ

**History:** Loetz is a type of iridescent art glass that was made in Austria by J. Loetz Witwe in the late 1890s. Loetz was a contemporary of L. C. Tiffany's, and he had worked in the Tiffany factory before establishing his own operation; therefore, much of the wares are similar in appearance to Tiffany products. The Loetz factory also produced items with fine cameos on cased glass.

**Marks:** Some pieces are signed "Loetz," "Loetz, Austria," or "Austria."

**Reference:** Robert and Deborah Truitt, *Collectible Bohemian Glass: 1880-1940*, R & D Glass, 1995.

Bowl, 9" w, 6-1/2" d, 5" h, rect amber glass bowl, papillon and swirled irid, crimped rim, polished pontil, Art Nouveau gilded and enameled bronze mount of entwined snakes and flowering tulip bulbs, c1900 ...... 1,725.00

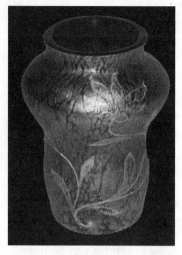

**Vase, blue irises, gilded flowers and leaves, 4" h, $475. Photo courtesy of Joy Luke Fine Art Brokers and Auctioneers.**

Bulb Vase, 4-3/4" h, mold blown, green, pulled magenta and pearl irid, rising to green bulbous top, small inside rim chips ................ 1,035.00

Candlesticks, pr, 11" h, 4-3/4" d, brilliant gold, blue highlights .... 595.00

Compote, 11" d, 10-1/2" h, ruffled rim, hobnailed bowl, mottled irid rose red and pale green, gilt metal Vienna Secessionist style tripart frame ............................................................................................. 265.00

Decanter, 11-1/4" h, bottle form, cobalt blue ground, silver blue luster, silver overlay, carved as foliate and scrolling dec, monogrammed, conforming silver overlaid stopper ....................................... 2,500.00

Ewer, 10-1/2" h, flared cylindrical form, brilliant blue papillon dec, silver overlay engraved as entwined grapes on vines, applied silver handle, polished pontil ........................................................................ 8,050.00

Inkwell, 3-1/2" h, amethyst, sq, irid, web design, bronze collar ... 125.00

Jack-In-The-Pulpit Vase, 13-1/2" h, freeblown floriform, colorless, striated gold amber pulled feather dec, gold and blue irid surface .......... 1,500.00

Lamp, desk, 17-1/4" h, double socket, raised gold irid festoons on linen-fold style shades, mounted on adjustable standard, ring-shaped finial, oval hammered brass base ............................. 1,495.00

Lamp Shade, mushroom shape, creamy irid ground, irid violet wavy swirled oil spot bands, pr ...................................................... 1,380.00

Pitcher, 8-1/2" h, pinched bulbous body, purple-green irid, applied handle, gilt metal mount with cast foliate motif ............................... 600.00

Rose Bowl, 3-1/4" h, raised ruffled rim, pinched squatty form, green with slight irid sheen, ext. draped with irid silver-blue threads, polished pontil, c1900 .......................................................................... 145.00

Sweetmeat Jar, cov, 5" h, irid silver spider web dec, green ground, sgd ......................................................................................... 400.00

Vase

4" h, blue irid ground, gilded flowers and leaves ................ 475.00

4-1/4" h, pinched oviform, raised rim, semi-opaque pink body, pulled purple swirls, silver spots, overall irid surface, spurious acid stamp in polished pontil, c1900 ............................ 2,645.00

4-1/4" h, pinched oviform, tricorn rim, light blue body, surface dec with knotted wood texture, overall light blue luster, polished pontil, few dark inclusions .................................................... 375.00

4-1/2" h, flared oval body, green glass, silver-blue oil spot irid, silver overlay of Art Nouveau styled clover, polished pontil ............ 815.00

5" h, Papillion Art, flared rim, cylindrical form, bulbed near base, colorless glass with irid Papillion dec, gold luster ground, polished pontil, early 20th C, burst bubbles ......................... 345.00

5-1/2" h, oviform, raised and flared rim, pale pink body, pulled and swirled silver irid threads and oval dots over gold oil spot luster surface, polished pontil .................................................. 1,495.00

6" h, double bulbed and pinched form, pale green ground with irid gold papillon dec, polished pontil ................................... 350.00

6" h, waisted form, flattened rim, cobalt blue, silver papillon irid, polished pontil .......................................................... 675.00

6-1/2" h, tapered form, cased glass with swirled irid green rising to pearly blue, Art Nouveau stylized silver overlay, polished pontil, rubbed marks on overlay, c1905 .................. 750.00

7" h, broad shouldered form, ruffled rim, colorless body with light blue papillon dec on dark gold luster surface, allover stylized iris silver overlay dec, c1900, burst bubble, loss to silver overlay ............................................................ 1,725.00

7-3/4" h, tricorn rim flaring to wide pinched base, irid green, pulled blue, purple, and green dec, polished pontil, sgd "Loetz Austria" ......................................................................... 1,035.00

8" h, oviform, raised rim, colorless cased to olive green, broad leaves of irid papillon dec, sgd "Loetz Austria" in polished pontil ....................................................................... 1,265.00

9" h, Persian bottle form, salmon pink, pulled silver blue leaves rising from base, descending from mouth, band of blue, amber, and white pulled swirls at base, polished pontil inscribed "Loetz Austria" c1900 .............................................................. 2,750.00

# LUSTER WIARE

**History:** Lustering on a piece of pottery creates a metallic, sometimes iridescent, appearance. Josiah Wedgwood experimented with the technique in the 1790s. Between 1805 and 1840 lustered earthenware pieces were created in England by makers such as Adams, Bailey and Batkin, Copeland and Garrett, Wedgwood, and Enoch Wood.

Luster decorations often were used in conjunction with enamels and transfers. Transfers used for luster decoration covered a wide range of public and domestic subjects. They frequently were accompanied by pious or sentimental doggerel as well phrases which reflected on the humors of everyday life.

Copper luster was created by the addition of a copper compound to the glaze. It was very popular in America during the 19th century, and collecting it became a fad from the 1920s to the 1950s. Today it has a limited market.

Pink luster was made by using a gold mixture. Silver luster pieces were first covered completely with a thin coating of a "steel luster" mixture, containing a small quantity of platinum oxide. An additional coating of platinum, worked in water, was then applied before firing.

Sunderland is a coarse type of cream-colored earthenware with a marbled or spotted pink luster decoration which shades from pink to purple. A solution of gold compound applied to the white body developed the many shades of pink.

The development of electroplating in 1840 created a sharp decline in the demands for metal-surfaced earthenware.

**Reference:** Michael Gibson, *19th Century Lustreware*, Antique Collectors' Club, 1999.

**Additional Listings:** English Soft Paste.

## Canary

Child's Mug, 1-3/4" h, "A Present for Charles," pink luster trim, minor wear ................................................................................... 625.00

---

## Reproduction Alert:

The market for copper luster has been softened by reproductions, especially creamers and the "polka" jug, which fool many new buyers. Reproductions are heavier in appearance and weight than the earlier pieces.

Creamer, 3-3/4" h, silver luster resist bands with floral dec, damage and repairs .................................................................... 125.00

Pitcher, 6-1/2" h, enameled red, green, blue and pink flowers, wear and crazing, hairline in spout ............................................ 650.00

## Copper

Bowl, 5-3/4" d, yellow band with enameled raised flowers ........... 50.00

Compote, 3-1/4" h, pedestal base, flared sides, wide blue band with copper luster house design ....................................................... 55.00

Creamer

  3" h, copper luster trim, marbleized, chips on spout ............. 75.00

  4-1/8" h, canary band with white reserves, purple transfer of woman and child in classical attire, polychrome enamel, repairs ...... 185.00

Goblet, 3-3/4" h, blue center band with red and brown enameled flowerhead, beaded ring on stem .......................................... 90.00

Hen on Nest, 10" h, 7" w, Italian ........................................... 225.00

Mug, copper luster body

  3-1/8" h, blue band, white polychrome cherubs and classical figures at play, scroll handle ........................................ 25.00

  3-1/2" h, medium blue center band, multicolored children and goat .................................................................................. 60.00

Pitcher

  4-1/4" h, cobalt blue lower band with yellow and brown enameled scene of dog, boy, and trees ......................................... 85.00

  5" h, polychrome badminton scene on canary band, copper luster body, unmkd ................................................................. 125.00

  6-1/2" h, cream center and neck band, pink luster streaks . 110.00

Salt, 2" h, pedestal base, yellow band, stylized luster leaves ....... 65.00

Tumbler, 2-3/4" h, blue band, polychrome molded flowers ......... 100.00

## Pink

Creamer, 3-7/8" h, light blue ground, alternating molded green acanthus leaves and pink and green floral springs, molded green grapevine border band, pink luster spout, rim, and handle ............... 120.00

Cup and Saucer, handleless, pearlware, pink luster reserve of trees and picket fence, pink luster stripes and banded rims ............... 20.00

Jug, 4-7/8" h, relief molded running hunting dogs, berried vine border, pink luster accents, Staffordshire, c1825 ................................. 450.00

Mug, 4-3/4" h, church pattern, fencing ................................... 500.00

Pitcher, 5-1/4" h, Masonic transfers "Protestant Ascendancy, Let Brotherly Love Continue," and statue of William of Orange on horseback, polychrome dec, glaze wear to spout and handle, wear to luster ........ 230.00

Teabowl and Saucer, landscape scene with villa, pink lustered rims, c1825 ............................................................................. 50.00

## Silver

Bough Pot, cov, 9" w, demilune shape, pierced cov, urn knob, pearlware, central panels of fruit flanked by molded columns and leaves, stylized floral reserves, ball feet, Staffordshire, c1820, pr ..... 2,100.00

Creamer, 4-3/8" h, helmet shape, overall luster ........................... 45.00

**Pitcher, silver luster, yellow ground, c1830, unmarked, restored, 5" h, $295.**

Cup and Saucer, hanging red painted flowerheads, green dots, silver luster scrolling leaves and borders ...................................... 110.00

Jug, 5-3/8" h, red and yellow owl seated on brown branch, silver resist leaves on body ................................................................. 750.00

Relish Tray, leaf design, Myott ............................................. 55.00

Teapot, 5-1/4" h, squatty, molded reeded borders, overall luster 140.00

Vase, 7-1/4" h, bulbous, floral dec on wide black band, cream ground, Wedgwood, 1920 ............................................................. 375.00

## Sunderland

Bowl, 11-3/4" d, Odd Fellows transfers and verses, splashed and wavy pink luster designs ......................................................... 1,250.00

Cream Pitcher, 3-1/2" h, paneled body, overall splashed pink luster ............................................................................. 115.00

Jug, 6-1/2" h, Battle of Wasp and Reindeer, "Constitution" on reverse, black transfers, pink luster trim, chips ................................. 400.00

Mug

  4" h, Mariners Arms, polychrome dec transfer ................... 125.00

  4-1/8" h, Sailor's Farewell, poem "The Sailor's Tears," polychrome highlights ...................................................................... 175.00

Plaque, pierced for hanging

  7" x 8-1/2", pink and silver luster frame, center with black transfer ship and "May peace and plenty on our nation smile and trade with commerce bless the British Isle" ............................... 175.00

  8-5/8" l, rect, *Flying Cloud, Boston,* black transfer, pink luster border, copper luster rim ...................................................... 450.00

  9-3/8" l, 8-1/4" w, rect, *Victoria and Albert Yacht,* black transfer, green water, pink splashed border, molded brown rim .................. 450.00

Pitcher, 7-1/4" h, transfer dec, pink luster, raised rim, bulbous body, dec under spout with Mariner's Arms, ship and two sailors, ships, lighthouse, and cannon in background, inspirational verse within floral border reserve on sides, England, c1840, chips ................. 635.00

Puzzle Jug, 6-1/2" h, pink luster house and landscape scene, lustered rim and nozzles, chips ...................................................... 750.00

Watch Stand, 11" h, figural tall case clock, flanked by two classical children, black, yellow, red, and green enamels, splashed pink luster on base, imp "Dixon, Austin" ............................................... 1,100.00

# LUTZ-TYPE GLASS

**History:** Lutz-type glass is an art glass attributed to Nicholas Lutz. He made this type of glass while at the Boston and Sandwich Glass Co. from 1869 until 1888. Since Lutz-type glass was popular, copied by many capable glassmakers, and unsigned, it is nearly impossible to distinguish genuine Lutz products.

Lutz is believed to have made two distinct types of glass: striped and threaded. The striped glass was made by using threaded glass rods in the Venetian manner, and this style is often confused with authentic Venetian glass. Threaded glass was blown and decorated with winding threads of glass.

Barber Bottle, 8" h, colorless ground, multicolored threaded latticino and opaque stripes ........................................................ 250.00

Beverage Set, 70-1/2" h tankard pitcher, four lemonade tumblers, four large tumblers, colorless ground, cranberry threading, engraved pattern of water plants and Grape Blue Heron on pitcher ..................... 650.00

Bowl, 3-1/4" d, 3" h, colorless, white, amethyst, and yellow latticino, goldstone border ................................................................ 75.00

Cake Stand, threaded, colorless, white threads ........................ 125.00

Compote, 7" h, colorless ground, lavender, pink, and opalescent swirls, entwined serpent stem .................................................... 275.00

Dish, 12" w, leaf shape, colorless, white latticino, goldstone and white waves .............................................................................. 175.00

Lemonade Tumbler, 5-1/2" d, colorless ground, cranberry threading, engraved dec, applied colorless handle ................................ 145.00

Marble

    1-3/4" d, colorless ground, green, red, white, and blue threaded twists, minor bruises, some roughness ...............................35.00

    2-1/8" d, colorless ground, cranberry and white swirl ...........95.00

    2-3/8" d, multicolored, minor roughness and bruises..........110.00

Pitcher, 10" h, colorless ground, pink threading..........................200.00

Plate, 6-1/4" d, threaded, rose shading to amber body, goldstone dec, ruffled ................................................................................125.00

Scent Bottle, 2-1/8" l, blown, colorless, figural sea horse, opaque white spiral ribs, applied blue rigaree ...............................................115.00

Syrup Pitcher, blue ground, white stripes, frosted handle...........175.00

Tea Service, creamer, cov sugar, two cups and saucers, colorless ground, light pink, blue, and white latticino ..............................250.00

Tumbler, colorless ground

    3" h, gold and white latticino, threaded, six applied strawberries, ftd ................................................................................115.00

    3-1/2" h, white, green, and orange latticino ........................120.00

Vase, colorless ground

    7" h, cylindrical, cranberry threading...................................125.00

    8" h, bulbous, white latticino, applied colorless handle.......150.00

Whimsy, 6-3/8" h, tiny Frozen Charlotte doll in colorless glass tube, latticino rings dec, bulbous finial, knob stem, colorless foot...375.00

# MAASTRICHT WARE

**History:** Petrus Regout founded the De Sphinx Pottery in 1836 in Maastricht, Holland. The firm specialized in transfer-printed earthenwares. Other factories also were established in the area, many employing English workmen and adopting their techniques. Maastricht china was exported to the United States in competition with English products.

Bowl
 6" d, ftd, Honc pattern, green transfer, polychrome accents. 40.00
 7-3/4" d, ftd, Slamat pattern, orange and green oriental scene with young boy, green Petrus Regout sphinx mark............ 45.00
 9" d, ftd, Honc pattern, green transfer, polychrome accents. 45.00
 9-1/2" d, 5" h, Timor pattern..................................................... 50.00
Charger, 13" d, rose, blue, and green flowers and lines in center, brown and yellow inner circles, border with blue triangles, cream ground, mkd "Maastricht, Made in Holland" ............................... 45.00
Coffee Set, 8-1/2" h coffeepot, 3-3/4" h creamer, 4-1/2" h cov sugar, Cambridge, Old England pattern............................................... 100.00
Cup Plate, 4-1/2" d, Lasso pattern, horse hunting scenes, red transfer, mkd "Petrus Regout & Co. Maastricht, Made in Holland".......... 20.00
Cup and Saucer
 Honc pattern, blue-black oriental design, orange accents.... 20.00
 Oriental pattern, overall floral design, red transfers, mkd "Societe Ceramique Maastricht"....................................................... 12.00
 Timor pattern, green, iron-red, blue, and luster dec.............. 38.00
Ginger Jar, cov, 11-1/2" h, white ground, blue florals, mkd "Petrous Regout, 1936" ....................................................................... 60.00
Plate
 6-1/2" d, Pajong, yellow and black, oriental scene of man and woman with umbrella, .......................................................... 20.00
 7" d, Tea Party pattern, brown transfer, rampant lion and "M. Maastricht" marks.................................................................. 25.00
 8-1/4" d, Timor ........................................................................ 30.00
 8-1/2" d, Canton pattern, multicolored .................................. 25.00
 9-1/8" d, red, blue, and yellow floral border band, sphinx mark .20.00
 9-1/4" d, Honc pattern, green, orange-red, and orange accents, crazing, stains ........................................................................ 25.00
 10" d, Abbey pattern ............................................................. 35.00
Pitcher, white, Royal Sphinx mark, c1941, two small chips ........ 200.00

**Bowl, Vlinder, gold luster trim, multicolored butterflies and florals, 6" d, 3" h, $65.**

Soup Plate, 9-1/8" d, Willow pattern, blue transfer, mkd .............. 45.00
Tea Set, 6-1/2" h teapot, creamer, cov sugar, four teacups, six saucers, six 7-7/8" d dessert plates, Art Deco concentric orange and black stripes on cream ground, back makers stamp on base, "N.V. De Sphinx" and "Petrous Regout & Co. Maastricht, Holland," c1925, crack, glaze flakes, minor chips ................................................. 80.00
Tureen, cov, matching ladle, white................................................ 170.00
Waste Bowl, 4" d, Pompeia pattern, c1875.................................... 65.00

# MAJOLICA

**History:** Majolica, an opaque, tin-glazed pottery, has been produced in many countries for centuries. It was named after the Spanish Island of Majorca, where figuline (a potter's clay) is found. Today, however, the term "majolica" denotes a type of pottery which was made during the last half of the 19th century in Europe and America.

Majolica frequently depicts elements of nature: leaves, flowers, birds, and fish. Designs were painted on the soft clay body using vitreous colors and fired under a clear lead glaze to impart the rich color and brilliance characteristic of majolica.

Victorian decorative art philosophy dictated that the primary function of design was to attract the eye; usefulness was secondary. Majolica was a welcome and colorful change from the familiar blue and white wares, creamwares, and white ironstone of the day.

**Marks:** Wedgwood, George Jones, Holdcraft, and Minton were a few of the English majolica manufacturers who marked their wares. Most of their pieces can be identified through the English Registry mark and/or the potter-designer's mark. Sarreguemines in France and Villeroy and Boch in Baden, Germany, produced majolica that compared favorably with the finer English majolica. Most Continental pieces had an incised number on the base.

Although 600-plus American potteries produced majolica between 1850 and 1900, only a handful chose to identify their wares. Among these manufacturers were George Morely, Edwin Bennett, the Chesapeake Pottery Company, the New Milford-Wannoppee Pottery Company, and the firm of Griffen, Smith, and Hill. The others hoped their unmarked pieces would be taken for English examples.

**References:** Susan and Al Bagdade, *Warman's American Pottery and Porcelain*, 2nd ed., Krause Publications, 2000; ——, *Warman's English & Continental Pottery & Porcelain*, 3rd ed., Krause Publications, 1998; Victoria Bergesen, *Majolica: British, Continental, and American Wares, 1851-1915*, Barrie & Jenkins, 1989; Leslie Bockol, *Victorian Majolica*, Schiffer Publishing, 1996; Helen Cunningham, *Majolica Figures*, Schiffer Publishing, 1997; Nicholas M. Dawes, *Majolica*, Crown, 1990; Marilyn G. Karmason and Joan B. Stacke, *Majolica, A Complete History and Illustrated Survey*, Abrams, 1989; Mariann Katz-Marks, *Collector's Encyclopedia of Majolica*, Collector Books, 1992, 2000 value update; Marshall P. Katz and Robert Lehr, *Palissy Ware: Nineteenth Century French Ceramics from Avisseau to Renoleau*, Athlone Press, 1996; *Price Guide to Majolica*, L-W Book Sales, 1997; Mike Schneider, *Majolica*, Schiffer Publishing, 1990, 1995 value update; Jeffrey B.

## Reproduction Alert:

Majolica-style pieces are a favorite of today's interior decorators. Many exact copies of period pieces are being manufactured. In addition, fantasy pieces incorporating late Victorian era design motifs have entered the market and confused many novice collectors.

Modern majolica reproductions differ from period pieces in these ways: (1) modern reproductions tend to be lighter in weight than their Victorian ancestors; (2) the glaze on newer pieces may not be as rich or deeply colored as on period pieces; (3) new pieces usually have a plain white bottom, period pieces almost always have colored or mottled bases; (4) a bisque finish either inside or on the bottom generally means the piece is new; and (5) if the design prevents the piece from being functional—e.g., a lip of a pitcher that does not allow proper pouring—it is a new piece made primarily for decorative purposes.

Some reproductions bear old marks. Period marks found on modern pieces include (a) "Etruscan Majolica" (the mark of Griffen, Smith and Hill) and (b) a British registry mark.

Snyder and Leslie J. Bockol, *Majolica: European and American Wares*, Schiffer Publishing, 1994.

**Periodical:** *Majolica Market*, 2720 N 45 Rd, Manton, MI 49663.

**Collectors' Club:** Majolica International Society, 1275 First Ave., Ste 103, New York, NY 10021.

**Advisor:** Mary D. Harris.

**Note:** Prices listed below are for pieces with good color and in mint condition. For less-than-perfect pieces, decrease value proportionately according to the degree of damage or restoration.

Basket, Rustic Tree, brown and green, pink interior ................... 275.00
Bowl
    Etruscan, 10" x 12", Oak Leaf, pink and green .................. 600.00
    Wedgwood, 6", bird and fan design .................................. 125.00
Bread Tray, Eat Thy Bread With Thankfulness, Begonia Leaf
    center ....................................................................... 400.00
Butter Dish, cov, Wheat and Flower design, white ground ......... 350.00
Butter Pat
    Etruscan, Smiilax, green and yellow ................................. 175.00
    Etruscan, Shell and Seaweed ........................................... 225.00
    Fielding, butterfly and bamboo, leaf ................................. 285.00
    Ruffled leaf, blue, green, and white .................................. 115.00
    Wedgwood, Shell and Waves, teal, yellow, and pink ......... 250.00
Cake Stand, 10" d, 5" h, Etruscan, conventional, green, brown, yellow,
    and white .................................................................... 500.00
Card Tray, 7" x 9", French wire basket, turquoise and brown ..... 150.00
Compote
    Begonia Leaf, 9" x 3", basketweave, yellow ground, green, pink,
      brown, and white leaf ............................................... 200.00
    English, Pineapple, 9" x 2", green, yellow, and brown ........ 300.00

Cheese Dish, cov, circular, argenta ground, molded relief of blossoming prunus blossoms, branch knob, imp "Wedgwood," c1882, slight stains, 8-1/4" h, $690. Photo courtesy of Skinner, Inc.

Etruscan, Daisy, 9" x 5", white ground, pink and yellow foliage,
    pink interior................................................................. 325.00
George Jones, 9" x 3", Horse Chestnut on napkin, green, white,
    and yellow ................................................................... 375.00
Rose and Rope design, turquoise and cobalt blue ............. 350.00
Cup and Saucer
    Bird and Fan design, turquoise ground, pink, yellow, and
      brown...................................................................... 200.00
    Holdcroft, quatrefoil shape, yellow ground, green bamboo leaves,
      blue interior ............................................................ 200.00
    Pineapple design, yellow and green ................................. 200.00
Dish, 9" x 12", Begonia Leaf, leaf shape, pink, green, and yellow ... 200.00
Humidor, cov
    Box, Dutch boy on top, cobalt blue ground, 7" x 6" x 4" ..... 200.00
    Frog dressed in pink jacket, holding pipe .......................... 400.00
    Man's head, wearing hat, smoking cigar, 9" h ................... 250.00
Mug
    Etruscan, Acorn, yellow ground, green and brown ............. 250.00
    French, Bunny, Choisey Le Roi ........................................ 300.00
    Turquoise, leaves and flowers ......................................... 150.00
Mustache Cup and Saucer, Etruscan, Shell and Seaweed ........ 450.00
Oyster Plate
    English, 10" d, pink and turquoise wells, green seaweed
      trim .........................................................................500.00
    French, Sarreguimes, 9-1/2" d, green and amber .............. 150.00
    Minton, 9" d, turquoise ................................................... 600.00
    Samuel Lear, 10" d, Sunflower, white ground, yellow sunflower,
      blue center ............................................................ 1,800.00
Pitcher
    English, 7" h, Corn, yellow and green................................ 175.00
    English, 10" h, figural, Owl, green and browns ................... 325.00
    Fielding, English, 8" h, Bow, white ground, blue bow, multicolored
      daisies and wheat ...................................................... 400.00
    French, 9" h, figural, Monk, sgd "Frie Onning," brown, gold, and
      black......................................................................... 175.00
    George Jones, 8" h, Stork, turquoise ground, cobalt blue and
      green ...................................................................... 1,500.00
    Reindeer, 7" h, yellow ground, brown reindeer, green trees175.00
    Shell & Coral, 8" h, white ground, pink scallop shells, green seaweed, blue water .................................................. 600.00
Plate
    Etruscan, 8", Cauliflower, yellow, green, and pink .............. 275.00
    Etruscan, 9", Leaf, pink and green leaf on basketweave ground,
      yellow border............................................................. 200.00
    Wedgwood, 9" d, Argenta series, fruit design..................... 225.00
    Wedgwood, 9" d, Naturalism series, leaves, green, brown, and
      yellow ...................................................................... 300.00
    Wedgwood, 9" d, Sunflower, all green ............................... 175.00
Platter
    English, 9" x 12", Begonia Leaf, red, green, and yellow ..... 175.00
    Wedgwood, 12", Argenta series, mum design.................... 450.00

Sardine Box, cov, Pineapple design, fish on lid, green, yellow, and
  brown ...................................................................................................675.00
Spooner, fence, floral design, white ground, pink flowers, green and
  blue leaves ..........................................................................................150.00
Sweetmeat Bowl, Wedgwood, 9" d, brown ground, green, thistle
  leaves, pink flowers............................................................................375.00

# MAPS

**History:** Maps provide one of the best ways to study the growth of a country or region. From the 16th to the early 20th century, maps were both informative and decorative. Engravers provided ornamental detailing, such as ornate calligraphy and scrolling, especially on bird's-eye views and city maps. Many maps were hand colored to enhance their beauty.

Maps generally were published as plates in books. Many of the maps available today are simply single sheets from cut-apart books.

In the last quarter of the 19th century, representatives from firms in Philadelphia, Chicago, and elsewhere traveled the United States preparing county atlases, often with a sheet for each township and a sheet for each major city or town.

**References:** *Antique Map Price Record & Handbook for 1996*, available from Spoon River Press (2319C W. Rohmann, Peoria, IL 61604), 1996; Melville C. Branch, *An Atlas of Rare City Maps: Comparative Urban Design, 1830-1842*, Princeton Architectural Press, 1997; Carl Morland and David Bannister, *Antique Maps*, Phaidon Press, 1993; K. A. Sheets, *American Maps 1795-1895*, available from Spoon River Press (2319C W. Rohmann, Peoria, IL 61604), 1995.

**Periodical:** *Antique Map & Print Quarterly*, P.O. Box 254, Simsbury, CT 06070.

**Collectors' Clubs:** Association of Map Memorabilia Collectors, 8 Amherst Rd, Pelham, MA 01002; Chicago Map Society, 60 W. Walton St., Chicago, IL 60610.

**Museum:** Hermon Dunlap Smith Center for the History of Cartography, Newberry Library, Chicago, IL.

**Notes:** Although mass produced, county atlases are eagerly sought by collectors. Individual sheets sell for $25 to $75. The atlases themselves can usually be purchased in the $200 to $400 range. Individual sheets should be viewed solely as decorative and not as investment material.

Africa, Heinrich Scherer, engraved folding map, wide margins, hand
  colored, in outline, Munich, 1700, matted, framed ...................350.00
America With Those Known Parts In That Unknowne Worlde, John
  Speed, Bassett and Chiswell, London, 1626, double page, engraved,
  395 x 520 mm, English text on verso, vertical fold reinforced with
  paper tape on verso, very slight browning along fold............3,910.00

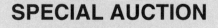

## SPECIAL AUCTION

Swann Galleries, Inc.
104 E. 25th St.
New York, NY 10010
(212) 254-4710

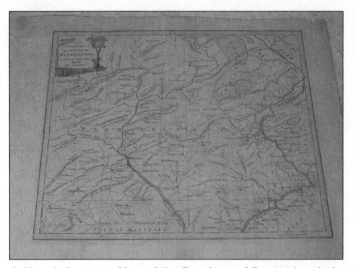

**A New & Accurate Map of the Province of Pennsylvania in North America from the Best Authorities, 13" x 16", folds, $275. Photo courtesy of Sanford Alderfer Auction Co.**

A New and Accurate Map of the North Pole, Emanuel Bowen, London,
  1747, double page, engraved, 380 x 430 mm, top margin trimmed to
  platemark, slight browning along vertical fold .........................230.00
A New and Accurate Map of the World, John Speed, Humble, London,
  c1627, double page, engraved, double hemispheric, 405 x 510 mm,
  margins trimmed, hand colored in outline, small tears..........2,530.00
England and Wales, embroidered, floral cartouche at upper right corner bearing title, date 1803, and initials, 19-7/8" w, 20" h ........815.00
Europe, Hartmann Schedel, Nuremberg, 1493, extracted from Latin
  edition of Nuremberg Chronicle, 395 x 580 mm image size, wide
  margins, Latin text on verso, vertical fold with expert closures, slight
  browning................................................................................2,990.00
Hydrographical Basin of the Upper Mississippi River, J. N. Nicollet,
  Washington, 1843, engraved, two joined sheets, folded, 970 x 800
  mm, scattered minor browning.................................................490.00
Louisiana, lithograph, "The Official records of the Union and Confederate Armies, 1861-65," plate CLVI of Jules Bien and Company, NY,
  unframed, 18" x 29"..................................................................90.00
Map of Ohio, Willis Thrall, Hartford, 1832, hand colored engraved roll
  map, wooden rollers top and bottom, linen backed, top third damp-
  stained, shellac very yellowed and browned, quote soiled ...3,680.00
Map of the Cities of Pittsburgh, Allegheny, and the adjoining Boroughs,
  G. M. Hopkins, Philadelphia, 1872, hand colored litho, folding, 475 x
  600 mm, folds into orig 12mo cloth case................................550.00
Map of the City of Albany, Oliver Steele, pocket type, engraved folding
  map, partially hand colored, New York, 1837, extensive separations
  along folds, several clean tears, most of map loose from binding, orig
  24mo roan case ......................................................................140.00
Map of the Republic of Switzerland, William Faden, London, 1820,
  double page, engraved, 575 x 830 mm, wide margins, partly hand
  colored, some browning .........................................................115.00
Map of the River Sabine from its Mouth on the Gulf of Mexico in the
  Sea to Logan's Ferry in Latitude 31°58'24" North, Haas, Washington, 1840, five sheet lithographed roll map with color, linen backed,
  top roller missing, bottom one intact, shellac quite yellowed, color
  subdued..............................................................................7,475.00
Map of the United States Projected by Olive Little Marshfield A.D.
  1830, pen, ink, and watercolor on paper, 27" h, 38-1/4" w, mounted to
  canvas, unframed, varnished, minor tears and creases .......2,530.00
Missouri River, engraved, higher parts of the Mississippi and Hudson
  Bay, 1789, framed in carved giltwood frame in Louis XVI taste, 19" x
  18" sight ..................................................................................175.00
Mitchell's Reference & Distance Map of the United States, J. H. Young,
  S. Augustus Mitchell, Philadelphia, c1855, large engraved roll map,
  insets of Texas and California, hand colored, wooden rollers top and
  bottom, linen backed, some dampstaining at top.................5,750.00

Northern hemisphere, John Churchman, published in Philadelphia 1790, dedicated "To George Washington President of the United States of America This Magnetic Atlas or Variation Chart is Humbly Inscribed" ................................................................. 3,450.00

Pennsylvania, lays out lot in Carnavan Township, Lancaster County, pen, ink, watercolor, laid paper, dated and sgd by surveyor, "Draft of Jesse Marche's Lands, 1827," red, blue, and black, stains and damage at fold lines, framed, 11-1/2" h, 7-1/2" w ........................... 440.00

State of New York, J. H. French, H. H. Lloyd & Co., unjoined four sheet hand colored engraved map, New York, 1865, scattered minor soiling and light browning, linen backed .......................................... 1,495.00

The Kindome of China, John Speed, Bassett and Chiswell, London, 1626, double page, engraved, 395 x 115 mm, English text on verso, map hand colored in outline, hand colored side figures, faintly evenly browned .................................................................................. 2,530.00

Tourist's Map of the State of New York, William Williams, pocket type, hand colored engraved folding map, Utica, 1828, scattered minor browning, some minor separation, folds into orig 24mo leather case ................................................................................... 400.00

Township Map of the State of Iowa, J. H. Colton, pocket type, hand colored engraved folding map, orig 12mo cloth case, New York, 1855 ................................................................................................ 420.00

World, J. H. Colton's Illustrated & Embellished Steel Plate Map of the World on Mercator's Projection, 20 section engraved map, New York, 1855, linen backed, orig half morocco covers, lacking backstrip, covers quite worn ........................................................................... 2,550.00

# MARBLEHEAD POTTERY

**History:** This hand-thrown pottery was first made in 1905 as part of a therapeutic program introduced by Dr. J. Hall for the patients confined to a sanitarium located in Marblehead, Massachusetts. In 1916, production was removed from the hospital to another site. The factory continued under the directorship of Arthur E. Baggs until it closed in 1936.

Most pieces found today are glazed with a smooth, porous, even finish in a single color. The most desirable pieces have a conventional design in one or more subordinate colors.

**Reference:** David Rago, *American Art Pottery,* Knickerbocker Press, 1997.

Bowl
2-1/2" h, slightly raised rim, squat shallow bowl, molded triangular linear pattern around rim and shoulder, matte brown glaze, green ground, imp ship mark, incised "H. T.," decorated by Hannah Tutt ...................................................................... 1,725.00
5" d, 6" d, blue speckled, imp ship mark ............................ 400.00
6" d, 3" h, red metallic glaze, imp sink mark ...................... 350.00
6-1/2" d, 2-3/4" h, dark blue ext., light blue int. .................. 375.00
7-1/2" d, 2" h, matte, mustard yellow, cream color int. ......... 450.00
8-1/2" d, 2-1/4" h, matte, two-tone blue, navy blue ext., light blue int. ................................................................................ 450.00
8-1/2" d, 3-1/4" h, flaring, emb lotus-leaf pattern, dark blue ext. glaze, light blue int., imp ship mark ................................. 375.00
Candlestick, 6" h, three handle form, green matte glaze, imp mark, slight damage .......................................................................... 75.00
Flower Pot, 5" h, 6" w at top, dark blue, imp ship mark .............. 400.00
Pitcher, handle
3-1/2" h, semi-gloss blue glaze, imp ship mark .................. 100.00

**Vase, ovoid, carved tall stylized flowers, umber, black, and cream, speckled matte green ground, by Hannah Tuff, imp ship mark, incised "HT," 6-3/4" h, 4" d, $120,750. Photo courtesy of David Rago Auctions.**

5" h, blue hi-glaze, incised dec of ship at sea, imp ship mark .......................................................................... 300.00
Tile, 5-3/4" sq, matte painted, silhouette landscape in blue and yellow, ship mark, several small edge nicks ..................................... 1,700.00
Vase
3-1/2" h, 3-1/2" d, matte painted, flying geese, two tones of blue-gray, speckled gray ground, stamped ship mark ........... 1,500.00
4-1/2" h, 5" d, cylindrical, blue speckled matte glaze, ship mark .......................................................................... 750.00
5-1/2" h, oval body tapering to base, matte blue-gray glaze, imp mark, crazing .................................................................. 345.00
6" h, cylindrical, four carved and painted dragonflies alternating in blue and grown, at top, green matte ground, imp mark, artist sgd "Hanna Tutt," small flake to base .......................... 1,600.00
6-5/8" h, wide mouth, swollen octagonal paneled body, horizontal ribbing, aqua semi-gloss glaze, artist sgd "A&B 26," imp mark ................................................................................ 230.00
8" h, 4" d, tapering, mottled green, brown, and blue matte glaze, stamped mark, paper label ............................................. 1,100.00
8-3/4" h, 3-3/4" d, cylindrical, blue speckled matte glaze, ship mark .......................................................................... 850.00
8-3/4" h, 4" d, cylindrical, gray-mauve speckled matte glaze, ship mark .......................................................................... 750.00
Vessel
3-1/2" h, 5" d, squatty, closed-in rim, blue speckled matte glaze, ship mark ................................................................................ 700.00
6-3/4" h, 3" d, squatty, gray and indigo grapevine dec, smooth matte speckled gray ground, Hannah Tuff, imp ship mark and HT" ...................................................................................... 1,300.00
8-1/2" h, 4" d, dark brown stylized peacock feathers, dark green matte ground, incised initials for Hannah Tutt, imp ship mark .......................................................................... 3,750.00
Wall Plaque, 4-5/8" w, 7-1/2" h, rect, profile portrait of Egyptian in relief, glossy turquoise glaze, imp mark and paper label, crazing, minor wear .................................................................................... 550.00
Wall Pocket, 6" h, 7" w, flaring, brown speckled matte ext., smooth ivory int., paper label, rim bruise ............................................. 400.00

# MARY GREGORY TYPE GLASS

**History:** The use of enameled decoration on glass, an inexpensive way to imitate cameo glass, developed in Bohemia in the late 19th century. The Boston and Sandwich Glass Co. copied this process in the late 1880s.

Mary Gregory (1856-1908) was employed for two years at the Boston and Sandwich Glass factory when the enameled decorated glass was being manufactured. Some collectors argue that Gregory was inspired to paint her white enamel figures on glass by the work of Kate Greenaway and a desire to imitate pate-sur-pate. However, evidence for these assertions is very weak. Further, it has never been proven that Mary Gregory even decorated glass as part of her job at Sandwich. The result is that "Mary Gregory type" is a better term to describe this glass.

**Reference:** R. and D. Truitt, *Mary Gregory Glassware*, published by authors, 1992.

**Museum:** Sandwich Glass Museum, Sandwich, MA.

Atomizer, cranberry ground, white enameled little girl, gold washed atomizer mounting.................................................345.00
Barber Bottle, 7-5/8" h, deep amethyst ground, white enameled young girl, landscape setting pr ........................................300.00
Beverage Set, pitcher and six tumblers, colorless ground, white enameled girl, garden setting..........................................295.00
Box, cov, 5-3/4" d, 4-3/4" h, sapphire blue ground, white enameled young girl holding basket of flowers on lid, multicolored enamel dec on base, fancy wire legs.......................................645.00
Calling Card Holder, 6" w, 8" h, powder blue ground, white enameled lass holding garland of blossoms, mounted in 15" h, 13" w shadow box frame ...............................................................750.00
Cologne Bottle, sapphire blue, white enameled child ................. 155.00
Cruet, orig stopper, 7-1/2" h, green, white enameled girl and trees ...............................................................................145.00
Decanter, stopper, 12" h, colorless, white enameled woman with basket ..............................................................................175.00
Dresser Set, pr 10-1/2" h perfume bottles, 7" h cov dresser jar, cobalt blue, white enamel dec of young children and angels, floral sprays, crown tops ........................................................900.00
Dresser Tray, 10-1/2" l, 8" w, oval, emerald green ground, white enameled boy and girl dancing white another girl plays the mandolin............295.00
Ewer, 10" h, 3-1/8" d, cranberry ground, white enameled girl in garden setting, applied colorless handle ...........................................225.00
Jewel Box, 10" l, 4" w, blue ground, white enameled boy and girl pulling cart, girl astride huge bottle, boy carrying goblet, floral garlands, SP edges, base and feet, sgd "Middletown Plate Co"..............850.00
Mug
  3" h, 2-1/8" d, cranberry ground, white enameled boy, applied colorless handle.............................................................85.00
  3-7/8" h, 2-1/4" d, amber ground, applied amber handles, white enameled boy on one, girl on other, pr............................150.00
Paperweight, 4" l, rect, black glass ground, white enameled little boy and girl in garden ..................................................300.00
Perfume Bottle

4-5/8" h, 2" d, cranberry ground, white enameled little girl dec, colorless bubble stopper .................................................165.00
5-3/4" h, 3" d, sapphire blue ground, white enameled boy chasing butterfly, tinted facial features, blue ball stopper ..............225.00
Pitcher
  6-1/2" h, blue ground, white enameled boy with boat.........150.00
  6-5/8" h, 4-1/4' d, lime green ground, bulbous, optic effect, round mouth, white enameled boy, applied green handle..........145.00
  12" h, 6-1/2" w, sapphire blue ground, bulbous, applied amber handle, white enameled young woman holding her hat and staff, standing in scenic spot, minor paint loss on front ............150.00
Rose Bowl, cranberry ground, crimped top, white enameled girl holding flower.........................................................................325.00
Tumble-Up, cranberry ground, white enameled girl on carafe, boy on tumbler .............................................................................415.00
Tumbler
  3-1/2" h, azure blue ground, white enameled Brussels town square fountain scene.....................................................100.00
  4-1/4" h, cranberry ground, white enameled girl holding basket of flowers......................................................................115.00
  4-1/2" h, sapphire blue ground, white enameled boy, ribbed body.................................................................................85.00
  5" h, 2-1/2" d, sapphire blue ground, white enameled girl carrying basket of flowers ................................................................90.00
  5-1/2" h, cobalt blue ground, white enameled girl picking flowers, narrow gold band at top .................................................115.00
Vase
  2-1/2" h, 1-1/2" w, cobalt blue ground, white enameled young man standing among foliage, gold trim ............................325.00
  6-3/4" h, 3 d, pale amber ground, white enameled young girl in forest scene, reverse with flowers and leaves, banded dec around neck and shoulder...............................................225.00
  7" h, cobalt blue ground, gilded rim, white enameled flowers and cupids................................................................................175.00
  7" h, 2-1/2" w, bud, white spatter over amber ground, white enameled young boy and girl among foliate, price for facing pr 550.00
  7-3/4" h, sky blue ground, white enameled dec of young girl with parasol and posy, c1890-95 .............................................90.00
  8" h, cylinder, sapphire blue ground, white enameled young boy .................................................................................195.00
  8-7/8" h, 4" d, cranberry ground, white enameled young girls carrying watering cans, facing pr .........................................425.00
  9" h, 4" d, frosted emerald green ground, white enameled girl holds flowers in her apron and hand...............................165.00
  9-7/8" h, cranberry ground, white enameled boy running with butterfly net, girl with bouquet of flowers, holding apron, colorless pedestal foot, facing pr.....................................................475.00
  10-1/4" h, 5" w, cranberry ground, large white enameled dec of young girl holding flower, paneled int. ..............................300.00

**Vase, honey amber ground, cobalt blue pedestal, white enameled girl and boy, facing pair, 6-3/4" h, $190.**

12" h, emerald green ground, finely white enameled scene of boy picking flowers..............................................190.00

Wine Bottle, 9" h, 3-1/8" d, cranberry ground, white enameled girl holding floral spray, orig colorless bubble stopper..........................195.00

# MATCH HOLDERS

**History:** The friction match achieved popularity after 1850. The early matches were packaged and sold in sliding cardboard boxes. To facilitate storage and to eliminate the clumsiness of using the box, match holders were developed.

The first match holders were cast iron or tin, the latter often displaying advertisements. A patent for a wall-hanging match holder was issued in 1849. By 1880 match holders also were being made from glass and china. Match holders began to lose their popularity in the late 1930s with the advent of gas and electric heat and ranges.

**Reference:** Denis B. Alsford, *Match Holders*, Schiffer Publishing, 1994.

Advertising

Arnold Stern Cookers, 7-1/8" h, 4-1/4" w, cardboard litho, Statue of Liberty image, detailed scene of bridges and boats in background, never used ..........................................400.00

Chef Spices, Berdan & Co., Toledo, OH, tin litho, wall type, wear on front basket, 4-7/8" h, 3-7/8" w, 1-1/4" d.......................375.00

Dr. Smith's Columbo Tonic Bitters, Scranton, PA, hanging, cardboard, litho of seated bear, match holder wood barrel between legs, sandpaper paws for striking, 7" h, 5-1/4" w .............300.00

Empire steam Laundry, figural frog, cast iron, 4" x 2-1/2" x 2" .225.00

Pointer Stoves and Ranges, figural fly, cast iron, 4" x 3-1/8" x 1-1/2"......................................................225.00

Bisque, 2-1/2" h, figural, dog in house ..........................................25.00

Composition Plaster, 8-1/2" h, Palmer Cox Brownie, holding bucket to side for matches, scratching spot on belly, paint worn, small chips ..............................................................275.00

Glass

5" l, cornstarch blue opaque glass, reeded and serrated detail, chip on one corner of base..............................................150.00

6" l, 2-3/4" h, white milk glass, Souvenir of Sacramento, CA, gold trim, blue enameled flowers, green leaves, worn gold trim .....30.00

Hanging, 2-7/8" h, 2-1/8" w, Cambridge Crest, Goss China .........25.00

Jasperware, 2-3/8" h, 2-1/2" w, light green and white classical scene, Wedgwood, England ..............................................30.00

Plated Metal, 3" h, figural, boot, open top, striker on base ...........10.00

Porcelain, figural, German

4-1/2" h, boy with backpack, floral dec .................................45.00

4-5/8" h, boy selling matches, green and white ....................20.00

**Salt Glaze, oversized, deeply imp and blue accents, "Crystal Springs Brewing Co., Syracuse, NY," three blue accent bands, tooled relief design, 5" h, $750. Photo courtesy of Vicki & Bruce Waasdrop.**

4-5/8" h, girl holding flags ......................................................60.00

Souvenir, 4-1/4" h, 3" base, Cunard Ship Lines, porcelain ..........40.00

# MATCH SAFES

**History:** Pocket match safes are small containers used to safely carry matches in one's pocket. They were first used in the 1840s. Match safes can be found in various sizes and shapes, and were made from numerous materials such as sterling, nickel-plated brass, good, brass, ivory, and vulcanite. Some of the most interesting and sought after ones are figurals in the shapes of people, animals and anything else imaginable. Match safes were also a very popular advertising means in the 1895-1910 period, and were used by both large and small businesses.

**References:** Denis Alsford, *Match Holders, 100 Years of Ingenuity,* Schiffer Publishing, 1994; Roger Fresco-Corbu, *Vesta Boxes,* Lutterworth Press, 1983; W. Eugene Sanders, Jr., and Christine C. Sanders, *Pocket Matchsafes, Reflections of Life & Art, 1840-1920,* Schiffer Publishing, 1997; Audrey G. Sullivan, *History of Match Safes in the United States*, published by author, 1978.

**Collectors' Club:** International Match Safe Association, P.O. Box 791, Malaga, NJ 08328-0791, e-mail: IMSA0c@aol.com

**Advisor:** George Sparacio

**Note:** While not all match safes have a striking surface, this is one test, besides size, to distinguish a match safe from a calling card case or other small period boxes. Value are based on match safes being in excellent condition.

AAONMS, Egyptian motif, figural fez, sterling silver, by Simons Bros., 2-5/8" x 1-7/8" ..........................................................350.00

Ally Sloper, figural, push button lid release, plated brass, 2-1/2" x 1-1/2" ......................................................................275.00

Anheuser Busch logo, locomotive with coal car motif, spring lids, nickel plated brass, 3" x 1-5/8" l .......................................235.00

## Reproduction Alert:

Reproduction, copycat, and fantasy match safes abound. Reproductions include Art Nouveau styles, figural/novelty shapes, nudes, and many others. Fantasy and fakes include Jack Daniel's and Coca-Cola. A fantasy nickel plated Jack Daniel's match safe, made in Italy, c1981, originally sold at their store for $17.50. Collectors today value these fantasy match safes at $50.

Many of the sterling match safes are marked "925" or "Sterling 925." Any match safe so marked requires careful inspection. Many period, American match safes have maker's marks, catalog numbers, 925/1000 or other markings. Period English safes have hallmarks. Beware of English reproduction match safes bearing the "DAB" marking. Always verify the date mark on English safes.

Check enameled safes closely. Today's technology allows for the economic faking of enamel motifs on old match safes. Carefully check condition of enameling for tell-tail clues.

Baden Powell, real photo, book shape, vulcanite, 2" x 1-1/2".....175.00

Battleship *Maine*, Havana Harbor, nickel plated brass, 2-5/8" x 1-3/4" ...............120.00

Billiards Motif
  Advertising, E. J. Riley, lithographed tin, 2-1/4" x 3-1/4".....150.00
  Circular, English, sterling silver, 1-1/2" d............900.00

Brunswick Blake Collender Co., slip top, gutta percha, 2-3/4" x 1" ...............185.00

Bryant & May, Sportsman Vesta, lithographed tin, 1-5/8" x 2-3/8" 65.00

Bust, woman, surrounded by scroll designs, Blake, sterling silver, 2-5/8" x 1-3/4"...............100.00

Candle Matches, Vesta socket, orig matches, by Roche Co., Belgium, 3-1/8" x 1-5/8"...............25.00

Champagne Bottle, figural, nickel plated brass, 2-1/4" x 7/8" .....125.00

Champagne Crate, Rd. #166171, nickel plated brass, 2" x 1-3/8" ...350.00

Columbian World's Fair, Ferris Wheel, Administration Building, plated brass, 3" x 1"...............150.00

Creel, figural, brass, 2-1/2" x 1-1/2" x 3/4"...............245.00

Devil Head, surrounded by snakes, sterling silver, 2-1/2" x 1-5/8" ...695.00

Dewey, bullet shaped, aluminum tip, brass body, by Metzger & Riedel, 7/8" x 2-5/8"...............135.00

Domino, figural, cream colored top, dark brown body, vulcanite, 1-7/8" x 1-1/8"...............135.00

Double Faced Man, one side drinking with smile, reverse frowning, sterling silver, 2-1/2" x 1-1/2"...............695.00

Dragon, with tama, figural, brass, 2-3/4" x 1-7/8"...............245.00

Ear of Corn, figural, Columbus medallion, nickel plated, 2-1/2" x 1"...............315.00

Fishing Motif, rod, creel, etc., nickel plated, push button lid release, 2-7/8" x 1-1/8"...............40.00

Geisha Girl, figural, Oriental, patinated brass, 2-1/2" x 1-7/8" ....585.00

Goldstone, rectangular, rounded end, brass trim, 3" x 1-5/8" .....150.00

Indian Chief, sterling silver, by Gorham, B2507, 2-7/8" x 1-3/4" .900.00

Irish Symbols, Iberian harp, shamrock, etc., book shape, bog oak, 2" x 1-1/2"...............115.00

Japanese Mask, figural, flat back, sterling silver, by Lawrence Emanuel, English hallmarks, 2" x 1-3/8"...............1,200.00

Knight in Armor, holding lance, castle background, sterling silver, 2-3/4" x 1-3/8"...............200.00

Lady of the Light, Washington, DC souvenir, brass, 2-1/2" x 1-1/2" ...95.00

Lion motif, sterling silver, saw tooth striker, 2-3/8" x 1-1/2".........210.00

Lisk Company, advertising, multicolored celluloid inserts, nickel plated brass, 2-3/4" x 1-1/2"...............495.00

London Souvenir, celluloid wrapped, color graphics, 2-3/8" x 1-3/8"...............125.00

Louisiana Purchase, 1803-1903, copyright by I.G.K., brass, 2-3/8" x 1-1/4"...............135.00

**Wedding Day/Three Weeks After, by J. Hynman, c1850, tin, 2-7/8" l, 1-7/8" h, $150. Photo courtesy of George Sparacio.**

Mastiff Dog, figural, brass, glass eyes, 2" x 1-3/8".....................395.00

McKinley for President, nickel plated brass, 2-7/8" x 1-1/2" .......250.00

Midnight Sun, applied enameled crest, nickel plated brass, 2-1/4" x 1-5/8"...............75.00

Never-Slip Horseshoes, celluloid wrapped, color graphics, by Whitehead & Hoag, 2-3/4" x 1-1/2"...............165.00

Order of Odd Fellows, insert type, nickel plated brass, 2-3/4" x 1-1/2"...............90.00

Padlock, figural, trick type, sterling silver, by A. Winston, English hallmarks, 2" x 1-1/8"...............475.00

Pants (overalls), figural, pewter, 2-7/8" x 1-1/4"...............125.00

Rattle Snakes, intertwined, bold design, by Kerr, sterling silver, 2-3/4" x 1-5/8"...............735.00

Royal Arcanum motif, insert type, by Aug. Goertz, nickel plated brass, 2-3/4" x 1-1/2"...............100.00

Saddle and Polo Mallet, quasi-figural, silver plate, 2-1/2" x 1-1/2" ...195.00

Scientific American Newspaper, figural, by Richardson, sterling silver with enameled stamp, 2-3/8" x 1-1/8"...............595.00

Shoe, figural, hobnailed type, .800 silver, 1-3/8" x 2-1/8"...........325.00

Skin-Like motif, by Pairpoint, silver plated, 2-1/2" x 1-1/2".........125.00

Teddy Bears, dancing, advertising, insert type, by Aug. Goertz, nickel plated brass, 2-3/4" x 1-1/2"...............250.00

Tiger Lady, sterling silver, by Gorham, #B3612, 2-3/4" x 1-1/2"..625.00

Unity, patented cigar cutter, by Horton Allday, sterling silver, 2" x 1-3/8"...............185.00

Venus Rising, German silver, 2-5/8" x 1-5/8"...............85.00

Washington/HMMBA, sterling silver, by Gorham #MDS, 2-1/2" x 1-5/8"...............250.00

Wedding Day, Three Weeks After, by J. Hynam, c1850, tin, 1-7/8" x 2-7/8"...............150.00

# McCOY POTTERY

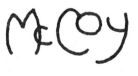

**History:** The J. W. McCoy Pottery Co. was established in Roseville, Ohio, in September 1899. The early McCoy company produced both stoneware and some art pottery lines, including Rosewood. In October 1911, three potteries merged creating the Brush-McCoy Pottery Co. This firm continued to produce the original McCoy lines and added several new art lines. Much of the early pottery is not marked.

In 1910, Nelson McCoy and his father, J. W. McCoy, founded the Nelson McCoy Sanitary Stoneware Co. In 1925, the McCoy family sold their interest in the Brush-

**Dewey, bullet shape, aluminum tip, brass body, by Mezger & Riedel, 2-5/8" l, 7/8" d, $135. Photo courtesy of George Sparacio.**

McCoy Pottery Co. and started to expand and improve the Nelson McCoy Co. The new company produced stoneware, earthenware specialties, and artware.

**Marks:** Most of the pottery marked "McCoy" was made by the Nelson McCoy Co.

**References:** Susan and Al Bagdade, *Warman's American Pottery and Porcelain*, 2nd ed., Krause Publications, 2000; Bob Hanson, Craig Nissen and Margaret Hanson, *McCoy Pottery, Collector's Reference*, Collector Books, Vol. I, 1996, Vol. II, 1999; Sharon and Bob Huxford, *Collector's Encyclopedia of Brush-McCoy Pottery*, Collector Books, 1996; ——, *Collectors Encyclopedia of McCoy Pottery*, Collector Books, Vol. I, 1980, 1999 value update; Martha and Steve Sanford, *Sanfords' Guide to Brush-McCoy Pottery*, Book 2, Adelmore Press (230 Harrison Ave., Campbell, CA 95008), 1996; ——, *Sanfords' Guide to McCoy Pottery,* Adelmore Press, 1997; Jeffrey B. Snyder, *McCoy Pottery,* Schiffer Publishing, 1999.

**Periodicals:** *NMXpress*, 8934 Brecksville Road, Suite 406, Brecksville, OH 44141-2318, http://www.members.aol.com/nmxpress./nmxpress.htm.

**Additional Listings:** See *Warman's Americana & Collectibles* for more examples.

Basket, 7-1/2" x 8-1/2", brown, detailed molding ........................... 25.00
Beanpot, cov, 6" d, 6" h, Suburbia Ware, brown, blue lid.............. 40.00
Bookends, pr, Yellow Dog, #205 ..................................................... 95.00
Bowl, blue, bird ................................................................................ 30.00
Candleholder, bisque, cobalt blue................................................... 40.00
Cookie Jar
    Bugs Bunny, cylinder ........................................................ 185.00
    Happy Face .......................................................................... 75.00
    Indian ................................................................................. 245.00
    Kissing Penguins ................................................................ 50.00
    Nabisco, some wear to paint at rim .................................... 70.00
    Puppy with sign, 1961 ......................................................... 60.00
    Teepee, slant lid............................................................... 350.00
    WC Fields .......................................................................... 250.00
Creamer and Sugar
    Elmer and Elsie................................................................... 90.00
    Sunburst, gold orig paper inventory tags .......................... 125.00
Decanter, Pierce Arrow ................................................................... 90.00
Dresser Caddy, buffalo..................................................................... 55.00

Flower Pot, saucer, hobnail and leaf............................................... 40.00
Frog, 8" l, naturalistically colored ................................................. 165.00
Hanging Basket
    Pine Cone Rustic ................................................................ 40.00
    Yellow, chain ....................................................................... 35.00
Hanging Strawberry Jar, chain......................................................... 40.00
Jardiniere
    Blended glaze, 12" h ........................................................... 90.00
    Nasturtiums, standard glaze, 7" w, 5" h .............................. 70.00
    Tulips dec, orange and yellow flowers, green leaves, dark to light brown standard glaze, ruffled top, 11" d, 11" h................. 280.00
    Tulips, standard glaze, mkd, 8" h, minor flaking to feet ...... 210.00
    Yellow, 4" h ......................................................................... 35.00
    White, 4" h .......................................................................... 35.00
Lamp
    Boot, no shade.................................................................. 100.00
    Cobweb, bedroom type, pink ............................................... 55.00
    Fireplace, green, #208 ........................................................ 85.00
Lamp Base, orange and yellow iris dec, green leaves, dark standard glaze, orig drill hole, 10" h ...................................................... 190.00
Mug, green...................................................................................... 24.00
Pitcher
    Blue Butterfly ................................................................... 235.00
    Hobnail, pastel blue, 48 oz ............................................... 120.00
    Souvenir, Nassau County G.O.P., 6-1/4" h ......................... 30.00
Planter
    Auto, Birchwood.................................................................. 35.00
    Driftwood, 8-1/2" l, c1957................................................... 40.00
    Duck with egg ..................................................................... 30.00
    Duck with umbrella ........................................................... 130.00
    Parrot, white........................................................................ 36.00
    Pelican, yellow .................................................................... 55.00
    Pirate head ....................................................................... 110.00
    Shoes, #135-1-2 ........................................................... 1,500.00
    Stretching Goat................................................................. 110.00
    Turtle, cold painted ............................................................ 45.00
    Umbrella Carriage, green ................................................. 177.00
    Umbrella Duck .................................................................. 130.00
    Water Lily and Pheasants ................................................... 95.00
Strawberry Jar
    Bird dec ............................................................................. 40.00
    Black, 7" h .......................................................................... 65.00
Tankard
    Green.................................................................................. 60.00
    Standard glaze, green and orange leaves, 11-1/2" h, 6" w. 210.00
Teapot, Leaf and Berry
    Blue................................................................................... 185.00
    Yellow............................................................................... 165.00
Tea Set, Daisy................................................................................. 70.00
Valet
    Eagle................................................................................... 75.00
    Smiling horse, tail brush missing ........................................ 70.00

## Reproduction Alert:

Unfortunately, Nelson McCoy never registered his McCoy trademark, a fact discovered by Roger Jensen of Tennessee. As a result, Jensen began using the McCoy mark on a series of ceramic reproductions made in the early 1990s. While the marks on these recently made pieces copy the original, Jensen made objects which were never produced by the Nelson McCoy Co. The best known example is the Red Riding Hood cookie jar which was originally designed by Hull and also made by Regal China.

The McCoy fakes are a perfect example of how a mark on a piece can be deceptive. A mark alone is not proof that a piece is period or old. Knowing the proper marks and what was and was not made in respect to forms, shapes, and decorative motifs is critical in authenticating a pattern.

**Tea Set, ivy dec, raised "McCoy USA" mark, nick to teapot finial, $45. Photo courtesy of David Rago Auctions.**

Vase and Flower Frog, Onyx ................................................ 50.00
Vase
    Antiqua, strap handle ................................................ 155.00
    Blossom Time, 6-1/2" h ............................................... 45.00
    Cornucopia, 7-1/4" h, green ....................................... 125.00
    Feather, maroon ........................................................ 55.00
    Flowers, green, yellow and orange flowers and leaves, dark
       brown to green ground, standard glaze, imp "232," 5" h, 8" w,
       base chip ............................................................. 80.00
    Pillow, orange and yellow floral dec, orange to brown ground, imp
       "#400," 5" h, 5" w ................................................ 120.00
    Springwood, large ..................................................... 40.00
    Swan, 9-1/2" h, white, gold trim ................................ 350.00
Wall Pocket
    Apple on leaf ............................................................ 50.00
    Bellows ................................................................... 40.00
    Cornucopia basket, green and white ............................ 40.00
    Fan, blue ................................................................. 45.00
    Fan, 24K overlay ...................................................... 40.00
    Fan, white, pink floral ............................................... 60.00
    Figure of woman in bonnet and bow, white, red trim .......... 40.00
    Leaf, blue and pink .................................................. 40.00
    Morning Glory .......................................................... 50.00
    Post Box, green ........................................................ 50.00
    Sunflower, blue ........................................................ 30.00
    Sunflower, yellow, with bird ....................................... 45.00
    Yellow, pink floral dec ............................................... 40.00
Window Box, Pine Cone Rustic ........................................... 35.00

# McKEE GLASS

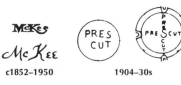

**History:** The McKee Glass Co. was established in 1843 in Pittsburgh, Pennsylvania. In 1852, it opened a factory to produce pattern glass. In 1888, the factory was relocated to Jeannette, Pennsylvania, and began to produce many types of glass kitchenwares, including several patterns of Depression glass. The factory continued until 1951 when it was sold to the Thatcher Manufacturing Co.

McKee named its colors Chalaine Blue, Custard, Seville Yellow, and Skokie Green. McKee glass may also be found with painted patterns, e.g., dots and ships. A few items were decaled. Many of the canisters and shakers were lettered in black to show the purpose for which they were intended.

**References:** Tom and Neila Bredehoft, *Fifty Years of Collectible Glass, 1920-1970, Volume 1, Volume II,* Antique Trader Books, 2000; Gene Florence, *Kitchen Glassware of the Depression Years,* 7th ed., Collector Books, 1995, values updated 1999; ——, *Very Rare Glassware of the Depression Years,* 5th Series, Collector Books, 1997.

**Additional Listings:** See *Warman's Americana & Collectibles* for more examples.

Animal Dish, cov
    Canary, nest base, milk glass .................................... 145.00
    Hen, milk glass, orig eyes ......................................... 140.00
    Rabbit, milk glass .................................................... 170.00
    Squirrel, split rib base, milk glass .............................. 150.00

**Candy Dish, fired orange dec, gold finial and trim, 7-3/4" d, $35.**

Basket, 15-1/2" h, 11" w, cut and pressed, floral and bird with butterfly ......................................................................... 50.00
Bird House, gray body, red roof ........................................ 165.00
Bottoms Up Tumbler, orig coaster, Seville Yellow .............. 180.00
Bowl, 10" l, 6" w, Autumn, Seville Yellow .......................... 85.00
Bread Plate
    Queen pattern, canary yellow .................................... 40.00
    Star Rosetted pattern, "A Good Mother Makes A Happy
      Home" ................................................................. 65.00
Butter Dish, cov
    Eureka pattern, heavy brilliant flint ............................. 75.00
    Gothic pattern, colorless, pyramid shaped finial ............ 50.00
    Queen pattern, canary yellow, domed lid ..................... 85.00
    Strigil pattern, colorless .......................................... 45.00
Cake Stand, Queen pattern, amber ................................... 65.00
Candlesticks, pr, 10" h, crucifix form, Christ figure and "INRI" plaque,
    hexagonal base, colorless ........................................ 125.00
Candy Dish, cov, 7-3/4" h, orange body, gold trim, gold finial, colorless
    pedestal base ......................................................... 35.00
Castor Set, 3 bottle, toothpick handle ............................... 270.00
Celery Vase, Eugenia pattern, heavy brilliant flint ............... 95.00
Cereal Bowl, Laurel, white, red trim .................................. 12.00
Champagne, colorless, heavy brilliant flint
    Eugenia .................................................................. 90.00
    Eureka ................................................................... 90.00
Cheese and Cracker Set, Rock Crystal, red ....................... 225.00
Clock, Daisy and Button pattern, tambour shape, blue .......... 495.00
Compote
    Queen pattern, apple green ....................................... 85.00
    Star Rosetted pattern, colorless, 8-1/2" d .................... 70.00
Cordial, colorless, heavy brilliant flint
    Eugenia pattern ....................................................... 90.00
    Eureka pattern ......................................................... 85.00
Creamer
    Comet pattern, colorless ........................................... 55.00
    Gothic pattern, ruby stain ......................................... 65.00
    Laurel, white, red trim .............................................. 15.00
    Masonic pattern, colorless ........................................ 45.00
    Queen pattern, canary yellow .................................... 45.00
    Strigil pattern, colorless ........................................... 35.00
Cup and Saucer, Laurel, white, red trim ............................. 15.00
Decanter Set, decanter, six whiskey glasses, pink ground,
    ring dec ................................................................. 125.00
Fruit Bowl, 12" d, Colonial pattern, caramel ....................... 140.00
Goblet
    French Ivory ............................................................ 40.00
    Gothic pattern, ruby stain ......................................... 65.00
    Puritan pattern, pink stem ......................................... 35.00
    Rock Crystal, amber ................................................. 30.00
Grapefruit Bowl, Rock Crystal, red .................................... 45.00
Grill Plate, Laurel, Skokie Green, 3 parts ........................... 25.00

Iced Tea Tumbler, Rock Crystal, red ............................ 35.00
Jelly Compote, Gothic pattern, colorless, scalloped rim ..... 20.00
Lamp
    Dance de Lumierre, green ..................................... 750.00
    Eugenia pattern, heavy brilliant flint, whale oil burner ........ 165.00
    Ribbed Tulip pattern, 9-1/2" h, colorless font, milk glass
      base ....................................................................... 125.00
Measuring Cup
    Glassbake, 4 cup, crystal, red lettering ................ 25.00
    Red ships, white ground ...................................... 28.00
    Seville Yellow, red dots, 2 cup ............................. 55.00
Mixing Bowl, 7" d, Red Ships ....................................... 40.00
Mug, Bottoms Down, Seville Yellow .............................. 150.00
Mustard Bottle, Eugenia pattern, heavy brilliant flint ....... 35.00
Pepper Bottle, Eugenia pattern, heavy brilliant flint ........ 30.00
Pickle Dish, oval
    Queen pattern, blue ............................................ 25.00
    Star Rosetted, colorless ...................................... 20.00
Pin Tray, hand shape, milk glass .................................. 20.00
Pitcher
    Aztec pattern, 5" h, colorless .............................. 20.00
    Gothic pattern, colorless ..................................... 75.00
    Queen pattern, blue ............................................ 85.00
    Yutec, Eclipse, marked "Prescut" ........................ 45.00
Plate
    Holly pattern, 8" d, Skokie Green ........................ 12.00
    Laurel, 9-1/2" d, white, red trim ........................... 20.00
    Serenade pattern, 6-3/8" d, opaque white ........... 60.00
Platter, 10-3/4" l, Laurel, white, red trim ...................... 30.00
Punch Bowl Set, bowl, 12 mugs, Tom and Jerry, red scroll dec ... 65.00
Reamer, Sunkist, Seville Yellow .................................... 95.00
Refrigerator Dish
    5" l, 4" w, Skokie Green, Greek Key design .......... 40.00
    8" l, 5" w, Skokie Green ...................................... 65.00
    Relish
    Hickman, 8" l, green, gold trim ............................. 30.00
    Prescut, milk glass ............................................. 25.00
Rolling Pin, Chalaine Blue, orig shaker ends and cork insert ........ 3,400.00
Salt and Pepper Shakers, pr
    Red Dots, Seville Yellow ground .......................... 75.00
    Roman Arches, black ........................................... 60.00
Sauce
    Gothic pattern, ruby stain .................................... 20.00
    Strigil pattern, colorless ....................................... 8.00
Sandwich Server, 10-1/2" d, Brocade, pink, center handle ........ 50.00
Soup Bowl, 7-7/8" d, Laurel, white, red trim .................. 45.00
Spooner
    Queen pattern, amber ......................................... 35.00
    Strigil pattern, colorless ...................................... 20.00
Sugar Bowl, cov
    Comet pattern, colorless ..................................... 55.00
    Laurel pattern, Skokie Green ............................... 15.00
    Masonic pattern, colorless ................................... 45.00
    Queen pattern, canary yellow .............................. 45.00
    Strigil pattern, colorless ...................................... 35.00
Sugar Shaker, Chalaine Blue ....................................... 125.00
Toothbrush Holder, Skokie Green ................................. 20.00
Toothpick Holder, figural, hat shape, vaseline ............... 35.00
Tumbler
    Gladiator pattern, cobalt blue, gold trim ............... 50.00
    Gothic pattern, colorless ..................................... 35.00
    Queen pattern, blue ............................................ 45.00
    Ribbed Palm pattern, colorless ............................ 70.00
    Sextec, colorless, 4" h, flat ................................. 20.00
Vase
    7-1/2" h, Brocade, crystal, two handles, gold trim ........ 50.00
    10" h, Hickman, green, gold trim .......................... 65.00
Vegetable Bowl, 9" l, oval, Laurel, white, red trim .......... 45.00
Window Box, 5" x 9", lion, Skokie Green ....................... 85.00

# MEDICAL and PHARMACEUTICAL ITEMS

**History:** Modern medicine and medical instruments are well documented. Some instruments are virtually unchanged since their invention; others have changed drastically.

The concept of sterilization phased out decorative handles. Handles on early instruments, which were often carved, were made of materials such as mother-of-pearl, ebony, and ivory. Today's sleek instruments are not as desirable to collectors.

Pharmaceutical items include those things commonly found in a drugstore and used to store or prepare medications.

**References:** A. Walker Bingham, *Snake-Oil Syndrome: Patent Medicine Advertising*, Christopher Publishing House, 1994; Douglas Congdon-Martin, *Drugstore and Soda Fountain Antiques*, Schiffer Publishing, 1991; Patricia McDaniel, *Drugstore Collectibles*, Wallace-Homestead, 1994; J. William Rosenthal, *Spectacles and Other Vision Aids*, Norman Publishing (720 Market St., 3rd Fl., San Francisco, CA 94102), 1996; Keith Wilbur, *Antique Medical Instruments*: Revised 4th ed., Schiffer Publishing, 2000.

**Periodical:** *Scientific, Medical & Mechanical Antiques*, 11824 Taneytown Pike, Taneytown, MD 21787.

**Collectors' Clubs:** Maryland Microscopical Society, 8621 Polk St., McLean, VA 22102; Medical Collectors Association, 1685A Eastchester Rd, Bronx, NY 10461.

**Museums:** Dittrick Museum of Medical History, Cleveland, OH; International Museum of Surgical Science & Hall of Fame, Chicago, IL; National Museum of Health & Medicine, Walter Reed Medical Center, Washington, DC; National Museum of History and Technology, Smithsonian Institution, Washington, DC; Schmidt Apothecary Shop, New England Fire & History Museum, Brewster, MA; Waring Historical Library, Medical University of South Carolina, Charleston, SC.

Advertising
    Diecut, 17" h, 11-1/2" w, emb cardboard, center young lady, message about painless dental extracting, matted, framed .... 800.00
    Poster, 16-1/4" h, 22" l, International Worm Powder, International Stock Food Co., MN, paper litho, multicolored illus with white horse in center ............... 1,100.00
    Print, 10-1/4" h, 6" w image, Use Dr. H. W. Clouds Invigorating Cordial (Ague tonic), Victorian lady in green dress holding flowers, framed .................. 50.00
    Tray, Hicks Capudine Liquid, flying cherubs around package .................. 75.00
Book
    *Leonard's Illustrated Medical Journal*, Vol. 5, No. 1, Quarterly, Illus. Medical Journal Co., Detroit, MI, c1884, 18 pgs, 11" x 16", all paper, illustrated articles on hare-lip, urinalysis, medication, Bright's disease, local medication, etc., lots of ads, , tears at binding, some tears at fold in horizontal center ............. 24.00
    *Pancoast's System of Anatomy,* Caspar Wistar, MD., Thomas, Cowperthwait & Co., Philadelphia, 8th edition, 1842, 5-3/4" x 6" .................. 85.00

*The History of the Great Plaque of 1665,* intro by Rev. H. Stebbing, printed by J. F. Dove, St. John's Square, London, 1832, 304 pgs .......................................................... 125.00

*Wilson's Human Anatomy,* Erasmum Wilson, MD., Lea & Blanchard, Philadelphia, 1849 ................................ 95.00

Box, 9" h, 6-1/2" w, Drs. Starkey and Panel Compound Oxygen, wood, dovetailed, brass catch, paper labels showing woman taking oxygen from a bottle ........................................................ 100.00

Display Case, 12-1/2" h, 22" l, 27" d, Dr. Johnson's Celebrated Remedies, Collins Ague Cure, Collins Bro's Drug Co., Sole Prop's Saint Louis, MO, curved corner German silver case, name etched on inside of glass, back door mirror missing ........................ 2,600.00

Dissectable Eye-Ball, composition, colorfully painted, celluloid tag reads "F. E. Becker and Co., Hatton Wall, London" ................ 575.00

Jar, colorless glass, orig stopper

6-1/2" h, "Dr. Pierce's Pleasant Pellets," squatty rect, etched name, three packages of "Pierce's Pleasant Purgative Pellets" ...................................................... 350.00

8-1/2" h, "Squibb's Brown Mixt. Lozenges," rect, recessed reverse painted on glass label, mkd "Pat'd Apr 2, 1889," ground stopper with flat top, minor discoloration to label ......................... 200.00

8-3/4" h, "Bromo Bracer Cures Headaches. Sold only by Albert Pick & Co.," rect, painted label, some chips on bottom of lid, minor lip roughness ........................................ 950.00

10-1/2" h, "Duff's Colic & Diarrhoea Remedy," cylindrical, recessed reverse painted on glass label, ground stopper matches pattern at base, some minor staining ................ 250.00

11" h, "Gono Pills - Man's Friend for Gonorrhea, City Drug, Johnson City, Tenn," cylindrical, etched label, ribbed pressed glass lid ............................................ 1,000.00

12" h, "Dent's Toothache Gum," tapered jar, etched label, ribbed pressed glass lid ............................. 550.00

12" h, "Dr. Simmon's Aspirin Laxative Tablets for Pain," beveled corner, reverse painted on glass label, chip on lid, small crack in glass label ...................................... 450.00

12" h, "Foley's Kidney Pills," reverse painted on glass label, black printing on orange background, orig contents, some color loss and fogging to label around edges, lid cracked ............... 600.00

16-1/2" h, "Dr. Miles Anti-Pain Pills Cure Headache," beveled corners, reverse painted on glass label, ground lid with swirled design, chip on upper rim, minor discoloration to corners of label ........................................ 650.00

Letter, from doctor to another doctor, 1835, describes use of leeches, politics, tools ...................................... 125.00

Magazine, 5-3/4"x 9",Wilmington Dental Mfg., Co., Philadelphia, PA, c1894, 102 pgs, Vol XVI, No. 6, June, "Items of Interest," monthly magazine of dental related items, plus cut of equipment and supplies-Snow's Spring Mallet, Kott's Hot Air syringe, gum lancets, dentimeter, dental cabinets, forceps, etc. ....................... 20.00

Pill Machine, 7-1/2" w, 15" l base, grooved wood top and base, brass construction, c1870 .......................................... 225.00

Portable Spittoon, 2" d, 4" h, Dr. Dettweiler's, cobalt blue glass body, nickel plate top and base, raised lettering on both sides, c1900 ...................................................... 375.00

Shadowbox Frame, containing chromolithograph advertising poster, "President Garfield and Cabinet, Warner's Safe Pills," two old business cards of B. F. Phillips, druggist and jeweler, North Jackson, Ohio, walnut frame, 9-1/4" h, 25-1/4" w ..................... 275.00

Sign

4-1/2" h, 5-1/2" w, Lavoris, emb tin, easel back, orig envelope, shows white jaw, red lettering, black background, white border ....... 300.00

9-1/4" h, 7" w, D. B. Cough Drops, D. Bacon Co., Harrisburg, PA, diecut, little girl leaning on counter .................. 140.00

12-1/2" h, 41" l, C. F. Hussey Optometrist, zinc, double sided, polychrome and gilt dec, figural eyeglasses, name and title in banner at base, late 19th C, imperfections ................ 2,650.00

17" h, 17" l, Dr. Drake's German Cough Remedy, two sided diecut cardboard, hanging, figural white duck ................ 1,600.00

18" h, 14" w, Dr. Trovillion, Skin Diseases and Skin Cancer, gold letters, black galvanized metal ground, double sided, worn decoration .......................................... 45.00

19" h, 16" w, Dr. L. Ray Temple, Dentist, gold letters, black sanded background, wood frame .......................... 35.00

20-1/2" h, 17-3/4" w, Dr. Sweet's Bone Setter Liniment, detailed graphics, matted and framed ............................ 500.00

21-1/4" h, 15-1/4" w, Humphrey's Specifics, framed tin, trademark bare breasted lady with lion, orig ornate frame emb "Humphreys" .................................. 4,700.00

22" h, 23-3/4" l, Dr. Bell Wonder Medicine Co., diecut cardboard, horse, some minor damage .......................... 190.00

25" h, 18-1/4" w, Dr. Pierce's Golden Medical Discovery, paper litho, two young Indian maidens preparing herbs for "Spring Time for the Blood," crude mortar and pestles, framed.... 350.00

26-1/2" h, 33" w, Perry Davis Pain Killer, paper litho, early graphics, some professional stain removal, orig frame, new matting ................................................ 425.00

Tin

3" l, 3" w, 1" h, Dr. Dick's Gail Cure, Pecan Oil Mfg. Co., Davenport, IA, farmer and plow horses in field ........................... 275.00

4" h, 2-1/4" w, 1-3/4" d, Skyes Comfort Talcum Powder, two little girls on front, nurse on back ................................ 275.00

4-1/2" h, 2-1/4" w, Hemstreet's Antiseptic Foot Powder, unused, black illus on tan ground ................................ 600.00

4-1/2" h, 2-1/2" w, Royce's Talcum Powder, Abner Royce Co., Cleveland, tin litho, baby in center .......................... 300.00

6" h, 3" w, 1/2" d, Dr. Tepper's Gum Lyke, Industrial Rubber Corp, shows dentures on front .................................. 500.00

8" h, 5-1/8" w, F. W. 5¢ Cough Tablets, Geo. Miller & Son, Phila., graphics of woman and ornate script, yellow ground, 1880's .................................................. 1,700.00

Tip Tray

3-1/2" d, Luden's Cough Drop, 5¢ package ...................... 400.00

4-1/4" d, titled "The Great Eye Remedy," cherub placing eye drops in lady's eye, H. D. Beach Co. Litho, minor rim chips .................................................. 110.00

5" l, 3-3/4" h, Sheldon Optical, titled "But the play that caused the biggest laugh was Teddy-G on a big giraffe," shows Roosevelt Bear humorously riding giraffe, scalloped rim with multiple Roosevelt Bears, copyright 1906 .................... 225.00

Trade Sign

26-1/4" l, 11-1/2" l, polychrome dec, cast iron and zinc, double sided, opthometrist's, shaped like pinz-nose glasses, "Glasses Fitted on one lens," "Eyes Tested" on other, wear, old paint retouches .......................................... 4,320.00

28" w, 17-1/2" h, "Dr. A. C. Daniels, Horse Cat Dog Medicines For Home Treatment," emb tin, white lettering on dark blue ground ............................................. 210.00

36" h, mortar and pestle, sheet zinc, old worn gilt paint, traces of black on top and bottom, dents, contemporary wood stand .............................................. 770.00

Veterinary Cabinet, counter type display case

27-3/4" h, 20" w, 10-1/4" d, Humphrey's Remedies, tin front lists remedies, seven different unopened remedies in cabinet, some damage ............................................ 400.00

33" h, 16-1/2" l, 7" d, Pratt Remedies, oak, emb tin front with trademark logo of horse's head, lists products, some damage ............................................ 700.00

Veterinarian Emergency Medicine Kit, 8" h, 12-1/2" l, 6-1/2" d, Dr. Daniel's, trimmed oak box, paper label inside describing contents, unused ...................................................... 1,200.00

# MEDICINE BOTTLES

**History:** The local apothecary and his book of formulas played a major role in early America. In 1796 the first patent for a medicine was issued by the U.S. Patent Office. At that time, anyone could apply for a medicinal patent; as long as the dosage was not poisonous, the patent was granted.

Patent medicines were advertised in newspapers and magazines and sold through the general store and at "medicine" shows. In 1907, the Pure Food and Drug Act, requiring an accurate description of contents on a medicine container's label, put an end to the patent medicine industry. Not all medicines were patented.

Most medicines were sold in distinctive bottles, often with the name of the medicine and location of manufacture in relief. Many early bottles were made in the glass-manufacturing area of southern New Jersey. Later, companies in western Pennsylvania and Ohio manufactured bottles.

**References:** Joseph K. Baldwin, *Collector's Guide to Patent and Proprietary Medicine Bottles of the Nineteenth Century*, Thomas Nelson, 1973; Ralph and Terry Kovel, *Kovels' Bottles Price List*, 11th ed., Three Rivers Press, 1998; John Odell, *Digger Odell's Official Antique Bottle and Glass Collector Magazine Price Guide Series*, Vol. 5, published by author (1910 Shawhan Rd, Morrow, OH 45152), 1995.

**Periodical:** Antique Bottle and Glass Collector, P.O. Box 187, East Greenville, PA 18041.

**Collectors' Club:** Federation of Historical Bottle Collectors, Inc., 88 Sweetbriar Branch, Longwood, FL 32750.

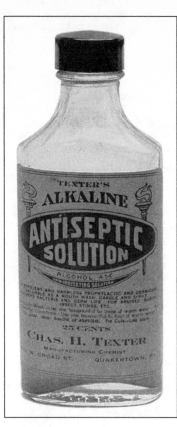

Texter's Alkaline Antiseptic Solution, 25 cents, Chas. H. Texter, manufacturing chemist, paper label, blue letters, 5-1/2" h, 2-1/4" w, $5.

Baker's Vegetable Blood & Liver Cure, Lookout Mountain Medicine Co. Manufacturers & Proprietors, Greenville, Tenn, oval, tooled mouth, smooth base, reddish amber, c1880-90, minor content stain, 9-7/8" h ............................385.00

Bateman's, hand blown cylinder, applied reverse painted label, some light crazing to label, 10" h, slight in-making imperfections in bottle ................................70.00

Bennetts Hyssop Cure Stockport, rect, aqua, sunken panel, 5-1/2" h ................................30.00

Black Swamp Syrup, colorless, light staining on orig label, orig contents, 7" h ................................50.00

Budwell's Emulsion of Cod Liver Oil No. 2 with Guaiacoil and Creosote Carbonate, Budwell Pharmacal Co., Lynchburg, Va, oval, tooled mouth, "W. T. & Co., U.S.A. Pat Jan 18 1898" on smooth base, deep cobalt blue, c1890-1900, 8" h, dug ................................190.00

Cook's Balm of Life, oval, strap sides, tooled mouth, smooth base, light cobalt blue, c1880-90, 8-1/4" h ................................175.00

Dr. Davis's Depurative, Phila, sq, beveled corners, applied sloping collar mouth, iron pontil, medium bluish-green, c1845-55, 9-3/4" h .....2,980.00

Dr. Henley's Celery, Beef and Iron, C B & I Extract Co., America, 1884-94, amber, tooled top, smooth base, 9-1/4" h ................................120.00

Dr. M. M. Fenner's Peoples Remedies, Fredonia, NY, Kidney & Backache Cure, oval, tooled mouth, smooth base, medium amber, c1890-1900, 98% orig label, contents, tax stamp, box, orig contents, 10" h ......385.00

Dr. Phelp's-Arcanum-Genuine, deep olive amber hexagonal form, blown molded, c1830-45, 8-1/4" h, chips to collar and base, mold roughness ................................3,450.00

Dr. R. Parker S. F., Indian Tla, Quillaugh's Balsam, cylindrical, applied mouth and smooth base, copper shading light to dark from shoulder, c1864-67, 8-1/2" h ................................ 11,650.00

Dr. Roback Swedish Remedy, C. W. Roback, MD, America, 1840-60, octagonal, bright aquamarine, applied sq collared mouth, pontil scar, 4-1/2" h ................................140.00

Dr. Rookes Rheumatic Lixile, dense cobalt blue, slope shouldered rect, double collar, three sunken panels, 5" h ................................50.00

Dr. S. Arnold's Balsam, eight sided, flared lip, open pontil, pale aqua, c1845-55, 2-3/8" h ................................180.00

Elipizone A Safe Cure For Fits & Epilepsy H. C. Root London, aqua, rect, emb front panel, 6-1/2" h ................................55.00

G. W. Stone's Liquid Cathartic & Family Physic, Lowell, Mass, rect, beveled corners, three identified panels, applied double collar mouth, smooth base, root beer amber, c1850-60, 8-7/8" h ............... 9,625.00

Hicks' Capudine Cure, brown cylinder, recessed reverse painted label with name, and man's head above trademark, ground stopper with flat top, 8-3/4" h, two cracks on label, some edge chips .......... 325.00

Iceland Balsam For Pulmonary Consumption, Iceland Balsam, America, 1830-50, rect, beveled corners, emb on 3 sides, yellow olive, short applied sloping collared mouth, pontil scar, 6-1/2" h, professionally cleaned, light emb lettering ................................ 5,500.00

Kimball's Anodyne Toothache Drops, Troy, NH, olive green, three pc mold, cylinder, pontil scarred base, 9" h ................................ 425.00

O. K. Plantation, triangular, amber, 11" h ................................ 200.00

Morrow's Kid-Ne-Oids, paper label showing man bent over with pain, cork closure, 2-3/4" h ................................ 50.00

Phelp's Arcanum Worcester, Mass, olive amber cylinder, blown molded, recess panel, c1830-45, 8-1/2" h, minor mold imperfection to base ................................ 1,380.00

Radium Radia, colorless, colorful graphic label wraps around 3 sides, orig contents, 5-1/4" h ................................ 210.00

Roshoton & Aspinwall, new York, Compound Chlorine Tooth Wash, golden olive, flared top, pontil, 6" h ................................ 250.00

Rushton Clark & Co, Chemist's New York, aqua, applied top, open pontil, 9-1/2" h ................................ 100.00

Sanderson's Blood Renovator Milton VT, America, 1840-60, oval, aquamarine, applied sq collared mouth, pontil scar, 8-1/8""h, very minor, ext. high point wear ................................ 650.00

Security Rheumatic Liniment, colorless, colorful graphic label wraps around 3 sides, orig contents, orig box (top missing), 7-1/2" h 325.00

Shaker Anodyne, NTH, Enfield, NH, aqua, front and rear labels, orig contents, 4" h ................................ 250.00

Shaker Digestive Cordial/AJ White New York, aqua, orig front and rear labels, orig contents, 5-1/2" h ................................ 110.00

Smith's Anodyne Cough Drops Montpelier, America, 1840-60, rect, beveled corners, aquamarine, applied sloping collared mouth, pontil scar, 5-7/8" l ................................ 140.00

Sun Drug Co, Los Angeles, CA, America, 1890-1905, light amber, tooled top, smooth base, winged mortar and pestle motif, 5-3/4" h ......... 175.00

Swaim's Panacea, Genuine, Philadelphia, rect, applied sloping collar mouth, open pontil, medium yellow-olive, c1840-50, 7-3/4" h..865.00
The Calqueur, Quehen & Smith, pillar with sunken panels on 4 sides, cobalt blue...............30.00
Thymo Borine, rect, emb "Thymo Borine" on one side, recessed reverse painted on glass label on other side adv "Thymo Borine The True Antiseptic," ground stopper with flat top, 5-1/2" h...........200.00
True Daff's Elixir, England, 1830-50, rect, beveled edges, yellow green, applied ring lip, bail pontil base, 4-7/8" h.............360.00
Use Pritchard's Teething Powders, aqua, rect, emb front panel, 3-1/2" l..............12.00
Warner's Safe Cure, London
    Olive green, pint...............90.00
    Yellow amber, heavy embossing, half pint...........45.00
Warner's "Tinct.Kino," pedestal cylinder, oval applied reverse painted label, pedestal emb "Pat'd Sept. 18, 1875, W. R. Warner & Co.," 9" h, crack, some chipping around edge of label............250.00
White Rose Extract, cylinder, colorful applied reverse painted label, pedestal base emb "W. R. Warner & Co., Pat'd Sept. 18, 1875," 10-1/2" h...........600.00
Whitwell's Liquid Improved Opodeloc, cylindrical, colorless, emb, sloping flanged lip, pontil, two part mold, 4-5/8" h...........110.00

# MERCURY GLASS

**History:** Mercury glass is a light-bodied, double-walled glass that was "silvered" by applying a solution of silver nitrate to the inside of the object through a hole in its base.

F. Hale Thomas of London patented the method in 1849. In 1855, the New England Glass Co. filed a patent for the same type of process. Other American glassmakers soon followed. The glass reached the height of its popularity in the early 20th century.

Atomizer, colored floral bud shaped glass stopper.........50.00
Bottle, 7-1/2" h, 4-1/4"d, bulbous, flashed amber panel cut neck, etched grapes and leaves dec, corked metal stopper, c1840..175.00
Bowl, 6" d, enameled white floral dec...........45.00
Candlesticks, pr, 6-1/4" h, gold, minor wear.........95.00
Carafe, 12" h, 5-1/2" d, mushroom stopper, dated 1909.........65.00
Compote, 7" h, 6-1/2" d, enameled white floral dec, gold luster int. ...65.00

**Candy Dish, silver, clear glass lid, 8-1/4" h, $35.**

Creamer, 6" h, etched grapevine dec, applied colorless handle. 115.00
Cup and Saucer, etched floral dec...........65.00
Curtain Tieback, 2-5/8" d, pewter fitting, starflower dec...........65.00
Garniture, 14" h, baluster, raised circular molded foot, everted rim, enameled foliate motif...........215.00
Goblet
    6-7/8" h, silver, etched Vintage pattern, gold luster int.........65.00
    7-1/2" h, Ivy pattern, engraved grape leaves and grapes...145.00
Mug, 2-7/8" h, silver, applied colorless handle...........35.00
Perfume Bottle, emerald green ground, cut and enameled dec, orig stopper...........225.00
Pitcher, 12-1/2" h, bulbous, applied colorless handle.........185.00
Reflecting Globe, 10" d, silver int., rests on white columnar form satin glass base, 19th C, minor silver loss, base chip, pr.........450.00
Salt, 3 x 3", price for pr...........100.00
Spooner, 4-1/2" h, silver, etched vintage dec, gold int. .........120.00
Sweetmeat Dish, cov, 4" d, 7-1/2" h, pedestal base, colorless cov....50.00
Tazza, 5-3/4" d, 2-3/4" h, etched birds and leaves dec............75.00
Toothpick Holder
    3-1/2" h, gold, pedestal base...........40.00
    5" h, gold, pedestal base, etched ferns...........45.00
Urn, 13" h, baluster, mkd "Harnish & Co. London"...........250.00
Vase
    6-1/4" h, cylindrical, ring dec at top and above pedestal foot, hp flowers, some loss of silvering...........125.00
    8" h, cut to show emerald glass ground, mkd "Harnish & Co. London Pat."...........115.00
    8-7/8" h, silver, minor wear...........145.00
    10-1/2" h, cylindrical, hand painted floral and leaf band around center...........125.00
    12" h, ribbed, emerald green, enameled floral and bird dec145.00
    12" h, 5" d, cylindrical, gold...........145.00
    13" h, trumpet shape, enameled panel of orange, yellow, green, and blue floral clusters and butterflies...........220.00
Walking Stick, 42-1/2" l, red, blue, yellow, and silver swirls, some wear to silvering...........200.00
Witch Ball, emerald green, attached base...........185.00

# METTLACH

**History:** In 1809, Jean Francis Boch established a pottery at Mettlach in Germany's Moselle Valley. His father had started a pottery at Septfontaines in 1767. Nicholas Villeroy began his pottery career at Wallerfanger in 1789.

In 1841, these three factories merged. They pioneered underglaze printing on earthenware, using transfers from copper plates, and also were among the first companies to use coal-fired kilns. Other factories were developed at Dresden, Wadgassen, and Danischburg. Mettlach decorations include relief and etched designs, prints under the glaze, and cameos.

**Marks:** The castle and Mercury emblems are the two chief marks although secondary marks are known. The base of each piece also displays a shape mark and usually a decorator's mark.

**References:** Susan and Al Bagdade, *Warman's English & Continental Pottery & Porcelain*, 3rd Edition, Krause Publications, 1998; Gary Kirsner, *Mettlach Book*, 3rd ed., Glentiques (P.O. Box 8807, Coral Springs, FL 33075), 1994.

**Periodical:** *Beer Stein Journal*, P.O. Box 8807, Coral Springs, FL 33075.

**Collectors' Clubs:** Stein Collectors International, 281 Shore Dr., Burr Ridge, IL 60521; Sun Steiners, P. O. Box 11782, Fort Lauderdale, FL 33339.

**Additional Listings:** Villeroy & Boch.

**Note:** Prices in this listing are for print-under-glaze pieces unless otherwise specified.

Beaker, #3883/553, 1/4 liter, German man leaning on rifle ........... 90.00
Bowl, 9-1/4" d, 4" h, six-sided, Secessionist-style, stylized trees, blue, ochre, and ivory, imp mark ..................... 500.00
Cigar Holder, figural, boy with basket on back, wearing pointed hat .................... 250.00
Coaster, #2820, etched, college boy holding stein ..................... 200.00
Mug, 5-1/2" h, #1028, half liter, brown tree-trunk ground, relief of may carrying hay while walking with woman, lids and thumbrests missing, set of 8 .................... 50.00
Pitcher
    8-1/2" h, trademark Hires Root Beer boy toasting with tall mug with same image on it, "Join Health and Cheer - Drink Hires Rootbeer," pewter thumb press lid with ceramic insert with image of oak leaf .................... 25,000.00
    13-1/2" h, quarter liter, brown tree-trunk ground, relief of may carrying hay while walking with woman, inlaid lid, pewter rim, and thumbrest, repainted handle .......................... 250.00
Plaque
    #1607, 11" d, etched, ladies representing summer and fall, sgd "Warth, 1893" ..................... 550.00
    #2875, 17-1/2" d, cameo, blue-green, white classical woman and man depicting industry .................... 775.00
Plate, #3096, octagonal, Art Deco design, burnt gold, ream, and royal blue .................... 75.00
Pokal, #2058, monkeys among branches, monkey on lid ........... 775.00
Punch Bowl, underplate, 13" d, 11" h, 16-1/2" d underplate, #2806, two handles, two cameo panels, cover missing ............................ 350.00
Stein
    No. 243B, musicians and dancers, pewter lid, 3.3 liter, pug, c1904, 12-3/4" h ..................... 250.00
    No. 1028, tree trunk body, relief of farmers, inlay lid, 2.3 liter, c1898, 13-1/2" h ..................... 175.00
    No. 1132, man fiddling, crocodile dancing in front of pyramids, inlay lid, half liter, c1896, 6-1/4" h ..................... 300.00
    No. 1675, Heidelberg scene, inlay lid, half liter, c1908, 7-7/8" h, restored .................... 90.00
    No. 1725, lovers scene, inlay lid, quarter liter, c1900, artist sgd "Warth," 5"h .................... 115.00
    No. 1972, four seasons in panels, pewter lid, half liter, c1889, 7-3/4" h, restored .................... 260.00
    No. 1997, George Ehvet Brewer, inlay lid, half liter, c1890, 7-3/4" h .................... 230.00
    No. 2025, cherubs carousing, inlay lid, half liter, c1894, 6-7/8" h .................... 300.00
    No. 2035, Bacchus carousing, inlay lid, half liter, c1891, 6-3/4" h .................... 250.00
    No. 2051, seven students drinking, inlay lid, half liter, c1891, 7-1/4" h .................... 460.00
    No. 2057, peasants dancing, inlay lid, 3/10 liter, c1901, 5-1/4" h .................... 115.00
    No. 2094, musicians and dancers, inlay lid, half liter, c1894, 7" h .................... 415.00
    No. 2107, Gambrinus on throne, jeweled base, inlay lid, 1-1/2 liter, artist sgd "Schlitt," c1897, 13-5/8" h .................... 850.00
    No. 2130, seated man with scepter drinking, inlay lid, half liter, c1895, 8-1/2" h .................... 150.00
    No. 2134, gnome seated in nest, holding two steins, inlay lid, half liter, c1894, 7" h .................... 1,610.00

    No. 2210, tavern and bowling relief scene, blue ground, inlay lid, 3.25 liter, artist sgd "H. Fuchs," 11-1/2" h .................... 200.00
    No. 2230, man and barmaid, inlay lid, half liter, c1910, 7-3/4" h .................... 350.00
    No. 2382, thirsty knight, conical lid, one liter, artist sgd "Schlitt," c1900, 11-1/8" h .................... 700.00
    No. 2401, Tannhouser in the Venusberg, inlay lid, half liter, c1899, 7-1/4" h .................... 575.00
    No. 2401, Tannhouser in the Venusberg, pewter lid, half liter, c1897, 8" h .................... 300.00
    No. 2530, boar hunt, cameo, inlay lid, one liter, early 20$^{th}$ C, 8-3/4" h, restored .................... 115.00
    No. 2607, three panels representing drinking, courting, and music, inlay lid, 2.15 liter, cameo, artist sgd "Schlitt," c1900, 11-7/8" h .................... 275.00
    No. 2639, blacksmith and cavalier drinking, inlay lid, one liter, c1900, 9" h .................... 525.00
    No. 2719, baker occupation crest, etched and glazed, inlay lid, half liter, 7-3/4" h .................... 1,160.00
    No. 2959, boy bowling, inlay lid, half liter, c1905, 7" h ........ 230.00
    No. 3091, knight drinking, inlay lid, one liter, artist sgd "Schlitt," c1906, 8-1/2" h .................... 500.00
Tumbler, #1191, old man in boat with windmill background, quarter liter, set of six, hairlines .................... 100.00
Vase
    9-1/2" h, detailed red and turquoise floral design, blue ground, imp arks .................... 300.00
    10" h, incised and painted geometric red and green design, cream ground, imp marks .................... 500.00
    11-1/2" h, #3040, emb maidens on each of four sides, sgd 200.00

# MILITARIA

**History:** Wars have occurred throughout recorded history. Until the mid-19th century, soldiers often had to provide for their own needs, including supplying their own weapons. Even in the 20th century, a soldier's uniform and some of his gear are viewed as his personal property, even though issued by a military agency.

Conquering armed forces made a habit of acquiring souvenirs from their vanquished foes. They also brought their own uniforms and accessories home as badges of triumph and service.

Saving militaria may be one of the oldest collecting traditions. Militaria collectors tend to have their own special shows and view themselves outside the normal antiques channels. However, they haunt small indoor shows and flea markets in hopes of finding additional materials.

**References:** Robert W. D. Ball, *Collector's Guide to British Army Campaign Medals*, Antique Trader Books, 1996; Thomas Berndt, *Standard Catalog of U.S. Military Vehicles*, Krause Publications, 1993; Ray A. Bows, *Vietnam Military Lore 1959-1973*, Bows & Sons, 1988; Nancy Britton, *A Splendid Little War: Collectibles and Commemoratives of the Spanish-American War, Volume I,* published by author, 1998, (215 N. 8th, Batesville, AR 72501-3404); Gary R. Carpenter, *What's It Worth: A Beginner Collector's Guide to U.S. Army Patches of WW II*, published by author, 1994; W. K. Cross, *Charlton Standard Catalogue of First World War Canadian Corps Badges*, Charlton Press, 1995; ——, *Charlton Standard Catalogue of First World War Canadian Infantry Badges*, 2nd ed., Charlton Press, 1995; Robert Fisch, *Field*

*Equipment of the Infantry 1914-1945*, Greenberg Publications, 1989; Gary Howard, *America's Finest: U.S. Airborne Uniforms, Equipment and Insignia of World War Two* (ETO), Greenhill Books, Stackpole Books, 1994; Martin Jacobs, *World War II Homefront Collectibles*, Krause Publications, 2000; Ron Menchine, *Propaganda Postcards of World War II,* Krause Publications, 2000; Marc Newman, *Civil War Knives,* Paladin Press, 1998.

**Periodicals:** *Men at Arms*, 222 W. Exchange St., Providence, RI 02903; *Militaria Magazine*, P.O. Box 995, Southbury, CT 06488; *Military Collector Magazine*, P.O. Box 245, Lyon Station, PA 19536; *Military Collector News*, P.O. Box 702073, Tulsa, OK 74170; *Military Images*, RD1 Box 99A, Henryville, PA 18332; *Military Trader*, P.O. Box 1050, Dubuque, IA 52004; *North South Trader's Civil War*, P.O. Box Drawer 631, Orange, VA 22960; *Wildcat Collectors Journal*, 15158 NE 6th Ave., Miami, FL 33162; *WWII Military Journal*, P.O. Box 28906, San Diego, CA 92198.

**Collectors' Clubs:** American Society of Military Insignia Collectors, 526 Lafayette Ave., Palmerton, PA 18071; Association of American Military Uniform Collectors, P.O. Box 1876, Elyria, OH 44036; Company of Military Historians, North Main St., Westbrook, CT, 06498; Imperial German Military Collectors Association, 82 Atlantic St., Keyport, NJ 07735; Karabiner Collector's Network, P.O. Box 5773, High Point, NC 27262; Militaria Collectors Society, 137 S. Almar Dr., Ft. Lauderdale, FL 33334; Orders and Medals Society of America, P.O. Box 484, Glassboro, NJ 08028.

**Reproduction Alert:** Pay careful attention to Civil War and Nazi material.

**Additional Listings:** Firearms; Swords. See World War I and World War II in *Warman's Americana & Collectibles* for more examples.

## French and Indian War

Enlistment Document, 1 page small oblong 8vo, Hampshire County, Massachusetts, April 6, 1759, for Ebenezer Warner who volunteered "in the present Expedition forming for the invasion of Canada" ............... 675.00

Powder Horn, scrimshaw dec, bottom of horn engraved "Jonathon Barker, Jonathon, His, A. D. 1760, Horn, Dated At Oswago, July 14, Aug, ...Montreal, September, the 8," other names of places, etc., many figural engravings, pie crust pattern base, base held on by wrought iron tacks, five iron tacks missing ............................ 4,500.00

## Revolutionary War

Autograph, Benedict Arnold, ALS, 2 pages folio, London, April 30, 1787, writing for assistance with business affairs, detailing travel plans from London to St. John, Canada, insight into scorn and financial difficulties .................................................................... 6,800.00

Broadside, 1 page small folio, Hartford, Nov. 29, 1780, printed by Hudson & Goodwin, recruiting Connecticut regiment of 575 soldiers ......1,200.00

Document Signed

    Bond, 1-1/3 pages small folio, Cambridge, Massachusetts, Nov. 4, 1777, to Seth Sumner to supply provisions to British brought to Boston Market, sgd by Sumner and several witnesses .....1,250.00

    Commission, 1 page oblong small folio, Boston, July 13, 1780, to David Holbrook as Captain of 4th Regiment of Foot, sgd by James Bowdoin as President of the Mass Provincial Council, intact MA paper seal ..................................................... 975.00

Oath of Allegiance, partially printed, 6-1/4" x 2-3/4" oblong, printed in Lancaster, PA, "...voluntarily taken and subscribed by the Oak Affirmation of Allegiance and Fidelity, as directed by an Act of General Assembly of Pennsylvania, passed the 13th Day of June, A.D. 1777" ........................................................ 275.00

Pay Voucher, part printed, part manuscript, approx. 6-1/2" x 7 1/2", sgd by "Jed[ediah] Huntington, Major General in the Continental Army," 1789 ............................................................ 75.00

Map, Battle of Long Island, William Faden, London, Oct. 19, 1776, double page, engraved battle plan, supporting letterpress text, 525 x 440 mm, sheet measuring 765 x 550 mm, wide margins, hand colored, browned along horizontal fold .................. 3,680.00

Powder Horn

    14-1/4" l, covered with scrimshawed scenes of shipping and buildings, long thin banner engraved "Prince Hamblen His Horn Made In The Year 1780," year going around at right angle, 2-3/4" wooden base plug well carved in swirled pattern ............ 1,200.00

    15" l, medium green color, plain wood base plug secured with early nails, wire staple strap holder inserted, tip end with octagonal carved raised ridge, side incised rect box with "Eliphas Hunt," light scroll carving, dark patina to wood, few bug bites, small crack at base edge ................................................. 400.00

Print, "View of the Battle Ground at Concord, Mass," titled and identified in margin, lithograph with hand coloring, after Fitzhugh Lane, 15-3/4" x 20-3/4" sheet size, framed ......................................... 6,350.00

Sword and Scabbard, 26" single edged slightly curved blade, brass hilt with stirrup guard, flat pommel, ribbed horn grip, brown leather scabbard, single brass mount ........................................................... 400.00

## Civil War

Autograph, Elziwah W. Langworthy, four letters, written 1862-54, 5th US Artillery Battery E, from Washington, Bristol Station, Chester, PA, and Rochester, NY hospital ...................................................... 40.00

Baldrick, US Officer, shoulder strap of tarred leather, gilt-cloth facing, brass mounts, tiger head chain and American shield applied, tarred leather brass bound box with spread winged American eagle on outer flap ............................................................................ 1,150.00

Belt and Buckle, period belt, oval US buckle plate, attributed to Pvt. Arthur E. Parker, Co. F., killed at Vicksburg, Miss 8/10/1863 ... 200.00

Broadside, Alexander H. Stephens, *Who Is Responsible For The War? Who Accountable For Its Horrors And Desolation? Extracts From A Speech...Delivered In The Secession Convention of Georgia...January 1861,* Boston, 1864, 11-1/2" x 9-1/4" .................................. 45.00

Cannonball, 6 lb., solid iron shot engraved in script "Gettsburg/1863," floral dec on wood base, breaks to base ................................ 350.00

Captains Epaulettes, 4-1/4" x 5-1/8", velvet ground, one pair with pressed brass surround, other with gold braid, provenance: reportedly belonged to MA Volunteers Captain A. J. Clough, 53rd Regiment, price for two pairs ................................................................. 250.00

Cartridge Box, woodburn, metal lined .......................................... 95.00

Cabinet Card

    Admiral Faragut, full dress, sword, Sarony ........................ 225.00

    Fort Marion, St. Augustine, FL, oversized ........................... 45.00

CDV, Admiral Foote ..................................................................... 65.00

Chair, camp, folding, orig carpet seat ......................................... 90.00

**Civil War, hat, ILL 63 inside triangle, purple hat band, $180. Photo courtesy of Joy Luke Fine Art Brokers and Auctioneers.**

Forage Cap, enlisted man's, tall, dark blue wool, tarred leather chip strap with two eagle "I" buttons, tarred leather visor with full sweat band and int., dark blue polished cotton lining, brown polished cotton body and crown ................................................................ 2,5,000.00

Kepi, GAR, dark blue wool, light blue silk lining, partially obscured mark's label, tarred leather visor, leather chip strap, two GAR buttons, late 7th US Cavalry brass insignia added to front, lining loose ................. 225.00

Map

    Appomattox Court House, War Dept., Washington, 1867, lithographed roll map, wooden rollers top and bottom, shellac slightly yellowed, linen backed ......................................... 490.00

    Battlefield in front of Franklin, Tennessee, War Dept., Washington, 1874, lithographed roll map, color, wooden rollers top and bottom, shellac slightly yellowed, linen backed ................ 350.00

    Bermuda Hundred, War Dept., Washington, 1867, lithographed roll map, color, wooden rollers top and bottom, shellac slightly yellowed, linen backed ....................................... 550.00

    Chancellorville, War Dept., Washington, 1867, lithographed roll map, color, wooden rollers top and bottom, shellac slightly yellowed and rubbed, linen backed ...................................... 635.00

    Map of the Seat of War! hand colored lithograph, Boston, 1861, map of Maryland and part of VA, map of railroad routes along east coast, map of Richmond, coastal chart of Norfolk Harbor, diagram of cap at Cairo (MS), view of Harper's Ferry, vignettes of Andrew Jackson and Winfield Scott, entirely backed, uneven toning, some soiling ......................................... 435.00

Muster Roll, Union, 28th Regiment of PA Volunteers, Company B, 1-1/2 pgs long oblong folio, Chancellorsville, VA, April 30, 1863, covers Feb 28 to April 30, lists 14 officers, 2 drummers, wagoner, 51 privates, 3 men discharged, chart form, 10 line record of events, fold wear ............................................................ 450.00

Newspaper, Daily Mirror-Extra, Manchester, NH, June 30, 1862, 12" x 6", special edition with headline "Startling Rumors! Reported Capture of Richmond! The Enemy Routed! A Four Days Fight!" ............. 40.00

Photographs, cartes des visites of three generals, identified in pencil as Kearny, Strong, and A. S. Williams, Brady imprint on verso, unidentified portraits of one general, two sergeants, and two corporals, also two tintypes of unidentified privates, two litho portraits of Generals Hancock and James Shields, published by L. Prang, set of 12 .................... 450.00

Shako, leather body, int. chin strap and visor, underside painted green, insignia missing, red, white, and blue rosette, mildewed, several creases ................................................................. 300.00

Stereoview

    Anthony, Rebel Artillery Soldier's, killed in trenches of Fort Mahone, two dead soldiers, horse .................................. 180.00

    Taylor, Brady view of Confederate prisoners on way to rear guard ..................................................................... 95.00

Surgeon's Kit, partial, 15 different surgical and doctor's tools, saws, scalpels, probes, stethoscope, knives, forceps, some mkd "Gemrig/Phila," some with tortoise shell handles, 16-1/2" x 6" x 4" walnut box, brass fixtures ........................................................ 600.00

Sword Belt and Plate, Union officer's, folded leather waist belt, both sets of sword hangers attached, model 1851 eagle belt plate . 325.00

Tintype

    1-7/8" x 2-1/16", head and shoulders of young lad in uniform, plastic case marked "S Peck & Co. A Union Case Improved" .......... 110.00

    3-3/8" x 3-3/4", soldier posing with unsheathed sword, Army tents in background, c1861, plastic case marked "S Peck & Co, The Crossed Cannons" .......................................................... 290.00

War Bond, Confederate, $500, issued 1864, $15 coupon, dry mounted and framed ................................................................ 20.00

**Spanish American**, canteen and strap, regular canvas covered ovoid shaped metal canteen, cork stopper, mkd on one side "US" and other with penciled name "JM Rudd," scattered blood spots, black strap with brass hooks and hangers mkd "Rock Island Arsenal," with inspector's marks .............................................................. 325.00

## World War I

Bayonet, Remington, case, 1917 ............................................. 90.00
Buckle, US Balloon Corps, emb hot air balloon ......................... 30.00

Flare Pistol, French, marked "Modele 1918" ............................ 125.00
Map Case, leather, strap, nine orig tour maps of France ............. 45.00
Measure, angle, US Army Engineer's Corps, case, 1916 ........... 45.00

Postcard

    Army and Navy Forever, patriotic salute to U. S. Soldiers, lyrics to "My country 'tis of Thee" at top ...................................... 40.00

    Fatal Wound, Brittannia bull dog wounds German Kaiser's backside, Belgian ............................................................... 50.00

    Well Done 77th, Homecoming, Statue of Liberty, 77th of Buffalo, sgd "Lawrence Wilber" .............................................. 75.00

Saddle Cloth, 7th Cavalry, yellow trim, blue felt, worn ............... 150.00

Sheet Music

    After the War is Over, 1917 .............................................. 5.00

    How 'Ya Gonna Keep 'em Down on the Farm After They've Seen Paree?, 1919 ............................................................... 8.00

    Madelon, I'll Be True to the Whole Regiment, 1919 ............... 6.00

    Since Katy the Waitress Became An Aviatress, 1919 ........... 8.00

Trench Knife, L. F. & C., 1917, stamped knuckle guard, wood handle, 9" blued triangle blade with green leather scabbard, metal tip and throat ...................................................................... 225.00

Uniform

    Army, wool blouse, 4th M.G. Battalion discs, machine gun, pin, trousers with ankle laces ............................................. 225.00

    Captain's, tunic and trousers, collar insignia, captain's bars, 2nd division patch ........................................................... 295.00

    Enlisted Man's, dress blues, tunic and trousers, no pockets ... 175.00

## World War II

Button, Royal Air Force, brass, emb wings and king's crown ......... 5.00
Field Glasses, German ......................................................... 100.00
Fighting Knife, 12-1/2" l, 1 pc blade and handle, 7-13/16" exposed spearpoint blade mkd "John Ek KNIFE/HAMDEN CONN," number "ID765" on left ricasso, 3-1/4" back grind, attached finger groove wood scales secured with three metal rivets, 3/4" exposed skull breaker accompanied by orig simple brown leather sheath ..... 310.00
Flyers Goggles, Japanese, gray fur lined cups, yellow lenses, boxed ...................................................................... 15.00
Knife, side, Imperial German, leather scabbard, well marked ...... 75.00
Medal, St. Christopher, USMC .............................................. 32.00
Paperweight, bronze, marked "Captured Japanese Material" from Yokosuka Naval Air Station, *USS Webster* .......................... 60.00
Plate, General Marshall surrounded by Allied Nations flags ......... 30.00
Poster, 17" w, 22" h, Protect Yourself Soldier, Use a Prophylaxis! Litho by Seventh Service Command for European barracks, orig fold lines ................................................................... 120.00

Wings

    Army Corp., sterling
    AVG, American Volunteer Group, Flying Tigers ................. 250.00
    WASP, Women Army Service Pilots ................................ 265.00
    Gunner's, 1st Model, open G ......................................... 100.00

# MILK GLASS

**History:** Opaque white glass attained its greatest popularity at the end of the 19th century. American glass manufacturers made opaque white tablewares as a substitute for costly European china and glass. Other opaque colors, e.g., blue and green, also were made. Production of milk glass novelties came in with the Edwardian era.

The surge of popularity in milk glass subsided after World War I. However, milk glass continues to be made in the 20th century. Some modern products are reissues and reproductions of earlier forms. This presents a significant problem for collectors, although it is partially obviated by patent dates or company markings on the originals and by the telltale signs of age.

Collectors favor milk glass from the pre-World War I era, especially animal-covered dishes. The most prolific manufacturers of these animal covers were Atterbury, Challinor-Taylor, Flaccus, and McKee.

**References:** E. McCamley Belknap, *Milk Glass*, Crown Publishers, 1949, out of print; Frank Chiarienza and James Slater, *The Milk Glass Book,* Schiffer, 1998; Regis F. and Mary F. Ferson, *Today's Prices for Yesterday's Milk Glass*, published by authors, 1985; ——, *Yesterday's Milk Glass Today*, published by authors, 1981; Everett Grist, *Covered Animal Dishes*, Collector Books, 1988, 2000 value update; Lorraine Kovar, *Westmoreland Glass*, 2 vols., Antique Publications, 1991; S. T. Millard, *Opaque Glass*, 4th ed., Wallace Homestead, 1975, out of print; Betty and Bill Newbound, *Collector's Encyclopedia of Milk Glass*, Collector Books, 1995, 2000 value update.

**Collectors' Club:** National Milk Glass Collectors Society, 46 Almond Dr., Hershey, PA 17033.

**Museum:** Houston Antique Museum, Chattanooga, TN.

**Notes:** There are many so-called "McKee" animal-covered dishes. Caution must be exercised in evaluating pieces because some authentic covers were not signed. Furthermore, many factories have made, and many still are making, split-rib bases with McKee-like animal covers or with different animal covers. The prices below are for authentic McKee pieces with either the cover or base signed.

Numbers in listings prefixed with a letter refer to books listed in the references, wherein the letter identifies the first letter of the author's name.

Animal Dish, cov
    Chick emerging from egg, basketweave base ...................... 90.00
    Deer, fallen tree base, sgd "E. C. Flaccus Co., Wheeling, WV" (F34) ...................... 185.00
    Hen, large, blue head, white body ........................................ 65.00
    Rabbit, patent date on base, Atterbury (F48) ..................... 175.00
Robin with Berry (F217) ...................................................... 75.00
Squirrel, acorn base (F15) .................................................. 175.00

**Animal Dish, cov, cat, ribbed base, 5-3/8" w, $120.**

Bon Bon, scoop shape, Eagle Glass Co., 1899 (F597) ................ 45.00
Bowl
    Arch Border pattern, 8" d, alternating wade curved arches and interlocking narrow pointed arches, Challinor, Taylor (B100a) ....... 50.00
    Cut Star pattern, 7-1/4" d, blue, scalloped edge, twelve rated stars (F289) .................................................... 75.00
Bread Tray, basketweave border, motto "Give Us Our Daily Bread" inscribed on rim, Atterbury (F345) .............................................. 75.00
Butter Dish, cov
    Crossed Fern pattern, 6"d, animal claw grasping ball feet and finial, scalloped edge, Atterbury (F232) .................... 75.00
    Gooseberry pattern, narrow beaded edges, band of fruit on cov and base, berry finial, Sandwich (F248) .......................... 120.00
Candlestick, 3-3/8" h, clown, bust rises from wide curved neck ruffle (F129) ................................................................. 75.00
Celery Vase, Burred Hobnail pattern ............................................. 45.00
Charger, Grape .......................................................................... 40.00
Child's Mug, Little Bo Peep (M-92) ............................................. 85.00
Compote
    Atlas, 8" h, figural stem, open weave border, attributed to Atterbury, c1865-1900 .................................................. 125.00
    Blackberry pattern, 9" h, large figural blackberry finial on cov, Hobbs Brockunier (B121) .................................................. 165.00
    Chick and Eggs, 11" h, pedestal, chick emerging from heaped eggs, finial cov, mounted on curved tripod, central support, rounded lacy edge base, emb Atterbury patent date, Aug. 6, 1889 inside cov (F362) ......................................... 195.00
    Prism pattern, 8" d, 5-1/2" h, wafer connection between Prism bowl and foot ................................................................. 155.00
Creamer
    Blackberry pattern ............................................................ 55.00
    Burred Hobnail pattern ..................................................... 50.00
    Forget Me Not pattern ....................................................... 45.00
    Paneled Wheat pattern, Hobbs Brockunier (F255) ............... 75.00
    Roman Cross pattern (F239) ............................................ 50.00
Cruet, Tree of Life pattern, blue .................................................. 80.00
Dish, cov, figural nut, white body, blue leaves, brownish red stripe around pedestal foot, dark brown nut finial, patent date "April 23, 1878" ....................................................................... 195.00
Epergne, 14" w, Paneled Grape, Westmoreland ........................ 345.00
Fish Set, figural fish platter, four serving dishes, Atterbury, emb patent date ...................................................................... 250.00
Glove Box, cov, rect, roses emb on top, scrolls emb on base, worn gold trim .................................................................. 125.00
Inkwell, horseshoe, circular inkwell in center, pen rests (F449) .... 55.00
Lamp, 20-1/4" h, clear and milk glass shade, clear font with cut stars, ovals, and strawberry point roundels, brass collar and connector, brass kerosene burner, milk glass base ................................... 275.00
Jar, cov, figural
    Eagle, "Old Abe," leafy base, "E. Pluribus Unum" on encircled banner, gray (F568) ........................................... 115.00
    Owl, glass eyes ............................................................... 85.00
Match Holder
    Indian Head (B219) ........................................................ 125.00
    Jolly Jester, patent date on rear (F201) ............................ 135.00
Miniature Lamp, 9" h, Chrysanthemum pattern, emb swirls and pink and yellow flowers, matching shade and base ......................... 290.00
Muffineer
    Gargolye, white ................................................................ 90.00
    Scrolls and bulging arches, rose dec .................................. 50.00
    Tapered cylinder, white, new lid ......................................... 30.00
Perfume Bottle, 7-1/2" h, Lightner's, emb cylindrical bottle, colorful oval recessed reverse painted label, bulbous shaped stopper
    Helitrope Perfume, very minor paint loss around label edge ... 275.00
    Lily of the Valley Perfume .................................................. 375.00
    Maid of the Mist Perfume .................................................. 375.00
    West End Perfume, crack in label, some discoloration ......... 175.00
Pitcher
    Birds on Branch pattern, trio of small birds on leafy branch, cold painted dec (F519) ......................................... 110.00

Dart and Bar pattern, 8" h, blue, rect handle, ftd (B85a).....100.00
Fish pattern, 71/4" h, finely detailed, Atterbury (F328).......185.00

Plate
Backward C with Lincoln.....................................................50.00
Contrary Mule ..................................................................25.00
Cupid & Psyche ...............................................................25.00
Easter Verse ...................................................................20.00
Gothic and Chain border, black .............................................35.00
Pinwheel, black................................................................20.00
Scroll and Waffle, McKee ...................................................20.00
Serenade, Greentown.........................................................55.00
Wicket ...........................................................................20.00

Platter, 13-1/4" l, Retriever, swimming dog pursuing duck through cattails, lily pad border (B53) ........................................................120.00

Salt Shaker
Atterbury Dredge, 3-3/8" h, combination octagonal paneled and pepper shapers shaped as small cov stein (F415) .............95.00
Diamond Point and Leaf pattern, 2-3/4" h, blue (F489) ........50.00

Spooner
Melon with Leaf and Net, Atterbury ......................................40.00
Paneled Flower, 4-5/8" h, ribbing separates six diamond point panels, stylized floral dec, scalloped edges, Challinor, Taylor (F284)......................................................................60.00

Sugar Bowl, cov
Almond Thumbprint, 7-1/2" h, large scalloped edges (F367)........................................................................120.00
Ceres pattern, 7-1/4" h, cameo profiles in beaded circles, leafy sprays, bust finial (B127) .............................................115.00
Forget Me Not pattern............................................................40.00
Melon with Leaf and Net pattern, Atterbury ...........................45.00
Roman Cross pattern (F239) ..............................................50.00
Sunflower pattern (B82b) ....................................................65.00

Sugar Shaker
Netted Oak pattern, 4-1/4" h, oak leaf centered on netted panels, green top band, Northwood (F495) ...................................85.00
Royal Oak pattern...............................................................90.00

Syrup, Pattern #87, Hobbs, orig top.........................................110.00
Tumbler, Louisiana Purchase...................................................55.00
Wine, Feather pattern ..........................................................42.00

# MILLEFIORI

**History:** Millefiori (thousand flowers) is an ornamental glass composed of bundles of colored glass rods fused together into canes. The canes were pulled to the desired length while still ductile, sliced, arranged in a pattern, and fused together again. The Egyptians developed this technique in the first century B.C. it was revived in the 1880s.

**Reproduction Alert:** Millefiori items, such as paperweights, cruets, and toothpicks, are being made by many modern companies.

Ashtray, biomorphic, smoky gray ground, silver mica flecks, pink, green, yellow, and aqua canes, attributed to A.V.E.M., Italy ......40.00
Bowl, 8" d, tricorn, scalloped, folded sides, amethyst and silver deposit................................................................................125.00
Bracelet, 8" l, long broad oval links separated by matching beads, burgundy, yellow, and blue ............................................................85.00
Creamer, 3" x 4-1/2", white and cobalt blue canes, yellow centers, satin finish ..............................................................................110.00
Cross, 2" l, 1-1/4" w, multicolored mosaic millefiori segments, brass setting ................................................................................115.00
Cruet, bulbous, multicolored canes, applied camphor handle, matching stopper ..............................................................................120.00

Cup and Saucer, white and cobalt blue canes, yellow center, satin finish ................................................................................90.00
Decanter, 12" h, deep black ground, all over multicolored flux and canes, including peachblow, and opal, enamel dec, Gundersen ..........1,450.00
Door Knob, 2-1/2" d, paperweight, center cane dated 1852, New England Glass Co. ................................................................395.00
Goblet, 7-1/2" h, multicolored canes, clear stem and base ........150.00
Lamp, 18-1/2" h, 8-1/2" d dome shade, glass base, electric.......650.00
Pitcher, 6-1/2" h, multicolored canes, applied candy cane handle ................................................................................195.00
Rose Bowl, 6" d, crimped top, cased, white lining .....................145.00
Slipper, 5" l, camphor ruffle and heal .........................................140.00
Sugar, cov, 4" x 4-1/2", white canes, yellow centers, satin finish 125.00

Vase
4" d, multicolored canes, applied double handles...............100.00
5-3/4" h, Czechoslovakian, pale vaseline urn shaped body, random yellow overlay stripes, red, blue, and yellow scattered millefiori flowers................................................................100.00

# MINIATURE LAMPS

**History:** Miniature oil and kerosene lamps, often called "night lamps," are diminutive replicas of larger lamps. Simple and utilitarian in design, miniature lamps found a place in the parlor (as "courting" lamps), hallway, children's rooms, and sickrooms.

Miniature lamps are found in many glass types, from amberina to satin glass. Miniature lamps measure 2-1/2 to 12 inches in height, with the principle parts being the base, collar, burner, chimney, and shade. In 1877, both

**Cut Glass, 8-1/2" h, $220. Photo courtesy of Joy Luke Fine Art Brokers and Auctioneers.**

L. J. Atwood and L. H. Olmsted patented burners for miniature lamps. Their burners made the lamps into a popular household accessory.

**References:** Marjorie Hulsebus, *Miniature Victorian Lamps*, Schiffer Publishing, 1996; Frank R. and Ruth E. Smith, *Miniature Lamps* (1981), Book II (1982, rev 2nd ed., 2000) Schiffer Publishing; John F. Solverson, *Those Fascinating Little Lamps: Miniature Lamps and Their Values*, Antique Publications, 1988, includes prices for Smith numbers.

**Collectors' Club:** Night Light, 38619 Wakefield Ct., Northville, MI 48167.

**Reproduction Alert:** Study a lamp carefully to make certain all parts are original; married pieces are common. Reproductions abound.

**Note:** The numbers given below refer to the figure numbers found in the Smith books.

#23-I, Time, clear, emb "Time and Light, Pride of America, Grand Vals Perfect Time Indicating Lamp," white beehive chimney, 6 5/8"h ...265.00
#36-I, Little Buttercup, amethyst, applied handle, nutmeg burner, 2-3/4" h.............................................................100.00
#109-I, Beaded Heart, green, six-toed foot, acorn burner, 5 3/8" h.............................................................315.00
#112-I, Bull's Eye, emerald green, acorn burner, 4 7/8" h...........100.00
#209-I, white milk glass, emb design and flowers, multicolored paint, nutmeg burner, 9-1/2" h.......................................150.00
#228-II, amber, 5 7/8" h .......................................125.00
#276-I, Pineapple in the Basket, white milk glass, fired-on brown paint, ruffled burner, 7 3/8" h..................................175.00
#279-I, pink cased.............................................135.00
#286-I, Cosmos, yellow cased .................................90.00
#288-I, red satin glass, emb designs, P & A Victor burner, 11-1/2" h.............................................................300.00
#317-I, white milk glass base and shade, green ground, pink and yellow daisy dec, nutmeg burner, 8 1/2" h ...................375.00
#385-I, peachblow, 6 7/8" h, chips on shade rim ...........440.00
#390-I, bright yellow, melon ribbed shade and base, glossy finish, nutmeg burner, 7" h.............................................525.00
#425-I, irid green, emb dec, nutmeg burner, 9-3/4" h ...........450.00
#458-II, white milk glass, heavily emb daisies and leaves, large white milk glass balls around base ...........................400.00
#467-II, blue opal, applied clear feet, foreign burner, 7-3/4" h ....325.00
#513-I, Swirl, blue opal, acorn burner, 4-3/4" h...........165.00

# MINIATURE PAINTINGS

**History:** Prior to the advent of the photograph, miniature portraits and silhouettes were the principal way of preserving a person's image. Miniaturists were plentiful, and they often made more than one copy of a drawing. The extras were distributed to family and friends.

Miniaturists worked in watercolors and oil and on surfaces such as paper, vellum, porcelain, and ivory. The miniature paintings were often inserted into jewelry or mounted inside or on the lids of snuff boxes. The artists often supplemented commission work by painting popular figures of the times and copying important works of art.

After careful study miniature paintings have been divided into schools, and numerous artists are now being researched. Many fine examples may be found in today's antiques marketplace.

**References:** Daphne Foskett, *Miniatures: Dictionary and Guide*, Antique Collectors' Club, 1999; Dale T. Johnson, American Portrait Miniatures in the Manney Collection, The Metropolitan Museum of Art, 1990.

**Museum:** Colonial Williamsburg Foundation, Williamsburg, VA; Gibbes Museum of Art, Charleston, SC.

1" w, 3/4" h, watercolor on ivory, American sailing vessel, unsigned, American School, 19th C, mounted as brooch in plated gold setting, minor fading, surface wear....................1,380.00
1-1/2" w, 2" h, watercolor on ivory, young child in white dress and bonnet, holding rattle, unsigned, American School, early 19th C, minor fading ...........................550.00
1-15/16" w, 2-1/4" h, watercolor on ivory, gentleman, sgd and dated "Weinedel, 1837" (Carl Weinedel, VA) on lower edge, gilded copper pendant case, reverse with empty hair compartment, dent, and gilding losses to case....................920.00
2-1/2" w, 3" l, watercolor and gum Arabic on paper, gentleman, unsigned, gilded copper pendant case, reverse with compartment containing clothing fragment, American School, 19th C, minor fading....................300.00
2-1/2" w, 3" l, watercolor on paper, gentleman in blue coat, unsigned, attributed to Rufus Porter, oval format, stamped brass frame, pigment loss, staining, toning....................460.00
2-5/8" h, watercolor on ivory, oval portrait of gentleman, blue eyes, minor wear and flaking, emb silver plated brass case ............330.00
2-3/4" w, 3-3/8" h, oval, oil on canvasboard, gentleman with lace collar, inscribed "Van Helst unbekannt" on label on reverse, Northern School, 17th C style, framed, retouched....................375.00
2-3/4" w, 3-1/4" h, watercolor on ivory, oval portrait of matron, lace bonnet, back mkd "Parcilaa Dean, Lynn, Mass," gilt insert, minor wear, incomplete leatherized case....................474.00
2-3/4" w, 3-1/2" h, facing pair, watercolor on thin paper, Tryphen Pomeroy and her brother Justus Pomeroy, stylized clouds to suggest halos and fanciful frames supported by yellow aureoles, painted by James Sanford Ellsworth, unframed, some staining and toning, price for pr....................4,025.00
3-1/8" h, watercolor on ivory, oval portrait of young woman, brown hair and eyes, white dress with red sash, leatherized case with dark burgundy velvet lining, edge uneven, colors worn ........................200.00
3-1/4" w, 3-7/8" h, watercolor on ivory, oval portrait of young woman, blond hair, white dress, blue, white, and green background, incomplete frame....................220.00
3-1/4" w, 3-7/8" h, watercolor on paper, woman in black dress, white bonnet, leatherized case ....................250.00

**Portrait of woman, painted in ivory, carved wooden frame, 1-1/2" h, 2" l, $120. Photo courtesy of Joy Luke Fine Art Brokers and Auctioneers.**

3-5/8" w, 4-1/8" h, on ivory, oval portrait of young child, blond hair, blue eyes, modern frame ................................................385.00

3-3/4" w, 4-3/8" h, on ivory, oval portrait of young woman, blond hair, white dress, blue accessories, blue background, brass fame with backing sgd "Painted by Rd. Mills, Birmm, 1829," minor edge damage .............................................................385.00

4" w, 5" h, oval, Empress Josephine, ruby and diamond parure, sgd "N. Ramier," period gilt-brass filigree frame, convex glass, French, c1885-95 ...............................................................330.00

4-1/8" w, 6-3/4" h, watercolor on ivory, lady, elegant dress, jewel and feather hairpiece, French school, rect gilt brass frame ...........400.00

4-1/4" h, on ivory, woman in large hat, elegant dress, indecipherable signature, oval gilt brass frame ..................................200.00

4-1/4" w, 5" h, on ivory, Napoleon, sgd "Hubert," boullework patri brass and shell frame, late 19$^{th}$/early 20$^{th}$ C....................................450.00

4-1/4" w, 6-1/2" h, on ivory en grisaille, Victorian officer in dress uniform, identified on reverse as Duke of Connaught, English, late 19$^{th}$/early 20$^{th}$ C, unframed......................................200.00

4-3/8" w, 5-1/8" h, on ivory, Josephine, sgd "Gerard," boullework patri brass and shell frame, late 19$^{th}$/early 20$^{th}$ C ..........................450.00

4-3/8" w, 5-3/8" h, on ivory, young child in white dress with blue ribbons, coral necklace, roses in her outstretched arm, roses at feet, pearl gray rose-tinted background, straw hat laying to side, orig hinged leather and velvet case, attributed to Moses B. Russell, sold with matching daguerreotype of same child, orig hinged leather and velvet 4-3/4" h x 3-1/2" case labeled "J. F. E. Prudhomme 663 Broadway, New York".........................................14,950.00

4-3/4" w, 5-1/4" h, on ivory, young woman, ebonized frame, late 19$^{th}$/20$^{th}$ C ......................................................275.00

4-3/4" w, 5-1/2" h, oblong, Renaissance ladies of fashion, matching period engraved ivory frames, Continental, c1885-95, price for pr, some loss to paint, one ivory stand broken and repaired.........120.00

4-3/4" w, 5-5/8" h, watercolor on ivory, oval portrait of woman, light brown hair, black dress, black lacquered frame with gilded fittings, chipped lens .......................................................200.00

5" w, 5-1/2" h, oval, early 19$^{th}$ C lady of fashion, sgd "Rosés," pierced ivory frame, Continental, c1875 ...............................125.00

5-1/2" w, 6-3/8" h, oval, painted with memorial urn in landscape, grieving man beside it, base of urn set with blue enamel oval framed with pears, set with lock of hair, memorial inscription dated 1902, framed, Regency, English, early 19$^{th}$ C..............................1,150.00

5-1/2" w, 7-1/2" h, oval, Mme de Pompadour, c1885-1895, French, elaborate period gilt-brass filigree frame fitted with rect matte striped in mother-of-pearl and ivory, convex glass..............................225.00

5-3/4" w, 5" h, watercolor on ivory, woman with long brown curls, dressed in riding attire, dark background, French, Menardi, 19th C, wood frame ............................................................450.00

6" d, circular, country girl, ebonized pierced wood frame with chased gilt-brass fillet, Northern European, 1820................................150.00

6-3/8" w, 7-1/4" h, watercolor on ivory, rect portrait of young cleric, black coat, black lacquered frame with gilded fittings, wear, frame loose...................................................................200.00

# MINIATURES

**History:** There are three sizes of miniatures: dollhouse scale (ranging from 1/2 to 1 inch), doll size, and child's size. Since most early material is in museums or is extremely expensive, the most common examples in the marketplace today are from the 20th century.

Many mediums were used for miniatures: silver, copper, tin, wood, glass, and ivory. Even books were printed in miniature. Price ranges are broad, influenced by scarcity and quality of workmanship.

The collecting of miniatures dates back to the 18th century. It remains one of the world's leading hobbies.

**References:** Nora Earnshaw, *Collecting Dolls' Houses and Miniatures*, Pincushion Press, 1993; Flora Gill Jacobs, *Dolls Houses in America*, Charles Scribner's Sons, 1974; ——, *History of Dolls Houses*, Charles Scribner's Sons; Constance Eileen King, *Dolls and Dolls Houses*, Hamlyn, 1989.

**Periodicals:** *Doll Castle News*, P.O. Box 247, Washington, NJ 07882; *Miniature Collector*, Scott Publications, 30595 Eight Mile Rd, Livonia, MI 48152; *Nutshell News*, 21027 Crossroads Circle, P.O. Box 1612, Waukesha, WI 53187.

**Collectors' Clubs:** International Guild Miniature Artisans, P.O. Box 71, Bridgeport, NY 18080; Miniature Industry Association of America Member News, 2270 Jacquelyn Dr., Madison, WI 53711; National Association of Miniature Enthusiasts, 2621 Anaheim, CA 92804-3883.

**Museums:** Colonial Williamsburg Foundation, Williamsburg, VA; Margaret Woodbury Strong Museum, Rochester, NY; Mildred Mahoney Jubilee Doll House Museum, Fort Erie, Canada; Museums at Stony Brook, Stony Brook, NY; Toy and Miniature Museum of Kansas City, Kansas City, MO; Toy Museum of Atlanta, Atlanta, GA; Washington Dolls' House and Toy Museum, Washington, DC.

**Additional Listings:** See Dollhouse Furnishings in *Warman's Americana & Collectibles* for more examples.

## Child or Doll Size

Blanket Chest
> 15-3/8" l, cherry, dovetailed case, dovetailed bracket feet, applied lid edge molding, till with lid, old finish, faint pencil inscription on bottom "Made by Mr. ___, in the year of 1847, Loudoun Co., Va., Presented to R. G. Axline by Mrs. Mary Axline".....3,575.00

Chair
> Hitchcock, Hitchocksville, CT, early 19th C, side, rolled crest above rect splat, rush seat, ring-turned legs, black painted ground, some graining, gold leaf dec, minor surface imperfections, 16" h seat, 21" h ....................................900.00
> Windsor, bow-back, painted, remnants of old ochre paint, New England, 19th C, minor imperfections, 13-1/4" h seat, 29" h .................................................................2,760.00

Chest of Drawers
> Classical, New England, 1835-45, painted and decorated, curving backboard with rolled top edge, small drawers on stepped out top drawer overhanging two lower drawers, flanked by scrolled serpentine columns ending in scrolled feet, orig brown and red paint, gold and olive highlights, orig turned pulls, very minor surface imperfections, 22" w, 14-1/8" d, 27-1/4" h ................750.00
> Cottage, America, 19$^{th}$ C, painted, arched swivel mirror flanked by two small drawers, lift-top box over three drawers with turned knobs and feet, painted green, floral dec, wear, minor crack, 14-1/4" l, 8-1/4" w, 16" h...................................1,495.00

Doll size chest of drawers, left: oak, 3 drawers, some spots on orig mirror, 24" h, 14" w, 7" d, $145; center: 3 drawers, chip carving around mirror, 15" h, 7-1/2" w, 5" d, $70; right: orig red paint, black pen striping, 2 drawers, 19" h, 13" w, 6" d, $60. Photo courtesy of Jackson's Auctioneers & Appraisers.

George III-Style, 19th C, mahogany veneered, five graduated drawers detailed with ebony stringing, each with diamond shaped ivory escutcheons and brass pulls, sides with two further handles, ogee bracket feet, 12-3/8" w, 7-3/4" d, 11-3/4" h ...............................................1,610.00

Grain Painted, America, 19th C, ochre grain on mustard ground, rect top, backsplash, pair of glove drawers, case with full blind drawer above two full drawers flanked by serpentine columns, wooden pulls, sides dec with incised concentric rings, scrolled skirt, minor paint loss, 8-3/4" w, 6" d, 9-3/4" h.............. 1,035.00

Sheraton, country, cherry and walnut, poplar secondary wood, two small over three graduated dovetailed drawers, paneled sides, scalloped apron, replaced turned feet painted black, turned wooden pulls, refinished, 14" w, 7-1/4" d, 17" h.................1,100.00

Cupboard

Step-back, Victorian, walnut, top section: doors with arched openings and scrolling, scalloped pie shelf surround, two dovetailed drawers with white porcelain knobs, scalloped apron, shaped base shelf, refinished, bottom section doors missing, one section of cornice missing, 17" w, 11-1/2" d, 27" h ................ 385.00

Wall, country, butternut and walnut, stepped-out dovetailed drawer, two mortised doors in base, sq nail construction, mellow refinishing, missing small section of back board, 10-3/4" w, 7-1/2" d, 11" h.............................................. 425.00

Desk, 19" w, 20-3/4" h, Queen Anne, New England, mid-18th C, cherry and tiger maple, slant lid opens to compartmented interior, cock-beaded case with two graduated drawers, bracket feet, old refinish, engraved batwing brasses appear to be orig, height loss, imperfections, 19" w, 20-3/4" h.......................................... 9,200.00

Rocker

9-1/2" h seat, 24-3/4" h back, New England, 1860-80, painted and dec, floral painted crest rail over spindles, natural arms, plank seat with rolled rail above rockers, old blue paint, surface imperfections............................................................... 350.00

23" h, 14" d, 16" d, red stained birch, New England, early 19th C, shaped back and sides, pierced handles, trapezoidal seat, cut-out skirt, seat replaced ..................................................... 425.00

School Desk and Chair, 29" h chair, 26" w x 26-1/2" h desk, wood, adjustable wrought iron base patented June 1896, polychrome scenic, scrolling devices, foliate dec, sgd "Peter Hunt from Cape Cod," surface imperfections ................................................ 450.00

Settee, New England, 1830-40, painted and decorated, orig red and brown grained surface highlighted with gold striping which outlines rect crest, horizontal splat above seat, rolled front rail, gold striping on turned tapering legs, minor surface imperfections, 25" l, 11" d, 21-1/2" h .................................................................. 1,610.00

Settle Bench, old green repaint with gold and black floral dec and striping, slat back, scalloped crest with floral detail, plank seat, rolled front edge, scroll arms, turned legs, stretcher base, arm repair, 26" w, 10" d, 16-3/4" h.............................................................. 935.00

Stand, Sheraton, walnut and pine, reddish brown finish, pegged construction, one board top, one nailed drawer with small dividers at back, wooden pull, turned legs, reconstruction, 13-3/4" w, 13-7/8" d, 18" h ...................................................................... 550.00

Storage Chest, painted dec, New England, 19th C, dovetail construction

6-3/4" h, 14" d, 7-1/4" d, lid and base with applied molded edge, dark umber on mustard ground dec, very minor wear, crack in top ......................................................................... 1,100.00

7-3/4" h, 14-1/2" 2, 7-3/4" d, lid and base with applied molded rim, black and white, red checked design, minor paint loss, crack in top ......................................................................... 1,495.00

Table, drop leaf, Sheraton, cherry, six turned legs, swing leg to support leaves, mellow finish, 30" w, 13-1/2" d, 9-7/8" leaves, 17-3/4" h.............................................................. 1,100.00

## Doll House Accessories

Candlesticks, pr, brass, 1" h, c1900.............................42.00
Christmas Tree, undecorated.......................................20.00
Coffee Grinder, wood base, iron fittings.........................90.00

Dresser Set, hp, china, 15 pcs.....................................35.00
Fireplace, Victorian, filigree metal, orig tools ...............95.00
Lamp, floor, Windsor style, 3-1/2" h...............................25.00
Plumbing Fixtures, white plastic, 1-1/2" h kitchen sink/stove combination, 2-1/2" l tub, 1-1/4" h bathroom sink, 1-1/4" toilet ..............20.00
Radio, floor model, 2-1/4" h, cardboard, 1950s .................6.00
Refrigerator, 2-1/4" h, white plastic .............................3.00
Sink, bathroom, pedestal, Renawal, 2-1/4" h.....................12.00
Sink, kitchen, Renwal, k-68, 2-3/4" h, 3" l.......................15.00
Tea Set, cov teapot, creamer, and sugar, English silver, Birmingham hallmarks, 1-1/4" h, 1906 ......................................... 160.00

## Doll House Furniture

Bed, maple, honey finish, scalloped head and footboard, 6-1/4" h, c1900 ................................................................. 110.00

Buffet, Ideal, brown marbleized plastic, opening drawer, 2-1/4" h, 4" l.........................................................................12.00

Cabinet, glass front, knob missing, wood, home made, 14" h ...... 90.00

Chair, carved wood, scrolled back and arms, blue velvet upholstery, 5-1/2" h, pr................................................................ 60.00

Desk, drop front, wood, metal knobs, 7-1/2" h.......................100.00

Nightstands, 1-1/2" h, price for pr................................ 10.00

Piano, upright, Marx, red plastic .................................15.00

Plant Stand, 1-3/4" h, cardboard, 1950s.............................6.00

Rocker, bentwood, matching stool with red material top.............. 12.00

Sofa

Marx, curved, red plastic........................................... 12.00

Regency, black walnut, green velvet upholstery, needlepoint and velvet pillows, 1840 styling, 9-1/2" l ................................215.00

Stove, Marklin, #1601, mint in orig box.....................................130.00

Suite

Baby Furniture, 4" h crib, 7-1/2" h wardrobe, 8" h high chair, bed, 6" h, litho tin, mkd "J. Chein & Co., Made in USA," c1940165.00

Dining Room Suite, maple, Art Nouveau style, rect extension table with two leaves, four matching scrolled back chairs, black leather seats and backs ................................................125.00

Living Room, cast iron 3-3/4" h side chair, wine colored tufted seat, 6-1/2" x 2-1/4" x 4-1/4" h sofa with wine colored tufted seat, pr 1-1/4" h footstools, carved wood 2-3/4" h table, some rust, sofa leg broken, table ornament missing ................... 65.00

Table, drop leaf, wood, home made, 7-1/2" l ..............................45.00

Wlardrobe, oak, golden finish, 1" scale, c1900........................100.00

# MINTON CHINA

**History:** In 1793, Thomas Minton joined other men to form a partnership and build a small pottery at Stoke-on-Trent, Staffordshire, England. Production

began in 1798 with blue-printed earthenware, mostly in the Willow pattern. In 1798, cream-colored earthenware and bone china were introduced.

A wide range of styles and wares was produced. Minton introduced porcelain figures in 1826, Parian wares in 1846, encaustic tiles in the late 1840s, and Majolica wares in 1850. Many famous designers and artists in the English pottery industry worked for Minton.

In 1883, the modern company was formed and called Mintons Limited. The "s" was dropped in 1968. Minton still produces bone-china tablewares and some ornamental pieces.

**Marks:** Many early pieces are unmarked or have a Sevres-type marking. The "ermine" mark was used in the early 19th century. Date codes can be found on tableware and majolica. The mark used between 1873 and 1911 was a small globe with a crown on top and the word "Minton."

**References:** Paul Atterbury and Maureen Batkin, *Dictionary of Minton*, Antique Collectors' Club, 1999; Susan and Al Bagdade, *Warman's English & Continental Pottery & Porcelain*, 3rd Edition, Krause Publications, 1998; Joan Jones, *Minton: The First Two Hundred Years of Design and Production*, Swan Hill, 1993.

**Museum:** Minton Museum, Staffordshire, England; Victoria & Albert Museum, London, England.

Bowl, 12-1/2" d, floral reserves, cobalt blue ground, gold trim, c1810 ...................................................1,450.00
Breakfast Set, plate with attached toast rack, salt and pepper shapers, Dejeuneau, green mark....................200.00
Bulb Planter, 10-3/4" l, majolica, emb brown fence, green leaves, turquoise lining, mkd ................150.00
Cup and Saucer, hp, bird vignettes and flower blossoms, aqua borders.................................55.00
Cup Plate, 3-7/8" d, central medium blue transfer floral design, zig-zag rim border, c1830 ..................100.00
Demitasse Cup and Saucer, scrolling reserves of flowers, gilt dec, cobalt blue ground, c1900.................295.00
Dish, figural, 7-3/4" h, majolica, modeled as cloth draped putto standing on coiled pedestal with blossoms, leaf dish on each sides, imp mark, c1871, restored rim chips.....................1,725.00
Floor Vase, 25" h, 12" d, Aesthetic Movement, squat, scalloped base, transfer-printed blue and yellow flowers, ivory ground, stamped "Minton's/Made in England".........500.00
Jardiniere, 22" h, two figural handles, multicolored floral design, navy blue ground, imp mark, minor glaze flaws, chip repair..........1,300.00
Marmalade Jar, butterflies, blue ground, c1920.........50.00
Oyster Plate, emb fish, white ground.........60.00
Plate
   8-7/8" d, multicolored, tortoise and hare in field near lake, basketweave molded border, loop pierced rim, Bernard Rischgitz.........75.00
   10-1/4" d, pate-sur-pate, blue border, white classical scenes, sgd "Birks".........160.00
   10-1/2" d, cream center, parcel gilt cornucopia, husk, and swag draping, retailed for Tiffany, set of 12.........1,840.00
Portrait Plate, 9-1/8" d, young woman, Victorian dress, multicolored, plique-a-jour border, sgd "A. Bouilemier," pr .........1,800.00
Tile Fireplace Surround, 43" x 37", seventeen enameled tiles depicting the seasons and other subjects, browns, yellow, and pale blue, late 19th C .........3,795.00

**Jardiniere and Stand, majolica, freeform oval shape, white ground, enamel dec foliage in relief, circular stand with four paw feet, unmarked, c1880, minor damage, slight glaze wear, 20-1/2" l, $2,990. Photo courtesy of Skinner, Inc.**

Tureen, cov, undertray, 14-1/4" w, Oriental garden scene, black transfers with enameled accents, ribbed handles, loop knob, c1882 .........400.00
Vase, 11-1/2" h, tapered cylindrical shape, flaring rim, Arts and Crafts style green and yellow flowerheads and stems, blue ground.....400.00
Wash Bowl and Pitcher, amethyst, ruby red, and yellow floral dec .........200.00

# MOCHA

**History:** Mocha decoration usually is found on utilitarian creamware and stoneware pieces and was produced through a simple chemical action. A color pigment of brown, blue, green, or black was made acidic by an infusion of tobacco or hops. When the acidic colorant was applied in blobs to an alkaline ground, it reacted by spreading in feathery designs resembling sea plants. This type of decoration usually was supplemented with bands of light-colored slip.

Types of decoration vary greatly, from those done in a combination of motifs, such as Cat's Eye and Earthworm, to a plain pink mug decorated with green ribbed bands. Most forms of mocha are hollow, e.g., mugs, jugs, bowls, and shakers.

English potters made the vast majority of the pieces. Collectors group the wares into three chronological periods: 1780-1820, 1820-1840, and 1840-1880.

**Marks:** Marked pieces are extremely rare.

**References:** Susan and Al Bagdade, *Warman's English & Continental Pottery & Porcelain*, 3rd Edition, Krause Publications, 1998.

**Reproduction Alert.**

Bowl
   7-1/2" d, 5-1/2" h, agate glaze, hairline, minor chips ..........575.00
   8-1/2" d, blue, white, and dark brown earthworm design, blue band, hairline on base.........385.00
Creamer, 2-5/8" h, bulbous, black seaweed, amber center band, brown and white stripes, ribbed leaf handle.........220.00
Milk Pitcher, 4-5/8" h, dark gray-blue band, black stripes, emb band, green and black seaweed, leaf hand .........440.00
Mug
   2-3/4" h, black and white, blue stripes, geometric band, applied ribbed handle with leaf ends, stains, minor damage........465.00
   3-1/4" h, brown, blue, and black stripes on white ground, molded beaded band, applied handle with leaf ends, stains, crazing, crow's foot hairline .........200.00
   3-1/2" h, center cream band with dark brown vertical stripes, dark brown ground, band of brown and cream circlets on rim, applied acanthus leaf handle.........325.00
   3-5/8" h, gray band, brown and white stripes, black seaweed dec, leaf handle.........165.00
   5" h, dark tan center band, blue, white, and dark brown earthworm design, dark brown and white stripe, leaf handle, hairlines...495.00
   5-1/2" h, earthworm design, impressed geometric border, dark brown, blue, and cream, pumpkin ground, hairlines, glaze wear to rim and handle, minute rim chips .........525.00
   6-1/2" h, two small blue bands flanking wide central gray band, four large stocks of seaweed, applied handle.........250.00
Mug Measure, 6" h, white ground, tan, blue, and black stripes and seaweed, leaf handle, mkd "Quart," stains and minor chips, short hairlines.........220.00
Mustard Pot, 4-1/8" h, bulbous, blue, tan, and white earthworm and cat's eye design, blue-gray center band, tan and white stripes, leaf handles, chips .........220.00

**Pitcher, yellow ware, brown and white banding, upper section with large band of blue seaweed dec on white ground, spout retouched, 7-3/4" h, $1,760. Photo courtesy of Sanford Alderfer Auction Co.**

Pitcher
- 5" h, Earthworm, tan and dark brown stripes, tan band, white, pale blue and brown earthworm, molded leaf ends handle, professional repair to handle ................................. 660.00
- 6-1/2" h, molded spout, leaf handle, machine tooled band, orange band with earthworm, white, light blue, pale green, and dark brown (black) bands and stripes, wear and chips, hairlines in foot ........................................................ 1,265.00
- 7-1/2" h, 9" w, incised green band, two bands of blue, brown, and white cat eyes on black ground, central band of brown, blue, white, and black spot mottled dec on gray ground, applied dec handle, molded spout, crack on bottom, discoloration at base, side crack ................................................... 1,750.00
- 7-7/8" h, Pearlware, pumpkin colored bands top and bottom, brown geometric and line dec on white ground, emb leaf dec on handle and spout, minor chips and wear, int. glaze flakes ............. 1,320.00
- 8" h, earthworm and polka dots, tooled band, white, gray, black, yellow, brown, and green stripes, blue in earthworm, wear and damage, old repairs to handle, spout, and rim ................. 880.00

Waste Bowl, 5-5/8" d, white, blue, and dark brown earthworm design, red-orange band, dark brown stripes, emb green rim, hairlines .......... 275.00

# MONT JOYE GLASS

**History:** Mont Joye is a type of glass produced by Saint-Hilaire, Touvier, de Varreaux & Company at their glassworks in Pantin, France. Most pieces were lightly acid etched to give them a frosted appearance and were also decorated with enameled florals.

**Note:** Pieces listed below are frosted unless otherwise noted.

Bowl
- 3-3/4" d, frosted ground, enameled floral dec, sgd ............. 275.00
- 12" d, folded rim, iris dec, four feet, unmarked ................... 150.00

Ewer, cov, cameo cutting, crystal, green, and gold, brass spout and handle, removable cover, artist sgd "Cristalle Rie Depantin" ... 550.00

Inkwell, green, enamel lavender flower dec ............................. 180.00

Jar, cov, 8" h, cylindrical, crystal ground, etched, enameled iris, gilt leaves, crystal knob, gilt factory mark, c1900 ......................... 275.00

Pitcher, 9" h, yellow iris dec, silver plate spout and handle, unmarked ............................................................... 300.00

Vase
- 5-3/4" h, green glitter body, gold leaf painted dec, applied opal glass spheres ............................................... 375.00
- 6-1/2" h, green frosted ground, cut poppies, crimson enamel and gilt trim ..................................................... 265.00
- 7" h, sq, yellow iris dec, sgd .............................. 250.00
- 7-1/2" h, dark green satin ground, enameled pink iris dec.. 400.00
- 8" h, light turquoise ground, etched iris dec, gold highlights, acid etched frosting, gold band around crimped edge ............ 395.00
- 8-1/2" h, cameo, icy frosted ground, enameled leaves, deep red poppies, sgd .................................................. 450.00
- 9" h, frosted ground, enameled purple orchids, green leaves .................................................... 200.00
- 9-1/2" h, 6" w, ovoid, acid etched, lilies outlined in gold, body slightly ribbed, indented fluted top with gold accents, sgd, c1900 .... 600.00
- 11" h, tomato red ground, lacy gold dec, enameled iris and foliage dec .......................................................... 250.00
- 13-3/4" h, flattened ovoid shape, cameo, crystal ground, etched, molded and enameled iris, gilt leaves, c1900 ................. 350.00
- 19-3/4" h, swollen at top, narrow stem, flared foot of transparent emerald green glass with textured acid finish, cameo-etched borders at top and bottom, enameled with silvered acorns, gold and silvered oak leaves on dark gilt ground, base with Mont Joye shield in gold enamel, France, c1900, minor wear to gilt .............. 3,200.00

Violet Vase, 6" h, frosted etched surface, colorless glass, naturalistic enameled purple violet blossoms, gold highlights, base mkd "Dimier Geneve" ..................................................... 260.00

# MOORCROFT

**History:** William Moorcroft was first employed as a potter by James Macintyre & Co., Ltd., of Burslem in 1897. He established the Moorcroft pottery in 1913.

The majority of the art pottery wares were hand thrown, resulting in a great variation among similarly styled pieces. Color and marks are keys to determining age.

Walker, William's son, continued the business upon his father's death and made wares in the same style.

**References:** Paul Atterbury, *Moorcroft: A Guide to Moorcroft Pottery 1897-1993, Rev. Ed.,* Richard Dennis and Hugh Edwards, 1990; Susan and Al Bagdade, *Warman's English & Continental Pottery & Porcelain*, 3rd Edition, Krause Publications, 1998; A. W. Coysh, *British Art Pottery, 1870-1940,* Charles E. Tuttle, 1976; Walter Moorcroft, *Walter Moorcroft Memories of Life and Living,* Richard Dennis Publications, distributed by Antique Collectors' Club, 1999; Frances Salmon, *Collecting Moorcroft*, Francis-Joseph Books, 1994.

**Collectors' Club:** Moorcroft Collectors' Club, Lipert International Inc., 2922 M. St., NW, Washington, DC 20007.

**Museums:** Everson Museum of Art, Syracuse, NY; Moorcroft Museum, Stoke-on-Trent, England; Victoria & Albert Museum, London, England.

**Marks:** The company initially used an impressed mark, "Moorcroft, Burslem"; a signature mark, "W. Moorcroft" followed. Modern pieces are marked simply "Moorcroft" with export pieces also marked "Made in England."

Bowl, 4-1/2" d, pink and yellow flower dec, green leaves, cobalt blue glaze.................................................................... 60.00
Bulb Bowl, 6-1-1/2" d, white and purple narcissus, dark blue and green ground, "Potter to the Queen" mark ......................... 150.00
Compote, 7-1/2" x 51/2", Cornflower pattern, mottled green ground, mkd "W. Moorcroft".................................................... 500.00
Creamer and Sugar, Pomegranate pattern, celadon ground, sgd in ink "W. Moorcroft" ........................................................ 1,900.00
Ginger Jar, cov, 6" h, tapered oval form, mauve flowers and green leaves, blue and blue-green ground, pond lilies, dragonfly on cov, green Moorcroft stamp, painted monograms of William J. Moorcroft and paintress Katherine Lloyd, imp candlestick mark .............. 800.00
Jardiniere, 5-3/4" h, multicolored panels, white ground, gilt trim, sgd "MacIntyre" ........................................................ 600.00
Lamp Base, 17" h, single-socket fixture, baluster shaped standard, blue, mauve, yellow, and green orchid blossoms and leaves, shaded brown ground, round metal stand with scroll relief dec above metal disk base, small edge nick, crack in metal base ...................... 290.00
Match Holder, 2-3/4" h, pink thistle flowers, mottled green ground, coat of arms, MacIntyre mark, green painted initials, "WM," printed "Redley Hall," c1897 ................................................ 350.00
Vase
   3" h, short flared rim, bulbous body, two mauve and purple anemone blossoms, cobalt blue ground, imp "Moorcroft" on base, mid 20th C .................................................................... 230.00
   3-1/4" h, raised rim, bulbous body, two mauve and purple anemone blossoms, cobalt blue ground, imp facsimile William Moorcroft signature and "Potter to H. M. The Queen," c1947 .. 260.00
   5-1/4" h, short rolled rim on globular body, ftd base, multicolored orchid blossoms, cobalt blue ground, imp marks, facsimile William Moorcroft signature and initials, second quarter 20th C......... 290.00
   5-1/2" h, flared rim, tapered oval body, ftd base, three large mauve and yellow hibiscus blossoms, shaded green ground, green stamp and paper label, mid-20th C ........................ 410.00
   6" h, 6" d, spherical, blue and green glaze, yacht design, sgd "William Moorcroft" .............................................................. 1,050.00
   7" h, ftd oviform, dark purple-red and orange-red clematis blossoms, reddish-orange tone ground, painted initials of Walter Moorcroft, imp mark, paper label, mid 20th C, small glaze scratch.................................................................. 490.00
   7-5/8" h, flared rim, tapered oval body, mauve and purple pomegranates and berries, dark cobalt blue ground, imp mark and painted signature, early 20th C, small repair on base ......... 460.00

7-3/4" h, slightly flared rim on extended neck, bulbous body tapering to base, purple, blue, and yellow orchid and flower blossoms, cobalt blue ground, imp factory mark, painted Walter Moorcroft initials and printed paper Royal Warrant label.......................... 350.00
8-1/4" h, raised flared rim, flattened spherical ftd body raised dec of finches, foliage, and fruit, shades of purple, green, and mauve, shaded cobalt blue ground, imp mark, bell and painted monograms of William J. Moorcroft and paintress Adrianne Wain, designed by Sally Tufflin, c1988 ........................... 900.00
9" h, 5-1/2" d, chalice shape, squeezebag red, garnet, and orange fruit, dark cobalt blue ground, paper seal "By Appointment/Moorcroft/Potter to H.M The Queen".................... 1,900.00
9-1/2" h, commemorative yacht, flared rim, tapered neck above flattened spherical body, slip trail dec with butterflies around rim and yachts at sea, one with 1897 flag, another with 1997 flag, shaded blue glossy glaze, small glaze imperfections ...... 500.00
9-3/4" h, flared rim, raised neck, wide shoulder tapering to flared base, purple, mauve, and yellow wisteria blossoms, cobalt blue ground, imp factory mark, blue painted signature, mid-20th C..................................................................... 435.00
17" h, raised flared rim, wide shoulder tapering to flared base, squeeze bag outline of grapes and leaves, glossy orange, red, purple, and mauve glaze, shaded rust and dark blue ground, imp "Moorcroft" on base, c1930 ................................. 4,890.00

# MORGANTOWN GLASS WORKS

**History:** The Morgantown Glass Works, Morgantown, West Virginia, was founded in 1899 and began production in 1901. Reorganized in 1903, it operated as the Economy Tumbler Company for 20 years until, in 1923, the word "Tumbler" was dropped from the corporate title. The firm was then known as The Economy Glass Company until reversion to its original name, Morgantown Glass Works, Inc., in 1929, the name it kept until its first closing in 1937. In 1939, the factory was reopened under the aegis of a guild of glassworkers and operated as the Morgantown Glassware Guild from that time until its final closing. Purchased by Fostoria in 1965, the factory operated as a subsidiary of the Moundsville-based parent company until 1971 when Fostoria opted to terminate production of glass at the Morgantown facility. Today, collectors use the generic term, "Morgantown Glass," to include all periods of production from 1901 to 1971.

Morgantown was a 1920s leader in the manufacture of colorful wares for table and ornamental use in American homes. The company pioneered the processes of iridization on glass as well as gold and platinum encrustation of patterns. It enhanced Crystal offerings with contrasting handle and foot of India Black, Spanish Red (ruby), and Ritz Blue (cobalt blue), and other intense and pastel colors for which it's famous. The company conceived the use of contrasting shades of fired enamel to add color to its etchings. It was the only American company to use a chromatic silk-screen printing process on glass, their two most famous and collectible designs being Queen Louise and Manchester Pheasant.

The company is also known for ornamental "open stems" produced during the late 1920s. Open stems separate to form an open design midway between the bowl and foot, e.g., an open square, a "Y," or two dia-

Vase, spherical, blue and green yacht design, sgd "Wm Moorcroft," 6" h, 6" d, $1,050. Photo courtesy of Joy Luke Fine Art Brokers and Auctioneers.

mond-shaped designs. Many of these open stems were purchased and decorated by Dorothy C. Thorpe in her California studio, and her signed open stems command high prices from today's collectors. Morgantown also produced figural stems for commercial clients such as Koscherak Brothers and Marks & Rosenfeld. Chanticleer (rooster) and Mai Tai (Polynesian bis) cocktails are two of the most popular figurals collected today.

Morgantown is best known for the diversity of design in its stemware patterns, as well as for its four patented optics: Festoon, Palm, Peacock, and Pineapple. These optics were used to embellish stems, jugs, bowls, liquor sets, guest sets, salvers, ivy and witch balls, vases, and smoking items.

Two well-known lines of Morgantown Glass are recognized by most glass collectors today: #758 Sunrise Medallion and #7643 Golf Ball Stem Line. When Economy introduced #758 in 1928, it was originally identified as "Nymph." By 1931, the Morgantown front office had renamed it Sunrise Medallion. Recent publications erred in labeling it "dancing girl." Upon careful study of the medallion, you can see the figure is poised on one tiptoe, musically saluting the dawn with her horn. The second well-known line, #7643 Golf Ball, was patented in 1928; production commenced immediately and continued until the company closed in 1971. More Golf Ball than any other Morgantown product is found on the market today.

**References:** Larry Baker, *The Morgantown Etching Plates, Vol. 1, Plates 1-100*, compact disc with patterns, 2000 (3929 Wyoming, Kansas City, MO, 64111); Tom and Neila Bredehoft, *Fifty Years of Collectible Glass, 1920-1970, Volume 1, Volume II*, Antique Trader Books, 2000; Jerry Gallagher, *Handbook of Old Morgantown Glass*, Vol. I, published by author (420 First Ave. NW, Plainview, MN 55964), 1995; ——, Old Morgantown, Catalogue of Glassware, 1931, Morgantown Collectors of America Research Society, n.d.; Jeffrey B. Snyder, *Morgantown Glass From Depression Glass Through the 1960s*, Schiffer Publishing, 1998; Hazel Marie Weatherman, *Colored Glassware of the Depression Era*, Book 2 published by author, 1974, available in reprint; ——, *1984 Supplement & Price Trends for Colored Glassware of the Depression Era*, Book 1, published by author, 1984.

**Collectors' Clubs:** Old Morgantown Glass Collectors' Guild, P.O. Box 894, Morgantown, WV 26507.

## Bowl

| | |
|---|---|
| #1 Berkshire, Crystal w/#90 Starlet Cutting, 8" d | 58.00 |
| #12-1/2 Woodsfield, Genova Line, 12-1/2" d | 545.00 |
| #14 Fairlee, Glacier decoration, 8" d | 525.00 |
| #19 Kelsha, Genova Line, 12" d | 425.00 |
| #26 Greer, Neubian Line, 10" d | 750.00 |
| #35-1/2 Elena, Old Amethyst, applied Crystal rim, 8" d | 425.00 |
| #67 Fantasia, Bristol Blue, 5-1/2" d | 75.00 |
| #101 Heritage, Gypsy Fire, Matte Finish, 8" d | 70.00 |
| #103 Elyse, Steel Blue, 7" d | 48.00 |
| #1102 Crown, Moss Green, 9" d | 45.00 |
| #1933 El Mexicana, console, Seaweed, 10" d | 385.00 |
| #1933 El Mexicano Ice Tub, Ice or Seaweed, 6" d | 210.00 |

| | |
|---|---|
| #4355 Janice, Ritz Blue or Spanish Red, 13" d | 445.00 |
| #4355 Janice, Crystal, Glacier Decor w/Snow Flowers, 13" d | 565.00 |
| #7643 Truman, Spanish Red, Crystal trim, rare, 10" d | 4,500.00 |

## Candleholders, pair

| | |
|---|---|
| #37 Emperor, Stiegel Green or 14K Topaz, 8" h | 625.00 |
| #80 Modern, Moss Green, 7-1/2" h | 70.00 |
| #81 Bravo, Peacock Blue, 4-1/2" h | 528.00 |
| #82 Cosmopolitan, Moss Green, slant, 7" h | 75.00 |
| #87 Hamilton, Evergreen, 5" h | 75.00 |
| #88 Classic, Nutmeg, 4-3/4" h | 55.00 |
| #105 Coronet, Ebony or Cobalt, slant, 8-3/4" h | 120.00 |
| #7620 Fontanne, Ebony filament, #781 Fontinelle etch | 1,000.00 |
| #7643 Golf Ball, Torch Candle, single, Ritz Blue, 6" h | 280.00 |
| #7662 Majesty, Randall Blue, 4" h | 750.00 |
| #7690 Monroe, Ritz Blue, 7" h, rare | 1,200.00 |
| #7951 Stafford, Crystal w/#25 gold band, 3-1/8" h | 685.00 |
| #9923 Colonial, Pineapple, 2-pc hurricane, 8-1/2" h | 140.00 |

## Candy Jar

| | |
|---|---|
| #14 Edmond, Danube Line, #4 cover, rare, 8-1/2" h | 625.00 |
| #16 Rachel, Crystal, Pandora Cutting, 6" h | 385.00 |
| #108 Bethann, Topreen Line, 5" h | 595.00 |
| #200, Mansfield, Burgundy matte, 12" h | 195.00 |
| #1212 Michael, Spanish Red, Crystal finial, 5-1/2" h | 1,000.00 |
| #7643-1 Alexandra, Randall Blue/Crystal Duo-Tone, 5" h | 825.00 |
| #9952 Palace, Ruby, 6-12" h | 60.00 |

## Champagne

| | |
|---|---|
| #7577 Venus, Ritz Blue, Pillar Optic, 5-1/2 oz | 55.00 |
| #7606-1/2 Athena, Ebony filament, #777 Baden etch, 7 oz | 75.00 |
| #7621 Ringer, Aquamarine, 6 oz | 55.00 |
| #7623 Pygon, D.C. Thorpe satin open stem, 6-1/2 oz | 165.00 |
| #7640 Art Moderne, Ebony open stem, 5 oz | 85.00 |
| #7643 Golf Ball, 5-1/2 oz , Spanish Red | 50.00 |
| #7660-1/2 Empress, Spanish Red | 45.00 |
| #7678 Old English, 6-1/2 oz, Ritz Blue | 50.00 |
| #7690 Monroe, Spanish Red | 45.00 |
| #7860 Lawton, Azure, Festoon Optic, 5 oz | 50.00 |

## Cocktail

| | |
|---|---|
| Chanticleer, Pink Champagne bowl, 4 oz | 45.00 |
| Mai Tai, Topaz stem, 4 oz | 50.00 |
| Old Crown, 6-1/4" h, 5-1/2 oz | 85.00 |
| #7577 Venus, Anna Rose, Palm Optic, 3 oz | 38.00 |
| #7577 Venus, Venetian Green, Palm Optic, 3 oz | 35.00 |
| #7620 Fontanne, Ebony filament, #781 Fontinelle etch, 3-1/2 oz | 135.00 |
| #7643 Golf Ball, 3-1/2 oz, Ritz Blue | 42.00 |
| #7643 Golf Ball, 3-1/2 oz, Stiegel Green | 42.00 |
| #7654-1/2 Legacy, Spanish Red, 3 oz | 45.00 |
| #7654-1/2 Legacy, Manchester Pheasant Silk Screen, 3-1/2 oz | 185.00 |

## Compote

| | |
|---|---|
| #201 Inverness, Meadow Green, Peacock Optic, 4-1/2" d, 7-1/2" h | 155.00 |
| #206 Colette, Burgundy, 7-1/2" h | 65.00 |
| #7556 Toledo, high with cover, Crystal, Forever Cutting, 4-1/2" d | 315.00 |
| #7654 Reverse Twist, Aquamarine, 6-1/2" d, 6-3/4" h | 195.00 |

## Cordial

| | |
|---|---|
| #7565 Astrid, Anna Rose, #734 American Beauty etch, 3/4 oz | 155.00 |
| #7577 Venus, Anna Rose, #743 Bramble Rose etch, 1-1/2 oz | 165.00 |
| #7643 Golf Ball, 1-1/2 oz, Pastels | 55.00 |
| #7643 Golf Ball, 1-1/2 oz, Spanish Red | 55.00 |
| #7643 Golf Ball, 1-1/2 oz, Stiegel Green | 52.00 |
| #7617 Brilliant, Spanish Red, 1-1/2 oz | 135.00 |
| #7654 Lorna, Nantucket etch, 1-1/2 oz | 105.00 |
| #7668 Galaxy, Mayfair etch, 1-1/2 oz | 87.50 |

#7673 Lexington, Ritz Blue filament, #790 Fairwin etch,
  1-1/2 oz ...........................................................................165.00
#7690 Monroe, Spanish Red ................................................68.00

## Goblet

#300 Festival, Gloria Blue, 8 oz ......................................35.00
#7568 Horizon, #735 Richmond etch, 10 oz ....................48.00
#7577 Venus, Anna Rose, Palm Optic, 9 oz ....................55.00
#7577 Venus, Crystal, #743 Bramble Rose etch, 9 oz ...............80.00
#7604-1/2 Heirloom, 14-K Topaz, #751 Adonis etch, 9 oz.........125.00
#7614 Hampton, Golden iris, Virginia etch, 9 oz ...........65.00
#7617 Brilliant, Spanish Red, 10 oz ................................95.00
#7624 Paragon, Ebony open stem, 10 oz ......................200.00
#7630 Ballerina, Aquamarine/Azure, Yukon cutting, 10 oz........120.00
#7637 Courtney, D.C. Thorpe satin open stem, 9 oz ......195.00
#7640 Art Moderne, Ritz Blue, Crystal open stem, 9 oz............155.00
#7643 Golf Ball, 9 oz, Alabaster ..................................150.00
#7643 Golf Ball, 9 oz, Pastels .......................................55.00
#7643 Golf Ball, 9 oz, Ritz Blue .....................................58.00
#7643 Golf Ball, 9 oz, Spanish Red ...............................56.00
#7643 Golf Ball, 9 oz, Stiegel Green ..............................52.00
#7644-1/2 Vernon, Venetian Green, Pineapple Optic, 9 oz .........55.00
#7659 Cynthia, #746 Sonoma etch, 10 oz ......................68.00
#7577 Venus, Palm Optic, Anna Rose .............................23.00
#7660 Empire, Spanish Red ............................................68.00
#7664 Queen Anne, Manchester Pheasant Silk Screen, 10 oz..275.00
#7665 Laura, Nasreen Etch, topaz .................................95.00
#7678 Old English, 10 oz, Spanish Red .........................55.00
#7690 Monroe, Golden Iris, Amber, 9 oz .......................80.00
#7690 Monroe, Spanish Red, 9 oz .................................68.00

## Guest Set

#23 Trudy, 6-3/8" h
    Alabaster........................................................175.00
    Baby Blue .......................................................85.00
    Bristol Blue......................................................125.00
    Opaque Yellow carafe, India Black tumbler .......195.00
#24 Margaret, 5-7/8" h
    Anna Rose, enamel decor ..............................170.00
    Azure/Aquamarine, enamel decor ...................575.00
    Jade Green .....................................................185.00

## Jug

#6 Kaufmann, #510 Doric Star Sand Blast, 54 oz ........275.00
#8 Orleans, #131 Brittany Cutting, 54 oz .....................385.00
#33 Martina, #518 Lily of the Valley Sand Blast dec, 46 oz, 7-piece
  set ............................................................................585.00
#36 Bolero, Pomona Two-Tone Line, 54 oz ..................985.00
#37 Barry, Anna Rose handle and foot, Palm Optic, 48 oz.........390.00
#303 Cyrano, #203 needle etch, 54 oz .......................385.00
#1933 LMX Del Rey, Randall Blue non-opaque, rare, 54 oz ......675.00
#1962 Ockner, Crinkle Line, 64 oz, Amethyst................145.00
#1962 Ockner, Crinkle Line, 64 oz, Pink Champagne, frosted ...165.00
#7622-1/2 Ringling, 54 oz, Golden Iris ........................650.00
#7622-1/2 Ringling, 54 oz, Spanish Red ......................695.00
#20069 Melon, Alabaster, Ritz Blue trim.....................1,250.00
Pilsner, Floret, etch #796, Lando, 12 oz ......................55.00

## Plate, #1500

Alexandrite, #776 Nasreen etch, dessert, 7" d...............135.00
Anna Rose, #734 American Beauty etch, dessert, 7" d.............55.00
Crystal, #765, Springtime, 6" d .....................................12.50
Crystal, #810 Sear's Lace Bouquet etch, dessert, 7" d..........25.00
Ritz Blue, Vernay decoration, dessert, 7-1/2" d .............135.00
Silk Screen, Queen Louise, cameo dec, c1928, 7-1/2" d...........120.00
Stiegel Green, salad/luncheon, 8-1/2" d ......................55.00
14-K Topaz, Carlton Madrid, liner, 6" d ........................35.00
14-K Topaz, #776 Nasreen etch, salad, 7-3/4" d ...........60.00

## Sherbet

#1962 Crinkle, 6 oz, Pink...............................................24.00
#3011 Montego, Gypsy Fired, 6-1/2" oz..........................38.00
#7620 Fontanne, #781 Fontinelle etch, 6 oz...................165.00
#7643 Golf Ball, 5-1/2 oz, Pastels.................................35.00
#7643 Golf Ball, 5-1/2 oz, Ritz Blue...............................65.00
#7643 Golf Ball, 5-1/2 oz, Spanish Red..........................40.00
#7643 Golf Ball, 5-1/2 oz, Stiegel Green.........................40.00
#7646 Sophisticate, Picardy etch, 5-1/2 oz....................48.00
#7654-1/2 Legacy, Manchester Pheasant Silk Screen, 6-1/2 oz 135.00
#7690 Monroe, Old Amethyst, 6 oz................................85.00
#7780 The President's House, 6 oz................................20.00
Torte Plate, Hollywood, crystal, platinum/ded band decor,
  14" d..................................................................400.00

## Tumbler

#1928 Ivy, Stiegel Green, ice tea, 15 oz ........................75.00
#1962 Crinkle, India Black, flat juice, 6 oz .....................85.00
#7622 Bracelet, Ritz Blue, ice tea, 14 oz .......................85.00
#7664 Queen Anne, Aquamarine/Azure, #758 Elizabeth etch,
  11 oz...............................................................115.00 -
#7668 Galaxy, #778 Carlton etch, 9 oz .........................22.00
#9051 Zenith, Venetian Green, Peacock Optic, bar, 2 oz............45.00
#9074 Belton, Primrose, Vaseline, Pillar Optic, 9 oz.........125.00

## Vase

#12 Viola, Rainbow Line, Spiral Optic, 8" d ...............120.00
#25 Olympic, #734 American Beauty etch, 12" h .........650.00
#26 Catherine 10" bud, Azure, #758 Sunrise Medallion etch ....250.00
#35-1/2 Electra, Continental Line, Old Amethyst, 10"...........1,000.00
#53 Serenade 10" bud, Opaque Yellow .....................430.00
#53 Serenade 10" bud, Venetian Green, #756 Tinker Bell etch .595.00
#67 Grecian, Ebony, Saracenic Art Line, 6" h.................1,200.00
#73 Radio, Ritz Blue, 6".............................................895.00
#90 Daisy, Crystal, Green and White Wash, 9-1/2" w...............450.00
#91 Lalique, Crystal Satin, 8-1/4" h ............................650.00
#1933 Gaydos, LMX Seaweed, 6-1/2"........................785.00
#7621 Ringer, 10" bud, Opaque Yellow .....................475.00

## Wine

#7565 Astrid, Anna Rose, #734 American Beauty etch, 3 oz.....125.00
#7577 Venus, Anna Rose, #743 Bramble Rose etch, 3-1/2 oz...145.00
#7643 Golf Ball, 3 oz, Alabaster ...............................145.00
#7643 Golf Ball, 3 oz, Ritz Blue ...................................65.00
#7643 Golf Ball, 3 oz, Stiegel Green............................55.00
#7640 Art Moderne, ebony stem, 3 oz ......................145.00
#7660-1/2 Empress, Spanish Red, 3 oz ......................85.00
#7668 Galaxy, #810 Sears' Lace Bouquet etch, 2-1/2 oz............48.00
#7690 Monroe, Spanish Red ........................................45.00
#7693 Warwick, Stiegel Green, 2-1/2 oz ......................55.00
#7721 Panama, Sharon decoration, 3 oz ....................225.00
#8446 Summer Cornucopia, Copen Blue bowl, 3 oz.................325.00

# MOSER GLASS

**History:** Ludwig Moser (1833-1916) founded his polishing and engraving workshop in 1857 in Karlsbad (Karlovy Vary), Czechoslovakia. He employed many famous glass designers, e.g., Johann Hoffmann, Josef Urban, and Rudolf Miller. In 1900, Moser and his sons, Rudolf and Gustav, incorporated Ludwig Moser & Söhne.

Moser art glass included clear pieces with inserted blobs of colored glass, cut colored glass with classical scenes, cameo glass, and intaglio cut items. Many inexpensive enameled pieces also were made.

In 1922, Leo and Richard Moser bought Meyr's Neffe, their biggest Bohemian art glass rival. Moser executed many pieces for the Wiener Werkstätte in the 1920s. The Moser glass factory continues to produce new items.

**References:** Gary Baldwin and Lee Carno, *Moser—Artistry in Glass*, Antique Publications, 1988; Mural K. Charon and John Mareska, *Ludvik Moser, King of Glass*, published by author, 1984.

Bowl, 7-1/4" d, 5-5/8" h, opalescent pink shaded ground, multicolored enameled oak leaves and foliage, applied lustered acorns, sgd in gold on base.............................................................. 1,200.00
Box, cov
   3" d, hinged, extensive gold dec, applied floral dec, wear .... 90.00
   3-3/8" h, circular, deep purple ground, gold enameled fauns and maidens, fitted cov, four ball feet, etched "Made in Czechoslovakia Moser Karlsbad" ................................................ 1,200.00
   4-1/2" l, red ground, enameled blue and white floral motif, gilt highlights .............................................................. 550.00
   6" d, 3-3/4" h, cranberry ground, white enameled woman carrying cornucopia and grapes, gold enameled vine and berries 650.00
Bride's Bowl, 12-3/4" d, 12" h, amber glass bowl with applied clear edge, two large enameled salamanders, additional floral and leaf dec, sgd Wilcox silver-plated holder with two young women carrying urn, castle and trees on base .............................................. 1,950.00
Cabinet Vase, 2" h, 2-1/2" w, bulbous, citron green ground, applied brass rim, three black glass acorns, gold and yellow florals and leaves, three flying insects, sgd "Moser Carlsbad" under base 200.00
Calling Card Holder, cranberry ground, turquoise jewels, gold prunts, four scrolled feet.................................................... 375.00
Chalice, cov, 9-1/2" h, amber and colorless ground, faceted, central landscape frieze, gold leaves outlined in white, gold and black dots, white dotted blossoms, neck, base, and orange stopper heavily gold encrusted ...................................................... 425.00

**Bud Vase, all over floral dec and gilding, sgd, 6-1/4" h, $350. Photo courtesy of Joy Luke Fine Art Brokers and Auctioneers.**

Cologne Bottle, 9-1/2" h, deep cobalt blue ground, enameled floral scene, matching stopper, script engraved "Moser" .................. 225.00
Compote
   4" h, 8-1/4" d, hollow base, pale amber ground, electric blue rigaree and four applied dec, int. deck of twelve painted leaves, brown branches, gold leaves, white cherries, matching branch on base ...................................................... 650.00
   9-1/2" h, quatraform, crystal ground, gilt enameled heavy scrollwork reserves, matching dec on pedestal foot, crystal stem, pr.... 400.00
Cordial, 1-3/8" h, cranberry bowl, colorless stem, multicolored enameled flowers, bee, and insect dec on base ............................... 100.00
Creamer and Sugar, cov, engraved branch and floral dec, gilt trim, sgd ........................................................................ 275.00
Cup and Saucer, green shading to clear, heavy gold dec........... 350.00
Decanter
   9" h, amber, matching glass, elaborate enameled dec ....... 200.00
   9" h, green, six matching liqueurs, elaborate enameled dec, sgd ........................................................................ 500.00
   15" h, cranberry, gold overlay dec, sgd.............................. 200.00
Ewer, 9" h, cov, horn shape, aquamarine ground, all over gold leaves, vines and flowers, pedestal base ............................................ 925.00
Fernery, 7" d, deep amethyst ground, inverted thumbprint, enameled florals, script sgd "Moser"........................................ 450.00
Goblet, 4-1/2" h, cranberry ground, enameled, gold overlay, wheel cut design, ftd stem with gold overlay on base, 6 pc set................ 500.00
Ice Cream Set, master bowl and four serving bowls, clear shading to gold ground, mermaid relief, gilt highlights................................ 395.00
Jar, cov, 8" h, flattened solid cover, raised rim, optic-ribbed ovoid body, translucent brilliant green, acid stamp on base, early 20th C, minor abrasions................................................................ 325.00
Jewelry Box, 3-1/2" d, dark cranberry, enameled stork, heavy gold dec ........................................................................ 225.00
Lamp, 18" h, 7-1/4" w globe, cranberry opaque ground, multicolored enamel floral dec, gilt scroll dec, finely cut pattern on globe and base, acid etched signature on base, c1920 ................................ 4,800.00
Liquor Bottle
   9" h, double sided, amber, heavy enameled dec............... 300.00
   11" h, blue, brass base, heavy enameled dec .................... 100.00
   13" h, double sided, amber, heavy enameled dec.............. 300.00
Mug, 4-1/4" h, topaz colored crackle ground, heavy gold handle and base edging, four applied insects with polychrome dec........... 345.00
Nappy, 5" w, 1-3/4" h, pastel green, yellow, blue, and pink, four enameled foxes, applied loop handle, polished disc base ................ 500.00
Pansy Vase, 14" h, colorless ground, multicolored dec ........... 1,000.00
Perfume Bottle, 6-1/2" h, 4-1/4" d, Malachite ground, molded bottle and stopper, slab polished sides and top ........................................ 295.00
Pitcher, 11-3/4" h, bright transparent blue ground, heavy gilding, enameled fern fronds, birds, and insects, applied salamander handle ....... 2,400.00
Plate, 7-3/8" d, amber ground, gold dec ...................................... 150.00
Pokal, cov, 8" h, cut, faceted, and enameled, amethyst body with cut panels, gold and high relief floral dec, wafer foot with cut stem........... 700.00
Scent Bottle, 5" h, emerald green ground,, multicolored leaves and berries, ball stopper.............................................................. 195.00
Sweetmeat Dish, round, cranberry ground, engraved, gold band ... 225.00
Toothpick, cranberry cased with clear, fancy gold band trim, acid etched signature.................................................................. 150.00
Tray, 12-7/8" l, cranberry, enamel foliate dec, gilt highlights, two handles.................................................................. 1,100.00
Tumbler
   3-1/2" h, octagonal, ruby cut to clear ground, gold dec ........ 85.00
   4" h, green, red, and blue, elaborately dec with floral, scrolled, beading, and gild, some beads missing, 9 pc set ........... 460.00
Vase
   4-1/4" h, amethyst, sgd.................................................... 400.00
   6-1/4" h, bud, allover floral dec, and gilding, sgd ............... 325.00
   6-1/4" h, hexagonal faceted body, heavy walled colorless glass, classical gilt frieze of Amazon women, acid stamp on base, c1925 ...................................................... 150.00
   6-1/2" h, Persian style dec of scrolls and flowers, lime green surface, cased opaque white lining, gold outlines................ 465.00

7" h, blue, applied crystal rigaree with drips, three feet, sgd ....250.00
8" h, dimpled, lavender, enameled bird and branch dec.....375.00
9" h, cranberry, gold beaded floral dec, sgd ......................425.00
10" h, flared cylindrical form, heavy walled smoky gray glass, Art Deco facet cut panels of four horizontal bands, unsigned, c1925, minute nicks ......................................................260.00
11" h, cranberry, gold beaded floral dec and Mary Gregory-type tree scene, sgd................................................................425.00
11" h, 7" w, fan shape, blue, heavy enameled dec .............450.00
12" h, 7-1/2" w, fan shape, apricot, enameled dec..............450.00
12-1/8" h, 3-7/8" w, flaring neck, stepped pedestal base, delicate gold all over fern and floral design on neck and body, 2-3/8" border with gold design, acid cutback dots above and below border, pink, white, purple, orange and magenta floral dec of pansies, bell flowers, mums, daisies and clematis, shaded green foliage all around base, orig paper label with design number, c1880 ................................................................2,800.00
15-1/2" h, clear and frosted ground, deeply etched thistles, inscribed "Moser/Karlsbad" ...............................................450.00

Wine
Rainbow glass, funnel shaped cup, Inverted Baby Thumbprint pattern, enameled grapes and leaves dec, applied row of gold knobs around top ......................................................365.00
Turquoise shading to clear ground, all over gold leaf dec, heavy applied prunts...............................................................425.00

# MOUNT WASHINGTON GLASS COMPANY

**History:** In 1837, Deming Jarves, founder of the Boston and Sandwich Glass Company, established the Mount Washington Glass Company in Boston, Massachusetts for his son, George D. Jarves. In the following years, the leadership and the name of the company changed several times as George Jarves formed different associations.

In the 1860s, the company was owned and operated by Timothy Howe and William L. Libbey. In 1869, Libbey bought a new factory in New Bedford, Massachusetts. The Mount Washington Glass Company began operating again there under its original name. Henry Libbey became associated with the company early in 1871. He resigned in 1874 during the general depression, and the glassworks was closed. William Libbey had resigned in 1872 when he went to work for the New England Glass Company.

The Mount Washington Glass Company opened again in the fall of 1874 under the presidency of A. H. Seabury and the management of Frederick S. Shirley. In 1894, the glassworks became a part of the Pairpoint Manufacturing Company.

Throughout its history, the Mount Washington Glass Company made different types of glass including pressed, blown, art, lava, Napoli, cameo, cut, Albertine, and Verona.

**References:** Kyle Husfloen, contributing editor Louis O. St. Aubin Jr., *Antique Trader's American & European Decorative and Art Glass Price Guide,* 2nd ed., Krause Publications, 2000; Edward and Sheila Malakoff, *Pairpoint Lamps,* Schiffer Publishing, 1990; John A. Shuman III, *Collector's Encyclopedia of American Art Glass,* Collector Books, 1988, 1994 value update.

**Collectors Club:** Mount Washington Art Glass Society, P.O. Box 24094, Fort Worth, TX 76124.-1094.

**Museum:** The New Bedford Glass Museum, New Bedford, MA.

**Additional Listings:** Burmese; Crown Milano; Peachblow; Royal Flemish.

**Advisor:** Louis O. St. Aubin Jr.

Basket, 8" l, 4-1/2" w, 9" h, satin, MOP, Herringbone pattern, sky-blue shading to pale blue, applied frosted camphor edge, sixty crimps, applied twisted frosted handle...................................675.00
Bowl
4-1/2" d, 2-3/4" h, Rose Amber, Swirl pattern, blue swirl bands, bell tone.................................................................295.00
8" d, 4" h, Cameo, blue over white, sq shape, ruffled edge, two winged griffins holding up scroll, spray of flowers .........1,475.00
Box, cov, 6-1/2" w, 4-1/2" h, Opal Ware, mint green background with deep pink roses and small red cornflowers, gold trim, blown-out floral and ribbon design, numbered "3212/20" ...............................1,750.00
Collars and Cuff Box, cov, shape of two collars with a big bow in the front, oriental poppies in shades of pink and orange, silver finial in the shape of a poppy with gold trim on cov, base with oriental poppies on white ground, gold trim, bright blue bow with white polka dots with a buckle on the back, sgd "Patent applied for April 10, 1894," numbered 2390/128 ...............................................................950.00
Cracker Jar, fancy metal work
6" h, 6-1/2" w, Opal Ware, pale green and white ground, panels of pink, white and orange poppies, gold trim, orig fancy silver-plated hardware has lion heads with rings for handles, Pairpoint trademark stamped in cover and numbered "3948," base mkd "3948/230".................................................................950.00
6-1/2" h, 6" w, 16 panels, gold/beige ground, white and deep pink roses, green leaves, cov sgd "Pairpoint-3932," base sgd "3932/222".................................................................595.00
Item M2160-Mt. Washington/Pairpoint cracker jar, 16 panels with a. Signed in cover and on base fancy metal work. 6-1/2" h by 6 "w. .................................................................595.00
9" h, 8" d, pagoda shape, blown-out mold, bright yellow ground, painted pink and white poppies, green leaves, orig silver-plated cov stamped "Pairpoint 3954," base numbered "230"... 1,200.00
9-1/2" h, 7-1/2" w, Opal Ware, bright yellow ground, pink oriental poppies, green leaves, blown out floral and leaf design on base, cov mkd "Pairpoint," base mkd "3930/230" ......................525.00
10" h, 6-1/2" w, egg-shape, deep burgundy ground, white, pink, yellow, and blue poppies dec, two-piece silver-plated top sgd with Pairpoint trademark and "3951," base numbered "3951/840"................................................................1,750.00
10" h, 6-1/2" w, egg-shape, deep green ground, white and yellow pond lily dec, two-piece silver-plated top sgd with Pairpoint trademark and "3951," base numbered "3951/849" ......1,750.00
Fruit Bowl, 10" w, 7" h, Napoli, solid green painted on clear glass background, outside is dec with pale pink and white pond lilies with green and pink leaves and blossoms against the dark green background, entire interior is dec with gold highlight traceries, silver plated base with pond lily design, two applied loop handles and four bud feet on base, mkd "Pairpoint Mfg. Co. B4704" ..................................2,200.00
Humidor, 6-1/2" h, 4-1/2" w, Opal Ware, shaded yellow ground, yellow and pink spider mums dec, silver-plated leaves finial on gold beaded top, base numbered "2382," int. edge flakes............................525.00
Jewel Box, cov
5-1/4" w, 3-1/4" h, Colonial Ware, pale pink base, 4 panels of painted purple and yellow pansies, fancy blown-molded blank with scrollwork, orig metal cover with orig cloth covered pin cushion, silver plated gold-washed metal mount, mkd "M.W."....................525.00
6" w, 3" h, heart-shape, Opal Ware, soft pink ground with gold highlights, cover with heart-shaped medallion with yellow and purple spider mum, orig lining, orig fancy gold-plated hardware, base numbered "4625"................................................1,200.00

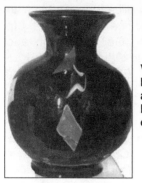

Vase, Lava Glass, jet black body, blue, jade, green, gray, white, red, and black imbedded designs, 5-3/8" h, 4-1/8" d, $1,950. Photo courtesy of Clarence & Betty Maier.

Nappy, 6" w, 2" h, crystal, gold pond lilies with buds, green stems and leaf, applied crystal loop handle ................................................ 375.00
Pitcher .......................................................................................................
    4-1/2" h, 3" w, satin, MOP, Polka Dot pattern, deep peachblow pink with white air traps, diamond quilted, unlined, applied frosted loop handle .......................................................... 325.00
    6" h, 3" w, satin, MOP, DQ pattern, frosted camphor shell loop handle ................................................................................ 325.00
    6" h, 4" w, satin, MOP, Polka Dot pattern, deep peachblow pink with white air traps, diamond quilted, unlined, applied frosted loop handle .......................................................... 475.00
    8" h, 5" w, tankard, crystal, white and purple spider mum dec, gold traceries, dec on handle ............................................. 895.00
    10-3/4" h, 5-1/4" w, Colonial Ware, white ground, heavy gold dec, fifteen gold ribbons with bows, roses, border of heavy raised scrolls and leaves, thorn handle, sgd in pontil with monogram and "1027" .................................................................. 1,200.00
Sugar Shaker, 5" h, 4" w, egg-shape, green shading to white ground, allover enamel white and pink flowers, orig metal cov in fair condition ................................................................................ 375.00
Vase
    5-3/4" h, 4-1/4" d, satin, MOP, Hobnail pattern, heavenly blue shading to white, white lining, four folded top ................. 675.00
    6" h, 3-1/4" d, satin, MOP, bulbous stick, flaring rim, DQ pattern, apricot shading to white, white lining ................................ 375.00
    6-1/4" h, 5-1/2" w, satin, Bridal White, MOP, Muslin pattern, melon ribbed, applied frosted edge, c1880 ................................. 425.00
    6-1/2" h, 3" d, satin, Bristol White, MOP, Raindrop pattern, applied frosted crimped edge, price for pr .................................... 550.00
    7-3/4" h, 7" w, satin, melon ribbed, MOP, Muslin pattern, deep gold, white lining, applied frosted edge ............................ 375.00
    8" h, satin, MOP, crimped top, butterscotch, Raindrop pattern, applied camphor edge ....................................................... 375.00
    8" h, 7" w, satin, MOP, bulbous, Alice Blue, Muslin pattern, applied frosted edge, three petal top ................................... 675.00
    8-1/4" h, 5" d, satin, MOP, amberina colored, red-orange with deep gold diamonds, white lining, slightly ruffed top ..... 1,250.00
    9" h, flaring gourd-shape, bright crystal, green Parrot tulips with gold leaves .............................................................................. 375.00
    9" h, 3-1/2" w at shoulder, satin, MOP, Raindrop pattern, deep gold, 1880s ............................................................................. 285.00
    9" h, 3-1/2" w, satin, wide swirl design, MOP, gold shading to pale pink-white .............................................................................. 425.00
    11-1/4" h, 6" neck, satin, gourd-shape, deep brown shading to gold, white lining, enameled seaweed dec ...................... 550.00
    12-3/4" h, 5-1/2" w, Colonial Ware, Persian water jug shape, bulbous body and pedestal base, loop handle on top, small spout, glossy white ground, pale pink and purple lilies, green leaves and stems, overlaid gold decoration of leaves, stems and daisies, scroll work, sgd, numbered #1022 ...................... 2,200.00

# MULBERRY CHINA

**History:** Mulberry china was made primarily in the Staffordshire district of England between 1830 and 1860. The ware often has a flowing effect similar to Flow Blue. It is the color of crushed mulberries, a dark purple, sometimes with a gray tinge or bordering almost on black. The potteries that manufactured Flow Blue also made Mulberry china, and, in fact, frequently made some patterns in both types of wares. To date, there are no known reproductions.

**References:** Susan and Al Bagdade, *Warman's English & Continental Pottery & Porcelain*, 3rd Edition, Krause Publications, 1998; Ellen R. Hill, *Mulberry Ironstone*, published by author, 1993; Petra Williams, *Flow Blue China and Mulberry Ware*, revised ed., Fountain House East, 1993.

**Collectors' Club:** Flow Blue International Collectors' Club, Inc., P.O. Box 168572, Irving, TX 75016.

**Advisor:** Ellen G. King.

**Athens,** Meigh, child's cup and saucer ..................................... 250.00
**Bouquet,** Wedgwood
    Charger Plate, 12-1/2" d ....................................................... 125.00
    Plate, 9" d ............................................................................... 65.00
**Bryonia,** Utzschneider
    Cake Plate, 14" d, stemmed ................................................. 375.00
    Demitasse Cup and Saucer ..................................................... 50.00
    Dessert Bowl, 4" d .................................................................. 35.00
    Fruit Compote, footed .......................................................... 220.00
    Plate, 8" d ............................................................................... 45.00
    Tea Cup and Saucer ............................................................... 65.00
**California,** Podmore & Walker, plate, 9-3/4" d ........................... 80.00
**Corean,** Podmore & Walker
    Plate, 7-3/4" d ........................................................................ 35.00
    Plate, 8-3/4" d ........................................................................ 55.00
    Plate, 9-3/4" d ........................................................................ 85.00
    Platter, 14" l ......................................................................... 200.00
    Platter, 16" l ......................................................................... 225.00
    Platter, 17" l ......................................................................... 300.00
    Platter, 18" l ......................................................................... 375.00
    Vegetable Tureen, cov .......................................................... 350.00
**Delhi,** M. T. & Co.
    Plate, 10-1/4" d .................................................................... 110.00
    Platter, 14" l ......................................................................... 185.00
**Flora,** Walker
    Cup and Saucer, handleless .................................................. 65.00
    Plate, 8" d ............................................................................... 55.00
**Genoa,** Davenport, platter, 13-3/4" l ....................................... 200.00
**Jeddo,** Adams
    Cup and Saucer, handleless .................................................. 80.00
    Platter, 12-1/4" l .................................................................. 225.00

Bryonia, demitasse cup and saucer, $50. Photo courtesy of Ellen G. King.

**Delhi, plate, 10-1/4" d, $110. Photo courtesy of Ellen G. King.**

| | |
|---|---:|
| Platter, 17-3/4" l | 300.00 |
| Sauce Tureen, footed, with tray | 475.00 |
| Teapot with lid | 450.00 |
| **Marble,** unknown maker | |
| Plate, 9" d | 65.00 |
| Vegetable Bowl, 9-1/2" d, open | 90.00 |
| **Medina,** Furnival, plate, 9" d | 75.00 |
| **Milan,** South Wales Pottery, platter, 14" l | 250.00 |
| **Rhone Scenery,** Mayer, tea cup and saucer | 75.00 |
| **Rose,** Challinor, plate, 8" d | 60.00 |
| **Rose,** Walker | |
| Cup Plate | 110.00 |
| Waste Bowl | 70.00 |
| **Royal,** Wood & Son | |
| Plate, 9-3/4" d | 85.00 |
| Tea Cup and Saucer | 65.00 |
| **Seaweed,** Ridgway, platter, 12" l | 135.00 |
| **Seville,** Wood & Sons, plate, 9-1/4" d | 50.00 |
| **Temple,** Podmore & Walker | |
| Bowl, 7" d | 125.00 |
| Cup Plate | 95.00 |
| Plate, 8-3/4" d | 70.00 |
| **Tillenburg,** Clementson, plate, 10-1/4" d | 80.00 |
| **Vincennes,** Alcock, relish dish, mitten shape | 300.00 |
| **Washington Vase,** Podmore & Walker | |
| Plate, 8" d | 55.00 |
| Platter, 16" l | 275.00 |
| **Wreath,** Furnival, plate, 9-3/4" d | 95.00 |

# MUSICAL INSTRUMENTS

**History:** From the first beat of the prehistoric drum to the very latest in electronic music makers, musical instruments have been popular modes of communication and relaxation.

The most popular antique instruments are violins, flutes, oboes, and other instruments associated with the classical music period of 1650 to 1900. Many of the modern instruments, such as trumpets, guitars, and drums, have value on the "used," rather than antiques market.

The collecting of musical instruments is in its infancy. The field is growing very rapidly. Investors and speculators have played a role since the 1930s, especially in early string instruments.

**References:** Tony Bacon (ed.), *Classic Guitars of the '50s,* Miller Freeman Books (6600 Silacci Way, Gilroy, CA 95020), 1996; S. P. Fjestad (ed.), *Blue Book of Gui-* *tar Values,* 2nd ed., Blue Book Publications, 1994; Alan Greenwood, *Vintage Guitar Magazine Price Guide,* 6th ed., Vintage Guitar Books, 1998; George Gruhn and Walter Carter, *Acoustic Guitars and Other Fretted Instruments,* GPI Books, 1993; ——, *Electric Guitars and Basses,* Miller Freeman Books, GPI Books, 1994; ——, *Gruhn's Guide to Vintage Guitars,* GPI Books, 1991; Philip F. Gura and James F. Bollman, *America's Instrument: The Banjo in the 19th Century,* Univ of North Carolina Press, 1999; Mike Longworth, *C. F. Martin & Co.,* 4 Maples Press, 1994; Paul Trynka (ed.), *Electric Guitar,* Chronicle Books, 1993; Michael Wright, *Guitar Stories, Vol. II,* Vintage Guitar Books, 2000.

**Periodicals:** *Concertina & Squeezebox,* P.O. Box 6706, Ithaca, NY 14851; *Jerry's Musical Newsletter,* 4624 W Woodland Rd, Minneapolis, MN 55424; *Piano & Keyboard,* P.O. Box 767, San Anselmo, CA 94979; *Strings,* P.O. Box 767, San Anselmo, CA 94979; *Twentieth Century Guitar,* 135 Oser Ave., Hauppauge, NY 11788; *Vintage Guitar Classics,* P.O. Box 7301, Bismarck, ND 58507.

**Collectors' Clubs:** American Musical Instrument Society, RD 3, Box 205-B, Franklin, PA 16323; Automatic Musical Instrument Collectors Association, 919 Lantern Glow Trail, Dayton, OH 45431; Fretted Instrument Guild of America, 2344 S. Oakley Ave., Chicago, IL 60608; Musical Box Society International, 887 Orange Ave. E., St Paul, MN 55106; Reed Organ Society, Inc., P.O. Box 901, Deansboro, NY 13328.

**Museums:** C. F. Martin Guitar Museum, Nazareth, PA; International Piano Archives at Maryland, Neil Ratliff Music Library, College Park, MD; Miles Musical Museum, Eureka Springs, AR; Museum of the American Piano, New York, NY; Musical Museum, Deansboro, NY; Streitwieser Foundation Trumpet Museum, Pottstown,

**Watercolor and gouache by Adolf Friederich Von Menzel (1815-1905), showing woman singing while standing next to early pianoforte, 10" x 12", $79,520. Photo courtesy of Jackson's Auctioneers & Appraisers.**

PA; University of Michigan, Stearns Collection of Musical Instruments, Ann Arbor, MI; Yale University Collection of Musical Instruments, New Haven, CT.

**Alto Saxophone**, A. Lecompte, Paris, c1920, bell stamped "A. Lecompte, 8, Cie, Paris," nickel plated body with double octave key, mouthpiece and case ............ 1,495.00

**Arch-Top Guitar**, John D'Angelico, NY, 1937 Model New Yorker, sunburst finish, stamped internally, two-piece medium curl maple back and sides, medium grain top with "X" bracing, strong medium curl neck, bound ebony fingerboard with split block inlay, 21-1/16" l back, 17-3/4" w at base, case .................... 21,850.00

**Baritone Horn**, Boston Musical Instrument Mfg., engraved "Made in The Boston Musical Instrument Manufy," brass, three keys, brass tubing in E flat .................................................. 260.00

**Baritone Saxophone**, Buescher Company, Elkhart, IN, stamped "The Buescher, Elkhart, Ind. USA" on the bell, case, music stand ... 920.00

**Bass Clarinet**, stamped "P. Gerard Paris" at the bell and on ebony body, nickel plated bell, neck, and keys, case ......................... 815.00

**Clarinet, French**

Chibonville Freres, multiple stamps "Chibonville Freres, B," boxwood, brass keys, ivory fittings, 26-1/6" l ....................... 575.00

J. Grandjon, Paris, bell stamped "J. Grandjion Boulevart De Sebastopol 105, Rue Reaunur, 48 Paris," boxwood, nickel plated keys, 27" l, 685 mm .............................. 375.00

**Fife**, English, unstamped, boxwood, five brass keys with round covers, ivory fittings, 11-3/4" l, 298 mm, loss to ivory ........................... 325.00

**Flute**

American, Heinrich Christian Eisenbrandt, Philadelphia, c1814, each piece stamped "Eisenbrandt, Philade," carved four-piece flute, silver fittings, four square ivory covered keys, 23-3/4" l, 602 mm .................................................. 6,325.00

American, Asa Hopkins, Litchfield, CT, 19th C, labeled "A. Hopkins, Litchfield, Conn," boxwood, one brass key with square cover, ivory fittings, 23-3/4" l, 605 mm, cap missing ..... 1,265.00

English, GX Astor & Co., London, 19th C, multiple stamps "GX Astor & Co. London," boxwood, ivory fittings, single brass key with square cover, 24-1/16" l, 610 mm ............................ 575.00

English, illegible mark, boxwood, ivory fittings, four brass keys with round covers, later cap, 24-1/4" l, 616 mm ............... 490.00

**Grand Piano**, Victorian, fourth quarter 19th C, Kirkman, London, burl walnut, massive tapering paneled legs, 86-1/2" w, 63" d, 40" h .......2,000.00

**Guitar**

Gibson Co., Kalamazoo, 1929, labeled "Gibson Nick Lucas Special," triple-bound two piece mahogany back, mahogany sides, medium grain spruce top, rosewood bound fingerboard with pearl inlay, custom "Florentine Banjo" style peghead, 19-3/8" l back, 492 mm, orig hardshell case ............................... 6,325.00

Gibson Co., Kalamazoo, 1964, labeled "Style Dove, Gibson Guitar, Number 178203, Is Hereby Guaranteed," etc., bound one-piece slab-cut medium curl maple back and sides, medium grain spruce top, mahogany neck, rosewood bound fingerboard with twin parallelogram pearl inlay, pickguard inlaid and engraved by Maudie Moore, 19-7/8" l back, 354 mm, orig hardshell case .......................................... 1,840.00

C. F. Martin & Co., Nazareth, PA, 1969, Model D-28, branded internally "C. F. Martin & Co., Nazareth, PA, Made in U.S.A., D-28, 244449, C. F. Martin & Co. Est. 1833," peghead decal, two-piece bound back and sides of Brazilian rosewood, medium grain spruce top, mahogany neck with ebony fingerboard inlaid with pearl eyes, 20" l back, 509 mm, orig hardshell case ............................2,415.00

C. F. Martin & Co., Nazareth, PA, 1938, Model 00-17, stamped internally "Model 00-17, C. F. Martin & Co. Est. 1833," peghead decal, two-piece mahogany back, mahogany sides and top, mahogany neck, rosewood bound fingerboard with inlaid pearl eyes, 18-7/8" l back, 479 mm, case ............................ 1,495.00

**Harp**, 66-1/2" h, Regency, first quarter 19th C, made in Paris, indistinctly signed, ebonized and giltwood, headed by floral garland and trio of dancing maidens .................................................... 4,850.00

**Oboe**

Austrian, M. Schuck, Vienna, c1900, stamped "H. Schuck Wien," maple, two silver keys with square covers, 22" l, 561 mm....575.00

German, Golde, Dresden, 19th C, stamped "Golde, Dresden" at the bell, boxwood, brass keys with round covers, ivory fittings, 21-7/8" l, 556 mm ...................................................... 4,600.00

**Plectrum Banjo**, Model Pete Seeger, Vega Co., Boston, labeled "The Vega Co. Boston 15 Mass., Patented U.S.A. No. A125547, Model Pete Seeger," laminated maple pot with 24 bracket rim, laminated maple neck with ebony faceplate inlaid with pearl star and VEGA, bound ebony fingerboard with pearl dot inlay, 11-3/8" d head, with stand.................................................. 1,725.00

**Resonator Guitar**, Dobro, c1970, sq neck, bound mahogany body, rosewood bound fingerboard with pearl eyes, 19-3/4" l back, case, steel, and fingerpicks .................................................. 490.00

**Ukulele**, C. F. Martin & Co., Nazareth, PA, c1950, Style I, stamped "C. F. Martin & Co., Nazareth, PA," mahogany back and sides, top bound in three-ply binding, mahogany neck, rosewood fingerboard with inlaid pearl eyes, 9-3/8" l back, 239 mm, with case ................ 875.00

**Viola**, Mittenwald, c1880, unlabeled, irregular curl one-piece back, narrow curl ribs and scroll, wide grain top, golden brown varnish, 15-1/2" l back, 393 mm, case ........................................2,070.00

**Viola Bow**

François Lotte, silver mounted, round stick stamped "François Lotte" at the butt, ebony frog with pearl eye, plain silver adjuster, 63 grams ............................................................. 1,150.00

Jean Jacques Millant, gold mounted, round stick stamped "Jean Jacques Millant A Paris" at the butt, ebony frog with Parisian eye, gold and ebony adjuster, 63 grams, without hair... 3,450.00

**Violin**

American, George E. Bryant, Lowell, 1926, labeled "Made by Geo. E. Bryant, Lowell, Mass, 1926," strong narrow curl one-piece back, similar ribs, faint curl scroll, medium grain top, golden varnish, 14-1/8" l, 359 mm, case ...................... 1,955.00

American, R. G. Hall, Portland, ME, 1916, labeled "R. G. Hall, Portland, Maine, 1916," narrow curl two-piece back, similar ribs and scroll, medium to wide grain top, red varnish, 14-1/16" l back, 357 mm, case ....................................................... 435.00

American, Jerome Bonaparte Squier, Boston, 1890, labeled "Jerome B. Squier, Maker, Boston, 1890, NO. 210," strong narrow curl two-piece back, medium curl ribs, narrow curl scroll, medium grain top, golden orange varnish, 14-3/16" l, 350 mm, bow and case ............................................................. 1,100.00

American, unlabeled, c1920, narrow curl one-piece back, similar ribs, plain scroll, medium to fine grain top, reddish-brown varnish, 13-7/8" l, 352 mm, case........................................ 1,265.00

English, possibly Charles Boullangier for Edward Withers, c1850, sgd internally "J. Panormo," strong narrow curl two-piece back, similar ribs and scroll, fine to medium grain top, golden red varnish, 14" l back, 355 mm............................................... 16,100.00

French, labeled "François Barzoni, Chateau Thierry," c1890, narrow curl two-piece back, similar ribs and scroll, fine grain top, amber varnish, 14-1/8" l, 359 mm, case ...................... 2,100.00

German, labeled "Copy of Joseph Guarnerius, by Rudolph Fischer 1899," medium curl two-piece back, narrow curl ribs and scroll, wide grain top, amber varnish, 14" l back, 356 mm, case..... 635.00

German, labeled "Bapt. Grancino, Fecit Milano An 19??," wide curl one-piece back, medium curl ribs and scroll, medium grain top, amber varnish, 14-1/8" l, 358 mm, case ................... 750.00

German, unlabeled, narrow curl one-piece back, medium curl ribs, irregular curl scroll, medium grain top, golden red varnish, 14" l back, 355 mm, case and two bows...................... 1,495.00

Italian, Giovanni Battista Guadagnini Parma, c1770, labeled "Joannes Baptista Guadagnini, Cremonensis Fecit Parma, Serviens C.S.R. 1770," narrow curl two-piece back, similar ribs and curl, medium grain top, golden amber varnish, 13-15/16" l back, 353 mm, case, certificate from Rembert Wurlitzer, June 13, 1950, and accompanying appraisals......................... 288,500.00

Italian, Pietro Sgarabotto, Parma, 1932, labeled "Petrus Sgarabotto Mediolani, Fecit Vicentiae Anno Domini, 1932, Parma," strong narrow curl one-piece back, medium curl ribs and scroll, fine to medium grain top, golden orange varnish, 13-7/8" l, 352 mm, case.................................................................. 23,000.00

Italian, Carlo Antonio Testore, Milan, 1721, stamped internally with maker's mark, labeled "Carlo Antonio Testore Figlio, Del Giuseppe Testore Fece In Contrada Larga Di, Milano L'Anno 1721," plain one-piece back, narrow curl ribs, plain scroll, fine grain top, golden brown varnish, 14" l, 357 mm .......... 79,500.00

Neapolitan, Ferdinando Gagliano, Naples, 1769, labeled "Ferdinandus Gagliano Figlius Nicolai Fecit Neap, 1769," narrow curl two-piece back, similar ribs and scroll, fine to medium grain top, amber varnish, 14-1/16" l back, 358 mm ..................... 68,500.00

Violin Bow

John Kew Dodd, gold mounted, octagonal stick stamped "Dodd" at the butt, ebony frog with pearl eye (loss), gold and pearl adjuster, 53 grams, without hair ..................................... 2,645.00

Grand-Adam, French, c1850, silver mounted, round stick unstamped, ebony frog with pearl eye, silver and ebony adjuster with Parisian eye, 62 grams ......................................... 14,950.00

William E. Hill & Sons, silver mounted, round stick stamped "W.E.H. & S." at the butt, ebony frog, plain silver adjuster, 66 grams ........................................................................ 2,185.00

Violoncello

English, Henry Lockey Hill, 1820, labeled "I. Hill, Violin & Violoncello Maker, Boro, London," narrow curl two-piece back, similar ribs, faint medium curl scroll, fine to medium curl top, golden varnish, 29-1/8" l, 740 mm, case ................................. 17,250.00

English, labeled "Made and Sold by John Johnson, at the Harp and Crown In Cheapside, 17 London 60," 1753, narrow curl two-piece back, irregular curl ribs and scroll, fine grain top, brown varnish, 29-1/8" l, 740 mm, case ...................... 10,350.00

French, Hugnes Emile Blondelet, Mirecourt, labeled "D'Apres A Stradivarius, E. Blondelet, No. 125 Annee 1912," strong curl two-piece back, narrow curl ribs and scroll, fine to medium grain top, brown varnish, 30" l, 761 mm, case .................... 10,925.00

French, labeled "Paul Lorange, Marseille 1966," strong narrow curl two-piece back, ribs similar, light curl scroll, fine to wide grain top, red varnish, 29-11/16" l back, 753 mm.......... 8,625.00

Italian, labeled "Opera Di Giacomo Rivolta Di 1835, Premiato Di Medagilia D'Argento…," strong narrow curl one-piece back, similar ribs and scroll, medium grain top, amber varnish, 29-3/16" l back, 742 mm ........................................ 10,350.00

# MUSIC BOXES

**History:** Music boxes, invented in Switzerland around 1825, encompass a broad array of forms, from small boxes to huge circus calliopes.

A cylinder box consists of a comb with teeth which vibrate when striking a pin in the cylinder. The music these boxes produce ranges from light tunes to opera and overtures.

The first disc music box was invented by Paul Lochmann of Leipzig, Germany, in 1886. It used an interchangeable steel disc with pierced holes bent to a point which hit the star-wheel as the disc revolved, and thus produced the tune. Discs were easily stamped out of metal, allowing a single music box to play an endless variety of tunes. Disc boxes reached the height of their popularity from 1890 to 1910 when the phonograph replaced them.

Music boxes also were incorporated in many items, e.g., clocks, sewing and jewelry boxes, steins, plates, toys, perfume bottles, and furniture.

**References:** Gilbert Bahl, *Music Boxes*, Courage Books, Running Press, 1993; Arthur W. J. G. Ord-Hume, *Musical Box*, Schiffer Publishing, 1995.

**Collectors' Clubs:** Music Box Society of Great Britain, P.O. Box 299, Waterbeach, Cambridge CB4 4DJ England; Musical Box Society International, 1209 CR 78 West, LaBelle, FL 33935.

**Museums:** Bellms Cars and Music of Yesterday, Sarasota, FL; Lockwood Matthews Mansion Museum, Norwalk, CT; Miles Musical Museum, Eureka Springs, AR; The Musical Museum, Deansboro, NY; The Musical Wonder House Museum, Iscasset, ME.

**Additional Listings:** See *Warman's Americana & Collectibles* for more examples.

Animated, 10" h, 7" w, composition grandmother sitting in chair grinding coffee in coffee mill, moves her lips and eyes as she churns, red printed dress, white apron, white bun hairdo, mounted on wood litho box, side crank handle ......................................... 1,400.00

Bells in Sight, litho paper label, list of eight tunes, mahogany veneer case, inlay and ebonized trim, 6" cylinder, 17-3/4" l ............. 1,320.00

Bells in Vue, Switzerland, litho paper label, list of ten tunes, mahogany veneer case, ebonized trim and clock in crest, 17-1/2" h, 11-1/2" d, 25-1/2" h ................................................................. 2,860.00

Columbia Grafonola, Deluxe, quarter sawed oak veneer case, lion handles, old finish, combination mechanism plays 78 records as well as Regina type metal disks, includes 28 disks, minor edge damage to case, 52" h ...................................................................... 12,650.00

Ideal Sublime Harmonie, Orpheus, labeled "Switzerland," patent dates 1885 and 1890, oak case

Molded detail and applied cast metal ornaments, two 11" d cylinders, needs some adjustments, 30-1/2" l ...................... 2,750.00

Relief carving, three 11" cylinders, storage drawer, 20-1/2" l... 5,225.00

Imperial Symphonion, 15-3/4" disc, stained mahogany case with cable and leaf tip lower borders, single comb, litho tune sheet, coffered lid, six discs, c1900, 23" w .......................................................... 3,500.00

Jacots, oak case, cylinder, Swiss, pat'd safety check Sept 22, 1886, refinished, applied filigree carving on front, 12 tunes, mechanism by Mermod Freres, late 19th C, plays well, 27" x 11" x 8" h case .................. 1,700.00

Kalliope No. 50, 9-1/8" disc, walnut case, bone inlaid lid, nine discs, 11-1/4" w .................................................................................. 900.00

Maliginon, cylinder, inlaid rosewood case, eight tunes, 13" cylinder, keywind, orig label inside outlining eight classical tunes, sgd "A. Maliginon," 20-1/4" x 6-1/2" ................................................... 1,650.00

Nichole Freres, keywind, line inlaid mahogany rect case, musical trophy, 8-1/8" cylinder, 15" w .............................................. 1,300.00

Olympia II, 11-5/8" disc, oak case with coffered lid, flanged base, molded and pressed repeating leaf tip and palmette dec, 22 discs, 15-1/4" w ............................................................................ 1,500.00

**Swiss, inlaid walnut case, 6" d cylinder, butterfly inside, 9-1/4" h, 11" d, 17" l, $700.**

Paillard, 13" cylinder, inlaid and rosewood grained case, eight air playing selection, zither attachment, late 19th C, 22-1/2" ........... 1,650.00

Polyphon, Karl Morat, Eisenbach, Braden, walnut, penny operated, crank handles, c1904, 21 tin discs, 24" w, 13" d, 43" h ......... 3,750.00

Regina, 11" inch, single cone box, old litho label on inside of lid, oak case, box restored, 14" x 12" x 9" ........................................ 1,400.00

Regina Style, works labeled "Scrutz-Marke. Made in Germany," retailer's label "Ilsen & Co. Cincinnati, O," mahogany case, base drawer holds 20 disks, 21" w, 17-1/4" d, 14" h ...................... 3,850.00

Swiss

    6" cylinder, inlaid rosewood grained case, litho tune sheet, eight air playing selection, late 19th C, 16-1/4" h .................. 1,200.00

    8" cylinder, ebonized case, litho tune sheet, 18" w ............. 950.00

Swiss Imperial, 11-1/2" disc, rect inlaid walnut and rosewood crossbanded case, 17 discs, late 19th C, 23-1/2" w ...................... 1,450.00

Thornes, 4-1/2" disc, silvered metal, engraved floral scrolling arabesque case, domed and colonnaded hinged upper section, divided drawer in base, 25 discs, 14" ............................................. 1,750.00

Troubadour, 8-7/8" disc, walnut case, single comb, four saucer bells, eight disks, 10-7/8" w .......................................... 1,200.00

Ultman, Charles, eight air playing selection, inlaid and rosewood grained case, stamped comb, gilt circular medallion behind cylinder, late 19th C, 21-1/4" w .......................................... 1,750.00

Zimbailist, Swiss movement, 42 disks, bright metal silver colored case shaped like bureau, cast machine tooled and engraved dec, 20th C, 12-1/2" l .................................................................... 500.0

# NAILSEA-TYPE GLASS

**History:** Nailsea-type glass is characterized by swirls and loopings, usually white, on a clear or colored ground. One of the first areas where this glass was made was Nailsea, England, 1788-1873, hence the name. Several glass houses, including American factories, made this type of glass.

Basket, 5-1/2" h, 5" w, pink loopings, white satin ground, applied frosted feet, applied frosted handle ........................................ 375.00
Bottle
   6-1/2" h, medium gray-blue ground, white loopings, pewter threading, pontil scar, cap missing, attributed to Germany, mid 18th C ................................................................. 1,750.00
   7-5/8" h, rect, beveled edges, medium sapphire blue ground, white loopings, pewter threads, pontil scar, attributed to Germany or Northern Europe, c1750 ................................. 1,250.00
   8-1/2" h, gemel, colorless ground, white loopings, sheared lip, pontil scar, 1860-80 ...................................................... 200.00
   8-3/4" h, gemel, cranberry ground, white loopings, applied rigaree ............................................................................ 275.00
Bowl, 4-1/4" d, 2-1/4" h, citron ground, narrow white looping, applied rigaree loop dec, rim, ground pontil ........................................ 200.00
Cologne Bottle, 5-3/8" h, opaque white body, blue and cranberry loopings, colorless stopper with white, pink, and blue loopings, pontil scar, New England, 1840-60 .................................................... 485.00
Creamer, 4" h, aqua, white and red spatter, applied handle, surface chips ...................................................................................... 125.00
Fairy Lamp, 6" h, blue shade, matching ruffled trifold rim base, colorless glass candle cup insert ...................................................... 750.00
Finger Bowl, 4-1/4" d, ftd, colorless ground, swirled streaks of deep blue ad white, foot drawn from body, applied colorless handles imp with cherub's face .......................................................................... 85.00
Flask
   6-1/2" h, 5" w, cranberry ground, white and deep pink feathering ................................................................................ 150.00
   6-3/4" h, colorless ground, white loopings, flattened round body, short sheared lip, small rough pontil, attributed to South Jersey ............................................................................. 185.00
   7-1/4" h, broad oval form, ruby red ground, white herringbone type loopings, applied double collared mouth, pontil scar 400.00
   7-3/4" l, clear cased in white, pink loops ............................. 200.00
   8-3/4" l, clear cased in white, pink loops ............................. 250.00
   8-3/4" l, clear cased in white, red and blue loops ............... 225.00
Mug, 5-1/4" h, 3-5/8" d, colorless ground, white and blue loopings, cylindrical, tapering slightly to rim, applied colorless solid handle, rough pontil .............................................................................. 375.00
Pipe, 18" l, white ground, red loopings, bulbous bowl, knopped stem ....................................................................................... 275.00
Pitcher, 9-1/2" h, cranberry ground, thick white loopings, applied clear handle with five crimps, applied colorless handle with five crimps, applied colorless foot, pontil scar, attributed to South Jersey, c1840-50 ............................................................... 4,100.00

**Fairy Lamp, ruby-red, white loopings, dome shaped shade, bowl shaped base, clear glass candle cup mkd "S. Clarke Patent Trade Mark Fairy," 5-1/2" d, 5" h, $985. Photo courtesy of Clarence & Betty Maier.**

Powder Horn
   11" h, colorless ground, blue and white loopings, tooled lip, pontil scar, ground lip, mid-19th C .............................................. 125.00
   13" l, colorless ground, white loopings and red stripes, stand ................................................................................... 250.00
Rolling Pin, 18" l, colorless ground, pink and white loopings ...... 265.00
Salt, open, 3-1/4" d, 1-1/4" h, colorless ground, white loopings, wide gauffered rolled rim, applied cobalt blue rim band, applied solid foot, polished pontil ........................................................................ 450.00
Vase
   9-3/4" h, medium blue ground, white loopings, hollow knop stem containing 1842 dime, applied foot, pontil scar, stem previously broken off and re-glued, attributed to Pittsburgh or South Jersey, 1840-50 ................................................................... 625.00
   9-7/8" h, bulbous, flaring neck, ftd, colorless ground, spiraling white bands, applied colorless swagging, applied colorless baluster stem, thick round base, attributed to New England, 19th C ................................................................................ 3,200.00
Witch Ball, 5-1/4" d, colorless ground, opaque white casing, red loopings, attributed to Pittsburgh ...................................................... 275.00

# NANKING

**History:** Nanking is a type of Chinese porcelain made in Canton, China, from the early 1800s into the 20th century. It was made for export to America and England.

Four elements help distinguish Nanking from Canton, two similar types of ware. Nanking has a spear-and-post border, as opposed to the scalloped-line style of Canton. Second, in the water's edge or Willow pattern, Canton usually has no figures; Nanking includes a standing figure with open umbrella on the bridge. In addition, the blues tend to be darker on the Nanking ware. Finally, Nanking wares often are embellished with gold, Canton is not.

Green and orange variations of Nanking survive, although they are scarce.

Bowl
   10" d, 5" h, cut corner, blue and white, minute rim chips .... 980.00
   15" l, oval, flat octagonal rim, blue and white, c1800 .......... 750.00
Chocolate Pot, 9" h, pear shape, blue and white, Buddhistic lion finial ........................................................................................ 775.00
Cider Jug, 7-3/4" h, blue and white, spearhead and lattice borders, coastal village scene, double entwined handle, molded flowers and leaves terminal, early 19th C, base rim chip ........................... 400.00
Mug, 6-1/8" h, blue and white water's edge scene .................... 350.00
Platter
   16-1/8" l, 13-3/8" w, eight-sided oblong, center dec with peafowl, rocks, and flower, rim with border of tight scrolls, flowers, and diaper patterns, 18th C, rim chips ................................... 575.00
   16-1/2" l, 13-1/2" w, eight-sided oblong, blue and white, late 18th C, glaze wear, minor rim chips ...................................... 690.00
   17-3/8 x 20", oval, blue and white, coastal village scene, spearhead and lattice borders, minor glaze wear, early 19th C ................................................................................ 875.00
   Sauce Tureen, cov, underplates, 8" l, blue and white, twin braided handles, floral knops, 19th C, base chips, price for pr .. 1,250.00
Serving Dish, cov, 11" l, two handles, blue and white, staple repair to lid ............................................................................................. 200.00

## Reproduction Alert:

Copies of Nanking ware currently are being produced in China. They are of inferior quality and are decorated in a lighter rather than in the darker blues.

Soup Bowl, 9-1/2" d, 19th C, hairline, rim chips, price for pr .......220.00
Sugar Bowl, cov, 6-1/2" h, cylindrical, blue and white, gilt highlights, strawberry knop finial .............................................................325.00
Tea Caddy, 5" h, blue and white, gilt trim ...................................750.00
Teapot, 5-1/2" h, lobed form, reeded strap handle, blue and white, gilt highlights, late 18th/early 19th C, minor chips, gilt wear .........525.00
Vegetable Dish, cov, 11-1/2" l, 4-1/2" h, oval, blue and white, mismatched cover, 19th C ...........................................................250.00

# NAPKIN RINGS

**History:** Gracious home dining during the Victorian era required a personal napkin ring for each household member. Figural napkin rings were first patented in 1869. During the remainder of the 19th century, most plating companies, including Cromwell, Eureka, Meriden, and Reed and Barton, manufactured figural rings, many copying and only slightly varying the designs of other companies.

**Reference:** Lillian Gottschalk and Sandra Whitson, *Figural Napkin Rings*, Collector Books, 1996.

**Reproduction Alert:** Quality reproductions do exist.

**Additional Listings:** See *Warman's Americana & Collectibles* for a listing of non-figural napkin rings.

**Notes:** Values are determined by the subject matter of the ring, the quality of the workmanship, and the condition.

## Silver

Chinese Export, early 20th C, engraved dragon and plain roundel, 1-3/4" d .........................................................................................100.00
Chinese Export, late 19th C, chased and emb with figures in landscape, plain central cartouche, 2" d .........................................125.00
Duhme Co., beaded rim, medallion of winged goddess, flanked by leafy scrolls, one monogrammed, other with inscription, dated 1873, price for pr ...........................................................................650.00
Gorham Co., Art Nouveau, band of slender entwined flowers, monogrammed, 1-1/2" h, 3 troy oz, price for pr ...............................460.00
Gorham Co., Art Nouveau style flowers, monogrammed ...........395.00
Pairpoint, seated cherub, back to napkin ring, draped attire, four ball feet support figure 8 base, c1885.............................................700.00
Simpson, Hall, Miller, twins on ladder, Greenaway type, rect tiered base, 3-1/2" h, c1870 ...............................................................700.00
Tufts, James W.
    Boy riding large dog, inscribed napkin ring, fancy rect ftd base, 3" h, c1876 .............................................................................700.00
    Dog, sitting next to barrel shaped ring, sgd "Tufts, #1531" ......125.00
Unmarked, bold flowers and leafy scroll, monogrammed, dated 1887 and 1912 ...............................................................................125.00

**Kate Greenaway-style girl, emb ring with florals, silver plated, $250.**

## Silver Plated

Apollo Silver Plate Co., bird, perched on top of ring, long tail, elaborately scrolled base ...............................................................185.00
Aurora
    Dog and bird, #27 .............................................................185.00
    Derby
    Chick and eggshell ...........................................................100.00
    Monkey, standing, oval base ..............................................295.00
    Meriden Brittania
    Bird, Boy and Dog, #199....................................................245.00
    Swan pulling wheeled napkin ring, c1896..........................600.00
    Vase, dark art glass vase with enameled flowers, supported by scrolls ending in rosettes, 6-7/8" h, c1860 ......................500.00
Middletown Plate Co.
    Naked boy pushing ring, ornate base ...............................395.00
    Turtle Doves, spread wings support base..........................200.00

# NASH GLASS

**History:** Nash glass is a type of art glass attributed to Arthur John Nash and his sons, Leslie H. and A. Douglas. Arthur John Nash, originally employed by Webb in Stourbridge, England, came to America and was employed in 1889 by Tiffany Furnaces at its Corona, Long Island, plant.

While managing the plant for Tiffany, Nash designed and produced iridescent glass. In 1928, A. Douglas Nash purchased the facilities of Tiffany Furnaces. The A. Douglas Nash Corporation remained in operation until 1931.

Bowl
    5-1/4" d, inverted rim, leaf design, sgd ...............................200.00
    8" d, aventurine Chintz, gold irid striping, base inscribed "Nash"................................................................................200.00
    8" d, rose petal Chintz, magenta stripes, base inscribed "Nash" ...............................................................................200.00
    15-1/2" d, Chintz amber, blue, and green opalescent, turned down rim..............................................................................325.00

**Console Bowl, Chintz, clear ground, pink and green chintz, sgd "501/DD/Nash," 11-1/2" d, 3-1/2" h, $230. Photo courtesy of David Rago Auctions.**

Candlestick, 5" h, Chintz blood red and silver dec...................... 550.00
Champagne, 5" h, pale irid amber, shallow cup splitting to three stems continuing to domed circular base .......................................... 750.00
Cologne Bottle, 6" h, cylindrical, Chintz paperweight stopper..... 275.00
Compote, 6" d, 2" h, fold over rim, Chintz, green-blue bowl, colorless pedestal foot, sgd .......................................................... 225.00
Creamer, 4-1/4" h, pale orchid and green design, applied colorless handle ............................................................................. 325.00
Dish, cov, 5" d, 2-1/2" h, internally molded leaf design, amber ground, lustrous gold irid, conforming cover, rim chips ......................... 260.00
Finger Bowl, 4-3/4" d, matching underplate, opalescent rays, cranberry rim, sgd ............................................................................ 225.00
Goblet, 6-1/2" h, Chintz ......................................................... 185.00
Perfume Bottle, 7-1/2" h, bulbous bottle shape over blown-in-mold apron, irid gold, conforming stopper with 7" l wand, sgd "Nash 523" ........975.00
Plate
    4-1/2" d, irid amber, scalloped edge, sgd and numbered ... 325.00
    6-1/2" d, Spiral pattern, orchid and clear spirals, sgd ......... 200.00
Salt, open, 4" d, 1-1/4" h, irid gold, ruffled rim, sgd and numbered ..350.00
Vase
    4-3/4" h, blue-gold irid, pedestal base, inscribed "Nash 644"...350.00
    5-1/4" h, Chintz, flared rim, oval colorless body, internally dec with orange stripes alternating with yellow-amber pulled threading .................................................................195.00
    6-1/4" h, 3-1/2" d, trumpet shade, Chintz, sgd and numbered ...............................................................375.00
    7-1/2" h, beaker, Chintz, blood red, sgd "Nash RD 1025"... 475.00
    7-3/4" h, baluster, brilliant irid pumpkin, lemon-yellow int. .....3,500.00
    8-1/2" h, Chintz, green, brown, and gold flecks .................. 325.00
    9-1/2" h, green and gold irid body, colorless irid circular base..................................................................................325.00
Wine, 6" h, Chintz, pink and green..................................... 175.00

# NAUTICAL ITEMS

**History:** The seas have fascinated man since time began. The artifacts of sailors have been collected and treasured for years. Because of their environment, merchant and naval items, whether factory or handmade, must be of quality construction and long lasting. Many of these items are aesthetically appealing as well.

**References:** E. H. H. Archibald, *The Dictionary of Sea Painters of Europe and America*, Antique Collectors' Club, 1999; Donald F. Kuhlstrom, *Sunday Sailors: A Beginner's Guide to Pond Boats & Model Yachting Until the 1950s*, Turner Publications, 1998; J. Welles Henderson, *Marine Art & Antiques*, Antique Collectors' Club, 1999; David Joel, *Charles Brooking and the 18th Century British Marine Painters*, Antique Collectors' Club, 1999.

**Periodicals:** Nautical Brass, P.O. Box 3966, North Ft. Myers, FL 33918; Nautical Collector, P. O. Box 949, New London, CT 06320.

**Collectors' Club:** Nautical Research Guild, 62 Marlboro St., Newburyport, MA 01950.

**Museums:** Chesapeake Bay Maritime Museum, Saint Michaels, MD; Kittery Historical & Naval Museum, Kittery, ME; Lyons Maritime Museum, St Augustine, FL; Mariners' Museum, Newport News, VA; Maritime Museum of Monterey, Monterey, CA; Museum of Science and Industry, Chicago, IL; Mystic Seaport Museum, Mystic, CT; Peabody Museum of Salem, Salem, MA; Philadelphia Maritime Museum, Philadelphia, PA; San Francisco Maritime National Historical Park, San Francisco, CA; U.S. Naval Academy Museum, Naval Academy, MD.

**Diving Helmet, shallow water type, home made, $200.**

Backstaff, wood, inlaid label "Made by William Hart in Portsmouth, NE/for 1767," 18th C ............................................................. 8,000.00
Bell, brass, 14" d, inscribed *SS Pacific Prince*............................ 500.00
Binnacle, 56" h, brass, mahogany base, complete..................... 750.00
Book
    Cram, W Bartlett, *Picture History of New England Passenger Vessels*, 8" x 10", dj, 414 pgs, 1980, 1st ed ...................... 75.00
    Spears, John, *Captain Nathaniel Brown Palmer, An Old-Time Sailor of the Sea*, 3" x 5", orig cloth, plates, 252 pgs, NY, 1922........ 20.00
Cane, 34-1/2" l, whalebone and ivory, five baleen bands at top of shaft, America, 19th C, age cracks..................................................... 1,265.00
Chronometer, 7-1/2" h, 4-3/4" d timepiece, two-day type, rosewood gimbal case, MOP plaque, flush brass carrying handles, Victor Kulberg, London, retailed by W. Bond and Son, Boston ............ 5,465.00
Clock, 11" h, nickel-plated, wall, outside bell ............................. 400.00
Foghorn, bellows operated, 1910 ............................................. 175.00
Half-Hull, 29" w, 6-1/2" h, carved wood, painted white above and green below the water line, mounted in black frame, ochre ground, America, late 19th C.......................................................... 2,875.00
Octant, 15-3/4" l, Spencer, Browning & Rust, London, 1787-1842, ebony, brass, and ivory, painted wood case............................. 575.00
Painting
    14" w, 21" h, oil on board, schooner at sea, sgd "WHPlummer 1881" lower left, tear, punctures, surface grime ............ 2,185.00
    20" w, 12" h, oil on canvas, two masted vessel at sea, unsigned, American School, 19th C, lined, minor retouch, scattered flaking and losses, craquelure ................................................. 6,440.00
    35-1/4" w, 21-3/4" h, oil on board, portrait of four masted schooner *Thomas S. Dennison*, sgd, inscribed, and dated "Antonio Jacobsen 1910 31 Paliade av West Hoboken NJ" lower left, vessel identified on bow, stern, and flag, prevalent flaking and loss, varnish inconsistencies...................................... 11,500.00
    42" w, 26" h, oil on canvas, portrait of ship *Republic*, unsigned, attributed to William Pierce Stubbs, vessel identified on bow and stern, mounted onto masonite, framed, retouched, scattered flaking and losses ............................................... 5,465.00
Porthole, 15"d, brass, storm cov.............................................. 120.00
Print, 34-1/2" l, 18-1/4" h, color lithograph, portrait of side-wheeler *C. Vanderbilt*, identified in inscription in matrix, Endicott & Co., 1852-86, descended in family of Commodore Vanderbilt to present owner, framed ................................................................................ 1,035.00
Quadrant, ebony, ivory inlays...................................................550.00

Sailor's Valentine, 9" h, 9-1/6" w, octagonal segmented case, various exotic shells, center reads "To One I Love" on left, heart center and initials on right panel, minor losses to case, 19th C ............. 2,185.00
Sea Chest, 37 l, orig green and brown paint and ropework beckets, 19th C ................................................................... 600.00
Sextant
    13" l, ebony, brass and ivory trim, mkd "J. Good, High St. Hull," damage to ivory ................................................. 450.00
    17" l, mahogany, engraved brass radial arm, ivory nameplate engraved "H Duren, New York," Gregory & Wright, London, 18th C ............................................................ 1,200.00
Ship's Block, 13 1/2" l, wood, one lignium vitae, one metal pulley ... 125.00
Ship's Log
    Bark *Petrea,* 65 pages folio, entries from March 17 to Dec 15, 1858, voyages from Le Havre to Portsmouth, New York, and Melbourne, details activities while in port, at sea, hourly speeds, courses, winds, weather, including near disaster, towing to Portsmouth, repairs, trying to save mud-covered cargo, mate with small pox ........................................................ 585.00
    Merchantman *Hanover,* 155 pages, manuscript journal for two Atlantic crossings, kept by Captain James Drummond, sailing from New Orleans to Le Havre and Cadiz in 1839 and 1841 ................ 815.00
    Shadow Box, 30" w, 26" h, carved and painted sailing yacht with two cut-out paper children on board, seascape background with lighthouse, framed, America, 19th C .......................... 920.00
Ship Model, 16" l, 6-3/4" w, 16" h, prisoner-of-war, bone, three masted war sip with sixteen brass cannons, scrimmed deck planking, stern quarters, pulleys and various decorations, oval blown glass dome mounted on black painted oval ftd wooden base, 19th C, some breaks in rigging .................................................. 8,050.00
Ship's Sternboard, carved and painted wood
    103" l, 6" h to 15" h at top of arch, from schooner *William West,* Essex, MA, 1869, gilt lettering on black asphaltum ground, arched form, molded to edge, sgd "C. I. Bedell Painters" on each end of conforming closure with red and black embellishments, edged in gilt on dark blue ground, orig paint, wear ........................... 1,725.00
    9'5" l, 5-1/2" h, from schooner *Mary-Elizabeth of New London,* white lettering on black ground, America, 19th C, normal wear ... 1,265.00
Speaking Trumpet, 17-1/2" l, nickel plated, applied spread eagle, inscribed "E. D. Hurlbut & Co. to Capt. Francis West," 19th C ... 1,400.00
Sternboard, 54" w, carved mahogany, gilded eagle, P Libbey, Maine, sgd on back .................................................... 1,500.00
Telescope
    4 3/4" h, brass, Swan, Hunter & Wingham Richardson Ltd., Neptune Works, dated 1840 ..................................... 750.00
    20-1/4" h, canvas cov brass, from ship *Edwina,* Capt. Francis West ...................................................... 1,200.00
Trailboard, 58 1/2" l, gilded, foliate scroll carving, black ground, 19th C ........................................................ 450.00
Watercolor, 9" h, 13-1/4" h, pen, ink, and watercolor on paper, sleek sailing ship flying American flag, minor stains, old 10-1/4" h, 14-5/8" w gilt frame ...................................................... 1,100.00

# NETSUKES

**History:** The traditional Japanese kimono has no pockets. Daily necessities, such as money and tobacco supplies, were carried in leather pouches, or inros, which hung from a cord with a netsuke toggle. The word netsuke comes from "ne"—to root—and "tsuke"—to fasten.

Netsukes originated in the 14th century and initially were favored by the middle class. By the mid-18th century, all levels of Japanese society used them. Some of the most famous artists, e.g., Shuzan and Yamada Hojitsu, worked in the netsuke form.

Netsukes average from 1 to 2 inches in length and are made from wood, ivory, bone, ceramics, metal, horn, nutshells, etc. The subject matter is broad based, but always portrayed in a lighthearted, humorous manner. A netsuke must have smooth edges and balance in order to hang correctly on the sash.

**Reference:** Raymond Bushell, *Introduction to Netsuke,* Charles E. Tuttle Co., 1971; George Lazarnick, *The Signature Book of Netsuke, Inro and Ojime Artists in Photographs,* first edition 1976, 2 volume second edition 1981.

**Periodicals:** *Netsuke & Ivory Carving Newsletter,* 3203 Adams Way, Ambler, PA 19002; *Orientalia Journal,* P.O. Box 94, Flushing, NY 11363-0094, http://members.aol.com/Orientalia/index.html.

**Collectors' Clubs:** International Netsuke Society, P.O. Box 471686, San Francisco, CA 94147; Netsuke Kenkyukai Society, P.O. Box 31595, Oakland, CA 94604.

**Notes:** Value depends on artist, region, material, and skill of craftsmanship. Western collectors favor katabori, pieces which represent an identifiable object.

Ivory, 18th C
    Chinese man holding musical instrument, sgd "Toshimitsu(?)," large ........................................................ 5,175.00
    Courtier discovering a demon hiding as a servant ........... 1,725.00
    Daikoku and Hoitei as sumo wrestlers ....................... 5,175.00
    Figure of boy sleeping on reclining buffalo ................. 635.00
    Hoitei with his bag of wealth, large ........................ 1,100.00
    Karako on back of elephant, deep amber coloring .......... 2,760.00
    Sciobo with branch of peaches and fan, sgd "Natosuke" 2,100.00
    Sennin holding jewel, three himetoshi ...................... 1,380.00
    Sennin in mugwort cape, double gourd, sgd "Sadayuki(?)" 865.00
    Sennin in mugwort cape, holding jewel ...................... 1,955.00
    Sennin with branch of peaches ............................. 520.00
    Shoki with a demon, sgd "Matsatomo" within cartouche . 1,150.00
Ivory, 18th/19th C
    European with small child holding drum, inlaid eyes ....... 1,265.00
    Fisherman holding net and weights, flowering branch coming out of enclosed net ........................................... 815.00
    Oni trapping shoki under old hat, sgd "Masakaza," Meiji period, 1868-1911 .............................................. 435.00
    Sennin, emaciated, double gourd, inlaid eyes ............... 415.00
    Sennin scratching his back ................................ 460.00
    Sennin with lobster, sgd "Masaka" ......................... 1,380.00
    Sennin with staff and double gourd ........................ 550.00
    Shoki with demon .......................................... 1,100.00
Ivory, 19th C
    Courtier with basket of fish and parasol, sgd "Tomoyuki" ... 575.00
    Daikoku and ebisu ......................................... 575.00
    Daikoku with his hammer and bug, an attendant fanning him, sgd "KO," line to back of attendant ........................ 635.00
    European with trumpet and small child, inlaid eyes and details ................................................... 690.00
    European with trumpet holding small boy, deep yellow color, sgd "Yasumasa" ............................................ 460.00
    Figure of blind man, stained details, sgd ................. 215.00
    Figure carrying Benkei's immense conch ................... 150.00
    Figure of foreigner with small child ...................... 375.00
    Figure of masked dancer, sgd "Osai(?)" ................... 635.00
    Figure of oni holding horn with smaller demon on it's shoulders, sgd "Tomoyuki," large .................................. 1,380.00

## Reproduction Alert:

Recent reproductions are on the market. Many are carved from African ivory.

Figure of two men wrestling at tug of war ........................... 260.00
Fisherman with basket of clams, stained details, large....... 175.00
Fukurokuji with court hat holding a peach, sgd "Tomokazu," Japan.................................................................230.00
Fukorokuji with large peach, moveable head, sgd "Tomokazu"...................................................................215.00
Gama sennin, stained deep amber..................................... 175.00
Gama sennin with three-legged frog.................................. 225.00
Group of seven masks, sgd .................................................. 290.00
Hoitei with his bag of wealth .............................................. 425.00
Monk arm wrestling with demon, sgd.................................. 520.00
Monk with oni ...................................................................... 600.00
Pair of wrestlers, sgd "Kogyoku"..................................... 1,265.00
Persimmon, finely carved and stained, sgd "Mitsuhiro," with kakihan .................................................................375.00
Reclining horse, sgd "Masaharu" ....................................... 550.00
Reclining ox, sgd "Tomotada" within sq cartouche........... 1,840.00
Shoki surrounded by six demons, sgd "Kogyoku" within cinnabar cartouche ................................................... 1,035.00
Tengu emerging from an egg .......................................... 2,530.00
Three figures in a tea cup, sgd "Minko," deeply colored, line to base of cup ..................................................... 115.00
Three figures, stained detail ............................................... 175.00
Three monkeys on a leaf, sgd "Shuzan" ............................ 865.00
Two performers, one wearing noh mask, sgd ..................... 230.00
Two priests fighting, sgd "Kogyoku" within cinnabar cartouche...................................................................460.00
Lacquer, 19th C, Kabuki actor, gold, silver, and vermillion surface .........................................................................575.00
Manju, 19th C
  Carved ivory in form of abalone shell, silver jump ring ....... 230.00
  Cloud carved stained ivory inset netsuke with enameled gold plaque with dragon and wave motif, sgd "Komei," gold chain holding a tobacco pouch embroidered with thunder god Raiken, gold lid weight of dragon with engraved silver plate, sgd with gold cartouche............................................................. 2,875.00
  Square form, carved bird and pomegranate tree, diapered ground ............................................................................ 260.00
  Two boys playing at tops, reverse with musical instruments, cinnabar lacquer ......................................................... 230.00
Marine Ivory, 19th C
  Figure of Hoitei carrying his bag of good fortune ................ 175.00
  Kappa carving large cucumber ............................................ 290.00
  Kettle transforming itself into a badger, deep amber color.. 415.00
Porcelain, sennin with double gourd, sgd with cartouche "Masakazu" ...................................................................115.00
Pottery, 19th C, Bizenware, figure of daruma............................ 230.00
Walnut Shell, 19th C, carved relief dec of treasure ship of the gods of luck, sgd "Hozan(?)".........................................450.00
Wooden, 18th C
  Blackwood carving of scholar holding bag with dyed horn oni head appearing from side, sgd "Gyokukei" ..................... 815.00
  Boxwood karako riding large double gourd ........................ 490.00
  Hanasaka jijii seated on tree stump, ivory inlay of flowering branches and cartouche, sgd "Gyokukei" ...................... 865.00
  Three monkeys, well worn ................................................... 115.00
  Two performers, one dancing, other playing drum, sgd "Shounsai" for Shounsai Joryu ..........................................................460.00
Wooden, 18th/19th C
  Figure of man stoking fire in hibachi with pipe .................... 490.00
  Figure of oni with tethered monkey, old loss to one foot, well worn ........................................................................ 1,610.00
  Figure of sennin with staff, well worn, large himetoshi........ 865.00
  Kuanyu with his halberd holding his beard, large himetoshi ....575.00
Wooden, 19th C
  Blackwood carving of Kiyohimi with bell of Dodoji, sgd "Mit-sushige(?)"" within seal ................................................. 345.00
  Blackwood carving of shishi with movable sphere in it's mouth, playing with brocade ball, inlaid eyes, one eye missing .............. 635.00

Boxwood carving of figure carrying an oni on a backpack, inlaid eyes and bone plaque, sgd "Kozan," ivory lined himetoshi (one missing) ........................................................................ 750.00
Carved as mask, dark patina, 19th C .................................. 260.00
Carving of oni startled by bee, inlaid details, sgd "Oyokusen," possibly for Tomochica, damage to fingers of one hand .. 435.00
Figure of child playing with ball, sgd "Masachiro," second character barely legible................................................... 215.00
Figure of boy playing flute, riding on ox, sgd "Toshio" ........ 290.00
Monk sleeping next to large mogokyu or temple bell, sgd "Gyokuzan" .....................................................................175.00
Mushroom with stem turned on itself as himetoshi............ 325.00
Puppy playing with sandal .................................................. 100.00
Rooster with horn inlays on top of rotten log ..................... 490.00
Shishi holding temple bell in it's front paws ....................... 260.00

# NEWCOMB POTTERY

**History:** The Sophie Newcomb Memorial College, an adjunct of Tulane University in New Orleans, LA, was originated as a school to train local women in the decorative arts. While metal working, painting, and embroidery were among the classes taught, the production of fine, hand-crafted art pottery remains their most popular and collectible pursuit.

Pottery was made by the Newcomb women for nearly 50 years, with earlier work being the rarest and the most valuable. This is characterized by shiny finishes and broad, flat-painted and modeled designs. More common, though still quite valuable, are their matte glaze pieces, often depicting bayou scenes and native flora. All bear the impressed NC mark.

**References:** Ralph and Terry Kovel, *Kovels' American Art Pottery*, Crown Publishers, 1993; Jessie Poesch, *Newcomb Pottery: An Enterprise for Southern Women*, Schiffer Publishing, 1984; David Rago, *American Art Pottery,* Knickerbocker Press, 1997.

**Collectors' Club:** American Art Pottery Association, P.O. Box 1226, Westport, MA 02790.

**Museum:** Newcomb College, Tulane University, New Orleans, LA.

**Advisor:** David Rago.

Bowl, 4-1/2" d, 2-1/2" h, hemispherical, matte, carved band of pink buds, green and blue ground, Sadie Irvine, 1927, "NC/IS/PV71".........1,100.00
Cabinet Vase
  3" h, 3-3/4" d, light blue bell-shaped flowers, green leaves, cobalt blue ground, Henrietta Bailey, 1929, "NC/HB3359/JM". 1,300.00
  3-3/4" h, 3-1/4" d, dark blue stylized strawberries, pale blue ground, Ester Elliott, 1902, mkd "NC/JM/EHE/R19"...... 8,000.00
Chamberstick, 5-1/4" d, 7" h, dripping green matte glaze over red clay body, "NC/JM/FR," restoration to handle.................................. 425.00
Charger, 13" d, three incised large blue crabs, blue ground, Sabrina Wells, mkd "NC/M/S.E.WELLS/YY64," short tight line on back .......... 25,000.00
Jar, cov, 6" d, 8" h, carved sweet peas, lid carved "Here are sweet peas on tiptoe for a flight," Marie T. Ryan, 1903, mkd "NC/M.T.R./W/MR/SS/64" ................................................ 37,500.00
Planter, 5-1/4" h, 6-1/2" sq, pale blue wild roses with yellow centers, denim-blue ground, Sadie Irvine, 1912, "NC/IS/FM90/B," restoration to several cracks ................................................................. 700.00

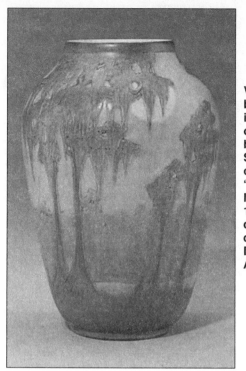

Vase, scenic, bulbous, Spanish moss, live oaks, full moon, by Anna Frances Simpson, 1916 or 1925, mkd "NC/150/IA?12/JM/AFS172," 10-1/4" h, 6-1/2" d, $17,250. Photo courtesy of David Rago Auctions.

Teapot, 4-1/4" h, 5-1/2" d, carved band of light pink and yellow wild roses, dark blue-green ground, Alma Mason, 1911, mkd "NC/EG44/A.M.B." ....................................................................3,000.00

Vase
> 7-1/4" h, 3-1/4" d, cylindrical, carved stylize primrose and tall stems, denim-blue ground, Mazie Ryan, 1904, "NC/SS12/M.T.RYAN" ......................................7,500.00
> 8-3/4" h, 4-3/4" d, Maude Robinson, 1904, painted light periwinkle wisteria blossoms, cobalt blue and celadon ground, mkd "NC/JM/Maude Robinson/XX41," restoration to hairline at rim ..........................................................12,000.00
> 11" h, 5" d, classical shape, carved by A. F. Simpson, 1927, tall oak tree, Spanish moss, full moon, deeply colored, mkd "NC/JM/AFS/QC35" .............................................13,000.00
> 12-1/4" h, 7-1/2" d, closed in rim, Harriet Joor, 1902, landscape of tall pines, mkd "NC/JM/HJ/U87/Q," restoration to line at shoulder.............................................................19,000.00

Vessel
> 4-1/4" h, 4-3/4" d, two handles, squatty, band of stylized teal and pink leaves and buds, denim-blue ground, "NC/NH75/254," artist mark illegible, minute nick to bottom ring at side ...... 1,700.00
> 5-1/2" h, 7" d, spherical, carved live oaks and Spanish moss under full moon, artist "FHF," c1939, "NC/Y38/FHF," very tight short rim line.................................................................3,000.00
> 8-3/4" h, 10-1/2" d, closed-in rim, white lilies, yellow centers, cobalt blue ground, Harriet Joor, 1903, mkd "NC/JM/X97/HJ," two rim repairs.......................................................12,000.00

# NILOAK POTTERY, MISSION WARE

**History:** Niloak Pottery was made near Benton, Arkansas. Charles Dean Hyten experimented with native clay, trying to preserve its natural colors. By 1911 he perfected Mission Ware, a marbleized pottery in which the cream and brown colors

predominate. The company name is the word "kaolin" spelled backwards.

After a devastating fire, the pottery was rebuilt and named Eagle Pottery. This factory included enough space to add a novelty pottery line in 1929. Mr. Hyten left the pottery in 1941, and in 1946 operations ceased.

**Marks:** The early pieces were marked "Niloak." Eagle Pottery products usually were marked "Hywood-Niloak" until 1934 when the "Hywood" was dropped from the mark.

**References:** Susan and Al Bagdade, *Warman's American Pottery and Porcelain*, 2nd ed., Krause Publications, 2000; David Edwin Gifford, *Collector's Encyclopedia of Niloak*, 2nd ed., Collector Books, 2000.

**Collectors' Club:** Arkansas Pottery Collectors Society, P.O. Box 7617, Little Rock, AR 72217.

**Additional Listings:** See *Warman's Americana & Collectibles* for more examples, especially the novelty pieces.

Ashtray, 3-1/2" w, Mission Ware ....................................................80.00
Bowl
> 4" d, Mission Ware............................................................100.00
> 5" d, Mission Ware..............................................................80.00
> 10" d, w, Mission Ware, imp mark......................................325.00

Box, cov, 5" d, Mission Ware, lid chip ..........................................190.00
Bud Vase, 6" h, Mission Ware, imp mark......................................180.00
Candlestick, 3-1/2" h, Mission Ware ............................................160.00
Chamber Pot, infant's, 5-1/2" w, Mission Ware...........................550.00
Cigarette Jar, cov, Mission Ware.................................................350.00
Drinking Cup, Mission Ware, set of six, various colors, minor flakes ................................................................................600.00
Flower Pot, 10" h, 9" w underplate, drainage hole, Mission Ware ..................................................................................950.00
Ginger Jar, 8-1/2" h, 5-1/2" d, marbleized terra cotta, brown, blue, and ivory clays, stamped "Niloak" ................................. 1,200.00
Humidor, cov, 6-1/2" h, tan, cream, and light beige Mission Ware, bell-bottom shape, rare mark ...................................... 1,300.00
Jardiniere
> 9" d, 8" h, marbleized terra cotta, teal, and gray clays, stamped "Niloak".....................................................................600.00
> 12-1/2" d, 11-1/4" h, marbleized brown, blue, and ivory clays, stamped "Niloak," paper label ......................................2,000.00

Jug, 6" h, Mission Ware ...............................................................325.00
Match Holder, 5" w, ashtray base, Mission Ware, paper label .... 400.00
Mug, Mission Ware
> 4" h, dark brown, dark cream, set of six, patent pending mark .......................................................................................900.00
> 5" h.....................................................................................230.00

Necklace, 18" l ............................................................................750.00
Pitcher, 10-1/2" h, Mission Ware, handle, early patent pending mark and imp mark ....................................................................950.00
Punch Bowl, 13" d, 9" h, glazed int., Mission Ware .................2,400.00
Rose Jar, 8" h, Mission Ware.......................................................850.00
Shot Glass, 2-1/2" h, Mission Ware, set of six, one chip ............425.00
Stem Holders, Mission Ware, set of three, 4-1/2" w, minor flakes.... 110.00
Tankard Pitcher, 10" h, brown, tan, cream, and turquoise Mission Ware, chip repair and line .....................................................290.00
Tile, 4" sq, Mission Ware, unmarked, minor flakes .....................110.00
Tobacco Jar, 5-1/2" w, 5-1/2" h, Mission Ware............................700.00
Toothpick Holder, 2" h, Mission Ware, cylindrical, imp mark.......110.00
Tray, Mission Ware
> 10-1/2" d, cream, beige, tan, red, and turquoise.................400.00
> 13" d, cream, tan, red, turquoise.........................................950.00
> Tumble-Up, 8-1/2" h, Mission Ware, imp mark ...................475.00

Umbrella Stand, Mission Ware
> 20" h, firing crack in base.................................................2,100.00

**Vase, Mission Ware, scroddled brown, blue, terra cotta, and ivory, stamped "Niloak," 9-1/2" h, 5-1/2" d, $375. Photo courtesy of David Rago Auctions.**

21" h, crack to base ........................................................ 1,500.00
Vase, Mission Ware
   3" h, cream, brown, blue, and red, closed cylinder form, imp
      mark ...................................................................140.00
   4-1/2" h, swelled ovoid, lip, imp mark ...............................130.00
   6" h, tapering ovoid with slightly flared base, slightly turned in
      shoulder, imp mark...........................................100.00
   6-1/2" h, waisted form, bulbous base..................................150.00
   8" h, baluster, wide flat top rim, imp mark ..........................130.00
   8-1/2" h, hourglass form.......................................................170.00
   10-1/4" h, 5" d, bottle shape, marbleized ivory, teal, and gray
      clays, stamped "Niloak".....................................425.00
   12" h, 5-1/4" d, corseted, marbleized brown, blue, green and ivory
      clays, stamped "Niloak".....................................600.00
   13" h, 7" d, bulbous, marbleized brown, blue, and ivory clays,
      stamped "Niloak"...........................................1,700.00
   16" h, baluster, wide flat top rim, imp mark ..................... 1,700.00
   18" h, baluster, wide flat top rim, orig paper label ............ 3,000.00
Violet Vase, 3-1/2" h, Mission Ware ...........................................375.00
Wall Pocket, 5-1/2" l, Mission Ware ...........................................375.00
Water Bottle, cov, 8" h, Mission Ware, top may not be orig, minor
   chip ..............................................................................250.00

# NIPPON CHINA, 1891-1921

**History:** Nippon, Japanese hand-painted porcelain, was made for export between 1891 and 1921. In 1891, when the McKinley tariff act proclaimed that all items of foreign manufacture be stamped with their country of origin, Japan chose to use "Nippon." In 1921, the United States decided the word "Nippon" no longer was acceptable and required all Japanese wares to be marked "Japan," ending the Nippon era.

**Marks:** There are more than 220 recorded Nippon backstamps or marks; the three most popular are the wreath, maple leaf, and rising sun. Wares with variations of all three marks are being reproduced today. A knowledgeable collector can easily spot the reproductions by the mark variances.

## Reproduction Alert:

Distinguishing Old Marks from New
   A common old mark consisted of a central wreath open at the top with the letter M in the center. "Hand Painted" flowed around the top of the wreath; "NIPP. O. Box N" around the bottom. The modern fake mark reverses the wreath (it is open at the bottom) and places an hourglass form not an "M" in its middle.
   An old leaf mark, approximately one-quarter inch wide, has "Hand" with "Painted" below to the left of the stem and "NIPP. O. Box N" beneath. The newer mark has the identical lettering but the size is now one-half, rather than one-quarter, inch.
   An old mark consisted of "Hand Painted" arched above a solid rising sun logo with "NIPP. O. Box N" in a straight line beneath. The modern fake mark has the same lettering pattern but the central logo looks like a mound with a jagged line enclosing a blank space above it.

The majority of the marks are found in three different colors: green, blue, or magenta. Colors indicate the quality of the porcelain used: green for first-grade porcelain, blue for second-grade, and magenta for third-grade. Marks were applied by two methods: decal stickers under glaze and imprinting directly on the porcelain.

**References:** Joan Van Patten, *Collector's Encyclopedia of Nippon Porcelain*, 1st Series (1979, 2000 value update), 2nd Series (1982, 1997 value update), 3rd Series (1986, 2000 value update), 4th Series, (1997), Collector Books; 5th Series (1998); 6th Series, 2000; Joan F. Van Patten and Linda Lou, *Nippon Dolls & Playthings*, Collector Books, 2000; Kathy Wojciechowski, *Wonderful World of Nippon Porcelain*, Schiffer Publishing, 1992.

**Collectors' Clubs:** ARK-LA-TEX Nippon Club, 6800 Arapaho Rd, #1057, Dallas, TX 75248; Dixieland Nippon Club, P.O. Box 1712, Centerville, VA 22020; International Nippon Collectors Club, 1417 Steele St., Fort Myers, FL 33901; Lakes & Plains Nippon Collectors Society, P.O. Box 230, Peotone, IL 60468-0230; Long Island Nippon Collectors Club, 145 Andover Place, W Hempstead, NY 11552; MD-PA Collectors' Club, 1016 Erwin Dr., Joppa, MD 21085; New England Nippon Collectors Club, 64 Burt Rd, Springfield, MA 01118; Sunshine State Nippon Collectors' Club, P.O. Box 425, Frostproof, FL 33843; Upstate New York Nippon Collectors' Club, 122 Laurel Ave., Herkimer, NY 13350.

**Additional Listings:** See Warman's Americana & Collectibles.

Biscuit Jar, 4-1/2" h, painted maroon and gold, blue maple leaf
   mark...............................................................................70.00

## SPECIAL AUCTION

Jackson's Auctioneers & Appraisers
2229 Lincoln St.
Cedar Falls, IA 50613
(319) 277-2256
e-mail:jacksons@corenet.net

Bowl

    7" d, ftd, raised nut design, green "M" in wreath mark .......... 85.00

    7-1/4" d, 4" h, tan and beige, hp chestnuts int., ext. with leaves and gold beaded dec, three legs, blue maple leaf mark ............100.00

    10" d, light green faded ground, yellow, red, and pink hp roses, gold dec rim, two small closed handles, blue maple leaf mark...100.00

Cake Plate, 11" d, floral design, gold trim, green "M" in wreath mark ....................................................................................40.00

Candlestick, 11" h, 5" base, hp gold highlights, light green ground pedestal base, green maple leaf mark .......................................... 115.00

Celery Tray, 10-1/4" l, scalloped edge, green "M" in wreath mark 75.00

Cheese Dish, cov, 7-3/4" l, slanted, floral design, gold trim, blue Komaro mark....................................................................................70.00

Chocolate Set, 9-1/2" h chocolate pot, four cups and saucers, orange and tan floral dec, white ground, gold highlights, green "M" in wreath mark ................................................................................ 100.00

Compote, 5-1/4" h, floral dec, green "M" in wreath mark .............30.00

Dish, 9" w, two section, handle, butterfly design, blue rising sun mark .................................................................................................50.00

Dresser Set, hair receiver, trinket box, powder box, Van Patten Book I, plate 65 ............................................................................ 375.00

Dresser Tray, 18" l, 6-1/4" w, delicate hp pink floral design, gold trim, closed handles, green "M" in wreath mark, minor gold wear......50.00

Egg Caddy, 4" h, 6" d, holds four eggs, handle over stopper, hp landscape scene, green "M" in wreath mark ....................................75.00

Hatpin Holder, shaped, raised beading..........................................65.00

Humidor, cov

    Bulldog.......................................................................................200.00

    Hand painted cottage landscape, trees, fence, green "M" in wreath mark ..........................................................................275.00

Lemonade Set, 6-1/2" h pitcher, four matching tumblers, grape design, gold trim, 5 pc, China JE-OH mark ............................................125.00

Milk Pitcher, cov, 7" h, lavender ground, Egyptian style boats, island with trees and buildings, brow handle, geometric devices, blue maple leaf mark ................................................................................185.00

Nut Set, master bowl and six nut cups, acorns dec ......................60.00

Pitcher

    6" h, lavender ground, hp scene of Mediterranean sailboats, island with trees and buildings, geometric beading around rim, applied hp brown handle, bulbous ribbed body................ 145.00

    6-1/2" h, 5" w, Moorage dec, tan ground, handle dec, green, and white beading, blue maple leaf mark................................50.00

Plaque

    Elk, blown-out .................................................................800.00

    Horses, 10-3/4" d, molded in relief, five tan and brown horses, fence and trees in back ground, green "M" in wreath mark.............550.00

    Indian Warrior, 10-1/2" d, molded in relief, full feather bonnet, hunter clad in buffalo cap, green "M" in wreath mark.......750.00

    Moose, blown-out .........................................................450.00

    Waiting by Shore, 10" d, Dutch mother and two children looking over bay, dec rim, blue "M" in wreath mark ......................100.00

Plate

    9-1/2" d, hp landscape of water, trees, and mountain in background, 1" w gold border with green and pink hp jewels, blue maple leaf mark...............................................................................70.00

Portrait Vase, 5" h, 4" w, hp, portrait of young lady on one side, hp floral scene on reverse, two open handles, ruffled top, unmarked ......325.00

Serving Tray, 11-3/4" l, swan dec, gold trim, blue "M" in wreath mark .................................................................................................110.00

Sugar Shaker

    Blue and pink pastel gooseberries, beaded gold swags and scrolls ..................................................................................100.00

    Cobalt band, roses dec, mkd .................................................. 140.00

    Ecru and white ground, blue and yellow butterfly ................80.00

    White, gold outlined pink and orange poppy dec, handle ... 125.00

Tankard, 10" h, 6" d, flared base, raised gold enameled dec, central hp floral medallion, green maple leaf mark, some wear to gold.......225.00

Tea Set, 6" h cov teapot, creamer, sugar, six cups and saucers, hp swans in pond, mill in background, gold highlighted beading, green

Vase, molded roses, mottled green ground with gold highlights, gold handles, white, light pink roses, green leaves, 9" h, $880. Photo courtesy of Jackson's Auctioneers & Appraisers.

"M" in wreath mark, wear to gold............................................... 150.00

Tiered Plate, 9" d, floral border, gold trim, magenta "M" in wreath mark .................................................................................................30.00

Vase

    5-1/4" h, bulbous, two handles, black, pink, red, and yellow roses, Royal Kinran mark.................................................................. 125.00

    6" h, four handles, scenic design, green "M" in wreath mark, pr .............................................................................................165.00

    6-1/2" h, hp, grapes on vines, gold dec, bulbous, green maple leaf mark .............................................................................................70.00

    7-1/2" h, 7" w, Madame Recamier portrait, handle, cobalt blue ground, three bright floral inserts, beaded, bulbous, pedestal ........................................................................................415.00

    8-1/2" h, double handles, Lilac pattern, gold trim, blue maple leaf mark .......................................................................................... 150.00

    8-1/2" h, double handles, scenic design, gold trim, green "M" in wreath mark, pr .....................................................................265.00

    8-1/2" h, 4-3/4" w, four sided, hp scenes of water views with trees, gold beading around each panel, green M in wreath mark...150.00

    8-3/4" h, double elephant trunk handles, florals, gold trim, green "M" mark, pr...............................................................................300.00

    9-1/2" h, 4-1/2" d, iris dec, two small handles, 2" heavy gold band around top, blue maple leaf mark....................................325.00

    10" h, black pottery, Gouda type design, green wreath mark ..200.00

    12-1/2" h, double handles, blue floral dec, gold trim, green "M" in wreath mark .......................................................................... 100.00

    13" h, two handles, hp flowers, gold painted griffins, black, red, and green, gold highlights, ruffled top, white and pink flowers, blue "M" in wreath mark .................................................................250.00

    13-1/2" h, two handles, small roses hp in portrait style, gold dec, two large ovals, green maple leaf mark, some minor gold wear, pr...............................................................................................450.00

    14" h, 6" d, hp white and red roses and leaves on one side, gold beaded highlights at rim and base, blue maple leaf mark, some wear to gold at rim.............................................................200.00

Vegetable Bowl, 10-1/4" d, two handles, scalloped edge, acorn design, green "M" in wreath mark ...........................................................90.00

Wall Plaque, 10" d, portrait ........................................................435.00

Wine Jug, monk portrait, Moorage stopper...............................750.00

# NODDERS

**History:** Nodders are figurines with heads and/or arms attached to the body with wires to enable movement. They are made in a variety of materials—bisque, celluloid, papier-mâaché, porcelain, or wood.

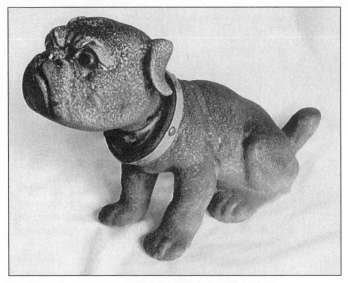

**Bulldog, brown, sand finish, 10" l, 6-1/2" h, $65.**

Most nodders date from the late 19th century, with Germany being the principal source of supply. Among the American-made nodders, those of Disney and cartoon characters are most eagerly sought.

**Reference:** Hilma R. Irtz, *Figural Nodders*, Collector Books, 1997.

**Collectors' Club:** Bobbin' Head National Club, P.O. Box 9297, Lakeland, FL 32120.

Black Boy, 24" h, papier-mâché, clockwork, felt and cotton outfit, c1900 ............................................................. 1,265.00
Black Woman, seated, holding removable watermelon, gray hair, head nods, salt shaker type ................................................. 75.00
Bull Dog Terrier, articulated head, papier-mâché, minor losses to paint .......................................................................... 375.00
Cat, 5" h, composition, black.......................................................... 75.00
Chinese figures, 4-3/4" h, male and female seated figure, floral enamel dec, articulated hands, heads, and tongues, Ernst Bohne Sons, Germany, 20th C, price for pr........................................................ 865.00
Donkey, 3" h, celluloid.................................................................. 48.00
Duck, 15-1/2" h, clockwork, yellow dyed rabbit fur, glass eyes, papier-mâché feet, articulated bill, French, early 20th C ..................... 690.00
Hobo, 3-1/2" h, 2-1/4" w, green coat, bottle in pocket, tan pants and hat, sitting in chair, holding stick................................................. 225.00
Little Orphan Annie, bisque, mkd "Germany".............................. 125.00
Monkey, 6-1/2" h, celluloid .......................................................... 70.00
Mother Goose, papier-mâché, old woman in red cape riding on back of white goose ........................................................................ 3,960.00
Oriental Lady, 6-3/4" h, bisque, seated, holding fan behind nodding head, Continental .................................................................... 200.00
Rabbit, 7" h, papier-mâché, glass eyes ........................................ 75.00
Turkey, 3-3/4" h, papier-mâché, male and female, orig black paint, polychrome trim, pewter feet.................................................... 120.00

# NORITAKE CHINA

**History:** Morimura Brothers founded Noritake China in 1904 in Nagoya, Japan. They made high-quality chinaware for export to the United States and also produced a line of china blanks for hand painting. In 1910, the company perfected a technique for the production of high-quality dinnerware and introduced streamlined production.

During the 1920s, the Larkin Company of Buffalo, New York, was a prime distributor of Noritake China. Larkin offered Azalea, Briarcliff, Linden, Modjeska, Savory, Sheridan, and Tree in the Meadow patterns as part of their premium line.

The factory was heavily damaged during World War II, and production was reduced. Between 1946 and 1948 the company sold their china under the "Rose China" mark, since the quality of production did not match the earlier Noritake China. Expansion in 1948 brought about the resumption of quality production and the use of the Noritake name once again.

**Marks:** There are close to 100 different marks for Noritake, the careful study of which can determine the date of production. Most pieces are marked "Noritake" with a wreath, "M," "N," or "Nippon." The use of the letter N was registered in 1953.

**References:** Aimee Neff Alden, *Collector's Encyclopedia of Early Noritake*, Collector Books, 1995, 2000 value update; Walter Ayars, *Larkin China, Catalog Reprint,* Echo Publishing, 1990; Joan Van Patten, *Collector's Encyclopedia of Noritake*, Collector Books, 1984, 2000 value update; David Spain, *Collecting Noritake, A to Z: Art Deco and More,* Schiffer Publishing, 1999,

**Collectors' Club:** Noritake Collectors' Society, 145 Andover Place, West Hempstead, NY 115532-1603.

**Additional Listings:** See *Warman's Americana & Collectibles* for Azalea pattern prices.

Ashtray, 4-3/4' w, tree trunk, relief molded raccoon, green "M" in wreath mark ........................................................................ 200.00
Bowl, 7" sq, 3 ftd, turned-in sides, autumn leaves, molded filbert nuts ........................................................................................ 80.00
Bread Plate, 12" l, ear of corn dec ............................................... 50.00
Butter Dish, cov, Tree in the Meadow pattern, orig insert ............. 65.00
Butter Tub, Azalea pattern ........................................................... 45.00
Cake plate, Baroda pattern .......................................................... 25.00
Candlesticks, pr, 3-1/2" h, 4-1/2" d, tan luster, blue roses, black handle and trim, three ftd base ............................................................. 75.00
Card Holder, Art Deco style, double handles, pedestal base, blue and orange luster, gentleman in checkered cape ........................... 225.00

**Cigarette Holder, Tree in Meadow, green ground, stamped mark, 3" h, $40.**

Celery Tray, 12" l, Azalea pattern....................................................45.00
Chocolate Pot, cov, Tree in the Meadow pattern ........................200.00
Compote, blue, gold, and white, fruit dec, 2 pcs ........................175.00
Condiment Set, figural, lady, pr salt and pepper shakers, and mustard
　pot, price for set ........................................................................85.00
Cookie Plate, 10-1/2" d, orange luster, vibrant sunflowers,
　handles .....................................................................................125.00
Cracker Jar, , cov, Tree in the Meadow pattern, melon ribbed....135.00
Creamer and Sugar, , cov, Tree in the Meadow pattern ..............70.00
Cup and Saucer, Chelsea pattern..................................................30.00
Dessert Set, Art Deco lady in cup, large geometric tray, blue
　luster ........................................................................................125.00
Dinner Service, partial
　Atlanta pattern, five dinner plates, six salad plates, three small
　　bowls, five cups, five saucers, creamer, sugar, gravy boat 70.00
　Caliban pattern, 89 pcs...........................................................175.00
　Juanita pattern, 43 pcs ...........................................................130.00
　Ramona pattern, creamer, sugar, two oval meat platters .....90.00
　Violet pattern, thirteen dinner plates, nine salad plates, nine bread
　　plates, sixteen cups, fifteen saucers, four cup plates, oval vege-
　　table dish, round vegetable dish, creamer .......................300.00
Dresser Set, orange luster, figural bird final on ftd powder box, match-
　ing tray ....................................................................................250.00
Jam Dish, gray luster, figural locust, multicolored emb fruits ........65.00
Lemon Dish, 5-1/2" d, Tree in the Meadow pattern ......................35.00
Napkin Ring, gentleman.................................................................50.00
Nut Bowl Set, 6" d bowl, open chestnut form, holds six 2" d nut dishes,
　painted nuts and leaves, earthtones, green mark ....................150.00
Plate, 8-1/2" d, Tree in the Meadow pattern .................................20.00
Potpourri Jar, 6" h , blue and white, pierced cov with red and yellow
　rosebud finial ............................................................................85.00
Salt and Pepper Shakers, pr, Art Deco style................................75.00
Sandwich Server, 8" d, pearlized center, fruit dec, bird finial ......175.00
Teapot, cov, Tree in the Meadow pattern ...................................100.00
Vase
　7" h, pink, flowers....................................................................42.00
　10" h, moriage dragon, two handles, green mark ...............175.00
　13" h, two handles, Tree in Meadow scene, green "M" in wreath
　　mark .....................................................................................125.00
Vegetable Dish, cov, 8-1/2" w, 5" h, floral design, heavy gold trim, mkd
　"Noritake China," "M" in wreath, Made in Occupied Japan (Mark
　#91), very slight wear to gold .................................................125.00
Wall Pocket, orange luster, figural bird peering over top.............180.00

# NORTH DAKOTA SCHOOL OF MINES

**History:** The North Dakota School of Mines was established in 1890. Earle J. Babcock, a chemistry instructor, was impressed with the high purity level of North Dakota potter's clay. In 1898, Babcock received funds to develop his finds. He tried to interest commercial potteries in the North Dakota clay but had limited success.

In 1910, Babcock persuaded the school to establish a Ceramics Department. Margaret Cable, who studied under Charles Binns and Frederick H. Rhead, was appointed head. She remained until her retirement in 1949.

Decorative emphasis was placed on native themes, e.g., flowers and animals. Art Nouveau, Art Deco, and fairly plain pieces were made.

**Marks:** The pottery is marked with a cobalt blue underglaze circle of the words "University of North Dakota/Grand Forks, N.D./Made at School of Mines/N.D. Clay." Some

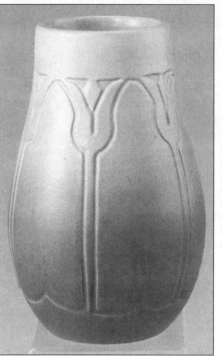

**Vase, incised tulips, matte gold to brown glaze, sgd "M. Cable" for Margaret Cable, circular ink stamp mark, $1,015. Photo courtesy of David Rago Auctions.**

early pieces are marked only "U.N.D." or "U.N.D./Grand Forks, N.D." Most pieces are numbered (they can be dated from University records) and signed by both the instructor and student. Cable-signed pieces are the most desirable.

**References:** Darlene Hurst Dommel, *Collector's Encyclopedia of the Dakota Potteries*, Collector Books, 1996.

**Collectors' Club:** North Dakota Pottery Collectors Society, P.O. Box 14, Beach, ND 58621.

Charger, 9-1/2" d, stylized flower motif, polychrome cuerda seca, dec
　by Margaret Cable, 1949, ink stamp, incised "M.Cable/1949/June
　Marks" ......................................................................................475.00
Vase
　3-3/4" h, 3-1/4" d, incised stylized flowers, celadon semi-matte
　　glaze, artist unknown, ink stamp "53H"...........................500.00
　5-3/4" h, 2-3/4" d, ovoid, incised cowboy and lasso, "Why Not
　　Minot," light periwinkle blue glaze, Julie Mattson, ink stamp
　　"JM/175" ...............................................................................375.00
Vessel
　3-1/2" h, 5" d, conical, incised geometric pattern, matte green glaze,
　　M. J. Arnegard, 1932, ink stamp "M.J. Arnegard/42132"......700.00
　3-3/4" h, 4-3/4" d, squatty, incised stylized flowers, matte green
　　microcrystalline glaze, by Flora Huckfield and student, ink
　　stamp "E. Ericson/Huck/1106"........................................450.00
　4" h, 5-1/2" d, squatty, band of pink prairie roses, green leaves,
　　pink ground, painted by Flora Huckfield and student, ink stamp
　　"Bridgeman/Huck/4248" ....................................................700.00
　4-3/4" h, 6-1/2" d, squatty, carved stylized flowers, around shoul-
　　der, matte caramel glaze, C. A. Sorbo, ink stamp "C. A.
　　Sorbo/196" ...........................................................................450.00
　4-3/4" h, 7" d, squatty, North Dakota Wheat, shades of brown,
　　carved by Flora Huckfield, ink stamp "Hoffman/Huck/1655/No.
　　Dakota Wheat" .................................................................1,200.00

# WALLACE NUTTING

**History:** Wallace Nutting (1861-1941) was America's most famous photographer of the early 20th century. A retired minister, Nutting took more than 50,000 pictures, keeping

10,000 of his best and destroying the rest. His popular and best-selling scenes included "Exterior Scenes" (apple blossoms, country lanes, orchards, calm streams, and rural American countrysides), "Interior Scenes" (usually featuring a colonial woman working near a hearth), and "Foreign Scenes" (typically thatch-roofed cottages). Those pictures which were least popular in his day have become the rarest and most-highly collectible today and are classified as "Miscellaneous Unusual Scenes." This category encompasses such things as animals, architecturals, children, florals, men, seascapes, and snow scenes.

Nutting sold literally millions of his hand-colored plain-otype pictures between 1900 and his death in 1941. Starting first in Southbury, Connecticut, and later moving his business to Framingham, Massachusetts, the peak of Wallace Nutting's picture production was 1915 to 1925. During this period, Nutting employed nearly 200 people, including colorists, darkroom staff, salesmen, and assorted office personnel. Wallace Nutting pictures proved to be a huge commercial success and hardly an American household was without one by 1925.

While attempting to seek out the finest and best early-American furniture as props for his colonial Interior Scenes, Nutting became an expert in American antiques. He published nearly twenty books in his lifetime, including his ten-volume *State Beautiful* series and various other books on furniture, photography, clocks, and his autobiography. He also contributed many photographs which were published in magazines and books other than his own.

Nutting also became widely known for his reproduction furniture. His furniture shop produced literally hundreds of different furniture forms: clocks, stools, chairs, settles, settees, tables, stands, desks, mirrors, beds, chests of drawers, cabinet pieces, and treenware.

The overall synergy of the Wallace Nutting name, pictures, books, and furniture, has made anything "Wallace Nutting" quite collectible.

**Marks:** Wallace Nutting furniture is clearly marked with his distinctive paper label (which was glued directly onto the piece) or with a block or script signature brand (which was literally branded into his furniture).

**Note:** "Process Prints" are 1930s machine-produced reprints of twelve of Nutting's most popular pictures. These have minimal value and can be detected by using a magnifying glass.

**References:** Michael Ivankovich, *Alphabetical & Numerical Index to Wallace Nutting Pictures*, Diamond Press, 1988; ——, *Collector's Guide to Wallace Nutting Pictures*, Collector Books, 1997; ——, *Guide to Wallace Nutting Furniture*, Diamond Press, 1990; ——, *Wallace Nutting Expansible Catalog* (reprint of 1915 catalog), Diamond Press, 1987; Wallace Nutting, *Wallace Nutting: A Great American Idea* (reprint of 1922 catalog), Diamond Press, 1992; ——, *Wallace Nutting General Catalog* (reprint of 1930 catalog), Schiffer Publishing, 1977; ——, *Wallace Nutting's Windsors* (reprint of 1918 catalog), Diamond Press, 1992.

**Collectors' Club:** Wallace Nutting Collectors Club, P.O. Box 2458, Doylestown, PA 18901.

**Museum:** Wadsworth Athenaeum, Hartford, CT.

**Advisor:** Michael Ivankovich.

A Little River, NH, 4" x 5", $95. Photo courtesy of Michael Ivankovich Antiques & Auction Co., Inc.

An Elaborate Dinner, Southbury, CT, copyright 1909, 22" x 28", $855. Photo courtesy of Michael Ivankovich Antiques & Auction Co., Inc.

A Dahlia Jar, orig copyright label o back, 8" x 10, $625. Photo courtesy of Michael Ivankovich Antiques & Auction Co., Inc.

## Wallace Nutting Furniture

Bed, maple, #809 ........................................ 600.00
Candle Stand, # 22, cross base ..................... 525.00
Foot Stool, #292 ......................................... 275.00
Chair
    Dutch Country, #461 ............................. 400.00
    Ladderback, #392 ............................... 350.00
    NE Ladderback, #490 ........................... 825.00
    NE Ladderback, arm, #492 ..................... 770.00
    Pilgrim, arm, #493 ............................ 1,050.00
    Wild Rose, side, #365 .......................... 440.00
    Windsor, side, #326 ............................ 850.00
Table
    Butterfly, #625 ................................ 2,200.00
    Ogee-top, #609 ................................. 625.00

## Wallace Nutting Pictures

A Berkshire Brook, 10" x 16" ........................ 110.00
A Book by the Window, 13" x 17" .................... 660.00
A Clogheen Bridge, 13" x 16" ........................ 715.00
A Garden Landing, 9" x 11" ........................... 300.00
A Highland Vale, 11" x 17" ........................... 410.00
A Little Dutch Cove, 14" x 17" ...................... 880.00
A Token in Remembrance, 13" x 16" .................. 440.00
A Willow Pastoral, 13" x 17" ........................ 825.00
An Arbor Arch, 13" x 16" ............................. 440.00
Blossoms on the Housatonic, 11" x 17" .............. 120.00
Boys at Postiano, 13" x 15" .......................... 770.00
Bride's Door, 13" x 16" .............................. 465.00
Bridesmaid's Procession, 10" x 12" .................. 110.00
Charles River Elm, 13" x 16" ......................... 165.00
Concord Banks, 11" x 14" ............................. 145.00
Crawford Notch Cascade, 10" x 12" ................... 120.00
Decked As A Bride, 16" x 20" ......................... 170.00
Disappearing in Blooms, 13" x 17" ................... 145.00
Dog-On-It, 7" x 11" ................................ 3,960.00
Flowering Time, 11" x 14" ............................. 80.00
Flume Falls, 11" x 14" ............................... 160.00
Grace, 12" x 15" ..................................... 155.00
Grandmother's Garden, 11" x 14" ....................... 85.00
Hollyhock Cottage, 17" x 22" ......................... 155.00
Honeymoon Stroll, 10" x 12" ........................... 80.00
Is The Fire Ready?, 13" x 16" ......................... 70.00
La Jolla, 13" x 15" .................................. 155.00
Larkspur, 15" x 19" .................................. 165.00
Locust Cottage, 16" x 20" ............................ 175.00
Mary's Little Lamb, 11" x 14" ........................ 250.00

Meadow Lilies, 13" x 16" ........................... 1,980.00
Morning Duties, 10" x 12" ............................ 155.00
Mossy Logs, 16" x 20" ................................ 285.00
New Hampshire in June, 13" x 16" ..................... 175.00
Newton Broads, 10" x 16" ............................. 140.00
On the Heights, 9" x 15" ............................. 740.00
Parlor Mantel, Keim House, 13" x 16" .............. 1,650.00
Pilgrim Hollyhocks, 9" x 11" ......................... 195.00
Reading from Arabian Nights, 14" x 17" ............ 2,200.00
Rose Gate, 8" x 10" .................................. 275.00
Roses and a Bud, 12" x 14" ........................... 685.00
Salisbury Shadows, 10" x 14" ......................... 285.00
Sea Ledges, 16" x 20" ................................ 410.00
Smothered in Flowers, 13" x 16" ...................... 330.00
Spinning at 84, 14" x 14" ............................ 355.00
Sunshine and Music, 10" x 16" ........................ 215.00
Tea for Two, 10" x 12" ............................. 2,145.00
The Cottage Beautiful, 11" x 13" ..................... 210.00
The Donjon Chenanceau, 14" x 17" ..................... 735.00
The Nutting Garden Corner, 9" x 11" .................. 320.00
The Pergola, Amalfi, 14" x 17" ....................... 465.00
The Way It Begins, 13" x 15" ......................... 465.00
Under The Blossoms, 13" x 16" ........................ 285.00
Venice's Chief Glory, 14" x 17" .................... 1,485.00
Village End, 14" x 20" ............................... 275.00
Westfield Water, 10" x 16" ........................... 155.00
Westmore Drive, 17" x 21" ............................ 210.00
Wissahickon Decorations, 13" x 15" ................... 300.00

# WALLACE NUTTING-LIKE PHOTOGRAPHERS

**History:** Although Wallace Nutting was widely recognized as the country's leading producer of hand-colored photographs during the early 20th century, he was by no means the only photographer selling this style of picture. Throughout the country, literally hundreds of regional photographers were selling hand-colored photographs from their home regions or travels. The subject matter of these photographers was comparable to Nutting's, including Interior, Exterior, Foreign, and Miscellaneous Unusual scenes.

Several photographers operated large businesses, and, although not as large or well-known as Wallace Nutting, they sold a substantial volume of pictures which can still be readily found today. The vast majority of their work was photographed in their home regions and sold primarily to local residents or visiting tourists. It should come as little surprise that three of the major Wallace Nutting-like photographers—David Davidson, Fred Thompson, and the Sawyer Art Co.—each had ties to Wallace Nutting.

Hundreds of other smaller local and regional photographers attempted to market hand-colored pictures comparable to Wallace Nutting's from 1900 to the 1930s. Although quite attractive, most were not as appealing to the general public as Wallace Nutting pictures. However, as the price of Wallace Nutting pictures has escalated, the work of these lesser-known Wallace Nutting-like photographers have become increasingly collectible.

A partial listing of some of these minor Wallace Nutting-like photographers includes: Babcock; J. C. Bicknell;

Blair; Ralph Blood (Portland, Maine); Bragg; Brehmer; Brooks; Burrowes; Busch; Carlock; Pedro Cacciola; Croft; Currier; Depue Brothers; Derek; Dowly; Eddy; May Farini (hand-colored colonial lithographs); George Forest; Gandara; Gardner (Nantucket, Bermuda, Florida); Gibson; Gideon; Gunn; Bessie Pease Gutmann (hand-colored colonial lithographs); Edward Guy; Harris; C. Hazen; Knoffe; Haynes (Yellowstone Park); Margaret Hennesey; Hodges; Homer; Krabel; Kattleman; La Bushe; Lake; Lamson (Portland, Maine); M. Lightstrum; Machering; Rossiler Mackinae; Merrill; Meyers; William Moehring; Moran; Murrey; Lyman Nelson; J. Robinson Neville (New England); Patterson; Own Perry; Phelps; Phinney; Reynolds; F. Robbins; Royce; Frederick Scheetz (Philadelphia, Pennsylvania); Shelton, Standley (Colorado); Stott; Summers; Esther Svenson; Florence Thompson; Thomas Thompson; M. A. Trott; Sanford Tull; Underhill; Villar; Ward; Wilmot; Edith Wilson; and Wright.

**References:** Carol Begley Gray, *History of the Sawyer Pictures*, published by author, 1995 (available from Wallace Nutting Collector's Club, P.O. Box 2458, Doylestown, PA 18901); Michael Ivankovich, *Collector's Value Guide to Early Twentieth Century American Prints*, Collector Books, 1998; —, *Guide to Wallace-Nutting Like Photographers of the Early 20th Century*, Diamond Press, 1991.

**Collectors' Club:** Wallace Nutting Collector's Club, P.O. Box 1536, Doylestown, PA 18901.

**Advisor:** Michael Ivankovich.

**Notes:** The key determinants of value include the collectibility of the particular photographer, subject matter, condition, and size. Exterior Scenes are the most common.

Keep in mind that only the rarest pictures, in the best condition, will bring top prices. Discoloration and/or damage to the picture or matting can reduce value significantly.

## David Davidson

Second to Nutting in overall production, Davidson worked primarily in the Rhode Island and southern Massachusetts area. While a student at Brown University around 1900, Davidson learned the art of hand-colored photography from Wallace Nutting, who happened to be the Minister at Davidson's church. After Nutting moved to Southbury in 1905, Davidson graduated from Brown and started a successful photography business in Providence, Rhode Island, which he operated until his death in 1967.

| | |
|---|---:|
| A Berkshire Jewel, 13" x 16" | 145.00 |
| A Vacation Seat, 12" x 16" | 85.00 |
| Beckoning Trail, 7" x 9" | 60.00 |
| Berkshire Sunset, 13" x 20" | 130.00 |
| Forest Lake, 12" x 14" | 65.00 |
| Gay Head, 13" x 15" | 100.00 |
| Grandpa's Marguerites, 7" x 9" | 100.00 |
| In The Making, 8" x 10" | 70.00 |
| Lover's Lane, 9" x 16" | 85.00 |
| Meeting House Lane, 7" x 9" | 80.00 |
| Neighbors, 10" x 13" | 300.00 |
| Profile Water Hazard, 12" x 15" | 105.00 |

**Davidson, Without A Ripple, 5" x 7", $60. Photo courtesy of Michael Ivankovich Antiques & Auction Co., Inc.**

| | |
|---|---:|
| Snow Bound Brook, 10" x 12" | 70.00 |
| Stone Arch, 8" x 10" | 70.00 |
| The Brook's Mirror, 12" x 16" | 120.00 |
| The Deacon's Parlor, 14" x 16" | 105.00 |
| The Lambs May Feast, 5" x 7" | 120.00 |
| The Match Makers, 13" x 16" | 125.00 |
| The Pergola Gate, 13" x 15" | 95.00 |
| The Spent Wave, 5" x 7" | 65.00 |

## Sawyer

A father and son team, Charles H. Sawyer and Harold B. Sawyer, operated the very successful Sawyer Art Company from 1903 until the 1970s. Beginning in Maine, the Sawyer Art Company moved to Concord, New Hampshire, in 1920 to be closer to their primary market—New Hampshire's White Mountains. Charles H. Sawyer briefly worked for Nutting from 1902 to 1903 while living in southern Maine. Sawyer's production volume ranks third behind Wallace Nutting and David Davidson.

**Sawyer, Mt. Lafayette, NH, 5" x 6", $85. Photo courtesy of Michael Ivankovich Antiques & Auction Co., Inc.**

A Rose Cottage, Cape Cod, 4" x 5" .........................................220.00
Among the Frost Flowers....................................................120.00
At the Water's Edge, 7" x 9"....................................................90.00
Bit of Mackerel Cove, 9" x 15" ............................................275.00
Bridge of Flowers, 10" x 13"................................................175.00
Clear Water Pond, 7" x 11"..................................................175.00
Crawford Notch in Box, 6" x 8" ...........................................155.00
Elk of the Mohawk Trail, 7" x 9"..........................................155.00
Gates of Yosemite, 13" x 15" ..............................................265.00
Joseph's Lincoln's Garden, 4" x 5".......................................105.00
Old Man of the Mts, 7" x 9" ...................................................90.00
Rainbow & Horseshoe Falls, 8" x 10" ................................120.00
Sunset on Rangley Lake, 9" x 11".......................................100.00
The Original Dension Plant, 14" x 17" .................................145.00
Up thro' Dixville Notch, 14" x 16" ........................................250.00

## Fred Thompson

Frederick H. Thompson and Frederick M. Thompson, another father and son team, operated the Thompson Art Company (TACO) from 1908 to 1923, working primarily in the Portland, Maine, area. We know that Thompson and Nutting had collaborated because Thompson widely marketed an interior scene he had taken in Nutting's Southbury home. The production volume of the Thompson Art Company ranks fourth behind Nutting, Davidson, and Sawyer.

Apple Tree Road, 11" x 17"....................................................60.00
Colonial Baby, 13" x 15".......................................................155.00
Deep Hole Brook, 10" x 15" ..................................................80.00
Flower Maid, 8" x 15" .............................................................60.00
Gay Head, 10" x 15" .............................................................300.00
Gay Head Cliffs, 10" x 15" ...................................................120.00
Hazy Morn, 7" x 9" ...............................................................160.00
Learning to Sew, 7" x 9".........................................................60.00
Miniature Interior, 3" x 4"........................................................60.00
Mirror with Interior Space, 4" x 13" .......................................60.00
Oceanside, 14" x 16"............................................................120.00
Old-Time Flowers, 7" x 9".......................................................60.00

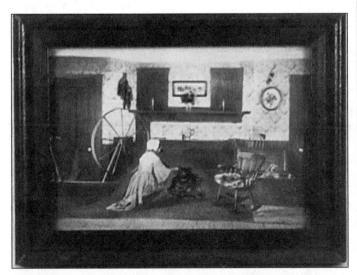

**Thompson, Interior, girl by fire, orig label on back, 3" x 4", $85. Photo courtesy of Michael Ivankovich Antiques & Auction Co., Inc.**

Paring Apples, 7" x 9" .............................................................60.00
Pond Cove, 7" x 11".................................................................60.00
Portland Head, 8" x 13"............................................................90.00
Roses and Reading, 8" x 16"...................................................85.00
Sunbonnet Days, 7" x 9"........................................................175.00
Whittier's Home, 8" x 13"........................................................230.00

## Minor Wallace Nutting-Like Photographers

Generally speaking, prices for works by minor Wallace Nutting-like photographers would break down as follows: smaller pictures (5" x 7" to 10" x 12), $10-$75; medium pictures (11" x 14" to 14" x 17"), $50-$200; larger pictures (larger than 14" x 17"), $75-$200+.

Bicknell, J. Carlton
    Double Head 8" x 12" .......................................................30.00
    Mirror with Exterior Scene, 8" x 11" ...............................85.00
    Sourduahump, 8" x 10".....................................................45.00
Burrowes
    A Country Road, 8" x 10"..................................................35.00
    Natural Bridge of Virginia, 8" x 12" ................................20.00
Carlock, Royal, Washington DC Monument, 5" x 7" ............30.00
Edson, Norman, Mt. Elephantic, 8" x 10" ............................45.00
Gardiner, H. Marshall, Bermuda, 12" x 15" .........................65.00
Gibson, A Rustic Bridge, 11" x 14"........................................30.00
Gourley, Rose Cloister, San Fernando, 8" x 10" ................65.00
Harris
    Approach to Limekiln Lake, 11" x 14" ...........................155.00
    Natural Bridge, VA, 12" x 22" ..........................................90.00
    St. Augustine, 9" x 16" .....................................................75.00
Higgins, Charles
    Fireside Reflections, 7" x 11"...........................................80.00
    Untitled Girl by Tree, 11" x 14".......................................145.00
Lamson
    Golden Hour, 7" x 11"........................................................60.00
    Willow Road, 8" x 15".........................................................60.00
LeBusch, A Country Road, 11" x 13".....................................25.00
McLead, N., Cabot Trail, Cape Breton, 10" x 16"................45.00
Meiers, J. W., Sunset on Flathead Lake, 11" x 15" .............65.00
Moosilauke Studio, Echo Lake, black and white, 8" x 10" ............25.00
Moran, In The Garden, 12" x 14"...........................................10.00
Payne, Cavern Cascade, 8" x 14".........................................60.00
Petty, George B., A Favorite Walk, 11" x 14" ......................35.00
Rogers, Stanley, Gay Head Cliffs, 9" x 12" ........................135.00
Sanger, Contemplative, 18" x 22".........................................80.00
Smith, Nature's Mirror, 11" x 14" ..........................................25.00
Sunsene, Storks, 7" x 9".........................................................35.00
Thompson, Florence
    June Blossoms, 7" x 11" ...................................................20.00
    Six Master, 7" x 11".........................................................320.00
Tillinghast, Untitled Cows, 9" x 11".......................................40.00
Unknown Photographers
    Close-Framed Fisherman, 8" x 10".................................40.00
    Cordova, Alaska, 14" x 20" ..............................................60.00
    Exterior Triptych, 7" x 16".................................................85.00
    German Photo- Nazi Flag, 9" x 11"..................................50.00
    Japanese Village, 14" x 24"..............................................65.00
    Men by Arches, 13" x 17" .................................................10.00
    Mirror with Canoe in Lake, 8" x 10" ................................70.00
    Schooner, 7" x 9" ...............................................................60.00
    Untitled Railroad Tracks, 16" x 19"..................................60.00
Villar, The Steps to the Road, 11" x 14".................................90.00
Winslow, R., The Outer Shore, Cape Cod, 11" x 14" ...........75.00
Woolford, J. P., Sentinel Pines, 14" x 16".............................65.00

# OCCUPIED JAPAN

**History:** The Japanese economy was devastated when World War II ended. To secure necessary hard currency, the Japanese pottery industry produced thousands of figurines and other knickknacks for export. The variety of products is endless—ashtrays, dinnerware, lamps, planters, souvenir items, toys, vases, etc. Initially, the figurines attracted the largest number of collectors; today many collectors focus on other types of pieces.

**Marks:** From the beginning of the American occupation of Japan until April 28, 1952, objects made in that country were marked "Japan," "Made in Japan," "Occupied Japan," or "Made in Occupied Japan." Only pieces marked with the last two designations are of major interest to Occupied Japan collectors. The first two marks also were used during other time periods.

**References:** Florence Archambault, *Occupied Japan for the Home,* Schiffer Publishing, 2000; Gene Florence, *Price Guide to Collector's Encyclopedia of Occupied Japan,* Collector Books, 1999 (updated prices for 5-book series *Collector's Encyclopedia of Occupied Japan*); Monica Lynn Clements and Patricia Rosser Clements, *Pocket Guide to Occupied Japan,* Schiffer Publishing, 1999; Carole Bess White, *Collector's Guide to Made in Japan Ceramics,* Book I (1996), Book II (1997), Collector Books.

**Collectors' Club:** The Occupied Japan Club, 29 Freeborn St., Newport, RI 02840.

**Additional Listings:** See *Warman's Americana & Collectibles* for more examples.

Ashtray, Niagara falls, hp, mkd "Occupied Japan" .........................20.00
Bank, 2" h, 3-1/4" l, piggy, "I'm A Little Piggy," blue ink mark "Made in Occupied Japan" ...................................................................15.00
Biscuit Barrel, hp, raised gold dec, Japanese characters painted on bottom and "Made in Occupied Japan" ...................................175.00
Box, cov, figural
    1-1/2" h, 1-3/4" w, chest of drawers, mkd "Made In Occupied Japan" ...........................................................................18.00
    1-1/2" h, 1-1/2" l, piano, mkd "Made in Occupied Japan" .....18.00

**Figure, black child, green hat, white shirt, blue pants, accordion, 3-3/4" h, $20.**

Child's Toy Plate, 2-3/4" d, hp floral pattern in center, mkd "PICO, Made in Occupied Japan" .............................................................8.00
Condiment Set, figural hen and rooster salt and pepper shakers, orig lids and spoon, mkd "Made in Occupied Japan" ....................125.00
Crib Toy, 3" h, composition, Mickey Mouse, mkd "Occupied Japan," c1945-52, tip of nose broken off.............................................125.00
Cup and Saucer, blue and white floral and dragon design, translucent ......................................................................................25.00
Demitasse Cup and Saucer, white, coat of arms with lion and dog supporters, shield, gold trim................................................................20.00
Figure
    2" h, Snow Birds, male in blue tie and black hat, female with brown scar, green hat, black mark ......................................7.50
    2-3/4" h, Colonial woman, sitting on bench with basket of fruit, mkd "Made in Occupied Japan" .......................................12.00
    2-7/8" h, Colonial man, mkd "Made in Occupied Japan" ......12.00
    3-1/4" h, baseball player, red mark "Made in Occupied Japan".12.50
    3-1/4" h, boy in pink checked shirt, blue pants, white overcoat, girl with pink checked skirt, red "Hand Painted Made in Occupied Japan" mark, pr ...................................................24.00
    3-1/2" d, boy with baseball bat, one eye on ball, other closed, black mark ..........................................................................22.00
    3-3/4" h, show girl, ethnic caricature, dark brown skin tone, red lips, side glance eyes, real fur tutu, green bandeaux, gold shoes, pink bow in black curly hair...................................65.00
    4" h, cat and kittens in basket................................................30.00
    4" h, Hummel type, golfer boy, golf clubs.............................25.00
    4" h, Oriental figure with basket, brown jacket, yellow sleeves, green paints, black mark......................................................12.00
    4" h, Victorian lady, black ink mark "Made in Occupied Japan" ......................................................................................12.50
    4-1/4" h, Hummel type, boy sitting on bench, violin, red stamp mark, minor paint loss .......................................................20.00
    4-1/4" h, 4" l, elf riding snail, green mark "Made in Occupied Japan" ......................................................................................35.00
    4-1/2" h, 5-1/2" w, cherub, pale pink, green highlights..........30.00
    5-1/4" h, Colonial couple, both mkd in red "Made in Occupied Japan" ......................................................................................35.00
    5-1/2" h, accordion player, red "Made in Occupied Japan" mark ......................................................................................18.00
    5-3/4" h, man, brown coat, blue vest, burnt orange pants, black mark ......................................................................................15.00
    7-3/4" h, lady with lute, white flowered dress, pink bodice, blue hat, black mark.......................................................................30.00
    8" h, 3-1/2" w, man holding flower, bright colors ...................40.00
Jar, 3" h, hp, gold detailing around mixed flower transfer, red "Hand Painted Made in Occupied Japan" mark ...................................10.00
Pin, 2" x 1-1/2", dog, celluloid ........................................................32.00
Planter
    3" h, dog, strolling outside basketweave planter, blue and tan, mkd "Occupied Japan"........................................................18.00
    5-1/4" h, 5-1/2" w, 5" d, bisque, girl with planter, red ink mark "Paulux Made in Occupied Japan" .....................................52.00
Platter, Kent, 18" l, 12-1/2" w, pink Spring willow dec on white ground..............................................................................................65.00
Salt and Pepper Shakers, pr
    2-3/4" h, Art Deco birds, black mark .....................................18.00
    3-1/4" h, Indians in Canoe, mkd "Made in Occupied Japan" .....30.00
    3-1/2" h, 3-1/2" w, pelicans, nesting, stand, bisque, green mark on stand "Urango China, Occupied Japan," red mark "Japan" on pelicans ...............................................................................35.00
    3-3/4" h, little Indian boy and girl, mkd "Made in Occupied Japan" ......................................................................................45.00
Scarf, 31-1/2" x 34", blue, brown, pink floral design on white, gray border, partial orig tag reads: "Pure Silk, a 'Top Hit' Fashion" (rest of tag is missing) .......................................................................................35.00
Shaker, 2-1/2" h, figural, preening duck, black head, yellow breast, gray feathers, rect blue base.............................................................15.00
Tea Set, teapot, 6 cups and saucers, 6 plates, cov sugar bowl, luster, paint dec..........................................................................................95.00

Toothpick Holder, 2-3/4" h, clown standing beside ivory toothpick holder, mkd "Made in Occupied Japan" ..................... 20.00

Toby Jug, 2-1/4" h, old woman, black bonnet, blue polka-dot dress, black mark ................................................................ 18.00

Toothbrush Holder, 4-1/4" h, Scotties playing cards, base mkd "Made in Occupied Japan" ........................................... 150.00

Toy, Baseball Catcher, NY, celluloid, wind-up, 5" h ..................... 60.00

Vase
  2-1/2" h, 1-3/4" d, seated Japanese official, Satsuma type dec, mkd "Made in Occupied Japan" ............................... 9.00
  5" h, white painting, blue rose on front, mkd "Made in Occupied Japan" ............................................................. 35.00
  7-1/2" h, Dragonware, green ink mark "Made in Occupied Japan Handpainted" with wreath and ferns mark ......................... 60.00
  8-1/2" h, Souvenir of Toronto, worn decal dec, bird mark, molded "Made in Occupied Japan" .................................... 15.00

Wall Plaque
  4-1/2" x 6", reclining woman with faun and cherub, scalloped ... 20.00
  4-1/2" x 7-1/2", Victorian gentleman on one, other with Victorian lady, mkd "Chase, Handpainted, Made in Occupied Japan," price for pr ........................................................... 95.00

# OHR POTTERY

**History:** Ohr pottery was produced by George E. Ohr in Biloxi, Mississippi. There is a discrepancy as to when he actually established his pottery; some say 1878, but Ohr's autobiography indicates 1883. In 1884, Ohr exhibited 600 pieces of his work, suggesting that he had been a potter for some time.

G.E.OHR, BILOXI.

Ohr's techniques included twisting, crushing, folding, denting, and crinkling thin-walled clay into odd, grotesque, and, sometimes, graceful forms. His later pieces were often left unglazed.

In 1906, Ohr closed the pottery and stored more than 6,000 pieces as a legacy to his family. He had hoped it would be purchased by the U.S. government, which never happened. The entire collection remained in storage until it was rediscovered in 1972.

Today Ohr is recognized as one of the leaders in the American art pottery movement. Some greedy individuals have taken the later unglazed pieces and covered them with poor-quality glazes in hopes of making them more valuable. These pieces do not have stilt marks on the bottom.

**Marks:** Much of Ohr's early work was signed with an impressed stamp including his name and location in block letters. His later work was often marked with the flowing script designation "G. E. Ohr."

**References:** Susan and Al Bagdade, *Warman's American Pottery and Porcelain*, 2nd ed., Krause Publications, 2000; Garth Clark, Robert Ellison Jr., and Eugene Hecht, *Mad Potter of Biloxi: The Art & Life of George Ohr*, Abbeville Press, 1989; Ralph and Terry Kovel, *Kovels' American Art Pottery*, Crown Publishers, 1993; David Rago, *American Art Pottery,* Knickerbocker Press, 1997.

Basket, 3" h, 6" d, flaring, serrated edge, mottled green, brown, and gunmetal glaze, stamped "G.E. OHR/Biloxi, Miss," restoration to small rim chip and base ............................... 1,400.00

Bottle, 7" h, 4" d, deep in-body twist, closed-in rim, unusual green, red, and teal leathery matte glaze, script sgd .............. 7,500.00

Bowl
  2" h, 5" d, free form, ext. covered in gunmetal, green, and ochre glaze, glossy raspberry int., imp "G. E. OHR/BILOXI" .. 4,250.00
  2-1/4" h, 4" d, folded rim, dimpled body, ext. cov with speckled brown-black glaze, black int., imp "G. E. OHR/Biloxi, Miss" ................................................................. 1,200.00
  2-1/4" h, 4-1/4" d, free-form, collapsed rim, ext. cov in glossy dripping green and purple glaze, int. with mottled ochre, imp "G. E. OHR/Biloxi, Miss," small restored base chip ................ 1,100.00
  4" h, 6" d, in-body twist, folded rim, glossy dark green and raspberry glazed ext., gunmetal green int., incised "OHR/1903," restoration to nicks and bruise at base ...................... 3,500.00

Chamberstick, 6" h, 4" d, sq dimpled base, ribbon handle, frothy raspberry and green matte glaze, script signature, stilt-pull to base ............................................................... 2,600.00

Inkwell, 7-1/4" l, 4-3/4" d, 4" h, mule head, small pot, tree, mottled green, brown, and gunmetal glaze, stamped "G.E.OH/BILOXI," touch-on on both ear tips ...................................... 4,000.00

Miniature, chamber pot, 3-1/2" d, sponge dec in green and brown, ochre colored ground, int. with realistic waste, imp maker's mark on base ............................................................... 865.00

Mug, Joe Jefferson
  4-3/4" h, 5-1/2" d, irregularly shaped rim, incised "Here's your good health...," mottled green and brown glaze, script signature and "3-18-96," restoration to two small areas on rim .............. 2,600.00
  6-1/2" h, 5-3/4" d, gourd shape, incised, "Here's your good health...," speckled and mottled blue-green glaze, script signature and "3-18-96" ..................................... 2,100.00

Pitcher
  2-1/2" h, 5" d, four-sided, cut-out handle, pinched side, light mauve glaze ext., chartreuse green int., mkd "GEO. E.OHR/BILOXI/MISS," minute nick to rim ..................... 2,000.00
  3" h, 5-1/2" d, squatty, closed-in rim, ear-shaped handle, amber, green, and gunmetal speckled glaze, mkd "G.E.OHR/Biloxi, Miss" ................................................................ 650.00
  3-3/4" h, 3-1/4" w, asymmetrical, deeply folded and pinched rim, gunmetal black glaze, imp "G. E. OHR/Biloxi, Miss" ..... 1,600.00

Puzzle Jug, 8" h, 6-3/4" d, incised wheat-sheaf and landscape dec, glossy brown and green glaze, script sgd "Biloxi/Miss/1899," and stamped mark ....................................................... 1,400.00

Tea Cup, 5" d, 2-1/2" h, crenulated rim, hand built handle, mottled mahogany glaze ext., gunmetal int., mkd "GEO E. OHR/BILOXI/MISS," minute rim nick ................................... 1,300.00

**Pitcher, beige bisque clay, asymmetrically pinched and folded, oxidized flashes, script sgd, several firing cracks to body and base, 5" h, 7-1/2" d, $2,650. Photo courtesy of David Rago Auctions.**

**Vessel, flaring rim, gunmetal brown glaze, script sgd, spider line to rim, 3-1/4" h, 3-1/4" d, $525. Photo courtesy of David Rago Auctions.**

Teapot, 4" h, 8-3/4" d, flat shoulder, snake spout, cobalt blue glossy glaze, stamped "G.E.OHR/Biloxi, Miss," natural abrasion around rim, small nick to tip of spout ........................... 10,000.00

Vase

4" h, 3-3/4" d, bulbous, cadmium yellow, lavender, green, and pink volcanic glaze, stamped "G. E. OHR/Biloxi, Miss". 2,700.00

4-1/2" h, 2-1/2" d, spherical base, dark speckled mirrored olive green glaze, cylindrical neck, folded rim, gunmetal, mkd "G.E.OHR/Biloxi, Miss" ..................................................... 2,300.00

4-1/2" h, 3-1/2" h, double gourd shape, amber and gunmetal glaze, mkd "G.E.OHR/BILOXI" ........................................ 950.00

4-1/2" h, 4-1/2" d, folded rim, collapsed side, covered in speckled amber and gunmetal glaze, sgd "G. E. OHR/Biloxi, Miss" ....................................................................... 5,550.00

4-3/4" h, 4-1/4" d, collapsed and dimpled shoulder, speckled amber glaze, mkd "G. E. OHR/Biloxi, Miss" .................. 3,250.00

6-1/4" h, 5" w, pillow, folded and scalloped rim, rare pink glaze, sponged on green and gunmetal band, stamped "G. E. OHR/Biloxi, Miss," small kiln kiss to body, minor glaze nick, few flakes inside rim ........................................................ 17,000.00

7-1/4" h, 3-3/4" d, bulbous, applied snake, dimpled rim, cobalt blue, amber, and raspberry sponged glaze, stamped "G.E.OHR/Biloxi, Miss," restoration to chip at base, firing lines to snake, few minute rim nicks .................................. 9,500.00

9-1/2" h, 5" d, spherical base, fluted, dimpled neck covered in mirrored cobalt blue and gunmetal glaze, script signature and "M," restored 1" chip at rim, typical abrasion line to body ..... 8,500.00

Vessel

3" h, 6" d, covered in mottled gunmetal and ochre glaze, imp "E. G. OHR/BILOXI" ....................................................... 3,500.00

3-1/4" h, 3-3/4" d, one side pinched and one side dimpled, dark brown and red bisque scroddled clay, tightly folded rim, incised "Biloxi" ............................................................... 550.00

3-1/2" h, 4-1/4" d, squatty, straight neck, green-speckled matte purple glaze, script signature, restoration to small rim chip, kiln kiss ....................................................................... 800.00

4" d, 3-3/4" d, collared rim, dimpled body, specked umber glossy glaze, stamped "G. E. OHR/Biloxi, Miss" ...................... 1,900.00

4-1/2" h, 5-1/4" d, collared rim, dimpled body, mottled brown and gunmetal glossy glaze, stamped "G.E. OHR/BILOXI,".. 2,800.00

# OLD IVORY CHINA

**History:** Old Ivory derives its name from the background color of the china. It was made in Silesia, Germany, during the second half of the 19th century.

OLD IVORY
84

**Marks:** Marked pieces usually have a pattern number (pattern names are not common), a crown, and the word "Silesia."

**References:** Susan and Al Bagdade, *Warman's English & Continental Pottery & Porcelain*, 3rd Edition, Krause Publications, 1998; Alma Hillman, David Goldschmidt & Adam Szynkiewica, *Collector's Encyclopedia of Old Ivory China,* Collector Books, 1998.

**Periodical:** *Old Ivory Newsletter*, P.O. Box 1004, Wilsonville, OR 97070.

**Collectors' Club:** Old Ivory Porcelain Society, Route 3, Box 188, Spring Valley, MN 55975.

Berry Set, master bowl and four serving bowls, 5 pc set
#11 ........................................................... 145.00
#84 ........................................................... 200.00
Biscuit Jar, cov, #15 ........................................ 350.00
Biscuit Barrel, 8-1/2" h, Yellow Rose ...................... 500.00
Bowl, 9-1/2" d, Yellow Rose ................................. 225.00
Cake Plate
#16, Clarion .............................................. 160.00
#XI, mkd "Germany Clarion: XI," 13" d, some wear to gold int. border ................................................... 150.00
Celery Bowl, #84, 11 x 5-1/2" .............................. 150.00
Chocolate Pot, 11, pedestal ............................... 410.00
Creamer
#16, Clarion .............................................. 165.00
#32 ......................................................... 48.00
Cup, Yellow Rose ........................................... 45.00
Cup and Saucer
Clarion, #16 ............................................... 75.00
Yellow Rose ............................................... 75.00
Demitasse Pot, cov, #16 .................................... 395.00
Dessert Plate, sgd "Old Ivory, Germany," 6 pc set ......... 75.00
Dinner Plate, 8-1/2" d, Yellow Rose, set of 6 ............. 400.00
Ladle Holder, #84 .......................................... 95.00
Luncheon Plate
7 1/2" d, Yellow Rose ..................................... 75.00
8-1/2" d, U30, Alice blank ................................ 22.00
Luncheon Set, No. 84, assembled 47 pc set, six small bowls, creamer, twelve cups, six small plates, six luncheon plates, 14 saucers, sugar, 12" rect tray, some mkd "Silesia No. 84" ....................... 1,000.00
Mustard Pot, cov, #16 ..................................... 100.00
Oyster Bowl, #11 ........................................... 175.00
Relish Dish, 8" l, 5" w, 1-1/2" h, #78, hp pink and white roses, white ground, gold trim .......................................... 45.00
Salad Plate, Clarion ....................................... 75.00
Salt and Pepper Shakers, #84, ftd .......................... 55.00
Serving Bowl, #84 .......................................... 100.00
Sugar, cov, #75 ............................................ 50.00
Tea Plate, pink and white daisies, gold trim, mkd "Old Ivory, Germany," set of 6 ................................................... 90.00
Teapot, cov, #15 ........................................... 395.00
Toothpick Holder, #84 ..................................... 285.00
Waste Bowl, mkd "Silseia & Ohme" .......................... 225.00

# OLD PARIS CHINA

**History:** Old Paris china is fine-quality porcelain made by various French factories located in and around Paris during the 18th and 19th centuries. Some pieces were marked, but most were not. In addition to its fine quality, this type of ware is characterized by beautiful decorations and gilding. Favored colors are dark maroon, deep cobalt blue, and a dark green.

**Urns, courting scene, gilded, 10-1/2" h, price for pr, $1,750.**

**Additional Listings:** Continental China and Porcelain (General).

Basket, reticulated, gold and white dec, c1825 ...................... 1,400.00
Bread and Milk Cup and Saucer, 3-1/2" d cup, 6-1/4" d saucer, neo-classical taste, cup inscribed "Fidelité Constance," c1835-40 .. 475.00
Cake Stand, Honore style, green border, c1845 ........................ 200.00
Figure, 18-3/4" h, Napoleon, standing, one arm tucked behind his back, other tucked into shirt, full military dress, gilt dec, low sq base, inscribed "Roussel-Bardell," late 19th C ................................... 650.00
Mantel Vase, bell-like flowered handles, blue ground, paneled enamel portraits of lovers, gilt trim, minor flower damage, price for pr . 325.00
Plate, 9-1/4" d, flower basket center, gilt line and borders, ochre ground, c1830, price for pr ...................................... 250.00
Tea Set, partial, enamel dec central medallions of portraits and musical instruments surrounded by gilt shields and spearhead border, 5-3/4" h cov teapot, creamer, compote, twelve coffee cans and saucers, 19th C, gilt wear, minor damage, price for 15 pc set ............. 2,875.00
Urn, cov, 14-1/2" h, painted hunting scenes, molded acanthus and palmette scrolled double handles, gilt border, sq plinth base, price for pr ............................................................... 1,200.00
Vase, 18" h, flared vasiform, shaped edge, elaborately dec in gilt enamel, applied tassel braid at waist, central ribbon accent, paneled body below, central portrait panel of young beauty with flowers, ovoid shaped edge base, scrolled feet, late 19th C, restoration, price for pr .......................................................... 4,900.00

# OLD SLEEPY EYE

**History:** Sleepy Eye, a Sioux Indian chief who reportedly had a droopy eye, gave his name to Sleepy Eye, Minnesota, and one of its leading flour mills. In the early 1900s, Old Sleepy Eye Flour offered four Flemish-gray heavy stoneware premiums decorated in cobalt blue: a straight-sided butter crock, curved salt bowl, stein, and vase. The premiums were made by Weir Pottery Company, later to become Monmouth Pottery Company, and finally to emerge as the present-day Western Stoneware Company of Monmouth, Illinois.

Additional pottery and stoneware pieces also were issued. Forms included five sizes of pitchers (4, 5-1/2, 6-1/2, 8, and 9 inches), mugs, steins, sugar bowls, and tea tiles (hot plates). Most were cobalt blue on white, but other glaze hues, such as browns, golds, and greens, were used.

## Reproduction Alert:

Blue-and-white pitchers, crazed, weighted, and often with a stamp or the word "Ironstone" are the most common reproductions. The stein and salt bowl also have been made. Many reproductions come from Taiwan.

A line of fantasy items, new items which never existed as Old Sleepy Eye originals, includes an advertising pocket mirror with miniature flour-barrel label, small glass plates, fruit jars, toothpick holders, glass and pottery miniature pitchers, and salt and pepper shakers. One mill item has been made: a sack marked as though it were old but of a size that could not possibly hold the amount of flour indicated.

Old Sleepy Eye also issued many other items, including bakers' caps, lithographed barrel covers, beanies, fans, multicolored pillow tops, postcards, and trade cards. Regular production of Old Sleepy Eye stoneware ended in 1937.

In 1952, Western Stoneware Company made 22- and 40-ounce steins in chestnut brown glaze with a redesigned Indian's head. From 1961 to 1972, gift editions were made for the board of directors and others within the company. Beginning in 1973, Western Stoneware Company issued an annual limited edition stein for collectors.

**Marks:** The gift editions made in the 1960s and 1970s were dated and signed with a maple leaf mark. The annual limited edition steins are marked and dated.

**References:** Susan and Al Bagdade, *Warman's American Pottery and Porcelain*, 2nd ed., Krause Publications, 2000; Elinor Meugnoit, *Old Sleepy Eye*, published by author, 1979.

**Collectors' Club:** Old Sleepy Eye Collectors Club of America, P.O. Box 12, Monmouth, IL 61462.

Mill Items
Advertising Sign, 24" h, 20" w, self framed tin, trademark picture of Chief Old Sleepy Eye, multiple Indian scenes on border, surface rust and staining on frame ..................................... 2,300.00

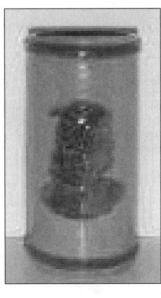

**Vase, Chief profile on one side, cattails on other, blue accents, professional restoration to small rim chip, imp "0" in base, 8-1/2" h, $275. Photo courtesy of Vicki & Bruce Waasdrop.**

Cookbook, Sleepy Eye Milling Co, loaf of bread shape, portrait of chief........150.00

Demitasse Spoon, roses in bowl ........140.00

Letter Opener, bronze, Indian head handle, marked "Sleep Eye Milling Co, Sleep Eye, MN"........750.00

Pinback Button, Old Sleepy Eye For Me, bust portrait of chief........165.00

Spoon, Unity SP ........110.00

Pottery and Stoneware

Cream Pitcher, 4" h, blue gray salt glaze, base imp "429," stenciled "Monmouth, Ill" in black diamond logo, small minor glaze flake on int. rim........125.00

Mug, cobalt blue on white, Indian head on handle, 1906-37 ...245.00

Pitcher, 8-1/2" h, blue gray salt glaze, very minor age crazing........150.00

Stein, 7-3/4" h, Flemish blue, gray stoneware ground, Weir Pottery Co, 1903........525.00

Tile, cobalt blue and white ........950.00

Vase, 8-1/2" h, blue gray salt glaze, Indian profile on one side, relief cattails on other side, blue accented, base imp "O," professional restoration to small rim chip........275.00

# ONION MEISSEN

**History:** The blue onion or bulb pattern is of Chinese origin and depicts peaches and pomegranates, not onions. It was first made in the 18th century by Meissen, hence the name Onion Meissen.

Factories in Europe, Japan, and elsewhere copied the pattern. Many still have the pattern in production, including the Meissen factory in Germany.

**Marks:** Many pieces are marked with a company's logo; after 1891 the country of origin is indicated on imported pieces.

**Reference:** Robert E. Röntgen, *Book of Meissen*, revised ed., Schiffer Publishing, 1996.

**Note:** Prices given are for pieces produced between 1870 and 1930. Early Meissen examples bring a high premium.

Bowl, 8-1/2" d, reticulated, blue crossed swords mark, 19th C...395.00

Box, cov, 4-1/2" d, round, rose finial ........75.00

Cake Stand, 13-1/2" d, 4-1/2" h ........215.00

Candlesticks, pr, 7" h ........80.00

Canister, marked "Prunes"........200.00

Centerpiece, 19" h, three-tier, reticulated........300.00

Compote, figural

17" h, rococo base with classical children figures surrounding body, crossed swords mark, late 19th C, damages, losses........2,415.00

18-3/4" h, male and female figures surrounding tree-form base, oval form reticulated bowl, crossed swords mark, late 19th C ...3,565.00

Creamer and Sugar, gold edge, c1900 ........175.00

Cup and Saucer, 2-3/4" h, 5-3/8" d, set of ten cups and eight saucers ........350.00

Demitasse Cup and Saucer, 2" h, 4-1/4" d, gold enamel dec, price for twelve cups and ten saucers........350.00

Fish Platter, 21-1/2" d, oval form with insert, gilt highlighted blue onion design, early 20th C ........490.00

Funnel, small........55.00

Hot Plate, handles........125.00

Ladle, wooden handle........115.00

Mold, melon, handle........45.00

Pie Crimper, wood handle........35.00

Plate

8" d, basketweave reticulated edges, gilt details, price for 22 pc set ........1,150.00

8-1/2" d, gilt details, price for 17 pc set........850.00

9-5/8" d, gilt details, price for 18 pc set........750.00

Platter, oval

12" l........95.00

13-1/2" l........120.00

18" l, oval, mkd "Meissen" in oval, pr........275.00

Pot de Creme........65.00

Salt and Pepper Shakers, pr........50.00

Serving Dish

9-1/8" l, sq, shallow, gilt details........200.00

9-7/8" l, 4-1/8" h, sq, notched corners, gilt details........265.00

Soup Plate, 9-1/4" d, gilt details, price for 17 pc set........900.00

Tea Set, teapot, creamer, sugar, four cups and saucers, tray.....400.00

Tea Strainer, wood handle........25.00

Tray, 17" l, cartouche shape, blue and white design, gilt edge...425.00

Vase, 6-1/2" d, bud........60.00

Vegetable Dish, cov, 10" w, sq........145.00

# OPALESCENT GLASS

**History:** Opalescent glass, a clear or colored glass with milky white decorations, looks fiery or opalescent when held to light. This effect was achieved by applying bone ash chemicals to designated areas while a piece was still hot and then refiring it at extremely high temperatures.

There are three basic categories of opalescent glass: (1) blown (or mold blown) patterns, e.g., Daisy & Fern and Spanish Lace; (2) novelties, pressed glass patterns made in limited quantity and often in unusual shapes such as corn or a trough; and (3) traditional pattern (pressed) glass forms.

Opalescent glass was produced in England in the 1870s. Northwood began the American production in 1897 at its Indiana, Pennsylvania, plant. Jefferson, National Glass, Hobbs, and Fenton soon followed.

**References:** Gary Baker et al., *Wheeling Glass 1829-1939*, Oglebay Institute, 1994, distributed by Antique Publications; Bill Edwards and Mike Carwile, *Standard Encyclopedia of Opalescent Glass*, 3rd ed., Collector Books, 1999; William Heacock, *Encyclopedia of Victorian Colored Pattern Glass*, Book II, 2nd ed., Antique Publications, 1977; William Heacock and William Gamble, *Encyclopedia of Victorian Colored Pattern Glass*, Book 9, Antique Publications, 1987; William Heacock, James Measell, and Berry Wiggins, *Dugan/Diamond*, Antique Publications, 1993; ——, *Harry Northwood* (1990), Book 2 (1991) Antique Publications; Eric Reynolds, *The Glass of John Walsh,* Richard Dennis Publications, distributed by Antique Collectors' Club, 1999.

## Blown

Barber Bottle, Swirl, ketchup bottle shape, cranberry........425.00

Basket, Daisy and Fern, vaseline, looped handle........190.00

Bowl

Ruffles and Rings, green ........40.00

Seaweed, white, 9" d ........80.00

Butter Dish, cov, Spanish Lace, blue ........265.00

Celery Vase
    Chrysanthemum Swirl, blue .............................................. 140.00
    Hobbs Hobnail, blue ......................................................... 90.00
    Seaweed, cranberry........................................................ 225.00
    Spanish Lace, vaseline ................................................... 135.00
    Stripe, white .................................................................... 90.00
    Windows, cranberry, ruffled rim ...................................... 115.00
Cheese Dish, Hobb's Swirl, cranberry ................................. 350.00
Compote, Ribbed Spiral, blue ................................................ 70.00
Creamer, Windows Swirl, cranberry..................................... 500.00
Cruet, orig stopper
    Hobb's Hobnail, blue ...................................................... 225.00
    Spanish Lace, canary yellow .......................................... 185.00
    Stripe, blue, applied blue handle .................................... 185.00
    Windows, Swirled, cranberry .......................................... 350.00
Finger Bowl
    Hobb's Optic Diamond, cranberry ................................... 70.00
    Spanish Lace, blue ......................................................... 50.00
Lamp, oil, Snowflake, cranberry........................................... 735.00
Miniature Lamp, Reverse Swirl, vaseline............................... 95.00
Pitcher
    Bubble Lattice, cranberry ............................................... 950.00
    Coinspot, cranberry, #127............................................... 300.00
    Coinspot, cranberry, #261, corner ruffle......................... 545.00
    Coinspot, cranberry, 3 tier.............................................. 1,375.00
    Fern, blue, square........................................................... 445.00
    Honeycomb & Clover, green ............................................ 325.00
    Poinsettia, blue, rare shape ............................................ 425.00
    Raised Swirl, cranberry, #79 ........................................... 685.00
    Seaweed, blue, square.................................................... 515.00
    Swag with Brackets, green .............................................. 200.00
    Thumbprint, 10" h, ruffled, colorless, white dots and rim, applied
        colorless handle ........................................................ 250.00
    Windows, blue, square.................................................... 485.00
    Windows, cranberry, #111, square................................... 485.00
Salt Shaker, orig top
    Coin Spot, cranberry....................................................... 200.00
    Reverse Swirl, blue ......................................................... 65.00
Spooner
    Bubble Lattice, cranberry ............................................... 145.00
    Ribbed Spiral, blue ......................................................... 110.00
Sugar, cov
    Bubble Lattice, cranberry ............................................... 195.00
    Spanish Lace, blue ......................................................... 175.00
Sugar Shaker
    Beatty Rib, blue .............................................................. 140.00
    Blown Twist, blue............................................................ 175.00
    Coin Spot, blue, tapered neck ......................................... 75.00
    Coin Spot, green, 9 panel mold ....................................... 150.00
    Daisy and Fern, cranberry, swirl mold.............................. 125.00
    Daisy and Fern, cranberry, wide waisted mold .................. 225.00
Syrup
    Coin Spot, 9 panel, blue ................................................. 200.00
    Leaf Umbrella, cranberry, heat check .............................. 395.00

**Cruet, white opalescent swirled body, sapphire blue handle and hollow stopper, 5-1/2" h, $285. Photo courtesy of Clarence & Betty Maier.**

Polka Dot, blue
    Bulbous .......................................................................... 245.00
    Tall ................................................................................. 315.00
Reverse Swirl, cranberry...................................................... 800.00
Tankard, Coin Spot, 3 tier, cranberry .................................. 1,375.00
Toothpick Holder, Ribbed Lattice, blue................................. 165.00
Tumbler
    Reverse Swirl, cranberry ................................................. 105.00
    Seaweed, cranberry........................................................ 150.00
    Spanish Lace, green ....................................................... 65.00
    Windows, cranberry ........................................................ 125.00
Vase, Stripe, vaseline .......................................................... 65.00

## Novelties

Basket
    4" h, 5" w, cranberry, white opalescent stripes and clear ribbing interspersed with silver mica, ruffled edge, applied clear twisted center loop handle.............. 150.00
    7-1/2" h, 5" w, rose bowl form, cranberry, deep white opalescent extends half way down, applied clear rigaree top, applied crystal five-footed base, small loop applied crystal handle.......... 200.00
Bowl
    Cashews, blue, crimped .................................................. 60.00
    Greek Key and Ribs, green .............................................. 75.00
    Jolly Bear, white.............................................................. 85.00
    Leaf and Beads, green, twig feet..................................... 60.00
    Many Loops, blue, crimped, fluted................................... 65.00
Compote
    Dolphin, vaseline ............................................................ 95.00
    Squirrel and Acorn, green, ruffled................................... 175.00
Dish, Lined Lattice, green .................................................... 85.00
Hanging Vase, 8-1/2" h, green opalescent vase with thorns, clear crystal vine as holder for vase, pressed green daisy-like flower on holder, Victorian .............. 115.00
Hat, Opal Swirl, white........................................................... 35.00
Mug, Singing Birds, blue ...................................................... 145.00
Plate, Wishbone and Drape, green........................................ 35.00
Rose Bowl. Cashews, white.................................................. 85.00
Vase, Lorna, blue................................................................. 60.00

## Pressed

Banana Boat, Jewel and Fan, green...................................... 115.00
Berry Bowl, master
    Alaska, blue ................................................................... 195.00
    Beatty Rib, white............................................................. 50.00
    Everglades, vaseline, gold trim........................................ 200.00
    Tokyo, green................................................................... 55.00
Berry Set, Wreath & Shell, blue, 7 pc ................................... 475.00
Bowl
    Beaded Stars, low base, green........................................ 45.00
    Beatty Rib, blue, rect...................................................... 65.00
    Jewel and Fan, blue........................................................ 35.00
    Peacock and Fence, blue ................................................ 300.00
Butter Dish, cov
    Argonaut Shell, white...................................................... 245.00
    Wreath & Shell, blue ....................................................... 255.00
Calling Card Receiver, Inverted Feather, vaseline..................... 225.00
Celery
    Beatty Swirl, blue ........................................................... 90.00
    Wreath & Shell, vaseline................................................. 225.00
Compote
    Intaglio, vaseline ............................................................ 70.00
    Tokyo, blue..................................................................... 60.00
Cracker Jar, cov, Wreath & Shell, blue ................................. 600.00
Creamer
    Alaska, blue ................................................................... 85.00
    Beaded Shell, green ........................................................ 165.00
    Paneled Holly, white........................................................ 70.00
    Scroll with Acanthus, green ............................................ 65.00
    Swag with Brackets, green .............................................. 90.00

Wild Bouquet, blue.................................................125.00
Wreath and Shell, vaseline, dec ......................135.00
Cruet
    Alaska, vaseline, enameled dec .......................275.00
    Christmas Pearls, white ....................................260.00
    Jackson, blue......................................................185.00
    Scroll with Acanthus, blue ................................200.00
Jelly Compote
    Diamond Spearhead, vaseline............................85.00
    Everglades, blue, gold trim .................................85.00
    Iris with Meander, vaseline.................................95.00
    Wild Bouquet, blue...........................................160.00
Match Holder, Beatty Rib, white ...............................35.00
Mug
    Diamond Spearhead, cobalt blue .......................85.00
    Stork and Rushes, blue .......................................90.00
Pitcher
    Beatty Swirl, canary yellow ..............................195.00
    Fluted Scrolls, vaseline....................................300.00
    Intaglio, blue .....................................................215.00
    Jeweled Heart, blue ..........................................250.00
    Swag with Brackets, vaseline ...........................225.00
    Wild Bouquet, blue...........................................300.00
Plate
    Palm Beach, blue, 10" d, set of 6......................895.00
    Tokyo, ftd, green ................................................70.00
    Water Lily and Cattail, amethyst ........................85.00
Rose Bowl
    Beaded Drape, blue.............................................60.00
    Fancy Fantails, cranberry, four clear applied feet..............650.00
    Fluted Scrolls, blue ..........................................125.00
    Water Lily and Cattails, amethyst .....................110.00
Salt and Pepper Shakers, pr, Everglades, vaseline...................400.00
Salt, open, individual
    Beatty Rib, white .................................................50.00
    Wreath & Shell, vaseline...................................120.00
Sauce
    Argonaut Shell, blue ...........................................40.00
    Circled Scrolls, blue ...........................................50.00
    Iris with Meander, yellow....................................25.00
    Water Lily and Cattails, white .............................35.00
    Wild Bouquet, blue..............................................40.00
Spooner
    Argonaut Shell, French Opal .............................170.00
    Beatty Rib, white .................................................45.00
    Flora, blue..........................................................110.00
    Iris with Meander, canary yellow ........................95.00
    Palm Beach, vaseline..........................................95.00
    Tokyo, blue ..........................................................85.00
    Wreath and Shell, vaseline ...............................120.00
Sugar, cov
    Alaska, vaseline.................................................155.00
    Circled Scroll, green ...........................................85.00
    Diamond Spearhead, vaseline..........................235.00
    Fluted Scrolls, blue ...........................................130.00
    Intaglio, blue .......................................................75.00
    Swag with Brackets, blue....................................95.00
    Tokyo, blue, gold trim .......................................115.00
Syrup, Flora, white, gold trim .................................275.00
Table Set, Wreath & Shell, vaseline.........................700.00
Toothpick Holder
    Diamond Spearhead, vaseline.............................80.00
    Flora, white, gold trim .......................................150.00
    Gonterman Swirl, amber top ..............................150.00
    Iris with Meander, blue......................................115.00
    Wreath & Shell, vaseline...................................245.00
Tumbler
    Alaska, vaseline ..................................................85.00
    Beatty Rib, white .................................................35.00
    Beatty Swirl, white ..............................................45.00

Everglades, vaseline...............................................50.00
Fluted Scrolls, vaseline...........................................75.00
Intaglio, white ........................................................45.00
Paneled Holly, blue ..............................................100.00
S-Repeat, blue........................................................45.00
Wreath and Shell, ftd, blue ..................................375.00
Vase
    Fluted Scrolls and Vine, blue ..............................70.00
    Inverted Fan and Feather, blue............................85.00
    Water Lily and Cattail, amethyst .........................75.00

# OPALINE GLASS

**History:** Opaline glass was a popular mid- to late 19th-century European glass. The glass has a certain amount of translucency and often is found decorated with enamel designs and trimmed in gold.

Basket, 6-1/2" h, 6" d, clambroth color, applied pink snake loop around handle, gold rim......................................................100.00
Bottle, 7" h, white, squatty bulbous body, trumpet neck, gilt scrolling vine dec, orig stopper, Continental, pr......................................................225.00
Box, cov, 4-1/4" l, 3-1/4" h, rect, blue, roundel studded brass strapwork, French, early 20th C ......................................................460.00
Bowl, 6-1/2" d, shallow, blue, gold painted trim, some wear to gold, set of six ......................................................100.00
Cache Pot, 7" h, blue, flamed lip, gilded flowerheads and vines dec, late 19th C ......................................................230.00
Candlestick, 7-1/4" h, white opaque clambroth body, rib molded 150.00
Cheese dish, cov, white opaque body, gold enamel dec ...........185.00
Child's Mug, 2-1/4" h, paneled scenes of Dutch children, pr ........65.00
Clock, 6" d, white opaque body, hanging type, circular frame, hand painted, Welch Company, Forestville, CT, clockworks, orig brass chain......................................................275.00
Cologne Bottle
    6" h, jade green opaque body, orig stopper .........................95.00
    8-3/4" h, jade green opaque body, gold ring dec, orig stopper ......................................................90.00
Creamer, shaded yellow to white opaque body, pink roses and blue forget me nots, SP rim and handle..........................................125.00
Cup Plate, Lee-Rose 258, white opaque body, minute rim roughage ......................................................75.00
Dish, cov, 6" d underplate, trefoil handles, lid with shaped edge, white cased glass snake handle, shaped edge and gilt enamel details on underplate, France, late 19th C ......................................................215.00
Ewer, 12-7/8" h, white frosted body, entwined with metallic green snake-form handle, gilt enamel scale detailing, France, late 19th C ......................................................300.00
Fairy Lamp, 17" h, French blue, four large faceted purple and dark blue jewels, filigree brass mountings ..............................................285.00
Garniture Stand, 7-1/2" h, white, probably orig fitted with colored opaline glass bowl or trumpets, French, c1825-40, pr ....................95.00
Lamp, 26-1/2" h, kerosene, hand painted, white ground, rococo taste, vieux-rose enframed floral cartouches, brass mounts, electrified, America, c1890-95 ......................................................200.00

**Box, hinged, pale green, gold enameling, French, 4" d, 2-1/2" h, $150.**

Match Holder, 1-3/8" h, blue opaque body, gold flowers and leaves.................................................................40.00

Perfume Bottle

2-3/4" h, blue opaque body, gold flowers and leaves, matching stopper .........................................................60.00

4" h, blue opaque body, gold, white, and yellow dec, matching stopper .........................................................75.00

Pitcher

4-1/4" h, pink opaque body, applied white handle ...............75.00

12" h, pink, applied ruby paste stones, beaded enamel swag, applied handle, French, 19th C .......................................110.00

Posy Holder, 8" h, blue opaque body, figural hand holding small vase, ruffled rim.............................................85.00

Sauce Stand, 7-3/4" w, 4-1/4" d, 6" h, shell form, parcel gilt, ftd, Louis Philippe, c1835-45 ...............................................50.00

Sugar, cov, shaded yellow to white opaque body, pink roses and blue forget me nots, SP cover, rim, and handle ............................150.00

Toothpick Holder, lavender opaque body, small ball feet..............85.00

Tumbler, white opaque body, enameled pink rose.......................25.00

Tumble-Up, carafe, tumbler, and underplate, pale green opaque body, gold beading, black and white jeweled dec, three pcs .............325.00

Urn, 13" h, blue opaque body, enameled blue flowers, gilt trim, flared rim, pr ..................................................................350.00

Vase

5" h, blue, platinum stars dec, Czechoslovakian ..................55.00

5-1/2" h, cased light blue opaline, blue applied ribbon handles, mkd "Czecho-slovakia".......................................................50.00

8" h, swirled and mottled colors over opaline, applied clear pinched handles, Czechoslovakian....................................35.00

9-3/8" h, milky white, crenellated edge, round funnel bowl, trumpet foot, applied apple green entwined snake, gilt details, France, late 19th C .........................................................150.00

11-7/8" h, milky white, ftd baluster, etched floral sprays on one side, gilt enamel dec, France, late 19th C, price for pr.................865.00

14" h, apple green, shaped edge, tapered vasiform, step allied with mint green entwined snake, gilt details, France, late 19th C .............................................................150.00

Violet Bowl, 3-1/2" d, 3" h, peachblow pink ground, blue and white enameled flowers, gray leaves and vines, base sgd, Mt. Washington 275.00

Whiskey Taster, white opaque clambroth colored body

Lacy, Sandwich, Lee, plate 150-5, minute rim nicks ......................45.00

Ten Panel, handle, small chip on bottom .....................................85.00

# ORIENTALIA

**History:** Orientalia is a term applied to objects made in the Orient, an area which encompasses the Far East, Asia, China, and Japan. The diversity of cultures produced a variety of objects and styles.

**References:** Sandra Andacht, *Collector's Guide To Oriental Decorative Arts*, Antique Trader Books, 1997; —, *Collector's Value Guide to Japanese Woodblock Prints*, Antique Trader Books, 1999; Carl L. Crossman, *The Decorative Arts of the China Trade*, Antique Collectors' Club, 1999; Christopher Dresser, *Traditional Arts and Crafts of Japan*, Dover Publications, 1994; R. L. Hobson and A L. Hetherington, *Art of the Chinese Potter*, Dover Publications, 1983; Duncan Macintosh, *Chinese Blue and White Porcelain*, Antique Collectors Club, 1994; Gloria and Robert Mascarelli, *Warman's Oriental Antiques*, Wallace-Homestead, 1992; Andrea and Lynde McCormick, *Chinese Country Antiques: Vernacular Furniture and Accessories, c1780-1920*, Schiffer Publishing, 2000; Nancy N. Schiffer, *Imari, Satsuma, and Other Japanese Export*

*Ceramics*, Schiffer Publishing, 1997; Jana Volf, *Treasures of the Chinese Glass Work Shops*, Asiantiques, 1997.

**Periodical:** *Orientalia Journal*, P.O. Box 94, Flushing, NY 11363-0094, http://members.aol.com/Orientalia/index.html.

**Collectors' Club:** China Student's Club, 59 Standish Rd, Wellesley, MA 02181.

**Museums:** Art Institute of Chicago, Chicago, IL; Asian Art Museum of San Francisco, San Francisco, CA; George Walter Vincent Smith Art Museum, Springfield, MA; Morikami Museum & Japanese Gardens, Delray Beach, FL; Pacific Asia Museum, Pasadena, CA.

**Additional Listings:** Canton; Celadon; Cloisonné; Fitzhugh; Nanking; Netsukes; Rose Medallion; Japanese Prints; and other related categories.

Altar Table

54" l, 16" d, 34-1/2" h, jui-shaped spandrels, everted edge, reeded leg, China, late 19th C ........................................425.00

98" l, 11" d, 34" h, elmwood, brown lacquer, everted rims carved with flowers, jui-shaped carved spandrels, China, 19th C 350.00

108" l, 15" d, 36" h, elmwood, everted rim, carved spandrels, apron carved with vase containing ling chih, China, early 20th C ..............................................................635.00

Bench, 39" l, 14" w, 19-1/2" h, elmwood, humpbacked stretcher with pillar struts, horse hoof feet, China, 19th C, price for pr.........460.00

Box, cov

4" l, 5" h, lacquer, gold ground, maki-e dec of various inro with their netsuke, ojime with coral, mother-of-pearl inlay, polychromes, edges of box mounted in silver, Japan, 18th C ...................4,025.00

6" l, 6" h, mixed metal, oval, four animal form feet, lid surmounted by pair of winged mythical animals facing gilt sphere, inlaid floral dec in gold, relief dec of sparrows in snowy bamboo grove, reverse with morning glories, minor losses, Japan, Meiji period, c1890 ..........................................................4,320.00

8-1/2" l, 9-3/4" h, inkstone, maki-e of bird in loquot tree, pewter leaves accents, Japan, 19th C.........................................490.00

9-1/2" l, 11" h, inkstone, basketry with mother-of-pearl and metal inlay, lacquer of deer and autumn grasses, sgd "Seiko(?)," Japan, 19th C, losses .................................................2,990.00

**Bowl, two handles, 3 legs, symbols around rim band, $200. Photo courtesy of Joy Luke Fine Art Brokers and Auctioneers.**

Bracelet, calcified jade or agate, carved with pair of single horned dragons, China, 19th C or earlier............................................200.00

Buddha

8-1/2" h, gilt bronze, syamatara, jeweled inlay, additional mineral pigments, Tibet, 19th C........................................................460.00

10-1/2" h, bronze, seated on lotus lozenge, hands in the lams bowl mudra, traces of gilt, China, 17th C...........................350.00

76" h, standing, carved, gessoed and gilt, inlaid eyes and minor details, Burma, early 20th C ......................................1,050.00

Buddhist Sculpture

8" h, three figures, one holding lotus flower, Gandhara, 4th C, A.D. ..............................................................................1,725.00

35" h, dark gray limestone with traces of pigment, figure of Mahasthamaprapta Boddhisattva, China, Northern dynasties, probably Liang Dynasty, 502-557..................................9,200.00

Cabinet

37" w, 24-3/4" d, 90" h, four section, elmwood, burgundy lacquer, four double doors, two drawers with moon brasses, China, 19th C....................................................................1,150.00

38" w, 17-1/2" d, 41" h, two part, ornate iron mounts, sides bootjacked, Sendai-type Tansu, Japan, 19th C ....................1,100.00

42" w, 19-1/2" d, 74" h, two doors, rosewood, round-corner type, brass mounts, China, 19th C .........................................450.00

42" w, 21" d, 80" h, elmwood, square-type corners, two doors over three drawers, China, late 19th C ............................750.00

43-1/4" w, 21-1/4" d, 84-1/2" h, elmwood, square-corner type, large character prosperity on back within red diamond, China, 19th C ....................................................................................700.00

Carving, 6-1/4" h, hardstone, lapis lazuli, god of longevity with an attendant, deep colored stone, Chinese, 20th C ..............175.00

Chair, arm

Bamboo, arched backrest, latticework, Chinese Export, late 19th C .......................................................................1,035.00

Chiang Chin work, vermilion ground with polychrome figures and formalized floral motifs, China, 19th C, 18-1/4" h seat......350.00

Yoke Back, elmwood, burgundy lacquer, black splats carved with basket and flowering tree, China, 18th C, 20" h, price for pr....................................................................................2,100.00

Clock, brass case, iron works, weight-driven, wooden frame, Japan, 19th C ...............................................................................4,315.00

Clothing Rack, 83" l, 65" h, elmwood with polychrome dec, carved birds and flowers, floral finials, China, early 20th C..................300.00

Desk, 26" sq top, 32-3/4" h, four drawers with brass mounts, maze pattern, foot rest, China, late 19th C, repairs.................................650.00

Doll Set, stylized figures in Heian-style costume, ivory heads, gold lacquer bodies, maki-e embroidery, cinnabar hakama and accents, lacquered box, Japan, 19th C ............................................2,415.00

Figure

9-1/2" h, stoneware, red robed daruma, holding fly whisk, Japan, late 19th/early 20th C .................................................200.00

11-1/2" h, gilt bronze, Shou Lao seated on deer, traces of gilt, Ming period (1368-1644)............................................3,335.00

19" h, stoneware, white robed daruma, bisque hands and face, Japan, early 20th C.................................................290.00

30" h, bronze, Deities, Nio figures, finely sculpted, holding lotus vases with swirling drapery around body, Japan, late 19th C, price for pr..................................................................2,415.00

Fireplace Crane, 12" h, heavy wood stained black, fitted iron stand, Japan, 19th C.......................................................................920.00

Garden Lantern, 50" h, granite, Japan, 18th C, price for pr......2,990.00

Hand Guard

Bronze, carved in the round as a dragon, gold inlay, Kinko school, 19th C ................................................................................865.00

Bronze, carved with shoki and inlay, Mito school, 19th C....750.00

Round, shakudo carved with prunus and clouds, surface textured, 18th C ................................................................................320.00

Steel, high relief carving, pierced, cherry blossoms design, sgd "Mitsuko," Japan, 19th C.................................................1,265.00

Hibachi, 6-1/2" d, black lacquer, gold maki-e of flowers, silvered copper ember holder, 19th C ...........................................................460.00

Incense Box, 4" d, lacquer, dark ground, polychrome lacquer of two women with water containers, mother-of-pearl, int. with seven small boxes with various brocade patterns, Japan, late 19th C......3,450.00

Incense Burner

4" d, koro with scrolling handles, three feet, procession and mille fleur pattern on green ground, sgd "Meizan" in gold on base within cartouche, Japan, Meiji period, 1868-1911, two small chips to inside of cover..................................................2,530.00

36" h, bronze and champleve enamel, dragon form, sculpted entirely in the round, supporting phoenix headed incense burner surmounted by rampant dragon, minor losses, Japan, 19th C ................................................................................1,150.00

Incense Table, 17-1/2" sq top, 31-1/4" h, elmwood, burgundy lacquer traces, single hidden drawer, archaic carving, cracked ice base, China, 19th C ..............................................................................550.00

Kimono, child's, brocade with gold threads, dragon design, Japan, early 20th C ...............................................................................225.00

Lectern, black lacquer, gold waves and cranes dec, Japan, 19th C, losses .............................................................................................300.00

Okimono

6-3/4" l, wooden, three carved kittens, inlaid horn eyes, 19th C, repair..................................................................................2,760.00

15" l, wave form bronze, three clear glass jewels, Japan, late 19th C ................................................................................1,035.00

Pedestal, 32" h, rosewood, lotus plants carved in high relief, China, late 19th C ........................................................................................750.00

Rice Container, 20" h, coopered, elmwood, brass stays, China, late 19th C ........................................................................................230.00

Robe

Brocade, deep purple, five clawed dragons, various imperial emblems, China, late 19th/early 20th C ..........................635.00

Dragon, blue silk embroidered with gold dragons, China, 19th C, losses ................................................................................1,150.00

Empress Dowager-Style, k'o ssu of butterflies and morning glory flowers, lemon yellow ground, morning glory flowers on black ground, k'o ssu borders, late 19th C, minor stains ........6,900.00

Silk, blue silk brocade embroidered with longevity emblems, birds, and flowers, China, 19th C........................................500.00

Winter, pale blue ground embroidered with flowers, fur lined, China, early 20th C.................................................................350.00

Scholar's Rock, 25" h, tai hu stone, white color, broad areas of black veining, rosewood stand........................................635.00

Scholar's Stone

10-1/2" l, mountainous form, striated, fitted stand .............230.00

26" l, gray ling pi, waxy texture in mounting form, fitted stand................................................................................2,300.00

Seal Box, 2-1/4" d, Peking enamel, copper with dec of man and child in garden scene, Ch'ien Lung four character mark and probably of the period, fitted stands, price for pr...........................................1,150.00

Stellar, 23" x 15", limestone, central Buddha flanked by seven attendants with two riders on horseback, back engraved, China, Northern Wei style, 386-557, repairs ...............................................865.00

Stem Cup, 6" d, 4-1/2" h, carved cinnabar lacquer over turned wooden frame, Buddhistic lions playing with brocade balls, China, 17th C, stress lines ...............................................................................2,990.00

Storage Jar, 15" h, green glaze, Tao Tieh masks in relief, cov possibly replaced, Han period, 206 B.C.-220 A.D.................................575.00

Sun Spot Incense Burner, 6-1/2" d, 5" h, bronze, pestle form, elephant head feet, sq handles with jui finials, dark bone with gold splash, three-character seal mark on base, China, 18th C ...............1,840.00

Sweetmeat Box, 21" d, tien ch'i lacquer, surface dec with five clawed dragons and cloud on red ground, six-character Ch'ien Lung mark, 1736-95, of the period .........................................................4,600.00

Sword, 12" l, tanto, lacquered tsuba inlaid with mother-of-pearl, shishi menuke, sgd "Harima Mori Kenataka," Japan...........................920.00

Sword Furniture, fuchi and kashira set, shakudo with mixed metal inlay of flowers, sgd "Yoshimasa" .....................................................490.00

Sword Guard

Armorers work tsuba, large iron guard, mokko form, per7ced work for no-dachi, Japan, 16th/17th C.........................................350.00

Steel, carved and inlaid with copper and gold, ship of wealth design, Soten school............................................375.00
Sword Mounts, fuchi and kashira, shakudo carved with waves with gold inlay, sgd "Omori Teruhide"....................................750.00
Table
    13" l, 8" d, 25" h, black lacquer with mother-of-pearl inlay, scholars in landscape, cash coin patterns, Ryuku islands, 17th C, repairs ..............................................................1,035.00
    48" l, 16" d, 36" h, rosewood, pierced legs, archaic-style carved aprons, China, 19th C...........................................1,035.00
    Tansu, 24" x 23" x 11-3/4", hinoki wood, two doors over six drawers, copper pulls, Japan, early 20th C ....................1,035.00
Tomb Figure
    8" h, 9" l, 9" w, ming chi of a farmhouse and barnyard with man and dog in house, numerous animals, green glazed, Han dynasty, 206 B.C.-220 A.D................................920.00
    33" h, San tsai glazed ming chi figure of attendant holding scarf, green and yellow glaze, head unglazed, Ming period, 1368-1644 ............................................................2,185.00
    33" h, San tsai glazed ming chi figure of attendant holding valise, green and yellow glaze, head unglazed, Ming period, 1368-1644 ............................................................2,670.00
Traveling Shrine, 3-1/4" h, miniature, sandalwood figure of Amida Buddha enclosed in black lacquer case with gold lotus flowers, Japan, 19th C ................................................................500.00
Tray, 10-3/4" x 7-1/2", black lacquer, maki-e of boats and pine trees, gold with togidashi, silver rim, Japan, 19th C .........................320.00
Tsuba, iron, rope design, sgd "Yamashiro Kuni Nishijin ju Umetada Saku," c1700 ..............................................................375.00
Wall Panel, 25-1/2" w, 48" h, carved in relief with vase of flowers, coral branch, resonance stone resting on low table, China, 19th C, price for pr ............................................................................230.00
Water Coupe, 3-3/4" d, 2-1/2" d, molded gourd, hexagonal form, shoe medallions and jui borders, lined with tortoiseshell, base marked "Enjoyed and admired Ch'ien Lung," China, 19th C ..............1,495.00
Wine Jar
    15" d, 15" h, Honan ware, faceted, bow string marks around base, tan-speckled black glaze, wave patterned int., China, 15th C ..............................................................1,350.00
    16" d, stoneware, Tzu Chou ware, cream colored glaze with black dec, inscription around top and on shoulder, Ming period, 1368-1644 ............................................................1,100.00
Wine Table, 51" l, 16" w, 31" h, rosewood, reeded legs, spandrels carved with ling chih swirls, China, 19th C ...............................575.00
Writing Box, 8-1/2" l, 7-1/4" w, lacquer, suzuribako with nashiji ground, two maki-e drums, int. dec with gold pines, ink stone, and suiteki intact, silver edges, Japan, late 19th C................................1,840.00

# ORIENTAL RUGS

**History:** Oriental rugs or carpets date back to 3,000 B.C.; but it was in the 16th century that they became prevalent. The rugs originated in the regions of Central Asia, Iran (Persia), Caucasus, and Anatolia. Early rugs can be classified into basic categories: Iranian, Caucasian, Turkoman, Turkish, and Chinese. Later India, Pakistan, and Iraq produced rugs in the Oriental style.

The pattern name is derived from the tribe which produced the rug, e.g., Iran is the source for Hamadan, Herez, Sarouk, and Tabriz.

**References:** J. R. Azizollahoff, *The Illustrated Buyer's Guide to Oriental Carpets,* Schiffer, 1998; Susan Gomersall, *Kilim Rugs: Tribal Tales in Wool,* Schiffer Publishing, 2000; Walter A. Hawley, *Oriental Rugs, Antique and Modern,* Dover Publications, 1970; Charles W. Jacobsen, *Check Points on How to Buy Oriental Rugs,* Charles E.

Tuttle Co., 1981; Robert Pinner and Murray L. Eiland, Jr., *Between the Black Desert and the Red Turkmen Carpets from the Wiedersperg Collection,* Fine Arts Museum of San Francisco, distributed by Antique Collectors' Club, 1999; Pamela Thomas, *Oriental Rugs,* Smithmark, 1996.

**Periodicals:** *HALI,* P.O. Box 4312, Philadelphia, PA 19118; *Oriental Rug Review,* P.O. Box 709, Meredith, NH 03253, http://www.rugreview.com/orr.htm; *Orientalia Journal,* P.O. Box 94, Flushing, NY 11363-0094, http://members.aol.com/Orientalia/index.html; *Rug News,* 34 West 37th St, New York, NY 10018.

**Reproduction Alert:** Beware! There are repainted rugs on the market.

**Notes:** When evaluating an Oriental rug, age, design, color, weave, knots per square inch, and condition determine the final value. Silk rugs and prayer rugs bring higher prices than other types.

Afshar, South Persia, last quarter 19th C
    Bagface, 2'7" x 2', small stepped medallions surrounded by geometric flowerheads, red, rose, sky blue, gold, ivory, aubergine-brown, and blue-green, midnight blue field, ivory palmette motif border, areas of wear, small corner gouge....................690.00
    Bagface, 2'9" x 2', stepped diamond medallion flanked by chevron oriented stepped lines, red, sky blue, gold, aubergine-brown, ivory, and blue-green, midnight blue field, ivory flowerhead border, even wear ...............................1,380.00
    Rug, 6'4" x 4'8", staggered rows of botch, red, royal blue, gold, brown, and blue-green, abrashed midnight blue field, red turtle variant border, even center wear....................2,530.00
Akstafa, East Caucasus, last quarter 19th C, 5'6" x 3'6", three gabled rect medallions flanked by eight peacocks, red, ice blue, ivory, gold, tan, and pale blue-green, navy blue field, ivory hooked sq border, slight even center wear, small tear.......................4,320.00
Bahktiari, West Persia, early 20th C
    6'8" x 5', large serrated medallion surrounded by large serrated botch and palmette motifs, red, royal blue, deep apricot, ivory, aubergine, and blue-green, midnight blue field, red crab border, even center wear, corner patch....................2,185.00
    16' x 14'6", sq grid of palmettes, cypress trees, weeping willow motifs, and floral groups, navy blue, red, rose, camel, gold, dark brown, and blue-green, ivory palmette and vine border, small areas of minor wear .......................................3,450.00
Bakshaish, Northwest Persia, last quarter 19th C, 6' x 4'10", stepped diamond medallion flanked by four botch variant motifs, red, rose, sky blue, red-brown, and blue-green, light camel field, sky blue spandrels, dark brown rosette and leafy fine border, small area of wear, outer border partially missing from both ends .....................4,900.00
Baluch, Northeast Persia, late 19th C
    Rug, 4'7" x 2'9", sq grid of paired serrated leaves and octagons, navy blue, red, rust, and light apricot, red curled leaf border, even center wear.......................................815.00
    Vanity Bag, 1'5" x 1'5", hooked octagonal medallion inset with cruciform motif, red, wine red, ivory, and dark blue-green, midnight blue field, ivory star border, moth damage, small rewoven area ...........................................250.00
Bordjalou Kazak, Southwest Caucasus, second half 19th C, 3'5" x 3'5", two connected diamond medallions surrounded by small geometric motifs, navy blue, ivory, gold, and blue-green, red field, two running dog borders, rewoven ends, areas of minor wear, other small repairs ...........................................3,450.00
Chi-Chi, Northeast Caucasus, last quarter 19th C, 6' x 4'2", rows of hooked polygons in abrashed navy blue, red, black, ivory, gold, and olive, midnight blue field, black rosette and diagonal bat border, rewoven areas, some moth damage, black corrosion..........2,990.00

Dahestan, Northeast Caucasus, dated 1881, prayer, 4' x 3'4", staggered rows of palmette motifs, navy and sky blue, red, gold, tan, and light blue-green, ivory field, navy blue crab border, even wear, small rewoven areas.......................................................................... 3,450.00

Ersari, West Turkestan, last quarter 19th C, 8'9" x 7'3", two columns of six octagonal gulli-guls, apricot, ivory, midnight, navy, and royal blue, rust-red field, compartmented rosette border, even center wear, areas of repiling................................................................... 5,750.00

Fereghan-Sarouk, West Persia, late 19th C, 6'6" x 4'3", lobed rosette medallions, matching spandrels and blossoming vines, midnight and navy blue, rose, brown, ivory, gold, olive, and blue-green, abrashed red field, midnight blue rosette border, small areas of minor wear ................................................................. 1,725.00

Heriz, Northwest Persia
    11'6" x 9'2", last quarter 19th C, small crenellated sq medallion surrounded by hooked diamonds, serrated leaves, numerous geometric motifs, midnight and sky blue, came, red-brown, ivory, and rose, terra cotta red field, sky blue rosette and serrated leaf border, even center wear, touch-up, guard stripe missing from one end.................................... 2,875.00
    12'4" x 9'2", early 20th C, gabled sq medallion surrounded by angular flowering vines, navy and sky blue, rose, ivory, came, red-brown, and blue-green, terra cotta red field, stepped ivory spandrels, red rosette and botch border, small areas of moth damage, end fraying, small repaired area..................... 8,100.00

Karabagh, South Caucasus, last quarter 19th C, column of six sq compartments each inset with cruciform medallion, navy and ice blue, red, cochineal, gold, pale apricot, brown, and blue-green, ivory flowerhead border, even center wear ......................................... 3,750.00

Kashan, Central Persia, second quarter 20th C
    Carpet, 10'4" x 8', gabled medallion surrounded by small medallions, sinuous blossoming vines, dark red, abrashed sky blue, ivory, rose, tan-gold, and blue-green, midnight blue field, apricot spandrels, dark red palmette and strapwork vine border ..................... 6,325.00
    Prayer, 6'4" x 4'6", birds perched in dense flowering trees, flanked by two architectural columns, navy, royal, and sky blue, rose, ivory, light brown, gold, aubergine, and blue-green, dark red field, ivory spandrels, navy blue flowering vine border........................ 3,565.00

Kazak, Southwest Caucasus, last quarter 19th C
    Long, 7'8" x 4'2", four small diamonds, rosy red field, red and ivory diagonal stripe border, abrashed navy blue and dark brown reciprocal trefoil outer and inner border, slight even wear, rewoven ends............................................................... 5,175.00
    Long, 13' x 4'6", dated 1903, column of five trees, surrounded by stars and octagons, navy and sky blue, ivory, orange, and aubergine, red field, abrashed sky blue, cross motif border, hole, moth damage, creases................................................ 1,265.00
    Prayer, 5'4" x 3'4", chevron oriented serrated stripes, red, royal blue, ivory, gold, aubergine, brown, and blue-green, ivory hooked diamond border, one end and other areas rewoven, small areas of wear, slight moth damage........................ 900.00
    Prayer, 8'6" x 4'2", dated 1902, large rect medallion inset with rows of plants, navy blue, gold, ivory, and blue-green, rust field, Turkoman-style pole tree inner border and Sainak outer border of similar coloration, slight center wear, creases ....................... 3,200.00
    Salt Bag, 1'7" x 1'5", two hooked diamonds and eight small stars, navy blue, ivory, gold, and blue-green, red field, narrow midnight blue sq motif border, slight moth damage ........... 1,265.00

Konya, Central Anatolia, second half 19th C, 3'5" x 2'6", hexagonal medallion and four octagons, red, royal blue, ivory, and gold, light blue-green field, red spandrels, ivory flowerhead border, gold elems, areas of wear, stain ............................................... 1,495.00

Kuba, Northwest Caucasus, last quarter 19th C
    9'4" x 4', three columns of hooked hexagons, red, sky blue, gold, ivory, aubergine, and blue-green, royal blue field, ivory octagon border, slight moth damage........................................ 6,325.00
    12'6" x 3', serrated hexagonal lattice of flowering plants, navy and sky blue, red, rose, gold, maroon, and blue-green, black field, ivory wineglass border, even center wear, black corrosion, slight moth damage .............................................. 4,025.00

Lesghi, Northeast Caucasus, last quarter 19th C, 4'9" x 3'4", three Lesghi stars, four small horses with riders, red, ivory, camel, gold, and blue-green, royal blue field, ivory octagon border, slight even center wear, black corrosion .......................................... 4,320.00

Luri Soumak, West Persia, late 19th-early 20th C, salt bag, 1'7" x 1'4", three rosettes and four serrated leaf motifs, red, ivory, gold, navy blue, aubergine, and blue-green, midnight blue field, ivory sq motif border, narrow pile elem, small repair ..................................... 520.00

Mahal, West Persia, second quarter 20th C, 18' x 12'2", overall design of rosettes, palmettes, serrated leaves, curved blossoming vines, navy blue, rose, gold, ivory, brown, apricot, and blue-green, terra cotta red field, midnight blue floral group border, small areas of wear, moth damage .................................................... 3,450.00

Malayer, Northwest Persia, second quarter 20th C, 6'6" x 4'9", overall Herati designs, sky blue, rose, ivory and light blue-green, abrashed terra cotta red field, sky blue spandrels, ivory botch and vine border, slight center wear .............................................. 550.00

Melas, Southwest Anatolia, last quarter 19th C, 5'8" x 4', columns of twelve small diamonds flanked by flowering, leafy vines, aubergine, sky blue, dark red, ivory, gold, apricot, and blue-green, red field, red radiating diamond and quatrefoil floral motif border, slight even wear, small rewoven area, small creases, small edge gouges ..................... 2,530.00

Meshed, Northeast Persia, second quarter 20th C, 19'6" x 11'6", overall design of palmettes, cloud bands, and flowering vines, midnight and royal blue, red, gold, dark apricot, and green, wine field, midnight blue palmette and arabesque vine border, slight moth damage......... 2,990.00

Qashqai, Southwest Persia, last quarter 19th C
    Bagface, 2'4" x 2'4", stepped and hooked diamond medallion flanked by four small hooked diamonds, red, navy blue, ivory, gold, aubergine, and sage green, midnight blue field, ivory floral meander border, even wear, rewoven center, slight end fraying .......... 290.00
    Kelim, 9' x 3'10", two columns of seven stepped diamond medallions, navy and medium blue, apricot, ivory, and blue-green, maroon field, multicolored reciprocal trefoil border, area of slight wear ................................................................. 1,035.00
    Rug, 8' x 4'8", stepped diamond medallion surrounded by small floral motifs, ivory, navy blue, gold, apricot, and red-brown, abrashed terra cotta red field, navy blue spandrels, red-brown paired triangle and serrated leaf border, small area of minor wear ................................................................. 1,150.00

Sarouk, West Persia, late 19th C, 6'5" x 4', large lobed medallion surrounded by blossoming vines, ivory, ice blue, rose, brown, gold, and dark blue-green, midnight blue field, rose spandrels, midnight blue rosette border, even wear, guard stripe partially missing from both ends .................................................................. 1,150.00

**Shirvan, staggered rows of snowflake flowerheads, red, abrashed royal blue, ivory, gold, brown, and blue-green, midnight blue field, gold crab variant border, 6' x 4', $1,265. Photo courtesy of Skinner, Inc.**

Serapi, Northwest Persia, last quarter 19th C, 12' x 9'6", large stepped medallion with palmette pendants and leafy vines, midnight and sky blue, ivory, tan, rose, and light blue-green, terra cotta red field, ivory spandrels, midnight blue turtle border, overall wear and moth damage ........................................................................................... 1,610.00

Shahsavan Soumak, Northwest Persia, last quarter 19th C, saddlebags, 4'6" x 1'10", single Lesghi star in red, royal blue, ivory, and gold, midnight blue field, ivory pinwheel border, several holes ........................... 1,380.00

Shirvan, East Caucasus, late 19th C

5' x 3'8", three stepped hexagonal medallions surrounded by small camel and other animal motifs, royal blue, maroon, rose, gold, ivory, tan, and blue-green on red field, gold interrupted vine border, very small hole .............................................. 4,370.00

6' x 4', staggered rows of snowflake flowerheads, red, abrashed royal blue, ivory, gold, brown, and blue-green, midnight blue field, gold crab variant border, even wear, guard stripe missing from both ends, small patch, touch-up ........................... 1,265.00

Tabriz, Northwest Persia, late 19th C

15' x 11'5", diamond medallion and overall lattice of palmettes, rosettes, and triple flowerheads, ivory, pale gold, midnight and slate blue, rust field, ivory turtle variant border, even wear, faded colors, small tear .......................................................... 35,650.00

24' x 11'10", overall rows of palmettes, rosettes, and blossoming vines, midnight, navy, and sky blue, red, rose, ivory, gold, brown, gold, and blue-green, deep wine red field, midnight blue rosette and floral group border, slight moth damage ................... 16,100.00

Talish, Southwest Caucasus, second half 19th C, 7'2" x 3'4", diamond lattice of quatrefoil circular motifs, royal blue, black, ivory, and gold on arrow terra cotta red field, ivory rosette and sq motif border, small areas of wear and moth damage, crease, end fraying .............. 1,150.00

Timuri, Northeast Persia, mid 19th C, 6' x 4', diamond lattice of quatrefoil motifs, midnight and navy blue, rust, red, and aubergine, ivory boat border, moth damage, crease repairs, aubergine and brown corrosion ....................................................................... 1,840.00

Ushak, West Anatolia, late 19th C

12'7" x 12'2", large serrated hexagonal medallion surrounded by small rosettes, navy and sky blue, gold, apricot, ivory, and olive, red field, olive spandrels, navy blue rosette and vine border, even center wear, small repairs ..................................... 5,175.00

13' x 10'6", three medallions surrounded by small floral motifs, red, rose, ice blue, deep gold, ivory, and pale violet, green-gold field, pale violet spandrels, ivory palmette and arabesque vine border, areas of wear ..................................................... 6,900.00

Veramin, North Persia, late 19th C, bagface, 3'10"x 2'9", large octagonal "Memling" guls, red, rose, royal blue, aubergine, gold, and blue-green, midnight blue field, two midnight blue and gold octagon borders, multicolored checkerboard elem, moth damage, small repairs, end and edge fraying ................................................................ 550.00

Yomud West Turkestan, late 19th C

Asmalyks, 3'6" x 2', lattice of concentric Ashik guls, red, navy blue, ivory, red-brown, and dark blue-green, ivory stylized flowerhead border, multicolored tassels, price for pr ............................. 875.00

Chuval, 4' x 2'6", twenty Chuval guls, red, navy blue, ovary, apricot, and blue-green, aubergine field, ivory shield motif border, plain aubergine elem, edges slightly reduced and machine reovercast, small repair, slight moth damage .................. 460.00

Okbash, 2' x 1'10", zig-zag serrated design, midnight blue, ivory, apricot, red, and brown, ivory cross motif border, small rewoven area along edge ...................................................... 350.00

Salatchak, 4'2" x 2'8", column of six stepped and hooked diamonds flanked by two columns of syrga motifs, midnight and royal blue, ivory, apricot, and red-brown, rust-red field, ivory "X" motif border, even wear, end fraying ................................. 980.00

# OVERSHOT GLASS

**History:** Overshot glass was developed in the mid-1800s. To produce overshot glass, a gather of molten glass was rolled over the marver upon which had been placed crushed glass. The piece then was blown into the desired shape. The finished product appeared to be frosted or iced.

Early pieces were made mainly in clear glass. As the demand for colored glass increased, color was added to the base piece and occasionally to the crushed glass.

Pieces of overshot generally are attributed to the Boston and Sandwich Glass Co. although many other companies also made it as it grew in popularity.

**Museum:** Sandwich Glass Museum, Sandwich, MA.

Basket, 10" h, 7-1/2" d, rect, shaded cranberry to crystal, applied crystal ruffled edge, applied thorn overshot handle ........................ 225.00

Biscuit Jar, cov, 7" h, 5" d, colorless melon ribbed body, applied cranberry overshot, coiled snake handle ....................................... 250.00

Bowl, 3-1/4" h, deep, colorless, attributed to Sandwich ................ 40.00

Bride's Bowl, 8-5/8" d, 6-5/8" h, shaded clear to blue ground, lobed, crimped edge, dec brass holder ................................................ 215.00

Compote

6-3/4" h, 8-3/8" d, cranberry shaded to clear bowl, applied clear scalloped and ruffled edge, fancy brass dome ftd pedestal base ........................................................................................ 125.00

9" h, 8-7/8" d, colorless ground, applied gold dec, cranberry serpent around stem .................................................................. 125.00

Custard Cup, pink ground, applied clear ground, Sandwich ......... 60.00

Decanter, colorless ground, ice bladder, orig stopper ................. 750.00

Dish, leaf form

1-1/4" l, colorless ............................................................... 30.00

2-3/4" l, green .................................................................... 35.00

Ewer, 13-1/2" h, trefoil top, colorless ground, twisted rope handle, Sandwich ................................................................................... 275.00

Finger Bowl, pink ground, fluted and swirled ............................. 115.00

Goblet, flint, cut cotton twist stem, American .............................. 300.00

Ice Cream Tray, 13" l, colorless, gold trim, Portland .................... 40.00

Jar, cov, 4-3/4" h, colorless body, metal cover ............................. 45.00

Lamp Shade, 7-7/8" d, 2-7/8" d fitter ring, sapphire blue shaded to clear ground, ruffled ............................................................... 125.00

Marmalade Jar, cov, matching underplate, green ground, gold snake entwined on cov, attributed to Boston and Sandwich Glass Co. ............................................................................................ 315.00

Mug, 3" h, colorless ground, applied colorless handle ................. 35.00

Pitcher

6" d, cranberry ground, bulbous, applied colorless reeded handle ...................................................................................... 125.00

8" d, bulbous, colorless ground, heavy enamel dec of white roses, blue forget me nots and green leaves, applied colorless handle ...................................................................................... 150.00

11" h, tricorn rim, ovoid body, overshot colorless glass, ice bladder, applied twisted rope handle, attributed to Sandwich ........... 145.00

Punch Cup, pink ground, applied colorless handle, attributed to Boston and Sandwich Glass Co. set of 8 ............................................. 300.00

**Compote, clear, flint, 7-3/4" d, 5-7/8" h, $165.**

Rose Bowl, 3-3/4" d, rubena ground, applied flowers and pale green leaves ..................................................................................... 165.00
Tazza, 5-3/4" h, 7-3/4" d, colorless ground, flint glass ............... 195.00
Vase, 7-1/2" h, bulbous base, slender neck, colorless ground, gold overshot, silver floral dec ............................................ 125.00

# OWENS POTTERY

**History:** J. B. Owens began making pottery in 1885 near Roseville, Ohio. In 1891, he built a plant in Zanesville and in 1897 began producing art pottery. After 1907, most of the firm's production centered on tiles.

Owens Pottery, employing many of the same artists and designs as its two cross-town rivals, Roseville and Weller, can appear very similar to that of its competitors, e.g., Utopian (brown glaze), Lotus (light glaze), Aqua Verde (green glaze).

There were a few techniques used exclusively at Owens. These included Red Flame ware (slip decoration under a high red glaze) and Mission (over-glaze, slip decorations in mineral colors) depicting Spanish Missions. Other specialties included Opalesce (semi-gloss designs in lustered gold and orange) and Coralene (small beads affixed to the surface of the decorated vases).

**References:** Paul Evans, *Art Pottery of the United States*, 2nd ed., Feingold & Lewis Publishing, 1987; Frank Hahn, *Collector's Guide to Owens Pottery*, Golden Era Publications (available from Green Gate Books, P.O. Box 934, Lima, OH 45802), 1996; Ralph and Terry Kovel, *Kovels' American Art Pottery*, Crown Publishers, 1993; Kristy and Rick McKibben and Jeanette and Martin Stofft, *Owens Pottery Unearthed*, published by authors (45 12th St., Tell City, IN 47586), 1996.

Bud Vase
6-1/4" h, 2-1/2" w, standard glaze, yellow roses, mkd "#804," initials for Harry Robinson ..................................................... 150.00
9" h, molded body under metallic glaze, hairline to body.... 160.00
Ewer, 10" h, brown high glaze, cherry design ........................... 200.00
Jug, 8" w, 4-1/2" w, standard glaze, ear of corn dec, mkd and sgd "Tot Steele" ..................................................................................... 230.00
Lamp Base
10" h, brown glaze, yellow daffodil dec, green leaves and stems, orig lamp hole in base ............................................... 190.00
10" h, 4-1/2" w, standard glaze, tulips and leaves, ftd form, mkd ............................................................................. 90.00
Mug, 7-1/2" h, standard glaze, cherries, mkd "#830," sgd "Henry R. Robinson," hairlines to int. ....................................... 110.00
Pitcher, 8-1/2" h, dark brown to green, orange and brown flowers, green leaves, mkd "JBO" intertwined, artist sgd "HK," crack in handle .................................................................................... 110.00
Tankard
7" h, brown high glaze, Indian design, incised signature, restored ....................................................................... 325.00
12" h, brown glaze, artist sgd, imp mark ........................... 210.00
Vase
....3-3/4" h, Utopia, dark brown, lighter brown, orange, and yellow floral dec, imp mark "#110," small base flake ............. 100.00
4" h, Lotus, bee flying above green blades of grass, ivory to blue ground, imp mark, artist initials ..................................... 400.00
4" h, Utopian, floral ........................................................... 135.00
4" h, 4" w, yellow chick surrounded by thinly painted grass, four feet, artist sgd ............................................................... 300.00

**Vase, Utopia, tall tapered form, yellow wild roses, green and brown leaves, stamped "Owens 014," 12-1/4" h, 4" d, $350. Photo courtesy of David Rago Auctions.**

5-3/4" h, brown flowers, mkd .............................................. 100.00
5-3/4" h, 3-3/4" w, brown clover, standard glaze, mkd "#232" . 100.00
6-3/8" h, Utopian Ware, silver overlay, flared rim on tapered oviform, glossy glaze, cream and brown rose blossoms and leaves, shaded brown ground, silver overlay imp "Utopian J. B. Owens 923" and "Phee F.N. Silver Co.," crazing, scratches, nicks .................................................................................... 290.00
7" h, fluted, Ida Steel, floral ................................................ 625.00
7-1/2" h, high glaze, orange, white, and green grapes, vines, and leaves, pink to green ground, imp "Owens #1260" .......... 300.00
8" h, Aqua Verdi, green matte, textured surface, incised geometrics, four handles around neck, unmarked ....................... 550.00
8" h, 8-1/2" w, ftd pillow, dark to light brown with yellow ground, Indian portrait, cream and red vest, blue in hair, imp mark, repaired top ................................................................. 1,100.00
8-1/2" h, standard glaze, yellow berry dec, green leaves, imp mark .................................................................................... 100.00
10" h, orange and yellow tulips, green leaves, brown ground, imp mark .................................................................................... 250.00
10" h, 5" w, standard glaze, mkd "Owens #010" ................. 210.00
10-3/4" h, 5-3/4" d, sgraffito, orange and blue irises, dark brown ground, Henri Deux, unmarked, pea sized burst bubble on shoulder ............................................................................ 650.00
11"h, Utopia, rose with green leaves, brown stems, orange and brown ground, mkd, artist sgd ....................................... 260.00
11-1/2" h, 5" w, Utopian, standard glaze, mkd "Owens Utopian #1031," sgd "Sarah Timberlake" ..................................... 375.00
12" h, molded flowers and heads, green matte glaze, hairline ................................................................................ 160.00
12-1/2" h, pink poppy, green stems and leaves, pink, ivory, and light blue ground, artist initialed, imp mark ..................... 600.00
12-1/2" h, 8" w, standard glaze, yellow flowers and petals, mkd "#8," minor roughness on bottom ..................................... 190.00
13" h, matte, Utopian ......................................................... 425.00
13-1/2" h, green, yellow, and brown leaves, swirling mahogany, yellow, and dark brown ground, artist initials "A. H.," incised bottom, sunburst "J. B. Owens" ........................................... 650.00
16-1/2" h, Lotus, rose, pink, purple, and yellow iris, green leaves, ivory, gray, and peach ground, artist sgd, imp mark ...... 1,400.00

# PADEN CITY GLASS

**History:** Paden City Glass Manufacturing Co. was founded in 1916 in Paden City, West Virginia. David Fisher, formerly of the New Martinsville Glass Manufacturing Co., operated the company until his death in 1933, at which time his son, Samuel, became president. A management decision in 1949 to expand Paden City's production by acquiring American Glass Company, an automated manufacturer of bottles, ashtrays, and novelties, strained the company's finances, forcing them to close permanently in 1951.

Contrary to popular belief and previously incorrect printed references, The Paden City Glass Manufacturing Company had absolutely no connection with the Paden City Pottery Company, other than their identical locale.

Although Paden City glass is often lumped with mass-produced, machine-made wares into the Depression Glass category, Paden City's wares were, until 1948, all handmade. Their products are better classified as "Elegant Glass" of the era as it ranks in quality with the wares produced by contemporaries such as Fostoria, New Martinsville, and Morgantown.

Paden City kept a low profile, never advertising in consumer magazines of the day. They never marked their glass in any way because a large portion of their business consisted of sales to decorating companies, mounters, and fitters. The firm also supplied bars, restaurants, and soda fountains with glassware, as evidenced by the wide range of tumblers, ice cream dishes, and institutional products available in several Paden City patterns.

Paden City's decorating shop also etched, cut, hand painted, and applied silver overlay and gold encrustation. However, not every decoration found on Paden City shapes will necessarily have come from the factory. Cupid, Peacock and Rose, and several other etchings depicting birds are among the most sought after decorations. Pieces with these etchings are commanding higher and higher prices even though they were apparently made in greater quantities than some of the etchings that are less-known (but just as beautiful).

Paden City is noted for its colors: opal (opaque white), ebony, mulberry (amethyst), Cheriglo (delicate pink), yellow, dark green (forest), crystal, amber, primrose (reddish-amber), blue, rose, and great quantities of ruby (red). The firm also produced transparent green in numerous shades ranging from yellowish to a distinctive electric green that always alerts knowledgeable collectors to its Paden City origin.

Rising collector interest in Paden City glass has resulted in a sharp spike in prices on some items. Advanced collectors seek out examples with unusual and/or undocumented etchings. Colored pieces which sport an etching that is not usually found on that particular color are especially sought after, and are bringing strong prices. In contrast, prices for common items with Peacock and Rose etch remain static, and the prices for dinnerware in ruby Penny Line and pink or green Party Line have inched up only slightly, due to its greater availability.

**References:** Jerry Barnett, *Paden City, The Color Company,* privately printed, 1979, out-of-print; Lee Garmon and Dick Spencer, *Glass Animals of the Depression Era*, Collector Books, 1993; Naomi L. Over, *Ruby Glass of the 20th Century*, The Glass Press, 1990, 1993-94 value update, *Book II,* 1999; Hazel Marie Weatherman, *Colored Glassware of the Depression Era 2*, Glassbooks, 1974.

**Advisor:** Michael Krumme.

Color is crystal (clear) unless otherwise noted.

Animal (made by Paden City for Barth Art)
- Dragon Swan, light blue .................................................... 495.00
- Squirrel ............................................................................ 30.00

Bowl, nappy
- #412 Crow's Foot Square, 5", ruby ...................................... 35.00
- 9-1/2" oval, ruby ............................................................... 45.00

Bowl, #888 12" low scalloped edge bowl, Floral Medallion etch... 59.00

Bowl, 2-handled serving
- #210 Regina, Black Forest etch ........................................ 110.00
- #215 Glades, Spring Orchard etch ...................................... 50.00
- #221 Maya, light blue ........................................................ 57.50

Cake Salver, footed
- #215 Glades, cutting .......................................................... 40.00
- #300 Archaic, Gothic Garden etch, topaz ............................ 99.00
- #300 Archaic, Peacock and Rose etch, Cheriglo ................. 95.00
- #300 Archaic, Lela Bird etch, green ................................... 125.00
- #411 Mrs. B., Ardith etch, yellow ........................................ 55.00
- #411 Mrs. B., Gothic Garden, green .................................... 46.00
- #695 Lucy, silver deposit ................................................... 40.00

Candy Box, cov, flat
- #411 Mrs. B., Ardith etch, green ....................................... 150.00
- #412 Crow's Foot Square, square shape, ebony w/crystal lid ...................................................................................... 60.00
- #412 Crow's Foot Square, square shape, ruby .................. 125.00
- #412-1/2 Crow's Foot Square, cloverleaf shape, cobalt ..... 225.00

Candy Dish, cov, footed
- #191 Party Line, ftd, Black Forest etch ............................. 149.00
- #412-1/2 Crow's Foot Square cloverleaf shaped covered candy, cobalt blue ...................................................................... 195.00
- #555 w/beaded edge, crystal with floral cutting ................... 85.00
- #555, w/beaded edge, ruby ................................................. 67.00
- #890 Crow's Foot Round, amber ......................................... 95.00

Candleholders, pr
- #210 Regina, Black Forest etch ........................................ 140.00
- #220 Largo, crystal, satin finish, silver deposit .................... 30.00
- #412 Crow's Foot Square, 6-1/2" keyhole style, ruby ........... 70.00
- #444 Vale three-light with cutting ........................................ 40.00
- #2000 Mystic double candleholders, ruby, pair .................... 92.00

Cheese and Cracker Set, #215 Glades, Spring Orchard etch ...... 35.00

Cocktail Shaker, orig strainer, rooster stopper .......................... 155.00

Comport, footed
- #411 Mrs. B, Gothic Garden etch, ebony, rolled edge .......... 89.00
- #411 Mrs. B, Gothic Garden etch, yellow, flared .................. 89.00
- #412 Crow's Foot Square, 6-1/2", ruby ................................ 70.00
- #412 Crow's Foot Square, 6-1/2", Orchid etch, ruby .......... 120.00
- #412 Crow's Foot Square, 6-1/2", Orchid etch, cobalt blue 135.00
- #412 Crow's Foot Square, 6-1/2", opal, silver overlay ........ 180.00
- #412 Crow's Foot Round, 9", ruby ....................................... 50.00
- #444 w/ball stem, ruby ....................................................... 40.00

Console Bowl
- #210 Regina 13" d, Black Forest etch, ebony .................... 185.00
- #220 Largo, three-footed, cupped up, light blue ................... 70.00
- #300 Archaic, 11" d, cheriglo, Cupid etch .......................... 230.00
- #411 Mrs. B., Gothic Garden etch, yellow ............................ 50.00
- #412 Crow's Foot Square, rolled edge, cobalt blue .............. 60.00
- #440 Nerva, 11" d, flat rim, light blue ................................. 50.00
- #881 Gadroon, Frost etch .................................................... 65.00

Console Set, bowl and pr candleholders, #412 Crow's Foot Square, keyhole style candleholders, amber .........................................62.00
Creamer, #90 Chevalier, ruby ...........................................18.00
Creamer and Sugar
    #191 Party Line, Cheriglo ........................................24.00
    #210 Regina, green, Black Forest etch ...........................115.00
    #412 Crow's Foot Square, ruby ...................................45.00
    #412 Crow's Foot Square, Orchid etch, ruby.....................265.00
    #881 Gadroon, ruby .............................................56.00
    #994 Popeye and Olive, ruby 70.00
Cream Soup, #412 Crow's Foot Square, ruby .........................25.00
Cup and Saucer
    #220 Largo, ruby..............................................22.50
    #411 Mrs. B., Ardith etch, topaz...............................15.00
    #412 Crow's Foot Square, ruby.................................17.50
    #991 Penny Line, ruby..........................................12.00
Decanter
    Georgian, cobalt blue, cobalt blue stopper ........................195.00
    Lobed shape decanter, five Penny Lane wines, Spring Orchard etch ............................................................80.00
    New Martinsville Radiance cordial decanter, Paden City's Trumpet Flower etching, with 5 plain cordials (unusual item)...250.00
Ice Bucket, metal bail, Cupid etch, pink, 225.00
Ice Tub, tab handles
    #191 Party Line, green ........................................19.00
    #895 Lucy, Blue Willow etch ...................................129.00
Mayonnaise, bowl and underplate:
    #215 Glades, Spring Orchard etch .............................33.00
    #300 Archaic, Cupid, Cheriglo, with orig ladle ...................125.00
    #300 Archaic, Nora Bird etch, Cheriglo .........................135.00
    #411 Mrs. B., Ardith etch, yellow, with orig ladle................48.00
    #555 beaded edge and "wing" handles, Gazebo etch ..........65.00
    #777 Comet, frosted rim, cut stars, with orig ladle...............25.00
Plate
    #210 Regina, Black Forest etch, 8"d ...........................35.00
    #412 Crow's Foot Square, 8-1/2", ruby.........................15.00
    #412 Crow's Foot Square, 11-1/2", ruby w/gold encrusted etch ............................................................90.00
Platter, oval, #412 Crow's Foot Square, ruby .........................45.00
Sugar Bowl, #411 Mrs. B., Gothic Garden etch, green ...............45.00
Sugar Pourer, #154 Rena, swirl pattern, metal top, Cheriglo......125.00
Syrup Pitcher, #180 with glass lid, floral cutting, green.................69.00
Tray, center handle
    #210 Regina, Black Forest etch................................78.00
    #215 Glades, Spring Orchard etch .............................35.00
    #220 Largo, ruby..............................................95.00
    #411 Mrs. B., Ardith, yellow ...................................58.00
    #412 Crow's Foot Square, Orchid etch, ruby.....................165.00
    #412 Crow's Foot Square, Delilah Bird etch, amber.............95.00
    #412 Crow's Foot Square, opal, rare ..........................350.00
    #701 Triumph, aquamarine blue with cutting ......................18.00
    #701 Triumph, Delilah Bird etch................................40.00
    #881 Gadroon, ruby ...........................................75.00
    #890 Crow's Foot Round, cupped up, floral etch..................50.00
    #1504 swan shaped handle, Gazebo etch .......................85.00
    #1504 swan shaped handle, silver overlay.......................95.00
Tray, two handle, #411 Mrs. B., Gothic Garden, ebony ...............40.00
Tumblers and Stemware
    #191 Party Line, tall footed soda, green .........................24.00
    #191 Party Line footed parfait, green ...........................20.00
    #215 cocktail, Spring Orchard etch..............................6.00
    #991 Penny Line, cordial, ruby w/platinum rings .................29.00
    #991 Penny Line flat ice tea, ruby .............................22.50
    #991 Penny Line wine, ruby ...................................7.00
    #991 Penny Line footed goblet, mulberry ........................18.50
    #991 Penny Line low footed sherbet, mulberry ..................12.50
    Blown tumbler, 5", Ardith etch, green...........................22.00
    Blown tumbler, 5-3/4" h, Black Forest etch, Cheriglo...........75.00

Vase
    #11, 9", box shape, Utopia etch, ebony .........................270.00
    #182 8" elliptical, Lela Bird etch, ebony ..........................200.00
    #182 8" elliptical, Cupid etch, Cheriglo .........................650.00
    #182 8" elliptical, gold encrusted Peacock and Rose etch, ebony............................................................335.00
    #184 10" bulbous-bottom, Lela Bird etch, ebony ...............150.00
    #184 10" bulbous-bottom, Utopia etch, ebony...................195.00
    #184 10" bulbous-bottom, Peacock and Rose etch, Cheriglo.......................................................165.00
    #184 10" bulbous-bottom, Rose Bouquet etch, green........158.00
    #184 10" bulbous-bottom, Lady with Grapes etch, Cheriglo.......................................................260.00
    #184, 10", Daisy etch, green...................................96.00
    #184 12" bulbous-bottom, Daisy etch, Cheriglo.................170.00
    #184 12" bulbous-bottom, Eden Rose etch, ebony ............142.00
    #184, 12", Gothic Garden etch, ruby ...........................205.00
    #184, 12", Utopia etch, ruby ..................................205.00
    #184, 12", Cupid silver deposit ................................230.00
    #210 Regina 6-1/2", Harvesters etch, ebony ..................145.00
    #210 Regina 6-1/2", Black Forest etch, green .................150.00
    #412 10" Crow's Foot Square, flared, ruby..........................96.00
    #412 10" Crow's Foot Square, Gothic Garden etch, ruby... 430.00
    #412, 12", Rose Bouquet etch ................................177.50
    Unknown #, small, bulbous, Orchid etch, ruby .................465.00
    Unknown #, 12" cylindrical, Rose Bouquet etch, green......305.00

# PAIRPOINT

**History:** The Pairpoint Manufacturing Co. was organized in 1880 as a silver-plating firm in New Bedford, Massachusetts. The company merged with Mount Washington Glass Co. in 1894 and became the Pairpoint Corporation. The new company produced specialty glass items often accented with metal frames.

Pairpoint Corp. was sold in 1938 and Robert Gunderson became manager. He operated it as the Gunderson Glass Works until his death in 1952. From 1952 until the plant closed in 1956, operations were maintained under the name Gunderson-Pairpoint. Robert Bryden reopened the glass manufacturing business in 1970, moving it back to the New Bedford area.

**References:** Kyle Husfloen, *Antique Trader's American & European Decorative and Art Glass Price Guide,* 2nd ed., Krause Publications, 2000; Edward and Sheila Malakoff,

**Vase, two handles, Jacqueminot pattern, 17-1/2" h, $3,000. Photo courtesy of Woody Auction.**

**Plate, china, painted harbor scene, artist sgd "L. Tripp," fuchsia-tinted rim, mkd "Pairpoint Limoges," 7-3/8" d, $385. Photo courtesy of Clarence & Betty Maier.**

*Pairpoint Lamps*, Schiffer Publishing, 1990; John A. Shumann III, *Collector's Encyclopedia of American Art Glass*, Collector Books, 1988, 1996 value update.

**Collectors' Clubs:** Mount Washington Art Glass Society, P.O. Box 24094, Fort Worth, TX 76124.-1094; Pairpoint Cup Plate Collectors, P.O. Box 890052, East Weymouth, MA 02189.

**Museum:** Pairpoint Museum, Sagamore, MA.

## Burmese

Bowl, 12-1/2" d, 3-1/2" h, ruffled, deep color, c1920 .................... 675.00
Plate, 10" d, orig glossy finish, c1920 ......................................... 275.00
Vase, 8-1/2" h, 6" d, corset-shape, c1920 .................................... 450.00

## Cut Glass

Ashtray, 5-1/2" w, Savoy pattern, sterling silver top .................... 100.00
Baked Apple Dish, 7-1/2" d, tab handles, engraved apple dec... 175.00
Bowl, 9" d, 4" h, flared, Silver Leaf pattern ................................. 750.00
Box, cov, hinged, 8" w, 7" h, brilliant sawtooth cut insert, brass plate metal ware, sgd "Pairpoint, #3969" ......................................... 950.00
Candlestick
    9" h, engraved floral design, rayed star base ..................... 175.00
    10" h, engraved Thistle pattern ............................................ 550.00
    10-1/4", Hampton pattern .................................................... 250.00
    11" h, Barrington pattern, hollow center, engraved, price for pr ........................................................................................ 475.00
    11" h, Tyrone pattern, price for pr ....................................... 600.00
Cheese and Cracker, 10" d, Urn and Flame pattern ................... 150.00
Cigarette Holder, 4" l, Chelsea pattern, silver plate dolphin base, sgd ........................................................................................ 75.00
Cigarette Holder and Ashtray Combination, 5", etched florals ...... 60.00
Clock, 5" h, Choelus pattern, dome shape ................................... 275.00
Compote
    6" x 8", green, Wickham pattern, sterling silver base ......... 275.00
    6-1/2" x 6-1/2", Veneti pattern, red and white candy swirl stem ................................................................................ 550.00
Plate, 7" d, Mortensen's Butterfly, border of flat stars and hobstars, center engraved with butterfly and daisy .................................. 200.00
Punch Bowl, 12" d, 12" h, bowl cut in hobstar, vesica, and prism motif, silver and marble base .......................................................... 1,750.00
Rose Bowl, 6" d, Sultan pattern ................................................... 175.00
Urn, 8-1/2" h, blue cut glass body with Pattern #37 cutting, fancy silver plate with two handles in shape of swan's heads, emb rose garlands, sgd ........................................................................................ 525.00
    9" h, green cut glass body with Pattern #37 cutting, fancy gold wash silver plate with two handles in shape of swan's heads, emb rose garlands, sgd ................................................... 650.00
Vase
    10-1/2" h, bulbous top, narrow body, Cactus pattern .......... 175.00
    12" h, Buchanan pattern, chalice shape, controlled bubble stem, price for pr ........................................................................ 250.00
Water Pitcher, 8" h, Ramona pattern, squatty, triple notched handle .................................................................................. 450.00

Wine, 5" h, red and white swirl stem, etched grapes, leaves and acorns ................................................................................... 50.00

## Miscellaneous

Bowl, 9" d, 2-1/4" h, broad rim, deep bowl, colorless glass, engraved daisies rising from star cur base, minor nicks at base ............ 400.00
Console Set
    12" d bowl, pr matching mushroom-type candlesticks with black bases, Flambeau, tomato red, applied black glass foot, c1915 ................................................................................ 1,950.00
    12" d bowl, pr 3" h matching candlesticks, Tavern or Potato Glass, red, white, and green bouquet of flowers ......................... 575.00
Candelabrum, pr, 10-1/2" h, three arms, controlled bubble stem, engraved toot and finial, silver plate arms and base, sgd .......... 75.00
Candlestick
    9" h, solid blue, controlled bubble base ............................. 200.00
    10-1/2" h, solid green, controlled bubbles at base ............. 400.00
    12" h, solid yellow, controlled bubbles at base .................. 175.00
Ice Bucket, 5-1/2" h, engraved rising sun and polar bear, silverplated rim .......................................................................................... 50.00
Martini Glass, 5" h, Flambeu pattern, red bowl, black stem, silver overlay ....................................................................................... 225.00
Presentation Goblet, 11" h, flared cup, knobbed stem, elaborate lamp worked handles, dome base, etched and engraved with ship amidst circle of laurel leaves, base inscribed "Pairpoint Silvia" .......... 450.00
Salt Shaker, 7" h, solid blue, engraved vintage motif, silver top . 175.00
Tumbler, 5-1/4" h, 3-3/4" w, Tavern Glass, whale dec, numbered "D1516-281" on base .............................................................. 275.00
Vase
    5-1/2" h, teardrop shape, one green, other amber, Pattern #37 cutting, brass griffin's heads and marble base, price for pr ........ 400.00
    6-1/2" h, Tavern Glass, small flared mouth, oval form, bubbled colorless glass, enamel dec with whale in water, scalloped and linear trim, pontil sgd "D1510-281," c1927 ...................... 300.00
    8" h, 6" w, flip, Tavern Glass, all over random bubbles, enameled flowers in a vase dec, base numbered "D1513/285" ........ 275.00
    9" h, cornucopia shape, Kenwood pattern, controlled bubble base .................................................................................... 125.00
    9" h, 5-1/2" w, Delft, dec opal ware with rare pink color, windmill with a person on front, gold trim on base and top ........... 375.00
    12" h, amethyst, rolled rim, swollen body, colorless trapped bubble ball connection to amethyst glass disc base, engraved bow and scroll pattern around rim, floral engraved body, attributed to H. G. Gulbranson, second quarter 20th C, minor rim nick 500.00
    12" h, green, ftd, copperwheel engraved Wickham pattern 200.00
    12" h, vaseline, trumpet shape, controlled bubble stem, Vintage pattern engraving ......................................................... 350.00
    14" h, trumpet shape, Waterford pattern, amethyst rim, ball stem .................................................................................. 100.00

# PAPER EPHEMERA

**History:** Maurice Rickards, author of Collecting Paper Ephemera, suggests that ephemera are the "minor transient documents of everyday life," material destined for the wastebasket but never quite making it. This definition is more fitting than traditional dictionary definitions that emphasize time, e.g., "lasting a very short time." A driver's license, which is used for a year or longer, is as much a piece of ephemera as is a ticket to a sporting event or music concert. The transient nature of the object is the key.

Collecting ephemera has a long and distinguished history. Among the English pioneers were John Seldon (1584-1654), Samuel Pepys (1633-1703), and John Bagford (1650-1716). Large American collections can be found at historical societies and libraries across the country, and museums, e.g., Wadsworth Athenaeum, Hartford, CT, and the Museum of the City of New York.

When used by collectors, "ephemera" usually means paper objects, e.g., billheads and letterheads, bookplates, documents, labels, stocks and bonds, tickets, and valentines. However, more and more ephemera collectors are recognizing the transient nature of some three-dimensional material, e.g., advertising tins and pinback buttons. Today's specialized paper shows include dealers selling other types of ephemera in both two- and three-dimensional form.

**References:** Edwin Barnes and Wayne Dunn, *Cigar-Label Art Visual Encyclopedia with Index and Price Guide*, published by authors (P.O. Box 3, Lake Forest, CA 92630), 1995; Joe Davidson, *Fruit Crate Art*, Wellfleet Press, 1990; Patricia Fenn and Alfred P. Malpa, *Rewards of Merit*, Ephemera Society, 1994; Robert Forbes and Terrence Mitchell, *American Tobacco Cards: Price Guide and Checklist,* Tuff Stuff Books, 1999; John Henty, *The Collectable World of Mabel Lucie Attwell*, Richard Dennis Publications, distributed by Antique Collectors' Club, 1999; Gordon T. McClelland and Jay T. Last, *Fruit Box Labels*, Hillcrest Press (3412-G MacArthur Blvd., Santa Ana, CA 92704), 1995; Gerard S. Petrone, *Cigar Box Labels: Portraits of Life, Mirrors of History,* Schiffer, 1998. Robert Reed, *Paper Collectibles*, Wallace-Homestead/Krause, 1995; Kenneth W. Rendell, *Forging History*, University of Oklahoma Press, 1994; Gene Utz, *Collecting Paper*, Books Americana, 1993.

**Periodical:** *Biblio,* 845 Willamette St, Eugene, OR 87401; *Paper & Advertising Collector,* P.O. Box 500, Mount Joy, PA 17552; *Paper Collectors' Marketplace,* P.O. Box 128, Scandinavia, WI 54977.

**Collectors' Clubs:** Calendar Collector Society, American Resources, 18222 Flower Hill Way #299, Gaithersburg, MD 20879; Cigar Label Collectors International, P.O. Box 66, Sharon Center, OH 44274; Citrus Label Society, 131 Miramonte Dr., Fullerton, CA 92365; Cook Book Collectors Club of America, Inc., P.O. Box 56, St. James, MO 66559-0056; Cookbook Collectors' Exchange, P.O. Box 3269, San Jose, CA 95152.

Ephemera Society, 12 Fitzroy Sq, London W1P 5HQ England; Ephemera Society of America, Inc., P.O. Box 95, Cazenovia, NY 13035; Florida Citrus Label Collectors Association, P.O. Box 547636, Orlando, FL 32854; International Seal, Label & Cigar Band Society, 8915 E. Bellevue St., Tucson, AZ 85715; The Ephemera Society of Canada, 36 Macauley Dr., Thornhill, Ontario L3T 5S5 Canada; National Association of Paper & Advertising Collectors, P.O. Box 500, Mount Joy, PA 17552; Society of Antique Label Collectors, P.O. Box 24811, Tampa, FL 33623.

**Additional Listings:** See Advertising Trade Cards; Catalogs; Comic Books; Photographs; Sports Cards. Also see Calendars, Catalogs, Magazines, Newspapers, Photographs, Postcards, and Sheet Music in *Warman's Americana & Collectibles*.

**Billhead, Edward Norton Co., Bennington, VT, dated July 6, 1896, 8-1/2" x 7", $70. Photo courtesy of Vicki & Bruce Waasdrop.**

## Account Books and Ledgers

7-1/2" x 9-1/2", Newbury Tax Log, Newbury, PA, 1755, booklet containing order by the assessors of Newbury to Anbros Berry, Constable, to collect taxes due to town and province, lists towns people, amount collector, tears, wear .............................................. 115.00
7-3/4" x 12-1/4", family type, James Short, Newbury, MA, 1743-96, leather bound, tears, staining, wear, descended in family ....... 230.00
11" x 7", Issac Manchester's Business Book, 1786 ................... 150.00
Receipts, 1824 to 1853, New York state, rents, repairs, shares of income for work performed, worn............................................. 150.00

## Bill Heads, Letterheads, Receipts

5-1/2" x 9-3/4", C. W. Cummins, 1897, Smyrna, DE, receipt for shipment of 6,200 bushels of yellow corn in good condition by C. W. Cummins on Schooner *Shipcarpenters*, lying in port of Smyrna, and mount for New York, March 19, 1857......................................... 14.00
8-1/2" x 7", Edward Norton Co., Bennington, Vt, dated Oct 1895, in the amount of $4.32 ........................................................... 70.00
8-1/2" x 7", Monmouth Pottery Co., Monmouth, Illinois, engraving of factory, orig company logo, dated Dec 23, 1897 ....................... 60.00

## Calendars

1899, Squeezers Playing Cards, NY Consolidated Card Co., foldout, 5-1/2" w, 6" h ................................................................ 375.00
1900, Try Star Eagle Cigars, diecut of pretty woman, 4-1/2" w, 11" h, professionally matted and framed, no calendar pages ............ 200.00
1907, Grand Union Tea Co, Brooklyn, NY, diecut, litho by Sackett & Wilhems, young girl with puppy color graphics, 10-1/2" w, 29-1/2" l, professionally framed, 14" w, 32" l ........................................ 350.00
1908, Grand Union Tea Co., Brooklyn, NY, diecut, little girl with doll, tea set on small table, 11" w, 29" h.............................................. 400.00
1913, Winchester, by American Litho, NY, artist Robert Robinson, bands top and bottom, November page only, dry mounted, 15-1/2" w, 30" l ..................................................................................... 850.00

## Cigar Labels

Affecionada. Faber, Coe & Gregg, Inc. ........................................ 8.00
Apter's Don-Remo ...................................................................... 6.50
Conning, Geo............................................................................... 8.00
Dolly Madison ............................................................................. 5.00
Golden Veil, Chas. L. Boak, Harrisburg, Pa............................... 10.00
Ideolo .......................................................................................... 8.00
La Estampa................................................................................... 3.50
La Favorita de Tampa ................................................................. 3.50
La Flor de Garcia y Vega, Fine Cigars Since 1882..................... 10.00
La Granda, Quality Cigar ............................................................. 3.50
La Saolo, Mild Blend .................................................................. 10.00
Marshall Field, Don't Bite - Just Lite .......................................... 10.00
Miss Primrose ............................................................................. 8.00
Natividad. El Primo Cigar Company, San Francisco, CA.............. 8.00
Our Kitties, black and white cat, white ground .......................... 10.00
Quaker Cigar................................................................................ 10.00
Reina Bella.................................................................................. 10.00
Senator Dixon .............................................................................. 7.00
Sonny Boy, Quality Cigar ............................................................. 3.50
Souvenir National Convention, 1948, Phila. Pa. ........................... 7.50

## Cook Booklets

Armour Ham, 60 Ways To Serve ham, 28 pgs, 1930s .................. 15.00
Baker's Choice, Choice Recipes, 64 pgs, 1926 ........................... 15.00
Betty Crocker, Your Share, 48 pgs, 1943 ..................................... 5.00
Bond Bread, Bond Bread Cook Book, 72 pgs, 1935 .................... 15.00
Crisco, Recipes For Good Eating, 64 pgs, 1944 .......................... 10.00
Del Monte, Del Monte Peaches, 11 Food Experts. 1927 ............. 15.00
Diamond Walnuts Menu Magic in Nutshell, 32 pgs, 1940 .............. 9.00
Dole Pineapple, Kingdom That Grew Out of Little Boy's Garden,
    1930 .................................................................................... 14.00
General Foods, Recipes For Today, 40 pgs, 1943 ...................... 10.00
Gold Medal Party Cakes, 24 pgs, 1931 ........................................ 8.00
Heinz, 57 Ways To Use Heinz Condensed Soups, 38 pgs, 1944 ... 6.00
Hellmann's, Salad Ideas, 16 pgs, 1929 ..................................... 16.00
Hershey Cocoa, Story of Chocolate and Cocoa, 24 pgs, 1934 .... 10.00
McCormack Cookbook; 5" x 7-7/8", 32 pgs ................................ 34.00
Spry, Aunt Jenny's Favorite Recipes, 48 pgs, 1943 ...................... 8.00
Standard Brands, The Bread Basket, 40 pgs, 1942 ...................... 7.50
Swans Down, How to Bake by Ration Book, 24 pgs, 1943 .......... 10.00
Worchester Salt Cook Book, 32 pgs, 1931 ................................. 12.50

## Drawing

5-1/2" h, 6-3/4" w, opaque watercolor on laid ledger paper, folksy
    rooster, red, green, yellow, blue, and black, dated 1812, stains, wide
    pine 9-3/4" h, 11" w frame ..................................................... 1,760.00
6" h, 5" w, watercolor and pencil on paper, red headed bird, blooming
    thistle, stains and ghost image of earlier mat, old 8-1/8" h, 6-3/4" w
    mahogany veneer frame ........................................................ 225.00
8-1/2" h, 6-3/4" w, watercolor on paper, lover's knot maze, two pairs of
    love birds flanked by heart arrangements, sgd "Miss Hannah E. Bill-
    ings Present from Orpah Sterns," framed, general toning, minor
    staining ................................................................................. 490.00
9" h, 7" w, watercolor on wove paper, bird on branch, shades of brown,
    blue, black, yellow, red, and green, minor fly specks and stains, old
    red and black sponged 11-3/4" h, 9-7/8" w frame ................... 350.00
9-1/8" w, 11-5/8" h, watercolor and graphite on heavy paper, full
    length profile portrait of Judge Green, Newark, Licking County,
    Judge seated in black wingback chair, fireplace, pocket watch,
    books and pictures in background, old paper label on backboard
    reads "John Green's likeness taken at the age of 80 by his grand-
    son Nath. E. Green 1841," sgd on front also, short biography of
    Judge on back, affixed to larger backboard, bird's eye maple
    veneer frame ......................................................................... 990.00

**Gus Becht Butcher's Supply, Calendar, 1891, full pad, litho by Gast, St. Louis & NY, 10" w, 14" l, $950. Photo courtesy of Past Tyme Pleasures**

Rule Book, *Rules Governing the Royal Game of Billiards,* Compliments of the Brunswick-Balke-Collender Co., Chicago, IL, 1914, 48 pgs, rules, colored picture of accessories and 8 cuts of various pool tables, 3-5/8" x 6-3/8", $215. Photo courtesy of Kenneth E. Schneringer

## Flyer

4" x 11-3/4", Howard Athenaum, 1861, "Flyer of E. L. Davenport Pre-
    sents Edwin Booth as the Duke of Gloster," announcements of the
    coming of Richard III and Census, see through paper ............... 15.00
5-1/2" x 8-1/2", Putnam Nail Co., Boston, MA, 1890, cut of their logo
    with horseshoe, nail and seven horseshoes inside larger shoe, brown
    paper .................................................................................... 20.00
6" x 9-1/2", James M. Taylor & Co., New York, NY, 1860, dry goods,
    broad black lettering ............................................................. 25.00
6-1/2" x 10-1/2", Cribb Carriage Co., Milwaukee, WI, c1900, "Flyer of
    our New Wheel the Cribb," cream paper, brown ink, highlighted with
    blue ink writing, two cuts of bicycles with prices of the "Cribb" .. 15.00
9" x 15-1/2", West Virginia Marconi Co., Clarksburg, WV, yellow and
    red ink on blue paper, products manufactured from Durim wheat
    semoina, samples, 39 illus ..................................................... 25.00
12" x 6-3/4", A. L. Tyler, Charlemont, MA, Feb 20, 1889, newsprint,
    closing out of boys, mens and youths overcoats and ulsters ....... 8.00

## Miscellaneous

Checks
    State Emergency Relief Board, Harrisburg, PA ..................... 3.50
    The State Bank of Belmont ................................................... 3.50
Cut-out, baptismal gift for god child, inscribed in ink, watercolor and pin-
    pick highlights, Europe, 19th C, minor imperfections, 12-1/2" d .... 375.00
Document, Monmouth Mutual Fire Insurance Company, policy, partly
    printed, 1846, filled out by hand ................................................ 75.00
Fan, McCormick Bee Brand Spices, 7" sq, wood handle, creased,
    bright colors ........................................................................ 100.00
Ink Blotter
    Geo. Amey, Richlandtown, PA, unused ................................. 5.00
    Gulf Fuel Oil, 5-3/4" x 2-3/4" ............................................... 28.00
    Kelly Heavy Duty Cord, 6-1/4" x 3-3/8", slight rubbing to cor-
        ners ................................................................................. 35.00
    Kelly Springfield Tires, ink blotter; 10" x 3-7/8" ................... 65.00
Menu, The Grist Mill Gazette, New York, NY, 1884, 4 pgs, 11-1/2' x 16-
    1/2", Vol. XVII, no. 22, heavy stock paper, Jimmy Denicola's Grist Mill
    Bill of Fare, plus history of mill ............................................... 28.00

## Newspaper Illustration,

Harper's Weekly, sight size

Scene on the Levee at New Orleans on the Departure of the Paroled Rebel Prisoners, Feb 20, 1863, sketched by Hamilton, 15-1/2" x 21"..................................................220.00
The Flood in the Mississippi, dated May 14, 1859, 10" x 14-1/2"150.00
The Sugar Harvest in Louisiana, drawn by A. R. Ward, 10" x 14"....250.00
Premium List, E. H. Pardee, New Haven, CT, c1888, 4 pgs, 10-3/4" x 16-1/4", folded, jewelry, silverware, novelties, 69 illus ...............26.00
Price List
    Albert C. Kuck, New York, NY, c1880, 5-1/2" x 8-1/2", 4 pgs, list of pistols, revolvers, and cartridges........................................25.00
    Dewitt Wire Cloth Co., Philadelphia, PA, c1880, 1 page, 10-3/4" x 13-1/2", broadside, galvanized wire netting for making your own poultry fencing, 7 illus........................................................20.00
    A. Zimmerman & Co., New York, NY, 1875, 1 page, 8-1/2" x 5-1/2", broadside, Blauvelt's Patent self locking and extension step ladders, two illus.........................................................12.00
Vaudeville Program, Jan 24, 1910, American Theatre, Daveport, Iowa, "The Pride of Davenport," 8 pgs, 8 vaudeville acts, ads for local merchants..................................................................................12.00
Wallpaper Book, Sears, Roebuck & Co., Chicago, IL, 62 pgs, 8-3/4" x 12-3/4", 1931 Style Book, "Certified Fadeproof Wall Paper & Colored Pages of Pressed Wall Hangings, Wall Hangings, Panel Binders, Art Cloth, etc." actual wall paper samples ........................................42.00

# PAPERWEIGHTS

**History:** Although paperweights had their origin in ancient Egypt, it was in the mid-19th century that this art form reached its zenith. The finest paperweights were produced between 1834 and 1855 in France by the Clichy, Baccarat, and Saint Louis factories. Other weights made in England, Italy, and Bohemia during this period rarely match the quality of the French weights.

In the early 1850s, the New England Glass Co. in Cambridge, Massachusetts, and the Boston and Sandwich Glass Co. in Sandwich, Massachusetts, became the first American factories to make paperweights.

Popularity peaked during the classic period (1845-1855) and faded toward the end of the 19th century. Paperweight production was rediscovered nearly a century later in the mid-1900s. Contemporary weights still are made by Baccarat, Saint Louis, Perthshire, and many studio craftsmen in the U.S. and Europe.

**References:** *Annual Bulletin of the Paperweight Collectors Association, Inc.*, available from association (P.O. Box 1263, Beltsville, MD 20704), 1996; Andrew H. Dohan, *The Dictionary of Paperweight Signature Canes: Identification and Dating*, Paperweight Press, 1997; Monika Flemming and Peter Pommerencke, *Paperweights of the World*, 3rd ed., Schiffer Publishing, 2000; Paul Jokelson and Dena Tarshis, *Baccarat Paperweights and Related Glass*, Paperweight Press, 1990; Edith Mannoni, *Classic French Paperweights*, Paperweight Press, 1984; Bonnie Pruitt, *St. Clair Glass Collectors Guide*, published by author, 1992; Pat Reilly, *Paperweights*, Running Press, Courage Books, 1994; Lawrence H. Selman, *All About Paperweights*, Paperweight Press, 1992; ——, *Art of the Paperweight*, Paperweight Press, 1988; ——, *Art of the Paperweight,* Perthshire, Paperweight Press, 1983; ——, *Art of the Paperweight, Saint Louis*, Paperweight Press, 1981 (all of the Paperweight Press books are distributed by Charles E. Tuttle Co., 1996); John Simmonds, *Paperweights from Great Britain*, Schiffer Publishing, 2000; Colin Terris, *The Charlton Standard Catalogue of Caithness Paperweights*, Charlton Press, 1999.

**Collectors' Clubs:** Caithness Collectors Club, 141 Lanza Ave., Building 12, Garfield, NJ 07026; International Paperweight Society, 761 Chestnut St., Santa Cruz, CA 95060; Paperweight Collectors Association Inc., P.O. Box 1059, Easthampton, MA 01027; Paperweight Collectors Association of Chicago, 535 Delkir Ct, Naperville, IL 60565; Paperweight Collectors Association of Texas, 1631 Aguarena Springs Dr., #408, San Marcos, TX 78666.

**Museums:** Bergstrom-Mahler Museum, Neenah, WI; Corning Museum of Glass, Corning, NY; Degenhart Paperweight & Glass Museum, Inc., Cambridge, OH; Museum of American Glass at Wheaton Village, Millville, NJ.

## Antique

Baccarat, France, 19th C
    Closely packed millefiori canes, 1-3/4" d, 1-1/4" h, minor wear................................................................635.00
    Double Garland, double trefoil garland of red and white canes centered by ring of blue canes, pink white and green cane, 3" d, 2" h, minor wear..............................................490.00
Clichy, France, 19th C
    Bottle, squat spherical body of colorless glass, dec internally with complex millefiori canes set concentrically on lace ground, 3-1/2" d, 3-1/2" h, stopper missing ....................................2,185.00
    Chequer, complex millefiori canes centered by pink and green Clichy rose, all divided by white latticinio twists, 2-3/4" d, 2" h......1,265.00
    End of Day, closely packed complex millefiori canes, including two pink and green Clichy roses, 3" d, 2-1/4" h, minor wear.......865.00
    Garland, trefoil of purple millefiori canes with seven complex canes interspersed including a pink and green Clichy rose, crystal ground, 2-1/2" d, 1-1/2" h, minor wear .......................635.00
    Millefiori, complex millefiori centered by pink and green Clichy rose set on colorless crystal, 3" d, 2-3/8" h, small inclusion, minor wear .............................................................1,380.00
    Millefiori, complex millefiori centered by pink and green Clichy rose set concentrically on green moss ground, 2-3/4" d, 2-1/8" h, minor wear ..........................................................13,800.00

Cristal D'Albret, John and Jacqueline Kennedy, emerald green ground, orig paper label, $200.

Millefiori, complex millefiori canes set in colorless crystal, 1-3/4" d, 1-3/8" h .................................. 375.00
Millefiori on Lace, complex millefiori canes set concentrically on white lace ground, 2-1/2" d, 1-7/8" h, inclusions, minor wear .......................... 865.00

Libbey
Frosted bust of woman, World's Fair 1893, 3" h ................. 600.00
Souvenir, showing Libbey Glass Company, 1893, 4" d ...... 275.00

New England Glass Company, MA, 19th C
Millefiori, concentric rings of millefiori canes, turquoise, blue, and white, centered by ten point star cane, 2-1/2" d, 1-3/4" h, off-center, minor wear .......................... 320.00
Millefiori, concentric rings of white and alternating turquoise, red, and blue canes centered by yellow cane, white latticinio cushion, 2-1/4" d, 1-1/2" h, inclusions, minor wear .................. 260.00
Pear, chartreuse with light blush color layering on colorless cooking glass base, 3" d, 2-1/4" h .......................... 690.00
Pink Flower, striated pink five-petal flowers, millefiori cane center, pink bud on deep green leafy stem, white latticinio bed, 2-1/4" d, 1-3/4" h, minor wear .......................... 690.00

Saint Louis, France, 19th C, concentric millefiori, five complex millefiori canes in blue centered by yellow, red, and blue cane, all surrounded by ring of pink and green millefiori canes, set on white latticinio bed, 2-1/2" d, 1-3/4" h, minor wear .................. 435.00

Sandwich Glass Company, Sandwich, MA, c1875
Dahlia, white flower, trapped air bubbles, centered by complex cane of red, yellow, and blue, two green leaves and stem, 3" d, 1-5/8" h, minor wear .......................... 1,265.00
Flower, poinsettia-type cobalt blue flower, trapped air bubbles, centered by whit rose-style cane, five light green leaves and stem, 2-3/4" d, 2" h .......................... 690.00
Fruit in Basket, symmetrical arrangement of pears and cherries, emerald green leaves, trapped air bubbles, white latticino ground, 2-1/2" d, 2" h, small inclusions, minor wear ........ 425.00

St. Louis
Faceted floral, upright bouquet, fourteen-point inside cane, recessed diamond-cut base, 3-1/8" d .......................... 2,000.00
Fruit, white latticino basket enclosing cluster of two green pears, striped apple, four cherries, green serrated leaves, 3-1/4" d .......................... 1,850.00

Sandwich
Cherries, two shaded red cherries pendent from green branch, four serrated leaves, 2-15/16" d .......................... 700.00
Poinsettia, flower composed of two rows of six overlapping red pointed petals, red, green, and white Clichy rose cane stamen, curved stem, four variegated leaves, one leaf off to side, 3-7/16" d .......................... 800.00

## Modern

Ayotte, Rick
Bird, compound weight, black-capped tan bird on blossoming branches, yellow cased to white ground, inscribed "Ayotte 1/1 '85," 3-1/2" d .......................... 575.00
Flower, fruit, seed pod, white, red, and purple cycle, green leafy stem, "Ayotte Ed. 50 '92," 3-3/4" d .......................... 550.00

Baccarat
Concentric ring, multicolored millefiore garlands, central cane of arrowheads, 2-1/2" d .......................... 250.00
Dahlia, pink and white fleur-de-lis center cane, twelve-petal white blossom, side bud, blue transparent ground, "B1970" cane, 3-3/8" d .......................... 150.00

Banford, Bob
Cornflower, blue flower, yellow center, pink and white twisted torsade, "B" cane at stem, 3" d .......................... 550.00
Flower bouquet, five red stemmed blossoms, "B" cane below, diamond cut recessed base, 3-1/4" d .......................... 475.00
Iris and rose, purple, blue, and pink irises, center pink roe, recessed diamond-cut base, "B" cane at stem, 3" d ........ 250.00

Banford, Bobbie, aquarium, three exotic green fish among sea plants

and shells, "B" cane on and, 3-3/8" d .......................... 350.00
Clichy, panel pattern, pink, white, and rose red clusters around central red on white cane, green cushion, fold at edge, 2-1/2" d ........ 475.00

Kaziun, Charles, MA, late 20th C
Millefiori, cluster of canes, one with gold "K," pink torsade, clear pedestal base, 1-1/2" h .......................... 500.00
Miniature, pedestal, small glass sphere, upright white spider lily with orange and yellow center, four green leaves, dark blue aventurine ground, gold "K" signature, 1-1/4" d, 2-7/8" h . 230.00
Yellow rose, upright flower, four green leaves, center "K" and seven hearts, star-cut base, 2-1/4" d .......................... 575.00

Rosenfeld, Ken
Bouquet, red and lilac blossoms among white flowers and buds, green leafy stems, translucent blue ground, signature cane, inscribed "4/25 Ken Rosenfeld '93," 3-1/4" d, 2-3/4" h ..... 500.00
Spray of exotic lavender bellflowers, dark centered yellow flowers on leafy stems, "R" cane, sgd "Ken Rosenfeld '94" at side, 3-3/8" d .......................... 500.00

Salazar, David, compound floral, lavender six-petal poinsettia star blossom, three-leaf stem over green and red wreath, white ground, inscribed "David Salazar/111405/Lundberg Studios 1991," 3-1/4" d ............ 225.00

Stankard, Paul, New Jersey
Blackberries, spray of yellow and pale blue wildflowers with three blackberries on yellow-green leafy stem, spirit and word canes underneath, signature cane, inscribed, "Paul J. Stankard F 44 '95," 2-3/4" d, 2-1/4" h .......................... 2,645.00
Jack-in-the-Pulpit, central green and maroon throated jack-in-the-pulpit over blueberries, flanked by four yellow flowers, pink blossoms, moss enclosing spirits and word canes, signature cane, inscribed, "Paul J. Standard N39, '96," 2-3/4" d, 2-1/4" h ..................... 2,300.00
St. Louis, Honeycomb, carpet of numerous hollow sienna canes, central red, white, and blue composite cane, sgd and dated "SL 1988" .......................... 1,200.00

Taristano, Debbie, MA, late 20th C
Floral bouquet, light blue, cobalt blue, pale pink, and yellow blossoms, upright yellow stamens, budded green leaf stems, signature cane underneath, star cut base, 3-3/4" d, 2-1/2" h ... 575.00
Pansy, two central blue and yellow pansies flanked by three rose-pink blossoms, three yellow blossoms, green leafy stems, signature cane underneath, 3-1/4" d, 2" h .......................... 920.00

Townsend, Milon, leopard frog, deep blue and opal, perched on oval weight of marbled tauge and cream with colorless bubble windows base inscribed with title, illegible signature, and date "1999," 2-1/4" d, 3-1/4" h .......................... 350.00

Trabucco, Victor, Buffalo, NY
Camellia, pink camellia bud and blossoms, upright yellow stamens, leafy green stems, inscribed "Trabucco 1982 6/50," 3" d, 2-1/4" h .......................... 350.00
Pear branch, yellow centered white blossom and buds, two red and yellow fruits, inscribed "Trabucco 1995" at lower edge, 3-1/4" d .......................... 650.00

Wheaton Village, Millville, NJ, upright lavender blossoming rising from mottled white pot, air trap center, air bubble patterned surround, base imp with "WV" monogram, 2-3/4" d, 2-3/4" h .......................... 65.00

# PAPIER-MÂCHÉ

**History:** Papier-mâché is a mixture of wood pulp, glue, resin, and fine sand which is subjected to great pressure and then dried. The finished product is tough, durable, and heat resistant. Various finishing treatments are used, such as enameling, japanning, lacquering, mother-of-pearl inlaying, and painting.

During the Victorian era papier-mâché articles such as boxes, trays, and tables were in high fashion. Banks, candy containers, masks, toys, and other children's articles were also made of papier-mâché.

Bread Tray, 14-1/4" l, cartouche shape, blood red, floral spray and butterfly dec, cavetto and shaped border, gilt edge, black under surface, England, c1820 ................................................500.00

Figure, 23"-1/4" h, comic male figure, brightly colored polychrome paint, spot welded high wheel bicycle, 20th C ......................1,750.00

Folio Cover, 16-1/2" l, MOP inlaid, painted, depicting Pliny Doves, foliate borders, Victorian, mid-19th C, losses ...............................200.00

Lap Desk, 14" w, 11" d, 4-1/2" h, painted and gilt stenciled, MOP inlaid, lid painted with still life of fruit, bombe sides resting on flattened feet, foliate gilt stenciling throughout ext. and int., minor losses to stenciling, Victorian mid 19th C .........................................................865.00

Match Safe, pill box-style
   2-1/2" w, large cathedral on cover .........................................95.00
   2-5/8", gilt design, name inside cover ....................................45.00

Milliner's Model, 13-1/2" h, papier-mâché shoulder head, molded and painted black hair with side wave brought back to molded braided bun, painted brown eyes, single stroke brows, closed mouth, kid body with wooden lower arms and lower legs, old pink print dress................475.00

Snuff Box, 3-3/8" d, 7/8" h, round, double lid, top lid with scene of hunter, attendant, and dog, inner lid with erotic couple, 19th C, wear ...............................................................................175.00

Table
   Games, 21-3/4" d, 18-3/4" h, circular top, mother-of-pearl inset, gilt dec, gaming board, paneled baluster support, shaped base, four scrolled feet, Victorian, mid 19th C.............................575.00
   Occasional, 20-1/2" w, 17" d, 28-1/2" h, shaped oval tilting top, gilt and mother-of-pearl inset border, center scene of two men gazing at ruins, conforming inlays, bulbous ebonized standard on molded base, scrolled feet on casters, gilt and polychrome accents, Victorian, fourth quarter 19th C ..........................750.00

Tea Caddy, 5-3/4" h, 7 2/3" w, MOP inlay, English......................200.00

Toy, Roly Poly, clown, 4-1/4" h, German ......................................90.00

Tray
   8" d, black lacquered and parcel gilt dec, imp mark, Jennens and Bettridge, Birmingham, c1850...........................................40.00

Tray on Stand
   20-1/2" l, 16" d, 20-1/2" h, rounded rect, elaborate oriental seascape, Victorian, third quarter 19th C, later ebonized faux bamboo stand with gilt accents ...............................................525.00
   25-1/2" l, 19" w, 21-1/2" h, serpentine outlined form, japanned and dec with gilt arabesques, imp "Jennens and Bettridge, Makers to the Queen," Victorian, second quarter 19th C, faux bamboo stand of a later date ....................................................1,320.00
   29" w, 22-1/2" d, 21-1/2" h, rounded rect top, elaborate figural oriental landscape, Victorian, third quarter 19th C, later ebonized faux bamboo stand with gilt accents ..................................825.00

Wine Coasters, 5-1/2" d, red lacquered, scrolled gilt foliage borders, English, 19th C, price for pr .....................................................260.00

# PARIAN WARE

**History:** Parian ware is a creamy white, translucent porcelain that resembles marble. It originated in England in 1842 and was first called "statuary porcelain." Minton and Copeland have been credited with its development; Wedgwood also made it. In America, parian ware objects were manufactured by Christopher Fenton in Bennington, Vermont.

At first parian ware was used only for figures and figural groups. By the 1850s, it became so popular that a vast range of items was manufactured.

**References:** Paul Atterbury, ed., *The Parian Phenomenon,* Shepton Beauchamp, 1989; Susan and Al Bagdade, *Warman's English & Continental Pottery & Porcelain*, 3rd Edition, Krause Publications, 1998; G. A. Godden, *Victorian Porcelain,* Herbert Jenkins, 1961; Kathy Hughes, *Col-*

**Figure, seated young girl with bird on shoulder, imp "Copeland," 13-1/2" h, $325.**

*lector's Guide to Nineteenth-Century Jugs* (1985, Routledge & Kegan Paul), Vol. II (1991, Taylor Publishing).

**Museum:** Victoria & Albert Museum, London, England.

Bust
   7-3/4" h, Mozart, torso resting on sq plinth, imp mark of R. & L. Robinson and Leadbeater, Hanley, third quarter 19th C ..............200.00
   7-3/4" h, Sir Walter Scott, torso resting on sq plinth, imp mark of R. & L. Robinson and Leadbeater, Hanley, third quarter 19th C ...200.00
   9-3/4" h, Sir Robert Burns, clothed in period attire, spreading socle base, third quarter 19th C........................................175.00
   15-1/2" h, Charles Dickens, waisted circular socle, England, 19th C .................................................................................575.00
   16" h, maiden, parian, garland of flowers in hair, black pedestal base ..............................................................................195.00

Figure
   8-1/2" d, Dying Gladiator, modeled on oval base, imp "Crystal Palace Art Union," factory mark for Bates, Brown-Westhead & Moore, England, c1860, rim chips....................................690.00
   13" h and 13-1/2" h, allegorical cherubs, Art and Literature, England, c1855-70, price for pr.......................................660.00
   13-1/4" h, child seated on trunk, England, 19th C, price for pr..............................................................................1,265.00
   22-3/8" h, Mercury, imp mark for Robinson and Leadbeater, England, late 19yh C, chips to base, hairline to wrist.......980.00
   22-1/2" h, fisherman, scantily clad man holding net, England, 19th C, restoration................................................................690.00

Pitcher
   2-5/8" h, gentlemen toasting, third quarter 19th C.................40.00
   3-1/2" h, modeled with shells, third quarter 19th C...............40.00
   4-1/2" h, floral motif, third quarter 19th C ..............................50.00

Vase
   5-1/4" h, modeled with a bird, third quarter 19th C...............45.00
   7" h, bud, bulbous, twin handles modeled as cattails and water lilies, third quarter 19th C ...................................................40.00
   7" h, large center upright shell, figures of children on either side, third quarter 19th C.........................................................50.00
   7-1/4" h, applied grape clusters, third quarter 19th C...........60.00
   11" h, figural, Paul and Virginia, harvesting grapes, third quarter 19th C, price for pr........................................................400.00

# PATE-DE-VERRE

**History:** The term "pate-de-verre" can be translated simply as "glass paste." It is manufactured by grinding lead glass into a powder or crystal

form, making it into a paste by adding a 2% or 3% solution of sodium silicate, molding, firing, and carving. The Egyptians discovered the process as early as 1500 B.C.

In the late 19th century, the process was rediscovered by a group of French glassmakers. Almaric Walter, Henri Cros, Georges Despret, and the Daum brothers were leading manufacturers.

Contemporary sculptors are creating a second renaissance, led by the technical research of Jacques Daum.

Ashtray, 6-1/4" l, 3-1/2" w, center medallion with Egyptian head, molded in reds and purples, small flower buds around edge, raised lattice work on bottom ......................................................... 1,650.00
Atomizer, 5-3/4" h, red berries, green leaves, molded signature "H. Berge" ........................................................................ 1,200.00
Bowl
    4-3/4" h, oviform, turquoise blue ground, molded green band of stylized flowers, molded "A. Walter Nancy" .................. 1,600.00
    9-3/4" d, 4" h, octagonal coupe, solid foot, dec by swags of stylized leafy purple and black branches, mottled colorless near transparent background, ext. molded "G. Argy Rousseau" ........... 6,500.00
    Dish, large, butterfly, script sgd "Daum Nancy, France" ...... 200.00
Inkwell, double, 6-1/2" l, 3" h, black and brown beetle, brilliant orange and yellow glass, central beetle motif, orig conforming covers, sgd "Walter" ................................................................................ 4,500.00
Jewelry
    Earrings, pr, 2-3/4" l, teardrop for, molded violet and rose shaded tulip blossom, suspended from rose colored swirl molded circle ....................................................................... 2,200.00
    Pendant, 2-1/8" x 2-1/4", pierced glass, butterfly, blue, green, red-orange wings, colorless and gray ground, inscribed "GAR" in design (G. Argy-Rousseau) .................................................. 2,415.00
Paperweight, 3-1/2" l, 1" h, swan, brown, green opalescent ground, sgd "A. Walter," some wear .............................................. 150.00
Plate, 9-1/2" d, pierced border, white slip dec cherub within raised gilt framed cartouche, one with salmon ground, other with brown ground, one signed for Albion Birks, imp and printed Minton marks, c1856, price for pair ......................................................................... 4,900.00
Sculpture
    8" h, Faune, man/goat, gray-green glass, inscribed "66/250" on base, mkd "Daum/J. P. Demarchi" on neck and plinth, 1980s............................................................................. 690.00
    10-3/4" h, seated cat, gray-green glass, inscribed "53/250" on base, mkd in mold, c1980 ................................................. 690.00
    Tray, 7" l, 5" w, angular mottled orange-yellow oval, full bodied black and brown center scarab, imp "A. Walter/Nancy" ............... 2,750.00
Vase
    5-1/8" h, striated aubergine purple and colorless cone shaped body, integrated disk foot molded with four repeating spiked devices, imp "Decorchemont" in horseshoe stamp, numbered C199 on base................................................................ 3,600.00
    5-1/4" h, 4-7/8" l, golden amber and brown ground, central conical bud vase in oval plinth base, molded and stylized birds of prey at each side, mkd "G. Argy-Rousseau" ......................... 4,025.00
    9" h, molded goblet form, yellow amber ground, shaded green to orange at base, highly detailed and realistic green-black lizard wrapped around stem, imp "A. Walter" and "H. Berge SC," orig thin rim area .................................................................. 6,325.00
Veilleuse, night light, 6-1/2" h, domed form, deep aqua blue glass, molded trailing vines, yellow flower, mounted on circular wrought-iron stand, removable domed cap molded "A. Walter Nancy" ...... 6,000.00
Vide Pouche, irregular shaped dish
    6-1/4" l, welled crescent shape, mottled tangerine shading to pale lemon, molded along with side with two spotted langoustines, one teal, the other burgundy, molded "A. Walter Nancy" and "Berge S.C." ......................................................................... 4,000.00
    6-3/4" l, 3-3/4" h, shallow oval, mottled orange and black, surmounted by green spotted black lizard molded in full relief, molded "A. Walter Nancy Berge" ...........................................4,500.00

# PATE-SUR-PATE

**History:** Pate-sur-pate, paste-on-paste, is a 19th-century porcelain-decorating method featuring relief designs achieved by painting layers of thin pottery paste one on top of the other.

About 1880, Marc Solon and other Sevres artists, inspired by a Chinese celadon vase in the Ceramic Museum at Sevres, experimented with this process. Solon emigrated to England at the outbreak of the Franco-Prussian War and worked at Minton, where he perfected pate-sur-pate.

**References:** Paul Atterbury and Maureen Batkin, *Dictionary of Minton,* Antique Collectors Club, Ltd., 1996; Susan and Al Bagdade, *Warman's English & Continental Pottery & Porcelain*, 3rd Edition, Krause Publications, 1998; Bernard Bumpers, *Pate-Sur-Pate,* Barrie & Jenkins, 1992; G. .A. Godden, *Victorian Porcelains,* Herbert Jenkins, 1961.

**Museums:** National Collection of Fine Arts, Smithsonian Institution, Washington, DC; Victoria & Albert Museum, London, England.

Book Stand, 16" l, walnut veneer, pate-sur-pate end panels with cupids playing badminton, Bettemann's patent, sold by Shreve Crump and Low.................................................................................... 500.00
Box, cov, 7-3/4" d, circular, white relief of figure on chariot, blue ground, cobalt blue rim band, gilt trim lines, illegible printed marks, Continental, late 19th/early 20th C ......................................... 175.00
Centerpiece, 11" l, cartouches with putti, ivory and gilt reserves, brown ground, imp and printed Minton factory m arks, dec by H Holls, c1872 ................................................................ 1,500.00
Lamp Base
    11-1/2" h vase, dark brown ground, white classical relief of female with cherub, gilt trim, Lawrence Birks, England, late 19th C................................................................................ 1,495.00
    15-3/4" h vase, dark brown ground, white classical relief, sgd "F Peyrat," France, c1875.................................................. 1,100.00
Pendant, 2-1/2" h, 2" w, oval, black and red cicada, purple ground, orig silk cord, incised "GAR" for G. Argy Rousseau ..................... 1,100.00
Plaque
    6" d, circular, Helios and his horses, white figures, celadon ground, inscribed monogram and "Limoges" .................. 120.00
    10-3/4" d, oval, blue ground, white dec of child reaching for bunch of grapes, dec and sgd "Taxile Doat, France, 1874" ..... 1,495.00
    19-1/4" d, brown and green Art Nouveau style, floral dec ground, five blue ground rect-form pate-sur-pate panels with classical genre scenes, sgd "Taxile Doat, 1901," marked "Sevres" .........29,900.00

**Box, cov, blue background, white classical figures, mkd "M. Limoges," 4-7/8" sq, $170.**

Portrait Vase, 9-1/2" h, Art Nouveau style, central mauve ground, portrait on teal blue ground, cherub in relief, gilt banded borders and foliate relief, France, late 19th C ................................................... 460.00
Tray, 5 x 3", elegant lady, cobalt blue ground, Limoges Barbatine 75.00
Vase, 13" h, porcelain, gilt banded and foliate borders, central relief of birds within landscape, France, 19th C, pr .............................. 920.00

# PATTERN GLASS

**History:** Pattern glass is clear or colored glass pressed into one of hundreds of patterns. Deming Jarves of the Boston and Sandwich Glass Co. invented one of the first successful pressing machines in 1828. By the 1860s, glass-pressing machinery had been improved, and mass production of good-quality matched tableware sets began. The idea of a matched glassware table service (including goblets, tumblers, creamers, sugars, compotes, cruets, etc.) quickly caught on in America. Many pattern glass table services had numerous accessory pieces such as banana stands, molasses cans, and water bottles.

Early pattern glass (flint) was made with a lead formula, giving many items a ringing sound when tapped. Lead became too valuable to be used in glass manufacturing during the Civil War; and in 1864 Hobbs, Brockunier & Co., West Virginia, developed a soda lime (nonflint) formula. Pattern glass also was produced in transparent colors, milk glass, opalescent glass, slag glass, and custard glass.

The hundreds of companies that produced pattern glass experienced periods of development, expansions, personnel problems, material and supply demands, fires, and mergers. In 1899 the National Glass Co. was formed as a combine of 19 glass companies in Pennsylvania, Ohio, Indiana, West Virginia, and Maryland. U.S. Glass, another consortium, was founded in 1891. These combines resulted from attempts to save small companies by pooling talents, resources, and patterns. Because of this pooling, the same pattern often can be attributed to several companies.

Sometimes various companies produced the same patterns at different times and used different names to reflect current fashion trends. U.S. Glass created the States series by using state names for various patterns, several of which were new issues while others were former patterns renamed.

**References:** Gary Baker et al., *Wheeling Glass 1829-1939*, Oglebay Institute, 1994, distributed by Antique Publications; George and Linda Breeze, *Mysteries of the Moon & Star*, published by authors, 1995; Sue C. Davis, *The Picture Book of Vaseline Glass,* Schiffer Publishing, 1999; Shirley Dunbar, *Heisey Glass, The Early Years, 1896-1924,* Krause Publications, 2000; Bill Edwards and Mike Carwile, *Standard Encyclopedia of Pressed Glass, 1860-1930,* 2nd ed., Collector Books, 2000; William Heacock, *Encyclopedia of Victorian Colored Pattern Glass: Book 1: Toothpick Holders from A to Z*, 2nd ed. (1976, 1992 value update) *Book 5: U. S. Glass from A to Z* (1980), *Book 7: Ruby Stained Glass from A To Z* (1986), *Book 8: More Ruby Stained Glass* (1987), Antique Publications; ——, *Old Pattern Glass*, Antique Publications, 1981; ——, *1000 Toothpick Holders*, Antique Publications, 1977; ——, *Rare and Unlisted Toothpick Holders*, Antique Publications, 1984; Kyle Husfloen, *Antique Trader's American Pressed Glass & Bottles Price Guide,* 2nd ed., Krause Publications, 2000; ——, *Collector's Guide to American Pressed Glass*, Wallace-Homestead, 1992; Bill Jenks and Jerry Luna, *Early American Pattern Glass—1850 to 1910*, Wallace-Homestead, 1990; Bill Jenks, Jerry Luna, and Darryl Reilly, *Identifying Pattern Glass Reproductions*, Wallace-Homestead, 1993; William J. Jenks and Darryl Reilly, *American Price Guide to Unitt's Canadian & American Goblets Volumes I & II*, Author! Author! Books (P.O. Box 1964, Kingston, PA 18704), 1996.

Minnie Watson Kamm, *Pattern Glass Pitchers*, Books 1 through 8, published by author, 1970, 4th printing; Ruth Webb Lee, *Early American Pressed Glass*, 36th ed., Lee Publications, 1966; ——, *Victorian Glass*, 13th ed., Lee Publications, 1944; Bessie M. Lindsey, *American Historical Glass*, Charles E. Tuttle, 1967; Robert Irwin Lucas, *Tarentum Pattern Glass*, privately printed, 1981; Mollie H. McCain, *Field Guide to Pattern Glass*, Collector Books, 2000; George P. and Helen McKearin, *American Glass*, Crown Publishers, 1941; James Measell, *Greentown Glass*, Grand Rapids Public Museum Association, 1979, 1992-93 value update, distributed by Antique Publications; Alice Hulett Metz, *Early American Pattern Glass*, published by author, 1958 (reprinted by Collector Books, 2000, with revisions); ——, *Much More Early American Pattern Glass*, published by author, 1965 (reprinted by Collector Books, 2000, with revisions);; S. T. Millard, *Goblets I* (1938), *Goblets II* (1940), privately printed, reprinted Wallace-Homestead, 1975; John B. Mordock and Walter L. Adams, *Pattern Glass Mugs*, Antique Publications, 1995.

Arthur G. Peterson, *Glass Salt Shakers*, Wallace-Homestead, 1970; Ellen T. Schroy, *Warman's Pattern Glass*, 2nd ed., Krause Publications, 2000; Jane Shadel Spillman, A*merican and European Pressed Glass in the Corning Museum of Glass*, Corning Museum of Glass, 1981; ——, *Knopf Collectors Guides to American Antiques, Glass*, Vol. 1 (1982), Vol. 2 (1983), Alfred A. Knopf; Doris and Peter Unitt, *American and Canadian Goblets*, Clock House, 1970, reprinted by The Love of Glass Publishing (Box 629, Arthur, Ontario, Canada NOG 1AO), 1996; ——, *Treasury of Canadian Glass*, 2nd ed., Clock House, 1969; Peter Unitt and Anne Worrall, *Canadian Handbook, Pressed Glass Tableware*, Clock House Productions, 1983; Kenneth Wilson, *American Glass 1760-1930*, 2 vols., Hudson Hills Press and The Toledo Museum of Art, 1994.

**Periodical:** *Glass Collector's Digest*, The Glass Press, P.O. Box 553, Marietta, OH 45750.

**Collectors' Clubs:** Early American Pattern Glass Society, P.O. Box 266, Colesburg, IA 52035; The National Early American Glass Club, P.O. Box 8489, Silver Spring, MD 20907.

**Museums:** Corning Museum of Glass, Corning, NY; Jones Museum of Glass and Ceramics, Sebago, ME; National Museum of Man, Ottawa, Ontario, Canada; Sandwich Glass Museum, Sandwich, MA; Schminck Memorial Museum, Lakeview, OR.

**Reproduction Alert:** Pattern glass has been widely reproduced.

**Additional Listings:** Bread Plates; Children's Toy Dishes; Cruets; Custard Glass; Milk Glass; Sugar Shakers; Toothpicks; and specific companies.

**Advisors:** John and Alice Ahlfeld.

**Notes:** Research in pattern glass is continuing. As always, we try to use correct pattern names, histories, and forms. Reflecting the most current thinking, the listing by pattern places colored, opalescent, and clear items together, avoiding duplication.

Items in the listing marked with an φ are those for which reproductions are known to exist. Care should be exercised when purchasing such pieces.

**Abbreviations:**

| ah | applied handle |
| --- | --- |
| GUTDODB | Give Us This Day Our Daily Bread |
| hs | high standard |
| ind | individual |
| ls | low standard |
| os | original stopper |

## Aberdeen

Manufacturer unknown, c1870.Made in clear, non-flint.

| Items | Clear |
|---|---|
| Butter Dish, cov | 55.00 |
| Compote, cov | 50.00 |
| Compote, open | 30.00 |
| Creamer | 42.00 |
| Egg Cup | 24.00 |
| Goblet | 30.00 |
| Pitcher, water, ah | 72.00 |
| Sauce, flat | 10.00 |
| Sugar Bowl, cov | 48.00 |
| Sugar Bowl, open | 24.00 |

## Adonis *(Pleat and Tuck, Washboard)*

Made by McKee & Brothers Glass Company, Pittsburgh, PA, in 1897. Made in canary, clear, and dark blue.

| Items | Canary | Clear | Dark Blue |
|---|---|---|---|
| Berry Bowl, 5" d | 18.00 | 12.00 | 24.00 |
| Berry Bowl, 8" d, master | 18.00 | 12.00 | 24.00 |
| Bowl, open, flat, beaded rim, 5" d | 18.00 | 12.00 | 24.00 |
| Butter Dish, cov | 85.00 | 410.00 | 95.00 |
| Cake Plate, 11" d | 30.00 | 24.00 | 40.00 |
| Cake Stand, 10-1/2" d | 55.00 | 36.00 | 60.00 |
| Celery Vase | 42.00 | 30.00 | 48.00 |
| Compote, cov, hs | 85.00 | 48.00 | 90.00 |
| Compote, open, hs, 8" d | 55.00 | 36.00 | 60.00 |
| Creamer | 210.00 | 25.00 | 40.00 |
| Jelly Compote, open, 4-1/2" d | 210.00 | 110.00 | 40.00 |
| Pitcher, milk, quart | 55.00 | 55.00 | 72.00 |
| Pitcher, water, ah | 55.00 | 55.00 | 72.00 |
| Plate, 10" d | 30.00 | 110.00 | 40.00 |
| Relish Tray | 110.00 | 18.00 | 24.00 |
| Salt and Pepper Shakers, pr | 48.00 | 42.00 | 55.00 |
| Sauce, flat, beaded rim, 4" d | 12.00 | 10.00 | 15.00 |
| Sauce, flat, beaded rim, 4-1/2" d | 12.00 | 10.00 | 15.00 |
| Spooner | 42.00 | 24.00 | 48.00 |
| Sugar Bowl, cov | 48.00 | 42.00 | 55.00 |
| Syrup, orig top | 180.00 | 60.00 | 180.00 |
| Tumbler | 24.00 | 110.00 | 24.00 |

## Amberette *(Ellrose, Daisy and Button-Paneled Single Scallop, Daisy and Button-Single Panel, Paneled Daisy, Panelled Daisy and Button)*

Manufactured by George Duncan & Sons, Pittsburgh, PA, 1885. Reissued by United States Glass Company, Pittsburgh, PA, c1892. Made in non-flint, clear with amber stain. Some ruby stained and solid canary and blue pieces are known.

| Items | Clear with Amber Stain |
|---|---|
| Bowl, cov, collared base, 7" d | 135.00 |
| Bowl, cov, collared base, 8" d | 130.00 |
| Bowl, open, collared base, 7" d | 90.00 |
| Bowl, open, collared base, 8" d | 85.00 |
| Bowl, open, flat, flared rim, 8" d | 95.00 |
| Bowl, open, flat, flared rim, 9" d | 85.00 |
| Bowl, open, flat, scalloped rim, deep, 8" d | 85.00 |

| Items | Clear with Amber Stain |
|---|---|
| Bowl, open, flat, scalloped rim, deep, 9" d | 110.00 |
| Bowl, open, flat, scalloped rim, shallow, 8" d | 85.00 |
| Bowl, open, flat, scalloped rim, shallow, 9" d | 115.00 |
| Bowl, oval, flat, 5" l | 72.00 |
| Bowl, oval, flat, 7" l | 90.00 |
| Bowl, oval, flat, 8" l | 85.00 |
| Bowl, oval, flat, 12" l | 130.00 |
| Bowl, square, flat, scalloped, 5" w | 55.00 |
| Bowl, square, flat, scalloped rim, 6" w | 65.00 |
| Bowl, square, flat, scalloped rim, 7" w | 90.00 |
| Bowl, square, flat, scalloped rim, 8" w | 85.00 |
| Bowl, square, flat, scalloped rim, 8" w | 115.00 |
| Bread Plate, 11" l | 90.00 |
| Butter Dish, cov, scalloped | 130.00 |
| Butter Pat, square | 55.00 |
| Cake Stand, hs, 10" d | 180.00 |
| Celery Tray | 65.00 |
| Celery Vase | 85.00 |
| Compote, open, hs, flared, scalloped rim, 8" d | 130.00 |
| Compote, open, hs, flared, scalloped rim, 9" d | 142.00 |
| Compote, open, hs, oval, scalloped rim. 9" d | 155.00 |
| Compote, open, hs, round, scalloped rim, 8" d | 130.00 |
| Compote, open, hs, round, scalloped rim, 9" d | 142.00 |
| Creamer, ah | 85.00 |
| Cruet, os | 190.00 |
| Finger Bowl | 55.00 |
| Goblet | 65.00 |
| Lamp Shade, 9" d | 110.00 |
| Olive Dish, scalloped rim, 6" l | 55.00 |
| Pickle Dish | 42.00 |
| Pitcher, milk, ah, 3 pint | 240.00 |
| Pitcher, water, ah, half gallon | 270.00 |
| Plate, dinner, 7" d | 55.00 |
| Salt Shaker, orig top | 55.00 |
| Sauce, collared base, square, 4" w | 30.00 |
| Sauce, collared base, square, 4-1/2" w | 30.00 |
| Sauce, flat, square, 4" w | 30.00 |
| Sauce, flat, square, 4-1/2" w | 30.00 |
| Spooner | 65.00 |
| Sugar Bowl, cov | 130.00 |
| Tumbler | 55.00 |

## Arched Ovals *Concave Almond*

Manufactured by United States Glass Company, c1908. This pattern was popular for souvenir wares. Made in clear, clear with gilt, cobalt blue, green, and ruby stained.

| Items | Clear | Cobalt Blue | Green | Ruby Stained |
|---|---|---|---|---|
| Berry Bowl | 15.00 | - | 110.00 | - |
| Bowl, cov, 7" d | 48.00 | - | - | - |
| Butter Dish, cov | 55.00 | - | 60.00 | 95.00 |
| Cake Stand | 42.00 | - | - | - |
| Celery Vase | 18.00 | 48.00 | 24.00 | - |
| Compote, cov, hs, belled, 8" d | 45.00 | - | - | - |
| Compote, open, hs, 8" d | 36.00 | - | - | - |
| Compote, open, hs, 9" d | 30.00 | - | - | - |

| Items | Clear | Cobalt Blue | Green | Ruby Stained |
|---|---|---|---|---|
| Creamer, individual | 24.00 | - | - | - |
| Creamer, table | 36.00 | - | - | - |
| Cruet | 42.00 | - | - | - |
| Goblet | 24.00 | - | 36.00 | 42.00 |
| Mug | 110.00 | 36.00 | 24.00 | 30.00 |
| Pitcher, water | 36.00 | - | 48.00 | - |
| Plate, 8" d | 24.00 | - | 30.00 | - |
| Punch Cup | 10.00 | - | - | - |
| Relish, oval, 9" l | 24.00 | - | - | - |
| Salt and Pepper Shakers, pr | 55.00 | - | 60.00 | - |
| Sauce | 9.00 | - | - | - |
| Spooner | 24.00 | - | 30.00 | 42.00 |
| Sugar Bowl, cov | 42.00 | - | 48.00 | - |
| Syrup, orig top | 42.00 | - | - | - |
| Toothpick Holder | 110.00 | 60.00 | 30.00 | 42.00 |
| Tumbler | 15.00 | 30.00 | 110.00 | 36.00 |
| Wine | 18.00 | - | 24.00 | 36.00 |

## Bamboo Edge *Bamboo*

Manufactured by LaBelle Glass Company, Bridgeport, PA, c1883. Made in clear and ruby stained.

| Items | Clear | Ruby Stained |
|---|---|---|
| Butter Dish, cov | 85.00 | 172.00 |
| Celery Vase | 36.00 | 66.00 |
| Compote, cov, hs, 7" d | 60.00 | - |
| Compote, cov, hs, 8" d | 72.00 | - |
| Compote, cov, hs, 9" d | 66.00 | - |
| Compote, open, oval, etched | 55.00 | - |
| Creamer | 42.00 | 75.00 |
| Pitcher, water | 75.00 | 180.00 |
| Relish, 7" l, 8" l, or 9" l | 24.00 | 55.00 |
| Salt and Pepper Shakers, pr | 310.00 | 75.00 |
| Sauce, flat, 4" d | 15.00 | - |
| Sauce, footed, 4" d | 15.00 | - |
| Spooner | 36.00 | 66.00 |
| Sugar Bowl, cov | 55.00 | 110.00 |
| Tumbler | 42.00 | 85.00 |

## Beatty Honeycomb *Beatty Waffle*

Manufactured by A. J. Beatty & Sons, Tiffin, OH, c1888. Reissued by United States Glass Company, Pittsburgh, after 1891, in a limited table service. Made in non-flint, blue opalescent and white opalescent.

**Reproductions:** Reproduced by Fenton Art Glass Company, Williamstown, WV, in green opalescent (basket, rose bowl, and vases) and milk glass.

| Items | Blue Opalescent | White Opalescent |
|---|---|---|
| Berry Bowl | 120.00 | 60.00 |
| Butter Dish, cov | 124.00 | 120.00 |
| Celery Vase | 85.00 | 55.00 |
| Creamer, individual | 42.00 | 24.00 |
| Creamer, regular | 36.00 | 30.00 |
| Cruet, os | 242.00 | 190.00 |
| Mug | 42.00 | 30.00 |
| Mustard | 72.00 | 55.00 |
| Pitcher, water | 360.00 | 240.00 |
| Salt and Pepper Shakers, pr | 66.00 | 55.00 |
| Sauce | 24.00 | 24.00 |
| Spooner | 48.00 | 36.00 |
| Sugar Bowl, cov, individual | 66.00 | 55.00 |
| Sugar Bowl, cov, regular φ | 85.00 | 66.00 |
| Toothpick Holder | 60.00 | 55.00 |
| Tumbler | 66.00 | 48.00 |

## Beatty Swirled Opalescent *(Swirled Opal)*

Manufactured by A. J. Beatty & Sons, Tiffin, OH, c1889. Made in non-flint, blue opalescent, vaseline opalescent, and white opalescent.

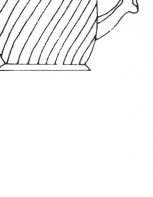

| Items | Blue Opalescent | Vaseline Opalescent | White Opalescent |
| --- | --- | --- | --- |
| Berry Bowl | 95.00 | 85.00 | 75.00 |
| Butter Dish, cov | 130.00 | 180.00 | 120.00 |
| Celery Vase | 60.00 | 55.00 | 55.00 |
| Creamer | 48.00 | 60.00 | 36.00 |
| Cruet, os | 124.00 | - | - |
| Lamp Shade | - | - | 100.00 |
| Mug | 30.00 | 48.00 | 36.00 |
| Pitcher, water | 180.00 | 165.00 | 48.00 |
| Sauce | 42.00 | 42.00 | 60.00 |
| Spooner | 60.00 | 55.00 | 48.00 |
| Sugar Bowl, cov | 55.00 | 120.00 | 60.00 |
| Syrup, orig top | 130.00 | 180.00 | 118.00 |
| Toothpick Holder | 60.00 | - | 55.00 |
| Tumbler | 60.00 | 130.00 | 55.00 |
| Water Tray | 124.00 | 130.00 | 135.00 |

## Bethlehem Star *(Star Burst, Bright Star)*

Made by Indiana Glass Company, Dunkirk, IN, c1907. Made in non-flint, clear.

| Items | Clear |
| --- | --- |
| Butter Dish, cov | 42.00 |
| Celery Vase | 30.00 |
| Compote, cov, hs, 5" d | 60.00 |
| Compote, cov, hs, 8" d | 72.00 |
| Creamer | 36.00 |
| Cruet, os | 42.00 |
| Goblet | 36.00 |
| Jelly Compote, cov, hs, 4-1/2" d | 60.00 |
| Pitcher, water | 55.00 |
| Relish | 18.00 |
| Sauce, flat | 12.00 |
| Spooner | 30.00 |
| Sugar Bowl, cov | 48.00 |
| Wine | 30.00 |

## Bridal Rosette *Checkerboard*

Manufactured by Westmoreland Glass Company, Grapeville, PA, in the early 1900s. Made in clear and ruby stained.

**Reproductions:** The pattern has been reproduced since the 1950s in milk glass. More recent reproductions are clear and clear with pink stain. The L. E. Smith Glass Company, Mount Pleasant, PA, introduced a milk white covered compote in 1961, which had a paper label. A seven-piece water set and four-piece table set were distributed by Levay Distributing Company, Edwardsville, IL, in 1983. Plum Glass Company, Pittsburgh, PA, issued a low standard compote made from the original Westmoreland molds in 1988, complete with the Westmoreland logo and the new PG in keystone mark for Plum. Additional Bridal Rosette molds have been sold to Plum Glass Company. Look for blocks that lack sharp detail and reproductions will usually feel heavier than original pieces.

| Items | Clear | Ruby Stained |
| --- | --- | --- |
| Bowl, shallow, 9" d | 24.00 | 60.00 |
| Butter Dish, cov φ | 48.00 | 120.00 |

| Items | Clear | Ruby Stained |
|---|---|---|
| Celery Tray | 24.00 | 60.00 |
| Celery Vase φ | 36.00 | 75.00 |
| Compote, open, ls, 8" d | 30.00 | 72.00 |
| Creamer φ | 30.00 | 72.00 |
| Cruet, os φ | 48.00 | 120.00 |
| Cup φ | 10.00 | 24.00 |
| Goblet φ | 36.00 | 75.00 |
| Honey Dish, cov, sq, pedestal φ | 48.00 | 120.00 |
| Iced Tea Tumbler | 18.00 | 42.00 |
| Pitcher, milk | 48.00 | 120.00 |
| Pitcher, water φ | 42.00 | 110.00 |
| Plate, 7" d φ | 18.00 | 42.00 |
| Plate, 10" d φ | 24.00 | 60.00 |
| Punch Cup φ | 6.00 | 12.50 |
| Salt and Pepper Shakers, pr φ | 48.00 | 120.00 |
| Sauce, flat | 6.00 | 12.50 |
| Spooner φ | 24.00 | 60.00 |
| Sugar Bowl, cov φ | 42.00 | 110.00 |
| Tumbler φ | 110.00 | 55.00 |
| Wine φ | 110.00 | 55.00 |

## Butterfly and Fan *(Bird in Ring, Butterfly with Fan, Duncan's Grace, Fan, Grace, Japanese.)*

Manufactured by George Duncan & Sons, Pittsburgh, PA, c1880. Also made by Richards and Hartley Glass Company, Pittsburgh, PA, c1888. Made in non-flint, clear only.

| Items | Clear |
|---|---|
| Berry Bowl, master | 36.00 |
| Bread Plate | 60.00 |
| Butter Dish, cov, flat | 120.00 |
| Butter Dish, cov, footed | 75.00 |
| Celery Vase | 75.00 |
| Compote, cov, hs, 7" d | 115.00 |
| Compote, cov, hs, 8" d | 115.00 |
| Compote, open, hs | 36.00 |
| Creamer, ftd | 55.00 |
| Goblet | 60.00 |
| Marmalade Jar, cov | 75.00 |
| Pickle Castor, silver plated frame and cov | 195.00 |
| Pitcher, water | 118.00 |
| Sauce, flat or footed, 4" d | 18.00 |
| Spooner | 36.00 |
| Sugar Bowl, cov | 60.00 |

## Cabbage Rose *(Central's No. 140, Rose)*

Manufactured by Central Glass Company, Wheeling, WV, c1870. The design was patented by designer John Oesterling (No. 4,263) on July 26, 1870. Made in non-flint, clear.

**Reproductions:** Mosser Glass Company, Cambridge, OH, made reproductions in clear and colors during the early 1980s.

| Item | Clear |
|---|---|
| Basket, 12" h | 130.00 |
| Bitters Bottle, 6-1/2" h | 130.00 |
| Bowl, cov, round, 6" d | 55.00 |
| Bowl, cov, round, 7" d | 72.00 |
| Bowl, cov, round, 7-1/2" d | 85.00 |
| Bowl, oval, 7-1/2" d | 42.00 |
| Bowl, oval, 8-1/2" d | 48.00 |

| Item | Clear |
|---|---|
| Bowl, oval, 9-1/2" d | 55.00 |
| Bowl, round, 6" d | 30.00 |
| Bowl, round, 7-1/2" d | 42.00 |
| Butter Dish, cov | 72.00 |
| Cake Plate, square, flat | 65.00 |
| Cake Stand, hs, 9" d | 42.00 |
| Cake Stand, hs, 9-1/2" d | 42.00 |
| Cake Stand, hs, 10" d | 48.00 |
| Cake Stand, hs, 11" d | 48.00 |
| Cake Stand, hs, 12" d | 55.00 |
| Cake Stand, hs, 12-1/2" d | 60.00 |
| Celery Vase, pedestal | 60.00 |
| Champagne | 60.00 |
| Compote, cov, hs, deep bowl, 6" d | 85.00 |
| Compote, cov, hs, deep bowl, 7" d | 115.00 |
| Compote, cov, hs, deep bowl, 7-1/2" d | 135.00 |
| Compote, cov, hs, deep bowl, 8" d | 118.00 |
| Compote, cov, hs, deep bowl, 8-1/2" d | 124.00 |
| Compote, cov, hs, deep bowl, 8" d | 130.00 |
| Compote, cov, hs, deep bowl, 10" d | 142.00 |
| Compote, cov, hs, regular bowl, 8" d | 110.00 |
| Compote, cov, hs, regular bowl, 9" d | 120.00 |
| Compote, cov, hs, regular bowl, 10" d | 135.00 |
| Compote, cov, hs, shallow bowl, 6" d | 90.00 |
| Compote, cov, hs, shallow bowl, 7" d | 95.00 |
| Compote, cov, hs, shallow bowl, 8" d | 115.00 |
| Compote, cov, ls, deep bowl, 7" d | 120.00 |
| Compote, cov, ls, deep bowl, 8" d | 120.00 |
| Compote, cov, ls, deep bowl, 9" d | 124.00 |
| Compote, cov, ls, regular bowl, 8" d | 135.00 |
| Compote, cov, ls, regular bowl, 9" d | 124.00 |
| Compote, cov, ls, regular bowl, 10" d | 135.00 |
| Compote, cov, ls, shallow bowl, 6" d | 115.00 |
| Compote, cov, ls, shallow bowl, 7" d | 120.00 |
| Compote, cov, ls, shallow bowl, 8" d | 135.00 |
| Compote, open, hs, 6-1/2" d | 65.00 |
| Compote, open, hs, 7-1/2" d | 90.00 |
| Compote, open, hs, 8-1/2" d | 85.00 |
| Compote, open, hs, 9-1/2" d | 120.00 |
| Cordial | 55.00 |
| Creamer, ah, 5-1/2" h | 55.00 |
| Egg Cup, with or without handle | 55.00 |
| Goblet φ (2 styles) | 55.00 |
| Mug | 72.00 |
| Pickle Dish | 42.00 |
| Pitcher, milk, quart | 180.00 |
| Pitcher, water, half gallon | 130.00 |
| Relish, 8-1/2" l, 5" w, rose filled horn of plenty center | 48.00 |
| Salt, master, ftd | 30.00 |
| Sauce, flat, 4" d | 12.00 |
| Spooner φ | 30.00 |
| Sugar Bowl, cov | 55.00 |
| Tumbler | 48.00 |
| Wine | 55.00 |

## Doyle's Shell *Shell #2, Cube and Fan #2, Knight*

Manufactured by Doyle and Company, Pittsburgh, PA, and continued by United States Glass Company, Pittsburgh, PA, c1892. Made in non-flint, clear, and emerald green.

| Items | Clear | Emerald Green |
|---|---|---|
| Berry Bowl | 18.00 | - |
| Butter Dish, cov | 55.00 | 55.00 |
| Cake Stand | 36.00 | - |
| Celery Tray, long, flat | 24.00 | 30.00 |
| Celery Vase | 24.00 | - |
| Creamer | 24.00 | 36.00 |
| Goblet | 24.00 | 36.00 |
| Mug | 18.00 | 24.00 |
| Nappy, handle | 18.00 | - |
| Pitcher, water | 55.00 | - |
| Pickle Dish | 18.00 | - |
| Salt Shaker | 18.00 | - |
| Spooner | 24.00 | 30.00 |
| Sugar Bowl, cov | 36.00 | 42.00 |
| Tumbler | 12.00 | 18.00 |
| Waste Bowl | 18.00 | 30.00 |
| Water Tray, 10" d | 42.00 | - |
| Wine | 24.00 | - |

## English *Diamond with Diamond Point*

Manufactured by Westmoreland Glass Company, Grapeville, PA, c1896. Made in non-flint, clear, emerald green, and milk white.

| Items | Clear |
|---|---|
| Butter Dish, cov | 42.00 |
| Celery Vase | 55.00 |
| Compote, cov, hs | 72.00 |
| Creamer, 3-1/2" h | 30.00 |
| Goblet | 36.00 |
| Pitcher, water | 48.00 |
| Spooner | 24.00 |
| Sugar Bowl, cov | 42.00 |
| Tumbler | 24.00 |

## Flat Diamond *(Lippman)*

Manufactured by Richards & Hartley, Tarentum, PA, c1880. Reissued by United States Glass Company, Pittsburgh, PA, after 1891. Shards have also been found at Burlington Glass Works, Hamilton, Ontario, Canada. Made in non-flint, clear.

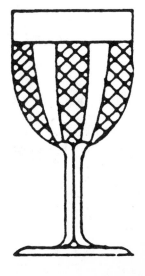

| Items | Clear |
|---|---|
| Apothecary Jar, os | 30.00 |
| Butter Dish, cov | 55.00 |
| Celery Vase | 42.00 |
| Creamer | 48.00 |
| Goblet | 30.00 |
| Marmalade Jar, cov | 36.00 |
| Pitcher, water | 55.00 |
| Sauce, flat | 6.00 |
| Sauce, footed | 6.00 |
| Spooner, pedestal | 24.00 |
| Sugar Bowl, cov | 55.00 |
| Tumbler, flat | 36.00 |
| Wine | 55.00 |

## Flower Band *(Bird Finial, Frosted Flower Band)*

Manufacturer unknown, c1870. Made in non-flint, clear, and clear with frosted band.

**Reproductions:** The goblet has been reproduced by Fenton Art Glass Company, Williamstown, WV, in amber, cobalt blue, sapphire blue, and several pastel colors.

| Items | Clear | Frosted Band |
|---|---|---|
| Butter Dish, cov, lovebirds finial | 120.00 | 180.00 |
| Celery Vase, handles | 72.00 | 85.00 |
| Compote, cov, hs, 8" d | 142.00 | 225.00 |
| Compote, cov, collared base, oval | 130.00 | 155.00 |
| Compote, cov, collared base, round | 118.00 | 142.00 |
| Creamer, 6" h | 65.00 | 115.00 |
| Goblet φ | 65.00 | 115.00 |
| Pitcher, milk, quart | 75.00 | 135.00 |
| Pitcher, water, half gallon | 115.00 | 130.00 |
| Sauce, flat | 12.00 | 24.00 |
| Sauce, footed | 12.00 | 24.00 |
| Spooner | 55.00 | 65.00 |
| Sugar Bowl, cov, lovebirds finial | 120.00 | 180.00 |

## Flower Pot *(Flower Plant, Potted Plant)*

Manufacturer unknown, c1870 and early 1880s. Made in non-flint, clear. Some rare pieces are known in amber, vaseline, and other colors.

| Items | Clear |
|---|---|
| Bread Plate, "We Trust In God" center | 55.00 |
| Butter Dish, cov | 60.00 |
| Cake Stand, hs, 10-1/2" d | 410.00 |
| Compote, cov, hs, 7" d | 55.00 |
| Compote, open, hs, 7-1/4" d | 24.00 |
| Creamer | 36.00 |
| Goblet | 42.00 |
| Pitcher, milk, quart | 48.00 |
| Pitcher, water, half gallon | 55.00 |
| Salt Shaker | 24.00 |
| Sauce, flat | 6.00 |
| Sauce, footed | 12.00 |
| Spooner, handles | 30.00 |
| Sugar Bowl, cov | 48.00 |

## Fluted Scrolls *(Klondyke, Jackson)*

Manufactured by Harry Northwood and Company, Indiana, PA, c1898. Made in blue opalescent, custard, vaseline opalescent, and white (clear) opalescent. Sometimes with burnished gold trim.

| Items | Blue Opalescent | Custard | Vaseline Opalescent | White Opalescent |
|---|---|---|---|---|
| Berry Bowl | 120.00 | 120.00 | 75.00 | - |
| Butter Dish, cov | 142.00 | 240.00 | 225.00 | 65.00 |
| Creamer | 75.00 | 120.00 | 130.00 | 55.00 |
| Cruet, os | 120.00 | 190.00 | 85.00 | - |
| Pitcher, water | 255.00 | 240.00 | 190.00 | - |
| Puff Box | 60.00 | - | 55.00 | - |
| Salt Shaker | 55.00 | - | 48.00 | 24.00 |
| Sauce | 36.00 | 55.00 | 30.00 | - |
| Spooner | 120.00 | 120.00 | 120.00 | 65.00 |
| Sugar Bowl, cov | 115.00 | 118.00 | 180.00 | 95.00 |
| Tray | 48.00 | - | 36.00 | 30.00 |
| Tumbler | 75.00 | - | 65.00 | - |

## Frances Ware

Manufactured by Hobbs, Brockunier & Company, Wheeling, WV, c1880. Made in non-flint. This pattern is a clear frosted hobnail or swirl pattern glass with amber stained top rims. It may be pressed or mold blown.

| Items | Clear | Frosted/Amber Stain, Hobnail | Frost/Amber Stain, Swirl |
|---|---|---|---|
| Barber Bottle | 65.00 | 130.00 | - |
| Bowl, oval, 7" l, 8" l, or 9" l | 60.00 | 75.00 | - |
| Bowl, round, 7-1/2" d or 8" d | 60.00 | 75.00 | 85.00 |
| Bowl, square, 7-1/2" w or 8" w | 60.00 | 75.00 | - |
| Box, cov, round, 5-1/4" d | 55.00 | 65.00 | - |
| Bride's Basket, orig silver plate holder | 135.00 | 180.00 | - |
| Butter Dish, cov, flanged rim | 95.00 | 135.00 | - |
| Butter Dish, cov, plain rim | 65.00 | 115.00 | - |
| Butter Dish, cov, underplate | - | - | 130.00 |
| Castor Set, orig silver plate holder | - | - | 720.00 |
| Celery Tray, oval | - | - | 65.00 |
| Celery Vase, flat | 42.00 | 65.00 | 85.00 |
| Creamer, ah | 60.00 | 85.00 | 55.00 |
| Cruet, os | 42.00 | 190.00 | 270.00 |
| Finger Bowl, 4" d | 48.00 | 60.00 | 72.00 |
| Lamp Shade, gas, bulbous or tall, scalloped rim | - | - | 120.00 |
| Miniature Lamp, orig shade | - | - | 495.00 |
| Mustard Jar, cov | - | - | 142.00 |
| Pickle Dish, oval | - | - | 85.00 |
| Pitcher, lemonade | 120.00 | 225.00 | - |
| Pitcher, milk, 8-1/2" h | 110.00 | 180.00 | - |
| Pitcher, water, 11" d | 180.00 | 225.00 | 180.00 |
| Plate, 5" d | - | - | 36.00 |
| Salt Shaker | 60.00 | 65.00 | 75.00 |
| Sauce, flat, oval | - | - | 30.00 |
| Sauce, flat, round, 4" d or 4-1/2" w | 18.00 | 36.00 | - |
| Sauce, flat, sq, 4" w or 4-1/2" w | 35.00 | 40.00 | - |
| Spooner | 55.00 | 72.00 | 65.00 |
| Sugar Bowl, cov | 72.00 | 85.00 | 85.00 |
| Sugar Shaker | 65.00 | - | 130.00 |
| Syrup, orig top | 85.00 | 360.00 | 190.00 |
| Toothpick Holder | 75.00 | 130.00 | 180.00 |
| Tray, leaf shape, 12" l | 75.00 | 130.00 | - |
| Tray, rect, rounded edges, 14" l, 9-1/4" w | 135.00 | 180.00 | - |
| Tumbler | 42.00 | 55.00 | 48.00 |

## Frosted Leaf

Manufacturer unknown, c1860-70. Made in flint, clear.

**Reproductions:** Imperial Glass Company, Bellaire, OH, was authorized by the Smithsonian Institution, Washington, DC, to reproduce several forms, including the butter dish, creamer, spooner, sugar bowl, and wine. These have been embossed with the "S. I." Mark.

| Items | Clear |
|---|---|
| Butter Dish, cov φ | 142.00 |
| Celery Vase, scalloped rim | 155.00 |
| Champagne | 172.00 |
| Compote, cov | 300.00 |

| Items | Clear |
|---|---|
| Compote open | 180.00 |
| Creamer φ | 360.00 |
| Decanter, os, pint | 350.00 |
| Decanter, os, quart | 300.00 |
| Egg Cup | 120.00 |
| Goblet, gentleman's | 115.00 |
| Goblet, lady's | 130.00 |
| Lamp, oil | 600.00 |
| Pitcher, water, ah | 495.00 |
| Salt, individual | 60.00 |
| Salt, master, ftd | 130.00 |
| Sauce, flat, 4" d | 30.00 |
| Spooner φ | 85.00 |
| Sugar Bowl, cov φ | 190.00 |
| Tumbler, flat | 180.00 |
| Tumbler, footed | 165.00 |
| Wine φ | 130.00 |

## Gonterman *(Duncan Pattern Line No. 95)*

Manufactured by George Duncan & Sons, Pittsburgh, PA, c1887-80. Made in non-flint, has an acid finished body with amber stain.

| Items | Acid Finish w/ Amber Stain |
|---|---|
| Bowl, cov, hs, 7" d | 85.00 |
| Bowl, cov, hs, 8" d | 110.00 |
| Bowl, open, ls, 7" d | 95.00 |
| Bowl, open, ls, 8" d | 85.00 |
| Butter Dish, cov | 130.00 |
| Cake Stand, hs, 10" d | 120.00 |
| Celery Vase, pedestal | 115.00 |
| Compote, cov, hs, 5" d | 120.00 |
| Compote, cov, hs, 7" d | 135.00 |
| Compote, cov, hs, 8" d | 124.00 |
| Compote, open, 5" d | 75.00 |
| Compote, open, 7" d | 95.00 |
| Compote, open, 8" d | 85.00 |
| Creamer | 135.00 |
| Goblet | 360.00 |
| Honey Dish, flat or footed | 24.00 |
| Pitcher, milk, quart | 142.00 |
| Pitcher, water, half gallon | 240.00 |
| Salt Shaker, orig top | 65.00 |
| Sauce, flat, 4" d or 4-1/2" d | 18.00 |
| Sauce, footed, 4" d or 4-1/2" d | 24.00 |
| Spooner | 75.00 |
| Sugar Bowl, cov | 120.00 |

## Gooseberry

Manufacture attributed to Boston and Sandwich Glass Company, Sandwich, MA, in the 1880s. Others also made this pattern. Made in non-flint, clear, and milk glass.

**Reproductions:** Reproduction goblets, mugs, and wines are found in clear and milk glass.

| Items | Clear | Milk Glass |
|---|---|---|
| Berry Bowl, master | 45.00 | 65.00 |
| Butter Dish, cov | 60.00 | 75.00 |
| Cake Stand, hs | 70.00 | - |
| Compote, cov, hs, 6" d | 72.00 | 65.00 |

| Items | Clear | Milk Glass |
|---|---|---|
| Compote, cov, hs, 7" d | 85.00 | 75.00 |
| Compote, cov, hs, 8" d | 75.00 | 110.00 |
| Creamer | 36.00 | 60.00 |
| Goblet φ | 42.00 | 55.00 |
| Honey Dish, cov | 55.00 | 65.00 |
| Lemonade Tumbler, ah | 42.00 | - |
| Mug, ah φ | 42.00 | 48.00 |
| Pitcher, water, ah | 165.00 | 270.00 |
| Sauce, flat | 12.00 | 18.00 |
| Spooner | 30.00 | 36.00 |
| Sugar Bowl, cov | 55.00 | 55.00 |
| Syrup, orig top, ah | 75.00 | 142.00 |
| Tumbler | 42.00 | 48.00 |
| Wine φ | 36.00 | 42.00 |

## Royal Ivy *(New Jewel, Northwood Pattern Line No. 287)*

Manufactured by Northwood Glass Company in 1889. Made in non-flint, clear with frosting (acid finish), rubena and frosted (acid finish) rubena. Also made were cased spatter, clear and frosted rainbow cracquelle, clear with amber, stained ivy, and clambroth opaline. These last mentioned were experimental pieces, not made in sets.

| Items | Clear Frosted | Rubena Clear | Rubena Frosted |
|---|---|---|---|
| Berry Bowl, master | 48.00 | 90.00 | 130.00 |
| Butter Dish, cov | 120.00 | 190.00 | 290.00 |
| Creamer, ah | 72.00 | 160.00 | 240.00 |
| Cruet, os | 110.00 | 230.00 | 330.00 |
| Finger Bowl | 30.00 | 60.00 | 75.00 |
| Marmalade Jar, silver plated cov | 130.00 | - | - |
| Miniature Lamp | 160.00 | 260.00 | 360.00 |
| Pickle Castor, silver plated frame | 130.00 | 240.00 | 390.00 |
| Pitcher, water, ah | 112.00 | 190.00 | 290.00 |
| Rose Bowl | 65.00 | 85.00 | 100.00 |
| Salt Shaker, orig top | 30.00 | 36.00 | 48.00 |
| Sauce, flat | 35.00 | 30.00 | 42.00 |
| Spooner | 55.00 | 85.00 | 115.00 |
| Sugar Bowl, cov | 160.00 | 175.00 | 195.00 |
| Sugar Shaker | 75.00 | 142.00 | 160.00 |
| Syrup, orig top | 135.00 | 230.00 | 360.00 |
| Toothpick Holder | 60.00 | 110.00 | 130.00 |
| Tumbler | 42.00 | 60.00 | 90.00 |

## Saint Bernard

Manufactured by Fostoria Glass Company, Fostoria, OH, c1894. Made in non-flint, clear.

| Items | Clear |
|---|---|
| Berry Bowl, 8" d | 45.00 |
| Butter Dish, cov | 90.00 |
| Cake Stand, hs | 48.00 |
| Celery Vase | 45.00 |
| Compote, cov, hs, 7" d | 65.00 |
| Compote, cov, hs, 8" d | 72.00 |
| Compote, open, ls, 6" d | 36.00 |
| Compote, open, ls, 7" d | 45.00 |
| Compote, open, ls, 8" d | 48.00 |
| Creamer | 45.00 |
| Cruet, os | 45.00 |
| Goblet | 45.00 |
| Marmalade Jar, cov | 65.00 |

| Items | Clear |
|---|---|
| Pitcher, water, bulbous | 65.00 |
| Pitcher, water, tankard | 72.00 |
| Salt Shaker | 24.00 |
| Sauce, flat | 12.00 |
| Sugar Bowl, cov | 90.00 |
| Tumbler | 24.00 |

## Saxon

Manufactured by Adams & Company, Pittsburgh, PA, c 1888. Reissued by United States Glass Company, Pittsburgh, PA, after 1891. Made in non-flint, clear. Copper wheel engraving was added to many pieces. Several items can be found in ruby stained and often with souvenir inscriptions. Prices listed below are for plain clear pieces.

| Items | Clear |
|---|---|
| Bowl, cov, flat, 5" d | 30.00 |
| Bowl, cov, flat, 6" d, 7" d, 8" d | 36.00 |
| Bowl, cov, flat, 9" d | 45.00 |
| Bowl, cov, ftd, ls, 5" d or 6" d | 30.00 |
| Bowl, cov, ftd, ls, 7" d or 8" d | 36.00 |
| Bowl, cov, ftd, ls, 9" d | 45.00 |
| Bowl, open, belled, scalloped rim, 5" d or 6" d | 12.00 |
| Bowl, open, belled, scalloped rim, 7" d or 8" d | 18.00 |
| Bowl, open, belled, scalloped rim, 9" d | 24.00 |
| Bowl, open, flared bowl, 7-1/2" d, 9" d, or 10" d | 24.00 |
| Bowl, open, flared bowl, 11-1/2" d | 30.00 |
| Bowl, open, ftd, ls, belled bowl, 5" d or 6" d | 12.00 |
| Bowl, open, ftd, ls, belled bowl, 7" d or 8" d | 18.00 |
| Bowl, open, ftd, ls, belled bowl, 9" d | 24.00 |
| Bowl, open, ftd, shallow bowl, 6-1/2" d | 12.00 |
| Bowl, open, ftd, shallow bowl, 7-1/2" d | 18.00 |
| Bowl, open, ftd, shallow bowl, 9" d | 24.00 |
| Bowl, open, ftd, shallow bowl, 10" d | 30.00 |
| Bowl, open, ftd, shallow bowl, 11-1/2" d | 36.00 |
| Bread Plate | 36.00 |
| Butter Dish, cov | 45.00 |
| Cake Stand, hs, 9"d | 48.00 |
| Cake Stand, hs, 10" d | 55.00 |
| Celery Vase | 30.00 |
| Claret | 30.00 |
| Compote, cov, hs, 5" d | 30.00 |
| Compote, cov, hs, 6" d | 36.00 |
| Compote, cov, hs, 7" d | 45.00 |
| Compote, cov, hs, 8" d | 48.00 |
| Compote, open, hs, belled bowl, 5" d or 6" d | 24.00 |
| Compote, open, hs, belled bowl, 7" or 8" d | 30.00 |
| Compote, open, hs, belled bowl, 9" d | 36.00 |
| Compote, open, hs, shallow bowl, 6-1/2" d | 24.00 |
| Compote, open, hs, shallow bowl, 7-1/2" d | 30.00 |
| Compote, open, hs, shallow bowl, 9" d | 36.00 |
| Compote, open, hs, shallow bowl, 10" d | 45.00 |
| Compote, open, hs, shallow bowl, 11-1/2" d | 48.00 |
| Creamer, 7" h | 30.00 |
| Cruet, os, ah | 60.00 |
| Dish, flat, oval, 7" l, 8" l, or 9" l | 18.00 |
| Dish, flat, round, 7" l, 8" l, or 9" l | 18.00 |
| Egg Cup | 24.00 |
| Finger Bowl | 45.00 |

| Items | Clear |
|---|---|
| Goblet | 36.00 |
| Mug | 24.00 |
| Pickle Tray, rect | 15.00 |
| Pitcher, milk | 48.00 |
| Pitcher, water | 55.00 |
| Plate, 6" d | 45.00 |
| Salt, individual | 24.00 |
| Salt, master | 36.00 |
| Sauce, flat, 3-1/2" d | 7.50 |
| Sauce, flat, 4"d or 4-1/2" d | 12.00 |
| Sauce, footed, 3-1/2" d | 12.00 |
| Sauce, footed, 4" d or 4-1/2" d | 18.00 |
| Spooner | 30.00 |
| Sugar Bowl, cov | 45.00 |
| Syrup, orig top | 45.00 |
| Toothpick Holder | 36.00 |
| Tumbler | 24.00 |
| Waste Bowl | 65.00 |
| Wine | 45.00 |

## Scalloped Swirl *York Herringbone*

Manufactured by unknown American maker in the late 1880s and by United States Glass Company, Pittsburgh, PA, after 1891. Made in non-flint, clear, and ruby stained. Often found with souvenir etching.

| Items | Clear | Ruby Stained |
|---|---|---|
| Berry Bowl | 30.00 | 72.00 |
| Butter Dish, cov | 60.00 | 90.00 |
| Cake Plate, hs, 10" d | 36.00 | 72.00 |
| Castor Set | 115.00 | 1,115.00 |
| Celery Vase | 24.00 | 60.00 |
| Compote, cov, 7" d | 55.00 | 90.00 |
| Creamer | 30.00 | 65.00 |
| Goblet | 30.00 | 48.00 |
| Pitcher, water | 65.00 | 110.00 |
| Spooner | 24.00 | 55.00 |
| Sugar Bowl, cov | 45.00 | 75.00 |
| Toothpick Holder | - | 55.00 |
| Tumbler | 30.00 | 55.00 |

## Scalloped Tape *Jewel Band*

Manufactured by unknown maker, c1880. Made in non-flint, clear. Occasionally found in amber, blue, canary-yellow and light green.

| Items | Clear |
|---|---|
| Bread Plate, oval, "Bread Is The Staff of Life" | 55.00 |
| Butter Dish, cov | 45.00 |
| Cake Stand, hs | 45.00 |
| Celery Vase, pedestal | 36.00 |
| Compote, cov, hs, 8" d | 65.00 |
| Compote, open, hs, 8" d | 48.00 |
| Creamer | 30.00 |
| Dish, rect, cov, 8" l | 55.00 |
| Egg Cup | 30.00 |
| Goblet | 30.00 |

| Items | Clear |
|---|---|
| Pitcher, milk, ph, quart | 45.00 |
| Pitcher, water, ph, half gallon | 65.00 |
| Plate, 6" d | 18.00 |
| Relish Tray | 12.00 |
| Sauce, flat, 4" d | 8.50 |
| Sauce, ftd, 4" d | 15.00 |
| Spooner | 24.00 |
| Sugar Bowl, cov | 45.00 |
| Tray, 6" x 7" | 30.00 |
| Wine | 24.00 |

## Scroll with Acanthus

Manufactured by Northwood Glass Company, Wheeling, WV, after 1903. Made in opalescent in clear (white) and shades of blue and canary-yellow. There is sometimes enameled decoration on the transparent pieces. Transparent colors are 20% less; purple slag, 50% higher.

| Items | Blue Opalescent | Canary Opalescent | White Opalescent |
|---|---|---|---|
| Berry Bowl | 72.00 | 75.00 | 45.00 |
| Butter Dish, cov, ftd | 130.00 | 112.00 | 60.00 |
| Creamer | 120.00 | 100.00 | 48.00 |
| Jelly Compote, 5" d | 60.00 | 55.00 | 36.00 |
| Pitcher, water | 2100.00 | 265.00 | 120.00 |
| Sauce | 30.00 | 30.00 | 24.00 |
| Spooner | 48.00 | 45.00 | 30.00 |

## Seashell

Manufacturer unknown, c1870. Made in non-flint, clear and clear with copper wheel engraving.

| Items | Clear |
|---|---|
| Butter, Dish, cov | 100.00 |
| Cake Stand, hs | 45.00 |
| Celery Vase | 36.00 |
| Champagne | 45.00 |
| Compote, cov, hs | 85.00 |
| Creamer | 30.00 |
| Goblet | 36.00 |
| Pitcher, water, ph, quart | 60.00 |
| Pitcher, water, ph, half gallon | 72.00 |
| Salt Shaker, orig top | 18.00 |
| Sauce, ftd | 18.00 |
| Spooner | 30.00 |
| Sugar Bowl, cov | 72.00 |
| Wine | 30.00 |

## Snow Band *Puffed Bands*

Manufacturer unknown, c1885. Made in non-flint, amber, blue, and clear.

| Items | Amber | Blue | Clear |
|---|---|---|---|
| Bowl | 25.00 | 30.00 | 20.00 |
| Butter Dish, cov | 55.00 | 60.00 | 48.00 |
| Cake Stand | 30.00 | 36.00 | 30.00 |
| Creamer | 36.00 | 45.00 | 30.00 |
| Goblet | 30.00 | 55.00 | 24.00 |
| Pickle Dish | 20.00 | 24.00 | 18.00 |
| Pitcher, water | 60.00 | 65.00 | 55.00 |
| Sugar Bowl, cov | 48.00 | 55.00 | 45.00 |
| Spooner | 30.00 | 36.00 | 24.00 |
| Tumbler | 36.00 | 45.00 | 30.00 |
| Wine | 24.00 | 30.00 | 20.00 |

## Star Rosetted

Manufactured by McKee & Bros. Glass Company, Pittsburgh, PA, c1875. Made in non-flint, clear.

**Reproductions:** Reproduced in color.

| Items | Clear |
| --- | --- |
| Bowl, flat, 7" d | 18.00 |
| Bowl, flat, 8" d | 18.00 |
| Bowl, flat, 9" d | 24.00 |
| Bowl, footed, ls, 7" d | 24.00 |
| Bowl, footed, ls, 8" d | 30.00 |
| Bowl, footed, ls, 9" d | 36.00 |
| Bread Plate | 60.00 |
| Butter Dish, cov | 55.00 |
| Compote, cov, hs, 7" d | 60.00 |
| Compote, cov, hs, 8" d | 65.00 |
| Compote, cov, hs, 8-1/2" d | 72.00 |
| Compote, cov, ls, 7" d | 60.00 |
| Compote, cov, ls, 8" d | 65.00 |
| Compote, cov, ls, 8-1/2" d | 72.00 |
| Compote, open, hs, 6-1/2" | 20.00 |
| Compote, open, hs, 7-1/2" | 24.00 |
| Compote, open, hs, 8-1/2" | 45.00 |
| Compote, open, ls, 6-1/2" d | 18.00 |
| Compote, open, ls, 7" d | 24.00 |
| Compote, open, ls, 7-1/2" d | 24.00 |
| Compote, open, ls, 8" d | 30.00 |
| Compote, open, ls, 8-1/2" d | 30.00 |
| Creamer | 45.00 |
| Goblet | 30.00 |
| Jelly Compote, cov | 65.00 |
| Pickle Dish | 18.00 |
| Pitcher, water | 60.00 |
| Plate, 7" d | 18.00 |
| Plate, 9" d | 24.00 |
| Relish, 9" l | 18.00 |
| Sauce, flat, 3-1/2" d, 4" d, or 4-1/2" d | 8.50 |
| Sauce, footed, 3-1/2" d, 4" d, or 4-1/2" d | 15.00 |
| Spooner | 30.00 |
| Sugar Bowl, cov | 55.00 |
| Sweetmeat, cov | 65.00 |
| Wine | 55.00 |

## Stippled Double Loop

Manufacturer unknown, c1870. Made in non-flint, clear and stippled.

| Items | Clear |
| --- | --- |
| Butter Dish, cov | 60.00 |
| Cake Stand | 48.00 |
| Celery Vase | 48.00 |
| Creamer | 36.00 |
| Goblet | 72.00 |
| Pitcher, water | 65.00 |
| Salt Shaker | 24.00 |
| Sauce, flat | 10.00 |
| Spooner | 24.00 |
| Sugar Bowl, cov | 30.00 |
| Tumbler | 36.00 |

## Stippled Peppers

Manufacture attributed to Boston and Sandwich Glass Company Sandwich, MA, in the 1870s. Made in non-flint, clear.

| Items | Clear |
| --- | --- |
| Creamer, ah | 45.00 |
| Egg Cup | 24.00 |
| Goblet | 36.00 |

| Items | Clear |
|---|---|
| Pitcher, water, ah | 90.00 |
| Salt, ftd | 18.00 |
| Sauce | 8.00 |
| Spooner | 30.00 |
| Sugar Bowl, cov | 45.00 |
| Tumbler, ftd | 24.00 |
| Wine | 45.00 |

## Sunburst *Flattened Diamond and Sunburst*

Manufactured by Burlington Glass Works, Hamilton, Ontario, Canada. Made in non-flint, clear with pieces occasionally found in amber or blue.

| Items | Clear |
|---|---|
| Bread Plate, 11" d, GUTDODB | 30.00 |
| Cake Stand | 36.00 |
| Creamer | 30.00 |
| Egg Cup | 20.00 |
| Goblet | 30.00 |
| Plate, 7" d | 18.00 |
| Relish | 15.00 |

| Items | Clear |
|---|---|
| Sauce | 7.50 |
| Wine | 24.00 |

## Swag with Brackets

Manufactured by Jefferson Glass Company, Steubenville, OH, c1904. Made in blue opalescent, canary-yellow opalescent, green opalescent and white (clear) opalescent. Also found in non-opalescent colors, gold trimmed, amethyst, blue, and vaseline.

| Items | Blue Opalescent | Canary Opalescent | Green Opalescent | White Opalescent |
|---|---|---|---|---|
| Butter Dish, cov | 190.00 | 190.00 | 160.00 | 120.00 |
| Creamer | 95.00 | 95.00 | 90.00 | 65.00 |
| Cruet, os | 160.00 | 160.00 | 112.00 | - |
| Jelly Compote | 55.00 | 55.00 | 65.00 | 36.00 |
| Pitcher, water | 200.00 | 200.00 | 240.00 | 136.00 |
| Salt Shaker | 60.00 | 60.00 | 48.00 | 45.00 |
| Spooner | 80.00 | 80.00 | 75.00 | 48.00 |
| Sugar Bowl, cov | 145.00 | 145.00 | 100.00 | 60.00 |
| Toothpick Holder | 130.00 | 130.00 | 100.00 | 48.00 |
| Tumbler | 75.00 | 75.00 | 60.00 | 45.00 |

## Swan *Plain Swan, Swan with Mesh*

Manufactured attributed to the Canton Glass Company, Canton, OH, c1882. Designed and patented by David Barker, Patent No. 12,887, on April 18, 1882. Made in amber, blue, canary-yellow, and clear. Rarely found in color.

**Reproductions:** Milk glass creamers and covered sugars are reproductions. Some sources suspect that the goblet has reproduced in clear.

| Items | Clear |
|---|---|
| Bread Plate, Bearded Head handles, oval | 100.00 |
| Butter Dish, cov | 130.00 |
| Compote, cov, hs | 130.00 |
| Compote, open, scalloped | 120.00 |
| Creamer φ | 90.00 |
| Goblet | 95.00 |
| Pickle Jar, cov, swan finial | 120.00 |
| Pitcher, water | 360.00 |
| Sauce, flat or footed, 4" d | 24.00 |
| Spooner, double handles | 115.00 |
| Sugar Bowl, cov, double handles φ | 190.00 |
| Wine | 110.00 |

## Teardrop and Tassel *Sampson*

Manufactured by the Indiana Tumbler and Goblet Company, Greentown, IN, c1895. Made in non-flint, clear, cobalt blue, emerald green, and opaque Nile green.

| Items | Chocolate | Clear | Cobalt Blue | Emerald Green | Nile Green Opaque |
|---|---|---|---|---|---|
| Bowl, 5-1/2" d | 650.00 | 40.00 | 60.00 | 55.00 | - |
| Bowl, 7-1/2" d | - | 48.00 | 65.00 | 60.00 | 90.00 |
| Butter Dish, cov | 1,200.00 | 65.00 | 115.00 | 165.00 | 330.00 |
| Celery Vase | - | 48.00 | - | - | - |
| Compote, cov, hs, 7" d | - | 90.00 | 110.00 | 95.00 | 130.00 |
| Compote, open, ls, 5" d | - | 24.00 | - | - | - |
| Compote, open, ls, 8" d | - | 36.00 | 55.00 | 45.00 | 75.00 |
| Creamer | 400.00 | 55.00 | 120.00 | 55.00 | 110.00 |
| Goblet | - | 112.00 | 130.00 | 190.00 | 115.00 |
| Jelly Compote, cov | - | 75.00 | - | - | - |
| Pickle Dish | 350.00 | 24.00 | 65.00 | 48.00 | 65.00 |
| Pitcher, water | - | 60.00 | 160.00 | 160.00 | 1,200.00 |
| Relish Dish, oval | 400.00 | 30.00 | 70.00 | 50.00 | 70.00 |
| Salt Shaker | - | 60.00 | 90.00 | 72.00 | 85.00 |
| Sauce, 4" d | 235.00 | 18.00 | 24.00 | 24.00 | - |
| Sauce, 4-1/2" d | 250.00 | 20.00 | 30.00 | 30.00 | - |
| Spooner | 350.00 | 36.00 | 55.00 | 45.00 | 75.00 |
| Sugar Bowl, cov | 565.00 | 72.00 | 145.00 | 85.00 | 110.00 |
| Tumbler | - | 48.00 | 60.00 | 55.00 | 75.00 |
| Wine | - | 75.00 | 95.00 | 85.00 | 112.00 |

## Tokyo

Made by Jefferson Glass Company, Steubenville, OH, 1905. Made in blue opalescent, green opalescent and white (clear) opalescent. Also found in apple green, blue, and clear, all with gold trim.

**Reproductions:** Some reproductions made by Fenton Art Glass, Fenton, OH. These were usually marked by Fenton.

| Items | Blue Opalescent | Green Opalescent | White Opalescent |
|---|---|---|---|
| Berry Bowl | 65.00 | 55.00 | 45.00 |
| Butter Dish, cov | 145.00 | 120.00 | 85.00 |
| Creamer | 95.00 | 72.00 | 60.00 |
| Cruet | 200.00 | 148.00 | 110.00 |
| Dish, 6-1/2" d | 48.00 | 55.00 | 36.00 |
| Jelly Compote | 48.00 | 55.00 | 45.00 |
| Pitcher, water | 200.00 | 160.00 | 120.00 |
| Salt Shaker | 60.00 | 48.00 | 36.00 |
| Sauce | 36.00 | 30.00 | 24.00 |
| Spooner | 55.00 | 48.00 | 36.00 |
| Sugar Bowl, cov | 115.00 | 90.00 | 72.00 |
| Toothpick | 112.00 | 95.00 | 60.00 |
| Tumbler | 60.00 | 55.00 | 45.00 |
| Vase | 72.00 | 72.00 | 55.00 |

## United States Regal

Manufactured by United States Glass Company, Pittsburgh, PA, c1906. One of the many imitation-cut patterns that were so popular. The bowls are slightly squared in shape. Made in non-flint, clear.

| Items | Clear |
|---|---|
| Basket, wide handle | 45.00 |
| Butter Dish, cov | 45.00 |

| Items | Clear |
|-------|-------|
| Creamer | 35.00 |
| Goblet | 30.00 |
| Sugar Bowl, cov | 42.00 |
| Spooner | 35.00 |
| Tumbler | 30.00 |

## Water Lily and Cattails

Manufactured by Fenton Glass Company, Williamstown, WV; Northwood Glass Company, Wheeling, WV, c1900; and Northwood-Diamond-Dugan Co. Made in amethyst, blue, chocolate, clear, and green opalescent. Also found in carnival glass.

| Items | Amethyst Opalescent | Blue Opalescent | Chocolate | Clear Opalescent | Green Opalescent |
|-------|---------------------|-----------------|-----------|------------------|------------------|
| Berry Bowl, 8" d, ruffled | 75.00 | 110.00 | 350.00 | 45.00 | 65.00 |
| Bon Bon, tricorn | 75.00 | 65.00 | - | 42.00 | 45.00 |
| Butter Dish, cov | 125.00 | 135.00 | 475.00 | 90.00 | 115.00 |
| Creamer | 110.00 | 85.00 | 295.00 | 65.00 | 80.00 |
| Pitcher, water | 275.00 | 295.00 | 1,350.00 | 90.00 | 135.00 |
| Plate | 45.00 | 45.00 | - | 35.00 | 42.00 |
| Relish, handle | 55.00 | 45.00 | - | 42.00 | 45.00 |
| Sauce | 45.00 | 42.00 | 85.00 | 30.00 | 35.00 |
| Spooner | 55.00 | 55.00 | 275.00 | 45.00 | 55.00 |
| Sugar Bowl, cov | 90.00 | 85.00 | 350.00 | 65.00 | 75.00 |
| Tumbler | 55.00 | 55.00 | 195.00 | 42.00 | 45.00 |

## Wedding Bells *Fostoria Pattern Line No. 789*

Manufactured by Fostoria Glass Company, Moundsville ,WV, c1900. Made in clear with gold trim, sometimes found with cranberry and rose blush.

| Items | Clear | Clear with Blush |
|-------|-------|------------------|
| Berry Bowl, 10" d | 90.00 | 110.00 |
| Butter Dish, cov | 75.00 | 135.00 |
| Celery Vase | 42.00 | 90.00 |
| Compote, cov, hs | 80.00 | - |
| Compote, cov, ls | 65.00 | - |
| Creamer, ah | 65.00 | 90.00 |
| Cruet, os | 80.00 | 135.00 |
| Custard Cup | 20.00 | 30.00 |
| Decanter, os | 110.00 | 120.00 |
| Finger Bowl | 42.00 | 55.00 |
| Pitcher, water, bulbous | 110.00 | 135.00 |
| Pitcher, water, tankard | 110.00 | 145.00 |
| Punch Bowl, 2 pcs | 135.00 | - |
| Punch Cup | 20.00 | - |
| Relish Tray | 30.00 | 45.00 |
| Salt Shaker, orig top | 42.00 | 65.00 |
| Spooner | 42.00 | 85.00 |
| Sugar Bowl, cov | 55.00 | 115.00 |
| Syrup, orig top | 85.00 | - |
| Toothpick Holder. | 42.00 | 65.00 |
| Tumbler | 35.00 | 65.00 |
| Waste Bowl | 42.00 | 55.00 |
| Whiskey | 30.00 | 55.00 |
| Wine | 45.00 | 75.00 |

# Wild Bouquet

Made by Harry Northwood Glass Company, Wheeling, WV, c1900-05, and other companies. Made in blue, green, and clear with white opalescence.

| Items | Blue Opalescent | Green Opalescent | White Opalescent |
|---|---|---|---|
| Berry Bowl | - | 115.00 | 75.00 |
| Butter Dish, cov | - | 250.00 | 225.00 |
| Creamer | - | 75.00 | 55.00 |
| Cruet | 350.00 | 350.00 | 250.00 |
| Cruet Set on Tray | 360.00 | 360.00 | 360.00 |
| Pitcher, water | 265.00 | 265.00 | 295.00 |
| Salt and Pepper Shakers, pr | 125.00 | 125.00 | 125.00 |
| Sauce | 42.00 | 35.00 | 35.00 |
| Spooner | 125.00 | 125.00 | 115.00 |
| Sugar Bowl, cov | 142.00 | 135.00 | 130.00 |
| Toothpick Holder | 135.00 | 130.00 | 125.00 |
| Tumbler | 75.00 | 55.00 | 55.00 |

# PAUL REVERE POTTERY

S.E.G.

**History:** Paul Revere Pottery, Boston, Massachusetts, was an outgrowth of a club known as The Saturday Evening Girls. The S.E.G. was composed of young female immigrants who met on Saturday nights to read and participate in craft projects, such as ceramics.

Regular pottery production began in 1908, and the name "Paul Revere" was adopted because the pottery was located near the Old North Church. In 1915, the firm moved to Brighton, Massachusetts. Known as the "Bowl Shop," the pottery grew steadily. In spite of popular acceptance and technical advancements, the pottery required continual subsidies. It finally closed in January 1942.

Items produced range from plain and decorated vases to tablewares to illustrated tiles. Many decorated wares were incised and glazed either in an Art Nouveau matte finish or an occasional high glaze.

**Marks:** In addition to an impressed mark, paper "Bowl Shop" labels were used prior to 1915. Pieces also can be found with a date and "P.R.P." or "S.E.G." painted on the base.

**References:** Susan and Al Bagdade, *Warman's American Pottery and Porcelain*, 2nd ed., Krause Publications, 2000; Paul Evans, *Art Pottery of the United States*, 2nd ed., Feingold & Lewis Publishing, 1987; Ralph and Terry Kovel, *Kovels' American Art Pottery*, Crown Publishers, 1993; David Rago, *American Art Pottery,* Knickerbocker Press, 1977.

**Collectors' Club:** American Art Pottery Association, P. O. Box 1226, Westport, MA 02790.

Bowl
   5-3/8" d, 2-1/4" h, border of repeating incised rim dec of three running rabbits in creamy white, blue ground, hairline, glaze imperfections ............................................................. 815.00
   8-1/2" d, 2-3/4" d, round tapering to base, matte brown ext., tan glaze int., sgd "S. E. G." .................................................. 175.00
Bread Plate, 9-3/4" d, white band dec in cuerda seca, "Give Us This Our Daily Bread," blue ground, ink mark "S.E.G. 11-21 FL," rim bruise ..................................................................... 550.00
Breakfast Set, cuerda seca dec, white running rabbits, blue ground, inscribed to "Bruce Learned," sgd and dated "12-18" in ink, 1918, hairline and chip repair to bowl, chip repair to plate ............. 1,300.00
Catalog Pamphlet, 9" h, 6-1/4" l, Paul Revere Pottery, Boston, colored and black and white photographic images of individual pottery items, breakfast, tea, and children's sets, minor wear .......................... 45.00

**Pitcher, blue-gray mottled glaze, frothy white glaze around rim, stamped "Paul Revere Pottery," 4-1/2" h, 4-1/2" d, $100. Photo courtesy of David Rago Auctions.**

Cereal Bowl, 6" d, 1-3/4" d, cuerda seca dec, yellow and white hen and chicks, inscribed "To Eliza," sgd and dated "241-4-09, F. L.," 1909, two short tight hairlines, slight surface wear ........................... 750.00
Plate, cuerda sec decoration
   5-1/2" d, pine cone dec, green, black, and brown, light cream ground, sgd, dated 5-22, artist sgd ................................. 170.00
   6-1/2" d, chicken and chicks, cream and yellow ground, sgd and initialed "EG," dated 9-13 ............................................... 350.00
   6-1/2" d, whimsical chick, outlined in black, cream and yellow ground, artist sgd and dated .......................................... 650.00
   7-1/2" d, green and brown trees, dark blue ground, ink sgd "7-14 S.E.G./A.M." 1914, tight hairline and minor touch-up to rim ............................................................................. 350.00
Tankard Set, 7-1/2" h, 9-1/2" d tankard, six mugs, blue-green mate glaze, imp Paul Revere mark ............................................. 650.00
Tea Caddy, cov, 4" h, 3-1/2" d, cuerda seca dec, indigo irises, brown and green ground, ink sgd "S. E. G. 11-14," small chips to lid, tight line on jar............................................................................. 1,200.00
Tile, 5" d, brown and green geometric, blue ground, black outline, sgd, framed in oak Arts & Crafts frame............................................. 250.00
Tray, 7" l, incised and painted tree, two tones of green, blue, and black, sgd, cracked and glued ............................................... 280.00
Vase
   4-1/2" h, 3-3/4" d, bulbous, band of lotus in cuerda seca, blue-gray ground, ink mark "SEG/Am/11-14" ......................... 1,100.00
   5-3/4" h, 4-1/2" d, bulbous, band of yellow tulips, matte green ground, Paul Revere stamp, illegible date ..................... 1,100.00
   6" h, small flared rim, bulbous body, matte drip glaze, shades of blue and gray, minor base flakes ....................................... 260.00
   6-1/2" h, 5" d, ovoid, dec in cuerda seca, yellow tulips, green leaves, blue ground, stamped Paul Revere mark ......... 1,300.00
   8-1/2" h, ovoid, rim dec with stylized petal forms, matte gray-blue, outlined in black, semi-glass dark blue ground, sgd "S.E.G." on base, hairline................................................................... 920.00

# PEACHBLOW

**History:** Peachblow, an art glass which derives its name from a fine Chinese glazed porcelain, resembles a peach or crushed strawberries in color. Three American glass manufacturers and two English firms produced peachblow glass in the late 1880s. A fourth American company resumed the process in the 1950s. The glass from each firm has its own identifying characteristics.

Hobbs, Brockunier & Co., Wheeling peachblow: Opalescent glass, plated or cased with a transparent amber glass; shading from yellow at the base to a deep red at top; glossy or satin finish.

Mt. Washington "Peach Blow": A homogeneous glass, shading from a pale gray-blue to a soft rose color; some pieces enhanced with glass appliqués, enameling, and gilding.

New England Glass Works, New England peachblow (advertised as Wild Rose, but called Peach Blow at the plant): Translucent, shading from rose to white; acid or glossy finish; some pieces enameled and gilded.

Thomas Webb & Sons and Stevens and Williams (English firms): Peachblow-style cased art glass, shading from yellow to red; some pieces with cameo-type relief designs.

Gunderson Glass Co.: Produced peachblow-type art glass to order during the 1950s; shades from an opaque faint tint of pink, which is almost white, to a deep rose.

**Marks:** Pieces made in England are marked "Peach Blow" or "Peach Bloom."

**References:** Gary E. Baker et al., *Wheeling Glass 1829-1939*, Oglebay Institute, 1994, distributed by Antique Publications; Sean and Johanna S. Billings, Peachblow Glass, *Collector's Identification and Price Guide*, Krause Publications, 2001. Neila and Tom Bredehoft, *Hobbs, Brockunier & Co. Glass*, Collector Books, 1997; Kyle Husfloen, *Antique Trader's American & European Decorative and Art Glass Price Guide,* 2nd ed., Krause Publications, 2000; James Measell, *New Martinsville Glass*, Antique Publications, 1994; John A. Shuman III, *Collector's Encyclopedia of American Glass*, Collector Books, 1988, 1994 value update; Kenneth Wilson, *American Glass 1760-1930*, 2 vols., Hudson Hills Press and The Toledo Museum of Art, 1994.

## Gunderson

Bowl, 4" d, 3-1/2" h, Paul Revere shape ..................................... 225.00
Candlestick
    8-1/4" h, classic Pairpoint shape, rolled edge on socket, pink shading to white, blush of color at base .......................... 375.00
    8-1/4" h, Morning Glory, bright pink and white, acid finish........275.00
Chalice, 7-1/4" h, 4" d, deep color, rare applied Burmese glass base ...............................................................................285.00
Creamer, 4" h, 5" w, pedestal, deep color, acid finish, applied reeded handle ...................................................................... 295.00
Cruet, 8" h, 3-1/2" d, matte finish, ribbed shell handle, matching peachblow stopper................................................................... 875.00
Cup and Saucer ......................................................................... 275.00
Decanter, 10" h, 5" d, acid finish, deep raspberry pink shading to brilliant white, peachblow ribbed handle, deep raspberry stopper, Pilgrim canteen form ...................................................... 950.00
Jug, 4-1/2" h, 4" w, applied loop handle, acid finish, bulbous ..... 450.00
Pitcher
    5-1/2" h, Hobnail, matte finish, hint of pink in int., orig label550.00
    6" h, 5-3/4" w, pink shading to white, strap handle, glossy finish.................................................................................395.00
Punch Cup, 2-3/4" h, 4" w, acid finish ........................................ 275.00
Tumbler, 3-3/4" h, matte finish ................................................... 275.00
Urn, 8-1/2" h, 4-1/2" w, two applied "M" handles, sq cut base, matte finish...............................................................................550.00
Vase
    4-1/4" h, 3" d, acid finish ..................................................... 225.00
    5" h, 6" d, ruffled top, pinched body ................................... 525.00
    8-1/4" h, 3-1/2" d, bulbous stick, orig glossy finish, deep fuchsia red to bright yellow ........................................................ 895.00
    9" h, 3-1/4" d base, Tappan, acid finish.............................. 425.00
Wine Glass, 5" h, glossy finish.................................................... 175.00

## Mt. Washington

Creamer, 5-1/4" h, ribbon edge, applied handle, orig paper label "Patented/Peach/Mt. W G Co/Blow/Dec 15 '85" ......................... 2,950.00
Cruet, 5-1/2" h, cylindrical ribbed body, blackberry vine dec, orig white faceted molded stopper with blue-gray tint, two small foot flakes on base ............................................................................ 1,000.00
Jack In The Pulpit, 9" h, bright pink shading to blue,, matte finish, c1880 ..................................................................................... 4,250.00
Sugar, cov, orig paper label ....................................................... 2,950.00

## New England

Celery Vase, 7" h, 4" w, Wild Rose, sq top, deep raspberry with purple highlights to white................................................................. 785.00
Cruet, 6-3/4" h, 4" d base, petticoat form, three lip top, acid finish ................................................................................... 1,950.00
Spooner, square top, acid finish.................................................. 825.00
Tumbler, 3-3/4" h, Wild Rose, shiny finish, thin walls................. 445.00

Vase
    6-1/2" h, 3" w, lily, Wild Rose, deep pink shading to white.. 650.00
    7" h, lily, Wild Rose, vivid crimson shading to deep pink to white .................................................................................785.00
    8" h, 3" d, baluster shape, applied base, flaring rim, glossy finish, deep color, price for pr ................................................. 1,275.00
    10-1/2" h, 5" d, Wild Rose, bulbous, tapering neck, cup top, glossy finish................................................................... 1,250.00
    10-1/2" h, 5" d, Wild Rose, bulbous, gourd-style, crushed raspberry shading to brilliant white, coloring extends two-thirds way down, four dimpled sides ............................................... 1,450.00
    12-1/4" h, lily, Wild Rose, deep raspberry to bright white, matte finish.............................................................................. 975.00

## Webb

Bowl, 3-3/4" d, folded and pinched rim, stamped on bottom "Queen's Burmese Ware Patented Thos Webb & Sons"........................ 425.00
Egg Cup Set, each holder is 2-1/2" h, peachblow cups with burnished gold blossoms and foliage on one side, gold butterfly on other, four spoons with English touch mark, 6-1/4" x 5" w x 6-1/2" h sterling silver stand................................................................................. 750.00
Scent Bottle, 2-3/4" d, acid finish, enameled blue, white, and yellow forget-me-nots, green leaves, creamy white lining, hallmarked SS screw-on dome top.................................................................. 695.00
Vase
    8" h, enameled gold prunus branch dec ............................. 275.00
    10-1/4" h, gold prunus branch dec, deep mahogany at top to pink to oyster white base ........................................................ 485.00

## Wheeling

Cream Pitcher, 3-1/8" h, deep mahogany to fuchsia to butter-cream, white lining, applied amber handle.......................................... 885.00
Milk Pitcher, 7-1/2" h, glossy finish, Hobbs Brockunier, c1890 1,000.00
Pear, 4-3/4" h, 3" d, matte finish, deep color, brilliant red and yellow, white lining, very tip of stem missing...................................... 900.00
Pitcher
    8" h, bulbous, quatrefoil top, glossy, deep coloration, white casing, applied amber handle............................................... 400.00
    11" h, acid finish, tankard, red to amber shading, opal glass int., applied amber reeded handle, Hobbs Brockunier......... 2,415.00
Punch Cup
    2-1/4" h, satin finish, chalk white lining, clear amber glass curled handle ................................................................................ 575.00
    2-1/2" h, Hobbs, Brockunier................................................. 535.00
Salt Shaker, large, satin ............................................................. 650.00
Sugar Shaker, 5-1/2" h, deep red shading to butter cream at base, screw-top oxidized to satiny gunmetal color ........................ 1,950.00
Vase, 13" h, gourd-shape, acid finish, light shaded ground........ 975.00

**Sugar Shaker, deep red shading to butter cream at base, satiny gunmetal cop, 5-1/2" h, $1,950. Photo courtesy of Clarence & Betty Maier.**

# PEKING GLASS

**History:** Peking glass is a type of cameo glass of Chinese origin. Its production began in the 1700s and continued well into the 19th century. The background color of Peking glass may be a delicate shade of yellow, green, or white. One style of white background is so transparent that it often is referred to as the "snowflake" ground. The overlay colors include a rich garnet red, deep blue, and emerald green.

Bowl
    3-1/2" d, white color, shallow, late 18th/early 19th C..............75.00
    6-1/4" d, cameo, green cut to white, squirrels and grapes, fitted with rosewood stand, 19th C, worn int............................175.00
    7" d, jade color, flaring form, carved with lotus plants, late 18th/early 19th C...........................................100.00
Jar, cov
    5-3/4" h, garnet red and white, lid carved with archaic dragon, globular body with two more chih lung, foo dog shaped jump rings on side, Ch'ien Lung mark and period, 1735-1796 .815.00
    14" h, cobalt blue, ovoid, carved fitted rosewood covers, Ch'ien Lung mark and period, 1735-94, price for pr.................5,750.00
Jewelry, bangle bracelet, round, hinged, saddles of green Peking glass within gilt silver chased and engraved mount, Chinese hallmark, price for pr..................................................260.00
Scholar's Seal, 2" l, sapphire blue glass carved with cat, seal impression intact, traces of cinnabar remaining, late 18th/early 19th C...........425.00
Snuff Bottle, heart shaped, color and markings of realgar, green glass stopper set in gilt metal, 19th C.................................690.00
Vase
    5" h, white, stylized foo dogs in low relief, two reserves of flowering branches in polychrome under clear glass layer, early 20th C.....................................................150.00
    7" h, pear shaped body, slightly flaring mouth, lemon yellow, carved birds on flowering branches, 19th C.....................815.00
    7-1/2" h, pear shaped body, ruby cut to snowflake ground, figures in palace garden, late 19th C..........................260.00
    9" h, bottle shape, pink color layered between white, carved lotus petals all around body, neck carved with lotus plants and birds, thunder meander around mouth, late 18th/early 19th C. 1,380.00
    9" h, ruby red, carved in relief, Ch'ien Lung mark, possibly of the period ..............................................750.00

**Vase, red floral pattern, white ground, 8" h, $225.**

11" h, mustard yellow, carved birds and flowering branches, 20th C, price for pr ..................................................250.00

# PELOTON

**History:** Wilhelm Kralik of Bohemia patented Peloton art glass in 1880. Later it was also patented in America and England.

Peloton glass is found with both transparent and opaque grounds, although opaque is more common. Opaque colored glass filaments (strings) are applied by dipping or rolling the hot glass. Generally, the filaments (threads) are pink, blue, yellow, and white (rainbow colors) or a single color. Items also may have a satin finish and enamel decorations.

Bowl, 6-1/2" d, 6" h, white ground, all over brown and yellow filaments, ribbed surface, three applied colorless thorn feet, eight point star top ..................................................325.00
Fairy Lamp, white ground, pastel filaments, undulating ruffled saucer base, colorless Clarke insert....................................365.00
Pitcher, 4-3/4" h, green filaments on colorless body.....................75.00
Plate, 7-3/4" d, colorless ground, blue filaments, enameled floral dec ..................................................125.00
Rose Bowl
    4" d, 4" h, bowl form, four pulled edges, sq shape, applied crystal edge and six shell feet, glossy finish blue shaded body, yellow, pink, white, red, and blue filaments.........................400.00
    5-1/2" w, 6" h, star shaped top with eight points, white lining, ribbed and swirled body, shades of brown filaments, applied crystal feet...........................................325.00
Toothpick Holder, 3" h, colorless ground, white filaments...........145.00
Tumbler, 3-3/4" h, colorless ground, yellow, pink, red, light blue, and white filaments ..............................................125.00
Vase
    4" h, 4-3/4" d, bulbous shape, folded over tricorn shape top, white ribbed cased body, pink, yellow, blue, and white applied filaments ..................................................290.00
    6" h, 4-1/2" d, shaded lavender to off-white opaque ground, cased in crystal, all over pink, white, yellow, blue, and red filaments, corset type shape, vertical ribs, tightly crimped top .........450.00
    6" h, 5" w, ribbed, bright pink ground, yellow, blue, white, red, pink, and purple filaments, white lining, two applied ribbed handles..................................................450.00

# PERFUME, COLOGNE, and SCENT BOTTLES

**History:** The second half of the 19th century was the golden age for decorative bottles made to hold scents. These bottles were made in a variety of shapes and sizes.

An atomizer is a perfume bottle with a spray mechanism. Cologne bottles usually are larger and have stoppers which also may be used as applicators. A perfume bottle has a stopper that often is elongated and designed to be an applicator.

Scent bottles are small bottles used to hold a scent or smelling salts. A vinaigrette is an ornamental box or bottle that has a perforated top and is used to hold aromatic vinegar or smelling salts. Fashionable women of the late 18th and 19th centuries carried them in purses or slipped them into gloves in case of a sudden fainting spell.

**References:** Jacquelyne Jones-North, *Commercial Perfume Bottles*, 3rd, Schiffer Publishing, 1996; —, *Perfume, Cologne and Scent Bottles,* 3rd ed., Schiffer Publishing, 1999; Jacquelyne Y. Jones-North, et. al., *Czechoslovakian Perfume Bottles and Boudoir Accessories, Revised Ed.,* Antique Publications, 1999; L-W Book Sales, *Diamond I Perfume Bottles Price Guide and other Drugstore Wares,* L-W Book Sales, 2000; Monsen and Baer, *A Century of Perfume: The Perfumes of François Coty,* published by authors, 2000; —, *Beauty of Perfume*, published by authors (Box 529, Vienna, VA 22183), 1996; —, *Legacies of Perfume*, published by authors, 1997; —, *Memories of Perfume,* published by authors, 1998; Jeri Lyn Ringblum, *Collector's Handbook of Miniature Perfume Bottles*, Schiffer Publishing, 1996.

**Periodical:** *Perfume & Scent Bottle Quarterly*, P.O. Box 187, Galena, OH 43021.

**Collectors' Clubs:** International Perfume Bottle Association, 3314 Shamrock Rd, Tampa, FL 33629, http://www.perfumebottles.org; Mini-Scents, 7 Saint John's Rd, West Hollywood, CA 90069; Parfum Plus Collections, 1590 Louis-Carrier Ste 502, Montreal Quebec H4N 2Z1 Canada.

## Atomizer

Baccarat, 5" h, 3-1/2" l, oval, etched crystal body, metal chrome top, marked ...................................................................... 125.00
De Vilbiss, 10" h, glass body with elongated neck, flaring at base, cobalt blue glass with orange gold heart and vine dec, strong irid purple-blue irid rising to gold and magenta, fitted with chased gilt metal atomizer fittings, base with DeVilbiss acid stamp, minor wear to metal finish, atomizer bag missing ...................... 1,495.00
Opalescent, 5-1/2" h cranberry striped, orig fittings .................. 125.00
Steuben, 4" h, Aurene ................................................................ 230.00

## Cologne Bottle

Boston and Sandwich, 5" h, vaseline, bull's eye motif ................ 150.00
Cameo Glass, 7" l, frosted snowflake background, cranberry cut floral scene, faceted cut stopper, St. Louis ...................................... 275.00
Cut Glass
    5" h, green cut to clear, hob and lace pattern, matching cut stopper ............................................................................. 425.00
    6-1/2" h, Atlas pattern, Eggington .................................... 200.00
    7" h, Genoa pattern, pattern cut stopper, by Clark ............. 450.00
Opalescent, 4-5/8" h, eight tooled panels, c1860 ...................... 150.00
Pairpoint, 7" h, clear, elaborate floral engraving, orig open red rose in paperweight stopper, Charles Kaziun signature cane .............. 750.00

**Cameo, citron body, white over red, crisscross pussy willow twig dec, push-on silver cap, Webb, 6-1/4" h, $1,250. Photo courtesy of Clarence & Betty Maier.**

Peachblow, 4-3/4" h, 3-1/2" d, ripe red at neck shading to yellow to pistachio green, polished pontil, screw-on sterling silver top and collar, mkd "Sterling," and silversmith's signature, English, minor dents on cap ...................................................................................... 585.00

## Perfume

Bohemian, 4-1/8" h, black glass, cut design, silver gilt fittings and rhinestones, clear stopper, paper label "Aristo, Genuine Bohemian Glass" ...................................................................................... 200.00
Brouseau, J. C., 11-3/4" h, flacon, octagonal press-molded colorless bottle, raised floral dec, frosted and polished to enhance design, frosted sphere stopper, base marked in mold "J. Brouseau, Made in France," c1925, minor staining .............................................. 290.00
Commercial
    Belter's New Mown Hay Perfume, 9-1/2" h, cylindrical bottle, oval applied reverse painted label with vintage lady, light staining and streaking to int. ..................................................... 150.00
    Jockey Club Perfume, 7-1/4" h, milk glass, rect, colorful recessed reverse painted label, stopper with flat top, Pat'd April 2, 1889 ......................................................................... 175.00
    Lightner's White Rose Perfume, 7" h, emb cylindrical bottle, colorful oval recessed reverse painted label, ground stopper with flat top, product inside ....................................................... 200.00
    Orange Flower Perfume, 7-1/4" h, milk glass, rect, colorful recessed reverse painted label, stopper with flat top, Pat'd April 2, 1889, two chips on bottle ........................................ 225.00
    Palmer's Bouquet Perfume, 9" h, emb cylindrical bottle, recessed reverse painted label, ground stopper with bulbous top, chip on stopper ................................................................... 325.00
    Palmer's Jockey Club Perfume, 9" h, emb, black, gold, white, and red reverse painted label, bulbous stopper ...................... 275.00
    Victorian King Edward, 9-1/2" h, cylindrical bottle, recessed colorful reverse painted label, ground stopper, ribbed top, Jasmine Perfume ....................................................................... 325.00
Cranberry
    2-1/4" h, round, cranberry, filigree, gilt collar ................... 695.00
    2-1/4" x 5-3/4", sanded gold enameled leaves, white enameled flowers, clear ball stopper, gold trim ............................. 135.00
Cut Glass, 6" h, cut glass, SS collar, cut stopper ....................... 180.00
Czechoslovakian
    4-1/2" h, clear and frosted, butterfly stopper, chip on stopper, incomplete applicator, mkd "Made in Czechoslovakia" .... 200.00
    5-3/4" h, amethyst cut and pressed body, clear stopper, Aristo paper label, mkd "Made in Czechoslovakia" ................... 250.00
    5-3/4" h, pale blue cut and pressed body, gilded filigree, blue glass stones and faux pearls, mkd "Made in Czechoslovakia" ....... 825.00
Galle, 4-1/2" h, frosted and green ground, green fern leaves scene, orig stopper, sgd .................................................................... 750.00
Moser, 4-1/2" l, lay down type, cranberry, white overlay, gold holly leaves and thistles ................................................................ 250.00
Mount Washington, 5-1/4" h, 3" w, Opalware, dark green and brown glossy ground, red and yellow nasturtiums, green leaves, sprinkler top ....................................................................................... 375.00
Opaline, 8" h, green, bell shaped base, tulip rim, enameled gold florals and dec, orig gold enameled stopper, polished pontil, c1870 .. 195.00
Staffordshire, 2-3/4" h, pillow shape, hp, garlands, gold dec, corner tassels, price for pr .............................................................. 250.00
Sterling Silver, 1-3/4", heart shape, monogrammed, mkd "…ffany Sterling" on one side, ".925" on other, c1920 ............................... 250.00

## Scent

Box, 4-1/2" l, glass, painted floral still lifes, gilt bronze foliate cast mounts, int. fitted with two bottles, French, early 20th C .......... 700.00
Cut Glass, 3-1/2" d, 5" h, Edwardian sterling silver top, hallmarked London, 1900, int. of top gilded ............................................. 350.00
Northwood, 1-3/4" h, pull-up design, eight horizontal bands, alternating stripes of rust, chartreuse, and white, SS cap ...................... 390.00
Opalescent, 3-1/4" l, horizontal and vertical ribs ......................... 85.00
Paris, 9-3/4" h, porcelain, figural, couple, slight restoration to lady, cracked to base of both .......................................................... 190.00

Porcelain, 3" h, German, second half 18<sup>th</sup> C, attributed to Kelsterbach, figural, young boy pulling horns of goat surrounded by grape vines, stopper attached with chains, gilt metal neck and base mount 900.00

Rock Crystal, 2-1/4" h, slightly bulbous swirled base, paneled neck with gold mouth chased leafage at neck, domed cov with translucent enameled royal blue over gillouche ground, moonstone thumbpiece, marked with initials of Workmaster "Henrik Wigstrom," 72 standard," incised signature of Fabergé in Cyrillic, St Petersburg, c1910 .................... 4,888.00

Satin Glass, sterling cap, slight dent to cap

4" d, globular, Bridal White, mother-of-pearl, white vertical stripes, sterling silver top engraved "Dora," stamped "CS, FS, STd SILr" ............. 400.00

7-1/2" h, Peacock Eye, mother-of-pearl, creamy yellow with hundreds of Peacock Eye airtraps, crown cap mkd "Sterling," cap joined by delicate sterling chain ...................... 750.00

## Vinaigrette

Cranberry, 2-1/2 x 1", rect, cut, enameled pink roses, green leaves, gold dec hinged lid, stopper, finger chain .................. 195.00

Cut Glass, oval design, 14kt rose gold lid with cabochon red stone, pierced floral design filter .................. 920.00

Enameled, 1-3/4" l, flattened rect flask, pale blue enamel over wave patterned metal surface, highlighted with pink enamel roses and blue ribbons on side and stopper, early 20<sup>th</sup> C .................. 95.00

Sterling Silver-Gilt

1" x 3/4", chased top, grill pierced and gilt, oval, English hallmarks on inside of cover "IT," attributed to Joseph Taylor, Birmingham ................................ 150.00

1" x 1-1/2", chased top, grill pierced and gilt, rect, bottom engraved "Anna," English hallmarks on inside of cover "IT," attributed to Joseph Taylor, Birmingham .................. 150.00

1-1/2" w, 1" d, "h, Victorian, maker Thomas Shaw, Birmingham, 1841 .................. 500.00

# PETERS and REED POTTERY

**History:** J. D. Peters and Adam Reed founded their pottery company in South Zanesville, Ohio, in 1900. Common flowerpots, jardinieres, and cooking wares comprised the majority of their early output. Occasionally art pottery was attempted, but it was not until 1912 that their Moss Aztec line was introduced and widely accepted. Other art wares include Chromal, Landsun, Montene, Pereco, and Persian.

**Pitcher, blue-gray matte glaze, frothy white glaze around rim, stamped "Paul Revere Pottery," 4-1/2" h, 4-1/2" d, $90. Photo courtesy of David Rago Auctions.**

Peters retired in 1921 and Reed changed the name of the firm to Zane Pottery Company.

**Marks:** Marked pieces of Peters and Reed Pottery are unknown.

Bowl

7" d, Moss Aztec, green and brown .................. 120.00

11-1/2" d, horizontal stripes inside and out .................. 160.00

Jug, 7-1/2" h, swirled form, brown glaze, portrait of Cavalier in yellow .. 50.00

Mug, 5 -3/4" h, high glaze, floral sprigs .................. 45.00

Nursing Feeder, grape and leaf garland dec around spout, glossy brown glaze .................. 45.00

Planter, 10-1/2" l, marbleized .................. 75.00

Pitcher, 4" h, brown glaze, yellow floral dec, unmarked, price for pr .. 70.00

Sand Jar, 21" h, molded design, maiden in forest with horse and rider, castle in trees, green wash over red clay, minor flaws ............. 700.00

Vase

6-1/2" h, blue, green, and brown dec, imp mark .................. 165.00

10" h, hexagonal, marbleized blue and gold, unmarked ..... 125.00

10" h, Moss Aztec, emb florals, green and red matte ......... 350.00

Wall Pocket

Floral, glossy .................. 135.00

Grapes and vines, molded design, bisque finish, brown and green, incised mark, 8" h .................. 100.00

# PEWTER

**History:** Pewter is a metal alloy consisting mostly of tin with small amounts of lead, copper, antimony, and bismuth added to make the shaping of products easier and to increase the hardness of the material. The metal can be cast, formed around a mold, spun, easily cut, and soldered to form a wide variety of utilitarian articles.

Pewter was known to the ancient Chinese, Egyptians, and Romans. England was the primary source of pewter for the American colonies for nearly 150 years until the American Revolution ended the embargo on raw tin, allowing the small American pewter industry to flourish until the Civil War.

**References:** Marilyn E. Dragowick (ed.), *Metalwares Price Guide*, Antique Trader Books, 1995; Donald M. Herr, *Pewter in Pennsylvania German Churches*, Vol. XXIX, The Pennsylvania German Society, 1995; Henry J. Kauffman, *American Pewterer*, Astragal Press, 1994.

**Collectors' Club:** Pewter Collectors Club of America, 504 W. Lafayette St., West Chester, PA 19380-2210.

**Museum:** The Currier Gallery of Art, Manchester, NH.

**Note:** The listings concentrate on the American and English pewter forms most often encountered by the collector.

Basin

7-3/4" d, Spencer Stafford, Albany, NY, c1820 .................. 325.00

8" d, Thomas Danforth Boardman, faint eagle touch .......... 225.00

9-1/8" d, Samuel Ellis, London, 18th C .................. 200.00

13-1/4" l, Samuel Pierce, Greenfield, MA, 1792-1830, faint eagle touch mark, edge damage, wear with dents and pitting ..... 220.00

Beaker, 3" h, J B Woodbury, Beverly, MA and Philadelphia, PA, 1830-38, handle, good mark .................. 400.00

Bowl

11-1/2" d, shallow, eagle touch with "TD" and "T. Danforth, Philadelphia," .................. 330.00

13-1/4" d, shallow, partial touch for Samuel Danforth, Hartford, CT ................................................................ 440.00

Candlesticks, pr

6" h, Rufus Dunham, Westbrook, ME, c1840, straight line touch, pr ......................................................................... 900.00

9-1/2" h, Plumey & Felton, Philadelphia, early 19th C, flaring around stems, circular base ............................................. 110.00

9-3/4" h, attributed to Horman, Cincinnati, unmarked ......... 225.00

9-3/4" h, unmarked American, married pair, one with slight battering, other with foot repair .................................................. 200.00

10" h, William Calder, Providence, RI, 1817-56, minor pitting on base ......................................................................... 325.00

Charger

13-3/8" d, Thomas Badger, Boston, MA, eagle touch, 13-3/8" d ...................................................................... 650.00

13-1/2" d, Nathaniel Austin, Charleston, MA, 13-1/2" d ...... 500.00

14-3/4" d, Charles White Leigh, London, England ............. 325.00

15" d, English, crowned rose touchmarks and "London," wear and battering ................................................................ 350.00

16-1/2" d, Richard King, London, England .......................... 375.00

Compote, 8-5/8" d, 6" h, unmarked .............................................. 420.00

Coffeepot, (tall pot)

Roswell Gleason, Dorchester, MA, 1822-1871, touch mark, minor pitting ................................................................... 425.00

Henry Horman (attributed to), Cincinnati, OH, 1847-65, tooled floral dec, acanthus leaf spout, scroll handle, grape finial, minor dents, 11-1/4" h ............................................................. 200.00

F. Porter, Westbrook, Maine, 1835-1860s, circular touch, 10-3/4" h ......................................................................... 470.00

John Whitlock, Troy, NY, 1836-44, touch mark, areas of pitting, well executed repair ......................................................... 330.00

Communion Flagon, 11-1/4" h, Reed and Barton, touch mark ... 660.00

Communion Plate, 13-1/8" d, Thomas Boardman, Hartford, CT, c1805-60, eagle touch mark ..................................................... 600.00

Compote, 5-1/4" sq, emb cherries, pierced, orig green glass liner, mkd "Tudric Pewter 0276/Made by Liberty & Co.," few nicks to feet ..1,600.00

Creamer, 4-1/2" h, Philadelphia, attributed to William Will ....... 6,900.00

Deep Dish, Samuel Hamlin, Hartford, CT, late 18th C ................. 600.00

Flagon, 12" h, Smith & Fletman, Albany ...................................... 350.00

Food Dome, 16-1/2" l, marked "James Dixon & Sons, Sheffield," traces of silver plating, one nut holding handle missing ..................... 125.00

Funnel, American, unmarked, ring handle, 6-3/8" l .................... 125.00

Lamp, 4-1/2" h, brass collar, fluid burner with snuffers, unmarked ... 115.00

Mug

Eddon, William, London, c1750, pint, tulip shape ............... 175.00

Whitmore, Jacob, Middletown, CT, c1758-90, quart, fair mark ...................................................................... 1,750.00

Lamp, double font, handle, Morey & Smith, Boston, 6" h, $300.

Pitcher

5-1/2" h, unmarked, American, pigeon breasted, reverse C-handle, removable lid ................................................... 325.00

6-1/2" h, Rufus Dunham, Westbrook, ME, c1845, cider type, two quart size ...................................................................... 350.00

11" h, Kayserzinn, Germany, early 20th C, long flaring neck, bulbous base, raised oak leaves and acorns, raised mark, wear ....... 320.00

Plate

7-3/4" d, Blakslee Barns, Philadelphia, 1812-1817, double touch marks with eagle and "B.B.," minor rim dents and wear .. 385.00

8" d, William Danforth, eagle touch, wear and scratches ... 275.00

8-1/2" d, Thomas Badger, Boston, 1787-1815, touch mark with eagle, bottom of bowl is pitted, wear ............................... 250.00

9" d, Thomas Danforth touch .............................................. 160.00

9-3/16" d, John Skinner, Boston, 1760-90, imp "EF" on rim, minor pitting and scratches ...................................................... 350.00

11-1/4" d, Blakeslee Barns, eagle touch with "Barnes, Phila" in rect, wear, scratches, and edge damage ......................... 300.00

Porringer

5" d, unmarked, attributed to David Mellville, Newport, RI, c1780-90, flowered handle initialed "FGW" ................................. 200.00

5-1/4" d, cast flowered handle, Calder, Provid. (William Calder, Providene, RI), eagle touch, minor dents ......................... 660.00

5-1/2" d, Samuel Green, Boston, MA, cast crown handle... 550.00

5-1/2" d, Samuel Hamlin, Providence, RI, c1790, flowered handle, minor int. pitting, good touch mark ................................. 500.00

Salt, Boyd, Parks, Philadelphia, PA, 1795-1819, beaded rim and base, ftd ....................................................................... 950.00

Spittoon, 4-3/4" h, handle, unmarked ........................................... 85.00

Sugar Bowl

Boardman & Hart, NY, c1835, orig lid, little minor denting, 8" h ........................................................................ 375.00

Unmarked, attributed to Boyd Parks, Philadelphia, PA, c1795-1819, beaded lid, rim and foot ..................................... 7,500.00

Tea and Coffee Service, Kayserzinn, Germany, late 19th/early 20th C, coffeepot, teapot, cov sugar, creamer, shaped oval 20" tray, all with raised stylized flowers and leaves, engraved initial "H," all with raised or imp marks and "4965," wear ........................................... 350.00

Teapot

6" h, Queen Anne, pear shaped, Israel Trask, Beverly, MA, 1807-1856, "I. Trask" touch, pitting, wear, old repair ................. 715.00

8-1/4" h, Horace C. and Dennis Wilcox, 1848-52, "H. C. Wilcox & Co." touch, soldered repairs where spout meets body ..... 110.00

8-1/4" h, Sellew & Co., mkd with name and "Cincinnati 12," damage, old repair to base .............................................. 300.00

8-3/4" h, Wm McQuickin, Philadelphia, 1845-53, domed lid, touch mark, handle restored, wooden finial missing, partial over varnish ..................................................................... 150.00

9" h, J. D. Locke, New York City, 1835-1860, touch mark .. 415.00

Tea Set, 4-1/2" h, 9-1/2" d squatty teapot with cane wrapped handle, creamer and open sugar, emb stylized fruit, stamped "Registered mark/Tudric" .............................................................. 425.00

# PHOENIX GLASS

**History:** Phoenix Glass Company, Beaver, Pennsylvania, was established in 1880. Known primarily for commercial glassware, the firm also produced a molded, sculptured, cameo-type line from the 1930s until the 1950s.

**References:** Tom and Neila Bredehoft, *Fifty Years of Collectible Glass, 1920-1970, Volume 1, Volume II,* Antique Trader Books, 2000; Jack D. Wilson, *Phoenix & Consolidated Art Glass,* Antique Publications, 1989.

**Collectors' Club:** Phoenix & Consolidated Glass Collectors Club, P.O. Box 159, Burlington, VT 05402-0159.

**Vase, Flying Geese, blue pastel ground, orig paper label, 9-1/2" h, 11-1/2" w, $150.**

Basket, 4-1/2" h, pink ground, relief molded dogwood dec...........65.00
Bowl, Bittersweet, relief molded, white ground, 9-1/2" d, 5-1/2" h ....165.00
Candlesticks, pr
    3-1/4" h, blue ground, bubbles and swirls.............................65.00
    4" h, blue ground, frosted.......................................................50.00
Canoe, 8" l, white ground, sculptured green lemons and foliage..95.00
Centerpiece Bowl, 14" d, opaque white ground, sculptured diving nudes, three colors..................................................................250.00
Charger, 14" d, blue ground, relief molded white daffodils..........100.00
Cigarette Box, Phlox, white milk glass, Wedgwood blue ............125.00
Compote, 8-1/2" d, butterscotch ground, relief molded dragonflies and water lilies dec.......................................................................85.00
Dish, cov, 8-1/2" l, oval, amber ground, sculptured lotus blossoms and dragonflies...............................................................................100.00
Ginger Jar, cov, frosted ground, bird finial .................................80.00
Lamp
    Boudoir, Wild Rose, brown highlights, milk glass ground ...150.00
    Table, 23" h, 16" d reverse painted shade, landscape with windmill, cottage, and barn, pale pink, yellow, and blue ground, green and brown landscape, minor edge flake ................650.00
Planter, 8-1/2" l, 3-1/4" h, white ground, relief molded green lion .95.00
Plate, 8-1/2" d, frosted and clear ground, relief molded cherries ..60.00
Powder Box, cov, 7-1/4" d, pale lavender ground, sculptured white violets .....................................................................................115.00
Rose Bowl, rose pink ground, relief molded starflowers and white bands .....................................................................................150.00
Tumbler, Lace Dew Drop, blue and white, set of 4 .......................75.00
Vase
    6" x 5", Goldware, emb birds on branch ...............................80.00
    8" x 5", Goldware, emb grasshoppers and grass....................125.00
    9" x 11", pillow shape, white, emb blue geese .....................240.00
    10-1/2" h, Dogwood, raised rim, molded ovoid body, colorless glass layered in dull yellow, overall dogwood blossoms, c1930.................................................................................115.00
    10-1/2" h, wide mouth, molded ovoid body, colorless glass layered in light blue, linear geometric dec outlining recessed panels of oriental-style flowers, c1930, minor nicks..............350.00

# PHONOGRAPHS

**History:** Early phonographs were commonly called "talking machines." Thomas A. Edison invented the first successful phonograph in 1877; other manufacturers followed with their variations.

**References:** Timothy C. Fabrizio and George F. Paul, *Antique Phonograph Gadgets, Gizmos, and Gimmicks*, Schiffer Publishing, 1999; —, *Discovering Antique Phonographs, 1877-1929*, Schiffer Publishing, 2000; —, *The Talking Machine: An Illustrated Compendium, 1877-*

*1929*, Schiffer Publishing, 1997; Neil Maker, *Hand-Cranked Phonographs*, Promar Publishing, 1993; Arnold Schwartzman, *Phono-Graphics*, Chronicle Books, 1993; Eric L. Reiss, *The Compleat Talking Machine*, 3rd ed., Sanoran Publishing, 1998.

**Periodicals:** *Horn Speaker*, P.O. Box 1193, Mabank, TX 75147; New Amberola Graphic, 37 Caledonia St., St. Johnsbury, VT 05819.

**Collectors' Clubs:** Buckeye Radio & Phonograph Club, 4572 Mark Trail, Copley, OH 44321; California Antique Phonograph Society, P.O. Box 67, Duarte, CA 91010; Hudson Valley Antique Radio & Phonograph Society, P.O. Box 207, Campbell Hall, NY 10916; Michigan Antique Phonograph Society, Inc., 2609 Devonshire, Lansing, MI 48910; Vintage Radio & Phonograph Society, Inc., P.O. Box 165345, Irving, TX 75016.

**Museums:** Edison National Historic Site, West Orange, NJ; Johnson's Memorial, Dover, DE; Seven Acres Antique Village & Museum, Union, IL.

**Advisor:** Lewis S. Walters.

Columbia
    BN, disc player.......................................................1,000.00
    BQ, cylinder player ................................................1,200.00
    HG, cylinder player ................................................2,400.00
Decca, Junior, portable, leather case & handle .....................150.00
Edison
    Amberola 30 ...........................................................350.00
    Army - Navy, World War I.........................................1,200.00
    Diamond Disc, VV-19, William & Mary......................500.00
    Excelsior, coin op....................................................2,500.00
    Fireside, original horn .............................................900.00
    Gem, maroon, 2 - 4 minute reproducer .....................1,700.00
    Opera, moving mandrel, fixed reproducer .................2,500.00
    Standard, Model A, oak case, metal horn..................550.00
    Triumph, cygnet horn, mahogany case......................2,500.00
    S-19 Diamond Disc, floor model, oak case................400.00
Graphone
    12.5 oak case, metal horn, retailer's mark, cylinder ...........450.00
    15.0 oak case with columns on corners, nickel plated platform, metal horn, stenciled cast iron parts ...............................725.00

**Standard Model A, Standard Talking Machine, red horn, $425.**

Home Grand, oak case, nickel-plated works #6, spring
motor ...................................................................... 1,300.00
Harvard, trumpet style horn ....................................... 300.00
Kalamazoo, Duplex -reproducer, original horns with decals, 1904
patent date .......................................................... 3,300.00
Odeon Talking Machine Co., table model, crank wind, brass horn,
straight tone arm ...................................................... 500.00
Silvertone (Sears), two reproducers ............................ 500.00
Sonora
Gothic Deluxe, walnut case, triple spring, gold plated parts, auto-
matic stop and storage ........................................ 400.00
Luzerne, Renaissance style case with storage .................. 200.00
Talk-O-Phone, Brooke, table model, oak case rope decorations, steel
horn .................................................................... 200.00
Victor
Credenza, crank ............................................. 1,100.00
Monarch, table model, corner columns brass bell horn ... 1,500.00
School House ................................................. 2,500.00
Victor I, mahogany case, corner columns bell horn ......... 1,500.00
Victor II, oak case, black bell horn .......................... 1,200.00
Victor II, oak case, smooth oak horn.......................... 5,500.00
Victor III, papier-mâché horn.................................. 1,400.00
Victor V, oak case, corner columns, no horn ................. 1,400.00

# PHOTOGRAPHS

**History:** A vintage print is a positive image developed
from the original negative by the photographer or under
the photographer's supervision at the time the negative
is made. A non-vintage print is a print made from an
original negative at a later date. It is quite common for a
photographer to make prints from the same negative
over several decades. Changes between the original
and subsequent prints usually can be identified. Limited
edition prints must be clearly labeled.

Vintage photography at auction has become quite
popular. Many auction houses are offering interesting
images in various forms, from tintypes to daguerreo-
types, albums, etc. Many of the high auction prices are
realized because of a famous photographer while others
are collected for their image or historical significance,
such as the Wild Bunch listed below.

**References:** Diane VanSkiver Gagel, *Ohio Photogra-
phers, 1839-1900: A History and Directory,* Carl Mautz
Publishing, 1998; Martin Gordon (ed.), *1999 Gordon's
Photograph Price Annual International,* Gordon and
Lawrence Art Reference, 1999; O. Henry Mace, *Col-
lector's Guide to Early Photographs,* 2nd ed., Krause
Publications, 1999; Susan Theran (ed.), *Leonard's
Annual Price Index of Posters & Photographs*, Auction
Index (30 Valentine Park, Newton, MA 02165), 1998;
Craig A. Tuttle, *An Ounce of Preservation, A Guide to
Care of Papers and Photographs,* Rainbow Books,
1995.

**Periodicals:** *CameraShopper*, 313 N. Quaker Lane,
P.O. Box 37029, W Hartford, CT 06137; *History of Photography*, 1900 Frost Rd, Suite 101, Tullytown, PA
19007; *On Paper*, 39 E. 78th St., #601, New York, NY
10021; *Photograph Collector*, 301 Hill Ave., Suite 2,
Langhorne, PA 18047.

**Collectors' Clubs:** American Photographic Historical
Society, Inc., 1150 Avenue of the Americas, New York,
NY 10036; Association of International Photography Art
Dealers, 1609 Connecticut Ave. NW #200, Washington,
DC 20009; Daguerrean Society, 625 Liberty Ave., Ste.
1790, Pittsburgh, PA 15222; National Stereoscopic
Association, P.O. Box 14801, Columbus, OH 43214;
Photographic Historical Society, Inc., P.O. Box 39563,
Rochester, NY 14604; Photographic Historical Society of
Canada, P.O. Box 54620, Toronto, Ontario M5M 4N5
Canada; Photographic Historical Society of New
England, P.O. Box 189, Boston, MA 02165; Western
Photographic Collectors Association Inc., P.O. Box
4294, Whittier, CA 90607.

**Museums:** Center for Creative Photography, Tucson,
AZ; International Center of Photography, New York, NY;
International Museum of Photography at George East-
man House, Rochester, NY; International Photographic
Historical Association, San Francisco, CA; National Por-
trait Gallery, Washington, DC.

**Additional Listings:** See *Warman's Americana & Collectibles* for more examples.

Album
Albumen Prints, 48 picturesque and diverse scenes of Japan, 12
prints of geishas, albumen prints in corners, most hand colored,
most 8" x 10-3/4" or reverse, numbers and captions in English,
1890s, oblong 4to, cloth, soiled, edges worn ............... 2,530.00
Carte-de-Visite, 11 photographs relating to Lincoln's assassination, two portraits of Lincoln, portraits of J. Wilkes Booth,
Edward Spangler, Samuel Arnold, David E. Herold, Michael
O'Laughlin, Payne, Hall, Lincoln family, tomb, two prints with
Hallett imprint, one with Fredericks imprint, mounted one per
page, all with handwritten notations, small 8vo, emb with gilt
stamped red leather, brass clasps, edges worn, contents loose,
all edges gilt, mid 1860s............................................. 2,530.00
Albumen Print
4-1/2" x 6-3/4", Curly, Custer's Crow Indian Scout, caption in pencil on mount verso, 1880s ........................................... 1,725.00
6-1/2" x 8-1/2", Eugene Atget, Omnibus, Paris, "Collection of
Berenice Abbott" handstamp and notation, 1898.......... 2,870.00
7" x 5-3/4", Richard Dykes Alexander, "Catherine Smart, her sister Eleza King and Eleven Pupils," clipper corners, orig mount,
photographer's credits and his handwritten identification on
back.................................................................... 1,725.00
8-3/4" x 6-1/2", Wilhelm Von Gloeden, classical couple, photographer's handstamp and numbered by hand, on verso,
c1900................................................................... 920.00
10" x 14", George N. Barnard, "The Front of Kenesaw Mountain,
Georgia," gold toned print, printed caption and caption on mount
back.................................................................... 2,300.00
13-3/4" x 11-1/4", Julia Margaret Cameron, "Elaine, the Lily-Maid
of Astolat," orig mount, framed, 1874......................... 14,950.00
Cabinet Card, 5-3/4" x 4", portrait of Nicholas II, Charles Berga-
mosco's London-St. Petersburg imprint on mounts recto and
verso, 1880s............................................................ 1,380.00

**Daguerreotype, half plate, bust view of gentleman, by McClees & Germon, Philadelphia, c1840-50, orig seal, some moisture and dirt under glass, leatherette half case, $220. Photo courtesy of Sanford Alderfer Auction Co.**

Carte-de-Visite, portrait, albumen print
  Brig. Gen. George Armstrong Custer, Brady's imprint and notations on back, 1865 ..................................................... 2,300.00
  Buffalo Bill, buckskins, Mora, New York, photographer's crest on mount recto, late 1860s................................................. 1,610.00
  Jesse James, copyright "Dick Parr 1901," printed caption below photograph, Kern Bros. New York imprint on mount, handwritten notations, 1882, printed 1901..................................... 10,250.00
Daguerreotype
  1-3/8" x 1-1/8", portrait of Daniel Webster, mid 19th C, oval gilt-metal pendant frame suspended from black ribbon ...... 1,100.00
  Quarter-plate, J. D. Cadwallader, group of men standing by large covered wagon, Ficklin building, Mason County, KY, in background, photographer's credit on mat, leather case, orig seal, 1858 ................................................................. 2,500.00
  Quarter plate, ambrotype, three young women, two men (one in military uniform), standing on log bridge over waterfall in Watkins Glen, NY, leather frame, late 1850s........................ 1,850.00
  Sixth-plate, female nude partially draped with gossamer fabric, delicately hand tinted, half leather case, 1850s ............ 2,760.00
  Sixth-plate, portrait of hansom cab driver wearing top hat, heavy blanket over shoulders, clay pipe in mouth, half leather case, 1850s ......................................................................... 1,150.00
  Sixth-plate, Wisconsin street scene of wagon parked in front of Babcock's Daugerrein Rooms, stamped floral mat, full leather case, late 1850s ........................................................... 8,825.00
Silver Print
  6-1/2" x 4-1/2", D. E. Barry, Crow King, photographer's signature in white ink, blindstamp on rect, period mat with caption label and blindstamp on mat recto, photographer's label and related articles affixed to mat verse, 1880s............................... 1,380.00
  6-1/2" x 8-1/2", John Swartz, The Wild Bunch, sitting left to right: Harry Longbaugh, Ben Kilpatrick, George Levy Parker, standing are Wm. Carver and Harvey Logan, all well attired in suits and a derby, photographer's address and handstamp, typewritten caption label on mount verso, c1900 .......................... 85,000.00

# PICKARD CHINA

**History:** The Pickard China Company was founded by Wilder Pickard in Chicago, Illinois, in 1897. Originally the company imported European china blanks, principally from the Havilands at Limoges, which were then hand painted. The firm presently is located in Antioch, Illinois.

**References:** Susan and Al Bagdade, *Warman's American Pottery and Porcelain*, 2nd ed., Krause Publications, 2000; Alan B. Reed, *Collector's Encyclopedia of Pickard China with Additional Sections on Other Chicago China Studios*, Collector Books, 1996, 2000 values update.

**Collectors' Club:** Pickard Collectors Club, 300 E. Grove St., Bloomington, IL 61701.

Bowl
  6" d, Autumn Blackberries, sgd "O. Goess" (Otto Goess), 1905-10 mark ................................................................. 200.00
  7-1/2" d, Poppy & Daisy pattern, ftd, sgd "Yeschek" (Joseph Yeschek), 1905-10 mark .................................................... 600.00
  8-1/2" d, shallow, handle, fish dec, sgd "Motzfeldt" (Andrew Motzfeldt), 1903-05 mark ................................................ 500.00
  9-1/2" d, 4-1/2" h, ftd, strawberries, white blossoms, and gooseberries dec, sgd "E. Challinor" (Edward Challinor), 1905-10 mark ................................................................. 300.00
  10" d, allover gold Rose & Daisy pattern, central scenic panel with bird, sgd "E. Challinor" (Edward Challinor), 1919-22 mark ... 250.00
  10" d, pink and blue flowers, gilding, unsigned, 1912-18 mark ...................................................................... 60.00
Chocolate Pot, white poppies and gilded band, sgd "Menges," (Edward Menges), 1905-10 mark ....................................... 350.00

**Chocolate Pot, white poppies and gilded band, sgd "Menges (Edward Mentges,)" 1905-10 mark, $350. Photo courtesy of Joy Luke Fine Art Brokers and Auctioneers.**

**Plate, white ground, violets and green leaves, gilded rim, sgd "H-H," 1903-05 mark, 8-3/4" d, $145. Photo courtesy of Joy Luke Fine Art Brokers and Auctioneers.**

Claret Set, Deserted Garden pattern, claret jug, five tumbles, 11-1/2" d round tray, each pc sgd "J. Nessy" (John Nessy), 1912-18 mark ......................................................................2,600.00

Coffee Set

Aura Argenta Linear pattern, coffeepot, creamer, cov sugar, six demitasse cups and saucers, two salt shakers, each pc sgd "Hess" (Robert Hessler), 1910-12 mark ......................1,300.00

Modern Conventional pattern, coffeepot, eight cups and saucers, coffeepot sgd "Hessler," 1910-12 mark, cups and saucers sgd "Hess" and "RH" (Robert Hessler), 1912-18 mark ........1,450.00

Creamer and Sugar

Deserted Garden pattern, sgd "J. Nessy" (John Nessy), 1912-18 mark ................................................................200.00

Violets dec, sgd "Z. Mac" (Zuie McCorkle), 1903-05 mark .100.00

White Poppies & Daisy pattern, 1912-18 mark ...................250.00

Creamer

4-3/4" h, red and yellow currants, green leaves, unsigned, 1905-10 mark ............................................................140.00

5-1/4" h, Tulip Conventional, sgd "Tomash" (Rudolph Tomascheko), 1903-05 mark ..............................................400.00

Demitasse Cup and Saucer

Gold Tracery Rose & Daisy pattern, sq, green band, 1925-30 mark .................................................................40.00

Poppy pattern, sgd "LOH" (John Loh), 1910-12 mark, price for pr ...........................................................................325.00

Lemonade Pitcher, Schoner Lemon pattern, sgd "Schoner" (Otto Schoner), 1903-05 ........................................... 1,700.00

Match Holder, Rose & Daisy pattern, 1925-30 mark.....................35.00

Plate

8-1/4" d, gooseberries dec, sgd "P.G." (Paul Gasper), 1912-18 mark ...............................................................40.00

8-1/4" d, scenic, unsigned, 1912-18 mark ..........................120.00

8-1/2" d, blackberries and leaves, sgd "Beitler," (Joseph Beitler), 1903-05 mark ...............................................80.00

8-1/2" d, Calla Lily pattern, sgd "Marker" (Curtis H. Marker), 1905-10 mark .........................................................225.00

8-1/2" d, chestnuts dec, unsigned, 1903-05 mark ...............60.00

8-1/2" d, Gibson Narcissus pattern, sgd "E. Gibson" (Edward Gibson), 1903-05 mark ............................................300.00

8-1/2" d, Lillum Ornatum pattern, sgd "Beulet" (F. Beulet) 1910-12 mark ........................................................100.00

8-3/4" d, Florida Moonlight pattern, sgd "E. Challinor" (Edward Challinor), 1912-18 mark..........................................200.00

8-3/4" d, orange flowers, sgd "F. James" (Florence James), 1905-10 ...............................................................100.00

8-3/4" d, violets and green leaves, gilded rim, sgd "H.H.," 1903-05 mark .........................................................125.00

9" d, Yeschek Currants in Gold pattern, sgd "Blaha" (Joseph Blaha) 1905-10 mark......................................................100.00

Pin Dish, violets dec.......................................................40.00

Tankard, 16" h, hexagonal, Chrysanthemums, Lustre & Matte Red pattern, sgd "Rean" (Maxwell Rean Klipphahn), 1905-10 mark ....950.00

Tea Set, Carnation Garden, teapot, creamer, cov sugar, each pc sgd "Yeschek" (Joseph T. Yeschek), 1903-05 mark .....................2,600.00

Vase

5-1/4" h, flying geese, three small feet, sgd "E. Challinor" (Edward Challinor), 1938-present mark.......................................550.00

8" h, Golden Pheasant, sgd "E. Challinor" (Edward Challinor), 1919-22 mark ........................................................500.00

8-1/4" h, scenic, sgd "E. Challinor" (Edward Challinor), 1912-18 mark ..............................................................425.00

11" h, Calla Lily pattern, sgd "Marker" (Curtis H. Marker), 1905-10 mark ..............................................................550.00

13-1/4" h, scenic with birch trees and gilding, two handles, sgd "E. Challinor" (Edward Challinor), 1912-18 mark...............1,920.00

16" h, Cherokee Rose, sgd "Walt" (Frederick Walters), 1910-12 mark ..............................................................2,100.00

Water Set, hand painted glass, Poppies pattern, lidded water pitcher, nine tumblers (2 different styles), sgd "Ross") "Carl Roessler), 1916-17 mark, minor chips on tumblers, gilding worn......................150.00

# PICKLE CASTORS

**History:** A pickle castor is a table accessory used to serve pickles. It generally consists of a silver-plated frame fitted with a glass insert, matching silver-plated lid, and matching tongs. Pickle castors were very popular during the Victorian era. Inserts are found in pattern glass and colored art glass.

Cranberry Glass

Insert with diamond quilted satin ground, enameled gild spider mums and leaves, ornate gold-toned frame with figural leaves holding jar in place, ftd, gold-tone cover, mkd "Rogers Smith".........................................................395.00

Insert with enameled dec, silver plate holder, lid, orig tongs..............................................................1,000.00

Insert with opalescent hobnail pattern, silver plate holder, lid, orig tongs ...........................................................550.00

Insert with thumbprint pattern, enameled florals, silver plate holder, lid, orig tongs.......................................................850.00

Double

Clear inserts, vertical panels, band of engraved leaves and vines, Wm Rogers frame .........................................................825.00

Clear inserts, vertical panels, unmarked resilvered frame ..750.00

Florentine insert, frosted blue, enameled dec...........................550.00

Mt. Washington

Satin, pink and frosted swirled opalescent stripes, polished pontil, SP frame, small chip under cov ......................................350.00

Seashell and Seaweed pattern insert, cased, pink to salmon, delicate enameled flowers, leaves, scrolls, Aurora frame, 9-1/2" h ...................................................................1,150.00

Opalescent, Daisy and Fern, cranberry .....................................450.00

**Lemonade Pitcher, Schoner Lemon pattern, sgd "Schoner" (Otto Schoner,) 1903-05 mark, $1,700. Photo courtesy of Joy Luke Fine Art Brokers and Auctioneers.**

Cranberry insert with diamond quilted satin ground, enameled gild spider mums and leaves, ornate gold-toned frame with figural leaves holding jar in place, ftd, gold-tone cover, mkd "Rogers Smith," $395.00. Photo courtesy of Joy Luke Fine Art Brokers and Auctioneers.

Pressed Glass, colorless insert
    Castle shaped insert, Warwick Castle, plated white metal stand, 10-1/4' h, 6" d, price for pr ............................................. 1,250.00
    Engraved flowers on each of six panels, F B Rogers #435 frame, resilvered, 9" h ................................................................ 350.00
    Satin
    Apricot mother-of-pearl insert, silver plate holder, lid, and tongs ............................................................... 1,300.00
    Blue, cased, egg shape, enameled dec, ornate holder, pickle shaped tongs hook ............................................... 700.00
    Rainbow, white to pink insert, Simpson, Hall, Miller frame, 12" h .................................................................... 1,395.00
Yellow-Amber, Button and Daisy insert, silver plate holder, lid, orig tongs .................................................................. 275.00

# PIGEON BLOOD GLASS

**History:** Pigeon blood refers to the deep orange-red-colored glassware produced around the turn of the century. Do not confuse it with the many other red glasswares of that period. Pigeon blood has a very definite orange glow.

Berry Bowl, Open Heart ................................................ 225.00
Biscuit Jar, cov
    Florette .......................................................... 295.00
    Little Shrimp ..................................................... 325.00
Butter Dish, cov
    Coreopsis ........................................................ 275.00
    Torquay, clear base ............................................. 195.00
Carafe
    Coreopsis ........................................................ 295.00
    Open Heart ....................................................... 295.00
Creamer
    Beaded Drape .................................................... 150.00
    Coreopsis ........................................................ 125.00
    Torquay .......................................................... 110.00
Pickle Castor
    Beaded Drape .................................................... 595.00
    Open Heart ....................................................... 375.00

Jelly Compote, Pink Slag, Inverted Fan & Feather pattern, orig Maude Feld paper label, 5" h, $685. Photo courtesy of Clarence & Betty Maier.

Pitcher, 6-3/8" h, applied handle, cut-out dec of strawberry diamonds and panels, English, minor wear, some pinpoint base flakes ..... 175.00
Salt Shaker, Periwinkle Variant ................................................... 110.00
Sugar Shaker, Bulging Loops pattern ........................................ 500.00
Syrup, Beaded Drape ................................................................... 595.00
Vase, 10-1/2" h, enameled flowers ............................................. 195.00

# PINK SLAG

**History:** True pink slag is found only in the molded Inverted Fan and Feather pattern. Quality pieces shade from pink at the top to white at the bottom.

Bowl
    9" d, ftd ............................................................... 600.00
    10" d .................................................................. 750.00
Butter Dish, cov, 7-5/8" d, 7" h cov, 2-1/4" h base with 4 molded feet, fiery opalescent coloring ...................................... 1,485.00
Creamer ..................................................................... 465.00
Cruet, 6-1/2" h, orig stopper ......................................... 1,300.00
Jelly Compote, 5" h, delicate pink bowl fades to off-white base, ribbed stem, four feet ................................................... 685.00
Marmalade Jar, cov ..................................................... 875.00
Pitcher, water .............................................................. 775.00
Punch Cup, 2-1/2" h, ftd ............................................... 275.00
Salt Shaker ................................................................. 300.00
Sauce Dish, 4-1/4" d, 2-1/2" h, ball feet ......................... 225.00
Spooner ..................................................................... 350.00
Sugar Bowl, cov .......................................................... 550.00
Toothpick Holder .......................................................... 825.00
Tumbler, 4-1/2" h .......................................................... 475.00

# PIPES

**History:** Pipe making can be traced as far back as 1575. Pipes were made of almost all types of natural and man-made materials, including amber, base metals, clay, cloisonné, glass, horn, ivory, jade, meerschaum, parian, porcelain, pottery, precious metals, precious stones, semiprecious stones, and assorted woods. Some of these materials retain smoke and some do not. Chrono-

## Reproduction Alert:

Recently, pieces of pink slag made from molds of the now-defunct Cambridge Glass Company have been found in the Inverted Strawberry and Inverted Thistle patterns. This is not considered true pink slag and brings only a fraction of the price of the Inverted Fan and Feather pieces.

logically, the four most popular materials and their generally accepted introduction dates are: clay, c1575; wood, c1700; porcelain, c1710; and meerschaum, c1725.

Pipe styles reflect nationalities all around the world, wherever tobacco smoking is custom or habit. Pipes represent a broad range of themes and messages, e.g., figurals, important personages, commemoration of historical events, mythological characters, erotic and pornographic subjects, the bucolic, the bizarre, the grotesque, and the graceful.

Pipe collecting began in the mid-1880s; William Bragge, F.S.A., Birmingham, England, was an early collector. Although firmly established through the efforts of freelance writers, auction houses, and museums (but not the tobacco industry), the collecting of antique pipes is an amorphous, maligned, and misunderstood hobby. It is amorphous because there are no defined collecting bounds; maligned because it is perceived as an extension of pipe smoking, and now misunderstood because smoking has become socially unacceptable (even though many pipe collectors are avid non-smokers).

**References:** Ben Rapaport, *Collecting Antique Meerschaum Pipes: Miniature to Majestic Sculpture,* Schiffer Publishing, 1999; R. Fresco-Corbu, *European Pipes,* Lutterworth Press, 1982; Benjamin Rapaport, *Complete Guide to Collecting Antique Pipes,* Schiffer Publishing, 1979.

**Periodicals:** *Agricultural and Mechanical Gazette,* P.O. Box 930401, Wixom, MI 48939, http://www.digiscape.com/a&mgazette/BriarPipes.html; *Pipes & Tobaccos,* 3000 Highwoods Blvd, Suite 300, Raleigh, NC 27604-1029, http://www.pt-magazine.com.

**Collectors' Clubs:** Chicagoland Pipe Collectors Club, 540 South Westmore, Lombard, IL 60148-3028; International Association of Pipe Smokers' Clubs, P.O. Box 930401, Wixom, MI 48393; New York Pipe Club, 440 East 81, Apt 1C, New York, NY 10028; North American Society of Pipe Collectors, P.O. Box 9642, Columbus, OH 43209-9642, http://www.naspc.org; Pipe Collectors Club of America, P.O. Box 5179, Woodbridge, VA 22194, http://www.pipesmoke.com; Pipe Club of London, 40 Crescent Drive, Petts Word, Orpington, Kent BR5 1BD; Society for Clay Pipe Research, 30 Ongrils Close, Pershore, Worcestshire WR10 1QE

**Museums:** Museum of Tobacco Art and History, Nashville, TN; National Tobacco-Textile Museum, Danville, VA; Pipe Smoker's Hall of Fame, Galveston, IN; U.S. Tobacco Museum, Greenwich, CT.

| | |
|---|---|
| Briar, 11" l, carved bearded man bowl, horn stem | 175.00 |
| Clay, 4 1/4" l, blue and white bowl, brown stem, Ohio | 165.00 |
| French, Williams Jenning Bryan, Gambier, 2-3/4" l, 2-1/4" h | 70.00 |
| Fraternal, c1927, carved, SS bands | 125.00 |
| Florida, carved folk art type, c1900 | |
| Black boy being swallowed by alligator, polychrome dec | 950.00 |
| Black boy in coat, detailed alligator on back attached to seat of boy's pants, red, green, and black polychrome dec | 1,150.00 |
| Snake and alligator | 175.00 |

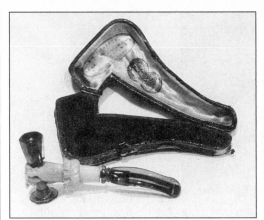

Meerschaum, carved hand holding goblet, amber stem and goblet, mkd "Wm Burnbaum, NY," 3-1/4" l, $295.

| | |
|---|---|
| Meerschaum, carved | |
| 6 1/4" l, girl with spinning wheel, cheroot holder, cracked amber stem, fitted case | 550.00 |
| 6 7/8" l, tavern scene, maid serving hunter, cheroot holder, amber stem, fitted case | 450.00 |
| 8" l, 6", laughing bearded soldier, map of France engraved on helmet and tunic, silver fitted case with turquoise | 2,650.00 |
| 10 1/2" l, hunting, maidens with wolves chase stag around rose, amber stem, fitted case | 1,400.00 |
| Porcelain, 31/2" h, Turkish gentleman bowl, bust head, jeweled and beaded turban, underglaze enamels, metal stem mount, hinged bowl cov, German, 19th C | 1,500.00 |
| Wood | |
| Civil War, folk art type, highly carved and detailed, emb "Union Forever" | 1,300.00 |
| Hand holding bowl | 85.00 |

# POCKET KNIVES

**History:** Alcas, Case, Colonial, Ka-Bar, Queen, and Schrade are the best of the modern pocket-knife manufacturers, with top positions enjoyed by Case and Ka-Bar. Knives by Remington and Winchester, firms no longer in production, are eagerly sought.

**References:** Jerry and Elaine Heuring, *Collector's Guide to E. C. Simmons, Keen Kutter Cutlery Tools,* Collector Books, 1999; Jacob N. Jarrett, *Price Guide to Pocket Knives,* L-W Books, 1993, 1998 value update; Joe Kertzman, *Knives 2001,* 21st ed., Krause Publications, 2000; Bernard R. Levine, *Levine's Guide to Knives and Their Values,* 5th ed., Krause Publications, 2000; Jack Lewis and Roger Combs, *The Gun Digest Book of Knives,* 5th ed., Krause Publications, 1997; Jim Sargent, *American Premium Guide to Pocket Knives & Razors,* 5th ed., Krause Publications, 1999; Ron Stewart and Roy Ritchie, *Big Book of Pocket Knives,* Collector Books, 2000; ——,*Cattaraugus Cutlery Co.,* Collector Books, 2000; ——, *Standard Knife Collector's Guide,* 3rd ed., Collector Books, 1993, 1999 value update; J. Bruce Voyles, *International Blade Collectors Association's Price Guide to Antique Knives,* Krause Publications, 1995; Richard D. White, *Advertising Cutlery,* Schiffer Publishing, 1999.

**Periodicals:** *The Blade,* 700 E. State St., Iola, WI 54990; *Knife World,* P.O. Box 3395, Knoxville, TN 37927.

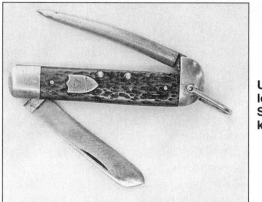

Union Cutlery, Boy Scout rigger knife, $55.

**Collectors' Clubs:** American Blade Collectors, P.O. Box 22007, Chattanooga, TN 37422; Canadian Knife Collectors Club, Route 1, Milton, Ontario L9T 2X5 Canada; National Knife Collectors Association, P.O. Box 21070, Chattanooga, TN 37421.

**Museum:** National Knife Collectors Museum, Chattanooga, TN.

**Additional Listings:** See *Warman's Americana & Collectibles* for more examples.

**Notes:** Form is a critical collecting element. The most desirable forms are folding hunters (one or two blades), trappers, peanuts, Barlows, elephant toes, canoes, Texas toothpicks, Coke bottles, gun stocks, and Daddy Barlows. The decorative aspect also heavily influences prices.

## Case

Case uses a numbering code for its knives. The first number (1-9) is the handle material; the second number (1-5) designates the number of blades; the third and fourth number (0-99) the knife pattern. Stag (5), pearl (8 or 9), and bone (6) are the most desirable handle materials. The most popular patterns with collectors are 5165 (folding hunters), 6185 (doctors), 6445 (scout), muskrat (marked muskrat with no number), and 6254 (trappers). In the Case XX series, a symbol and dot code is used to designate a year.

| | |
|---|---|
| 265 | 200.00 |
| 928R Tested, cracked ice | 350.00 |
| 2137, sod buster | 25.00 |
| 4200, melon taster, serrated blade | 165.00 |
| 5111 1/2 L, SSP Cheetah, 4" | 700.00 |
| 5165SAB | 660.00 |
| 5172, 1965-70, XX series | 150.00 |
| 254, 1965-70, XX series | 90.00 |
| 5375, stag | 75.00 |
| 5391 Tested, red stag | 2,000.00 |
| 5452 | 300.00 |
| 6143, 1965-70, XX series | 45.00 |
| 6261 | 125.00 |
| 52131, canoe | 200.00 |
| 61093 Tested, green bone | 550.00 |

## Ka-Bar, Union Cutlery Co, Olean, NY

Ka-Bar knives have many stampings, including Union (inside shield); U-R Co. Tridoute (variations); Union Cutlery Co, Olean NY; Alcut, Olean, NY; Keenwell, Olean, NY; and Ka-Bar. The larger knives with a profile of a dog's head on the handle are the most desirable. Pattern numbers rarely appear on a knife prior to the 1940s.

| | |
|---|---|
| 6191, knife, fork, spoon | 625.00 |
| 6260, KF | 100.00 |
| 21107, Grizzly | 2,000.00 |
| 61161, composition handle | 125.00 |
| 62191, dog's head trapper, bone | 1,450.00 |

## Keen Kutter, Simons Hardware, St. Louis, MO

| | |
|---|---|
| K1771 3/4", Daddy Barlow | 150.00 |
| K1898 3/4", toothpick | 100.00 |
| K8464 1/4", Kattie | 65.00 |

## New York Knife

| | |
|---|---|
| 20, office, celluloid | 170.00 |
| 142, hawkbill, wood | 150.00 |
| 223, sowbelly, bone | 470.00 |
| 251, rooster comb, celluloid | 300.00 |
| 2077, peanut, pearl | 270.00 |
| 2515, cigar, wood | 750.00 |

## Remington, last made in 1940

| | |
|---|---|
| R181, teardrop jack, wood | 255.00 |
| R273, Texas Jack | 200.00 |
| R303, one blade trapper, bone | 400.00 |
| R315, two blade trapper, celluloid | 435.00 |
| R718, hawkbill, wood | 220.00 |
| R945-M, toothpick, celluloid | 520.00 |
| R982, peanut, rubber | 320.00 |
| R1253, bullet lockback hunter, bone | 2,610.00 |
| R1303, bullet trapper, bone | 2,320.00 |

## Winchester

| | |
|---|---|
| 1613, speying, wood | 115.00 |
| 1701, Barlow | 125.00 |
| 1920, hunter | 1,000.00 |
| 2070, doctor's | 95.00 |
| 2078, serpentine pen, celluloid | 75.00 |
| 2363, congress, pearl | 225.00 |
| 2380, doctor's, pearl | 515.00 |
| 2879, jumbo sleeveboard | 515.00 |
| 3022, whittler | 250.00 |

## Wostenholm

| | |
|---|---|
| 3B, Art Nouveau, bronze | 100.00 |
| 5010A, plumber's, wood | 75.00 |
| B181X, stock, imitation ivory | 100.00 |
| B133, premium stock, bone | 180.00 |

# POISON BOTTLES

**History:** The design of poison bottles was meant to serve as a warning in order to prevent accidental intake or misuse of their poisonous contents. Their unique details were especially helpful in the dark. Poison bottles generally were made of colored glass, embossed with "Poison" or a skull and crossbones, and sometimes were coffin-shaped.

John H. B. Howell of Newton, New Jersey, designed the first safety closure in 1866. The idea did not become popular until the 1930s when bottle designs became simpler and the user had to read the label to identify the contents.

**References:** Ralph and Terry Kovel, *Kovels' Bottles Price List*, 10th ed., Crown Publishers, 1996; Carlo and Dorothy Sellari, *Standard Old Bottle Price Guide*, Collector Books, 1989.

**Periodical:** *Antique Bottle and Glass Collector,* P.O. Box 187, East Greenville, PA 18041.

**Collectors' Club:** Federation of Historical Bottle Collectors, Inc., 88 Sweetbriar Branch, Longwood, FL 32750.

Ammonia around shoulder, three sets of ribbing, Poisonous then ribbing and "Not To Be Taken," 6-1/2" h, cylinder ....................4.00
Bowker's Pyrox Poison, colorless ................................................30.00
British Household Ammonia, "Poisonous Not To Be Taken," 6-1/2" h, aqua, name around neck, panel with emb lettering ...................20.00
Burdalls Manufacturing Chemists Sheffield "Not To Be Taken Internally," 6" l oval, aqua, row of ribbing each side of lettering ....22.00
Coffin, 3" h, irregular hexagonal, emerald green, glass stopper, ribbed ................................................30.00
Figural, skull, America, 1880-1900, cobalt blue, tooled mouth, smooth base. 2-7/8" h, small hole in nose area ...................................475.00
Foultsons Crescent, 5" h, cobalt blue, sunken ribbed front panel, "Not To Be Taken" and ribbing on side ................................................65.00
Hobnail, 3-1/2" h, cobalt blue ................................................40.00
Ikey Einstein Poison, rect, ring top, colorless, 3-3/4" h ................25.00
Killgerm Disinfectant, oval, aqua, front panel with "Poisonous Not To Be Taken" 6-1/2" l ................................................25.00
Kill Pest Non Poisonous Disinfectant, 5" h, aqua, hexagonal, emb lettering on three panels ................................................20.00
Imperial Fluid Co. Poison, 1 gallon, colorless ................................95.00
J Wilson Bonsetter, light cobalt blue, rect ................................65.00
Lysol, 3-1/4" h, cylindrical, amber, emb "Not To Be Taken" ...........12.00
McDonalds Steam System, 5-1/2" h, aqua, Poisonous across shoulder ................................................20.00
"Not To Be Taken," cobalt blue, hexagon, 3" h ................................10.00
Not To Be Taken Gordon Grand Lysol, 5" h, amber jug shape, emb around neck, cross hatching on 2 sides ................................32.00
Owl Drug Co., three sided, emb "Poison" on one side, owl, mortar and pestle on other side, name on third, tooled lip, smooth base, cobalt blue, c1900-10, 4-7/8" h ................................................90.00
Poison, embossed
    Down the side, rect, beveled ribbed corners, cobalt blue, 4-1/4" h ................................................45.00
    Three sided, diamond lattice design, tooled mouth, smooth base, turquoise blue overlay, orig coffin-shaped pills each mkd "Poison," c1890-1910, slight wear, 5-1/4" h ................135.00
    Three sided, emb on one side, skull and crossbones on other sides, orig paper label, ABM, cobalt blue, c1915 .............145.00
Poison-Gift, six-sided, emb skull and crossbones panels alternating with name, ABM lip, smooth base, olive green, Germany, c1910-20, 9-3/4" h ................................................360.00
Poison-Wyeth, cylindrical, emb, orig front and back paper labels, ABM lip, smooth base, amber, c1890-1910, 2-1/4" h ...................220.00
Strychinia Poison, cylindrical, tooled top, some exterior striations, clear, 2-1/2" h ................................................45.00
Sulpholine, 4" h, rect, colorless ................................................10.00
Sun Drug Company, rect, ribbed beveled corners with "Poison" on one back, name on front, green, 4" h ................................235.00
Tinct Gelsem Poison and Hydrag Subchlor Poison, 5-1/2" h, green ribbed cylinder, orig label in rect panel, pr ................................150.00
Towle's Chlorodyne, 4-1/2" h, colorless ................................40.00
Trioloids Poison, triangular, blue, c1900, 3-5/16" h ................25.00
Vapo Cresolene Co, 4" h, sq, bumps on 2 panels, cobalt blue .....48.00

# POLITICAL ITEMS

**History:** Since 1800, the American presidency has been a contest between two or more candidates. Initially, souvenirs were issued to celebrate victories. Items issued during a campaign to show support for a candidate were actively being distributed in the William Henry Harrison election of 1840.

There is a wide variety of campaign items—buttons, bandannas, tokens, pins, etc. The only limiting factor has been the promoter's imagination. The advent of television campaigning has reduced the quantity of individual items, and modern campaigns do not seem to have the variety of materials that were issued earlier.

**References:** Herbert Collins, *Threads of History,* Smithsonian Institution Press, 1979; Theodore L. Hake, *Encyclopedia of Political Buttons, United States, 1896-1972* (1974), *Book II, 1920-1976* (1977), *Book III, 1789-1916* (1978), revised prices for all three books (1998) Americana & Collectibles Press, (P.O. Box 1444, York, PA 17405); ——, *Hake's Guide to Presidential Campaign Collectibles,* Wallace-Homestead, 1992; Margaret Brown Klapthor, *Official White House China: 1789 to the Present,* 2nd edition, Harry N. Abrams, Inc., 1999; Edward Krohn (ed.), *National Political Convention Tickets and Other Convention Ephemera,* David G. Phillips Publishing (P.O. Box 611388, N. Miami, FL 33161), 1996; Keith Melder, *Hail to the Candidate,* Smithsonian Institution Press, 1992; James W. Milgram, *Presidential Campaign Illustrated Envelopes and Letter Paper 1840-1872,* David G. Phillips Publishing (P.O. Box 611388, N. Miami, FL 33161), 1996; Edmund B. Sullivan, *American Political Badges and Medalets, 1789-1892,* Quarterman Publications, 1981; ——, *Collecting Political Americana,* Christopher Publishing House, 1991; Mark Warda, *100 Years of Political Campaign Collectibles,* Sphinx Publishing (P.O. Box 25, Clearwater, FL 34617), 1996; ——, *Political Campaign Stamps,* Krause Publications, 1998.

**Periodicals:** *Political Bandwagon,* P.O. Box 348, Leola, PA 17540; *Political Collector,* P.O. Box 5171, York, PA 17405.

**Collectors' Clubs:** American Political Items Collectors, P.O. Box 340339, San Antonio, TX 78234; Ford Political Items Collectors, 18222 Flower Hill Way #299, Gaithersburg, MD 20879; NIXCO, Nixon Collectors Organization, 975 Maunawili Cr., Kailua, HI 96734; Third Party & Hopefuls, 503 Kings Canyon Blvd., Galesburg, IL 61401.

## Reproduction Alert:

Campaign Buttons
The reproduction of campaign buttons is rampant. Many originated as promotional sets from companies such as American Oil, Art Fair/Art Forum, Crackerbarrel, Liberty Mint, Kimberly Clark, and United States Boraxo. Most reproductions began life properly marked on the curl, i.e., the turned-under surface edge.
Look for evidence of disturbance on the curl where someone might try to scratch out the modern mark. Most of the backs of these buttons were bare or had a paper label. Beware of any button with a painted back. Finally, pinback buttons were first made in 1896, and nearly all made between 1896 and 1916 were celluloid covered. Any lithographed tin button from the election of 1916 or earlier is very likely a reproduction or fantasy item.

## SPECIAL AUCTION

Hake's Americana & Collectibles
P.O. Box 1444, Dept. 344
York, PA 17405
(717) 848-1333

**Museums:** National Museum of American History, Smithsonian Institution, Washington, DC; Western Reserve Historical Society, Cleveland, OH.

**Additional Listings:** See *Warman's Americana & Collectibles* for more examples.

**Advisor:** Theodore L. Hake.

Brooch, 13/16" x 1", Harrison & Reform, sulfide, 1840, brass frame holds sulfide with black and white image ................................. 400.00
Bust, 5-1/2" h, black vinyl, John F. Kennedy, inscription on front, name , birth and death dates 1917-1963, c1963 ................................. 40.00
Button
    5/8" d, For President Warren G. Harding, browntone photo, white letters, dark blue rim ..................................................... 10.00
    7/8" d, Theodore Roosevelt, multicolored portrait, Spanish-American war uniform, gold background ..................................... 125.00
    7/8" d, Willkie Minuteman, graphic red, white, and blue Uncle Sam hat .................................................................... 20.00
    1-1/4" d, red, white, and blue rim, black and white photo, 1" x 3" red, white, and blue fabric ribbon, attached to pinback is 3" d yellow fabric sunflower, white plastic elephant, "Landon For President" .................................................................... 50.00
    2-1/2" red, and white, black and white illus of Truman with button sewn on his lip, red inscription reads "I'm For Stevenson," text underneath Truman illus reads "How We'd Like Harry," c1952 .................................................................... 25.00
    3-1/2", black type on white outside rim, large black and white center photo of Franklin D. Roosevelt, c1938-40 ..................... 40.00
    3-1/2" d, red, white, and blue, pinktone coloring over portrait, "Jacqueline Kennedy" ...................................................... 120.00
    4" d, Willkie, black and white litho ...................................... 40.00
    6" d, red, white, and blue, large bluetone center photo, Re-Elect Nixon, yellow cardboard easel back .................................. 15.00
Button with Ribbon
    1-3/4" d, red, white and blue, black and white photo button, Franklin D. Roosevelt, attached to 2" x 5" linen-like white fabric ribbon, gold inscription on ribbon "Inauguration President Franklin D. Roosevelt/Washington, D. C./Jan 20, 1937" ................. 80.00
    1-3/4" d, black and white button, attached 2" x 6" red fabric ribbon, 1-1/2" long gold colored plastic donkey on chain, John F. Kennedy Presidential Visit, c1961-63 ............................... 45.00

**Plate, National Convention, San Francisco, CA, 1956, mkd "Vernon Kilns," 12-3/4" d, $70.**

3" d, "U.S. For Ike," red, white, and blue with black and white photo at center, cardboard back, 2" x 9" red, white, and blue fabric ribbon with slogan "The People Want Ike" .............. 90.00
Campaign Envelope
    Stephen A. Douglas, 1860, shows Douglas with quotation "The People Alone are Sovereign" ............................................ 45.00
    Lincoln and Hamlin, 1860, jugate, black image on cream, 2-5/8" x 4-3/4" ................................................................................ 65.00
Campaign Medalet
    1-1/2", white metal, Lincoln portrait on front "For President Abraham Lincoln Of Illinois," reverse eagle with wings standing on section of globe depicted with the United States shield on his chest, holding arrows and olive branch in his talons, scroll in beak inscribed "E. Plurbius Unum" .................................. 175.00
    1-9/16" white metal, Henry Clay "Native American" 1844, full figure of man holding large American flag, torn and tattered, observe slogan "Our Flag Trampled Upon" referring to Philadelphia riots, reverse with eagle flying with long ribbon in beak "Natives/Beware of Foreign Influence/1844" .................... 225.00
Cartoon Art, orig
    11-1/2" x 14-1/2", Wilson and Bryan, by T. E. Powers, black ink, caricature of Wilson and Bryan on stage with Uncle Sam peeking around corner of building, c1912 ................................. 115.00
    15" x 18", Woman Suffrage, Frank A. Nankivell, black ink, Cleaning House, office boy in bellhop-like outfit wears "1905" cap, uses broom to sweep out objects and papers representing "Imperialism," "Yellow Peril," "Dave Hill," "Tom Taggart," and "Campaign Oratory 1904," 18 inscriptions on wall regarding Woman Suffrage, Hearst vs. Everything Continued..., Case of Watson Against Bryan, Big Stick, Explorers vs. North Pole, etc., 1905 ................................................................................. 110.00
Christmas Card
    4" x 5-3/4", Franklin D. Roosevelt, 1945, white card stock, 2" x 2-3/4" black and white illus of "The White House North Front," inscription in gold, emb mistletoe leaf and two accompanying red emb berries, "With Christmas Greetings And Our Best Wishes For A Happier Nineteen Forty-Five The President And Mrs. Roosevelt" .......................................................... 225.00
    4-1/2" x 6-1/2", John F. Kennedy, glossy full color photograph of Creche in East Room, The White House, inside message with gold emb presidential seal above and facsimile signature at bottom of John F. Kennedy and Jacqueline, inscription "With Our Wishes For A Blessed Christmas And A Happy New Year," made by Hallmark, cards arrived at the White House the same day as assassination, never used, few examples saved by assistant to President Kennedy ....................................... 350.00
Clothing Button, 5/8" d, ferrotype, Grant, thin brass rim, angled ridges surrounding clear ferrotype portrait ...................................... 200.00
Coloring Book, 8-1/2" x 11", full color caricature cover of Watergate figures leading a parade of people with US, flags, carrying crayons as if they were rifles, "Join the Fun-Color The Facts!," sealed in plastic bag .................................................................................... 10.00
Earrings, 5/8" h, rhinestone, slight blue tint, silver metal mountings, orig 2-1/4" x 2-3/4" stiff card, IKE, 1956 ................................. 25.00
Ferrotype, 15/16", Lincoln and Hamlin, Lincoln side with full name and date 1860 with bright and clear ferrotype portrait, Hamlin portrait on reverse ................................................................................ 400.00
Flag, For President Grover Cleveland, 15" x 24" silk flag, red stripes faded to light pink, hand stitched to slightly larger piece of cardboard for displaying under glass, some damage, c1888 ................. 1,350.00
Inauguration Button
    6" d, red, white, and blue, large black and white photo of John F. Kennedy and LBH, Presidential seal in gold and white between two photos, easel back ...................................................... 65.00
    6" d, red, white, and blue, with black and white photo of Lyndon B. Johnson and Hubert H. Humphrey, bluetone image of John F. Kennedy at center on dark blue background, gold presidential seal at bottom just above the words "The Great Society," easel back .................................................................................... 40.00

Inauguration Medal, 3" d, Franklin D. Roosevelt, second, bronze, Medallic Art, raised image of Franklin D. Roosevelt on one side, "John Nance Garner" on other, dated Jan. 20, 1937............225.00

Inauguration Pennant, 4-1/2" x 12" l, red and yellow felt, white image of Franklin D. Roosevelt, Capitol dome, and inscription "I Was At The 1st Third Term Inauguration January 20, 1941".........80.00

Japanese Lantern, Hayes, 1876 campaign, each side with "Hayes & Wheeler," dark blue and deep pink design, 8-3/4" d closed, pulls open to 14" h, tin candle holder mounted in base, wire handle attached to rim ........................300.00

Jugate
7/8" Parker/Davis, black and white photos, gold rim, accented by red, white, and blue stripe....................30.00
1-1/4" d, Grant, hard rubber, black disk, very detailed raised jugate portraits of Grant and Colfax in center, reverse with names and tiny star design ....................75.00
1-1/4" d, Bryan, black and white photo surrounded by blue rim with white stars, "Bryan/Sewall/Free Silver"....................100.00
1-1/2", Roosevelt/Truman, browntone, with photos of both, 1944 ....................400.00
1-3/4" d, Bryan/Stevenson, black and white photos against bright red, white, and blue shield, bright silver background .........80.00

Lapel Stud, McKinley, Protection 96, sepia photo, red, white, and blue flag background....................15.00

License Emblem
4" x 4-1/2", Willkie, heavy steel, red and blue, tan ground, orig heavy paper envelope with illus o front ............100.00
5" x 10", Win with Truman and Barkley, red, white, and blue metal, 1948 ....................150.00

Match Holder, 3" h, Teddy and the Bear, three dimensional figure of Teddy Roosevelt on his knees in Rough Rider outfit, bear figure clinging to tree stump, front base inscribed "Jamestown, NY," white ceramic, green and gold accents, German, c1904 ..................125.00

Menu, 7" x 10", Franklin D. Roosevelt, from return trip from Portland to Washington, D.C., red, white, blue, and gold flag design at top of cover, titled "The President Of The Untied States of America and Party/In Route Via The Chicago & Northwestern Railway/August 8-9, 1934"....................125.00

Paperweight, 2-1/2" x 4", 1" thick glass, sepia photo of Teddy Roosevelt ....................70.00

Photo, McClelland, military uniform, c1864, 3/4" x 1" brass frame held by pair of slots with folded brass tabs on the reverse to a 2-1/4" x 4" beige card with ornate frame design in light green ..................250.00

Pin
Cleveland, figural, diecut aluminum, silver luster, four-leaf clover, raised lettering "Our Four Leaf Clover/Grover" ..................40.00
Harrison, figural, diecut aluminum, silver luster, five petal pansy, raised lettering "Protection/Reciprocity/Our Nation's Pride/Harrison" reverse with orig pin....................50.00

Pocket Watch, Reagan Inaugural, 4-1/2" x 5" blue felt fitted box with blue presidential seal in gold on inside lid, brass watch with 14" l brass link chain, raised image of Reagan and inscription "40th President" on hinged lid, full color illus of eagle, garland and cross flags on dial, raised image of White House on reverse, Swiss made watch by Nicolet ....................75.00

Postcard
Taft, real photo, sepia campaign photo of Taft speaking from back of rail car, inscribed "Taft 10/3 '08 Newtown," by Cyko ......40.00

**Button, Inauguration Harry S. Truman, Wash DC, Jan 20, 1949, black image, cream ground, red, white, and blue border, $175. Photo courtesy of Hake's Americana & Collectibles.**

Teddy Roosevelt, pen and ink drawing printed postcard, artist "Alla," captioned "Shooting From A Blind," elephant on left with initials "G.O.P." on forehead, large container on back inscribed "Prosperity in Michigan," Theodore Roosevelt crouches behind donkey labeled "Democracy," blank reverse, c1904 ..........30.00

Poster
11" x 16", Win With Ike!, black, white, and light brown, stiff cardboard, large 9-1/2" x 10-1/4" black and white photo of Eisenhower ....................40.00
20-1/2" x 27", Bryan and Kern, black and white, facsimile signatures, slogan "Shall The People Rule" ....................95.00

Press Badge, 1-1/2" x 5", National Republican Convention, Philadelphia, 1900, white metal, fabric, and celluloid with McKinley portrait.......135.00

Program, 11" diecut football, 8 pgs, "Republican Victory Kick-Off Dinner," cover program for Convention Hall, Philadelphia, PA, Oct 1955 dinner, diecut pages include sepia illus of Ike, dinner addressee G. W. Humphrey, introduction speech by Thatcher Longstreth.......25.00

Ribbon, fabric
2" x 5", blue and white, "Bull Moose/Watcher," Teddy Roosevelt, coattails type, 1912, 1-1/4" sq at top with blue illus of Bull Moose figure on fabric, reads "Vote Under This Emblem," names Roosevelt, Johnson, Strauss, and Davenport ....................125.00
2-1/8" x 5-1/8", Delegate, Democratic Convention, 1895, blue on white fabric, inscription "Democratic Society of Utah, Delegate, Convention 1895"....................15.00
2-1/2" x 10", red, silver type "I'm For Roosevelt in '44".......50.00

Ribbon, silk
2" x 6-1/2", black on light gray silk, McKinley Calendar, memorial, 1902 ....................45.00
2-1/4" x 5-3/4", black and white, Republican Candidate for President, Col. J. C. Fremont, The Champion of Liberty, scattered and light small areas of spotting....................350.00
2-1/2" x 4", Harrison & Morton, 1888, red, white, and blue, fringe on sides....................50.00

Sheet Music, *The Road Is Open Again,* FDR, 9" x 12", 4 pgs, red, white, and blue glossy paper, lyrics by Irving Kahal, music by Sammy Fain, sung by Dick Powell in NRA short film, large 5" x 8" bluetone photo of FDR on front cover....................20.00

Silk, woven, 1-3/8" x 3-1/2", black and white image of Eisenhower at top, white silhouette of state of New York on yellow background, inscription "We Like Ike!," made in Austria, c1956 ....................50.00

Souvenir Card Deck, John F. Kennedy, Air Force One, two sealed decks of playing cards enclosed in gold cardboard box with blue flocking slip case lid, cards have black, white, and gold design, presidential seal, plane, and world background....................450.00

Souvenir Key, 3-3/4" l, brass, March 4, 1909 inauguration of Wm. H. Taft, reads "Key Of The White House," full luster....................50.00

Stereo Card
3" x 7", Hayes & Wheeler, jugate sepia toned, c1877, photo inset surrounded by white lace and fern design ....................35.00
3" x 7", Mrs. President Hayes, sepia toned, c1877, photo inset surrounded by white lace and fern design ....................20.00
3-1/2" x 7", Rough Riders on Parade, stiff cardboard, black and white photos, pinkish colored sky on left, bluish colored sky on right, c1898 ....................25.00

Stickpin
7/8", Bryan, black on cream, vertical, real photo ..................40.00
2-1/2" l, Cleveland, 1" d brass frame mounted with clear glass dome covering sepia cardboard photo, 1888....................150.00
2-1/2" h, Harrison, flat tin 1" x 1-3/4" American flag at top, stenciled blue field, every other stripe is stenciled in red, alternating stripes and star design unpainted, silver luster, blue lettering "American Tin/Protection/Reciprocity"....................100.00
2-1/2" h, Wm. H. Taft, brass, facsimile diecut signature at top, full luster, 1908....................25.00
2-3/4" h, Grants Tomb Dedication, 1898, white metal diecut, image of Grant with shield below, full bright brass plating .45.00

Mechanical, red, white, and blue tin shield dated "1888," sides of shield are held and then pin is pulled down to reveal sepia paper on tin diecut head of Cleveland, brass stickpin mounted to reverse ....................250.00

Ticket Stub

1-3/4" x 5", Truman Inauguration, light orange card stock, black printing, humorous, reverse reads "Compliments of Lafayette Smoke Shop" ............................................................ 20.00

2" x 4-1/2", Roosevelt-Garner Inaugural Parade, missing stub, orange stock, black type, for address on Pennsylvania Ave. second floor window seat ................................................... 15.00

2-1/2" x 4-1/2", Truman and Barkley, red, white, blue, and gold, with black and white photo insets on front, seating information on reverse ........................................................................ 25.00

Tintype, 1/2" x 7/8", Abraham Lincoln on orig card mount, photo surrounded by black lines and stars, caption reads "Patent'd Oct 13, 1863, S. Wing 290 Washington Sq, Boston," white background has faint traces of soiling ................................ 600.00

Watch Chain Charm, 5/8" sq, glass cube, tin band surrounding side edge, loop for fastening, black and white paper illus on front with red, white, and blue flag design, McKinley, 1896 ................. 125.00

Watch Fob

1-1/4" d, Wm. H. Taft, black and white button with photo image attached to 5-1/2" l black leather strap, c1908 .................. 60.00

1-3/8" x 1-1/2", brass with incised black lettering "Roosevelt 1904 Fairbanks/Washington" ..................................................... 30.00

# POMONA GLASS

**History:** Pomona glass, produced only by the New England Glass Works and named for the Roman goddess of fruit and trees, was patented in 1885 by Joseph Locke. It is a delicate lead, blown art glass which has a pale, soft beige ground and a top one-inch band of honey amber.

There are two distinct types of backgrounds. First ground, made only from late 1884 to June 1886, was produced by making fine cuttings through a wax coating followed by an acid bath. Second ground was made by rolling the piece in acid-resisting particles and acid etching. Second ground was made in Cambridge until 1888 and until the early 1900s in Toledo, where Libbey moved the firm after purchasing New England Glass works. Both methods produced a soft frosted appearance, but fine curlicue lines are more visible on first-ground pieces. Some pieces have designs which were etched and then stained with a color. The most familiar design is blue cornflowers.

**Cruet, second ground, Cornflower dec, amber irid on base and ball stopper, 7-1/4" h, $335. Photo courtesy of Clarence & Betty Maier.**

Do not confuse Pomona with Midwestern Pomona, a pressed glass with a frosted body and amber band.

**References:** Joseph and Jane Locke, *Locke Art Glass*, Dover Publications, 1987; Kenneth Wilson, *American Glass 1760-1930*, 2 vols., Hudson Hills Press and The Toledo Museum of Art, 1994.

Bowl

4-1/2" d, 3" h, first ground, rich amber staining .................. 275.00

5" d, Rivulet pattern, second ground, fluted, blue stain ........ 95.00

5-1/4" d, Cornflower pattern, second ground, fluted ............. 45.00

Celery Vase, 6-1/2" h, 4" d, Inverted Thumbprint pattern, scalloped amber rim ............................................................. 125.00

Champagne Glass, 5" h, second ground, rich amber staining.... 245.00

Cream Pitcher, 3-1/4" h, first ground, amber stain, three dainty applied feet, applied handle with heat check ............................. 245.00

Cruet, 7-1/4" h, Cornflower, second ground, petaled base with hint of amber irid, ball stopper............................................. 335.00

Finger Bowl, 2-1/2" d, first ground, gold stain ............................ 75.00

Lemonade Tumbler, Leaf pattern, first ground, ring handle ......... 85.00

Nappy, 5-1/4" d, Cornflower pattern, first ground, blue stain, applied handle ....................................................................... 125.00

Pitcher, 7-1/2" d, honeycomb pattern frosted body, quatraform rim, twisted rope applied necklace and handle, hp polychrome floral dec, polished pontil ................................................... 700.00

Punch Cup

Cornflower, first ground, blue staining, ring handle............. 145.00

Cornflower, second ground, blue staining........................... 110.00

Inverted Thumbprint pattern, first ground, amber staining.. 145.00

Spooner, 5" h, Inverted Thumbprint pattern, second ground, red stemmed blueberry dec, crimped base .................................. 140.00

Toothpick Holder, triangular rim, second ground, amber staining at top ...................................................................................... 120.00

Tumbler, 4" h, Cornflower, second ground, blue staining, DQ ...... 95.00

Vase, 5-1/4" h, Cornflower pattern, first ground body, ruffled amber rim, gold and blue floral belt at waist, applied wishbone feet .......... 375.00

# PORTRAIT WARE

**History:** Plates, vases, and other articles with portraits on them were popular in the second half of the 19th century. Although male subjects, such as Napoleon or Louis XVI, were used, the ware usually depicts a beautiful, and often unidentified, woman.

A large number of English and Continental china manufacturers made portrait ware. Because most was hand painted, an artist's signature often is found.

Box, cov

3" d, Court woman on lid, artist sgd "H. Patine," enamel dec, French ............................................................................. 900.00

7" d, portrait of Queen Louisa, green ground, pink floral dec, sgd "Nakara" ..................................................................... 2,000.00

Cup and Saucer, 2-1/2" h, cup with Marie Antoinette portrait in gilt medallion, cobalt blue ground, polychrome pastoral scene on saucer, Sevres, 18th C ................................................ 300.00

Dresser Tray, 10-1/2" l, porcelain, portrait of Flossie ................... 45.00

Ewer, 7-1/4" h, 6-1/2" d, Celeste blue ground, five damsels by a brook, maroon, purple, green, and blue gowns, gold Rococo handle, scalloped opening and pedestal, Royal Saxe Germany ................ 300.00

Jewel Box, 10-1/2" x 5", blown-out florals, ribbons on cov, center multi-colored portrait of seated woman, 18th C attire, beige ground, gold highlights, marked "Mt. Washington" ...................................... 950.00

Plaque, painted porcelain

6-1/4" w, 8-1/4" h, partially reclining woman with flowing tresses, boldly scrolled giltwood frame, Continental, late 19th C 4,315.00

8" w, 9-1/2" d, seated young woman in draped robe, floral giltwood frame, Continental, late 19th C .......................... 1,150.00

Plate, Lebrun II portrait, green ground, floral border, unmarked RS Prussia mold 29, 11-1/2" d, $1,500. Photo courtesy of Woody Auction.

### Plate

8" d, bust length portrait of Anmuth, Vienna style, gilt scroll, diaper, and foliate pattern border, sgd "Wagner," framed......850.00

9-1/2" h, Vergissmeinnicht (Forget Me Not), gilt and enameled border, jeweled details, sgd "Sittrick," Viennese, framed.........1,150.00

9-3/4" d, bust length portrait of Ariadne, Vienna style, wide gilt foliage border, metallic red ground, lobed rim, sgd "Wagner" ........1,225.00

10-1/2" d, Rape of Sabine Woman, wide cobalt blue border, gilt floral filigree and trellis pattern, artist sgd "C Landutrut," blue Royal Vienna beehive mark .............................................. 865.00

13" d, lobed circular plate,-3/4 length portrait of woman, mountainous landscape, thick gold band border surrounded by russet border, sgd "M Wantzel," Limoges ................................... 110.00

17 d, woman, jade green border, gold trim, marked "Victoria, Austria" ....................................................................225.00

### Vase

16-1/4" h, opaline glass, oviform, circular cushioned foot, parcel gilt, enameled, turquoise blue opaque body, gilt rimmed molded border and handles, oval panels with artists' portraits, one with Raphel, other Van Dyke, brown, claret, white, and flesh tones, gilt borders with scrolling foliate edges, French, 19th C, pr...................2,500.00

20-1/4" h, molded infants and scrolled foliage handles, body with matte blue ground, central circular cartouche of classical female, Paris, France, 19th C ........................................... 675.00

# POSTERS

**History:** Posters were a critical and extremely effective method of mass communication, especially in the period before 1920. Enormous quantities were produced, helped in part by the propaganda role posters played in World War I.

Print runs of two million were not unknown. Posters were not meant to be saved; they usually were destroyed once they had served their purpose. The paradox of high production and low survival is one of the fascinating aspects of poster history.

The posters of the late 19th and early 20th centuries represent the pinnacle of American lithography. The advertising posters of firms such as Strobridge or Courier are true classics. Philadelphia was one center for the poster industry.

Europeans pioneered posters with high artistic and aesthetic content, and poster art still plays a key role in Europe. Many major artists of the 20th century designed posters.

**References:** George Theofiles, *American Posters of World War I*, Daffram House Publishers; Susan Theran (ed.), *Leonard's Annual Price Index of Posters & Photographs*, Auction Index (30 Valentine Park, Newton, MA 02165), 1995; Jon R. Warren, *Collecting Hollywood*, 3rd ed., American Collector's Exchange, 1994; Bruce Lanier Wright, *Yesterday's Tomorrow*, Taylor Publishing, 1993.

**Periodicals:** *Biblio,* 845 Willamette St., Eugene, OR 87401; *Collecting Hollywood*, American Collectors Exchange, 2401 Broad St., Chattanooga, TN 37408; *Movie Poster Update*, American Collectors Exchange, 2401 Broad St., Chattanooga, TN 37408; Plakat Journal, Oskar-Winter Str. 3 D30160 Hannover, Germany.

**Museum:** Museé de la Publicité, 107 Rue de Rivoli, Paris, France.

**Additional Listings:** See *Warman's Americana & Collectibles* for more examples.

**Advisor:** George Theofiles.

### Advertising

Corsets Le Furet, Roger Pérot, Art deco lingerie poster, adv "The Woman's Dream," showing stylized silhouette of woman in Merry

**Red Belt 5¢ Cigar, professionally framed, 15" w, 20" h, $750. Photo courtesy of Past Tyme Pleasures Auction.**

Widow-type corset, bright orange and yellow background, 1933, 39" x 55" ................................................................................500.00

"Do It Electrically, Comfort, Convenience, Efficiency in the Home…Save Fuel, Food, Time, Money -By Wire," image of angel holding electric motor, period electrical appliances, full color, blue background, expert restoration to edges ,c1915, 27" x 35"......600.00

Ferry's Seeds, full color image of pretty young lass amid towering hollyhocks, light fold lines, restoration to edges, thin tears, 1925, 21" x 28" .................................................................................325.00

Granite Iron Ware, paper, woman carrying milking pail, cow, "For Kitchen and Table Use," 12-1/2" x 28"........................................75.00

House of Kuppenheimer, J. C. Leyendecker, "Clothes for Men," bold placard showing dandy in white tie and tails, 1919, 14" x 22"..425.00

Lady Esther Face Cream, , printed on board, beautiful young woman in oval vignette, "A Skin Food-An Astringent," c1920, 23" x 36" ..325.00

Lucite Hosiery, Coles Phillips, full color car, woman pointing horizon at sea net to handsome naval vet in wheelchair, c1918, 21" x 11", damp stain upper right, some border bites...........................................90.00

Kix Cereal, Lone Ranger 6-shooter ring, General Mills premium, "Only 15 cents plus Kix box top," c1948. 17" x 22" ............................225.00

Miles Shoes, anonymous, "The Best Thing On Foot," yellow and black, detailed locomotive, c1900, 17" x 11", some light residue to small sections of surface, small tack holes........................................100.00

Popcorn Starch, packages and little girl, color litho, c1900, 10" x 13"................................................................................200.00

Royal Portable Typewriter, dark green detailed manual portable typewriter against leafed red and green ground, c1940, 24" x 36" .................285.00

Shamrock Tobacco, canvas, seated man holding knife and tobacco, "Plug Smoking -10 cents a Cut," c1900, 17" x 23" ....................190.00

Waterman's Ideal Fountain Pen, paper, Uncle Sam at Treaty of Portsmouth, early 1900s, 41-1/2" x 19-1/2" ......................................950.00

**Life and Adventures of Buffalo Bill, stone litho by Riverside Printing Co., Milwaukee, 29" w, 43" h, $1,650. Photo courtesy of Past Tyme Pleasures Auction.**

## Circus, Shows, and Acts

Barnum and Bailey Circus, Strobridge Litho, Co., "Jockey Races," 1908, 19" x 28".............................................................900.00

Carson & Barnes Circus, anonymous, clowns of all types, full color offset with removable date sheet, white margin wear, 1950s, 42" x 36" ...75.00

Clyde Beatty-Cole Bros Combined Circus, The World's Largest Circus, "Clyde Beatty in Person," Roland butler, lion tamer, multicolored, 19" x 26".................................................................90.00

Cole Brothers Circus - Miss Allen with Her Five Gaied Palomino, anonymous, brilliant 1930s-type litho of Miss Allen and her horse, removable date sheet at bottom, 1945, 21" x 35" ............................165.00

Downey Bros Big 3 Ring Circus, "Leaps-Revival of that Astounding and Sensational exhibition," group of elephants, camels, and horses in line, aerial artist leaping overhead, audience background, c1925, 41" x 27" .............................................................125.00

Hoxie Bros Old Time Circus Land, One Mile West of Walt Disney World, multicolored view of circus grounds and big top, 20" x 27"..............65.00

Larry Breener's Fantasies of 1929, vaudeville and dance revue, Donaldson Litho, 14" x 22".........................................................80.00

Ringling Bros and Barnum & Bailey Circus, Alfred Court, Master Trainer, G. H., litho image of leopard draped over shoulders of trainer, bears and lions in background, full color, removable data sheet somewhat worn, c1943, 28" x 21", some tape stains and tears to upper edge ........................................................125.00

Ringling Bros Barnum & Bailey Liberty Bandwagon, color litho, ornate wagon with Merle Evans portrait, 1943, 30" x 19"....................225.00

Tim McCoy's Wild West, circle of riders around red circle, on canvas, 1938, 54" x 41".........................................................900.00

## Magic

Buddha and Heartstone, Polish magician performing tricks, English and Polish text, c1914, 14" x 26" ............................................100.00

Carter the Great-A Baffling Chinese Mystery- The Elongated Maiden, Otis Litho, "A pretty Chinese girl tied to a torture rack without seeming discomfort..," life-sized Chinese nobleman looking down on vignettes of complicated rack, stretched maiden, banshees, imps, devils, in color, c1920, 41" x 81" ............................................650.00

Friedlander Stock Magic, Adolph Friedlander #6966, smiling devil holds card-like vignettes of magic acts in one hand, wand in other, yellow ground, c1919, 14" x 19"..............................................150.00

Kar-Mi Swallows a Loaded gun Barrel, National, "Shoots a cracker from a man's head," Kar-Mi with gun in mouth blasts away at blindfolded assistant, crowd of turbaned Indians, 1914, 42" x 28" ..350.00

## Movie

"African Queen," French release of classic Bogart and Hepburn film, color portraits of both above steamy jungle setting, c1960, 22" x 31"....150.00

"Amazing Transparent Man," Miller Consolidated, D Kennedy, Marguerite Chapman, sci-fi silhouette against blue, 1959, 27" x 41"..............125.00

"Anthony Adverse," Warner Bros., Frederick March, Olivia de Havilland, embracing among panorama of runaway coaches and dancing girls, 1936, 27" x 41" ............................................................300.00

"Atlantic City," Republic, Constance Moore, Jerry Colonna in drag, by James Montgomery Flagg, 1941, 14" x 36" ............................200.00

"Blondie in the Dough," Columbia Pictures, Penny Singleton, Chick Young's Blondie cartoon film, full color, 1947, 27" x 41" ...........95.00

"Bad Boy," James Dunn and Louise Fazenda,, Fox, 1934, 27" x 41"................................................................................150.00

"Buck Privates," Relart re-release, Bud Abbott, Lou Costello, the Andrews Sisters, full-color montage, 1953, 27" x 41" ................95.00

"Cheaters At Play," Thomas Meighan and Charlotte Greenwood, Fox, 1931, 27" x 41".......................................................275.00

"Double Danger," Preston Foster and Whitney Bourne, RKO, 1938, 27" x 41"................................................................110.00

"Dr. No," United Artist, Sean Connery, Ursula Andress, 1962, 27" x 41"................................................................................325.00

"13 Rue Madeleine," Fox, James Cagney, Annabella, Cagney coming from behind looming door, printed in US for So American market. 1947, 27" x 41" ..................................................................225.00

"Farmer's Daughter," RKO, Loretta Young, Joseph Cotton, Ethel Barrymore, Cotton kneeling to pick up blond Young in maid's outfit, 1947, 27" x 41" ...................................................................... 125.00

"Fear Strikes Out," Paramount, Anthony Perkins, Karl Malden, full color, 1957, 27" x 41" ........................................................ 150.00

"Fly, The" Vincent Price, Fox, "The Monster Created by Atoms Gone Wild!," red, black, yellow, and puce, 1958, 27" x 41" ........... 325.00

"Goodbye Mr. Chips," Robert Donat and Greer Garson, MGM, 1939, 27" x 41" ...................................................................... 450.00

"I'll Be Seeing You," Ginger Rogers, Joseph Cotton, and Shirley Temple, United Artists 1945, 27" x 41" ...................................... 150.00

"Letter of Introduction," Universal, Charlie McCarthy, Edgar Bergen, Andrea Leeds, full-color dummy. 1938, 27" x 41" .............. 300.00

"Love Takes Flight," Bruce Cabot and Beatrice Roberts, Grand National, 1937, 22" x 28" .............................................. 135.00

"Mule Train," Columbia Pictures, Gene Autry, Champion, full-color portraits, 1950, 27" x 41" .............................................. 150.00

"New York, New York," United Artists, Robert DeNiro, Liza Minnelli, 1977 ....................................................................... 35.00

"One-Eyed Jacks," Paramount, Marlon Brando, Karl Malden, full color, 1959, 27" x 41" ........................................................ 85.00

"Pursuit Of The Graf Spee," John Gregson and Anthony Quayle, Rank, c1955, 22" x 28" .............................................................. 150.00

"Roll Along Cowboy," Guaranteed Pictures, Smith Ballew, Zane Gray Story, full color, c1940, 27" x 41" ...................................... 75.00

"Smoldering Fires," Pauline Frederick and Laura La Plante, Universal, 1925, 14" x 22" .................................................................... 125.00

"Streets of Laredo," Paramount, William Holden, Macdonald Carey, full color, 1949, 27" x 41" ................................................ 125.00

## Political and Patriotic

America Lets Us Worship As We Wish - Attend The Church Of Your Choice, for American Legion sponsored "Americanism Appreciation Month," full color image of praying Uncle Sam, family at dinner table behind him, c1945,20" x 26" .................................. 225.00

Bridge of Peace, Venette Willard Shearer, anti-war poster from American Friends Service Committee, National Council to Prevent War, in color, children of all nations play beneath text of song of peace, c1936, 16" x 22" ........................................................ 125.00

Confidence, large color portrait of Roosevelt over yacht at sea, "Election Day was our salvation/Franklin Roosevelt is the man/Our ship will reach her destination/Under his command…Bring this depression to an end…," c1933, 18" x 25" ...................................... 250.00

Taft, William H. - James S. Sherman, anonymous, presidential election poster, monochromatic photo images of both, 1908, 28" x 21" 110.00

United Nations Day, blue and white U.N. banner waves over airbrushed stylized brown and yellow globe, minor edge crumple, 1947, 22" x 23" .................................................................. 250.00

Willkie for President, anonymous, "The New America Needs," detailed photo image, orange and white background, 1940, 37" x 48", some repairs at edges .................................................................. 165.00

## Theater

Black Dwarf, Beck & Pauli Litho, Milwaukee, detailed stag set with 9 strutting players, cat-like character, a knight, ladies, etc., folio fold, expert restoration to upper cream border, c1870, 28" x 21" ..... 325.00

Bringing Up Father, McManus, "Jiggs, Maggie, Dinty Moore-George McManus's cartoon comedy with music," early newspaper cartoon characters against New York skyline, c1915, 41" x 81" .......... 425.00

Colette Andris, Sierre Thiriot, Art Deco image of Parisian dancer, stylized nude portrait, blue-greens, black, and white, c1930, 30" x 46", minor crumpling ............................................................... 525.00

Gregory Et Sa Panthere, Harfort, semi-nude muscle guy and beautiful female in sky-tight leopard outfit, tussle behind background of palms, yellows, golds, greens, blue, and white, c1938, 20" x 25" ........ 275.00

Les Amours D'Eve, Paul Colin, c1947, 16" x 24", silhouette of blond Eve, serpent, and apple, multicolored, blue background, surrounded by attractions for cabaret, including costumes by Erté and Les Mayfair Lovelies Girls ............................................................ 90.00

No No Nanette, Tony Gibbons, Theatre Mogador, Paris, European production of American musical, c1925, 15" x 22" .................. 375.00

## Transportation

Air France - North Africa, Villemot, stylized imagery of mosques and minarets, lave3nders, yellow, and blues against sky blue background, plane and Pegasus logo, c1950, 24" x 39" ................ 225.00

Cie De Navigation Transatlantique, Vittorio Grassi, Italian placard, string hanger at top, color image of huge hull of liner plying toward viewer, motif of gulls at borders, c1930, 10" x 17", light scratches at lower blue border, some corner bumps .................................. 95.00

Cosulich Line Trieste, Dondou, steamer plies foaming waves, spied on by American Indian chieftain in foreground, c1930, 26" x 35".. 475.00

French Line - Ile De France Returns, Mimouca Nebel, impressionist view of New York Harbor, full color, c1950, 20" x 27", light dampstain left edge .................................................................... 150.00

Grace Line - Caribbean South America Cruises, David, stylized natives, sea, and sun, 1959, 28" x 41" ...................................... 225.00

Royal Mail Atlantis, Padden, tourists in Royal mail motor launch approaching harbor village, mountains in background, c1923, 25" x 38" .................................................................. 675.00

SS France, Bob Peak, launching of French ocean liner, champagne and confection in front of huge, night-lit bow of ship, 1961, 30" x 46" .................................................................. 450.00

SS Michelangelo and SS Raffaello, Astor, detailed cutaway of Italian ocean liners, designed for use in travel office, printed on plasticized stock, metal frame, 1964, 54" x 22" ...................................... 300.00

## Travel

Arizona - Fly TWA, Austin Briggs, full color western lass in 1950s style, c1955, 25" x 40" .................................................................. 300.00

Boston - New Haven Railroad, Nason, full color, stylized montage of Historic Boston by day and night, faint folio folds, c1938, 28" x 42" ... 275.00

Britain in Winter, Terence Cuneo, color rendering of horseman, hunters, and tourists outside rustic inn, 1948, 19" x 29" ................ 125.00

Come to Ulster, Norman Wilkinson, sailboats and fishermen in front of lighthouse, full color, c1935, 50" x 40" ...................................... 450.00

Fly to Britain by Clipper, Mark von Arenburg, 1948, full color image of coronation carriage and footmen, Buckingham guard at right, 28" x 42" .................................................................. 300.00

Mexico, C. Uruelá, idealized Mexican children in typical 1930s primitive style, c1938, 18" x 27" ...................................................... 250.00

Nassau - Jet BOAC, Hayes, beautiful Bahamian dancer, sharp detail and color, c1953, 27"x 41" ...................................................... 275.00

Paradise Valley - Mount Ranier National Park, anonymous, Chicago, Milwaukee, St. Paul and Pacific Railroad, painted image of hotel in foreground, snow covered peak in background, c1927, 28" x 22" ...... 325.00

Paris, Paul Colin, doves floating above stylized Eiffel tower and Arc de Triumph, 1946, 24" x 39" ........................................................ 600.00

Pistany Spa, Hempel, grand spa imagery, male bathers taking the waters in front of ornate gate, golfers and tourists behind, full color, c1935, 24" x 20" .................................................................. 375.00

San Remo - Gold - All Sports, L. Polo, Italian Riviera resort, smiling blond lass holds armful of flowers, resort landscape background, c1935, 24" x 38" .................................................................. 375.00

Travel Flashes - New Fast Bus Service East, Union Pacific Stages, "Direct, Through - 3 Nights Only to Chicago," bright yellow design against black, bus shown at bottom, schedule from "Los Angeles to Salt Lake, Cheyenne, Denver, Omaha, Chicago," silk-screen and offset, c1936, 12" x 18" ...................................................... 200.00

Visit Spain, Morell, stylized image of signòrita, c1948, 25" x 39" 250.00

## World War I

Beat Back The Hun, F. Srothmann, large Hun lurks on horizon, bloody bayonet, burning city, c1918, 20" x 29", wear to margins, thin tears, edge bites ............................................................................ 200.00

Buy Buy Buy, anonymous, red, white, and blue typographic image for Victory Liberty Loan, c1918, 14" x 21" ...................................... 75.00

Clear the Way!, Howard chandler Christy, Columbia points the way for Naval gun crew, c1918, 20" x 30" ................................................ 250.00

Follow The Flag - Enlist in the Navy, James Daugherty, sailor plants flag on shore, 1917, 27" x 41" .............................................. 450.00

Foods From Corn - Corn Products Are Plentiful - Use Them, Lloyd Harrison, corn cakes, pies, soups, fillings, etc., tins of corn products all against corn yellow and blue ground, 20" x 30", c1918............225.00

For Every Fighter A Woman Worker, Adolph Treidler, woman worker holds detailed biplane and projectile aloft, 30" x 40", expert corner restoration, faint center folio folds ............................................275.00

Treat 'Em Rough - Jon The Tanks, A. Hutaf, window card, electric blue-black cat leaping over tanks in fiery battle, white border, c1917, 14" x 22"............................................................................900.00

You Wireless Fans - Help The Navy Get A Hun Submarine - A Thousand Radio Men Wanted, C. B. Falls, wireless operator reaching up to grab lightening bolt, starry night background, blue, green, red, and white, 1918, 27" x 44"............................................................550.00

## World War II

A National Emergency Is Upon Us - Arise Americans, anonymous, for Naval reserve, big flag atop red, white, and blue letters, June 1941, 29" x 42" ...............................................................................150.00

Army Air Forces Want You! WACS Keep 'Em Flying, anonymous, "Go to your U. S. Army recruiting station now," WAC inspects propeller and motor while AAF pilot walks towards her, c1943, 19" x 27" ...........125.00

Be A Marine...Free A Marine To Fight, D. Dickson, "The Marshalls - First pre-war Japanese territory to be conquered in WWII..." charging Marines on beach of jungle stoll, 1945, 29" x 40" .....................225.00

Ideas Will Help Beat The Promise, anonymous, worker peers into robot-like brain in curious, futuristic design, bright color, black ground, c1943, 18" x 22" ........................................................125.00

Keep 'Em Flying - Air Crews Are Vital, Ivan Dimitri, bomber pilots study maps under panoramic flyover of B-17s, full color, very light folio folds, 1942, 25" x 36" ...................................................................150.00

Pass The Ammunition - OK Soldier That's Our Job!, Frederick Stanley, brilliantly light image of soldier rushing to line of artillery with ammo, 1943, 28" x 40" ....................................................................275.00

# POT LIDS

**History:** Pot lids are the lids from pots or small containers which originally held ointments, pomades, or soap. Although some collectors want both the pot and its lid, lids alone are more often collected. The lids frequently are decorated with multicolored underglaze transfers of rural and domestic scenes, portraits, florals, and landmarks.

**Whimbleton, July 2nd, 1880, Pratt, 4" d, $190.**

The majority of the containers with lids were made between 1845 and 1920 by F. & R. Pratt, Fenton, Staffordshire, England. In 1920, F. & R. Pratt merged with Cauldon Ltd. Several lids were reissued by the firm using the original copper engraving plates. They were used for decoration and never served as actual lids. Reissues by Kirkhams Pottery, England, generally have two holes for hanging. Cauldon, Coalport, and Wedgwood were other firms making reissues.

**Marks:** Kirkhams Pottery reissues are often marked as such.

**References:** Susan and Al Bagdade, *Warman's English & Continental Pottery & Porcelain*, 3rd Edition, Krause Publications, 1998; A. Ball, *Price Guide to Pot-Lids and Other Underglaze Multicolor Prints on Ware*, 2nd ed., Antique Collectors' Club, 1991 value update.

**Note:** Sizes given are for actual pot lids; size of any framing not included.

Alexandra Toothpaste, Dr. Ziemer's Matchless for Beautifying and Preserving The Teeth & Gums, London, portrait of Queen Alexandra, facing left, black and gray on white, outer gold band, 3-1/2" d.................250.00

Areca Nut Tooth Paste

Army and Navy Co-Operative Society Limited, two military men shaking hands and holding flags, black on white, 3 1/16' d, rust stains........90.00

Barclay and Sons, Farmingdon St, London/A Fleet Marriage Party From a Print Of The time, gold border, black on white, 3-1/2" d.............2,400.00

For Cleansing and Whitening The Teeth and Gums/Timothy White Company Chemists, Portsmouth, geometric center, black on brown, 2-13/16" d................................................................................100.00

Cherry Tooth Paste, Patronized by the Queen/For Beautifying and Preserving The Teeth, Prepared by John Gosnell 7 Co, London, young head profile of Queen Victoria facing left, shades of blue, and black on white, gold band, 3 3/16" d.................................................125.00

Cold Cream, R Lemmon, Chemist, The Pharmacy Hythe, geometric border, gray on white, 2-1/2" d.................................................110.00

Higgin's Cherry Tooth Paste/For Cleansing Beautifying and Preserving The Teeth & Gums/Trademark R Higgins, Chemist 235 Strand Next Temple Bar, London, street scene, black on white, 2-3/4" d....185.00

Napoleon Price & Cos., Cherry Toothpaste For Beautying & Preserving The Teeth & Gums, 27 Bond St., London, bust of Queen Victoria and Prince Albert, shades of yellow, black, white ground, 3-3/16" d....900.00

Otto of Rose Cold Cream, SF Goss Chemist, 460 Oxford St., red rose center, green leaves, black letters, white ground, 2 5/8" d.......115.00

Rimmels Cherry Tooth Paste, bunch of cherries, deep yellow and pink cherries, green leaves, yellow-orange black band, white ground, 3" d.........................................................................950.00

Saponaceous Shaving Compound, Prepared by X Bazin, Perfumer, Philadelphia, geometric stars border, black and white, 4 3/8" d...........250.00

Victoria Carbolic Toothpaste/For Preserving and Beautifying The Teeth/Perfumes The Breath, Strengthens The Gums/A. B., warrior with shield lying against lion, black on white, sq, rounded corners, 2-1/2" l................................................................................250.00

Worsley Wholesale Perfumer, Philadelphia, Capitol at Washington, linear border, view of Old Capitol Building, violet on white, 3-1/2" d .........................................................................475.00

# PRATT WARE

**History:** The earliest Pratt earthenware was made in the late 18th century by William Pratt, Lane Delph, Staffordshire, England.

PRATT
PRATT
FENTON

From 1810 to 1818, Felix and Robert Pratt, William's sons, ran their own firm, F. & R. Pratt, in Fenton in the Staffordshire district. Potters in Yorkshire, Liverpool, Sunderland, Tyneside, and Scotland copied the products.

The wares consisted of relief-molded jugs, commercial pots and tablewares with transfer decoration, commemorative pieces, and figures and figural groups of both people and animals.

**Marks:** Much of the early ware is unmarked. The mid-19th century wares bear several different marks in conjunction with the name Pratt, including "& Co."

**References:** Susan and Al Bagdade, *Warman's English & Continental Pottery & Porcelain*, 3rd Edition, Krause Publications, 1998; John and Griselda Lewis, *Pratt Ware 1780-1840*, Antique Collectors' Club, 1984.

**Museums:** City Museum & Art Gallery, Stoke-On-Trent, England; Fitzwilliam Museum, Cambridge, England; Potsdam Public Museum, Potsdam, NY; Royal Pavilion Art Gallert & Museum, Brighton, England; Royal Scottish Museum, Edinburgh, Scotland; Victoria & Albert Museum, London, England; William Rockhill Nelson Gallery of Art, Kansas City, MO.

**Additional Listings:** Pot Lids.

Bank, 5" h, house shape, coin slot in roof, open chimney, two figures, faces in windows, professional repair ...................................... 650.00
Box, cov, 5-1/8" d, man on horseback, trees, deer, river, large white house in background, titled "Strathfieldsay," crazing and hairline, rim chips on base ...................................... 250.00
Creamer, 4-3/4" h, children at play, heart shaped cartouche, underglaze blue, green, and brown .................................... 250.00
Finger Vase, 7" h, four colors, leaves and flowers, minor wear, slight hairline, pr ...................................... 990.00
Model, 4-1/2" l, baby in cradle, underglaze yellow and blue enamels, early 19th C, nick to bonnet ...................................... 350.00
Money Box, 5" h, modeled as house, two children peering from windows, flanked by man and woman, blue, ochre, brown, and green, base and chimney restored, c1820 ...................................... 650.00
Pipe, c1800
    5" h, sailor form, stem formed as large fish swallowing male figure supporting a mask-head bowl, restored at mouthpiece and bowl stem ...................................... 890.00
    8-1/2" l, 4-1/8" h, monkey form, bowl molded as bird's head, stem and bowl restored...................................... 650.00

Plaque, Christ in the wheat field, sgd "J. Austin," c1851, 13" d, $195.

9-1/4" l, coiled snake, bowl extending from snake's mouth, stains, hairline, and repair ...................................... 400.00
13-1/2" l, coil, underglaze enamels, molded figural bowl, staining ...................................... 920.00
Pitcher
    7-1/4" h, pearlware, molded dec of children in heart shaped devices, titled "Mischievous Sport" and "Sportive Innocence," yellow, green, tan, blue, and brown, chips on handle and spout.................. 535.00
    7-1/2" h, relief busts and floral dec, six colors, minor glaze wear and stains...................................... 470.00
Pomade Jar, cov
    3-3/4" d, Philadelphia World's Fair, minor roughness to under edges of lid...................................... 200.00
    4" d, Walmer Castle, roughness to edge of lower lid .......... 185.00
Relish Bottle, 7-3/4" h, triangular shape, enameled transfers, one with "The Fishbarrow," other with "The Poultry Woman," mid-19th C, minor gilt rim wear, pr...................................... 500.00
Sauce Boat, 5" h, 7" w, orange-ochre fox's head as body and spout, white with sponged brown wings swan forming handle, yellow-green acanthus leaves on white wide body base, c1790, body reglazed ............... 850.00
Sugar, cov, 5-34" h, almond shaped relief medallion of woman and child, figural swan finial, stains, minor wear and chips............ 415.00
Tea Bowl and Saucer, 5-1/4" d, peafowl perched on leafy branch, blue, yellow, green, and ochre ...................................... 300.00
Tea Caddy, 5-1/4" h, applied and glazed floral dec, early 19th C 275.00
Toby Jug, 9-1/2" h, seated Mr. Toby, holding jug, wearing tricorn hat, jacket, vest, knee breeches, manganese, soft green, brown ochre, yellow, and orange-ochre, 18th C, pipe bowl by chair missing, small flake on one hand.............................. 1,540.00
Watch Stand, 10" h, tall case clock flanked by two children wearing yellow crowns, applied sq base with mound beneath their feet, blue, orange-ochre, yellow, brown, and green, small shallow chip on base ....... 500.00

# PRINTS

**History:** Prints serve many purposes. They can be a reproduction of an artist's paintings, drawings, or designs, but often are an original art form. Finally, prints can be developed for mass appeal rather than primarily for aesthetic fulfillment. Much of the production of Currier & Ives fits this latter category. Currier & Ives concentrated on genre, urban, patriotic, and nostalgic scenes.

**References:** Jay Brown, *The Complete Guide To Limited Edition Art Prints,* Krause Publications, 1999; William P. Carl, *Currier's Price Guide to American and European Prints at Auction*, 3rd ed., Currier Publications, 1994; Clifford P. Catania, *Boudoir Art*, Schiffer Publishing, 1994; Karen Choppa, *Bessie Peace Gutmann,* Schiffer Publishing, 1998; Karen Choppa and Paul Humphrey, *Maud Humphrey*, Schiffer Publishing, 1993; Max Allen Collins and Drake Elvgren, *Elvgren: His Life & Art,* Collectors Press, 1998; Erwin Flacks, *Maxfield Parrish Identification & Price Guide*, 3rd ed., Collectors Press, 1998; Patricia L. Gibson, *R. Atkinson Fox & William M. Thompson Identification & Price Guide*, Collectors Press, 1994; Michael J. Goldberg, *Maxfield Parrish Vignettes,* Collectors Press, 1998; Martin Gordon (ed.), *Gordon's 1999 Print Price Annual*, Gordon and Lawrence Art Reference, 1999; William R. Holland, Clifford P. Catania, and Nathan D. Isen, *Louis Icart*, Schiffer Publishing, 1994; William R. Holland and Douglas L. Congdon-Martin, *Collectible Maxfield Parrish*, Schiffer Publishing, 1993; Robert Kipp, *Currier's Price*

*Guide to Currier & Ives Prints*, 3rd ed., Currier Publications, 1994; Stephanie Lane, *Maxfield Parrish*, L-W Book Sales, 1993; Coy Ludwig, *Maxfield Parrish*, 2nd ed., Schiffer Publishing, 2000; *Maxfield Parrish*, Collectors Press, 1995; Ian Mackenzie, *British Prints*, Antique Collectors' Club; Rita C. Mortenson, *R. Atkinson Fox, His Life and Work*, vol. 1 (1991, 1994 value update), Vol. 2 (1992), L-W Book Sales; Norman I. Platnick, *Coles Phillps*, published by author (50 Brentwood Rd., Bay Shore, NY 11706); Tina Skinner, *Harrison Fisher: Defining the American Beauty*, Schiffer Publishing, 1999; Kent Steine and Frederick B. Taraba, J. *C. Leyendecker Collection*, Collectors Press, 1996; Susan Theran and Katheryn Acerbo (eds.), *Leonard's Annual Price Index of Prints, Posters & Photographs*, Auction Index, published annually; Naomi Welch, *The Complete Works of Harrison Fisher Illustrator,* Images of the Past, 1999.

**Periodicals:** *Illustrator Collector's News*, P.O. Box 1958, Sequim, WA 98382; *Journal of the Print World*, 1008 Winona Rd, Meredith, NH 03253; *On Paper,* 39 E. 78th St., #601, New York, NY 10021; *Print Collector's Newsletter*, 119 East 79th St., New York, NY 10021.

**Collectors' Clubs:** American Antique Graphics Society, 5185 Windfall Rd, Medina, OH 44256; American Historical Print Collectors Society, P.O. Box 201, Fairfield, CT 06430; Gutmann Collector Club, P.O. Box 4743, Lancaster, PA 17604; Prang-Mark Society, P.O. Box 306, Watkins Glen, NY 14891.

**Museums:** American Museum of Natural History, New York, NY; Audubon Wildlife Sanctuary, Audubon, PA; John James Audubon State Park and Museum, Henderson, KY; Museum of the City of New York, NY; National Portrait Gallery, Washington, DC.

**Additional Listings:** See Wallace Nutting.

## Reproduction Alert:

The reproduction of Maxfield Parrish prints is a continuing process. New reproductions look new, i.e., their surfaces are shiny and the paper crisp and often pure white. The color on older prints develops a mellowing patina. The paper often develops a light brown to dark brown tone, especially if it is acid based or was placed against wooden boards in the back of a frame.

Size is one of the keys to spotting later reproductions. Learn the correct size for the earliest forms. Be alert to earlier examples that have been trimmed to fit into a frame. Check the dimensions before buying any print.

Carefully examine the edges within the print. Any fuzziness indicates a later copy. Also look at the print through a magnifying glass. If the colors separate into dots, this indicates a later version.

Apply the same principles described above for authenticating all prints, especially those attributed to Currier & Ives. Remember, many prints were copied soon after their period introduction. As a result, reproductions can have many of the same aging characteristics as period prints.

## SPECIAL AUCTION

Michael Ivankovich Antiques & Auction Co., Inc.
P.O. Box 1536
Doylestown, PA 18901

Phillips Fine Art Auctions
406 E. 79th St.
New York, NY 10021

Skinner Inc.
Bolton Gallery
357 Main St.
Bolton, MA 01740

Swann Galleries, Inc.
104 E. 25th St.
New York, NY 10010

**Note:** Prints are beginning to attract a wide following. This is partially because prices have not matched the rapid rise in oil paintings and other forms of art.

Arms, John Taylor
 Bark *Metis* Making Harbor, 1923, etching, aquatint, printed in colors, sgd "John Taylor Arms" in pencil lower right, inscribed "Artist's Proof" in pencil lower left, 12-1/8" x 18", framed ....... 805.00
 Oviedo, the Holy, 1937, etching on laid J. Whatman paper with watermark, third state, sgd and dated "John Taylor Arms 1937" in pencil lower right, numbered "Ed. 100 III" in pencil lower left, 12-1/4" x 4-1/2" ............... 320.00
Audobon, John James, etching, engraving, aquatint and hand-colored, wove paper with J Whatman watermark, Blue Gray Flycatcher, 1830, Havell edition, full typographical inscription, 19-3/8" x 12-1/4", good condition, taped edge tears, mount staining, scattered foxing and tape residue, creasing ....... 450.00
Bacon, Peggy B., The Sights of the Town, sgd "Peggy Bacon" in pencil lower right, titled in pencil lower left, lithograph on paper, watermark "Basingwerk Pap...," image size 8-3/8" x 10-3/8", matted, deckled lower edge ....... 320.00
Baumann, Gustave
 Indiana Red Gum, 1909-16, sgd "Gustave Baumann" in pencil, hand to heart chop lower right, numbered "48 125" in pencil lower right, titled in pencil lower left, color wood block on cream wove paper, hand-in-heart watermark, edition of 125, image size 9-3/8" x 11-1/4", framed ....... 5,465.00
 Summer Clouds, sgd "Gustave Baumann" in pencil, hand-in-heart chop lower right, titled in pencil lower left, numbered "No. 53 of 100" in pencil lower left, color woodcut on cream laid paper, shield or crest watermark, 10-3/4" x 9-5/8", framed ....... 9,775.00
 Sycamore Salt Creek, 1916, sgd "Gustave Baumann" in pencil, hand-in-heart chop lower right, numbered "no. 37 of 120" in pencil lower center, titled in pencil lower left, color woodcut on oatmeal paper, image size 9-1/2" x 11-1/4", framed ..... 3,740.00
Benson, Frank Weston
 Ducks in the Rain, 1918, sgd "Frank w. Benson" in pencil lower left, stamped "Childs Boston" on reverse, etching on paid paper with partial watermarks, published state, edition of 100 plus proofs, plate size 7-7/8" x 6", framed, deckled edges, annotations to margins and reverse ....... 1,265.00
 Log Driver, 1924, sgd "Frank w. Benson" in pencil lower left, drypoint on laid paper with watermark, "FJ Head & Co.," published state, edition of 150, plate size 9-3/4" x 11-7/8", deckled lower edge, pale mat burn, annotations to lower margin ....... 1,150.00
 Wild Goose Drinking, 1915, sgd "Frank W. Benson" in pencil lower left, numbered "1/50" in pencil lower right, label from Holman's Print Shop, Boston, on reverse, etching on Shogun paper with watermark, plate size 7-7/8" x 5-7/8", framed, deckled edges, annotations to lower margin, staining ........... 750.00

**Benton, Thomas Hart**

Instruction, 1940, sgd "Benton" in pencil lower right, within matrix lower left, lithograph on paper, edition of 250, published by Associated American Artists, image size 10-1/2" x 12-3/8", framed ...................... 1,725.00

Nebraska Evening, 1941, sgd "Benton" in pencil and within matrix lower right, lithograph on paper, edition of 250, published by Associated American Artists, image size 10" x 13", matted, deckled edges to 3 sides, pale fox marks .................... 2,300.00

**Berry, Carroll Thayer**, Petunia, color woodcut on paper, sgd "Carroll Thayer Berry" in pencil lower right, titled in pencil lower left, 8-5/8" x 6-1/2" d, framed .......................... 230.00

**Birch, William Russell**, High Street from the Country Marketplace, Philadelphia-Procession of the Death of George Washington, engraving, 8-1/4" x 11" .......................... 250.00

**Calder, Alexander**, Circus, sgd "Calder" in pencil lower right, numbered "84/125" in pencil lower left, color lithograph on paper, sight size 25-1/2" x 37-3/8", framed.......................... 690.00

**Chagall, Marc**, Solomon, sgd in pencil, color lithograph, numbered 34/75, 1956, cream wove paper, full sheet printed to edges, 14" x 10-1/4" .......................... 1,500.00

**Currier and Ives**, hand colored lithograph

A Mansion of the Olden Time, C#3969, framed 13-1/4" h, 16-1/4" w, minor stains, white painted stop on top margin .......... 150.00

American Autumn Fruits, C#106, 24" h, 30" w, old gilt frame, margins slightly trimmed, minor stains .................................. 935.00

Apples and Plums, 16" x 12".......................... 50.00

A Race on the Mississippi, 12" x 15" .......................... 990.00

A Summer Landscape, Haymaking, C#5867, margins slightly trimmed, very minor stains, tape repair, old gilt frame. 13"h, 17-1/4" w .......................... 360.00

Bombardment & Capture of the Forts at Hatteras Inlet, NC, C#594, stains and minor damage, 11-7/8" h, 15-7/8" w, matted and framed .......................... 110.00

Bound Down the River, copyright 1870, 9-1/2" x 13-1/2". 1,100.00

Home on the Mississippi, copyright 1871, 12" x 16"..........615.00

Little Snowbird, C#3719, minor stains, 15-11/16" h, 12-1/8" w, matted and framed, 20" h, 16" w .......................... 365.00

Maiden Rock, 12" x 16".......................... 475.00

Midnight Race on the Mississippi, 9-1/2" x 13-1/4"..........440.00

Partridge Shooting, C#4719, margins trimmed, 10" x 14", old 12-1/2" x 16-1/4" frame.......................... 275.00

Perry's Victory on Lake Erie, C#4754, damage and some repair, 9-7/8" h, 13-7/8" w, matted and framed.......................... 440.00

Queen of the Garden, 13-3/4" x 10".......................... 90.00

Rarus-The King of Trotters, 21" x 28", antique tiger maple frame .......................... 150.00

Steam Ship Bothnia, C#5730, minor stains, 13-1/2" h, 17-3/4" w, matted and framed, 17-1/2" h, 21-3/4" h .......................... 325.00

The Battle of Gettysburg, Pa, July 4d, 1863," C#407, minor stains, 11-9/16" h, 15-7/16" w, matted and framed.......... 110.00

The Fall of Richmond, 13-15/16" w, 10" h, margins trimmed, minor damage, one corner repaired, matted and framed, C#1823.......................... 110.00

The Nosegay, 13-1/4" x 9-3/4" .......................... 80.00

View of Harpers Ferry, Va., C#6395, good margins, some minor corner damage, rosewood veneer frame with gilded liner, 27" h, 30-1/2" w .......................... 550.00

View on the Harlem River, NY, 1852, C#6441, identified in inscription in matrix, hand coloring on paper, 18-1/2" x 22-1/2" sheet size, framed.......................... 750.00

Washington from the President's House, 10-1/2" x 15" ......550.00

**Currier, N.**, McDonough's Victory on Lake Champaign," C#4096, hand colored lithograph, minor damage, taped repair, 10-7/8" h, 15-1/2" w, shadowbox frame, 13" h, 17-1/2" h .......................... 110.00

**Curry, John Steuart**, Elephants, 1936, sgd "John Steuart Corry" in pencil lower right, titled and dated in pencil lower left, initialed within the matrix lower right, identified on the AAA label affixed to reverse, lithograph on BFK Rives paper with watermark, edition of 250, published by Associated American Artists, image size 9" x 12-5/8" ......... 750.00

**Darley, F.O.C. and A. H. Ritchie**, On The March To The Sea, hand colored, sgd in pencil by both artist and engraver, artist's proof before title, General Sherman mounted watching his troops burn, pillage, and destroy rail tracks, telegraph poles, etc., freed slaves coming in, American flag held high, bridge in distance being destroyed, 42" x 27" plus frame, publisher's description and copy of invoice for hand coloring included .......................... 1,300.00

**Endicott & Company**, handcolored litho, New Bedford Fifty Years Ago, 1858, after William Allen Wall, identified within matrix, diagram of figures and view affixed to reverse, 19-1/2" x 26-1/4", period frame, staining, tears.......................... 460.00

**Fox, R. Atkinson**

An Approaching Storm, 14" x 20" .................................... 110.00

Flowerland, 18" x 30".......................... 215.00

Garden of Hope, 10" x 12".......................... 145.00

Heart's Desire, 12" x 18".......................... 185.00

Shower of Daisies, 10" x 14" .......................... 195.00

**Gardiner, Eliza Draper**

In The Big Bank, sgd and numbered "Eliza D. Gardner 8/5..." in pencil lower left, titled in pencil lower center, inscribed "no. 8" in pencil lower right, color woodcut on Japan paper, image size 11-7/8" x 10".......................... 350.00

Wading, Low Tide, sgd "Eliza D. Gardiner 2" in pencil lower right, color woodcut on tissue, image size 9" x 7", framed........ 375.00

**Gutmann, Bessie Pease**

A Double Blessing, 14" x 18" .......................... 1,045.00

A Little Bit of Heaven, 14" x 14".......................... 115.00

Come Play with Me, 3" x 5".......................... 55.00

Daddy's Coming, 14" x 18".......................... 440.00

Friendly Enemies, 11" x 14".......................... 155.00

Lorelei, 14" x 17".......................... 1,650.00

Mighty Like a Rose, 14" x 18".......................... 155.00

On the Up and Up, 14" x 18".......................... 140.00

Our Alarm Clock, 14" x 20".......................... 220.00

The Message of the Roses, 14" x 20".......................... 360.00

**Hall, H. B., Jr.**, Washington at Home, hand colored lithograph, 27" h, 22" w, George seated in chair, Martha and children, stains, soiling, minor paper damage, ornate gilded frame with minor damage, 38" h, 33" w .......................... 275.00

**Hassam, Frederick Childe**

The Church Tower, Portsmouth, 1921, monogrammed and inscribed "…imp" in pencil lower right, monogrammed and dated within the plate lower left, identified on label from H. V.

Harrison Fisher, The Alternative, girl in yellow dress, black dog, framed, 8" x 10", $65. Photo courtesy of Michael Ivankovich Antiques & Auction Co., Inc.

Allison & Co., New York, on reverse, etching on thin laid paper, pate size 8-3/8" x 6" .................................................. 1,610.00

Union Square, 1896, monogrammed and inscribed "...imp" in pencil lower right, monogrammed, dated, and inscribed "New York..." within plate center right, identified on label from William MacBeth, New York, on reverse, etching on wove paper, plate size 4-1/4" x 5-3/4", framed.......................................... 8,525.00

Henry, Michel, serigraph, titled "Delphinums," still life with blue flowers in vase, viewed through window, sgd in pencil "Michel Henry, #144/250" lower right, framed, 45" x 62" ................................. 225.00

Icart, colored etching on paper, lady at flower vender, Arc de Triomphe in background, sgd "Louis Icart," glued between mat and backboard with emb windmill mark partially covered, matted and framed, 26-1/2" h, 21" w ...................................................................... 1,155.00

Kasimir, Luigi, New York - Fog and Mist, 1936, sgd "Luigi Kasimir" in pencil lower right, numbered "20/100" in pencil lower left, dated within the plate, color etching on paper, plate size 12-1/2" x 14-3/4", framed ..................................................................................... 575.00

Kellogg & Comstock, Amelia, hand colored lithograph, 14" h, 10" w, refinished curly maple frame ....................................................... 330.00

Kent, Rockwell, Diver, 1931, wood engraving on paper with Japan watermark, edition of 150, sgd "Rockwell Kent," 7-7/8 x 5-3/8", matted, unframed ............................................................................. 980.00

Kloss, Gene, Summer Evening in New Mexico, 1941, sgd "Gene Kloss" in pencil lower right, titled in pencil lower left, aquatint and drypoint on paper, edition of 75, plate size 8-7/8" x 12", matted ................... 1,840.00

Lane and Scott, View of New Bedford. From the Fort Near Fairhaven, 1845, identified within the matrix, lithograph on paper, 19-3/8" h x 27-1/4" w, unframed ................................................................. 1,265.00

Marsh, Reginald, Loco - Going Through Jersey City, etching on heavy paper, from the Whitney Museum edition of 100, 1969, Whitney Museum drystamp lower right, annotated in lower margin, unmatted, unframed, 1930, 4-7/8 x 9-7/8".............................................. 250.00

**Maxfield Parrish, The Little Peach, bookplate print, framed, 8" x 10", $65. Photo courtesy of Michael Ivankovich Antiques & Auction Co., Inc.**

Mucha, Alphonse, color lithograph on silk, 33-1/2" h, 8-1/2" w, framed, c1896

Lady in long green outer garment, holding bird, three birds sit on snow covered branch .................................................. 3,750.00

Lady with long brown hair, sitting on rock, feet in stream, red flowers in hair .............................................................. 3,750.00

Lady with long flowing hair, five birds on harp ................ 3,500.00

Maiden picking berries in forest ...................................... 3,750.00

Parrish, Maxfield

Christmas Eve, 8" x 11" ................................................... 525.00

Circe's Palace, 10" x 12"................................................. 175.00

Garden of Allah, 15" x 30" .............................................. 275.00

Hilltop, 18" x 30" ........................................................... 715.00

The Lantern Bearers, 9" x 11"......................................... 550.00

The Page, 10" x 12" ....................................................... 175.00

The Prince, 10" x 12" ..................................................... 185.00

Patterson, Margaret Jordan, color woodcut on paper

In The High Hills, sgd "Margaret Patterson" in pencil lower right, indistinctly inscribed in pencil lower left, 11" x 8-3/4", framed ...................................................................... 1,380.00

Morning Glories, edition of 100, sgd "Margaret J. Patterson" in pencil lower right and lower center, titled in pencil lower right, numbered "#4/100", 10" x 7-1/4", framed...................... 1,380.00

Thayer & Co, Boston, Lithographers, View of the Grand Mass Washingtonian Convention on Boston Common,, on the 30th of May, 1844, lithograph, handcolored on paper, full typographical inscription below image, 8-1/2" x 13-1/2" image, period burl frame, minor staining and fading ..................................................................................... 225.00

Thornton, Dr. Robert, The Scared Egyptian Bean, 1804, from *The Temple of Flora,* identified within the plate, color aquatint on paper, sheet size 20" x 14", framed ...................................................... 690.00

Wengenroth, Stow, Along the Canal, 1949, sgd "Stow Wengenroth" in pencil lower right, lithograph on paper, edition of approx. 50, image size 7-7/8" x 13-3/9", orig folder, text from Society of American Etchers, Gravers, Lithographers, and Woodcutters, Inc................... 350.00

Whistler, James Abbott McNeill

Annie Seated, unsigned, inscribed "Annie" in the plate lower center, etching on thin laid paper, second state, plate size 5-1/8" x 3-3/4", matted................................................................ 865.00

Billingsgate, c1859, sgd and dated "Whistler 1859" in the plate lower center, etching on J. Whatman laid paper with partial watermark, eighth state, plate size 6" x 8-7/8" ................. 980.00

Drouet, sgd and dated in the plate lower right, titled in the plate lower center, etching on paper, second state, plate size 9" x 5-7/8" ............................................................. 1,035.00

The Winged Hat, butterfly monogram within the matrix, Birnie Philip stamp on reverse, lithograph on paper with watermark "R. Munn & Co. 1824," 1890, edition of approx. 25, matted, unobtrusive soiling, annotations lower left, image size 7" x 6-3/4" ..................... 1,265.00

Wood, Grant, Approaching Storm, 1940, sgd "Grant Wood" in pencil lower right, litho on paper, published by Associated American Artists, 11-3/4" x 8-7/8", framed........................................................ 4,320.00

Zorn, Anders, Anatole, France, 1906, sgd "Zorn" in pencil lower right, sgd and dated in the plate, etching on laid paper, partial shield watermark, 8-3/8" x 6-1/4", unmated ................................................. 750.00

# PRINTS, JAPANESE

**History:** Buying Japanese woodblock prints requires attention to detail and abundant knowledge of the subject. The quality of the impression (good, moderate, or weak), the color, and condition are critical. Various states and strikes of the same print cause prices to fluctuate. Knowing the proper publisher and censor's seals is helpful in identifying an original print.

Most prints were copied and issued in popular versions. These represent the vast majority of the prints found in the marketplace today. These popular versions should be viewed solely as decorative since they have little monetary value.

A novice buyer should seek expert advice before buying. Talk with a specialized dealer, museum curator, or auction division head.

The following terms are used to describe sizes: chuban, 7-1/2 x 10 inches; hosoban, 6 x 12 inches; and oban, 10 x 15 inches. Tat-e is a vertical print; yoko-e a horizontal one.

**Reference:** Sandra Andacht, *Collector's Value Guide to Japanese Woodblock Prints,* Antique Trader Books, 1999.

**Collectors' Club:** Ukiyo-E Society of America, Inc., FDR Station, P.O. Box 665, New York, NY 10150.

**Periodical:** *Orientalia Journal,* P.O. Box 94, Flushing, NY 11363-0094, http://members.aol.com/Orientalia/index.html.

**Museum:** Honolulu Academy of Fine Arts, Honolulu, HI.

**Note:** The listings below include the large amount of detail necessary to determine value. Condition and impression are good unless indicated otherwise.

Chikanobu, triptych of women watching young boy on hobby horse, framed, faded, stained ......................... 210.00
Eisen, triptych, three women before bramble, good impression, framed, faded ......................... 690.00
Gekko, eight framed prints from Gekko's Miscellaneous Drawings series, good impression, some fading and toning ............. 300.00
Harunobu, woman on veranda, intricately carved frame, small print, some fading and soil ............................. 260.00
HasuiTemple snow scene, framed ........................... 350.00
    Woman crossing bridge during rain storm, faded ............... 230.00
Hiroshi Yoshida
    Abuto in the Morning, very good impression, color, and condition, Jizuri seal, unframed ....................... 920.00

**Hiroshige III, harbor scene, c1885, Arts & Crafts style frame, 6-1/4" h, 9" h, $145. Photo courtesy of David Rago Auctions.**

Evening in Nara, very good impression, color, and condition, Jizuri seal, unframed ....................... 690.00
Fuhiyama from Kawaguychi Lake, faded and toned .......... 350.00
Kuto in Tomonoura, very good impression, color, and condition, Jizuri seal, unframed ....................... 920.00
Hiroshige
    Fujikawa, from *The Hoeido Tokaido,* good impressions, good margins .......................... 1,380.00
    Hirokoji Street, Shitayo, from *100 Famous Views of Edo,* framed ............................ 200.00
    Shono, from *The Hoeido Tokaido,* c1832, travelers climb hill in rain, very good impression, fading ................. 7,500.00
    The Sea off Satta in Suruga Province, from *36 Views of Fuji,* 1858, large wave crashes in foreground, Fuji in distance, very good impression, some fading, tape marks to edges ............... 1,840.00
Hiroshige II
    Horsemen from series of 100 Famous Views, framed, good impression, faded, c1860 ...................... 260.00
    Townspeople from "Thirty-six Views of Fuji," 1860, very good impression and color, album backing ............... 290.00
Hiroshige III, watery landscape from series of One Hundred famous Views, good impression, faded, c1860 ............. 200.00
Hokusai, landscape, framed, fading, signature trimmed ............ 350.00
Kiyoshi Saito, woman, framed, glazed, woodblock, 20th C ......... 415.00
Koitsu, good impression and color, framed
    Boats on lake, 20th C ...................... 320.00
    Forest scene ...................... 200.00
    Night scene ...................... 115.00
Koryusai
    Chuban of two woman in an interior, c1770, good impression, some fading and soil ...................... 1,495.00
    Chuban of two women in garden, c1780, framed, fading, damage ...................... 230.00
Kunichika, portrait of Nakamura Shika, moon in distance, very good impression, good color, some soil to margins, 1860s ............. 200.00
    Kunimasu, hanshi-bon, actor, c1850, good impression and color ...................... 320.00
Kunisada
    Fan print of Genji on shore with two women, fair impression, worn ...................... 60.00
    Figures in front of stations modeled after Hiroshige, from Tokaido series, c1835, framed, good impression and condition .... 320.00
    Kakemono of woman holding towel to her face, faded, toned ...................... 290.00
    Kakemono of woman with elaborate hat, framed, faded, slightly trimmed ...................... 175.00
Okiie Hashimoto, girl with flowers, pencil sgd in lower margin, dated 1952, artist's seal within image, printed character to right margin, 15-1/2" x 21-1/2" ...................... 805.00
Sadanubo, chuban yoko-e of snowy landscape, mid-19th C, good impression and color, stain to left third ...................... 145.00
Shigemitsu, triptych of warriors on hill overlooking lake, Fuji in distance, framed, very good impression and color ...................... 350.00
Shiro, woman in bath house, published by Watanabe, fading, mat burn ...................... 260.00
Shoson, oban of two carp, published by Watanabe, long seal in margin ...................... 815.00
Shuncho, courtesan and her attendants standing beneath lanterns, poem slips hanging from vines, laid down on cardboard, fading ...................... 425.00
Terauchi Manjiro, woman with parasol, watercolor, framed, glazed ...................... 215.00
Toyokuni, four people before waterfall, framed, faded ............... 115.00
Toyokuni II, woman and child, framed ...................... 140.00
Toyokuni III, triptych
    Genji playing flute, four women in int. setting, c1850, framed, faded ...................... 230.00
    Theatrical fight scene, framed, some fading ...................... 230.00
Utamaro, woman on tortoise with fan, toned, faded ................. 175.00

Yasuharu, Meiji period

    Koban size winter landscape, framed.............................200.00
    Small landscape of walk along river, framed......................115.00
    Small winter landscape, framed.......................................175.00
    Winter landscape with temple, koban size, framed.............175.00
Yoshida, landscape with cherry trees...........................................230.00

# PURPLE SLAG (MARBLE GLASS)

**History:** Challinor, Taylor & Co., Tarantum, Pennsylvania, c1870s-1880s, was the largest producer of purple slag in the United States. Since the quality of pieces varies considerably, there is no doubt other American firms made it as well.

Purple slag also was made in England. English pieces are marked with British Registry marks.

Other slag colors, such as blue, green, and orange, were used, but examples are rare.

**Reference:** Ruth Grizel, *American Slag Glass,* Collector Books, 1998.

**Additional Listings:** Greentown Glass (chocolate slag); Pink Slag.

**Reproduction Alert:** Purple slag has been heavily reproduced over the years and still is reproduced at present.

Animal Dish, cov, duck, Atterbury, ridged base with diamond motif ...85.00
Bowl, 8" d, Dart Bar...........................................................................50.00
Butter Dish, cov, cow finial ............................................................145.00
Cake Stand, plain.............................................................................125.00
Celery Vase, Jeweled Star, Challinor-Taylor, 1880s ....................125.00
Compote, Beaded Hearts .................................................................95.00
Match Holder, dolphin head .............................................................75.00
Mug, Bird In Nest, cat on base.......................................................105.00
Plate, 10" d, lattice edge .................................................................75.00
Rose Bowl, ribbed, Northwood .........................................................90.00
Sauce Dish, Majestic Crown, Challinor-Taylor, 4" d......................25.00
Sherbet, Majestic Crown, Challinor-Taylor, 4" d............................35.00
Sugar, cov, Fluted ..........................................................................195.00
Toothpick, Scroll with Acanthus .....................................................150.00
Vase

    4" h, flared rect form, four columns dec, striated purple and
      white ......................................................................................85.00
    4-5/8" h, slender rect formed ftd body, raised parrot dec, striated
      purple and white................................................................... 115.00
    5-1/8" h, flared neck, four paneled rounded body, striated purple
      and white................................................................................95.00
    9" h, Dance of the Veils, Fenton, blue and white ................500.00

# PUZZLES

**History:** The jigsaw puzzle originated in the mid-18th century in Europe. John Spilsbury, a London map maker, was selling dissected-map jigsaw puzzles by the early 1760s. The first jigsaw puzzles in America were English and European imports aimed primarily at children.

Prior to the Civil War, several manufacturers, e.g., Samuel L. Hill, W. and S. B. Ives, and McLoughlin Brothers, included puzzles in their lines. However, it was the post-Civil War period that saw the jigsaw puzzle gain a strong foothold among the children of America.

In the late 1890s, puzzles designed specifically for adults first appeared. Both forms—adult and child—have existed side by side ever since. Adult puzzlers were responsible for two 20th-century puzzle crazes: 1908-1909 and 1932-1933.

Prior to the mid-1920s, the vast majority of jigsaw puzzles were cut out of wood for the adult market and composition material for the children's market. In the 1920s, the die-cut, cardboard jigsaw puzzle evolved and was the dominant medium in the 1930s.

Interest in jigsaw puzzles has cycled between peaks and valleys several times since 1933. Mini-revivals occurred during World War II and in the mid-1960s, when Springbok entered the American market. Internet auction sites are impacting the pricing of puzzles, raising some (Pars, Pastimes, U-Nits, figure pieces) but holding the line or even reducing others (Straus, Victory, strip cut). As with all auctions, final prices tend to vary depending upon the time of yea and the activity of at least two interested bidders.

**References:** *Dexterity Games and Other Hand-Held Puzzles*, L-W Book Sales, 1995; Jack Matthews, *Toys Go to War*, Pictorial Histories Publishing, 1994; Chris McCann, *Master Pieces, The Art History of Jigsaw Puzzles,* The Collectors Press, 1998; Jerry Slocum and Jack Botermans, *Book of Ingenious & Diabolical Puzzles*, Time Books, 1994.

**Collectors' Clubs:** American Game Collectors Association., P.O. Box 44, Dresher, PA 19025.

**Advisor:** Bob Armstrong.

**Note:** Prices listed here are for puzzles which are complete or restored, and in good condition. Most puzzles found in attics do not meet these standards. If evaluating an old puzzle, a discount of 50% should be calculated for moderate damage (1-2 missing pieces, 3-4 broken knobs,) with greater discounts for major damage or missing original box.

**Dissected A.B.C.,** J. Ottmann Litho. Co., c1910, 11-1/2" x 10", 24 pcs, $50.

## Cardboard, pre-1950

Consolidated Paper Box/Perfect

Mt. Shasta, 1930s, 13-3/4" x 10-1/4", 250 pcs, diecut, round knob stripe, partially interlocking, orig box, 1 pc replaced .......... 12.00

Wilderness Retreat, 1940-50, 19-1/2" x 15-3/4", 375 pcs, diecut, round knob strip, partially interlocking, orig box, 1 pc replaced............ 12.00

Winter on the Farm, 1940-50, 15-1/2" x 10-1/4", 275 pcs, diecut, round knob strip, partially interlocking, orig box, 1 pc replaced............ 12.00

Einson-Freeman, Every Week, untitled, dog with peasant, Pope artist, 1930s, 14" x 10", 200 pcs, diecut, sq knob, edge-interlocking, replaced orig box.................... 12.00

Happy Hour, Indian Village, American News distributor, 1933, 13-1/4" x 10," 300 pcs, diecut, round knob, push fit, edge-1, orig box, 1 pc replaced .................... 14.00

Milton Bradley, Mayfair Jig, Spirit of Progress, 1930s, 12" x 15, 200 pcs, diecut, round knob strip, partially interlocking, orig box...... 14.00

Pilgrim Jig, Love tha Keeps, 1930s, 15-3/4" x 11-3/4", 300 pcs, diecut, long/line, edge-interlocking, orig box, 1 pc replaced .................. 12.00

Viking/Picture Puzzle Weekly, The Poor Poet, American News distributor, 1932, 13-3/4" x 10-1/4", 185 pcs, diecut, push fit, orig box ..... 15.00

## Wood and/or Handcut, pre-1930

Ayer, Isabel/Picture Puzzle Exchange, The Last Load, Victor Anderson artist, 1910, plywood, 23-1/2" x 18-1/4", 623 pcs, push fit, color line cutting, orig box.................... 300.00

Damon, Treasures, Norman Rockwell artist, 1920s, solid wood, 11" x 9", 101 pcs, push fit, color line cutting, 24 figures, orig box ....... 50.00

Leisure Hour Puzzle Co., The Gossips, 1909, solid wood, 13-1/4" x 8-3/4", 252 pcs, angular push fit, color line cutting, orig box ....... 120.00

Parker Brothers, Pastime

A Brook in the Swiss Alps, c1928, plywood, 19-3/4" x 15-3/4", 350 pcs, curve ftd knobs, color line cutting, interlocking, 46 figures, sawed by #83, orig box .................... 185.00

Mountain, Lake, and Rill, D. Soyrin artist, 1915s, plywood, 12" x 17", 305 pcs, curl knob, color line cutting, interlocking, 45 figures, well cut by #15, orig box.................... 160.00

Strawberries and Cream, 1920s, plywood, 11-3/4" x 7-3/4", 150 pcs, random, color line cutting, partially interlocking, 14 figures, sawed by #31, 2 replaced pcs, orig box............................ 70.00

The Three Gallants, 1910s, plywood, 8-3/4" x 12-3/4", 200 pcs, push fit, color line cutting, 24 figures, sawed by #21, orig box ....... 100.00

Untitled, clipper chip, 1910s, plywood, 9-3/4" x 7-3/4", 108 pgs, sq knob, color line cutting, semi-interlocking, 18 figures, replaced box .................... 40.00

Thompson, Peter G., Queen City, steamboat, 1870-90, cardboard, 16" x 12", 25 pcs, diecut, straight line, replaced box ........................ 35.00

Unknown Maker

Ready for the Hunt, J. S. Sanderson Wells artist, 1909, solid wood, 5-3/4" x 8", 146 pcs, push fit, color line cutting, orig box, 2 pcs replaced.................... 60.00

Scene of 1776, 1910-20, plywood, 14" x 10", 205 pcs, long, large, round, color line cutting, partially interlocking, orig box, thick wood, 1 pc replaced .................... 70.00

Untitled, drafting Declaration of Independence, Moran artist, 1910-20, plywood, 24-3/4" x 15-1/2", 292 pcs, push fit, some of part color line cutting, 2 figures, orig box ........................ 110.00

## Wood and/or Handcut, 1930s-40s, all plywood

Browning James, U-Nit, 1940-50

Sister and Brother, Roth artist, 19-1/2" x 23-1/2", 60 pcs, 100 figures, round knob, jagged, interlocking, orig box, 3 replaced box ...250.00

Untitled, across the bridge, 16-1/4" x 13-1/2", 268 pcs, random knob, interlocking, 40 figures, mahogany back, replaced box, 6 replaced pcs.................... 90.00

Clift, Lloyd, Miloy, Ben Hur's Chariot Race, 1930s, 21-1/4" x 9-1/4", 410 pcs, sq knob, some of part color line cutting, interlocking, 6 figures, orig box .................... 135.00

Crosby, A. T. Puzzler Picture Puzzle, Sunrise, R. Atkinson Fox artist, 1930s, 16" x 12", 361 pcs, round knob, interlocking, 5 figures, orig box, 2 replaced pcs .................... 150.00

Hayter, Victory

A Tall Tale, M. Dovaston artist, 1940-50, 23-3/4" x 17-3/4", 800 pcs, round knob strip, interlocking, orig box, loose cut, 1 replaced pcs.................... 100.00

Low Tide, 1930-50, 19-3/4" x 14", 500 pcs, round knob strip, interlocking, 30 figures, loose cut, orig box............................ 125.00

Madmar/Interlox, 1930s

A Peasant Home, E. Zampig… artist, 15-1/2" x 12-1/4", 350 pcs, large curl knob, interlocking, orig box, 2 pcs replaced........ 100.00

The Duet, 5" x 7", 80 pcs, earlet, curve knob, interlocking, orig box.................... 30.00

Parker Brothers, Pastime, Fresh Horses, 1933, 15" x 11", 261 pcs, random, color line cutting, interlocking, 33 figures, orig box, sawed by #97 .................... 120.00

Par Co., Murounder in the Making, stained glass window, 1930-40, plywood, 18-1/2" x 21", 750 pcs, earlet, jagged, interlocking, 20 figures, orig box, Par Time, 9 hrs .................... 700.00

Proudfit, Albert D., The Tavern, 1930s, 15-3/4" x 11-1/4", 314 pcs, random, color line cutting, interlocking, orig box, 3 replaced pcs ......... 90.00

Schwartz, F. A. O., Spec. Cut, Doorway to the Sea, well cut by Straus, 1940-50, 19-3/4" x 15-3/4", 500 pcs, round knob, interlocking, 16 figures, orig box .................... 120.00

Simonds, Don, Jolly Jigsaws, An Empire Bulwark, Dovaston artist, 1930s, 18-1/4" x 14", 419 pcs, long, knobby, some of part color line cutting, interlocking, 10 figures, orig box, 1 replaced pc .......... 140.00

Straus, Joseph K.

Nature's Paradise, Frederick D. Ogden artist, 1930s, 23-3/4" x 17-3/4", 750 pcs, sq knob, interlocking, orig box ............... 85.00

Rockport Elms, 1930s, 19-3/4" x 14-1/2", 500 pcs, curve knob, interlocking, orig box .................... 60.00

Tri-Ply Wood Puzzle, Good Story by Bad Shot, 1930s, 10" x 7", 136 pcs, sq knob, angular, interlocking, 10 figures, orig box.......... 40.00

Unknown Maker

Road Thru Winter Woods at Sunset, Thompson artist, 1930s, 12" x 10", 538 pcs, 1-by-1, scroll, color line cutting, interlocking, orig box, 2 replaced pcs .................... 150.00

The Fountain of Youth, Van Nortwick artist, 1930s, 10" x 13", 152 pcs, sq knob, interlocking, replaced box .................... 40.00

Untitled, cottage by the shore, 1930s, 20" x 16", 530 pcs, random knob, interlocking, 30 figures, 1 pc replaced, replaced box .. 125.00

What the Neighbors Brought, L. A. Crow artist, 1930s, 8" x 8-3/4", 166 pcs, scroll, interlocking, orig box, 1 pc replaced.......... 50.00

Zig-Zag Puzzle Co., Departure of the Stage Coach, Eugene Chaperone artist, 1930-40, 16" x 11-1/2", random knob, interlocking, tight cut, orig box 1 pc replaced .................... 80.00

## Wood and/or Handcut, post-1950, all plywood

Atlantic/Kingsbridge, untitled, stream, old bridge, 1950-60, 15-1/4" x 11-1/2", 400 pcs, round knob strip, interlocking, loose cut, photo, 3 replaced .................... 35.00

Guiles, Glencraft/Glendex, Winter Scene, Otto Ellersten, artist, 1970-80, 19-1/2" x 13-1/2", 512 pgs, round knob strip, interlocking, orig box, rounded corners .................... 65.00

Hayter, Victory/Poplar, untitled, river, snow capped mountain, artist Frederick D. Ogden, 1950-60, 19-3/4" x 15-3/4", 500 pcs, round knob strip, interlocking, orig box .................... 60.00

Hodges, William, Clipper Ship Three Brothers, Currier & Ives artist, 1960s, 13-1/2" x 8-1/2", 1-by-1 round knob, interlocking, orig box, "H" signature piece.................... 100.00

Straus, Joseph K.

The Delta Queen, 1950-60, 23-3/4" x 17-3/4", 750 pcs, round knob strip, interlocking, orig box.................... 110.00

The Grand Canyon, 1950-60, 27-3/4" x 21-3/4", 1,000 pcs, round knob variation stripcut, interlocking, orig box, 11 figures....... 150.00

# QUEZAL

**History:** The Quezal Art Glass Decorating Company, named for the quezal—a bird with brilliantly colored feathers—was organized in 1901 in Brooklyn, New York, by Martin Bach and Thomas Johnson, two disgruntled Tiffany workers. They soon hired Percy Britton and William Wiedebine, two more Tiffany employees.

The first products, which are unmarked, were exact Tiffany imitations. Quezal pieces differ from Tiffany pieces in that they are more defined and the decorations are more visible and brighter. No new techniques were developed by Quezal.

Johnson left in 1905. T. Conrad Vahlsing, Bach's son-in-law, joined the firm in 1918 but left with Paul Frank in 1920 to form Lustre Art Glass Company, which copied Quezal pieces. Martin Bach died in 1924 and by 1925 Quezal had ceased operations.

**Marks:** The "Quezal" trademark was first used in 1902 and was placed on the base of vases and bowls and on the rims of shades. The acid-etched or engraved letters vary in size and may be found in amber, black, or gold. A printed label which includes an illustration of a quetzal was used briefly in 1907.

Bowl, 9-1/2" d, gold calcite ground, stretch rim, pedestal foot, sgd "Quezal" .................................................................. 800.00
Candlesticks, pr, 6-1/2" h, white opal ground, orange-green King Tut irid dec, flared bobeches rim, ringed hollow baluster, sgd........ 950.00
Compote, 4-5/8" h, pale pastel blue ground, pedestal foot, sgd and numbered ............................................................ 525.00
Creamer, 2-1/2" h, irid gold ground, applied lip and handle ........ 550.00
Cruet, white opal ground, green pulled feather design, yellow stopper, applied handle ....................................................... 2,500.00
Cup and Saucer, 2-1/2" h, 4-1/2" d, irid gold with purple highlights, sgd ................................................................ 950.00

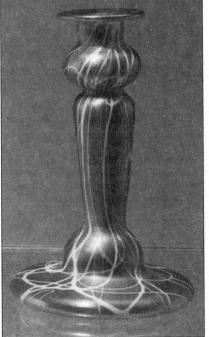

**Candlestick, white King Tut dec, blue irid ground full sgd, 7" h, $900. Photo courtesy David Rago Auctions.**

Desk Lamp, 13" h, 16" l, figural, bronze lion reclining on faceted weighted pedestal foot, offset curved lamp shaft fitted with gold, white, and green pulled feather dec glass shade inscribed "Quezal" ..................... 1,100.00
Flask, 8-1/2" h, brilliant irid rainbow ground, finely chased silver overlay carnations, inscribed "Quezal," Alvin Corp. mark stamped on silver................................................................ 1,200.00
Floor Lamp, 58" h, 10" d, bell shaped shade with green and gold damascene dec, adjustable base, shade sgd, base has been polished.............................................................. 2,100.00
Jack in the Pulpit Vase
   8-3/4" h, squatty bulbous base, tapering to tall slender neck, ending in widely flaring and ruffled rim, int. with gold irid, ext. with tightly drawn mint green and gold striated pulled feather designs, continuing down to base, sgd "Quezal P663" . 2,950.00
   9" h, broad mouth, tapering stem, bulbous foot, brilliant orange and salmon irid, inscribed "Quezal"................................. 750.00
   11-3/4" h, squatty bulbous base, tall slender stick neck, widely flared and ruffled rim, int. with deep amber irid, ext. with pearly opalescent, wintergreen striated feathering edged in amber irid, continues down neck and base, additional amber irid feathering on base, ext. rim with amber irid chain dec, sgd........... 4,000.00
Lamp Base, 12" h, elaborate pulled and hooked gold feather on green glass, cream ground, pulled gold feather at top, gold int. ........ 750.00
Lamp Shade, 5-1/4" h, 2-1/4" fitter ring, pulled feather, gold to white opalescent with green feather edge, gold irid int., sgd inside top fitter rim .................................................................. 350.00
Salt, 2-1/2" d, irid gold, pr .......................................... 325.00
Sconce, 16-1/2" drop, bronze, round domed wall mount, raised arch and dart border dec from which extend a cornucopia shaped arm holding swivel harp and domed shaped shade mount, bell form shade with scalloped rim, creamy white glass with irid amber pulled feather motifs, sgd "Quezal" on rim, attributed to Handel, early 20th C ..................... 1,380.00
Student Lamp
   15" d base, green with yellow swirls shade, orig lamp base, sgd .............................................................. 1,000.00
   21-1/4" h, brass, carved double arms ending in quatraform sockets, raised linear dec, slender adjustable standard, round stepped base, two opalescent yellow shades with irid luster, etched "Quezal," chips to shades.................................... 575.00
Table Lamp, 18-1/2" h, cast metal lamp base, Art Nouveau woman and quatraform swirling platform base, gold irid squared glass shade inscribed "Quezal" at rim, pr................................... 2,550.00
Vase
   4" h, compressed bulbous base, wide shoulder, narrow flaring neck, dec with bands of silvery amber, green and blue lappets, rich emerald green irid ground at base, pearly white neck, sgd "Quezal 901" ............................................... 1,650.00
   5" h, four-edged top, gold irid, inscribed mark ................... 550.00
   5" h, pedestal form, ruffled top, lined with irid gold, green pulled feather with gold border, white ground, inscribed mark, #838 ................................................................ 1,000.00
   5-1/2" h, long flaring body, flared top, gold body, rose and blue irid highlights, inscribed mark................................... 375.00
   6-1/2" h, baluster, slightly flared foot, blue, orange, and gold irid pulled and hooked swirling dec, sgd ........................... 1,000.00
   7" h, trumpet form, lobed body, amber irid neck, lower section dec with striated amber irid lappets edged in green, reserved against opalescent ground, inscribed "Quezal A982," c1925................................................................ 1,500.00
   8-3/4" h, scalloped rim, slender body over bulbed stem of opal glass, int. with stretched gold irid, ext. with five gold outlined pulled green feathers rising from applied gold irid domed foot, polished pontil sgd "Quezal"......................................... 3,450.00
   9-1/2" h, bottle form, opal white dec, reverse pulled gold irid feathers above symmetrical spider web criss-cross designs, sgd "Quezal C269".......................................... 1,500.00
   9-5/8" h, ovoid body, tapering to slender waisted stick neck, lower section dec with amber irid lappets and silvery blue irid striated feathering reserved against caramel irid ground, fine int. ribbing, creamy white neck and shoulder, sgd "Quezal A465," c1920 ........................................... 3,500.00

10-3/4" h, pyriform body, squatty foot, rich opalescent sides dec with brilliant amber irid striated feather devices below amber irid lappets, edged in lime green, sgd "Quezal 937," c1920 2,200.00

12-1/2" h, wide ovoid body, low flared neck, ext. with creamy irid ground, trailing gold vines interspersed with green flowers, large pulled feather design around bottom, sgd .................... 3,500.00

# QUILTS

**History:** Quilts have been passed down as family heirlooms for many generations. Each one is unique. The same pattern may have hundreds of variations in both color and design.

The advent of the sewing machine increased, not decreased, the number of quilts which were made. Quilts are still being sewn today.

**References:** Cuesta Benberry, *Always There: The African-American Presence in American Quilts*, Kentucky Quilt Project, 1992; Deborah Harding, *Red & White, American Redwork Quilts and Patterns*, Rizzoli, 2000; Patricia T. Herr, *Quilting Traditions*, Schiffer Publishing, 2000; Carter Houck, *Quilt Encyclopedia Illustrated*, Harry N. Abrams and Museum of American Folk Art, 1991; Donald B. Kraybill, Patricia T. Herr, Jonathon Holstein, *A Quiet Spirit: Amish Quilts from the Collection of Cindy Tietze & Stuart Hodosh*, UCLA Fowler Museum of Cultural History (405 Hilgard Ave., Los Angeles, CA 90024); Elizabeth Kurella, *The Complete Guide To Vintage Textiles*, Krause Publications, 1999; Jeanette Lasansky et. al., *On the Cutting Edge*, Oral Traditions Project, 1994; Nancy and Donald Roan, *Lest I Shall be Forgotten*, Goschenhoppen Historians, Inc. (P.O. Box 476, Green Lane, PA 18054), 1993; Robert Shaw, *The Art Quilt*, Hugh Lauter Levin Associates, Inc., 1997; Shelly Zegart, American Quilt Collections/Antique Quilt Masterpieces, Nihon Vogue Ltd., 1996.

**Periodicals:** Quilt Journal, 635 W. Main St., Louisville, KY 40202; Quilters Newsletter, P.O. Box 4101, Golden, CO 80401; Vintage Quilt Newsletter, 1305 Morphy St., Great Bend, KS 67530.

**Collectors' Clubs:** American Quilt Study Group, 660 Mission St., Ste 400, San Francisco, CA 94105; American Quilter's Society, P.O. Box 3290, Paducah, KY 42001; National Quilting Assoc., Inc., P.O. Box 393, Ellicott City, MD 21043; Textile Group of Los Angeles, Inc., 894 S Bronson Ave., Los Angeles CA 9005-3605.

**Museums:** Colonial Williamsburg Foundation, Colonial Williamsburg, VA; Doll & Quilts Barn, Rocky Ridge, MD; Museum of the American Quilter's Society, Paducah, KY; National Museum of American History, Washington, DC; New England Quilt Museum, Lowell, MA.

**Notes:** The key considerations for price are age, condition, aesthetic appeal, and design. Prices are now level, although the very finest examples continue to bring record prices.

## Appliqué

Carolina Lily, appliqué and pieced, goldenrod and green calico, white ground, cut-out corners, small stamped ink maker's label on back, 72" x 79" ................... 375.00

Double Fleur-de-Lis, cotton, printed navy blue and white patches, white ground, double sawtooth border, feather wreath and diamond quilting, MI, c1860-70, 78" x 80" ......................................... 2,250.00

Floral medallions, stylized, red flowers with green and gold leaves, green, gold, and red star blocks, blue and red Flying Geese border, dark green borders, wear, frayed fabric, stains, 87" x 107" ...... 250.00

Floral medallions with pollen, nine stylized medallions, medium blue and red on white, PA, well quilted, stains and minor overall wear, 78" x 80" ............. 770.00

Flowering Vines, appliqué and pieced, bands of flowering vines and birds alternating with bands of flying geese within stripes, cotton, red, yellow, and taupe, 19th C, imperfections, 76" x 78" ................. 500.00

Missouri Rose variant, stylized potted flowers, meandering vine border, yellow, green, and red patches, white ground, conforming heart, tea cup and flowerhead quilting, Catherine Jane McPeak Stults, 1858, minor discoloration and fiber loss, 91" x 72" ........................... 900.00

Nasturtiums, red and green, white ground, scalloped border, America, early 20th C, staining, 90" x 76 ............................................... 200.00

Oak Leaf Variant, red, green, and yellow calicos, white ground, crib size, 36" x 28-3/4", America, 19th C ....................................... 575.00

Poinsettia and Christmas cactus, red and green, white ground, dated "March 14, 1934," 68-1/2" x 62" ............................................. 250.00

Pots of flowers, nine pots, red, beige, and goldenrod, well quilted with white pots of flowers between appliqués, PA, wear and stains, colors slightly faded, 70" x 78" ......................................................... 550.00

Potted Tulips, border of birds among foliage, green and red calicos, white ground, minor staining, scattered fiber wear, 92-1/2" x 94-1/2" ........................................................................... 980.00

Rose and Bud, pink calico, green, and red, white ground, America, mid 19th C, 90" x 73", top only ......................................... 460.00

Rose Medallion, nine medallions, pink, medium green, and pale pink, white ground, vining border, well quilted, light staining, 84" x 85" ............................................................................ 220.00

Rose of Sharon and heart design, scrolling foliate border, green calico and red cotton, white ground, toning, minor fading, America, second half 19th C, 84" x 82-1/2" ............................................... 900.00

Rose Wreath, similar borders, cut corners, red and teal green, America, mid 19th C, 84" x 82", fading, very minor staining ............. 250.00

Star of Bethlehem, various appliquéd potted flowering plants, plain and printed cottons, white ground, 85" x 88", staining, fading, scattered fiber wear ........................................................................ 750.00

Stylized floral medallions, teal blue, red, and burnt orange, minor stains, 86" x 90" ...................................................................... 690.00

Stylized floral medallions, vining border, two shades of green, red, and orange, stains, 78" x 81" ................................................. 715.00

Sunburst and Eagle, green, terra-cotta, and red, white ground, America, mid 19th C, 88" x 90", fading, staining, minor areas of fiber wear ........................................................................... 250.00

Sunburst and Rose of Sharon with Birds, variant, red, green, and terra-cotta, white ground, America, mid-19th C, very minor staining to reverse ................................................................................ 2,415.00

**Crazy,** knotted crazy quilt center, multicolored solids, quilted border of faded blue and maroon crepe, Kalona, Iowa, origin, very worn, holes, and stains ............................................................................ 110.00

## Pieced

Barn Rising, log cabin variant, calicos and other materials, America, late 19th C, fading, minor fiber wear, 69-1/2" x 68" .................. 375.00

Baskets, red baskets, white ground, red block borders, crib size, wear and stains, few small holes, 41-1/4" x 27-3/4" ........................... 55.00

Bow Tie, multicolored colored prints, white ground, stains, one corner with minor damage, 70" x 80" ............................................... 220.00

Crown of Thorns, blue and black calico on white, alternating squares of olive green calico, overall wear, some repair and stains, 74" x 88" ....................................................................... 220.00

Double Irish Chain, pink calico and white, double borders, PA, minor stains, 76" x 76" ...................................................................... 330.00

Fence 'Round Field, green and goldenrod, brown center, Holmes County, Ohio, minor stains and overall wear, 81" x 82" ........... 325.00

**Flying Geese, green calico ground, multicolored stripes, black and white floral printed backing, 79-1/2" x 72-1/2", $440. Photo courtesy of Sanford Alderfer Auction Co.**

Flower Garden, printed cotton patches, red floral roller printed border, cut-out corners, mid-19th C, 81" x 90-1/4" ............................... 400.00

Flying Geese, red and white, reversed with pieced bars backing, 75" x 82" .................................................................................................. 650.00

Goose Chase, indigo blue print and white, PA, minor wear and stains, 78" x 78" ......................................................................................... 660.00

Hour Glass, blue and white prints, PA, minor stains, 68" x 68" ......... 110.00

Irish Chain

    Blue and white print, white ground, machine and hand stitching, mid-20th C, stains, crib size, 33-1/2" x 52" ....................... 200.00

    Green and white, quilted trapunto floral sprays in white center blocks, green sawtooth border, late 19th C, fading, light staining, 100-1/2" x 101-1/4" ........................................................... 980.00

    Medium blue and mauve, PA, initials "KR," well quilted with feather design borders, minor stains, 84" x 84" .............. 475.00

LeMoyne Star, calicoes, red and green ground, America, late 19th C, very minor staining, 80" x 66-1/2" .................................................. 375.00

Log Cabin, concentric diamond design, multicolored prints, solids, and white, red border, machine sewn, hand quilted, minor stains, 83" x 88" .............................................................................................. 330.00

Lone Star, red, medium blue, goldenrod, and white, small black stains and age stains, machine sewn binding, 80" x 82" ..................... 385.00

Mosaic, pinwheel stars, blue, black, green, and yellow, lavender ground, fish scale quilted border, machine sewn binding, Cochranton, PA, origin, overall wear, some stains, 67" x 80" ................ 250.00

Navajo Rug design, green, blue, red, and orchid cotton, white ground, fading, minor staining, America, late 19th/early 20th C, 77" x 69" ...... 300.00

Nine Patch Irish Chain Variant, pierced in red printed and white fabric, triple border of rose pink and green, America, mid-19th C, minor staining, 74-1/2" x 87-1/4" ........................................................... 350.00

Pinwheel and Sunburst, diamond latticework, pinwheel within starburst within quatrefoil in diamonds, pieced triangle border, solid and printed cotton fabrics, green, squash brown, and cream, conforming parallel line quilting, mid 19th C, some discoloration, 92" x 98" ........................ 900.00

Postage Stamp Squares, brightly colored prints alternating with white, red binding, corner embroidered "Allie," wear and some loose seams, 66" x 78" .............................................................................................. 450.00

Rob Peter to Pay Paul, indigo blue print and white, PA, 75" x 74" ... 440.00

Stained Glass Window, solid and printed fabric, diagonal red lattice with solid blue, pink, white print, plaid triangles within, narrowed border, wide blue print outer border, Berks County, PA, c1885, minor fading, 71" x 70-1/2" ................................................................. 350.00

Star of Bethlehem Variant, red, blue, green, and white printed cotton, paisley printed border, America, late 19th C, 76" x 791/2" ....... 850.00

Sunshine and Shadow Log Cabin, diagonal bands of red, blue gray and pink contrasted with white, wear and stains, 65" x 73" ..... 220.00

Sunset over Mountain, multicolored prints, black and white gingham, double wide pink calico border, PA, some wear and stains, 65" x 84" ............................................................................................. 330.00

Tumbling Blocks, red, light mustard, and white blocks, inner red and outer white border, quilted clam shell border, c1900, minor staining, 82-3/4" x 82-1/2" ..................................................................... 420.00

# QUIMPER

**History:** Quimper faience, dating back to the 17th century, is named for Quimper, a French town where numerous potteries were located. Several mergers resulted in the evolution of two major houses— the Jules Henriot and Hubaudière-Bousquet factories.

The peasant design first appeared in the 1860s, and many variations exist. Florals and geometrics, equally popular, also were produced in large quantities. During the 1920s, the Hubaudière-Bousquet factory introduced the Odetta line which utilized a stone body and Art Deco decorations.

The two major houses merged in 1968, the products retaining the individual characteristics and marks of the originals. The concern suffered from labor problems in the 1980s and was purchased by an American group.

**Marks:** The "HR" and "HR Quimper" marks are found on Henriot pieces prior to 1922. The "Henriot Quimper" mark was used after 1922. The "HB" mark covers a long time span. Numbers or dots and dashes were added for inventory purposes and are found on later pieces. Most marks are in blue or black. Pieces ordered by department stores, such as Macy's and Carson Pirie Scott, carry the store mark along with the factory mark, making them less desirable to collectors. A comprehensive list of marks is found in Bondhus book.

**References:** Susan and Al Bagdade, *Warman's English & Continental Pottery & Porcelain*, 3rd Ed., Krause, 1998; Sandra V. Bondhus, *Quimper Pottery: A French Folk Art Faience,* printed by author, 1981, Revised Edition, 1995; Millicent Mali, *French Faience*, United Printing, 1986; Millicent Mali, *Quimper Faience,* Airon, Inc., 1979; Adela Meadows, *Quimper Pottery, A Guide to Origins, Styles, and Values,* Schiffer Publishing, 1998; Ann Marie O'Neill, *Quimper Pottery, 2nd Edition,* Schiffer Publishing, 1998; Marjatta Taburet, *La Faience de Quimper*, Editions Sous le Vent, 1979, (French text).

**Collectors' Club:** USA Quimper Club, 2519 Kansas Ave., Suite 108, Santa Monica, CA 90404.

**Museums:** Musee des Faiences de Quimper, Quimper, France; Musee Departemental Breton, Quimper, France; Victoria and Albert Museum, French Ceramic Dept., London, England.

**Advisors:** Susan and Al Bagdade.

Additional Terms:

A la touche border decor—single brush stroke to create floral.

Breton Broderie decor—stylized blue and gold pattern inspired by a popular embroidery pattern often used on Breton costumes, dates from the Art Deco era.

Croisille—criss-cross pattern.

Decor Riche border—acanthus leaves in two colors.

Fleur de lys—the symbol of France.

Ivoire Corbeille pattern—red dots circled in sponged blue with red touches forming half a floral blossom, all over a tan ground.

Quintal—five fingered vase.

Bookend, 8" h, 5" w, figural seated little boy wearing violet shirt, green pants, black vest and hat, brown shoe on base, or seated little girl wearing black dress, yellow overdress, with red trim, brown shoes, dark brown bench, medium brown base, sgd "B. Savigny HB Quimper" marks, pr .................................. 750.00

Bud Vase, 8-1/2" h, bulbous base with band of red flowers, green leaves, and blue dot flowers with yellow centers, blue semicircle and dot border, yellow band on shoulder with blue zigzag, slender neck with turned female peasant holding bunch of flowers, orange and blue band rim, "HenRiot Quimper France 116" mark ................ 95.00

Chamberstick, 7" w x 6" w, yellow ground, peasant man with florals on base, square nozzle with red crosshatching or florals, blue outlined shaped rim and handle, "HenRiot Quimper 118" mark ............. 200.00

Charger, 12-3/4" d, Modern Movement of busts of male and female peasants, white, black, lt. Blue, and yellow clothes, red open flowerhead border with green leaves, blue sponged rim, "HB Quimper" mark ............................................................. 295.00

**Cruets and Stand, 8-3/4" h, black, red, blue, and yellow male or female peasant, black "V" or "H," band of red, blue and green floral border on base, blue striped handles, blue banded borders, glaze skips, "HB Quimper" marks, $350. Photo courtesy of Susan and Al Bagdade.**

Cheese Dish, Cov, 11" x 10" w, round cov with seated peasant woman holding distaff, dark blue décor riche border, figural brown pipe handle, figural pink bows and brown pipes on base, "HenRiot Quimper" mark ............................................................. 495.00

Cider Pitcher, 6-1/2"h, male peasant on front, floral sprays and 4 blue dot design, blue lined spout and rim, blue dashed overhead and side handle, "HB Quimper" mark ...................................... 175.00

Coffeepot, 7-3/4" h, male peasant on one side, female on reverse, a la touché flowers on sides, dark blue knob with small flower sprays, dark blue handle, "HB Quimper" mark ................................... 375.00

Cruets and Stand, 8-3/4" h, black, red, blue, and yellow make or female peasant, black "V" or "H," band of red, blue and green floral border on base, blue striped handles, blue banded borders, glaze skips, "HB Quimper" marks ......................................... 350.00

Cup and Saucer, hex shape, blue outlined panels, male peasant, female peasant, or single stroke red flowers, green leaves, blue dot flowers in panels, gold outlined blue dash handle, blue outlined indented saucer with scattered florals, "HR Quimper" mark 50.00

Dish

4-1/2" d, female peasant holding bouquet, green grass, blue and yellow banded border, scalloped rim, "HenRiot Quimper France 93" mark ...................................................... 35.00

4-5/8" w, shell shape, female peasant with florals in center, blue dash border, gold-yellow handle, "HenRiot Quimper France" mark ........................................................................ 85.00

10" l, figural fish shape, female peasant holding umbrella in center, red, blue, and green florals at side, yellow fish head, blue lined shape, red, and green streaked fins and tail, "HenRiot Quimper" on front ............................................... 130.00

11-1/2" w, figural bagpipe dancing couple in center with overhead floral spray, dark blue décor rich border, yellow and pink figural bow at top, brown figural bagpipe handle, "HR Quimper" mark ....................................................... 600.00

Egg Cup, 2" h, 3-3/4" d, attached underdish, figural chick, yellow body, blue hatched wings, blue outlined scalloped rim, "HenRiot Quimper France" mark .................................................... 100.00

Figure

4" h, male peasant playing bagpipe, orange pantaloons, cobalt jacket, sq. base with orange and blue stripes and geometrics, "LAOW" on base, "HenRiot Quimper 135" mark ............. 385.00

8-1/2" 1, shoe, male peasant on green grass, 4 blue dot design, lt blue border with dark blue loops, "HB Quimper" mark ..... 275.00

10" h, St. Yves, standing figure in cobalt garb with white and gold trim, holding gold cross, black and white money bag, red and blue trimmed oct base, "HenRiot Quimper" mark............ 400.00

12-1/2" h, dancing couple, male peasant in black suit and hat, lt and dark blue sash, gold vest, female with hand on hip, pink dress with blue, dark red and gold lower stripes, black vest, white coif, sgd "R. Micheau-Vernez" on circ base, "HenRiot Quimper 78" mark ......................................................... 495.00

Fish Platter, 24" l, peasant man playing flute, female with wrap over arm, lt green trees in background with large green pine tree, scattered 4 blue dot designs, blue loop border, "HBQuimper" mark..................... 1,300.00

Holy Water Font, 10-1/4" blue outlined figural fleur de lys, girl kneeling at wayside cross, scattered red, green, yellow, and blue florals, scattered 4 blue dot designs, red and green lattice bowl, "HR Quimper" on front ............................................................. 495.00

Inkwell, 7-1/4" l, crescent shape, reclining female peasant holding basket or reclining male peasant blowing horn, green décor riche border with crest, Porquier Beau ....................................... 1,350.00

Knife Rest, 3-1/4" l, triangle shape, male peasant, blue dash edges, blue sponged ends, "HB Quimper" mark................................... 75.00

Match Safe, 3-1/4" h, male peasant on front with bluet florals, blue lattice background with red dots, "HR Quimper" mark ................ 200.00

Melonnier, 14-1/2" handle to handle, dancing couple in meadow in center, dark blue décor riche border with crest of Brittany at top, green sponged handles with yellow-gold trim, "HenRiot Quimper" mark ............................................................................. 450.00

Menu, 7" h, male peasant blowing horn, raised yellow fleur de lys, "Menu" with snake head, blue outlined wavy rim, Porquier Bveau ............ 770.00

Mirror Frame, 10-1/2" h x 8-1/2" w, rect, curved indentations, female peasant at shore on left, male peasant with bagpipe on right, crest of Brittany at top and base, green décor riche on lt green ground border, unmkd ............................................................... 1,100.00

Mustard Jar, cov, 4-1/2" h, attached underplate, slotted cov, bulbous shape with cut corners, male peasant scattered florals, dashes at cut edges, blue scalloped and dot design on underplate, "HenRiot Quimper France" mark ............................................. 130.00

Pitcher
    5-1/2" h, bulbous, female peasant under spout, scattered florals, yellow and blue striped base and shoulder, "HenRiot Quimper France 94" mark .............................................. 60.00
    8" h, bulbous shape, female peasant on front with dark red and blue single stroke vert florals, blue dash spout, dark blue band on shoulder and base, yellow striped rim and handle, "HB Quimper France" mark ....................................... 75.00

Planter, 9-7/8" l x 5-3/8" w, diamond shape, blue, yellow, reed and black peasants, red, blue, green and yellow scattered florals, black ermine tails, large red and yellow cabbage rose on reverse with red, yellow, green, and blue horizontal florals, red, blue and green cross hatched ends, blue lined borders, 4 small feet, "HR Quimper" on reverse .................................................... 600.00

Plate
    8-1/2" d, blue, red, and yellow crowing rooster in center, scattered florals at sides, blue and yellow striped border, unmkd.... 225.00
    8-3/4" d, center scene of peasant woman holding basket, fence and meadow in background, cobalt acanthus border, crest of Britanny at top, 12 pointed star shaped rim, "HR Quimper" on front and reverse .............................................. 467.00
    9-3/4" d, red, blue and yellow bird in center, red and blue cabbage rose and florals, orange sponged border, "HenRiot Quimper France" marks, pr ............................................... 450.00
    11" d, Modern Movement, medium blue, white, yellow, and orange bust of female peasant in dark blue and orange inner circle, border of dark blue stylized flowerheads on lt blue ground between orange stripes, "HB Quimper" mark ................... 150.00

**Planter, 9-7/8" l x 5-3/8" w, diamond shape, blue, yellow, red and black peasants, red, blue, green and yellow scattered florals, black ermine tails, large red and yellow cabbage rose on reverse with red, yellow, green, and blue horizontal florals, red, blue and green cross hatched ends, blue lined borders, 4 small feet, "HR Quimper" on reverse, $600. Photo courtesy of Susan and Al Bagdade.**

**Platter, Ivorie Corbeille, orange apron and pantaloons, green blouses, dark red trim, orange outlined blue sponged circles with dark red centers, inner border of green sponged circles with dark red centers on yellow band, dark red single stroke stylized flowers, blue sponged rim, "HenRiot Quimper" mark, 15" l, $400. Photo courtesy of Susan and Al Bagdade.**

Platter, 15-1/4" l, oval, blue and red strutting peacock in center, red, blue, and green florals at sides, band of red, blue and green floral border, blue outlined shaped rim, "HB Quimper" mark ............. 710.00

Porringer, 5-1/2" handle to handle, male peasant in center, yellow and blue banded border, blue wings handles, "HenRiot Quimper France 93" mark ................................................... 75.00

Quintal, 5" h, ball shape, gold outlined quatrefoil with seated female peasant with basket of eggs, band of gold and dark blue geometrics, blue ground, "HenRiot Quimper France 119" mark ................. 165.00

Ramekin, 1-1/4" h, 3" d, male or female peasant on int, vert fluting, band of red, blue, and green flowers, blue lined rim and base, "HB Quimper" mark, pr ......................................................... 75.00

Snuff Bottle, 2-3/4" h, figural bagpipe, yellow figural bow and pipe on side, male peasant on front, red and yellow-centered blue flowers, green leaves and 4 blue dot designs on reverse, blue dash rim, "HR Quimper" mark ........................................................ 200.00

Soup Tureen, 12" handle to handle, 11" h, female peasant holding blanket and staff, male with walking stick, fence in background, vert green trees on cov, scattered floral sprays and 4 blue dots, molded seashell and swag handles, molded yellow apple knob, "HB" mark ............... 2,200.00

Vase, 6" h, oval shape, circ base, Modern Movement style dark blue, orange, and white sailor and maiden with blue waves and stylized gulls behind, orange and blue squiggles, dots and frame lines, orange base, "HB Quimper" mark ........................................... 350.00

Vegetable Bowl, cov, 13" handle to handle, oval, overall single stroke blue bachelor buttons and 4 red dot designs, yellow banded rims, blue dash handles and knob, Adolphe Porquier ...................... 770.00

Wall Pocket, 7-1/2" h, figural bagpipe, frontal view of female peasant holding flower, figural blue bow at top, brown mouthpieces, scattered, red, green, red, and blue florals, "HenRiot Quimper, France 45" mark ............................................................... 220.00

# RADIOS

**History:** The radio was invented more than 100 years ago. Marconi was the first to assemble and employ the transmission and reception instruments that permitted the sending of electric messages without the use of direct connections. Between 1905 and the end of World War I, many technical advances affected the "wireless," including the invention of the vacuum tube by DeForest. Technology continued its progress, and radios filled the entertainment needs of the average family in the 1920s.

Changes in design, style, and technology brought the radio from the black boxes of the 1920s to the stylish furniture pieces and console models of the 1930s and 1940s, to midget models of the 1950s, and finally to the high-tech radios of the 1980s.

**References:** Robert Breed and Marty Bunis, *Collector's Guide to Novelty Radios, Book II,* Collector Books, 1999; Marty and Sue Bunis, *Collector's Guide to Antique Radios*, 4th ed., Collector Books, 1997; ——, *Collector's Guide to Transistor Radios*, Collector Books, 1994, 1996 values; Marty Bunis and Robert Breed, *Collector's Guide to Novelty Radios*, Collector Books, 1995; Philip Collins, *Radio Redux*, Chronicle Books, 1992; Harold Cones, and John Bryant, *Zenith Radio: The Early Years, 1919-1935,* Schiffer Publishing, 1997; Chuck Dachis, *Radios by Hallicrafters*, 3rd ed., Schiffer Publishing, 1999; Alan Douglas, *Radio Manufacturers of the 1920s*, Vol. 1 (1988), Vol. 2 (1989), Vol. 3 (1991), Vestal Press; Roger Handy, Maureen Erbe, and Aileen Farnan Antonier, *Made in Japan*, Chronicle Books, 1993; David and Betty Johnson, *Guide to Old Radios, Pointers, Pictures and Prices*, 2nd ed., Wallace Homestead/Krause, 1995; Mark Stein, *Machine Age to Jet Age, Radiomania's Guide to Tabletop Radios—1933–1959*, published by author (2109 Carterdale Rd., Baltimore, MD 21209); Eric Wrobbel, *Toy Crystal Radios,* published by author, 1997 (20802 Exhibit Court, Woodland Hills, CA).

**Periodicals:** *Antique Radio Classified*, P.O. Box 2, Carlisle, MA, 01741; *Horn Speaker*, P.O. Box 1193, Mabank, TX 75147; *Radio Age*, 636 Cambridge Road, Augusta, GA 30909; *Transistor Network*, RR1, Box 36, Bradford, NH 03221.

**Collectors' Clubs:** Antique Radio Club of America, 81 Steeplechase Rd, Devon, PA 19333; Antique Wireless Assoc., 59 Main St., Bloomfield, NY 14469; New England Antique Radio Club, RR1, Box 36, Bradford, NH 03221; Vintage Radio & Phonograph Society, Inc., P.O. Box 165345, Irving, TX 75016.

**Museums:** Antique Radio Museum, St. Louis, MO; Antique Wireless Museum, Bloomfield, NY; Caperton's Radio Museum, Louisville, KY; Muchow's Historical Radio Museum, Elgin, IL; Museum of Broadcast Communication, Chicago, IL; Museum of Wonderful Miracles, Minneapolis, MN; New England Wireless and Steam Museum, Inc., East Greenwich, RI; Voice of the Twenties, Orient, NY.

**Additional Listings:** See *Warman's Americana & Collectibles* for more examples.

**Advisor:** Lewis S. Walters.

**Note:** Prices of Catalin radios are dropping by about 10 to 15%. Collectors and dealers feel prices for these radios have reached their high side and are falling into a more realistic range.

Admiral
| | |
|---|---|
| Portable, #33-35-37 | 30.00 |
| Portable, #218, leatherette | 40.00 |
| Portable, #909, All World | 85.00 |
| Y-2127 - Imperial 8, c1959 | 45.00 |
| Air King, tombstone, Art Deco | 3,000.00 |

Arvin
| | |
|---|---|
| Rhythm Baby #417 | 275.00 |
| Hoppy with lariatenna | 575.00 |
| Table, #444 | 100.00 |
| Table, #522A | 65.00 |
| Tombstone, #617 Rhythm Maid | 215.00 |

Atwater Kent
| | |
|---|---|
| Breadboard Style, Model 9A | 550.00 |
| Breadboard Style, Model 10, with orig tags | 1,300.00 |
| Breadboard Style, Model 10C | 930.00 |
| Cathedral, 80, c1931 | 380.00 |
| Table, #55 Keil | 225.00 |
| Table, #318, dome | 115.00 |
| Tombstone, #854 | 155.00 |
| Type R Horn | 200.00 |

Bulova, clock radio
| | |
|---|---|
| #100 | 40.00 |
| #110 | 25.00 |
| #120 | 40.00 |

| | |
|---|---|
| Colonial, New World Radio | 1,000.00 |
| Columbia, table radio, oak | 125.00 |

Crosley
| | |
|---|---|
| ACE V | 170.00 |
| Bandbox, #600, 1927 | 80.00 |
| Battery Operated, #4-28 | 130.00 |
| Dashboard | 120.00 |
| Gemchest, #609 | 425.00 |
| Litfella, 1N cathedral | 175.00 |
| Pup, with box | 350.00 |
| Sheraton, cathedral | 290.00 |
| Showbox, #706 | 100.00 |
| Sleigh | 125.00 |
| Super Buddy Boy | 125.00 |

| | |
|---|---|
| Dumont, RA346, table, scroll work, 1938 | 110.00 |

Emerson
| | |
|---|---|
| AU-190 Catalin Tombstone | 1,200.00 |
| BT-245 | 1,200.00 |
| #274 Brown Bakelite | 165.00 |
| #400 Aristocrat | 475.00 |
| #409 Mickey | 1,400.00 |
| #411 Mickey | 1,400.00 |
| #570 Memento | 110.00 |
| #640 Portable | 30.00 |
| #888 Vanguard | 80.00 |
| Snow White | 1,200.00 |
| Dealer Sign, porcelain | 150.00 |

Fada
| | |
|---|---|
| #43 | 240.00 |
| #53X | 200.00 |
| #60W | 75.00 |
| #115 bullet shape | 1,000.00 |
| #136 | 1,000.00 |
| #252 | 575.00 |
| #625 rounded end, slide rule dial | 700.00 |

| | |
|---|---|
| #1000 red/orange bullet | 1,100.00 |
| #L56 maroon and white | 2,600.00 |

Federal
| | |
|---|---|
| #58DX | 500.00 |
| #110 | 550.00 |

General Electric
| | |
|---|---|
| #81, c1934 | 200.00 |
| #400, 410, 411, 414 | 30.00 |
| #515, 517 clock radio | 25.00 |
| K-126 | 150.00 |
| Tombstone | 250.00 |

Grebe
| | |
|---|---|
| CR-8 | 500.00 |
| CR-9 | 650.00 |
| CR-12 | 600.00 |
| MU-1 | 250.00 |
| Service Manual | 50.00 |

Halicrafters
| | |
|---|---|
| TW-600 | 100.00 |
| TW-200 | 125.00 |

Majestic
| | |
|---|---|
| Charlie McCarthy | 1,000.00 |
| #59 Wooden Tombstone | 375.00 |
| #92 | 125.00 |
| #381 | 225.00 |

Metrodyne Super 7, 1925 | 265.00

Motorola
| | |
|---|---|
| #68X11Q Art Deco | 75.00 |
| Jet Plane | 55.00 |
| Jewel Box | 80.00 |
| M logo | 25.00 |
| Pixie | 45.00 |
| Ranger, Portable | 60.00 |
| Ranger #700 | 30.00 |
| Table, plastic | 35.00 |

Olympic, radio w/phonograph | 60.00

Paragon
| | |
|---|---|
| DA-2 table | 475.00 |
| RD-5 table | 600.00 |

Philco
| | |
|---|---|
| T-7 126 transistor | 65.00 |
| T1000 clock radio | 80.00 |
| #17, 38 cathedral | 250.00 |
| #20 Cathedral | 200.00 |
| #551, 1928 | 145.00 |
| #37-62, table, two tone | 60.00 |
| #37-84, Cathedral, 1937 | 175.00 |

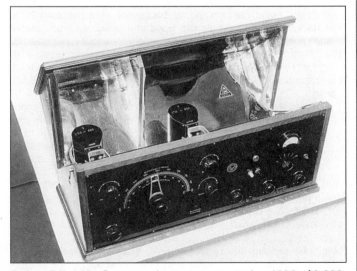

**Reico RF 144, German, battery operated, c1926, $2,833. Photo courtesy of Auction Team Breker,**

| | |
|---|---|
| #40-180, console wood | 150.00 |
| #46-132, table | 20.00 |
| #49- 01, Boomerang | 475.00 |
| #49-506, Transitone | 35.00 |
| #52-544, Transitone | 40.00 |
| #60-Cathedral | 125.00 |

Radiobar, with orig glasses and decanters | 1,500.00

Radio Corporation of America, RCA
LaSiesta550.00
Radiola
| | |
|---|---|
| #17 | 120.00 |
| #18, with speaker | 125.00 |
| #20 | 165.00 |
| #24 | 170.00 |
| #28, console | 200.00 |
| #33 | 60.00 |
| #6X7 table, plastic | 25.00 |
| 8BT-7LE portable | 35.00 |
| 40X56 Worlds Fair | 1,000.00 |

Silvertone, Sears
| | |
|---|---|
| #1 table | 75.00 |
| #1582 cathedral, wood | 225.00 |
| #1955 tombstone | 135.00 |
| #9205 plastic transistor | 45.00 |
| Clock Radio, plastic | 15.00 |

Sony, transistor
| | |
|---|---|
| TFM-151, 1960 | 50.00 |
| TR-63, 1958 | 145.00 |

Sparton
| | |
|---|---|
| #506 Blue Bird, Art Deco | 3,300.00 |
| #5218 | 95.00 |

Stewart-Warner, table, slant | 175.00
Stromberg Carlson, # 636A console | 125.00
Westinghouse, Model WR-602 | 50.00

Zenith
| | |
|---|---|
| #500 transistor - owl eye | 75.00 |
| #500D transistor | 55.00 |
| #750L transistor, leather case | 40.00 |
| #6D2615 table w/boomerang dial | 95.00 |
| Trans-Oceanic | 90.00 |
| Zephyr, multiband | 95.00 |

# RAILROAD ITEMS

**History:** Railroad collectors have existed for decades. The merger of the rail systems and the end of passenger service made many objects available to private collectors. The Pennsylvania Railroad sold its archives at public sale.

**References:** Stanley L. Baker, *Railroad Collectibles*, 4th ed., Collector Books, 1990, 1999 value update; Richard C. Barrett, *Illustrated Encyclopedia of Railroad Lighting*, Vol. 1 (1994); Vol. 2 (1999), Railroad Research Publications; Barbara J. Conroy, *Restaurant China: Restaurant, Airline, Ship & Railroad Dinnerware,* Collector Books, Volume 1 (1998), Volume 2 (1999); Don Stewart, *Railroad Switch Keys & Padlocks*, 2nd ed., Key Collectors International, 1993; Joe Welsh, et. al., *The American Railroad,* MBI Publishing, 1999.

**Periodicals:** *Key, Lock and Lantern*, 3 Berkeley Heights Park, Bloomfield, NJ 07003; *Main Line Journal*, P.O. Box 121, Streamwood, IL 60107.

**Collectors' Clubs:** Chesapeake & Ohio Historical Society, Inc., P.O. Box 79, Clifton Forge, VA 24422; Illinois Central Railroad Historical Society, 14818 Clifton Park,

Midlothian, IL 60445; Railroad Enthusiasts, 102 Dean Rd, Brookline, MA 02146; Railroadiana Collectors Assoc., 795 Aspen Drive, Buffalo Grove, IL 60089; Railway and Locomotive Historical Society, P.O. Box 1418, Westford, MA 01886; Twentieth Century Railroad Club, 329 West 18th St., Ste 902, Chicago, IL 60616.

**Museums:** Baltimore and Ohio Railroad, Baltimore, MD; California State Railroad Museum, Sacramento, CA; Frisco Railroad Museum, Van Buren, AR; Museum of Transportation, Brookline, MA; National Railroad Museum, Green Bay, WI; New York Museum of Transportation, West Henrietta, NY; Old Depot Railroad Museum, Dassel, MN.

**Additional Listings:** See *Warman's Americana & Collectibles* for more examples.

**Notes:** Railroad enthusiasts have organized into regional and local clubs. Join one if you're interested in this collectible field; your local hobby store can probably point you to the right person. The best pieces pass between collectors and rarely enter the general market.

Ashtray, 3-1/2" d, Cotton Belt Route, copper, logo on bottom....... 25.00
Baggage and Brass Check
    1-1/4" d, key tag, GN Ry ...................................................... 12.00
    1-1/2" x 2", SOU PAC RR, 794, strap ................................. 45.00
Bell, 25" h, 15-1/2" h at yoke, nickel plated, mounted on modern mahogany base................................................................. 2,145.00
Book, *Colorado,* Chicago, Milwaukee & St. Paul Railway, c1910, illustrated travel guide .................................................................. 28.00.
Button, Erie, large silver dome, Scovill Mfg. Co., Waterbury, CT.... 7.50

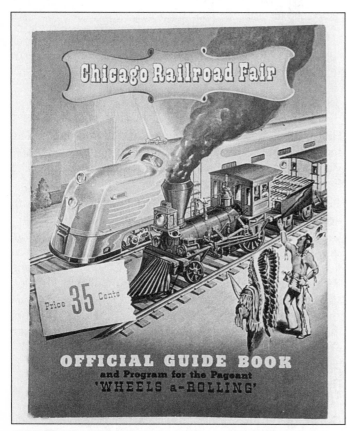

**Guide Book,** *Chicago Railroad Fair,* **1948, 16 pgs, 8-1/4" w, 10-3/4" h, $20.**

Calendar
    10" w, 22" l, 1931, Great Northern Railway, litho by Louis Dow, St. Paul, Indian wearing hat with feather, May calendar page only .................................................................................. 115.00
    14" w, 34" l, 1948, Great Northern Railway, Lazy Boy, Blackfeet Medicine Man, Glacier park, unused, orig top and bottom bands.................................................................................. 100.00
Catalog, Pennsylvania Steel Co., Steelton, PA, 1906, 96 pages, 4-1/4 x 6-3/4", hardcover, black, gold emb, spirals, street railway curves, formulas, tables, illus...................................................... 45.00
Check, Atlantic City & Shore Railroad Co..................................... 10.00
Children's Book, *Union Pacific's Half Pint,* David L. Tank author, illus by Forrest Wallford, distributed by Union Pacific ........................... 35.00
China
    Atchinson, Topeka & Sante Fe, gravy boat, Syracuse China, no backstamp ............................................................................ 165.00
    Atlantic Coast Line, butter pat, 3-1/2" d, Flora of the South, Buffalo China backstamp............................................................ 100.00
    B & O (Baltimore & Ohio)
        Creamer, 4-1/2" h .......................................................... 75.00
        Plate, dinner .................................................................. 75.00
        Platter ............................................................................ 175.00
    C & O (Chesapeake & Ohio), plate, 4-3/4" sq, Silhouette, Martha and George Washington dancing with hands up, Syracuse China, no backstamp ............................................................ 250.00
    Delaware & Hudson, Canterbury, platter, 10-1/4" x 7", Syracuse China, no backstamp ....................................................... 120.00
    Florida East Coast, Carolina, bowl, 5-3/4" d, Buffalo China backstamp ................................................................................. 75.00
    Mimbreno, platter, 9-1/4" l, oval, dear motif ...................... 175.00
    New York Central, Albany, compote, 7-1/4" d, Shenango China backstamp ............................................................................ 275.00
    Norfolk & Western, plate, 6-1/4" d, , Syracuse China, no backstamp ...................................................................................... 80.00
    UP (Union Pacific), plate, 8-1/4" d, circus theme, monkey, clown, bareback rider ..................................................................... 125.00
    Wabash Banner, cup and saucer, logo, Syracuse China, no backstamp ................................................................................ 250.00
Glassware
    Canadian Pacific, wine, 4" h, etched script logo on side, ornate facets................................................................................... 40.00
    Lehigh Valley, highball, 4-1/2" h, maroon and white train, map of northeastern US marking route ......................................... 75.00
    Sante Fe, cordial, 4-1/2" h, applied Sante Fe white script logo . 60.00
    Union Pacific, goblet, 5-1/2" h, etched name inside shield ... 20.00
Hat
    Missouri Pacific, two silver bands, silver "Missouri Pacific Lines" buttons on each side, red cap badge with buzz saw logo, "Missouri Pacific Lines" and "Trainman" ................................. 165.00
    Penn Central, red logo and cap badge with "Station Master" 75.00
Hat Rack, overhead type, coach, wood and brass, six brass double sided hooks ...................................................................... 200.00
Head Rest, Pennsylvania, 15" x 16" tan linen-type fabric, brown PRR logo and electric train ................................................................ 15.00
Lamp, caboose interior side, C & O, c1920, price for pr ............. 350.00
Lantern
    Great Northern Railway, Adams & Westlake, double horizontal guard, twist-off pot and burner, 5-3/8" h clear globe, patent date Nov 30, '97 ........................................................................... 175.00
    Penn RR, Dressel, short clear globe ................................. 100.00
    Southern Railway, red globe............................................... 150.00
    Lock, brass
    Boston & Maine Railroad, switch type, marked "B&M RR LS S," made by "Sherburne & Co/Boston, Mass" ....................... 150.00
    B & O, orig key................................................................. 45.00
Illinois Central Railroad, six lever round style, "ICRR" cast over front side............................................................................... 200.00
Map, "Map shewing the Location of the N. Y. & Oswego Midland R.R.," Weed, Parsons, Albany, 1869, lithographed roll map, color, wooden rollers top and bottom, linen backed, various routes identified by different colors, inset of Great Lakes region ............................... 435.00

Oil Can, Locomotive Oil ............................................. 100.00
Paperweight, New York Grand Central Station, 2-1/2" w, 4" l, rect, view of station, adv 5 limited trains, Barnes & Abrams Co, light scratching to top glass ....................................................... 150.00
Pinback Button, 1-1/4" d, celluloid, "Brotherhood of Locomotive Firemen & Enginemen and Ladies' Society, Second Annual Tri-State Union Meeting, Duluth, Minnesota, Aug 17-19, 1931," blue on white, mkd "courtesy of the Hamilton Watch Co." .................................. 12.00
Print, 25" h, 33" w, American Express Train, Currier & Ives, hand colored large folio lithograph, minor soiling and stain, margins trimmed, shadowbox frame with gilded liner ........................................ 3,190.00
Playing Cards
    Louisville & Nashville, engine, six scenes............................. 50.00
    Norfolk & Western, N & W in circle, blue and black .............. 50.00
    Union Pacific, river scene, two horses and riders in foreground, c1910, 52 cards, joker, extra card, booklet ......................... 65.00
Ruler, Soo Line, 12" l, tin, map and logo, red letters, white ground .... 10.00
Sign
    Chicago, Rock-Island & Pacific Railway, intricate mother-of-pearl inlay on reverse painted glass, 137 engine and tender, United States express car, five passenger cars, promoting railroad between Chicago and California, switchman in forefront, view is 3 miles east of LaSalle, ornate frame, 32-1/2" h, 43-1/2" l, minor loss to black background and gold border ....................... 275.00
    Railway Express Agency, set of three matched porcelain signs, tan and red letters, green ground, each 4" h, length varies from 26" to 30-1/4" ................................................................ 425.00
    Railway Express Agency, tin over cardboard, men unloading early railroad car while truck comes for pickup, H. D. Beach Co. litho, 13-1/2" h, 19-1/2" d, some minor scratching ........... 500.00
Silver Flatware, top marked
    Lackawanna, fruit knife, Cromwell pattern, International Silver ...................................................................... 25.00
    NPR (North Penn Railroad), iced tea spoon, Winthrop pattern, Gorham ................................................................ 35.00
    PRR (Pennsylvania Railroad), teaspoon, Kings pattern, International Silver .................................................... 30.00
    Reading, fork, Kings pattern, International Silver ................. 30.00
    Soo Line, fork, Windsor pattern, Reed & Barton................... 35.00
Silver Hollowware
    Chesapeake & Ohio, sugar tongs, 5-1/4" l, Waverly pattern, Albert Pick, top marked, no backstamp ...................................... 165.00
    Pennsylvania, creamer, hinged lid, raised PRR keystone logo on side, Gorham, backstamp with name of railroad .............. 175.00
    Southern Pacific, teapot, 12 oz, Reed & Barton, backstamp reads "S.P. Lines" .................................................................. 145.00
    Western Pacific, cheese scoop, 8-1/4" l, Belmont pattern, Reed & Barton, top mark reads "W P Ry" ..................................... 125.00
Stamp Set, Atlantic Coast Line, Jacksonville, FL, freight office, wooden drawer, seventy city stamps, c1950 ....................................... 150.00
Step Stool, SP Co, marked "Morton" ........................................ 325.00
Stock Certificate
    New York Central, vignette of engine 3404 pulling passenger train .......................................................................... 20.00
    Western Maryland Railway, Mercury standing in front of diesel locomotive .................................................................... 6.00
    Western Pacific Railroad, male and female flanking streamlined train ............................................................................ 8.00
Tea and Coffee Service, Ball, Black & Co., c1868, Greco-Roman Revival, sterling silver, coffeepot, teapot, cov creamer, cov two-handled sugar, waste bowl, helmet-form finial with beading above scroll engraved lid, 10-1/2" h coffeepot with elaborately engraved body centering reserve of locomotive, reverse with identical center reserve with "1868," beaded handles surmounted by neoclassical heads, anthemion leaves, circular molded base, 9-3/4" h teapot inscribed "Presented to Addison Day Esq. By the Employees of the Rome, Watertown & Ogdensburg Railroad Co., Dec 1st, 1868," minor loss to one teapot ivory spacer, 98 troy oz ................................... 3,450.00
Time Table, Union Pacific, 1945.................................................. 12.00

Travel Guide, Carlsbad Caverns, New Mexico, 1930, Santa Fe Railroad, 54 pages .............................................................. 15.00
Watch Fob, brass, Oklahoma International Petroleum Expo, train, oil wells, plane .......................................................... 45.00

# RAZORS

**History:** Razors date back several thousand years. Early man used sharpened stones; the Egyptians, Greeks, and Romans had metal razors.

Razors made prior to 1800 generally were crudely stamped "Warranted" or "Cast Steel," with the maker's mark on the tang. Until 1870, razors were handmade and almost all razors for the American market were manufactured in Sheffield, England. Most blades were wedge shaped; many were etched with slogans or scenes. Handles were made of natural materials: horn, tortoiseshell, bone, ivory, stag, silver, or pearl.

After 1870, razors were machine made with hollow ground blades and synthetic handle materials. Razors of this period usually were manufactured in Germany (Solingen) or in American cutlery factories. Hundreds of molded-celluloid handle patterns were produced.

Cutlery firms produced boxed sets of two, four, and seven razors. Complete and undamaged sets are very desirable. The most-popular ones are the seven-day sets in which each razor is etched with a day of the week.

**References:** Ronald S. Barlow, *Vanishing American Barber Shop*, Windmill Publishing, 1993; *Safety Razors: A Price Guide*, L-W Book Sales, 1995; Roy Ritchie and Ron Stewart, *Standard Guide to Razors,* 2nd ed., Collector Books, 1999 value update; Jim Sargent, *American Premium Guide to Pocket Knives & Razors*, 5th ed., Krause Publications, 1999.

**Periodical:** *Blade Magazine*, P.O. Box 22007, Chattanooga, TN 37422.

**Additional Listings:** See *Warman's Americana & Collectibles* for more examples.

**Notes:** The fancier the handle or more intricately etched the blade, the higher the price. Rarest handle materials are pearl, stag, sterling silver, pressed horn, and carved ivory. Rarest blades are those with scenes etched across the entire front. Value is increased by the presence of certain manufacturers' names, e.g., H. Boker, Case, M. Price, Joseph Rogers, Simmons Hardware, Will & Finck, Winchester, and George Wostenholm.

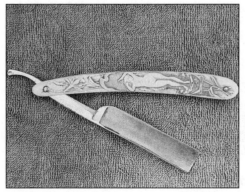

**Geneva Cutlery Co., Geneva, NY, carved bone handle, 6-1/4" l, $70.**

Boker & Co., H., etched blade with American Lines *S. S. St. Louis* ship scene, black celluloid handle .................................................. 130.00

Challenge Cutlery Co., Bridgeport, CT, blade etched "Rince," black peacock pattern.................................................. 70.00

Country Club, #76, black handle, orig box ................................. 25.00

Kinfolks Straight Razor, good condition ...................................... 45.00

Lecourtre, Jacques, Swiss, frameback, wafer blade, tang stamped "M. M. & Co.," engraved plated steel blade, "William Ernest Barnes Dec 30th 1869".................................................. 45.00

Morley & Sons, W. H., German, silver overlay hunting scene ...... 55.00

Novelty Cutlery Co., Canton, OH, rounded point blade, handle with cow, horse, train, and owner's name and address, front dated "1921," German silver ends .................................................. 85.00

Saffa, John S., St. Louis, scene of two gold covered camels, scroll on blade with "Silver Sheet," ivory colored handle .......................... 40.00

Sears Craftsman, celluloid handle, orig box ................................. 45.00

Set, boxed, four bone and steel strop razors, calamander and brass box, int. fitted with orig Imperial purple velvet lining, late Victorian, c1890 .................................................. 100.00

Three Admirals, one medallion with Admiral Dewey, inscribed "Dewey-Manilla," other with Admiral Sampson, inscribed "Sampson-Santiogo," third with Admiral Schley, inscribed "Schley-Santiogo," gold dec .................................................. 175.00

Turniss Cutler & Stacey Sheffield, unusual shaped point blade, tang stamped "For Use," two pressed intertwined snakes on mottled horn handle .................................................. 650.00

Union razor Cutlery Co., Union City, GA, banded tobacco pattern handle.................................................. 50.00

Wade & Butcher, hollow ground blade, engraved and ornate escutcheon plate, two inlaid engraved star shaped metal dec, mottled horn handle, blade etched "The Celebrated Hollow Ground Razor," c1850 .................................................. 90.00

Westfield Mfg. Co., hollow ground blade, checkered raised shield, ivory handle.................................................. 60.00

Wostenholm & Sons, George, Celebrated I'XL Razor Washington Works, wedge blade, etched spread American eagle and "The Congress Razor," notched point, black horn handle, five sided pewter end cap ends, c1930.................................................. 120.00

Yankee Cutlery, celluloid handle, nude woman, orig box.............. 75.00

# RECORDS

**History:** With the advent of the more sophisticated recording materials, such as 33 1/3 RPM long playing records, 8-track tapes, cassettes, and compact discs, earlier phonograph records became collectors' items. Most have little value. The higher-priced items are rare (limited-production) recordings. Condition is critical.

**References:** Mark Allen Baker, *Goldmine Price Guide to Rock 'n' Roll Memorabilia,* Krause Publications, 1997; Mark Brown, Thomas Conner and John Wooley, *Forever Lounge,* Antique Trader Books, 1999; John Clemente, *Girl Groups, Fabulous Females That Rocked The World,* Krause Publications, 2000; Les Docks, *American Premium Record Guide, 1900-1965,* 5th Edition, Krause Publications, 1997; Goldmine Magazine, *Goldmine's 1997 Annual,* Krause Publications, 1996; ——, *Goldmine Roots of Rock Digest,* Krause Publications, 1999; Ron Lofman, *Goldmine's Celebrity Vocals,* Krause Publications, 1994; William M. Miller, *How to Buy & Sell Used Record Albums,* Loran Publishing, 1994; Tim Neely, *Goldmine Christmas Record Price Guide,* Krause Publications, 1997; ——, *Goldmine's Country & Western Record Price Guide,* 2nd ed., Krause Publications, 2000;

——, *Goldmine Jazz Album Price Guide,* Krause Publications, 2000; ——, *Goldmine's Price Guide to Alternative Records,* Krause Publications, 1996; ——, *Goldmine's Price Guide to 45 RPM Records,* Krause Publications, 1996; ——, *Goldmine Standard Catalog of American Records 1950-1975,* 2nd ed., Krause Publications, 2000; Tom Neely and Dave Thompson, *Goldmine British Invasion Record Price Guide,* Krause Publications, 1997; Jerry Osborne (comp.) *Rockin' Records, 1998 Ed.,* Antique Trader Books, 1997; Charles Szabala, *Goldmine 45 RPM Picture Sleeve Price Guide,* Krause Publications, 1998; Neal Umphred, *Goldmine's Price Guide to Collectible Jazz Albums,* 1949-1969, 2nd ed., Krause Publications, 1994; ——, *Goldmine's Price Guide to Collectible Record Albums,* 5th ed., Krause Publications, 1996; ——, *Goldmine's Rock 'n' Roll 45 RPM Record Price Guide,* 3rd ed., Krause Publications, 1994.

**Periodicals:** *Cadence*, Cadence Building, Redwood, NY 13679; *DISCoveries Magazine*, P.O. Box 309, Fraser, MI 48026; *Goldmine*, 700 E. State St., Iola, WI 54990; *Jazz Beat Magazine*, 1206 Decatur St., New Orleans, LA 70116; *Joslin's Jazz Journal*, P.O. Box 213, Parsons, KS 67357; *New Amberola Graphic*, 37 Caledonia St., St. Johnsbury, VT 05819; *Record Collectors Monthly*, P.O. Box 75, Mendham, NJ 07945; *Record Finder*, P.O. Box 1047, Glen Allen, VA 23060.

**Collectors' Clubs:** Association for Recorded Sound Collections, P.O. Box 453, Annapolis, MD 21404; International Association of Jazz Record Collectors, P.O. Box 75155, Tampa, FL 33605.

**Additional Listings:** See *Warman's Americana & Collectibles* for more examples.

**Note:** Most records, especially popular recordings, have a value of less than $3 per disc. The records listed here are classic recordings of their type and are in demand by collectors.

Annette, Country Albumn, last LP, sealed..................................... 50.00

Atomic Rooster, Save Me/Close Your Eyes, Spain....................... 15.00

Beach Boys

    Good Vibrations/Let's Go Away For Awhile, Germany ......... 20.00

    I Can Hear The Music/All I Want, France ........................... 20.00

Beatles

    A Hard Days Night, 7" promo, UA Interview .................. 10,000.00

    Introducing the Beatles, stereo ........................................ 6,000.00

    The Beatles & Frank Field, portrait cover ....................... 4,500.00

Blue Barons, Twist to the Greatest Blues Hits ............................. 18.00

Booker T & the MG's, in the Christmas Spirit ............................ 400.00

David Bowie, Alabama song/Space Oddity, Germany ................. 20.00

Burke Solomon, If You Need Me.................................................. 50.00

Dave Clark Five, Weekend in London .......................................... 30.00

ELO, Strange Magic/Down Home Town, Germany....................... 12.00

Fabian, Good Old Summertime ................................................... 20.00

Fleetwoods, Buried Treasures ..................................................... 20.00

Nina Hagen, Spirit in the Sky/My Way, promo, Spain ................. 25.00

Hollies, Stop, Stop, Stop, Spain ................................................. 45.00

Jefferson Airplane, Mexico, 3 promo stamps, Brazil.................... 40.00

Lennie Kravitz, Stand By My Woman/Flowers, France................. 8.00

Los Shakers, Break it All.............................................................. 20.00

Barry Manilow, Let's Hang On, promo, Spain .............................. 20.00

Rod McKuen, Mr. Oliver Twist...................................................... 12.00

Meatloaf, Dead Ringer for Love, promo, Spain............................ 15.00

Monkees, Daydream Believe, promo, Japan ............................... 60.00
Willie Nelson, Help Me Make It, Spain.................................... 10.00
Donny Osmond, When I Fall In Love, Spain................................ 15.00
Elvis Presley, Sun Singles, 2-volume set................................ 80.00
Rolling Stones, Emotional Rescue, France ................................ 20.00
Royalettes, It's Gonna Take a Miracle .................................. 30.00
Silhouettes, Working Hard, sealed....................................... 12.00
Slade, Bangin Man/She Did It To Me, Germany ............................ 15.00
Bruce Springsteen, Tenth Avenue/Freeze Out, Germany............. 75.00
Cat Stevens, Two Fine People/A Bad Penny, France................... 8.00
Supremes, Baby Love, France ............................................ 75.00
Ike & Tina Turner, The Great Hits ...................................... 185.00
Sammy Turner, Lavender Blue Moods....................................... 70.00
Valentine, T., Hello Lucille ........................................... 10.00
Del Vikings, Come Go With the Del Vikings............................... 400.00
Gene Vincent, A Gene Vincent Record Date ............................... 130.00
Who, My Generation, Czech .............................................. 20.00

# REDWARE

**History:** The availability of clay, the same used to make bricks and roof tiles, accounted for the great production of red earthenware pottery in the American colonies. Redware pieces are mainly utilitarian—bowls, crocks, jugs, etc.

Lead-glazed redware retained its reddish color, but a variety of colored glazes were obtained by the addition of metals to the basic glaze. Streaks and mottled splotches in redware items resulted from impurities in the clay and/or uneven firing temperatures.

Slipware is the term used to describe redwares decorated by the application of slip, a semi-liquid paste made of clay. Slipwares were made in England, Germany, and elsewhere in Europe for decades before becoming popular in the Pennsylvania German region and other areas in colonial America.

**References:** Susan and Al Bagdade, *Warman's American Pottery and Porcelain*, 2nd ed., Krause Publications, 2000; William C. Ketchum Jr., *American Pottery and Porcelain*, Avon Books, 1994.

Bank, 6-1/2" h, 5-3/4" d, beehive shape, peg finial clear lead glaze, slight greenish int. ...225.00
Basin, 18" d, tin glaze ...75.00
Basket, 3-1/4" h, 6" d, hanging type, red and white, yellow slip, green and brown glaze, notched rim, pot and saucer, three pierced holes, restored ...1,300.00
Bottle, 11-3/4" h, donut shape, amber glaze, brown flecks ...140.00
Bowl
   6" d, running brown glaze, wear and minor glaze flaking on back...110.00
   11-3/4" d, brown and green striped glaze, cream ground, Continental, 19th C, minor chips, glaze wear...635.00
   12-1/2" d, shallow, very worn int., yellow slip bird on branch and edge design, green and brown glaze, chips...250.00
   13-1/2" d, 2-1/2" h, shallow, coggle edge, three line yellow slip dec, worn, center badly chipped ...400.00
   18" d, 9-1/2" h, unglazed ext with flared rim and tapered sides, glazed int. has small brown running streaks, old chips ....250.00
   Charger, coggle edge
      11-3/8" d, four line slip dec...1,200.00
      13-3/4" d, yellow slip combware dec...1,350.00
Chestnut Dish, 13-1/2" d, oval, slip dec, rim chips...425.00
Colander, 9-3/4" x 7", clear glaze, brown flecks, orange-ground ground, rim handles, three applied feet...350.00

Creamer, 4" h, incised band, four vertical lines of black irid glaze....125.00
Crock, 9" h, clear glaze, brown splotches, applied handles........190.00
Cuspidor, 3-7/8" h, 7-1/2" d, red and white slip, green and brown sponged glaze under clear lead glaze, foot chips and wear ....100.00
Custard Cup, 2 3/8" h, incised "TS Stahl, Sept 1, 1940"..............60.00
Desk Set, 5-1/2" l, 6-1/2" h, molded edges, hollow int., dog with urn, black brushed design, clear glaze...525.00
Dish
   4-1/2" d, 2-1/4" h, brown fleck glaze, brown sponging around rim, wear and small chips...90.00
   7 5/8" d, dark glaze, yellow slip spots, rim flake ...275.00
   8" d, yellow slip dec, wear and chips ...200.00
   Figure
      7-3/4" l, 7-1/4" h, poodle, in style of Staffordshire spaniel, brown glaze, reverse inscribed "H. McD," 19th C, minor loses, cracks, kiln imperfections ...200.00
      8-3/4" l, lion, rect base, mottled tan and cream colored unglazed surface, incised label "12-6-'31, WADS, O., L.E." ...385.00
      9-1/2" h, seated dog, tooled coat, open front legs, solid casting, chips around base, worn black stain...420.00
Flask, 8" h, brown splotches, clear glaze, orange ground, New England...275.00
Flower Pot
   5" h, 6-1/8" d, red and white slip, brown sponge dec, clear lead glaze ext., attached undertray imp "John Bell/Waynesboro"...200.00
   7-5/8" h, 8-1/8" d, white slip, applied brown slip and dabbed green glaze swag design dec, double roulette rim attached ruffled undertray, imp "Solomon Bell"...450.00
Foot Warmer, 6-3/4" h, 13-1/2" l, ram-form, glazed, 19th C, very minor chips...520.00
Jar, ovoid
   6" h
      Brown sponging, ribbed strap handle, chips...135.00
      Light amber, brown splotches, ribbed strap handle, minor chips...300.00
      Well defined brown and amber glaze, minor flakes...220.00
   6-1/2" h, dark ground, brown splotches, minor chips...275.00
   9-1/2" h, dark green amber glaze, incised initials "SB" on side, ripped strap handle, wear, chips ...315.00
   9-3/4" h, pumpkin orange glaze, brown brushed floral dec, poorly restored flared lip, chips...360.00
   10-1/2" h, ovoid, applied shoulder handles, dark brown running glaze, chips...500.00
Jug, America, 19th C
   8" h, minor hairlines, minor chips to base...2,645.00
   9-5/8" h, glazed, very minor chips and cracks ...400.00
   9-3/4" h, gonic glaze, minor chips...775.00
   Lamp, 23" h overall, 9" h jar drilled and mounted as lamp base, incised lines, applied ribbed shoulder handles and clear glaze, tan color, dark brown splotches, wear and chips, wooden base, old burlap shade...265.00
Loaf Pan, 13" l, rect, coggle edge, three line yellow slip dec, worn, old chips ...425.00
Meat Roaster, 12" l, scoop shape, applied finger crimped rim, strap handle, end spout, greenish amber glaze ...220.00
Milk Bowl, 8-1/2" d, 2-3/4" h, interior glaze with yellow, green, and brown slip floral dec, wear, chips, hairline...200.00
Milk Pitcher, 4-1/4" h, green and yellow slip dec, tooled lines and applied ribbed strap handle...500.00
Miniature, bottle, 3-1/2" h, red sponge dec, orig "Mohawk Rock Rye" paper label ...35.00
Mug, 4-3/8" h, 4-1/4" d, brown sponging, clear lead glaze, top and bottom thumbnail grooves, imp "John Bell"...550.00
Pie Plate, coggle edge
   9-3/4" d, three line yellow slip dec ...220.00
   10" d, three line yellow slip dec, very worn, chips and scratches ...100.00
   10-1/4" d, brown sponged "X," wear and damage ...220.00
   10-1/4" d, yellow slip dec, very work, damage...200.00
   12-1/4" d, yellow slip dec, wear and old chips ...315.00

**Whistle, five birds, applied yellow and brown Rockingham glaze, c1880, professional restoration to top cross bar and 2 birds, 9" h, $275. Photo courtesy of Vicki & Bruce Waasdrop.**

Pitcher
    5" h, pinched spout, white slip, mottled brown glaze ............ 95.00
    7-1/2" h, red and white overall slip, brown spattered dec, clear lead glaze, bold handle ...................................... 325.00
Plate
    8-1/2" d, zigzag and parallel line yellow slip dec, reddish brown glaze, chips ........................................................ 225.00
    9-1/4" d, coggled rim, yellow slip dec, initials "S. B.," glaze wear, chips .................................................................. 460.00
    10-1/4" d, yellow slip dec, parallel zigzag lines and commas, reddish brown glaze, rim chip and roughage ........................ 325.00
    11-1/4" d, glazed face, unglazed back, applied yellow slip dec reads "Lafayette," yellow slip squiggles above and below name, coggle edge, professional restoration to 6" l rim hairline ............... 2,750.00
Pot, cov
    6" h, 5-1/2" w with handle, four bands of yellow slip, bulbous body, applied handle, attributed to CT ...................................... 400.00
    6" h, 7-1/2" w with handle, splotched dec, four vertical swipes, pouring spout, small finial on matching lid, applied handle with thumb print, two chips on lid ............................................ 450.00
Preserving Jar
    5-3/4" h, orange spots, dark green and brown glaze, flared rim, emb tin lid with shield and "Banner Jelly," glaze hairlines ............. 150.00
    8" h, applied shoulder handles, flared lip with gallery for lid, greenish-cream colored slip, reddish tan mottled glaze, brown squiggles, paper label from the "George McKearin Collection of American Pottery," chips ............................................. 2,860.00
    9-3/4" h, brick red glaze, imp label "A. Wilcox, West Bloomfield," chips on lid finial, pot stone on side ............................. 425.00
    10-1/2" h, dark brown splotches, minor edge damage ....... 550.00
Shaving Mug, 5-3/4" h, brown-green mottled glaze, strap handle .... 290.00
Stirrup Cup, 4-1/2" h, hound form, glazed, English, late 18th C ....... 300.00
Turk Mold, 10" d, 3-1/2" h, mottled red and dark brown glaze, c1830 ................................................................................ 150.00
Vase, 3 5/8" h, sgraffito, birds and flowers, tricolor, bulbous base, marked "DDR, June 5, 1828, PA" ....................................... 1,750.00
Washboard, 12" w, 24" h, alkaline glaze with dark sponged accents, overall wear to wood frame, attributed to OH area, c1870 ....... 650.00
Whistle, 9" h, five birds, applied yellow and brown Rockingham glaze, c1800, professional restoration top cross bar and 2 birds perched there ............................................................................. 275.00

# RED WING POTTERY

**History:** The Red Wing pottery category includes several potteries from Red Wing, Minnesota. In 1868, David Hallem started Red Wing Stoneware Co., the first pottery with stoneware as its primary product. The Minnesota Stoneware Co. started in 1883. The North Star Stoneware Co. was in business from 1892 to 1896.

The Red Wing Stoneware Co. and the Minnesota Stoneware Co. merged in 1892. The new company, the Red Wing Union Stoneware Co., made stoneware until 1920 when it introduced a pottery line which it continued until the 1940s. In 1936, the name was changed to Red Wing Potteries, Inc. During the 1930s this firm introduced several popular patterns of hand-painted dinnerware which were distributed through department stores, mail-order catalogs, and gift-stamp centers. Dinnerware production declined in the 1950s and was replaced with hotel and restaurant china in the early 1960s. The plant closed in 1967.

**Marks:** Red Wing Stoneware Co. was the first firm to mark pieces with a red wing stamped under the glaze. The North Star Stoneware Co. used a raised star and the words "Red Wing" as its mark.

**References:** Dan and Gail DePasquale and Larry Peterson, *Red Wing Collectibles*, Collector Books, 1985, 1997 value update; ——, *Red Wing Stoneware*, Collector Books, 1983, 2000 value update; B. L. Dollen, *Red Wing Art Pottery*, Collector Books, 1997; B. L. and R. L. Dollen, *Collector's Encyclopedia of Red Wing Art Pottery*, Collector Books, 2000; ——, *Red Wing Art Pottery Book II*, Collector Books, 1998; Ray Reiss, *Red Wing Art Pottery Including Pottery Made for Rum Rill*, published by author (2144 N. Leavitt, Chicago, IL 60647), 1996; ——, *Red Wing Dinnerware,* published by author, 1997.

**Collectors' Clubs:** Red Wing Collectors Society, Inc., P.O. Box 50, Red Wing, MN 55066; RumRill Society, P.O. Box 2161, Hudson, OH 44236.

**Additional Listings:** See *Warman's Americana & Collectibles* for more examples.

Bookends, pr, polar bears, jet black glaze, Rumrill ..................... 525.00
Bud Vase, 8-1/2" h, cactus, pale blue-green ............................. 345.00
Candleholders, pr, 1-1/2" h, fluted, green ................................. 35.00
Child's Feeding Dish, figural, clown, orange-pink glaze, Hankscraft ................................................................................ 35.00
Console Bowl, 13" l, mottled green, trumpet flowers dec .......... 290.00
Cooler, stoneware, two gallon, cobalt blue flourish and mark, 11" h, c1900 ................................................................................ 250.00
Cookie Jar, cov
    Dancing Peasants, white stoneware ................................... 45.00
    Katrina, tan and brown .................................................... 80.00
Crock, 18-1/2" h, 15 gallon, leaf design, some design fry on thick blue dec, c1880 ...................................................................... 660.00
Dinner Service, bird dec, 54 pcs ............................................. 350.00
Figure, elephant
    Nokomis finish, mottled matte surface of brown, tan, teal, bronze, and rust .......................................................................... 800.00
    Pale Yellow, 4" h, #236A ................................................. 430.00
Mason Jar, 7" h, stoneware, screw top, metal lid, mkd "Stone Mason Fruit Jar, Union Stoneware Co., Red Wing, Minn" .................. 300.00

**Cooler, 2 gallon, c1900, professional restoration to crack and one handle, 11" h, $200. Photo courtesy of Vicki & Bruce Waasdrop.**

Planter

    Duck, #439.................................................385.00
    Giraffe, Murphy, repairs, tight hairline ................330.00
    Muses reclining, bronze finish, Deluxe line, small chip.........55.00
    Seal, #941.................................................90.00
    Swan, #440, mustard yellow, Rumrill ....................60.00
Plaque, Minnesota Centennial, maroon, 1958...........100.00
Souvenir Jug, 1992 Red Wing Collectors Society .........55.00
Urn

    #252, 11" h, pale yellow glaze, blue circle stamp mark ......290.00
    #852, large .............................................80.00
Vase

    4" h, green, elongated tulip shape ......................95.00
    7" h, Nokomis finish, mottled matte surface of brown, tan, teal, bronze, and rust .........................300.00
    7" h, #175, yellow.......................................75.00
    8" h, Tropicana series, Bird of Paradise, mkd "B-2000," designed by Belle Kogan, 1950 ......................65.00
    10" h, 6-1/4" d, light drab green, mkd "Redwing USA M-1461," factory flaw .....................................65.00
    11" h, Art Deco.........................................100.00
    15" h, #157, green and white, drilled for lamp base............235.00
    Two handles, trumpeting elephants, pale yellow ...............135.00

# RELIGIOUS ITEMS

**History:** Objects used in worship or as expression of man's belief in a superhuman power are collected by many people for many reasons.

This category includes icons since they are religious mementos, usually paintings with a brass encasement. Collecting icons dates from the earliest period of Christianity. Most antique icons in today's market were made in the late 19th century.

**Reference:** Penny Forstner and Lael Bower, *Collecting Religious Artifacts (Christian and Judaic)*, Books Americana, 1995.

**Collectors' Club:** Foundation International for Restorers of Religious Medals, P.O. Box 2652, Worcester, MA 01608.

**Museum:** American Bible Society, New York, NY.

**Reproduction Alert:** Icons are frequently reproduced.

**Additional Listings:** Judaic, Russian Items.

Alms Box, 10-3/4" w, 16" h, oak, old brown grained repaint, Gothic style, English, wear and one incomplete scalloped bracket.....145.00
Altar Cabinet, 18" w, 14" d, 23" h, giltwood, carved columns, masks, foliage, and architectural niches, Italian Renaissance, attributed to Sansovino, late 15th/early 16th C, losses, restorations ........3,105.00
Altar Stick, 29-1/2" h, carved wood, celadon painted and parcel gilt, carved paw feet, Louis XVI taste, Italian, c1900-1915, mounted as table lamp..................................................420.00
Autograph

    Autographed letter signed, Peter Boehler, Nov. 27, 1763, Bethlehem, (Pennsylvania) to inner conference of the Moravian Brotherhood, in German, relating Bishop's trip to Philadelphia and the hostile attitude there against missionaries and treatment of Indian delegation, mentions well known colonial figures, such as Franklin, Logan, Daniel, 3-1/2 closely written pages, with translation..................................................1,495.00
    Deed of Conveyance, partially printed, granting Brigham Young 99 square feet of land in Salt Lake City for $1.55, sgd by Daniel H. Wells, Mayor, January 10, 1873, 1 page, folio, affixed gold seats of Salt Lake City, notary James Pack .....................375.00

**Monstrance, enamels of saints, center requilary, part of 3 pc set, $20,700. Photo courtesy of Jackson's Auctioneers & Appraisers.**

Document Signed, Pope Pius IV, sgd "El Cardinal di Medici," Nov 23 1555, appointment to Church in Cassano, action approved by Duke of Florence and King of England, 1 full page, tall 4to ..920.00
Buddha

    5-1/2" h, gilt bronze, seated on double lotus throne, fired gilded with applied cold gold paste to face, blue pigment to hair and unisha, offering plate cover with double vajra, Tibetan, 17th/18th C.................................................1,035.00
    16-1/2" h, bronze, seated, hands in teaching position, seated on pierced double lotus throne, detachable halo at back, Nepal, late 19th/early 20th C.....................................300.00
    Bust, 11-1/2" h, Our lady of Lourdes, carved alabaster, amethyst veining, oval plinth, reverse sgd "Causse" for Julian Causse ..................................................865.00
Chalice

    9-1/4" h, gold-washed copper, Ecclesiastical, bell-shaped bowl embellished with cut card work featuring bull rushes, grapes, and wheat, emb baluster stem, domed foot emb and inset with images of Mary................................................460.00
    9-1/4" h, sterling silver and gold-washed base metal, Ecclesiastical, silver bowl with gold-washed lip and int., stem with central gothic-style knop, plain hexafoil foot with emb cross .......140.00
    9-1/2" h, silver, Ecclesiastical, slightly flared bowl engraved to one side with stylized sunburst and "IHS," knopped stem with central applied foliate band, spreading repousse foot with foliate edge, gold washed int., former gold wash to ext. removed, 20 troy oz ...................................1,150.00
    9-7/8" h, silver, Ecclesiastical, slightly flared bowl with gold-washed int., stem with egg-shaped knob flanked by compressed knops, gold-washed ribbing, spreading foot with ribbed band and engraved flat leaves and flowers, French, first quarter 19th C, 14 troy oz...........................................460.00
    9-7/8" h, silver-gilt, bell-shaped bowl embellished with gothic-style cut card work, stem with central hexafoil knob, hexafoil base, stamped gothic-style detailing, three painted porcelain plaques depicting religious vignettes, maker's mark Chevron Freres, French, late 19th C.....................................1,495.00
    10" h, silver, Ecclesiastical, plain bell-shaped bowl, int. gold-washed, stem with central egg-shaped knop between flared knobs with bands of guillouche, domed foot stamped with cartouches of grapes, bull ruses, and wheat between roundels depicting biblical images, French, marker's mark H. Puchs, late 19th/early 20th C, 9 troy oz.............................475.00

Chasuble, velvet, crimson, orphrey embroidered colored silks, metal thread, roundels of Madonna and Child, four Saints within strapwork, Spanish, 16th C...................2,750.00

Crucifix, 8-1/4" l, carved ivory, mounted on 21-1/4" l wooden cross, engraved ivory plaque, stepped plinth, southern Germany, 18th C ...................2,070.00

Ecclesiastical Scepter, 29-1/2" l, carved ivory, hexagonal faceted knob mounted with figural plaques, stem carved with fruiting leafy foliage, Continental, losses...................4,025.00

Figure

15" h, Madonna and Child, painted and gilt gesso, crowned virgin, naturalistic tones, shaped base, Continental, 19th C ....1,265.00

26" h, pilgrim, standing female with hands raised in prayer, closed in floral dress and cloak, silk head covering, hands, face, and feet painted composition, body filled with excelsior, carved wooden socle with gilt detailing, Continental, 19th C, fabric losses...................450.00

30" h, painted wood, Madonna & Child, c1700, Baroque, South German, benign expression, hair falling in long tresses over her shoulders, wearing long gown, heavy mantle falling into deep folds, infant Christ delivers blessing and supports gilt orb, both with gilt-metal crowns, ornate plinth base with acanthus leaves and winged cherubs, some worming and cracks, most of polychrome intact, overall patina and craquelure, flat back...................5,100.00

33-1/2" h, St. Peter, high relief carving, tiara on head, stylized hair connecting to stylized hobnail-type beard, left hand holds key, right holds gospels, cape deeply carved folds, painted wood, Continental, 19th C, later paint, flat back...................920.00

42-1/2" h, Lindenwood, Ecco Homo, finely carved, high relief, curly cascading hair, fine facial and anatomical features, circle of "Der Rasso-Meister," South German, 16th C, hallowed back, some losses, worming, cracks, and restored nose.......4,035.00

64" h, female saint, finely carved, delicately sculpted hair, elaborately draped brocade mantle and tunic, orig "estafado" paintwork, Italian, early 18th C, minor restoration, some worming, orig gilt plinth...................650.00

Incense Burner

9-1/2" h, bronze, archaic-style tripod, Tao Tich masks and frieze of mythical animal on cloud background, animal form handles, dark chocolate brown patina, sgd, Chinese, 18th/19th C.250.00

9-1/2" h, 10" w, bronze, tripod shaped with handles, tall highly elongated feet and understated handles, surface finely inlaid with gold and silver emblems, mons, thunder meander ground, Japanese, 19th C...................1,500.00

Icon, Greek, 11-1/2" x 8", Hodigitra Mother of God, 19th C, angels crown Mary as Christ delivers blessing, custom fitted shadow box kit, mother of pearl inlays and double headed eagle at top...................1,555.00

Icon, Russian

10-1/2" x 12-1/4", The Lord Almighty, 19th C, finely executed, Vsederzhitel, Christ delivers blessing with right hand, left hand holds open Gospels to Matthew, entire image overlaid with finely fashioned gilt-metal repousse riza, attached halo, embellished with faux gemstones, executed in 16th C style...................1,450.00

10-1/2" x 12-1/2", Christ Immanuel, 17th C, finely detailed on ochre ground, ivory highlights, overlaid with applied gilt-metal halo embellished with faux gemstones and gilt metal open riza...................3,335.00

10-1/2" x 12-1/2", The Dormination of the Mother of God, 17th C, Christ stands behind recumbent Mary, receives her soul in the form of an infant, Apostles stand around her, fanatical Jewish priest tires to bush the bier over, hand cut off by sword-welding angel, borders and background with traces of orig gilding, double kovcheg, some early restoration...................2,300.00

12" x 10-1/4", St. Paraskeva Paitnista, 18th C, finely executed painting done on gold leaf ground, two angels place a crown upon her head, right hand delivers blessing, left hand supports scroll which begins, "I believe in One God the Father, The Almighty Maker of Heaven and Earth...," borders with Guardian Angel left and St. Paul the Confessor Archbishop of Constantinope on right, image overlaid with well crafted gilt repousse metal riza...................1,840.00

Monstrance, 19-1/4" h, gilt-brass, Gothic-style, spires with central glass holder for host, small angel-form handle, stem with flattened knob, hexagonal foot, fitted case...................690.00

Painting

16-1/2" x 10-1/2", gouache and watercolor on paper, Portrait of a Cleric, sgd "Spy" in pencil lower left, identified on presentation plaque, titled and identified on label on reverse, painted by Sir Leslie Ward, framed...................300.00

37-1/2 x 27-1/2", oil on canvas, "St. Jerome Reading Before A Crucifix," unsigned, Italian School, 17th C, lined, retouched, flaking and losses, craquelure...................2,100.00

41" x 68", Congregation Watching the Baptism at the River, Henry Sanderson, oil on canvas, framed, background retouched...................8,625.00

78" x 52", oil on canvas, Last Communion of St. Jerome, unsigned, inscribed, "G. H. Thomson Rome 1858" on stretcher, framed, repaired, retouched punctures plus additional retouch, craquelure...................4,900.00

Panel, 20" h, 14-1/2" w, carved walnut, Madonna and Child, traces of polychrome dec, Italian, 17th C...................1,150.00

Pendant

18k gold, ivory carved Madonna, diamond accented hallow, pink plique-a-jour background, turquoise and seed pearl frame, pearl and diamond accents...................980.00

18k gold, Maltese cross, c1900, designed as pin/pendant, reeded and beaded accents, sgd "T. B. Starr"...................550.00

Plaque, 8-1/4" h, 11-1/4" h, carved cameo alabaster relief, St. Rose of Lima holding Christ Child aloft on a branch, flanked by buildings in the distance, seated dog and rose to one side, black stained detailing, 19th C, restorations...................1,265.00

Prei-dieu (kneeling bench), 23-1/4" w, 20-1/2" d, 34-1/2" h, walnut, Italian Renaissance, restorations...................1,610.00

Refectory Table, early 20th C, mahogany, rounded planted top, five large turned legs, brass caps and casters, 140" l, 36" d, 30" h...................1,320.00

**Painting, St. John Nepomuil, oil on copper, 9" x 11", $4,370. Photo courtesy of Jackson's Auctioneers & Appraisers.**

Reliquary, 20-1/2" h, Gothic Revival, silver and gilt metal, upper section in two parts, spires and figures within niches, int. lined with amber glass, faceted and shaped stem on arched foot, 19th C ......................5,175.00

Reliquary Cross, 9-1/2" x 6-1/2" panel, 2-1/2" x 2-1/4" cross, Russian, 18th C, silver, hollow construction, front engraved with crucifixion, end of each cross bar with hand made silver screws to fasten the lid, final screws pierced for suspension, 2 pc wood cross inside, 6 to 8 relics on front suspended in resin or wax, mounted in wood panel with receptacle for cross, later silvered metal riza with opening for cross to show through, reverse inscribed with names of Saint's relics contained within cross, and other indistinguishable names....................................1,265.00

Santos, 11-3/4" h, carved and painted wood, robed figured, stepped base, Continental, 19th/20th C..................................................425.00

Stele, 19-1/2" w, 31-3/4" h, carved gray limestone, Buddhist Trinity, Northern Wei style, central standing robed Buddha, two standing bodhisattvas on either side, lotus plinths being held up by animal heads, low relief carved floral motifs on flat ground, reverse with rows of Buddhas, inscriptions, wood stand, repairs.......................1,100.00

Triptych, 14-1/4" l, 10-1/8" h, carved ivory, opens to reveal Madonna and Child flanked by four apostles on each side, each figure in gothic arch, panel pediments carved with shields, central shield on double-headed eagle, German, 19th C, mounted in frame ...............2,415.00

# REVERSE PAINTING ON GLASS

**History:** The earliest examples of reverse painting on glass were produced in 13th-century Italy. By the 17th century the technique had spread to central and eastern Europe. It spread westward as the center of the glass-making industry moved to Germany in the late 17th century.

The Alsace and Black Forest regions developed a unique portraiture style. The half and three-quarter portraits often were titled below the portrait. Women tend to have generic names while most males are likenesses of famous men.

The English used a mezzotint, rather than free-style, method to create their reverse paintings. Landscapes and allegorical figures were popular. The Chinese began working in the medium in the 17th century, eventually favoring marine and patriotic scenes.

Most American reverse painting was done by folk artists and is unsigned. Portraits, patriotic and mourning scenes, floral compositions, landscapes, and buildings are the favorite subjects. Known American artists include Benjamin Greenleaf, A. Cranfield, and Rowley Jacobs.

In the late 19th century, commercially produced reverse paintings, often decorated with mother-of-pearl, became popular. Themes included the Statue of Liberty, the capitol in Washington, D.C., and various world's fairs and expositions.

Today craftsmen are reviving this art, using some vintage looking designs, but usually with brighter colors that their antique counterparts.

## Portraits

Eleanor, young woman, "Eleanor" in white title bar, blue dress, red cape, gold trim, green, blue, and red hat with white feather, shaded blue ground, 10" h, 7-1/2" w, some wear, late black 11-5/8" h, 9" w frame .......................................................................440.00

Pastoral scene of cottage, sgd "L. Ray," wood, plaster, gilt frame, 16" x 20-1/8", $80.

Gentleman, blue coat, gold detail, red vest, high collar shirt, shaded blue-green ground, 10" h, 7-1/2" w, late black 11-5/8" h, 9" w frame............................................................................220.00

Josephina, red, green, white dress, red hair ribbon, green background, 11-1/2"h, 9-1/4" w, wear and white margin retouched, orig frame....................................................................220.00

Man and woman, oval gilded frames, 7" h, 6" w, price for pr.........275.00

Sylvia, woman in red dress, blue ground, orig frame, 7-3/4" x 10-1/2" ..................................................................120.00

Washington, George, oval portrait, white border, sky blue background, mahogany veneer frame, 12-1/4" h, 10-1/4" w, paint flaking....220.00

Woman and child seated in chair, small white dog, blue oval background with marbleized spandrels, 14" h, 12" w, some minor wear and flaking, one corner damaged, old gilded frame.................350.00

## Scenes

Adoration of the Magi, later carved giltwood frame, Italian, 27" x 18-1/2"....................................................................425.00

Blarney Castle, forest scene, castle on right, touches of mica and abalone, 20" x 27".....................................................................150.00

Landscape, pink, gray, white, green, and brown, Chinese Export School, 10" x 8"......................................................................175.00

Man and woman in landscape, Chinese Export School, late 18th or early 19th C, 15-1/4" x 11-1/2".............................................2,750.00

Rock of Ages, gold, white, red, blue, and green, black ground, tinsel highlights, orig oak frame, 20-3/4" h, 17-3/4" w ........................115.00

Summer-Winter, winter landscape with woman in velvet coat, summer landscape with young woman in straw bonnet carrying sickle, sprays of wheat, Chinese Export School, 19th C, 10" x 14-1/2", price for facing pr...............................................................900.00

Titanic, sinking with life rafts in water, 15-1/2" h, 19-1/2" w, silver dec frame, some paint loss ..........................................................75.00

**Sign,** 7-3/4" l, 4-1/2" h, "No Hard Liquor Allowed On Premises," dark ground, orig frame, metal backed chain hanger.......................325.00

# RIDGWAY

**History:** Throughout the 19th century the Ridgway family, through a series of partnerships, held a position of importance in the ceramics industry in Shelton and

Hanley, Staffordshire, England. The connection began with Job and George, two brothers, and Job's two sons, John and William. In 1830, John and William dissolved their partnership; John retained the Cauldon Place factory and William the Bell Works. By 1862, the porcelain division of Cauldon was carried on by Coalport China Ltd. William and his heirs continued at the Bell Works and the Church (Hanley) and Bedford (Shelton) works until the end of the 19th century.

**Marks:** Many early pieces are unmarked. Later marks include the initials of the many different partnerships.

**References:** Susan and Al Bagdade, *Warman's English & Continental Pottery & Porcelain*, 3rd Edition, Krause Publications, 1998; G. A. Godden, *Ridgway Porcelains*, Antique Collectors' Club, 1985.

**Museums:** Cincinnati Art Museum, Cincinnati, OH; Potsdam Public Museum, Potsdam, NY.

**Additional Listings:** Staffordshire, Historical; Staffordshire, Romantic.

Beverage Set, 12-3/8" x 6-1/2" tankard, pitcher, six 4-1/4 x 5" mugs, Coaching Days, caramel ground, black scene, silver luster top bands and handles, price for 7 pc set .................. 400.00
Bowl
    6" d, Shakespeare .................. 35.00
    8-1/2" w to handles, Coaching Days.................. 40.00
Cheese Dish, cov, light brown floral transfer.................. 75.00
Child's Teapot and Creamer, Dickensware, Humphrey's Clock, blue and white, c1891-1903.................. 165.00
Coffeepot, cov, 7-1/2" h, Coaching Days, silver luster.................. 95.00
Cup Plate, Marmora.................. 45.00
Mug
    4" h, Shakespeare .................. 45.00
    4-3/4" h, Coaching Days, silver luster.................. 40.00
Pitcher, 10-1/2" h, earthenware, blue glaze, molded and enameled foliate dec, pewter lid, base sgd "William Ridgway & Co., Hanley, October 1, 1835," minor chip to handle .................. 115.00
Plate, 9" d, Coaching Days.................. 25.00
Tankard Pitcher, 12" h, Coaching Days, In A Snowdrift.................. 300.00
Tea Caddy, cov, 4" x 5-3/4" h, Coaching Days, scenes on all sides .................. 175.00
Tile, 6" d, round, Coaching Days .................. 115.00
Tray, 8-1/4" d, Bank of Savannah, handles.................. 185.00
Vase, 4-7/8" h, egg shape, Coaching Days, caramel ground, black scenes, silver luster top band and handle.................. 75.00

**Creamer and Sugar, white ground, gray dec, heavy gold trim, $80.**

**Porcelain, hand painted, mkd "Germany," 3-3/4" d, $35.**

# RING TREES

**History:** A ring tree is a small, generally saucer-shaped object made of glass, porcelain, metal, or wood with a center post in the shape of a hand, branches, or cylinder. It is a convenient object for holding finger rings.

Bronze, 5" h, figural, parrot.................. 48.00
Fenton, 4-1/2" h, yellow, figural owl .................. 15.00
Hand Painted China, center hand, saucer base, rose dec, maple leaf mark and "Hand Painted".................. 55.00
Jasperware, 3-1/4" h, deep blue ground, white relief classical bust medallions .................. 50.00
Limoges, hand shaped, gilding .................. 25.00
MR France, blue flowers .................. 20.00
MZ Austria, pink flowers.................. 20.00
Nippon, purple violets dec, gold band, shallow base, maple leaf mark.................. 65.00
Silver, Sheffield, maker's mark, chased base, fluted rim, Victorian, c1900, 2 troy oz.................. 115.00
Unmarked, hand shaped, blue flowers, gilding.................. 25.00

# ROCKINGHAM and ROCKINGHAM BROWN-GLAZED WARES

**History:** Rockingham ware can be divided into two categories. The first consists of the fine china and porcelain pieces made between 1826 and 1842 by the Rockingham Company of Swinton, Yorkshire, England, and its predecessor firms: Swinton, Bingley, Don, Leeds, and Brameld. The Bramelds developed the cadogan, a lidless teapot. Between 1826 and 1842, a quality softpaste product with a warm, silky feel was developed by the Bramelds. Elaborate specialty pieces were made. By 1830, the company employed 600 workers and listed 400 designs for dessert sets and 1,000 designs for tea and coffee services in its catalog. Unable to meet its payroll, the company closed in 1842.

The second category of Rockingham ware includes pieces produced in the famous Rockingham brown glaze that became an intense and vivid purple-brown when fired. It had a dark, tortoiseshell appearance. The glaze was copied by many English and American potteries. American

Pitcher, yellow ware body, relief hunting dogs and deer design, applied hound handle, relief grapes and vine design around top half, attributed to American Pottery C., Jersey City, c1860, 9-3/4" h, $550. Photo courtesy of Vicki & Bruce Waasdrop.

manufacturers which used Rockingham glaze include D. & J. Henderson of Jersey City, New Jersey; United States Pottery in Bennington, Vermont; potteries in East Liverpool, Ohio; and several potteries in Indiana and Illinois.

**References:** Susan and Al Bagdade, *Warman's American Pottery and Porcelain*, 2nd ed., Krause Publications, 2000; Susan and Al Bagdade, *Warman's English & Continental Pottery & Porcelain*, 3rd Edition, Krause Publications, 1998; Mary Brewer, *Collector's Guide to Rockingham*, Collector Books, 1996.

**Museum:** Bennington Museum, Bennington, VT.

**Additional Listings:** Bennington and Bennington-Type Pottery.

Bowl, 14" d, 6-1/2" h, emb ext.......................................... 75.00
Cup and Saucer, enamel painted tulip and poppy dec, white ground, barbed rim, 1826-30 ............................................... 550.00
Figure
    6-5/8" h, 9-1/2" l, lion, rect base, good detail and glaze, price for pr ..................................................................... 525.00
    12-5/8" h, 16" l, bull, flint enamel glaze, 19th C, minor losses, restoration .......................................................... 300.00
    18-1/2" h, 36-1/2" w, bulldog, overall brown glaze, finely modeled, glass eyes, late 19th C, restoration to tail ...................... 2,180.00
Flask, 7-1/4" h, molded hunting dogs, hairline in bottom ............ 330.00
Food Mold, 8-1/2" d, Turk's head, brown glaze, green flint enamel....85.00
Goblet, 5-3/8" h ................................................... 525.00
Inkwell, 4-3/4" l, lion ................................................ 185.00
Mixing Bowl, 16-1/2" d, 6-5/8" h, 1849 mark ........................... 2,500.00
Pitcher
    7-1/4" h, detailed emb scenes of camel and elephant, imp mark "R Bew, Bliston".............................................. 75.00
    7-3/4" h, Paneled Grapevine pattern, brown glaze .......... 1,100.00
    11-1/2" h, lion, Rockingham glaze, tail molded to form handle.............................................................. 220.00
Plate, 9-1/4" d, Woodnook, Wentworth Park, Yorkshire, man holding game bird, river and wooded scene, scrolling vine and scattered insects band, 1926-32 ........................................... 520.00
Scent Bottle, 6" h, onion shape, applied garden flowers, gilt line rims, 1831-40 ......................................................... 450.00
Spittoon, 4-1/2" d, brown glaze, sgraffito inscription "L. J. Underwood Barberton, Ohio, July 24, '09," base inscribed "L.J.U. 7-24-1909"............................................................ 95.00
Teapot, 8-1/4" h, emb design, portrait of lady ....................... 75.00
Tobacco Jar, 8" h, molded oval floral medallions, dark brown glaze, small rim chip ..................................................... 80.00
Toby Snuff Jar, 4-1/8" h, flint enamel glaze, 19th C, minor glaze wear to rim ................................................................ 375.00
Wall Pocket, toby shape, brown glaze ................................. 375.00

# ROCK 'N' ROLL

**History:** Rock music can be traced back to early rhythm and blues. It progressed until it reached its golden age in the 1950s and 1960s. Most of the memorabilia issued during that period focused on individual singers and groups. The largest quantity of collectible material is connected to Elvis Presley and The Beatles.

In the 1980s, two areas—clothing and guitars—associated with key rock 'n' roll personalities received special collector attention. At the moment, the market is highly speculative and driven by nostalgia.

It is important to identify memorabilia issued during the lifetime of an artist or performing group as opposed to material issued after they died or disbanded. Objects of the latter type are identified as "fantasy" items and will never achieve the same degree of collectibility as period counterparts.

**References:** Jeff Augsburger, Marty Eck, and Rick Rann, *The Beatles Memorabilia Price Guide,* Antique Trader Books; Mark A. Baker, *Goldmine Price Guide to Rock N' Roll Memorabilia,* Krause Publications, 1997; John Clemente, *Girl Groups, Fabulous Females That Rocked The World,* Krause Publications, 2000; Goldmine Magazine eds., *Goldmine Roots of Rock Digest,* Krause Publications, 1999; ——, *The Beatles Digest,* Krause Publications, 2000; Marty Eck, *The Monkees Collectibles Price Guide,* Antique Trader Books, 1998; Dr. Anthony J. Gribin and Dr. Matthew M. Schiff, *The Complete Book of Doo-Wop,* Krause Publications, 2000; Joe Hilton and Greg Moore, *Rock-N-Roll Treasures,* Collector Books, 1999; David Loehr and Joe Bills, *The James Dean Collectors Guide,* L-W Book Sales, 1999; Tom Neely and Dave Thompson, *Goldmine British Invasion Record Price Guide,* Krause Publications, 1997.

**Periodicals:** *Beatlefan,* P.O. Box 33515, Decatur, GA 30033; *Good Day Sunshine,* 397 Edgewood Ave. New Haven, CT 06511; *Instant Karma,* P.O. Box 256, Sault Ste. Marie, MI 49783.

**Collectors' Clubs:** Beatles Connection, P.O. Box 1066, Pinellas Park, FL 34665; Beatles Fan Club of Great Britain, Superstore Productions, 123 Marina St., Leonards on Sea, East Sussex, England TN 38 OBN; Elvis Forever TCB Fan Club, P.O. Box 1066, Pinellas Park, FL 34665; Graceland News Fan Club, P.O. Box 452, Rutherford, NJ 07070; Working Class Hero Club, 3311 Niagara St., Pittsburgh, PA 15213.

**Additional Listings:** See The Beatles, Elvis Presley, and Rock 'n' Roll in *Warman's Americana & Collectibles* and *Warman's Flea Market Price Guide.*

Autograph

Motley Crue, sgd "Theatre of Pain" album, sgd by Mick Mars, Vince Neil, Tommy Lee, Nikky Sixx ................................... 300.00

Pink Floyd, sgd "Animals" album, sgd by all four ............... 425.00

Jerry Garcia, sgd 8" x 10" color photo, close-up with guitar 400.00

Janis Joplin, 5" x 6" tan album page, bold signature ....... 1,200.00

John Lennon, Yoko Ono and Geraldo Rivera, eight-page contract sgd for film and TV rights for One to One concert......... 5,000.00

Los Lobos, sgd drum head, sgd "Cesar Rosas, Louie Perez, Conrad Lozano," and others, 1997 ........................................ 150.00

Jim Morrison, check endorsed "J. Morrison," drawn on his management company account ........................................... 1,500.00

Rolling Stones, sgd "Tattoo You" album, sgd by all five ...... 425.00

The Grateful Dead, sgd "Shakedown Street" album cover, sgd by Jerry Garcia, Bobby Weir, Phil Lesh, Mickey Hart, Rob Hunter, and Brent Mydland, 1978................................................. 600.00

Frank Zappa, sgd "Sheik Yerbouti" album, 12" x 12" .......... 295.00

Backstage Pass, cloth

Aerosmith, Pump, stage hand, 1989 ................................... 10.00

Billy Idyl, photo pass, large ............................................... 15.00

Black Sabbath, 1974 Civic Arena ...................................... 75.00

Fleetwood Mac, Behind The Mask, dressing room ............ 25.00

Gloria Estefan, Into the Light ............................................ 15.00

Kiss, Kiss Alive, 1983 ........................................................ 20.00

Madonna, Like A Virgin, 1985............................................ 25.00

Backstage Pass, laminated

Metallica, Snakepit .......................................................... 15.00

Pink Floyd, film crew, 1986 ............................................... 25.00

Banner, Beatles, printed nylon, four Beatles in black, large blue print heading "The Beatles," Memphis, 1966 ...................... 1,150.00

Bubble Gum Cards, Elvis Presley/Bubbles, Inc., set of 66 color cards, plastic protectors, 1956 ....................................... 1,000.00

Concert Clothing

James Brown, stage vest, black leather, gold round buttons, lined in white felt, front left wide cut white leather initials "JB," white leather letters "Mr D" on other side .............................. 1,840.00

Madonna, stage shorts, low waisted, high-cut purple shorts, ribbed stretch knit, legs lined in black satin, completely decorated with purple sequins, 1992 Girlie Tour................... 1,725.00

Concert Pin, Elvis Presley, 1978, 25" silver chain.......................... 35.00

Concert Poster

Bill Graham Series, marked "Six Days of Sound - Dec 26-New York's Eve 1967," design by Bonnie MacLean, includes The Doors, Chuck Berry, Big Brother & the Holding Co., Winterland ......125.00

Grateful Dead, Skull in Sand, 1981 European Fall tour, design by Stanley Mouse, 22-1/2" x 27"............................................. 85.00

Hells Angels Party, featuring Big Brother, God, Main Squeeze & Janis Joplin, May 21, 1970, design by Don Moses, toned, minor damage ........................................................................... 345.00

Led Zeppelin, July 23-24, 1977, Oakland Stadium, design by Randy Tuten & William Bostedt................................... 175.00

The Supremes, Trude Heller and G. Keys present - The Supremes - Lincoln Center, Philharmonic Hall, Friday, Oct. 15, 1965, design by Eula, 25" x 38" ........................................ 500.00

Concert Program

Aerosmith, World Tour, 1953/54............................................. 15.00

Eric Clapton, N. America, 1995 ............................................. 10.00

Deep Purple, Royal Albert Hall, London ............................... 20.00

Page & Plant, USA Tour, 1998............................................... 20.00

Rolling Stones, Japan, 1995.................................................. 30.00

Crew Shirt

Grateful Dead, white, "Grateful Dead - Crew 1994," drawing of cargo plane over pocket area........................................... 30.00

Metallica, black, "Staff 85/86," drawing of wild Father Time and metal babies................................................................... 30.00

Display, Beatles, Wings, Back to the Egg, promotion, 3-D .......... 35.00

Guitar Pick, custom

Guns N Roses, Slash ......................................................... 25.00

Ozzy Osbourne, Zac Wilkd ................................................. 25.00

Rolling Stones, Richard's/Blamehound................................ 30.00

ZZ Top, Dusty Hill ............................................................... 25.00

Guitar, sgd

Aerosmith ...................................................................... 1,100.00

Vince Gill .......................................................................... 650.00

Kiss, orig 4 ........................................................................ 995.00

Fleetwood Mac ............................................................... 1,250.00

Rolling Stones, all 5 ........................................................ 2,200.00

Bob Seger ......................................................................... 850.00

Jacket, Rolling Stones, Varsity Tour, red wool body, black leather sleeve, chenille Stones logo on back, breast, and sleeves...... 225.00

Lobby Card

Elvis Presley, Blue Hawaii, 1961, 11" x 14", full color ........... 40.00

Led Zeppelin, John Paul Jones playing bass ....................... 12.00

Lyrics

Alice Cooper, handwritten for song "Trash," composed in studio, 1989, three verses in black ink, corrections in blue ball point pen, two additional verses in blue ball point pen, written on yellow legal size paper.............................................................. 300.00

Paul McCartney, handwritten for song "When I'm 64," 1967 Sgt. Pepper album, lyrics and revisions ............................ 40,250.00

Magazine, Sixteen, 1966, Beatles cover and article .................. 15.00

Make Up Kit, Kiss, sealed in package, showing group in make-up....................................................................................10.00

Medallion, Beatles, St. Peppers, US promo 30th anniversary ...... 50.00

Mousepad, Kiss, showing group in make-up.............................. 10.00

Newspaper, Memphis Press, August 17, 1977, announcing death of Elvis Presley.............................................................................. 35.00

Patch

Bon Jovi .............................................................................. 10.00

David Lee Roth, Charlotte, 1986 ......................................... 15.00

Pen, Elvis Presley, Tickle Me Feather, mkd "Elvis Presley In Tickle Me It's Your Summer/Block Buster For Release June 30th Allied artists," 1965 ............................................................................................ 50.00

Perfume Bottle, Elvis Presley, Teddy Bear, 1965 photo of Elvis on label, gold top, orig contents ...................................................... 100.00

Pinback Button

7/8" d, Elvis Presley, Hound Dog, 1956 ............................... 40.00

1" d, Fabian Fan Club, blue on white, litho, late 1950s......... 15.00

3-1/2" d, Monkeys, black and white photo, red and white logo, 1966 .................................................................................. 25.00

4" d, Jackson Five, black and white photo, bright red ground, copyright 1971, Motown Record Corp............................... 40.00

Poster

Guns and Roses, Use Your Illusion World Tour, 1993, 24" x 36".............................................................................20.00

Oldfield Mike, Tubular Bells, two album cover artwork, 24" x 36".............................................................................20.00

Queen, Rocks Volume I, band name and two coats of arms, 36" x 24".............................................................................20.00

Savage Garden, Affirmation album cover artwork, 24" x 27"..... 18.00

Press Kit Video, Brian Wilson, Imagination.................................. 15.00

Promo Tape, Doors, Live At The Hollywood Bowl, advance VHS tape, sealed in MAC Video box .......................................................... 15.00

Radio Interview Tape

Celine Dion, Special Radio Event........................................ 75.00

Dire Straits, in studio for Brothers in Arms, 2 CDs, radio interview tape ................................................................................... 20.00

Elton Jon, King Biscuit, 2 CDs and question sheet.............. 65.00

Yes, Live at the Universal, aired 5/95 .................................. 15.00

Record Award

Bob Dylan, Greatest Hits, RIAA Double Platinum LP Award, 2nd hologram ......................................................................... 700.00

Peter Frampton, Frampton Comes Alive, RIAA Platinum LP Award for 6 Million Sales.................................................. 500.00

Honey Droppers, Volume One, RIAA Gold LP Award, first hologram ................................................................................. 450.00

Whitney Houston, Whitney Houston, RIAA Platinum LP, for 12 million sales...................................................................... 700.00

Dire Straits, RIAA Platinum LP ............................................ 700.00
The Doors, Dance on Fire, RIAA Gold Video Award .......... 375.00
The Eagles, Hell Freezes Over, RIAA Gold LP........................... 600.00
Road Sign, Led Zeppelin, Walking into Clarkesdale, green and white,
    12" x 16" .................................................................... 35.00
Sweatshirt, Rolling Stones, white, "Rockware by Brockum," four dif-
    ferent Stones logos ................................................... 40.00
Ticket Stub, Bob Dylan, Tom Petty, Greek Theater, Berkeley, CA,
    6/13/86 ....................................................................... 12.00
Tour Book
    Joe Crocker, Power & The Passion, 1990 ............................ 10.00
    Culture Club, A Kiss Across the Ocean, Japanese Tour, some
      cover wear................................................................. 60.00
    Deep Purple, Moments of Abandon.................................... 15.00
    Def Leppard, Euphoria Tour................................................ 20.00
T Shirt
    Aerosmith, Get A Grip, XXL ............................................... 15.00
    Guns N Roses, tie dye........................................................ 25.00
    Rolling Stones, Bablylonian Tongue, tan ............................ 20.00
    Van Halen, Right Now......................................................... 15.00

# ROGERS & SIMILAR STATUARY

**History:** John Rogers, born in America in 1829, studied sculpture in Europe and produced his first plaster-of-paris statue, "The Checker Players," in 1859. It was followed by "The Slave Auction" in 1860.

His works were popular parlor pieces in the Victorian era. He produced at least 80 different statues, and the total number of groups made from the originals is estimated to be more than 100,000.

Casper Hennecke, one of Rogers' contemporaries, operated C. Hennecke & Company from 1881 until 1896 in Milwaukee, Wisconsin. His statuary often is confused with Rogers' work since both are very similar.

**References:** Paul and Meta Bieier, *John Rogers' Groups of Statuary*, published by author, 1971; Betty C. Haverly, *Hennecke's Florentine Statuary*, published by author, 1972; David H. Wallace, *John Rogers*, Wesleyan University, 1976.

**Periodical:** *Rogers Group*, 4932 Prince George Ave., Beltsville, MD 20705.

**Museums:** John Rogers Studio & Museum of the New Canaan Historical Society, New Canaan CT; Lightner Museum, Saint Augustine, FL.

**Notes:** It is difficult to find a statue in undamaged condition and with original paint. Use the following conversions: 10% off for minor flaking; 10%, chips; 10 to 20%, piece or pieces broken and reglued; 20%, flaking; 50%, repainting.

## Rogers

Campfire ........................................................... 650.00
Challenging Union Vote ........................................ 1,100.00
Charity Patient, 1866 .......................................... 665.00
Courtship Sleepy Hollow...................................... 750.00
Elder's Daughter ................................................ 950.00
Favored Scholar, 1873........................................ 425.00
Faust and Marguerite.......................................... 800.00
Fighting Bob........................................................ 1,800.00
First Ride............................................................ 1,800.00
Ha, I Like Not That ............................................. 500.00

**Rogers-Type, First Love, $200.**

One More Shoot.................................................. 500.00
Pews .................................................................. 600.00
Phrenology.......................................................... 750.00
Politics............................................................... 1,300.00
Private Theatricals ............................................. 700.00
Referee .............................................................. 900.00
You Are A Spirit.................................................. 750.00
We Boys.............................................................. 800.00
Why Don't You Speak ........................................ 600.00
Wrestlers............................................................ 1,600.00

## Rogers Type

Croquet Player.................................................... 200.00
Evening Devotion................................................ 300.00
Family Cares....................................................... 120.00
First Love............................................................ 200.00
Lost & Found....................................................... 150.00
Red Riding Hood................................................. 350.00
Welcome, alabaster............................................ 300.00

# ROOKWOOD POTTERY

**History:** Mrs. Marie Longworth Nicholas Storer, Cincinnati, Ohio, founded Rookwood Pottery in 1880. The name of this outstanding American art pottery came from her family estate, "Rookwood," named for the rooks (crows) which inhabited the wooded grounds.

Though the Rookwood pottery filed for bankruptcy in 1941, it was soon reorganized under new management. Efforts at maintaining the pottery proved futile, and it was sold in 1956 and again in 1959. The pottery was moved to Starkville, Mississippi, in conjunction with the Herschede Clock Co. It finally ceased operating in 1967.

Rookwood wares changed with the times. The variety is endless, in part because of the creativity of the many talented artists responsible for great variations in glazes and designs.

**Marks:** There are five elements to the Rookwood marking system—the clay or body mark, the size mark, the decorator mark, the date mark, and the factory mark. The best way to date Rookwood art pottery is from factory marks. From 1880 to 1882, the factory mark was the name "Rookwood" incised or painted on the base. Between 1881 and 1886, the firm name, address, and year appeared in an oval frame. Beginning in 1886, the impressed "RP" monogram appeared and a flame mark was added for each year until 1900. After 1900, a Roman numeral, indicating the last two digits of the year of production, was added at the bottom of the "RP" flame mark. This last mark is the one most often seen on Rookwood pieces in the antiques marketplace.

**References:** Anita J. Ellis, *Rookwood Pottery*, Schiffer Publishing, 1995; Herbert Peck, *Book of Rookwood Pottery*, Crown Publishers, 1968; ——, *Second Book of Rookwood Pottery*, published by author, 1985; David Rago, *American Art Pottery,* Knickerbocker Press, 1997.

**Collectors' Club:** American Art Pottery Association, P.O. Box 834, Westport, MA 02790-0697, http://www.amartpot.org.

Bookends, 5-1/2" h, molded trees, mottled brown matte glaze, 1929, imp mark #6020, also imp "W. P. McDonald" ............................ 500.00
Bowl
    3-3/8" h, three repeating lily of the valley sprays, vellum glaze, E. T. Hurley, 1919 ............................................. 1,400.00
    9-1/4" d, light orange, clover dec, cameo glaze, 1869 ........ 385.00
    13-1/8" d, blue roses, repeating patterns dec, blue tinted high glaze, Sara Sax, 1926 ...................................................... 850.00
    Box, cov, decorated by Elizabeth Lincoln
    5" d, #XXIII 2660E, six sided, butterfly dec ..................... 2,400.00
    5-1/2" d, #XXII 2009 ......................................................... 950.00
Bust, 9-3/4" h, young boy, matte glaze, 1913 ............................. 750.00
Candlestick, 6" h, oval column-form, standard glaze with green leaf dec on base, dec by Amelia Browne Sprague, 1889, imp mark and "508 S.," inscribed "A.B.S./I" on base, small hairline ................ 260.00

Cane Handle, 3-3/8" l, dragonfly dec, iris glaze, c1905 ............. 375.00
Charger, 12-5/8" d, young Indian boy, standard gales, titled on back "Moki Rabbit Hunter," Grace Young, 1898 ........................... 6,000.00
Chocolate Pot, 9-3/8" h, baluster, jonquils dec, standard glaze, Elizabeth Lincoln, 1904 ................................................................ 600.00
Creamer, 2-1/4" h, pansy dec, standard glaze, Olga Reed, 1891 .... 190.00
Cup and Saucer, daisy dec, cameo glaze, Ed Abel, 1891 .......... 325.00
Ewer, 7" h, Chrysanthemum, standard glaze, folded spout on broad rimmed ovoid vessel, delicate "C" handle, pale orange chrysanthemum blossoms and green leaves, brown ground, dec by Harriet Elizabeth Wilcox, c1888, Rookwood logo, 443 C, and artist's initials ................ 750.00
Figure, elephant, 4" h, #6488, 1934, white matte, flat flake on ear .. 180.00
Jar, cov, 6" d, #1349, incised geometric design, red and green matte glaze, 1908, minor flake to inner rim ....................................... 375.00
Jardiniere, 10-1/2" h, grape and leaf dec, standard glaze, Albert Valentien, 1888 ................................................................... 1,400.00
Match Holder, 1-3/4" h, forget-me-not dec, matches and cigarettes dec, standard glaze, Carl Schmidt, 1898 ............................... 385.00
Pitcher, 8-3/4" h, 6-1/4" d, cameo, dec in Limoges style, white narcissus, salmon pink ground, A. M. Valentien, 1890, flame mark/343/W/A.M.V. .................................................................. 400.00
Plaque, 16" w, 14" h, vellum, scenic, Evening, trees by path at dusk, dec by Fred Rothenbusch, Cincinnati, 1927, artist's cipher lower left corner, Rookwood mark and date on reverse, framed ........ 19,550.00
Tea Set, porcelain, Shipware, teapot, creamer, sugar, trivet, cups, saucers, and luncheon plates for six, flame mark ...................... 1,100.00
Tile
    4" sq, pink flower in brown vase, cream ground, Arts & Crafts oak frame ................................................................................ 325.00
    5-3/4" sq, raised dec of Dutch mother holding baby, little girl at side, by shore with windmill, matte glaze in shades of blue, green, pink, and tan, imp mark, c1924 ............................. 320.00
    6" h, cuenca dec, pink Glasgow rose, green leaves, Arts & Crafts frame, imp "Rookwood Faience/1281Y" ........................... 1,300.00
    Urn, 12-3/4" h, 9-1/2" d, mustard microcrystalline glaze, 1910, flame mark/X/339B ........................................................... 1,300.00
Vase
    3" h, #1186, four-sided top, incised geometric design, green and blue matte glaze, 1904 ...................................................... 400.00
    4" h, #942F, incised geometric design, green matte glaze, imp mark, 1904 ......................................................................... 425.00
    4-1/2" h, matte blue glaze, slightly flared rim, ovoid vessel, border of raised berry dec, blue drip glaze, slight crystalline effect, imp mark, date 1928 and "212" on base ............................... 290.00
    5" h, 4-1/2" h, vellum, blue, green, pink, and purple stylized flowers and leaves, medium blue ground, Margaret Helen McDonald, 1923, flame mark/XXIII/1343/HMH ................ 600.00
    5-7/8" h, Honeysuckle, raised rim, tapered oval form, two small angled handles at shoulder, honeysuckle blossoms on standard glaze, shades of gold and brown ground, dec by Adeliza Drake Schon, Cincinnati, 1900, imp marks, inscribed artist's initials, crazing and minor scratches ............................................. 490.00
    6-1/2" h, Iris, standard glaze, flared rim over wide neck and bulbous body, yellow iris and dark green leaves, golden, green, and brown ground, dec by Amelia Browne Sprague, c1889, imp mark and "C. W.," inscribed artist's initials ...................... 575.00

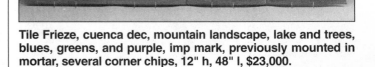

**Tile Frieze, cuenca dec, mountain landscape, lake and trees, blues, greens, and purple, imp mark, previously mounted in mortar, several corner chips, 12" h, 48" l, $23,000.**

7" h, 3-1/4", scenic vellum, purple and apricot landscape of birch trees by lake, Elizabeth McDermott, 1917, flame mark/XVII/30F/EFM...................................... 1,400.00

7" h, 6" d, porcelain, brown and cobalt blue geometric pattern, ivory ground, W. Rehn, 1930, flame mark/XXX/1780/WR ..........1,200.00

7" h, 7" d, jewel porcelain, spherical, gray and white birds and magnolia blossoms, amber ground, Jens Jensen, 1946, flame mark/XLVI/6204/artist's cipher...................................... 1,800.00

7-3/4" h, vellum, white roses, ivory and gray ground, M. H. McDonald, 1914, flame mark/XIV/1861/V/M.H.MD..........750.00

7-3/4" h, marine scenic vellum, painted sailboats, aqua water and sky, uncrazed, Carl Schmidt, 1923, flame mark/XXIII/CS/901D....................................................3000.00

7-3/4" h, 3" d, marine scenic vellum, sailboats on water, E. T. Hurley, 1943, uncrazed, flamemark/XLIII/932E/E.T.H.........2,400.00

8" h, 4" d, tapering, painted matte, pink flower, charcoal ground, O. G. Reed, 1911, flame mark/1655E/OGR...................1,300.00

8" h, 4-1/2" d, jewel porcelain, bottle shape, brown and red, figures of Adam and Eve, with flowers, fish and fowl, cobalt blue butterfat glaze, Jens Jensen, 1933, flame mark/XXXIII/5/artist's cipher .......................................................................... 2,600.00

8" h, 6" d, jewel porcelain, brown and blue covered figures of Eve, flowers, fish, and fowl, sheer ivory butterfat glaze, Jens Jensen, 1945, flame mark/XLV/8005/64/artist's cipher...............1,900.00

8-1/4" h, 3-3/4" d, ovoid, iris glaze, yellow, purple, and blue gooseberry leaves and fruit, shaded gray ground, Ed Diers, 1902, flame mark/II/732/ED ......................................... 1,200.00

8-1/4" h, 4" d, scenic vellum, silhouetted seagulls in flight against pink sky, over gray waves, E. T. Hurley, 1905, flame mark/V/845d/V/E. T. Hurley.......................................... 1,300.00

8-1/2" h, #1297, molded poppies dec, two-tone blue matte glaze, 1912 ................................................................................550.00

8-1/2" h, 3-1/2" d, carved matte, tooled indigo irises and green leaves, red and green ground, Rose Fescheimer, 1906, flame mark/VI/932D/P.F................................................................5,500.00

8-3/4" h, 3-3/4" h, marine scenic vellum, sailboats at dust, purple and green sky, Fred Rothenbusch, 1910, flame mark/X/1660D/V/FR, two hairlines ...................................650.00

8-3/4" h, 5" d, Iris, painted yellow water lilies, dark gray ground, Constance Baker, 1902, flame mark/II/CAP/935c.........2,100.00

9-1/2" h, carved vellum, three orchids on branch, coffee colored ground, Ed Diers, 1905, flame markVX/942D/ED ......... 4,250.00

**Vase, Jewel Porcelain, Chinese style, four panels of birds and hollyhocks, blues and greens, ivory butterfat ground, by Lorinda Epply, 1929, flame mark/XXIX/2933/LE, 12" h, 5" d, uncrazed, $3,925. Photo courtesy of David Rago Auctions.**

9-1/2" h, 4" d, wax matte, red flowers, green leaves, shaded orange ground, Eliz. Lincoln, 1923, flame mark/XXIII/614D/LNL"................................................1,400.00

10" h, two loop handles at shoulder, standard glaze, flared rim on extended neck over ovoid body, cream colored wild roses on leafy stems, dec by Albert Valentien, 1891, imp mark, "610C W," inscribed with artist's initials ......................................... 1,380.00

10" h, 4-1/2" d, Marine Scenic vellum, sailboats in Venetian harbor, Carl Schmidt, 1925, flame mark/XXV/1121C/V/CS, uncrazed ....................................................................... 6,500.00

10-1/4" h, 4" d, marine scenic vellum, baluster, small sailboats against dusk sky, Carl Schmidt, 1920, imp flame marl/XX/937/V/CS ...................................................... 3,750.00

10-1/2" h, geometric design at shoulder, pink and green matte glaze, #2033D, 1912 ......................................................400.00

10-1/2" h, 5" d, vellum, large mushrooms on shaded pastel ground, Carl Schmidt, 1905, flame mark/V/939B/V/CS, uncrazed ..................................................................... 11,000.00

10-1/2" h, 5-1/4" d, wax matte, painted brown and red poppy pods and blossoms, red butterfat ground, Eliz. Lincoln, 1922, flame mark/XXII/614D/LNL ..................................................... 2,400.00

10-3/4" h, 5-1/4" d, wax matte, purple flowers, green foliage, turquoise butterfat ground, Eliz. Lincoln, 1928, flame mark/XXVIII/614D/LNL..................................................... 1,700.00

12" h, 3" d, bottle shape, bisque, Aerial blue, mother and child amidst crashing waves, William McDonald, 1895, flame mark/242D................................................................. 11,000.00

12-1/4" h, 5" d, painted matte, crisply pained, band of ochre dogwood blossoms on orange ground, violet body, H. Wilcox, 1906, flame mark VI/950B/HEW ............................................. 3,750.00

12-1/2" h, 5-1/2" d, Scenic vellum, sunset landscape of silhouetted trees, pink ground, Sara Sax, 1920, flame mark/XX/2032C/SX ................................................. 12,000.00

16" h, 6-1/2" d, Scenic vellum, birch landscape at dusk, E. T. Hurley, 1912, flame mark/XII/1660/A/E.T.H. ...................... 6,500.00

# ROSE BOWLS

**History:** A rose bowl is a decorative open bowls with a crimped, pinched, or petal top which turns in at the top, but does not then turn up or back out again. Rose bowls held fragrant rose petals or potpourri which served as an air freshener in the late Victorian period. Practically every glass manufacturer made rose bowls in virtually every glass type, pattern, and style, including fine art glass.

**Reference:** Johanna S. Billings with Sean Billings, *Collectible Rose Bowls,* Antique Trader Books, 1999.

**Collectors' Club:** Rose Bowl Collectors, P.O. Box 244, Danielsville, PA 18038-0244.

**Reproduction Alert:** Rose bowls have been widely reproduced. Be especially careful of Italian copies of satin, Mother of Pearl satin, peachblow, and Burmese, and recent Czechoslovakian ones with applied flowers.

**Additional Listings:** See specific glass categories.

**Advisor:** Johanna S. Billings.

## Glass

Carnival

Beaded Cable, Northwood, aqua opalescent, 4 toes, lightly ruffled top ...............................................................................500.00

Concave Flute, Westmoreland, green, ruffled top, collar foot.. 135.00

Honeycomb, Northwood, peach opalescent ......................... 80.00

Horse Medallion, Fenton, marigold, three toes, ruffled top . 175.00

Cameo, over Mother-of-Pearl satin, blue, white lining, Diamond Quilted pattern, white floral cameo pattern, ground pontil, 3-1/2" h, 4" w, $1,500. Photo courtesy of Johanna Billings.

Cameo, 3-1/2" h, 4" wide, over Mother-of-Pearl satin, shaded deep rose to red, white lining, Diamond Quilted pattern, white floral cameo pattern, ground pontil ............................................................ 1,500.00

Cased, 5" h, 4-1/2" w, pink over white, ribbed, with 5 triangular crimps, 2 white applied glass flowers ........................................................ 85.00

Fenton, 2-1/2" h, 3" w, Burmese miniature "Love Bouquet" with a rose, rosebud, lily of the valley and forget me nots, embossed butterfly in the bottom, sgd "Mary Walrath, 1986," also sgd "Handpainted by Pam Miller" ................................................................................... 75.00

Moser, 2-1/2" h, 2-1/2" w, green, intaglio engraved with lily, polished pontil, 6 delicate crimps ............................................................... 250.00

Opalescent
    Button Panels, Northwood, clear with white opalescence .... 45.00
    Inverted Fan and Feather, Northwood, footed, clear with white opalescent ........................................................................... 90.00

Pattern Glass, Heart with Thumbprint pattern, 5" h, 5" w, hearts and bulls-eye centers repeat 4 times around bowl, starburst bottom ............ 170.00

Porcelain, 5" h, 5" w, heart shaped with large yellow roses on a brown background, ruffled top, no markings ......................................... 45.00

Satin
    3-1/2" h, 4" w, blue to white, white lining, "Niagara Falls" ......... 150.00
    3-1/2" h, 4" w, yellow to white, white lining, ground pontil ........... 40.00
    4" h, 4" w, pink blown out petals in "Cabbage Rose" design, white lining, rough pontil ............................................................... 225.00
    4" h, 4" wide, Shell & Seaweed pattern, enamel decoration, ground pontil .................................................................................. 150.00

# ROSE CANTON, ROSE MANDARIN, and ROSE MEDALLION

**History:** The pink rose color has given its name to three related groups of Chinese export porcelain: Rose Mandarin, Rose Medallion, and Rose Canton, and Rose Medallion.

Rose Mandarin, which was produced from the late 18th century to approximately 1840, derives its name from the Mandarin figure(s) found in garden scenes with women and children. The women often have gold decorations in their hair. Polychrome enamels and birds separate the scenes.

Rose Medallion, which originated in the early 19th century and was made through the early 20th century, has alternating panels of figures and birds and flowers. The elements are four in number, separated evenly around the center medallion. Peonies and foliage fill voids.

Rose Canton, which was introduced somewhat later than Rose Mandarin and was produced through the first half of the 19th century, is similar to Rose Medallion except the figural panels are replaced by flowers. People are present only if the medallion partitions are absent. Some patterns have been named, e.g., Butterfly and Cabbage and Rooster. Rose Canton actually is a catchall term for any pink enamel ware not fitting into the first two groups.

**Periodical:** *Orientalia Journal*, P.O. Box 94, Flushing, NY 11363-0094, http://members.aol.com/Orientalia/index.html.

## Rose Canton

Bowl, 14-3/4" d, 6" h, mandarin scenes, edge repair .................. 825.00
Creamer, 4" h, gilt dec, double twisted handle ........................... 215.00
Dish, 10-1/2" l, shell shape, gold dec, c1850 ............................ 450.00
Plate, 8-1/2" d, Thousand Butterfly border, gilt highlights, 19th C .... 110.00
Platter, 18-7/8" l, well and tree, mkd on base, late 19th C, very minor rim chips ................................................................................... 550.00
Punch Bowl
    21" d, very minor gilt and enamel wear ........................... 3,450.00
    13-3/8" d, 5-3/8" h, minor gilt and enamel wear .................. 900.00
Vase, 12-1/2" h, mandarin scenes, drilled and mounted as lamp, chip on base ring .......................................................................... 390.00

## Rose Mandarin

Cache Pot, 8-1/2" h, reserves of court figure, squirrel and grape border, 19th C, restoration, lid missing, minor chips ..................... 700.00
Hot Water Dish, 9-1/4" d, gilt highlights ..................................... 545.00
Platter
    14-3/4" l, gilt and enamel wear, minute rim chips, knife marks ................................................................................ 635.00
    14-3/4" l, 12" w, some wear .............................................. 700.00
    15-3/4" l, gilt and enamel wear, minor chips .................... 1,100.00
    17-1/2" l, well and tree, restoration, gilt and enamel wear 1,150.00
Dish, cov, 12-1/2" l, 2-1/2" w, 8-1/2" h, bronze ftd mount with swing handle, embellished with floral and foliate motifs, gilt, China, 19th C, gilt wear .................................................................................. 865.00
Teapot, 8-1/4" h, domed cover, China, 19th C, crack in lower cover, minor spout chip .................................................................... 815.00
Vase
    12-3/8" h, 7-3/4" d, Ku-form, raised acanthus leaf ribbing, gilt archaic dragon design, blue ground, first half 19th C, pr ............... 3,350.00
    13-5/8" h, Ku-form, chips and cracks, pr .......................... 1,035.00
    15-1/4" h, 10" d, Ku-form, very minor rim chip, gilt and enamel wear, 19th C .............................................................................. 575.00

Rose Medallion, vegetable, nut finial, c1775, 8-1/4" l, $725.

## Rose Medallion

Basin
16" d, 5" h, multiple alternating Mandarins avian/floral reserves, c1850-65 ............................................................. 495.00
18-3/4" d, 5-3/4" h, hairline, wear, 19th C ............................ 805.00

Bowl
9-1/8" d, 3-3/4" h, Chinese Export, mid 19th C, discoloration...375.00
10" d, 4-3/4" h, minor wear, mid-19th C ............................ 450.00

Brush Box, cov, 7-1/2" l, 3-3/4" w, 2-7/8" h, rectangular, interior divider, China, late 19th C ................................................ 635.00

Brush Holder, 4-1/2" h, 4-3/4" h, hairlines, chip, wear, 19th C, price for pr ................................................................. 290.00

Bun Tray, 13-1/2" x 7" x 1-3/4" h, rect ........................................ 800.00

Candlestick
9-3/4" h, minor chips, enamel wear .................................... 300.00
10-1/4" h, minor gilt and enamel wear, pr ...................... 1,000.00

Center Bowl, 10-3/8" d, 6-1/2" h, paneled, scalloped rim, ftd, two very minor rim chips, minor gilt and enamel wear....................... 2,875.00

Chamber Pot, 9-5/8" d, minute rim chips ................................... 635.00

Charger, 18" d, scenes of people............................................. 200.00

Compote, 7-5/8" d, 3-5/8" h, reticulated, pr................................ 700.00

Creamer
3-1/4" h, 7" w, repaired........................................................ 60.00
4-1/2" h, curved spout........................................................ 225.00

Dish, cov, 10-1/2" l, 4-1/4" h, oval, China, 19th C, rim chips ....... 490.00

Fruit Basket, 9-3/8" h, 9-7/8" l undertray, reticulated basket, very minor chips, minor gilt and enamel wear....................................... 950.00

Garniture Vase, cov, 15" h, tall neck, elaborate alternating Mandarins avian/floral reserves, Mongol Hat cover, c1835-50 .................. 715.00

Garniture Vase, open, 8" h, baluster, alternating Mandarins avian/floral reserves, c1835-50, price for pr ...................................... 350.00

Jar, cov, 14-1/2" h, domed lid, flower bud finial, oval form, leafy branch handles, China, 19th C, glaze flakes ................................. 1,495.00

Plate, dinner, 9-3/4" d
Alternating Mandarins and avian/floral reserves, c1835-50, price for six of eight ........................................................ 500.00
Large avian centers and floral cartouche borders, Chinese Export, c1840, price for 4 pc set ..................................... 525.00

Platter
13-1/2" l, 11" w .................................................................. 300.00
14-1/2" l, 11-3/4" w ............................................................ 250.00
15-1/2" x 11-1/2" w ............................................................ 350.00
16" l, 13" w ........................................................................ 300.00
16-1/2" l, 13-1/4" w, cabbage leaf center .......................... 625.00
18" l, 14-1/2" w, oval ........................................................ 350.00
18-3/4" l, well and tree, panels of red flowers and butterflies................................................................... 800.00

Punch Bowl, 15-1/2" d, 6-3/4" d, China, 19th C, minor glaze wear, gilt retouch ............................................................... 1,725.00

Rice Bowl and Spoon, 4-3/4" d x 2-1/4" h bowl, 5" spoon ........... 45.00

Sauce Tureen, 8-1/8" l, mismatched undertray, gilt and enamel wear ............................................................................... 575.00

Soap Dish, cov, 6" l, 4-3/4" w, 2-1/2" h, rectangular, drainer, China, 19th C, chips, paint retouches............................................. 435.00

Soup Bowl, 10" d, China, 19th C, edge chips, wear, hairlines, some glaze retouches, price for set of eight ................................. 980.00

Teapot, 8-3/4" h, domed cover, China, 19th C, repairs, chips, crack ....................................................................... 1,200.00

Umbrella Holder, 24" h, 9-1/2" w, twelve panels of people in int., setting birds and butterflies with flowers, reeded type molded side.. 1,650.00

Vase
17" h, 8" d, baluster, handles modeled as pair of Foo dogs en face, paired gilded dragons in relief at shoulders, c1840-60, price for pr ................................................................ 660.00
18" h, 9" d, baluster, alternating Mandarins and avian/floral reserves, Kuang, c1835-50, price for pr.......................... 900.00

Vegetable Dish, cov, 8-1/2" l, 6-1/2" w, 5" h, rect, China, mid-19th C, chips, glaze wear .............................................................. 375.00

Wash Basin and Pitcher
15-7/8" d basin, 13-1/4" h pitcher, mismatched, restoration, minor gilt and enamel wear............................................... 1,100.00
16" d basin, 14-3/4" h pitcher, heavy enamel wear to basin .... 650.00

Water Bottle, cov
14-1/2" h, hairline, minute chip to lid, minor gilt and enamel wear........................................................................... 435.00
15" h, minor chips to lid, minor gilt and enamel wear, hardwood stand ............................................................................ 890.00

# ROSENTHAL

**History:** Rosenthal Porcelain Manufactory began operating at Selb, Bavaria, in 1880. Specialties were tablewares and figurines. The firm is still in operation.

**Reference:** Dieter Struss, *Rosenthal,* Schiffer Publishing, 1997.

Bowl, 10-3/4" d, pink, strawberries and leaves, scalloped gold trim, scroll handle, red glazed underside, artist sgd ........................... 85.00

Cake Plate, 10" d, multicolored roses, cobalt blue and gold border... 55.00

Coffee Cup and Saucer, white porcelain cup, .800 silver holder and saucer, Art Nouveau dec, initials, price for 6 pc set ................. 750.00

Creamer and Sugar, gold trim, sgd "Donatello" ........................... 45.00

Cup and Saucer, Maria pattern, heavy silver overlay .................. 65.00

Dessert Set, Maria pattern, teapot, creamer, cov sugar, six cups, saucers, and dessert plates, 1908-48, price for 23 pc set ...350.00

Dinner Service, Regina pattern, gold trim, price for 101 pc set..... 1,000.00

Dresser Set, lavender flowers, gold trim, price for 3 pc set .......... 75.00

Figure
Bird on branch, artist sgd, 6" h........................................... 155.00
Harem Dancer, 10" h, artist sgd .......................................... 600.00
Springer Spaniel, basket, 1932, 71 /2" h ........................... 200.00
Rabbit, dark brown, 3" h ....................................................... 165.00
Woman in 18th C dress, walking hound, oval base, 10-1/2" h ..................................................................... 200.00

Fruit Set, 10" d bowl, six 8" d plates, blue, green, yellow, and pink, pink roses, gold dec, price for 7 pc set ....................................... 395.00

Luncheon Service, partial, cobalt blue ground rims, and gilt borders, twelve: 6-1/4" d plates, 7-3/4" d plates, 10-1/8" d plates, 5-1/4" d sauce dishes, 8-1/4" d soup bowls, saucers, eleven teacups, 12-3/4" l oval platter, 14-3/4" oval platter, oval 9-3/4" l serving dish, cov vegetable bowl ...................................................................... 2,300.00

**Dinner Service, partial, Sunburst pattern, designed by Raymond Loewry, price for 50 pc set, $95. Photo courtesy of David Rago Auctions.**

Nappy, brown nuts and flowers on gold ground, ruffled rim .......... 50.00

Nut Set, master bowl, six 3-1/2" d serving bowls, Pompadour pattern, cream ground, ornate gold scrolled rim, price for 7 pc set ......... 65.00

Place Card Holder, small multicolored floral dec .......................... 15.00

Plaque, 10" x 12", snow covered mountain, lake in foreground, orig frame .................................................................... 700.00

Plate

    8" d, pastel daisies, price for 6 pc set ................................... 95.00

    11" d, Ivory, floral center, claret inner border, palmette gilded edge, c1920-25, price for set of 12 ................................. 330.00

Sculpture, 16" h, 9-1/2" d base, white, two tropical fish swimming among rising seaweed, wood base, artist sgd "F. Heidenreich," small in-making fracture on seaweed leaf .................................. 200.00

Tea Cup and Saucer, Donatello pattern, price for 12 piece set..... 50.00

Vase

    7" h, crackle, rust foliage, artist sgd "Stockmayer," 1946.... 125.00

    17-1/2" h, Studio Line, bisque ext., glazed int., cylindrical, flaring neck, molded bands of figures supporting ribs of flowers, designed by Bjorn Winblad ................................. 275.00

# ROSEVILLE POTTERY

**History:** In the late 1880s, a group of investors purchased the J. B. Owens Pottery in Roseville, Ohio, and made utilitarian stoneware items. In 1892, the firm was incorporated and joined by George F. Young, who became general manager. Four generations of Youngs controlled Roseville until the early 1950s.

A series of acquisitions began: Midland Pottery of Roseville in 1898, Clark Stoneware Plant in Zanesville (formerly used by Peters and Reed), and Muskingum Stoneware (Mosaic Tile Company) in Zanesville. In 1898, the offices also moved from Roseville to Zanesville.

In 1900, Roseville introduced Rozane, an art pottery. Rozane became a trade name to cover a large series of lines. The art lines were made in limited amounts after 1919.

The success of Roseville depended on its commercial lines, first developed by John J. Herald and Frederick Rhead in the first decades of the 1900s. In 1918, Frank Ferrell became art director and developed more than 80 lines of pottery. The economic depression of the 1930s brought more lines, including Pine Cone.

In the 1940s, a series of high-gloss glazes were tried in an attempt to revive certain lines. In 1952, Raymor dinnerware was produced. None of these changes brought economic success and in November 1954, Roseville was bought by the Mosaic Tile Company.

**References:** Mark Bassett, *Bassett's Roseville Prices,* Schiffer Publishing, 2000; John and Nancy Bomm, *Roseville In All Its Splendor,* L-W Book Sales, 1998; Virginia Hillway Buxton, *Roseville Pottery for Love or Money,* updated ed., Tymbre Hill Publishing Co. (P.O. Box 615, Jonesborough, TN 37659), 1996; John W. Humphries, *Roseville Pottery by the Numbers*, published by author, 1999; Sharon and Bob Huxford, *Collectors Encyclopedia of Roseville Pottery*, 1st Series (1976, 2001 value update), 2nd Series (1980, 2001 value update), Collector Books; —, *The Roseville Pottery Price Guide, #12,* Collector Books, 1997; James S. Jen-

kins, Jr., *Roseville Art Pottery, 1998-1/2 Price Guide, Volume II,* Clinical Pharmacology Consultants, 1998; Gloria Mollring, *1999 Roseville Price Guide, 5th ed.,* published by author (P.O. Box 22754, Sacramento, CA 95822); Randall B. Monsen, *Collectors' Compendium of Roseville Pottery*, Monsen and Baer (Box 529, Vienna, VA 22183), 1995; —, *Collectors' Compendium of Roseville Pottery, Volume II,* Monsen and Baer, 1997; David Rago, *American Art Pottery,* Knickerbocker Press, 1997; Betty Ward and Nancy Schiffer, *Weller, Roseville, and Related Zanesville Art Pottery and Tiles,* Schiffer Publishing, 2000.

**Collectors' Clubs:** American Art Pottery Association, P.O. Box 834, Westport, MA 02790-0697, http://www.amart-pot.org;; Roseville's of the Past Pottery Club, P.O. Box 656, Clarcona, FL 32710.

**Additional Listings:** See *Warman's Americana & Collectibles* for more examples.

Ashtray

    Silhouette, red, 799................................................ 130.00

    Wincraft, blue, 240-7 ........................................... 135.00

Basket

    Apple Blossom, 309-8.......................................... 250.00

    Blackberry, 7" w, minor flake to top..................... 650.00

    Bushberry, blue, 8" h, 370-8 ................................ 210.00

    Bushberry, blue, 8-1/2" h, 369-6.5 ...................... 175.00

    Monticello, arched handle, incised mark, 6-1/2" h ... 550.00

    Pine Cone, 11"...................................................... 700.00

Bookends, pr

    Freesia, delft blue, relief mark ............................. 250.00

    Magnolia, blue ...................................................... 250.00

    Water Lily, pink and green, mkd, 5" w, 5" h.......... 180.00

    Zephyr Lily, brown to green, 5-1/2" ..................... 210.00

    Zephyr Lily, orange and yellow, #16, 5" h ........... 190.00

Bowl

    Baneda, low form, two handles, 11" l.................... 475.00

    Donatello, 10" d .................................................... 110.00

    Luffa, two handles, horizontal wavy lines, large green leaves, small white flowers, 7" d.................................... 200.00

    Monticello, low, two handles, black and white geometric design, rust, camel, and tan ground, green border, 13" w, 3" h... 375.00

    Pine Cone, blue 321-9 .......................................... 600.00

    Pine Cone, brown, 425-8 ...................................... 200.00

    Topeo, two-tone red hi-glaze, paper label, 9" d, minor flakes .. 100.00

    Water Lily, 663, pink............................................. 45.00

    Windsor, maroon, orig black paper label ............ 575.00

    Zephyr Lily, rust, green int., #810 ....................... 125.00

Candleholders, pr

    Carnelian II, aqua and lilac, 1059-2-1/2"............... 150.00

    Ixia, 3-1/4" h, low, pink, imp mark ....................... 220.00

    Moss, 1107-4-1/2", blue ...................................... 415.00

    Tuscany, 3-1/2" h ................................................. 65.00

Candlesticks, pr

    Ming Tree................................................................ 80.00

    Pine Cone, green, 1099-4-1/2" ............................ 200.00

Celery Dish, Raymor, brown, #177 ................................ 65.00

Child's Feeding Dish

    Baby Bunting, rolled edge.................................... 150.00

    Chick dec, stamp mark, 8" d ................................ 110.00

Child's Mug, Chicks ....................................................... 130.00

Compote, Silhouette, white, 722 ................................... 110.00

Conch, Peony, pink, 436 ................................................ 150.00

Console Bowl

    Bushberry, green, 385-10 .................................... 155.00

    Columbine, pink, 405-12" ..................................... 165.00

Gardenia, green, 632 .......................................... 70.00
Pine Cone, blue, 263-14", rect, two handles, rolled edge 1,870.00
Pine Cone, green, 322-12" ............................... 350.00
Poppy, 10" d, pink ............................................ 175.00
White Rose, 393-12 .......................................... 225.00
Console Set, Apple Blossom, blue............................ 275.00
Cookie Jar, cov
Freesia, brown, 4-8 .......................................... 425.00
Magnolia, blue, 2-8 .......................................... 475.00
Magnolia, orange to green, white and pink flowers, mkd,
8" h ................................................................ 300.00
Water Lily, brown ............................................ 440.00
Cornucopia, Silhouette, 8" ...................................... 85.00
Creamer, Juvenile Ware, chicks .............................. 135.00
Egg Cup, Juvenile Ware, chicks .............................. 280.00
Ewer
Clematis, blue, 18-15" ...................................... 365.00
Columbine, 7" h, blue, 18-7 .............................. 195.00
Freesia, blue, 21-15 ........................................ 350.00
Iris, pink, 926-10" ............................................ 300.00
Ming Tree, 10" h, white .................................... 150.00
Peony, green, 7-6" ............................................ 125.00
Pine Cone, brown, 909-10 .............................. 450.00
Snowberry, mauve, 6" h .................................... 90.00
Zephyr Lily, green and brown, 24-15 ................ 300.00
Floor Vase
Bittersweet, #888-16 ........................................ 900.00
Iris, 929-15 ...................................................... 650.00
Rozane Woodland, 19" h, 8-1/2" d, Art Nouveau style portrait of
woman on one side, other side with brown, ochre, and green iris,
Rozane wafer, couple of small glaze base flecks .......... 8,500.00
Flower Bowl, low, Florentine, 8" ............................... 85.00
Flower Pot
Clematis, blue, saucer base .............................. 140.00
Thornapple, pink, unmarked, 5" h .................... 250.00
Hanging Basket
Bittersweet, green, orange berries, 5" h ............ 210.00
Clematis, blue .................................................. 250.00
Pine Cone, blue ............................................... 550.00
Pine Cone, brown, unmarked .......................... 385.00
Snowberry, raised rim, wide shoulder tapering to base, two han-
dles, dusty rose glaze, c1946, 4-3/4" h ............ 115.00
Vista, molded landscape design, flower underneath, 7" w . 210.00
Wisteria, brown, rim chip .................................. 660.00
Humidor, Dutch .................................................... 275.00
Jar, Carnelian, blue, brown, and speckled gold underglaze, 7-3/4" x 5-
1/2", minor chip repair .......................................... 50.00
Jardiniere
Bleeding Heart, blue, 651-3 ............................. 100.00
Bushberry, blue, 657-3...................................... 120.00
Cosmos, blue, 649-3 ........................................ 100.00
Freesia, brown, 669-8" ...................................... 385.00
Futura, two handles, multicolored leaf design, orange to green
ground, 14" d .................................................. 400.00
Futura, two handles, stepped base, shoulder flake ........... 415.00
Old Ivory, 6"d .................................................... 50.00
Persian, stylized orange colored fruit, green leaves, white matte
ground, 7" d .................................................... 400.00
Pine Cone, raised rim, bulbous body, two branch handles in high
relief, matte green, brown, and cream glaze, blue ground, imp
"Roseville 632-8" on base, c1930, 8-1/4" h ........... 550.00
Primrose, blue, 634-6" ...................................... 225.00
Jardiniere and Pedestal
Larose, 30" h...................................................... 900.00
Peony, broad body with two handles, molded with white peonies
on sea green and brown ground, matching stand, raised marks,
c1942, 24-1/2" h, 12" d, hairlines to jardinière base......... 600.00
Vintage, dark brown ground, yellow and orange design, 13-1/2" d
jardiniere, 30-1/2" h, minute flakes ................ 1,100.00
Lamp Base, Vista, landscape dec, 15" h, drill hole in side......... 350.00

Mug
Cornelian, ornate handle, elaborate relief designs, 4" h ....... 50.00
Della Robbia, incised and painted Dutch girls, blue, white, and
brown, cut-back ground of dark green bordered by olive green,
artist initials "F. B.," 4-1/2" h ........................ 750.00
Juvenile Ware, chick, large .............................. 145.00
Pedestal, Clematis, 8" h........................................ 250.00
Pitcher
Boy with horn .................................................. 400.00
Bushberry, blue, green branch handle, mkd #1325, 9" h .... 375.00
Holland, 12" h .................................................. 480.00
Planter
Artwood, 10", yellow, 1056-10 ........................ 125.00
Bushberry, #383, browns, 6" .............................. 60.00
Bushberry, #384, browns, 8" ............................ 120.00
Cosmos, blue, 381-9" ...................................... 250.00
Rhead design, squeezebag dec of yellow and black water lilies,
pale green ground, orig liner, 5" h, minor flakes .......... 250.00
Planter Bookends, Pine Cone, green........................ 575.00
Rose Bowl, Foxglove, 6" h, pink ............................ 210.00
Sand Jar, Florentine, ivory ground, rust panels and green design,
21" h, minor chips........................................ 260.00
Strawberry Jar, Earlam, green, blue, and peach matte glaze, 8" h,
glaze imperfection to side ................................ 325.00
Sugar, Magnolia, blue .......................................... 95.00
Teapot
Apple Blossom, blue .......................................... 300.00
Magnolia, #4, brown ........................................ 160.00
Zephyr Lily, green, emb mark ............................ 340.00
Tea Set, teapot, creamer and sugar
Magnolia, brown .............................................. 425.00
Persian, ivory matte glaze, tapering handles and tops ....... 550.00
Wincraft, green, 7" h teapot, creamer and sugar each 3" h 130.00
Zephyr Lily, green ............................................ 475.00
Tobacco Jar, cov, ivory ground, two American colonists enjoying long
stemmed pipes, 6" x 5", restored finial ................ 220.00
Umbrella Holder, 20" h, 10" d, cylindrical, raised floral design, matte
green glaze, unsigned........................................ 600.00
Urn
Bittersweet, green, 842-7................................... 150.00
Panel, brown.................................................... 125.00
Pine Cone, blue, 623-3 .................................... 250.00
White Rose, blue, 388-7 .................................... 170.00
Vase
Apple Blossom, 15" h, pink .............................. 360.00
Apple Blossom, 382-7, pink .............................. 155.00
Baneda, 7-1/2" h, green.................................... 475.00

**Vase, Wisteria, corseted, strong mold and color, 10-1/4" h, 7" d, $2,415. Photo courtesy of David Rago Auctions.**

Blackberry, 6" h ................................................... 585.00
Carnelian I, green, 9" h ........................................ 300.00
Carnelian II, raised flared rim, bulbous body, angled scrolled
　handles, mottled matte, mauve, drip glaze, partial paper label,
　1915 .................................................................. 550.00
Cherry Blossom, blue, ball shape ........................ 535.00
Chloron, green suspended matte glass, three legs,
　12-1/4" h ........................................................... 900.00
Clemana, two handles, 6-1/2" h ............................ 200.00
Clematis, 12" h, green, 112-12 ............................. 350.00
Dahlrose, 10" h, brown, orig black paper label ................. 295.00
Della Robbia, cut-back and incised floral design, shades of blue,
　aqua, olive green, brown, and yellow, 10-1/2" h, restoration to
　top and bottom .............................................. 8,000.00
Della Robbia, flaring waisted form, incised and cut-back olive
　green tulips, cut-back aqua background, Rozane wafer, artist
　sgd ................................................................. 1,300.00
Donatello, 5" h ....................................................... 60.00
Egypt, green suspended matte glaze, six arched linked to each
　other, 5-3/4" x 5-1/4" .......................................... 600.00
Foxglove, pink and green, 54-15 ........................... 900.00
Fuchsia, brown, 255-B ........................................... 215.00
Futura, #380-6 ..................................................... 485.00
Imperial I, 71-8 ..................................................... 165.00
Iris, blue, 9" h, 924-9 ........................................... 255.00
Iris, tan, 923-8 ..................................................... 170.00
Jonquil, 523-3 ....................................................... 240.00
Luffa, brown, 683-6 ............................................... 325.00
Magnolia, blue, 86-4 ............................................. 100.00
Magnolia, brown, 184-6 ......................................... 125.00
Montacello, 5-1/4" h, raised rim, oval body, two handles, stylized
　fleur-de-lis motif, cream within brown band, dark blue ovals on
　streaked light green and tan ground, c1931 .................... 435.00
Morning Glory, white, 7" ....................................... 525.00
Mostique, 8" h, incised geometric design, two open
　handles ......................................................... 1,300.00
Mostique, 21" h, stylized white floral design, red center, peach
　ground, dark and light green incised dec ...................... 950.00
Pauleo, 19" h, iris dec, artist sgd "Josephone Imlay" ....... 3,300.00
Pine Cone, blue, 705-9 ......................................... 400.00
Pine Cone, blue, ftd, 425F-5 ................................. 575.00
Pine Cone, blue, 10" h, handles at top, 848-10 ................. 825.00
Pine Cone, blue, 12" h, orig foil label, 712-12 ................. 800.00
Pine Cone, brown, triple bud type, 113-8" .................... 275.00
Pine Cone, brown, 704-7 ....................................... 350.00
Pine Cone, green, 10" h, 749-10410.00 .................... 585.00
Pine Cone, green, 12" h ........................................ 395.00
Rosecraft Panel, 8-1/8" h, raised rim, tapered cylindrical body,
　disk foot, four panels of burnt orange berry and flower laden
　vines, olive green-brown ground, dark blue "R" ink stamp,
　c1920, chip on base ......................................... 230.00
Rozane Fudji, 10" h, 3-3/4" sq, twisted four sided shape,
　squeezebag dec, stylized cobalt blue, green, and ochre flow-
　ers, Rozane wafer seal and "20," small surface abrasion at
　base ............................................................. 2,600.00
Rozane Mongol, three handles, red hi-glaze, wafer mark,
　6-1/4" h ........................................................... 550.00
Rozane Royal, floral dec, hi-glaze, imp mark, artist sgd "M.
　Timberlake," 11" h .............................................. 160.00
Russco, blue, 108-7 ............................................. 145.00
Savona, 6" ........................................................... 150.00
Silhouette, #710-10 ............................................. 325.00
Silhouette, Nude, #74206 .................................... 600.00
Sunflower, 5" h, two long open handles ........................ 400.00
Sunflower, 6" h, 7-1/2" w, broad shouldered form ............ 750.00
Sunflower, 6" w, two open handles ......................... 650.00
Sunflower, 7" h ................................................... 650.00
Thornapple, brown, 813-7 .................................... 140.00
Thornapple, pink, 824-15" .................................... 525.00

Vista, 17-3/4" h, slightly flared rim, bulbed cylindrical body, tropi-
　cal green trees, light blue ground, obscured marks on base,
　c1920, imperfections ....................................... 1,150.00
White Rose, blue, 985-8 ....................................... 235.00
Wincraft, green, 282-8 .......................................... 175.00
Wincraft, tan, 241-6 ............................................. 150.00
Wisteria, 6" h, tan ............................................... 375.00
Wisteria, brown, 631-6 ......................................... 630.00
Woodland, 8-7/8" h, incised and glazed floral and leaf dec, brown
　and gold on stippled unglazed ground, raised ceramic seal,
　c1905, hairlines .............................................. 175.00
Zephyr Lily, 12" h, blue ........................................ 250.00

Wall Pocket
Apple Blossom, green, #366-8" .............................. 185.00
Blackberry, remnant of foil label ......................... 1,450.00
Carnelian I ......................................................... 250.00
Cherry Blossom, unmarked, 6" x 9" ...................... 1,450.00
Corinthian, 8-1/2" h ............................................. 150.00
Dahlrose, 9" h ..................................................... 170.00
Dogwood, 8-1/2" l, unusual form, minor flakes ......... 275.00
Dogwood, 9-1/2" l, stamp mark ............................. 325.00
Egypto, fan shape, unmarked, 8" x 12", glaze nicks ....... 1,045.00
Futura, geometric design, 8" l, minor chip .............. 250.00
Gardenia, brown, #666-8" ..................................... 150.00
Maple Leaf, 8-1/2" ................................................ 75.00
Ming Tree, green, raised mark .............................. 360.00
Mostique, 10" h, tapered cone shape, stylized yellow and brown
　flowers, green leaves, blue band on gray ground, c1915, chips,
　price for pr ...................................................... 400.00
Pine Cone, double, brown, imp mark ...................... 500.00
Snowberry, blue, #1WP-8 ..................................... 180.00
Sunflower, flower pot shape ............................... 1,760.00
Tulips, white ........................................................ 60.00
Wisteria, blue, 7" x 9" ........................................ 1,210.00

Window Box
Tourist, 13" x 7" x 7", three tight hairlines inside corners ....... 1,760.00
Vista, 11-1/2" l, orig liner, molded landscape dec, minute flake to
　top ................................................................. 1,200.00

# ROYAL BAYREUTH

**History:** In 1794, the Royal Bayreuth factory was founded in Tettau, Bavaria. Royal Bayreuth introduced its figural patterns in 1885. Designs of animals, people, fruits, and vegetables decorated a wide array of tablewares and inexpensive souvenir items.

Tapestry wares, in rose and other patterns, were made in the late 19th century. The surface of the piece feels and looks like woven cloth. Tapestry ware was made by covering the porcelain with a piece of fabric tightly stretched over the surface, decorating the fabric, glazing the piece, and firing.

Royal Bayreuth still manufactures dinnerware. It has not maintained production of earlier wares, particularly the figural items. Since thorough records are unavailable, it is difficult to verify the chronology of production.

**Marks:** The Royal Bayreuth crest used to mark the wares varied in design and color.

**References:** Susan and Al Bagdade, *Warman's English & Continental Pottery & Porcelain*, 3rd Edition, Krause Publications, 1998; Mary J. McCaslin, *Royal Bayreuth*, Antique Publications, 1994.

**Collectors' Club:** Royal Bayreuth Collectors Club, 926 Essex Circle, Kalamazoo, MI 49008; Royal Bayreuth International Collectors' Society, P.O. Box 325, Orrville, OH 44667-0325.

Bowl, Dutch children, 6" d .............................................. 65.00
Candlestick, Basset, marked ....................................... 600.00
Cigarette Holder, Oak Leaf, pearl, marked ................. 275.00
Coffeepot, 8" h, 7" w, Brittany girl with draft horse, scene of trees and meadow, blue mark, lid not orig ............................... 450.00
Creamer
    Alligator, white, unmarked............................ 550.00
    Apple............................................................ 250.00
    Bull, red, marked........................................ 150.00
    Butterfly, open wings, brown, orange, gray, and green, 3-1/2" h, blue mark ...................................... 325.00
    Chick, unmarked.......................................... 225.00
    Coachman.................................................... 385.00
    Cow, red...................................................... 300.00
    Crow ............................................................ 300.00
    Dachshund, unmarked................................. 145.00
    Eagle, marked............................................. 450.00
    Fish Head, blue mark.................................. 250.00
    Frog, green, blue mark ............................... 300.00
    Monkey, green, marked ............................... 575.00
    Mountain Goat, marked ............................... 450.00
    Oak Leaf, green luster, Depoinert................ 125.00
    Orange, marked........................................... 175.00
    Parakeet, red, unmarked............................. 275.00
    Pelican ........................................................ 275.00
    Pig, gray, blue mark ................................... 495.00
    Poodle, gray, blue mark .............................. 275.00
    Robin ........................................................... 280.00
    Rococo style, tropical bird scene, blue mark ...................... 125.00
    Rural landscape, figure and turkeys, 4-1/4" h, blue mark ... 115.00
    Seal, blue mark........................................... 400.00
    Scenic, dogs hunting moose scene, 3-1/2" h, mkd............. 100.00
    Shell, purple, seahorse handle ................... 225.00
    St. Bernard, unmarked................................ 350.00
Creamer and Sugar, figural, oyster and pearl ............ 475.00
Cup and Saucer, Shell, ftd, blue mark ....................... 165.00
Dresser Box, cov, 3" x 4-1/2", 3 gold feet, peacock dec ............. 250.00
Ferner, ftd, ornate, Hunter with Dog, in Tree, gold trim, blue mark...450.00
Hair Receiver, Mountain Goat scene, ruffled, blue mark ........... 156.00
Humidor, cov
    Coachman, blue mark................................. 795.00
    Gorilla, black, blue mark ........................... 1,075.00
Lamp, 9" h, porcelain base, seated semi-nude Fairy, brass fittings, figural dolphin feet............................ 400.00
Letter Rack, cows, unmarked ..................................... 465.00
Match Holder
    Arab on horseback, another horse beside him ............... 175.00

**Creamer, Bull, $195.**

Elk, brown .................................................................. 250.00
Milk Pitcher, snail ...................................................... 300.00
Pitcher
    3-1/4" h, Highland Goats............................ 165.00
    4" h, Little Jack Horner............................... 165.00
Plate, Strawberry, 8" d .............................................. 165.00
Playing Card Box, ship scene .................................... 150.00
Salt and Pepper Shakers, pr, radish, figural ............. 350.00
Shoe, figural, black, mkd, price for pr ....................... 300.00
String Holder, rooster, marked ................................... 500.00
Sugar, cov
    Orange, figural, blue mark .......................... 375.00
    Pansy, purple, tiny rim flake....................... 225.00
Sugar, open, double rooster, unmarked...................... 425.00
Teapot, cov, figural, pansy, purple, blue mark ........... 625.00
Tea Trivet, Sand Babies, sgd .................................... 95.00
Toothpick, ovoid, side handle, Dutch boy and goose, mkd........ 200.00
Vase, 4" h, scenic, boy sitting between two donkeys, blue mark .. 95.00
Water Pitcher, Pelican................................................ 1,400.00

## Patterns
Devil & Cards
    Candy Dish .................................................. 195.00
    Creamer........................................................ 250.00
    Cup and Saucer........................................... 175.00
    Dresser Tray ................................................ 250.00
    Milk Pitcher ................................................. 500.00
    Salt, master.................................................. 175.00
Grape Cluster
    Cracker Jar, cov, white pearl, blue mark...... 675.00
    Creamer and Sugar, purple .......................... 395.00
    Salt and Pepper Shakers, pr, purple............ 165.00
    Wall Pocket.................................................. 500.00
Lobster, red
    Ashtray......................................................... 60.00
    Bowl, 8" d, blue mark.................................. 375.00
    Creamer........................................................ 75.00
    Radish Bowl, 5" d, blue mark....................... 275.00
Poppy
    Cake Plate, white pearl, open handles ......... 225.00
    Creamer, red................................................ 145.00
    Match Holder, standing, red.......................... 550.00
    Sugar, cov.................................................... 225.00
Red Clown
    Ashtray, blue mark ...................................... 345.00
    Candlestick, 6 1/2 x 4-1/2".......................... 525.00
    Creamer, blue mark ..................................... 450.00
    Match Holder, hanging, blue mark ................ 425.00
    Mug, unmarked............................................ 435.00
Red Devil
    Ashtray, blue mark ...................................... 165.00
    Creamer, blue mark ..................................... 550.00
Snowbabies
    Cereal Set, sledding .................................... 175.00
    Plate, 6" d, babies playing .......................... 85.00
    Salt Shaker ................................................. 120.00
    Trivet, Snowbabies, blue mark...................... 110.00
Sunbonnet Babies
    Bell, sewing, unmarked................................ 400.00
    Candlestick, babies ironing.......................... 300.00
    Creamer and Sugar, open, price for pr ......... 475.00
    Cup and Saucer, babies sewing ................... 155.00
    Hatpin Holder............................................... 250.00
    Plate, 9" d, washing clothes......................... 245.00
Tomato
    Biscuit Jar, cov............................................ 200.00
    Bowl, 5-1/2" d, green leaf............................ 35.00
    Creamer and Sugar ..................................... 75.00
    Cup and Saucer........................................... 115.00
    Mustard Jar, lettuce leaf underplate, blue mark.......... 100.00

**Pitcher, pastoral scene, blue mark, 5" h, $365.**

| | |
|---|---|
| Salad Bowl, large | 395.00 |
| Tea Set, 4-1/2" h cov teapot, 3" h creamer, 5-1/2" d plate with open handle, 3-1/2" h sugar, 3" h x 4" d cov waste bowl | 250.00 |
| Water Pitcher, marked | 315.00 |

## Tapestry

Basket

| | |
|---|---|
| 3" h, three colored roses | 400.00 |
| 5" h, reticulated base, three colored roses | 440.00 |
| Boot, three colored roses | 550.00 |
| Box, cov, round, dome lid, three color roses, shape #1187 | 400.00 |
| Candleholder, three color roses, shape #1251 | 860.00 |
| Chocolate Set, chocolate pot, four matching cup and saucers, three color roses, blue mark, price for 10 pc set | 2,800.00 |

Creamer

| | |
|---|---|
| 2-1/2" h, red roses | 250.00 |
| 3-1/2" h, The Bathers, shape #1038 | 285.00 |
| 3-3/4" h, lady's portrait | 350.00 |
| 4" h, multicolored roses, mkd | 150.00 |
| 4" h, pinched spout, Hounds and Stag | 350.00 |
| Cup and Saucer, three color roses | 400.00 |
| Dish, Colonial Couple, maple leaf shape | 225.00 |

Dresser Tray

| | |
|---|---|
| Japanese chrysanthemum dec, leaf shape | 225.00 |
| Roses, large, blue mark | 350.00 |
| Hair Receiver, roses | 325.00 |

Match Holder, hanging

| | |
|---|---|
| Roses | 365.00 |
| Sheep, shape #1059 | 485.00 |
| Mug, 3-3/8" h, roses, gold handle, blue mark | 325.00 |
| Nappy, 5" w, clover shape, handle, multicolored roses, mkd | 75.00 |

Plate

| | |
|---|---|
| 7-1/2" d, goats scene, mkd | 150.00 |
| 7-3/4" d, pink roses, mkd | 150.00 |
| Powder Dish, cov, 5-1/2" x 3-1/2", colonial couple dancing | 495.00 |
| Relish, 8" l, Chrysanthemum, handles | 375.00 |

Shoe

| | |
|---|---|
| Roses and figures dec | 550.00 |
| Three colored roses | 550.00 |
| Sugar, cov, pink roses, shape #1310 | 220.00 |
| Sugar, matching underplate | 450.00 |
| Teapot, three color roses | 650.00 |

Vase

| | |
|---|---|
| 4-1/2" h, Christmas Cactus | 325.00 |
| 7-1/2" h, Pheasant Tapestry, gold handles, blue mark | 425.00 |

# ROYAL BONN

**History:** In 1836, Franz Anton Mehlem founded a Rhineland factory that produced earthenware and porcelain, including household, decorative, technical, and sanitary items.

The firm reproduced Hochst figures between 1887 and 1903. These figures, in both porcelain and earthenware, were made from the original molds from the defunct Prince-Electoral Mayence Manufactory in Hochst. The factory was purchased by Villeroy and Boch in 1921 and closed in 1931.

**Marks:** In 1890, the word "Royal" was added to the mark. All items made after 1890 include the "Royal Bonn" mark.

| | |
|---|---|
| Biscuit Jar, 6 5/8" h, 5-1/4" d, floral dec, beige and cream color ground, rose, purple, and yellow flowers, green leaves, emb scrolls | 210.00 |
| Bowl, 9-1/2" d, cream, floral dec, metal rim, c1760 | 195.00 |
| Cachepot, 10" w, 7" h, vasiform, Aesthetic taste floral design, sgd, c1891-1900 | 300.00 |
| Celery Tray, floral dec | 85.00 |
| Cheese Dish, cov, pink, floral design | 125.00 |
| Cup and Saucer, blue and white, wild roses dec | 45.00 |

Ewer

| | |
|---|---|
| 6-1/2" h, gold handle, floral tapestry, scene with brick fence | 150.00 |
| 10-3/8" h, large red and pink flowers, raised gold, fancy handle | 75.00 |
| Garniture Vase, 12-1/2" h, enameled and parcel-gilt, ivory porcelain, baluster form, c1890-95 | 150.00 |
| Mug, 4" h, blackberries and flowers, shaded green ground | 65.00 |
| Spittoon, two cartouches with Oriental scenes | 150.00 |
| Teapot, 4-1/2" x 9-1/2", cream, red, black, and blue florals, gold trim, marked "1755" | 125.00 |
| Urn, 15-1/2" h, two handles, floral still life, gilded mask-form handles, paw feet, shaped base, c1900 | 320.00 |

**Vase, pink and lavender orchids, green foliage, gold outlines, 8" h, $100. Photo courtesy of Joy Luke Fine Art Brokers and Auctioneers.**

Vase
    5-1/2" h, Victorian boy and girl sledding, shaded fuchsia ground .............................................................. 150.00
    7" h, globular, Boucher scenes, blue transfers, 1850 ......... 125.00
    8" h, pink and lavender orchids, gold outlines .................... 100.00
    8-1/4" h, portrait type, artist sgd .......................................... 795.00
    9-1/2" h, floral and gilt dec, blues and greens .................... 100.00
    11" h, green glossy ground, blue floral enameled dec ........ 450.00
    11-1/2" h, gourd shape, hp, numbered, orchids dec, gold border, c1900 .................................................................. 155.00
    13" h, baluster form, gilt loop handles, bulbous shaped neck, floral cartouche, green, royal blue, and gilt ground, pr.550.00

# ROYAL COPENHAGEN

c1889    c1923

**History:** Franz Mueller established a porcelain factory at Copenhagen in 1775. When bankruptcy threatened in 1779, the Danish king acquired ownership, appointing Mueller manager and selecting the name "Royal Copenhagen." The crown sold its interest in 1867; the company remains privately owned today.

Blue Fluted, Royal Copenhagen's most famous pattern, was created in 1780. It is of Chinese origin and comes in three styles: smooth edge, closed lace edge, and perforated lace edge (full lace). Many other factories copied it.

Flora Danica, named for a famous botanical work, was introduced in 1789 and remained exclusive to Royal Copenhagen. It is identified by its freehand illustrations of plants and its hand-cut edges and perforations.

**Reference:** Robert J. Heritage, *Royal Copenhagen Porcelain: Animals and Figurines,* Schiffer Publishing, 1997.

**Marks:** Royal Copenhagen porcelain is marked with three wavy lines (which signify ancient waterways) and a crown (added in 1889). Stoneware does not have the crown mark.

**Additional Listings:** Limited Edition Collector Plates.

Bowl, 4-1/2" d, orange blossoms, green leaves ........................... 115.00
Box, cov, egg shape, seagulls on cov ......................................... 195.00
Chocolate Cup and Saucer, Flora Danica, raised paneled border, enamel dec botanical design, titled on reverse, 20th C, set of 12 ............ 4,325.00
Crocus Pot, 8-1/2" l, armorial dec, white and gilt ground, red highlights, lion form mounts, 19th C .......................................... 400.00
Cup and Saucer, Blue Fluted Full Lace ...................................... 100.00
Cup, covered, stand, 3-1/4" h, Floral Danica, triangular, raised paneled border, enameled dec botanical design, titled on reverse ........ 865.00
Dessert Service, blue floral imbricated border, coffeepot, creamer, cov sugar, cake tray, fruit bowl, 12 cake plates, cups, and saucers ..... 450.00
Dinner Service
    Blue fluted half lace pattern, service for 8, cups and saucers, dinner plates, bread and butter plates, teapot, sq vegetable, meat platter, serving bowl, nappy, tri-part dish, butter pats, creamer, sugar, and waste bowl, price for 43 pc set .................... 1,600.00
    Blue foliate sprays, molded basketweave borders, dinner, luncheon, bread and butter, salad plates, tea, coffee, and demitasse cups and saucers, tea set, soup bowls, 19 additional pieces, price for 175 pc set ............................................. 2,645.00

Figure
    Boy, sitting on rocks, whittling stick, sgd on back of rocks, #905, 7-1/2" h ............................................................ 275.00
    Goose Girl, #528 ............................................................... 210.00
    Mouse, sugar cubes ............................................................ 65.00
    Nude on Rock, #4027 ........................................................ 150.00
    Pan, sitting on column, holding flute, rabbit at base, 8-1/2" h .. 375.00
    Pekinese, tan and white, begging on haunches, #1776 ..... 150.00
    Satyr, holding snake, sitting, #1712, 3 x 5" ........................ 225.00
    Siamese Cat, #3281, seated, 7-3/4" h ............................... 195.00
    Witch and soldier, #1112, 8" h .......................................... 500.00
Fruit Compote, Floridian pattern, "Potentilla Nivea L." inscribed underneath bowl .................................................................. 550.00
Jardiniere, 13" h, anemones dec, 1890s ...................................... 275.00
Luncheon Service, partial, Floral Danica, 11-1/2" d cov tureen, twelve 9" d luncheon plates, fourteen coffee cups and saucers, two 3" d butter pats, 20th C .................................................... 14,950.00
Monteith, 13-1/8" l, painted with botanical specimens, printed inscriptions, modern, hairline ................................................... 980.00
Plate
    Blue Fluted Full Lace
    Bread and butter ................................................................ 40.00
    Dinner ............................................................................... 85.00
    Salad ................................................................................. 60.00
Flora Danica, raised paneled border, enamel dec botanical design, titled on reverse, 20th C
    5-3/4" d, set of 12 ........................................................ 2,875.00
    7-3/4" d, set of 12 ........................................................ 3,680.00
    9" d, set of 12 .............................................................. 5,575.00
    10" d, set of 12 ............................................................ 7,590.00
Platter, 17-1/4" l, oval, Flora Danica pattern, marked and numbered .............................................................................. 450.00
Serving Dish, 14-1/4" d, raised paneled border and enamel dec botanical design, titled on reverse ................................................. 1,610.00
Tea Set, Fluted Lace pattern, blue and white, price for 5 pc set . 295.00
Tray, 6-1/2" d, round, rose, fish swimming ................................... 150.00
Vase
    7" h, mermaid on rocks, gazing into harbor .......................... 95.00
    7-3/4" h, floral and dragonfly dec, c1890 .......................... 150.00
    11-3/8" h, swollen cylindrical shape, green, blue, white, and brown wildflowers, hilly landscape in background, blue shaded ground, #2549/1148 ....................................................... 300.00

# ROYAL CROWN DERBY

**History:** Derby Crown Porcelain Co., established in 1875 in Derby, England, had no connection with earlier Derby factories which operated in the late 18th and early 19th centuries. In 1890, the company was appointed "Manufacturers of Porcelain to Her Majesty" (Queen Victoria) and since that date has been known as "Royal Crown Derby."

Most of these porcelains, both tableware and figural, were hand decorated. A variety of printing processes were used for additional adornment. Today, Royal Crown Derby is a part of Royal Doulton Tableware, Ltd.

**References:** Susan and Al Bagdade, *Warman's English & Continental Pottery & Porcelain*, 3rd Edition, Krause Publications, 1998; John Twitchett, *Dictionary of Derby Porcelain 1748-1848*, Antique Collectors' Club; John Twitchett and Betty Bailey, *Royal Crown Derby*, Antique Collectors' Club, 1988.

**Museums:** Cincinnati Art Museum, Cincinnati, OH; Gardiner Museum of Ceramic Art, Toronto, Canada; Royal Crown Derby Museum, Osmaston Road, Derby; Derby Museums & Art Gallery, The Strand, Derby; Victoria & Albert Museum, London, England.

**Marks:** Derby porcelains from 1878 to 1890 carry only the standard crown printed mark. After 1891, the mark includes the "Royal Crown Derby" wording. In the 20th century, "Made in England" and "English Bone China" were added to the mark.

Bowl, Chinoiserie dec, four small feet ......................................... 145.00
Creamer and Sugar, cov, Dublin shape, Imari pattern ................ 300.00
Cup and Saucer ............................................................................. 60.00
Demitasse Cup and Saucer .......................................................... 50.00
Dessert Service, eleven 9-1/4" d plates, three 9-1/2" ftd plates, each painted with varying foliate sprays, last quarter 19th C ......... 2,415.00
Ewer, 7-1/2" h, raised gold dec on reticulated cobalt blue neck and handle, enameled flowers on gold ground ............................... 675.00
Figure, 10-1/4" h, young man, foot on lap of woman, polychrome and gilt, edge chips on foliage ......................................................... 300.00
Jar, cov, 12" h, globular form, enamel and gilt dec floral design, c1890 ....................................................................................... 1,150.00
Plate, 8-1/4" d, Japan pattern, No. 2451, price for 8 pc set ........ 115.00
Tea Cup and Saucer, 2-1/4" h cup, Japan pattern, price for 14 pc set ............................................................................................... 115.00
Urn, cov, 5" h, yellow ground, leaves and butterflies, molded mask handles, 1887 ............................................................................ 425.00
Vase, cov, 12" h, 8" w, bulbous, raised fruit and leaf dec around handles on body, irregular gilt edge at top resembles waves, raised fruit and gilt bows around neck, delicate gilt flowers on green ground, line drawings of leaves and flowers with some raised leaves on body, raised gilt wavy design around base, round green cov with raised gilt flowers, orange mark 3718786, incised 786D/D, made for J. E. Caldwell and Co., Philadelphia, c1891 ....................................... 3,800.00
Vase
    8" h, 6" w, bulbous, Imari pattern, cobalt border at top with gilt dec, 1-1/4" band of cobalt blue with geometric designs in white and orange, gilt panels and cobalt blue panel with white flower with orange lines alternating, center cartouche in cobalt blue with gilt swirls and white flowers with orange accents, cobalt blue base with gilt leaf design, mkd "Royal Crown Derby, England" in orange, incised numbers, c1911 .................. 875.00
    8-1/4" h, bottle form, enamel and gilt dec fruits, flowers, and foliage, c1887 ................................................................................. 450.00

# ROYAL DOULTON

**History:** Doulton pottery began in 1815 under the direction of John Doulton at the Doulton & Watts pottery in Lambeth, England. Early output was limited to salt-glazed industrial stoneware. After John Watts retired in 1854, the firm became Doulton and Company, and production was expanded to include hand-decorated stoneware such as figurines, vases, dinnerware, and flasks.

In 1878, John's son, Sir Henry Doulton, purchased Pinder Bourne & Co. in Burslem. The companies became Doulton & Co., Ltd. in 1882. Decorated porcelain was added to Doulton's earthenware production in 1884.

Most Doulton figurines were produced at the Burslem plants, where they were made continuously from 1890 until 1978. After a short interruption, a new line of Doulton figurines was introduced in 1979.

Dickens ware, in earthenware and porcelain, was introduced in 1908. The pieces were decorated with characters from Dickens's novels. Most of the line was withdrawn in the 1940s, except for plates which continued to be made until 1974.

Character jugs, a 20th-century revival of early Toby models, were designed by Charles J. Noke for Doulton in the 1930s. Character jugs are limited to bust portraits, while Royal Doulton toby jugs are full figured. The character jugs come in four sizes and feature fictional characters from Dickens, Shakespeare and other English and American novelists, as well as historical heroes. Marks on both character and toby jugs must be carefully identified to determine dates and values.

Doulton's Rouge Flambé (Veined Sung) is a high-glazed, strong-colored ware noted primarily for the fine modeling and exquisite colorings, especially in the animal items. The process used to produce the vibrant colors is a Doulton secret.

Production of stoneware at Lambeth ceased in 1956; production of porcelain continues today at Burslem.

**Marks:** Beginning in 1872, the "Royal Doulton" mark was used on all types of wares produced by the company.

Beginning in 1913, an "HN" number was assigned to each new Doulton figurine design. The "HN" numbers, which referred originally to Harry Nixon, a Doulton artist, were chronological until 1940, after which blocks of numbers were assigned to each modeler. From 1928 until 1954, a small number was placed to the right of the crown mark; this number added to 1927 gives the year of manufacture.

**References:** Susan and Al Bagdade, *Warman's English & Continental Pottery & Porcelain*, 3rd Edition, Krause Publications, 1998; Diana and John Callow and Marilyn and Peter Sweet, *Charlton Price Guide to Beswick Animals*, 2nd ed., Charlton Press, 1995; Jean Dale, *Charlton Standard Catalogue of Royal Doulton Animals*, 2nd ed., Charlton Press, 1998; ——, *Charlton Standard Catalogue of Royal Doulton Beswick Figurines*, 6th ed., Charlton Press, 1998; ——, *Charlton Standard Catalogue of Royal Doulton Beswick Jugs*, 5th ed., Charlton Press, 1999; ——, *Charlton Standard Catalogue of Royal Doulton Beswick Storybook Figurines*, 5th ed., Charlton Press, 1999; ——, *Charlton Standard Catalogue of Royal Doulton Figurines*, 4th ed., Charlton Press, 1994; ——, *Charlton Standard Catalogue of Royal Doulton Jugs*, Charlton Press, 1991; Jean Dale and Louise Irvine, *Charlton Standard Catalogue of Royal Doulton Bunnykins,* Charlton Press, 1999; Doug Pinchin, *Doulton Figure Collectors Handbook*, 4th ed., Francis-Joseph Books, 1996.

**Periodicals:** *Collecting Doulton*, BBR Publishing, 2 Strattford Ave., Elsecar, Nr Barnsley, S. Yorkshire, S74 8AA, England; *Doulton Divvy*, P.O. Box 2434, Joliet, IL 60434.

**Collectors' Clubs:** Heartland Doulton Collectors, P.O. Box 2434, Joliet, IL 60434; Mid-America Doulton Collectors,

P.O. Box 483, McHenry, IL 60050; Royal Doulton International Collectors Club, 700 Cottontail Lane, Somerset, NJ 08873; Royal Doulton International Collectors Club, 850 Progress Ave., Scarborough Ontario M1H 3C4 Canada.

Animal
Cat, HN2580 .................................................. 50.00
Cocker Spaniel with pheasant, HN1137 ........... 475.00
Duck, flambé, #7, 3-1/2" h ........................... 150.00
Pheasant, HN2577 ....................................... 325.00
Biscuit Jar, cov, 6" x 7-3/4", ribbed cream ground, band of turquoise with birds and animals, SP top, rim, and handle, marked "Doulton, Burslem Pottery" .................................................. 225.00
Bowl, 8-7/8" x 4-1/4", blue, brown geometric borders, grazing cows and horses, sgd "Hannah Barlow, 1885" ................................... 675.00
Dinnerware
Creamer, Glamis Thistle ................................. 30.00
Cup and Saucer, Glen Auldyn ........................ 30.00
Plate, bread and butter, Glen Auldyn ............... 12.00
Plate, dinner, Glen Auldyn ............................. 25.00
Plate, salad, Glen Auldyn .............................. 20.00
Sugar, open, Glamis Thistle ........................... 30.00
Ewer, 9" h, Babes in Wood Series, girl with cape in woods ..... 1,250.00
Figure
Adirenne, HN2152 ....................................... 160.00
Ascot, HN2356 ............................................ 175.00
Autumn, HN2087 ......................................... 450.00
Balloon Man .............................................. 200.00
Bess, HN2002 ............................................ 350.00
Blithe Morning, HN2021 ............................... 245.00
Blue Beard, HN2105 .................................... 650.00
Bonnie Lassie, HN1626 ............................... 550.00
Bridesmaid, M12 ........................................ 425.00
Bunny, HN 2214, 5-1/4" h ............................ 160.00
Camelia, HN2222 ........................................ 225.00
Carolyn, HN2112 ........................................ 350.00
Carrie, HN2800 .......................................... 225.00
Celeste, HN2237 ........................................ 240.00
Christmas Time, HN2110 .............................. 425.00
Cookie, HN2218 ......................................... 150.00
Coralie, HN2307 ......................................... 140.00
Daffy-Down Dilly, HN1712 ............................ 425.00
Darling, HN1319 ......................................... 190.00
Day Dreams, HN1731 .................................. 300.00
Dinky Do, HN 1678, 4-1/2" h ......................... 400.00
Emma, HN2834 .......................................... 225.00
Faith, HN3082 ............................................ 175.00
First Dance, HN2803 ................................... 215.00
Fleur, HN2368 ........................................... 200.00
Gail, HN2937 ............................................. 325.00
Goody Two Shoes, M81 ............................. 1,275.00
June, HN2027, restored ............................... 575.00
Kathy, HN2346 .......................................... 160.00
Laura, HN2960 ........................................... 175.00
Laurianne, HN2719 ..................................... 175.00
Lilac Time, HN2137 ..................................... 385.00
Marguerite, HN1928 .................................... 475.00
Maureen, M85 ......................................... 1,400.00
Melaine, 8" h, fully signed, 1964 ................... 150.00
Merely a Minor, HN2531, gray, 12" h, orig sticker ..... 750.00
Midsummer Noon, HN2033 ........................... 625.00
Pauline, HN2441 ........................................ 200.00
Penelope, HN1901 ...................................... 360.00
Primroses, HN1617 .................................. 1,100.00
Roseanna, HN1926 ..................................... 425.00
Silks & Ribbons, HN2017 ............................. 250.00
Solitude, HN2810 ....................................... 250.00
Sonia, HN1692 ........................................ 1,600.00
Spring Flowers, HN1807 .............................. 350.00

Spring Morning, HN1922 .............................. 275.00
Suitor, HN2132 .......................................... 385.00
Susan, HN2952 .......................................... 185.00
Symphony, HN2287 ..................................... 250.00
The Ballerina, HN 2216, 7-1/4" h ................... 120.00
The Last Waltz, HN 2315, 8" h ...................... 225.00
Top of the Hill, HN1849 ............................... 190.00
Vanity, HN2475 .......................................... 120.00
Victorian Lady, M1 ...................................... 400.00
Wizard, HN2877 ......................................... 400.00
Jug, large
Auld Mack, "A" ............................................ 85.00
Catherine Parr .......................................... 135.00
Jane Seymour ........................................... 115.00
Leprechaun ............................................... 125.00
Ringmaster ............................................... 175.00
Romeo ..................................................... 100.00
Scaramouche, 2nd version ........................... 125.00
Sir Thomas Moore ...................................... 160.00
Trapper .................................................... 100.00
Jug, miniature
Bacchus .................................................... 50.00
Eli ........................................................... 55.00
Falconer ................................................... 50.00
Falstaff ..................................................... 50.00
Gone Away ................................................ 55.00
Henry VIII .................................................. 75.00
John Peel "A" ............................................. 80.00
Lobsterman ............................................... 45.00
Long John Silver ......................................... 50.00
Merlin ...................................................... 50.00
N. A. Indian ............................................... 55.00
Tam O Shanter ........................................... 75.00
Jug, small
Arman ...................................................... 86.00
Earl Mountbaten of Burma ........................... 100.00
Lumberjack ................................................ 60.00
Neptune .................................................... 50.00
N. A. Indian ............................................... 55.00
Pearly King ................................................ 65.00
Pearly Queen ............................................. 65.00
Poacher, flow rim ........................................ 50.00
Rip Van Winkle ........................................... 55.00
Sailor ....................................................... 65.00
Sleuth ...................................................... 55.00
Smuggler ................................................... 60.00
Soldier ...................................................... 65.00
Tam O Shanter ........................................... 65.00
Trapper ..................................................... 55.00
Viscount Montgomery of Alamein ................... 100.00

**Plate, horse motif, deep gold glaze, 1907, 9-3/4" d, $75.**

Mustard Pot, 3-1/2" h, handle, brown and tan stoneware, relief dogs and figurals, Lambeth, lid damaged ......................................... 175.00
Plate, 10-3/4" d, bone china, crinolated edge, fluted molding, central floral dec, turquoise ground, gilt accents, 20th C, price for 14 pcs..........300.00
Salt Cellar, 3-1/8" l, stoneware, hexagonal, stepped foot, sgd "Emily J. Edwards," imp mark, c1872, foot rim chips ............................. 115.00
Spittoon
    European landscape, blue and white, sgd "Geneva" ..........275.00
    Landscape scene, brown and green luster ........................ 160.00
    Poppies, inner border with grapes and leaves.................... 110.00
Teapot, two pansy reserves and pale flowers dec, gilt handle, marked "Doulton Burslem," late 19th or early 20th C ........................... 190.00
Toby, large
    Auld Mac, "A" ........................................................ 115.00
    Lumberjack ............................................................ 150.00
    Neptune ................................................................ 125.00
Toothpick Holder
    Doulton Burslem, flowers, gold trim ............................. 90.00
    Gamp .................................................................... 510.00
Umbrella Stand, 24" h, 9" w, cylinder, tapering top, blue birds and flowers, ivory ground, imp and printed mark.................................500.00
Vase
    6-1/2" x 9", double handle, Margueterie pattern, blue/gray ground, gold leaf.............................................................. 475.00
    9" h, Welsh Ladies ................................................ 295.00
Water Filter, cov, 13-3/4" h, Silicon stoneware, brown ground, light blue, gray/blue, and white imp and applied foliate and floral relief below white classical dancing figures, imp Doulton Lambeth mark, c1885, nick to cover rim .......................................... 500.00

# ROYAL DUX

**History:** Royal Dux porcelain was made in Dux, Bohemia (now the Czech Republic), by E. Eichler at the Duxer Porzellan-Manufaktur, established in 1860. Many items were exported to the United States. By the turn of the century Royal Dux figurines, vases, and accessories, especially those featuring Art Nouveau designs, were captivating consumers.

**Marks:** A raised triangle with an acorn and the letter "E" plus "Dux, Bohemia" was used as a mark between 1900 and 1914.

Bust, 18-1/2" h, woman adorned with flowers, Czechoslovakia, c1915 ......................................................................460.00
Calling Card Receiver, 4", figural, frog standing on large open shell, beige, matte finish, pink triangle mark...................................... 125.00
Candlestick, 13" h, figural, boy wearing knickers.......................... 175.00
Centerpiece, 11 x 4-1/4" x 7-3/4", pr of kneeling nudes, central flared base, creamy white, cobalt blue, and gold trim ...................... 450.00
Compote, 20 5/8" h, three dancing female figures, emb bowl and base, sgd ........................................................................ 750.00
Dresser Mirror, 25" x 14", figure of two cupids, shell dish holding beveled mirror ...............................................................1,600.00
Figure
    Bulldog, raised pink triangle "Royal Dux Bohemia," blue stamped circle "Czech Republic," #6, #652, #536 ..........................120.00
    Elephant, 10" x 13", trunk up ................................................. 190.00
    Fox, 4" x 8", glossy glaze, post-war mark ........................... 180.00
    Gentleman, simulated ivory colored ground, early 20th C, 16-3/4" h ..............................................................575.00
    Grecian Woman, 8-1/2" h, classic Greek-style clothing, pre-war "E" mark .................................................................. 335.00
    Hunting Dogs, 7-1/2" h, 11-1/4" l, hp, natural colors and pose..........................................................................255.00

Lady, sedan chair, 2 courtiers, hound, 14" x 8-1/2" x 15-1/2" ..800.00
Male, 12" h, bird in right hand, hp ...................................... 110.00
Male, 12-1/2" h, 4-1/2" w, playing flute, imp #198.............. 135.00
Peasant Couple, 12" h, matte glaze, pre-war marking, male damaged and repaired.....................................................395.00
Polar Bear, 10" h, 13" l, detailed expression, back stamp numbered 3/8/4.66.16 with "R" and pink triangle with Royal Dux Bohemia D, circle with triangle inside mkd "Hand Painted, Made in Czech Republic" .............................................. 250.00
Retriever, duck in jaws, 14" l, matte finish ......................... 400.00
Sled Dog Team, 9" x 8", three tethered dogs, pre-war "E" mark .................................................................. 1,295.00
Stork, 8" h, orig sticker, mkd "353" and "82" ...................... 65.00
Woman, 9" h, bright colors, high gloss, "Made in Czechoslovakia," pink triangular mark............................................. 285.00
Pin Tray, figural, Art Nouveau maiden on wave ................. 325.00
Serving Dish, 8-1/2" h, open shell-shape, maiden and lovebirds dec ........................................................................230.00
Tobacco Jar, 8" h, figural, man's head, wearing nightcap, smoking pipe ........................................................................200.00
Vase
    6-1/2" h, 3-3/4" l, Art Deco, orig gold sticker, back stamp "Royal Dux Bohemia, Hand Painted, Made In Czech Republic," raised, pink triangle. #11295, 3, 6 numbers under glaze, designed by V. Serak.................................................................. 70.00
    16" h, 5-1/2" d, Grecian maid with drapery on front, heavily gold embellished, creamy white, rust colored vines, leaves, and flower on back, 1arge raised pink triangle mark "Royal Dux Bohemia" with an "E" in center, c1900-18, some glaze wear, wear to gold edging, minor repair to hand........................ 700.00

# ROYAL FLEMISH

**History:** Royal Flemish was produced by the Mount Washington Glass Co., New Bedford, Massachusetts. The process was patented by Albert Steffin in 1894.

Royal Flemish is a frosted transparent glass with heavy raised gold enamel lines. These lines form sections—often colored in russet tones—giving the appearance of stained-glass windows with elaborate floral or coin medallions.

**Collectors' Club:** Mount Washington Art Glass Society, 60 President Ave., Providence, RI 02906.

**Advisors:** Clarence and Betty Maier.

Biscuit Jar, cov, 8" h, ovoid, large Roman coins on stained panels, divided by heavy gold lines, ornate SP cov, rim, and bail handle, orig paper label "Mt. W. G. Co. Royal Flemish"........................... 1,750.00
Box, cov, 5-1/2" d, 3-3/4" h, swirled border, gold outlined swirls, gold tracery blossoms, enameled blossom with jeweled center on lid ......................................................................... 1,500.00

**Ewer, sepia colored body, eight vertical panels framed in heavy raised gold, four panels tinted pale mauve, alternating with four smoky-gray panels, raised gold tendril laden with multi-petaled blossoms of encrusted gold and tinted autumn leaves, raised gold stylized floral dec on cerise spout, frosted clear-glass handle, very slight loss of gold on rim and raised lines, 12" h, 5-1/2" d, $7,500. Photo courtesy of Clarence & Betty Maier.**

**Ewer**

10-1/2" h, 9" w, 5" d, circular semi-transparent panel on front with youth thrusting spear into chest of winged creature, reverse panel shows mythical fish created with tail changed into stylized florals, raised gold dec, outlines, and scrolls, rust, purple, and gold curlicues, twisted rope handle with brushed gold encircles neck, hp minute gold florals on neck, burnished gold stripes on rim spout and panels ..................................................... 4,950.00

12" h, 5-1/2" d, sepia colored body, eight vertical panels framed in heavy raised gold, four panels tinted pale mauve, alternating with four smoky-gray panels, raised gold tendril laden with multi-petaled blossoms of encrusted gold and tinted autumn leaves, raised gold stylized floral dec on cerise spout, frosted clear-glass handle, very slight loss of gold on rim and raised lines .................. 7,500.00

**Jar**, 8" h, classical Roman coin medallion dec, simulated stained glass panels, SP rim, bail, and cov, paper label "Mt. W. G. Co. Royal Flemish" ................................................... 1,650.00

**Vase**

4-1/2" h, 5-1/2" d, raised rim, applied angular handles, bulbous transparent colorless body, overall gold and silvered metallic coin medallions, raised gold enamel outlines and accents, partial label .................. 2,650.00

6-1/2" h, 6" d, stylized scrolls of pastel violet, two tiny handles at neck, realistically tinted sprays of violets randomly strewn around frosted clear glass body, gold lines define violet nosegays and frame scrolls, gold daubed accents, logo and "0583" ............................ 2,200.00

7-1/2" h, 7-1/2" d, squatty, smaller squatty form as collar, 14 pastel pansies, clear frosted ground, 4 rayed suns, painted foliage-like gold tracery .................. 1,400.00

13" h, classic handled oval body, gilt enameled panels and medallions, center star-studded scene of cameo with ethnic-costumed rider, body guard with scimitar, Mid-Eastern scrolls and devices on reverse .................. 13,800.00

## ROYAL RUDOLSTADT

**History:** Johann Fredrich von Schwarzburg-Rudolstadt was the patron of a faience factory located in Rudolstadt, Thuringen, Germany, from 1720 to c1790.

In 1854, Ernst Bohne established a factory in Rudolstadt.

The "Royal Rudolstadt" designation originated with wares which Lewis Straus and Sons (later Nathan Straus and Sons) of New York imported from the New York and Rudolstadt Pottery between 1887 and 1918. The factory manufactured several of the Rose O'Neill (Kewpie) items.

**Marks:** The first mark of the original pottery was a hayfork; later, crossed two-prong hayforks were used in imitation of the Meissen mark.

"EB" was the mark used by Ernst Bohne.

A crown over a diamond enclosing the initials "RW" is the mark used by the New York and Rudolstadt Pottery.

**Bowl**

7-1/4" d, white roses, green leaves, yellow centers, light green to white shaded int., 3 gold feet, crown and "B" mark ............ 70.00

9-1/8" d, paneled, hummingbird with blue wings, yellow tail, green branch chrysanthemums and peonies on int., black outlined blue luster border, yellow luster int. rim ............................. 20.00

**Cake Plate**

10-1/4" d, hp, white flowers ................................................. 75.00

12" w, large roses, open handles ........................................ 195.00

**Celery Dish**, 13" l, handles, hp, yellow roses, gold trim, artist sgd ................................................. 90.00

**Creamer and Sugar**, cov, purple pansies, cream ground, gold trim .................. 85.00

**Dresser Set**, tray, hatpin holder, hair receiver, hp camellias, green leaves, pastels, gold trim, imp mark "Royal Rudolstadt Coronet B Prussia" .................. 250.00

**Ewer**, 13-1/4" h, cream and light pink shell body, pebbled ground, brown worm type handle .................. 195.00

**Figure**, 3" h, seated Chinese figures, blue and white garb, late 19th C, pr .................. 120.00

**Hair Receiver**, hp, pastel florals ........................................ 50.00

**Pitcher**, 15-1/2" h, jeweled, inlaid gold leaves ............................ 315.00

**Plate**, 8-1/2" d, chickens and roosters ..................................... 75.00

**Sweetmeat Jar**, cov, 5-1/2"x 8", pink florals, green and rust leaves, cream ground, SP holder, marked "Middletown" .................. 150.00

**Urn**, 25-1/2" h, floral dec, imp mark ................................... 595.00

**Vase**

5-1/2"h, two children in Victorian winter clothes, stone wall, oval rocky base, polychromed, Ernest Bohne Sons Rudolstadt 90.00

11" h, center medium blue band, painted purple flowerheads, raised enameled centers, molded gilt outlined shoulder and foot, two scroll handles, matte beige ground, c1910 ........ 250.00

## ROYAL VIENNA

**History:** Production of hard-paste porcelain in Vienna began in 1720 with Claude Innocentius du Paquier, a runaway employee from the Meissen factory. In 1744, Empress Maria Theresa brought the factory under royal patronage; subsequently, the ware became known as Royal Vienna. The firm went through many administrative changes until it closed in 1864. The quality of its workmanship always was maintained.

1749 -1864

**Marks:** Several other Austrian and German firms copied the Royal Vienna products, including the use of the "Beehive" mark. Many of the pieces on today's market are from these firms.

**Bone Dish**, center gilt dot cartouche, multicolored period courting couple, wide gold border, gold flowerheads and gold drops, pale green ground, blue shield mark, set of 4 ............. 100.00

**Charger**, 20-1/2" d, titled "Columbus Triumphant Return," landing party, Indians, bountiful scene ....................... 1,500.00

**Compote**, 9-1/2" d, two handles, portrait dec, cobalt blue ground, gold trim .................. 165.00

**Cup and Saucer**, 3-1/2" d cup, 5-1/2" d saucer, green and gold dec, center scene of colorful rooster in landscape, saucer with similar gold and greed dec, center reads "quand ce coq chantera mon anmite finira" Bindenschild mark .................. 250.00

**Ferner**, 7-3/4" w, 4" h, portrait of lady on side, portrait of different lady on other side, burgundy, green, gold, beaded, ftd, scalloped edges, sgd, mkd "Royal Vienna, Austria" .................. 425.00

**Figure**, 8-5/8" h, man playing mandolin and other man playing hurdy-gurdy, one with pink jacket and striped trousers, other with yellow coat and purple trousers, blue shield mark, pr ....................... 300.00

**Plate**

6" d, multicolored scene of seated Cupid and Dido, dark red and gold border .................. 395.00

9-1/2" d, two girls feeding birds in garden setting, multicolored intricate raised border, beehive mark .................. 400.00

**Plate, classical scene, pink, maroon, blue border, artist sgd, beehive mark, 10" d, $415.**

Portrait Plate, 15" d, cobalt blue border, gilt lily stylized flowers, center with emerald green ground, pr of facing portraits of young woman, one with orchid shawl on her hair with flowers and stars, red and blue design, other with long blond hair, elaborate hair dec and rose shawl, underglaze beehive mark on back of each, c1890, pr .......... 3,200.00

Portrait Vase, 8-1/2" h, 4" d, bottle shape, cobalt blue, gold beading and flowers, beautiful woman portrait ...................................... 235.00

Stein, 6" h, seated monk with stein, cobalt blue ground, gold trim, artist sgd "Wagner"................................................................................ 900.00

Urn, 8" h, maidens dancing, small cherub, beehive mark........... 175.00

Vase, 10" h, irid purple ground, three ornate gilded handles and feet, oval portrait panel, band of roses dec ................................... 1,100.00

# ROYAL WORCESTER

**History:** In 1751, the Worcester Porcelain Company, led by Dr. John Wall and William Davis, acquired the Bristol pottery of Benjamin Lund and moved it to Worcester. The first wares were painted blue under the

glaze; soon thereafter decorating was accomplished by painting on the glaze in enamel colors. Among the most-famous 18th-century decorators were James Giles and Jefferys Hamet O'Neale. Transfer-print decoration was developed by the 1760s.

A series of partnerships took place after Davis's death in 1783: Flight (1783-1793); Flight & Barr (1793-1807); Barr, Flight & Barr (1807-1813); and Flight, Barr & Barr (1813-1840). In 1840, the factory was moved to Chamberlain & Co. in Diglis. Decorative wares were discontinued. In 1852, W. H. Kerr and R. W. Binns formed a new company and revived the production of ornamental wares.

In 1862, the firm became the Royal Worcester Porcelain Co. Among the key modelers of the late 19th century were James Hadley, his three sons, and George Owen, an expert with pierced clay pieces. Royal Worcester absorbed the Grainger factory in 1889 and the James Hadley factory in 1905. Modern designers include Dorothy Doughty and Doris Lindner.

**References:** Susan and Al Bagdade, *Warman's English & Continental Pottery & Porcelain*, 3rd Edition, Krause Publications, 1998; Anthony Cast and John Edwards, *Charlton Price Guide to Royal Worcester Figurines*, Millenium Ed., Charlton Press, 2000; G. A. Godden, *Victorian Porcelain,* Herbert Jenkins, 1961; Stanley W. Fisher, *Worcester Porcelain,* Ward Lock & Co., Ltd., 1968; David, John, and Henry Sandon, *Sandon Guide to Royal Worcester Figures*, Alderman Press, 1987; Henry Sandon, *Flight & Barr Worcester*, Antique Collectors' Club, 1992; Henry Sandon and John Sandon, *Dictionary of Worcester Porcelain*, Vol. II, Antique Collectors' Club, 1995; ——, *Grainger's Worcester Porcelain*, Barrie & Jenkins, 1990; John Sandon, *The Dictionary of Worcester Porcelain*, Vol. I, Antique Collectors' Club, 1993.

**Museum:** Charles William Dyson Perrins Museum, Worcester, England; Roberson Center for the Arts and Sciences, Binghamton, NY.

Biscuit Jar, cov, 7" h, vertical ribbing, cobalt blue bamboo leaves and stems.......................................................................355.00

Bowl, cov, stand, 6-1/8" d, gilt and enamel floral dec, fluted body, c1890 ........................................................................................ 350.00

Cache Pot, 8" d, 7" h, circular, lug handles, Kakiemon style dec, Chamberlain, price for pr ...................................................... 5,995.00

Candlestick, 7-3/8" h, lotus, frog mounted to leaf-form base, shape 687, c1879 ..................................................................... 425.00

Cheese Dish, 9-3/4" h, modeled bamboo body, brown and gilt dec, dec relief bamboo leaves, printed factory mark and "Richard Briggs Boston," c1879, slight rim nick, minor wear................................... 635.00

Claret Jug
    8-1/4" h, gilt, bronze, and enamel floral design, late 19th C .....275.00
    10-1/4" h, blossoms in relief, shape 1047, late 19th C ........ 300.00

Cup and Saucer, Blue Arundel..................................................... 95.00

Dinner Service, partial, bone china, Regency pattern, c1930-35, price for 47 pc set .............................................................. 250.00

Ewer
    10-1/4" h, bulbous, stylized scroll handle, fern dec, shape 1227, late 19th C ..................................................................... 750.00
    13-1/8" h, porcelain patent metallic, floral dec, 19th C ........ 635.00

Fern Pot, 7" h, figural, boy standing by wood simulated pot, printed mark, c1887, brim of hat restored, gilt wear........................... 345.00

Figure
    6-1/2" h, young girl, holding fan, standing by pedestal based urn, shape 944, c1883............................................................. 425.00
    17" h, water bearers, green, gilt, and brown, c1896 and 1897, price for pr .................................................................. 1,380.0

Ice Cream Set, enamel dec stylized floral and leaf designs, gilt trim, twelve sq shaped 6-1/4" w plates, 14-3/8" l rect tray, printed marks, c1883, glaze scratches, one plate restored, minor damage, price for 13 pc set............................................................. 115.00

Jardiniere
    6-3/4" h, leaf molded and basketweave body, scrolled handles, enamel and gilt dec, printed mark, c1897 ...................... 345.00
    8-1/4" h, enamel and gilt dec floral sprays with foliate borders, printed mark, c1891, gilt wear......................................... 460.00

Jug, 7-1/8" h, melon, bronzed and gilt dec, shape 1111, c1888 ......................................................................... 350.00

# ROYCROFT

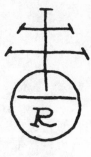

**History:** Elbert Hubbard founded the Roycrofters in East Aurora, New York, at the turn of the century. Considered a genius in his day, he was an author, lecturer, manufacturer, salesman, and philosopher.

Hubbard established a campus which included a printing plant where he published *The Philistine*, *The Fra*, and *The Roycrofter*. His most-famous book was *A Message to Garcia*, published in 1899. His "community" also included a furniture manufacturing plant, a metal shop, and a leather shop.

**References:** Kevin McConnell, *Roycroft Art Metal*, 2nd ed., Schiffer Publishing, 1994; The Roycrofters, *Roycroft Furniture Catalog, 1906*, Dover, 1994; Paul Royka, *Mission Furniture ,from the American Arts & Crafts Movement,* Schiffer Publishing, 1997; Marie Via and Marjorie B. Searl, *Head, Heart and Hand*, University of Rochester Press (34 Administration Bldg, University of Rochester, Rochester, NY 14627), 1994.

**Collectors' Clubs:** Foundation for the Study of Arts & Crafts Movement, Roycroft Campus, 31 S. Grove St., East Aurora, NY 14052; Roycrofters-at-Large Assoc., P.O. Box 417, East Aurora, NY 14052.

**Museum:** Elbert Hubbard Library-Museum, East Aurora, NY.

**Additional Listings:** Arts and Crafts Movement; Copper.

**Pitcher, hp polychrome flowers, cream ground, gold handles and trim, purple ink stamp, 6-1/2" h, 5-1/4" w, $125. Photo courtesy of David Rago Auctions.**

Lamp, 11" d, 5-1/2" h, 27" to top of harp, inverted funnel shape, floral, gilt, scrolled handles ................................................................. 165.00
Muffineer, young boy, hands in pocket, wearing boater hat ........ 300.00
Plate
    8-3/8" d, shell shape, gilt rim, enameled floral dec, c1889, four with restored rim chips, three with rim chips, price for 15 pc set ..345.00
    9" d, fruit dec, gilt border on cobalt blue ground, sgd "Albert Shuck," pattern no. W8346, printed marks, c1928, price for 18 pc set ............................................................................ 8,100.00
Potpourri Vase, cov, 14-1/2" h, wicker basketweave molded bodies, raised enamel and gilt dec water lilies, pierced borders, printed mark, c1883, finials restored, price for pr ........................................... 920.00
Salad Bowl
    6-3/4" w, square-form, leaf molded, scalloped edge, pierced gallery, enamel and gilt dec floral sprays with butterflies, printed mark, c1884 .................................................................... 230.00
    9-1/4" d, molded foliate body, enamel floral sprays, gilt trim, printed marks, c1892 ..................................................... 345.00
    Service Plate, 10-3/8" d, band of Neoclassical gilt enamel, border with raised gilt enamel with scrolls and urns, lapis blue ground, c1918-25, price for 18 pc set ....................................... 2,185.00
Tray, 14-1/2" d, Royal Lily pattern, gilt trim, printed and imp mark, c1878 .............................................................................. 190.00
Urn, 12-1/2" h, painted reserve of two ravens, moonlit landscape, gild trim, c1875-80, lines, chips ..................................................... 175.00
Vase
    6-1/8" h, figural, cornucopias set on backs of swans, imp mark, c1870, one neck restored, rim chips, price for pair .......... 200.00
    9-3/8" h, lotus-form, patent metallic dec, printed mark, late 19th C, gilt wear, rim chips restored ............................................ 635.00
    12-7/8" h, bottle-form, two scrolled foliate handles, floral dec, shape 1491, c1892 ............................................................ 550.00

Ashtray, 13-3/4" l leather strap with small squat hammered 2-1/4" d copper vessel riveted to strap, tooled and weighted ends, tooled orb and cross mark ............................................................................ 275.00
Book
    *Abe Lincoln and Nancy Hanks,* unusual binding, 5-1/2" w, 8-1/2" h .............................................................................. 50.00
    *Little Journeys*, volumes one through fourteen, set ........... 100.00
    *The Book of Business*, leather bound ............................... 100.00
    *The Dog of Flanders*, leather bound ................................ 120.00
    *The Ebert Hubbard Scrapbook*, leather bound .................. 100.00
    *The Notebook of Ebert Hubbard,* leather bound ............... 115.00
    *The Philosophy of Ebert Hubbard,* leather bound ............. 110.00
Bookends, pr, hammered copper, orb and cross mark
    2-1/2" x 3-3/4" x 2-3/4" orig box, Ivy pattern, plaster block printed with motto "I love you because you love the things I love" .......... 500.00
    4" h, 6-1/2" d, hammered copper, rect, emb owl, pristine orig patina, orb and cross mark ............................................... 475.00
    5" h, 3-3/4" w, trefoil motif, orig dark patina, small dent on one curl ...................................................................................... 250.00
    5" h, 5" w, owl motif, riveted corners, heavy gauge, orig dark patina, ............................................................................... 400.00
    5-1/4" h, 4" d, hammered copper, riveted strap hinge, ring pull, Secessionist style, orig patina, orb and cross mark ......... 450.00
    5-1/2" h, 5" w, poppy, orig patina ....................................... 850.00
Bowl, 10" d, 3-3/4" h, three ftd, acid-etched silver-washed hammered copper, orb and cross mark, light wear .................................... 425.00
Box, cov, 7" w, 3-1/2" d, 1-3/4" h, hammered copper, rect, quatrefoil emb on lid, orig patina, orb and cross mark ............................. 900.00
Calendar, 7-1/2" w x 3" h, hammered copper, lightly cleaned patina ............................................................................... 100.00
Calling Card Tray, 6-1/4" l, hammered copper, blue patina, emb stylized flowers ........................................................................... 100.00

**Jardiniere, hammered copper, ftd, riveted band at rim and base, orig patina, orb and cross mark, 11" h, 10" d, $9,200. Photo courtesy of David Rago Auctions.**

Candleholders, pr, 20-1/2" l, hammered copper, eight candle holders, arranged on hammered length with curled ends, brass wash, orb and cross mark ..................................................... 1,400.00

Chest, 23" l, 12" d, 9-1/4" h, mahogany, hinged lid, rect, hammered patinated metal latch, corner brace and handles, carved Roycroft orb and cross on lid, imp on handles, reddish brown finish, small losses, joint separation ..................... 575.00

Compote, 8-3/4" d, 2-3/4" h, brass-washed hammered copper, floral design, heavy gauge, orb and cross mark, wear to brass-wash ...600.00

Crumb Tray and Knife, 8-1/2" l, 5" w, brass-washed copper, emb Trillium design, orb and cross mark ............................................... 175.00

Dressing Table, 39" w, 18" d, 58" h, bird's eye maple, single drawer, orig copper pulls, swivel mirror, Mackmurdo feet, refinished. 5,500.00

Foot Stool, 17" w, 12" d, 15" h, mahogany, drop-in cushion, refinished, orb mark ........................................ 425.00

Goodie Box, 26" w, 9" h, mahogany and hammered latch, trim, and handles, orb signature, slightly worn orig finish, minor split to top .......700.00

Humidor, cov, 4-3/4" d, 3-3/4" h, hammered copper, riveted handle, orig patina, orb and cross mark, small blemish on lid .............. 475.00

Inkwell, 3-1/2" h, 15" l, hammered copper pen tray, pair of glass inkwells on each end, orig patina, orb and cross mark.................. 600.00

Lamp, table

14-1/2" h, 10" d, hammered copper, traces of brass wash, acanthus dome shade, orig mesh and celluloid panel, orb and cross mark, break to celluloid ................................................. 2,300.00

23-1/2" h, 18" d, brass-washed copper, three sockets, conical shade designed by Dard Hunter, opaque green and lavender leaded glass, orb and cross mark ............................... 30,000.00

Lantern, porch, 22-3/4" h, 7" d, hammered copper, light and dark green channeled slag glass, orig reticulated copper cap, paper clip chain, ceiling mount, designed by Dard Hunter, c1912, from the entrance of Hubbard Hill, home of Elbert Hubbard, damage to two thin panels, normal dirt and corrosion to orig patina............................... 25,000.00

Library Table, 74" l, 37-1/2" w, 30" h, rect, sq posts, straight apron, lower stretchers, new ebonized finish, carved orb and cross 6,500.00

Motto, 15" w, 19" h, *Resolve,* hand illuminated, mounted in orig Roycroft oak frame, orig finish....................................... 500.00

Nut Bowl, 10-1/2" d, 4" h, hammered copper, three ftd, orig patina, orb and cross mark.................................................. 1,900.00

Picture Frame, 38" l, 11" h, *Little Journeys,* individual renderings of Leonardo da Vinci, Thomas Gainsborough, Bellini, Velasquez, Thorwaldsen, Cellini, by Samuel Warner, orig finish, carved orb and cross mark .......................................... 2,500.00

Plate, 10" d, hammered copper, emb trefoils against verdigris panels, some pitting to patina, orb and cross mark ............................ 300.00

Poker Chip Holder, 6-1/2" h, 4-1/2" d, hammered copper, orig patina, imp mark ....................................................... 375.00

Rocker

19" w, 30" d, 34" h, sewing, five vertical backslats, tacked-on hard leather seat, orig finish and leather, carved orb and cross mark, splits to seat ................................................. 1,300.0

29" w, 35" d, 36" h, open arms, five vertical backslats, tacked-on leather seat, orig finish, new leather, carved orb and cross mark ................................................ 1,500.00

Sample Book, fifty mottos, many hand-illuminated, spine split, some foxing and wrinkles to pages................................. 4,500.00

Smoking Stand, 29" h, 10" d, mahogany, hammered copper match holder and ashtray riveted to wood base, tapering shaft, orb and cross mark, cleaned patina ...................................... 450.00

Tabouret, 11-1/4" sq, 18-3/4" h, flaring legs, sq overhanging top, orig ebonized finish, carved "Roycroft" on apron ........................ 2,600.00

Tray

10" d, brass-washed hammered copper, emb Trillium pattern, orb and cross mark, bent rim, wear to brass-wash ................ 100.00

15-1/2" d, brass-washed hammered copper, two riveted handles, orb and cross mark, slight rim dents, significant wear to brass wash............................................................. 225.00

22-1/4" l, 9-1/2" w, brass-washed hammered copper, oval, emb stylized motif, medium patina, orb and cross mark ......... 225.00

Vase

6" h, 3-3/4" d, silver-washed hammered copper, leaf shaped prongs holding orig green bubbly glass Steuben liner, orb and cross mark, light wear to wash........................................ 250.00

7-1/4" h, 3-1/2" d, American Beauty, hammered copper, orig dark patina, orb and cross mark............................................ 2,500.00

21" h, 8-1/2" h, American Beauty, hammered copper, orig patina, made for Grove Park Inn, stamped "The G.P.I. American Beauty Vase Made Exclusively For Grove Park Inn by The Roycrofters"..........................................................6,000.00

Wastebasket, 14" sq, slatted, orig ebonized finish, carved orb and crown mark.................................................... 2,100.00

# RUBENA GLASS

**History:** Rubena crystal is a transparent blown glass which shades from clear to red. It also is found as the background for frosted and overshot glass. It was made in the late 1800s by several glass companies, including Northwood and Hobbs, Brockunier & Co. of Wheeling, West Virginia.

Rubena was used for several patterns of pattern glass including Royal Ivy and Royal Oak.

Basket, 3-1/2"x 5-1/2", threaded dec, clear applied twisted handle ................................................................125.00

Carafe, Aurora .......................................................... 150.00

Celery Vase, Inverted Thumbprint, ruffled rim ............................. 85.00

Compote, 8-1/4" d, Honeycomb, low standard ............................. 75.00

Creamer, Medallion Sprig, clear applied handle ......................... 165.00

Creamer and Sugar, Royal Oak, frosted................................... 200.00

**Vase, coralene floral dec, gold trim, 5" h, $395.**

Cruet

    IVT, tee pee shape, trefoil spout, faceted stopper, Hobbs, Brocku-nier ...................................................................................... 550.00
    Royal Oak ............................................................................ 300.00
Finger Bowl, matching underplate ................................................ 85.00
Jar, cov, sq, Royal Oak, frosted ................................................ 100.00
Lamp Shade, 3-7/8" h, applied ribbed petals, opalescent rim, chips at base, one petal glued ............................................................ 50.00
Peg Lamp, 15-1/4" h, 5-1/8" d, fluted top, frosted rubena center shades to cranberry, flowers and scrolls patterning, frosted rubena font with flowers dec, brass candlestick base ........................................ 325.00
Pickle Castor, Royal Oak, frosted insert, orig tongs ................... 395.00
Rose Bowl, 6" d, Hobnail ............................................................ 230.00
Salt and Pepper Shakers, pr, Royal Oak, frosted ...................... 175.00
Sugar Bowl, cov, Royal Oak, frosted ......................................... 155.00
Sugar Shaker

    Royal Oak, frosted .............................................................. 240.00
    Swirl, threaded ................................................................... 175.00
Table Set, Royal Oak, frosted .................................................... 425.00
Toothpick Holder, Royal Oak, frosted......................................... 115.00
Vase, 6" h, bud, enameled floral dec, diamond band.................... 75.00
Water Set, acid etched storks, Hobbs, price for 7 pc set ............ 700.00

# RUBENA VERDE GLASS

**History:** Rubena Verde, a transparent glass that shades from red in the upper section to yellow-green in the lower, was made by Hobbs, Brockunier & Co., Wheeling, West Virginia, in the late 1880s. It often is found in the Inverted Thumbprint (IVT) pattern, called "Polka Dot" by Hobbs.

Bowl, 9-1/2" d, IVT, ruffled............................................................ 175.00
Butter Dish, cov, Daisy and Button ............................................. 250.00
Celery Vase, 6-1/4" h, IVT........................................................... 225.00
Cruet, IVT, orig stopper............................................................... 225.00
Creamer and Sugar Bowl, cov, Hobnail, bulbous, applied handle....550.00
Finger Bowl, IVT .......................................................................... 95.00
Jack In The Pulpit Vase, 8" h ...................................................... 250.00
Pickle Castor, Hobb's Hobnail, SP frame, cov, and tongs........... 500.00
Pitcher, 4-1/4" h, applied handle and feet .................................. 110.00
Salt and Pepper Shakers, pr, IVT ............................................... 210.00
Tumbler, IVT................................................................................. 125.00
Vase, 9-1/4" h, paneled body, enameled daises dec ................... 85.00
Water Pitcher, Hobb's Hobnail .................................................... 395.00

# RUSSIAN ITEMS

**History:** During the late 19th and early 20th centuries, crafts-men skilled in lacquer, silver, and enamel wares worked in Russia. During the Czarist era (1880-1917), Fabergé, known for his exquisite enamel pieces, led a group of master crafts-men who were located primarily in Moscow. Fabergé also had an establishment in St. Petersburg and enjoyed the patronage of the Russian Imperial family and royalty and nobility throughout Europe.

ВРАТЬЕВЪ

Baterin's factory
1812-1820

КорНИЛОВЫХЪ

Korniloff's factory
c1835

Almost all enameling was done on silver. Pieces are signed by the artist and the government assayer.

The Russian Revolution in 1917 brought an abrupt end to the century of Russian craftsmanship. The modern

Soviet government has exported some inferior enamel and lacquer work, usually lacking in artistic merit. Modern pieces are not collectible.

**References:** Joel A. Batech, *Kremlin Gold: 1000 Years of Russian Gems & Jewels,* Harry N. Abrams, 2000; Martin J. Goodman, *Lenin's Legacy,* Schiffer Publishing, 2000; Vladimir Guliayev, *Fine Art of Russian Lacquered Minia-tures,* Chronicle Books, 1993; P. Hare, *The Art & Artists of Russia,* Methuen & Co., 1965; L. Nikiforova, compiler, *Russian Porcelain in the Hermitage Collection,* Aurora Art Publications, 1973; Marvin Ross, *Russian Porcelains,* University of Oklahoma Press, 1968; A. Kenneth Snow-man, *Fabergé,* Harry N. Abrams, 1993; John Traina, *The Faberge Case: From the Private Collection of John Traina,* Harry N. Abrams, 1998; Ian Wardropper, et. al., *Soviet Porcelain,* The Art Institute of Chicago, 1992.

**Museums:** Cleveland Museum of Art, Cleveland, OH; Forbes Magazine Collection, New York, NY; Hermitage, Leningrade, Russia; Hillwood, The Marjorie Merri-weather Post Collection, Washington, DC; Russian Museum, Leningrad, Russia; Virginia Museum of Fine Arts, Lillian Thomas Pratt Collection, Richmond, VA; Walters Art Gallery, Baltimore, MD.

## Bronze

Angel, 3-1/4" x 1-3/4", cast bronze, 16th C................................. 400.00
Encolpion Cross, 3-3/4" x 2-1/4", cast bronze, 16th C............... 750.00
Figure

    19" w, 19" h, Cossack Plunder, by Eugene Lanceray, c1874, blackish patina ............................................................. 6,900.00
    23-1/4" l, 11-1/2" h, peasants in wagon, by Eugene Lanceray, c1877, blackish patina............................................... 2,990.00
Sculpture, 6-1/4" h, 7" l, Resting Peasant, detailed, pensive expression, inscribed "Possen" Worffel found mark, dark brown patina........ 1,850.00

## Enamel Ware

Bowl, each handle realistically chased bear's head, set with jeweled eyes, sides with multicolored enamel floral dec, moss green base, silver-gilt, base hallmarked "Moscow," 1899-1907, Cyrillic makers mark "F. R." for Fyodor Rückert.............................................. 9,500.00
Box, cov, 2-1/2" d, low, silver, round, hinged lid, five colors of enamel, St. Petersburg, Cyrillic makers mark "D. O." ........................... 575.00
Cream Spoon, 5" l, wooden, enameled handle, hallmarked......... 50.00
Kovsh, 3" h, 8-1/2" l, 5" w, blue, red, white, and gold flowers, gold wash to silver areas, int. bowl with enamel circle, base hallmarked "T K" with "84", touch mark under handle ..................................... 3,300.00
Match Box Cover, enamel on gold gilt silver, 2-3/8" x 1-1/8" x 1-3/16", I. S. Lebdkin, Moscow Assayers mark, illegible maker's mark, mkd with .875 and star and letter "M," 84 standard mark, assayer's initials, some enamel missing ........................................................... 300.00
Napkin Ring, silver, bright enamels, c1908, hallmarked "84," Cyrillic makers mark "D.O.," set of 12............................................... 1,840.00
Pencil, 5" l, no maker's mark ........................................................ 25.00
Salt, open

    1-1/4" d, hallmarked, artist CMW ...................................... 100.00

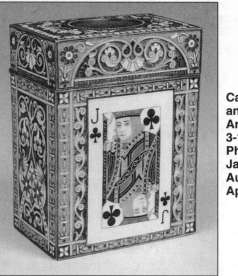

**Card Case, silver and enamel, 11th Artel, c1908-17, 3-1/2" h, $13,440. Photo courtesy of Jackson's Auctioneers & Appraisers.**

2-1/4" d, ftd, hallmarked 84-1893 Gustan Gustavovich Klingest.....................................................170.00
Sugar Container, 5-1/2" h, water bucket form, gilt metal, multicolored enamel dec, 19th C ......................200.00
Sugar Scoop, 5-1/2" l, silver-gilt and plique-a-jour enamel, scratched inventory no. ...............................520.00

## Icon

7" x 8-3/4", St. Nicholas, c1900, detailed image, gold leaf background, faux enamel borders ................................575.00
9" x 10-3/4", The Kursk Sign Mother of God, c1842, Old Testament figures such as King David, King Solomon, Moses, Daniel, Elijak and others all surrounding central image, overlaid with fine silver repousse and chased riza, attached halo and porcelain title plaques, riza hallmarked "84" and dated 1842 with Cyrillic makers' mark "P. N." for Pavel Nikitin .................................3,220.00
10-1/2" x 12", The Lord Almighty, c1900, Christ delivers blessing with right hand, while left hand holds open Gospels to John 13:34, overlaid with very fine silver engraved riza and champleve enamel Gospel text and title plaque, attached halo with 8 colors of cloisonné enamel, hallmarked "84, Moscow," Cyrillic makers mark "D. G." (Dimitriy Gorbonov) .........................3,165.00
10-1/2" x 12-1/4", The Image Not Made By Hands, 19th C, so-called first icon, Christ's face seen as was miraculously transferred onto cloth or napkin, finely executed, gold leaf ground, entire image overlaid with finely crafted silver-gilt, repousse, and chases riza, attached halo, hallmarked "84 Moscow," dated 1864, Cyrillic makers mark "I. G." ...................................3,165.00
10-3/4" x 12-1/2", Kazan Mother of God, 18th C, double raised border (kovcheg), silver-gilt riza starts a flat piece of silver, gemstone dec riza, hallmarked Moscow and dated 1781, Cyrillic stamp "Ya. F." (Ya. Frolov) ...................................6,440.00
10-3/4" x 12-1/2", St. Seraphim of Sarov, c1903, finely executed with each hair individually painted, entire image overlaid with silver-gilt repousse and chased riza, applied multicolored enamel corner plaques, multicolored enamel halo, hallmarked "84, Moscow," Cyrillic makers mark "S. E." (Semion Yegornov), title at bottom identifies subject as "The Holy Starets Seraphim" ...............................4,890.00
11" x 12-3/4", Svyenskaya-Percherskaya Mother of God, 18th C, shows Mother of God seated with Christ in her lap, Saints Antoniy and Feodosiy stand beside her holding scrolls, overlaid with later very fine silver repousse and chased riza, attached halo, embellished with river pearls, riza hallmarked "84" city mark of Kirov, Cyrillic makers' mark "L. G." ...............................3,450.00
11" x 14", The Dormition, c1890, Abramstervo School, Christ at center in mandrola receives soul of his mother in form of an infant, 12 Apostles gather around her, reverse inscribed in Cyrillic script "Abramtsrvo August 15, 1890," borders overlaid with silver engraved riza, hallmarked "84, Moscow," makers mark of Imperial silver smith Ivan Gubkin ...............................1,725.00
11-1/2" x 13", Smolensk Mother of God, 17th C, double kovcheg panel, attributed to Yaroslavi-Kostroma region, overlaid with fine detailed gilt-metal riza, halo dec with angles and seraphim ...............4,890.00
12" x 14-1/4", Joy To All Who Suffer, 19th C, crowned Mother of God stands at center, infant Christ on her left arm, scepter in right hand, suffering humans gathered on both sides, angels among them, open scrolls with petition of the people, inscription below her is kotakion "O All-Hymed Mother," additional row of stains added, God delivers blessing from above, entire image overlaid with elaborate gilt metal repousse and chased riza ...................................1,995.00
12-1/4" x 10-1/2", The Kazan Mother of God, c1893, 20 individual pieces of gold plated silver decorated with 7 colors of enamel and faux gemstones, finely crafted silver-gilt riza cover, from workshop of Nicholay Vasilevich Alexeyev, Moscow .................................6,440.00
13-1/2" x 11-1/4", The Resurrection, c1800, Christ standing on fallen gates of Hades, reaches down to grasp hand of Adam, Eve kneels at right, other old Testament Prophets and Patriarchs seen in background preparing to walk forth from bondage, overlaid with fine silvered metal repousse riza ...................................1,495.00

## Miscellaneous

Candelabrum, 29-1/2" h, 16-light, silver plated, Baroque taste, c1900 .................................................3,000.00
Cuff Links, pr, round, applied anchors, gold ropetwist accents, Russian hallmark for St. Petersburg, c1890, partially obliterated maker's mark, 9.5 dwt...................................460.00
Humidor, 12-1/2" w, 5-1/2" d, 6-1/2" h, fold-out, engraved brass inlaid birchwood, lid, façade, and rear inset with engraved brass equestrian plaques in English taste, int. fitted with fold-out trays for 32 cigars, later chrome ashtray and compartments for two reamers and cigar cutter, c1905-15 ...................................1,650.00
Samovar, 20-1/2" h, brass, urn, chimney, and underliner, late 19th C...................................................300.00
Tea Set, hand dec porcelain, teapot, coffeepot, and cream pitcher, attributed to Gardner Factory, minor war to gilding, hairline in creamer ...................................................300.00

## Niello

Beaker, 3-1/2" h, 3" w, gilt and niello, hallmarked "B. C. 1865 BC," Moscow assayers' mark for Viktor Savinkov, attributed to Vasiliy Semenov ...................................................375.00
Box, 3-3/4" l, 1-1/2" h, domed trunk, allover floral scroll niello, enameled straps, tack heads, hinged lid, gold washed int., late 19th C, .875 fine, 4 troy oz...................................................635.00

**Icon, Christ, heavily enameled riza, from workshop of Andrei Postnikov, c1908, 10" x 9", $20,160. Photo courtesy of Jackson's Auctioneers & Appraisers.**

Cigarette Case, 3-1/2" l, niello and silver, indistinguishable makers mark, c1900 .......................................... 350.00

Snuff Box, shoe shape, hallmark 84 ........................................... 400.00

Spoon, 4-7/8" l, three with ovoid bowls engraved to reverse with trefoil roundels and stylized script, two with rounded bowls, niello city scenes to back of bowl, engraved frame, all with twisted stems, gold washed, c1860-80, 4 troy oz, price for set of five..................... 250.00

## Silver

Baptismal Cross, 2-1/4" x 1-3/4", 18th C ..................................... 490.00

Beaker, 6" h, Moscow, early 19th C, bulbous foot, chased and emb with stylized rocaille, tapered conical cup chased and emb with eagles on pediments bearing floral swags and sprays, two rococo cartouches centered by engraved crosshatching and fish scaling, 7 troy oz ........ 815.00

Cigarette Case, 4-1/4" l, lid with 2 swans, makers mark of Aleksandr Ivanovich Peskarev, Moscow, c1908........................................ 435.00

Cream Jug, 4-3/4" h, ovoid, low foot, reeded lobing to lower section of body, applied floral band at girdle, carved ivory ear handle, gadrooned rim, gold washed int., 1829, 6 troy oz ................... 375.00

Fruit Service, five 6-1/2" l fruit forks, five 7" l fruit knives, Louis XVI taste, Peter Carl Fabergé, Moscow, c1900, fully hallmarked, 12.7 troy oz ............................................................................. 1,100.00

Place Setting, 11" dinner knife, dinner fork, place spoon, First Empire style, Peter Carl Fabergé, Moscow, c1900, workmaster Julius Rappaport, fully hallmarked, 9.7 troy oz ........................................ 550.00

Priestal Cross, 4-1/4" x 2-1/4", corpus in relief, reverse inscribed with Cypher of Nicholas II, hallmarked "84, Moscow" and dated 1896, Cyrillic makers initials "V. Z.," suspension loop mission .......... 260.00

Snuff Box, 3-1/4" l, niello, hinged lid with Peter the Great, side with Russian cottages, back with scene of St. Petersburg, hallmarked "84 Moscow," dated 1932, makers mark of Fedor Maximov ......... 350.00

Vodka Cup, 2-1/2" h, bright cut floral dec, fleur-de-lis rim band, mkd "CK," set of six........................................................................ 300.00

# SALOPIAN WARE

**History:** Salopian ware was made at Caughley Pot Works, Salop, Shropshire, England, in the 18th century by Thomas Turner. At one time, the product was classified "Polychrome Transfer" because of the method of decoration, but the ware is better known by the more popular name "Salopian." Much of the output was sold through Turner's Salopian warehouse in London.

**Marks:** Pieces are impressed or painted under the glaze with an "S" or the word "Salopian."

Bowl
    9-1/4" d, 4" h, pearlware, blue and white Oriental dec, "S" mark, wear and slightly yellowed rim repair ............................... 165.00
    11" d, Bird on Branch pattern, blue and white ..................... 415.00
Cann, 5-3/4" h, transfer dec, foliate devices and reserves of archers, 19th C, hairlines, minor transfer wear ........................................ 90.00
Creamer and Sugar, man and woman having tea in garden, black and white transfer ................................................................................. 450.00
Cup and Saucer, handleless, girl with sheep, small rim chip ...... 385.00
Cup Plate, 4-1/2" d, Deer pattern, polychrome dec ................... 450.00
Mug, 4" h, Bird on Branch pattern ............................................... 250.00
Pitcher, figures in garden, polychrome dec ................................ 220.00
Plate
    7-1/2" d, Oriental design ...................................................... 360.00
    7-3/4" d, polychromed Creil scene of man, woman, and child, hut and church in background, black transfer with applied yellow, blue, red, and blue-green highlights .................................... 45.00
    8-1/4" d, harvest scene, polychrome dec .......................... 300.00
    8-1/2" d, Double Deer, green, yellow, black, and white ...... 225.00
    8-3/4" d, octagonal, Oriental scene, blue and white .......... 195.00
Saucer, pearlware, deep
    Birds, 5-1/2" d ..................................................................... 100.00
    Birds and animal views, set of three .................................. 225.00
    Country cottage views, set of four ...................................... 275.00
    Floral dec, restored .............................................................. 50.00
    People views, set of three .................................................. 250.00
Teapot, 4" x 8-1/4", boy carrying lamb, blue and white .............. 475.00

# SALT and PEPPER SHAKERS

**History:** Collecting salt and pepper shakers, whether late 19th-century glass forms or the contemporary figural and souvenir types, is becoming more and more popular. The supply and variety is practically unlimited; the price for most sets is within the budget of cost-conscious collectors. In addition, their size offers an opportunity to display a large collection in a relatively small space.

Specialty collections can be by type, form, or maker. Great glass artisans, such as Joseph Locke and Nicholas Kopp, designed salt and pepper shakers in the normal course of their work.

**References:** Larry Carey and Sylvia Tompkins, *1006 Salt & Pepper Shakers,* Schiffer Publishing, 2000; Melva Davern, *Collector's Encyclopedia of Figural & Novelty Salt and Pepper Shakers,* Collector Books, First and Second Series, 2000 value updates; Helene Guarnaccia, *Salt & Pepper Shakers,* Vol. I (1985, 1999 value update), Vol. II (1989, 1998 value update), Vol. III (1991, 1998 value update), Vol. IV (1993, 2001 value update), Collector Books; Mildred and Ralph Lechner, *World of Salt Shakers,* 2nd ed., Collector Books, 1992, 1998 value update; Arthur G. Peterson, *Glass Salt Shakers,* Wallace-Homestead, 1970, out of print; Sylvia Tompkins and Irene Thornburg, *America's Salt and Pepper Shakers,* Schiffer, 2000.

**Collectors' Clubs:** Antique and Art Glass Salt Shaker Collectors Society, 2832 Rapidan Trail, Maitland, FL 32751-5013, http://www.cbantiques.com/ssc; Novelty Salt & Pepper Shakers Club, P.O. Box 3617, Lantana, FL 33465, http://members.aol.com/jlfuller1/jdf1.htm.

**Museum:** Judith Basin Museum, Stanford, MT.

**Additional Listings:** See Warman's Americana & Collectibles and Warman's Flea Market for more examples.

**Notes:** The colored sets, in both transparent and opaque glass, command the highest prices; crystal and white sets the lowest. Although some shakers, e.g., the tomato or fig, have a special patented top and need it to retain their value, it generally is not detrimental to replace the top of a shaker.

The figural and souvenir types are often looked down upon by collectors. Sentiment and whimsy are prime collecting motivations. The large variety and current low prices indicate a potential for long-term price growth.

Generally, older shakers are priced by the piece; figural and souvenir types by the set. Pricing methods are indicated in the listings. All shakers included below are assumed to have original tops unless otherwise noted. Reference numbers are from Arthur Goodwin Peterson's *Glass Salt Shakers*. Peterson made a beginning; there are hundreds, perhaps thousands, of patterns still to be cataloged.

Prices below are for individual shakers unless otherwise noted.

**Burmese, Mt. Washington, shading to lemon-yellow base, two part metal top, 4-1/2" h, $265. Photo courtesy of Clarence & Betty Maier.**

## Art Glass (priced individually)
Cased
    Bulging Petal, pink, pr ........................................... 45.00
    Flower Band pink ................................................. 30.00
    Palm Leaf, pink .................................................. 48.00
    Pineapple, pink .................................................. 55.00
Mount Washington
    Four lobe shape, white body, violet nosegays, minor corrosion to salt .............. 235.00
    White opaque, large pink blossom with yellow center ........ 100.00
    White opaque, orange bird with black wings, pale blue background ................... 100.00
Peachblow, Wheeling, orig top ...................................... 325.00
Spatter, vaseline and cranberry spatter, Leaf Mold, orig top ........ 85.00
Wavecrest, dark cream ground, swirled ribbed body, forget-me-nots, 2-1/2" h ............ 285.00

## China (priced by set)
Bartender, 3 condiment barrels on base ..................... 50.00
Black Bears, Rosemead ...................................... 60.00
Bendel Bugs, green ......................................... 60.00
Chickens, 3, egg cup base .................................. 40.00
Dutch Children and Dutch Shoe .............................. 40.00
Old McDonald, boy and girl, Regal China .................... 75.00

## Cut Glass
4" h, crosscut diamond, prism and fan motif, sterling silver tops, sgd "P & B" .......... 225.00

## Figural and Sets (priced by set)
Billiken, white, opaque and crystal, gilt, Buddha shape, inscription on base "The God of things as they ought to be," patent 1908, tin top ......... 75.00
Dogs, cast metal, 3" h, green paint, amber glass eyes, pr ........... 85.00
Metal Frame, tapered panels, pr, marked "C. F. Monroe" ........... 205.00

## Opalescent (priced individually)
Argonaut Shell, blue ....................................... 65.00
Fluted Scrolls, canary, orig top ........................... 65.00
Reverse Swirl, white, orig top ............................. 45.00
Windows Swirl, cranberry ................................... 110.00

## Opaque (priced individually)
Bulging Petal, green, pr ................................... 45.00
Ear of Corn, jade green opaque ............................. 60.00
Forget Me Not, rose opaque, Challinor ...................... 110.00
Guttate, green ............................................. 30.00
Rib & Swirl, blue .......................................... 45.00
Square Scroll, pink ........................................ 25.00

## Pattern Glass (priced individually)
Acorn, pink, orig top ...................................... 45.00
Banded Portland, maiden's blush ............................ 35.00
Klondike, amberette, pr .................................... 225.00
Nestor, amethyst, dec ...................................... 55.00
Nevada ..................................................... 30.00
Red Block .................................................. 60.00
Thousand Eye, vaseline ..................................... 40.00
Wheat and Barley, blue ..................................... 35.00
Whirligig, orig tip top .................................... 35.00

# SALT-GLAZED WARES
**History:** Salt-glazed wares have a distinctive pitted surface texture made by throwing salt into the hot kiln during the final firing process. The salt vapors produce sodium oxide and hydrochloric acid which react on the glaze.

Many Staffordshire potters produced large quantities of this type of ware during the 18th and 19th centuries. A relatively small amount was produced in the United States. Salt-glazed wares still are made today.

**References:** Susan and Al Bagdade, *Warman's English & Continental Pottery & Porcelain*, 3rd Edition, Krause Publications, 1998; A. & N. Harding, *Victorian Staffordshire Figures, 1835-1875, Book Three*, Schiffer Publishing, 2000; Arnold R. Mountford, *The Illustrated Guide to Staffordshire Salt-Glazed Stoneware*, Barrie & Jenkins, 1971; Louis T. Stanley, *Collecting Staffordshire Pottery*, Doubleday & Co., 1963.

**Museums:** American Antiquarian Society, Worcester, MA; City Museum, Stoke-On-Trent, England; British Museum, London, England, Colonial Williamsburg Foundation, Williamsburg, VA; Fitzwilliam Museum, Cambridge, England; Museum of Art, Rhode Island School of Design, Providence, RI; Victoria & Albert Museum, London, England; William Rockhill Nelson Gallery of Art, Kansas City, MO.

Batter Pail, 8-1/2" h, relief oak and vine design, imp "4" under spout, attributed to Whites, Utica, NY, factory ................... 330.00
Bean Pot, 9-1/2" d, orig lid, relief and blue accented, children eating beans on one side, relief and blue accented "Boston Baked Beans" on opposite side, minor clay separation near handle in the making .......... 450.00
Bottle
    7-1/2" h, James E. Pepper Est. 1780 Lexington KY Geo. H. Smith Distributor, Utica, NY, relief and blue accented rose design on opposite side, also "Purest & Best," relief and blue accents in shield at shoulder, professional restoration to handle ........ 440.00
    7-1/2" h, White Rose Rye Whiskey P. J. Bowlin Liquor Co. St. Paul Minn, Bristol glaze, relief and blue accents, "Pure Rye" at shoulder, back with relief and blue accented rose bouquet design, handle, attributed to Whites, Utica, NY, factory ........ 450.00
Butter Crock, cov
    4-3/4" h, relief peacock design, palm tree relief repeated on orig matching lid ............. 500.00
    7" h, J. B. Shattuck's Creamery Cherry Creek, NY, opposite side imp and blue accented "This package manufactured by the Central NY Pottery Utica NY," both impressions deep and very detailed, tooled accents band top and bottom with blue accents, extensive chipping, hairlines, some glaze flaking ........... 500.00
Charger, 13-1/8" d, white, scalloped rim, molded geometric design, English ............. 425.00
Figure, man and woman seated on pew, cream, brown, black, Staffordshire, 1704s, damaged, incomplete ................... 216,750.00
Humidor, 6-1/2" h, hunting dog design, Bristol glaze, orig lid, very minor clay separation in the making ................. 190.00
Jar
    3-3/4" h, Bovox Makes Real Strength, relief, blue accented tooled band, checker band along bottom, Bristol glaze ............. 190.00
    4" h, L. A. Delicatesse a Confection in Cheese, blue relief, fitted replacement lid, attributed to Whites, Utica, NY, factory .... 90.00
    6" h, Malted Beef, double sided decoration, relief over wheat sheaf design, Bristol glaze ............. 220.00
Match Safe
    3" h, American Brew Co. Rochester, NY, blue accents, imp eagle inside badge logo design which is also repeated on back, quarter size chip at rim on one side ................ 50.00

**Butter Crock, orig lid, relief peacock and palm tree design, 4-3/4" h, $500. Photo courtesy of Vicki & Bruce Waasdrop.**

3" h, tooled pattern, one blue accent band, mold mark #1, attributed to Whites, Utica, NY, factory, very minor rim surface roughness................................................50.00

5" h, Crystal Spring Brewing Co. Syracuse, NY, deeply imp and blue accents, three blue accent bands, tooled relief design, attributed to Whites, Utica, NY, factory............................750.00

Mug, handle, imp and blue label, attributed to Whites, Utica, NY, factory

4" h, Bayle's St. Louis, Pretzels are the Best, two blue accent bands top and bottom, overall diamond relief pattern......590.00

4" h, Pan American Exposition 1901 Buffalo NY, USA, imp and blue accents, tree bark-type ground, mkd "Whites Pottery Utica NY"......................................................................275.00

4-3/4" h, Compliments of Crystal Spring Co., Syracuse, NY, Crystal Lager, relief and blue accented design of two women filling jug........................................................................275.00

5" h, Iroquois Brewing Co., Buffalo, NY, center Indian logo, Bristol glaze, blue accent bands, blue accent at handle.............200.00

5" h, Jos. Schlitz Brewing Co., Milwaukee, Schlitz logo between name, imp and blue accented German verse on opposite side, short faint lines all around rim which occurred in the making200.00

5" h, 25 Bezirks Turnfest West New York Dodgeville, NY 1894, base back also imp "C. N.Y. Pottery Utica, NY," blue accent bands top and bottom, blue accent on handle, tight glaze in-making separation line at handle.....................................175.00

Pitcher

6-3/4" h, Paul Revere, Bristol glaze, blue accents, relief bark handle, attributed to Whites, Utica, NY, factory, mold mark #2 in base, minor surface chipping at spout............................250.00

8" h, grazing cows design in relief........................................200.00

8-1/2" h, diffused design, blue shades to white then back to blue, in-making clay separation under handle..........................165.00

Salt Box, hanging

5-3/4" h, stenciled vine and wildflower design....................100.00

5-3/4" h, 6" d, relief apricot and honeycomb design, very minor surface chip in orig lid.............................................150.00

Stein, 7" h, imp and blue accented "Pan American Exposition 1901, Buffalo, NY, USA," relief and blue accented standing buffalo on opposite side, Bristol glaze, pewter top, base imp "Whites Pottery, Utica, NY"..............................................................................365.00

Syrup Pitcher, 5-1/2" h, pewter lid, blue, green, and brown three color accented relief of children pulling log, attributed to Whites, Utica, NY, factory, surface wear at blue accented spout, some minor age crazing to glaze............................................................500.00

Toby Mug, 4" h, Bismarck, attributed to Whites, Utica, NY, factory, short hairline at rim...................................................................450.00

Water Cooler, 10" h, 3 gallon, orig brass spigot, later sponged lid...120.00

Water Cooler Base, 12" d, 4-1/4" h, relief medallion clam shell designs all around, blue accented relief tooled bands top and bottom, Bristol glaze, imp "6" on bottom, attributed to Whites, Utica, NY, factory.............190.00

# SALTS, OPEN

**History:** When salt was first mined, the supply was limited and expensive. The necessity for a receptacle in which to serve the salt resulted in the first open salt, a crude, hand-carved, wooden trencher.

As time passed, salt receptacles were refined in style and materials. In the 1500s, both master and individual salts existed. By the 1700s, firms such as Meissen, Waterford, and Wedgwood were making glass, china, and porcelain salts. Leading glass manufacturers in the 1800s included Libbey, Mount Washington, New England, Smith Bros., Vallerysthal, Wave Crest, and Webb. Many outstanding silversmiths in England, France, and Germany also produced this form.

Open salts were the only means of serving salt until the appearance of the shaker in the late 1800s. The ease of procuring salt from a shaker greatly reduced the use of and need for the open salts.

**References:** Mr. And Mrs. A. E. Coddington, *Old Salts,* privately printed, 1940 (available in reprint from *Salty Comments,* 401 Nottingham Rd, Newark, DE 19711); William Heacock and Patricia Johnson, *5,000 Open Salts,* Richardson Printing Corporation, 1982, 1986 value update; Allan B. and Helen B. Smith have authored and published ten books on open salts beginning with *One Thousand Individual Open Salts Illustrated* (1972) and ending with *1,334 Open Salts Illustrated: The Tenth Book* (1984). Daniel Snyder did the master salt sections in volumes 8 and 9. In 1987, Mimi Rudnick compiled a revised price list for the ten Smith Books; George and Carolyn Tompkins, *Gorham Silver Salts,* privately printed; Kenneth Wilson, *American Glass 1760-1930,* 2 vols., Hudson Hills Press and The Toledo Museum of Art, 1994.

**Periodical:** *Salty Comments,* 401 Nottingham Rd, Newark, DE 19711.

**Collectors' Clubs:** Central Mid-West Open Salt Society, 10386 Fox River Drive, Walnut Springs, Newark, IL 60541; Mid-West Open Salt Society, 9123 S Linden Rd, Swartz Creek, MI 48473-9125; New England Society of Open Salt Collectors, 6-2 Clear Pond Drive, Walpole, MA 02081; Open Salt Collectors of the Atlantic Region, 71 Clearview Lane, Biglerville, PA 17307-9407; Open Salt Seekers of the West (Northern Chapter), 84 Margaret Drive, Walnut Creek, CA 94596; Open Salt Seekers of the West (Southern Chapter), 2525 East Vassar Drive, Visalia, CA 93292; Salt Collector's South East, 1405 N Amanda Circle, Atlanta, GA 30329-3317.

**Note:** The numbers in parenthesis refer to plate numbers in the Smiths' books.

## Condiment Sets with Open Salts

Porcelain, light pink with gold trim, leaf shaped holder, mkd "Made in Bavaria" (388)................................................................130.00

Silver Plated, 3 pcs, emb pattern around bowls, Oriental (481)....65.00

## Individuals

Agate, carved hardstone, orange, slight pedestal.......................120.00

Basket, metal frame, cobalt blue liner, pierced ribbon handles, mkd "E. P. N. S." (413)...........................................................................40.00

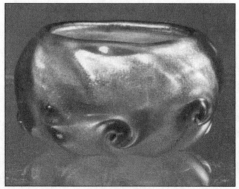

Tiffany, gold Favrile, twisted prunt, sgd "LCT," orig paper label, 1-3/4" d, 1" h, $315. Photo courtesy of David Rago Auctions.

Belleek, ruffled rim, hp roses, gold trim, Lenox palette mark ........ 60.00
Cameo Glass, Webb, red ground, white lacy dec around bowl, sgd, matching spoon .................... 650.00
Copper, heavy, pedestal base, deep maroon enamel (414) ........ 35.00
Cranberry 2-1/2" d, cut to clear, elongated punties and star base....200.00
Cut Glass
    2-1/2" d, tab handle, hobstar, strawberry diamond and fan 125.00
    3-1/2" h, Anglo-Irish, tapered boat shape, tapered diamond stem, oval foot, serrated edge, cut with straight and angled flutes, 19th C, price for set of four ................... 275.00
Heisey, octagonal paneled bowl, sloping octagonal base, H in diamond mark (475) ................... 40.00
Meissen, double salts, floral dec int. and ext., crossed swords and crown mark (460) ................... 85.00
Opaline, blue, boat shape, white garland and scroll enamel dec...90.00
Peking Glass, orange-red cut back to white ................ 170.00
Steuben, Aurene, calcite, gold, pedestal base.......... 290.00
Tiffany & Co., silver
    1-3/8" d, 1" h, ovoid, low foot, allover floral repousse, monogrammed, c1875-91, price for pr .................. 225.00
    1-7/8" d, 1-1/8" h, ovoid, three ball feet, gold washed int., c1891-1902, price for pr ................ 195.00
Vallerystahl, turquoise milk glass, double, sgd "Vallerystahl, Made in France" (460) ................. 50.00

## Figurals

Cupid driving reindeer pulling sleigh, SS, mkd "Made in Germany" (352) ...................... 420.00
Donkey, painted, pulling colorful painted cart (458) .............. 35.00
Flower, 2" w, 3-1/4" l, 3" h, petal top, green swirl glass insert, SP leaf border ................. 135.00
Swan, 4-7/8" h, swan, mottled cranberry and clear, pressed flint glass base, New England Glass Co, 19th c, price for pr............. 150.00

## Masters

Bronze, Belle Epoque, patinated and gilded, form of ancient Roman tripodal bearer, c1890-1895, bowl fitted with blown cobalt glass liner, 7-1/8" h ................... 100.00
Cranberry Glass
    2-3/4" d, 1-3/4" h, applied colorless and vaseline shell trim, SP standard ................. 140.00
    3" d, 2-1/4" h, fluted top, colorless wafer foot .......... 80.00
Cut Glass, Diamond pattern on top of bowl, ribbed base (404) .... 50.00
Glass, lacy
    Neal, EE2, colorless, 3" l, chips .............. 125.00
    Neal JY2b, medium green, 3" l, chips ................. 200.00
    Neal, LE1, colorless, 3-1/4" l ................. 150.00
    Neal LE3, deep blue, one foot glued, 3-1/8" l ........ 220.00
    Neal Og 7, New England Glass Co, colorless, chip on inside of base ................. 85.00
    Neal OP4, green, 3-5/8" l.............. 400.00
    Neal SL1a, amber, 31/8" l, corner crack ............. 150.00
Mercury Glass, 2-3/4" d, 2-1/4" h, vintage etching, pedestal base, gold int. ................ 90.00
Pewter, pedestal base, cobalt blue liner (349) ............. 85.00
Pressed Glass
    Dewdrop, 3-3/4" d, ftd, pressed six-point star in base, c1875-1890, price for set of four ............... 100.00
    Eyewinker, pedestal base (346) ............... 85.00
    Hamilton, pedestal base (344) ............... 45.00
    Hobnail pattern, round (407) ............... 35.00
    Palmette pattern (471) ............... 60.00
    Paneled Diamond, pedestal base (331) .............. 50.00
    Square Pillared pattern (341) ............... 30.00
    Vintage pattern (340) ............... 40.00
Silver
    Aesthetic Movement, third quarter 19th C, unmarked, 1-1/2" h, tapered ovoid form, four stylized saber legs, two small angular handles, mounted to side with realistically modeled fly....295.00

Aesthetic Movement, third quarter 19th C, Whiting Manuf Co, 1-1/8" h, three-sided cylindrical form, one side with plain gold-washed rect plaque, other two sides with fish and water plants engraved on gold washed ground................... 275.00
Chinese Silver, late 19th C, ovoid, three ball feet, applied dragon around circumference, glass liner, 1-1/2" h, price for pair.. 90.00
Continental, circular, ribbed, c1890, 2" l, 1.8 troy oz, price for pr ................. 40.00
Georgian, oval, ftd, London, c1745, maker's mark, date letter, and silver hallmark obliterated, 4.2 troy oz, price for pr ........... 70.00
Scottish, Edinburgh, 1796, quaich-form, int. gilded, .8 troy oz.................165.00

# SAMPLERS

**History:** Samplers served many purposes. For a young child, they were a practice exercise and permanent reminder of stitches and patterns. For a young woman, they were a means to demonstrate skills in a "gentle" art and a way to record family genealogy. For the mature woman, they were a useful occupation and method of creating gifts or remembrances, e.g., mourning pieces.

Schools for young ladies of the early 19th century prided themselves on the needlework skills they taught. The Westtown School in Chester County, Pennsylvania, and the Young Ladies Seminary in Bethlehem, Pennsylvania, were two institutions. These schools changed their teaching as styles changed. Berlin work was introduced by the mid-19th century.

Examples of samplers date back to the 1700s. The earliest ones were long and narrow, usually done only with the alphabet and numerals. Later examples were square. At the end of the 19th century, the shape tended to be rectangular.

The same motifs were used throughout the country. The name of the person who stitched the piece is a key factor in determining the region.

**References:** Ethel Stanwood Bolton and Eva Johnston Coe, *American Samplers*, Dover, 1987; Elizabeth Kurella, *The Complete Guide to Vintage Textiles,* Krause Publications, 1999; Glee Krueger, *Gallery of American Samplers*, Bonanza Books, 1984; Jack L. Lindsey, *Worldly Goods, The Arts of Early Pennsylvania, 1680-1758,* Pennsylvania Museum of Art, distributed by Antique Collectors' Club, 1999; Betty Ring, *American Needlework Treasures*, E. P. Dutton, 1987; Anne Sebba, *Samplers*, Thames and Hudson, 1979.

**Museums:** Cooper-Hewitt Museum, National Museum of Design, New York, NY; Smithsonian Institution, Washington, DC.

**Note:** Samplers are assumed to be on linen unless otherwise indicated.

1773, floral border surrounding bands of practice patterns, central section bearing names and initials with floral sprays above, Northern European origin, framed, 21-1/4" w, 21-1/2" h ......... 575.00
1776, "Rebeckah RSS Tainton 1776," various alphabets and numbers, toning, fading minor losses and holes, 12" x 8-3/4", framed .... 450.00
1784, Catharine Walton Born July 5, 1784, alphabets and geometric borders, bands with bird perched on flowering tree in lower center, inspirational verse on left, geometric flowering fine and sawtooth bor-

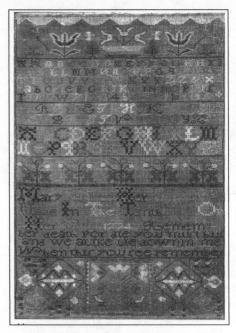

**1794, Mary Tufts her sampler made in the tenth year of her age, memory verse, stylized flower band, three bands of alphabets, flowering shrubs, lower panel centered with birds and free flanking diamond shaped devices, framed, toning, facing, minor losses, 15-3/4" w, 22-1/4" h, $1,380. Photo courtesy of Skinner, Inc.**

ders, MA, late 18th C, 21-1/2" w, 21" h, unframed, general toning, fading, small losses ............................................... 1,495.00

1786, "Mary Greenleaf born in July the 16 1786," Newbury or Newburyport area, MA, upper panel of alphabets and pious verse above lower panel with vase of flowering vines flanked by parrots and various fruit, foliate, and animal motifs, geometric floral border, 21-1/8" h, 16-1/4" w, unframed, toning, fading, minor staining ........... 10,925.00

1789, "Sarah Starrs work done in her 13 age 1789," alphabet and geometric bands above inspirational verses, central parrot flanked by urns of flowers, above row of geometric tulips, cottage with trees, flora, and fauna, various other animals, floral, and foliate devices, surrounded by geometric floral vine border, fabric losses, staining, toning, 14-1/4" w, 17-1/4" h .................................................. 1,150.00

1794, "Lucy Deweys sampler wrought in the eleventh year of her age 1794," upper panel with flowering vine with box, lower panel with potted flowering plant flanked by foliate devices, flowering fine border, unfinished, unframed, 15-1/2" h, 17" w ................................. 2,100.00

1795, "Nabey Bradley born Dec 23 in the year of our Lord 1785. This wrought in the 10 year...," Essex County, MA, upper panel of alphabets with geometric borders, lower panel centered with inspirational verse flanked by fruitful tree, basket, and bouquet of flowers, well-dress people, birds, and animal devices in landscape, toning, some silk thread loss, 12-1/2" w, 15" h, sampler accompanied by several genealogical charts of Bradley family................................. 18,400.00

1796, "Havervill Auguft 29 Betsey Gage Plummer Born AD 1782 this wrought in the 14 year of her age...," MA, upper panel of alphabets and pious verse above lower panel of scrolling grape vines, birds, and other foliate devices, checkered basket, flowering vine border, 19-3/8" h, 15-3/4" w, framed, toning, fading, tack holes, very minor staining.......................................................................... 10,925.00

1809, "Sarah Jubb, Aged 9 Dec 4, 1809," inspirational verse above Solomon's Temple, panel with gentleman and lady, animal, flora, and foliate devices, geometric flowering vine border, framed, toning, staining, scattered fabric loss, 18" w, 20" h ............................. 690.00

1810, Anne Clarance, silk on finely woven linen homespun, small precise stitches with vining floral border, alphabets, stylized flowers, verse, name and date, shades of green, blue, brown, white, small holes and wear, rebacking on linen, old gilt frame, 14-1/2" h, 14-1/4" w ...................................................................................650.00

1814, "Martha James Aged 11 1814," upper panel of pious verse, lower panel of architectural, animal and floral motifs, geometric floral border, 16" x 12-3/4", framed, losses, fading, minor toning...... 520.00

1820, "Mary Barker Her Work in the MIDD Society School Aged 11 Years 1820," inspirational verses flanked by trees with birds above trees, flowering devices with geometric floral border, framed, toning, minor staining, 13" w, 21-1/2" h.................................................. 1,150.00

1823

"Martha Mary Miller Newport August 25, 1823," alphabet panels above inspirational verse above name and date in wreath, various other devices, surrounded by stylized floral border, minor toning, 17-1/4" w, 17-1/4" h.............................................. 1,955.00

Harriet Williams, silk on linen homespun, meandering flower border, large house with double chimneys, tree, small building, several birds, alphabets, verse "Trust in Providence," and "Harriet Williams, Aged 10 Years, Orange, September 19, 1823," blue, green, brown, yellow, black, and white, stains, 18" h, 14-5/8" h, old 19-1/4" h, 15-5/8" w frame............................................. 990.00

1824, "Elizabeth Downess work Aged 12 1824," upper panel of alphabets and pious verse, lower panel of figural foliate and animal motifs, Greek key border, 12-3/4" h, 12-3/4" w, framed, minor repairs, toning..... 700.00

1827, "Sarah Marie Child aged 9 1827," alphabets above inspirational verse, baskets of fruit flanking name and date, with surround wreaths of flowers, sawtooth border, framed, toning, fading, minor staining, 14" w, 19" h .................................................................... 2,760.00

1828, "Jane Thomas Ended this Sampler July the 25th in the 14 year of her age in 1828," inspirational verse above two panels of various symbolic devices above another inspirational verse surrounded by meandering vine border, England, small areas of fabric loss, toning, 12-1/2" w, 14-1/2" h.................................................................. 750.00

1832, "Sarah T. Root, Pittsfield Aug 23 1832 Aged 12 Year," cartouche flanked by baskets of flowers and floral devices, beneath alphabet panels and inspirational verse, surrounded by wave bordertoning, fading, 17-1/4" w, 15" h ........................................................... 1,495.00

1833, family register, "Wrought by Harriet A. Newell Aged 11 Pluma Loomis Instructress," alphabet panels above family register, scenic panel with two buildings, tree and flowering shrubs bordered with geometric devices, meandering vine, framed, staining, toning, fading, 17" x 18"..................................................................................... 2,760.00

1835, "Catherine S. Tirrell, 7, Boston, September, 1835," silk on linen homespun, alphabets faded blue, olive, and brown, minor war and stains, framed, 17-1/2" h, 10-1/2" w ........................................ 650.00

1836, "Worked in the Town of Cordon by Catherine Farquar, March the 31st, 1836," silk on loosely woven homespun linen, blue, white, brown, and faded green alphabets, attributed to Indiana, minor stains, modern frame, 25" h, 20-14" w .................................... 550.00

1837

"Emma Nunns Aged July 18, 1837," alphabet variations, 7-7/8" h, 12-1/2" w, framed .......................................................... 400.00

"Margaret Craigs Sampler done in the 10th year of her age 1837," upper panel with basket of fruit flanked by various human, foliate, animal, and angelic motifs, middle panel with basket of flowers flanked by pious verse, lower panel with neoclassical memorial flanked by human, animal, and foliate motifs, foliate border, edges glued down, toning, minor staining, 22" x 20-1/2" l, framed ....................................................................... 1,200.00

183-, "Eliza Riddell, January, —, 183-," silk on linen homespun, vining floral border with stylized flowers, house, birds, verse, names of parents, faded blue, green, red, white, and black, wear, some missing floss, old mahogany veneer frame, 28-1/2" h, 24-1/2" w ...... 1,760.00

1845, wool on canvas, vining floral border with house, flowers, angels, birds, teapot, several sets of initials and date, strong colors, shades of red, green, blue, yellow, brown, wear, stains, damage to canvas, missing floss, old frame back in very worn Dutch American newspaper, 25-3/4" h, 27" w ............................................................... 660.00

1847

Elizabeth Billing 1847 Dear God and Honour the Queen, alphabet panels above pious verse above Federal building surrounded by birds, pair of cherubs, foliate, floral, animal, and various other devices, framed, toning, fading, minor thread loss, 18-1/2" sq ............................................. 1,150.00

Initialed "ECD 1847," alphabet panels above initialed floral wreath above two church buildings flanking flower basket, surrounded by geometric borders, framed, creased, fabric loss, minor staining, toning, 14-1/2" w, 16-1/2" h ........................................ 1,035.00

1854, "Elizabeth Wheel Finished this work 1854," upper panel of alphabet and pious verse, lower panel of animal, foliate, and architectural motifs, geometric floral border, 20-1/4" h, 15-3/8" w, framed, toning, minor staining, minor holes, insect damage .................. 460.00

1865, 17" h, 12-3/4" w, silk and wool on loosely woven canvas, blue and green leaf border, "God is Love…" verse in black, period pen and ink n paper presentation paper on back "This sampler was given…Easter Day, 1865, Cawthorne, near Barnsley," orig stretcher loose at corners, wear damage, some missing damage .......... 350.00

1867, "Ebth Pashley, Maxborough, 1867," wool, vining floral border, stylized flowers, brick house, verse, birds, butterflies, Adam and Eve, lion and unicorn, red, green, yellow, brown, violet, and pink, wear and damage, stains, bleeding, large hole on right side, modern 29-1/2" h, 30-1/2" w frame ............................................................ 385.00

Undated

10-1/2" h, 16-1/2" w, silk on linen homespun, alphabets, numerals, "Mary Anne Godlonton," shades of red, blue, brown, gold, and green, wear and damage, 15-3/4" h, 18-3/4" w frame.......... 385.00

17-1/4" h, 17-3/4" w, silk on linen homespun, vining floral border, alphabets, house and trees and "Eleanor C. Chambers," faded blue, white, green, brown, and red, wear, small holes, some loss of floss, modern frame ............................................ 750.00

20-5/8" w, 20-5/8" h, Dutch, floral border, central Dutch-style house with windmill above, mermaid below, motif of flower urns, peacocks, dogs, caged birds, crowns, and putti in flight, sgd "Elizabeth Poth," late 18th/early 19th C, framed ............... 575.00

# SANDWICH GLASS

**History:** In 1818, Deming Jarves was listed in the Boston Directory as a glass factor. That same year, he was appointed general manager of the newly formed New England Glass Company. In 1824, Jarves toured the glass-making factories in Pittsburgh, left New England Glass Company, and founded a glass factory in Sandwich.

Originally called the Sandwich Manufacturing Company, it was incorporated in April 1826 as the Boston & Sandwich Glass Company. From 1826 to 1858, Jarves served as general manager. The Boston & Sandwich Glass Company produced a wide variety of wares in differing levels of quality. The factory used the free-blown, blown three mold, and pressed glass manufacturing techniques. Both clear and colored glass were used.

Competition in the American glass industry in the mid-1850s resulted in lower-quality products. Jarves left the Boston & Sandwich company in 1858, founded the Cape Cod Glass Company, and tried to duplicate the high quality of the earlier glass. Meanwhile, at the Boston & Sandwich Glass Company, emphasis was placed on mass production. The development of a lime glass (non-flint) led to lower costs for pressed glass. Some free-blown and blown-and-molded pieces, mostly in color, were made. Most of this Victorian-era glass was enameled, painted, or acid etched.

By the 1880s, the Boston & Sandwich Glass Company was operating at a loss. Labor difficulties finally resulted in the closing of the factory on January 1, 1888.

**References:** Raymond E. Barlow and Joan E. Kaiser, *Glass Industry in Sandwich*, Vol. 1 (1993), Vol. 2 (1989), Vol. 3 (1987), Vol. 4 (1983), and Vol. 5 (1999), distributed by Schiffer Publishing; ——, *A Guide to Sandwich Glass: Cut Ware, A General Assortment and Bottles*, Schiffer Publishing, 1999; ——, *Price Guide for the Glass Industry in Sandwich Vols. 1-4*, Schiffer Publishing, 1993; Ruth Webb Lee, *Sandwich Glass Handbook*, Charles E. Tuttle, 1966; ——, *Sandwich Glass*, Charles E. Tuttle, 1966; George S. and Helen McKearin, *American Glass*, Random House, 1979; Catherine M. V. Thuro, *Oil Lamps II*, Collector Books, 1994 value update; Kenneth Wilson, *American Glass 1760-1930*, 2 vols., Hudson Hills Press and The Toledo Museum of Art, 1994.

**Museum:** Sandwich Glass Museum, Sandwich, MA.

**Additional Listings:** Blown Three Mold; Cup Plates.

Basket, 5-1/2" w, 5-1/2" h rose bowl type base, White Burmese, candy pink shading to pale yellow, ruffled box-pleated top, applied thorn frosted handle ............................................................ 795.00

Bowl

6-1/2" d, Peacock Eye, lacy, slightly clambroth, RWL pate 115 ............................................................ 175.00

7-1/4" d, Oak Leaf, lacy, colorless ...................................... 45.00

7-1/2" d, Tulip and Acanthus, lacy, colorless ........................ 45.00

Candlestick, 7" h, Pleat & Loop, vaseline, flint............................ 425.00

Celery Vase, 7" h, 4" d, Hobnail pattern, peachblow, satin finish, 11 rows of pointed hobnails ............................................ 475.00

Cologne Bottle, 5" h, vaseline, bull's eye motif .......................... 150.00

Compote

6-1/8" d, 7 1 /2" h, cov, Lincoln Drape, colorless ............... 250.00

7-1/4" d, Plume, lacy, colorless ......................................... 175.00

Creamer, Heart & Scales, lacy........................................... 135.00

Dish, ftd, 10-5/8" l, 6"h, Princess Feather, medallion and basket of flowers, canary, leaf foot, 1840-45, base of foot ground, base chips, small rim chips, annealing mark.......................... 20,700.00

Goblet, Sandwich Vine.......................................... 16,500.00

Honey Dish, Roman Rosette, flint.......................................... 25.00

Lamp

Astral, 33" h, wheel cut and acid etched shade with Gothic arches, overlay cut red to white standard, gilt and polychrome foliate and scroll devices, scrolling gilt brass base, electrified, one prism missing, gilt wear, very minor chips to shade, provenance indicates lamp was owned by Deming Jarvis, then George McKearin who sold it to Ruth Webb Lee ...................................... 3,450.00

Oil, white overlaid glass cut with leaves and berries font, semi-translucent starch blue base with three dolphins, c1870 ........... 4,700.00

Miniature, tureen, cov, 3" l, cobalt blue, lacy................................ 415.00

Molasses Jug, 5-1/8" h, Bellflower pattern, fiery opalescent, hollow applied handle, Britannia metal collar, hinged lid, c1860, slight handle check .............................................................. 3,500.00

Pitcher, 6-3/4" h, 7-1/2" d, Hobnail pattern, peachblow, ten rows of pointed hobnails, bulbous, sq top, applied frosted handle ....... 550.00

Salt

Figural, boat, blue opaque ............................................. 1,450.00

Figural, crown, 2-1/8" h, 3-1/8" l, fiery opalescent, c1830-50, chips............................................................ 260.00

Master, 3-1/4" l, Barlow/Kaiser #1471, flint.......................... 95.00

**Salt, master, scalloped, hexagonal pedestal, flint, $95.**

Sauce Dish, Crossed Swords, lacy, flint ..............45.00
Spill Holder, Sandwich Star, opaque white ...............300.00
Spooner, Ribbed Grape pattern, sapphire blue, c1860............7,750.00
Toothpick Holder, 2-1/4" h, 1-5/8" d, hp orange crane, green marsh
 stalks ..................................500.00
Vase
 9-1/2" h, Bull's Eye and Diamond Point, colorless..............175.00
 9-7/8" h, Tulip, pressed, dark amethyst, octagonal base, Barlow
  3021b, minute base chips, rim roughness ....................1,035.00
 10" h, Tulip, pressed, light amethyst, octagonal base, Barlow
  3021b, minute rim chips, pr..........1,850.00
 10-1/2" h, tulip, scalloped rim, eight paneled vase, pedestal base
  of deep green glass, mid-19th C, minor nicks to base......690.00
Whiskey Taster
 Flute, canary ..........................195.00
 Lacy, colorless ..........................200.00

# SARREGUEMINES CHINA

**History:** Sarreguemines ware is a faience porcelain, i.e., tin-glazed earthenware. The factory which made it was established in Lorraine, France, in 1770, under the supervision of Utzschneider and Fabry. The factory was regarded as one of the three most prominent manufacturers of French faience. Most of the wares found today were made in the 19th century.

**Marks:** Later wares are impressed "Sarreguemines" and "Germany" as a result of changes in international boundaries.

Asparagus Dish, 9" l, majolica, naturalistic colors..........................95.00
Basin, 16" d, 5-1/4" h, Napoleon III, Calcutta pattern, blue and white,
 c1860-70, several hairline cracks descending from rim ..........420.00
Box, cov, heart shape, floral dec, ormolu mount, c1760 .............150.00
Character Jug, 7-1/2" h, Scotsman, red hair, blue and red hat.....95.00
Creamer, 5" h, ducks and frogs, flower border..........................75.00
Ewer, 10" h, tan, gold butterflies and flowers ...............85.00
Luncheon Set, majolica, cov strawberry dish, sq basket, 6 different fruit
 plates..................................650.00
Oyster Plate, price for 4 pc set..........................200.00

**Vase, green ground, oil drop finish, imp mark and "115/227," stamped "Etna," 6-1/2" h, $175.**

Plate
 7-3/4" d, NY World's Fair, 1939 ..........................45.00
 8-1/2" d, majolica, strawberries and floral trim, aqua ground 85.00
Tea Service, florals, ornate shapes, c1840, price for 14 pc set ..625.00
Tobacco Jar, cov, relief masks, brown, yellow trim ...............95.00
Toby Pitcher, 8-1/4" h, toothy grin, polychrome dec, marked "Sarreguemines, Made in Germany," stains and crazing.................45.00
Vase
 8-1/2" h, majolica, gargoyles and lizards ..........................150.00
 17" h, incised lilies, intricate design of leaves and stems in yellow,
  brown ground, imp marks, minor flakes at top .................250.00

# SATIN GLASS

**History:** Satin glass, produced in the late 19th century, is an opaque art glass with a velvety matte (satin) finish achieved through treatment with hydrofluoric acid. A large majority of the pieces were cased or had a white lining.

While working at the Phoenix Glass Company, Beaver, Pennsylvania, Joseph Webb perfected mother-of-pearl (MOP) satin glass in 1885. Similar to plain satin glass in respect to casing, MOP satin glass has a distinctive surface finish and an integral or indented design, the most well known being diamond quilted (DQ).

The most common colors are yellow, rose, or blue. Rainbow coloring is considered choice.

**Additional Listings:** Cruets; Fairy Lamps; Miniature Lamps; Rose Bowls.

**Reproduction Alert:** Satin glass, in both the plain and mother-of-pearl varieties, has been widely reproduced.

Basket
 4-1/2" w, 7" h, pouch shaped basket, satin, MOP, shaded rose to
  pink to white, Diamond Quilted pattern, applied frosted loop
  handle ..................................550.00
 7-1/4" w, 7-1/4" h, bright orange int., mint green ext., applied
  wishbone thorn handle ..........................275.00
 10-3/4" w, 9" w, 9-1/2" h, solid rose int., white ext., large Raindrops pattern, applied clear frosted edge, applied frosted thorn
  loop handle..................................750.00
Bowl, 10-1/4" d, 4-5/8" h, pink and white loops, ruffled rim, gold and
 yellow encrusted floral dec..................................470.00
Bride's Bowl, 9-1/2" d, MOP, blue, moiré pattern, SP holder with strawberries and leaves applied to handle, marked "Simpson, Hall, Miller
 Co" ..................................375.00

**Cup and Saucer, pink shading to white, Raindrop, MOP, 3" h cup, 5" d saucer, $285. Photo courtesy of Clarence & Betty Maier.**

Candlesticks, pr, 8-3/4" h, yellow, brown roses, dark painted rims and bases ......................170.00

Cup and Saucer, 3" h, 5" d, pink to white MOP, Raindrop pattern....285.00

Ewer
  9" h, blue, yellow enameled dec, handle ...............................75.00
  9-1/4" h, delicate gold floral sprays, blue and violet enamel petals, golden-brown handle, brushed gold highlights, sgd "10" in pontil......................485.00

Finger Bowl, 5" d, red, DQ ......................200.00

Jam Dish, 6-3/4" h, 5" d, shaded pink, white lining, frosted shell trim applied around top, dark color berries, leaves, and bird dec, SP holder ......................175.00

Lamp, 19-3/4" h, peg, pale pink shading to deep pink, ribbed base, matching ribbed shades with ruffled rims, orig brass burners, brass base, price for pr ......................990.00

Miniature Lamp, 9-3/4" h, 3-1/2" d, soft green and blue, enameled purple and white flowers, gold leaves, pedestal............285.00

Mug, barrel shape
  2-3/4" h, 2-1/4" d, deep rose to amber DQ, creamy white lining, frosted loop handle......................175.00
  3-1/2" h, pink and gold looping, white ground, applied frosted reeded handle ......................175.00

Mustard, cov, 4-1/8" h, melon ribs, yellow shaded to pale pink, SP fittings, sterling spoon with enameled bowl................190.00

Nappy, 6" l, 2-1/2" w, triangular shape, MOP, white, DQ, allover gold dec, deeply crimped edge, applied frosted handle...................425.00

Perfume Bottle, 5-1/2" l, teardrop shape, lay down type, mother of pearl shaded blue, DQ, Webb ......................575.00

Pickle Castor, Heart Arches pattern insert, white, enameled rose color apple blossoms and green leaves, silverplated frame ............395.00

Pitcher
  5" h, blue, ribbed, swirled......................175.00
  5-1/2" h, scalloped top, gold shaded to white, applied frosted handle, sgd "Webb"......................265.00

Plate, 7" d, shaded rose to lighter pink, Drape MOP, marked "Patent" in glossy letters on base ......................200.00

Rose Bowl, 4" d, shaded blue to white, mezzotint cherub dec ...175.00

Salad Set, 8" d x 4-1/2" d bowl, shaded gold ribbon MOP bowl, silver plated top rim, matching silver plated salad fork and spoon, gold ribbon MOP glass handles ......................900.00

Sugar Shaker
  Bulbous, blue colored ground, Raindrop pattern, mother-of-pearl ......................500.00
  Bulbous, blue, Raindrop pattern, mother-of-pearl, butterfly and berries dec ......................750.00
  Bulbous, butterscotch colored ground, Raindrop pattern, mother-of-pearl ......................300.00
  Bulbous, Coinspot pattern, apricot shading to white, lavender floral dec, mother-of-pearl......................600.00
  Egg shape, blue, yellow and rust colored floral dec, Mount Washington......................350.00
  Egg shape, multicolored coleus leaf dec, Mount Washington .400.00
  Melon shape, pink and blue ground, blue floral dec. Gillinder .150.00
  Ostrich egg shape, yellow ground, beaded pink and blue floral dec ......................350.00

Sweetmeat jar, 6 h, 5" d, shaded blue, DQ, MOP, white lining, white enameled flowers, brown leaves, SP top ................565.00

Tumbler
  3-1/4" h, pink herringbone, MOP ......................55.00
  3-1/2" h, vertical rainbow bands of vivid pink, blue, and yellow, DQ, MOP, floral dec, applied enamel branch of three white and pink singled petal blossoms, partially opened buds, four leaves, stylized stems, gold highlights and rim............885.00

Vase
  6" h, 5" w, pinched pouch shape, Bridal white, flower and acorn pattern, English ......................750.00
  7-1/4" h, 4" w at shoulder, flaring top, broad shoulder with tapered body, Rainbow MOP, shades of pink, yellow, blue, and white, DQ, glossy white int., sgd "Patent"................1,250.00
  8" h, gourd shape, blue, DQ ......................150.00

9" h, elongated neck on bulbous base, cream colored ground cased to yellow green, air trap diamond pattern, gray, rust, and maroon enameled flowers and bee, minor wear to enamel ...............900.00

10-1/2" h, 5-1/2" w, bulbous, stick neck, pale blue shading to white, creamy white lining, English ......................265.00

11-1/2" h, 4" w, bulbous, four petal top, deep blue to white, orange branches and white floral dec, Victorian ......................185.00

11-1/2" h, 5-3/4" w, 6" h stick neck, Bridal White MOP, Herringbone pattern, shocking pink int., allover clear threading on entire surface, Victorian ......................750.00

# SATSUMA

**History:** Satsuma, named for a war lord who brought skilled Korean potters to Japan in the early 1600s, is a handcrafted Japanese faience (tin-glazed) pottery. It is finely crackled, has a cream, yellow-cream, or gray-cream color, and is decorated with raised enamels in floral, geometric, and figural motifs.

Figural satsuma was made specifically for export in the 19th century. Later satsuma, referred to as satsuma-style ware, is a Japanese porcelain also hand decorated in raised enamels. From 1912 to the present, satsuma-style ware has been mass-produced. Much of the ware on today's market is of this later period.

**Reference:** Nancy N. Schiffer, *Imari, Satsuma, and Other Japanese Export Ceramics,* Schiffer Publishing, 1997.

**Periodical:** *Orientalia Journal*, P.O. Box 94, Flushing, NY 11363-0094, http://members.aol.com/Orientalia/index.html.

Belt, 36" l, twelve 1-1/2" Satsuma buttons, figures, butterflies, dragons, flowers, two 1-3/4" buttons of dragons at ends ........................300.00

Biscuit Jar, cov, 6-1/2"x 6", orange, bamboo type handles, diaper border......................125.00

Box, 4" d, round, tripartite feet, two panels painted as hanging scrolls, one with plants and flowers, the other with people in garden, remaining surface cov in gold dec on cobalt blue ground, sgd "Kinkozan," orig label......................1,265.00

Bowl
  6-1/2" d, foliate form, gilt net and butterflies dec, sgd "Nichimitsu," 19th C ......................230.00
  9-3/4" d, Hundred Buddhas pattern, various figures of Buddhist vanities with gasu-blue robes, dragon borders, imp Jyusho with Satsuma mon and seven-character inscription starting with "Tai nihon Satsuma," late 19th C ......................635.00

Creamer and Sugar, cov, floral pattern ......................350.00

Cup and Saucer, flowers and butterflies, c1900 ......................50.00

Dish, 9-7/8" h, Kannon, arhats and dragon, int. dec, scalloped, gilt ground, c1900 ......................275.00

**Incense Burner, courtesans on one side, mandarins on other, c1875, 4" w, 3-3/4" h, $275.**

Incense Burner, 4" h, ovoid, three arrow form molded flowerhead reserves, cream glaze, tripod feet, reticulated cov, Meiji period ....175.00

Jar, cov, 5" h, prunus branch with bird, diaper border neck band and handles..................................................................................250.00

Koro, 17-1/2" h, earthenware covered, blue field, birds and flowers dec, green foo dog handles to lid and sides, three green foo dog feet, 18th/19th C............................................................................425.00

Miniature

Box, 1-1/4" h, drum-shape, cov dec with court scene of eight people, body with landscape of flowering cherry blossoms, sgd "Yabu Meizan" in gold, gold ground ..............................1,725.00

Teapot, 3-3/4" h, diamond shaped, four reserves of figures in garden settings, blue ground with gold flowers, cracked ice pattern, sgd "Kinkozan" in gold on back cartouche, orig paper label........690.00

Plate, 9" d, mother and children in garden, flowers and butterflies border, Japanese..................................................................300.00

Tea Bowl, 5" d, 33/4" d, high sides, int. dec with hexagons, dragonflies, and butterflies surrounding central medallion of children flying kite, brocade borders, ext. with four medallions of court scenes, brocade ground, landscape around base, two-character Fuzan mark, Meiji period ....................................................................1,955.00

Tea Caddy, cov, 5-1/2" d, blooming prunus tree, bird, brocade ground, handles..................................................................................195.00

Teapot, cobalt blue ground, gilt floral dec, two panels with women and children in palace scenes, sgd "Ryuzan," Japan, late-19th C......425.00

Vase

8-1/2" h, hexagonal, cobalt blue ground, gilt dec, two reserves, one of women, other warriors, sgd "Tai Nihon Koku Satsuma," Japan late 19th/early 20th C, rubbing...............................350.00

12" h, globular body, jump ring handles, garlic bulb mouth, cobalt blue ground strewn with diaper patterns and flowers, two fan-shaped medallions, one with sun goddess, other with dragon king with two dancing girls, two other reserves on brown ground, one with butterfly and grape vine, other wisteria and peony flowers, imp "Kinkozan" mark, Meiji period, c1880 .....................5,500.00

12" h, women and children, polychrome dec, gilt trim, late 19th C, losses ......................................................................230.00

15" h, parrot, handled basket of flowers, brocade borders, sgd "Dai Nihon Kyoto Kinkozan Sei," late 19th C ................1,150.00

24" h, courtiers and warriors, polychrome dec, gilt trim, early 20th C....................................................................................1,150.00

25" h, mouth molded in form of leaves, tan body with blue clouding, design of doves in cherry tree, sgd "Kinkozan," Japan, late 19th C ....................................................................550.00

Wine Bottle, sake tokuri, hexagonal, reserves of various figures, sgd with Satsuma mon in blue, Japan, late 19th C ........................575.00

# SCALES

**History:** Prior to 1900, the simple balance scale was commonly used for measuring weights. Since then, scales have become more sophisticated in design and more accurate. There are a wide variety of styles and types, including beam, platform, postal, and pharmaceutical.

**Reference:** Bill and Jan Berning, *Scales: A Collector's Guide,* Schiffer Publishing, 1999.

**Collectors' Club:** International Society of Antique Scale Collectors, 300 W. Adams St., Suite 821, Chicago, IL 60606.

## Reproduction Alert:

Many "fake" Schlegelmilch pieces are appearing on the market. These reproductions have new decal marks, transfers, or recently hand-painted animals on old, authentic R. S. Prussia pieces.

**French, Jouan, brass, lab type, with microscope, wood and glass case, marble base, 20-1/2" h, 17" w. $550. Photo courtesy of Joy Luke Fine Art Brokers and Auctioneers.**

Apothecary, 9" h, 19-1/2" l, 6" d, oak base, window in side to show balance, marble top, matching brass weighing bowls...................250.00

Balance, 18" h, 12-1/2" w, balance, brass pans suspended from painted tin arm, two paper and ink registers, red grain painted pine glazed case with lower single drawer, salmon color int., New England, 19th C, minor paint wear ......................................1,265.00

Brass, 23" h, central stand with ribbed knop, suspending bracket and two pans, mahogany base, N. & L. Avery, Birmingham, England, late 19th C ...............................................................................260.00

Candy

Anderson Computing Scale Co, 2 lb...................................300.00

Enterprise Manufacturing Co, Phila, PA, tin scoop, brass slide.........................................................................145.00

National, decal, restored.....................................................350.00

Computing, 31" h, 19" w, 18" d, painted, top plate reads "The Computing Scale Co./Dayton, Ohio, U.S.A." ......................................400.00

Country Store, 14" h, cast iron, large hopper, some orig paint and stenciling.....................................................................................150.00

Egg, 8-1/2" x 6-1/2" x 3", aluminum weight indicator, brass head screw, red weighing arm......................................................................50.00

Feed, red and white checked top, blue and cream bottom, metal pan, "Purina Feed Saver and Cow Culler" adv ..................................80.00

Home, 8" h, cast iron, porcelain dial printed backwards, when side is angled down it exposes mirror to read scale, 0 to 270 lbs .......300.00

Pharmacy, oak case, beveled glass and marble top, 1800s........300.00

Postal, Hanson Bros. Scale Co., c1925.......................................48.00

# SCHLEGELMILCH PORCELAINS

**History:** In 1861, Leonard Schlegelmilch (1823-1898) founded the first porcelain factory ever established in Suhl, Prussia, the Erdmann Schlegelmilch (ES) Porzellanfabrik, which was named to honor Leonard's father, Erdmann (1782-1844). The factory continued in production until the 1935 era. Leonard's son, Carl (1855-1920) founded the Carl Schlegelmilch (CS) Porzellanfabrik in 1882 in Suhl's neighboring village of Mäbendorf. This factory was, in reality, an extension of the original ES facility, but failed in 1915 and was sold to the Matthes und Ebel Porzellanfabrik which continued production as an independent (non-ES related) facility until 1937. Another one of Leonard's sons, Oscar (1862-1938) founded the Oscar Schlegelmilch (OS) Porzellanfabrik in 1892, in Langewiesen. This facility was separate, distinct and independent from the original ES facility and the CS facility. However, it continued in OS and ES family hands until being nationalized by East German officials after the end of WWII. It then continued until 1972, when it ceased to function as an independent East German state-managed facility.

In 1869, Reinhold Schlegelmilch (1837-1906), (not a blood relation to Erdmann, Leonard, Carl or Oscar,) founded his own porcelain factory in Suhl, the Reinhold Schlegelmilch (RS) Porzellanfabrik. This facility continued production until 1915, being then closed because the Suhl labor force was dedicated to the production of firearms in support of the WWI German war effort. Prior to this, in 1894, Reinhold through his sons—Otto (1863-1916), Erhard (1866-1934) and Arnold (1868-1934)—opened a second factory in Tillowitz, Upper Silesia, Prussia, Germany. Both the Suhl and Tillowitz facilities maintained simultaneous production under the overall management of the Suhl facility until it closed. At that time (1915), all management and production activities were centered in the Tillowitz facility which was then under the shared ownership of Arnold and Erhard until they both died in 1934. The facility ownership then shifted to Lothar (1904-1940), son of Arnold, until Lothar died. The factory was then inherited by Brigitte Koch (1923-1991), grand-daughter of Arnold. She retained ownership until the end of WW-II (1945). The Tillowitz facility was essentially abandoned during the period 1945 until 1947, when the factory was nationalized by the Polish government. The Tulowice (Polish name for Tillowitz) Factory continued as a Polish government-managed facility until the 1991-92 time frame, then privatized as a Polish company when the Polish economy was restructured into a free-market economy. It is still in production, producing items primarily for the hotel and restaurant business on a world-wide basis.

**Marks:** ES factory marks usually incorporated the initials ES into whatever mark used. CS and OS also incorporated their own initials. These related facilities used approximately 14 basic marks with many variations. The RS facilities used well over 25 different marks, not counting special added marks put on by various decorating studios and import companies—the result being that literally hundreds of variants have been noted and documented!

**Note**: The most common RS mark is a Wreath in many, many variants—the original being the so-called "RSP or RS Prussia" mark—this having been registered in the

German Trademark System in 1905. Although not proven, the RS Wreath markings may have been designed by the brothers, Erhard, Arnold and Otto, in honor of their father, Reinhold. It should be noted that most of the RS Wreath marks were used simultaneously by both the Suhl and Tillowitz facilities. This definitely applies to all items marked with either the "RS Prussia" or "RS Germany" markings. However, those items with the wreath annotated with either Suhl or Tillowitz should be considered to have been produced only by those respective factories. All in all, there are literally hundreds of variant marks which have been attributed to these two RS factories.

**References:** Susan and Al Bagdade, *Warman's English & Continental Pottery & Porcelain*, 3rd Edition, Krause Publications, 1998; R. H. Capers, *Capers' Notes on the Marks of Prussia*, Alphabet Printing, 1996 (P.O. Box 695, Crownsville, MD 21032); Mary Frank Gaston, *Collector's Encyclopedia of R. S. Prussia and Other R. S. and E. S. Porcelain*, 1st Series (1982, 1993 value update), 2nd Series (1986, 1994 value update), 3rd Series (1994), 4th Series (1997, 2001 value update), Collector Books; —, *R. S. Prussia Popular Lines,* Collector Books, 1999; Leland and Carol Marple, *R. S. Prussia: The Art Nouveau Years,* Schiffer, 1998; —, *R. S. Prussia: The Early Years,* Schiffer Publishing, 1997; —, *R. S. Prussia: The Wreath and Star,* Schiffer Publishing, 2000; A. Zydek, *Tillowitz Porcelain,* ADAN Silesian Publishing, 2000 (P.O. Box 695, Crownsville, MD 21032).

**Collectors' Club:** International Association of R. S. Prussia Collectors Inc., 212 Wooded Falls Rd, Louisville, KY 40243.

## Reproduction Alert:

Dorothy Hammond, in her 1979 book *Confusing Collectibles*, illustrated an R. S. Prussia decal which was available from a china-decorating supply company for $14 a sheet. This was the first of several fake R. S. Prussia reproduction marks that have caused confusion among collectors. Acquaint yourself with some of the subtle distinctions between fake and authentic marks as described in the following.

The period mark consists of a wreath that is open at the top. A five-pointed star sits in the opening. An "R" and an "S" flank a wreath twig in the center. The word "Prussia" is located beneath. In the period mark, the leg of the letter "P" extends down past the letter "r." In the reproduction mark, it does not. In the period mark, the letter "I" is dotted. It is dotted in some fake marks but not in others.

The "R" and the "S" in the period mark are in a serif face and are uniform in width. One fake mark uses a lettering style that utilizes a thin/thick letter body. The period mark has a period after the word "Prussia." Some fake marks fail to include it. Several fake marks do not include the word "Prussia" at all.

The period mark has a fine center line within each leaf of the wreath. Several fake marks do not.

## E. S. Germany

Bowl, 14" l, oval, large re roses, orange shaded rose sprays, gold tracery, scalloped, mkd "E. S. Germany Prov. Saxe" .............125.00

Candy Dish, 7-1/4" d, lobed body, white camellias, green leaves, gold sponged rim and handle, red "E. S. Germany Prov. Saxe" mark20.00

Chocolate Pot, Napoleon portrait, mkd "E. S. Prov Saxe" .........375.00

Demitasse Cup, Napoleon and Recamier, portrait, mkd "E. S. Prov Saxe"..............................................................................................135.00

Dish, basket type, ruffled edge, Josephine and Hortense portraits, mkd "E. S. Prov Saxe" .........................................................................175.00

Portrait Plate, 10-1/2" d, Madame DuBarry in center, luster burgundy border, four cartouches of women..........................................400.00

Urn, 6-3/4" h, 3 feet, two Victorian women with cupid, gold beading, cobalt blue ground..............................................................195.00

Vase, 9-1/2" h, Lady with Swallows, turquoise and gold beading, white ground ........................................................................475.00

## R. S. Germany

Basket
    Peafowls and Asian pheasants................................150.00
    Scallop & Fan, 5" x 3".............................................225.00

Cake Plate, 11-1/2" d, leaf shape, white and dark green, rose dec, steeple mark...........................................................................60.00

Celery Tray, 10-1/2" l, 5" w, pink flowers, green ground .............65.00

Creamer and Sugar, Art Deco dec.................................................135.00

Cup and Saucer, Art Deco, blue silhouette of dancing girl and scarf, beige luster ground, blue, black, and white bands....................90.00

Dish, 13" l, oval, open handles, pink and yellow roses .................45.00

Hatpin Holder, 4-1/2" h, large white rose at top, long green stem, shaded brown to green ground, green mark............................150.00

Demitasse Cup and Saucer, muted greens and gold, blown roses ...75.00

Luncheon Set, partial, seven 6" d plates, creamer, sugar, cov sweetmeat, light lavender ground, blue iris dec, heavy gold trim, price for set .......................................................................................100.00

Pitcher, 5" h, hidden images ........................................................265.00

Plate, 11-1/4" d, lilacs on white, green, and pink shaded ground, green and gold trim, gold rim....................................................110.00

Shaving Mug, Poppy pattern, with soap holder, scalloped base.100.00

Smoke Set, blue borders, match holder and pipe.......................295.00

Toothpick Holder, white daisies, blue ground, gold handles and top, slight wear to gold ...................................................................95.00

Tray, 15-1/4" l, white and green poppies, handles ......................250.00

Vase, 5-3/4" h, pheasant women, one with wheat gathering scene, other with sheep tending scene, mkd "RS Made in Germany/Poland," price for matched pair ..............................................................750.00

## R. S. Poland

Bowl, 10-1/2" d, Heart mold, poppies, satin finish.......................245.00

Candlestick, 6' h, violets, lily of the valley dec, shiny finish ........125.00

Hair Receiver, violets, lily of the valley dec.................................100.00

Hatpin Holder, 6" h, garland of red roses and green leaves, pale green band below with gold geometrics, pale green pierced top .......125.00

Powder Jar, violets, lily of the valley dec.....................................100.00

Server, 11" d, 8" h, center handle, lavender and orange roses...515.00

Vase

    7-1/4" h, large white roses, yellow centers, green foliage, shaded brown to cream ground ......................................................85.00

    8-3/4" h, cream ground, pink and white roses, gold band around top, garlands of gold roses and leaves ...........................195.00

## R. S. Prussia

Berry Set, 10-1/2" d berry bowl, six matching individual dishes, cream color, pink rose dec, luster finish ............................................350.00

Bowl
    9" d, jewel mold, light green, pink rose dec, opal jewels..... 140.00
    10" d, iris mold, pink and yellow, pink poppy dec...............225.00
    10-1/2" d, iris mold, cream center, dark green border, poppy dec ...........................................................................200.00
    11" d, scalloped mold, yellow, pink poppy dec...................140.00

Bowl in a Bowl, 10-1/2" d, dark green, yellow and brown, pink rose dec ...........................................................................................325.00

Cake Plate
    10" d, icicle mold, light green, water lily dec ......................150.00
    10-1/2" d, cabbage mold, light green, rose dec .................100.00
    10-1/2" d, carnation mold, green, white magnolia dec........130.00
    10-1/2" d, iris mold, light green, pink rose dec...................125.00
    10-1/2" d, iris mold, light pink, rose dec.............................150.00
    11" d, iris mold, light blue, pink rose dec...........................150.00
    11" d, iris mold, light green poppy dec ..............................140.00
    11" d, plume mold, browns, spilled basket dec ..................175.00
    11" d, point and clover mold, yellow and green, snowball and rose dec ...........................................................................180.00
    11" d, sunflower mold, white ground, pink rose dec...........125.00
    11-1/2" d, thistle mold, light green, pink poppy dec, luster finish...........................................................................75.00
    12" d, mold 38, rose dec, Tiffany finish border....................210.00

Celery Tray, 12" l, iris mold, yellow and blue, pink rose dec .........75.00

Chocolate Pot
    10" h, point and clover mold, pink and white rose dec, heavy gold, blue opals ...........................................................................350.00
    12" h, carnation mold, light green, pink and white rose dec380.00

Dresser Tray
    Carnation mold, pink poppy dec, heavy gold border ..........250.00
    Iris mold, rose dec, dark green border................................150.00
    Jewel mold, pink and white rose dec, heavy gold, Tiffany border......................................................................................225.00

Fernery Bowl, cabbage mold, cream and green, pink rose dec....50.00

Pin Tray, 5-1/2" l
    Medallion mold, water lily dec............................................100.00
    Point and clover mold, light green, glass bowl dec..............90.00

Plate, 9" d, swan scene, satin finish ...........................................150.00

Relish Tray, 9" l, stipple mold, dark green, rose dec.....................60.00

## R. S. Suhl

Bowl, 10" d, sheepherder scene, cottage, red mark ...................500.00

Compote, 4-1/2" d, ftd, creamy roses, gold stencil design, green mark.............................................................................................225.00

Cracker Jar, mold #628, spring season portrait, 7" h, $3,300. Photo courtesy of Woody Auction.

Sugar Bowl, cov, poppies and white flowers dec, shaded ground, 5" h, $90.

**Relish Dish, divided, green ground, white flowers, gold trim, mkd "R. S. Tillowitz, Silesia," 7-7/8" l, $45.**

Hatpin Holder, 5" h, hp pink roses, satin shaded blue to yellow ground, wreath mark ......................................................... 85.00
Pitcher, 5-1/2" h, white ground, red roses, unmarked ................ 115.00
Vase, 9-1/2" h, Gibson Girl portrait, red mark ........................... 850.00
Spittoon, pale green, pink roses ................................................. 275.00

## R. S. Tillowitz

Bowl, 10" x 6-1/4", oval, hp, pheasant hen and cock, blue mark 295.00
Cheese and Cracker Dish, 8-1/2" d, 2-1/2" h, blue mark, "Germany" in green .......................................................................... 65.00
Chocolate Pot, Art Nouveau dec, glossy finish ........................... 55.00
Dish, 8-1/2" l, oval, handle, gold trim ......................................... 38.00
Marmalade, cov, underplate, floral dec ....................................... 85.00
Plate, 7" d, stylized butterfly border, gold rim and handles, blue mark ............................................................................ 65.00
Relish, basket handle, bird of paradise ...................................... 350.00
Tray, five sided, roses dec .......................................................... 45.00

# SCHNEIDER GLASS

**History:** Brothers Ernest and Charles Schneider founded a glassworks at Epiney-sur-Seine, France, in 1913. Charles, the artistic designer, previously had worked for Daum and Gallé. Robert, son of Charles, assumed art direction in 1948. Schneider moved to Loris in 1962.

Although Schneider made tablewares, stained glass, and lighting fixtures, its best-known product is art glass which exhibits simplicity of design and often has bubbles and streaking in larger pieces. Other styles include cameo-cut and hydrofluoric-acid-etched designs.

**Marks:** Schneider glass was signed with a variety of script and block signatures, "Le Verre Francais," or "Charder."

Bowl, 6" h, spherical, colorless glass with mottled lime green and crackled dec, circular foot, sgd "Schneider," polished pontil, c1925 ............. 400.00
Box, cov, 5" d, 4-1/8" h, flattened spherical form, applied pointed knob, mottled white and orange layered in rose and purple, acid etched sign stylized berries and honeycomb border, base inscribed "Charder Le Verre Francais," c1925, cover loose ................... 500.00
Center Bowl, 10" d, 4-1/2" h, shaped orange bowl, layered with tortoiseshell brown, etched as five scarab beetles alternating geometric elements, lower edge inscribed "LeVerre Francais France/Ovington New York" .................................................... 700.00
Compote, 8" d, 5" h, blue rim on broad bowl of mottled yellow, applied bulbed stem and disk foot of mottled amethyst, foot sgd "Schneider," polished pontil, c1925 .................................... 750.00

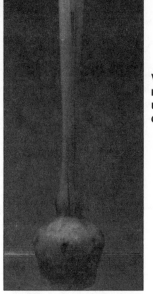

**Vase, 12" h, Jade Berluze, muted oranges and blues, sgd, urn mark, $460. Photo courtesy of David Rago Auctions.**

Rose Bowl, 4" d, 3" h, flattened spherical form, mottled red over mottled yellow and colorless glass, inscribed "Schneider France" near base, c1925, polished pontil ....................................... 320.00
Vase
6-1/2" h, ovoid with raised rim, mottled pink glass layered in maroon, rising to bright orange-red, etched stylized foxgloves, illegible signature at base, c1925 .................................... 690.00
6-3/4" h, swollen form, cushion base, deep purple over mottled lavender, inscribed "Schneider," polished pontil with distributor's paper label, minor abrasions, c1920 ............................. 650.00
9-5/8" h, swollen cylindrical, bulbed stem, cushion base, mottled red-orange and yellow, layered in striated maroon, cameo etched stylized clusters of grapes on vines, inscribed "Le Verre Francais," c1925, rough rim ........................................... 350.00

# SCHOENHUT TOYS

**History:** Albert Schoenhut, son of a toy maker, was born in Germany in 1849. In 1866, he ventured to America where he worked as a toy-piano repairman for Wanamaker's in Philadelphia, Pennsylvania. Finding the glass sounding bars inadequate, he perfected a toy piano with metal sounding bars. His piano was an instant success, and the A. Schoenhut Company had its beginning.

From that point on, toys seemed to flow out of the factory. Each of his six sons entered the business, and it prospered until 1934, when misfortune forced the company into bankruptcy. In 1935, Otto and George Schoenhut contracted to produce the Pinn Family Dolls.

The Schoenhut Manufacturing Company was formed by two other Schoenhuts. Both companies operated under a partnership agreement that eventually led to O. Schoenhut, Inc., which continues today.

Some dates of interest:

| | |
|---|---|
| 1872 | toy piano invented |
| 1903 | Humpty Dumpty Circus patented |
| 1911-1924 | wooden doll production |
| 1928-1934 | composition dolls made. |

**References:** E. Ackerman and F. Keller, *Under the Big Top with Schoenhut's Humpty Dumpty Circus*, published by author (P.O. Box 217, Culver City, CA 90230), 1997; Carol Corson, *Schoenhut Dolls*, Hobby House Press, 1993; Elizabeth Stephan (ed.,) *O'Brien's Collecting Toys*, 9th ed., Krause Publications, 1999.

**Collectors' Clubs:** Schoenhut Collectors Club, 1003 W. Huron St., Ann Arbor, MI 48103; Schoenhut Toy Collectors, 1916 Cleveland St., Evanston, IL 60202.

Animal, jointed wood construction
- Alligator, painted green, red mouth, white teeth, leather feet, 13" l ..............500.00
- Brown Bear, hand painted shades of brown, leather ears, 7-1/2" l on hind legs ..............275.00
- Buffalo, glass eyes, hand painted dark brown, leather horns, rope tail, 8" l ..............200.00
- Bulldog, painted white, black spot over eye, leather collar and tail, 5" l ..............410.00
- Camel, painted brown, black hoofs, rope tail, double hump back, 7-1/2" l ..............250.00
- Cat, olive brown, black stripes, white underbelly, leather tail, 4-1/4" h ..............770.00
- Cow, glass eyes, hand painted brown, leather collar, rope tail, horns, and ears, 8-1/2" l ..............265.00
- Donkey, glass eyes, painted brown, gray nose, fabric mane, price for pr ..............90.00
- Elephant, glass eyes, hand painted dark gray, rope tail and tusks, large leather ears, orig box ..............635.00
- Giraffe, painted ..............320.00
- Goat, glass eyes, hand painted black and white, leather ears, horns, beard and tail, 8" l ..............220.00
- Goose, glass eyes, painted white, orange beak and feet, 7" l .360.00
- Gorilla, painted brown, leather ears, 11" arm span ..........3,410.00
- Hippo, painted eyes, dark brown, leather tail and ears, wooden carved front teeth, 10" l ..............185.00
- Horse, glass eyes, painted brown, leather ears and saddle, 8" h, missing stirrups, price for pr ..............110.00
- Hyena, Teddy Roosevelt safari animal, hand painted gray with stripes, leather ears, rope tail, 6" l ..............1,430.00
- Kangaroo, painted shades of brown, white underbelly, leather ears, stands on rear legs and tail, 10-1/2" l ..............440.00
- Leopard, painted yellow with brown spots, rope tail, 7-1/4" l ...360.00
- Pig, glass eyes, painted light brown, leather ears, 8" l .........55.00
- Polar Bear, painted white, short rope tail, leather ears, 8" l 660.00
- Poodle, glass eyes, painted white, rope tail, 7" l ..............55.00
- Rabbit, painted brown, leather ears and tail, 5-1/4" l ..........715.00
- Rhino, painted eyes, hand painted olive brown with black spots, rope tail, leather ears, 9" l, one ear missing ..............110.00
- Seal, painted dark brow, leather flipper hands, 9" l............290.00
- Show Horse, glass eyes, ring tail, leather ears, wooden platform mounted on back, 10" l, price for pr ..............360.00
- Tiger, hand painted orange, brown spots, rope tail, 7-1/2" l, some paint flaking ..............230.00

**Circus Tiger, painted wood, 7-1/2" l, $185.**

- Wolf, painted shades of brown, red mouth, long carved wooden tail, leather ears..............1,980.00
- Zebra, painted light brown with dark stripes, leather ears, rope tail, 7-3/4" l ..............330.00
- Balancing Bar, painted wood and metal..............550.00
- Cage Wagon, 12" x 12", wood, red, gray bars, blue wheels, top mkd "Schoenhut's Humpty Dumpty Circus," contains lion with full mane, rear door opens..............990.00
- Camera, Spirit of America, wood, painted black, movie camera clicks when turned, 10" h, orig box ..............935.00
- Circus Animal in Cage, wood animal, wire cage
  - 7-1/2" h, brown bear, leather ears, hand painted, shades of brown..............220.00
  - 8" l, lion, rope tail, carved head, body painted light to medium brown ..............415.00
  - 11" h, giraffe, leather ears, wood short horns, rope tail, natural colors..............770.00
- Circus Pedestals, painted wood and litho paper, price for 5 pc set.. 470.00
- Figure, jointed wood construction
  - Barney Google and Spark Plug, wood hat, fabric suit, yellow blanket with name on Spark Plug ..............550.00
  - Black Dude, hand painted face, leather ears, long purple coat, yellow vest, checkered pants, white top hat, 8-1/2" h ......315.00
  - Circus Acrobat, bisque head, hand painted, fabric suit, blue and yellow felt suit, red shorts..............300.00
  - Farmer, straw hat, bucket and rake, 7" h..............110.00
  - Felix the Cat, black and white, large leather ears..............470.00
  - Hobo, hand painted face, leather ears, felt jacket and hat, fabric pants and scarf around neck..............140.00
  - Maggie and Jiggs, cloth and fabric suits, animated appearance, Maggie holding rolling pin ..............525.00
  - Mary and Her Lamb, cloth outfit, straw hat, white lamb, school desk, feeding trough..............1,430.00
  - Ringmaster, hand painted face, red tails, vest, and pants, orig top hat and whip..............250.00
- Golf Game, indoor, 36" l long wooden handles with golfers, tee area, putting green, sand trap, water well, balls..............1,320.00
- Pull Toy, Hood's Milk Wagon, jointed Schoenhut figure, painted, decal on wooden wagon, hide-covered platform horse, wear to hide, feet missing from driver, 23"..............1,000.00
- School Desk, painted wood, for Mary and her lamb set .............190.00
- Weights, painted wood, lift weights, 50 lb barbells, 100 lb barbells, price for 4 pc set..............990.00

# SCIENTIFIC INSTRUMENTS

**History:** Chemists, doctors, geologists, navigators, and surveyors used precision instruments as tools of their trade. Such objects were well designed and beautifully crafted. They are primarily made of brass; fancy hardwood cases also are common.

The 1990s have seen a keen interest in scientific instruments, both in the auction market and at antique shows. The number of collectors of this mechanical wonders is increasing as more and more interesting examples are being offered.

**References:** Florian Cajori, *History of the Logarithmic Slide Rule and Allied Instruments*, Astragal Press, 1994; Gloria Clifton, *Directory of British Scientific Instrument Makers 1550-1851*, P. Wilson Publishers, 1994; William H. Skerritt, *Catalog of the Charles E. Smart Collection: Antique Surveying Instruments*, published by author, (12 Locust Ave., Troy, NY 12180), 1996; Gerard L. E. Turner, *Scientific Instruments 1500-1900: An Introduction*, University of California Press, 1998.

**Periodicals:** *Tesseract*, P.O. Box 151, Hastings-on-Hudson, NY 10706; *Scientific, Medical & Mechanical Antiques*, P.O. Box 412, Taneytown, MD 21787, http://americanartifacts.com/smma.

**Collectors' Clubs:** International Calculator Collectors Club, 14561 Livingston St., Tustin, CA 92680; Maryland Microscopical Society, 8261 Polk St., McLean VA, 22102; The Oughtred Society, 2160 Middlefield Rd, Palo Alto, CA 94301; Zeiss Historical Society, P.O. Box 631, Clifton, NJ 07012.

**Museum:** National Museum of American History, Smithsonian Institution, Washington, DC.

**Adder**, 6-3/4" l, 4-7/8" w, brass, mahogany backer, brass wall fasteners, mkd "C. H. Webb N.Y. 'The Adder' PATd March 10, 1868, B1108".............................................................520.00

**Anemometer**, 6 register, 8 blade, 2-5/8" d fan derives 2-1/4" d silvered dial with six registers from 1 to 9,999,999 cubic feet, brass construction, mounting bracket, softwood case, c1875 . 350.00 **Artificial Horizon,** unsigned, mercury reservoir with two glass covers, 6-1/4" l, 3-7/8" w, 3-7/8" h, mercury filled container locks into dovetailed mahogany case, c1900 ..................................................... 490.00

**Batson Sketching Case**, 10-1/2" l, 7" w overall, 4-1/2" x 6-1/8" plotting surface, 5" d graduated plotting scale, 2" l rotating trough compass, 2 paper rollers, varnished hardwood and lacquered brass, sgd "W. & L. E. Gurley, Troy, NY," patent Sept. 28, 1897 ................ 750.00

**Chronometer**

Hamilton Watch Co., Lancaster, PA, model 36, 21 jewel, 5 position, motor barrel, double roller, 56 hour, 5" mahogany cube, double lid, gimballed deck case, nickel silver finish, 2-3/4" d bezel, c1918............................................................... 1,495.00

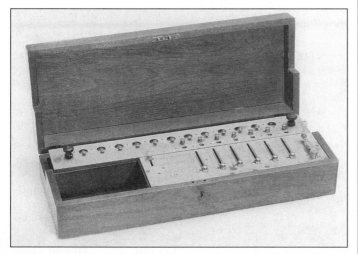

**Arithmomètre, by Thomas de Colmar, c1870, $4,530. Photo courtesy of Auction Team Breker.**

Waltham Watch Co., 8 days, 4-7/8" cube mahogany double lid desk case, weighted brass case in brass gimbals, second hand, winding register, 15 jewels, c1913 .................................. 635.00

**Circumferentor**, 5-1/4" h, 9" outside diameter, brass, 4-1/8" compass in center, attached to rotating sight vane/vernier arm, inset vial, silvered dial, outer ring engraved with 8 point star, 2 outer fixed sight vanes, Dollond London, c1825............................................. 1,955.00

**Drawing Instruments**, cased, 6" l ivory and brass sector, 6" l ivory scale, 6" ebony and brass parallel rule, 1-3/4" brass protractor, six brass and iron drafting tools with ram's head screws, 6" l x 3" w black shagreen cov wood case, unsgd, c1800 .................................. 400.00

**Fowler's Calculator**, Fowler & Co. Manchester, England, 6978, two 11/16" d x 1-1/2" thick with circular logarithmic scales on both faces, two stems for rotating faces and cursor, nickel plated, sq velvet lined case, c1920............................................................... 375.00

**Globe**, 39" h, Cram's, floor model, wooden stand with tripod snake feet................................................................... 1,550.00

**Lords Patent Pocket Calculator**, 2-1/2" d pocket watch style, three stems move inner dial and its cursor, center ring and minute hand type cursor, three circular logarithmic scales engraved on silvered dial, c1920................................................................... 920.00

**Microscope, Binocular,** T. W. Watson, 4 Pall Mall, London, No. 287, 18-1/2" h, mounted on case board, 12-1/4" l binocular tubes, single focus for both ubes, fine focus on eyep. End, rect mechanical stage on 4-3/8" d rotating stage with degree scale to 1/2º, gimballed mirror yoke, lacquered brass, "H. B. Gelb," 1879 .............................. 750.00

**Microscope, Cary Type**

Paul Roescler, New Haven, Ct, 7-3/4" h, rack and pinion focus of 2-1/8" d glass stage, horiz. and vert. adjustable eyep. Arm, single mirror, lacquered brass, 4-1/2" w x 6-1/2" l x 2-7/8" h mahogany case, c1875 ..................................................... 920.00

Unsigned, 7" h, rack and pinion focus of 2" d glass stage, vert. and horiz. adjustable lens holder, 3 lenses, single mirror, dissecting knife and tweezers, lacquered brass, mahogany case, c1875 ................................................................... 750.00

**Microscope, Compound Monocular**

Bausch & Lomb Optical Co., Rochester, NY

#1761, Family, 13-3/4" h, 9-5/8" l, 1-1/8" d tube with single obj., rack and pinion focus, rect table, 4 hole diaphragm, single mirror, 1 eyep., 2 obj., japanned and lacquered brass, case, c1882 1,100.00

#11737, 12" h, 8-1/2" l, 1-1/8" d tube with 1 object., fine focus on arm, rect stage, 5-hole diaphragm, double mirror on rotating arm, extra eyep., orig case, japanned and lacquered brass, sgd "Wm. H. Armstrong & Co., Indianapolis, Ind ," c1893 ...... 635.00

#13668, 13-1/4" h, 9" l, 1-1/2" d single nosepiece tube, 3-1/2" d stage, condenser and double mirror revolve on arms centered on stage, against graduated vertical circular silvered dial, 4 obj. and 3 eyep., lacquered brass, orig case, mkd "Pat. Oct 13, 1885, c1894" ............................................................... 1,840.00

Boston Optical Co., Boston, 17-1/4" h, 12" l, 1-3/16" d tube with double nosepiece and calibrated draw tube, fine focus on tube, 4-1/4" d rotatable stage table, condenser with double mirror on rotating arm, lacquered brass, case, c1870 .................. 5,175.00

Boston Optical Works Tolles, SN 140, 14-1/4" h, 9-1/4" l, 1-1/8" d tube with single obj., fine focus at bottom of tube, mechanical stage, 4 hole diaphragm with tube, double mirror, 3 eyep., 2 obj., slides, case, c1870............................................ 1,380.00

Spencer, Buffalo, folding, 10-1/4" h, 6-1/4" l x 1-1/2" d tube, triple nosepiece, micrometer drum fine focus on arm, calibrated draw tube, rect stage, condenser, double mirror, japanned and lacquered brass, heavy metal case, c1900 .......................... 750.00

Tolles, Boston, 272, 15-1/2" h, 10-1/2" l, 1-1/4" d tube, single nosepiece, fine focus on front of tube, 4-1/2" d stage, 2 substage condensers, double mirror, detachable parabolic mirror, extra 8" l, 1-1/" d, draw tube, detachable stand condenser lens with "bug" holder, prism eyep., 2 objt., 2 eyep., lacquered brass, orig case, c1875............................................................ 2,070.00

Zentmayer, J., Philadelphia, 726," hospital style stand, 15" h, 10-3/4" l, 1-1/2" d, single obj. with fine focus on tube, rect table, slide holder, 4 hole tube diaphragm, double mirror, 4 eyep., 2 obj., lacquered brass, case, condenser stand, c1879 ...... 980.00

**Microscope Compendium**, Wilson, 3-1/4" l x 1-1/8" d, screw barrel, brass construction with socket for ivory handle (missing), spring loaded under specimen plate, 11/16" d eyep., detachable simple microscope with six numbered lenses, four with lens caps, four hole brass slide holder, mahogany case, unsigned, c1925 ............. 575.00

**Miner's Dial**, hanging, 8-1/4" l, 5-1/2" h, 4" d gimballed 3" compass, silvered dial and outer ring, lacquered bright brass, Otto Fennel Cassel, c1900 ........................ 635.00

**Nystrom's Calculator,** "Patented March 4, 1851, Made by W. J. Young, Philada," No. 754, 9-1/2" d, 5-1/4" l, "A" and "B" arms, "C" dial with 1" long arrow pointer, brass construction, silver plate scale face, engraved lines, numerals, and letters, c1855 ..................... 10,350.00

**Octant**
    Bassnet, Liverpool, 12-3/4" l, 10-1/2" w, ebony arms, circle, and "T" cross brace, brass accessories, ivory scale, vernier, and nameplate, 3 sun glasses, scratch pad and pencil missing............520.00
    F. W. Lincoln Jr. & Co., Boston, 13" x 11-1/2" case, ebony and ivory, brass fittings, ivory scale to 105 degrees, paper label on case.................................... 700.00
    Simon Robinson, 16" l, 13" w, 14" rad. ivory circle, ivory vernier with 1' least count, ivory nameplate and scratch pad, adjustable mirrors, brass arm and fittings, ebony arms and braces, 3 smoked glass, pie shaped case, labeled "Richard Patten, NY," c1820 ...................... 750.00

**Palmer's Computing Scale/Fuller's Time Telegraph**, two 8-1/2" d scale wheels with finger grommets, on 10-7/8" sq outer scale board, computing scale logarithmic, Time Telegraph Scale is liner, gold, brown, black, and pastel green, mkd "Aaron Palmer/John F. Fuller," engraving by Geo. G. Smith, c1846 ...................... 1,035.00

**Railroad Compass**
    Pocket, 7-1/4" l, 6" w, 10" h, 4-1/2" l hinged sight vanes, 4 screw leveling adaptor, 3-1/2" d silvered compass card and ring with declination vernier, 1' single vernier horiz circle, bronzed brass finish, orig case with paper label, made by W. & L. E. Gurley, Troy, NY, c1880 ......................... 2,185.00
    Vernier, 15-7/8" l, 71/2" w, 3-7/8" h, without sight vanes, crossed vials, outside 30º, 1' declination vernier, outside 7" d, 1', 2 vernier horizontal scale, needle floats over 5-1/2" d silvered dial engraved with 8-point star, edge engraved out ring, darkened brass, dovetailed mahogany case, sgd "James Meneely made Janry. 1838," Meneeley & Oothout, West Troy, NY, Warranted No. 674.............................. 2,300.00

**Sperry Pocket Calculator,** Keuffel & Esser Co., NY, Pat. Dec 26, 11, 777, 2-1/8" d pocket watch style, dual faces, 2 knob stem rotates the dials with logarithmic scale and minute hand style cursors, German silver finish ........................... 920.00

**Telescope**
    39" l closed, 52" l extended, brass, French, engraved "Telegraphe No. 22…Bardou Rue St. Martin No. 171…A Paris," brass ends, wood center, wood split.................................... 350.00
    95" h extended, 59" l telescope, pedestal mounted, counter weighted equatorial mount, mahogany telescope case with 10 eyep., 5 colored lenses, lens caps, sgd "J. H.Steward Ltd , 406 Strand, London," c1910, including both handwritten and typed copies of approx. 250 pgs *Southern Stars for Small Telescopes…,* by G. V. Hudson, F.R.S.N.Z., 1925.............. 4,600.00

# SCRIMSHAW

**History:** Norman Flayderman defined scrimshaw as "the art of carving or otherwise fashioning useful or decorative articles as practiced primarily by whalemen, sailors, or others associated with nautical pursuits." Many collectors expand this to include the work of Eskimos and French POWs from the War of 1812.

**References:** Stuard M. Frank, *Dictionary of Scrimshaw Artists*, Mystic Seaport Museum, 1991; Nina Hellman

and Norman Brouwer, *Mariner's Fancy*, South Street Seaport Museum, Balsam Press, and the University of Washington Press, 1992; Martha Lawrence, *Scrimshaw*, Schiffer Publishing, 1993.

**Museums:** Cold Spring Whaling Harbor Museum, Cold Spring Harbor, NY; Kendall Whaling Museum, Sharon, MA; Mystic Seaport Museum, Mystic, CT; National Maritime Museum, San Francisco, CA; New Bedford Whaling Museum, New Bedford, MA; Old Dartmouth Historical Society, New Bedford, MA; Pacific Whaling Museum, Waimanalo, HI; Sag Harbor Whaling & Historical Museum, Sag Harbor, NY; San Francisco Maritime National Historical Park, San Francisco, CA; South Street Seaport Museum, New York, NY; Whaling Museum, Nantucket, MA.

**Bracelet,** five oval scrimshaw plaques, three depicting nautical scenes, all sgd "Howard Weyahok," joined by 14kt yellow gold trace link chain ...................................................................60.00

**Buggy Whip,** 82" l, whale ivory and whalebone sections, baleen rings, two rope carvings, mid 19th C.................................................. 2,000.00

**Busk**
    11-1/4" l, whale bone, engraved compass, stars, tree, flags, hot air balloon....................................................500.00
    11-1/2" h, whalebone, whale, lighthouse, and American eagle, 19th C...........................................................550.00
    12-1/2" h, whalebone, heralding angel, harp, and two story house, 19th C, repaired crack.............................. 230.00
    13-1/4" h, baleen, panels of floral and geometric design, 19th C, minor chipping to one side ............................. 200.00
    13-1/2" h, baleen, panels of palm trees, three story building, ship, 19th C, age cracks and worming...................................... 230.00
    14-1/4" h, panels of woman, plants, and heart, 19th C, in two pcs.................................................................225.00

**Butter Mold,** 5-1/8" h, circular, wood, carved rosette, whale ivory handle, early to mid-19th C ........................................................... 275.00

**Cane**
    31-17/8" h, wood and whalebone, whale ivory and baleen rings, 19th C................................................................. 295.00

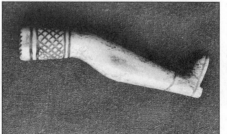

**Pipe Tamp,** serrated tamp end, engraved high button shoe, lattice garter, 2-1/2" l, $200.

37-1/2" l, wood, whale ivory tip and knob, partially wound baleen and ropework, diamond shape wood inlays, 19th C ........275.00

Chest, 20-3/4" x 9-1/2" x 9", walnut or mahogany and pine, hinged top, three inlaid abstract whalebone figures on front panel and initials "G. W. T." .....................................................550.00

Cribbage Board, 18-1/2" d, walrus tusk, 7 walruses ...................300.00

Ostrich Egg, engraved sailor, sweetheart, eagle, flag, stars, and ship, orig ropework hanger .............................................................275.00

Sewing Box
   6-3/4" l, engraved baleen, stuffed brocade pin cushion lid, 19th C, small losses ...................................................1,100.00
   8" sq, island wood, geometric wood inlays, inlaid whale ivory and abalone shell compass rose, diamonds and spandrel dec, mid-19th C.....................................................650.00

Snuff Box, 3 x 1-1/2" l; shaped oval, top diamond inscribed "R. N.," (Royal Navy) and anchor, other side inscribed "Capt. N. C. Norten," dates of service, 1831, 1841, on ends, fluting, highlighted with lamp-black ...................................................450.00

Watch Fob, whale ivory, book form, engraved colored Masonic symbols, mid-19th C ...................................................395.00

Whale's Tooth, 19th C
   4" l, engraved fashion portrait of lady, holding flower sprig, polychrome dec, age cracks ...................................................675.00
   4-1/8" l, engraved fashion portrait of lady, holding flower bouquet, polychrome dec, age cracks ...................................................700.00
   4-1/4" l, engraved and polychromed, woman wearing cape and hat, holding flowers and basket, yellow, red, and brown tones, reverse with parrot in tree with red and yellow highlights, minor chips to edge, age cracks ...................................................865.00
   5-1/2" l, one side with eagle and shield over cannon barrel, surrounded by flowering vine and butterfly, reverse decorated with rooster, age cracks.....................................................2,415.00
   5-3/4" l, both sides engraved with British Ship *Calliope* at sea with flags flying, "G. Wozencroft" inscribed below and "Calliope" in banner above, reverse with "Calliope" in an oval above ship, touches of red sealing wax.....................................................3,450.00
   6" l, engraved young lady in mid 19th C costume and bonnet, age crack.....................................................920.00
   6" l, woman seated on sea serpent, banner inscribed "The Queen of the Sea," costumed man and woman holding flag "United States Secret Service," and woman wearing mid-19th C dress, age cracks .....................................................2,415.00
   6-1/4" l, obverse engraved with American three-masted sailing vessel, intaglio cut hull, reverse faintly scribed with two-masted sailing ship, lighthouse in background beneath an eagle, surface imperfections .....................................................2,070.00
   8" l, obverse with polychrome dec of native woman picking fruit from tree, hut, palm trees, and mountains, other side with lady, anchor, and trees on shire, marine scene in distance, minor age cracks.....................................................2,300.00
   15-1/2" l, engraved women wearing a hat, two-masted fishing vessel, two husky dogs, man sluicing for gold, inscribed "Nome, Alaska, 1901," reverse with *S. S. Oregon*, age cracks.....575.00

# SEVRES

**History:** The principal patron of the French porcelain industry in early 18th-century France was Jeanne Antoinette Poisson, Marquise de Pompadour. She supported the Vincennes factory of Gilles and Robert Dubois and their successors in their attempt to make soft-paste porcelain in the 1740s. In 1753, she moved the porcelain operations to Sevres, near her home, Chateau de Bellevue.

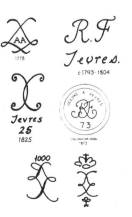

The Sevres soft-paste formula used sand from Fontainebleau, salt, saltpeter, soda of alicante, powdered alabaster, clay, and soap. Many famous colors were developed, including a cobalt blue. The wonderful scenic designs on the ware were painted by such famous decorators as Watteau, La Tour, and Boucher. In the 18th century, Sevres porcelain was the world's foremost diplomatic gift.

In 1769, kaolin was discovered in France, and a hard-paste formula was developed. The baroque gave way to rococo, a style favored by Jeanne du Barry, Louis XV's next mistress. Louis XVI took little interest in Sevres, and many factories began to turn out counterfeits. In 1876, the factory was moved to St. Cloud and was eventually nationalized.

**References:** Susan and Al Bagdade, *Warman's English & Continental Pottery & Porcelain*, 3rd Edition, Krause Publications, 1998; Carl Christian Dauterman, *Sevres Porcelain, Makers and Marks of the Eighteenth Century,* Metropolitan Museum of Art, 1986; Linda Humphries, *Sevres Porcelain from the Sevres Museum 1740 to the Present,* Hund Humphries, 1997; George Savage, *Seventeenth & Eighteenth Century French Porcelain,* Hamlyn Publishing Co., Ltd., 1969.

**Museums:** Art Institute of Chicago, Chicago, IL; British Museum, London, England; Frick Collection, New York, NY; Gardiner Museum of Ceramic Art Museum, Toronto, Canada; J. Paul Getty Museum, Los Angeles, CA; Metropolitan Museum of Art, New York, NY; Musee de Louvre, Paris, France, Musee National e Ceramique, Sevres, France; Victoria & Albert Museum, London, England; Wadsworth Atheneum, Harford, CT.

**Marks:** Louis XV allowed the firm to use the "double L" in its marks.

**Reproduction Alert.**

**Urn, cov, courting scene of couple walking, pastels, artist initials, metal handles, rim, and base, mkd, 12" h, $335.**

**Bowl**

8-3/4" d, 3-1/4" h, exotic bird and swags of flowers, early blue mark ...................................................................... 500.00

11-1/4" d, 4-1/4" h, inside of bowl dec with large spray of flowers, outside medium blue, one large panel of colorful flowers, another with cherub flanking Louis Philip seal, crown over intertwined L & P surrounded by wreath mark ........................ 400.00

**Box, cov**

3" w, sq, hinged, cobalt blue, courting scene on lid, gold dec ..300.00

5-1/2" l, shell shape, hinged lid, center scene of figures in landscape, sgd "Max" in scrolled gilt cartouche, sides dec with small landscape scenes in similar cartouches, late 19th C ........ 635.00

**Bust**, 9-3/4" h, Napoleon, bisque, cobalt socle base, stamp for 1870 ................................................................................920.00

**Cabinet Plate**

9-1/2" d, central painted portrait bust of Mme Elisabeth, sgd "Debrie" in bluette surround, gilt dec, mkd for Chateau de St. Cloud, c1846 ...................................................................... 195.00

9-1/2" d, central painted scene of courting couple, sgd "O. Brun" in celeste blue surround, gilt dec, mkd for Chateau des Tuileries, c1844 ........................................................................ 175.00

10" d, central portrait of Mme de Maintenon, jeweled surround, cobalt blue border with floral cartouches on white ground, gilt scrollwork and further jewelling, identified on back, second half 19th C ............................................................ 1,150.00

**Cache Pot**, 5-1/2" h, figural cartouche of putto, sky blue ground, silver overlay floral and swag dec........................................................ 800.00

**Center Bowl**, 12-3/4" d, painted reserves of courting couple, landscape, cobalt blue ground, gilt metal mounts, sgd "Guy," c1900 .............. 400.00

**Compote**, 10-5/8" d, center portrait medallion of Louis XVI, gilt scroll and floral border, pink ground, two gilt lined flat handles ......... 275.00

**Cup and Saucer**, gilt and floral panels, apple green ground ......... 75.00

**Dresser Box**, cov, 5-3/4" l, oval, portrait medallion of lady o cov, floral side dec, gold bronze mounts .............................................. 350.00

**Garniture Vase**, 22" h, gilt-brass mounted, obverse with gallants reserve, reverse with bucolic landscape reverse, Belle Epoque, c1900-15, now mounted as lamps, price for pr ...................... 1,100.00

**Inkwell**

9" l, floral swag dec, sky blue and gilt ground, attached to quatrefoil dish .......................................................................... 550.00

10-1/2" l, gondola-form, green painted hull, gilt rim and prow ..250.00

**Magnifying Glass**, 14-1/2" l, porcelain handle with figural cartouches, gilt and cobalt blue ground ........................................................ 700.00

**Lamp Base**, 24-1/4" h, made from urns, green, gold trim, oval reserves of romantic couples, pr............................................................ 375.00

**Patch Box**, 6" l, cobalt blue ground, painted Napoleonic scene, sides painted with landscape panels, gilt scrolls, sgd "Henet," late 19th C .....................................................................................980.00

**Plate**

8" d, embracing couple, garden setting, yellow dec, scalloped gold dec rim, artist sgd, marked "Chateau St. Cloud" ........ 95.00

11" d, two putti, monogram, celeste blue borders, factory marks, sgd "Bruny," Louis-Philippe, 1846 .................................. 225.00

**Portrait Plate**, 9-3/4" d, set of three, each with shaped cobalt blue edge, gilt dec Napoleonic devices, central painted porcelain portrait busts sgd "Gaby," of Napoleon, Josephine, and "Roi de Rome," price for three pc set .............................................................. 1,100.00

**Urn**, 18th C courting couples within cartouche, cobalt ground, ormolu mounts, electrified, pr............................................................ 500.00

**Vase**, 5" h, ovoid, figural and landscape cartouches, cobalt blue and gilt ground ................................................................................ 250.00

# SEWING ITEMS

**History:** As recently as 50 years ago, a wide variety of sewing items were found in almost every home in America. Women of every economic and social status were skilled in sewing and dressmaking.

Iron or brass sewing birds, one of the interesting convenience items which developed, were used to hold cloth (in the bird's beak) while sewing. They could be attached to a table or shelf with a screw-type fixture. Later models included a pincushion.

**References:** *Advertising & Figural Tape Measures*, L-W Book Sales, 1995; Elizabeth Arbittier et al., *Collecting Figural Tape Measures*, Schiffer Publishing, 1995; Carter Bays, *Encyclopedia of Early American Sewing Machines*, published by author, 1993; Ruth Miller Clark, *Carnival of Iridescent Luster Buttons, 1986; Book II, 1992 (*2100 Dawn Dr., Georgetown, TX 78628)*; Book III (*Alan G. Perry, 7614 McKenry St., Houston, TX 77087-3834), 1997; Jane O. Dinkins, *Sketchbook of Little Carnival Glass Buttons,* (1100 Ridgeley Dr., Houston, TX 77055) 1996; Fink & Ditzler, *Buttons, The Collector's Guide To Selecting, Restoring and Enjoying New & Vintage Buttons, 1993;* Edith M. Fuoss and Nora O. Jones, *Black Glass Buttons,* 1945 (reprint by New Leaf Publishers); Edith M. Fuoss and Caroline Smith, *Black Glass Buttons, Return Engagement,* 1952; Elizabeth Hughes and Marion Lester, *The Big Book of Buttons,* 1981 (reprint by New Leaf Publishers); Lori Hughes, *A Century of American Sewing Patterns, 1860-1959,* C & B Press, 1998; Frieda Marion, *China Half-Figures Called Pincushion Dolls*, published by author, 1974, 1994 reprint; Averil Mathis, *Antique & Collectible Thimbles and Accessories,* Collector Books, 1997; Bridget McConnel, *The Story of Antique Needlework Tools,* Schiffer Publishing, 1999; Wayne Muller, *Darn It!,* L-W Book Sales, 1995; Florence Zacharie Nicholls, *Button Handbook, with three supplements, 1943-1949,(*reprints by New Leaf Publishers); James W. Slaten, *Antique American Sewing Machines*, Singer Dealer Museum (3400 Park Blvd., Oakland, CA 94610), 1992; Glenda Thomas, *Toy and Miniature Sewing Machines* (1995, 1997 value update), Book II (1997), Collector Books; Helen Lester Thompson, *Sewing Tools & Trinkets,* Collector Books, 2000; Debra J. Wisniewski, *Antique & Collectible Buttons,* Collector Books, 1999; Estelle Zalkin, *Zalkin's Handbook of Thimbles & Sewing Implements,* Warman Publishing Co., 1988, distributed by Krause Publications, http://www.krause.com.

**Collectors' Clubs:** Buckeye State Button Society, 251 Pfeiffer Ave., Akron, OH 44312-4137; Denton Button Club, 500 El Paseo, Denton, TX 76205-8502; International Sewing Machine Collectors Society, 551 Kelmore St., Moss Beach, CA 94038, http://ismacs.net; National Button Society, 2733 Juno Place, Apt. 4, Akron, OH 44313-4137; Pioneer Button Club, 102 Frederick St., Oshawa, Ontario L1G 2B3 Canada; The Button Club, P.O. Box 2274, Seal Beach, CA 90740; Thimble Collectors International, 2594 E Upper Hayden Lake Road, Hayden, ID 83835; Thimble Guild, P.O. Box 381807, Duncanville, TX 75138-1807; Toy Stitchers, 623 Santa Florita Ave., Millbrae, CA 94030.

**Periodicals:** *Button Bytes,* http://www.tias.com/articles/buttons; *That Darn Newsletter,* 461 Brown Briar Circle, Horsham, PA 19044; *Thimbletter,* 93 Walnut Hill Road, Newton Highlands, MA 02161-1836.

**Museums:** Antique Sewing Machine Museum, Oakland, CA; Button Bytes, http://www.tias.com/museum/clothing buttons.html; Fabric Hall, Historic Deerfield, Deerfield, MA; Frank Smith's Sewing Machine Museum, Arlington, TX, http://rampages.onramp.net/~arlprosv/museum.htm; Museum of American History, Smithsonian Institution, Washington, DC; Shelburne Museum, Shelburne, VT.

**Additional Listings:** See Thimbles and *Warman's Americana & Collectibles* for more examples.

Basket, cov, round, birch bark and quill, two bears, damaged...... 25.00
Bodkin, sterling silver, engraved, floral dec, hallmarked .............. 35.00
Booklet
    Singer, "The honor of your company is most respectfully requested at the Exhibition of the latest Novelties in Art Needle Work and Home Decoration, now open at the Singer Office…" .............. 14.00
    Wrights Bias Tape & Trimming, Idea Booklet, 6" x 9" .......... 10.00
Caddy, 8-1/4" w, 5-5/8" d, 8-1/4" h, grain painted, shaped pierced carved galleried top, sixteen spool holders, one drawer, shaped base, America, 19th C.............................................................. 250.00
Chatelaine
    Leather, three straps connect to scissors and case, thimble holder and pencil, English, c1900 ................................................ 215.00
    Sterling Silver, ring top, chains connect to note pad, thimble and thimble case, buttonhook, English ..................................... 575.00
Color Chart, Wrights Bias Tape & Trimmings, emb areas that look like fabric samples, 9" x 12-1/4"....................................................... 20.00
Crochet Hooks, whale bone, carved, price for 3 pc set ............. 245.00
Darning Ball, Nailsea, blown glass, blue, white pulled loops ...... 115.00
Hemming Clamp
    2-1/2" l, 7/8" w, 4" h, carved ivory and bone, three applied ivory diamond motifs, chip-carved edge dec, iron screw, America, 19th C, hairline................................................................. 575.00
    4-1/2" l, carved American shield with red and blue coloration, carved ivory star thumbscrew, America, 19th C, chip....... 690.00
    5-3/4" h, carved, two contrasting ivory triangles and polka dots, baleen dec, turned wooden screw, America, 19th C, age cracks ............................................................................... 635.00
    8" h, carved ivory dolphin figure, baleen eyes, whale bone C-clamp and thumbscrew, America, 19th C, minor age cracks......... 2,990.00
Knitting Needles, 12-3/4" to 15" l, three pairs, ivory, exotic wood, baleen and whalebone, minor cracks, some insect damage. 1,650.00
Label, diecut, New Home Sewing Machine Company, multicolored, white lettering
    Butterfly............................................................................... 30.00
    Heart ..................................................................................... 18.00
    Leaf ....................................................................................... 18.00
Needle Cabinet, Standard Sewing Machine, dark brown, black and gilt lettering, one long compartmentalized drawer, six small drawers ..1,050.00
Needle Case, ivory, book shape, fabric pages............................ 125.00
Pin Cushion Box, 3" d, 2-1/2" h, cylindrical, padded green silk covered top, green, dark red, and black floral pattern wallpaper covered cardboard sides, America, 19th C, wear, loss to wallpaper ............. 460.00
Punch, 3-1/8" l, ivory, turnings on top .......................................... 40.00
Quilt Frame, 36" h, two 111" l rails, two 100-1/2" l rails, curly maple, old soft brown patina, four turned legs and posts, all wooden clamps 660.00
Scissors, 6-1/2" l, dagger shaped, nacre inlay, emb maker's name, steel.................................................................................... 175.00
Sewing Bird, 4-1/2" h, nickel plated brass, purple velvet pin cushion................................................................................. 175.00

Sewing, Federal, mahogany veneer, 3 drawers, ornately carved pedestal base, $900. Photo courtesy of Joy Luke Fine Art Brokers and Auctioneers.

Sewing Box
    7" w, 10" l, 4-3/4" h, Neoclassical, America, 19th C, mahogany, chamfered hinged lid with contrasting dark veneer border and inset at center, hand painted scene of house beside river, int. fitted with mirror on lid, lift-out tray with divided compartments, floral emb brass feet, wear, scratches ............................. 1,100.00
    7-1/2" w, 5-1/4" d, 7" h, carved and painted, three tiered rect, carved and pierced scalloped border at top, glass bead and carved spire finials, pierced diamond and scallop motifs, drawer below, painted dark blue, red, and yellow, PA, 19th C, lacking one carved spire at side, minor paint loss........................ 750.00
    14-5/8" w, 10-3/4" d, 6-3/4" h, black lacquer, paneled rect with canted corners, case dec with gilt cartouches of Chinese figures, floral sprays, carved giltwood dragon's head feet, hinged lid, removable segmented tray, single front drawer, Chinese Export, late 19th C ......................................................... 690.00
Sewing Clamp, carved ivory, America, 19th C
    4-1/2" h, pair of carved ivory horse heads with studded brass eyes, wiretwist reigns flanking carved horn clip, clamp body dec with pierced star, heart-shaped thumbscrew, minor age cracks .................................................................................815.00
    4-3/4" h, carved and incised crested bird on oval platform with carved edge, pierced heart motif below, brass thumb screw, cracks ................................................................................ 980.00
    5-1/4" h, closed-fisted hand screw, clamp body dec with incised leaf and stippled tulip motifs, metal heart-shaped thumbscrew, age cracks............................................................................ 1,495.00
Sewing Stand, 17-3/4" x 18" top, 29" h, Sheraton, mahogany and mahogany veneer, pine secondary wood, one board top, two dovetailed drawers with turned pulls, beaded edges, top drawer with divided compartments, well turned and tapered legs with ring turned tops, biscuit corners, old ink label with some provenance in drawer, refinished.......................................................................... 1,980.00
Sewing Table
    26-1/2" l, 17-1/4' d, 29-1/2" h, Classical, mahogany veneer and grained drop-leaf, stencil label "J. & J. W. Meeks Makers No. 4 Vesey St., New York" on inside of sectioned drawer, sewing bag fitting, pierced, shaped medial shield flanked by faux bois scrolled supports, serpentine legs with castors, old refinish, c1840 ................................................................................ 1,150.00
    34" l, 22" d, 27" h, curly maple, molded edge top made from six narrow boards, turned edge, folding, early 20th C .......... 330.00
Spool and Cutter Clamp, 3-1/2" h, turned ivory finials hold two metal cuttings blades flanked by two whalebone spool holders, diamond-shaped abalone inlay dec on clamp, iron thumb screw, America, 19th C, cracks ........................................................................... 635.00

Spool Cabinet, counter top

    7-1/2" h, 22" w, 15-1/2" deep, two drawers, Clark's O. N. T. Spool Cotton ...............................................................................150.00

    18" h, 18" w, 14" d, five drawers, Hemingway & Sons, divided drawers, some damage to wood case ...........................350.00

    22" h, 18" d, cylindrical, wood and glass, columns rotate by turning spindle at top, "Merrick's Six Cord Soft Finish Cotton" stenciled in gold on glass in two locations, top plaque reads "Pat'd July 20, 1897," some glass missing on one curved panel 850.00

Spool Caddy, 10-1/4" h, turned wood, old dark repaint over earlier red, three tiers with wire pins, several pins missing .......................250.00

Spool Winder, 6-1/2" h, carved ivory, triple-spool holder with ivory finials, scored heart-shaped thumb screw, America, 19th C, age cracks ..815.00

Spool Winder Clamp, 6" h, carved ivory, America, 19th C ..........520.00

Tape Measure, figural

    Baseball player, celluloid ...............................................225.00

    Black man, celluloid ........................................................125.00

    Cat, in boot, metal ..........................................................400.00

    Cello, metal .....................................................................285.00

    Chick, hatching from egg, celluloid .................................200.00

    Dancing Girl, porcelain, sashed dress ...........................185.00

    Dog and puppy on cushion, celluloid ..............................110.00

    Drum, metal ....................................................................300.00

    Dutch Boy, porcelain ......................................................145.00

    Eiffel Tower, metal ..........................................................375.00

    Fruit Basket, celluloid .....................................................120.00

    Girl, with muff, celluloid ..................................................100.00

    Golfer, celluloid ..............................................................425.00

    Groom, porcelain ...........................................................225.00

    Indian, boy, wearing headdress, celluloid ......................110.00

    Man, with monocle, celluloid ..........................................375.00

    Turtle, metal ......................................................................85.00

Thread Caddy, 8-1/2" d, 8-3/4" h, treen, walnut, old varnish finish, turned detail, spire finial, pin cushion inside lid, age crack .......260.00

Yarn Swift, 16" d, 17" h, ivory, bone, and wood, turned ivory cup above whalebone shaft and expanding slats, natural mahogany barrel shaped clip with turned ivory thumb screw, America, 19th C, minor wear, minor cracks ...............................................................1,850.00

# SHAKER

**History:** The Shakers, so named because of a dance they used in worship, are one of the oldest communal organizations in the United States. This religious group was founded by Mother Ann Lee, who emigrated from England and established the first Shaker community near Albany, New York, in 1784. The Shakers reached their peak in 1850, when there were 6,000 members.

Shakers lived celibate and self-sufficient lives. Their philosophy stressed cleanliness, order, simplicity, and economy. Highly inventive and motivated, the Shakers created many utilitarian household forms and objects. Their furniture reflected a striving for quality and purity in design.

In the early 19th century, the Shakers produced many items for commercial purposes. Chairmaking and the packaged herb and seed business thrived. In every endeavor and enterprise, the members followed Mother Ann's advice: "Put your hands to work and give your heart to God."

**References:** Edward Deming Andrews and Faith Andrews, *Masterpieces of Shaker Furniture,* Dover Publications, 1999; Christian Becksvoort, *The Shaker Legacy:* *Perspectives on an Enduring Furniture Style,* The Taunton Press, 1998; Michael Horsham, *Art of the Shakers,* Apple Press, 1989; John T. Kirk, *The Shaker World: Art, Life, Belief,* Harry N. Abrams, 1997; Charles R. Muller and Timothy D. Rieman, *The Shaker Chair,* Canal Press, 1984; June Sprigg and Jim Johnson, *Shaker Woodenware,* Berkshire House, 1991; June Sprigg and David Larkin, *Shaker Life,* Work, and Art, Stewart, Tabori & Chang, 1987; Timothy D. Rieman, *Shaker: The Art of Craftsmanship,* Art Services International, 1995; Timothy D. Rieman and Jean M. Burks, *Complete Book of Shaker Furniture,* Harry N. Abrams, 1993.

**Collectors' Clubs:** Shaker Heritage Society, 1848 Shaker Meeting House, Albany-Shaker Road, Albany, NY 12211, http://www.shakerworkshops.com/waterv.htm; Western Shaker Study Group, 1700 Pentbrooke Trail, Dayton, OH 45459; http://www.shakerwssg.org.

**Periodical:** *Shaker Messenger,* P.O. Box 1645 Holland, MI 49422; *Shakers World,* P.O. Box 1276, Manchester, CT 06045.

**Museums:** Canterbury Shaker Village, Canterbury, NH; Hancock Shaker Village, Pittsfield, MA; Shaker Historical Museum, Cleveland, OH; Shaker Museum and Library, Old Chatham, NY; Shaker Museum at South Union, South Union, KY; Shaker Village of Pleasant Hill, Harrodsburg, KY 40330.

Advertisement, newspaper

    "Canterbury Shakers' World Renowned Sarsaparilla...," The Canaan Reporter, Sept. 17, 1880, front page adv with engraving of Shaker brother ................................................................ 15.00

    "The Tall Shakers' Concert," The Age, ME, June 18, 1846, re traveling apostate performers .....................................................20.00

Basket, 19-1/4" h, 14-3/4"" h, splint, four handle, 19th C, minor losses ..............................................................................1,495.00

Bed, single, wooden wheels ........................................................920.00

Blanket Chest, 48-1/2" w, 23-3/4"" d, 29-1/2" h, pine, orig red paint, applied edge molding top, dovetailed case, dovetailed bracket feet, stenciled label on back "H. B. Bear," attributed to Ohio Community, some wear and edge damage................................................770.00

Bonnet, 7-1/4" h, striped iridescent silk, attributed to Enfield, NH, 19th C, splits, minor tears ...............................................................435.00

Book

    Allen, Catherine, *Biographical Sketch of Daniel Fraser of the Shaker Community of Mt. Lebanon,* Columbia County, NY, Weed, Parsons & Co, Albany, 1890, 38 pgs .......................75.00

    Anderson, Martha Jane and others, Social Gathering Dialogue, between Six Sisters of the North Family of Shakers, Mt. Lebanon, Columbia County, N. Y., Albany, 1873, 18 pgs, 8vo, orig letterpress wrappers, sewn ...................................................70.00

    Anderson, Martha Jane, *Social Life and Vegetarianism,* Mt. Lebanon, Guilding Star Printing House, Chicago, 1893, 27 pgs, small stains on cov ......................................................................80.00

    Chandler, Lloyd, *A Visit To the Shakers of East Canterbury,* NH, printed by the Shakers, 1894, 11 pgs................................65.00

    Green, Calvin and Seth Wells, *A Brief Exposition of the Established Principles and Regulations of the United Society of Believers Called Shakers,* New York, 1879, 32 pgs, 8vo, orig letterpress wrappers ...............................................................70.00

    Green, Calvin and Seth Wells compilers, *A Summary View of the Millenial Church, or United Society of Believers, (Commonly called Shakers),* Albany, 1823, 12mo, orig tree sheep, presentation inscription from Sister Mildred Bonher, dated 1960, on front free endpaper................................................................100.00

Mace, Aurelia Gay, *The Aletheia: Spirit of Truth...by Aureilia*, Farmington, ME, 1899, plates, 8vo publisher's cloth, inscribed, "Caroline Helfrich, West Pittsfield, Mass. From Sabbathday Lake Friends," front flyleaf missing .................................. 140.00

Mace, Fayette, *Familiar Dialogues on Shakerism,* Portland, ME, 1838, 12mo, orig letterpress wrappers, darkened, owner's signature on front cover ..................................................... 140.00

Wells, Seth Young, compiler, *Millennial Praises,* Hancock, 1813, 12mo, orig tree sheep, contemporary label..................... 150.00

Box, cov

4-3/4" l, bent wood, oval, finger construction, copper tacks, old worn green paint, C. Hersey type.................................... 570.00

6" w, 4-1/2" d, 21/4" h, oval, brown stain, base with two fingers, one finger on top ............................................................. 150.00

7" w, 5" d, 2-1/2" h, oval, reddish-orange stain, base with four fingers, copper tacks, one finger on top................................ 850.00

8" d, round, light brown finish, single finger construction, slight reduction to top of base.................................................... 155.00

9" l, bent wood, oval, finger construction, copper tacks, cleaned down to worn natural patina, two fingers on base, one on lid, edge damage ............................................................... 330.00

11-5/8" l, 8-5/8" w, 4-7/8" h, bent wood, oval, finger construction, copper tacks, four left facing lapped fingers, painted blue, splitting, wear .................................................................. 2,185.00

18" l, dovetailed, canted sides ......................................... 7,015.00

Broadside, *The Shaker Museum,* Founded 1931, Sabbathday Lake, Poland Spring, Maine, c1970 ............................................. 10.00

Bucket, 10-7/8" w, 11-1/2" d, 6-7/8" h, butternut, rect box-form, canted sides, iron bale handle attached with hammered copper pins, 19th C ....................................................................... 1,150.00

Candlestand, two tier ......................................................... 2,875.00

Carrier, three finger construction

11" l, 6-1/2" h, painted yellow, attributed to Canterbury, NH, even wear, cracks ................................................................. 2,990.00

11-1/4" l, 7-1/4" h, painted yellow, fixed int. handle, Mt. Lebanon, NY, 19th C, minor break lower edge ............................. 8,625.00

Catalog, Catalog of Fancy Goods Made At Shaker Village, Alfred, York County, Maine, Fannie Casey, Trustee and General Manager, 1908, 10 pgs ................................................................................ 135.00

Chair, dining, production, No. 4, Mount Lebanon, NY, late 19th/early 20th C, low back, tapering stiles with ball to finials, joined by two turned horizontal spindles, tape seat, tapering turned legs joined by double stretchers, left back leg mkd "Shaker's No. 4 Trademark Mount Lebanon," gold lettered decal, old dark brown varnished stain, 17-1/4" h seat, 28" h................................................................. 520.00

Chair, side, ladderback

33-1/2" h, old dark finish, Mt. Lebanon, NY label on bottom slat, "3" imp on top slat, replaced woven blue and gray tape seat .....470.00

35-1/8" h, 17" h seat, red stain, two arched slats, splint seat jointed by double stretchers, tilters, early 19th C, minor imperfections ............................................................................ 1,840.00

39-1/4" h, 16" h seat, old red paint, three slat back, old splint seat, good turned finials, worn patina, seat missing some splint ...250.00

41" h, 16" h seat, Watervliet, NY, c1850, maple stained, arched slats flanked by lightly tapered stiles, taped seat, turned legs, double stretchers, rear tilters refinished, minor imperfections ...........920.00

Clock, tall case, poplar, old red paint, base molding, overlapping door, simple bonnet, wag-on-the-wall works, painted wooden face, brass gears, wooden plates, old inscription "Repaired by Smith Mar 11, 1910 Tiffin O, Written by A.L. Norris," other unreadable notations, 78" h ...............................................................................5,100.00

Desk, rect overhanging top, two long drawers, tapered legs, Canterbury ............................................................................ 37,950.00

Dipper, 7-1/4" round, 8-1/2" handle, wood, turned handle, copper tacks, good old staining, 8" horizontal crack to side................. 250.00

Dust Pan, tin ........................................................................ 1,840.00

Essay

Blinn, Henry, *What Shall I Do To Be A Shaker?* East Canterbury, 1885, printed on both sides of single sheet................... 125.00

Hollister, Alzono, *Joyful Tiding,* Mt. Lebanon, 1886, 4 pgs . 165.00

Embroidery Hoop, 6-1/4" d, walnut and cherry, table clamp, hand made .................................................................................. 145.00

Foot Bench, production, No. 0, Mt. Lebanon, NY, c1875, maple, sq top, slanted stool raised on turned and incised legs, dark brown varnish finish, decal affixed, 11-1/2" l, 11-1/2" d, 6-1/2" h ........... 220.00

Foot Stool, production, No. 1, Mount Lebanon, NY, late 19th/early 20th C, maple, four turned tapering posts joined by tape seat, turned stretchers, mkd "Shaker's No. 1 Trademark Mount Lebanon, NY" with gold lettered decal, old brown stain, 12-3/4" w, 9-1/2" d, 9-1/2" h..................... 490.00

Grain Sack, 37-1/2" l, 18-1/2" w, Enfield, NH, woven, stenciled, staining, patches .......................................................................... 115.00

Hymnal, *Shaker Hymnal By The Canterbury Shakers,* East Canterbury, NH, Stanhope Press, Gilson Co, Boston, 1908, 273 pgs, pencil inscription, stamped "North Family, Mt. Lebanon, NY".............. 65.00

Label, canned goods, Butter Beans ad Fresh Tomatoes, Anna Case Trustee South Family Shakers, West Albany, Mt. Lebanon, NY, chromolithographic labels, matted and framed, 15" h, 20" w .......... 315.00

Letter

Canterbury, NH, March 24, 1798, concerning death of a sister, 12" x 7", splits, minor losses, toning, staining ................. 225.00

New Lebanon, NY, July 15, 1849, from Sister Hannah Treadway to her biological sister Nancy Lucks, 6 pgs ...................... 525.00

Magazine, The Shaker Herbalist, No. 1, Spring, 1975................. 15.00

Peg Board, 38-3/4" l, pine and cherry, old patina, one peg missing... 50.00

Photograph, albumen portrait, cabinet card form, three elderly Shaker sisters doing needlework, cozy indoor setting, orig unmarked mount, reverse filled with two manuscript religious poems, sgd by Nellie J. Watts .................................................................................. 175.00

Rocking Chair, production

No. 1, Mount Lebanon, NY, late 19th/early 20th C, maple, tape backrest joining tapered stiles with acorn finials, tape seat, turned legs and double stretchers, on rockers, int. of left rocker mkd "Shaker's No. 1 Trademark Mount Lebanon NY" with gold lettered decal, old brown varnish stain, minor imperfections, 12-3/4" h seat, 28" h............................................................ 575.00

No. 3, Mount Lebanon, NY, late 19th/early 20th C, maple, tape backrest joining tapering stiles, acorn-form finials, crescent-shaped arms with circular pommels, vase and ring-turned supports, tape seat, double stretchers, rockers, int. of left rocker mkd "Shakers No. 3 Trademark Mount Lebanon, NY" with gold lettered decal, old brown stain, 15-1/2" h sea, 33-1/2" h.................................... 490.00

No. 7, Mount Lebanon, NY, late 19th/early 20th C, maple, stiles surmounted by acorn finials, tape back, tape seat over turned double stretchers, turned front legs, on rockers, old finish, imperfections, 16" h seat, 42" h ...................................... 600.00

Sander, 3" to 3-1/2" h, wooden, 19th C, staining, price for 3 pc set . 230.00

Seed Box, 14-3/4" l, unfinished pine, black and white paper label "Shakers' Garden Seeds, Raised at New Lebanon, NY," broken leather hinges......................................................................... 1,100.00

Sewing Box, 8-1/2" l, oval, hard wood and pine, finger construction secured with copper tacks, three fingers on base, one on lid, swivel bent wood handle, int. lined with old blue brocade, two accessories, refinished............................................................................. 275.00

Sewing Cabinet, red painted pine, cherry and butternut, six drawers, dated 1846 .................................................................. 230,000.00

**Seed Box, Mt. Lebanon, NY, c1890, 23-1/2" l, 11-1/2" d, $1,650.**

Sewing Carrier, cov, 3-1/2" x 9-1/2", oval, three finger lapped construction, swing handle, interior lined with royal blue silk, fitted with straw pin keep and needle book, fabric pincushion, emery and wax block, mid-20th C ...........................................................................690.00

Sewing Desk, 25" d, 28" h work surface, 40" h overall, top with central paneled door, flanked by three lip molded drawers on either side, top drawers with keyhole escutcheons, mushroom-shaped walnut pulls on lower drawers, lower portion with three large similar drawers in front, side with paneled door above full length lip molded drawers, delicate turned legs, chestnut work surface, refinished soft wood, small chip on one small drawer ......................................10,000.00

Sieve, 6-7/8" l, 3-5/8" h, stained wood, 19th C, minor imperfections 115.00

Spit Box, 10" d, yellow painted, Mt. Lebanon, NY, 19th C, crack, even paint wear ......................................................................1,955.00

Step Stool, 11" h, label "Sister Ednah E. Fitts," Canterbury, 1846-1924 ...............................................................................16,100.00

Stove Set, 17-1/2" l shove, 22" l tongs, wrought iron, attributed to Canterbury, NH ..............................................................................495.00

Swift, 15" h, worn orig yellow varnish, minor crack in table clamp, attributed to Hancock, MA ..........................................................220.00

Tailor's Counter, six dovetailed lip molded drawers, top with large swing-over work surface, orig iron supports on side, short simple turned legs, each of drawer fronts fitted with walnut mushroom shaped pulls, old mellow patina, 72" w, 40" deep when open, 38" h..........................21,000.00

Utility Bucket, cov, 17" d, 15-1/2" h, stave, wire, and metal band construction, wire attached turned wooden handles, painted dark green, 19th C, lid cracked ................................................................920.00

Wood Box, 37-1/2" w, 21" d, 31" h, pine, old mellow finish, bin top with hinged lid with breadboard ends, one dovetailed overlapping drawer, sq corner posts, chamfered feet, red stain int., wear from kindling, purchased from Shakers in Canterbury, NH, in 1940s, old pierced repair to one end of drawer front.............................................880.00

Work Table, New Lebanon, NY, mid-19th, cherry and pine, pine top with breadboard ends overhangs single drawer with molded lip, turned tapering legs, leg "boots," old surface, 58" w, 27-3/4" h, 30" h ............3,325.00

# SHAVING MUGS

**History:** Shaving mugs, which hold the soap, brush, and hot water used to prepare a beard for shaving, come in a variety of materials including tin, silver, glass, and pottery. One style, which has separate compartments for water and soap, is the scuttle, so called because of its coal-scuttle shape.

c1908

Personalized shaving mugs were made exclusively for use in barber shops in the United Sates. They began being produced shortly after the Civil War and continued to be made into the 1930s.

Unlike shaving mugs that were used at home, these mugs were personalized with the owner's name, usually in gilt. The mug was kept in a rack at the barber shop, and it was used only when the owner came in for a shave. This was done for hygienic purposes, to keep from spreading a type of eczema known as barber's itch.

The mugs were usually made on European porcelain blanks, that often contained the mark of "Germany," "France," or "Austria" on the bottom. In later years, a few were made on American-made semi-vitreous blanks. The artwork on mugs was done by decorators who worked for major barber supply houses. Occasionally, the mark of the barber supply house is also stamped on the bottom of the mug.

After a short time, the mugs became more decorative, including hand-painted floral decorations, as well as birds, butterflies, and a wide variety of nature scenes, etc. These are classified today as "decorative" mugs.

Another category, "fraternal mugs," soon developed. These included the emblem of an organization the owner belonged to, along with his name emblazoned in gold above or below the illustration.

"Occupational mugs" were also very popular. These are mugs which contained a painting of something that illustrated the owner's occupation, such as a butcher, a bartender, or a plumber. The illustration might be a man working at his job, or perhaps the tools of his trade, or a product which he made or sold.

Of all these mugs, occupationals are the most prized. Their worth is determined by several factors: rarity (some occupations are rarer than others), size of mug, and size of illustration (the bigger the better), quality of artwork, and condition. Although rare mugs with cracks or chips can still be valuable if the damage does not affect the artwork on the mug. Generally speaking, a mug showing a man at work at his job is usually valued higher than that same occupation illustrated with only the tools or finished product.

The invention of the safety razor by King C. Gillette, issued to three and one-half million servicemen during World War I, brought about changes in personal grooming—men began to shave on their own, rather than visiting the barber shop to be shaved. As a result, the need for personalized shaving mugs declined.

**References:** Susan and Al Bagdade, *Warman's English & Continental Pottery & Porcelain*, 3rd Edition, Krause Publications, 1998; Ronald S. Barlow, *Vanishing American Barber Shop*, Windmill Publishing, 1993; Keith E. Estep, *Shaving Mug & Barber Bottle Book*, Schiffer Publishing, 1995.

**Collectors' Club:** National Shaving Mug Collectors Association, 320 S. Glenwood St., Allentown, PA 18104.

**Museums:** Atwater Kent History Museum, Philadelphia, PA; Barber Museum, Canal Winchester, OH; Lightner Museum, Saint Augustine, FL.

**Note:** Prices shown are for typical mugs which have no damage and show only moderate wear on the gilt name and decoration.

## Decorative

| | |
|---|---|
| Bunch of violets | 50.00 |
| Butterfly hovering over water lily | 75.00 |
| Humorous, frog fishing | 275.00 |
| Windmill scene | 150.00 |

## Fraternal

| | |
|---|---|
| Foresters of America, emblem over flags | 125.00 |
| Independent Order of Redmen, luster ware, 24K gold trim, mkd "Made in Germany," 3-3/4" d, 3-3/4" h | 100.00 |
| Knight Templar, man standing in uniform | 400.00 |
| Knights of Pyhtias, shield of organization | 100.00 |
| Loyal Order of Buffaloes, buffalo head with flowers | 450.00 |
| Odd Fellows, chain emblem with eye | 100.00 |
| 32nd Degree Mason, emblem over name | 175.00 |

United Mine Workers of America, bright luster finish, 24K gold and enamel dec, mkd "Made in Germany," 3-3/4" d, 3-3/4" h ........ 210.00
Woodman of the World, ax, stump, and bird .............................. 175.00

## Occupational

Automobile, old touring car ..................................................... 850.00
Bartender, man serving two customers at bar ........................... 400.00
Baseball Game, player sliding into home plate, shows entire field .................................................................................... 1,000.00
Brick Mason, man laying a brick wall on side of house .............. 650.00
Butcher Tools, saw, sharpener, and cleaver ............................. 175.00
Cabinet Maker, man working at wood-working bench ................ 500.00
Cowboy, man roping a steer ................................................... 800.00
Dentist, man working on a patient in dental chair .................... 700.00
Glass Blower, man blowing glass bottle .................................. 750.00
Hat Maker, man's hat in center of floral decorations ................ 400.00
Horse-Drawn Ice Wagon ....................................................... 550.00
House Painter, man painting house on scaffold ....................... 550.00
Painter, can of paint and brush .............................................. 250.00
Railroad Locomotive .............................................................. 250.00

# SHAWNEE POTTERY

**History:** The Shawnee Pottery Co. was founded in 1937 in Zanesville, Ohio. The company acquired a 650,000-square-foot plant that had previously housed the American Encaustic Tiling Company. Shawnee produced as many as 100,000 pieces of pottery a day until 1961, when the plant closed.

Shawnee limited its production to kitchenware, decorative art pottery, and dinnerware. Distribution was primarily through jobbers and chain stores.

**Marks:** Shawnee can be marked "Shawnee," "Shawnee U.S.A.," "USA #——," "Kenwood," or with character names, e.g., "Pat. Smiley" and "Pat. Winnie."

**References:** Jim and Bev Mangus, *Shawnee Pottery*, Collector Books, 1994, 2000 value update; Mark Supnick, *Collecting Shawnee Pottery*, L-W Book Sales, 2000; Duane and Janice Vanderbilt, *Collector's Guide to Shawnee Pottery*, Collector Books, 1992, 1998 value update.

**Collectors' Club:** Shawnee Pottery Collectors Club, P.O. Box 713, New Smyrna Beach, FL 32170.

Ashtray, Indian Arrowhead .................................................... 580.00
Bank, Howdy Doody ............................................................. 395.00
Bookends, pr, Flying Mallards ................................................ 110.00
Bowl, cov, Lobsterware, #907 ................................................. 45.00
Candlesticks, pr, 6-1/2" h, hand dec gold trim .......................... 25.00
Casserole, cov, Fruits ............................................................ 95.00
Cookie Jar, cov
    Cinderella ...................................................................... 125.00
    Cottage, figural ............................................................. 900.00
    Drum Major .................................................................. 275.00
    Dutch Boy .................................................................... 275.00
    Dutch Girl .................................................................... 275.00
    Great Northern Boy, mkd "Great Northern U.S.A. 1025" .... 395.00
    Jo-Jo The Clown, mkd "Shawnee, U.S.A." ....................... 300.00
    Little Chef .................................................................... 120.00
    Mugsy .......................................................................... 650.00
    Puss 'n Boots ............................................................... 225.00
    Sailor Boy .................................................................... 325.00
    Smiley, gold paint, orig decals ...................................... 550.00
    Winnie, green collar ..................................................... 275.00
Creamer
    Elephant ........................................................................ 40.00
    King Corn, No. 70 .......................................................... 25.00

Planter, Wishing Well, green, mkd "710," 8-1/2" l, 5-1/4" h, $40.

    Lobster, Kenwood, 13 oz .............................................. 100.00
    Puss N Boots, green and yellow ...................................... 85.00
Cup and Saucer, King Corn, cup marked "90," and saucer marked "91" ....................................................................................... 45.00
Figure
    Raccoon ........................................................................ 65.00
    Squirrel ......................................................................... 80.00
Hors d'oeuvre Holder, Lobster, Kenwood ............................... 265.00
Lamp, emb flowers ................................................................ 45.00
Lady's Head Planter, girl with doll .......................................... 60.00
Mixing bowl, King Corn
    5" d .............................................................................. 37.00
    6-1/4" d ........................................................................ 45.00
Pie Bird ............................................................................... 45.00
Pitcher
    Ball style, blue .............................................................. 20.00
    Chanticleer, figural rooster ........................................... 125.00
    Fruits, ball shape ......................................................... 110.00
    Little Bo Peep, blue hat, pink coat ................................. 135.00
    Little Boy Blue, large .................................................... 150.00
    Smiley Pig, pink flower .................................................. 150.00
Planter
    Bird, blue, yellow beak, 6" l, 4-1/2" h ............................. 45.00
    Buddha, #524 ................................................................ 25.00
    Dog and jug .................................................................. 24.00
    Fawn, gold trim ............................................................. 20.00
    Girl at gate ................................................................... 25.00
    Ram, #515 ..................................................................... 25.00
    Water Trough, #716 ....................................................... 20.00
Plate, King Corn, 8" d ............................................................ 40.00
Range Shakers, pr, Smiley, red bib ........................................... 5.00
Relish Tray, King Corn, marked "Shawnee 79" .......................... 35.00
Salt and Pepper Shakers, pr
    Chef ............................................................................. 35.00
    Dutch Boy and Girl, medium size ................................... 95.00
    Fruits, small .................................................................. 35.00
    Lobsters, small .............................................................. 50.00
    Smiley Pig ................................................................... 125.00
Sugar, cov
    King Corn ..................................................................... 42.00
    Lobster, Kenwood ......................................................... 65.00
Teapot, cov, hp blue flowers ................................................... 85.00
Vase
    #805, green ................................................................... 25.00
    #827, green ................................................................... 25.00
Wall Pocket
    Birdhouse ..................................................................... 40.00
    Grandfather Clock, #1261 .............................................. 45.00

# SILHOUETTES

**History:** Silhouettes (shades) are shadow profiles produced by hollow cutting, mechanical tracing, or painting. They were popular in the 18th and 19th centuries.

The name came from Etienne de Silhouette, a French Minister of Finance, who cut "shades" as a pastime. In America, the Peale family was well known for the silhouettes they made.

Silhouette portraiture lost popularity with the introduction of the daguerreotype prior to the Civil War. In the 1920s and 1930s, a brief revival occurred when tourists to Atlantic City and Paris had their profiles cut as souvenirs.

**Marks:** An impressed stamp marked "PEALE" or "Peale Museum" identifies pieces made by the Peale family.

**Museums:** Essex Institute, Salem, MA; National Portrait Gallery, Washington, DC.

## Children

4-3/8" h, 3-1/2" w, hollow cut, boy, good detail or hair and bow at neck, old brown ink beneath "Robt. Watson," partial Peale emb mark at bottom, margin stains, black cloth backing, mahogany veneer 7" h, 6" w frame with corner chips ...................385.00

4-3/4" d, girl, hollow cut, turned frame, stains ...........................115.00

4-3/4" l, 3-5/8" w, boy, hollow cut, black cloth backing, discolored and stained paper, old black molded frame ....................220.00

5" h, 3-7/8 w, boy, hollow cut, black velvet backing, ink inscription "take When A Child, George A. Cushing," printed "Certificate of Merit" on back of frame from Boston school, "Master G. A. Cushing," old frame, wrinkles, taped tears ..............................90.00

10-1/2" h, 9-1/2" w, boy, painted, flaked white coating, mahogany veneer frame, gilded liner...........................60.00

## Groups

5-1/4" x 4-1/2", 5-1/4" x 4-1/2", 3-1/4" x 2-1/2", hollow-cut, ink embellishments, Wheelock family, Francis, Nancy, and Emily, Sturbridge, MA, 1826, unsigned, identified on reverse, stamped brass and giltwood frames, price for set of three.......................1,495.00

7-1/8" h, 9-1/8" l, eight hollow-cut silhouettes, cut-work background, men and woman, framed together in common period frame, attributed to PA...................................575.00

18-3/4" x 15-1/2", pen and ink, two men and women, seated on chairs, pencil room int., sgd "Aug Edoart, fecit 1840," bird's eye maple frame ....................................650.00

## Men

4-3/4" h, 3-1/2" d, young man, gilt highlights, back labeled "J. I. Maginn Artist," black oval frame.............................115.00

5-1/8" h, 4" w, young man, hollow cut, black cloth backing, modern frame, stains.........................................140.00

6" h, 5-1/8" w, gentleman, ink on heavy paper, black on black, white detail, old black reeded frame with gilded liner .......................350.00

7-1/2" h, 5-1/2" w, Henry Clay, faded black cloth backing, minor stains, tear at edge, later mat and frame...............................95.00

8" h, 6-1/4" w, full length profile of stocky man, top hat, old inscription on back of frame "Silhouette of Doctor Johnson," cut from heavy black colored paper, gray paper background, framed.............275.00

8-1/4" x 6-3/4", slave, praying pose, rosewood frame, 19th C....575.00

11-3/4" h, 5-1/4" w, full length portrait, Lt. Edward M. Yard, U.S. Navy Boston 1st March 1842 on *John Adams* Sloop of War, unsgd, attributed to August Edouart, framed ...............................750.00

## Pairs

3-1/2" h, 2-3/4" w, man and woman, penciled highlights in hair and bonnet, man identified on back as Cornelius Wheeler, oval brass and wood frames, pr ....................................200.00

4-1/2" h, 3-1/4" w, pair, Captain Braddock and Martha Bourne Nye of Sandwich, marked on reverse "Gallery of Cuttings cut by Master Hankes with Common Scissors," one with bronze highlights, named on reverse, framed, toning, staining, fold creases ...................475.00

4-1/2" x 5-3/4", girl and boy, cut, titled "Agnes and Lindsey," sgd "Auguste Edouart, 1831" .......................................450.00

5-1/2" h, 4-1/2" h, woman and child, hollow cut, black cloth backing, worn eglomise glass, price for pr .............................275.00

5-1/2" h, 8-5/8" w, double, hollow cut man and woman, pen and ink detail, eglomise glass with gilded frame, some damage and stains, black paper backing .................................350.00

6-5/8" h, 5-5/8" w, man and woman, hollow cut, black cloth backing, old mahogany veneer frames with black finish, minor stains, pr....220.00

7-5/8" h, 10-7/8" w, facing pair of men in top hats, sgd in pencil on backing paper "Mary D. Smith," cherry frame, minor stains.....345.00

8-1/2" h, 7-1/4" w, man and woman, hollow cut, matching emb brass frames with cardboard backs, stains, and damage, pr.............200.00

8-3/4" w, 10-1/4" h, lithograph on paper with ink and watercolor, hollow cut silhouettes of man and wife, black highlights, joined by strip of green silk ribbon, with birth record of William Stebbins, Aug 12, 1806 and Eliza Perrin, Oct 20, 1808, married March 23, 1829, their daughter's birth June 5, 1830, framed, staining and toning ...........1,495.00

## Women

3-1/2" h, 2-3/4" w, woman, penciled hair, illegible identification on back, oval brass and wood frame .......................................100.00

3-5/8" h, 2" w, hollow cut, watercolor details, woman wearing bonnet and blue dress with puffy sleeves, holding floral sprig, gilt frame, America, 1830-31, minor creases .........................................4,887.50

3-3/4" h, 2-1/8" w, hollow cut, lady with book, backed with woven fabric, black watercolor costume and embellishments, framed, 19th C, minor toning .....................................................1,350.00

4" h, 3-1/4" w, hollow cut, young lady, black embellishments, oval eglomise mat, giltwood frame, toning, minor paint loss ..................550.00

4-3/8" h, 3-1/2" w, hollow cut, young lady, well executed, ribbon at top of bonnet, stains and tears, black cloth backing, period mahogany 6-5/8" h, 5-5/8" w frame......................................................275.00

5-3/8" h, 5-1/8" w, ink silhouette old woman in bonnet, old guilt frame, stains.........................................................................70.00

5-3/4" h, 4-7/8" w, hollow cut, young lady, gilt frame, minor stains 85.00

5-7/8" x 6-5/8", hollow cut, young woman, paper with emb mark "Museum," (Peale Museum), black cloth backing, minor stains and creases, mahogany veneer frame.........................................225.00

6-1/4" h, 4-1/2" w, hollow cut, black cloth ground, molded pine frame.......................................................................100.00

**Woman, hollow cut, sgd "Elizabeth Baker Boston, 1724," 6" x 5", $210.**

# SILVER

**History:** The natural beauty of silver lends itself to the designs of artists and craftsmen. It has been mined and worked into an endless variety of useful and decorative items. Pure silver is too soft to be fashioned into strong, durable, and serviceable utensils. Therefore, a way was found to give silver the required degree of hardness by adding alloys of copper and nickel.

Silversmithing in America goes back to the early 17th century in Boston and New York and the early 18th century in Philadelphia. Boston artisans were influenced by the English styles, New Yorkers by the Dutch.

**References:** Jill Bace, Alexis Butcher, Juliet Nusser, *Miller's Collecting Silver,* Miller's Publications, 1999; Louise Belden, *Marks of American Silversmiths in the Ineson-Bissell Collection*, University of Virginia Press, 1980; Frances M. Bones and Lee Roy Fisher, *Standard Encyclopedia of American Silverplate,* Collector Books, 1998; Frederick Bradbury, *Bradbury's Book of Hallmarks*, J. W. Northend, 1987; Bonita Campbell and Nan Curtis (curators), *Depression Silver*, California State University, 1995; Janet Drucker, *Georg Jensen: A Tradition of Splendid Silver,* Schiffer Publishing, 1997; Stephen G. C. Ensko, *American Silversmiths and Their Marks*, Dover Publications, 1983; Rachael Feild, *Macdonald Guide to Buying Antique Silver and Sheffield Plate*, Macdonald & Co., 1988; *Fine Victorian Gold-and Silverplate, Exquisite Designs from the 1882 Catalog of the Meriden-Brittania Co.,* Schiffer Publishing, 1997; Tere Hagan, *Silverplated Flatware*, 4th ed., Collector Books, 1990, 1999 value update; —, *Sterling Flatware, L-W Book Sales, 1999;* Stephen J. Helliwell, *Understanding Antique Silver Plate, Reference and Price Guide,* Antique Collectors' Club; William P. Hood Jr., *Tiffany Silver Flatware, 1845-1905, When Dining Was An Art,* Antique Collectors' Club, 1999; Kenneth Crisp Jones (ed.), *Silversmiths of Birmingham and Their Marks*, N.A.G. Press, 1981, distributed by Antique Collectors Club; Henry J. Kaufman, *Colonial Silversmith*, Astragal Press, 1995; Ralph and Terry Kovel, *Kovels' American Silver Marks,* Crown Publishers, 1989; *Daniel Low and Co., Gold and Silversmiths Catalogue, 1901,* reprinted by Bridgham Antiques, 1998; (Box 28204, San Diego, CA 92198); Everett L. Maffett, *Silver Banquet II,* Silver Press, 1990; Penny C. Morrill, *Silver Masters of Mexico,* Schiffer Publishing, 1996; Harold Newman, *An Illustrated Dictionary of Silverware,* Thames & Hudson, 2000; Richard Osterberg, *Silver Hollowware for Dining Elegance,* Schiffer Publishing, 1996; ——, *Sterling Silver Flatware for Dining Elegance,* Schiffer Publishing, 1994; Ian Pickford, *Jackson's Silver and Gold Marks of England, Scotland & Ireland,* Antique Collectors' Club; ——, *Silver Flatware, 1660-1980,* Antique Collectors' Club; Dorothy T. Rainwater, *Encyclopedia of American Silver Manufacturers,* Revised 4th ed., Schiffer Publishing, 1998; Dorothy T. and H. Ivan Rainwater, *American Silverplate,* Schiffer Publishing, 1988; *Sterling Silver, Silverplate, and Souvenir Spoons,* revised ed., L-W Book Sales, 1987, 1994 value update; Charles Venable, *Silver in America 1840-1940,* Harry Abrams, 1994; Peter Waldron, *The Price Guide to Antique Silver,* Antique Collectors' Club; Joanna Wissinger, *Arts and Crafts Metalwork and Silver,* Chronicle Books, 1994; Seymour B. Wyler, *Book Of Old Silver,* Crown Publishers, 1937 (available in reprint).

**Periodicals:** *Silver & Gold Report,* P.O. Box 109665, West Palm Beach, FL 33410, http://www.wessinc.com; *Silver Magazine,* P.O. Box 9690, Rancho Santa Fe, CA 92067, http://www.silvermag.com; *Silver Update* and *Sterling Silver Hollowware Update,* P.O. Box 2157, Ellicott City, MD 21041-2157.

**Collectors' Clubs:** International Association of Silver Art Collectors, P.O. Box 28415, Seattle, WA 98118-8415; New York Silver Society, 242 E. 7th St., #5, New York, NY 10009; Society of American Silversmiths, P.O. Box 704, Chepatchet, RI 02814, http://www.silversmithing.com.

**Museums:** Bayou Bend Collection, Houston, TX; Boston Museum of Fine Arts, Boston, MA; Colonial Williamsburg Foundation, Williamsburg, VA; Currier Gallery of Art, Manchester, NH; Yale University Art Gallery, New Haven, CT; Wadsworth Antheneum, Hartford, CT.

**Additional Listings:** See Silver Flatware in *Warman's Americana & Collectibles* for more examples.

## American, 1790-1840

### Mostly Coin

Coin silver is slightly less pure than sterling silver. Coin silver has 900 parts silver to 100 parts alloy. Sterling silver has 925 parts silver. American silversmiths followed the coin standards. Coin silver is also called Pure Coin, Dollar, Standard, or Premium.

Beaker, 3-1/2" h, E & D Kinsey, Cincinnati, 1840-61, reeded top and bottom rim, cylindrical tapering form, mark in two straight lines, 5 troy oz .................................................................................. 415.00

Cann, 5-1/8" h, William Swan, Boston, 1757-74, bulbous form, molded rim, applied molded circular foot, cast hollow scroll handle, molded body drop at upper joining, mkd on base, initialed "CTL," dents, 11 troy oz .............................................................................. 1,850.00

Communion Cup, 6-1/4" h, Boston, early 19th C, straight-sided bowl, rounded foot, applied disc, engraved "Presented by David Goodwin to the First Baptist Church in Charlestown 1802" within bright-cut swag, 8 troy oz ................................................................. 1,380.00

Creamer

4-7/8" h, Joseph Lownes, Philadelphia, 1859-1820, neoclassical form, applied reeded banding, strap handle, monogrammed, mkd twice on base, 5 troy oz .......................................... 460.00

6" h, Thomas Fletcher, Philadelphia, 1813-15, baluster form, applied foliate banding, mkd on base, 10 troy oz ............... 350.00

6-1/4" h, America, mid-19th C, baluster form, foliate chasing, applied geometric banding, molded circular base, mkd "Pure Silver Coin," and "T & W," 4 troy oz ............................... 325.00

Cream Jug, 8-1/4" h, Harding & Co., Boston, mid 19th C, urn form, beaded stepped foot, beading at girdle and rim, loop handle, engraved name under spout, 10 troy oz .................................. 225.00

Cream Pitcher, 6-1/2" h, Geradus Boyce, New York, c1820-57, "G. Boyce" in rectangle mark, baluster form, applied floral banding, scrolled handle, lower body with lobed paneling, monogrammed, 8 troy oz ....................................................................... 480.00

Crumber, 13-1/8" l, Geradus Boyce, NY, 1820-57, engraved with reserve of castle, scrolling foliage devices, minor dents .......... 175.00

Fruit Set, maker's mark "H.M. +S.," mid-19th C, twelve fruit spoons, gold washed bowls engraved with fruit, shaped edge, twisted stem with fiddle shaped handle engraved with flat leaf and monogrammed shield, matched pierced ladle, matching serving spoon, 13 troy oz, price for 14 pc set .................................................. 520.00

Goblet, 7-1/4" h, Robert & William Wilson, Philadelphia, mid-19th C, beaded rim, 14 troy oz, price for pr ......................................... 575.00

Ladle, 13-3/4" l, Joseph Richardson, Jr. and Nathaniel Richardson, Philadelphia, 1785-91, molded handle, V-slashed, double molded bowl, mkd three time on handle, monogrammed and dated "1782," 7 troy oz .................................................................................. 875.00

Mug, 3-1/2" h, J. E. Caldwell & Co., Philadelphia, mid 19th C, octagonal, chased and emb with floral sprays and C-scrolls, plain central cartouche, reeded top and bottom band, angular handle, 5 troy oz ........ 230.00

Napkin Ring, 2-1/8" d, unidentified American maker, bas relief foliate design, inscribed "Charles Codman" ...................................... 200.00

Porringer, 7" l, Heinrich Boelen, New York, mid-18th C, single pierced handle, monogrammed, 5 troy oz ......................................... 1,035.00

Powder Box, 2-7/8" h, 4" d, low round form, butterfly finial, domed cov, engraved monogram, Gorham, some dents, 6 troy oz ............. 230.00

Presentation Mug, 3-1/4" h, unmarked, engraved "Albert Henry Minot from his Grandmother L.A.M. 1851," tapering cylindrical form, reeded top and bottom rim, 5 troy oz ................................................... 200.00

Punch Ladle, 13" l, marked "J. Einstein," Philadelphia retailer, elliptical bowl, upturned fiddle handle, monogram, 8 troy oz ................. 230.00

Salt, 1-1/4" l, 1-1/4" w, mid-19th C, sq, beaded lower edge, sides engraved rectangles centered by stylized flower, small well offset at edges with further stylized engraving, 3 troy oz, price for 6 pc set ...................... 325.00

Spoon
 Serving, 12" l, George Alexander and Peter Riker, New York, 1797-1800, bright cut dec, monogrammed, mkd twice, 3 troy oz...825.00
 Teaspoon, 5-3/4" l, Pelletreau, Bennett & Cook, NY, 1825-28, basket of flowers, outlined shell on bowl, monogrammed, 3 troy oz, price for set of six ....................................................... 275.00

Sugar Bowl
 6" d, Jones, Ball & Co., Boston, 1952-54, 4-1/2" h, navette-form, applied beaded rim, chased C-scroll and foliate design, ftd, handle, monogrammed, mkd on base, 7 troy oz .................... 450.00
 7" h, Thomas Fletcher and Sidney Gardner, Boston, 1808-25, acorn finial, domed lid, baluster form body, applied foliate and star banding, sq molded base, monogrammed, mkd twice on base, minor dents, 22 troy oz ...................................... 350.00
 7-3/4" h, Jonathon Stodder and Benjamin Frobisher, Boston, 1816-25, two handles, strawberry finial, molded circular lid, baluster form bowl, acanthus leaf chasing, applied scroll and foliage banding, circular molded base, applied gadrooning, monogrammed, mkd on base, minor dents, 23 troy oz .... 425.00

Teapot, cov
 10" h, Henry Ball, Erastus Tompkins, and William Black, NY, 1839-1851, basket of fruit finial, domed lid, baluster form, applied grape and foliate banding, scroll handle, oval molded base, engraved, mkd on base, 32 troy oz ........................ 700.00
 10-1/2" h, Baldwin Gardiner, Phila and New York, 1814-46, basket of flower finial, domed lid with foliate chasing, baluster form body, applied foliate banding, ornately chased foliate and cornucopia handle, spout with similar chasing, open hands motif, circular molded base, 43 troy oz ......................................... 990.00

**Teaspoon, J. M. Mitksch, Bethlehem, PA, 6" l price for two, $180.**

Tea Service, 4-1/2" h teapot, cream jug, and sugar (slightly later date), marked "Lincoln and Reed, Boston," 1838-48, foliate form lid, baluster finial, melon-form body, engraved scroll and foliate dec, minor dents, 26 troy oz....................................................................... 980.00

Tray
 8-3/4" x 12", oval, Gorham and Co., 1848-65, gadrooned border, enclosing engraved design of flanking vases containing floral and foliate scrolls, four scrolled feet, monogram, 7 troy oz .......... 375.00
 10" d, Jones, Shreve, Brown & Co., Boston, 1854, beaded border, engraved scrolled foliate design, three scrolled feet, monogram, slightly misshapen, 6 troy oz ............................................ 490.00

Water Jug, 10-7/8" h, America, second quarter 19th C, baluster form, applied foliate banding, molded circular foot, scrolling handle, inscribed "Presented to Esek Saunders. A token of esteem Jany 1st 1833," 30 troy oz, very minor dents.......................................... 890.00

Water Pitcher
 9-1/4" h, Fletcher & Gardinier, Philadelphia, 1811-25, baluster form, applied foliate banding, scrolling handle with eagle's head, molded circular base, mkd on base, minor dents on base, 32 troy oz ................................................................................ 1,500.00
 10-1/4" h, James Ward, Hartford, CT, 1768-1856, lobed baluster, applied foliate banding, scrolling handle, molded circular base, inscribed "The Boston Light Infantry to their respected past Commander Henry Codman Esquire 1820," mkd "Ward" twice on base, 36 troy oz........................................................ 1,200.00

Wine Ewer, 10-7/8" h, Lows, Ball & Co., Boston, 1841-47, baluster form, engraved C-scroll and foliate design, monogrammed on base, "S. C. Jan 1, 1845," base mkd, minor dents, 16 troy oz........... 575.00

## American, 1840-1920

### Mostly Sterling

There are two possible sources for the origin of the word sterling. The first is that it is a corruption of the name Easterling. Easterlings were German silversmiths who came to England in the Middle Ages. The second is that it is named for the sterling (little star) used to mark much of the early English silver. Sterling is 92.5 percent per silver. Copper comprises most of the remaining alloy. American manufacturers began to switch to the sterling standard about the time of the Civil War.

Asparagus Tongs
 Bailey & Co., mid/late 19th C, bright-cut engraved leafy floral dec on handle, pierced grips, 6 troy oz ................................... 375.00
 Mulford, Wendell & Co., mid/late 19th C, teardrop-shaped pierced dec, 6 troy oz................................................................. 375.00

Basket
 Towle, early 20th C, 13" d, open pierced flower shape, reeded rim, base, and handle, two balls finial, monogram, 26 troy oz ..... 800.00
 Reed & Barton, 1946, 13" d, sterling, leaf motif double bowls, central entwined vine handle, 14 troy oz......................... 250.00
 Watson Co., c1926, engraved neoclassical dec, garlands and leaves, openwork border under rim, low ftd base, monogram on handle, 28 troy oz......................................................... 650.00

Bonbonniere, 7" d, 6-1/4" h, Ellmore, c1945, ftd, reticulated edge, slightly miss-shaped.................................................................. 50.00

Bread Tray, 14-1/2" w, 9-1/4" d, 2-1/2" h, Gorham, rococo taste 175.00

Cake Plate, 9" d, Black, Starr & Frost, early 20th C, low tapered foot, plates with wide edge stamped with classical wreaths and husk swags, reticulated ground, guilloche reticulated rim, monogrammed center, 17 troy oz, price for pr ............................................ 750.00

Candelabra, three-light
 9-1/8" h, Redlich, 20th C, spreading circulars base, removable bobeches, weighted, pr................................................... 435.00
 11-1/2" h, Gorham, 20th C, sterling, central tapering column, S-curve reeded arms, weighted........................................... 350.00

Candlesticks, pr
 6-1/8" h, Gorham, retailed by Foster & Co., 20th C, pointed oval spreading base with fluted detail, paneled stems, fluting under receded nozzle, weighted .............................................. 400.00
 8-1/4" h, Gorham, retailed by Bigelow, Kennard & Co., 1905, Corinthian columns, removable bobeches, weighted....... 750.00

10" h, International, Royal Danish pattern, elongated teardrop body, decorative motif under nozzle and above base, monogram, weighted................................520.00

10-1/4" h, Gorham, 1907, Corinthian column style, removable bobeches, sq pedestal base with beaded detail, weighted ...980.00

Celery Vase, 10-3/8" h, cast stag head handles, Greek key border, mid-19th C............................................980.00

Center Bowl, 10" d, Whiting for Gorham, 1925, everted rim, engraved with scrolls, bellflowers, and floral drops, four scroll-reticulated cartouches, engraved and dated center, 9 troy oz .......................300.00

Centerpiece

6-15/16" h, 16-3/8" l, Gorham, 1860s, navette-form, engraved inscription and date .......................................1,380.00

9" d, Durgin, late 19th/early 20th C, central circular mirror with four scroll arm candle holders, openwork leaf dec, engraved leaf and bow design on candle nozzles, four ball feet .....................1,265.00

Child's Cup, 3" d, 3-1/4" h, Wood and Hughes, c1865-75, Japonesque taste, engraved, 4.5 troy oz.....................................75.00

Cocktail Fork, 5-1/2" l, Wallace, Dorchester pattern, c1905, price for set of six ..............................................70.00

Cocktail Shaker

4" d, 9-1/2" h, Poole, c1930-40, Colonial taste, 11.5 troy oz ....315.00

4" d, 12" h, International Silver, c1939, Royal Danish, 25 troy oz ..............................................275.00

Coffee and Tea Service

Hirsch, M. F., c1940, Danish Modern taste, coffeepot, teapot, two-handled cov sugar basin, ftd cream pitcher with gilded int., 74.5 troy oz ..........................................825.00

Reed & Barton, 20th C, 8-1/2" h coffeepot, 13-1/2" h kettle on stand, teapot, creamer, cov sugar, open sugar, plain shaped vasiform bodies, shaped ovoid foot, rocaille scroll uprights on stand, silver burner, together with matching electroplated scroll ftd tray, all pieces monogrammed, approx 124 troy oz .......................2,300.00

Smith, Frank M., c1920-30, hand chased, ribbed, bearing floral repousse ornament, ftd coffeepot, ftd teapot, two handled ftd open sugar basin, ftd waste bowl, ftd cream pitcher, 72 troy oz.....900.00

Whiting, Frank M., late 19th C, 10-1/2"h coffeepot, squat baluster form, spreading foot, scrolled shaped edge, flat leaf ear handles, bodies chased and emb with scrolled leaf cartouche, topped by floral swags, flanked by vertical scroll bands, domed lids, gadrooned ball finials, monogrammed, 137 troy oz .............................2,100.00

Compote, 2-3/4" h, Baltimore Sterling Silver Co., late 19th C, trumpet foot with repousse, bowl with wide band of floral repousse, 8 troy oz ..200.00

Creamer and Sugar Set, Gorham, c1894, 6" l, 3-1/2" h creamer, 8-1/2" l, 5-1/2" h sugar, squat ovoid, scroll feet topped by anthemion, vertical fluting, shaped scrolled edge, tapered ear handles with flat leaves at terminals, domed fluted lid with rocaille scroll finial, monogrammed, 27 troy oz ...................................395.00

Dresser Set, Gorham, c1900-10, floral repousse, period script monogram, three hair brushes, clothes brush, baby's hair brush .....275.00

Entrée Dish, cov, 12" l, Gorham, c1909, cover finial modeled as two dolphins, 31 troy oz .........................................425.00

Fish Server, 11-5/8" l, Albert Coles, engraved floral border on blade, central engraved fish, engraved scroll foliate design on handle, monogram, 3 troy oz .........................................175.00

Flask, 5-1/2" h, Gorham, early 20th C, sterling, cigar case shape, hidden twist-off corner spout, 6 troy oz ..........................325.00

Flower Basket, 22-1/2" h, Alvin Corp, early 20th C, tapered trumpet foot engraved with floral sprays and swags, tapered stem, engraved with floral drops and lappets suspending husk drops, wide rim applied with four floral roundels flanked by engraved floral sprays and linked by husk swags, shaped rim, high upright handle pierced with flat leaves and bat's wing fluted roundels, 23 troy oz.................1,035.00

Fruit Basket, 10-1/2" l, 7-1/2" w, 6-1/2" h, Whiting Manufacturing Co, c1900-1910, reticulated, stationary handle, 10.8 troy oz .........200.00

Fruit Bowl, 11-1/2" d, Gorham, c1900-15, Chrysanthemum edge, 28.6 troy oz ..............................................225.00

Goblet, water, 6-1/2" h, Manchester, c1945-60, price for set of twelve................................................770.00

Ice Bucket, Poole, Georgian taste, thermos-lined, two handles, Silver-craft tongs, c1950-55 ..........................................350.00

Jar, cov, 4-1/4" h, Gorham, late 19th C, Aesthetic Movement, tapered urn form, rounded lid, allover hammered surface, body and lid applied to one side with gold washed Japonesque prunus blossoms on engraved branches, 6 troy oz.....................................980.00

Jelly Spoon, 8" l, Gorham, Versailles, reticulated circular blade.195.00

Julep Cup, 3-3/8" h, mkd "E. & D. Kinsey" (Edward and David Kinsey, 1836-50, Newport, Kentucky, Cincinnati, OH), tooled rings on rim and base ..............................................425.00

Kettle and Tray, Dominick & Haff, retailed by Shreve, Crump & Low, early 20th C, sterling, round kettle with fluted detail, scroll design joints, sq tray with band of fluting under reeded rim, 48 troy oz .........................650.00

Kettle on Stand, 14-1/2" h, Gorham, Plymouth pattern, shaped oval, cut corners, oval molded foot and base, four ball feet, scrolling supports, angular wooden over handle, burner unmarked, 42 troy oz.........800.00

Ladle, 12-1/2" l, Gorham, retailed by Tiffany & Co., third quarter 19th C, profile medallion of classical woman, ovoid bowl, regilded int., 8 troy oz ..............................................690.00

Loving Cup, 7" h, Frank W. Smith, Art Nouveau taste, c1900-10, three handles, 7 troy oz .........................................275.00

Mayonnaise Bowl, 4-1/2" w, 3-1/2" d, 2-1/2" h, Watson Company, c1910, 2 troy oz.........................................35.00

Mug

3-5/8" h, Gorham, 1870, barrel shape, reeded borders and handle, monogram, 5 troy oz ................................200.00

4-1/4" h, Colin V. G. Forbes, reeded rim and base borders, scroll handle, monogram, 12 troy oz .........................800.00

Nutmeg Grater

2-1/8" h, shell form, engraved "Winslow," minor loss and corrosion to grater .........................................325.00

4-3/8" h, Jacobi & Jenkins, c1900, cov compartment, exposed grating surface, monogram, 2 troy oz .............................865.00

Pastry Basket, 8" w, 7-1/2" d, Galt and Brother, c1910-15, reticulated, swing handle .........................................150.00

Patch Box, late 18th C, engraved basketweave design, gold wash int., repaired, 2 troy oz .........................................115.00

Peacock Dish, Gorham, 20th C, cast body, chased tail feathers, pr, 16 troy oz ..............................................2,300.00

Pepper Grinder, 3-1/2" h, Gorham, 1898, cylindrical, chased floral dec, monogram ..............................................115.00

Photograph Frame, Haut-Relief, Beaux-Arts style, double, cobalt blue velvet back and double easels, 13-1/2" w, 10-1/2" h................150.00

Pitcher, 7-3/4" h, Gorham, third quarter 19th C, baluster form, domed foot, body chased and embossed on lower section with dense floral sprays, plain cartouche on one side, monogrammed on other side, serpentine handle with flat leaves at bottom, 35 troy oz, price for pr............1,610.00

Porringer, 4-5/8" d, Gorham, retailed by Spaulding & Co, low relief band under rim, nursery rhymes, pierced scroll design handle, monogram, 7 troy oz .........................................350.00

Powder Jar, 4" h, Black, Starr & Frost, 20th C, chased floral border on top, monogram, cut glass base ....................................175.00

Presentation Bowl, 9-7/8" d, 3-3/4" h, Gorham, 1880, sterling and mixed metal, four raised feet, hammered surface, applied birds and plants, two applied medallions, owl and bird in trees, inscription on base, 46 troy oz..............................................4,600.00

Presentation Cup, 11-1/2" h, Bigelow, Kennard & Co., late 19th C, reticulated domed foot, diapering, rocaille scrolls, and roses, shaped rim, two horn handles set on stylized horn sockets, engraved on one side with initials and date 1899, 60 troy oz....................................3,110.00

Presentation Pitcher, 8" h, Gorham, 1880, sterling and mixed metal, hammered surface, applied leaf and fruit motifs, four lower panels with chased figures of mythological women, branch-form handle, inscription on base, 36 troy oz .........................................10,350.00

Punch Bowl

9" d, 5" h, Barbour Silver Co., c1915-20, Georgian taste, ftd, engraved, 21 troy oz ....................................315.00

11" d, 5-1/2" h, Stieff, c1930-40, Revere form, 30.9 troy oz 250.00

Punch Ladle, 14-1/2" l, S. Kirk & Son, 20th C, floral repousse pattern, 8 troy oz ..............................................350.00

Ramekin, 3-1/2" d, Hamilton & Diesinger, circular, pierced, trellis, scrolls, and flowers, handles with pierced terminals, monogram, French porcelain liners, set of twelve, 31 oz, 4 dwt ................ 850.00

Salt and Pepper Casters, 1-5/8" d, 5-3/4" h, Anco, NY, Georgian taste, c1920-27, price for pr ................................................................. 50.00

Sandwich Tray, 18" d, S. Kirk and Son, cavetto engraved with multiple facsimile signatures of US Congress colleagues of Hon. John Taber of NY, retailed by Galt and Brother, Washington, DC, hallmarked, c1960, 72 troy oz .............................................................................. 350.00

Salver, 10-1/4" d, John B. Jones, Boston, 1816-37, applied shaped foliate rim and feet, monogrammed, minor surface abrasions, 22 troy oz ........................................................................................ 635.00

Serving Fork, 9" l, engraved "Ovulo," 3 troy oz ........................... 110.00

Serving Spoon, 8-1/8" l, Gorham, design attributed to George Wilkinson, third quarter 19th C, Egyptian Revival "Isis" pattern, pierced pointed gold washed bowl, 2 troy oz ...................................... 690.00

Serving Tongs, 7" l, Reed & Barton, La Perle, reticulated bowl, claw terminals .................................................................................... 175.00

Sweetmeat Basket, 5" w, 9" l, 11" h, Simpson, Hall, Miller Company, c1900-15, reticulated, stationary handle, 16.4 troy oz ............. 315.00

Sweetmeat Jar, cov, 6" d, 6" h, Gorham, 1908, floral engraved, int. gilded, 12 troy oz .................................................................... 150.00

Sweetmeat Tray, Wallace, c1925-30, Egyptian taste, circular, ftd ...... 90.00

Tazza, 6-1/2" d, 3-1/4" h, S. Kirk & Son Co., early 20th C, trumpet foot partially chased and emb with flowers on stippled ground, shaped edge, bowl with further chased and emb rim, shaped edge, 20 troy oz, price for pr ......................................................................... 635.00

Tea and Coffee Set
  Aldelphia, 20th C, 9-7/8" h coffeepot, teapot, creamer, cov sugar, waste bowl, melon baluster-form, repousse floral and scroll motif, 66 troy oz ...................................................................... 1,380.00
  Durgin, retailed by Grogan Company, late 19th C, 9-3/4" h coffeepot, kettle on stand, teapot, creamer, cov sugar, waste bowl, paneled baluster-form, ftd base, ivory finials, monogram, 148 troy oz .......................................................................................... 3,450.00
  Gorham, 1912-51, sterling, coffeepot, teapot, creamer, cov sugar, waste bowl, baluster form, spreading circular base, reeded borders, baluster finials, monogram, 67 troy oz ......................... 875.00
  Redlich & Co., retailed for Shreve, Crump and Low, late 19th C, sterling, tea and coffee pots, kettle on stand, creamer, cov sugar, waste bowl with strainer, and tray, baluster-form, chased floral design, 302 troy oz .................................................... 9,200.00

Tea Set, Towle, Symphony pattern, 8-3/4" h teapot, creamer, sugar, baluster form, engraved lobing to lower portion of bodies, serpentine handles and spouts, domed lids, slender acorn finials, 53 troy oz total ................................................................................... 550.00

**Sugar Basket, Reed & Barton, c1868, red glass liner, 4-1/4" w, 4" h, $125.**

**Bud Vase, corseted, three split handles, spade-shaped ends, attributed to Charles Clement Pilling, 1903, hallmarks, 6" h, 2-1/2" d, pr, $850. Photo courtesy of David Rago Auctions.**

Tray, 29-1/2" l, Gorham, 20th C, oval, shaped gadrooned rim, handles raised on C-scrolls, 119 troy oz ........................................... 2,530.00

Vase, 22" h, Lebkuecher & Co., Newark, late 19th C, four scrolled feet, round base with husk border, trumpet foot applied with flat leaves, inverted baluster form body chased and emb with horizontal band at girdle with paterae within cartouches, scroll and bellflower swags below band, scrolls and anthemion above, applied center Renaissance Revival style shields, applied monogram, topped by grotesque mask, everted rim applied with four further masks, gadrooned border, 80 troy oz ............................................................................. 4,600.00

Vegetable Serving Spoon, 10" l, Towle, Olde English, int. bowl gilded, 3 troy oz .................................................................................... 115.00

Water Pitcher, 9" h, 6" d, Poole, c1930-35, Georgian taste, Plain Gadroon, 26 troy oz ................................................................. 275.00

Wine Coaster, 4-3/4" d, Gorham, 1897, ftd, openwork sides, monogram, 4 troy oz ........................................................................ 250.00

## Arts & Crafts

Silver of the Arts & Crafts movement encompasses several styles and features well-made craftsmanship. The movement encouraged crafts people to express themselves in whatever medium they were using, thus creating some exciting silver items for today's collector to enjoy. As craftsman, they often chose to hammer and adorn pieces with unique trims and borders, as well as free-flowing forms. Most pieces have impressed marks. Because the Arts & Crafts movement was international, guilds were located in the United States, Great Britain, Germany, and Austria, creating many forms.

Bowl, 6" w, 9-1/2" l, 1-1/2" h, Kalo, Chicago, quatrefoil rolled rim, lobed shallow bowl, hammered surface, imp "Sterling Handwrought at The Kalo Shops Chicago and New York 413," 9 troy oz ................ 875.00

Candlesticks, pr, 12" h, Kalo, hammered, initials on base, imp mark .............................................................................................. 2,900.00

Cocktail Shaker, 8" h, LeBolt, hammered, detailed rim, imp mark ... 700.00

Compote
  5-1/2" d, Gorham, hand-hammered, imp mark ................... 150.00
  6" d, Kalo, hand-hammered, five-lobed bowl ..................... 550.00

Creamer and Sugar, 4" h, Kalo, hammered, imp mark .............. 750.00

Demitasse Cup, John O. Bellis, hammered, scalloped rim, imp mark, set of six ................................................................................ 125.00

Gravy Boat, undertray, ladle, Alan Adler maker, 4-1/8" h gravy boat with open wirework foot, plain ear handle, allover hammered surface, 7-1/8" l hammered oval undertray, 6" l ladle with ovoid bowl, stylized Onslow stem end, 18 troy oz total ...................................... 1,380.00

Pitcher, 10-1/2" h, 8" d, Kalo, hand hammered, emb sections, monogrammed "B," stamped "Sterling/Handwrought/The Kalo Shop/Chicago/USA/5 Pints" .................................................................. 2,600.00

Presentation Bowl, 11" d, 5-3/4" h, Gebelein, Boston, 1938, flared rim, circular stepped base, engraved "Charles Pendleton Lewis '33 from the Spee Club July 1 1938," imp makers marks on base .........350.00

Serving Spoon, 9-1/2", Kalo, hammered....................................275.00

Shaker, 7" h, Woolley, hammered, pierced holes in top, finely tooled center floral design, mkd ............................................................450.00

Shoe Horn, 4-3/4" l, Kalo, Chicago, hammered surface, raised stylized initial "S," imp "Sterling Kalo P114S" ..................................550.00

Tea Caddy Spoon, 2-1/2" h, 1-1/2" w, Handicraft Guide, hand hammered, c1895, cut-out handle, die-stamped...........................150.00

Tea Set, LeBolt, hammered, 7-1/2" h teapot, 3-1/2" h creamer, 3-1/2" h sugar, 13" d tray, imp marks ...............................................1,000.00

Tray

9-1/2" d, Kalo, hand-hammered, five-lobed rim, imp mark .500.00

10-1/2" l, 5" w, hammered, handled, glass bottom, imp mark..325.00

Vase

5-5/8" h, Unger Brothers, Newark, NJ, ruffled and flared rim tapering to swollen base, hand hammered surface, imp marks and "B2295," minor scratches .....................................................490.00

7" h, Kalo, Chicago, bud, flared rolled rim, cylindrical body tapering to round disk base, hammered surface, imp "Sterling Kalo 377G" on base, 7 troy oz, price for pr ...........................1,850.00

# Continental

Generally, Continental silver does not have a strong following in the United States, but Danish pieces by Georg Jensen are early sought. As the antiques marketplace continued to expand globally, Continental silver has become more popular.

## Austrian

Bowl, 5-1/8" d, repousse floral design, two medallions of pastoral scenes with cow and horse, spreading circular base, 4 troy oz.....................................................................................175.00

Box, cov, 9" h, mid-19th C, bombe form, engraved design, mark's mark "WH," 9 troy oz ...........................................................425.00

Candlesticks, pr, 12" h, 19th C, Rococo Revival style, floral repousse baluster form standard, molded socle, cast scrolls and wave work feet, 26 troy oz ...............................................750.00

Chalice, 7-7/8" h, c1910, raised repeating geometric and medallion pattern, trumpet base with raised repeating pyramid pattern, imp "WMFM," wear to finish .............................................250.00

Chinese Export, kettle on stand, 14-5/8" h, kettle with chased landscape scenes and figures, floral and plant panels, extensive inscriptions, bamboo finial, handle, and stand, c1900, 44 troy oz ......865.00

## Denmark

Cigarette Lighter, 3-1/2" h, lamp-form, leaf dec foot, bud finial, Georg Jensen, 1925-30, 5 troy oz................................1,380.00

Coffeepot, 11-1/8" h, pear-shape, fluted band on bottom of pot and on lid, ball in fluted cup finial, lightly hammered surface, part-wood scroll handle, applied ball and scroll dec, Georg Jensen, 29 troy oz...............................................................2,185.00

Condiment, 5-1/4" h, Andress Holm, Copenhagen, 1795, hinged lid, cobalt blue glass liner ...............................................295.00

Service Plates, 10-1/4" d, C. C. Hermann, 20th C, beaded rim, monogrammed on edge, 238 troy oz, price for 12 pc set............4,320.00

## France

Chocolate Pot, 8-1/4" h, baluster, turned wooden side handle, three pad feet, hinged swing finial, Paris, 1781, 18 troy oz .........2,000.00

Creamer, 5-1/2" h, hinged lid, Rococo detail, monogrammed, indistinct mark .........................................................................140.00

Egg Cup Set, 19th C, engraved egg-form container, two pedestal bases, 950 fine, 3 troy oz ...............................................300.00

Planter, 14" l, 5-1/2" h, Neoclassical, late 18th/19th C, ovoid, pierced scroll and shell feet, bowl with chased and emb husk swags on pierced guilloche ground, ribbon-tied undulating edge, two cast scroll handles, fitted metal liner, 27 troy oz .........................1,725.00

Platter, 17-1/2" l, 11-3/8" w, late 19th C, made for Theodore B. Starr, NY, shaped ovoid, concave reeded rim with small shells and floral sprays, monogrammed center, .950 fine, 32 troy oz ...........700.00

Sauceboat and undertray, J. C. Camier, Paris, 1809-19, oval, attached undertray, flying handle, foliage and applied figural mask, 23 ox...........................................................................2,500.00

Tumbler, 4" h, spreading circular base, gadrooned border, Paris, 18th C, some dents, 3 troy oz ..................................................300.00

Urn, cov, 9-3/4" h, 1819-38, four ball feet, square base, trumpet foot with flat leaf edge, short stem with ribbed shoulder, urn pierced to one side with putto with tambourine, other with cupid borne by swans, flat leaf trim, cast grotesque herm handles, slightly domed lid with beaded edge, egg-shaped foliate finial, .950 fine, 16 troy oz........................................................................575.00

## Germany

Box, cov, 7-1/2" l, 4-3/8" w, 3-3/4" h, late 19th/early 20th C, rect, hinged lid chased and emb with military scene of foot soldiers and cavalary officers, edge band of fruit and leaves, sides chased and emb with cornucopia and flower-filled urns, stippled ground, gold-washed int., monogrammed, .800 fine, 13 troy oz ...............980.00

Coffee and Tea Service, Belle Epoque, rococo taste, c1900-10, ftd coffeepot, ftd teapot, ftd cream pitcher, ftd cov two-handled sugar basin, lobed tray, .800 fine ...............................1,760.00

Coffeepot, cov, 9-1/2" h, 18th C style, c1915, .800 fine, 20 troy oz .........................................................................................400.00

Coffeepot and Sugar, cov, 12" h coffeepot, 7-1/2" h sugar, Rococo Revival, late 19th C, pear shaped ovoid coffeepot with four scroll feet, chased and emb allover with Rococo style scrolls and flowerheads, serpentine handles, short spout, domed lids with plain and diapered scroll cartouches, open rocaille finials, sugar with trefoil open scroll and rocaille handles, monogrammed, .800 fine, 45 troy oz total.........................................................................815.00

Platter, Louis XV taste, c1900, circular, .800 fine, 27 troy oz...385.00

Sauce Boat, Belle Epoque, in the Louis XVI taste, c1900-15, reticulated, int. fitted with conforming blown crystal liner, 6" w, 3-3/4" d, 4" h..............................................................................150.00

Solitaire, Louis XVI taste, c1900-15, rect tray, cov coffee pot, ftd cream pitcher, open two handled sugar bowl, gilded int., .800 fine, 13 troy oz......................................................................200.00

## Italian

Fruit Bowl, 10-1/2" d, rococo taste, ftd, leaf engraving, hallmarked "R. Miracoli and Cir.," .800 standard ...............................125.00

Garniture Vase, 16-3/4" h, baluster, two handles, maker Gorcia, c1950, hallmarked, .800 standard, 37 troy oz .................850.00

Sweetmeat Bowl, 4" w, 8" l, sterling, ftd, two handles, bateau form, c1925-30 ..........................................................................50.00

Tea Strainer and Stand, Coppini, 20th C, strainer chased and emb at rim with fruit, stem with beaded roundel, tripod stand, paw feet, legs topped by floral baskets, medial beaded bowl with foliate rim, .800 fine, 4 troy oz.............................................230.00

Russian, goblet, 5-5/8" h, banded in black with turquoise, white, and gilt foliate motifs, post 1958 Soviet period, 8 troy oz...............250.00

## Scandinavian

Platter, Gadroon and Shell, ovoid, c1900, 24 troy oz .........400.00

Sauce Ladle, 8-1/2" l, Palmette and Leaf pattern, oviform bowl with gilded int., Carlsson, Stockholm, maker, c1875..........75.00

Tablespoon, 9" l, Palmette and Leaf pattern, maker F. Holm, c1875 .....................................................................................40.00

Tray, 16-1/2" l, 12" w, rect, c1920 ......................................500.00

Vodka Cup, 2" d, 2" h, gilded int., c1830-35, price for pr ......45.00

# Sterling, English, Irish, Scottish

From the 17th century to the mid-19th century, English silversmiths set the styles which American silversmiths copied. The work from the period exhibits the highest degree of craftsmanship. English silver is actively collected in the American antiques marketplace.

Apple Corer, 5-7/8" l, Victorian, H & T makers, Birmingham, 1870, turned handle, 2 troy oz .........................................................460.00

Asparagus Tongs, Victorian, Messrs. Eady makers, London, 1861, beaded borders with openwork, scroll design, 7 troy oz .........750.00

Beaker, 4-1/4" h, George III, Henry Chawner and John Emes, London, 1799, tapered cylindrical form, engraved with heraldic crest, reeded rim, two applied card handles, price for pr, 8 troy oz ............. 1,150.00

Berry Spoon, George IV, Glasgow, 1820, engraved floral handles, chased pear and grape gold wash bowls, monogrammed, price for pr, 5 troy oz ................................................................. 175.00

Bowl, 6" d, George V, maker's mark partially rubbed, London, 1911, domed foot with leafy scroll reticulated band, applied scrolled edge, bowl fully reticulated with further leafy scrolls, matching applied edging, cobalt blue glass liner, 8 troy oz ................................ 320.00

Brandy Pitcher, 15" l, Georgian, c1765, sterling and barley-twist carved ebony ...................................................................... 60.00

Candlestick

10-1/4" h, Georgian, Dublin, late 18th/early 19th C, chased and engraved scroll foliate dec, removable bobeches with engraved heraldic device, set of four, 96 troy oz .......................... 4,025.00

13-1/4" h, George III, IWFK makers, London, 1767, fluted Corinthian columns, sq stepped base with bands of ovolos, removable nozzles with canted corners, beaded rim, one engraved with heraldic symbol, base with wood mounts, price for pr ..................... 1,495.00

Caddy Spoon, George III, George Baskerville maker, London, 1798, engraved dec, .5 troy oz ................................................. 175.00

Cann, London hallmarks for 1770-71, 3-7/8" h, very minor dents .... 575.00

Caster

6-1/2" h, London, 1837, baluster, pierced cover, molded foot, 7 oz, 2 dwt ............................................................ 200.00

9" h, Thomas Bradbury & Sons, London, 1895-96, octagonal, waisted reeded band and foot, pierced cover ................... 350.00

Center Bowl, 13" l, 7" h, Victorian, George Fox maker, London, 1996, domed foot with fluted rim, reticulated with candle and flame, chased and emb with husk swags and paterae, boat-shaped bowl similarly pierced and emb, monogrammed cartouches on each side, rim pierced and applied with paterae roundels, scrolls, and husk swags, 29 troy oz .................................................................. 2,415.00

Chamberstick, 7" h, George III, attributed to Ebenezer Coker, London, 1761, scroll handle, tapered socket, applied rocaille scroll and flowerhead rim, snuffer, extinguisher missing, 13 troy oz ................. 520.00

Cheese Knife, 8-1/2" l, Scottish, Eider and Company, Edinburgh, 1857, King's Shell, engraved with coronet-surmounted cipher ........... 75.00

Cheese Scoop with Pusher, 8-1/2" l, George III, JT maker, Birmingham, 1803, Stilton, carved palmette-shaped ivory handle ....... 375.00

Cigar Case, 5-1/4" l, 3-1/8" w, Victorian, maker's mark "GHJ," London, 1886, four-fingers, engraved presentation initials and date 1889, gold washed int., 5 troy oz .............................................. 520.00

Coffeepot

6-1/4" h, George III, TK & RS makers, London, 1804-05, cylindrical, wooden handle and finial, gadroon border on lid, engraved crest under spout and on lid .......................................... 700.00

11-3/4" h, George III, maker's mark illegible, London, 1774, baluster-form, spreading circular base, beaded and fluted dec, garland swags under rim, scroll rattan handle, later dec, repairs to back under handle, 22 troy oz ......................................... 750.00

Condiment Set, J. C. Ltd. maker, Birmingham, 1922, mustard pot and salt with cobalt blue glass liners, pepper aster, two condiment spoons, fitted case, 4 troy oz ................................... 190.00

Cream Pitcher

4" h, Irish, Georgian-style, Dublin, 1913, hallmarked and produced for Harrods, London, baluster, ftd, 6 troy oz ......... 225.00

4" h, Victorian, Georgian-style, London, c1891, markers J.P./P.P. with "flower basket" repousse mark, ftd, 2 troy oz ........... 360.00

4-1/2" h, George III, London, 1780, ftd, floral repousse of a later date, 3 troy oz ......................................... 250.00

Diary, 4" l, weekly type, gold and silver, Japonesque taste, William and John Barnard makers, London, 1881, int. fitted with seven ivory diary pages, lined in compartmented period royal-blue silk ............. 900.00

Egg Stand, 7-5/8" h, George III, illegible maker's mark, possibly William Elliot, London, 1817, raised rect shape, double scroll lifting handle, four paw feet, rosette and scroll detail, gadroon borders on frame, six round cup holders, six egg cups with gadroon rim and silver-gilt int., six spoon slots on frame, six George IV egg spoons, four

1823 with maker's mark, other two 1820, attributed to R. Peppin maker, all King's pattern, silver-gilt bowls, same engraved heraldic symbol, repairs to frame base, 34 troy oz ........................... 1,265.00

Entree Dish, George III, Richard Cooke maker, London, 1804-05, cushion-shape, deep body, cov, removable liner, cast lion's head handles and scroll finial, gadroon rims, engraved coat of arms on cover and body, paw feet, 168 troy oz ................................ 4,325.00

Epergne, George III, Matthew Boulton maker, Birmingham, 1804, four detachable branches, band around rim with vine motifs, cast lion's masks on each of four supports, bottom incurving quatrefoil plinth, gadroon rim, cast fluted finial, four paw feet, large 11-1/8" d central cut glass dish and four smaller dishes, 98 troy oz ............. 8,925.00

Fish Knife, Victorian, Hy. Wilkinson & Co. makers, Sheffield, 1880, engine-turned surface dec on handle, beaded border, bright-cut engraved blade, 4 troy oz ............................................ 150.00

Fish Server, Regency, John Emes maker, London, 1800, heraldic device surrounded by open wrigglework, 7 troy oz ................. 575.00

Fish Set, Victorian, FE maker, Birmingham, 1876, service for five, ivory handles, floral engraved blades, fitted case ........................ 200.00

Fruit Basket, 10-1/4" d, William IV, Robinson, Edkins and Astor makers, Birmingham, c1831, round, raised central foot, fluted dec overlay, reeded openwork entwined body with vine and grape design draped rim, swing handle, scroll foliate dec and central flower, 22 troy oz ......................................................... 1,200.00

Fruit Spoon, Regency, G. T. maker, London, 1814, repousse fruit dec gold washed bowls, engraved floral handle, price for pr, 4 troy oz ..... 7,475.00

Glove Stretcher, 8-5/8" l, Victorian, D & S maker, Birmingham, 1888, mosaic pattern handle, 2 troy oz ................................... 175.00

Goblet, 6-1/4" h, George III, Henry Chawner and John Emes makers, London, 1796, lower body repousse with leaves, circular molded foot, engraved armorials, pr, 22 oz 8 dwt ......................... 1,200.00

Gravy Boat, George III, London, R. Peaston maker, 1774-75, gadroon border, flying scroll handle, engraved stag, three shell feet, minor dents on one, 26 troy oz ............................................. 2,185.00

Gravy Ladle, 7" l, Fiddle Thread pattern, maker George Angell, London, 1874 ................................................................. 90.00

Hot Milk Jug, 5-3/4" h, George IV, London, 1938, tapering cylindrical, domed lid, reeded rim and foot, wood handle, engraved crest, 11 oz, 7 dwt .............................................................. 350.00

Hot Water Urn, 21" h, George IV, Daniel Holy & Co., Sheffield, 1925, beehive form, waisted foliate band centering two crested cartouches on shaped sq base, four paw supports issuing from foliage, four paw feet, reeded and foliate handles, dome cover, scrolling foliate finial, with liner, 165 oz ..................................................... 11,000.00

Inkstand, 13-1/4" l, Victorian, Birmingham, Robinson, Edkins and Astor makers, 1840, rect, shell and scroll border, four scrolling shell feet, two pen dips, crystal bodied inkwell and pounce pot, central sealing wafer pot, 31 troy oz ................................................ 980.00

Inkwell, traveling, 2" h, Edwardian, illegible maker's mark, London, 1902, cylindrical, twist-off lid, inner glass ink chamber, ext. engraved checkerboard dec, ............................................... 260.00

Ladle

7-1/8" l, George III, Hester Bateman maker, London, 1780, 1 troy oz .......................................................... 350.00

13" l, Irish, maker's mark "W.W.," Dublin, 1762, barbed rectangular punch ovoid bowl with tapered back tipt stem, monogrammed, 5 troy oz ..................................................... 320.00

13-1/2" l, English, George III, Peter and Ann Bateman, London, 1795, ovoid bowl, plain back tipt handle, 5 troy oz ........... 290.00

14-1/8" l, 3-7/8" d, George II, Elias Cachart maker, London, 1746, rat tail handle, engraved coat of arms, 6 troy oz ............. 300.00

Marrow Scoop, 9-1/2" l, Georgian, c1735, hallmarks obliterated, double-end .............................................................. 100.00

Mote Spoon, 5-1/2" l, George II, London, 1715, reticulated bowl . 80.00

Napkin Ring

George V, Birmingham, 1920, round, engine-turned surface dec, central monogram, pair in fitted case, 2 troy oz .............. 125.00

Victorian, JR maker, London, 1861, floral repousse design, set of six in fitted case, individually numbered, 6 troy oz ........... 800.00

Nutmeg Grater, George III, Matthew Linwood maker, Birmingham, 1809-10

Cushion-shape, lined surface dec, 1 troy oz .......................760.00
Rect hinged box, 1 troy oz ................................................760.00
Pepper Caster, 6-1/8" h, George II, attributed to Samuel Wood maker, London, 1737, tall bulbous shape, pierced dec on cov, minor dents, 5 troy oz ...........................................................................300.00
Photograph Frame, Elizabeth II, Edwardian style
7-1/2" w, 10" h, London maker, Guillouche pattern, blue velvet easel and back ...............................................................175.00
8-1/2" w, 7-1/2" h, faux tortoiseshell trim, blue velvet easel and back.................................................................................200.00
9-1/2" w, 8-1/2" h, London maker R C., emb, blue velvet easel and back ...............................................................225.00
Presentation Trowel, 12-1/2" l, Victorian, maker's mark partially rubbed, possibly Francis Higgins, London, 1887, stylized heart shaped blade engraved with presentation inscription dated 1889, acanthus engraving above and below, beaded handle, tapered faux ivory handle ending in single bead ...........................................300.00
Punch Bowl, 12-1/8" d, 5-3/4" h, Paul Storr, letter date for 1827, London, marked near rim, opposed by engraved heraldic device, further marks for John Samuel Hunt, 1852, marked to underside of foot, ovoid form, spreading foot, everted rim, bowl chased and emb allover with scenes of village revelry, gold-washed int., 44 troy oz ...8,100.00
Salt
1-1/2" d, circular, Victorian, F. V. maker, 1888, fitted with conforming blown cobalt blue glass liner, price for pr .....................50.00
1-3/4" h, 3-1/2" l, George III, Robert and David Hennell, London, 1765, ovoid, pad feet, scroll legs topped by shells, spiral fluting and small cartouche engraved with heraldic crest, edge with gadrooned rim, worn gold-wash int., 11 troy oz, price for set of four ....................................................................................490.00
Salver
10-1/2" d, George II, Paul Lamerie maker, London, 1745, engraved scroll foliate detail, central cartouche, engraved rampant lion, four scroll feet, segmented outer fluted border, 26 troy oz ......................................................................... 16,100.00
12" d, George III, John Carter maker, London, 1775, gadroon border, central engraved coat of arms, three ball and claw feet, 30 troy oz ........................................................................... 1,265.00
12-1/4" l, George III, Edward Jay, London, 1781, oblong, molded edge, four scroll feet, engraved center mottoed coat of arms, 34 troy oz ........................................................................... 2,650.00
13" d, George III, John Carter maker, London, 1771, gadroon border, engraved coat of arms with heart-shaped shield, floral dec, four feet, 32 troy oz ..............................................................2,070.00
Sauce Boat, 7" w, 4" d, 4" h, George V, George III-style, c1915, tripodal, price for pr .............................................................125.00
Sauce Tureen
9" l, 6-1/4" h, George III, Jos. Craddock and William Reid, London, 1819, ovoid, four hairy paw feet topped by rocaille shells flanked by acanthus, two acanthus handles centered by shells, body engraved to one side with heraldic device, applied rim cast as stylized continuous hunting scene with stags and hunting dogs, domed lid with band of vertical reeding, finial formed as entwined snakes on leafy ground, 34 troy oz .................2,100.00
10-3/8" l, 5-3/4" h, John Schofield, London, 1784, boat shape, oval beaded foot, beaded edge, loop handles, engraved on one side with heraldic crest over husk swag, coat of arms on other side, 15 troy oz.............................................................1,265.00
Spoon, 7-1/2" l, early, partially illegible London marks, trifid end, rat-tail handle, engraved crest and monogram, 1-1/2 troy oz ............250.00
Straining Spoon, 12" l, George III, William Eley, William Fearn, and William Chawner makers, London, 1911, plain Fiddle pattern, engraved heraldic animal, vertical straining device in center of bowl, 5 troy oz ........................................................................230.00
Stuffing Spoon, 12" l, George III, Thomas Ollivant maker, London, 1795, 3 troy oz ...............................................................175.00
Sugar Basket, 3-3/4" h, Georgian-style, International Silver, early 20th C, bail handle, cobalt blue glass liner, 2 troy oz ........................50.00

Sugar Tong
5-1/2" l, Georgian, London maker H.C./M.J., 1811, Fiddle Thread, oviform terminals, 1 troy oz ...............................................70.00
6" l, Scottish, William Alexander and Son maker, Glasgow, 1865, King's Shell, palmette terminals ......................................200.00
Sweetmeat Box, 2-1/2" l, Victorian, makers Yapp and Woodward, Birmingham, 1846, one side with engraved armorial, engine-turned rect....................................................................500.00
Tablespoon, George III, Richard Crossley maker, London, 1787, engraved figure of rampant horse on handle, set of eight, 18 troy oz ..........750.00
Tankard, 7-1/2" h, George I, Thomas Tearle, London, 1725, tapered cylindrical form, applied ribbed foot, body with single applied girdle, engraved plain rococo cartouche, serpentine handle, domed hinged lid with volute thumbpiece, 26 troy oz ...................................3,220.00
Tea and Coffee Service, George IV, Rebecca Emes and Edward Barnard, London, 1829, oblong bodies, ball feet, band of vertical reeding at girdle, engraved on one side with heraldic crest, applied gadrooning and rocaille shells at rim, angular fruitwood handles on teapot and 8" h, coffeepot, oblong finials, flying flat leaf scroll handles on open creamer and sugar, regilded interiors, 67 troy oz .........2,185.00
Teapot
6" h, Victorian, Jas. Dixon & Sons, Sheffield, 1869, shaped ovoid, engraved with plain foliate roundel on sides, top with band of floral vine, short serpentine spout, flat topped ear handle, slightly domed hinged lid with mushroom finial, 22 troy oz...........................575.00
10-3/4" l, George III, Peter, Anne, and William Bateman makers, London, 180-2, compressed cylindrical form, gadrooned rim, circular foot, wood finial and loop handle, 212 oz ............950.00
Tea Set
Regency, J. McKay maker, Edinburgh, 1819-20, teapot, creamer, open sugar, oblong oval form, four ball feet, gadroon rims, engraved floral and leaf dec, gold washed int. in creamer and sugar, curving leaf-shape handles, repair and split to lid, spout damage, 40 troy oz .......................................................750.00
Victorian, GR maker, London, 1850, 9-1/2" h teapot, creamer, open sugar with gold wash int., rounded baluster form, spreading circular base, scroll handles, engraved plain scroll dec, central monogram, molded scroll border, ornate bell finial, 47 troy oz ...........................................................................750.00
Victorian, Walter and George Sissons, makers, London, 1876, 12-1/2" h coffeepot, teapot, creamer, two handled open sugar, plain baluster shape, beaded rims, circular foot, leaf-capped loop handle with applied beads, bombe hinged cover, baluster finial, monogrammed, 69 oz.........................................1,200.00
Tea Urn
19-3/4" h, George III, London, 1764, chased floral and scroll dec, gadroon rims, four raised ball and claw feet, some dents, missing finial on lever, 83 troy oz.........................................2,070.00
20-1/2" h, George III, Charles Wright maker, London, 1775, center with beaded details, ivory handle, monogrammed, 78 troy oz.......................................................................2,415.00
Tray, 20-3/8" d, William IV, London, Paul Storr maker, 1831, cast scroll and floral border, engraved scroll foliate dec, central coat of arms, three foliate feet, 110 troy oz..............................................6,900.00
Wine Coaster, 5-3/4" d, George IV, Matthew Boulton maker, Birmingham, 1824, repousse scroll foliate design, curved petal shaped rim .......................................................................500.00

**Tray, scroll center, emb edge, 19-1/4" d, $535.**

## English, Sheffield

Sheffield Silver, or Old Sheffield Plate, has a fusion method of silver-plating that was used from the mid-18th century until the mid-1880s, when the process of electroplating silver was introduced. Sheffield plating was discovered in 1743 when Thomas Boulsover of Sheffield, England, accidentally fused silver and copper. The process consisted of sandwiching a heavy sheet of copper between two thin sheets of silver. The result was a plated sheet of silver, which could be pressed or rolled to a desired thickness. All Sheffield articles are worked from these plated sheets. Most of the silver-plated items found today marked "Sheffield" are not early Sheffield plat. They are later wares made in Sheffield, England.

Argyle, 6-3/8" h, c1830, cylindrical, beaded rim, raffia wrapped handle, sell terminal, faceted ovoid knob ...............................................295.00
Basket, 13-1/4" l, boat shape, ovoid foot, rim with band of rect piercing, applied reeded edge, tapering swing handle, engraved heraldic device on int. ..........................................................................375.00
Candlestick
    7" h, 4-1/2" d, c1815-25, dunce-cap snuffers, cylindrical glass shades missing, price for pr ...............................................75.00
    11" h, sq loaded base with beading, engraved band of husk drops, columnar stem engraved with spiraling band of husks, flat leaf capital sconce, sq beaded nozzle, 19th C, price for set of four .................................................................................1,965.00
Compote, 4-1/2" d, Martin Hall & Co., Ltd. Makers, made for Tiffany & Co., 1911, ftd, pierced fretwork band under rim, price for pr, 13 troy oz .............................................................................................460.00
Dessert Service, Walker and Hall, c1925-30, service for twelve, orig fitted case, price for 24 pc set ......................................................175.00
Entree Dish, 12-3/4" l, applied rim of shells and scrolling foliage, foliate handles, four paw feet, liner ...........................................750.00
Epergne, 16" w, 16" d, 13-3/4" h, George IV, c1825-30, central cut glass bowl surrounded by four sweetmeat bowls, each on dependent arm, one bowl cracked and repaired ...............................................825.00
Fish Slicer, 13" l, ivory handle, maker's mark, 1906 ...................175.00
Fruit Bowl, 10" d, 4-1/2" h, Edwardian, c1900-10, Shell and Flower relief border, lined with conforming cork disc .........................115.00
Ice Tongs, 5-3/4" l, Victorian, maker's mark, bird claw grips, central monogram, 2 troy oz .......................................................................115.00
Magnum Coaster, 6-3/4" d, Old Sheffield style, center cavetto fitted with Sheffield plate boss, reticulated sides, gadroon edge, fruitwood .......................................................................................150.00
Pen Tray, 9" l, c1830, oblong, gadroon edge, armorial engraved in cavetto ........................................................................................70.00
Sauce Tureen, cov, 10-1/2" w, 4-1/4" d, 5-1/2" h, oval, two handles, neoclassical taste, c1800-10 ...............................................250.00
Sconces, pr, 12-1/2" h, 14" w, 8" d, Edwardian, Tonks & Company, Sheffield, Charles II inspiration, c1900-10, three-light .............150.00
Serving Tray
    18-1/4" d, oval, central engraved crest of arms, reeded border and handles, four feet .............................................................275.00
    21" d, Henry Wilkinson maker, c1800, gadroon border, two engraved dogs on rim ......................................................300.00
Tea Caddy, c1815-20, 5" w, 3-1/2" d, 5-1/2" h, rect, chamfered corners, silvering renewed ...................................................................350.00
Tea Set, Regency style, 19th C, 6" h, teapot, reamer, and sugar, mkd "TM"......................................................................................300.00
Wine Cooler, 10-3/4" h, c1810, campana form, applied grapevine dec at shoulder, waist and rims, foliate handles, molded circular foot, liner and collar, monogrammed.....................................................2,500.00

## Silver, Plated

Englishmen G. R. Elkington and H. Elkington are given credit for being the first to use the electrolytic method of plating silver in 1838.

Argyle, 6-1/2" h, late Georgian, late 19th C, compressed urn form, cut engraved tapered body, raked spout, stepped oval cov with ball finial, wood loop handles, oval reeded scole ...................................500.00
Biscuit Box, 6-1/2" d, 7-1/4" h, English, Neo-Grecque style, c1860-70, ram's head feet and goat mask ring handles ...........................615.00

**Syrup, floral relief, mkd "Samson, Hall, Miller & Co.," 7-1/2" h, $85.**

Bowl, Elkington & Co., Birmingham, c1850, shaped oval form, stag head handles, scrolled feet, three pc set ...............................800.00
Butter Dish, cov, 5-1/2" d, 5" h, English, c1890, dome ribbed roll-top, period pierced silverplate drain plate, four hairy paw feet........100.00
Candelabra, pr, 23-3/8" h, Elkington & Co., 1950, lobed and fluted baluster stems, serpentine branches, campana shaped detachable scones...................................................................................2,400.00
Candlesticks, pr, 12" h, English, 20th C, sq molded loaded base, stamped with band of flowers and scrolls, baluster form stem with four panels stamped with flower sprigs, shaped sq floral knop above and below, plain sconce, removable floral stamped shapes sq nozzle ..........420.00
Collar Button Box, 2-1/4" d, emb sides, figural collar button o lid with engraving "Here's Your Collar Button," marked "Homan Silver Co.," four SS buttons inside ................................................................65.00
Dish Cross, Edwardian, c1900-10, mid-Georgian style, one foot broken, 12" l .......................................................................................40.00
Entrée Dish, 14" w, 10-1/2" d, 6" w, William Adams, Louis XV taste, c1925-35, ovoid, foliate scroll finial removes to permit reverse of cover and use as separate open vegetable dish........................50.00
Entree Dish, Elkington & Co., Birmingham, c1850, shaped oval, stag head handles, scrolled feet, orig liner, nested seven pc set..1,200.00
Marrow Scoop, Edwardian, c1900-10, double end, 9-1/2" l..........45.00
Monteith, 12" d, Ellis Barker, early 20th C, round fluted body, spreading circular base, scroll rim, two medallions surrounded by scroll detail, two applied lion's head ring handles, detachable rim to convert to punch bowl ..........................................................................2,990.00
Muffin Basket, 13" l, oval, pierced ribbed sides, twin scrolled handles ...................................................................................95.00
Muffin Warmer, 9-1/2" h, Edwardian, c1900-10, gilded int., fold-down outer panels in form of ribbed shells ......................................110.00
Napkin Ring, child's, narrow, engraved cupid being drawn on chariot by butterflies................................................................................25.00
Pitcher on Stand, 22" h, Derby, foliate scroll dec, insulated, swing type, period detachable drip pan, c1880-85....................................275.00
Plateau
    14" d, 5-1/4" d, American, c1890-1900, Old Sheffield style, circular, upper surface fitted with period mirror plate ...............625.00
    20" d, American, Victorian, rococo taste, reticulated, mirror plate with scallop beveled edge ...............................................275.00
Sandwich Tray, 11-1/2" d, Belle Epoque, Dutch taste, circular, marked "Denmark," c1890-1915 .........................................................50.00
Service Plate, 12" d, Gadroon and Shell pattern, Regency-style of 1800-15, price for set of twelve ...............................................550.00
Serving Bowl
    15-1/2" d, W. & S. Blackington, c1930-40, shell shape, Old Sheffield style ...............................................................................100.00
    20-1/2" w, 14-1/2" d, 3" h, Sheffield, c1920-25, oval, ftd, Shell and Scroll pattern, Bakelite handles.......................................160.00

Sweetmeat Server, 14-1/2" w, 7" d, 9-1/2" h, American, c1875-80, double-bowl, each bowl surmounted by full figure of bird in flight, bowl cavettos with floral relief ornament.........................................200.00

Tea and Coffee Service, Reed & Barton, 12-1/4" h coffeepot, teapot, creamer, two handled open sugar, baluster-form, lobed at intervals, chased, scroll and foliate cartouche, loop handle, four scroll feet, flower, and bud finial ...............................................................200.00

Tray
　21-1/4" l, oblong, pierced gallery rim, engraved scroll foliate dec, two side handles, four ball feet, c1900.............................175.00
　30" l, shaped rect, repousse with flowers and leaves border, monogrammed cartouche flanked by flowers and foliage, two scrolling foliate handles, Pairpoint.....................................475.00

Trophy Goblet, Edwardian, dated 1905, Celtic Revival taste, 4" d, 7-3/4" h .........................................................................................50.00

Vase
　18-1/2" h, 9-1/2" d, Rogers, c1905-10, reticulated, Wedding Basket form, stationary hoop handle.......................................50.00
　20-1/2" h, 9-1/2" d, America, c1905-10, paneled, Wedding Basket form, swing handle, flaring reticulated lip ........................110.00

Vegetable Dish, cov, 14" l, shaped oval, applied scroll dec, scrolling handles, Sheffield, price for pr....................................................150.00

Wine Cooler, 11-1/4" l, oblong, gadrooned rims, two leaf-form side handles, two removable bottle compartments, Portugal, 20th C .........325.00

# SILVER DEPOSIT GLASS

**History:** Silver deposit glass was popular at the turn of the century. A simple electrical process was used to deposit a thin coating of silver on glass products. After the glass and a piece of silver were placed in a solution, an electric current was introduced which caused the silver to decompose, pass through the solution, and remain on those parts of the glass on which a pattern had been outlined.

Bowl, 5-1/2" d, vines and leaves dec, scalloped edge..................45.00
Compote, 7" d, floral dec...............................................................85.00
Creamer and Sugar, cov, floral dec...............................................90.00
Decanter, 9" h, emerald green, hollow stopper...............................75.00
Serving Plate, 12-1/2" d, dark amethyst, floral dec.......................75.00
Toothpick Holder, 2" h, amber ground.........................................50.00
Tumbler, 4-5/8" h, flared top........................................................25.00
Vase, 10" h, baluster, black ground, twin handles, parrot on branch dec .............................................................................................50.00

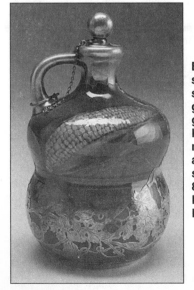

**Bottle, double gourd shape, ear of corn dec, sterling silver overlay in grapevine motif, monogrammed "GWC," Rookwood flame mark/S976/W/illegible artist's cipher, silver stamped "Sterling/R321," 8-1/2" h, 4-3/4" d, $2,300. Photo courtesy of David Rago Auctions.**

# SILVER OVERLAY

**History:** Silver overlay is silver applied directly to a finished glass or porcelain object. The overlay is cut and decorated, usually by engraving, prior to being molded around the object.

Glass usually is of high quality and is either crystal or colored. Lenox used silver overlay on some porcelain pieces. Most designs are from the Art Nouveau and Art Deco periods.

**Reference:** Lillian F. Potter, *Re-Introduction to Silver Overlay on Glass and Ceramics*, published by author, 1992.

Basket, 11-3/4" h, angular handle, narrow waisted transparent green lime glass body, silver overlay of roses, foliate border, silvered handle, berry prunts, La Pierre Mfg Co. hallmark, polished pontil, minor repair to silver overlay ..........................................................2,415.00

Bottle
　6" h, spherical form, colorless glass body, chased silver floral and scroll design, orig stopper, monogrammed, price for pr...325.00
　8" h, pinch style, colorless glass body, men, birds, dragons, silver marked "YTK"..................................................................50.00
　10-1/4" h, colorless glass body, floral overlay, heavy floral center medallion, monogrammed, matching stopper..................800.00

Claret Jug, 13" h, baluster form, colorless glass body, base cut with calyx, faceted neck with applied silver mount, hinged shell lid with spout, applied chased handle reaching down to silver mounted base, circular dome foot, repousse and chased floral and foliate design, unclear hallmark................................................................1,100.00

Coffee and Tea Service, 10-1/4" h coffeepot, 7-1/4" h teapot, 5-1/4" h creamer, 5" h sugar, bright green glazed porcelain bodies, Art Deco stylized dec silver overlay, Metalporzellanfabrik Schwabisch Gmund Gmbh, Germany, c1935, hallmarked "MSG," minor wear1,150.00

Cruet
　7" h, green glass body, cornstalk pattern overlay, orig stopper ...................................................................................1,100.00
　8-1/4" h, bulbous form, colorless glass body, base cut with calyx, chased silver floral and foliate design, applied handle, orig stopper, stamped "Black, Star & Frost, 4000".........................200.00

Decanter
　7-3/4" h, square form, chamfered corners, colorless glass body, chased silver floral and foliate design, base with cut calyx, faceted stopper .....................................................................440.00
　10-1/2" h, bulbous form, shaped base, colorless glass body, chased floral and foliate pattern, rim with tri-spout, applied handle, pinched stopper, monogrammed, unclear stamp mark.......................770.00
　11-1/2" h, baluster form, colorless glass body, faceted neck, chased grape and foliate design, orig stopper, monogrammed, stamped "Thaihfimer & Frank" .......................................715.00

Flask, 4-1/4" h, colorless body, overlaid with silver foliate dec, rubbed silver marks and hallmarks.......................................................200.00

Lamp, 10-1/2" h, 8-3/4" d shade, pierced bronze shades with floral motifs, three-arm spider over bulbous bronze base, floral motifs in silver, paper foil labels, Heintz Metal Shop, Buffalo, NY, early 20th C, price for pr, one shade lacking silk liner ...............................2,645.00

Perfume Bottle, 3" h, colorless glass body, squat pear shape, everted rim, plain ball stopper, 19th C .....................................................90.00

Vase
　3-1/8" h, tri-corn rim, pinched oval body, ambergris glass, foliate silver overlay over light blue irid surface, polished pontil, silver mkd "Sterling" and faint hallmark, possibly La Pierre, Loetz, late 19th C, irregular edges to overlay....................................750.00
　4" h, bronze, trumpet form tapering to flared base, green patina, silver overlay of leaves and berries, paper retailers label, Smith Carroll Company, Lexington, KY, early 20th C..................175.00
　6" h, bud, black, silver over, Wedgwood, c1900 .................360.00

7-1/2" h, flared neck, ovoid, emerald green diamond quilted satin glass, dec with stylized floral silver overlay, maker's mark for "La Pierre Mfg. Co.," rim monogrammed and dated "M. W. June 1909" ....................................................................... 750.00

10-1/2" h, ruffled rim of four curve panel colorless body, silver overlay of stylized poppies, polished pontil, shallow base chip ........................................................................... 575.00

12-3/4" h, cylindrical, inverted rim, swollen base, bronze, pebble textured surface with green patina, silver overlay of iris blossoms on stem .................................................................. 325.00

12-3/4" h, elongated swollen mold blown pale green glass body, acid etched surface with silver overlay in Secessionist-Style geometric design, Austria, late 19th/early 20th C, minor wear ............... 520.00

# SMITH BROS. GLASS

**History:** After establishing a decorating department at the Mount Washington Glass Works in 1871, Alfred and Harry Smith struck out on their own in 1875. Their New Bedford, Massachusetts, firm soon became known worldwide for its fine opalescent decorated wares, similar in style to those of Mount Washington.

**Marks:** Smith Bros. glass often is marked on the base with a red shield enclosing a rampant lion and the word "Trademark."

**References:** Kenneth Wilson, *American Glass 1760-1930*, 2 vols., Hudson Hills Press and The Toledo Museum of Art, 1994.

**Reproduction Alert:** Beware of examples marked "Smith Bros."

Bowl, 9" w, 4" h, melon-ribbed, beige ground, pink Moss Rose dec, blue flower, green leaves, white beaded rim ............................. 675.00

Bride's Bowl, 9-1/2" d, 16" h overall, opal glass bowl, painted ground, 2" white and gray band dec with cranes, fans, and flowers, sgd silver-plated Pairpoint holder, sgd and numbered "2117" ............... 1,450.00

Cologne Bottle, 11" h, 7-1/4" w, green and white ground, bright yellow and orange spider mums, orig glossy finish, rare orig matching stopper ....................................................................... 595.00

**Rose Bowl, creamy ext. with bold beaded rim, floral leaf and vine dec, sgd, 3-3/4" d, 2-1/2" h, $175. Photo courtesy of David Rago Auctions.**

Cracker Jar
7" h, 5" w, barrel shape, beige ground, seven deep brown, rust, maroon, green, and gold pansies, metal cov mkd "S. B. 4412," base also sgd .......................................................... 750.00

7" h, melon-ribbed, cream ground, green and brown English ivy and vines dec, gray traceries, gold trim, fancy metal work .......... 975.00

Creamer and Sugar
3-1/2" d, 3-1/2" h creamer, 3-3/4" d, 4-1/2" h cov sugar, painted Burmese ground, portrait of young girl with wind-blown hair, in heavy raised gold, lid sgd "SB" ....................................... 785.00

3-3/4" d, 3-1/2" h creamer, 3" d, 4" h cov sugar, blue and beige shaded ground, multicolored violet and leaves dec, fancy orig silver-plated metal ware .................................................... 750.00

Dresser Jar, cov, 5-1/2" d, melon ribbed, multicolored pansy dec .............................................................................. 300.00

Ferner, 10" d, melon ribbed, glossy white, violets and leaves, orig metal insert, sgd ................................................................... 675.00

Humidor, cov, 6-1/2" h, 4" w, cream ground, eight blue pansies, melon-ribbed cov ............................................................................. 850.00

Mustard Jar, 3-1/4" h, heron dec, SP top ................................. 85.00

Perfume Bottle, 5" h, enameled floral dec, emb flower cap, sgd 350.00

Plate, 8" d, Santa Maria, brown anchored ship, three people on deck, pale blue sky and water, 1893 World's Fair Souvenir ............. 600.00

Sugar Shaker, 5-3/4" h, pillar ribbed, white ground, wild rose and pale blue leaves, blue beaded top ................................................. 495.00

Toothpick Holder, 2-1/4" h, pillar ribbed, white ground, wild rose and pale blue leaves, blue beaded top .......................................... 250.00

Vase
4-1/4" h, 4" d, pansy blossoms, cream colored ground, row of raised rim dots, rampant lion signature ........................... 385.00

4-3/4" h, three dented sides, cream ground, enameled garland of daisies clinging to tendril draped around shoulder, raised enamel dots, rim dots, lion-in-shield signature ................ 445.00

5-1/4" h, 3-1/2" w, pinched-in form, apricot ground, white wisteria dec, gold highlights, sgd ................................................ 375.00

7" h, soft pink ground, white pond lily, blue-green/black leaves, brown stems, maroon trim, price for matched pr ............. 375.00

7-3/4" h, 5" w, Winter Scene, shades of brown, gray and white, orig sgd "Pairpoint" silver-plated stand, rare early stamp "Smith Brothers, New Bedford, Mass." ....................................... 785.00

8" h, 4-1/2" w, soft pink ground, white clematis blossoms, green, brown and gray leaves, stems and vines, gold beaded top .. 785.00

8-3/4" h, 6-1/2" w, temple, soft beige ground, pink and yellow chrysanthemum dec, with green and gold leaves, gold beaded top with pale green trim ................................................. 1,675.00

8-3/4" h, 7" w, canteen, white ground, pink roses and blue forget-me-nots dec, gold beaded top, glossy finish .................... 575.00

9-3/4" h, 7" w, pillow, glossy shaded green ground, bright pink wild roses, green and brown leaves, gold beaded top ..... 795.00

10-1/4" h, 4-3/4" w, brilliant emerald green, two stems of white lilies, one with five flowers and leaves, other with three unopened blossoms, heavy gold enamel trim ................................. 450.00

# SNOW BABIES

**History:** Snow babies, small bisque figurines spattered with ground porcelain that resembles snow, were made originally in Germany and marketed in the early 1900s. One theory about their origin is that German doll makers copied the designs from the traditional Christmas candies. While sales were modest at first, demand increased after the birth of Admiral Peary's daughter in Greenland in 1893 and her subsequent popularity as the "Snow Baby," so-named by the Eskimos.

Hertwig and Company, a German manufacturer of china doll heads and bisque figurines, was the first to make these small figures dressed in hooded snowsuits and posed in a variety of positions. They reached their greatest popularity between 1906 and 1910, when they were manufactured by a variety of German firms and imported by many American companies.

**Reference:** Mary Morrison, *Snow Babies, Santas, and Elves: Collecting Christmas Bisque Figures*, Schiffer Publishing, 1993.

**Reproduction Alert:** During the 1940s and as late as the 1970s, many inferior Japanese-made snow babies entered the market, some marked with an impressed "Japan," others with a paper label. Their crudely painted features, awkward poses, and coarser "snow" make them easy to distinguish from the original German examples. Since 1977, Dept. 56® has been marketing a line of products called The Original Snow Village.

Angel, sitting, arms outstretched, 1-3/4" h ................................. 195.00
Baby
    Arms outstretched, 1-1/4" h .............................................. 115.00
    Holding baton.............................................................. 115.00
    Kneeling on one knee, 1" h............................................ 85.00
    Laying on side, 1-1/2" l.................................................. 75.00
    Laying on tummy, 1" l.................................................... 70.00
    Sitting, hole in head for small birthday candle .................... 45.00
    Sitting, snow covered cardboard box, 2-1/4" h .................. 135.00
    Skating, red suit and hat, sgd, marked "Germany," 2" h ..... 130.00
    Standing, dog licking cheek, marked "Germany," 2" h........ 200.00
    Standing, wooden skies, pink cheeks, marked "Germany,"
      1-1/2" h...................................................................115.00
Carolers, three standing in snow, lantern, marked "Germany,"
  2-1/4" h .........................................................................185.00
Penguin, marked "Germany," 4" h..............................................100.00
Snow Pup on skies, marked "Germany" .................................... 150.00

# SNUFF BOTTLES

**History:** Tobacco usage spread from America to Europe to China during the 17th century. Europeans and Chinese preferred to grind the dried leaves into a powder and sniff it into their nostrils. The elegant Europeans carried their snuff in boxes and took a pinch with their finger tips. The Chinese upper class, because of their lengthy fingernails, found this inconvenient and devised a bottle with a fitted stopper and attached spoon. These utilitarian objects soon became objets d'art.

Snuff bottles were fashioned from precious and semi-precious stones, glass, porcelain and pottery, wood, metals, and ivory. Glass and transparent-stone bottles often were enhanced further with delicate hand paintings, some done on the interior of the bottle.

**Collectors' Club:** International Chinese Snuff Bottle Society, 2601 No Charles St., Baltimore, MD 21218.

Amethyst, round, high relief carving of plum blossoms and branches,
  well hollowed, amethyst stopper, 19th C. 2" h...........................400.00
Boulder Opal, pearl gray with flashes of color, double gourd form, high
  relief carved carp and waves, 2-1/4" h ....................................350.00
Carnelian
    Heart shaped, well hollowed, silver mounted jade stopper,
      19th C ......................................................................115.00
    Well marked orange hue stone with darker veining, allover carv-
      ing of flowers and vines, matching carved stopper, fitted stand,
      19th C, 2-1/2" h ........................................................250.00

Chalcedony, cylindrical form, carved with goldfish and bamboo, gray
  colored stone with orange and tan inclusions, 2" h................. 175.00
Cloisonné, high shouldered flattened form, indented sides, design of
  hundred antiques on turquoise ground, heavily gilded borders,
  matching stopper, Ch'ien Lung mark, early 20th C, 2-1/2" h.... 115.00
Coconut Shell, carved, relief seal characters on textured ground,
  inscription on both sides, Chinese, 19th C, 2" h...................... 700.00
Glass, interior painted
    Cylindrical, two scholars and serving boy on one side, reverse
      with extensive inscription, int. heavily stained with snuff,
      2-1/2" h...................................................................290.00
    Oblong flattened form, dec with bird, flowering prunus, vase of
      flowers, and incense burner, 2-1/4" h...............................250.00
Horn, carved all over with dragons and clouds, tortoiseshell coloring,
  20th C, 3-1/2" h .................................................................. 115.00
Ivory
    Polychrome, male and female figures seated on elephants, late
      19th C, price for pr......................................................375.00
    Small boy and large Chinese cabbage, 4" h...................... 115.00
    Small boy with large bitter melon with leaves, matching stopper,
      2-1/2" h...................................................................115.00
Jade
    Celadon colored, flattened spade shape, carved tied brocade panel
      around center, apple green jadeite stopper, 2-1/2" h ...........500.00
    Even toned celadon stone, spade shape, carved with two fisher-
      man, gilt brass stopper, 2" h...........................................500.00
    Off-white stone with veils of emerald green, natural veins of color
      used to accent carving of dragonflies, butterflies, rocks, and
      flowers, rounded flask form, Peking glass stopper, 2" h 1,380.00
    Pale green stone, yellow markings, flattened rounded form,
      brighter green clouds, twenty-character inscription, reverse with
      children playing, 2-1/4" h................................................ 350.00
    Pale greenish-white stone, carved with orchid plant on one side,
      pebble shape, coral stopper, late 18th/early 19th C .......... 490.00
Lapis Lazuli
    Deep blue stone, double-gourd form, matrix carved as tiger and
      gourd with leaves, matching stopper, 2" h ...................... 550.00
    Flattened flask form, deep blue stone, veins of gold and white,
      carved single relief woman with fan and flowing dress, matching
      high domed stopper, 3" h ............................................... 460.00
Opal, vasiform, relief carving of Kuan Yin and lotus, lion mask handles,
  1-3/4" h............................................................................... 290.00
Peking Glass
    Amber ground, surrounded with gilt framed repousse dec, filigree set
      with garnets, turquoise, and glass, Mongol-style, 3-1/2" h....300.00
    Cranberry colored overlay, snowflake ground, covered with scroll-
      ing chih lung dragons. 2-1/2" h ....................................... 175.00
    Flattened round form, foot rim, coral colored glass carved with
      carp and crashing waves, reverse with flowering plant and but-
      terfly, dyed ivory top, 2-1/2" h.......................................... 175.00

**Peking Glass, red floral motif on amber, 21/2" h, $145.**

Pear form, high foot, tortoiseshell colored overlay on bubble diffused yellow ground, finely carved wreathes of chih lung dragons enclosing Shou characters, tied fillets and rui for sides, 19th C, 2-3/4" h ...450.00

Ruby cut to milk white, one side with scrolling archaic dragon, reverse with bats and clouds, tourmaline glass stopper, late 18th/early 19th C ....................................635.00

Pewter and cinnabar, five musicians on one side, reverse with two sages, one on water buffalo, other on mule, two character Ch'ien Lung mark, 20th C, 3" h ..........................350.00

Porcelain, mei ping shape, celadon ground, enameled in famille rose colors, tourmaline-colored Peking glass stopper, 3" h .............150.00

Pottery, unglazed turquoise, form of winged carp ridden by dragon, coral colored glass stopper as celestial pearl, 3-1/2" h ............115.00

Rhodochrosite, deep pink stone with white markings in concentric circles, flattened oblong, relief carved pines and ornamental rocks, 2-1/2" h ....................................575.00

Rock crystal, hexagonal, well hollowed, remaining skin of stone carved with flowering plum and pine branches, bud, monkey, bee, and deer, Chinese, 19th C, 3" h ...........................400.00

Rose Quartz
    Carved with birds and flowering branches, matching stopper .150.00
    Flattened spade shape, pale pink color, carved birds, trees, and flowering plants, matching cover, 2-3/4" h........................400.00

Shadow Agate
    Flattened oblong form, even dove gray colored stone infused with black and brown markings resembling plants and rocks, finely hollowed, turquoise stopper, 19th C, 2-1/2" h ..................550.00
    Rounded flattened flash form, well hollowed, delicately carved pair of birds, and tree, agate stopper, 2-3/4" h, 2-1/2"d 1,265.00

Shagreen, shagreen covered bottle and stopper, demilune ribbed form, China, 19th C..............................................225.00

Silver, Mongol-style dec, two archaic dragons confronting each other on both sides, further dec with coral cabochons, turquoise mounted in cloisons, coral set top, 19th C, 2-3/4" h................................115.00

Tourmaline, elongated heart shape, pink rubelite material with apricot shadings, carved pine tree and three seals, 2-3/4" h...............350.00

# SOAPSTONE

**History:** The mineral steatite, known as soapstone because of its greasy feel, has been used for carving figural groups and designs by the Chinese and others. Utilitarian pieces also were made. Soapstone pieces were very popular during the Victorian era.

**Reference:** *Soapstone,* L-W Book Sales, 1995.

**Vase, chrysanthemums, foliage, and bird, 9-1/2" h, $255.**

Bookends, pr, elephants, c1890...................................65.00
Box, 3 x 5", inlaid pearl dec, artist sgd..........................45.00
Carving, 4" h, figure of sleeping monk, white colored stone, yellow and red markings, China, 19th C......................................230.00
Figure
    5" h, pomegranate .............................................25.00
    7" h, two boys riding water buffalo, mottled brown and cream color stone, 19th C .....................................230.00
    16 1/2" h, Shoulao, holding dragon headed staff and peach, Chinese ....................................................225.00
Incense Burner, 8" h, black, 19th C ..........................350.00
Inkwell, geometric carving on sides ........................150.00
Match Holder, elaborate carving ............................70.00
Paperweight, three carved monkeys..........................75.00
Pillow, 12" l, carved in the form of small boy, China, 19th C........660.00
Sculpture
    7" h, four chilongs and two toads carved in relief, ovoid form stone, chestnut and light green colored stone, 19th C.....460.00
    28" h, angel, Raymond Coins ............................4,950.00
Toothpick Holder, carved monkey ...............................70.00
Urn, 7-1/4" d, 10-1/4" h, carved figures, buildings, florals, and trees, elephant head handles, wood stand ........................175.00
Vase, 9-1/4" h, carved flowers, birds, and leaves, Oriental.........150.00

# SOUVENIR and COMMEMORATIVE CHINA and GLASS

**History:** Souvenir, commemorative, and historical china and glass includes those items produced to celebrate special events, places, and people.

China plates made by Rowland and Marcellus and Wedgwood are particularly favored by collectors. Rowland and Marcellus, Staffordshire, England, made a series of blue-and-white historic plates with a wide rolled edge. Scenes from the Philadelphia Centennial in 1876 through the 1939 New York World's Fair are depicted. In 1910, Wedgwood collaborated with Jones, McDuffee and Stratton to produce a series of historic dessert-sized plates showing scenes of places throughout the United States.

Many localities issued plates, mugs, glasses, etc., for anniversary celebrations or to honor a local historical event. These items seem to have greater value when sold in the region in which they originated.

Commemorative glass includes several patterns of pressed glass which celebrate persons or events. Historical glass includes campaign and memorial items.

**References:** Pamel E. Apkarian-Russell, *A Collector's Guide to Salem Witchcraft & Souvenirs,* Schiffer Publishing, 1998; Monica Lynn Clements and Patricia Rosser Clements, *Popular Souvenir Plates,* Schiffer Publications, 1998; Barbara J. Conroy, *Restaurant China, Volume 2,* Collector Books, 2000; Bessie M. Lindsey, *American Historical Glass,* Charles E. Tuttle Company, 1967; David Weingarten and Margaret Majua, *Monumental Miniatures,* Antique Trader Books, 1998; Lawrence W. Williams, *Collector's Guide To Souvenir China,* Collector Books, 1998.

**Periodicals:** *Antique Souvenir Collectors News*, Box 562, Great Barrington, MA 01230; *Souvenir Building Collector*, 25 Falls Rd, Roxbury, CT 06783.

**Collectors' Clubs:** Souvenir Building Collectors Society, P.O. Box 70, Nellysford, VA 22958; Statue of Liberty Collectors' Club, 26601 Bernwood Rd, Cleveland, OH 44122.

**Additional Listings:** Cup Plates; Pressed Glass; Political Items; Staffordshire, Historical. Also see *Warman's Americana & Collectibles* for more examples.

Cup and Saucer, Jasper Park, English bone china, Myott, luster worn .................................................................20.00
Demitasse Cup and Saucer, Scammeli, Harry Stevens................35.00
Dish, York Minster, Prince Edward Islands, shell shape ..............12.00
Mug, University of Pennsylvania, c1905, football player............250.00
Pin Tray
    Alaska, husky dog, mkd "Queen Anne China, Made in England"8.00
    HMS *Canopus*, 4-3/4" d, red and pink transfer dec of ship, rope scalloped edge, mkd "Spode" ...........................................15.00
Pitcher, 7-1/4" h, hp porcelain, bust of Lincoln on one side, U. S. Grant in uniform on other, molded leaf panels with worn gilt decal, spout chip, hairline .......................................................................1,045.00
Plate
    DAR, Greenwood China ...............................................10.00
    Denver, Rowland & Marsellus............................................125.00
    Dickens, Charles, 10" d, rolled edge, Rowland & Marsellus . 40.00
    Maritime Provinces, Royal Doulton.....................................24.00
    Niagara, Royal Doulton.......................................................24.00
    Oakwood, OH, transfer dec of pumpkins and berries, mkd "Dresden China" on back ........................................................30.00
    Rochester, 8" d ..................................................................45.00
    Roosevelt, Theodore, blue, rolled rim, Rowland & Marsellus65.00
    Texian Campaigne, light blue transfer, Anthony Shaw, restored ......................................................................300.00
    Yale College, 9-1/2" d, light blue transfer, Charles Meigh, chip on foot rim ..............................................................100.00
Shoe, china
    Denver, CO, white, gold trim, 4" l, 2" w, c1940 .....................20.00
    Omaha, NE, luster finish, rose pink, yellow, and white, 6" l, 2-3/4" w, c1940 ..........................................................................30.00
Stein, Cedar Rapids, IA, 2-3/4"" h.............................................75.00

**Plate, Gettysburg, General Meade's Headquarters, blue and white, mkd "F. Winkle & Co., England," 10" d, $55.**

## Glass

Badge, paperweight type, cannonball dec, Oldest House, St. Augustine, FL ...................................................................45.00
Bowl, Detroit, 1910, Elks, Fenton, amethyst carnival glass ........650.00
Bust
    4-3/4" h, frosted, Abraham Lincoln, raised name on front of base, "Centennial Exhibition" and "Gillander & Sons Inc." on back, chip on corner of base.................................................425.00
    5-1/4" h, frosted, Columbus, raised "World's Fair" and "1893" on back, minor chips .......................................................275.00
    6" h, frosted, Benjamin Harrison ........................................250.00
    6" h, milk glass, George Washington, raised name on front of base, "Centennial Exhibition" and "Gillander & Sons Inc." on back....................................................................................470.00
    6-1/2" h, frosted glass, James A Garfield, raised name on front of base ...................................................................300.00
Butter Dish, cov, 6-1/2" x 5-3/4", Lancaster Fair, 1916, Button Arches pattern, ruby stained ...........................................175.00
Candlestick, 8" h, gold script "Souvenir of World's Fair" ..............35.00
Creamer, Atlantic City, NJ, ruby stained ....................................45.00
Cup, Akron Ohio, custard, Heisey mark, 2-1/2" h ........................25.00
Goblet, Gettysburg, 1863, Button Arches, ruby stained, 4" h .......35.00
Mug, Pacific Grove, Button Arches pattern, ruby stained ............25.00
Paperweight, Plymouth Rock......................................................65.00
Pitcher, Ocean City, NJ, 1912, King's Crown pattern, ruby stained ...95.00
Plate
    Niagara Falls, transfer dec....................................................50.00
    Spectors Dept. Store, marigold carnival glass ................1,100.00
Platter, Newark 1952 Sesq, Twist pattern, Heisey .....................145.00
Statue
    Boy with dog, frosted, 1876 Expo .......................................215.00
    Woman, standing, holding child, 14-1/2" h, raised mark of Gillander, division of United States Glass Co, 1891-1900, on back of base.................................................................850.00
Toothpick Holder
    Belle Plaine, KS, ruby stained, 3-1/2" h ...............................35.00
    Omaha Expo, 1899, Colorado pattern ..................................35.00
Tumbler
    Grand Rapids, ruby stained, 3-7/8" h....................................40.00
    Halstad, MN, custard, 4" h ...................................................95.00
    Lowell, IN, Colorado pattern, 3-1/2" h...................................35.00
Tray, Old State House, 12" d, blue.............................................225.00
Water Set, 7" h pitcher, three 3-3/4" h tumblers, pink shading to clear, hp dec of Whittier Birthplace, Haverhill, MA............................150.00

# SOUVENIR and COMMEMORATIVE SPOONS

**History:** Souvenir and commemorative spoons have been issued for hundreds of years. Early American silversmiths engraved presentation spoons to honor historical personages or mark key events.

In 1881, Myron Kinsley patented a Niagara Falls spoon, and in 1884 Michael Gibney patented a new flatware design. M. W. Galt, Washington, D.C., issued commemorative spoons for George and Martha Washington in 1889. From these beginnings a collecting craze for souvenir and commemorative spoons developed in the late 19th and early 20th centuries.

**References:** Wayne Bednersch, *Collectible Souvenir Spoons,* 2nd ed., Collector Books, 2000; George B. James, *Souvenir Spoons (1891),* reprinted with 1996 price guide by Bill Boyd (7408 Englewood Lane, Raytown, MO 64133), 1996; Dorothy T. Rainwater and

Donna H. Fegler, *American Spoons*, Schiffer Publishing, 1990; ——, *Spoons from around the World*, Schiffer Publishing, 1992; *Sterling Silver, Silverplate, and Souvenir Spoons with Prices*, revised ed., L-W Book Sales, 1987, 1994 value update.

**Collectors' Clubs:** American Spoon Collectors, 7408 Englewood Lane, Raytown, MO 64133; Dallas Souvenir Spoon Collectors Club, 9748 Broken Bow Road, Dallas, TX 75238; Northeastern Spoon Collectors Guild, 8200 Boulevard East, North Bergen, NJ 07047-6039; Southern California Souvenir Spoon Collectors Club, 3832 Denwood Ave., Los Alamitos, CA 90720; The Scoop Club, 84 Oak Ave., Shelton, CT 06484; Washington State Spoon Collectors, 1992 S. Elger Bay Road, Box 151, Stanwood, WA 98292.

**Additional Listings:** See *Warman's Americana & Collectibles* for more examples.

Boston Tea Party............................................................60.00
Calgary, Alberta, Canada, 3-1/2" l................................30.00
Camp Sheridan, soldier on handle...............................40.00
Carnaval De Quebec, Canada, orig box........................30.00
Chicago, four engraved vignettes ................................35.00
Coronation, Canadian, mkd "Birks Sterling," 4" l...........35.00
Edmonton, Canada, engraved bowl, 3-1/2" l ................35.00
Elk's Temple, Erie, PA, on bowl, SS.............................40.00
Innsbbruck, enamel illus of Maria Theresa, mkd "Sterling .900"...35.00
Kaiser Wilhelm II, SP, bust handle, crest, flag, Army and Navy figures, mkd "Deutschland," plain bowl ...................................70.00
Kentucky, state seal .....................................................35.00
Lethbridge, Canada, 3-1/2" l.........................................30.00
Mackinaw Island, MI, Indian Chief, demitasse..............35.00
Maligne Lake, Canada, 3-3/4" l.....................................30.00
Massachusetts, Falmouth engraved in bowl, sterling ....40.00
Medicine Hat, Alberta, Canada, Indian head on handle, scene in bowl .....................................................................30.00
Mount Hekla, showing eruption, mkd ".800," 3-1/2" l....30.00
Niagara Falls, Indian head handle ................................45.00
New York City, city hall, engraved bowl, Bridal Rose figural handle...30.00
Observatory Peak, Ogden, Utah, in bowl, sterling.........45.00
Pan American Exposition, 1901, sterling .......................30.00
Quebec City, Quebec, Canada, skyline on handle, sterling..........30.00
Santa, SP, ornate handle, demitasse ...........................70.00
Seattle, WA, Indian figures, 4-1/8" l..............................30.00
Struck it Rich, minor, view of state capitol, Sacramento, CA, sterling silver, 1-1/4" w, 4" h......................................................75.00
Toledo, engraved bowl, lily handle, Whiting Manuf Co, c1902......35.00
Utah, bowl engraved "Mae March 11, 98".....................30.00
Vassar College, Poughkeepsie, NY, scene in bowl.......40.00

Watson County, Texas, Houston engraved in bowl, Wallace Silversmiths, late 1890s ....................................................45.00
Winnepeg City Hall, Manitoba enameled on handle.....................40.00

# SPANGLED GLASS

**History:** Spangled glass is a blown or blown-molded variegated art glass, similar to spatter glass, with the addition of flakes of mica or metallic aventurine. Many pieces are cased with a white or clear layer of glass. Spangled glass was developed in the late 19th century and still is being manufactured.

Originally, spangled glass was attributed only to the Vasa Murrhina Art Glass Company of Hartford, Connecticut, which distributed the glass for Dr. Flower of the Cape Cod Glassworks, Sandwich, Massachusetts. However, research has shown that many companies in Europe, England, and the United States made spangled glass, and attributing a piece to a specific source is very difficult.

Basket
5-1/2" d, pink, crimped handle, clear reeded twisted thorn handle ..185.00
10" l, 8-1/2" w, 9-1/2" h, pink, yellow, brown, and green, silver flecks, white ext. lining, applied crystal edge, clear twisted rope handle...........325.00
Bowl
3-3/4" d, 3-7/8" h, cranberry, three clear scroll feet, embossed heads, clear stars with berry centers applied around bowl, large mica flakes ...165.00
5-3/4" d, 4-1/2" h, olive green blue stripes, clear applied rigaree around top, clear dripping appliqué, mica flakes in bowl, clear berry prunt, applied clear feet.......................................................................240.00
8-1/2" d, 3" h, shaded pink overlay, clear ruffled edge, melon rib, white lining .........................................................................................175.00
Bride's Basket, 10" h, pink shaded to white, silver flakes, ruffled edge, shiny finish ...............................................................................85.00
Candlesticks, pr, 8" h, green and maroon, gold mica flakes, white lining ...........................................................................................115.00
Condiment Set, 2" x 5-1/2" x 6" h, cov pepper pot, cov mustard pot, cruet with orig stopper, cranberry and green spatter, mica flecks, SP covers, orig SP holder.............................................................275.00
Ewer
6-7/8" h, 2-3/4" d, blue overlay, white lining, mica flakes, applied clear handle, price for pr ................................................135.00
8-3/8" h, 3-1/2" d, apricot, white lining, mica flakes, applied thorn handle ..........................................................................145.00

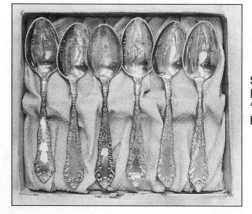

Set, Great White Fleet, mkd "Standard," orig box, 4-1/4" l, $85.

**Miniature Lamp, green, brown, and white spatter, emb swirls and beaded trim, burner mid "P & A Hornet," 8-1/2" h, $290.**

Fairy Lamp, 3-5/8" h, 2 7/9" d, embossed swirl pyramid cranberry shade with mica flakes, embedded green threading on clear marked "Clarke" base ............................................................. 155.00

Jack in the Pulpit Vase, 5-3/4"h, white ext., pink int., clear edging, mica flakes, ruffled rim ......................................................... 150.00

Pitcher, 8" h, 5-1/2" w, bulbous, six wide rib blowouts, silver mica, rose ground, hp flowers and leaves, white lining, gold trim, patented 1883, applied clear handle, Hobbs Brockunier ............................... 500.00

Rose Bowl, 3-1/4" d, eight crimp top, shaded blue ext., white int., mica flecks ..................................................................................... 115.00

Tumble-Up, 7-1/2" h decanter, matching tumbler, cobalt blue, mica flecks, white enamel and gilt dec ........................................... 220.00

Vase

8-1/2" h, flattened oval, applied cranberry rigaree, copper aventurine flecks, scroll handles, c1880 ............................ 320.00

9-1/2" h, 6" d, squatty bulbous base, tapering to slender cylindrical body, flaring rolled and crimped rim, pink, cased in clear, white lining, silver mica flecks, clear shell trim down each side .......... 175.00

# SPATTER GLASS

**History:** Spatter glass is a variegated blown or blown-molded art glass. It originally was called "End-of-Day" glass, based on the assumption that it was made from batches of glass leftover at the end of the day. However, spatter glass was found to be a standard production item for many glass factories.

Spatter glass was developed at the end of the 19th century and is still being produced in the United States and Europe.

**References:** William Heacock, James Measell and Berry Wiggins, *Harry Northwood*, Antique Publications, 1990.

**Reproduction Alert:** Many modern examples come from the area previously called Czechoslovakia.

Basket

5" w, 7-1/2" w, triangular shape, white ground, bright pink and yellow spatter, ruffled edge, applied clear twisted thorn handle ....... 225.00

6" h, 6" h, star shape, sapphire blue ground, white spatter, applied blue thorn handle ................................................... 225.00

6" l, 7-1/2" h, tall sides, ruffled star-shaped edge, white ground, brown and jade green spatter, applied clear thorn handle, Victorian, c1890 ...................................................... 275.00

7" l, 6-1/2" h, yellow shading to white ground, deep brown and green spatter, ruffled edge with applied crystal edge, applied rope twisted handle ......................................... 195.00

Bowl, 8-1/4" d, 5-1/4" h, crimped rim, peach and white spatter, ornate ftd ormolu base ....................................................... 245.00

Candlestick, 7-1/2" h, flared socket, twisted hourglass stem, domed ribbed base, yellow, red, and white spatter ...................... 50.00

Creamer, 4-1/2" h, 2-3/4" d, blue and light blue opaque, embossed swirl, applied blue reeded handle ....................................... 95.00

Cruet, 8-3/4" h, 3-1/2" d, blue ground, white spatter, clear applied handle, clear heart-shaped stopper ....................................... 135.00

Darning Egg, red, yellow, and green, clear applied handle ........ 125.00

Dish, cov, 4-1/4" d, 5-3/4" h, pink and green spatter, white lining, clear applied leaves on sides, clear applied feet, cover with applied clear finial ................................................................................ 80.00

Finger Bowl and Underplate, 6" d, 3-1/4" h, Tortoise Shell, ruffled bowl and plate ................................................................... 275.00

Jack in the Pulpit Vase, 7-1/4" h, green, peach, yellow, and white spatter, green DQ body ......................................................... 75.00

Jar, cov, 3-3/4" x 6-1/2", maroon, white, yellow, and green, white cased int., clear applied feet and finial ........................................ 85.00

Pitcher, amber and white, square top, IVT ............................. 185.00

Rolling Pin, 16" l, clear ground, red and blue spatter ................ 200.00

Rose Bowl

3-1/2" d, egg shape, cased, red ground, mica flakes .......... 110.00

6-1/2" d, 6" h, transparent amber ground, white spatter, purple flowers, gold leaves, sgd in pontil with propeller mark and numbered "171.8 V517" ........................................... 475.00

Sugar Shaker

Leaf Umbrella, cranberry, satin finished .......................... 400.00

Leaf Umbrella, vaseline ............................................... 175.00

Ring Neck, cranberry and white ...................................... 125.00

Tumbler, 3-3/4" h, IVT, pink and cream spatter ...................... 45.00

Vase, 8" h, baluster, ringed neck, flared mouth, red, yellow, and green spatter, brown lining .......................................................... 90.00

# SPATTERWARE

**History:** Spatterware generally was made of common earthenware, although occasionally creamware was used. The earliest English examples were made about 1780. The peak period of production was from 1810 to 1840. Firms known to have made spatterware are Adams, Barlow, and Harvey and Cotton.

The amount of spatter decoration varies from piece to piece. Some objects simply have decorated borders. These often were decorated with a brush, requiring several hundred touches per square inch to achieve the spatter effect. Other pieces have the entire surface covered with spatter.

**Marks:** Marked pieces are rare.

**References:** Susan and Al Bagdade, *Warman's English & Continental Pottery & Porcelain*, 3rd Edition, Krause Publications, 1998; Kevin McConnell, *Spongeware and Spatterware*, Schiffer Publishing, 1990.

**Museum:** Henry Ford Museum, Dearborn, MI.

**Notes:** Collectors today focus on the patterns—Cannon, Castle, Fort, Peafowl, Rainbow, Rose, Thistle, Schoolhouse, etc. The decoration on flatware is in the center of the piece; on hollow ware it occurs on both sides.

Aesthetics and the color of spatter are key to determining value. Blue and red are the most common colors; green, purple, and brown are in a middle group; black and yellow are scarce.

Like any soft paste, spatterware is easily broken or chipped. Prices in this listing are for pieces in very good to mint condition.

Bowl, 11-1/8" d, stamped foliage border, center reserve of hp drapery swags and foliage devices, English, 19th C, hairline, very minor enamel loss, staining ................................................... 200.00

Child's Cup and Saucer, handleless, four-color ...................... 5,720.00

Child's Tea Set, teapot, two handleless cups and saucers, cream jug, green and blue spatter, repairs to all pieces ....................... 1,100.00

## Reproduction Alert:

Cybis spatter is an increasingly collectible ware in its own right. The pieces, made by the Polishman Boleslaw Cybis in the 1940s, have an Adams-type peafowl design. Many contemporary craftsmen also are reproducing spatterware.

**Plate, repeated red, green, and brown design, c1880, overall staining, 8-1/2" d, $125. Photo courtesy of Vicki & Bruce Waasdrop.**

Creamer
    Cluster of Buds, blue spatter, 4" h ........................ 770.00
    Double-sided red, yellow, blue, green, and black rooster, purple spatter, repaired spout ................................. 1,870.00
    Rose, red and green spatter, bulbous creamer, 4" h, repaired spout ............................................................. 330.00
Cup and Saucer, handleless
    Acorn, red spatter, hairline crack on the cup ...................... 660.00
    Peafowl, blue, green, black, and red, red spatter, saucer imp "Adams," hairline in saucer ................................ 350.00
    Rainbow, red and blue spatter stripes, red center ............. 200.00
    Thistle, maroon and red flower, green foliate, minor stains, hairline on cup ................................................. 385.00
Cup, handleless, School House, red, blue, and yellow, blue spatter, minor rim roughness ............................................. 385.00
Cup Plate, 5 1/8" d, blue morning glory in center, yellow spatter ... 3,245.00
Pepper Pot, 5-1/8" h, dome top, purple and blue rainbow spatter ..................................................................... 5,500.00
Pitcher
    7-3/4" h, Tulip, paneled, yellow spatter ......................... 2,200.00
    10-1/2" h, Rainbow, red, green, yellow, black, and blue spatter ........................................................... 14,850.00
    10-3/4" h, Cluster of Buds pattern, blue spatter, red buds, green leaves, bulbous ........................................... 5,390.00
Plate
    5" d, Double Acorn, blue spatter ................................ 2,860.00
    8" d, Rainbow, red, blue, and green, red rose and green foliage in center, scalloped rim, imp "Adams" on back, minor rim wear .......................................................... 495.00
    8-1/2" d, stick, repeated red, green, and brown pattern, overall crazing ........................................................ 125.00
    8-1/2" d, Peafowl, ironstone ..................................... 880.00
    9-1/4" d, Schoolhouse, paneled, blue spatter .................. 3,740.00
    9-1/2" d, Triple Acorn, flake on edge ........................... 1,870.00
    9-5/8" d, Fort and Castle, blue spatter ........................... 330.00
    9-3/4" d, Cockscomb, paneled, yellow spatter ................. 5,775.00
    9-3/4" d, Dahlia, purple ........................................... 385.00
Saucer, 6" d
    School House, red, green, and black, blue spatter, rim flake and wear .......................................................... 770.00
    Tulips, red, green, and black, chip on one table ring, price for pr ............................................................... 550.00
Sugar Bowl, cov
    Double-Loop, four-color rainbow spatter, 4" h ................ 3,520.00
    Hollyberry covered sugar bowl, blue spatter, small chip to the rim ............................................................. 545.00
    Peafowl, red, blue, yellow, and black, blue spatter, 4" h, chips and repair .......................................................... 550.00
Teapot, cov
    Cluster of Buds pattern teapot, blue spatter ................. 1,210.00
    Windmill, purple spatter, 5-3/4" h .............................. 2,750.00
Toddy, 5-3/4"" d, red design spatter border, blue stripe, purple, green, yellow ochre, and black viola, pinpoint flakes ....................... 290.00
Tray, 11-1/4" l, maroon, very worn and stained ...................... 200.00
Wash Bowl and Pitcher, 12-5/8" d, 10-3/4" h, red and green four part flower, edge chip on bowl ...................................... 1,375.00

# SPONGEWARE

**History:** Spongeware is a specific type of decoration, not a type of pottery or glaze.

Spongeware decoration is found on many kinds of pottery bodies—ironstone, redware, stoneware, yellowware, etc. It was made in both England and the United States. Pieces were marked after 1815, and production extended into the 1880s.

Decoration is varied. On some pieces the sponging is minimal with the white underglaze dominant. Other pieces appear to be solidly sponged on both sides. Pieces made between 1840 and 1860 have circular or horizontally streaked sponging.

Blue and white are the most common colors, but browns, greens, ochres, and a greenish blue also were used. The greenish blue results from blue sponging with a pale yellow overglaze. A red overglaze produces a black or navy color. Blue and red were used on English creamware and American earthenware of the 1880s. Other spongeware colors include gray, grayish green, red, dark green on stark white, dark green on mellow yellow, and purple.

**References:** Susan and Al Bagdade, *Warman's American Pottery and Porcelain*, 2nd ed., Krause Publications, 2000; ——, *Warman's English & Continental Pottery & Porcelain*, 3rd Edition, Krause Publications, 1998; William C. Ketchum, Jr., *American Pottery and Porcelain*, Avon Books, 1994; Kevin McConnell, *Spongeware and Spatterware*, Schiffer Publishing, 1990.

Baking Dish, 10-1/2" d, 3-1/2" h, blue and white ...................... 155.00
Bowl, blue and white
    10-1/4" d, 4-1/2" h, relief exterior column design, extension interior glaze wear, 3" glaze spider line on side that goes through ..... 70.00
    11" d, 4-1/2" h, relief ribbed column exterior, 3" faint hairline extending up from base .................................... 80.00
    11" d, 5-1/4" h, white center band, extensive surface chipping around rim, two 4" hairlines extending from rim, third extends from bottom .................................................. 35.00
    13-1/4" d, 6-1/2" h, relief exterior column design, scalloped blue decoration, few minor interior scratches .................. 325.00
    14" d, 6-1/4" h, two blue accent bands, stained and glaze use crazed interior, few minor rim and base chips ................ 110.00
Butter Crock, cov, 3-3/4" h, blue and white, "Butter" stenciled on front, navy blue chicken wire pattern, orig matching lid, two filled rim chips ......................................................... 250.00
Chamber Pot, handle
    9" d, 5" h, light blue and white, blue accent bands around middle, handle, 2" tight hairline extending from rim near handle .... 45.00
    10" d, 5-1/2" h, blue and white ................................. 125.00
Cookie Jar, 9" h, blue and white, orig matching lid, footed .......... 65.00

**Pitcher, deep blue, half dollar size int. glaze spot missing on bottom, 9" h, $525. Photo courtesy of Vicki & Bruce Waasdrop.**

**Serving Bowl, relief exterior column design, few minor int. scratches, 13-1/4" d, 6-1/2" h, $310. Photo courtesy of Vicki & Bruce Waasdrop.**

Cup, 2-3/4" h, blue and white, surface wear at rim, int. glaze crazing, hairline extending from rim ......................................................... 50.00

Deep Dish, 9" d, 1-1/2" h, blue and white, scalloped relief molded edge, deep blue diffusion .......................................................... 175.00

Honey Pot, cov, 4-1/2" d, blue and white, matching orig lid, deep navy color ............................................................................................... 250.00

Mug, 3-1/2" h, blue and white, black accent bands top and bottom .225.00

Nappie, 3-1/4" x 10", blue and white ........................................... 250.00

Oversized Cup and Saucer, 7" w, 4" h cup, blue and white, applied ring handle, dark blue sponging, gilt edge on plate slightly worn .... 125.00

Pitcher

    6-1/2" h, blue, white, and green, blue accent bands top and bottom, very minor surface chip at bottom ........................... 110.00

    8-3/4" h, blue and white, bulbous, 3-1/2" l hairline extending from rim, 1" hairline at base, overall age glaze crazing ............ 165.00

    9" h, blue and white, half dollar size interior glaze spot missing on very bottom inside .................................................. 525.00

    9" h, blue and white, heavily sponged in blue, three very tight hairlines extending from rim ................................................ 385.00

    9" h, blue and white, relief wild rose pattern with blue accents, very minor surface rim chip ............................................. 450.00

    9-1/2" h, blue and white, relief daisy and vine design, sponged gold accents applied around body, rim, and handle, interior stained, 5" l tight hairline extending from rim near handle, few minor surface chips on bottom ......................................... 175.00

    9-3/4" h, blue and gray, blue accent bands top and bottom, bulbous ...................................................................................... 650.00

Plate

    7-1/2" d, blue and white, molded rim ................................... 85.00

    9-1/4" d, blue and white, molded rim ................................. 115.00

    10" d, blue and white, molded rim handles ......................... 125.00

    10-1/4" d, blue and white, molded rim ............................... 120.00

Platter, 15" l, blue and white ....................................................... 325.00

Salt Crock, cov

    5-3/4" h, blue and white, molded basketweave and vintage, hairline ........................................................................................... 80.00

    6-3/8" h, blue, yellowware ground, lid missing ..................... 65.00

Spittoon

    4-1/2" h, blue and white, blue accent bands at rim and shoulder ............................................................................................ 100.00

    5" d, blue and white, blue accent bands at shoulder and base, int. glaze crazing, 3" crack on side .......................................... 75.00

Teapot, 6-1/2" h, bluish green and white, small chips ................. 385.00

Toothbrush Holder, 5-1/4" h, blue and white ............................... 45.00

Tray, 9-1/2" l, leaf shape, blue and white .................................. 115.00

Umbrella Stand, blue and red sponge dec .................................. 715.00

Vase, 7-1/2" h, bulbous, blue and white, relief ribbon design, interior rim chip ........................................................................................ 110.00

Water Cooler, 9" h, dark brown sponge design over cream colored Bristol glaze, one gallon, orig bale handle, spigot, and matching stoneware lid, stenciled leaf and "Western Stoneware Co. Monmouth, Ill" above spigot, c1920 ............................................. 400.00

# SPORTS CARDS

**History:** Baseball cards were first printed in the late 19th century. By 1900, the most common cards, known as "T" cards, were those made by tobacco companies such as American Tobacco Co. The majority of the tobacco-related cards were produced between 1909 and 1915.

During the 1920s, American Caramel, National Caramel, and York Caramel candy companies issued cards identified in lists as "E" cards.

During the 1930s, Goudey Gum Co. of Boston (from 1933 to 1941) and Gum Inc. (in 1939) were prime producers of baseball cards. Following World War II, Bowman Gum of Philadelphia (B.G.H.L.I.), the successor to Gum, Inc., lead the way. Topps, Inc. (T.C.G.) of Brooklyn, New York, followed. Topps bought Bowman in 1956 and enjoyed almost a monopoly in card production until 1981.

In 1981, Topps was challenged by Fleer of Philadelphia and Donruss of Memphis. All three companies annually produce sets numbering 600 cards or more.

Football cards have been printed since the 1890s. However, it was not until 1933 that the first bubble gum football card appeared in the Goudey Sport Kings set. In 1935, National Chickle of Cambridge, Massachusetts, produced the first full set of gum cards devoted exclusively to football.

Both Leaf Gum of Chicago and Bowman Gum of Philadelphia produced sets of football cards in 1948. Leaf discontinued production after their 1949 issue; Bowman continued until 1955.

Topps Chewing Gum entered the market in 1950 with its college-stars set. Topps became a fixture in the football card market with its 1955 All-American set. From 1956 thorough 1963 Topps printed card sets of National Football League players, combining them with the American Football League players in 1961.

Topps produced sets with only American Football League players from 1964 to 1967. The Philadelphia Gum Company made National Football League card sets during this period. Beginning in 1968 and continuing to the present, Topps has produced sets of National Football League cards, the name adopted after the merger of the two leagues.

**References:** *All Sports Alphabetical Price Guide*, Krause Publications, 1995; Mark Allen Baker, *All-Sport Autograph Guide,* Krause Publications, 1995; —, *Collector's Guide to Celebrity Autographs,* 2nd ed., Krause Publications, 2000; Tol Broome, *From Ruth to Ryan*, Krause Publications, 1994; *Charlton Standard Catalogue of Canadian Baseball & Football Cards*, 4th ed., The Charlton Press, 1995; Jeff Kurowski and Tony Prudom, *Sports Collectors Digest Pre-War Baseball Card Price Guide*, Krause Publications, 1993; Mark Larson, *Complete Guide to Baseball Memorabilia,* 3rd ed., Krause Publications, 1996; —, *Complete Guide to Football, Basketball & Hockey Memorabilia,* Krause Publications, 1995; —, *Sports Collectors Digest Minor League Baseball Card Price Guide*, Krause Publications, 1993; Mark Larson (ed.), *Sports Card Explosion*, Krause Publications, 1993; Bob Lemke, ed., *2001 Standard Catalog of Baseball Cards,* 10th ed., Krause Publications, 2000; Bob Lemke and Sally Grace, *Sportscard Counterfeit Detector*, 3rd ed., Krause Publications, 1994; Michael McKeever, *Collecting Sports Cards*, Alliance Publishing, 1996; Tom Mortenson, *Standard Catalog of Sports Auto-*

*graphs,* Krause Publications, 2000; Alan Rosen, *True Mint,* Krause Publications, 1994; Sports Collectors Digest, *Baseball Card Price Guide,* 14th ed., Krause Publications, 2000; ——, *Baseball's Top 500 Card Checklist & Price Guide,* Krause Publications, 1999; ——, *Premium Insert Sports Cards,* Krause Publications, 1995; ——, *2001 Standard Catalog of Basketball Cards,* 4<sup>th</sup> ed., Krause Publications, 2000; ——, *2001 Standard Catalog of Football Cards,* 4<sup>th</sup> ed., Krause Publications, 2000; ——, *Standard Catalog of Football, Basketball, & Hockey Cards,* 2nd ed., Krause Publications, 1996; http://www.krause.com.

**Periodicals:** *Allan Kaye's Sports Cards News & Price Guides,* 10300 Watson Rd, St Louis, MO 63127; *Baseball Update,* Suite 284, 220 Sunrise Hwy, Rockville Centre, NY 11570; *Beckett Baseball Card Monthly,* 15850 Dallas Pkwy, Dallas, TX 75248; *Beckett Football Card Magazine,* 15850 Dallas Pkwy, Dallas, TX 75248; *Canadian Sportscard Collector,* P.O. Box 1299, Lewiston, NY 14092; *The Old Judge,* P.O. Box 137, Centerbeach, NY 11720; *Sport Card Economizer,* RFD 1 Box 350, Winthrop, ME 04364; *Sports Cards Magazine & Price Guide,* 700 E. State St., Iola, WI 54490; *Sports Card Trader,* P.O. Box 443, Mt. Morris, IL 61054; *Sports Collectors Digest,* 700 E. State St., Iola, WI 54990; *Tuff Stuff,* P.O. Box 1637, Glen Allen, VA 23060; *Your Season Ticket,* 106 Liberty Rd, Woodsboro, MD 21798.

# Baseball

### Bowman
1948

| | |
|---|--:|
| 8, Ruzzoto, PSA Grade 9, MT | 2,500.00 |
| 17, Slaughter, PSA Grade 7, NM | 110.00 |
| 18, Spahn, PSA Grade 7, NM | 300.00 |

1949

| | |
|---|--:|
| 46, Roberts, PSA Grade 7, NM | 200.00 |
| 84, Campanella, PSA Grade 8, NM-MT | 1,250.00 |
| 224, Paige, PSA Grade 7, NM | 950.00 |

1950

| | |
|---|--:|
| 94, Boudreau, PSA Grade 8, NM-MT | 150.00 |
| 112, Hodges, PSA Grade 8, NM-MT | 275.00 |
| 148, Wynn, PSA Grade 7, NM | 75.00 |
| 178, Fitzgerald, PSA Grade 8 | 125.00 |
| 215, Lopat, PSA Grade 8, NM-MT | 175.00 |
| 217, Stengel, PSA Grade 7, NM | 125.00 |
| 219, Bauer, PSA Grade 8 | 275.00 |

1951

| | |
|---|--:|
| 3, Roberts, PSA Grade 7, NM | 85.00 |
| 58, Slaughter, PSA Grade 8, NM-MT | 125.00 |
| 254, Exeter, PSA Grade 7, NM | 65.00 |
| 305, Mayes, PSA Grade 7, NM | 3,000.00 |

1952

| | |
|---|--:|
| 1 Berra, PSA Grade 7, NM | 595.00 |
| 21, Fox, PSA Grade 7, NM | 80.00 |
| 158, B Harris, PSA Grade 8 | 175.00 |
| 196, Musical, PSA Grade 7, NM | 550.00 |
| 218, Mays, PSA Grade 7, NM | 1,095.00 |

1953, color

| | |
|---|--:|
| 61, Keil, PSA Grade 8, NM-MT | 250.00 |
| 63, McDougald, PSA Grade 8 | 395.00 |
| 73, Pierce, PSA Grade 8, NM-MT | 250.00 |

| | |
|---|--:|
| 1954, 66, Williams, PSA Grade 7, NM | 3,500.00 |

1955

| | |
|---|--:|
| 23, Kaline, PSA Grade 8, NM-MT | 225.00 |

| | |
|---|--:|
| 102, Thomson, PSA Grade 8 | 65.00 |
| 179, Aaron, PSA Grade 7, NM | 225.00 |
| 252, Smalley, PSA Grade 8 | 50.00 |

1957

| | |
|---|--:|
| 1, Williams, VG | 60.00 |
| 2, Berra, PSA Grade 7 | 150.00 |
| 30, Reese, NM-MT | 70.00 |
| 55, Banks, NM-MT | 50.00 |
| 115, Gillam, NM-MT | 12.00 |
| 258, Gromak, NM | 23.00 |

### Cracker Jack
1911

| | |
|---|--:|
| 81, Delehanty, PSA Grade 7, NM | 225.00 |
| 122, Bush, PSA Grade 7, NM | 225.00 |
| 128, Evans, PSA Grade 7, NM | 225.00 |
| 131, Baumgardner, PSA Grade 6, EX-MT | 125.00 |
| 140, Murphy, PSA Grade 7, NM | 225.00 |

1915

| | |
|---|--:|
| 4, Doyle, PSA Grade 7, NM | 225.00 |
| 9, Hoffman, PSA Grade 6, EX-MT | 125.00 |
| 21, Zimmerman, PSA Grade 7, NM | 225.00 |
| 45, Luderus, PSA Grade 5, EX | 70.00 |
| 124, Moore, PSA Grade 7, NM | 225.00 |

### Diamond Stars, 1934-36

| | |
|---|--:|
| 41, Hendrick, PSA Grade 7, NM | 75.00 |
| 43, Lyons, PSA Grade 7, NM | 175.00 |
| 44 Hornsby, PSA Grade 7, NM | 500.00 |

### Fleer
1961

| | |
|---|--:|
| 14, Cobb, EX-MT | 22.00 |
| 31, Gehrig, MT | 55.00 |
| 154, Young, NM | 24.00 |

1963

| | |
|---|--:|
| 5, Mays, EX-MT | 90.00 |
| 29, Persal, EX | 6.00 |
| 42, Koufax, NM | 140.00 |

### Goudey
1933

| | |
|---|--:|
| 6, Dykes, PSA Grade 7, NM | 200.00 |
| 14, Johnson, PSA Grade 7, NM | 225.00 |
| 59, Miller, PSA 7, NM | 175.00 |
| 139, Cantwell, PSA Grade 8, MN-MT | 350.00 |
| 182, High, PSA Grade 7, NM | 125.00 |

1934

| | |
|---|--:|
| 18, Manush, PSA Grade 7, NM | 300.00 |
| 22, Vaghan, PSA Grade 8, NM-MT | 700.00 |
| 61, Gehring, PSA Grade 4, VG-EX | 1,500.00 |
| 75, Werber, PSA Grade 6, EX-MT | 150.00 |
| 90, Coyler, PSA Grade 6, EX-MT | 275.00 |

### Miscellaneous Vintage Cards

| | |
|---|--:|
| 1895, Anson, Mayo Cut Plug, PSA Grade 4, VG-EX | 2,250.00 |
| 1909-11, T206, Cobb, white border, PSA Grade 7 | 4,750.00 |
| 1910, E93, Standard Caramel, Young, PSA Grade 6 | 795.00 |
| 1910-11, T206, Magie, white border, PSA Grade 3 | 6,500.00 |
| 1911, T205, Tinker, gold border, PSA Grade 7 | 895.00 |
| 1914, D303, General Baking, Wagner Throwing, PSA Grade 3 | 595.00 |

### Sporting Life, 1911

| | |
|---|--:|
| Baker, PSA Grade 8, MN-MT | 800.00 |
| Delehanty, PSA Grade 6, EX-MT | 50.00 |
| Demmitt, PSA Grade 8, NM-MT | 300.00 |
| Tinker, PSA Grade 7, NM | 350.00 |

### Topps
1951, blue back

| | |
|---|--:|
| 3, Ashburn, PSA Grade 8, NM-MT | 395.00 |
| 6, Schoendenst, PSA Grade 9, MT | 395.00 |
| 37, Doerr, PSA Grade 8, NM-MT | 175.00 |
| 50, Mize, PSA Grade 8, NM-MT | 225.00 |

| | |
|---|--:|
| 1952, 261, Mayes, PSA Grade 5, EX | 395.00 |

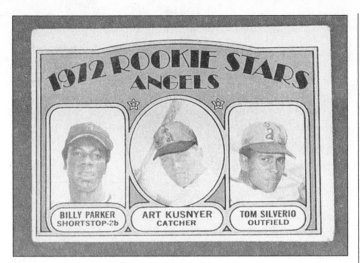

**Topps, #213, 1972 Rookie Stars, $2.**

1953
    27, Campanella, PSA Grade 9, MT .................................. 495.00
    258, Gillam, PSA Grade 7, NM........................................... 295.00
1954
    32, Snider, PSA Grade 8, NM-MT .................................. 695.00
    54, Banks, PSA Grade 7, NM........................................... 895.00
    102, Hodges, PSA Grade 7, NM-MT ............................. 275.00
1955
    123, Koufax, PSA Grade 7, NM........................................ 795.00
    155 Matthews, PSA 8, NM-MT ....................................... 295.00
    177, Robertson, PSA Grade 8 .......................................... 145.00
1964
    7, Ford, PSA Grade 8 ......................................................... 85.00
    24, Howard, F, PSA Grade 7 ............................................. 20.00
    25, Mantle, PSA Grade 8 ................................................. 225.00
    41, Gibson, PSA Grade 8 ................................................... 35.00
1978, T. Molitor/Trammel, PSA Grade 10 ....................... 2,000.00
1982, Ripken, PSA Grade 8.............................................. 140.00
1985, Clemens, PSA Grade 8............................................. 40.00

## Football
### Bowman
1948
    7, Van Buren, PSA Grade 7, NM ...................................... 150.00
    250, McAfee, PSA Grade 8, NM-MT ............................... 250.00
1950
    6, Groza, PSA Grade 7, NM ............................................ 120.00
    8, Speedia, PSA Grade 7, EX-MT ...................................... 10.00
    37, Layne, PSA Grade 7, NM .......................................... 150.00
    45, Graham, PSA Grade 8, NM .................................... 1,295.00
    53, Huffman, PSA Grade 7, NM......................................... 35.00
    108, Lilywhite, PSA Grade 8, NM-MT ................................ 85.00
    137, Kavanaugh, PSA Grade 8, NM-MT ............................ 85.00
1954
    7, Rote, PSA Grade 8, MT................................................. 28.00
    22, Reid, Grade 8, MT....................................................... 15.00
    53, Layne, Grade 8, MT................................................... 105.00
    85, Creekmar, Grade 8, MT............................................... 35.00
    102, Tunnell, PSA Grade 8 .............................................. 125.00
    113, Connelly, Grade 8, NM-MT ....................................... 25.00
1995, McNair, PSA Grade 10............................................ 100.00
1996, McNair, PSA Grade 8................................................ 20.00
1998, C. Batch, chrome, PSA Grade 10 .............................. 50.00
**Leaf**, 1948, 36 Dudley, PSA Grade 7, NM................................. 125.00
### Topps
1981, Montana, PSA Grade 8.......................................... 125.00
1984
    Elway, PSA Grade 8 ......................................................... 55.00
    Marino, PSA Grade 7......................................................... 225.00

# SPORTS COLLECTIBLES

**History:** People have been saving sports-related equipment since the inception of sports. Some was passed down from generation to generation for reuse; the rest was stored in dark spaces in closets, attics, and basements.

In the 1980s, two key trends brought collectors' attention to sports collectibles. First, decorators began using old sports items, especially in restaurant decor. Second, card collectors began to discover the thrill of owning the "real" thing. By the beginning of the 1990s, all sport categories were collectible, with baseball items paramount and golf and football running close behind.

**References:** Mark Allen Baker, *Sports Collectors Digest Complete Guide to Boxing Collectibles*, Krause Publications, 1995; Don Bevans and Ron Menchine, *Baseball Team Collectibles*, Wallace-Homestead, 1994; David Bushing, *Guide to Spalding Bats 1908-1938*, published by author; ——, *Sports Equipment Price Guide*, Krause Publications, 1995; Dave Bushing and Joe Phillips, *1996 Vintage Baseball Glove Pocket Price Guide*, No. 4, published by authors (217 Homewood, Libertyville, IL 60048), 1996; ——, *Vintage Baseball Bat 1994 Pocket Price Guide*, published by authors, 1994; Bruce Chadwick and David M. Spindel authored a series of books on major-league teams published by Abbeville Press between 1992 and 1995; Duncan Chilcott, *Miller's Soccer Memorabilia*, Miller's Publications, 1994; Douglas Congdon-Martin and John Kashmanian, *Baseball Treasures*, Schiffer Publishing, 1993; Ralf Coykendall, Jr., *Coykendall's Complete Guide to Sporting Collectibles*, Wallace-Homestead, 1996; Sarah Fabian-Baddiel, *Miller's Golf Memorabilia*, Millers Publications, 1994; Chuck Furjanic, *Antique Golf Collectibles, A Price and Reference Guide, 2nd Edition*, Krause Publications, 2000; John F. Hotchkiss, *500 Years of Golf Balls*, Antique Trader Books, 1997; Kevin Keating and Michael Kolleth, *The Negro Leagues Autograph Guide*, Tuff Stuff Books, 1999; Mark K. Larson, *Complete Guide to Baseball Memorabilia*, 3rd ed., Krause Publications, 1996; Mark Larson, Rick Hines and David Platta (eds.), *Mickey Mantle Memorabilia*, Krause Publications, 1993; Carl Luckey, *Old Fishing Lures and Tackle*, 5th ed., Krause Publications, 1999; J. L. Mashburn, *Sports Postcard Price Guide*, Colonial House, 1998; Kevin McGimpsey and David Neach, *Golf Memorabilia*, Philip Wilson Publishers, distributed by Antique Collectors' Club, 1999; Tim Mortenson, *2000 Standard Catalog of Sports Memorabilia*, Krause Publications, 1999; Dudley Murphy and Rick Edmisten, *Fishing Lure Collectibles*, 1995, 2000 value update, Collector Books; *1996 Vintage Baseball Glove Catalog Source Book*, The Glove Collector (14057 Rolling Hills Lane, Dallas, TX 75240), 1996; John M. and Morton W. Olman, *Golf Antiques & Other Treasures of the Game*, Market Street Press, 1993; George Richey, *Made in Michigan Fishing Lures*, published by author (Rte. 1, Box 280, Honor, MI 49640), 1995; George Sanders, Helen Sanders, and Ralph Roberts, *Sanders Price Guide to Sports Autographs*, 1994 ed., Scott Publishing, 1993;

Harold E. Smith, *Collector's Guide to Creek Chub Lures & Collectibles,* Collector Books, 1996; Mark Wilson (ed.), *Golf Club Identification and Price Guide III*, Ralph Maltby Enterprises, 1993.

**Periodicals:** *Baseball Hobby News*, 4540 Kearney Villa Rd, San Diego, CA 92123; *Beckett Focus on Future Stars*, 15850 Dallas Pkwy, Dallas, TX 75248; *Boxing Collectors News,* 3316 Luallen Drive, Carrollton, TX 75007; *Boxing Collectors Newsletter*, 59 Boston St, Revere, MA 02151; *Button Pusher*, P.O. Box 4, Coopersburg, PA 18036; *Diamond Angle*, P.O. Box 409, Kaunakakai, HI 97648; *Diamond Duds*, P.O. Box 10153, Silver Spring, MD 20904; *Fantasy Baseball*, 700 E. State St., Iola, WI 54990; *Golfiana Magazine*, P.O. Box 688, Edwardsville, IL 62025; *Old Tyme Baseball News*, P.O. Box 833, Petoskey, MI 49770; *Sports Collectors Digest*, 700 E. State St., Iola, WI 54990; *Tuff Stuff*, P.O. Box 1637, Glen Allen, VA 23060; *US Golf Classics & Heritage Hickories*, 5407 Pennock Point Rd, Jupiter, FL 33458.

**Collectors' Clubs:** Antique Ice Skating Collectors Club, 70-104 Scott St., Meriden, CT 06450; Boxiana & Pugilistica Collectors International, P.O. Box 83135, Portland, OR 97203-0135; Collectors' League, 575 Hwy 73 N, West Berlin, NJ 08091-2440, http://www.gartlanusa.com; Eastern PA Sports Collectors Club, P.O. Box 3037, Maple Glen, PA 19002; Golf Club Collectors Association, 640 E. Liberty St., Girard, OH 44420; Golf Collectors Society, P.O. Box 241042, Cleveland, OH 44124, http://www.golfcollectors.com; International Hot Rod Association, 9-1/2 E. Main St., Norwalk, OH 44857, http://www.ihra.com; International Pin Collectors Club, 602 Chenango St., Binghamton, NY 13901-2029; Logo Golf Ball Collector's Association, 4552 Barclay Fairway, Lake Worth, FL 33467; Professional Skaters Association, International, 1821 2nd St. SW, Rochester, MN 55902; Society for American Baseball Research, 812 Huron Rd, E., #719, Cleveland, OH 44115; Sports Hall of Oblivion, P.O. Box 69025, Pleasant Ridge, MI 48069-0025; The (Baseball) Glove Collector, 14507 Rolling Hills Lane, Dallas, TX, 75240; Tennis Collectors Society, Guildhall Orchard, Mary Lane North, Great Bromley Colchester, Essex C07 7TUWorld Logo (Golf) Ball Association, P.O. Box 91989, Long Beach, CA 90809, http://www.hyperhead.com/wlba2.

**Museums:** Aiken Thoroughbred Racing Hall of Fame & Museum, Aiken, SC; International Boxing Hall of Fame, Canastota, NY; Kentucky Derby Museum, Louisville, KY; Metropolitan Museum of Art, The Jefferson Burdich Collection, New York, NY; Naismith Memorial Basketball Hall of Fame, Springfield, MA; National Baseball Hall of Fame & Museum, Inc., Cooperstown, NY; National Bowling Hall of Fame & Museum, St. Louis, MO; New England Sports Museum, Boston, MA; PGA/World Golf Hall of Fame, Pinehurst, NC; University of New Haven National Art Museum of Sport, W Haven, CT.

## Baseball
Autographed Baseball
    Babe Ruth, 1948 ............... 3,750.00
    Tigers Team, 1926 ......... 5,750.00
    Yankees Team, 1935, includes Gehrig, Crosetti ............ 1,895.00
Autographed Photo, Babe Ruth, 1935, spring training, avoiding pickoff attempt at first base by Cincinnati rookie Johnny Mize, International News wire photo inscribed on back, "To My Friend John from Babe Ruth" ............ 7,500.00
Bank, 3" x 6" x 7", Cleveland Baseball Club, china, figural, Cleveland Baseball Club copyright, Gibbs-Sonner & Co., mid-1950s ...... 225.00
Baseball, orig box, Goldsmith's #97 Official League Ball, 2-3/4" x 2-3/4" x 3" box, unopened ............ 155.00
Book, *History, World's Tour, Chicago White Sox, New York Giants,* Ted Sullivan, 1913-14, 90 pgs, inscribed in front, "To Charles W. Murphy From His Friend Ted Sullivan" ............ 895.00
Booklet, Chicago Daily News, World Series, player profiles, 1910, 48 pgs ............ 795.00
Box, 6-7/8" w, 9-1/4" l, 2-3/8" h, New York Champions Chocolates, paper label, wooden box, inside with illus of uniformed baseball players ............ 650.00
Candy Bar Wrapper, 7-7/8" w, 7" l, wax paper, Bit Hit 10¢ Babe Ruth, Universal Candy Co., Oconto, WI ............ 160.00
Jersey, autographed
    Eddie Murray ............ 325.00
    Pete Rose ............ 250.00
    Lawrence Taylor ............ 195.00
Medallion, 1-1/2" d, Babe Ruth Shrine, Ruth at bat on one side, Baltimore birthplace on other ............ 60.00
Pennant
    Baltimore Orioles League Championship, 29-1/2" l, black, 1969 ............ 30.00
    New York Mets, 29-1/2" l, blue, white, and orange inscription and design, late 1960s ............ 20.00
Press Pin, New York Yankees, 1938 World Series, two crossed bats, raised baseball, red, white, and blue border mkd "World Series Yankee Stadium" ............ 850.00
Program
    New York Giants, 1892, 24 pgs ............ 1,250.00
    St. Louis Browns vs. Detroit Tigers, 1908, 24 pgs ............ 750.00
    World Series, 1929, plus ticket stubs, Wrigley Field ........ 2,500.00
Souvenir Booklet and Game Ticket, World's Tour, 1914, 64 pgs, New York Giants and Chicago White Sox ............ 1,500.00
Toy, Baseball Catcher, NY, celluloid, wind-up, Occupied Japan, 5" h 60.00
Yearbook, Yankees, 1951 ............ 120.00

## Boxing
Autographed Photo, Mohammad Ali, sgd in gold marker, Ali in suit with his arm around Elvis Presley, framed, 16" x 20" ............ 450.00
Game, Championship Fight, Frankie Goodman copyright and design, US National & Intercollegiate Champion, 1940-50 ............ 48.00
Playing Cards, James J. Jeffries Championship, boxer photo on each card, complete deck, 1909 copyright ............ 120.00
Program, 1964 Ali vs. Liston, Boston, MA, sgd "Muhammad Ali" 150.00

## Fishing
Fish, 31-1/2" l, wood, paint dec, America, early 20th C, minor paint wear and losses ............ 1,495.00
Folk Art, 25" h, 40-1/4" l, wood carving, titled "Two Fish and a Frog," sgd "L. A. Plummer, 1904" in lower right, polychrome dec, minor cracks ............ 17,250.00

Trout Reel, Edw. Vom Hofe, NY, size #2, Perfection Model, hand made, German silver and hard rubber, $4,290. Photo courtesy of Lang's Sporting Collectables, Inc.

Painting, 13" x 16", oil on canvas, still life with fish and creel, monogrammed and dated "1882" upper right, American School, framed, lined, retouched .................................................................. 1,265.00
Reel, B. F. Meek & Sons, #33 Bluegrass ................................... 200.00
Rod
    F. E. Thomas, three piece fly rod, extra tip, metal case, mkd "Special, Bangor, Maine," 8-1/2' ............................................... 275.00
    Hardy's of England Salmon Deluxe Rod, extra tip, aluminum case, 9' ..................................................................................... 175.00
    H. L. Leonard, fly, Leonard Tournament, extra tip, metal case, 9' ...................................................................................... 300.00

## Football

Ashtray, 7-1/2" d, Baltimore Colts Championship, china, white, blue cartoon illus, dated Dec. 29, 1958, orig box .............................. 75.00
Autographed Miniature Helmet
    Derrick Brooks ...................................................................... 50.00
    Duce Stanley ......................................................................... 60.00
    Ray Lucas .............................................................................. 65.00
    Joe Namath .......................................................................... 150.00
Glass, 5-1/4" h, Ohio State University Football, Champions Western Conference, Appreciation Banquet, Nov 25, 1968 ..................... 18.00
Nodder, 6-1/2" h, LA Rams, composition, c1961 .......................... 55.00
Pennant
    Chicago Bears, 28" l, black, dark orange lettering and design .. 42.00
    San Diego Chargers, 29-1/2" l, felt, yellow-gold and white lettering and helmet design, blue ground, American Football League insignia, late 1960s .......................................................... 18.00
Program, Chicago Tribune All-Star Charity Football, College All-Americans and Chicago Bears, Soldiers' Field, Chicago, c1935 ......... 30.00

## Fox Hunting

Place Card Holders, 1-3/4" h, porcelain, scarlet coated master of hounds on leafy base, matching open salt, German, early 20th C, price for 9 pc set ....................................................................... 265.00
Print, 26" w, 11" h, fan shaped images, The Chase and the Death, etchings with aquatint and hand coloring on paper, French School, 19th C, sgd "Susse Fils Paris" in the plate, framed, toning, price for pr ..... 450.00

## Golf

Beer Mug, 5" h, cut glass, punties and prism motif, engraved "C.A.C. Gold Class A, 1898," sterling silver rim, stag bone handle, cut by Dorflinger ................................................................................ 475.00
Bowl, Old Foley-Wileman .......................................................... 225.00
Decanter, silver overlay, dark amethyst glass body, figure of golfer . 300.00
Doorstop, 8" h, cast iron, figural, wear to old polychrome ........... 770.00
Miniature Cup and Saucer, Old Foley-Wileman .......................... 225.00
Mug, white stoneware, hp golfer, Scotland, c1950 ..................... 140.00
Plate, small, Old Foley-Wileman ................................................. 85.00
Tray, 12" d, golfer and caddy on golf course, plane flying overhead pulling banner adv "Famous Beverwyck Beers and Ales," Electro-Chemical Engraving Co. litho, © 1934 ..................................... 225.00

## Hunting

Box
    2-1/4" w, 2-1/4" d, 2-1/2" h, Peters High Velocity .410ga, empty, one pc box ............................................................................ 125.00
    3-1/2" w, 2-1/2" d, 3-1/2" h, Winchester Repeater, 24ga black powder, empty, two pc box .................................................. 250.00
    4" w, 4" l, 2-1/2" h, Sears Sport Loads, 12ga, bright image of goose in flight, empty, two pc box .......................................... 180.00
    4" w, 4" l, 2-1/2" h, Straitline Shot Shells, by Eley/Nobel, 12ga, empty, two pc box, scrapes on front and top of label ....... 135.00
    4" w, 4" l, 2-1/2" h, US Cartridge Co., Climax, 12 ga, empty, two pc box .................................................................................... 70.00
Calendar, 15" w, 27" h, 1928, Remington, artist Henry Watson, fireside scene with hunter and dog, 14 calendar pages, top 2" glued to matte board ....................................................................................... 600.00
Catalog, F. C. Taylor Fur Co., hunting, trapping, camping supplies, 2 page full color ad for Remington Game Load boxes, 54 pages, 1923-244 ........................................................................................... 90.00
Compass, 1-3/4" d, celluloid, Dave Cook Sporting Goods Co., Denver, CO, litho by Parisian Novelty, Chicago, red lettering, cream ground ....................................................................................... 60.00
Counter Stand-up, diecut cardboard
    11" w, 21" h, Western Super X Shells, cut-away of shell .... 585.00
    14" w, 16" h, American Field Hunting Garments, mallard, c1940 ................................................................................... 125.00
Cover, unused
    6-1/2" l, 3-1/2" h, Winchester Rifles and Cartridges ........... 100.00
    6-1/2" l, 3-3/4" h, Dupont Sporting Powders, dated 1907 ... 160.00
    6-1/2" l, 3-3/4" h, Hazard Powder, dated 1905, mallard duck .. 100.00
Painting, orig oil on canvas for King's Powder Quickshot adv, unsigned, c1890, 20" w, 28" h, orig frame, professionally cleaned and revarnished ............................................................................ 9,100.00
Pinback Button, Peter's Cartridges, 3/4" d, celluloid, by Bastian Bros., Rochester, NY .......................................................................... 60.00
Poster
    12-1/2" w, 19-1/2" h image, Dead Shot, by George A. Walker & Co., Boston, matted and framed, matte glued down to litho ......... 450.00
    15-1/4" w, 25-1/2" h, Cock of the Woods, Winchester, 1905, top and bottom bands missing, 3" tear mid left ...................... 760.00
Target Ball
    2-1/2" d, medium blue, ribbed pattern, French ................... 115.00
    2-1/2" d, 3" h, cobalt blue glass, mkd "A. St. Quentin" basketweave design, Van Cutsem ....................................................... 115.00
Tin
    2-1/2" w, 1" d, 2-7/8" h, Hazard Indian Rifle Gunpowder, litho tin, lb size, bright colors, back mkd "FFFG," c1890 ............... 600.00

Painting, oil on canvas, created for King's Powder Quickshot, c1890, orig frame, professionally cleaned and revarnished, 20" w, 28" h, $9,100. Photo courtesy of Past Tyme Pleasures Auction.

2-3/4" w, 1" d, 4-3/4" h, Winchester Talc, Jolind Dist., NY, graphics of hunter and seated dog .................................................. 180.00

4" w, 6" h, Dupont Superfine HFG Powder, 1 lb size, bright red ground ......................................................................... 40.00

# STAFFORDSHIRE, HISTORICAL

**History:** The Staffordshire district of England is the center of the English pottery industry. There were 80 different potteries operating there in 1786, with the number increasing to 179 by 1802. The district includes Burslem, Cobridge, Etruria, Fenton, Foley, Hanley, Lane, Lane End, Longport, Shelton, Stoke, and Tunstall. Among the many famous potters were Adams, Davenport, Spode, Stevenson, Wedgwood, and Wood.

**References:** David and Linda Arman, *Historical Staffordshire* (1974), 1st Supplement (1977), published by authors, out of print; Susan and Al Bagdade, *Warman's English & Continental Pottery & Porcelain*, 3rd Edition, Krause Publications, 1998; A. W. Coysh and R. K. Henrywood, *Dictionary of Blue and White Printed Pottery* (1982), Vol. II (1989), Antique Collectors' Club; Mary J. Finegan, *Johnson Brothers Dinnerware*, published by author, 1993; N. Hudson Moore, *The Old China Book,* Charles E. Tuttle, Co., second printing, 1980; Jeffrey B. Snyder, *Historical Staffordshire American Patriots and Views*, Schiffer Publishing, 1995.

**Museums:** American Antiquarian Society, Worcester, MA; Cincinnati Art Museum, Cincinnati, OH; City Museum & Art Gallery, Stoke-on-Trent, England; Colonial Williamsburg Foundation, Williamsburg, VA; Elverson Museum of Art, Syracuse, NY; Henry Ford Museum, Dearborn, MI; Hershey Museum, Hershey, PA; Metropolitan Museum of Art, New York, NY; The National Museum of History & Technology, Washington, DC; The Henry Francis DuPont Winterthur Museum, Winterthur, DE; William Rockhill Nelson Gallery of Art, Kansas City, MO; Yale University Gallery of Fine Arts, New Haven, CT.

**Notes:** The view is the most critical element when establishing the value of historical Staffordshire; American collectors pay much less for non-American views. Dark blue pieces are favored; light views continue to remain under-priced. Among the forms, soup tureens have shown the largest price increases.

Prices listed below are for mint examples. Reduce prices by 20% for a hidden chip, a faint hairline, or an invisible professional repair; by 35% for knife marks through the glaze and a visible professional repair; by 50% for worn glaze and major repairs.

The numbers in parentheses refer to items in the Armans' books, which constitute the most detailed list of American historical views and their forms.

## Adams

The Adams family has been associated with ceramics since the mid-17th century.

W.ADAMS&SONS    ADAMS

In 1802, William Adams of Stoke-on-Trent produced American views. In 1819, a fourth William Adams, son of William of Stoke, became a partner with his father and was later joined by his three brothers. The firm became William Adams & Sons. The father died in 1829 and William, the eldest son, became manager. The company operated four potteries at Stoke and one at Tunstall. American views were produced at Tunstall in black, light blue, sepia, pink, and green in the 1830-40 period. William Adams died in 1865. All operations were moved to Tunstall. The firm continues today under the name of Wm. Adams & Sons, Ltd.

Cup and Saucer, handleless, Home in the Woods, blue transfer, luster trim, imp "Adams," minor wear, pinpoint flakes ......................... 220.00

Cup Plate, 4" d, Fair Mount, Hudson River Series, pink transfer (459) .................................................................................. 90.00

Plate

7-3/4" d, St. Paul's School, London, dark blue transfer, imp "Adams" .................................................................. 175.00

9" d, "Mitchell & Freeman's China & Glass Warehouse, Chatham Street, Boston," dark blue transfer, imp "Adams," wear, chip on back of rim, scratches ...................................................... 385.00

Platter

15-1/2" l, Fountain Scenery, blue transfer, wear and scratches, imp "Adams" .............................................................. 200.00

17" l, Jedburgh Abbey, Roxburghshire, dark blue transfer, imp "Adams," wear and deep knife scratches ........................ 360.00

Soup Plate, 10-1/2" d, US Views, Catskill Mountain House, light blue transfer (445) ........................................................................ 85.00

Vegetable Bowl, open, 8-1/4" l, Hanover Terrace, Regents Park, dark blue transfer, imp "Adams" ...................................................... 385.00

Waste Bowl, Log Cabin, medallions of Gen. Harrison on border, brown transfer (458) .......................................................................... 265.00

## Clews

From sketchy historical accounts that are available, it appears that James Clews took over the closed plant of A. Stevenson in 1819. His brother Ralph entered the business later. The firm continued until about 1836, when James Clews came to America to enter the pottery business at Troy, Indiana. The venture was a failure because of the lack of skilled workmen and the proper type of clay. He returned to England, but did not re-enter the pottery business.

Cup and Saucer, handleless

Going to the Well, dark blue transfer, imp "Clews," pinpoint flakes ........................................................................ 150.00

Young couple in forest, dark blue transfer, imp "Clews," minor wear .............................................................................. 250.00

Cup Plate, 4-5/8" d, winter view of Pittsfield, MA, dark blue transfer, imp "Clews," chips and hairlines .............................................. 200.00

Pepper Pot, Landing of Lafayette, dome top, dark blue transfer 1,155.00

Pitcher, 7-7/8" h, "Landing of Gen. LaFayette," dark blue transfer, imp "Clews," wear and glaze flakes .............................................. 1,100.00

Plate

8" d, America and Independence, two story building, curved drive, States border, dark blue transfer, imp "Clews" ................. 330.00

8-7/8" d, Landing of Gen. Lafayette, dark blue transfer, imp "Clews," minor wear .......................................................... 440.00

9-7/8" d, blue and white transfer, Italianate landscape with ruin, imp underglaze mark, c1825-35......................140.00

10" d, Landing of Gen. Lafayette, dark blue transfer, imp "Clews," minor knife scratches and wear ......................440.00

10-1/4" d, Landing of Lafayette, dark blue transfer, imp Clews385.00

10-1/2" d, Winter View of Pittsfield Elm, dark blue transfer 300.00

Platter

14-3/4" l, America and Independence, dark blue transfer, scene of mansion with small boat and flag, imp "Clews," minor wear and scratches ......................1,210.00

16-1/2" l, 13-1/4" w, Sandusky, dark blue transfer, misnamed "Detroit," Cities series, minor staining on back..............4,500.00

17" l, Peace & Plenty, dark blue transfer, imp "Clews," wear, small edge flakes and deep scratches ......................715.00

18-1/2" l, 15-1/2" w, Winter View of Pittsfield Mass, dark blue transfer, scalloped edge, minor staining on back.........3,000.00

Sauce Boat Tray, 9-3/4" l, "Landing of Gen. LaFayette," dark blue transfer, imp "Clews" ......................965.00

Sauce Tureen, 6" h, 7-3/4" w handle to handle, Hudson River, Fort Montgomery, light blue transfer, Picturesque Views series ......350.00

Saucer, English scene with church and fisherman, dark blue transfer, imp "Clews," wear ......................75.00

Toddy Plate, 5-1/2" d, "Landing of Gen. LaFayette," dark blue transfer, imp "Clews" ......................425.00

Tureen, cov, 16" l, 10" h, 3-3/4" d, 11" ladle, "Landing of Gen. Lafayette at Castle Garden in New York, 16th August 1824," dark blue transfer, imp "James and Ralph Clews," some damage......................5,175.00

Vegetable Dish, cov, 12-1/2" d, 6-1/2" h, Peace and Plenty, dark blue transfer, imp "James and Ralph Clews," some damage........1,725.00

## Goodwin, Thomas, 1830-40

Plate, 9-1/4" d

Schuykill Water Works, 9 1/4" d plate, American Views series , brown transfer ......................160.00

William Penn's Treaty American Views series, dark blue transfer......................85.00

Platter, Crystal Palace, mauve transfer, deteriorating repair to 2" chip, staining......................50.00

Soup Plate, 10 1/2" d, William Penn's Treaty American Views series , green transfer ......................90.00

Vegetable, open, 8" l, oval, William Penn's Treaty American Views series, red transfer ......................250.00

## Hall, Ralph, Tunstall, 1800-29

Bowl, 9-3/4" d, Select Views, Biddulph Castle Staffordshire, medium blue transfer, glaze wear, minor chips......................300.00

Compote, Rode Hall, Cheshire, 3-1/2" x 12" w, ftd, Foliage border series, dark blue transfer, underglaze title, shell and scroll emb handles, four tiny peg feet, light center, dark border, three stilt marks on face, two shallow rim chips ......................350.00

Plate, 7-1/2" d, Sheltered Peasants, dark blue transfer, wear and scratches, pr......................400.00

Waste Bowl, 6 1/4" d, dark blue transfer, imp "Nest, R. Hall"......200.00

**Heath, Joseph & Co.**, pitcher, 6-1/4" h, Residence of the Late Richard Jordan, New Jersey, black transfer, crack to handle ...............250.00

## J. & J. Jackson

Job and John Jackson began operations at the Churchyard Works, Burslem, about  1830. The works formerly were owned by the Wedgwood family. The firm produced transfer scenes in a variety of colors, such as black, light blue, pink, sepia, green, maroon, and mulberry. More than 40 different American views of Connecticut, Massachusetts, Pennsylvania, New York, and Ohio were issued. The firm is believed to have closed about 1844.

Plate

6-1/4" d, Girard's Bank, Philadelphia, one green, one black, two mulberry, 4 pcs......................350.00

8-1/4" d, Library, Philadelphia, Beauties of America series, floral border, blue transfer......................200.00

8-1/2" d, Dumb Asylum, blue transfer.................160.00

9" d, The Race Bridge, Philadelphia, black transfer ...........100.00

10" d, Water Works, Philadelphia, oak leaf and acorn border, blue transfer......................600.00

10-1/4" d, The President's House, Washington, Jackson's Warranted, red transfer......................315.00

Platter, 9-3/4" , Upper Ferry Bridge, Philadelphia, red transfer...500.00

## Thomas Mayer

In 1829, Thomas Mayer and his brothers, John and Joshua, purchased Stubbs's Dale Hall Works of Burslem. They continued to produce a superior grade of ceramics.

Cup Plate, 4" d, Arms of South Carolina, Arms of States series, dark blue transfer, unmarked ......................700.00

Plate, 8-1/2" d, Arms of Rhode Island, Arms of the American States series, dark blue transfer, minor staining ......................600.00

Soup Plate, 10" d, Arms of New York, Arms of States series, dark blue transfer, wear, shallow rim flakes, pinpoints on table ring........635.00

Sugar Bowl, Lafayette at Washington's Tomb, cov, dark blue transfer (511) ......................750.00

Vegetable Dish, 11-3/4" l, Arms of Georgia, Arms of States series, dark blue transfer (500)......................3,000.00

## J. & W. Ridgway and William Ridgway & Co.

John and William Ridgway, sons of Job Ridgway and nephews of George Ridgway who owned Bell Bank Works and Cauldon Place Works, produced the popular Beauties of America series at the Cauldon plant. The partnership between the two brothers was dissolved in 1830. John remained at Cauldon. William managed the Bell Bank Works until 1854. Two additional series were produced based upon the etchings of Bartlett's American Scenery. The first series had various borders including narrow lace. The second series is known as Catskill Moss. Beauties of America is in dark blue. The other series are found in light transfer colors of blue, pink, brown, black, and green.

Bowl, urn shaped, 10" d, Oriental, medium blue transfer, gilt trim, mkd "Ridgways" ......................275.00

Cup Plate, Exchange Building, Baltimore, Beauties of America series, dark blue transfer (254) ......................450.00

Gravy Tureen Ladle, 6" l, Portions of a View, College series, dark blue, transfer, repairs to handle ......................325.00

Gravy Tureen, cov, 6-1/4" h, 8-1/4" w, Trinity Hall, Cambridge, College series, dark blue transfer, underglaze mark, emb handles, floral finial......................600.00

Plate

7-1/8" d, Insane Hospital, Boston, Beauties of America series, medium to dark blue transfer ......................350.00

8-1/2" d, City Hall, New York, Beauties of America series, dark blue transfer, mkd "J. & W. Ridgway," Hanley, 1814-30 ......200.00

9" d, Fairmount Gardens, Catskill Moss series, 1844...........90.00

9-1/2" d, Meredith, Catskill Moss series (307) ......................65.00

9-3/4" d, City Hall, New York, Beauties of America series, medium to dark blue transfer, imp mark, tiny factory flaws around rim ......................300.00

Platter

16" l, Almshouse, New York, Beauties of America series, dark blue transfer (255) ......................625.00

18-1/2" l, Pennsylvania Hospital, Philadelphia, Beauties of America series, dark blue transfer, octagonal......................1,400.00

20-3/4" l, 15-1/2" w, Capitol Washington, Beauties of America series, medium to dark blue, staining, 12" crack, wear to face ......................200.00

Soup Plate

    8-1/4" d, Straughton's Church, Philadelphia, Beauties of America series, dark blue transfer, pr............................................. 350.00

    10" d, Kosciusko's Tomb, Catskill Moss series(305)............. 75.00

    10" d, Octagon Church, Boston, Beauties of America series, dark blue transfer(A-271) ........................................ 275.00

## Rodgers, John & Son, Longport, England

John Rogers and his brother George established a pottery near Longport in 1782. After George's death in 1815, John's son Spencer became a partner, and the firm operated under the name of John Rogers & Sons. John died in 1916. His son continued the use of the name until he dissolved the pottery in 1842.

**ROGERS**

Cup and Saucer, Boston Harbor, dark blue transfer (441).......... 650.00

Plate, 10" d, Boston State House, dark blue transfer (442) ........ 150.00

Platter, 14" l, Boston State House, dark blue transfer (442) ....... 495.00

Set, Boston State House, c1815-42, blue and white, 29 dinner plates, 19 luncheon plates, 11 soup plates, 4 bread and butter plates, 10 platters, pierced insert, soup tureen with undertray and ladle, 4 sauce tureens, 3 undertrays, 4 cov serving dishes, sq center bowl, all mkd "Rogers," some with staple and other repairs, minor cracks, chips, staining, price for set ........................................... 16,500.00

Sugar Bowl, Boston Harbor, dark blue transfer (441) ................. 675.00

## Stevenson

As early as the 17th century, the name Stevenson has been associated with the pottery industry. Andrew Stevenson of Cobridge introduced American scenes with the flower and scroll border. Ralph Stevenson, also of Cobridge, used a vine and leaf border on his dark blue historical views and a lace border on his series in light transfers. The initials R. S. & W. indicate Ralph Stevenson and Williams are associated with the acorn and leaf border. It has been reported that Williams was Ralph's New York agent and the wares were produced by Ralph alone.

**R. S. W.**

Cup and Saucer, New Orleans, Lace border series (387) .......... 150.00

Plate

    5-1/2" d, Baltimore Exchange, Acorn and Oak Leaves border series, dark blue transfer (348) ........................................ 775.00

    6-1/4" d, Columbia College, New York, Acorn and Oak Leaves border series, dark blue transfer, minor staining and rubbing to edge .......................................................................... 600.00

    7" d, City Hall, New York, Floral and Scroll border series, dark blue transfer (397).......................................... 1,200.00

    8-3/8" d, Harvard College, Acorn and Oak Leaves border series, dark blue transfer .......................................... 295.00

    10" d, Harvard College, Acorn and Oak Leaves border series, medium to dark blue transfer, hairline on front................ 300.00

    10" d, Park Theater, New York, Acorn and Oak Leaves border series, dark blue transfer(357) ........................................ 195.00

    10-1/4" d, New York from Brooklyn Heights, Floral and Scroll border series, dark blue transfer ........................................ 995.00

Platter, 18-3/4" l, New York from Weehawk, dark blue transfer, imp "Stevenson," wear, knife scratches, hairline.......................... 1,210.00

Soup Plate, 10" d

    Capitol, Washington, Vine border series(370) .................... 425.00

    Erie Canal at Buffalo, Lace border series (386)................. 195.00

Tureen, cov, 9-1/4" sq, 5-1/2" h, Pennsylvania Hospital, int. with flowers and Charleston Exchange, Vine border series, leaf molded rim corners, leaf molded base corners with carved feet, base incorrectly painted New York Battery, imp "Stevenson," clover leaf Ralph Stevenson mark, blue and white ........................................... 7,000.00

**Upper Ferry Bridge over the River Schuylkill, Joseph Stubbs, 13" d bowl 10" h pitcher, $ 1,495; platter, 19" l, 15-1/2" w, $1,495. Photo courtesy of Skinner, Inc.**

## Stubbs

In 1790, Joseph Burslem Stubbs established a pottery works at Burslem, England. He operated it until 1829, when he retired and sold the pottery to the Mayer brothers. He probably produced his American views about 1825. Many of his scenes were from Boston, New York, New Jersey, and Philadelphia.

Pitcher, 6-1/2" h, 7-1/4" w, Boston State House/City Hall, New York, dark blue transfer, small lip chip................................. 800.00

Plate

    6-5/8" d, City Hall New York, Spread Eagle border series, medium blue transfer, ........................................ 300.00

    8-3/4" d, Upper Ferry Bridge Over the River Schuykill, Spread Eagle border series, dark blue transfer ........................... 160.00

    8-7/8" d, Nahant Hotel, Near Boston, Spread Eagle border series, medium to dark blue transfer, restored ........................... 300.00

    10-1/4" d, Fairmount Near Philadelphia, Spread Eagle border series, medium to dark blue transfer, ........................... 200.00

Platter

    10-5/8" l, Woodlands Near Philadelphia, dark blue transfer 650.00

    14-1/2" l, 12" w, Boston State House, Spread Eagle border series, dark blue transfer, professional restoration ...................... 900.00

    16-1/2" l, 13-1/2" w, Menden Hall Ferry, Spread Eagle border series, dark blue transfer, stained, couple of small pits on front and back, wear to face ................................. 1,100.00

    18-1/2" l, Upper Ferry Bridge Over the River Schuykill, Spread Eagle border series, dark blue transfer ...................... 1,350.00

    20-1/2" l, Fairmount Near Philadelphia, Spread Eagle border series, dark blue transfer........................................ 1,750.00

Sauce Tureen, underplate, oval, Upper Ferry Bridge Over the River Schuylkill, Spread Eagle border series, brown transfer ............ 275.00

Soup Plate, 9-7/8" d, Fairmount Near Philadelphia, dark blue transfer, imp "Stubbs" on base, hairlines, very minor base chips, glaze wear, set of three ............................................................ 500.00

Soup Tureen, cov, 9-1/4" h, 14" w, Birds and Fruit, dark blue transfer, large shell emb scroll handles, four paw feet, floral finial, replaced finial, restoration to lid ............................................. 1,300.00

Vegetable Dish, open, 9-1/8" l, oval, Upper Ferry Bridge Over the River Schuylkill, Spread Eagle border series, brown transfer ........... 575.00

## Unknown Maker

Caster, 4-5/8" h, "Landing of Gen. Lafayette At New York 1824," medium blue transfer ........................................... 300.00

**Creamer**

6" h, scene of horse drawn sleigh, dark blue transfer, filled in rim flake..................................................................440.00

Lafayette at Franklin's Tomb, dark blue transfer.................400.00

**Cup Plate**

3-7/8" d, scene of three men, dark blue transfer.................110.00

4" d, Hyena, dark blue transfer, stains, some glaze wear...175.00

**Pepper Pot**, 4-5/8" h, Landing of Lafayette, domed top, dark blue transfer, shallow chip and flakes on top........................2,750.00

**Pitcher**

6-1/8" h, scroll and foliate devices, spread eagle, "E. Pluribus Unum," blue and white transfer, spout chip, hairlines......750.00

6-1/4" h, City Hall New York and Insane Asylum, New York, flower and foliage border, dark blue transfer, rim and spout edge wear, circular hairline in base.................................................660.00

6-1/4" h, Landing of Gen. Lafayette, scrolled handle, scalloped rim, dark blue transfer, stained.................................1,760.00

6-3/8" h, Boston State House, spread eagle mark in base, dark blue transfer, restoration to spout, chip, hairlines to base 750.00

6-1/2" h, The Landing of the Fathers at Plymouth, dark blue transfer, minor chips, star crack, glaze wear............................350.00

**Plate**

7" d, New York Battery, dark blue transfer, wear, stains, and scratches.............................................................110.00

7-5/8" d, View of Trenton Falls, dark blue transfer, wear and scratches.............................................................95.00

8-1/2" d, American Villa, dark blue transfer, fruit, and flower border, stained, dings, wear and scratches......................150.00

9-1/8" d, Transylvania University Lexington, dark blue transfer, wear and some kiln damage.......................................325.00

9-3/4" d, Boston State House, medium blue transfer, wear and scratches.............................................................125.00

10" d, Arms of New York, dark blue transfer, chip on table rim 500.00

10" d, Baltimore Exchange, dark blue transfer, fruit and flower series, minor staining and rubbing to rim......................500.00

10" d, The Dam & Waterworks, Philadelphia, stern wheeler, dark blue transfer, stains and minor wear..............................445.00

10-1/4" d, Fair Mount Near Philadelphia, medium blue transfer, wear and scratches.....................................................150.00

**Platter**

15-3/8" l, Harper's Ferry, red transfer, scalloped rim, eagle signature on back...........................................................440.00

18-3/4" l, Christianburg Danish Settlement on the Gold Coast, Africa, dark blue transfer, wear, small glaze flakes, and hairline...1,265.00

19" x 15-3/4", Hanibal Crossing the Alps, light to medium blue, minor staining............................................................250.00

20-1/4" l, lakeside scene of fisherman hanging nets out to dry on tree, blue transfer, attributed to Robert Hamilton Stoke, 1811-26, very minor rim chips, glaze wear, knife marks...........575.00

**Sauce Boat**, 7-3/4" l, Hoboken, New Jersey, dark blue transfer, stains, hairline, foot chip...................................................220.00

**Sauce Tureen**, 3 pc, 8" x 5-3/4" x 6-1/2" h, Boston Mails, Gentleman's Cabin, brown transfer, tureen with attached undertray, lid, and ladle, base restored.............................................................450.00

**Saucer**, 5-7/8" d, 1-1/8" deep, Railroad, dark blue transfer, floral border, stained, cracks...................................................400.00

**Soup Plate**, 9-7/8" d, Fair Mount near Philadelphia, medium blue transfer, pinpoint flakes, short scratch, crow's foot.............275.00

**Sugar**, cov, 6-1/4" h, Landing of Gen. Lafayette, dark blue transfer, chips on rim and lid..........................................................650.00

**Teapot**, 8-1/2" h, 12-1/2" w handle to spout, young girl with basket of flowers, floral border, dark blue transfer, stained, spider crack to side, minor chips on spout, lid damaged, finial replaced..................400.00

**Under Tray**, 10-1/4" l, pearlware, blue transfer of English castle, reticulated rim, chips, surface flakes.....................................440.00

**Vegetable Bowl**, cov, 9-1/2" h, 9-1/2" l, "A Ship of the Lines in the Downs," mismatched lid with unidentified verse, dark blue transfer, both have repaired hairlines (139)..................................715.00

**Waste Bowl**, 7" d, 3-5/8" h, Boston Harbor, dark blue transfer, wear and hairline..............................................................825.00

## Wood

Enoch Wood, sometimes referred to as the father of English pottery, began operating a pottery at Fountain Place, Burslem, in 1783. A cousin, Ralph Wood, was associated with him. In 1790, James Caldwell became a partner and the firm was known as Wood and Caldwell.

In 1819, Wood and his sons took full control. Enoch died in 1840. His sons continued under the name of Enoch Wood & Sons. The American views were first made in the mid-1820s and continued through the 1840s. It is reported that the pottery produced more signed historical views than any other Staffordshire firm. Many of the views attributed to unknown makers probably came from the Woods. Marks vary, although always include the name Wood. The establishment was sold to Messrs. Pinder, Bourne & Hope in 1846.

**Coffeepot**, dome lid, 12" h, Commodore MacDonnough's Victory, dark blue transfer.........................................................3,410.00

**Cream Pitcher**, 3-1/2" h, Commodore MacDonnough's Victory barrel shape, Floral border series, dark blue transfer (154)............1,850.00

**Cup and Saucer**, handleless, Lafayette at Franklin's Tomb, dark blue transfer, saucer imp "Wood and Sons" with eagle mark, hairline and repair on cup.............................................................440.00

**Cup Plate**

3-5/8" d, English brick bridge, dark blue transfer, imp "Wood".150.00

3-5/8" d, cottage in the woods, dark blue transfer, imp "Wood," under glaze "A" on back.............................................165.00

3-3/4" d, Cadmus, dark blue transfer, imp "Wood," chip on table ring.....................................................................330.00

3-3/4" d, Castle Garden Battery New York, dark blue transfer, imp "Wood," minor wear and stains.................................385.00

**Gravy Boat**, 7" w, 2-3/4" d, 4-1/4" h, Pass in the Catskill Mountain, dark blue transfer, Shell border series, crack in handle, very minor staining.............................................................400.00

**Plate**

7-1/2" d, Pass in the Catskill Mountains, dark blue transfer, imp "Wood & Son".............................................................330.00

7-1/2" d, The Landing of the Fathers at Plymouth, Dec 22, 1620, medium blue transfer, imp "Wood," wear and scratches, small flake.....................................................................50.00

7-1/2" d, Trenton Falls, dark blue transfer, shell border series.350.00

**Niagara from the American Side, Enoch Wood & Sons, 14-1/2" h, 11-1/2" w, $2,070. Photo courtesy of Skinner, Inc.**

8-3/8" d, Fall of Montmorenci, Near Quebec, dark blue transfer, imp "Wood," wear and scratches ................... 175.00

9-1/4" d, Gilpin's Mills, dark blue transfer, shell border series .. 450.00

9-1/4" d, Transylvania University Lexington, dark blue transfer, imp "Wood" ................ 250.00

9-1/4" d, View de Chateau Ermenonville, dark blue transfer, imp "Wood" ................ 300.00

9-1/2" d, B & O Railroad, inclined view, dark blue transfer, shell border series, imp "Wood & Sons," minor staining and hairline crack ................ 550.00

9-7/8" d, Albany, dark blue transfer, shell border series .. 1,800.00

9-7/8" d, London Views Hanover Lodge Regent's Park, Enoch Wood & Sons, knife marks ................ 200.00

10" d, Naval Battle, Constitution and the Guerriere, shell border, minor staining ................ 1,200.00

10-1/8" d, The Landing of the Fathers at Plymouth, Dec 22, 1620, medium blue transfer, transfer mark "Enoch Wood," wear and small edge chips ................ 50.00

10-1/4" d, American Independence, Landing of the Fathers at Plymouth, medium blue transfer, very minor staining and wear to front ................ 300.00

10-1/4" d, Commodore MacDonnough, dark blue transfer, shell order series ................ 375.00

10-1/4" d, Table Rock Niagara, dark blue transfer, imp "Wood" ................ 300.00

10-1/2" d, Fisherman, red transfer, imp "Wood," pinpoint rim flakes ................ 220.00

Platter

12-1/2" d, Highlands, Hudson River, steam boat, dark blue transfer ................ 1,650.00

16-1/2" l, 13" w, Lake George, NY, Shell border series, dark blue transfer, imp "Wood," 2" crack to rim ................ 1,900.00

18-3/4" l, 14-1/2" w, Castle Garden, Battery, NY, Shell border series, dark blue transfer, three minor stain spots on back ............ 2,600.00

Saucer, MacDonnough's Victory, dark blue transfer, imp "Wood" .... 150.00

Sauce Tureen and Tray, Boston State House, medium blue transfer, tureen unmarked, tray imp "Wood," stains and chip on table ring of tray ................ 715.00

Soup Tureen, cov, 15" l, 11" h, Dix Cove on the Gold Coast Africa, dark blue transfer, imp "Enoch Wood & Sons, Burslem," int. staining 4,890.00

Sugar Bowl, cov, 6-3/4" h, 6-1/2" w handle to handle, Commodore MacDonnough's Victory, dark blue transfer, teapot lid, repair to bottom rim, cracks in base ................ 500.00

Teapot, 8" h, 11" w handle to spout, Franklin's Tomb, dark blue transfer of Lafayette at Franklin's Tomb, imp "Enoch Wood & Sons," cracks, replaced rim chip ................ 500.00

Toddy Plate

5-1/4" d, Panoramic Scenery, R.S.W., dark blue transfer, wear and some glaze imperfections ................ 175.00

5-3/4" d, House in the woods, dark blue transfer, imp "Woods" ................ 150.00

# STAFFORDSHIRE ITEMS

**History:** A wide variety of ornamental pottery items originated in England's Staffordshire district, beginning in the 17th century and still continuing today. The height of production took place from 1820 to 1890.

These naive pieces are considered folk art by many collectors. Most items were not made carefully; some even were made and decorated by children.

The types of objects are varied, e.g., animals, cottages, and figurines (chimney ornaments).

**References:** Susan and Al Bagdade, *Warman's English & Continental Pottery & Porcelain*, 3rd Edition, Krause Publications, 1998; Pat Halfpenny, *English Earthenware*

*Figures*, Antique Collectors' Club, 1992; Adele Kenny, *Staffordshire Spaniels*, Schiffer Publishing, 1997; Griselda Lewis, *A Collector's History of English Pottery*, 5th ed., Antique Collectors' Club, 1999; Arnold R. Mountford, *The Illustrated Guide to Staffordshire Salt-Glazed Stoneware*, Barrie & Jenkins, 1971; Clive Mason Pope, *A-Z of Staffordshire Dogs*, Antique Collectors' Club, Ltd., 1996; P. D. Gordon Pugh, *Staffordshire Portrait Figures of the Victorian Era*, Antique Collectors' Club, 1987; Dennis G. Rice, *English Porcelain Animals of the 19th Century*, Antique Collectors' Club, 1989. Louis T. Stanley, *Collecting Staffordshire Pottery*, Doubleday & Co., 1963.

**Museums:** American Antiquarian Society, Worcester, MA; Brighton Museum, England; British Museum, London, England; City Museum and Art Gallery, Stoke-on-Trent, England; The Detroit Museum of Arts, Detroit, MI; Fitzwilliam Museum, Cambridge, England; Victoria & Albert Museum, London, England.

**Note:** The key to price is age and condition. As a general rule, the older the piece, the higher the price.

ABC Plate, 7" d, dancing figures in center, raised alphabet border, discolored ................ 75.00

Animal Dish, cov, 8" l, hen, black and white, light brown basketweave base ................ 275.00

Bank, 5" h, cottage, white snow on roof, two chimneys, black outline, c1885 ................ 225.00

Bowl, 11" d, creamware, mottled brown lead glaze, irregularly depressed interior center glazed in green and yellow, late 18th C, restored rim ................ 1,265.00

Box, 3-5/8" l, primrose ground, emb, painted sprays of flowers, gilt metal mounts ................ 275.00

Cheese Dish, cov, 10" l, 8-1/2" w, 7" h, blue and white Parrot Tulip, William Ridgeway ................ 125.00

Chimney Piece

8-1/2" h, Eva and Uncle Tom, polychrome and gilt, crazing and repair ................ 200.00

10-3/8" h, Uncle Tom with Little Eve on shoulder, polychrome, crazing ................ 450.00

## Reproduction Alert:

Early Staffordshire figurines and hollowware forms were molded. Later examples were made using a slip-casting process. Slip casting leaves telltale signs that are easy to spot. Look in the interior. Hand molding created a smooth interior surface. Slip casting produces indentations that conform to the exterior design. Holes occur where handles meet the body of slip-cast pieces. There is not hole in a hand-molded piece.

A checkpoint on figurines is the firing or vent hole, which is a necessary feature on these forms. Early figurines had small holes; modern reproductions feature large holes often the size of a dime or quarter. Vent holes are found on the sides or hidden among the decoration in early Staffordshire figurines; most modern reproductions have them in the base.

These same tips can be used to spot modern reproductions of Flow Blue, Majolica, Old Sleepy Eye, Stoneware, Willow, and other ceramic pieces.

Coffee, Tea, and Dessert Service, partial, Johnson Brothers, Garden Bouquet, six after dinner coffee cups, eight after dinner coffee saucers, oval open bowl, six cake plates, two oval condiment dishes, four coffee cups, eight dessert bowls, circular party tray with handle, cream pitcher, two handled cov sugar basin, ten teacups, six saucers, teapot, oval tray, three underplates ................................. 300.00

Creamer, 6" h, girl with flower basket, floral border, dark blue transfer, chips and cracks .................................................. 150.00

Figure

4" h, horse, flat back, polychrome dec ............................... 330.00

4" h, rooster, red, yellow, and green-yellow, white ground, chip on neck, minor flaking, early ..................................... 250.00

4-1/4" h, seated cat, sponged black and yellow, white ground, wear and chips ....................................................... 275.00

4-1/2" h, seated cat, sponged black and brown, white ground, glazed over crack at seam ..................................... 275.00

5" h, zebra, polychrome, late, repair ................................. 150.00

6-1/2" h, girl with oversized dog, red, white, blue, pink, and black, crazing ........................................................... 1,595.00

7" h, seated dog, black and white, polychrome dec, wear, chips on base and nose.................................................. 330.00

7-7/8" h, Scottish couple, very minor chip and loss ........... 230.00

9-1/2" h, earthenware, child with cornucopia, overglaze enamel dec, cornucopia rim chips restored, some retouched painting, early 19th C ....................................................... 225.00

11-1/2" h, English sailor, c1845-60 ..................................... 250.00

11-3/4" h, woman holding basket and flower bouquet, dog at her side, 19th C, minor chips, hairlines, glaze wear .............. 230.00

12-1/2" h, soldier at rest, leaning on musket, c1855-70...... 140.00

Fork, 6-7/8" l, agate, steel tines, c1760, handle broken and glued...230.00

Mug, 3-7/8" h, molded scenes, white, int. yellow frog with black spots, red eyes, rim chips ......................................................... 250.00

Pastille Burner, 4-3/8" h, house, yellow sides, gray windows, roofed ochre door, olive green roof, two yellow chimneys with brown edging, green grassy mount base, c1790 ............................................. 695.00

Plate, 10-1/2" d, Sevres pattern, Myott, c1915-25, price for set of ten ...................................................................... 175.00

Platter, 14-5/8" d, scrolling foliate border, reserves of manor houses, center reserve of game birds, blue and white transfer, second quarter 19th C .................................................................. 635.00

Spill Vase, 12" h, cow with calf, brightly colored ......................... 275.00

Stirrup Cup, 5-3/8" h, ironstone, fox head, shaded iron-red and ochre mask, gray and black muzzle and eyes, green collar edged in black and white, gilt center square, c1810 ...................................... 595.00

Sugar Bowl, cov, 5-1/2" h, genre scene of figures in foreground of manor house, ring handles, blue and white transfer, 19th C, minor chips, glaze wear ................................................................ 100.00

Tea Set, 6-1/2" x 11" teapot, creamer, sugar, seven handleless cups, ten saucers, basket of fruit and flower motif, dark blue transfer on pearlware, unmarked .................................................. 2,185.00

Vegetable Dish, 11-5/8" l, blue transfer scene of polar bears, imp "Enoch Woods," some edge wear ................................................ 990.00

Wash Bowl and Pitcher Set, 11" h pitcher, 13" d, 4" h bowl, light blue transfer, Aladdin pattern, basket weave edging ...................... 220.00

# STAFFORDSHIRE, ROMANTIC

**History:** In the 1830s, two factors transformed the blue-and-white printed wares of the Staffordshire potters into what is now called "Romantic Staffordshire." Technical innovations expanded the range of transfer-printed colors to light blue, pink, purple, black, green, and brown. There was also a shift from historical to imaginary scenes with less printed detail and more white space, adding to the pastel effect.

Shapes from the 1830s are predominantly rococo with rounded forms, scrolled handles, and floral finials. Over time, patterns and shapes became simpler and the earthenware bodies coarser. The late 1840s and 1850s saw angular gothic shapes and pieces with the weight and texture of ironstone.

The most dramatic post-1870 change was the impact of the craze for all things Japanese. Staffordshire designs adopted zigzag border elements and motifs such as bamboo, fans, and cranes. Brown printing dominated this style, sometimes with polychrome enamel highlights.

**Marks:** Wares are often marked with pattern or potter's names, but marking was inconsistent and many authentic, unmarked examples exist. The addition of "England" as a country of origin mark in 1891 helps to distinguish 20th-century wares made in the romantic style.

**References:** Susan and Al Bagdade, *Warman's English & Continental Pottery & Porcelain*, 3rd Edition, Krause Publications, 1998; Jeffrey B. Snyder, *Romantic Staffordshire Ceramics*, Schiffer Publishing, 1997; Petra Williams, *Staffordshire: Romantic Transfer Patterns* (1978), *Staffordshire II* (1986), *Staffordshire III* (1996), Fountain House East (P.O. Box 99298, Jeffersontown, KY 40269).

**Museums:** City Museum & Art Gallery, Stoke-on-Trent, England; Henry Ford Museum, Dearborn, MI.

Arabesque, gray-blue, Edwards & Son

Creamer............................................................. 60.00

Gravy Boat......................................................... 50.00

Relish, small, oblong.......................................... 35.00

Vegetable Dish, open.......................................... 45.00

Waste Bowl......................................................... 40.00

Balantyre, J Alcock

Bowl, 8" d............................................................ 45.00

Cup Plate ............................................................ 55.00

Creamer.............................................................. 50.00

Plate, 10-1/2" d ................................................... 35.00

Teapot ................................................................. 195.00

Caledonia, William Adams, c1800-65

Bowl..................................................................... 45.00

Creamer............................................................... 55.00

Cup and Saucer................................................... 45.00

Plate, 8-1/2" d, pink.............................................. 75.00

Soup Plate, red transfer, 10-3/4" d, imp "Adams," stains, bruise on table ring ......................................................... 150.00

Sugar, cov........................................................... 85.00

Canna, platter, red transfer, 18" l, edge wear, minor stains ........ 385.00

Canova, T. Mayer

Platter, 17-1/2" x 14-1/2", black transfer, minor staining ..... 300.00

Tureen, Underplate, brown transfer, 13-1/2" x 9" x 9-1/2" h tureen, 15" x 10-3/4" underplate, staining, chips, crack to underplate, lid missing ........................................................... 100.00

Vegetable, cov, red transfer, 12-1/2" l, Mayer, stains, chips 225.00

Etruscan Vase, blue and brown, Thomas, John, Joseph Mayer, c1843-55

Bowl, 7" d............................................................ 45.00

Plate, 10-1/2" d ................................................... 55.00

Platter, 16 x 11-1/2" ............................................ 145.00

Relish, 5" l ........................................................... 45.00

Soup Plate, wide flange....................................... 65.00

Fairy Queen, pitcher, 9-1/2" h, purple transfer, edge wear, small flake on foot .............................................................. 275.00

Garden Scenery, pink, Mayer

Bowl, 4" d............................................................ 35.00

Cup and Saucer................................................... 65.00

**Cup and Saucer, Venus, Podmore, Walker & Co., pink, $45.**

Cup Plate .................................................... 45.00
Plate ........................................................... 55.00
Sauce Dish ................................................. 35.00
Soup Plate .................................................. 75.00
Teapot ....................................................... 175.00
Vegetable Bowl, open ................................ 85.00
Ivanhoe, Podmore Walker & Co, 1834-1859
Bowl ........................................................... 40.00
Creamer ...................................................... 60.00
Plate ........................................................... 45.00
Sugar, cov .................................................. 80.00
Oriental, Ridgway, c1830-34
Creamer ...................................................... 75.00
Cup and Saucer, handleless ....................... 75.00
Cup Plate .................................................... 60.00
Plate ........................................................... 85.00
Tureen, cov, octagonal .............................. 225.00
Park Scenery, G. Philips, platter, 18" x 15", brown and white,
staining ....................................................... 255.00
Priory, Edward Challinor and Co, c1853-1862
Bowl ........................................................... 45.00
Creamer ...................................................... 65.00
Cup and Saucer, handleless ....................... 45.00
Plate ........................................................... 55.00
Platter ......................................................... 95.00
Soup Plate .................................................. 85.00
Toddy Plate, 5" d, light blue ....................... 45.00
Royal Cottage, sauce tureen, underplate, 8-3/4" l, light blue transfer,
plain white ladle ......................................... 250.00
Undina, black and blue, J Clementson, registered Jan 7, 1852
Plate ........................................................... 45.00
Relish, oval, shell shaped ........................... 65.00
Wash Bowl and Pitcher ............................... 295.00

# STAINED and/or LEADED GLASS PANELS

**History:** American architects in the second half of the 19th century and the early 20th century used stained- and leaded-glass panels as a chief decorative element. Skilled glass craftsmen assembled the designs, the best known being Louis C. Tiffany.

The panels are held together with soft lead cames or copper wraps. When purchasing a panel, protect your investment by checking the lead and making any necessary repairs.

**Reference:** Web Wilson, *Great Glass in American Architecture,* E. P. Dutton, New York, 1986.

**Periodicals:** *Glass Art Magazine*, P.O. Box 260377, Highlands Ranch, CO 80126; *Glass Patterns Quarterly,*

P.O. Box 131, Westport, NY 40077; *Professional Stained Glass*, P.O. Box 69, Brewster, NY 10509; *Stained Glass*, 6 SW 2nd St., #7, Lees Summit, MO 64063.

**Collectors' Club:** Stained Glass Association of America, P.O. Box 22462, Kansas City, MO 64113.

**Museum:** Corning Museum of Glass, Corning, NY.

Leaded Door Panel
32" w, 70" h, leaded and stained, Arts & Crafts multicolored florals, fold and white striated background minor flaws .... 4,000.00
36" w, 78" h, rect, art glass and striated glass segments, large stylized iris blossoms and buds in foreground, yellow, orange, blue, and green, stylized pink hydrangea blossoms, striated pink and green background, wooden frame, few cracked segments ................................................... 5,000.00
Panel
18" h, 36" w, Art Nouveau lily pads in pond motif, framed, some bowing in glass, few pieces cracked ................................. 850.00
25-1/8" w, 44-1/2" h, rect, multicolored transparent and leaded glass segments arranged to depict seated woman holding a book, flanked by two pillars, leafy vines with red berries in background, wood frame, America, late 19th C, few cracked segments ................................................................ 4,025.00
31-1/4" w, 56" h, Egyptian-Revival, scarab over two rows of stylized papyrus, polychrome hammered and slag glass with clear glass panels, wood frame, ring mounting hooks, few minor cracks ................................................................. 3,000.00
Window
15-3/4" w, 31-3/4" l, oval, transparent and slag glass segments on ground of segmented transparent blue glass arranged to depict two stylized fleur-de-lis centered with round floral medallions, one medallion lifts and rotates to reveal round colorless glass window, oval window frame, attributed to Belcher Mosaic Glass Co., some cracks to frame ............................................. 1,610.00
16" w, 36" h, rect shaped, Arts & Crafts stylized flowers on stems, three buds of striated pink and green glass, yellow striated glass center, surrounded by geometric shaped colorless glass panels, oak window frame, price for pr ......................................... 600.00
31-1/2" w, 45" h, rect border segments of bottle green, aqua slag, and amber glass, center square of colorless glass with beveled edges, transparent green glass ground with geometric arranged octagon and lozenge shaped segments, John Lafarge, from Thomas Elwood Grover house, Canton, MA, some cracked segments ................................................................ 635.00

**Window, Tiffany, garden scene, stream, irises, trees, multicolored, $112,000. Photo courtesy of Fontaine's Auction Gallery.**

## Stained

Panel

14-3/8" w, 12-1/8" h, female saint, framed with lead caning, Continental ........................................................................ 320.00

25" w, 40" h, multicolored panels, stenciled boar's head and stenciled horse's head, three large clear panels, several round amber jewels on side ......................................... 375.00

Roundel, 11-3/4" d, wealthy woman in beaded necklace, caned surround, Continental, late 18th/early 19th C, old repair to one chip .............. 200.00

Window

18-1/2" w, 31-1/2" h, stained pattern of curtains pulled back revealing owl on tree branch, moon and stars, showing books and glowing candle, curtain glass raised to further illustrate a further pulled back curtain, tied with tieback ................. 3,450.00

30" w, 44-1/2" h, scenic view at twilight with trees, path leading across meadow to forest, framed, two glass panels cracked ....................................................... 1,600.00

# STANGL POTTERY BIRDS

**History:** Stangl ceramic birds were produced from 1940 until the Stangl factory closed in 1978. The birds were produced at Stangl's Trenton plant and either decorated there or shipped to its Flemington, New Jersey, outlet for hand painting.

During World War II, the demand for these birds, and other types of Stangl pottery as well, was so great that 40 to 60 decorators could not keep up with the demand. Orders were contracted out to be decorated by individuals in their own homes. These orders then were returned for firing and finishing. Colors used to decorate these birds varied according to the artist.

**Marks:** As many as ten different trademarks were used. Almost every bird is numbered; many are artist signed. However, the signatures are used only for dating purposes and add very little to the value of the birds.

**References:** Harvey Duke, *Stangl Pottery*, Wallace-Homestead, 1992; Robert C. Runge, Jr., *The Collector's Encyclopedia of Stangl Dinnerware,* 1998, 2000 value update; Mike Schneider, *Stangl and Pennsbury Birds*, Schiffer Publishing, 1994.

**Collectors' Clubs:** American Art Pottery Association, P.O. Box 834, Westport, MA 02790-0697, http://www.amart-pot.org; Stangl/Fulper Collectors Club, P.O. Box 538, Flemington, NJ 08822.

**Additional Listings:** See *Warman's Americana & Collectibles* for more examples.

**Advisor:** Bob Perzel.

**Note:** Several birds were reissued between 1972 and 1977. These reissues are dated on the bottom and are worth approximately the same as older birds if well decorated.

3250, Gazing Duck, Antique Gold ................................................ 60.00
3250, Preening Duck ............................................................. 125.00
3273, Rooster, 5-3/4" h ......................................................... 650.00
3274, Penguin ..................................................................... 500.00
3275, Turkey ....................................................................... 475.00
3276, Bluebird ..................................................................... 80.00
3285, Rooster, 4-1/2" h, early blue green base ......................... 100.00
3286, Hen, 4-1/2" h, late lime green base ................................. 50.00
3285, 3286, Rooster and Hen shakers, late, pr ......................... 100.00

**#2376, blue and yellow, $75.**

3400, Lovebird, old, wavy base ................................................ 120.00
3400, Lovebird, revised leaf base ............................................. 60.00
3402, Pair of Orioles, revised ................................................. 125.00
3402, Pair of Orioles, old ...................................................... 250.00
3404, Pair of Lovebirds, old ................................................... 400.00
3404, Pair of Lovebirds, revised .............................................. 125.00
3405, Pair of Cockatoos, revised, open base ............................ 175.00
3406, Pair of Kingfishers, blue ............................................... 150.00
3407, Owl .......................................................................... 325.00
3431, Duck, standing ........................................................... 500.00
3432, Rooster, 16" h ......................................................... 2,000.00
3443, Flying Duck, teal ......................................................... 350.00
3444, Cardinal, pink, glossy .................................................. 100.00
3445, Rooster, yellow .......................................................... 220.00
3446, Hen, gray .................................................................. 225.00
3449, Parakeet ................................................................... 200.00
3450, Passenger Pigeon ..................................................... 1,300.00
3451, William Ptarmigan ..................................................... 2,500.00
3453, Mountain Bluebird ..................................................... 1,100.00
3454, Key West Quail Dove, single wing up ............................. 350.00
3454, Key West Quail Dove, both wings up .............................. 750.00
3455, Shoveler Duck .......................................................... 2,300.00
3457, Walking Pheasant ...................................................... 1,800.00
3458, Quail ....................................................................... 1,200.00
3459, Falcon/Fish Hawk/Osprey .......................................... 3,000.00
3490, Pair of Redstarts ........................................................ 225.00
3492, Cock Pheasant ........................................................... 225.00
3518, Pair of White Headed Pigeons ....................................... 650.00
3580, Cockatoo, medium ...................................................... 165.00
3580, Cockatoo, medium, white 350.00
3581, Group of Chickadees195.00
3581, Group of Chickadees, black and white ............................ 250.00
3582, Pair of Green Parakeets ............................................... 200.00
3582, Pair of Blue Parakeets ................................................. 275.00
3584, Cockatoo, large .......................................................... 300.00
3590, Chat ......................................................................... 165.00
3591, Brewers Blackbird150.00
3595, Bobolink ................................................................... 150.00
3596, Gray Cardinal .............................................................. 85.00
3597, Wilson Warbler, yellow .................................................. 45.00
3599, Pair of Hummingbirds ................................................... 300.00
3625, Bird of Paradise, large, 13-1/2" h ............................... 2,000.00
3627, Rivoli Hummingbird, with pink flower .............................. 150.00
3634, Allen Hummingbird ....................................................... 75.00
3635, Group of Goldfinches ................................................... 200.00
3715, Blue Jay with peanut .................................................... 650.00
3717, Pair of Blue Jays ...................................................... 3,500.00
3746, Canary, rose flower ...................................................... 225.00
3749, Scarlet Tanager .......................................................... 350.00
3750, Pair of Western Tanagers ............................................. 425.00
3751, Red Headed Woodpecker, pink glossy ............................ 225.00
3752, Pair of Red Headed Woodpeckers, red matte .................. 350.00
3754, Single White Winged Crossbill .................................... 2,500.00

3754, Pair of White Winged Crossbills, pink glossy.................... 350.00
3755, Audubon Warbler ...................................................................... 200.00
3756, Pair of Audubon Warblers.......................................................... 500.00
3757, Scissor-tailed Flycatcher....................................................... 650.00
3758, Magpie Jay.................................................................................. 1,250.00
3810, Blackpoll Warber ....................................................................... 165.00
3811, Chestnut Chickadee...................................................................... 85.00
3812, Chesnut Sided Warbler............................................................. 150.00
3813, Evening Grosbeak ...................................................................... 150.00
3814, Blackthroated Green Warbler....................................................... 165.00
3815, Western Bluebird ........................................................................ 400.00
3848, Golden Crowned Kinglet ............................................................ 100.00
3850, Yellow Warbler .......................................................................... 150.00
3852, Cliff Swallow.................................................................................. 125.00
3853, Group of Golden Crowned Kingfishers ............................. 600.00
3868, Summer Tanager ......................................................................... 600.00
3921, Yellow-headed Verdin ....................................................... 1,250.00

# STATUES

**History:** Beginning with primitive cultures, man created statues in the shape of people and animals. During the Middle Ages, most works were religious and symbolic in character and form. During the Renaissance, the human and secular forms were preferred.

During the 18th and 19th centuries, it was fashionable to have statues in the home. Many famous works were copied for use by the general public.

**Reference:** H. Nicholas B. Clark, *A Marble Quarry: The James H. Ricau Collection of Sculpture at the Chrysler Museum of Art*, Hudson Hills Press, 1997.

**St. Joseph and infant Christ, carved and painted wood, late 19th C, 84" h, $7,250. Photo courtesy of Jackson's Auctioneers & Appraisers.**

6-3/4" h, 5-3/4" w, 3" d, Verde Antico marble, seated wolf gazing upward, rockwork base, Continental, c1900, loss to one ear... 200.00

11-5/8" h, 7" l, bronze, sgd and dated "A. Rodin Pinx. 1905," inscribed "Alexis Rudier. Fondeur," late casting, marble base................. 400.00

12-1/2" h, 7-1/8" w, 4" d, patinated bronze, Muses Trepischore and Erato, Napoleon III, third quarter 19th C, scattered corrosion spots......... 900.00

14" h, 11-1/2" w, 8-1/2" d, black patinated bronze, youthful Alexander the Great mounting war horse, Russian, 4th quarter 19th C, sgd at right façade corner of base in Cyrillic ...................................... 900.00

16" h, bronze, woman, parcel gilt, bare breasted, standing on leopard skin, holding staff, mounted on revolving base .................... 1,650.00

17" h, painted metal, The Marley Horse, after Guillaume Coustou, wood base ............................................................................................ 90.00

17-5/8" h, bronze, Thesee et le Minotaure, (Thesesus Slaying the Minoraur), base inscribed Barye (Antoine-Louis Bayre), dark green-ish-brown patina .............................................................................. 12,075.00

17-3/4" h, 6-3/4" l, bronze, Hoop Girl, sgd "G. Gorin," dark brown patina with golden brown highlights, variegated marble base .............. 1,700.00

18-1/4" h, alabaster, Water Nymph, seated on rock with maskhead fountain, sgd "G Pochini," Italian, c1880 ............................. 1,725.00

19-3/4" h, carved black stone, ancient female torso, polished smooth, resting on salmon color sq plinth............................................... 300.00

20" h, patinated bronze, semi-nude Atlas shouldering the world, Italian, Baroque-style, circular patinated bronze base...................... 1,200.00

22-1/2" h, 16" w, 9" d, patinated bronze, The Rattlesnake, Frederick Remington, c1909-10, sgd on base, copyright 09 and edition stamped "15/100," mounted on later gray oval marble base with brass title plaque ................................................................... 1,100.00

24-1/8" h, bronze, L'Armour, rich reddish-brown patina, sgd "Auguste Moreau Sept" .......................................................................... 1,800.00

25" h, patinated bronze, nude Apollo after the antique, 4th quarter 19th C, fig leaf detached, but present ........................................... 2,530.00

27-1/2" h, 26-1/2" w, carved and stained wood, seated cherub, arms outstretched, Continental, mid-19th C ................................... 1,955.00

29" h, 19" w, 10" d, white metal, unicorn on angled rock outcropping, black finish, sgd "T. J. Pairpoint, SD" .................................... 5,000.00

31-1/2" h, 11-1/2" w, carved and polychromed wood, bearded semi-nude angel, Colonial Spanish, mid-19th C, wear to polychrome ............ 920.00

32-1/2" h, carved, polychromed, and parcel-gilt wood, Blackamoor gondolier, Venetian, in 18th C style, c1900, elaborately gilded and polychromed costume ...................................................................... 2,530.00

33-3/4" h, bronze, Aurora, Art Nouveau style, holding scarf and diaphanous gown, standing in chariot, cupid and doves, Auguste Moreau, late 19th C.......................................................................................... 2,750.00

35-1/4" h, marble, Cupid, sgd "A. Bassetti Fec," 1876............. 3,300.00

36" h, bronze, Oyster Girl, medium brown and greenish patina, sgd "E Rousseau," French, 20th C ...................................................... 1,265.00

39" h, bronzed plaster, Dante, sculptor unknown, 19th C........... 350.00

41" h, marble, mythological Diana Being Birthed from the Water, unsigned, well executed, minor roughness, 3 broken fingers 6,000.00

42-1/2" h, 11-1/2" d, carved and polychromed wood, St. Sebastian, Colonial Spanish, second quarter 19th C, mounted on custom steel stand, damage and some elements missing ............................. 750.00

56" h, cast stone, polychrome, semi-nude female, laurel wreath, one hand clasping draped cloth, circular base, 18th C style, one raised hand incomplete ................................................................................. 750.00

61" h, iron, Allegorical Figure of Winter, sculptor unknown, 19th C ............................................................................................. 2,500.00

82" h, black patinated bronze, Atlas, mounted with armillary openwork sphere with German terrestrial globe, half size ................... 6,325.00

# STEIFF

**History:** Margarete Steiff, GmbH, established in Germany in 1880, is known for very fine-quality stuffed animals and dolls, as well as other beautifully made collectible toys. It is still in business, and its products are highly respected.

The company's first products were wool-felt elephants made by Margaret Steiff. In a few years, the animal line was expanded to include a donkey, horse, pig, and camel.

By 1903, the company also was producing a jointed mohair teddy bear, whose production dramatically increased to more than 970,000 units in 1907. Margarete's nephews took over the company at this point.

Newly designed animals were added: Molly and Bully, the dogs, and Fluffy, the cat. Pull toys and kites also were produced, as well as larger animals on which children could ride or play.

**Marks:** The bear's-head label became the symbol for the firm in about 1907, and the famous "Button in the Ear" round, metal trademark was added.

**References:** Peter Consalvi, Sr., *2nd Collector Steiff Values*, Hobby House Press, 1996; Margaret and Gerry Grey, *Teddy Bears*, Running Press, Courage Books, 1994; Dee Hockenberry, *Steiff Bears and Other Playthings Past and Present,* Schiffer Publishing, 2000; Margaret Fox Mandel, *Teddy Bears and Steiff Animals*, 1st Series (1984, 2000 value update), 2nd Series (1987, 2000 value update), 3rd Series (2000), Collector Books; ——, *Teddy Bears, Annalee Animals & Steiff Animals*, 3rd Series, Collector Books, 1990, 1996 value update; Dee Hockenberry, *Big Bear Book*, Schiffer Publishing, 1996; Linda Mullins, *Teddy Bear & Friends Price Guide*, 4th ed., Hobby House Press, 1993; Ken Yenke, *Teddy Bear Treasury,* Collector Books, 2000.

**Collectors' Clubs:** Steiff Club USA, 31 E. 28th St., 9th Floor, New York, NY 10016, http://www.steiff-club.com; Steiff Collectors Club, 5001 Monroe St., Toledo, OH 43623, http://www.toystorenet.com.

**Additional Listings:** Teddy Bears. See also Stuffed Toys in *Warman's Americana & Collectibles* for more examples.

**Notes:** Become familiar with genuine Steiff products before purchasing an antique stuffed animal. Plush in old Steiff animals was mohair; trimmings usually were felt or velvet. Unscrupulous individuals have attached the familiar Steiff metal button to animals that are not Steiff.

Cat, 7" h, plush cotton, green glass eyes, orig red rayon bow, c1930 ............................................................100.00
Circus Bear, 8-3/8" h, roly-poly, brown mohair, black steel eyes, shoe button nose, excelsior stuffing, wooden stick and metal chair, weighted wood base, c1897, base repair..............................1,265.00
Dog
   Airedale Terrier, glass eyes, c1951-61................................100.00
   Dachshund, 18" l, black and brown wool, fully jointed, black shoe button eyes, embroidered nose, mouth and claws, c1930, some fiber loss and repairs......................................................350.00

**Bambi, 1939, 32" h, $450.**

Fox Terrier, 11" l, rayon fur, mohair face and muzzle, glass eyes, black embroidered nose, mouth, and claws, leatherette collar, paper tag, 1930s, spotty fur loss and yellowing ...............175.00
   German Shepherd, 20" l ......................................................125.00
Elephant, 17-1/2" l, black button e yes, pull cord sound box, four wood wheels, c1920 ........................................................................295.00
Fish, 12" l, mohair, eye and fin missing ......................................230.00
Fox, 10-1/4" l, 5-1/2", mohair, fully jointed, glass eyes, embroidered nose, mouth, and claws, excelsior stuffing, c1913, ear button missing, slight moth damage ........................................................435.00
Lamb, 4-5/8" l, pile wool, felt face, ears, and legs, black bead eyes, pink embroidered nose and mouth, c1913..............................575.00
Monkey, Jocko, 6-1/2" h, orig hang tag........................................60.00
Teddy Bear
   3" h, buff mohair, fully jointed, black bead eyes, black embroidered nose and mouth, ear button, no pads, c1905 ........690.00
   3" h, white mohair, fully jointed, black bead eyes, rust embroidered nose and mouth, ear button, no pads, c1905
   3-3/4" h, yellow mohair, fully jointed, black embroidered nose and mouth, c1905 ................................................................420.00
   5-1/2" h, light golden mohair, fully jointed, black steel eyes, black embroidered nose and mouth, no pads, excelsior stuffing, c1905, minor fur loss.....................................................1,035.00
   5-1/2" h, yellow mohair, fully jointed, glass eyes, black embroidered nose and mouth, no pads, c190u, overall traces of fur, no button ...............................................................................435.00
   9-1/2" h, blond mohair, fully jointed, black steel eyes, brown embroidered nose, mouth, and claws, felt pads, excelsior stuffing, c1905, button missing, spotty moth damage, needs stuffing............550.00
   9-1/2" h, light apricot mohair, fully jointed, black steel eyes, brown embroidered nose, mouth, and claws, felt pads, excelsior stuffing, c1905, button missing ................................................865.00
   12-1/2" h, golden mohair, fully jointed, black steel eyes, brown embroidered nose, mouth, and claws, felt pads, excelsior stuffing, c1909, ear button, spotty fur loss ..........................1,380.00
   13" h, light yellow mohair, fully jointed, black steel eyes, black embroidered nose, mouth, and claws, replaced felt pads, c1905, spotty fur loss, new nose stitching....................1,495.00
   15" h, light golden mohair, fully jointed, black steel eyes, black embroidered nose, mouth, and claws, tan felt pads, excelsior stuffing, c1905, button missing......................................3,220.00
   15-1/2" h, golden apricot mohair, fully jointed, black steel eyes, brown embroidered nose, mouth, and black claws, felt pads, excelsior stuffing, blank ear button, c1905, cotton jacket, spotty fur loss, pad damage......................................................1,610.00
   16" h, golden mohair, fully jointed, black steel eyes, brown embroidered nose, mouth, and claws, felt pads, excelsior stuffing, c1905, button missing ...........................................7,475.00
   16" h, light apricot mohair, fully jointed, black steel eyes, dark brown embroidered nose, mouth, and claws, felt pads, excelsior stuffing, c1905.............................................................4,325.00
   19" h, long curly golden mohair, fully jointed, black steel eyes, brown embroidered nose, mouth, and claws, excelsior stuffing, c1905, replaced pad, fiber unstable on muzzle, button missing ....1,850.00
   20" h, cinnamon mohair, fully jointed, center seam, black steel eyes, black embroidered nose, mouth, and claws, tan felt pads, c1905, some fur loss on muzzle...................................12,650.00
   24" h, ginger mohair, fully jointed, center seam, black steel eyes, brown embroidered nose, mouth, and claws, excelsior stuffing, c1905, button missing, fiber loss on muzzle ................4,600.00

# STEINS

**History:** Steins, mugs especially made to hold beer or ale, range in size from the smaller 3/10 and 1/4 liter to the larger 1, 1-1/2, 2, 3, 4, and 5 liters, and in rare cases to 8 liters. (A liter is 1.05 liquid quarts.)

Master steins or pouring steins hold 3 to 5 liters and are called krugs. Most steins are fitted with a metal hinged lid with thumb lift. The earthenware character-type steins usually are German in origin.

**References:** Susan and Al Bagdade, *Warman's English & Continental Pottery & Porcelain*, 3rd Edition, Krause Publications, 1998; Gary Kirsner, *German Military Steins*, 2nd ed., Glentiques (P.O. Box 8807, Coral Springs, FL 33075), 1996; ——, *Mettlach Book*, 3rd ed., 1994; Gary Kirsner and Jim Gruhl, *The Stein Book, A 400 Year History,* Glentiques, 1990.

**Periodicals:** *Regimental Quarterly*, P.O. Box 793, Frederick, MD 21705; *The Beer Stein Journal,* P.O. Box 8807, Coral Springs, FL 33075.

**Collectors' Clubs:** Stein Collectors International, P.O. Box 5005, Laurel, MD 20726-5005; Sun Steiners, P.O. Box 11782, Fort Lauderdale, FL 33339.

**Museum:** Milwaukee Art Center, Milwaukee, WI.

Anheuser Busch, Ceramarte, color
    Half Liter, City series, Stuttgart ............................................ 350.00
    Liter, Pilique .................................................................... 990.00
Capo-di-Monte, 8-1/4" h, painted pottery, lion finial, body with continuous hunt scene, late 19th C .................................................... 345.00
Character, half liter, porcelain
    Indian, E Bohne & Sohne, inlaid lid, chips on feathers ....... 340.00
    Munich child on barrel, Schierholz, porcelain lid, 5" h ........ 395.00
    Skull, E Bohne & Sohne, inlaid lid .................................... 465.00
    Von Motlke, tan, brown, Schierholz ................................ 1,250.00
Character, half liter, pottery, black man in white striped jacket, glazed finish No. 138, inlaid lid .................................................... 445.00
Earthenware, 7-7/8" h, polychrome dec earthenware, bird perched on branch, pewter lid and rims, illegible imp mark, Germany, 19th C .690.00
Glass, blown, third liter, beige, enameled cavalier, matching glass inlaid lid .................................................................... 215.00
Mettlach
    #1527, half liter, continuous scene of drunken men and musicians.................................................................... 320.00
    #2025, half liter, inlaid lid, carousing cherubs .................... 250.00
    #2182, quarter liter, PUG printed design of maiden with stem, 6-1/2" h .................................................................... 200.00
    #2752, half liter, two men drinking in tavern scene, sgd "Schlitt" .................................................................... 200.00
    #2782, Rookwood type, man drinking, shades of green and brown, mkd "Villeroy & Boch," imp number, transfer number 6127, hinged pewter lid, 18-3/4" h.................................. 900.00
    #3395, blue, bowling ball and scene, 12" h, 7" w................ 350.00
Military, half liter, stoneware, transfer and enamel dec, 8 Bavarian Infantry, Munchen, center scene, pewter lid with relief initials on top, large lion thumblift .................................................... 350.00
Musterschutz , 7" h, porcelain, pig form, German...................... 475.00
Occupation, half liter, porcelain, transfer and enamel dec
    Coach Driver, named to Diermeier, large scene of horses pulling coach, pewter lid, pewter tear and repair, base chip repaired .................................................................... 565.00
    Farming, named to Josef Fusseder, central scene, pewter lid.480.00

Salt Glazed Stoneware, blue accents, emb "Empire Theatre Wed. Ev March 30th, 100th Performance, The Conquerers," relief design of elves on front and back, relief design of children at play around bulbous base, mold mark #39, $525. Photo courtesy of Vicki & Bruce Waasdrop.

    Jockey, relief pewter lid of horse jumping stone wall with jockey, scratches on handle, base and pewter strap .................. 440.00
Regimental, half liter, porcelain
    9-1/2" h, 1 Chevauleger, Nurnberg 1904-07, named to Chevauleger Fischer, two side scenes, roster, lion thumblift, prism inlaid lid with scene of Chevauleger painted on underside, strap repoured, base chip repaired .......................................... 580.00
    10-1/2" h, 171 Infantry, Ludwigsburg, named to Musketier, name removed, pewter lid...................................................... 200.00
    11" h, 22 Infantry, Zweibrucken 1902-04, named to Res. Conrad, two side scenes, roster, lion thumblift ............................. 465.00
    12" h, 23 Infantry, Saargemund 1909-11, named to Res. Schwarz, two side scenes, roster, lion thumblift with stanhope, wear on roster.................................................................... 415.00
Salt Glaze
    8" h, bust of Washington on one side, framed German verse on opposite, blue accented gargoyle handle, attributed to Whites, Utica, NY, factory, mold mark #44 .................................. 350.00
    8" h, relief and blue accented profile of Nathan Hale on one side, framed German verse on opposite, relief and blue accented gargoyle handle, attributed to Whites, Utica, NY, factory, mold mark #43 .................................................................... 325.00
    10-1/4" h, Empire Theatre Wed. Eve March 30th, 100th Performance, The Conquerors, imp and blue accented, relief design of elves front and back, relief design of children at play around bulbous bottom, attributed to Whites, Utica, NY, factory, mold mark #39 .................................................................... 525.00
    10-1/2" h, thread relief of ducks, birds, and swans in wooded pond scene, relief rathskeller tavern scene on opposite side, both scenes heavily blue accented, attributed to Whites, Utica, NY, factory, mold mark #6, two very short in-the-making clay separations at rim .......................................................... 600.00
    12-1/2" h, relief design of woman playing tuba, vines and acorn in thread relief on opposite side, cobalt blue and brown accents, attributed to Whites, Utica, NY, factory, mold mark #5 ..... 800.00
    13" h, thread relief of medieval tavern scene, relief vine design on opposite side, brown and blue accents, attributed to Whites, Utica, NY, factory, mold mark #7 .................................... 475.00
    13-1/2" h, thread relief medieval tavern scene, vine and acorn design on opposite side, cobalt blue and brown accents, attributed to Whites, Utica, NY, factory, mold mark #7 ............. 365.00
    14-3/4" h, relief design of man toasting, child toasting on opposite side, blue accented bands on vine designs, attributed to Whites, Utica, NY, factory, mold mark #8, 1" very faint hairline at rim 475.00
    15" h, relief thread design of brown white, blue, and green man toasting, design of brown and blue child toasting on opposite side, green vine designs, attributed to Whites, Utica, NY, factory, mold mark #8 ................................................................ 700.00
    15-1/2" h, detailed heavy pewter lid, blue, brown, and green three color accents of man and woman reading on one side, framed German verse on opposite side, blue accented deep relief Northwind pouring spout, attributed to Whites, Utica, NY, factory, mold mark #00...................................................... 1,200.00
Stoneware
    7" h, Bristol glaze, relief and blue accented tavern scene on front, framed German verse on back, gargoyle handle, attributed to Whites, Utica, NY, factory, mold mark #43 ...................... 110.00

9" h, Bristol glaze, The Prince of Pilsen at shoulder, relief of man and woman dancing on one side, framed verse on opposite "Here's to the heart that beats for me," imp and blue accents, attributed to Whites, Utica, NY, factory............................ 250.00

10-1/2" h, relief design of man and woman drinking at table, upper half of woman accented in very dark green, brown accents in hair and background, additional cobalt blue accents, vine design with blue accents on opposite side, attributed to Whites, Utica, NY, factory, mold mark #6, professional restoration to short hairline........................................... 550.00

13" h, Bristol glaze, pewter lid, relief and blue accented design of Washington crossing the Delaware, attributed to Whites, Utica, NY, factory, mold mark #5, several in-the-making glaze misses . 160.00

Tin Glazed Earthenware, 8" d, polychrome dec of horse in landscape, pewter lid and rims, Germany, late 19th C ............................. 1,150.00

# STEUBEN GLASS

1903–32

**History:** Frederick Carder, an Englishman, and Thomas G. Hawkes of Corning, New York, established the Steuben Glass Works in 1904. In 1918, the Corning Glass Company purchased the Steuben company. Carder remained with the firm and designed many of the pieces bearing the Steuben mark. Probably the most widely recognized wares are Aurene, Verre De Soie, and Rosaline, but many other types were produced.

The firm is still operating, producing glass of exceptional quality.

**References:** Thomas P. Dimitroff, Charles R. Hajdamach, Jane Shadel Spillman, and Robert F. Rockwell III, *Frederick Carder and Steuben Glass: American Classic*, Schiffer Publishing, 1998; Paul Gardner, *Glass of Frederick Carder*, Crown Publishers, 1971; Kyle Husfloen, *Antique Trader's American & European Decorative and Art Glass Price Guide,* 2nd ed., Krause Publications, 2000; Paul Perrot, Paul Gardner, and James S. Plaut, *Steuben*, Praeger Publishers, 1974; Kenneth Wilson, *American Glass 1760-1930*, 2 vols., Hudson Hills Press and The Toledo Museum of Art, 1994.

**Museums:** Corning Museum of Glass, Corning, NY; Rockwell Museum, Corning, NY.

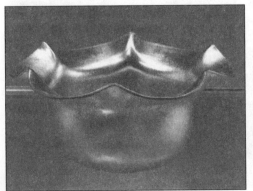

Aurene, bowl, gold, ruffled edge, sgd "Aurene" in silver, 5" d, 2" h, $230. Photo courtesy of David Rago Auctions.

## Aurene

Bowl

6" d, undulating ruffled rim, polished pontil, mkd "Aurene Haviland" within, early 20th C, minor nick edge of pontil ......... 460.00

6" d, 2-1/4" h, flared rim, gold irid finish, sgd "F. Carder, Aurene" in script on base................................................................ 520.00

9-5/8" d, 2-3/4" h, opaque white Calcite ext., irid gold int., polished pontil............................................................................... 230.00

10" d, flared rim, stepped bowl of opal glass, int. with strong gold irid, c1925, uneven irid, wear .......................................... 175.00

Centerbowl, 3-1/4" h, 12" d, catalog no. 2879, planter-form, inward curved rim, red-gold irid surface and int., polished base, inscribed "Aurene 2879," wear scratches on base ................................. 450.00

Jar, cov, 3-1/2" h, 5" w, blue ground, silver, blue, and purple irid, sgd "Aurene #1616" ...................................................................... 750.00

Lamp Shade, 4-1/8" h, 2-1/4" d top rim, gas, ten ribbed bell form, inverted and flared rim, silver fleur-de-lis stamp, c1915, light wear............. 230.00

Perfume Bottle, 7-1/2" h, gold, orig stopper, sgd "Aurene #1414," small flake to lip ................................................................................ 600.00

Potpourri Jar, cov, 5-3/4" h, catalog no. 2812, bright gold irid, oval body, conforming cov with three drilled fragrance holes, applied finial ... 650.00

Stemware, 7" h, deep gold, blue irid, flaring bowl, twisted stem, sgd "Aurene" and numbered, six pc set ...................................... 2,300.00

Tumbler, 4-1/2" h, gold, brilliant irid, sgd "Steuben #2361" ......... 120.00

Vase

5" h, flared ten-rib oval body, blue-purple irid luster, mirror bright near base, inscribed "Steuben" ..................................... 1,100.00

5-1/2" h, catalog no. 913, ten-ribbed flared body, blue, base inscribed "Steuben" .......................................................... 600.00

5-3/4" h, 6-1/4" w, gold, bulbous, irid blue and green highlights ......................................................................950.00

12" h, Catalog 2683, strong gold irid, base inscribed "Steuben Aurene 2683," polished pontil, c1928, minor scratches 3,750.00

## Bristol Yellow

Urn, cov, 9" h, 4" d, swirled yellow cover and body, optic base, green cone shaped finial, rough pontil, block and fleur-de-lis marks . 260.00

Vase, 7" h, 6-3/4" d, flared rim, cylindrical swirled body, circular foot, polished pontil, fleur-de-lis mark, c1925, some base wear ...... 175.00

## Calcite

Bowl

6" d, 2-5/8" h, wide flared rim, gold aurene int., unmarked. 220.00

13-3/4" d, 3-1/2" h, gold aurene int., unmarked .................. 250.00

Parfait, gold, matching underplate .............................................. 165.00

Sherbet, gold, matching underplate ............................................ 155.00

Salt, 2-5/8" d ............................................................................... 85.00

## Cluthra

Vase

4-3/4" h, 6-7/8" d, wide mouth, angular body, bubble glass shading from green to white, polished pontil fleur-de-lis mark on base...........................................................................690.00

10-1/4" h, Catalog 2683, raised flared rim over broad shouldered ovoid vessel, mottled light green and white cluthra, polished pontil, acid fleur-de-lis mark on base, c1927, minor wear ........ 700.00

## Crystal

Animal

Eagle, catalog no. 1172, David Dowler design ................. 2,315.00

Fox, catalog no. 8260, Lloyd Atkins design, seated with tail wrapped, inscribed "Steuben" on base, c1971.............. 1,265.00

Gazelle, catalog no. 7399, leaping Art Deco figures, molded rect plinth, stylized curvilinear Frederick Carder and Sidney Waugh design, base inscribed "Steuben," price for pr .............. 1,150.00

Geese, catalog no. 8519, 5-1/4" h gander, 4" h preening goose, Lloyd Atkins design, price for pr ...................................... 350.00

Horse, catalog no. 7727, Sidney Waugh design, stylized Clydesdale, base inscribed "Steuben," 1930s.......................... 1,035.00

Koala, catalog no. 8268, Lloyd Atkins design, base inscribed "Steuben," 1976 ....................................................... 1,100.00
Owl, catalog no. 8064, Donald Polland design, frosted eyes, base inscribed "Steuben," smoothed base edge ...................... 300.00
Squirrel, catalog no. 8291, George Thompson design, upright, tail extended, inscribed "Steuben" ........................................ 900.00

Bowl

10" d, Trillium, slightly tri-corn shaped bowl, trillium shaped foot, inscribed "Steuben," design created 1958, Madigan 8089....345.00
10" d, 4-1/2" h, flared, colorless body, four scrolled feet, disk base, inscribed "Steuben," design created 1940, Madigan 7884....260.00

Creamer and Sugar, catalog no. 7907/7906, John Dreves design, each inscribed "Steuben," price for pr..................................575.00
Decanter Set, trapped bubble stopper, teardrop shaped vessel of colorless glass, two matching cordials, bases inscribed "Steuben," design by Samuel Ayres, 1939, Madigan 7736........................260.00
Paperweight/Doorstop, catalog no. 7257, solid, controlled bubbles and silvered cushion, center bright pink Cintra five-petaled lily blossoms, fleur-de-lis stamp on base, 4" h, 4-1/2" d ................................300.00
Vase, 12-1/2" h, masterwork, exhibition piece designed by Sidney Waugh to commemorate Paul Revere's ride, three vignettes, base inscribed "Steuben" ............................................... 3,450.00

# Ivrene

Candleholders, pr, 3-1/2" h, 4" l, catalog no. 7564, Grotesque, irid white, oval ribbed and folded bobeche cups, base inscribed "Steuben," one ruffle rough ...................................... 435.00
Centerbowl, 7" h, 12" l, 7-1/2" w, catalog no. 7449, Grotesque, four-rib oval, lustrous opaque white, manipulated undulating rim, base evened, minor chips ................................................ 350.00
Lamp Shade, 4-1/2" h, 3-1/2" d, opaque white glass, slight irid finish, acid etched medallion and swag design, fleur-de-lis mark on edge........90.00
Vase

5" h, 5" d, wide mouth, flared rim, rippled texture to bulbous base, circular foot, sgd in script on base "F. Carder Steuben" ...350.00
8" h, Catalog 8453, flared rim, classic form, opal white body, faint irid sheen, polished pontil, c1920, later signature ............ 800.00

# Jade

Bowl

4-5/8" d, 2-1/2" h, flared rim, semi-opaque yellow jade, polished pontil................................................................350.00
11-1/4" d, 4" h, green, wide flat rim, bulbous body, circular foot, polished pontil, fleur-de-lis mark on base, wear to base..520.00

Candlestick, 8" h, 4-1/2" d, attributed to Catalog #2956, green jade rim and candle cup, turned paler green stem raised on wide circular foot, stem repair, crack int. of candle cup........................................ 150.00
Compote, 7" d, 23/4" h, shallow green jade bowl and stem, alabaster foot, polished pontil, edge roughness ...................................... 260.00
Lamp, 32-1/2" h, Catalog 7008, urn form body, green jade glass with acid etched design in Sculptured pattern of stylized chrysanthemums, gilt metal lamp fittings, c1925 ...................................... 920.00
Plate, 8-1/2" d, green, wide rim, overall swirl design, block letter mark on one, set of four ................................................................260.00
Vase

6" h, Catalog Variant 6287, ribbed fan body of green jade glass, alabaster knobbed standard and disk foot, polished pontil, c1920, dark inclusions....................................................800.00
6-7/8" h, 6-7/8" d, green swirl, wide mouth, cylindrical form on circular foot, polished pontil, fleur-de-lis mark on base........375.00
7" h, Catalog 5007, elongated and flared neck, bulbous body, dark yellow, applied handles at sides suspending twisted rings, polished pontil, c1925, minor inclusion ......................... 2,100.00

# Miscellaneous

Bowl, 7-7/8" w, 4-3/4" h, Alabaster, Catalog Variant 6415, gently flared and shaped rim, broad pillared bowl, c1925 .......................... 1,495.00
Cologne Bottle, Catalog 6917, faceted stopper, heavy walled crystal bottle

7" h, internally dec with white and black cluthra glass and trapped bubbles, ext. deeply engraved with cross hatch and arched recesses, rubbed fleur-de-lis acid mark on base, c1930, few nicks ................................................................. 4,350.00
7-1/4" h, internally dec with silver flecks, pale green cintra and trapped bubbles, ext. deeply engraved with cross hatch and alternating facets, arched recesses, rubbed fleur-de-lis acid mark on base, c1930, few nicks, minor staining to air traps at top ................................................................. 4,600.00

Compote

7" d, 5" h, Silverina, pinched rim, shallow bowl, clear amethyst glass stem with median disc, circular foot with edge folded under, amethyst glass bowl and foot with mica flakes enclosed in diamond shaped air traps, rough pontil, fleur-de-lis mark near edge, c1925 .................................................................. 825.00
7-1/4" d, 4-7/8" h, ruffled edge of colorless glass with green threading on underside, trapped bubbles within shallow bowl, large tear shaped bubble in colorless glass swollen stem, circular foot, polished pontil .................................................. 175.00

Lamp, 33" h total, Catalog 8496, possibly Crest, Pegasus, gold Aurene drips over glass base of yellow jade layered with black and cameo etched scene of flying horses in Art Deco-style sky, cameo fleur-de-lis mark, minor bubble burst ................................................. 4,025.00
Lemonade Mug, 6" h, Matsu Noke catalog no. 3329, optic ribbed colorless goblet form, Pomona green cintra rim, handle, and three fan-shaped dec.................................................................. 230.00
Perfume Bottle, opal, light blue stopper, #5203 ...................... 700.00
Salt, 2-1/8" d, clear, blue threading.................................... 85.00
Torchere, 68" h, 9" shade, Oriental Poppy, internally striped pink-opal flared shade, pale green receding under flared rim, inserted into elaborate floor lamp with ram's heads, tassels, and beading above twisted metal shaft ................................................. 2,875.00
Vase

6-1/4" h, 8-1/4" d, Catalog 7565 variant, Wisteria, free form oval body with pillar lines, knob and domed foot of dichroic pink/blue glass, c1925, minor white inclusions............................... 635.00
10" h, amethyst, flared oval, pattern molded in swirled design, small sand grain dot.............................................. 350.00
12" h, Black Matsu, catalog no. 6391, flared rim, mirror black oval body, three full-length acid etched Ming trees, stylized cloud formations, triangular foil label ......................................... 1,100.00

# Rosaline

Boullion Cup and Saucer, alabaster handles ............................. 150.00
Bowl, 12-1/2" d, 6" h, deep rolled rim, sgd.................................. 575.00
Console Set, compote with wide, petal shaped rim on Rosaline bowl, circular alabaster foot, pr of Rosaline candlesticks with petal shaped rim and candle-cup, alabaster stem with median disc, whole raised on white circular Rosaline foot, all marked on foot.............. 2,415.00
Cup and Saucer, alabaster handle........................................... 150.00
Goblet, 6" h, flaring rim ..................................................... 135.00
Sherbet, matching underplate................................................ 175.00

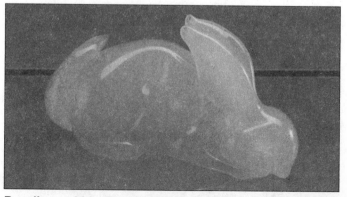

**Rosaline, rabbit, Rosaline body, alabaster ears, feet, and tail, 4-1/4" l, $310. Photo courtesy of David Rago Auctions.**

Vase

7" h, 5-3/4" d, short flared rim, bulbous Rosaline body, circular alabaster foot, polished pontil ..........................................250.00
12" h, cone shape, acid etched floral design, alabaster base, rough pontil, burst hole in alabaster petal ....................1,035.00

## Threaded

Bowl, 5-3/8" h, Catalog 6778 variant, flared colorless body, diamond optic pattern, blue threaded dec around rim, fleur-de-lis acid stamp, polished pontil, c1920 ................................................230.00
Compote, 7" h, shallow blue bowl with yellow threading around underside, long stem on circular folded foot, fleur-de-lis mark ..........200.00
Vase, 7-1/2" h, 5" d, wide mouth barrel form, quilted colorless glass body, black threading on top third, fleur-de-lis mark on base...150.00

## Verre de Soie

Bowl, 9-3/4" d, 2" h, wide squat bulbous form, polished pontil, abrasions ..........................................................................350.00
Tazza, 8" d, 3-1/2" h, irid, stretched edge ...................................395.00
Vase

3-1/4" h, 4" d, wide flaring rim with blue reeding, narrow neck flaring to bulbous base, faint fleur-de-lis mark, some reeding disconnected..................................................................130.00
7-7/8" h, 4" d, wide mouth, narrow rim, tapering cylindrical form, copper wheel engraved floral design, polished pontil ......460.00
8" h, Catalog 6813, ruffled and flared rim, molded quilt verre de soie glass, red threading, c1925 ......................................260.00
8-3/8" h, narrow etched rim on wide shoulder, cylindrical form, tapering to foot, copper wheel engraved floral design .....490.00
11-1/2" h, Catalog 676 variant, ruffled rim, goblet shape body, slender stem, disc foot, dec at top with stretched irid over pulled and swirled green band, early 20th C ...........................2,185.00

# STEVENGRAPHS

**History:** Thomas Stevens of Coventry, England, first manufactured woven silk designs in 1854. His first bookmark was produced in 1862, followed by the first Stevengraphs, perhaps in 1874, but definitely by 1879 when they were shown at the York Exhibition. The first portrait Stevengraphs (of Disraeli and Gladstone) were produced in 1886, and the first postcards incorporating the woven silk panels in 1904. Stevens offered many other items with silk panels, including valentines, fans, pincushions, and needle cases.

Stevengraphs are miniature silk pictures, matted in cardboard, and usually having a trade announcement or label affixed to the reverse. Other companies, notably W. H. Grant of Coventry, copied Stevens' technique. Their efforts should not be confused with Stevengraphs.

Collectors in the U.S. favor the Stevengraphs with American-related views, such as "Signing of the Declaration of Independence," "Columbus Leaving Spain," and "Landing of Columbus." Sports-related Stevengraphs such as ""The First Innings" (baseball), and "The First Set" (tennis) are also popular, as well as portraits of Buffalo Bill, President and Mrs. Cleveland, George Washington, and President Harrison.

Postcards with very fancy embossing around the aperture in the mount almost always have Stevens' name printed on them. The two most popular embossed postcard series in the U.S. are "Ships" and "Hands across the Sea." The latter set incorporates two crossed flags and two hands shaking. Seventeen flag combinations have been found, but only seven are common. These series generally are not printed with Stevens' name. Stevens also produced silks that were used in cards made by the Alpha Publishing Co.

Stevens' bookmarks are longer than they are wide, have mitered corners at the bottom, and are finished with a tassel. Many times his silks were used as the top or bottom half of regular bookmarks.

**Marks:** Thomas Stevens' name appears on the mat of the early Stevengraphs, directly under the silk panel. Many of the later portraits and the larger silks (produced initially for calendars) have no identification on the front of the mat other than the phrase "woven in pure silk" and have no label on the back.

Bookmarks originally had Stevens' name woven into the foldover at the top of the silk, but soon the identification was woven into the fold-under mitered corners. Almost every Stevens' bookmark has such identification, except the ones woven at the World's Columbian Exposition in Chicago, 1892 to 1893.

**References:** Geoffrey A. Godden, *Stevengraphs and Other Victorian Silk Pictures*, Associated University Presses, 1971; Chris Radley, *Woven Silk Postcard*, privately printed, 1978; Austin Sprake, *Price Guide to Stevengraphs*, Antique Collectors' Club, 1972.

**Collectors' Club:** Stevengraph Collectors' Association, 2829 Arbutus Rd, #2103, Victoria, British Columbia, V8N 5X5, Canada.

**Museums:** Herbert Art Gallery and Museum, Coventry, England; Paterson Museum, Paterson, NJ.

**Note:** Prices are for pieces in mint or close-to-mint condition.

## Bookmarks

Assassination, Abraham Lincoln.................................................395.00
Centennial, USA 1776-1876, General George Washington, The Father of Our Country, The First in Peace, The First in War, The First in the Hearts of Our Countrymen!, few small stains........................125.00
Forget-Me-Not, Godden #441 ....................................................350.00
Happy Birthday, framed ...............................................................50.00
I Wish You A Happy New Year, small stain at bottom..................50.00
I Wish You A Merry Christmas and A Happy New Year................65.00
Lord Have Mercy.........................................................................400.00
Mail Coach ..................................................................................225.00
Mother and Child, evening prayers, 10-1/2" l, 2" w, 1-1/2" silk tassel ......................................................................................400.00
Mourning, Blessed Are They Who Mourn, 9-1/2" l, 2" w, 2" silk tassel ......................................................................................450.00
Old Armchair................................................................................150.00
Prayer Book Set, five orig markers attached with small ivory button, cream colored tape fastened to orig frame, Communion, Collect, Lesson I, Lesson II, Psalms, gold lettering, gold silk tassels, orig mount, c1880-85 .............................................................................3,400.00
To One I Love, Love me little, love me long is the burden of my song, Love that is too hot and strong, burneth soon to waste, Still I would not have thee cold, not too backward or too bold; Love that lasteth till this old fadeth not in haste ..........................................................75.00

### Postcard

RMS *Arabic,* Hands Across the Sea .........................................465.00
RMS *Elmina*...............................................................................225.00
RMS *Franconia*..........................................................................175.00
RMS *Iverina*...............................................................................165.00
USMS *Philadelphia*....................................................................185.00

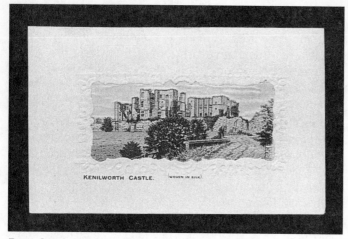

**Post Card, Kenilworth Castle, orig mat, $90.**

## Stevengraph

Betsy Making the first Untied States Flag, Anderson Bros, Paterson, NJ, 5" x 8-1/2" ...................................................................... 50.00
Buffalo Bill, Nate Salsbury, Indian Chief, orig mat and frame, 8" x 7" ................................................................................. 500.00
Chateau Frontenac Hotel, Quebec, silver filigree frame .............. 75.00
Coventry, 7-1/4" x 13", framed ..................................................... 100.00
Death of Nelson, 7-1/4" x 2-1/2" .................................................. 200.00
Declaration of Independence ....................................................... 375.00
Dick Turpin's last ride on his Bonnie Black Bess ....................... 175.00
For Life or Death, fire engine rushing to burning house, orig mat and frame ....................................................................... 350.00
Good Old Days, Royal Mail Coach, 5-3/4" h, 8-1/2" l, orig frame 200.00
God Speed the Plow ..................................................................... 175.00
H. M. Stanley, famous explorer ................................................... 300.00
Jeyhanne d'Arc, F. Lematte, 12-1/2" x 6-1/2" w .......................... 50.00
Kenilworth Castle, 7-1/4" x 13" framed ....................................... 100.00
Landing of Columbus .................................................................... 350.00
President Cleveland ...................................................................... 365.00
Oxford, Cambridge, Are You Ready, 5-3/4" h, 8-1/2" l, orig frame.... 300.00
The Water Jump ............................................................................ 195.00
Untitled, crew boats ..................................................................... 175.00
Untitled, life saving boat .............................................................. 175.00

# STEVENS and WILLIAMS

**History:** In 1824, Joseph Silvers and Joseph Stevens leased the Moor Lane Glass House at Briar Lea Hill (Brierley Hill), England, from the Honey-

19th C

Borne family. In 1847, William Stevens and Samuel Cox Williams took over, giving the firm its present name. In 1870, the company moved to its Stourbridge plant. In the 1880s, the firm employed such renowned glass artisans as Frederick C. Carder, John Northwood, other Northwood family members, James Hill, and Joshua Hodgetts.

Stevens and Williams made cameo glass. Hodgetts developed a more commercial version using thinner-walled blanks, acid etching, and the engraving wheel. Hodgetts, an amateur botanist, was noted for his brilliant floral designs.

Other glass products and designs manufactured by Stevens and Williams include intaglio ware, Peach Bloom (a form of peachblow), moss agate, threaded ware, "jewell" ware, tapestry ware, and Silveria. Stevens and Williams made glass pieces covering the full range of late Victorian fashion.

After World War I, the firm concentrated on refining the production of lead crystal and achieving new glass colors. In 1932, Keith Murray came to Stevens and Williams as a designer. His work stressed the pure nature of the glass form. Murray stayed with Stevens and Williams until World War II and later followed a career in architecture.

**Additional Listings:** Cameo Glass.

Bowl, 6" d, 3" h, Matsu No Ke, applied dec, creamy yellow satin glass bowl, twisted, knurled, and thorny frosted crystal branch winds around permimeter of bowl and forms feet, 36 florets, inscribed registry number "Rd 15353" .......................................................... 985.00
Decanter, 13" h, pink cut to clear, long neck cut to represent crackle glass, floral engraving, pattern cut stopper, cut by Joshua Hodgetts, c1897 .......................................................................... 4,100.00
Dish, 3-1/2" d, 2-1/4" h, Jewel, ruffled rim, deep bowl, zipper style trapped air dec on ribs, polished pontil, set of five, four amber, one light blue .................................................................... 115.00
Ewer, 10-1/4" h, 5-1/2" w, MOP satin, Jewell Pattern, deep rose shading to white, 25 rows of jewels, each row contains 60 jewels (air traps), applied handle ............................................................. 695.00
Perfume Bottle, 6-1/2" h, 3-3/4" d, Pompeiian Swirl, deep gold and brown/red, turquoise blue lining, orig cut frosted stopper ........ 895.00
Pitcher, 6-1/2" h, ribbed, yellow and opal vertical stripes, clear ground shell reeded handle ..................................................... 225.00
Plate
    6" d, cranberry cut to clear, finely engraved teardrops with floral motifs .................................................................................. 900.00
    8" d, tricolor, green cut to yellow to clear, engraved floral and acorn motif ...................................................................... 1,100.00
Vase
    3-3/4" h, pink opaline, footed base, mkd "S & W England"... 90.00
    5-1/2" h, 5" d, cameo, pink flowers and leaves, frosted ground ................................................................................ 850.00
    6" h, 6" w, applied Matso Nuke dec, pink-peach colored ground, bright cream-yellow lining, crystal applied shell like rigaree at top, three rosettes, three large 5-1/4" leaf feet, applied raspberry prunt over pontil, price for pr ................................. 750.00
    7-1/2" h, Striped Swirl pattern, frosted deep rose pink, yellow stripes, frosted ground, 36 vertical ribs ............................ 425.00
    7-3/4" h, 3-3/4" w, Pompeiian Swirl, gourd shape, light brown to gold .................................................................................. 475.00

**Vase, cameo, pink flowers and leaves, cut back to frosted white ground, 5-1/2" h, 5" d, $825. Photo courtesy of Joy Luke Fine Art Brokers and Auctioneers.**

10-1/4" h, flared rim, narrow neck, cylindrical for, dome foot, opal white glass cased to purple ext., engraved with sprays of flowers and berries, highlighted by dec borders at neck and foot, polished pontil, price for pr ............................................. 2,185.00

10-3/4" h, Pompeiian Swirl, MOP satin, pale lime green solid color, white lining, very bulbous shape, pedestal base .. 850.00

11" h, 6-1/2" w, Pompeiian Swirl, bulbous stick, amber to bright red ..................................................................................... 950.00

12" h, 6-1/2" w, Pompeiian Swirl, gourd shape, brilliant blue with brown swirls, bright yellow lining ................................... 1,750.00

Wine, 5-1/4" h, one apricot, other green, both cut to clear, engraved apple blossoms, spiderweb design, cut by Frederick Carter, authenticated by Rockwell, price for pr ............................................. 1,700.00

# STICKLEYS

**History:** There were five Stickley brothers: Albert, Gustav, Leopold, George, and John George. Gustav often is credited with creating the Mission style, a variant of the Arts and Crafts style. Gustav headed Craftsman Furniture, a New York firm, much of whose actual production took place near Syracuse. A characteristic of Gustav's furniture is exposed tenon ends. Gustav published *The Craftsman*, a magazine espousing his antipathy to machines.

Originally Leopold and Gustav worked together. In 1902, Leopold and John George formed the L. and J. G. Stickley Furniture Company. This firm made Mission-style furniture and cherry and maple early-American style pieces.

George and Albert organized the Stickley Brothers Company, located in Grand Rapids, Michigan.

**References:** David Cathers, *Furniture of the American Arts and Crafts Movement: Revised Edition*, Turn of the Century Editions, 1996; —, *Stickley Style: Arts and Crafts Homes in the Craftsman Tradition*, Simon & Schuster, 1999; Donald A. Davidoff and Stephen Gray, *Innovation and Derivation: The Contribution of L. & J. G. Stickley to the Arts and Crafts Movement*, Craftsman Farms Foundation, (2352 Route 10-W, Box 5, Morris Plains, NJ 07950), 1996; Donald A. Davidoff and Robert L. Zarrow, *Early L. & J. G. Stickley Furniture*, Dover Publications, 1992; *Furniture of the Arts & Crafts Period*, L-W Book Sales, 1992, 1995 value update; Thomas K. Maher, *The Kaufmann Collection: The Early Furniture of Gustav Stickley*, Treadway Gallery (2029 Madison Rd., Cincinnati, OH 45208), 1996; Paul Royka, *Mission Furniture, from the American Arts & Crafts Movement*, Schiffer Publishing, 1997.

**Periodical:** *Style 1900*, 333 Main St., Lambertville, NJ 08530.

**Collectors' Club:** Foundation for the Study of Arts & Crafts Movement, Roycroft Campus, 31 S. Grove St., East Aurora, NY 14052.

**Museum:** Craftsman Farms Foundation, Inc., Morris Plains, NJ.

**Notes:** Gustav denotes Gustav Stickley and Craftsman Furniture.

L & J G denotes L. and J. G. Stickley Furniture Company.

Bed, 45-1/2" l, 35-1/2" h, single, five broad vertical slats on head and foot boards, orig finish, L. and J. G. Stickley Handcraft decal, some restoration ............................................................................. 1,700.00

Bookcase

36" w, 14" d, 58" h, single door, designed by Harvey Ellis, orig glass in three vertical panes, leaded glass panels, pilaster details, arched and overhanging top, orig int. finish, faded orig ext. finish with traces of whitewash in grain, red Gustav Stickley decal, two small pilasters replaced, one replaced shelf 9,500.00

48" w, 14" d, 58" h, double doors, designed by Harvey Ellis, c1902-03, overhanging top, four leaded glass panels over vertical panes, arched toe-board, casters, large red Gustav decal, wear to orig finish ...................................................... 13,000.00

48" w, 13" d, 56-1/2" h, double doors, eight panes in each door, gallery top, hammered copper V-pulls, mortised through sides, medium brown finish, large paper Gustav label ............ 8,500.00

60" w, 13-1/2" d, 48" h, double doors, nine glass panes in each door, arched apron, hammered copper pulls, orig finish, branded "The Work of L. and J. G. Stickley," some scratches to top ..................................................................................... 6,500.00

Candlesticks, pr, 11-3/4" h, 4-1/2" d, hammered copper, applied brass bands and bobeches, orig patina, Stickley Bros., mkd "131" in pencil, minor dents to upper arms and cups ...................................... 2,000.00

Cellarette, #86, Gustav, copper lined, pull-out shelf over single drawer, paneled door, orig iron hardware, int. divided compartment, orig finish, red decal, 22" w, 16" d, 40" h .......................................... 4,000.00

Chest of Drawers

#913, Gustav, Harvey Ellis, nine drawers, overhanging rect top, six small drawers over three long graduated drawers, bowed sides, orig wooden knobs, lightly cleaned orig finish, red decal, slight veneer split, 36" w, 20" d, 51" h ......................... 7,000.00

L. & J. G., two small drawers over three long drawers, V-backsplash, chamfered sides, large faceted wooden pulls, orig dark finish, 36" w, 20' d, 43" h ............................................... 13,000.00

Chiffonier, #111, L. & J. G., two door, four small drawers over four wide drawers, paneled doors, orig finish, branded "The Work of...," 40" w, 19" d, 48" h ........................................................................... 16,000.00

China Cabinet

#729, L. & J. G., two doors, each with sixteen leaded panes of glass, two cabinet doors, orig hammered copper hardware and straps, eight panes on each side, lightly cleaned orig finish, some glass replaced, branded "The Work of...," numbered, 43" w, 16" d, 66" h ..................................................................... 18,000.00

#814, Gustav, two doors, each with eight panes of glass, orig brass hardware, straight tow board with thru-tenon construction, eight panes to sides, lightly cleaned orig finish, branded and paper label, minor distress to top, 42" w, 15" d, 64" h... 8,000.00

Stickley Bros., two doors, each with eight panes of glass, four panes on sides, orig copper hardware, plate rail at back, three adjustable shelves, orig finish, illegible number, 42" w, 17" d, 64" h ..................................................................... 3,250.00

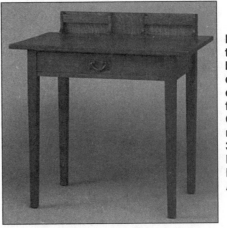

**Desk, postcard type, two letter backsplash, single drawer, hammered copper V-pull, orig finish, branded Gustav Stickley mark, 32" l, 30" d, 33-1/4" h, $4,200. Photo courtesy of David Rago Auctions.**

Costumer, double, 71" h, tapering posts, six bronze double hooks, orig finish, unmarked ............................................................ 2,200.00

Desk

Drop Front, 30" w, 11-1/4" d, 44" h, designed by Harvey Ellis for Gustav Stickley, overhanging top, three panels inlaid with stylized flowers, full gallery int., refinished, unmarked ...... 22,500.00

Postcard, 38" l, 23" d, 37" h, designed by Harvey Ellis, gallery top fitted with letter slots and drawers, two drawers with hammered copper pulls, paper label and branded Gustav mark, orig finish ............................................................ 3,250.00

Desk Set, hammered copper, perpetual calendar frame, inkwell, letter opener, stamp box, and ashtray, Gustav Als Ilk Kan mark .... 1,700.00

Dining Chair, Charles Stickley, Stickley and Brandt, c1918, oak, arm chair, five side chairs, waisted shaped crest rail over three back slats, shaped front stretcher, two side stretchers, upholstered drop-in seat, refinished, some repairs, 37" h side chair, 39" h arm, price for set of six ...................................................................... 1,840.00

Dining Table

Charles Stickley, Stickley and Brandt, c1918, 48-1/2" d, 29-1/2" h, oak, round top, two leaves, five sq post legs, minor wear and separation, top has clear coat finish .................................. 815.00

L. and J. G. Stickley, 48" d, 29-1/4" h, split pedestal, four footed base, orig finish, branded "The Work of...," some minor stains to top .............................................................................. 3,500.00

Stickley Brothers, 54" d, 29-3/4" h, split pedestal, buttressed feet, casters, paper label, new finish ........................................ 1,600.00

Drink Stand, 20" d, 25-1/2" h, circular overhanging top, cloud-lift cross-stretchers, skinned finish, paper Gustav label ...................... 1,700.00

Foot Stool

16" w, 12" d, 9" h, orig tacked-on Japan leather, orig finish, unmarked ...................................................................... 950.00

16" w, 12" d, 9-1/2" h, orig tacked-on leather seat, orig finish, paper Craftsman label, branded Gustav mark ................. 700.00

Gout Stool, 12" sq, 4-1/2" h, orig dark leather cover, orig finish, branded Gustav mark ...................................................... 1,000.00

Lamp, table, 24" h, 18" d shade, tapering hammered copper standard, period silk-lined wicker shade, orig patina, Ala Ik Kan, Gustav stamp, replaced silk, small dent in base ........................................ 5,000.00

Lantern, 14-1/2" l, 9" w, hammered copper, cut-out panels on sides and top, yellow hammered glass inserts, orig hanging chain and ceiling plate, unmarked, attributed to Gustav Stickley ................ 2,100.00

Library Table

Model No. 637, trestle, tacked-on brown leather top, keyed through tenon lower shelf, light orig finish, branded Gustav mark, Craftsman paper label, 48" l, 30" d, 30" h .......... 9,000.00

Model No. 675, Gustav, oak, rect top over two drawers, v-shaped hammered copper drawer pulls, medial shelf with pegged through tenons, sq post legs, medium brown finish, red decal and paper manufacturers label, 47-1/2" l, 29-3/4" w, 30" h, stains, scratches, joint separation .................................. 1,840.00

Magazine Stand

16" w, 13" d, 31-1/2" h, gallery top, slatted sides and back, three shelves, orig finish, remnant of Stickley Bros tag .......... 1,200.00

19" w, 12" d, 45" h, four shelves, chamfered back, arched apron, unmarked, L. and J. G. Stickley/Onondaga Shops, model no. 45, refinished ................................................................ 2,400.00

26-1/2" w, 12-1/2" d, 31" h, three shelves, three spindles on each side, orig finish, stamped number on base, Stickley Bros .. 1,100.00

27" w, 12" d, 38-1/2" h, three shelves, slatted sides, branded Gustav mark, paper label .............................................. 2,300.00

Morris Chair

Bow arm, arched seat rails, loose seat and back cushions, orig finish, small red Gustav Stickley box mark, replaced reclining peg, normal war to arms, accompanied by formal photograph of Cliffdale, Poughkeepsie, NY, home where piece originated, 31-1/2" x 34" x 38" h ...................................................... 42,500.00

Drop arm, broad scooped back arms, seven flats to floor, new leather upholstery on orig drop-in spring seat, orig finish, L. and J. G. Stickley Handcraft label, 32-1/2" w, 38" d, 40" h . 14,000.00

Drop arm, slats under arms, drop-in spring seat and back cushion, reupholstered in tan leather, orig finish, red Gustav decal, 38" h ...................................................................... 22,500.00

Flat arm, No. 332, five vertical slats, short corbels under each arm, orig worn leather seat and back cushion, orig finish, branded Gustav mark, 31" w, 38-1/4" d, 40" h ........... 11,000.00

Music Cabinet, #70, Gustav, single panel door, orig iron hardware, thru-tenon construction, two orig int. shelves, orig light finish, paper label, 20" w, 16" d, 48" h .................................................... 4,500.00

Occasional Table, Gustav, New York, c1902, round top, four sq post legs with arched cross stretchers, orig dark brown finish, large red decal, 35-3/4" d, 29" h, minor edge wear, stain .................... 3,740.00

Rocker, 22-1/2" w, 30-1/2" d, 45" h, high back, spindled, long corbels under flat arms, drop-in spring seat recovered in dark brown leather, red Gustav decal, orig finish with very thin overcoating ........ 6,500.00

Rug, 72" x 37", drugget, charcoal gray twining design, aqua squares, oatmeal ground, Gustav, minor discoloration .......................... 350.00

Sconce, #830, Gustav, hammered iron lantern, six sq cut-outs at top over hammered amber glass, supported by L-shaped brackets, orig patina, replaced glass, 6" w, 11" d, 12" h ............................ 4,200.00

Server, Stickley Brothers, 48" w, 20" d, 36" h, backsplash, two small drawers over linen drawer, orig pulls, lower shelf, orig condition, Quaint metal tag, decal, and brand ...................................... 2,100.00

Settle, 85" l, 33-1/4" d, 36-1/2" h, knock-down style, broad horizontal back rail, sq posts, four vertical slats to each side, drop-in leather upholstered seat cushion, unmarked, attributed to Charles Stickly, refinished, replaced pins, replaced seat cushion ................. 5,000.00

Settee, 77" l, 28" d, 36-3/4" h, drop-arm, broad slats under wide arms, scooped crest rail, drop-in spring seat recovered in dark brown leather, The Work of L. and J. G. Stickley label, cleaned orig finish ........ 6,000.00

Shaving Mirror, 26" w, 21-1/2" h, beveled glass, iron ring hardware, shoe feet, orig finish and mirror, branded Gustav mark ........ 1,600.00

Sideboard

Charles Stickley, Stickley and Brandt, c1918, oak, mirrored back, rect top, three center drawers flanked by two cupboards, lower long drawer, arched apron, bronze patina on pulls, Stickley and Brandt decal, 48" d, 18" d, 51-1/4" h, clear coat finish on top .......................................................... 2,070.00

L. and J. G. Stickley, plate rail, two doors, orig strap hardware, four drawers over linen drawer, Handcraft decal, refinished, 54" l, 24" d, 47-1/4" h ........................................................ 5,000.00

Side Chair, Model 350, curved crest rail over three vertical slats, wide front and back stretchers, two narrow side stretchers, medium brown finish, branded Gustav Stickley mark, replaced red vinyl upholstered seats, c1912, wear, some losses, 39" h, price for set of eight .......................................................... 2,645.00

Tabourtet

15" sq, 17" h, octagonal, legs mortised through top, arched cross stretchers, orig finish, remnant of L. and J. G. Stickley Handcraft label, wear to top .................................................. 900.00

16" w, 18" h, clip-corner, through-tenon cross-stretchers, red Gustav decal, top refinished, orig finish to base ........... 1,400.00

18" sq, 20" h, #561, clip-corner, straight apron, arched stretchers, orig finish, label "The Work of L. and J. G. Stickley," some wear, minor stains, scratches on top ...................................... 1,400.00

18" sq, 20-1/2" h, octagonal, legs mortised through top, arched cross stretchers, top refinished, orig finish to base, L. and J. G. Stickley Handcraft label .................................................. 1,400.00

25-3/4" w, 15" d, 20-1/2" h, oval, mortised cross-stretchers, orig finial, Stickley Bros. Quaint metal tag .............................. 1,700.00

Tea Table, 50" d, 30" h, #699, circular top, cloud-lift, mortised cross-stretchers, topped by finial, remnants of paper Gustav label, 1909-15, orig finish, some scratches on top .................................. 3,000.00

Tray

11-1/8" w, 23-1/8" l, Model 355, c1910, Gustav, hammered copper, elongated oval form, fold-over rim, riveted strap handles, medium brown patina, stamped with joiner's compass mark, scattered spotting, dent ................................................ 490.00

23" l, 11" w, oval, hammered copper, riveted handles, new dark patina, "Als Ik Kan" stamp .................................................. 700.00

Umbrella Stand

#100, Gustav, flaring slatted form, riveted to int. iron hoops, cleaned orig finish, unsigned, drip-pan missing, 12" d, 24" h .......... 1,600.00

**Umbrella Stand, hammered copper, six sided, applied brass riveted band, single knob on each panel, orig patina, stamped "Stickley Brothers," 26-1/2" h, 10-1/2" d, $5,175. Photo courtesy of David Rago Auctions.**

#382, Gustav, hammered copper, repousse design, riveted handles, new dark patina, 13" d, 24" h ................................. 1,300.00

Urn, 18" h, 10" d, L & J. G., hammered copper, riveted sinewy handles, orig patina, imp LJGS shield and F15 .................................. 4,000.00

Vase

    10" h, Stickley Bros., hammered copper, applied handles at shoulder, rolled rim, three emb designs, recent patina, imp #20 ...850.00

    17-1/2" h, L. & J. G. hammered copper, vertical lobes at base, cleaned patina, imp mark, drilled at base, dent to one side ............................................................. 2,000.00

Wall Shelf, 25" l, 6-1/4" d, 13-3/4" h, Stickley Bros., hanging, sectional, heart-shaped cut-out top, light overcoat on orig finish, Quaint metal tag ........................................................... 1,400.00

Wardrobe, child's, 59-1/2" h, Gustav, two paneled doors with hammered copper V-pulls, eight int. drawers, four shelves, remnants of paper label, new medium brown finish .................................. 5,000.00

Wastebasket

    L. & J. G., flaring sides, cut-out handles, scalloped rim, orig medium finish, 13" sq, 16" h ............................................. 1,300.00

    Stickley Bros., five slats on each side, refinished, numbered, 14" w, 14" d, 16" h ...................................................... 425.00

# STIEGEL-TYPE GLASS

**History:** Baron Henry Stiegel founded America's first flint-glass factory at Manheim, Pennsylvania, in the 1760s. Although clear glass was the most common color made, amethyst, blue (cobalt), and fiery opalescent pieces also are found. Products included bottles, creamers, flasks, flips, perfumes, salts, tumblers, and whiskeys. Prosperity was short-lived; Stiegel's extravagant lifestyle forced the factory to close.

It is very difficult to identify a Stiegel-made item. As a result, the term "Stiegel-type" is used to identify glass made during the time period of Stiegel's firm and in the same shapes and colors as used by that company.

Enamel-decorated ware also is attributed to Stiegel. True Stiegel pieces are rare; an overwhelming majority is of European origin.

**References:** Frederick W. Hunter, *Stiegel Glass*, 1950, available in Dover reprint; Kenneth Wilson, *American Glass 1760-1930*, 2 vols., Hudson Hills Press and The Toledo Museum of Art, 1994.

**Reproduction Alert:** Beware of modern reproductions, especially in enamel wares.

## Enameled

Bottle

    4-1/2" h, rect, colorless, enameled girl and flowers ............ 265.00

    5" h, oval, colorless, enameled deer, flowers, and verse, pewter top, dated 1770 ................................................... 625.00

    6-1/4" h, octagonal, colorless, enameled reserve of bird on each side, pewter top, 18th C ............................................ 925.00

Decanter Set, painted heraldic unicorn dec, decanter with stopper, twelve glasses, four tumblers, each with different painted heraldic dec, Bavarian ...................................................... 1,500.00

Flip, 3-7/8" h, clear, blown, enameled flower and running deer .. 175.00

Mug, 3-3/4" h, enameled "Forget Me Not," in blue diamond medallion, forget me nots and other flowers, "C" handle, ribbed base ...... 150.00

Tumbler, 3-1/2" h, 3-1/2" w, colorless, enameled connected hearts, clasped hands, German writing, dated 1708, open pontil, wear marks ........................................................................ 600.00

## Etched

Flip, 6" h, colorless, flaring shape, floral and leaf etch ............... 175.00

Mug, 6-1/2" h, colorless, floral and leaf etch, applied flat "C" handle 375.00

Nursing Bottle, 3-1/8" h, blown half-post type, clear, pontil, bow and leaf dec ................................................................ 195.00

Tumbler, 3-5/8" h, colorless, etched and ribbed blown, early 19th C 130.00

## Other

Baptismal Bowl, 4-1/4" h, blue, diamond mold, ftd, base repaired 75.00

Bowl, 3 x 2-1/8", blown mold, Expanded DQ, deep cobalt blue, applied foot ............................................................... 1,200.00

Creamer, 3-5/8" h, blue, diamond mold, loop handle, circular ftd base, 18th C .................................................................... 450.00

Cup, 3" h, colorless, inverted pear shape, diamond mold, circular base ................................................................... 350.00

Flask, 5" h, 4" w, amethyst, Daisy and Hexagon pattern, globular, short cylindrical neck and plain lip, two lateral rows of hexagons start at central bottom part and continue up, second horizontal band curves up the neck, terminates at top of shoulder, open pontil, McKearin 435. 6,500.00

Finger Bowl, 4" d, deep amethyst, diamond mold, 18th/19th C, price for 4 pc set ................................................................. 700.00

Salt, blown mold, Expanded DQ, cobalt blue, ftd ....................... 750.00

Scent Bottle, 2-3/4" l, swirled, deep cobalt blue ......................... 195.00

Sugar Bowl, cov, 3-1/4" h, blue, circular, rimmed base, 18th C .. 500.00

# STONEWARE

**History:** Made from dense kaolin and commonly salt-glazed, stonewares were hand-thrown and high-fired to produce a simple, bold, vitreous pottery. Stoneware crocks, jugs, and jars were made to store products and fill other utilitarian needs. These intended purposes dictated shape and design—solid, thick-walled forms with heavy rims, necks, and handles and with little or no embellishment. Any decorations were simple: brushed cobalt oxide, incised, slip trailed, stamped, or tooled.

Stoneware has been made for centuries. Early American settlers imported stoneware items at first. As English and European potters refined their earthenware, colonists began to produce their own wares. Two major North American traditions emerged based only on location or type of clay. North Jersey and parts of New York comprise the first area; the second was eastern Pennsylvania spreading westward and into Maryland, Virginia, and West Virginia. These two distinct geographical boundaries, style of decoration, and shape are discernible factors in classifying and dating early stoneware.

By the late 18th century, stoneware was manufactured in all sections of the country. This vigorous industry flourished during the 19th century until glass fruit jars appeared and the use of refrigeration became widespread. By 1910, commercial production of salt-glazed stoneware came to an end.

**References:** Susan and Al Bagdade, *Warman's American Pottery and Porcelain*, 2nd ed., Krause Publications, 2000; Jim Martin and Bette Cooper, *Monmouth-Western Stoneware*, published by authors, 1983, 1993 value update; Don and Carol Raycraft, *Collector's Guide to Country Stoneware & Pottery*, 1st Series (1985, 1995 value update), 2nd Series (1990, 1996 value update), Collector Books; —, *Stoneware*, Wallace-Homestead, 1995, —, *Wallace-Homestead Price Guide to American Country Antiques,* 16th ed., Krause Publications, 1999; Terry G. Taylor and Terry and Kay Lowrance, *Collector's Encyclopedia of Salt Glaze Stoneware*, Collector Books, 1996, 2001 value update.

**Collectors' Clubs:** American Stoneware Association, 208 Crescent Ct, Mars, PA 16066; Federation of Historical Bottle Collectors, Inc., 1485 Buck Hill Drive, Southampton, PA 18966.

**Museum:** Museum of Ceramics at East Liverpool, East Liverpool, OH.

Advertising
Crock, 13" h, six gallon, imp and blue accented "O. Vaupel 11 Union Ave, Williamsburg, NY," cobalt blue chicken pecking corn, extensive ground cover, unsigned, c1870, professional restoration to full length cracks on front and back................... 1,050.00
Jar, 9" h, half gallon, imp and blue accented "Made Expressly for C. D. Brooks Boston," unsigned, c1870, glaze spider on side, minor surface chipping and staining................................ 110.00
Jug, 9-1/2" h, two quart, blue stenciled "John H. Seehan 27 White St. Cohoes, NY," c1870, minor surface wear ................... 275.00
Jug, 11" h, cobalt blue quill work label "Gillig Bros, 273 Washington St. Buffalo, N.Y.," gray salt glaze, brown pebble highlights ...220.00
Jug, 14" h, two gallon, ovoid, blue stenciled "John H. Lalor Wholesale Liquor Dealer 27 to 31 Charlotte St. Utica NY," long spout and half the handle dipped in cobalt blue, attributed to Whites Utica, c1880, couple of long spider lines, over glazing at shoulder.................................................................................325.00
Jug, 14" h, two gallon, "Moore & Hubbard, Syracuse, NY" in blue script, Fort Edward Stoneware Co., Fort Edward NY, c1880, minor glaze drips on back, two minor stone pings on front, all in the making......................................................................220.00
Preserve Jar, 11-1/2" h, tall cylinder, "J. Reitzel, Newark, NJ" in heavy blue slip, c1870, some over glazing, large deep rim chip.................................................................................200.00

**Advertising Crock, 6 gallon, chicken pecking corn dec, imp and blue accented "O. Vaupel 11 Union Ave. Williamsburg NY," c1870, professional restoration to full length cracks, 13" h, $1,050. Photo courtesy of Vicki & Bruce Waasdrop.**

**Batter Pail, 3 quart, running bird dec, unsigned, attributed to Whites Utica factory, orig bale handle, c1865, 8" h, $1,050. Photo courtesy of Vicki & Bruce Waasdrop.**

Batter Pail, orig bale handle
8" h, three quart, cobalt blue running bird dec, imp "3" at shoulder on back, unsigned, attributed to Whites Utica, c1865, very minor surface chip under spout, minor glaze spider along handle on back.................................................................. 1,050.00
9-1/2" h, one gallon, slip blue oak leaf design below spout, orig tin lid, unsigned, attributed to Whites Utica, c1865 ............... 580.00
9-1/2" h, six quart, large brushed and drooping cobalt blue flower on back, E. W. Farrington & Co., Elmira, NY, c1890, professional restoration to chips at spout and long hairline on side.................................................................................475.00
11" h, two gallon, two cobalt blue brushed flowers on either side of front spout, large double flower dec on back, extensive blue accenting at ears, handle, and spout, Cowden & Wilcox, Harrisburg, PA, c1870, some surface chipping, 7" hairline extending from rim just touching flower on back...........................1,210.00
Bottle
9-1/2" h, imp and blue accented "Smith & Snow/White Root/White Root/Pat. July 17, 66/Ltd. & Co. 1873," label fills entire shoulder, in making glaze burn on front.........................................210.00
9-3/4" h, imp and blue accented "G. R. Gate," incised and blue accented stripes at shoulder above and below name, minor surface chip at top.................................................................. 180.00
10" h, imp and blue accented "J. Francis Hop Beer," repairs to hairline, base chip ................................................................. 70.00
Butter Churn
16" h, four gallon, brushed blue puppet-like man design, side with brushed blue cattail design, unsigned, c1850, rim chip 2,650.00
19" h, six gallon, orig churn guide, vine and floral design starts at bottom and ends at top, W. Roberts, Binghamton, NY, c1860, professional restoration to damage area on right side ..... 800.00
Cake Crock
10" d, 5-3/4" h, cobalt blue brushed swag design, blue accents under ears, unsigned, c1850, some signs of over glazing, large glaze burn on back........................................................ 275.00
10-1/4" d, 6-5/8" h, cobalt blue brushed floral dec, applied handles, imp label "E. B. Norton & Co. Worcester, Mass," 1-1/2," minor chips and wear........................................................ 525.00
Canning Jar
5-1/2" h, A. P. Donaghho, Parkersburg, WV, c1880............ 250.00
6" h, one quart, three brush cobalt blue stripes going half way around, unsigned, c1850................................................ 360.00
8" h, half gallon, seven cobalt blue stripes, inscription under glaze on bottom "From Aunt Bell," c1850 ................................. 550.00
Cream Pot, 8" h, one gallon, cobalt blue dotted horse head dec, Whites Utica, c1865, some cobalt blue loss to thick blue dotted design, full length glued crack on back ................................. 5,060.00

**Butter Churn, W. Roberts, Binghamton, NY, orig churn guide, vine and floral design starts at bottom and ends at top, c1860, professional restoration, 19" h, $800. Photo courtesy of Vicki & Bruce Waasdrop.**

**Crock, 1 gallon, thick blue "singing bird" dec, unsigned, c1870, 7-1/4" h, $525. Photo courtesy of Vicki & Bruce Waasdrop.**

Crock, cov, 11-1/2" h, four gallon, cobalt blue airy dotted floral design, C. W. Braun, Buffalo, NY, c1870, orig lid ................................. 425.00

Crock, open

7-1/4" h, one gallon, cobalt blue running bird, Whites Utica, c1865 ................................................................................... 965.00

8" h, ovoid, applied handles, imp label "Penn Yan," cobalt blue floral dec and dots on handles, Penn Yan Pottery, Yates County, NY ........................................................................................ 385.00

9" h, boldly dec in dark cobalt blue with squiggles and date "1840," applied handles, imp "2," chips and hairlines ....... 385.00

9-1/2" h, cobalt blue brushed label "N. G. Humil Newport, Ohio," hairlines .................................................................................. 440.00

9-1/2" h, two gallon, cobalt blue singing bird with long tail, sitting on dotted plume design, Haxstun & Co., Fort Edward, NY, c1870, surface chip at rim on side, few light grease stains from use ....................................................................................... 690.00

10-1/2" h, three gallon, cobalt blue long tailed bird on stump, Brady & Ryan, Ellenville, NY, c1880, professional restoration to tight line on back, some staining, overglazed in the making .................... 200.00

10-3/4" h, applied handles, cobalt blue stenciled label "Jas. Peterson, Hopewell, Muskingham Co. O. 3," stains ................ 580.00

11-1/2" h, four gallon, cobalt blue reclining dog, flying birds and tree dec, West Troy Pottery, NY, c1880, professional restoration to glaze flaking and one handle, rim chip on front ........... 915.00

11-1/2" h, four gallon, bold cobalt blue fan tailed bird, Whites Utica, c1865, 2" hairline at rim, int. surface chip at rim on back ...... 500.00

11-1/2" h, three gallon, ovoid, brushed cobalt blue flower design, blue accents at handles, Cowden & Wilcox, Harrisburg, PA, c1870, extensive int. lime staining .................................. 525.00

11-1/2" h, stenciled cobalt blue dec, "James Hamilton & Co. Greensboro, Pa. 3," double handles, raised rim, minor stains and chips ......................................................................... 385.00

12" h, applied shoulder handles, cobalt blue quill work spotted bird on branch, imp label "Edmands & Co. 2," chips and hairlines ........................................................................................ 450.00

12-3/4" h, applied handles, stenciled cobalt blue label "Neff Bros. Manufactures Taylorsville, O. 5," gray salt glaze with brown and yellow highlights ............................................................. 1,540.00

13-1/2" h, applied handles, brushed cobalt blue floral designs with "6," out of round ............................................................. 200.00

13-1/2" h, six gallons, cobalt blue dotted double flower design, C. W. Brawn, Buffalo, NY, c1870, three tight old hairlines . 2,640.00

18-1/2" h, cobalt blue stenciled label "Harris Bros. Brownsville, Ohio," double handles, incised ring around rim, cracks ..... 50.00

Cup, 3-1/2" h, brown Albany slip, sgraffito inscription "Mr. Isaac Stevens" in scroll work cartouche, chips .................................. 275.00

Grease Lamp, 4-3/4" h, greenish gray salt glaze, applied handle, open font with spout, saucer base, attributed to Tennessee ............. 475.00

Jar, cov

10-3/4" h, 2 gallon, cobalt blue starburst design fills entire front surface, Jordan, c1850, orig stoneware lid .................... 1,650.00

13" h, three gallon, large triple brushed flowers covering entire front, blue accents at applied handles and "3" in brush blue, T. Harrington Lyons, c1850, chip at knob of fitted stoneware lid, professional restoration to rim chip at front ...................... 750.00

Jar, open, ovoid, applied shoulder handles

11-1/2" h, incised crane with fish, in filled with cobalt blue, blue at handles and imp "2," minor wear .................................. 3,410.00

13-1/2" h, boldly brushed cobalt blue floral dec, faint imp label, some wear, small chips ..................................................... 150.00

13-3/4" h, cobalt blue stenciled and free hand floral dec, "Hamilton & Jones, Greensboro, Pa, 3," chips on handle .......... 525.00

16-1/2" h, cobalt blue brushed floral dec, stenciled label "John Borgundshal, Pouhatun, Ohio 5," hairlines ..................... 500.00

17-1/2" h, cobalt blue brushed floral dec with "S," hairlines .. 1,045.00

18-1/2" h, cobalt blue stenciled dec, label "Jas Hamilton & Co. Greensboro, Pa," chips and base hairline ....................... 385.00

24-1/2" h, cobalt blue brush work dec with free hand flowers and vining, stenciled roses at base, sgd "Hamilton & Jones, Greensboro, Pa, 15," hairline damage ...................................... 1,980.00

Jug

10" h, ovoid, one gallon, incised and blue accented antlers design, imp circles forming grapevine design, blue accents at handle, I. Seymour & Co., Troy, NY, c1825 ................... 1,815.00

11" h, ovoid, one gallon, simple cobalt blue brush flower design, blue accent at handle, Clark & Fox, Athens, NY, c1830, small stone ping on front and back, both in the making ........... 550.00

11-1/2" h, applied strap handle, cobalt blue quill work pecking chicken, imp label "West Troy N.Y. Lottery" .................. 1,650.00

13" h, ovoid, two gallon, incised and blue accented signature clam shell design, Commeraw's Stoneware, Commeraw's Corlears Hook, New York, c1800, cobalt blue accents the 6 line name down the front, blue accents at handle, professional restoration to tight freeze line around back, dime size stone ping on front ................................................................................ 1,925.00

13-1/2" h, strap handle, cobalt blue stenciled label "C. W. Weaver Stoneware Depot, Cincinnati, O, 2," hairline in handle, small chips ................................................................................. 110.00

14" h, cobalt blue slip bird with tail feathers fanned on branch, strap handle, imp label "White's Utica 2," shallow chip on base, hairline, pot stone with spider hairline .............................. 330.00

14" h, ovoid, two gallon, cobalt blue brush flower with accents above and below, S. H. Addington, c1830, some design fry, stack marks on side in the making ................................... 690.00

14" h, ovoid, strap handle, raised rings around spool, cobalt blue stenciled floral dec around arched signature for "Hamilton and Jones Greensboro, Pa. 2," spout chip, minor chips ......... 265.00

14" h, two gallon, standing deer design, J. & E. Norton, Bennington, VT, c1855, mottled clay color in the making, professional restoration to numerous stone pings ............................. 6,600.00

14" h, strap handle, cobalt blue quill work branch with bird with hooked beak, blue highlights on imp label "New York Stoneware Co. Ft. Edward, N.Y. 2," chips ........................................... 450.00

14" h, two gallon, cobalt blue wreath dec, gallon designation and dots highlight center, Jordan, c1850, minor surface chip at spout, orange peel texture due to over glazing ............... 660.00

14" h, two gallon, cobalt blue poppy dec, John Burger, Rochester, c1865 ..................................................................................... 450.00

14-1/4" h, applied strap handle, cobalt blue slip dec bust of man with mustache, coat, and string tie, imp "M. & T. Miller, Newport, Pa. 2" ................................................................................. 4,300.00

14-1/4" h, cobalt blue bird slip dec, strap handle, imp "2" ... 495.00

14-1/2" h, applied strap handle, cobalt blue stenciled label "Jas. Hamilton & Co. Greensboro, Pa. 2," rose dec, chips ....... 200.00

14-1/2" h, two gallons, dated 1853, apple perched on top of leafy branch, fine point slip, Jordan, 1853, very minor stack mark on front, stone ping on front ............................................. 11,275.00

15" h, three gallon, centennial date "1776" in bold blue, attributed to Hastings & Belding, early 1850s ................................... 350.00

16" h, applied handle, cobalt blue quill work foliage dec, imp label "Bullard & Scott, Cambridgeport, Mass," shallow lip chip 200.00

**Jug, 2 gallon, apple perched on top of leafy branch, dated 1853, fine point slip, Jordan, 14-1/2" h, $11,275. Photo courtesy of Vicki & Bruce Waasdrop.**

**Water Cooler, unsigned, blue bird dec and lid, 4 incised and blue accented lines, minor chip on orig lid, attributed to Fulper Bros., NJ, c1880, 14" h, $315. Photo courtesy of Vicki & Bruce Waasdrop.**

16" h, three gallon, cobalt blue double bull's eye flower at top and bottom, illegible maker's name, NY origin, c1870, chip at spout, small stone ping in design, long surface chip on handle..600.00

17-1/2" h, four gallon, "Bennington Blue" cobalt stylized floral design, E. & L. P. Norton, Bennington, VT, c1880, dime size surface chip at spout, stack mark ....................................... 1,045.00

18" h, four gallon, simple cobalt blue brushed leaf design, T. Harrington Lyons, c1850, some glaze crazing and staining... 250.00

18" h, five gallon, Whites Utica, NY, signature ribbed orchid design, c1865 ........................................................... 1,925.00

Milk Pan, 9-1/2" d, 3-1/4" h, formed spout, simple cobalt blue swag designs all around, unsigned, c1860, stone ping in the making, minor surface chip at spout ................................................ 275.00

Pitcher, 13" h, cobalt blue stenciled and free hand label "Williams & Reppert, Greensboro, Pa, 2," wear and hairlines ..................... 935.00

Preserve Crock, 8-3/8" h, three emb lines around center, brushed cobalt dec above and below, hairlines and small flakes ........... 315.00

Preserve Jar, cov, 12" h, three gallon, heavily dec with thistle floral design, J. & E. Norton, Bennington, VT, c1855, glued freeze crack on back, overall glaze crazing suggesting piece was once painted white....415.00

Preserve Jar, open
9" h, cobalt blue quill work monogram, imp label "A. P. Cook, Brooklyn, Mich, Dealer in All Kinds of Dry Goods, Groceries, Drugs, Medicines, Wooden Ware, Grain, Pork & Produce" ..............265.00

9" h, one gallon, cobalt blue brushed flower design and gallon designation, blue accents under ears, gray clay, Lyons, c1860, extensive professional restoration to hairlines and chipping at one ear ....................................................................... 135.00

9-3/4" h, cobalt blue brushed and stenciled label "James Hamilton, Greensboro, Pa," with fan, hairlines .......................... 220.00

10-1/8" h, cobalt blue brushed floral dec, on two sides, incised ring around body, flared lip .......................................... 200.00

10-1/2" h, two gallon, tall cobalt blue dotted flower and leaf, Brewer & Halm, Havana, NY, c1852, surface chipping at ears from use, staining.............................................................. 385.00

10-1/2" h, tooled rings, flared lip, cobalt blue brushed floral dec, minor rim flakes............................................................... 250.00

13" h, three gallon, cobalt blue large compote of flowers, J. & E. Norton, Bennington, VT, c1855, minor glaze flaking ........ 880.00

Sign, 23" l, 13" h, "Pottery," two individual stoneware panels framed to create double sided sign, relief letters accented in Albany glaze, found in MA, wood frame, one panel with full length glaze separation in center ............................................................................ 1,540.00

Spittoon, 9" d, 4-1/2" h, cobalt blue swag design, imp "1" in circle at rim, unsigned, c1850, minor surface chips.............................. 250.00

Table Top Churn
12-1/2" h, applied shoulder handles, cobalt blue brushed floral dec, imp "1-1/2," orig wooden lid and dasher, chips......... 425.00

12-3/4" h, two gallons, slip blue "2," and squiggles on front, overall cinnamon clay color, unsigned, attributed to Midwest potter, c1840, minor glaze wear, short clay separation at rim on back, surface chip at rim on front................................................. 200.00

# STRETCH GLASS

**History:** Stretch glass was produced by many glass manufacturers in the United States between 1915 through 1935. The most prominent makers were Cambridge, Fenton (which probably manufactured more stretch glass than any of the others), Imperial, Northwood, and Steuben. Stretch Glass is pressed or blown-molded glass, with little or no pattern, that is sprayed with a metallic salt mix while hot, creating a iridescent, onionskin-like effect, that may be velvety or shiny in luster. Look for mold marks. Imported pieces are blown and show a pontil mark.

**References:** John Madeley and Dave Stetlar, *American Iridescent Stretch Glass,* Collector Books, 1998; Berry Wiggins, *Stretch Glass*, Antique Publications, 1972, 1987 value update.

**Collectors' Club:** Stretch Glass Society, P.O. Box 573, Hampshire, IL 60140.

Bon Bon, Florentine green, dolphin handles, Fenton....................50.00
Bowl
   9-1/2" d, Treebark, ftd .........................................................65.00
   11" d, ftd, frosty white, Imperial #600B, iron cross mark..... 150.00
Breakfast Creamer and Sugar, ice green, cobalt blue handles, Fenton...................................................................................275.00
Candlesticks, pr, 9-1/2" h, green irid, c1920 ..............................90.00
Candy Jar, Interior Panel, US Glass, celeste blue, large ..............55.00
Compote
   4-3/4" x 2-3/4", vaseline, Northwood ................................. 135.00
   8" d, ftd, frosty white, Imperial #600, iron cross mark ......... 125.00
Lemonade Glass, hourglass shape, celeste blue, cobalt handles, Fenton.....................................................................................65.00
Perfume Bottle, tall, flower formed stopper, ice green, Fenton ... 900.00
Plate, 8-1/2" d, Aurene, gold............................................................75.00
Powder Jar, cov, ice blue .................................................................50.00
Roundel, 10" d, emerald green, free-blown, lustrous gold, blue, and purple irid surface, mounted in three-prong metal holder for hanging, each with edge chip, pr ......................................................... 350.00
Tumbler, Concave Diamond, Northwood, vaseline..................... 180.00
Tumble-Up, celeste blue, Fenton................................................. 110.00
Vase, swung, 9-1/2" h, swung Interior Panels, Imperial, red....... 350.00

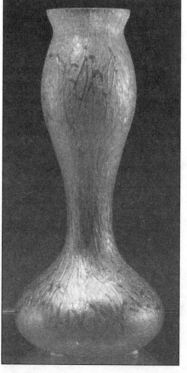

**Vase, double gourd shape, gold irid, polished rim, Bohemian, $200. Photo courtesy of David Rago Auctions.**

# STRING HOLDERS

**History:** The string holder developed as a useful tool to assist the merchant or manufacturer who needed tangle-free string or twine to tie packages. The early holders were made of cast iron, some patents dating to the 1860s.

When the string holder moved into the household, lighter and more attractive forms developed, many made of chalkware. The string holder remained a key kitchen element until the early 1950s.

**Reference:** Sharon Ray Jacobs, *Collector's Guide to Stringholders*, L-W Book Sales, 1996.

## Ceramic

| | |
|---|---|
| Bear Cub, bee on tummy | 230.00 |
| Bird, scissors forms beak, Royal Copley | 50.00 |
| Cat | |
|     Black, head only, white markings, red bow | 95.00 |
|     White, pearlized, string out extended paw | 150.00 |
| Dutch Girl, flowered hat | 95.00 |
| Flapper Girl, head, black, orange, and green hair | 170.00 |
| Fox, wearing glasses | 160.00 |
| Mammy | |
|     Polka dot scarf | 400.00 |
|     Red scarf, gray face | 425.00 |
| Owl, dark brown | 60.00 |
| Pumpkin, winking | 180.00 |
| Scotty Dog | 220.00 |

## Chalkware

| | |
|---|---|
| Apple, bird chasing worm | 110.00 |
| Bride, groom, one bridesmaid | 170.00 |
| Bride and two bridesmaids | 120.00 |

**Beehive, cast iron, 6-1/2" d, 4-1/2" h, $25.**

| | |
|---|---|
| Bridesmaid | 85.00 |
| Cat, pink collar | 150.00 |
| Clown, comical expression | 230.00 |
| Dog, head, sad expression | 160.00 |
| Dutch Girl, red hat | 50.00 |
| Lemon | 130.00 |
| Pear | 45.00 |
| Pineapple, smiling | 150.00 |
| Strawberry | |
|     Face | 50.00 |
|     With blossom | 65.00 |
| Tomato, wearing hat | 140.00 |

## Glass

Cut, 3-1/2" h, vertical flutes and stepcutting, Gorham sterling silver top, Straus ......... 350.00

Etched, colorless glass dome, cobalt blue band around rim and base, engraved flowers around side, America, mid-19th C minor chips . 175.00

## Tin, advertising

Cornell White Lead, 13-3/4" w, 19-3/4" h, double sided diecut tin, Dutch Boy painting in opened window ......... 1,000.00

Heinz, 17" l, hanging, double sided diecut pickle suspended from marquee labeled "57 Varieties" on one side, "Pure Foods" on reverse, spool of thread mounted on top of pickle ......... 5,940.00

Lipton's Tea, 13-1/3" w, 19-1/2" h, hanging, double sided diecut litho tin ......... 1,665.00

# SUGAR SHAKERS

**History:** Sugar shakers, sugar castors, or muffineers all served the same purpose: to "sugar" muffins, scones, or toast. They are larger than salt and pepper shakers, were produced in a variety of materials, and were in vogue in the late Victorian era.

**Reference:** William Heacock, *Encyclopedia of Victorian Colored Pattern Glass*, Book III, Antique Publications, 1976, 1991-92 value update.

| | |
|---|---|
| Custard Glass, Maize, Libbey, colored leaves | 200.00 |
| Cut Glass | |
|     5" h, notched prism cutting, sterling silver cap | 200.00 |
|     6" h, Birkshire pattern, Pairpoint, silver top | 375.00 |
| Figural, egg shape, yellow and orange, leaf dec, 4-1/2" h | 375.00 |
| Findlay Onyx | 400.00 |
| Gillander, satin glass, melon shape | |
|     Blue and white floral dec | 140.00 |
|     Blue ground, rust-orange floral dec | 125.00 |
| Mount Washington | |
|     Satin, egg shape, red-violet leaves, white buds dec | 300.00 |
|     Satin, pink shaded to blue, bulbous | 125.00 |
| Opalescent | |
|     Poinsettia, light blue | 250.00 |
|     Poinsettia, cranberry | 250.00 |
|     Ribbed Lattice, cranberry | 300.00 |
|     Spanish Lace, blue, wide waist | 210.00 |
|     Spanish Lace, white, wide waist | 200.00 |
|     Stripe, white, new lid | 25.00 |
|     Swirl, blue | 125.00 |
|     Windows, blue, swirled | 300.00 |
| Opaque | |
|     Acorn pattern, reverse shaded pink | 125.00 |
|     Alba pattern, blue | 100.00 |
|     Argus pattern, white, orange wild rose dec | 25.00 |
|     Chrysanthemum Base Swirl, turquoise satin finish | 200.00 |
|     Chrysanthemum Base Swirl, white | 150.00 |
|     Cone pattern, shiny opaque blue | 50.00 |
|     Cone pattern, squatty, pink | 80.00 |

Satin Glass, royal blue, Raindrop, MOP, coralene dec, stepple shaped metal fittings, mkd "Patent," 6" h, $1,085. Photo courtesy of Clarence & Betty Maier.

Diamond Quilted and Paneled, green, dome top.................. 40.00
Forget-Me-Not pattern, Challinor, blue ............................. 125.00
Forget-Me-Not pattern, Challinor, pink.............................. 70.00
Gargoyle pattern, white milk glass ......................................... 90.00
Leaf Umbrella, blue cased ................................................. 250.00
Little Shrimp, shiny rich blue ................................................ 40.00
Melligo, blue.......................................................................... 40.00
Parian Swirl, white milk glass, rose and leaves dec ............. 50.00
Quilted Phlox, light green........................................................ 60.00
Scrolled Rib, green, new lid ................................................. 25.00
Pattern Glass
 Daisy and Button with diamond point panels, clear .............. 25.00
 Leaning Pillars, blue .......................................................... 50.00
 Pineapple and Fan variation, new top ................................. 15.00
 Rope and Ribs, amber......................................................... 30.00
 Rope and Thumbprint, blue.................................................. 50.00
 Snail, ruby stained ............................................................ 300.00
 Utopia Optic, cobalt blue, beaded enamel dec .................. 150.00
 Zipper & Stars, clear........................................................... 40.00
Peachblow-Type
 Argus Swirl pattern, pink satin ........................................... 100.00
 English, blue and white prunus blossom enamel dec......... 200.00
Rubena
 Medallion Sprig, new top ................................................... 150.00
 Royal Ivy, frosted .............................................................. 125.00
Satin Glass
 Fig shape, pink blossoms, beige leaves dec ................... 1,500.00
 Ostrich egg shape, light blue ground, blue and magenta violet
   dec ................................................................................. 400.00
 Ostrich egg shape, yellow ground, pink cherry blossom dec...475.00
 Tomato shape, green and beige fern dec, ornate metal lid with
   dragonflies and daisies dec............................................. 400.00
Spatter
 Leaf Mold pattern, vaseline................................................ 175.00
 Royal Ivy, shiny, cased...................................................... 325.00

# SWANSEA

**History:** This superb pottery and porcelain was made at Swansea (Glamorganshire, Wales) as early as the 1760s, with production continuing until 1870.

**Marks:** Marks on Swansea vary. The earliest marks were "Swansea" impressed under glaze and "Dillwan" under glaze after 1805. "Cambrian Pottery" was stamped in red under glaze from 1803 to 1805. Many fine examples, including the botanical series in pearl-

## Reproduction Alert:

Swansea porcelain has been copied for many decades in Europe and England. Marks should be studied carefully.

Plate, floral dec, sgd , c1815, 8-1/2" d, $125.

ware, are not marked but may have the name of the botanical species stamped underglaze.

**References:** Susan and Al Bagdade, *Warman's English & Continental Pottery & Porcelain*, 3rd Edition, Krause Publications, 1998; W. D. John, *Swansea Porcelain,* Ceramic Book Co., 1958.

**Museums:** Art Institute of Chicago, Chicago, IL; Glynn Vivian Art Gallery, Swansea.

**Note:** Fine examples of Swansea often may show imperfections such as firing cracks. These pieces are considered mint because they left the factory in this condition.

Cup and Saucer, sq handle, purple and green sprig designs, worn ..25.00
Cream Jug, 4-1/2" h, printed and multicolored, Mandarin pattern, gilt scroll
  border int., rim with panels of trees and foliage, red mark............. 265.00
Dessert Tray, 9-1/2" l, hp, creamware, gilding, polychrome, underglaze
  mark, c1780 .................................................................................... 285.00
Goblet, 4-3/8" h, copper luster ground, multicolored molded putti riding
  lions on blue band, c1820 ................................................................ 80.00
Plate
  7-1/4" d, pearlware, yellow, orange, brown, blue, and green bird
    on brown branch, green spatter tree, blue emb shell edged scal-
    loped rim ................................................................................... 775.00
  7-3/4" d, hp, creamware, flowers, reticulated, mkd "Dillwyn,"
    c1805 ......................................................................................... 200.00
Spill Vase, 10-1/2" h, figural, dog standing in blue and white uniform,
  orange epaulets, blue and white striped pants, black hat with feather,
  holding drum, brown and green mottled rock spill holder and base,
  imp "Bibi Tapin," c1860-70 ............................................................ 395.00
Sugar, cov, 6" h, painted pink roses, gilt line, leaf borders, c1820 ...190.00
Teacup and Saucer, 3-5/8" h, 6" d saucer, floral dec, c1815 ...... 125.00

# SWORDS

**History:** The first swords used in America came from Europe. The chief cities for sword manufacturing were Solingen in Germany, Klingenthal in France, and Hounslow and Shotley Bridge in England. Among the American importers of these foreign blades was Horstmann, whose name is found on many military weapons.

New England and Philadelphia were the early centers for American sword manufacturing. By the Franco-Prussian War, the Ames Manufacturing Company of Chicopee, Massachusetts, was exporting American swords to Europe.

Sword collectors concentrate on a variety of styles: commissioned vs. non-commissioned officers' swords, presentation swords, naval weapons, and swords from a specific military branch, such as cavalry or infantry. The type of sword helped identify a person's military rank and, depending on how he had it customized, his personality as well.

Following the invention of repeating firearms in the mid-19th century, the sword lost its functional importance as a combat weapon and became a military dress accessory.

**References:** *Swords and Hilt Weapons*, Barnes & Noble Books, 1993; Gerald Welond, *Collector's Guide to Swords, Daggers & Cutlasses*, Chartwell Books, 1991.

**Museum:** Fort Ticonderoga Museum, Ticonderoga, NY.

**Note:** Condition is key to determining value.

## American

Naval Cutlass, 1861 Pattern handle with large basket, brass handguard, riveted to single knuckle bow, 26" l slightly curved iron bade with wide unstopped fuller, completely unmarked on ricasso or spine, pommel cap mkd "13," quillion mkd "11M/644" ........................ 300.00

Presentation, Pattern of 1860 Staff Officer's sword, 31" narrow double edge blade etched on both sides or 13-1/2" with pattern of s rolls, eagle, and trophy of arms, obverse ricasso stamped "Ridabock & Co/New York" within oval plus "Made in France" within curved banner, reserve with maker's mark "FBD" combined with vase and torch, all within an oval, very detailed brass hilt with lion head quillion, openwork guard with raised eagle clutching olive branches and arrows, pearl grips would with twisted brass wire, folding langet handsomely engraved "Presented to/Genl. Stillman F. Kneeland/By a few of his friends/Jan. 1st 1897," German silver scabbard with very elaborate cast gilded brass mounts, accompanied by papers relating to Kneeland's military service................................................ 2,000.00

Springfield Armory Light Infantry, late ceremonial type, 30" x 7/8" blade, etched both sides with usual pattern, four branch handguard and finger groove wood grip, all nickel plated, orig scabbard, langet and quillion bent, one branch of knuckle guard missing .......... 150.00

US Civil War Non-Regulation Staff and Field Officer, 32-1/2" l single edged straight blade with etched panels having US and spread-winged eagle ricasso mkd "Clauberg" and "Schuler Hartley & Graham, New York," iron half basket guard with eagle over US, fish skin wrapped grip with twisted brass wire, iron scabbard, uncleaned blade, medium gray patina, lightly pitted hilt and scabbard............................................600.00

US Model 1833, Foot Artillery, 19" l double edge wide blade mkd "N. P. Ames/Springfield" and dated 1835, cast brass hilt with fish scale grip eagle on pommel, black leather scabbard with brass mounts, leather belt and frog with two pc US belt plate ....................................950.00

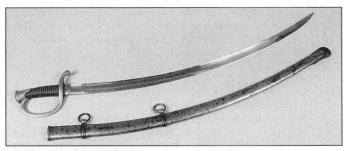

**Ames, US Model 1840, mounted artillery saber, $924. Photo courtesy of Jackson's Auctioneers & Appraisers.**

US Model 1840

Light Artillery, 32-1/2" curved single edged blade, manuf by Ames, dated 1863, cast brass D-guard leather and twisted wire wrap grip, iron scabbard with two carrying rings and throat...................600.00

Non Commissioned Officer, 32" single edged straight blade, cast brass hilt, clam shell guard, leather scabbard with brass mounts, manuf by Ames, dated 1864 .............................500.00

US Model 1850

Foot Officer, 31-1/4" l single edged blade with bold etching, military and floral motifs, US and spread-winged eagle, cast brass half basket hilt with leather wrap grip and twisted wire, leather scabbard with brass mounts, manuf. By C. Roby & Co., W Chelmsfort, MA ................................................... 1,050.00

Staff and Field, 31-1/2" l single edged blade etched with US American eagle, military and floral motifs, unsigned blade, large cast brass floral half-basket guide with US fish skin and twisted wire grip, solid brass scabbard gold plated with line engraved mounts, blade retains most of its frosty etched appearance, hilt has been cleaned, scabbard fine with untouched patina, no dents ......................................................... 2,500.00

Staff and Field, presentation grade, 31-3/4" l imported German blade by W. Clauberg of Soligen, standing knight logo, one side floral engravings with "US" in center panel, other side with floral engraving with eagle and "E. Pluribus Unum," some dark spots, overall good condition, etching crisp, hilt gilted brass with some areas of gilt remaining, "US" with floral work to guard, quillion in form of eagle's head, brass drip with wire wrap comprised of small chain link, metal 2 ring scabbard with fancy throat, brass drag and hanger mounts................................. 2,000.00

US Model 1860

General, Staff and Field, 30" double edged straight bade, etched panels covering 75% of length, dec in gold, spread-edged winged eagle, US on one side, presentation "Brig. Gen'l Hunter C. White" on other side, Soligen-made blade etched "The M. C. Lilley & Co., Columbus, Ohio," double clam shell pierced cross guard in high relief, sterling silver American eagle applied to one side, pierced guard on reverse having oak leaf clusters with US in raised oval panel, heavily encrusted two branch D-guard with vines, roses, acanthus leaf, and other dec, standing urn-shaped pommel with relief cast suit of armor on cross swords, two pc mother-of-pearl grips with fancy triple laid brass wire wrap, gilt cloth blackened gold sword knot attached, bright nickel plated steel scabbard with heavy gilt and pierced floral mounts ............................................. 5,000.00

Light Cavalry, 35" l, single edge curved blade, manuf by Ames, mkd "US" and inspected "G. G. S" on ricasso, dark uncleaned blade, c1860.................................................................725.00

US Model 1862 Pattern, Cavalry, saber, belt, and buckle, standard configuration, 34-3/4" blade, single wide fuller, mkd on right ricasso "R&C" left mkd "IRON/PROOF," 3 branch brass handguard with twisted wire wrapped handle, iron scabbard, black suede textured sword belt and hangars, rect brass spread-winged eagle buckle with applied silver laurel leaves, inside of belt and hangers are light buff colored, with mark "W. Kinney/Newark, N.J.".........................1,000.00

**French,** Dragoon Cavalry Officer, 38" l single edged curved blade by Glingenthal, dated 1823, right face of blade engraved "Donne Par Le Roi," cast brass fore branch dec guard with laurel leaf dec on pommel, underside of guard stamped "Manceaus A Paris," leather grip with twisted brass wire, iron scabbard with two carrying rings, bright blade ...................................................................... 950.00

**Indian,** talwar with heavy 3-1/2" w blade, carved with parrots, tigers, figures, and deities in watered steel inlaid with gold, kottgari hilt of steel inlaid with gold, leather covered wooden scabbard, 19th C........1,150.00

## Japanese

8-1/2" l, tanto, suga-kuchi gai hai, carved with san character and two barely legible characters, two mekugi-ana, copper mounts with shakudo inlay, silver, and gold frogs, centipedes, spider, and snake, sgd "Shoami".....................................................................3,750.00

9-3/4" l, kwaiken, diamond shaped double edge blade with suga-hamon and mokume grain, engraved silvered copper mounts, 19th C ..........................................................................650.00

# TEA CADDIES

**History:** Tea once was a precious commodity and was stored in special boxes or caddies. These containers were made to accommodate different teas and included a special cup for blending.

Around 1700, silver caddies appeared in England. Other materials, such as Sheffield plate, tin, wood, china, and pottery, also were used. Some tea caddies are very ornate.

Chinese Export

Black lacquer, canted corners, cushion sloped top, gilt dec Chinese scenes, int. with lidded pewter canister, mid 19yh C ..........1,100.00

Black lacquer, rect, gilt grape vines, florals, and diapered ground, two handles, hinged lid opening to int. fitted with two pewter caddies, stippled floral dec to ext. lid, int. drop-in lid, 19th C, flaking, 15-3/8" w, 11" d, 10-1/2" h ........................................ 460.00

Brown lacquer, floral form, gilt dec Chinese scenes, dragon form feet, 19th C, 9-1/2" l ...................................................... 2,760.00

Brown lacquer, floral form, gilt dec Chinese scenes, cov interior pewter liner, mid-19th C, 6" w, 5-1/2" h........................... 1,100.00

Red lacquer, gilt scenes of figures, dragons, and foliage, carved paw feet, int. with two lidded pewter canisters, key, 19th C........2,185.00

Ivory, 4" w, 4-1/2" h, George III, early 19th C, silver mounted, tortoiseshell and mother-of-pearl inlay, faceted sides, lidded and foil lined interior.................................................................................. 2,760.00

Persian Export, 8-1/4" w, 5-3/4" h, lacquer, canted corners, cushion top, polychrome paisley design, two lidded int. wells, orig key, 19th C ................................................................................. 1,380.00

Silver

4-1/2" h, Tiffany & Co., early 20th C, ovoid, central band of scrolling leaves and flowerheads, cylindrical lid with similar central band, int. set lid with small bead finial, gold washed int., monogrammed lid, re-silvered, 7 troy oz .................................. 490.00

4-3/4" h, George III, Thomas Robins, London, 1794, ovoid, body reeded to lower section, engraved on front with heraldic crest, flush hinged lid with carved ivory egg-shaped finial, 17 troy oz.................................................................................... 1,495.00

Tôle, 13" d, 16" h, two carrying handles and spout, front dec with gilt scrolls, Edwardian, first quarter 20th C .................................... 220.00

Tortoiseshell

4-1/4" w, 5" h, raised faceted lid, canted corners, allover pierced rococo style silver mounts, int. with lidded well, Victorian, Birmingham, c1840............................................................................. 4,600.00

4-3/4" w, 4" h, stepped top with ivory ball finial, tapered sides, ball feet, orig key, late George III, early 19th C ........................ 980.00

5-3/4" w, 5-1/2" h, faceted shaped top, serpentine case, ivory dec, two lidded int. wells, ball feet, George III, 19th C........... 1,495.00

Tunbridgeware

4-1/2" w, 4" h, inlaid rosewood, checker cross-banding, inlaid butterfly, English, 19th C ...................................................... 865.00

9" w, 5-1/4" h, cross banded mahogany, tapered rect form, block feet, Victorian, 19th C ...................................................... 395.00

Wood

3-3/4" w, 4-1/2" h, boxwood, cross banded and strung rosewood, twelve sided, lined foil and paper interior, Regency, early 19th C.................................................................................750.00

4-3/8" w, 5-3/8" h, silvered metal mounted rosewood, flush corner mounts, top inset with foliage, key, Asian Export ............. 550.00

4-1/2" h, fruitwood, apple form, angled stem, shaped base, George III style, 20th C...................................................... 635.00

4-1/2" w, 5-3/8" h, fruitwood and boxwood inlaid mahogany, late George III, early 19th C, cross-banded and string inlaid borders, inlaid paterae, lidded int. and key.................................. 1,610.00

4-3/4" h, fruitwood, apple form, oval metal escutcheon, upright stem, hinged lid, lock missing, George III, late 18th C ....1,265.00

4-3/4" h, fruitwood, pear form, angled stem, light yellow tone, remnants of red stain, George III style ............................. 920.00

**Wood, sarcophagus form, brass lion's head and ring handles, paw and ball feet, ivory inlaid escutcheon, int. with 3 compartments, lids with ivory handles, center compartment with later glass bowl, 12" w, 6" d, 7" h, $360. Photo courtesy of Sanford Alderfer Auction Co.**

4-3/4" w, 3-1/2" h, mahogany, miniature, traveling, sarcophagus form, silvered metal mounts, plaque, lion mask, and ring handle, ball feet, lidded int., Edwardian, 19th C ............................ 625.00

4-3/4" w, 4" h, penworked fruitwood, cov with gondola scene, side with flower filled baskets, turned feet, German, 20th C .... 250.00

5" h, fruitwood, apple form, silvered metal escutcheon, late George III, early 19th C ............................................... 2,875.00

5-1/2" h, fruitwood, apple-form, lobed panels, orig pigment remaining, late George III, early 19th C........................ 4,900.00

5-1/2" w, 4-3/4" h, fruitwood, marquetry inlaid satinwood, oval, floral inlay, Turnbridge cross banding, George III, early 19th C...... 980.00

5-3/4" h, fruitwood, pear form, stylized trefoil metal escutcheon, hinged lid with foil int., George III, late 19th C, stem off, but present ................................................................................ 3,220.00

6-1/2" h, fruitwood, apple form, silvered metal escutcheon, mellow yellow color, late George III ..................................... 4,320.00

7" h, fruitwood, pear form, angled stem, steel escutcheon, light yellow color with mottling, orig key, late George III, early 19th C ................................................................................4,600.00

7-1/2" w, 5" h, fruitwood inlaid burl, cross banded, inlaid panels of insects and shells, Victorian, 19th C.............................. 1,150.00

8-1/4" l, 4-1/4" w, 4-1/4" h, walnut, rect, canted lid inlaid with oval cartouche of butterfly, rect flattened block feet, George III-style........................................................................................260.00

10-1/2" h, fruitwood, cross-banded rosewood, knife urn form, faceted sides, turned stem, sq feet, turned ivory finial, faceted lid, lidded int., George III/Regency, early 19th C, price for pr ..............7,475.00

10-3/4" l, 5-7/8" d, 6-1/4" h, rosewood, sarcophagus shape, lid with mother-of-pearl diamond inset, round ivory escutcheon, int. with two foil lined compartments, central mixing well, flattened bun feet, English, early 19th C........................................... 250.00

12" w, 7" h, amboyna and fruitwood inlaid sycamore, late Georgian, 19th C, inlaid with foliage and oval panels, two lidded int. compartments ............................................................. 4,600.00

12-1/8" l, 6" d, 7-1/4" h, bird's eye maple and inlaid, inlaid with ebonized banding to perimeter and with scrolled banding to front, lion's head pendant handles on sides, int. fitted with two lidded foil-lined compartments with central mixing well, Regency, England, early 19th C, bowl missing................. 700.00

12-1/2" w, 7-1/2" h, fruitwood, marquetry inlaid mahogany, tapered rect form, inlaid with fans and foliage, int. fitted with twelve silver spoons, cut glass mixing bowl, two lidded wells, attributed to Nathaniel Munroe, c1777, George III, early 19th C ............ 1,850.00

14-1/2" w, 8-1/4" h, rosewood, sideboard form, ivory pulls and feet, brass mounts, int. fitted with three wells, Empire.............2,415.00

14-1/2" l, 6-1/4" d, 11-1/2" h, mahogany veneer, sideboard form, hinged lift top opens to cylindrical container flanked by two shallow compartments over two deep pull-out lead-lined drawers, English, 19th C, veneer losses, cracks.............................980.00

# TEA LEAF IRONSTONE CHINA

**History:** Tea Leaf ironstone flowed into America from England in great quantities from 1860 to 1910 and graced the tables of working-class America. It traveled to California and Texas in wagons and down the Mississippi River by boat to Kentucky and Missouri. It was too plain for the rich homes; its simplicity and durability appealed to wives forced to watch pennies. Tea Leaf found its way into the kitchen of Lincoln's Springfield home; sailors ate from it aboard the *Star of India*, now moored in San Diego and still displaying Tea Leaf.

Contrary to popular belief, Tea Leaf was not manufactured exclusively by English potters in Staffordshire. Although there were more than 35 English potters producing Tea Leaf, at least 26 American potters helped satisfy the demand.

Anthony Shaw (1850-1900) is credited with introducing Tea Leaf. The most prolific Tea Leaf makers were Anthony Shaw and Alfred Meakin (1875-present). Johnson Bros. (1883-present), Henry Burgess (1864-1892), Enoch Wedgwood, and Arthur J. Wilkinson (1897-present), all of whom shipped much of their ware to America.

Although most of the English Tea Leaf is copper luster, Powell and Bishop (1868-1878) and their successors, Bishop and Stonier (1891-1936), worked primarily in gold luster. Beautiful examples of gold luster were also made by H. Burgess; Mellor, Taylor & Co. (1880-1904) used it on children's tea sets. Other English potters also were known to use gold luster, including W. & E. Corn, Thomas Elsmore, and Thomas Hughes, companies which have been recently identified as makers of this type of ware.

J. & E. Mayer, Beaver Falls, Pennsylvania, founded by English potters who immigrated to America, produced a large amount of copper luster Tea Leaf. The majority of the American potters decorated with gold luster that had no brown underglaze beneath the copper luster.

East Liverpool, Ohio, potters such as Cartwright Bros. (1864-1924), East End Pottery (1894-1909) and Knowles, Taylor & Knowles (1870-1934) decorated only in gold luster. This also is true of Trenton, New Jersey, potters, such as Glasgow Pottery, American Crockery Co., and Fell & Thropp Co. Since no underglazing was used with the gold, much of it has been washed away.

By the 1900s, Tea Leaf's popularity had waned. The sturdy ironstone did not disappear; it was stored in barns and relegated to attics and basements. While the manufacture of Tea Leaf did experience a brief resurgence from the late 1950s through the 1970s, copper lustre Tea Leaf didn't recapture the hearts of the American consumer as it had a generation before.

Tea Leaf collectors recognize a number of "variant" decorative motifs as belonging to the Tea Leaf family: Teaberry, Morning Glory, Coral, Cinquefoil, Rose, Pre-Tea Leaf, Tobacco Leaf, Pepper Leaf, Pinwheel, Pomegranate, and Thistle & Berry, as well as white ironstone decorated with copper lustre bands and floral and geometric motifs. Once considered the stepchildren of Tea leaf, these variants are now prized by collectors and generally bring strong prices.

Today's collectors eagerly seek out Tea Leaf and all of its variant motifs, and copper-lustre decorated white ironstone has once again become prized for its durability, beauty, simplicity, craft, and style.

**References:** Annise Doring Heaivilin, *Grandma's Tea Leaf Ironstone*, Wallace-Homestead, 1981, 1996 reprint distributed by L-W Book Sales; Jean Wetherbee, *White Ironstone, A Collector's Guide*, Tea Leaf Club International (324 Powderhorn Dr., Houghton Lake, MI 48629), 1996.

**Collectors' Club:** Tea Leaf Club International, 324 Powderhorn Dr., Houghton Lake, MI 48629.

**Museums:** Lincoln Home, Springfield, IL; Ox Barn Museum, Aurora, OR; Sherman Davidson House, Newark OH.

**Advisor:** Dale Abrams.

**Notes:** Tea Leaf values have increased steadily for the last decade, but there are some general rules of thumb for the knowledgeable collector. English Tea Leaf is still more collectible than American, except for rare pieces. The earlier the Tea Leaf production (1850s-1860s), the harder it is to find pieces and, therefore, the more expensive they are. Children's pieces are highly collectible, especially those with copper lustre decorative motifs. Hard-to-find Tea Leaf pieces include mustache cups, eggcups, covered syrup pitchers, ladles, oversized serving pieces, and pieces with significant embossing. Common pieces (plates, platters) of later production (1880-1900) need to be in excellent condition or should be priced accordingly as they are not that difficult to find.

Bone Dish
   Meakin
      Crescent shape .............................................. 55.00
      Scalloped edge............................................... 65.00
   Shaw, fluted edge .............................................. 60.00
Brush Vase
   Burgess, Pagoda ............................................... 215.00
   Meakin, Fishhook............................................... 200.00
   Shaw
      Basketweave ................................................. 425.00
      Plain round, drain hole ................................... 225.00
Butter Dish, 3pc, base, cover, liner
   Meakin, Fishhook............................................... 185.00
   Wedgwood, simple square ................................. 185.00
Butter Dish Liner, sq.................................................. 25.00
Butter Pat, Meakin
   Square ................................................................ 15.00
   Round, Chelsea .................................................. 25.00
Cake Plate
   Edwards, Peerless (Feather), sq, handles.......... 185.00
   Meakin, Bamboo, 8-3/4" with handles ................. 85.00
   Wilkinson, Senate shape, oval........................... 150.00

Chamber Pot, Meakin
  Bamboo, 2 pc.............................................265.00
  Scroll, 2 pc.............................................285.00
Children's Dishes
  Mug, child's, Shaw.....................................375.00
  Tea Set, Knowles, Taylor & Knowles, 4 cups and saucers, teapot, creamer and sugar....................................850.00
  Tea Set, Mellor-Taylor, round bottom, gold luster, 6 cups and saucers, 6 plates, teapot, creamer, sugar, waste bowl.......1,850.00
Coffeepot, cov
  Furnival, Gentle Square (Rooster).....................325.00
  Meakin, Chelsea.......................................300.00
  Shaw, Lily-of-the-Valley...............................475.00
Compote
  Mellor Taylor, sq, ridged..............................325.00
  Red Cliff, simple square, 1960s.......................150.00
  Shaw, plain, round.....................................310.00
  Unmarked, unusually deep bowl, 8" d, 5" h..........435.00
Creamer
  Edwards, Peerless (Feather)..........................285.00
  Meakin, Bamboo........................................185.00
  Red Cliff, Chinese shape, 1960s.......................80.00
  Shaw, Cable...........................................250.00
Cup and Saucer
  Adams, Empress shape, 1950s...........................30.00
  Meakin.................................................65.00
  Shaw, Lily-of-the-Valley...............................125.00
Egg Cup
  Meakin, Boston Egg Cup, 4" d, 1-3/4" h...............395.00
  Unmarked, 3-1/2" h.....................................325.00
Gravy Boat
  Johnson Bros, Acanthus, with stand....................160.00
  Mayer, American........................................90.00
  Meakin, Bamboo.........................................85.00
  Shaw, Basketweave, with stand........................185.00
  Wedgwood, simple square................................65.00
Mug
  Meakin, Scroll.........................................195.00
  Shaw
    Chinese shape........................................115.00
    Lily-of-the-Valley...................................350.00
Mush Bowl, Meakin........................................85.00
Nappy
  Meakin, Fishhook, 4-1/4" sq............................20.00
  Wedgwood, 4-1/4" sq, scalloped edge...................24.00
Pitcher and Bowl Set
  Furnival, Cable........................................495.00
  Meakin, Fishhook.......................................285.00
  Shaw, Cable............................................525.00
Pitcher/Jug
  Meakin
    Chelsea..............................................375.00
    Fishhook.............................................285.00
  Shaw
    Cable shape, 7" h....................................295.00
    Chinese shape, 7-1/2"................................500.00

Plate
  Furnival, plain, round, 8-1/4".........................12.00
  Johnson Bros., Acanthus, 9" d..........................22.00
  Meakin, plain, round, 6-3/4" d.........................10.00
  Shaw, plain, round, 10" d..............................25.00
  Wedgwood, plain, round, 9-1/4" d.......................17.00
Platter
  Meakin
    Chelsea, 10" x 14", oval.............................65.00
    Plain, 9" x 13", rect................................35.00
  Shaw, Lily-of-the-Valley, 13".........................150.00
Punch Bowl, Shaw, Cable.................................525.00
Relish Dish, Shaw, Chinese shape........................265.00
Sauce Tureen
  Furnival, Cable, 3 pc.................................185.00
  Meakin, Bamboo, 4 pc, including ladle................425.00
  Red Cliff, 4 pc, including ladle......................175.00
Serving Bowl, open
  Grindley, round, scalloped edge......................135.00
  Meakin, sq, scalloped edge, 6" sq.....................45.00
Soap Dish, cov
  Grindley, Bamboo, 3 pc, liner, rect..................225.00
  Shaw, Cable, 3 pc, liner, oval.......................300.00
Soup Bowl, Meakin, plain, round, 8-3/4" d...............25.00
Soup Plate, Meakin, plain, round, 10" d.................50.00
Soup Tureen, Meakin, Bamboo, 4 pc with ladle..........1,500.00
Sugar Bowl, cov
  Meakin
    Bamboo...............................................95.00
    Fishhook.............................................85.00
  Shaw
    Bullet..............................................135.00
    Cable shape.........................................145.00
Vanity Box, cov, Furnival, Cable, horizontal............325.00
Vegetable, cov
  Meakin, Bamboo........................................165.00
  Shaw
    Basketweave.........................................325.00
    Hanging Leaves......................................450.00
  Wilkinson, Maidenhair Fern...........................275.00
Waste Bowl
  Meakin, plain, round..................................110.00
  Shaw, Niagara Fan.....................................120.00

# TEAPOTS

**History:** The origins of the teapot have been traced to China in the late 16th century. Early Yixing teapots were no bigger than the tiny cups previously used for drinking tea. By the 17th century, tea had spread to civilized nations of the world. The first recorded advertisement for tea in London is dated 1658 and is called a "China drink,...call Tcha, by other Nations Tay, alias Tee..." Although coffee houses were already established, they began to add tea to their selections.

While the Chinese had long been producing teapots and other tea items, the English were receiving these wares along with shipments of tea. By the early 1700s, British china and stoneware producers were manufacturing teapots. It was in 1706 that Thomas Twining bought his own coffee house and thwarted the competition of the many other such establishments by offering a variety of quality tea. Coffee houses were exclusively for males, thus women would wait outside, sending their footmen inside for purchases. For the majority of the 1700s, teapots were Oriental imports. British factories continued

Cup and Saucer, 2-1/4" d cup, 5-3/4" d, saucer, $65.

experimenting with the right combination of materials which would make a teapot durable enough to withstand the daily rigors of boiling water. Chinese Export Porcelain was an inspiration to the British and by the end of the 1700s, many companies found the necessary combinations of china clay and stone, fired at high temperature, which could withstand boiling water needed to brew precious pots of tea.

From the very first teapots, figural shapes have always been a favorite with tea drinkers. The Victorian era saw a change from more utilitarian teapots toward beautiful, floral, and Rococo designs, yet figural pots continued to be manufactured.

Early American manufacturers mimicked Oriental and British designs. While the new land demanded sturdy teapots in the unsettled land, potteries were established steadily in the Eastern states. Rockingham teapots were produced by many companies, deriving this term from British companies manufacturing a strong, shiny brown glaze on heavy pottery. The best known are from the Bennington, Vermont, potteries.

By the 1800s and the turn-of-the-century, many pottery companies were well established in the U. S., producing a lighter dinnerware and china including teapots. Figural teapots from this era are highly desired by collectors while others concentrate on collecting all known patterns produced by a company.

The last 20 years has seen a renewed interest in teapots and collectors desire not only older examples, but high-priced, specialty manufactured teapots such as those from the Lomonosov factory in Russia or individual artist creations commanding hundreds of dollars.

**References:** Edward Bramah, *Novelty Teapots,* Quiller Press, London, 1992; Tina M. Carter, *Teapots,* Running Press, 1995; —, *Collectible Teapots, Reference and Price Guide,* Krause Publications, 2000; Robin Emmerson, *British Teapots & Tea Drinking,* HMSO, London, 1992.

**Periodicals:** *Tea, A Magazine,* P.O. Box 348, Scotland, CT 06264; *Tea Talk,* P.O. Box 860, Sausalito, CA 94966; *Tea Time Gazette,* P.O. Box 40276, St. Paul, MN 55104.

**Reproduction Alert:** Teapots and other ware with blurry mark of shield and two animals, ironstone, celadon colored body background, design made to look like flow blue, are new products, possibly from China. Yixing teapots have been reproduced or made in similar styles for centuries, study this type of teapot to help determine the old from the new.

**Advisor:** Tina M. Carter.

Automobile, figural, shaped like Austin, Carlton Ware, England. 500.00
Belleek, sea urchin and coral, Echinus Tea Ware, Ireland, first black
   mark ....................................................................... 850.00
Cadogan, brown Rockingham style pottery, no mark, possibly made in
   England, late 1800s ............................................... 195.00
Blue Canton, reproduction of Chinese export porcelain, 1970s.. 150.00
Clarice Cliff, teepee, 1946.......................................... 850.00
Cloisonné, panel with butterflies and flowers, Chinese, late
   19th C .................................................................. 450.00
Copper, spun, E. W. Allen, 1940s ................................. 550.00
Flow Blue, Scinde pattern, Alcock, octagonal, 8 1/2" h ............. 950.00
Graniteware, large teapot with pewter handle, lid and spout, Manning
   Bowman & Co. Manufacturers, called Perfection Granite Ironware,
   West Meriden, Connecticut ...................................... 325.00
Lenox, Art Deco, applied sterling silver dec, c1930, 3 pc set ..... 400.00
Majolica, fish, multi-colored, Minton, no mark, late 1800s ........ 2000.00
Old Worcester, first period, Old Japan Star, 1765-70 .............. 5,250.00
Parian Ware, Brownfield, Mistletoe pattern.......................... 450.00
Porcelain, pink and gray luster swirls, Surf Ballet, by California artist,
   Sascha Brastoff. mark includes artist name and chanticleer (rooster)
   used since 1953, especially large teapot ................. 250.00
Rockingham Style, triple-spouted teapot, brown pottery, relief design,
   late 1800s, early 1900s ......................................... 2,000.00
Sheffield, silver and ebony details, c1912................................ 1,500.00
Silver, repousse, S. Kirk & Sons, 6 pc set............................... 8,000.00
Wedgewood
     Earthenware, cabbage, lettuce, melon, various designs....... 650.00
     Jasperware, unglazed porcelain with decoration in white relief,
       modern set includes creamer and sugar, mark, Wedgwood,
       England, set ..................................................... 295.00
Yixing
     Bamboo handle, Chinese "chop mark" or signature, c1880 450.00
     Padded storage box, fixed handle, all over Chinese writing,
       imported by Midwest Importers, made in China, orig pamphlet
       explaining centuries old tradition, modern.......................... 75.00
Zurich porcelain, dragon spout, china series, rococo style,
   c1770 .................................................................... 6,000.00

# TEDDY BEARS

**History:** Originally thought of as "Teddy's Bears," in reference to President Theodore Roosevelt, these stuffed toys are believed to have originated in Germany. The first ones to be made in the United States were produced about 1902.

Most of the earliest teddy bears had humps on their backs, elongated muzzles, and jointed limbs. The fabric used was generally mohair; the eyes were either glass with pin backs or black shoe buttons. The stuffing was usually excelsior. Kapok (for softer bears) and wood-wool (for firmer bears) also were used as stuffing materials.

Quality older bears often have elongated limbs, sometimes with curved arms, oversized feet, and felt paws. Noses and mouths are black and embroidered onto the fabric.

The earliest teddy bears are believed to have been made by the original Ideal Toy Corporation in America and by a German company, Margarete Steiff, GmbH. Bears made in the early 1900s by other companies can

Copper Luster, raised scene of girl in red dress playing with brown and white dog, green ground, unmarked, 5-1/2" h, $90. Photo courtesy of Susan and Al Bagdade.

be difficult to identify because they were all similar in appearance and most identifying tags or labels were lost during childhood play.

**References:** Shawn Brecka, *Big Book of Little Bears*, Antique Trader Books, 1999; Dee Hockenberry, *Steiff Bears and Other Playthings Past and Present*, Schiffer Publishing, 2000; Constance King, *The Century of the Teddy Bear*, Antique Collectors' Club, 1999; Margaret Fox Mandel, *Teddy Bears and Steiff Animals*, 1st Series (1984, 2000 value update), 2nd Series (1987, 2000 value update), 3rd Series (2000), Collector Books; ——, *Teddy Bears, Annalee Animals & Steiff Animals*, 3rd Series, Collector Books, 1990, 1996 value update; Ken Yenke, *Bing Bears and Toys*, Schiffer Publishing, 2000; ——, *Teddy Bear Treasury, Identification & Values*, Collector Books, 2000.

**Periodicals:** *Antique & Collectables*, P.O. Box 12589, El Cajon, CA 92022, http://www.collect.com/antiqueandcollectables; *Beans & Bears!* P.O. Box 3070, Richmond, VA 23228, http://www.beansmagazine.com; *National Doll & Teddy Bear Collector*, P.O. Box 4032, Portland, OR 97208; *Teddy Bear & Friends*, 741 Miller Drive, SE, Suite D2, Harrisburg, PA 20175; http://www.cowles.com/maglist.html; *Teddy Bear Review*, 170 Fifth Ave., 12th Floor, New York, NY 10010; *Teddy Bear Times*, Avalon Court, Star Road, Partridge Green, West Sussex RH13 8RY, http://www.teddybeartimes.com.

**Collectors' Clubs:** Good Bears of the World, P.O. Box 13097, Toledo, OH 43613; My Favorite Bear: Collectors Club for Classic Winnie the Pooh, 468 W. Alpine #10, Upland, CA 91786; Steiff Club USA, 31 E. 28th St., 9th Floor, New York, NY 10016, http://www.steiff-club.com; Teddy Bear Boosters Club, 19750 SW Peavine Mountain Road, McMinnville, OR 97128.

**Museum:** Teddy Bear Museum of Naples, Naples, FL.

**Additional Listings:** See Steiff.

**Notes:** Teddy bears are rapidly increasing as collectibles and their prices are rising proportionally. As in other fields, desirability should depend upon appeal, quality, uniqueness, and condition. One modern bear already has been firmly accepted as a valuable collectible among its antique counterparts: the Steiff teddy put out in 1980 for the company's 100th anniversary. This is a reproduction of that company's first teddy and has a special box, signed certificate, and numbered ear tag; 11,000 of these were sold worldwide.

Bing, 15" h, white mohair, fully jointed, black shoe button eyes, rust embroidered nose, mouth, and claws, white felt pads, 1910......1,265.00
Bruin, 28" h, golden mohair, fully jointed, glass eyes, tan felt pads, excelsior stuffing, pink silk and mohair jacket, worn, detached partial cloth label, c1907 ............................................................. 6,325.00
Herman, 19" h, golden mohair, no side seams, fully jointed, shoe button eyes, fabric nose, embroidered mouth, excelsior stuffing, replaced pads.......................................................................... 175.00
Ideal
   10-1/2" h, golden mohair, fully jointed, black shoe button eyes, black embroidered nose, mouth, and claws, beige pads, excelsior stuffing, c1919, remnants of red felt tongue, minor fur loss ........425.00
   12" h, white mohair, fully jointed, black shoe button eyes, tan embroidered nose, mouth, and claws, felt pads, well loved ............575.00

19" h, golden mohair, fully jointed, black steel eyes, tan felt pads, black embroidered nose, mouth, and claws, c1905, fur flattened on back........................................................................5,750.00
20" h, golden mohair, fully jointed, glass eyes, fabric nose, embroidered mouth and claws, felt pads, excelsior stuffing, early 1920s.................................................................... 350.00
Schuco
   4-3/4" h, Yes/No, yellow mohair, fully jointed, black steel eyes and eye glasses, early 20th C, minor fur loss ......................... 435.00
   5" h, dancing, gold mohair, black steel eyes, embroidered nose and mouth, arm jointed at shoulders, red felt beret and trousers, black metal feet, key, 1930, 5" h ..................................... 290.00
Steiff
   9-1/2" h, blond mohair, fully jointed, felt pads, black steel eyes, dark brown embroidered nose, mouth, and claws, excelsior stuffing, blank ear button, c1905, well loved ................... 500.00
   22" h, golden mohair, few signs of moth damage, c1905 ...10,065.00
Unknown Maker
   5-3/4" h, 7-1/2" l, light brown velveteen, glass eyes, wooden platform base, metal wheels, early 20th C, some pile loss ...... 225.00
   12" h, polar, off-white mohair, glass eyes, composition nose and open mouth with teeth, Distler key, French clockwork........ 980.00
   13" h, yellow mohair, fully jointed, shoe button eyes, tan embroidered nose and claws, excelsior stuffing, well loved .......... 290.00

# TEPLITZ CHINA

**History:** Around 1900, there were 26 ceramic manufacturers located in Teplitz, a town in the Bohemian province of what was then known as Czechoslovakia. Other potteries were located in the nearby town of Turn. Wares from these factories were molded, cast, and hand decorated. Most are in the Art Nouveau and Art Deco styles.

**Marks:** The majority of pieces do not carry a specific manufacturer's mark; they are simply marked "Teplitz," "Turn-Teplitz," or "Turn."

Bowl, 5-1/2" d, girl pulling rooster's tail, marked "Stellmacher"..... 75.00
Candlestick, 5-1/4", figural, woman wearing flowing gown ......... 150.00
Compote, 6" d, Art Nouveau woman, high relief florals, marked "Amphora-Teplitz" .................................................................... 400.00

**Vase, two handles, brown, gold highlights, mkd "Stellmacher, Teplitz, Austria," 7-1/2" h, $165.**

Ewer
   10" h, Art Nouveau, scrolled and gold beaded handle, reticulated ruf-
      fled collar, goldfish lip spout, raised gold outlined flowers .....425.00
   11-1/2" h, flower dec, ornate handle, marked "Turn Teplitz Bohe-
      mia" ...................................................................................225.00
Figure, 18-1/2" h, young woman, elaborate dress ......................450.00
Loving Cup, 15" h, 9-3/4" w, reticulated outer wall, turquoise, amber,
   opal, and cobalt blue jewels, gold scalloped rim, foot, and twisted
   branch handles..........................................................................350.00
Pitcher, 9-1/2" h, green and pink, lily pad dec, c1895 .................225.00
Vase
   7" h, enameled caped gentleman, mkd "Teplitz Stellmacher"..165.00
   8-1/2" h, molded intricate design, gold highlights, cram ground,
      blown-out stylized design at top, pink centers, designed by Paul
      Daschel, stamp mark ........................................................700.00
   13" h, 5-1/4" d, Art Nouveau-style, woman's head with flowing
      hair and blossoms, stems form two asymmetrical handles,
      ochre and green, ink stamped mark...................................450.00
   14" h, 6" d, corseted, bulbous top, Secessionist-type dec, emb
      stylized white roses and gilded leaves, blue-gray ground 600.00
   15" h, winged gold and ivory creature at neck, reticulated top with
      applied flowers, bulbous ribbed bottom with painted flowers out-
      lined in gold, stamped mark, minor chips and repairs ..........290.00

# TERRA-COTTA WARE

**History:** Terra-cotta is ware made of hard, semi-fired ceramic. The color of the pottery ranges from a light orange-brown to a deep brownish red. It is usually unglazed, but some pieces are partially glazed and have incised, carved, or slip designs. Utilitarian objects, as well as statuettes and large architectural pieces, were made. Fine early Chinese terra-cotta pieces recently have sold for substantial prices.

Figure
   19" h, two young satyrs by statue of Bacchus, light brown colora-
      tion, incised signature "Gamma" on rocky base, 20th C...425.00
   29-1/2" h, woman, peasant dress, holding basket of fruit and veg-
      etables, painted, 19th C, needs restoration ......................265.00
Garden Urn, cov, 22" d, 61" h, grapevine molded lid, acorn finial, molded
   edge lip, body dec with clusters, circular and leaf molded standard, socle
   base, acanthus shaped handles, price for pr.............................1,980.00
Medallion, 3-1/2" w, 4-3/8" h, oval, white classical relief of children with
   sheep, imp Wedgwood & Bentley mark, rim chips................1,100.00
Olive Jar, 42" h, bulbous, French, 19th C ....................................650.00
Plaque, 13-1/4" w, 7-1/2" h, rect, relief carved darrodila, incised signature "S. D. Chapman," deep beveled mahogany frame, repair and
   some chips, early 20th C.............................................................325.00
Tile
   10-1/4" w, 14-1/4" h, wedge shaped tile, raised dec of centaur
      with bow and arrow, ornate vine in background, unglazed, imp
      "3859 11" on side, chips, firing bursts ..............................385.00
   12" w, 8-1/2" d, 19-1/2" h, rect shape, molded high relief dolphin,
      mouth fitted with fountain hole over shell form basin, unglazed,
      attributed to Grueby Pottery, Boston, early 20th C, chips ...1,200.00
Urn, cov, 45" h, 20" d, bulbous, foliate and fruit swagged body, spiral
   fluted socle, surmounted fruit cov, pr....................................4,000.00

# TEXTILES

**History:** Textiles is the generic term for cloth or fabric items, especially anything woven or knitted. Antique textiles that have survived are usually those that were considered the "best" by their original owners, since these were the objects that were used and stored carefully by the housewife.

Textiles are collected for many reasons—to study fabrics, to understand the elegance of a historical period, for decorative purposes, or to use as was originally intended. The renewed interest in antique clothing has sparked a revived interest in period textiles of all forms.

**References:** Dilys E. Blum, *The Fine Art of Textiles: The Collection of the Philadelphia Museum of Art,* Philadelphia Museum of Art, 1997; M. Dupont-Auberville, *Full-Color Historic Textile Designs*, Dover Publications, 1996; Loretta Smith Fehling, *Terrific Tablecloths from the '40s and '50s,* Schiffer, 1998; Frances Johnson, *Collecting Household Linens*, Schiffer Publishing, 1997; Elizabeth Kurella, *The Complete Guide To Vintage Textiles,* Krause Publications, 1999; Sheila Paine, *Embroidered Textiles: Traditional Patterns from Five Continents, With a Worldwide Guide To Identification,* Thames & Hudson, 1997; Mildred Cole Peladeau, *Art Underfoot: The Story of Waldoboro Hooked Rugs,* American Textile History Museum, 1999; Raffaella Serena, *Embroideries and Patterns from 19th Century Vienna,* Antique Collectors' Club Ltd., 1998; Jessie A. Turbayne, *Hooked Rug Treasury*, Schiffer Publishing, 1997.

**Periodicals:** *HALI*, P.O. Box 4312, Philadelphia, PA 19118; *International Old Lacers Bulletin*, P.O. Box 554, Flanders, NJ 07836; *Textile Museum Newsletter*, The Textile Museum, 2320 S. St. NW, Washington, DC 20008.

**Collectors' Clubs:** American Needlepoint Guild, Inc., P.O. Box 1027, Cordova, TN 38088-1027, http://www.needle-point.org; Colonial Coverlet Guide of America, 5617 Black-stone, La Grante, IL 60525-3420; Costume Society of America, P.O. Box 73, Earleville, MD 21919, http://www.costumesocietyamerica.com; Stumpwork Society, 55 Ferncrest Ave., Cranston, RI 02905-3510; International Old Lacers, Inc., P.O. Box 554, Flanders, NJ 07836, Rug & Textile Society of Indiana, 8940 Sassafras Court, Indianapolis, IN 46260; Textile Group of Los Angeles, Inc., 894 S. Bronson Ave., Los Angeles CA 9005-3605.

**Museums:** Cooper-Hewitt Museum, New York, NY; Currier Gallery of Art, Manchester, NH; Ipswich Historical Society, Ipswich, MA; Lace Museum, Mountain View, CA; Museum of American Textile History, North Andover, MA; Museum of Art, Rhode Island School of Design, Providence, RI; Philadelphia College of Textiles & Science, Philadelphia, PA; Textile Museum, Washington, DC; Valentine Museum, Richmond, VA.

**Additional Listings:** See Clothing; Lace and Linens; Quilts; Samplers.

Blanket, homespun wool, two-piece construction
68" x 76", black checks on natural white, wear and holes ..........330.00
70" x 84", navy blue and natural white, small holes and wear ....175.00
72" x 78", blue and tomato red plaid, small holes and repairs ....200.00
Bolster Cover, 18" x 58", blue and white homespun, hand sewn
   seams..........................................................................................150.00
Coverlet, chintz, cotton, 90-3/4" x 79", shades of brown and red on nat-
   ural ground, hand quilted, constructed of three panels with urns,
   birds, and flowering vines, mid 19th C, minor stain ...............2,100.00
Coverlet, jacquard, one piece, single weave
   73" x 86", navy blue and white, snowflake corner blocks, double
      urns of flowers border, flowering plants on central ground, ini-
      tialed "A. C. 1859," minor stains....................................210.00

82" x 96", twenty divided panels with four flowers each, flowering plant borders, star corner blocks with "E. K." and "1845," green, gold, navy blue, and tomato red, wear and stains............ 325.00

Coverlet, jacquard, two piece, single weave

66" x 83", rose and buildings borders, urns of flowers in center, olive green, red, and dark natural white, sgd "Peter Uhl, Portage County, Ohio, 1852," wear and some fringe loss ............. 360.00

69" x 86", grapevine border, leaf and heart medallions, red, medium blue, natural white, and navy blue, pattern slightly off where sections are sewn together, light stains.................. 200.00

72" x 89", sixteen leaf panels surrounded by flowers and intricate double foliage borders, 1834, four snowflake corner blocks, navy blue and natural white, stains, wear, small holes .... 440.00

74" x 80", basket of flowers border with small houses, stars, tulips, and foliage in central ground, sgd "Sebastian Hipp, 1854," (Richland County, OH), salmon, green, natural white, and navy blue, two holes, light stains, loss to bottom edge .................................250.00

76" x 88", eagle and tree borders, stars and four rose medallions, corner signature blocks "Martin B. Brenemen, Washington Twp. York Co. Pa 1836," brick red, light blue, navy blue, and natural white, minor moth damage and stains ............................. 550.00

Coverlet, overshot, linsey woolsey, blue and white geometric pattern, America, 19th C, minor staining, two corners cut for bed posts, 92" x 90-1/2".................................................................................... 175.00

Flag, 60" x 100", handsewn wool, thirteen double appliquéd cotton stars, canvas hoist with pierced holes, mid 19th C, soiled, fabric loss ....................................................................................2,185.00

Hooked Rug

19" h, 32" l, bridge in background, pine trees and road, maple leaves in corners, minor damage ..................................... 110.00

22" h, 37" l, red, green, brown, and yellow poppies, foliage scroll border ...................................................................................... 110.00

30" h, 55" l, rag, crossed logs and leaves, shades of red, green, brown, light gray and cream, old rebinding ...................... 175.00

31-1/2" h, 55-1/2" l, wool, cotton, silk yarn and ribbons, bowl of flowers, shades of red, blue, and green, outlined in black, ochre ground surrounded by meandering borders of purple, cream, and shades of brown and ochre, America, late 19th C, mounted on frame, minor imperfections......................................5,175.00

**Beadwork, picture, vase and flowers on silk ground, cobalt blue, pink, greens, and red, framed, w/orig 1906 bill of sale, stains, loss, 14" w, 18" h, $990. Photo courtesy of Sanford Alderfer Auction Co.**

**Needlework Picture, silk, chenille, watercolor, and ink on silk, woman seated in chair making wreath, sheep in background, black painted frame, gilt liner, reverse painted mat, 12-1/4" x 9-3/4", $660. Photo courtesy of Sanford Alderfer Auction Co.**

33" h, 65" l, log cabin pattern, multicolored wool, shades of yellow, browns, red, green, gray, and black, America, c1900, repairs .................................................................................... 250.00

35" h, 54" l, brightly colored tulips, daffodils, lilies, and iris, white central oval ground, gray border ..................................... 425.00

35-1/2" h, 59" l, oval, burgundy and pink roses, cream colored ground, burgundy border.................................................... 90.00

37" h, 58-1/2" l, rust, tan, and gray tree of life dec with blue, salmon, yellow, orange, and tan flowers, leaves, etc., gray ground, maroon and black borders ................................. 220.00

41-1/2" h, 48" l, flowering tree in pot flanked by two red leaping stags on black ground, horse at each corner, wide border of hit or miss geometric shapes, mounted on frame, America, 19th C, minor imperfections...................................................... 5,465.00

43-1/2" l, 28" h, seated black and white dog watching over black and white hens, chicks, and ducks, red highlights on tan ground, two black borders, hooked in various fabrics and yarns, mounted on frame, America, 19th C, minor imperfections......................... 865.00

Lap Robe, velvet and silk embroidered, dated and initialed "1885 CLH," pierced in Windmill Blades variant, corners with embroidered flora and fauna, border with padded silk roses and chenille embroidered leaves, pieced scalloped shaped edge with silk embroidery fans and tassels, decorative embroidery throughout, backed with olive green velvet, minor losses, 56" x 58-1/2" h .................. 4,320.00

Needlework Panel, 18-1/4" h, 20-1/4" w, silk on silk, landscape scene, shades of green, brown, yellow, white, and black, old label "The handwork of Miss Chloe, a school teacher...born in Abington, now Rockland, Mass in 1786...," wear, tear in sky, matted and reframed ............. 385.00

Needlework Picture

6-1/4" w, 9-1/4" h, solidly stitched in silk threads, watercolor features and sky, oval format, young lady gathering roses in landscape, oval frame, eglomise mat, framed, England, 19th C, losses to toning, mat restored ......................................... 425.00

6-1/2" w, 9" h, solidly stitched in silk threads, watercolor features and sky, oval format, pensive young lady, black and white dog seated in landscape, tacked to padded backing, egiomise tablet, early 19th C, framed, minor toning, tablet restored ............................... 460.00

15-1/2" w, 13" h, The Anglers Delight, young lady and gentleman with their catch, dog and child catching butterflies, buildings in landscape, watercolor features, horizon and sky, solidly stitched silk threads, green, gold, and blue, oval floral in foliate border, eglomise mat, framed, America or England, early 19th C, minor toning and fading....................................................2,875.00

16-1/4" w, 18" h, solidly stitched in silk threads, watercolor features and sky, oval format, young lady and dog standing at well, large trees and foliage, silk and chenille threads, framed, splits to silk ground.........................................................520.00

16-1/2" w, 16-1/2" h, "by Anna Margaret Houghtling aged 9 years 1835," church and Federal house flanked by trees, fenced garden and duck pond, gentleman walking with his dog, surrounded by floral meandering vine border, unfinished, toning, fading.............................................................2,875.00

Penny Rug, 19-1/4" w, 33" l, dark green, tan, light green, orange, and blue circles, tan ground, staining and minor damage..............220.00

Rag Runner
  32-1/4" x 90", blues, black, gray, purple, charcoal end binding, PA....................................................................165.00
  33" x 120", red, green, white, and black woven stripes, PA 220.00

Show Towel, linen, homespun
  15" w, 72" l, hearts in stars, pots of flowers, ladies, birds, "1848 Seaver," fringed bottom, staining ...................................300.00
  17-5/8" w, 61" l, embroidered pink and blue diamonds, trees, urns of flowers, crowns, and hearts, "1806," six embroidered line dividers beneath with triple fringed bottom, several small holes and minor stains..............................................200.00

Silk, 24-3/4" h, 29-1/2" w, printed bust of Washington in medallion, crossed flags, bugles, oak leaves, acorns, eagle and "First in War, First in Peace," battle ship border, black, olive green, mustard yellow, and red, minor stains, framed ...............................1,450.00

Spread, Candlewick, woven, three-piece, dated and initialed "1824 PT," center with vase and floral arrangement surrounded by scrolled leaves and flowers, staining, fabric loss, 104" x 84"................460.00

Tapestry
  Brussels Verdure, 17th/18th C, wooded landscape with parrot perched in tree, eagle attaching dog, river and castle in background, 100" x 90".................................................9,200.00
  Flemish Verdure, 17th/18th C, wooded landscape with thistles and hydrangeas, pair of fowl by stream, flower filled border, separation, thread weakness, 135" x 104" .............................9,775.00

# THREADED GLASS

**History:** Threaded glass is glass decorated with applied threads of glass. Before the English invention of a glass-threading machine in 1876, threads were applied by hand. After this invention, threaded glass was produced in quantity by practically every major glass factory.

Threaded glass was revived by the art glass manufacturers such as Durand and Steuben, and it is still made today.

Basket, 3-1/2" d, rubena, clear applied twisted handle ...............135.00

Bowl, 8" d, 3-3/4" h, triangular shape, Tartan, blue, white, and pale pink plaid, clockwise swirl on ext., reversed swirls on int., attributed to Wordsley Flint Glass Works, Stourbridge, small chip off one applied foot .................................................................485.00

Cheese Dish, cov, 7-1/2" d, light blue opal threading on upper half of bell shaped dome, faceted knob .............................................125.00

Cocktail Set, 9-1/2" h colorless decanter, applied mirror black threads, stopper and jug monogrammed "H.W.N.," six matching handled cups, Steuben fleur-de-lis mark on jug base, Steuben catalog no. 7056 ..............................................................450.00

Epergne, 9-1/2" d, 15" h, four orange to clear threaded vases, petal scalloped tops, clear branches, orange threaded base ..........675.00

Finger Bowl, 5" d, yellow-green, scalloped rim, price for set of eight .................................................................200.00

Perfume, 5-1/2" h, blown, machine applied threads ..................250.00

Pitcher, blue rim, applied handle.....................................65.00

Rose Bowl, 2-1/4" d, , clear glass ovals, sgd "Rd 81951," English
  Cranberry.............................................................275.00
  Olive Green...........................................................275.00

Salt, 2-3/4" x 1-1/2", opaque white threads, cranberry ground, clear applied petal feet ...................................................75.00

Sugar Shaker, Rubena Swirl...........................................175.00

Tumbler, 4-1/4", aqua threads, clear ground............................200.00

Vase, 7-1/4" h, tapered, pinched top, irid satin finish, applied threading ..............................................................110.00

# TIFFANY

**History:** Louis Comfort Tiffany (1849-1934) established a glass house in 1878 primarily to make stained glass windows. In 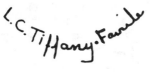 1890, in order to utilize surplus materials at the plant, Tiffany began to design and produce "small glass" such as iridescent glass lamp shades, vases, stemware, and tableware in the Art Nouveau manner. Commercial production began in 1896.

Tiffany developed a unique type of colored iridescent glass called Favrile, which differs from other art glass in that it was a composition of colored glass worked together while hot. The essential characteristic is that the ornamentation is found within the glass; Favrile was never further decorated. Different effects were achieved by varying the amount and position of colors.

Louis Tiffany and the artists in his studio also are well known for their fine work in other areas—bronzes, pottery, jewelry, silver and enamels.

**Marks:** Most Tiffany wares are signed with the name "L. C. Tiffany" or the initials "L.C.T." Some pieces also are marked "Favrile" along with a number. A variety of other marks can be found, e.g., "Tiffany Studios" and "Louis C. Tiffany Furnaces."

**References:** Victor Arwas, *Glass, Art Nouveau and Art Deco*, Rizzoli International Publications, 1977; Alastair Duncan, *Louis Comfort Tiffany*, Harry N. Abrams, 1992; William P. Hood Jr., *Tiffany Silver Flatware, 1845-1905, When Dining Was An Art*, Antique Collectors' Club, 1999; Robert Koch, *Louis C. Tiffany, Rebel in Glass*, Crown Publishers, 1966; David Rago, *American Art Pottery*, Knickerbocker Press, 1997; John A. Shuman III, *Collector's Encyclopedia of American Art Glass*, Collector Books, 1988, 1996 value update.

**Museums:** Chrysler Museum, Norfolk, VA; Corning Glass Museum, Corning, NY; University of Connecticut, The William Benton Museum of Art, Storrs, CT.

**Book,** *Character and Individuality in Decorations and Furnishing,* Tiffany Studios, New York, 1913, paperboard cover, photo plates tipt to mounts, tear to spine, 9" h ...............................................750.00

## Bronze

Bookends, pr
  4-3/4" w, 4-7/8" d, 6-1/2" h, shaped top over sq panel of gilt bronze, relief dec with framed vegetation and shield elements, stamped "Tiffany Studios New York 1056," early 20th C...................920.00

## Reproduction Alert:

A large number of brass belt buckles and badges bearing Tiffany markings were imported into the United States and sold at flea markets and auctions in the late 1960s. The most common marking is "Tiffany Studios, New York." Now, more than 25 years later, many of these items are resurfacing and deceiving collectors and dealers.

A partial list of belt buckles includes the Wells Fargo guard dog, Wells Fargo & Company mining stage, Coca-Cola Bottling, Southern Comfort Whiskey, Currier and Ives express train, and U.S. Mail. Beware of examples that have been enhanced through color enameling.

An Indian police shield is among the fake Tiffany badges. The badge features an intertwined "U" and "S" at the top and a bow and arrow motif separating "INDIAN" and "POLICE."

Vase, floriform, ruffled rim, orange through green pulled leaf design, pedestal base, etched "LCT M8155," $3,620. Photo courtesy of Joy Luke Fine Art Brokers and Auctioneers.

4-3/4" w, 6-1/4" h, wide rect form, Venetian pattern, recessed in red, blue, and green enamel, imp "Tiffany Studios, New York, 1683," minor wear ............................................................ 920.00

Candlesticks, pr, bulbous cup holder raised on three prong support, tall slender standard, wide circular base, textured gilt dore surface, imp "Tiffany Studios New York 1213" on base, wear and spotting ..................................................................... 2,530.00

Clock, mantel, 9-3/4" h, domed case, early 20th C .................. 1,035.00

Desk Box, 5-5/8" l, 1-5/8" h, shaped rect lid, gilt bronze box, top and sides etched with arabesque patterns, curlicue border, lattice ground, central quatrefoil medallion with blue enameled recesses, imp "Tiffany Studios, New York 2035," enamel loss, gilt wear ............. 375.00

Desk Set, Zodiac pattern, blotter ends, blotter roller, large perpetual calendar, 12" x 14" picture frame, cov inkwell with glass liner, orig patina, stamped "Tiffany Studios/New York" ........................ 2,200.00

Dish
6-1/2" d, shallow, foliate border, textured gilt surface, stamped "Tiffany Studios New York 1677," minor spotting ............. 150.00
8" d, shallow round ftd dish, imp markers mark and "1742," spotting ................................................................................. 90.00
9" d, shallow stepped bowl, scrolled geometric border, gilt, stamped "Tiffany Studios New York 1707," minor spotting ................... 115.00

Inkstand, 3" h, 5-1/4" w, 4-1/4" d, Nautical, dark green patina, shell cov, dolphin corners, imp "Tiffany Studios New York 1842" .......... 1,400.00

Lamp Base
52-3/4" h, floor type, single socket, reeded shaft ending in round radiating ribbed base, imp "Tiffany Studios, New York, 684," minor spotting ................................................................. 2,100.00
54-1/2" h, bridge type, adjustable balanced arm, swivel socket on slender shaft supported by five spade feet, dark brown patina, imp "Tiffany Studios New York 468," lacking shade ring 3,750.00

Letter Holder, 4-1/2" h, single-tier, Venetian pattern, lower border of ermine, mature dore bronze patina, imp "Tiffany Studios New York 1634" ................................................................................. 575.00

Letter Opener, 3-1/4" l, grape metal overlay over green slag glass, brown-green patina, imp "Tiffany Studios New York 872," loss to celluloid weight chart .................................................................. 490.00

Magnifying Glass, 8-3/4" l, bronze handle in Zodiac pattern, brown patina, imp "Tiffany Studios 928" ............................................. 690.00

Note Pad, molded design, heavy bronze, dark patina, green coloration, base imp "Tiffany Studios New York 1120" ............................ 750.00

Picture Frame, desk type
6-1/4" h, 7-1/2" w, etched bronze, blossom pattern, dark patina, beaded edges, green slag, easel back, notched back plate, imp "Tiffany Studios New York" .................................................. 920.00
9" h, 7" w, dore, Abalone pattern, shaped vertical frame, some green patina, shell inserts, easel back, imp "Tiffany Studios New York 1178" ..................................................................... 1,500.00

Stamp Box, hinged lid, rect
2-1/8" w, 4-1/8" l, 1-5/8" h, Grapevine pattern, caramel slag glass, flattened ball feet, imp "Tiffany Studios New York 801" on base, spotting ..................................................................................... 350.00
3-1/2" w, 2" d, 1" h, Zodiac pattern, zodiac design on lid, three stamp compartments, brown-green patina, base stamped "Tiffany Studios New York 802," early 20th C ............................... 375.00

## Glass, Favrile

Basket, 7" h, 7" d, pastel yellow Favrile bowl, opal laurel leaf design, fitted into dore bronze "Tiffany Furnaces" handled holder #516, bowl inscribed "LCT Favrile 1925" .............................................. 875.00

Bowl
4-1/2" d, ruffled rim, eight-ribbed form, amber glass, overall gold irid, polished pontil inscribed "L.C.T.," damage, loss, price for set of six ..................................................................... 1,725.00
4-1/2" d, 2-1/2" h, pinched and ruffled rim, gold irid, ground and polished pontil, sgd "L. C. T." on base ........................... 290.00
6-1/4" d, 2-1/4" h, shallow, ruffled rim, applied ribbed disc base, amber irid, inscribed "L.C.T.," wear ...................................... 360.00
7-1/4" d, 2-1/2" h, scalloped rim, lobed ten ribbed shallow bowl, stepped base with strong gold irid, base inscribed "X-129 L.C.T. Favrile" ..................................................................... 490.00
8" d, 3" d, scalloped rim, ten ribbed bowl, pale amber glass, strong irid gold luster, sgd "L. C. T. Favrile" around polished pontil, nicks, scratches ..................................................... 920.00
8" d, 3-1/4" h, flared rim over ribbed bowl, pale green at rim shading to colorless with opal glass at ribs, irid luster, base inscribed "L. C. Tiffany Favrile 263 V," paper label, polished pontil. 900.00
10-1/4" d, 8" h, raised bronze handle, mottled green enameled channel dec, rust brown stained ground, bronze rim encircling green and opalescent glass bowl, pulled feather dec, stretched irid at rim, underside of bronze rim sgd "Louis C. Tiffany Furnaces Inc. Favrile 507" and Tiffany monogram ............... 2,415.00

Cabinet Vase, 3-5/8" h, raised rim, pinched eight-ribbed swollen form, amber glass with overall gold irid, mkd "L.C.T. M 6734" around polished pontil, c1900, light wear ................................................ 375.00

Candlesticks, pr, 5" h, broad cups over spiral-ribbed shafts flared at base, amber glass ext. with gold irid, reinforced button pontils, each base inscribed "L.C.T." ................................................... 1,380.00

Compote
6" d, 3-3/4" h, scalloped rim, ten-ribbed shallow bowl, bulbous stem, ribbed disk foot, amber glass with overall gold irid, inscribed "5-L.C.T. Favrile" around pontil ..................... 1,100.00
7" l, 5-1/2" d, 3-3/8" h, flared rim on optic ribbed pale yellow oval bowl, stem, circular foot, stretched irid at rim, inscribed "1893 L.C.T. Favrile O" around polished pontil ......................... 690.00

8" d, 2-1/8" h, irid gold glass rim, shallow cobalt blue bowl, applied cobalt blue glass foot, base inscribed "L. C. T. Favrile" ......1,495.00

Cordial, 4-1/2" h, irid gold, base inscribed "L.C.T.," some color variation in set of five ...................................................... 950.00

Cup and Saucer, cup sgd "L. C. Tiffany Favrile #1157," saucer sgd "L. C. T. Favrile #1246" .................................................. 650.00

Decanter, 9-1/2" h, gold, engraved wheat dec, sgd "L. C. Tiffany #1272" ........................................................................ 2,800.00

Dish, 3" d, ruffled rim, amber glass with overall gold irid, inscribed "L.C.T." ..................................................................... 230.00

Dish, cov, 5-3/4" d, 6" h, pointed spiral finial, spiral ribbed cover, squatty dish, three applied coiled shell feet, strong gold luster, button pontil, inscribed "2319J L.C.Tiffany Favrile," c1915, repairs to two feet ......................................................................... 1,150.00

Finger Bowl, 5" d, 1-7/8" h, flared rim, optic ribbed bowl of colorless glass with pastel aqua and stretched irid at rim, opalescent ribs, base inscribed "1777 L.C.T. Favrile" .................................... 690.00

Finger Bowl and Undertray, 4-3/4" d bowl, 2" h, 5-3/4" d plate, amber, irid gold luster int., both inscribed "L.C.T." around polished pontils......300.00

Goblet
  5-1/8" h, swollen cylindrical, amber glass with overall gold irid, flared pedestal stem, band of gold threading and pulled prunts, paper label .......................................................... 865.00
  6-1/2" h, flared optic ribbed bowl, gold glossy ext., irid int., base inscribed "L.C.T. Favrile" .................................... 350.00

Paperweight, 1-1/2" l, scarab, deep blue and purple irid ........... 150.00

Plate, 8" d, slightly scalloped broad rim, fourteen-ribbed dish, opalescent and colorless glass, stretched gold irid at rim, inscribed "1775 L.C.T. Favrile," polished pontil .................................... 635.00

Salt, 1-1/4" d, irid gold, four-ftd serving pots, each inscribed "LCT" and numbered, two small foot chips, price for matched set of four.......900.00

Toothpick Holder
  1-3/4" h, raised rim, small pinched oval body, amber glass with overall gold irid, inscribed "L.C.T. Favrile"" on pontil," minor wear .......................................................... 290.00
  2" h, slightly flared rim over four pinched sides, light amber glass with overall gold irid, mkd ""LCT" in polished pontil ...........320.00
  2-1/2" h, slightly flared rim over four pinched sides, light amber glass with overall gold irid, mkd "LCT O 2607," polished pontil, c1901 .......................................................... 290.00

Vase
  5" h, double bulbed gourd-form amber body, green leaves and amber vines, darker gold blossoms, base inscribed "L. C. Tiffany Favrile 8246B" ...................................................... 1,900.00
  5-1/4" h, bulbous oval, dark green favrile covered by swirling pulled and coiled irid dec, irregular cypriot surface, base inscribed "L. C. T. K378".................................................. 2,550.00
  8-1/2" h, small flared rim, ovoid body, amber glass, dec with brown hearts and vine, irid gold surface, sgd "L.C.T. 840B" around reinforced button pontil, minor wear.................. 1,955.00
  16-1/2" h, floriform, gold favrile insert, bronze base mkd "Tiffany Studios New York 1686"" and monogram ..................... 1,320.00
  18-1/2" h, ruffled flower form of opalescent glass with pulled green leaves, int. with stretched gold irid, pale clear green stem, inserted into bronze base with bulbed stem over disk foot, imp "Tiffany Studios New York 25695, 9433," Tiffany mark, wear to base .......................................................... 6,325.00
  20" h, tapering form, gold Favrile, blue/purple irid pulled feather at bottom, sgd "L. C. Tiffany Favrile #3570L" .................... 2,600.00

Wax Seal, 1-3/4" h, gold Favrile, three scarabs.......................... 210.00

## Lamps

Bridge, 58" h, 12" d shade with amber mottled dichroic glass with green acorns, adjustable harp, slender standard raised on five-leg spade form base, shade sgd "Tiffany Studios, New York, #1410," base sgd twice "Tiffany Studios New York #423" ................ 18,500.00

Chandelier
  6" drop, 5-1/2" d shades, flush mounted bronze fixture over three fleur-de-lis ornaments radiating from center dome, green patina,

**Lamp, bronze, double branch, holding t6 irid shades, central bronze stem hollowed on one side to hold candle snuffer (not present), base imp "Tiffany Studios 10456," each shade sgd "LCT," minor roughness on base of shades, 15-1/2" h, 22" w, $12,500. Photo courtesy of Joy Luke Fine Art Brokers and Auctioneers.**

imp "972," three flared floriform vaseline and opalescent glass shades with scalloped rim, early 20th C ....................... 3,750.00

  21" l drop, 16" d inverted dome, two amber-brown borders, clusters of mottled yellow daffodils, blue-green spike leaves, amber fractured glass ground, closed center with leaded symmetrical circlet, int. fitted with four hooks at later date by Tiffany Studios, metal rim rags imp "Tiffany Studios New York 144...," all suspended from patinated metal ceiling mount with four chains................32,200.00

  58" l drop, 22-1/2" d domed shade, bronze chain with gold favrile glass ball connector, shade of radiating rows of quadrangular and rectangular striated yellow-green glass segments with horizontal band of irid blue glass balls, six-socket fixture, rim tag imp "Tiffany Studios New York," crazed segments, one glass ball broken, corrosion to metal ................................... 41,400.00

Desk
  14-34" h, pierced shade cap over domed etched metal openwork shade in Pine Needle pattern, single-socket fixture on slender reeded shaft, round stepped base with five simulated miniature pottery vessels, bronze with green patina, imp "Tiffany Studios New York 724," minor wear........................................... 1,265.00
  18" h, dark patina on spun bronze dome shade, silver color reflective int., two-socket base, reticulated finial cap, flared fluted shaft, conforming base, imp "Tiffany Studios New York 617" ...........2,000.00

Floor
  57" h, 12" d green and gold damascene shade suspended from bell shaped harp, swivel mount, slender swollen standard, attached ashtray with match holder, round walnut tray, magazine rack, whole terminating in floriform base with paw feet, brownish green patina, stamped "Tiffany Studios New York 552," patina wear ....................................... 12,650.00
  78" h, 24-1/2" d domed shade with mottled shades of amber brickwork tiles over stylized geometric border, deep drop apron of amber and opalescent, rippled, vertical rect glass tiles, perforated serpentine cap, six-socket gilt bronze standard, cushion shaped base, shade tag imp "Tiffany Studios New York 1616," base imp "Tiffany Studios New York 877," some cracked segments, wear, spotting on bronze ................................ 74,000.00

Student
  24-5/8" h, 10" d shade, slender shaft of bronze supporting adjustable oil canister, applied scrolled wire dec, bronze ring supporting ribbed white opal favrile glass shade with wavy irid gold dec, domed base with applied pebble texture, shade inscribed "S2881," base stamped "1539," electrified, small nick to shade rim .......................................................... 9,775.00

29-1/4" h, 28-1/4" w, 10" d shade, bronze, wire twist dec central font between double post frame, adjustable arm mechanism, beaded spiral dec on twin burners, one cased green over white glass shade, verdigris and brown patina, imp "3896" on one foot, minor wear ..............................................3,750.00

Table, leaded glass and bronze

Dogwood, white, lavender, and green petals, blue background, fracture, striated, rippled, and mottled glass segments, two bands of rippled greenish opalescent glass, bronze pumpkin-type base, rich brown/green patina, fuel canister, fire-arm shade supports, wired for electricity, micro tag on shade "Tiffany Studio, New York," fuel canister sgd "Tiffany Studio, New York, #21218" ..............................................39,000.00

Narcissus, 25" h, 29-1/2" d shade, golden yellow mottled daffodils, deep yellow/green mottled foliate, yellow/green stems, grayish pinpoints outlined in deep rich blue/purple background, bronze base inverted trumpet-form, cast with radiating leaves, finial cap with reticulated swirl top and single large finial, shade sgd "Tiffany Studio New York #1919," base sgd "Tiffany Studio, New York #368"..............................................52,500.00

Pomegranate, 22-1/4" h, 18" d dome shade, radiating mottled amber and green tile segments, border of mottled orange and amber pomegranates, metal rim tag imp "Tiffany Studios New York 1457," three-socket fixture over slightly swollen paneled shaft with flared circular base, dark brown patina, stamped "Tiffany Studios New York 534," minor spotting to base..............................14,950.00

Pond Lily, 25" h base, 20" d shade, pattern of green and white striated lily pads, mottled glass, clear glass tinged with green background, lower border of faceted emerald green glass, bronze base with cylindrical standard cast with over lapping leaf tips at top, shallow incised loops around middle, cushion-form circular base cast with two rows small alternating bosses, bands of loops with raised centers at outer edge, four petal-form feet, cap swirling reticulated shallow cap with small finial, shade sgd "Tiffany Studio, New York," base imp "Tiffany Studios New York #359," some fractures, deep brown/green patina ..............................39,000.00

## Silver

Asparagus Tongs, 10" l, sterling, leaf pattern handle, teardrop shape openwork grips, 5 troy oz .....................................................350.00

Basket, 9" h, stepped oval foot, pierced body, applied with floral sprays to shaped edge, tapered upright handle, monogrammed int., c1902-07, 12 troy oz ..............................................980.00

Bonbon Dish, 7-1/2" d, ovoid, shaped edge applied and pierced, monogram at side, c1891-1900, price for pr .............................690.00

Bowl

6" d, 2" h, conical, three ball feet, optical ribbing, c1938-47, 7 troy oz ..............................................230.00

7-3/8" d, 2-1/8" h, lobed round form, applied silver bead on rim and at each interval, ftd, base, hammered surface, imp "Tiffany & Co. 19100 Maker's 5263 Sterling Silver 925-1000 M.," "Special Hand Work," minor wear, 14 troy oz .......................980.00

Bowl and Undertray, 9-1/4" d, 2-3/4" bowl, 10-1/4" d underplate, Art Deco style lobing on sides, slightly everted scalloped rim, undertray with conforming edge, c1938-47, 37 troy oz .........................1,100.00

Candelabra, pr, 16" h, 12" w, two arm, center candleholder, monogrammed, mkd "Tiffany & Co. Makers Sterling Silver, 925-1000"..............................................2,200.00

Cigar Box, 6-1/4" x 3-3/4" x 2-5/8", blue dec, hinged metal box, monogrammed "CH" on cov, int. engraved "1852 D.S. 1922," base inscribed "Louis C. Tiffany Furnaces Inc./350," worn silver plating ..............................................900.00

Child's Setting, presentation type, 8" d plate, 3-1/4" h cup, saucer, napkin ring, knife, rims with applied grapevine on squiggle stipple ground, napkin ring with allover vine dec, vine on handle of monogrammed ftd cup with vines and applied birds, presentation inscriptions dated 1870 and 1943, 24 troy oz..............................3,450.00

Creamer and Sugar, sterling, 2-1/2" h, rounded rect shape, low foot, leaf design handles, beaded border around body, chased scattered flowers, c1873, 7 troy oz ..............................................400.00

Desk Box, 8" w, 6-1/2" d, 2" h, rect, presentation, lid engraved to Wm. J. Kenny, showing tower of Metropolitan Life Building, NY, engraved with signatures of colleagues, divided int. lined in sandalwood, c1949 ..............................................200.00

Dresser Set, ten piece, 1891-1902, repousse scroll foliate design, hairbrush, three clothes brushes, hand mirror, shoe horn, comb, buttonhook, nail file, buffer handle, monogrammed, some wear........575.00

Fruit Bowl, 8-7/8" d, round, ftd base, openwork band below reeded rim, handle, 1907-38, 16 troy oz ..............................................250.00

Goblet, 6-3/4" h, 1865-75, applied fretwork band on rim, fretwork border around base, 7 troy oz ..............................................400.00

Ladle, 11" l, sterling, Audubon pattern, fluted edge, rect form bowl, 1871, 7 troy oz ..............................................1,265.00

Pitcher

7-1/2" h, paneled tapered form, panels outlined in etched bands of paterae, foliate scrolls, and husk drops, short spout, angular handle with further etched details, monogrammed at side, c1907-38, 22 troy oz ..............................................1,495.00

10-3/4" h, squat baluster form, foot chased and emb with shells and seaweed, body partially fluted, overhanging girdle chased and emb with shells and dolphins on stippled ground engraved with cattails, foliate ear handle, rim rolled at spout and everted at sides with half leaves, c1875-91, 55 troy oz .............4,025.00

Porringer, 7-1/4" l, ovoid, shaped and pierced handle, engraved detailing, c1902-07, 6 troy oz..............................................415.00

Salt, pr, Chrysanthemum pattern, 1907, 5 troy oz .....................875.00

Salver, 16" l, ovoid, four scroll and trefoil feet, molded edge, engraved center with presentation inscription dated 1978, surrounded by engraved signatures, 20th C, 42 troy oz..............................815.00

Sandwich Tongs, 8-1/4" l, sterling, engraved handle, openwork grips, 5 troy oz ..............................................400.00

Sauce Ladle, beaded handle, cast head of mythological figure on back of gold wash bowl, fitted case, 2 troy oz ..............................175.00

Tablespoon, 8-1/2" l, Chrysanthemum pattern, late 19th C, 30 troy oz total, price for set of nine..............................................1,265.00

Tazza, 9-1/4" d, round, low ftd base, acid-etched floral and fine border, 16 troy oz ..............................................300.00

Tea Service

4-3/8" h teapot, creamer, cov sugar, chased floral design, eagle finial, monogrammed, mkd "Tiffany, Young & Ellis," 27 troy oz..............................................1,150.00

13-1/4" h kettle on stand, teapot, open sugar and pitcher, four lion law feet on kettle, Greek revival style with bands of fretwork, wooden handles and finials on kettle and teapot, 1854-70, 96 troy oz ..............................................4,025.00

Tea Strainer, 5-3/8" l, round, two pierced scroll handles, c1907-38, 2 troy oz ..............................................350.00

Traveling Toilet Kit, gentleman's, brush, comb, cov soap box, lidded jar, shaving brush in jar, razor box with Gillette razor and blades, powder dispenser, all monogrammed, fitted leather carrying case, 1907-38, approx 12 troy oz ..............................................520.00

Trophy, 9-3/4" h, urn form, two handles, spreading circular base, engraved inscriptions, c1923, 48 troy oz..............................800.00

Vase, 15-1/4" h, low round foot with flat leaf band, tapered body engraved to one side with presentation inscription, incised with horizontal reeding at shoulder, everted neck with flat leaf rim, presentation inscription, 1907-38, 65 troy oz ..............................................3,450.00

Waste Bowl, 5-3/16" d, 2-13/16" h, applied rim border, monogram, c1866, 8 troy oz..............................................200.00

Whistle, sterling silver mouthpiece, bulbous naturalistic motif center, mother-of-pearl handle, c1900, sgd "Tiffany & Co." .................450.00

## TIFFIN GLASS

**History:** A. J. Beatty & Sons built a glass manufacturing plant in Tiffin, Ohio, in 1888. On January 1, 1892, the firm joined the U. S. Glass Co. and was known as factory R.

c1960

Fine-quality Depression-era items were made at this high-production factory.

From 1923 to 1936, Tiffin produced a line of black glassware called Black Satin. The company discontinued operation in 1980.

**Marks:** Beginning in 1916, wares were marked with a paper label.

**References:** Fred Bickenheuser, *Tiffin Glassmasters*, Book I (1979, 1994-95 value update), Book II (1981, 1994-95 value update), Book III (1985), Glassmasters Publications; Tom and Neila Bredehoft, *Fifty Years of Collectible Glass, 1920-1970, Volume 1, Volume II*, Antique Trader Books, 2000; Gene Florence, *Glass Candlesticks of the Depression Era*, Collector Books, 1999; Bob Page and Dale Fredericksen, *Tiffin Is Forever*, Page-Fredericksen, 1994; Jerry Gallagher and Leslie Piña, *Tiffin Glass*, Schiffer Publishing, 1996; Ed Goshe, Ruth Hemminger, and Leslie Piña, *Depression Era Stems & Tableware: Tiffin,* Schiffer Publishing, 1998.

**Collectors' Club:** Tiffin Glass Collectors Club, P.O. Box 554, Tiffin, OH 44883.

Basket
  Satin, #9574 .......... 65.00
  Twilight, 9" h, 5-1/2" w .......... 300.00
Bon Bon
  Killarney, #6281, crystal applied handle .......... 65.00
  Twilight, #7 .......... 95.00
Bowl
  Swedish Modern, Copen blue and crystal, 5-1/4" h, ftd .......... 65.00
  Twilight, 9-1/4" w, ftd, sq .......... 200.00
Bud Vase
  Cherokee Rose, 6" h .......... 25.00
  Etched roses, crystal and smoke .......... 190.00
  Fuchsia, #14185, 10-1/2" h .......... 40.00
  June Night, 8" h .......... 30.00
  Swedish Modern. #17350 .......... 35.00
  Twilight, #85 .......... 150.00
Candlesticks, pr
  #319, 8" h, red satin .......... 175.00
  Cherokee Rose, #5902, 2-lite .......... 160.00
  Classic .......... 250.00
  Fuchsia, #5902 .......... 125.00
  June Night, #5902 .......... 95.00
  Killarney, #6364, green .......... 100.00
  Satin, #315, emerald green, flat foot .......... 55.00
Candy Dish, cov
  Conic, emerald green .......... 55.00
  Deerwood, #15320, black, gold encrusted dec, 6" d .......... 750.00
Celery Tray, Fuchsia .......... 48.00
Centerpiece, 13", #8153
  Fontaine, green, light use .......... 95.00
  La Fleure, yellow .......... 125.00
Champagne
  Athens Diana .......... 25.00
  Cherokee Rose, #17403 .......... 35.00
  Empire, optic, pink .......... 20.00
  Fuchsia, #15803 .......... 12.00
  June Night, #17403 .......... 30.00
  Killarney, #15074, green .......... 25.00
  Le Fleur .......... 25.00
  Majestic Twilight, #17507 .......... 35.00
  Persian Peasant, #17358 .......... 25.00
  Twilight, #17524 .......... 35.00
Cheese and Cracker, Flower Garden with Butterflies, amber, gold trim .......... 225.00

Claret
  Cherokee Rose, #17399, 4 oz .......... 55.00
  Persian Peasant, #17358 .......... 50.00
Cocktail
  Athens Diana .......... 18.00
  Cherokee Rose, #17399 .......... 16.00
  Classic .......... 35.00
  Flanders, pink .......... 45.00
  Fuchsia, #15083 .......... 20.00
  June Night, #17358 .......... 20.00
  Majestic Twilight, #17507 .......... 40.00
  Persian Peasant, #17358 .......... 20.00
Comport, open
  Cherokee Rose, blown, beaded, tall .......... 150.00
  Deerwood, #15320, black, gold encrusted dec, 7" h, ftd .... 350.00
  Juno, yellow, 6-1/2" h .......... 65.00
  Killarney, #17394 .......... 65.00
Console Bowl, Flanders, 8" w, 4-1/4" h, blown, pink .......... 800.00
Console Set, #8088, 7" d bowl, #320 10" h candlesticks, black . 250.00
Cordial
  Cameo etching, #17594 .......... 70.00
  Celestial, #17707, ebony .......... 30.00
  Celestial, #17707, turquoise .......... 30.00
  Cherokee Rose, #17399 .......... 55.00
  Classic, #185 .......... 70.00
  Coventry, #17623 .......... 30.00
  Fantasy, #17687 .......... 40.00
  Flanders, crystal .......... 55.00
  June Night, #17358 .......... 45.00
  Majal, #17594 .......... 30.00
  Persian Pheasant, #17392 .......... 65.00
Creamer and Sugar
  Cherokee Rose, beaded .......... 60.00
  Luciana, green trim .......... 225.00
Cup and Saucer
  Athens Diana .......... 25.00
  Rosalind, yellow, blown .......... 40.00
Dahlia Vase
  Black Satin, cattails dec .......... 65.00
  Carrara, 12" h, ftd, Delft blue .......... 145.00
  Ebony, two tone gold parrot dec .......... 175.00
  Flanders, pink, 8" h .......... 800.00
  Ships dec, two tone gold .......... 125.00
Decanter, #3700, globe stopper, carved dec
  Jonquil, sgd "Franz Grosz" .......... 300.00
  Roses .......... 260.00
Dessert Plate, Luciana, green, 8" d .......... 30.00
Figure, pheasant, head down .......... 195.00
Flower Basket, Copen, blue and crystal, 13" h .......... 165.00
Goblet, luncheon, June Night, #17358, low .......... 35.00
Goblet, water
  Chalet .......... 50.00
  Cherokee Rose, #17403 .......... 35.00
  Classic, #185 .......... 35.00
  Fuchsia, #15083, 7-1/2" h .......... 22.00
  June Night, #17358 .......... 35.00
  Killarney, #15074, green .......... 35.00
  Rosalind, yellow .......... 30.00
  Twilight, #17492 .......... 45.00
Grapefruit, Flanders, yellow, crystal insert .......... 250.00
Iced Tea Tumbler
  Cherokee Rose, #17403 .......... 35.00
  Flanders, pink, 12 oz .......... 75.00
  Flying Nun, crystal, green base .......... 60.00
  June Night, #17358 .......... 35.00
  Killarney, #15074, green .......... 30.00
  King's Crown, ruby flashed, 12 oz .......... 14.00
  Majesty, #17507, wisteria .......... 35.00

Jug, #128
Athens Diana ................................................................260.00
Rosalind, yellow ..........................................................350.00
Juice Tumbler, King's Crown, ruby flashed, 4 oz, ftd ..................12.00
Lamp Shade, Jack Frost, amber..........................................150.00
Martini Jug, Twilight, 11-1/2" h .......................................450.00
Nut Dish, June Night ......................................................45.00
Oyster Cocktail, Athens Diana ...........................................18.00
Parfait
Classic, #185 ................................................................70.00
Flanders, pink, handle ...............................................150.00
Pitcher, Cherokee Rose, ftd ............................................700.00
Plate
Classic, 10-1/2" d, dinner .............................................125.00
Fuchsia, #8814, 7-7/8"....................................................12.50
June Night, crystal, 6" d ...............................................17.50
Juno, yellow, 9-1/2" d, dinner .........................................40.00
La Fleure, Mandarin, 7-1/4" d .........................................15.00
Rosalind, yellow, 8" d ...................................................12.00
Rosalind, yellow, dinner ................................................50.00
Salt and Pepper Shakers, pr, Parakeet Twin, Reflex Green, enameled
dec, wear to chrome tops .................................................85.00
Sandwich Tray, Brilliancy, amber, handle................................28.00
Server, center handle, Deerwood, #15320, black, gold encrusted dec,
10-1/2" d ..................................................................250.00
Sherbet, Cherokee Rose, #17399, low ...................................25.00
Sherry, June Night, #17403 ..............................................30.00
Sugar, cov, Fuchsia, #5902, bead handle................................24.00
Torte Plate, King's Crown, ruby flashed, 14" d...........................70.00
Tumbler
Classic, 8 oz, flat.........................................................44.00
Fuchsia, 12 oz, ftd .......................................................22.00
June Night, #17403, 10-1/2 oz, ftd.....................................20.00
Vase
Canterbury, roses dec, 10" h .........................................190.00
Cerise, 10" h, #14185, gold encrusted dec..........................60.00
Cherokee Rose, 10-1/2" h .............................................40.00
Empress, #6551, red and crystal, 12" h.............................190.00
Fuchsia, 11" h, trophy shape, handles..............................230.00
Swedish Modern, #17383, urn, bubble stem .......................75.00
Wedding Bowl, cov, King's Crown, ruby flashed, 7-1/2" d............90.00
Whiskey
Classic, #185, ftd, 2 oz ................................................75.00
Flanders, yellow, 2-3/4" h.............................................175.00
Wine, Chalet ...................................................................55.00

# TILES

**History:** The use of decorated tiles peaked during the latter part of the 19th century. More than 100 companies in England alone were producing tiles by 1880. By 1890, companies had opened in Belgium, France, Australia, Germany, and the United States.

Tiles were not used only as fireplace adornments. Many were installed into furniture, such as washstands, hall stands, and folding screens. Since tiles were easily cleaned and, hence, hygienic, they were installed on the floors and walls of entry halls, hospitals, butcher shops, or any place where sanitation was a concern. Many public buildings and subways also employed tiles to add interest and beauty.

**References:** Susan and Al Bagdade, *Warman's American Pottery and Porcelain*, 2nd ed., Krause Publications, 2000; ——, *Warman's English & Continental Pottery & Porcelain*, 3rd Edition, Krause Publications, 1998; Norman Karlson, *American Art Tile, 1876-1941*, Rizzoli Publications, 1998; Ralph and Terry Kovel, *Kovels' American Art Pottery*, Crown Publishers, 1993; Richard and Hilary Myers, *William Morris Tiles*, Richard Dennis (distributed by Antique Collectors' Club), 1996; David Rago, *American Art Pottery*, Knickerbocker Press, 1997; Betty Ward and Nancy Schiffer, *Weller, Roseville, and Related Zanesville Art Pottery and Tiles*, Schiffer Publishing, 2000.

**Periodical:** *Flash Point*, P.O. Box 1850, Healdsburg, CA 95448, http://www.aimnet.com/~toolson/pages/tileorgs.thfinfo.htm.

**Collectors' Clubs:** Tiles & Architectural Ceramics Society, 36 Church St., Stony Stratford, Milton Kaynes MK11 1BD, UK, http://www.aimnet.com/~toolson/webtiles.htm

**Museums:** Boymans-van Beunigen Museum, Rotterdam, Holland; City Museum, Stoke-on-Trent, England; Iron Bridge Gorge Museum, Teford, England Lambert Van Meerten Museum, Delft, Holland; Mercer Museum & Tile Works, Doylestown, PA; Victoria & Albert Museum London, England.

**Notes:** Condition is an important factor in determining price. A cracked, badly scuffed and scratched, or heavily chipped tile has very little value. Slight chipping around the outer edges of a tile is, at times, considered acceptable by collectors, especially if these chips can be covered by a frame.

It is not uncommon for the highly glazed surface of some tiles to have become crazed. Crazing is not considered detrimental as long as it does not detract from the overall appearance of the tile.

American Encaustic Tile Co, Zanesville, OH
3" sq, portrait of President Wm McKinley, blue glazed intaglio, 1896, biography pasted on back ......................................225.00
3" sq, portrait of William Jennings Bryan, blue-gray glazed intaglio, biography pasted on back ......................................195.00
4" sq, Oriental junque, pagoda in background.....................45.00
6" sq, cherub and dog, small repair .................................35.00
18 x 6", hunting dogs, high relief, sponged pale aqua and honey brown glossy glaze........................................................250.00
Arts & Crafts
4" w, sq, raised outline of seagull in flight in clouds, mottled matte glazes, white, green, and rust, oak frame .........................30.00
5-1/2" sq, yellow flowers, green leaves, cut-back brown ground, Arts & Crafts oak frame.................................................200.00
6" w, 12" h, two tiles, squeezebag dec, stylized light green flower, aqua ground, Arts & Crafts oak frame.............................600.00
Batchelder, 4" sq
Hunter and dog in woods, bas relief, reddish brown clay, high gloss light blue rubbed into background..............................90.00
Landscape of trees, water, and bridge, deeply imp, red clay, light chalky blue brushed into recessed areas............................95.00
Beaver Falls, 6" sq, standing squirrel, incised and outlined in black, squirrel and border medium blue, Kelly green ground, marked .65.00
DeMorgan, William, 6" sq, hedgehog, ruby luster glaze .............400.00

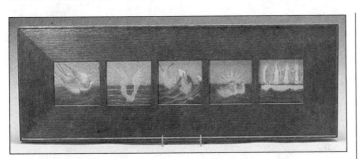

**Grueby, 5-tile frieze, dec in cuenca, seagulls, ducks, and penguins, greens, blues, and browns, new Arts & Crafts frame, each tile 4" sq, $11,500. Photo courtesy of David Rago Auctions.**

Grueby
    4-1/2" sq, landscape, trees, stream and mountain, green, blue, yellow, and brown, marked "Architectural" ...................... 600.00
    8" sq, mocha brown galleon, billowing white sails, choppy powder blue sea, medium blue sky, black wood frame, sgd "EH," partial black stamp ................... 850.00
Hartford Faience, attributed to, 8-1/2" h, 35" l, mosaic pieces forming landscape with two owls, house, full moon, mounted on wood, framed, no visible mark, several cracks ................ 4,500.00
Low, J. & J. G., Chelsea, MA
    4" sq, bearded man, laurel wreath, green gloss ................. 165.00
    6" x 5", cupid on flying bird, olive gloss, 1883.................... 175.00
    7" x 7-1/2", flowers, brown shaded to amber ....................... 50.00
Marblehead, 6" x 6", scenic, house and trees, deep blue and green, imp ship mark, minor nicks...................... 1,265.00
Minton China Works, 6" sq, transfer printed
    Adam and Eve driven out of Eden, blue cream ground ........ 45.00
    Farmyard scene, sheep, brown on white, sgd "W. Wise," 1879 ...................80.00
    Hancock House, brown on white ......................................... 35.00
    Romeo and Juliet, sepia ..................................................... 35.00
Moravian Pottery & Tile Works, Doylestown, PA
    4" sq, Aladdin Lamp..............................................................70.00
    7-1/4" x 4", Knight in armor on horseback, ochre and blue...85.00
Mosaic Tile Co, Zanesville, OH
    4" sq, German Shepherd dec ........................................... 120.00
    6" sq, Little Bo Peep, blue, tan, and cream, Walter Crane.. 100.00
    6" sq, ship at sea, yellow sail, blue water, imp mark........... 250.00
Pardee, 4" sq, houses and trees, matte glaze, brown and green, 1910 ...................225.00
Pewabic Pottery, Detroit, MI
    2-3/4" sq, bird of paradise, gray-taupe bird, cranberry red ground, high luster finish ................................................... 65.00
    3" sq, Detroit Skyline, round, emb, brown on blue ............... 75.00
Richards, H, 6" sq, Art Nouveau flower, tube lined, red and green, cream ground ...................................................................... 75.00
Robertson, 8" sq, scenic, cloisonné dec, brown road winding through green hills, fortress ............................ 1,300.00
Robineau, Adelaide, 4-3/4" sq, carved rabbit, matte celadon glaze, carved "AR," several minute nicks to edges, slight surface abrasion ....................................................................... 1,100.00
Rookwood Faience, 6" sq, geometric, matte ochre glaze, wood box frame, no visible mark .............................................. 100.00
Solon, 5-1/2" sq, ship at sea, blue against camel ground, Arts & Crafts oak frame ...................................................................... 500.00
Tiffany, 4" sq, blue-black glass, molded fire-breathing dragon in circular reserve, overall luster irid ......................... 375.00
Trenton Tile Co, Trenton, NJ
    4-1/4" sq, portrait of woman, brown glaze ........................... 65.00
    6" sq, flower, tan glossy glaze............................................... 25.00
US Encaustic Tile Co
    6" sq, birds, framed ............................................................. 75.00
    18" x 6", Dawn, woman, emb green glaze .......................... 175.00

# TINWARE

**History:** Beginning in the 1700s, many utilitarian household objects were made of tin. Because it is nontoxic, rust resistant, and fairly durable, tin can be used for storing food; and because it was cheap, tinware and tin-plated wares were in the price range of most people. It often was plated to iron to provide strength.

An early center of tinware manufacture in the United States was Berlin, Connecticut, but almost every small town and hamlet had its own tinsmith, tinner, or whitesmith. Tinsmiths used patterns to cut out the pieces, hammered and shaped them, and soldered the parts. If a piece was to be used with heat, a copper bottom was added because of the low melting point of tin. The industrial revolution brought about machine-made, mass-produced tinware pieces. The handmade era had ended by the late 19th century.

**References:** Dover Stamping Co, *1869 Illustrated Catalog*, Astragal Press, 1994 reprint; Marilyn E. Dragowick (ed.), *Metalwares Price Guide*, Antique Trader Books, 1995; John Player, *Origins and Craft of Antique Tin & Tole*, Norwood Publishing, 1995 (available from Christie & Christie Association, P.O. Box 392, Cookstown, Ontario, Canada LOL 1LO).

**Museum:** Cooper-Hewitt Museum, New York, NY.

**Additional Listings:** See Advertising; Kitchen Collectibles; Lanterns; Lamps and Lighting; and Tinware, Decorated.

Candle Sconces, pr, 12" h, oval backs, crimped drip pans, holes from electrification .............................................................. 250.00
Candle Tray, 9-1/4" x 19" x 12-3/4", rect, formed strap handle, holds 24 candles ..................................................................... 650.00
Canteen, 5 5/8" h, punched star and circle dec ........................... 95.00
Centerpiece, 14-1/2" d, whimsey, tiered, traces of green paint... 175.00
Chandelier, 24-1/2" h, four branch, crimped drip pans ........... 1,155.00
Churn, 21-1/2" h, wooden dasher ............................................... 200.00
Coffee Grinder, hanging, Parker .................................................. 45.00
Cookie Cutter
    8-1/2" h, man with pipe, hat, and frock coat with tails, punched circle around hole, light rust............................................... 525.00
    9" h, woman with hat and long dress ................................ 525.00

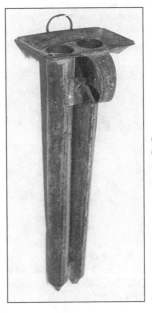

**Candlemold, two tubes, late 19th C, $175.**

Figure, 29" h, 24-1/2" l, rooster, silver gilt, carved wood rockery base, Continental .......... 1,025.00
Food Grater, 14-1/4" l, punched, wood frame, mortised and turned handle .......... 95.00
Foot Warmer, 7-3/4" x 8-1/2", punched heart designs in side, punched Maltese cross on door, tin, mortised birch frame, turned posts, old dark finish, some soldered repair, mismatched pan in base .... 315.00
Mistletoe Ball, 6-1/4" d, hinged .......... 450.00
Quilt Pattern, rose .......... 20.00
Spice Canisters and Carrier, 8-1/2" x 8-1/2" x 5-3/4", crimp dec 275.00
Tinder Box, 4-1/4" d, America, late 18th/early 19th C .......... 100.00

# TINWARE, DECORATED

**History:** The art of decorating sheet iron, tin, and tin-coated sheet iron dates back to the mid-18th century. The Welsh called the practice pontypool; the French, tôle peinte. In America, the center for tin-decorated ware in the late 1700s was Berlin, Connecticut.

Several styles of decorating techniques were used: painting, japanning, and stenciling. Designs were done by both professionals and itinerants. English and Oriental motifs strongly influenced both form and design.

A special type of decoration was the punch work on unpainted tin practiced by the Pennsylvania tinsmiths. Forms included coffeepots, spice boxes, and grease lamps.

**Reference:** Marilyn E. Dragowick (ed), *Metalwares Price Guide*, Antique Trader Books, 1995.

Basket, 10-1/2" x 9", crimp and curl dec .......... 825.00
Box, dome top, orig dark brown japanning
6-3/4" l, white band, floral dec, red, green, and yellow stripes, wear, one hinge loose .......... 115.00
    7" l, white band, yellow, red, green, and black floral dec, hasp end broken .......... 125.00
Candlestick, 6" h, domed sq base, orig yellow on worn brown japanning, push-up .......... 175.00
Chestnut Jar, cov, 7" w, 5-1/2" d, 12" h, Scattered Flowers dec, pale green sponged ground, ringed lion mask handles, Georgian form, English, c1920-25 .......... 450.00
Coal Hod, 23-3/4" h, old black paint, worn gilt and floral transfers, rack in back for tools, marked "GD Manf. Co." .......... 225.00
Coffeepot, 10-3/4" h, worn orig dark brown japanning, red, yellow, white, and dark green floral dec, some old touch up repair ..... 715.00
Deed Box, 9-1/4" l, dome top, orig yellow paint, stenciled bowl of fruit and foliage on front, green stripe on lid, wear, front panel dec crazed .......... 500.00

**Tray, rect, rounded corners, cut-out handles, red paint, stenciled dec, scrolled border, banded and floral design I center, minor loss and retouch, 30-1/2" I, 22-1/2" w, $275. Photo courtesy of Sanford Alderfer Auction Co.**

Fruit Basket, 13" w, 8-1/2" d, 5-1/2" h, bateau form, black and gold, reticulated, Georgian, c1810-20 .......... 385.00
Hat Box, 15" d, 15" h, hinged top, heraldic dec, Edwardian, first quarter 19th C .......... 250.00
Lamp, 20-1/2" h, adjustable candle socket and shade, old paint, red and gold dec, brass post and finial .......... 615.00
Lantern, 16" h, old yellow japanning, hinged door, added candle socket, reflector slot .......... 115.00
Nutmeg Grater, 6" l, brown japanning, hand crank .......... 175.00
Patch Box, 1-1/2" l, 1" w, 1/2" h, curved rect shape, 3/4 hinged top, colorful flower dec .......... 75.00
Tea Caddy, rect bombe shape, floral dec, black ground, ornate bronze bail, scroll feet, three compartment int., 19th C .......... 425.00
Teapot, 8-1/4" h, worn orig red paint, yellow, white, and dark green floral dec, resoldered handle .......... 330.00
Tray
    15" w, 9-7/8" d, 17" h, cartouche form, center polychromed oval of Galatea and her attendants, Victorian, c1840-50, later parcel gilt black lacquered stand .......... 850.00
    26" w, 20-1/2" d, 21-3/4" h, oval, two carring handles, raised edge, gilt and polychromed grapevine dec, idyllic country landscape, later ebonized faux-bamboo stand with gilt accents, Victorian, third quarter 19th C .......... 2,860.00
    30" w, 22-1/2" d, 21-1/2" h, oval, two carrying handles, elaborate foliate scrolling center design, conforming border, later ebonized faux-bamboo frame with gilt accents, Victorian, third quarter 19th C .......... 1,430.00
Verrières, Belle Epoque, c1900-1910, price for pair
    11" w, 8" d, 5" h, Louis XVI taste, milk-blue painted finish, parcel gilding .......... 360.00
    14-1/2" w, 10" d, 4" h, Restauration taste, yellow ground with black stylized berry vine painting, ringed mask handles .. 375.00

# TOBACCO CUTTERS

**History:** Before pre-packaging, tobacco was delivered to merchants in bulk form. Tobacco cutters were used to cut the tobacco into desired sizes.

Ax Shape, cast iron, wood handle and base, 18" l, 7-1/2" h .......... 225.00
Dexter, wood base, metal slide and cutter, measures plug .......... 100.00
Enterprise Manufacturing Co., Philadelphia, OA, cast iron, emb "E. W. Venables Tobaccos" adv, patented April 15, 1875, 16-1/2" l, 7" h .......... 150.00
European, wrought iron, fancy marking on blade and hinge, wood base with dark patina, dated "1773," some insect damage to base, 35" l .......... 250.00
John Finzer & Brothers, Louisville, KY, cast iron, emb adv, 17" l, 7" h .......... 140.00
P. J. Song Co., spear head, cast iron, red, black lettering, 16-1/2" l .......... 170.00
R. J. Reynolds Co., black japanned finish .......... 125.00

# TOBACCO JARS

**History:** A tobacco jar is a container for storing tobacco. Tobacco humidors were made of various materials and in many shapes, including figurals. The earliest jars date to the early 17th century; however, most examples seen in the antiques market today were made in the late 19th or early 20th centuries.

**Reference:** Joseph Horowitz, *Figural Humidors, Mostly Victorian,* published by author, 1997 (FTJ Publications, 3011 Fallstaff Rd, Baltimore, MD 21209).

**Collectors' Club:** Society of Tobacco Jar Collectors, 3011 Fallstaff Rd., Baltimore, MD 21209.

**Stoneware, Bristol glaze, relief hunting dog design, orig lid, very minor clay separation in the making, 6-1/2" h, $180. Photo courtesy of Vicki & Bruce Waasdrop.**

Alpine Man, 5" h, bisque, white, green and brown trim............... 150.00
Blackamoor, 7-1/2" h, majolica.................................................... 250.00
Boy, 5" h, majolica, earflap hat, realistic coloring....................... 175.00
Cat, 6" h, majolica, wearing yellow straw hat, mkd "Made in Austria," raised "J. S." in shield, numerals on base .............................. 450.00
Cigar Man, 8-3/4" h, terra cotta, mkd "J. M. 3625, Made in Bohemia, Czech".................................................................................. 350.00
Cylinder, 7-1/2" h, pewter, claw and ball feet .............................. 95.00
Dog, 5" h, majolica, boxer's head ............................................... 450.00
Englishman, 7" h, majolica, night hat, mkd "6567" and "48" incised in bottom..................................................................................... 250.00
Indian, 5-1/2" h, porcelain, polychrome dec, set-on lid, E Bohne & Sohne..................................................................................... 235.00
Man, 10" h, full figure, wearing swallowtail coat, white vest, skull cap, terra cotta............................................................................... 220.00
Monk, majolica
    6-3/4" h, high gloss, c1950 ................................................ 100.00
    6-3/4" h, realistic coloring, incised "2585" over "27"........... 225.00
    8" h, realistic coloring......................................................... 350.00
Owl, 7" h, pottery, high glaze, cobalt blue, yellow, and brown .... 350.00
Skull, bisque, sitting on book, wearing golfing cap .................... 150.00

# TOBY JUGS

**History:** Toby jugs are drinking vessels that usually depict a full-figured, robust, genial drinking man. They originated in England in the late 18th century. The term "Toby" probably is related to the character Uncle Toby from *Tristram Shandy* by Laurence Sterne.

**References:** Susan and Al Bagdade, *Warman's English & Continental Pottery & Porcelain*, 3rd Edition, Krause Publications, 1998; Vic Schuler, *Collecting British Toby Jugs,* 2nd ed., Kevin Francis Publishing Ltd., 1987.

**Museums:** American Toby Jug Museum, Evanston, IL; City Museum & Art Gallery, Stoke-on-Trent, England; Victoria & Albert Museum, London, England.

**Additional Listings:** Royal Doulton.

6-1/8" h, Benjamin Franklin, seated figure, pipe, wine goblet, mottled brown Rockingham glaze, Bennington, 1849-58 ..................... 550.00
7-1/4"h, Huntsman, Royal Doulton, c1910................................. 350.00

**Pitcher, stoneware, Rockingham glaze, c1880, 6" h, $110. Photo courtesy of Vicki & Bruce Waasdrop.**

8" h, salt glaze stoneware, cobalt blue accents facial features, man perched on barrel inscribed "Old Tom" with blue accents, Albany glaze int., attributed to Norton, Bennington, VT, c1850 .................... 1,320.00
8-1/4" h, Prattware-type, underglaze palette, restorations to hat brim, handle, and one foot, late 18th C .............................................. 375.00
9-1/8" h, Mr Toby, seated, holding jug, tricorner hat, jacket, vest, knee breeches, manganese, soft green, brown ochre, yellow, and orange-ochre, Prattware, 18th C, pipe bowl missing, slight damage...... 1,540.00
9-1/8" h, seated man, blue and yellow mottled coat, yellow pants, brown hair, hat, and shoes, holding jug on left knee, pipe between legs, Leeds type, c1800 ....................................................... 850.00
9-1/2" h
    Derbyshire, standing man, yellow-tan glaze, dark brown splashes, mid-19th C ......................................................... 125.00
    Staffordshire, seated man, blue coat, yellow breeches, foaming jug on left knee, late 18th C ............................................. 900.00
    Wood, Ralph, seated man, green waistcoat, gray jacket, dark hat, one hand raised to mouth ................................................ 950.00
10-1/2" h, Sailor, seated, tricorn hat, holding jug in one hand, pipe in other, Staffordshire, 19th C, repairs ............................ 345.00
10-3/4" h, Napoleon, ironstone, multicolored enamel, marked "Napoleon Jug-patent applied for Alfred E Evans, Philadelphia, PA"........... 400.00
11" h, Coachman, wearing tassels, Rockingham glaze, Bennington, 1849 mark ............................................................................ 450.00
11-1/2" h, Hearty Goodfellow, full figure man, tricorn hat, coat, waistcoat, knee breeches, carrying pitcher and ale glass, rockwork base, manganese, green, pale blue, tan, brown-ochre, olive green, Staffordshire, attributed to Ralph Wood, 18th C, professional restoration............................................................3,575.00

# TOOLS

**History:** Before the advent of the assembly line and mass production, practically everything required for living was handmade at home or by a local tradesman or craftsman. The cooper, the blacksmith, the cabinet maker, and the carpenter all had their special tools.

Early examples of these hand tools are collected for their workmanship, ingenuity, place of manufacture, or design. Modern-day craftsman often search out and use old hand tools in order to authentically recreate the manufacture of an object.

**References:** Ronald S. Barlow, *Antique Tool Collector's Guide to Value*, L-W Book Sales, 1999; Kenneth L. Cope, *American Machinist's Tools*, Astragal Press, 1993; Martin J. Donnelly, *Catalogue of Antique Tools*, published by author (31 Rumsey St., Bath, NY 14810), 1998; Garrett Hack, *The Handplane Book,* Taunton Press, 1997; Jerry and Elaine Heuring, *Collector's Guide to E. C. Simmons, Keen Kutter Cutlery Tools,* Collector Books, 1999; Herbert P. Kean and Emil S. Pollak, *Price Guide to Antique Tools*, Astragal Press, 1992; ——, *Collecting Antique Tools*, Astragal Press, 1990; Kathryn McNerney, *Antique Tools, Our American Heritage*, Collector Books, 1979, 2000 value update; Emil and Martyl Pollak, *Guide to American Wooden Planes and Their Makers,* 3rd ed., The Astragal Press, 1994; ——, *Prices*

Realized on Rare Imprinted American Wood Planes, 1979-1992, Astragal Press, 1993; John Walter, *Antique & Collectible Stanley Tools, Guide to Identity & Value,* 2nd ed., The Tool Merchant, 1996; C. H. Wendel, *Encyclopedia of American Farm Implements & Antiques,* Krause Publications, 1997; John M. Whelan, *The Wooden Plane,* Astragal Press, 1993; Jack Wood, *Early 20th Century Stanley Tools,* L-W Book Sales, 1996 value update; ——, *Town-Country Old Tools,* 6th ed., L-W Book Sales, 1997, 1999 value update.

**Periodicals:** *Fine Tool Journal,* 27 Fickett Rd, Pownal, ME 04069, http://www.FineToolJ.com; *Plumb Line,* 10023 St. Clair's Retreat, Fort Wayne, IN 46825; *Stanley Tool Collector News,* 208 Front St., P.O. Box 227, Marietta, OH 45750, http://www.thetoolmerchant.com; *Tool Ads,* P.O. Box 33, Hamilton, MT 59840-0033.

**Collectors' Clubs:** American Barbed Wire Collectors Society, 1023 Baldwin Rd, Bakersfield, CA 93304-4203; Blow Torch Collectors Club, 3328 258th Ave. SE, Issaquah, WA 98027-9173, http://www.indy.net/~toper/BTCA; Collectors of Rare & Familiar Tools Society, 38 Colony Ct, Murray Hill, NJ 07974; Collectors of Rare & Familiar Tools Society of New Jersey, 38 Colony Street, New Providence, NJ 07974-2332, http://www.craftsofnj; Early American Industries Association, 167 Bakersville Rd, South Dartmouth, MA 02748-4198, http://www.eaiainfo.org; Early American Industries-West, 8476 West Way Dr., La Jolla, CA 92038; Long Island Antique Tool Collector's Association, 31 Wildwood Drive, Smithwotn, NY 11787-3452; Mid-West Tool Collectors Association, P.O. Box 8016, Berkley, CA 94707-8016; Missouri Valley Wrench Club, 613 N. Long St., Shelbyville, IL 62565; New England Tool Collectors Association, 11-1/2 Concord Ave., Saint Johnsburgy, VT 05819; Ohio Tool Collectors Association, P.O. Box 261, London, OH 43140-0261; Pacific Northwest Tool Collectors, 5022 Erskine Ave., Seattle, WA 98136, http://www.tool-timer.com/PNTC.htm; Preserving Arts & Skills of the Trades, 2535 Grambling Way, Riverside, CA 9250y, http://www.tooltalk.org; Potomac Antique Tools & Industries Association, 6802 Newbitt Pl, McLean, VA 22101; Richmond Antique Tool Society, 2208 Lochwood Court, Richmond, VA 23233; Rocky Mountain Tool Collectors, 1435 S Urban Way, Lakewood, CO 80028; Society of Workers in

**Beader, Windsor, brass, ebonized wood, Patent March 10, 1885, June 2, 1885, cutter missing, $135.**

Early Arts & Trades, 606 Lake Lena Blvd., Auburndale, FL 33823; Southwest Tool Collectors Association, 712 S. Lincoln Lane Court, Mustang, OK 73069-4141, http://www/swtca.org; Three Rivers Tool Collectors, 310 Old Airport Road, Greensburg, PA 15601-5816; Tool Group of Canada, 7 Tottenham Rd, Ontario MC3 2J3 Canada; Western New York Antique Tool Collector's Association, 3162 Avon Road, Genesco, NY 14454, http://physics.sci.genesco.edu/WNYATCA/info.htm.

**Museums:** American Precision Museum Association, Windsor, VT; Barbed Wire Museum, La Crosse, KS; Living History Farms, Urbandale, IA; Mercer Museum, Doylestown, PA; National Agricultural Center & Hall of Fame, Bonner Springs, KS; Post Rock Museum, La Crosse, KS; Shelburne Museum, Shelburne, VT; Winchester Mystery House, San Jose, CA; World of Tools Museum, Waverly, TN.

Awl, 5-1/4" l, stag horn, old worn patina........................................100.00
Beader, Stanley No. 66, full set of replacement blades, fences, 70%
   plating...............................................................................................100.00
Bit Gauge, Stanley No. 49, orig box, early SR & L label...............22.50
Brace and Bit, wood, inlaid pewter..................................................500.00
Buck Saw, 8-1/2" l, miniature, dated "1859"..................................150.00
Butt Gauge, Stanley No. 95G, yellow box with reinforced corners 22.50
Calipers, Goodell Pratt, No. 505, outside spring, 8", faded red
   box ....................................................................................................25.00
Carving Tools, Miller Falls, No. 1, set of 6, rosewood handles, orig oak
   box with inside paper label........................................................ 110.00
Clapboard Maker, Stanley 88, adjustable, orig box, early SR & L
   label....................................................................................................40.00
Dowel Jig, Stanley No. 59, 6 drill guides, orig box........................ 40.00
Dowel Machine, Stanley No. 77, 3/8" cutter, blue finish, orig instructions and cardboard box..................................................................395.00
Drill, Miller Falls type, 90% orig red detail painting, 96%
   japanning ......................................................................................... 110.00
Grooving Router, Preston, adjustable, three cutters, three fences, 80%
   japanning...........................................................................................85.00
Gouge, Ibbotson Peace & Co, graduated set of 9, cast steel.....225.00
Hammer
      Adz head, Cheney No. 777....................................................65.00
      Snowball, wrapped handle, fancy brass clip........................35.00
Hatchet, 10-3/4" l, hand forged, old hickory handle, mkd "AH"...250.00
Level
      Goodell Pratt, 18", cast iron, double plumb, one dry vial......15.00
      Stratton Brothers No. 10, brass, bound 12", rosewood, 1908 Barber quarter dollar inlaid in side .........................................195.00
Molding Plane, 11" l, adjustable gate, rosewood and boxwood, ivory
   and brass trim, stamped "Casey & Co. Auburn, N.Y.," wedge
   replaced ..........................................................................................425.00
Parallel Ruler, Carrington's Patent, manufactured by William Hill, Wallingford, CT, wood, paper label ....................................................65.00
Pipe tongs, 17-1/4" l, wrought steel, incised dec and "Fort W. M. Henry
   Capt. B. Williams 1756".............................................................9,200.00

Plane
    Bedrock, 604, bench, type 9, orange frog, Sweet Hart blade, 93% japanning.............................................................145.00
    Spiers Ayr, rosewood filled, 2 1/8" inch iron, polished ........325.00
    Stanley
        No. 47, dado, type 5, 60% japanning .............................395.00
        No. 50, combination, 15 cutters, B casting, 70% plating 110.00
        No. 97, chisel, 60% japanning........................................395.00
        No. 278, rabbet, 85% japanning, wrong fence ..............125.00
Ratchet Brace
    Consolidated Tool Works, Inc., No. 808, knob controlled, hardwood handles, 85% plating .................................................45.00
    Keystone, W A Ives Mfg Co, Wallingford, CT, lever controlled, hardwood handles......................................................65.00
Sash Router, Preston.........................................................40.00
Saw, Disston, right angle ..................................................30.00
Saw Set, Stanley 42, orig box.............................................15.00
Screwdriver, 18-1/2" l, Cowles Hardware Co, Warranted Superior, sold by T.H.E. Co., cabinet maker's type ..........................................48.00
Sharpening Stone, 13-3/4" l, mounted on block, carved designs and "James N. Rosser, 1826" ..........................................385.00
Socket Set, PS & W Co, set of 12 in orig wood box, 9 apple wood handles, 3 with replaced handles.................................................325.00
Tool Box, 24-1/2" l, narrow pine tongue and groove bead board, out varnish finish, brass hardware, lock with key ..............................70.00
Wrench, W & C Wynn & Co, Patent, combination wrench, pliers, buggy wrench, hammer, and screwdriver ..........................................75.00

# TOOTHPICK HOLDERS

**History:** Toothpick holders, indispensable table accessories of the Victorian era, are small containers made specifically to hold toothpicks.

They were made in a wide range of materials: china (bisque and porcelain), glass (art, blown, cut, opalescent, pattern, etc.), and metals, especially silver plate. Makers include both American and European firms.

By applying a decal or transfer, a toothpick holder became a souvenir item; by changing the decal or transfer, the same blank could become a memento for any number of locations.

**References:** Neila and Tom Bredehoft and Jo and Bob Sanford, *Glass Toothpick Holders,* Collector Books, 1999; William Heacock, *Encyclopedia of Victorian Colored Pattern Glass*, Book I, 2nd ed., Antique Publications, 1976, 1992 value update; —, *1,000 Toothpick Holders*, Antique Publications, 1977; —, *Rare & Unlisted Toothpick Holders*, Antique Publications, 1984; National Toothpick Holders Collectors Society, *Toothpick Holders*, Antique Publications, 1992.

**Collectors' Club:** National Toothpick Holder Collectors, P.O. Box 417, Safety Harbor, FL 34695-0417, http://www.collectoronline.com/clubNTHCS.html

**Additional Listings:** See *Warman's Americana & Collectibles* for more examples.

Amberina, 2-1/4" h, IVT, tricorn folded top ..................................285.00
China, three handles, silver deposit design, sgd "R. S. Tillowitz" . 65.00
Cut Glass, 2-1/2" h, Little Lobe, Libbey, tiny blue flowers and ivy leaves, pink tinted base, blue tinted upper half, sgd "Libbey Cut Glass Toledo O" ..........................................................300.00
Opaque Glass
    Beggar's Hand, white, green base.............................45.00

Cut Glass, pedestal base, $100. Photo courtesy of Joy Luke Fine Art Brokers and Auctioneers.

    Burmese, 2-1/2" h, soft blush of pink, soft yellow rim and base, Mt. Washington ................................................335.00
    Burmese, 3" h, 3" d, matte finish, naturalistic pine cone and branches dec, 7 pine cones, 1880s, Mt. Washington ......675.00
    One-O-One, pink ...................................................80.00
    Palm Leaf, green ...................................................45.00
Porcelain, figural, nude girl in shell, mkd "Glen Falls, NY"............45.00
Pattern Glass
    Block, hat shape, vaseline......................................55.00
    Box in Box............................................................32.00
    Cat on a Pillow, amber............................................60.00
    Frances Ware, 2-1/2" h, 1-1/2" d, bright golden yellow rim, frosted hobnail base...............................................170500??
Royal Bayreuth
    Coal Shuttle, Dutch Boy and goose, unmkd......................200.00
    Ovoid, side handle, Dutch boy and goose, mkd ................200.00
Ruby Stained
    Daisy and Button, red buttons and rim ...........................65.00
    Scroll with Cane band............................................65.00
    Sunk Honeycomb ................................................45.00
Silver Plate, figural
    Bird sitting next to goblet, engraved "Take Your Pick" ........100.00
    Boots, pair on base, Aurora...................................125.00
    Rat crouching next to pouch, Derby ...........................85.00

# TORTOISESHELL ITEMS

**History:** For many years, amber and mottled tortoiseshell has been used in the manufacture of small items such as boxes, combs, dresser sets, and trinkets.

**Note:** Anyone dealing in the sale of tortoiseshell objects should be familiar with the Endangered Species Act and Amendment in its entirety. As of November 1978, antique tortoiseshell objects can be legally imported and sold with some restrictions.

**Also** see *Celluloid* for imitation tortoiseshell items.

Bowl, 7-3/4" d, one turned up side, applied amber feet ..............115.00
Box, cov, round, small round watercolor of gentleman on top, early 19th C..................................................................300.00
Cabinet Door, 28-1/2" h, 18" w, repousse silver scene of descent from cross, reverse with incised giltwood designs, Continental, 19th C, losses .................................................................3,850.00
Dance Program Holder, 5-3/4" x 3-1/8", rect, Continental silver, tortoise shell, and enamel, floral and shell engraved silver frame, one side with oval-3/4" portrait of damsel, Victorian, mid-half 19th C.....350.00
Glove Box, 9-3/4" l, 2-7/8" w, 2-3/4" h, silver inlay, int. lined in period claret plush and silk, c1875-1890.............................................660.00

Hair Ornament, Art Nouveau
- Back Comb, gilt grass, turquoise glass accents ................ 135.00
- Side, applied metallic dec, simulated gemstones ................ 75.00

Hairpin, carved poppy blossom, heavy shell ............................ 135.00

Inkstand, 8" x 16", three cut glass bottles, brass inlay, shaped handles ................................................................................ 400.00

Letter Opener, sterling silver, stylized spear design, sterling shaft, tortoiseshell blade, hallmark for William Spratling, Taxco, Mexico ..... 690.00

Match Box Cover, applied red coral trim ...................................... 65.00

Match Safe, 2-3/8" l, silver trim, felt lined, octagonal, push button opening .................................................................................. 200.00

Necessaire, 10" l, tortoiseshell and ivory, rect, fitted int. with sewing implements, ball feet, Victorian, mid-19th C ......................... 865.00

Patch Box, 3-1/4" d, brass inlaid, scrolled foliate and bird design, Continental, 19th C, minor breaks ............................................. 150.00

Snuff Box, 1-3/8" d, ivory medallion with miniature watercolor painting of gentleman in blue coat, Anglo/American School, 18th C ..... 375.00

Tea Caddy
- 5" w, 5-1/2" h, George III, silver mounts, ivory inlay, late 18th C ............................................................................ 1,375.00
- 6" x 8" x 5-1/2", William IV, oblong top, bread front outline, twin canisters, conforming case resting on molded base, second quarter 19th C ............................................................. 900.00

# TOYS

**History:** The first cast iron toys began to appear in America shortly after the Civil War. Leading 19th-century manufacturers include Hubley, Dent, Kenton, and Schoenhut. In the first decades of the 20th century, Arcade, Buddy L, Marx, and Tootsie Toy joined these earlier firms. Wooden toys were made by George Brown and other manufacturers who did not sign or label their work.

Nuremberg, Germany, was the European center for the toy industry from the late 18th through the mid-20th centuries. Companies such as Lehman and Marklin produced high-quality toys.

**References:** Ronald S. Barlow (ed.,) *The Great American Antique Toy Bazaar, 1879-1945: 5,000 Old Engravings from Original Trade Catalogs*, Windmill Publishing, 1998; Robert E. Birkenes, *White Knob Wind Up Collectible Toys*, Schiffer Publishing, 1999; Larry Bloemker, Robert Genat, and Ed Weirick, *Pedal Cars*, MBI Publishing, 1999; Bill Bruegman, *Toys of the Sixties*, Cap'n Penny Productions, 1991; Dana Cain, *Collecting Monsters of Film and TV*, Krause Publications, 1997; Brad Cassity, *Fisher-Price Toys*, Collector Books, 1999; Jurgen and Marianne Cieslik, *Lehmann Toys*, New Cavendish Books, 1982; Christopher Cook, *Collectible American Yo-Yos, 1920s-1930s*, Collector Books, 1997; Don Cranmer, *Collectors Encyclopedia, Toys—Banks*, L-W Books, 1986, 1993 value update; Greg Davis and Bill Morgan, *Collector's Guide to TV Toys and Memorabilia*, 2nd ed., Collector Books, 1999; Phillippe De LeSpinay, *Vintage Slot Cars*, MBI Publishing, 1999; Judith Anderson Drawe and Kathleen Bridge Greenstein, *Lithographed Paper Toys, Books, and Games, 1880-1915*, Schiffer Publishing, 2000; Antoni Emchowicz and Paul Nunneley, *Future Toys*, New Cavendish, distributed by Antique Collectors' Club, 1999; Edward Force, *Corgi Toys*, Schiffer Publishing, 1984, 1997 value update; —, *Dinky Toys*, Schiffer Publishing, 1988, 1992 value update; —, *Lledo Toys*, Schiffer Publishing, 1996; —, *Solido Toys*, Schiffer Publishing, 1993; Jurgin Franzke, *Tinplate Toys: From Schuco, Bing & Other Companies*, Schiffer Publishing, 2000; Tom Frey, *Toy Bop: Kid Classics of the 50s & 60s*, Fuzzy Dice Productions, 1994;

Bill Gallagher, *Japanese Toys*, Schiffer Publishing, 2000; Kurt Guile, Mike Willyard and Gary Konow, *Wyandotte Toys Are Good and Safe*, Wyandotte Toys Publishing, 1996; Ted Hake, *Hake's Price Guide To Character Toys*, 3rd ed., Collector Books, 2000; Tom Heaton, *The Encyclopedia of Marx Action Figures*, Krause Publications, 1999; Andrew Gurka, *Pedal Car Restoration and Price Guide*, Krause Publications, 1996; Don Hultzman, *Collector's Guide to Battery Toys*, Collector Books, 1998; Alan Jaffe, *J. Chein and Co., A Collector's Guide to an American Toymaker*, Schiffer Publishing, 1997; Dana Johnson, *Matchbox Toys 1947-1996*, 3rd ed., Collector Books, 1999; Michele Karl, *Composition & Wood Dolls and Toys: A Collector's Reference Guide*, Antique Trader Books, 1998; Sharon Korbeck and Elizabeth Stephan, *Toys & Prices, 2001*, 8th ed., Krause Publications, 2000.

Kathy and Don Lewis, *Talking Toys of the 20th Century*, Collector Books, 1999; David Longest, *Antique & Collectible Toys 1870-1950*, Collector Books, 1994; —, *Character Toys and Collectibles* (1984, 1992 value update), 2nd Series (1987), Collector Books; —, *Toys*, Collector Books, 1990, 1994 value update; Rex Miller, *The Investor's Guide to Vintage Character Collectibles*, Krause Publications, 1999; Richard O'Brien, *Collecting American Made Toy Soldiers*, Krause Publications, 1997; —, *Collecting Foreign-Made Toy Soldiers*, Krause Publications, 1997; Bob Parker, *Hot Wheels*, 4th ed., Schiffer Publishing, 2000; —, *Marx Toys*, Schiffer Publishing, 1996.

Vincent Santelmo, *The Complete Encyclopedia to G. I. Joe*, 3rd ed., Krause Publications, 2001; Carole and Richard Smith, *Pails by Comparison*, published by author (P.O. Box 2068, Huntington, NY 11743), 1996; Michelle Smith, *Marx Toys Sampler, Playthings from an Ohio Valley Legend*, Krause Publications, 2000; Elizabeth Stephan, ed., *O'Brien's Collecting Toys, Ninth Ed.*, Krause Publications, 1999; —, *Collecting Toy Cars & Trucks*, 3rd ed., Krause Publications, 2000; —, *Today's Hottest Die-Cast*, Krause Publications, 2000; —, *Toy Shop's Action Figure Price Guide*, Krause Publications, 2000; Craig Strange, *Collector's Guide to Tinker Toys*, Collector Books, 1996; Glenda Thomas, *Toy and Miniature Sewing Machines*, Collector Books, 1997;; Stuart W. Wells, III, *Science Fiction Collectibles: Identification & Price Guide*, Krause Publications, 1999; Harry A. and Joyce A. Whitworth, *G-Men and FBI Toys and Collectibles*, Collector Books, 1998; Neil S. Wood, *Evolution of the Pedal Car, Volume 4*, L-W Book Sales, 2000; Myra Yellin and Eric B. Outwater, *Cast Iron Automotive Toys*, Schiffer Publishing, 2000.

**Periodicals:** *Antique Toy World*, P.O. Box 34509, Chicago, IL 60634; *Canadian Toy Mania*, P.O. Box 489, Rocanville, Saskatchewan SOA 3LO Canada; *Collectors Gazette*, Fleck Way, Thornsby, Stockton-On-Ters,

Cleveland, T617 9J2, UK, http://www.icn.co.uk/cg.html; *Die Cast & Tin Toy Report*, 559 North Park Ave., Easton, CT 06612; *Master Collector*, 225 Cattle Barron Park Drive, Fort Worth, TX 76108; *Model & Toy Collector Magazine*, 137 Casterton Ave., Akron, OH 44303; *Plane News*, P.O. Box 845, Greenwich, CT 06836; *Robot World & Price Guide*, P.O. Box 184, Lenox Hill Station, New York, NY 10021; *Toy Cannon News*, P.O. Box 2052-N, Norcross, GA 30071; *Toy Collector & Price Guide*, 700 E. State St., Iola, WI 54990; *Toy Collector Marketplace*, 1550 Territorial Rd, Benton Harbor, MI 49022; *Toy Gun Collectors of America Newsletter*, 312 Starling Way, Anaheim, CA 92807; *Toy Shop*, 700 East State St., Iola, WI 54990; *Toy Trader*, P.O. Box 1050, Dubuque, IA 52004; Toybox Magazine, 8393 E. Holly Rd, Holly, MI 48442; *U.S. Toy Collector Magazine*, P.O. Box 4244, Missoula, MT 59806; *Yo-Yo Times*, P.O. Box 1519, Herndon, VA 22070.

**Collectors' Clubs:** A. C. Gilbert Heritage Society, 1440 W. Rolley, Suite 252, New Haven, CT 06515, http://www.acghs.org; American Game Collectors Association, P.O. Box 44, Dresher, PA 19025; Antique Engine, Tractor & Toy Club, Inc., 5731 Paradise Rd, Slatington, PA 18080; Antique Toy Collectors of America, 13th Floor, Two Wall St., New York, NY 10005; Canadian Toy Collectors Society, 67 Alpine Ave., Hamilton, Ontario L9A1Z7, Canada; Capitol Miniature Auto Collectors Club, 10207 Greenacres Dr., Silver Spring, MD 20903; Diecast Exchange Club, P.O. Box 1066, Pineallas Park, FL 34665; Ertl Collectors Club, Highways 136 & 120, Dyersville, IA 52040; Farm Toy Collectors Club, P.O. Box 38, Boxholm, IA 50040; Ideal Toy Co. Collector's Club, P.O. Box 623, Lexington, MA 02173; Majorette Diecast Toy Collectors Association, 13447 NW. Albany Ave., Bend, OR 97701; Miniature Piano Enthusiast Club, 633 Pennsylvania Ave., Hagerstown, MD 21740; San Francisco Bay Brooklin Club, P.O. Box 61018, Palo Alto, CA 94306; Schoenhut Collectors Club, 45 Louis Ave., West Seneca, NY 14224; Southern California Toy Collectors Club, Ste. 300, 1760 Termino, Long Beach, CA 90804.

**Museums:** American Museum of Automobile Miniatures, Andover, MA; Eugene Field House & Toy Museum, St. Louis, MO; Evanston Historical Society, Evanston, IL 60201; Forbes Magazine Collection, New York, NY; Hobby City Doll & Toy Museum, Anaheim, CA; Margaret Woodbury Strong Museum, Rochester, NY; Matchbox & Lesney Toy Museum, Durham, CT; Matchbox Road Museum, Newfield, NJ; Museum of the City of New York, New York, NY; Smithsonian Institution, Washington, DC; Spinning Top Exploratory Museum, Burlington, WI; Toy & Miniature Museum of Kansas City, Kansas City, MO; Toy Museum of Atlanta, Atlanta, GA; Washington Dolls' House & Toy Museum, Washington, DC; Western Reserve Historical Society, Cleveland, OH.

**Additional Listings:** Characters; Disneyanna; Dolls; Schoenhut. Also see *Warman's Americana & Collectibles* and *Warman's Flea Market* for more examples.

**Notes:** Every toy is collectible; the key is condition. Good working order is important when considering mechanical toys. Examples in this listing are considered to be at least in good condition, if not better, unless otherwise specified.

## Arcade, USA

Auto Transport, painted cast iron, restored, 24" l ......................... 350.00

Bus

    A Century of Progress, Chicago, 1933, Greyhound Lines, worn orig paint, mkd "A.M.C. 1933," 11-1/2" l ........................... 220.00

    A Century of Progress, Chicago, 1933, Greyhound Lines, worn orig paint, mkd "A.M.C. 1933," 14-1/4" l ........................... 330.00

    Double Decker, painted cast iron, four passengers, 8" l ..... 300.00

    Fageol, some restoration, 12-1/4" l ................................... 225.00

    Greyhound Lines, New York World's Fair, worn orig paint, 10-1/2" l ................................................................. 385.00

Car Carrier, four cars, old paint, some rust, 11-1/4" l ................. 275.00

Chevy Coupe, painted cast iron, 8" l...........................................750.00
Chevy Sedan, replaced tires and spare, 8-1/4" l........................550.00
Coupe, painted cast iron, some roof and hood blemishes,
6-1/2" l........................................................................................225.00
Dump Truck, International Harvester, old worn repaint, labeled inside
cab, rubber tires also marked "Arcade," 9" l.............................90.00
Farm Truck, orig driver, very worn orig paint, traces of decal, light rust,
also labeled inside cab, 10-1/4" l............................................425.00
Farm Wagon
    Arcade, two horses, driver, two wooden legs, 11" l.............350.00
    McCormick Deering, two horses, orig paint, minor wear, orig
    decal, 12-1/2" l...................................................................250.00
    Fire Truck, cab and trailer, worn orig paint, decal label, tires mkd
    "Arcade," accessories missing, 16" l .......................................95.00
Ford Coupe, painted cast iron, orig condition, 6-1/2" l...............400.00
Gas Tanker, painted cast iron, steel tank, new tires, incorrect driver,
12-1/2" l.......................................................................................425.00
Hathaway Bread Truck, restored, 9-1/2" l...................................400.00
Ice Truck, Mack, six blocks of glass ice, old worn repaint, incomplete,
labeled inside of cab, 8-1/2" l...................................................200.00
Model T, coupe, minor wear to orig black paint, driver missing, mkd
"Arcade Mfg Co.," 6-1/2" l...........................................................55.00
Plow
    Arcade, old worn paint, nickel finish trim, labeled with "AC" mono-
    gram, 5-3/4" l.....................................................................100.00
    McCormick Deering, minor wear to orig paint, orig decal,
    7" l ......................................................................................220.00
    Oliver, minor wear to orig paint, decal label, black rubber wheels
    labeled "Arcade Balloon," 5-1/2" l........................................75.00
Railroad Transport, Pullman Railplane, worn orig paint, labeled inside
body, 8-3/4" l...............................................................................80.00
Show Boat, painted cast iron, repair to front deck, 11" h ...........400.00
Stake Truck, 1931 International, orig driver and gate, replaced wheels,
12" l...........................................................................................325.00
Tanker Truck, 2 piece, painted cast iron, 5-1/2" l.......................135.00
Taxi, cast iron
    Brown and white paint, restored, 7-3/4" l.............................170.00
    Old repaint, wheels replaced, driver, labeled on inside of
    frame ..................................................................................200.00
T-Bar Dump, painted cast iron and steel, restored, 12" l ...........300.00
Thresher, McCormick-Deering, orig red paint, intact decal,
9-1/2" l.......................................................................................275.00
Tractor
    Allis-Chalmers, worn orig paint, rust, orig rusty driver, decals, 7-
    1/4" l .....................................................................................55.00
    Arcade, worn orig paint, decal labels "Arcade" and "Row Crop,"
    black rubber tires labeled "Arcade Balloon," 5-1/4" l..........45.00
    Farmall, worn partial repaint, mismatched driver, orig decal, 7-
    1/4" l .....................................................................................90.00
    Ford, dump wagon, worn old paint, 15-1/4" l ......................360.00
    McCormick-Deering, traces of orig paint, rust, worn decal, mis-
    matched driver, 7-1/4" l.........................................................55.00
Yellow Cab, cast iron, 7-3/4" l....................................................300.00
Weaver Wrecker, cast iron, restored, 9" l...................................225.00

## Arnold, West Germany

Howdy Doody Acrobat, tin litho, cloth, and plastic, lever action..225.00
Motorcycle, tin litho, key-wind, working headlight, cover missing, 7-
1/2" l...........................................................................................150.00
Tin Lizzy, tin litho, composition figures, steering mechanism, wind-
shield missing, 9-3/4" l ..............................................................135.00

## Automatic Toy Co.

Alpine Express, tin litho, key-wind, some damage to orig box, 20"
l.....................................................................................................90.00
Union Station, tin litho, key-wind, 20" l......................................150.00

## Bell Toy, unknown makers, cast iron

Buster Brown and Tige, old worn silver paint, red wheels,
7-1/2" l.......................................................................................275.00

Convertible, litho tin wind-up, 6-1/2" l, $300. Photo courtesy of Richard Opfer Auctioneering, Inc.

Daisy, worn old polychrome paint, wheels not painted, some rust,
8-1/2" l.......................................................................................680.00
Elephant Cart, old worn repaint, old worn nickel finish on driver,
7-3/4" l.......................................................................................200.00
Landing of Columbus, very worn old gold paint, bell loose,
7-1/2" l.......................................................................................110.00
Monkey and Coconut, worn old polychrome paint, wheels incomplete,
6" l..............................................................................................250.00
Push, two bells with double head clapper, replaced heart design
wheels, worn nickel finish, light rust, wooden handle, 6" l.........70.00
Wild Mule Jake, very worn polychrome paint, front wheel damaged,
rear axle replaced, 9" l ..............................................................420.00

## Bing Toy Works, Germany

Airplane Tower, tin litho, mechanical, partial orig box with label,
scratches and blemishes, 20" l, fair to good condition .............275.00
Amphibian Airplane, hand painted tin, overhead engines, clockwork
housing in fuselage, painted silver and brown, 16" wingspan, some
silver over paint .........................................................................800.00
Convertible, litho tin, mechanical, working, 6-1/2" l ...................300.00
De Dion Runabout, hand painted tin, white, gold trim, red upholstered
emb finish, two open seats, front head lamp and curved running
boards, 8" l..............................................................................2,310.00
Limousine, litho tin, clockwork, red body, black roof, full running
boards, seated driver, spare mounted on side, gold finished grill,
spoke wheels, partial orig box, 10-1/2" l................................2,100.00
Pigmyphone, litho tin wind-up, tin container, illus of Little Red
Riding Hood, Wolf, Seven Dwarfs, two black banjo players, Little
Wonder record plays "The Alcoholic Blues," extra box of needles,
6" x 6" x 3-1/2".............................................................................90.00
Sedan, tin litho, mechanism missing, 6-1/2" h..............................95.00
Taxi limousine. beveled-glass windows, carriage lights, bright red,
orange, and green paint with black trim; 14-1/4" l...............21,850.00
Tug Boat, hand painted tin, red and black hull, upper deck painted yellow, pilot's house, mast with rigging, stack on cabin, two support
beams, clockwork mechanism, 9-1/2" l.................................1,350.00

## Bliss, USA

Buffalo Floor Train, 45" long, litho paper on wood, alphabet blocks
cargo and connecting rod missing, c1900..............................7,190.00
Horse Drawn Chariot, wood, paper lithography, drawn by wheeled
horse, ornate details, stamped cardboard seat, "C" shaped chariot
with curtained back window graphics, covered roof, 15-1/2" h,
23" l........................................................................................1,540.00

## Brown, George, USA

paddle wheeler, tin, hand painted, stenciled, light blue boat, red top
deck roof, cast iron spoke wheels, two stacks, stenciled "Monitor" on
sides, American tin flag on bowl, ball pole on stem, clockwork..........
5,280.00

## Buddy L, USA

Aerial Tower Tramway, pressed steel, restored, 34" h................625.00
Air Mail Truck, painted pressed steel, restored, 22" l..............1,250.00
Air Plane and Hanger, painted pressed steel, restored, catapult
hanger, partial repaint, 10" w wingspan ..................................550.00
Concrete Mixer, painted pressed steel, restored, 18" l ..............400.00
Crane, painted pressed steel, restored...................................225.00
Dump Truck, painted pressed steel, restored, 24" l.................1,700.00

International Harvester Pick-Up Truck, painted pressed steel, restored, 23" l ..................................................................1,100.00

Moving Van, No. 204, black cab, red body, 1926, 25" l, decals missing ..............................................................................575.00

Parcel Delivery Truck, pressed steel, brown and beige paint, large slant black body, rear doors, decals on sides, solid rubber wheels, 24" l, pull bar and one headlight missing ..................................990.00

Passenger Bus, pressed steel, light green, 22 chair seats, two benches, spare tires on sides, 29" l, shellacked ...................3,300.00

Pickup Truck, Red Baby, painted pressed steel, orig but crazed, 24" l..............................................................................1,150.00

Railway Express, pressed steel, 1938 International cab, painted yellow and green duo-tone, van body with removable top, opening rear doors, large side decals adv "Wrigley's Spearmint Chewing Gum," rubber tires, emb spoke wheels, 24" l ...............................715.00

Road Roller, painted pressed steel, restored, 18-1/2" l............2,200.00

Robotoy, pressed steel, red tractor, green dump body, black chassis, electrical, moves forwards and backwards to automatically dump cargo, orig transformer and box, 21-5/8" l............................2,310.00

Shell Oil Truck, pressed steel, International model cab, orange and red duo-tone, decals on tank body "Shell Fuel Oils," rubber wheels, red centers, 20-3/4" l, dent to grill...................................................360.00

Station Wagon, all wood, maroon front, hood fenders, side panels, and roof with simulated wood graining, opening front and rear doors, side decals "Buddy 'L' Station Wagon," orig box, 19" l..................1,100.00

Steam Shovel, Improved, painted pressed steel, restored, 22" l 800.00

Town and Country Car, wooden, convertible, retractable roof, fine orig condition, very minor wear, 18-1/2" l .......................................550.00

Truck Loader, painted pressed steel, partial chain replacement, 18-1/2" h...............................................................................225.00

## Carrette, Germany

Gun Boat, hand painted tin, brown, red hull stripe, railed deck, pilot's house, two stacks, two guns and mast, 16" l, mast loose ........660.00

Limousine, hand painted tin, clockwork, maroon, orange trim, two head lamps, two side lanterns, glass windows, opening doors, detailed molded seats, full running boards, rubber tires, 12-1/4" l, professionally restored.......................................................................2,750.00

Limousine, litho tin, clockwork, deep green, brown and yellow trim, black full running boards, nickel plated head lamps, side lanterns, opening side doors, glass windows, seated hand painted chauffeur, rubber tires, spoke wheels, roof rack, 16" l, replaced lights.................7,150.00

River Boat, hand painted tin, red and cream hull, yellow corrugated deck simulating wood flooring, cabin deck with curtained corners, stairs lead to upper deck, railed bow and stern, twin screw activated by clockwork mechanism, 17" l, stairs railway missing ...........660.00

## Champion, USA

Motorcycle

    With policeman, worn orig paint, worn and cracked white rubber tires, 5" l ...................................................................... 110.00

    With cop in sidecar, wear to orig paint, 5" l .........................220.00

Tow Truck, worn old paint, rust, 9-1/4" l ......................................110.00

## Chein, USA

Alligator, litho tin wind-up, native riding on back, wear, working, 15" l...............................................................................150.00

Popeye, litho tin wind-up, wear, 6-1/4" h......................................420.00

## Citroen, France

Aviation Fuel Truck, pressed steel, clockwork, painted red, enclosed cab with opening driver's door, tanker body with filler cap and brass drain valve, electric headlights, rear decal "AVIA," 18" l.....................1,320.00

Coupe, pressed steel, clockwork, painted maroon, black roof and trunk, chromed grill, molded seats, 11-1/2" l, replaced tires, clockwork and lights missing ...........................................................495.00

Delivery Truck, litho tin, friction, green, black highlights, covered body, exposed tail end, curved fenders, 9" l .....................................825.00

Fire Engine, painted tin, clockwork, red, open bench seats, removable hose reel, ladders mount on rear body, disc wheels, rubber tires, orig box, 19" l............................................................................2,860.00

**Carousel, Converse 5 wooden seats with lithographed horses, 5 matching 10" h German dolls in orig clothing, 15" h, 36" w, $1,500. Photo courtesy of McMasters Doll Auction.**

Flat Bed Truck, litho tin, friction, enclosed green cab, nickeled front grill, black flat bed body, removable stake side rear, pulley bar, body hooks, 12-1/4" l ........................................................................1,045.00

Race Car, pressed steel, clockwork, blue, molded seated figure with hand painted composition head, rubber tires, decal "Petite Rosalie," 12-1/4" l ............................................................................440.00

Sedan, litho tin, clockwork, bright orange and red, molded black seats, full running boards, dummy headlights, opening driver's door, 11-1/2" l, repainted lights ..................................................................1,210.00

Stake Truck, litho tin, flywheel on rear axle, enclosed cab painted red, yellow highlights, blue stake side body, curved venders, 9" l .....990.00

## Converse

USA, open car, painted steel, mechanical, working, overpainted, 15" l. 650.00

## Courtland

Checker Cat, tin litho, key-wind, working, scratches, 7" l .............85.00

Ice Cream Cart, litho tin wind-up, working, 6-1/2" l.....................200.00

## Dent

Fire Wagon, cast iron, red paint, yellow wheels, orig figures and horses, two ladders, 15" l..........................................................150.00

Taxi, painted cast iron, yellow, replaced figure, 8-1/4" l ..............200.00

**Distler,** Germany, limousine, litho tin, clockwork, deep blue, aqua blue trim, full running boards, opening repair box on each side, two brass plated headlights, folding rear rack, c1920, 12" l ..................1,320.00

## Doepke

MG, painted pressed steel, 15" l.................................................360.00

Sports Car, painted pressed steel, restored, 17-1/2" l ................300.00

## Erbl, Hans, Germany

Comic Convertible Car, litho tin, clockwork allows car to rollover onto it's roll bar, extensive graphics of faces in spirited patterns, seated tin clown driver, 10" l, fair condition................................................550.00

**Ocean Liner, Fleishman painted tin wind-up, minor flakes, two lifeboats missing, 18" l, $1,250. Photo courtesy of Richard Opfer Auctioneering, Inc.**

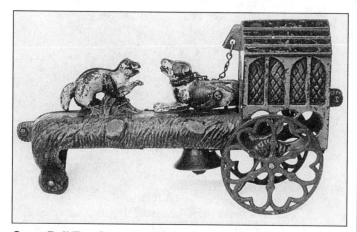

**Gong Bell Toy Co., cat and dog bell toy, $1,450.**

Delivery Truck, litho tin, clockwork, blue and red body, black roof, overhead luggage rack, full running boards, spoked metal wheels, seated driver in doorless open cab, 8" l, fair condition..........................660.00
Delivery Truck, litho tin, clockwork, red and black body, black roof, open rear door, open side door, seated driver, sides read "Strawbridge & Clothier," spoke wheels, 7-1/2" l, paint cracked ...... 1,320.00

## Fischer, Heinrich, & Co., Germany, penny toy
Fire Engine, pumper truck.............................................145.00
Roadster, open, sloping hood .....................................2,650.00

## Fleischmann, Germany
Cargo Ship, hand painted tin, red and black, upper deck features railed cat walks from pilot's house to cabins and observation deck, three funnels, railed sides, multi leveled cabins, clockwork mechanism, 19-1/2 l, missing masts ...................................725.00
Ocean Liner, painted tin, mechanical, working, minor flakes, missing tow lifeboats, 18" l .............................................. 1,250.00
Tanker, hand painted lithograph tin, some flaking, 20" l..............850.00

## Gunthermann, Germany
Bugle Player, hand painted tin, soldier with bugle in hand, circular base, plans "Soldier to Arms Call" when clockwork activated, 7-7/8" h ......................................................................990.00
Convertible Touring Car, litho tin, clockwork, blue, gray trim, brown seats, front head lamps, full running boards, simulated top down model, seated driver behind glass windshield, 9-3/4" l ......... 1,100.00
Monkey and Darkey Minstrels, hand painted tin, clarinet playing minstrel, seated monkey violinist, mounted on base, music stand, clockwork mechanism activates movement and rhythmic notes, 7-1/2" h x 6" w ......................................................1,320.00
Open Touring Car, litho tin, clockwork, blue, white, silver trim, unit "V" shaped hood, tow front lanterns, curved running boards, tin driver, two tin seated lady passengers, 10" l, repainted figures, new headlights..........................................................................4,620.00
Saloon, litho tin, red, yellow trim, opening doors, glass windows, seated hand painted tin driver, curved running boards, fifth wheel on rear used with clockwork mechanism, 9-1/2" l .....................4,675.00
Vis-A-Vis, hand painted and litho tin, clockwork, open seat, railed arm rest and backrest, lamps on front, modeled after Peugeot motor car, rubber tires, spoked wheels, 10-1/4" l, new lamps, figure, two new tires ....................................................................1,650.00
Vis-A-Vis, litho tin, clockwork, open seat car, seated driver, railed seat with backrest, rubber tires, spoked wheels, 6-1/2" l, replaced figure, mud guards, and lamps.............................................1,540.00

## Hot Wheels, USA
Drive-In Set ................................................................30.00
FAO Gold Series, collection #1 .................................400.00
Hot Rod Magazine Set................................................35.00
Porsche, 50th Anniversary ..........................................40.00
Voodoo Highway ........................................................28.00

## Japan, various manufacturers
Airport Cab, tin litho, friction, working, Bandai, 7" l.......................75.00
Bulldog, tin litho, friction, working, 6" l......................................95.00
Douglassworld Air Line, tin litho, friction, propellers spin, working, Bandai, 7" l.........................................................................120.00
Fishing Bear, tin litho, wind-up, working, orig box, 7-3/4" h ........135.00
Greyhound Bus, tin litho, friction, orig box, 6-1/4" l.....................90.00
Highway Patrol Car, friction, siren, working, one light missing, 11-1/4" l..................................................................................65.00
Issetta Car, tin litho, friction, Bandai, 7" l ...............................160.00
Mercedes Sedan, tin litho, friction, working, 12" l .....................100.00
Merry Go Round Truck, tin litho, friction, working, 8" l...............150.00
Mouse Barber, tin litho, wind-up, working, 5" h.........................160.00
Navy Jet, tin litho, friction, fold-up wings, scratches, Yone, 8-1/2" l...................................................................................50.00
Santa, long neck, tin litho, celluloid, and cloth, mkd "T. N. Japan" 70.00
Sedan, tin litho, working, mkd "C. K. Japan," flaking, dents, slight rust, 7" l, fair condition...................................................................80.00
Sports Car, tin litho, friction, working, man and dog, 8" l ...........100.00
Telephone Truck, tin litho, rubber wheels, KTS, dents and scratches, 8" l......................................................................................40.00
Thunderbird Convertible, tin litho, friction, rubber wheels, minor scratches, 9" l...........................................................................150.00

## Hubley, Lancaster, PA
Airplane, painted cast iron, black and orange, flat tires, 4-1/2" l.......180.00
Bell Telephone Truck, cast iron, orig paint with minor wear, deteriorated white rubber tires, mismatched accessories, mkd "Made in USA," 10" l.............................................................................385.00
Champion Motorcycle, painted cast iron, 5" l..............................150.00
Coupe, painted cast iron, 4-1/4" l.................................................80.00
Crash Car, motorcycle with cart, cast iron, orig worn blue paint, nickel wheels, 4-3/4" l........................................................................220.00
Dump Truck, cast iron, worn orig paint, light rust, 6-3/4" l .........160.00
Fire Truck, cast iron
    Ladder Truck, painted, no ladders, 5" l ...............................30.00
    Pumper, electric head lights, worn repaint with rust, worn rubber tires, 10-1/4" l.......................................................................95.00
    Water tower, orig paint, some gold touch up on wheels, 10-3/4" l.............................................................................110.00
Grasshopper, cast iron, worn orig paint, decal label, antenna loose, wheels possibly replaced, 11-1/2" l........................................360.00
Lindy Airplane, painted cast iron, 4-1/2" l..................................140.00
Motorcycle Cop, cast iron, electric lamp with possibly orig battery, worn orig paint, very worn rubber tires, 6-3/8" l ..................................90.00
Motorcycle, painted pot metal, rubber wheels, flaking, 8" l.........100.00
Motorcycle, sidebar, passenger, painted cast iron, iron wheels, 4" l..................................................................................135.00
Patrol Wagon, cast iron, early example, worn orig paint, light rust, 6-3/4" l..................................................................................125.00
Police Motorcycle, painted cast iron, electric headlight, 6-1/4 l ..350.00
Roadster, painted cast iron, black and gold, 5" l........................120.00
Speedboat, painted cast iron, 4-3/4" l........................................100.00
Steam Roller, with driver, "Huber," wear to orig paint, chains missing, 8" l......................................................................................330.00
Studebaker Roadster, cast iron, worn orig paint, nickel trim, patent date, 6-5/8" l..........................................................................330.00

## Kenton, Kenton, OH
Bakery Wagon, two horses, old repaint, driver missing, 13-3/4" l ....150.00
Beer Wagon, two horses, driver, wear to orig paint, light rust, 15" l......................................................................................420.00
Buckeye Ditcher, labeled "Kenton Toys, Kenton, Ohio," repainted, 5" h......................................................................................250.00
Coupe, cast iron, restored, 8" l .................................................550.00
Dray Wagon, two horses and wagon, cast iron, very worn paint, tin sides on wagon with worn paper covering, driver, assortment of mismatched cargo, wear, rust, 23-1/2" l.......................................825.00
Engine, stationary, wear to old repaint, labeled in three places, 8" l......................................................................................360.00

Farm Wagon, two horses, wear to orig paint, driver missing, 15" l...150.00

Hanson Cab, one horse, driver, passenger, orig paint with minor wear, 16" l..........................................................................200.00

Jaeger Cement Mixer, minor wear, 7-1/2" l.....................275.00

Nodders, The, cart with driver, cast iron, very worn paint, replaced parts, 6-1/4" l.........................................................200.00

Overland Circus, wagon with two horses and outriders, driver, six musicians, worn orig paint, 16" l...............................425.00

Sand & Gravel, dump wagon, two horses, wear to orig paint, driver missing, 15" l.........................................................175.00

Sedan, painted cast iron, Sears, 12" l.............................450.00

Touring Sedan, painted cast iron, damage to lady passenger, 9" l..............................................................................1,150.00

## Keystone Mfg. Co., Boston, MA

Bus, pressed steel, gray, cream hinged roof, wooden handles on top of roof for steering, simulated headlights and tail lights, rear railing decal on grill "Packard," side decals "Coast-to-Coast Keystone Bus," large door decals lists 15 cities, greyhound decal on side, 31" l, fair condition ...................................................................1,430.00

Dump Truck, pressed steel, black open bench seat cab and chassis, red dump body, hand lever for tilting body, disc wheels, rubber tires, 26" l, over painted ..................................................300.00

Packard Dump Truck, painted pressed steel, restored, 26" l......375.00

Ride 'Em Plane, pressed steel, fighter plane, child's seat and handle bars on fuselage, propeller revolves, painted gray, red wings, rubber tires, disc wheels on front, 27" wingspan, fair condition...........275.00

Ride 'Em Steam Shovel, sheet steel, worn orig paint, label, 20" l......75.00

## Kilgore, USA

Gullwing Airplane, painted cast iron, slight rust, 4-3/4" h............275.00

Sea Gull, repainted, welded repair, 8-1/4" w wingspan...............110.00

Tat, painted cast iron, 11" l.............................................1,450.00

Tat Passenger Plane, painted cast iron, 5-3/4" wingspan...........125.00

Travel Air Mystery Plane, painted cast iron, 6" l .......................500.00

## Kingsbury Toys, USA

Chrysler Airflow, pressed steel, painted brown, chromed grill, clockwork and battery box...........................................................2,640.00

Convertible, painted pressed steel, working, steering wheel missing, scratches, 13" l, fair condition .................................110.00

Golden Arrow Racer, Major Segrave as driver, working mechanism, gold paint, 95% orig Kingsbury decal, orig paper tag, 20" l...1,200.00

Hook and Ladder Truck, painted pressed steel, restored, 30" l..950.00

Ladder Truck, painted pressed steel, rubber tires, 31" l ............950.00

Sedan, mechanical, working, restored, 12" l........................600.00

Water Pumper Truck, painted pressed steel, restored, 22-1/2" l...1,000.00

## Lehmann, Germany

Autin, litho and hand painted tin, clockwork, boy in pedal car, 4-1/4" l....................................................................615.00

Autohutte, litho tin

One car, Stiller, yellow and black sedan, clockwork mechanism parked in cottage style garage with silhouette of children at play on back, ornate graphics, 6" l.......................................2,860.00

Two car, red scalloped roof, large opening front doors stores sedan EPL No. 760 and the Galop, both included, orig box 6-1/4" x 7" w, missing box lid..............................................2,320.00

Baker and Sweep, litho and hand painted tin, clockwork, baker with spoon in hand, chimney sweep in charcoal, 5-1/2" l ............4,400.00

Balky Mule, litho and hand painted tin, clockwork, comical clown, cart, and donkey, fabric suit, orig box, 8" l.......................550.00

Buster Brown, litho and hand painted tin, friction, seated in open auto, 4" l......................................................................1,650.00

Coco, string pull toy, man climbing palm tree, paper leaves, 14-1/2" h.....................................................................1,045.00

Convertible, litho tin

Berolina, navy blue, red trim and int., tan cloth top, 6-3/4" l ..1,380.00

Chromed grill, bumpers, and spare, orig box, 4" l..............360.00

Crawling Beetle, litho tin, clockwork, light green wings, wings move, crawls, 4" x 4-1/2" l...........................................................440.00

Crocodile, litho tin, clockwork, animated, simulated real life colors, walks and jaw moves, 9-1/2" l.................................................500.00

Dancing Sailor, Columbia on hat, 1903, 7-1/2" h, repairs to box 690.00

Dump Truck, litho tin, red cab, green stationary dump body, chromed grill, rubber tires, orig box, 4-1/4" l.........................................250.00

Express, litho and hand painted tin, clockwork, porter wearing blue jack, pulling trunk carrier, 6" l...............................................660.00

Flying Bird, hand painted tin, paste board bird suspended by two strings, wings, orig box, 10" wingspan, missing box lid............660.00

Galop, litho tin, clockwork, cowboy rider pulled by zebra, c1954, orig box, 7-1/4" l.......................................................................990.00

Garage and Car, litho tin, mechanical car, 6" l.............................500.00

Going to the Fair, litho and hand painted tin, flywheel, woman seated in promenade chair, 5" h, 6-1/2" l..........................................3,190.00

Gustav the Miller, litho tin, string pull, figure climbs long shaft to mill, orig box, 18" h.......................................................................440.00

Hansom Cab, litho and hand painted tin, clockwork, 5-1/2" l... 1,980.00

Kadi, litho and hand painted tin, clockwork, two Chinese figures with tea chest, 7" l...................................................................2,310.00

Kamerun, litho tin, string wind drive, ostrich drawn cart, black boy seated on open bench seat, 6" l.......................................1,100.00

Mandarin, litho and hand painted tin, clockwork, Chinese in sedan chair, pulled by two servants, 7" l.......................................2,750.00

Mars Motorcycle, litho and hand painted tin, clockwork, motorcycle, 3" x 4-3/4" l.........................................................................660.00

Masuyama, litho and hand painted tin, clockwork, rickshaw, floral design on umbrella, 6-3/4" l.................................................3,190.00

May Beetle, litho tin, clockwork, brown wings, 8" l.....................660.00

Mensa Delivery Van, litho tin, clockwork, 5-1/4" l.....................2,530.00

Mikado Family, Japanese litho and hand painted tin, clockwork, rickshaw with seated woman holding baby, pulled by China man, 7" l......................................................................1,430.00

Mixtum, litho and hand painted tin, clockwork

Black driver, 4-1/4" l.........................................................1,760.00

White driver, 4-1/4" l.........................................................2,420.00

Motor Car, litho tin, steering by front wheels, 5" l, replaced key handle ..............................................................................925.00

Naughty Boy, litho and hand painted tin, clockwork, car, driver, and boy, 5" l..............................................................................1,430.00

New Century Cycle, litho tin, mechanical, working, orig box, 4-1/2" h.............................................................................1,150.00

Nina, Cat and Mouse, litho tin, large black and white cat chases mouse ..............................................................................1,650.00

Nu-Nu, litho and hand painted tin, clockwork, Chinese with tea chest, 5" l......................................................................1,210.00

Oho, litho tin, clockwork, open cab automobile, 3-3/4" l .............550.00

Paak-Pak, litho tin, clockwork, duck cart and ducklings, 7" l ......715.00

Paddy and the Pig, litho and hand painted tin, clockwork, figure riding large scaled pig, 5" l...........................................................1,100.00

Performing Sea Lion, litho tin, clockwork, orig box, 8" l.............600.00

Race Car, tin litho, key-wind, patent date 1913, scratches and dents, 6" l......................................................................225.00

Shell Filling Station, litho tin, two pumps, orig box, 5-1/2" w, 4" d ....990.00

Suzi Turtle, litho tin, clockwork, boxer turtle, walking motion, orig box, 5" l......................................................................715.00

Swing Doll, litho tin, clockwork, seated china doll, cloth dress, 7-1/4" h.............................................................................2,970.00

Tap-Tap, litho and hand painted tin, clockwork, walking gardener, wheelbarrow and shove, 1920s, 7" l .....................................1,045.00

Tut-Tut, litho and hand painted tin, clockwork, automobile and driver, 6-1/2" l ....................................................................1,100.00

Tyras Walking Dog, litho tin, clockwork, 6" l...............................715.00

Uhu, litho and hand painted tin, clockwork, amphibian auto, simulated lights on sides of high windshield, propeller bladed wheels for water travel, 9" l .......................................................................1,320.00

Zig-Zag, litho tin, clockwork, rocking car, 4-1/4" h.........................................................................3,080.00

Zikra-Dare Devil, litho tin, clockwork, cart with driver pulled by kicking zebra, orig box, 7-1/4" l.......................................................1,650.00

## Linemar, Japan

Bubble Blowing Popeye, battery operated, 12-1/2" h ................ 950.00
Sleeping Baby Bear, battery operated, orig box, 9" l .................. 125.00

## Marklin, Germany

Airplane, tin litho, mechanical, #1980, orig box, 15" l ................ 600.00
Construction Set, boxed, Chassis Set No. 1101, clockwork motor and light, all complete, orig instructions, 13" x 18" ..................... 2,250.00
Coupe, #1903, new in orig box, 15" l ..................................... 350.00
Coupe, #19021, new in orig box, 15" l ................................... 350.00
Delivery Truck, #C-9320, new in orig box, 13" l ....................... 175.00
Delivery Wagon, #1989, new in orig box, 15" l ........................ 275.00
Farmer with Sickle, hand painted tin face, lead feet and hands, farmer wears cloth suit, hold long handled sickle, simulates cutting motion when clockwork activated, 7-1/2" l, new jacket .................... 1,045.00
Fire Truck, #1991, new in orig box, 15" l ................................. 450.00
Gullwing, #1952, key wind, new in orig box, 13" l ..................... 300.00
Limousine, #19032, new in orig box, 15" l ............................... 450.00
Mystery Ball, litho tin, ball with standing figure, travels down spiral band ball opens and then climbs to top for another descent, 12" h ................................................................................. 925.00
Race Car, #1947, new in orig box, 12" l .................................. 150.00
Rheinland Battleship, hand painted tin, olive green hull, deck painted in simulated wood flooring, railing throughout, four guns on each side, six deck cannons, with turrets, observation deck, two masts, chained anchors, lifeboats supported on rods, two deck cranes, extensive details, stenciled "Rheinland," clockwork mechanism, 26-1/2" l ......................................................... 6,600.00

## Marx, Louis & Co., New York

Airplane, tin litho, key-wind, scratches, 6" l ............................... 90.00
Army Plane, tin litho, key-wind, working, scratches, 18-1/2" l ..... 225.00
Big Parade, tin litho, key-wind, runs, but needs string, 24" l ....... 170.00
Bull Dozer, litho tin wind-up, orig box, wear, damage to box, 10-1/2" l .............................................................................. 115.00
Busy Miners, tin litho, key-wind, orig box, minor scratches ........ 175.00
Charlie McCarthy, Benzine Buggy, litho tin wind-up, minor wear, working, 7-1/8" l ................................................................. 450.00
Coupe, tin litho, key-wind, working, soiling and blemishes, 9" l .. 300.00
Cowboy with Lasso, tin litho, key-wind, working, minor scratches, 9" l ...................................................................................... 210.00
Donkey Cart, tin litho, key-wind, working, 8-1/2" l ...................... 65.00
G-Man Automatic Pistol, tin, key-wind, working, orig box missing one end, 4" l ............................................................................ 85.00
Honeymoon Express, tin litho, key wind, working, early version, minor scratches, 9-1/2" l .................................................... 350.00
Hopping Cary the Crow, tin litho, wind-up, working, orig box, 4-1/4" h .................................................................................. 80.00
Jumpin' Jeep, tin litho, key wind, working, 5-1/2" l .................... 120.00
Looping Plane, tin litho, key-wind, dents and scratches, mechanism skips, 5" l ............................................................................... 40.00
Pluto Watch Me Roll Over, litho tin wind-up, mkd "Walt Disney Productions 1939," worn, ears missing, working, 9" l .................. 110.00
Race Car Set, tin litho, key-wind, 2 cars, 16 track sections, minor dents and scratches, 30" l ................................................... 180.00
Race Car #7, tin litho, key-wind, working, scratches, fading, paint loss, 5" l ..................................................................................... 50.00
Son of Garloo, tin litho and plastic, wind-up, working, 6" h .......... 60.00
Speed Racer, tin litho, mechanical, working, orig box, 6-1/4" l ... 450.00
Tiger Trike, tin litho and plastic, wind-up, working, orig box, 4-1/2" h ................................................................................... 90.00
Wacky Taxi, tin friction car, mkd "Marx," 7-3/4" l ...................... 110.00
Wonder Cyclist, tin litho, mechanical, working, orig box, top and side torn, 9" l .............................................................................. 225.00

## Metal Craft, USA

Coca Cola Truck, painted metal, rubber tires, electric headlights, stenciled, fixed adv logo on top, holds 10 bottles, 11" l ................ 1,015.00
Goodrich Tires Service Truck, painted sheet metal, open bed with tires and winch, adv along side rail, 12" l, minor wear ..................... 275.00
Heinz 57 Truck, painted sheet metal, rubber tires, electric lights, 12" l, grill missing headlamp brackets .............................................. 440.00
Meadow Gold Medal Butter Truck, painted sheet metal, rubber tires, electric lights, 13" l ......................................................... 1,650.00
Samarkand Ice Cream Truck, painted sheet metal, rubber tires, adv on van body, 10-3/4" l ........................................................ 3,250.00
Shell Motor Oil Truck, painted sheet metal, rubber tires, 8 orig cans, 12" l ...................................................................................... 825.00
Standard Stake Truck, painted shell metal, rubber tires, white stake body, red company name on side, 12" l ................................. 1,870.00
St. Louis Truck, painted sheet metal, disc wheels, company name on van body, 11-1/2" l ............................................................... 360.00
Sunshine Biscuit Truck, painted sheet metal, rubber tires, adv on van body, 12" l ....................................................................... 1,210.00

## Orkin Craft

Motor boat, tin, clockwork, painted maroon, white and red hull, cabin deck, fully appointed, deck level open seat, trimmed windows, pilot's doors, funnels, railway, 31" l, chip off rear deck ................... 3,025.00

## Orobor, Germany

Cargo Plane, litho tin, three propellers, wood grain simulated cargo, intricate double clockwork mechanism allows propellers to spin while other activates wheel motion, 14-1/4" l .............................. 1,540.00
Packard Coupe, litho tin, clockwork, red, black top, rumble seat opens, full running boards, disc wheels, spare attached to trunk, "Packard" written across radiator, missing one great ............................. 2,860.00

## Penny Toy, miscellaneous makers, tin litho, good or very good condition unless noted

Beetle, minor scratches, 3" l ..................................................... 40.00
Cat and Dog, 4" l .................................................................... 425.00
Chinaman, minor flaking and rust, 2-1/2" l .............................. 450.00
Delivery Boy, minor flaking, 3" l ........................................... 1,100.00
Delivery Truck, minor blemishes, 3-1/2" l ................................. 325.00
Goose, nodder, 2-1/2" l ........................................................... 120.00
Hansom Cab, minor flaking and rust spots, 3-1/2" l, fair to good condition ................................................................................ 220.00
Hay Wagon, minor rust spots and blemishes, 4-1/2" l, fair to good condition .................................................................................. 60.00
Horse and Tank Wagon, rust spots throughout, 4-1/2" l ............ 110.00
Military Wagon, minor blemishes and flaking, 4-1/2" l .............. 150.00
Motorboat, minor rust spots, 4-1/2" l ...................................... 325.00
Open Car, minor flaking ........................................................... 500.00
Racecar, #948, minor flaking, 3-1/2" l ..................................... 600.00
Red Cross Truck, rust spots and flaking, 3-1/2" l ...................... 325.00
Sheep Truck, rust spots, 3-1/2" l ............................................. 425.00
Touring Car, rust spots, 3-1/2" l .............................................. 300.00
Trapeze, flaking and paint loss, poor condition, 2-1/2" l .............. 70.00
Trolley Car, minor flaking, 3" l ................................................ 375.00

## Pratt and Letchworth, USA

Hanson cab, cast iron, light brown horse with white blanket, gold bridle, yellow and black cab, yellow wheels, driver missing, c1880 .................................................................................. 685.00

## Schuco, trademark of Schreyer and Company, Germany

BMW, #00012, new in orig box, 10" l ...................................... 160.00
Motorcycle Rider, litho tin, dressed in felt and mohair, working, 5" l ...................................................................................... 225.00

## Steelcraft, USA

Airplane, US Navy Patrol, pedal car, silver, red and blue trim, spring belt driver propeller, mid-20th C, 48" l ................................. 2,990.00
Dump Truck, painted pressed steel, restored, 26" l .................... 350.00
U. S. Mail Truck, painted pressed steel, restored, 22" l ............. 300.00

## Strauss, USA

Santee Claus, litho tin, mechanical, working, 11" l .................. 1,450.00
Yell-O-Taxi, 8-1/2" l, one wheel repaired ..................................... 410.00

## Structo, USA

Loom, pressed steel, free standing, working model, 12-1/2" l .... 210.00
Transport Truck, pressed steel, painted red and gray, enclosed cab, semi trailer body, additional flat bed trailer, rubber tires, chromed hubs, side decal reads "Hi-Way Transport," 25" l ..................... 320.00
Vista Dome Horse Van, sheet steel, orig box, 20" l ................... 360.00

## Sturditoy, USA

US mail truck, 25-1/2" l, 11" h, green, black, and red pressed steel, paint scratched on edges, 1920s ......................................... 2,300.00

## Tipp Co., Tipp & Co., Tipco, Germany

Ambulance, litho tin mechanical, orig drivers and wounded on stretcher, 9" l ................................................................................ 1,000.00
Army Truck and Cannon, litho tin wind-up, opening door, composition soldiers, well articulated cannon with working lever auction, elevation device, camouflaged, 16" l ....................................................... 100.00
Bomber Airplane, litho, clockwork mechanism drops lead cap bombs from wings underside while in motion, tan, red and blue graphics, 14-1/2" wingspan, replaced bombs ......................................... 1,650.00
Club Sedan, litho tin, clockwork, bright orange and gray, two opening doors, elaborate int., seated driver, rear trunk lid opens, electric lights, full running boards, 1933, 17" l .................................. 1,540.00
Fuhrerwagon, litho tin, clockwork, Mercedes Benz, black, six different lights, two horns, side mounted muffler pipes, spares mounted on full running boards, convertible model, molded seats, 9" l ............. 825.00
Limousine, litho tin, clockwork, green, luxury model, molded seats, tin dashboard with graphics, seated tin chauffeur, opening passenger doors, chromed front grill with hood ornament, 1920s, 15-1/2" l ............................................................................................ 4,125.00
Luxury Sedan, litho tin clockwork, maroon and brown, full running boards, opening doors, seated tin driver, luggage compartment, electric headlights, 19-1/2" l ...................................................... 2,100.00
Motorcycle, litho tin friction, headlight missing, 11" l .................. 200.00

## Tonka, USA

Ace Hardware Semi Truck, red, decals, 1955 ........................... 425.00
Army Troop Carrier, 1964 ........................................................... 150.00
Bulldozer, orange, rubber treads, 1960 ....................................... 75.00
Car Hauler, yellow, 1961 ........................................................... 250.00
Carnation Milk Van, white, decals, 1955 .................................... 200.00
Deluxe Fisherman, boat and trailer, 1960 .................................. 225.00
Dump Truck, 1949-53 ................................................................. 135.00
Fire Dept Rescue Van, 1950s .................................................... 150.00
Fire Truck, hydraulic aerial ladder, 1957 ................................... 200.00
Gasoline Tanker, red, 1957 ........................................................ 400.00
Green Giant Transport Truck, white, green lettering, 1953 ......... 200.00
Hi-Way Mobil Clam, orange, 1961 .............................................. 225.00
Hi-Way Sign Set, 1959 ............................................................... 250.00
Livestock Van, red, 1952 ............................................................ 150.00
Log Hauler, red cab, orig logs, 1953 .......................................... 150.00
Pickup Truck, 1955 .................................................................... 195.00
Road Grader, orange, 1953 .......................................................... 75.00
Star-Kist Tuna Box Van, red cab, blue body, 1950-53 ............... 180.00
Steam Shovel, red, 1949 ............................................................ 130.00
Tonka Air Express, black, decals, 1959 ..................................... 300.00
Wrecker Truck, blue, 1949-53 .................................................... 175.00

## Tootsietoy, USA

Chrysler Convertible, '50, red, replaced windshield .................... 150.00
Ford Station Wagon, '52, gray and blue, 4-1/4" l .......................... 45.00
GMC Box Truck, '39, green, 4-1/2" l, repainted ............................ 40.00
Jumbo Sedan, '47, #1018, green .................................................. 35.00
Mercedes, '56, #995, red ............................................................ 195.00

German, Goose Girl, painted tin wind-up, 11-1/2" l, $1,000. Photo courtesy of Richard Opfer Auctioneering, Inc.

## Unique Art, Newark, NJ

Bombo, tin litho, key-wind, orig box with tear, 9-1/2" h ................ 70.00
Clown, tin litho, wind-up, worn surface, works with reluctance, labeled, 10-1/2" h ................................................................................... 170.00
Dogpatch Band, tin litho, key-wind, working, minor scratches, 8-1/2" h ................................................................................... 300.00
G. I. Joe and K-9 Pups, tin litho, wind-up, working, 9" h ............. 120.00
Lincoln Tunnel, tin litho, key-wind, scratches, 24" l .................... 180.00
Rodeo Joe, tin litho, wind-up, working, 7" l ................................ 120.00
Sky Ranger, tin litho, key-wind, working, minor scratches, 28" l . 150.00
Unique Artie, tin litho, mechanical, working, hat tip separated, 7" l ...................................................................................... 240.090

## Unknown Maker

Bicycle, string toy, tin litho, 6-1/2" l ............................................ 125.00
Blacksmith, tin litho, steam operated, flaking, 5" h, fair to good condition ........................................................................................ 60.00
Bobsled, painted tin, steam operated, crank mechanism, minor flaking, 5-1/2" l ..................................................................................... 175.00
Ferris Wheel, painted tin, steam operated, paint loss throughout, 13" h, poor to fair condition .................................................................. 350.00
Grinder, steam toy, painted tin, paint loss throughout, 5" h, poor to fair condition ..................................................................................... 90.00
Hobo, string toy, tin litho, 8-1/2" l ............................................... 100.00
Spirit of St. Louis, airplane, tin litho, electric, scratches and blemishes, 13-1/2" l ................................................................................... 375.00
Velocipede, clockwork, early American, redressed .................... 450.00

## Williams, A. C., USA

Ford Wrecker, '29, cast iron, dark blue ...................................... 375.00
Fuel Truck, cast iron .................................................................. 225.00
Sedan
    Desoto Airflow, blue, white rubber tires, red hubs, 1937, 6-7/8" l ............................................................................... 635.00
    Pierce Arrow, 1933, cast iron, take apart type ................... 275.00
Truck, 6-3/4" l, stake body, red body, green chassis, balloon tires, nickel plated radiator, late 1920s ............................................. 635.00

## Wolverine Supply & Mfg. Co.

Jet Roller Coaster, tin litho, key-wind, minor scratches, 12" l ..... 180.00
Ocean Liner, tin litho, key-wind, working, scratches, 14-1/2" l .... 110.00

# TRAINS, TOY

**History:** Railroading has always been an important part of childhood, largely because of the romance associated with the railroad and the prominence of toy trains.

The first toy trains were cast iron and tin; wind-up motors added movement. The golden age of toy trains was 1920 to 1955, when electric-powered units and high-quality rolling stock were available and names such as Ives, American Flyer, and Lionel were household words. The advent of plastic in the late 1950s resulted in considerably lower quality.

Toy trains are designated by a model scale or gauge. The most popular are HO, N, O and standard. Narrow gauge was a response to the modern capacity to miniaturize. Its popularity has decreased in the last few years.

**References:** Paul V. Ambrose, *Greenberg's Guide to Lionel Trains, 1945-1969*, Vol. III, Greenberg Publishing, 1990; Paul V. Ambrose and Joseph P. Algozzini, *Greenberg's Guide to Lionel Trains 1945-1969*, Vol. IV, *Uncatalogued Sets* (1992), Vol. V, *Rare and Unusual* (1993), Greenberg Publishing; Tom Blaisdell and Ed Urmston, St., *Standard Guide to Athearn Model Trains*, Krause Publications, 1998; John O. Bradshaw, *Greenberg's Guide to Kusan Trains*, Greenberg Publishing, 1987; W. G. Claytor Jr., P. Doyle, and C. McKenney, *Greenberg's Guide to Early American Toy Trains*, Greenberg Publishing, 1993; Joe Deger, *Greenberg's Guide to American Flyer S Gauge*, Vol. I, 4th ed. (1991), Vol. II (1991), Vol. III (1992), Greenberg Publishing; Cindy Lee Floyd (comp.), *Greenberg's Marx Train Catalogues*, Greenberg Publishing, 1993; John Grams, *Toy Train Collecting and Operating*, Kalmbach Publishing, 1999;

Bruce Greenberg, *Greenberg's Guide to Ives Trains*, Vol. I (1991), Vol. II (1992), Greenberg Publishing; —— (Christian F. Rohlfing, ed.), *Greenberg's Guide to Lionel Trains: 1901-1942*, Vol. 1 (1988), Vol. 2 (1988), Greenberg Publishing; ——, *Greenberg's Guide To Lionel Trains: 1945-1969*, Vol. 1, 8th ed. (1992), Vol. 2, 2nd ed. (1993), Greenberg Publishing; *Greenberg's Lionel Catalogues*, Vol. V, Greenberg Publishing, 1992; *Greenberg's Marx Train Catalogues*, Greenberg Publishing, 1992; *Greenberg's Pocket Price Guide, American Flyer S Gauge*, Kalmbach Publishing, 1998; *Greenberg's Pocket Price Guide, LGB, 1969-1996*, 3rd ed., Kalmbach Publishing, 1996; *Greenberg's Pocket Price Guide, Lionel Trains, 1901-1999*, Kalmbach Publishing, 1998; *Greenberg's Pocket Price Guide, Marx Trains*, 7th ed., Kalmbach Publishing, 1999; George Horan, *Greenberg's Guide to Lionel HO*, Vol. II, Greenberg Publishing, 1993; George Horan and Vincent Rosa, *Greenberg's Guide to Lionel HO*, Vol. I, 2nd ed., Greenberg Publishing, 1993; John Hubbard, *Story of Williams Electric Trains*, Greenberg Publishing, 1987; Steven H. Kimball, *Greenberg's Guide to American Flyer Prewar O Gauge*, Greenberg Publishing, 1987; Roland La Voie, *Greenberg's Guide to Lionel Trains, 1970-1991*, Vol. I (1991), Vol. II (1992), Greenberg Publishing.

Lionel Book Committee, *Lionel Trains: Standard Of The World, 1900-1943*, Train Collectors Association, 1989; Dallas J. Mallerich III, *Greenberg's American Toy Trains: From 1900 with Current Values*, Greenberg Publishing, 1990; ——, *Greenberg's Guide to Athearn Trains*, Greenberg Publishing, 1987; Eric J. Matzke, *Greenberg's Guide to Marx Trains*, Vol. 1 (1989), Vol. II (1990), Greenberg Publishing; Robert P. Monaghan, *Greenberg's Guide to Marklin OO/HO*, Greenberg Publishing, 1989; John R. Ottley, *Greenberg's Guide to LGB Trains*, Greenberg Publishing, 1989; Peter H. Riddle, *America's Standard Gauge Electric Trains*, Antique Trader Books, 1998; Robert Schleicher, *Fun with Toy Trains*, Krause Publications, 1999; ——, *N Scale Model Railroading*, Krause Publications, 2000; Alan R. Schuweiler, *Greenberg's Guide to American Flyer*, Wide Gauge, Greenberg Publishing, 1989; Gerry & Janet Souter, *The American Toy Train*, MBI Publishing, 1999; Elizabeth A. Stephan, *O'Brien's Collecting Toy Trains*, 5th ed., Krause Publications, 1999; Robert C. Whitacre, *Greenberg's Guide to Marx Trains Sets*, Vol. III, Greenberg Publishing, 1992.

**Periodicals:** *Classic Toy Trains*, 21027 Crossroads Circle, P.O. Box 1612, Waukesha, WI 53187, http://www2.classtrain.com; *Collectors Gazette*, Fleck Way, Thornsby, Stockton-On-Ters, Cleveland, T617 9J2, UK, http://www.icn.co.uk/cg.html; *LGB Telegram*, 1573 Landvater, Hummelstown, PA 17036; *Lionel Collector Series Marketmaker*, Trainmaster, P.O. Box 1499, Gainesville, FL 32602; *O Gauge Railroading*, P.O. Box 239, Nazareth, PA 18064.

**Collectors' Clubs:** A. C. Gilbert Heritage Society, 1440 W. Rolley, Suite 252, New Haven, CT 06515, http://www.acghs.org; American Flyer Collectors Club, P.O. Box 13269, Pittsburgh, PA 15234; Ives Train Society, P.O. Box 59, Thompson, OH 44086; LGB Model Railroad Club, 1854 Erin Drive, Altoona, PA 16602; Lionel Collectors Club of America, P.O. Box 479, LaSalle, IL 61301; Lionel Operating Train Society, 18 Eland Ct, Fairfield, OH 45014; Marklin Club-North America, P.O. Box 51559, New Berlin, WI 53151; Marklin Digital Special Interest Group, P.O. Box 51319, New Berlin, WI 53151; The National Model Railroad Association, 4121 Cromwell Road, Chattanooga, TN 37421; Toy Train Collectors Society, 109 Howedale Drive, Rochester, NY 14616-1534; The Toy Train Operating Society, Inc., Suite 308, 25 West Walnut St., Pasadena, CA 91103; Train Collector's Association, P.O. Box 248, Strasburg, PA 17579, http://www.traincollectors/org.

**Museums:** Delaware Train and Miniature Museum, Wilmington, DE; Toy Train Museum of the Train Collectors Association, Strasburg, PA.

**Additional Listings:** See *Warman's Americana & Collectibles* for more examples.

**Notes:** Condition of trains is critical when establishing price. Items in fair condition and below (scratched, chipped, dented, rusted or warped) generally have little value to a collector. Accurate restoration is accepted and may enhance the price by one or two grades. Prices listed below are for trains in very good to mint condition unless otherwise noted.

American Flyer, railway set, engine, 3 cars, restoration, $275. Photo courtesy of Richard Opfer Auctioneering, Inc.

## American Flyer

Car

Baggage, #1202, eight wheel, litho, blue ............................... 90.00
Box Car, #9713, New York Central, orig box ........................ 25.00
Flat Car, #9005, New York Central, with vans, orig box ........ 15.00
Gondola, #9005, New York Central, orig box ........................ 15.00
Observation, #9912, aluminum, black lettering, 10-1/8" l ..... 60.00
Tank Car, #9106, New York Central, orig box ........................ 20.00

Locomotive

Silver Bullet, #356, streamlined, chrome, yellow and blue decals, 1953 ................................................................. 145.00
Steeple Cab, #1218, black, 1920-21 .................................. 165.00

Set

O gauge, cast iron wind-up engine, litho tin tender, #1106 Union Pacific coach, curved track, damaged box ...................... 500.00
Standard gauge, Minnie-Ha-Ha, #964-T, locomotive with built-in tender, two coaches, observation car, 1935 ..................... 200.00
Standard gauge, Missouri Pacific Passenger, #49601, orig box .................................................................. 350.00

## Ives

Car

Baggage, #550, litho, four wheels, emerald green, black roof, 1913-30, 6-1/2" l ................................................. 50.00
Parlor, #72, NY and Chicago, litho steel, brown sides, 1914-20, 12" l ................................................................. 375.00

Locomotive, steam, #1122, diecast boiler, black boiler and tender, brass trim, 1929-30 ........................................... 320.00
Set, boxed, #14 passenger set, O gauge, windup black cast iron engine, litho tin #11 black tender, #62 red Limited Vestibule Express parlor car, #60, red Limited Vestibule Express Baggage/Mail car, some wear to orig box ............................................ 4,025.00

## Lionel

Accessory

Bridge Section, bright green, standard, set of four sections, 13-3/4" l ................................................................. 200.00
City Station, #114, green roof, cream building, green and cream trim, 8-1/2" h, 19-1/2" w, 9-1/8" d ............................. 1,150.00
Freight Station Platform, maroon roof, green stations, orange platform, 18" l ..................................................... 375.00
Manual Switch, #210, bright green, 15-1/2" l, some rust on track ................................................................. 20.00
Mountain, papier-mâché, houses and trees, 36-1/2" l ........ 550.00
Platform and Garden, #129, flowers and lawn, 13" l .......... 575.00
Train Station, #116, red and cream tin, 9" h, 19" l, repainted ........................................................... 460.00

Car

Caboose, lighted, #6456 ................................................. 40.00
Cattle Car and Corral, operating, #3656 ............................ 55.00
Flatcar, #3830, blue car, gray submarine, 1960-63 ............. 90.00
Gondola, #6462, painted red .......................................... 25.00
Refrigerator Car, #6472, orig box ................................... 25.00
Stock, #802, green, Union Stock Line, 1915-28 .................. 45.00
Sunoco Tank Car, #6555, orig box ................................... 35.00
Wells Fargo Sheriff & Outlaw, #3370 ............................... 35.00
W & ARR, US Mail Car, #1876 ......................................... 55.00

Locomotive

Berkshire and Tender, #736, c1950, orig box .................... 400.00
Diesel, Texas Special, 210AA .......................................... 100.00
Electric, #250, terra cotta body, maroon frame, 1934 ......... 250.00
Steam, #1681E, red, red frame, 1934-35 .......................... 120.00
Switcher, #625, Lehigh Valley, GE 44 ton, blue, yellow lettering, 1969 ................................................................. 150.00

Set

Freight, #385E gun metal steam engine, #5 tender, #515 cream tank car, #516 red gondola, #513 orange and green cattle car, #514 cream refrigerator, #511 flatbed with lumber, #65 whistle controller, 1933-39 ............................................... 700.00
Freight, #392E black steam engine, #384T black tender, #214 cream and orange box, #212 maroon gondola with eight wooden barrels, #219 green and red crane, #217 red and green caboose, 1932-39 ............................................... 1,150.00
Passenger, #10 peacock electric engine, #339 peacock Pullman, #341 Observation, #332 Railway Mail, 1926-30, paint slightly dull ................................................................. 435.00

## Marklin

Locomotive and Tender, steam, O gauge, wind-up, black and red, green, and gold trim, 8-3/4" l engine, early 20th C ........ 4,315.00
Set, #5751, complete orig box, 30" l ............................... 600.00

# TRUNKS

**History:** Trunks are portable containers that clasp shut and are used for the storage or transportation of personal possessions. Normally "trunk" means the ribbed flat- or domed-top models of the second half of the 19th century.

**References:** Roseann Ettinger, *Trunks, Traveling Bags and Satchels,* Schiffer, 1998; Helenka Gulshan, *Vintage Luggage,* Phillip Wilson Publishers, 1998; Martin and Maryann Labuda, *Price & Identification Guide to Antique Trunks,* published by authors, 1980; Jacquelyn Peake, *How to Recognize and Refinish Antiques for Pleasure and Profit,* 3rd ed., Globe Pequot Press (P.O. Box 833, Old Saybrook, CT 06475), 1995.

**Notes:** Unrestored trunks sell for between $50 and $150. Refinished and relined, the price rises to $200 to $400, with decorators being a principal market.

Early trunks frequently were painted, stenciled, grained, or covered with wallpaper. These are collected for their folk-art qualities and, as such, demand high prices.

Canvas Covered, 24" l, 13-1/2" w, 13" h, whimsical pen and ink lettering, illus on int., "Ephraim Warren, Chelmsford, County, Middlesex, State, Massachusetts, Ward No. 5, March 6th, 1810, AE, 17," lid with tale of "The Hermit," "On A Sudden Arose A Violent Storm," and "The Hermit's Cave," box illus tale of "The Old Man and His Ass," partial newspapers including The Middlesex Gazette, Concord, MA, Aug 12, 1817, line the trunk beneath these illus, newspaper clipping from the Boston Globe, Fall River, MA, June 15, 1926, relates the story of the trunk, staining, lid unattached ............................................. 16,100.00
Dome
    12" l, worn dec black oil cloth and leather trim, brass tacks, lined with 1844 newspaper, hasp missing ................................. 45.00
    12-1/4" w, 30" l, black and red grain paint, plain int., early 19th C ............................................................................................. 325.00
    18" w, 16" d, 12" h, leather, alligator texture, strapwork...... 200.00
    23-1/4" x 30-3/4" x 19-1/2", tooled leather covering, int. with two lift-out trays, very bright chromolithograph decorations, some wear to oil cloth, edge wear, handles missing ................... 225.00
    24-1/4" l, pine, orig graining in imitation mahogany, line inlay, dovetailed, age cracks in lid, some wear and edge damage, wrought iron lock .............................................................. 200.00
    25-3/4" w, 12-3/4" d, 13-1/4" h, grain and fancifully painted, various foliate devices in sienna paint, ochre ground, Vermont, 19th C, cracks, minor paint wear, surface abrasions ............ 3,000.00
    36" w, 22" d, 31" h, America, fourth quarter 19th C, body mounted with oak staves joined at corners by metal brackets, decorative paper lining........................................................................ 135.00
    46" l, immigrant's, pine, old red paint, ornate dec wrought iron strapping, tooled detail, int. with cov till, shelf along hinge rail, three dovetailed drawers, some edge damage, age cracks ........... 160.00
    47-1/2" l, immigrant's, white oak, old red repaint, dovetailed, orig iron hardware, age cracks and repair in bottom ............... 145.00

Dome top, dovetailed joints, wrought metal handles, 39" w, $290. Photo courtesy of Joy Luke Fine Art Brokers and Auctioneers.

Pitcher, both sides painted in rose, iron-red, yellow, purple, blue, and green with floral cluster, gilt dec under spout, initials "SR," neoclassical foliate motifs on spout and neck, band borders on shoulder, foot, and rims, 9-3/8" h, $2,500.

Flat Top
    7" sq, leather cov, label "George W Tukey Portland, ME"..... 80.00
    11-3/4" h, 18-1/2" l, grain painted, red and brown raised molded plinth base, inscribed in red "1856, PWS"........................ 175.00
    27-1/2" l, pine, dec, bowed side and lid, worn light blue repaint int., orig brown graining, orig wrought iron lock and hasp 200.00
Leather Bound, 26" l, worn black leather, brass tack trim, flattened seat on lid, engraved brass plaque "J. D. Warner Canandaigua" .... 110.00
Louis Vuitton, 43-1/2" w, 21-1/2" d, 13" h, late 19th/early 20th C, surface wear........................................................................ 575.00

Oriental
    31-1/4" w, 13" h, pigskin covering, hinged rect top, conforming case, metal carrying handles, Chinese ........................... 150.00
    15" l, leather covered wood, worn painted scenes with figures, brass hardware ................................................................. 275.00

Traveler's, poplar, dovetailed, dark red mahogany stain, fitted int. with doors and drawers, some repair, int. door rehinged, 24 x 13-1/4" x 34-3/4"................................................................................. 200.00

# TUCKER CHINA

**History:** William Ellis Tucker (1800-1832) was the son of a Philadelphia schoolmaster who had a small shop on Market Street, where he sold imported French china. William helped in the shop and became interested in the manufacture of china.

In 1820, kaolin, a white clay which is the prime ingredient for translucence in porcelain, was discovered on a farm in Chester County, Pennsylvania, and William earnestly began producing his own products with the plentiful supply of kaolin close at hand. The business prospered but not without many trials and financial difficulties. He had many partners, a fact reflected in the various marks found on Tucker china including "William Ellis Tucker," "Tucker and Hulme," and "Joseph Hemphill," as well as workmen's incised initials which are sometimes found.

The business operated between 1825 and 1838, when Thomas Tucker, William's brother, was forced by business conditions to close the firm. There are very few pieces available for collectors today, and almost all known pieces are in collections or museums.

**Museum:** Pennsylvania Historical Museum, Harrisburg, PA.

Coffee Cup and Saucer, large size, floral spray, green band dec, gilt edges and handle, from set made for Atherton family of Chester County, PA, monogrammed "A"............................................ 1,500.00

Creamer and Sugar, black transfer dec, landscape with house, c1830, sugar bowl repaired, pr ........................................... 400.00

Fruit Dish, 11" l, oval, serpentine, gilt border, c1830................ 1,150.00

Perfume Vial, 1-1/2" h, heart shape, basket of flowers and floral bouquet dec, gilt trim................................................... 450.00

Pin Box, cov, circular, floral dec, gilt trim, wear............................ 50.00

Pitcher
9-1/4" h, polychrome dec, foliate reserves, gilt highlights, cracks, gilt wear.......................................................... 200.00
Large, polychrome river scenes with sailboats, scrolling, gilt highlights........................................................... 16,240.00
Large, floral dec, chip to spout........................................... 815.00
Small, gold fern dec, gilt highlights, squared handle ......... 700.00

Plate, luncheon, landscape, monogram....................................... 95.00

Urn, 11-3/4" h, classical shape, square plinth, Blanc de Chine glaze, twin scroll handles, c1830, slight damage to one, pr .............. 4,750.0

# VAL ST.-LAMBERT

**History:** Val St.-Lambert, a 12th-century Cistercian abbey, was located during different historical periods in France, Netherlands, and Belgium (1930 to present). In 1822, Francois Kemlin and Auguste Lelievre, along with a group of financiers, bought the abbey and opened a glassworks. In 1846, Val St.-Lambert merged with the Socété Anonyme des Manufactures de Glaces, Verres à Vitre, Cristaux et Gobeletaries. The company bought many other glassworks.

Val St.-Lambert developed a reputation for technological progress in the glass industry. In 1879, Val St.-Lambert became an independent company employing 4,000 workers. The firm concentrated on the export market, making table glass, cut, engraved, etched, and molded pieces, and chandeliers. Some pieces were finished in other countries, e.g., silver mounts were added in the United States.

Val St.-Lambert executed many special commissions for the artists of the Art Nouveau and Art Deco periods. The tradition continues. The company also made cameo-etched vases, covered boxes, and bowls. The firm celebrated its 150th anniversary in 1975.

Box, cov, round, faceted knob applied to cylindrical cov
   6-1/2" d, 3-3/4" h, colorless glass, layered in lavender, etched flowering wisteria vines, frosted and textured ground, c1920 .........865.00
   9" d, 4" h, colorless glass, layered in lavender, etched flowering wisteria vines, frosted and textured ground, c1920..........980.00
Cabinet Plate, 8" d, famous artist series, price for set of four.......50.00
Champagne Pitcher, 14" h, royal blue cameo cut florals, triple notched cut glass handle, sgd ............2,750.00
Cologne Bottle, 5-1/4" h, transparent green cylinder, overlaid in ruby red, double etched blossoms, swags, and gold accents, fitted with threaded rim, screw top, hallmarks at rim and within, wear to cover.............375.00
Decanter, 12" h, triangular shaped body, notched neck, Ariane, cranberry cut to clear, matching stopper ........................800.00
Stemware Set, twelve 8-1/4" h goblets with waisted bucket-form bowl, twelve 5-5/8" h wide champagne/sherbet glasses with conical-shaped bowl, eleven 6-5/8" h wide glasses with waisted bucket form bowl, all with faceted triple-knopped stems, hexagonal feet, late 19th C, price for 35 pc set ............1,840.00
Toothbrush Holder, clear, amber stain, sgd..................65.00
Vase, 8" h, flared, colorless glass layered in cobalt blue, engraved fan dec on martele ground, geometric borders, faceted near ftd base, c1920 ...................350.00

**Paperweight, intaglio etched nude holding flame, script sgd, 4" d, $65.**

# VALENTINES

**History:** Early cards were handmade, often containing both handwritten verses and hand-drawn pictures. Many cards also were hand colored and contained cutwork.

Mass production of machine-made cards featuring chromolithography began after 1840. In 1847, Esther Howland of Worcester, Massachusetts, established a company to make valentines which were hand decorated with paper lace and other materials imported from England. They had a small "H" stamped in red in the top left corner. Howland's company eventually became the New England Valentine Company (N.E.V. Co.).

The company George C. Whitney and his brother founded after the Civil War dominated the market from the 1870s through the first decades of the 20th century. They bought out several competitors, one of which was the New England Valentine Company.

Lace paper was invented in 1834. The golden age of lacy cards took place between 1835 and 1860.

Embossed paper was used in England after 1800. Embossed lithographs and woodcuts developed between 1825 and 1840, and early examples were hand colored.

There was a big revival in the 1920s by large companies, like R. Tuck in England, which did lots of beautiful cards for its 75th Diamond Jubilee; 1925 saw changes in card production, especially for children with paper toys of all sorts, all very collectible now. Little girls were in short dresses, boys in short pants, which helps date that era of valentines. There was an endless variety of toy types of paper items, many companies created similar items and many stayed in production until World War II paper shortages stopped production both here and abroad.

**References:** Robert Brenner, *Valentine Treasury,* Schiffer Publishing, 1997; Dan & Pauline Campanelli, *Romantic Valentines*, L-W Book Sales, 1996; Roberta B. Etter, *Tokens of Love*, Abbeville Press, 1990; Katherine Kreider, *One Hundred Years of Valentines,* Schiffer, 1999; ——, *Valentines with Values*, Schiffer Publishing, 1996.

**Collectors' Club:** National Valentine Collectors Association, P.O. Box 1404, Santa Ana, CA 92702.

**Advisor:** Evalene Pulati.

Animated, large
   Felix, half tone, German .....................................25.00
   Jumping Jack, Tuck, 1900 .....................................65.00
Bank True Love note, England, 1865 ..........................75.00
Bank of Love note, Nister, 1914...............................38.00
Charm String
   Brundage, 3 pcs...............................................45.00
   Four hearts, ribbon ............................................45.00
Comic
   Sheet, 8" x 10", Park, London...............................25.00
   Sheet, 9" x 14", McLoughlin Co., USA, 1915.................20.00
   Woodcut, Strong, USA, 1845.................................25.00
Diecut foldout
   Brundage, flat, cardboard ....................................25.00
   Cherubs, 2 pcs.................................................40.00
   Clapsaddle, 1911..............................................60.00

**Novelty, oblong, satin, celluloid, linked horseshoes of puffed silk, easel, 16" x 10-1/2", $65. Photo courtesy of Evalene Pulati.**

Documentary
    Passport, love, 1910 ...................................... 45.00
    Wedding certificate, 1914 ............................... 45.00
English Fancy, from "Unrequited Love Series"
    8" x 10", aquatint, couple, wedding................... 135.00
    8" x 10", aquatint, girl and grandmother............... 95.00
Engraved
    5" x 7", American, verse.................................... 35.00
    8" x 10" sheet, English, emb, pg....................... 65.00
    8" x 10" sheet, English, hand colored ................ 45.00
Handmade
    Calligraphy, envelope, 1885............................. 135.00
    Cutwork, hearts, 6" x 6", 1855 ......................... 250.00
    Fraktur, cutwork, 1800 .................................... 950.00
    Pen and ink loveknot, 1820 ............................. 275.00
    Puzzle, purse, 14" x 14", 1855......................... 450.00
    Theorem, 9" x 14", c1885 ................................ 325.00
    Woven heart, hand, 1840.................................. 55.00
Honeycomb
    American, kids, tunnel of love........................... 48.00
    American, wide-eyed kids, 9".............................. 40.00
    German, 1914, white and pink, 11".................... 75.00
    Simple, 1920, Beistle, 8"................................... 18.00
Lace Paper
    American, B & J Cameo Style
        Large ................................................... 75.00
        Small, 1865 .......................................... 45.00
    American, layered, McLoughlin Co., c1880 ......... 35.00
    Cobweb center, c1855 ................................... 250.00
    English, fancy
        3" x 5", 1865 ....................................... 35.00
        5" x 7", 1855 ....................................... 75.00
        8" x 10", 1840 .................................... 135.00
    Hand Layered, scraps, 1855............................. 65.00
    Layered, in orig box
        1875, Howland ..................................... 75.00
        1910, McLoughlin Co. .......................... 45.00
    Orig box, c1890 ............................................ 55.00
    Simple, small pc, 1875................................... 22.50
    Tiny mirror center, 4" x 6" ............................... 75.00
    Whitney, 1875, 5" x 7"..................................... 35.00

Novelty, American Fancy, c1900, originally sold in a box
    5" x 7-1/2", mat, fancy corners, parchment, orig box ............ 32.50
    7-1/2" x 10", rect, panel with silk, celluloid, orig box ............ 45.00
    10-1/2" x 10", star shape, silk rushing, orig box ................ 55.00
    16" x 10-1/2", oblong, satin, celluloid, orig box .................... 65.00
Pulldown, German
    Airplane, 1914, 8" x 14" .................................... 175.00
    Auto, 1910, 8" x 11" x 4" .................................. 150.00
    Car and kids, 1920s......................................... 35.00
    Dollhouse, large, 1935..................................... 45.00
    Rowboat, small, honeycomb paper puff................ 65.00
    Seaplane, 1934, 8 x 9"...................................... 75.00
    Tall Ship, 8" x 16" ........................................... 175.00
Silk Fringed
    Prang, double sided, 3" x 5" ............................. 24.00
    Triple layers, orig box...................................... 38.00
Standup Novelty
    Cupid, orig box.............................................. 45.00
    Hands, heart, without orig box .......................... 35.00
Parchment
    Banjo, small, with ribbon ................................. 65.00
    Violin, large, boxed......................................... 125.00

# VALLERYSTHAL GLASS

**History:** Vallerysthal (Lorraine), France, has been a glass-producing center for centuries. In 1872, two major factories, Vallerysthal glassworks and Portieux glassworks, merged and produced art glass until 1898. Later, pressed glass animal-covered dishes were introduced. The factory continues to operate today.

Animal Dish, cov
    Hen on nest, opaque aqua, sgd............................ 75.00
    Rabbit, white, frosted ........................................ 65.00
    Swan, blue opaque glass.................................. 100.00
Box, cov, 5" x 3", cameo, dark green, applied and cut dec, sgd . 950.00
Butter Dish, cov, turtle, opaque white, snail finial...................... 100.00
Candlesticks, pr, Baroque pattern, amber.................................. 75.00
Compote, 6-1/4" sq, blue opaque glass .................................... 75.00
Dish, cov, figural, lemon, opaque white, sgd............................. 70.00
Mustard, cov, swirled ribs, scalloped blue opaque, matching cover with slot for spoon.................................................................. 35.00
Plate, 6" d, Thistle pattern, green .......................................... 65.00
Salt, cov, hen on nest, white opal ........................................... 65.00
Sugar, cov, 5" h, Strawberry pattern, opaque white, gold trim, salamander finial........................................................................ 85.00

**Novelty, star shape, heart shaped satin pad center, hp dec, silk ruching, 10-1/2" x 10", $55. Photo courtesy of Evalene Pulati**

**Dish, cov, squirrel finial, blue opaque, $95.**

Tumbler, 4" h, blue ............................................................ 40.00
Vase, 8" h, flared folded burgundy red rim, oval pale green body,
matching red enamel berry bush on front, inscribed "Vallerysthal" on
base .......................................................................................... 490.00

# VAN BRIGGLE POTTERY

**History:** Artus Van Briggle, born in 1869, was a talented Ohio artist. He joined Rookwood in 1887 and studied in Paris under Rookwood's sponsorship from 1893 until 1896. In 1899, he moved to Colorado for his health and established his own pottery in Colorado Springs in 1901.

Van Briggle's work was heavily influenced by the Art Nouveau schools he had seen in France. He produced a great variety of matte-glazed wares in this style. Colors varied.

Artus died in 1904. Anne Van Briggle continued the pottery until 1912.

**Marks:** The "AA" mark, a date, and "Van Briggle" were incised on all pieces prior to 1907 and on some pieces into the 1920s. After 1920, "Colorado Springs, Colorado" or an abbreviation was added. Dated pieces are the most desirable.

**References:** Richard Sasicki and Josie Fania, *Collector's Encyclopedia of Van Briggle Art Pottery*, Collector Books, 1993, 2000 value update; David Rago, *American Art Pottery,* Knickerbocker Press, 1997.

**Collectors' Club:** American Art Pottery Association, 125 E. Rose Ave., St. Louis, MO 63119.

**Museum:** Pioneer Museum, Colorado Springs, CO.

Bowl
  6" d, 3" h, squatty, light turquoise matte glaze, mkd "AA/VAN
    BRIGGLE/1905/50B".................................................. 800.00
  8 1/2" d, emb tulip dec, turquoise blue glaze, incised logo, name,
    Colorado Springs, No. 40, orig flower frog ........................ 50.00
Candlesticks, pr, 7-1/2" h, handled form, purple and maroon matte
  glaze, c1913 ................................................................ 120.00
Chalice, 11 1/2" h, stylized mermaid embracing fish, velvety light green
  matte glaze, incised logo, name, ate 1902, Roman numeral III, shape
  No. 1, repaired ................................................................ 14,300.00
Console Set, jet black drip glaze, sgd "Anna Van Briggle, Colorado
  Springs" ............................................................................ 70.00
Dish, 5 1/2" d, #491, circular, emb stylized black spider, dark green matte
  ground, incised "AA/Van Briggle/1906/Colorado Springs/491" ...... 450.00
Figure
  Dragonfly, mulberry, 6-3/4" h, #792, dated 1920 ................ 200.00
  Hopi Maiden, blue, c1940 ................................................. 165.00
Flower Frog, triple, dated 1914 ............................................ 250.00

Jardiniere, 5 1/4" h, emb stylized tulips, mottle blue glaze, incised logo,
  name, Colorado Springs, shape No. 625 ............................. 715.00
Night Light, 5" h, grape leaf form, light crystalline mulberry
  glaze ............................................................................. 150.00
Pitcher, 8-3/4" h, waisted oval, conforming molded handle, matte Persian Rose glaze, incised marks............................................ 200.00
Plaque, 5 1/4" d, spider, green-black matteglaze, incised logo, name,
  date 1908, shape No. 491 ................................................. 770.00
Plate, 8-1/2" d, grapes and leaves, deep burgundy and blue matte
  glaze, incised marks, c1907-12 ......................................... 210.00
Sign, 15" h, cat shape, stylized Art Deco, green, Colorado
  Springs............................................................................... 225.00
Vase
  3-3/4" h, 4-1/2" d, spherical, turquoise matte glaze, mkd "AA/VAN
    BRIGGLE/1903/III"........................................................ 800.00
  3-3/4" h, 5" d, squatty, emb butterflies, green and red matte glaze,
    mkd "AA/VAN BRIGGLE/Colo. Spgs./626," overfired, restoration to rim chip........................................................... 450.00
  4-3/4" h, 3-3/4" d, bulbous, emb leaves, blue-green matte glaze,
    mkd "AA/VAN BRIGGLE/Colo. Spgs./730" ....................... 475.00
  5-1/4" h, 3-1/2" d, ovoid, emb crocus, green and pink matte glaze,
    sgd "823/AA" ................................................................. 420.00
  5-3/4" h, 3-3/4" d, trumpet shape, matte mustard glaze, mkd
    "AA/VAN BRIGGLE/COLO. SPRINGS/825" .................... 465.00
  6" h, 4" d, trumpet shape, emb medallions of wheat sheaves,
    leathery matte green glaze, mkd "AA/VAN BRIGGLE/1905/X/347" ........................................................ 1,900.00
  7" h, 6-1/2" d, emb butterflies, cobalt blue and turquoise matte
    glaze, mkd "AA/1916".................................................... 500.00
  7-1/4" h, 3-1/2" d, bottle shape, emb poppy pods, purple matte
    glaze, mkd "AA/VAN BRIGGLE/830/1915" .................... 1,000.00
  7-1/4" h, 4" d, bottle shape, emb stylized flowers, leathery purple
    matte glaze, mkd "AA/VAN BRIGGLE/287/1905" ......... 2,800.00
  7-3/4" h, 5" d, gourd shape, emb stylized flowers at rim, wide ribs
    on body, fine teal glaze, mkd "AA/VAN BRIGGLE/Colo.
    Spgs.,/864/1912," tight 2" hairline to rim ........................ 650.00
  8" h, 5-1/2" d, classic shape, turquoise matte glaze, mkd "AA/VAN
    BRIGGLE/1906/269"...................................................... 450.00
  8-1/2" h 3-1/2" d, classical shape, lavender matte glaze, mkd
    "AA/VAN BRIGGLE/1905/N/343C"................................. 900.00
  9" h, 4" d, corset shape, emb daffodils, blue-green matte glaze,
    dirty bottom incised "AA/VAN BRIGGLE/120," two small flat
    base chips, small rim bruise............................................. 500.00
  11" h, 9-1/2" d, figural, Lady of the Lily, brown and green mottled
    matte glaze, dirty bottom mkd "AA/VAN BRIGGLE/Colo. Spgs.,"
    c1930 ......................................................................... 1,900.00

**Vase, bottle-shape, emb stylized flowers and row of leaves, feathered dark matte green glaze, incised "AA/Van Briggle/Colo. Springs," c1908-11, 6-1/2" h, 3-3/4" d, $1,035. Photo courtesy of David Rago Auctions.**

Vessel
    3" h, 6-1/2" d, squat, emb pods, sheer frothy light bleu glaze, brown clay showing through, incised "AA/VAN BRIGGLE/1905/288" ........................................................ 850.00
    3-1/2" h, 4-1/4" d, squat, emb leaves, matte frothy brown glaze, incised "AA/VAN BRIGGLE/COLO. SPGS" .................. 1,100.00
    4" h, 4-1/2" d, spherical, emb mistletoe under sheer frothy dark green glaze, brown clay showing through, incised "AA/VAN BRIGGLE/Colo. Spg" ........................................ 700.00
    6" h, 4-1/2' d, bulbous, curdled blue matte glaze, incised "AA Van Briggle/1905/XV/349" ...................................................... 425.00

# VENETIAN GLASS

**History:** Venetian glass has been made on the island of Murano, near Venice, since the 13th century. Most of the wares are thin walled. Many types of decoration have been used: embedded gold dust, lace work, and applied fruits or flowers.

**Reference:** Sheldon Barr, *Venetian Glass, Confections in Glass, 1855-1914,* Harry N. Abrams, Inc., 1998.

**Periodical:** *Verti: Italian Glass News,* P.O. Box 191, Fort Lee, NJ 07024.

**Reproduction Alert:** Venetian glass continues to be made today.

Bowl, 11" l, free form, cased, ice blue swirl with aventurine over white opaque and pulled clear handles ................................ 25.00
Candlesticks, pr, 6-5/8" h, sunflower form, clear amber petals with black specks, twisted ribbed clear glass stem and petals, rough pontil, early 20th C ........................................ 150.00
Center Bowl, 13" d, free form, amberina, elongated pulled edges, green partial Murano label ........................................ 30.00
Chandelier, 48" d, 58" h, threaded and blown cranberry glass shaft, clear glass scrolled rods suspend faceted swags, 14 scrolled candle arms with molded drip pans ........................................ 825.00
Cornucopia, 15-1/2" h, free form, emerald green shading ............ 75.00
Epergne, 19-1/2" h, pale yellow, large central trumpet shaped vase surrounded by ten smaller vases, ruffled base, 20th C ......... 1,150.00
Figure
    11" h, swan, amber and green, elongated neck, ground and polished base, pr ........................................ 50.00
    12" h, bird, black sommerso, aventurine encased in clear and shaded amber, applied cobalt blue tail ........................ 35.00
    13" h, dolphin, clear, shaded electric blue back, bullicante dec, free form base ........................................ 90.00
Perfume Bottle, 5-5/8" h, pear form, twist-turned body, green, gold flecks ........................................ 115.00
Pitcher, 3-1/2" h, green, gold trim ........................................ 95.00
Vase
    11" h, banjo shape, pale green, hand blown, folded foot, rough pontil ........................................ 115.00
    13-3/4" h, banjo shape, Celeste blue, hand blown, folded foot, rough pontil ........................................ 115.00

# VERLYS GLASS

**History:** Originally made by Verlys France (1931-1960), this Lalique-influenced art glass was produced in America by The Holophane Co. from 1935 to 1951, and select pieces by the A. H. Heisey Co. from 1955 to 1957. Holophane acquired molds and glass for-

mulas from Verlys France and began making the art glass in 1935 at its Newark, Ohio, facility. It later leased molds to the Heisey Co., and in 1966 finally sold all molds and rights to the Fenton Art Glass Co.

The art glass was made in crystal, topaz, amber, rose, opalescent, and Directorie Blue. Heisey added turquoise. Most pieces have etched (frosted) relief designs.

**Marks:** Verlys France marked the glass with mold impressed "Verlys France" and "A Verlys France." Holophane (also known as Verlys of America) marked pieces with the mold-impressed "Verlys" and a scratched-script "Verlys" signature. The A. H. Heisey Co. used only a paper label which reads, "Verlys by Heisey."

**Reference:** Carole and Wayne McPeek, *Verlys of America Decorative Glass,* revised ed., published by authors, 1992.

Bowl
    Chinois ........................................ 80.00
    Cupid ........................................ 125.00
    Cuspidon ........................................ 90.00
    Orchid ........................................ 175.00
    Pinecone
        Blue ........................................ 175.00
        Opal ........................................ 175.00
    Poppies ........................................ 200.00
    Tassels ........................................ 150.00
    Thistle, topaz ........................................ 250.00
    Tripartite design, frosted
        6-1/4" d, pinecones and needles ........................ 135.00
        8-3/4" d, thistle design ........................ 75.00
    Water Lily, dusty rose ........................................ 500.00
    Wild Duck ........................................ 175.00
Box, cov, band of flowers ........................................ 75.00
Candleholders, pr, Eagle ........................................ 500.00
Charger, dragonfly ........................................ 135.00
Dish, cov, 8" d, 1-1/2" lid, three moths and glass knob ........... 225.00
Vase, 10" h, mermaids, dolphins, crystal and frosted ............... 750.00
Vase, 8-3/4" h, 9" d, flared colorless oval, press molded Alpine Thistle dec frosted on ext., base inscribed "Verlys" ........................ 250.00

# VILLEROY & BOCH

**History:** Pierre Joseph Boch established a pottery near Luxembourg, Germany, in 1767. Jean Francis, his son, introduced the first coal-fired kiln in Europe and perfected a water-power-driven potter's wheel. Pierre's grandson, Eugene Boch, managed a pottery at Mettlach; Nicholas Villeroy also had a pottery nearby.

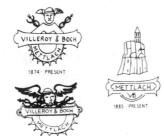

In 1841, the three potteries merged into the firm of Villeroy & Boch. Early production included a hard-paste earthenware comparable to English ironstone. The factory continues to use this hard-paste formula for its modern tablewares.

**References:** Susan and Al Bagdade, *Warman's English & Continental Pottery & Porcelain,* 3rd Edition, Krause Publications, 1998; Gary Kirsner, *Mettlach Book,* 3rd ed., Glentiques (P.O. Box 8807, Coral Springs, FL 33075), 1994.

**Beaker, #2327, flute player dec, $70. Photo courtesy of Joy Luke Fine Art Brokers and Auctioneers.**

**Additional Listings:** Mettlach.

Beaker, quarter liter, incised white florals, brown leaves, light green ground, Mettlach #2834 ............................................................ 90.00

Bowl
    8-1/2" d, spatter, gaudy floral dec, polychrome, mkd "Villeroy & Boch" ................................................................................. 45.00
    10-1/2" d, blue floral dec, handles ..................................... 175.00
Coffeepot, cov, Virginia pattern ........................................................ 95.00
Cruet, 8-1/2" h, blue and white, orig stopper ............................... 85.00
Demitasse Cup and Saucer, Patermo .......................................... 25.00
Dinner Service, partial, Alpina pattern, black transfer print on creamware, four bread and butter plates, four cups and saucers, three dinner plates, four salad/dessert plates, c1955-60 ........................ 45.00
Mug, 3-1/2" h, tan, leaf and twig dec, twig handle ....................... 65.00
Pitcher, 10-5/8"h , six sided, dark gray raised scrolls, leaves, pods, and birds, gray ground, white int., beige crest mark ...................... 275.00
Plaque, 12 h, reticulated lilies of the valley dec .......................... 225.00
Plate
    9-1/2" d, blue florals, white ground ..................................... 35.00
    12-1/2" d, Chintz pattern, marked "Villeroy & Boch," price for 8 pc set ................................................................................... 120.00
Stein, 6-1/2" h, half liter, #171, five white figures, blue ground, Mercury mark ...................................................................................... 225.00
Teapot, 6-1/4" d, blue and white ................................................. 135.00
Tray, 11" x 16", cavalier, PUG ..................................................... 165.00
Turkey Set, 22-1/2" l platter, ten 10" d plates, blue transfer of turkeys, floral border, few minor flakes ................................................. 440.00
Vase, 11-1/4" h, flared rim, double bulbed base, brown and black exotic birds and geometric dec, matte robin's egg blue ground, imp "V&B, Luxembourg" and "298," c1935 ..................................... 400.00

# WARWICK

**History:** Warwick China Manufacturing Co., Wheeling, West Virginia, was incorporated in 1887 and remained in business until 1951. The company was one of the first manufacturers  of vitreous glazed wares in the United States. Production was extensive and included tableware, garden ornaments, and decorative and utilitarian items.

Pieces were hand painted or decorated with decals. Collectors seek portrait items and fraternal pieces from groups such as the Elks, Eagles, and Knights of Pythias.

Some experimental, eggshell-type porcelain was made before 1887. A few examples are found in the antiques market.

**Reference:** John R. Rader Sr., *Warwick China,* Schiffer Publishing, 2000.

Ale Set, tankard pitcher, seven matching mugs, BPOE emblem and elk dec, shaded brown ground............................................325.00
Bone Dish, flow blue scenic dec ......................................45.00
Bowl, 4" d, flower and stems dec ....................................72.00
Chocolate Pot, cov, 10-1/2" h, Pansy pattern, flow blue dec, c1893-98 ..........................................................300.00
Cider Pitcher, fruit dec, brown glaze .............................100.00
Cream Soup Bowl, underplate, white, gold trim.................20.00
Creamer, speckled blue and white, gold trim, raised leaves around rim, marked "Warwick China"......................................40.00
Demitasse Cup and Saucer, 2-3/4" h cup, 5" d saucer, muted floral pattern, pink, brown, and gold, wear........................20.00
Humidor, cov, portrait of woman, brown ground, marked "IOGA".....215.00
Lemonade Pitcher, portrait dec, brown glaze...............175.00
Mug
    BPOE emblem and elk dec.................................35.00
    Monk drinking from mug ....................................60.00
Portrait Plate, 10" d, Indian, yellow shading to brown ground.......75.00
Restaurant Ware
    Salad Plate, 7" d, white, brown wave border ...........5.00
    Saucer, 6" d, Indian Tree, mkd "Warwick, Made in U.S.A. 1950" ................................................................5.00
    Soup Bowl, 8" d, white, brown wave border, dated 1948......10.00
Spittoon, beige ground, red roses...............................140.00
Tankard, 13" h, portrait of monk and mug of ale ........250.00
Vase
    8" d, ftd, portrait of woman, large hat with peacock feathers, holding rose to her lips, shaded brow to cream ground, marked "IOGA" ..........................................................125.00
    10" h, amaryllis dec, orange blossoms, brown ground, marked "IOGA" ..........................................................95.00
    11-1/2" h, ring handles, marked "10 GA Madam LE Brun" . 285.00

# WATCHES, POCKET

**History:** Pocket watches can be found in many places—from flea markets to the specialized jewelry auctions. Condition of movement is the first priority; design and detailing of the case is second.

Descriptions of pocket watches may include the size (16/0 to 20), number of jewels in the movement, whether the face is open or closed (hunter), and the composition (gold, gold filled, or some other metal). The movement is the critical element since cases often were switched. However, an elaborate case, especially if gold, adds significantly to value.

Pocket watches designed to railroad specifications are desirable. They are between 16 and 18 in size, have a minimum of 17 jewels, adjust to at least five positions, and conform to many other specifications. All are open faced.

Study the field thoroughly before buying. There is a vast amount of literature, including books and newsletters from clubs and collectors.

**References:** T. P. Camerer Cuss, *Antique Watches,* Antique Collectors' Club, 1999; Roy Ehrhardt, *European Pocket Watches*, Book 2, Heart of America Press, 1993; Roy Ehrhardt and Joe Demsey, *Cartier Wrist & Pocket Watches*, Clocks, Heart of America Press, 1992; ——, *Patek Phillipe*, Heart of America Press, 1992; ——, *American Pocket Watch Serial Number Grade Book*, Heart of America Press, 1993; Alan Sherman, *Pocket Watches of the 19th and 20th Century,* Antique Collectors' Club, 1999; Cooksey Shugart and Richard E. Gilbert, *Complete Price Guide to Watches*, No. 20, Collector Books, 2000.

**Periodicals:** *The Premium Watch Watch,* 24 San Rafael Drive, Rochester, NY 14618; *Watch & Clock Review*, 2403 Champa St., Denver, CO 80205.

**Collectors' Clubs:** American Watchmakers Institute Chapter 102, 3 Washington Sq, Apt 3C, Larchmont, NY 10538; Early American Watch Club Chapter 149, P.O. Box 5499, Beverly Hills, CA 90210; National Association of Watch & Clock Collectors, 514 Poplar Street, Columbia, PA 17512.

**Museums:** American Clock & Watch Museum, Bristol, CT; Hoffman Clock Museum, Newark, NY; National Association of Watch and Clock Collectors Museum, Columbia, PA; The Time Museum, Rockford, IL.

**Abbreviations:**

| | |
|---|---|
| gf | gold filled |
| j | jewels |
| S | size |
| yg | yellow gold |

## Lapel, lady's

Niello, white porcelain dial, black Roman numerals, niello checkerboard pattern, European hallmarks, c1900, some surface scratches........................................................................460.00

Patek Philippe & Co., Geneve, 1905-10, 18kt yellow gold, white dial, black and gold Arabic numerals, fancy scroll hands, rose-cut diamond-set bezel, back cover with black enamel rhombic-shaped panels with white painted fleur-de-lis, suspended from shell-form brooch, black and white enamel and rose-cut diamonds, triple signed, Swiss hallmarks, movement needs restoration ................................. 5,750.00

Tiffany & Co., c1900, 18kt yellow gold, white dial, black Arabic numerals, sgd, gold case, back cov set with foil-backed round cabochon sapphire framed in old European-cut diamonds, suspended from open box motif pin with sapphires and old European-cut diamonds in platinum topped gold mount, sgd ......................................... 3,220.00

## Pendant, lady's

Bucherer, round silvertone dial, black Roman numeral indicators, sterling silver marcasite bezel, pendant case with engraving and millegrain dec, suspended from metal trace-link chain spaced by clear stones, 23" l, several marcasites missing, minor nicks to crystal ...................................................................................... 115.00

Mers Mann, Art Deco, hexagonal form, blue guillouche enamel, applied silver and marcasite flower basket surmounted by silver and marcasite top, suspended from silver and tracery enamel bar pin by trace link chains ...................................................................... 325.00

## Pocket, gentleman's

Bovel & Courvoisier, Neuchatel, 14kt gold, hunter case, matching no. 64795 on movement, dust cover, and case, white porcelain dial, black Roman numerals, subsidiary seconds dial, engraved case, gold-filled 48" l rope chain with seed pearl slide ....................... 290.00

Chopard, Geneve, open face, 17 jewels, goldtone engraved foliate dial with black Roman numeral indicators, 18kt yellow gold engine-turned and engraved case ................................................................... 290.00

Elgin, open face, porcelain dial, black Roman numerals, subsidiary seconds dial, plastic crystal, 18 size, minor dents.................... 230.00

Frodsham, Arnold Chas, hunting case, no. 01220, 14kt yg, white porcelain dial with black Roman numerals, subsidiary dial, engraved dust cover "Agnes I. Greene, January, 1863," keywind, 22 dwt, 6 size .......... 635.00

Guinand, C. L., 14kt gold, open face, no. 31175, creamtone porcelain dial, black Arabic numerals, gold fleur-de-lis hands, subsidiary minutes and seconds dial, triple sgd, engraved gold case ............ 800.00

E. Howard Watch Co., Boston, openface, 14kt yellow gold, 17 jewels, nickel movement, white porcelain dial, black Roman numerals, subsidiary seconds dial, small gold filled watch chain, minor cracks to dial....................................................................................... 200.00

Illinois Watch Co., 14kt tricolor gold, white dial, black Roman numerals, subsidiary seconds dial, female portrait on dust cover, case dec with seascape and lighthouse, monogrammed crest, box hinge case...................................................................... 1,495.00

Lodel, Edouard Lerregaux, open face, no. 6322, 18kt yg, white porcelain dial, black Roman numerals, subsidiary seconds dial 16 size ....... 375.00

Patek Philippe & Co., Geneve, hunting case
Case #14981, 18 kt yg, engraved "HBG," interior of case engraved "Teachers & employees to Horatio G. Bent 1911, Bloomington Public Schools," movement marked "Patek Philippe & Co. #

**Patek Philippe & Co., 18k yg, open face, engraved "HGB," int. of case engraved "Teachers & Employees to Horatio G. Gent 1911, Bloomington Public Schools," patent Jan. 13, 1891, 8 adjustments, 20 jewels, hairline to dial, $1,050. Photo courtesy of Joy Luke Fine Art Brokers and Auctioneers.**

149891 pat. Jan 13 1891," eight adjustments, twenty jewels, hairline crack on dial ................................................................... 1,050.00

Case #26586, white porcelain dial, black Roman numerals, subsidiary seconds dial, 18kt gold monogrammed case with inscription, crystal missing........................................................ 635.00

Silvertone dial with both Arabic and abstract indicators, subsidiary seconds dial, platinum case with monogram, platinum rectangular box link chain and 14kt white gold pocket knife, orig fitted box mkd "Spaulding-Gorham"..................................... 2,415.00

S. Silverthau & Sons, 18kt yellow gold, openface, repeater, white dial, black Arabic numerals, subsidiary seconds dial, 14" l fancy link watch chain with swivel hook and T-bar .......................................... 2,415.00

Smith, Patterson & Co., Boston, 18kt gold, openface, 23 jewels, white porcelain dial, black Arabic numerals, subsidiary seconds dial, blue Arabic minute indicators, monogrammed case, 14kt yellow gold seal set on black grosgrain lapel ribbon, 14kt yellow gold swivel hook............ 920.00

Vacheron ET Constantin, Geneve, 18kt yellow gold, hunter, 13 jewel, white porcelain dial, black Roman numerals, chased gold case ... 750.00

Waltham, American, 14kt gold
Hunter case, creamtone dial, black Roman numerals, subsidiary seconds dial, diamond accent on case, 19" l goldtone fancy link chain.................................................................... 1,380.00

White dial, Arabic numerals, subsidiary second dial, 19 jewels, fleur-de-lis design on cover, diamond accents, monogram on back, suspended from bow pin with center diamonds ..... 490.00

## Pocket, lady's

American Waltham, 14 kt yg, hunting case, porcelain dial, black Roman numerals, subsidiary seconds dial, case no. 109032, dec with "S" monogram in rose diamonds, verse with engraved star set with rose diamonds, 0 size, dial cracked.................................. 320.00

Elgin, 14kt yg, hunting case, white porcelain dial, black Roman numerals, subsidiary seconds dial, case engraved with Gothic-revival griffin motif, 0 size ........................................................................ 375.00

# WATCHES, WRIST

**History:** The definition of a wristwatch is simply "a small watch that is attached to a bracelet or strap and is worn around the wrist." However, a watch on a bracelet is not necessarily a wristwatch. The key is the ability to read the time. A true wristwatch allows you to read the time at a glance, without making any other motions. Early watches on an arm bracelet had the axis of their dials, from 6 to 12, perpendicular to the band. Reading them required some extensive arm movements.

The first true wristwatch appeared about 1850. However, the key date is 1880 when the stylish, decorative wristwatch appeared and almost universal acceptance occurred. The technology to create the wristwatch existed in the early 19th century with Brequet's shock-absorbing "Parachute System" for automatic watches and Ardien Philipe's winding stem.

The wristwatch was a response to the needs of the entrepreneurial age with its emphasis on punctuality and planned free time. Sometime around 1930, the sales of wristwatches surpassed that of pocket watches. Swiss and German manufacturers were quickly joined by American makers.

The wristwatch has undergone many technical advances during the 20th century including self-winding (automatic), shock-resistance, and electric movements.

**References:** Hy Brown and Nancy Thomas, *Comic Character Timepieces*, Schiffer Publishing, 1992; Gisbert L. Brunner and Christian Pfeiffer-Belli, *Wristwatches, A Handbook and Price Guide*, Schiffer Publishing, 1997; James M. Dowling and Jeffrey P. Hess, *The Best of Time: Rolex Wristwatches, An Unauthorized History*, Schiffer Publishing, 1996; Roy Ehrhardt and Joe Demsey, *Cartier Wrist & Pocket Watches, Clocks*, Heart of America Press, 1992; ——, *Patek Phillipe*, Heart of America Press, 1992; ——, *Rolex Identification and Price Guide*, Heart of America Press, 1993; Sherry and Roy Ehrhardt and Joe Demesy, *Vintage American & European Wrist Watch Price Guide*, Book 6, Heart of America Press, 1993; Edward Faber and Stewart Unger, *American Wristwatches*, revised ed., Schiffer Publishing, 1996 Anton Kreuzer, *Omega Wristwatches*, Schiffer Publishing, 1996; Heinz Hampel, *Automatic Wristwatches from Switzerland*, Schiffer Publishing, 1997; Fritz von Osterhausen, *Movado History*, Schiffer Publishing, 1996; ——, *Wristwatch Chronometers,* Schiffer Publishing, 1997; Cooksey Shugart and Richard E. Gilbert, *Complete Price Guide to Watches*, No. 17, Collector Books, 1997.

**Periodical:** *International Wrist Watch*, 242 West Ave., Darien, CT 06820.

**Collectors' Clubs:** International Wrist Watch Collectors Chapter 146, 5901C Westheimer, Houston, TX 77057; National Association of Watch & Clock Collectors, 514 Poplar St., Columbia, PA 17512; The Swatch Collectors Club, PO Box 7400, Melville, NY 11747.

**Museums:** American Clock & Watch Museum, Bristol, CT; Hoffman Clock Museum, Newark, NY; National Association of Watch and Clock Collectors Museum, Columbia, PA; The Time Museum, Rockford, IL.

## Gentleman's

Akron, lady's, Retro, 14kt white gold, ruby, and diamond, cov sq coppertone dial, black Roman numerals, red abstract indicators, raised cover set with faceted rubies and diamonds, flanked by ruby and diamond scroll motif, double snake link bracelet ................. 575.00
Arenbe Watch Co., platinum and diamond, 17 jewels, rect, cream dial, black Arabic numerals, watch and bracelet set with baguette, round and marquise diamonds, platinum mount with millegrain accents.....1,610.00
Audemars Piguet, Geneve, man's, 18kt yellow gold, sq silvertone dial, goldtone applied and Arabic numeral indicators, subsidiary seconds dial, brown leather strap, box, crystal chipped ...................... 1,100.00
Bailey, Banks & Biddle Co., lady's, dress, platinum and diamond, C. H. Meylan movement, 18 jewels, silvertone dial, black Roman numerals, diamond bezel flanked by diamond and platinum foliate motif, rose-cut diamond crown, floral engraved back, 14kt white gold bracelet................................................................1,035.00
Baume & Merier, Geneve, 18kt yg, double time zone, gold and cobalt blue dial, Roman numerals, black alligator-lizard strap, Swiss assay marks, 8-3/4" l ..................................................... 1,725.00
Cartier, Santos Automatic, stainless steel and gold, white dial, Roman numerals, blue-steeled bands, deployment buckle ................ 1,100.00
Hamilton, 14kt yg, rect goldtone dial, abstract and Arabic indicators, subsidiary dial, verso inscribed, later gold bracelet, repair evident......350.00
Hermes, silver, bracelet-type, Swiss movement, silvertone dial, date aperture and abstract indicators, framed in twisted silver wire freeform design, same style sectioned bracelet, hallmarked.........290.00
Juvenia, Retro, 14kt yellow gold, round dial, slightly curved triangular cover centered by prong set sapphires and diamond, heavy mesh bracelet ...................................................................... 575.00

LeCoulture, Futurematic, 17 jewels, auto wind, power reserve window, subsidiary seconds dial, 10kt gold-filled case, black leather band, scratches to crystal .............................................................. 320.00
Movado
     Kingmatic, 14kt gold, 28 jewels, sq silvertone dial, goldtone indicators, leather strap ....................................................... 345.00
     Moonphase triple calendar, Swiss movement, cream dial, applied goldtone abstract and Arabic numeral indicators, month, day, date, subsidiary seconds dial with moon phase, 14kt yellow gold bracelet, scratches to crystal........................................ 2,875.00
Omega, Seamaster DeVille, automatic, 14kt gold, silvertone dial with gold abstract indicators, reverse inscribed to "Manual Zung 1925-1965 from Colleagues and Trustees, Boston Symphony Orchestra," leather band ........................................................................ 300.00
Patek Philippe, Geneve, 18kt yellow gold
     Round silvertone dial, goldtone abstract indicators, black leather strap, boxed ................................................................2,185.00
     Square silvertone dial, goldtone indicators, subsidiary seconds dial, 18 jewels, black leather strap ...............................2,645.00
Rolex
     Cellini, 18kt yellow gold, white rect dial, black Roman numeral indicators, brown crocodile strap, Rolex gold buckle .... 1,610.00
     Chronometer, 1950s, 18kt yellow gold, goldtone dial with alternating Roman numerals and abstract indicators, subsidiary seconds dial, leather strap with Rolex gold plated buckle, boxed ...........3,335.00
     Oyster Perpetual Day-Date, 18kt yellow gold and stainless steel, goldtone dial, abstract indicators, sweeping seconds hand, magnifying glass on date aperture, jubilee bracelet, polished yellow gold central links, minor scratches to crystal.........690.00
     President Oyster Perpetual Day-Day, 18kt yellow gold, automatic winding, silvertone Florentine dial, magnifier over date aperture, oyster bracelet with deployment clasp ......................... 4,255.00
Piaget, rectangular face with champagne dial, 18kt yg bracelet composed of carved brick links, deployant buckle, orig box and warranty ..2,875.00
Vacheron and Constantine, Geneve, round silvertone dial with gold abstract indicators, subsidiary seconds dial, 18kt yg with integral mesh band ........................................................................ 1,265.00

## Lady's

Bucherer, floral matte finish case, 17 jewel movement, sgd ....... 200.00
Cartier
     No. 12912, 18kt electroplate, tank style, white dial with black Roman numerals, sapphire winder, black leather strap .................... 290.00
     No. 3046843, tank-style, black enameled dial with white Roman numerals, sgd "Must de Cartier," orig box ........................ 200.00
     Quartz movement, circular gold plated, cram dial with black enameled Roman numerals, synthetic sapphire winder, sgd "Must de Cartier" ........................................................... 575.00
     Vendome, silvered dial with black Roman numerals, blue steel baton hands, gold integral bracelet, quartz movement . 4,600.00
Concord, Saratoga, 18kt yg, goldtone dial, Roman numerals, date, diamond bezel, deployment buckle, Swiss assay mark............. 2,990.00
Corum, 18kt yg, round goldtone dial with black Roman numerals, textured gold bezel with sapphire winder, integral woven mesh band......... 425.00
Cresaux Watch Co., 14kt gold, 17 jewels, goldtone dial signed "H. W. Beattie and Sons," black abstract indicators, round yellow diamond and diamond-set bezel, yellow gold mesh band ...................... 800.00
Elgin, dress, 18kt gold and diamond, 15 jewels, whitetone dial, blacktone Arabic numerals, engraved bezel, flanked by geometric design, diamond and bead accents, black silk cord band .................... 175.00
Exor, Retro, round goldtone metal dial, Roman numerals, scallop-shaped clipped shoulders accented with ten single-cut diamonds, snake-link straps, French assay marks, 7-1/8" l...................... 425.00
Girard-Perregaux, Swiss, 14kt white gold, silvertone dial with abstract indicators, round bezel framed with 22 single-cut diamonds, fancy chain strap, Swiss assay marks, 6" l ...................................... 425.00
Gubelin, 18kt yg, silvertone dial with abstract indicators, back wind, textured gold curb-link straps ................................................. 375.00

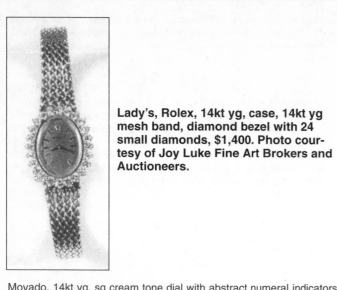

**Lady's, Rolex, 14kt yg, case, 14kt yg mesh band, diamond bezel with 24 small diamonds, $1,400. Photo courtesy of Joy Luke Fine Art Brokers and Auctioneers.**

Movado, 14kt yg, sq cream tone dial with abstract numeral indicators, diamond bezel, integral textured mesh strap, dated 1966, monogrammed ...................................................................... 525.00
Omega, 14kt yg, square silvertone dial with abstract indicators, Swiss hallmarks, leather band............................................ 300.00
Piaget, 18kt white gold, round lapis lazuli dial, sapphire and diamond bezel, intregal gold textured band, Swiss assay marks, 6-1/4" l.................................................................... 1,035.00
Rhone Watch Co., Art Deco, 18 jewels, cream dial, black Arabic numerals, framed in diamonds, diamond-set box link bracelet, heavy lead solder........................................................... 230.00
Rolex
    Art Deco, 15 jewels, silvertone dial with black Arabic numerals, diamond bezel, 18kt white gold case, leather band ...... 1,035.00
    Oyster Perpetual, 14kt yg, mechanical movement, 14kt yg bracelet, sgd............................................................... 1,955.00
    Precision, 14kt white gold, silvertone dial with abstract indicators, round bezel framed with 16 circular-cut diamond melee, accented with two diamond baguette shoulders, snake chain strap, Swiss assay mark, 6-3/4" l ........................... 825.00
    Precision, 18kt yg, circular dial, hinged lid of open-work 0.35 ct diamond set design, gold mesh bracelet, sgd "Rolex"............. 750.00
Smith Patterson, ESEF Watch Co., Swiss, Art Deco, platinum and diamond, 16 jewel movement, three adjustments, white metal dial with Arabic numerals, 24 single-cut diamonds set in millegrain bezel, engraved case................................................ 550.00

# WATERFORD

**History:** Waterford crystal is high-quality flint glass commonly decorated with cuttings. The original factory was established at

Waterford, Ireland, in 1729. Glass made before 1830 is darker than the brilliantly clear glass of later production. The factory closed in 1852. One hundred years later it reopened and continues in production today.

Ashtray, 7" d, 5 lb ......................................................... 125.00
Brandy Snifter, Lismore pattern ....................................... 45.00
Butter Dish, cov, mushroom finial ................................... 250.00
Candlesticks, pr, 7" h, pear shape, hollow center, horizontal oval cuts on wafers between fluted top and rayed base, looped cross cuttings in two sizes, downward spray with star cut .............................. 175.00

Centerpiece Bowl, 10" d, ftd, master cutter, Archive Collection .... 1,395.00
Champagne, Castletown, 1972, set of 6.................................... 200.00
Cocktail, Kylemore pattern.................................................... 35.00
Compote, ftd
    Colleen, large, #3821371200.......................................... 100.00
    Glandore, 5-1/4" h, #3814341200...................................... 90.00
Cordial
    Ashling pattern............................................................ 30.00
    Clare pattern .............................................................. 34.00
    Kinsale pattern............................................................ 28.00
    Kylemore pattern ......................................................... 28.00
    Lismore pattern ........................................................... 31.00
Creamer and Sugar, Powerscourt pattern ............................... 115.00
Decanter
    Alana pattern .............................................................. 195.00
    Kenmare pattern .......................................................... 195.00
    Lismore pattern, captain's type....................................... 195.00
    Powerscort pattern........................................................ 335.00
Goblet
    Boyne pattern ............................................................. 35.00
    Lismore pattern ........................................................... 35.00
Hock, Alana pattern, long stem............................................ 45.00
Ice Bucket, Powerscort pattern............................................ 195.00
Liqueur, stemmed, Colleen pattern, set of 12 .......................... 335.00
Pen Tray, 10" l, small chips................................................ 100.00
Pitcher, water, Powerscort pattern........................................ 195.00
Ring Holder, mkd............................................................... 20.00
Stemware, Lismore pattern, leaded glass, twelve water goblets, ten wines, sixteen cordials .............................................. 800.00
Tumbler
    Boyne pattern ............................................................. 32.00
    Clare pattern .............................................................. 50.00
Vase, master cutter, Noah, limited edition, no. 21 of 250, sgd "T. Cooke," 1973............................................................... 1,800.00
Wine
    Kildare pattern ............................................................ 35.00
    Kylemore pattern ......................................................... 40.00

# WAVE CREST

**History:** The C. F. Monroe Company of Meriden, Connecticut, produced the opal glassware known as Wave Crest from 1898 until World War I. The company bought

**WAVE CREST WARE**

**c1892**

the opaque, blown-molded glass blanks from the Pairpoint Manufacturing Co. of New Bedford, Massachusetts, and other glassmakers, including European factories. The Monroe company then decorated the blanks, usually with floral patterns. Trade names used were "Wave Crest Ware," "Kelva," and "Nakara."

**References:** Wilfred R. Cohen, *Wave Crest*, Collector Books, out-of-print; Elsa H. Grimmer, *Wave Crest Ware*, Wallace-Homestead, out-of-print; Kyle Husfloen, *Antique Trader's American & European Decorative and Art Glass Price Guide*, 2nd ed., Krause Publications, 2000; Carrol Lyle and Whitney Newland, *The C. F. Monroe Co. Catalogue No. 11, 1906-1907*, L & N Associates (P.O. Box 2013, Santa Barbara, CA 93120.)

Bon Bon Dish, 7-1/4" w, 7" h, swirl mold, alternating panels of light green and white, blue purple asters with white enamel, fancy silver-plated hardware, pale yellow int., pink banner mark................ 750.00

Box, cov, hinged

5" d, 4-1/2" h, cobalt blue ground, emb and hand painted floral dec, clock on lid, brass feet, repair .................................. 400.00

6-1/2" d, 3-3/4" h, swirl mold, multicolored ground, storks flying in sunset scene, enameled floral and gold border, sgd "Wavecrest" .................................................................. 2,500.00

6-1/2" d, 6-1/2" h, egg crate mold, sq, ftd, cream ground, floral dec and cupid scene on lid ........................................ 3,100.00

7" d, puffy mold, white ground, pink floral dec, enameled beads, unmarked ...................................................................... 500.00

7" d, sq, white ground, blue highlights and tapestry dec, unmarked ...................................................................... 900.00

7" d, swirl mold, light pink ground, pink and blue floral dec, sgd .......................................................................... 450.00

7" d, swirl mold, white ground, pink floral dec, sgd ........... 400.00

7" d, swirl mold, white ground, pink morning glory and ribbon design, ftd, sgd "Wavecrest" ......................................... 700.00

7" d, 3-1/2" h, round, dark green, emb pink floral wreath dec, "Birthday Cake," sgd ................................................. 1,700.00

7" d, 6" h, swirl mold, cream ground, blue and white floral dec .............................................................................. 900.00

7" d, 6-1/2" h, wave mold, gray ground, goldfish scene, sgd "Wavecrest" .................................................................. 9,500.00

7-1/2" d, 6" h, ftd, pink and yellow ground, portrait of woman on lid, sgd "Nakara" ......................................................... 3,000.00

8" d, green and pink ground, pink floral dec, unmarked ..... 900.00

8" d, light pink and blue ground, blue floral dec, unmarked 550.00

8" d, sq, apricot ground, blue iris dec, sgd "Nakara" ........ 1,900.00

8" d, white ground, pink floral, brass feet, unmarked .......... 400.00

9-1/2" l, 7-1/4" w, 6" h, rect, ftd, royal blue ground, yellow rose dec, emb scroll mold border, sgd "Wavecrest" .............. 4,500.00

Candlestick, 7-1/2" h, pink floral dec, brass top and base, sgd "Wavecrest" ............................................................... 275.00

Cigarette and Match Holder, 7" h, blue floral dec, sgd ............... 550.00

Cigar Humidor, enameled "Cigars"

4-3/4" d, 6-1/2" h, scroll-type mold, milk white ground, floral dec, sgd "Wavecrest" ..................................................... 850.00

6" h, shell mold, white and pink ground, blue floral dec, sgd "Wavecrest" ................................................................ 700.00

6-1/2" d, 6-1/2" h, egg crate mold, square, cream ground, floral dec, silver plate feet ................................................. 600.00

Collars and Cuffs Box, cov, hinged, 7-1/2" d, 5-1/4" h, light blue and white ground, pink and yellow floral dec, sgd "Nakara" ......... 1,800.00

Cracker Jar, silver plate lid and bail handle

Light blue ground, pink floral, ruffled mold, unmarked ........ 200.00

Light yellow ground, violet dec, sgd "Wavecrest" ............... 225.00

White and cream ground, pink and yellow floral dec, sgd "Wavecrest" ................................................................ 225.00

White ground, blue floral dec, unmarked ........................... 225.00

White ground, pink rose dec, swirl mold ............................ 400.00

Dresser Box, hinged

4" d, emb floral mold, blue and white ground, pink floral dec, sgd "Wavecrest" ......................................................... 325.00

4" d, emb floral mold, cream ground, blue floral dec, sgd "Wavecrest" ................................................................ 190.00

**Dresser Box, hinged, blue mottled background, pink poppy dec, sgd "Kelva," 8" d, $1,500. Photo courtesy of Woody Auction.**

4" d, scroll type mold, floral dec, sgd "Wavecrest" ............. 150.00

4" d, shell mold, floral dec, sgd "Wavecrest" ..................... 225.00

4" d, swirl, white ground, yellow floral dec, unmarked ........ 175.00

5-1/2" x 6" x 9", fancy scroll mold, white and pink ground, chrysanthemum dec, brass feet ........................................ 1,300.00

6" d, swirl mold, cream ground, enameled morning glory and blue ribbon dec, orig paper label ................................... 600.00

6" d, white ground, scene of woman on fence, sgd ........... 475.00

7" d, branch and leaf mold, blue and white ground, pink floral dec, brass feet, sgd ................................................ 1,100.00

7" d, egg crate mold, white and blue ground, floral dec, sgd "Wavecrest" ...................................................... 1,300.00 1,300.00

7" d, swirl mold, enameled daisy dec ................................. 700.00

8" d, wave mold, pink and white ground, blue floral dec, brass feet, sgd "Nakara" ...................................................... 2,400.00

Fernery

5" l, scroll mold, light blue ground, pink floral dec, sgd "Wavecrest" ............................................................... 250.00

8" l, rope mold, pink ground, blue floral dec, brass rim and feet, sgd "Wavecrest" ..................................................... 300.00

Hair Receiver

4-1/2" w, green ground, pink floral dec, attached beveled mirror, sgd "Nakara" ......................................................... 600.00

5-1/2" w, sq, green ground, pink floral dec, brass top, sgd "Nakara" ................................................................... 250.00

Jewel Box, hinged

4" d, green ground, portrait of woman, sgd "Nakara" .......... 525.00

6" d, cream ground, blue highlights, enameled tapestsry, paper label .......................................................................... 500.00

6" d, pink ground, scene with four sailboats, sgd "Nakara" ... 2,400.00

Lamp, 17" h, cream ground, pink floral dec, castle and farm scene, sgd "Wavecrest" ............................................................. 400.00

Letter Holder, 5" x 6", egg crate mold, blue and white ground, floral dec, brass feet, sgd "Wavecrest" ...................................... 325.00

Mayonnaise Set, 5" d, pink ground, blue floral dec, gilt holder, sgd "Nakara" ....................................................................... 200.00

Pin Dish

3" l, pink ground, blue floral dec, swirl mold, unmarked ........ 70.00

3" l, white ground, blue floral dec, swirl mold, unmarked ...... 60.00

3" l, white ground, white floral dec, swirl mold, unmarked .... 50.00

4" x 3-3/4", oval, light green and white ground, pink floral dec, emb scroll mold, sgd "Wavecrest" ................................... 75.00

Planter, 6-1/2", high gloss, leaf dec, sgd "Nakara" .............. 175.00

Plaque, fancy mold

7-1/2", iris dec, gilt frame, orig paper "Wavecrest" label ........ 3,600.00

8" x 10", light blue ground, pink floral dec, scroll mold, gilt frame ......................................................................... 4,100.00

10", fancy royal blue, white sailboat scene, gilt frame, unmarked .................................................................... 4,800.00

Plate

7" d, pond lily dec, shaded blue ground, reticulated border 750.00

8" d, lake and farm scene, gold trim, paper label ................ 125.00

Powder Box, cov

3-1/2" w, 3-1/4" h, sq, pink and yellow ground, portrait of woman on lid, sgd "Nakara" ................................................... 800.00

4" w, 3" h, sq, blue mottled ground, emb pink and yellow maple leaf on lid, mkd "Kelva" .............................................. 1,200.00

4-1/2" d, 2-1/2" h, round, green ground, portrait of woman on lid, sgd "C. F. Monroe" ..................................................... 1,000.00

Ring Box, 2-1/2" d, round

Beige, portrait of woman on lid, sgd "Nakara" ................. 1,300.00

Blue ground, portrait of woman on lid, mkd "C.F.M. Co.". 1,200.00

Salesman Sample

Dresser Box, 7", hinged, different colored lids combined to demonstrate varieties .......................................................... 325.00

Vase, 5" h, blue and white ground, floral dec, brass top and feet .......................................................................... 325.00

Vase, 6-1/2" h, blue and white ground, pink floral dec, brass handle and frame, unmarked .............................................. 250.00

Salt and Pepper Shakers, pr, Meriden silver plate holder ........... 125.00

Tobacco Box, cov, hinged

    5", egg crate mold, white ground, pink floral dec, enameled "Tobacco," unmarked ...................................................... 750.00

    5-1/2", sq, egg crate mold, cream ground, pink floral dec, enameled "Tobacco," sgd "Wavecrest"................................... 1,100.00

Vase

    10-1/2" h, light blue ground, floral dec, scroll type mold, brass feet, sgd "Wavecrest" ...................................................... 450.00

    11" h, two handles, royal blue and white ground, pink rose dec, fancy mold brass handles, dolphin feet, sgd "Wavecrest"........... 4,400.00

    12" h, two handles, red, green, and white ground, floral dec, brass handles and feet, sgd "Wavecrest"................................ 2,000.00

    12-1/2" h, light pink ground, sailboat scene, fancy scroll mold, brass feet, unmarked .................................................... 2,500.00

    13-1/2" h, pink mottled ground, iris dec, brass feet, sgd "Kelva" ................................................................................ 1,800.00

    14" h, two handles, red mottled ground, white morning glory dec, silver plated handles and feet, sgd "Kelva" ................... 2,200.00

    16" h, two handles, light blue ground, pink floral dec, puffy wave mold, brass handles, mkd "Nakara" .............................. 2,600.00

    17" h, two handles, ftd, light blue ground, royal blue highlights, pink floral, orig paper label .......................................... 1,500.00

    18" h, two handles, Guba duck dec, brass dolphin handles and feet, sgd "Wavecrest" ...................................................... 6,500.00

    18-1/2" h, two fancy metal handles, ftd, green ground, large pink iris dec, sgd "Wavecrest"................................................ 5,000.00

Whisk Broom Holder, hanging type, light pink ground, floral dec, fancy brass frame, unmarked ......................................... 1,000.00

# WEATHER VANES

**History:** A weather vane indicates wind direction. The earliest known examples were found on late 17th-century structures in the Boston area. The vanes were handcrafted of wood, copper, or tin. By the last half of the 19th century, weather vanes adorned farms and houses throughout the nation. Mass-produced vanes of cast iron, copper, and sheet metal were sold through mail-order catalogs or at country stores.

    The champion vane is the rooster—in fact, the name weathercock is synonymous with weather vane—but the styles and patterns are endless. Weathering can affect the same vane differently; for this reason, patina is a critical element in collectible vanes.

    Whirligigs are a variation of the weather vane. Constructed of wood and metal, often by the unskilled, whirligigs indicate the direction of the wind and its velocity. Watching their unique movements also provides entertainment.

**References:** Robert Bishop and Patricia Coblentz, *Gallery of American Weathervanes and Whirligigs*, E. P. Dutton, 1981; Ken Fitzgerald, *Weathervanes and Whirligigs*, Clarkson N. Potter, 1967; A. B. & W. T. Westervelt, *American Antique Weathervanes* (1883 catalog reprint), Dover Publications, 1982.

**Reproduction Alert:** Reproductions of early models exist, are being aged, and then sold as originals.

Angel, 35" l, wood, tin trumpet, brown and yellow paint........... 2,500.00

Arrow, 42-1/4" l, 17-1/2" h, copper, allover verdigris patina, traces of gilt, America, late 19th C, slight bend to feather edge .......... 2,070.00

Arrow and Banner

    37" l, 24-5/8" h, copper, scrollwork, banner pierced with SMITH at center, some verdigris patina, traces of gilt, small loss, solder repairs ........................................................................ 1,840.00

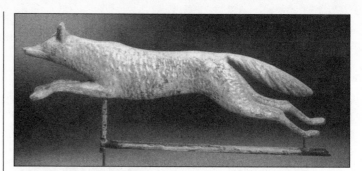

**Running Fox, L. W. Cushing & Sons, Waltham, MA, c1883, copper, traces of gilding, surface wear, 22" l, $5,750. Photo courtesy of Skinner, Inc.**

    68" l, 13" h, gilt zinc, cutout scalloped banner, weathered gilt surface, America, late 19th C, gilt loss ............................... 2,070.00

Bull, 42" l, 30-1/8" h, molded and applied copper, attributed to A. L. Jewell & Co., Waltham, MA, c1875, fine verdigris, bullet holes, minor dents, seam splits ................................................ 34,500.00

Bull Dog, 30" l, 1920s, tail missing........................................... 1,100.00

Car, 23" l, 12" h, carved and painted wood and copper, white open roadster, gray wheels, copper driver, steering wheel, fenders, running board, hub caps and lamps, iron shaft, America, early 20th C, minor paint loss ....................................................... 6,900.00

Cow, 33" w, 8" d, 21" h, gilt molded copper, full bodied, weathered gilt surface, America, late 19th C, minor imperfections ............. 13,800.00

Eagle

    16" h, 17" wingspan, copper and cast zinc, worn old gilding and green patina, hollow body, cast and emb detail, modern stand........................................................................ 2,300.00

    19" h, 32-1/2" l, molded copper, America, late 19th/early 20th C, fine verdigris, traces of gilt, old weathered gold paint, minor dents .................................................................. 2,650.00

    21" h, 24-1/2" l, gilt molded copper, America, early 20th C, regilt, minor dents and holes................................................. 1,850.00

    21" h, 25-1/2" l, molded copper, A. L. Jewell & Co., Waltham, MA, 1855-67, areas of verdigris, losses to ball, gilt wear, minor dents......................................................... 3,800.00

    27-1/4" h, 30-3/4" l, gilt molded copper, America, early 20th C, regilt, minor dents.................................................... 950.00

Horse

    24-1/2" l, 15-1/4" h, running horse, molded gilt copper, directionals, dents, America, late 19th C, gilt loss, seam separations ....2,530.00

    25" l, 17-1/2" h, Black Hawk, copper molded, allover verdigris surface, America, 19th C, minor dents ............................... 3,220.00

    25-3/4" l, 18-1/2" h, Black Hawk, flattened full bodied copper, veridgris patina, grades of gilt, seam splints, dents, some solder repairs ........................................................................ 4,025.00

Horse and Jockey

    26" l, 16" h, full bodied gilt copper, old ochre painted surface, attributed to Cushing & White, Waltham, MA, late 19th C, illegible maker's label attached to shaft, minor paint loss............. 8,050.00

    26-3/4" l, 16 h, full bodied copper, old ochre painted surface, traces of gilt, imp maker Cushing & White, Waltham, MA, tag on rod, minor seam splits ................................................ 13,800.00

Indian, 49" h, sheet metal, wrought iron framework, old polychrome repaint, riveted and ark welded, modern wall mount rack........ 750.00

Rooster

    27-1/2" l, 36-1/2" h, sheet iron, reinforced with riveted iron strapwork.......................................................................... 980.00

    38" l, 39-1/2" h, gilt molded copper, full bodied, perched on arrow, America, late 19th C, minor gilt loss ........................... 12,650.00

Sailing Ship, 25" w, 32" h, gilt-copper and iron, three directionals, America, late 19th C, from Gloucester, MA area, gilt loss, imperfections.................................................................... 2,300.00

## Whirligig

Soldier, 17-1/2"h, painted wood, red tunic, late 19th/early 20th C, repairs, repainted ........................................................ 865.00
Santa and reindeer, 32" l, painted wood, some repair and restoration ......................................................................... 175.00
Two men and mule, 21"l, painted wood ....................... 110.00
Uncle Sam, 72" h, 48" w, 28" d, carved wood and sheet metal, Uncle Sam sawing log, American flag on flagpole, polychrome dec, Henry Wilson Sargent (Henny Penny), Wilmington, MA, dated 1900 ........... 12,650.00

# WEBB, THOMAS & SONS

**History:** Thomas Webb & Sons was established in 1837 in Stourbridge, England. The company probably is best known for its very beautiful English cameo glass. However, many other types of colored art glass were produced, including enameled, iridescent, heavily ornamented, and cased.

**References:** Charles R. Hajdamach, *British Glass, 1800-1914*, Antique Collectors' Club, 1991.

**Additional Listings:** Burmese; Cameo; Peachblow.

Basket, 4" w, 5-1/4" h, rose bowl type base, bright yellow-green ground, white casing, heavily raised passion flowers, leaves, vines, and buds, applied clear V-shaped thorn handle, sgd in pontil with spider web and large "E" .................................................. 495.00
Flask, 5-3/4" l, cameo, figural swan's head, ruby red glass overlaid in opalescent white, intricately carved, sgd "Rd. 11109," gold washed sterling silver cap mkd "Gorham," other hallmarks ................. 9,200.00
Pitcher, 10-1/2" h, cream ground, red floral dec ........................... 125.00
Sugar Shaker, satin, herringbone pattern, mother-of-pearl, pink 350.00
Toothpick Holder, 3-1/2" h, egg shape, three small feet, cream ground, gold leaf design ........................................................ 300.00
Vase
    4-1/4 h, satin, amberina, maidenhair fern dec, flared crimped rim .................................................................. 475.00
    6" h, 6" w, shaded sky blue to pale white cream base, applied crystal edge, enameled gold and yellow flowers and leaves, 7 buds, butterfly, acid-cut basket weave design on body .... 425.00
    6" h, cased, orange color, enameled wild floral dec ............ 125.00
    6-1/2" h, Alexandrite, floriform, violet blush shading to sapphire blue, pale amber body with eight optic ribs, round base ............. 1,345.00
    7" h, 5-1/2" w, satin, bulbous, basketweave, MOP, deep brown to tan to gold shading to cream, creamy white lining ........... 850.00
    8" h, 4" w, satin finish, pink and white stripes, frilly top, bulbous base, unlined, c1885 ................................................ 425.00

**Vase, floriform, Alexandrite, violet blush scalloped top shading to sapphire-blue tip, pale amber body, 6-1/2" h, $1,345. Photo courtesy of Clarence & Betty Maier.**

9-1/4" h, 6" w, satin, MOP, DQ, emerald green shading to chartreuse, creamy white lining, green, brown, lavender, and white painted and enameled floral and leaf design, two in-flight bees ............... 950.00
10-1/2" h, satin, gourd shape, bright spring yellow shading to pale yellow ground, creamy white lining, bleed-thru in pontil ........ 285.00
10-1/2" h, 4" w, satin, bulbous, Jules Barbe gold floral prunus blossom, leaves, pine needles, and branch dec, shaded brown to gold, creamy white lining ............................................. 450.00
20" h, 7" d, banjo shape, satin, bright yellow-green ground, pink and white azalea dec, green and white leaves, gold highlights, allover small enameled flowers on neck, pained and enameled collar, dome foot, two applied thorn handles .................... 895.00
Vessel, 3-1/2" h, 5-1/2" w, satin, MOP, Bridal White, Flower and Acorn pattern, small gold flowers and leaves .................................... 650.00

# WEDGWOOD

**History:** In 1754, Josiah Wedgwood and Thomas Whieldon of Fenton Vivian, Staffordshire, England, became partners in a pottery enterprise. Their products included marbled, agate, tortoiseshell, green glaze, and Egyptian black wares. In 1759, Wedgwood opened his own pottery at the Ivy House works, Burslem. In 1764, he moved to the Brick House (Bell Works) at Burslem. The pottery concentrated on utilitarian pieces.

Between 1766 and 1769, Wedgwood built the famous works at Etruria. Among the most-renowned products of this plant were the Empress Catherina of Russia dinner service (1774) and the Portland Vase (1790s). The firm also made caneware, unglazed earthenwares (drab-wares), piecrust wares, variegated and marbled wares, black basalt (developed in 1768), Queen's or cream-ware, and Jasperware (perfected in 1774).

Bone china was produced under the direction of Josiah Wedgwood II between 1812 and 1822 and revived in 1878. Moonlight luster was made from 1805 to 1815. Fairyland luster began in 1920. All luster production ended in 1932.

A museum was established at the Etruria pottery in 1906. When Wedgwood moved to its modern plant at Barlaston, North Staffordshire, the museum was expanded.

**References:** Susan and Al Bagdade, *Warman's English & Continental Pottery & Porcelain*, 3rd Edition, Krause Publications, 1998; Diana Edwards, *Black Basalt*, Antique Collectors Club, 1994; Robin Reilly, *The New Illustrated Dictionary of Wedgwood*, Antique Collectors' Club Ltd., 1995; —, *Wedgwood Jasper*, Thomas Hudson, 1994.

**Periodical:** *ARS Ceramica*, 5 Dogwood Court, Glen Head, NY 11545.

**Collectors' Clubs:** Wedgwood International Seminar, 22 DeSavry Crescent, Toronto, Ontario M4S 212 Canada; The Wedgwood Society, The Roman Villa, Rockbourne, Fordingbridge, Hants, SP6 3PG, England; The Wedgwood Society of Boston, 28 Birchwood Drive, Hampstead, NH 03841; The Wedgwood Society, of New York, 5 Dogwood Court, Glen Head, NY 11545; Wedgwood Society of Southern California, Inc., P.O. Box 4385, North Hollywood, CA 91617.

**Museums:** Art Institute of Chicago, Chicago, IL; Birmingham Museum of Art, Birmingham, AL; Brooklyn Museum, Brooklyn, NY; Cincinnati Museum of Art, Cincinnati, OH; City Museum & Art Gallery, Stoke-on-Trent, England; Cleveland Museum of Art, Cleveland, OH; Henry E. Huntington Library and Art Gallery, San Marino, CA; Jones Museum of Glass & Ceramics, East Baldwin, ME; Nassau County Museum System, Long Island, NY; Nelson-Atkins Museum of Art, Kansas City, MO; Potsdam Public Museum, Potsdam, NY; Rose Museum, Brandeis University, Waltham, MA; Victoria & Albert Museum, London, England; Wadsworth Atheneum, Hartford, CT; Wedgwood Museum, Barlaston, Stoke-on-Trent, England.

## Agate Ware

Vase, 14-7/8" h, two white glazed scrolled handles terminating at goat masks at shoulders, foliate borders and festoons, mounted on sq black basalt plinth, imp Wedgwood and Bentley lozenge mark, 18th C, cover missing, restored throughout ................................. 1,380.00

## Basalt

Bulb Pot, cov, 6-1/2" h, brown glaze, oval form, bird molded handles, oval disc cov with two fitted bulb wells flanked by pierced holes, green glazed scroll border and stiff leaves at foot, imp mark, early 19th C, restored cover ........................................... 575.00

Bust, black

    3-7/8" h, Ariadne, mounted on waisted circular socle, 19th C, bust glued at joint ................................................................... 230.00

    4-1/2" h, Minerva, mounted on waisted circular socle, imp mark, early 20th C, shallow chips under helmet brim ................. 520.00

    5-1/2" h, Locke, mounted on waisted circular socle, spurious mark, late 19th C ..................................................... 320.00

    5-3/4" h, Voltaire, mounted on waisted circular socle, imp title and mark, early 19th C ......................................... 350.00

    6" h, Shakespeare, mounted on raised circular plinth, imp title and mark, 19th C ................................................. 490.00

**Figure, Winter, modeled on circular base, imp title and mark, late 19th C, 10" h, $2,415. Photo courtesy of Skinner, Inc.**

**Figures, reclining boys, overglaze enamel dec, rect bases, imp marks, attributed to Ralph or Enoch Wedgwood, c1800, minor restoration to both, 7-3/8" h, price for pr, $2,185. Photo courtesy of Skinner, Inc.**

    8-1/2" h, Byron, mounted on waisted circular socle, imp title and mark, 19th C ............................................................. 575.00

    18-1/4" h, Mercury, mounted on waisted circular socle, imp title and mark, late 19th C, wings restored ........................... 1,035.00

Candlestick

    6-5/8" h, black, Egyptian-style, sconce set on stem molded with three sphinx figures, triangular base, imp mark, 19th C, sconce restored at base ........................................................ 1,100.00

    9" h, black, dolphins, raised rect base, molded shell border, imp mark, c1972, price for pr ............................................ 1,100.00

    9-1/2" h, black, foliate and figural molded body trimmed in gilt, imp mark, 19th C ......................................................... 1,265.00

Coffee Cup and Saucer, 5" d saucer, black, engine turned body, imp mark, early 19th C, price for pr ................................................. 435.00

Crocus Pot, 6-1/2" h, black, figural hedgehog, imp mark, early 19th C, repairs to feet ...................................................................... 520.00

Figure, black

    4-1/2" h, cat, modeled by E. W. Light, glass eyes, imp mark, c1913 ........................................................................... 375.00

    4-1/2" l, sleeping boy, rect base, imp mark, 19th C ............. 575.00

    4-7/8" l, sleeping boy, head on basket of fruit, imp lower case mark, late-18th C, shallow foot rim chips ...................... 1,100.00

    5" h, classical female, feeding large bird, raised circular plinth, imp mark, mid-19th C, arm restored at shoulder ............. 750.00

    6-1/8" h, crane, pierced rocky base, modeled by E. W. Light, glass eyes, imp mark, nick to top of beak, c1915 ........... 460.00

    8-3/4" h, Cleopatra, nude seated on freeform rock, imp title and mark, late-19th C ............................................................. 980.00

    9-1/4" h, Sphinx, seated, stepped rect base, molded with taper sconce atop head, imp mark, 19th C, chip under one wing .. 820.00

    10" h, Winter, circular base, imp title and mark, late-19th C .. 1,035.00

    11" h, Nymph at Well, reclining, holding shell, oval base, imp title and mark, mid-19th C .................................................... 2,415.00

    16-1/4" h, Faun, standing, scantily clad, supporting dead game on crossed sticks set on his shoulders, imp title and mark, mid-19th C ...................................................................... 1,725.00

    16-1/4" h, Milton, standing, leaning on pedestal, holding scroll, imp title and mark, c1870, repair at wrist ..................... 1,100.00

    16-5/8" h, Faun and Flute, standing, supported by tree trunk, rect base, imp title and mark, 19th C .................................... 2,185.00

    21-1/2" h, Faun and Goat, standing, supported by tree trunk, rect base, imp title and mark, early-20th C .......................... 2,185.00

Inkwell, black, applied rosso anico foliate relief, insert inkpot

    5-1/4" l, modeled as lantern, beadwork borders, imp mark, early-19th C, slight chip to scroll handle ................................... 490.00

    7-1/4" l, modeled as oil lamp, imp mark, early-19th C, restorations ...................................................................... 350.00

Ink Stand, black

    3-1/4" h, two handled oval tray with central urn shaped bottle, circular inkwell and sand pot, imp lower case mark, late-18th C, restored chips to stand rim .............................................. 575.00

    6" h, oval, molded bird head handles, two fitted ink pots, imp mark, early-19th C, one pot restored at cover seam ........ 980.00

8" l, enameled floral dec, rect form with cut corner, molded with two oblong pen wells, three wells for fitted pots, imp mark, mid-19th C, one pot missing, slight ext. rim chip ..................... 520.00

Jar, cov, 12" h, Auro, black, slip dec gold leaf design, imp mark, c1886 .........................................................................2,530.00

Jug, black

6-1/8" h, enamel "capri" floral dec, ropetwist handle, imp mark, late-19th C ........................................................290.00

6-3/4" h, enameled floral dec, hinged pewter lid, imp mark, mid-19th C ...............................................................460.00

7-1/4" h, Kenlock Ware, black, tapered sides, ropetwist handle, enamel dec, foliate border, squid motifs, titled and imp mark, c1900 .........................................................................5,465.00

7-1/2" h, club, black, enameled floral dec, imp mark, c1870....490.00

7-3/4" h, central Bacchanalian boys frieze bordered with engine turning, grotesque mask at handle terminal, silver mounts, imp mark, c1800, slight chip to mask.................. 1,725.00

Orange Bowl, 9" d, black, circular form, raised foot, floral festoons and basket weave dec, imp mark, mid to late-19th C ............... 750.00

Pipe, black, applied classical figures within foliate frames, imp mark, 19th C .......................................................................... 375.00

Plant Pot and Stand, 4-1/2" d, black, circular pierced sides, imp mark, mid-19th C .....................................................................420.00

Plant Pot, cov, 7-3/8" h, engine turned body, scrolled foliate handles, cover with grass molded relief, imp mark, early-19th C, hairline to pot ................................................................................... 750.00

Plaque, black, framed

4-7/8" w, 6-3/8" h, oval, one with Venus and Cupid as night, other as Day, imp marks, 19th C, price for pr ............................ 575.00

7-1/2" l, Hercules Strangling the Nemean Lion, oval, imp mark, late 19th/early 20thC, mounted in gilt wood frame .......... 815.00

10-7/8" l, oval, Lioness and Cupids, imp title and mark, mid-19th C................................................................................. 2,300.00

11-3/4" l, oval, Judgment of Hercules, imp mark, 19th C, mounted in gilt wood frame .......................................... 1,610.00

Plate, 7-1/2" d, black, applied rosso antico fruiting grapevine border, imp mark, 19th C, price for pr ....................................... 460.00

Portrait Medallion, black, 3-1/2" d, John Wesley, foliate molded border, central crown supported by two angels above portrait bust, imp mark, 19th C .......................................................................... 320.00

Root Pot, cov, 7-1/2" l, black, rect form, paneled sides, relief of cherubs supporting laurel garland, cov fitted with three pots, imp mark, early-19th C, slight rim chips ........................................... 2,415.00

Tankard, 5-3/4" h, black, engine turned body, central frieze of children hunting, imp lower case marks, late-18th C........................... 1,495.00

Tea Kettle, cov, black

6-1/4" h, bamboo-molded body, imp retailer "Mortlock" and factory mark, c1897 ................................................................. 575.00

9" h, fruiting grapevine finial, imp mark, 19th C, shallow chip on spout ................................................................................. 420.00

Teapot, cov, 8-1/4" h, black, enamel floral dec, imp mark, mid-19th C .................................................................................520.00

Tea Set, cov teapot with sybil finial, 2-5/8" h creamer, 4" h cov sugar, 13-7/8" l oval tray, black, enameled floral designs and engine turning, mid-19th C, restorations, chips ............................................. 1,035.00

Vase

4" h, black, enameled floral sprays, lion masks at handles, imp marks, mid-19th C, price for pr ...................................... 1,150.00

4-5/8" h, black, four spout, bamboo type, molded on encrusted freeform oval base, imp mark, 19th C, restored foot rim chip................................................................................980.00

5" h, black, enamel floral dec, molded lion mask handles, imp mark, mid-19th C, wear to enamel................................... 520.00

5-7/8" h, black, Encaustic dec, two handles terminating in lion masks, iron-red and black classical figural dec, imp mark, artist monogram and date 1859, slight chip at mask handle.......2,300.00

6-1/4" h, black, enamel floral dec, late-19th C....550.00

6-5/8" h, figural, modeled as central seated child flanked by three cornucopia-form spouts, imp mark, 19th C...................1,725.00

7-1/4" h, black, Encaustic dec, two handles, classical figures, anthemion dec, iron-red, black, and white, spearhead and dot border, imp mark, early-19th C ................................. 3,220.00

7-1/2" h, black, applied rosso antico florets, Greek key and foliate borders, imp mark, early-19th C, restored chips............... 550.00

8-1/2" h, black, Encaustic dec, upturned loop handles, iron-red dec, black and white trim, one with classical male subject, other with classical female subject, imp mark, early-19th C, restored through socle on male, price for pr............................... 4,900.00

9-1/2" h, black, body with molded central arabesque floral band above ribbed lower body, four paw-form feet, male mask handles, imp mark, c1900 ...................................................... 800.00

9-3/4" h, black, Cybele, two grapevine molded handles terminating at Bacchus heads, trophy relief to neck, "Triumph of Cybele" on one side, reverse with Cybele in car drawn by lions, imp mark, early-19th C ...................................................... 1,380.00

9-3/4" h, black, Encaustic dec, two handles, classical figures in white and black enamels, foliate and lattice borders in iron-red, blue, and white, imp mark, early-19th C ...................... 4,025.00

10-1/2" h, black, two handles, engine turned body below drapery festoon border in relief, imp Wedgwood & Bentley wafer mark, 18th C, cover missing, handle damage, rim and plinth repairs, slight rim chips ................................................................. 320.00

13" h, black, Encaustic dec, two handles, iron-red and black enamel classical figures, imp mark, c1800 .................. 4,900.00

Vase, cov, black, two handles

5-3/8" h, black, fruiting grapevine festoons in relief, terminating at horned male mask handles, engine turned shoulder, imp Wedgwood & Bentley mark, 18th C, cover missing, handles restored .................................................................................920.00

8-1/4" h, black, orange peel body, oval classical medallions between laurel festoon terminating at goat masks, engine turned neck, imp mark, 19th C, cover missing.................. 520.00

9" h, classical figures and foliate borders, imp mark, 19th C. 1,035.00

9-1/4" h, relief of children at play, central frieze bordered with foliage and zodiac signs, imp Wedgwood & Bentley mark, 18th C, restorations ............................................................................. 2,100.00

Vestal Lamp, cov, 8-7/8" h, black, seated female, oval lamp, relief acanthus leaves and bellflowers, imp mark, 19th C ............. 1,495.00

Wine Ewer, 14" h, gilt and bronzed black basalt, modeled by Satyr seated on shoulders, holding horns of ram's head below spout, imp mark, late 19th C, handle restored, hairline to shoulder, mounted to later marble plinth.................................................................. 575.00

## Caneware

Fruit Basket, stand, 10-7/8" l, oval, pierced biscuit body, imp mark, early 19th C .......................................................................... 1,265.00

Game Pie Dish, cov

7" l, oval, inset liner, molded body, dead game between fruiting grapevine festoons, rabbit finial, imp mark, c1872, int. rim chip, inset dish missing........................................................ 435.00

8-1/4" l, oval, inset liner, molded body, dead game between fruiting grapevine festoons, rabbit finial, imp mark, c1863..... 435.00

9-1/2" l, oval, inset liner, molded body, dead game between fruiting grapevine festoons, rabbit finial, imp mark, mid-19th C, surface staining................................................................... 320.00

10-1/2" l, oval, cauliflower form finial, fruiting grapevine relief, imp mark, early-19th C, rim chips to cov, insert dish missing....... 350.00

Mug, 3-3/8" h, bamboo molded foot rim and handle, classical relief of children in landscape, blue enamel trim and banded anthemion border, imp lower case mark, 18th C, shallow surface chip........ 1,265.00

Potpourri Vase, cov, 8" h, upturned loop handles, pierced disc, lid, applied blue glazed classical relief, imp mark, c1830, handles restored, insert lid missing ...................................................... 290.00

Serving Dish, 12-1/4" l, rect form, raised foot, double foliate molded handles, imp mark, early-19th C ...................................... 1,150.00

Tea Cup and Saucer, 5" d saucer, red enamel anthemion turned border, cup with children at play in relief, engine turned foot, saucer with engine turned ext., 18th C, slight chip to foot rim of cup........... 865.00

## Diceware

Bell Pull, 2-3/4" h, three-color jasper, engine turned green ground, yellow quatrefoils, white foliate borders, imp mark, early-19th C, restored at top .................................................................................. 635.00

Bowl, 8-1/4" d, oval, scrolled handles, three-color jasper, dark blue ground, white bamboo strapping and scrolled border, yellow basket weave lattice and acanthus leaves at handles, imp mark, early-19th C, one handle restored........................... 6,900.00

Coffee Can and Saucer, 2-1/2" h, three-color jasper, engine turned black ground, yellow quatrefoils, white foliate borders, imp mark, mid-19th C, firing line to handle ................................... 1,955.00

Cream Jug, cov, 4" h, three-color jasper, engine turned dark blue ground, green quatrefoils, white foliate borders, imp mark, early-19th C.......................................................................... 4,320.00

Cup, cov, Saucer, 3" h cup, three-color jasper, engine turned ground, yellow quatrefoils, white foliate borders, imp mark, early-19th C, restored finial, handle, and saucer center ..................... 1,495.00

Jardiniere, 3-3/8" h, three-color jasper, engine turned lilac ground, green quatrefoils, green and white foliate borders, imp mark, early-19th C, slight rim nicks, relief loss ......................... 1,610.00

Jug, cov, 2-3/4" h, three-color jasper, engine turned lilac ground, yellow quatrefoils, white foliate borders, imp mark, mid-19th C, base hairline.................................................................... 1,955.00

Teapot, cov
    3-5/8" h, three-color jasper, solid blue ground, green quatrefoils, white foliate borders, imp mark, 19th C ........................ 4,600.00
    4" h, three-color jasper, engine turned lilac ground, green quatrefoils, white foliate borders, imp mark, mid-19th C, slight nicks to spout, stains ................................................................ 3,740.00

Vase, 6-1/2" h, three-color jasper, engine turned green ground, yellow quatrefoils, white foliate borders, imp mark, early-19th C, cov missing, mark altered ............................................... 865.00

Vase, cov, 8" h, three-color jasper, black ground, applied white classical and foliate relief, yellow quatrefoils on engine turned dicing, imp mark, 19th C, slight nick to cover and rim............................... 3,450.00

## Drab Ware

Cup and Saucer, 5-3/8" d, glazed, enamel dec of birds and flowers, imp mark, c1830, rim loss to one saucer, price for pr............... 300.00

Incense Burner, pierced cover, 5-7/8" h, glazed, dolphin tripod base, imp mark, c1830, restored foot rim, chips ............................... 490.00

Tea Set, applied white stoneware floral band, 3-5/8" h creamer, 6" h cov teapot with sybil finial, 5" h cov sugar bowl with sybil finial, imp marks, c1830.................................................................. 460.00

## Earthenware

Chamber Set, each with wide band of enamel dec flowers and foliage, 9" d chamber pot, 9-7/8" h pitcher, 16" d wash bowl, 5-5/8" d cov soap dish with insert straining, 5" h tumbler, imp marks, c1931, price for 5 pc set ..................................................................... 300.00

Charger, 12-3/8" d, enameled landscape with flowering branch and bird in foreground, imp mark, c1876, slight stains.................... 115.00

Crocus Pot, hedgehog
    9" l tray, blue glaze, imp mark, c1860 ............................. 1,380.00
    12-1/4" l tray, drab glaze, imp and printed marks, glaze scratches to tray ........................................................................... 1,035.00

Soup Tureen, cov, stand, 12-3/8" l, brown transfer printed sunflower pattern, gilt trim, imp mark, late 19th C, glaze wear to rim, lightly stained int. ..................................................................... 225.00

Tray, 16-3/4" l, enameled dec landscape with birds surrounding fairy figure, imp mark, 19th C, slight stain ....................................... 460.00

Vase, 4-5/8" h, slip dec, mustard yellow ground, brown slip banding, field of dots, raised floral border, imp mark, early 19th C.......... 490.00

## Jasper

Barber Bottle, 10" h, three-color dip, green ground, oval lilac medallions, applied white classical relief between fruiting grapevine festoons, foliate borders, Bacchus heads at shoulders, imp mark, 19th C, missing cover, foot rim chip ......................................... 490.00

Biscuit Jar, silver plated rim, cover, and handle
    5" h, three-color dip, applied white classical, floral, and foliate relief to central green ground, wide lilac ground borders, imp mark, late-19th C, slight relief loss.................................... 460.00
    5-1/4" h, black dip, applied white stylized Egyptian motifs, imp retailed "W. T. Lamb & Son" and factory mark, c1911, cover restored ................................................................................ 350.00
    5-3/8" h, three-color dip, green ground with yellow latticework alternating with white scrolled bands below zigzag border, imp mark, late-19th C ...................................................................... 500.00
    5-1/2" h, three-color dip, central black ground with applied white classical relief framed within bands of yellow, imp mark, c1900.......................................................................................... 635.00
    5-3/4" h, three-color dip, central black ground with applied white classical relief framed within bands of yellow ground, imp mark, late-19th C, rim nicks ..................................................... 825.00

Bough Pot, pierced lid
    2-5/8" h, solid pale blue, applied white stiff leaves in relief, foliate border, imp mark, slight nick to cov rim........................... 375.00
    5" h, green dip, square, each side with recessed oval cartouche, dec with applied white relief of cherubs representing the seasons and garden urns, imp marks, c1830, covers missing, one with foot repaired, one with rim nick, price for pr............. 490.00
    5" h, yellow dip, applied blue relief, foliate borders with cherubs representing seasons within framed panels, pierced grid, imp mark, mid-19th C ...................................................................... 1,610.00
    5-1/2" h, solid light blue, orange peel ground, applied white Dancing Hours above foliate borders, pierced grid cover with applied florets, imp mark, 19th C............................................... 1,265.00
    6" h, solid light blue, cylindrical, orange peel ground, applied white Dancing Hours above foliate borders, pierced grid cover with applied florets, imp mark, 19th C............................. 1,380.00
    6" h, solid pale blue, cylindrical, applied white columns below borders of floral festoon terminating at fox heads, scrolled florets on scalloped rim, mounted on attached stand, imp lower case mark, late 18th C, grid cov missing, restoration to rim chip, hairline to body.................................................................. 350.00
    7-1/8" h, pale blue dip, applied white Blind Man's Bluff relief and foliate borders, fluted engine turning, cylindrical, mounted on solid jasper hexagonal base, imp marks, c1790, pierced grids missing, rim nicks, hairline to one, chips, price for pr... 1,725.00
    7-1/8" h, solid light blue, applied white acanthus and bellflowers with foliate borders, pierced grid cover with applied florets, imp mark, 19th C ................................................................. 1,610.00

**Portland Vase, solid black, white classical relief shaded with black enameling, half-length figure wearing Pyragian cap under base, unmarked, late 18th C, $4,600. Photo courtesy of Skinner, Inc.**

7-3/4" h, solid pale blue, sq form, fluted base, each side with arched panel framed in applied white foliate with cherub representing each season, pierced white jasper grid lid, imp mark, late-18th C, rim chips restored to top and foot..............2,300.00

Bowl, 10-1/8" d, black dip, applied white classical Dancing Hours figures, foliate banding, imp mark, c1962 ...................................460.00

Box, cov

2-3/4" l, lilac dip, white slip floral dec, imp mark, artist sgd "Harry Barnard," c1900 .....................................................................920.00

3-5/8" l, yellow dip, scalloped body, applied black classical and floral relief, imp mark, c1930...............................................350.00

Cachepot, 4-1/2" d, 3-1/2" h, blue dip, two handles, white relief dec, imp mark, c1920-25 ............................................................150.00

Candlestick

6" h, lilac dip, applied white classical medallions between fruiting festoons terminating at ram's heads, engine turned banding, imp mark, mid-19th C, price for pr ..................................1,380.00

7" h, lilac dip, applied white classical relief, foliate and arabesque floral borders, imp mark, late-19th C, price for pr .............980.00

10-1/4" h, light blue and white, figural, female holding cornucopia fitted with floral form candle sconce, mounted on fluted pedestal set on sq plinth, imp mark, c1800, restored .....................375.00

Ceiling Fixture, 9-7/8" d, lilac dip, pierced ground between circular cartouches, white relief figures depicting four seasons, imp mark, applied registry mark, c1868 ..................................................2,100.00

Chamber Stick and Snuffer, 2-5/8" h, black dip, applied white classical relief with foliate borders, imp mark, c1876, rim chip to sconce ....635.00

Cheese Dome and Underplate, 10-1/2" d, 7-1/2" h, blue dip, white classical relief dec, foliate on top and around base of underplate with well for chilled water, imp mark, c1855-70 ...............................660.00

Cigar Rest, 4" l, yellow dip, applied blue classical relief, floral border, imp mark, c1868.......................................................................490.00

Clock Case

8-1/2" h, dark blue dip, rect form, mounted on urn, applied white classical and foliate relief, imp mark, c1900.....................460.00

13-1/8" h, light blue dip, applied white classical and foliate relief, imp mark, c1900, edge chips, restoration to relief, mark partially removed ........................................................................690.00

Coffee Can and Saucer

2-1/2" h can, three-color dip, light blue ground with white trophy drops alternating with green medallions between applied white floral festoons terminating at ram's heads, imp mark, mid-19th C, line to saucer restored ................................................ 1,380.00

2-1/2" h can, three-color dip, lilac ground with white trophy drops alternating with green medallions between applied white floral festoons terminating at ram's heads, imp mark, mid-19th C ...1,725.00

2-5/8" h can, three-color dip, light green ground, white trophy drops alternating with lilac medallions between applied white floral festoons terminating at ram's heads, imp mark, mid-19th C ...1,265.00

5-1/8" d saucer, dark blue dip, applied white classical relief panels, foliate and floral borders, imp mark, c1800 ............ 1,035.00

5-3/8" d saucer, three-color, solid white ground, lilac medallions and berries, green foliate festoons and borders, imp marks, late-19th C .................................................................... 1,495.00

Coffeepot, cov, 9-3/4" h, dark blue dip, applied white classical relief, spaniel finial, imp mark, c1830...............................................2,100.00

Cup and Saucer, 5-1/8" d, green dip, applied classical figures above engine turned bands, imp mark, 20th C, marks partially altered ....200.00

Custard Cup, cov, 3" h, solid pale blue, applied white foliate relief, imp mark, c1790, one with hairline and cov chip, price for pr .........750.00

Dessert Plate, 9-1/2" d, blue dip, applied white classical relief of figures and trees, imp marks, c1920-25, price for 8 pc set ..................385.00

Frieze, 17-3/8" l, 3-1/4" h, rect, dark blue dip, applied white scrolled foliate dec, imp mark, mid-19th C ...............................................320.00

Incense Burner, cov, 4-1/4" h, three-color, solid white ground with lilac and green applied foliate relief, bowl mounted on three dolphin feet, imp mark, mid to late-19th C, piece work missing from cov, slight relief loss, shallow foot rim flake .........................................375.00

Inkstand

2" h, solid pale blue, cylindrical pot attached to under-dish, applied white foliate relief, imp mark, c1790 ...................920.00

5" h, light blue dip, each medallion with applied white classical relief, brass mounts, late-19th C......................................350.00

6-1/2" h, light green dip, applied white classical relief, imp mark, c1900, insert missing ......................................................320.00

Jardiniere

7-7/8" h, lilac dip, applied white Muses in relief below fruiting grapevine festoons terminating at lion masks and rings, imp mark, late-19th C, surface blemish at rim .......................690.00

8" h, crimson dip, applied white classical relief, imp mark, c1920, slight relief loss...............................................................2,415.00

Jardiniere, stand, 3-3/8" h, solid blue, applied white foliate border above basket weave engine turning, imp lower case marks, late-18th C, hairlines and rim chip to jardiniere, slight hairlines to stand.............1,100.00

Jug

3-3/4" l, yellow dip, tapering sides, ropetwist handle, applied black classical relief, imp mark, slight relief loss .......................375.00

4-1/2" h, 6" h, 7" h, crimson dip, each with white applied classical relief, imp mark, c1920, price for 3 pc set ....................2,645.00

4-5/8" h, yellow dip, applied white classical relief below floral festoons and scrolled rosette borders, imp mark, c1900 ......575.00

6-3/4" h, yellow dip, Etruscan, applied black classical relief, imp mark, c1930 ..............................................................................865.00

7-5/8" h, three-color, green ground with applied yellow trellis between white scroll banding and foliate borders, hinged pewter lid, imp mark, late-19th C, slight relief loss, stained ground...375.00

Letter Box, 9" l, light blue, casket-form calamander wood, brass mounts, central oval medallion with applied white classical figures in relief, c1900, brass loss to back................................................230.00

Match Box, cov

3-3/4" l, yellow dip, oval, applied blue classical relief and oak leaf border, imp mark, c1900, slight chip to cover, box repaired ...................................................................................350.00

3-7/8" l, black dip, oval, white slip floral dec, artist sgd "Harry Barnard," imp mark, c1900 ...................................................800.00

Medallion, oval

2-5/8" x 3-1/4", solid pale blue, applied white classical female figure, imp Wedgwood & Bentley mark, c1775, rim chips, price for pr.......................................................................................1,265.00

2-5/8" x 3-1/2", pale blue body, dark blue garland dip, applied white classical female in relief, polished edge, imp mark, 18th C, edge chips....................................................................................815.00

Mug

5-1/4" h, black dip, applied white drapery and acanthus borders, central slip motto "Fill what you will, Drink what you fill," imp mark, c1900 ......................................................................435.00

5-1/4" h, dark blue dip, applied white fruiting grapevine border, slip dec motto "Drinke Faire, Don't Sware" above foliate band, imp mark, c1900...............................................................320.00

5-3/8" h, crimson dip, applied white classical relief, imp mark, c1920 ...................................................................................1,265.00

5-1/2" h, dark blue dip, applied white slip floral dec, imp mark, attributed to Henry Barnard, c1900.................................320.00

Music Box, light blue dip, walnut veneer casket-form case, applied chased brass hardware and jasper medallions with applied white classical relief, late-19th C, plays four tunes, veneer loss and damage to case.......................................................................................575.00

Mustard Pot, cov, 3-5/8" h, three-color, applied white classical relief on central green ground, wide lilac borders, silver plated rim, cov, and handle, imp mark, late 19th/early 20th C..................................750.00

Necklace, 15-1/2" l, thirty assorted beads including white relief on dark blue, light blue, and black ground, light blue relief on white ground, 20th C ......................................................................................1,035.00

Pedestal Base, 6-1/4" h, dark blue dip, applied white relief with fruiting grapevines terminating at leopard masks and trophy drops, imp mark, 19th C, relief loss .............................................................550.00

Pin Tray, 6" l, rect with cut corners, yellow dip, applied white classical relief, oak leaf banded border, c1900.......................................460.00

Pipe Stand, 5-1/4" l, dark blue dip, applied white relief of crossed pipes and tobacco pouch, imp mark, late-19th C, slight in-making dec flaw ..................................................260.00

Planter, 6-1/4" h, dark blue dip, applied white classical relief of Muses within foliate frames, imp mark, 19th C ......................................490.00

Plaque

4-1/2" h, 3-1/2" d, oval, solid black, applied white relief depicting Justice and Liberty, inscribed "Sgt. C. Bevington R. G. Artillery," imp mark, c1919, mounted in oak frame ..........................260.00

5" d, circular, solid light blue, applied white relief, raised title "The Sentry Box," inscribed "A. B. Wyon SC, and C. R. Leslie R.A.," imp mark, c1880.......................................................1,495.00

5-3/4" d, circular, solid light blue, applied white relief of Cupid, imp mark, late-19th C, brass frame .....................................550.00

6-3/8" h, 5-5/8" w, oval, black dip, Infant Academy, applied white relief, imp mark, 20th C, mounted in mahogany and ebonized wood frame ......................................................575.00

7" d, circular, solid blue, applied white relief of child playing horn while riding goat, imp mark and oval "O," early 20th C, slight rim chip..............................................................290.00

7-1/4" l, 2-1/2" w, rect, black dip, applied white relief of Dancing Hours, imp mark, 19th C...............................................350.00

8-1/8" l, 5-3/4" w, rect, light blue, applied white relief of classical female, imp mark, early-19th C, gilt wood frame ..............550.00

8-1/2" l, 6-1/2" w, rect, solid light blue, applied white relief of classical male, imp mark, 19th C ...........................................1,610.00

9-1/8" l, 6-1/8" w, oval, solid black, applied white classical relief of Venus and Cupid, imp mark, 20th C, attributed to Bert Bentley, mounted in brass frame, edge chips along back, relief painted.........................................................520.00

10" l, 4" w, rect, solid light blue, applied white Muses, imp mark, 19th C ..............................................................490.00

11" l, 4" w, rect, three-color dip, central green ground, light blue border, applied white classical figures within a foliate frame, imp mark, mid-19th C .......................................1,495.00

12" l, 5-7/8" w, rect, three-color dip, central light blue ground with green border, applied white Dancing Hours figures within foliate frame, imp mark, mid-19th C, crazing, hairline .............1,380.00

15-1/4" d, round, self framed, light blue, applied white relief of Centaur and Bacchante, imp mark, 19th C, relief and rim restored, craze lines.....................................6,325.00

15-1/2" l, 6" w, black dip, Achilles in Scyros among the Daughters of Lycomedes, applied white classical relief, imp mark, early-19th C, mounted in gilt wood frame ................................2,990.00

17-3/4" l, 5-3/4" w, green dip, rect, applied white relief of Hector taking leave of Andromache, imp mark, early-19th C, mounted in gilt lined wood frame .............................................2,760.00

22-7/8" l, 7-5/8" w, rect, black dip, applied white relief of Orestes and Pylades, imp mark, 19th C.....................................2,415.00

Potpourri Vase, pierced cover

5" h, dark blue dip, applied white foliate festoons and borders, bowl supported on three dolphin feet, imp mark, early-19th C....1,495.00

5" h, light blue dip, applied white foliate border and festoon in relief, bowl supported on three dolphin feet, imp mark, early-19th C, feet repaired ....................................................1,150.00

5-1/4" h, solid black, applied white foliate festoons and borders, bowl supported on three dolphin feet, imp mark, 19th C1,955.00

6-5/8" h, light blue dip, two handles, applied white classical relief above foliate borders, drum base with white relief of fruiting festoons terminating at ram's heads, imp mark, c1864 ........450.00

7-1/8" h, pale blue dip, cylindrical, applied white Blind Man's Bluff relief with foliate borders, fluted engine turning, mounted on solid jasper hexagonal base, imp marks, c1790, pierced cov missing, rim nicks, hairline to one, numerous chips to feet, price for pr..................................................................1,725.00

14-1/4" h, solid light blue, orange peel ground, applied white goat head handles, classical figures in relief about foliate borders, insert lid, imp mark, c1862 ...........................................1,840.00

Salad Bowl

8-1/4" d, yellow dip, applied black classical relief, raised foot, imp mark, c1930 .....................................................460.00

8-7/8" d, three-color dip, central green ground with lilac borders, applied white classical figures below floral festoons terminating at ram's heads, acanthus leaves on rim, silver plated bowl rim and serving utensils, imp mark, late 19th C ......................920.00

Salt, master, 2" h, solid pale blue, cylindrical, polished interior, applied white relief of children at play on ext., imp mark, c1790, shallow foot rim and int. rim chips .......................................375.00

Spill Holder

3" h, three-color dip, dark blue ground, lilac medallions, applied white portraits and drapery swags, imp mark, c1900, stain, firing line to foot ............................................................635.00

3-7/8" h, yellow dip, applied blue foliate dec, imp mark, mid-19th C .................................................................980.00

Sugar Bowl, cov, 3-3/4" h, three-color, white ground, applied lilac medallions and berries, white classical figures and green grape leaf festoons and foliate borders, imp mark, late-19th C ..............1,035.00

Tea Canister, cov, 5-3/8" h, pale blue, applied white classical relief of children above engine turned band, imp lower case mark, late-18th C, chips and hairlines to foot rim............................................435.00

Tea Plate, 6-1/2" d, blue dip, white relief dec, imp mark, c1920-35, price for set of 8 pcs................................................................250.00

Teapot, cov

4-1/8" h, green dip, applied white relief of children at play, floral and foliate borders, imp mark, early to mid-19th C........1,150.00

4-1/4" h, three-color, solid white ground with lilac medallions, ribbons and grapes, green foliage and flowers, imp mark, early-19th C, crazing, top of spout restored..............................865.00

4-1/2" h, black dip, applied white classical and foliate relief, imp mark, late-19th C ...........................................................1,150.00

5-1/8" h, dark blue dip, silver-form, octagonal shape, applied white classical figures in oval medallions, trophy drops and foliate borders, imp mark, early-19th C, cov damaged, loss to relief, spout chip..................................................................400.00

Tea Set, 3 pcs

Pale blue dip, applied white classical relief of Lady Templeton subjects above fluted engine turning, 4-1/2" h cov teapot, 4" h cov creamer, 4-3/8" h cov sugar, two 5-1/8" d saucers, imp mark, c1790, slight chips, and hairlines .......................2,990.00

Three-color, applied green medallions, ribbons, grapes, and foliage, green foliage, 4" h cov teapot, 2-5/8" h creamer, 3-7/8" h cov sugar, imp mark, mid- to late-19th C, slight chip to teapot spout .................................................................1,840.00

Yellow dip, applied black classical relief, 4-3/8" h cov teapot, 2-3/4" h creamer, 3-1/2" h cov sugar, imp marks, c1930 .................1,150.00

Tobacco Jar, cov, 7" h, dark blue, applied white relief of tavern figures and acanthus leaf borders, slip motto "For Rich or Poor, in Peace or Strife, It Soothes the Rugged Path of Life," imp mark, c1900 ....................690.00

Tray, 12-5/8" l, 10" w, oval, three-color, solid pale blue ground, applied white sunflower centering scrolled ribbon and vinework border, green florets, imp mark, late 18th/early 19th C, rim chip, slight relief loss .............................................................1,150.00

Trophy Cup and Saucer, 5-1/2" d saucer, solid black, applied white relief of trophy drops and classical figures between floral festoons terminating at ram's heads, imp mark, early 20th C .................920.00

Trophy Plate, 8-3/4" d, solid black, applied white classical relief with figural group centering border of trophy drops and figures between floral festoons terminating at ram's heads, imp mark, early 2th C ..........1,265.00

Vase

5-1/8" h, three-color, yellow ground, black classical relief with column framed panels of floral festoons below oval medallions, raised white banding, imp mark, late-19th C, damage under base ................................................................525.00

6-1/2" h, black dip, portrait, applied white relief with framed portraits centering foliate festoons, Greek key and foliate borders, beadwork trim, imp mark, mid-19th C..............................990.00

6-1/2" h, light blue dip, two handles, applied white relief depicting Blind Man's Bluff, foliate borders, imp mark, mid-19th C.......435.00

10" h, dark blue, Portland, applied white classical relief, base molded with man wearing Phrygian cap, imp mark, 19th C.............1,725.00

10-1/2" h, dark blue, Portland, applied white classical figures, base molded with man wearing Phrygian cap, imp mark, mid-19th C, firing line under base........................................1,725.00

Vase, cov

6-1/2" h, black dip, applied white relief torch dec, foliate borders, pierced cover, imp mark, cover restored.......................1,100.00

7" h, lilac dip, applied white relief bands of arabesque floral designs between anthemion and shell borders, lovebird finial, imp mark, mid-19th C....................................................1,610.00

8-1/8" h, black dip, two handles, applied white relief, classical figures, foliage borders, drum base with fruiting festoons terminating at ram's heads, imp mark, mid-19th C, cov restored..............1,150.00

8-1/4" h, four-color dip, two handles, central black ground with applied white drapery swags and Greek key band surrounding oval dark blue medallions with classical subjects, socle, and shoulder, and cover with yellow ground and foliate relief, imp mark, c1900 ....................................................2,990.00

8-3/4" h, light blue dip, Apollo, applied white relief and raised Latin verse "CC Post Natum Conditorem Anno Viget Ars Eturiae Redintegrata," designed by John Goodwin to commemorate 200th anniversary of the birth of Josiah Wedgwood, imp mark, c1930, mounted to ebonized wood plinth, fair surface hairline.........865.00

9-1/4" h, black dip, two handles, Bacchus mask head handles, applied white Dancing Hour figures, foliate borders, imp mark, mid-19th C ..................................................................1,495.00

9-3/4" h, three-color dip, central dark blue ground, applied white Dancing Hours figures and foliate borders, wide light green borders, imp mark, late-19th C, socle, handles, and finial restored..............................................................1,035.00

10-3/4" h, solid blue, urn finial, upturned loop handles, applied white Blind Man's Bluff relief centering foliate borders, imp mark, late-18th C, cov rim restored, slight relief loss to handle, firing lines in relief, slight foot rim ..............................1,100.00

11" h, black dip, two handles, applied white classical medallions and trophy drops between laurel festoons terminating at circular tie backs and ribbons, foliate borders, imp mark, mid-19th C, cov restored, finial missing .....................................435.00

11" h, light green dip, Bacchus mask handles, applied white relief of Dancing Hours, foliate borders, imp marks, c1900, marks partially removed, price for pr...........................................990.00

11-1/2" h, pale lilac dip, two handles, applied white classical relief, snake-form handles terminating at Medusa masks, Cupid finial, imp mark, early-19th C, rim chip on cov ............................920.00

12-1/2" h, three-color dip, two handles, black ground, engine turned central band with yellow quatrefoils, white foliate and figural borders, imp mark, mid-19th C, restored cover, handles, and socle...................................................................1,495.00

13-1/4" h, green dip, two handles, applied white classical relief with foliate borders, imp mark, 19th C ............................1,265.00

14" h, solid black, applied white classical subject frieze bordered within foliate design, imp mark, late-19th/early-20th C, handles restored..................................................................1,610.00

19" h, solid light blue, two handles, Pegasus, white classical relief depicting Apotheosis of Virgil, banded borders of running anthemion and foliate designs, inscribed "Made for Charles Bellow," imp date "1910," and mark, handles restored, chips to plinth, crazing on cover.....................................................2,990.00

19-1/2" h, solid pale blue, two handles, Borghese, applied white classical figures in relief centering foliate, gadroon, and fruiting grapevine borders, imp mark, c1780, minor relief loss to cover, restoration to socle and plinth ....................................10,350.00

20-5/8" h, three-color, solid white body with wide central green panel dec with white Dancing Hours figures, foliate borders alternating with green and pale mauve, imp mark, c1900, missing ball finial, restored socle, firing lines to handles, chip under foot ....................................................................4,025.00

## Lustres

Bowl

7-1/4" d, Dragon, Pattern No. Z4825, octagonal, mottled orange/red int., mottled blue/purple int., printed mark, c1920.................825.00

8" d, Hummingbird, Daventry, Pattern Z5294, hummingbirds with flying geese border, mottled blue ext., mottled orange int., printed mark, c1920, gilt wear.........................................750.00

8-1/8" d, K'ang His, Pattern Z4832, butterflies, mother-of-pearl ext., mottled orange/red int., printed mark, c1920, wear..............460.00

8-7/8" d, Fairyland, Pattern Z5125, Castle on Road ext., Fairy in a Cage int., printed mark, c1920, gilt wear.......................4,025.00

Candlesticks, pr, 7-3/4" h, Powder Blue, polychrome fruit band dec, printed mark, 20th C ......................................................550.00

Inkstand, 6-5/8" h, Moonlight, oval, molded bird's head handles, attached undertray, inkpot insert, imp mark, c1805...............2,185.00

Melba Cup, Butterfly, Pattern No. Z4827, Chinese ornaments on mottled ruby ext., mother-of-pearl int. with butterfly centers, printed marks, c1920, light surface wear, set of 8............................1,610.00

Plate

10-1/8" d, Pattern Z4970, central floral medallion and border of Chinese motifs, mother-of-pearl ground, printed marks, c1920, light surface wear, set of 8 ..........................................2,300.00

10-5/8" d, Powder Blue, each with band of vibrantly enameled flowers, printed mark, 20th C, price for set of 12.............825.00

Vase

7-1/2" h, Powder Blue, Pattern Z4612, globular form, gilt dragon and wave motif, printed mark, c1920 .............................690.00

8" h, Dragon, Pattern Z4829, trumpet form, mottled blue ext., mother-of-pearl int., Oriental panel and diaper border, printed mark, c1920 ..............................................................435.00

Vase, cov, 8-5/8" h, Dragon, Pattern Z4831, Shape 2046, mottled green/blue ground, printed marks, c1920, price for pr ..........1,100.00

## Pearlware

Bidet, 16-1/4" l, blue transfer printed botanical floral dec, imp mark, early-19th C ............................................................825.00

Bough Pot, cov, 10-3/4" h, body with engine turned bands alternating pearl ground with mottled buff and gray glaze, pierced cover, imp mark, late-18th C, ball finial missing, glaze loss, rim chip on cover .........435.00

Foot Bath, 17-1/2" h, two handled oval form, enamel dec, panels of pink with green trim, imp mark, early-19th C, minor surface scratches......................................................................460.00

Fruit Cooler, cov, 7-1/2" d, insert bow, enamel colored Chinese flowers, yellow honeycomb ground, gilt trim, imp mark, c1815 .............825.00

Garniture, pair of 6" h vases, 6-7/8" h center vase, rouletted border above applied drapery swags and fluting, traces of gilding, lower case marks, late-18th C, price for set of 3 ............................1,150.00

Luncheon Service, partial, each shell molded, green and black enamel shell and vegetation dec, two 6" h cov "Anornia" cream bowls and stands, 5-7/8" l ladle, six 7-5/8" d plates, two 9" l shaped serving dishes, c1800, imp marks, chips, hairlines.............................2,760.00

Vase

5-1/8" h, slip dec, brown slip on engine turned bands above green glazed basket weave, rope handles, imp marks, c1800, lids missing, rim and foot rim chip restored, foot rim chips.....520.00

5-3/8" h, slip dec, rouletted border above drapery swags and fluting, apricot colored slip, imp lower cast marks, late 18th C, price for pr.......................................................................1,380.00

## Queen's Ware

Bottle, cov, 9-3/4" h, molded lizard on neck, enamel dec figural landscapes, sgd by artist Emile Lessore, imp mark, c1870, shallow foot rim chips, cover chip, price for pr .........................................1,035.00

Bowl, 11-1/2" d, black transfer print, ext. scenes with hunt, lover's group and mythological sea scenes, int. with foliate border and central sailing ship, imp lower case mark, late-18th C, several restored rim hairlines......................................................................1,265.00

Bowl, cov, 5-1/2" d, set on three fluted feet, enamel dec of children in landscape, sgd by artist Emile Lessore, imp mark, c1870, restoration to side of bowl ..................................................................230.00

**Platter, armorial, green oats border with gilt berries, enameled Irish papal coat of arms, imp mark, minor surface stain spot, slight glaze pitting, late 18th C, 20-5/8" l, $575.**

Center Bowl, 11-5/8" d, scalloped rim, relief fruiting festoons, enamel dec fruiting grapevine borders, imp mark, c1914, foot rim chip 320.00

Centerpiece, 5-1/2" d, central footed cup surrounded by four compartmented dish, set on raised stand, imp mark, early-19th C, rim and foot rim chips ................................................ 865.00

Chimney Ornament, 7" h, enamel dec cartouches of children in landscapes, sgd by artist Emile Lessore, imp mark, c1875, restored under base ............................................ 1,035.00

Clock, mantel, 12-1/2" h, architectural, gilt trim, underglaze blue painted landscape panels, arched top and verse "Eheu Fugaeces Labuntur Anni" below model of a globe, enameled dial, imp mark, late-19th C, light gilt rim wear .................................... 575.00

Condiment Stand, 10-1/4" l, boat form, molded ends of horned male head, swan rear, int. with three fitted compartments, two inserts, inserts enameled with fisherman in landscape, imp mark, mid-19th C .............................................. 520.00

Cruet Set, 7-1/4" h, assembled, pierced circular stand fitted with two bottles and covers, two shakes, covered jar, imp mark, early-19th C, glaze and rim chips .............................. 3,105.00

Dinner Service, partial, brown enameled laurel and dot border, twelve 9-3/4" d plates, two 10-3/8" l platters, two 11-1/4" d circular platters, three 13-1/4" l oval platters, 8-3/4" l sauce boat, two oval 9-3/4" l vegetable bowls, two sq 10" w vegetable bowls, imp marks, early-19th C, enamel wear, chips .............................. 865.00

Dish

    7-1/2" l, oval, compartmented interior, cherubs in landscape setting, sgd by artist Emile Lessore, imp mark, c1861, rim restorations .......................................... 320.00

    8-3/4" l, shell shape, enamel dec of nude boys supporting tray of wine glasses, landscape setting, sgd by artist Emile Lessore, imp mark, c1860 ............................................ 1,035.00

Incense Burner, 8-3/8" h, pierced cover, Emile Lessore-style enameled scenes of children in landscapes, molded ram's heads on tripod hoofed feet supporting circular bowl, imp mark, c1871, cover damaged, hairline to one leg ............................... 520.00

Inkwell, 5-3/4" h, molded tripod dolphin feet supporting fluted circular bowl, inkpot insert, black and iron-red enamel trim, imp and printed mark, c1900, finial reglued, inkpot stained, rim chips ............. 550.00

Jardiniere, 8-1/4" h, globular form, octagonal base, transfer printed Peacock and Landscape pattern in Oriental style, imp mark, c1875, rim nick .................................................... 490.00

Lamp, oil, 5-7/8" l, circular form, enamel dec of cherub in landscape, sgd by artist Emile Lessore, imp mark, c1869, cover stained ............... 635.00

Orange Bowl, cov, 8-1/2" h, scrolled and entwined handles, pierced body with molded foliate design, printed and imp mark, c1971 ............. 350.00

Plate, 9-7/8" d, black transfer print, monogrammed, foliate border, central sailing ship, yellow enamel dec flag, imp mark, c1800, slight rim nick, glaze wear ...................................... 435.00

Strawberry Dish, stand, 10-1/2" l, Pattern No. 1029, enamel floral and foliate borders, imp mark, c1800, slight foot rim chip to stand ........... 575.00

Tea Infuser, 13-1/4" h, red transfer printed foliate dec, metal spigot, insert metal strainer, imp marks, Beane's Patent, c1880 ...... 1,100.00

Vase

    5-1/2" h and 6" h, bottle form, enamel dec figural landscapes, sgd by artist Emile Lessore, imp marks, c1870, price for pr .............. 575.00

    7-3/4" h, baluster, enamel dec cherubs, sgd by artist Emile Lessore, imp marks, c1862, restored rim chips .................... 750.00

    7-3/4" h, ewer shape, double spouts, yellow ground, hp oval cartouches of children harvesting, landscape settings, scrolled handles terminating in satyr masks, sgd by artist Emile Lessore, imp mark, c1862, one vase with restored handles and spout, price for pr ......................................................... 520.00

    7-3/4" h, ewer shape, double spout, enamel dec of figural scenes, titled below base "Old Age and Infancy" and "Youth and Manhood," scrolled handles terminating in satyr masks, sgd by artist Emile Lessore, imp mark, c1870, price for pr ................ 1,265.00

    8-1/4" h, gilt trim, scrolled handles, enamel dec landscapes with cherubs and children, sgd by artist Emile Lessore, imp mark, c1863, slight gilt rim wear .................................... 980.00

    10-1/2" h, two handles, enamel dec of scrolled snake and vine framed cartouches, children in landscape on one side, reverse with village gathering, sgd by artist Emile Lessore, imp marks, c1862, restored handle, foot rim .................................... 690.00

    11-3/4" h, two handles, enamel dec putti, sgd by artist Pepin, imp marks, c1866, restored handles and foot rim chip, glaze scratches ................................................... 690.00

    12-1/2" h, flat sided vase modeled with mermaid handles, enameled scene of two children in landscape, reverse with butterfly and foliate, modeled by Hugues Protat, painted by Pepin, imp mark, c1875 ................................................... 1,840.00

## Rosso Antico

Basket, 4-5/8" h, basket weave molded loop handle, sides with applied black basalt form florets within foliate frames, imp mark .......... 920.00

Candlesticks, pr, 7-1/8" h, enameled floral dec, imp marks, mid-19th C, shallow rim restored ............................................ 690.00

Coffeepot, cov, 7-1/2" h, enameled floral sprays, imp mark, c1850, slight chip to handle, firing line to side of spout ...................... 260.00

Ewer, 6-3/4" h, eagle loop handle, applied black basalt classical relief, imp mark, early-19th C ............................................ 690.00

Hot Water Pot, cov, 9" h, sybil finial, engine turned body, imp mark, early-19th C, slight chip to finial ................................. 920.00

Incense Burner, pierced cover, black basalt dolphin tripod base,

    5-1/8" h, foliate relief, imp mark, early-19th C ................. 2,415.00

    5-1/2" h, inset disk, imp mark, early-19th C, restored piercing to cover, chips ................................................... 980.00

Jug

    6" h, club, applied black basalt arabesque floral relief, imp mark, early-19th C ............................................... 1,100.00

    7-1/2" h, Egyptian, club form, black, iron-red, and white enamels, sphinx on either side of bird in flight, imp retailer and Wedgwood mark, c1880 ................................................ 980.00

Lamp, 5-3/8" l, applied black basalt classical relief, scrolled handle, foliate design on spout, imp mark, early-19th C ....................... 575.00

Miniature, tea set, 2-1/2" h cov teapot, 1-1/8" h creamer, 1-1/4" h sugar, enamel dec floral designs, imp marks, mid- to late-19th C ........... 460.00

Potpourri Vase, pierced cover

    5-1/4" h, applied black basalt foliate relief, bowl supported by three dolphin feet, imp "Josiah Wedgwood Feby 24 1805," rim chip, cover restored ....................................... 1,495.00

    6" h, applied black basalt classical frieze bordered with foliate design, imp mark, early-19th C ............................... 1,265.00

Tea and Coffee Set, Cambridge Ware, each piece with white inlaid banding, 6" h cov coffeepot, 4" h cov teapot, 2-1/8" h creamer, 3-1/4" h cov sugar, imp marks, chips, restorations ............................ 460.00

Teapot, cov, 7-1/4" h, spaniel finial, molded body with arabesque floral dec, imp mark, early-19th C ..................................... 575.00

## Stoneware

Incense Burner, cov, 5-1/2" h, dolphin tripod base, pierced cover, inset disc, imp mark, early-19th C, restored finial, slight rim chip ..... 435.00

Jardiniere and Stand, 6" h, brown, gilded kylin's mask handles, herringbone banding and trim, enameled dec Oriental floral designs, imp mark, mid-19th C, minor gilt wear ............................... 690.00

Teapot, cov, white smear glaze, molded body with arabesque floral banding, stippled ground, spaniel finial, imp mark, c1830, nick to spout ......................................................................................215.00
Vase, 4-1/8" h, Portland, black glaze, molded body, white classical relief, half figure wearing Phrygian cap under base, imp mark, c1870, fitted stand with mirrored base .............................................865.00
Vase, cov
    3-5/8" h, 5" h, white smear glaze, applied lilac classical relief, foliate borders, imp marks, covers missing, price for 3 pcs .............260.00
    5-5/8" h, white, loop handles terminating in satyr masks, imp marks, one finial reglued, light stain spots, price for pr ......................750.00

# WELLER POTTERY

**History:** In 1872, Samuel A. Weller opened a small factory in Fultonham, near Zanesville, Ohio. There he produced utilitarian stoneware, such as milk pans and sewer tile. In 1882, he moved his facilities to Zanesville. Then in 1890, Weller built a new plant in the Putnam section of Zanesville along the tracks of the Cincinnati and Muskingum Railway. Additions followed in 1892 and 1894.

In 1894, Weller entered into an agreement with William A. Long to purchase the Lonhuda Faience Company, which had developed an art pottery line under the guidance of Laura A. Fry, formerly of Rookwood. Long left in 1895, but Weller continued to produce Lonhuda under the new name "Louwelsa." Replacing Long as art director was Charles Babcock Upjohn. He, along with Jacques Sicard, Frederick Hurten Rhead, and Gazo Fudji, developed Weller's art pottery lines.

At the end of World War I, many prestige lines were discontinued and Weller concentrated on commercial wares. Rudolph Lorber joined the staff and designed lines such as Roma, Forest, and Knifewood. In 1920, Weller purchased the plant of the Zanesville Art Pottery and claimed to produce more pottery than anyone else in the country.

Art pottery enjoyed a revival when the Hudson Line was introduced in the early 1920s. The 1930s saw Coppertone and Graystone Garden ware added. However, the Depression forced the closing of the Putnam plant and one on Marietta Street in Zanesville. After World War II, inexpensive Japanese imports took over Weller's market. In 1947, Essex Wire Company of Detroit bought the controlling stock, but early in 1948 operations ceased.

**References:** Sharon and Bob Huxford, *Collectors Encyclopedia of Weller Pottery*, Collector Books, 1979, 1999 value update; Betty Ward and Nancy Schiffer, *Weller, Roseville, and Related Zanesville Art Pottery and Tiles*, Schiffer Publishing, 2000.

**Collectors' Club:** American Art Pottery Association, P.O. Box 1226, Westport, MA 02790.

**Museum**: On-Line: http://www.weller.com.

**Additional Listings:** See *Warman's Americana & Collectibles* for more examples.

Bowl
    Burntwood, lions with wings......................................125.00
    Coppertone, green and brown matte glaze cov flower frog on end, 10" l, 5" h, minor bruise ...........................................375.00
    Glendale, molded design of seagulls, flower frog with molded eggs, sgd, 15" d, 3" h, small flake on frog .......................700.00
    Squirrel, small base chip...........................................115.00
    Woodland, ftd, 7-1/2" d .............................................70.00
Box, cov, Sicard, crimped and twisted form, irid green, blue, green glaze, gold floral dec, mkd, 6" h, bottom and lid repaired ........375.00
Bud Vase, Eocean, 6" ......................................................150.00
Candlestick, 14" h, Woodcraft, owl .................................260.00
Clock
    10" h, curvilinear stylized five-point star shape, dec with orange and yellow chrysanthemum blossoms, standard glaze brown ground, artist initials "ER" on side, round white enamel clock face with Roman numerals, imp "Louwelsa Weller," minor foot chip ....................................................................865.00
    11" h, 11" w, mantel, Louwelsa, rose dec............................600.00
Console Bowl, Ardsley, kingfisher flower frog, 16-1/2" d.............700.00
Cookie Jar, Mammy ...................................................2,495.00
Ewer, Dickensware
    Pears on brown branches, green leaves, blue yellow to brow, painted and incised dec, incised mar, incised initials "B.L." ..425.00
    Two colonialists playing board game, peach to blue, imp mark, 5" h ...................................................................200.00
Figure
    Brighton Woodpecker, 6" h, orig base ...............................375.00
    Coppertone, turtle, green and brown matte glaze, 5" l .......240.00
    Drunken Ducks, yellow, Coppertone base, stamped mark, 15" h, small flake to bottom edge ......................................3,250.00
    Hen, six chicks around base, incised mark, 8" h, restored minor flakes.................................................................1,600.00
    Muskota, fishing boy, 7" h, repaired chip ..........................150.00
Floor Vase, Eocean, white tea roses, shaded blue ground, Mae Timberlake, hand incised "Eocean Weller," artist sgd, couple of minor base flake .........................................................6,500.00
Flower Frog, Muskota
    Crab, 7"..................................................................375.00
    Woman on Rock, 7" h, minor flakes..................................180.00
Garden Ornament, fisher Boy, multicolored, Coppertone base, 20" h, some restoration ..........................................................500.00
Jardiniere
    Hudson, 8" x 10".......................................................390.00
    Louwelsa, 9" h, raised on swollen cylindrical form, glossy glaze, yellow iris among green leaves, brown and ochre ground, imp half-circle Weller Louwelsa mark, glaze scratched ..........290.00
Jug
    Dickensware, tan to green, incised and painted fish swimming through waves, imp mark, artist initial, 5-1/2" h ...............325.00
    Dickensware, yellow, green, orange, and brown berry and leaf dec, mkd, initialed "R. G.," 10-1/2" h, minor scratches.....270.00
    Mt. Vernon Bridge, Upjohn..........................................4,150.00
Lamp
    Blue Ware, dark blue, girl and yellow garlands, 11" h, 5" w, hairline...................................................................200.00
    Bronzeware, green and gold metallic glaze, l" h................400.00
Pitcher, Woodcraft, three fox heads, tree trunk form, 12-1/2" h..500.00
Planter, 10-1/2" w, 6-1/2" h, molded landscape with sheep and flowers, matte green glaze, minor chip repair......................................375.00
Umbrella Stand, 20" h, 10" d, matte dark green glaze, emb poppies and sunflowers on long stems.............................................1,700.00
Vase
    Ardsley, 9" h............................................................90.00
    Aurelian, standard glaze, dragon in fire, mkd and sgd "Edward Abel," 12-1/2" h, 5" w ...........................................600.00
    Blue Ware, 10" h, blue ground, female figure, minor flake..200.00
    Blue Ware, 12" h, 6" w. blue ground, several figures,.........475.00
    Bonito pattern, 11-1/2" h, artist Myrtle Vorhees .................280.00
    Bronzeware, metallic red textured glaze, 11" h...................800.00

**Vase, Coppertone, 2 frog handles, ink kiln mark, short tight line to rim, 7-1/2" h, 9" d, $1,620. Photo courtesy of David Rago Auctions.**

Camelot, 4" h, cream geometric design, yellow matte glaze, mkd.................................................................225.00
Chase, 9" h .........................................................375.00
Chengtu, 8" h ......................................................125.00
Claywood, 9" h ....................................................150.00
Coppertone, 7" h, 8-1/2" w, green and rust matte glaze, two closed handles, incised signature ...................600.00
Eocean, 6-1/2" h, green, pink, and cream carp, green to pink background, incised signature .....................1,500.00
Glendale, brown and green, bird nest dec, mkd, 9" h, 8" w ..1,000.00
Glenwood, 8-1/4" h, 2 birds with nest .............................1,100.00
Greora, 9" h .......................................................190.00
Hudson, 7" h, blue, multicolored floral dec, sgd "McLaughlin," orig label, stamp mark........................................375.00
Hudson, 8-1/4" h ...............................................1,800.00
Hudson, 15" h, 7" w, blue ground, white and pink peonies, painted and sgd by Pillsbury, mkd .............................4,500.00
Hudson Pictorial, 11-1/2" h, landscape with snow laden road, brown fence running alongside tree line, painted and sgd by McLaughlin, incised mark..................................4,250.00
Jewel, incised fern fronts, swirling blue jewels, dec front and back, blue, green, and light pink ground, imp mark, 7-1/2" h..........700.00
LaSa, 4" h, bulbous...........................................250.00
Louwelsa, 7-1/2" h, holly berries and leaves, shades of blue, imp mark ...........................................................900.00
Louwelsa, 10-1/2" h, stylized yellow roses, deep emerald green ground, sgd "H. Pillsbury," incised mark........................2,400.00
Louwelsa, 12" h, matte, deep ruse oak leaves and acorns, tan matte ground, sgd "Hester Pillsbury," incised and imp marks ......1,100.00
Marvo, 7" h.......................................................90.00
Perfecto, pink and purple peonies, brown centers, green leaves, Dorothy England decorator, 9" h, 9" w ...........................650.00
Scandia, incised black vertical stripes, 9-1/4" h.................280.00
Sheaves of Wheat, 12" h, 4-1/2" d, ovoid, emb sheaves of wheat, green and periwinkle-blue leathery matte glaze, stamped "Weller"........................................................1,800.00
Sicard, 8-1/2" h, 5-3/4" d, gourd shape, swirling poppies on lustrous gold, blue, green, and purple glaze, sgd "Sicardo".............2,600.00
Sicard, 14-1/2" h, 7" d, celadon poppies, purple narceous ground, mkd "Sicard/Weller," restored drill hole in base 2,600.00
Tutone, Art Deco, 9"..........................................285.00
Warwick, double, 5" .........................................60.00
Woodcraft, 5-1/2" h, #156-2/4 ...........................100.00
Woodcraft, chalice shape, 9" h ...........................175.00
Wall Pocket
   Ardsley, double, 12" l ....................................190.00
   Klyro, 8" h .................................................110.00
   Tutone, 11" l...............................................170.00
   Woodcraft, 11" h, 5-1/2" w, owl, tapered, naturalistic tree trunk, leafy branch, relief owl head, imp "Weller," painted "N" on back, c1928 .......................................................400.00
   Woodland...................................................120.00
   Woodrose...................................................110.00

# WHALING

**History:** Whaling items are a specialized part of nautical collecting. Provenance is of prime importance since collectors want assurances that their pieces are from a whaling voyage. Since ship's equipment seldom carries the ship's identification, some individuals have falsely attributed a whaling provenance to general nautical items. Know the dealer, auction house, or collector from whom you buy.

Special tools, e.g., knives, harpoons, lances, and spades, do not overlap the general nautical line. Makers' marks and condition determine value for these items.

**References:** Nina Hellman and Norman Brouwer, *Mariner's Fancy*, South Street Seaport Museum, Balsam Press, and University of Washington Press, 1992; Martha Lawrence, *Scrimshaw*, Schiffer Publishing, 1993.

**Museums:** Cold Spring Harbor Whaling Museum, Cold Spring Harbor, NY; Kendall Whaling Museum, Sharon, MA; Mystic Seaport Museum, Mystic, CT; National Maritime Museum Library, San Francisco, CA; New Bedford Whaling Museum, New Bedford, MA; Pacific Whaling Museum, Waimanalo, Hawaii; Sag Harbor Whaling & Historical Museum, Sag Harbor, NY; South Street Seaport Museum, New York, NY.

**Additional Listings:** Nautical Items; Scrimshaw.

Bag, 19-1/2" l, 11" w, linen, whaleship *Ohio*, holds ship's mail, mkd "Ship Ohio/Letter Bag" ........................................800.00
Blubber Hook, 44-1/2" l, wrought iron, carved wooden handle, America, mid-19th C.......................................................150.00
Book
   *Etchings of a Whaling Cruise*, J Ross Browne, first edition, New York, 1846 ......................................................575.00
   *Whale Ships and Whaling*, George Francis-Dow, Marine Research Society, Salem, MA, 1925.............................125.00
   Bookplate, aquatint engraving of whaling scenes, framed, French, 19th C, pr .................................................225.00
Box, H & E Howland Whaleship Agents, New Bedford, rosewood, brass bound, lift-out tray, two cut glass ink bottles, scrimshaw pen .....1,200.00
Busk, whalebone, engraved
   12-11/16" l, dec with various geometric devices, plants, three-masted ship under sail, crack, minor chips, minor insect damage ...........................................................150.00
   14-1/8" l, dec with neoclassical urn with willow, "Love," ship under sail, coconut tree, and lighthouse, polychrome highlights, faded, slightly warped, minor crack, 19th C ..........................250.00

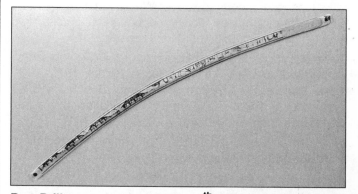

**Bow Drill, carved walrus, Inuit, 19th C, $3,080. Photo courtesy of Jackson's Auctioneers & Appraisers.**

Caulking Tool, 4-1/2" l, boat maker's, whale bone ..................... 385.00
Crew List, whaleship *Montpelier,* Sept 6, 1853, names, position, number of shares in voyages to be received .................................. 150.00
Harpoon Gun, 37" l, US Springfield Trapdoor model 1873, inspector mark "SWP 1889," including bronze harpoon, cleaning rod, and wrench in wooden carrying case ................................................ 575.00
Log Book, bark *Pioneer,* Captain James S Hazard, departed New Bedford, August 5, 1869, held by US Consol at Mauritins, released and returned by New Bedford on Dec 1, 1872, sent home 232 barrels of sperm oil .................................................................................. 3,500.00

Print
    "Right Whaling in Behring Straits and Arctic Ocean with its Varieties," Benjamin Russell, publisher, John H. Bufford, lithographer, 1871, identified within matrix, chromolithograph on paper, framed, sheet size 19-1/8" h, 35-1/4" l, tears and losses to margins, staining, not examined out of frame ....................... 525.00
    "The Whale Fishery, Attacking a 'Right' Whale and 'Cutting In'," Currier and Ives, John Cameron, lithographer, (Conningham 6623), identified in inscriptions in the matrix, litho with hand coloring on paper, sheet size 21-1/8" h, 28" l, unframed, tears and punctures, staining, toning ............................................. 1,035.00

Receipt, whale oil purchase, William Rotch & Sons, New Bedford, dated 1811 and 1813, framed, pr ....................................... 80.00
Sailor's Fid, 11" l, whale bone, old worn surface......................... 200.00
Seam Rubber, whalebone, engraved "T. D. C.," mid 19th C....... 325.00
Ship's Block, 5-1/2" l, double, brass shims, iron hanger, imp metal cross dec on each side ............................................................ 120.00
Sugar Nippers, 12" l, scribe line dec, whalebone handle, wrought iron nippers, mounted on rect wood base, late 18th C, corrosion, cracks to handle ................................................................................. 575.00
Try-Square, 11-13/16", whalebone, 19th C ................................. 635.00
Whale's Tooth, engraved, late-19th C, minor crack
    5-1/8" l, dec with elegant lady, seated nude woman, initialed "OM" ...................................................................................... 950.00
    6-1/4" l, dec with sailor....................................................... 450.00
    6-1/4" l, dec with spiraling design of various ships under sail, whaling scene, stained.................................................... 1,20.00
    7" l, dec with elegant lady ................................................. 1,110.00
Whale's Tooth, mounted
    5-1/4" l, plaque reads "This tooth taken from a sperm whale that made 125 barrels of oil. The oil was brought into Nantucket, June 1797," contemporary wood stand............................ 450.00
    19" h, pair of teeth mounted with baleen, naturalistically carved wood base, 19th C, some insect damage to baleen ..... 2,990.00

# WHIELDON

**WHIELDON**

**History:** Thomas Whieldon, a Staffordshire potter, established his shop in 1740. He is best known for his mottled ware, molded in the shapes of vegetables, fruits, and leaves. Josiah Spode and Josiah Wedgwood, in different capacities, had connections with Whieldon.

Whieldon ware is a generic term. His wares were never marked, and other potters made similar items. Whieldon ware is agate-tortoiseshell earthenware, in limited shades of green, brown, blue and yellow. Most pieces are utilitarian items, e.g., dinnerware and plates, but figurines and other decorative pieces also were made.

Cream Jug, 3-1/2" h, baluster, Cauliflower, scrolled foliage handle, silver shape rim, dark green glazed leaves, cream glazed florets, Whieldon/Wedgwood/Greatbatch, c1790............................. 2,250.00
Dish, 14" l, molded border, scrolls and basketwork, panels, trellis pattern, shaped rim, tortoise shell glaze, hairline, 1760............. 1,650.00

Figure
    2-3/4" h, two nude children resting arm in arm on shrub, applied bird and foliage, translucent brown, green, and gray-blue glazes, c1765, repair to bases, pr.................................. 1,035.00
    5" h, cow, standing on freeform base, creamware, translucent brown, yellow, and green glazes, c1780, repairs .......... 2,300.00
Jar, cov, 2" h, creamware, cylinder shape, mottled gray-green and blue glazes, c1760 .................................................................... 1,265.00
Plate
    8" d, brown tortoise shell glaze, green and yellow splashes, unmarked ........................................................................... 140.00
    9-3/8" d, trellis diaper molded rim, separated by pairs of feathers, gray splashed glaze with yellow and green splotches, c1760, 9 pc set.................................................................................. 3,100.00
    9-1/2" d, black tortoise shell glaze, green, blue, and brown splashes, emb diapered border.......................................... 390.00
Platter, 17-1/4" l, oval, paneled border, threaded rim, manganese-brown, green, and blue splashes, cream ground ..................... 290.00
Soup Plate, 9-1/4" d, black tortoise shell glaze, green, blue, brown, and yellow splashes, emb diapered rim .......................................... 550.00
Sugar, cov, 3-5/8" h, 4-3/8" d, Cauliflower, dark green glazed leaves, cream glazed florets, stains ..................................................... 3,245.00
Tea Canister, 4-1/2" h, Cauliflower, dark green glazed leaves, cream glazed florets, Whieldon/Wedgwood, c1765 ......................... 1,250.00
Teapot, cov
    2-1/2" h, creamware, globular, straight spout, loop handle, mottled brown, blue, and green glazes, c1760 .................... 1,265.00
    4" h, Cauliflower, molded lower body and handle, dark green glazed leaves, cream glazed florets, Whieldon/Wedgwood, c1765, base rim chips ...................................................... 1,000.00
    5-3/8" h, molded pineapple form, mold green leaves base, handle, and spout, ochre pineapple body, c1770, restored cracks .............................................................................. 1,035.00

# WHIMSIES, GLASS

**History:** During lunch or after completing their regular work schedule, glassworkers occasionally spent time creating unusual glass objects known as whimsies, e.g. candy-striped canes, darners, hats, paperweights, pipes, and witch balls. Whimsies were taken home and given as gifts to family and friends.

Because of their uniqueness and infinite variety, whimsies can rarely be attributed to a specific glass house or glassworker. Whimsies were created wherever glass was made, from New Jersey to Ohio and westward. Some have suggested that style and color can be used to pinpoint region or factory, but no one has yet developed an identification key that is adequate.

Glass canes are among the most collectible types of whimsies. These range in length from very short (under one foot) to ten feet or more. They come in both hollow and solid form. Hollow canes can have a bulb-type handle or the rarer C- or L-shaped handle. Canes are found in many fascinating colors, with the candy striped being a regular favorite with collectors. Many canes are also filled with various colored powders, gold and white being the most common and silver being harder to find. Sometimes they were even used as candy containers.

**References:** Gary Baker et al., *Wheeling Glass 1829-1939*, Oglebay Institute, 1994, distributed by Antique Publications; Joyce E. Blake, *Glasshouse Whimsies*, published by author, 1984; Joyce E. Blake and Dale

Murschell, *Glasshouse Whimsies: An Enhanced Reference*, published by authors, 1989; Wayne Muller, *Darn It,* published by author (P.O. Box 903, Pacific Palisades, CA 90272.)

**Collectors' Club:** Whimsey Club, 2 Hessler Court, Dansville, NY 14437.

Baton
    59-1/2" l, clear, maroon swirls .............................. 330.00
    87" l, hollow, blue and maroon twist .................................. 220.00
Bird Fountain, 5-3/4" l, colorless, blown three mold, pontil scar, New England, 1825-40, McKearin GI-12, inner stain ...................... 280.00
Cane
    36-3/4" l, clear, square, twisted handle and tip, chips at tip ...... 100.00
    41" l, amber, square, twisted shepherd's crook handle, twisted tip, chips at both ends .......................... 140.00
    41" l, opaque white, cased in amber, chips at handle, tip ground .................. 120.00
    45" l, clear, mahogany triple swirl, tip chipped .................. 220.00
Darner, 5-1/2" l, 2-1/4" d, gold Aurene ........................ 850.00
Hat, blown three mold, New England, 1825-40
    McKearin GII-18, colorless, pontil scar, 2" h ...................... 110.00
    McKearin GIII-3, colorless, pontil scar .............................. 1250.00
    McKearin GIII-23, deep sapphire blue, pontil scar, 2-1/4" h ..... 850.00
Hatchet, 6" l, clear, worn painted dec.................... 30.00
Horn, sapphire blue, hunting shape, folded over rim, two flat flakes on rim ...................................... 525.00
Pen Holder, 3" h, 3-1/2" d paperweight base, blown spatter glass, cobalt blue, red, and white solid round sphere, pulled into six coils to hold pen .................... 200.00
Powder Horn, 11" h, Nailsea type blue and white loopings, colorless ground, ftd, tooled ground lip, pontil scar .................. 135.00
Vase, 4" h, blown, witch ball cover, amber, wear, small flake on ball ........................ 165.00
Witch Ball and Stand
    9-1/2" h, free blown, deep sapphire blue, pontil scar, attributed to South Jersey, mid-19th C .................. 1,400.00
    9-3/4" h, Nailsea type white loopings, colorless ground, pontil scar, attributed to South Jersey or Pittsburgh area, 1840s ........... 400.00

# WHISKEY BOTTLES, EARLY

**History:** The earliest American whiskey bottles were generic in shape and blown by pioneer glass makers in the 18th century. The Biningers (1820-1880s) were the first bottles specifically designed for whiskey. After the 1860s, distillers favored the cylindrical "fifth" design.

The first embossed brand-name bottle was the amber E. G. Booz Old Cabin Whiskey bottle which was issued in 1860. Many stories have been told about this classic bottle; unfortunately, most are not true. Research has proven that "booze" was a corruption of the words "bouse" and "boosy" from the 16th and 17th centuries. It was only a coincidence that the Philadelphia distributor also was named "Booz." This bottle has been reproduced extensively.

Prohibition (1920-1933) brought the legal whiskey industry to a standstill. Whiskey was marked "medicinal purposes only" and distributed by private distillers in unmarked or paper-labeled bottles.

The size and shape of whiskey bottles are standard. Colors are limited to amber, amethyst, clear, green, and cobalt blue (rare). Corks were the common closure in the early period, with the inside screw top being used between 1880 and 1910.

Bottles made prior to 1880 are the most desirable. When purchasing a bottle with a label, condition of that label is a critical factor. In the 1950s, distillers began to issue collectors' special-edition bottles to help increase sales.

**References:** Ralph & Terry Kovel, *Kovels' Bottles Price List*, 11th ed., Three Rivers Press, 1998; John Odell, *Digger Odell's Official Antique Bottle and Glass Collector Magazine Price Guide Series*, Vol. 8, published by author (1910 Shawhan Rd, Morrow, OH 45152), 1995 Carlo and Dorothy Sellari, *Standard Old Bottle Price Guide*, Collector Books, 1989.

**Periodicals:** *Antique Bottle and Glass Collector*, P.O. Box 187, East Greenville, PA 18041; *Bottles & Extras*, P.O. Box 154, Happy Camp, CA 96039.

**Museum:** The Seagram Museum, Waterloo, Ontario, Canada.

**Additional Listings:** See *Warman's Americana & Collectibles* for a listing of Collectors' Special Edition Whiskey Bottles.

Arch Cowan Mason & Co Leith, applied green, rect shape, blob top, emb front panel, 8" h ........................ 40.00
Bininger's Travelers Guide, A. M. Bininger & Co, No. 19 Broad St., NY, 1860-80, teardrop form, golden amber, applied double collared mouth, smooth base, 6-3/4" h ...................... 200.00
C. A. Richards & Co., 18 & 20 Kilby St., Boston, Mass, 1860-90, sq, beveled corners, applied sloping collared mouth m, smooth base, yellow amber, slug plate address, 9-1/2" h ................. 90.00
Chestnut Grove Whiskey, 1840-60, flattened chestnut form, applied handle, golden amber, applied mouth with ring, pontil scar, 9" h ......... 110.00
Chickenrock Pure Rye Whiskey, clear, tin cap, 7-1/2" h, 4-1/2" w ..... 25.00
E. G. Booz's Old Cabin Whiskey, Whitney Glass Works, Glassboro, NJ, 1860-80, cabin form, golden amber, applied sloping collared mouth, smooth base, qt, McKearin GVII-4, 3/8" x 1" shallow vertical chip has been replaced on sloping collar mouth ...................... 650.00
Four Aces American Rye Whiskey, clear, emb with name and playing cards, 7-1/2" h, 3-3/4" w ....................... 10.00
Freeblown Jug, applied handle, America, 1840-60
    6-1/8" h, pear form, red amber, applied sloping collared mouth, pontil scar........................ 220.00
    8" h, cylindrical corseted form, golden amber, applied double collared mouth, pontil scar.................. 350.00
Golden Wedding Has Had No Peers for 50 Years, irid marigold, 8" h, 4" w................................... 10.00
Potter & Bodine, yellowish olive amber, cylindrical, lady's leg shaped neck, applied mouth, base emb "Patent," 11-1/2" h ................. 220.00
Revd. J. E. Melhuish on black glass seal, cylinder, olive amber, applied mouth, H. Ricketts & Co. Glass Works Bristol on pontil scarred base, 1830-40, 10-7/8" h.................... 400.00
Royal Iron Ship Co. Whisky, emb sailing ship *Thomas W*, 1905, red, brass spout, 24" h ..................... 350.00
Something Good In A Hog - He Won't Squeal, pig shape, colorless smooth base, tooled lip, 4-3/8" l............... 120.00
Wharton's Whiskey 1850 Chestnut Grove, amber, applied handle, tooled lip, pour spout, 10" h..................... 185.00

**White Rose Rye Whiskey, P. J. Bowlin Liquor Co. St. Paul, Minn., Bristol glaze stoneware, handle, relief and blue accented "Pure Rye" at shoulder, relief and blue accented rose bouquet on back, 7-1/2" h, $440. Photo courtesy of Vicki & Bruce Waasdrop.**

# WILLOW PATTERN CHINA

**History:** Josiah Spode developed the first "traditional" willow pattern in 1810. The components, all motifs taken from Chinese export china, are a willow tree, "apple" tree, two pagodas, fence, two birds, and three figures crossing a bridge. The legend, in its many versions, is an English invention based on this scenic design.

By 1830, there were more than 200 makers of willow pattern china in England. The pattern has remained in continuous production. Some of the English firms that still produce it are Burleigh, Johnson Bros. (Wedgwood Group), Royal Doulton (continuing production of the Booths' pattern), and Wedgwood.

By the end of the 19th century, production of this pattern spread to France, Germany, Holland, Ireland, Sweden, and the United States. Buffalo Pottery made the first willow pattern in the United States beginning in 1902. Many other companies followed, developing willow variants using rubber-stamp simplified patterns, as well as overglaze decals. The largest American manufacturers of the traditional willow pattern were Royal China and Homer Laughlin, usually preferred because it is dated. Shenango pieces are the most desirable among restaurant-quality wares.

Japan began producing large quantities of willow pattern china in the early 20th century. Noritake began about 1902. Most Japanese pieces are porous earthenware with a dark blue pattern using the traditional willow design, usually with no inner border. Noritake did put the pattern on china bodies. Unusual forms include salt and pepper shakers, one-quarter pound butter dishes, and canisters. The most desirable Japanese willow is the fine quality NKT Co. ironstone with a copy of the old Booths pattern. Recent Japanese willow is a paler shade of blue on a porcelain body.

The most common dinnerware color is blue. However, pieces can also be found in black (with clear glaze or mustard-colored glaze by Royal Doulton), brown, green, mulberry, pink (red), and polychrome.

The popularity of the willow design has resulted in a large variety of willow-decorated products: candles, fabric, glass, graniteware, linens, needlepoint, plastic, tinware, stationery, watches, and wall coverings. All this material has collectible value.

**Marks:** Early pieces of Noritake have a Nippon "Royal Sometuke" mark. "Occupied Japan" may add a small percentage to the value of common table wares. Pieces marked "Maruta" or "Moriyama" are especially valued.

**References:** Mary Frank Gaston, *Blue Willow*, 2nd ed., Collector Books, 1990, 2000 value update; Jennifer A. Lindbeck, *A Collector's Guide to Willow Ware,* Schiffer Publishing, 2000.

**Periodicals:** *American Willow Report*, P.O. Box 900, Oakridge, OR 97463; *The Willow Transfer Quarterly, Willow Word*, P.O. Box 13382, Arlington, TX 76094.

**Collectors' Clubs:** International Willow Collectors, P.O. Box 13382, Arlington, TX 76094-0382; Willow Society, 39 Medhurst Rd, Toronto Ontario M4B 1B2 Canada.

**Note:** Although colors other than blue are hard to find, there is less demand; thus, prices may not necessarily be higher priced.

Berry Bowl, 5-3/4" d, mkd "Japan" ................................................8.00
Bone Dish, 6-1/4" l, pink, Bailey Walker........................................20.00
Bowl
    4" d, mkd "Societe Ceramique Willow" ................................60.00
    5-1/4" d, mkd "Allerton"".........................................................10.00
    9" d, mkd "Royal" ....................................................................20.00
Butter Dish, cov, mkd "Societe Ceramique Willow"......................90.00
Butter Pat, 3" sq, mkd "Booth's Real Old Willow" .........................25.00
Cake Plate, pierced sides ............................................................65.00
Children's Dishes
    Dinner Service, four plates, cups and saucers, creamer, cov sugar, cov teapot, platter, cov casserole, gravy boat, mkd "Japan"...........................................................................295.00
    Tea Set, mkd "Occupied Japan," price for 18 pc set...........375.00
Creamer, mkd "J. & G. Meakin" ....................................................30.00
Cream Soup, 5" w, red, mkd "Swinnertons," c1930 .....................30.00
Cup and Saucer
    Mkd "Adams".........................................................................25.00
    Mkd "J. & G. Meakin"............................................................20.00
    Mkd "Japan"...........................................................................25.00
    Mkd "Royal China" ................................................................15.00
Demitasse Cup and Saucer, mkd "Allerton"..................................15.00
Egg Cup, 3-3/4" h, mkd "Japan," price for set of six ...................145.00
Fish Platter, 12" l, 11-1/2" w, dated 1886, mkd "Minton" ............650.00
Fruit Bowl, mkd "J. & G. Meakin" ..................................................10.00
Gravy Boat, mkd "J. & G. Meakin" .................................................30.00
Hot Water Plate, 11-1/2" w, mkd "Semi-China Warranted," c1830...475.00
Jardiniere, 6-1/4" h, 8" d, horizontal ribbing, brown transfer, yellow glaze..................................................................................400.00
Jug, 6" h, octagonal, blue, serpent handle, Mason's crown mark with "Patent Ironstone China" ...........................................................360.00
Mug, 4" h, mkd "Doulton" ..............................................................95.00
Mustard Pot, cov, 3" h, unmarked, few rough edge spots...........110.00
Oil Lamp, 8-1/2" d, blue and white ceramic base, 1950s.............85.00

**Egg Cup, mkd "Made in Japan," 2-1/4" h, $17.50.**

**Gravy Boat, Buffalo Pottery, dated 1911, $55.**

Pepper Toby, 5" h, orig lid, red jacket, yellow breeches .............. 625.00
Pitcher, 8-1/2" h, mkd "Willow England" ..................................... 140.00
Plate
    5-3/4" d, mkd "Allerton" ............................................................ 9.50
    6" d, green, mkd "Royal Venton Ware" ................................. 15.00
    8-1/2" d, black, mkd "Royal Albert Mikado," 1920s, crack .... 75.00
    8-1/2" d, ivory ground, scalloped edge, light brown daisy border, blue allover willow pattern, gold bands on edge and base of border .................................................................................. 65.00
    9" d, pink, mkd "Allerton" ...................................................... 10.00
    10" d, blue, Two Temples pattern, butterfly border, mkd "W. T. Copeland" ........................................................................... 40.00
    10" d, red, mkd "Johnson Brothers" ..................................... 25.00
    10-1/2" d, grill, mkd "Moriyama" .......................................... 48.00
Platter
    12" d, round, mkd "Royal China" .......................................... 25.00
    12" l, 9" w, red, mkd "Royal Venton Ware, John Steventon & Sons, Ltd." ........................................................................... 50.00
    12-1/4" l, mkd "J. & G. Meakin" ........................................... 35.00
    13" d, round, mkd "Allerton" ................................................. 95.00
    14" l, mkd "J. & G. Meakin" .................................................. 65.00
    14" l, 9" w, mkd "Allerton" ................................................... 125.00
    16" l, 12-1/2" w, mkd "Warranted Staffordshire" .................. 225.00
    16-3/4" l, 12" d, black white, mkd "M & T Co.," slight nick .. 250.00
    18" l, mkd "Allerton" ........................................................... 150.00
    19" l, 14-1/2" w, mkd "Copeland" ........................................ 200.00
    20" l, English ...................................................................... 200.00
Pudding Mold, 5-3/4" d ............................................................... 60.00
Relish Dish, 11" l, divided into three sections, mkd "Booth," c1906 ...................................................................................... 275.00
Sauce Boat with Underplate, 14" l ............................................. 115.00
Soup Plate, 7-3/4" d, mkd "J. & G. Meakin" ................................. 25.00
Sugar, cov, mkd "J. & G. Meakin" ............................................... 35.00
Teapot, cov
    Blue, 5" h, mkd "Sadler, England" ....................................... 100.00
    Pink, mkd "Royal" ................................................................. 45.00
Tile, 8" sq, mkd "Steele & Wood" ............................................... 145.00
Toothpick Holder, 1-3/4" h, border at top, English ....................... 45.00
Tray, 17-1/4" l, rect, cut corners, blue, gilt rim, mkd "Wedgwood" ..... 315.00
Tumbler, 5-1/8" h ........................................................................ 30.00
Vegetable Bowl, cov, round, mkd "J. & G. Meakin" ..................... 75.00
Vegetable Bowl, open, round, mkd "J. & G. Meakin" ................... 65.00

# WOODENWARE

**History:** Many utilitarian household objects and farm implements were made of wood. Although they were subjected to heavy use, these implements were made of the strongest woods and were well cared for by their owners.

**References:** Arene Burgess, *19th Century Wooden Boxes,* Schiffer Publishing, 1997; Jonathon Levi and Robert Young, *Treen for the Table,* John Campbell, *Fire & Light in the Home Pre 1820,* Antique Collectors' Club, 1999; George C. Neumann, *Early American Antique*

*Country Furnishing,* L-W Book Sales, 1984, 1993 reprint.

**Additional Listings:** See *Warman's Americana & Collectibles* for more examples.

**Note:** This category serves as a catchall for wooden objects which do not fit into other categories.

Apple Box, 71/2" x 7-1/2" x 3-1/4" h, old worn salmon red paint, laced panels in sides and bottom ..................................................... 275.00
Band Organ Figure, 31" h, carved and painted, British officer, articulated arm, blue and white uniform, shako with red plume, black boots, orig paint, late-19th C, loss to base, paint loss ..................... 5,750.00
Barber Pole, 76" h, well turned, red and white repaint, filled age cracks and chips, on base, tin top cover, early .............................. 550.00
Bowl, cov, 5-3/4" d, 4-1/2" h, burl, ash, good figure, mellow finish, turned foot and ring around side, domed top with finial, ext. crack in bottom ....................................................................................... 1,650.00
Bowl, burl
    14" d, 4-1/2" h, ash, old soft patina ................................. 1,430.00
    21" d, 8-1/2" h, ash, scrubbed finish, two age cracks, old putty repair, wear from use .................................................... 1,650.00
Box, cov
    3-7/8" w, 2-1/2" d, 1-5/8" h, carved burl, old varnish finish, made from one piece of wood, hinged lid, brass closure, relief rococo border on lid with initials "S. K." and shells, incised lines and relief border on front, Greek key design on sides, bottom initialed "F.G.S.R." ...................................................................... 330.00
    5-5/8" d, bentwood, round, old dark reddish brown paint, dark yellow striping and label "Rice," some edge damage .......................... 330.00
Bucket, 14-1/4" h, painted blue-green, stave and lapped wooden band construction, curved swing handle with pegged joinery, America, 19th C ............................................................................................... 1,150.00
Butter Churn, 47-1/4" h, stave and wooden band construction, dasher and lid, painted gray-green, America, 19th C, wear, minor paint loss ... 435.00
Churn, cov, 14-1/2" w, 13-3/8" d, 24" y, poplar and ash, black circle graining on red ground, white striping, stenciled labels "E. H. Funks, Champion Churn, Sturgis, Mich," 1868 patent, missing dasher .............. 770.00
Cribbage Board, 5" w, 15" l, mahogany and beech, inlaid geometric designs on case and top, one dovetailed drawer, three mismatched metal pins ................................................................................... 275.00
Document Box, 16" l, 8" d, 7" h, rect, Tunbridge marquetry, Chevrons pattern, int. lined in later cobalt blue velvet, Edwardian, c1900 .......... 200.00
Keg, 7-1/4" h, 10" d, stave construction, old reddish brown paint .... 115.00
Knife Box, 12" w, 8" d, 5-1/2" h, pine, very worn orig brown grained dec, canted sides, pierced opening for handle, sq nail construction ..... 250.00
Niddy-Noddy, 17-1/2" l, 14-1/4" w, carved walnut, detailed chip carved dec, initialed "O.P.," dated 1798, small age splits .................... 420.00

**Sugar Bucket, painted, mkd "C. S. Hershey," 9" h, 9-1/2" d, $165.**

Noah's Ark, 18-1/2" l, Converse, orig polychrome screened dec with label, thirteen animals and assortment of various wooden blocks, some damage .................................................................385.00

Pantry Box, cov, 9" d, bentwood, hardwood and pine, lapped seams, compass star and heart piercings, steel and copper tacks, old patina, few breaks and age cracks ......................................770.00

Peg Board, 59-1/2" l, pine, old dark worn finish, beaded edges, nine turned pegs .........................................................................440.00

Pipe Rack, carved mahogany, farm gate frame, fitted to hold seven pipes, Edwardian, c1900-10.......................................45.00

Sign, 21-1/2" d, 17-1/4" h, oval, both sides depicting eagle in black holding banner with "2190 Main St" in mustard and red on black, whole on mustard colored ground, red and black border with gilt stars, America, late-19th/early-20th C, paint wear ....................435.00

Spice Box, 9-1/4" d, bent wood, round, eight matching canisters, orig varnish finish, tin edge bands, black stenciled labels, imp label with patent date and "Made in New Jersey" ...................................440.00

Spoon, 8" l, carved pierced handle, carved hook on shallow bowl, America, 19th C, age crack.......................................................550.00

Spoon Rack, 17-1/4" h, 8-3/4" w, ash, old red repaint, arched top with cornice, scalloped center section, three pierced racks for spoons, scalloped base, rose head nails.............................................660.00

Storage Box, 11-1/2" d, 7-3/4" h, round, worn orig yellow paint with polychrome stenciled bird and flowers, matching lid with handle, wear, fading to dec, age cracks............................................1,760.00

Watch Hutch
  7-1/8" h, 4-1/2" w, 2-1/2" d, America, 19th C, carved and red painted, carved scalloped crest above case with pierced hanger, glazed door, with Georgian silver pair cased verge pocket watch with fusee movement, sgd "G. Mowlsworth, London," bull's eye crystal and enamel dial, imperfections......................................1,380.00
  12" h, 7-1/2" w, 5-5/8" d, hanging, pine with worn orig bittersweet paint, shaped crest with sq nail and screw construction, beveled base and top with one pane of glass in door.................1,320.00

Wine Cooler, 29-1/2" h, George III, England, c1700, brass bound mahogany, bell form top, cylindrical body, tripod base, brass paw casters............................................................................900.00

# WORLD'S FAIRS and EXPOSITIONS

**History:** The Great Exhibition of 1851 in London marked the beginning of the World's Fair and Exposition movement. The fairs generally featured exhibitions from nations around the world displaying the best of their industrial and scientific achievements.

Many important technological advances have been introduced at world's fairs, including the airplane, telephone, and electric lights. Ice cream cones, hot dogs, and iced tea were first sold by vendors at fairs. Art movements often were closely connected to fairs, with the Paris Exhibition of 1900 generally considered to have assembled the best of the works of the Art Nouveau artists.

**References:** *Crystal Palace Exhibition Illustrated Catalogue* (London, 1851), Dover Publications, n.d.; Robert L. Hendershott, *1904 St Louis World's Fair Mementos and Memorabilia*, Kurt R. Krueger Publishing (160 N. Washington, Iola, WI 54945), 1994; Joyce Grant, *NY World's Fair Collectibles: 1964-1965*, Schiffer Publishing, 1999; Frederick and Mary Megson, *American Exposition Postcards*, The Postcard Lovers, 1992; Howard M. Rossen, *World's Fair Collectibles: Chicago, 1933 and New York 1939*, Schiffer Publishing, 1998.

Mug, salt glazed, "World's Fair Chicago 1893," deep impressions, blue accents, attributed to Whites, Utica, NY, factory, 1-1/2" hairline extending from rim on left, 1" hairline extending from rim on right, 4-3/4" h, $525. Photo courtesy of Vicki & Bruce Waasdrop.

**Collectors' Clubs:** 1904 World's Fair Society, 12934 Windy Hill Drive, St. Louis, MO 63128, http://www.inlink.com/~terryl; World's Fair Collectors' Society, Inc., P.O. Box 20806, Sarasota, FL 34276.

**Museums:** Buffalo & Erie County Historical Society, Buffalo, NY; California State University, Madden Library, Fresno, CA; 1893 Chicago World's Fair Columbian Exposition Museum, Columbus, WI; Museum of Science & Industry, Chicago, IL; Presidio Army Museum, San Francisco, CA; The Queens Museum, Flushing, NY.

## 1876, Centennial Exposition, Philadelphia

Paperweight, glass, exposition buildings ......................................90.00

Textile, 19" h, 25-1/2" l, printed in black and red, "Memorial Hall Art Gallery, Centennial 1776-1876," age stains, some purple stains..........90.00

Ticket, United States International Exhibition Package, 3-7/8" x 2-3/8", minor edge discoloration ..............................................30.00

## 1893, Columbian Exposition, Chicago

Advertising Trade Card
  Halveda Milk, evaporated milk and other milk products, fold-out type ...................................................................................50.00
  McLaughlin's Coffee, "Opening of World's Fair," President Cleveland's picture on lower right corner, 7" x 5-1/4" .................45.00

Badge, red, white and blue ribbon, eagle and hanging token, one side "World's Columbian Exposition Souvenir, Chicago, IL, 1892-93," other side with illus of Administration Building ...........................85.00

Bank, 4-1/2" h, salt glaze, globe shape, relief, blue accents "World's Fair My Expenses to Chicago, pat Applied for," central relief design of train and track with blue accents, attributed to Whites, Utica, NY, factory ...................................................................3,750.00

Bell, 4-1/2" h, cut glass
  Engraved "Worlds Fair 1893," emb "Columbia Exposition 1893 World's Fair" on inside of bell...........................................125.00
  Swirl frosted handle, mkd "The World's Columbian Exposition 1893"...............................................................................125.00

Book
  *Artistic Guide to Chicago and the World's Columbian Exposition*, Charles E. Banks, illus, hard bound ................................110.00
  *In Remembrance of the World's Columbian Exposition*, Chicago, Zum Andenken-En Memoire, 1893, 5" x 6", red, hard bound, illus of buildings.................................................................45.00
  *Official Guide of the World's Columbian Exposition*, compiled by J. Flinn, illus, soft bound, dark maroon cov........................40.00
  *World's Columbian Exposition at Chicago 1492-1892*, 1893, hard bound, drawings illus, red, 6-1/4" x 9-1/2"........................55.00
  *World's Columbian Fair*, Chicago, red, hard bound, illus, 7" x 5" ..........................................................................30.00
  *World's Columbian Fair*, Chicago, 1893, 9" x 5-1/2", tan, black, and gold, pictures of buildings, worn...............................35.00

Booklet
  ""White City by Lake Michigan," Albertype, black and white photos of buildings .................................................................35.00
  "World's Fair and Midway Scenes," midway scenes, Government Bldg., German Bldg., Old Vienna, German Exhibit, etc. .......6.00

"World's Fair Souvenir," given out by "Eric Preserving Co., Finest Canned Goods, Buffalo, N. Y., U.S.A.," green cover, pictures of fair, 6-1/4" x 3-1/2" ............ 40.00

Bookmark, woven, 10" l, The Star Spangled Banner, woven on the Exposition Grounds by Phoenix Manufacturing, tassel, mounted on orig paper backing, 6" x 20" walnut frame ............... 200.00

Bottle, pottery, pig shaped, 7-1/4" l, incised "From the World's Fair/ With a little good Old Rye in 1893/ Cut Rates/ To All Points East," Kirkpatrick Bros., Anna, IL ............ 1,760.00

Bowl, 8-1/2" d, porcelain, sq shape, Machinery Bldg and Electric Bldg on inside ............ 100.00

Cream Pitcher, 2-1/2" h, blue satin glass, made and dec by Mount Washington Glass Co., sgd "1893 World's Fair" ............ 435.00

Glass, 3" h
    Etched Art Palace and lake ............ 75.00
    Etched flowers and M.B.F., other side "World's Fair 1893" ... 75.00

Hatchet, 8" l, solid gold glass, etched "1893 World's Fair," Libbey ...275.00

Mug, 4-3/4" h, salt glazed, "World's Fair Chicago 1893," deep impressions, blue accents, attributed to Whites, Utica, NY, factory, 1-1/2" hairline extending from rim on left, 1" hairline extending from rim on right ............ 525.00

Paperweight, rect, colorful, Machinery Hall, dated ............ 35.00

Pin, 2-1/2" x 1-3/4", Queen's head in foreground, sailing masts in background ............ 65.00

Pin Box, cov, 1-1/2" x 1/4", Columbian Souvenir 1492-1892, silver finished metal, Columbus landing on cov ............ 100.00

Plaque, 23" h, 24" w, bronzed three-dimensional plaster relief bust of Shitting Bull, detailed face and head dress, sgd under shoulder, gold lined dec wood frame, attributed to Rupert Schmid ............ 900.00

Pocket Mirror, Model Ranges and Heaters, Providence, RI, World's Best at World's Fair, Chicago, Il, 1893, Sicer Stove Co. ............ 50.00

Token, metal
    Columbus on one side, other with three presidents, ring for chain ............ 45.00
    Columbus on one side, other with building and "World's Fair, Chicago, 1893," ring for chain ............ 15.00
    "Souvenir of World's Columbian Exposition" around edges, info about Chicago in center, other side picture of Landing of Columbus ............ 18.00
    "World's Columbian Exposition," given out at the U.S. Treasury Dept. Exhibit, 1893, dollar size ............ 25.00

Watch Fob
    "Compliments of the Keystone Watch Case Co.," figural ...... 35.00
    "World's Columbian Exposition Chicago 1893," Columbus landing on one side, other "Chicago 1893," small chain with three small squares with saying on one side, illus on other ............ 85.00

**1899, Omaha Exposition,** toothpick holder, Colorado pattern, etched "Omaha Expo, 1899" ............ 35.00

## 1901, Pan American Exposition, Buffalo

Bookmark, celluloid, pansy at the top, "Souvenir," fair emblem, "Libby, McNeill & Libby, Chicago," list of food products on back ............ 55.00

Button, 2" w, "Northwestern Consolidated Milling Co.'s Pan-American Souvenir, Cresota Flour, Standard of Excellence" ............ 48.00

Card, 2" x 3-1/2", metal, City Hotel, back with illus of fair, "Pan-American Exposition, Buffalo, 1901, Temple of Music," where President McKinley was shown, Sep 6-died Sep 14th, 1901 ............ 50.00

Letter Opening, gold washed white metal, detailed figural buffalo at top, 9" l ............ 95.00

Mug, 6-1/2" h, Bristol glazed stoneware, pewter top, imp, blue accents "Pan American Exposition, 1901, Buffalo, NY, U.S.A.," relief and blue accented tavern scene on opposite side, base imp "Whites Pottery Utica, NY" ............ 365.00

Paperweight
    Rect, Fine Arts Building, black and white ............ 65.00
    Rect, "I was at [buffalo] in 1901," black and white ............ 95.00
    Rect, 2-1/2" x 4", glass, photograph of Temple of Music, Electric Tower and Administration Building, small hole in center of photo ............ 80.00

Round, "I was at [buffalo] in 1901," multicolored, made by Empire Art Co. ............ 95.00

Playing Cards, "Official Pan-American Exposition Souvenir Playing Cards," different fair scenes ............ 95.00

Ticket, Buffalo Day, Oct 19, used ............ 25.00

Token, 1-3/4" d, man standing in clouds, one leg bent, resting on another cloud, reaching above his head, wearing hat with sunrays, back with fair emblem, name, and date ............ 25.00

Tray
    Oval, metal, flowers and birds border, Electricity Building in center, back "Electricity Building at Buffalo, U.S.A., 1901," tarnished ............ 28.00
    Oval, metal, flowers and birds border, U. S. Government Building in center, back "U. S. Government Building at Buffalo, U.S.A. 1901," tarnished ............ 28.00
    Round, 3" d, ornate border, center globe and banner "Niagara Falls, Pan-American Exposition 1901," silvered colored metal ........ 48.00
    Round, 4" d, flowers and scroll work edges, "1901 Pan American [buffalo] Exposition, Buffalo," brass ............ 65.00

## 1904, Louisiana Purchase Exposition, St. Louis

Calendar, Coca-Cola, 1909 ............ 8,050.00

Card, signed by Geronimo, pencil annotations of orig owner .. 3,300.00

Creamer, glass, colorless, Star of David pattern, ruby stained top, etched "World's Fair St. Louis, 1904" ............ 130.00

Fan, Keen Kutter Kuttlery advertisement ............ 50.00

Plate, clear, open edge, gold center dec ............ 50.00

Salt and Pepper Shakers, pr, opaque white ground, Palace of the Liberal Arts dec, 2-1/2" h ............ 175.00

Serving Tray, tin, oval, young woman enjoying Coca-Cola ............ 3,450.00

Stereo Cards, curved card
    Canadian Exhibition Agricultural Building, Replica in Wheat of the Parliament Library at Ottawa, H.C. White Co. ............ 20.00
    Electricity Building, lithographed ............ 10.00
    Festival Hall from Cascade Gardens H. C. White ............ 15.00
    Grace and Beauty, Italian Section, B.W. Kilburn ............ 15.00
    Tip tray, illus of Festival Hall and Cascades, 3-1/4" h, 5" l .... 80.00

Tray, 12" d, Duesseldorfer Beer, baby sucking on bottle of beer, titled "Grand Prize Winners," St. Louis 1904 World's Fair, Chas. W. Shonk Co. litho, rim chips, come overall crazing ............ 500.00

## 1905, Lewis & Clark Centennial

Match safe, 2-3/4" h, plated metal with insert, "The Lewis & Clark Centennial, Portland, Oregon, 1905," reverse "Forrestry Building, Lewis and Clark Exposition," minor wear ............ 145.00

## 1915, Panama Exposition, San Francisco

Bell, metal, bear on Oriental gate, mkd "1915 Panama Exposition" on one side of gate, "1915 San Francisco, Los Angeles, San Diego" on other side, bell mkd "1761, El Camino Real," stamped "Pat. Apld For".... 75.00

Sample Bag, Sperry's Flour, 3" l, 1" d, 2" h ............ 50.00

Tip Tray, Buffalo Brewing Co., children of the world paying homage to Italy, 4-1/4" d ............ 175.00

Tray, Buffalo Brewing Co., titled "San Francisco Exhibition 1915 The Nations Paying Homage to San Francisco," children of the world paying homage to Italy, Kaufmann & Strauss Co. litho, 12" d, overall soiling, rim chips ............ 225.00

## 1933, Century of Progress Chicago, 1933

Bank, 4" h, wood, barrel, circular removable tin coin slot, burnt brown lettering ............ 40.00

Bottle, 6" h, 6" d, glass, colorless, GM Building in center, log cabin, teepee ............ 45.00

Compact, 2" d, silvered metal, white enamel accents ............ 50.00

Plate, china, blue ground, Science Hall scene, Pickard ............ 25.00

Thermometer, 5-1/4" x 7-1/4", glass, Golden Temple of Jehol by Night, brass frame, hanging cord ............ 40.00

Tray, copper, rect, engraved dec ............ 95.00

# YARD-LONG PRINTS

**History:** In the early 1900s, many yard-long prints could be had for a few cents postage and a given number of wrappers or box tops. Others were premiums for renewing a subscription to a magazine or newspaper. A large number was advertising items created for a store or company and had calendars on the front or back. Many people believe that the only true yard-long print is 36 inches long and titled, "A Yard of Kittens," etc. But lately collectors feel that any long and narrow print, horizontal or vertical, can be included in this category. It is a matter of personal opinion.

Values are listed for full-length prints in near-mint condition, nicely framed, and with original glass.

**References:** C. G. and J. M. Rhoden and W. D. and M. J. Keagy, *Those Wonderful Yard-Long Prints and More*, Book 1 (1989), Book 2 (1992), Book 3 (1995), published by authors (605 No. Main, Georgetown, IL 61846).

**Reproduction Alert:** Some prints are being reproduced. Know your dealer.

**Advisors:** Charles G. and Joan M. Rhoden, W. D. and M. J. Keagy.

**Note:** Numbers in parentheses below indicate the Rhoden and Keagy book number and page on which the item is illustrated, e.g. (3-52) refers to Book 3, page 52.

**Pompeian, lady in pink dress, blue ribbon in hair, blue flower at bosom, seated in front of fireplace with handsome young man, date 1914 and info on back (BK 1-22), $350. Photo courtesy of Joan Rhoden.**

## Animals

A Yard of Kittens, sgd Guy Bedford (BK 1-50)............................450.00
Piggies in Clover, by The Art Interchange Co., New York, copyright 1904, (BK 3-25)........................................................800.00
Yard of Chickens, sgd C. L. VanVredenburgh, by J. Onmann Lith. Co., N.Y., copyright 1905 (BK 2-19)...............................................400.00
Yard of Puppies by Guy Bedford, Chicago (BK 2-26) ................375.00

## Calendar

1910 American Beauty Souvenir Clay, Robinson & Co., calendar and advertising at bottom, also advertising on back (BK 3-44).......550.00
1911 Pompeian Beauty by Forbes, calendar and advertising on back (BK 2-78)....................................................................450.00
1917 dark haired lady with left hand entwined in the pearls around her neck and pink roses at her waist, calendar on back (BK 2-90) 400.00
1918 Selz Good Shoes, copyright Selz, Schwab & Co., lady in black dress, long stem pink rose in right hand (BK 2-83) .................500.00
1921 Fairbanks and Morse Quality 100% on logo at left, lady in sleeveless dark blue dress, light yellow shawl around arms, calendar and advertising at bottom (BK 3-49) ..............................................550.00
1924 John Clay & Company Live Stock Commission by Frank H. Desch, lady sitting on porch railing with hat in right hand and umbrella across lap, calendar at bottom, advertising on front and back (BK 3-52) .......................................................................550.00

## Flowers and Fruits

A Shower of Pansies by Muller Lutchsinge & Co., N.Y., copyright 1895 (BK 2-41)..................................................................300.00
A Yard of Chrysanthemums by Maud Stumm (BK 2-33) ...........300.00
Carnations by Grace Barton Allen, basket of red carnations (BK 2-30).....................................................................250.00
Water Lilies by R. LeRoy, yellow bowl with white and yellow water lilies (BK 3-38).....................................................................350.00
Yard of Cherries and Flowers by LeRoy (BK 2-70)....................300.00

## Long Ladies

Alluring, Pompeian Art Panel, sgd Bradshaw Krandall, advertising on back (BK 2-99) .........................................................300.00
Barbara, 1912, sgd C. Allan Gilbert, by Brown and Bigelowe, St. Paul, USA and Sault Ste. Marie, Ont., lady in purple dress arranging yellow roses (BK 2-93) ..........................................................450.00
Beatrice, by J. Baumgarth Co. Chicago, advertising "Belle of Drexel," Chicago's best 5 cent cigar, copyright 1911 (BK 3-41)............550.00
Indian Maiden in native attire, bowl of flowers in left hand, right hand at neck holding braids, river and trees in background (BK 3-89) .450.00
Liberty Girl, Pompeian Beauty, by Forbes, verse by Daniel M. Henderson, date 1919 and information on back (BK 1-28)..................400.00
Lovely lady in floppy hat, seated on bench with dog at side, sgd H. Dirch, "The Clay, Robinson & Co. Army of Employees" shown on back (BK 2-91) ..........................................................400.00
The Stockman Bride, 1912 National Stockman & Farmer Magazine. bride in wedding dress, advertising on back (BK 1-12)............550.00

# YELLOWWARE

**History:** Yellowware is a heavy earthenware which varies in color from a rich pumpkin to lighter shades, which are more tan than yellow. The weight and strength varies from piece to piece. Although plates, nappies, and custard cups are found, kitchen bowls and other cooking utensils are most prevalent.

The first American yellowware was produced at Bennington, Vermont. English yellowware has additional ingredients which make its body much harder. Derbyshire and Sharp's were foremost among the English manufacturers.

**References:** Susan and Al Bagdade, *Warman's American Pottery and Porcelain*, 2<sup>nd</sup> ed., Krause Publications,

**Butter Crock, cov, off-white and dark brown accent bands, matching orig lid, few tight hairlines extending from rim, 4-3/4" h, $220. Photo courtesy of Vicki & Bruce Waasdrop.**

2000; William C. Ketchum, Jr., *American Pottery and Porcelain*, Avon Books, 1994; Joan Leibowitz, *Yellow Ware*, Schiffer Publishing, 1985, 1993 value update; Lisa S. McAllister, *Collector's Guide to Yellow Ware*, Collector Books, 1996, 2000 value update; Lisa S. McAllister and John L. Michael, *Collecting Yellow Ware*, Collector Books, 1993.

Bank, 3-1/2" x 6", figural pig, brown and green sponging, pierced eyes, coin slot on top .......................................................... 215.00
Bowl
    9" d, 4" h, blue sponge dec inside and out, rim glaze wear from use, minor staining and glaze crazing ................................ 50.00
    10-1/2" h, 4-1/4" h, relief petal design with dots, Rockingham glaze, one very minor surface chip at rim, other glaze flake spots ............................................................................. 80.00
    14" d, 6-1/2" h, two slip blue accent bands, blue mocha designs all around on cream white background, c1870, overall age crazing to glaze .................................................................... 470.00
    14-1/2" d, 6-1/2" h, base stamped "USA," c1890 ................. 70.00
Butter Crock, cov, 4-3/4" h, off-white and dark brown accent bands, conforming dec lid, few extremely tight hairlines extending from rim, some glaze crazing around base ............................................. 220.00
Colander
    9-1/4" d, 4" h, relief diamond pattern at rim, relief panels and diamonds around body, white Bristol glaze int. ...................... 250.00
    12" d, 5-1/4" h, applied cream colored Bristol glaze, ext. with relief arch panel design, full length hairline extending from rim 180.00
Creamer, 3-3/4" h, mottled Rockingham glaze, pin head size glaze flake at rim ............................................................................. 80.00
Custard Cup
    2-1/4" h, Rockingham glaze, c1900, set of nine, three with short hairlines ............................................................................. 90.00
    2-3/4" h, light brown Rockingham glaze, c1870 .................... 20.00

Deep Dish
    9-1/2" d, 3" h, Rockingham glaze, bottom imp "195," overall glaze crazing, short hairline from rim ......................................... 60.00
    10-1/2" d, 3-1/2" h, relief column and dot design around rim, Rockingham glaze, bottom imp "195," c1860, overall glaze crazing, couple of short hairlines extending from rim ............... 70.00
Dish, cov, 5" x 8", Rockingham glaze, c1910 ............................... 80.00
Food Warmer, 13-1/2" l, 6-1/2" d, 3-3/4" h, green and brown mottled glaze, attributed to Morton Pottery Factory, imp "Pat. Apl. For The Jiffy Product Company," c1930, few breaks along scalloped edge ................... 110.00
Inkwell, 5-1/2" l, Rockingham glaze, c1880, attributed to Bennington, surface rim chip ...................................................................... 250.00
Miniature
    Chamber Pot, 2" h, slip white accent stripe, underglaze brown lettering "Wild Water Sport, Pan American 1901," in the making rim chip ............................................................................. 220.00
    Pitcher, 3" h, chicken wire sponging in brown and green ........ 225.00
Mixing Bowl, 14" d, 7" h, one light blue and two white accent bands, base imp "Wattware," minor crazing to ext. glaze, 4" tight hairline extending from rim ................................................................... 50.00
Nappie, 14" d, 3-1/2" h, four molded relief lines, c1850, few minor mold imperfections in the making ................................................... 110.00
Pie Plate
    9-1/2" d, 1-1/2" h, c1850, some staining from use ............... 45.00
    12" d, 1-3/4" h, c1850, some staining from use .................. 200.00
Pitcher
    3" h, figural, smiling man's face, Rockingham glaze, late 19th C .............................................................................. 65.00
    5" h, relief tulip design, Rockingham glaze, c1890 ............. 125.00
    7" h, relief swag design at shoulder, c1800, one minor stone ping and some surface roughness around base ...................... 100.00
    7-1/4" h, relief pillar and scroll design, mottled Rockingham glaze .............................................................................. 70.00
    8" h, relief grapes design, overall green glaze ..................... 60.00
    8-1/2" h, relief barrel design, Rockingham glaze, c1900 ...... 90.00
    9-1/4" h, relief lattice design, brown and green sponging, some chipping at spout, minor surface chips .............................. 90.00
    9-3/4" h, relief hunting dogs and deer design, applied hound handle, relief grapes and vine design around top half, Rockingham glaze, attributed to American Pottery Co., Jersey City, c1860 ......... 550.00
Toby Pitcher, 6" h, Rockingham glaze, c1880 ............................ 115.00
Washboard, 12" w, 22" h, yellow and brown Rockingham glaze, wood frame with overall wear from use, attributed to East Liverpool, OH, area, c1870 ......................................................................... 650.00
Waste Jar, cov, 10" h, relief scroll design at top with gilt trim, blue sponge dec, 3" very tight hairline extending from rim ............... 90.00

# ZANE POTTERY

**History:** In 1921, Adam Reed and Harry McClelland bought the Peters and Reed Pottery in Zanesville, Ohio. The firm continued production of garden wares and introduced several new art lines: Sheen, Powder Blue, Crystalline, and Drip. The factory was sold in 1941 to Lawton Gonder.

**Reference:** Jeffrey, Sherrie, and Barry Hersone, *Peters and Reed and Zane Pottery Experience*, published by authors, 1990.

**Additional Listings:** Gonder; Peters and Reed.

Bowl, 5" d, brown and blue ..............................................50.00
Figure, 10-1/8" h, black cat, green eyes ...................... 600.00
Jardiniere, 14-1/2" h, variegated green semi-matte glaze, two handles, Montene ............................................................165.00
Lamp, 11-1/2" h, 5-1/2" w, white ground, green and rust drip .....500.00
Vase
    8" h, ivory glaze, molded roses, foliage, long stems with thorns, cylindrical with flared top .................................125.00
    9" h, yellow, green, and black drip over brown ...................150.00
    10" h, red clay .........................................................275.00
    10-1/2" h, peach dec................................................60.00
    12" h, black, yellow, green, and brown drip over rust .........210.00
    12" h, Persian blue..................................................275.00
    12" h, Shadow Blue, gray semi-matte glaze, bulbous ........115.00
    18" h, molded grapes, tan matte.......................................125.00

# ZANESVILLE POTTERY

**LA MORO**

**History:** Zanesville Art Pottery, one of several potteries located in Zanesville, Ohio, began production in 1900. At first, a line of utilitarian products was made; art pottery was introduced shortly thereafter. The major line was La Moro, which was hand painted and decorated under glaze. The firm was bought by S. A. Weller in 1920 and became known as Weller Plant No. 3.

**Marks:** The impressed block-print mark "La Moro" appears on the high-glazed and matte-glazed decorated ware.

**References:** Louise and Evan Purviance and Norris F. Schneider, *Zanesville Art Pottery in Color*, Mid-America Book Company, 1968; Evan and Louise Purviance, *Zanesville Art Tile in Color*, Wallace-Homestead, 1972, out-of-print.

Bowl
    5-1/2" d, 2-1/4" h, emb floral design between four buttressed handles, brown glazed int. ...............................165.00
    6-1/2" d, mottled blue, fluted edge.................................45.00
Jardiniere, 9" h, brown and gold glaze.............................140.00
Paperweight, A. E. Tiling Co., Ltd., 1896, calendar on back.........40.00
Tankard, floral dec, artist sgd..........................................320.00
Tile, elk, needlepoint-type technique, "Mosaic" in oval, round circle mark, set of sixteen .....................................300.00
Vase
    7-1/2" h, 7" w, white, molded peony dec, classical shape.....75.00
    8-3/4" h, cone top and neck, bulbous base, two handles, La Moro 375.00
    9" d, matte green glaze, cylindrical, fan flare to top ...........200.00
Wine Decanter, figural, monk..........................................85.00

# ZSOLNAY POTTERY

**History:** Vilmos Zsolnay (1828-1900) assumed control of his brother's factory in Pécs, Hungary, in the mid-19th century. In 1899, Miklos, Vilmos' son, became manager. The firm still produces ceramic ware. The early wares are highly ornamental, glazed, and have a cream-colored ground. Eosin glaze, a deep rich play of colors reminiscent of Tiffany's iridescent wares, received a gold medal at the 1900 Paris exhibition. Zsolnay Art Nouveau pieces show great creativity.

**Reference:** Susan and Al Bagdade, *Warman's English & Continental Pottery & Porcelain*, Third Edition, Krause Publications, 1998; Federico Santi and John Gacher, *Zsolnay Ceramics: Collecting a Culture*, Schiffer Publishing, 1998.

**Marks:** Originally, no trademark was used; but in 1878 the company began to use a blue mark depicting the five towers of the cathedral at Pécs. The initials "TJM" represent the names of Miklos' three children.

**Note:** Zsolnay's recent series of iridescent glazed figurines, which initially were inexpensive, now are being sought by collectors and are steadily increasing in value.

Bowl
    6" d, multicolored floral pattern, gold trim ..........................150.00
    6-1/2" w, 2-1/4" h, shell shape, hp, floral dec, gold highlights and edging, blue Zolsnay Pecs mark, castle mark, "Patent" over top, imp factory mark, form #2004, incised "27," gold painted "71," underglaze crazing, some darkening of cream ground at base .........................................................150.00
    7-1/2" h, 5" h, fully reticulated, flower and leaf dec, steel blue, rust, yellow, and pink, 4 feet..............................................260.00
Box, cov, 4" l, 3" d, 4" h, domed trunk shape, Old Ivory dec, incised form #2688, mkd "Zsolnay Pecs," additional incised numbers, minor edge flakes........................................................................300.00
Cachepot
    4-1/2" h, 5" d, metallic eosin glaze, high style Secession design, form #5897, c1900, round raised trademark, minor glaze flakes.......................................................950.00
    6-3/4" h, multicolored courting couple in landscape scene, incised "ZW Pecs," hp blue steeple mark, c1880, Armin Klein artist .......................................................1,650.00
    8" d, Titiana theme, walking through birch tree forest followed by deer, full moon, form #8389, c1910, designed by Sandor Pillo Hidasy, sgd and dated.......................................7,500.00
    13" d, young girls dancing around stylized tree, Labrador blue, pale silver, and pale lilac glaze, form 7770, 1904 .........8,500.00
Chalice, 6" h, four flower stems as handles, relief flowers and berries, green and blue eosin glaze, red int., form #5668, c1899, millennium factory mark, ext. rim chip, repaired ....................................1,650.00
Coffee Set, 8-1/2" h coffeepot, six cups, saucers, and dessert plates, creamer, sugar, cake plate, white ground, cobalt blue and gold rim, 1940s .........................................................................600.00
Ewer
    8-1/2" h, 8" d, gold dec, c1895-1920, repair to base of handle....................................................................300.00
    10" h, reticulated, Persian form, crescent finial, minor chips to lip.........................................................................220.00
    12-1/2" h, 6-1/2" d, reticulated handle, neck, body, and foot, Art Nouveau florals, majolica tin glazes with pale robin's egg blue base, yellow, light cranberry pink, told trim, form #2567, five steeple stamp mark, small flake and glaze wear .............575.00

**Coffeepot, yellow ground, reticulated, teardrop motif, multicolored castle mark, 9-1/2" h, $425.**

Figure

Anonymous, 13-1/2" h, 14-1/2" l, 10-1/4" d, vibrant blue eosin glaze against mottled green seat, minor glaze losses, small corner restoration to edge of chair ..................... 3,500.00

Cat, 9-1/2" h, modernist design .......................................... 115.00

Caterpillar, 2-3/4" h, Eosine glaze...................................... 165.00

Cello Player, 8-1/2" h, designed by Gygory Furtos ............. 350.00

Deer, 2-1/4" x 3-1/2", green eosin glaze ............................... 85.00

Duck in Flight, 20" w, 20" d, 16" h, 1906, multiple repairs, price for pr ................................................................................. 9,500.00

Elephant, 3" h, 2-1/2" w, 3-3/4" l, gold, green, and blue ..... 145.00

Female, reclining, 10" l, partially clad, green, gold, and pink luster glaze, blue and green irid clothing and platform, stamp mark .............................................................................. 900.00

Fox, 4" h, eosin glaze, current production ............................. 75.00

German Shepherd, 5-1/4" h, red glaze, artist sgd .............. 100.00

Girl with Basket, 4-3/4" l, 3-1/2" h, irid blue glaze................. 65.00

Mallard Duck, 7" h, 7" w, two naturally colored ducks on white oval base, c1940 ................................................................ 200.00

Nude, female with charger under arms, c1930, 5 steeple mark, slight in-making paint slip ................................................ 175.00

Owl, 3" h, green eosin glaze, unmarked ............................... 45.00

Polar bear .......................................................................... 385.00

Spaniel, 5" h, green eosin glaze .......................................... 95.00

Inkwell, 4-1/4" h, figural conch shell, crimson and black lustered glazes, repair to handle ........................................... 300.00

Jar, cov, 7" h, blue and cream snowflake design, coral ground, painted millennium mark, c1894 ..................................... 1,650.00

Jardiniere, 18" h, majolica glaze, thistle dec, form #5454, 6" glaze line on int. ..................................................... 6,500.00

Jug, 16" h, iron gray matte around high luster gold band, enameled highlights, form #564, c1879, int. label from Wahliss Shop, numerous later white paint flakes............................. 1,750.00

Pitcher

5-1/2" h, metallic cream dec, purple-blue metallic ground, millennium mark, c1865....................................................... 1,250.00

8" h, Old Ivory line, rose and pink, gold highlights, form #2953 ............................................................................. 650.00

13-1/2" h, organic form, blue, green eosin glaze, form #5517, c1899, round raised factory mark............................... 9,500.00

15" h, Persian pattern ....................................................... 300.00

15-1/2" h, high relief acorns, oak leaves, several large red beetles, eosin glaze, form #4115, factory mark, base glaze line .....5,500.00

18" h, cock, form #1132, c1883, raised mark, minor restoration to beak .............................................................................. 4,950.00

Planter, 17-1/2" h, sq, branch form supports, reticulated, irid, molded leaf and vine dec, gold highlights ......................................... 1,000.00

Plaque, 15-1/4" w, 10-1/4" h, rect, yellow, pink, green, and brown Dutch windmill and horse scene, irid Art Nouveau border, mkd........... 1,000.00

Plate, 11-1/2" d, 1-3/4" d, pink and yellow carnation flowers, cream ground, 1870s mark ...................................................... 800.00

Portrait Plate, 6-1/2" d, glossy glaze, man and woman in period costumes, blue, green, purple, yellow, and brown, textured gilt ground, gilt highlights, blue stamped mark, early 20th C, crazing, one of pair damaged .............................................................. 400.00

Stein, half liter, relief design of shield on front, flowers and ribbons on sides, pink glaze, pink glass inlaid lid, crackled finish, Zsolnay Pecs mark ...................................................................................... 235.00

Vase

4-1/2" h, Secessionist era, gold-green undulating glaze, faintly metallic purple ground, form #5330, c1900.................. 3,850.00

4-3/4" h, Secessionist era flowers, vines and leaves in contrasting metallic red and blue eosin glazes, deep metallic blue eosin ground, millennium factory mark, repaired rim................. 950.00

7-3/4" h, Egyptian, bright gilt metal mounts enclose mottled purple, gold, blue, and green Labrador glaze, c1905, sgd "Osiris"".................................................................... 2,250.00

7-3/4" h, landscape, rainbow metallic eosin glaze, form #5288, c1898, vertical hairline crack........................................ 5,000.00

8" h, elaborate red, tan, and gold florals, overall irid, wafer mark ............................................................................. 1,100.00

8-1/2" h, landscape dec with trees, highly lustrous eosin leaves, high style dec, Nabis school of design, form #6011, c1906....... 6,500.00

8-3/4" h, tulip form, Secessionist era, form #6173, c1900 .... 6,500.00

9" h, classic shape, large looping ribbon-like handles, blue and yellow stylized flowers, strong red ground, form #6171, designed by Sandor Abt, c1900 ................................... 3,000.00

9" h, ewer shape, ribbon handles, highly lustrous maroon ground, faint eosin glaze, form #5338, c1898, printed millennium mark.................................................................. 2,500.00

9" h, high style Art Deco shape, metallic blue glaze, form #8513, round raised factory mark, repair to side...................... 2,650.00

9-1/4" h, double gourd form, highly metallic luster surface, blue, green, and silver Labrador glaze, millennium mark, c1896................................................................................. 1,350.00

10" h, mottled cream globular glaze, deliberate burnt spots, Secessionist gilt and orange painted dec, form #?024, round raised factory mark, c1902, rim repair........................ 10,000.00

10" h, stylized relief flowers, putty colored ground, form #7926, c1906, round raised factory mark, minor rim repair .... 12,500.00

10-1/2" h, red and putty dec, white glaze, form #3939, c1893, Iznik design ................................................................. 2,750.00

10-3/4" h, Leopard Vase, form #8589, Sandor Pillo Hidasy, c1912................................................................................. 17,500.00

11-3/4" h, Aztec-style dec, millennium factory mark, form #933, c1882 .............................................................................. 3,850.00

11-3/4" h, blue painted flower and leaf Secessionist dec, deep burgundy ground, form #7804, round raised steeple mark, lip repair............................................................................... 1,750.00

11-3/4" h, metallic gold and blue painted dec, deep burgundy ground, flower and leaf dec, high style Secession design elements, form #7804, round raised steeple mark, lip repair.............. 1,750.00

13" h, completely reticulated, double walled, Persian pattern type dec .................................................................................... 1,500.00

15-3/4" h, Goose Girl, green, blue, and gold eosin glazes, raised relief design, maiden sitting under tree with geese, setting sun, clouds, form #5561, Sandor Apati Apt, c1898............ 17,500.00

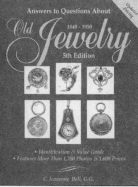